D1219022

*British*
*Parliamentary Papers*

SILK TRADE

Industrial Revolution

Textiles 5

IRISH UNIVERSITY PRESS SERIES

OF

# British Parliamentary Papers

REPORT FROM THE
SELECT COMMITTEE
ON THE
SILK TRADE
WITH MINUTES OF EVIDENCE
APPENDIX AND INDEX

*Industrial Revolution*

*Textiles*

5

SHANNON · IRELAND

© 1968

*Irish University Press Shannon Ireland*

*Microforms*

*Microfilm, microfiche and other forms of micro-publishing*
© *Irish University Microforms Shannon Ireland*

SBN 7165 0164 3

*Irish University Press Shannon Ireland*
DUBLIN CORK BELFAST LONDON
*Captain T M MacGlinchey Publisher*

PRINTED IN IRELAND AT SHANNON
BY ROBERT HOGG PRINTER TO IRISH UNIVERSITY PRESS

# REPORTS

FROM

## COMMITTEES:

*EIGHTEEN VOLUMES.*

---

—(15.)—

SILK TRADE.

---

### Session
6 December 1831—16 August 1832.

## VOL. XIX.

# REPORTS FROM COMMITTEES:

## 1831-2.

*EIGHTEEN VOLUMES:—CONTENTS OF THE*

FIFTEENTH VOLUME.

---

---

# REPORT

FROM

## SELECT COMMITTEE

ON THE

# SILK TRADE:

WITH

## THE MINUTES OF EVIDENCE,

AN APPENDIX,

AND

## INDEX.

———

*Ordered, by* The House of Commons, *to be Printed,*
2 *August* 1832.

———

### Jovis, 1° die Martii, 1832.

*Ordered,*

THAT a Select Committee be appointed to examine into the present State of the Silk Trade, and to inquire what effects have been produced by the changes in the Laws relating to it, since the Year 1824; and whether any, and what Legislative Measures, compatible with the general interest of the Country, may be advisable, in order to promote it, or to check Smuggling in Silk Manufactures; and to Report their Observations thereupon to The House :—And a Committee is appointed of

| | |
|---|---|
| Earl Grosvenor. | Mr. Fowell Buxton. |
| Mr. Henry L. Bulwer. | Sir Michael Stewart, Bart. |
| Mr. Poulett Thomson. | Mr. Strutt. |
| Sir Robert Peel, Bart. | Mr. Heywood. |
| Mr. Alderman Venables. | Mr. Stewart Mackenzie. |
| Mr. Courtenay. | Mr. Edward Stewart (of Wigton.) |
| Mr. G. Bankes. | Mr. Sheil. |
| Mr. Hume. | Lord Dudley Stuart. |
| Mr. Alexander Baring. | Mr. Ayshford Sanford. |
| Sir H. Parnell, Bart. | Mr. James Morrison. |
| Mr. Frankland Lewis. | |

*Ordered,* That the said Committee have Power to send for Persons, Papers and Records.

*Ordered,* That Five be the Quorum of the Committee.

### Martis, 6° die Martii, 1832.

*Ordered,* THAT Mr. Alderman Waithman be added to the Committee.

### Mercurii, 7° die Martii, 1832.

*Ordered,* THAT all Petitions presented in the present Session, on the subject of the Silk Trade, be referred to the Committee.

### Jovis, 15° die Martii, 1832.

*Ordered,* THAT Mr. Wynn Ellis be added to the Committee.

### Lunæ, 26° die Martii, 1832.

*Ordered,* THAT the Petitions of Silk Throwsters of Blockley, and of the Vicar, Churchwardens, Guardians, Overseers and Inhabitants, Owners of Property in the parish of Foleshill, complaining of the distressed state of that Trade, and praying for relief, be referred to the Committee.

*Ordered,* That the Petition of Silk Manufacturers and Throwsters in Manchester, against any alteration of the Laws relating thereto, be referred to the said Committee.

### Lunæ, 9° die Aprilis, 1832.

*Ordered,* THAT Accounts of Drawback on Silk Manufactures exported in 1830 and 1831, and of Raw and Waste Silk imported and entered for Consumption, in each year, from the year 1814 (presented 9th April), be referred to the said Committee.

# R E P O R T.

THE SELECT COMMITTEE appointed to examine into the present State of the SILK TRADE, and to inquire what effects have been produced by the changes in the Laws relating to it, since the Year 1824; and whether any, and what Legislative Measures, compatible with the general interest of the Country, may be advisable, in order to promote it, or to check Smuggling in Silk Manufactures; and to report their Observations thereupon to The House; and to whom the several Petitions, presented to The House in the present Session of Parliament on the Silk Trade, were referred; and who were empowered to report the MINUTES of the EVIDENCE taken before them, to The House:——HAVE examined the Matters to them referred, and have agreed to submit to The House the Evidence already taken before them.

YOUR COMMITTEE regret that they are unable to make any General or full Report on the several Matters submitted to their consideration; but the various Interests involved, and the extent of the Subjects brought before the Committee, as well as the great number of Witnesses they have had to examine, and the knowledge that many others still remain to be examined, compel them, at this late period of the Session, only to lay the Evidence before The House.

2 *August* 1832.

## LIST OF WITNESSES.

## LIST OF WITNESSES—*continued.*

# MINUTES OF EVIDENCE.

*Veneris, 16° die Martii,* 1832.

## THE RIGHT HON. THE EARL GROSVENOR,

IN THE CHAIR.

*James Deacon Hume,* Esquire, called in; and Examined.

1. **Y**OU are Joint Secretary to the Board of Trade?—I am.

2. The Committee have desired your attendance in order to state the changes which have taken place in the laws relating to silk, and also to put in certain Custom-house Accounts, which you can furnish from the proper office; the first change that took place was in 1824, was it not?—Yes, in April 1824.

3. Were you employed in 1824, in preparing the Act of Parliament of that year, relating to the silk trade?—I drew the Bill.

4. And afterwards in framing the Tables of Duties on the Act of Parliament of 1826?—I was.

5. Have the goodness to state to the Committee on what principles these Acts of Parliament and the Table were constructed?—The intention of the Act of 1824 was to substitute a protecting duty of 30 per cent. in lieu of total prohibition.

6. Then the Committee are to understand, that it was upon the principle of substituting a duty of 30 per cent. that the rated duties were fixed in the Act of Parliament of 1826?—The Committee will remember, that two years or rather more was given before the Act came into operation, and in the progress of that time the

*James D. Hume, Esq.*

16 March, 1832.

678. trade

*James D. Hume*, Esq.

16 March, 1832.

trade became of opinion that an *ad valorem* duty would not be effectual; they therefore begged and suggested, that certain rates of duty, by weight, should be computed, so as to give the 30 per cent. as nearly as such rates could be made to do so; and it was upon that principle, and in consequence of the change of opinion in the trade, that the Tables of 1826 were prepared before importation commenced, and I was employed in preparing them.

7. They were prepared strictly with the view to give 30 per cent.?—That was the intention; and I have good reason to believe, that according to the value of silks at that time the intention was not frustrated, and that the Table then gave 30 per cent. as nearly as rated duties possibly could give it; the articles could only be classed in descriptions, but there will be varieties of values of the same description; a fixed rate will give different per centages on the different values of the same sorts of goods; it will be a heavier duty on the inferior and a lighter duty on the superior articles; the average on each description was supposed to be 30 per cent. as nearly as possible, by the Tables of 1826.

8. That was the principle which regulated the construction of the first Tables?—It was considered at that time by the Government that 30 per cent. should be the maximum of protection to any trade when they were relinquishing prohibition and prohibitory duties, and changing to the protective system. At that time the Government kept two points in view, one was the facility of smuggling, the other was the giving an adequate protection to home industry; 30 per cent. was deemed a maximum for protection, and in respect of silk it was supposed to be the minimum of smuggling.

9. The correctness of that Table was afterwards destroyed by the changes in the value of the goods, was it not?—Very considerably so; the goods generally became of less value than when the Table was framed, and some in a greater degree than others; the value of silk, the material had fallen.

10. And an attempt was made in 1829, when the duty was again altered, was it not, to adjust the rates of duties again to the original scale?—The Table was then re-constructed, with a view in great measure to such adjustment; but the previous principle was not quite strictly adhered to; some articles were found to be less liable to smuggling than others, and where smuggling did not interfere there was rather more protection given; so far one of the principles may be said to have been departed from in the second Table, that is the fixing of a maximum of protection.

11. The other principle, namely, the fixing the duty at the minimum cost of smuggling was attempted to be adhered to?—It was attempted and fully intended, for on one article, plain silk, the duty was put at 25 per cent. because at that time it was understood that that was the article chiefly smuggled, certainty and quickness of arrival being less important in plain than in fancy silks.

12. Can you state, from the Returns you have brought, how the importation of raw silk has gone on since the repeal of the prohibition declared in the Act of Parliament of 1824?—Yes.

13. Do I understand you to mean, that the duty in 1829, was in any case intended to be more than 30 per cent.?—Yes; the fact is, that velvets, for instance, were allowed to remain at more, and there was no reduction on several of the other articles, although their values had fallen. I also think that crape was conceived not to be so easily smuggled as the plain silks.

14. Are we to understand that you conceive that the principle of the arrangement of 1829 was, that the minimum of smuggling would be attained by taking 30 per cent., or 25 per cent., or any other rate of per centage as the rate of protection of the trade?—According to the best of my opinion, the minimum of smuggling was believed to be attained in 1829, as much as in 1826, the intention was to stop smuggling at all events.

15. And that was supposed to be 25 per cent.?—25 per cent. on plain goods, and there was some variation in regard to some others; in some it was conceived that the risk of smuggling did not create a necessity for reduction, although the rated duties gave much more than 30 per cent.

16. With the exception of velvets and peculiar articles of that nature, was not 25 per cent. taken in 1829, as 30 per cent. had been taken in 1824 and 1826?—Only for plain goods: the Tables will show that, in the option given to the officers.

17. As far as I understand, I think the reduction did not take place in consequence of the desire to reduce the duties; but the reason of it was, because the goods had fallen in price, and, consequently, the duty on them was relatively higher then than

it

it was in 1824?—The duty had become higher relatively to the prices at that time. The Table of 1829 was conceived to give higher *ad valorem* duties than the Table of 1826. The change when reduction was made was forced on us by the apprehension of smuggling. We went no further than the necessity required.

*James D. Hume,*
*Esq.*

———

16 March,
1832.

18. Have you an account of the Table of Duties as fixed by the law in 1826?—Yes.

19. I have understood you to say, that the duties were determined on in April 1824, but that they were not brought into operation until April 1826?—They were altered in 1826, and before they came into operation, which was not till the 5th July 1826.

20. I wish to know whether the duties brought into operation in 1826 were the same duties that were decided on in the year 1824?—The duty in 1824 was stated in one word—simply 30 per cent. The Table which was prepared in 1826 meant to give the same, and the principle was to be the same. It had been arranged in the year 1824 that the duty should be 30 per cent.

21. But were not the officers of the Customs allowed, in the year 1826, to take the same *ad valorem* if they chose it?—No, not in 1826: in 1829 they were, and that was with a view to the getting the full 30 per cent. in case that any goods of very great value should be introduced at that rate of duty which applied to them.

22. Another alteration was made in the Tables in the year 1829?—Yes.

23. Are the Committee to understand that these alterations were intended to be equal on the whole to 30 per cent.?—I have meant to be understood, that the alterations in 1829 departed, in some degree, from the original intention; some articles, in particular the plain goods, were so much smuggled, that it was intended the duty on them should be only 25 per cent., and on others it was left unchanged, with a consciousness that they were more than 30 per cent. The Table in 1829 was not, like that in 1826, framed upon one single direction: in the former instance the direction was to make it 30 per cent.; in the second there was a modification; 25 per cent. was adopted in some cases, and even more than 30 per cent., in other cases, was consented to by the manufacturers.

24. Then am I to understand you to say that this modification was applied to the different qualities f goods, but still it was intended to be in the same proportion of 30 per cent. as it was originally?—I meant to say, that I considered it was not so intended.

25. Was it intended to be more than 30 per cent. or less than 30 per cent. on the average?—I do not exactly feel the application of an average. The duty on one article does not average with the duty on another; each pays by itself. Some goods, as I have said, were placed at 25 per cent. and others at 30 per cent., and some at much more than 30. In the last case, it was not a raising of the duty, for the duty might be said to have been left, rather than fixed, at more than 30 per cent.

26. In 1824, do you mean that the articles rated at an *ad valorem* of 30 per cent., which you say were plain goods, were in 1829 considered to be taken at 25 per cent.?—The rate in 1829 was meant to give 25 per cent. on plain goods.

27. Was not there an arrangement in 1829, that the officers should be allowed to take an *ad valorem*, or a duty per pound, at their pleasure?—The officers were allowed, at their sole option, to take the *ad valorem* duty instead of the rate; that is to say, to the parties who were the owners of the goods, you shall enter their goods at value, and as the option was only on their side, and was of course given for the protection of the revenue, they would only do that when the goods were of very great value, and were entered at a rate, which in the judgment of the officers, would not give the intended per centage, whether it was 25 or 30; but there is no instance in which the officers had a right to demand more than 30 per cent. if they required the goods to be entered at value.

28. In 1826 there was no *ad valorem* duty at all?—There was no choice; there were some goods that could not be rated; but there was no choice except in instances of millinery, or some things of that sort.

29. And 25 per cent. was the maximum, previously it had been 30?—Yes; on plain goods.

30. Then the Committee understand, that in 1829, with the exception of the plain goods, which were reduced from 30 to 25 per cent., there was no alteration in the rating; but in consequence of the goods having decreased in value, and the same rating being continued, it operated so as to produce a higher rate of duty?—There were alterations in the rating of many of the articles, and in some there was none. The plain silk which had been 15 s. the lb. was reduced to 11 s. the lb.; that 15 s. was understood to be 30 per cent. in the former case, but in the latter case the

678.

11 s.

*James D. Hume,*
*Esq.*

——————

16 March,
1832.

11 *s.* was understood to give only 25 per cent; then there came the figured and the satin, they were reduced, but still they were meant to give 30 per cent. ; others were left at the original duties, with the knowledge that they gave more than 30 per cent.

31. In fact, according to your account, it seems that there were three divisions of silk goods, some where the principle of 30 per cent. was adhered to, others where it was taken at 25 per cent. which is a reduction, and others for which certain duties were assessed, amounting to more than 30 per cent.?—Yes; but these last were not alterations.

32. Did you draw out both Schedules?—Yes.

33. What were your instructions in drawing up the Schedule of April 1826?—To adhere strictly to 30 per cent.

34. What were your instructions for drawing up the Schedule for 1829?—Certainly not such instructions as in the former case, because it was agreed that there should not be an universal rule; it was rather a matter of discussion through the whole time of drawing up the Tables. In the first case there was an universal rule, in the other there was constant discussion without a fixed rule.

35. The effect of the Table of 1829 was to reduce the protection of the silk trade?—I should certainly say it increased the protection as compared with that of 1826, except on one article.

36. The Table of 1829, the duty was fixed at the minimum cost of smuggling in all cases?—That was the intention of the government of that day; it was believed, that the articles, on which they left the higher duty unreduced, were less likely to be exposed to smuggling than those on which they had reduced the duties.

37. Was not there an understanding at that time, on the part of the silk trade, that a duty of 30 per cent. was absolutely necessary for their protection, and was not that stated in their communications with the government?—I conceive that the silk trade thought a great deal more than 30 per cent. was necessary.

38. Was not the result of their negociations, if we may call them so, with the government, that they were to have that protection?—They were to have 30 per cent. if practicable. I stated at first that two principles were acted on, one of these was to give the maximum of protection, which was agreed on not merely for silk but any goods; to give that maximum to silk, provided the minimum of smuggling would admit of it; therefore when 30 per cent. was agreed on, and might be considered as a compact with the trade, it was likewise accompanied with the condition of the practicability of it in preventing smuggling; consequently the 30 per cent. would give way whenever it was found necessary to go lower in order to undersell the smuggler.

39. Was it not believed that such an arrangement could be made on the part of government as would ensure the collection of 30 per cent.?—There may be various opinions as to the stopping of smuggling. I believe when the temptation to smuggling is great it is very difficult to put an end to; it was intended to use every salutary endeavour that could be devised to prevent the continuance of smuggling.

40. Did you, from the knowledge you then possessed, believe that 30 per cent. could be collected, so as to prevent smuggling?—In 1826 I certainly entertained a very strong hope, as far as my opinion is worth any thing, that it could be collected, because accounts had been given of the price of smuggling, which led us to believe it would be collected; smuggling, like every thing else, has been lowered in price.

41. In 1829 you were convinced that that opinion had been an erroneous one?—I conceive that before 1829 the erroneousness of that opinion had been proved.

42. Be good enough to hand in a Table of the Duties of 1826, and also a Table of the Duties of 1829?—They are in columns, with observations as to the per centages.

[*The Witness delivered in the following Paper.*]

DUTIES on the Importation of MANUFACTURED SILKS; showing the RATES of the DUTIES, and the Amount of the same upon the Value of the ARTICLES.

James D. Hume, Esq.

16 March, 1832.

| BROAD SILKS. | These Rates gave at the time, 30 per Cent. on the Value. Act of 1826. | These Rates gave at the time, and still give, various per-centages. Act of 1829. | | |
|---|---|---|---|---|
| | £. s. d. | £. s. d. | Per-centage intended at the time. | Present per-centage. |
| Silk, plain - - lb. | – 15 – | – 11 – | 25 per cent - | 30 per cent. |
| —— figured - - lb. | 1 – – | – 15 – | - - - | 35 – |
| Satin, plain - - lb. | – 16 – | – 11 – | - - - | 30 – |
| —— figured - lb. | 1 1 – | – 15 – | 30 per cent. | - - - |
| —— tissue or bro- caded - lb. | 1 – – | – 15 – | - - - | 20 to 30 per cent. |
| Gauze, plain - - lb. | – 17 – | – 17 – | - - - | 30 to 35 – on Broad Goods. |
| —— striped, figured or brocaded, lb. | 1 7 6 | 1 7 6 | 30 to 35 p' ct. | 40 to 70 – on Ribbons. |
| Crape - - - - lb. | – 16 – | – 16 – | - - - | 40 to 45 – |
| —— Lisse - - lb. | – 17 4 | – 18 – | - - - | 30 to 40 – on plain crape, Lisse. 20 only – on printed. |
| —— China, plain or figured - lb. | – 18 – | – 18 – | 30 to 35 p' ct. | 30 to 40 – |
| Velvet, plain - - lb. | 1 2 – | 1 2 – | - - - | 40 to 45 – |
| —— figured - lb. | 1 7 6 | 1 7 6 | 35 per cent. | - - - |
| RIBBONS: | | | | |
| Silk, plain - - lb. | – 15 – | | | |
| —— figured - - lb. | – 17 – | | | |
| Satin, plain - - lb. | – 16 – | Ribbons charged as Broad Silks of similar descriptions. | | |
| —— figured - lb. | – 18 – | | | |
| Gauze, plain or figured, lb. | 1 14 6 | | | |
| Velvet, plain - - lb. | 1 2 – | | | |
| —— figured - lb. | 1 7 6 | | | |

43. Have you a Table showing how the importation of raw silk has gone on since the repeal of the prohibition was declared in 1824, and how it was in the previous years?—I have prepared a Table of that description.

44. How far back does that Table go?—To the origin of the prohibition.

45. When did the prohibition take place?—Partly in 1765 and partly in 1766; some prohibition was imposed in 1765, and then it was made complete in 1766.

46. What was the amount of the importation of raw silk at that time?—I have the average of 1765, 1766 and 1767, 352,000 pounds weight.

47. And of thrown silk?—Three hundred and sixty-three thousand.

48. Will you state the progress of the trade from the paper you hold in your hand?—I have the average from 1785, 1786 and 1787, which is a period of 20 years after the prohibition. The raw silk was then raised from 352,000 to 544,000, and the thrown silk was reduced from 363,000 to 337,000, that is at the end of 20 years after prohibition had been enforced. I then have taken the average of 12 years, from 1801 to 1812, to show the progress in a term of 30 years, between the last and the next triennial average. The raw silk, in those 12 years, was 760,000; the thrown silk 350,000; then I have taken three years again, 1815, 1816 and 1817, which is a period of 50 years after prohibition and the first years of peace, 1,095,000 of raw silk and 293,000 of thrown. I then take the *three* last years prior to the change of the law, 1821, 1822 and 1823, the raw silk was then 1,970,000, the thrown silk was then 355,000. I then take the *three* last years, 1829, 1830 and 1831; and the raw silk was then 3,075,000 the thrown silk 374,000.

49. In the account of raw silk, do you include waste during the last three years?—I do not; there were four years in which they paid the same duty, and were not distinguished. I have made a deduction, to the best of my judgment, for the waste in

678. those

*James D. Hume, Esq.*

———

16 March, 1832.

those four years, from 1826 to 1829. In this account I have also the progress of the waste silk which may be worth stating; I have not the account for any distant period, only from 1815. In the three years 1815, 1816 and 1817 the quantity of waste silk, including any " knubs or husks" was 27,000 pounds : and the next three years 1821, 1822 and 1823, it rises to 74,000, and in the next three years 1829, 1830 and 1831 it was 515,000. In 1831 it was 762,000, therefore rising from the year 1815 from 27,000 to 762,000, in addition to the necessarily great increase of the produce of our own throwing mills.

50. What duty was paid upon it in the year 1815?—Until 1824 the duty was 4 *s.* the pound, then 3 *d.* a pound, afterwards a penny, in common with raw silk, and now it is 1 *s. per* hundred weight.

[*The Witness here delivered in the following Return.*]

QUANTITIES of RAW SILK, WASTE SILK, and THROWN SILK, Imported at certain periods.

| In 1765 and 1766, Prohibitions on Manufactures enacted. | Raw Silk. | Waste Silk. | Thrown Silk. |
|---|---|---|---|
| | Lbs. | Lbs. | Lbs. |
| AVERAGE IMPORT of 1765-6-7; Commencement of Prohibition  - | 352,000 | - - - | 363,000 |
| of 1785-6-7; being a period of 20 years after Prohibition  - - - - - | 544,000 | - - - | 337,000 |
| of 1801 to 1812  - - - - - | 760,000 | - - - | 350,000 |
| of 1815-16-17; being 50 years after Prohibition, and the first years of peace - - - - | 1,095,000 | 27,000 | 293,000 |
| of 1821-2-3; being the last three years prior to the change of the Law - - - - | 1,970,000 | 74,000 | 355,000 |
| of 1829-30-31; being the three last years  - | 3,075,000 | 515,000 | 374,000 |
| of 1830-31; being the two last years  - - | 3,353,000 | 623,000 | 475,000 |
| of 1831 - - - - - - - - | 3,036,000 | 762,000 | 514,000 |

51. Have you a Return of every year since 1814?—Yes; every year from 1814.

[*The Witness here delivered in the following Return.*]

AN ACCOUNT of the Quantities of RAW, WASTE and THROWN SILK Imported into the UNITED KINGDOM, from 1814, to the present time; with the Quantities entered for HOME CONSUMPTION, and the Quantities re-exported during the same period.

| YEARS | RAW SILK: Imported. | Entered for Home Consumption. | Exported. | KNUBS OR HUSKS, AND WASTE SILK: Imported. | Entered for Home Consumption. | Exported. | THROWN SILK: Imported. | Entered for Home Consumption. | Exported. Foreign Thrown. |
|---|---|---|---|---|---|---|---|---|---|
| | Lbs. | Lbs. | Lbs. | Lbs. | Lbs. | Lbs. | Lbs. | Lbs. | Lbs. |
| 1814 | 1,636,183 | 1,504,235 | 10,000 | 27,208 | 29,234 | - - | 646,338 | 586,505 | 2,273 |
| 1815 | 1,443,533 | 1,069,596 | 75,106 | 30,457 | 27,921 | - - | 359,588 | 377,822 | 488 |
| 1816 | 944,168 | 873,414 | 269,155 | 3,668 | 4,162 | - - | 194,509 | 208,014 | 5,495 |
| 1817 | 932,102 | 1,343,051 | 55,326 | 48,777 | 49,055 | 18 | 247,599 | 294,553 | 2,257 |
| 1818 | 1,646,477 | 1,444,881 | 78,208 | 98,604 | 86,940 | 1,685 | 460,924 | 391,166 | 4,345 |
| 1819 | 1,486,676 | 1,446,097 | 27,996 | 67,905 | 71,331 | 1,293 | 293,389 | 331,125 | 2,698 |
| 1820 | 2,215,692 | 1,621,590 | 5,612 | 92,538 | 96,092 | 1,947 | 333,636 | 309,953 | 4,820 |
| 1821 | 2,119,743 | 1,864,425 | 7,257 | 81,298 | 105,135 | 968 | 341,154 | 360,248 | 152 |
| 1822 | 2,060,292 | 1,993,509 | 15,612 | 117,481 | 65,176 | 837 | 502,795 | 382,878 | 122 |
| 1823 | 2,453,167 | 2,051,895 | 8,012 | 58,997 | 52,362 | 597 | 368,470 | 363,864 | 5,105 |
| 1824 | 3,051,979 | 3,414,520 | 2,258 | 83,665 | 133,257 | 101 | 342,005 | 463,271 | 1,341 |
| 1825 | 2,855,793 | 2,848,506 | 129,051 | 261,448 | 195,910 | - - | 777,529 | 559,642 | 24,554 |

| YEARS | Imported. | Entered for Home Consumption. | Exported. | Imported. | Entered for Home Consumption. | Exported. | Imported. | Entered for Home Consumption. | British Thrown. | Foreign Thrown. |
|---|---|---|---|---|---|---|---|---|---|---|
| 1826 | 2,487,820 | 1,814,188 | ⎱ 257,254 | 150,000 ⎱ | 150,000 | - - | 177,405 | 289,325 | 160 | 22,258 |
| 1827 | 3,146,926 | 3,559,138 | * 34,961 | 200,000 * | 200,000 | - - | 463,801 | 454,015 | 5,882 | 8,988 |
| 1828 | 4,256,423 | 3,912,550 | 22,530 | 250,000 | 250,000 | - - | 508,818 | 385,262 | - - | 9,421 |
| 1829 | 3,594,754 | 2,419,962 | ⎰ 221,412 | 300,000 ⎰ | 300,000 | - - | 211,179 | 172,239 | 6,671 | 26,715 |
| 1830 | 3,440,638 | 3,771,969 | 59,191 | 463,703 | 485,013 | - - | 413,840 | 436,535 | 7,773 | 5,196 |
| 1831 | 3,221,910 | 3,036,107 | ⎱ 14,348 3 qrs. to 10 Oct. | ⎱ 758,226 | 762,258 | ⎱ 3,512 3 qrs. to 10 Oct. | 629,141 | 514,240 | ⎱ 175 3 qrs. to 10 Oct. | 19,841 |

* In these Years, Waste Silk was included with the Raw Silk; assumed Quantities have therefore been transferred from one Account to the other.

52. YOU

*James D. Hume,*
*Esq.*

16 March,
1832.

52. You have not stated what the alterations were in the duty on raw and thrown silk since the year 1824; will you be good enough to state what alterations have taken place in the law relating to thrown silk since that period?—The duty on raw silk, prior to the 25th March 1824 from British India was 4s. the pound, from other places 5s. 6d. On the 25th March 1824, and afterwards, raw silk 3d., from all places. On 5th July 1826 1d. from all places; then thrown silk, prior to 25th March 1824, all sorts 14s. 8d.; 25th March 1824, 7s. 6d.; 5th November 1825, 5s. on all sorts; 5th July 1826, 5s. on organzine and crape, and 3s. on tram and singles; 5th July 1829, 3s. 6d. on organzine and crape, and 2s. on tram and 1s. 6d. on singles.

*[The Witness here delivered in the following Return.]*

AN ACCOUNT of the DUTIES payable on the Importation of RAW and WASTE SILK, and of THROWN SILK; showing the Changes which have been made therein, in and since the Year 1824.

### RAW AND WASTE SILK:

| DATES. | FROM BRITISH INDIA. | | FROM OTHER PLACES. | |
| --- | --- | --- | --- | --- |
| | Raw. | Waste. | Raw. | Waste. |
| | s. d. | s. d. | s. d. | s. d. |
| Prior to 25th March 1824 - - - | *per lb.* 4 — | *per lb.* 3 9 | *per lb.* 5 6 | *per lb.* 4 — |
| — 25th March 1824 - - - | — 3 | — 3 | — 3 | — 3 |
| — 5th July - 1826 - - - | — 1 | — 1 | — 1 | — 1 |
| — 5th July - 1829 - - - | - - - | *per cwt.* 1 — | - - - | *per cwt.* 1 — |

### THROWN SILK:

| DATES. | DYED. | | | NOT DYED. | | |
| --- | --- | --- | --- | --- | --- | --- |
| | Organzine and Crape. | Tram. | Singles. | Organzine and Crape. | Tram. | Singles. |
| | £. s. d. | £. s. d. | £. s. d. | s. d. | s. d. | s. d. |
| Prior to 25th March 1824 - | *per lb.* 2 5 6 | 2 5 6 | 2 5 6 | *per lb.* 14 8 | 14 8 | 14 8 |
| — 25th March 1824 - | - - - | - - - | - - - | 7 6 | 7 6 | 7 6 |
| — 5th July - 1825 - | — 7 6 | — 7 6 | — 7 6 | — | — | — |
| — 5th Nov. - ,, - | - - - | - - - | - - - | 5 — | 5 — | 5 — |
| — 5th July - 1826 - | — 6 8 | — 4 — | — 4 — | - - - | 3 — | 3 — |
| — 5th July - 1829 - | — 5 2 | — 3 — | — 3 — | 3 6 | 2 — | 1 6 |

53. You have stated, that the duties upon thrown silk were reduced in 1824, again in 1825, again in 1826, and again in 1829; by the Papers which you have given in, it appears, that in spite of that great reduction, the import of thrown silk did not increase in any material degree, certainly not in the least degree in proportion to the increase of raw silk?—By no means; because in 1765 the thrown silk was 363,000, and the average of 1829, 1830 and 1831 is only 374,000, while the raw silk has increased from 352,000 to 3,355,000.

54. While you were at the Board of Trade have you had occasion to hear, in the consultations you have had with the Board, the frequent complaints of the silk trade during the time the prohibition was in force?—I am aware of the applications made by the trade, for a considerable length of time, and of the character of those applications.

55. What account did they give of the cause of the distress, and the nature of it at that time?—In 1817 an application was made, very numerously signed by the throwsters, complaining of the duty then on raw silk, and that it was not drawn back, which consequently prevented them from exporting thrown silk. This application was backed by a similar application from the East India Company, and the

representation

*James D. Hume,*
*Esq.*
———
16 March,
1832.

representation was that " if the silk thrown in this country could be discharged from all duty imposed on the raw silk, that they could export thrown silk for the use of other countries, and that they looked at the progress, as they stated, which had been made in the exportation of cotton yarn, and they anticipated an ability to carry on a trade by the export of thrown silk similar in a great degree to that which was carried on in the export of cotton yarn;" that was the case of the throwsters. It was signed by seventy-seven throwsters. The East India Company presented a memorial at the same time to the same tenor ; they also used the expression in their application that, " they believed that we could export thrown silk like cotton yarn." A petition, in some degree similar, was presented in 1818, by the manufacturers, and several others in 1819, stating " that the demand of manufactured goods had for some time past so decreased as to afford serious ground of alarm to the manufacturers, and to threaten the existence of the silk manufactory of this country."

56. From what part of the country did this come?—From the London district; the Spitalfields district.

57. Was the Coventry district united with the Spitalfields?—That was from Spitalfields ; then there was one from Nottingham and another from the Dublin silk trade. In the first petition, after what I have quoted, they in another part say, " The principal cause is the duty preventing competition with foreigners," meaning the duty on the raw and thrown silk, and of course alluding to exportation. In 1818 the trade of Nottingham made a similar representation : they stated in their petition, " that the trade was in great distress, and that men who used to earn from 30 s. to 40 s. a week, now can only earn 10 s. or 11 s." this was in 1818. They state, " that their dependence is on an export trade ; that the trade was stopped for want of a sufficient drawback of the duty on the Piedmontese thrown silk, which alone can be used in the articles that they make."

58. Do they state the articles?—Plain point silk net; they, like the others, look to relief from exportation. The Dublin silk trade complain of the " insufficient drawback of the duty on the raw material, as the reason why the British manufacturer cannot compete with the French in the foreign market." In June 1819 a similar application came from Spitalfields. It proceeds on the assumption that British silk, fairly discharged from the home consumption duty on the raw material, by a sufficient drawback, can compete with French silks in the Foreign markets.

59. Does it distinguish what branch of manufacture it was that made this application?—No, I do not think it does ; I took these extracts from the memorials in the books in our office.

60. Are these all entered in your books?—Yes, they are; according to their complaint, a sufficient drawback not being given a sort of transit duty remained on the goods, and that must always be considered to be a great impediment to a foreign trade. I should say that the general complexion of these applications was this : That the home trade was saturated, and that therefore it was time they looked, like the cotton spinners and the cotton manufacturers, to a foreign trade ; and they described, that if the foreign trade was not interrupted or opposed in any way by any duty, that is, if an adequate export drawback were given on the manufactured goods, equal to the duty on the materials, if that was done then like cotton, (for they constantly refer to the great success of cotton), silk also might have an ample export trade, and in some places they say that it would become one of the staple commodities of export from this country. In consequence of these representations, as I presume, the Act of 59th of Geo. 3, c. 112, dated the 12th of July 1819, gave the following additional bounties, 3 s. 4 d. a pound on ribbons, and 5 s. 4 d. on broad silks, in addition to the bounties which had long been in force before, and which, though called bounties, were in reality drawbacks.

61. You do not know what those bounties were, do you?—No; I have not brought a memorandum of them.

62. Do any of these petitions complain of the introduction of contraband silks?—No, they were on a very different subject; the petitioners were then asking only for a fair stage, in order that they might compete with foreign silks on equal terms; but in 1810 there was an association of the silk trade formed to prevent smuggling, and the papers, with their proceedings, were laid before the government of the day. The title of it is " To stop the alarming introduction of foreign manufactured silks." I have not perceived, in looking over the books for the other petitions, that the subject of smuggling was formally complained of again after that, but the complaints out of doors were constant and notorious.

63. They have made no complaint since then?—I am not aware of any presented in writing.

writing, perhaps they might; but such subjects are often mentioned at interviews or in conversation.

64. Have you any other papers you wish to give in?—Yes.

*James D. Hume, Esq.*

16 March, 1832.

[*The Witness delivered in the following Papers.*]

AN ACCOUNT of all SILKS and RIBBONS (separately) Imported from July 1826, to the present time.

SILK MANUFACTURES IMPORTED INTO THE UNITED KINGDOM FOR HOME CONSUMPTION.

| | 1826: from 5th July Lbs. | oz. | Year 1827 Lbs. | oz. | Year 1828 Lbs. | oz. | Year 1829 Lbs. | oz. | Year 1830 Lbs. | oz. | Year 1831 Lbs. | oz. |
|---|---|---|---|---|---|---|---|---|---|---|---|---|
| **SILKS of EUROPE:** | | | | | | | | | | | | |
| Silk or Satin | 20,228 | 11 1/4 | 38,549 | 6 1/4 | 61,323 | 2 1/4 | 64,612 | 3 1/2 | 51,417 | 6 1/2 | 82,400 | 5 |
| —— in Ribbons | 7,682 | 1 1/2 | 20,958 | 11 1/2 | 35,516 | 14 | | | | | | |
| Gauze | 5,282 | 14 1/4 | 6,504 | 5 1/4 | 4,600 | - 1/4 | 20,052 | 3 3/4 | 30,241 | 3 | 33,488 | 7 3/4 |
| —— in Ribbons | 3,617 | 15 | 16,210 | 14 1/4 | 21,917 | 13 | | | | | | |
| Crape | 5,496 | 13 3/4 | 16,381 | 1 | 24,951 | 13 | 22,786 | 11 1/2 | 28,880 | 4 | 19,669 | 5 |
| —— in Ribbons | | | | | | | | | | | | |
| Velvet | 5,518 | 8 1/2 | 15,403 | 15 3/4 | 18,470 | 7 | 13,743 | - | 14,847 | 6 | 12,264 | 13 |
| —— in Ribbons | 52 | 10 | 242 | 2 | 2,101 | 10 3/4 | | | | | | |
| Ribbons embossed or figured with Velvet | | Not entered under this denomination until 5th July 1829. | | | | | 317 | 2 | 529 | 3 | 345 | 14 |
| Fancy Silk Net or Tricot | 27 | 14 | 223 | 5 | 11 | 4 | 3 | 12 | 42 | 11 | 95 | 12 |
| Silk, mixed with Metal | 339 | 8 | 583 | 10 1/4 | 512 | 7 1/4 | 438 | 12 1/2 | 412 | 7 | 464 | 8 |
| —— in Ribbons | 54 | 1 | 220 | 13 | 125 | 1 | | | | | | |
| TOTAL entered by Weight | 48,301 | 1 1/2 | 115,278 | 5 1/4 | 169,530 | 9 | 121,953 | 13 1/4 | 126,370 | 8 1/2 | 148,729 | - 3/4 |
| Plain Silk Lace or Net called Tulle *(Square yards)* | 40,676 1/4 | | 122,238 1/4 | | 171,005 1/2 | | 109,729 1/2 | | 114,381 1/4 | | 54,164 1/4 | |
| Millinery; viz. Turbans or Caps *(Number)* | 113 | | 326 | | 295 | | 383 | | 368 | | 199 | |
| —— Hats or Bonnets | 119 | | 428 | | 414 | | 528 | | 535 | | 412 | |
| —— Dresses | 44 | | 213 | | 275 | | 330 | | 298 | | 200 | |
| —— at Value *(Declared value)* | - | | £.50 12 - | | £.13 10 - | | £.30 12 - | | £.154 4 - | | £.27 16 - | |
| Manufactures of Silk, or of Silk and any other Materials not particularly enumerated | £.21,489 5 - | | £.54,128 9 10 | | £.77,189 - 8 | | £.85,258 19 5 | | £.44,923 15 10 | | £.35,722 - 9 | |
| **SILKS, of INDIA:** | | | | | | | | | | | | |
| Bandannoes, Romals and Silk Handkerchiefs *(Pieces)* | 208,066 | | 55,183 | | 69,628 | | 67,465 | | 77,953 | | 101,023 | |
| Silks and Crapes in Pieces *(Pieces)* | 32,754 | | 18,150 | | 15,577 | | 10,164 | | 2,978 | | 3,796 | |
| Crape Shawls, Scarfs, Gown Pieces and Handkerchiefs *(Number)* | 77,776 | | 24,200 | | 4,789 | | 1,959 | | 17,620 | | 16,157 | |

*Note:*—THE distinction in the Rates of Duty between Silks and Ribbons having ceased to exist in 1829, on the passing of the Act 10 Geo. 4. c. 23, both Articles have since been entered at the Custom House under the general denominations of Silk or Satin, Gauze and Velvet, and are necessarily stated in the same manner in the above Return.

*James D. Hume*, Esq.

————

16 March, 1832.

AN ACCOUNT of the OFFICIAL VALUE of MANUFACTURED SILKS Imported in each Year since the Repeal of the Prohibition in 1826; distinguishing *European* from *East Indian*.

| YEARS. | OFFICIAL VALUE OF MANUFACTURED SILKS Imported into the United Kingdom. | | |
| | European. | East Indian. | TOTAL. |
| --- | --- | --- | --- |
| | £. | £. | £. |
| 1826 - - | 172,176 (from 5th July.) | 275,525 (from 5th January.) | 447,701 |
| 1827 - - | 380,202 | 176,210 | 556,412 |
| 1828 - - | 545,925 | 131,293 | 677,218 |
| 1829 - - | 425,231 | 170,416 | 595,647 |
| 1830 - - | 410,500 | 124,599 | 535,099 |
| 1831 - - | - - - - - | - - - - - | say 550,000 |

AN ACCOUNT of the Amount of BOUNTY and DRAWBACK paid in the United Kingdom on *British* Manufactured SILK GOODS Exported.

| YEARS | £. | s. | d. | |
| --- | --- | --- | --- | --- |
| 1814 - - | 23,973 | 6 | 2 | |
| 1815 - - | 30,134 | 12 | 10 | |
| 1816 - - | 30,214 | 12 | 5 | |
| 1817 - - | 20,889 | 13 | 5 | |
| 1818 - - | 23,710 | 7 | 4 | |
| 1819 - - | 21,335 | 10 | 6 | |
| 1820 - - | 23,601 | 4 | 6 | |
| 1821 - - | 32,172 | 3 | 3 | } - - - Bounty. |
| 1822 - - | 33,353 | 6 | 2 | |
| 1823 - - | 32,446 | 9 | – | |
| 1824 - - | 34,252 | 7 | 7 | |
| 1825 - - | 565 | 12 | 2 | } Arrears. |
| 1826 - - | 56 | 16 | 6 | |
| 1827 - - | 61 | 19 | – | |
| 1828 - - | — | | | |
| 1829 - - | 4,844 | 1 | 7 | } - - - Drawback. |
| 1830 - - | 36,690 | 8 | 7 | |
| 1831 - - | 46,658 | 17 | 8 | |

AN ACCOUNT of the OFFICIAL VALUES of *British* Manufactured SILKS Exported in each Year from 1821 to 1830, both inclusive.

| YEARS | OFFICIAL VALUES OF BRITISH MANUFACTURED SILKS Exported from the United Kingdom. | | | | | | | | |
| | Manufactures of Silk only. | | | Silks mixed with other Materials. | | | TOTAL. | | |
| --- | --- | --- | --- | --- | --- | --- | --- | --- | --- |
| | £. | s. | d. | £. | s. | d. | £. | s. | d. |
| 1821 - - | 104,124 | 10 | 7 | 32,717 | 8 | 6 | 136,841 | 19 | 1 |
| 1822 - - | 102,707 | 3 | 3 | 38,467 | 14 | 3 | 141,174 | 17 | 6 |
| 1823 - - | 104,934 | 19 | 2 | 35,525 | – | 3 | 140,459 | 19 | 5 |
| 1824 - - | 95,038 | 9 | 5 | 64,632 | 8 | 1 | 159,670 | 17 | 6 |
| 1825 - - | 57,499 | 8 | 9 | 93,387 | 11 | – | 150,886 | 19 | 9 |
| 1826 - - | 53,155 | 19 | 3 | 53,775 | 10 | 10 | 106,931 | 10 | 1 |
| 1827 - - | 78,665 | 15 | 10 | 94,927 | 8 | 8 | 173,593 | 4 | 6 |
| 1828 - - | 81,636 | 6 | 6 | 97,417 | 13 | 5 | 179,053 | 19 | 11 |
| 1829 - - | 141,686 | – | 6 | 80,312 | – | 9 | 221,998 | 1 | 3 |
| 1830 - - | 348,761 | 10 | 8 | 79,087 | 14 | 11 | 427,849 | 5 | 7 |
| 1831 - - | - | - | - | - | - | say | 500,000 | – | – |

65. You

*James D. Hume,*
Esq.

———

16 March,
1832.

65. You have not mentioned particularly any memorials presented from Coventry, prior to 1824?—I am not aware that there are any.

66. Do you think that the prohibition was more effectual against smuggling than the protecting duty?—Yes; I think that the smuggling of an article that cannot be legally possessed within the country at all may be more effectually guarded against than that of one which is admissible, however high the duty; no doubt a more rigid rule may be adopted, and the severity of the law may be applied with more decision, so as to make it more effectual.

67. You gave us the years 1829, 1830 and 1831; could you give the average of the import of raw silk in the years 1826, 1827 and 1828?—Every year, singly, from 1814, is included in the other Return which I have handed in.

68. When you say that you think that, in the event of a prohibition fewer goods would be imported, or a more effectual prevention of smuggling take place, that would depend on the power of distinguishing the French manufactured goods from the English manufactured goods?—I understand they are not so distinguishable as they were some years ago, and of course if that is the case, the success in detection would be less than it has been previously.

69. You have stated, that 30 per cent. was fixed by those who made the law which you have alluded to in a former answer; was that as high a protection as should have been fixed with any chance of keeping out the smuggler?—I stated, that the 30 per cent. was at the first established on two principles; one was, that it was hoped it would be the minimum of smuggling; but it was not intended to give more than 30 per cent. originally, in any case whatever, when it was considered how large a portion of the value of silk consist of the material itself, perhaps half, 30 is perhaps 60 per cent. on the industry, which was the subject intended to be protected.

70. In point of fact was it discovered that this protection did not operate in the way that was expected?—We were told that smuggling took place, and the alterations were made to prevent smuggling.

71. Do you conceive that these alterations have, in point of fact, in any degree prevented smuggling?—I understand that those articles on which the duty was reduced, the plain goods, are not now smuggled, except sometimes, in conjunction with other articles on which the duty is so excessively high, that the payment on the one helps to cover the other; gauzes for instance. An assortment may be made where the gauze, being subject to 60 or 70 per cent., would carry with it some other silks which would not have paid more than 25 or 30 per cent., such as plain silks, and which would not have been smuggled by themselves.

72. That is your opinion?—My opinion is, from all the information I have been able to obtain on the subject, that plain silks by themselves are not much smuggled.

73. Explain why there is an advantage in bringing plain silks over with gauze, when, as you state, there is no advantage in smuggling a plain silk by itself?—The advantage is in the assortment; and in occasional opportunities of bringing a variety of things together at a low price. If some of them are subject to a very high duty, it may answer the purpose to unite with them a portion of goods which are subject to a moderate duty, and so smuggle the whole; the high duty on one article covering as it were, or extending a portion of its advantage to the other, which is subject to a low duty.

74. I do not comprehend in what way there is an advantage in smuggling the plain with the silk crape and lighter articles; it appears to me the advantage would be greater if a certain sized package was to be brought over, the whole consisting of lighter articles rather than that you should include in that package a grosser fabric on which they say there is no advantage whatever in smuggling?—On which there is no advantage in smuggling singly; the advantage, as described to me by the trade, consists in buying an assortment together, and in the better purchase thereby made of the whole.

75. In saying that the advantage is in the purchase; do you mean that in France these articles of different kinds are purchased from the same manufacturers?—I do not mean to say that there or are not; but I believe it is so in ribbons. There may be middle dealers in France as there are in England; I am speaking from what has been represented to me; I am only stating the impression on my own mind, and what I have brought my belief to—the value of that belief the Committee will judge of. I cannot give specific information or evidence on such subjects, and I may have been misled by others; but I think that large purchases are made of many sorts of goods in lots; and made much more advantageously than by buying one particular sort separately, and having bought such lots, the party is anxious to

678. bring

*James D. Hume,*
Esq.

----

·16 March,
·1832.

bring them all into this country upon the best terms he can ; he accordingly compares the duty and the payment for smuggling as per centages on the goods, and if he finds an advantage on the whole in smuggling, he smuggles his whole parcel ; what I mean to say is this, that the duty on some articles is so excessive, that they may actually become the vehicles of smuggling other articles in their company, which, were it not so high, would be very little, or not at all smuggled alone.

76. Then I understand it to be the result of your opinion, that the plain silks are in no instance smuggled solely with a view to the benefit the smuggler can gain on this particular article ?—I do not mean to say no instance. I mean to say, that smuggling in the sense in which it is understood to be important, does not take place as I am told, and believe, in plain silks, it occurs chiefly in inferior gauzes ; but that 25 per cent., may not lead to occasional smuggling of plain silks, by themselves, I do not mean to deny. It is a near race between smuggling and regular entry, and the mixture of some high dutied gauzes will decide the question in favour of smuggling.

77. Do you conceive that smuggling upon the whole has increased or diminished, comparing this period with the period of 1826 ?—I am induced to think there has been more smuggling of late, but really it must be like the greatest part of my evidence, only matter of opinion, formed in the best manner I am able.

78. When you say that you think smuggling has increased of late, do you mean that it has increased continually since 1829, or that it has been greater within a very short period now passed ?—I mean particularly recently ; I should say since the latter end of 1830. Since the distress and difficulties at Lyons the temporary loss of trade in France was supposed to have thrown a great quantity of goods on the market, those which were sold at less than their cost of manufacture, and were purchased by the smugglers.

79. You say that since the distress in France a great quantity of goods have been thrown on the market at a low price ?—I meant it to be understood, that a great quantity of goods were thrown on the French market, and that made an opening for persons who intended to smuggle to buy at very low prices, which reduced the risk of smuggling as compared with the duty ; the lower you purchase the goods the less your stake at risk compared with the prize, which is the duty.

80. You say it is not worth smuggling articles under 25 per cent. ?—It is so understood ; the trade will always pay considerably more to the revenue than to the smuggler, equal to five or six per cent.

81. Do you consider that there is a disposition generally in the trade that they would, supposing they have the option, rather pay five per cent. more on the goods to the revenue than they would save themselves to that amount by smuggling ?—I certainly think that they would ; the regular importer can give his order, and can have it executed immediately ; he knows when his goods will arrive, and we must also allow something I suppose for a man's wishing to comply with the laws of his country. These considerations, put together, are supposed to be sufficient to induce men rather to give, say 25 per cent. to the revenue, than 20 or even 19 to the smuggler.

82. Then in the answers you have given, when you said 25 per cent. would be a sufficient protection, you have spoken on that impression, have you not ?—Yes, certainly, against smuggling at 20 per cent. ; I conceive that they would give 25 per cent. in duty for any such goods, rather than smuggle them at 20.

83. You do not consider that it would be advisable to reduce the duty below 25 per cent. ?—I conceive that you may always keep the duty rather above the cost of smuggling ; but I am not prepared to say that 25 per cent. or any other per centage would be the proper sum. I must be understood to speak from the impression which my mind has received in consequence of those inquiries which, in my situation I feel it my duty to be perpetually making. The price of smuggling is variously stated, and whatever it is now, it may become lower.

84. You have put in an account of the quantity of British silk exported in the last year?—Yes.

85. Has the quantity increased since the year 1826 ?—Yes, it has.

86. State what it was in 1826 ?—In 1826 the total quantity was 106,931.

87. What was it in the last year ?—The last year is not made up ; but I can give you a tolerable good estimate. In 1830 it was 427,860 ; in 1831 it was not less than 500,000.

88. Since the change of the law in 1829, has not the exporter had the advantage of the debentures that have been received ?—Yes ; it could not be supposed that they could export any manufactured goods, and not get back the duty they had paid on the material.

89. Has

*James D. Hume,*
Esq.

16 March,
1832.

89. Has not the change of law had the effect of stimulating exportation?—It has at least removed the impediment from a certain description of goods, inferior articles.

90. And that has operated very beneficially?—I conceive the effect of that to be this; that the fine Italian silks are made into superior goods for the use of this country, and that the East India silks are made into inferior articles which suit the export trade.

91. Your opinion is, that that state of the law is very beneficial as regards the exportation of goods?—I think it has done good; the home silk being dearer by reason of the duty on the foreign silk; the exporter requires the drawback for the one as well as the other.

92. Of course in the proportion in which it is beneficial to the exporter, it is injurious to the consumer or worker of the fine silk in this country on which the duty is paid?—No, it is a benefit to him; if it does any injury it is to the throwster of the fine silk; the rate of export is sold for the benefit of the importer at some price in the market; the quantity of import is so large, compared with the export, that the price is now at a very low rate, almost nominal; to whatever extent it went it would go to the reduction or alleviation of the duty on foreign thrown silk, and so be beneficial to the worker-up of that material.

93. Not to the manufacturer of the fine silk, as he manufactures an article which is charged with the duty?—I am speaking of the drawback; I assume the duty that exists, whether there be a drawback or not, and then the question is, what effect the drawback has. I have shown that it is beneficial to the manufacturer, who uses the duty-paid thrown silk.

94. Suppose it should appear that the duty levied on thrown silk falls chiefly on Coventry and Spitalfields, and that the drawback is allowed on goods manufactured at Macclesfield and Manchester, if the export trade be beneficial to the two latter, the duty would be injurious to the former ones?—The duty is a direct evil to those who work up the description of thrown silks liable to it; the drawback is an indirect alleviation of that evil, and is a direct benefit to those who work up a different description of thrown silks for exportation; while there is the duty the drawback must work beneficially on the whole trade. I conceive that the question put to me was, how it worked at the different districts of the trade; the duty is injurious to Coventry and Spitalfields, and the drawback is beneficial to Macclesfield and Manchester; these were the places named in the question.

95. Is there any party to whom the drawback is other than beneficial?—I should imagine not; except, as before observed, to the throwsters of Italian raw silk. I do not conceive that any fine silk goods whatever are exported; there is no export, or very little, of goods made from the Italian thrown silk, or from British thrown silk of similar quality.

96. Supposing there had been an export of silk made up from Italian silk, how would that be?—They would receive the drawback, but the prices of the foreign market will not enable them to export such goods.

97. Supposing the export to take place, is the drawback injurious to any party?—To none, if the practical reduction of the duty by debenture sales does not operate as a lessening of the protection to the throwster.

98. If it is an injury to any party, it is no benefit to the manufacturer, who sees the article charged with the duty, because you state, that in point of fact the articles on which the silk is used are for export?—It is a benefit to any manufacturer to whatever amount the debentures sell.

99. You stated that the debentures now sell for nothing?—I am told very little; it depends on the quantity; the sum received on thrown silk is so large, and it is so unlikely that the quantity exported will draw hard on the fund, that the right of exporting is very trifling.

100. The value of the debenture, in point of fact, would depend on the proportion of thrown silk imported, as compared with the quantity of British goods exported?—Precisely so.

101. Could any export trade exist without the advantage of debentures?—I should almost doubt it.

102. The duty is paid upon the silk used in this country?—Yes.

103. Then the debenture upon the silk gives a drawback upon a different quality of silk?—Identification is not insisted on.

104. It gives a drawback on silk that in fact pays no duty?—It does so; but then the law assumes, that the price of the one silk to the manufacturer is so much the greater by reason of the duty on the other, and therefore the exporter stands in need of a drawback, just as much as if he used the same that had paid the duty.

It

*James D. Hume,*
Esq.

———

16 March,
1832.

It is assumed, but perhaps falsely, that the throwster here enhances the price by force of the duty.

105. The fact, as I take it, is, that the duty is paid upon a silk, and the drawback is allowed, not on the silk that pays the duty, but on another inferior description of silk that pays no duty?—Yes, certainly.

106. Is not that a bounty?—Very like it, abstractedly considered.

107. May he not have paid the duty in the shape of enhanced price?—There is the qualification which I have before pointed out.

108. Can you make any thing else but a bounty?—I put this position; there is a certain duty on thrown silk imported; it is assumed that British thrown silk is the dearer by reason of the duty to the exporter; therefore he feels the weight of the duty, even though he exports the article made of that which did not pay it; therefore identification is not required, and, so far as the money which is received is not exceeded, Parliament has consented to let it be returned in drawbacks upon either sort of silk, indifferently.

109. The consumer of the silk on which the duty is paid of course must pay the duty, and the drawback operates as a bounty on the other silk that pays no duty; is not the fact so?—The person here has the silk so much the dearer.

110. Who has the silk the dearer?—The manufacturer who works up the British silk has the price so much the higher to him, because there is the duty on the foreign silk.

111. Did not the drawback originate in a representation of the manufacturers of English thrown silk that their power of exporting was impeded by the duty?—Certainly they felt that the export trade was impeded by the duty on the imported thrown silk.

112. In point of fact, it produced the effect intended, increasing the export of silk?—The intention was to make the export possible.

113. If the duty be paid on Italian silks, which silks are used in this country, and if the drawback be allowed on Bengal silks which are exported, is it not a tax on the manufacturer of Italian silk, and a bounty to the manufacturer of Bengal?—The duty is a tax on the manufacturer of Italian silk, which tax is eased to the extent of the sum for which he can sell his right of exportation, and therefore the drawback is not an evil to him; to the manufacturer of Bengal silk, which is thrown here, the drawback, I should say, is rather a compensation than a bounty.

114. The value of the drawback has been hitherto nominal to the importer?—It has, at times, been of some value, but I believe it is now very low.

115. If Italian silks, on which the duty is paid, are chiefly used in Spitalfields and Coventry, and the drawback allowed on British silks manufactured at Macclesfield and Manchester, is it not a tax upon Spitalfields for the benefit of Manchester?—The duty is a tax on Spitalfields and Coventry, but not the more so because of the return of it to Macclesfield and Manchester, but rather the less, to the extent of the sum given for the right of exportation.

116. As the law now applies, it is an encouragement to the use of Bengal silks, in preference to the Italian?—I do not know as to the preference. The home consumption takes the Italian; the export takes the other.

117. If there was no bounty, there would not be so great an importation of Bengal silk?—There would be a less export, and perhaps a less demand and the less import.

118. Was not the effect of the duty to raise the price of British thrown silk?—Yes; it is supposed to do so.

119. And does not that apply to Macclesfield and Manchester, as well as to other places?—It certainly applies to all.

---

*Lunæ,* 19° *die Martii,* 1832.

### THE RIGHT HON. THE EARL GROSVENOR, IN THE CHAIR.

Mr. *William Brunskill,* called in; and Examined.

Mr.
*William Brunskill.*

———

19 March,
1832.

120. WHAT are you?—A broad silk manufacturer in Spitalfields, and a ribbon manufacturer at Coventry; and since the Ports have been opened, I have been an importer and dealer in foreign goods to a considerable extent.

121. What is the state of the ribbon trade at present?—Great distress, arising entirely, in my opinion, from foreign competition, the demand being very good, but supplied by foreigners.

222. Suppose

Mr.
*William Brunskill.*

19 March,
1832.

122. Suppose foreign ribbons were prohibited, what effect would it produce on the ribbon manufacture?—It would at once cause a large outlay of capital in jacquard looms, which are necessary to make the figured gauze ribbons, of which an immense quantity are imported.

123. In what does your distress at the present differ from that which existed in 1817?—In 1817, the Princess Charlotte died, that caused a great stagnation in the trade; but there might have been other causes. I think there was an over supply of goods as well as a want of demand.

124. Does fashion operate injuriously upon the ribbon trade?—Yes; and on this point hangs the most important part of this case; so powerfully does it operate, that in my opinion, the ingenuity of man will never be able to devise a plan by which we can get over it, except by a total prohibition. I should state that this applies more particularly to fancy goods.

125. Are not the present duties a sufficient protection?—No; if they were 20 per cent. higher, then a larger quantity would still pay the duty; the reason why they would pay the duty is, that expensive fancy goods cannot be delayed upon their passage.

126. Do you mean that they would sell if they paid 20 per cent. higher duties than they do now?—Yes, I do.

127. In preference to English ribbons of any fashion, or any beauty, do you mean that French ribbons, however expensive, would sell in preference to English ribbons, however beautiful?—Yes.

128. What kind of ribbons are principally imported?—Plain satins, figured satins, figured and striped gauzes.

129. If they were prohibited, could you make that description of ribbon at Coventry?—Yes; they are all made to a certain extent, and they would be immensely increased under a prohibitory system.

130. What is the rate of duty upon those ribbons?—Upon plain satins, from 15 to 20 per cent., according to the way they are bought; sometimes perhaps they are 22½, that is when the duty is collected by weight, which the officers invariably do.

131. What is the duty on figured satin ribbons?—From 15 to 16 per cent.

132. The duty on gauze ribbons?—Our striped gauzes from 30 to 45 per cent., according to the way they are bought also.

133. On figured gauzes?—From 25 to 35 per cent., depending upon the manner in which they are bought, and the quality.

134. Would not an *ad valorem* duty be better?—An *ad valorem* duty would not do at all in my opinion; so much depends upon the immediate sale, that the importer might give in a very low value, knowing that the officer durst not seize them, being aware that the fashion would be gone by before he could bring them into the market, and even if he could bring them into the market directly, he could not make near so much of them as the importer.

135. Then you think they might be considerably undervalued?—Yes.

136. So that if an officer were to detain ribbons entered to pay the duty, *ad valorem*, in the month of April, he would not be able to sell them till September or October; and they would be reduced in value at least 30 per cent. by the change of fashion; is that your opinion?—Yes.

137. Has smuggling increased since the ports were opened, and why has it increased?—Yes; if the smuggler had been consulted what would tend most to his interest, I should think he would have recommended the very course that was adopted; yet, strange to say, the getting rid of smuggling was assigned as one of two principal reasons for the adoption of the measure.

138. Adopted, when?—In 1824; the Chancellor of the Exchequer assigned that as a reason.

139. Do you mean the measure that came into operation in 1826?—Yes.

140. Why has smuggling increased?—Because of its operating as a license. The smuggled goods which were already in the country could then be shown as goods that had paid duty, there being no distinction between them and those which had paid the duty.

141. In that case they would have been previously introduced?—Yes; but you could smuggle to any extent afterwards, and not be detected; previously you were obliged to keep them in secret places, and showed them only to persons you had confidence in.

678.

142. You

Mr.
*William Brunskill.*

19 March,
1832.

142. You mean to say, since the ports have been opened, goods, however introduced, might be offered for sale without risk?—Yes.

143. Before, that could not be done?—No.

144. There was great danger in attempting to dispose of smuggled goods before? —Yes; the goods being liable to be seized wherever found, and the parties liable to be exchequered for three times the amount, as well as the loss of the goods.

145. Do you think it possible to prevent smuggling?—In a great degree I do; by a total prohibition, and making the offence personal degradation to the principal and agent, and giving a large portion of the fine to the informer.

146. Do you not think there are other modes by which smuggling might be prevented, even supposing that goods were still allowed to be sold in this country?— I think it might be checked; the same principle would operate very much in the absence of total prohibition.

147. Have the debentures or drawback facilitated the export of ribbons?—I am not aware of any quantity having been exported.

148. What is the present price of debentures, valued at 3 s. 6 d.?—Three halfpence to two-pence.

149. Then a debenture, that would entitle the exporter to 3 s. 6 d. a pound drawback, now fetches three halfpence and two-pence; is that so?—Yes.

150. What would be the effect of lowering the present rate of duty to a rate at which there would be no inducement to smuggle?—Total destruction to all the finer branches of the trade.

151. Do you know what is the present rate of smuggling; what goods can be introduced for?—Generally, I believe, from 20 to 25 per cent.

152. You are not of opinion that goods have been introduced at a much lower rate than that?—Except in one instance that has been so much before the public, I do not believe it has been done at a much lower rate than that.

153. At what rate do you imagine the house, to which you have alluded, imported?—It would be mere surmise; I cannot tell what they paid the superior men, but it was a mere trifle they paid for the landing; I should think five to ten per cent.

154. You mean in the case of Messrs. Leaf's?—Yes.

155. Where the goods were handed over the side of the vessel?—Yes.

156. How do you found that calculation?—I ascertained the fact of their only paying 2 s. per cartoon on the landing, which a regular importer must have paid about 4 l. 4 s. to 6 l. for.

157. What is the cartoon?—A box of ribbons, containing twelve or eighteen garnitures or pieces of 36 yards each.

158. Do you mean to say that that was the whole expense incurred?—No, but a very small sum was paid for the landing of those cartoons; if they only paid the other men after the same rate, it could not amount to more than I have stated.

159. What other men do you allude to?—There were, for instance, the captain of the vessel; he would require remunerating for the risk he took; and three superior servants I should more properly have stated.

160. Do you mean men employed on board the vessel?—No, employed by the house.

161. In addition to the captain of the vessel, you have no reason to suppose any body else was paid but their own servants?—Certain individuals that had the doing of the transaction; I cannot say to what extent they were paid.

162. What was the employment of those individuals?—The one had a barge, which he would require being paid for; and he employed another individual under him, I think.

163. You did not, in point of fact, mean any Custom-house officer, or any officer of Government?—No, I did not.

164. Is it your custom to prepare a stock of goods before each season commences?—It used to be done to a very large extent.

165. Is it so now?—No; fatal experience has taught us all to act with the greatest caution, and therefore we are obliged to leave the people unemployed in the winter months.

166. Why is that?—Because of foreign competition entirely in my opinion.

167. What is the consumption of silk at Coventry; is it as large as formerly?— Much the same.

168. Then the consumption of silk at Coventry being much the same, how do you reconcile that fact with your statement of the distress?—A commoner article is made now, upon which a very small amount of labour is paid.

169. You

Mr.
*William Brunskill*

19 March,
1832.

169. You mean plain goods?—Yes, a very heavy description of goods.

170. There is a great consumption of raw material, but with a small amount of wages paid upon it?—Just so.

171. Are you of opinion, that English manufacture is improved in consequence of French goods being admitted?—In some cases, particularly in country places, where the manufacture was in its infancy; but in the finer branches I do not think any improvement has taken place at all.

172. Do you confine your answer to plain silks?—I speak generally.

173. And ribbons?—Ribbons may have improved a little.

174. Is it your opinion there would be any difficulty in finding hands at this moment to make goods of the character you formerly made in the broad trade principally?—No, I think we should have no difficulty in finding as much skill as they have in France in the broad trade.

175. But in the ribbon trade, should you have any difficulty in procuring hands?—At present we are not quite equal to them in skill.

176. Do you consider that you have less skill than formerly?—No, not less; but the ribbon trade certainly was very inferior indeed to the foreign ribbons.

177. Are you of opinion, that in the broad trade the hands are employed in plainer works than formerly?—Decidedly so.

178. Then of course there is no need for the exercise of that skill they formerly exercised?—No, certainly.

179. With regard to the ribbon trade, do you think that in the ribbon trade the hands have improved in skill; that is, that they make a better description of fabric?—Yes, in a slight degree; but they have been very short of machinery for the purpose of making the higher articles.

180. Is the improvement that as so taken place been in machinery principally, or do you mean that the hands make your goods in a superior style?—I cannot say that there may have been any great increase of skill, but they have since obtained machinery to enable them to make the goods required that could not be made formerly by the old mode.

181. Was that machinery unknown to them formerly?—It was known to them in 1823.

182. Not previously to that period?—I think not, in Coventry; in London we had it two years earlier.

183. What machinery do you allude to principally?—The jacquard loom, principally.

184. Any other description of machinery?—The bar loom has been imported, but it has not been used at Coventry.

185. Will you explain what it is?—It is called a la bar loom; it is a description of power loom that may be carried by power; I have never seen it worked by power.

186. Is it a later machine than the jacquard?—No; it has been used in France for a long time.

187. Is it used at St. Etienne?—Yes.

188. Where has it been used in England?—It has been used at Coggleshall; at Battersea they have a large quantity, and some other places; it is used, I believe, also at Evesham, and I understand they have some at Manchester, I am not sure that it is so.

189. Would a return to the prohibitory system increase the price of silks and ribbons?—In a slight degree, where labour is not remunerated.

190. What do you mean by slight degree?—Perhaps five per cent.

191. How would that increase of price be distributed?—It would never be perceived by the purchaser.

192. Who would obtain the advantage of it?—It would be distributed among the various operatives employed in the trade, dyers, winders, weavers and warpers.

193. Do you not think that increase, to the extent of five per cent., would injure the sale?—Not materially.

194. Do you think it would at all injure it?—In the higher branches it would not.

195. How has foreign competition operated upon the morals of your work people?—A deplorable change for the worse has taken place, owing to the extreme poverty to which they have been reduced.

196. You are engaged in the manufacture of broad silks as well as ribbons?—Yes, in Spitalfields.

197. What is the state of that trade?—Extreme distress.

678.

Mr.
*William Brunskill.*

19 March,
1832.

198. Do you mean at the present moment ?—Yes ; I am not aware that any great improvement has taken place in Spitalfields.

199. Is not this the season at which you ought to be very busy ?—Yes ; we used to be preparing very largely for the spring trade.

200. How do you account for the want of that business ; does it arise from foreign competition ?—Yes ; I should say almost entirely ; the weavers of Spitalfields having been accustomed to make almost exclusively the finer kinds of goods, which are now imported from France.

201. Do you not think that the Spitalfields trade has been very much injured by Manchester and other provincial manufactures ?—Very little since the ports were opened.

202. State your reason for this?—They make much commoner goods at Manchester and elsewhere, with few exceptions.

203. Do you consider, at present, Spitalfields is struggling rather against Manchester, than Manchester against Spitalfields ?—Yes, I do.

204. You consider, that from the fact of the operatives in Spitalfields having lost that superior employment they were accustomed to, they are now struggling against the plainer fabrics of Manchester that they did not formerly care about ; is that your opinion ?—Decidedly.

205. Is the Spitalfields trade affected in any thing but fancy goods ?—Yes.

206. I have understood that foreign plain goods have been beaten out of the market ; is it so ?—No ; they are not.

207. Have you imported any plain goods yourself recently ?—Yes ; we cleared a case the other day, upon which we paid 32½ per cent. duty.

208. What was the value of that case ?—About 370 *l.* exclusive of duty.

209. What description of goods ?—Plain Gros de Naples.

210. When you have so paid that duty, are they dearer or cheaper than English plain goods ?—They are dearer ; but there are certain connections that will have foreign goods so long as they are to be obtained.

211. Even plain goods ?—Yes.

212. How much dearer are they ?—About 10 per cent. having paid the duty.

213. And yet they sell in preference to English of greater cheapness ?—Yes, decidedly so.

214. What is the reason of it ?—I suppose it is prejudice ; but it exists, and we cannot control it.

215. You have so sold them ?—Yes.

216. In preference to English goods you had in your stock ?—Yes.

217. Supposing a piece of English goods of the same quality as the French, and ten per cent. lower, do you mean you can sell the French article in preference to the English ?—Yes, decidedly.

218. You have said in certain channels ; what do you mean by certain channels ? —I sell them to parties that supply milliners, who must sell foreign articles, or they will not sell at all.

219. Suppose an English manufacturer had been permitted to make those goods, what amount would he have paid for labour ?—At least 100 *l.* in that particular case.

220. Do you believe that a considerable quantity of these goods are now coming into the market ?—Yes ; I have reason to know that large quantities of these and other kinds are being imported, peculiarly adapted to the Spitalfields manufacture.

221. Have you an idea of the quantity ?—No ; I cannot state the quantity.

222. Do you mean that there are a certain number of ells in a case, and that you calculated the cost per English yard, in making it ?—Yes.

223. And therefore you arrive at a certainty, or near a certainty, of what you would expend in making them ?—Yes.

224. Do you know the number of ells in that case ?—No ; I have not the particular numbers.

225. Do you also import velvets from Germany ?—Yes.

226. What quantity did you import last season ?—Between four and 5,000 yards, as well as many yards of plush.

227. Did you sell them when you imported them ?—The plush were all sold, but not the whole of the velvets.

228. How much would you have paid for labour in Spitalfields, had you been permitted to make them there ?—Between thirteen and fourteen hundred pounds.

229. The two together ?—Yes.

230. What

230. What is the rate of duty you pay upon velvets?—From 40 to 50 per cent. according to the quality and make.

231. And yet with those duties, you still sell foreign velvets?—Yes; we have hitherto.

232. What is the rate of duty upon plushes?—Thirty per cent. *ad valorem.*

233. You pay about 20 or 25 per cent.?—No; they manage some how or other to prevent that; they are rated at so much a yard, so that they get it up to 33 per cent. with the expenses.

234. That rather proves that an *ad valorem* duty can be collected?—Yes; in a case of that kind it is a heavier article, but not on fancy articles.

235. Are not these duties sufficiently high to protect you?—If they had been, I should have made the goods instead of importing them.

236. Are you of opinion that trade would revive in Spitalfields, if prohibition were granted?—I have no doubt of it.

237. You have stated that the superiority of the French goods depends upon being made by machinery in France?—That is a particular species of ribbon, the light figured ribbon.

238. Does that give them the principal advantage?—Yes.

239. And you think if prohibition took place, that you would immediately have an increase of machinery in Coventry to meet the demand?—Decidedly so; an amazing increase of machinery would take place immediately.

240. Are you aware of any effort having lately been made in Coventry to use machinery?—Yes; I use it myself to a certain extent, but it is at a very great discount notwithstanding.

241. Is not there a great objection in Coventry to use machinery?—Not at all; the weavers get much the best wages in machinery.

242. Are you aware of a mill having been burnt down in 1831, in Coventry?—That is, as to the power-looms, there is an objection to them.

243. What kind of articles would those looms have made?—I am not aware what they might have been applied to, but they were making plain goods, but they might have been applied to other kinds.

244. Do you conceive the wages in France are cheaper than the wages of England for the making of narrow goods, or is it in the machinery that the French have the advantage?—Their wages are much cheaper for those kinds of articles.

245. Can you state to the Committee what took place when Messrs. Woodhouse's mill was nearly finished in Coventry, what led to its destruction?—I am not very well acquainted with that circumstance; but I believe it was entirely owing to its being a power-loom, that the weavers were determined not to have it there.

246. Were not there meetings of the workmen held, protesting against the use and introduction of machinery?—The power-looms; we must confine ourselves to power-looms; they have not the slightest objection to the jacquard looms; on the contrary.

247. Are you aware that that loom would have been moved by steam, and have made five or six pieces where one only is now made?—No, I am not aware of it; nor can I believe it till I have strong evidence of the fact.

248. Are you aware that a list of prices now exists at Coventry, below which the people will not work?—Yes; the list was made by the masters, not the men.

249. Have you ever seen those lists [*handing two Papers to the Witness;*] the prices for single-hand work and engine loom-work?—Yes, I think I have; those are the last regulated lists that were made.

250. Are you aware, whether the goods may be made cheaper by an engine than by the hand?—Certain kinds of goods can.

251. Are you aware that those lists make the same price paid for engine as for hand-labour?—No, I am not.

252. Take one; the first list, letter (A.): by that list, what is the rate charged for work, called " Sixteen-penny?"—Five shillings is the printed mark.

253. That is the wages?—Yes.

254. Now look on the other paper, the Engine List (B.), and see what is charged for the same article?—Three shillings and sixpence.

255. In the first list is not there the preparatory process, including winding, weaving and warping?—Yes.

256. If you deduct that, which is 1 *s.* 6*d.*, from the 5*s.*, what is left?—Then they would be upon a par nearly.

257. Then on the one list, the charge for winding and warping is included in the

678.

Mr.
*William Brunskil..*

19 March, 1832.

5*s.*; in the other for 3*s.* 6*d.* they are not included; are they not on a par; does not the piece turn out to be made at the same expense by the engine and the hand?—It depends upon what the engine would cost winding and warping.

258. Supposing it is 1*s.* 6*d.*?—Yes; but it is not so.

259. Can you tell how much it is?—No, I cannot; but there is always a saving to the undertaker in the winding and warping, or he would not do it.

260. Assuming that to be the price, the cost of the article, whether done by the engine or the hand would be the same?—Decidedly.

261. You are aware that a committee was appointed in November, by the masters and men, to fix this Table?—Yes.

262. Were you a party to that settlement?—I was.

263. Were you present at any of the meetings?—Yes, some of them.

264. Are those wages higher or lower than wages for the same article in any other part of the country where silk articles are made?—It is very likely they are higher than where they are made by power-looms; there are a few ribbons made in some parts of the country by power-looms, but a very small quantity; I mean any where but in Coventry.

265. But if higher, will not that operate against Coventry being employed to make the article?—Yes, unquestionably; if they produce an article equally good.

266. Have they any regulated prices at any other places of the same nature?—I cannot speak to that.

267. Was there not a great difficulty in agreeing to those tables, between the masters' committee and the committee of the men?—No very great difficulty; the masters made up their minds to pay those prices, and the weavers were obliged to accept them.

268. Do you mean that they considered them as low as they could have the work done for in other parts of the country, or did they make up their minds without entering into that consideration?—They considered them at that time such prices as the circumstances of the times would afford, and the weavers, I suppose, thought so too; they accepted without much hesitation.

269. You have made a great many ribbons at Coventry?—Yes.

270. You have stated that the French excel; will you state whether they excel in the article by putting more work into the article, or in what way?—They use a better commodity; their silk is of a very superior kind, and they have always been in the habit of using a superior kind of silk to what the Coventry people generally do, there are very few Coventry manufacturers that make those kinds of goods.

271. Do they not also put more work into the article?—Yes; they get more labour in.

272. That makes the article superior?—Yes.

273. Have you not been very anxious to make the manufactures of Coventry equal, if possible, to the French?—Yes; as far as I possibly could.

274. Great exertions have been made?—Some alterations have been made certainly.

275. Have you not been able, in some instances, to bring the article so near that it requires a practical man to distinguish them?—Yes, in some instances I have been very successful, such as striped gauzes.

276. Have you not known Coventry garnitures sold occasionally as French garnitures?—No, I cannot say that ever I did; I am not aware that I ever knew it.

277. You think they are not so good?—We seldom can get them done up in so complete a way.

278. Do you remember last year your giving directions in Coventry that the quantity of work which is now done in which 80 are put in should be increased to 100 in a certain sort of fancy work; will you state whether it was done, or objections were taken by the workmen to it?—I accompanied it with a condition, that I should fine them if they did not do it.

279. Then in your anxiety to obtain a superior work, what were your instructions?—To put a certain quantity of shoots.

280. How much?—In some cases 90 shoots; I always instructed them to put that quantity, but could not get it done.

281. It was 90 shoots to an inch?—Yes.

282. Were those instructions complied with?—No, they were not; they did not like the idea of being fined; they would not submit to it.

283. They would not make the article as fine as you wished?—No, I imagine they would not; they protested very strongly against it.

284. Then

Mr.
*William Brunskill.*
———
19 March,
1832.

284. Then they would not exert themselves to complete the article you were anxious to have to compete with the French?—I should say, that they had reason on their side; in some respects the quantity of labour I required them to put in would give them very little wages; I required a good deal of silk to be put in, and very rich, and they have only scanty wages; I could get the labour if I was to give them more wages, but I have the foreign competition to look to and cannot afford it.

285. As there is a committee of masters to protect the trade of Coventry, did you call that committee together, and claim their assistance to have that work done?—No.

286. Did you not apply to the masters to assist you to get that work done?—Yes, I applied to them; but I found a reluctance in some to meddle with it; they approved of the plan, but did not wish to adopt that particular system at that particular moment.

287. On what account?—They have been in the habit of conducting their business on a particular principle, and did not choose to alter it.

288. It did not arise from any supposition on their part, that you were pressing too much upon the people for what they earned?—No, not at all; I was paying the same per piece, but perhaps getting more done for my money.

289. Your neighbours would not insist upon the same quantity of labour?—No, in some instances they did not.

290. Did they think it putting too hard upon the men?—No, they perfectly justified me.

291. In what way did you ascertain from the committee that they would not support you?—I never applied to the committee, only to individual manufacturers; I had a desire to accomplish it, and applied to them.

292. Has not every innovation and improvement in Coventry been a matter of some difficulty?—Yes, I dare say it has; the weavers have got a very good living generally, and have been in a certain degree uncontrollable.

293. Do they get a good living now?—No.

294. As long as they can get a good living, they have not paid attention to introducing any improvement in the goods they make?—I cannot speak to it generally; I have always endeavoured, as far as I could, to get my goods made as well as possible, and as near the French as possible.

295. Is not this an example of your endeavouring to get a better article, and being prevented by the workmen refusing?—Certainly; I should say the manufacturers do not attempt so high an article.

296. But in this instance you could not obtain the improvement you desired?—Not at this moment.

297. Why did not the masters unite as the men were without employment, why should not the masters unite?—I cannot say I pressed them much; I called upon one or two, they did not seem inclined to adopt the same course, and I am very sure if I did, I should get much obloquy, and I thought it better to drop it at present; I do not mean to give it up altogether.

298.—From whom would you get obloquy?—From the weavers, it created a very strong feeling at the time.

299.—Did you take any trouble to explain to them, if you could get work done in this way, you could come nearer the French?—Yes, I took all the pains I could, and had all the men up; I stated to them that they were more interested in adopting it than I was.

300. What objections did they state at that time to it?—That their wages would not afford such a quantity of labour, and particularly not afford their being fined; and they thought it arbitrary to be fined.

301. Are you aware that at St. Etienne, or in France, novelties are introduced almost every year, and great efforts made to vary the fashions, and study the taste of their customers?—Undoubtedly, more frequently than every year.

302. That is done by the manufacturers themselves?—Yes; the same thing is done in England, only the goods are of a different cast altogether.

303. Have you ever been at St. Etienne yourself?—No.

304. You are not aware whether they find any difficulty in varying their work, or putting what portion of labour they please into the article?—No, I am not; I know they get it for all that.

305. But you know in Coventry you cannot get it?—I do not know whether we shall be able to get it; I hope we shall.

678.

306. You

Mr.
*William Brunskill.*

19 March,
1832.

306. You do not mean to say you cannot get your patterns changed as often as you wish it?—Certainly not; I understood the question to allude to the quantity of labour.

307. Did you make more than one effort to persuade them it would be for their advantage to take this work?—No, I was down there the whole time.

308. In consequence of not getting that work done, have you been obliged to increase your orders for French articles?—I do not know that I have; it is too late.

309. But as you cannot get them made at Coventry, you must get them somewhere?—I can get any quantity made, but not the same amount of labour.

310. Will that oblige you to increase your orders elsewhere?—Not at present, certainly; although I, as a manufacturer, can distinguish the difference between the quantity of labour that a weaver would give me, and the quantity I require, it would not be so with every body. It is a minute distinction, but it makes the article perfect and complete.

311. And makes the article better?—Yes.

312. Does not the public require a fine article?—Yes.

313. Does not every obstacle to that check the mode of supply?—Yes.

314. Was this case you have mentioned a single case, or had it happened to you in two or three other cases?—I never tried it before.

315. That was the only instance in which you met with any disappointment from the people?—Yes.

316. Previous to that you had always found the men conformable to your wishes?—We cannot always say that.

317. You have stated the difference in the value between the French and the Coventry manufacturers in price?—No, I have not.

318. Will you state the difference in value between the same article made in France and at Coventry; two or three leading articles?—I have not got the calculation with me; I cannot give the precise per centages, but I can state generally, that the English goods are cheaper than the foreign goods, I mean they cost me less than those I import.

319. That is supposing you pay the duty?—Yes.

320. In the case of plain satin ribbons, of which a duty of about twenty per cent. is paid, when you have so paid that duty, would the commodity you make at home be cheaper than the French ribbon?—If I was to make it of the same material the French would be cheaper, because the duty is so low.

321. Now the gauze ribbons, made from silk of an equal quality, having paid the duty of 30 per cent., would your commodity you make at home be cheaper or dearer than the French?—Mine would be cheaper; our labour upon plain gauze ribbons is very low.

322. Is your labour very low upon figured gauze ribbons?—No; it is owing to a short supply of machinery.

323. Why have you not more machinery?—The original cost is so very great, we do not see our way to get our money back.

324. There is very considerable difference between the wages of plain work and fancy work?—Yes, of certain kinds.

325. Are you aware, that at St. Etienne the wages for both kinds are the same?—They approach much nearer than ours do.

326. Are you not aware, that since the introduction of the jacquard loom, the skill required for doing the work is much less than formerly existed, and consequently the wages have equalized, the same person being able of nearly doing the same work?—That has certainly lowered the price of those goods, they used to cost a great deal more.

327. Do they not in Coventry keep the distinction between plain and fancy goods?—Yes.

328. If a man can do the plain and fancy goods by the same machine, is there any reason why there should be a difference in the price of labour?—That is not the case; it requires considerably more of skill in the work of a fine article.

329. I wish to ask you as to the quality; how much per cent. are your goods worse than the French?—It is a very difficult question; I should say, perhaps five per cent.

330. As the value of the goods must consist in the quantity of work, suppose you could get the weavers to throw in 90 instead of 80 shoots, or 100 instead of 90,

would

Mr.
*William Brunskill,*

19 March
1832.

would not that bring them nearly upon a par?—In that description of goods I hope we shall soon be equal to the French, that is in the striped gauzes.

331. Supposing that difficulty got over with the men, to put in the quantity of work you require?—They would do it if I could give them more money, but I cannot afford it.

332. Are you able to state what wages per week, the rate you would pay them, would give?—No, I have not made a calculation, but they vary according to the different widths, some will earn 4*s.* 5*s.* or 6*s.* or 8*s.* per week.

333. You mean each individual of a family?—Each individual at a loom; in the narrow descriptions they would not get more than 3*s.* 6*d.*

334. Is that the price by those tables?—Yes, that is the price I pay.

335. What is the highest wages you pay to clever workmen?—We have men that can earn from 2*l.* to 3*l.* per week, one or two instances.

336. Are they by hand looms?—No, jacquard looms; it depends upon his exertions, they vary very much indeed.

337. Have you many such weavers as those?—No, very few; there are very few that earn those kind of wages.

338. What are the kinds of work in which the men can earn upwards of 2*l.*?—Upon figured gauzes; they are very skilful industrious men, that will work a great many hours per day; by working extra hours.

339. You state extreme distress exists, do you mean among the single-hand work, or among the engine weavers?—I ought to have qualified it in this way, it existed to a much greater degree a month ago than it does now; but this is a season of the year in which, if they have ever employment at all they have it now; but there is much distress.

340. Among which class is the greatest distress?—The single-hand weavers are the most distressed I think; in the latter part of January an estimate was taken, and I think out of about 10,800 single-hand looms, there were 8,600 totally out of employment.

341. The Coventry trade has been liable to these changes for years?—I think less so than any other trade in the kingdom.

342. How have they been employed to your own knowledge in 1827, 1828, 1829 and 1830, have they not been pretty well employed?—Up to 1828 they were very well employed, since that time they have, perhaps, been only half employed, not more.

343. What is the difference in work that a single-hand loom and an engine loom can do, supposing the same article; and how much of the same article can an engine make in comparison with the single-hand loom?—I should think nearly three times as much.

344. Are you not aware, that the engine loom, in which the shuttle is thrown by machinery, can make five or six pieces where one is done by the hand loom?—Yes.

345. It is one to five?—Yes; but that is not the way to make the calculation, there is a large quantity of silk to manage, and the man is only shooting half his time.

346. If a table of wages should be so constructed, to enable a man with the single-hand work to earn the same as engine loom work, must not that necessarily check the production of the engine loom work?—There is no objection to anybody increasing their engine looms, and of course they do so as their interest directs them; of course a man can earn more money, a good deal, in an engine loom than in a single hand loom.

347. But if the effect of that Table of Prices should make work done by single hand or engine loom the same, must not that stop the quantity made by the engine loom?—Certainly, to a certain degree.

348. Will not that drive it to the places where it can be got cheaper?—It never has yet; we have no facts to guide us in that opinion.

349. You are not able to state to what extent the branches of Coventry have been copied in other places?—No; but I can state positively it is to a very small extent.

350. At Congleton, do they not make a great quantity of plain common black ribbon?—Not a great quantity; they make very good goods, I believe.

351. Jent and Smeaton, do they not supply a great portion of the trade with an article that was formerly made at Coventry?—Undoubtedly; they have a very good trade, but it is to a very small extent compared to the Coventry trade.

678.                                                           352. Has

Mr.
*William Brunskill.*
———
19 March,
1832.

352. Has not the black been a trade in which the workmen were employed when the other fancy articles were not required, was not it an article on which the workmen were frequently employed in the winter?—No, I do not think that is the case; it is very seldom a plain weaver has any thing to do with fancy weaving.

353. In Coventry?—Yes.

354. You have stated the difference in price; are you aware whether in France the raw article, the article used in the ribbon, costs more or less than what we are able to purchase it for at Spitalfields or Coventry?—Their market is almost always a little lower than ours, exclusive of the 3 s. 6d.

355. You are aware that the Italian thrown silk introduced into this country, is principally used in Spitalfields and Coventry?—Yes.

356. Do you know the proportion used in any other part of the country?—No, I cannot speak to that; it is much the same as usual, by the annual returns.

357. If you are unable to give wages, which you say you are unable to give, in order to compete with the French, if you had the article cheaper should you not be able to give better wages?—In the fancy branch of the trade very little; because fancy goods will come to a very great extent, so long as they are permitted to do so.

358. Supposing you pay now 22s. 6d. upon fancy goods, and you could get it for 19s. would not that enable you to give better wages?—Yes, upon plain goods it would.

359. Why not upon fancy goods?—Upon fancy goods it all depends upon the newness of them.

360. You mean to say that the difference is not a question of price?—No.

361. Matter of fashion?—Yes, decidedly.

362. Have you ever made a calculation to know what proportion of the value of 100 l. of your fancy goods you pay for labour, and what is the proportion you pay for material?—No; I never made a calculation, but the weavers always get the best wages upon fancy goods.

363.—Suppose 100l. value of plain goods made at Spitalfields, to be thus divided, 70½ for material, 11½ including dying, winding and warping, and about 18 for weaving, supposing that to be the case, if you could get that 70l. reduced to 67, would you not be able to produce an article cheaper?—Unquestionably; I should be able to produce it so much cheaper, but as I said before, we cannot govern fashion.

364. Does not the duty now levied upon the importation of Italian thrown become, as the Italian thrown is principally used in Spitalfields and Coventry, as far as the amount of 3s. 6d. goes, a burthen on the manufactures of those two places?—Unquestionably it does.

365. Is the foreign thrown silk used principally at Coventry and Spitalfields?—Yes.

366. Would not the reduction of that duty now paid enable you to produce your article cheaper, or give higher wages?—Yes; I should say that that is a question of extreme difficulty, for it would affect all our stocks, the removal of it to that extent; the throwsters know best how it would operate upon them; I think it would operate very injuriously, and my opinion is, sooner or later we must return to a total prohibition, which would obviate the necessity of the removal of that.

367. Can you inform the Committee, what proportion of British thrown silk and Foreign thrown silk is used at Coventry and Spitalfields?—Really I cannot say; I cannot give an opinion. We have from four to 500,000 lbs. of foreign to dispose of, and that is principally disposed of in those two places.

368. Do you know the quantity of British?—No.

369. Are you aware of the whole quantity used in those two places?—No, I am not; I could not give a probable opinion as to what is used at Spitalfields.

370. Could you at Coventry?—Yes; we have some idea of the total consumption; I have not the document with me; it is from four to 500,000 lbs. dyed, which would be one-third more, or 600,000 weight.

371. Did they use the foreign thrown tram for the shoot?—Not to a very great extent; they generally are inferior.

372. Is not some English thrown silk superior to any Italian thrown?—I am not aware that it is so.

373. Not the organzine?—For certain purposes we have English thrown silks that we cannot get foreign to answer so well.

374. Do

Mr.
*William Brunskill.*

19 March,
1832.

374. Do you not think that the effect of removing those duties on foreign thrown silk would destroy the production of that commodity here?—I cannot say how it would operate; I should imagine not.

375. Are the Committee to understand that it is your opinion, that the difficulties in competing with the French manufacture arise not so much from the difference in the price of labour and material, in the two countries, as the superiority of the French goods, as to fashion?—It is not only the superiority; generally I should say they are superior, but not in all cases; but it is the style more particularly; they bring out new styles continually that are sold immediately.

376. Can any protecting duty affect the fashion?—I do not think that any duty could protect the fancy branch.

377. You say the patterns in France are very fine, and if you had time you could imitate them?—I think we could produce as good patterns; but as they govern the fashions entirely, we have no inducement.

378. You have stated that the distress arising in Coventry is owing to the decreased number of looms?—No, I did not say that, because they have a large number of jacquard looms; it is not that they are decreased, they are increased; but if they have a larger number, there would be more employment.

379. Did you not say there was as much work done in Coventry, as when the trade was open?—Yes, as much silk consumed.

380. Are you aware of the increase that has taken place in the number of weavers in the last ten years?—There has been an increase, no doubt, as population has materially increased, and of course principally the silk manufacturers.

381. You do not consider that the silk manufacture has increased in proportion to the population?—Not at all.

382. That may account for the difficulty?—Partly so, perhaps.

383. If prohibition was to take place, are you quite sure you could distinguish the French goods from the English?—Quite sufficiently so; we had a long experience of that kind of thing previous to the opening of the ports in 1826; I was, previous to that time, connected with a house, where we used to make 50 or 60,000 *l.* a year to order, for the principle fashionable houses at the west end of the town, made entirely from patterns that were smuggled by these people; and therefore it was no injury to us, but a good to that extent.

384. Do you recollect the house at Depolier?—Yes.

385. Do you recollect a large seizure on his premises?—Yes.

386. Alleging they were French goods?—Yes.

387. Were you one of the party selected to report whether they were French?—No.

388. Do you know the facts of that case?—No.

389. Were the goods seized as French, and detained and examined as French, and afterwards given up proved to have been manufactured in Spitalfields?—I should have a strong suspicion there was a very small portion manufactured in Spitalfields.

390. Are you not aware that some of the most experienced Manufacturers' Committee in London were appointed by the Government to examine into that point, and they declared they could not distinguish?—I have already stated that I believe we have as much skill in Spitalfields as they have in France.

391. How are the public to distinguish the foreign goods from the home, when such an instance as that has taken place?—There might be difficulties at times, but we had a long experience of those things previous to the measure taking effect in 1826; and we felt no sort of inconvenience from the smuggling, but we rather approved of the extent to which it was done.

392. Was not it a fact, that the silk was introduced into this country previously dyed and warped ready to put into the loom; and being made from silk dyed in France, the difficulty of stating where it was woven was not to be surmounted?—I believe it was a fact, but I should not say that the winding and warping could have much to do with the ultimate finishing of the goods; there is no difficulty in the winding and warping; we can do that in any way we think fit.

393. Is not the dyeing the essential thing?—I think our dyers have been quite equal to the French for some time past.

394. Suppose that a warp is made of silk, and that it is then separated into two parts, and the silk which is intended to be used in shoot is divided also, and a part is sent to this country, and the other part is dyed at Lyons, would it be impossible to ascertain

678.

Mr.
*William Brunskill.*

19 March,
1832.

ascertain which was the French and the English piece?—If the manufacturer wished to imitate the French, then it could not be distinguished.

395. Do you know whether it was so?—Yes; I believe it was, whilst Depolier had a license to import the silk dyed without duty.

396. That would account for the difficulty, and explain the mistake made when the parties said the goods were made in Spitalfields, when they were made in France?—Yes, certainly.

397. You do not think there is any difficulty in ascertaining which is made in Spitalfields and France, except where the silk is dyed in France?—Yes, I should say there may, at times, be great difficulty in distinguishing.

398. Where the silk is dyed here?—Yes; it is immaterial where it is dyed.

399. Do you think, upon the whole matter, you are capable of distinguishing between the French and British manufactures at present?—Not in all cases.

400. Does this apply to all species of goods?—In fancy goods we can distinguish rather better; but still we are liable to be deceived in them.

401. Supposing two bales of Italian thrown silk, one dyed at Lyons and the other in London, would there be just the same difference as if both were dyed at Lyons, one being wove here, and the other being wove in France; are our colours exactly like the French?—Yes; but we do not make our goods in the same way. In plain Gros de Naples there is generally a distinction that may be known by an accurate judge, but still it is not to be depended upon.

402. But in mere colour there is no such distinction?—No.

403. Are you aware, when Mons. Depolier established his warehouse in London, that we were at that time supposed not to dye so well as the French?—Yes, that was the case at that time.

404. But since the opening with France, we have copied the same colours, and dye quite as well as the French?—Yes, I think we have dyed quite as well for a longer period.

405. Is not the Italian mode of dyeing superior to the English and the French?— I am not aware that it is; but I am not acquainted with the Italian mode of dyeing.

406. You have said, that the morals of the weavers have been deteriorated by foreign competition?—I am alluding more particularly to Spitalfields in that case.

407. May not the competition at home have lowered the wages as much as competition abroad, as you admit the price is not so much an object as fashion?— I think, with respect to Spitalfields, owing to the skill in working the finer kinds of goods, that the competition with France is the principal cause of their distress.

408. You think there is no competition between Spitalfields and Manchester as to the finer sorts of goods?—If there is a competition it is Spitalfields against Manchester, rather than Manchester against Spitalfields, because they were not formerly accustomed to make those sorts of goods.

409. May not that competition produce the distress as much as the introduction of foreign goods?—If they are to be deprived of the finer branches altogether it would be so.

410. If they leave Spitalfields and go to other parts of the country, that would be the effect produced?—Yes, but they do not do so.

411. Do the operatives get as good a price for the work now made in Spitalfields as they did for the fancy work which was formerly done in Spitalfields?—No, certainly not

412. You say, that workmen in Spitalfields get better wages than the workmen in Manchester?—Yes, but they make a better article and use more skill.

413. You mean to say, that at Manchester they never have made the fancy goods that were formerly made at Spitalfields?—No, certainly not, to any extent.

414. In point of fact, they have never made at Manchester what was made at Spitalfields?—Not of the rich goods.

415. But they have made latterly, in Spitalfields, goods that were the staple of Manchester?—Yes.

416. Are not figured poplins made at Manchester to a great extent?—I am not aware whether any quantity of it is made any where.

417. Is it not the fact, that in Manchester they make figured goods as well as at Spitalfields?—Yes, a very common article; but not such as they make at Spitalfields.

418. Do you know whether they are now making more fancy goods at Manchester?—Yes; but that of a very common kind.

419. Supposing

Mr.
*William Brunskill.*

19 March,
1832.

419. Supposing that a prohibition entirely excluded foreign goods, and there was a demand for fancy goods, do you not think that the Manchester people would immediately compete with the Spitalfields weavers?—They could not make the finer sorts of goods.

420. Are you not aware, that in Manchester they make plain Gros de Naples quite as well as at Spitalfields?—I do not think they do; I never saw any such.

421. Are you not aware that a great number of weavers that were employed in Spitalfields, are thrown out of employment by the same article being made at Manchester?—I am not aware of that.

422. You have stated that the Spitalfields weavers were endeavouring to get back the inferior part of the trade they had formerly abandoned, in consequence of now having lost the better sort of trade?—I think they never made any great quantity of these inferior goods in Spitalfields.

423. The distress they are now in obliges them to endeavour to get back a part of that trade?—Yes.

424. Is it not the fact, that taking the whole of the goods now made in Spitalfields, that the quality is much better than it was a few years ago?—I should say not; I can say that we made much better goods ten years ago than now.

425. Do you mean plain Gros de Naples?—Yes, Levantines and plain Gros de Naples were better ten years ago than now in Spitalfields; but then we made them with boiled off shoot, which produced a better article than we can do with supple shoots.

426. You have been questioned a good deal as to the competition Spitalfields receives from Manchester and other places, and whether that competition, if it takes any hands from London, must not be injurious to it; if that be the case, the Committee wish to know whether the letting in a large quantity of foreign manufactures must not greatly add to that injury?—Unquestionably.

427. A good deal has been said with respect to fashions; in all fancy trades almost, does not a manufacturer prepare a quantity of goods for a particular season?—Yes.

428. In order to procure new patterns adapted for the season, is it not necessary that he should be remunerated by a larger profit?—Certainly; his risk is greater than on plain goods.

429. Is that risk owing to a great loss falling upon the goods after the season is over?—Yes, in case they should not take.

430. Then if a manufacturer is to be met in his own market by foreign goods, and a prejudice in favour of those goods exists, must it not deter him from coming into competition with those goods?—Decidedly.

431. Then on the whole, must not this competition very greatly diminish the profits of the manufacturer?—Most decidedly.

432. And he consequently reduces the wages of his labourers?—Yes, certainly; they may have been reduced nearly 50 per cent. since the opening of the ports.

433. You have been asked a good deal upon this point, whether, if there was a reduction on the thrown silk, the manufacturer would not bring his goods cheaper into the market; if that was the case, would it confer a benefit upon the manufacturer and the labourer?—It might, so far, if we confine our consideration to the manufacturer and the labourer, because it would be a check to smuggling to that extent.

434. If you have a reduction of duty, and you bring your goods to market at a cheaper rate, would there not be a lower price put upon foreign goods that were to come into competition with you?—It is more than probable, when they found the English competition too much for them, they would lower their price immediately; we have found that the case it plain goods.

435. Have you not had to contend constantly with a glutted market?—Yes; which is one of the greatest evils we can possibly have.

436. You could manufacture more goods if there was a demand for them?—Certainly.

437. If you have to contend with a glutted market, must not that oppress any trade where it happens?—Unquestionably; that is the effect of forcing into the market large lots of goods at reduced prices; they interfere afterwards with the regular trade.

438. Do you happen to know whether the manufacturers, who have been rather bold in bringing out new things, have been compelled to make very large sacrifices?—Yes; I know that has been the case to a very large extent.

678.

439. That

439. That is sufficient to deter them from repeating the same ?—I should think it would.

440. You have stated that fashion has a great influence upon the price of an article; is there not always in the upper ranks of society, at least, a great preference for foreign articles, although inferior to English ?—That is my opinion.

441. You have generally observed it ?—I have ; and as an instance I would remark, that at the time to which my observation applied, that we made better gros de Naples ten years ago, they were made with boiled-off silk ; yet the French introduced the common supple article, which is of a very inferior kind and much cheaper certainly, and the English immediately adopted it, and it has been followed up ever since.

442. Will you explain to the Committee what is meant by supple and boiled-off ?—The supple comes in from the dyer's the same weight, or a little heavier than it is sent to them ; but owing to there being a gum upon the silk when it is boiled off, it reduces it one-fourth.

443. You think you could make as good patterns, but as you have this competition to meet, you say it would be useless ?—Yes, we find it so.

444. You say there is as much silk consumed, but not nearly so much labour upon it ?—Yes, decidedly ; all the lighter and finer articles are made by the French.

445. There is what you call the round or coarse silk, that is not near so long? —Yes.

446. And which takes only half the labour ?—Yes.

447. You thought that the smuggling which existed before these laws passed, rather favourable than unfavourable to you ?—Yes ; we used to consider it very serviceable to us, it supplied us with patterns and styles that we immediately copied.

448. At that time the principal and most respectable houses were not much concerned in smuggling ?—No.

449. It was done in small quantities ?—Yes, generally in dress lengths.

450. It was done by private families ?—Yes, the couriers used to bring them.

451. Do you know that there is great distress existing at Congleton, Manchester and Macclesfield, and other places where weaving has been carried on ?—I believe it is very general, and has been throughout the winter.

452. Do you know that there has been good a deal of distress among the throwsters ?—Yes, there has.

453. Supposing you could be relieved by the reduction of the duty upon certain manufactured goods, although it would be relieving one party, would it not be throwing a greater burthen on the other party, the throwster?—I should think it very probable.

454. Would the condition of the people, in a general point of view, be bettered? —No, not altogether.

455. With respect to the degree of distress existing at Coventry, are there other persons better acquainted with it who can state it more particularly ?—There are several other persons who can go into it more minute particulars, and who have come up with all the calculations.

456. You have stated that out of ten thousand and odd looms there were eight thousand and odd out of employment?—Yes, in January.

457. Was the trade generally progressive before the prohibition was removed? —Yes.

458.—In general, was the trade increasing?—Yes ; from the year 1814 to 1826, there was an increase of imports to the amount of 140 per cent. and during the whole of that period or nearly so, the manufacturers were well remunerated for their capital and labour.

459. If you had gone on without interruption, and these laws had not passed, do you think the trade would have been in a state of progressive improvement ?— I have no doubt, instead of the increase of imports being about from 20 to 25 per cent. I am inclined to think it would be double that.

460. At the time you speak of up to 1826, though the silk trade had been progressing as to the quantity of pounds weight, was not the raw material worked at a very heavy expense ?—Yes.

461. That must have retarded its improvement?—Yes, certainly.

462. In the year 1824, when you were told there was to be this remission of duty, and that it was to lead to such extraordinary success in your manufacture, and

an

Mr.
*William Brunskill.*

19 March,
1832.

an increase of foreign trade, should you reckon it a very foolish thing for people to make mills and extend their concerns when such an expectation was held out at that time?—I suppose they might be induced to do so under the representation of the Government, but I confess I should not have done it; I had a very bad opinion of the measure from the beginning.

463. Did you find an immediate alteration after the prohibition was removed?—Yes; we were obliged to put down all our jacquard looms immediately, and we were thrown on to a commoner or coarser article, while the French supplied the finer articles; when our customers found it difficult to obtain finer things by smuggling, they gave us the orders, but when they could get them as they now do, they ceased giving us orders.

464. Have you been able to export many goods?—No; I never exported any.

465. With respect to exportation, is it not found that the debentures assist very materially?—I should think there would be very little exportation without it.

466. Do you not find them particulary useful when there is a glut in the trade?—In what way.

467. In assisting the exportation?—They only assist in exporting certain very common goods; then the next question is, whether, nationally speaking, there is much profit in them; the labour upon the article exported is very small indeed.

468. Would they not be sold lower in this country?—I am not aware that they would.

469. Are you not aware there has been a change in the fashions to such an extent, that instead of silks, cottons are now generally substituted?—We have had the trade a little interfered with by printed muslins, and an article called shally.

470. And there has been a great change among the weavers, in consequence of an alteration of fashion, going from the coarser kinds of silks into finer woollens and mixed goods?—Yes, I dare say there has.

471. Do you happen to know, that the goods that have been exported, have been Bengal silks; the coarser silks, the bandannas, and goods mixed with silk and cotton, and silk and worsted?—Yes; that was the observation I was making, that the original cost was so small, and the amount of labour expended upon them was so trifling, that it was of very little importance in a national point of view.

472. Then in point of fact, the price of weaving a piece of grey bandannas being two shillings and three pence, and as two pieces would weigh a pound, the labour on those two pieces would amount to four and six pence, and the drawback upon the exportation would be three and sixpence out of that?—Yes, so that there is very little profit.

473. That is the description of article?—Yes.

474. You mean to say that the superior silk is not exported at all?—No, it is not, except in a very trifling degree.

475. Is it not your opinion, that in consequence of reducing the price of fancy silk goods, and silk goods generally, that as a matter of necessity all cotton articles must be reduced in price, because the public would naturally take the superior commodity if they could get it for a lower price, and those cotton manufacturers would be compelled to lower the price of their fancy commodities, in order to sell them?—Yes.

476. You stated, that the lowering of the duty upon cotton goods last year had interfered with the consumption of silk?—No, I did not say anything about that; but I said that the fancy cotton goods had interfered with the sale of silks; they were fashionable last summer.

477. They were worn last year more than they had previously been?—Yes.

478. Were not there some mixed goods also that came into competition with the inferior silks?—Yes.

479. That was in consequence of the reduction of the duty on cotton goods, was not it?—I am not aware of that; I dare say it might be the case.

480. You stated that smuggling is usually done now at from 20 to 25 per cent.?—Yes.

481. But in the particular instance it was supposed to have been done at five per cent.?—Yes, from five to ten per cent.

482. If it could be done in that singular instance, why do not all those persons who are engaged in smuggling transactions adopt the same principle?—I hope we never shall hear of another transaction like that, it was so very barefaced; it was a case of that wholesale kind of smuggling I had never heard of before.

678.

483. Were

Mr.
*William Brunskill.*

19 March,
1832.

483. Were you at all aware that such transactions were going on before it was found out?—We had a strong suspicion they had some channel by which they got their goods through at a very low rate.

484. Can you conceive any reason why another tradesman should not adopt the same plan?—It might so happen, but we never heard of such a thing before; the ports have been opened six years.

485. Then it only comes to this, that no one has ever been detected?—Certainly; we have strong reason for supposing it never has been done before.

486. You stated there would be an increase of price in the case of a prohibition, what do you imagine that increase would be?—Not more that five per cent. upon the goods.

487. What are the wages a workman can earn, at the list of prices put in?—That would be a very complicated question; some can earn only 3 *s.* per week, and others from 2 *l.* to 3 *l.*; but it is a very rare circumstance for a man to earn so much as the latter sum.

488. Does it depend upon the loom at which they work?—Yes.

489. Does it require a better workman to work a jacquard loom?—Yes; he must be a skilful weaver to work at a jacquard loom.

490. The high wages apply only to the jacquard looms?—Yes.

491. What is the average price of working at a jacquard loom?—I should think under 1 *l.* per week.

492. Do you think there are 100 weavers at Coventry earning more than 1 *l.* a-week?—I should think not.

493. What is the difference of wages between an English workman and a foreign workman, both working at a jacquard loom?—I should think that the English is very nearly double, generally speaking.

494. Is the jacquard loom employed for plain as well as fancy work?—No, fancy work only.

495. You have stated that the weavers were well employed up to 1828?—Yes.

496. The prohibition was removed in 1826; how do you account for their being well employed in those two years between 1826 and 1828?—It took some time before the foreigner found out the channels of trade, and up to that time it was not so much felt; but since they have found out those channels, we feel it the more.

497. You are aware of the number of pounds of raw silk, and the number of pounds of thrown silk introduced into the country?—Yes.

498. As far as the information of the Committee goes, the number of pounds of thrown silk in the last three years was 374,000 pounds, but the raw silk was 3,075,000 pounds; what, in your opinion, would be the effect upon the price of thrown silk introduced into this country, supposing the duty of 3 *s.* 6 *d.* was removed?—Ultimately it would lower the price of silk to that extent.

499. Do you not think the event of a greater demand in the foreign market would have the effect of raising the price?—The foreigner must still pay the same price as we do; if it rose here, it would rise abroad.

500. If the 3 *s.* 6 *d.* protecting duty that the throwster has was removed, and that removal had the effect of reducing the throwster's profits so much that he must give up his trade, what would be the effect upon the foreign market?—It would certainly make the trade of a foreign throwster a very good one, but still the price would be the same all over Europe, or very nearly so.

501. Would the English manufacturer gain in that case the whole profit of the 3 *s.* 6 *d.* which he would be supposed to gain by the removal of the duty?—No, it is very likely he would not; but it would not matter as the foreigner would have to pay a higher price also.

502. What effect has the duty upon foreign silk on the price of ribbons?—Five or six per cent. upon ribbons if a light make.

503. Upon ribbons of heavy make?—I have no calculation by me.

504. Would the silk trade be in a more advantageous state generally, if the supply of thrown silk was foreign?—Speaking as a manufacturer, I should prefer it so.

505. Why so?—We always prefer foreign thrown, if we can get it, with few exceptions.

506. Have not the English thrown silks improved of late years?—I cannot say that they have, although we have some good throwsters.

507. What proportion of British thrown silk do you use compared with foreign?—We use a large proportion of foreign.

508. What

Mr.
*William Brunskill.*

19 March,
1832.

508. What proportion?—I have not ascertained that fact.

509. Do you chiefly use, in your manufacture, English or foreign?—We use a great deal of foreign.

510. Do you use chiefly English or chiefly foreign in your manufacture?—About half each.

511. In what part of this kingdom do you consider that the silk is best thrown?—I think that the best throwster we have in England is at Manchester.

512. If the duty was taken off foreign thrown silks, and the duty on foreign manufactured silks were taken off in an equal proportion, would that have an equally beneficial effect?—Yes, to that extent, because it would be an attack upon smuggling.

513. If the duty was taken off foreign thrown silk, and the duty lowered upon foreign manufactured silks, you would consider that a benefit?—Yes, speaking merely as a manufacturer; because it would reduce the inducement to smuggle to that extent.

514. Are there not occasions when you are in want of an immediate supply of thrown silk which you might not be able to obtain if you depended upon a foreign supply?—No, I should think not.

515. You say the price paid for smuggled goods is from 20 to 25 per cent., do you not know, that generally speaking they are introduced at a much lower rate?—No, I should think not. I know that they are not introduced at a lower rate to any extent.

516. But that a larger quantity is introduced now at that rate?—Yes.

517. In point of fact, they order with great confidence, knowing they will be subject to a duty to that extent; they do not regard the smuggler as the importer?—Certainly not.

518. Are there not people there who regularly insure the delivery of the goods here?—Yes, responsible people.

519. Who, for a certain per centage, agree to deliver the goods?—Yes.

520. Are there not many persons in town, who import their goods in that way, instead of having recourse to the measure that Messrs. Leaf resorted to?—I should think there is no house in the habit of doing it as Messrs. Leaf did; all the smuggling is carried on in that way.

521. Did you formerly manufacture the goods that you now do?—Yes, except figured gauzes were never very much made in this country; but the striped gauzes were very commonly manufactured.

522. How many looms would the 5,000 yards of velvet you have spoken of, have employed?—I do not recollect that exactly.

523. What is the rate paid upon the insurance on smuggling in the mode you have adverted to?—From 20 to 25 per cent.

524. That is the general rate?—Yes.

525. Does that apply to the heavier goods as well as the lighter?—Yes.

526. There is a difference in the insurance between the lighter and the heavier goods?—Sometimes that is the case. I do not know that it is now.

527. Do you know whether that practice of insuring was in existence before 1826?—Yes; but I do not think that the same channels were made use of.

528. Has it not been found that goods have been landed, and been detained three months before they could be delivered?—Yes.

529. On account of the risk?—Yes.

530. And that a respectable man, with one or two exceptions, would not run the risk of having smuggled goods in his possession?—He would not.

531. Do you consider that smuggling has increased at this period, as compared with the period prior to 1826?—I should say amazingly.

532. You have said that for your own part you had a bad opinion of the experiment of the change that took place in the year 1826?—Yes.

533. There were some manufacturers that thought better of it?—Yes.

534. Are you aware of any manufacturers who thought well of the scheme when it was first proposed, who have since altered their opinion?—Yes, I have reason to think several have; some of those who held those opinions have left the trade altogether.

535. Could you instance any in particular?—Yes, if it was not invidious to do so; if the Committee desire an answer I will give it.

536. Not if you think it any secret, or that you shall hurt any body's feelings?—I believe I may mention the name of Mr. Beckwith as one.

537. You stated that it was in November last that the Table of wages was adopted?—Yes.

678.

538. Was

Mr.
*William Brunskill.*

19 March,
1832.

538. Was it before or since that the circumstance occurred, you have adverted to, of your endeavouring to get the workmen to consent to a greater increase of labour on a particular manufacture; did that happen before or after the settlement of the wages?—It happened about a month ago.

539. Consequently since what happened in November?—Yes.

540. Do the Committee understand you right, that what you desired of the workmen was, that they should give a greater quantity of labour at the same rate of wages?—I did not exactly ask them for more labour than I had been requiring them to give previously, but I wished to bring them all up to the same point, which I could not do without I fined them.

541. You wished to impose a fine?—Yes.

542. Was that a new proposition?—Entirely.

543. Had any thing been said about fines at the time the Table of wages was settled?—No.

544. This was new?—Yes.

545. Was that the main reason of the work-people objecting?—Yes; that was the principal reason.

546. You said that the small proportion of foreign organzine was chiefly used at Coventry and Spitalfields?—Yes.

547. But that is only used for the warp?—Only for the warp.

548. Therefore half of it must be British organzine?—No, the rest is not organzine.

549. It is British thrown silk?—It is what we call " Shute."

550. The warp is foreign?—Yes; we have foreign trams also, but not to a great extent.

551. Is not a very large proportion of the shute used in plain goods at Coventry, Brutia singles, and is that affected by the duty on foreign thrown silk?—If the duty was taken off foreign thrown silk it would very likely be reduced a little in value.

552. It is your opinion that a duty of 25 per cent. can be collected, without much risk from smuggling?—Yes, most decidedly.

553. Could a higher duty than 25 per cent. be collected?—Yes, if you are willing to throw more difficulties in the way of the smuggler.

554. Is it not your opinion that a protection of 25 per cent., as far as regards any difference in labour there may be, and any difference in price in the two countries, would be an ample protection to the manufacturer?—I should think on all plain goods it certainly would, but it would not do, in some cases, upon ribbons.

555. Then do you mean that the difference between the labour and the material in France, and the labour and material in England, is more than 25 per cent. in some cases?—Yes, their labour on light articles is so much lower than ours.

556. As there is very little difference in the cost of the material, there must be a difference of 25 per cent. upon the labour done?—No, I did not say there was very little difference in the cost of the material.

557. You think that that increase of duty would not be sufficient to afford protection to the English manufacturer, as far as fancy goods are concerned?—Yes; nothing but prohibition will answer.

---

*Martis,* 20° *die Martii,* 1832.

### THE RIGHT HON. THE EARL GROSVENOR, in the Chair.

Mr. *William Brunskill,* again called in; and further Examined.

Mr.
*William Brunskill.*

20 March,
1832.

558. HOW much did you allow in your prime cost of the goods imported from France, for the necessary expenses, beyond what you would incur in purchasing them in Spitalfields and Coventry?—You mean freight and commission, and Custom-house charges altogether?

559. Yes?—I am not exactly prepared to say; indeed it must always vary very much according to the size of the package.

560. How much per cent.?—It must vary per cent. according to the size of the packages.

561. Suppose you take any certain sum in the course of the year, how much upon the average would it come to?—I think two per cent. for expenses, and two per cent. more for commission upon purchasing the goods in France.

562. Do

Mr.
*William Brunskill.*

20 March,
1832.

562. Do you not believe, in round numbers, it amounts to five per cent., including all the expenses, beyond what you would have to pay in Spitalfields?—No, not quite five per cent.; I should think from three to four per cent., about four per cent.; I speak from recollection.

563. Whatever it is, it must be so much additional protection to the English manufacturer?—Unquestionably.

564. Having stated that a duty of 25 per cent. may be collected, do you mean that 29 per cent. is not a sufficient protection to the English manufacturer for the difference of labour in France and England?—No, I do not think it is a sufficient protection, on account of fashion; on account of labour generally, it would be so; in some cases it would not; it would not be a protection in all cases.

565. It would be a protection against the difference in the cost of labour and the material?—I think not in light gauze ribbons.

566. Then you mean in some instances, the cost in France is more than 30 per cent.; that is to say, that the cost in England is more than 30 per cent. beyond what it is in France?—Yes, I do.

567. When therefore you state that the difference of the cost is more than 30 per cent., do you state that upon any knowledge you possess of the prices of wages in the two countries, or the materials?—Yes, it is from calculations I have made from time to time; but it varies at different times of the year; it will vary from 10 to 15 per cent. in the course of a year.

568. You mean wages in France vary to that extent?—Yes.

569. But in some instances more than 30 per cent. difference?—Yes.

570. You have never been at St. Etienne?—No.

571. Have you had an opportunity of comparing the price of labour in the same article, at St. Etienne and Coventry?—Yes, I have found in some instances 100 per cent.

572. In what instances?—In cut gauzes.

573. Can you state the actual prices paid in each instance?—Yes, in England we pay 12 s., and in France 6 s. for the piece.

574. What would be the price of the article?—They are sold by the garniture, I have not made the calculation in that way; I am speaking of the particular width of the ribbon; but then the French always put a narrower width with a wide width; I am speaking of thirty-penny ribbon.

575. When you speak of a hundred per cent., do you not mean upon the value of the article?—No, in the labour.

576. What proportion of the whole value would that be; would it be more than 30 per cent. upon the value of the article?—Yes, in our case considerably more than 30 per cent., and in theirs, not quite so much; it would not be quite so much on theirs.

577. Would it be less than 18 s. a piece; would it be three times the labour?—No, I should think not in France.

578. But 30 per cent. upon the value of the article would cover perhaps 100 per cent. in wages, in most instances?—No, I think it would not do that; 30 per cent. would not cover 100 per cent. in the labour, but it requires a very minute calculation upon that; I could have given it, had I been aware of the question.

579. What proportion of the wages enter into the cost of the articles made at Coventry?—They vary so very much, I could hardly state it.

580. If you take a piece of gauze ribbon, the value of which when you shall sell it shall be 40 s., what amount of wages would you pay for making that piece, taking what you call the thirty-penny gauze?—About a pound, no not quite so much as that, I do not know any article that embraces that price, for a thirty-penny width usually sold for 36 s., we calculate that the weaver should receive 18 s., that is at first hand.

581. Supposing the price of that article to be in England 18 s., and in France 9 s., that is one half, an extreme case; it would be 25 per cent. upon the cost of the article, would it not?—Upon the selling price it would, but that is for weaving labour alone; there are other descriptions of labour that would have to be included.

582. But as far as regards the weaving, 25 per cent. would be sufficient?—Yes, except in light articles.

583. Do you happen to know whether France imports large quantities of thrown silk from Italy?—No, I am not aware that they do; I have understood but a small quantity.

584. You have understood that they do import?—Yes; but it decreases every

678.                                                                    year,

Mr.
*William Brunskill.*

20 March,
1832.

year, as they find it answers their purpose to produce their own silk, which is the best silk produced in any country.

585. The two articles offered to the manufacturers at Lyons, the one Italian, and the other French, of equal qualities; they would fetch equal prices, would they not?—Yes, I suppose they would.

586. And it is equally true that the Italian thrown silk must sell for the same price at Lyons as it does in London?—Yes, with the exception of 3 *s.* 6 *d.* duty.

587. Independent of the duty?—We generally pay a little more, our merchants have sundry charges that raise it to us a little.

588. You mean the French manufacturers buy better than you do?—Yes; they are not subject to so many changes as we are.

589. There is a small difference of carriage?—Yes.

590. If, therefore, the English manufacturer is to pay 1 *s.* 10 *d.* more duty than the French manufacturer has to pay, it follows as a matter of course, does not it, that the English manufacturer must pay that additional price for his silk beyond what the French manufacturer does?—Yes, he must pay that, at all events, if not more.

591. One shilling and ten pence upon a pound of Piedmont silk would be about eight per cent.?—Yes, eight or nine per cent.

592. Consequently the duty in England obliges the manufacturer to pay eight per cent. more for his silk than is paid by the French manufacturer?—Yes, at the least.

593. You stated yesterday that the labour in France, you had reason to suppose, was 50 per cent. cheaper than it was in England?—I am not aware that I stated it; in some cases it is so.

594. You do not mean that as a general answer, but only to apply to particular cases?—Yes, certainly.

595. What would you state to be the average difference?—I really do not recollect at this moment, but it can be easily ascertained.

596. Should you say 20 per cent.?—In May last I made the calculation upon plain gros de Naples; the English were then 40 or 50 per cent. higher, but that was owing to their labour being then exceedingly low, and ours rather higher than usual.

597. Not looking to particular instances, what, in your opinion, is the average difference in labour in the two countries?—In confining my observation to labour, I cannot speak precisely; my calculations have generally applied to the cost of goods, and I do not remember it.

598. Do you think that the labour in France is one-fifth cheaper than that of England?—Yes, more than that.

599. Should you say one-fourth?—Yes, I should say full that.

600. Twenty-five per cent., in your opinion?—I cannot speak positively to the point; I should think more than that.

601. You stated yesterday, you had imported a particular parcel of goods from France that cost you 370 *l.*?—Three hundred and seventy pounds French cost.

602. Do you mean you have ascertained that that was what you paid in France?—Yes, or thereabouts.

603. And you say there would have been 100 *l.* paid upon the same goods for labour?—Yes, at least.

604. What did you pay duty upon it?—About One hundred and sixteen pounds.

605. Consequently, if the French had made them for nothing they would have been liable to a difference of 16 *l.*, the English manufacturer would have had a protection to that extent?—Yes; but the Committee is aware we are subject to a duty of 3 *s.* 6 *d.*; I stated yesterday I could make the goods cheaper.

606. You said, with reference to those goods, they were 12½ per cent. dearer?—Ten per cent.

607. And yet that they sold in preference?—Yes, in certain channels.

608. What was the amount of duty in this case?—One hundred and sixteen pounds.

609. What would have been the amount of labour to be expended?—About 100 *l.*, it might be a little more or less.

610. How have you taken your cost, at the par of exchange, or at 25?—We have taken the cost as they have drawn upon us, which I think is rather favourable to us just now.

611. You stated yesterday that wages in Spitalfields had been reduced 50 per cent. since 1826?—Yes, or thereabouts, from 40 to 50 per cent.

612. Do you attribute that reduction to the introduction of goods from France?—Yes, mainly.

613. Is

Mr.
*William Brunskill.*

20 March,
1832.

613. Is gros de Naples one of the articles you meant?—Yes, we used to pay 11 *d.* or 1 *s.* and we now pay from 7 *d.* to 6 *d.*

614. Were any of the goods in this parcel gros de Naples?—All plain gros de Naples.

615. You think that the importations from France have reduced the wages on plain gros de Naples from 11 *d.* and 1 *s.* to 6 *d.* or 7 *d.*?—I do not attribute it entirely to that; it may not have produced all that effect, but it must have produced a considerable alteration.

616. You have taken an instance of 100 *l.* and 116 *l.*?—Yes, that is at the present rate of wages.

617. The importations cannot have reduced wages, taking that as an example, to that extent?—We have had a continual glut of goods.

618. Do you know that gros de Naples are manufactured at Manchester?—Yes.

619. Are you acquainted with the Manchester goods?—Not particularly.

620. Do you know the prices paid there?—From 3½ *d.* to 5 *d.*

621. Those are not the goods you pay 6 *d.* or 7 *d.* for?—No, 5 *d.*; the article may be what we pay 6 *d.* for.

622. Do you not think that the competition at Manchester has reduced the price of weaving gros de Naples?—It may have had its share, but Spitalfields would have been employed principally in the higher description of article, had it not been for the importation.

623. You mean to say, that formerly the Spitalfields people did not care about the inferior fabrics being made in the country; they had sufficient employment in making velvets, and a superior description of silks; but having now lost that, they are struggling against Manchester, and other towns in the country, to gain back that trade they did not care about formerly?—Yes, in the absence of all other employment.

624. France having taken up all those superior branches of the manufacture, or having supplied us with those articles which used to be made in Spitalfields?—Yes, certainly.

625. Do you know that it is so?—Yes, I know it within myself, to a very considerable extent; I have been a large importer all along.

626. You are aware that the silk manufacture has increased at Manchester since 1826?—Yes; a low description of goods has been made, to an immense extent, there.

627. Do you not know that they make also very good goods?—Yes, in a few instances, I believe.

628. Have you not seen goods made at Manchester and Macclesfield, quite as good as any you have seen at Spitalfields?—No, not the richer goods; they are not equal in texture.

629. Did you ever hear of velvets made at Manchester?—No.

630. Did you ever hear of satins made at Manchester?—No, I never did.

631. And in few instances only have figured silks been made at Manchester?—Excepting the common kinds, and those have been made to a considerable extent.

632. Are velvets imported from France?—Yes, of the richest kind.

633. Many?—No, not a very large quantity; the largest quantities are imported from Germany.

634. Are satins imported from France in any quantities?—Yes, rich ones.

635. Broad satins?—Yes; the principal part used are French.

636. Are there many figured silks made at Spitalfields now?—No.

637. What have been made lately have been made at Manchester?—Yes, low goods.

638. Are there not a great many fancy goods now making at Manchester?—I really cannot speak to that.

639. But the figured goods made at Manchester are of a lower description?—Yes.

640. You spoke yesterday of importing a considerable quantity of velvets?—Yes.

641. You said you had not sold them?—Not the whole of them; I have sold the principal part of them.

642. You know that the importation has fallen off generally?—No, I do not know it; I know the contrary is the fact. Last year was the largest importation we ever had.

643. Have you been at Elverfeld and Crifeld?—No, I have not.

644. Do you happen to know that the manufacture of velvets there, differs materially from the manufacture here?—No, I am not aware that it does; I am aware that an impression is gone abroad that they make two at once, but I do not think that is the fact; they do of ribbons a little.

' 678.                                                                   645. Can

Mr.
*William Brunskill.*

20 March,
1832.

645. Can you say it is not the fact?—I have been told it is not the fact by the manufacturers themselves; they make ribbons in that way, but not that to any great extent.

646. Ribbon velvets?—Yes.

647. You stated you made striped gauze ribbons quite equal to French?—Perhaps not quite equal, but we make them so near, we sell a great quantity.

648. But you have not the material so beautiful for making them?—No, we are a little short of that material.

649. And that material they grow at home?—Yes.

650. And prevent the export of it?—Yes, they do not allow it to be exported.

651. That is cheaper than in England?—Yes, the maraboo.

652. That is what you use in gauze ribbons?—Yes, that is one of the material articles.

653. If that was obtained from France, you could make them as good?—Yes, I think so.

654. You think it of great importance to the manufacturer to have those materials from France?—Yes.

655. Do not the English manufacturers copy the French patterns?—Yes.

656. And after having copied them, they cease to import them from France?—I do not import the stripe gauze ribbons at all; all we sell we make ourselves.

657. Are they not out of fashion before you can imitate them?—Yes, the figured ones are; but in stripes, we make our patterns.

658. You say you copy French patterns, and when you have done so, it does not pay to bring them from France?—No, that is not the case in stripe gauzes; we do not copy the patterns at all.

659. Speaking generally of fancy goods?—They are generally stale in a short time.

660. But when copied, it does not answer to bring them?—No.

661. Do you know whether or not the Swiss ribbons continue to be imported in such large quantities as they were?—I am told not.

662. The improvement here has shut them out?—No, I am told that they can sell cheaper than we can; but the distance is so great, the stocks get unassorted, and the warehousemen feel great inconvenience in that, and they therefore do not depend upon a supply from that quarter.

663. In point of fact, they are not brought in such quantities as they were?—No, they are not; I used to import them myself.

664. The duty is collected upon them, upon per pound weight?—Yes.

665. If the English and Swiss ribbon fell in price, and the duty remained the same, the duty would be much higher in England?—Yes.

666. The duty may be 50 per cent., that is now 60 for that reason?—Yes.

667. Do you know the duty?—It used to be from 40 to 50 per cent. I have not ascertained the fact lately.

668. When do you mean that was the duty?—Three or four years ago.

669. When you state that English fancy goods are worse by five per cent. than French goods, do you mean that that is owing to the difference of material or the difference of labour?—It is owing partly to the inferior skill on our part, and partly to the material.

670. Have you ever been at Lyons?—No.

671. Have you ever seen the French raw silk?—Yes.

672. Is it not superior to any thing you get from Italy?—Yes, it is a lighter bodied silk than we get from any other place.

673. Have not the English manufacturers improved very much in the last five or six years at Coventry?—I think some improvement has taken place, but I think it has been very much retarded in consequence of the harassing competition.

674. Do you not think, in a very few years, we shall be quite equal to the French?—No, I think not, because I do not see any prospect of increasing the quantity of machinery.

675. Machinery may be increased for throwing the silk; but you think the machinery to be used for the production of fancy goods will not be increased?—No, being too expensive for any profits that can be obtained upon the goods, whilst we are exposed to foreign competition.

676. Persons will not engage their capital in it?—No.

677. Does that observation apply to both branches of the trade?—Yes; the fancy branch we have almost abandoned.

678. Is there any encouragement for embarking capital in the throwing machinery?—I should think not.

679. Do

Mr.
*William Brunskill.*

20 March,
1832.

679. Do you mean there has been no considerable increase of machinery in the manufacture of ribbon in Coventry since 1821?—Yes; there has been an increase, but it has been found to be a bad speculation, I have bought figured looms at a third, and sometimes half their original cost.

680. Are there not better goods making for the summer trade at Coventry than have been made before?—I should say, generally, that that is the case, owing to the list made in November, when the manufacturers were bound down to pay a particular price; and they can have a richer piece of goods made at the same price as a poor one.

681. Did you never make as good goods before as you are now making?—Yes, we have, certainly.

682. It is no new thing to make goods as beautiful as you are now making them at Coventry?—No, it is not new.

683. Are not the goods manufactured at Coventry now much better than they were ten years ago?—I should think they are a little better.

684. You stated yesterday, that Leaf & Company had smuggled goods at five per cent.?—From 5 to 10 per cent., I imagined; but I stated that opinion in a very doubtful shape.

685. You mean, that it is a conjecture of yours?—Yes, it is

686. When you were asked whether you did not imitate the French goods, you stated you could not go to the expense of the machinery; does that arise from the French goods, when first introduced, obtaining better prices than the goods made here?—They obtain quite as high prices as we get.

687. If you were to imitate the patterns, and after you imitated them they ceased to import them, would that arise from your selling them at a less price?—No; from their having gone out of fashion.

688. Can you obtain as good prices when they are gone out of fashion?—No, we can sell them cheaper.

689. When you receive a pattern from France, of the finest and most difficult fabric, in point of execution, how long will it take you to prepare your loom, so as completely to imitate the pattern?—From a week to ten days, I should say; that is, supposing we have a loom that would make that kind of article.

690. What would be the expense of setting the pattern?—It depends upon the extent of it; they vary from 2*l.* to 5*l.* or 6*l.*, or more than that, according to the extent of them.

691. You stated yesterday, that the consumption at Coventry of silk was 600,000 lbs. annually; can you state how much of that quantity is foreign thrown silk?—No; but if the Committee wish me to give a probable opinion, I should say, perhaps, about 150,000 lbs.

692. Are there not large quantities of Bengal and China organzine used at Coventry?—Yes, very large.

693. Is not the organzine used for the warp?—Yes.

694. Are not the following sorts of silk used as shute: Italian tram?—In small quantities at Coventry.

695. Bengal tram?—Also in very small quantities.

696. China tram?—In very small quantities.

697. China singles?—That to a very considerable extent.

698. Bengal singles?—Yes; that to a considerable extent.

699. Brutia singles?—Yes; that is used to a very large extent.

700. Is there much Italian tram used?—No, very little indeed; it is hardly used at all.

701. What proportion of Italian tram is foreign thrown?—That I cannot tell; not a very large proportion; a very small proportion.

702. Can you tell what proportion the Italian tram used in Coventry bears to all the other sorts?—I should say it is the smallest proportion imaginable.

703. What number of looms do you employ in Coventry?—I cannot say at this moment.

704. All the observations you have made in regard to the duty, apply to the small proportion of foreign thrown silk used at Coventry?—Not in allusion to Coventry only, but the broad trade as well.

705. When you say that the duty of 1 *s.* 10 *d.*, the actual protecting duty, occasions the manufacturer of Coventry to pay eight per cent. more for his silk, that applies to the small proportion of foreign organzine he uses?—Yes.

706. It is not correct to say he pays it generally?—No, not generally.

678.

707. Yesterday

Mr.
William Brunskill.

20 March,
1832.

707. Yesterday you stated, in your own particular manufacture you used a very large proportion of foreign thrown silk?—About half.

708. You stated, that since 1826 there has been a considerable addition to the machinery at Coventry and elsewhere?—I said, not a very considerable addition. There has been an addition, but it has been found a bad speculation; for instance, in the factory sold at Battersea, in the early part of February, they had laid out about 14,000*l*. in machinery, which did not sell for one penny.

709. Was that Ames & Atkinson's?—Yes; the building cost more than it fetched, including the machinery.

710. Has there been any increase in the quantity of machinery, or any improvement in it since 1828?—I am not aware of any material improvement.

711. To what do you impute this cessation?—I am not aware that the French have made any improvement of theirs since that.

712. Did you not say that the English machinery was not quite so perfect as the French?—No, I said it was quite as perfect.

713. You said, that the arrangements made in 1826 for the prevention of smuggling were very incorrect; you said, that if the smuggler had been consulted, he would have recommended the very course adopted by Government?—I did.

714. Do you think that you could upon consideration, or that the trade can, point out means by which the duty might be collected, and the revenue, and consequently the manufacturer, effectually protected?—I stated yesterday, if personal degradation for principal and agent was adopted, it would go a great way, in my opinion.

715. That is matter of opinion?—Yes, that is my opinion.

716. Was Ames & Atkinson's machinery the best?—Yes, the very best.

717. You mentioned that the best throwster in England was at Manchester?—Yes, that is my opinion.

718. Are you acquainted with the machinery used by that throwster?—I am not a judge of machinery; I judge of the work; and I have understood his machinery is of a very perfect kind.

719. Does this throwster make use of the same machinery that Ames and Atkinson used?—They have no throwing machinery at all.

720. You stated you are an importer yourself?—Yes.

721. Is it to a considerable extent?—Yes.

722. In what way, speaking generally, do you make your purchases in France; do you purchase an assortment of goods?—Yes, we employ agents to buy whatever we require, in some cases, and in other cases we give our orders direct to the manufacturers; sometimes the one way and sometimes the other.

723. Have you any different rule as respects the particular sort of goods, or do you do it indifferently as to all goods; sometimes you go to the manufacturer and sometimes through agents?—The ribbons have generally come direct from the manufacturer.

724. Is it the practice with yourself, or any others who are importers, to buy up the whole quantity of any particular sorts of ribbons or any other silk fabric?—It is very seldom that the manufacturers have any ribbons ready manufactured in France; they do not do as we do; first of all they make patterns and show their patterns, and take their orders, and then work to order, and send them off when ready; but the reverse is the fact of the English manufacturer; he makes the goods, and offers them ready made for sale.

725. At what period of the year do you usually give the orders?—We give for the spring the order in December, or sometimes as early as November.

726. Do they send over to you the patterns?—They bring them over and expose them for sale, and we order what we like, and have them delivered in any month we please in the spring.

727. Supposing a particular ribbon brought over from France, which should become peculiarly fashionable in this town, what time would it take you to get your looms set at Coventry, and introduce the same article into this town, so as to be able to rival that ribbon of foreign manufacture?—It would depend very much upon the kind of ribbon it was; but a portion might be introduced in a month.

728. Do you think it might be done sooner in some cases?—Yes; if it was easy to make.

729. The question applies to those articles where labour constitutes so great a part of the value, and consequently is more difficult to make, and which takes more time?—Not much earlier than a month, certainly not any quantity.

730. Do

Mr.
*William Brunskill.*

20 March,
1832.

730. Do you consider that, in point of fact, it will generally answer to make the imitation such as has been referred to, of a French article which has already found its way into this country and got into general use and fashion?—In fancy articles they generally become stale by the time that the English manufacturer could get any quantity round; and therefore it seldom happens he does imitate them now.

731. You mentioned before, you could set your looms for a pattern to produce it in a week or ten days?—Yes; then the goods would be to be produced.

732. You were understood to say, that you could set a loom in the course of a week or ten days?—Yes.

733. But to manufacture an article in any quantity, would take, in the case of goods requiring much skill and labour, a period of not much less than a month?—Not less.

734. Then in point of fact it appears to be the result of what you have said, that the introduction of these French articles of fabric to any very great extent indeed, excludes the introduction of English fabrics, which might otherwise have led the fashion of which the French have now the advantage?—Decidedly so.

735. That is the ground upon which you consider nothing short of prohibition sufficient to protect the fancy articles made in England?—Yes.

736. Under the present system of protection of 30 per cent., those articles are brought in at a considerable expense by smuggling; and they are brought in because you stated that a number of the rich and more tasty persons in this country choose foreign fancy articles?—Yes.

737. Then do you not expect that smuggling will be at a greater premium, and foreign articles be still brought in, if that is a taste that is to be satisfied only by foreign articles?—We can judge best of that from the experience we had before those laws passed; the smuggling we used to consider then as a benefit instead of an injury, it supplied us with styles and patterns useful to us.

738. Then the prohibition is not to be entire, but it is to be subject to that degree of smuggling?—My opinion is, we can never stop smuggling entirely, but we can reduce it to so small extent as not to suffer by it, we should receive some goods, but not to any great extent.

739. Did you not say you had as good patterns here as they had in France?—Yes.

740. At the same price?—They are cheaper, speaking of good.

741. On those goods that most interfere with your trade, the regular duty is generally paid?—Yes.

742. Because that does not amount to 30 per cent. upon the value of the cost?—About that.

743. That is the rich figured gauzes?—Yes.

744. The reason why the public will have those things is, because they are French?—Yes.

745. Do you mean to say that the rich gauze ribbons of France are decidedly superior in price, having paid the duty of 30 per cent.?—They are quite a high or higher than ours.

746. Do you mean to say it is a matter of taste?—Entirely so.

747. You state, that in France they do not manufacture stocks on hand, but receive orders, and make them to order?—Yes.

748. Is that the case here, or do you make stocks on hand?—We make stocks on hand, and run the risk of the stock ourselves.

749. Do you labour under great disadvantage from being subject to change of fashions, that the French manufacture is not?—Yes.

750. You receive orders as well as manufacture?—Yes, occasionally.

751. Is not it more the case now than formerly?—No. I should think when ribbons were much in demand, the orders were tenfold what they are now.

752. How far can you go back?—To 1827 or 1828.

753. There were more orders then?—Yes.

754. In your opinion, is it a competition of price, or a competition of fashion only?—It is a competition of fashion decidedly; we could sell as cheap or cheaper than they could, and the public would not pay more for their goods if we had prohibition.

755. You said there were large imports just now, this is the season for it?—Yes, I spoke of a large quantity of goods of the description I have been speaking of, the plain gros de Naples that were coming, peculiarly suited to the Spitalfields manufacture.

678. 

Mr.

Mr. *Anthony Cheeper*, called in ; and Examined.

756. WHERE do you live ?—At Coventry.

757. What are you ?—A ribbon manufacturer.

758. Do you know what are the relative proportions of the value of labour in making ribbons ?—I have made a calculation, with the assistance of one or two other manufacturers, which I will explain, if the Committee will allow me.

759. Will you state to the Committee the proportion of labour ?—The proportion of labour on narrow plain sarsnett ribbons, amounts to 35¼ per cent. on the whole cost of producing them ; on broad sarsnets from 16 *d.* width to 40 *d.*, the proportion of labour on the whole cost of producing them amounts to 40 per cent. ; on narrow satins 37 per cent. ; on broad eight-leish satins 38¼ per cent. ; on orientals and small pattern leys, rather a cheap fancy ribbon, 37½ per cent. ; on satin striped gauzes, 43 per cent. ; on rich figured gauzes, 58 per cent. ; on damask figures 47 per cent. ; on satin figures, 49 per cent. ; on rich lutestrings, 31¼ per cent.; on plain pads (that is waist ribbons) 32 per cent. ; and on rich figured pads, 45 per cent. In all these calculations the proportion of the cost of labour is always considered in reference to the whole of the cost of the ribbons when completed, and the average of the whole of the articles enumerated is 41½ per cent. ; that is to say, it would cost 41 *l.* 10 *s.* for labour, and 58 *l.* 10 *s.* for dyed silk to make 100 *l.* worth of ribbons, in an equal proportion of all the articles stated.

760. That is supposing equal quantities of each ?—Yes ; there are twelve articles, and the average of the twelve is 41½.

761. From what quality of goods is this calculation made ?—This is on the better qualities ; the rich goods, generally speaking.

762. Made by the better description of manufacturers ?—Yes. If they were inferior goods, the proportion of labour would be very much greater to the silk.

763. The same workmen are employed ?—Yes, to make the light weights or the heavier.

764. Does this include all sorts of labour ?—It includes winding, warping, draught drawing, clipping, and all the labour, except that of the dyeing and throwsters.

765. On what description of these works are the hands at Coventry principally employed in the ribbon manufacture, as far as you are acquainted with it ?—I should say on lutestrings, satins and orientals, and small figures and eight-leese of that kind.

766. That is the description of labour that is of the least value, compared with the commodity ?—Yes, the bulk would be.

767. So that those articles on which you would pay 43, 45, 47, 49 and 58 per cent. are less made than the others ?—Yes ; in small proportions, certainly.

768. Do these take up more silk ?—Generally speaking they do ; the gauzes, which pay the highest rate in proportion to any thing else, there is less silk in.

769. The coarser goods, where there is less wages, take the most silk ?—Yes.

770. So that there may be a great consumption of the material, and yet a very little amount of wages paid ?—Certainly, and *vice versâ*.

771. Do you know the quantity of gauze ribbons imported in the last quarter, ending the 10th of October 1831, according to the official statement ?—I have the official statement for that period. The amount imported in the quarter ending the 10th of October 1831, of stripe gauzes, amounts to 10,913 lbs. weight ; there is an entry above, of 252 lbs. which I allow for broad gauze, not ribbons at all.

772. Is it stated in value ?—No, it is pounds weight.

773. What was the amount of duty paid upon it?—£. 14,995. 6. 9.

774. Do you know the quantity of other ribbons imported ?—I have the quantity of other ribbons imported ; but they are mixed with the general description of silks that are imported, and I can only arrive by calculation at what proportion are ribbons ; I take the ribbons to be two-thirds ; the amount of the whole is stated together at 26,636 lbs. 5 oz.

775. Of the whole quantity, you take the proportion to be two-thirds of ribbons? —Yes ; I consider of the whole quantity imported, 17,758 are ribbons.

776. Have you given the amount of duty collected, or can you state the duty collected ?—No, I cannot ; I have the amount stated here of the whole ; it would be a work of time to divide it.

777. What is the amount there stated ?—It is about 15,000 *l.* ; it is in two items.

778. Does

Mr.
*Anthony Cheeper.*

20 March,
1832.

778. Does the present duty that is paid by the pound show clearly that those goods, in some instances, pay no more than from 15 to 22½ per cent. ?—Yes, most certainly; on the article most consumed during the season; these goods were brought in, and the duty paid was not more than 16 per cent.; I mean French satin figures.

779. Was not it understood that 30 per cent. was the duty to be collected?—That was the idea we received from Mr. Huskisson's statement.

780. You have a protection less by that difference ?—Yes, 14 per cent.

781. There is no smuggling in those goods that pay 14 per cent. ?—No, I should think not; the smuggling is in the article of gauze alone.

782. You think the duty could be raised on those articles ? —Yes; and collected very easily.

783. And beneficially to the trade ?—Yes; as far as there could be any benefit by duty.

784. Do you think that a duty of 25 per cent. could be collected ?—Yes.

785. Do you think that smuggling could take place under laws prohibiting the importation of foreign manufactured silks?—Under prohibitory laws I should think it would be impossible to smuggle to any extent; from the circumstance, that if their goods were different from ours, by that difference they would be detected, which a manufacturer can immediately detect; and if they followed our styles and designs, we should be now in the situation in which they are placed, we should have that advantage; if we should set the fashion, we should not mind their following us; they would be in the situation in which we now are.

786. They would follow you, instead of your being obliged to follow them at a disadvantage ?—Yes.

787. Have not the English always followed the French ?—Yes; the French decidedly set the fashion; most decidedly.

788. If their goods come in here in great quantities, and the public will consume them, they must displace so many fancy goods that might be made at home?—Decidedly.

789. You say, that the patterns would be known; that supposes that the people of Coventry, either by themselves, or agents employed for that purpose, would look out for the goods ?—Yes, I should say that they would; their interest would be at stake.

790. Therefore they would not be exhibited in the warehouses ?—No.

791. That would not prevent their being sold by private houses, milliners and others, where they would not be exposed?—I do not see how the milliners are to obtain them.

792. By smuggling?—They are not, generally speaking, the class that would smuggle.

793. Are you aware that a great quantity of goods are sold by them?—Yes; but not smuggled by them.

794. In the event of prohibition, do you not consider that they would smuggle?—Yes, to a certain extent, but not injuriously to the trade.

795. Others might smuggle for them ?—Yes; smuggling might take place to a small extent, but not to an extent injurious to the trade.

796. The exposure would not prevent their being sold privately, in the way suggested, nor prevent their being sold in the large country towns?—I think that would do every good; a lady wearing a bonnet trimmed with a ribbon of French manufacture, would lead to inquiry where it was obtained.

797. You mean, that the manufacturers at Coventry, who could alone know where the ribbon was made, would stop that lady, and inquire where it was obtained?—I do not say that they would do that; but they would attend to their interests.

798. Under a state of prohibition, the moment goods are landed here they are seizable?— I believe they are.

799. There is great risk in bringing them from the coast to London?—Yes.

800. And bringing them to the country towns ?—Yes.

801. Do you know that they were sold principally in bathing rooms and hair-dresser's shops?—Yes.

802. The quantity sold was very considerable?—Very slight.

803. So that, when you were first exposed to competition with France, you were quite surprized at the style of goods you had to contend with?—We had no idea, from the smuggling that had taken place, of the extent of their manufactures, or the style or pattern they would produce.

678.

804. If

804. If that smuggling had been extensive, previously to the free importation of foreign silks, you would have known what goods you had to contend with?—Yes.

805. But you did not know?—No, we could not know.

806. That clearly proves there was no considerable extent of smuggling?—No, there was not.

807. Would not the difficulty of smuggling before 1826, compared with the present time, in your opinion, be measured by the difference of the premium paid then in London and now; before prohibition and since prohibition?—I could not form an idea upon that point.

808. The cost of smuggling being now 25 per cent., if it was shown that the premium paid before 1826 was not more than 25 per cent., you would not say that the difficulties were greater then than now?—No.

809. Independent of the rate paid for smuggling into this country, was not there considerable difficulty in disposing of those goods?—Every difficulty they had to contend with; the tradespeople having to contend against the laws, they were innumerable.

810. Supposing a person had smuggled goods into London, would he not find great difficulty in disposing of those goods in the country or elsewhere?—Very great indeed.

811. So that he had not only the cost of smuggling, in the first instance, but the risk of disposing of them afterwards?—Yes.

812. And was always at the mercy of his servants?—Certainly.

813. Supposing, in the event of prohibition, that a manufacturer was to obtain a commission in France, and put it to work there and in London at the same time, for the spring trade, if he manufactured 10 pieces here, might he not manufacture 100 in France, and introduce them here without the risk of detection?—I question whether it would answer his purpose, if he could do so.

814. If the goods are made cheaper there than here, it would answer his purpose to bring them out at the same time?—Yes; I know nothing of the rate of labour in France.

815. In the event of prohibition, you stated you should be able to detect the French goods by the pattern being different; supposing that a manufacturer in England to make 10 pieces, and to import from France 100 pieces, might he not import those without detection?—I should think he might.

816. You know, that during the prohibition, all French goods found upon a person's premises were liable to seizure?—Yes.

817. That must have left a man not only at the mercy of informers and his customers, but even of his servants?—Yes.

818. Do you also know that the proof of those goods not being contraband by our Custom Laws, rested with the person on whose premises they were found?—I was not aware of that.

819. If that was the case, must not that, with the other circumstances mentioned, deter at least respectable dealers from entering into smuggling transactions?—It certainly would.

820. You live at Coventry?—Yes.

821. How is the state of trade at Coventry; are the manufacturers reduced in their profits?—Yes, very much.

822. And the trade depressed?—Yes, very much indeed.

823. How were they with respect to the operatives?—The price of labour is very much less than it was before the introduction of French goods.

824. Is there great want of employment?—Taking the whole district, there is not half employment.

825. Do you happen to know anything of the state of the poor?—I know very little of the state of the poor.

826. Independently of the influence that fashion has, and the influence that price has, so as to affect the interests of the home manufacturers, is there not also a very great injury by having constantly a great glut of goods in the market?—Certainly.

827. Then even if you could manufacture goods here as cheap as they could in France, and even had no prejudice existing against you as to fashion, would not that itself tend to depress trade, and lower the profits?—I should say, if we were not exposed to the coming in of a quantity of French goods, when the market became overstocked, the manufacturer would decrease giving out, thereby bringing the thing to a level.

828. It has been stated, that in France the goods are generally made to order?—I believe it is so universally.

829. They

Mr.
*Anthony Cheeper.*

20 March,
1832.

829. They do not run the risk of having large stocks on hand ?—No.

830. Is that the case with the English manufacturer ?—Invariably the English make almost all on speculation.

831. Does not the success of the manufacturer a great deal depend upon the advanced price he gets at the commencement of the season?--In a great degree it does ; as there is almost certain to be a loss at the end of the season.

832. Is that loss occasioned by the preference of French fashions?—Yes, certainly ; to nothing else do we attribute it.

833. Then previous to the admission of foreign goods, had the trade been, generally speaking, not looking to any particular casual circumstances, a flourishing and increasing trade?—Decidedly ; it was an increasing trade, and progressively increasing up to 1828, I should say.

834. Has it been as thriving and increasing since ?—It has been falling off since 1828.

835. Do you apprehend if it was not for the introduction of foreign manufactured goods meeting you in the market, your trade would have continued to flourish as it had done from 1814 to 1826?—I think it would have increased still more ; the improvement in the machinery, and beauty in the style of goods, would have increased the consumption and the fashion for them.

836. If you had the prospect of leading the fashions, and had no French competition, could you produce good patterns, and a variety in goods?—Yes, equal to the French.

837. You would be relieved from a good deal of the hazard you now have ?—Yes.

838. If French goods are introduced, and you imitate them afterwards, the fashion, before you could come into the market, must have gone by ?—Always.

839. Can you obtain equal profit from those imitations ?—I should think the English manufacturer never gets half the profits that the Frenchman does on any one article ; they take the cream of the market, and they could afford to sell much lower than they do.

840. Does the manufacturer of fancy goods depend a good deal upon his success in introducing new and fancy goods at the commencement of the season ?—I think he generally provides for any loss that may arise from change of fashion.

841. When the most fashionable people are supplied at a higher rate, the public at large were benefited by having goods at a lower rate ?—Yes, to a certain degree.

842. The tide comes in afterwards?—Yes ; it frequently happens that an article that has been produced for the rich and more opulent class of society is imitated and made of an inferior style, which also affects the value of that previously made.

843. In consequence of all those difficulties you have to contend with, and the risk of manufacturing goods upon speculation, and having to meet with foreign competition, are not the manufacturers frequently subject to great losses by their stocks on hand, and obliged to job at a low rate ?—Yes ; certainly it is the case.

844. You have known instances of it ?—I have experienced instances of it.

845. And great sacrifice and loss attending it ?—Yes, with a stock over produced.

846. Then you are of opinion, that if foreign goods were prohibited altogether, the smuggled goods would come in in such small proportions that they would not affect your interest?—If it affects them, it would affect them beneficially.

847. Are you aware of the price at which smuggled goods were sold before the prohibition was removed, in comparison with the home made goods?—No, I am not ; I think the article smuggled was generally gauzes, and I do not make them.

848. Does not the fancy article lose much of its value if not rapidly brought into consumption?—Certainly.

849. Suppose the case of a manufacturer here under the prohibitory laws that should make 100 pieces of goods here, and he should give an order for 1,000 pieces to be made in France, if a delay of two or three months was to take place between the time of their being first landed or hovering round the coast before they could be brought into the capital, what would be the effect upon that 1,000 pieces?—A very serious loss indeed.

850. It would cure him of a second speculation?—I think it would.

851. So that you consider, that in case of prohibition, the insurance payable on smuggling transactions would be at a higher rate than it is, according to the law as it now exists?—I should think double, in consequence of the increased risk ; I have no data to go upon ; it is mere matter of opinion.

678.

852. Comparing

852. Comparing the present period with that prior to 1826, do you consider that there is a very great difference in the amount of smuggling at present to what it existed prior to 1826?—It has increased to an enormous extent.

853.—Can you give any estimate of the rate at which it has increased?—I can only give an estimate according to my own opinion; when I learn that two-thirds of the quantity of French gauzes have come through illegal channels, I must believe that the smuggling has increased to a degree I hardly dare state.

854. You have stated there were 10,913 lbs. of gauze ribbons imported through the Custom House in the quarter ending the 10th of October last?—Yes.

855. And you have now stated that you think a great deal more was smuggled than paid the duty?—I have no doubt of it.

856. What would be the amount of labour that would have been employed in the production of that 10,913 lbs. of gauze ribbons?—The produce for English labour would be 26,191 l. 4s.

857. You consider that upon that particular article alone Coventry lost the whole of that amount of wages?—Yes, and the proportion also that was smuggled.

858. You have stated that you would consider smuggling to be beneficial to the silk trade, supposing the prohibitory system was introduced; will you have the goodness to explain to the Committee how you consider it would operate beneficially?—I think an opportunity of seeing the style of goods that the French were making would be advantageous to us.

859. Therefore you still think, that the French taste, and French patterns, would be preferred in this country?—I am not clearly of that opinion.

860. What other benefit is to arise from the degree of smuggling that you have been alluding to?—Benefit would arise from the simple fact of seeing them; the manufacturers, in putting together articles of taste, refer, very frequently, to old pattern cards for general ideas and mixture of colouring, and so forth, not with any view of bringing the old pattern in again.

861. Is it not the fact, that in what are called fancy houses, it is the custom to keep pattern books for 50, 60 or 100 years, for the purposes you have alluded to?—Yes, I believe it is so.

862. Supposing you had entire prohibition, is it your belief that you could supply fancy articles to the satisfaction of the public in this country?—I have no doubt of it.

863. Do you not think if prohibition was to take place, that the standard of taste in this country would cease in a great measure to be regulated by France?—I certainly think we have sufficient national taste.

864. You think that the Coventry people would make speculations, and that some article of their manufacture would be the fashion?—Yes; but I have no idea that the fashion in ribbons would be affected by prohibition; I think they would be as much worn, and as tastefully made.

865. Are there not more fancy ribbons made now than there were prior to 1820?—Certainly, there are more fancy ribbons made; the fashion then was, for twelve-penny and sixteen-penny satins, or articles at all events much narrower and simpler than those manufactured now.

866. Do you not attribute that improved taste, and change of fashion, to the importations from France?—I cannot say so entirely, because I have myself seen patterns of ribbons made from 50 to 100 years ago in England, wider, richer and of larger figure, than were made just prior to the introduction of French ribbons.

867. Do you not know, that 100 years ago, or nearly so, the French had an acknowledged superiority in taste?—I am not aware of that; I do not know that circumstance. I have seen patterns of ribbons, forty penny widths, made in this country a great many years ago, and therefore I cannot suppose that it is to the French we are entirely indebted.

868. But then those might have been copied from France?—Yes, they might.

869. Is it not the fact, that the French have set the fashions generally almost all over the world?—Almost invariably, I believe.

870. Would it not be useful to the manufacturers of fancy goods in England generally, and especially to the manufacturers of Coventry, that they should have the benefit of the taste of all civilized countries, in order to improve the patterns of their own goods after having seen those of other countries?—I think there is an advantage derived from seeing a variety of patterns.

871. You

Mr.
*Anthony Cheeper.*

20 March,
1832.

871. You are aware that foreign colours have been very beneficial in that respect?—I am not aware of that; I am not aware that they have superseded ours.

872. They have increased the numbers of them?—I do not know that they have; in the very last autumn trade the French introduced a very old colour that had been long known in England, and I should give it as my opinion, that if it had been made by the English it would not have been sold at all.

873. Is there not a greater variety of colours now than there was ten years ago? —I do not think there is, myself.

874. You spoke of the large quantity of goods which you thought were smuggled, have you any knowledge upon that subject yourself?—No other knowledge than the admission at the Board of Trade to that extent, to the extent of nearly two-thirds; Lord Auckland admitted that two-thirds of what was imported were imported illegally.

875. You state it upon the opinion of Lord Auckland?—Yes, I so understood him distinctly to state; it was stated by one of the members of our deputation to Lord Auckland, and by him, as I understood it, admitted.

876. Do you found your opinion of the extent to which smuggling prevails, from what you heard at the Board of Trade alone, or upon information derived from other sources?—I do not found it upon that circumstance entirely, because the public newspapers have asserted the same fact over and over again, and our own local papers have stated it.

877. You have given the proportion of labour upon a variety of articles, is it not your opinion, that as far as respects the price of labour, a duty of 25 per cent., which it is admitted might be collected, would be an ample protection for any probable difference there may be in that respect between the two countries?—I do not know the rate of labour in France, but from what I see I think we could sell ribbons as cheap or cheaper than in France, but the fashion prevents it; when the French ribbons are introduced, they supersede us.

878. It is not a question of price, but a question of fashion?—As I said before, I am not aware of the rate of wages in France; I am not aware that they can make cheaper than we do: but my opinion is, that we could, if permitted, make them as cheap as they are sold; I am not speaking of as cheap as they are manufactured.

879. Has not this competition the great effect of bringing down the prices in each market?—I do not know how it affects their own market.

880. You know there has been great distress at Lyons?—Yes, by public report I know it.

881. Must not that have arisen from competition with England?—That applies only to the broad trade.

882. It has been stated, that part of the distress here arises from competition with Manchester, Macclesfield, Congleton and other places?—I have heard it.

883. Then it cannot mend the matter to have a foreign competition introduced also?—Certainly not; but I am not aware that we have any competition in those places.

884. Do you imagine that the competition at Macclesfield, Manchester and other places, is any thing more than that fair competition which is necessary to protect the public?—Certainly not; and I am of opinion that a fair competition is always necessary to protect the public.

885. Do you not think that that is sufficient here already, without the introduction of foreign competition?—Certainly, there is sufficient capital in this country; if the trade was monopolized, it would immediately be obviated.

886. Does foreign competition tend to overload the market, and occasion universal depression?—Yes, and throw our operatives out of employment.

887. What is the difference of price at present, compared with the period when the prohibition was taken off the gauze ribbons?—I am not aware of that.

888. You resort either to duty or prohibition?—Certainly.

889. You say you prefer prohibition to duty for two reasons, the one is, in case of prohibition you could distinguish the French goods from English, and the other is, that in the case of prohibition the French would have to follow the English, whereas now the English have to follow the French?—Yes.

890. Those are the only two reasons why you prefer a prohibition to a duty, or are there any other reasons?—The question of price would not arise if French goods are admitted; it does not affect the British manufacturer at what price they are admitted, or what duty is imposed; I think the taste for them is so paramount, that the price is not a consideration with the parties consuming them.

678.

891. Is

Mr.
*Anthony Cheeper.*

20 March,
1832.

891. Is not a third reason why you wish for a prohibition, that you wish to exclude the quantity of foreign goods that now press upon your market?—Yes, certainly.

892. You would exclude the French goods either by prohibition or duty?—I have not said that duty would exclude them at all; I do not think any amount of duty would.

893. Nor do you think prohibition would?—It would more effectually than any other mode.

894. More effectually, for two reasons; the first is, that it is more easy to distinguish French goods in case of prohibition?—I did not say it was more easy to distinguish them because of the prohibition; I could distinguish the one from the other; now they are distinguishable to any body, not merely manufacturers alone.

895. Then, if the amount imported at present be one million sterling per annum, what proportion of that do you consider would come in under a state of prohibition; do you think a fourth or a tenth would be brought into the market of this country by smuggling?—Any thing I could say would be mere matter of opinion; I should say that there could not be smuggling carried on to the extent of 100,000*l*.; I do not believe there could be one twentieth.

896. Then you believe there are two millions smuggled?—I do not know the amount.

897. You have said before, that the manufacturers, by having a large stock in hand, and being met by foreign goods, are frequently subject to great losses?—Yes.

898. And obliged to job off their goods, as it is called?—Yes.

899. Has not that a very pernicious effect upon the general and fair trader?—It affects every one, more or less.

900. Do you not find that some of your customers are often ruined by this jobbing?—There are repeated instances of men being ruined by jobbing.

901. Are you not aware that those jobbings go on every day in London?—Yes; I have understood so.

902. There was a Committee of the House of Commons, which sat in 1766, to inquire into the condition of the Spitalfields weavers, and it was there stated, that a very great injury was sustained, as it could be only a very few houses that could be importers, and of course it was an injury to the great body of traders, by causing a monopoly; do you apprehend that that is the case now?—Certainly not; there are a great number of people in a situation to be importers to a very large extent.

903. Do you mean to say there are more than 15 or 20 large importers?—I do not know the number, but I believe there is sufficient capital embarked in the silk trade; and if importing ribbons was at all desirable to a greater extent, it would be immediately done.

904. How long have the weavers of Coventry been in the distressed state that they are now in?—All this winter they have been in a state of dreadful distress.

905. Do you remember, in November last, an advertisement appearing in the Coventry papers, from a silk manufacturer at Manchester, for weavers to work a certain description of work that could be easily done?—I saw an advertisement of the description alluded to, but not last November.

906. Do you recollect when it was?—No, I do not; but I am confident it was some time previous; as far as my impression goes, it was some time in the summer.

907. You are aware, that not a single application was made in consequence?—I do not know that; I certainly saw the advertisement; I forget what article it was to make.

908. Are you aware that, whilst prohibition was the law, if silks which were then contraband goods were found on board any vessel, that vessel was forfeited?—I am aware of that.

909. Do you not consider that that circumstance forms a most essential difference between what is prohibited and what is only chargeable with duty, let the duty be ever so high?—It must make a very great difference.

910. In the rate of insurance?—Yes; in the calculation of the difficulties, that amounts to a very considerable proportion.

911. Consequently, in the case put of a person who should fabricate ten pieces in this country, and order 100 of the same kind from France, to be produced in this market at the same moment, that circumstance would operate, supposing there was a prohibition, to enhance most enormously the sum paid upon the hundred pieces to be introduced from France?—Certainly.

912. You

Mr.
*Anthony Cheeper.*

20 March,
1832.

912. You do not know the premium paid on smuggling then or now?--No.

913. Do you not think you can manufacture goods at the present time in Coventry, quite as well as in France?—I believe there are goods in Coventry, produced quite equal to any thing produced in France.

914. You have no doubt of it?—No.

915. Supposing that to be the case, and supposing the same pattern to be made in France and England, could you readily distinguish the one from the other?—Generally speaking, I think I could.

916. But you do not think that any person could, who is not engaged in the trade?—I should say that a factor could, as well as a manufacturer.

917. Parties not engaged in the trade could not distinguish the one from the other?—I think not; certainly not so well as manufacturers; there might be some who could distinguish them.

918. In the event of a suit in the Exchequer for smuggling, the juries, composed as they always are, would not be able to distinguish the one from the other, so as to convict the party charged?—In that case I think the jury decide upon the evidence produced, whether they are French or English.

919. You do not know of any instance occurring of that kind?—No.

920. If you were told that in the case of Depolier, the manufacturers in London could not distinguish the difference, your opinion would be different?---I should doubt it, certainly.

921. You would have very little difficulty in deciding between two pieces of English and French ribbon?—I think I could decide without any difficulty.

922. Every dealer could tell?—Yes, I should think so.

923. You do not know anything about Depolier's case?—I do not.

924. Suppose a buyer at Coventry, who was there every week, and familiar with every manufacturer's goods, do you think he would be able to distinguish the same pattern made by different manufacturers, the one from the other?—Yes, I do.

925. It is just in the same way you would distinguish between the manufacture of this country, and the manufacture of France?—There might be slight differences in style.

926. Is it not the fact, that an experienced eye can tell when he sees two pieces of silk, where they are made?—Yes, it is very easy to do so; and in French articles the superiority of the silk would detect them.

927. Any experienced man would tell you where they were made, though made of the same silk?—I think so, certainly.

928. It would be also easy to vary them in two or three months, so that it might be ascertained at once; and if the French imitated you, you might almost have a certain guide?—I cannot anticipate any difficulty in it.

929. If you were told that previously to the admission of French goods in 1826, a slip had been cut away of some English goods, showing the leesure, and sent over to France, and accurately copied, leesure and all, should you not think it rather difficult to distinguish the one from the other?—I think the manufacture would detect itself; the French would tell itself from the English, even though the leesure should be exactly the same.

930. You have stated the value of labour upon different ribbons, and the average was 41½ per cent.?—Yes.

931. If 25 per cent. were to be collected upon foreign silks, that would leave only 16½ per cent. for the labour of the foreign manufacturer?—Yes; it would be so, if that was the case.

932. Is that a higher amount or a lower amount than you think the wages would amount to?—I have no idea of the amount of the wages. I heard a statement the other day that would reduce it to very much less than that; I heard a statement the other day of a quantity of ribbons made in this country, upon which the labour amounted to 16s., whereas the same quantity was produced in Switzerland for 18d.; but I wish to be understood as not vouching for this fact, though I believe it.

933. You have stated enough to induce the Committee to believe that you think the great difficulty is in the patterns that rule the market being always from France, and the impossibility of your being able to get them?—Yes; that applies to fancy goods.

934. You do not make the same description of fancy goods or plain goods that you made before the importation of foreign manufactured silks was allowed, but you can perhaps tell the Committee whether you consider your manufactures to have materially improved?—I have known manufacturers in the Coventry trade,

678.

that

Mr.
*Anthony Cheeper.*

———

20 March,
1832.

that in the years 1815 and 1816 made better goods than I have ever seen since; the article I allude to is the black sarsnets, that Green of Nuneaton made.

935. Did not the house of Adams & Co. in Bread-street, make things far more beautiful than are made now?—I am not aware of that; they certainly made beautiful goods.

936. You are not aware of any great improvement intrinsically, setting aside the question of difference?—There is an improvement since that period; we have now the jacquard loom that produces different patterns; setting that aside, there is no advantage gained at present.

937. That is an advantage gained since the opening of the trade?—They were in existence in Coventry before that circumstance took place.

938. For how long before were they in existence at Coventry?—Two years, I believe.

939. Have they increased much?—Yes, they have.

---

*Veneris, 23° die Martii,* 1832.

———

## THE RIGHT HON. THE EARL GROSVENOR, IN THE CHAIR.

———

*Benjamin Poole,* called in; and Examined.

*Benjamin Poole.*

———

940. WHERE do you reside?—At Coventry.

941. What are you?—I am a ribbon weaver.

942. How long have you resided at Coventry?—I was born at Coventry, and have resided there ever since, 32 years.

943. Have you any knowledge of the condition of the working classes of society there?—I have; and my knowledge enables me to say, that the condition of the working classes of Coventry is one of the most complete distress; and in my recollection it has never been so great as at the present time, particularly affecting persons in the ribbon trade.

944. How long have you perceived that distress to exist?—More particularly these last three years.

945. What are the particular descriptions of manufacture carried on at Coventry?—The two principal branches of manufacture are the ribbon trade and the watch trade.

946. On which of those branches are the greatest number of persons depending for a livelihood?—Decidedly the ribbon trade.

947. Have any improvements taken place lately in the manufactures of Coventry?—Not in the last three, four or five years, or beyond that time, I do not remember any that have taken place within seven years.

948. Do you mean that no improvements have taken place since the introduction of foreign manufactured ribbons?—There have not, to my knowledge; the machinery we have now in use, was in use prior to that time, for a considerable length of time.

949. Has it increased?—Not latterly; the machinery used in the fancy branch of the ribbon trade has not increased.

950. Is there any indisposition shown by the working classes to the introduction of machinery at Coventry?—Never; the improvements that have taken place were received with alacrity by the working hands at Coventry, at the time of their introduction.

951. What is the reason that the machinery you already possess, has not been more generally adopted?—The manifest reason appears to me to be, that the very low profits of the manufacturers will not warrant them in speculating, by laying money out in machinery; and the poverty of the working classes is so great, they cannot procure it on their own account.

952. Then to what do you attribute the want of employment you have alluded to, if that machinery did not interfere with you?—I attribute the want of employment to the fact that ribbons of a certain description are in great demand in this country, and those ribbons are supplied by foreign artizans, and that we have artizans destitute of employment, competent and anxious to supply that demand by their own hand labour.

953. Is it not your belief that the introduction of foreign manufactured goods has given a stimulus to the improvements in machinery you know to exist in Coventry?—My opinion is, it has rather prevented it than otherwise of late years.

954. Is

*Benjamin Poole.*

23 March,
1832.

954. Is it your opinion, that if foreign manufactured ribbons had not been introduced, the machinery would have been extended in quantity?—I believe it would have been in more general use than at this time.

955. About what is the general rate of wages in Coventry?—In the plain branches from 9 s. to 12 s. 6 d. per week, and that is the greatest extent that any ribbon weaver can earn by employment.

956. In the fancy branches, will you say what it is?—From about 14 s. to 16 s. the extent of the earnings in the fancy branch.

957. You are speaking of the wages that they can earn?—Yes, with full employment.

958. Do they find employment at that rate of wages?—By no means the whole number.

959. Has any considerable reduction of wages taken place in the last few years? —A very considerable reduction has taken place in the wages of ribbon weavers since 1826.

960. Was the rate of wages generally uniform and steady previous to that time? —Yes, generally so; and, as a proof of it, I may say that the rate of wages from 1804 to 1824 was not diminished more than four or five per cent.

961. Do you recollect whether any particular distress existed in Coventry about 1816 and 1817?—Yes, there was very great distress prevailing at that time in Coventry.

962. To what do you attribute that distress?—In the ribbon trade, about 1812, a considerable demand arose for ribbons, and an increase of hands was in requisition, and brought into exercise; a depression, to my knowledge, took place about 1815, and in addition to this depression, a disbanding of the militia occurred, which sent home a great many men who had no other resource to look to but the ribbon trade, they having been brought up to it in their younger years; this, added to the depression occasioned by the diminution of the demand, increased the distress, and it continued up to 1816 and 1817, when it was further protracted by the decease of the Princess Charlotte.

963. You first perceived the distress about 1815?—Yes.

964. Were the poor-rates of Coventry high at that time?—Very high.

965. What is the amount of poor-rates at present in Coventry?—The total amount of poor-rates for the year ending April 1831, was 17,792 l. 7 s. 9 d.

[*The Witness delivered in a Paper.*]

AN ACCOUNT of the Sums expended in the United Parishes of the City of *Coventry*, by WEEKLY PAYMENTS to the Permanent and Casual OUT POOR of the same City, in each of the Years ending April, from 1815 to 1831, with the Gross Amount of Parish Expenditure for each Year; also the Average Price of Wheat.

| YEAR. | Permanent Poor. | | | Casual Poor. | | | Gross Parochial Expenditure. | | | Average Price of Wheat. | |
|---|---|---|---|---|---|---|---|---|---|---|---|
| | £. | s. | d. | £. | s. | d. | £. | s. | d. | s. | d. |
| 1815 - | 3,586 | 18 | 3 | 1,299 | 11 | 9 ½ | 12,081 | — | 8 | 63/8 | |
| 1816 - | 3,671 | 10 | — | 1,480 | — | 11 | 10,856 | 9 | 11 | 76/2 | |
| 1817 - | 3,886 | 15 | 2 | 7,818 | — | 8 ½ | 17,547 | 14 | 4 | 94/. | |
| 1818 - | 4,516 | 9 | 10 | 6,324 | 18 | 1 | 18,015 | 14 | 5 ½ | 83/8 | |
| 1819 - | 4,357 | 4 | 10 | 4,236 | 10 | 2 | 16,142 | 1 | 9 | 72/3 | |
| 1820 - | 4,275 | 17 | 4 | 4,253 | 1 | 6 | 15,684 | 1 | — ½ | 65/10 | |
| 1821 - | 4,650 | 8 | 11 ½ | 4,084 | 11 | 3 | 14,891 | 17 | 9 ½ | 54/5 | |
| 1822 - | 4,366 | 7 | 8 | 3,575 | 16 | 7 | 14,583 | 15 | 5 | 43/3 | |
| 1823 - | 4,199 | 5 | 7 | 2,389 | 11 | 5 | 12,734 | 5 | 5 | 51/9 | |
| 1824 - | 3,762 | 1 | 2 | 2,394 | 4 | — | 12,352 | 1 | 2 ½ | 62/. | |
| 1825 - | 3,740 | 18 | 9 | 2,127 | 12 | 10 | 11,280 | 2 | 6 | 66/6 | |
| 1826 - | 3,676 | 18 | — | 2,069 | 2 | 3 | 11,868 | 9 | 7 | 57/. | |
| 1827 - | 4,132 | 13 | 10 | 2,829 | 15 | 7 | 13,783 | 17 | 10 | 56/9 | |
| 1828 - | 3,917 | 13 | — | 2,056 | 16 | — | 11,877 | 6 | 9 | 60/6 | |
| 1829 - | 4,001 | 4 | 4 | 2,885 | 1 | — | 13,789 | 11 | 4 | 65/3 | |
| 1830 - | 4,305 | 4 | 4 | 9,278 | 10 | 10 | 23,138 | 17 | 4 | — | |
| 1831 - | 4,305 | 5 | 3 | 4,087 | 4 | 10 | 17,792 | 7 | 9 | — | |
| Three Quarters | 2,920 | 18 | 6 | 2,776 | 3 | 1 | 12,569 | 11 | 9 | — | |

12 March 1832.  (Examined)  *Rob* Abbott.

*Benjamin Poole.*

23 March,
1832.

AN ACCOUNT of the AVERAGE WEEKLY EARNINGS of WEAVERS, *having full employment* in the PLAIN RIBBON TRADE, including SATINS and SARSNETTS, from the Year 1815 to 1832.

| YEARS. | Per Week. | |
|---|---|---|
| | s. | d. |
| 1815 - - - | 18 | 1 ½ |
| 1816 - - - | | |
| 1817 - - - | 14 | 6 |
| 1818 - - - | | |
| 1819 - - - | 18 | 1 ½ |
| 1820 - - - | — | — |
| 1821 - - - | — | — |
| 1822 - - - | — | — |
| 1823 - - - | — | — |
| 1824 - - - | 17 | — |
| 1825 - - - | — | — |
| 1826 - - - | 14 | — |
| 1827 - - - | — | — |
| 1828 - - - | — | — |
| 1829 - - - | 10 | 10 |
| 1830 - - - | — | — |
| 1831 - - - | — | — |
| 1832 - - - | — | — |

Various prices paid in these years, but not correct; average about 14/6 - - { 1816, 1817, 1818 }

In putting in the above Statements, the Witness feels called upon to say, that the average is somewhat higher than would otherwise be, in consequence of including satin ribbons, and that the proportion of plain satin looms to those of plain sarsnett, is not more than as one to twenty. Also, that in addition to a reduction of wages of about twenty-five per cent. since 1824, the income of a weaver is further diminished by the charge of 1 s. per week loom hire. This, however, is included in the average as given above.

966. Do the working classes at Coventry, particularly the ribbon-weavers, contribute to the poor-rates?—Of late years they have not, and by far the greatest proportion do not at this time, and have not for some time.

967. It appears that the poor-rates for the year ending April 1830, in Coventry, were much higher than at present; how do you account for this?—When I obtained the statement, I observed a manifest difference between the year ending April 1830 and the last year; I gave myself the trouble to inquire how it occurred, and I went to a director, who was in office in 1829. The explanation he gave me was this: that at that time they had what was denominated a very liberal board, and they distributed the rates more liberal than was usual, and at the close of the year they found themselves upwards of 3,000l. in debt. A choice of directors took place in April 1831, and a resolution was determined upon, to adopt a different system, a more saving mode of distributing the poor-rates, in order to liquidate the debt, and make the rates collected spend according to the applications for relief; and in consequence of this determination, the rate per head allowed to the poor was very greatly diminished; and this will be explained, in a great measure, by stating the amount paid to the casual poor in the quarter ending April 1830, and the quarter commencing April 1830. The sum distributed by public payments to the casual poor in the city of Coventry, for the quarter ending April, 21st, 1830, amounted to 2,818l. 8s. The sum distributed to the same class of persons, for the quarter ending the 21st of July 1830, was 1,134l. 6s. 3d., a little more than one-third of the amount paid in the previous quarter.

968. You have stated that the distress never was so great in Coventry; in what trade is it, in the engine or the hand loom trade?—The engine trade is the prevailing trade at Coventry; there are very few single hand looms in Coventry.

969. You speak of the engine loom trade?—Yes.

970. You have stated that you have been thirty-two years in Coventry; do you recollect a Committee of this House in 1818, appointed to inquire into the ribbon-trade?—I know there was a Committee at that time.

971. Are you aware whether the distress as stated then, or now, is the greatest?—My opinion is, that the distress as stated now is the greatest; for this reason, that the distress at that time was not confined to the ribbon-trade, but to the watch-trade also; and by referring to the records of The House of Commons, it will be

found

found there is the Report of a Committee appointed to inquire into the distressed state of the watch trade, which was instituted at the same time.

*Benjamin Poole.*

23 March, 1832.

972. Was it a protracted distress?—It was; it continued for two or three years in the watch trade; their petition was forwarded to The House of Commons in 1816.

973. How long was the ribbon trade in a state of distress then?—The distress in that trade began in 1815, continued through 1816, and also through 1817, for the reason I have assigned, the death of the Princess Charlotte, and the consequent mourning; but in 1819 the ribbon trade had recovered itself, and a considerable rise of wages took place.

974. When did the present distress commence?—In the ribbon trade alone it has existed without intermission, I may say, I will not say always in the same degree, but there has been a vast number of hands out of employment, to my certain knowledge, for the last three years.

975. Are you aware that in 1818, Mr. Carter stated before a Committee of this House, that the ribbon weavers had suffered great privations and distress, in consequence of the inadequate wages paid for labour, which had the effect of reducing hundreds of them to seek relief from the poor rates, instead of contributing as formerly?—I am not aware of the nature of Mr. Carter's Evidence, but I am ready to admit such might be the fact.

976. You were understood to say in 1818, the distress had been less; that it began in 1815, and continued in 1816, but was lessened in 1818?—Yes.

977. Then the Evidence at that time taken could not be correct, or your Evidence now is not consistent with that Evidence?—I am not exactly certain as to the object of the question.

978. Were you understood to say, that in 1818 the distress had disappeared?—It had considerably diminished.

979. That it was greatest in 1817?—Yes; and by reference to the poor rates at that time, so far as it can be considered Evidence, it will bear me out in that opinion.

980. You have stated that the wages are from 9 s. to 12 s., will you state what part of the year you receive those wages; do you speak of the average of the whole year?—I speak of the average of the whole year, provided that a man has full employment at the present rate of wages; but in addition to this, we have a vast number of hands entirely destitute of employ, and who cannot earn any thing.

981. How many hours work do you consider them to perform?—From fourteen to sixteen; and I believe in some parts of the year, it extends so far as eighteen hours a day.

982. Are you aware that William Pears, in 1818, when asked this question, what can a man earn in a single hand loom? said, in a single hand loom, upon sarsnets, a man cannot earn more than 6 s. if he works from twelve to fourteen hours a day, each day alike; you say he can earn from 9 s. to 12 s.?—The witness there alludes to the single hand trade; I am speaking of the engine loom.

983. Then you are not able to say what the single hand looms now can earn?—No, I am not.

984. Samuel Makin was asked, " What does the engine weaver now earn upon an average?" the answer is, " There is a great deal of difference; but, according to the nearest calculation, I should say about 10 s.; that is as near as I can tell?"—That refers to the plain trade, engine weavers.

985. Did you not allude to the plain work, when you said that a plain weaver got from 9 s. to 12 s.?—I did.

986. Then, if 10 s. at that period only was paid, you do not mean to say the wages are now decreased, and less than they were at that time?—I am certain, so far as the price paid for different articles is concerned, that they have considerably diminished since that time; I cannot speak to the correctness of the Evidence of 1818, but I can certify to the correctness of what I say myself; I have made my calculation accurately, with an intention not to underrate the truth.

987. If it was stated by Mr. Makin that from 10 s. to 18 s. a week was the average wages for an engine weaver, you do not consider that that was correct?—I will not vouch for the correctness of it; I can only certify to my own statement; but I think that at the time that was given in evidence, that there were no hands out of employment; if you refer to the evidence of Peter Gregory, Mr. Fletcher and Mr. Dalby, you will find that stated.

988. Do you receive any assistance in the earning of these wages, from 9 s to 12 s.?—No, not in the plain trade.

989. Do you pay any thing out of it to any body to assist you?—There is nothing regularly to be deducted from it.

678.

990. Have

*Benjamin Poole.*

23 March,
1832.

990. Have you any thing to pay for quill winding?—I have deducted it.

991. Are there more people out of employment now than there were in 1818?—I do not know that there were any out of employment at that time, but my own knowledge is, that there are a great number destitute of it now.

992. Are you sure that there were not thousands out of employment at that time?—I cannot speak to that.

993. Do you speak of wages received from the undertakers or the manufacturers?—When I speak of the engine trade, I speak of the wages received from the manufacturers.

994. What is the difference between the wages received direct from the manufacturers and the undertakers?—The wages received by the journeymen from the undertakers is the same as received by the journeyman from the manufacturer.

995. Explain what is the nature of the undertaker at Coventry?—The undertaker is the individual who receives the silk as it comes from the dyers; he receives it from the manufacturers; his business is to get it manufactured into certain articles, as directed by the manufacturer; in doing which he employs what is denominated the journey hand. The undertaker is answerable that they are produced of such quality and nature as the manufacturer prescribes, for which he finds looms, tackling and room for the machinery employed in the manufacture; he receives it from the manufacturer, and returns it to him.

996. Do you know what proportion of the work is done in Coventry by undertakers?—Very little in Coventry; I am not aware of any.

997. Is not the system of undertaking abolished in Coventry by the engine looms?—Yes.

998. They are principally used?—Yes.

999. In the engine looms the master finds the warp, and gives out to the men the article ready for manufacture?—Yes.

1000. And your observation is made upon the engine receiving the material so prepared?—Yes.

1001. Are the undertakers more employed in the villages round Coventry?—Yes, entirely in the single-handed branch.

1002. You have stated that no improvement has taken place in the ribbon trade in the last three years at Coventry?—I say the last seven years in the machinery.

1003. Are you aware whether improvements have taken place in any other parts of the country in weaving ribbons?—I am not aware of any.

1004. The loom you speak of is the engine loom commonly called the Dutch loom?—Yes; I believe it is called the Dutch loom, not exclusively; the Dutch loom is used in the plain branches of the engine trade.

1005. How many widths can an engine loom make, from 3 to 40?—From 4 to 28; and there formerly used to be some of the number of 36. They made an article called halfpenny Chinas, but there are very few of that number now.

1006. You mean that kind of narrow ribbon which was usually sold for 3 s. 6 d. a gross?—I do not know what it was sold for, but the 24 or 28 is generally now used for twopenny sarsnett.

1007. Do you know what the a-la-bar loom is?—I do not know exactly the nature of the a-la-bar loom, except that it is an extraordinary power applied to machinery for weaving ribbons, but I am not acquainted with it.

1008. You are not aware that it is an engine by which ribbons can be woven by steam or other power?—I have heard that engine looms have been worked for ribbons by steam.

1009. You say, no indisposition has been shown to receive improvements in Coventry, by the men?—Yes.

1010. Do you know Mr. Woodhouse there?—Yes.

1011. Did not Mr. Beck attempt to set up a manufactory for Messrs. Woodhouse?—I am not aware exactly who Mr. Beck acted for; but I know there was a Mr. Beck in Coventry, who set up engine looms, to work by steam.

1012. Were not those looms destroyed by the workmen?—Looms were destroyed about November last.

1013. Was not there a public meeting of the workmen on some early day in November; were you one of those assembled?—There was a meeting on the 7th of November, in the morning, and I attended it.

1014. Are you one of the committee appointed there?—I am not.

1015. What was the object of that meeting of the workmen?—I will take the

liberty

liberty of briefly stating the circumstances that induced that meeting, which were these; but I will first state my reason for saying what I have in reference to improvements in machinery. In 1819, 1820, 1821, and in 1822, at various periods in one or other of those years, three different improvements in the ribbon machinery were introduced, one by Mr. Thompson, one by Mr. Sawbridge, and another by a Mr. Goddard; and finally, in 1822 or 1823, the jacquard machines were introduced, which are now generally used in the figured trade; and in none of those cases was any opposition shown to the introduction of that machinery, but it was cheerfully and readily adopted by all whom it was set before.

*Benjamin Poole.*

23 March,
1832.

1016. What was the nature of those improvements; the Committee know what was the nature of the jacquard?—I am not aware of the nature of them any further than that they were considered a great improvement upon the manufacture of figured ribbons.

1017. Do you mean that they improved the figure, or increased the quantity of work?—Improved the quality of goods manufactured, and afforded greater facility for their production.

1018. Did these improvements save labour in the manufacture of ribbons as well as improve the quality?—In some instances I believe the labour was considerably saved.

1019. Have you ever yourself worked with any of those improvements?—I am not particularly conversant with the nature of them. The circumstances which induced the meeting were these; a very great number of hands were entirely destitute of employment at that time, and a great reduction of wages had taken place in the prices for weaving articles, particularly in the single hand loom, and in the greater widths in the engine loom; a list of prices was in existence which had never been abandoned fairly by either the masters or workmen, and generally it was thought desirable to come to some understanding, either to obtain a reason why the list of prices should be departed from, or to endeavour to get a list of prices that should introduce an equality of wages for the same article throughout the trade, so that one manufacturer might not be manufacturing the same article at half the price for making as another; this was the only object of the meeting which took place upon the morning of the 7th of November; a provisional committee was then appointed to wait upon the manufacturers to know their opinions upon the subject, and to obtain, if possible, something like an equal rate of wages; by no means was any rise of wages contemplated. The persons then present at the meeting, which was not a very numerous one, were requested to go round the trade to inform those hands not present at the meeting, that a meeting would be held at five in the afternoon to receive the report of the provisional committee appointed in the morning, and thereby to know the opinion of the manufacturers as to the regulated rate of wages. In the course of the afternoon the person who was the proprietor or superintendent of this factory, was met by the weavers who were going about the town to inform their fellow workmen of the meeting to take place in the afternoon, and some complaints were made, but of the nature of which I am not aware; I was at work myself, but some observations were made at the time, and some complaints uttered with regard to making articles by steam while they were destitute, and those complaints were caused principally for this reason, from the certain knowledge that the cost of weaving those articles by steam was considerably more than the rate of wages they had been working at by hand. They were then taken down to the factory by the superintendent of the factory, or in other words, Mr. Beck, who has been mentioned; but from what circumstances the factory was set on fire I do not know; my conviction is, that the thing was never a premeditated act, and my knowledge enables me to say, that such a thing was never adverted to at the meeting in the morning.

1020. Do you allude to the meeting in Little Park-street?—Yes.

1021. Do you mean that they did not adjourn from that to meet at three o'clock at Cross Cheaping?—Yes; to receive the report of the provisional committee appointed to wait upon the masters, but it was at five o'clock, and not three.

1022. Did not, from that meeting, a body of 200 and upwards proceed to the premises and gut it, to use a common phrase, and destroy the machinery, and set the house on fire?—Decidedly not from that meeting, the meeting broke up about half past eleven in the morning.

1023. Did it not break up in the morning in Little Park-street, and agree to assemble at Cross Cheaping?—Yes, at five o'clock.

1024. After that, did not a collection of people proceed to the manufactory, and destroy it?—No, not after the meeting, because the meeting never took place, in consequence of the burning of the factory, it having occurred before that time.

678.                                                                      1025. You

*Benjamin Poole.*

———

23 March,
1832.

1025. You do not know by whom the factory was burnt?—Certainly not; I have not the most distant knowledge.

1026. If the factory would have given more wages, as you say, why should the factory have been destroyed; would not more wages have been beneficial to them? —I am not aware that the factory would have given more wages; there were hands employed; and my own knowledge enables me to say, that the cost of manufacturing articles in that place, by steam, was greater than the weavers had been in the habit of receiving previous to that time.

1027. If so, what possible reason could there have been for destroying the machinery, if the men were getting low wages?—I can give no explanation of that sort; but I can conceive that the knowledge of that fact produced an irritation that overcame the better judgment, perhaps, of some persons at that time; but how it operated I cannot tell.

1028. The knowledge of what fact?—That they were at play, and destitute of the means of supplying their families with food, while more money was paid for producing the articles by steam than they had received for supplying by the hand.

1029. Was not this machinery intended to produce a greater quantity of goods in a given space of time?—Certainly; my opinion is, that the cost of manufacturing twenty pieces of a certain article by the steam looms then at work, was greater than had been paid for manufacturing twenty pieces of the same article by the hand.

1030. But the twenty pieces would have been produced in a shorter space of time?—Yes, they would have been produced in a shorter space by the steam loom than by the hand.

1031. How do you estimate the expense of making by the steam-loom?—I am not prepared to give any detailed proof of the expense; but according to all the information I have been able to gather, the cost of the machinery, and the maintaining it and keeping it at work, and the sum allowed to the hand which is always necessary to superintend even a steam loom; that those costs, put together, were considerably more than had been afforded, previous to this time, to the hand loom weaver.

1032. Then you do not speak from your own knowledge, but from the information you have generally received?—Yes.

1033. Do you mean that a cause of discontent among the people arose from the circumstance of this machinery doing more labour and at more wages than they were receiving?—That was the conviction, that it was making by steam what they were waiting to make; and provided they had been enabled to get even a very moderate livelihood, they would have had no objection to steam.

1034. If they got less wages, that was one cause of discontent; but you were understood to say, that this loom would manufacture a considerable quantity more goods in the same time?—Yes.

1035. That would throw them out of employ?—Yes.

1036. Was that one cause of dissatisfaction?—It was their opinion that it did, in some measure, contribute to the depriving them of employment; but although they had been working at a less rate of wages, they had nothing to do, and consequently, nothing to receive.

1037. You mean to say, that the cost of producing the commodity by that machine would have been expended in coals, and the wear and tear of the machinery, rather than the cost of manual labour?—Yes.

1038. And no saving in the cost?—No.

1039. That was the first introduction of weaving by steam?—Yes, I believe it was.

1040. The workmen thought it would displace their labour?—It had been in existence some time, and I do not believe one quarter of the people knew it was in existence.

1041. Have you any doubt that that was the cause that it was destroyed?— I have no doubt that some such feeling operated upon the people; but as a matured prejudice, I do not think any such objection exists to the introduction of machinery, provided a man can get a very moderate livelihood.

1042. Have you any doubt that the prevalence of that feeling among the men led to the destruction of the machinery?—At the moment I believe it did.

1043. Will you state, whether at that meeting there was not a general expression of dissatisfaction at the existence of those looms?—I am certain no such expression was manifested at that meeting.

1044. Do

*Benjamin Poole.*

23 March,
1832.

1044. Do you know Joseph Wright and Richard Holmes in Coventry ?—I do not know them that I know of.

1045. Are you aware, that a short time after the destruction of those machines in Coventry, a letter was sent by Joseph Beck, stating, that as the public opinion was against him, he sacrificed his private views to that of the general voice, and requests it may be stated to Coventry and the public at large, he will not apply the power of steam to the weaving of ribbons in Coventry?—I have some recollection of something of that kind appearing in the papers.

1046. No attempt has been made since that time to introduce machinery by steam ?—I do not know that there has, there may be, but I do not know it.

1047. Do you know, that in 1816, sarsnett ribbons, as narrow as twelve-penny, and plain satin ribbons as narrow as eight-penny, were made in single-hand looms at that time ?—I will not undertake to say there was no small breadths, but I will say it was nothing like the general make of ribbons; there might be an instance, I will admit.

1048. Are there many of these now made in single hand looms; are they not all made in engine looms?—Six-penny, eight-penny and twelve-penny are.

1049. In the engine loom?—Yes; I am not aware of any making in the single hand looms.

1050. You do not know when they ceased to be made in that loom?—I cannot state when they ceased to be made; but that they have been making in the engine loom I know. I made a twelve-penny sarsnett myself in an engine loom, as far back as 1814.

1051. Will you have the goodness to state, what arose out of that meeting; was not a committee appointed to meet the masters to arrange a Table of Prices ?—A provisional committee was appointed for that purpose.

1052. Was not the purpose of that meeting to fix such a rate of wages as should give to the single hand weaver what was considered fair wages, nearly approximating to the engine weavers?—The object of the conference of the weavers' committee and the manufacturers' committee, was to arrange such a rate of wages for the engine and the single hand loom, which under the circumstances of the trade were considered fair and equitable to both parties.

1053. You stated there was a previous Table existing at that time ; do you speak of the Table of 1816 ?—I allude to the Table of Wages adopted by the manufacturers and workmen conjointly in 1829.

1054. You are aware that Tables of Wages were made in 1816?—Yes.

1055. And after 1816, were there any before 1829?—Yes, there was another List of Prices adopted in 1819; but from the list of 1816, in consequence of the distress that existed at that time, and to which I have before referred, that list was departed from generally; it was lowered; but as I have before stated, the trade recovered itself, and in 1819 the same list was re-adopted by the unanimous consent of the masters and workmen; the same lists, or very nearly so, uniformly so, with the exception of one or two articles, the same list was adopted in 1819, that was in existence in 1816.

1056. Will you state the comparative prices of 1816 and 1819 and 1829, according to those Tables ?—The list of 1816 was as near as possible the same rate of wages that had been paid in the ribbon trade from 1804. Some diminution of wages took place in consequence of the distress in 1816 and 1817. The list of 1819 was, with the exception of one or two articles, a mere ratification of the list of 1816: the list of 1819 continued in force up to 1824, when another list of prices was agreed to by the manufacturers and workmen, and at about five or six per cent. reduction from the list of 1819, or, I may say, from the list of 1804. Another list was adopted by the same parties in 1826, which was a reduction of about 10 per cent. from the list of 1824, in addition to the loss sustained in 1824, which makes about 15 per cent. from 1804. The list of 1829 was a reduction of 15 per cent. from 1826.

1057. That is a reduction of 30 per cent. ?—Yes.

1058. What was the list of the 10th of November 1831, as compared with the list of 1829?—The list of November 1831 was a ratification of the list of 1829.

1059. A continuation of that list?—Yes; it was re-adopted in consequence of its having been departed from in many instances on no reasonable grounds that could be given, and it was re-adopted by the unanimous consent of the masters and workmen, under all the circumstances of the trade at that time.

1060. Can you, from your own recollection, state that the list of 1816 was no sooner made than departed from by some of the masters, and the same in each
successive

successive list, soon after the agreement, that the list was departed from?—I know that the list of 1816 was, for a very short time, abided by, by the whole number of masters; the trade was in a very bad state at that time, but the list that was adopted in 1819, which was a renewal of the list of 1816 to my own knowledge, continued to be uniformly paid for some years.

1061. Do you mean to say, that as long as the trade is flourishing and there is plenty of work, no attempt is made to alter the Tables, and that it is only when they are distressed, as in 1816, the list is departed from?—As the demand diminishes, we naturally expect some reduction of wages follows.

1062. Between 1829 and 1831, have not the wages of the hand loom weavers, in the neighbourhood of Coventry, decreased much more in proportion than the engine weavers?—I have before stated, that the rate of wages in a single hand loom have been most grievously low; so low as not, even with work, to afford a single hand loom weaver a morsel of bread.

1063. What have they earned, compared with former times?—Compared with former times, of many years past, I am not prepared to say; but I know this much, that for many articles made previous to November 1831, in the single hand loom not more than half the price was given which was recorded upon the list of 1829. In many instances I know that to be the fact; but in others it was still kept up by the manufacturers, which produced a great deal of discontent.

1064. Just state in figures what the reductions in single hand looms had come to, before this Table of 1831, as far as any papers you have will enable you to state. Do you believe those are the lists made at the time, both for single hand looms and the engine looms? [*handing the two following Papers to the Witness:*]—Yes, I believe they are.

## RIBBON TRADE.

LIST of PRICES of ENGINE LOOM WORK, agreed to at a Meeting of Manufacturers, held at the Castle Inn, in the City of Coventry, on Thursday November 10th, 1831, and to commence the following day.

| SARSNETTS, per Piece. | s. | d. |
|---|---|---|
| 1 dy. | — | 6 |
| 2 | — | 7 |
| 4 | — | 9 |
| 6 | 1 | — |
| 8 | 1 | 3 |
| 10 | 1 | 7 |
| 12 | 1 | 11 |
| 14 | 2 | 3 |
| 16 | 2 | 7 |
| 20 | 3 | 4 |
| 24 | 4 | 1 |
| 30 | 5 | — |

No Pads to be made at a less price than Sarsnetts.

| LOVES and SATINS, 5-Leish. | s. | d. |
|---|---|---|
| 1 dy. | — | 8 |
| 2 | — | 10 |
| 4 | 1 | 1 |
| 6 | 1 | 3 |
| 8 | 1 | 7 |
| 10 | 1 | 10 |
| 12 | 2 | 3 |
| 14 | 2 | 8 |
| 16 | 3 | — |
| 20 | 3 | 10 |

| SATINS, 8-Leish. | s. | d. |
|---|---|---|
| 1 dy. | — | 10 |
| 2 | 1 | — |
| 4 | 1 | 3 |
| 6 | 1 | 6 |
| 8 | 1 | 11 |
| 10 | 2 | 4 |
| 12 | 2 | 9 |
| 14 | 3 | 2 |
| 16 | 3 | 6 |
| 20 | 4 | 4 |

| SATIN LOVES, 8-Leish. | s. | d. |
|---|---|---|
| 1 dy. | — | 9 |
| 2 | — | 11 |
| 4 | 1 | 2 |
| 6 | 1 | 4 |
| 8 | 1 | 8 |
| 10 | 2 | — |
| 12 | 2 | 5 |
| 14 | 2 | 10 |
| 16 | 3 | 2 |
| 20 | 4 | — |

| SATIN GAUZES. | s. | d. |
|---|---|---|
| 12 dy. | 2 | 9 |
| 16 | 3 | 6 |
| 20 | 4 | 4 |
| 24 | 5 | — |
| 30 | 6 | — |

| VELOM and FLORET GAUZE. | s. | d. |
|---|---|---|
| 16 dy. | 4 | 3 |
| 20 | 5 | 6 |
| 24 | 7 | 6 |
| 30 | 10 | 6 |

| CLIPT and DOUBLE FLORET GAUZE. | s. | d. |
|---|---|---|
| 16 dy. | 5 | — |
| 20 | 6 | 6 |
| 24 | 8 | 6 |
| 30 | 12 | — |
| 40 | 15 | — |

| COMMON LUTESTRING FIGURES. | s. | d. |
|---|---|---|
| 16 dy. | 5 | — |
| 20 | 6 | — |
| 24 | 8 | — |
| 30 | 11 | — |
| 40 | 14 | — |

CLIPT

### CLIPT LUTESTRING FIGURES. *s. d.*

| | *s.* | *d.* |
|---|---|---|
| 16 dy. | 5 | 6 |
| 20 | 7 | – |
| 24 | 9 | – |
| 30 | 12 | – |
| 40 | 15 | – |

### DAMASK FIGURES.

| | *s.* | *d.* |
|---|---|---|
| 20 dy. | 7 | – |
| 24 | 8 | 6 |
| 30 | 12 | – |
| 40 | 15 | – |

### DAMASK FIGURE PADS, (New Standard.)

| | *s.* | *d.* |
|---|---|---|
| 24 dy. | 11 | – |

### SHUTE FIGURE PADS, (New Standard.)

| | *s.* | *d.* |
|---|---|---|
| 6 dy. | 4 | – |
| 20 | 14 | – |
| 24 | 15 | – |

### FIGURED SATINS.

| | *s.* | *d.* |
|---|---|---|
| 20 dy. | 7 | 6 |
| 24 | 8 | – |
| 30 | 12 | – |
| 40 | 15 | – |

AT a Meeting of the Committee of Ten appointed at the General Meeting to make a new Standard, held at the Castle Inn on the 9th of November 1831, it was Resolved, That the following deviations from the Standard of 1822 be made, and that the following be the width of Sarsnetts.

| | | | | | | | |
|---|---|---|---|---|---|---|---|
| 1 dy. | – | – | quarter of an inch. | 14 | – | – | 1 & 10–12 of an inch. |
| 2 | – | – | 7–16 - ditto. | 16 | – | – | 2 & 1–12 - ditto. |
| 4 | – | – | 5–8 - ditto. | 20 | – | – | 2 & 7–12 - ditto. |
| 6 | – | – | 10–12 - ditto. | | | | |
| 8 | – | – | 1 & 1–12 ditto. | 24 | – | – | 3 & 1–12 - ditto. |
| 10 | – | – | 1 & 4–12 ditto. | 30 | – | – | 3 & 10–12 - ditto. |
| 12 | – | – | 1 & 7–12 ditto. | 40 | – | – | 4 & 7–12 - ditto. |

Resolved, That Satins, Satin Loves, Satin Figures, Sarsnett Figures, Orientals and all dressed goods, excepting Gauzes, be 1–12 of an inch wider than Sarsnetts; that fine Gauzes be 2–12 of an inch wider than Sarsnetts; that Pads be the same width as Sarsnetts; that on the Standard, Gauzes be named as undressed; that the Standard be marked Coventry 1831. If any manufacturer requires a weaver to make any breadth exceeding the standard width, it is to be paid for as the next width wider.

## RIBBON TRADE.

LIST of PRICES of SINGLE HAND WORK agreed to at a Meeting of Manufacturers held at the Castle Inn, in the City of Coventry, on Thursday, November 10th, 1831, and to commence the following day.

### LUTESTRINGS.

| | *s.* | *d.* |
|---|---|---|
| 20 dy. | 5 | – |
| 24 | 6 | – |
| 30 | 7 | 6 |
| 40 | 9 | – |

with 1 *s.* per piece extra for Grogram.

### 8-LEISH SATINS.

| | *s.* | *d.* |
|---|---|---|
| 12 dy. | 4 | – |
| 16 | 5 | – |
| 20 | 6 | – |
| 24 | 7 | – |
| 30 | 8 | 6 |
| 40 | 11 | – |

5-Leish Satins and Satin Loves 2 *s.* per gross less than 8-Leish Satins.

### SATIN GAUZES.

| | *s.* | *d.* |
|---|---|---|
| 16 dy. | 4 | 6 |
| 20 | 5 | 6 |
| 24 | 6 | 6 |
| 30 | 8 | – |
| 40 | 9 | 6 |

### PADS, New Standard.

| | *s.* | *d.* |
|---|---|---|
| 8 dy. and narrower | 3 | – |
| 10 | 3 | 6 |
| 12 | 4 | – |
| 14 | 4 | 6 |
| 16 | 5 | – |

all other breadths in proportion.

678.

### ORIENTALS.

| | *s.* | *d.* |
|---|---|---|
| 16 dy. | 5 | – |
| 20 | 6 | – |
| 24 | 7 | – |
| 30 | 8 | 6 |
| 40 | 11 | – |

standing course leys at the same price.

All Tyer Sarsnett figures, not exceeding 80 shoots, with or without Satin, to be paid for 2 *s.* per piece extra if exceeding 80 shoots, according to trouble.

### SATIN FIGURES.

| | *s.* | *d.* |
|---|---|---|
| 20 dy. | 8 | – |
| 24 | 10 | – |
| 30 | 12 | – |
| 40 | 15 | – |

not exceeding 80 shoots; if exceeding 80 shoots, according to trouble.

All other articles not enumerated in this list, to be paid for according to trouble.

1065. Were

*Benjamin Poole.*
--- ---
23 March,
1832.

1065. Were not they settled in Coventry at a meeting at the George Inn, as well for the single hand looms, although few were used in Coventry, as the engine looms?—Not at the George Inn; that was a meeting of the weavers exclusively; the lists of prices were agreed to at the Castle Inn by the committee of masters and weavers.

1066. At this meeting was not there a resolution come to, that a committee should be appointed by the workmen to co-operate with the masters, to form a list of prices?—Yes; these are the lists agreed to by the weavers' committee and the master manufacturers.

1067. Those apply to the single hand looms and the engine looms?—Yes; the one is a list of the single hand looms, and the other of the engine looms.

1068. Can you state to what rate the wages of the single hand weavers have been reduced?—My belief is, on many articles they could not earn more than 2 s. or 2 s. 6 d. a week with work.

1069. While the engine loom weaver was receiving from 9 s. to 12 s.?—In my reason I assigned for the convening of the meeting in November, many of the articles common to the engine loom, as well as the single hand loom, had suffered a considerable reduction; but the rate of wages I have stated as being from 9 s. to 12 s. a week, applies to the rate of wages, presuming that the hand receives the price given in the list, which at that time was not the case.

1070. Before this list was renewed on the 10th of November 1831, state in figures what the engine weaver earned, and what the hand loom weaver earned by the week, equally employed?—In reference to some articles, not more than 7 s. or 7 s. 6 d. in an engine loom, and about 2 s. or 2 s. 6 d. in the single hand loom. Many of the country weavers were not earning more than that; I confine my remarks to those articles only that were common to the single hand loom and the engine loom, the greater number of articles made in the engine loom were paid for according to the list of 1829.

1071. You stated that all the reductions that have taken place amount to about 30 per cent.?—Yes.

1072. Was there an effort between 1829 and 1831 to reduce it still lower?—A partial one there was, and that gave rise to general discontent.

1073. Some of the masters insisted upon a reduction?—Yes, some of them.

1074. You mean to say that those wages, having been reduced in 1829 to 30 per cent., you became dissatisfied in 1831 because many of you were paid still lower?—Yes; paid still lower than the list agreed upon as an equitable list, for certain articles, and no reason had been shown for such a reduction; and there was no proof that any increase of supply was afforded to the working hand.

1075. You were asked just now the amount received by the engine loom weaver and the single hand loom weaver; you say one will receive 7 s. 6 d. per week, and the hand loom weaver 2 s. 6 d.?—I referred to the period immediately before the 7th of November, not to the present time, or any time before that.

1076. And those comparative amounts are correct?—Yes, to the best of my knowledge; but as there was no list, I am not able to say exactly.

1077. What is the amount that would be paid to the engine loom weaver, for the highest rate of wages he could receive, and the highest rate of wages paid to the hand loom weaver?—I believe the highest rate of wages I can state, in the plain trade and in an engine loom, is 12 s. a week, and not exceeding 12 s. 6 d., and varying down to 9 s. in the plain trade.

1078. Now state the highest amount paid to a single hand loom weaver?—I am not acquainted with those wages.

1079. They are almost exploded?—Not by any means.

1080. Are there not goods made in the engine looms that cannot be made in a single hand loom?—I am not aware there are any made in an engine that cannot be made in the hand loom. I know there are articles made in the hand loom that cannot be made in the engine loom.

1081. At those rates of wages, was the employment constant?—By no means; a vast number of hands were out of employment at that time.

1082. Look at List A., which is the single hand list of wages; does that include the preparatory process of winding and warping?—Yes, this includes the winding and warping.

1083. Now look at List B., which is the engine work; that does not include the winding and warping?—No.

1084. Previous

*Benjamin Poole.*

23 March,
1832.

1084. Previous to those lists, the wages were as 2 *s.* 6 *d.* to 7 *s.* 6 *d.* for a week's labour ?—Yes.

1085. How many pieces more could a man in an engine make than in a single hand loom, take eight-leish satins, sixteen-penny ?—A weaver in an engine loom, making sixteen-penny eight-leish satin, would perhaps make them in a ten-shuttle loom, but he would not make ten pieces to the single hand weaver's one.

1086. How many on the average ?—I should say, that an engine loom weaver would make double the quantity of the single hand loom weaver.

1087. Not more than two to one ; where a single hand would make one piece, would not the engine make more than two ?—I would rather decline answering that question, because, not being acquainted with the single hand trade, I am not aware of the quantity they can make.

1088. How many can you make in an engine of that description ?—About five pieces.

1089. Were you not paid by the piece, as you are now, before that Table of Wages was agreed upon ?—Yes, in the engine loom.

1090. Did not the engine weaver receive increased wages, because he made more pieces than in the single hand loom ; was not that the cause of the difference of wages ?—I conceive that the engine weaver receives less per piece than the single hand weaver.

1091. How much less : the question supposes that a man is employed all the week in a single hand loom, and at an engine loom ; now the difference of wages was as 2 *s.* 6 *d.* to 7 *s.* 6 *d.*, what was the difference of work made by the one in proportion to the other ; you say, only two to one ; now, no man would pay 7 *s.* 6 *d.* for two pieces in an engine, when he could get it made for 5 *s.* in the single hand loom ?—I am not acquainted with the single hand weaving.

1092. Was not the object of those two Tables to bring the wages that the single hand weaver should earn as nearly as possible to the wages an engine weaver should earn ?—I was not aware of that ; the object of the list is to include all the articles made in the single hand loom and in the engine loom.

1093. If there is the same charge in the single hand list as in the engine list, for making a piece, surely the intention was to make them equal ?—They are not equal, whatever the intention might be ; the price paid in the single hand loom is more than the price paid in the engine loom.

1094. Take the eight-leish satin, sixteen-penny wide ; look at the list, and see what is to be paid for making it ?—Five shillings per piece ; that includes winding and warping.

1095. How much would you deduct for winding and warping ; would it amount to 1 *s.* 6 *d.* ?—No, not 1 *s.* 6 *d.*

1096. How much should you think ?—About 1 *s.*

1097. That would bring down the price to 4 *s.* ?—Yes, in a single hand loom.

1098. If it was 1 *s.* 6 *d.* for winding and warping, that would bring it down to 3 *s.* 6 *d.* ?—Yes.

1099. Look at list B. ; where you see the same kind of work made by an engine loom, where the winding and warping is previously done by the master, and where the labour only is stated ; what is the rate there stated ?—Three shillings and six-pence for a piece.

1100. If the winding and warping was 1 *s.* 6 *d.* that deducted from 5 *s.* would leave 3 *s.* 6 *d.* for a single hand loom and the same for an engine ?—Yes ; but I have stated it does not amount to 1 *s.* 6 *d.*, it is about 1 *s.*

1101. That would make 4 *s.* at the single hand and 3 *s.* 6 *d.* at the engine ?—Yes.

1102. Is it the same proportion throughout the other articles ?—To the best of my judgment it is.

1103. Then the intention of that list for the hand loom was to bring the rate of wages for one piece of eight-leish sixteen-penny to 4 *s.* whilst the engine was to receive 6 *d.* less ?—I never heard such a view taken of the reasons for arranging the list.

1104. Is not that the fact you have now stated ; will not that be the effect ?—That the single hand weaver has about 6 *d.* in 4 *s.* more than the engine weaver for making the same article.

1105. That is the effect of it ?—I believe it is.

1106. Has not, since those Tables were agreed upon, a large portion of the work that was formerly done by the single hand weaver been done by the engine-weaver ?

678.                                                                        —I am

*Benjamin Poole.*
————————
23 March,
1832.

—I am not aware that any difference has been made in the number of single hand looms and engine looms since these lists were made.

1107. Do you mean to say that the distress or difficulty in the single hand weaver has not increased of late?—Not any more than the proportion has in the engine trade.

1108. Do you mean to say that they have been employed to make twelve-penny and eight-penny, and a great variety of other articles that the engines can make; has the single hand looms that employment, continued as before?—The single hand weaver when he can get any thing better than those articles, for they are not very lucrative, is glad to do it if he can.

1109. Putting it to you not now as a workman, but as a manufacturer, would you pay 4 s. for making a piece to the hand loom weaver when you can get the same piece made for 3 s. 6 d. by an engine?—In regard to many articles the article is made better, so much better in the single hand looms as to induce me to give the additional price.

1110. Are there any articles much better in the engine than in the single hand loom?—I am not aware of any.

1111. Your opinion is that the single hand would turn out better articles, so that you could afford to pay 4 s. instead of 3 s. 6 d. ?—Yes, on some articles.

1112. State those articles?—Eight-leish satin, and on satin figures of the greatest width.

1113. State what articles can be made as good in the engine as in the single hand loom?—There are some that can be made as good, but there are few that can be made equal in richness.

1114. Do you not consider, that in a regulation by which the master is called upon to pay more for making by hand looms than by the engine, must necessarily stop employment to the hand loom?—I am not aware of any such effect, because whenever such an effect is likely to arise, the manufacturers have it in their power to call their hands together without it, and by general knowledge of the state of the trade, to regulate the prices according as the circumstances of the trade require.

1115. As long as that list continues, you consider the rates ought to be paid accordingly?—Yes, as long as the list continues, we presume there is no good reason shown for its being departed from.

1116. And you think it perfectly right, that the hand loom weaver under the circumstances stated, should continue to receive that increased rate of wages over the engine weaver?—Yes; I think it right so far as the manufacturers agree, such a price is equitable.

1117. Are the articles on which you have now been questioned, articles much in demand?—Not being acquainted with that branch of the trade, I am not aware.

1118. Does that difference between the engine and single hand looms occur in any other article in the list?—I believe something like a uniform proportion is observed in all the articles.

1119. As to the price of winding and warping?—Yes.

1120. You say the quality of hand loom articles is preferable, in your estimation, to the other?—In some articles.

1121. Is that quality paid for by the purchaser in an increased price?—I am not aware of the prices paid by the purchaser.

1122. Whenever there is any depression in the trade, the hand-weavers feel it first; it presses upon them with more severity?—It depends more particularly upon the articles upon which that depression falls, and the majority of the articles made in the engine loom belong to it, and are apart from the single hand loom.

1123. Is it not the fact, that the single hand loom weavers feel it first?—I am not aware of that.

1124. Are there any such tables of wages existing at Congleton or Reading, or any other places where ribbons are made?—I do not know whether there are or are not, but my belief is that the articles made at those places are not the same as those made at Coventry; those made at Coventry are finer than those made at those places.

1125. You have stated that the wages are low, by competition with the French goods?—My belief is so.

1126. Are there any of those plain goods imported from France of which we have been speaking?—I am not aware that the importation of foreign goods is in the plain articles of ribbons.

1127. You believe that that kind of plain ribbons are also imported, as well as the

the fancy goods?—No, I do not know that the plain goods are imported to any amount.

1128. Do you know any thing, except by the official accounts?—No, I have not observed any thing as to plain ribbons.

1129. If an engine loom can make goods as well, and perform a great deal more work in a certain time than the hand loom, must not it displace labour, and cause distress?—In reference to those articles which can be made as well in the engine loom as in a single hand loom, my opinion is that they would; that the engine loom would supersede the single hand loom, if the article was in demand.

1130. Must not that throw persons out of employ, and cause distress?—Except they can find that those articles that are in demand can be preferably made in the single hand loom.

1131. Is not there a greater consumption of silk than was ever known?—I believe it is so.

1132. Can you give a reason when that is the case, why wages are so much reduced?—I think I have stated, that the manifest cause is, that those goods that are in demand are supplied by foreign artizans, that might be supplied by our own, being fully competent to make them.

1133. The fine fancy goods pay the workman and the manufacturer more than plain goods?—Yes, more than plain goods, it pays something more; but the profits on even the fine fabrics are so impoverished, as not to warrant the manufacturers speculating in the making of them.

1134. Does not foreign competition compel the manufacturer and workmen to go to a much lower description of goods?—Decidedly.

1135. You mean that lutestrings would be as well made in the engine loom as in the single hand loom?—Yes.

1136. Would you say so of satins?—I have said, that the preference given to single hand looms is in eight-leish satins, and broad satin figures.

1137. So that the engine loom will not make so beautiful an article in satin goods as the single hand?—No.

1138. Do you know the proportion of gauze made in Coventry now, compared with 1824 and 1825?—I do not know that.

1139. You have spoken with regard to machinery, are you aware, that at Reading machinery has been introduced for many years, which makes articles to come in competition with Coventry?—I am not aware of the nature of the machinery; I believe they are chiefly blacks, India, and other sorts of goods, of which there are not many making in Coventry.

1140. Do you know, that there are any a-la-bar looms worked by a long pole in Coventry?—No, I do not.

1141. Are there any called the Swivel looms that are used in Reading?—I have heard that there may be one or two, but they are not to any considerable amount I am certain.

1142. Have you ever heard of what is called the San or the Swiss loom, that is an improvement on the a-la-bar loom?—No.

1143. You are not aware how it makes an improvement in the fancy work?—No.

1144. Then are the Committee to understand, that the only machines for weaving in Coventry, are the engine loom and the jacquard machine?—Yes; those are the two principal machines in use in Coventry.

1145. You were asked why the machinery was not increased, and you stated that the low profit prevented it?—Yes.

1146. If the machinery used in other parts of the country and in France were introduced at Coventry, would not you be able to compete with the foreigner?—I am not aware there is any superior machinery used in France to that we have in Coventry; the jacquard loom is the machine used in Coventry, and I am informed it is of the same description in France.

1147. You know nothing but what you have been told about France?—No.

1148. You have spoken of Mr. Beck's machine, or Woodhouse's machine?—Yes.

1149. You were understood to say that it would make 20 pieces where a man would make one?—No.

1150. Can you state the proportions?—It might make 15 where a man would make 10; on the whole, perhaps, produce 15 pieces to 10.

1151. But then it employed the power of steam instead of manual labour?—Yes;

Benjamin Poole.

23 March, 1832.

*Benjamin Poole.*
————————
23 March,
1832.

Yes; the steam, in some degree, produced quicker than manual labour, but manual labour was combined with it.

1152. But yet there was steam power used to a considerable extent?—Yes, it facilitated the production.

1153. Do you know that in 1817 there was general distress pervading all parts of the country?—·I am not aware of what distress pervaded all parts of the country; I know it affected all Coventry.

1154. Do they allow to the poor in Coventry so much as they used to do formerly?—No, much less.

1155. Whether the amount of the poor rates have increased or not, has the number of the poor increased?—I believe that the number of the poor in Coventry, so far as refers to the silk trade, and the number of applicants for relief, has considerably increased.

1156. The number is stated to have increased from 147 to 323?—The number in the house varies; sometimes it may be more and sometimes less.

1157. Do you know that the casual poor have increased much?—Yes, very much indeed.

1158. Have they reduced their allowance?—Yes; I know many individuals who have been in the habit of receiving 4*s*. 6*d*. a week, who do not receive now more than 2*s*. or 2 *s*. 6*d*., a man and his wife and two or three children.

1159. Do you know the amount per pound of the poor rate in the year for which you have given the returns?—I am not aware of the assessment, or how the directors have managed it; I only know what is collected and expended, and I know that a vast number of those who formerly contributed to the poor rate are unable to do it now.

1160. You say that the distress began in 1815 and continued down to 1818, are you aware that the poor rates for those years were 10,000*l*., 12,000*l*. and 15,000*l*., how do account for the distress beginning when the poor rates were so low?—Trade had not declined so materially in 1815.

1161. You stated that trade began to decline in 1827, 1828 and 1829, and that it has been gradually getting worse?—Particularly 1829. I do not say any thing about any particular decline in 1827 and 1828, for this reason, that previous to the 5th of July, the time appointed for the introduction of foreign goods, the manufacturers' warehouses were completely empty; after that time they went on with a desire to keep their hands employed, and they concluded in 1828 with their warehouses full.

1162. Do you consider that the paper you have given in marks the deficiency of employment in Coventry?—I conclude that it is a pretty fair criterion of the condition of the poor.

1163. If, in 1818, 1819, and 1820, the poor rates were 18,000 *l*., 15,000 *l*., and 16,000 *l*., and in 1826, 11,000 *l*., in 1827, 13,000 *l*., and in 1828, 11,000 *l*., in 1829, 13,000 *l*. ought not those to be taken as a proof of the trade being brisk when the rates were so low?—Provisions were much dearer in the former years; money would not go so far.

1164. Taking the latter years, there has not been any great variation?—No.

1165. You spoke of the distress; are you aware, or have you brought any statement showing the increased number of weavers in Coventry, between the period of 1821 and 1831?—I do not know the increased number of weavers from 1821 to 1831; but, from the best information we have been able to obtain, the number has diminished considerably in the last three or four years.

1166. You are not aware that the population has increased from 21,000 to 27,000 in Coventry?—I am aware that a great addition has been made to it.

1167. Is it not the rule in Coventry for the father to bring up his sons to the same trade as himself?—Generally it is; he has no other alternative; he cannot bring them up to any other trade.

1168. Do you mean to say that the number of weavers in the last year has decreased?—Yes, upon the whole I believe they are; there are fewer now than three years ago.

1169. Have you any criterion to go by in forming that opinion?—The number of weavers in Coventry is about 4,400, according to the statement obtained when they petitioned Parliament.

1170. In this year?—Yes.

1171. Do you know the number five or ten years back?—No, I am not aware of it.

1172. You

*Benjamin Poole.*

———

23 March,
1832.

1172. You cannot say whether it has increased or not?—I have no doubt that it increased for the former part of the last ten years, from 1819 to 1825, or 1826 or 1827.

1173. You have no account of what they were in 1826?—No.

1174. You are an engine weaver?—Yes.

1175. You have stated an account of the number of looms?—Yes.

1176. Were you engaged in making that inquiry?—No, I was not.

1177. What was the number taken?—Four thousand four hundred and sixty-one, I think, was the number.

1178. Are you able to state the average rate of wages paid in the year stated in the list you have handed in for single loom work and for engine loom work?—I cannot say for single hand work; I am unacquainted with that branch of the trade.

1179. But you can for engine loom work?—Yes.

1180. In giving in the rate of wages, is it to be understood you give it in as the wages a man can earn when employed?—Yes.

1181. In the course of the last year, how many weeks do you think the men have been unemployed?—It sometimes happens that the individuals in work at one time are out at another; but on the whole I should think, dividing the quantity among the whole number, that they had not more than seven months' employ in the year, full work.

1182. So that 12 s. per week is, when reduced by that scale, only 7 s. per week?—Yes; the whole sum distributed among the weavers would not amount to more than that.

1183. Do you mean the head of a family or each individual in the family?—I mean the weaver, and he has a family dependent upon him; if a man has five or six children, I do not mean to say that no one of them is able to afford him assistance to the amount of one or two shillings per week, that must depend upon circumstances; in my own case, I have five children, and the oldest is not eight years of age, and cannot earn any thing.

1184. Your five children do not produce anything?—Not a farthing.

1185. Have you got a list of the prices for the years 1816, 1819, 1824, 1826, and 1829?—Yes.

[*The Witness produced the same, and they were delivered in.*]   Vide Appendix.

1186. In making a piece of gauze ribbon, you will probably consume five ounces of silk, and perhaps be paid 15 s. for making it?—Perhaps so.

1187. You may consume a pound of silk in making a piece of ribbon, for which you will not be paid more than 5 s. wages, is that the fact?—Yes.

1188. So that the gross consumption and weight of silk is no proof that the operative is beneficially employed?—No.

1189. Can you state the ordinary proportion of sarsnett and pad ribbons?—No, I am not aware of that; I have a statement here of certain articles taken at two periods, which will elucidate the question. A weaver employed, having full work on a twelve of twelve-penny sarsnetts at 2 s. 4 d. per piece in 1824, making four lengths in five weeks, paying 2 s. 6 d. a week to the filler, would earn 19 s. 11 d. per week. A weaver employed, and having full work on a six of twenty-four penny sarsnetts or lutestrings at 4 s. 1 d. per piece in 1832, having full work and making four lengths in six weeks, paying 2 s. 6 d. a week to the filler, and 1 s. a week loom hire, would earn 12 s. 8 d. a week. In the first case, that is in 1824, the weaver earns 19 s. 11 d., and works up 24 ounces of silk, and in the second he earns 12 s. 8 d. and works up 32 ounces of silk.

1190. Both those are plain articles?—Plain sarsnetts made by an engine-loom, twelve-penny sarsnett in 1824, was as common a work at that time as the twenty-four penny is at this time.

1191. A piece of gauze ribbon would weigh five ounces, and you would now not consider yourself over paid in procuring 15 s. for the making of that five ounces into a piece of ribbon?—Fifteen shillings per week is about the rate of wages in the gauze figure trade.

1192. Do you know the number of engine-looms employed in 1826?—I do not know; considerable pains have been taken to ascertain it, but in consequence of no statement having been taken at the time, we have not been able to ascertain it.

1193. You have stated, that there is at this present time the number of 4,461 engine-looms in Coventry?—Yes.

1194. Do you mean to say, that all those looms are at the present time employed?—By no means.

1195. What

*Benjamin Poole.*
———
23 March,
1832.

1195. What number do you consider are out of employment at the present time?—According to the last statement taken, when our petition was sent in, and no accurate account has been taken since, according to the number then obtained, it was about 2,000 entirely without employment.

1196. Out of of the number you have stated?—Yes, out of the 4,461.

*Edward Goode,* called in; and Examined.

*Edward Goode.*
———

1197. YOU are engaged in the ribbon trade?—I am.

1198. In Coventry?—Yes.

1199. How long have you been so employed?—About 21 years.

1200. How many branches of the ribbon trade are there?—There are two, generally denominated the single hand loom and the engine loom; that is the one shuttle loom and the many shuttle loom, each embracing two parts, plain and fancy.

1201. To which of those branches do you belong?—The engine plain.

1202. Are there any persons besides weavers who are engaged in the plain branch of the ribbon trade?—Yes, there are warpers, winders and fillers.

1203. Do you know the number of those warpers, winders and fillers who are dependent upon the plain branch of the ribbon trade?—There are about 1,000 winders, 1,000 fillers and about 320 warpers.

1204. What is the state of those branches of the trade at present?—Unprecedently depressed; very much distressed indeed.

1205. Do you know the number of those various descriptions of persons who are consequently unemployed?—According to the most accurate census that can be taken, I believe the numbers to be 1,800 weavers, 450 fillers, 450 winders and, I think, about 160 warpers.

1206. In consequence of this want of employment, is there considerable distress at the present moment?—There is.

1207. In your opinion what is it that has produced this distress?—Want of employment and low wages.

1208. Has this depression been of long duration?—Yes, it has extended over the three past years.

1209. You have stated that low wages are one cause of this distress; what are the average earnings, in your branch of the trade, at the present time?—The most correct average that can be obtained, shows that the average earnings are 10 s. a week; there are some few men who can earn more under particular circumstances, but there are many who earn less; therefore I should say that 10 s. is the most correct average that can be stated.

1210. Can you state what has been the amount of the reduction of wages in the plain branch of the ribbon trade?—As near as I can ascertain, it is 30 per cent.

1211. Since when?—One thousand eight hundred and nineteen.

1212. Are the Committee right in understanding you to say, that you consider that there is a difference to their disadvantage of 30 per cent., comparing this period with 1819?—Yes, I might say from 1804, we have sustained a reduction of 30 per cent.

1213. Then during what space of time, according to your experience, did the wages continue steady?—From 1804 to 1812 there was one and the same price uniformly paid; in 1812 we had an extraordinary trade, and then there was a very extraordinary price given; and we had a higher price given. Upon the return to peace in 1815, there having been an influx of hands from disbanding the army, and the general depressed state of the country, things reverted back to their old channel; and there was a list of prices in 1816, which was little more than a copy of 1804; there have been periods between the making of the different lists, when different individuals of the manufacturers (for I am sorry to say there are some that are very ready to make reductions) have made encroachments upon the list; but when I speak from the list of prices, I mean the established list.

1214. Whatever price is fixed, whenever there is a depression, there will be a departure from it by the manufacturers; is not that the case?—Yes, in some cases.

1215. And when there is a very brisk trade it is departed from on the other side?—No.

1216. Was not that the case in 1812?—It was at the option of the manufacturers; it was not forced upon them.

1217. To what circumstances do you attribute these great reductions in the wages of the ribbon weavers of Coventry?—The importation of foreign manufactured ribbons, most undoubtedly; that is my opinion.

1218. Does

*Edward Goode.*

23 March,
1832.

1218. Does this importation of foreign ribbons operate injuriously in any other respect besides reducing your wages?—It robs us of our labour.

1219. In what manner do you know, or how do you form your notion, of the quantity of foreign ribbons imported?—I am not able to state the quantity imported, but the first reduction of which we complain was made in 1824; just at the time the law was anticipated in 1826 comes another reduction; in 1829, when there was an alteration in the import duty, came these reductions, and no entreaty on our part has ever got us an advance.

1220. How do you account for the reduction in 1818; there was no import then?—It was only a partial departure; the Committee will find that in the evidence it is acknowledged that at that time all manner of prices were paid; the list of 1816 was one established rule, and though it was partially departed from, there was no uniform price paid till 1819.

1221. You do not agree with the last witness, that the distress began in 1815, and gradually increased down to 1818, when the prices were the lowest?—Yes; I agree it commenced in 1815, and extended over three or four years; and extended over the country at large; but at the time when low wages were paid in 1818, they were not paid by any general acknowledged scale, but all the reductions effected under this late system are regular adopted scales, that are acknowledged and paid, and every fresh succeeding scale comes lower and lower; that was not the case antecedent to 1826.

1222. Did you attribute the fall that took place in 1818, to importation also?—Certainly not.

1223. Did you attribute the fall in 1824 to importation?—Yes, in the prospective.

1224. In 1822, 1823 and 1824 they were depressed?—There was no reduced list, although there were partial deviations.

1225. You are employed upon plain ribbons?—Yes.

1226. Just state the kind of work which you make, and which you conceive to be met by importation from abroad?—I have, in my employment, two or three kinds of work; but the kind of work I have under my superintendence and care is not the kind imported.

1227. You are understood to be in the plain trade?—Yes.

1228. And you say the wages have gradually decreased; and you stated that it is importation that has decreased your wages; you are asked now to state the kind of articles brought in competition with your work?—In the first place, at the commencement of the legalizing system in 1826, a great many plain ribbons were imported that brought down our prices to a certain scale, beyond which the manufacturers could not give it if they sold at all. I admit, to the best of my knowledge, the importations in the plain articles have not been so great as in 1826, 1827 or 1828, or 1829, but the engine trade embraces two parts, the fancy and the plain, they are like twin sisters, the one is so connected with the other, the one cannot suffer without the other suffering too; the importation may take place on one particular article, and if that affects one part of the trade it is sure to affect the other.

1229. Your trade is affected by the importation of fancy goods?—Yes.

1230. And those hands who have been employed in fancy goods are now compelled to make plain goods?—Yes, in some instances.

1231. And they press upon those employed in making plain goods?—Yes; and if the foreigners did not import fancy articles, the scores of plain hands now out of employment would be employed in making fancy ribbons.

1232. How do you know that people would buy English fancy goods if there were no French imported?—I think it is fair to infer, if there was nobody to import them and they were wanted, we should supply them.

1233. Did you make figured gauzes before 1826?—Yes; they were making before that.

1234 Do you make them now?—They are made in Coventry.

1235. Do you believe there are more gauzes now made in Coventry than were made in 1824?—I do believe there is now making in Coventry more fancy goods; there are some articles that were making a few years back that are now obsolete.

1236. If there are more gauzes made now than were made in 1824, the trade has not decreased?—Not in the fancy branch in Coventry.

1237. What is your opinion as to the increase of hands in that branch; are there not more weavers now for that branch than in 1824?—Yes, unquestionably; if there is more work, there must be more hands to do it.

1238. If

1238. If there is more work how do you account for the distress?—The fashion has undergone a change; the fashion favours the fancy goods, the plain goods are not so much in demand; but if the fancy goods were not supplied from abroad, the plain hands would have that employment here.

1239. You mean that plain goods were much more used formerly?—Yes.

1240. You make now fancy goods as you used to do?—Yes.

1241. But those coming in from abroad have thrown the hands at Coventry out of employment?—Yes.

1242. Are not the fancy goods made by machinery?—Yes, the jacquard looms.

1243. Must not the nation that has the machinery most in perfection supply the most?—I am not aware that our machinery is inferior to the French.

1244. Are you not aware that the jacquard loom is superseded at St. Etienne?—I am not.

1245. You say that if the fancy goods were not used, the plain goods would come in?—Yes.

1246. Before, when plain goods were wanted, did you not find serious competition at Manchester and other places?—My firm conviction is, that the plain trade has declined in more places than it has grown up.

1247. Has the machinery, in the plain branch of the trade, declined in value since the importation?—Decidedly; looms that were worth 12 *l.* or 15 *l.* are knocked down at public auction for 2 *l.* and 3 *l.* a-piece.

1248. The number of fancy looms has increased greatly at Coventry?—Yes; there are more than 600, and in 1826 there were between 200 and 300.

1249. You think there would be more fancy work at Coventry if it was not interfered with by foreigners?—Twice the quantity.

1250. But at present the manufacturer does not choose to invest his capital in it?—Certainly not; it would be a ruinous speculation.

1251. Can you make as good ribbons in Coventry as at France?—I believe we can.

1252. Are you aware, whether Tables of Wages, such as exist in Coventry, are established at Manchester or Congleton, or any of those places?—I am not aware of that.

1253. Has it not been the anxious wish of the workmen to keep to the Tables as closely as possible?—Yes; although the Tables do not allow us a living price for ourselves, or for our families.

---

*Lunæ, 26° die Martii*, 1832.

### THE RIGHT HON. THE EARL GROSVENOR, in the Chair.

*David Smith*, called in; and Examined.

1254. WHAT are you?—A figured ribbon-weaver, from Coventry.

1255. In what department of the ribbon-trade do you operate yourself?—In the figure department.

1256. How long have you done so?—The greater part of eighteen years.

1257. How many belong to that department at Coventry?—From 650 to 700 Jacquard weavers.

1258. What is the present state of that department of the trade?—There is employment, but it is very uncertain and irregular; consequently, the operatives are very much distressed.

1259. What are the average earnings of a Jacquard loom weaver?—The average earnings, if in full employ, would be from fourteen to fifteen and sixteen shillings per week.

1260. Can you state how many weeks in the last year you think, generally, the Jacquard loom weavers were unemployed?—I should say, generally, from ten to fourteen weeks.

1261. Was there the same want of employment the year before?—No.

1262. Then you mean to say, that that branch of the business was worse during the last year than the preceding one?—Yes.

1263. Does the making of figured ribbons require more skill and attention than the making of plain ribbons?—Yes, on account of the extra machinery and harness that is required to make the figured ribbon.

1264. How many Jacquard weavers were there previously to the importation of foreign ribbons?—In 1823 there were five Jacquard looms, and in the early part of 1826 there were two hundred and nineteen.

1265. Has

*David Smith.*

26 March,
1832.

1265. Has there been any increase in the last year?—There has been but very little increase for the last two years and a half.

1266. What is that owing to?—I conceive it is owing to the advantage that the foreigner has in our market; that is, that although the goods are in demand, they are supplied from other quarters than from our own manufactures.

1267. Can a figured weaver, under any circumstances, earn from 2*l.* to 3*l.* a week?—Decidedly not.

1268. What are the largest wages you ever knew a figured loom weaver earn?—I should say from 24*s.* to 28*s.*

1269. At what date was that?—In 1826.

1270. In what part of 1826?—The early part of 1826.

1271. Then you mean that the trade was better in the early part of 1826 than you have ever known it?—I should say, that the Jacquard trade might be as good at that time as at any other.

1272. Can you state what quantity of persons there were out of employment in 1831?—The articles were in demand, and I am not aware of any great number of Jacquard looms that were destitute of employment during that year.

1273. Do you know whether, in the year 1826, there were many Jacquard loom weavers out of employ?—No, I do not.

1274. Then in 1826, the 219 Jacquard looms were very generally employed, and in 1831, the 650?—The 219 were generally employed in 1826, and the articles being in demand in 1831 for the 650, the operatives had something to do; but in consequence of the constant variation of pattern, a great deal that they had to do was merely to alter for the exchange of pattern, which was tantamount to no employ to them.

1275. Were the Jacquard looms fully employed in 1827?—Partially.

1276. And in 1828?—In 1828 I think they were better employed than in 1827.

1277. In 1829?—Then they were worse off again.

1278. In 1830?—I should say 1830 was worse than 1829.

1279. In 1831?—That was worse still.

1280. You were understood to say that they were employed in 1831?—The employment was of the nature I stated, that the article was in demand; but the employment that the men had was principally to alter from one pattern to another.

1281. When was the first Jacquard loom introduced into Coventry?—In the year 1823.

1282. Before that time what machinery was used previously for making the same articles that are now made by the Jacquard looms?—There were no similar articles made.

1283. Do you know what was the number of looms in Coventry prior to 1823?—No.

1284. Did the men who in 1826 worked at the Jacquard looms, before that time work at another species of loom?—Yes.

1285. Did the introduction of the Jacquard looms cause the discontinuance of other machinery in Coventry?—The improved figure loom, which had been employed before the year 1823, still continued to be employed when the Jacquard looms were introduced, and in 1826, when there were 219 Jacquard looms employed.

1286. Is not the figured loom still in use?—I cannot answer whether there are any other figured looms in use now, except the single hand loom, not in the engine branch, other than the Jacquard loom.

1287. When the Jacquard machinery was introduced, was it applied to machinery before in use, or was the introduction of the Jacquard machinery, in fact, the introduction of an entirely new loom?—Of an entirely new machine.

1288. Can the Jacquard machine, such as was introduced in 1823, be applied to looms of the former construction?—Yes.

1289. In point of fact, was the improvement of the Jacquard applied to looms before in existence?—There were new looms made for the purpose of employing the Jacquard machine, and in very many instances since that, the Jacquard machine has been applied to plain looms; plain looms have been altered into Jacquard looms.

1290. That is to say, the Jacquard machine has been placed upon the loom?—Yes.

1291. Has not the Jacquard machine been applied both to the single hand and the engine loom for making patterns?—Yes.

1292. Then when you refer to the number of Jacquard looms, as you have stated increasing in the year 1826 to 219, and afterwards increasing at the present period 678.　　　　　　　　　　　　　　　　　　　　　　　　　　to

*David Smith.*

———

26 March,
1832.

to between six and seven hundred, do you mean that those were new machines that were constructed, or that the Jacquard machinery was applied to looms previously in existence?—Both ways.

1293. Since you have used the Jacquard machinery, has the old mode of figure weaving been abandoned?—I believe it has.

1294. Then it is merely a change?—Yes.

1295. Do you know whether any improvement has taken place in Coventry in the Jacquard loom since its first introduction?—I am not aware of any improvement.

1296. Are you aware whether any improvement has taken place at Congleton or Reading or Battersea, or any other places where fancy goods are made? —No.

1297. Are not the Jacquard looms included under the head of engine looms?—Yes.

1298. Do you know how many engine looms there were in 1826, as distinguished from hand looms?—No; all I know as to the numbers is, that in 1826 there existed 219 Jacquard looms, and that in 1831 the total number of engine looms, I think, was about 4,000 and upwards.

1299. As the Jacquard looms increased, did the employment in looms which had not the Jacquard machine decrease, in consequence of the application of the Jacquard machine being found to make goods of a superior quality?—Yes.

1300. You do not mean to say that there are more figured goods making now than there were in 1823 or 1826, but that it is merely another mode of making figured goods?—Exactly so.

1301. You were understood to say that the fancy trade has fallen off since 1826?—Yes.

1302. Is there less employment now for the weavers in fancy work than there was from 1824 to 1826?—There are less fancy goods made, but the hands are employed a great deal in altering patterns.

1303. Does that alteration of patterns pay as well as making goods?—No, we have nothing for altering patterns.

1304. When you say that the number of Jacquard looms increased from 200 to 600, is it to be inferred that the fancy work has increased to that amount?—Certainly not.

1305. Then, when you say that those looms increased from 200 to 600, you mean by that, that the work is transferred from those looms that were before employed in fancy work to those in the engines?—Yes; I mean to say that the men that operated upon the improvements from 1820 to 1823, now operate upon Jacquard looms.

1306. You were understood to say that there is rather a decrease of employment, and less wages?—Yes.

1307. And that a considerable part of the year you are out of employment?—Yes.

1308. Is there much distress in Coventry?—Yes.

1309. How do you account for that?—Because the articles that we can make are supplied from another source, and therefore, though the figured ribbon is in demand, the constant variation of fashion, in consequence of the introduction of foreign patterns, fills up a great deal of the operative's time, and that he really is not employed during that time in earning any thing for himself and his family.

1310. Why cannot you have new patterns, and make variations and lead the fashions?—We could have new patterns and we could make variations, but we could not lead the fashions, I apprehend, because there is a general feeling and a desire to know what patterns will come from abroad.

1311. Are the wages lessened in consequence of that; cannot the manufacturers afford to give as good wages in consequence of having the cream of the trade taken away from him?—Certainly not.

1312. Do you mean to say that the 650 jacquard looms now employed, are merely an exchange for the former looms?—There are some additional looms; the greater part of Jacquard looms in existence, are looms that have been altered from some other kind of loom, but there have been some new ones made.

1313. Are the 650 looms now employed in the Jacquard apparatus, in addition to the former employment afforded to the trade?—No.

1314. Do you mean to say that when those engines were increased from 200 to 600, it was merely an alteration in the mode of doing the work by a different engine, but not increasing the employment?—Yes; it did not increase the employment.

1315. When

David Smith.

26 March,
1832.

1315. When those Jacquard looms were introduced, were the old looms gradually turned to these?—Yes.

1316. That increase from 200 to 600 is not an increase of the quantity of persons employed, but a change from one mode of making those goods to another?—Yes.

1317. You mean to say that the Jacquard apparatus makes fancy goods so much better than the old machine, that you use the Jacquard apparatus instead of the other?—It produces a different article.

1318. Does it produce a better article as well as a different one?—Not as to quality.

1319. Then why is it used?—Because the Jacquard loom will produce a longer and a more beautiful pattern.

1320. If it is longer and more beautiful, may not it be said to be better?—It is better in point of taste, but not as to quality.

1321. Are not the patterns that come from France, all made in the Jacquard loom?—I believe they are.

1322. Would it not be quite vain for you to produce a commodity that is unlike the French, and are you not therefore compelled to use the Jacquard loom?—Yes.

1323. What time does it take to change the pattern?—From two to five weeks, according to the article.

1324. What time does it take to set a pattern originally?—From a month to six weeks.

1325. What is the highest wages you have known any individual in the fancy work earn in any one week within the last two months?—I should say 23 s. in one week.

1326. You are sure that none have received 34 s.?—I have no knowledge of any such fact.

1327. Do you believe that there have been 100 instances in the last year of persons having earned 23 s. in a week?—No; the 23 s. is in one week when the loom is fully prepared.

1328. But during the preceding weeks, when he was setting the pattern in, he was earning nothing?—No.

1329. If you had employment for six weeks, could not you earn the same every week?—No; because it is not usual for us to have warps long enough to last us for regular weaving six weeks.

1330. Who sets the pattern for you?—We put the pattern in ourselves.

1331. What is the nature of the preparation, that prevents you from earning as much in one week as in another, if you have full employment?—The getting in fresh warps, and the altering the patterns.

1332. What time does getting in the warps take?—It takes sometimes a week, and sometimes a fortnight, to get a fresh set of warps, and put them in the loom.

1333. How long will they last?—When they are in, they can be wove for a month.

1334. Is not that the case with all kinds of work, that it requires time to prepare it?—Not so much time as that.

1335. Before the introduction of the Jacquard looms, did not you also take some time to prepare the warp, and put the work in readiness?—Yes.

1336. Is there any additional labour of that sort, in consequence of the application of the Jacquard machine?—Yes, there is a greater variety of stripes; there is additional labour to get the warps in, over and above the labour that was required to get in a figured warp upon the old plan.

1337. When you say 23 s. a week, you mean when the loom is fully at work?—I say in one week, when the loom is fully prepared, and the man has nothing to do but to weave from Monday morning till Saturday night.

1338. Must not all the time that is employed in the preparation of the work be a deduction from those wages?—Yes.

1339. In addition to the time you take in putting the work into the loom, you ave stated that you occasionally suffer from the want of work altogether?—Yes.

1340. Are the Committee to understand that if you have a frequent change of patterns there is a great portion of your time lost to you?—Yes.

1341. What proportion does the time you lose in changing patterns bear to the time you are employed in making them?—In certain articles it would take as long to alter the pattern as it would to make 12 pieces of the article.

1342. How long does it take you to make 12 pieces after the pattern is prepared?—A month.

1343. Are there many articles that you so make that do in fact require a month?—There are.

1344. What

1344. What articles are they?—Twenty-four-penny figured gauzes, the broad satin figures, and damask figures.

1345. Those, of course, are in the fancy line?—All in the fancy line.

1346. You are speaking now of the best employment in your trade?—Yes.

*Joseph Marston,* called in ; and Examined.

1347. WHERE do you reside?—At Foleshill.

1348. What are you?—I am an operative, in the single hand, in the ribbon business.

1349. Are you overseer of Foleshill?—I am the guardian of the poor.

1350. How long have you been in the ribbon trade?—About 18 years.

1351. Are you an undertaker?—Yes.

1352. What do you mean by an undertaker?—I am the person that takes the silk from the manufacturer in the hank, and we have to wind it, to warp it, to find the harness and the machinery of all descriptions.

1353. What number of operatives are there in your parish?—There are 2,691 operatives; of whom 1,062 are employed, and 1,629 unemployed, according to the account we have taken through the parish, since the time of the distress, to find the exact number of people unemployed; that was in December last.

1354. How did you take that?—By going from door to door; that is the number of persons in the parish that are employed in the business, that is of weavers, winders and warpers, and all the persons employed in the business.

1355. When you say 2,691, do you mean that all those persons are or should be employed in the ribbon trade?—Yes.

1356. Do you count the women and children?—We count the women because they attend the business.

1357. Do you count the children who are too young to attend the business?—No; only those that are employed in the business.

1358. What is the state of that branch of the trade at this time?—Very bad indeed.

1359. Is not this the season when you are generally well employed?—Generally it has been; but the last two seasons, and more particularly the present, it has been so depressed as I never knew it at this season of the year.

1360. How long has your trade been so depressed?—It has been on the decline the last four years, but more particularly the last two years.

1361. What number of persons are there out of employment?—In December there were 1,629 destitute of any employment whatever.

1362. Were the others fully employed?—No, only partially; and I do not think they averaged two days' work a week through the winter season, for such was the state of the trade that those that had employment were worse off considerably than those that had parochial relief.

1363. What are the present average earnings in that branch of the ribbon trade? —Five and sixpence when at work; that I have ascertained from the rate of wages specifying the article, and then taking the average on it.

1364. When you say 5 s. 6 d., do you mean to say that those that were employed only two days in the week earn, in those two days, 5 s. 6 d.?—No, I take the week when fully employed.

1365. So that those who are employed only two days earn only one-third of 5 s. 6 d.?—Yes.

1366. Can you state how many days in a week they are employed now?—A great portion of them are out of employment now.

1367. Are they more employed now than they were in December?—There may be a little more employment, but it is so trifling that we have never perceived it to any extent.

1368. Do men, women and children earn this?—No; this is for men and women, operatives that are capable of doing any kind of work, not children.

1369. What were the average earnings prior to the making the lists in November last?—From 4 s. 3 d. to 3 s. 8 d.

1370. Is the distress very great among the weavers in your parish?—Very great.

1371. To what cause do you attribute that distress?—The introduction of foreign ribbons; I have positively seen French goods sold in Coventry for less than we formerly had for manufacturing them.

1372. What kind of goods do you allude to?—They were gauzes that I allude to, which we were pretty well paid for in 1824 and 1825 and 1826.

1373. Have

1373. Have the poor rates in your parish increased ?—A great deal.

1374. To what amount?—I have the amount from the parish from the year 1821, which I received from the vestry-clerk.

*[The Witness delivered in the same, which was read as follows :]*

Parish of Foleshill, March 24th, 1832.

AN ACCOUNT of Monies actually paid to the Permanent and Casual Poor.

| | | £. | s. | d. |
|---|---|---|---|---|
| For the Year ending Lady Day - - 1820 - - - | | 1,561 | 12 | 1 |
| Ditto - - - - - - 1821 - - - | | 1,481 | 17 | 7 |
| Ditto - - - - - - 1822 - - - | | 1,437 | 6 | 9 |
| Ditto - - - - - - 1823 - - - | | 1,075 | 10 | 2 |
| Ditto - - - - - - 1824 - - - | | 1,307 | 10 | 3½ |
| Ditto - - - - - - 1825 - - - | | 1,058 | 16 | 5 |
| Ditto - - - - - 1826 - - - | | 1,030 | 11 | 11½ |
| Ditto - - - - - 1827 - - - | | 1,040 | 11 | 11 |
| Ditto - - - - - - 1828 - - - | | 964 | 12 | 10 |
| Ditto - - - - - 1829 - - - | | 1,083 | 3 | 4 |
| Ditto - - - - - 1830 - - - | | 2,192 | 19 | 3 |
| Ditto - - - - - 1831 - - - | | 1,499 | 16 | -½ |
| Eleven months, ending 29th February 1832 - - - | | 1,933 | 10 | 11½ |

The above is a correct Return.          (signed)     J. Johnson,
                                                      Vestry Clerk.

(signed)     { Wᵐ Masser, Churchwarden.
             { Richᵈ Richardson, Overseer.
             { Richᵈ Owen, Guardian.

---

1375. Why was the list established in November last?—The prices varied so much that a part of the manufacturers did not think proper to carry on their business under the unsettled circumstances of the prices, and they were solicited, and the price was offered us.

1376. Do you consider that a fair remuneration for your labour?—By no means.

1377. Did you express that opinion?—Yes ; but we were assured that the manufacturers, under the present depressed state of things, could not give us a better.

1378. Do you consider the evils you labour under, as single hand weavers, to be ascribed to the introduction of the jacquard engine?—By no means.

1379. Have you not improvements in the single hand engine, independent of the Jacquard engines?—Yes.

1380. Do you believe that they would be greatly increased if foreign ribbons were excluded?—Yes.

1381. Are there any descriptions of goods made in the single hand loom which cannot be made in the engine loom?—Certainly.

1382. Are they numerous?—They are an article that prevails very much in the present day, as far as the demand goes for them ; it is a double shute satin, made with three shuttles ; I have seen patterns with four colours at one time, and I never knew them attempted to be made in the engine loom.

1383. Can you state what the population of your parish was in 1821?—No, I cannot.

1384. Are you aware that the population of that parish has increased since 1821 from 4,900 to 6,900?—I know that there is an increase, but I do not know exactly to what amount.

1385. Have you had reason to think that it is very considerable?—Yes, I have.

1386. Was there any want of employment for the increase up to a certain period?—There was not up to the end of 1827.

1387. Then when you took the account there were 2,691 persons capable of working, and only 1,629 without employment, leaving a remainder of 1,062 who were employed?—Partially.

1388. Are you aware that that is a greater number than the whole population of 1821?—Very probably it is a greater population.

1389. Do you think that the increase of population has taken place since 1827, or between 1821 and 1827?—I do not know at what period, but it has been a regular increase for the last 15 or 16 years.

1390. Do you think it increased more from 1824 to 1827, than it has done from 1827 to this period?—It might have done so, I cannot tell.

1391. Were they employed in 1821?—Yes.

1392. Were

*Joseph Marston.*

26 March,
1832.

1392. Were the 1,062 well employed in 1831?—No, there was very partial employment.

1393. Do you recollect what was the cause of the distress that took place in 1818, or what proportion it bore to the present state of distress?—I recollect that we had a bad trade about two years after the disbanding of the army, a number of hands were thrown upon the trade, and I account for the depression of it by that circumstance, and partly by an article prevailing then, that each operative made a great length of.

1394. You mean to say, that the fashion of making different articles has varied?—Yes.

1395. Do you recollect whether, in the year 1818, there was any distress occasioned by the death of the Princess Charlotte, and the change of fashion in consequence?—We have had several depressions in consequence of deaths in the Royal Family; as that happened at that time, I believe that was part of the cause.

1396. Do you not recollect the cause of that distress to have been considered by the workmen to be the half-pay apprentices?—There never was much of that prevailed in the parish I have been speaking of.

1397. In what state was the trade in 1827?—In the former part of it I never witnessed a better; it gradually declined towards the latter part of it.

1398. In 1828 what kind of trade was it?—The trade was still worse, but not so bad as it has been since.

1399. If the poor rates of that year were 964*l.* 12*s.* 10*d.*, whilst in 1820 and 1821 they were 1,561*l.* 12*s.* 1*d.* and 1,481*l.* 17*s.* 7*d.*, how do you account for that difference?—I had nothing to do with the accounts of the parish in those years.

1400. In 1829 how was the trade?—In 1829 it was bad.

1401. And yet are you aware that the poor-rates were only 1,083*l.* in that year, being as little as they have been, except in one year, for fifteen years before?—It might depend upon the management of the affairs of the parish.

1402. Do you remember that the poor, in the years 1828 and 1829, were paid less when out of employ, than they had been in the years 1826 and 1827?—Very probably they might, but not being in office, I cannot state.

1403. Can you state how many shillings in the pound was the rate in each year?—I can state to the present year; in the present year we shall not have more than 12*s.* in the pound, but I can account for this. About two years ago, so great was the distressed state of the parish, that the overseers of the poor applied to the House of Commons, and they obtained a local Act, by which they rated the proprietors of houses instead of the occupiers, so that our rate is now almost double what it was formerly, because they make almost every cottage of the parish pay; the owner is responsible for the payment.

1404. Do you mean by the word double, that the gross amount collected is double the amount that used to be collected, or that it extends over a greater number of persons?—It extends over a greater number of people; there are twice the number pay now that used to pay formerly.

1405. Within the last ten years, has there been any increase of houses in your parish?—Yes, there was a great quantity of newly-erected houses in 1825, 1826 and 1827; but we have had very few since.

1406. You say there have been a great many houses newly built; are there many uninhabited houses in that neighbourhood?—At the time the Census was taken of the parish, in the latter end of last year, there were upwards of 100.

1407. How many houses do you think have been built since the year 1827?—I should think not ten.

1408. In the year 1827, how many houses were uninhabited?—Perhaps not five.

1409. Have the allowances made to the poor not in the workhouse much increased?—There are a great number.

1410. Do you allow them as much individually as you used to do?—No.

1411. How much used you to allow?—I have heard of their having 2*s.* to 2*s.* 6*d.* a head; but in the present day, not more than 1*s.* 6*d.* is allowed to them.

1412. If you made the same allowance now that you had before done, would not the amount of your rates be much higher?—Undoubtedly.

1413. Then the increase in the amount of the rate is not in proportion to the increase of the number of persons?—No.

1414. Do you know how the weaving trade went on with the exception of casual depression, for any given period, from 1814?—No; in the year 1814 I left the trade for a time.

1415. Did it increase at that time?—No.

1416. Was

*Joseph Marston.*

26 March,
1832.

1416. Was it not depressed from 1814 to 1818, in consequence of the revulsion from the war to peace?—Yes.

1417. From that time did it increase?—It increased generally up to that time.

1418. You are in the plain trade, do any of the other branches pay as well as they used to do?—By no means.

1419. Does the depression in the figured trade throw an additional depression upon you in the plain trade?—I have not worked in the plain trade, though I belong to it, I work in the fancy, and there is a general depression both in the fancy and plain articles.

1420. Is the reason why you are so depressed in wages in consequence of the depressed profits of the manufacturer?—I believe it is.

1421. What do you consider to be the cause?—I cannot attribute it to anything else but the introduction of goods that we were not accustomed to formerly.

1422. Do you imagine that if half a million of foreign goods were not introduced into this market, you would have more employment and better prices?—I have no doubt about it.

1423. If half a million of goods were not made by foreigners, and introduced here, do you think that you should have some of them to make?—Yes, I should indulge myself with that expectation.

1424. If half a million of goods were not imported in a year, would that circumstance lessen or increase the trade?—Increase it, undoubtedly.

1425. What proportion of work can an engine machine do compared with a single hand?—I am not prepared to answer many questions respecting the engine, for the depressed state of the trade, since the introduction of it, has prevented our having much to do with it.

1426. At one time you were actively employed; will you mention any one year when that was the case?—1826.

1427. What did you make in that year?—Brocade gauzes.

1428. Do you make any of them now?—I have not seen an article of the sort these two years, or upwards.

1429. Do you happen to know whether they are used?—There are plenty of them in use.

1430. Do you know where they are manufactured?—I do not, but I see them brought into this market manufactured.

1431. Do you know whether any of them are made in any other part of England? —I never heard that they were.

1432. Do you know the prices at which they are made?—I know what they were when I was employed upon them.

1433. Can they be made in an engine?—No, they can be made in a jacquard machine, but not in an engine loom.

1434. Then how is it made?—It is made by a jacquard or other machinery, with a single hand loom.

1435. Are they made in Coventry?—No; I have not heard of the article being made in Coventry.

1436. Do you know where they are made?—No; unless they are made in a foreign country.

1437. Suppose they made them cheaper in an engine loom than in the single hand, would not that account for a manufacturer employing persons to do it in the way in which he can get it cheapest done?—Yes, that is the cause.

1438. You were understood to ascribe it to the importation of French goods?— I was speaking of the gauzes; there is no doubt there is an increase in the engine looms.

1439. If you were a manufacturer, and could get your plain ribbons made by an engine for 1 s. 3 d. less than by the hand loom, would you not employ the engine? —Most likely.

1440. Can you not suppose that the manufacturers are adopting that mode, and therefore that the single hand weavers are less in demand?—It may in a small degree.

1441. Might not that account for the single hand loom weavers being so much distressed at the present time?—I cannot think so altogether.

1442. Before the Table of Wages of the 10th November 1831, were not the single hand weavers employed in making a variety of goods which have since ceased to be made by them?—No, I cannot speak to any thing positive as to that; I do not know that any thing has declined in the employment of the single hand branch, except the gauzes which have been lost.

678.

1443. Is

*Joseph Marston.*
———
26 March,
1832.

1443. Is there any article in Coventry that the single hand loom and the engine can both make?—The sarsnetts more particularly than any thing else.

1444. Take thirty-penny lutestrings, the rate of which is put down by the November Table at 7 s. 6 d.; can that be made both in single hand and in engine looms?—Exactly so.

1445. If you were working the single hand loom, and another man was working the engine loom, how many could you make, and how many could he make?—I think the number of shuttles in an engine is about four, and that man would make two pieces; perhaps a single hand weaver would not make above a piece and a half.

1446. Then it would not be twice as much?—No, not quite.

1447. Do you think that the engine loom, in making plain sarsnett or lutestring ribbons, within the last six years, has materially affected the hand loom weaver?—I do not think it has materially, for the reason that there are rich articles made which the manufacturers always prefer putting in the single hand loom.

1448. With regard to the Table of Wages, were you a party to that?—I never was a party in establishing the list, or soliciting the manufacturers to establish a list.

1449. What was the rise that took place after that Table was agreed to?—We got an advance, I think, to 5 s. 6 d.; I believe we got that advance upon the lutestrings and satins and the satin figures.

1450. Of what width?—The widths prevailing in the satin figures are chiefly thirty-pennies.

1451. Have you made as many thirty-penny ribbons since that as you did before?—I have not found any decrease, but so far as there is any alteration, rather an increase.

1452. Your trade has been better since November 1831?—There has been more work in that one branch, being a prevailing article.

1453. In what other branch have you fallen off?—I cannot say that we have fallen off in any thing since December, but there has been little alteration in the satin figures.

1454. If the same things are made to the same amount, how do you account for the increase of the distress?—The longer it exists the worse it gets; we have so little employment that we can scarce perceive any amendment, and it is so partial that the trade is now in a very bad state indeed.

1455. What is the season of the year in which your trade is generally most fully employed?—This at the present day.

1456. Has there been so much improvement as there has been generally in former years at this present season?—No, by no means.

1457. Then if you are only stationary now, as compared with last December, you are in fact worse off than in former years?—Yes.

1458. Can you account for that?—I cannot account for it, for I can see the haberdasher's windows in this metropolis elegantly dressed with ribbons of a foreign manufacture, whereas before, I could have owned some of those patterns as made in my own neighbourhood.

1459. Have you any difficulty in distinguishing between the Foreign and the British made brocade gauzes and figured satins?—None; people that have been as long in the business as I have been can distinguish them perfectly.

1460. How do you distinguish them?—By the colour in a great measure.

1461. What was the object of the list made in November, was it not to raise the wages of the hand loom to an equality with the engine weaver?—It was to equalize the wages; and so unsettled was the trade before, that some of the manufacturers quite declined altogether finding any employment. The consequence was at last to have an understanding as to the rate of wages; the operatives thought it was in consequence of the unsettled state of the wages; so that an adjustment took place in November, and they have obtained that fair understanding of what we were to have for that portion of work that we might have to manufacture.

1462. Then was it your opinion that by this Table, which raised the wages, the manufacturer would be better able to pay them?—Certainly; they were upon a safer ground with reference to the goods manufactured for their spring stock; they were upon an equality with others.

1463. Can you really suppose that if the manufacturers were unable to give the wages which were low before November, they would be better able to give them by raising them according to those Tables?—In the face of a season like the present, we thought it a duty to ask them; but as to giving an answer whether they could better afford it or not, I can only say that they have willingly come forward and raised the wages a trifle.

1464. Since

*Joseph Marston.*

26 March,
1832.

1464. Since these Tables were made which raised the wages, have those prices been kept to?—I have not heard of a deviation in one instance.

1465. Do you recollect former Tables being made in 1829 and 1826, and 1824?—Yes.

1466. Were the rates by those Tables generally fixed?—I never knew so much uniformity in a list as in the present one. The manufacturers and the operatives have had an understanding, and it gives a great deal of satisfaction on both sides.

1467. Now for the work that is done, do the single hand weavers and the engine weavers get nearly the same?—With a small distinction.

1468. To what amount may the difference be?—It may be from 1 s. in the pound to 1 s. 6 d.

1469. You have stated the average of wages to be 5 s. 6 d., do you mean the average wages of every person employed?—I mean a man when he is full employed as a regular man in the business.

1470. Have you heard of the resolution of November 1831, by which the masters agreed that they would give out no work for the single hand looms but by undertakers?—I have heard of it; but I had nothing to do with the deputation that waited upon the manufacturers.

1471. Did you not work under it?—I did.

1472. To what extent are you an undertaker?—I have about 10 people under me when I have full work.

1473. How many children do they employ under them?—Ten workmen would employ three or four children.

1474. Are you able to state the amount that is allowed you for winding, warping and superintending; what proportion of it is reserved for the undertaker?—We do not realize more than 6 d. to 8 d. upon a piece of satin, and in some cases, where the pattern is rich work, we do not get a farthing upon it; at the present rate of wages, for instance, upon rich pads, we do not get a farthing more than the price of winding, warping and paying the journeyhand.

1475. Suppose 50 s. is allowed you by the master, do you mean that you would only get 3 s. out of that?—Not more.

1476. Do you employ any apprentices?—Yes, I have one apprentice.

1477. What do you tax him to do a week?—I am sorry to say, latterly I could not tax my boy as I used to do, for want of employment; and when we have a bit of work, we are forced to work as much as we can, and to work longer than is lawful, because we are so long and so frequently without.

1478. Is there not a rule for apprentices generally?—I always had one till I was forced to deviate from it.

1479. Has it been the practice of the trade generally to tax the apprentices to earn 16 s. a week?—No, by no means; and we generally set them a length. I could not boast, in the present day, of my apprentice earning me more than 5 s. when employed, when I take the necessary expenses for winding, warping, and filling out; and then a great portion of the time he has no work to do.

1480. Do you mean to say, that no apprentices are taxed above 5 s. 6 d.?—They must be better off than I am to find employment, to get much more wages at the present day, although I work for a very respectable manufacturer, and upon as good work as any that the trade make.

1481. Is there any rule for taxing apprentices?—I never heard of any rule being permanent amongst them; where there are many undertakers in the different neighbourhoods, they may be employed upon different articles, one a lutestring weaver, and another a guaze weaver.

1482. What has been the rule that you yourself have followed formerly?—I have set my apprentice formerly to get me 9 s. a week; that is, the boy in the latter part of his apprenticeship, when he is capable of working with a journeyman.

1483. In what year did you do that?—In the years 1826 and 1827; previous to that, I had not any thing to do with apprentices.

1484. In 1828 and 1829, what was the rate?—I should have been well satisfied if I had got 4 s. a week paid through those years.

1485. Had you to keep that apprentice out of the 4 s. a week?—Yes; and washing and lodging.

1486. When you taxed your apprentice at 9 s., in 1826, what could an able workman earn in the week?—I had then 14 s. and 15 s. earnings by a journeyman, a good workman; in some cases more.

1487. Is it in consequence of the want of work, or low wages?—It is the two

things

things together; the one thing always accompanied the other in our market; if we are short of work, we are short in price also.

1488. Then are the Committee to understand, that the rate of wages made in November last, though it made a considerable rise, is not sufficient?—No, it is quite inadequate to keep a decent house, in the closest way possible.

1489. Do you know what wages are paid at Congleton and Manchester to weavers?—I know nothing about them whatever.

1490. Do you know what rate of wages is paid at Reading, or in any other part where silk is made?—No.

1491. Do you know the rate of wages of our cotton manufacturers, or any other manufacturers?—Nothing whatever.

1492. You have been asked whether engine looms would not perform more work; if they would perform more work, and you were generally to use them, would not that throw more persons out of employment?—Certainly it would, partially, under the present distressed state of trade.

1493. Would the importing of foreign goods assist you in that case?—Undoubtedly not.

1494. Did you ever know any persons who had any thing to leave behind them, or to support them in case of infirmities and old age, upon the wages you have mentioned?—Formerly.

1495. Could you do it now?—By no means.

1496. Have you any other prospect but the workhouse before you?—Nothing else; there is not one in a thousand that can keep their house.

1497. Has your reduction in wages, within a few years, been as much as one or two shillings a week?—A good deal more.

1498. In 1819, what did the single hand loom weaver earn?—There was as much as 11 *s.* 6 *d.* got in that period.

1499. What is the price of making a twenty-penny lutestring?—I think it is 5 *s.* 6 *d.* a piece.

1500. What does the piece weigh?—About six ounces.

1501. In 1827, you have said, there were only five houses in the parish unoccupied, and you say that now there are 100 houses unoccupied, with a population as large in 1827 as it is now?—The population might not be quite so large as it is, since some people have gone, through distress, to other parishes.

1502. Are there not men employed upon the roads in your parish?—We have fifty able-bodied men employed upon the roads, and they are paid out of an extra composition rate granted for that purpose. We have a separate rate called the Composition, for the use of the highways, and the proprietors of the houses pay that the same as the poor's rate.

1503. Is that stated in the return you have given in of the poor's rate?—It is not included in that return.

1504. How long have you adopted that system?—Within the last two years.

1505. Then, in point of fact, the whole amount of the money collected for the relief of the poor, is much greater than is stated in the return you have given in?—Yes, because we shall spend the composition rate in addition to the poor's rates; and I have got an account from the overseer which says, that 20 *l.* a week is paid at the present day for that purpose.

1506. Are the single hand weavers worse now than they were in 1818, when Samuel Makin stated in evidence, that " a single loom could only earn about 5 *s.* 6 *d.* or thereabouts. It does not vary but a mere trifle one way or the other; perhaps some weeks they do not earn more than three or four shillings?"—I mean to say, that we are not so well off for employment now as we were then.

1507. Although the rate of wages may be 5 *s.* 6 *d.* when you are employed, you mean to say, that you are not employed more than one-third of the week, and consequently you earn only 1 *s.* 10 *d.*?—That is the case.

1508. Was there not a list of prices agreed to in 1816?—I have heard of such a thing.

1509. What description of silk do you use in your manufacture?—We always have it in a dyed state; but as to its name and its nature I am not conversant enough with it to answer that.

1510. How many years have you been in the habit of manufacturing the fine gauzes you have alluded to?—The first I recollect of them was about the year 1820.

1511. Have you any other observations to make to the Committee?—I wish to
show

show to the Committee the difference in the nature of the work as accounting for the consumption of the silk.

*Joseph Marston.*

26 March, 1832.

[*The Witness produced some samples of silk.*]

1512. What article do you call this?—A rich belt or pad.

1513. What is the weight of a piece of that?—Eighteen ounces.

1514. What is the price paid for weaving it?—Nine shillings.

1515. What do you call that ribbon? (*Another specimen being pointed out.*)—A gauze. That is a thirty-penny gauze figure.

1516. What are you paid for weaving it?—Eighteen shillings.

1517. What does it weigh?—About four ounces and a half.

1518. Here is a gauze not so wide. (*Another specimen.*) What do you call this? —That is a satin gauze figure.

1519. What are you paid for weaving this?—From 15s. to 16s.

1520. What does it weigh?—About four and a half to five ounces.

1521. Is that made in any engine?—No, those are all single hand goods.

1522. Can that be made in an engine?—Yes.

1523. Would you get the same price for making them in an engine as you get for making them in a single hand loom?—About the same.

1524. Will you produce any one which cannot be made in an engine loom?— Here is a thirty-penny brook-edge gauze. (*pointing it out.*)

1525. Why cannot you make this in an engine loom?—That is made with a shuttle, and a shuttle is a fixture; but that is forced to be shifted by the hand.

1526. Do you mean to say that that cannot be made by the Jacquard?—It could be made by the Jacquard by a single hand.

1527. Do you make any thing as large and as beautiful as that without the Jacquard?—That I have made without the Jacquard; I never was in possession of a Jacquard.

1528. Does not the labour upon an ounce of silk cost as much as the labour upon a pound in some instances?—It does.

### James Perkins, called in; and Examined.

1529. WHAT are you?—A Jacquard engine loom weaver at Coventry.

*James Perkins.*

1530. How long have you been employed in using the Jacquard engine?—I have been in the figure trade nearly ten years.

1531. When did you first use the Jacquard loom?—About two or three years ago.

1532. Do you know whether the use of the Jacquard engine is to be considered as an addition to the fancy looms employed, or merely a change from one to the other?—Most decidedly only a change.

1533. Are the other engines that you formerly used nearly abandoned, and the Jacquard engine substituted in its stead?—They are quite abandoned.

1534. Do you know the number of looms used in 1822 or 1823?—No.

1535. Are you aware how many of the former figured looms were superseded by the Jacquard looms?—I think a greater number than the number of Jacquard looms now in use.

1536. Do you mean to say that the total number of looms employed in making fancy ribbons was as great formerly as the total number now employed of the Jacquard and the common looms?—No; I mean that there were more engine looms that made figures previous to the introduction of the Jacquard machine than there are Jacquard machine looms at work at this time.

1537. Do you know how many Jacquard machines there are now at Coventry?— Between 650 and 700.

1538. Do you know how many other figured looms there are at work now at Coventry?—I should not think there was one.

1539. Do you then imagine that there were not as many as 700 looms employed before the year 1823?—I imagine there were more making figured ribbons, but I do not know how many.

1540. Can the Jacquard apparatus be applied to the engine loom?—Yes.

1541. Are you aware that in 1818 there were 3,000 engine looms at Coventry? —I am aware it was so stated.

1542. How many are there now?—Four thousand four hundred was the last account.

1543. And of that number there are 650 that have the Jacquard apparatus applied?—Yes.

678.

1544. What

*James Perkins.*

26 March,
1832.

1544. What is the total number of looms now employed in making fancy ribbons? —Between 650 and 700; the additional quantity to make up the 4,400 are employed in making plain ribbons.

1545. Then all the looms now at Coventry, making fancy ribbons, have the Jacquard apparatus applied to them?—Yes.

1546. Did you examine the new mill that was built for Mr. Woodhouse?—No.

1547. Do you know whether it was for applying the Jacquard apparatus?—I do not know; but I should not expect that it was; I am of opinion that it was to be applied to making of plain goods, but I did not see it at all.

1548. Have you ever seen the a-la-bar loom?—No.

1549. Have you ever been at Reading?—No.

1550. Have you ever been at Congleton to see the apparatus there?—No.

1551. Then you do not know anything of any other machinery but the engine loom and the Jacquard machine?—No.

1552. What proportion of work can you do upon an engine loom figured in comparison with a single hand-loom?—I heard the last witness give his evidence, and I am decidedly of opinion that he gave a correct evidence in that respect.

1553. About one-fourth more?—Yes.

1554. What wages have you earned in the last year when at full work?—I should think the average earnings, if we had had full work, would have been from fourteen to sixteen shillings.

1555. In any one week what have you earned?—In one week we have perhaps earned 23 s. or 24 s., but we are not in the habit of having warps in a loom that will last us above four or five weeks.

1556. In 1829 were your wages better?—Yes, they were something better, and the alterations were not quite so frequent.

1557. Are you employed now principally in imitating French patterns, or in making patterns from what the manufacturers give you?—The manufacturers on all occasions give us the patterns.

1558. On paper or on silk?—The manufacturer provides drafts and card papers that are used, and those are got ready for us, so that we have nothing to do with either the design or the pattern, those cards are prepared for us, and we put them in in the proper place, and they make the pattern.

1559. Is there a class of men at Coventry called designers?—There are a few, I know two or three.

1560. Are those employed by manufacturers to put on the figures?—Yes.

1561. Are you oftener employed to make new figures than you are to imitate French patterns?—In all cases they are new figures to us, we do not know whether they are French patterns or any other patterns.

1562. Have you that piece sent, or a card?—On all occasions cards.

1563. What time do you lose in getting the work into the loom?—About two weeks in six.

1564. You say that you earn fourteen shillings a week for those six weeks?—Yes.

1565. Were you idle for want of work any part of last year?—Yes.

1566. How many weeks in the year were you absolutely idle?—I should suppose nine or ten.

1567. Did you serve an apprenticeship?—Yes.

1568. How long?—Seven years.

1569. What were you taxed to do during the time you were an apprentice?—It varied according to the work. I have been taxed in the course of my apprenticeship to 16 s. a week, but that was on quite a different nature of article from what we work on now; that was on a figured loom; it was satin figures, and they had not near the labour in them, because there was not the great quantity of work that we now use, and fewer shutes were then put in, consequently they were of a nature that we could earn more upon than we can at present.

1570. Do you make any of those articles now?—There are satin figures making, but of a different style and quality.

1571. What work are you engaged upon when at home?—On the Jacquard machine, in making satin figures, at present.

1572. Of what width?—Thirty-penny.

1573. Have you been long upon it?—About a year and a quarter; I have had four or five alterations of the pattern within that time.

1574. What quantity do you make in a width?—When I have no alteration, I generally make about four half lengths in the six weeks; in the six weeks I make about ten pieces.

1575. What

*James Perkins,*
26 March, 1832.

1575. What is the price paid for each piece?—Twelve shillings.

1576. Then that is 20*s.* a week, at six weeks?—Yes; mine is a five-shuttle loom; but there are as many made in a four-shuttle loom.

1577. Does that six weeks include the setting up of the pattern?—No, it does not include the setting up of the pattern; merely the getting in of the warps.

1578. Do you mean to say, that when the loom is fitted up, that you are in the habit of earning 20*s.* a week?—Yes; but besides the time lost in getting in the warps, there are other losses in alterations, and so on.

1579. Have you any thing to pay for shute-filling out of what you earn?—Yes, half a crown.

---

## *Mercurii, 28° die Martii, 1832.*

### THE RIGHT HON. THE EARL GROSVENOR, IN THE CHAIR.

Mr. *William Jacombs*, called in; and Examined.

Mr. *William Jacombs.*
28 March, 1832.

1580. YOU reside in Nuneaton, and are a ribbon manufacturer?—Yes.

1581. Have you got an account of the poor-rates in your parish?—I have here a statement of them, which I believe to be correct, and which I assisted myself in preparing from the parish books.

[*The Witness delivered in the same, which was read, as follows:*]

GENERAL EXPENSES of the Parish of *Nuneaton.*

| PERIOD. | COUNTY RATES. £. | s. | d. | Nº of Poor Rates. | Workhouse Expenses. £. | s. | d. | Nº of Persons relieved, besides those in the Workhouse. | Amount of MONEY Paid to, and in respect of the Poor. £. | s. | d. | TOTAL. £. | s. | d. | |
|---|---|---|---|---|---|---|---|---|---|---|---|---|---|---|---|
| From Lady-day 1818 to Lady day 1819 | 192 | – | – | 11½ | 782 | 12 | 11½ | 1,836 | 2,964 | – | – | 3,938 | 12 | 11 | (1) |
| To Lady-day 1820 | 235 | 16 | 8 | 12 | 732 | 12 | 7½ | 1,912 | 3,224 | 9 | 5½ | 4,192 | 18 | 9 | (1) |
| To Lady-day 1821 | 215 | 12 | 3½ | 7¾ | 511 | 10 | 2 | 1,548 | 2,225 | 5 | 2 | 2,952 | 7 | 7½ | (2) |
| To Lady-day 1822 | 189 | 2 | 9½ | 7 | 440 | 1 | 7 | 1,232 | 1,754 | 1 | 7½ | 2,383 | 6 | – | (2) |
| To Lady-day 1823 | 135 | 4 | 8½ | 5 | 283 | 15 | 1½ | 1,088 | 1,463 | 13 | 3½ | 1,882 | 13 | 1½ | (2) |
| To Lady-day 1824 | 107 | 16 | 2 | 6 | 432 | 1 | 5½ | 1,168 | 1,842 | 11 | 2½ | 2,382 | 8 | 10 | (2) |
| To Lady-day 1825 | 202 | 2 | 9½ | 6 | 378 | 17 | 8½ | 920 | 1,639 | 5 | 8¼ | 2,220 | 6 | 2¼ | (2) |
| To Lady-day 1826 | 202 | 2 | 10 | 5 | 443 | 2 | 2½ | 888 | 1,353 | 8 | 10 | 1,998 | 13 | 10½ | |
| To Lady-day 1827 | 215 | 12 | 4½ | 6½ | 510 | 3 | 8½ | 936 | 1,785 | 16 | 1 | 2,511 | 12 | 2 | (3) |
| To Lady-day 1828 | 188 | 17 | 3½ | 6 | 460 | 4 | 9 | 972 | 1,551 | 16 | 8¾ | 2,200 | 18 | 9¼ | (3) |
| To Lady-day 1829 | 202 | 2 | 10 | 5½ | 419 | 15 | –½ | 1,008 | 1,685 | 4 | 7 | 2,307 | 2 | 5½ | (3) |
| To Lady-day 1830 | 215 | 12 | 4 | 11½ | 667 | 3 | 7½ | 2,980 | 3,769 | 5 | 6 | 4,652 | 1 | 5½ | (3) |
| To Lady-day 1831 | 229 | 9 | 5 | 7½ | 589 | 10 | 7 | 1,998 | 2,800 | 5 | 11¾ | 3,619 | 5 | 11¾ | (3) |
| — 1832 | 296 | 9 | 5½ | 12 | 726 | 11 | 3 | 3,240 | 3,759 | 8 | –½ | 4,782 | 8 | 9 | |

OBSERVATIONS:

(1) 1819 & 1820.—During these years there was no Select Vestry. A tradesman had a salary of £. 150 a-year to collect the levies and pay the poor; and very much of the parish money went into the shop, even before it was paid from the Workhouse, and many were most improperly relieved. In short, there was great mismanagement; for in 1820, 1,912 Paupers cost the parish £. 3,224. 9. 5½. or about 34*s.* 9*d.* per head; whereas in 1832, 3,240 Paupers were supported for £. 3,759. 8. 0½. or about £. 1. 3. 2. per head, although in 1819 and 1820 the trade was very fair, and the prices tolerably good.

(2) In 1821, Select Vestry apointed for the parish of Nuneaton.

The Five years' expenses, before the importation of French ribbons was allowed - - - - - - - - - - - - - - - - is } £. 11,821. 1. 9½.

(3) The Five years' expenses, after the importation of French ribbons was allowed - - - - - - - - - - - - - - - is } £. 15,291. 1. 8.

In the year 1830, soup was given to about 2,500 poor inhabitants, four days each week, raised entirely from voluntary contributions.

In the present year, soup and bread has been given to at least 3,000 of the inhabitants, three days each week, from the middle of November to the present time, including many families who did not receive parochial relief; all raised by voluntary contributions.

There is much more accommodation in the Workhouse than in 1819 and 1820; and, in the present year, there has been at least one-third more Paupers supported in it than in the first-mentioned two years, although the expenses have been less.

At Lady-day 1831, the Overseer of the Poor has £. 200 in hand, which makes the present expenditure £. 4,982. 8. 9.



1582. Does

1582. Do you know how many persons there are in the parish of Nuneaton depending upon the ribbon trade for support?—Upwards of 6,000.

1583. How many looms are there?—There are upwards of 3,000 in the whole, besides winders and warpers.

1584. Can you state what number of those are single hand looms?—I cannot exactly say that, but the greater portion of them are single hand looms.

1585. How many looms are there?—There are about 3,000 looms.

1586. You said that there were 6,000 persons depending upon the ribbon trade, do you mean to say that there is that number of persons employed in the ribbon trade?—No; that includes children not able to work; children of weavers.

1587. But there are upwards of 4,000 persons actually employed?—Yes; if they could get it to do.

1588. Has there been any material reduction in wages since 1826?—Yes, very great. I myself paid from 2*l.* 10*s.* to 3*l.* 4*s.* for the manufacturing of sixteen ounces (a pound of silk) into ribbons; and now the price, for the same article and the same quantity of silk, is only from 20*s.* to 24*s.*

1589. Do you mean that that silk is consumed in the same description of work? —It is.

1590. Has machinery much depreciated in value?—Yes, very much; many looms have been sold under distress for rent, for less than one-fourth of the cost.

1591. What description of looms were those?—Various descriptions, single hand as well as engine looms.

1592. Do you think any looms have been sold under their value besides what had been sold under distress for rent?—Yes; I purchased jacquard engine looms myself, in May last, for 18 *l.* each, which I should suppose cost from 40*l.* to 50*l.* each.

1593. When did they cost that?—If they were built in the year 1827 or 1828.

1594. Did you buy them of a weaver, or some one who was compelled to sell them?—No; I bought them of a ribbon manufacturer, Mr. James Jenkins, of Coventry.

1595. What do you suppose induced him to sell them?—He told me the reason was, because he was giving up the fancy trade, for he could not obtain any profit on fancy ribbons, and I bought them myself on speculation; under the impression, that some efficient relief would be given to the ribbon trade, and thereby we should be able to employ them to advantage.

1596. Have you used them yet?—We have, to a small extent.

1597. Did he make any remark to you, about his reasons for selling them?— He stated that the reason he was selling them was, that he was giving up the fancy trade; that he could get nothing upon that article.

1598. To what do you attribute the present distress?—To the introduction of French ribbons, decidedly.

1599. Do you think there was any improvement in the manufacture of ribbons previous to 1826?—Yes, very great.

1600. Do you think that that improvement would have continued to as great an extent, without the introduction of foreign ribbons, as it has with them?—Yes, certainly to a greater extent; but now there is no encouragement to improve; if we introduce ever so beautiful an article the French fashion is preferred, and our goods are considered as unsaleable and useless, if not exactly like theirs.

1601. Is not Mr. Jenkins disposing of his machines to you for so much less than they cost him, a proof that there is no great inducement to invest much money in machinery?—Yes.

1602. Can you not get the patterns of those articles that the French are making, and make them in time to bring them into the market as soon as they can? —No; the French take orders from patterns, but we have no means of knowing what those patterns are, till they are actually imported and presented for sale.

1603. Do you know any thing of the mode of buying ribbons in the French market, and are you aware whether the principal sales are made by persons coming here to exhibit the pattern, or whether, in fact, the English houses do not send over buyers to St. Etienne there to make the purchases?—I believe many of the English houses send over their buyers to St. Etienne for that purpose.

1604. Cannot you sell your new fancy ribbons before the French houses import theirs?—No; the buyers wait to know what the French patterns are before they will look at our new fancy ribbons; and if there should happen to be some trifling difference ours are considered unsaleable and useless.

1605. Was that the custom formerly?—Certainly not; we were enabled to make

our

Mr.
*William Jacombs.*

28 March,
1832.

our own patterns from original designs, and when the season commenced to intro-duce them for sale, and we were able to lead the fashion.

1606. Did you on many occasions sell your goods before they were cut off the loom, from the patterns so made?—Generally so, prior to the introduction of French ribbons.

1607. That is, the practice with you was what it now is in France?– Exactly so.

1608. Then you think that the taste has changed here, that they prefer French ribbons to English ribbons?—Decidedly, be the price what it may.

1609. Then, of course, where the manufacturer executed his orders from patterns, he did it without loss or risk?—Yes.

1610. What would be the expense of putting to work a French pattern?—It depends upon the size and nature of the pattern; from 5*l*. to 8*l*. is the average. We have patterns at the present time making that have cost us from 12*l*. to 14*l*., but that is an extraordinary large pattern; but I reckon that the average cost of those alterations on our Jacquard looms is from 12*l*. to 13*l*. per annum on each loom, for the mere changing of patterns, and the alterations necessary for such changes.

1611. Do you think ribbons are as much worn as they formerly were?—They are more generally worn, no doubt.

1612. Do you yourself know from observation and in fact, that ribbons are absolutely more worn upon bonnets than formerly?—Most assuredly they are, in my opinion.

1613. Where have you been in the habit of selling your goods?—From 1823, when we commenced business, to 1826, we had a very excellent connection among the town haberdashers, where we sold all the ribbons that we made; but at that time, when French ribbons were introduced, we felt convinced of the consequences that would follow, that they would be able to purchase French ribbons and we then turned our whole attention to seek a connection in the country.

1614. Did you send out a traveller?—We did, and also myself and my partner travelled to most of the towns in England where we did establish a connection, and for the first two years we could sell most of the goods we made; but in 1829 we found that French ribbons were so rapidly circulating through the country, that eventually we were completely shut out from both town and country connections.

1615. Then is the result of all this, that you are making very few fancy goods?—Very few, indeed.

1616. Do you not suppose that steam may be applied with advantage in the manufacture of fancy ribbons?—Certainly not; for fancy ribbons being of so fine a texture, and the complicated machinery requisite to make fancy ribbons being compressed into so small a space, it will always require the same personal attention as it would if the machine was propelled by manual power.

1617. You are aware that steam power is applied to the manufacture of ribbons in Manchester?—Yes, I have seen it; but they were only plain ribbons of a common sort, made from strong coarse silk.

1618. Have you any patterns to show to the Committee?--Yes, I have. (*The Witness produced the same.*)

1619. What is your object in showing these patterns?—I wish to make this remark, and to show the result of the introduction of French ribbon; some of these patterns were put into the express order of a certain house, from an original design, who promised to take all we made of the pattern, provided we would confine it to themselves; we did so, and put it in according to their order, and in the month of September we had a small assortment made ready to show them; but it happened so that the French had brought in their new ribbons before we showed ours (or about the same time), and there was a trifling difference in the style; the conse-quence was that they would not take our goods, because they were perfectly useless, the preference being given to the French fashions.

1620. When you say a trifling difference, do you mean that they were the same description of article, but varied in some degree?—Ours were figured bonnet ribbons; their's were two-coloured satin figures for bonnet ribbons.

1621. What do you call this?—This is a double figure upon ground with satin stripe.

1622. And yet they consider that trifling difference as fatal to that pattern?—They did; in consequence of which they would not take it, and we felt satisfied in our minds that others would buy it, as the pattern was generally admired; but, however, others made the same objection, and the consequence is that we have the

whole

Mr.
*William Jacombs.*
———
28 March,
1832.

whole of the goods in our drawers, and should be glad to sell them considerably under cost price.

1623. Did you make a contract with that house?—We did not make a contract, because we did not know what price the ribbons would be.

1624. Did you make them at your own risk?—In a certain sense, but not altogether; we were told they would take the pattern, if we made it to their order.

1625. Is not the custom with the trade, that when parties say we will take the pattern, it is presumed that there will be a fair dealing between you, and the parties are considered bound to take that pattern?—Decidedly so.

1626. Then their refusal to take that pattern was a departure from the usual custom of your trade?—Certainly it was.

1627. Why did you not proceed to compel them to take the pattern?—Because at that time we felt sure that as the pattern was so much admired that we should sell it to others, and we did not wish to offend the house by taking legal proceedings.

1628. If a customer is whimsical and throws the patterns up, would it be prudent for you always to proceed to law?—Most assuredly not.

1629. Have you any other patterns to show?—I have some patterns of gauze ribbons to show the improvement we have made, and the money we paid for manufacturing a pound of silk into gauze ribbons in 1823 and 1824, and what we should pay at the present time if we made them.

1630. Do you now make any of those gauze ribbons?—None of them since 1828.

1631. Will you state what you paid prior to 1824, and what you should now pay if you made those ribbons?—As I said before, from 2*l.* 10*s.* to 3*l.* 4*s.* we paid in the year 1823 and 1824, and now if we were making the same article we should pay only from 20*s.* to 24*s.*

1632. Was there any material reduction in 1826?—There was.

1633. What rate per cent.?—I have not made that calculation; but I think a similar calculation has been made by others.

1634. Have you now abandoned the manufacture of gauze fancy ribbons?—Entirely, since 1828.

1635. Speaking of patterns, have you any artists that provide you patterns?—Yes, we have.

1636. Before the prohibition was removed, were you in the habit of imitating the French patterns?—Sometimes we were, not regularly; we could make our own, and they were generally approved of.

1637. Do you rely now entirely upon your own artists for your patterns?—Yes; for it is of no use to copy the French pattern, we should not have it in time, and we do not know the pattern they will bring until the goods are brought in.

1638. Do you never copy any French patterns?—We have done it, I am sorry to say, and lost seriously by them.

1639. Would they not sell, though they may not take the first of the market here?—They perhaps might sell at a loss of 30 or 40 per cent. which we have often done.

1640. You have stated, that there are 3,000 looms at Nuneaton, how many of those are Jacquard, and how many engine and how many hand looms?—I do not know how many are engine looms, nor how many are Jacquard looms.

1641. How did you get that amount?—It was a census taken in December.

1642. Was there no distinction made between the different kinds of looms?—There was not.

1643. Do you know what number of looms there were at Nuneaton in 1818?—I do not.

1644. Are you aware, that it is stated before this Committee, that there were 500 engine looms, and 1,000 single hand looms?—I am not.

1645. If that account was correct, has not the number of looms doubled in Nuneaton in that time?—I cannot say what it was since 1818, that was before I had any thing to do with the business on my own account.

1646. Whatever might be the number, were they all well employed?—They were.

1647. Up to what period were they well employed?—Up to 1828.

1648. Do you mean that there was no interval of bad trade between 1818 and 1828?—There might be some intervals of slack trade, but it was quite a temporary thing.

1649. To what period can you speak to your own knowledge?—Not further back than 1820.

1650. Were

Mr.
*William Jacombs.*

28 March,
1832.

1650. Were there no periods of bad trade between 1820 and 1828 ?—Most assuredly we had short intervals of slack trade ; but we were employing our weavers pretty well, because we knew we should sell them in the next season ; for instance, we made spring ribbons in the winter months.

1651. Was not 1827 a very good year ?—Yes ; it was partly owing to the French not being aware of what sort of a connection they were to fall into, and they were not prepared with the right sort of goods.

1652. In 1828, was not your trade very good ?—It was not so good in 1828 as in 1827.

1653. In the spring of 1830, was not the trade at Nuneaton very brisk ?—It was not very brisk, it was better than it was in 1831.

1654. Do you recollect how it was in the winter of 1830 ?—It was bad.

1655. In the spring of 1831 again, how was it ?—Very bad, but better than this spring.

1656. And this year it is now worse than it has been since you recollect ?—Much worse ; here are some patterns that we made last spring, which we were in the full expectation of selling, but which unfortunately were superseded by the French gauzes; these are bonnet ribbons (*pointing out the same*) ; and the consequence was, that they were left on our hands unsold, and we have this spring sold them at 30 per cent. loss. In those goods there are at least sixteen ounces in the piece, and in former years we have made fancy ribbons such as we have sold with five to seven ounces each, but we have been driven out of that branch of the trade.

1657. Is that made from a pattern drawn by an artist of your own ?—It is.

1658. You stated that you bought Jacquard looms in 1831 at a great depreciation of price, and to work them at Nuneaton ?—Yes.

1659. Cannot you state how many Jacquard looms there are at Nuneaton ?—I cannot.

1660. How many have you got ?—From 45 to 50.

1661. Were those you bought of the best kind ?—I know of no improvement upon the Jacquard machine, the Jacquard machine is the best kind for fancy ribbons.

1662. You mean that they were not sold for less money, as being inferior things ? —Certainly not ; they are the same sort that are made at the present time.

1663. Have you any knowledge of the fall that has taken place in the price of machinery generally, cotton and every other kind of machinery, within the last four years ?—I am not acquainted with it.

1664. Do you know what would be the cost of such a machine at the present moment?—I should think that if we were to purchase the machine and the loom altogether from the manufacturer, it would be as much as from 28 to 32 *l.*, including the mounting, &c.

1665. Have not the machines you bought been made since 1826?—I should think they were, but I cannot tell when they were made.

1666. You are understood to state that before 1826, before the introduction of French ribbons, great improvements had taken place in the quality of the ribbons of Coventry, but that none have taken place since?—I did not say that none have taken place since, but not to so great an extent as prior to 1826.

1667. But there were more improvements between 1820 and 1826 than between 1826 and this time ?—Upon the article that we worked there was a greater improvement up to 1826 than since 1826, that was gauze ribbons.

1668. When were gauze ribbons first introduced?—I cannot say, we made them first in 1823.

1669. Were there any made from 1820 ?—I should think very likely there were.

1670. You stated that you paid a high price, might not that high price be owing to its being a new article in 1823 ?—I think others were paying quite as high as ourselves.

1671. Was it a new article in Coventry ?—No ; because I suppose it was made before 1820 in Coventry to some extent.

1672. What proportion of fancy and of plain goods did you make ?—We have generally been entirely upon fancy goods.

1673. Do you continue that ?—We continue making fancy goods, what we do make.

1674. What sort of persons are they that design the patterns?—They are persons that we call designers.

1675. Have you not understood that in France they employ a superior class of persons for that purpose ?—I consider ours a superior class of persons.

678.                                                          1676. The

Mr.
*William Jacombs.*

28 March,
1832.

1676. The word artist would imply a person taught in some skill of drawing; is that the case with the persons employed at Coventry?—I cannot say how they get a knowledge of it, I only know they bring the patterns or designs to us.

1677. Is it not understood that the French have a class of people for that purpose, superior to the same persons generally employed in this country?—I never understood it.

1678. You have stated that ribbons are much more worn now than formerly; will you state what is the price now, and what was the price in 1824 and 1825, of a ribbon of the same quality?—I am not prepared to answer the question; I have not referred to our books to notice that.

1679. You have stated the great reduction in the price of labour; cannot you state what is the reduction in the price of the article?—There is a great reduction no doubt; we buy our silk much cheaper than we used, but I cannot state accurately to what extent.

1680. Cannot your recollection enable you to state the difference of price in any one article, between now and 1823?—I should say there was a considerable reduction, perhaps 30 per cent.

1681. When you prepare a number of fancy goods for the spring, ought you not to obtain a larger profit upon them, in order to cover the losses after they go out of fashion?—We certainly ought, and we expect it.

1682. Are not the spring goods that are sold after the fashion is gone by, sold at a very great loss?—We frequently sell them at less than half price.

1683. Upon many of those fancy goods, if a person in the trade was to cast his eye upon a new fancy article, could he tell the precise value of it within 10 per cent.?—I should think not.

1684. Are there not cases with respect to some of the light fancy articles, new things that have not been seen before, upon which a person in the trade would not know the value within 10 or 20 per cent?— I should think so.

1685. If a ribbon were brought out in the first week in April, in a time of good trade, would it not probably sell for 60 s.; whereas if you did not bring it out until the first week in May, it might probably not sell for 40 s.?—Yes.

1686. Then the great loss you speak of is not a general depreciation upon the market article, but the general loss owing to those fluctuations, and having your goods thrown upon you in consequence of competition?—Just so.

1687. And that is a check to ingenuity, and prevents you from going to expense for new patterns?—Yes.

1688. Do the designers you speak of draw patterns?—They do.

1689. Are they clever ingenious men?—Yes.

1690. Is it their particular business?—It is; they follow it exclusively.

1691. Does not the fluctuation in the trade affect the designers very much; does not it disable you from employing them?—We do not profess to employ them; they prepare them on speculation, and offer them to us for sale.

1692. Does not it often happen that when the market is over-done, some particular individual that has good connections may do pretty well, when his neighbours are badly off?—It is very often the case.

1693. Then when you speak of the depression of trade, you speak from your general knowledge of the state of trade?—Yes; I apply it to all who are situated similarly with myself.

1694. When you bring out new things, and have to enter into competition with your neighbours who bring out a thing as good as yours, do not you run a race as to price?—Yes.

1695. And of course that does not help you much, to let the Frenchman in to compete with you?—I should say very little.

1696. Then the competition against you or any other individual may be both home competition and foreign competition?—Just so.

1697. You have stated that you found yourself shut out at every place; were you shut out by competition at home, or by competition abroad, or by the difference of price, or by difference of taste?—I stated that we were shut out from both town and country connection; when we went round our journies, we were invariably asked by our customers if we had French ribbons; "No; our's are British," was the answer; "Then we can do nothing with you," would be the answer our customers gave us.

1698. Did you ascertain whether the French colours were considered prettier or

more

Mr.
*William Jacombs,*

28 March,
1832.

more varied, or what was the reason?—I cannot say the reason, only that there was a prejudice in favour of French goods.

1699. Have they not introduced into the French patterns generally a greater variety of colours?—There may have been instances where they have introduced a great variety of colours, but I think we have introduced quite as great a variety ourselves.

1700. Do you think your goods have been as varied in colour as the French?—I think so.

1701. Can you state at what comparative price you could bring goods to market, as compared with the French?—I cannot.

1702. Are you able to state the extent of competition in your line from manufacturers in other parts of England?—No, I do not know that.

1703. What do you reckon is the amount of labour paid on one hundred pounds worth of fancy goods?—I have not made any such calculation, and I am not able to answer it.

1704. Are you not able to state, when one hundred pounds worth of gauzes has been finished, how many pounds has been paid for labour?—I have not made that calculation.

1705. Take the card of gauzes you have produced; have you ever made the calculation as to how much any one article should cost you for material, and how much for labour?—I should say, that upon the first article here, the labour would have cost us as much as 75 per cent. at the period we made it, in 1823; but I am not prepared to answer that accurately.

1706. What is the article?—The twelve-penny gauzes.

1707. What would the labour now be upon the same article, if manufactured this year?—I cannot say exactly, because it depends upon the quantity of silk in each pattern, and we have not made them for the last four years.

1708. Taking that particular article, and suppose the same quantity of silk that was then put in was put in now?—I should say it would be about 50 per cent. upon that precise article; but I cannot give any accurate account, having never made the calculation, and would therefore rather decline answering such questions.

1709. Will the same proportion apply to any or all of those gauzes you have produced, or is there any great difference?—There is certainly a material difference, according to the pattern.

1710. Is there any one of those articles upon that card you are now making?—None; I have stated we have not made them for the last four years.

1711. Is that an article you are now making *(a sample being shown to the Witness)*?—We made that article last spring; it is a double figure, upon ground with satin stripe.

1712. Can you state to the Committee what proportion in the cost of that article the material would be?—About 43 or 44 per cent., I should suppose, upon a rough calculation.

1713. How much do you pay for actual labour upon that piece?—I cannot recollect that at the present time, because it is 12 months since we made it.

1714. Is that above or below the average rate of wages you would have to pay in the fancy work generally?—It is rather above the average.

1715. Could you state any average amount of labour upon that kind of ribbon; would it be as low as 25 per cent.?—I should think not, but I cannot state accurately.

1716. Did you find the objection to your goods depend upon the price at which you were able to offer them, or upon the peculiar patterns that your customers wanted?—Nothing but the pattern and style, or the fashion.

1717. Have you any means of knowing whether you can manufacture as cheap as the French, setting taste and fashion aside?—I should not suppose that we can.

1718. Have you ever made any calculation, or seen any calculation that enables you to judge?—None whatever.

1719. In point of fact, have you found that your difficulty in selling your goods has not been owing to the price, but owing to the style?—Owing to the style, on account of the difference of the pattern, though our ribbons are equally good and beautiful, in quality and pattern.

1720. Have not the profits of the manufacturer been much decreased of late years?—I should think they have.

1721. Do you consider that that decrease of profits has arisen from the competition of our own manufacturers, or from the competition of the French?—I consider that the competition of the French is the cause of the competition at home in a great measure.

1722. Is

Mr.
*William Jacombs.*

28 March,
1832.

1722. Is not the competition between English manufacturers the cause of the reduction of price?—When British manufacturers know they have a large stock on hand which are unsaleable, in consequence of the French goods being preferred to theirs' they are compelled to sell them at a great loss.

1723. Would not that induce a smaller quantity to be made, after one or two trials?—A smaller quantity is made,

1724. If the looms that have been formerly employed in making gauze ribbons are no longer so employed, would they not endeavour to find employment in making heavier goods?—Certainly.

1725. And that, of course, would create a pressure upon the market, and a conflict between manufacturers, where no conflict had before existed?—Yes.

1726. Suppose the French were entirely out of the market, do you think the profits would be greater, with the competition of machinery now existing in England?—We certainly should not have so much competition to contend with, and we should have some encouragement to make ribbons from original designs.

1727. Are there not, at the present moment, many more weavers, and many more manufacturers, than can find employment?—There are certainly many more weavers than are employed.

1728. Do you think, that if the quantity of French goods that now enters this market were stopped, that would give employment to the English manufacturers and workmen?—It would certainly better our trade, if we were to make all the ribbons that are now worn.

1729. Are the Committee to understand from you, that it is not so much a matter of price as of fashion that you think the trade suffers under?—Certainly not so much of price as fashion.

1730. Have you any doubt in your mind, that if French ribbons were altogether excluded from the market, there would not be employment for all the looms?—I have no doubt that there would.

1731. Have you any doubt that smuggling would recommence if French goods were prohibited from coming in?—To no extent to injure us.

1732. Will you state what is your opinion with regard to the exclusion of French goods; would you increase the duty, or have a prohibition?—Nothing short of a prohibition would relieve us, in my opinion.

1733. You give that opinion deliberately, believing it to be a matter of taste, not a matter of price?—That is my opinion, and I have given that part of the subject a good deal of consideration.

1734. Do you conceive that an entire prohibition of the importation of foreign ribbons would raise the price of English ribbons?—If we had the material for the same price that we now have, certainly it would not raise it very much; because there is enough competition amongst us at home, independently of the French manufacturers, to keep the article from being at a very exorbitant price.

1735. Do you believe that there would be more general employment?—No doubt of it.

1736. Could such a prohibition raise the profits of the manufacturer?—Supposing that to be the case, no doubt every manufacturer of any taste would be able to make ribbons from superior designs, and to sell them at a profit.

1737. And the superior taste of that manufacturer would carry the market?—To a certain extent it would.

1738. What kind of silk do you use principally in your fancy articles, is it the Italian thrown or English thrown?—I should think about one-tenth of what we use is Italian thrown.

1739. Is that the case generally in Coventry?—I should think it is.

1740. Do you consider the thrown silk that comes from Piedmont, or the Italian silk that is thrown in England, best suited for your manufacture?—Some that is thrown in England is quite as well calculated for our trade as the foreign thrown.

1741. Is not, on the average, the best silk that is thrown in England, as serviceable for your manufacture as the Piedmont silk?—I have never used much of the Piedmont silk, therefore I cannot say much as to what that is calculated for; we have generally used the foreign thrown Italian silk, and the English thrown.

1742. Which do you prefer?—Certainly we find the English thrown as good as the Foreign in some instances, but it entirely depends upon the quality of the silk.

1743. Have you any means of judging, whether, if you had the silk at the same price as the manufacturer at Lyons has it, whether you could, as regards price,

compete

Mr.
*William Jacombs.*

28 March,
1832.

compete with him?—Nothing will enable us to compete with the French manufacturer, in my opinion, because there is a prejudice in favour of the French fashions, let ours be ever so elegant.

1744. You speak of fancy articles?—I speak of fancy ribbons; I do not go into the plain trade.

1745. Do you think there is only one-tenth of the foreign thrown silk used in the fancy trade in Coventry?—I suppose upon the average there is not more than one-tenth.

1746. Do you mean one-tenth of all that is imported or one-tenth of all that is worked up?—I mean one-tenth of all we work up in the manufacturing of ribbons.

1747. Therefore, if the duty was taken off the Italian thrown silk, you would only be benefited to the extent of one-tenth of the material?—Certainly not.

1748. If goods are to be admitted on a duty, have you formed any opinion what would be a protecting duty for you?—No duty would be a protecting duty, in my opinion; because, as I before said, they will buy them at any price, the preference being given to the French fashion.

1749. You have been asked whether a lowness of price would not be introduced by a competition at home; if foreign goods were not admitted, would not you meet such competition on equal terms, without any prejudice?—Certainly.

1750. Is that the case now?—It is not the case now, on account of the prejudice in favour of the French goods.

1751. Are the Committee to understand, that your great complaint is, that the market is so overdone that there are so many more goods manufactured than there is a demand for, that you cannot find adequate profit or a due remuneration for labour?—Certainly it is.

1752. If you were able to manufacture as cheap as the French, or even cheaper, would not the throwing into the market an undue proportion of goods depress wages and lower profits?—Certainly.

1753. You have stated, that you began manufacturing in 1823; at that time had not the silk trade began to improve, and had been improving for some short time before?—It had.

1754. Was not that improvement mainly owing to the introduction of French patterns?—I am not aware of it.

1755. Is it not a fact, that when you went into the trade French patterns were fashionable?—I never saw any quantity of French ribbons worn at that time.

1756. Had not the style of ribbon changed a short time before that considerably?—Yes, decidedly; there was a great improvement from 1823 to 1826.

1757. But you never understood that that was owing to the importation of French patterns?—Certainly not.

1758. Have you not reason to suppose that there has been an increased consumption of ribbons altogether since you became a manufacturer?—Yes; I think there has been an increased consumption, the population has increased.

1759. Have they not become better?—They have been better no doubt, they have been broader and of a better quality.

1760. You have stated that you do not attribute the improvement in the trade in in 1823 to French patterns, to what do you attribute it?—There was a spirit of improvement among the manufacturers at home.

1761. What occasioned that spirit?—I can only say it has always been the case in most fancy branches, there is a spirit of emulation amongst us, one trying to outvie another.

1762. Do you endeavour to get houses to engage your goods as they engage the French goods?—Yes; but we find very few willing to do it at present.

1763. Do not you consider that the profits of the manufacturers at any place, Leicester for example, are determined by the competition between the manufacturers generally at Leicester?—I do not know any thing of the Leicester trade.

1764. Do not you suppose that the profits of any trade are determined by competition amongst themselves?—No doubt competition amongst themselves affects their profits to a great extent.

1765. Is not that the general law?—It is a general rule certainly.

1766. Do not you imagine, that the profits of the manufacturers at Coventry must be equal to those of the manufacturers at Birmingham or Leicester?—No.

1767. Would not the capital go out of the ribbon manufacture into other branches of trade, if the profits were higher in other branches?—I think the ribbon manufacturers are very ill prepared to go into any other branch of business.

678.                                                                1768. If

Mr.
*William Jacombs.*

28 March,
1832.

1768. If their capital is invested in machinery, and mills and looms, is it a very easy matter to remove that capital when it is depreciated about 75 per cent.?—No, it is very difficult.

1769. It has been stated in evidence, that prior to 1816 there were 219 Jacquard looms at Coventry, and that now there are between 650 and 700; do you know whether that is the case?—I dare say it is.

1770. If that be true, must not the capital invested in the purchase of this machinery have been introduced since 1826?—A part of it, not all; some of them have been purchased at a lower rate from other manufacturers.

1771. Do you happen to know whether the additional 450 that have been brought into use since the year 1826 were new looms, or whether the Jacquard principle was applied to old looms?—Generally the Jacquard machine applied to the old looms.

1772. Do you think there have been any additional Jacquard looms put up within the last few years?—Very few.

1773. Has there been any depreciation in value since the number was increased in 1826?—Very much.

1774. So that it is possible that the 200 looms that were put up in 1826 might be worth what the whole 600 are worth now?—Very likely.

1775. You stated, that you make use of the best Jacquard loom; is that the same description of engine that you used in 1823?—So far as the Jacquard applies, which is merely a part of the loom, it is the same.

1776. What rate of wages can a fancy weaver earn, upon the average, in full employment, in a single hand loom?—I should say, from seven to nine shillings per week, upon the best articles, with a Jacquard single loom.

1777. Upon what article could he earn that?—Thirty-penny figured satins.

1778. Do they get regular employ at those wages, or do they lose some time in preparing the work?—Certainly not; they lose a great time in preparing the work.

1779. How many yards would he make of that in a week?—He will make, on the average, three quarters of a piece, that is, 27 yards in a week.

1780. How much would a man, with a Jacquard machine applied to an engine loom, earn in making the same article?—It would vary from 14 to 16 shillings per week.

1781. How many yards would he make in that case?—Perhaps he would make a piece and a half, not more than that; he would make from 48 to 54 yards.

1782. Would it be equally as well made in either machine?—About the same; there are articles made in the single hand loom that cannot be made in the engine; I should say, that the goods we make ourselves, in the single hand loom, are preferable to the engine loom, in point of quality.

1783. What would that cost you for wages a yard?—I cannot say.

1784. At that rate, does not the engine make it cheaper?—Very little; we pay a man with the engine nearly the same price per piece as the single hand.

1785. You know there is a Table of Wages at Coventry; is that in use at Nuneaton also?—It is; we conform to that.

1786. Were you one of the committee that met to form that Table?—I met the Coventry committee upon that occasion.

1787. What was the object of those Tables; was it to equalize, as much as possible, the rate of wages by the single hand and the engine loom?—I apprehend the object was, for the respectable manufacturers to agree with each other all to pay the same price, because some were paying not more than half what the others were.

1788. Were you a party to the Table of Wages in 1829, did you work by that?—Yes.

1789. Before the Table of 1831, had you departed, or had many of the manufacturers departed, from that Table?—We did not, nor did any manufacturer in Nuneaton depart from that Table.

1790. Then the reduction of wages to the single hand loom had not taken place at Nuneaton?—Certainly not.

1791. But you are aware that it had taken place in other parts?—Yes.

1792. And the object of the Table was to put all on an equality?—It was to equalize the rate of wages.

1793. Do you know whether the same rate of wages is paid in any other part of the country where similar articles are made?—I am not aware that similar articles are made in any other part of the country; plain ribbons may be, to a certain extent, in other parts.

1794. Do

Mr.
*William Jacombs.*

28 March,
1832.

1794. Do you consider it beneficial to the manufacturer, that he should be obliged to pay the same rate of wages upon all occasions, whether the article is well finished or not?—The manufacturer is not compelled to receive any article from the weavers that is not well finished.

1795. Having fixed a certain amount for the thirty-penny and so on, is it not the fact, that you do not make any of those articles unless you pay the rate fixed by the Table?—We do not do it.

1796. Are there not workmen willing to work at a less rate than that which the Table fixes?—Yes; but I should suppose they might at once as well be receiving parochial relief.

1797. Are there not a large proportion idle?—There are.

1798. Would they rather remain idle than work below the Table?—They are not offered work below the Table, there is no inducement to the manufacturer to do it.

1799. Are the masters allowed to do it if they are willing?—They are not compelled to do any thing.

1800. Have they not signed an agreement that they would not do it?—There is no compulsion, but they agreed to that Table.

1801. Do you know whether there are instances of persons receiving a higher amount of parish relief than the amount paid to a man that is in work?—I have known that to be the case in many instances.

1802. Therefore a man would prefer working at less wages than the parish would allow him, in order to keep himself out of the parish relief if he could?—That spirit is manifested amongst the poor generally.

1803. And when they receive those wages, are they too high, and more than a man could fairly live upon?—I should fancy he must live very poorly to live upon those prices.

1804. Would there be any reason or any justice in trying to make a man work at a lower rate?—I think not.

1805. You have said that engine looms do more work than the others, and that they make the goods a little cheaper, are there any engine loom weavers out of employ?—A great many.

1806. Is not the warp entrusted to a weaver, valuable?—It is.

1807. Is not it necessary that he should have a decent room to put that warp into?—It is.

1808. And in cold weather to have a fire, as it will not work without warmth?—It will not.

1809. Must not he also pay for soap and candles?—Yes.

1810. What would you put down for rent, and coals and candles?—I should say at least from 3 s. 3 d. to 3 s. 6 d. a week.

1811. So that if a man earns 5 s. 6 d. a week, he would make but a miserable saving of it after all?—I should think he would.

1812. And with regard to Jacquard looms, which earn about 14 s. a week when their warps are out, what time do they lose in getting fresh warps in and changing the pattern?—Getting fresh warps in alone, we generally take from 10 days to a fortnight.

1813. How often are those warps changed?—Every six weeks.

1814. What wages would you consider adequate, under the circumstances you have just stated, for a man's reasonable support, taking into account the rent you stated, and other expenses?—I should think they ought to earn at least from 2 s. to 3 s. a week more than they can earn, that would be at least 12 s.

1815. With that rate of wages, do you consider that the price of the French fancy ribbons would be so very much cheaper than yours, that you would be unable to come into competition with them?—Certainly, we could not compete at such a price.

1816. Then if you were to pay an adequate amount of wages to the workmen, it would make it requisite to increase the price of your ribbons?—Certainly.

1817. Therefore a prohibition of the French ribbons would of course increase the price of the home made fancy ribbons?—Most assuredly, because under a prohibitory law, I should hope to sell the ribbon at some trifling profit.

1818. And you would hope to give the workmen rather a larger amount of wages?—Yes.

1819. If a man earned 3 s. a week extra, which was distributed over 54 yards of a rich thirty-penny ribbon, what difference of price would it make to the consumer?—Very trifling, rather more than a halfpenny a yard.

678.                                                              1820. And

Mr.
*William Jacombs.*

28 March,
1832.

1820. And you are speaking of a description of goods which are now sold generally* at about 3 s. a yard, and upon which the public will indulge their taste, if they even pay one shilling a yard more?—No doubt.

1821. Is the protecting duty sufficiently high to enable you to enter into competition with the French, as far as price is concerned?—In some few articles, but not in all; for example, in gauze ribbons we cannot; but I know it is not often the case that we can make ribbons as cheap, for they can live so much cheaper than we can.

1822. Were not the profits in 1827 and 1828 as good as they have been at any time?—They were certainly better in 1827 and 1828 than they now are (in 1827 particularly), but they were better still in 1824 and 1825.

1823. Are you not aware that there were great complaints of distress in Coventry in the Christmas of 1825?—I do not recollect that.

1824. Are the Committee to understand that by the Table of Wages, a man can only earn from 7 s. to 9 s. a week if fully employed upon a single hand loom?—Yes.

1825. Is it your opinion, that it would be better for a man to work even at a lower rate than to be altogether unemployed, and receive relief from the poors rates?—It might be better in a certain sense, as it would relieve the parish from some burthens, but even where they were working at a lower rate, they have been receiving parochial relief at the same time.

1826. Have any persons worked at a lower rate since that Table was made?—I believe not.

1827. Has the parish been relieved by that?—We have not had time to feel the effect of it.

1828. Has not the amount of the poor rates increased since that Table of Wages was made?—I think not.

1829. Do you conceive, that if the rate of wages was reduced, and by that means the price of ribbons increased, you would be enabled to give greater employment to your weavers?—Certainly not.

Mr.
*Cleophas Ratliff.*

Mr. *Cleophas Ratliff*, called in; and Examined.

1830. WHERE do you reside?—At Coventry.

1831. You are a ribbon manufacturer?—Yes.

1832. Have you been so for some years?—Since 1817.

1833. Can you state the quantity of silk dyed in Coventry in the years 1824, 1825, 1830 and 1831, being two years before the importation of foreign ribbons and the last two years?—Yes; in 1824, 413,693 pounds weight; in 1825, 448,165 pounds weight; in 1830, 537,335 pounds weight; and in 1831, 508,375 pounds weight.

1834. Were the same descriptions of ribbons made at Coventry in 1830 and 1831 as in 1824 and 1825?—Certainly not, as leading articles; the chief goods manufactured in 1824 or 1825 were gauze ribbons; the chief articles now made are bonnet ribbons and waistbands; I speak of the Coventry trade, they are given out from Coventry, but made in the adjacent villages.

1835. To what do you attribute the present distress of the ribbon trade?—The very great importation of French ribbons.

1836. Do you know the quantity of ribbons imported lately, and have you estimated the employment that the making of them would have given to the British manufacturers?—I can. In the Custom House returns for the quarter ending the 10th of October 1831, it stands thus: 252 lbs. weight of plain gauze, 10,913 lbs. weight of gauze ribbons; they are styled striped, figured or brocaded; I mention these collectively, because they are not separated; there are very few broad gauzes, and I deduct the 252 lbs. in the calculation for broad gauzes, this would leave 10,913 lbs. weight of ribbons, and produce, at four ounces to the piece or garniture, 43,652 pieces. I calculate the latter at 12 s. the piece in the following way; that is, 9 s. 3 d. weaving and filling, 2 s. 9 d. winding, warping, clipping, draft, cards and loom mounting, will amount to the sum of 26,192 l. quarterly, yearly 104,764 l., or weekly 2,015 l. If the above ribbons were made in Jacquard engine looms at a calculation of two pieces per week for a loom, they would require 1,680 looms, and employ 1,680 weavers, 420 fillers, 420 winders, 140 warpers, clippers, draftsmen and card-stampers, exclusive of designers, loom and harness makers, dyers and throwsters, the whole amount of employed population would be 2,660, if made in the most improved Jacquard engine loom. With the permission of the Committee

I will

I will read the importation of other descriptions of silk. The silk imported in the quarter ending the 10th October 1831, exclusive of gauzes, stands thus: 21,446 lbs. weight of silk or satin plain, 5,189 lbs. brocades, the whole amounting to 26,635 lbs. I assume that half of them were ribbons, which would be 13,317 lbs. I take them at 5,189 lbs of brocaded, which at 10 ounces per piece will produce 8,302 pieces quarterly, and 8,128 lbs. of plain satin at 6½ ounces average to the piece, will produce 20,007 pieces. The brocaded will be 8,302 pieces quarterly, or 638 weekly. I make this calculation for the single hand loom, with the jacquard engine fixed upon it. Brocaded satin figures, at 20s. per piece to the undertaker, who pays 13s. ¼d. per piece to the weaver, and retains 6s. 8d. himself for winding, warping, drafting, mounting cards, looms, harness, and being responsible for the work. A weaver upon this work, can only make half a piece per week, and earn 6s. 8d. per week. The number of pieces would have given employment to 1,277 weavers weekly, 410 undertakers, winders, warpers, draftsmen, mounters and card stampers; 20,007 pieces quarterly, 1,539 weekly of satins, which at an average of wages at 6s. 6d. per piece to the undertaker, would amount to 6,502l. quarterly, 500l. weekly. The undertaker pays the weaver 4s. 4d. per piece, and finds looms, harness, winding, warping, &c. &c. for the remaining 2s. 2d. The number of pieces would have given employment to 1,026 weavers weekly, 415 undertakers, winders and warpers, at 1¼ pieces to the weaver, who would earn 6s. 6d. per week.

1837. How do you obtain the account of plain satins?—It is merely assumption; I can take it in no other way; the brocaded parts are distinguished, they are called brocades, and I have no doubt that I have apportioned them correctly in that respect.

1838. Did you look at any former years when they used to be kept separately, in the Custom House Returns?—I cannot fancy that it would at all bear upon the question; because I think more plain satins are introduced into England at present than there ever were before.

1839. You stated, that a great quantity of gauze, brocade and satin ribbons had been imported, do you mean to say, that the English weavers could have made those articles?—Certainly; the same description of goods.

1840. Do you wish the Committee to understand that the English manufacturers can make as good ribbons as the French?—I think, with the same advantages, they can.

1841. And at as low a price?—Certainly not; if they were in the same relative situation they could, but not without; if they had the same labour, the same material, the same climate and the same means of existence throughout, but not otherwise. I was requested by a very ingenious manufacturer to submit to the Committee the samples he has sent to me, which are the production of his looms at the present moment, and as they are equal to what are coming from France of the best description, he is desirous of having them exhibited. With the permission of the Committee, I will read the remarks that the gentleman makes himself, respecting them; they are made by Mr. Henry Atkins, of Coventry:—he says, " These patterns are produced in the single hand loom; one loom cannot produce any more than half a piece per week, which costs 10s. making. The cost of putting one of these patterns to work will be 14l. and before I am remunerated for the expense, the French introduce something fresh and mine becomes unfashionable, and it will not answer my purpose to cultivate this trade:" this is matter of speculation.

1842. What is the price of those articles?—Two shillings a yard I believe; the French articles of a similar description have been sold in the shops at 3s., or even at 4s. 6d. a yard. He says, " these patterns are our own drawing and designing."

1843. Do you consider that these are as good as any that the French can make?—As a matter of skill they are equal; as to matter of taste, I cannot say.

1844. Would the abolition of 3s. 6d. per lb. import duty upon foreign thrown silk, enable you more successfully to compete with the foreign manufacturer?—It is a question I can scarcely entertain for a moment; I do not conceive that there are any means short of a prohibition that would enable us to make goods at all.

1845. If you get your silk 3s. 6d. cheaper than you now pay for it, could you make your goods cheaper?—I have no hesitation in saying that we could.

1846. Do you conceive, that by reducing the duty 3s. 6d. upon foreign thrown silk, it would be sold 3s. 6d. per lb. less?—I do not conceive it would.

1847. Will you explain to the Committee the advantage that the French have in their satin ribbons?—I have examples of satin ribbons; two of French and two

Mr.
*Cleophas Ratliff.*

28 March,
1832.

of English; they are corresponding widths, and I can state, that with reference to the quantity of silk worked into the English satin, compared with the foreign, there appears, on the average, to be $19\frac{1}{4}$ per cent. silk more used to make the same articles, and the effect of that I will leave the Committee to judge.

1848. Is the same kind of silk used, or is yours all Italian silk?—It is the produce of Italy; but the silk from which this is made is thrown in England.

1849. If you were shown some plain satin, English made, and some plain satin, French made, should you have any difficulty in ascertaining in a moment which were the foreign and which were the English manufacture?—Not the least in the world.

1850. Have you ever seen any that you found difficult to distinguish the one from the other?—Never, in the article of satin ribbons.

1851. Have you seen it in any other article?—I cannot precisely state that there might not be some difficulty, but I think I might venture to say that I have not.

1852. Could not you tell another manufacturer's goods from your own?—Not precisely; there would be some description of work I could tell in a moment, by the pattern, but in the plain article there would be hardly sufficient to distinguish; but I could readily distinguish between the French and the English.

1853. Does that arise from the nature of the silk?—I think chiefly.

1854. Is the French silk a superior silk to yours?—The French silk is superior to any other silk grown in the world, I have no doubt.

1855. Have the French any advantage over us in the manufacture of gauze silk?—Certainly, they have a very much superior article at a much lower price; the French Marabout hard, used in the gauze ribbons, would cost $22s. 3d.$ per pound, and English, for a very much worse material, would cost $32s.$; that is to say, the French manufacturer gives $22s. 3d.$ per pound for the Marabout hard, for which we give $32s.$

1856. You are now speaking of the material before it is manufactured, and you are speaking of the article which you consume in the manufacture of gauze ribbons, and which the French also consume?—Yes.

1857. How does that difference arise?—I cannot possibly say how it arises; I dare say there are a variety of causes conspiring. I am stating what is an absolute fact as to the price.

1858. Have they a great abundance of that silk?—As much as they can possibly require.

1859. How have you ascertained the French prices?—From the best authenticated information I ever received in my life: it was obtained by two gentlemen perfectly conversant with the trade in every respect. They were not manufacturers; they obtained those prices from three or four different channels on the same day, without any concert whatever, and they corresponded in every particular.

1860. Have the French a superior mode of dressing their ribbons?—They have.

1861. Will you state what proportion of this kind of gauze is made in Coventry?—I could not possibly state that; but I will endeavour to ascertain it.

1862. What per centage would that be in the price of the article?—Not being a gauze maker, I have it not in my power to state that.

1863. In point of fact, is not the gauze trade nearly abandoned at Coventry, on account of this very difficulty?—On account of this and other difficulties.

1864. Has the French manufacturer any advantage over you in the price of labour comparative, separately and collectively paid on the description of ribbons?—I will read the calculations upon one description of articles formed on the most accurate principles, which I have obtained from two persons, of the comparative prices of weaving in France and England; I will state, first, the prices paid at Saint Etienne for the French clipt figured gauzes made in the Jacquard looms; the price for sixteen-penny per piece at thirty-six yards, is $2s. 6d.$; the price of twenty-penny is $3s.$; the price of twenty-four-penny is $4s$; the price of thirty-penny is $5s. 6d.$; the price of forty-penny is $7s. 9d.$ The weaver in France has only half this sum; the undertaker takes the other half for finding shop, looms and harness, the manufacturer finds draft, cards, winding and warping. I mention this particularly to show, that the undertaker, by receiving so large a portion of the amount paid, is enabled to invest his capital in the improved machinery of the day, which, in the case of England, the manufacturer is compelled to do. I will next state the prices paid in England for clipt figured gauzes, made in the Jacquard looms; the price of sixteen-penny per piece of thirty-six yards is $5s.$; the price of twenty-penny is $6s. 6d.$; the price of twenty-four penny is $8s. 6d.$; the price of thirty-penny is $12s.$; the price of forty-penny is $15s.$ This is the price actually paid to the

weaver,

Mr.
*Cleophas Ratliff.*

28 March,
1832.

weaver, who does not find anything but quil winding or filling; the manufacturer finds looms, winding, warping, draft and cards; then there are other advantages which a manufacturer has in France; the clipping gauzes in France costs 6 *d*. per piece; in England the clipping gauzes cost 1 *s*. 6 *d*, per piece, or 200 per cent. higher.  In France the winding costs 1 *s*. 3 *d*. per pound, the English winding is 2 *s*. per pound. The French silk, native produce of France, organzines, costs 29 francs or 24 *s*. 2 *d*. English, for the French pound of 17 ounces 10 drams, subject to 11 per cent. discount, which leaves the cost for the English pound of sixteen ounces 19 *s*. 4 *d*.  In England Fossombrone organzine, the same size, and the nearest in quality we can arrive at, though it is still very far inferior, I take at 25 *s*. per pound, it is from 24 *s*. 6 *d*. to 26 *s*., subject to a discount of 2½ per cent., which leaves the cost 24 *s*. 4½ *d*.

1865. Are those the prices now?—They were the prices in the last week in December; the general calculation upon all the articles, the expense of English weaving more than the French, is 108 per cent. average.  I will state the particulars of the calculation upon which I have come to this result.

[*The Witness delivered in the following Statement, which was read.*]

### COMPARATIVE PRICES of LABOUR in *England* and *France*.

| PRICES for Weaving in France. | PRICES for Weaving in England. | GAUZES. |
|---|---|---|
| *d.* 16 per p⁵ of 36 yards - 2/6 | *d.* 16 per p⁵ of 36 yards - 5/ | 100 per cent. more in England than France. |
| 20 - - „ - - 3/ | 20 - - „ - - 6/6 | 116¾ „ |
| 24 - - „ - - 4/ | 24 - - „ - - 8/6 | 112½ „ |
| 30 - - „ - - 5/6 | 30 - - „ - - 12/ | 118 „ |
| 40 - - „ - - 7/9 | 40 - - „ - - 15/ | 93½ „ |
| | | 540¾   Average, 108 p'cᵗ. |
| Clipping Gauzes in France, 6 *d*. per pˢ. | Clipping Gauzes in England, 1/6 per pˢ. | 200 per cent. higher in England than France. |
| Winding, in France, 1/3 per lb. | Winding in England, 2/ per lb. | 60 per cent. higher in England than France. |
| French organzine, native produce, 19/4. | English organzine, 24/4½. | 26 per cent. higher in England than France. |
| French Marabout, hard, 22/3. | English Marabout, 32/0. | 44 per cent. higher in England than France. |

It is fair to assume that a French gauze ribbon would be made with a much less quantity of material from the superiority of the silk, but we take the same weight in both cases for an example.

| FRENCH. | | ENGLISH. | | |
|---|---|---|---|---|
| | *s. d.* | | *s. d.* | |
| 1 pˢ of Gauze Ribbon, 4 oz. silk, av. 1/3½ - 5 2 | | 4 oz. silk, av. 1/9 - 7 — | | So that the English cost for the article will be 78⅜ per cent. more than the French. |
| Weaving - - - 4 3 | | Weaving - - 9 3 | | |
| Winding - - - 3¾ | | Winding - - - 6 | | |
| Clipping - - - 6 | | Clipping - - 1 6 | | |
| | 10 2¼ | | 18 3 | |

In this calculation, no mention is made of the difference in cost to the English manufacturer, in making of looms, designing, draft drawing, card stamping, card making, mounting, dyeing and warping.

The French prices are given to a medium-man, who pays half to the weaver and retains the other half for finding looms, harness and shop; this enables him to invest a large sum in machinery.

1866. Have you any idea of the profit that the French manufacturer obtains upon his fancy goods?—When I know that the prices are often greater than the English, and when I see that the cost is 78⅓ per cent. less, he must have an enormous profit, and I think they would be very silly not to have it when they always have so many orders for months beforehand.

1867. Must not they always have the advantage you have stated of being able to make as much with four ounces as the English manufacturer can with five ounces?—They must as long as they have the exclusive possession of that description of silk.

1868. You stated that the prices you have mentioned were the prices in last December, are they the same at present?—I have no doubt that they are the same, for I obtained the prices from another source yesterday, and they correspond precisely; I might add, that the French prices have advanced since 1825, and it may be fair to remark, that ours have been declining.

1869. You have shown that French manufacturers have a great advantage over you in the cost of silk and of labour, have they any other advantage over you?—A very decided one in the preference given to the articles they produce; they have a decided advantage in receiving orders many months before the goods are required; they manufacture upon a certain principle, without chance of loss.

1870. Is it not the custom in France, that manufacturers will make 600 or 700 garnitures of a pattern without any difficulty?—I believe it is.

1871. If you were making a rich fancy ribbon, what number of pieces would you think a fair speculation?—From 40 to 50 pieces would be the utmost extent I should make.

1872. If you had, as the Frenchman has, customers from America, from Germany, from Poland, from Russia, from England, and from his home market, might you not make a very much larger quantity, and divide it between those different countries, without selling the same pattern to more than one person in one country?—Yes; I have understood that it is a principle with the French manufacturer, when he has shown a pattern to an English house, not to sell that pattern to any other English house; but if he can obtain an order from the German, and from the Russian, and from the American especially, he does so, and thereby of course lessens the cost of putting in the pattern, by distributing it over a large quantity.

1873. Have you yourself been at Lyons and at Saint Etienne?—Not at Saint Etienne, I have been at Lyons.

1874. Did you enquire into the state of the trade, and did you examine the silk?—I went there in November 1824, with a view to ascertain what chance I should have in attempting to compete with that nation, and on my going there, I was introduced by a gentleman to many manufacturers; I saw the silk, I saw the nature of the principle and business altogether; and it quite determined me that I should have no real chance in prosecuting the trade at home.

1875. Do you think a reduction in the price of English goods would drive the French goods out of the market?—Certainly not; I do not think that any reduction of price in the world could do it.

---

*Veneris, 30° die Martii,* 1832.

## THE RIGHT HON. THE EARL GROSVENOR, IN THE CHAIR..

Mr. *Cleophas Ratliff,* called in; and further Examined.

1876. IN your former Evidence, you stated that you went to Lyons in 1824, and you had made up your mind in consequence of what you saw, not to pursue certain branches of the trade; what particular branches were they?—That branch of the trade that required a very expensive machinery to prosecute, that is, a newly introduced machinery; and I have not purchased a loom, or invested any capital in it since.

1877. Did you observe the quality of the silk at Lyons?—I did, and believe it is the best silk in the world.

1878. Have you ever seen any such in England?—Never; I had in company with me at that time, a throwster of considerable information, who had been so from his earliest years; he saw the silk in the warehouse of a manufacturer, and was immediately attracted by its beauty, and the attraction was so great that he could

not

Mr.
*Cleophas Ratliff.*

30 March,
1832.

not resist it; and he went to examine it very injudiciously, because we were introduced as Americans into the warehouse, with a particular wish that we should not expose ourselves as Englishmen; he went and examined the silk, and untwisted it to examine the degree of throw upon it, as a throwster; and the man at the scale, with a quickness distinguishing a Frenchman, said that was a manufacturer " Un Fabricant," and of course we were very soon shown out, we were not allowed to see much more upon that occasion, but we had frequent opportunities afterwards from the gentleman using more prudence.

1879. You said that you made up your mind, in consequence of what you saw at Lyons, not to go to the expense of machinery; should you have gone to that expense if there had been a prohibition of French ribbons?—Unquestionably, to a very great extent; I have always had the means, but deemed it inexpedient to do so.

1880. Have not Jacquard looms been put up in considerable numbers in this country?—I believe they have, very much to the regret of the parties who have put them up.

1881. Do you know whether there has been any considerable number of jacquard looms put up within the last two or three years?—I believe not, I think a very small number.

1882. Was the silk which you stated you inspected in the manner you have described, accompanied by a throwster, native French silk, and consequently that sort of silk, the exportation of which is strictly prohibited from France?—Certainly, all silk is prohibited from France.

1883. Do you get this silk in spite of the prohibition?—Never.

1884. What description of silk do you manufacture?—Chiefly from Italian, on the organzine thrown in this country, from Italian raw.

1885. Where do you procure it from?—From a variety of sources, chiefly from the throwsters, or through the agency of brokers in London.

1886. Do you consider the Foreign thrown silk superior to English?—I think there are some Foreign thrown silks very superior indeed; but there is a description of silk thrown in this country, superior to any I have been able to obtain from Italy.

1887. In what does that superiority consist?—In the throw; there is a patent taken out by Courtauld and Taylor, which throw is superior to any foreign silk we procure.

1888. Is that superior British silk used in any particular goods?—It is used in the satin ribbons I exhibited the other day.

1889. Do they use in France any but the native thrown silk?—A very small proportion.

1890. Can you inform the Committee what quantity of Italian silk is used in French goods?—I cannot, but I should fancy a very small proportion.

1891. Do not the French, in making their plain goods, use Piedmont silk as the shute, in the same manner in which the English manufacturer uses the China?—I think not, they use their own trams and their own shutes.

1892. Are their own trams the produce of France, or the produce of Italy?—They may use some from Italy; but my opinion is, that the principal consumption of France is the native French, that is a part organzine and a part tram, and part marabout hard.

1893. Do you think if you had the French silk you could enter into competition with the French manufacturer?—Not with one advantage alone, that would be but one small component part of the advantages we should require.

1894. Then you think there is a superiority in the fashion as well as in the manufacture?—There is a prejudice in favour of the French; as to the superiority of the fashion, that is an ideal question.

1895. Might not that be obviated by employing better artists in England?—I think we can scarcely have better artists.

1896. Do you think that the superiority of the French fashion depends merely upon the quality of the French ribbons, or upon something extraneous, in the way in which they are made up?—I think it depends very much in the way in which they are introduced.

1897. For instance, if a cap were made in a particular way in France, will not the cap being made in that way in France, give to a ribbon an additional value, independent of its value if not so employed?—Unquestionably.

1898. Therefore, even if you could make a ribbon as beautiful and as cheap as the French, still that advantage which the French milliner has over our milliner in

setting

setting the fashions to this country, would still give them an advantage, in point of fashion, which the quality of your ribbon would not enable you to compete with?—Certainly.

1899. Do you not think that an English sarsnett ribbon is superior to a French sarsnett ribbon?—There are very few French sarsnett ribbons come into this country, and very few made, in comparison with others; the Swiss manufacturers supersede the make of France in that.

1900. Is the English manufacture of sarsnett ribbon equal to the Swiss manufacture?—I think it is; but there is a neatness and a fineness derived from the power of putting in a certain quantity of labour at much less price; and, of course, from labour being cheap, they can give a great deal more labour than we have the power to do.

1901. Are you aware, whether those Swiss ribbons you speak of are prohibited from being sent into France?—I understood when I went to France first, in 1818, that they were prohibited under very severe laws.

1902. Do you understand whether they are prohibited now?—I do not know; I think the French Government would do anything to support their own trade; and I think if the French manufacturer wished to have them prohibited, for the sake of the trade, they would do it.

1903. Are you aware, whether the sarsnett made in Switzerland, is made with Swiss grown silk, or from Italian silk?—I think from Italian grown silk; I have not had an opportunity of ascertaining the relative prices between Switzerland and in England; but when I know that they take the trade from the French, I fancy that they labour at a much lower rate; and I should be very glad to have the means of knowing the relative prices of labour in Switzerland and in this country.

1904. Have you any way of suggesting to the Committee, the manner in which that can be obtained?—By sending over a person competent to obtain it.

1905. Do you imagine that much Swiss goods come here?—They have done till lately; I think they do, even now.

1906. Do you think the English weaver can exist upon the same amount of earnings as a French weaver?—Certainly not; the various disadvantages under which the English labourer has to contend, would take almost a volume to enumerate. A Frenchman can exist upon a much less quantity of food, and of course the expense of producing that is much less in France. The climate of England requires a more expensive description of sustenance; in fact, I could not give a better authority, upon this subject, than the celebrated work under the name of Dr. Lardner, who gives an excellent answer to that question.

1907. Is not the weather so warm in the neighbourhood of Lyons, that they are able to work without fires in the middle of December?—I think so; I recollect being there the latter end of November, and I could have borne my coat off in walking; there is a passage in Dr. Lardner, which so clearly illustrates this point, that, with the permission of the Committee, I will read it. Speaking of expense, he says, " But while the expense of living is higher in Great Britain, than it is in those countries whose political and financial circumstances place them in a less artificial state, the wages of labour ought to be, and will be, higher in something like an equal ratio. Greater comforts are needed by the English artizans, in consequence of the less favourable nature of our climate; and if, after taking all these circumstances into calculation, it is yet found that the labouring classes here are not all sunk so deeply into the abyss of poverty and wretchedness, as those of some neighbouring states may be, it will not thence be argued, that their situation is too favourable, and that the principle of buying in the cheapest market should, as is sometimes insisted on, be carried to so extreme a length, as would lower them to the same miserable level, and reduce them to the procurement of a bare subsistence." That is precisely my opinion.

1908. Are you aware that the French import, very largely, Piedmont silk?—I am not aware of it; I do not think they do.

1909. If it should appear that they do import to the extent of twenty millions of francs, in what way, in your opinion, would they use them?—If they import twenty millions, they must have an enormous trade, because the native produce is very extensive.

1910. What do you consider the best protection against smuggling ribbons?—Prohibition is the only protection.

1911. Do you consider that smuggling can be prevented, so long as foreign ribbons are allowed to be imported?—It is totally impossible; while foreign goods

are

Mr.
*Cleophas Ratliff*.

30 March,
1832.

are legally imported, any quantity of goods can be smuggled and blended with them; and when once they are in the houses of the merchants that import them, they never can be separated and ascertained; and I think while they are admitted, although a certain rate per cent. may be paid to some respectable houses, I have no doubt there are so many channels through which they can pass them, that it is impossible to attempt a detection of them.

1912. Is it your opinion that smuggling ribbons could take place to any extent under prohibitory laws?—Quite impossible; I conceive, that under prohibitory laws there are so many points to contend with, a man without capital could not enter into the trade, and a man with capital would not have the hardihood to do it. I have no doubt there would be as many smugglers as candidates to bring them in, but I do not know who would receive them. Under the legal importation, a man can employ twenty or thirty servants; he exposes his goods for sale, and he facilitates the consumption of them in every way possible; whereas, under prohibitory laws, he must keep them in a garret, or a place unconnected with his own, and be at the mercy of his servants every hour.

1913. Is not he as much at the mercy of his servant now, if he is a smuggler? —I think not, I think he can avoid his servants knowing, in a degree, that he could not do if there were prohibitory laws.

1914. Can he do that if he is in a large way of business?—He might divide the confidence between them in a way he could not do under prohibitory laws.

1915. Do not you think that very large dealers might be buyers and sellers of smuggled goods, without being aware of the fact?—Unquestionably.

1916. So that if a warehouseman in London were to send to a Foreign house and buy goods, day after day, he would never know that those goods were smuggled, though every piece of them might be smuggled?—It would not be his business to inquire.

1917. Do you speak of all ribbons, when you talk of prohibition?—Every description of ribbon, plain as well as figured; such is the omnipotence of the French in making any thing fashionable, that if fancy goods were prohibited, the next year they might make plain goods fashionable, and produce a little variety of colour, that would injure the sale of all we had prepared.

1918. Have you any goods you wish to show to the Committee?—I observed in the house of a considerable importer, two descriptions of ribbons selling; the young man, the chief superintendant of the concern, was showing them to me without thinking it a matter of any consequence; and he said, now what a shame it is, here is a French ribbon I can sell currently with ease for 48 s. per piece, here is an English one of superior manufacture, and equally good taste, which I cannot sell for more than 36 s., and if I were to ask 38 s. for it, they would say I imposed upon them; but when I ask 48 s. for the French, they purchase it with avidity.

1919. Supposing a prohibition again took place upon the importation of French ribbons, do you suppose that persons would then be prevented from exposing them to public view?—Unquestionably they would; the French could only have a preference from its being entirely new, and different from what we were producing, and by that character and mark it would be known in a moment.

1920. Then you think the quality of the English ribbon is equal to the quality of the French?—It would not be the quality; but what I mean to say is, that if any different pattern were introduced from France, that would mark it in a moment as being French.

1921. Suppose they imitated and made a ribbon after your patterns?—They would then be in the same relative situation as we are now, they would have the dregs of the trade instead of the better part of it; if they were to imitate us, they would be so far behind the period when the goods would be required for sale, that they would be almost valueless.

1922. And if any delay took place in the delivery of those goods, there would of course be a serious loss sustained?—Yes.

1923. Supposing they made goods different from yours, in order to get the precedence in point of fashion, they would then be distinguished by the difference, whereas if they imitated you, they would be so far behind you in the market that they would give you that advantage over them which they at this moment possess over you?—Yes.

1924. Do you mean to say, that the Coventry people would be able to say that a particular pattern must be French, not being made at Coventry?—Yes.

1925. But if that particular pattern were made here to a small extent, as a blind,

678.                                                                              would

would not that prevent you from being able to detect it in that manner?—I think if they were to make a small quantity of a certain description of ribbon here, and a large quantity abroad, the length of time it would take to get them in under smuggling would drive them past the season, so that the goods made in France, instead of being blended and sold immediately, would be jobbed off in any way they could.

1926. Is it not the case at the present moment, that a vessel with silks on board may come up to the Custom House, and if they have an opportunity of throwing them overboard at night they can do so; and if there is any fear of detection they can enter them for exportation, whereas under a prohibitory law there would be no opportunity of doing so; but if they were found, the goods might be seized and the vessel also?—The goods would be seized, and I believe the vessel also.

1927. Do you imagine there is less difficulty now, from the state of inter-course between France and this country, to the smuggler to bring goods here than there was during the period of the prohibitory law?—The facilities are greater, from a larger connection being established in the smuggling way; but I think they would return back to the original difficulty if the prohibitory laws were again re-enacted; but the intercourse is much greater cetainly now, and therefore the facility is greater on that account.

1928. Do you know when goods are seized in a man's house, as prohibited articles, that it rests with a person to prove that he has paid the duty?—I think it does.

1929. Do you happen to know, that when they enter a man's house and make a large seizure of goods, if only a single piece is found that is contraband, that will justify his entering the house?—I should think it would; but I do not exactly know the law upon that subject.

1930. You mean to say, that if a quantity of goods came into this country from France, they could not be sold unless they were exhibited, and if they were not so sold, they would not interfere with you?—Yes.

1931. And that the difficulties of selling them would be very great; inasmuch as persons importing foreign manufactures would be afraid to exhibit those goods, and consequently they could not interfere with you?—Exactly so.

1932. Can you form any estimate of the proportion of ribbons sold in this town which are smuggled?—It is merely opinion; I have heard it estimated at two-thirds.

1933. Do you consider that any considerable proportion of smuggled ribbons is sent from this city to supply the country trade?—I have no doubt a very large quantity are; because I understand that in the remotest parts of England French goods are equally desired as in the most fashionable circles at the West end of the town.

1934. If there were a prohibition of French ribbons, would it not be advantageous to a great many individuals, who would then sell British goods at a higher price as smuggled?—I do not know whether they would attempt such a deception as that, it would not be necessary; I think the British goods would pass well enough on their own merits.

1935. Under a state of prohibition, would it not cost as much to introduce French goods into this country as it does now?—It would cost much more.

1936. In addition to that, must not the dealers in this country have a much larger profit to pay them for the risk?—No doubt.

1937. And that would, of course, enhance the price, and afford a greater pro-tection to your trade?—No doubt it would.

1938. One of the evils of which you now complain, being that the French manu-facturer receives a certain number of orders regularly, almost from the English market; do you think he would receive the same number of orders, if there were a state of prohibition, and if he, therefore, depended merely upon the smuggling sale?—I do not conceive that orders would be given under such circumstances; I conceive that the only species of smuggling that would take place, would be from the French depôts, of persons who order goods upon the same principle that we do now from St. Etienne.

1939. And you think that they would then make only for chance and speculation, whereas they now make upon a certainty, and that to a very large extent?—If they made at all, it would be in that way; but I do not think they would make upon chance and speculation.

1940. Is it your opinion, that there was much smuggling before 1826?—Very inconsiderable indeed.

1941. And that it is much larger now?—Yes.

1942. Is

Mr.
*Cleophas Ratliff.*

30 March,
1832.

1942. Is not that merely matter of opinion?—I do not think the last is merely matter of opinion; I think we have public documents which give us an idea that it is much greater than it was.

1943. If a warehouseman dealt in foreign silks to the extent of 100,000 *l.* a year, would not he be obliged to keep a stock of at least 10,000 *l.* in his house?—At least.

1944. Do you believe that, before the importation was allowed of foreign manufactured silks, any house ever had, at any one time, 5,000 *l.* worth of foreign goods in their house?—I do not believe that any house ever had 5 *l.* worth of foreign goods in their house; I think they kept them in other houses, in the most clandestine and secret way they could.

1945. You have mentioned the difference of price between an English ribbon and a French ribbon, of about the same quality; have not you reason to suppose that the profit upon both articles is the same?—Upon the English I know, from my own experience, that there is scarcely any profit; upon the other, there must be an enormous profit.

1946. The question refers to the dealer's profit in London?—No; the dealer gets from seven and a half to ten per cent. more upon the foreign article exhibited, than the English one; that was stated to me yesterday.

1947. With that difference, would not the English be cheaper than the French?—It would.

1948. Is not the result of your evidence, that the question between the English and the French ribbons is a question of fashion and not a question of price?—I think I have shown, that it is a question of price also; I think the calculation I gave the other day, showing that the expense of manufacturing in France is 78$\frac{1}{8}$ per cent. less than in England, establishes, that it is a question of price; if you were to put on a duty of 40 per cent. upon the article, I calculate that the manufacturer in France could afford to take off from 32 to 40 per cent. and still have a much larger profit than the Englishman.

1949. Do you consider that there has been a great increase in the manufacture of Coventry?—There has been an increase in the manufacture of silk, but there are fewer pieces made.

1950. Can you take upon yourself to say, that there has been more distress in the five years since 1826, than there was in the five years before 1826?—I think there was more distress in the year 1831 than ever was known in Coventry before.

1951. The question refers to the five years before, taking into account the year 1818?—If I were asked whether there has been greater distress since 1826 than in the five years previous to it, I should say, yes.

1952. Has the manufacture increased or decreased since that time?—The manufacture in the number of pieces has decreased, in the consumption of silk it has increased.

1953. Do you mean to say that there are fewer looms and less work, although there may be more silk consumed, than there were in the five years before 1826?—Yes; I have no doubt much fewer looms.

1954. Notwithstanding the great increase of the population of Coventry since 1826, which appears by the returns, do you really think that there has been less work done at Coventry than there was during the preceding five years?—There has been less amount of wages paid, there is more silk consumed, but there has been less amount of work done.

1955. Are the Committee to understand that you attribute the diminution of work and the decrease of wages to the French competition alone, or to any other causes also?—To the French competition.

1956. Do you consider competition at home to have had any effect?—Competition at home has been caused by competition abroad, much larger quantities of goods have been brought in than can be sold, and of course that would increase the competition at home.

1957. Is there any thing peculiar in the competition in the silk trade as distinguished from the competition in the cotton or any other trade?—I know nothing of the cotton or any other trade; I have devoted all my attention to my own peculiar trade.

1958. You have stated that, in your opinion, no relief can be afforded unless a complete exclusion of French manufacture shall take place?—I think it impossible, and to that point sooner or later the Government of this country must come.

678.

1959. Would

1959. Would you exclude all imports from abroad, or would you confine the exclusion to silk goods?—I would allow those things to be exported or imported, that the trade of the country can bear; I would allow the exuberance of those manufactures to be exported upon any branch that could bear it, but I would not subject any branch of trade to it that could not bear it.

1960. What do you mean by bearing it, do you mean with reference to the expenses of manufacture, or what do you mean?—I mean that if in this country we have the power of producing an article at a lower rate than the foreigner, we have the power to export that article, and it is fair to put it into competition, but if from a variety of circumstances we are unable to effect that competition, I think it unfair to compel us to it.

1961. Is it your opinion that we cannot obtain silk as cheap in England as the French can at Lyons?—We cannot, unless we could induce the French Government to allow it to come here, and not even then unless the duty is made sufficiently low.

1962. With regard to the cost of production, you stated that the average of the difference in the cost of production was 78 per cent.; from whom have you got that table of the French rates?—It is from the most respectable source I ever had a document in my life, and it was obtained by a gentleman adverse to the English silk trade, he had obtained it for a very different purpose from that to which it is now applied, and with the liberality which distinguishes him, in order to facilitate the ends of truth, he has given up that document, and I have had it corroborated by another authority equally respectable.

1963. Have you any objection to state from whom you obtained that document? —It has been given to me in confidence, and I must beg leave to ask permission before I can do it.

1964. Do you believe that this information was obtained with a view to this or any other inquiry?—Unquestionably not; but to satisfy the party of the correctness of his own views upon the subject.

1965. As you state that 78 per cent. is the average difference of wages between the English manufacturer and French, exclusive of the looms, design, warping, &c. can you state how much should be added for looms, design and warping, which you excluded upon the former occasion?—I thought I had gone far enough in showing so great a difference, but I will make an estimate of that, and it would make a considerable per centage in addition to the other; I do not say that it is 78 per cent. upon the wages alone, but upon the article when produced; upon the average rate of wages the difference would be 108 per cent., but it is 78 per cent. upon the article when produced.

1966. What would the average rate of wages more in England than in France be?—The average rate of wages more in England than in France would be 108 per cent.

1967. What would the average increased cost of material be?—There are many other things; although I have excluded a number, I have included winding, clipping and the cost of the silk. It is 26 per cent. upon the silk, 60 per cent. in winding, 44 per cent. upon another description of silk (marabout hard), and 200 per cent upon clipping.

1968. What proportion of Italian thrown silk that pays duty do you use in those articles?—My English calculation is upon an article that does not pay any duty at all, except a penny a pound.

1969. If there were a reduction of the duty on thrown silk, would that affect your calculation or affect your manufacture?—It would, to a trifling amount; but it would be a positive evil to a large population in this country without any commensurate good to us.

1970. Has any trouble been taken by you or by other manufacturers to lessen wages, as they appear to be so much higher in England than in France?—I think it is sufficiently manifest that we have.

1971. Has there not been a constant struggle between the manufacturers and the men, the one wishing to reduce and the other to keep up their amount?—It is natural that the weaver should endeavour to obtain all he can, and it is equally so that the manufacturer, if he is a fair man, should give all that is right.

1972. What has been the result of that state of things, has it been to keep wages higher in Coventry than in any other part of the country?—I cannot say as to that, but the wages in Coventry have not been too high.

1973. Do you think the present wages will admit of diminution, and still support the weaver?—I do not.

1974. Is

Mr.
*Cleophas Ratliff.*

30 March,
1832.

1974. Is not the price of provisions and house-rent, and every thing of that sort, higher at Coventry than in France?—Yes.

1975. Were you a party to any settlement of wages, either in 1819 or in 1821, or in 1826?—I do not recollect them; but I was in 1831.

1976. Have not you been generally one of the committee, settling those disputes between the masters and the men?—No.

1977. Have you not concurred in the arrangements that have been made?—In last November, when the list was established, I was one of the committee, and have been so since for the maintenance of it.

1978. Will you state what object you had in view at that meeting?—Prior to the establishment of the list, the wages given by some few houses in Coventry for working were at so low and ruinous a rate, that a man was in a worse situation than if he had received relief from the parish; the article of thirty-penny lutestring, which is now fixed at 7 s. 6 d. a piece, was then paid for at half-a-crown. Now a man, working from twelve to fourteen hours a day, could not earn half-a-crown a week upon that work. The object of establishing this list was not to establish a high list, but to establish one that could be maintained and paid, giving ample scope to anybody, that had the power to do so, to give a higher price.

1979. Do you mean to say, that if there had not been that meeting and that resolution, those prices would have been paid generally by the trade?—They were paid higher by many persons; but the object was to make the distribution of wages equal and fair.

1980. Do you think there is any thing to prevent the master and the men now from agreeing upon any rate they please?—Unquestionably not.

1981. Do you think it tends to lower wages by compelling a man to pay more than he otherwise might bargain for?—I think it equitable that a man should not be allowed to reduce his wages, by working at a rate below existence. It would be possible that in cases of severe distress, a weaver depending for his existence upon the work he receives from his warehouse, might offer to make it at a lower price, but a virtuous manufacturer ought to resist such a temptation.

1982. Is not the object of the manufacturer to make his wares as good as he can, and as cheap as he can?—Certainly.

1983. Do you think it consistent with the principles of trade, that any master should be dictated to, as to what he should pay, or how he should regulate his business?—I am not aware that any thing of the sort takes place.

1984. Is it not done by that Table?—So far from dictating, it was made by mutual agreement.

1985. Can any manufacturer depart from that Table without risk?—He could not do it in common justice and honesty; but there could no possible risk attend it, unless he was to get into disrepute with the manufacturers with whom he had agreed, nothing further could attend it.

1986. Has not it often taken place at Coventry, that men that have been anxious to reduce the rate of wages have been threatened, and had their property destroyed in consequence?—No; I do not recollect an instance.

1987. Do you recollect any trials in 1822?—No.

1988. Do you recollect the King against Kean and others, where twelve journeymen weavers were tried?—No.

1989. Do you recollect a person of the name of Carver?—No.

1990. Then you do not recollect the trial that took place in the King's Bench, of the King against Kean and others, for unlawful combinations?—I dare say it did take place, but I have no recollection of the circumstance.

1991. You were in business then?—Yes.

1992. Could such a transaction, which affected the whole of Coventry, take place without your knowing it?—Certainly not; I must have known it at the time, but not applying immediately to myself, it has not been impressed upon my memory.

1993. Do you happen to know, whether any regulation of the price of wages exists at St. Etienne or at Lyons?—Yes, there does; there is a positive rate of wages existing at St. Etienne, to which all the manufacturers agree.

1994. Do you mean to say, that the effect at Coventry, of making these Tables, is not to keep wages higher than they otherwise would be?—I think the Table is so regulated that it could not, by possibility, be brought to a lower scale of wages.

1995. Inasmuch as the wages were lower before the Table was made, is not the effect of such Tables, in point of fact, to increase the wages?—I have no doubt

678.                                                                                                    that

that they keep them at a higher price; but when I have stated that a reduction from that list would render the people in a worse than pauperized state, I think it fair to assume that they ought not to go below it.

1996. Do not the persons that receive wages under that list, receive also a considerable amount from the poor's rate?—Not when they are employed; if they are employed they are not allowed relief of any description.

1997. Do you not conceive, that it is desirable not to reduce the wages so low as not to compel a man to use that haste in making his work by which he might injure the work?—Certainly; there would be no cheapness in it, although it would appear to be a reduction of wages, it would be nothing of the kind.

1998. Has it not a tendency to enable certain houses, who make inferior commodities, to sell those commodities nominally cheaper, but in fact dearer to the consumer?—Certainly; and very much injuring the trade.

1999. Speaking as an individual manufacturer, how can you suffer by paying your men lower wages?—I do not suffer directly, but I do indirectly, because if I were to pay lower wages one week, another man would follow me immediately.

2000. If in any other part of the country lower wages are paid, and equally good work done, will not that individual have an advantage over you in the market?—Certainly, if he can do so, but I dispute the possibility.

2001. Do you not think it best, that every master and man should be allowed to make what scale of wages they please?—Up to a certain point.

2002. What point would you go to?—To the bare existence of the weaver.

2003. Supposing you could manufacture goods, and get a bare living profit, paying 3 s. 6 d. wages for a certain piece, and that 4 s. 6 d. should be demanded from you for wages for that work according to that Table, would you go on manufacturing, or would you stop?—If I could not sell at a profit, I would not go on manufacturing.

2004. In that case would not the workmen suffer greatly from a total want of work?—The effect of it would be this, that those that took the work at 3 s. 6 d. would make goods of an inferior description, and supersede the use of better goods.

2005. Why should they be inferior?—I assume that they would be inferior if men were not allowed an existence upon making them.

2006. Is not the rate of wages determined by the demand for his labour in the market?—In a great measure.

2007. How then can you come to a conclusion, that any such regulation of the rate of wages, can do otherwise than to interfere with a fair scope of capital and labour?—I would not allow of any interference beyond a certain point; I think there is ample scope for a man paying above the list price, but no consideration in the world ought to allow him to go below it.

2008. Suppose a man is willing to work for 3 s. 6 d. rather than have no work, would you allow him to go to the poor rates rather than work for 3 s. 6 d.?—I should not like him to go to the poor rate under any circumstances, but as it regards the interests of the trade, it would be better that he should, than to take wages below a certain point.

2009. Does not the rate of wages depend upon the number of individuals seeking work?—Of course, if there is an exuberance of labour, there will be a depreciation of price; if the contrary, the reverse would be the case.

2010. If there should be 2,000 workmen, and employment only for 1,000, do you mean that you would not divide the work, or allow any man to work for less than the fixed sum?—No; it is the custom with us to apportion it in the best way we can, and to give a certain amount to each man, and I think it is a very good principle.

2011. On every occasion, when there has been a Table of Wages at Coventry, has not the object been to make some manufacturer pay higher wages than he was willing to give?—It would have been very proper that it should have been so, it was in the late case unquestionably.

2012. Is not that the intention of it in every case, or if not, why should it be made?—The object is to make all payers pay as nearly equal as possible.

2013. Do you think it fair, that one person should dictate to another what he should pay, or how he should carry on his trade?—Not upon a general principle.

2014. Do not that Table, and the resolutions go to that precise point?—This Table and resolution goes to the point of allowing a man, if he is fully employed, to get a rate sufficient for his subsistence, and below that point he ought not to go.

2015. Is

Mr.
*Cleophas Ratliff.*

30 March,
1832.

2015. Is it your opinion, as you would not give below the rate fixed by this Table, that if the master is not able to do that, it is better to allow the party to go to the poor rate?—If the wages were as low as you can allow a man to exist upon, I would prefer any thing to going below that.

2016. There appears attached to these resolutions a list of 45 or 50 manufacturers. Do you not think it possible, that one of those manufacturers may possess more capital, and better machinery than others, and that he will have an advantage in his manufacture over a man who is obliged to raise money to a great disadvantage, and who has inferior machinery; and would you compel a man with those disadvantages to pay the same as the other?—I think they would be advantages derived from a very proper source; and it is an advantage that capital should always give to a man.

2017. If a man is to have the advantage of capital, should he not also have the advantage of judgment to determine the rates of wages he would pay, and to whom he should give his wages?—I think if he has not the one to accompany the other it will be of very little use to him.

2018. Does not this Table deprive a man of those advantages, because he is obliged to give the same sum to all?—Certainly not; and you will find no man of capital desirous of departing from such a principle as that. It is a voluntary act upon the part of every manufacturer to subscribe to that, and if he were to depart from it, it would have this effect, that if he were to pay a very low rate, a vast quantity of goods would be accumulated in the market at a low price.

2019. Do you not, by this scale, secure yourself against bad work?—You do.

2020. Supposing it to be a question between 4 s. 6 d. and 3 s. 6 d. a piece, do you believe that a reduction in the wages of 1 s. a piece, would make any difference in the sale of that commodity to the consumer?—Certainly not; it might induce the warehouseman to buy it, and take it into stock, but the public would not benefit by it on that account.

2021. You think, that when from the severity of competition the wages of the workman have been reduced so low as to give him a bare subsistence, it is not advantageous either to him or to the public to go lower?—Certainly not.

2022. Supposing you were to go even lower than that, and to give a man an addition to his wages out of the poor's rate, would not the effect of it be to increase the quantity of goods in the market, and thereby to continue the depression?—If you were to keep men employed when you could not sell the goods, of course it would create an addition to the stock in the market.

2023. Does not it follow, that it would be better for the men not to work at all than to lower the wages?—As a matter of interest to the trade I have no doubt.

2024. Would not it be also more beneficial to the public?—That is another question, if you include, in considering the interests of the public, the burthens that necessarily arise from the poor rates.

2025. Would not the goods be thrown into the market at a loss?—At a loss to the manufacturer.

2026. Is not one of your great complaints, that too great a quantity of goods is thrown into the market?—It is a matter of complaint with us, that too great a quantity of foreign goods is thrown into the market.

2027. Have the profits of the manufacturers, and the wages of the weavers been lower or higher since 1826, than they were before?—As regards myself, I have no objection to state, that my profits have not been near so good, and I am sure the wages of the weavers have not: with respect to profit, it is not to be found now; we only know it in name.

2028. If the profits to the manufacturer are only in name, is the way of increasing them to give higher wages?—With respect to the competition at home, if you make upon the same terms as your neighbour, you can sell upon the same terms.

2029. If you have no profits now, do you think you would increase them by reducing the wages?—I think not; because the price of the goods of course will come down with it.

2030. When you say at home, do you mean the competition in Coventry, or in other parts of England?—We do not fear any competition in England; I should be happy to hear that the trade could be carried on profitably in any part of England.

2031. Is it not your opinion, that the price of raw silk should be left to find its own level in the market, without interference?—I think it will do so.

2032. Supposing the merchants of London were to unite together and say, "We will not sell silk under 25 s." when perhaps the price may be 23 s., do you think

that

Mr.
*Cleophas Ratliff.*

30 March,
1832.

that would be injurious to the manufacturers?—I think it is what the manufacturers have often experienced, and of course it is an evil.

2033. Would not a combination of the men have the same effect as a combination of the merchants?—A combination of the men would be resisted immediately; it could have no possible effect against the general interests of the trade.

2034. Is there such a thing in existence as a combination of the men?—I think not.

2035. Is there not an agreement now existing to pay a certain rate of wages?—There is; but such an agreement would not be suffered to exist, nor would it be established upon any principle but an equitable one.

2036. Do you not think that wages ought to be left to find their level, according to the number seeking work and the capital to employ them, in the same manner as the price of silk or any other article?—They always do find the level; but our object in this is not to confine the rate of wages to that rate, but to prevent it going lower.

2037. Your object is to prevent any one who wishes to manufacture his goods cheaper, in order that he may sell more of them, from doing so?—That is the object of it; but it is the voluntary act of all.

2038. How can it be necessary to enter into an agreement of any kind, if it is voluntary?—Unless a general agreement took place of that kind, one manufacturer, perhaps, meaning well, as they all do, might, in ignorance, be paying a lower price than his neighbour, without being desirous of doing so.

2039. If a man out of employment comes to a manufacturer, and he can give him employment at half the rate of those Tables, should not he be allowed to do it?—I should be very sorry for the feeling that permitted him to do it; but, in fact, though this is an agreement, every man has the power of departing from it if he wishes.

2040. Do you know that every agreement, from 1816, downwards, has been departed from very soon after it has been made, by some one or other?—I think, in large communities there must be some black sheep; I can scarcely imagine that in a large community like Coventry, you will not find some few desirous of taking an advantage over their neighbours.

2041. It was stated to a former Committee of this House by Mr. Peter Gregory, that the Table of 1816, was not conformed to uniformly for a single week, and that very soon they departed from it altogether; do you know whether any of the other Tables have been more attended to than that of 1816?—From recollection I cannot state that; I am free to admit that they have been departed from in most cases.

2042. Is it probable, that if any manufacturer departed from that agreement, his goods would be worse in consequence?—I think they would be made worse.

2043. Do you recollect the following resolution which took place in 1819: " At a public meeting, resolved, That this meeting are firmly persuaded, that to the system of half pay apprenticeships may justly be ascribed the greater part of the distress which has been so long felt amongst the weavers, and that from henceforth they will denounce with their most public disapprobation and censure, all persons who shall hereafter take any apprentice under any other engagement."—I dare say it might be so.

2044. Then no cause of complaint, arising from apprentices has, to your recollection, existed in Coventry?—As I have had nothing to do with them I cannot say, it is a question more for the weavers than the manufacturers.

2045. Have you at all visited other manufactories, where power has been applied to the manufacture of silk?—I never saw the power loom, as applied to silk, I have seen it applied to some other articles of very fine fabrics.

2046. Do you think that any advantage would be derived from the application of the power loom to the manufacture of silk?—I think it would be impossible to apply it with any effect; I will give an example with respect to sixteen-penny eight-leish satins; a loom necessary to put it in, for an engine loom, would be a ten shuttle loom; now it consists of a vast number of threads, introduced into a very small compass; the sixteen-penny satin made in one shuttle, would have 960 threads, and it would require a great deal of attention to keep those 960 threads in their proper place; whereas if it were put into an engine loom of ten shuttles, there would be 9,600 threads to superintend; and my opinion is, that as much manual labour would be required to superintend and keep in place 9,600 threads, and the man might propel the machine at the same time.

2047. Have you seen it applied?—No, I have not; but I draw my conclusions

from

from the intricacy of the work that requires to be made; I speak of the finer fabrics. I think perhaps in the courser fabrics it might be applied.

Mr.
Cleophas Ratliff.

30 March,
1832.

Mr.
Richard S. Cox.

### Mr. *Richard Saurey Cox*, called in; and Examined.

2048. WHAT is your trade, and where do you reside?—I reside in Saint Paul's Churchyard, I am a ribbon manufacturer at Coventry.

2049. How long have you been a ribbon manufacturer?—I have been in business on my own account about 20 years.

2050. What branch of the business does your house apply itself to particularly? —To the gauze and finer fancy branches of the trade.

2051. Has your business undergone any change since the introduction of foreign goods?—Certainly.

2052. In what respect?—Inasmuch as we have lost a most respectable and very valuable connection were we used to vend those goods, there were five or six houses with which we did a vast deal of business, previous to the present laws; there was one house that we did from six to eight thousand a year with entirely in the finer branches of goods, and our business is now nearly closed with that house; there are five or six other houses which in the aggregate might make up 20,000 *l.* more, and our business has nearly gone with all those houses.

2053. What number of gauze looms had you in 1826?—In 1826, we had about 300 gauze looms.

2054. What number had you in 1831?—We had 19 looms.

2055. What number of looms and what number of persons do you suppose are employed upon the whole?—When they are employed, when our business is active we have about 600 looms, and I suppose from 900 to 1,000 persons taking one and a half to each loom, we are not in activity at this moment, but there are that number of hands depending upon us.

2056. Did you only employ at the rate of one and a half to those 19 looms in 1831?—Those 19 looms are only a portion of the looms I employed, my total number of looms is 600.

2057. In 1831 had you the whole 600 employed?—Partially, but there were only 19 then employed in making gauze ribbons.

2058. What is the decline of price at the present period as compared with 1824? —The average reduction according to my calculations in satins, are 33 per cent. that is one-third, and in lutestrings one-third, in figured and fancy goods they are reduced from 40 to 50 per cent., nearly one-half, and in gauzes the reduction is from 50 to 65 per cent.

2059. What do your plain engine weavers earn a week when employed?— Eleven shillings and sixpence.

2060. What do your Jacquard weavers earn when employed?—From 18 *s.* to 30 *s.* average 24 *s.*, play two weeks in six weeks, making 16 *s.*

2061. What number of jacquard looms have you?—About 60.

2062. How many had you in 1824?—We had 30 in 1826, but I do not know how many we had in 1824, some few certainly.

2063. Are the Jacquard weavers constantly employed?—No.

2064. Do they loose any time in putting in their work?—Certainly.

2065. What proportion of time do they loose?—My information is from my manufacturer at Coventry, I depend upon what he states to me, he says they are idle two weeks out of six, that is to say, the warps come down and must be renewed in the loom.

2066. That is to say, there is a necessary loss of time of two weeks in six to enable them to earn the sum you have mentioned in the other four weeks?—Yes.

2067. Are there any other reductions to make from the man's earnings?—There is the filling of the quills; and I believe it is the custom with some masters to charge them something for the use of the loom, but we do not.

2068. Is it necessary that a person in a Jacquard loom should receive assistance? —It is not necessary; but of course if he receives assistance he will do more work, and it is not uncommon.

2069. Is not your average made upon the principle of a man that does receive assistance?—Their assistance is very partial; the wives come to pick the warps.

2070. When you say from 18 *s.* to 30 *s.* do you mean, that the man has nothing to pay for assistance in any shape, or that he is not assisted?—I think that

678.

assistance

Mr.
Richard S. Cox.

30 March,
1832.

assistance is not generally paid for; but that if a man has a wife or daughter, he takes them to help him.

2071. Have they assistance or have they not, in point of fact, to enable them to earn 16 s. a week?—When I say 16 s. a week and deducting 2 s. for filling, I take it without assistance.

2072. In addition to this necessary loss of time, have any of your men been out of employment?—Yes, frequently; many of our looms have been out of employment for two months.

2073. Is there not some advantage in the manufacture, in the application of engine looms over the single hand looms, in the cost of production?—Yes; the master employing these engine looms puts himself in the situation of the under-taker, the intermediate man, and therefore he gets the profit which that undertaker would get; and I think that profit appears to range at from two and a half to five per cent. in favour of the master on the total cost.

2074. In the case of engine work, does the master supply the looms?—Yes, we do so; and I fancy it is the general custom.

2075. Is the master subject to the wear and tear of harness, and other expenses?—Yes.

2076. With respect to the Jacquard loom, do you conduct that also upon the journeywork system?—Yes.

2077. Can you state what is the expense of your Jacquard looms in the course of a year, for change of patterns?—For change of patterns, for remounting the looms and other necessary expenses, during the year 1827, our sixty Jacquard looms cost us 647 l. 4 s. 4 d.

2078. Can you state the average per loom, per year?—It is about 12 l. a loom.

2079. Do you consider the style and quality of your goods improved since the admission of French goods?—I do not consider the quality at all improved; with regard to the style, it is such a complete matter of taste and opinion, that I can scarcely answer, but I should say not; I think we made far more beautiful things from the year 1821 to 1825 than we have ever made since.

2080. Were those from French designs?—Partially so.

2081. Were any of those English designs?—Yes.

2082. Were the majority?—I do not know.

2083. Do you consider that any of the distress now complained of in Coventry and its vicinity is attributable to the introduction of French ribbons?—Yes; I naturally infer that to be the cause, from what I have said as to my own connection, and the manner in which it has been superseded by the French; when I state the extensive connection I had, not only in London but in various other places, Edinburgh and Dublin, and so on, and that they are now entirely served with French goods, I must infer, of course, that I am under a disadvantage from that cause.

2084. Then the duty on foreign fancy goods is no protection to your manufacture?—Certainly not.

2085. Do you consider that prohibition would protect it?—I conceive that if we had a prohibition, we should be pretty much in the same state that we were in when we had it before.

2086. Did you happen at that time to manufacture, for a celebrated fashionable house at the West end of London, any considerable quantity of these gauze or rich fancy ribbons?—Yes, very largely.

2087. Do you so manufacture now for them?—I scarcely make a piece for them, although I am upon the very best terms with the house, and have the honour of the friendship of it.

2088. Do you know whether that house is now supplied with French ribbons?—I am sure it is.

2089. If that house had sold as many French ribbons in 1824, or before the introduction of French ribbons, would you have supplied them with so many of your fancy articles?—Certainly not.

2090. Did you find your trade with them decline from the moment of the opening of the trade?—Not immediately, because the French were not in a precise situation to meet the demand of this market.

2091. Have you any objection to state the extent to which you manufactured for that house prior to the introduction of the French goods?—The amount was very similar to the amount I mentioned in the case of another house.

2092. Can you state the proportion of your present supply to that house, as compared with what it formerly was?—I think perhaps about one sixteenth.

2093. And

2093. And you supplied the house almost exclusively with rich fancy ribbons?—Yes.

2094. Do you still do any work for them in gauzes?—Not in gauzes.

2095. To what cause do you attribute your disadvantage in competing with the French in gauze ribbons more particularly?—I should suppose that a very material cause must be the difference in the price of labour; and there is no question that there is a great difference in the price of silk also, because I have seen goods cleared from the Custom House; I have seen the invoice of the sellers of the goods, and I have seen every expense added to it, and fifty per cent. duty added to the cost, and the total came as near our cost price as may be.

2096. And yet you suppose the Frenchman obtains a profit before he sends these goods out of the country?—I do not know; a great many may come without profit, no doubt.

2097. Do you know any thing of the relative difference of wages between France and England?—Not of my own knowledge.

2098. Is the sale of French ribbons confined to London and other large towns?—No, they find their way every where, and more particularly in the large towns; it is not at all uncommon for my traveller to write to me from Edinburgh, or from Glasgow, that there are six or seven French agents in that city with loads of French goods, and of course his sales are superseded.

2099. What proportion of foreign organzine do you use in your manufacture, compared with the total quantity of silk consumed?—I have taken it out for eight years, and presuming it is half warp and half shute, we use one-tenth of foreign organzine.

2100. Do you speak of the total amount of silk consumed by you?—The total amount of silk which we use.

2101. Is there any difficulty in ascertaining whether fancy or figured goods are of foreign or home manufacture?—No, I should have no difficulty in ascertaining it.

2102. In the event of French goods being prohibited, you would have no hesitation in pronouncing?—I should be directed very materially by the patterns; I think we see every fancy pattern that comes into London, and if I was undecided in my opinion, I could in 24 hours know whether it was made in England or not.

2103. Do you know what is the proportion of the value of labour to the value of silk?—I have got it upon separate articles, I have taken ten pieces of different kinds; upon ten pieces of lutestring, beginning with sixteen-penny and ending with thirty penny, I make the value of the silk 128 *s.*, and the labour I make 60 *s.* 3 *d.* ; upon ten pieces of satins, I make the silk 132 *s.*, and the labour 60 *s.* : I make the value of the silk of ten pieces of figured lutestrings 230 *s.*, and the labour 132 *s.*; so that the value of the labour is 50 per cent. upon the lutestrings, 50 per cent. upon the satin, and 60 per cent. upon the figured lutestring; then as to striped gauzes, the silk is 62 *s.* 6 *d.* and the labour is 40 *s.* 2 *d.*, that is 66 per cent.; then upon figured gauze ribbons, the value of the silk is 80 *s.*, and the value of labour is 114 *s.* which is 145 per cent.

---

*Lunæ, 2° die Aprilis,* 1832.

EDWARD AYSHFORD SANFORD, ESQUIRE, in the Chair.

Mr. *Richard Saurey Cox*, called in; and further Examined.

2104. WHAT do your single hand weavers earn per week when employed?—My manufacturer has written me a letter which I have received this morning, stating that on Saturday last, on taking an average of the 156 looms of the best works which are now making, and all fully employed, the average is 6 *s.* 9 *d.* per week.

2105. Is it to be assumed, that the alleged increase in the consumption of silk has proportionably benefited the labourer?—I conclude certainly not; because the distress has been greater since a larger quantity of silk has been consumed.

2106. That is, the silk is consumed in articles which absorb a greater quantity of the commodity, and there is less of labour expended?—Yes; in fact the loss of the gauze trade very much accounts for it, inasmuch as that those looms have been now filled with heavier goods.

2107. What is the cost of labour upon one pound of silk at the present time, compared with 1824, or any other succeeding year?—According to the average of our consumption of silk the payment for labour, beginning in 1824, was 38 *s.* per pound.

2108. Was

2108. Was that the average you paid for all the silk you consumed?—Yes, when it was mixed with a larger portion of gauze ribbons; in 1825 it was 38 s. a pound; in 1826, 31 s.; in 1827, 30 s.; in 1828, 30 s.; in 1829, 23 s.; in 1830, 20 s.; in 1831, 19 s.; and from August 1831 to February 1832, it was down to 15 s.

2109. Is this the average upon all you make?—It is, upon all work of every kind.

2110. Are the same articles now worked by you that were in 1824?—No, we now make articles that take four times the silk for the same looms.

2111. The statement you have just given in, is the amount of money expended in labour upon a pound of silk, does that include the whole of the silk consumed by you in your manufactory?—Decidedly.

2112. Do you know what is the difference between the price of labour in France and England in the manufacture of ribbons?—Not to speak with certainty to it; but I have no doubt it is very considerable, because I have known when 50 per cent. duty is added to the French gauze ribbons, they are sold at about the same that our gauze ribbons cost us; therefore I infer that labour must be cheaper, and the silk as well.

2113. Are you able to give to your hands any thing like full employment?—Certainly not.

2114. Therefore, from the average of weekly earnings already stated, there will be a great deduction to be made in taking the average earnings of the men throughout the year?—Certainly. I will state some information I have received this morning from my agent at Coventry; he has taken out the amount of the earnings of 470 single hand weavers from the 1st of August to the 1st of February, and there appears paid to each hand at a loom 3 s. 10 d. per week. They certainly did not play half the time; but had they been fully employed I should suppose they would get from 5 s. to 6 s. per week. It should be remembered, that we pay rather a higher price for our fancy single hand goods than the generality of the trade, so that our weavers will average rather higher than others.

2115. Is that price higher than the list that has been referred to?—There is no list of prices for figured ribbons that I know of; there is a list of prices for the Jacquard figures, but I do not allude to those, they are undefined articles that no man can make up a list for.

2116. Do you mean to say, that those articles, for which there is no list, cannot be made in the Jacquard loom?—Yes; they could be made on the Jacquard engine; but when we can get those goods made for 4 s. or 5 s. a piece single hand, it would never answer to put those articles in the Jacquard loom, because the Jacquard machine is for things of a more complicated nature.

2117. Does not the list for Jacquard looms regulate the single hand looms?—No, I do not believe it does. The letter from my agent also states, that the average of 156 single hand looms, fully employed last week, was 6 s. 9 d. per loom.

2118. Are those fancy goods or plain ribbons?—It is possible that there may be some plain belt ribbons, but the majority of them are fancy ribbons.

2119. What is the highest and the lowest?—The highest is 9 s. and the lowest is 3 s. 6 d.; upon the last day, I was asked what was the amount of the profit to the master upon giving out engine work instead of single hand work, and I stated that it was from two and a half to five per cent.; I have since written to Coventry, that I might be sure to be correct, and I find that the amount of the advantage derived by the master finding the silk, and taking the profit of the undertaker, is three and three-quarters per cent. on the cost; it is 10 per cent. on the labour.

2120. What does he do for that?—He winds and warps, and generally I should say, supplies the loom.

2121. What is your advantage in employing an undertaker instead of doing it yourself?—We very much lessen our own risk and trouble; upon the 156 looms I have mentioned, the silk is taken out by 22 undertakers.

2122. Do you mean to say that you prepare the work for any single hand looms?—No.

2123. Is there not a resolution in Coventry, that all the work to be done by the single hand looms should be done by undertakers?—I do not know that there is, but we never transacted the single hand work in any other way than through an undertaker.

2124. In the event of a return to the prohibition of French ribbons, do you think there would be any difficulty in ascertaining which were of English and which were of foreign manufacture?—I am certain not.

Mr.
*Richard S. Cox.*

2 April,
1832.

2125. Supposing they were of the same pattern?—I think that that could rarely occur, but if it did, I have no doubt I could ascertain it; if goods of any quantity came to supply this market, of course they would be very evident, and then our attention would be directed to the nature of the patterns, and I should detect it in a moment.

2126. Do you mean that you should know it from the quantity?—If I had an interest to serve in ascertaining it, I should know it as well by one piece as by a quantity, because I should immediately send down to the manufacturer to know if any such goods had been made.

2127. Supposing a manufacturer at Coventry made 100 pieces, and somebody else got 1,000 pieces made abroad, and they were brought into the market at the same time, do you think that the manufacturer would not be able to tell whether he had made 100 pieces of that pattern, or 1,100?—No doubt, if I were the person that made the smaller quantity, and found a larger quantity in the market, I should have no difficulty in ascertaining that there was a much larger quantity made than I had made, and I should direct my attention to ascertain where the rest was made.

2128. If you could not distinguish them, what remedy would you find?—I would leave that to the law.

2129. Can you suggest any means by which it could be done?—I should recur to the system we had before we had the present; I found no inconvenience then from smuggling.

2130. What was that system?—A prohibition.

2131. Supposing that to be done, and that an article were introduced from France in imitation of the English, how could you distinguish between them?—I should speak from my general impression; I do not mean to say that I could swear whether a piece of goods were French or English.

2132. Do you know what was the state of the law under the prohibitory system?—If they were seized, you must prove that they are English goods.

2133. Is not your trade chiefly a town trade?—Very much so.

2134. Suppose a manufacturer here for the purposes of fraud, was to make 100 gauzes here, and to import 1,000 of the same pattern, and that the goods were distributed over the country, should you have any means of ascertaining whether what you had heard of in the country was part of that 100 pieces, or might not the 1,000 pieces be distributed without it being discovered?—Such a thing might occur, but I do not think it would be often repeated, because the hazard would be so great.

2135. Have you ever heard of such a case under the former prohibitory law, as that ribbons or silks have been made here, and imitated in France, and distributed in this country, and any difficulties arise to ascertain it?—No.

2136. Did you ever hear of a seizure being made of ribbons, in which they could not ascertain at once whether they were of English or foreign manufacture?—Never.

2137. Under the prohibitory system, do you not apprehend there was much greater risk and hazard in smuggling than there is now?—Of course.

2138. Do you not know that when any article was seized, the officer would be justified in making a seizure if he could discover any proportion, however small, of smuggled goods, and that it would rest with the person to whom those goods belonged, to prove that they were of British manufacture?—That was the law.

2139. Would not that circumstance prevent houses of respectability in a large way ever having a large quantity of foreign goods in their possession?—I should think no house of respectable character would venture to have a large quantity.

2140. Do not you know that the goods smuggled before were generally in small quantities, and often by private families?—I know it by general repute, I never heard of any large importations.

2141. Is it not well known, that large houses in a considerable way did not keep large stocks of prohibited goods in their possession?—I never heard of their keeping any.

2142. Do not you know that there are people who import and smuggle largely, and supply the large houses with those goods?—I have so understood.

2143. Is not that generally understood with respect to most of the houses?—I think it is.

2144. Do you know that there are houses that have very large stocks of French goods on hand that do not appear to be importers to any amount?—Not having paid any attention to what amount they import I cannot speak to it.

2145. Looking at the state of the trade in general, do you believe that there could be a sufficient quantity and variety of goods manufactured at home to supply

678.                                                                              this

this market?—I am quite sure there could be, and it would be a most advantageous thing to this country, because it would take up a great deal of unemployed labour.

2146. Can you point out any possible equivalent that we can have by introducing a large quantity of foreign goods brought into competition with our own manufactures in the home market?—Certainly not, it only terminates in bad stock, and bad debts in our own country.

2147. Do not you know, that the consequence of having a continual glutted market with goods, subjects the manufacturer to great loss; and that he is often compelled to job his goods, which all tends to the injury of the fair trader?—Unquestionably; I know that to my sorrow; we have to job some thousands of pieces of fancy ribbons every year.

2148. What do you mean by the word job?—Selling them under prime cost.

2149. Do you mean to say, that those things are only jobbed when the fashion goes by?—Some of those, which are termed jobbed goods, never came into fashion; they are made for a certain season, but they do not happen to assimilate with those introduced by the French, and never are sold at all.

2150. Do not you know, that a large quantity of those goods are brought into the market, and in consequence of the market being over done, the manufacturer is obliged to sell them at an immense disadvantage?—In the case of our own house we have, I should say, as good an insight into what the French are likely to introduce as any house can have; but we frequently make mistakes, and after having made a large quantity of fancy goods we find that we have made them of a wrong colour or style, and we sell them at a loss.

2151. If that happens with your house, must it not operate in full as great a degree with the manufacturers of less capital?—I dare say it does.

2152. Are the Committee to understand, that in expectation of a demand in the spring you prepare goods, and that when the spring comes you find some other fashion takes place, and the goods are shut out?—Yes.

2153. Did not that happen before the opening of the trade?—No, we used to work to order before, because the people that now import French goods, instead of going to St. Etienne and Paris, used to come to my warehouse, and other warehouses, in October and November, and say, now we must arrange something for the spring, what have you got to show us; but now we are precluded from that advantage.

2154. You mean to say, that they prefer the foreign patterns to yours?—They buy them. I mean to say, that under the prohibitory law we used to receive orders, as the French do now, and that therefore they are precisely now in the advantageous situation that we were in before that was the case, because the large dealers in ribbons here go over regularly to St. Etienne and Lyons to order their goods in October and November for the next spring.

2155. Can you state, what proportion of the goods manufactured at Coventry, are made by order, and what are not made by order?—I have no idea; I should think that not one-hundredth part of what we make are ordered.

2156 You sometimes now do make goods to order?—We do.

2157. And you sometimes make them from French patterns, which are furnished you by the warehousemen?—Yes.

2158. When you used to make ribbons to order for those houses, did you make them from French patterns that they supplied you with, or did you furnish the patterns?—In both ways; I used to go over to Paris once or twice a year.

2159. The houses did not furnish you with the patterns, so as to lead you to suppose that they had any intention of importing a quantity of French ribbons to mix up with yours?—No; at the time I allude to, when they gave me the orders, they had no opportunity of having French ribbons, because the time I allude to was the months of October and November.

2160. In point of fact, would they have had any interest in bringing French goods in when they gave you that order, inasmuch as French goods would be dearer than yours?—I do not know whether they would be dearer, it depends upon what they paid for smuggling.

2161. When you find the houses you have been used to supply full of French goods, does not it put you under the power of those houses?—We dispose of our goods in the best manner we can, in other channels.

2162. Do you, in fact, sell your goods to the large houses?—Yes, we do sometimes. With the permission of the Committee, I will state a conversation at which I was present. Early in the month of December I had an interview with Lord
Auckland,

Mr.
Richard S. Cox.

2 April,
1832.

Auckland, in company with Mr. Howell: in discussing different points about the silk trade, as to the relative quantity of French broad silks and English broad silks, of which the sales of his trade are composed, it was stated by Mr. Howell, with regard to broad silks, that 13-20ths were French and 7-20ths were English. My Lord Auckland said, "Then, Mr. Howell, how is the state of your ribbon trade?" Mr. Howell said, that English ribbons, as Mr. Cox knew to his cost, were perfectly out of the question with him : he said, " I told Lord Auckland that he had just been to Paris, having returned in the month of November, where he had had designs and patterns submitted to him of French ribbons, and he had ordered all his goods for the spring." I then asked Mr. Howell, " Supposing I had shown you, to prevent your journey to Paris, patterns and designs which you should have admitted were beautiful goods, would you have favoured me with your order in November to set my looms going, instead of going to Paris to order your goods :" he said, " Certainly not, it is impossible; because the fashion is not under my control; you know very well that every milliner, as well as ladies of rank, import the fashions, and that I could not sell any goods but what were in strict accordance to the French taste, and if I ordered goods of you, I might order things directly opposite to what the French introduce, and thereby, of course, not meet a sale for them."

2163. You stated, that broad silks were referred to in the conversation, and also the ribbon trade, did you understand Mr. Howell to speak generally ?— With reference to the general ribbon trade, more particularly in the elegant and superior sort of ribbons, he said that the English ribbons were quite out of the question.

2164. Was there any other part of the ribbon trade to which that conversation referred also?—No other part.

2165. The Committee collect from what you said, that there are certain parts of the silk trade that you conceive it necessary to protect by prohibition, do you conceive that the whole of the silk trade requires that protection?—The fancy trade unquestionably does; I suppose that the plain trade might be protected by a certain duty, if that duty were collected.

2166. Do you believe that such a duty could be collected by the Government as would be a protection to the plain trade ?—It is impossible for me to say what means they might take to prevent smuggling; and I think they might take much stronger means than have been taken at present.

2167. Suppose the cost of smuggling to be 25 per cent., could not a duty be collected to that amount ?—Certainly.

2168. If, therefore, it should be manifest that the cost of manufacturing plain goods in other countries is not 25 per cent. less than ours, would they not be shut out by a duty to that amount?—Yes.

2169. Can you state the proportion of the quantity of silk you manufactured in 1825 or 1826, as compared with the quantity you manufactured in 1831 ?—I can state the proportion between 1824 and 1831 ; we have used more than double the amount of silk in 1831 than we used in 1824.

2170. Can you state the kind of goods you principally manufactured in 1824, and the changes that have taken place since then, and the proportion ?—I think that in 1824, 1825, 1826 and 1827, we made pretty much the same quantity of gauze ribbons every year.

2171. Were you not the largest manufacturer of gauze ribbons?—I think there was a house or two that made a larger quantity, but not of the excellent quality we particularly directed our attention to.

2172. Can you state in 1824, what the proportion of the whole work of Coventry and its neighbourhood, the gauzes constituted ?—I could not state it.

2173. Are there as many gauzes made now as there were then ?—I should think very far short of it.

2174. Can you state the proportion that the gauzes now form to the whole manufacture?—No, it would be impossible.

2175. You stated that the gauzes predominated up to 1827, what change took place in 1828 and 1829?—We progressively discontinued making gauzes, we made less in 1828 and 1829 progressively, as the French seemed to import more.

2176. Do you confine your observations chiefly to gauzes ?—To gauzes.

2177. Have you found them meet you in the plain satins also ?—We never made much of plain satins, the French satins are certainly preferred in all the fashionable circles ; I fancy there is no such thing as English satin used by the West-end milliners.

2178. Have

Mr.
*Richard S. Cox.*

8 April,
1832.

2178. Have not you known fashions produce great alteration, even before 1826 ? —Yes.

2179. Have not you known articles entirely discontinued, and new articles introduced?—Certainly.

2180. Has the change been as great in any other article as what has taken place in the case of the gauzes?—Gauzes are still in fashion as much as ever.

2181. Might not the change of fashion in favour of the French have produced as great a change if the trade had not been open?—We do not lose the trade because the article is out of fashion, the quantity that is worn is immense, but the French have them to make instead of our having them to make.

2182. But the Coventry manufacture is out of fashion as compared with the French?—It is.

2183. Have not you known very considerable changes effected by fashion prior to the opening of the trade?—There is a change of fashion every season almost.

2184. Have not you known before 1826 individuals prepare patterns, and not succeed, when the season came, in selling them?—Yes, I have.

2185. How did you manage to get rid of the goods on those occasions, did you job them in some manner?—Certainly, but they were in small quantities in proportion to what we have to job now.

2186. What is your opinion with regard to the increase of silk ribbons generally in this country?—I should think ribbons were never more worn, I have seen a greater quantity of ribbon put upon an individual bonnet in 1826 and 1827 than now, but they are more universally worn about the country.

2187. Must not the speculations to provide for the season be in proportion to the increased demand?—I should think the speculation must be less when the market is large.

2188. Will not there be greater provision made for the market for the season?—Yes; but there would be less speculation attending it, it would be a natural provision for the trade when the trade was extended.

2189. Do you mean to say that fashion has not so much effect as it formerly had in the sale of ribbons?—I think it has more.

2190. If the market change according to the fashions, and there are more frequent changes of fashion, must not the speculations be more hazardous now than formerly?—Yes; but there is a large consuming part of the community that are not so much regulated by fashion.

2191. Are your observations, with respect to the risk run, confined to the higher branches of the business?—Yes.

2192. What proportion does that branch of trade bear to the whole trade in ribbons?—I should think it is one-third, because those higher branches of goods are sold in every principal city and large town in England, as well as in the Metropolis, and also in Ireland.

2193. Then your proposition of a prohibition would extend to that one-third of the trade which is of a superior kind?—My proposition would extend to all the goods; I do not see how you can draw a line to exclude a particular style of goods which is undefinable.

2194. You were understood to state, that the competition which you met with was in the higher branches, constituting about one-third of the whole ribbon trade; and that there were not such frequent changes of fashion in the other two-thirds of the trade, which goes among the mass of the community. Would you recommend, that the prohibition should extend also to those two-thirds of the trade, in which there are not those frequent changes of fashion?—I should recommend, that all French fancy ribbons, which at present supply this country, should be excluded, and that we should supply it ourselves.

2195. Then you would not recommend that prohibition because the French are cheaper than yours, but merely on account of the fashion?—Decidedly.

2196. In all fancy trades, does not a prudent man calculate upon the demand he is likely to have for his goods?—Yes.

2197. Does not a prudent man, in every branch of the trade, make the same calculation?—He ought to do.

2198. When you go to expense and trouble to produce new patterns to meet the spring trade, do you calculate upon the profit you get to enable you to make a sacrifice afterwards when the great bulk of the customers are to be supplied?—Yes; we endeavour to prepare for that sort of equalization which must take place occasionally.

2199. Is

Mr.
*Richard S. Cox.*

2 April,
1832.

2199. Is it not generally the case, that the advantage gained in the spring trade enables you to supply the great body of the people afterwards at a cheap rate?— We do not make any of our goods with that view. I think the lower classes of the people are supplied by persons in that particular line of trade; it does so happen, when we job our goods, that those goods may get into those channels, but we do not lay ourselves out for the supply of that description of trade.

2200. If there are at present a great many weavers out of employ, and they get very inadequate wages, can you point out any good end that can be answered by introducing foreign goods?—I know no good end certainly.

2201. Could you state what increase in the number of manufacturers, and the amount of capital there is now in the trade, as compared with what it was in 1826?—I cannot say, but I think there have been a number of them broke since 1826. I am not much acquainted with Coventry, but I know they broke by half a dozen at a time.

2202. Have there been more failures since the introduction of foreign goods than prior?—Certainly; my impression is, that there have been more failures in Coventry within the last three or four years than there were in the previous four years.

2203. From what you know of the state of trade generally, if the French goods were entirely shut out, do you think the competition of one English manufacturer with another, would not bring down the rates of profits as much as the other competition now does?—Any competition will bring down the profits; but when I hold in my hand a paper, stating at a moderate computation the number of pieces of French ribbons that have come into this country by one means or the other; and when I see that there have been 176,000 pieces of ribbons, I naturally infer that if we had had that quantity to make, that it would have taken up our great redundancy of labour, I do not think that we should have been in a state of competition.

2204. You admit that the use of ribbons has greatly increased; you admit also that the prices are much reduced, may not those two changes have led to the great consumption now which would not otherwise have taken place?—I may concede that in part, but we certainly could have made these 176,000 pieces in our looms, and they would have occupied 4,230 hands.

2205. Could you have persuaded the public to buy them if they had not been equally cheap and equally good?—I conceive the preference is owing to the taste, not the price.

2206. Do you conceive that the introduction of the French ribbons into England has had any material effect in compelling the British manufacturer to improve his article?—I think it has produced a great many worse goods than ever I saw made before; at least such is the fact, that there have been a larger quantity of inferior goods than I ever knew made.

2207. Have there not been also a quantity of superior goods than were ever made before?—I stated before, that we made more beautiful goods in the year 1822, 1823, 1824 and 1825, than we have ever made since, and I could mention other houses that did the same.

2208. It has been stated, that there has been a great increase in the use of ribbons; do you consider that that has been from the improved quality of the ribbon, or from the French fashion of using more ribbons?—I think we are very dependent upon the French fashion.

2209. Supposing that a fashion came from Paris, that French bonnets were trimmed with a very small quantity of ribbon, would not that have the effect of materially reducing the quantity of ribbons worn?—Certainly; I am afraid so.

[*A pattern of fancy ribbon was shown to the Witness.*]

2210. Before the French goods were introduced, could any thing like that be made in England?—It could not be made without a Jacquard.

2211. In consequence of the introduction of French patterns, have they not been much improved?—I do not call them an improvement; it is a change; and we are apt, in speaking of fashion, to think every change an improvement; but I mean to say, that in the years 1822, 1823, 1824 and 1825, we made far more beautiful goods in my opinion that what are made now.

2212. Is it not a fact, that there are more men of capital employed in the business now than formerly?—I think not.

2213. Are not the English goods cheaper than the French, supposing that the smuggler or the Custom House imposes 25 per cent. upon the importation?— I think it is very doubtful.

2214. Have

Mr.
Richard S. Cox.
_____

2 April,
1832.

2214. Have you any doubt of it, except with respect to the gauzes?—Yes; I have heard it stated so by other manufacturers; that with regard to plain satins, the present duty is by no means a protection.

2215. If English goods are in reality cheaper than the French, when subject to that expense, would not a competition here be more injurious than a competition with France?—I cannot conceive why it should be.

2216. The Committee have had two articles exhibited to them, the one English, the other French; the one at 36s. and the other at 48s.; now would not the English article, costing 36s. be a more formidable competitor than the French, at 48s.?—The English would produce them all at the same price, unless advantage might be given to those that have capital and skill.

2217. Would you rather have as an opponent a man whose article cost 48s. than one that cost 36s.?—I should not have him as an opponent at 48s.; because I think the people would buy the goods at 36s.

2218. Supposing that French goods were absolutely prohibited, and supposing the consumption of fancy goods to be the same as it now is, would not the speculations in England, on the part of manufacturers, be much larger than they now are?—I think they would, certainly; I think there would be a vast number of Jacquards set up, and a great deal of machinery.

2219. Would there not, at the end of the season, be a vast quantity of goods for sale in the way you have stated?—If the supply was greater than the demand, that must be the effect.

2220. Would not a man of good taste make a good profit upon his goods, while the people who did not possess good taste would have to dispose of their goods at a loss?—Unless there was a class of persons to buy those.

2221. Would not the quantity of goods jobbed be greater in that case than it is now?—I do not know that that would be the case.

2222. Supposing that those 176,000 pieces that now come from France were prohibited and thereby excluded, would not the increased demand, that would be created in this market, probably occasion more than 176,000 pieces to be made?—I think it is possible.

2223. Did you experience the ill effect of this competition, previous to 1826?—I am not aware that we did.

2224. Supposing such a competition to exist as has been referred to, and you were a loser by the rivalry of another manufacturer, still would it not be a British manufacturer who would be gaining by your loss?—Of course.

2225. At present, what you complain of is, that it is the foreign manufacturer that is gaining by your loss?—Unquestionably.

2226. And therefore in the case supposed, although the injury to the individual master might be as great as it is now, it is clear that the operative weaver must benefit?—Of course.

2227. Could the rate of wages be raised unless there was additional employment for all the persons now out of employment?—Wages always follow the demand.

2228. Would it not be the effect of such a competition as has been supposed, at least to keep up, if not to raise the wages of the operatives?—I think it is likely that it would; unless there were a great redundancy of goods produced, it would not lessen the wages.

2229. When you say that it would better the manufacturer, do you mean the weaver?—Yes.

2230. Do you know that the goods imported from France are paid for by British labour, although not by weavers?—I am not aware that it is the case; I do not know what British labour goes to France.

2231. How do you suppose the silk is paid for that is produced from France --I know how a great deal of it is paid for, because there are bills drawn upon London and paid here.

2232. How is it paid for?—I do not know how it is paid for.

2233. What are those bills drawn for?—For a debt owing in this country.

2234. Are you aware that we can pay for them in no other way but by British labour?—I am sure we do pay the French in British labour, because the French receive a great deal of gold and bullion.

2235. Does not the jobbing of ribbons depend upon there being more in the market than is required?—If they were of a kind that are wanted, there might not be too many, but the jobs arise principally from their being goods unsuited to the market.

2236. Why

Mr.
*Richard S. Cox.*

2 April,
1832.

2236. Why do you not make those gauze ribbons now?—Becasue we have no chance in the market with French gauzes, they are produced cheaper in the market than ours are after paying 50 per cent. duty.

2237. Then it is not a mere question of taste alone?—No; when you come to mere coloured striped gauzes, it is an every day article.

2238. You stated that you have almost discontinued to manufacture gauze ribbons do you not know that although you have declined in the manufacture of gauze ribbons, others have increased very much?—I do not know that, but it is possible.

2239. If the French can manufacture cheaper than we can, and pay a duty of 50 per cent., would any one manufacture gauzes in England?—I would not.

2240. If therefore persons are manufacturing gauzes, and increasing the manufacture of gauze ribbons, can it be true that the French are underselling them?—It may be true, but the fact is, that we make a good quality, and perhaps the question may allude to inferior gauzes that we could not sell.

2241. Have you seen any English gauze ribbons of such a description as you could neither make nor sell if you had made them?—Yes; and if they were generally made, they would ruin the trade.

2242. Does not every manufacturer make what he thinks he can sell best?—No doubt about it.

2243. Do you mean to say that nobody is to make any thing but the best of each article?—What I mean to say is, that if the ribbons made in this country were generally of that inferior quality, the French would soon supply the whole country, because the English would get so bad a character that nobody would buy the English at all.

2244. Will not the price of the article correspond with its quality?—It ought to do.

2245. May not those inferior kinds of goods suit the American, or a foreign market?—Yes.

2246. Do you mean to say, that it may not be equally advantageous to the country to manufacture that inferior class of goods for exportation?—Yes; but I am not aware that there is any exportation.

2247. Are you not aware that this low quality of ribbons have been exported lately?—Not in any quantity; I know that we have exported 500*l.* worth, and I think we received 240*l.* for them; but in what I said just now, I was speaking of the home trade; it had no reference to foreign trade.

2248. You have stated, that you used in 1831 double the quantity of silk that you used in 1824, what description of silk was it you used in this year?—It was Italian silk (Brussa) and China, and different kinds of silk.

2249. What was the proportion of Italian, and of the other kinds of silk?—I think the proportion of Italian would be about one-half.

2250. What proportion of the Italian was thrown in Italy, and what proportion was thrown in England?—One-fifth of the warp was thrown in Italy, one-tenth of the gross consumption of silk.

2251. Then about half of your whole warp is Italian thrown?—Half of the silk we consume is warp, and half of it shute; of the warp, one-fifth is foreign and four fifths is English thrown; it is therefore one-tenth of the whole, and one-fifth of the warp. The whole of the shute is British thrown; therefore nine-tenths of the whole is British thrown silk.

2252. What other descriptions of silk are used for warps in Coventry?—Of China silks, we use some which are thrown in England, China organzines no other warps.

2253. What are the principal sorts of shute used in Coventry?—China and Brussa.

2254. Is there any Bengal used?—Very little.

2255. Is there any Italian shute used?—Very little, if any.

2256. Then are the Committee to collect, that upon a very large proportion of the silk used at Coventry, that is, upon all the China, the Bengal and the Brussa silk, the duty upon foreign thrown silk can have no effect whatever, inasmuch as they pay none?—Certainly.

2257. Therefore it is paid upon one-tenth alone of the silk used in the making ribbons?—As far as our house is concerned.

2258. What is your opinion with regard to the comparative quality of the foreign thrown silk and the English thrown silk?—The best answer I can give is to refer to the preference we give to the English thrown; I believe in one of those years we did not use an ounce of foreign thrown silk, and never above one-tenth.

2259. Of

Mr.
Richard S. Cox.

2 April,
1832.

2259. Of the different sorts that are thrown in this country, which do you conceive to be the best?—The Italian is the superior silk; but we can get Chinese and Bengal as well thrown as the Italian; but then they are an inferior silk.

2260. Which is the next best?—It depends upon what purpose they are to be applied to; the China organzine is exceedingly good for the purpose for which it is appropriated, but the China is a coarser silk; the Brussa is never organzine; it is all single.

2261. For what particular purposes is the best thrown silk used?—For the finer purposes.

2262. Do you think it desirable for the silk manufacturers of Great Britain to encourage the throwing of Italian silk in this country?—Unquestionably.

2263. Do you like the British thrown Italian silk better than the Italian thrown?—Certainly.

2264. Why do you buy Italian thrown silk when the British is better?—We never do, unless it happens that we cannot, at the moment, meet with British thrown that we approve of.

2265. Do you mean to say, that there has been any difficulty in obtaining British thrown silk for your own manufacture?—We confine ourselves to particular kinds of silk certain persons throw, and if the market happened to be bare of that, instead of speculating in silks that we are not acquainted with, we may buy foreign thrown.

2266. Do you mean to say, that the Italian raw silk may be thrown better by some persons than by others?—Certainly.

2267. What is the superior throwing owing to, is it owing to superior machinery?—I do not know by what means the perfection is obtained, but I know what the perfections are that I require; in the first place the cleaning of the silk is a material thing, and the sizing of the silk is material.

2268. Has there been much improvement in the quality of British thrown silk since 1823 or 1824?—No; I think for the last 15 years there has been pretty much the same average consumption in favour of the British; I believe there has been some patent obtained for throwing organzine.

2269. Are you aware that the very quality of the silk as imported now is better than it was formerly?—No.

2270. Supposing any alteration of the law were to cause the throwing of silk to be abandoned in this country, what effect do you think that would have upon the silk manufacturers?—I should think we should be completely in the hands of the Italian silk throwster, and the effect of that I can only collect from the consideration, that every body that has a monopoly of the market makes the best of the market that he can.

2271. Are there any kinds of silk thrown out of England that are superior to the British thrown silk?—I think not; there is a peculiar silk, the Piedmont, which we have nothing to do with, which I believe has some qualities which rather oblige those parties who make particular articles, to give a preference to that silk; but we never use it, it is bought by velvet makers, I believe, and other persons.

2272. Do not you think, that if you were entirely dependent upon the Italian for thrown silks, they might very often send you an inferior quality?—They would send us what they liked, and I should think charge us what they liked.

2273. Do not they send what they like to you now?—Yes; and if we do not like it we do not buy it.

2274. Are not you obliged to buy the raw now?—Yes; but I think they would keep the raw at home if they could sell the thrown here.

2275. Is there not a particular kind of silk called marabout, that you use?—Yes.

2276. By whom is that silk thrown?—It is thrown by a great many houses.

2277. Is there a fair competition in the price of that?—Yes, I think there is now; there used not to be, but there is now.

2278. When did that competition begin?—Perhaps two or three years ago.

2279. Before that, used there not to be a considerable difference in the price of that, as compared with marabout abroad?—A greater difference than there is now, but I am sure that there is considerable difference now.

2280. Is there not a considerable improvement in the marabout silk?—No, I think it has retrograded very much.

2281. Do you know where the marabout silk, now used in the manufacture of gauzes, comes from?—It is fine Italian white gum silk.

2822. You mentioned that you exported a small quantity of ribbons, what per centage

centage did you find the drawback to amount to on the cost of those goods ?—We frequently make small shipments to our home colonies; the drawback averages as nearly as possible five per cent. upon the invoice, and allowing that there is a profit upon the invoice, it is of course something more upon the cost.

2283. Do you think that in this country as much trouble is taken to employ superior artists in designing patterns as there is in France ? — I am not sure whether there is quite so much trouble taken, we have not quite the encouragement, they have so many markets to manufacture for; the English market, the German market, the American market, the Polish market, and others.

2284. Would it not be worth the application of capital here, as well as in France, to have superior artists, seeing that fashion governs the sale ?—We have very good artists here.

2285. Are not the French patterns admitted to be superior for beauty and variety of colours, to those here ?—I think the French employ artists rather of a superior class to ours.

2286. How do you account for that?—Because they are compensated by the large sales they obtain.

2287. Of late years has there been any great increase of designers in this country as compared with what there was before ?—Yes, certainly.

2288. Does that enable you to come nearer the French?—No; when we make any designs, it is not with a view of getting nearer the French, but it is to make the best of our own ideas.

2289. Has there not been, since you have manufactured at Coventry, very little of that invention, and very few artists of that class ?—Very few.

2290. May not that in some degree have contributed to prevent your being equal to the French in fashion and style?—I think we are equal; I think no Frenchman in Paris can show a better set of patterns than those I have produced.

2291. Must not the principal source of encouragement to artists be from their having the run of the market with a new pattern for a considerable time ?—Yes, as I stated.

2292. And have you not been excluded from that of late?—Decidedly.

2293. Can you give the Committee any idea of the average value per pound of the silk used at Coventry?—I think it is about 18 s. undyed thrown silk, warp and shute altogether.

2294. You have been asked some questions as to the fashion prevailing at present with respect to ribbons, and it has been supposed that that fashion has been derived from it being a fashion to wear them in France. During the war in the years 1813 and 1814, when what are called the large pearl ribbons were worn, do not you think that ribbons were quite as much worn as now?—There were a greater number of yards of ribbon worn then, but they were not so wide or so heavy; I think there were as many pieces of ribbon used.

2295. Has not the Jacquard loom been introduced since the period you allude to?—I think the first we had was in 1824.

2296. Are you not aware that in the Jacquard loom 12 pieces of twelve-penny figured gauze ribbons can be made at one time .—Yes; I have no doubt that can be done; but we do not make any thing so narrow.

2297. In the description of ribbons worn at that time, would the Jacquard looms have been of any use to you?—Very little; the French did not use the Jacquard at that time.

2298. Can you now make many more pieces by the use of the engine loom, as compared with the single hand machine formerly?—The engines were very much used before. I do not conceive if you exclude the Jacquard, that the engine looms are very considerably increased.

2299. Are you aware to what extent engine looms have been increased; how many more pieces, and how much greater breadths can be made now than were made then?—The breadths were not required then; if they had been, they could have been as easily made then as they are now.

2300. Are you aware, that in the best constructed looms a weaver can make at once 24 pieces of twopenny or fourpenny?—Yes.

2301. Could they do that formerly?—Yes; I have seen thirty twopennies made in 1816.

2302. Are you aware that they have increased to the extent of 40?—No; I never knew more than 30, but they are more commonly 20.

2303. Before the introduction of the Jacquard loom, how many figured satin

678.                                                             ribbons

Mr.
*Richard S. Cox.*

2 April,
1832.

ribbons could you make at once?—The Jacquard does not apply to quantity; it is only applicable to particular descriptions; because we could make as many figured ribbons twenty years ago as we can now in the Jacquard loom.

2304. What is the greatest number you can make with a Jacquard machine?— I suppose you might put up a dozen shuttles, but there is no particular advantage in it, because the man's attention is taken off to his warps, which are constantly breaking threads.

2305. Has the application of the Jacquard engine enabled you to make a greater number of warps in the common engine loom than before?—Certainly not; it is for nothing but peculiar patterns.

2306. You have stated that the duty upon foreign thrown silks applies only to a small proportion of the trade of Coventry, do you think that any relief would be afforded by reducing that duty?—No material relief; the relief would be no further than to the extent of its respective quantity upon the whole consumption.

2307. Supposing the duty were taken off Italian silk, which is now 3s. 6d. a pound, how much would that reduce the price of that silk to the manufacturer?— It would depend upon the price the Italian put upon it; there are generally some limits of prices, and therefore I do not take it that we should benefit more than one-half at all events.

2308. You mean that the Italian would get 1s. 9d. more for the silk than he now gets, and you would get it 1s. 9d. cheaper?—Yes.

2309. If the price were reduced to you 1s. 9d., would not that occasion an equal reduction in the English thrown Italian?—I do not know that; I should think the Italian would keep his raw silks at home and throw them himself.

2310. If you got the Italian 1s. 9d. cheaper, would you not get the English 1s. 9d. cheaper?—If we had it in the market; but I take it that we should be in the Italian's hands.

2311. Do you consider that the price of the English thrown silk depends upon the price of the Italian, or that the price of Italian depends upon the price of English?—I think that the price of English thrown always depends very much upon what the English throwster gives for the raw silks.

2312. If the thrown silk were entirely in the hands of the Italian, is not there the probability that he would increase his price, and probably to a greater extent than the duty now paid?—That is a matter of opinion; nothing would surprise me in that respect if we were in their hands.

2313. Might not it have the effect of throwing many of the throwsters here out of employment?—I should think so.

2314. Must not the price of Italian thrown silk depend upon the price of the Italian raw?—I think they are very frequently at variance; we can frequently buy Italian thrown silk cheaper than we can buy the Italian raw and throw it, and sometimes vice versâ.

2315. Is not the price then dependent on the British thrown silk?—I think the Italian merchant, in selling his thrown silks, will not attempt to undersell the English silk throwster; he will get the best price he can.

2316. As he ought to have the same profit upon the Italian thrown as upon the Italian raw, how do you account for the difference of price between the Italian raw and the Italian thrown?—I do not know how to account for that; I believe there is a small duty put by the Italians upon the Italian raw silks.

2317. Are you not aware that there is a duty in Italy of 10d. upon raw, and of 5d. upon Italian thrown exported?—I was not aware that there was a duty of 5d. upon Italian thrown silk; I thought there was a bounty upon the thrown.

2318. To what do you attribute the difference of price which you stated to exist in the market occasionally, between raw and thrown Italian?—I fancy the scarcity of one or the other.

2319. Is it not the policy of the Italian government to encourage the exportation of their organzine silk, and to discourage the exportation of the raw?—Certainly it must be the policy of every state to send out the manufactured article instead of the raw.

2320. Did you ever manufacture broad silk goods?—Yes.

2321. When was that?—We manufactured broad silks from about the year 1814 to about 1827.

2322. What description of goods were they?—All fancy goods.

2323. How many looms did you employ?—From 60 to 100.

2324. Where was the manufacture carried on?—At Spitalfields.

2325. Have

Mr.
*Richard S. Cox.*

2 April,
1832.

2325. Have the answers you have given, respecting the ribbon branch, had any reference to broad silk ?—Certainly not.

2326. What was the amount of wages you paid for those goods ?—We paid from 60 *l.* to 100 *l.* a week, in proportion to the number of looms we had going: about a pound upon each loom.

2327. Have you discontinued to make those goods ?—Yes, in 1827.

2328. For what reason ?—We found our goods entirely superseded by the French fancy goods; I prepared to discontinue it in 1826.

2329. Do you consider that you were at all interfered with by Manchester, or any other branch of manufacture in England ?—Certainly not.

2330. Did they, at that time, make that description of goods at Manchester ?—No.

2331. Do they make that description of goods now ?—No.

2332. When you say broad goods, what kind of goods do you mean ?—A great many figured terries and figured velvets, and a variety of figured broad goods, figured satins and figured lutestrings.

2333. Are the goods you so made now imported from France ?—Not of that kind; they change every season.

2334. In the shutes you used for those goods, did the gum remain, or was it boiled out ?—Boiled out.

2335. That is to say, the public had not an artificial article ?—No; they had twelve ounces instead of sixteen.

2336. Are not the articles that come from France, which superseded yours, made with the gum in ?—Most of the French goods are made with the gum in.

2337. They therefore intrinsically are not so good as those you made at the time you speak of ?—Certainly not.

2338. You are understood to say that they have been superseded by goods of a similar kind ?—These kind of goods change almost every season.

2339. Is that the change of fashion and not of fabric ?—Yes, of both.

2340. Is it not the fact, that the principal goods imported from France in that branch of the trade, are crapes ?—I do not know, I have so lost sight of the broad silk trade, that I know very little about it.

2341. Are there not a great many other fancy articles imported from France besides crapes ?—Yes, figured broad silks; and every season there is something constantly coming in new, and in very large quantities.

2342. Supposing there were a demand for figured broad silks, would they not probably be made at Manchester ?—I should think not; the class I allude to are so dependent upon fashion, that the Manchester manufacturer would have no idea what goods to make, because they are only required at a particular season.

2343. Supposing the French goods were shut out by a prohibition, do not you suppose that those manufactures would take place at Manchester ?—I think it is very likely.

2344. Have that description of goods ever been made at Manchester ?—Never.

2345. Have you been in the habit of seeing the goods made at Manchester ?—At that time I knew more about them than I do now, and at that time there was nothing of that kind made at Manchester.

2346. You were asked whether formerly the practice was not to manufacture goods without gum, do you not know that the practice of supleing is carried to a much greater extent than it was before ?—Yes, it was unknown till the French taught us.

2347. To what extent will the dyers weight goods ?—I cannot state; we never exceed the weight of the silk in our suples, we do it to the extent of fourteen and a half.

2348. Do the French do more than that ?—I am told that the French do it to the extent of 20; I ought to state that the suple only applies to the shute.

2349. Has not the importation of French silks increased very much lately ?—Yes.

2350. Do you happen to know that 30 cases were imported on Thursday last ?—I am not aware.

2351. Is not this a time of year when the importation of the French takes place to a large extent ?—It is.

2352. Were not the silk trade very anxious in a negociation that took place with the Board of Trade, to make regulations to prevent smuggling ?—Certainly they were, they suggested means to prevent it by stamping, &c.

*Mercurii, 4° die Aprilis,* 1832.

## THE RIGHT HON. THE EARL GROSVENOR, in the Chair.

Mr. *Thomas Sawer,* called in ; and Examined.

Mr.
*Thomas Sawer.*

4 April,
1832.

2353. WHERE do you reside ?—In Aldermanbury.

2354. What are you?—A ribbon manufacturer at Coventry.

2355. Do you employ any travellers to sell goods for you in the country ?—Yes, I do.

2356. Do you find French ribbons to be in such demand in the country as to injure your own manufacture?—Very materially ; there is scarcely a shop they go into, though the ground they go over is very extensive, but what they are opposed in every place by French goods ; when they come to show their patterns, they are objected to, because they say they are not to our taste, we cannot buy them ; in consequence of that, it has made me reduce my looms very considerably ; I had for a long time a particular objection to dealing in any thing that was French, but I was persuaded by my travellers to get them, or that I should sell very few goods of the fancy kind, and at last I yielded to their desires ; and recently I bought a large quantity of French ribbons, and I find that they sell in preference to my own ; indeed I have ordered the whole of my looms almost to be taken down, except upon two articles which the French do not send us, those are some few black and white striped gauzes, and the rest I have discharged.

2357. Then you do not employ so many hands in the fancy trade as formerly ?—I do not.

2358. Were you ever connected with machinery in the manufacture of ribbons? —Yes, unfortunately I was.

2359. When did you cease to be the owner of machinery ?—At Christmas 1829 ; we had looms upon an improved principle, bar looms, and to them were attached the Jacquard ; but I found it would not answer our purpose, we could not produce goods such as would sell ; I made a proposition to my partner that I would rather get rid of them, to which he assented, and with that, I had other machinery which I was very desirous of getting rid of, and he took the whole, and we dissolved partnership, and I have rejoiced ever since that I got rid of them, and I have put up no machinery since.

2360. Did you sell your machinery to him at a sacrifice?—Yes, I did.

2361. Is he using that machinery now?—He has been using it hitherto, but to what good purpose I cannot say; all I know is, that he would be glad to get rid of it if he could, even at a sacrifice.

2362. In point of fact you have not found any benefit from the use of machinery? —I have not.

2363. Have you been in any other way connected with machinery ?—In a throwing mill.

2364. Are you now a throwster?—I am not, I ceased to be a throwster at the same time that I gave up the looms, for the same cause that they were doing no good.

2365. Did you sell that at a sacrifice?—They all went in one lot.

2366. Did the person that took them succeed in benefiting himself ? —I am afraid not, but I cannot speak positively as to that.

2367. Are you not an assignee under the estate of Thompson & Co. at Stratford-le-Bow?—Yes.

2368. Had they any machinery or mills?—I was co-trustee with Mr. Pearce, of the house of Halling, Pearce & Stone, and among the rest of the assets we had to pay the creditors, was a silk mill in most excellent condition ; some of it I believe had not been used at all.

2369. Have you sold the mill property?—I have not sold it ; I put it up to auction at one time to ascertain the value, and I think there was a bid of 1,000*l.*

2370. Did the offer include the machinery ?—The whole of the premises altogether ; it was a rental of 40*l.* a year, the whole in complete order, and it stands upon half an acre of ground altogether ; and since that, I have repeatedly offered it for sale, and even no later than this morning I offered it for 600 *l.* and I could not get it.

2371. Do

2371. Do you know what it cost?—Six thousand four hundred pounds or six thousand five hundred pounds.

2372. When was it erected?—About 1824 or 1825.

2373. You have stated that you found your goods objected to on the ground of taste, was there any objection also on the ground of price?—I bought them at lower prices that what I manufactured for.

2374. Did you find the French goods you bought, cheaper than those you manufacture, or were they dearer?—In some instances they were cheaper.

2375. What particular kind of French goods did you buy?—Gauzes.

2376. What kind of gauzes?—Rich figured gauzes, such gauzes as I never made; I made the small figured gauzes.

2377. Therefore you found a taste for richer gauzes than you had been in the habit of making, and that therefore you could not sell yours?—Yes.

2378. What kind of goods had you been in the habit of making whilst you was a manufacturer, can you state what proportion of gauzes you made?—I cannot say that.

2379. Where was the a-la-bar mill you had?—At Coggeshall, in Essex.

2380. Did you reside there?—No, in London.

2381. Was it erected by a French artist?—Yes.

2382. Do you mean to say that you had a manufactory at Coventry, and another at Coggeshall?—Yes.

2383. Who superintended the manufactory at Coggeshall?—We had a Frenchman to assist the latter part of the time.

2384. What kind of goods did you make at Coggeshall?—We have attempted to make satins, but we did not succeed with them.

2385. How long did you make the attempt?—I cannot say exactly how long.

2386. Was the Frenchman that superintended it a partner in the business?—He was not.

2387. Had you no other superintendent than that Frenchman?—We had assistants, we looked upon him as the principal man to direct that part of the business.

2388. At Coventry, what machinery had you?—We had no machinery, it was given out to the weavers in common; when I say we had none, we had a few looms, but very trifling in comparison.

2389. Do you know whether it is a practice generally at Coventry for people to superintend their own machinery, or to employ others to do it?—I can speak as to our house for the last 16 or 17 years, it has been superintended by a servant; my former partner originally resided there, but when he died, it was superintended by a servant.

2390. Can you state what proportion of gauzes, and what proportion of plain goods, you made at Coventry?—No, I cannot.

2391. Do you know whether it is the practice at Manchester, and other places where machinery is used, for the parties interested to superintend the manufactory themselves, or employ agents?—I cannot answer that question.

2392. At any rate you did not superintend your own machinery?—I supplied it with silk, and that was all I did.

2393. If a manufacturer leaves the management of his business entirely to a servant, do you think any business is likely to succeed in England in that way now?—I know that it has succeeded.

2394. You mean formerly?—Yes.

2395. Was there as much competition formerly as there is now?—I have always found competition in the trade, and I do not know that there is any great difference; the greatest competitor we have as to fancy ribbons, is the foreigner.

2396. You do not consider that there is competition amongst the British?—Yes I do, and there always was such a competition as would keep down prices; I do not think it possible that a monopoly could be formed.

2397. What is the competition you fear from France?—The competition I fear is what I see, which is the French goods coming in whether they are smuggled or not; I consider that as long as they come in, my trade will be destroyed.

2398. Were you employed in figured gauzes?—Very trifling.

2399. Did your travellers state to you, that the French goods were preferred in consequence of superior patterns, or on what ground?—I cannot state that they stated precisely what it was, but the fact was, that they did not buy ours, but bought the French.

678.

2400. Do

Mr.
*Thomas Sawer.*

4 April,
1832.

2400. Do you employ any artists for making new patterns?—Having no machinery of the Jacquard description, I did not think it was necessary.

2401. Have you never employed the Jacquard machine?—I employed the Jacquard machine while at Coggeshall, but I found it anwer so badly that I was glad to get rid of it.

2402. What were the advantages you expected by substituting the a-la-bar loom for the engine looms?—I expected that we should produce them quicker and better, but we failed in that.

2403. Had you any evidence before, or have you been informed what had been the result of the trial of that loom anywhere else?—No, it was an experiment.

2404. Did you make this experiment without ascertaining what was the result of any prior experiment any where else?—Being given to understand that the Swiss use the same branch of machinery, I had a mind to attempt it.

2405. Had the person that superintended it ever been in Switzerland to see how that loom was employed?—I believe not.

2406. Was any person employed upon that loom in Coggeshall who had been in Switzerland to see it in operation?—I believe not.

2407. Who was the person that made it?—He was a Frenchman.

2408. Had he been in Switzerland?—I am not aware that he had.

2409. You stated that you parted with your machinery on that account, and that you found no advantage from any machinery?—Not there.

2410. Did you find advantage from machinery any where else?—Only from the common looms I employed in the neighbourhood of Coventry, and I have no other machinery but that.

2411. Is there not a great deal of very excellent work done by the hand looms?—A great deal.

2412. Was not your house connected with a very old house in the trade?—It was.

2413. Did not you use to do a great deal of country business?—Our business mainly depended on the country trade.

2414. When you used to pursue the country trade, yours being an established house, did you find that you could get a fair and ready sale for your goods?—Generally.

2415. When you say that the competition at home kept down prices, do you mean to say that it gave the public the security of having the articles on reasonable terms, or did you mean to say that it affected you so, that yours became a losing trade?—In order to keep up our trade we sold our goods lower.

2416. Do not you think that that sort of competition at home gives a fair security to the public?—Certainly.

2417. Without being injurious to the manufacturer?—I think the competition amongst ourselves is sufficiently great to keep the prices down.

2418. And at the same time to allow you a scope to get a fair profit?—Certainly.

2419. And when you sent your travellers about for orders, you found the introduction of foreign goods to interfere so as to obstruct your business?—Very greatly, so much so, that even last autumn I had manufactured a quantity of fancy goods, and I thought they were such things that I might fairly anticipate would be sold in the course of the autumn at a fair remunerating profit; I sold a portion of them, and the rest I have got lying by me now.

2420. Do not you conceive that there is a prejudice in favour of all foreign articles, particularly French, and that people are often guided more by fashion and caprice than price?—From the quantity that appears to be worn, it appears to me evidently so.

2421. If you could make goods here equally good and equally cheap, would not this prejudice still be very injurious to you?—It certainly would be injurious.

2422. Do you conceive also, that when the competition keeps down prices, the letting in a quantity of foreign goods also, and with this prejudice in favour of foreign goods, must be very detrimental?—I consider that where the supply exceeds the demand, we have not the least occasion for any foreign goods to be brought in; and I think our supply is equal to the demand.

2423. Will not too large a quantity thrown into the market, whether home goods or foreign goods, be injurious?—I conceive so.

2424. Do not you conceive that there could be more goods manufactured than
there

Mr.
*Thomas Sawer.*

4 April,
1832.

there could be possibly a demand for ?—I know I could manufacture a great many more if I had a protection, and I believe that we could supply the whole demand.

2425. Have not the markets generally been overloaded for some time past ?—I believe they have.

2426. Has not the fancy trade always been somewhat speculative; have not those who provide the best pattern been the most successful?—I consider it has always been somewhat speculative, but rendered ten times more so by the introduction of the French.

2427. Do you consider that the French can make better goods than we ?—In certain fancy goods I think they can.

2428. In what does the superiority consist ?—As far as my knowledge goes, I think the marabout that they use is better, and I think they have a greater encouragement for fancy than we have, and a greater protection than we have.

2429. Did you make any effort to rival them by means of artists to design patterns as they do in the French?—I had no opportunity of doing so.

2430. You say you now buy French goods, do you know what similar goods would cost to make them in this country ?—I cannot say exactly, because I have not the machinery.

2431. Is the price such as to induce you not to make the attempt ?—I dare not make the attempt.

2432. When the last reduction of duties took place, did not you understand that it was done to put a stop to the smuggling by coming down to the smuggler's price?—I understood that that was the intention.

2433. Has it had any such effect ?—I cannot find that it has; I know nothing about smuggling, either direct or indirect, all that I know is, that goods are laid before me, and if I can purchase them, and make a profit upon them, I do so, and that is all I have to do with them.

2434. Have you ever seen the power loom at work ?—I have; but it did not answer the purpose.

2435. You are now a manufacturer, making simple works in the old manner ?—Yes.

2436. Do you use the Italian thrown silk or the English thrown silk ?—I use both.

2437. Which do you consider the best?—That depends upon the purposes I require it for.

2438. Do you use a larger proportion of English thrown or foreign thrown ?—The English thrown.

2439. Is not a large proportion of the silk used at Coventry, China, Bengal and Brussa ?—Yes.

2440. Are those imported in a thrown state ?—No.

2441. Has the duty on foreign thrown silk any effect whatever upon a larger proportion of the silk used at Coventry, namely, upon all the China, Brussa and Bengal ?—It has no effect upon that.

2442. Do you think it desirable for the silk manufactory of Great Britain, to encourage the throwing of Italian silk in this country ?—Yes, I do.

2443. You did not then reside in Coventry?—No.

2444. Have you looked accurately into the proportion of silk used there ?—I have not minutely.

2445. In what way does the encouragement of the throwster here benefit the manufacturer ?—I could not get Italian thrown that would answer for some purposes, and then I must resort to the British.

## Mr. *William Merry*, called in; and Examined.

2446. YOU are of the firm of Merry & Brown ?—Yes.

2447. Where do you reside ?—At 26, Wood-street, Cheapside.

2448. Have you a manufactory at Coventry ?—We have.

2449. Have you been extensively engaged in the fancy branch of the ribbon trade?—We have for fourteen years.

2450. Through what channel did you formerly dispose of your goods ?—To the fashionable retailers at the West end of the Town and the City.

2451. Do they continue to deal with you as extensively as in former years ?—No, they do not; we have entirely lost the retail trade, and I have taken three

Mr.
*William Merry.*

678.                                                                                      accounts

Mr.
*William Merry.*

4 April,
1832.

accounts out of our ledger to show the comparison from the year 1826 to the year 1831.

[*The Witness delivered in the same, which was read as follows :*]

No. 1.—Retail Account.

| 1826. | 1827. | 1828. | 1829. | 1830. | 1831. |
|---|---|---|---|---|---|
| £.   *s.*   *d.* | £.   *s.*   *d.* | £.   *s.*   *d.* | £.   *s.*   *d.* | £.   *s.*   *d.* | £.   *s.*   *d.* |
| 1,138 19 – | 1,091 7 – | 952 4 – | 349 13 – | 29 17 – | 37 11 – |

No. 2.—Wholesale and Retail Account.

| | | | | | |
|---|---|---|---|---|---|
| 4,318 19 – | 4,635 9 – | 5,662 9 – | 3,952 16 – | 1,547 1 – | 572 10 – |

No. 3.—Wholesale Account.

| | | | | | |
|---|---|---|---|---|---|
| 1,244 12 – | 755 17 – | 247 17 – | 137 16 – | 7 18 – | 4 6 – |

2452. Are the houses from which those purchases are made still in existence?—They are.

2453. Are they in the habit of purchasing goods now to the same extent, although they do not purchase them of you?—Yes; and they have every disposition to purchase them of us.

2454. Have you reason to think, that the parties alluded to in that paper do now buy English manufactured ribbons from other parties?—Certainly not. I believe they are supplied by the French.

2455. Have the parties alluded to given you any reason for withdrawing their custom?—They have very frequently, when I called upon them for orders, said, they could not buy a piece of my goods for their demand was for French; and I know that at least nine-tenths of the stocks at the West end of the Town are French; I have looked through several of them, and I believe that to be the fact.

2456. You allude particularly to fancy French ribbons?—Yes; we are in the fancy trade entirely.

2457. Have you particularly directed your attention to the improved machinery?—We have.

2458. At what time prior to the introduction of French goods?—In the year 1820 we began to make our improved looms; in fact we contested a patent; an action was brought against us for introducing a new invention, which was brought forward by a man named Thomson. The plaintiff proceeded against a Mr. Goddard, and afterwards against us, and he was nonsuited.

2459. What description of ribbons were there made in 1826?—We were making gauzes in 1825 and 1826.

2460. Were they rich cut gauzes?—Yes.

2461. Do you continue to make them?—No; we have not a loom going.

2462. For what reason did you discontinue the making of those ribbons?—We found the French interfere so much with us, that we were obliged to abandon them altogether; we could not get material to make them as good as the French.

2463. When you say, that you could not get material so good as the French, do you mean as to quality?—As to quality.

2464. Do you know any thing of the price in France?—No.

2465. Have you any reason to think, from the price at which the French ribbons come here, that they must produce the commodity at a lower price than you do?—I have.

2466. What do you now make?—We make lutestring ribbons.

2467. Do the French interfere with you in that branch?—Yes; because they introduce gauzes, which are more fashionable at the West end of the Town, and the moment their goods are introduced our goods are laid aside.

2468. Have you sustained any loss from that circumstance?—I have.

2469. When did you first use the Jacquard engine?—In February 1825. It

made

made the figures much larger, and in fact it cut to a thread, which was very superior work to that made before by the old description of looms.

2470. Do you happen to know when the Jacquard loom was first introduced into England?—I think it was introduced in the year 1820 by a Mr. Wilson; he obtained a patent for the engine in this country.

2471. You have stated that the Jacquard loom enabled you to make figures of a larger size, was that the only advantage?—Yes; and cutting the figures finer.

2472. Could you make handsome goods before that time?—Yes.

2473. You have shown patterns of lutestring figured ribbons to the Committee, when did you make those patterns?—In the spring of 1831.

2474. Did they afford you a profit?—They did in the spring, and in consequence of our being successful in the spring we were induced to continue making those goods in the autumn; we have now seventy looms going, and the expenses of the alterations are so considerable that it would not answer our purposes to do so, we went on making the same patterns in autumn colours; and those goods we were compelled, in consequence of the French introducing satin figures, to job off at ruinous prices; and at the end of the year, instead of gaining money by our trade we were considerable losers.

2475. And you think that if those French goods had not been introduced you would have sold those goods at a profit?—Yes.

2476. Did you sustain a serious loss?—A very serious loss.

2477. How much per cent. do you think you lost by them?—Forty-five per cent.

2478. What prevented your immediately altering your looms and making satin figures?—The expense of the alteration is too considerable; we consider that the looms will cost from 10 *l.* to 12 *l.* annually; if we were to go to the expense of altering every season it would entirely destroy the profit, and we are obliged to give up the trade.

2479. Do you mean to say that you intend to discontinue the manufacture?—We are going to dissolve partnership, and to break up our establishment entirely.

2480. Have you not found any sale this spring?—Yes; we were equally fortunate this season, but I am sorry to say that we shall be compelled to stop every loom by the 1st of May.

2481. To whom have you sold those ribbons which you have made for this spring?—We have sold them to warehousemen in town.

2482. Do you know what they do with them?—They sell them to the country houses chiefly.

2483. Does what you have said apply to the plain lutestring as well as to the figured?—No, we confine ourselves entirely to the fancy trade, and principally to the Jacquard machinery.

2484. The ribbons you have made this spring you have sold to the large wholesale houses; do you think it likely that you could have sold them to the houses at the West end of the Town if the French goods had not been introduced?—Certainly.

2485. Do not your connection admire them, and think them very pretty?—Yes, they do; in fact we have been very fortunate in making our patterns.

2486. Therefore when you speak of breaking your establishment up, it is not in consequence of having failed this spring, but in the apprehension of your failing hereafter?—It is in consequence of having failed these last three years, although we have succeeded in the spring, at the end of the year we have lost money.

2487. Is not the preparation of fancy goods confined to the spring, and do not prudent manufacturers generally stop in May?—Not with machinery like ours, they do with single hand goods.

2488. Is it not the fact that manufacturers do prepare in May for the autumn?—Not quite so early as May. To show the trouble and expense we are obliged to go to in producing the patterns, I will show a draft of a Jacquard pattern before it is made [*producing the same.*]

2489. How many cards are applied to this pattern?—Eight hundred and sixteen cards. The draft writing and stamping of this pattern cost 10 *l.*

2490. Have you been in France to see how the figures are got up there?—I have been to France, but I never saw a loom put up there.

2491. Are not the French put to the same expense?—Yes, but they get positive orders for the goods which we do not, they provide patterns and show them to the buyers, and they generally get orders upon those patterns.

678.                                                                              2492. Cannot

Mr.
*William Merry.*
———
4 April,
1832.

2492. Cannot you show patterns to the buyers also?—We have tried it, but we did not succeed.

2493. Do you fail in taste?—I think not, when we have sold all our goods, although made on speculation.

2494. Is it on account of price then that you fail?—No.

2495. What do you consider to be the difference in price between the French and yours?—I do not think price has any thing to do with the fancy articles.

2496. Will you state what is the reason why the French is preferred in your opinion?—I think prejudice in a great measure, for I do maintain that if we had prohibition we could make as good goods in this country as the French can. I think if we had encouragement by protection, the manufacturers in this country are disposed to go to every expense they can to produce quite as good goods as the French.

2497. What do you mean by the word protection?—I mean prohibition; we nave invested a great deal of money in machinery; we have been going on the last three years at considerable loss, so much so that we are now going to give up the trade.

2498. Do you find that the French have more beautiful patterns than you have, or that they change them oftener than you do?—I do not think they change them so often, they have a foreign market, and they continue their patterns much longer than we do.

2499. Do you know any thing of what foreign markets they have?—I believe they send their goods to the American market, but I am not acquainted with those things.

2500. If your goods are equally good, why should you not get hold of the American market as well as they?—I have tried the American market and other markets, and we have goods out now at several places, but we do not get 10 s. in the pound from our foreign trade.

2501. Have the Americans also had some prejudice in favour of the French?—I cannot say.

2502. Do not you believe that the French goods can be sold in America cheaper than yours?—I do believe the satins are much cheaper.

2503. Do not you require a 30 per cent. duty as a protection in this country?——Certainly.

2504. Then the answers you have given have reference to a duty of 35 or 40 per cent. being added to the French articles when brought here?—Yes; but I do not think that price is an object, it is the fashion.

2505. After paying the duty on the French goods, such as you manufacture, are they dearer or cheaper than yours?—I think they are higher in price.

2506. What is the duty upon French figured satins?—I believe it is 15 s. per pound weight.

2507. Do you know what it is per cent.?—About 16 or 20 per cent.

2508. Do you find that you can make them at as low a price as the Frenchman, when he pays a duty of 20 per cent.?—No; we require more than 20 per cent.

2509. Are you undersold by the French in this market?—I cannot say; the French are not introducing the article similar to ours.

2510. Comparing French lutestrings with similar goods made by yourself, which were the cheapest after the duty had been paid?—I think ours have been as low, but we could get no profit by them.

2511. Are they not in fact lower than the French?—In some instances they are, and in some not.

2512. For what would you sell a similar article to that?—[*A French pattern being shown to the Witness.*]—I could not say, unless I knew the weight of it; this would require at least a 1200 engine to be placed upon the loom.

2513. Do you believe that that is as good as you make them in England?—No, it is not so good.

2514. Therefore if they should be lower in price, that would be no surprising matter?—No.

2515. What is the value marked upon it?—Fifty-nine shillings and five-pence.

2516. What is the duty upon it?—Ten shillings.

2517. What do you suppose would be the price of a similar article to that, if made by you at Coventry?—I do not know.

2518. Could not you make a better article for less than 50 s.?—Not to get a living profit by it.

2519. Are

2519. Are not these better?—[*Some patterns being shown to the Witness.*]—They are.

2520. Could not you sell them for 50 s. ?—Yes, they are sold for less than that; if we could employ our looms through the year it would answer our purpose very well; but on account of the continued change of patterns that is required, this price does not give us a remunerating return for our labour.

2521. Are then the English cheaper than the French?—Yes; but the French are too wise to send in things of this sort; they send in gauzes that supersede our manufacture.

2522. Could not you in point of fact manufacture goods cheaper than the French, when the duty has been paid on French goods?—Those heavy goods; but if they are not fashionable, where is the use of manufacturing them.

2523. Taking goods of the same quality, are not the English goods cheaper than the French?—Those lutestrings are cheaper than the French.

2524. Looking at those two goods before you, French and English, which are the cheapest after the duty is paid upon the French?—I consider the English the cheapest.

2525. You said you could not get marabout from France; supposing that silk could be obtained, could you make your articles as cheap and as well as the French?—No; we labour under very great disadvantages, our price of labour is much greater, although it is reduced to the lowest ebb that it is possible to be reduced.

2526. What is the proportion of labour in the manufacture of your gauzes, and what is the proportion of silk ?—I cannot say, we have not made a piece of gauze this four years.

2527. If you had not the French fashions to interfere with you, could not you advantageously employ machinery which now you cannot employ?—We could, certainly.

2528. You mean to say that there is so much prejudice in point of fashion in favour of French goods, that whenever they come into this market they lead the fashions, and supersede the English even if better ?—They do.

2529. Is not one advantage the French have, that they receive orders for the goods?—I believe they do.

2530. When those goods are ordered, and the houses have those stocks in hand, must not that prejudice you in the sale of your goods, and also in your profits?—Certainly.

2531. Does not every man engaged in the fancy trade look for an extra profit in the spring, in order to enable him to sustain a depreciation of price afterwards ?—Yes.

2532. You are understood to say, that in consequence of this competition you are not able to do that ?—We are not.

2533. You have been asked about exportation, have not the French the raw material themselves?—They have.

2534. If this country were to enter into competition with France in the export trade to America and other places, would it not naturally induce the French to lower their commodity, and would they not always have the means of superseding ours ?—I believe they would.

2535. Would not the effect be, that they would lower the prices both of the raw material and other things?—Yes.

2536. Is there not always a natural prejudice amongst foreigners in favour of that particular country, which has the reputation of excelling in an article?—Generally there is.

2537. The French having the advantage of having received orders, do they not avoid a great deal of that risk that you are liable to ?—They do.

2538. And when they have set their looms, cannot they do a great deal more work without being at the expense of changing the pattern?—Certainly, they can do it at less expense than we can.

2539. If the working of your looms would pay you, would not you do it immediately?—Yes; we have tried it for the last three years, and we have been unfortunate.

2540. Was not one of the reasons urged against prohibition in 1826, the prevention of smuggling?—Yes.

2541. Do you think the present system has answered that purpose, or has smuggling increased ?—I believe that smuggling has increased very much since the duties were lowered.

Mr. *William Merry.*

4 April, 1832.

2542. Another

2542. Another reason stated for the admission of French goods was, that it would expand our commerce; that it would open fresh channels, and give us a large import trade; has it had that effect?—Quite the reverse.

2543. It was stated in 1826, that the admission of French goods would have the effect, in less than six months, of raising the price of the wages of all the persons concerned in the silk trade 25 per cent.; has that been the case?—Wages have been very much depressed since 1826. I will state the money we have been paying for labour. In the years 1823, 1824 and 1825 we paid for labour 40,714 *l*; the average, yearly, was 13,571 *l.* 6 *s.* 8 *d.*; the weekly payments, 261 *l.* for those three years. In 1829, 1830 and 1831, the payments were 20,411 *l.* 6 *s.* 2 *d.*; the average yearly payments were 6,803 *l.* 15 *s.* and the weekly payments, 131 *l.*

2544. Was that always upon the same description of work?—Yes; in fancy goods principally.

2545. You have stated, that before the admission of French goods, you sold goods to a large extent to some of the fashionable houses in London, but that since that time those houses have almost entirely ceased to deal with you; are you on good terms with those houses, and are they willing to transact business with you if they could do it?—They are.

2546. Have they given you any reason why they could not do their former business with you?—Yes; they have told me, that the prejudice is so much in favour of French goods that they cannot buy my goods.

2547. Has there been any want of exertion, on your part, to employ designers and produce good patterns?—Not at all. I think we are now producing very good patterns at home.

2548. If there was proper encouragement, could you produce as many novelties, and employ as many designers as they do in France?—Yes; if we had prohibition, we should have encouragement.

2549. Was your business upon the increase before this measure passed?—Yes; progressively increasing.

2550. Do you imagine it would have continued to increase?—I have no doubt at all it would.

2551. Do you think now if there was a prohibition, you could have carried on your own concern profitably?—I have no doubt of it.

2552. Can you point out any new channel for the sale of goods than this admission of French goods has opened?—Not for the ribbon manufacture of this country; we have given it all to the French, and our people are now in a state of destitution.

2553. Is there sufficient capacity in this country to supply any quantity that might be required?—I think so.

2554. Then the favourite maxim, that wherever you displace labour it can be employed more profitably, does not hold in this place?—Certainly not.

2555. Has it not been thrown into the workhouse and upon the roads?—Yes, thrown into the workhouse.

2556. If there are manufacturers sufficient and labourers sufficient to supply any demand that may occur, must it not be very injurious to let in a quantity of foreign labour in competition with it?—Certainly it is.

2557. Have you any doubt that that is the cause of the present distress in the trade?—I am certain it is the cause; ribbons never were so fashionable as they are at the present moment.

2558. Are not silks generally used by ladies, as well as in waistcoats, and furniture, and a variety of articles?—They are.

2559. You have stated that the French have the material for the manufacture, do you know what proportion of silk the French import from Italy?—I do not.

2560. What opportunity have you had of knowing that there is considerable smuggling now?—From common report.

2561. Has any particular instance come to your knowledge in which you have known whether goods that have been imported have paid duty or been smuggled?—No; but I believe from the quantity of goods entered at the Custom House returns, and from the quantity of goods I see in every shop that I used to supply, that they must come through other channels than the regular channels.

2562. You have stated that the distress is very great at the present moment, have they not a fixed rate of wages, below which none of them will work at Coventry?—They have a regular list.

2563. Do you abide by that list?—Yes.

2564. Do

Mr.
*William Merry.*

4 April,
1832.

2564. Do you approve of a man remaining idle rather than working below that list?—Yes; I do not approve of any one running down the weavers to such a low price that they are obliged to apply to the parish.

2565. Of those who are now on the poor rates distressed, could any of them obtain work at a lower rate if there was no table of wages?—At the present moment I do not think they could be employed by the trade, not even at a lower rate of wages.

2566. You have stated that it would be difficult for you to continue your business in consequence of the great expense you are at more than the French?—In consequence of the great expense we are at in producing those patterns, we cannot go on.

2567. Can you state to the Committee any estimate of the amount you pay for material, the amount for labour, and the amount for machinery?—The annual expense of 70 looms that we now employ would be 700 *l.* a year.

2568. What value of goods will that turn out?—Seventy looms would not make more than 100 pieces a week, but they are not always employed, there is some time taken up in changing the patterns. The cottage pattern I have shown would take a man a month to prepare.

*[Some patterns were shown to the Witness.]*

2569. In a pattern of that description, can you state what the value of the material would be, and what would be the expense of the labour?—I think the labour is about one-third of the value.

2570. Does that include the dyeing?—No.

2571. What do you call the article now before you?—It is a forty-penny lute-string.

2572. What are the wages for making that article?—I think it is 14 *s.* a piece.

2573. How many pieces would a man make in a month?—He would make four lengths, that is, eight pieces in six weeks.

2574. What time does he lose in putting in those eight pieces?—Every warp that he makes he has to twist in his warps, which will take him at least a week to do; it would take him six weeks to work and put in his warps; I have taken the average of six of our weavers, and the earnings are 17 *s.* 11¾ *d.* a week, taking the whole year, and they have 2 *s.* or 2 *s.* 6 *d.* to pay for filling, out of that; but the men employed upon that work are the best artisans, and very stout men.

2575. Are there any other kinds that you pay more for?—Those are the only kinds of goods we make at present.

2576. Do you mean that that is the average, supposing them to work on one pattern only for six weeks, and to change the pattern every six weeks?—No, he does not change it every six weeks; if the pattern suits a single loom, he may change the pattern in half an hour, but there is a certain preparation necessary for that; we have other artisans employed in draft-drawing, stamping and reeding, and all that to prepare for the looms.

2577. Does the average you have stated apply to the case of the pattern being changed once in six weeks?—No; it is when the men are fully employed upon the loom.

2578. What may be the average number of pieces you make of a good pattern?—If we think it a good pattern we mak 100, if it is not a good one we only make 40 or 50; sometimes, we do not make more than eight pieces.

2579. How many pieces of figured ribbons does a man with a Jacqnard loom make at once?—These broad forty-penny ribbons are made in four shuttle looms; the thirty-penny are fours, fives and sixes, and the twenty-four are sixes. The sixteen-penny are tens and twelves.

2580. What are the respective quantities that a man can make, working in a single hand loom, with a Jacquard figure applied, and working at an engine loom?—It depends upon the pattern.

2581. Take the same pattern in each case?—He would make a piece and a half in the engine, and a piece in the single hand loom.

2582. What description of goods does that apply to?—I am speaking of forty-penny.

2583. How many of that forty-penny can he make in a engine loom at once?—Four.

2584. And he can only make one in a single hand loom?—Yes.

2585. How much more work can a man do making four pieces in an engine loom above what he can do making one in the single hand loom?—Half a piece.

2586. How

2586. How much could he make of the twelve-penny in the engine loom, and how much in the single hand loom?—There are very few twelve-pennies made in the single hand loom, it would not answer the purpose.

2587. Do you consider the work turned out of the Jacquard looms equal to that in the single hand, or better?—The single hand looms cannot make those patterns unless they apply the Jacquard engine to the loom.

2588. Supposing they apply the Jacquard machine to the single hand loom, which is best?—The expense would be very considerable to apply the Jacquard engine to the single hand loom, and I think the engine would beat it.

2589. Generally speaking, is it your opinion, that the engine loom to which the Jacquard engine is applied, can do the work better than where the engine is applied to the single hand loom?—No; I think they can make very superior work in the single hand loom if they have an engine large enough; because a man in a single hand loom has not so much silk to attend to as in the Jacquard loom.

2590. Have you ever made any plain satins?—We have made them but we found it a bad trade, and gave them up; we have not made any for the last four or five years.

2591. You were understood to say, that the French receive orders for goods, and therefore have an advantage over you; do the English manufacturers never receive orders?—Very seldom indeed.

2592. Have they never received orders?—I mean to say that they do not at the present moment. I showed an English buyer those patterns, and he said they were very good things, but he could not order them; but he would see them when they were made, and therefore we were compelled to make a quantity of them, and take the risk ourselves.

2593. Did you use to receive orders before 1826?—We used to receive orders then, frequently.

2594. Do you never receive orders now?—Scarcely ever till we have produced the goods; we take the risk entirely upon ourselves.

2595. Will you undertake to say, that the practice differs now very materially from what it was before 1826, in respect to orders?—Yes, very materially, though there may be orders given now sometimes.

2596. Are you acquainted with the saw loom?—I never heard the term before.

2597. Have you ever been at Battersea?—I have seen the bar looms at Battersea.

2598. Have you ever been at Reading?—No.

2599. Do you know what machinery is used there?—I believe there are no ribbons made there except galloons and doubles.

2600. You have stated, that you manufactured gauzes formerly, but that you do not make them now; are not other people making gauzes although you are not?—I believe they are, but in a very small proportion to what they were making in 1824, 1825, and in 1826. I believe there are not more than two or three houses now, and at that time I should think there were a dozen making them.

2601. Have you any doubt that the parties who are making gauzes are obtaining profits?—I do not know what profits they are making.

2602. When you make gauzes what price do you pay for your marabout?—I cannot state that, but I can ascertain.

2603. Is not the price of marabout very much reduced?—Very much reduced.

2604. You have stated, that as far as regards price, the English lutestrings are cheaper than the French?—Those heavy goods are cheaper, and if it was not for the prejudice I think they would be sold; but we have absolutely lost the trade, although we are producing as good things as any in the trade.

2605. Have you any doubt that as many fancy goods have been made since 1826 at Coventry, as there were made in the same number of years before?—There were more more made in 1826 than there were before; they were getting very fashionable indeed, and there was a great demand for fancy ribbons in 1826.

2606. In the five years since 1826, have not more fancy goods been made at Coventry than were made in the previous five years?—No; before 1826 they were of a different description; narrower goods; and there was not so much silk consumed on that account.

2607. Speaking of value, has not there been a greater value of ribbons made in the last five years than in the three years before?—Yes; because the goods have been made much richer than they were in 1821, 1822 and 1823.

2608. Is

Mr.
*William Merry.*

4 April,
1832.

2608. Is not the general fashion of the country people to wear a more expensive ribbon?—Yes.

2609. Has the increase of the value of ribbons, made since 1826, been chiefly in respect of the material?—Much more in respect of the silk than of the labour.

2610. Do you mean, that fewer men have been employed since 1826 than in the last five years before?—No; I should think there have been more employed, but at less wages.

2611. Have they been as constantly employed?—No.

2612. You stated, that wages at Coventry were very low; did you mean to apply that to gauze ribbons?—No, I do not know any thing about gauze ribbons; I was only speaking of our own trade; we have not made a piece of gauze for the last four years.

2613. Are not the principal part of the ribbons imported from France, gauze ribbons?—They are.

2614. You have been asked as to the price of silk in France; are you aware that the French import silk from Italy?—I believe they do.

2615. Must not the price there be the same as it is here, having both markets open?—I do not know any thing about that.

2616. Would not the same quality of silk bear the same price at Manchester and at Coventry?—Yes.

2617. Must it not be the same at Lyons and at Coventry?—I think the charges of carriage, and so on, would be less in France than they are here; but not having been there, I cannot speak of what is done in France.

2618. What is your opinion as to the effect of the introduction of French silk goods into this country, with reference to the improvement of our own manufactures in consequence?—I think we were improving our own manufactures before the introduction of French silks.

2619. Has there been a corresponding improvement since that period?—We have been gradually improving our machinery from 1825 to the present time.

2620. Are you now making better goods this year than you ever made before?—I think we made as good last year.

2621. Were the goods you made last year and the present better than you ever made before?—The men have got more used to the work, and they now make them very good.

2622. Before the introduction of the Jacquard machine, were there not by the hand looms as good goods manufactured as there are now?—Quite as good.

2623. Then does this improvement in the quality extend further than to the introduction of other machinery?—That is all; it enables us to make the patterns much larger.

2624. Is the machinery materially improved since 1826?—No, we are using the same machinery as we were in 1825; but the men are more used to it, and they are better able to manage it.

2625. You have stated the wages earned by a man in full work; are there not often interruptions for the want of work, and so on?—Very frequently.

2626. Do they work over hours?—No, about 12 hours a day.

2627. Must not the persons that earn those wages be skilful superior men?—Yes, they are the best weavers.

2628. Are there a great number of them that can obtain such wages as that?—No, there are not 700 Jacquard engines in the town.

2629. When you stated the average earnings of six of your men, after making the necessary deductions, to be at 15 s. 11 d. per week, do you mean to say that they earn 15 s. 11 d. per week upon the average of the whole year?—Yes; those men have been employed the whole year.

2630. Previous to 1820 or 1821, when those improvements began, did you not make an inferior article, chiefly called lays?—Yes.

2631. Have you any doubt that but for the introduction of French goods, which took place soon after 1821, by smuggling and bringing our patterns from France, the English trade would not have been in the state that it now is?—There was sufficient emulation among the manufacturers in Coventry to improve, and we were progressively improving.

2632. Did not the improvement depend mainly upon copying the French style?—Not altogether; we of course copied our patterns from the best source we could.

2633. Did

2633. Did you not find the French patterns to be the best source?—They have been the most fashionable here; but we have not followed them altogether.

2634. Was it not the case, that after the peace the English manufacturers had an opportunity of going over to France and bringing with them patterns, so as to enable them to improve their manufactures quite as much during the existence of the prohibition as they have been able to do since?—Quite as much; I went over myself in 1819 and obtained patterns.

2635. And did not the Treasury allow the patterns to be imported through the Custom House?—Yes.

2636. Consequently there was every facility for improving by means of French patterns during the prohibition as much as there is now?—Yes.

*Mr. George Stephens,* called in; and Examined.

2637. WHERE do you reside?—I belong to the house of Halling & Company, in Cockspur-street.

2638. Have you lived with them for some time?—I have been in their London house for about five years; I have been in their service 15 years.

2639. Do you know any thing of the proportions that French and English ribbons bear to each other in the purchases of that house, for any considerable number of years?—I cannot speak from any reference we have made to our books further back than the present year, from the 1st of January to the present time; in the purchases of this year, the proportion the French have borne to the English has been 400 per cent.; when I buy 100*l.* worth of French fancy ribbons, I buy but 25*l.* of English fancy ribbons.

2640. Do you think the proportion has greatly increased in the last six months?—Not very much.

2641. Have you any idea of what the proportions were in the year 1826, the first year of allowed importation?—I should think the proportion of the English over the French would not be above 35 to 40 per cent.

2642. Do you sell any English fancy ribbons?—We sell very few English fancy ribbons; the proportion the English gauze ribbons bear to the French is not five per cent.

2643. Do you consider that the price of the commodity is an object with your customers?—Not altogether.

2644. Do you not sometimes sell English goods very cheap?—Yes.

2645. Generally speaking, do you find that a rich and expensive commodity will be bought by some persons at any price?—Yes.

2646. Do you find a disposition on the part of the public to follow the great leading houses in point of fashion?—Yes.

2647. Perhaps you consider yourselves one of the leading houses?—We are not the leading house for fashions in London.

2648. Are you employed in selling yourself?—I am a buyer, I do not sell in the shop.

2649. If you are not a seller, how do you know that the ladies prefer French to English ribbons?—By the daily report of the young men that sell them; I have a report every night of what will sell and what will not sell.

2650. Do they ever make any particular remarks to you?—They have said that the sale of English ribbons declines daily, that they have no chance of selling them now.

2651. Do you conceive that the preference of the French arises from any particular beauty in the French?—I think in gauzes it does.

2652. Do you mean that if you produce two articles of equal goodness in beauty and quality, the French will be preferred?—In gauzes we have not lately seen any thing so good in the English as the French, but in lutestring a lady will generally ask the young man whether it is English or French.

2653. Do you make many purchases of English ribbons?—Very few.

2654. As you have been 15 years in this business, have you any knowledge of the quantity of French goods that were sold before they allowed importation?—I recollect in 1823, 1824 and 1825, I was then engaged in selling goods in Bristol, and we used then occasionally to receive boxes of goods that were smuggled; those goods were always such as had been taken from private individuals, and had been seized and stamped at the Custom House, and sold there at public sale, exported and brought into England again at other places.

2655. Did

Mr.
George Stephens.

4 April,
1832.

2655. Did you sell any quantity of them?—Not any quantity of them; and I do not think that one haberdasher in 500 sold any.

2656. You say that they were seized from private individuals, have you any doubt that they were intended as a matter of trade?—Yes; I do not believe that they were, because they were in such detached pieces.

2657. You have stated that you sold very few French goods; had you any opportunity of getting them?—I think we could always get them if we wrote for them.

2658. Could you get them immediately?—Not immediately.

2659. What was the proportion of French goods in your stock?—We never kept any by us.

2660. Had you not then great difficulty in selling them?—Great difficulty, great fear and great trouble; they were never kept on the premises, and they were mostly sold within a few days from the time we heard of their being in the city.

2661. Do you think that where you sold 50 l. of English you sold 5 l. of French?—No, we did not sell two and a half per cent. of French.

2662. How did you get the French goods when you wanted them?—If we wrote for some things, " over the left" as it was termed, we could have them in a fortnight or three weeks.

2663. Did you write to London or to France?—To London.

2664. Did you write to the house of Halling & Company, or to some other house?—Not to Halling's house.

2665. When you procured them, was it generally for some customer that wanted them?—We never wrote for them, unless we were sure that we could get persons to purchase them.

2666. Do you believe that the house of Halling & Company in London sold any?—I only know that a young man was discharged for having a piece of bandanna in his possession; I do not believe they sold any.

2667. Could you yourself tell French from English goods?—Yes, I could tell them.

2668. Could you tell now?—I cannot tell from a pattern, I can tell from a lot of goods.

2669. Have you seen much improvement in English fancy goods since 1826?—Not any in gauzes, and very little in lutestrings.

2670. Is it merely a change of fashion?—Merely a change of fashion, scarcely any improvement.

2671. Do you consider that there was as much beauty in the patterns manufactured at home as in those procured from abroad?—In lutestrings.

2672. Did the French gauzes come in in 1830 and 1831 very cheap?—There has not been, for the last four years, any great difference in the price of gauzes, but the trade always suffers from what are called "jobs," which come in after the beginning of the season; after they have been picked in Paris, they come in at about one-third of the price, that is a practice which quite interrupts the regular trade; I have brought with me some patterns of goods of the description.

*[The Witness produced some patterns.]*

2673. Are those goods that have come over to England after they have stood the day of the fashion at Paris, and which, upon coming here, have interfered with the same kind of goods you had previously ordered?—Such is the case, the Paris houses always get a greater profit on new goods than any house in London; they can sell about one-third of a parcel of goods at an immense profit, and then rather than sell the other part in Paris, they will send it over here.

2674. Is not there a good deal of that done in England?—There is very little of it now.

2675. Did you observe that in 1830 or 1831, that kind of goods became cheaper than they were before?—Just after the French Revolution there were a great many, but not on any other particular occasion.

2676. Are you in the habit of going to Paris?—I go occasionally.

2677. Do you not know that after the Revolution, and during the year 1831, there was a great glut of those goods in France?—Not more in France than in London; there were a great many in London after the Revolution, and that was in consequence of a want of confidence in the minds of the St. Etienne manufacturers, in the stability of the Paris houses.

2678. Have you any reason to know what difference there was in the prices of
    678.                                                                    the

Mr.
George Stephens.

4 April,
1832.

the same articles in 1831, and in the preceding year before the Revolution?—I cannot tell.

2679. Was there not a very considerable reduction?—Yes, very considerable, I think.

2680. Are you acquainted with the export of those articles to other countries?—I have heard from French manufacturers, that they have a trade with Spain, Portugal, Italy, Germany, and all the countries of Europe.

2681. Do you know whether their trade with the North of Europe was not much interrupted in 1831?—I do not know; but I have heard that they sent a great quantity to London immediately after the Revolution, in order to obtain the money for them more readily.

2682. Do you find goods dearer this year than last?—No, not at all.

2683. Then the prices have not been raised since, although they were lowered then in consequence of the state of alarm?—No; the goods that came in consequence of the alarm were jobs. Those which they had orders for came regularly.

2684. When were you in Paris last?—In July and August last year.

2685. Did you find the French goods in great quantities there?—No; there were not a great many goods in Paris then.

2686. Do you know how they are now?—I have been told by a gentleman who left Paris on Sunday morning, that the goods are scarce: the report of the cholera morbus has, however, had such an effect upon the holders of goods, that they would sell without a profit.

2687. Do you go to St. Etienne to purchase?—No.

2688. Do you usually give your orders in the spring or in autumn?—Generally in the beginning of January for the spring goods, and about July for winter goods.

2689. Did you give orders last January?—Yes; for goods which will be here in the course of this month.

2690. Did you give any orders for English goods?—Not any worth notice.

2691. Did you formerly give orders for English goods?—Yes; during the prohibition, if they brought patterns to us.

2692. Did they bring patterns to you then?—Yes.

2693. Do they bring patterns now?—They do not bring patterns now; it would be a foolish speculation in manufacturers to lay out money for patterns.

2694. If they did bring the patterns, would you give an order?—We should not.

2695. Why not?—We must wait till we see what the French bring over; indeed I have suffered lately, for ordering two patterns to be made from the French patterns, because I found that the fashions had been changed, and I shall be obliged to sell them at a loss.

2696. Are you not subject to the same chance of loss in the case of French goods?—No; because we can sell them as French goods, and our customers will accept them as new goods.

2697. Do not the fashions often succeed each other quickly in Paris?—Yes.

2698. Then you are obliged to get rid of your stock as quickly as possible?—Yes.

2699. Under the prohibition, did the English fashions follow the French so much as they do now?—They did not.

2700. Were you in London before 1826?—I was, for one year.

2701. Had you any experience of the state of things except as to that year?—No, except that we had the first fancy trade in Bristol.

2702. Was it the custom for the manufacturers to go to country towns?—Yes; we saw patterns of ribbons as regularly as patterns of muslins or anything else, we generally saw the patterns a month before the goods were made.

2703. You say that the English people prefer French goods because they are French; do not you believe that in this country a large quantity of goods are sold as French which were never made in France?—I do not think that such is now the case.

2704. Is there not a great temptation to offer English goods as French?—I cannot see that there is any temptation.

2705. Are not the English lutestrings cheaper than the French after paying the duty?—In the sort of articles which do not require much labour upon them, but I think not the figured lutestrings of the best quality, such as we sell.

2706. What are their respective prices?—The English do not always make lutestrings so good as those we sell of the French, they do not make ribbons so good as these of the French [*producing some patterns.*]

2707. Cannot

Mr.
George Stephens.

4 April,
1832.

2707. Cannot they make as good?—I only know one person that attempted it last winter, and he told me that he lost 50 l. by it, but if an English manufacturer got a French pattern and imitated it, he could make it cheaper than the French.

2708. Do you believe it ever happens that when purchasers who wish to patronize British manufactures ask for English goods, the French are sold to them as English?—I think that does often happen.

2709. Do you apprehend that if there were equal ingenuity and equal cleverness in the formation of patterns, and equal perfection in the quality of the goods made in England, that even in that case the French article would not have the preference? —It would have the preference.

2710. Have you any idea as to the extent of smuggling of late?—There was a little smuggling before 1826, but I know since that time it has been very extensive.

2711. Has it been gradually increasing from that time to this?—I think it has.

2712. Can you state from your own knowledge that it has been carried on to a very great extent?—I know as a buyer that large houses in the city of London have been in the habit of smuggling goods, indeed nearly all they sold; there are scarcely any bounds to the amount of goods they smuggle.

2713. Have you not frequent occasion to know when you are buying a large quantity of goods in the city of London, that those goods have been smuggled?— I know that smuggling has not ceased, but that it still exists to a great extent.

2714. Are there not very large houses in the city of London who do not smuggle them directly themselves, but who do it through an agent, who insures the safe delivery of the goods to them?—That is the way it is generally done, that is not the way in which it was done in the Old Change.

2715. Do you know that goods to a very large amount were smuggled previous to this discovery of Leaf's?—To a very large amount.

2716. Was not it notorious in the trade, as a matter of conversation, that goods were invoiced, and that duplicates were made up, and that they were regularly, to a most extensive degree, smuggled in?—Yes; it is well known to persons in the trade, and not only was it known that they did smuggle goods but the rate they did it at.

2717. Can you state what was the rate?—It was generally 18 per cent.

2718. Did that include freightage and every thing?—Yes.

2719. Are you aware what the insurance was for smuggled goods before the prohibition was removed?—My observation never enabled me to know that smugglers would have insured them at any rate at that time.

2720. Is it not generally very notorious in the trade, who are the houses that smuggle?—Amongst buyers it is pretty well understood which are the houses that smuggle, and those that do not.

2721. Do they make any secret of it in telling you confidently that the goods have been smuggled?—They do not make any secret to persons that they know would discover it without.

2722. Do not the goods bought in this way bear a large proportion of the business?—They do.

2723. Does the smuggling apply to any particular part of the silk manufacture more than any other?—I think it does to gauze ribbons more than any thing else.

2724. Do you happen to know, that before foreign goods were admitted here, there was considerable risk in this respect; that if a single piece of smuggled goods was found upon a man's premises, the officer would be justified in making a seizure of the stock, and you had no remedy against him?—I believe he was justified in seizing all the stock upon the premises.

2725. Do you know that when a person's goods were seized it rested with him to prove that the goods were not smuggled?—I believe that was the law.

2726. You keep a great many men in your house?—Yes.

2727. Would it not be too hazardous for you, under those circumstances, to have a quantity of prohibited goods brought into your house?—My employers would not risk an article.

2728. Are there not very few scruples of that sort now among the trade generally, but they think the goods are safe when they are once deposited?—That is the principle generally acted upon, certainly.

2729. Do you apprehend, that there is a sufficient quantity of goods of home manufacture to supply this market, and a sufficient display of ingenuity and excel-

678.                                                                        lence

Mr.
George Stephens.

4 April,
1832.

lence of quality without the introduction of any foreign goods?—There would be quite enough.

2730. When the English manufacturers have to make goods upon speculation, which are to meet in the market the goods ordered from France, is it likely that they should be inclined to go to the expense for looms and machinery and proper wages?—I think there is not any encouragement now to lay any money out with a view of producing novelties, and we should not buy them if they were to produce them.

2731. In the spring trade is it not the case, that after you have got the cream you must make a reduction?—That is the case, without the fancy trade can command the taste of the consumer it is not profitable.

2732. Then, generally speaking, with the ordinary competition, that has happened; is not a man enabled to make adequate sacrifices upon what remains, without it being attended with that ruin that it now is?—Before the prohibition was removed good profits were got by fancy goods.

2733. Do not you find that the market is always over done with goods?—About the middle of the season it is always over done.

2734. Have you not known, formerly, that a person in the fancy trade has been obliged to look about him, and to order before hand, in order to secure a good selection of goods?—Yes.

2735. Is that the case now?—Not with English goods.

2736. Must not the market, being constantly glutted, tend to depress the prices?—It does, and I will show these patterns as a proof of that ; we have jobs of French ribbons, we likewise buy a few English ribbons ; but the jobs of the French ribbons prevent the sale of the English goods.

2737. You have stated that the French, having a home trade and an export trade, they take care, when they have goods that they want to job off at a lower price, not to job them in their home market?—Such is the general principle in Paris; for instance, I was in Paris in July last, I then could have bought goods from French houses, who rather than make a sacrifice in their own trade, they would sell them to me 10 per cent lower than they would sell them in Paris.

2738. But that was upon the condition that they must go out of their own market?—Yes.

2739. When those goods are brought over here, in addition to all the disadvantages that the English manufacturers labour under, must not it be a serious injury to them?—It is the entire ruin of the English fancy ribbon maker.

2740. Looking to the retail trade in general, do not you think that this glut of goods and this inundation of foreign goods, tend to the injury and the ruin of a great body of the retailers?—A very great many.

2741. Do not you attribute a great many of the failures and the compositions to that circumstance?—Yes, I do.

2742. Do you happen to know, that if there is a manufacturer who has six or eight, or 10,000 l. worth of goods, and if he is under acceptances or in any way pinched in his circumstances, that there are houses in London where he can immediately go, and by a reduction of 20 or 25 per cent. send those goods into the market?—In one hour.

2743. Then what becomes of the great body of retailers that have been giving 25 or 30 per cent. more?—They must suffer from it.

2744. Have there not been an immense number of compositions among traders generally in this business?—A great many.

2745. Is not the embarrassment very much increased by the overstock in the market, and the introduction of foreign goods to interfere with our own?—It is very much increased by it.

2746. Do you know any new channel of trade that the introduction of French goods has opened to us?—I do not know any.

2747. Do you know any new employment that it has furnished for the weavers thrown out of work by it?—I do not.

2748. Suppose the case of some ribbons manufactured at Lyons, which shall cost the manufacturers there 30s. ; they are consigned to Paris, and a large profit made upon a considerable quantity of them, and the remainder of them jobbed to an English house at 20s. ; those goods may be introduced here by smuggling at 20 per cent. ; may it not therefore happen that those goods would cost in London 24s., which actually cost at Lyons 30s.?—Yes ; every season that is the case.

2749. Is

Mr.
George Stephens.

4 April,
1832.

2749. Is it not impossible, under such a state of things, that the English manufacturer can exist?—It is.

2750. If the duty were paid upon such goods, would not it amount to 60 or 70 per cent. ?—I have known cases where it would amount to cent. per cent.

2751. Within the last few years, have not a great many of the little manufacturers been induced to withdraw from business ?—A great many; when I first took the department I now hold, our ribbon account was with 30 houses, it is now reduced to as few as 12; and I imagine that six out of the 30 have failed; the others have gone out of the business; the little manufacturers are quite broken up.

2752. When silks are ordered from French houses in the regular way, is not the duty generally paid upon all that come at the commencement of the season ?—Yes.

2753. Are not goods in a similar style sent to Paris, many of which are jobbed, as in the case of the ribbons ?—Yes; I have seen goods come in at 2 s. 6 d. the ell, such as we had paid four francs seventy-five centimes for, at the beginning of the season.

2754. So that you have had them in the month of February at about 4 s. 9 d. and 5 s.; and then they have come here in June at 2 s. or 3 s. ?—Yes, at half the original price.

2755. Is not that very destructive to the English manufacturer?—Yes.

2756. Do you believe that such a case is of common occurrence ?—It happens every season.

2757. Although your house is in a very large way, and you sell a great many French goods, it appears by a paper before the Committee, that your house is at the bottom of the list of the great importers ?—It is very likely, for we buy a great many French goods in London.

2758. Can you buy them cheaper in London than you can import them ?—Much cheaper.

2759. You have stated that the greatest smuggling transaction which has been known to have occurred of late years, has been carried on, as you conceive, by introducing the foreign article at a rate of no more than 18 per cent. into this town, such being the case, do you conceive that if the duty on the foreign articles were lowered to 20 per cent., smuggling would or would not still be carried on ?—It would be carried on in some things, many goods would still be smuggled.

2760. Would prohibition lessen smuggling in your opinion?—It would lessen smuggling; with what I call proper prohibition I think smuggling could be stopped.

2761. What is the duty paid upon French gauze ribbons?—Nominally, it is 30 per cent., but it is actually from 20 to 45 per cent.

2762. What do you suppose would be a sufficient reduction of duty to prevent smuggling in that article ?—If the duties could be levied according to the value of the article, I would say 15 per cent. would be low enough to prevent smuggling.

2763. Do you know any thing of a recent case of smuggling which has not come before the public, of goods being illegally introduced ?—I have seen smuggled goods within the last week.

2764. What description of goods were they ?—Gauze ribbons.

2765. Do you know what rate of insurance was paid upon them?—I believe it was a little more than 18 per cent.; it was under 20 per cent.; I bought part of those ribbons, and I have a couple of pieces of them here [producing the same.]

6766. Did the 18 per cent. include all charges of carriage?—No, I think all was included in 20 per cent. The importer told me that in the month of January he had 5,000 pieces of nines and sixteens at Calais, and he should have them over as occasion required; that he had 5,000 pieces of about ten patterns, about 500 pieces of a pattern, and I believe about 100 pieces of each pattern, came into the Custom House, and all the rest " over the left" as they call it.

2767. Do you know that that amount included insurance in case of seizure?—It did.

2768. Do you make any difference as to the different kinds of silks, or do you mean the answer you have given to apply to gauzes?—I have spoken only of gauzes; I have not answered any question as to silks generally.

2769. Are you sure that in the 18 or 20 per cent. there was any sum included for insurance in case of seizure?—It included every thing; the owner ran the risk of seizure after landing.

2770. When you speak of 18 per cent. being paid to the smuggler, you mean 18

678.                                                                                        per

Mr.
*George Stephens.*

4 April,
1832.

per cent. ad valorem upon the goods?—Yes; he insures that they should be safely landed for 18 per cent.

2771. Did the owner only run the risk from the place of landing to his own house?—Exactly so.

2772. Are you in the habit of going to Paris to purchase goods for the house you belong to?—I have been only once in the last fall.

2773. Have you understood that any persons who may have gone there before you, have had offers made to them at Paris to deliver the goods at Charing Cross, at a certain rate of charge?—I am not aware that they have, but offers were made to me at last fall.

2774. Are there not companies that insure goods regularly?—Yes.

2775. Was it the agent of a company of that kind that applied to you?—No, it was the seller of the goods; he offered to sell me those goods for francs in Paris, or to deliver them in our house in London for shillings, that is to say, if the article he offered me was 25 francs, he offered to deliver them in London for 25 s.

2776. Did you understand that if the goods were not delivered at your house in London, you were not to pay for them?—Not a farthing.

2777. And therefore the difference between francs and shillings included the insurance in that case?—Yes.

2778. What goods were those?—Ribbons, and broad silks likewise.

2779. What was the duty you had to pay upon them?—If the ribbons had come through the house they would have been about 9 s. or 10 s. a garniture, that is about 50 per cent.

2780. Do not you know that persons sometimes enter French goods at considerably less than the value?—I believe that often occurs; I have seen goods sold in London which from their condition I believe came in through the Custom House, for I have seen enough of ribbons to enable me to distinguish generally those that are smuggled from goods that come through the Custom House, and I believe that ribbons come in paying under 15 per cent., upon which we should pay 30 per cent. or more than that.

2781. How do you account for that difference?—They must be entered under their value, or else they are never weighed, or something of that sort.

2782. Why should a person receive 20 per cent. for smuggling them in, when they can get them through the Custom House at 15 per cent.?—That must be accidental at the Custom House.

2783. Do you mean that it depends upon the officers at the Custom House?— I do not wish to charge the officers at the Custom House with neglect of duty, but I believe that goods sometimes come cheaper than they do at others.

2784. Is not the duty levied by weight?—They can be weighed or valued as the officer pleases, but I imagine they are never really weighed at all; I believe they are taken by valuation.

2785. Do you believe that inaccuracies take place at the Custom House with respect to weight?—That is my impression.

2786. Can you suggest any means of preventing that inequality in levying the duty?—The only means would be, for a person always to be present in whom confidence would be placed who would be a judge of the goods.

2787. Could any man tell the value of those fine fancy goods to 10 or 15 per cent.?—It can only be done by getting patterns from Paris at the approach of each season.

2788. You alluded just now to a transaction in which the party had smuggled a quantity of goods into London, and you were asked whether the 18 per cent. paid to the smuggler included the insurance?—I believe it included the insurance up to the time of landing the goods.

2789. Is it not understood that it is the custom of persons that smuggle goods in Paris, to order them to be delivered at some particular place in London?— I believe it is the custom.

2790. And therefore when you speak of their being delivered at London, you mean delivered at that particular place?—Yes.

2791. Are you able to distinguish out of that 18 per cent. how much would be the premium of the smuggler?—I cannot say that.

2792. Is not the freight included in the 18 or 20 per cent?—Every expense is included.

2793. Supposing the duty were lowered considerably, might it not still be worth
the

Mr.
*George Stephens.*

4 April,
1832.

the smuggler's while to continue his trade, though of course with a great reduction of profit?—I think he would still continue.

2794. In the goods smuggled by the house of Leaf & Company, were there not other goods besides gauzes smuggled?—Yes.

2795. And at the rate you have stated of 18 per cent.?—Yes; in stating that rate I cannot say that that was what it really cost them; but I can only say that that was the understanding in the trade, that they imported them at that rate.

2796. Have you had an opportunity of knowing the rate at which plain goods were smuggled?—I believe that plain goods were smuggled; I heard a smuggler offer within a short time, to do silks generally at 15 per cent. in piece, ribbons at 20 per cent., and lace at 10 per cent.

2797. Did you ever ask about gloves?—I do not think gloves are smuggled.

2798. Do you know from your intercourse at Paris, and with buyers of those articles, that there is much smuggling in gloves?—I do not think there is.

2799. Do you know many that buy gloves?—Yes, I do.

2800. Did it often come to your knowledge in conversation, that any great quantity was smuggled?—I have asked the question repeatedly, and I have never been led to believe that gloves are smuggled.

2801. Do you import gloves?—We do.

2802. Do French goods admit of much profit?—There is a profit.

2803. How much is the wholesale profit?—About five per cent.

2804. Do you get larger profits upon French goods than upon the English?—Yes, larger profits.

2805. Then you have no particular interest to wish for the exclusion of the French?—I have not; but it would not surprise me if the large haberdashers of London generally were to petition for the continuance of the present system, knowing that their returns are greatly increased by admitting foreign goods.

2806. As it is not the ordinary description of houses that can be going over selecting that description of goods abroad, does not it throw a great monopoly into few hands?—It does.

2807. Does that necessarily lead to a monopoly in the home market?—I think it does; it has increased the returns of large houses more than it has increased the returns of small houses.

2808. Must not that increase tend to lessen other channels?—No doubt it does.

2809. Do you mean to say, that there are now, in that trade, houses of great capital who monopolize the market?—I do.

2810. Do not those houses compete with each other in the home market?—They do.

2811. Will not that be sufficient to prevent a monopoly?—It would prevent such a monopoly as would injure the public.

2812. Have they any thing in common to concert about the prices?—No, they have not.

2813. Then must not each be desirous to get as much business as he can?—Yes.

2814. Will not that competition bring down the profits to a reasonable rate?—Yes, in certain articles; but it does not answer the purpose of all houses to import the richer kind of goods.

2815. Does not the extent of business regulate the degree of profit at which it can be carried on?—Yes.

2816. Cannot a great capitalist buy the goods upon better terms than a small capitalist?—Yes.

2817. Is not that the case in the trade with England as well as with France?—Yes.

2818. You have stated, that there have frequently been jobs of French goods; are there not as many goods jobbed belonging to English manufacturers as French?—Not in proportion to the capital employed in the trade.

2819. What proportion of the silk trade of your house consists of the fine and figured gauzes?—I suppose the broad gauzes amount to about 20 or 30 per cent.; the English gauze ribbons, in proportion to the French, only amount to about five or six per cent.

2820. Can you state what proportion of your plain goods are French, and what proportion English?—I could not answer that.

2821. You have stated that many of the small retail dealers have, of late years

Mr.
*George Stephens.*

4 April,
1832.

been greatly injured, has the business of large houses extended of late?—Very considerably.

2822. Are there not greater facilities now in the supply to the retail dealers, in comparison with what they were before?—No, I do not think it. I imagine that the retail houses would have bought of large houses before the prohibition was removed.

2823. Do you suppose that there are fewer retail dealers now than there were? —No; but I suppose they have not increased in number so much as the large houses have increased the amount of their returns.

2824. Has not the consumption of ribbons very much increased?—Yes.

2825. You have stated, that the present low jobs have been very ruinous to the dealers; have not the prices in this country very much decreased?—They have.

2826. Have not the consumers benefited very much?—I do not think they have benefited by it.

2827. Then who gets the profit?—I do not know that any body has got it.

2828. If the consumers buy them cheaper must not they have the advantage?— I think they have been injured by some means to more than that amount.

2829. If the wages of a labourer are reduced from 10s. a week to 8s. so that a lady who goes to Court will have that part of her dress for 8s. instead of giving 10s. will not she be benefited?—She will be benefited in the purchase of the article.

2830. Then if there be any description of people benefited, it will be those fashionable people who buy those dresses so much cheaper?—That is the class that benefit most.

2831. Then that benefit of the reduction of wages, and the reduction of profits goes to them?--Yes.

2832. As you are a buyer, do you not happen to know many instances, where, if a small buyer was to go with his ready money in his hands, he could not buy the goods as cheap by five per cent. as some of the large houses?—I know it is the case.

2833. Do you not know that there are agents in London selling for the manufacturers, who, if fifty persons were to go to them with 50l. each, they would not sell to them, unless they paid five per cent. more than what they charged the large houses?--I know it is the case.

2834. Are the retailers generally, or the public at large, better served than when there was a more open competition?—They are not better served now.

2835. Do you mean to say that the manufacturers will refuse to sell to the small houses at the same price at which they supply the large houses?—They would rather serve large houses.

2836. Do you mean at cash prices, or on credit account?—On credit accounts.

2837. Do not you consider that that arises from the difference in the risk of being paid by a small house or by a large capitalist?—I have seen instances where mall houses have been refused that have offered to pay cash.

2838. Was there plenty of the article on sale?—They went to a large house with a view of having it cheap, but they could have got it perhaps at another place.

2839. How do you account for a man that carries on business refusing to deal with one man unless he pays five per cent. more than another?—Because it is better to have a few good customers than a great many little ones.

2840. Do not you know that there is another reason, that if they were to sell those goods to the small house at the same price that they did to the large customer, they would offend the large customer?—I believe that is often the case; I believe that instances of that occur daily.

2841. Do you not know it to be the fact, that there are houses where goods come from the manufacturers, and where persons go with the money in their hands, but they cannot buy those goods without giving five per cent. more than they sell them to the large houses, on account of the fear of giving offence to those houses? —Such things occur almost daily.

2842. Your house is one of the largest houses at the West end of the Town; do you buy goods five per cent. cheaper than your neighbours?—Not in all instances five per cent., but generally we have an advantage.

2843. Is not your business, being larger than that of your neighbours, owing to your serving the public better?—I do not know that we serve the public better, it is supposed we do it.

2844. Why

2844. Why do people come to you in preference to other houses, if they cannot buy the goods cheaper?—Because they can always see a great variety.

2845. Have you within the last fortnight seen any cases of silk handkerchiefs smuggled from France?—No, not silk handkerchiefs.

Mr.
*George Stephens.*

4 April,
1832.

---

*Veneris, 6° die Aprilis, 1832.*

## THE RIGHT HON. THE EARL GROSVENOR, IN THE CHAIR.

### Mr. *William Merry*, called in; and further Examined.

2846. IN all your answers on a former day, when speaking of the value of English and French ribbons, you speak of your cost price and the selling price of the French, but you know not what profit may have been obtained by the French?—Yes, just so.

2847. Your answers refer chiefly to two patterns which were exhibited?—Yes.

2848. One of them, an English pattern, was manufactured by yourself?—It was.

2849. You sold that at 48 s. 6 d.?—Yes.

2850. As to the other pattern which was exhibited, at what price was that?—It was marked 59 s. 9 d.

2851. Your answers apply to those two patterns?—Those goods were sold under particular circumstances, and I think that I ought not to be referred to as regards those goods; the answer I have given to the question just put is, that I cannot tell what the French manufacture cost; my idea is that they cost much less, and that their profit is much larger than ours; but I am not a manufacturer, only a seller, and I do not know what would be the cost of the French pattern, because I do not know what machinery it would require to make it.

2852. You have been asked some questions respecting gauze ribbons, have you any information to which you think any importance or value may be attached?—The wages in Coventry are lower than they were in 1825, which affects the other fancy articles; I applied my answer to the weavers being starving, to the single handed weaving especially; I was asked on a former day, whether there had been a corresponding improvement since the year 1825; I wish to correct my evidence, by saying there has not been any improvment in machinery, but that the men have been better able to attend to the work, but the machinery is the same as it was in 1825; the men being more used to machinery, are making better goods.

2853. Do you know whether the machinery has been employed abroad?—I do not know.

Mr.
*William Merry.*

### Mr. *George Stephens*, called in; and further Examined.

2854. YOU stated on a former day that you have lived with your present employers 15 years, five years of that time in London?—Yes.

2855. So that you came to London in the beginning of 1827?—I was in London before that time; if I said five years, I was wrong; I came up to London in the spring of either 1825 or 1826, I think 1826, it was before the prohibitions were removed.

2856. The prohibition was removed in 1826?—Yes.

2857. Consequently the only knowledge you have of the existence of smuggling during the prohibitory system, was what you knew at Bristol?—That is all, except that which I have learned from persons engaged in it in London before the prohibitions were removed.

2858. Had those from whom you learned that, themselves carried on any of those smuggling transactions?—I had part of the information I possessed from an individual who saw the goods at the only house that smuggled at that time in London, he saw all the smuggled goods which came through that house.

2859. Do you believe that there was only one house smuggled before 1826?—I mean to say that only one house used to import to any extent, to sell goods.

2860. That is your opinion?—That is the result of the information I have obtained.

2861. The goods you were in the habit of purchasing at Bristol, had been, as you

Mr.
*George Stephens.*

678. understood,

understood, bought at Custom House sales here for exportation, and subsequently smuggled into this country?—They had.

2862. If they could smuggle in those goods they could have smuggled in any other goods which had not been purchased at Custom House sales, could not they?—No they could not; those goods were always damaged more or less, and it would have injured new goods 50 per cent.; I should think so from the damage new goods would have received if they had been subjected to the same treatment.

2863. To what do you allude when you speak of the treatment of the goods?— They had been exposed to wet, and bore evident marks of having been injured by sea water.

2864. Did they bear the appearance of having been put into an improper place, pressed and injured by being squeezed into a bag, or a lady's trunk, or under her petticoat?—Yes, they always had a damaged appearance.

3865. Did this arise from the bringing them in on the first occasion?—Partly, and partly on the second.

2866. They were smuggled in the second time, at some other place?—Yes.

2867. Might not they have smuggled in other goods?—Not in the same way. I think that the damage arose generally in the second time of smuggling.

2868. Do you mean the smuggling of those goods took place prior to the year 1826?—Yes; and I understand that they were shipped to Calais, and brought back again.

2869. You are aware there are two premiums on smuggling at present; one by which the party receives a certain sum of money on delivering the goods in London, and that if he does not deliver them he does not obtain his payment, but if they are lost the loss falls upon the importers here: and in the other case, the party engages to deliver them, and in the event of their being lost, to pay their value?— I am aware there are two such systems existing.

2870. When you speak of an offer to smuggle at 20 per cent. made to you at Paris, which of the modes did you understand that person alluded to?—The latter; that is, that I should not pay for the goods if I did not receive them safely in London.

2871. When you speak of 18 per cent., which you understood had been paid in London, to which of the modes did you allude?—The latter; that is, that the smuggler would be at the loss, if they were not delivered safely, and not the importer.

2872. Were they to be delivered in London, in either case?—Yes; in both cases.

2873. When you spoke of 15 per cent. what did you refer to?—I do not recollect speaking of 15 per cent.

2874. You said a person had very recently offered to smuggle at 15 per cent.?— That was silk goods only.

2875. In relation to those rates of 20 and 18 per cent., which you have stated as payable for smuggling, do you mean to say, they were paid on the same goods or goods of a different quality, and what kinds were they?—The circumstance I spoke of, as occurring in London, was on gauze ribbons only; that which passed at Paris, was on gauze ribbons and fancy silks.

2876. Do you state that 15 per cent. was, to your knowledge, paid?—No; I stated that a smuggler offered to do goods at 15 per cent.; those were silk goods.

2877. You understood that to include the insurance?—Yes.

2878. How much extra is paid as the insurance in case of loss?—In this case of the offer, nothing extra would be paid.

2879. How much of that 15 per cent. do you suppose was intended for insurance?—I cannot say.

2880. Do you know what is paid for freightage of French goods from Paris, regularly passed through the Custom House?—It is almost impossible to answer; they pay by weight.

2881. As to the extent of smuggling at present, do you mean to state, that the first of every fashion of goods are often smuggled, or that they come in paying the duty; that smuggling is principally in the jobs, after the fashion is over?—I think fashionable articles, when new, pay the duty; that bulks and jobs come smuggled.

2882. Do you mean that the bulk of the goods imported are jobs?—Yes.

2883. You

Mr.
George Stephens.

6 April,
1832.

2883. You think more of that class of goods are smuggled than of the new goods?—Yes.

2884. You stated, that in the case of some new goods, amounting in number to 5,000 pieces, only 500 paid the duty?—Yes.

2885. They were not jobs?—They were not.

2886. What reason have you for thinking then that new goods should not be smuggled?—I spoke of the very fashionable, and the newest goods.

2887. Those goods, you understood, were kept in stock at Calais?—Yes; kept in warehouses there.

2888. And they would be smuggled in as the demand required?—Yes.

2889. Do you know, absolutely, that they were at Calais; they might be at Havre?—That is possible; but I believe they were at Calais.

2890. You produced two pieces of ribbon, of which you stated 5,000 pieces were at Calais, that those had paid the duty, and you believe the others would be brought over, while those which had paid the duty were a blind; can you state whether those 5,000 have been smuggled?—I said that they were at Calais in January; they are not now there; they have all come to London.

2891. You think that the small portion which came first is the only part which has paid the duty?—Yes.

2892. Are those fashionable goods, or otherwise?—They are not first-rate fashionable goods; they are low-priced goods, but new.

2893. With respect to those who have been in the practice of smuggling, are you able to state what would be the lowest rate of duty which would put an end to their speculations?—I think that if the duty were fixed at 15 per cent. the smuggling would go down to 10 per cent.

2894. Do you mean for silk goods generally, or only for gauzes?—For silk goods generally.

2895. Do you mean to say there is so much competition, even among smugglers, that you think they would run that risk for 10 per cent.?—Yes.

2896. Do you think that would cover insurance also?—Yes; if no other precautions were taken than now exist, to prevent smuggling.

2897. What other precautions should you suggest to prevent it?—Nothing short of prohibition.

2898. Do you not believe if that prohibition took place smuggling would be still continued?—Yes; if some precautions were not taken which have never yet existed.

2899. What are those precautions which have never yet existed?—I would offer 1,000 l. to any person who would give information where smuggled goods were to be found, and I would fine the holders of those goods 1,000 l.

2900. Would you fine the wearer of those goods?—No, I do not think that would be a just thing; the wearer may buy them without knowing they are French.

2901. May not a merchant be in possession of goods without knowing whether they are French?—No, I think not.

2902. You think there is no possibility of mistaking the French for English manufacture?—Not by a person accustomed to buy goods.

2903. Do you apply that to all French goods?—I think all but plain gros de Naples.

2904. You think that it is not possible for the English manufacturer to imitate the French so as to prevent you or any person acquainted with the business knowing it?—In all but plain goods.

2905. If you bought goods at a manufacturer's house, that would be a fair presumption that they were made in England?—Yes.

2906. If you got them of a warehouseman you would look at them more circumspectly?—Certainly.

2907. If you saw the goods at a warehousman's house, you would feel it your duty to examine them more minutely?—Certainly.

2908. Have you known of any considerable purchase, where a French manufacturer has offered to deliver them without any expense to the purchaser?—Not by manufacturers, but I know of the merchants having made that offer; I have seen a gentleman who left Paris not more than four days since, who having bought a small parcel at a house for four or five thousand francs, an offer was made him that if he would increase it to twelve or fourteen thousand francs, the goods should be delivered in London without any commission or duty.

678.

2909. Was

Mr.
*George Stephens.*
———
6 April,
1832.

2909. Was the seller a manufacturer?—He was not.

2910. Was it a shopkeeper or a warehouseman?—A warehouseman.

2911. Were those job goods or first fashion goods?—First fashion goods.

2912. Was that done with a view to raise money through the distress of the parties?—No; with a view to sell goods.

2913. They must have been responsible persons to make such an engagement?—Certainly they were.

2914. How long were you in Paris?—I was there two months.

2915. What was your object in staying there?—I went with the view of buying goods and of establishing myself in Paris, if I thought there was any probability of our being able to sell English goods to the French people.

2916. Had you a pretty good introduction to persons in Paris connected with trade?—Yes, in my own station in life, I had the best possible introduction; I knew eight young men who had lived in our house, who are in commercial houses there.

2917. Had you a free access and introduction to the first houses in consequence?—Yes, to all houses in business.

2918. Did you avail yourself of those circumstances, and make every possible inquiry as to the nature of the trade carried on there?—Yes, I made every possible inquiry, it occupied two-thirds of my time; I went with a view to establish myself as a seller of English goods, thinking the French would open their ports to our trade.

2919. If you had seen a probability of the introduction of English goods, you would have settled there?—Yes, in connection with a Frenchman who had left our house shortly before, and who went with the same object.

2920. You stated on a former day, that the shops here are crowded with French goods, that you see them in all directions?—Almost every shop contains French goods.

2921. Did you look much at the shops in Paris, and if so, did you find any English manufactures?—Yes; I found a few common worsted stuffs, such as we had been selling here at sixpence a yard, and a few printed Bandanna handkerchiefs.

2922. You did not see any English silks selling in the shops?—Never any English silks.

2923. Did you see any English silks besides Bandannas exposed for sale in the shops?—I do not think I saw a single piece.

2924. Did you see exposed in the different shops in Paris, a great many English goods manufactured of other sorts?—No, I did not.

2925. Had you any conversation with Frenchmen upon the subject, of the reason why they would not admit our goods?—I had much conversation on that subject, in company with the Frenchman to whom I have referred, with all classes, with the consumer, the retail dealer, the wholesale dealer, the manufacturer, and with a member of the Chamber of Deputies; and the result was, that it was in vain to wait with such expectation, we found that there are three interests in the Chamber of Deputies; the one the iron, the other the cotton, the other the silk, that the iron and cotton united were too strong for the silk; and that France would rather lose our custom for silk goods than take our iron and cotton goods.

2926. What made you so very particular to avail yourself of this information; was it because you had a distinct object in view, to settle there if you could find it to be for your interest?—Yes.

2927. Did you see any English goods of a mixed quality there, a mixture of silk and worsted?—I think in one shop I saw the article called Norwich crape, a mixture of silk and cotton, a low priced article of about 1 s. a yard.

2928. Did you see any printed cottons and chintzes?—Not in shops.

2929. Do you imagine that the French, on their fine sorts of goods which come over here, get large profits?—Yes, I have no doubt of that; I am satisfied that is the case.

2930. Printed cottons and chintzes are prohibited in France, are they not?—I believe they are.

2931. Are you aware of any of those goods being smuggled into France?—In single lengths I know they are for ladies' wear, but not in large quantities.

2932. Taking into consideration that the French have the silk there, and that labour is lower, and the high profits they get, do you believe that if the English goods were reduced 20 per cent. in price, the French would not reduce theirs also?
—I think

Mr.
*George Stephens.*
_____
6 April,
1832.

—I think the fashionable houses would reduce the prices of their goods in order to sell them.

2933. That would be their profit?—Yes, that must be their profit.

2934. You think that if the English goods were reduced 20 per cent. the French would still find it answer their purpose to reduce their goods, and come in competition?—In some goods it would answer perhaps.

2935. Do you not think that would occasion a reduction in the raw material?—I cannot go so far into the manufacturing part of it as that.

2936. Do you know any thing about the profits got by the manufacturers or dealers in France?—I only know from hearing manufacturers and dealers speak.

2937. Did the manufacturers and dealers say they had very large profits?—I have heard manufacturers of St. Etienne and Lyons say, that they would never undertake it without getting something by it.

2938. What amount?—From 7½ to 10 per cent.

2939. Did you ever hear any particular one of them say that themselves?—No, I cannot say that I have.

2940. Is it not the practice, when new goods come from Lyons to the warehousemen at Paris, for them to show invoices, to have bills, and to allow the advantage, as they would call it, of allowing the customer to take the goods net, from which they have obtained a discount of 14 per cent.?—Yes, often with a commission of two per cent. in addition to the 14.

2941. Is 14 per cent. the discount allowed upon ribbons at St. Etienne to the buyer in Paris?—On some fancy ribbons; I do not know that it is on all ribbons.

2942. What is the lowest you have known?—I have known it down to eight.

2943. You mean that you were asked 16 per cent. profit upon those goods?—I do not mean that it was to myself, but I have heard buyers say that that was the case.

2944. You being the buyer in the house you have spoken of, and having been at Paris for the distinct object you state, and having been in intercourse with so many Frenchmen there who have been in commercial houses, do you speak with confidence from the information you have gained from those channels?—Where I have spoken I have spoken with confidence; but when I am asked about such things as goods sold at the invoice price, I should say with a commission over that of two per cent.

2945. When you state this, is it entirely from hearsay, or is it from the information you derived from those particular sources through the connection of these young men, and those commercial houses in which you place confidence?—It is from the persons so situated in Paris in whom I can place confidence.

2946. And from what you have generally heard and understood, you have no doubt that the commissioners, on their new fashionable goods, obtain very large profits?—I have no doubt of it.

2947. Your house is not the only house which does business to a large extent there, is it?—It is not.

2948. The Committee could obtain the same information you think from other houses?—I think so.

2949. Do you think the trimmings the ladies wear in their bonnets are supplied cheaper to them than if they were made in England?—No, they are not.

2950. What description of ribbons do they use now?—Gauzes principally.

2951. Does the supply of gauze ribbons this year, from France, exceed that of former years?—I think it will when they all arrive.

2952. The French fashions have not all arrived yet?—No.

2953. Do you think the large wholesale houses have been increasing their stocks of French goods of late?—Yes, they have, and likewise their returns on French goods; I know an instance in the city of London where, in 1828, a house made a return of a million and a half, and that they sold only 100,000 pounds worth of French goods; in 1831 the returns were 1,200,000 l. and the French goods sold in that year were 200,000 l.

2954. That you know from your own knowledge?—I was not in the house, but I had it from a person who lives in the house and knows it well.

2955. Whence do you conceive this increase has arisen?—It has arisen from the fashions having gone into the country, which did not happen immediately on the ports being opened; the English country ladies will not wear them till they become pretty well known; they did not in 1827 and 1828 use so many fashionable goods as they now do.

2956. When

Mr.
*George Stephens.*
—————
6 April,
1832.

2956. When you speak of a certain description of goods, are there any other French articles besides silk to which a great preference is given ?—There are other kinds of French goods ; I have put patterns into my pocket of two other articles Côte Palè and printed muslins of French manufacture.   [*The Witness produced them.*]

2957. Is there any particular beauty in the colour of French goods, which makes them preferred to British, or is it only because they are French ?—It is because they are French goods, some of the patterns I have produced are very ugly.

2958. Are you able to discover on what the preference depends ?—It is because these French goods are not comeatable by vulgar people.

2959. Because they are scarce ?—Yes.

2960. Because they are high priced and rare ?—Yes.

2961. It is not because of the colour or the quality ?—No, the colours are generally very ugly.

2962. Do you not then think, if they were prohibited altogether, the articles would become scarcer, and therefore in fact be more in general demand ?—That would be the case unless there were some further measures against smuggling.

2963. You stated, on a former day, that the respectable men would not keep them in their houses if there was a prohibition, on account of the danger of smuggling ?—Yes.

2964. You stated that the house you were in before 1825, sold the articles which had been smuggled ?—Yes, which had the Custom House mark upon them, but not publicly.

2965. They were sold by the young men ?—Yes.

2966. Messrs. Halling discharged a young man because he had a piece of Bandanna, did they not ?—Yes, they did.

2967. Would there be any danger of having those goods introduced to any great extent ?—If the Government would give a reward to the informer, it would be almost impossible to do it.

2968. Is it your opinion that the respectable persons who buy goods of the description you have just produced, would be content with the English if they did not see these ?—Yes, I think they would be, with the best English goods.

2969. You have been asked as to 200,000 *l.* returned by a certain house in French goods, do you mean to say that consisted of silks ?—Silks, gloves, ribbons and a few things of this kind.

2970. Do you think there was any material portion of the sum in these cotton goods ?—No, a very small portion.

2971. You have been asked as to the rates of bringing goods from Paris which come first into the French market, they are of higher value than afterwards ?—Yes.

2972. So that it may be worth a Frenchman's while to smuggle at 10 per cent. though afterwards he may require 20, in order to realize the same profit to himself upon the transaction ?—Yes.

2973. You said they had paid a duty at the Custom House frequently in consequence either of the neglect or ignorance of the officer, considerably under the per centage intended by law to be levied ?—The duty stated on ribbons in particular.

2974. Do you suppose they do not weigh the goods at the Custom House, or that any connivance exists between the importer and the officer ?—I cannot say that connivance exists, but the facts came before me which prove that a duty of 30 per cent. has not been levied in all instances.

2975. Are the French now producing any particular colours which are fashionable ?—Yes, I have brought samples of two or three, all of which are very ugly [*producing them.*]

2976. You suppose it to be the intention of the law that 30 per cent. should be levied, do you mean that 18 per cent. only is levied ?—As low as 10 per cent. has been paid.

2977. Can you account for that ?—I cannot.

2978. Do you suppose the officers actually weigh the goods ?—They can value them or weigh them.

2979. Do the officers generally take them at the *ad valorem* duty ?—I cannot state whether they actually do, they may do which they please, I believe.

2980. Have you seen goods which ought to have paid 30 per cent. which did no pay above ten?—I have.

2981. Do

Mr.
George Stephens.

6 April,
1832.

2981. Do you know whether those were taken at the *ad valorem* duty, or weighed? —I cannot say.

2982. Do these goods, samples of which you have just produced, sell currently now?—They do.

2983. If these were made in England, do you believe that ladies would buy them?—I think not, they are very ugly.

2984. With reference to the goods on which you state 30 per cent. ought to have been paid, and on which only 10 per cent. was paid, is it your belief that they actually passed through the Custom House?—I cannot swear that they passed through the Custom House, but their condition induces me to believe that they did.

2985. Can you state how it is that you suppose they had paid only 10 per cent.? —That I can tell from what the goods would be worth in France and what tney would be worth here, by adding the duty.

2986. You mean to say those goods you are alluding to, if they had been weighed, and if they had paid the duty according to the Table of 1829, would have paid 30 per cent. duty?—They should have paid that duty.

2987. And that if they had been regularly weighed they would have paid that? —Yes.

2988. Do you mean to impute any fraud on the Custom House?—No.

2989. You think it is done by a trick upon them?—Yes.

2990. Are they always weighed?—They are not.

2991. Do they take them on an *ad valorem* duty?— Sometimes they do.

2992. Do they ever take the duty on the word of the importer?—I cannot say.

2993. Have you ever cleared any goods at the Custom House?—I have been there when they have been cleared by our agent, they generally put them into scales and weigh them.

2994. Did you ever see them pass goods without putting them into the scales?— —No.

2995. Of what particular kind of goods are you speaking?—Gauze ribbons.

2996. Are they not also weighed at the Custom House?—I do not know that they are always weighed.

2997. You stated that you formerly purchased of thirty houses in the ribbon trade, and that you purchase now of about six?—Of about twelve I believe.

2998. At what time are you speaking when you state that you bought of thirty? —The accounts were existing when I took the department I now hold; it was in the beginning of 1827.

2999. Do you mean to say that your house bought of thirty?—They had accounts opened with thirty Coventry houses.

3000. Were they in the habit of going to Coventry?—No.

3001. You bought of houses having establishments in London?—Yes.

3002 You now purchase of only twelve?—No more.

3003. Were they all manufacturers?—Not all of them.

3004. Do you buy the larger proportion of your goods of manufacturers, or of warehousemen?—Of manufacturers.

3005. Do you buy a larger proportion of manufacturers now than formerly, or a less proportion?—I think the same proportion.

3006. The custom is to buy of manufacturers more than formerly?—Yes, with us generally.

3007. Is it not the fact that a considerable number of the larger manufacturers have no establishments in London?—I am not aware of that.

3008. You spoke of having purchased goods at four francs in Paris, and at the end of the season at much less in London; you were then speaking of broad silks? —Yes, figured silks.

3009. Those who smuggle have an advantage over those who do not?—Yes, I think they have.

3010. All who do not smuggle, therefore, have an interest in putting down smuggling?—I think they have an interest in doing so.

3011. Supposing that in consequence of the prohibition increased smuggling took place, all those in the habit of smuggling are interested in the prohibition?—Yes, unless there are further means to prevent smuggling.

3012. Do you believe that if we were to return to a state of prohibition there would be any smuggling at all?—I think that means might be taken to prevent smuggling altogether.

3013. Do you think if any increased means were taken, that persons would

engage

engage in smuggling, the parties being subjected to the old law?—I think that smuggling would then exist.

3014. Do you think it would exist to the extent of one-tenth of the quantity now sold in this country?—Not an hundreth part.

3015. You were asked as to buying French silks at four francs in Paris, and afterwards buying them at less; you stated that you bought them at first at Paris at five francs, and afterwards at a less price there?—That they were offered in Paris.

3016. You were asked as to your buying from 30, and afterwards 12, Coventry houses; your purchases of English ribbons have greatly declined?—They have.

3017. Whether you buy of 30 or of 12 is of no consequence, but the quantity has declined?—Yes, it has, very greatly.

3018. Were there not a great many houses five years ago which were commission houses, agents for manufacturers, and some of them manufacturers?—Yes, there were then a great many of such persons.

3019. Those were the sort of houses that you meant when you stated that they had disappeared?—Yes.

3020. You think the prevailing system has annihilated a great part of those houses?—It has eaten them up.

3021. Are you aware whether any smuggling exists coastwise, whether any ships coming to an English port, with a certain quantity of silks entered on their papers do not on board take goods from ships at sea of much greater value, without increasing the number of their packages?—I cannot say.

Mr. *Vernon Royle*, called in; and Examined.

3022. WHAT are you?—I am a silk throwster and a manufacturer at Manchester.

3023. Are you a mill-owner?—I am.

3024. To what extent?—If I include the weavers and winders, and their children, as well as the throwsters and their children, who receive employment and bread from my mills, I think the number may be taken from four to five thousand persons.

3025. When were your throwing mills erected?—My first throwing mill was built in 1819 or 1820.

3026. Was not that the first mill erected in Manchester?—Another was building in the same year, but mine I think was finished first.

3027. What increase was there in mills between the years 1819 and 1823?—I think there was no increase.

3028. How many mills were there in 1823?—There were two erected in 1819 or 1820; there might have been one or two more before 1823; I know what mills are now there, but I cannot fix the dates of their erection.

3029. Between 1823 and the present time, what increase has taken place in the number of mills?—There are now twelve which may be called Manchester mills, one in the parish of Ashton, and another in the parish of Eccles, but belonging to parties living in the town.

3030. It is usual to estimate the size of the mills by the power of steam engine; what is the power employed in those mills at the present time?—The power is 342 horse power, but that requires a very considerable qualification; if I was to say the Manchester mills were driven by 342 horse power, that would give an idea that they were all in full operation, which is not the case; two were completed only last autumn, and are now filling with machinery, and in the course of perhaps this year or the middle of the next the whole of the horse power will be at work, and all the engines will be loaded.

3031. What is the number of horse power out of the 342 not at work?—I cannot tell; one is a very large mill, I think it will require 60 horse power.

3032. Of the 342, how many horse power are now working?—It is impossible to say; I should think about two-thirds; that is, one-third are now running without a load, or have not begun to work. It has been said in the House of Commons, that the Manchester people were working their silk mills with steam engines of 342 horse power, but it is not so.

3033. Can you form any estimate of the probable quantity of thrown silk which those mills would produce in the course of a year?—I have an opinion as to what
the

the horse power is capable of doing, but I do not think I am justified in stating that opinion, for I have not sufficient facts to enable me to state it accurately.

Mr
*Vernon Royle.*

6 April,
1832.

3034. Are those all throwing mills?—They are for throwing and manufacturing silk.

3035. When were the first weaving mills introduced?—I cannot tell when Mr. William Harter first began weaving, perhaps seven years ago.

3036. Of those 12 mills, how many are throwing, how many weaving, and how many both?— They are all throwing silk; that is, two-thirds of the 342 horse power are employed in throwing silk.

3037. What do you conceive to be the value of those 12 mills, with their machinery?—The value I am enabled to come at in this way; when I retired from the manufacturing part of the business, two young men, who had been my servants, succeeded for one of my mills, and became my tenants; and for the purpose of finding the rent the machinery was valued; the mill-work was valued, and the buildings and land were valued by professional men; and considering the mill and its machinery as good as others in the town, if I include the value of the land on which they stand, the value of the whole 12 is much more than 200,000*l.*; they have cost considerably more.

3038. You state, that the first mill for throwing silk in Manchester was erected in 1819; do you know how many looms were employed in Manchester at that time, in weaving articles in silk and in mixed articles of silk and other articles?— I think, in 1819, there were not 50 all silk or broad silk weavers in Manchester.

3039. How many for mixed goods?—I think about 1,000.

3040. Do you know how many are so employed now?—It must be mere matter of opinion; the fact can be ascertained only by going from house to house; it has been stated in the House of Commons that there are 15,000, but I think that is above the number.

3041. Are you a manufacturer?— I manufacture by steam looms; I am becoming a manufacturer.

3042. On what authority has the statement as to the number of silk looms being 15,000, been made?—I cannot say.

3043. What, in your belief, is the number?—I believe there are about 12,000.

3044. Do you mean for silk, or for silk and mixed together?—For the whole.

3045. Are you able to divide those?—No, I am not.

3046. Have the goodness to state in what year the increase of the mills took place, how many in each year, so far as you are able to state it?—There were two built last year. 1831.

3047. How many in 1830?—I think there were none in 1830.

3048. How many in 1829?—I cannot say when they came into work; one or more mills were built in the prosperity year, the year 1825.

3049. Were any built in 1826?—I cannot say when each mill came into work.

3050. Can you tell how many before, and how many since 1826?—I cannot tell with any certainty at the present moment.

3051. Will you give a progressive statement of the silk manufacture in Manchester, from the period of its introduction in 1819 to the last year?—I cannot mark the progress of every year.

3052. Can you state whether it has increased?—Certainly it has increased.

3053. Cannot you describe the state of the silk trade in previous years?—No, we have had depressions in the silk trade; but when the silk trade has been depressed in Lancashire, it has been from a general cause.

3054. Has it been in a variable state from July 1830?—I believe it has been more unsteady than at any previous time.

3055. Do you mean that it laboured under depression?—The depression was exceedingly severe from November 1831 to the middle of January 1832; the circulation of the Bank of England in January last was only sixteen millions and a half, and that was the time we suffered the most.

3056. Was it in a state of depression or in a state of activity from 1830 up to this time last year?—I think in the beginning of 1831 we had a fair and reasonable demand, as much so as we could expect under the circumstances of the country, but the prices were gradually sinking from June till Christmas; I think about Christmas 1831 the pressure was at the worst.

3057. What in your opinion was the cause of that depression?—I think there are various causes which may be mentioned; I think for one thing, the Yorkshire manufacturers made an article called Merino Cloth, which perhaps interfered with

678.                                                                                                    silks;

Mr.
*Vernon Royle.*

6 April,
1832.

silks; and from the continued varying of the standard of value by the Bank of England, the pressure was general, it was on the cotton trade as well as on the silk trade.

3058. Would not the state of the currency affect all trades alike?—Yes.

3059. What effect do you think taking off the duty on cotton prints had upon the silk trade?—I think it had an effect certainly; I think that it affected the trade during the summer of the last year.

3060. In what way do you think it affected the trade?—I think that from the noise made about cheap prints made people buy them; there was in fact a demand for prints, which may have injured the silk trade in some degree.

3061. What is the state of the silk trade at Manchester at the present moment? —The silk trade at the present time I think would be in a very fair state of demand if this Committee had never been called together, and at this present time I think the demand as good as we can reasonably expect under the circumstances of the country; I have no doubt that the circulation of the Bank of England is now twenty-one or twenty-two millions.

3062. You think that the appointment of this Committee has injured the trade? —I think it has; I think that the shopkeepers are afraid of buying silks, lest they should be cheaper.

3063. Are the demands for home trade or foreign consumption? —I know nothing of the foreign trade; the silk trade is chiefly home trade.

3064. On what sort of silks are the mills in Lancashire working?—Bengal silks, China silks, Italian silks, and generally as other mills in the North are.

3065. What is the proportion in your own mills, of the Italian and other silks you throw?—We do not throw one-tenth of Bengal silk, nine-tenths may be Italian, and one-tenth Bengal and China.

3066. Do you throw it on commission, or is it all your own?—It is all our own, with very trifling exceptions.

3067. Do the regulations under which the silk trade is now proceeding, in your opinion, require any alteration?—If I am asked my opinion, or only as to the drawback, I should say, No.

3068. Is it your opinion that prohibition would be beneficial to the silk trade?— I have never found fault with the present regulations; if prohibition is given, I will never find fault with it certainly.

3069. It will do you no injury?—Certainly not.

3070. Do you think it will do Manchester any benefit?—I would rather avoid the question.

3071. Do you think that prohibition would benefit the cheaper branches of the silk trade in Manchester?—I think it might, perhaps.

3072. Do you feel much competition in Manchester?—Yes; such as is felt elsewhere.

3073. Are you not desirous of being freed from restrictions as a manufacturer, rather than have more put upon you?—I cannot answer that question exactly, I have but a choice of evils; I have said that the present regulations satisfy me.

3074. As a throwster?—Yes.

3075. As a throwster, you think the present protecting duties sufficient?— I would not ask for more, though I think other men may have a different opinion, and that their opinion is entitled to as much attention as mine is.

3076. What, in your opinion, is the real amount of duty now paid on foreign thrown silk?—Raw silk coming from the Austrian States and from Lombardy, pays twice as much as thrown silk; I think the duty at present paid on thrown silk is about 2s. 10d. a pound English, the sale of the debenture may be 2d. or 3d.; the people in Lombardy protect their throwsters by taxing raw silk going out of the country.

3077. If the duty paid on Foreign thrown silk were discontinued, what in your opinion would be the consequence to the English throwster?—I think it would ruin a great many of them, particularly those in remote places; for we find as the import duty has decreased, the import of thrown silk has increased, and in the face too of a falling market, for 1831 was a falling market from first to last, or nearly so; I think the Italian mills are capable of throwing off double what they do at present; I have been in many of them.

3078. What has been the difference in point of quantity?—In 1831, the quantity of thrown silk imported was 514,000 pounds; in 1830, it was 437,000 pounds.

3079. Do you think this would be partial or would it be an entire destruction

to

to the British throwster?—Indeed I can hardly say; my opinion is, that I might perhaps survive the wreck, but I think that very few others could.

3080. Do you mean if the duty was wholly taken off?—Yes.

3081. Have the mills which you think would be affected, as good machinery as yours?—I do not know anything of the machinery of any mills but my own.

3082. Are you not able to state, whether their machinery is on a better principle than yours?—No, for I have never seen them.

3083. Then how do you think that they would be more affected than you?—Because I think that throwsters, in large towns, would become manufacturers, and would convert their mills to manufacturing purposes as well as for throwing.

3084. Confining your answer to throwing, do you think, supposing the duty were removed, you would continue to throw Italian silk?—Yes, possibly; but not to sell to manufacturers. I will beg to read an extract from a letter from my partner on this subject. " March 26th. This morning Mr. ———, who is a customer of " ours, bought four bales of beautiful foreign tram at 19s. 6d. from Mr. ———, for " raws; to make such tram they ask 18s. How is it?" Then he says lower down : " To day we commenced working a short time, in winding and cleaning, (four days " and a half per week)." We cannot make fine tram at 19s. 6d.; we cannot make tram so cheap as was bought of the foreigners on this occasion.

3085. Are the Committee to understand there is only that difference between the raw and the thrown?—Yes.

3086. Can you suppose such a price will continue; do you think the manufacturers of Piedmont charge only 1s. for throwing it?—No, I do not suppose that; nor can I explain why such a circumstance takes place.

3087. Do you not conceive this is an exception to the general rule?—Yes, I think it is; but it is important to this inquiry to know, that tram may have been brought to England when prices were much better; the merchant here may have written out to his correspondent there, that things were mending, that discounts were in plenty, and before it comes here the Bank has changed its policy, has contracted its issues, and it must be sold for whatever it will fetch; it is one of those anomalies which will happen in all places, it is brought here when the Bank of England is filling the country with notes, and is sold when she has withdrawn them.

3088. You do not think you could throw silk so as to supply manufacturers with it?—It would not answer our purpose to throw silk to sell, we should be obliged to manufacture it ourselves on the premises if we are to exist, that would be the only way in which we could do so.

3089. You have stated, that if the duty was taken altogether off Foreign thrown silk, that many throwsters would be ruined; but you think you yourself could live through it?—Yes, by becoming a manufacturer.

3090. Would not that answer apply to most of the manufacturers now at Manchester?—I apprehend it would.

3091. Then they would survive it as well as yourself?—I think they would.

3092. Do you consider that you throw silk as well as the Italians?—Yes.

3093. In case the duty on foreign thrown silk were taken off, do you consider that the purchaser of thrown silk here, or the Italian throwster, would gain the difference; would the whole charge be still made upon you to the amount of the duty paid?—I think the profit would be increased to the Italian throwster, certainly; I think the Italian throwster would gain the greatest part.

3094. The manufacturers in this country, in your opinion, would gain a very small part of it?—I think so.

3095. Supposing you were to throw entirely for your own consumption, to which branch of the trade should you direct your efforts?—We should direct our efforts to that branch which has the least fancy about it, to the manufacturing of plain goods.

3096. Are you aware, that other countries are supplied with thrown silk besides England?—Yes, I am.

3097. What would regulate the price of the silk, would the small quantity sent to England, or the large quantity sent to the rest of Europe?—I do not know, it depends so much on circumstances. England, for a time, might be a very good market, and a good deal would come in, then when we were supplied it would go elsewhere.

3098. You mean to say, that it would not come to England unless they could sell it at a profit?—I will relate a conversation with a gentleman of the name of

678. Steiner,

Mr.
Vernon Royle.

6 April,
1832.

Steiner, at Bergamo.   He said, that sending silk to England was perfect gambling, for that they never knew what they should get for it at all.   Sometimes they had a profit of 15 per cent.; sometimes they lost 15 per cent.   That when they sent silk to the Rhine, or to Vienna, or St. Petersburgh, they could always tell to five per cent. what they should get; but when they sent to England they never knew what they should get; sometimes they got a large profit, and sometimes they lost a great deal.   He inquired how the matter was, and it was explained, viz. by the increase and decrease of Bank of England notes.

3099. Do you not suppose a great number of the speculators in England, speculating in that trade, produce that?—Yes, certainly.

3100. You think it would not continue as long as the trade was going on increasing?—I think, that with regard to the importation of the thrown silk it is a matter of great consequence.   I am hardly competent to give an opinion as to the power of the Italian mills; but they can do more perhaps by one-half than they do; their water falls are tremendous, and they have no factory time Bills there to rule them and lop off one day in six.

3101. You consider that any such regulation is against you?—Decidedly so; one day in the week from our productive industry would totally ruin us.

3102. If the variation of the price of silk, which is stated to exist in England, is owing to speculation or competition, is the silk trade this year in a more healthy state than it was any year since 1826, as far as men of capital are now in it?—I think there is not much alteration in that respect, it is much as usual.

3103. If the same speculation exists here, you think the same uncertainty will continue?—We know from whence men are able to speculate, viz. from the excessive issues of the Bank of England.

3104. You conceive that supposing the duty were removed, the quantity of thrown silk imported would of necessity be abundant?—I think so.

3105. And that the greater number of those persons now employed in it would be ruined?—Yes, they would be driven to the parish and to poor houses.

3106.   What do you conceive to be the proportion between the fixed property of the throwster, and the fixed property of the manufacturer?—The difference is so great that I can hardly state it; the manufacturer begins trade with his outlay, with his silk and his bobbins, and his reeds and harness, &c. &c.; and I apprehend if a man has 1,000 weavers in Spitalfields, his fixed capital in those materials will be perhaps two or three hundred pounds.   I apprehend that the worst silk mill is worth more as old materials than all the reeds and harness in Spitalfields.

3107. The business of the throwster depends upon the manufacturer notwithstanding?—Yes.

3108. You mean that there is a greater quantity of capital in the mills of the throwsters?—Yes.

3109. You have stated the Manchester mills to be of the value of more than 200,000 *l.*; do you know how many operatives they employ?—I can tell how many they will employ when they are all in full operation; they will employ 5,850 operatives who would tend the frames; besides these are to be added the mechanics, &c. &c.

3110. Have you made a calculation, supposing the building of a mill cost 4,000 *l.*, how much of that has been paid for taxes on materials?—I have not a calculation by which I could show how much money was expended in labour, and how much in materials; but if a mill cost 4,000 *l.*, I think it may safely be said that 1,000 *l.* has been paid to the King for taxes.   The bricks are taxed at 5 *s.* 10 *d.* the 1,000; the timber is taxed 100 per cent.; the glass 500 per cent.

3111. Then of course if your trade was destroyed, you would naturally look for compensation?—Certainly; if the silk throwster is to be stripped of his protection for the public good, I think he is entitled to compensation; for a reasonable compensation is that which every man has a right to expect, inasmuch as he sees nearly all trades protected; the cotton spinner is protected, the corn grower is protected, the wool grower is protected.

3112. Do you think the present protection given to the silk throwster is equivalent to that given to the cotton spinner?—I think it is nearly the same; the cotton spinner has a protecting duty of 10 per cent., and 3½ *d.* for every square yard of printed cotton in addition.

3113. Are you aware of the protection the French give to their throwsters?—They will not allow the raw silk to be exported at all; and they tax thrown silk coming from Piedmont about 10½ *d.* on every pound English.

3114. Organzine pays 10 *d.* per pound?—Yes.

3115. The

Mr.
*Vernon Royle.*

6 April,
1832.

3115. The duty on importation being 2 *s.* 10 *d.* ?—Yes.

3116. What do you think would be the effect on the British silk manufacturer, supposing the throwster was destroyed?—He would require a protecting duty against foreign manufactured goods, as heretofore.

3117. Can you give any rule by which a protecting duty might be imposed?—I really cannot; if I knew what the issues of the Bank would be for the next two years, I could give a rule, but I cannot without that.

3118. Can you explain how it is, that the importation of raw silk has increased so considerably, whilst the importation of thrown silk has increased only in a trifling degree?—I attribute it to the decrease of protecting duty; the last two years there has been more thrown silk imported than in the two former years; and I attribute that to the reduction of the protecting duty; till that time it was really a protecting duty, it enabled the mill-owner to increase his mills, and to make a tolerable living.

3119. The quantity of raw silk has considerably increased?—Yes, and the English throwsters have thrown it into different articles.

3120. There has been a complaint in the country that the throwster has been in a state of distress?—That is very true, and the throwsters have been branded as being very imprudent men.

3121. Can you give an explanation of the alleged distress; has it arisen from an increase of raw produce, without a corresponding increase in the manufacture?—I can only say for myself, I have never complained of distress, it is true we are obliged to reduce our wages when severe pressure has been upon us.

3122. It appears from a letter you have just read, that your mills are not in full employment?—In consequence of this Committee, we trim our vessel, not knowing how the storm may come upon us.

3123 You made no complaint to the Board of Trade?—No; I wrote a letter to the Board of Trade, which I will explain, there is no complaint of distress in that, the word " distress " I believe is not in it.

3124. Do the master throwsters and manufacturers in Manchester, in conjunction with the operatives, form lists such as are formed at Coventry so as to prevent wages being reduced unreasonably low?—Never.

3125. Have such lists been formed at Macclesfield?—I am not aware that lists have been formed there, but there is a society of masters there, and they have a secretary, and they meet to tell of their experience, and the circumstances of their trade, and so on.

3126. What, in your opinion, are the effects of such lists upon the operatives in Macclesfield?—If there are such lists at Macclesfield, I should think that they are more calculated to keep wages down than any thing else, that the more jealous the masters are of each other the better for those whom they employ.

3127. You have visited the silk mills of Italy, and you have had an opportunity therefore of observing the machinery, and the power there is of working mills?—I have.

3128. Do you know what is the difference between the wages paid in the Italian and the English mills?—The wages in Italy I think are about one-third of the wages we pay in England, or thereabouts; of course the wages are governed by the demand for the silk, or whatever the article may be, they rise and fall with the demand.

3129. Are you able to calculate the rate of wages, in proportion to the want of silk?—I am not able to answer that question, in passing through a silk mill we hear what such a person has per week.

3130. Have you any means of knowing what those persons do?—They are all paid by the day.

3131. Have you any means of stating to the Committee what may be the difference of labour in those mills as compared with the manual labour in English mills?—I think that it is about the same; I am not aware of any great difference, the Piedmontese are extremely intelligent, and are like English people.

3132. Are you aware that English machinery of the most approved principle has been sent from England into Lombardy?—It has.

3133. Can you state the circumstances under which that machinery was sent from England into Lombardy?—A silk throwster came to Manchester in, I think, the year 1830, he had no letter of introduction to me, but called upon me; I was civil to him, having been received very politely by his countrymen; his object in coming to England was to obtain machinery of the best description; he brought a correct

678.                                                                              plan

plan of his mill, and came prepared to purchase machinery; he purchased several frames of the first description, which were sent to Lombardy. I am not prepared to say that the Government gave him permission to export them, but he did export them, and they are now there; he was frequently at my office.

3134. Have you any reason to suppose that the Italians keep the best raws to be thrown at home?—The large throwsters in Italy reel a great deal of silk for themselves; they buy the cocoons, but they do not reel all they use, they are very careful to buy the best; I do not mean to say that all the best remains there; but they reel with great care that which they work in their own mills.

3135. Have you information that there is a system carried on in that country of selecting the best silk for their own use?—No; the merchants of England are very desirous to obtain silk on consignment, and promise the Italian growers that they will get them good prices; the silk is brought here certainly, and they get, when it comes, what they can.

3136. Have you ever petitioned the Board of Trade, or Parliament, to export your own machinery?—I applied to Mr. Huskisson, a few years ago, in consequence of the alterations continually making, not being disposed to endure much of it, I applied for permission to carry my machine out of the country, but it was not attended to.

3137. How many years ago was that?—About five or six years ago.

3138. Was it since the year 1826?—Mr. Huskisson was at our mill the year before he died; that would be, I should think, 1827.

3139. Have you ever since made application to the Government relative to the state of the silk trade?—A gentleman from Macclesfield, came to my house on a Sunday, and was anxious for me to join in a petition, describing the trade there to be in the greatest distress, but I would not do so.

3140. At what period was this?—In January 1832, it was the first Sunday in the year. I said we have part of our mill not employed. This gentleman said to me, whenever we talk of a depression of trade, they say at the Board of Trade the trade is all gone to Manchester. I said I will state the simple fact, that we have part of our machinery not employed; I have no objection to state it, if it is wished, to Mr. Poulett Thomson, for I want to have a fling at him, for encouraging Hobhouse in his Bill, and Sadler's Bill, and so I wrote a letter which will speak for itself.

3141. Have you any objection to that letter being read?—No, not the least; it was a private letter to Mr. Poulett Thomson, but I wish it should be read; it has gone too far, too much has been said about it for me not to wish to have it read now.

3142. It appears that you addressed a private letter to the Vice President of the Board of Trade in January last; did that letter contain any intimation that you considered it might be a desirable provision to introduce into some law, to allow manufacturers to quit this country, carrying with them their machinery and their labourers?—Looking at Mr. Hobhouse's Bill, and Mr. Sadler's, I asked, in effect, for permission to go away from such oppression, and such unreasonable enactments.

3143. Had you made a similar application to Mr. Huskisson?—Yes, some years before that; that was not by letter.

3144. Has it appeared to you, having given your attention to subjects connected with the manufacture in which you are engaged, that other countries in Europe protect their own manufacturers, and more particularly those who lay out large sums of money in mills and buildings, and fixed property, to a degree not offered to manufacturers in this country?—I think that they do protect the manufacturers to a much greater degree; the reason is this, that when a man builds a mill, it is considered a real or national property, and an addition to the means of employing the poor in the kingdom or country; a manufacturer merely may take his capital and walk away to Paris or elsewhere, but when he has built a mill, he is almost always obliged to stay with it, and so promote the welfare of his poorer neighbours; this is considered of great consequence in all countries, and it is of great importance; if a man, for example, builds a mill of the value of 100 *l.*, and that employs five people, to each of those he supplies 20 *l.* worth of tools; he lends to them 20 *l.* worth of tools to work with, and that is the reason why property of that description is considered deserving of protection; it is proposed now to strip the English throwster of his protecting duty. I think that as almost every other trade is protected, the cotton trade, and the agriculturist, and almost every other, the silk

throwster

Mr.
*Vernon Royle.*

6 April,
1832.

throwster then ought to be protected also, or to have a fair compensation made to him for his loss.

3145. You are understood to say, that in Manchester laws introduced for the regulation of work in factories tends, in your opinion, considerably to embarrass the manufacturers?—Yes; and to injure the operatives grievously.

3146. Have the goodness to explain in what respect you conceive such laws have an injurious tendency?—The silk trade hitherto has not been under such laws; but from the strength of the party who support Mr. Sadler's Bill, I have no doubt it will come under the law; and if the Bill passes into a law, as it stands now, the silk throwster, who now obtains from his mill 600 lbs. weight of silk per week, will only obtain 500 lbs. and the operatives will loose, out of their wages, one shilling in six; and looking at the Bill, as it now stands, the mill owner or manufacturer is delivered over, bound hand and foot, to the common informer and to the law-making justice.

3147. Have you ever been to the Board of Trade for advice or information respecting your trade?—Yes; I have once, and only once.

3148. Did you obtain the advice you were in need of?—Certainly most imperfectly.

3149. At what period was that?—At the beginning of last year. I went there for advice and instruction, as I was entitled to do, knowing that the gentlemen there are very well paid for their attendance; but in place of having instruction there, I had to give instruction, and particularly as to an Act of Parliament.

3150. Do you conceive that the prosperity of the silk manufacture, in any certain year, is shown by the importation of thrown silk in that same year?—Not by any means; when it is thought necessary to explain to the country how the silk trade is going on, they say the trade must be in prosperity, because the importation is so large, the manufacturer must have been busy: such is not the fact; for if it happens, as in 1831, that the issues of the Bank are 20 or more millions for three months, there is for that time a great importation, but it may remain over in the London Docks for many months, or until there is another or a greater issue of notes; therefore the quantity coming in, in one year, is no proof that it is manufactured in that year.

3151. In the present state of the law, from the ease with which the English machinery is obtained by foreigners, do you conceive it possible for this country to retain for any considerable period, any superiority in respect of its machinery?—Not for one day.

3152. How long is it since our silk machinery was superior to the French?—I do not know that it is superior even now.

3153. You have stated that the best machinery was sent out in 1830; do you mean for throwing?—Yes.

3154. How long is it since our throwing machinery was superior to the Italian?—I do not know that it is superior at all; the English frames are superior in form; they are superior, being in cast iron, and they are more durable; but the Italian machinery does the work quite as well.

3155. The Committee are to understand that it is more durable?—Yes; and stands in less compass.

3156. Is it cheaper?—No, I think not.

3157. Do you then think the Italians would want it dearer?—The form is the principal thing; but machinery made mostly of wood would last a great many years.

3158. Are the Committee to understand that the machinery used in England is equal, taking the form and duration together, to that used in Italy?—Certainly.

3159. Have you any means of judging whether it is equal to that used in France?— I think it is much the same.

3160. Do you think that either the Italian or the French have any advantage over you in throwing?—No, I think not.

3161. But you think they have in wages?—Yes.

3162. Can you give an estimate of the expense of throwing in England?—No, I cannot.

3163. Is it 4s.?—I must decline answering any questions respecting my own business.

3164. You state that the wages in Italy are much lower?—I think only about one-third, but they vary of course.

3165. Do

3165. Do you mean the wages of per day, or what they turn out of hand?—They are employed by the day.

3166. Have you any means of judging what the charge per pound weight is in Italy?—I have not.

3167. Is it not probable that a man may have in Italy 1 s. a day, and an Englishman 3 s., and yet the Englishman's labour be cheaper than the Italian's?—Yes, it may be; but it is not so in Piedmont, they understand very well what they do there, they understand the division of labour as well as we do.

3168. How do you know it was a third?—Because I asked work people in the mills one or more, of what they earned, and I know how many spindles they tended.

3169. What were the hours?—The hours were more than ours.

3170. Can you state the expense upon a pound of silk?—When I see a machine at work, and see how many spindles or places an operative tends, I know what difference there is between the price of labour in England and in Italy.

3171. Can you not then state the expense per lb.?—It depends so much on circumstances, one shall employ ten men at 3 s. a day, another shall employ the same number at 4 s. yet these latter shall be less productive than the former.

3172. As you have given a decided opinion, was that opinion formed on learning the result, or merely on casual observation in going through the mills?—In the mills in Italy I have seen as much order, as much application of industry and ingenuity, as much looking after the work, as in England; the Piedmontese are well known for their application and industry.

3173. Having seen all that, did you ever hear what was the charge per lb. for throwing?—That depends upon the sort of silk, and the quality of silk; fine or coarse silk will make a difference.

3174. Take the average?—I cannot give the average; I think if I had a mill in Piedmont, and you had mine in Manchester, I could ruin you in a few years.

3175. You have been asked about a private letter, do you mean with reference to that private letter that the Committee should understand that the constant change in the law, which regulates the silk trade, and the rights of interference with the application of that labour, are the principal grounds of the complaint stated in your letter?—Yes, they are.

3176. Do you not consider that all interference of that kind must be detrimental to British manufacture?—Yes, I do certainly.

3177. That is the sole ground on which you state you would rather leave the country than remain in it, subject to such restrictions and changes?—Yes, I would rather do it even at my age; I would rather leave the country than be subject to Mr. Sadler's Bill.

3178. Do you not consider it of essential necessity to the silk trade, whether applicable to the throwsters or weavers, that the rate of duty should be settled once for all?—I do.

3179. You have been asked, if the duty on the import of Italian thrown silk were taken off, what the consequence would be, and you were understood to say, that a great increase in the import of foreign thrown silk would take place?—I think so.

3180. Are you aware that in 1824 the duty on thrown silk was 14 s. 8 d. up to the 25th of March in that year?—I have no memorandum of the amount, but the duty upon raw silk was then 5 s. 6 d. per lb.

3181. Are you aware that on the average of ten years prior to that, the quantity never exceeded 400,000 lbs. weight?—Yes, it may be so.

3182. Are you aware that the duty was reduced to 7 s. 6 d., and in 1825 to 5 s.?—Yes, I am.

3183. Are you aware in the year 1826 there was only 289,000 lbs. weight, and in the year 1829 only 172,000 lbs. weight; and if so, how do you reconcile the fact that from the time the heavy duty was taken off, there was less thrown silk imported than while the duty was 14 s. 6 d., with the opinion you have given?—My opinion is, that the duty down to 5 s. was really a protecting duty. Some manufacturers thought that foreign thrown would answer the purpose best, and they would have it; probably our throwsters are not so competent; it is only within the last few years that the English thrown silk has been as good as the foreign thrown.

3184. Are you aware that since the year 1765 up to the year 1831, the quantity of Italian thrown silk, on the average of any number of years, has never exceeded 10,000 lbs. weight?—It may be so.

3185. In

Mr.
*Vernon Royle.*

6 April,
1832.

3185. In 1765 there were 363,000 lbs. imported; in the years 1829, 1830 and 1831, the last year, only 374,000 lbs.?—I cannot state the quantities.

3186. You have stated, that if the duty was taken off altogether, which is 2 s. 8 d. we should be overwhelmed with foreign silk; how can you expect an increase to take place now, if it has not increased, when the duty has so far decreased?—The English throwster at the time spoken of, I think, did not pretend to throw Italian silk into organzine; I am old enough to know when they would not throw Italian raw silk if they could help it. Until now, the duty was a protecting duty; the 7 s. 6 d. and 5 s. kept the distance greater between the English and Foreign throwster. I have said, that I think the Italian mills are capable of throwing twice as much as they do at present, from their immense water-falls, and from being allowed to work night and day, as they may think proper.

3187. If you take the average of any five years, for the last fifty years, does not that prove that the quantity of Italian thrown silk entered for home consumption has undergone little change?—The importation of a particular year is no guide; those circumstances take place from various causes which I cannot explain; such as fashions, and various circumstances. The last two years, when the duty was reduced to 3 s. 6 d., there was a higher import than in any two former years; and if the duty was taken off altogether, the quantity would increase still more.

3188. Can you state what were the prices of Italian thrown silk in the English market in each of the last five years?—I cannot.

3189. Do you know whether it has been cheaper the last two years than in preceding years?—I have no memorandum at all of the prices; prices are governed by the issues of the Bank of England.

3190. What have you paid for Italian thrown silk in 1827 and 1828?—I have no memorandum.

3191. Or in 1829 and 1830?—I have no memorandum; I can only say, that silks are rather improving in value now.

3192. Can you say whether it was cheaper the last two years than the three preceding years?—I cannot speak to that without memorandum.

3193. Are you able to state the price of organzine in the last five years?—It is lower now than five years ago.

3194. Must not the price of thrown silk, whether Italian or English, depend on the general price of silk in the market?—There are anomalies: sometimes thrown silks are scarce, sometimes they are abundant; sometimes looking at the price of raw in the English market, and foreign thrown in the English market, it would appear that the foreign throwster has thrown his silk for less than nothing.

3195. May not that affect the quantity of Italian thrown silk?—There are so many circumstances, I cannot answer to that.

3196. But you are clearly of opinion, that if the duty was taken off, that would increase the quantity which comes in?—Yes.

3197. From what you know of Italian thrown silk and English thrown silk, which do you think the best article; can you throw as well in England as they do in Italy?—I never felt satisfied with what I did myself; I always thought any body could do it better, or as well.

3198. You were asked before, whether you could not make it as well as the Italians, and you said, Yes?—Yes, I think we can; we ought, certainly.

3199. You have stated, that you were very well satisfied with things as they are; that, individually, you sought no change?—Just so, speaking of the regulations.

3200. That may happen with one individual, and not apply generally?—It may not apply generally; I apply it to myself.

3201. Is there not something peculiar in the Manchester trade, do not they make the lower description of articles and mixed goods, which consume a quantity of silk, with a view to effect large sales, and to meet a great and extended consumption without attempting to guide or influence the fashions?—I do not know; when I was a manufacturer we endeavoured to make such patterns as we thought would sell.

3202. Formerly a great many white dresses of plain muslin were worn by ladies, they are not worn now?—That may be so.

3203. Has not a great change taken place by the manufacturing of different kinds of articles, and persons now turning again more to the silk trade than formerly?—If I am asked how it is that the silk trade has increased so much, I can explain it; probably the silk trade of Manchester has increased mostly towards Bolton in Lancashire; formerly they wove in that part of the country fustians by hand, now those fustians are mostly woven in mills and by power, consequently the weavers who

worked

worked them have been seeking other employment, and the weaving silk has been of the last importance to them; they would have been very greatly distressed but for that; the manufacturers have found weavers ready to take work at very reasonable terms, and they are very easily led to make such goods as the manufacturer wants; the silk trade being better for them than the cotton.

3204. A good deal of the Bengal and China silk is used at Manchester, is it not; is there not a good deal of waste also?—Yes; there is a good deal spun and made into handkerchiefs.

3205. There has been 40,000 *l.* drawback paid the last year?—I am glad that that circumstance is mentioned, because the Committee must have some knowledge of that circumstance.

3206. Has not that been one reason why the Manchester people have fared rather better than their neighbours, being encouraged by this drawback?—It may be so, and I beg to state that the drawback which applies to spun silk requires revision.

3207. How is the drawback regulated?—The waste silk which is bought from 2 *s.* 10 *d.* to 3 *s.* 6 *d.* a pound is spun into thread, manufactured into goods, and receives a drawback of 3 *s.* 6 *d.* a pound, the original cost of the materials not being so much as the drawback; so in mixed goods one ounce of silk may be so mixed as to receive twice its value in drawback; and that was the complaint I made to Mr. Huskisson the last time I saw him, and he promised that he would look into it.

3208. Is not a large part of the goods made at Manchester similar to and equal in quality to the Spitalfields, and not exported?—Certainly; I should think three-fourths at least.

3209. Are they equal in quality?—If I was a manufacturer I should never be easy if I thought any man could make better goods than I did at the same prices, and I believe that spirit generally prevails.

3210. How long were you a manufacturer?—Up to 1826.

3211. In what respect does the drawback require revision?—It is the same on a material which costs 3 *s.* as on a material which costs 20 *s.*; an ounce of silk of the value of 1 *s.* 3 *d.* may be made up with cotton, the silk may be worth only 1 *s.* 4 *d.*, and it shall receive a drawback of 2 *s.* 4 *d.*, that is what I mentioned to Mr. Huskisson.

3212. Is it not the fact, that those debentures are bought at very low prices, and that they get a drawback which is intended to promote the shipping trade, an allowance to the extent of 3 *s.* 6 *d.* a pound on the silk bought at the low rate you have spoken of?—Yes; my motive for mentioning this circumstance is, that I wish the silk trade to be put on such a basis that no party should hereafter complain.

3213. Are you aware that the regulations of drawback require that the silk goods shall be worth 14 *s.* a pound?—Yes; but we know how declarations are made at the Custom House. I can contemplate cases where a debenture of 3 *s.* 6 *d.* may be worth 4 *s.*, then the English throwster would have a bounty against him.

3214. How would you propose that the drawback should be applied to those circumstances?—That is a matter which requires great consideration.

3215. Notwithstanding you have got a tolerable trade in Manchester, and a demand for those things, could you manufacture more goods if you had a demand for them?—We could manufacture a great deal more if we had a demand; they could manufacture much more certainly.

3216. Some of those perhaps are exporters and participate in the bounty?—I think not.

3217. Have you any means of knowing the fact at this moment that there is a great deal of depression of the trade; a great deal of want of employment among the labouring classes in the districts carrying on the silk trade?—I have no doubt there is or has been a great deal of distress in Macclesfield and elsewhere, and we feel it in degree in Manchester, and perhaps from the same causes; but we do not complain of it so much; we bear our sufferings with more patience perhaps.

3218. If there was a prejudice in favour of certain goods introduced against your's, that would affect you?—We should meet the pressure by making as good goods and as handsome goods as we could, and overcome it if possible.

3219. You have been asked respecting the quantity of raw silk brought in different years, formerly there was very little silk consumed in proportion to what has been consumed the last 15 or 20 years; are you not aware that some of the fluctuations in the quantities of thrown silk imported have arisen from a determination on the part of some of the throwsters to make an effort to prevent its intro-

duction;

Mr.
*Vernon Royle.*

6 April,
1832.

duction; that they have lowered their prices and wages to meet the competition?
—We never think about that; we buy our raw silk as low as we can, and look after
our mill as well as we can.

3220. Do you think the Macclesfield and Congleton manufacturers have not
reduced their profits to meet the competition?—I wish we had an Act of Parliament
to give us regular profits; I wish we could always make a profit.

3221. At this moment are you working at a profit?—Yes.

3222. What has been the effect upon the silk trade in Manchester of the changes
which have taken place in the law?—The silk trade have nothing to thank the
Government for; for the duty on raw silk was kept on till we were pointed at by
every government in Europe; they took it off at last, and there has been in consequence a great increase of trade. If the regulations which have been called
Mr. Huskisson's Regulations, had not been carried into effect, we should have had
no silk trade to talk of; they became necessary.

3223. Do you refer to the duty of 5 s. 6 d. on the raw material?—I mean the
regulations generally.

3224. Has the trade in Manchester generally been a prosperous trade?—Yes, it
has generally.

3225. Do you call to mind many failures among those connected with it in
Manchester?—Not many, only one or two; there have been very few failures in
that trade.

3226. Do you think there would have been any complaints from Manchester
unless they had been instigated from other quarters?—I think that some gentlemen
in the room would answer that question better than I can; I think they would not
have complained unless they had been stimulated to it.

3227. You have no particular complaint to make of the state of your own
trade?—No.

3228. You can sell all you make, and as fast as you make it?—That is rather
too far; I have no complaint to make; that should be a sufficient answer.

3229. You are now extending your work, are you not?—Yes; but then we are
all imprudent men in Lancashire, that has been stated in the House of Commons;
I am sure if I am increasing my throwing machinery now I am an imprudent man,
and looking to Mr. Sadler's Bill, and other Bills.

3230. Is the distress in Manchester greater than it has ever been before?—
My neighbours have said nothing about distress in their petition, nor have I said
anything about it.

3231. Do you think that the distress in the silk trade in Manchester is greater
than it has been previously?—I have said nothing of distress at this moment.

3232. Do you consider the silk trade in Manchester to be in a distressed state?
—I think it is not; I feel no distress, and my neighbours say nothing about it in
their petition; and if there was distress I think that they would say so.

3233. Did you not complain of the trade being unsteady since July 1830?—
I did.

3234. You said that was owing to their being only sixteen millions and a half
Bank notes in circulation?—No; if I am asked what I mean by saying the trade
is now more unsteady, I say, that since July 1830 the exchange has been often
unfavourable to this country, that the circulation of the Bank of England since
May the 1st, 1830, has diminished gradually to January the 7th last, it has gone
on decreasing all the while, until it was then 16¼ millions; but I have no doubt that
the circulation is now more than 21 millions, and that it will remain so some
months, till July or August perhaps.

3235. Do you found that opinion on this document?—Yes.

[*The Witness delivered in the following Account.*]

ACCOUNT

ACCOUNT of all PROMISSORY NOTES and POST BILLS of the Governor and Company of the Bank of *England* in Circulation at the close of the Business on Saturday in every Week, from the 10th of April 1830 to the 7th of January 1832.

| 1830: | | £. | s. | d. | 1831: | | £. | s. | d. |
|---|---|---|---|---|---|---|---|---|---|
| April | 10 | 21,284,023 | 10 | 3 | March | 5 | 19,357,578 | 14 | 3 |
| — 17 | | 21,701,858 | 4 | 5 | — 12 | | 18,866,649 | 12 | 11 |
| — 24 | | 22,073,311 | 3 | 1 | — 19 | | 18,638,738 | 16 | 9 |
| | | | | | — 26 | | 18,896,416 | 3 | 5 |
| May | 1 | 22,080,493 | 13 | 10 | | | | | |
| — 8 | | 22,064,560 | 6 | 10 | April | 2 | 19,032,536 | 8 | — |
| — 15 | | 21,622,506 | — | 5 | — 9 | | 19,715,850 | 5 | 4 |
| — 22 | | 21,211,869 | 3 | 6 | — 16 | | 19,846,314 | 1 | 11 |
| — 29 | | 21,078,650 | — | 2 | — 23 | | 19,468,091 | 16 | 3 |
| | | | | | — 30 | | 19,268,750 | 9 | 8 |
| June | 5 | 20,268,254 | 7 | 4 | | | | | |
| — 12 | | 19,827,280 | 19 | 10 | May | 7 | 18,810,175 | 16 | 2 |
| — 19 | | 19,854,267 | — | — | — 14 | | 18,663,780 | 6 | 2 |
| — 26 | | 19,978,507 | 12 | 4 | — 21 | | 18,438,640 | 16 | 2 |
| | | | | | — 28 | | 18,224,093 | 18 | 7 |
| July | 3 | 19,886,620 | 8 | 4 | | | | | |
| — 10 | | 22,016,045 | — | 6 | June | 4 | 17,969,488 | 7 | 1 |
| — 17 | | 22,551,170 | — | 2 | — 11 | | 17,773,148 | — | 6 |
| — 24 | | 22,612,106 | 2 | 5 | — 18 | | 17,499,591 | 19 | 11 |
| — 31 | | 22,549,249 | 13 | 2 | — 25 | | 17,716,586 | 6 | 10 |
| August | 7 | 22,605,713 | — | 9 | | | | | |
| — 14 | | 21,842,953 | 11 | 11 | July | 2 | 17,626,238 | 18 | 4 |
| — 21 | | 21,855,950 | 6 | 6 | — 9 | | 19,403,893 | 2 | 7 |
| — 28 | | 21,082,324 | 14 | 10 | — 16 | | 19,601,773 | 9 | — |
| | | | | | — 23 | | 19,812,924 | 1 | 2 |
| September | 4 | 20,764,925 | 1 | 2 | — 30 | | 19,632,112 | 3 | 4 |
| — 11 | | 20,058,749 | 1 | — | | | | | |
| — 18 | | 20,076,602 | 5 | 6 | August | 6 | 19,527,560 | 12 | 11 |
| — 25 | | 19,717,795 | 15 | 5 | — 13 | | 19,137,136 | 18 | — |
| | | | | | — 20 | | 18,627,537 | 17 | 8 |
| October | 2 | 20,142,976 | 17 | 2 | — 27 | | 18,465,335 | 13 | 4 |
| — 9 | | 19,446,592 | 15 | 10 | | | | | |
| — 16 | | 20,751,818 | 12 | 5 | September | 3 | 18,396,570 | 2 | 2 |
| — 23 | | 20,721,540 | 15 | 1 | — 10 | | 18,607,059 | 8 | 11 |
| — 30 | | 20,534,836 | 6 | 11 | — 17 | | 17,722,554 | 12 | 5 |
| | | | | | — 24 | | 17,661,219 | 11 | 6 |
| November | 6 | 20,266,363 | 10 | 7 | | | | | |
| — 13 | | 20,176,052 | 12 | 1 | October | 1 | 17,923,457 | 18 | 7 |
| — 20 | | 19,833,238 | 3 | 4 | — 8 | | 17,679,398 | 13 | 9 |
| — 27 | | 19,300,086 | 11 | 1 | — 15 | | 18,670,660 | 15 | — |
| | | | | | — 22 | | 18,671,660 | 1 | — |
| December | 4 | 19,022,276 | 8 | 5 | — 29 | | 18,721,210 | 19 | 11 |
| — 11 | | 18,398,535 | 10 | 9 | | | | | |
| — 18 | | 18,122,172 | 12 | 4 | November | 5 | 18,514,548 | 11 | 11 |
| — 25 | | 18,237,925 | 3 | 5 | — 12 | | 18,161,765 | 13 | 1 |
| | | | | | — 19 | | 17,873,824 | 19 | 7 |
| 1831: | | | | | — 26 | | 17,396,665 | 4 | 5 |
| January | 1 | 18,331,402 | 2 | 2 | | | | | |
| — 8 | | 19,397,394 | 1 | 5 | December | 3 | 17,082,619 | 3 | 1 |
| — 15 | | 20,436,258 | 15 | — | — 10 | | 16,901,847 | 17 | 9 |
| — 22 | | 20,345,503 | 18 | 10 | — 17 | | 16,704,594 | 8 | 9 |
| — 29 | | 20,341,818 | — | 10 | — 24 | | 16,756,865 | 6 | 3 |
| | | | | | — 31 | | 16,890,093 | 2 | 7 |
| February | 5 | 20,399,391 | 13 | 6 | | | | | |
| — 12 | | 20,069,260 | 7 | 6 | 1832: | | | | |
| — 19 | | 19,758,448 | 18 | 7 | | | | | |
| — 26 | | 19,650,846 | 1 | 6 | Jannary | 7 | 16,495,053 | 5 | 6 |

A true Extract from two Parliamentary Papers, dated respectively Bank of England, August 4th, 1831, and February 7th, 1832, and signed respectively,

*William Smee,*

Chief Accountant.

3236. Did

Mr.
*Vernon Royle.*

6 April,
1832.

3236. Did you not say there was a great deal of depression in the autumn of 1831?—Yes.

3237. By what was that caused, was it by the contraction of the Bank circulation?—I think so, and that affected the cotton trade as well.

3238. You speak of Manchester?—Yes, of course.

3239. Are not wages lower in Manchester than you have ever before known them in the silk trade?—I think they are, and I think they have been so since Christmas.

3240. Are not the wages in the silk trade regulated in some degree by the wages paid in the cotton trade?—Yes, there is a good deal of influence in that respect; we cannot depress our wages below a certain point, or the operatives will go to the cotton mills.

3241. If the rate of wages is lower, then the earnings of the people are in the same proportion lower?—The operative silk hands are mostly paid by the week.

3242. Your observation is applied to throwing?—Yes.

3243. Are you able to state whether the wages of weaving silk are not affected by the wages in the cotton trade?—No doubt; the wages in November and January were as low as at any time; but I believe they have since advanced somewhat.

3244. Was there the same depression in other trades?—Yes, certainly; but the amount of poor's rate for the last six years shows the condition of the operatives.

[*The Witness delivered in the following Paper:*]

### POOR's RATES for the Township of *Manchester.*

| RATE on the RENTS. | | £. s. d. |
|---|---|---|
| 5 s. in the Pound | Collected from 25th March 1826 to 25th March 1827 | 59,216 16 8 |
| 5 s. - ditto - | Ditto - - 25th March 1827 to 25th March 1828 | 70,159 - 5¾ |
| 4 s. - ditto - | Ditto - - 25th March 1828 to 25th March 1829 | 55,704 6 6 |
| 4 s. - ditto - | Ditto - - 25th March 1829 to 25th March 1830 | 52,247 16 4½ |
| 0 s. - ditto - | Ditto - 25th March 1830 to 25th March 1831 | 9,760 15 4½ |
| 3 s. - ditto - | Ditto - - 25th March 1831 to 1st March 1832 | 44,080 - 4 |

| | | |
|---|---|---|
| Population of the Township of Manchester | - - - | 142,026 |
| Ditto - of the Parish of Manchester | - - - | 270,963 |
| Ditto - of the Hundred of Salford | - - - | 612,414 |
| Ditto - of the County of Lancaster | - - - | 1,335,600 |

Manchester Town's Office,⎱
    March 14th, 1832.   ⎰                    *Geo. Single.*

To Mr. Vernon Royle.

3245. Do you attribute the depression to the introduction of French manufactures?—My acquaintance with the French goods is so confined I am not prepared to give an answer upon that, it is merely my opinion that the French goods have not interfered with the Manchester goods.

3246. They have not interfered with the goods you have made at Manchester?—No, I think not.

3247. Do not the wages of weaving the silk goods depend upon the wages paid to persons engaged in weaving cotton?—If a particular description of cotton goods is in demand, a weaver can turn from silk to cotton and then by that means get a better price, and they do so; silk is the more clean and comfortable work, and they all prefer it, and it is better paid generally.

3248. Is it usual, when there is a want of employment in the silk trade, for the same hands to work in the cotton trade?—Yes, when driven to extremities they do so.

3249. The wages paid are very much the same?—Yes, sometimes there is not silk work to be had, then the men will take the other.

678.                                        3250. You

3250. You stated that the wages in Italy in throwing are one-third of those paid in Manchester?—Yes.

3251. What is the value of the plat, supposing a mill in England which would let for 500 *l.* a year, what would be the rent for that in Italy?—I cannot state that.

3252. You think that they do their work as well and as expeditiously as those in England?—Yes, as well.

3253. So that in point of fact, as far as the operative workmen are concerned, they could do as much for 100 *l.* as you can do for 300 *l.* at Manchester?—Yes, I think so.

3254. Are you aware of a Memorial that was sent from Manchester to the Board of Trade in the month of January last, about the time when you addressed your letter to the Vice-President of the Board of Trade?—Yes, I am.

3255. Perhaps you will know the names of the gentlemen if they are read to you?—Yes, of course I shall.

3256. Was there the name of Messrs. Broadbents?—Yes.

3257. That is a house of considerable eminence, is it not?—A very respectable house.

3258. Rothwell & Molineaux?—I know them by name.

3259. J. & J. Occleston, Kay & Co., Longworth & Co., William Walker, J. & G. Smith, Benjamin Williams, Harrop, Taylor & Co., Bindlosses & Preston, do you think that those gentlemen, or any of them, could be instigated to put their names to any memorial which they did not honourably and conscientiously approve of?—That is a very trying question indeed, it is calling upon me to place a mark upon them as long as they live; I must beg to decline answering that question.

3260. Have you seen the Memorial referred to?—I saw a copy of it at the house of the honourable Member for Lancashire. I never knew of it till then.

3261. Is that now shown to you the Memorial?—It is.

*[The same was delivered in and read, as follows :]*

" To the Right Honourable The Lords Commissioners for Trade and Plantations.

" Your Lordships,

" It having been represented at your Board, that the throwing trade of Macclesfield and elsewhere has come from those places to Manchester, we, the Undersigned, some principal mill owners of Manchester, beg to remove this erroneous impression: our throwing mills have been unprofitable, and we have, ever since the reduction of duty, 1829, considered their cost a total loss of the capital used in their erection; and beg to add, that the silk trade at Manchester, and its vicinity, is in a very depressed and ruinous state; that we cannot make goods at a price at which they can be exported, but that an increase of debenture might ultimately enable us to do so; without some effectual relief of this kind we are convinced a great part of the silk trade must speedily be abandoned, and the hands thrown out of employment; already at Middleton, and elsewhere, they are chiefly supported by private subscription.

" We have the honour to be, your Lordships' obedient servants,

| | |
|---|---|
| " *Broadbents.* | *William Walker.* |
| *Rothwell* & *Molineaux.* | *J.* & *G. Smith.* |
| *J.* & *J. Occleston.* | *Benjamin Williams.* |
| *Kay* & *Co.* | *Harrop, Taylor* & *Co.* |
| *Longworth* & *Co.* | *Bindlosses* & *Preston."* |

3262. Have those same individuals since signed a Petition, which was presented on the 26th March to the House of Commons, expressing different sentiments?—It seems so.

*[The Petition was read, as follows :]*

" To the Honourable The Commons of the United Kingdom of Great Britain and Ireland
in Parliament assembled.

" THE humble Petition of the several persons whose names are hereunto
subscribed, being Silk Manufacturers and Throwsters in Manchester, in
the County of Lancaster:

" Showeth,

" THAT your Petitioners are deeply interested in the result of an inquiry into the Silk
Trade which has lately been instituted, and is now carrying on by Your Honourable House :

" That Your Petitioners humbly beg leave to express their opinion, that it is inexpedient
to alter the laws which now exist relative to the Silk Trade.

" Your Petitioners therefore humbly entreat Your Honourable House, that the said laws,
relative to the Silk Trade, may be allowed to continue as now in force.

" And Your Petitioners will ever pray, &c.

| | |
|---|---|
| " *Henry & Edward Tootal.* | *William Harter.* |
| *Morley & Bindloss.* | *Ashworth, Gould & Whitworth.* |
| *Bosley, Smith & Bosley.* | *John Clegg.* |
| *Barker, Lyddall & Co.* | *Henry Farrington.* |
| *Longworth & Co.* | *Joseph Kay.* |
| *Thomas Cole & Co.* | *John Barton.* |
| *Louis Schwabe.* | |
| *George & James Smith.* | *W. Walker.* |
| *Aughton & Ashworth.* | *Thomas Lomas.* |
| *J. & J. Broadie.* | *White & Bentley.* |
| *Harrop, Taylor & Pearson.* | *Wentworth & Proctor.* |
| *J. Broadbent & Sons.* | *Molineaux, Rothwell & Co.* |
| *Levyssohn, Astbury & Co.* | *Bindlosses & Preston."* |

3263. Your letter, addressed to the Vice-President of the Board of Trade, does
not appear from the Minutes; but some questions have been put to you, in eliciting
some portions of the letter, which will appear upon the Minutes; have you
any objection to state, whether there appeared in this letter a Statement to this
effect:—" I have heard that it has been stated to the Board of Trade, that the
" severe distress, under which the silk trade of Macclesfield is labouring, arises in
" consequence of a transfer of a part of that trade to Manchester, and that the silk
" trade of Manchester is in comparative prosperity; I respectfully beg leave to state
" my belief that such is not the fact; for in the silk throwing establishments in this
" place, of which I am the principal proprietor, we have more than 10,000 spindles
" totally unemployed since August last: this fact, at all events, will show rather,
" that our throwing mills at Manchester are in as bad condition as any at Maccles-
" field ?"—Certainly, that was the fact at the time; but there is no statement made
of the cause of that depression. The word distress is never used in the letter; that
letter was written entirely to oblige a gentleman of great learning and great discretion, and but for his application (on a Sunday too) that letter would never have
been written at all; that letter was written entirely with a view to having a fling at
Mr. Thomson for not opposing the time Bills. I told the gentleman I would
make a complaint to that effect, and that only; and that I would say nothing as to
the cause of the spindles being unemployed, which indeed were unemployed for
prudential considerations merely; and although they seem a considerable number,
yet they are but a small portion of the whole.

*Lunæ, 9° die Aprilis,* 1832.

## THE RIGHT HON. THE EARL GROSVENOR, IN THE CHAIR.

Mr. *Vernon Royle,* called in; and further Examined.

3264. ARE you a manufacturer now ?—I am by power looms.

3265. You disposed of one of your manufactories to two persons formerly in
your employment ?—I did.

3266. You have stated that there are at Manchester 12,000 looms on silk and
silk mixed goods, can you give the Committee an opinion how many of those looms

are

are employed on all silk ?—I should think perhaps two-thirds, but that is merely an opinion.

3267. You have stated that there were not above fifty looms engaged in the weaving broad silk in Manchester in 1819 ?—Yes, broad silks for garments.

3268. Are you aware that in 1796 there was a List agreed upon in Manchester for regulating the prices for weaving silks, signed by fifteen manufacturers?—It might be so, but after that almost all the silk trade went to Macclesfield.

3269. You have stated, that had not Mr. Huskisson brought about a change of system, there would have been no trade to quarrel about?—Just so.

3270. Do you mean by that, to express an opinion that the silk trade was not prosperous and increasing before that change?—I do not mean to say that, but I say that the trade could not have borne the duty of 5s. 6d. a lb. on raw silk much longer.

3271. Your statement applied to the raw silk, not to the admission of silk goods, when you state that it had regularly increased up to 1824, though burthened with heavy duties?—I think it had increased, and was increasing slowly.

3272. Do you think the raw silk being freed from that duty of 5s. 6d. in 1824, had the prohibition of foreign silk been continued, the prosperity of the silk trade would not have continued also?—I am hardly able to answer that question, it involves so many principles, and requires so much consideration as to the full effect of prohibition and its consequences; it is true it had prospered, I think in spite of the regulations.

3273. You do not think that the prosperity of the silk trade has been promoted by the admission of silk goods?—That is a very nice point; I think the competition raised in the minds of our manufacturers by having excellent patterns, and having excellent colours, and improved qualities, and figures shown to them, has not done any harm, I think it has rather done them good.

3274. Is not the employment of people in the silk manufacture a very clean and a healthful occupation?—I have a certificate of a medical man who inspected one of my mills or works in 1831, one of the ablest physicians in Europe, his certificate was given after an examination of the mills; he describes the nature of the employment, the temperature, the hours of employment, and the general appearance of the hands or operatives.

3275. You are giving in evidence a copy of the certificate of Dr. Carbutt?—I am.

[*The same was delivered in and read, as follows :*]

" Manchester, 7th April 1831.

" I have this day made a general examination of the silk mill of Messrs. Royle & Crompton, in Great Bridgewater-street, Manchester, and found the work-people, whether adults or children, to have a very healthy appearance indeed, quite as much so as could be expected in persons whose employment is not entirely in the country. Many of the children whom I questioned have been in the business three or four years, and have a healthy cheerful aspect, with a sufficient alertness of manner. The temperature I found to range from 60° to 70° of Fahrenheit, which I do not consider too high for health. The labour appears very light and easy, and the hours I found from inquiry are, for the women and girls 63½ per week, and for the men and boys 68½ per week, which period is certainly not too long.

*Edward Carbutt*, M.D.
Physician to the Manchester Infirmary and Dispensary,
Fever Wards, &c. &c.

3276. You have stated that you visited the silk mills in Italy, and you found that the wages there were but one-third of the amount in England?—Thereabout.

3277. You have stated that the price of labour in the silk mills in Italy is very much cheaper than in England, that the mills of Italy are capable of turning off twice their present quantity, and that the Italians take every improvement in machinery from England which is introduced here; have the goodness to state what chance, under these circumstances, you think the throwster of Italian silk in England would have provided the duty on Italian thrown silk were taken off?—I have answered that question on a former day, that if a person had my mill in Manchester, and the best machinery that money would purchase, and I had a mill on one of the streams in Piedmont, that being called to sell at my prices, I would ruin the person carrying on the concern at Manchester in a very few years.

3278. You mean to say that an English throwster would have no chance against an Italian?—That is my opinion.

3279. If

Mr
*Vernon Royle.*

9 April,
1832.

3279. If a greater reduction of duty on foreign thrown silk were to take place, would it not very much diminish, if it did not destroy, the value of mill property in this country?—My opinion is that it would do so.

3280. Do you contend for further reduction?—Certainly not; it would be attended with great loss to every one, and increase the poor's rates most seriously.

3281. Do you think you shall be able to survive the storm by adding the business of a manufacturer to that of a throwster?—I have stated that I think I could, by manufacturing upon the most economical principle, by manufacturing inside our own buildings.

3282. That manufacture you would apply by power?—Chiefly.

3283. Do you think of making fancy goods by power?—I think it is very possible; greater improvements have been made in my time than that would be.

3284. You are understood to have stated, that there is a power equal to 342 horses in the silk mills at Manchester, that one-third is out of work, and one-third is not now loaded?—No; that one-third has not yet begun to work, two mills were built only last year, one is a very large mill, and not yet come into work.

3285. How many of them are at work?—Two-thirds of them are now at work.

3286. Do you mean in full work?—Yes.

3287. Can you give the Committee the particulars on which your estimate is founded?—I hardly can; the two mills which have not begun to work will be 75 horse power; one mill is not loaded to the full extent it will bear, I believe I am pretty correct in saying, that one-third is not employed.

3288. You furnished to Mr. Hume of the Custom House an account?—I did.

3289. Will you have the goodness to state, whether this is nearly a correct statement of what is now at work, Longworth's at work six?—I cannot give a nearer statement than I have given.

3290. You say if the duty were taken from the foreign thrown silk you should begin manufacturing to save you from loss. If your trade as a throwster had become unprofitable by the competition of the foreign throwster, would it not be more for your advantage as a manufacturer, to buy the cheap silk of the foreign throwster, rather than to throw silk at a dearer rate at your own mill?—I would rather not answer that question; if I am pressed upon the subject I must answer it; but I may be exposing my intentions or my views of trade.

3291. How do you account for it that there are only two-thirds of your power at Manchester at work when the importation of raw silk is so large, and the machinery is situate at a place where the manufacture of silk is in so prosperous a state?—Two of the mills have not yet begun to work, because they are not completed.

3292. You think they will be set to work?—Certainly in as short a time as possible.

3293. Is not a considerable quantity of silk thrown at your mill afterwards worked up by manufacturers at Coventry and Spitalfields?—I believe it is.

3294. You were understood to state at your last examination that the persons employed to work up the silk produced at your mill were from four to five thousand? —No; I said that if you reckoned the throwsters and their children, the weavers and winders and their children who weave the silk thrown at our mills, our mills furnish employment and bread to nearly 5,000 people.

3295. Are you to be understood, that the persons dependent on your mill with their whole families constitute from four to five thousand?—I said with the children who depend for their bread upon their parents, many of them, though fed from the mill, are too young to work.

3296. You are understood to say, that the families of persons you employ who may be considered dependent upon that employment, amount to about 4,000? —Yes.

3297. Do you believe that any of those persons, constituting those families, are employed in any other mills than yours?—No; that our mills furnish employment and bread for that number.

3298. You mean to say, that the families at present employed in your mill and the persons employed in the mill together, make an aggregate of 5,000?—Yes; those who are employed and fed.

3299. Your mill finds bread for so many persons?—Yes.

3300. Those persons are not employed elsewhere?—Certainly not.

3301. Does that number include the weavers?—Yes.

3302. Do you include in those the weavers employed in Manchester, or the

678.                                                                          weavers

weavers whom the silk employs where that is elsewhere, in Coventry, and so on ?—When it goes elsewhere also.

3303. How many persons in Manchester are dependent upon your mills ?—I think about 3,000 in Manchester and the neighbourhood ; throwsters about 1,400, and weavers and their children, and winders, about the same number.

3304. Are those persons employed by you ?—They are employed by my tenants and myself.

3305. Where are the remainder of the four or five thousand resident ?—Most of them in Manchester, but some in Coventry and Spitalfields.

3306. You have stated, that in 1827 you applied for permission to remove your machinery and the works out of the kingdom, and you have also stated, that you were influenced in making a similar application in January last, to the Vice President of the Board of Trade, by the desire to escape from such laws as were proposed by Mr. Sadler ; what was your reason for wishing to remove from this country at the former period ?—It regarded the continual change of the protecting duty, and shifting policy of those that had the direction of the silk trade ; and we were threatened then with being stripped of the duty, as we are at present.

3307. You have also stated, that you considered you were really protected then ?—It was a fair and a better protecting duty than now.

3308. You approved of the change made in 1824, when the duties were reduced ?—Yes ; the duty on raw silk.

3309. Do you know of any change in 1827 ?—I do not know that there was at that time ; I said, you had better pass an Act of Parliament to allow us to go away ; that was the only remark I made at the time.

3310. There being no change in 1827, why did you wish to remove ?—Because I anticipated the stripping of the throwster and the manufacturer together.

3311. You approved of the reduction of duty, but you did not approve of the admission of French silks ?—I approved of the reduction of duty on raw silk, but I disapproved of the protecting duty on thrown silk being taken off manufactured goods.

3312. You would not like the whole duty being taken off from the foreign silk ?—I disapproved of it being taken off ; it was spoken of, and a sort of notice was given by Mr. Grant at the time, to that effect.

3313. You apprehended that the whole of the duty on foreign thrown silk would be taken off ?—I did ; and I was inclined to keep it on then, as I am now.

3314. Are you aware of the amount paid by Government in the shape of debentures, on the export of English manufactured silk ?—Not of my own knowledge.

3315. Do you know whether any part of any debenture is received by the people of Manchester ?—I think a considerable part is received by them ; I am not prepared to say how much.

3316. Do you know for what goods they receive that debenture ?—I think mostly for mixed goods, and goods made from what we call spun silk, an article of silk made from waste silk.

3317. What is the first cost of that waste silk ?—It depends upon the quality of it : it would range from 2 s. 6 d. to 3 s. 6 d., or it may be rather more, for any thing I can tell ; I do not know what we obtained for the last we sold.

3318. Do you think that any considerable quantity, Gros de Naples or silks not made from spun silk, is exported from Manchester, and receives any amount of the drawback ?—I am not aware how much.

3319. Do you think there is a considerable quantity ?—I think there is not a considerable quantity.

3320. Are you aware that there are some goods sold to houses in London and elsewhere, for exportation, in consequence of those debentures which they have ?—I am not aware that they are sold particularly to London.

3321. You have stated that the goods exported, on which bounty is paid, are principally mixed goods ?—I think so.

3322. Do any of the Lombardy silks enter into those goods ?—I think not ; but to a very limited degree indeed, if at all.

3323. Is it your opinion, that that silk on which the debenture is paid, has never paid any duty in England ?—Except one penny a pound.

3324. Are you able to state what effect the withdrawing that bounty would have upon that trade ?—I am not aware that waste silk is spun anywhere but in England ; if it is, it can be but an inconsiderable quantity.

3325. What

Mr.
*Vernon Royle.*

9 April,
1832.

3325. What effect would the withdrawing that bounty have upon that kind of trade which is carried on by the debentures?—I think it would regulate it in such a way as may be required. The debenture, at present, is more in amount than the original cost of the raw material, which could never be the intention of the legislature.

3326. Would it put an end to that trade or not?—I think it would alter the character of it; it might possibly derange it for a little time only.

3327. Are the Committee to understand that the Lombardy silk, which pays a 3*s.* 6*d.* duty on importation, is not worked up in goods exported to receive the bounty?—I do not think that it is.

3328. You have stated, that if the duty was taken off the import, the throwster's interest would be very much injured?—I think so.

3329. What effect would it have upon the weavers if they could buy their silk 3*s.* 6*d.* a pound cheaper, would not that rather improve the condition of the weaver?—Of course it would, if they could indeed have the material less by about 2*s.* 8*d.* a pound.

3330. Of your knowledge, have the silk weavers generally at Manchester, or in that neighbourhood, been slack of work?—There was a considerable scarcity during the latter part of last year, up to about the second week in January, I think it then began to revive considerably.

3331. Are not you aware, that there was a pressure on the muslin trade last year as well as the silk?—Certainly there was, and the cotton spinning as well.

3332. Is it within your knowledge, that at Bolton, and different places up to Manchester, a great many people who had been employed in the cotton trade were actually employed in the silk trade in the course of last year?—Certainly there were a great number of people in the neighbourhood of Bolton got employment in the silk trade last year.

3333. When the cotton trade was slack?—Yes; or when the silk was better than the cotton trade.

3334. You think you are correct in stating, that the workmen in cotton and silk change from hand to hand, as the work may be better or worse?—Certainly.

3335. Is it your opinion that the work in silk and cotton will have a tendency to equalize?—Certainly.

3336. Is that more the case now than it formerly was?—No, I do not think it is; many cannot turn their hands to both, but many can.

3337. What per centage on the price of silk imported would 3*s.* 6*d.* be?—That depends upon the quality of the silk; there is silk from 10*s.* to 20*s.*

3338. Take the bulk of Italian silk?—I suppose about 10 per cent.

3339. What is the price of thrown Lombardy now?—That depends on the quality; there are various qualities and prices.

3340. What is the range?—Five or six shillings a pound, I suppose.

3341. Does the price now exceed 24*s.*?—I think very seldom.

3342. What proportion is 3*s.* 6*d.* to the price?—The duty is not exactly 3*s.* 6*d.* but about 2*s.* 10*d.* deducting the debenture.

3343. Will not it be 10 per cent.?—Rather more.

3344. Do you not think it a matter of importance to any trade to be supplied with the raw material 10 per cent. cheaper?—It is certainly a matter of consideration, it depends on circumstances altogether; it may or may not.

3345. Can there be an hesitation in your mind, that if you are a manufacturer, and are making plain or fancy silks, if you can get the material 10 to 15 per cent. cheaper, you can bring them to market cheaper?—Certainly; if I can buy the material cheaper, I can make my goods cheaper.

3346. Can you state where the imported raw silk is principally used?—It is used in various parts of the Kingdom; in Spitalfields, in Coventry and Manchester also.

3347. Have you any means of knowing what proportion is used in Manchester? —No; but a small proportion comparatively.

3348. If the weavers of Spitalfields and of Coventry are subject to an additional tax of from 10 to 15 per cent. on the material they use, would you not consider that a great hardship compared with other manufacturers of silk?—No; I should not, because if the weaver is benefited by the 10 per cent. the throwster is paid out of the parishes where the throwing mills are situated, and that which is gained in one way is lost in another.

3349. Supposing the throwing to be in Manchester and its neighbourhood, and

678. the

the weaving to be in London and Coventry, can you have a doubt that the weaving in both those places must be injured by that tax?—If I am asked, whether a man can make cheaper silks from silk at 20 s. than 21 s. of course he does; but the question is as to the extent of good to be done to the whole of the silk trade.

3350. Can you have a doubt that the effect of keeping the 3 s. 6 d. on thrown silk is injurious to the weaver?—If I am asked, whether taking off the duty from thrown silk will do good to the Spitalfields weaver, I should say it would not.

3351. Have not the Spitalfields weavers considerable competition from Manchester in different sorts of work?—Perhaps they have; they would certainly have more trade if there was no Manchester at all.

3352. If, in Spitalfields, they consume an article taxed at 3 s. 6 d. do you not think that they manufacture under a disadvantage to that amount?—Yes; but the consideration does not exactly rest upon that; the interest of the whole trade must be looked at, and if the throwster is stripped of his duty he will be compelled to be a manufacturer, and so increase the competition with Spitalfields. In the abstract, the weaver might make the goods cheaper if there was no duty, and if really he could be served at 2 s. 10 d. per lb. less than at present.

3353. The Spitalfields weaver and the Coventry weaver pay from 10 to 15 per cent. more for the raw material than they would do if the duty was off?—I do not know that exactly; thrown silks are sold very often in England, without reference at all to the cost.

3354. Are you able to explain why Italian silk should be thrown here, without reference to prime cost?—I will give my opinion why it is so: when the Bank makes her issues, very abundant supplies are brought here, in expectation of finding a good market; but they are often sold when she has withdrawn those issues, and, in consequence, at a loss.

3355. Speaking of trade, during the period of five or six years, you cannot expect the Italian merchant to send silk here to sell it at a loss?—The Italian merchant is often induced to send it, hoping for a profit but getting none.

3356. If the duty is kept up to favour the throwing, it is kept up at an expense to the weaver?—I am not prepared to say that it is, for the considerations I have mentioned before must be looked to, with a view to that; viz. whether it would be a real gain to sacrifice the throwster for the sake of giving the weaver a trifling reduction in the cost of his raw material; the weaver cannot exist for a moment without a protecting duty against foreign goods, even if the throwster was destroyed.

3357. Have you not expressed an opinion, that a bounty should be paid only on that silk on which duty has been paid?—No, I have said no such thing; but I mean to say that the drawback should be in some proportion to the cost of the raw material, and should never exceed the cost of the raw material. I complain that the drawback is greater than the cost of the raw material; if the drawback of 3 s. 6 d. is paid upon silk of the value of 12 s. per lb., then the drawback upon silk of the value of 3 s. 6 d. per lb. should be less in proportion.

3358. If the drawback on the debentures received, as you state, is exclusively on goods in which no Italian or French silk are worked up, is not this a direct bonus on the use of Bengal and China raw silk?—Certainly it is a bounty; the duty received is given back as a bounty on the silk of our own colonies, and it was so intended, as well as to extinguish the duty upon thrown silk gradually; as the export trade increased, the duty upon thrown silk would decrease; that was the intention of those who made the present regulations under which the silk trade is proceeding.

3359. You were asked, on a former day, whether other countries do not protect their throwsters, what protection is given to the French against the Italian throwster?—Four francs on a kilogram; the duty on thrown silk going into France from Italy is about 10½ d. the English pound.

3360. Are the Committee to understand, that whilst the French Government afford only the protection of 10½ d. to their throwsters, you would think it right to afford the English throwster 2 s. 10 d.?—Certainly I would.

3361. On what ground would you give that preference?—Because there is that difference in the cost of living in this country and in France.

3362. That is three times?—I think a man may live in France on one-third of the sum he can live in England.

3363. Is not silk more dependent on machinery than on labour?—No, certainly not;

Mr.
*Vernon Royle.*

9 April,
1832.

not; silk is a thread made to our hands, of course the silk has less work upon it than upon cotton, there is less scope for the application of machinery.

3364. If the French weaver can obtain his silk, with only a duty of 10½ $d$. a lb., do you think it fair to the English weaver that he should pay 34 $d$. per lb. ?—The English weaver has greater reason to complain of the corn laws; and the French Government will not allow silk grown in France, the best silk when thrown, to be exported, and the French silk grower is obliged to take such price as the French manufacturer will give him.

3365. Are you aware what proportion the foreign Italian silk, made into fabrics, bears, as compared with the produce of France ?—No, I have no information upon that subject.

3366. The question does not apply to the exportation of raw silk, but to the working up of thrown silk in France; in that view do you not think it unjust to the English weaver to be placed on disadvantageous terms as compared with the French weaver ?—I do not think he is placed on disadvantageous terms.

3367. Do not the same expenses of wages apply to the weaver here as to the throwster ?—Yes ; the same charges of taxes, and so on.

3368. If the English weaver has the disadvantage of increased price for his food, do you think it fair he should have also the disadvantage of paying three times more for his silk than the foreigner does ?—I deny that he does, for the French silk throwster is obliged to sell his silk to the French manufacturer ; it is not allowed to be exported at all, he is obliged to take such price as he can get; they import but a small proportion.

3369. That is principally Piedmontese silk ?—Yes.

3370. You think it right that the French weaver should get his Piedmontese silk at 10½ $d$. per lb., while the English weaver pays 34 $d$. ?—That is not exactly the fact, because the raw silk is thrown into organzine in England, often at a very low price indeed.

3371. The question is, whether you think it fair to the weaver of England, that he should pay three times as much duty on the raw silk he uses as the French do ?—That depends on other considerations.

3372. You mean to say that it is fair ?—I do, that it is fair he should pay a higher price.

3373. State why the English weaver should pay three times as much duty on the silk to manufacture goods likely to come into competition with the foreigner's goods ?—I do not think he does pay three times as much.

3374. Is not 34 $d$. three times 10½ $d$. ?—The interest of the whole silk trade must be taken together; the silk going into France from Italy forms but a very small proportion.

3375. Suppose an English weaver to work up an cwt. of Italian thrown silk, on which he has paid 34 $d$. duty, and the French weaver to work up an cwt. of the same silk on which he has paid only 10½ $d$. duty, is it not unfair to the English weaver to be placed in that situation ?—If the English weaver were supplied only with thrown silk from Italy, something might be said upon that subject, but that is not so.

3376. Allowing the English weaver to be supplied partly from English thrown silk, what reason would you give ?—I cannot answer that question, because it is one which involves so many considerations; it is not in my power to answer it; there is the interest of the throwster to be considered, his taxed bread corn, the benefit his property is of to the country, the interest of the weaver ; it is the business of a statesmen to look at these matters, and say what had best be done for the whole trade.

3377. Suppose you were a weaver, and that you had to manufacture an cwt. of Italian silk ?—I say the whole question must be looked at by a statesman, and settled, whether it shall be the interest of the whole community that the trade shall be so dealt with.

3378. Has not the French weaver, working 100 lbs. weight of Italian silk, upon which he has paid a duty only of 10½ $d$. an advantage over an English weaver working the same quantity of the same article, he paying 34 $d$. ?—I have answered that by saying, that in the abstract they may make cheaper goods paying 10½ $d$. than 34 $d$.

3379. The last question you have been asked, has been, whether the French weaver, subject to so much less duty upon the silk, has not had an advantage over the English weaver, must not that depend upon the market where they carried their

manufactured

Mr.
*Vernon Royle.*

9 April,
1832.

manufactured goods, and the sort of competition they have to encounter?—Yes, it does depend upon that; if the markets are protected and regulated by the laws, of course that would make a difference to the manufacturer.

3380. You have said that depends upon circumstances, is not one of those circumstances very material, that the French bring their manufactured goods into the home market while we are precluded from it?—That is an important consideration no doubt.

3381. If we had to go into that market and they were shut out from ours, that would make a great difference, would it not?—Perhaps it might, but the smuggler does business very cheaply.

3382. If we had to meet them in the London market it would be necessary we should meet them on equal terms?—I may say, abstractedly, yes; but the matter requires so much consideration I cannot answer decisively.

3383. Do they meet the English weavers on equal terms when they are allowed to bring their goods here and we are not allowed to send ours there?—I cannot say any thing to that.

3384. Suppose the English and French weavers desire to sell their goods in America, would you, as an English manufacturer, not consider it hard that you should pay 34$d.$ per pound duty on silk, while the French weaver only pays 10$\frac{1}{2}d.$, if you two have to come in competition in the American market?—Abstractedly I should; but the fact is not exactly so I think.

3385. Are you aware that the Americans purchase silk from France?—Yes, I believe they do; but more from China.

3386. Is there any reason, other than difference of price, why the English cannot meet the French manufacturer in the American market?—Yes, there may be plenty of other considerations besides that; the Americans can tax the goods of one country and give a bounty upon those of another.

3387. You are understood to say, that as far as it goes, the 3$s.$ 6$d.$ being taken off, would of course be a relief to the manufacturer; but that you think it necessary, as you have before stated, that the whole question should be considered, as it is not a question whether one branch of the trade should be destroyed or not, but the question of the whole trade?—Yes; that is what I said over and over again.

3388. Taking it in one general view, you think such a protection is necessary?—I do, because if the throwster was unprotected the weaver or manufacturer could not exist a single day without a protecting duty upon foreign goods.

3389. Do you in the price you charge for your thrown silk, consider in any way the profits the manufacturer in Spitalfields is to have on his work?—Never; nor does he consider mine.

3390. Do not the throwster and the manufacturer each carry on their trade with reference to their own profit?—Certainly.

3391. Have you fully considered this with reference to its bearing on the weaving and the throwing trade?—Very cursorily, I am not a statesman.

3392. Does the price of the Italian thrown silk regulate the price of the English, or do you think that the price of the English thrown silk regulates that of the Italian?—I think the price of the Italian thrown silk regulates the English.

3393. Do you think that the competition between the English throwsters has a greater effect in fixing the price, than the competition of the Italian throwster with the English?—I think that the English throwster who throws Italian silk, has a competition with the Italian throwster more than with the English throwster.

3394. Have you paid any attention to the relative prices of the raw and thrown Italian in the market?—I have.

3395. Have you not often found the difference between the two prices will not afford any profit to the Italian throwster?—Sometimes the prices are such as would make it appear at first sight that the Italian throwster has thrown his silk for less than nothing.

3396. Do you think, speaking as a tradesman, that the throwster in Italy would continue to work for nothing, that he will continue to send his Italian silk here thrown if he cannot get a better price here for it?—Not always, it depends upon circumstances.

3397. Do you not draw a conclusion from that, that the price depends upon the throwsters in England?—In some degree it does; the price of raws in England enter into the consideration.

3398. Do you think the Italian throwsters get much larger profits than the English, or less?—I cannot tell what may be their profits.

3399. Has

Mr.
*Vernon Royle.*

9 April,
1832.

3399. Has not the French manufacturer a great advantage from the exclusive use of the native grown silk?—Certainly, the French grower is dependent upon the home market only.

3400. So that if France should continue to increase her growth of silk, there is no saying to what extent of advantage the French manufacturer may not be benefited?—Certainly.

3401. Will he be in a situation to undersell the rest of the world?—Certainly; as the grower would have no other market, he can only get the best price he can in the home market.

3402. Do you know the relative price of Italian and French silk?—I do not.

3403. Can you say there will be that advantage if it be dearer?—It was assumed that the quantity would be increased, and that the silk would be consigned to France only.

3404. It is the fact, that French silk of native growth is not permitted to be exported?—It is, I have always so understood.

3405. Is silk, the produce of France, lower than other silk?—I have no means of knowing that.

3406. If the French grower has no other consumer for the commodity than the home manufacturer, he must always submit to take such a price as he can obtain for his silk?—Yes.

3407. Are you able to say whether the prices at which it is sold are lower than that of Italian silk or not?—I cannot answer that question.

3408. Is the principle of manufacture at Manchester similar to that of Spltalfields?—I think not exactly similar.

3409. In what do they differ?—In Spitalfields they make a larger quantity of more valuable goods than they make at Manchester.

3410. Is not the Manchester manufacture altogether of a coarser kind than that of Spitalfields?—Not altogether.

3411. Is it in a great measure confined to Bengal silk?—No.

3412. What proportion of Bengal silk, in comparison with Italian, is used there?—That is a difficult question to answer.

3413. Do they work figured goods?—Yes.

3414. Have you any idea how many looms they have?—No, but I know they have a good many.

3415. Do you believe there are 1,000 looms there?—I know there are a very considerable number.

3416. Are you aware there are some manufacturers of silk damask in Manchester?—Yes.

3417. Are you aware that they have succeeded in providing an article which has been preferred to that of Spitalfields, for the furnishing of Windsor Palace?—I have heard that fact.

3418. They use Italian silk?—Yes, for the best qualities of course; if they wish to make an article as good as can be made, it will be of Italian silk.

3419. Do you consider the protection given to the English throwster equivalent to that given to the French?—I am not prepared to answer that question exactly.

3420. Do you think that it would be an advantage to the British weaver to be entirely dependent upon the Italian throwster?—Certainly not.

3421. You are understood to have stated that you are adding to your machinery and extending your mills, is that the case?—Yes, we are completing our mill.

3422. You are doing that in expectation of carrying on an increased trade with advantage?—We intended to complete our mill, a mill will not pay unless it is filled with machinery; we had prepared frames or skeletons for the purpose, and we are finishing them off; we have nearly done all our machinery.

3423. Does that embrace the weaving?—No, I refer to the throwing.

3424. Are you not extending your works for weaving?—Yes, we are.

3425. Notwithstanding the bad times?—Yes.

3426. It appears that the name of Longworth & Company is signed to the Memorial put in on a former day, is that the same as appears to the petition from Manchester?—Yes.

3427. Are the names of Broadbent & Company, Rothwell & Molyneaux, and Occleston, the same on the two?—They are; there are some other names added to the petition.

3428. Are you aware what was the state of distres existing in January last,

when

Mr.
*Vernon Royle.*

9 April,
1832.

when the Memorial was presented ?—I think the trade at that time was exceedingly depressed.

3429. More so than at present ?—Yes.

3430. Had you thoughts of abandoning your works at that time ?—Certainly not.

3431. The Memorial states that it would be necessary to abandon the works ?—I did not sign the Memorial.

3432. Had you to do with either ?—No.

3433. Have you commenced weaving? —Yes.

3434. How many weavers have you at work ?—I decline answering that question.

3435. Supposing the duty upon thrown silks to be taken off, must not that be followed by the reduction of wages ?—Yes, certainly; the throwster would endeavour to meet the difficulties, and the first thing he would do would be to reduce the wages as low as he could.

3436. Are the people in a situation to bear further reduction ?—I think not.

3437. Should you have gone on increasing your machinery if you had supposed that the 3 s. 6 d. duty on the throwster was about to be removed ?—Certainly not; not one spindle more would be set up.

3438. The Committee understand there are some observations you wish to make with reference to certain questions put to you, upon a letter referred to in your examination ?—I have ; when I was requested to sign the petition to the House of Commons, describing the distress of the silk trade, I said to the gentleman, I will do no such thing ; I cannot perceive that there is the slightest reason for the complaints which are made by the silk trade, and I cannot see that the Government can relieve the silk trade by any thing they can do, and such are my opinions at this moment; to oblige the gentleman, I wrote that letter, and I did so referring to the Factory Time Bills, and not intending to make any complaint against the regulations under which the silk trade was proceeding.

### Mr. *Thomas Brockwell,* called in ; and Examined.

Mr.
*Thomas Brockwell.*

3439. ARE you concerned in the silk trade ?—I am.

3440. In what manner ?—As a silk broker.

3441. How long have you been a broker ?—Between four and five years.

3442. Is your experience grounded on so short a period ?—No.

3443. Where do you reside ?—In Bishopsgate churchyard ; we have also a house in Manchester, my partner resides there, we carry on business as brokers in both places.

3444. Do you import ?—No.

3445. How many years have you applied yourself to the knowledge of silk, and been concerned in that trade ?—Between fifteen and sixteen years.

3446. Have you been in London all that time ?—No, nine years of the time in Italy.

3447. Were you a silk broker in Italy ?—No.

3448. What were you in Italy ?—A silk merchant.

3449. In what part of Italy ?—Established at Genoa, in the King of Sardinia's dominions.

3450. Were you residing in Italy during the high duty of 14 s. 8 d. a pound ?—Yes ; during the last six or seven years of its existence, with the exception of two or three visits to England of a few months duration at each period.

3451. What was the price of throwing fine organzine in Italy at that time ?—Upon the average 3 s. a pound, exclusive of waste.

3452. What is the price now in Italy for the same thing ?—Upon the average 2 s. 6 d. a pound, exclusive of waste also.

3453. What! no greater difference in the price of throwing organzine in Italy, when the duty was 14 s. 8 d. a pound, than when it was only 3 s. 6 d. a pound ?—No.

3354. Does not the price of silk in England regulate the price of silk in Italy? —No.

3455. Why not ?—Because England is not her largest customer.

3456. Who are her largest customers ?—Germany, and her own people.

3457. Is not France a large customer ?—To the King of Sardinia, France is the largest customer.

3458. What is the quantity of silk produced in Italy ?—I estimate the quantity produced in all Italy, including Piedmont, at seven millions of English pounds.

3459. In

Mr.
*Thomas Brockwell.*

9 April,
1832.

3459. In what year ?—It averages for a variety of years, taking an estimate of the product of the whole States.

3460. What proportion of that quantity is thrown in Italy ?—I estimate the quantity thrown at five millions and a half pounds.

3461. The one million and a half pounds remains over in raw silk ?—Yes.

3462. England then is her largest customer for raw silk ?—Hitherto she has been.

3463. What do you mean by saying hitherto?—Because I find the importation of raw silk diminishing.

3464. You allude to Italian raw silk ?—Most assuredly, I am at this time referring to no other kinds of raw silk than those which are produced in Italy.

3465. Can you state when you have observed Italian raw silk diminishing in the amount of imports ?—I find in 1830 the importation was 4,558 bales, and in the year 1831, 3,784 bales.

3466. You do not mean to infer, by comparison of the two last years, that the importation of Italian raw silk will show a decrease, compared with two or three preceding years?—The fact is so, the average for the three preceding years was 4,945 bales, and the average for the two last years 4,171 bales.

3467. How do you obtain those numbers?—They are obtained by the importations through the Custom House, and deliveries into the respective merchants' warehouses, and then journalized ; the government documents are in pounds weight, comprising the great mass of raw silk, and it is next to impossible to legislate for the English throwster by mere reference to the great mass of raw silk coming from all countries ; for our own information and government, we journalize the Italian from the other sorts of raw silk.

3468. Are you not aware that there are separate heads, first raw silk, and then waste silk, in the public accounts?—Yes; but the raw silk should be journalized into the different denominations of raw silk, and not having a public document of that kind, I am under the necessity of framing my own.

3469. It appears, then, that Italian raw silk is evidently going lower in the scale of imports into this country ; can you state the imports from Italy of thrown silk ?— I find the importation of thrown silk to have augmented considerably within the last year, the quantity amounting to 2,780 bales, whereas in the year before, 1830, the quantity did not exceed 1,776 bales.

3470. Taking the average of 1830 and 1831, how will that compare with the average of 1827 to 1829 as concerns thrown silk ?—The average of 1827 to 1829 I find to be 1,682 bales, and the average of 1830 and 1831 resulting 2,278 bales, there is an increased importation evident by comparison, amounting to 35 per cent.

3471. You say that Italy throws five millions and a half pounds of silk, are you of opinion she could throw the remaining million and a half of raw silk?—Yes, I am of that opinion.

3472. Would such a circumstance as a further reduction in the duties on thrown silk move Italy to throw more silk, thereby reducing the present surplus which you estimate she retains in raw silk ?—I have a great opinion of the capabilities of Italy to throw silk, and I consider she is gradually gaining ground over England with the present duties, and so soon as the competition amongst the throwsters in this country is abated by the ruin of some few more, the trade would become more conspicuously in the hands of the Italian.

3473. Why so?—Because the remainder who desire to work at some profit, and having already reduced labour to its lowest suffering point, would not go on to the inevitable destruction of the remaining part of their property.

3474. Are you of opinion, that as the throwns increase, the raws will decrease in the amount of their importations into Italy?—Yes, I am of that opinion.

3475. On what reasoning do you establish that opinion?—I take the surplus quantity of raw at one million and a half, and I divide it into the exports to England, France and Switzerland ; to England I portion 1,250,000 lbs., to France and Switzerland the remaining 250,000 lbs. : I now divide the thrown silk to its respective channels ; to Vienna and her own (Italian) people, 2,000,000 ; to Germany and Switzerland, and the North of Europe, 2,000,000 ; and to France and England, one million and a half ; the portion to France 1,050,000 lbs. to 1,100,000 lbs., and the portion to England 400,000 or 450,000 lbs. : I then arrive at this conclusion, that the question turns upon taking away from the 1,250,000 lbs. of raw to add to the 400,000 or 450,000 lbs. of thrown, presuming the other customers of Italy to go on in their wonted manner.

3476. Do

Mr.
*Thomas Brockwell.*
———
9 April,
1832.

3476. Do you portion off to England according to the importation, or according to the consumption of thrown silk?—According to the consumption.

3477. What was the consumption last year of foreign thrown silk?—Of organzine 428,745 lbs., and of tram 90,770 lbs.

3478. When you speak of the year, when do you commence it?—The 1st of January to the 31st of December of any year of which I speak.

3479. What was the consumption of the year before?—Of organzine 412,295 lbs., and of tram 35,909 lbs.

3480. What was the consumption for the year 1829?—Of organzine 165,416 lbs., and of tram 11,419 lbs.

3481. What was it for 1828?—Of organzine 350,790 lbs., and of tram 15,379 lbs.

3482. There seems particularly a large increase in the consumption of foreign tram in England?—There is.

3483. Was it not generally believed, and very confidently stated, that the reduction of the duty on foreign tram to 2s. a pound, would not affect the throwing of Italian tram in England?—I have heard such opinions, but I never found there was any foundation for them.

3484. Is it your opinion the increased importation, and consequently consumption of foreign thrown trams in England, has taken place upon the reduced duty of 2s. a pound?—I am perfectly of the opinion that the duty of 2s. per pound is not sufficiently high to enable the English throwster to buy the raws, and get his throwing cost for them, in competition with the Italian.

3485. What are the prices for throwing Italian silk in England?—We now hear of very low prices.

3486. What are the low prices you hear of?—Three shillings and nine-pence a pound for fine Italian organzine, and two shillings and sixpence a pound for fine Italian tram, exclusive of waste.

3487. Do you think those prices can be reduced any lower?—I apprehend that they are ruinous prices already, but that question I consider can be better answered from Manchester, Macclesfield, Congleton, Derby, and the West of England, where throwsters reside.

3488. Why cannot you answer it?—Because I am not a throwster, and can judge only from the results.

3489. What results do you speak of?—That the throwsters, when they want silk, make the best bargain they can to take it, to throw at any price to keep their mill going, until I hear that the mill is closed, or that the man is ruined.

3490. How many throwsters have failed lately?—The year just expired was a direful period, and many of them failed.

3491. How many?—It is impossible to say how many; we hear, as brokers, of mercantile failures, but there are a variety of compositions that never come to our knowledge: if it is an object to have a list, perhaps I can obtain one.

3492. Did manufacturers fail last year as well as throwsters?—Yes, they generally fail together.

3493. How is that?—The throwster's ruin is progressive, so is the manufacturer's; depreciation upon the thrown silk causes depreciation on manufactured silk goods.

3494. You are of opinion, that it is the interest of the manufacturer that the throwster shall gain instead of lose?—Unquestionably I am of that opinion, and for this reason, that the manufacturer's thrown silk then does not depreciate in value during the progress of its manufacture.

3495. There is a class of manufacturers anxious to have foreign thrown silk without the duty?—I believe there is, but in my opinion they would be the first to suffer from the destruction of the English throwster.

3496. They conceive it will turn to their individual advantage?—I am not of that opinion; I rather think they would find their error, as others have already, who fancied the same thing in 1829.

3497. Do this class of manufacturers form a large proportion of the invested interests of the silk trade?—Certainly not, I conceive they have very small invested interests in the silk trade.

3498. Who have the invested interests?—The manufacturer who is a throwster, and the throwster or mill-owner, who in many instances is not a manufacturer.

3499. You are of opinion, that the silk trade in this country must die away or flourish as the throwster be protected by such a rate of duties on thrown silk as will

produce

produce a large importation of Italian and the finer kinds of raw silk?—I am decidedly of that opinion.

Mr.
*Thomas Brockwell.*

9 April,
1832.

3500. Do you consider a large importation of Italian, and the finer kinds of raw silk, as indispensable to the silk trade at Manchester as elsewhere?—Quite as indispensable.

3501. Is there any mode which, in your judgment, might be beneficially adopted towards the silk trade, short of a positive law of prohibition?—Should a o sitive law of prohibition be inadmissible, I am of opinion that a system, differing from that now in force, may be advantageously adopted towards the silk trade.

3502. What is that system?—To regulate the importation upon thrown silk, and to regulate the importation of silk manufactured goods upon a remodelled scale of duties, with a clause respecting those countries concerned in the production of the raw material.

3503. How should you propose to regulate the importation of thrown silk?—By a duty of 5 s. per lb. on organzine, and 3 s. per lb. on tram, imported from all countries producing and exporting raw silk.

3504. How should you propose to regulate the importation of foreign manufactured silk goods?—By sufficient rates of duty, and those duties most rigidly enforced, and by the prohibition of imports from all countries producing and not exporting raw silk.

3505. In point of fact it would come to this, that if France would not allow you to have her raw and thrown silk, you would not have her manufactured silk goods?—Just so.

3506. You would compel her, either to supply this country with the raw and thrown silk of native growth, or we should cease to import French manufactured goods, and that by her own act?—Decidedly so; because the importation of manufactured silk goods, being conditional on the import of raw silk, France would either export her raw silk, or abandon her trade to England in silk goods.

3507. You would think that fair?—Yes; if they determined to export their raws, the manufacturers of England generally, and Coventry in particular, would have fairer competition; and should France determine to keep her raw silk, I should think it but fair that she should also keep her manufactured silk goods.

3508. Do you think that would tend to equalize the prices of raw and thrown silk?—Unquestionably it would to a very much greater degree than at present.

3509. As matters now stand, the French grower has but one customer; that is to say, the home manufacturer?—Just so; it is the greatest security for the manufacturer in this country that the price of the raw material should be equalized, and at present it is not so.

3510. If the French manufacturer has influence enough with the French Government to prevent the export of their own raw and thrown silk, you think he ought to be punished by not being allowed to send his goods to this country?—Certainly.

3511. In your former answer do you refer to the manufacturer of silk goods?—I consider all the interests as connected, and that one cannot exist for any long period without the other.

3512. Do you mean by manufacturer the manufacturer of silk goods, or the manufacturer of raw into thrown silk?—Both of them would be advantaged.

3513. Do you refer to the operative weaver?—He would be advantaged when his master was advantaged.

3514. If the French manufactured silk goods were not imported into this country, that would be by the prohibitory laws of France, and not by the prohibitory laws of England?—Certainly.

3515. The same reasoning would apply to the thrown silk of Piedmont?—Most unquestionably it would, so long as the King of Sardinia prohibited the exportation of his raw silk.

3516. With respect to the exportation trade in silk manufactures, it is not desirable for the country it should be encouraged?—Very desirable in my opinion, for so much exported not only allows of so much more labour, but tends to uphold the price of labour upon the remainder.

3517. The additional import duty of 1 s. 6 d. per lb. on organzine, and 1 s. per lb. upon tram, would be given in drawback upon the exportation of silk manufacture, and serve two good purposes, aid the throwster, and advantage the export trade?—The effect would be precisely as stated, by the trade working in that manner, and the throwing and weaving population would be the earliest to experience their proportion of its benefits.

678.

3518. You

Mr.
*Thomas Brockwell.*

9 April,
1832.

3518. You say if France would allow the exportation of her raw material you would admit her manufactured goods, have you taken into consideration the difference of the price of labour in France in the manufacture of their goods?—I think that is a question which would afterwards have to be adjusted by the legislature in conjunction with the manufacturer for his protection.

3519. You are of opinion that at present there is a difference existing beyond the mere difference of labour?—Unquestionably.

3520. Do you believe that silk is cheaper in France than in Italy?—I will endeavour to explain how these countries work : as France does not allow of the exportation of her raw material, of course the manufacturer of silk goods, according to the price which he obtains for his goods, legislates on two sides, with the grower on one side, and with the weaver on the other; but this country being under the necessity of buying its raw silk from the Italian (the Hibernian Company not having succeeded), has no other resource than the levying of its losses upon the artisan or weaver.

3521. What do you mean by the French manufacturer legislating?—He directs his loss to two parties, one towards the grower and the other towards the artisan.

3522. Does he throw his losses on these two parties or one?—He endeavours to do his best, and divides them accordingly, and in any case he has two parties to divide them with, whereof in England there is but one.

3523. Suppose he gains, does he divide that equally?—That is another question, I suppose that is not usual.

3524. If the French manufacturer were to buy from the grower of silk at 24 francs per lb., and he should not succeed in making a profit upon his goods from any external opposition, he would take care, next year, to give a lower price, and to that lower price the grower of French silk must submit?—Unquestionably, having no other customer.

3525. If it is not the case, that the difference in labour is to be counterbalanced by some regulation, would it not give France an advantage of the export trade in the foreign market?—My feeling is, that the point of labour becomes a question between the legislature and the manufacturers; and the duties should be established according to the price of labour between the two countries; my views go no further than to equalize, as near as practicable, the price of the raw material in all the manufacturing markets of the world.

3526. Are there not various qualities of Italian thrown silk in Piedmont?—Not so great a variety in Piedmont as in the other parts of Italy.

3527. Has the manufacture in Piedmont improved or deteriorated of late?—I should think the manufacture of Piedmont was always the best, as it throws particularly for France; and France being particular in her thrown silk, I should say, taking the mass of thrown silk exported from Italy, the Piedmont silk is the best.

3528. Do they manufacture silk as well now as they did formerly?—Unquestionably; *i. e.* throwing of silk.

3529. To what countries are the best qualities sent from Piedmont?—To France.

3530. Do you mean to say, that the best quality of Piedmont silk is not sent to England?—In a small proportion.

3531. Taking the proportion of 400,000 to 450,000, do they bear the same proportions?—I should think the proportion of Piedmont silk coming to England out of 400,000 or 450,000 thrown, might be one-sixth, one-eighth or one-tenth, then I should divide that proportion of one-sixth, one-eighth or one-tenth, to one-quarter for the best kind, the other three quarters being of a very ambiguous sort; the quantity as well as the quality varying at times in different years.

3532. Does France receive a greater proportion of fine than we do?—Certainly, in the whole she must, because Piedmont produces a very large quantity of fine silk, and so small a proportion comes here. France being her largest customer, she must receive the remainder.

3533. Can you state what have been the prices of the raw and thrown Italian silks in this market for the last few years?—I think I can. I have an account where the variations of the year are made into an average for that particular year.

3534. State the prices of 1831 of the raw and thrown?—To understand this it is necessary to state, that I have taken the best kinds of raw silk that come from Milan, and that I have not put Piedmont into the calculation. The account I have made bears more upon the English throwster's question; the throwns being of the

best

Mr. *Thomas Brockwell.*

9 April, 1832.

best kinds thrown at Milan, and of 20 to 26 deniers, and the raws being of the best kinds usually sent upon consignment and sold in London. In 1831 the raws were 17*s.* 4*d.* per lb., and the thrown 23*s.* 3½*d.* per lb. averaged for that year.

3535. What were they in 1830?—17*s.* 6*d.* and 24*s.* 6*d.*

3536. What were they in 1829?—18*s.* 3½*d.* and 26*s.* 9¼*d.*

3537. What were they in 1828?—Raw 21*s.* 11½*d.* and the thrown 29*s.* 9¾*d.*

3538. What were they in 1827?—21*s.* 2½*d.* for the raws, and 29*s.* 1¼*d.* for the thrown.

3539. Will you state the preceding years?—In 1826, 20*s.* 3*d.* for the raw, and 28*s.* 3¾*d.* for the thrown; in 1825, 22*s.* 11¾*d.* for the raw, and 36*s.* 10*d.* for the thrown; in 1824, 20*s.* 7½*d.* for the raw, and 33*s.* 7*d.* for the thrown; in 1823, 26*s.* 9¾*d.* for the raw, and 40*s.* 4¾*d.* for the thrown; in 1822, 30*s.* 4*d.* for the raw, and 47*s.* 2¾*d.* for the thrown; in 1821, 28*s.* 6¾*d.* for the raw, and 44*s.* 11½*d.* for the thrown; in 1820, 27*s.* 2¼*d.* for the raw, and 41*s.* 7½*d.* for the thrown; in 1819, 36*s.* 0½*d.* for the raw, and 52*s.* 7¾*d.* for the thrown.

[*The Witness delivered in the Statement, which was read as follows:*]

THROWNS. Best kinds, Milan 20/26 den. thrown in ITALY.

| YEARS | London Price. | | Less Consignees Charges, at 6*f.* % | | Duty. | | Less Duty. | | Less Austrian Duty, 5*d.* f. lb. | |
|---|---|---|---|---|---|---|---|---|---|---|
| | *s.* | *d.* | *s.* | *d.* | *s.* | *d.* | *s.* | *d.* | *s.* | *d.* |
| 1819 | 52 | 7¾ | 49 | 6¼ | 14 | 8 | 34 | 10¼ | 34 | 5¼ |
| 1820 | 41 | 7½ | 39 | 1½ | - | - | 24 | 5½ | 24 | -½ |
| 1821 | 44 | 11½ | 42 | 3¼ | - | - | 27 | 7½ | 27 | 2½ |
| 1822 | 47 | 2¾ | 44 | 4¾ | - | - | 29 | 8¾ | 29 | 3¾ |
| 1823 | 40 | 4¾ | 37 | 11¾ | - | - | 23 | 3¾ | 22 | 10¾ |
| 1824 | 33 | 7 | 31 | 7 | 7 | 6 | 24 | 1 | 23 | 8 |
| 1825 | 36 | 10 | 34 | 7½ | - | - | 27 | 1½ | 26 | 8½ |
| 1826 | 28 | 3¾ | 26 | 7½ | 7 | 6 | 19 | 1½ | 18 | 8½ |
| | | | | | 5 | – | 21 | 7½ | 21 | 2½ |
| 1827 | 29 | 1¼ | 27 | 4½ | - | - | 22 | 4½ | 21 | 11½ |
| 1828 | 29 | 9¾ | 28 | -½ | - | - | 23 | -½ | 22 | 7½ |
| 1829 | 26 | 9¼ | 25 | 2 | 5 | – | 20 | 2 | 19 | 9 |
| | | | | | 3 | 6 | 21 | 8 | 21 | 3 |
| 1830 | 24 | 6 | 23 | -½ | - | - | 19 | 6½ | 19 | 1½ |
| 1831 | 23 | 3½ | 21 | 10¾ | - | - | 18 | 4¾ | 17 | 11¾ |

RAWS. Best kinds, Milan Raws sold in LONDON.

| YEARS | London Price. | | Less Consignees Charges, at 6*f.* % | | DUTY. | | Less Duty. | | Less Austrian Duty, 10*d.* f. lb. | |
|---|---|---|---|---|---|---|---|---|---|---|
| | *s.* | *d.* | *s.* | *d.* | *s.* | *d.* | *s.* | *d.* | *s.* | *d.* |
| 1819 | 36 | -½ | 33 | 10¾ | 5 | 6 | 28 | 4¾ | 27 | 6¾ |
| 1820 | 27 | 2¼ | 25 | 6¾ | - | - | 20 | -¾ | 19 | 2¾ |
| 1821 | 28 | 6¾ | 26 | 10¼ | - | - | 21 | 4¼ | 20 | 6¼ |
| 1822 | 30 | 4 | 28 | 6¼ | - | - | 23 | -¼ | 22 | 2¼ |
| 1823 | 26 | 9¾ | 25 | 1¾ | - | - | 19 | 7¾ | 18 | 9¾ |
| 1824 | 20 | 7½ | 19 | 4½ | – | 3 | 19 | 1½ | 18 | 3½ |
| 1825 | 22 | 11¾ | 21 | 7¼ | - | - | 21 | 4¼ | 20 | 6¼ |
| 1826 | 20 | 3 | 19 | -½ | – | 3 | 18 | 9½ | 17 | 11½ |
| | | | | | – | 1 | 18 | 11½ | 18 | 1½ |
| 1827 | 21 | 2½ | 19 | 11¼ | - | - | 19 | 10¼ | 19 | -¼ |
| 1828 | 21 | 11½ | 20 | 7¾ | - | - | 20 | 6¾ | 19 | 8¾ |
| 1829 | 18 | 3½ | 17 | 2½ | - | - | 17 | 1½ | 16 | 3½ |
| 1830 | 17 | 6 | 16 | 6 | - | - | 16 | 5 | 15 | 7 |
| 1831 | 17 | 4 | 16 | 4 | - | - | 16 | 3 | 15 | 5 |

| YEARS | THROWN. | | RAW. | | DIFFERENCE. | |
|---|---|---|---|---|---|---|
| | *s.* | *d.* | *s.* | *d.* | *s.* | *d.* |
| 1819 | 34 | 5¼ | 27 | 6¾ | 6 | 10½ |
| 1820 | 24 | -½ | 19 | 2¾ | 4 | 9¾ |
| 1821 | 27 | 2½ | 20 | 6¼ | 6 | 8¼ |
| 1822 | 29 | 3¾ | 22 | 2¼ | 7 | 1½ |
| 1823 | 22 | 10¾ | 18 | 9¾ | 4 | 1 |
| 1824 | 23 | 8 | 18 | 3½ | 5 | 4½ |
| 1825 | 26 | 8½ | 20 | 6¼ | 6 | 2¼ |
| 1826 | 18 | 8½ | 17 | 11½ | – | 9 |
| | 21 | 2½ | 18 | 1½ | 3 | 1 |
| 1827 | 21 | 11½ | 19 | -¼ | 2 | 11¼ |
| 1828 | 22 | 7½ | 19 | 8¾ | 2 | 10¾ |
| 1829 | 19 | 9 | 16 | 3½ | 3 | 5½ |
| | 21 | 3 | 16 | 3½ | 4 | 11½ |
| 1830 | 19 | 1½ | 15 | 7 | 3 | 6½ |
| 1831 | 17 | 11¾ | 15 | 5 | 2 | 6¾ |

3540. It appears from that statement, that whereas in 1819 the Italian grower had 6*s.* 10½*d.*, his difference between the raw and the thrown, now he has only 2*s.* 6¾*d.*?—Just so.

3541. How do you account for that?—In 1819 the silk trade in this country was in comparative infancy, it was shortly after the war, during which the Continent was closed,

Mr.
*Thomas Brockwell.*
___
9 April,
1832.

closed, and the profits are very much reduced since; I mean to say that he gained money in that year; that the Italian throwster was very well satisfied with the prices in 1819.

3542. Do you think that the low price of Italian thrown silk has produced the low price of English thrown silk, or that the price of English thrown silk determines the price of Italian thrown silk?—The low price of Italian thrown silk acts upon the price of the British thrown silk.

3543. You do not think the price of English thrown silks acts upon the price of Italian thrown silk?—Certainly not.

3544. Can you suppose that the prices of 1830, the difference between 17 s. 4 d. and 23 s. 3 d. can continue in this country, and allow any profit to the throwster?—Yes, certainly.

3545. You consider that the 2 s. 6 d. will be sufficient?—Yes, he is satisfied with it.

3546. Then that difference may be expected to continue?—With the local advantages the Italian has, I question whether he could not continue this trade even with a greater reduction.

3547. Do you state that 3 s. was formerly the price of throwing and 2 s. 6 d. now?—Yes.

3548. And that the throwing in England is now 3 s. 9 d. for fine organzine, and 2 s. 6 d. for tram?—Yes.

3549. The difference you make between the expense of throwing fine organzine in England and Italy, is 1 s. 3 d.?—The 2 s. 6 d. in Italy is a remunerating price, now I very much doubt whether 3 s. 9 d. or 4 s. is a remunerating price to the throwster here, the 3 s. 9 d. is the price of depression, and 2 s. 6 d. in Italy is a price which satisfies the Italian.

3550. How do you know that?—I certainly know that the Italian is perfectly satisfied with 2 s. 6 d., and I know that the Englishman is not satisfied with 3 s. 9 d.; the British throwsters take the silk at any price to keep their mills going till they are ruined, whereas we have an increasing supply of Italian thrown silk to this country going on all the time.

3551. Then does the importation of foreign thrown silk reduce the price in the English market?—Unquestionably.

3552. Do you conceive that the prices the Italian silk has sold for in those years, has been a remunerating price to the Italian?—The Italian stands on a much better ground than the throwster in this country, because he has the raw material, and has an opportunity of selecting it for his mills; and although he may as a matter of calculation appear to lose sixpence or a shilling or even two shillings a lb. on the price of his thrown silk, yet from his power of selecting the raw on the spot, his local advantages are so great, that in effect he may be a gainer, and regulates himself accordingly; whereas at the same time the English throwster has to sell his thrown silk at a lower price to compete with the foreigner, and is obliged to give a higher price for the raw silk.

3553. If the Italian raw silk is 17 s. 6 d. in Italy, the thrown will be 20 s., 2 s. 6 d. being added?—Yes.

3554. Do you consider, that the Italian will throw his silk if he cannot obtain that 2 s. 6 d., will he not prefer sending the raw here to throwing it there?—No, I do not think he would.

3555. You think he would rather lose the advantage for the purpose of throwing it, than send the raw here?—That is not the way in which the trade works.

3556. Do the Italians retain their silk for sale at home, or consign it to England and other places for sale?—The greatest trade in Italy for silk is, perhaps, the execution of orders for France and Germany, the trade with England is chiefly on consignment, consequently by being chiefly on consignment, and the parties in Italy taking advances upon those consignments, in nine instances out of ten they regulate the price and limit the price.

3557. Does not your observation apply to thrown only?—To both.

3558. How can the German market affect the raw?—The proportion of raw silk is now diminishing in consequence of the increase of thrown silk, and as we find the one increase the other will diminish.

3559. The competition of Germany cannot affect the quantity of raw sent here?—Yes, it does, because they require a large quantity of thrown silk; in effect, acting against the throwsters in this country by lessening the supplies of raw.

3560. Have you not said, that the prices of raw silk will rise in this country as
compared

compared with thrown?—From scarcity, and not from profit upon buying and throwing them in England.

3561. Will not that bring, instead of the present quantity, a larger quantity to London, where the highest price will be given for the raw?—It may or it may not.

3562. If raw will produce a higher price in England than in Italy, will it not find its market here?—It may for the instant, but I have my doubts whether the price of raw silk can be maintained against a customer who is losing his money upon the thrown; that customer for the raw silk being positively dwindling by degrees in consequence of the competition with the foreigner.

3563. What is the capability of Italy to increase the cultivation of silk?—I do not reckon upon its capability to increase much, therefore I reduce the point to its present surplus, being about a million and a half; and as thrown silk increases in amount of importation into this country, the raws necessarily will be diminished.

3564. Do you mean, that the capability of Italy to increase the raw material is limited, while the capability of increasing the thrown is greater?—Decidedly so.

3565. And in that way you think the quantity of thrown silk may be increased to this country considerably if the duty was taken off?—Decidedly.

3566. Does the increased quantity of tram, which you have stated to have been produced of late years, arise from an increased quantity of tram in Italy, or does it arise from the tram manufactured in Italy not having found a market elsewhere, and been sent to England?—The tram imported into England is principally prepared for this market, and displaces so much raw silk, and goes towards the establishment of my argument, that it reduces the quantity of raw. I am sure that is the way the trade between Italy and England is now working, and to the prejudice of the English throwster.

3567. Is there a great increase in the importation of China silk?—A very large increase of late compared with former years.

---

*Mercurii, 11° die Aprilis, 1832.*

---

THE RIGHT HON. THE EARL GROSVENOR, in the Chair.

---

Mr. *Thomas Brockwell*, called in; and further Examined.

3568. IF the British throwster will throw silk at a less price than the Italian, must not that affect the price of Italian thrown silk in the British market?—It may affect it in a slight degree, but the large importations from Italy would shortly overwhelm the English throwster, and replace the Italian in his permanent state in the English market.

3569. Do you mean a large increased import of the raw or the thrown?—I mean of thrown silk.

3570. Do you contemplate that an increase can possibly take place of thrown silk from Italy, when there is no remunerating price for the thrown, the British underselling him here?—In appearance, by calculation, of the price perhaps there may be no remunerating price, or no profit; but the local advantages of the Italian are sufficient to keep the Italian in perfect hold of this market, with the duty of 3 s. 6 d. per lb.

3571. Do you think it possible, under any circumstances, that the British throwster can undersell the Italian throwster without producing absolute ruin to the business of the British throwster?—Certainly not.

3572. Will you state what are the advantages which the Italian possesses in throwing, over the English, which will enable him to undersell the British throwster?—I am to understand that to refer to local advantages, reeling his own silk, selecting the best kinds of others reeling for his own mills, assorting silk at the time of purchasing, and putting aside all which does not precisely correspond with the sample, in size as well as goodness, or making a second price for the objectionable part, less waste, and the raw silk retaining a quality upon it, advantageous to the price when thrown, a more intrinsic article when in organzine or tram, more uniform in size; more valuable to an intelligent manufacturer, because the thread has not been overstrained by speed; all those are advantages of no small importance in skilful hands; the Austrian government too lends him their aid, so far as to cede to

him

Mr.
*Thomas Brockwell.*

11 April,
1832.

him 5 *d.* per lb. below the duty charged upon the raw silk exported to other countries, the raw silk paying 10 *d.* a pound, and the thrown 5 *d.*

3573. Are not the raw and the thrown sold separately and distinctly from each other, and is there not a regular price for the raw in this country as well as in Italy?—Certainly there is; there is a difference of price, a man if he wishes to buy raw silk, makes his bargain in buying raw silk; if he wishes thrown he makes his bargain in buying thrown.

3574. Has not the British throwster the same advantage of buying raw silk as the foreign throwster?—Certainly not; if he was to reside in Italy he would have the same local advantages, but as he cannot bring those local advantages into England, he cannot have them.

3575. Does not a merchant who imports, endeavour to assort in equal qualities?—He is the man who sells it, it is a different thing for the man selling to assort, and the man buying to assort.

3576. Has not the British throwster an opportunity of buying equally good raw silk with the Italian throwster?—No.

3577. Why?—The Italian has all those advantages around him which the British throwster has not, or any one engaged in the silk trade residing in England, compared with any one in the silk trade residing in Italy.

3578. Is raw silk sent to this country on consignment by the Italian merchants chiefly, or purchased there by the British merchant on his own account to send here?—The trade in England is considered an agent's trade, but I believe there are parties here who buy silk in Italy, and import it into this country for sale.

3579. Do you ever buy?—No, never; we are brokers only.

3580. Do you know of any merchants who do?—I have seen a gentleman in this Committee who has imported raw silk.

3581. Is the major part of the raw silk consigned to England on commission, or purchased by merchants on their own account?—I am not able to tell; I think there is a great deal on joint account, a great deal of consignment, a great deal on their own account; brokers are not acquainted with those circumstances.

3582. Would the silk merchant in Italy sell to the British merchant either by consignment or otherwise, wherever he can get the best price?—I am not able to tell you.

3583. Can you have any doubt of it?—Yes, I have very many doubts upon this subject.

3584. Can you doubt whether a man will sell where he can get the best price?—I have many doubts upon the subject, because although high prices may have been quoted to Italy from England, the Italian may apprehend a disappointment.

3585. Do the bales of silk imported into this country always contain the same quality of silk throughout the whole bale?—No, very rarely.

3586. Is it necessary to assort the silk after it is imported?—The bales which come into this country contain a mixture which the trade are accustomed to see, and to pass over, which an Italian throwster would not think of doing, and that is one of the advantages an Italian has in buying silk, and assorting it; that is one of the disadvantages of the English throwster being obliged to buy in this country, and one of the advantages which the Italian has of being able to select his raw silk at home.

3587. You mean to say that the Italian has an obvious advantage in the selection of the silks the best suited for his purpose?—Unquestionably; and every man who has resided in Italy, and has had any experience of the subject, knows it to be the case.

3588. You mean to say the inferior qualities are sent to this country after he has made his selection?—In nine instances out of ten.

3589. Are not many sorts of silk worked with less waste than others?—In respect of waste, there is a very great local advantage to the Italian, and I have placed that as one, perhaps I have not placed it so conspicuously as it might be placed; it perhaps might arrive in some instances to a very apparent difference in favour of the Italian.

3590. The Italian, in his selection, pays a particular attention to the taking such silks as are not subject to great waste?—Of course.

3591. And that gives him the advantage?—That gives him a great advantage; I should consider the present duty of 3*s.* 6 *d.* per lb. about an equivalent to the local advantages I have enumerated.

3592. There are some silks sent here on consignment, are there not?—Yes.

3593. You

Mr.
*Thomas Brockwell.*

11 April,
1832.

3593. You say sometimes they are sent on joint account ?—Yes.

3594. You mean that the person consigning, and the merchant here, divide the profit?—Yes, they divide the profit or share the loss; sole account is the man in Italy sending it here on consignment, or the party whom I have referred to, importing it on his own account.

3595. Do you consider that we get from Italy any great proportion of their best quality silks ?—No, a very small proportion from the throwing districts.

3596. Taking the whole import from Italy into this country, do you consider that a great proportion is of inferior quality as far as regards Italian silks?—Of inferior quality; the Italian naturally reserves until the last period of the year, until the new reeling begins, his best silk, not knowing but he may have demands for it for the various markets of the Continent, in thrown.

3597. What effect would the reduction of duty on thrown silk have upon the price of Italian raw silk?—It would advance the price of raw silk in this market.

3598. Would it diminish the quantity?—Decidedly, it would diminish the quantity, one thing bearing on the other.

3599. Do you mean to say that if the price of raw silk in England should rise nigher in proportion to what it now is, the supply would be decreased?—If the duty upon thrown silks remained the same as it is now, it depends upon the protection given to the throwster.

3600. Supposing the duty taken off, and the price of raw silk to increase, would the supply notwithstanding that, decrease?—It would be destroyed; the Italians would have the whole of the throwing trade in their own hands, if the duty on thrown silk were reduced; but little would be here, and that would unquestionably be very dear.

3601. What is the average difference between the same quality of Italian silk, raw and thrown; take the quality of Bergamo?—We are not accustomed to see in England the best qualities of Bergamo, and we are accustomed to see the best qualities of thrown.

3602. Are you able to state what is the average difference between the same quality of Italian raw silk and thrown?—We can buy in this country a raw silk at 17 s. 6 d. per pound; the cost of throwing that silk I have stated to be 3 s. 9 d. a pound.

3603. The question applies not to the component parts, but to the price at which they are selling in this market?—This being regulated by the quantity of raw and the quantity of thrown, we now find that raw silks of the most accredited throwing districts of Italy are very scarce, whereas the thrown silk from the same districts is not so scarce, consequently the prices do not bear the relative proportion; to illustrate this, I will state, that to-day a man must give 18 s. per pound for a good pound weight of Italian raw silk, and a throwster would be obliged to give that price; but he might go into a merchant's warehouse, and buy a better article in organzine foreign thrown for 22 s. 3 d. or 22 s. 6 d., which shall have paid the duty of 3 s. 6 d. a pound.

3604. You have stated that the best silk is worked up into organzine, in Italy?—Yes a proportion, not the whole.

3605. And that, generally speaking, the worst raw is sent here?—Yes, decidedly.

3606. You mean to say that the difference between the best Italian thrown in this country, and the indifferent raw silks which come from Italy, is only 4 s. 3 d. or 4 s. 6 d. per lb. ?—That would be the exact difference to-day.

3607. Out of that 22 s. 3 d., what has been paid for duty?—Three shillings and sixpence.

3608. Then the difference between the price of the thrown, and the duty taken off, is exactly nine-pence?—Yes.

3609. Do you consider that the nine-pence can pay the throwster in Italy?—In this way it pays him; as I stated in a preceding answer, that I consider the present duty of 3 s. 6 d. per pound, about an equivalent for the local advantages of the Italian over the English throwster; consequently the Italian having all those local advantages, which I believe I have explained, he may in appearance lose nine-pence per pound by those comparative prices, and continue his trade and be satisfied.

3610. Is it not more probable that the Italian throwster in that case suffers?—No; I should not think he suffers, because he sends us his raw.

3611. Do you mean to say that the Italian throwster will continue to send to this country thrown silk, and sell it here at only nine-pence more than the raw silk?—I think it very likely, having in hand all those local advantages.

678.

3612. Do

Mr.
*Thomas Brockwell.*

11 April,
1832.

3612. Do you mean to say that he generally sells for only nine-pence a pound more ?—No, I am only stating that which is the case this very day.

3613. Is that the rule, or the exception?—It is the exception, for I have given averages which show a different result.

3614. Do you mean to say that Italian silks generally are or will be exported to this country, with that difference of nine-pence only ?—No.

3615. You have stated that large quantities of the seven millions of thrown are sent to Germany, France, and other countries, are you able to state the relative difference of price between the same quality of silk in France and here ?—No, I am not able to state the prices comparatively between foreign countries.

3616. Are the Committee to understand that thrown silk, of the same quality, is sent to England, as to Germany and other places ?—I should think that Germany takes a proportion of the same kind of silk which comes into this country, and every country consumes partially a different style of thrown silk.

3617. Are you able to state the difference of price between thrown and raw silks in France ?—No, I am not.

3618. You do not know whether the proportion which you have now stated to prevail here holds at this moment in any part of the Continent ?—I do not.

3619. How do you explain the opinion you have given, that if the duty is taken off organzine, the raw will decrease, and the thrown will be increased ?—I find that in 1824 and 1825 the importations of raw silk averaged 6,286 bales, and thrown silk averaged 2,491 bales ; in 1827 and 1828, the averaged importation of raws was 5,872 bales, and of thrown 2,092 bales; in 1830 and 1831, the averaged importations of raw were 4,171 bales, and of thrown 2,278 bales, which show, that in 1824 and 1825, the proportion between raw and thrown was 152 per cent. more raws than thrown ; in 1827 and 1828, 180 per cent. more raws than thrown ; and in 1830 and 1831, only 85 per cent. more raws than thrown.

3620. Is not the weight of a bale of silk more now than it was in the year 1824 ? —It might be in some instances a little more now than formerly.

3621. Do you not know how much it is ?—I do not believe anybody can tell.

3622. Do they vary?—They vary in some degree, but on reference, the bale for any one year will bear an equal reference to the bale or bales for other years ; it will not make a difference of five per cent. in the weight.

3623. Does the weight of the bale the same year apply in an equal degree to the thrown and to the raw?—No, I do not know that it does ; but I will explain my position by figures, in pounds weight, which will perhaps put aside anything like the inquiry of the weight of a bale.

3624. Will you state what was the proportion of raw to thrown in 1826?—My object has been to put aside those years in which the changes of the duty have taken place, considering that a fairer way to arrive at the information.

3625. Do you not consider that it would be fairer to take a larger average for the importations ?—I think it would be unfair to mix up those years in which the changes in the duty were made. In the year 1826, there were imported of Italian raw, 1,590 bales ; and 849 bales of thrown.

3626. What per centage is that?—I will give, if it is wished, the amount in pounds weight.

3627. Will you state what are the comparative importation and consumption of foreign thrown silk in the respective years, averaged for the 14 s. 8 d. duty, the 5 s. duty, and the 3 s. 6 d. duty?—I will begin at the year 1819, and end with the year 1823 ; the average importation for those five years is 368,000 lbs. weight, and the average consumption is 350,000 lbs. weight during the 14 s. 8 d. duty.

3628. Can you state the amount in 1825, when the 7 s. 6 d. duty prevailed?— The year 1825, which was the year of 7 s. 6 d. duty, the importation was 777,529 lbs. and the consumption was 559,642 lbs., showing, immediately that the duty was reduced from 14 s. 8 d. to 7 s. 6 d., how the Italian increased his exportation to this country even by that reduction.

3629. It appears by the returns, that in the year 1826, when the duty was changed to 5 s. the amount imported was 177,405 lbs. consumed 289,325 ; will you state what were the quantities in the succeeding years ?—The average importation for the two years 1827 and 1828, was 486,310 lbs., and the consumption 420,000 lbs., that was during the 5 s. per pound duty.

3630. It appears that in 1829, when the duty of 3 s. 6 d. commenced, the quantity imported was 211,179 lbs., consumed 172,239 lbs., will you state the amount in 1830 and 1831 ?—In 1830 and 1831, when the duty was working effectually,
the

Mr.
*Thomas Brockwell.*

11 April,
1832.

the average importation amounts to 522,000 lbs. of thrown, and the consumption to 475,400 lbs., showing in the result, that during the 14 s. 8 d. duty, the consumption of thrown silk was about 350,000 lbs. per year, during the 5 s. duty, 420,000 lbs. per year, and during the 3 s. 6 d. duty, 475,000 lbs. a year.

3631. If you take the years 1825, 1826 and 1827, and the years 1829, 1830 and 1831, are not the averages nearly the same?—I have not taken it that way, conceiving that not the way of reasoning on the duties, those being years of change.

3632. Knowing the great changes which have taken place in the silk trade, do you think you should take any one year?—No.

3633. Would it not be better to take five years?—If there had been five years where they had been working on the same duty, I should say so, but that is not the case.

3634. If it should appear that there is very little more consumed in the three years at the 3 s. 6 d. duty than there was in the three years at the 7 s. 6 d. duty, how will you support your opinion, that if the duty was taken off, the quantity would increase?—I think my opinion is sufficiently supported, even by seeing what I see every day; I produce these figures to reason with men who do not see what I see.

3635. You were understood to put these figures forward as facts?—Yes, and I put them forward to show how the trade is working between Italy and England.

3636. Do you found the opinion you have given, that if the duty were taken off, the quantity would increase upon those quantities of imports and consumptions you have given?—They are founded on these facts of imports, connected with the daily experience I have had in the silk trade in Italy and in England, one thing confirming another.

3637. You have spoken of the advantages of Italy in throwing, have you visited the mills there?—I have seen many mills in Italy.

3638. Are they like the Derby mills, or like the Manchester mills?—I do not understand mills or machinery, I think there will be some persons better able to give opinions upon them; I have been connected with the silk trade, and can give mercantile opinions, but I had rather not give an opinion on mills and machinery.

3639. You have entered into the advantages which the Italian has in Italy, is that from inspection?—I have been interested in the reeling of silk very frequently.

3640. Have you never examined mills?—I have seen many mills; but not being a man of mechanical genius, I had rather not go into questions of the comparative excellence of mills in one country and another.

3641. Are the mills in Italy better for throwing than the new mills in England?—My opinion is, that we can throw silk in this country as well as in any country in the world; I can judge of thrown silk when I see it, and I have seen as good thrown silk in this country as I have ever seen in Piedmont.

3642. Are the mills better?—I repeat, that I am not able to give an opinion on the different construction of mills, but one thing I am convinced of, that the English mill can produce an organzine silk as good as I have ever seen an organzine silk of Italy.

2643. You come to the opinion, that the throwsters would be entirely ruined here by importations of thrown silk, if the duty was reduced?—Certainly, they would.

3644. If they can throw better in England, might they not throw cheaper also?—I maintain that they can throw as well if you give them the silk, but that must be produced as cheap to them, and be remunerative, which is the very question we are at issue upon.

3645. Can the labour in this country be reduced as low as in Italy?—I should think not, they cannot live so cheaply in this country.

3646. Do you know for what tram can be thrown in England, exclusive of waste?—I have stated 2 s. 6 d. a pound, and I understand that is not a remunerating price to the throwster here; but I repeat, that questions of price will be better answered by throwsters; I find that the throwsters are ruining themselves upon these prices, the Italian is getting forward.

3647. How can you form an opinion which will throw the silk cheapest if you do not know what they cost?—I stated that the Italian was satisfied with half a crown a pound, and the English was not satisfied with 3 s. 9 d. per lb. for fine organzine.

3648. Are you aware that tram is thrown here for 2 s.?—I cannot say I know that; throwsters will take throwing at any price to keep their mills going, but

678.                                                          I must

Mr.
*Thomas Brockwell.*

11 April,
1832.

I must disbelieve many men to suppose that others make it worth their while to take tram at 2 s. a pound.

3649. If tram can be thrown here from 1 s. 8 d. to 2 s. per lb. do you consider it necessary to continue the present duty which you say ought to be continued or rather increased ?—I do not believe tram can be thrown at 1 s. 8 d. to 2 s. per lb.

3650. In reference to an answer you gave to a former question, that tram cannot be thrown in England at 2 s. with a remuneration to the throwster, is it your opinion that a duty of 3 s. should be laid on to protect him ?—Decidedly so, to equalize the advantages which I conceive the Italian throwster has, and which I enumerated in a former part of my evidence ; I see the English throwster ruined by taking the prices they are taking. I was not aware that tram was taken at 2 s. a pound ; this is a lower price than I have known it reduced to.

3651. Is the opinion you have now given, that the British throwster cannot come into competition with the Italian, founded on your having seen a great many English throwsters ruined ?—Having heard of their ruin.

3652. Do you found it upon that alone ?—No ; I state that the local advantages of the Italian constitute every thing ; I give my opinion founded on an experience of eight or nine years in Italy, and I am not aware that there is any man in England who has had so many opportunities of knowing the various bearings of the subject.

3653. Do not you know that labour is lower in Italy than here ?—Of course it is, 2 s. 6 d. per lb. being the price which compensates the Italian for organzine, and 3 s. 9 d. not being the price which compensates the English throwster.

3654. You are understood to have said, that you think the Italian can throw the silk cheaper in consequence of the local advantages which he possesses, and among those local advantages you say labour is one ?—No ; I have never mentioned labour in those local advantages. I consider, and I repeat, that 3 s. 6 d. per lb., which is the present duty on organzine, may be esteemed or regarded as about an equivalent to those local advantages ; and if I was to suggest the additional duty to be placed upon thrown silk, it is just that difference between the present 2 s. 6 d. per lb., and at what the British throwster can afford to throw his silk. I should then put the 3 s. 6 d. per lb. (present duty) by the side of the local advantages possessed by the Italian, which I have enumerated, and which I conscientiously think equal to 3 s. 6 d. per lb., and adding to this 3 s. 6 d. the difference of cost of throwing between the two countries, I should fix that as the future duty. Its being otherwise accounts for the Italian carrying on trade in this country apparently losing, but really gaining.

3655. You have given your opinion, that 3 s. 9 d. would give a profit to the English throwster in this country ?—No ; I say that 2 s. 6 d. a lb. compensates the Italian throwster, and 3 s. 9 d. per lb. does not compensate the English throwster.

3656. What do you think would compensate the English throwster ?—I conscientiously think he would have a difficulty to contend against 5 s. per lb. for organzine, and 3 s. per lb. for tram in the very fine sizes of Italian silk which comes from abroad, and would find, at times, that 5 s. per lb. would not be a sufficient protection for him.

3657. Do you mean the old mills at Derby or the new mills, such as have been erected by Mr. Grant and Mr. Royle ?—I apply to the best machinery in the country ; I think it would be very unfair to tax any manufacture to give protection to very bad machinery.

3658. Have you ever had put into your hand a statement by any of the mill owners what are their expenses of throwing ?—I have seen a statement which shows that a good raw silk, and an inferior raw silk, or a middling sort of raw silk, shall make a difference of 9 d. or a 1 s. per lb. in the throwing of it.

3659. Which of the raw silks do you apply your observations to as most beneficial for the English throwster ?—I am supposing 5 s. per lb. duty would produce a larger importation of raw silk, which importation of raw silk should be of a better kind, and the throwster would find his benefit in having excellent raw silk.

3660. You have stated that the price of silk gives a difference of only 4 s. 3 d. ; how do you reconcile the fact, that the English throwster should buy raw silk at 18 s. and expend 5 s. upon it, how would the prices then correspond, at what would he then be able to sell it ?—Those are questions formed on the incongruities trade which perpetually occur.

3661. Is

Mr.
*Thomas Brockwell.*

11 April,
1832.

3661. Is not the Fossembrone silk, which comes to this country, of very good quality ?—Yes, it is.

3662. Is the whole of that sent to England ?—The greater part of it is sent to England.

3663. Some comes in the thrown state, does it not ?—No.

3664. If the duty on thrown silk were taken off, do you think that would continue to be sent ?—Fossembrone, at present, having no throwing mills, and having been accustomed for so many years to send her raw silk to this country, I have no doubt that will be the last raw silk which we should find retained in Italy ; but as it is decidedly good silk, the Italians, by having a greater trade in thrown silk would direct themselves into this market during the fairs of Sinegalia, and procure it for their throwing mills, consequently that would tend ultimately to deprive this country of that supply of raw silk (small as it is) which at present comes to England.

3665. That is peculiarly valuable, is it not ?—It is rendered so in this country because it is our habit, but the Piedmontese prefer their own, and so do I.

3666. When it is thrown in this country is it not considered superior to the Piedmontese organzine ?—I think it is for various purposes. Fossembrone silk will take a peculiar white in the dye, which renders it valuable, but I think it is more from that peculiarity than from the intrinsic value, for the Piedmont raw silk is very much more even and more intrinsically valuable, in my estimation, than any other silk.

3667. Still in general estimation it has a peculiarity which renders it valuable ? —Yes ; trade having formed itself upon that particular silk, not having the Piedmontese raw silks in this country ; but it is my opinion if we had a large supply of Piedmontese raw silk here, Fossembrone would fall considerably in the scale of value.

3668. Is it not your opinion that the importation of thrown silk would have materially increased at the different periods of the reductions of duty, had it not been for the circumstance, that such importation has been checked by ruinous reduction on the part of the English throwster, both as to his charge for throwing and in the wages of the persons employed ?—I think there is no question that when the English throwster is so pressed as he has been in those particular years it has been destruction to him, and the Italian has kept a little back in his supplies, but then he comes forth again with overwhelming quantities, and I am convinced in my own mind, that he is pursuing a profitable trade, though he appears by figures to be losing money.

3669. Is it your opinion that the importation has been checked by distress amounting almost to ruin at those particular periods ?—Yes.

3670. Do you conceive there would be a very extensive increase to the importation of Italian thrown silks ? —Very great.

3671. You say that the importation of raw silk has been checked at particular periods by the state of the British throwster ; do you mean by that that the price of thrown silk has been reduced in this market by the competition of the English throwster ?—At certain times I have no doubt the ruin of the English throwsters have had the effect of showing that the Italian had much better abstain for a few months from supplies of either raw or thrown.

3672. The question does not apply to ruin, but to the prices at which thrown silk could be supplied by the British throwster at those periods ?—A competition, founded upon equalization of price, I am perfectly persuaded the Italian will never fly from, but it is a competition of desperation which he certainly at times will allow to go on for a certain period of months, and keep his raw and his throwns, and it will appear in a small year of importation, the raw and the thrown will be proportionate.

3673. Was it not therefore the competition in price by the British throwster that prevented the increase of import of Italian thrown ?—At various times I have no doubt it is so.

3674. Do you not know that at particular times the English throwster, in order to keep his mills going and employ his men, has so reduced his prices and the wages of those men, that it has had the effect of preventing the importation of foreign thrown silk ?—Such causes I have observed to produce such effects.

3675. That accounts probably for the small importations of silk at particular periods?—There is no doubt of that.

3676. During the last ten years has the quality of raw silk from Italy

678.                                                                 improved ?

improved ?—I have been about four years a broker in England, and I rarely see Italian raw silk which pleases me, although I see the greater part of the importations into the country, but in the preceding seven years I was in Italy, and very frequently sent from Italy at those times the best raw silk.

3677. Has the raw silk lately been better than what was formerly imported ?—Certainly not, from throwing districts.

3678. From Italy generally ?—No, from Fossembrone perhaps, and from Naples also, some little improvement has taken place.

3679. In what has that improvement been ?—A more even silk generally, but silk of these districts forms a small proportion of the great mass of raw silk. I think Trent and Friuli also have improved their reeling of silk.

3680. Are you aware whether the expense of throwing good silk is greater than of inferior silk?—I think I have answered that question by stating that I have seen accounts of a throwing mill where the price has been perhaps nearly 1 s. a pound in favour of good over indifferent sorts of raw silk.

3681. Can you state the average pecuniary earnings of operatives in Italy ?—No; but I know that the throwster, taking it in a mercantile view, is compensated with 2 s. 6 d. a pound, and continues the trade.

3682. You consider the Italian as invariably keeping the best silk at home for his own throwing?—Yes.

3683. Is not another advantage that the new silk winds better ?—No doubt; and that forms a part of the local advantages belonging to the item of less waste.

3684. If the duty were taken off foreign thrown silk, do you mean that in this market there will be less or more difference between the price of raw and the price of thrown, than there is now after deducting the duty now paid on the thrown silk ? —I should think that the thrown silk, if the duty was taken off, would be quite or nearly the price it now is, the raw silk would rise the difference, and there would eventually be about that difference between the raw and the thrown determined upon by the Italian.

3685. Supposing the price of raw silk to be now 17 s. a pound, and thrown silk of the same sort 23 s. 6 d., if the duty of 3 s. 6 d. were to be repealed, the latter ought to be sold at 20 s.; but will it be sold for more than that, or may it not happen that the thrown silk will still sell for 23 s. 6 d. though the 3 s. 6 d. duty may have been repealed ?—I think I have already answered that question.

3686. That is what you mean when you say that raw silk will rise, the Italian getting nearly all the advantage of that repeal ?—There is no question about that in my mind.

3687. Do you conceive that the throwster, and his operatives, are now at the lowest point in respect of the remuneration of wages?—I think the distress we perceive and hear of in all the throwing districts, is quite enough to answer that question.

3688. In case of a greater reduction of duty, would not the importation of thrown silk greatly increase, and the destruction of the English throwster, and the distress of his work people, be consequently completed?—I am of opinion, that if the duty on raw silk is taken off, the largest mills and the greatest capital in the country will be taken out of the trade.

3689. Which, in your opinion, is the most likely way to obtain a large supply of the best Italian raw silk for the use of the English mills, by taking off the duty on thrown silk, or by leaving a considerable duty thereon?—By increasing the present duties.

3690. Has there been a great increase in the importation of China and Turkey silk ?—Turkey silk has greatly increased in the amount of imports into this country ; for instance, preceding the reduction of the duties, the average for the last five years, namely, 1819 to 1823, was only 955 bales, increased in the average of 1824 to 1826 to 1,492 bales, and since going on at the average rate of 2,500 bales ; as concerns China silk, the average from 1827 to 1829 exceeds the average from 1824 to 1826 by 48 per cent., and the average of the two last years, 1830 and 1831, exceeds the preceding average by another 25 per cent.

3691. Has there been so great an increase upon the import from Bengal?—Not so great.

3692. Taking the Bengal, Turkey and China together, there has been a great increase?—Yes.

3693. Is that likely to continue ?—Putting aside Bengal, I should think so ; there are no throwing mills in those countries ; though we see those amounts placed

Mr.
*Thomas Brockwell.*

11 April,
1832.

*en masse*, as raw silk coming into this country, and without journalizing the Italian silk, from this great mass of raw silk, the country generally is inclined to believe that so long as the amount of importation is large, the British throwster must be doing well.

3694. There has been a great increase of waste silk, has there not?—There has been a very large increase of Italian waste silk.

3695. Has there been within the last six months?—No.

3696. How are the China, and Turkey, and waste silk generally applied; on what description of articles?—That would be more a question for the manufacturer; I do not feel myself competent to say how the various descriptions of silk are applied beyond this, that I think the very large importations of China silk, which have given rise to a large manufacture at Manchester, certainly create a great necessity for a large importation of the best kinds of Italian raw silk to work up with that China silk, and that I apprehend, unless the throwster is protected by the rate of duties to introduce into this country a large supply of the best raw silks of Italy, the manufactures of Manchester will experience in a very few months a very serious inconvenience, because that manufacture is founded principally upon China silk from which they make organzine, and to work up which they require the best kinds of Italian raw silk, to throw by their own mills, into tram.

3697. You think that has given rise to a great part of the goods manufactured at Manchester?—I consider that the trade at Manchester is a new trade that has taken its foundation upon China and other silks.

3698. The use of coarser silks will require the finer to be mixed in certain proportions?—That is my opinion.

3699. They are greatly aided in the manufacture at Manchester by having the bounty of 3 s. 6 d., are they not?—Of course the trade at Manchester is very materially formed for an export trade, and the debenture is a very valuable consideration for them; indeed without the debenture there would be no export trade.

3700. They use a great deal of waste silk there, do they not?—I believe they do.

3701. Do you know the price per pound when manufactured?—No, I do not; the application of waste silk, to manufacture in this country, has increased in a very great degree since the debenture has been attached to thrown silk.

3702. If the raw waste is bought at 3 s. 6 d. or 4 s. per lb. and it receives a bounty by reason of this debenture, that must give a very preponderating advantage?—Without the debenture no export trade could have existed to any extent in this country; a drawback must have been given in form of debenture, or there must have been a fund for the purpose.

3703. Mr. Hume, of the Custom House, having stated that there can be no trade without that, you concur in that opinion?—Yes, decidedly.

3704. Do you buy debentures for a house in Manchester, who export?—We buy some for Manchester; but our largest purchases of debentures are for houses not Manchester houses.

3705. There are shipping houses in town who buy those debentures, and they order the goods from Manchester to export, in order to receive the drawback?—Yes; supposing an agent has a thousand weight of debentures from the Custom House here, he lodges those debentures, and he opens a credit, similar to a banking credit, at the Custom House at any out-port, and in making the sale of goods he gives an order to pass those goods through those respective Custom Houses, and to debit them with so much weight on his account, he having deposited so many debentures.

3706. From whence does the waste silk come principally?—From the throwing districts of Italy.

3707. Is there any from Turkey?—No, there is a different kind of waste; there may be knubs and cocoons, and so on; but throwing waste comes from the throwing countries.

3708. What are the kinds of waste which are imported?—There is waste in reeling silk, there is waste from the bur and the husk, and all kinds of waste; but that which I consider referred to, as having established a branch of manufacture, is the throwing waste.

3709. When was that first introduced into this country?—It has always come into this country ever since I can remember; but it was on a very high duty at one period. I think duty was paid last year on 700,000 weight of waste. In 1828 the waste was 238,088 lbs. In 1829 it was 163,465 lbs. In 1830 it was 490,980 lbs., and in 1831 it was 705,330 lbs.

3710. What

3710. What was it in 1819?—Seventy-seven thousand eight hundred lbs.

3711. Do not you think the principal inducement to go into that trade is the opportunity of obtaining the debentures?—If there is any branch of manufacture where the material is a cheap one, and there is a large drawback upon it, there is no doubt but that manufacture will rise upon such a protection.

3712. Did not the imports of foreign thrown silk greatly increase in the years 1830 and 1831, after the duty had been reduced from 5 *s.* to 3 *s.* 6 *d.* in 1829?—Certainly; and if the duty remains as it is, the Italian having hold of the throwing trade, will become more and more conspicuous.

3713. Are you not aware, that the peculiar state of the Continent, in the last two years, has thrown a larger quantity of that silk into England than would otherwise have come?—The peculiar state of the Continent may at one time have had that effect; but it has righted itself, and the consumption of silk has gone on in the interim, and, at the present time, the market is very bare of Italian silk, it having been consumed.

3714. During the last two years has not the price been very low?—Very low.

3715. Are you not aware, that the state of Europe, from disease and otherwise, has taken off a less quantity than usual, and that a larger quantity has come here in consequence?—No, I do not think so; for though at the period we had a large quantity, the manufacturers on the Continent are going on consuming, and the trade in England is now at a loss for good Italian raw silk at a moderate price.

3716. The duty was first reduced in 1824, was it not, from 14 *s.* 8 *d.* to 7 *s.* 6 *d.*, that was not immediately followed by a large importation, but it was in 1826, when the Italian had time to prepare his consignment?—No; in 1825 there was a large importation from Italy.

3717. The Italian is not in a situation always to avail himself of reduction within a month?—No; if the duty was wholly taken off, the stock of silk is so small in Italy there could not be a large supply for several months, but then it would come.

3718. Do you mean to say that Italy is barer of silk now than usual?—Yes.

3719. How long has that been the case?—It is becoming less every week now, until they have a fresh supply from their new Raccoltà.

3720. What was their stock last year?—I am not able to say.

3721. Was not it a very large stock?—No, I think not above the average.

3722. Notwithstanding the state of Europe the last two years, the stock of silk in Italy is now lower than usual?—I understand it is very low at present.

---

*Mercurii*, 18° *die Aprilis*, 1832.

## THE RIGHT HON. THE EARL GROSVENOR, in the Chair.

Mr. *Lamech Swift*, called in; and Examined.

3723. YOU are a silk throwster?—I am.

3724. Where do you carry on your business?—At Milverton, in the county of Somerset, and at Church Stanton, in the county of Devon.

3725. How many years have you been engaged in the throwing of silk?—Upwards of thirty years; my father was a silk throwster and brought me up in his own business.

3726. In what part of England?—At Derby; my father occupied the mill erected by Sir Thomas Lombe, which was the first mill built in England for throwing organzine; Sir Thomas brought from Italy the models for the machinery for which he had at first a patent, and afterwards a sum of 14,000 *l.* was voted him by Parliament, so anxious was the government of that day to render the silk manufacture of England independent of Italy for thrown silk, which seems to me a much wiser policy than that pursued by the present government, whose wish seems to be to destroy that throwing trade which so much pains had been taken to introduce, and to make us again dependent on Italy for Italian thrown silk.

3727. How long have you occupied your present mills?—I entered upon the mill at Milverton in 1819, and upon that at Church Stanton in 1822.

3728. Did you build the mills?—I did not; the one at Milverton was already fitted up with machinery, which I took from parties in London, the other at Church
Stanton

Mr
*Lamech Swift.*

18 April,
1832.

Stanton had been a clothing factory, and I adapted it to the silk throwing; but it has never been thoroughly completed with machinery, because, before I had time to complete it, the operation of 1824 alarmed me, and I ceased putting in machinery, so that it has never been fully set going to the present hour.

3729. Your mills are entirely worked by water?—Entirely.

3730. Is the machinery in your mills on the most improved principles?—I have been gradually improving my machinery since 1822, and I consider it now as good as any in the kingdom. I have had some from Manchester upon the principle of machinery used in the throwing mills there, but I consider it to be no improvement at all, and decidedly prefer my own; I am quite sure that Manchester has no superiority in this branch of the trade over the West of England, and that I can throw silk quite as cheap as any body at Manchester can; and I beg leave to add, that silk is now frequently sent into the West of England from Manchester to be thrown for the use of the Manchester manufacturer.

3731. What description of silk is sent from Manchester to be thrown?—I believe mostly Italian, but as I have not thrown any myself for Manchester, I cannot speak with so much certainty.

3732. Any China?—I am not aware; as I have not thrown any for Manchester myself, I cannot say what they receive, but I know that silk comes from Manchester to the West of England to be thrown.

3733. To what mills does it come?—To some mills within three or four miles of me, some comes I know to Taunton and to the neighbourhood of Taunton, Mr. Jones of Taunton I know has received some from Manchester.

3734. In what year?—Within the last twelve months.

3735. Do you throw silk on your own account, or for other persons?—Not on my own account; I receive raw silk from manufacturers in London, Coventry and other places, and throw it for them; I certainly have tried the working of silk on my own account, and have suffered most severely from it, and have therefore discontinued it.

3736. What description of silk do you chiefly throw?—Chiefly fine Italian silks, I throw them into organzine and into tram, the proportions of each vary according to circumstances.

3737. Do you throw any Bengal or China?—I throw a little occasionally, my connection is with that class of manufacturers, who chiefly use Italian silks.

3738. Were your mills fully employed previous to 1826?—They were; I at that time employed about 300 hands, and had about 5,500 spindles constantly at work.

3739. Are they fully employed at present?—No, by no means, more than half of the spindles have been standing for the last twelve months, and for two months of that time I had not one of them at work, and during the last twelve months I have been able to employ only about sixty hands, and those occasionally have been limited to three and four days a week.

3740. To what do you attribute the difference between the present and the former state of your trade?—To the low prices of thrown silk in this market, occasioned by the reduction of the duty on foreign thrown organzine from 5 s. to 3 s. 6 d. and on foreign thrown tram from 3 s. to 2 s. which took place in 1829, and to the great influx also of foreign silk goods.

3741. Are the prices charged for throwing much lower now than they were?— Yes, considerably, especially since the last reduction in 1829, and are such as by no means remunerate the throwster.

3742. Have you lost by continuing to carry on your business, and employ your hands?—Yes, I have very seriously lost.

3743. What is the average of the wages you pay your hands?—I cannot speak positively to that point, but I think it is between 2 s. 6 d. and 2 s. 9 d., I have them from 15 d. to 5 s., and I think it does average from 2 s. 6 d. to 2 s. 9 d. per week of six days.

3744. Persons of what age?—I have them from eight or nine years of age upwards, till they get married and leave me.

3745. They are chiefly females?—Entirely so.

3746. That is the average when they are in full work, at the common labour of six days to the week?—Yes.

3747. What used those wages to be?—We had then a greater proportion of higher priced hands than we have at the present moment, and therefore the average

678.

would

Mr.
*Lamech Swift.*

18 April,
1832.

would have run higher; the same childen who now have 15 *d.* per week, would have had 1 *s.* 6 *d.* or 1 *s.* 9 *d.* formerly.

3748. Give the lowest and the highest you used to pay formerly ?—We used to go as high as 6 *s.*

3749. For the same quantity of work which they now do, what were the wages in 1826?—Our wages were so low, we have not been able to reduce them sufficiently to meet the times, and therefore we have increased the work.

3750. They do now more work than they did in 1826?—Decidedly.

3751. How many hours did they work in 1826?—Our working hours were the same then as they are now, when fully employed, eleven hours and a quarter a day.

3752. How do you mean that they work double now?—Because we have speeded the machinery much faster, and have made them look after a greater quantity; the time is from six in the morning to seven in the evening in summer, giving them three quarters of an hour for breakfast, and one hour for dinner out of that time.

3753. The greater quantity of work they now do is done by the improvement of machinery, and by their attending to a greater quantity of machinery, not by working a greater number of hours?—We do not work a greater number of hours, but they have more work to attend to.

3754. The speed of your machinery is increased?—Yes.

3755. By which, in the same number of hours, a greater quantity of silk is thrown off?—Certainly.

3756. In what degree is the labour increased by the additional work given?—They are obliged to give greater attention to it, and cannot rest between; the labour is incessant, because the machinery going with that velocity, they are subjected to a constant attendance upon it.

3757. From the increased velocity of the machinery, the threads are more continually breaking, and they are constantly employed to tie them up?—Yes, they had before an opportunity of sitting down.

3758. Is the staple of the silk you receive now, improved?—Not at all, some of the East India silks were of better quality than they are at present.

3759. How is it with respect to the Italian?—We do not get better Italian than we used to; I have not of late worked so much of the East India silks as I did when at Derby, I cannot speak therefore with so much certainty as to that, as I could with respect to the Italian.

3760. You do not conceive the Italian silk you received improved in quality?—Not at all, that I have been in the habit of receiving.

3761. Can you state of what growth the silk you receive is?—I have all descriptions, but not being a purchaser, I do not know the names they go by, but I know the Fossembrone from the Bergam or Piedmont; we have silk that will waste two or three per cent., and we have silks that will make 20 per cent. waste. A few months back I received some Italian silk from London, being very much distressed to employ my people, and after working about 20 or 30 lbs. of it I returned the bale to London, and sent all my people home; if I had gone on I should have lost from 30 *l.* or 40 *l.* in working that bale, from the quality turning out so bad.

3762. Did you ascertain what kind of silk that was?—It was a silk reeled in imitation of Novi, it was a very inferior Genoese silk, that was got up in imitation of the Novi silks; it was not a white one, it is in a similar proportion to silk reeled in Ancona, in imitation of the real Fossembrone, one is superior to the other.

3763. Do you think, that by any improvement in machinery, by reducing still lower the wages of the hands, or any other means, it will be possible for the English throwster still further to reduce his charges for throwing?—No, I do not think it possible; the wages are so low, that to reduce them still lower is quite out of the question.

3764. Under these circumstances, do you think if the import duty on foreign thrown silk should be taken off, an English throwster of Italian silk will be able to carry on his business?—I have no doubt it would cause the ruin of many throwsters, for I do not conceive it possible to bring down the charges of throwing any lower than they are at present. I would in explanation of that say, that there are many charges of throwing that we cannot, by possibility reduce, however we may reduce our labour, or however we may improve our machinery, there are other charges we cannot control, such as the carriage to and from London or other places, the whole carriage falling on the throwster.

3765. What distance are you from London?—About 160 miles.

3766. Have

Mr.
*Lamech Swift.*

18 April,
1832.

3766. Have you any water-carriage?—We have water-carriage, but it is too tedious; we have waggon and van, and so on; van carriage is higher, and the prices are so low we cannot afford it.

3767. How far are you from Coventry?—I send my silk to Coventry by way of London, for expedition; but our nearest road is by Bristol.

3768. What do you pay per pound?—The waggon carriage to London I believe, at the present moment, is about 7s. per cwt., that makes 14s. the cwt. taking it both ways, that is from and to London; the actual carriage upon the thrown silk is increased, because we have the same carriage to pay on what is made into waste, and also the package, but which we get no remuneration for.

3769. Upon a hundred weight sent down to you, and returned, it would amount to about 15s. perhaps?—Yes, that at least.

3770. What is the carriage to Coventry?—I cannot exactly say; part of it is water carriage from London, and I am not aware at this moment of the charge.

3771. What other charges are there you cannot get rid of?—Our expense in travelling, as also for oil, candles, and so on.

3772. What is the amount of the house and window tax?—We have no tax on our factories except poor rates.

3773. What is your inducement to have your mills at such a distance from London, is it owing to the cheapness of labour?—It is for obtaining water power and cheap labour.

3774. Does that compensate for the expense of carriage?—The expense of carriage to Manchester is nearly the same as we have, they have no advantage over us, nor we over them in that respect; the prices do not compensate us.

3775. Have you made any calculation of what those additional charges you have mentioned amount to in the throwing?—I have not.

3776. Is it fair for you to give an estimate of what you formerly could throw silk for, and what you can now throw silk for?—Before I can sufficiently and properly answer that, it will be necessary for me to consider the sort of people I must work with.

3777. Taking the same sort of people you now have?—The fact is, we are giving such inadequate wages that the parishes are compelled to allow something to the parents to maintain the children, so that we are partly working with paupers.

3778. Do the persons who receive from you wages of 2s. 6d. and 2s. 9d. per week, receive any allowance from the parish?—Some of them may, but I cannot speak to the proportion or amount from my own knowledge.

3779. Are the Committee to understand, that the rate of wages you have fixed is a fair average of those who do not receive parish relief?—Yes, so far as some of my principal hands go; the parents of some younger children receive from the parish, but I cannot say to what extent.

3780. Have the poor's rates of your parish varied much within the last ten years?—I would explain, that my people come from a circuit of several miles round me, and not entirely from the parishes in which the mills are situate, therefore it is not a business, nor carried on to that extent materially to affect the poor's rates in any one parish in particular.

3781. Are there any other silk mills in that immediate circuit?—No

3782. Are there any woollen mills?—Very extensive woollen mills a few miles from me, but not immediately in my own parish.

3783. Do any of the hands employed in the woollen mills work with you when the trade is slack, or do your hands go to the woollen sometimes?—No; the trade is very different, we cannot afford to pay the same wages and instruct them.

3784. Is there any cotton factory in your neighbourhood?—No.

3785. Then the hands you employ have no means of obtaining employment in any other line?—No.

3786. Do you state, that you cannot reduce the wages you now pay unless you employ paupers?—I cannot reduce the sum; I have hands from 1s. 3d. to 5s., there are not so many at high wages as there ought to be; I have not advanced them as they ought to have been advanced.

3787. The parents of some of them receive allowances from the parish?—They do.

3788. Would it be possible for you to reduce the wages to a lower rate without compelling those persons to resort to the parish?—No, they cannot maintain themselves for less than they receive.

678.

3789. Can

Mr.
*Lamech Swift.*

18 April,
1832.

3789. Can you state what amount on the whole year may be paid by the parish to those you employ?—I cannot say.

3790. Did any of those, before 1824 or 1826, receive allowance in the same manner?—I cannot say; if they come to me and have been previously receiving parish relief they would receive from me 1 *s.* 6 *d.* to 1 *s.* 9 *d.* per week, which is more than the parish allowance, and therefore the parish would immediately strike off the allowance.

3791. Of the 300 hands you employ, how many are under ten years of age?— A great many of the hands that I employ work at their own houses, the wives and mothers who could not come to the factory; they wind the silk and prepare it for the mills, and they employ perhaps younger children in their own families living at too great a distance to send them to the factory.

3792. In the factory how many persons are actually present?—I had about 150 out of that 300, the remainder were working at home in the manner I have described.

3793. Of those 150 how many are above 15 years of age?—I should say three-fourths of them are under 15.

3794. Are there any above 20?—There may be a few, of course there are, for they generally stay with me till they get married, and that is according to circumstances.

3795. How many males are there?—Not one, except my carpenter and foreman, we employ no males, except a few small boys.

3796. Supposing you were to manufacture with that population you now have, are you able to state what the remunerating charge for throwing would be, putting carriage out of the question, that being an extra charge altogether?—That is a question I should wish not to answer at random; with the present state of taxation we are labouring under, which tends to increase our prices, as whatever charges are incurred upon our business, if we are to live by it, we must put it upon the article we work, I do not see how the throwster of Italian organzine can be remunerated under 5 *s.* 6 *d.* to 6 *s.* if the people are to be paid adequate wages.

3797. Is there not a great deal of difference in the silks with respect to the prices?—Unquestionably, there are silks on which will waste two or three per cent., and some that will waste from 20 to 30.

3798. Are not the fresh silks less liable to waste than the old?—Yes, the Italians have a great advantage over us, their silks are not injured by carriage and friction.

3799. Do you apprehend that the Italian will reserve the best silks for himself? —Unquestionably, I should select the best for my own use, if I had them, and export the other.

3800. You have mentioned one charge, that of carriage, which is greater to you than to a person in the neighbourhood of London; is there any other peculiar charge to which you are subjected?—We have a longer coach carriage to pay if we have to come up to London.

3801. If you were assured of 5 *s.* or 5 *s.* 6 *d.* per pound for throwing organzine silk, would that enable you to raise the wages of your people, or would it only enable you to continue them as you now pay them?—If I could get the proper price of my throwing, I should give them proper wages.

3802. Would it enable you to increase the wages?—Yes, certainly; because we are now throwing at 3 *s.* 6 *d.*; if we got 5 *s.* to 5 *s.* 6 *d.* or 6 *s.*, we should give our hands wages adequate to maintain them.

3803. Do you happen to know that there have been several silk mills in the neighbourhood of London, within the last few years?—Yes, I know it, and that many of them have failed.

3804. Do you know any that have succeeded?—I do not know of one, they have been in a worse situation than we have been.

3805. Can you state what are the wages paid generally when fairly employed, to the agricultural labourer in your neighbourhood?—Not employing any myself I cannot speak to it accurately; but I believe it is 7 *s.* a week with cider, if they have only two children they maintain them, but if they have more then they receive about a shilling per week for each off the poor's rate.

3806. Is yours a town or a village?—A small town.

3807. Are there many shopkeepers and others dependent upon those work people?—Unquestionably, because whatever I pay them goes to the shops, and is engaged before they earn it.

3808. Are

Mr.
*Lamech Swift.*

18 April,
1832.

3808. Are the shopkeepers great losers by the depreciation of wages?—My hands, coming from a circuit of a mile or two round, it does not fall on the shopkeepers in the town so materially.

3809. The reduction of 1 s. a week on each will make a great difference in the aggregate to the shopkeepers?—No doubt.

3810. Can you state the average wages of artizans?—I give my carpenter rather more than carpenters in general have, because he is an ingenious man and very useful to me, I give him 18 s. a week, he is a man that serves me as a blacksmith, carpenter or whatever I may require; a common carpenter would get from 10 s. to 12 s. a week.

3811. Have you thrown that kind of silk called marabout?—Yes, I have been in the habit of throwing it ever since early in the year 1826.

3812. To what manufacture is marabout applied?—To the manufacture of gauze, but chiefly gauze ribbons.

3813. In what way is marabout thrown?—It is in fact a very hard thrown tram, generally composed of three threads, that is the better article, but unlike common tram, when it has received a part of the throw it is returned to London to be dyed, and is then sent back to the throwster to receive the remainder of the throwing, and be finished. On that article I have to pay greater wages.

3814. How many turns to an inch do you put on your marabout?—That depends upon the size of the silk.

3815. Do you go to 70 on the average?—Yes.

3816. What is the range?—From 60 to 80 or 90, according to whether it is a very fine article or not.

3817. Does it require a superior kind of silk?—Yes, the very best white Novi's.

3818. Can you throw Bengal, or any other kind of silk except Italian, into marabout?—Bengal is not at all fit for the purpose, China is sometimes used for inferior purposes.

3819. What inferior purposes in that manufacture do you allude to?—An inferior article, used for some purposes of black goods, that the best is not applied to.

3820. Do you throw marabout from Italian single?—No, from the very fine white Novi; we have no single silk in this country of a proper size for it that I know of.

3821. Has not some been introduced of late years applicable to that?—I have never seen any.

3822. Do you ever make it from tram?—This is a tram; we throw it in the first instance into a tram, and send it to London, that the manufacturer may dye it to the colour he may require.

3823. Is not that less expense than your former operation?—It is the same operation that we apply to silk used in the broad trade of Spitalfields, called tram.

3824. Do you obtain a better price for throwing marabout than other silks?—Yes; there is so much more work upon it, that the throwing one pound of marabout is equal to throwing two pounds of organzine.

3825. Do you mean the process before and after dyeing?—Yes, I mean the whole together; that taking it from the raw, it is worth a double price than for throwing organzine.

3826. What is your average number of circles in the inch, in organzine?—It undergoes two processes of throwing.

3827. In what respect is marabout more expensive in its process than organzine?—Silk to prepare organzine from, comes down to the throwster in its raw state; it is wound on bobbins, goes to the mill in a single thread to have a spin or twist put upon it, it is then doubled two threads, and is twisted again the contrary way; a tram silk undergoes only one process of twisting, it comes down in the raw state, is wound and put on bobbins, and doubled two or more threads together as the manufacturer may desire, it then receives a slighter twist than organzine, and is returned.

3828. What is the process of marabout?—The marabout has the same quantity of work put upon it as tram in the first instance; it is then dyed and has to be re-wound, and the finishing twist put upon it to bring it up to the required quantity of turns to the inch, there is a great deal of trouble, and great care required on account of the colour in that article.

3829. Does the operation of dyeing increase the trouble?—No, only we have to have it re-wound before we can apply it to the mill, and therefore more expense is incurred.

3830. What

3830. What do you receive for throwing organzine?—If I were to quote a price, I should say a catch price, it is not a price remunerating us, it is from 3 s. 6 d. to 4 s., it is not often we can get more than 3 s. 6 d.

3831. What is the average price for throwing marabout?—About double that price, about 7 s. 6 d.

3832. Before 1826, what did you receive for organzine?—About 7 s. to 8 s. or 9 s., according to the demand.

3833. What did you receive for marabout?—About double, but we had a great many experiments to try; not being conversant with the article, we got it dyed in the raw and tried some experiments, it fluctuated as the price of organzine fluctuated.

3834. Will you state what you charge for tram?—The present price for tram is somewhere about 2 s. 6 d.

3835. What was it in 1826?—We had 3 s. 6 d. and 4 s., and up to 5 s.; we used at times to get 6 s. for trams, and it has gone down to 2 s. 6 d. now.

3836. The French who make marabout must put the same additional labour into it as you do, must not they?—I believe, from the inquiries I have been making, and the information I have obtained, the French have a peculiar advantage over us, which will account in some measure for the great difference in their price from ours.

3837. Do you require different machinery for throwing marabout?—The machinery applied to other branches of throwing is easily adapted to this.

3838. Is marabout imported?—I believe not.

3839. It has been stated to this Committee, that marabout is about 22 s. or 23 s. per lb. in France, and about 32 s. or 33 s. in England, can you account for this great disproportion?—I am not sure that I can; I cannot say whether I am correctly informed upon this point, but from the best information I have been able to collect, I believe that France has in this article two very great advantages over us; first, that from the prohibition of the export of her raw silk she has it at a lower rate, and of superior quality, than we can buy Italian for, especially such fine Italian as is necessary to make marabout; secondly, that the silk she uses for marabout, is reeled for the purpose in one thread, of a sufficient size, so that while the English throwster is working three fine threads together to compose one of the necessary thickness, she has one already formed in one operation, and this very much lessens to France the cost of throwing.

3840. Can you in England get none of that single thread which the French use? —I believe not; I am not aware that any description of silk is brought to England sufficiently good and even for that purpose.

3841. You are not aware that Italian silk of that description is brought to England?—No.

3842. Are you aware that any Italian silk is used in the single thread in France? —No, I am not; but I believe having the filatures, they can obtain the article to their own size; but in England we cannot do that. According to the healthiness of the season, I believe the worm will spin a stronger or more feeble thread, so that if we sent out an order from this country to Italy to reel so many cocoons, it might come back heavier or lighter than we wanted it.

3843. Do you ever send out to Italy to order any particular kind of silk for this article?—No, I am not aware that any orders have ever gone out to Italy for that purpose.

3844. Is not a merchant at liberty to select from the Italian silks received in this market that which will best suit him?—The manufacturer, or person wishing to throw this particular silk, examines certain samples, and selects that which he thinks best adapted, when three threads are put together, for that purpose.

3845. You think no Italian silk can be got for marabout, equal to the French silk?—No, for the worm, according to the healthiness or sickliness of the season, will spin a finer or a thicker thread; therefore if the order was sent out to Italy in a particular way, it might come at one time much finer, and at another time much stouter than was wanted.

3846. Are the Committee to understand that the difference of marabout in France and England arises from the difference of quality of material, or the greater labour in one case than another?—It resolves itself into two points, into a matter of difference in the price of labour, and a difference in the price of silk.

3847. In point of fact, what quantity of marabout in one year have you made? —It fluctuates of course, being applied entirely to the fancy trade; I have thrown from 100 to 120 lbs. per week of it for a month together; every month is not alike

certainly

Mr.
*Lamech Swift.*

———

18 April,
1832.

certainly, there are some seasons of the year I do not throw any, from the stagnation of trade.

3848. Have you ever thrown four or five thousand, or ten thousand pounds, in a year?—No, the last year I threw only 500 lbs. in the year; in the month of May the preceding year, I threw 430 lbs.

3849. Did you ever throw 1,000?—Yes, I have thrown 3,000 lbs. in a year.

3850. Did you throw only that proportion from the want of demand, or the want of the article to throw it from?—From the want of demand.

3851. Did this arise from the gauze not being manufactured to a greater extent?—The marked was glutted with French goods of the same kind.

3852. Does the throwing marabout give to the throwster much larger profit than the other descriptions of organzine?—It does not, the manufacturer if he cannot get a little more for a fancy thing where he has so much more trouble and increased risk, will not undertake it.

3853. Taking the risk into consideration, do you think you get a larger profit?—No, not in a difficult time like this; it has been valuable to throwsters as employing a great many of their hands and a considerable portion of machinery for a small parcel of silk, having to work it twice over; 1 cwt. is equal to two.

3854. The price at which the foreign throwster sells, compels you to reduce your profits of labour?—Unquestionably.

3855. Do you know the cost of raw silk?—I believe it varies from 19s. to 20s. for the best, applicable to this purpose.

3856. You say the throwing is now 7s. 6d.?—That is the price I am receiving for it.

3857. Do you know what the charge for waste would be?—It depends on circumstances, according whether the raw is a very good winding silk or not; they fluctuate very much, I should think from a shilling to eighteen-pence, including the second operation.

3858. Do you know the expense of dyeing?—That depends upon the colour; I should suppose from 2s. 6d. to 3s., taking the average of colours.

3859. What was the price of throwing fine superior tram in 1821 to 1824?—It fluctuated from 4s. 6d. to 5s. 6d., or 6s.

3860. What was the price of throwing organzine at the same period?—That also fluctuated from 8s. to 7s. 6d., according to the quality, for there is always a difference between a very fine article and a coarse article; the superior fine are of course at a higher rate, from 8s. downwards.

3861. The finer silk is not only of greater length, but more subject to accidents?—The fine silk in a general way takes more precision, independent of their being a greater number of yards in length, and it will not take off the same quantity in weight.

3862. You cannot have the same celerity in motion, because it is more apt to break?—It is a more tender article to deal with, and we cannot apply at all times the same velocity to it.

3863. Of course if you were driven from the use of the finer silks to a coarser material, there is more silk and much less labour?—A greater quantity of silk, and less labour.

3864. So that you may appear to increase your quantity, while you are decreasing the amount?—Yes, for the same quantity of machinery which will turn off 100 lbs. of fine Italian, will turn off two or three hundred of coarser silk; 150 lbs. of Bengal in the article of singles, for instance, appears on paper the same as 150 lbs. of Italian; in point of weight it is the same, but not in the proceeds.

3865. What difference does it make in point of wages?—A very great difference; if I was entirely on that description of coarse silks, I should not want nearly the number of hands I have for fine silk.

3866. If you are driven to use the coarse article, you must diminish your number of hands?—Yes.

3867. What are the articles of thrown silk principally sent from abroad, are they the finer description or the coarser?—The Italian organzines are mostly of the finer descriptions.

3868. Are you aware who else throws marabout in England besides yourself?—Messrs. Courtauld & Taylor, in Gutter-lane; they were I believe the first marabout throwsters, they were throwing it twelve months before I was.

3869. Have you at all any idea of the quantity of silk thrown into marabout in this country?—I have not.

678.                                                                  3870. You

3870. You have not exceeded in any year 3,000 lbs. yourself?—I have thrown in one year 3,000 lbs. weight, last year I did not throw above 400 or 500 lbs.

3871. The importation of raw silk having increased, to what do you attribute the distress of the throwsters?—The importation of raw silk last year very much fell off, and the thrown increased; a large quantity of raw is used in an unthrown state; of the raw silk imported, a larger proportion than formerly, is the Turkey and other coarse kinds, which require little throwing; and also the throwsters distress arises as much from the lowness of price, occasioned by the last reduction of duty, as from the want of work.

3872. If the quantity of silk from Bengal and Turkey had been abundant within the last six years, would you have found any increased improvement more than would have been afforded by half the quantity of Italian raw?—That must depend upon how the trade could have consumed it.

3873. The question refers to the time occupied in throwing it?—Certainly not.

3874. What duty, in your experience, would be a protection to the British throwster?—I should say 5 s. organzine, and 3 s. tram.

3875. The coarse silk does not give half the employment of the fine?—No.

3876. The marabout has been an advantage to the throwster?—Yes; the marabout gives an immense employment for the lower classes, with a very small consumption of silk.

3877. You are aware that the protection now given is equal to the whole labour of throwing?—I would say if that is taken off, the manufacturer will not reap the advantage of it; we are throwing at 3 s. 6 d., because we cannot obtain a better price, but it is not a price that will remunerate the throwster.

3878. Do you think that the low price is occasioned by the Italian thrown silk being imported, or by the competition among the manufacturers?—It may be remarked, the very small quantity of Italian thrown silk which has come into this market since the reduction of duty; after the duty was once reduced from 9 s. 2 d. to 7 s. 6 d., and subsequently to 5 s., the throwster by increased exertion, by screwing down his people, and reducing his charges, kept the Italian in a great measure out of the market; but when it came down to 3 s. 6 d., we could not decrease our expense in proportion, and the consequence is, there has been an increased importation of thrown silk.

3879. In your opinion, has the reduction of the profit of the throwster arisen from competition at home, or from that small increase of thrown silk?—It has arisen in some measure from the competition at home, that the manufacturer has been forced into, with the foreigner.

3880. The reduction from 5 s. to 3 s. 6 d. you complain of, took place in 1829?—Yes, in 1829.

3881. What has been the state of the trade from 1829?—We have been in a constant state of distress from the period French goods were admitted; it has varied only in degree.

3882. Do you mean to say that in 1829 the throwing was a bad trade?—Yes, and it has been gradually getting worse.

3883. Do you speak of yourself, or of others?—I speak of myself as an old throwster, and knowing that my mills cannot be in a bad state without others feeling a like depreciation.

3884. You have been principally employed by the London and Coventry manufacturers?—Yes.

3885. At the time when your throwing trade was a good one, had any manufacturers mills of their own?—Yes, some have had mills of their own for many years; they have increased of late years.

3886. Have not the number of mills in the hands of manufacturers considerably increased?—Certainly, but not so as to injure the trade.

3887. Have not mills also been established within short distances of London?—I believe there have.

3888. Cannot you account for a decrease in your trade, and your employment, by the expense of carriage, by the establishment of new mills, and by manufacturers who formerly employed you also throwing their own silk?—Unquestionably; every throwster who has been engaged in throwing to a large extent, for a particular house, suffers a loss if that house establishes a mill of their own, and he loses the connection; but as it refers to the mills established in the neighbourhood of London, though there have been many established, they have not succeeded, they have not drawn away our business from us.

3889. They

Mr.
*Lamech Swift.*

18 April,
1832.

3889. They have affected you probably for the moment?—Yes, they may have done so.

3890. It is the increase of Italian silk which affects you, the increase from 350,000 to 500,000 lbs. ?—I do not mean to say it has affected us to that extent.

3891. There were 4,000,000 of lbs. imported the last year into this country, of which only 500,000 were thrown, being only one-eighth; do you think the proportion of one-eighth thrown in Italy, affected the price of the seven-eighths thrown here?—Yes, because it is the quotation they go by; though it is not a quantity for the trade to go on, they will still argue upon it.

3892. You were understood to say that the price of throwing had been depressed by the great increase of importation of Italian thrown?—Yes, the importations from Italy have certainly affected the mills of this country.

3893. What amount do you put down as imported for home consumption of Italian thrown silk the last two years?—It is impossible for me to say what I put down for home consumption, it may be exported again without my knowledge, and though some part of the increase may be in train, it deprives the throwster of throwing tram equally with organzine, and affects his price; if a single pound is imported, there is a pound less of British organzine or tram wanted.

3894. Do you know the proportion of tram imported in those two years, less than was imported before?—I have not those returns by me.

3895. Can Bengal be thrown into tram?—Certainly, but it will not produce the same article as Italian tram.

3896. Are you aware that tram has been imported only of late years?—It was, I believe, a contraband article prior to the reduction of duty in the first instance in 1826, when the duty was 9 *s.* 2 *d.*

3897. Are you aware that of the increased import of thrown silk from Italy, one-fourth of it has been tram?—I am not aware of the respective quantities of tram and organzine.

3898. Are you aware that the importation of organzine silk, for the last fifty years, has never varied 30,000 lbs. on the average of years?—I am aware of that, but I think that is to be explained, because the Italian has had a better market than here; but if you take off the duties, he will send less raw and more thrown to this country.

3899. Have not the difficulties of the throwster really commenced and increased since the removal of the protection given him by the alteration of the duties?—Unquestionably.

3900. If the protection given to him were further removed by lowering the duties, would it not increase their difficulties?—Unquestionably.

3901. You mean to say that the introduction of foreign thrown silk at the duty which made it only to the extent of 3 *s.* 6 *d.*, depressed you very much?—Yes.

3902. If 500,000 lbs. came into this country, where 300,000 only had come in, that would be so much additional, and you conceive that with the reduced amount of protection, the Italian would send more thrown silk into this country, and less raw?—I think there is no doubt upon that.

3903. You think he can throw silk much cheaper than you can?—Yes; as a question of labour upon a question of machinery, the same machinery in England will throw as good organzine or tram as any machinery they have got in Italy, suppose the quality of silk the same, but then it resolves itself into the difference of labour.

3904. You conceive it is the difference in the rate of labour which makes protection necessary to you?—The Italian has also a decided advantage in selecting the best silks; in this country we cannot do that, being obliged to take that which is sent.

3905. One cause of the advantage they possess is in the cheapness of foreign labour?—Yes.

3906. If you were not to reduce your profits and labour so as to meet the foreign competition, would it not occasion a much larger quantity to be imported?—There is no doubt of that; it is the increased exertion and the decreased prices we have worked at that has kept the importation of thrown silk so low as it is.

3907. If there were even a less quantity of Italian thrown silk it would still compel you to work at low prices?—We must be compelled to work at low prices, unless our manufacturers had an increased remuneration for their goods, we are dependent one upon another.

3908. If you suffer from home competition, is not that an evil that generally remedies

Mr.
Lamech Swift.

18 April,
1832.

remedies itself?—Unquestionably, because, if we have not the foreigner to contend with, those things will always adjust themselves in some way or other, by a little reduction for a time; if the manufacture is depressed, we right ourselves, but we cannot guard against the importation of the foreigner, we cannot prevent his glutting our market.

3909. Do you mean to say that it is the cheapness of foreign labour against which you want protection, and what do you suppose is that difference of labour between England and Italy?—I am not in possession of the exact price of labour in Italy, but the wages of Italy and their rate of taxation altogether, enable them to work cheaper than we can in England.

3910. You admit that they can work cheaper than in England; take the 2 s. 8 d. you have here protection from the 3 s. 6 d. what will remain for the throwing?—Only 10 d.

3911. Can you suppose that in Italy they can throw for 10 d.?—I do not suppose that they can work exactly as we do here; I can speak as to their rate of wages, but if you reduce the protection here they will very soon glut our market.

3912. The apparent difference is 10 d., but if it were to be merely for the labour it would be impossible of course for the Italian throwster to throw for 10 d. a pound, but has not he other advantages which enables him to throw at that reduced price, and still compete with the English throwster?—There are silks come into my hands that I would not throw at twice the price that I throw others for, yet they both shall go under the denomination of Italian silks.

3913. Has he any other advantages beyond the lowness of wages, which will enable him to enter into competition with the English throwster even at that low price?—He has wonderful advantages in the selection of the best raws above what we can procure in this country.

3914. Are you aware of any disadvantages he has in coming to the English market with the English throwster?—I do not know of any disadvantage he has in coming to the English market.

2915. Do you know that thrown silks sustain greater damage in shipping and landing than raw silks?—I do not, I know that raw silks sustain great injury.

3916. You think he has great advantages in the selection of his silk, and probably that he will send to this country only those silks he does not find it conducive to his interest to work up?—He sends to this country what he does not require for his own use.

3917. Would it not often answer the purpose of the Italian, for the sake of selling his silks, to send them here, even though he got no profit upon the throwing?—I believe it would, because, in the balance of his account with this country, by sending a part thrown and part raw, it answers his end.

3918. He would rather send it thrown than raw?—Yes, he has employment for his people.

3919. Then he is not like a man who depends altogether on the profit of throwing?—No, he has other advantages.

3920. Does he not often work the produce of his own district?—I believe that there are many cases where the filature and the throwing are combined, but never having been in Italy I am not able to speak correctly to those points.

3921. Are you not aware that there are a great many persons in Italy who purchase silk, and have no throwing mills?—I cannot speak decidedly to that.

3922. Are not raw silks injured in their transit from Italy to England?—Very seriously.

3923. Are thrown silks subject to the same injury?—That I cannot speak to, thrown silks not coming into my hands as a throwster.

3924. You mention, that there are some Italian silks which you would require to be paid twice as much for throwing as other silks?—Yes.

3925. Do those silks bear a higher price in the markets of Italy?—I cannot say, but they do not in this market.

3926. Is that owing to the Italian throwster having the choice of silks in that market?—Yes; I have thrown silks at 4 s. per pound, that I have got a better remuneration for than some Italians that I have thrown at 8 s.

3927. Are you acquainted with the nature of the power used in Italy, so as to form a comparison between the situation of the English and Italian throwster?—I understand their power is mostly water; I am not aware, exactly, of the power they use.

3928. Of the raw Italian silks you throw, are the great proportion of finer or inferior

inferior qualities?—There is a distinction; there are very good coarse raws and very bad ones, and the same in fine; it is not the degree of fineness which constitutes the superiority or inferiority, it depends upon the care with which they are reeled; some fine silks of the same number of deniers, will waste, perhaps, twice as much as others, the coarser the silk, if it is well reeled, the less waste.

Mr.
*Lamech Swift.*

18 April,
1832.

3929. You have been asked, whether one cause of the distress of the throwster was not the manufacturers having established mills of their own; you say they have established mills of their own?—Some of them have, and some of them have abandoned them from the serious losses they sustained; they did not reap that advantage from having throwing mills of their own they anticipated.

3930. Have not as many mills, not belonging to manufacturers, discontinued working their mills as belonging to manufacturers?—A great many mills not belonging to manufacturers, have discontinued; a great many have not been set to work at all; led away by the prosperity that was promised to the trade by the alteration of the duties, they were induced to rush into the trade, and many of the mills were created in consequence; but a skein of silk was never, I believe, put into many of them, the trade became so depressed before they could get to work.

3931. Were those mills established by the manufacturers?—No; by parties who rushed into the trade, who were induced to go into it by the state of prosperity they expected the trade would be put into.

3932. What year do you speak of?—Previous to 1826, from 1824 to 1826; the late Mr. Huskisson stated in the House, that he would put the silk trade into such a state of prosperity it was never in before; in consequence of that, persons who could realize a few thousand or hundred pounds, put it into silk mills, anticipating a rich harvest, and some of them have not even commenced working.

3933. It was foretold that it would increase the wages of labour 25 per cent. in six months, had it that effect?—No; but the contrary effect.

### Mr. *John Sharrer Ward*, called in; and Examined.

3934. WHERE do you carry on the throwing business?—At Bruton, in Somersetshire, and the surrounding villages.

Mr.
*John S. Ward.*

3935. How long have you carried on this business?—My father and myself 65 years.

3936. What induced you to extend your business to the villages?—I have been, in all cases, solicited by the overseers of the parishes, or by the principal inhabitants to do so to employ the poor.

3937. What number of hands do you now employ?—At the present moment about 230.

3138. What number did you employ in 1823?—From eight to nine hundred, or perhaps to one thousand, the children often working at their own houses with their parents.

3939. What is the average of your wages?—The average, as well as I can make out at present is 2 s. 3 d. for women and children; but it is a very difficult thing to give an average, for I had used at Easter to raise all my children's wages, which I have omitted to do the last two years.

3940. What was the average of your wages in 1823?—About 3 s.

3941. What was the average of your wages in 1829?—Nearly as at present, 2 s. 3 d., I have made no great alteration since.

3942. What number of spindles have you now at work?—At present about 7,000, but only working four days in the week.

3943. What number had you in 1823?—Fifteen thousand seven hundred, and they were then in full work.

3944. What number in 1825?—About the same.

3945. What was the number in 1828 and 1829?—They varied a little in 1828 and 1829, in 1828 nearly the same, in 1829 somewhat less; I began to buy my own silk about that time; I began indeed in 1828.

3946. Do you throw Italian silk?—Principally fine Italian.

3947. What was the price of throwing in 1823 for organzine and tram?—From 9 s. to 10 s. per lb. for organzine, tram 5 s. 6 d.

3948. What was the price of throwing in 1829?—From 4 s. 6 d. to 5 s., and tram about 3 s.

3949. What is the price now?—I understand the price is 4 s. for organzine,

and

Mr.
John S. Ward.
————
18 April,
1832.

and 2 s. 6 d. for tram ; but I have thrown none for hire, but for myself, paying me nothing.

3950. By what means have you been able to make that reduction in price ?—By lowering the wages, and submitting to great loss.

3951. Has there been, since 1823, any important improvement in the principle of throwing machinery ?—No, very trifling ; there was no necessity with me, because my machinery was very perfect.

3952. Are some parts of the machinery now turned faster than they used to be ?—I have increased the speed of my spinning mills occasionally, according to the quality and strength of the silk.

3953. To what parts of the machinery does this apply ?—To the spinning mills chiefly.

3954 Can you state the difference of increased rapidity ?—I should suppose about one-twentieth I have increased my speed ; then I formerly worked at a greater velocity than others I believe.

3955. Can you state how many revolutions there were before 1823 ?—It is about 3,000 now, having been increased about a twentieth.

3956. Is this increased speed a great saving in the cost of throwing ?—It is inconsiderable, inasmuch as there must be more hands employed to attend our mills, particularly if the silk be of fine or inferior quality, and tender fibre.

3957. Does the portion of additional hands make up for the increased speed, or what is the difference ?—In some cases, as matter of experience, we try what velocity the silk will bear, and are obliged to relax occasionally.

3958. What induced you to increase the speed of your machinery ?—I had heard that other persons had increased, and I tried the experiment.

3959. Were you, previous to the alteration you speak of, to the extent of a twentieth part, working more rapidly than a great many other mills ?—Certainly.

3960. Are you now working with as great velocity as any others ?—I understand there are greater velocities used, but I have not found them of advantage to myself ; I have the power of doing so.

3961. You consider that the increased number of hands, in consequence of the increased velocity, is not in the proportion of a twentieth ?—No.

3962. That is very inconsiderable ?—It is very inconsiderable.

3963. What advantage does the Italian throwster possess over the English ?—Lower wages ; I have no difficulty in asserting that they have cheaper plant and power, meaning their water wheel and their mill ; I have been told by a friend of my brother, who had been in Italy to superintend a factory, that a mill can be rented in Italy for 60 l. a year, English money, that would turn off four cwt. a week ; the very coal that a steam engine in England would require, would amount to three or four hundred a year.

3964. What do you pay for coals ?—About nine-pence a hundred.

3965. Do you use steam or water ?—Both.

3966. You say a mill can be rented at 60 l. a year which would throw off at the rate of four hundred a week, what would a mill in this country which would perform the same quantity of work, cost a throwster ?—Reckoning interest of money, it would cost eight or ten thousand pounds to build a mill, that at five per cent. would be four hundred a year.

3967. Would not the site of the mill cost something in addition to the 8,000 l. ?—No doubt.

3968. Supposing silk throwing did pay, and that a person required a mill, what would a mill throwing 400 lbs. a week let for ?—From four to five hundred a year ; certainly there is one other matter which is more important still, their silk is in a better condition, and of better quality.

3969. What do you mean by better condition ?—In the transit from Italy here, it gets rubbed and so on ; I should think that makes about two per cent. difference.

3970. Do you think the circumstance of the Italian being able to make a selection of his raws, a great advantage ?—An incalculable advantage.

3971. Is not the circumstance of silk making more or less waste, of great importance ?—Decidedly of great importance.

3972. Do you think those advantages are counterbalanced by the present import duty ?—By no means, certainly not.

3973. What has been the effect of lowering the import duty in 1829 from 5 s. to 3 s. 6 d. a pound ?—To reduce the price to the throwster, and consequent lowering

the

the wages to the workpeople, which has brought great distress upon the labouring classes.

3974. What would be the effect of still lowering the duty?—Absolute ruin to the English throwster.

3975. You have stated that ruin would follow a further diminution of duty, on what do you found that opinion?—As the duties have been varied, so has the price of throwing been varied, and it is rather singular it has kept pace exactly with the price of throwing; in 1823 the duty was 9s., the price for organzine was 9s.; at the next reduction of duty to 5s., organzine was 5s., and trams in proportion; now it is 3s. 6d., and I have known trams taken within this three months at 2s. 3d. per pound, the person who sent it said he knew the throwster would not pay himself, but he said I can do no better.

3976. There being so large a proportion of fixed capital, is a constant inducement to the mill owner to throw?—Yes, my inducement is to keep my hands together, hoping trade would revive, by which I have lost thousands.

3977. What is the number of mills in your town and neighbourhood?—I really do not know, there were eighteen, but I believe they are now reduced to twelve.

3978. How many have been erected since 1823?—I believe none of those twelve.

3979. Has it been a total loss to the proprietors, the mills being thrown out of employ supposing it to be permanent?—Yes, the loss of our capital; my mill cost me between 20 and 30,000l., it would be perfectly useless if I were to give up throwing; there is no manufacture in the neighbourhood to employ it about, they must go back to be flour mills I suppose.

3980. Do you know, generally, the value of the mills?—I cannot say that I do; but it must be very considerable.

3981. Are the hands employed in this winding dependent on the poor rate?—They partly have been.

3982. Are there many hands out of employ?—The greater part of them are out of employ.

3983. What is the state of the town and neighbourhood of Bruton, as to poor's rate?—I believed they have increased about one-fourth in the town of Bruton.

3984. What proportion of the mills and spindles in your neighbourhood are now at work?—In my own mill about one-half of the spindles are at work; but they work only two-thirds of the usual time.

3985. You say, one of the disadvantages under which the silk throwster laboured was, that the Italian silk throwster got his silk of better quality?—Certainly he does.

3986. Will you explain to the Committee how it occurs, that the merchants, of whom you buy silk, have not been able to procure silk of equal quality to that they have in Italy?—I can only reason by analogy, if I were an Italian throwster I would work the best silks and send the worst to England, which it is a notorious fact they do.

3987. If an additional price were given, might not the best be procured here?—It is not the fact that it is procured.

3988. You state, that there is injury to raw silk in the transit?—Yes; about equal to two per cent.

3989. Are you able to inform the Committee, whether Italian raw silk, or organzine be subject to the same injury?—I cannot say, I never imported it.

3990. If the duty on thrown silk is lowered, is it not probable that the Italians will keep at home, and throw it?—I apprehend so.

3991. Do you think it is the most likely way to obtain a good supply of Italian raw silk to keep the duty at present existing on foreign thrown silk?—I should hope it would be increased.

3992. Have you been in the habit of working on commission or otherwise?—I never began working my own till about 1826 or 1827.

3993. Which do you find most profitable, working by commission, or your own silk?—I should say, bad as it is, on commission, and for this reason; in 1829 I sold a large quantity of thrown silk at less than it cost me in the raw; also, in 1829 I almost supplied myself by my own means; there is one gentleman I used to earn 3,000l. a year of, and I can get no work from him, except a bale now and then; but what was I to do, either buy my own silk, or turn off my work people; in 1829 a very large quantity of silk I sold which did not pay me 1s. 6d. per lb. for working into organzine, after deducting for waste and broker's commission.

678.

3994. What

3994. What induced you then to work for yourself?—It may appear vain to say so, but it was the love of my poor people, who worked 60 years for my father and myself.

3995. Should you have worked for yourself if you had been able to obtain silk to work on commission?—Certainly not; and I would return to commission to-morrow if I could.

3996. Did you ever go to Manchester?—Never.

3997. Your attention has been directed to the circumstance of some establishments being made at Manchester for the throwing of silk?—I am aware there are.

3998. Are you aware of any advantage which exists at Manchester beyond that possessed by you?—I know of none; I believe the gentlemen who employ me and employ the Manchester mills, will say that there has no better organzine ever been made than that I have made.

3999. Are you aware of any advantages they possess over yourself and other manufacturers in your neighbourhood?—No.

4000. Do you think you are able to throw silk as low as they can do it?—I should think I am, our labour is cheaper.

4001. The Committee are to gather from your evidence, that you are of opinion you can throw silk as cheap as they can do at Manchester?—Yes.

4002. Do you think the expense of carriage down to you is compensated by the cheapness of your labour, and other advantages?—Yes.

4003. Do you think you could manufacture it within 20 miles of London cheaper than you do?—Certainly not; labour is dearer; our carriage does not exceed three farthings a pound.

4004. Are you aware of any silk having been sent from Manchester, within the last twelve or eighteen months, to be thrown in your neighbourhood?—I believe not; not to me in Bruton.

4005. A large proportion of people employed in the mills are females?—Almost all.

4006. Is the employment healthy?—Perfectly so.

4007. Is the employment domestic?—I had 500 employed at their own houses.

4008. Do you know of any means by which the poor children could be subsisted, if you should be obliged to dismiss them?—I do not.

4009. You have been obliged to dismiss your labour from the surrounding villages, have you not?—Yes, I have only 230 out of the 800 now.

4010. What protection do you conceive it necessary the throwing interest should have?—I should say at least 5 *s.* organzine, and 3 *s.* tram.

4011. What would such a mill as you now use, if built at the present time in the best manner, cost you?—I cannot tell, I suppose 20,000 *l.*

4012. If you wanted to let it, what would it let for?—I do not know any body who would take it, I can reason by analogy; I know a gentleman who laid out more than 16,000 *l.* in a mill and machinery, the most that was bid for it was 2,600 *l.*; and all the machinery, which cost I suppose 8,000 *l.*, the person who succeeded him, bought for 200 *l.*

4013. How can such a state of things exist where there is such an increased supply of Bengal silk to be thrown?—I never worked Bengal, mine is entirely fine Italian silk.

4014. Can you at all account for the distress of the throwster, there being such a great increased importation of raw silk?—I believe the great importation consists in a great measure of Bengal, which is put into the loom at Manchester, I believe without any throwing at all; it is worked in the single.

4015. A bale of Bengal would afford very little employment for your people, as compared with a bale of Italian?—Very little.

4016. Can you give the Committee any idea of the difference of employment between working up a bale of ordinary sized Bengal, and a bale of ordinary sized Italian?—No, I can do it in this way, by the price; I work very little Bengal, the last I had, I did it at 1 *s.* 6 *d.* per lb. for single, merely wound and twisted.

4017. So that in point of fact there may be a very great increase of Bengal, and China, and Turkey silks, and yet the mills of this country may be very inadequately supplied with silk to throw?—Yes, the mills in the West of England, they are calculated for Italian silk.

4018. You have stated that yourself and your father have been engaged in this manufacture for sixty-five years?—Yes, I have been in it four-and-forty.

4019. Has

4019. Has there not within that period been a progressive improvement in silk throwing?—Yes.

4020. By those means you have been able to compete with the disadvantage occasioned by the successive lowering of the protecting duty you have had to encounter?—Yes.

4021. And by throwing the employment and all the materials into unfavourable situations?—Yes.

4022. Are not all the mills of England, unfavourably situate, thrown out of employment?—Yes.

4023. Whether they are in the neighbourhood in which the labour is not very cheap, or where they have not the advantage of water power, and where coals are not very cheap?—Yes, in some neighbourhoods I suppose not one half of them have been able to stand.

4024. Would 1,000 lbs. weight of Bengal silk find as much employment for the people as 500 weight of Italian?—I should think not.

4025. How do you account for there being so little increase in the quantity of thrown silk imported, considering the several reductions of duty which have taken place?—I suppose that the Italian throwster, as well as ourselves, is getting very little profit, but he has a profit on the raw also.

4026. Is he the grower?—I believe in a great part of Italy he is; I should say also, we have been driven to work at such low wages, that it falls on the throwster.

4027. The wages at which you have been working are such as you cannot continue to work at?—I cannot.

4028. The Italian having a profit on his raw silk, he might be induced to send it over here, though he got nothing on the throwing?—I apprehend he might.

4029. Do not you think that the introduction of so many foreign manufactured goods must have operated very materially to depress the throwster, and also to throw people out of employment?—Certainly so; gentlemen engaged in silk weaving, who gave me considerable employment, do not now, being thrown out of their means of working it.

4030. Do you know any great opening to export, that the importation of foreign manufactured goods as obtained for this country?—No, that is out of my line.

*Mr.
John S. Ward.*

18 April,
1832.

---

*Mercurii, 11° die Aprilis,* 1832.

EDWARD AYSHFORD SANFORD, ESQ., in the Chair.

Mr. *Alexis James Doxat*, called in; and Examined.

4031. YOU are a silk merchant in the city of London?—I am.

4032. How many years have you been engaged in that business?—I entered the business in the year 1798.

4033. Have you been in the habit of importing silks from other parts of the world besides Italy?—No, Italy only.

4034. You import thrown silk as well as raw?—We do.

4035. Are you able to state from your inquiries and observations, the general effect produced on the silk trade in this country, in consequence of the alterations of duties on foreign raw and manufactured silks?—I am.

4036. In the course of your inquiries into the state of the silk trade of this country, have you made some statements of the progress, at various periods, of the quantities of raw and thrown silk, waste, knubs and husks, consumed by our manufacturers; and also the amount of duties, wages and profits, accruing from those quarters; and have you likewise taken some comparative view of those progresses with those which have taken place in the cotton trade, and if so, will you state what have been the results of your inquiries in those respects?—I will begin by giving in a Tabular Statement I have made, of all the imports and consumption of silks in this country, from the year 1814 to the year 1831; I have endeavoured to separate all the qualities which are placed together in the Parliamentary Returns, duty paid, and I have balanced my accounts ultimately by the Parliamentary Returns [*producing the same, Vide No.* 1.] Being much interested in the silk trade, I have made, at various periods, inquiries into all which relates to that branch of industry, as much as it has been in my power; I have made every inquiry in my

*Mr.
Alexis J. Doxat.*

11 April,
1832.

Appendix (F.)

Mr.
*Alexis J. Doxat.*

———

11 April,
1832.

Appendix (F.)

power into its various parts, and have endeavoured to make a comparatives tate-ment of the situation of the silk trade, before the alterations of 1824 and 1825, when the new duties commenced, likewise its situation since the importation of foreign manufactured silks ; leaving the details of points which are seen in all those columns, I will take the per centages of the silk trade, as compared with the cotton trade in this statement [*producing the same, Vide No.* 2.] The cotton trade has often been adverted to of late years, as without parallel in its progress ; and the silk trade has as often been mentioned in contradiction as "dwindling, sickly, &c." previously to the alterations in our laws relative to this branch of our national industry, obser-vations so contrary to the real state of the case would not have been offered, had a relative comparative view of the respective progress of the silk and cotton trades been taken, as will appear by the statements and recapitulations as I have men-tioned ; they differ from year to year ; I have contented myself with inquiries in that branch of industry, and likewise made statements of its progress. Last year, a friend of mine, who is a principal broker in the cotton line, sent me a Report of the West India Trade ; and every time that a paper is sent to me of that kind, I read it with great interest ; every branch of industry has some point of comparative analogy ; when I came to the page of cotton, I saw the progress very rapid, but those numbers struck me immediately as less rapid than I was acquainted with, and which were familiar to me in the silk trade ; I placed those numbers in comparison, and I found the result to be in this way, taking the average of three years, 1815, 1816 and 1817, and the subsequent three years, 1818, 1819 and 1820, I found the increase to be in the silk trade 31½ per cent., the increase in the relative period in the cotton trade, 22 per cent. The next three years, 1821, 1822 and 1823, the increase in the silk trade was 70 per cent. over the starting point of 1815, 1816 and 1817, the comparative three years in the cotton trade was 48 ; I would state here, that during those periods of nine years I have been mentioning, the duty on raw and thrown silks, without fractions, was from 25 to 30, 40, 50, 60, 70, 80, and even 90 per cent. upon the value of the raw article, and the article (the thrown) which has received some preparation towards its manufacture. In the average of the years 1824 and 1825, compared with the same years in the cotton trade, the increased consumption of the silk trade was 156, and in the cotton 83 ; I should mention that on cotton I do not know professionally, but I believe the duties were merely scale duties ; there has been lately a duty on raw cotton, but at those periods the duty on raw cotton was next to nothing during the whole of that period. The numbers I have given are 31½ silk, 22 cotton ; 70 silk, 48 cotton ; 156 silk, 83 cotton ; during those last two years, 1824 and 1825, the duties were consider-ably reduced ; the average duty of 5s. per lb. on raw silks was reduced to 3d. a pound, that on thrown silk from 14s. 8d. to 7s. 6d. per lb. ; I will avoid further details for the present ; I should add with respect to the years 1815 to 1824 and 1825, our wages then were at the rate of about 10½d. per yard for weaving a certain description, with trifling variations, during those periods ; there was scarcely any alteration in the wages during that long period ; the silk trade was a rapidly increas-ing trade, and sustained those wages, which were only moderate wages under all circumstances ; the medium numbers of 1821, 1822 and 1823, and 1824 and 1825, that is the medium of those two points compared with 1815, 1816 and 1817, still the starting point is, on silk 113, the corresponding numbers in the cotton 65 ; taking the whole of that period previously to the repeal of the laws of 1766, the numbers abstractedly were these, 31½ silk against 22 cotton ; 70 silk against 48 cotton ; 156 silk against 83 cotton, and 113 silk against 65 ; taking the various quantities in 1826, 1827, 1828, 1829 and 1830, I find the numbers to be 17 per cent. increase in silk over the five preceding years 1821–23, 1824–25, whereas the increase on cotton during the same period was 36¾ per cent.

4037. Do you include 1826 and 1830 together, or is it exclusive of those years ?—The years 1826, 1827, 1828, 1829 and 1830, that is to say, that from 1815 to 1825, the respective progress of the silk trade was thus compared with the cotton ; the silk increased in proportion of seven to four of the cotton trade, the progress has been inverted since ; comparing the last five years with the preceding five years, the silk trade has been as six to thirteen in the cotton ; this alteration has taken place notwithstanding low duties, duties reduced from the average of 5s. on raws, as I mentioned before, to 1d. per lb.; and the 14s. 8d. on thrown, as compared with 7s. 6d. to 3s. 6d., so that the amount of duty in 1821, 1822 and 1823, was 729,000l. upon the average ; the average of 1824 and 1825, was 272,000l., and the amount of the five following years 1826, 1827, 1828, 1829 and 1830,

were

Mr.
*Alexis J. Doxat.*

11 April,
1832.

were 82,000*l.*, 128,000*l.*, 111,000*l.*, 45,000*l.*, and 90,000*l.* While upon this subject, I should state that I believe there is no branch of trade in this country upon which the duty was levied with less expense than upon the silk ; upon that subject I would appeal to Mr. Hume of the Board of Trade, who might state that the whole of the silks imported during those periods, were landed in a small space near the Custom House, hardly as large as this room ; the remaining duties were collected at the East India House, under their own lock, so that the expense in collecting those duties was very inconsiderable ; I have mentioned that during the former periods 1815, 1816 and 1817, to 1824 and 1825, the wages were, taking a certain point, 10 ½ *d.* for weaving well and neatly gros de Naples of a description called 10 to 1100 three doubles, and that the differences from year to year were extremely trifling during those periods ; on the whole, I believe they were fully as high from 1821 to 1825 as from 115 to 123 ; since the year 1826 inclusive, the rate of wages has ranged thus, having been previously upon the average 10½*d.* ; from 1815 to 1825 with very trifling variations, about 7½*d.*, 8*d.*, 7*d.*, 6*d.*, 6¼*d.*, and 6*d.*, speaking in round numbers ; having spoken of the quantities, and the rate of wages, I will proceed to the amount of dutes, wages, profits, &c. that I conceive to have been earned in the respective periods I will take in this case.

4038. Are the Committee to understand you to take the rate of wages for the whole of the silk, as that you have taken for the gros de Naples ?—No ; I take that as the pivot on which to proceed to other branches, but that would detain the Committee considerably longer ; I take that point as forming a large basis in the trade, it seems to be a central point, the amount of duties and wages, profit, &c. are stated collectively in this paper ; the average of 1815, 1816 and 1817, I have stated at 2,073,000*l.* ; in 1818, 1819 and 1820, the three following years, 2,719,000*l.* ; in 1821, 1822 and 1823, 3,514,000*l.* ; in 1824 and 1825, 4,263,000*l.* ; the medium of 1821, 1822, 1823, and of 1824 and 1825, part with the old duties and part with the new duties, and with the same rate of wages, 3,888,000*l.* I will now proceed to the five following years : In 1826 the amount was 1,941,000*l.* ; in 1827, 3,647,000*l.* ; in 1828, 2,922,000*l.* ; in 1829, 1,832,000*l.* ; in 1830, 3,182,000*l.* The average of those five years appears to be 2,705,000*l.* As I have mentioned the quantities consumed in the silk and the cotton branches by per centages, I will mention likewise those per centages with relation to the amount of duties, wages, profits, &c. I find the progress from 1815, 1816 and 1817, to the following three years 1818, 1819 and 1820, in the silk trade, with respect to the amount of duties, wages, profits, &c. was 31 per cent., whilst in the corresponding period, in the cotton, it is only 8 per cent. ; the following three years 69½ of silk, 13½ of cotton ; in 1824 and 1825, 105 of silk against 28¼ of cotton ; the medium of 1821, 1822, 1823 and 1824, and 1825, was 87 of silk against 21⅛ of cotton. The following five years 1826 to 1830, as compared with 1821, 1822, 1823, 1824 and 1825, was 30 of silk minus the preceding five years, and the cotton 4¾ per cent. above the said period of 1821–23, 24–25. Taking the single year 1831, comparing the cotton with respect to the quantities, the increase in the silk has been 32⅔ per cent. over the average of five years 1821, 1822, 1823, 1824 and 1825, and the relative increase in the cotton trade has been 67, that is to say, 67 of cotton and 32⅔ of silk. With respect to the wages, comparing 1831 with the cotton trade, the silk trade presented a difference of 33½ per cent. minus the five preceding years, whereas the increase in the cotton has been 7 per cent. plus ; and in the period between 1826 to 1831, being a period of six years, the state of the silk trade has been 31 per cent. minus 1821, 1822, 1823, 1824 and 1825, whereas the cotton has been 5 per cent. above ; that is, silk 31 per cent. *under*, against cotton 5 per cent. *above.* I have mentioned before, that with respect to quantities consumed, the proportions were as silk 7, to 4 of the cotton trade previously to 1826 ; and since then the relation is as silk 6, to 13 cotton. In respect to duties, wages, profits, &c. taking the same view of the subject, the increase from 1815, 1816 and 1817, to 1824 and 1825, is 8 per cent. per annum *in favour* of the silk trade as compared with cotton. Since that the progress has been *inverted*, the relative progress of 1826 to 1830, as compared with 1821 to 1825, has been 7 per cent. *against* the silk trade ; whereas before it was 8 per cent. per annum *in favour* of the silk trade, showing an inversion. I have mentioned, when I was speaking of the amounts of wages and duties drawn from the silk trade during the years 1826, 1827, 1828, 1829 and 1830, that the variations were very considerable from year to year, as will appear by the amounts which I will read over again, because they are very important. In the year 1826, 1,941,000*l.*,

678.                                                                                    the

Mr.
*Alexis J. Doxat.*

11 April,
1832.

the next year, 1827, 3,647,000 *l.*; in 1828, 2,922,000 *l.*; in 1829, 1,832,000 *l.*; in 1830, 3,182,000 *l.*; not only have the collective amounts, in the respective years, varied exceedingly in 1826, 1827, 1828, 1829 and 1830, but the amounts *in the years* have varied considerably. I have here a statement of the year 1831, it can be only an approximating statement; but I have supposed this in 1831, taking round numbers, to be 2,600,000 *l.* The point I wish particularly to look to is, not only have the greatly reduced returns of 1826, 1827, 1828, 1829 and 1830, averaging 2,700,000 *l.* per annum, and those of 1829, 1830 and 1831, 2,534,000 *l.*, greatly fluctuated from year to year during that period of six years in which we have been open to foreign competition, but the variations in the course of the *same year* have been extreme; it is estimated, for example, that the variations in 1831 have been as follows, always speaking approximatively: the first quarter at the rate of about 3,100,000 *l.* per annum; the second quarter at the rate of 2,900,000 *l.* per annum; the third quarter at the rate of 2,600,000 *l.* per annum; the fourth quarter at the rate of 1,800,000 *l.* per annum; the medium of that year 2,600,000 *l.* per annum, the amount at which I have over stated the result of 1831. Then I proceed to observe, if 2,600,000 *l.* in one year be miserable for our industrious classes engaged in this branch of our manufactures, what must be the intensity of their sufferings when working at the rate of 1,800,000 *l.*!

4039. How do you assume that that is miserable?—I will endeavour to show that; there are some points which I know of my own knowledge; others, that must, in some respects, be hypothetical; I have endeavoured to inquire into those points; " Figures cannot convey any adequate idea of such a state of things; and that in winter months;" it can only be conceived by personal inspection in Spitalfields and other silk manufacturing districts. The intensity of such wretchedness can only be compared in degree with " the exemplary patience, and peaceable forbearance, and loyal demeanour, with which the poignancy of those sufferings is borne." Considerations these, which make it a duty, an imperative duty, in those acquainted with that state of things, to intreat the attention of His Majesty's Government towards it, and towards the causes to which it is referrible. I have mentioned before, the valuation in quantities, and in amount of wages; and I will add one observation besides, which is, that according to various comparative estimates, grounded on every antecedent, whilst the average amount of wages in 1821, 1822, 1823, 1824 and 1825, the medium of those two periods, which was about 3,900,000 *l.*, would have been more than 6,000,000 *l.* in 1829 to 1831, instead of 2,530,000 *l.*, which is the actual result of these three years. I should state here, that when I mentioned 3,900,000 *l.* as the average amount of the years 1821, 1822, 1823, 1824 and 1825, I have taken the average of those five years at very reduced estimates.

4040. Are the Committee to understand, from this last statement, that it is your opinion, that if the duty of 14 *s.* 8 *d.* had not been taken off, and the prohibition continued against the importation, the amount of your manufacture in silk would now have been six millions instead of three, as it appears?—I have endeavoured to make comparative statements of what the progress might have been with the continuation of high duties, and the same rate of wages; and likewise, what that progress might have been with a considerable reduction of duties, which is a benefit to the trade. There is no knowing to what extent the trade might have been carried, with the low duties of 1 *d.* per lb. on the raw silk, and 5 *s.* per lb. on the thrown, and a continuance of protection from the imports of foreign manufactured silks, that is, of a continuance of the protective laws of 1766; but taking the rate of 10½ *d.* per yard, for weaving gros de Naples, and the other charges of manufacture in proportion; taking the rate of duties, such as they existed in the previous years, without taking entirely by itself the great increase in 1824 and 1825, I find by taking it with those old duties, as they then existed, and taking it with the low duties, and at the rate of 8½ *d.* for weaving, I arrive at nearly the same result, *i. e.* six millions, or thereabout. Then, in the latter period, the advantage is this, that with low duties, a larger proportion of wages would go to the industrious class of this country, so that less would go directly to the Exchequer, but it would go in the most beneficial way to the industrious employment of our lower classes.

4041. Have you made any statement of what the prices of the silk manufacture would have been, supposing this state of things to have existed?—Yes, I have for the year 1830, where I assume the weaving at 8½ *d.*, and with the low duties I have even made an addition to the price of the raw silk, corresponding to 2 *d.* per yard; because I believe, that if this country had gone on working at the rate it should

have

Mr.
*Alexis J. Doxat.*

11 April,
1832.

have worked at, with low duties, and a small decrease in the wages, the silk trade in this country would have been so considerable, that it would have had an influence upon the price of silk, not only in this country, but in foreign countries: and I will show that; I made a statement at the rate of 3*s*. 1*d*. a yard, which I have called 3*s*. 3*d*., supposing, that had we gone on manufacturing under such circum-stances, the trade would have been so greatly extended, as to have had some influence on the prices of the raw material.

4042. Is it your opinion, that if the price of the raw material had been kept up by that great additional duty, the increase would have been in the proportion you state?—The amount of wages and duties, &c. would have been the same, that is, 6,000,000 *l*.; the material would not have been so great; it would have been much less labour, with infinitely more wages for labour to the lower classes.

4043. What would have been the effect upon the price of the raw material, provided the 14*s*. 8*d*. duty had been continued?—I have not extended my calcula-tion to that at present.

4044. You estimate the wages as founded on one article, the gros de Naples? —Yes.

4045. Do you understand that silk will follow a different rule from that of any other article?—That answer would require developement. I will beg, at present, if the Committee will permit me, to go through the papers before me, which may answer some of the questions the Committee may be pleased to propose. Three or four days ago I was requested, by an Honourable Member of this Committee, to present a Table, in which the amount of duties should be separated from the amount of wages, and this [*producing the same, Vide* No. 3.] is the result; taking the amount of wages and profit alone, in the years 1818, 1819 and 1820, as com-pared with 1815, 1816 and 1817, the increase in those years, in wages and profit, was 32 per cent.; the following three years, 1821, 1822 and 1823, over 1815, 1816 and 1817, 74 per cent. in wages and profit; in 1824 and 1825, over 1815, 1816, 1817, 142 per cent., the medium of 1821, 1822 and 1823, 1824 and 1825, as compared with the three first years, 1815, 1816 and 1817, was 108 per cent.; in the year 1826, as compared with 1824 and 1825, the decrease has been 53 per cent.; in 1827 the decrease upon 1824 and 1825 was 12 per cent.; in 1828, 30 per cent., under the same years 1824 and 1825; in 1829, 55 per cent.; in the year 1830, 23 per cent. under 1824 and 1825; the average of 1826, 1827, 1828, 1829 and 1830, has been 34 per cent., in respect of wages and profits, under the average of 1824 and 1825; taking the year 1831 alone, that decrease has been 40 per cent.; taking the six years, from 1826 to 1831, as compared with 1824 and 1825, the decrease has been 35 per cent.; this is the only statement in which I took the point of comparison between the latter years, and 1824 and 1825; in every other paper I have placed the comparisons with 1821, 1822, 1823, 1824 and 1825, for reasons I will state.

Appendix (F.)

4046. Where are the Committee to learn the component parts of the sum of 1,608,000*l*.?—It will be my duty to show that. I have taken a comparative view of five years, five years and five years, that is, 1816, 1817, 1818, 1819 and 1820; 1821, 1822, 1823, 1824 and 1825, and 1826, 1827, 1828, 1829 and 1830. I have taken a comparative view of the quantities consumed in the three periods of five years each; the increase of 1821, 1822, 1823, 1824 and 1825, over 1816, 1817, 1818, 1819 and 1820, was 79½ per cent. in quantities, and in 1826, 1827, 1828, 1829 and 1830, as compared with 1821, 1822, 1823, 1824 and 1825, was 17 per cent. increase.

4047. Why do you take the comparison from 1816, when all the other Tables begin with 1815?—Because I have taken it in periods of five years, that the Com-mittee may have it in every possible view, to show the various points of comparison; then if we deduct the 17 per cent. increase in the last five years from 79½, the increase in the preceding five years, there is a balance against the silk trade of 62½ per cent.; the quantities in cotton will be found thus: 45 per cent. increase in 1821, 1822, 1823, 1824 and 1825, over 1816 to 1820, and the increase in the last five years 1826 to 1830, over 1821 to 1825, 36¼ per cent., making a decrease in progress of quantities of 8¼ per cent., whereas the decrease in the relative period in the silk trade was 62½ per cent. in quantities. With respect to the amount of wages the comparison is thus: the amount of wages, duties, profits, &c. in the silk trade in 1821, 1822, 1823, 1824 and 1825, as compared with the five preceding years, was 58 per cent. increase; since that an *inversion* has taken place the last five years of 30 per cent. decrease; if we add the increase to the inversion of 30 per

cent.,

cent., it will give a balance against the silk trade of 88 per cent. in respect of wages and duties. Taking the same view of the cotton trade, the progress from 1821 to 1825, over the five preceding years, from 1815 to 1820 was $15\frac{1}{2}$ per cent., and the progress the last five years, 1826 to 1831, as compared with 1821 to 1825, was 5 per cent., that is a less increase; the balance of those two increases shows a less rapid progress in the cotton of $10\frac{1}{2}$ per cent., whereas the decrease in the silk trade was 88 per cent. during the same period. I should observe, in addition to these various points of comparison, I have drawn comparisons of the increases and decreases per annum, not only periodically but per annum, which will form points of reference. I have prepared a paper to show the principle on which I have made those estimates.

Appendix (F.)

*[The Witness delivered in the same, Vide No. 4.]*

4048. You produce this for the purpose of showing the Committee the principle on which you have made out these estimates?—Yes; we made formerly more waste on silks than we do now, I have taken that into the account.

4049. Do any of your statements show the proportion of silk made up into plain goods and fancy goods?—Yes, I have assumed that; in the former years we manufactured one-fifth in figured and fancy goods, that is an assumption of course, there can be no exact statement of that sort. I have assumed, that in the last six years we have manufactured at the rate of one-tenth and one-eighth of those higher branches; but I find, by various information I have lately obtained, that the proportions in figured and fancy goods is considerably less than I had made it of late years; I have reckoned one-fifth in former years, and from one-eighth to one-tenth of late years; but I find, that in latter years, it has been considerably less; I refer to the period since the foreign competition has come against us.

4050. On what do you ground your information that the portion of fancy goods has decreased?—There can be nothing precise upon that point; but I believe I have been enabled to obtain correct information.

Appendix (F.)

4051. What do you consider a good proportion of figured and fancy goods?—I should consider one-fifth as a good proportion. I have prepared another Table, [*producing it, Vide* No. 5.] This is a comparative view of various respective costs of manufacture at London and Lyons, of good gros de Naples, of common colours, "10 to 1100, three double," neat make; when I mention neat make, I should explain what it is I mean; one man having to make a gros de Naples, and another man having to make, comparatively speaking, a common sacking; an inexperienced hand may work a gros de Naples at $9d.$, another at $1s.$ I take my estimate on good work, well made; I compare London with Lyons. I then go to other parts of Europe, in which this article may be made cheaper, as it may be in other parts of England, as also of the most excellent manufacture in various parts of England; but London and Lyons I consider as giving the proper point of comparison, I take it at the best average quality.

4052. Are those actual prices, and in what years are the prices fixed?—This Table is a comparative range of variations, at present it may be applicable to any year since the alteration of the system, with the exception, that I have assumed a rate of wages in column No. 1, $8\frac{1}{2}d.$ weaving, which it is necessary to introduce in figures; but which, I am sorry to say, has not existed since the competition brought against us, and that $8\frac{1}{2}d.$ is, in itself, a considerable reduction on former years. I beg to say, that I have been requested, at various periods, to publish these statements, but I have never done so; they are printed for the use of the Committee; I consider them as entirely for their use.

---

*Veneris, 13° die Aprilis, 1832.*

---

## THE RIGHT HON. THE EARL GROSVENOR, in the Chair.

---

Mr. *Alexis James Doxat*, called in; and further Examined.

4053. WILL you proceed in your explanation of Paper No. 5?—When I had the honour to be here last, I stated to the Committee, that one object in printing this statement, in fact, my only motive was to save as much as possible, trouble to the Committee; to bring every element of the question as much as possible under the view of the Committee, and to condense every part as much as it was in my

power

Mr.
*Alexis J. Doxat.*

13 April,
1832.

power so to do. The utility of analytical statements is this, that they furnish a clue to all the elements of the question that it is intended to bring under review; an analysis is a point of reference; I am bound to show from every one of these papers, the materials from which I have derived what I have set down; it is not easy to wade through an immense mass of papers, but when these documents and calculations are brought to one focus, reference can be made to any one, two, or twenty points which may be desired, with the utmost facility; an immense mass of papers, if it be not condensed into analysis, is worth nothing; a man may either deceive himself, or he may deceive those before whom he is called; I have here two boxes, the result of my researches for the last ten years; having employed my leisure time in those inquiries, I have spent the interval since the Committee met, in endeavouring to condense still more the information I then gave; but a misfortune happened at seven this morning, the press of the lithographer broke, and I am not able to present it in that shape; the last three or four hours have been occupied in repairing the loss. In the course of the examination with which I was honoured the day before yesterday, I had frequent occasion to recur to various rates of wages, at various periods; and as that forms a very important part of the question, I will beg to detain the Committee a few minutes upon that subject; I have endeavoured at various periods to make inquiry of the amount of wages which may be earned per day and per week in various articles of silk manufacture; but leaving the lowest and highest branches of the subject for the present, I will confine myself to this, on which my statement is grounded. I have been informed by various persons, and by various classes in the silk trade, that taking the average of circumstances, taking the average of material, taking the average of time that is lost by the man obtaining his work, and carrying it back, likewise the circumstance whether a man works with much quickness, or is a slow hand; I have been informed, that under all those circumstances, the average quantity of the description of silk called gros de Naples, 10 to 1100 three double, is about three yards and a half per day; taking the chance whether the warps be good or bad, or whether the delays be greater or less, I make those calculations on the labour of twelve hours per day, inclusive of the usual interruptions for meals, &c.; I am aware that if a man works sixteen or eighteen hours in the twenty-four, he can do more work than that.

4054. From what places have you derived this information?—London and different parts of the country.

4055. Do you refer to Spitalfields?—Yes, but I have made comparative views; if a man works sixteen hours per day here, he can do the same at Lyons; if he can work eighteen hours here, he can do the same at Lyons; if a man has a small family here, he may have a small family there; every thing ought to be parallel, not what one bachelor can get in this country, in comparison with a man of less ability, but every thing should be relative; in stating that the average of that quantity of work well done, neatly got up, is three yards and a half, which at the rate of $10\frac{1}{2}d.$, it will produce $3s.\ 0\frac{3}{4}d.$ If they require frequently the work to be done more quickly, it may be badly done; and I am told that hands that work moderately fast, if they are steady and able at their work, will turn out work worth some pence more per yard in value than work hurried; if a man can do four or five yards here, he can do the same at Lyons; again I submit, all is relative. At $10\frac{1}{2}d.$ per yard I find that the gross amount per week is $18s.\ 4\frac{1}{2}d.$, from that, various deductions are to be made, they are technical deductions called quilling, loom standing, candles, fire, soap, utensils, twisting on and turning in; altogether I find those charges were, at the rate of $10\frac{1}{2}d.$,; $5s.$ to be deducted from $18s.\ 4\frac{1}{2}d$, leaving $13s.\ 4\frac{1}{2}d.$ as the nett amount of wages per week, arising from the rate of $10\frac{1}{2}d.$ per yard; this was the rate paid from 1815 to 1824 and 1825, with some small variations; and I believe the average rate of wages in 1821, 1822, 1823, 1824 and 1825, the five years preceding the alteration of our laws, was fully as high as in the preceding years. I will descend to the statement, on which I have established the point to which our labourers in this class of industry ought at least to be entitled, that is $8\frac{1}{2}d.$ for the same class of work.

4056. Do you conceive that a man at $8\frac{1}{2}d.$ now, is doing so well as a man was formerly at $10\frac{1}{2}d$?— Not quite, but that is a rate ($8\frac{1}{2}d.$) which our labourers have not enjoyed, or with very few exceptions, since our change of laws; the gross amount for the said good class of plain work, $14s.\ 11d.$, the average expenses to be deducted from that $4s.\ 5\frac{1}{2}d.$, leaving $10s.\ 5\frac{1}{2}d.$ per week as the nett amount of wages referrible to the rate of $8\frac{1}{2}d.$ per yard; I will now proceed to that point which has been frequently introduced in my statement for late years, which is $6d.$ per yard; I find at

678. that

Mr.
*Alexis J. Doxat.*

13 April,
1832.

that rate, the gross amount in 10*s*. 6*d*. per week, from which, deducting 3*s*. 6*d*. for the charges, there remains 7*s*. nett wages per week; contrasted with the former point of 13*s*. 4½*d*. nett per week.

4057. Why do you allow only 3*s*. 6*d*. for quilling, loom standing, candles, &c., when it was 5*s*. before?—It is against myself; by doing so, the smaller I place the charges to the reduced amount, the greater I make the nett amount of the wages of the weaver.

4058. Is the relative deduction 3*s*. 6*d*. now, the wages being 10*s*. 6*d*., as the relative deduction was 5*s*. when the wages were 18*s*.?—I have taken it at that, but I think I have rather under-rated the deductions to be made from the gross amount of wages; rents and other things are rather diminished, candles are cheaper, soap is cheaper, loom standing is cheaper; still I do not consider that the actual reduction in the charges which bear on the weaver, are quite so much as the ratio of 5*s*. to 3*s*. 6*d*., which I have taken as the basis of that calculation. On their general expenses, *i. e.* for food, &c., there is not that reduction.

4059. Do you conceive 5*s*. cheaper than it really was?—No; I think that was about the mark; the nett wages of the labourer are now as 7*s*. compared with 13*s*. 4½*d*.; but there is another view of this question; that, at the former period, our weavers had a large proportion of figured and fancy goods, which went in assistance; for example, in a house in which there were five looms, there might be one employed in figure and fancy goods; which loom, being worked by workmen of more ability, afforded altogether, being a higher branch of manufacture, not only a larger rate of wages, but a larger amount of wages; consequently there was a larger distribution of wages throughout the silk districts. I have assumed, in my comparative Estimates, the quantity of figured and fancy goods to be at one-fifth of the whole, during the periods of 1815–17 to 1824–25. I have assumed, in subsequent stages, that it has been one-eighth and one-tenth, but I find that I have considerably understated the case; that the proportion of figured and fancy goods has been, of late years, considerably under the proportion of one-eighth and one-tenth. If we look at the difference existing between 7*s*. and 13*s*. 4½*d*., we shall find a difference of 48 per cent. against our labourers, for the same quantity of work; if to that we add the considerable diminution which has taken place in figured and fancy goods, and that that was spread over the whole trade, we shall find a greater diminution still in the relative amount of wages accruing from this branch of industry. I have only stated 48 per cent. with reference to plain goods.

4060. The result is, that between 1815 and 1830, the reduction of wages is 48 per cent., there being no alteration between 1815 and 1825?—I am aware that there have been variations in the payment for industry, and I wish to call the attention of the Committee to the causes which have operated to produce that.

4061. The same rate of wages had continued from 1815 to 1825?—Pretty nearly so.

4062. Then, between 1815 and 1830, the reduction has been 48 per cent.?—Not from 1815 to 1831, but actually from the period of 1826, that is, subsequently to the period of 1824–25; the introduction of foreign manufactured silks commenced in 1826, the reduction, which I have stated at 48 per cent., may be 50 or 55 according to the circumstances. Since I made the statement, if I have mis-stated, it is my duty to correct it on behalf of those more particularly concerned, *i. e.* the lower classes. I am told that where I introduce the point of comparison as 10½*d*. is to 6*d*., the point of comparison is greater still; taking the proportion of figured and plain goods, there are many species of manufacture, both plain and figured, in which there is a greater difference than from 10½*d*. to 6*d*., *i. e.* many in the ratio of 9*d*. to 4½*d*., &c. I would call the attention of the Committee to one point; that since the removal of the protective laws of 1766, which took place in 1826, the changes in this branch of industry have been so considerable and so sudden, from year to year, in every branch of the silk trade, that the lower classes particularly. have experienced the greatest inconvenience from the alterations. Not only has the average amount of wages been considerably less in 1826 to 31, than in 1821–23 to 1824–25, but the variations have been very great from year to year, and even in the same year; and such is the pressure of foreign competition on this branch of industry, that it happens, not unfrequently, that our people when working at the wretched rate of 6*d*. per yard, have only half-work; the lowest rate of wages have frequently been accompanied with a great diminution of work, the same causes depressing the wages, and occasioning an enormous diminution

in

Mr.
*Alexis J. Doxat.*

13 April,
1832.

in the quantity of work, at various periods of the year; so that when they have been working at 6 *d.* a yard, the nett proceeds of which was 7 *s.* per week when in full-work, being at half-work on low wages, their nett wages have been only 3 *s.* 6 *d.* per week.

4063. Has it not been the fact, that while trade was good at Manchester it was bad at Coventry, and so on; do you mean to say that the silk trade has been uniform in every place, and that Macclesfield is equally distressed with Coventry?— Every thing tends, among ourselves, to regulate itself; there cannot be a great activity in Manchester without a corresponding activity in Spitalfields; there may be demands for particular kinds of goods, but whenever the silk trade at Manchester has been in a state of prosperity, a correspondent prosperity has existed in Spitalfields, and Coventry, and Macclesfield, and in other parts of the country.

4064. Is not there at the present moment great distress in Spitalfields and Coventry, and, at the same time, is not the state of the trade in Manchester satisfactory?—A large proportion of goods made at Manchester are low goods and mixed goods, to take advantage of an enormous bounty accruing to that class of goods, from debentures, which are sold on the market at various prices, from 1 *d.* to 7 *d.* per lb., although they entitle the exporter of those goods to an allowance of 3 *s.* 6 *d.*, 1 *s.* 2 *d.* and 7 *d.* per lb.; and that in most cases those goods have been manufactured from raw silks, which have only paid 1 *d.* per lb. duty, and from waste silks, on which the duty is only 1 *s.* per 112 lbs.; but even those goods are manufactured at very low wages to the labourers; and speaking generally of Manchester, I understand that the state of the silk trade there has been very far from satisfactory, often wretched, in the last few years. I believe that in the country, both at Manchester and at Macclessfield—at Macclesfield I know, from my personal inspection of the goods, it is the case—there are some establishments that would do honour to any part of Europe, but in every place there are distinctions; there is in one place a larger proportion of goods of the higher class; and the class of goods manufactured at Manchester altogether is of a lower, and a considerably lower standard than the goods manufactured in Spitalfields, which yield a much larger proportion of labour; this brings me to the very point in question. I will mention a case, to which I would most respectfully draw the attention of this Honourable Committee; I understand that in former periods, taking 1821, 1822, 1823, 1824 and 1825, large quantities of goods were manufactured at Macclesfield, in the higher branches, that is to say figured and fancy goods; and I understand that the weaver who worked 16 to 20 ounces per week, in those higher branches of the trade, earned from 20 *s.* to 30 *s.* per week, they are branches which require much ability, the average of those was 25 *s.* per week; I understand that the average charges to be deducted were 6 *s.* 3 *d.*, leaving a nett amount of 18 *s.* 9 *d.* per week, which 18 *s.* 9 *d.* spread over 18 ounces, would give 1 *s.* 0½ *d.* nett, per oz. I understand that a very considerable proportion of those works in the higher branches have been lost to Macclesfield, not from want of ability, because there is very excellent manufacture, as I shall mention, at Macclesfield. I will mention in particular, the name of Messrs. Samuel Pearson & Brothers, because when I was requested, some years ago, to make particular inquiries, I had all the samples of their goods, I showed them to foreigners, and they were extremely admired. I understand that of late a very large proportion of those higher branches of silks have been lost to that town, and that large proportions of low goods, such as low bandannas, and other low descriptions of goods are manufactured, from 40 to 60 ounces of which are worked up in the course of a week, at the rate of 6 *s.* to 9 *s.* per week; the average of that gross amount per week is 7 *s.* 6 *d.* from which deducting 2 *s.* 6 *d.*, a nett amount of 5 *s.* per week remains for the labour; which amount of 5 *s.* per week, spread over 50 ounces, the average, leaves 1¼ *d.* per ounce, contrasted with 1 *s.* 0½ *d.* nett, per ounce.

4065. The Committee are to understand, that the prices you have given in the Paper No. 5, from 1815 to the present time, are the prices which are paid to the Spitalfields weavers?—Yes.

Appendix (F.)

4066. You state, in Paper No. 5, that the silk trade in France is subject, from the causes you adverted to, to great fluctuations?—Yes.

Appendix (F.)

4067. From what causes have the fluctuations in the silk trade at Lyons arisen?—Lyons manufactory, being principally for export, is subject to very great and sudden variations; for eight or nine months they will be working at the rate of 70 to 75 centimes per ell (aune); the orders for America will be diminished, or something will occur on the Continent to diminish the demands for export;

678.                                                                                              for

Mr.
*Alexis J. Doxat.*

13 April,
1832.

for instance, a war between Russia and Turkey, also the demand for home consumption arising from a disturbed state of things. At Lyons, if any thing occurs to diminish the demand of their manufactures for four or five months or less, there is a fall of wages and a fall of silk, and if they have a great abundance of goods on hand the manufacturer is willing to throw off the profit, interest and incidentals, in order to get rid of his goods; they find England a considerable and a rich market, at which they could get their money at once, whether by immediate sale or by way of consignment; and consequently we are overwhelmed with large quantities at considerable reductions; and the more they are depressed from any contingent cause, the more they press upon our industry to a calamitous degree, beyond the usual and already very detrimental course of their competition on our wages of labour, and consumption of our own manufactures.

Appendix (F.)
4068. Will you explain the object you have in giving in Paper No. 5?—The same object I am endeavouring to develope, that the French manufacturers having always great quantities of goods to distribute all over the world, greater proportions of them are sent here in times of pressure with them.

4069. Taking the years between 1815 and 1825, when you state that the nett wages to the manufacturer were 13 s. 4½ d., are you enabled to give the Committee information, what was the nett wages to the Lyons weaver for the same description of goods?—I can state the comparison for the last five years of the relative wages of weaving in London and at Lyons in 1821, 1822, 1823, 1824 and 1825. I have mentioned, that the rate of wages in London was 10½ d.; the relative price at Lyons was, I understand, 6¼ d., but I should mention here, that out of that the weaver winds his shute, which is not done here by weavers, which occasions him an expense of a halfpenny, so that it is reduced to 5¾ d.

4070. Is he supposed to make the same quantity as the London weaver?—I am assuming, that a man in France can make the same quantity as a man in England, I am supposing an equality of quality; we have made great improvements, and they have made great improvements; this difference between 10½ d. and 5¾ d., made 83 per cent. In all my comparative Estimates, I assume an equality of perfection, although the French possess some advantages peculiar to themselves, on which I will not detain the Committee at the present moment.

4071. Have the goodness to state what was the amount when you say it cost 8½ d.?—I have before stated, that our weavers have of late years worked mostly at the rates of 7 d. to 6 d. per yard; but I consider 8½ d. as a very moderate remuneration for the description of work alluded to in all my estimates, and that to which they are at least entitled. I understand, on the other hand, that 5½ d. is the usual rate at which the French weavers work of late years, when they have an usual quantity of employment; deducting a halfpenny (as before mentioned) for winding the shute, there remains 5 d. per yard, which compared with 8½ d., presents a difference of 70 per cent. only, whilst the former relative rates of 10½ d. and 6¼ d., equal to 5¾ d. presented 83 per cent. higher at London than at Lyons. Consequently, the highest point which I take in my present statement (No. 5.) and in all my comparative statements, as the rate to which our weavers are at the least entitled to, is lower relatively than that which existed in 1821-25.

Appendix (F.)

4072. Can you state the comparative wages when in this country it is at 6 d.?—I have taken 6 d. as our lowest range, although I am told I might have taken it still lower. I am comparing it with the price of their very low wages; that is, when they are at 4 d. per yard, which is equal to 3½ d., taking off a halfpenny for winding the shute; comparing the relative rate of 6 d. per yard with us for the class of goods I have been mentioning, with the very depressed rate of 3½ d. at Lyons, I find the difference to be 71 per cent.; the prices in France apply not to a particular period, but to the variations they are continually exposed to, and over the contingent effects of which we can have no control.

4073. If it does not relate to any particular period, what conclusion are the Committee to draw from this?—It is another element of the question, because the French are exposed to continual variations, not only in the rates of wages for weaving, and all other processes of manufacture, but in the price of their silks also; all these causes combined, occasion an enormous variation in the price of the goods they send to this country; and the greater the depression, the larger masses of goods they press upon us; feeling, besides, willing to sacrifice their profits, interest and charges for incidentals, to send away their goods to a market.

4074. At what do you estimate the quantities and produce of thrown and raw silk consumed by the French manufacturers, and other Continental manufacturers, to the competition of which we are open ?—I have no exact collective data upon that subject ; I will mention what I understood to be the French consumption, and I will proceed to what I believe to be the Swiss and Rhenish consumption. In France 5,500,000 lbs. English per annum. I will mention here, as it is a question connected with this point, that the French work on a higher standard of silk than the English ; they work upon the average of 40 deniers, whereas we work upon 60 deniers, which is a coarser standard by 50 per cent.

4075. That 5,500.000 averages 40 deniers ?—Yes.

4076. Have you any means of knowing the quantity used in Switzerland ?— I have drawn out a statement of the quantities of foreign silk imported and consumed in France in the years 1825, 1826, 1827 and 1828 ; of the quantity imported in 1829, 1830 and 1831, I have not the particulars. The average of 1825, 1826, 1827 and 1828, I find to be 380,000 pounds of raw silks ; the imports of France in raw silk, are composed mostly of the coarse descriptions ; that is to say, the Brussa and other Levant silks, also of the coarser descriptions from Naples ; if it were not for that the standard would be higher.

4077. What is the quantity of thrown imported ?—Six hundred and ninety-three thousand pounds English on the same average of years, principally of Piedmont organzine, which I understand is required for particular purposes, velvets, &c.

4078. Are not silks of French growth suitable to the manufacture of those descriptions of goods ?—Their silks, as I have before mentioned, are of very good qualities ; but they import Piedmont organzines more particularly for certain works. The total amount, as I have stated before in answer to inquiries, is 1,073,000 pounds of raw and thrown silk. I have reason to believe that the imports of France from foreign ports of silks, both raw and thrown, in 1829, 1830 and 1831, has decreased, whereas the produce of their own silks has increased correspondingly. I find that they consume large quantities of waste, not only in the raw state, but in a spun state ; the average quantity of the raw waste imported for consumption into France in 1825 to 1828, was 146,000 pounds English weight ; the average of spun was 287,000 pounds ; the collective quantity was 433,000 pounds of waste. I have thought it right to state this quantity, because I am not certain whether it has been included in the statement of 5,500,000 lbs. or exclusive of it.

[*The Witness delivered in the following Statement.*]

678.                                                                                    Paper,

## Paper, No. 16.

### FRENCH SILK MANUFACTURES.

A STATEMENT of the Quantities of Raw and Thrown Silks, as also of Waste Silk, in the Rough, and in a Spun State, Imported into *France* from *Italy* and other Parts, for Consumption.

| | | 1825: | 1826: | 1827: | 1828: |
|---|---|---|---|---|---|
| Raw Silks | Kilogrammes | 145,000 = w$^t$ 319,000 Eng. | Kils. 285,000 = w$^t$ 627,000 | Kils. 130,000 = w$^t$ 286,000 | Kils. 131,000 = w$^t$ 288,000 |
| Thrown Silks | - - - | 337,000 = 741,000 - | 343,000 = 755,000 | 338,000 = 740,000 | 242,000 = 534,000 |
| | Kils. - - | 482,000 = w$^t$ 1,066,000 Eng. | 628,000 = w$^t$ 1,382,000 | 468,000 = w$^t$ 1,026,000 | 373,000 = w$^t$ 822,000 |

| | RAW SILK. | THROWN SILK. | TOTALS of Raw and Thrown. |
|---|---|---|---|
| 1825 | w$^t$ 319,000 Eng. | w$^t$ 741,000 Eng. | w$^t$ 1,060,000 |
| 1826 | 627,000 | 755,000 | 1,382,000 |
| 1827 | 286,000 | 740,000 | 1,026,000 |
| 1828 | 288,000 | 534,000 | 822,000 |
| | (¼) w$^t$ 1,520,000 | 2,770,000 | 4,290,000 |
| 1825–28, Averages per Annum | w$^t$ 380,000 | 693,000 | 1,073,000 |

Averages per Annum; 4 Years, 1825 to 1828.

Raw - - w$^t$ 380,000 { The major part consists, I understand, of Brussa (Turkey) and other coarse silks.

Thrown - - 693,000 { Piedmont Organzine, and small portions of other descriptions.

Total - - w$^t$ 1,073,000

Average of 1825–28 - - 4 years.

---

Exclusive of Waste Silk, in the Rough, and in a Spun State; as follows:

| | WASTE (Raw.) | WASTE (Spun.) | TOTALS OF WASTE. |
|---|---|---|---|
| 1825 | Kil. 55,000 = w$^t$ 132,000 | Kil. 105,000 = w$^t$ 252,000 | Kil. 160,000 = w$^t$ 384,000 Eng. |
| 1826 | 67,000 = 161,000 | 115,000 = 276,000 | 182,000 = 437,000 |
| 1827 | 54,000 = 130,000 | 130,000 = 312,000 | 184,000 = 442,000 |
| 1828 | 67,000 = 161,000 | 128,000 = 307,000 | 195,000 = 468,000 |
| | (¼) Kil. 243,000 = w$^t$ 584,000 | Kil. 478,000 = w$^t$ 1,147,000 | Kil. 721,000 = w$^t$ 1,731,000 |
| 1825–28, Averages per Annum | Kil. 61,000 = w$^t$ 146,000 | Kil. 119,000 = w$^t$ 287,000 | Kil. 180,000 = w$^t$ 434,000 |

Averages per Annum, 4 Years, 1825–28; WASTE SILK.

Raw - - Kil. 61,000 = w$^t$ 146,000 Eng.

Spun - - 119,000 = 287,000 -

Kil. 180,000 = w$^t$ 433,000 -

Average of 1825 to 1828 - - 4 Years.

April 1832.     (Errors excepted.)     (signed)     *Alexis James Doxat.*

Mr.
*Alexis J. Doxat.*

13 April,
1832.

4079. Can you state the average quality of French silk?—The silk of French growth is in general of a fine description; every year they improve the reeling of their silks, and I believe they reel them gradually on a finer standard. That improvement in reeling French silks has been very great within the last twenty years. I entered into business in 1798, I had occasion to see a great deal of French silk at that period, and the improvement of the French silk within that period, has been extraordinary.

4080. What is the quality of the thrown Piedmont organzine imported into France, in comparison with the organzine silk imported into this country?—I do not know exactly what is the range of the sizes, but I should think that they import rather a coarser size from Piedmont; I have seen statements grounded rather on size 28 to 30. The fine sizes of French silks are so beautifully reeled that the sort of articles I have alluded to in my statements, that is good gros de Naples, double warp, are almost entirely made of their own silks of the size of 22 deniers; I understand they make their velvet principally with 28 to 30 deniers. I suppose the consumption of Piedmont organzine in France rests upon a coarser standard than that of the Piedmonts imported here, which are from 18–20 to 26–27, the average of our Piedmont size is 24 to 25 deniers compared with the consumption of Piedmontese in France, 28 to 30; to their finer fabrics they apply their own silks.

4081. Will you state the importations into other foreign countries?—I have no exact statements, but I can mention them approximately. I believe in the town of Zurich (one of the largest manufacturing towns in Switzerland) and its neighbourhood, there are about 12,000 looms employed. Those gentlemen who are engaged in manufacture, will understand the relation which that number of looms bears to the silk consumed; it is supposed there are about 15,000 to 16,000 looms at work in Spitalfields, when our manufacture is well employed.

4082. You are not able to state the quantity of silk thrown in Switzerland?—No, not exactly; but there are on the whole considerable manufactures and very large manufactures of ribbons at Basle, there are also very large manufactures at Creveldt and Elberfeldt, and other places on the Rhine, &c.; these manufactures are in such a perfect state, and their wages so low, that they sell considerable quantities of velvets in France, although France excels in the highest descriptions of velvets. From Switzerland I understand large quantities of plain goods are sent to France; plain goods from Zurich, and plain ribbons from Basle, though there is a duty of about 10 per cent.; their aptness to manufacture these goods is so great, and their wages so low, they can afford to send them to France, but they do not send figured ribbons or goods, because France has a peculiar taste and ability in the manufacture of those articles; besides the silk of its own growth is particularly applicable to them.

4083. Is the duty levied by weight or by valuation?—I understand by weight, but I am not certain.

4084. Do you know the duty levied on the importation of velvets?—I do not.

4085. Do you know whether there is any duty levied?—I make no doubt there is.

4086. In speaking of the quantity of silk imported from Italy into France, are you able, from any documents in your possession, to state the total amount of raw and thrown silk exported from Italy?—I have no exact information; I have had very various accounts; I have endeavoured to draw up statements from them, but I found the accounts vary so much that I did not think I could lay them before the Committee with satisfaction.

4087. Are you aware that at the Custom House of Milan and Bergamo, from which the silks principally come, regular accounts are kept?—Yes, of course; but those accounts are by no means sufficiently comprehensive as to the total produce of Italy and Piedmont.

4088. Is the silk of which the plain ribbons sent from Switzerland to France are made, the produce of Switzerland or silk imported from Italy?—Silk imported from Italy, and part from Turkey; Switzerland does not produce silk, with the exception of some trifling quantities, in the parts contiguous to Italy.

4089. Do the Swiss import any but organzine silk from Italy?—Both organzine and tram; they have for some time past established some mills, but they find it mostly answer their purpose better to import it ready thrown from Italy.

4090. Are you able to state whether the quality of organzine and tram

678.

Mr.
Alexis J. Doxat.

13 April,
1832.

imported into Switzerland is better than that imported into France, or is better than that imported into England?—The thrown silks which are imported into France from Italy are, as I have before stated, almost entirely from Piedmont, whereas the Swiss manufacture rest their consumption principally on Lombardy thrown silks, because Switzerland does not manufacture velvets, and some other descriptions to which Piedmonts are more suitable; and I believe the importations of thrown silk from Piedmont into France are principally for velvets, &c.

4091. What is the quality of that silk exported from Lombardy into Switzerland compared with that we import?—I should suppose very much the same range, with this exception, that we import almost entirely organzine, whereas Switzerland imports one-half thrown and one-half tram.

4092. As to the relative quality of our English imported organzine, is it superior or inferior to the imported organzine in Switzerland?—It is of the same ange.

4093. Are the Committee to understand that the Swiss can manufacture plain ribbons which they send into France from that kind of silk?—They manufacture their ribbons with Lombardy silk, but in their figured ribbons they do not equal France at all.

4094. Why are those ribbons imported from Switzerland preferred in France?—They are very well made; I should say equally well made and cheaper; labour in Switzerland being still cheaper than in France. I allude to Basle; the establishments at Basle are so enormous, so considerable, that it is not only their wages, but as they work on a large mass, they produce their goods very cheap.

4095. Are you able to state the quantity of those goods imported into France?—No, I am not, I am told by some of the agents who sell manufactured goods here, that it is so considerable that houses both at Zurich and Basle have regular agents in France, and have depôts in Paris.

4096. Do you know the relative prices?—No; but when they pay about 10 per cent., there must be a difference in the cost.

4097. Is there any duty paid on the importation of thrown silk into Switzerland?—Merely a scale duty.

4098. Is there any duty paid on the importation of thrown silk into Germany?—Merely a scale duty; they have no mills to protect; there are some throwing mills which they are establishing, but their wages and other expenses of building, &c. are so very low, that I suppose they have not thought it necessary to levy a duty to protect their throwing interest.

4099. Will you go on to state the quantity of silk sent to Vienna or Saxony?—I should suppose the manufacture of Vienna is considerable. I have no exact data upon that subject, but I know the principal banking houses at Vienna are much engaged in the silk branch, and that in their establishments they have a separate establishment for the silk; and that it would not be worth their while, if it were not considerable, to interfere in it; but it is fair to say that I do not think there are any goods from Vienna sent here; the manufactures which press upon us essentially are France with plain goods and ribbons of superior descriptions, and figured and fancy goods and ribbons of every kind, besides some velvets, &c. &c. From the Rhenish manufactures we receive velvets and various other goods in which they excel; and from Switzerland, various plain goods and ribbons with some figured ribbons; but on this subject I can speak but generally, our house never having had the least concern in the importation of any kind of foreign manufactured silks.

4100. Do they manufacture for exportation, (alluding to Vienna)? —I think they partly provide Poland and parts of Russia and Greece, the Levant, &c.; they manufacture considerably for their own consumption, but they manufacture for other parts in a degree.

4101. What description of goods do they manufacture for exportation?—I cannot state that exactly.

4102. Do you happen to know the wages of the workmen at Basle?—Not exactly.

4103. Is not a great part of this silk wrought with gold for the Turkish dresses and other things?—At Vienna probably they work that class of goods which goes to the Levant.

4104. Will you state comparatively the quality of silk imported into France and into England?—The consumption of France in foreign organzines rests principally, as I have repeatedly mentioned, on Piedmont organzine; the standard of
those

Mr.
*Alexis J. Doxat.*

13 April,
1832.

those organzines, I believe to be about 28 to 30 deniers on the average, whereas our importations of silk consist principally of Lombardy organzines, and the quantity of Piedmont which we consume averages 24 to 25 deniers.

4105. Will you explain how the quality is regulated, by English terms?—In almost every silk establishment there is an assay machine, upon which they place six small skeins, taken out promiscuously from a bale, on the reel; they wind off 400 French ells, which are weighed with a weight called deniers; after those six smaller skeins of 400 French ells each have been wound off, they are weighed separately, and again together; we consider that the assay is not exact unless it is done on 24 skeins; in Piedmont it is mostly done on 24 skeins; there are other modes of assaying, the time required to make an assay of 24 skeins, may be about three quarters of an hour.

4106. The Committee understand that the lighter the 400 ells weigh, the finer you consider the silk?—Certainly.

4107. Does that mark the equality of the thread?—Yes; the respective weights of each assay, whether of six or of twenty-four small skeins, indicates the degrees of equality, besides the aggregate standard or size.

4108. How do you compare the equality of the thread?—It is a matter of judgment both in regard to quality and equality; but the assay machine is often used, besides the judgment, in regard to equality.

4109. Comparing the quality of thread sent into England with that sent to other countries, which is the best?—I am not aware that there is a distinction; the French require their 28 to 30 deniers reeled with great care; I understand the standard of 28 to 30 deniers, sent to them from Piedmont, is generally of as good qualities as those sent to us in the 24–25; but the qualities being of equal goodness, and our standard of Piedmont organzines finer on an average, the prime cost is correspondingly higher.

4110. Is it your opinion that we get as good Italian thrown silk in England as any other country gets?—No doubt; the market is open to us.

4111. What is the comparative statement of the quality of silk used in England, and the quality of silk used in France, both as to the home product of France, and as to her import?—I have endeavoured to make an approximating statement upon that subject, of which the following is a rough memorandum.

MINUTE intended to show the degrees of fineness (" size " or " titre ") all calculated on the double-thread, on which the Silk Manufacturers have worked during the last Six Years—1826 to 1831.

| | AVERAGES of Quantities consumed per Annum. | Estimated Sizes. |
|---|---|---|
| Thrown Silks (Italian) - | lbs. 375,000 | |
| Raw - ditto - ditto, &c. - | 1,006,000 | Numbers. |
| | 1,471,000 a' 30 deniers × = | 44,130,000 |
| Ditto - Bengal and China - | 1,611,000 a' 80 ditto × = | 128,880,000 |
| Ditto - Turkey - - | 365.000 a' 100 ditto × = | 36,500,000 |
| | 3,447,000 | 209,510,000 |
| Average 1826 to 1831 - | | 61 deniers. |

4112. The standard in France being forty, the standard in England is sixty?—I believe the standard in France is forty; it is, I have reason to believe, at least of that fineness; so that if we calculate our number of pounds by sixty, and theirs by forty, their proportion is much larger than ours, the numbers sixty being fifty per cent. coarser than the forty.

4113. In France they do not use any Bengal silk?—No, or very trifling quantities occasionally; they work on an average on a finer standard than us; they do not make bandannas; their silk manufacture is mostly employed in the superior plain goods, and in figured and fancy goods of all descriptions; comprehensively speaking, in the higher branches of the manufacture.

4114. Are the Committee to understand that the Bengal silk is worked up to make the same kinds they make in France, or a coarser sort of goods?—A coarser kind of goods; for example, those which yield five farthings per pound at

678.                                                                 Macclesfield,

Mr.
*Alexis J. Doxat.*

13 April,
1832.

Macclesfield, contrasted with silks worked in the higher branches, worked at 1 s. 0¼ d. a pound; this is mentioned of course as a conspicuous point.

4115. The coarser require a certain proportion of fine with them?—Some description of goods do. In addition to our working on a lower standard, the standard of 60, and France working on the standard of 40, I should observe, that a silk of the same quality and fineness, for example, an Italian silk of 24 deniers, can be applied either to make plain goods of a second class and a first class, or to make figured and fancy goods; which various descriptions yield respectively 12 s., 20 s., 40 s. or 50 s. and more per pound weight of the raw material. But the effect of foreign competition, being to press still more on the high than on the low descriptions of goods, the more we labour under the baneful influence of that competition, the more we must retreat on the low and lowest descriptions of goods; because there enters in their composition a smaller and much smaller proportion of wages of labour. Hence it is, that of late years Italian silks themselves have, on an average, been worked into much lower classes of goods than previously to the admission of foreign manufactured silks: and in this essential point of view also the standard of English works has become lower yet than would appear by the relative numbers of 60 deniers in England as compared with 40 deniers in France; goods of inferior quality.

4116. At the present moment, which is the highest price raw silk in London, that which will make the clean, even organzine used by the French, *viz.* 28 to 30 deniers, or the finer sorts usually sent from Lombardy, of a size 24 to 28 deniers?—Twenty-eight to thirty deniers; that is the size of Piedmont silk mostly imported into France; but that is very excellent silk. The Piedmontese do not allow of the exportation of their raw silks, so that it is sent to us in the thrown state, in that respect their throwsters have a great advantage. The Piedmontese raw silk is very good silk, well reeled; but if I were to speak of silk of equal quality with Piedmont silk of 28 to 30 deniers, I should say I suppose that silk, from its great superiority, would be worth not less than 18 s. 6 d. per lb. at the usual credit of five months, though not of fine size. The next question is, what is the size of the finer sorts usually sent from Lombardy of the size of 24 to 28 deniers, I should say from 17 s to 18 s.

4117. In this market they would fetch the same price?—Yes, nearly so, but one is finer than the other.

4118. Which bears the highest price at this time in London?—I cannot answer that question, for we do not get the Piedmontese raw silks here.

4119. In what does the superiority of the French home grown silk consist over the Italian silk?—The French silk has a peculiar brilliancy; some French silks have a texture superior to that of Italy, it is susceptible of being reeled exceedingly fine; they keep up the thread of three to four cocoons better in France than in many parts of Italy, owing to the goodness of their cocoons. I have been reminded that silk of 28 to 30 deniers, where it is reeled with great precision, is as valuable as silk of a finer description, because it is wanted for a particular purpose. There is a silk called Turina in Lombardy, and others which are not so fine, but sell for as high a price, because they are reeled with great precision.

4120. The silk imported into France being of 28 to 30 deniers, but being reeled with great precision, you conceive equivalent to some finer sizes of 24 and 25, to which the same attention in reeling has not been paid?—Yes.

4121. Why does one manufactory reel the silk better than another?—For the same reason that every thing is done better or worse in various establishments in every country, according to the degree of ability and industrious application of the principals, &c.

4122. You do not mean to say that the French silk is not better than any other?—No; I mean to say that French silk, as a mass, its texture and its brilliancy, is superior to that of Italy. Piedmont silk that is sent to Lyons of the size 28 to 30, is required for particular purposes; for example, in the highest branches of velvets, they require that particular size. The silk of 28 to 30, sent from Turin to Lyons, is very good.

4123. Is that prepared entirely for the French market?—I am not aware that it is; but the 28 to 30 Piedmont I believe is reeled with the same as the 24 to 25; but there are some ulterior processes of throwing it into organzine.

4124. Are the Committee to understand that in France they can wind better than in England, they having the same quality of silk?—No, not at all; when we consider the relation of wages we have in this country as compared with France

and

and with Italy, our throwing is done relatively lower in this country than it is in France and in Italy; that is to say, that our wages in that branch of industry, are by no means analogous with the wages given in France and Italy. The "reeling" of silk is winding it from the pod or cocoon; the reeling off the silk to convert it into tram and organzine is quite a separate question. The throwster in this country, whether it arises from smaller profits and lower relative wages, or from greater ability, which I will suppose, does his work much cheaper relatively than France and Italy; consequently we have no right to complain of the throwster in this country, as he has been working at such wages as are miserable.

4125. The importation of raw silk into this country appears to have increased very much since 1826, will you state why you conceive the quantity of silk imported has increased in a greater degree than the quantity of thrown, and why, under those circumstances, the throwsters of this country have any reason to complain?—I will beg to give in a statement I have drawn out upon this subject.

Mr.
*Alexis J. Dorat.*

13 April,
1832.

*[The Witness delivered in the following Paper.]*

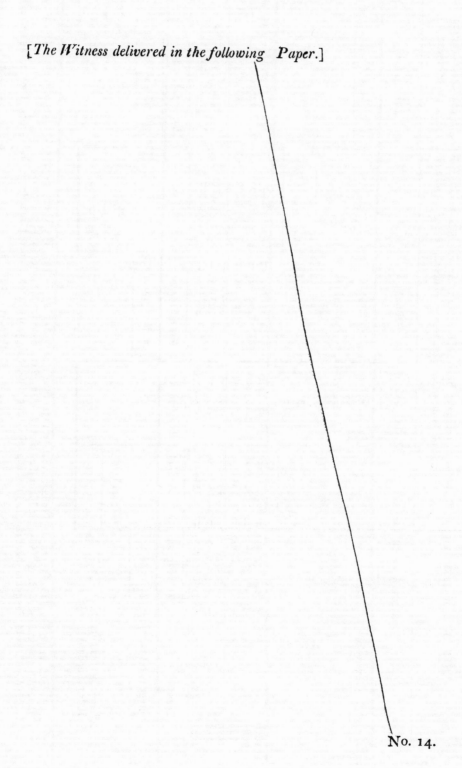

678.                                                                    No. 14.

## No. 14.

### MINUTE MADE RELATIVE TO THROWSTER'S WORK.

ESTIMATE of QUANTITIES of RAW SILKS consumed by our Manufacturers in 1824-25, and in 1826 to 31 ; computed at various Rates, with regard to the Rates of Labour and Profit which those respective descriptions yield, on an average, to the Throwster.

| | BENGAL and CHINA. (85 deniers) | | TURKEY. (100 deniers) | | ITALIAN, &c. (39/2 deniers) | TOTAL of all Descriptions. | TOTALS, Computed into one Standard, that of Fine Italian Silks. |
|---|---|---|---|---|---|---|---|
| | | Computations. at 1/3d | | Computations. at 2/5ths | | | |
| 1824-25, Averages of | lbs. 1,349,000 | lbs. 450,000 | lbs. 334,000 | lbs. 133,000 | lbs. 1,269,000 | lbs. 2,952,000 | lbs. 1,852,000 — Average of 1824-25. |
| 1826 | lbs. 1,173,000 = | lbs. 391,000 | lbs. 221,000 = | lbs. 88,000 | lbs. 718,000 | lbs. 2,112,000 | lbs. 1,197,000 |
| 1827 | 1,862,000 = | 621,000 | 405,000 = | 162,000 | 1,463,000 | 3,730,000 | 2,246,000 |
| 1828 | 1,456,000 = | 485,000 | 429,000 = | 172,000 | 1,340,000 | 3,225,000 | 1,997,000 |
| 1829 | 1,471,000 = | 490,000 | 338,000 = | 133,000 | 834,000 | 3,249,000 | 1,457,000 |
| 1830 | 2,055,000 = | 685,000 | 493,000 = | 197,000 | 1,297,000 | 3,845,000 | 2,179,000 |
| 1831 | 1,632,000 = | 554,000 | 338,000 = | 135,000 | 1,026,000 | 2,996,000 | 1,715,000 |
| 6 Years | lbs. 9,649,000 | lbs. 3,226,000 | lbs. 2,224,000 | lbs. 887,000 | lbs. 6,678,000 | lbs. 19,148,000 | lbs. 10,791,000 |
| Average per Ann. 1/6th | lbs. 1,608,000 | 1/6th lbs. 538,000 | 1/6th lbs. 371,000 | 1/6th lbs. 148,000 | 1/6th lbs. 1,113,000 | 1/6th lbs. 3,191,000 | 1/6th lbs. 1,798,000 |

Average per Annum of Italian standard — Average of 1826-31, per Ann. = 3 per Cent. under the average of 1824-25.

Qy. How much lower the Wages and Profits in 1826 to 1831, than in 1815 to 1825?—Ans. The Wages estimated at less, and much less in most cases, than one-half.

Qy. What quantities of Bengal Silks used in a Raw State?—Ans. Some considerable portions of late years.

Qy. What loss of Capital in this Branch, (fixed capital) during the last six years, to be deducted from the profits?—Ans. Those losses enormous.

| | On Organzine. | On Tram. |
|---|---|---|
| Duty, | 5/ - | and 3/ in June |
| Reduced to | 3/6 - | and 2/ 1829. |

N.B.—The Imports of Thrown Silks in 1829 - - lbs. 163,000
1830 - - lbs. 437,000
1831 - - lbs. 514,000

It is no use to take an "average" of three years, so very dissimilar in the very circumstance which forms the essence of the question; and to say, the Average of 1826, 27, & 28, was - - - lbs. 376,000
and that of 1829, 30, & 31 - - - - lbs. 370,000

*Alexis James Doxat.*

March 1832.

Mr.
*Alexis J. Doxat.*

13 April,
1832.

4126. Will you explain that statement you have just given in?—I shall endeavour to show there is a great difference between the quantities of silks imported, and the work accruing to the throwster, and that of late the quantity of foreign thrown silks has increased considerably; but I will touch that question afterwards. Speaking generally, I should say, it has been occasioned by gradual improvement in our mills, and great depression in our wages and profits; mills are a fixed property, of no value except in activity; when standing still they become an actual loss; hence the necessity to work them under the most unfavourable circumstances to the throwster, which has been mitigated only by miserable and wretched wages. Of late years, that is 1826 to 1831, the quantity of throwsters' work has however actually decreased as compared with 1824 and 1825, notwithstanding those calamitous wages; although we have worked at very low wages, and wages the extreme of wretchedness, the quantity of throwsters' work has actually decreased since 1824–25. The quantity of foreign thrown silk has greatly increased since June 1829, when the duties of 5s. on thrown silk, and 3s. 6d. on tram, were reduced in the June of that year to 3s. 6d. on organzine, and 2s. on tram. We were working before that on very low wages; in the last year, we have been working on wages of wretchedness, speaking of the poor labourers; but the gentlemen who come from the throwing establishments, will be able to give answers more satisfactory upon that subject.

4127. How do you account for there being less imported in 1828 and 1829, although the duty was lower than the 7s. 6d. duty?—I will show a statement bearing upon that subject.

4128. Has the quantity of raw silk imported into this country increased?—Yes.

4129. Why then have the throwsters reason to complain?—I have made a minute respecting the throwsters' work. An "Estimate of quantities of raw silks consumed by our manufacturers in 1824–25, and in 1826 to 1831, computed at various rates with regard to the rates of labour and profit, which those respective descriptions yield on an average to the throwster." In 1824–25, the averages of Bengal and China silk, 1,349,000 lbs. 85 deniers; the average of Italian, &c. silk, 1,269,000 lbs., $\frac{30}{32}$ deniers; the averages of Turkey silk, 334,000 lbs., 100 deniers; total of all descriptions, 2,952,000 lbs. I have endeavoured to get information upon these subjects, and I find that the average quantity of labour afforded by the winding and twisting of Bengal and China silk, as compared with Italian silk, is one-third only; to the Turkey silk I have assigned already 100 deniers; I have called that two-fifths, because being a very long reel, it is wound but slow; to the Italian I do not assign any, because it is my standard; then computing the quantities of Bengal and Italian, and Turkey, consumed in 1824 and 1825, I find the computation of Bengal and China to be 450,000 lbs., bringing it to the standard of Italian; and the computation of Turkey is 133,000 lbs., relative to Italian; and if we add to that, the number of Italian which I have already stated to be 1,269,000 lbs., I have an aggregate of 1,852,000 lbs. of the Italian standard, with relation to the throwsters' work. I have gone through the same process for 1826 to 1831; I have analysed the quantity of work which the throwster has had to do. I proceed to the dissection I have made of the quantities of various silks consumed in those six years; I will not read over all the annual numbers; the average of the six years from 1826 to 1831, has been of Bengal and China 1,608,000 lbs. compared with 1,349,000 lbs. in 1824–25, making a considerable increase of the coarse silks in 1826 to 1831. Then with respect to Italian, I find that the average quantity upon the same six years is, per annum, of Italian 1,113,000 lbs. compared with 1,269,000 lbs. in 1824–25, which was greater; and with respect to Turkey silks, I find the average of the last six years to be 371,000 lbs., which is greater than the corresponding quantity of 334,000 lbs. in the former period; then by computing all those quantities by the same standard, I make this estimate for the last six years to be 1,798,000 lbs. of Italian standard; whereas in the former period, the amount is 1,852,000 lbs., showing a difference of three per cent. less employment for the mills in that point of view in 1826 to 1831, than in 1824–25, although there appears an increase in the gross quantity.

4130. Do you infer that there has been three per cent. less employment for the mills?—Yes, as I understand it in that point of view; there is another point to which I cannot speak practically, but I know that of late years large quantities of Bengal silks have been used in a raw state; that many of the low goods we make, principally for export, are made of very coarse silk, only wound off, and the first operation of winding off coarse silk is very inconsiderable; in that state it

678.                                                                                    gives

gives extremely little employment, it is merely the operation of winding off; the throwster has thus to work on a smaller quantity; the goods are produced after the raw silk has been merely wound off; and then there is that which forms the element of the whole question, which interests particularly this branch of industry; how much lower the wages and profits were from 1826 to 1831 than in 1815 to 1825? the answer, as far as I understand it, is this; the wages are estimated at less and much less in most cases than one-half; I have seen statements considerably under that; I state this, not that I know it of my own knowledge, but I know it from gentlemen much better qualified than I am to speak to it. Another reason they have to complain is, the loss of fixed capital during the last six years, and this is again a most important point: I am surrounded by many gentlemen who are throwsters and many manufacturers; one gentleman whom I have in view may employ 500 weavers, or he may employ 200 weavers only; if his trade is pressed upon, he dismisses part of his people; his capital is not decidedly fixed, it is a great loss of capital, a great inconvenience when he is forced to discharge his weavers; but as to the throwster, the major part of his capital is fixed in machinery on which the whole of his business rests; wages constitute the floating part of his capital, and this part of it is returned many times in the course of the year; but when his machinery is stopped, there is not only an end to wages, but there is an absolute loss of capital, his machinery becomes of little or no value; the same causes which bring disability upon the weaver bring disability upon the throwster, but the loss of capital to the throwster is more absolute; his machinery, which is the basis of his business, becomes useless and deteriorated, his people must disperse, the whole of his establishment is gone. The next point for consideration is, how the foreign throwster has been able to grow upon us so considerably during the last two years, notwithstanding the low and wretched wages at which the English throwsters have worked. I find that in 1829, the imports of thrown silks were 169,000 lbs.; the duty, which was 5s. on organzine and 3s. on tram, was reduced to 3s. 6d. on organzine and 2s. on tram, in June of that year. In the next year, 1830, the importation was 437,000 lbs., and in the following year 514,000 lbs. I should observe, however, that 1829 was a low year for the silk trade altogether; the year 1830, an increased year, with a little improvement in wages, but the year 1831 has been a decreasing one, and with wages of extreme wretchedness (particularly in the throwing branches), lower than at any period since this country has worked silks; notwithstanding which, the quantity of foreign thrown silks, which had been 437,000 lbs. in 1830, increased to 514,000 lbs. in 1831. I find that those quantities of thrown silks, viz. 159,000 lbs. in 1829, 437,000 lbs. in 1830, and 514,000 lbs. in 1831, as compared with the quantities of Italian raw silks, (which silks are worked for analogous purposes,) were 20 per cent. in 1829, 36 per cent. in 1830, and 50 per cent. in 1831. Bengal raw silks are worked for various purposes, many of which purposes have no analogy with those of Italian.

4131. Are the Committee to understand that you consider the great increase of thrown silk during the two last years to have arisen from the duty being reduced from 5s. to 3s. 6d.?—Yes, as far as I can understand the question, and I have given it all the attention possible.

[*The Witness delivered in the following Paper.*]

No. 10.

Mr.
*Alexis J. Doxat.*

13 April,
1832.

### No. 10.

A COMPARATIVE VIEW of the QUANTITIES of FOREIGN (ITALIAN) THROWN SILKS, and of ITALIAN RAW SILKS, consumed at various Periods from 1815-17 to 1829-30 and 31.

| THROWN SILKS. | Duties on | | DATES of Alterations. | Proportions of Thrown, per Cent. | Italian Raw SILKS. | DUTY. |
|---|---|---|---|---|---|---|
| | Organzine. | Tram. | | | | |
| | *s. d.* | | | | | *s. d.* |
| 1815–17 - lbs. 295,000 | 14/8 | | - - | 125 | lbs. 236,000 | 5/6 |
| 1818–20 - 343,000 | - - | - - | - - | 86 | 400,000 | - - |
| 1821–23 - 389,000 | - - | - - | - - | 62 | 632,000 | - - |
| 1824–25 - 481,000 | 14/8 | | - - | 38 | 1,269,000 | 5/6 |
| (a) - - - | (a  7/6 | | { 25 March 1824. } | - - - | - - - | ./3 |
| (b) - - - | (b) 5/· | | { 25 Nov. 1825. } | — | — | — |
| 1826 - - 289,000 | - - | | - - | 40 | 718,000 | - - † |
| (c) - - - | 5/. | (c) 3/. | { 5 July 1826. } | - - | - - - | ./1 |
| 1827 - - 453,000 | - - | - - | | 31 | 1,463,000 | - - |
| 1828 - - 385,000 | - - | - - | | 29 | 1,340,000 | - - ‡ |
| 1829 - - 169,000 | - - | - - | | 20 | 825,000 | - - § |
| (d) and Debentures | 3/6 | (d) 2/. | { 2 June 1829. } | — | — | — |
| 1830 - - 437,000 | - - | - - | - - | 36 | 1,202,000 | - - ‖ |
| 1831 - - 514,000 | - - | - - | - - | 50 | 1,026,000 | - - ¶ |

### NOTES.

(a) Duty on Organzine and Tram, and Raw Silks, lowered in March 1824.
(b) Ditto - Organzine and Tram - - ditto - ditto - November 1825.
(c) Ditto - - - - - - Tram and Raw - - ditto - July 1826.
(d) Ditto - Organzine and Tram - - ditto - ditto - June 1829.
And Debentures of 3 *s.* 6 *d.* per lb. on Organzine} granted from June 1829.
Silks, and of 2 *s.* per lb. on Tram, ditto - -} 

* 1815–17}
     to } Rapid decrease in the relative qualities of Foreign Thrown.
  1824–25}
† 1826 - - - A slight Increase.
‡ 1827–28 - - Some decrease.
§ 1829 - - - A large decrease. (Wretched Wages.)
‖ 1830 - - - Unparalleled increase. (Some improvement in Wages.)
¶ 1831 - - - Further considerable increase (notwithstanding wretched Wages.)

And this calamitous depression in the Throwing Branch has been unattended with any advantage to the other Branches of the Silk Manufacture; the state of which has been miserable in 1831, and aggravated still during the three last months.—(Minute, 7th April 1832.)

4132. Are

4132. Are the Committee to understand that you consider the taking off the duty on organzine silk has increased the quantity of imports of thrown silk?—Yes.

4133. Do you find that that has been the case after every reduction of duty?—No, it has not.

4134. Are you aware that, since the year 1765, the importation of thrown silk for consumption has varied, taking the average, between 350 and 400,000 lbs. ?—I am told it was only 20 years after 1765, that any organzine silk was made in this country; I have not looked into the whole statement, but there is a point which will meet that. The question I apprehend to be, when we had high protecting duties in favour of the throwsters (that is, at 14s. 8d. on organzine and tram, as compared with 5s. 6d. for the raw, from 1815 to 1824, and at 7s. 6d., as compared with 3d. on raw, in 1824–25), whether they remained sleeping over their spindles, and made no improvements. I have a statement, by which I will show that the internal competition of British mills in various parts of the country, had, during those periods, the effect of reducing considerably the quantity of foreign thrown silks, in proportion to the raw; it is apprehended, in all cases in which we do not alter duties, we keep up charges, but it will be found that those latitudes have not been taken. I will refer to paper No. 10; it appears that the average quantity of thrown silk we imported in 1815 to 1817, was 295,000 lbs., that the proportion was 125 per cent.; that the thrown organzine silks, in the three following years 1818, 1819 and 1820, their relative quantity was diminished to 88 per cent.; in the years 1821, 1822 and 1823 that relative quantity had further decreased to 62 per cent.; in 1824 and 1825 I find the relations altered, in a still greater degree, say, to 38 per cent. in 1824 and 1825, compared with 125 per cent. in 1815, 1816 and 1817; consequently it appears that, in those periods, the throwster did his duty towards his brother at the loom; for I consider this as a question affecting one family, it applies to all the silk family, as one family. I find that the quantity of foreign thrown silk consumed in 1826, was 289,000 lbs.; the duties were lowered by an Order in Council, on the 25th November 1825, to 5s. on organzine and tram, and 1d. on raw; I find a slight re-action in the import of thrown silks in 1826, that is, to 40 per cent., instead of 38 in 1825. In the subsequent years, 1827, 1828 and 1829, we went on lowering our wages and profits, and by so doing, jointly with further improvements—(we have seen the effects of material improvements during high duties) —I find the relative quantities of thrown silks reduced from 40 per cent. in 1826, to 31 per cent. in 1827, to 29 per cent. in 1828, and to 20 per cent. in 1829. It is but fair to notice here again, that which I have mentioned before, that 1829 was a very bad year for the silk trade altogether, and that the manufacturers in such years turn more particularly to the lower branches, and work at a lower standard, because they can employ their people at less loss. But what has been the apparent effect, when we come to 1830? we find the operation of the duty, lowered from 5s. to 3s. 6d., is, jointly with the debentures, although small, to come against the throwster; for the value of those debentures, although given for 3s. 6d., has varied from 1d. to 7d. or 8d., so that the duty has been virtually reduced nearly to 3s. or 3s. 1d., from 5s.; and the consequence appears to be, that in 1830, notwithstanding low wages, the wages in 1830 were not so low as in 1831; we find that the quantity of foreign thrown silk has increased to 36 per cent.; then in 1831, which was a declining year, and particularly a year of wretchedness with the throwing interest, we find an increase to 50 per cent.

4135. It appears that in the year 1830, 1,202,000 lbs. of raw silk were imported; in 1831 only 1,026,000 were imported; during the year 1830 the quantity of foreign thrown was less than in 1831; if this had been the consequence of distress or failure on the Continent which had compelled the foreigner to send it into this country, would he not have been impelled to send an equal quantity of raw?—Certainly; if a man was afraid of his property he would send the one as well as the other.

4136. Is it not the fact that Germany and other places principally import thrown?—Yes.

4137. If from disease and other circumstances on the Continent in the two last years an interruption to the trade took place there, would that necessarily alter the proportion between thrown and raw, and leave a larger quantity of thrown on the hands of the Italian merchant?—I feel that that question cannot be answered without explanation, and we now touch the minute at which the Committee are going to adjourn.

4138 Has not a larger quantity been consigned to you from Italy?—Certainly.

4139. Has

Mr.
*Alexis J. Doxat.*

13 April,
1832.

4139. Has it not been stated to you that the state of the European market has been the reason for so much being sent?—I cannot do justice to so important a question without going into an explanation.

4140. You consider that the alteration of the proportion has arisen from the state of the law, not the state of Europe?—Yes, just so; but I respectfully repeat, that the moment of adjournment does not allow of the requisite developement.

---

### *Martis*, 17° *die Aprilis*, 1832.

---

## THE RIGHT HON. THE EARL GROSVENOR, in the Chair.

---

Mr. *Alexis James Doxat*, again called in; and made the following Statement.

Mr.
*Alexis J. Doxat.*

17 April,
1832.

I AM particularly anxious to take up two points in answer to questions before put: first, as to the prosperity that is supposed to have existed in the silk manufacture at Manchester, at the time that great misery was existing in the silk manufacture in Spitalfields; and the second point is this, whether the misery that existed in Spitalfields in so many instances during the last few years, is analogous, or arises from the same causes as the transient misfortunes that weighed on that industrious part of the community from 1815 to 1825. With respect to the first point, I claim the indulgence of the Committee, because it is very important. Manchester is more particularly engaged in the manufacture of silk goods, and of silks mixed with cotton of low descriptions, which are well made in their various kinds, and likewise some mixed figured and fancy goods; goods which have been manufactured however at very low wages, and which have the benefit of the bounty before alluded to, which is an immense bounty. Many of those goods are entitled to a bounty of 3 *s.* 6 *d.* per lb. whilst most of them have paid only the lower duty of 1 *d.* per lb., and I believe many of them are manufactured even with waste which has paid only 1 *s.* per cwt.; consequently it is a bounty to the highest extent. But, returning to the abstract question of the prosperity of Manchester, I would beg leave to read a letter dated the 2d of January 1832, addressed to the Board of Trade, which I had heard something of before, but of the contents of which I was not fully aware, and which has been sent to me by a friend since my last examination.

[*For the Letter and the various signatures attached to it, vide
Mr. Royle's Evidence, p.* 166–7.]

The silk family is one family all over the kingdom. But I speak of those particularly that I am acquainted with; and I feel anxious that nothing I shall say shall throw a cloud upon them. That letter presents a most lamentable picture of the state of the silk trade at Manchester; it speaks in every sense for itself. I am aware that another letter signed, I understand, by some of the same parties, was addressed subsequently from Manchester to the Board of Trade, dated 26th March, praying, that no alteration might be made in the laws relative to the silk trade; I understand that it was written under the impression which was conveyed in the House of Commons by the Right honourable the Vice President of the Board of Trade, not as a threat, but it was received almost as such, that the duties would be taken off on foreign thrown silk, and the corresponding drawbacks (bounties) granted on the export of manufactured goods would cease. The manufacturers in Manchester having mostly mills of their own, it is a question which would concern them doubly; in this way, if the duty were taken off thrown silk their mills which, "since 1829 have become worth next to nothing," would become, notwithstanding the very low wages at which they have been working the last two or three years, if I may so express it, worth less than nothing, and not only that, but they would lose the advantage peculiar to Manchester, of having an enormous bounty, in some cases 50 per cent. on the duty paid, in some cases 100 per cent. taking the duty on the waste, and comparing it with the bounties; so that it would fall on Manchester twofold. It appears that they have been carrying on the manufacture on very low wages, and that the exportation has taken place essentially, and mostly on account of the immense bounty. With respect to Spitalfields, I was anxious to submit these points, because there is an impression that Spitalfields is behindhand in point of industry, that there is a disability in Spitalfields; and that does not exist; there is in this district amazing industry and assiduity; the work is well done there, and

comparatively

Mr.
*Alexis J. Doxat.*

17 April,
1832.

comparatively cheap with regard to its excellence; and I believe it can be shown from step to step, that Spitalfields remains what it has long been, the eldest brother of the silk trade in this country. With respect to the distress in Spitalfields, I will beg leave to read a paragraph of a letter which I addressed to the Right honourable Vesey Fitzgerald on the subject of the silk trade, dated the 28th of April 1829;— I could dwell here at great length.

" Sir,

" On the subject of that part of our industrious population, engaged in the silk trade, with " which I am more particularly acquainted; but again, I should trespass too much on your " time, when inquiring into a state of things which requires the immediate application of " every remedy that can be recommended by His Majesty's Government to the Legislature, " I will only repeat here, the expression of my deep conviction that there does not exist in " these realms, or in any part of the world, a class of people more industrious, more moral, " and in every sense more deserving the protecting hand of a government, than the Spital- " fields weavers; I speak as I conscientiously believe from experience, and close and inti- " mate and continued observation, which has been most fully corroborated by persons " perfectly foreign, by their professions, to every kind of trade or commerce, but who have " made the subject of the industrious man, and of all that can contribute to his comfort and " his moral improvement, a subject of deep and solicitous study; and hence, when I hear " it expressed as a regret, that we should have in one part of this metropolis fifty thousand " such people, I would say, by whom should we reimplace such people, such industrious, " such assiduous, and such peaceable and loyal members of our social family? Admitting " that at some periods, namely, in 1792 and in 1815, much distress prevailed among them, " owing to a change of fashion in the former period, and a change from war to peace in the " other, and that a benevolent public held out a truly charitable hand to those industrious " sufferers, can the amount of subscriptions during those periods, however great and how- " ever beneficent, be considered, in a pecuniary point of view, otherwise than as a mite, " compared to the benefit accruing (in a pecuniary point of view alone) to the country from " the possession, within itself, of such industrious classes? And as to some trifling sub- " scriptions, which, at some other periods, have occasionally been made to furnish those " industrious people, under the pressure of very inclement seasons, or some circumstances " of general pressure to the country, with some blankets and soup, the amounts occasion- " ally expended in such relief, would not deserve to be mentioned, but as proofs of the " kindness with which British beneficence is ever found to flow on all occasions calling for " its exertion. And has the silk trade stood alone in receiving occasionally the fruits of " such beneficence? Have not other portions of our industrious classes had to lament much " more frequently, during the said period of 1792 to 1823, far greater vicissitudes than those " experienced by the silk trade? Have we not seen, in particular, immense masses of " workmen, employed in the cotton and in other trades, suddenly thrown out of employ, to " a degree that even endangered the tranquillity of great districts? Can some occasional " relief, afforded formerly to the silk trade by means of soup societies, &c., be for a moment " placed in comparison with such calamitous occurrences, incident to trades dependent in a " great measure on exports for employment?"

Every thing in trade and commerce must be comparative; I have mentioned that the silk trade was prosperous from 1815 to 1825, notwithstanding the enormous duties in most of these years, and it has since been exposed to as great vicissitudes as possible. The reason why I wished to introduce the comparative numbers of seven to four as regarded the progress of the silk trade from 1815–17 to 1821–23, 1824–25, compared with that of the cotton trade, was, because I was asked, whether the silk trade had not been exposed to contingencies as well as the cotton and other trades during the periods anterior to 1826. The cotton trade has been considered as without parallel in its progress, whereas I have found that during that period of eleven years, the progress of the silk trade had far exceeded that of the cotton, that is, in the ratio of seven to four; and that from 1826 to 1830, those progresses had been *inverted* in the ratio of four the silk, to nine the cotton.

---

4141. What in your opinion has been the effect of the alteration of the laws relative to the silk trade since 1826, on the trade of Spitalfields?—A material reduction of the rate of wages for a certain description of goods which I have taken the whole way through as my standard; a reduction of wages from 10 ½ d. to 8 d., 7 ½ d., 7 d., 6 ½ d. and 6 d. The rate of wages in 1821, 1822, 1823, 1824, 1825, for that class of goods I understand to have been 10 ½ d.

4142. What is the article on which the wages have been so reduced?—It is 10 to 1100 three double gros de Naples, neat made and well got up.

4143. Has that reduction of price arisen from competition of foreign silks or competition of home silks at Manchester?—I believe from foreign silks; the pressure has originated from abroad, from the period I have referred to; I believe
that

that the wages from 1821 to 1825 were the same, on the average, that they were in 1815 to 1817, because it was a rapidly increasing trade, a trade entirely of luxury which afforded those wages, and which were only fair and moderate wages; by no means extraordinary wages.

4144. Do you know the quantity of foreign gros de Naples which has been imported in the different years since 1826?—I do not, because a very large proportion is imported by the smugglers, I believe.

4145. What means have you of showing that there has been the introduction of a large quantity from France?—I am told of it generally from various quarters; our business is in raw and thrown silk, and we are foreign bankers; our business is banking and silk; we have, in almost every week, men that come from the Continent for their silk goods here, and drafts to large amounts pass through our hands upon various houses; but there are agents coming over frequently, they enter freely upon their business when they come to the counting-house, one says I am following a parcel of goods which I have sold, another says I am come to take orders; I cannot follow the smugglers to know what they do, but I understand that immense quantities are smuggled. I could have known every particular about it, over and over again, but the moment that I find the agents conversing about private business with me, I tell them I do not want to hear any secrets; I do not know whether you are aware that for the last few years I have endeavoured to do all in my power by applications to Government, to induce them to re-consider the changes that took place in 1826, in regard to the silk trade of this country: I wish to hear nothing private upon those matters; any thing you tell me respecting your prices of weaving, of winding, throwing, &c., I shall be glad to hear, I hear that they are bringing over very great quantities of goods, and that a large proportion are smuggled.

4146. Have you reason to believe from your transactions that that is the case? —Yes; from the drafts that go through our bill books, and also from what I hear continually in various ways, and from various quarters on this subject.

4147. Do you know from any bills which pass through your hands as a banker, that the goods which are paid for have been introduced into this country in an illicit manner?—There is scarcely a week passes but some bills drawn for silk goods pass through our hands.

4148. Are such bills to a large amount?—They are sometimes.

4149. Were they so in the year 1826?—I cannot speak to that particular date.

4150. Have you any means of knowing the particular amount drawn for from Lyons on England?—No, it is impossible for me to speak with any degree of precision on this subject.

4151. Do you know for what the bills are drawn?—They are drawn on silk mercery houses.

4152. Are you certain they may not be for silks which have paid duty?—Some of them may be, no doubt.

4153. Bills drawn at Lyons upon London cannot be for raw silk can they?— For raw silk they are upon us sometimes, and upon other merchants; the silk is sent to Lyons, if it does not sell there, it is forwarded to London; consequently bills on silk merchants we know to be for raw silk, as also occasionally for thrown silk.

4154. But those bills you refer to are drawn by manufacturing houses on warehousemen in London?—Yes.

4155. May they not be drawn for other goods besides silk manufactures?— I would say distinctly, I believe they are for silk goods.

4156. Was the description of goods such as was made in Manchester in 1825, such as was likely to interfere with the manufacture in Spitalfields?—This question I am not sufficiently informed upon, and would rather leave it to others.

4157. Do you know whether they now make in Manchester such goods as they used to make in Spitalfields?—I believe not; that a very large proportion are low goods, well made for that class, but goods made essentially to have the benefit of that immense bounty given to them; and that they have been made at very low wages. I would beg to draw the attention of the Committee to one point, I was at Malvern in Worcestershire, for two or three months last summer with my family; I heard a great deal of the distress of the glove trade; sometime after I had been there, some gentleman of the neighbourhood called upon me, and

678.                                                                              told

Mr.
Alexis J. Doxat.
————
17 April,
1832.

told me there was a gentleman from Manchester who said that the distress of the glove trade was nothing to that of the silk trade in Manchester, and he entered into various particulars on the subject; this was I think in August last.

4158. Was the gentleman in the silk trade?—Yes, he was; I asked who he was, and they told me, he was a manager in one of the first concerns in Manchester, with whom we had transacted business for 32 or 33 years. He told me the situation of the silk weavers at Manchester was dreadful; I did not ask him minutely the rates at which they were weaving, but he mentioned them generally.

4159. Is it your opinion that the competition of Manchester making any goods, such as are made in Spitalfields, does not affect the Spitalfields wages?—Every competition may affect wages, but every thing within ourselves tends to regulate itself; the Spitalfields weaver is not afraid of the competition of any fellow labourer; on the contrary I believe that the Spitalfields weaver does his work as cheap as any, considering the perfection of his workmanship, speaking as a whole.

4160. Do you think that the silk manufactured at Manchester tends, by competition, to lower wages in Spitalfields?—It may in some degree, but the pressure is from abroad; I might say Spitalfields presses on Manchester, and it does press upon Manchester in various respects.

4161. Are not the goods coming from abroad, of a class and description more likely to interfere with Spitalfields than those made in Manchester?—Generally speaking, certainly; but superior goods press always directly and indirectly on low goods.

4162. Then independently of that, if there is a competition which may injure the manufacturer, must not the bringing in a large importation of foreign goods tend still further to press upon the market and injure it?—Yes.

4163. You are understood to state, that notwithstanding any occasional vicissitudes in trade, the silk trade of Spitalfields from 1815 to 1825, was in a progressive state of improvement?—An extraordinary state of improvement, notwithstanding the high duties from 30 to 40, 50 and 60, and 70, and 80 per cent. upon the raw material, and upon the prepared material, and with fair moderate wages to our labourers in every department of that manufacture.

4164. Since 1826, has there been the same improvement, or has it suffered a depression?—It has suffered a calamitous depression in these years, upon the whole; and there is besides an essential consideration, that the largest masses of foreign goods, most frequently come in at the most depressed prices; so that although our labourers retreat from very low, to wretched wages, they are, at these, often reduced for a time to half work; and over such contingencies, with our foreign competitors, they have no control.

4165. There has not only been great distress in reduction of wages, but also great numbers of individuals out of employ?—The unsteadiness of the trade has been unparalleled; I have taken the whole way through, the former standard of $10\frac{1}{2}d.$ against $6d.$ for plain goods, but I am told by various members of the manufacture, that if I were to take the average of plain goods, the average difference would be more than that of $10\frac{1}{2}d.$ to $6d.$

4166. When you state gros de Naples, did you merely take that as a criterion to form an estimate of the general depression?—Yes, I take it as a centre.

4167. If you have taken that as a criterion, the introduction of any foreign article of the same description, whether smuggled or otherwise, would not matter, because the different kinds of silk introduced, must cause a further depression?—Upon some articles, I have said before, that the depression was as $10\frac{1}{2}d.$ to $6d.$ upon the wages; I understand it goes further still, and thus in taking the proportion of $10\frac{1}{2}d.$ to $6d.$, I under-rate the average of depression.

4168. It is the general operation on a large quantity of goods?—Yes, if we extend the comparison to figured and fancy goods, of course it will be higher.

4169. Does the competition of French goods with Spitalfields, depend on the price and quality of the goods?—In all the calculations I have made, I assume an equality of perfection in the goods made here and abroad. By referring to my Appendix (F.) Tables No. 4 and No. 5, it will be seen that I assume we make the same article in this country, as well as they do abroad, in all the departments of manufacture; that our dyeing is equal, our brilliancy is equal, and our ability in every respect equal. I assume an equality. Then as to the differences of prices between Lyons and this country, I estimate that there are the differences I have stated.

4170. You suppose the quality to be equal?—No, I do not suppose that, I assume that.

4171. What

Mr.
*Alexis J. Doxat.*

17 April,
1832.

4171. What is the difference of price between the Lyons and Spitalfields manufactures, first in materials, secondly in wages?—If our weavers were to work at 8½ d. per yard, and other charges of manufacture in proportion, the price of the article would be 3 s. 1 d. when we have retreated from step to step, and are brought down to the wretched wages of 6 d. a yard, we come to 2 s. 8 d. For the same goods at Lyons, the usual rate for the last few years has been 5¼ d. which is equal to 5 d. per yard, as the weaver there winds his shute. When they are manufacturing at that rate, which is a rate of ease with them, and considering the relative circumstances, is equal to our 8½ d.; and supposing the price of silk with them at the highest relative point, the price of the manufactured silk at Lyons will be 2 s. 4 d. and ⅞ths.

4172. What would be the cost in England under those circumstances?—Three shillings and one penny, as stated before.

4173. What per centage would that be?—The difference between 3 s. 1 d. and 2 s. 4 d. ⅞ths. is 30 per cent.

4174. Are the Committee to understand, that the expense of weaving and manufacturing plain silks at Lyons, is 30 per cent. lower than in England?—It varies continually.

4175. Give the variation; what is the lowest, and what is the highest?—I have not the last price of goods at Lyons, but I will mention what I understand to be the variations in the course of the year, at Lyons; whether they are working on high prices, or at very low prices of silk; and whether their wages be much depressed, or fair wages; and whether the manufacturer wishes to effect the sale of his goods, when he has few orders from America, &c. or whether any thing occurs in France, to diminish the sale of his goods; I understand the variations may be from 2 s. 4 d. and ⅞ths. to 1 s. 9 d. and ⅞ths. If I take the extremes from 3 s. 1 d. to 1 s. 9 d. and ⅞ths., the extreme is as much as 70 per cent. It is frequently the case, that when we are working here at tolerable wages, a sudden fall happens at Lyons, which depresses the silks; and that an enormous difference, as much as 40 or 50 per cent., takes place in a short time, without our having any control over it, under contingent circumstances with the French and other foreign manufacturers. The rate of 6 d. per yard does not at all shelter us from those contingencies.

4176. Are you able to state the rate of wages for weaving a neat made gros de Naples at Lyons, and a neat made gros de Naples at Spitalfields?—Not at this moment.

4177. When was the last account you heard?—I have had no recent account, except that there is great activity at Lyons; but I believe that a great deal of gros de Naples made there in the last year, was so low as 4 d. a yard for weaving, and I believe, in some cases, even lower.

4178. What did it cost here?—Sixpence per yard, which is a low and wretched rate of wages here.

4179. Has not gros de Naples been down at 5 d. in England?—It has of late, but not for the same description of goods; and 6 d. for these does not shelter us from those contingencies.

4180. How low do you know it to have been in France?—When I say 4 d. in Lyons, it is equal to 3½ d.; and I mention that, as the lowest point at which I have taken my calculations; I believe that, not unfrequently, at the rate I have been alluding to at Lyons, of 4 d. equal to 3½ d., goods are manufactured, and even lower; that is to say, the rate of 4 d. is equal to 53 centimes, and I believe that when very much depressed, they have been lower than that; for example, that before the riots at Lyons, the rate of wages was even lower than 53 centimes.

4181. Do you know the prices at which work of that kind has been done at Manchester, or at Spitalfields?—I believe it has been done so low as 5 d.; it is done under circumstances of extreme wretchedness; and when goods are turned out from abodes of misery, they cannot be suitably got up, goods deserving the denomination of superior class—of goods to be compared to those produced at Lyons.

4182. Does not wretchedness exist at Lyons, as well as here?—They are open to frequent and material changes, they manufacture for export principally.

4183. You mean to say, the wages have been depressed from 10 d. to 6 d., and under, and that that has been in consequence of the competition?—Yes.

4184. What do you estimate the total value of the silk manufacture of England?—It has varied extraordinarily the last five or six years.

678.

4185. What

4185. What do you understand to be the difference between the price of silk in Lyons and London?—The price of the raw material varies continually.

4186. Take the average?—The question is not one of averages; the business of the merchant, or the man who deals in goods, is to avail himself of differences existing between one period and another; when those differences subside into what may be called an average, less importations take place; but when prices are very low, the merchant's business is to operate under the averages; that is the very point they are continually looking after.

4187. It is the business of the merchant to look out for an opportunity of making a profit by the difference in price?—Yes; he imports more or less according to the price.

4188. In your opinion, can the price of silk at Lyons and in London differ more than the cost of transport from one place to the other?—There are frequently considerable differences existing at Lyons in the price of the major part of the silks, arising from this; that the consumption of silks in France has been, upon the average of the last few years, 5,500,000 lbs., and I have submitted a paper, in which it appears, that the quantity imported into France is about a million of pounds; of that million of pounds, a large proportion, that is six or seven hundred thousand pounds of thrown silks, principally Piedmont organzine; the remainder, three or four hundred thousand raw, are principally Levant silks, and other coarse silks; out of those three or four hundred thousand pounds of raw silks imported into France, I believe a small proportion, an hundred thousand, or an hundred and fifty thousand pounds, consists of fine silks. I have stated, that the quantity consumed in France is 5,500,000 lbs., and that the quantity of silk imported there from various foreign parts, is about 1,000,000 lbs., and the remaining quantity, referrible to the trade of France, would appear to be 4,500,000; the largest proportion of that is fine silk; so that it is 4,500,000, contrasted with 1,000,000 lbs. imported into France, being a small proportion; consequently the manufacture of the French rests, in a very great measure, on their own silk, on some portion of foreign thrown, and a little coarse raw; with some very small quantities of fine Italian silk, when they are in a state of great activity; and then they can import Italian silk at cheaper rates than us, being nearer the Italian markets, and their import charges being a trifle lower than ours; but when they become depressed, they obtain their own fine silks (that is the great basis of their manufacture) much lower than we can import from Italy; and they have their own silks lower, under general circumstances.

4189. Not having an export for the raw material when trade is low, the raw material must fall?—Yes.

4190. Have there been any years in which they have not imported more or less? —No; in my statements laid before the Committee, I have assumed that the price of raw silk at Lyons varies from 17 s. to 14 s. 6 d. per lb. I have two statements here, from two respectable houses at Lyons, dated the 19th and 22d April 1831, before which period there had been a great depression; the one mentions, that French organzines of 21-22 deniers, which in February could not be sold at 28 francs (equal to 17 s. 6½ d. per lb. English), or at most at 27 francs, 50 cents. (equal to 17 s. 2½ d.) were then easily saleable at 32 francs (equal to 20 s. 4 d.) The other, that good current French organzines, of 22 deniers, which a month previous were fallen to 28 francs, (equal to 17 s. 6½ d.,) had got up to 32 francs (equal to 20 s. 4 d.;) that rise was attributed to orders from America. All those quotations in French money are with their usual discount of 12½ per cent. I should observe that the size of 21-22 deniers, is finer than that of 22-24, upon which I have grounded all my calculations at London and at Lyons. The lowest point I have taken in my Lyons estimates of costs (" 4. 4," in Tables No. 5, 6, 7, and 18,) for organzines of 22-24 deniers, and tram of 24-26 deniers, collectively, has been 17 s. 7 d.

4191. What was the distance of time between the price of 17 s. 6 d. and the 20 s. 4 d.?—They say from February and March to April: they say that the Lyons manufacture had been very much depressed, and that when they receive orders from America, that immediately raised the price of the article, and raises the wages.

4192. This is to mark the great and sudden variations in the price of French produce?—The variations are sometimes greater still; I was going to compute from that the price of French raw silk; in one case I had 17 s. 6½ d.; the price of throwing in France is generally for that size 3 s. 9 d., but we will assume that they

were

were depressed in their price of throwing; I will assume that they were working the raw at 3 s. per lb. into organzine, that the waste upon that was about 8 d., I must then deduct the price of the throwing and the waste from the price of the organzine, to come to that of the raw.

4193. The Committee wish to know the actual result when you have known a great variation in the price of raw?—We can judge of the price of the raw only from the price of the thrown. I quote the prices of the French organzine silk, from which I deduce the price of the French raw, as we but seldom get quotations of French raw.

4194. Does the price of the Italian organzine vary as much as the price of the French organzine?--Not so much, because they consume Piedmont for some particular purposes, for peculiar articles; but the great mass of their manufactures rests on fine French silks.

4195. Can you state the price of Italian organzine in April 1831?--It was by no means so depressed.

4196. Can you make a comparison between the price of the Italian organzine at Lyons and in England at the same time?—I cannot at this moment, not having the quotations with me.

4197. Can you furnish the Committee with a list, during a series of years, of the prices of Piedmont organzine at Lyons and in London, taking the same qualities?—Yes; certainly.

4198. Can you furnish the Committee with a Table showing the price of French organzine at Lyons, and of Italian organzine in London, or English organzine in London, made from Italian silk, at the same periods?—Taking Piedmont organzine and English organzine collectively of the same description, I have the price of 22 s. 10 d., but that is for a class a little inferior; I should say from 23 s. to 24 s., corresponding with that I have referred to as 17 s. 6 d. and 17 s. 2 d.

4199. What was the relative price with the 17 and 24?—The French were depressed at that period.

4200. Did the price of Italian and English organzine in London rise or fall equally with that, or did they maintain their price?--They were not influenced by that; the French were going on working on their low prices, they were consuming nine-tenths of their own silk at that period.

4201. Can you take an average of two or three years of the same quality of silks at Lyons and in London, and thus come to some general conclusion, avoiding or embracing the different variations?—I can draw the average, but that average is departing from the very question now under the consideration of the Committee, which is, to see the extraordinary variations we are exposed to from foreign competition; and how far we are pressed upon generally by the comparative low rate of wages; but I repeat that low and wretched wages do not shelter us.

4202. What influences the price of Italian organzine silk in this market, is it the competition of the English organzine, or the price which organzine bears in the rest of Europe?—There are two distinctions; France consumes its own silk, and rests essentially on silk grown at home; frequently the difference in price is very considerable; they are usually under the proportion of the price of silk in other parts of Europe, silk of French produce being retained entirely for her own consumption, France cannot equalize itself in that respect.

4203. Do you mean to say that in times of depression the manufacturer at Lyons can buy his silk at an extremely reduced price, which silk he can manufacture up at wages also reduced and send the goods into this country, to the great injury of the manufacturer here?—Yes.

4204. When he procures large orders from America, silk will naturally rise in the Lyons market, wages will rise, and he ceases to send goods to this country for a time?—Comparatively less quantities; the intensity of foreign competition varies much.

4205. Italian silks sent into this country are to a certain extent protected; you have limits as to price?—Yes.

4206. An Italian merchant has the option of withdrawing the silk consigned to you and consigning it to France or Germany or to other countries, and he will not admit of this reduction of price, when there is a better state of trade elsewhere?—No.

4207. Therefore the English manufacturer in that state of trade has no chance with the French?—No; on every pound of Italian silk imported into France, the export and import duties and charges, inclusive of commission, are about 2 s. 1 d.

678. The

Mr.
*Alexis J. Doxat.*

17 April,
1832.

The charges to this country, although more distant, are about 2 *s.* 2 *d.* to 2 *s.* 3 *d.* sending them forward, packing them, and so on, including the export and import duties ; the import duty at Lyons is 5 ½ *d.* and 1 ⅓ *d.* at London.

4208. Will you state the component parts of that 2 *s.* 1 *d.* ?—The charges of brokerage and packing 2 *d.* a pound ; export duties 9 *d.* ; carriage to Calais and putting on board for London 3 ¼ *d.* ; the import duties here are called one penny ; but there is a city due which makes a penny and one third of a penny, including the scavage ; then there are the various charges, insurance, freight, entries, landing charges, stamps, &c., commission and brokerage in London, 1 *s.* 0 ½ *d.*, making 2 *s.* 4 *d.*, it may range from 2 *s.* 2 *d.* to 2 *s.* 4 *d.*

4209. Does the 1 *s.* 0 ½ *d.* include the freight from Calais to London ?—Yes, and other port charges.

4210. Those are the whole charges from Lombardy to London on a pound of raw silk ?—Yes, the charges being a little more or less, according to the price of the silk.

4211. What do they pay at Lyons for the same articles ?—The charges at Lyons are 2 *d.* for the packing, brokerage, &c., the export duty 9 *d.* ; the waggon charge to Lyons is 1 ¼ *d.* ; the import duty at Lyons 5 ½ *d.*, they have no charges of freight and insurance, &c. the commission and brokerage 7 *d.*, and one quarter, as compared with our 1 *s.* 0 ½ *d.*, making 2 *s.* 1 *d.* ; every pound of silk that France imports from Italy costs them 2 *s.* ; besides which the Italian markets are nearer to them, which constitutes a relative cheapness ; and they have the silk of their own growth, which forms the great mass of their consumption.

4212. Whilst the same article to us costs 2 *s.* 4 *d.* ? —Yes ; 2 *s.* 2 *d.* to 2 *s.* 4 *d.* besides some difference, owing to our market being further from the sources.

4213. What does the home grower in France save out of this, is there any part of the charge which falls upon him ?—Comparatively trifling ; the produce of silk is spread all over the South of France, and there are no duties on it.

4214. Can you state the charges on the thrown imported into France ?—Yes ; I will take it from Piedmont organzine, because that is the largest quantity, as France consumes principally Piedmont organzine ; I will take the relative charges in respect to Piedmonts, to London and to Lyons ; first to London, packing, brokerage, &c. at Turin at per pound of organzine silk, three pence and a quarter, the export duty 6 ½ *d.* ; (Piedmont does not allow an exportation of its raw, consequently we have no comparison of that) ; carriage to Calais, and putting on board 3 ¼ *d.* our import duties 3 *s.* 7 *d.* per lb., including the penny for the scavage, insurance, freight entries, landing charges, stamps, &c. ; commission and brokerage in London, 1 *s.* 7 *d.* making together about 6 *s.* 3 *d.*

4215. How much of that does the Lyons merchant pay per lb. on silk from Piedmont ?—The brokerage, packing, &c. remains the same, 3 ¼ *d.*, the export duty remains the same, 6 ½ *d.*, the carriage is 1 ¼ *d.*, the import duty 11 *d.*, commission and brokerage 10 *d.*, making the total of about 2 *s.* 8 *d.*

4216. Do you know that which is stated in this letter to be the fact ; " I learnt that the custom of sizing a bale of silk is attained in this way, to obtain the number of deniers in a bale of silk we take out ten hanks, and measure from each 400 aunes, French ells, weighing the 400 aunes, which divided by ten, will give the average length of the bale ; the persons who perform this are not paid in money, they keep for themselves the silk thus weighed ; when trade is brisk they gain from eight to ten francs per day, sometimes from 15 to 20 ?"—I know that the employment is one of great confidence ; it is an assay, and they depend upon the correctness of the assayers ; I know at Turin, there are many respectable ladies who maintain themselves in assaying silk.

4217. From the statement you have given of the expense of charge of a pound of Piedmont thrown silk, from Piedmont to Lyons and Piedmont to London, it appears that the charge is 2 *s.* 8 *d.* as compared with 6 *s.* 3 *d.* ?—Yes ; we are more distant from the source.

4218. Deducting the amount of import duty and scavage from that, the English manufacturer receives his Piedmont silk only at an increased price of one penny more than the Lyons manufacturer ?—Yes, it is one penny all but the duty ; that is, that the Lyons manufacturer, for that part which he imports in thrown silk, has it so much cheaper.

4219. Of the organzine which arrives in London, what portion of it is sent to Spitalfields for their manufacture, what portion to Coventry, and what portion to the rest of England ?—Speaking of an average, except the last two years in which

the

Mr.
*Alexis J. Dorat.*

17 April,
1832.

the importation has been so much greater, Spitalfields for some years past has consumed for the far greater part English organzine; our imports of thrown silks are mainly the Milan and Bergam, that is, Lombardy silks, of which a very small part is disposed of in Spitalfields, I should think not above one-sixth in Spitalfields, and still a less proportion where there is a common degree of activity in Coventry, and a common degree of activity in Spitalfields; I believe we sell ten bales of Lombardy organzines to Coventry to one in Spitalfields. That brings me back to the point, that Spitalfields consumes but a small proportion of Piedmont thrown silk, and consumes principally English organzine.

4220. Do you think nine-tenths goes to Coventry?—When there is a fair degree of activity the Piedmont are principally sold in Spitalfields, three-fourths of the Piedmont thrown are sold in Spitalfields; there were immense quantities sent in some years to Norwich; this depended upon what particular works were going on.

4221. Do you draw a distinction between the Piedmont and the Lombardy?—Yes; for example, in one year we sold one hundred bales of thrown silks to Norwich; the same year only fifty to Spitalfields, but the following year it was reversed; if speaking to the average, we say one-fifth of the thrown imported is sent to Spitalfields; that I think will be near the mark.

4222. Where do the other four-fifths go?—To Coventry principally.

4223. The largest proportion of foreign thrown silk goes to Coventry?—Yes.

4224. One-fifth to Spitalfields, and the rest is spread about to Norwich and Kidderminster and other places?—Yes; there is some sent to Manchester, but mostly of the finest description, to be mixed with cotton to hold the cotton threads together, to receive the drawback.

4225. The English weaver having 3 s. 7 d. more to pay than the Lyons weaver, can he possibly meet him in the foreign market without some bounty?—The Lyons manufacturer has a proportionably higher price to pay throughout the year for Piedmont organzine, for specific and limited purposes, than for the great bulk of his own produce, on which rests the very major part of his manufacture. The English weaver has likewise on some fractional part, on some proportion of his goods, to pay a higher price for the Piedmont than for the English organzine; for the English throwsters most frequently are found to work under protection, otherwise they would be overwhelmed. It must not be taken that our weavers pay generally a difference of 3 s. 6 d.

4226. Take the prices of Italian thrown silk in England for the year 1830 or 1831, what proportion per cent. of the price paid by the manufacturer does the import duty of 3 s. 7 d. bear?—I have made out a Table which comprises the prices of various descriptions of Bengal and China silks and Italian silks, both raw and thrown. This Table of comparative prices of various descriptions of silks, we fill up at the periods of the East India Company's sales. I commenced it in June 1824, after the period of our alteration in the import duties. In February 1830, this Table being for 26 and 28 deniers, Milan and Bergam organzines, which form a large feature in our trade, the average of that size was 22 s. 9 d.

4227. What was the portion of duty in that?—Three shillings and seven-pence, contrasted with the Lyons at 11 d.; and I should mention that organzine silk here pays 3 s. 7 d., at Lyons it pays 11 d.; at Lyons tram pays 11 d. likewise, here it pays 2 s, We import, generally speaking, extremely small quantities of tram; the imports of the last four years have not averaged 40,000 lbs.

4228. Will you state the per centage which 3 s. 7 d. forms?—It varies according to the fluctuation in the prices, as may be seen by the following quotations of Milan and Bergam organzine of 26–28 deniers, taken from a paper before me. In June 1830, the price was 23 s. 8 d.; in October 1830, 24 s. 4 d.; in February 1831, 23 s. 4 d.; in June 1831, 22 s. 4 d.; in October 1831, 21 s. 10 d.; in February 1832, 21 s. 9 d.

4229. The Committee understand this all to be Milan organzine?—Yes; Milan and Bergam of 26 to 28 deniers; I could have taken a comparison with Piedmont, but that it forms so small a proportion, and the Piedmontese do not allow their silks to go out in raw; then there is another point of view connected with this, which I should wish to mention, that although the duty in France on tram and organzine is only 11 d., still as the throwster has the whole surface of French raw silk to work upon, and the exportation of that article is prohibited, he has all the advantage of the difference that exists between the price of Italian raws and French raws, which is very considerable; sometimes two or three shillings, some-

678.

times more. Although the French have only a duty of 11 *d.* both upon tram and organzine to protect their mills, their raws being frequently 1 *s.*, 2 *s.* and 3 *s.* lower than they can import from Italy, their throwsters have all that difference, as a protection beyond the duty of 11 *d.* a pound both on tram and organzine. Upon this very point, I have mentioned before, that every pound of Italian raw silk imported into France, bears about 2 *s.* or 2 *s.* 1 *d.* charges, so that the French manufacturers start with an advantage of about 2 *s.* 1 *d.* on their raw silks; and *primâ facie*, there is thus an advantage to them of 2 *s.* 1 *d.*, supposing the raw silks in Italy and in France both grown on the same terms; but beyond that they have those enormous variations alluded to before in respect of 21–22 deniers French organzine, which was 17 *s.* 2½ *d.* to 17 *s.* 6½ *d.*, when the import cost at the same period of 23–24 deniers Piedmont at Lyons, would have been 20 *s.* 6 *d.* to 21 *s.* The same protection which our weavers require, our throwsters require. On this very point I am anxious to show that the throwster in this country does his work cheaper, " *relatively,*" than the French and Italian throwsters.

4230. Do you mean to say that you would give to the throwster the same protection for the Bengal and China silk he throws, as for the Italian?—Bengal and China silks are only imported in a raw state; and the expense of working a pound of Bengal and China, is not more than one-third, on an average, of that of the fine Italian; there is so little labour in working those coarser descriptions.

4231. As it appears by the prices you have given, that the 3 *s.* 7 *d.* duty, when the price was 22 *s.* 9 *d.*, amounts to 15 per cent., and when at 21 *s.* 9 *d.*, it amounts to 16 per cent. must not that affect the weaver by increasing the cost of the material to him, and prevent his competition with the French weaver?—Of course partially.

4232. Will it not to the whole extent?—No, not to the whole extent, because we consume a small proportion only of foreign thrown; and we have seen that the French manufacturers only import a small proportion also of the thrown silk that they consume. We must take the surface on the French side, and on this side; we must see what is the bulk of goods that France comes upon us with, and what is the relative quantity made here; besides which, as I have observed before, our throwsters work mostly under protection; and again, the duty on tram is only 2 *s.* in this country; goods are made half of tram and half of organzine. Moreover we must notice here, that the purchaser of foreign thrown, has the advantage of the debentures of 3 *s.* 6 *d.* on organzine, and 2 *s.* on tram; for which he can obtain some market value, if he does not use them himself for export.

4233. You have been asked whether the English weaver would not be afraid of coming into competition with the French, do you mean in this market, or in the foreign market?—Not at all in this market, if we are not pressed upon by foreign competition.

4234. At present there is no competition with the French in any foreign market, is there?—No, except those goods we export with an enormous bounty.

4235. If the thrown silk was admitted here free of duty, do not you think that the English weaver would still be enabled to meet that competition in this market? —The duty laid upon thrown silk is only intended as a protection to one of the brethren in the silk trade; and I have endeavoured to show before to this Committee, that the throwster in this country does his work as cheap *relatively* as all his brethren in the trade, and that he does it even cheaper, which can be accounted for: (and I would feel pleasure in following the subject step by step) so that we shall find that the work is not relatively done cheaper abroad. If we dismiss the throwster, then we must next dismiss the dyer, then the warper, and the winder successively; and then we shall come to the whole weight of the question, which is, that the labouring classes in this country require certain protection from the beneficent hand of the law, and that without that protection they cannot sustain competition.

4236. If the duty be taken off the foreign thrown silk, would that enable our weavers to meet the French competition in this market?—No.

4237. Would it not have the effect to destroy the throwster?—Yes; it would be an imaginary advantage, for we should be entirely in the hands of the foreigner for our supply of thrown silk, and should have to pay variations incident on various contingencies, instead of a competition between throwster and throwster, in this country, between Congleton, Macclesfield and Somersetshire, and various other parts of the country, which is always active enough, and takes care that the profits shall not be too high. It is not only a competition amongst our throwsters, as it stands at present, but between our throwster and the foreign throwster; the effect of which is to supply our manufacturers with thrown silks, at the lowest possible

point

Mr.
*Alexis J. Doxat.*

17 April,
1832.

point under the relative circumstances of this country, in regard to wages, &c. Laying aside the desolation, which the withdrawal of a protecting duty for our throwsters would occasion on that important branch of our silk manufacture, the manufacturer himself (speaking abstractedly) would lose many important advantages, attendant on his having the throwing done in this country, and we should expose ourselves to all contingencies of foreign supply, and occasionally to differences much more considerable, than the fractional one, which it causes on the total cost of the goods; I say fractional, because it is in fact, speaking comprehensively, much less than would appear from the rates of 3*s.* 6*d.* on organzine and 2*s.* on tram; all which points are susceptible of minute developement.

4238. Supposing we were entirely dependent upon the foreign throwster, you think there would be greater variations in the price than there are at present?— Much greater occasionally.

4239. Do you find in practice, that the Swiss who depend altogether on the foreign throwster, are exposed to great changes?—They are exposed to all the variations; but being nearer the sources, they are not liable to the same contingencies.

4240. Do they not receive their silk cheaper than we do?—They have nothing to protect; the wages in Switzerland are cheaper even than those of France; they are so cheap, that with their cheap labour they send large quantities of their own plain manufactured goods and plain ribbons for sale in France.

4241. If the duty on Italian thrown silk be further reduced, will there be an increased importation of Italian thrown silk?—Yes.

4242. What proportion of the thrown silk which Italy exports does she send to England?—A very small proportion.

4243. Can Italy with her present mills and machinery throw more silk than she now does?—Certainly, considerably; beside that, there is no difficulty in establishing mills in Italy.

4244. If Italy should send more of her thrown silk to England, is it likely she will send as many raws as she does?—No, she will retain still more of the higher descriptions of raws than she does at present for her mills.

4245. What are the advantages which you think the Italian throwster possesses over the English throwster, either in respect of wages or in any other respect?— The wages in Italy are considerably lower, I cannot say exactly how much; but I have been told that a common labourer, with 10*d.*, considering the lower prices of food, the climate and the habits of the people who use very coarse bread and garlic, &c. that 10*d.* is relative to 30*d.* in this country.

4246. Do the Italians keep their best raws to work at home?—Decidedly; many of them never part with their raws. An enormous difference in price might extract some portion of those filatures which are invariably retained, but even then, I believe there are some filatures, a large proportion of filatures, which never come out, being exclusively reserved for the use of their own mills, the regular employment of which, and with the same silk from year to year, is to them of the most material importance.

4247. Does that custom operate to a sufficient extent to be an advantage to them? —It does; it gives an amazing advantage to them; as they take the silks from their filatures they dry them and put them carefully at once into large boxes; and from those boxes they are taken out as required all through the year, and put at once on the mill, so that not a thread is broken, nor any other deterioration whatever occasioned.

4248. Since the reduction of the duty on thrown silk in 1829, has there been a tendency to the importation of a larger quantity of thrown silks and less raw?— Yes; I find that in 1829 the quantity of Italian thrown silk, as compared with Italian raw, was only 20 per cent.; and in the succeeding year, 1830, the quantity increased to 36 per cent.; and in 1831, the quantity of thrown silk, still in relation to Italian silk, was 50 per cent., an increase of such magnitude I do not find any example in any previous case.

4249. What proportion of the thrown silk imported is Piedmont organzine?— It varies much; some years, one eighth, some, one quarter, &c.

4250. Will not a further reduction of the duty, and a consequent increased importation of foreign thrown silk which you have stated you expect will happen, have the immediate effect of throwing out of employment some of the mills of this country, and of eventually transferring the throwing of Italian silks from this country to Italy?—Yes.

4251. Will the British manufacturer be as well supplied, in your opinion, when

he

he is wholly dependant on foreign thrown silk, as he now is having the thrown silk both of Italy and England, as well as a general choice of raw silk which he can have thrown to suit his own purposes?—If such a thing were to take place, it could not take place without the demolition and destruction of the throwing interest of this country, which is a most essential and important part of its silk manufacture. If it were to take place, we should lose the immense advantage, which our manufacturers possess, in having near them, their right hand; that is, the throwster here; and we should thereby expose ourselves, as I have before stated, to all contingencies. In case of war, or of any interruption, we should then unavoidably depend upon the foreign throwster; we can put up a loom, but cannot put up a mill, in an hour.

4252. Are the prices of silk in France generally higher or lower than in England, independent of the duty?—The prices of silk in France are decidedly lower; that is to say, that every pound of Italian raw silk, imported into France, pays about 2 s. charges; and when a depression takes place in the French manufactures, the silk of their own produce sinks under the level of the Italian raw, making a still greater difference.

4253. Do you attribute the fact of silk being lower in France than in England to the circumstance of France herself producing a large proportion of the raw silk used in her manufactures?—Yes; she has every advantage that Italy can possess in regard to the cultivation of silk; she has the whole produce of Italy to select from at first hand; and in addition to that, she has *exclusively* the whole of her immense home growth, which is, as a whole, of excellent quality, and rather preferable to that of Italy, particularly in regard to texture and brilliancy.

4254. Is Italian raw silk of the same quality, thrown as well in England as in Italy?—Mr. Royle's mill at Manchester, and Mr. Ward's mill at Bruton, Somersetshire, with all their care, and all the perfection of their machinery, do not produce better organzine than we receive from good mills in Italy, where the mills are more bulky, but still producing excellent organzine. All we have been endeavouring to attain, and in which we have succeeded for a number of years past, has been an equality in throwing with those mils, which are called by many over bulky.

4255. Are the Committee to infer, that in your opinion raw silk is thrown as well in England as in Italy?—Yes; there are good and indifferent mills in this country as well as in Italy, but there is no disability in this country.

4256. Is it customary to buy raw silk in Italy, or does it come to this country on consignment?—I can only speak of our own house, in which I have been ever since 1798, and we never have imported, to my knowledge, a single bale of silk on our own, or on half account, either thrown or raw.

4257. Do we get any raw silk from Piedmont at all?—None whatever, its export is strictly prohibited.

4258. Can you state what is the comparative price of Italian thrown silk, and Italian silk thrown in England at Mr. Royle's or Mr. Ward's mills?—I cannot, exactly; I can do it only approximately; we do not sell English organzine; I can only state what foreign organzine sells for.

4259. The French grower of silk sells only to the French manufacturer; so long as he supplies him with all he requires, of course none need be imported from Italy? —Certainly not, except as I have mentioned before, some portion of foreign thrown, principally Piedmont organzine for particular purposes, and some small quantities of foreign raw silks, principally Levant coarse silks, for particular purposes also.

4260. That might continue for some time, might it not?—Without doubt.

4261. By possibility it may continue, if the growth of French silk should be increased in quantity there will be no necessity to import from Italy at all?—I can produce some letters showing, that every year the quantity of her produce increases, and her imports decrease; and we should not lose sight of the fact, that her produce, as a whole, is not only excellent, but of a fine standard.

4262. Can you show, by Table, the progressive imports of Italian silk into France?—I have given that for the years 1826, 1827, 1828 and 1829. Ten or twenty years ago the quantity of Italian silks imported into France was much larger; the quantity imported gradually diminishes, I understand, each year.

4263. Are you able to state, whether the silk manufacture in France, as a manufacture, has decreased or not?—I am not able to state that exactly; but I have every reason to believe, that in the last ten years it has, on an average, increased materially.

4264. It

Mr.
*Alexis J. Dorat.*

17 April,
1832.

4264. It is your opinion, that the silk may be very much lower at Lyons than in Italy?—Certainly; I have mentioned before, as an example of great depression in silks the produce of France, that in February and March, of last year, that good French organzine of 21–22 deniers, was only worth 17 s. 2 d. and 17 s. 6 d., that is 27 francs 50 cents., and 28, with the usual discount of 12½ per cent.

4265. Has the price of silk in Italy any thing to do with the price of silk in France?—Not as a whole, but partially only, that is in regard to small quantities, and mostly of particular descriptions, for particular purposes.

4266. What do you think has been about the average difference?—When good thrown silk of 21–22 deniers was at Lyons, 17 s. 2 d. to 17 s. 6 d., I believe the same quality here was worth 23 s. 6 d. to 24 s.

4267. That is an extreme case, is it not?—I mentioned it as an extreme case: I have not taken my comparative statement from it, but it was in my memory, and I referred to it about a fortnight ago; I went to our old book of prices current, and found those prices.

4268. What do you think is about the average of the difference of price between Lyons and Italy?—I cannot say at this moment, but I might easily by reference.

4269. Do you think it is ten per cent.?—Upon the raw silk it is often more than ten per cent.; the duties and import charges upon it into France are more than that, although the market prices at Lyons of French raw silks come occasionally in contact with those of Italian raw silks.

4270. What do you think is the difference of price at which the manufacturer in London and in Lyons is supplied with the material necessary for his manufacture?—The difference will vary from three to four, five and six shillings and more; I am alluding to thrown silks; the thrown silk made in France is with extremely small exceptions, made from raw silks of their own produce.

4271. Do you think that the duty on Italian silk imported into France raises or not the price of French silk?—I do not think it does; for they will only pay for those specific articles they want, their manufacture rests essentially upon their own produce in the first instance; and they have all the advantage of the fall, but no inconvenience from rise, for when they come occasionally in contact with Italian silks, they have them a little under us.

4272. To what extent does the duty levied on Italian organzine silk imported into this country affect the price of organzine thrown here?—That is a question which has been answered before; it is a complex question; if you look at figures merely, you would say it affects it, 3 s. 6 d. with regard to organzine, and 2 s. on tram, but that is not the case; we import usually but a small proportion of foreign thrown silks, and it is the same at Lyons; but the great mass of our manufacture is carried on with British thrown silks, worked at rates under the protection; for although the protecting duties on thrown silks have been reduced of late to a miserable point (jointly with the effects of the debentures) for the English throwster, he has participated beyond that, in the calamitous pressure of foreign manufactured silks, on every constituent part of our silk manufacture, of which the throwing forms a very important branch. On this subject I shall have the honour to submit hereafter some particulars to the Committee.

4273. You mean to say we have no raw Italian silk imported to be thrown in England, of the same quality as that thrown in Italy?—No, that is not so.

4274. Take the same quality of thrown silk imported into England as that thrown in Italy, and state the effect the duty on the organzine thrown in Italy when imported into this country will have upon the price of that imported raw and thrown here?—Three shillings and sixpence is the duty, but it does not operate to the extent of 3 s. 6 d.

4275. To what extent then does the duty on foreign organzine thrown silk affect the price of British organzine?—To answer this, we must see what difference exists between the relative quality of raw and of thrown silk in this country; I will go to the comparison between Bergam and Milan raw silks of four to five cocoons, and thrown silk from the same countries of 26–28 deniers. I began this statement many years ago, I placed Milans of 4–5 and 5–6 cocoons against 26–28 deniers, but the more exact comparison should be between 4–5 cocoons and 26 to 28 deniers. I have now made a statement reducing this Table alone to 4–5 cocoons Milans and Bergam raw silk, against 26–28 deniers organzine, which correspond as nearly as can be; I reckon about six deniers to the cocoon; multiplying the four-and-half by six will give 26. I find that in February 1831, the

678. average

Mr.
*Alexis J. Doxat.*

17 April,
1832.

average price of Milan and Bergam raw silk was 18 s. 1 d. taking the average of 26–28 deniers thrown silk, Milan and Bergam at the same period, I find that the average was 23 s. 4 d. each at five months credit; I find the difference between these two prices is 5 s. 3 d. The value of the debenture has varied greatly, from one penny to 6 d. and 7 d. which is to be deducted, because the manufacturer who buys a bale of foreign thrown silk is entitled to a debenture; the value of the debenture is 3 s. 6 d., but the export is so little that its value in the market is from one, two, three, four, and up to seven pence. I have taken the average market value of it at four pence; I deduct 4 d. from the difference of 5 s. 3 d. that will leave 4 s. 11 d., which remains for work and waste, interest and profit, besides the risk of alterations in the market, whilst the raw silk is under work, risk of the buyers and some charges for agencies. If the manufacturer comes to us to buy foreign thrown silk it is all at hand; we have only to take it out of dock; in the course of three or four hours it may be had up. The man who buys raw silk to work it into organzine or tram, must take all the chances of the market; and no man will run the risk without some consideration for that particular. Then the ultimate difference is 4 s. 11 d. (it has even been reduced to 4 s. 5 d. from January of this year), for work and waste and chance of market, and a comparatively inferior choice of raw silk. Besides this we make rather more waste in this country than they do on the spot; if from 4 s. 11 d. we deduct the waste, say 10 d. or 11 d., there remains 4 s. a pound (and even only 3 s. 6 d. if from 4 s. 5 d. as just mentioned) abstractedly of all other considerations. The rate of 4 s. per lb. is considerably lower here relatively than the charges for similar work in France and in Italy respectively; that can be demonstrated step by step; and on this subject I shall have the honour to submit to this Committee, two Statements marked (D.) and (E.) furnished in April 1829 at his request, to the Right honourable Vesey Fitzgerald. The rate of 4 s. per pound has been obtained only by extremely low and wretched wages; the same will be found in regard to weaving, warping and winding; the same in the dyeing, which requires much manual labour; the quantity of manual labour in dyeing properly, so that the silk shall be neatly turned out and retain its colour, is very considerable; the same exists in regard to every process of the silk manufacture; there are analogies through every part of it.

4276. Do you mean to say that we actually do manufacture cheaper?—Relatively cheaper; that is to say, a labouring man in Italy lives, as I understand, on tenpence compared to thirty-pence, in this country; and those proportions have been stated to this Honourable Committee by a gentleman who went from Manchester to make inquiries into every thing relating to the throwing of silk in Italy; he said the inquiries he had made, led him to the conclusion that the difference was as three to one. Then there are other elements in this question; we suppose that our steam engines give us a great advantage of power; water power costs a great deal in this country; for example, a mill that shall turn out a certain quantity of silk, will occasion an expense of one hundred pounds for turning power, whether by steam or by water, or part one and part the other. In the north of Italy, all that is to be done, is to direct the currents of water; there are so many small rivers come down from the Appenines and the Alps, that it will cost them in the proportion of 1 d. to 5 d. per lb. of organzine, that is 20 l. per annum, as compared with 100 l. with us. We have here coals; and for some branches of industry it is to us an incalculable advantage; but this very point, in which it is imagined we have a great advantage in silk throwing, that is the mota, the moving power, costs in Italy in the proportion of 1 d. to 5 d. here.

4277. They have more mill sites than are occupied?—Yes; there is a stream in the neighbourhood of Turin, which is divided to irrigate a large portion of that district; it is divided off to various sites in small currents, at a very trifling expense; the whole of the north of Italy is one receptacle for water.

4278. Are you able to give the Committee information as to the quantities of silk imported from our own possessions abroad?—Yes; our importations of Bengal silks, exclusive of China, I think form about one-third of the whole of our consumption of raw and thrown silks, exclusive only of foreign waste.

4279. Has there been any improvement in the quality of silk imported from Bengal since you have been acquainted with the silk trade?—I apprehend that that answer will occupy more time than the Committee can now afford me, I beg to be permitted to defer answering that question, as the Committee is going to adjourn.

[*The Witness delivered in the following Paper.*]

No. 6.

Mr.
*Alexis J. Doxat.*

17 April,
1832.

## No. 6.

## PLAIN SILK GOODS.

ABRIDGED RECAPITULATION of the foregoing COMPARATIVE ESTIMATES of COSTS, at *London* and *Lyons*, of good PLAIN GOODS, in common Colours.

| AT LONDON — Rates of Wages for Weaving, and others in about the same Ratio. (Per Yard. d.) | Cost of 1 lb. Fine Raw Silk. (Estimate at London. s. d.) | Cost of good Plain Manufactured Silks in common Colours, per lb.=16 Yards. (s. d.) | Cost per Yard of 16 Drams. (s. d.) | TOTAL Differences of Cost per Cent. between London and Lyons. | Cost per Yard of 16 Drams. (s. d.) | Cost of good Plain Manufactured Silks in common Colours, per lb.=16 Yards. (s. d.) | Cost of 1 lb. Fine Raw Silk. (Estimate at Lyons. s. d.) | AT LYONS — Rates of Wages for Weaving, and others in about the same Ratio. |
|---|---|---|---|---|---|---|---|---|
| Between usual moderate Wages, from 1821 to 1825 { 10½ to 8½ } | (1) - 17  6 | 49  3 | 3  1 | 30 per Cent. | 2  4⅜ | 37  10 | 17  - | 5½d. per Yard.  — = 72 c. per Aune. (6½d. to 5½d. per Yard, i.e. about 85 to 72 Cents per Aune, were the usual rates in former Years.) |
| And wretched Wages - 6 |  |  |  | 40 | 2  2⅜  Cost less Profit, &c. | 35  3 | 17  -  (1.1) | 5½  - |
| Low - 7½ | (2) - 17  6 | 47  1 | 2  11⅜ | 31 | 2  2⅞ | 35  10 | 16  - | 5¼  -  — = 69 c. per Aune.  (usual rates for some years.) |
|  |  |  |  | 41 | 2  1  - ditto. | 33  4 | 16  -  (2.2) | 5¼  - |
| Very low - 7 | (3) - 17  6 | 44  11 | 2  9⅝ | 33 | 2  1⅜ | 33  10 | 15  6 | 4¾  -  } low rates - = 63 c. per Aune. |
|  |  |  |  | 43 | 1  11⅝  - ditto. | 31  6 | 15  6  (3.3) | 4¾  - |
| Wretched - 6 | (4) - 17  6 | 42  7 | 2  8 | 37 | 1  11⅜ | 31  1 | 14  6 | 4  -  } very low - = 53 c. per Aune. |
|  |  |  |  | 47 | 1  9⅝  - ditto. | 28  11 | 14  6  (4.4) | 4  - |

(*continued.*)

Mr.
*Alexis J. Doxat.*

17 April,
1832.

No. 6.—*continued.*

## ILLICIT IMPORTS.

| LONDON, Cost of 1 lb. of Manufactured Plain Silks, in common Colours. | LYONS, Cost of 1 lb. of Manufactured Plain Silks in common Colours, inclusive of 4 per cent. for Charges of Purchase, &c. at Lyons, and of transmission to Paris, where the Smuggler takes up the Goods. | Differences of Cost and Charges per lb. of those Descriptions of Plain Silks, assuming the Colours and Qualities to be in every respect equal. |
|---|---|---|
| *s. d.* | *s. d.* | *s. d.* |
| 49 3 | 39 4 / 36 8 | 9 11 = 25 per Ct. / 12 7 = 34 |
| 47 1 | 37 3 / 34 8 | 9 10 = 25 / 12 5 = 35 |
| 44 11 | 35 3 / 32 9 | 9 8 = 27 / 12 2 = 38 |
| 42 7 | 32 4 / 30 1 | 10 3 = 32 / 12 6 = 42 |

*Query*—What is the Charge of the Smuggler on Plain Goods?

## LEGAL IMPORTS.

| LONDON, Cost of 1 lb. of Manufactured good Plain Silks in common Colours. | LYONS, Cost of 1 lb. of Manufactured good Plain Silks in common Colours, inclusive of 6 per Cent. for Charges of Purchase, &c. at Lyons, and of transmission to London. (Estimate at Lyons.) | Differences of Cost and Charges per lb. of those Descriptions of Plain Silks. | Our Import Duty on Manufactured Plain Silks, per lb. | Differences on Legal Imports: in favour of \| against the Lyons Manufacturer. |
|---|---|---|---|---|
| Estimate at London. | | *s. d.* PerCt. | *s. d.* per Ct. | |
| (1) Raw - 17 6, Weaving - 8¼ } 49 3 | Raw - 17 -, Weaving - 5½ } 40 1, Cost less Profit, &c. 37 4 (1.1) | 9 2 = 23 / 11 11 = 32 | 11 - = 27* / 11 - = 30 | 4 per Ct. - / - 2 per Ct. |
| (2) Raw - 17 6, Weaving - 7½ } 47 1 | Raw - 16 -, Weaving - 5¼ } 37 11, Cost less Profit, &c. 35 4 (2.2) | 9 2 = 24 / 11 9 = 33 | 11 - = 29 / 11 - = 31 | 5 per Ct. - / - 2 per Ct. |
| (3) Raw - 17 6, Weaving - 7 } 44 11 | Raw - 15 6, Weaving - 4¾ } 35 11, Cost less Profit, &c. 33 5 (3.3) | 9 - = 25 / 11 5 = 34 | 11 - = 31 / 11 - = 33 | 6 per Ct. - / - 1 per Ct. |
| (4) Raw - 17 6, Weaving - 6 } 42 7 | Raw - 14 6, Weaving - 4 } 32 11, Cost less Profit, &c. 30 8 (4.4) | 9 8 = 30 / 11 11 = 39 | 11 - = 33 / 11 - = 36 | 3 per Ct. - / - 3 per Ct. |

* On the Lyons Cost and Charges of Purchase & Transmission.

March 1832.     Errors excepted.     (signed)   *Alexis James Doxat.*

*Mercurii, 18° die Aprilis, 1832.*

THE RIGHT HON. THE EARL GROSVENOR, IN THE CHAIR.

Mr. *Alexis James Doxat,* called in; and further Examined.

4280. YOU stated in your examination yesterday, that early in 1831, the market price of good French organzine of the size of 21–22 deniers, was 17 s. 4½ d.; have the goodness to state what the cost of Italian raw silk of the same kind would have been, if imported into Lyons at the same period?—Seventeen shillings and four-pence.

4281. The price in fact of the two articles would have been precisely the same?—With this difference, that the raw silk with which the organzine silk in France was made, was rather superior to the quality of Italian silk on which I have made the calculation.

4282. In point of fact, French organzine of rather superior quality as to raw silk, was at the same price there, within one halfpenny, of the Italian raw silk at the same period?—Yes, the 17 s. 4 d. as compared with 17 s. 4½ d.

4283. How do you arrive at the fact of the price of Italian raw silk in Lyons?—At that period there was no Italian raw silk consumed in France to my knowledge; the French silk was so considerably cheaper, the export of the French silk not being allowed, they worked upon that; that is, upon a produce of 4 to 4,500,000 lbs., mostly of fine descriptions.

4284. Do you know whether at that time there was any Italian raw silk in the city of Lyons?—There was, in transit for this country; but it was not touched by their manufacturers.

4285. It is supposed that because France finds it necessary to buy some Italian silk of a particular description, and for particular purposes, the price at which that silk is sold in Lyons must have an influence, and must regulate the whole of the silk of France of the native growth sold in Lyons; are you quite certain that such is or is not the fact?—I have answered that question before; if it is the wish of the Committee, I will go again through the subject; it forms one element of the question; a certain quantity of Piedmont organzine is imported throughout the year for particular purposes, but it forms but a small part.

4286. Do you know whether that has sold at a higher price than French silk of similar quality?—Yes, for those particular purposes; but the great bulk consumed in France is sold considerably under; I understand the consumption of France is, upon the average, 5,500,000 lbs.; the importation of Italian thrown silk, principally Piedmont organzine, about 600 to 700,000 lbs.; the importation of foreign raw silks, 350 to 400,000; and of those 350 to 400,000, a small part only is fine silk, the large bulk is Turkey silk and coarse Neapolitan and Venetian silks; I believe upon the average the quantity of fine Italian silk consumed in France, is about 150,000, as compared with about 4,500,000 lbs. of their own growth.

4287. Are you aware whether there is any importation of marabout into this country?—I am not aware that there is; I do not know that it is thrown in Italy.

4288. What do you consider to be the various degrees of competition against which our silk manufacturers have to contend?—I had the honour to state yesterday abstractedly, that taking the standard, which I consider to be but fair moderate wages for the description of manufactured silks, I have been alluding to in all my calculations, that is gros de Naples, 10 to 1100 three double neatly made, at the moderate wages of 8½ d. for weaving, and other work in proportion, would be 3 s. 1 d.; whilst when we manufacture at the rate of sixpence per yard for weaving and other charges in proportion, then it is depressed to 2 s. 8 d. per yard. I have made a comparative statement of the cost of the same article with France, and I find the following variations. When they work at moderate wages, and at the same time at the highest relative point for the cost of the raw silk, the comparative point between Lyons and this country, that is the relative price under those circumstances, is 2 s. 4 d. and three-eighths, as compared with 3 s. 1 d. with us; then they descend rapidly if there is for some time a want of orders for America, or any other particular cause of depression, a war on the Continent, or any internal disturbance in France, upon any occurrence which checks the vent of their goods, they reduce their price of weaving, and their price of throwing, and of every operation; and

678.                                                                                                   the

Mr.
*Alexis J. Doxat.*

18 April,
1832.

Mr.
*Alexis J. Doxat.*

18 April,
1832.

the silk falls also in price gradually; and they go beyond that, they will do what the manufacturer will do here to get rid of their goods; they will sacrifice the items of incidentals, interest and profit. Taking into consideration all those circumstances to which they are continually exposed, I find the difference to be from 2 *s.* 4 *d.* and $\frac{3}{4}$ths down to 1 *s.* 9 *d.* $\frac{4}{5}$ths.

4289. Then it is comparing 3 *s.* 1 *d.* down to 2 *s.* 8 *d.* in this country with 2 *s.* 4 *d.* $\frac{3}{4}$ths. down to 1 *s.* 9 *d.* $\frac{4}{5}$ths in France?—Yes.

4290. You have stated, that under a certain state of things silk falls in Lyons as well as labour and other things. If the grower of silk in France were allowed to export that silk would it sell so low?—It would not; it would in some measure equalize itself; still the French would retain a great advantage over us, as they have no charge on their own silk, while every pound they import from Italy has about 2 *s.*, and we about 2 *s.* 2 *d.* besides our being more distant from the source; consequently they would yet start witn a comparative material advantage of about 2 *s.*

4291. You conceive it would be a very material point if we could induce the French government to allow us to have a free importation of their raw silks?—Certainly, in many respects; but there are many points of importance in the whole of this question; and it is a matter of such great moment to France to have the possession of our vast and rich markets, both under ordinary and contingent circumstances, that they might possibly be induced to that course if pressed so to do by an apprehension of losing such benefit; but there are so many other causes of disability besides, with respect to this branch of industry which requires so much of manual labour, and hence employs such considerable numbers of our population, that the privation of so good a material, and at prices comparatively low, forms one part only, among many, of this momentous question. And we could not fall into a more baneful error, than that of allowing ourselves to be drawn into such an arrangement; whereby we should confirm, as it were, by our own act, the state of misery in which has been placed, of late years, a manufacture of such vast importance, in every sense, to Great Britain; a manufacture which operates as a direct and most beneficent transfer from the superfluities of the rich, to industrious employment.

4292. You think that the French manufacturer considers it a very material point if he has sufficient influence with the French government to prevent their acceding to our wish upon that subject?—It has often been a subject of consideration, it was so two or three years ago, and again three or four months ago.

4293. The effect of keeping it at home is to compel the grower to submit to the reduced price whenever they have a bad trade?—Yes; a fall in wages takes place, and the price of silk falling to, they work therefore with some degree of safety; but if good times do not speedily return they make some sacrifice on those low cost prices of their goods, as I have before stated, and this accounts for the intensity of their pressure on our industry, to degrees of extreme misery, under contingent circumstances with them.

4294. You do not imagine that if we had the finer raw silks of France imported here, there is any thing to prevent our manufacturers from making as good an article of any sort?—No, there is a peculiar taste in France; but in respect of quality there is no doubt we can make as good articles; there is every possible means in this country to do every thing which can be done there; it is not want of ability in our manufacturers and labourers; the question is one of wages, that is the basis of all; the French materials form one part.

4295. The question referred to the possibility of the manufacturer in this country to have the best quality of French silks, from their skill in making as good articles in every respect as the French?—I repeat, that our manufacturers and their labourers, are capable of doing every thing that is done by foreign manufacturers; but our progress in improvements has been, as a whole, considerably impeded by the discouraging and calamitous effects of foreign imports; we have been compelled, for the very major part of our manufacture, to confine ourselves to plain goods, and in these to *retreat* mostly on low, and very low descriptions, for the sake of cheapness, which classes afford but small amounts of wages to our labourers.

4296. Do you consider the silk manufacture exotic?—Not at all; I find in cotton only one-nineteenth part is the produce of our Colonies; whereas of the silk, one-third is the produce of our Colonies.

4297. To what manufacture is the silk which is grown in our own possessions applied?—Very principally to low and coarse goods.

4298. Can

Mr.
*Alexis J. Doxat.*

18 April,
1832.

4298. Can you, at all, state the proportion of wages paid upon the silk grown in our own Colonies and the silk grown in Italy?—The proportions, I should suppose, from inquiries, to be from 5 *s.* to 12 *s.* per lb. on the Bengal, and from 14 *s.* to 40 *s.* and more per lb. on the Italian.

4299. Can you state the relative increase, since the alteration of the duty in the importation of Italian, with other silks?—Yes; in 1826 the quantity of foreign thrown silk, as compared with the quantity of Italian raw silks, was 40 per cent.; in 1827, 31 per cent.; in 1828, 29 per cent.; in 1829, it fell so low as 20 per cent. The last alteration of duty took place on the 2d of June 1829, from 5 *s.* to 3 *s.* 6 *d.* on organzine thrown silk, and from 3 *s.* on tram to 2 *s.*; in addition to which the debentures, to which I have often had occasion to allude to in the course of my examination, have been granted from that period to the purchaser of foreign thrown silk. I have stated, that in 1829 the number was 20 per cent., that is the relation between foreign thrown silk imported into this country and Italian raw silk. I find, that the following year that ratio was increased to 36 per cent.; and the following year, 1831, to 50 per cent.

4300. You refer to the relative proportions of raw and thrown silk imported from Italy; the question referred to the increase of the quantity of Italian silk imported into this country since the removal of the duty between the importation of Italian silks and other silk?—In 1824 and 1825 the importation of Italian raw silk, as compared with other silks, was 75 per cent.; in 1831 that proportion was 52 per cent., showing a greater relative proportion of Bengal, China and Turkey silks, that is, a much greater proportion of coarse silks in 1831. In 1824 and 1825 the quantity of Italian thrown silk imported was 38 per cent. relatively with Italian raw; in 1831 it was 50 per cent.

4301. You would infer from that, that our manufacture as to quality, has certainly declined?—They have worked on a much lower standard; and beyond that, silks of similar standard have been applied, of late years, to much lower classes of goods, on an average.

4302. Has not the China and Bengal improved of late years?—I think that our importation of China silks of late years has been, on an average, of a finer standard, and we apply them very usefully. With respect to Bengal silk it is not so; taking the average of the last ten years, and the previous ten years, as to Bengal, I think there is not any great alteration; some filatures have improved and others may have gone back.

4303. Is there any doubt that since the year 1825 the proportion of coarse goods made in the silk manufactures of this country has been relatively much larger than at any former period?—Incomparably larger.

4304. Has that proportion been gradually increasing?—It has been gradually increasing.

4305. Has not the effect of that been, to employ a much smaller number of persons to produce the same number of yards?—Very much so; I gave in a statement the second day I was before the Committee, showing that one kind of silk gave ten times the labour which the other did, so that one pound of Italian silk worked into some high branches of the manufacture, gave ten times the amount of wages of labour than coarse Bengal, applied to low works. I mention that not as an extreme point, but as a conspicuous point, because it occurs on a large surface.

4306. Has there been a diminution in the price of silk in the home market, corresponding with the reduction of duty on imported thrown silk?—Yes; every time that the duty has been reduced, the difference between raw and thrown silk has been diminished, even beyond the amounts of the respective deductions in duties; and there has been a greater proportionate quantity of thrown silk imported during the last two years. I have a statement made from year to year since 1824, of the comparative points between a certain quality of fine Italian raw silk, and a certain quality of foreign organzine silk; the difference has been this, applying it to the Milan and Bergam raw silk of 4–5 to 5–6 cocoons, and Milan and Bergam organzine silk of 26 to 28 deniers, the results are as follows: 11 *s.* 3 *d.*, 13 *s.* 9 *d.*, 18 *s.* 9 *d.*, 12 *s.*, 10 *s.* 9 *d.*, 9 *s.*, 7 *s.* 3 *d.*, 7 *s.* 5 *d.*, 7 *s.* 6 *d.*, 7 *s.* 2 *d.*, 7 *s.*, 8 *s.* 5 *d.*, 6 *s.* 8 *d,* 7 *s.* 1 *d.*, 7 *s.* 1 *d.*, 7 *s.* 3 *d.*, 6 *s.* 1 *d.*, 6 *s.* 2 *d.*, 6 *s.* 9 *d.*, 6 *s.* 5 *d.*, 5 *s.* 7 *d.* 5 *s.* 4 *d.*, 5 *s.* 4 *d.*, 5 *s.* 1 *d.*

4307. Those are the differences between raw and thrown?—Yes; from June 1824 to April 1832, both inclusive, specified at distinct periods three times a year. I should observe on this subject, that from June 1829, in addition to those differences so considerably diminished, that the debenture comes against the British

678.                                                                              throwster;

throwster; though the debentures are worth nominally 3 s. 6 d. they have been sold in the market from 1 d. to 7 d., I will take the average at 4 d. which will come pretty near the mark. The manufacturer who purchases the foreign organzine, has the benefit of the debenture; he has it in two ways; if he exports he uses it; if not, it is a marketable commodity.

4308. You have alluded to the lamentable and overwhelming pressure of foreign competition in the silk manufacture, the effect of which has been to reduce the wages of the labour to a low and wretched rate; have the same reductions taken place in regard to other manufactures?—No, they have not; I will take as a relative point, one I have frequently alluded to. It appears by statements I have submitted to the Committee, that from 1815 to 1830 the difference in the amount of wages per pound weight of cotton wool, has been about 50 per cent.; but those reductions have not been absolutely in the rate of wages, but composed of various elements; one part has arisen from reductions in the rate of wages to our labourers, another from gradually larger quantities of cotton exported in a spun state only to the Continent, &c. which have become very considerable of late years; in addition to these, considerable quantities of work have been done in the cotton manufacture with power looms, diminishing the amount of wages; so that if the whole range of diminution of wages which has occurred in the cotton trade from the manufacture of one pound of cotton appear as 5 s. to 2 s. 6 d. from 1815, 1816 and 1817 to 1830, that diminution has not only been gradual during that period, but composed of various elements; whereas the diminution of wages in the silk manufacture has taken place entirely since 1826, that is, subsequent to the periods of 1821–1823 and 1824–1825. I take the surface of the country, and find, that whether I take the average wages of Spitalfields, or the average wages at Manchester, or at other silk manufacturing places the same relation, with some variations from year to year, on the goods manufactured, exists. I have taken it in my various statements in the ratio of 10 ½ d. to 6 d. on plain goods, but I find that I have underrated it.

4309. You have stated that the wages in the cotton manufacture began to decline from the year 1815, did the wages in the cotton manufacture decline at Manchester from 1815?—I believe so, and prior.

4310. Did they decline in the silk trade from 1815?—I am not aware that they did; there were some trifling fluctuations, but I believe the wages in 1821, 1822, 1823, 1824 and 1825, were the same, or as nearly the same as possible, as in 1815, 1816 and 1817.

4311. So that that proves that the wages in one branch of trade in the same town may decline, and not in another?—I will even go further, and submit that even in the same branch of trade there is no equality of wages. I understand from minute inquiries I have made, that the wages earned by a man in the cotton spinning mills, are from 18 s. to 21 s. per week, and that the price of weaving in the same town and in the same street, whether by power or by hand loom, is from 6 s. to 7 s. and 8 s. a week, as compared with 18 s. and 21 s. I understand that in spinning cotton, our machinery gives us immense advantages; the spinning of cotton is performed almost as a metamorphosis by the extraordinary power of our machinery, and we export immense quantities of cotton yarn to foreign nations; whereas the looming, whether by hand or by power, depends much more upon manual labour. Machinery has immense power in the conversion of cotton wool into yarn. We export upwards of sixty millions of pounds per annum of this article, from which large quantities of goods, manufactured by foreign nations with cheap labour, meet in various parts of the world our own goods, although the looming part of our work has been done at such very low rates of wages; and that on the spun cotton sent to them (on which our labourers have had good wages,) the foreigners have had to pay various charges of agency and transmission. So that, notwithstanding all those peculiar advantages which we possess in this manufacture, in its very basis and very important parts, we meet at every step the ultimate effects of cheap foreign labour, whether the looming abroad be done by hand or by power. If we are thus pressed upon with regard to a manufacture in which we possess such paramount advantages of every description, and which in the aggregate so greatly depends upon the operation of machinery; what must be our relative situation with France, &c. in regard to the silk manufacture in which our foreign competitors possess material advantages, and in which manual labour obtains of necessity, in such considerable ratio, as ten to one with machinery in its most improved application. With respect to the latter point, I made three years ago, at the request of the Right honourable Vesey Fitzgerald, some statements, showing the dissection of every process and charge in

the

the silk manufacture. I have had copies of those Statements printed for this
Honourable Committee, and I beg leave to submit them to their consideration
(*Vide,* Tables Nos. 8 and 9, marked originally D. and E. April 1829); and also
the printed Paper No. 18, which I mentioned on the second day of my examination
had been destroyed by an accident under the Lithographic press.

*Mr.*
*Alexis J. Daxat.*

18 April,
1832.

[*The Witness delivered in the same. Vide Papers* Nos. 8, 9 *and* 18.]

Appendix (F.)

---

### Jovis, 19° die Aprilis, 1832.

### EDWARD AYSHFORD SANFORD, ESQUIRE, IN THE CHAIR.

#### Mr. *Alexis James Doxat*, called in; and further Examined.

4312. HAVE you any observations to make on the prices of silk at Lyons, in
addition to your former evidence?—I observed, in the course of my examination
yesterday, that in the early part of last year the market price at Lyons for French
organzine of 21–22 deniers was 17 *s.* 4½ *d.* on the average; and that the importation
of Milan and Bergam raw silk of the same size, that is the same fineness, but not of
quite so good a quality, would have been 17 *s.* 4 *d.* I have looked this morning
at our own price currents, that is to the price currents in London at the same
period, for the same description of Milan and Bergam raw silk, and I find its
price 18 *s.* on an average, at the usual credit of five months, equal to 17 *s.* 6½ *d.*,
deducting the customary discount of 2½ per cent. for cash. I have thought it right
to state this to the Honourable Committee, in order to complete this view of the
subject. I shall only add, that in looking through also the quotations received
from Lyons for the same period, I have found various quotations of French raw
silks, which fully corroborate the low prices of French organzine so distinctly
quoted to us by two respectable houses at Lyons at that period. But I will not
further detain the Committee on these particulars.

*Mr.*
*Alexis J. Doxat.*

19 April,
1832.

4313. Will you state the price of organzine in London at the same time?—I do
not know exactly what was the price of English organzine at that period, but the
average price of Piedmont and of Milan and Bergam organzine of 21–22 deniers
was then 24 *s.* 8½ *d.* at the usual credit of five months, equal to 24 *s.* 1 *d.* for
cash.

4314. What was the price of French raw silk of the same quality at the same
period at Lyons?—I find the range of prices that may be referrible to the same
quality, rather higher yet, 14 *s.* 6 *d.*, 15 *s.* 9 *d.*, 14 *s.* 2¼ *d.*, 15 *s.* 1½ *d.*, 13 *s.* 10½ *d.*
and 13 *s.* 3 *d.*, averaging 14 *s.* 5½ *d.*

4315. How many deniers weight is that?—Eight to ten deniers against eight
to ten deniers, 10 to 12 deniers, 10 to 12 deniers, 9 to 10 deniers, and 10 to 11
deniers; that is, corresponding to rather a finer standard than 21–22 in organzine.

4316. You have stated that the consumption of foreign thrown silk in France is
700,000 lbs. per annum, principally Piedmont organzine and low Italian trams, are
you to be understood to say, that this is the average consumption of foreign thrown
silk, and that much less of foreign raw silk is consumed in France during the
periods of frequent occurrence in which there exists some considerable depression
in the prices of organzine worked in France from raw silk, the produce of their
own growth?—The quantity just mentioned of 700,000 lbs. of foreign thrown silk
imported into France, has reference, as I have upon a previous occasion observed,
to the average of the years 1825, 1826, 1827 and 1828; the respective quantities
were in 1825, 741,000 lbs., in 1826, 755,000 lbs., in 1827, 740,000 lbs., and in
1828, 534,000 lbs.

4317. Can you state how you get at the fact of that importation?—By the
French official Custom House Returns; the gradual improvement taking place in
France in her throwing mills, some of which have attained great perfection, and
the cultivation of silk gradually increasing in that country every year, I have
reason to believe that the importation of foreign thrown silks has been less on the
average during the years 1829, 1830 and 1831, than during the former period.

4318. Have you any Return?—I have not the Returns of the last three years;
and with respect to the second part of the inquiry, I should answer, that the Pied-

678.
mont

mont organzines imported into France are in general applied to specific purposes to which they are more particularly suitable ; many of those purposes are supplied by French organzine when some material difference exists between the price of French and Piedmont organzines.

4319. Do you consider the general trade in silk in France, including the manufacture, to be in a state of improvement, or the reverse?—As far as I can answer the question, I will do so. In the figured and fancy branches, and in the higher classes of plain goods, they are, I understand, without rivals. Then with respect to the secondary class of goods, and all plain ribbons, they are pressed upon by lower wages in other parts of Europe; that is to say, in Switzerland and on the Rhine. I have had the honour to state before, that although the Swiss and Rhenish manufacturers have not the advantage of silks of their own growth, their wages are so much lower than in France that they send, I believe, some large quantities of plain goods and of plain ribbons into that country; in addition to this, I believe that the Rhenish manufacturers send some quantities of secondary velvets, very well made in their class.

4320. Do you consider the silk trade of France, in the year 1831, larger than it was in the year 1825?—I should say in 1831 not; because it has been impeded by various causes.

4321. Take the average of 1823, 1824 and 1825, and 1829, 1830 and 1831? —The last four or five years there was an increase, I apprehend, on the previous years; but I have no exact information upon that point. The silk trade in France is, I believe, in a state of progressive increase, though the manufacturers are occasionally much depressed, owing to various circumstances to which I have before alluded.

4322. Why do you make the exception of last year?—The cholera on the Continent, and the war in Poland, and so on; natural and political causes.

4323. May not the same causes that prevented the trade of France with the rest of Europe to which you have referred, have tended to throw a large quantity of organzine silk from Italy into England, than had previously taken place?—The same causes would operate upon the bulk; that is, they would have sent us more raw silk from Italy than of thrown, whereas there has been a considerable quantity of thrown sent in the last year, and a decrease in raw.

4324. Do not those countries take only thrown silk, and as the impediments to those countries took place, would not naturally there be a surplus of raw silk, which would find its way to England?—The operation of the lowering the duties on thrown silks has, in my opinion been, that of inducing them to send us large quantities of thrown silks; and had it not been for that, we should have had larger quantities of fine raw sent here instead of thrown.

4325. Might not the causes which impeded the French trade in silk, such as cholera and war in Poland, influence the supply of organzine silk from Italy here? —I said before, it may have had some influence ; but even then we are not to suppose they send to us all, and that they do not send to other countries ; after all, the thrown which they send to us is but fractional ; and if the circumstances of the Continent were such as to influence their sending of thrown silks to us, the same causes would send us here large quantities of manufactured goods at reduced prices.

4326. Were not the prices of manufactured silk goods lower in France in the year 1831, than they had been for many years past?—I believe so, but still I believe that in 1829 the depression was as great.

4327. Do you believe from the prices at which French manufactured silk goods were sold in England, in the course of the last year, that it is possible the manufacturer could have obtained any profit or any remunerating price for them?—I do not think so ; France depends I believe essentially upon export for her manufactures ; whenever manufacturers are impeded in the sale of their manufactured goods, they are very happy to throw off one, two, or three pence a yard ; it is an advantage to them to have a market, and not only a market, but a rich and very considerable market, where they can not only effect sales by dropping the price, but they can immediately draw upon account on consignment ; so that if they have England at hand, it is an immense advantage to them, England being the largest market for silk goods ; for there is no country in which silk goods of every description are so generally used. It has been supposed by a portion of the British public, that the changes effected in late years in our laws, relative to the silk trade, impeded the progress of the French manufacture. I cannot for a moment imagine

how

Mr.
*Alexis J. Doxat.*
———
19 April,
1832.

how such an idea can have been entertained; the condition of the labourers at Lyons, which was very lamentable some months ago, would have been much more so, but for the immense quantities of goods which the opening of our ports since 1826, enabled them to send to this country, both in figured and plain goods. France presses upon us at all times, she depresses the whole surface of our wages, deprives us of the manufacture of the very major part of the higher branches; and keeps us pinned down in all the branches of our silk manufacture to low and wretched wages under the ordinary range of her competition; but even the extremes of wretchedness in wages, cannot shelter us from the overwhelming and calamitous effects of their contingencies, that is of their much increased sendings of figured and plain goods at very reduced prices, as I have had occasion to mention before. I should take here the opportunity to observe that, important as are the advantages to foreign manufactures accruing from the opening of our markets to them, those advantages constitute only a fraction of the blighting effects of foreign competition, on this branch of our national industry, under ordinary circumstances, and of its calamitous effects from contingencies with them.

4328. Do you know whether manufactured silk goods have risen in price since the period of depression in November last at Lyons?—Yes; there has been extraordinary activity at Lyons. I am told the quantity of silk sold at Lyons in the last month, was greater than it had been for a long time previous.

4329. Do you know that those silks so sold were ordered at the period of depression, and that cheap as silks were in November, they may be purchased at Lyons at the same or even lower prices?—I know nothing about the value of goods at the present moment.

4330. Can you give the Committee any notion, from your own knowledge, of the comparison between the quantity of manufactured goods exported from France, with what they actually consume within themselves?—I cannot; there are some returns, but whether those returns comprise the immense quantities smuggled to this country, I do not know. With respect to raw and thrown silk, the quantities of silk raw and thrown imported into France, that is not subject to error; but in respect to manufactured goods, I believe that cannot be given with the same distinctness, and a great deal depends upon the class of goods exported.

4331. You have given in evidence, that at the time Italian raw silk was 17s. 6¼d. per lb. cash price in London, the French raw in Lyons ranged from 15s. 9d. to as low as 13s. 3d. averaging 14s. 5½d., is that difference so much more in favour of the French throwster and the French manufacturer, over the English throwster and the English manufacturer?—I consider the question to be in this way; the duty on foreign thrown silks, whether organzine or tram imported into France, is 11d. a pound, they make no distinction between the one and the other. But the French throwster having the whole of the French native produce reserved to him, which is reckoned at 4,500,000 lbs. of fine standard, he has beyond the duty of 11d., all the advantage by this protection of the difference in price at which raw silk can be imported from Italy into France, and the actual price of French raw silk. Italian silk could not be imported at the period alluded to, under 17s. 4d., whereas the average of French silk was at the same period 14s. 5½d. and rather of superior description; the throwster has not only the duty, but all the differences in price of raw silks in his favour, so that the actual protection is not only 11d., but it is generally more, for the average difference in the prices of raw silks is at least 1s., it would be like 11d. and 1s., or I might begin at 6d.; it is as 11d. and 1s., and 11d. and 2s., and 11d. and 3s., so that the French throwster has all that advantage reserved to him, and in addition to that, he is much nearer to Italy; and the condition of the labourer in the South of France and in Italy, has infinitely more analogy than that of the labourer here.

4332. How do you account for that permanent difference in price between the French silk and the Italian; why should they pay 3s. more for the same quality of Italian silk than they can get their own French silk for?—That is not the case; they do not purchase Italian raw silks under those circumstances. The consumption of France, I understand, is about 5,500,000 lbs.; the imports into France are about 1,000,000 lbs., of which about 600,000 or 700,000 lbs. in thrown silk, and 300,000 to 400,000 lbs. in raw silks; of the 300,000 to 400,000 raw silks, a very large proportion consists in Brussa and other coarse silks; the remainder will be 100,000 to 150,000 lbs. of fine silks; these

678. are

Mr.
*Alexis J. Doxat.*

19 April,
1832.

are further compared with 4,500,000 of fine French raw ; so that the quantity of Italian fine silk consumed, is about 100,000 to 150,000, compared with four millions and a half pounds. When a great demand occurs in France, that raises altogether the price of French silk; the Lyonese having a large entrepôt of foreign silks, they have a certain quantity always at hand ; if they find that the French growers avail themselves too much of such a demand, and that the price of silk rises for example to sixteen and seventeen shillings, they will come in such instances, in contact with Italian raw, and a certain quantity of fine Italian raw silk is then drawn into the French consumption; but it will run in general only in the proportion of one hundred or one hundred and fifty thousand pounds, compared to the four millions and a half, so that it is just like keeping a rod over the growers in France. If you will not let us have your raw silks at a fair price, we will bring in the Italian.

4333. Is the Italian raw silk of the same quality with the French silk, higher or lower in price at Lyons, speaking generally ?—It is always higher ; it is higher in the proportion as 150,000 is to 4,500,000, and it is only now and then that they come into contact.

4334. Is it one franc or two francs ?—It happens occasionally that they come in contact ; that is, the price is nearly the same, but it is seldom that that does happen ; and on an average it happens only in the proportion as an hundred or an hundred an fifty thousand is to 4,500,000 lbs,

4335. The export duty from Italy being but 10 d. for the raw, why should the Italian silk be more than 10 d. above the price of the French silk ?—This question is answered by the evidence I have given the day before yesterday, in which I was asked particularly what were the relative charges of bringing one pound of Italian raw silk into this country, and one pound of Italian raw silk into France. I found that every pound of silk imported into France was about 2 s., whereas here it is about 2 s. 1 d. and 2 s. 2 d. As respects the export duty from Lombardy and the import duty in France, the one is about 9 d. per lb. and the other $5\frac{1}{2}d.$ together $14\frac{1}{2}d.$

4336. You are understood to say, that silk at Lyons varies from 1 s. to 2 s. per pound, differing in price from Italian silk in England ?—Even more, as I have previously stated circumstantially

4337. Lyons being merely a place of transit, if the quantity of French native silk is so considerable and the native grower can only sell it to the native consumer, if it is so considerable that the price keeps lower than the average of that passing through France to any part of the world, the Frenchman does not consume it, is that so ?—Yes, it is so.

4338. If the quantity of French silk from the extreme briskness of trade at Lyons, should become short, and the Frenchman be compelled from necessity to resort to the Italian, he will stop it in transitu, and buy it at the price at which it will be sold in England, is that so ?—Yes ; rather under that, owing to the import charges being a little lower, besides that the Lyons market is contiguous to the sources.

4339. If French silks were imported into a country where the expenses of throwing were equal, there will be nothing for that importing country to fear ? —No.

4340. If you resided at Lyons, and you were a throwster, and if the manufacturer imported into Lyons, or if he stopped in the course of transit a quantity of Piedmont silk for any particular purpose of manufacture, you do not conceive that the small quantities so imported would interfere with or regulate the price at which the whole of the silk of native growth would be sold ?—I do not.

4341. You conceive that French silk is cheaper in France than Italian of the same quality in England, by reason of the French grower of silk supplying only the native manufacturer ?—Yes.

4342. Do you conceive that the introduction of the dearer Italian silk into the cheaper country of France, would have the effect of raising the price of the silk of native growth ?—No.

4343. Supposing the home grown silk in France is dearer than Italian silk at Lyons, what will be the effect upon the market by the introduction in transit of the cheaper Italian silk on the price of the home growth ?—It will naturally have the effect to lower the price of the French silk.

4344. Why should not the reverse take place with the Italian silk ?—Because
the

Mr.
Alexis J. Doxat.

19 April,
1832.

the French silk cannot come out either in a raw or a thrown state, so that French silk may be depressed.

4345. Do you believe that any manufacturer of goods at Lyons will give 16*s.* for a pound of Italian silk, when he can buy the French silk of the same sort for 14*s*?—No one would buy it under such circumstances; they will only be bought when they come into contact, even at the highest point of contact, which happens but seldom on an average; that is in the proportion of 100 to 150,000 to 4,500,000.

4346. Is it not the fact, that the French silk of native growth, may supply the manufacturer for eleven months in the year by possibility; so long as the native silk of France supplies the home manufacturer, he must sell to that manufacturer because he has nobody else to sell to; and in the next place the price of that commodity will not rise till it becomes scarce from the consumption of the manufacturer; but when the native silk is so consumed by the trade at Lyons, they must then have recourse to the Italian silk passing in transit through Lyons; of course, as the silk of France becomes scarcer it will become dearer, and will ultimately reach that point where it would have stopped; and that stop is the price of the Italian silk so passing in transit through Lyons, is that just the fact? —Yes.

4347. That happens every year?—Some part of the year.

4348. You are understood to say, that France does not grow every quality of silk, is that so?—Yes.

4349. It may be necessary for the French manufacturer to have silk from Piedmont for a particular purpose?—Yes.

4350. If the Piedmontese grower can obtain a greater price in Germany, in Switzerland, in Austria, or in England, will he sell that commodity at a lower price to the Frenchman?—Certainly not.

4351. Whatever that price may be for particular purposes, it is essential that the French manufacturer should have it, is it not?—Yes.

4352. It sometimes also happens, that the Frenchman may, for a particular purpose, require a silk even inferior to his own; and that it would answer his purpose better to pay a somewhat dearer price relatively, for an inferior commodity for which his own silk is not applicable, and that he will not pay for that a price beyond its real value?—Yes, that is the case.

4353. Is raw silk dearer in England than in France?—Yes, it is, generally speaking.

4354. How much does it differ occasionally?—From 6*d.* to 3*s.* and even more.

4355. Is thrown silk dearer in England than at Lyons?—Yes, it is.

4356. How much, occasionally?—3, 4, 5 and 6*s.* to 6*s.* 6*d.*

4357. Italian silk passes through Lyons on its way to England?—Yes, the major part.

4358. The silk of native growth in France must be consumed at home?—Yes.

4359. Therefore, if the silk manufacturers at Lyons have a bad state of trade they will consume less silk?—Yes.

4360. The silk falls as a matter of consequence?—Yes.

4361. Does it happen that the Italian silk falls at the same time?—Not at all proportionably; it is sent on to other countries.

4362. Is it limited in other countries as to the price at which it shall be sold?—Mostly; speaking as a commission merchant, I should say it is frequently.

4363. When the French manufacturers shall, from an increased business, have consumed the whole of the silk of native growth, they will touch the Italian?—They will.

4364. They must then pay the price for that Italian silk which it would realize in other countries?—Yes, with the exception of the differences of charges.

4365. It does sometimes happen, that though silk may be cheaper of native growth in France, it is not always applicable to the purpose for which the manufacturers require it?—Just so.

4366. Therefore he will pay for Piedmontese silk, or any other he may require, and for which silk of native growth is not applicable, a higher price proportionably than for the silk of France?—Yes, that is perfectly the case.

4367. Do you suppose any Italian silk can ever be sold at Lyons, but when the price of French grown silk rises on a level to that of Italian?—Speaking generally,

678.

Mr.
*Alexis J. Doxat.*

19 April,
1832.

generally, not; the French cocoons are mostly of very good qualities, and they do not apply them to coarse silks, except in very small proportions, and the quantity of raw silk imported into France is very small; it is for the major part, of coarse, and very coarse descriptions, that is from 70, 100, and even up to 200 deniers, descriptions of silks to which they apply their cocoons in very small quantities; they are too good to be applied to inferior purposes. They find it worth their while to import certain coarse silks, that they may reserve their own cocoons for fine silks. I will repeat that there are some periods in each year in which the Italian silk and the French silk come in contact; I will suppose that contact to be 17 *s.*; that the French silk, by particular circumstances, is raised to 17 *s.*; at that price some fraction, and a very small fraction, in the average of the year, will be taken out of entrepôt and brought into consumption; so that the range shall be sometimes in contact at 17 *s.*; but taking the average of years, it will range in this way: I will suppose that the Italian silk shall be at the highest point, namely, 17 *s.* and that the French will fluctuate, according to various circumstances, from 16 *s.* to 15 *s.* and 14 *s.* 6 *d.* and even rather under. The French consumer never touches the Italian raw silk, except when it comes in contact; thus the large mass of his consumption of fine raw silks rests on the produce of France, which is of about 4,500,000 lbs., compared with 100,000 to 150,000 lbs. of fine Italian raw silks, consumed per annum, on an average.

4368. Are there not sales of Italian raw silk at Lyons, of the same quality as that which is grown in France during every portion of the year?—Lyons being a transit market, there are quotations at Lyons the whole year through for Italian silks; they are frequently purchased to be sent on to this country, and thus they enter but very partially into the consumption of France.

4369. Are the Italian silks of the same quality as that grown in France purchased by the French manufacturer, in every month in the year, at Lyons, for consumption?—Certainly not.

4370. During the whole period of the year, you say you can quote the prices at Lyons, how are those prices at Lyons calculated; is it in relation to the use made of it in England and in Germany, and in other parts of the Continent?—The entrepôt at Lyons is an open market; the French silk is a close market, reserved to themselves alone; there are at Lyons 25 silk merchants, more or less; we are in correspondence with about 20 of them; they go to the entrepôt; if they find a difference in the price currents of this market of 6 *d.* or 1 *s.* beyond their prices, they purchase the silk, and send it on for sale.

4371. It is not that they are not actually disposed of, but that they are not disposed of in the Lyons market for French use?—Just so.

4372. Are those quotation prices of Lyons regulated by the markets of England and Europe generally?—With reference to Europe generally; but particularly the English market as respects raw silks.

4373. Those quotation prices are made up by the 20 or 25 merchants at Lyons? —By the effect of the buying and selling; it is a buying and selling market for export; but at some periods of the year they come into contact; I should observe here again, that some descriptions, such as Piedmont organzines and coarse Levant raw, sell more or less throughout the year for specific purposes.

4374. Can you state the difference of price in the market of Lyons between the organzine grown and thrown in France and the organzine imported?—I will take the same period I have already taken, of the early part of last year; at that period I find the prices at Lyons, of 23 to 24 deniers Piedmont organzine, were depressed to about 19 *s.* to 19 *s* 6 *d.*, owing to the great depression of the French organzines; when I mention the great depression of French organzine, I refer to the average price of 17 *s.* 4½ *d.* for 21–22 deniers, which is a rather finer size; while the import cost of Piedmontese, was 20 *s.* 6 *d.* to 21 *s.*; that is the price at which Piedmont organzine of 23–24 deniers would have stood in France; at that time the great depression in French silks dragged down to a certain degree even the Piedmont. As I have mentioned before, when French silk is much depressed, when it falls greatly, then the price of Piedmont organzine is lowered by it; for then they only touch a small quantity, for those particular purposes to which it is absolutely necessary.

4375. Can you state the price in London at the same period?—I believe at that period, that is in February and March last, Piedmont organzine was at about 24 *s.* and 24 *s.* 6 *d.*

4376. Was

Mr.
*Alexis J. Doxat.*

19 April,
1832.

4376. Was it sold in England at that time?—It was; we were then in a state of activity in England, and they were in France in a state of great depression.

4377. The 17s. 4½d. silk of France was as good as the Piedmontese, the import cost of which was 20s. 6d. to 21s.?—Yes; the great bulk of their own manufacture rested on silk of their own growth at 17s. 4½d.

4378. Can you state what is the quantity of Piedmont organzine silk consumed in this country in a year?—Yes, about 100,000 lbs. on an average.

4379. You have spoken of the sale of raw silk formerly in France imported from other countries, are they always the fine Italian raw or sometimes the coarser kind from Modena and Naples, such as the French do not accustom themselves to reel, but which they must have sometimes?—Yes; the coarser descriptions have a sale throughout the year to a certain extent.

4380. Are not those silks sometimes sold as low as 11s. and 12s.?—Yes, and below that.

4381. What do you consider to be the effect of the price of foreign thrown silk coming into this country and being sold here, upon the throwster in England?—The quantity of thrown silk imported into this country varies from 200,000 to 500,000 pounds weight; it has the effect to depress the whole of the throwing interest; and the quantity imported in 1830 and 1831 has increased considerably as compared with 1829.

4382. When you sell the Italian silk sent to you on commission, do you, in selling it, pay any attention to its prime cost, or do you not get what the silk market will give you?—We pay continual attention to the prime cost, and the instructions we have; sometimes we use our discretion if we see that the market will not afford a better price, or a better prospect for our principals; I allude to the cases frequent, in which we are requested to act according to our own judgment; but we always consider the prime cost of the article, as also the state of foreign markets, in order to do the best for our correspondents.

4383. Do you not, in all cases, endeavour to get the best price for your consignees?—It is our duty so to do.

4384. If you have cheap silk sent to you, do you not sell it at the average price of the same silk in the market?—If it is very cheap, the effect of competition is naturally to depress it in our market also.

4385. Are the Committee to understand, that the silk sent to you is sold with reference to the price abroad, whatever the price in England may be, or are you limited in the sale to a certain standard?—Some correspondents limit us, others do not; but we always take into consideration the state of the markets abroad, and likewise the state of the market here.

4386. It is your opinion that the amount of four or five hundred thousand pounds weight of Italian thrown silk depresses the price of the whole of the British silk?—It is; and I can show that, step by step, by a Paper now in my hand.

4387. You have stated that you sell your silk frequently with reference to the price in foreign countries; when Italian thrown silk is quoted to you at Lyons at 17s. 6d. do you immediately sell your Italian thrown silk at 17s. 6d. in England?—No; we should not be doing justice to our correspondent; but if the market at Lyons is heavy, it will in some degree influence the market here.

4388. You always take care to keep a distance from the price at Lyons?—Certainly, as much as possible.

4389. If it was not so your friends would be dissatisfied with your sales, and not send you the Italian silk, as they might send it either to Switzerland or Germany, or some other country?—Yes.

4390. Do you not sometimes send from England Italian silk to Lyons when the market is depressed?—Seldom to Lyons; we have sent some to Russia; we have sent some to the Rhine; and some sent to our market not suitable to our consumption, we have occasionally sent back to Lyons.

4391. Whenever the price of Italian raw silk is below the price in other places, you ship it to other places?—That does happen occasionally, seldom, however, in regard to raw.

4392. Thus the price of Italian silk approximates to its level?—The price of Italian thrown silk in entrepôt at Lyons approximates sometimes to their own; but generally speaking, the case of France is distinct from that of other countries, in consequence of her own very considerable and good produce.

4393. Are the Committee to understand, that the sale price of Italian silk here is often or generally regulated by what the price of that silk may be at Lyons, or

other

other parts of the world?—Not at Lyons, properly speaking, with regard to its consumption; but in some measure with its entrepôt as a general market; in which I should observe here again, that the French manufacturers have the first and the cheapest choice, in addition to their other considerable advantages relative to the silks of their own produce.

4394. The Lyonese must pay for the quantity of silk he requires, of either the growth of Piedmont or Italy, nearly the same price as any other part of the world must pay?—Quite so; except with the difference of duties and the difference of charges.

4395. That does not at all go to say, that he pays the same price for the rest of the silk he may require, and of which the Italian forms but a small proportion?—By no means; it has nothing to do with it. Some questions were asked me incidentally yesterday, whilst I was placing before the Committee this Paper, (No. 18.) which diverted my attention from it at the time. The purport of this Paper is to show, in one distinct view, all the elements of the various costs of manufacture of one yard of good plain gros de Naples, in common colours, (which I take as the basis of all my calculations), " of 10 to 1100, three double," of superior make, at London and at Lyons, respectively; both in regard to the raw material, and to the various processes of manufacture; also what are the amounts per cent. of those differences between our manufactures and those of Lyons, which (as well as other foreign manufactures) are greatly dependent on export, and hence continually exposed to sudden and considerable variations, over which our manufacturers have no control; thus greatly aggravating the degrees of intensity with which foreign competition presses on this branch of our national industry, in which the *wages of labour alone*, independently of other charges of manufacture, obtain in the ratio of at least *ten* to *one* of the charges referrible to machinery in its most improved application (respecting which *see* Papers D. and E. Nos. 8 and 9.) Such is the range of those contingent variations, even in the prices of foreign plain manufactured silks, with which our manufacturers have to contend, that their *retreat from step to step*, down to very low and wretched wages, to wages of absolute misery, cannot shelter them from the calamitous pressure of such competition, as may be seen by the graduated scale of per centages, set forth in the margin on the right of this Paper; as also of Papers, No. 5, 6 and 7; and still more by the *inverted* scale of those variations (placed under the graduated scale,) even without taking the extreme points of this *inverted* scale. I should observe, in regard to the *starting point* which I have taken on the London side, of 8½ *d.*, for weaving, well and neatly, one yard of that description of plain goods, that it is only a very moderate remuneration for work well done; and considering the great value of the commodity placed under the entire control of the weaver, upon whose skill and care greatly depends the marketable value of so delicate and valuable an article. The rate of wages for weaving the same description of silks was, on an average, 10½ *d.* per yard from 1815–17 to 1824–25, with very little variation; and I have reason to believe that the rates of wages in this branch of our national industry, so rapidly increasing previously to 1826 were, on an average, quite the same in 1824–25 as in 1815–17. I should add, that in taking 8½ *d.* per yard, for weaving the said description of good plain goods, and the other charges of manufacture in proportion, compared with the usual rate at Lyons, of late years, that is 5¼ *d.*, equal to 5 *d.* per yard; I take a lower relative stand than that of 10½ *d.* against 6¼ *d.*, equal to 5¼ *d.* which obtained from 1821 to 1825; 5 *d.* per yard against 8½ *d.* presenting 70 per cent., whilst 5¼ *d.* per yard against 10½ *d.* presented 83 per cent. From all these data, it will appear that low and very low wages afford us no effectual shelter in respect to plain goods, from the range of ordinary variations with our foreign competitors, nor even the extremes of wretchedness from particular contingencies with them. These estimates and comparative views relate to good plain goods, neatly made, in common colours. The differences in the respective costs of plain goods of high colours, and of figured and fancy goods are much greater; and the duties on them, as also the charges for smuggling, are proportionably lower, with regard to their higher costs. I have endeavoured to condense this Paper (No. 18) still more; I have condensed all the charges at Lyons and here, showing, at one view, side by side, every charge at Lyons and in London, at various periods. The object of my making out this Paper, besides the great facility of comparison it affords in every respect, is to show that the wages of labour in our silk manufacture is considerably lower than the range which existed in this country in 1821 to
1825.

Appendix (F.)

Appendix (F.)

Appendix (F.)

Appendix (F.)

1825.  I naturally ask, Why is it that since the opening of our ports to foreign manufactured goods, our labourers have scarcely or never enjoyed the rate of 8½ $d$. for weaving gros de Naples, neat make, 10 to 1100, three double, nor proportionable rates for other work; but that they have been mostly pinned down to 7 $d$. 6½ $d$. and 6 $d$.? notwithstanding which latter miserable rate, we have frequently not been able to keep out overwhelming quantities of foreign manufactured plain goods; that is, quantities beyond the usual sendings to our markets of those descriptions?  To which I answer, it is consequently not from calculations alone, that is, calculations made on paper, that I deduce the fact, that wages even of wretchedness *do not shelter us*, in good plain goods, under contingent circumstances, with our foreign competitors.

Thus when our weavers are reduced to 6 $d$. for superior gros de Naples, and their masters to sacrifices on the cost of their goods, although manufactured at such lamentable rates, we find,—we find even then!—our poor labourers reduced, not unfrequently to half work, that is, to 3 $s$. 6 $d$. nett per week.  And if a man, in order to save his family from starvation, work eighteen hours per day, work till he drop, if such labour continue for any length of time, his extra and harassing labour deprives another man of what might otherwise have been his share of the scanty pittance arising from work under such melancholy circumstances.

Thus the man who is fortunate enough to obtain some work, exhausts himself; and his neighbour is obliged to seek at the workhouse door, or worse—in the workhouse, for that which cannot be called relief!

The poor rates cannot provide for such a state of things; they are only intended for the common course of casualties; not for such general and awful calamities, to which the hand alone of the Legislature can and may apply effectual remedy.

And here it is my duty to recal to the recollection of this Honourable Committee, sitting on so interesting and so important an inquiry, as that relative to the welfare and very existence of immense numbers of our fellow beings; that the changes which were made in the laws respecting this branch of our national industry, have over and over, and at various periods (which the very last clause of the Act of 10th Geo. 4. c. 23. sufficiently indicates,) been mentioned as

### " An Experiment."

I will add the expression of my intimate conviction, that could the lamented Right Honourable Gentleman, the principal projector of those alterations, have been able to see the full extent of the calamitous results with which they may have been attended; and have been present at the developement, by various witnesses, brought before this Honourable Committee, of the causes of those results, he would have been the first to take the beneficent course of recommending to the Legislature the reconsideration of those measures.

> [*Whilst reading this paragraph, Mr. Doxat interrupted Mr. Gurney in the trouble which he was taking of putting down his words, observing that they might be taken from the printed Paper* (No. 21), *which he was then giving in.*]

The Paper I now beg to deliver in, will bring all these various points more distinctly before the Committee, showing, as it does, the usual charges in London and in Lyons, at the periods of 1821 to 1825, and the relation drawn out in per centages, in which they stood with each other; the usual rates of those charges at Lyons, in 1826 to 1831, compared in the same column, with such as our labourers are at the least entitled to.  And the last column, under the head of 1831, presents the rates of wages to which they fall at Lyons when depressed by any contingent circumstances; exclusive of the fall in the raw and thrown silks of their own produce, which contributes to enable their manufacturers to make goods at very low prices.  (Weaving at Lyons falls sometimes under 4 $d$., equal to 3½ $d$. for the said description of goods.)  And with respect to London, the same column shows the rates of wages to which we are frequently obliged to retreat, owing to the pressure, varying in its intensity, of foreign competition; but which retreat to wretched wages does not afford us any effectual shelter, as may be seen by the various parts of this Paper (No. 21), and by the whole series of my other comparative statements, but more particularly by the recapitulation of the costs of good plain goods, adjoined to the printed paper No. 5, which I put in on the first day of my examination.

[*The Witness delivered in the following Paper.*]

Mr.
*Alexis J. Doxat.*

19 April,
1832.

Appendix (F.)

## No. 21.

Appendix to Table No. 18.—Being an ABSTRACT VIEW of the various Rates of Wages, &c. at *London* and at *Lyons*, as particularly set forth in that Paper.

| | 1821–25. Usual Charges at that Period. | 1826–31. *Usual at* LYONS; also such as our Labourers are at the least entitled to. | 1831. Very low at L Y O N S, (a) and wretched at L O N D O N. (b) |
|---|---|---|---|
| | *s. d.*    *s. d.* | *s. d.* | *s. d.* |
| Throwing good Organzine of 22–24 deniers | At London 9 0 - 7 6 <br> At Lyons † - - 4 0 } =87 p' Ct. | 6 0 <br> 3 9 } = 60 p' Ct. | 4 6 <br> 3 0 } = 50 p Ct. |
| Ditto of good Tram of 22–26 deniers | At London 5 6 - 4 6 <br> At Lyons † - - 2 5 } =86 p' Ct. | 3 6 <br> 2 3 } = 56 p' Ct. | 2 10 <br> 1 10 } = 55 p' Ct. |
| Dyeing, Common Colours | At London - - 2 8 <br> At Lyons - - 1 2 } =121 p' Ct. | 1 8 <br> 1 1 } = 54 p' Ct. | 1 5 <br> 0 11 } = 65 p Ct. |
| Winding Warp | At London 3 3 - 2 9 <br> At Lyons † - - 1 8 } =65 p' Ct. | 2 6 <br> 1 7 } = 58 p' Ct. | 1 6 <br> 1 3 } = 20 p' Ct. |
| Winding Shute | At London 3 0 - 2 6 <br> At Lyons † - - 0 0 § } 0 per Ct. | 2 3 <br> 0 0 § } 0 p' Ct. | 1 4 <br> 0 0 § } 0 p' Ct. |
| Weaving | At London - - 0 $10\frac{1}{2}$ <br> At Lyons 0 $6\frac{1}{4}$ = 0 $5\frac{3}{4}$ § } =83 p' Ct. | 0 $8\frac{1}{2}$ <br> *d.*   *d.* <br> $5\frac{1}{2}$ = 5 § } = 70 p' Ct. | 0 6 <br> *d.*   *d.* <br> 4 = $3\frac{1}{2}$ § } = 71 p' Ct. |
| Collective Amount of Wages, Profit, &c. | At London 0 $10\frac{1}{2}$ - 27 3 <br> At Lyons 0 $6\frac{1}{4}$ - 14 4 } =90 p' Ct. | 21 10 <br> 13 0 } = 68 p' Ct. | 16 3 <br> 10 1 } = 61 p' Ct. |

† The actual Charge for throwing good Organzines of 22-24 drs. in $\left.\begin{smallmatrix}1821-23\\1824-25\end{smallmatrix}\right\}$ was 9 s.; but for the reasons stated in my printed Paper, marked No. 4, I have introduced, at 7 s. 6 d. only, that Charge in my Estimates for that period.— And the same with regard to the Work of fine good Tram, 4 s. 6 d. instead of 5 s. 6 d.—Also of winding Warp, 2 s. 9 d. instead of 3 s. 3 d.—And of winding Shute, 2 s. 6 d. instead of 3 s.

(*a*) Rates of Wages to which they fall at Lyons, when depressed by any contingent circumstances; exclusive of the fall in the Raw and Thrown Silks of their own produce, which contributes to enable their Manufacturers to make Goods at very low prices.—Weaving at Lyons falls sometimes under 4 d.=$3\frac{1}{2}$ d., for the said description of Goods.

(*b*) Rates of Wages with us, to which we are frequently obliged to retreat, owing to the pressure, varying in its intensity, of Foreign competition; but which retreat to wretched Wages, does not afford us any effectual shelter, as may be seen by the annexed Remarks.

§ The Weaver at Lyons winds his own Shute.

Query ?—

Mr.
*Alexis J. Doxat.*

19 April,
1832.

Query ?—Why is it that since the opening of our Ports to Foreign manufactured goods, our Labourers have scarcely, or never, enjoyed the rate of 8½ d. for weaving good gros de Naples, neat make, 10 to 1100 three double,—nor proportionable rates for other work; but that they have been mostly pinned down to 7 d., 6½ d. and 6 d.? notwithstanding which latter miserable rate, we have frequently not been able to keep out overwhelming quantities of Foreign manufactured plain goods—that is, quantities beyond the usual sendings to our market of those descriptions.

It is consequently not from calculations alone,—that is, calculations made on paper,— that I deduce the fact, that wages even of wretchedness *do not shelter us,* in good plain goods, under contingent circumstances with our Foreign competitors.

---

N. B.—I should observe, in regard to low, cheap plain goods, that although manufactured at low and wretched wages with us, they are ultimately depressed and beaten down by the importation of Foreign manufactured plain goods of superior classes, at comparatively cheap prices. I will suppose a very low gros de Naples, of British manufacture, single warp, at 2 s. 2 d. per yard, weighing 16 drams,—

(there are lower priced goods, but they are as *brown paper* is to *white,*)

against which, a Lyons gros de Naples of double warp, of first class, and same weight per yard, shall come in, according to circumstances, at the respective

COSTS OF

| (First Class of Lyons Gros de Naples.) | | (First Class of Lyons Gros de Naples.) |
|---|---|---|
| s.    d. | | s.    d. |
| 2    11¾ per yard on our Market   -   -   -   -   - | | 2    2⅝ |
| that is   2    4⅛ highest prime cost at Lyons on my Table No. 18, and others, of comparative costs   -   -   - { lowest prime cost at Lyons } | | 1    9⅝ |
| —    1¼ Charges of purchase at Lyons, and of transmission to Paris, where the smuggler takes up the goods { -   -   -   - | | —    1 |
| —    5½ for 18 per cent. on cost and charges, which I assume as the Estimate of the charge for smuggling plain goods inclusive of insurance { -   -   -   - | | —    4 |

Thus when our weavers are reduced to 6 d. for superior gros de Naples, and their masters to sacrifices on the *cost* of their goods, although manufactured at such lamentable rates, we find,—we find even then!—our poor labourers reduced, not unfrequently to half-work—that is, to 3 s. 6 d. nett per week. And if a man, in order to save his family from starvation, work 18 hours per day,—work till he drop, if such labour continue for any length of time, —his extra and harassing labour deprives another man of what might otherwise have been his share of the scanty pittance arising from work under such melancholy circumstances.

Thus the man who is fortunate enough to obtain some work, exhausts himself; and his neighbour is obliged to seek at the workhouse door,—or worse,—in the workhouse,—for that which cannot be called relief!

The Poor Rates cannot provide for such a state of things,—they are only intended for the common course of casualties :—not for such general and awful calamities, to which the hand alone of the Legislature can and may apply effectual remedy.

And here it is my duty to recal to the recollection of this Honourable Committee, sitting on so interesting and so important an inquiry, as that relative to the welfare and very existence of immense numbers of our fellow-beings, that the changes which were made in the Laws respecting this branch of our national industry, have over and over, and at various periods, (which the very last clause of the Act of 10th Geo. IV. c. 23, sufficiently indicates,) been mentioned as

" AN EXPERIMENT."

I will add the expression of my intimate conviction, that could the lamented Right Honourable Gentleman, the principal projector of those alterations, have been able to see the full extent of the calamitous results with which they have been attended; and have been present at the developement, by various witnesses, brought before this Honourable Committee, of the causes of those results, he would have been the first to take the beneficent course of recommending to the Legislature the reconsideration of those measures.

18th April 1832.        Errors excepted.        (signed)    *Alexis James Doxat.*

---

4396. In 1825, the difference of throwing organzine in England and in Lyons, was 87 per cent., and in 1831, only 50 per cent., how do you account for the reduction?—I account for it by the extreme depression of wages, and loss of profit;

for

Mr.
*Alexis J. Doxat.*

19 April,
1832.

Appendix (F.)

for it will be seen by a note at the foot of my said Paper No. 21, that in the column 1821–1825, I introduce the charge for throwing good organzine of 22–24 deniers at 7 s. 6 d., instead of 9 s. which was the actual charge at that period, for the reasons stated in my printed Paper No. 4.

4397. Has there been a diminution in the price of raw silk corresponding with the reduction of duty on imported thrown?—I have here a comparative view of the market prices at London, of Milan and Bergam raw silks of four to five cocoons, and of Milan and Bergam organzine of 26 to 28 deniers, at various periods from June 1824 to February and April 1832; from which it appears, that with a difference in price of 12 s. 2 d., there is a difference in duty of 7 s. 3 d.; with 13 s. 6 d., 7 s. 3 d.; with 7 s. 9½ d., 4 s. 9 d.; with 7 s. 1 d., 4 s. 11 d.; with 6 s. 10¼ d., 4 s. 11 d.; with 7 s. 0¾ d., 4 s. 11 d.; with 6 s. 9 d., 4 s. 11 d.; with 6 s. 4 d., 3 s. 5 d.; with 5 s. 9¼ d., 3 s. 5 d.; with 4 s. 9 d., 3 s. 5 d.; with 4 s. 5 d., 3 s. 5 d.; inclusive of the market value of the debenture granted since June 1829, taken at the average of 4 d. for the 3 s. 6 d. duty.

[*The Witness delivered in the same.*]

No. 22.

## No. 22.

A COMPARATIVE VIEW of the MARKET PRICES at *London*, of *Milan* and *Bergam* RAW SILKS of 4 to 5 Cocoons, and of *Milan* and *Bergam* Organzine of 26 to 28 deniers, at various Periods, from June 1824 to February and April 1832.

| | | | | MILAN AND BERGAM. | | | DUTIES. | | | DATES of alteration in Duties. |
|---|---|---|---|---|---|---|---|---|---|---|
| | | | | Raw. (Averages.) | Organzine. | Difference in Prices. | Difference in Duties. | Raw. | Organzine. | |
| | | | | s. d. | s. d. | s. d. | s. d. | s. d. | s. d. | |
| 1824 | - - | June | Oct<sup>r</sup> | 19 10½ | 32 -½ | 12 2 | 7 3 | - 3 | 7 6 | |
| 1825 | February | June | Oct<sup>r</sup> | 23 10 | 37 4 | 13 6 | 7 3 | - 3 | 7 6 | 5th November 1825 (*By Order in Council.*) |
| 1826 | February | June | - - | 21 1 | 28 10½ | 7 9½ | 4 9 | - 3 | 5 - | |
| 1826 | - - | - - | Oct<sup>r</sup> | 20 5 | 27 6 | 7 1 | 4 11 | - 1 | 5 - | 5th July 1826 |
| 1827 | February | June | Oct<sup>r</sup> | 21 3¼ | 28 2 | 6 10¾ | 4 11 | - 1 | 5 - | |
| 1828 | February | June | Oct<sup>r</sup> | 22 - | 29 -¾ | 7 -¾ | 4 11 | - 1 | 5 - | |
| 1829 | February | - - | - - | 21 8 | 28 5 | 6 9 | 4 11 | - 1 | 5 - | |
| 1829 | - - | June (19th) | Oct<sup>r</sup> | 17 8 | 24 - | 6 4 | 3 5 | - 1 | 3 6 | 2d June 1829 |
| 1830 | February | June | Oct<sup>r</sup> | 17 5¾ | 23 7 | s. d. 6 1¼ | | | | |
| | | | | | | deduct - 4 | - - | for Sale of the Debenture of 3s. 6d. per lb.* | | |
| | | | | | | remain - - | 5 9¼ | 3 5 | - 1 | 3 6 |
| 1831 | February | June | Oct<sup>r</sup> | 17 5 | 22 6 | 5 1 | | | | |
| | | | | | | deduct - 4 | | | | |
| | | | | | | remain - - | 4 9 | 3 5 | - 1 | 3 6 |
| 1832 | February & April } | - - | - - | 17 - | 21 9 | 4 9 | | | | |
| | | | | | | deduct - 4 | | | | |
| | | | | | | remain - - | 4 5 | 3 5 | - 1 | 3 6 |

* The purchasers of Foreign organzine silks have had, since the 2d June 1829, the benefit of a debenture of 3s. 6d. per lb.; of which, if they do not avail *themselves* for the purpose of export, they can effect the sale on the market, to other manufacturers who export; and the market value of these debentures having fluctuated from 1d. to 7d. per lb., I have introduced the average of 4d., as above, in deduction of the differences existing between the prices in our market of Italian raw silk and Italian organzine.

April 19th, 1832.     (Errors excepted.)     (signed)     *Alexis James Doxat.*

## NOTES RELATIVE TO THE ANNEXED TABLE.

       s. d.

In 1824, the throwster had not only a difference of 7 3 in regard to the respective duties on raw and thrown silks, but of   -   -   -   4 11 beyond that, as may be seen by the annexed Table; constituting a total difference of 12 2, *within* which to ground his operations.

       s. d.

He has now only 3 5 in regard to the duties,

       and 1 0 beyond that; constituting a total difference

       of only 4 5, for work of 26–28 deniers organzine thrown silk; waste, interest, profit, risk of differences in markets (while the silk is under work), and of the buyers, besides some expenses of agencies.

Whilst every charge, inclusive of the *del credere*, is comprised in the Account of Sales rendered of Foreign thrown silks; which, besides, are always ready at hand to supply the demands of our manufacturers, two or three hours being sufficient to enter silks for home consumption from the docks.

    It

Mr.
*Alexis J. Doxat.*

19 April,
1832.

It is not likely that, under the calamitous circumstances in which our throwsters are placed, by the *collective* influence of the present very reduced duties on organzine and tram (besides the debentures), and of the general pressure of foreign manufactured silks, on every constituent branch of our silk manufacture, of which the throwing is a very important one,—it is not, I say, likely that our throwsters can keep any thing like stocks, assortments, and regular supplies of organzine and tram, whereon our manufacturers are to provide themselves. Thus the more our throwsters become discouraged and depressed in their operations, notwithstanding the wretched rates of wages to which their labourers have been reduced of late, the more we shall decline in that important branch, the support of which I consider so necessary for the well-being of the whole silk manufacture of Great Britain, and the more foreign throwsters will get possession of our consumption.

I might offer a variety of other important details on this subject, but I will confine myself at present to the foregoing.

---

4398. You mean to show by that document that the whole pay of the throwster is 4*s*. 5*d*.?—Yes; the ultimate difference existing between those two periods, the *absolute* difference, is as 4*s*. 5*d*. now, to 12*s*. 2*d*. in 1824. There are two points of view to be considered in this Paper, the absolute difference, and the ultimate difference between the two differences; the absolute difference is as 12*s*. 2*d*. to 4*s*. 5*d*. and then the ultimate difference between the two differences, is considerably less now than it was formerly. The throwster now works very near to the amount of the protecting duty, which is very much reduced; whereas in former times, he had a large protecting duty, and beyond that, a large margin; therefore the ultimate, the total difference on which the throwster now works, that is work, waste, &c. &c., is 4*s*. 5*d*. per lb.

4399. When he had a higher price for work he had a higher protecting duty, and when he has a lower price he has at the same time a lower protecting duty?—Yes; and the throwster has gone even nearer to the duty; this shows the enormous pressure which exists against the throwster.

4400. By the statement that you have now given, the difference in 1824 between the thrown and the raw, both duties paid, was 12*s*. 2*d*., from which deducting the tax on raw, 11*s*. 11*d*. remained, being an inducement to the English throwster to throw?—Yes.

4401. In 1832 the difference was 4*s*. 9*d*., from which the debenture of 4*d*. and the tax on raw a penny being deducted, leaves 4*s*. 4*d*., the inducement stands therefore, in 1824, 11*s*. 11*d*. in 1832, 4*s*. 4*d*.?—No, not exactly so; the actual and total difference is this, as 12*s*. 2*d*. to 4*s*. 5*d*.; not only has the duty been considerably lower, but the throwster is driven to work nearer to the duty than he did before, for the reasons stated in the Notes to my Paper, No. 22.

4402. On what principal do you deduct the 4*d*. debenture?—Because the manufacturer who comes to us to purchase a bale of foreign thrown silk, has the benefit of that debenture; consequently that virtually lowers the price of foreign thrown silk, and depresses still further the throwing interest in this country, that is beyond the effect of the lower protecting duties. The purchaser of foreign thrown silk asks for that which he can use to the extent of 3*s*. 6*d*. a pound if he exports, or which he can sell in the market at the average of 4*d*. This makes the foreign thrown silk so much the cheaper; therefore the British throwster works now with a total difference of only 4*s*. 5*d*., whereas formerly that difference was 12*s*. 2*d*. and more. There are many other points of importance which bear upon this part of the question, and others of great importance generally, which I have not had the honour to submit to the Committee in order not to detain them.

I beg leave to deliver in a Paper (No. 7,) which belongs to the first series of my Papers, and which it had escaped me to deliver in on the second day of my examination.

*[The Witness delivered in the following Paper.]*

No. 7.

Inverted Scale of Costs.)

## No. 7.—PLAIN SILK GOODS.

The preceding Abstract of Comparative Costs of good *Plain* Manufactured Silk in Common Colours, shows a *graduated* Scale of Variations at LONDON and at LYONS.
And the following presents those Variations in an inverted order, which is of frequent occurrence.
By means of these Two Tables, may be seen at one view the various differences in Costs (in those *Plain Goods* alone) against which we have to contend with our Foreign Competitors:—differences incident on contingencies with them, over which we have no control.
The difference in the respective Costs of Plain Goods of high Colours, and of Figured and Fancy Goods, are much greater;—and the Duties on them, as also the Charges for Smuggling, are proportionably lower, with regard to their higher Costs.

| LEGAL IMPORTS. | | | | | | ILLICIT IMPORTS. | | | |
|---|---|---|---|---|---|---|---|---|---|
| LONDON<br>Cost of 1lb. of manufactured good plain Silks, in common Colours. | LYONS<br>Cost of 1lb. of manufactured good Plain Silks, in common Colours, inclusive of 6 per Cent. for Charges of Purchase, &c. at Lyons, and of transmission to London. | Differences of Costs and Charges per lb. of those descriptions of Plain Silks. | Duty on manufactured Plain Silks per lb. | Differences on Legal Imports against | in favour of the Lyons Manufacturer. | LONDON<br>Cost of 1 lb. of manufactured Plain Silks, in common Colours. | LYONS<br>Cost of 1lb. manufactured Plain Silks, in common Colours, inclusive of 4 per Cent. for Charges of Purchase, &c. at Lyons and of transmission to Paris, where the Smuggler takes up the Goods. | Differences of Cost and Charges per lb. of those descriptions of Plain Silks. | |
| Estimate at London. *s.* *d.* | Estimate at Lyons. *s.* *d.* | *s.* *d.* p' cent. | *s.* *d.* p' cent. | | | Estimate at London. *s.* *d.* | Estimate at Lyons. *s.* *d.* | *s.* *d.* p' cent. | |
| (1) Raw - 17 6<br>Weaving - 8½ } 49 3 | (4.4) Raw - 14 6 } 32 11 (*d*)<br>Weaving - 4 } 30 8 | 16 4 = 50<br>18 7 = 61 | 11 - = 33<br>11 - = 36 | -<br>- | 17 p' cent<br>25 " | (1) Raw 17 6<br>Weaving - 8½ } 49 3 | (4.4) Raw - 14 6 } 32 4<br>Weaving - 4 } 30 - | 16 11 = 52<br>19 3 = 64 | Query—What is the charge of the Smuggler on plain goods. |
| (2) Raw - 17 6<br>Weaving - 7½ } 47 1 | (3.3) Raw - 15 6 } 35 11 (*c*)<br>Weaving 4¾ } 33 5 | 11 2 = 31<br>13 8 = 40 | 11 - = 31<br>11 - = 33 | -<br>- | —<br>7 p' cent | (2) Raw 17 6<br>Weaving - 7¼ } 47 1 | (3.3) Raw - 15 6 } 35 3<br>Weaving - 4¾ } 32 9 | 11 10 = 33<br>14 4 = 44 | |
| (3) Raw - 17 6<br>Weaving - 7 } 44 11 | (2.2) Raw - 16 - } 37 11 (*b*)<br>Weaving 5¼ } 35 4 | 7 - = 18<br>9 7 = 27 | 11 - = 29<br>11 - = 31 | 11 p' cent<br>4 " | —<br>— | (3) Raw 17 6<br>Weaving - 7 } 44 11 | (2.2) Raw - 16 - } 37 3<br>Weaving - 5¼ } 34 8 | 7 8 = 21<br>10 3 = 29 | |
| (4) Raw - 17 6<br>Weaving - 6 } 42 7 | (1.1) Raw - 17 - } 40 1 (*a*)<br>Weaving 5½ } 37 4 | 2 6 = 6<br>5 3 = 14 | 11 - = 27<br>11 - = 29 | 21 "<br>12 " | —<br>— | (4) Raw 17 6<br>Weaving - 6 } 42 7 | (1.1) Raw - 17 - } 39 4<br>Weaving - 5½ } 36 8 | 3 3 = 8<br>5 11 = 16 | |

(*See* annexed Notes relative to these Tables.)

Our relative situation during the last 4 or 5 months, (*i. e.* from December 1830 to April 1831,) in respect of good Plain Goods of common Colours, appears to have been as follows:—which difference of Costs are consequent on a little improvement in Wages, &c. with us, and a great depression at Lyons, jointly with very low prices of the Silks of their own produce. (Some accounts show yet greater differences.)

| | | | | | | | | | |
|---|---|---|---|---|---|---|---|---|---|
| *s.* *d.*<br>(3) 44 11 (Raw - 17 6<br>Weaving - 7<br>* Per Yard - 2 9⅝ | (4.4) *s.* *d.* 32 11 (*s.* *d.* 14 6 Raw -<br>- 4 Weaving<br>1 11⅜ p' yard. | *s.* *d.* p' cent.<br>12 - = 37 | *s.* *d.* p' cent.<br>11 - = 33 | - - | 4 p' cent | (1) *s.* *d.* 44 11 - - - | (4.4) *s.* *d.* 32 4 - - - | *s.* *d.* p' cent.<br>12 7 = 39 | Query—What is the charge of the Smuggler on plain goods. |
| | 30 8 (14 6 Raw -<br>- 4 Weaving<br>and loss of Profit, &c.<br>1 9⅝ p' Yard. | 14 3 = 46 | 11 - = 36 | - - | 10 " | - - - - | 30 1 - - - | 14 10 = 49 | |

* In this Estimate (3) the throwing of good fine organzine is cast at 5*s.*, and of good fine tram at 3*s.* with the rate of waste assumed in this, as in all my Estimates, at 4½ %, *i. e.* ¾ of an ounce in lb. 1. 0¾; whilst those charges for throwing and waste have been higher during the last few months; but, on the other hand, our manufacturers have been able to meet partly those higher charges by purchases of foreign organzines and trams (inclusive of the advantage of the debentures,) at rates lower than the increased cost of English thrown silks in this period.—Minute made in April 1831.

March 1832. Errors excepted. (signed) *Alexis James Doxat.*

*Lunæ, 7° die Maii, 1832.*

---

EDWARD AYSHFORD SANFORD ESQUIRE, IN THE CHAIR.

---

Mr. *William Banbury*, called in ; and Examined.

Mr.
*William Banbury.*

———

7 May,
1832.

4403. YOU are a silk merchant, are you not?—I am.

4404. In what house are you a partner?—In the house of James Vere, Nephew & Company.

4405. Is not that a house which has been very long established in the silk trade?—Upwards of an hundred years, it was established in 1720, I believe.

4406. How many years have you personally known the silk trade?—Fifty-two years next October, but for about seven or eight and thirty years I was a broker, I served my time to a silk broker, and when the late Mr. Vere retired from business, I joined that house as a merchant and silkman in the latter end of the year 1817.

4407. You are acquainted with the laws which have been passed at different times in regard to the silk trade?—Yes; when the contemplated measure of the repeal which had so long protected the silk manufactory took place, I took pains to collect all the information I possibly could, presuming that at that period we should have got a hearing in defence of the system that worked so favourably for us, but Parliament refused that, and I am very sorry for it, for the result has been extremely prejudicial to my interest.

4408. You are now speaking of the alteration of the law in 1824?—I am.

4409. Will you state the several Acts which have passed to prohibit the importation of foreign wrought silks?—The Act for prohibiting the importation of foreign wrought silk and velvets, passed (the 6th of George the Third,) in May 1766, and came into operation the 17th of June the next month; but ribbons were then, and had been prohibited upwards of 260 years, they were prohibited in the 19th of Henry the seventh, chapter 21; the Act passed in 1503.

4410. What led to the prohibition in the 6th of George the Third?—That refers to the broad silks and the velvets; it appears that that was owing to the introduction of so many foreign silks, which injured our own manufacture, that was the apparent cause.

4411. Do you consider that the prohibitory laws had a beneficial effect on the silk manufacture of Great Britain?—I have no more doubt of it than I have of the baneful effects which have resulted from the repeal of those salutary laws.

4412. In the year 1766, was not a Committee appointed in consequence of complaints then made, and was not the effect the prohibition?—Yes, it took place as an experiment for five years, I think the government wished it to be three years, but I believe Mr. Pattison pressed for five years, to give it a more fair trial.

4413. The effect of it was extremely beneficial in your opinion?—No doubt of it, I have felt the good effects of it myself.

4414. Did the manufactures very much increase under the operation of those laws?—It wonderfully increased; at the time of those laws taking place, the importation of raw silk was not above 6 or 700,000 lbs. and of thrown silk about 360,000 lbs.

4415. Were the operatives in general employed in the manufactures, both in Spitalfields and Coventry, well employed and fairly paid during the prohibition? —Generally they were; but of course at different periods they were not so well employed, they were at times extremely brisk; Coventry used to be very well employed in the spring season, they used to say that where a person came to make goods thin, and who had not employed them in other times of the year, they called them cuckoo masters.

4416. Did the throwing trade extend very much during the same period, and can you state the degree in which it extended?—The comparative state of the trade in 1766 and 1826 will prove it; at the former period there were only seven mills in the kingdom that threw organzines, and those were in trifling quantities compared with the late returns of our mills, I should say perhaps not a fiftieth or even an hundredth part of that which has been lately thrown in this country.

4417. Can you state to the Committee what was the duty on foreign thrown silk in 1765?—Yes, I have an account from the year 1660 to the present time.

4418. What was the duty on foreign thrown silk in 1765?—Four shillings and

five-pence

Mr.
*William Banbury.*

7 May,
1832.

five-pence and $\frac{17}{20}$ths, it may be called 4*s.* 6*d.* on thrown silk, and 1 *s.* 3 *d.* the pound on raw.

4419. Have you a general statement of the duty on foreign thrown silk in 1765, and the changes afterwards made in that duty?—Yes; in 1765 it went up to 4*s.* 9*d.*, there was 6*d.* additional duty put on in the year 1765, and they took off 6*d.* off raw silk, to encourage the throwing trade.

4420. Have you any objection to put in that statement for the information of the Committee?—None at all.

*[The Witness delivered in the same, which was read as follows :]*

### AN ACCOUNT of the PROGRESSIVE increase of DUTY on THROWN SILK, from the Year 1660 to the present time.

| | DUTY, the Pound of 16 Ounces. £. s. d. | | s. d. |
|---|---|---|---|
| Nett Duty, in the year 1660 - - - - - | — — 9 $\frac{10}{20}$ | 1784 to 1787 } | - 7/4. |
| 1692 - - - - | — 1 6 $\frac{17}{20}\frac{1}{2}$ | | |
| 1699 - - - - | — 2 4 $\frac{7}{20}\frac{1}{2}$ | 1797 to 1801 } | - 8/. |
| 1703 - - - - | — 2 7 $\frac{16}{20}\frac{5}{6}$ | | |
| 1704 - - - - | — 3 1 $\frac{17}{20}\frac{1}{2}$ | 1805 | - 11/5. |
| 1747 - - - - | — 3 11 $\frac{17}{20}\frac{1}{2}$ | 1807 | - 12/2. |
| A. - - - - - - 1765 - - - - | — 4 5 $\frac{17}{20}\frac{1}{2}$ | 1814 to 1823 } | - 14/7. |
| 1779 - - - - | — 4 8 $\frac{11}{20}\frac{3}{8}$ | | |
| 1781 - - - - | — 4 10 $\frac{16}{20}$ | 1824 | - 7/6. |
| 1782 - - - - | — 5 1 $\frac{12}{20}$ | 1825 | - 5/. |
| B. - - - - - - 1784, and at present, 1786 | — 7 4 | | |

It must be observed, that except at the periods marked A. & B. the duty on most other goods was increased in proportion to their rate, or supposed value in the Book of Rates, in an equal degree with thrown silk. In 1765, the period marked A. the additional duty imposed was 6*d.* per pound; but it was in consideration of a material reduction then made in the duty on raw silk, for which see the Table; in 1784, the period marked B., the increase of duty was not on goods in general imported, but applied to silk only; for the increase on raw silk see the Table.

### AN ACCOUNT of the PROGRESSIVE variation of DUTY on RAW SILK, from the Year 1660 to the present time 1786.

| | CHINA, the Pound of 24 oz. £. s. d. | BENGAL, the Pound of 24 oz. £. s. d. | ITALIAN, &c. the Pound of 24 oz. £. s. d. |
|---|---|---|---|
| Nett Duty in the Year 1660 - - - | — — 11 $\frac{8}{20}$ | — — 5 $\frac{14}{20}$ | — — 5 $\frac{14}{20}$ |
| 1690 - - - | — 1 10 $\frac{13}{20}$ | — — 11 $\frac{6}{20}\frac{1}{2}$ | — — 5 $\frac{14}{20}$ |
| 1699 - - - | — 2 10 $\frac{1}{20}$ | — 1 5 $\frac{0}{20}\frac{1}{2}$ | — — 11 $\frac{8}{20}$ |
| 1703 - - - | — 3 1 $\frac{17}{20}$ | — 1 6 $\frac{18}{20}\frac{1}{2}$ | — 1 1 $\frac{6}{20}$ |
| 1704 - - - | — 3 9 $\frac{9}{20}$ | — 1 10 $\frac{14}{20}\frac{1}{2}$ | — 1 5 $\frac{2}{20}$ |
| 1747 - - - | — 4 9 $\frac{9}{20}$ | — 2 4 $\frac{14}{20}\frac{1}{2}$ | — 1 11 $\frac{2}{20}$ |
| 1750 - - - | — 1 11 $\frac{2}{20}$ | — 2 4 $\frac{14}{20}\frac{1}{2}$ | — 1 11 $\frac{2}{20}$ |
| 1765 - - - | — 1 3 | — 1 3 | — 1 3 |
| 1779 - - - | — 1 3 $\frac{15}{20}$ | — 1 3 $\frac{15}{20}$ | — 1 3 $\frac{15}{20}$ |
| 1782 - - - | — 1 4 $\frac{10}{20}$ | — 1 4 $\frac{10}{20}$ | — 1 4 $\frac{10}{20}$ |
| 1784, and at present 1786 - - - } | — 4 4 $\frac{16}{20}$ | — 4 4 $\frac{16}{20}$ | — 4 4 $\frac{16}{20}$ |

The

Mr.
*William Banbury.*

7 May,
1832.

The Duty was now paid on Raw, by the lb. of 16 oz.

|  | £ | s. | d. | £ | s. | d. | £ | s. | d. |
|---|---|---|---|---|---|---|---|---|---|
| Nett Duty in the Year 1784 to 1787 - - - | - | 3 | - | - | 3 | - | - | 3 | - |
| 1797 - - - | - | 3 | 3 | - | 3 | 3 | - | 3 | 3 |
| 1801 to 1805 - - - | - | 5 | 1 | - | 3 | 9 | - | 5 | 1 |
| 1807 - - - | - | 5 | 5 | - | 4 | 9 | - | 5 | 5 |
| 1814 - - - | - | 5 | 7 | - | 3 | 9 | - | 5 | 7 |
| 1817 to 1823 - - - | - | 5 | 6 | - | 3 | 6 | - | 5 | 6 |
| 1824 - - - | - | - | 3 | - | - | 3 | - | - | 3 |
| 1825 - - - | - | - | 1 | - | - | 1 | - | - | 1 |

It must be observed, that until the year 1750, the duty on most other articles was increased (in proportion to their rate, or supposed value in the Book of Rates) in an equal degree with raw silk; and that in the year 1765, when the general reduction of duty on raw silk took place, an addition was made to the duty on thrown silk of 6 *d.* the pound of 16 ounces.

---

(Mr. *Banbury.*)—There is one circumstance may be observed; there was a duty of 2 *s.* in the pound laid on in the year 1824, on both raw and thrown; that was at the suggestion of the trade; Mr. Pitt, on the winding up of the American war and then funding the outstanding debts, among other taxes, proposed to levy 120,000 *l.* by a stamp on ribbons and gauzes; the trade felt that would be extremely vexatious and troublesome, and it was suggested by them to Mr. Pitt, that if he took 2 *s.* a pound on all the silk imported it would produce that revenue, or perhaps 30,000 *l.* more, making 150,000 *l.*; and when they offered that, he took it directly.

4421. Up to the period when the prohibitory laws were repealed, had there been any very large amount of capital invested in silk mills and machinery?—An immense quantity in both, as by reference to the mills in Cheshire, Somersetshire, Essex, Norfolk, Berkshire, &c. will appear.

4422. Has not that capital been subsequently very much deteriorated?—In many instances totally sunk, and in every instance seriously injured.

4423. From what period do you date that deterioration?—From 1826; the throwing trade until that period was a progressively improving trade.

4424. Was not the silk trade during your experience, setting aside any casual circumstances, a generally progressive improving trade?—Exactly so.

4425. Then you say that this increase of capital, which took place during the progress of prosperity, has been deteriorated since the year 1826?—Precisely so.

4426. It appears by the papers you have delivered in, that in 1784 the duty was raised from 5 *s.* 1 *d.* to 7 *s.* 4 *d.*; that was done on consultation with the merchants?—It was.

4427. Can you state that, at any of the subsequent periods, when the duty was laid on and increased to 14 *s.* 10 *d.*, on each of those operations the merchants were consulted?—No, never on any other occasion; the duties were laid on at different periods; during the late war, the silk trade very much increased, then the duties still continued to be augmented; but the general feeling was, silk is an article of luxury; the minister must have taxes; and therefore with what face can we go before the minister, and ask him to take off taxes on an article of luxury, when it would be much more useful for them to be taken off necessaries, and we always submitted to it without a word.

4428. The trade went on progressively increasing notwithstanding those heavy duties?—Yes, wonderfully.

4429. Did you complain to the Government that it was a falling trade?—No.

4430. Though it was burthened with heavy duties it increased?—Yes.

4431. By the trade, do you mean the whole of the persons employed in the silk manufacture?—Yes, I mean the silk trade generally.

4432. Do you mean the merchant, the throwster and the manufacturer?—Certainly, the whole of the trade; if Government wanted any information from the silk trade, the merchants were generally consulted, and they first of all consulted the manufacturers.

4433. Recurring to the capital invested in mills and machinery, what is the present condition of the throwing trade in this country?—It is miserably bad;

many

Mr.
*William Banbury.*

7 May,
1832.

many of the mills are now shut up, and only dragging on their operations partially at ruinous and starving prices, alike destructive of the comfort and even necessaries of life to both master and servant; it is miserably bad.

4434. Have there been many failures in the throwing trade since the repeal of the prohibitory laws?—Enormous.

4435. You mentioned that several mills had been thrown out of employment, can you give any description of them or their situations?—There are several mills at Reading, which are all shut up; Mr. Billings, a very capital mill at Twyford, and others; I am told Mr. Kay's is shut up.

4436. Have not all the mills been thrown out of employment that are in unfavourable situations, where, being worked by steam, they are not near coals, or where they are in a situation where they cannot get cheap labour?—I know that Macclesfield and Congleton used to be considered very favourable situations; but that half of them have been shut up.

4437. You mentioned that Mr. Kay's mill is shut up?—I have been told so.

4438. Where is that situate?—At Tring, in Hertfordshire.

4439. Do you know when that mill was built?—I should think about six or seven years ago.

4440. Was not that built in the year 1826?—I believe it was; we too were unfortunate; we erected a mill ourselves for the benefit of an old clerk, who wanted a situation for his son; he thought a silk mill would be a very good employment for him, and would yield him a comfortable subsistence; and in consequence of that we agreed to advance him four or five thousand pounds; and that was just built in 1824, when Mr. Robinson brought forward the contemplated alterations; I wished to knock it on the head then, and shut it up; but they thought that he would not persevere in his plan.

4441. To what do you attribute this reverse in the throwing trade?—The diminished consumption of thrown silk that would have been required to make ribbons and broad silks for our own use, and which have been supplanted by foreign, brought in legally and illegally, to the injury of every branch of the silk trade; the importation of trams, which were formerly prohibited, and the reduction of the duty on organzines to 3 s. 6 d. a pound.

4442. You of course conclude that mills in the worst situations would naturally decline first, were they to charge more than mills more favourably situate would be obliged to charge?—I think that is the natural cause.

4443. You do not mean to say, that the mills in Congleton and other places, which have decreased, were under disadvantageous circumstances?—No, only from the depressed state of the trade.

4444. Arising only from the general depression and want of employment?—Yes.

4445. Of course, in either way, the weakest would go first to the wall?—Yes.

4446. If one mill had an advantage over another to the extent of 1,000 l. a year, that would last longer than the one which had no such advantage?—These are difficult questions to answer; but, generally speaking, I should say, there is no profit at all now, but a loss.

4447. What has been the specific effect of the reduction of the duty upon organzine from 5 s. to 3 s. 6 d.?—It does no good to the manufacturer, for he is as bad off as ever he was; and it is an injury to the throwsters, for it has still further tended to reduce the wages and his own charge, which was before ruinously low.

4448. What do you conceive would be the effect upon the throwing trade of this country if the duty on thrown silk should be still further reduced?—Bad as it is at present, that must naturally, if possible, make it still worse.

4449. What effect was produced upon the trade by the sudden reduction of the duty on thrown silk from 7 s. 6 d. per lb. to 5 s. per lb. in November 1825 by a Treasury order?—That was a dreadful event; the trade, from the recent alterations was then in a very ticklish feverish state, and that was an unexpected reduction of duty which nobody could contemplate, for it was done by a Minute of the Treasury, in consequence of a representation from Mr. Jaques, a silk dyer. In the Act passed for the admission of thrown silk 7 s. 6 d. was the duty; but it was the same both on the silk in the gum, and that which was dyed. Mr. Jaques went up to the Board of Trade and made a representation that that would be very injurious to his trade, though I do not suppose there would have been five cwt. of silk imported in the dyed state in the next twelve months; but in consequence of his representation the Government altered the duty from 7 s. 6 d. to 5 s., the trade was

678. at

Mr.
*William Banbury.*

7 May,
1832.

at that time in such a ticklish feverish state, that it gave us a complete damper, I will venture to say, our house lost from four or five thousand pounds by that event, and the trade in general four or five hundred thousand pounds; we had three and forty bales consigned to us, which had paid the 7 s. 6 d. duty; we memorialized the Board of Trade to put these in the same situation as if they had been still in the Docks; it was mere matter of accident whether they were in the one or the other, and we thought it very hard that our friends should suffer; those silks being on consignment, we memorialized the Board of Trade, or the Treasury, and I think we never got an answer for five months, whether they would or would not allow it; but about two or three days before Parliament met, they gave us an answer that they could do nothing in the business, so that those forty-three bales stood waiting the result of the determination of Government, and then had to pay half-a-crown more than other silks, and our friends sustained a serious loss upon them in consequence.

4450. Who was Chancellor of the Exchequer at that time?—I believe Mr. Robinson.

4451. Do you mean to say the trade had no previous notice until the Treasury order appeared?—They have not above two or three days at all events.

4452. This change took place to protect the dyer, the duty being 7 s. 6 d. both on dyed and undyed thrown silk?—Yes.

4453. To protect the dyer, the duty of 7 s. 6 d. on thrown silk was lowered?— Yes; and the duty of 7 s. 6 d. remains on the dyed by way of protecting the dyer; the silk, in dyeing, loses about four ounces—about one quarter.

4454. At the time of issuing the Order in Council for the reduction of duties, did the throwsters take any steps to represent to the Government the effect of such a change?—I do not recollect whether they did or did not; Mr. Bull, a considerable throwster, was very much alive to that matter; but whether the throwsters made any representation I cannot say.

4455. You say, that no answer was received for five months to your representation?—Yes; that is speaking as near as I can recollect.

4456. Do you consider it essential to the prosperity of the silk manufacture that the throwing of Italian silk in this country should be encouraged?—I do consider it a most important part of the silk manufacture in this country, one of its essential parts, independent of the employment it gives to women and children, who are as competent to perform the requisite labour in a silk mill, or perhaps more so, than the most athletic men; that circumstance, and the peculiarly clean delicate nature of the article, renders it a very desirable occupation for those interesting classes of society.

4457. You have stated, that the silk trade had been increasing in prosperity up to 1826?—I have.

4458. Do you believe, that but for the law which was then passed, it would have continued to increase in prosperity?—I think it would have increased in prosperity and in extent, it was progressively improving with the large duty of 14 s. 7 d. on thrown, and 5 s. 6 d. on raw; at 14 s. 7 d. the duty amounted, not unfrequently, to cent. per cent.; when we have had a few bales of silk, not of very marketable quality, when they have lain in our warehouses for two or three years, the duty and charges have amounted to more than the nett proceeds; there was perhaps interest for two or three years on the duty. We sold silk at ten months; there was our and the broker's commission, and the *del credere*.

4459. At what credit do you sell now?—At five months; it is a most extraordinary circumstance; I was very extensively employed as a broker towards the latter end of the last century and the beginning of the present; I have sold for Mr. Doxat 150,000 l. a year, and other houses in proportion; I went on for ten years and never made a bad debt for a friend; and now latterly we cannot sell three bales of silk but there is a bad debt; probably from one, if not two.

4460. Those were good old times?—They were good old times indeed.

4461. Do you find your neighbours much better off than you?—I have known a terrible rot among other trades, for instance, the cotton, and we have been as sound as an acorn.

4462. What duty do you think would be a sufficient protection to the throwster? —That is a consideration a good deal with manufacturers; my opinion has always been, that about 4 s. would be a fair protection to the throwster, and not injurious to the manufacturer.

4463. That

Mr.
*William Bunbury.*

7 May,
1832.

4463. That is an advance of 6 *d.* on the present?—Yes, and I would make it the same on tram and on organzine.

4464. Do you give that opinion with reference to the manufacturer having to compete with the French?—I do not think we can do that.

4465. Do you found your opinion that the manufacturer could easily bear 4 *s.*, on a supposition of a prohibition taking place, or on a supposition of the English coming into competition with the French manufacturer?—I ground it more on the old system.

4466. What do you conceive would be the effect upon the throwster, of the duty remaining at 3 *s.* 6 *d.* as it is?—The throwster is very much injured by the reduction to 3 *s.* 6 *d.* in my opinion.

4467. What would be the ultimate effect of the duty remaining at 3 *s.* 6 *d.*?—He certainly will not be in a very enviable situation at that price.

4468. Do you think he will be able to exist with it?—It will be a miserable existence. I think; unless we have prohibition we shall never do any good; and I am determined, unless something of that kind is done before the end of this year, I will leave the silk trade.

4469. What effect will keeping the duty at 3 *s.* 6 *d.* or increasing it to 4 *s.* produce upon the manufacturer in this country, looking at it not as you have said, with reference to prohibition, but as entering into competition with the foreign manufacturer?—In the present situation we are placed in with respect to the admission of foreign goods, I think it is of very little importance whether it is 3 *s.* 6 *d.* or 4 *s.*

4470. Do you mean to say that the English manufacturer cannot the better meet in competition with the French by having the silk 3 *s.* 6 *d.* cheaper than he now has it?—I do not know that he would get it cheaper; because if the duty was to be taken off, that would knock up the mills in this country, I should think; and they would take advantage of us abroad, and would make us pay for it.

4471. What do you conceive would be the rise of price of foreign thrown silk in this country, supposing the throwster in this country was entirely destroyed?—I think it is very likely it would rise 2 *s.* 6 *d.* or 3 *s.* 6 *d.*; last Thursday we had a letter from Bergamo, from the house of Piatzoni & Co.; they stated the prices, so that they would stand here for us to sell, of 18–20 deniers at 28 *s.*, and of 20 to 24 at 27 *s.*, we paying duty 3 *s.* 6 *d.*; the price here at this moment I have sold that silk at, is 23 *s.* 6 *d.*, so that we are considerably under the prices abroad, that is owing to the competition among our throwsters, who are selling their silks at a loss.

4472. Have you lately received any consignments?—We had 5,000 weight of trams consigned to us a fortnight ago.

4473. Do those houses who send you those prices send you any silk?—Not an ounce; we used to receive hundreds of bales from them; we have received some from Milan, on a supposition that the duty was about to be taken off; but we never gave them that information I am sure.

4474. What do you put as the expense from thence to London?—About five or six shillings, with the duty, and every thing; the commission, the *del credere*, the brokerage, and so on, five per cent. more; five months credit, that would be about 1 *s.* 6 *d.* besides the duty.

4475. You have stated that the mills would be all knocked up; are you aware that during the year 1831, the whole of the mills for Italian in England have been obtaining only 3 *s.*, between the price of raw and of thrown; that the prices of Italian and Bergamo silks have been on the average 18 *s.* 6 *d.* raw and 25 *s.* thrown?—No, the thrown has been lower than that; the raw, I should suppose was upon the average about 16 *s.* 6 *d.* Bergamo raws, and the thrown about a guinea or 21 *s.* 6 *d.*

4476. What has been the difference in 1831 between raw and thrown?—About 4 *s.* 6 *d.*

4477. Deducting the 3 *s.* 6 *d.* duty from that, all that the throwster had was 1 *s.*?—That is all.

4478. Do they get more now; is the difference greater between the raw and the thrown?—They are selling at such prices, it is impossible to tell; I saw beautiful organzine the other day sold at 21 *s.* 3 *d.*

4479. Has that reduction of price been effected, in your opinion, by the competition among our own merchants?—Yes, and the want of demand; there has been more silk thrown.

4480. Has not the operation been of a ruinous nature, and not of a remunerating nature?—Quite so.

4481. When

Mr.
*William Banbury.*

7 May,
1832.

4481. When you place the duty on thrown silk at 4s. a pound, as a sufficient protection, you mean for tram and organzine together?—Yes.

4482. So that, presuming that half and half are imported, that would make 5s. for the organzine, and 3s. for the tram?—Yes, there is more organzine comes than tram.

4483. You do not conceive that 4s. on organzine alone would be a sufficient protection?—I am doubtful of that, it would do very well if we were under the old system, which I hope we shall be.

4484. Considering the ruinous price at which the Italian thrown silk has been sold here, has there been less imported the last twelve or eighteen months than there was before?—There was a great deal imported in the latter part of 1830 and the beginning of the year 1831, but the latter end of last year there has not been nearly so much.

4485. Do you think the difference of price has made the quantity of Italian thrown fall off?—Yes.

4486. Still there is some comes?—Very little; I am offering trams at this moment at a guinea; I sold the same man's silk at 19s. last week, but they were very superior raw; the tram paid 2s. duty, so that the throwing is given away.

4487. Of what country?—Milan silk.

4488. How do you account for men going on sending a manufactured article to sell at the same price as the raw article?—Ten months ago we were a little lively, and then they inundated us with silk.

4489. Does it not arise from this, that the silk throwsters in England being in close competition with each other, are obliged to buy raw silk to keep their mills going, and that they drive down their people to a pitch of suffering, and thus undersell the Italians?—Yes.

4490. Are not some of the families employed in the silk mills, partially supported by the poor's rate?—I do not know that fact.

4491. Is it your opinion, that it is the competition amongst our own throwsters that regulates the price, and not the importations from abroad?—Yes, it is from the want of demand for the thrown article.

4492. Do you think that the last eighteen months, in the silk throwing, the expense and the manufacture has been paid out of capital, or out of profit?—Out of capital; profit is an obsolete term.

4493. Are you aware that in 1831, there were 456,345 lbs. of organzine not dyed, and 170,645 lbs. of tram not dyed, imported, notwithstanding the great reduction of price which you state?—Yes, they imported a great deal; that has been the reason we have been selling at such a loss; they wrote us word that formerly our market was the best market in Europe, and they now find it is the worst.

4494. Do you mean to say that our market here is not so good as other markets in Europe?—No, it certainly is not.

4495. Then why do they send it here?—They do not send the same quantity, and there has lately been many bales of thrown silk sent back.

4496. Has the effect of the alteration in 1829 been to increase the quantity of thrown, and to decrease the quantity of raw silk imported from Italy?—I think it did increase it, but they sent in a great deal in the year 1831; but they are not sending now, there is nothing coming to our house but two or three bales from Piedmont.

4497. If there is a great diminution of silk from Italy, how comes it that the throwsters are supplied with Italian silk, so as to compete with each other?—At present there is no good raw silk coming.

4498. What is the raw silk which comes now?—There is some very good in the country, but now is getting scarce; some has been sold; I was only offered 18s. at Christmas, and would not then take it.

4499. Is there, in your opinion, a diminution of importation within the last six months of the finer qualities of raw silk from Italy?—Yes.

4500. Is there, in your opinion, a great increase of thrown silk from Italy?—No, there is a reduction of late.

4501. What silk are the throwsters generally throwing now?—Some of last years; there has been very little come in of late.

4502. Do you not know that during the last eighteen months, the state of disease and so on, on the Continent, influenced the export?—I cannot say, the trade is remarkably good on the Continent; it is very good in Germany; it is very good in Switzerland, and is very good at Lyons; it is better here within the last ten days

than

than it was, but after this and next month I expect we shall revert again to our old miserable state.

4503. Do you think that the distress of the throwster arises more from the introduction of manufactured goods than the importation of foreign silk?—From the importation of manufactured goods, there is where the mischief lies.

4504. Will you state how the importation of manufactured goods affects the throwster?—Every yard which is imported diminishes the manufacture in this country.

4505. Are you acquainted with the condition of the silk manufacturer in England?—I have had a long and intimate acquaintance with persons residing in Spitalfields, but a manufacturer would be able to answer that question better than I can; I have had frequent communications with them, and a tolerable knowledge of their trade.

4506. What is their condition now as compared with that in which they were previously?—It has been latterly very bad; there has been very little demand for goods, and no sales of consequence made without a great sacrifice, but if they submit to it, then the great monopolizing or slaughter-houses (as they are called) are always ready to grapple with their unfortunate victim.

4507. What do you mean by slaughter-houses?—That is the term for those great houses which are always ready to buy any goods when they can get them 10 or 15 per cent. under cost—great houses with large capital.

4508. They buy at all prices?—Yes, I dare say they do; but as low as they possibly can.

4509. When the distresses of others oblige them to sell they buy?—Yes.

4510 But that will not continue when the distresses of those persons must oblige them to discontinue their trade?—I should think not.

4511. Can you devise any plan by which the silk manufacturers of Spitalfields can get rid of their goods without selling them in the best market, the whole trade being open to them they will naturally take the best price they can get?—No doubt.

4512. Those slaughter-houses are resorted to in such cases probably?—Yes.

4513. The silk manufacturers sell to those houses at the prices the trade generally will give, do they not?—They sell as much in the regular way as they possibly can, but when they get distressed, those gentlemen are generally, as they suppose, aware of that.

4514. Do not you suppose those persons who keep those which you call slaughter-houses are holders of large stocks, and that they have no true interest in beating down the manufacturer, but that in self defence they are compelled to buy at the cheapest market?—I cannot say.

4515. Are the Committee to understand, that the sellers of goods have any better market than those slaughter-houses?—They have no other now.

4516. Do you consider that that may be beneficial to them?—That is a new system; formerly the manufacturers gave credit, and when they gave credit there was a profit on goods, but now when they sell for money there is never any profit.

4517. It is a ready money trade?—The next thing to a ready money trade.

4518. Therefore the commodity comes forth to the public not taxed with those long credits which used to be given?—I suppose that is the case, but when there was credit given, there was a deal more profit.

4519. Must not that be beneficial to the operative, as the public will consume more of a cheap than of a dear commodity?—We can only judge of things by the results; during my experience, which has been pretty extensive, since this system has been adopted, of selling at short credit to those houses, we have made enormous bad debts, and they have, I believe, very much participated in them.

4520. You have shortened your own credit?—Yes, we have been obliged to do it.

4521. Is not the result of that system of short credit and small charge beneficial to the consumer?—It may make it a little cheaper, but those great houses are nothing but middle houses, they buy of the manufacturer and then sell to the shops after that.

4522. Why does not the manufacturer sell to the shop-keeper?—Some of them do; and those who do so, do best.

4523. Are they not at liberty to go to those slaughter-houses or to retail shops?—Certainly.

4524. If those wholesale houses absorb a great portion of the trade, is not that to be taken as a proof that the manufacturers sell to them because they get the best market by that mode?—They are almost the only buyers now.

4525. Are

Mr.
*William Banbury.*
_____

7 May,
1832.

4525. Are the dealings of those large houses sufficient to fix the price in the market?—I should think they would materially influence it.

4526. When the trade was more divided, and there were not those very large houses existing, was there not great competition, and had not the manufacturers a better chance of deriving a fair profit by their trade?—There is no question of that, the trade has never flourished since that system ceased.

4527. There being but few buyers, and those being very large buyers, have they it not in their power frequently to rule the market by raising or depressing the prices to suit their interest?—I do not think they much raise them, they depress them as much as they possibly can, but manufacturers in constant communication with those houses will give a much better answer on that point than I can, as I have no communication with them direct.

4528. You have been asked whether, if manufacturers were ruined, they would leave off selling; do you not know a great many individuals who have been so ruined compelled to leave off selling?—Yes, when they have broken they have nothing to pay beyond 1 s. to 2 s. 6 d. and when they have failed they have no goods.

4529. Have you known any silk manufacturers who, when they have wanted money, have gone and sold at an immense sacrifice to raise money?—Frequently that has been done; I could mention instances, if necessary; there have been two or three actions brought against the purchasers of those goods. I received a dividend last Friday from Marshall, of Watling-street, he had goods consigned to him from Manchester, he was to sell at such and such prices, he sent them to those slaughter-houses as they are termed in the trade; there were actions brought against two or three of them; they compromised, and I got 5 s. 7 ½ d. in the pound on my debt, in consequence, or I should not perhaps have got sixpence but for that.

4530. Has it not been notorious to the trade that there have been disputes between the creditors of those persons who have failed, and some of those houses who have been purchasers?—This is a case in point.

4531. And all those persons have compromised the matter by making that payment?—Yes, instead of standing the trial.

4532. You could name the houses?—I could if it were necessary.

4533. In which actions had been threatened against persons who had purchased of other houses' agents, who had received goods to sell by commission?—Yes.

4534. Do you not know, that recently there have been actions brought against individuals, and that those individuals have been ruined in consequence of verdicts being obtained against them?—I recollect something about it.

4535. You have been asked whether those very large purchasers, by buying low, do not benefit the consumer; however these great monopolists may benefit the public by cheapness, do they not do essential injury to those individuals who manufacture the goods?—That is my impression.

4536. You mention these things merely to illustrate the distressed state of the trade, which gives to large buyers an advantage which they would not have under a more prosperous state of things?—Yes.

4537. When a manufacturer has been buying goods on credit, and has bills out for those goods, is there not a great inducement when he is pressed for money, to sell goods for cash, to meet his demands which are coming due?—Yes.

4538. So that he may go on for a considerable time in the hope of recovering himself?—Yes.

4539. Does not an operation of that sort ultimately very much increase the mischief arising from his insolvency?—Yes.

4540. The observations you have made are not intended to apply unfavourably to large businesses?—Certainly not; I only mention that a manufacturer told me, when the trade was bad, we cannot sell our goods in the regular way; but if we choose to make a sacrifice, we can sell all we have got.

4541. The extensive operations of those houses have grown out of the importance of the trade?—Yes, they have.

4542. Does the mischief of which you complain, arise from the manufacturer making more goods than he can sell to a profit, or is it not very much aggravated by the pressure of French goods upon the market?—That certainly magnifies the evil.

4543. Have the same sort of compromises you refer to, taken place in the Manchester trade?—I believe they have.

4544. Do

Mr.
*William Banbury.*

7 May,
1832

4544. Do you know that there is a possibility of a fraudulent debtor conniving with fraudulent assignees, to allow such sort of transactions ?—I am not aware of such a circumstance, but it is possible.

4545. Do you mean to apply that charge of making those compromises to all the great dealers in the city ?—I believe it is pretty general with them, they all buy as cheap as they can.

4546. Are the parties who sell, at liberty to sell where they please ?—Yes, certainly.

4547. You state that a number of persons are breaking every day ?—Not now.

4548. Are there more in the silk business now than there were some years ago ? —I should think not half.

4549. There have been too many in the business to find a living ?—Yes ; there has been such an immense quantity of foreign goods come in, it has tended, I have no doubt, very greatly to the distress which they now feel.

4550. Do you mean to say that trade is in a more wholesome state than formerly ? —Yes, I think there is more care ; we have not had a bad debt of late.

4551. Is there larger capital in the trade than formerly ?—I think not.

4552. They give more credit than in the cotton trade, do they not ?—I cannot say.

4553. Are you not aware that raw cotton is sold at a very few days' credit ?— I do not know the customs of that trade.

4554. Are you not aware that the credit in Coventry is generally one week ?— I have no doubt Mr. Cope gives a credit.

4555. Why do you merchants trust the little houses ?—We trust very little now, that evil is pretty well cured.

4556. Has there been any alteration in the credits given by merchants to manufacturers of late years ?—I forget how long it is since the last alteration was made ; I think four or five or six years ago we used to give ten, then eight, and now it is five months.

4557. How much discount ?—Two and a half per cent. now ; half a per cent. per month.

4558. Do not the manufacturers now generally take the discount ?—Some of them do and some do not, the majority to whom we sell do not.

4559. The throwsters do not ?—Some of them do, and some do not.

4560. What credit do you get on China and Bengal silks ?—That is ready money article.

4561. You purchase of the East India Company on ready money ?—Yes.

4562. What is the credit given on the Turkey silk ?—That used to be seven months, now I believe they generally allow five per cent. and sell for money ; the broker gets that I believe.

4563. You sell a great deal more silk to the throwster than you were in the habit of doing, do you not ?—Formerly the throwsters did not buy at all, they were not buyers of silk.

4564. Do you find the throwsters pay ready money more frequently than manufacturers ?—I think not.

4565. Upon British thrown silk, what is the credit ?—Five months, the same as Italian.

4566. Has not this curtailment of credit had the effect, that many of the brokers, instead of acting fairly as brokers, and being content with the commission, advance the money and guarantee it at a certain per centage ?—I believe there is a great deal done in that way now, but I am not acquainted exactly with that business.

4567, Do you charge 5-8ths brokerage now ?—Yes, we pay that charge.

4568. You say that the British thrown silk and the Foreign are sold at the same credit ?—Yes.

4569. Many of the brokers guarantee the debts, and charge a per centage now, do they not ?—Yes, I believe so.

4570. That was not formerly within the line of the broker's duty ?—It was always done more or less.

4571. But persons who have large capital engross the trade by holding out this inducement to manufacturers ?—Yes, capital will have its advantage.

4572. You have been asked whether the British thrown silk was not sold at four months, with the discount of three per cent. for ready money, whilst Italian

678.

was

was sold at five months and two and a half?—No, we sell at five months, and allow three per cent., whereas the foreign is five months, allowing two and a half.

4573. Do the merchants take a guarantee for the security of their debts now as before?—Precisely the same.

4574. What is the per centage allowed to brokers?—Five-eighths.

4575. What for the guarantee?—We say such a man owes a good deal of money, and I should rather not sell him any more unless you will guarantee; he says, I will guarantee, and we allow him accordingly.

4576. Has any change taken place in that respect since 1826?—There has been no alteration in that respect that I know of.

4577. You do not mean to say that the guarantees have not been carried to a greater extent than formerly?—I cannot say, I am out of that line now.

4578. Is that system of guarantee a system you approve of?—I cannot say indeed.

4579. You avail yourselves of the custom?—Yes, occasionally.

4580. Do you, looking at your general business, do you guarantee those who consign goods to you on the sale?—Uniformly; they would not send silk to us without, to be sold on their credit; such an experiment was tried before my time, and it did not succeed; there were bad debts made, and the Italians will not send their silk here to come and look after it.

4581. What effect had the Berlin and Milan Decrees on the silk trade?—We had very little connexion with the Continent during that time; we had very little silk in our market in consequence, there was no Italian thrown silk to be got, and our manufacturers at the time were obliged to have recourse to any expedients to make a few goods, they even threw singles hard, wove and used them as warp, and tram they threw hard and used that as warp for the time; certainly those times were good for the throwster.

4582. Having been accustomed to depend on Italy for their organzine, and being deprived of that, they were reduced to considerable distress?—Yes, the manufacturers were.

4583. The price rose very much?—Yes, to 100 s. I believe.

4584. Was not there some smuggled through Holland?—Yes, it used to come in little bags, sometimes pushed into butter firkins and come as butter; it was not smuggled in here, but smuggled out of Holland, because they could not let us have it from Italy, owing to the Berlin and Milan Decrees.

4585. It was so scarce, was it not, as to influence the operations of trade?—Yes.

4586. All the operations used were not sufficient to supply the want of it?—No, there were not mills at that time sufficient, mills have much increased since that period, that gave a stimulus; there were enormous profits made at that time on the silk thrown in this country; my partners told me that in one year about that time, they got no profit as merchants, but that they cleared about 10,000 l. upon their British silks.

4587. Did the high price and the difficulty of getting silk, produce the effect of drawing more attention to the throwing?—I think it did, it gave a great stimulus.

4588. It increased the throwing of silk in this country?—Yes; and the high duty on organzines was another stimulus to induce persons to erect mills.

4589. If England were chiefly dependent on Italy for her supply of silk, would not an interruption of trade with the Continent cause much greater inconvenience to this country than if we threw the greater part ourselves?—There is no doubt of that; the consequence would of course be very serious, but if there were plenty of mills to throw organzines and every description of silk, the inconvenience would not be so much, there is always a great quantity of China and Bengal which can be substituted.

4590. The result of your long experience and extensive information is, that it is quite necessary for the prosperity of the silk manufacture of this country, that it should continue to protect its thrown silks?—Yes, I think it is.

4591. Was it not considered of so much consequence that Parliament voted Sir Thomas Lombe 14,000 l.?—Yes, that was before my time; I have the Evidence in my pocket of Mr. Pattison, the father of the highly gifted director of the East India Company.

4592. What, in your opinion, would be the most effectual remedy for the existing evils of the silk trade?—I am of the old school; I speak with the greatest sincerity from the conviction of my mind, that the only effectual remedy for the present

Mr.
*William Banbury.*

7 May,
1832.

present distress of the silk trade is to return to that state under which it so long flourished, prohibition and nothing but prohibition.

4593. Is not the exportation of raw silk from Piedmont prohibited?—Yes, it has been for many years.

4594. For what reason?—It was generally supposed that when Sir Thomas Lombe got the secret of throwing in this country, the King of Sardinia was so exasperated he prohibited the exportation of raw silks. In regard to the raw silks of Bergamo and Brescia, those countries were formerly under the government of the republic of Venice, and during that period we never saw any silks from those countries but organzines, as the raws were prohibited; but for the last thirty years there has been an immense quantity of those silks imported, and also Bolognas; those we never used to see but in the thrown state, they come now raw.

4595. To what is that to be attributed?—Because they (Bergamo and Brescia) are under the Austrian government now.

4596. Whatever was the cause of prohibition, the Piedmontese government have continued it?—Yes, I believe the Grand Duke of Tuscany.

4597. We get none of the finest of the raw silks from France or Piedmont?— No; France prohibits all silk, except manufactured, to be exported.

4598. Do you think it would be of any importance that the silk trade should be able to avail itself of the raw silk of France?—Yes.

4599. That would tend to equalize the prices?—Yes; as they have no vend for their silk to a foreign country, they depend entirely on their own manufacturers; when that manufacture is flat they must of course comparatively give it away, or sell it at very low prices.

4600. Therefore the French manufacturer is placed in a situation to undersell the English manufacturer who purchases from Italy now, Italy having three or four other markets?—Yes.

4601. You state that the only remedy is prohibition?—I think so.

4602. Have you considered well the effect of prohibition?—Yes, I have both considered it and felt it; the prohibitory law for silks and velvets passed in 1766, was tried as an experiment for five years, and at the end of those five years it had answered so well, that it was renewed every time it was about expiring, till Mr. Perceval's administration, when it was made perpetual without any question about its propriety and usefulness.

4603. Who was in administration at that time?—It was a Whig administration that gave us the prohibition, the Marquis of Rockingham.

4604. That was a very powerful administration?—Yes.

4605. England is a manufacturing commercial country, would you propose to extend prohibition to any other trade?—I cannot say, I want only the benefit I had when I was a youth.

4606. When silks sold for 32s. the duty and charges amounted to half of that? —Yes.

4607. Did you receive at that time your commission on the whole gross amount?—Yes, because we sold it, and paid all the charges and ran the risk.

4608. Every diminution of duty lessened your commission?—Yes; but I should not regard that if I saw the manufacture flourish.

4609. You think the manufacturer can flourish best with dear silk?—We did formerly well; under the duty of 14s. 7d. and 5s. 6d. trade was as prosperous as possible, I went on for ten years and never made a bad debt.

4610. You propose an increase of duty now?—I do not think an increase of duty would do any good, because they would smuggle in manufactured goods.

4611. What are your ideas about smuggling, if we prohibit the importation, should we be in danger of smuggling?—No, it was particularly mentioned by the Custom House officers, and people who were examined in 1765 and 1766, that the extension of duty would not prevent smuggling, and that nothing less than an absolute prohibition would.

4612. What do the Custom House officers say now?—I cannot say.

4613. Are you not aware that considerable smuggling takes place now?—Yes.

4614. What is the inducement to smuggling?—To get in their goods cheaper, I suppose.

4615. Can you state what is the charge for smuggling?—Not being engaged in that line I cannot say; I never had a transaction of the kind in my life.

4616. Do you not consider, that if French goods were prohibited now, there would be a considerable increase of smuggling?—No, I think not; I remember,

678. for

Mr.
*William Banbury,*

———

7 May,
1832.

for many years, during the prohibition, when the duty was very high, and I never heard any thing about smuggling.

4617. Goods may be admitted now at a duty of 25 or 40 per cent., and yet smuggling takes place, that must be because they get the goods cheaper?—Yes.

4618. If prohibition was to take place what do you conceive would be the effect?—Then the houses would be afraid to deal in prohibited articles, they could not keep them.

4619. There is much greater facility to smuggling now than under prohibition, in your opinion?—Certainly, no doubt there is; when the duty was 14 *s.* 8 *d.* on organzine silk I know there was a little smuggling of that article, it was too high, and had not the duty been lowered there would probably have been more smuggling in it; prohibited articles it is that people are afraid to deal in.

4620. You think, that if prohibition was to take place to-morrow our manufacturers would be better employed, trade would be improved, and no smuggling take place?—Exactly so.

4621. The goods smuggled are made of the finer qualities of French silk?—No doubt they use French silk.

4622. If there is at this moment a demand for those smuggled goods depending on their being of better quality, in the opinion of those who receive them, do you imagine, under the prohibitory system, you can manufacture those goods without having the raw material?—I apprehend, if the French discover any very material alteration or improvement, it is very likely we could get their goods over to see how they make them; and I think there is capital and ingenuity enough in this country to imitate them.

4623. Is it or not, in your estimation, in the power of this country to command the raw silk?—I do not know, we cannot interfere with other Governments to make them alter their laws.

4624. We cannot get the raw silk from France?—No.

4625. It is a manufactured article from France of a superior quality and fineness that takes in this market; if you cannot get the raw material to make them, and there is a prohibitory system, how can you meet the French manufacturer?—I do not know that there is any article for which Italian might not be substituted.

4626. You could make goods in this country from the Piedmont silk, or Italian silks imported, equal to those imported from France, which now command the market?—Yes; but they certainly have an advantage by growing the silk, and keeping it for their own use.

4627. You are of opinion, that Piedmont and Italian silks can be substituted for the French silk which we cannot obtain?—Yes; in my opinion.

4628. Do you mean to say, that the French manufacturers have a decided advantage over you in the quality of their silk, or is it more an advantage in price?—I do not know; some few years ago we had a vast deal of French silk over soon after the revolution, but I never saw any French silk that was better than some Italian.

4629. What advantage has the French manufacturer over the English?—I suppose because he prohibits the exportation of his raw silk, he must have it cheaper than we have it, as Italy is open to all the world.

4630. Is there any thing peculiar in the quality of the silk?—I do not know any thing peculiar in the quality of any silk, but that we can find something similar to it in Italian; a great quantity of it came here in the early part of the revolution.

4631. Had you an opportunity of examining it?—Yes, it was not well selected; it was not sent over so well sorted; and I said, at the time, these Frenchmen are an hundred years behind the Italians; the Italians are extremely neat in their packing, the French came higgledy piggledy, like a bundle of sticks almost.

4632. Were they smuggled?—No, they let them come out I believe at that time.

4633. Do any French silks come here now?—I have not seen them for some years.

4634. What was your opinion of its quality?—There are some of the Italian silks superior to any French I have ever seen.

4635. Have you ever been at Lyons?—Never, I have never been out of this country.

4636 You

Mr.
*William Banbury.*

7 May,
1832.

4636. You suppose the advantage the French manufacturer has, is in the cheapness of the article he uses?—Yes, certainly that is an advantage.

4637. Your opinion is founded upon your knowledge of the French silk which you saw introduced into this country, about forty years ago.

4638. Have you known from any late quotations, the price of French silk in that country?—No.

4639. Do not you think that these French silks are superior to some of the silks of Italy?—No, I think not; there is a new filature started on the Piedmontese principle at Naples, they send over a great deal of very excellent silk, which probably approximates more nearly to that of Piedmont.

4640. Have you ever known in this market thrown silk sold at less price than the raw silk?—I have.

4641. In what year was that?—That must have been before 1787 or 1790; at that time there was an immense demand for gauze made of raw silk; I think at that period there was not less than 1,500 to 2,000 bales a year used for gauze; when the muslins came into use, about the year 1788, that began to dwindle.

4642. Is the Italian silk thrown in England as well thrown as the thrown silk you have bought from Italy?—I think there are some mills in this country equal, if they had the raw material, to the Italian.

4643. Is Italian silk thrown in England as well thrown as that in Italy?—Yes, if the silk is similar, I think we can do it as well here as there; in Piedmont they do throw the silk most beautifully.

4644. What is the relative price of Italian and British thrown silk, both of the same material?—They must approximate pretty nearly to each other; if the manufacturer can buy good English thrown silk at eighteen-pence less than the Italian, he will buy it, and *vice versâ*.

4645. Is there is any difference in the goodness of the thread in our own thrown?—I think that we clean their silks in our mills better than the Milan or Bergamo people do at theirs.

4646. Has the thrown silk much improved, or deteriorated, in your opinion?—I think it has improved, but Mr. Pattison had a beautiful mill at Congleton, and he used to work Fossembrone silk, he used to send it out as Bologna; I recollect when that silk would fetch eighteen-pence a pound more than the best Piedmont of the same size.

4647. How many years ago?—Forty years ago.

4648. You mean to say we have been able for forty years to throw as well as the Italians?—Mr. Pattison could; but forty years ago we could not get the Bergamo or the Bolognas in the raw state.

4649. Are the Committee to understand, that since 1824, any decided improvement in the throwing of silk has taken place?—Two or three mills have got a great credit, Mr. Brawns at Colchester for instance; but his is on the principle of Mr. Cortauld and Mr. Royle of Manchester; there are excellent mills in the West of England; if you give them a good raw silk they do as well as possible.

4650. Has there been a considerable improvement in the throwing of silk since 1824?—No, I do not think there has been a considerable improvement; there was never any better thrown silk than Mr. Pattison's.

4651. Has Bengal silk improved in quality since 1824?—No, nor never since I have been in business. I believe they began to reel it after the Italian fashion about the year 1770. I have known it well since the year 1780; I have heard it said there was never any better silk than Mr. Weiss first sent to this country; he was sent over by the Company to establish their filatures, and I do not think they have at all improved since that time.

4652. Has China silk improved in quality since 1824?—We have had a good deal more of the fine qualities, there are very nice silks among them.

4653. It appears that in the years 1823 and 1824 the amount of waste imported was between fifty and eighty thousand pounds weight, and now it amounts to 752,000 pounds; do you know to what particular manufacture that is applied?—I am not very well acquainted with that article, I understand a good deal of it is exported now; we sell a little now and then.

4654. Is it exported in the thrown state?—It is carded and spun like cotton.

4655. With respect to the cheapness of silk in France, do you mean that they have their raw silk cheaper, in consequence of the prohibition of the export of that article?—I have no doubt of that.

4656. You think that they have raw silk cheaper in France than they have in Italy or in England?—I should think at times they have; generally I should say.

4657. Have you any doubt about that?—No, I have not.

4658. Would your observation apply to thrown, as well as to raw silk?—Yes.

---

*Mercurii, 9° die Maii,* 1832.

## EDWARD AYSHFORD SANFORD, ESQUIRE, in the Chair.

---

Mr. *Thomas Willmott,* called in; and Examined.

4659. HOW long have you been engaged in the silk trade?—I have been 32 years engaged in it.

4660. Where?—At Sherborne in Dorsetshire.

4661. Do you throw Italian silks?—Principally; I throw Italian silks, trams and organzines; my mills are principally calculated for throwing such descriptions of silks.

4662. Do you throw those silks on your own account?—No, I throw them on commission.

4663. When were the mills erected, and what is their power?—One of my mills was erected about 80 years ago, two others were erected 18 or 20 years ago; the power is water.

4664. Are there any other mills in your town?—There is one other mill, formerly employed in throwing organzines and trams, but which has been discontinued, in consequence, as I suppose, of the low and ruinous prices of throwing silk.

4665. What was the condition of the silk trade in that neighbourhood before 1826?—The throwster was constantly employed, and at prices by which he could live himself as well as his hands.

4666. What number of spindles had you then at work?—About 8,000.

4667. How many work people did you then employ?—About 600.

4668. How many spindles have you now at work?—Not more than 3,000.

4669. How many people do you now employ?—Not more than 150.

4670. Has this decrease in the number of spindles and hands been of long duration?—Yes, I have been gradually decreasing the number both of spindles and hands since 1829.

4671. What was the cause of your thus decreasing them?—I found it difficult, if not impossible, to obtain as formerly, a regular supply of silk, and the prices of throwing became so low as to leave me no profit.

4672. Have the poor rates in your parish increased in consequence of the want of employment?—Yes; the poor rates within a few years have increased in the parish of Sherborne about 1,000 *l.* per annum.

4673. What were they before, and what are they now?—In the year ending at Easter 1825, they were 1,590 *l.* In the year ending at Easter 1831, they were 2,340 *l.* In the year ending at Easter 1832, they were about 2,450 *l.*

4674. Have you the other years?—I have some.

4675. What was the year 1821?—One thousand seven hundred and thirty pounds. I have an account from the year 1816.

4676. How did you become possessed of that account?—From the vestry clerk of Sherborne.

4677. Did you see the extracts made?—No, I did not see the extracts made, but they came from him.

4678. You are a rate-payer in the parish?—I am.

4679. That consists, with your own knowledge, of the facts?—Yes.

[*The Witness delivered in the same, which was read, as follows:*]

AMOUNT

Mr. *Thomas Willmott.*

9 May, 1832.

AMOUNT of ASSESSMENTS for POORS' RATE, for *Sherborne.*

| | £. | s. | d. | | £. | s. | d. |
|---|---|---|---|---|---|---|---|
| For the year ending 25 March 1816 - | 1,439 | 4 | – | For the year ending 25 March 1825 - | 1,597 | 5 | 6 ¾ |
| — 1817 - - | 1,711 | 6 | 11 | — 1826 - - | 1,726 | 2 | 9 ½ |
| — 1818 - - | 1,973 | 2 | 7 | — 1827 - - | 1,825 | 13 | 2 ¼ |
| — 1819 - - | 1,779 | 17 | 8 ¾ | — 1828 - - | 1,766 | 6 | 9 ¼ |
| — 1820 - - | 1,706 | 9 | 6 ¼ | — 1829 - - | 1,760 | 6 | 4 |
| — 1821 - - | 1,729 | 19 | 8 ¾ | — 1830 - - | 2,108 | 7 | 9 ½ |
| — 1822 - - | 1,616 | 1 | 7 ¼ | — 1831 - - | 2,359 | 18 | 8 ½ |
| — 1823 - - | 1,448 | 6 | 6 ¾ | — 1832 - - | 2,450 | – | – |
| — 1824 - - | 1,575 | 9 | 11 ¼ | | | | |

4680. What is the population of the parish?—I believe nearly 4,000.

4681. What increase has there been in the population?—No very material increase; I speak at random, but I do not suppose the increase was 300 in the 20 years.

4682. Were all the people you employed belonging to the parish?—No, not half of them belong to Sherborne.

4683. Are you aware whether the people employed in the other mills which have been shut up, belonged to the parish?—A great many of them, some of them from the surrounding country.

4684. Are the persons you now employ inhabitants of your parish?—Mostly.

4685. Have you reduced the wages of your work people as well as diminished their number?—Yes, I have been compelled to reduce their wages, something more than 30 per cent.

4686. Since what period, have you made the reduction of 30 per cent.?—Principally since 1829.

4687. What was the average of your wages in 1829; were your work people divided into classes?—Children and grown women.

4688. Will you state the rates of the women and the children?—Our payments have been 5*s.* per week for that class of girls we call mill hands.

4689. How many hours per day?—Our people work about ten hours and a half.

4690. What do the common hands receive?—Gradually diminishing to 1*s.* 3*d.* and down to 1*s.* for the young children.

4691. What do you pay to the same description of hands now?—The reduction of wages bears no proportion to the reduction of the price of throwing, it was impossible to reduce the wages of our hands in an equal degree to the reduction of the price of throwing.

4692. Have the goodness to state in what way wages are reduced 30 per cent.?—The mill hands at present are paid 4*s.* 6*d.* there has been a reduction of 6*d.* upon them.

4693. How long do they work now?—The same hours.

4694. Do they do more work now in those hours?—No, the average that I speak of is taken upon the aggregate of wages, women and children.

4695. How long do you pay the others, or on what class is there the greatest reduction?—That is the greatest reduction per cent.; the way in which I have taken the average has been by taking the amount for a certain quantity for six months.

4696. Do any receive under 1*s.* a week?—No; but I include in wages that which I pay for winding silk on which there is a very great reduction.

4697. That comes also into the throwing department?—Yes.

4698. How much a pound did you pay in 1829 for winding?—For fine silks as much as 2*s.* 3*d.*

4699. What do you pay now?—One shilling.

4700. Did you include the winding in the 600 you mentioned?—Yes.

4701. What proportion were employed upon that?—I suppose 400.

4702. Then there were two-thirds winders, and one-third for your mills?—Yes.

4703. That you say was for the finest silk?—Yes.

4704. What was paid for the average of silk?—Two shillings.

4705. What is the average now?—For any silk we give out we give but 1*s.*



4706. How

Mr.
*Thomas Willmott.*

———

9 May,
1832.

4706. How much a week can a good hand wind?—I will explain why it is impossible to give a definite answer to that question. Here is a mother with a family, takes silk to her own home, if her children are ill she cannot do so much.

4707. How much can a girl wind per week?—That depends upon the quality of the silk; it depends first, upon the length of time she devotes to it, which being a domestic employment may be uncertain.

4708. Supposing a hand employed at home in winding silk, and her attention not distracted, how many pounds per week would she wind?—I should think from two pounds and a half to three pounds per week, according to the quality of the silk. I have taken the average in this way, the total amount paid for six months in 1831, and then I have taken the last six months.

4709. You do not mean to say, that a person earned only a shilling a week in winding?—Certainly not; I said that it of course depended upon circumstances, such as whether there was a family in the way, or illness.

4710. You mean to say, that they now earn 1 s. per lb. for winding silk, and that they wind 2½ lbs. of that silk per week?—Yes.

4711. You mean to say, that they earn 2 s. 3 d. a pound for winding silk, and that they can then wind off the same quantity?—Yes; but the 2 s. 3 d. was for the finer silks, the average was about 2 s.

4712. The people you employ are divided into two classes, the people in the mill and the winders?—Yes.

4713. Which of them are the most skilful; the people in the mill are the best workpeople, are they not?—They are the most important.

4714. The winding is done in their own houses?—Principally.

4715. Those persons have other employment to attend to besides silk winding, have they not?—Certainly, agricultural employment; they are not confined to us; they are not under any engagement.

4716. The sum they would earn per week would be the same probably they would earn in other employments?—That I cannot say.

4717. When there is other employment, they will not work for you, if they can obtain higher wages at other employments?—Of course not.

4718. Supposing they were not employed in the silk trade, is there any other employment in that neighbourhood to which they could apply themselves?—They lie under the same state of distress as the glovers do; there is a great deal of gloving in our neighbourhood, but they are reduced nearly in the same proportion.

4719. What kind of silk do you principally work upon?—Principally Italian tram and organzine.

4720. Do you undertake to say, that there is a want of employment in other lines, and that the wages of labour are lowered?—There is a very great want of employment, and the wages are lowered.

4721. You have an account of the wages you have paid of late, and you have compared it with what you have paid before, and there has been, you say, a reduction of at least 30 per cent. in the wages according to your calculation, is that so?—Yes.

4722. You are quite confident that the reduction, looking at the whole of the persons employed by you, is to the extent of 30 per cent.?—Certainly.

4723. Is there less employment than there used to be?—Yes.

4724. That, in your business as well as in the glovers and others, has occasioned a great increase of the poor rate?—Yes, certainly. I stated just now that whereas I used to employ 600 hands, I have employed only about one-fourth part of that number lately.

4725. To what do you attribute this loss of trade and depression?—To the introduction of foreign thrown silks; to the introduction of manufactured silks, which both oppress the throwster and the manufacturer, from having goods brought in, the manufacturer has less demand for manufactures, and the throwster has again to compete with the introduction of the foreign silks.

4726. Is there not a greater quantity of the coarser silks now used than there used to be?—I am not competent to speak upon the application of the silks to the manufacturers' purposes.

4727. You happen to know, probably, that the coarse silks require less labour than the fine silks?—Certainly.

4728. Should there be a decrease in the finer silks, and an increase in the coarser, that would of course lessen labour?—The purposes for which the fine

silk,

Mr.
*Thomas Willmott.*

9 May,
1832.

silk, and the purposes for which the coarse silks are used, are so different that one cannot be substituted for the other in the employment of my machinery.

4729. The coarse silks would require less labour than the fine?—Certainly.

4730. They would not employ so many hands?—Certainly not.

4731. Are there not as many fine silks thrown in this country as formerly?—I suppose there are, when the mills are in a state of activity.

4732. Are there not as many imported now as formerly?—I am quite unconnected with the import; I cannot speak to that.

4733. Up to 1826 was there not a gradual increase in the consumption of the finer silks?—There was an increase in the quantity which we were called upon to throw.

4734. You found a gradual increase up to that time?—Up to 1826.

4735. From the year 1815 up to the year 1826, you found a gradual increase of your trade?—Yes, with very little exception, arising from temporary causes, momentary depressions.

4736. Since that period you have found a decrease?—Yes, a very material one.

4737. What do you think would relieve the throwing trade from its present difficulties?—Government affording us the same protection, or something like the protection it used to do, probably a return to the duties of 1826.

4738. The duties of 5 s. and 3 s.?—Yes.

4739. What do you think would be the consequence of lowering the present duties?—I have no hesitation in answering that, the total ruin of the throwster without any relief to the manufacturer; I consider that such a measure would be a total destruction of my property, vested in buildings, machinery, and so on; and the still further pauperizing of the already poor people I employ, and in fact ruin of the English throwsters altogether.

4740. Did not the reduction of the duty from 5 s. 6 d. to 3 s. 6 d. cause a reduction of profits and labour to that extent?—Yes; the prices of throwing were lowered in proportion.

4741. Of course that must fall, either upon the manufacturer or his labourers, or upon them together?—Yes; when the term manufacturer is used, I suppose it refers to the throwster.

4742. A reduction from 5 s. 6 d. to 3 s. 6 d. must cause an equal reduction either in the profits of the throwster, or his labourer, or the two together?—Yes.

4743. You say your trade has diminished in the fine goods, but independently of that, was not that reduction in wages a great loss, and did it not cause great distress in the trade?—Very great distress among the poor people.

4744. You now complain that with the duty of 3 s. 6 d. you have not an adequate protection, so as to enable you to give fair wages and to pursue your trade with a fair profit?—It is not sufficient, it does not enable us to give remunerating wages to our work people.

4745. You have just stated, that since 1829, there has been a reduction in the wages of 30 per cent., has there within that same period been a similar reduction in agricultural and other branches of labour?—I am not in possession of sufficient data to speak positively to that.

4746. Do you believe there has been anything like a reduction of 30 per cent. in the wages of agricultural labour?—I think it is probable, but I cannot speak decidedly to that.

4747. You have said that on the reduction of the duty from 5 s. to 3 s. 6 d. the working classes have been reduced to distress; are the Committee to understand that since 1826 the wages have been bad the whole of the time?—The trade, I apprehend, has been gradually getting worse since 1826; but in 1829, the period when a further reduction took place, our distress increased in proportion, we were deprived of the fair remunerating prices we used to have.

4748. The question before asked was, whether on a reduction of duty in 1826, a reduction of wages took place; you say the distress of the poorer classes took place from that time, has that distress continued all that time?—It increased materially in 1829.

4749. After the duty was reduced in 1826, what was the effect?—In 1826, when the duties were reduced there was a corresponding lowering of our prices of throwing, consequently a gradual reduction in our wages.

4750. Do you mean to say that the throwing trade has been bad since 1826?—Yes.

678.

4751. Who

4751. Who used to supply you with goods, did you throw on your own account or obtain the silk from others?—Italian silks I always have thrown on commission.

4752. From whence were those silks sent you?—From different houses, either silk men or manufacturers.

4753. Where were they situate?—My principal house has been for many years the house of Vere & Company, in London.

4754. What are the expenses of carrying the silk backwards and forwards, from the time the raw silk leaves the house of Vere, until you return it thrown to Messrs. Vere again?—That would require me to go into so minute and elaborate a calculation, I do not know how to answer the question at the moment.

4755. Are you aware that other mills have been erected since that time, and that they may have been more convenient in point of situation for the throwing than yours?—I never found that our distance was considered a disadvantage on the part of our friends who sent us the silk.

4756. At what time was the machinery in your mills erected?—In one, eighty years ago.

4757. Does that mill contain all the late improvements in throwing?—The mills have been gradually, from time to time altered, so as to suit the improvements whenever any improvement has taken place.

4758. How many revolutions in a minute do your spindles perform?—Really I cannot say.

4759. One thousand five hundred or 3,000?—Not so many as 3,000 I should think, but I really cannot answer the question.

4760. Are you aware what is the greatest number of revolutions performed by any of the lately erected mills in England?—I am not.

4761. Are you aware of the quantity they will perform in the same time, and whether they can throw a greater quantity in the same time than you?—Not materially, I believe.

4762. You are not aware whether your loss of trade has been owing to others doing the throwing cheaper than you?—Certainly not.

4763. Do you suppose that less silk has been thrown in England since 1826 than formerly, because you have thrown less?—I cannot speak precisely to that point.

4764. Do you conceive less is thrown in England, or that it has changed hands?—I have no reason to suppose that it has materially changed hands, houses that used to give me large quantities of silk per week have ceased to do so, my services are not wanted by them.

4765. Are the Committee to conclude that you conceive there has been less manufactured of later years because you have had less to do?—Yes.

4766. There have been some new mills erected of late years, if the quantity were not increased they could not be all employed in the same manner as the smaller number had been employed before, it is possible therefore, is it not, that some of the new mills have taken part of that employment you used to receive?—Yes; but still other mills may be in a state of distress, if there has been an increase in the demand for thrown silks those additional mills would not account for the depression of the throwsters.

4767. Will you explain your own view of the cause of the depression?—I view it as connected with the importation of foreign thrown silks and of foreign manufactured silks; that we were placed beween two fires.

4768. Are you aware that since 1826 there has been more silk thrown in England?—I think it is possible; I am not in possession of any fact to know that it is so.

4769. Have you ever seen any of the new throwing mills?—Yes, I have, at Congleton.

4770. Have you seen those in Reading?—No; but I believe in the West and the South our mills, generally speaking, are as well appointed as most others, I have not seen any of late years.

4771. Have you, within the last ten years, visited any of those erected at Congleton and Manchester?—No.

4772. Do you believe that any have been erected on a construction superior to your own?—There may be improvements, but I conceive not essentially.

4773. The speed may have been increased?—Yes.

4774. Do

Mr.
*Thomas Willmott.*

9 May,
1832.

4774. Do you conceive the speed may have been increased without injury to the silk?—It is possible.

4775. Are you to be understood to say, that the throwing trade in the West of England has been getting considerably worse since 1826?—Yes, gradually.

4776. That it was better before 1826 than it is now?—Yes, certainly.

4777. When you allude to 1826, you refer to the introduction of thrown silk, by the lowering the duty in the July of that year?—Yes, I allude generally to that period, as marking it by the alteration of the duty.

4778. Do you mean to state that the throwing trade was good in the winter of 1825, and the spring of 1826?—In 1825 it was getting worse, but we did not feel it so much, because perhaps at the time the alteration took place, my warehouse perhaps was full of silk; I had a stock in hand that would have carried me through the winter of 1825.

4779. You did not petition the House of Commons in the spring of 1826 on the distress of the trade?—I do not recollect that I did.

4780. You have stated, that up to 1826 there was an increase in the throwing trade?—When I referred to 1826, I meant as marking the time of the alteration of the duties.

4781. There have been of course intervals of distress, but independently of those, you are understood to say that the trade up to 1826 was an increasing and prosperous trade?—Yes, I considered it so.

4782. All this was done under the high duties on the raw material?—It was.

4783. Were not you taught to expect that the duty being taken off the raw silk would give an increase of trade to the throwster?—That idea was held out, but that was never realized.

4784. After that period, you say there was a reduction of your profits and wages?—Yes.

4785. Were not you after the taking off those duties, led to expect that there would be a great increase in the trade?—I do not recollect.

4786. Do you believe that if it were not for those laws, the trade would have continued to have increased as it had before done to 1826?—I think it would.

4787. Have you any doubt of that?—I have no doubt of it, because of the vast increase of consumption in silks as an article of dress.

4788. You have been asked how you could account for the depression, did you not charge 5s. 6d. for throwing at one time?—Yes.

4789. What do you charge for throwing now?—Two shillings and nine-pence for the same article; just half.

4790. Do you mean that you would restore the duty on the raw material?—I am of Mr. Banbury's opinion, that when the trade was the most taxed, it was the most flourishing.

4791. Therefore you would restore the duties to enable the throwster to revive the trade?—I should have no objection to it as a throwster.

4792. When you speak of 2s. 9d., do you mean for tram, or for organzine?—For tram.

4793. How much for organzine?—Three shillings and nine-pence, and four shillings.

4794. You are understood to state that your trade of a throwster is very materially injured, and that at this moment you throw at 2s. 9d., whereas you used formerly to throw at 5s 6d.; and by way of improving that trade, that you would increase the price of the raw material?—Then there would be a corresponding duty upon the thrown silk; place us in the same situation as we were before Government interfered, and that would satisfy us.

4795. You stated that by a return to the duties of 2s. 6d., and 5s., and 3s., there would be a protection to yourself?—That we might live.

4796. Do you mean that without enacting a prohibition against the importation of manufactured silks, or do you include a prohibition of the importation of manufactured fine silks?—The prohibition would prevent smuggling, as was stated.

4797. You include in your view of return to the state before 1826, also a return to the prohibitory system of importation of manufactured silks?—Yes, I think that would place us in a state of prosperity.

4798. Do you conceive that with the taste for the finer quality of silks of France, you can by any prohibitory laws prevent their introduction?—The introduction of manufactured silks, so far as I can understand it, would be prevented, because they dare not be exhibited.

678.                                                                          4799. You

Mr.
*Thomas Willmott.*

9 May,
1832.

4799. You think that smuggling would not increase under a prohibitory system? —No, I should think not.

4800. Are the Committee to understand, that it is your opinion, the increase of poor rates has arisen from the decrease of employment in the silk mills?—Certainly.

4801. Were there any other trades carried on at Sherborne, were not gloves manufactured, and were not silk shirt buttons manufactured?—No; gloving was like the winding of silk, given out; there is no establishment of the kind, of a glover, in the town; but at Yeovil, and at Milborne Port, there are a great number, so that they are sent over.

4802. In 1826 and 1827, were there any great number of people employed in sewing gloves?—Not in Sherborne, in fact nothing beyond a few straggling hands; because frequently some connexion of one family to another at Yeovil might occasion some work.

4803. Are the people employed in the glove trade now as they were before?— Certainly not.

4804. Was there any other employment for them at Sherborne?—Not in my recollection. With respect to the duties, I think that I ought to state, as a country throwster, I am not prepared on the spur of the moment to give an opinion upon it, it not being a thing which comes under our observation.

## Mr. *Thomas Field Gibson*, called in; and Examined.

Mr.
*T. F. Gibson.*

4805. HOW long have you been a silk manufacturer?—I have known the trade ten years.

4806. How long have you been employed in it connected with the trade?— I have been employed as a manufacturer ten years, with the exception of one year, when I was not manufacturing.

4807. In what branches, and where, do you now carry on your manufacture? —In Spitalfields, in the broad silk trade.

4808. How has the alteration of duties in 1826 affected the trade of Spital-fields, in your opinion?—I think the reduction of duties on raw and thrown silk has had a very beneficial effect, and the admission of French goods has certainly not been advantageous to the trade.

4809. Do you mean, that the reduction of duties has been advantageous to the manufacturer by his obtaining the material cheaper, or in what other way?—Prin-cipally by his obtaining it cheaper.

4810. What kinds of silk are principally used in the Spitalfields manufacture? —The largest quantity used is Italian silk.

4811. Are the Committee to understand, that the finest kinds of plain goods are manufactured in Spitalfields?—Yes.

4812. Are there any other parts of the country where goods of the same de-scription are made?—Various other parts.

4813. What are the principal parts?—In Lancashire the trade is most ex-tensive.

4814. As the principal part of the silk you use is Italian silk, the reduction of duty which has taken place has enabled you to obtain it cheaper?—Very much cheaper.

4815. It is in that way you think the change of the duties has done your ma-nufacture good?—We have been enabled to manufacture goods at a much cheaper rate and have brought them within a much larger range of consumers.

4816. Has of late years the competition between the Lancashire and Spitalfields manufacturers increased?—Very greatly of late years.

4817. What has been the effect of that competition on the goods and on the profits of the master manufacturers in Spitalfields?—The effect of the competition on the labouring class of people has been to reduce their wages very materially, the competition with the master manufacturers has had the effect of diminishing their profits.

4818. In Spitalfields at present are you aware that there are any fixed rates of wages for any particular branches, or is that open?—It is entirely open.

4819. Is there no fixed rate for velvets?—Not fixed by law.

4820. Is there any fixed by the masters and the workmen under them, are there any exceptions to the rule?—The rate of wages is entirely open to mutual agreement between the masters and the labourers.

4821. There

Mr.
T. F. Gibson.

9 May,
1832.

4821. There is no general conventional agreement ?—There is a conventional agreement, but it is entirely unrestricted by law.

4822. There is no list similar to that which formerly existed ?—No.

4823. The manufacture of velvets is confined to Spitalfields, is it not ?—Entirely.

4824. Is the manufacture of satins ?—Principally.

4825. What was the book price for weaving velvets ?—That varied according to the quality, from 4 s. 6 d. to 5 s.

4826. What is it now ?—It varies now from 3 s. to 4 s.

4827. Can you state the proportions of the different kinds of silks which are used in Spitalfields, Italian, China and Bengal ?—I should say about two-thirds of Italian and one-third of the others, but this is quite a vague statement.

4828. Every reduction of the amount of duty in Italian silk must benefit the manufactures of Spitalfields ?—I consider so.

4829. If the duty of 3 s. 6 d., which now exists, was taken off, you, as a manufacturer, would consider yourself likely to be benefited ?—Looking at my competition with the foreigner.

4830. The question was asked, supposing you had competition with the French manufacturer in the goods you make ?—Certainly.

4831. Have you any means of judging of the quality and prices of the goods made by you in Spitalfields as compared with goods of the same kind made in France ?—I see the goods occasionally that come from France.

4832. You have stated that the profits of the master have been reduced, do you attribute that reduction in the profits to the competition with the French manufacturer entirely or conjointly with the competition you have met with from Lancashire ?—I think conjointly with the competition from other parts of the country.

4833. Are you able to give an opinion as to the proportion of that reduction arising from one cause and the other ?—I should say that the competition at home was the most important.

4834. Have you ever calculated the increase per cent. on the value of goods which the duty of 3 s. 6 d. now adds ?—Yes, I have; and I marked it to be between eight and nine per cent.

4835. That is to say the organzine silk you use, being subject to 3 s. 6 d. duty, adds eight or nine per cent. to the value of the goods you turn out ?—Yes.

4836. A reduction of the duty would lower the price of goods to that amount ?—Provided the price of the silk were reduced to that amount.

4837. What do you think will be the effect on the price of silk if that duty were taken off ?—I think the great effect would be, to equalize the prices in this market and the foreign market.

4838. Do you mean to put the manufacturers upon the same footing ?—Yes.

4839. Do you mean to say, that at the present moment you are not on an equal footing with the manufacturer abroad, in the prices of silk ?—Certainly not.

4840. Is it to the extent only of the duty, or is there any other cause ?—There are other causes.

4841. Wherein is the manufacturer differently situated ?—The French have a very important advantage, in being large growers of raw silk, by which they are able to supply themselves much better than we who are limited to the Italian market, the trade of France has been of much longer standing than the trade in this country; it has been more fostered by government, and the climate is more favourable to it, and all the operations of the manufacture are cheaper in consequence of the cheaper rate of labour in France than in England. All those are advantages the French manufacturers possess.

4842. Are you able to state, what are the wages which you consider to afford an advantage in France as compared with those in England ?—The price of dyeing is lower, the price of weaving is somewhat lower.

4843. Can you state the price of dyeing there, and the price of dyeing here, of your own knowledge ?—Only from what I have learnt from dyers; the last account I got was a difference of 10 per cent.

4844. All colours, or only one colour ?—All colours. In weaving, the present tariff is very nearly the same as our actual prices of weaving plain goods; but I believe it is ascertained that the tariff is not adhered to.

4845. The weaver winds his own shute, does he not ?—Yes.

4846. Will you state the price as now fixed at Lyons and here for weaving the

same

Mr.
T. F. Gibson.

9 May,
1832.

same articles?—The price of weaving three single or three double gros de Naples by the tariff, is precisely the same there as in England.

4847. Assuming that the tariff is adhered to the prices would be equal?—Yes.

4848. What is your opinion of the quality of English thrown silk as compared with the Italian thrown silk imported?—I am of opinion that there is as good thrown silk produced from English mills as can be imported from Italy.

4849. Has the quality of the Italian thrown silk improved of late years, or not? —Decidedly not, in my own experience.

4850. Has the quality of English thrown silk improved?—The operation of throwing has been improved within the last five or six years.

4851. Is the quality of raw silk imported better now than formerly?—Yes.

4852. Therefore you are able to make a better thrown silk?—Yes.

4853. What is the quality of silk imported from Italy here?—We have some of all descriptions.

4854. Which are the best, the raws or the thrown?—We have the best raws and the best throwns from Italy; and we have the worst raws and the worst thrown.

4855. Have you ever been in Italy?—I have been there.

4856. Have you attended to throwing silk?—I have been in many mills.

4857. Have you ever superintended the throwing it there?—No, I have not.

4858. Are you able to state what the expense of throwing there is as compared with the expense of throwing here?—The cost of throwing organzine in Lombardy was 2s. 6d. per lb. three years ago when I was there.

4859. Does that include the waste?—No, that would be 6d. more, making 3s.; from the best kinds of raw silk.

4860. Have you any throwing mills in England?—Yes; I am interested in a throwing mill here.

4861. Can you state what the expense of throwing here is?—The actual price of throwing organzines in this country, of the same quality now, is about 4s.

4862. Do you mean, in speaking of 4s. that that is the actual cost?—That is the actual price. I speak of the *actual* price in Italy, and the *actual* price in England.

4863. Is that your cost for throwing?—It would be difficult to state what the cost is.

4864. Treating it as a question of price in both instances?—Yes.

4865. Do you throw for any other persons?—No.

4866. If you threw for others should you receive 4s.?—I should be very sorry to throw for 4s.; but I am afraid I could not get more.

4867. Is that a losing or a gaining price?—It would be a losing price to me.

4868. Are you aware whether it has been done for less?—It certainly has.

4869. Do you include in the 4s. waste?—That would depend upon the kind of silk.

4870. What addition would that be?—Perhaps 9d.

4871. Do you mean that the difference is between 3s. in Italy, and 4s. 9d. here?—Yes.

4872. Why should the waste here be 9d. and in Italy 6d.?—Because the waste made from silk thrown immediately is much less than it is after it has been kept long.

4873. The result is, that the price is 3s., including waste in Italy, and 4s. 9d., including waste in this country?—Yes.

4874. You do not know whether it pays in Italy or not?—I do not, but it is an established price.

4875. It does not pay here?—I should be sorry to throw for this price.

4876. And yet others do throw it?—Yes, they do.

4877. How do you account for that?—Because they would rather throw it than shut up their mills, and wages are lower in some places than in others.

4878. If the duty was entirely thrown off must not the consequence be, that they must shut up their mills?—No, I think not.

4879. At present they cannot obtain more than 4s., and they cannot afford to throw it at less, how would they be able to carry on their business if the 3s. 6d. duty was taken off foreign thrown?—The question would take for granted, that there would be a much greater import of foreign thrown silks.

4880. You are understood to say, that the price now of throwing silk here is 4s., and that you should be sorry to do it for that; you consider that a losing price,

Mr.
T. F. Gibson.

9 May,
1832.

price, though there are some individuals who, rather than shut up their mills, do throw for less ?—Yes.

4881. If that be their present condition, that they are throwing silk at less than they can afford to do it, how would they be able to conduct their business, if the 3 s. 6 d. was taken off foreign thrown ?—They would conduct it as they do now.

4882. They must either go on at a loss or shut up their mills ?—Yes, unless they can get a better price.

4883. Are they likely to get a better price when 3 s. 6 d. is taken off the thrown, than when 3 s. 6 d. is paid ?—I think it probable they may, in altered circumstances of the trade.

4884. Is it your opinion that the price of Italian silk regulates the price o English silk, or that the price of the English thrown silk regulates the price of the Italian ?—I conceive that the price of the English thrown silk regulates the price of the Italian. With regard to the profit of throwing at 4 s., I speak of my own experience at my own mills; there are mills at which the wages have been latterly extremely reduced in amount, as has been stated before this Committee; the persons who employ hands at lower wages, are much more able to work at 4 s. than I am.

4885. How do you explain to the Committee the opinion you have given, that the price of silk in this country regulates the price in Italy ?—I think that the very much greater quantity of English than of foreign thrown silk will regulate the market price; the large amount of silk used in this country being thrown in England, will regulate the amount of the smaller quantity imported from Italy.

4886. Is it your opinion that a reduction of the duty heretofore on organzine silk has led to an increase of import or not ?—The facts do not show that it has.

4887. Is it your opinion, that if the duty was taken off organzine silk, we should have a larger quantity of organzine thrown ?—Yes, I think we should have a larger quantity, but not to an important amount.

4888. If hitherto the reduction of the duty has not led to any great increase, what reason have you for supposing that a still further reduction of duty would lead to any increase ?—I have no reason to suppose it.

4889. As you have stated that silk can be thrown at 3 s., including the waste in Italy, and it is 4 s. 9 d. in this country, on what do you found that opinion that there would not be a very large increase of Italian thrown silk imported, in case of the duty being removed ?—Because there are other markets for Italian thrown silk, which already take off a great quantity of it, and would continue to take off the same quantity.

4890. Have not the Italians the means of throwing at least double the quantity they now do ?—I am not aware of that.

4891. Have they not it in their power to throw every pound they grow ?—Certainly not.

4892. Is it your opinion, from what you observed on the spot, that they have the power of doubling, or increasing, even to any considerable extent, the quantity they now throw ?—They could certainly increase the quantity, but not rapidly, nor to any considerable extent.

4893, Are you aware that for the last two years, the difference of price between raw and thrown in this country, has not afforded to the foreign throwster there, any thing whatever for throwing ?—It would appear from the prices of thrown silk, that he has obtained a very small amount.

4894. What is the difference you have made between the raw and the thrown the two last years; what has been left for the throwster ?—It is very difficult to state averages, they must depend so much on the different qualities of silk; I have seen averages lately, and have seen that they do not at all correspond one with another; but the difference has not been equivalent to the cost of throwing in Italy, added to the charges made by the merchant here.

4895. Are you aware whether the difference, deducting the duty between the thrown and the raw, has been more than from 2 s. to 4 s. a lb. ?—No, I should think not.

4896. You have stated that the expense of throwing in Italy, including waste, is 3 s.; it has been stated, that the expense of transport would be about 3 s. 11 d. per lb., making the two together 6 s. 11 d.; do you conceive that all the difference between the raw and the thrown, below that sum, is a loss to the throwster ?—If the statement made with regard to the 3 s. 11 d. be correct, it must be so.

678.

4897. Do

4897. Do you expect that the Italians will continue to send their silk here unless they receive a fair return for the labour in throwing?—I should conceive not.

4898. Is it your opinion from that, that if those relative prices of raw and thrown continue, the quantity of thrown will be diminished?—That it will not increase and would diminish either in quantity or quality.

4899. You have employed people in Italy, have you not?—Yes, in reeling silk.

4900. What wages did you pay there?—They varied very greatly; the wages obtained in Italy during the reeling season are no criterion for the general wages of the country.

4901. What does a woman earn per day at reeling in Italy?—The women were receiving 10 d. per day.

4902. Did they earn that during the reeling season?—Yes; girls of fourteen to fifteen, and women.

4903. In the winter time wages are lower?—Very much lower.

4904. It is in the winter time they throw the silk principally?—Yes.

4905. At what time is the reeling?—In the summer and autumn.

4906. Then the silk would be in the hands of the English throwster here as soon as it would be in the hands of the Italian throwster, would it not?—No, there must intervene the time of transport and sale.

4907. He does not throw his silk till the wages are low?—He cannot throw his silk during the time of its being reeled, but he may begin immediately afterwards.

4908. The reeling and throwing would then go on together, the early produce might be in the course of being thrown, while the latter would be reeling?—The advantage of winding silk immediately after it is reeled is so great that those reelers who have large filatures and are throwsters likewise, wind the silk immediately and keep it on bobbins till they want to throw it.

4909. When you state that the price of throwing silk in Italy is 3 s. a pound, you do not mean that they pay 10 d. a day wages to the women?—No.

4910. What do they then pay?—I have no means of stating that.

4911. On what ground do you state that the price of throwing is 3 s.?—That is the market price.

4912. Do you mean that the difference between raw and thrown is to that amount?—If I were to offer to an Italian throwster silk to throw for me, he would throw it at 3 s. including waste.

4913. Do you consider that it is more profitable for an Italian, supposing him to be a merchant, and also a throwster under the existing laws, to import his article here in a raw state or in a thrown state?—In a raw state.

4914. Do you consider that, according to the existing law, the duty at present comes out of the pocket of the Italian?—I hardly understand the question.

4915. You say it would be more profitable for the party to introduce the silk raw than to throw it there on account of the duty?—Yes, on account of the duty and charges which thrown silk pays in this market.

4916. Does not the duty form a material part of your calculation?—It forms a part, to the amount of 3 s. 6 d.

4917. Supposing that duty were taken off, would it or not alter your view of the case?—If the price of thrown silk remained the same it would be more advantageous than it is now to import thrown silk.

4918. It would then place the question in a totally different point of view, would it not, as to the merchant possessed of a quantity of raw silk, whether he should then introduce that in the raw or the thrown?—Supposing the prices remained the same, certainly.

4919. Do you not conceive, supposing the prices to remain the same, that might so far alter the view of the case as that it might become more to his advantage to introduce it in the thrown state entirely, and to forbear from introducing any in a raw state?—I think that the total abolition of the duty (for which I am not an advocate) would have the effect of placing much greater advantages in the hands of the Italian spinner.

4920. In case of a repeal of the duty on the organzine silk, whilst it gives an advantage, would that advantage be more than counterbalanced by the effect of competition from the English throwster here with regard to price?—I think the English throwster can never produce his organzine or tram at the same price as the Italian, other things remaining the same in this country.

4921. What amount would you think necessary to place them upon the same
footing

Mr.
T. F. Gibson.

9 May,
1832.

footing?—I should say, that if he had 2 s., the prices remaining as they are, that would be a protection.

4922. Do you mean on organzine and tram?—On organzine; I am not prepared to say what amount of protection should be given on tram.

4923. According to your statement just now the difference was 1 s. 6 d., leaving out the waste?—I do not say that 4 s. 9 d. is an advatageous price to the English throwster.

4924. Do you consider that 3 s. to the Italian throwster to be a remunerating price?—I consider that a price that satisfies him.

4925. Do not you suppose that a reduction of 1 s. 6 d. would tend to increase the quantity of foreign thrown silk imported into this country?—I do not think it would have any important ultimate effect.

4926. Would a diminution of 3 s. increase it materially?—It would have a greater tendency certainly, and by how much you go on to decrease the scale of duty the greater the amount that would be imported.

4927. You think the difference of 2 s. would be necessary to put them on an equality?—Not less than 2 s.

4928. Is the machinery in England worse than in Italy?—Better.

4929. Are the wages higher in England than in Italy?—Very considerably.

4930. Can you state what is paid there as compared with what is paid in this country?—I cannot.

4931. Are you aware, that the weekly wages in throwing silk are less on an average than 2 s. 9 d. in Italy, taken the different wages?—I should not think they were less.

4932. What did you pay during the time you were there?—I did not throw silk, the wages I paid were for reeling from the cocoon.

4933. Judging from the 5 s. per week you paid for reeling, do you think that those employed in throwing would have been satisfied with 2 s. 6 d.?—I cannot think that the price is lower than 2 s. 6 d. I have no certain knowledge.

4934. At what time are the cocoons reeled off, are they reeled immediately?—Immediately, for the most part.

4935. Was there not a considerable increase in the quantity of foreign thrown silk imported after the reduction from 5 s. to 3 s. 6 d.?—That does not appear to have been the case, with the exception of the last year, when it was much larger than in the previous years.

4936. If foreign thrown silk, paying a duty of 3 s. 6 d. per lb., is sold here for 22 s., do you suppose that if the duty of 3 s. 6 d. per lb. were to be repealed, the silk, without such charge of 3 s. 6 d., would be sold for more or less than 18 s.?—For more.

4937. So that the reduction of 3 s. 6 d. would not be all in favour of the manufacturer, which is the case supposed?—No.

4938. If the Italian now finds it to his interest to throw a considerable quantity of silk, and send it into this country where it is charged with a duty of 3 s. 6 d., would he not find it much more for his advantage to send it here when it was not charged with the 3 s. 6 d.?—Certainly, I consider that the Italian, for the last few years, has sent silk here at a sacrifice; that he has not obtained a remunerating price, and that if the duty is reduced, the price would not be reduced in the same proportion.

4939. If the duty were repealed he might be induced to increase his means of throwing, and might throw every pound he sent to this country, might he not?—It is not physically impossible.

4940. Inasmuch as he can do that for 3 s. which it appears from your evidence, you cannot do for less than 4 s. 9 d., would it not be to his interest to throw that silk rather than send to this country raw?—That would depend entirely upon the amount of duty imposed by the English Government upon foreign thrown silk.

4941. Would he not rather buy it of the Italian throwster if he could get it 1 s. 9 d. per lb. cheaper?—If he could buy foreign thrown silk for 1 s. 9 d. less than he could buy it of the same quality from the English, he would buy of the Italian, no doubt.

4942. What is the cause of the Italian throwster losing in this market by sending his silk here?—My own opinion is, that it is the competition of the English throwsters.

4943. If the duty were withdrawn, he would then be able to introduce it into this country at a profit, would he not?—Yes, the prices being the same.

678.

4944. You

Mr.
T. F. Gibson.
———
9 May,
1832.

4944. You have stated what you think would be a protecting duty for thrown silk; have you formed any opinion what would be a proper protecting duty for the manufacturer of plain goods in Spitalfields as against the French manufacturer?—The duty remaining as it does now I think 25 per cent. would be sufficient.

4945. Supposing the duty taken off, what would it be?—It would be less by eight per cent.

4946. Have you formed any opinion how that duty could be efficiently collected?—No, I have not.

4947. Are you aware of any scheme by which that duty might be efficiently and *bonâ fide* collected. Is it your opinion that the duty of 25 per cent. could be collected?—Yes; I state that from the opinion of others.

4948. Are you aware whether the smuggling has been carried to any extent in plain goods?—I have no information on the question of smuggling. I do not believe that the smuggling of plain goods has been of greater amount than might have been expected where a duty is collected to the extent of 30 per cent.

4949. What is the protection on plain goods you manufacture under the present law?—Thirty per cent.

4950. Do you think the duty should be decreased?—I think it would be better to make it 25, that the smuggler might have less inducement.

4951. You believe that the manufacturer is protected to the extent of 25 per cent. and no more than that?—Yes; I would add, that the cost of smuggling may be very greatly augmented by the regulations of the Government.

4952. Has the importation of thrown silk, in point of fact, increased or decreased during the last two years?—It has not greatly increased, as appears by the official returns, with the exception of the last year.

4953. You think that the Italian throwster has persisted in introducing his thrown silk to an increased amount, though at a loss?—Yes.

4954. Have you any solution for that which appears a singular problem?—I conceive that the general condition of the continental market for the last two years has been unfavourable to the Italian throwster, and that he has sent it to the best market he could find, though a bad one.

4955. Do you know whether, in point of fact, the number of throwing mills in England has increased or diminished during the last five years?—I should think within the last five years they have not increased much, but the previous five years they increased enormously.

4956. You think the last five years they have not increased much?—They have increased, but not greatly.

4957. The importation of foreign thrown silk has increased during the last two years?—Yes.

4958. Then the increased distress that has arisen to the throwing trade during the last five or six years, it will follow that that must arise, not from the home competition from the mills having been increased, but from the increase of the foreign thrown goods which have been imported?—No, I think not; the increased amount of foreign thrown silk is not such as to have caused the distress of the throwster; but although the number of English mills has not increased materially during the last five years, the quantity of silk which the same number of mills has produced, has greatly increased, in consequence of the greater speed at which the machinery is worked.

4959. Supposing the quantity produced from the foreign mills had not found its way into this country, do you not conceive that the trade of the English throwster would at this time have been in a different situation from that in which it is at present unhappily placed?—If there were no importation of thrown silk from Italy, we should have a much greater demand for our own mills.

4960. Do you conceive it probable, that the foreigner has continued to import, though as you state at a loss, looking forward to the probable abolition or reduction of duty, when he might import not at a loss but at a profit?—I have no reason to suppose so; I have no reason to suppose the foreigner has ever had such an expectation; one other reason why the foreigner may have continued to send silk here under a sacrifice of price is, that this market is one which has formerly been very advantageous to him, and some time will elapse before a man will give up a favourite market, and forsake his connexions.

4961. Do you know about what quantity is thrown annually in Italy?—No, I do not.

4962. Do

Mr.
*T. F. Gibson.*

9 May,
1832.

4962. Do you know what quantity they grow?—According to the best information I could get, it was about four millions of pounds weight.

4963. Do the mills work all the year round?—No.

4964. Then they are capable of increasing their production?—Yes.

4965. Do they send their silk thrown to Austria?—Yes.

4966. Do they also send their silk thrown to Switzerland?—Yes.

4967. Do they send much of it thrown to France?—The Piedmontese do. It is reckoned that the Piedmontese send half their thrown silk to France.

4968. Do they send it thrown to any other countries?—To Germany.

4969. What do you think is the aggregate amount of the silk so sent to those countries?—I have no means of forming an opinion.

4970. Have you the means of knowing the quantity they send unthrown?—France and England are the only countries to which they send any raw.

4971. Have you any means of knowing the quantities sent to France?—I have not.

4972. Do you conceive they have the means of throwing more than two millions of pounds now?—I should think not.

4973. At what period of the year are the mills still?—I do not think there are any certain times; they would be standing still perhaps during the reeling season in consequence of the working people being better employed in reeling.

4974. When you calculate eight per cent., are you speaking of the whole of the duty being repealed?—Yes.

4975. You are supposing if there were a diminution in the price of foreign thrown silk, that would operate to that extent on the British thrown silk?—I am not supposing that the reduction of duty would effect a reduction to the same amount in the price of silk, but that 3 s. 6 d. is eight per cent. upon the manufactured article.

4976. You are supposing, that the reduction of the duty, taking the whole of the duty of 3 s. 6 d. off, would effect a reduction of eight per cent. on the manufacture?—Rather it would have the effect of equalizing the price of thrown silk, so that the French manufacturer would be put upon the same footing as ourselves.

4977. Supposing that to be the effect, from your calculation, would it or not effect a reduction of 3 s. 6 d. on the British thrown silk?—It would effect an equalization in price between France and England.

4978. Would not that give a bounty on the importation of foreign thrown silk, because of the existence of the duty on the exportation of raw silk from Piedmont?—Raw silk is not imported from Piedmont.

4979. There is a duty imposed in Italy upon the exportation of raw silk?—There is.

4980. If the whole of the duty paid here on the importation of foreign silk was removed, would there not be a bounty, in fact, existing upon the introduction of foreign raw silk, supposing the duty still to continue on foreign raw silk in Italy?—There is a greater advantage in exporting thrown silk from Italy than raw, by the difference of 10 d. and 5 d. in the pound weight.

4981. If that duty on foreign thrown silk remained in this country, they would have a bounty?—They would have an advantage of 5 d. per lb.

4982. You have stated it as your opinion, that the peculiar situation of the Continent induced the Italians to send an increased quantity of thrown silk here the last two years, would not the same causes induce them to send raw silk?—That would depend very much upon the stock in hand.

4983. If they sent the one in consequence of distress or alarm, would they not equally send the other?—The same causes would not operate, inasmuch as this country being the only great market for raw silk, the alarm or distress on the Continent would not affect the quantity of raw.

4984. You stated that the throwsters are obliged to throw at less than 4 s. rather than shut up their mills, you stated since that you think 2 s. would be a fair protection, will you explain why, if 3 s. 6 d. is not a sufficient protection to ensure them a remunerating price, 2 s. would be?—But I do not admit that the fact of their throwing for 4 s. is owing to the very great increase of the import of foreign thrown silk.

4985. You say the Italians have sold their silk here at a price which did not pay them, owing to the competition here?—Yes.

4986. That competition would of course exist if there was a reduction of the duty on the Italian thrown?—Yes.

4987. If the competition at present is a strong competition, so that the throwsters

cannot

Mr.
T. F. Gibson.

9 May,
1832.

cannot afford to do it at the price, how can they afford to do it at all, if the duty were reduced to 2 s. ?—I do not see how the alteration of duty will affect the price, if it be admitted that the competition of the English mills governs the price of throwing.

4988. Do you mean to say that the low price of silk is owing to competition here ?—Yes.

4989. And not at all owing to the foreigner ?—Not at all more so now than it has always been.

4990. Formerly you were protected by a higher duty, do you mean to say that the reduction of duty on thrown silk has not caused a greater competition than existed before ?—I mean to say, that when the amount of duty was high, the quantity imported was as large, with the exception of the last two years.

4991. If there is already such a competition, that the foreigner to meet that, sold at a price which does not remunerate him, how is it that the reduction to 2 s. will not put him on a better footing ?—It will put the foreigner on a better footing.

4992. Then that is giving an advantage to him over the home throwster ?—It would be giving him a greater advantage than he has at present.

4993. You admit that that portion of duty which you say ought to be re-mitted——I do not say ought.

4994. Which you say might safely be remitted is at present paid by the Italian throwster ?—A portion of it is a loss to him.

4995. Consequently to that amount he would be a gainer ?—Certainly.

4996. The home throwster says, that owing to the home competition, he cannot get a profit; you say, owing to this competition he cannot get a remunerating price ?—Yes.

4997. Will not that reduction of duty give an advantage to the foreigner as against the home throwster ?—It will certainly give a greater advantage to the foreign throwster than he possessed before.

4998. Then if there is that advantage given to the foreigner, that it destroys the throwing trade at home, would you put the trade into the hands of the foreigner? —If the reduction of duty would destroy the trade at home, I would not recommend it.

4999. Would it not be the destruction of immense property ?—If the trade is destroyed there will also be destroyed a large quantity of property.

5000. You stated that the competition at home has been beneficial to the manufacturer ?—I stated the reverse.

5001. You stated that the introduction of the foreign goods has been injurious, but that the reduction of duties has been beneficial to the manufacturer ?—Yes.

5002. Since all those laws have come into full operation since 1829, has the prosperity of the manufacturer, and also their workmen depending upon them, increased or not ?—The prosperity of the workmen is not so great as it was, because their wages are very materially reduced, speaking of Spitalfields.

5003. By the reduction of goods, which are the particular class of persons benefited ?—Those persons who use them.

5004. The consumer ?—Yes.

5005. Does not the profit of the manufacturer depend upon the amount of his returns, does it depend upon the number of pieces ?—The amount of his profit depends on the rate he gets upon his return.

5006. Does not the manufacturer calculate upon the amount of his returns; does not a man calculate on more by selling 100 l. worth of goods than 50 l. ?—It depends upon whether he sells at a five per cent. profit in one case, or at 10 per cent. profit in the other.

5007. Does not a man estimate his profits on the amount of his returns, if you are getting 10 per cent. upon 100 l. worth of goods, if you sell only one half, will not your profit be decreased ?—If the rate of profit is the same, of course the amount of profit will be reduced.

5008. Does not a tradesman or a manufacturer generally regulate his profits by a certain per centage upon his returns ?—He ought to get as much as he can.

5009. If a man returned 50,000 l. a year in his concern, if his returns are reduced to half would he get the same profit ?—That depends upon the rate of profit.

5010. If a manufacturer gets 10 per cent. upon the goods he sells, if his trade is reduced to one half, must not his profits be diminished, supposing that he continues to sell at the same rate of profit ?—Nothing can be more clear.

5011. When the duty upon thrown silk was reduced from 14 s. 7 d. to 3 s. 6 d.
and

Mr.
T. F. Gibson.

9 May,
1832.

and the duty upon the raw material from 7 s. 6 d. to 1 d. per pound, and profits and labour are also reduced, has not that had the effect of lowering the returns of the manufacturer?—I think it has increased the returns.

5012. Do you mean to say, that in point of amount, there are more goods selling now than in 1826?—In quantity, certainly.

5013. The question refers to money?—The same amount of goods does not come to the same amount of money.

5014. If the prices of goods are reduced, the returns must also be reduced?—Yes, unless the returns are made up by an additional quantity.

5015. There must be double the quantity sold if the price is reduced to half?—Yes.

5016. Is there double the quantity sold?—I do not know.

5017. Do you not know, that the great increase has been in Chinese and Bengals and articles manufactured out of waste?—No, not out of waste.

5018. You have also stated, that there is a saving in the dyeing at Lyons of 10 per cent., but you say the wages are the same; if that is the case, how can you make it out that plain goods are manufactured there 15 or 20 per cent. cheaper than here?—I cannot make it out.

5019. Do you suppose there is a greater difference in the price of silk than that which arises from the difference of duty?—I really know nothing on the subject of French manufactures.

5020. Do not the French derive an advantage, first, from the cheapness of labour; secondly, by their growing a great deal of the raw material in their own country; thirdly, by manufacturing their goods to order; do not you know that fancy goods are manufactured chiefly by order from this country?—The fancy good are, I believe.

5021. Does not that give them a great advantage?—Yes.

5022. If a manufacturer has to manufacture goods on his own risk, and to meet goods which are ordered, does not that give him a great advantage?—It gives him an advantage, certainly.

5023. Do not you know that there is a great taste for foreign fashions?—Yes.

5024. Have you not heard that one house has lost connexions to the amount of several thousands in a year from that cause?—No.

5025. Have you been in the habit, as a manufacturer, of receiving orders for goods?—Not of late.

5026. The French derive an advantage, first, from the cheapness of their labour; secondly, from having an excellent raw material growing in their own country; thirdly, from their manufacturing many of their goods to order; and fourthly, from the prejudice in favour of French fashions?—Yes.

5027. Do not those circumstances give them a great advantage in this market?—Yes.

5028. You state that you think that the depression in prices and lowness of labour is occasioned, not by foreign but by home competition?—Yes, principally.

5029. Could not our own manufacturers supply the demand of this market without any foreign goods?—Yes.

5030. Do not you think there would always be a sufficiency of goods in the market to meet the demand?—I think so.

5031. Do not you think there would be a considerable competition among our own manufacturers?—Yes.

5032. Does not that competition in all trades generally regulate itself according to the demand, that if men over-manufacture they draw in?—The supply is generally proportioned to the demand.

5033. Must not the introduction of French goods into this market in large quantities, tend exceedingly to depress the prices in this market?—I think the French goods which have been imported into this market have had a partial effect, as I stated before, of increasing the competition amongst ourselves.

5034. Do not you know, that when the market is full of goods buyers keep back, and regulate the market almost to their own demand?—That depends upon the number of buyers there may be.

5035. When there is a large quantity of goods on hand, are not buyers a little shy and cautious, and careful to beat down the prices?—This seems to me to be the same as stating, that when there is a glutted market prices will always decline.

5036. Must

Mr.
*T. F. Gibson.*

9 May,
1832.

5036. Must not the quantity of French goods, with all the prejudices existing on their behalf, greatly depress the prices of goods here, and thereby lower labour? —The effect is to increase competition and to keep down prices.

5037. Can you state any new channel which has been opened by the introduction of foreign manufactured silks?—I am not a merchant, and therefore cannot say, but I have no doubt that foreigners do not send their goods to this market without obtaining an equivalent.

5038. Can you state any new channel that the introduction of French goods has opened to the trade of this country?—No; I have no knowledge upon that subject.

5039. Were we not told that it would give us an export trade?—I never heard it said.

5040. What class of consumers have been benefited by the reduction of duty? —The persons who buy the cheaper articles.

5041. Are you not aware, that a great part of the wages of the weavers and labourers are paid in taxes?—Certainly; I am sorry to say that is so.

5042. Do you think it fair and just that the duty should be taken off for the benefit of the consumer of the articles, while taxes on labour are continued?— I think the alteration of the corn laws would be a most beneficial measure. If I am asked, whether the taxes that press on labour ought not to have been taken off at the same time that the duties on silk were taken off, I should say, yes. If the lowering of those duties were a mischief to the labouring man I should be opposed to it; but I think the labouring man has not been prejudiced by the removal of the restrictions, although it would have been far more just to have made other alterations at the same time.

5043. Do you think that the introduction of foreign goods has been beneficial to the manufacturer and to the weaver?—No; there is nothing that would be so agreeable to me, as a manufacturer, as to have a strict monopoly of my trade.

5044. Is there not, in this country, always sufficient competition among the manufacturers of silk and other fancy goods, to insure to the public a plentiful supply at a reasonable profit?—Quite a sufficient competition.

5045. Is there not a sufficient supply to give the manufacturer a fair advantage? —If you ask me as a manufacturer, I should say certainly, if it were less I should be satisfied.

5046. Do you mean to say that persons concerned in manufacture and trade have an undue advantage, and are getting too much?—Not at all, I should like to get more.

5047. Do you think it is necessary for foreign competition to come in and put down prices?—No, but the reverse.

5048. Is not the competition among manufacturers sufficient to ensure to the purchaser goods at a fair rate of profit?—I do not know what would be considered a fair rate of profit.

5049. You have stated that the prices of throwing silk is determined by competition in England; do you not believe that the profits of manufacture and the wages of labour are mainly determined by the same circumstances?—Yes.

5050. Of 100*l.* worth of goods in Spitalfields, what proportion is labour of weaving?—The value of the article is increased from 45 to 50 per cent. by the operations of dyeing, winding, warping and weaving.

5051. What article do you speak of?—Plain gros de Naples.

5052. Do you think it possible to exclude French goods by prohibition?— Not entirely.

5053. Are you aware that smuggling took place to a considerable extent before 1826?—Yes.

5054. Do you not believe that would be resorted to again if there were a prohibition?—Yes, I think it would.

5055. Do you think there has been more or less smuggling since 1826?—More.

5056. What advantages do you imagine the Italian throwster has over the English, independent of the cost of throwing?—I know of no other advantages. The only advantages I know that the Italian possesses over the English throwster, are these, that he is able to work his silk at less waste, that he procures his labour at a less price, and that his mill and machinery cost him much less money.

5057. You state that the price charged in Italy for throwing is 3*s.* a lb., he has probably some other advantages beyond that of buying his silk on the spot; what are those advantages?—I do not know of any other advantages.

5058. In

Mr.
T. F. Gibson.

9 May,
1832.

5058. In point of fact, you believe there are no advantages beyond those you mention?—None whatever.

5059. The Italian silk throwster is accustomed to work his mills at certain periods of the year?—Yes.

5060. The people are employed at other seasons of the year in other occupations?—Yes.

---

*Veneris, 11° die Maii,* 1832.

---

## THE RIGHT HON. THE EARL GROSVENOR, IN THE CHAIR.

---

Mr. *Thomas Field Gibson,* called in ; and further Examined.

Mr.
T. F. Gibson.

11 May,
1832.

5061. WHAT kind of thrown silks are imported from Italy?—Organzines and trams.

5062. From what parts of Italy?—The principal importations are from Piedmont and Lombardy.

5063. To what uses are they applied?—To the manufacture of all kinds of silk goods.

5064. Of fine silk goods?—Principally to the manufacture of broad silk goods.

5065. Therefore, chiefly used in Spitalfields?—Chiefly in Spitalfields.

5066. To what use is the Piedmont silk applied?—The largest portion of Piedmont silk which is imported, is consumed in the manufacture of broad silks, such as the richest kinds of gros de Naples, also in velvets, and the richest kind of satins. I am not aware of any other appropriation of it in Spitalfields.

5067. What description of broad goods are imported from France?—The richest kind of plain silks principally.

5068. Such as are manufactured here from those fine silks?—Yes.

5069. The taking off the duty upon thrown silk, or materially reducing it, would in your opinion materially benefit Spitalfields?—I conceive it would.

5070. That it would increase the demand for goods?—It would place us more nearly on an equality with the French manufacturer.

5071. It would increase the consumption?—I think the small amount of duty which might be taken off would have no great effect in increasing the consumption.

5072. It would have some effect?—I think that every deduction of price has a proportionate effect in increasing the consumption.

5073. And consequently increasing the demand for labour?—Yes.

5074. Have you reason to suppose that any considerable part of the goods manufactured in Spitalfields are exported?—I think none whatever.

5075. What kind of goods do you believe are exported?—The greatest proportion is of the lowest kind of silks, principally handkerchiefs.

5076. Where are they manufactured?—At Manchester and Macclesfield.

5077. From what kind of silk are they made?—From Bengal and China.

5078. So that the duty is levied on the fine goods made in Spitalfields, and the drawback allowed on the common goods made at Manchester and Macclesfield?—Undoubtedly.

5079. What is the price of the debentures now?—They are worth scarcely any thing, one penny, I believe.

5080. What is the difference, at present, between the price of Italian thrown and raw silk of the same quality?—From 5 s. to 6 s.

5081. That would, after paying the duty, leave the Italian from 1 s. 6 d. to 2 s. 6 d.?—Yes.

5082. Have you reason to suppose he can continue to send thrown silks here?—I should think he could not send them profitably.

5083. So that if the difference between thrown and raw silk continues as it is at present, we shall get very little Italian thrown silk?—I am of opinion, that it would be a continually decreasing quantity, supposing the law to remain as it is.

5084. If the imports of thrown silk diminished, or if the exports of manufactured silk increase, the debentures would rise in price?—Undoubtedly.

5085. In that case they would probably reach, ultimately, somewhat about 3 s. 3 d. a pound?—There would be very little advantage to the buyer of the debenture if they ever arrive at that price.

5086. The

5086. The advantage to him would be only 3 d., and he will not buy unless he has some advantage; would not 3 d. be sufficient to induce him to buy?—That would be a very small inducement in such a case. The advantage upon the value of the silk he exports would not be very important.

5087. Supposing the price to rise to 3 s., in that case the throwster would not be benefited, because he would get in the sale of his debenture so large a proportion of the amount of the duty he had paid?—Yes.

5088. Therefore the protection would be diminished?—Yes.

5089. Supposing the debenture to sell at 3 s. the throwster would have a protection of only 6 d.?—Just so.

5090. In that case, without any benefit to the throwster, it would be a material injury to Spitalfields; and the only party who would benefit would be the manufacturer at Manchester and Macclesfield?—The Spitalfields manufacturer would have obtained the 3 s. for his debenture, he would have bought his silk nearly without duty.

5091. You mean to say, that if foreign thrown silk is imported, and a duty of 3 s. 6 d. paid for it, if the debenture sold for 3 s., the manufacturer would pay only 6 d. duty?—Just so.

5092. And that the benefit of that debenture would go to the manufacturer?—Yes.

5093. Then if we continue to export the same quantity of coarse made goods from Manchester and Macclesfield, that would be decidedly beneficial to the manufacturer of the finer articles, who use the foreign thrown silk without injury to the maker of coarse goods, if he continued to export the same quantity he now does?—The effect of such a state of things would be to destroy the protection of the throwster.

5094. There would be the machinery and collecting the duty, and allowing the drawback, without any benefit?—Just so.

5095. Have the goodness to state what are the terms on which the manufacturers of Spitalfields generally sell their goods?—They generally sell them for a two months' bill at the end of the month in which the goods are sold.

5096. There is a settlement at the end of the month?—Yes.

5097. Can you state the probable number of considerable buyers in Spitalfields?—From twenty to thirty.

5098. Have the goods been sold on those terms ever since you have been in the business?—Certainly not.

5099. Formerly, what was the credit given?—It was either six months or twelve months.

5100. The consequence of that change has been, that the manufacturer, instead of having his capital in his books, is enabled to pay cash for his silk, for which he formerly used to obtain credit?—The effect of the alteration has been, to give him a much larger money capital.

5101. It has had the further effect, has it not, of excluding the middle-man, the speculating jobber in silks in a great measure?—I am not aware that it has had that effect.

5102. The manufacturer now buys direct from the merchant, and has his silk thrown?—Yes.

5103. Was not he in the habit formerly of buying from middle-men?—Yes, he was.

5104. Of what class were those persons you called middle-men, between the manufacturer and the merchant?—The middle-man who was just referred to, was a person between the manufacturer and the silk merchant; he was called a silk-man, a dealer in raw and thrown silk.

5105. Are the Committee to understand, that the effect of the alteration has been entirely to destroy that class of persons, so that they no longer exist?—The fact is, at this moment there exist very few of such middle-men, and six years ago there existed a large number.

5106. There is one class of persons which it appears has been nearly annihilated by this alteration of the law?—No, I do not mean to say that it has been by the alteration of the law.

5107. In point of fact, there was a class of persons getting their livelihood in the silk trade some years ago, which class has now almost ceased to exist?—Yes.

5108. You are understood to say, that the manufacturer goes immediately to the merchant in a greater degree than he did formerly?—Yes.

5109. You

Mr.
T. F. Gibson.

11 May,
1832.

5109. You are understood to have stated, that you conceive, supposing the law should continue precisely in its present state as relates to the duties, there will be found a decreasing quantity of imported foreign thrown silk?—Yes.

5110. Is not that supposition of yours contrary to the fact, with reference to the experience of the last two years?—Yes.

5111. Upon what grounds do you form that supposition?—Upon the acknowledged fact, which will be confirmed by every person who is well informed in the trade, that the foreign throwster has for the last few years been losing by the silk he has sent to this market.

5112. For how many years do you suppose any foreigner has been thus importing at a loss?—I should wish to avoid that question, not being a merchant; but to the best of my belief, for three or four years.

5113. Are you enabled to give a general statement of the portion of foreign thrown silk imported into this country during the last year, as compared with the Italian silk thrown in this country, speaking generally of the quantity?—I should think the raw silk imported from Italy during the last two years, has been from double to treble the amount of silk imported thrown.

5114. Can you state in what degree that proportion has varied, either one way or the other, during the last three or four years?—I do not think it has varied importantly, except in the last year.

5115. In the last year, on which side has the balance of variation been?—In favour of the thrown.

5116. Can you state from recollection, the amount of Italian thrown silk that was imported in the last year?—I cannot say; there is one circumstance I would state, which has increased the quantity of thrown silk last year, which did not operate in the preceding year; during the last year, a very large quantity of foreign thrown tram was imported into this market. An article which had never been imported (or to a very small extent) in previous years; I believe that the persons who imported this silk, invariably lost by it.

5117. Are you enabled to give any statement to the Committee of what might be the proportion of home thrown silk in the market during the last year, as brought in competition with this large quantity, which it appears was imported?—I can only make an estimate from the published reports, of the whole amount of raw and thrown silk which was brought into the market. The whole amount of raw silk imported was nearly 4,000,000 and the amount of thrown was 500,000, therefore there was 3,500,000 lbs. speaking roundly, of silk to be thrown in this country.

5118. Did not the price of trams in this market, fall considerably at the end of the year 1830 and the beginning of the year 1831, in consequence of so large a quantity of foreign tram coming into the market about that time?—The price of trams fell, but I do not think it fell in consequence of the large amount that came in, there was a slackness of demand for trams generally. The British mills had been very actively employed on trams, and there is no doubt that the large importation of foreign thrown trams operated conjointly with the glut, from the working our own mills in reducing the price.

5119. You stated on a former day, that though there are not more mills at work in England than there were five or six years ago, yet you consider that the mills which are in existence turn off more work than they used to do, will you state whether, in your opinion, all the silk mills now at work turn off more silk of a certain fineness than all the mills at work did five or six years ago?—Most undoubtedly they do, they are capable of doing so.

5120. Do they, in point of fact, turn off more?—I believe they do.

5121. Seeing that the foreigner has, during some years, as you state, imported and continued to import, in the face of discouragement and disadvantage and actual loss, do you not suppose that if the law was so far altered as to give him even a very small certain remuneration upon his import, the quantity imported would not only be increased, but very considerably increased?—I think that every reduction of duty on foreign thrown silk is *pro tanto* an advantage to the Italian throwster.

5122. Do you not conceive that taking off the whole duty would be a very serious evil, amounting almost to ruin to the English mills?—It would be a very serious evil.

5123. The Committee are to collect from your evidence, that according to that opinion it is a question of degree as to how far it would be expedient to relax the duty, and that you would not consider it politic or safe with reference to the

existence

Mr.
T. F. Gibson.

11 May,
1832.

existence of the English throwster, to remove the whole duty?—Speaking as a throwster, I should say so.

5124. Do you think, from what you know of the existing state of throwing in this country, that if the whole duty was off, the Italian organzine would for any length of time keep the market against the British organzine?—I think the advantage would be so much in favour of the Italian throwster, that we should have a very small part of the raw silk to throw if the whole duty were taken off.

5125. It being in your mind a question of degree, do you not think it would be a dangerous experiment to make any considerable alteration in the rate of duty, speaking with reference to the throwster?—I think the alteration I before mentioned of 1 s. 6 d. would not be productive of serious inconvenience. I observe from evidence which has been given before this Committee by a gentleman in every way qualified to give the best information, Mr. Doxat, that the amount of charges paid by the Italian merchant, including the duties and all expenses on thrown silk imported into this country is 6 s. 3 d. If to this sum we add 3 s. as the cost of throwing in Italy, we have total of 9 s. 3 d. The charges upon raw silk are stated to be 2 s. 4 d. by the same witness, and this amount being deducted from 9 s. 3 d. leaves 6 s. 11 d. as the sum which the Italian throwster must now obtain on thrown silk more than on raw to remunerate him in this market. Now if the duty were lowered by 1 s. 6 d. there would remain 5 s. 5 d. as a protection to the English throwster.

5126. Taking the importation of Italian raw silk at 1,021,000, what proportion do you consider may be thrown for sale against the competition of the foreign throwster of organzine?—I really have no means of stating that at the moment, I should very much doubt the fact of there being only 1,021,000, I conceive the quantity is more than that.

5127. Taking the quantity of Italian raw imported during the last year at the amount stated, 1,021,000, and the greater part of that being bought up by throwsters who were also manufacturers, is it not very likely to be the fact that there would be but a small quantity of British thrown actually in the market in competition with this 600,000 lbs. of foreign thrown imported?—No, I should not think so.

5128. Is it not the fact that a very considerable quantity of this raw imported silk was in the hands of those throwsters who were also manufacturers?—There is always a large market for raw silk as well as for thrown silk. It would be a question with the purchaser of silk whether he should buy it raw, and throw it, or buy it thrown, according as the advantage might appear to him to be.

5129. You stated that you have been in business about ten years, when you first entered trade, was it by yourself or in partnership with any other?—In partnership with my father.

5130. At the time when you entered into partnership with your father, was he a manufacturer in any considerable degree of fancy silks?—Yes; in as great a proportion as other persons in the trade at that time.

5131. He was in a very large way, was he not?—In a considerable way.

5132. He was selling many of his goods in the fancy line to the great houses at the West end of the Town, was he not?—Certainly.

5133. Was it not the fact, that your father's trade and your's was a very prosperous and profitable trade in that line at the time of the opening of the ports to the foreign silk goods?—It was as advantageous as that of other persons employing capital in that trade.

5134. How long after that period did your father and yourself continue in that line of business?—My father left trade about three years ago, and I have always continued in the same line of business.

5135. Are the Committee to understand, that you continue precisely in the same line, that is, as much engaged in the manufacture and sale of fancy articles as you were when you first engaged in business?—I am not a manufacturer now of fancy articles, because there is but little demand for fancy articles of the description referred to.

5136. Do you conceive that that want of demand may, in any degree, be attributed to the opening of the ports and the admission of foreign goods?—It was to be expected that the opening of the ports would have had a contrary effect; but the fact is, that the public are not disposed to use the kind of articles which were made ten years ago—fancy silks.

5137. Do you mean that the public do not, in point of fact, now purchase fancy articles of the general description you manufactured when first in trade?—Only to a very small extent.

5138. Are

Mr.
T. F. Gibson.

11 May,
1832.

5138. Are the Committee to understand, that the taste is so totally changed in this country, that articles which fell under the class of fancy articles when you first entered trade, are considered quite out of fashion, and entirely gone by; or that the public taste may be changed with reference to colour and pattern?—It is the taste of the public to use plain silks much more than it was ten years ago.

5139. Have you not lately been copying some French figured silks?—Yes.

5140. You have told the Committee, that the taste of the public is not for those goods, but that you expected that when the ports were opened the public taste would have been for those goods?—It was to have been expected I think.

5141. On what do you found your opinion that there is no taste among the public for that description of goods?—From the fact of there not being any demand.

5142. Do you know that very large quantities are imported from France, and sold in this country, and that they have entirely superseded the English, because you have been unable in your attempts to cope with them in price?—I am not aware, that with the duty we now enjoy, we are unable to cope with them in price.

5143. Have you lately made any article, which you have given up, because you cannot compete with the French?—No.

5144. Have you not abandoned the article you were in the habit of making?—I made it much cheaper than the French.

5145. How do you know that?—From what I was informed by the person for whom I made it, Mr. Ellis.

5146. At what did you make it?—I made it at 3 s. 9 d. a yard, and I understand that it cost 4 s., imported, with the duty.

5147. Did you get a fair tradesman's profit by that article when you sold it at 3 s. 9 d. a yard?—I got more by it than I could have got by the plain silk.

5148. Then why did you decline continuing to make it?—Because the person for whom I made it refused to take it.

5149. Was this article made only for a particular house?—It was made only for a particular house; the pattern was given me by that house.

5150. Is it the understanding of the trade, that when a pattern is given by a particular house, it is considered that the order is to be executed for that particular house exclusively by whom the pattern was given; that it would be considered improper in the manufacturer to furnish that particular pattern to other houses?—Certainly.

5151. When this particular article was declined by the warehouseman, do you conceive it was declined because the public taste had declined, and the article had become unsaleable; or because an article of the same description could be procured from another quarter, and the public taste supplied at a cheaper rate in another manner?—My own belief was, that the demand for the article had ceased.

5152. You have stated, that taking the French tariff for your guide, the rates of wages at Lyons and in Spitalfields are the same, or nearly so; what are the wages now paid in Spitalfields for the principal works manufactured there?—The price in London of making three single gros de Naples is 5 d. per yard, the tariff of Lyons is, as nearly as possible, the same; the price of weaving three double gros de Naples is 6½ d. per yard, and the price at Lyons, by the tariff, is the same; in the price of weaving figured gros de Naples the greatest difference appears to exist in Spitalfields, the price would be from 1 s. to 2 s. 6 d.; the price in Lyons is from 7½ d. to 11½ d..

5153. How can you account for that difference?—I conceive it is to be accounted for by the use of the Jacquard machine, which has been employed in Lyons for a much longer time than it has been in London.

5154. For how long a time has the Jacquard been in general use in London?—In general use about six years.

5155. What are the articles you speak of as being at so high a rate as 2 s. 6 d.?—The most expensive kinds of figured satins woven in the Jacquard machines; but I am not myself a weaver of these articles, therefore I do not speak with great certainty.

5156. Can you state what was paid for the same works in Spitalfields in the year 1826?—The works which are now made at 1 s., in 1826 would have been made at 18 d., speaking from the information I have gained; I am not myself a large figured weaver.

5157. There is about a difference of one-third upon the former price?—Yes.

5158. You have stated, that the difference in the price of dyeing between London and Lyons is about 10 per cent., can you state to the Committee the

respective

respective prices of the leading colours?—The following is a comparative List of prices:—

|                                              | London. | Lyons. |
|----------------------------------------------|---------|--------|
| White and light colours - - - -              | 1/3     | 1/.    |
| Middle and dark colours - - - -              | 1/9     | 1/3.   |
| Black supple and 16 ounce coloured ditto -   | 2/      | 1/3.   |
| Black soft - - - - - - -                      | 1/3     | 1/.    |

[Note.—*The Witness not having this list before him during his examination, made the statement of difference of* 10 *per cent. between the prices at London and Lyons erroneously.*]

5159. Upon what is it you found your opinion as to the difference of price being 10 per cent.?—From the statement given to me by an English dyer connected with a Lyonese dyer.

5160. Is there any particular colour that you are more particularly concerned in in your manufactory, is your manufactory generally applicable to all colours, or is it to any one in particular?—To all colours alike.

5161. Do you conceive that there is any peculiar advantage that the foreigner has in dyeing in any particular colour?—I am not aware that there is any advantage whatever.

5162. Is there any advantage that the English dyer has in dyeing of any particular colour?—No, except in the article of white; I believe in that we have a decided advantage over the French dyer.

5163. Have not we now an advantage in black?—Not materially in the price of dyeing. But I think our black goods are, upon the whole, superior in colour to the French blacks I have seen.

5164. Is it not the fact that there is less pressure on the English black goods from foreign competition than upon many other colours?—I know no reason why there should be.

5165. Is it the fact that the importation of black foreign goods is in as large proportionate quantities as in other colours?—I believe not.

5166. The importation not being so large, is it not a fair inference, that the English have an advantage in that colour which they have not in others?—In the mode of dyeing I think it would be a fair inference; for although the price of dyeing in black more nearly approaches to the French than in many other colours, the difference is not very important.

5167. Are you aware of the amount of duties paid on dyeing stuffs introduced into France as compared with the duties paid on their introduction into this country?—No.

5168. You stated on a former day, that you conceive at the present day smuggling is undoubtedly carried on to a greater extent than it was during the existence of the prohibition?—Yes, the smuggling now takes place principally in the lighter description of manufactured articles.

5169. It is a fact that there is also some smuggling carried on in the plain silks?—To a very small extent now I believe.

5170. Do you imagine there is much in the figured broad silks?—I should think the quantity is larger than that of plain silks.

5171. With respect to the lighter articles there can be no doubt that it is carried on to a great extent?—I do not know that of my own knowledge, but I judge so from the conjoint belief of those persons who have made inquiries.

5172. Was it your opinion, prior to the opening of the ports, that this would have been one of the consequences of the introduction of foreign silks, that the smuggling would be increased instead of diminished?—I did not then form any opinion.

5173. How many years were you in Italy?—I was there two successive summers.

5174. Two crops?—Yes.

5175. Were you at all engaged in the throwing trade?—Not at all.

5176. Had you an opportunity of examining their mills?—Yes.

5177. And the general system of the trade of the throwster?—Yes.

5178. You state that you do not think the throwsters there possess any peculiar advantage over the throwster in this country?—No other advantages than these, that the wages are less, the waste is less, and the throwster has his plant and machinery at a less cost.

5179. Does

Mr.
T. F. Gibson.

11 May,
1832.

5179. Does not the Italian throwster reel his own silk?—Some of the throwsters reel the silk from the cocoon, and also possess machinery.

5180. Do not you conceive that is a very great advantage?—No, I do not.

5181. Do not you conceive it is a very great advantage that he should be able to select his raws upon the spot?—I think the English throwster has as good a market for raw silk as the Italian throwster; in fact, he has a better market. In England he sees the produce of every part of Italy at one view, whereas an Italian throwster can only make a selection from the silk of the district in which he resides.

5182. Has not he an opportunity of assorting his silk better than in any market here?—No.

5183. You do not consider the Foreign thrown silk at all better than the English thrown silk?—Of the same quality of raw silk, I do not.

5184. Being thrown in Italy before it is transported to this country, you conceive it possesses the same advantages, after having crossed the sea in a raw state that it does when thrown in Italy?—I can state from my own experience, that the silk thrown in England from the same quality of raw is as good silk as the silk thrown in Italy.

5185. Are you aware of the rapidity with which the mills are worked abroad?—I do not know it precisely, it is much less than that of the mills in this country.

5186. As a throwster, do you not conceive, that silk thrown in a mill which does not go at the same rate of speed lately attempted in this country, is better than the silk which has undergone the operation with that speed?—I am able to say from my experience as a manufacturer, that the increased speed of throwing is no injury to the silk.

5187. You state that the removal of the duty in your opinion, would be very injurious to the throwster?—Yes, the removal of the entire duty.

5188. Do you think that if removed it would afford any equivalent advantage to the manufacturer?—I have to speak both as a manufacturer and throwster; as a manufacturer I should like to say the duty entirely off, as a throwster I should wish it on.

5189. Are you able to say, that supposing the whole of the duty was removed, that would give an equivalent protection to the manufacturer?—No, I think the protection which may be afforded to the English manufacturer, against French silk goods, will be sufficient to cover 2 s. of protecting duty to the throwster.

5190. Has your last answer reference to the existing protection to the manufacturer, or do you contemplate any variation of that protection?—If the present duty were really collected, there would be an ample protection.

5191. You are aware that in point of fact it is not collected?—I believe that it is not collected.

5192. You state that you think 25 per cent. might be collected as a duty to exclude the smuggler?—Yes.

5193. Have you purchased cocoons in Italy the same way that the Italian would do?—Yes.

5194. You have had the silk thrown in Italy on commission for yourself?—Yes.

5195. Has not your trade lately been principally in black?—My trade for the last year and a half has been divided betwen blacks and colours.

5196. Are not your goods principally of a low description?—No, they are not.

5197. Not of a quality principally for the consumption of the lower class?—No, they are fitted for all classes.

5198. Are you not aware that the largest throwsters in Italy have reeling houses and reel their own silk?—It is a very common case for the owner of a large filature to be also a throwster, but it is not the general practice.

5199. Can you give the Committee an average of the earnings of the workmen, or any given number of workmen, employed by you at present?—I took an average of their earnings a very short time since, and found that for the last three months the earnings of the head of the family were 13 s. 9 d. per week, and the earnings of the women and children in the family varied from 8 s. 6 d. to 9 s. 6 d.

5200. When you say women and children, do you mean a woman or child?—A woman or young person.

5201. Did you ever take the average of such earnings previous to the repeal of the prohibitory laws?—I do not remember to have done so; there is no doubt that at the time when the laws relating to the silk trade were altered, the earnings of the work peope were larger than they are now.

5202. Did

5202. Did you make a very extensive average of your work people lately?—I took an average of twenty.

5203. On what goods were they employed?—On three double gros de Naples.

5204. Not on velvets?—On velvets they would be larger.

5205. What deductions has a weaver to pay out of that 13s. 9d.?—I think one shilling should be deducted as the necessary expense for quill winding.

5206. During how many weeks in the year does he lose time?—He must lose two days in every change of his work.

5207. What price do you pay for that work on which those persons are employed, three double gros de Naples?—Sixpence halfpenny.

### *John Benjamin Heath,* Esq. called in; and Examined.

5208. YOU are a silk merchant?—I am.

5209. How long have you been engaged in that trade?—More than twenty years.

5210. Your house has been established longer than that in London, has it not? —We have had our house in London since the year 1805.

5211. Can you state the gross produce of silk in Italy, on an average of years, in the different States of Piedmont, Lombardy, the Tyrol, Tuscany, Fossembrone and Naples?—Yes; I can state the average of the three last years of the production of Lombardy, the Tyrol, the Frioul, and other Italian States.

5212. From what documents do you take that statement?—From documents which I have collected, that have been transmitted to me by my correspondents in Italy from time to time, chiefly founded on official returns.

5213. You have been for years past in the habit of having regular returns of every thing connected with the silk trade?—I have the average from Lombardy, the Tyrol, and the Frioul, for the last three years 1829, 1830 and 1831; it was 17 to 18,000 bales, weighing 4,250,000 lbs. Italian, or about 3,000,000 of lbs. English; Piedmont I estimate 1,250,000 lbs. English; the Roman States, Naples and Sicily, 3,000 bales, of 200 lbs. each, together 600,000 lbs.; making a grand total of between 5 and 6,000,000 lbs. English, the whole produce of Italy.

5214. Is the quantity capable of any great increase in any or all of those countries?—In most of them, certainly.

5215. Has it within the last eight or ten years much increased?—It has increased very much.

5216. In what proportion?—I cannot state precisely; it has diminished in some parts, and very much increased in others. My last journey to Italy was in 1825, I remained there eight months, and made many inquiries on this subject; there were great complaints, that the general produce of the soil was not remunerating to the grower, and that the only thing which paid the agriculturist, was silk; and the result was, that a very great increase in the plantation of mulberry trees was taking place.

5217. Were the prices for silk higher than they are now?—They were.

5218. The price of the silk would depend upon the proportionate profit from growing silk, as compared with the other produce of the soil?—Yes, no doubt of it.

5219. Can you state how much of that is made into organzine and tram in each country?—That depends entirely upon the demand in the foreign markets for organzine and tram; there is no datum by which that can be ascertained.

5220. Can you state the average quantity in the three years you have alluded to?—No, I cannot.

5221. By reference to your papers will you be able to do so?—No, I fear not, as there are no official returns.

5222. Can you state to what countries that silk is exported, and in what proportion, particularizing that to France and England?—I can state what the export from the Lombardy States alone was in 1831; to Berlin and Vienna, 335,000 lbs.; to Russia, 120,000 lbs.; to Switzerland, 200,000 lbs.; to the different manufacturing places on the Rhine, 500,000; to England, 2,250,000 lbs.; making in the whole, 3,405,000 lbs. of export.

5223. In what way is the silk that remains over and above the exports worked up in that country, is it worked up for manufactured goods for export, or for home consumption?—I am not able to answer that question; I should think there is no export of silk stuffs from the North of Italy; from the Tuscan States there is.

5224. Any velvets?—The velvets are chiefly from Genoa.

5225. Can

*John B. Heath,*
Esq.

———

11 May,
1832.

5225. Can you state generally the quality of the silk produced by each of those States?—Each State produces a silk different from the other; in Lombardy, for instance, there are a great variety of sizes of silk, but it is of the same description; Tyrol the same; and in the Frioul the same; the manufacturers are better able to speak as to the application of the silk that they manufacture.

5226. Are you able at all to state the expenses in either of those States, attendant on the throwing?—I have notes which show that.

5227. When you were in Italy yourself, did you attend particularly to that branch; did you take the notes then, or is it information since received?—I have notes which I took then, and I have received information since.

5228. Take the most important place from which the greatest quantity is sent, can you state what is the expense of the different branches, from the cocoons to the finishing of the organzine?—I can state what the expense of throwing was, but the actual expense of the reeling varies according to the season, and other circumstances.

5229. Are you able to state the prices at which the cocoons are purchased in that country?—They vary every year according to the season, and to the state of the different silk markets.

5230. Will you state generally what you know of the expense of throwing in Italy?—In Piedmont, an organzine of 22 to 24 deniers, which is a fine size, including the waste, is thrown at the price of 3 livres to 3 livres. 5. of that country, which I consider to be equal to 4s. to 4s. 4d. of our pound English weight; the second and third sizes, which I class under the head of 24 to 30 deniers, from 3s. 6d. to 4s. the English pound.

5231. Waste always included?—Yes, in Lombardy; the finest size which is 18 to 20 deniers, 3s. 6d.; 22 to 24 deniers, 3s. 4d.; 28 to 30 deniers 3s. per pound English.

5232. At what period was that price given?—For several years past; my last note on the subject is dated about eighteen months ago.

5233. Have you reason to believe that those prices charged are the average prices of the country?—They were so at the time this list was furnished me, and I believe are so still.

5234. With regard to tram, will you state the information you have of the expense attending the throwing that?—My information with regard to tram is more limited, I have merely the average expense of throwing trams from 22 to 26 deniers, and 26 to 30 deniers, without the waste, 1s. 9d. to 2s.

5235. Can you state what are the wages the parties employed in that receive?—I cannot.

5236. Have you yourself visited the machinery for throwing in Italy and in this country?—I have visited mills in Italy on various occasions, but never with any other view than that of satisfying my curiosity; I did not take any notes respecting the mechanical part.

5237. Have you visited mills in this country?—I have seen mills in this country.

5238. Will what you have seen enable you to form any comparison between the state of machinery there and here?—No; I have not made sufficient observations to answer that question satisfactorily.

5239. What duties are levied in each of those States on the export of raw and thrown?—The export duty in Piedmont upon organzine is 50 centimes the pound of that country, which is equal to 62 centimes and a half the pound English, making a small fraction above 6d.

5240. Is that for organzine?—Yes; the exportation of raw from Piedmont is prohibited; in Lombardy the export duty on raw silk is 241 Austrian livres and a fraction for every 100 kilogrammes, which is equal to about 9d. a pound English; the export duty on organzine from Lombardy is half that amount, 120 Austrian livres and a fraction for 100 kilogrammes, equal to 4½d.; and in the kingdom of Naples the export of raw silk is free.

5241. Is there none thrown in Naples?—Very little indeed; what is thrown is for the use of their own manufactures; there is a large export of sewing silk, but none of organzine.

5242. From what part is the sewing silk exported?—It is exported from different parts of Italy, but chiefly from Naples; there is a very considerable trade carried on between Naples and the United States in sewing silk; the silk is shipped generally through Leghorn, and the proceeds come through London.

678.

5243. Does

*John B. Heath,*
Esq.

———

11 May,
1832.

5243. Does any of that sewing silk find its way to England ?—I should say not. My house received, two or three years ago, a box containing various samples of sewing silk of that country, for which we could not find a sale here.

5244. The Committee are to understand, that from Naples generally nothing but raw silk is imported ?—Nothing.

5245. From whence do we import our largest quantity of thrown silk?—The largest quantity from Lombardy, some from Piedmont, a little from the Duchy of Modena and the Roman States, but the latter quantity scarcely worth mentioning.

5246. Can you state the proportion which on any average number of years we have received from Lombardy and Piedmont?—I can put in a document to that effect.

5247. Does all the silk which is imported from Italy now come through France? —Not the whole of it.

5248. How long is it since silk was brought through Lyons ?—I do not recollect precisely the period, but not very long after the peace. A considerable quantity used to come through the ports, Leghorn and Genoa, but it was found more advantageous to let it have the double chance of the markets of Lyons and London.

5249. It is distinguished as Italian silk, is it not ?—It is put into depôt at Lyons as Italian silk.

5250. What are the qualities of the silks that find their way to England, is it of the superior or the middling quality ?—There is some of all sorts; a great deal of indifferent raw silk finds its way into this country.

5251. Is there any difference in the quality of the thrown ?—They are of different qualities, from 18 to 20 deniers up to 36 and 40.

5252. Does England receive a greater proportion of fine than any of the other countries you have stated ?—That depends on circumstances ; I do not think there is any general rule by which to answer that question satisfactorily.

5253. Are the Committee to understand, that it will vary according to the different prices ?—I think so ; the market of Norwich used to consume a quantity of the finest organzine, while Coventry always used that that was coarser from 26 to 30 deniers ; the consumption of Norwich has almost entirely ceased, and where I used to sell 50 bales of silk for that city I do not now sell two.

5254. Of the silk you import from Italy can you state where it is principally manufactured ?—It is a difficult thing to answer that question ; there is generally a large assortment of bales in the market, and the manufacturer selects that which suits him, and is adapted to his particular purposes.

5255. Can you state to the Committee what quantity of silk is exported from Italy to France, and what are its qualities ?—The quantity of silk imported into France from Italy, Spain and Turkey, in the documents I have, is stated thus : The average of foreign raw and thrown silk imported into France from 1825 to 1830, both inclusive, is 540,390 kilogrammes, making 1,186,719 pounds English ; the average duty on which, as stated by a deputy to the Chamber at Paris, was 1,034,800 francs.

5256. Of that how much is Italian ?—I should say seven-eighths of it, or more ; the consumption of foreign organzine in Lyons is about 700,000 lbs. weight annually, the greater part of which comes from Piedmont ; France employed three-fifths of the organzine silk thrown in Piedmont.

5257. Is that she employs of a finer quality than that which other countries receive ?—That will depend, I should think, entirely upon the stuffs for which they are employed ; they have the Piedmont thrown silk of all sizes from the finest to the coarsest.

5258. Have you any returns to show where the other two-fifths go to ?—A great deal comes to England ; I should think very nearly the whole.

5259. You do not state that there is much Piedmont in the quantities exported to Germany and other countries ?—What I stated was only the exports from Lombardy.

5260. From what document do you state the amount to be upwards of a million of pounds ?—I procured the information partly at Lyons and partly from Paris.

5261. Under what date ?—I do not recollect the precise date ; but I got part of it when I was at Lyons last July.

5262. Did that come in the raw or the thrown state?—According to the statement I have given, it appears to be about two thirds thrown, and one third raw silk.

5263. Can you state what duties are paid on the import of foreign silks into

France ?

France ?—The duty on foreign raw silks is 1 franc and two-thirds per kilogramme, equal to about 8 *d.* per pound English.

5264. Does all raw silk pay the same duty, or is that Italian ?—Every kind of raw silk except India ; if India silk is imported direct it pays 55 centimes, about 2½ *d.* an English pound.

5265. Coming indirect, what does it pay ?—It is not admitted ; the duty on foreign thrown silks is two francs and 42 centimes per kilogramme, equal to about 1 *s.* a pound.

5266. Do they import any silks from Spain ?—Yes, they do, but very few.

5267. Does that pay the same duty ?—Precisely ; all foreign raw silks pay the same duty, except those from India.

5268. Are you able to state the prices of silks for different years in Italy, and the prices of the same silks at Lyons, and the prices of the same silks in England ? —I have not the document with me, being informed that those prices had been given to the Committee ; I can put the document in if it is wished.

5269. Will you lay before the Committee the prices on the average of as many years as you can of the Italian raw and thrown silks in Italy at one or two of the principal markets, the prices of the same at Lyons, and the prices of the same in England, as nearly as possible of corresponding quality and at corresponding times ?—I will.

5270. Will you further state, if you can, the amount of the sale of Italian silks at Lyons ?—I have not any document to enable me to do that here ; but I can get it from Lyons in eight days ; the sales are all registered by persons appointed for the purpose, and the returns are easily procured.

5271. In what manner is the registry kept of the quantity of silk consumed at Lyons ?—I have never seen the registry, therefore I am ignorant of the manner in which it is done, but I very frequently find it mentioned in letters, that the monthly sale has been such a quantity.

5272. That you believe to comprehend the whole of the silk ?—Yes.

5273. Do the French import any fine Italian raw silks ?—Yes, they do.

5274. Under what circumstances is it that the French resort to the use of Italian raws, when they grow silk themselves ?—They do not perhaps grow enough for their consumption when the demand is very brisk.

5275. Do they ever resort to those till their own stocks are exhausted ?—That depends in some measure on the prices ; the prices of their very best are generally 10 per cent. dearer than the Italian of the same class.

5276. Is there any duty paid on the import of organzine silk into Switzerland, or any other of the places to which you have stated the exports of Italy to be sent ? —I have a note here, that at Zurich, which is one of the principal places in Switzerland for the manufacture of silk, the manufacture has increased there in a most extraordinary manner ; in the year 1792 they had only 1,000 looms and now they have 12,000, and both raw and thrown silk are imported there free of duty.

5277. Is there any duty paid at Vienna, or Berlin or Moscow, or any of those places ?—I believe there is, but I do not know the fact.

5278. Have they any silk mills in Switzerland ?—At Zurich they throw very little indeed, and that little is, I believe, tram ; they get the thrown silk free of duty, and therefore they have probably no inducement.

5279. From what part of Italy do they get their silk ?—They get it from Lombardy and from other parts. I suppose for some particular kinds of goods they may get a little from Piedmont also.

5280. Are you aware whether the same thing exists at Basle ?—I do not know.

5281. Can you state for what purposes the silk is sold at Zurich ?—As they have the number of looms I have stated, I take for granted it must be in stuffs, in broad goods of some description, but I have no information upon that subject.

5282. How much silk would 12,000 looms use up ?—I am not able to answer that question, I am not acquainted with the details of manufacture.

5283. Probably you would think, that if we had no throwing interests to protect in this country, the best way would be to repeal all duties on raw and thrown silks ? —That is a question I cannot satisfactorily answer, it is necessary I should know something connected with the throwing in England, which I do not.

5284. Have you yourself been interested in throwing silk in Italy ?—Never.

5285. Have the relative prices of raw and thrown silk in this country afforded what you consider remuneration to the foreign throwster of late years ?—If by

that

*John B. Heath,*
Esq.

11 May,
1832.

that question I am to understand that the foreign throwster is the person sending his silk to be sold in this market, I should say not.

5286. Taking the price of raw Italian silk, and the price at which the thrown silk of the same qualities has been sold in the English market, has the difference between those afforded what you consider to be the expense of throwing the article in Italy?—According to the evidence which I have upon the subject of throwing in Italy, I should say not; the persons who have of late years sent the thrown silk to be sold in this country, have generally lost by it.

5287. Are the persons who send the thrown silk, the throwsters, or persons who buy it of those who have separate establishments?—There are some of both.

5288. For what period do you consider that the importer of foreign thrown silk has been a loser?—That is a question I cannot answer with precision; but for the last four or five years, I conceive the person who has sent Italian thrown silks to this market, has not been remunerated.

5289. Do you conceive that he has not only not been remunerated, but has been a loser?—Naturally the non-remuneration is a loss.

5290. Can you state from your local knowledge of Italy, and the observation thereon made, whether the throwster in Italy has any advantages over the throwster in England, and to what extent, and in what those advantages consist?—I am not aware that he has any other advantages than that of having a better climate to work in; I believe that they prove of some importance.

5291. Do they work there in the open air?—No, the mills are constructed in the same way as those in this country.

5292. It has been stated to this Committee, that the Italian throwsters have an advantage equal to the payment of 3 s. 6 d., the amount of the present duty on the English throwster?—I should doubt that very much; if I knew the evidence upon which that supposition is founded, I might perhaps better explain it.

5293. This question was put to Mr. Brockwell, " Will you state what are the advantages which the Italians possess in throwing, over the English, which will enable him to undersell the British throwster?" to which he answered, " I am to understand, that to refer to local advantages, reeling his own silk, selecting the best kind of others reeling for his own mills, assorting silk at the time of purchasing, and putting aside all which does not precisely correspond with the sample, in size as well as goodness, or making a second price for the objectionable part, less waste, and the raw silk retaining a quality upon it advantageous to the price when thrown, a more intrinsic article when in organzine or tram, more uniform in size, more valuable to an intelligent manufacturer, because the thread has not been over-strained by speed; all those are advantages of no small importance in skilful hands; the Austrian Government too lends him their aid, so far as to cede to him 5 d per pound below the duty charged upon the raw silk exported to other countries, the raw silk paying 10 d. a pound and the thrown 5 d. ;" then, when afterwards stating what the amount of the advantages is, the answer is repeated, that 3 s. 6 d. a pound, which is the present duty on organzine, is about an equivalent to the local advantages enumerated?—If I may be allowed to answer this question by an explanation, I should say, that comparing the English with the Italian throwster, the English throwster has perhaps the better chance of the two in the selection of silk, because when the English throwster wishes to make a purchase, he has the produce of all the different countries of Italy before him to make his selection; the Italian has only the silk of his own country before him, and not that of the other States, as Fossembrone, Naples, and so on ; I do not at all understand what is meant here by local advantages, nor do I see on what ground it can be that the foreign throwster has the advantage of 3 s. 6 d. over the English throwster; I do not see that he has any.

5294. How do you account for so many English throwsters failing of late?—Because I think many English throwsters have set up mills who had no capital to support them, and as there is no trade so susceptible of variations from the caprices of fashion, and from the state of the national prosperity as the silk trade, a throwster should possess means. As long as it is a remunerating trade, they will go on; but the moment a check comes, they naturally fail, not being able to support themselves till a reaction takes place,

5295, Are you aware what time is taken to throw silk?—It depends entirely on the nature of the machinery; if the machinery is good, it will of course go with greater speed.

5296. Do they throw in Italy in the winter or the summer?—It depends on
circumstances;

*John B. Heath,*
Esq.

11 May,
1832.

circumstances; in the summer time they are principally employed in spinning the silk; in the winter time they throw according to the demand; I have known mills in Piedmont, going the whole winter, as long as there was a supply of water; the whole of the mills in Italy are turned by water; here there is in many cases the expense of steam.

5297. The Piedmont thrown silk is the best silk of Italy, is it not?—It is in general.

5298. Those throwsters are not in the habit of going out of their own market, are they?—I have known instances, where, on account of a deficiency in the crop, Lombardy silk has been imported into Piedmont to be thrown.

5299. Does the superiority of the Piedmontese arise from the growth of the silk of Piedmont, or from its being thrown immediately after the growth?—I should think it operate both ways; in the first place, any person at all acquainted with the conduct of the filature and spinning of silk, knows that the temperature, the weather, has a great influence; besides the utmost care is taken in the reeling. With respect to throwing, the government of Piedmont have always taken great pains that proper persons should be appointed to examine the organzine, in order to preserve the character of the thrown silk of that country; it is done with a great deal more care than in other parts.

5300. Are not those advantages you have enumerated just now, which the throwster there possesses over the English throwster?—They are advantages as far as they go, they render the organzine perfect certainly; but I do not see that as a matter of remuneration to them, they are advantages. If the English throwster excels in his work, he will be remunerated by a better price for his article.

5301. Are you of opinion that there are too many mills in this country already, and that the competition is too great?—As a matter of opinion I should say so, but I have no precise information upon that subject.

5302. You state that the foreign throwster has been sending here at a loss?—I conceive that is the case.

5303. How has the market been in other parts of Europe at the period at which he has been sending here at a loss, has he equally sent to other markets at a loss?—That I am not able to answer.

5304. Has the importation of the foreign thrown silk into this market regulated the price of the market here, or has the competition of the English throwster regulated the market?—I think they both have operated, it depends very much on circumstances.

5305. Taking for granted that you are correct in supposing that the importer of foreign thrown silk has imported at a loss for some years past, how do you reconcile that with the fact, that the importation has increased in quantity, particularly during the last two years?—I am not able to answer the question, except in this way. I can in some measure account for the increase since July 1830, because I know from the nature of the letters I received from several correspondents at that period, that when the Revolution broke out in France they felt that there was no knowing how far it might spread, and a great deal of silk was sent here with a view to its being placed in greater security.

5306. When you state that you believe that the number of throwing mills in this country is too large, do you give that opinion without reference to the increased and increasing quantity of the importation of foreign thrown silk?—I merely judge from this fact, that we have unfortunately had a great many failures in the silk trade; the majority of those failures now, and in 1826, was among the throwsters, unfortunately I was interested in some of those failures, and it turned out on investigation of the bankrupts' accounts, that they were mostly persons who had set up mills without the least means of resisting the pressure of trade.

5307. Has the number of throwing mills, in point of fact, increased within the last five or six years?—Judging from what I hear, I conceive it has.

5308. You state that you conceive silk has been sent here in the raw state for security?—I conceive it was upon the occasion to which I have referred.

5309. Why has not the quantity of thrown silk sent to this country increased in the same proportion?—I have not investigated that fact.

5310. In 1830 the quantity of thrown silk introduced was about 437,000, the quantity of foreign raw 200,000, whereas last year the quantity introduced was 514,000 thrown, and the raw was 1,026,000, diminishing by 200,000 in the raw state, and increasing in the thrown?—I cannot give a positive answer to that, further than to say that I have observed that when anything has occurred at Lyons,

678.                                                                                                  in

*John B. Heath*,
Esq.
———
11 May,
1832.

in the shape of commercial or political convulsion, silk has been often forwarded in the same way.

5311. Do not you conceive that would have an effect equally upon raw?—Yes, I conceive so.

5312. There is no reason why it should not have produced the effect on raw?—No; when I stated that the import was great, from a political cause in 1830, it should be stated that that was in July at the very commencement of a new crop when the amount of raw silk on hand would be low.

5313. Is not England the principal mart for the raw silk of Italy?—That is shown by the return of the exports of silk from Lombardy, to which I have before alluded; by that it appears that while the largest export to other countries, which is that to the Rhine, is 500,000 pounds, that to England has been 2,200,000 pounds.

5314. You account for the large import in July 1830 by the effects of the French Revolution?—Yes, I do in some measure.

5315. How do you account for the larger import in November, December, January, February and March following?—I have not had the opportunity of seeing the returns.

5316. Is not the export of raw silk from Piedmont prohibited, and also exports of organzine from France prohibited?—Not that I know of: the export of organzine from France is not prohibited, for I have seen some here, but it was not approved, and I returned it a month ago.

5317. Have you any raw from Piedmont here for the English market?—We have, but it is smuggled.

5318. For what purposes is the raw of Piedmont principally required?—There is no purpose that I am aware of that renders the raw of Piedmont indispensably necessary; there is a quality of silk from the Piedmontese States called Novi, the principal place of consumption of which is England, it is smuggled out of the country, and brought here.

5319. Does that belong to the Genoese?—To the King of Sardinia.

5320. Could you obtain any greater quantity than now comes, if you had a market for it?—Novi silk is not of current sale in quantities.

5321. Could you obtain a greater quantity from Piedmont, if there was a sale?—The Piedmontese States are placed in a very different situation from the rest of Italy; the export being prohibited, there is no encouragement to increase the cultivation of the mulberry tree; the consequence is, that Novi, which produces the silk the most sought for in this country, is the place from which the principal smuggling takes place.

5322. Are you aware at what expense that smuggling is performed?—It is a per centage upon the value of the article, but I cannot say exactly what it is.

5323. To what place is it smuggled generally?—The mode in which it is done is extremely curious; the persons undertaking to get the silk beyond the frontiers, deposit the value of the silk with the individual who sends it out; he does not restore the money, or pay the man his agency till he is advised that it has passed the frontier.

5324. Is that of Novi used in the manufacture of marabout in this country?—I believe it is.

5325. Has any considerable improvement in the quality of raw silk in Italy taken place since 1824?—In some places, certainly.

5326. What places principally?—Chiefly Lombardy and Naples.

5327. In what respect has the improvement been?—In reeling the silk with a great deal more care, and cleaning it more.

5328. You have stated in a former answer, that the best silks in Lyons, the produce of France, bear an increased price of 10 per cent. above the best silks from Italy?—Some of the very best qualities.

5329. Are you acquainted with the qualities of the silks generally produced in France?—Not with the whole; I have seen a great many of them; a fair average.

5330. Have you brought some silks of French growth with you?—I have.

[*The Witness produced the same.*]

5331. Do equal qualities of Italian and French silks obtain equal prices at Lyons?—There are some qualities among the French which, as I said before, are worth 10 per cent. more; I have stated to the Committee that last July when I was at Lyons, I made some inquiries upon the subject, and procured those samples I

have

*John B. Heath,*
Esq.

11 May,
1832.

have now laid upon the table; at that period there was some notion that the French Government intended to take off the restriction on the French raw silks, and I took these samples with a view to having them examined here, to see whether some business might not be done between the two places, but I found on inquiry that they were so much above what we could get for them here, it would not answer.

5332. Have you received consignments of French organzine here?—I have of French thrown; I do not know whether the raw silk of which it was made was grown in France.

5333. Can you obtain the French silk used in making marabout?—That is prohibited among the rest.

5334. Is any of it smuggled here?—I have never seen any; if the price at Lyons is higher than it is here, there could be no inducement to bring it here.

5335. Do you know that French silk, of the native growth, and thrown in France, is allowed to be exported into this country?—I cannot answer that question; all I can say is, that I have received silks thrown at Lyons which passed through the regular channel.

5336. Did your correspondent inform you that it was French thrown silk?—Yes.

5337. Have you ever heard of the growers of French silk having petitioned that Government to allow the exportation of it to this country?—When I was there I heard that they had petitioned to be allowed to export it, but the manufacturers opposed it on the ground that they possessed certain qualities which gave them a superiority in manufacture which would be attained by others if the export was permitted.

5338. If it is not allowed to be exported through the Custom House, must not there be a considerable expense in smuggling it through France?—I should think very considerable expense and great risk; but I am not sufficiently acquainted with the subject to speak positively.

5339. Will you state to the Committee through what channel this silk, which was consigned from Lyons, reached you?—It came to me through Calais, in the ordinary way, with all my Italian silks. This skein of silk I hold in my hand is one of the qualities they use for making the article they call marabout; this is a silk which in the month of July last was worth, in the market of Lyons, 59 francs the kilogramme, which, deducting 12½ per cent. discount for cash payment, made that silk cost at Lyons 18 s. 10 d. the English pound, in addition to which there would be the charges to add, supposing it brought here. In July last we had great difficulty in being able to sell Lombardy silk of the best quality at 17 s. to 18 s.

5340. Are the Committee to understand, that the silk you exhibit is silk of French growth?—Yes, it is; I got these six skeins through a French silk merchant; they were sent by the diligence. I did not bring them with me; there was no difficulty in sending mere samples.

5341. What is the comparative quality, judging from your knowledge of silk, between that which was 18 s. 10 d. at Lyons, and that which was selling from 17 s. to 18 s. here?—The best answer to that would be, to exhibit another sample which comes nearer the Lombardy silk; that silk, No. 748, which would make an organzine of 18 to 24 deniers, cost 54 francs the kilogramme at Lyons at that period, that would stand in about 17 s. 4 d.; for the parallel quality to this, as nearly as possible in London, at that time it would have been difficult to have obtained more than 17 s., all the charges being paid.

5342. What are the charges of transport per pound of raw silk from Lyons here?—I have the account of charges on a bale of raw silk weighing 288 lbs. English.

| | £. | s. | d. |
|---|---|---|---|
| Carriage from Lyons to Calais, 45 centimes per kilogramme, f⁵ 58. 27. making - - - - - - - - | 2 | 5 | - |
| Freight to London, and Charges at Calais - - - | - | 12 | - |
| Duty, entry, scavage and expenses - - - - - | 2 | 10 | 4 |
| In all - - | £.5 | 7 | 4 |

making 4¼ d. per pound.

5343. You mean that the French manufacturer at Lyons was in a situation to procure silk at 17 s. 4 d. per lb., equal to that you could sell in England of Italian growth at 17 s. to 18 s.?—Yes, within a fraction.

678.

5344. Have

*John B. Heath,*
Esq.

11 May,
1832.

5344. Have you any samples of French thrown silk?—No.

5345. You know nothing of the comparative prices in July?—I do not recollect them.

5346. Would the silk you now produce have made marabout?—I am not acquainted with the details of the manufacture, but those are the silks which I was told at Lyons were used for that purpose.

5347. Is Lombardy silk as well adapted for making marabout as the French silk?—I should think not, it is not the quality used for that purpose here.

5348. You have stated that the best raw silk of France is 10 per cent. higher than the best raw of Italy?—Yes, in the Lyons market; at least in was in July last; I should think the same difference exists now.

5349. Why does not the French manufacturer buy the imported Italian raws, until the raws of France fall to a par with the price of Italian?—I can only answer that, by stating that there is a very strong prejudice in the French manufacturers' minds in favour of silks of their own country; they have been always used to employ that silk in their manufactures, and they have not been so accustomed to use Italian raw silk.

5350. The French manufacturers prefer their own silk, though it is 10 per cent. higher? So it appears.

5351. You say that they frequently resort to the Piedmont silk on account of their own being 10 per cent. higher?—I did not state that it was on that account, but that it was the fact that the great consumption of foreign organzine at Lyons was chiefly confined to Piedmont thrown.

5352. Are there any other places in Switzerland besides Zurich where silk is manufactured?—Yes, I believe there are; I do not know it of my own knowledge.

5353. You are not able correctly to state what quantity of silk a loom will take?—No, I am quite ignorant of all details of manufacture.

5354. Can you say that a loom on the average might use one or two pounds per week?—I have not the smallest knowledge upon that subject.

5355. Supposing the looms to consume from one to two pounds per week, there being as you state 12,000 looms in operation in Zurich, allowing only one pound to a loom, it appears that there would be 600,000 pounds of silk used in a year at Zurich alone; even supposing there were no other place in Switzerland having looms, it appears from the account you have given, that you portion to Switzerland no greater quantity than 200,000 pounds of silk as exported from Italy to that quarter, how do you explain that?—The 200,000 pounds I alluded to were the export from Lombardy alone. The remainder is probably derived from the produce of the other parts of Italy and Turkey.

5356. But you are not able to state from whence they derive the remainder of the quantity?—Not with accuracy.

5357. Are you aware whether in Switzerland there have ever been throwing mills to any extent?—I have heard that they throw very little in Zurich, and that that is tram chiefly.

5358. Are you aware whether there have been throwing mills there to any extent?—As matter of opinion I should say there have not.

5359. Are you aware that there are other throwing establishments?—I do not know it of my own knowledge.

5360. Is it your impression that there have not been?—I have not considered the subject and have no impression, but finding that silk is admitted duty free into that country, that the increase in the manufacture has taken place since the peace, that they could obtain thrown silks on a more reasonable footing than others, I conclude, therefore, that they had not the same inducement to set up throwing mills which persons have in other places.

5361. There is not that inducement which exists in this country, where we have silks from all parts of the world?—No.

5362. Is there any China or Bengal imported through this country into Switzerland?—There has been in small quantities.

5363. It is not your opinion that the price of Italian silk produces an effect upon the price of the French silk at Lyons?—That is a question which does not apply generally; what I have stated respects certain qualities not to be equalled by any silk I have seen in any other part of the world; it is that which is ten per cent. higher, there is a great deal much more moderate in price and inferior in quality in France.

5364. Do you think that the price of the quality in which the Italian may
come

come in competition, is regulated by the quantity introduced from Italy?—No doubt it is.

*John B. Heath,*<br>*Esq.*

11 May,<br>1832.

5365. That amounts in France to about two millions pounds weight?—As I before stated to 1,200,000 pounds. I have a document here showing the average production in France for the last three years, including the season of 1832. It is estimated at 10,000 bales, weighing 826,000 kilogrammes, or 1,750,000 pounds English. I have reason to believe that what I have stated is correct, for it was the information collected for the Committee who were appointed by Government to ascertain whether they should permit the exportation of the silks of France.

5366. Can you state how many looms there are in France?—No, I do not possess that information.

5367. In what do you imagine the superiority of the French silk consists?—I conceive that it depends upon the elasticity of the thread, and that greater care is taken in the cleaning of it.

5368. Are you able to state what proportion of silk of that superior quality bears to the whole produce of silk?—I cannot say accurately, but I should think a very moderate proportion.

5369. Can you state what is the average consumption of silk in France?—No, I have no document here to show that.

5370. Is the proportion of the best kind of raw silk, as compared with the whole produce of silk, greater in France than in Italy?—I am not able to answer that question, I have never considered it; a great deal will depend upon season.

5371. Can you state the total quantity of foreign silk imported into France?—I have before mentioned, that the average quantity of raw and thrown silk imported into France from 1825 to 1830, both inclusive, is 540,390 kilogrammes or 1,186,719 pounds English annually.

5372. Is the superior quality of the French raw to be attributed to the difference in the quality of the cocoon, or to greater skill in reeling?—I have before stated that there is a great quantity of French raw silk which is not of superior quality, but that if allusion is made to the best quality, I should say the temperature has a great deal to do with the giving the thread of silk a greater elasticity; I should also add that greater care is generally taken in the reeling of the silk and cleaning it.

5373. Has the increase of production of silk in Italy been since 1826?—There has been a gradual increase ever since the peace.

5374. Has it been progressive in the same degree?—I should say not latterly so much as before.

---

*Martis, 15° die Maii, 1832.*

---

### J. A. S. MACKENZIE, ESQUIRE, in the Chair.

---

#### Mr. *Andrew Martin*, called in; and Examined.

Mr.<br>*Andrew Martin.*

15 May,<br>1822.

5375. HAVE the goodness to state the name of the firm to which you belong? Morris, Prevost & Company, in London.

5376. Can you inform the Committee the gross produce of silk in Italy?—I have put down the information which I got in Italy in 1824; the quantity at that time, which was produced in Italy, was about four millions of pounds English; the crop was rather abundant that year.

5377. Have you the detail of the countries in which it was produced?—I have; in Piedmont, 1,100,000 pounds English; in Lombardy and Tyrol, 2,300,000 pounds, English weight; these I believe are pretty correct; the following are not so accurate, as it is difficult to get at the account of the quantity produced; Naples and Sicily 400,000 pounds, the Roman States about 300,000 pounds, Tuscany and Lucca about 100,000 pounds.

5378. Have you any reason to think the produce has much increased since 1824?—Taking the average of the last three years, I should say in Piedmont it has not increased materially, that it is still about the same, 1,100,000 pounds; in Lombardy and Tyrol, about 3,000,000; Naples and Sicily, 450,000 pounds; the Roman States and Tuscany, and Lucca, the same.

5379. The increase appears to be in Lombardy?—Yes.

5380. That makes the average of the last three years 4,900,000 pounds?—Yes.

678.　　　　　　　　　　　　　　　　　　　　　　　　5381. Have

5381. Have you reason to suppose that any of those countries can materially increase their produce, and what countries?—I should say there has been no increase in Piedmont, nor is there likely to be any material increase, as the production is rather discouraged by the prohibition to export of raw silks.

5382. How do you obtain those returns?—I got those returns in Italy, and by conversing with the first silk merchants in that country; I am not aware of any official returns; there are returns of the exports, but I believe none of the production.

5383. It is as a general merchant in silk, that you obtained the information you now give, as to the produce of silk in Italy?—It is. In the Roman States I should think there is no increase; there might be an increase there, as they grow very good silk, particularly in Fossembrone, but they want capital, they cannot easily get advances from foreign merchants; they find it very difficult on account of the badness of the laws in that country, where the creditor is not sufficiently protected against the dishonesty of his debtor.

5384. The Committee understand that the exportation of raw silks is prohibited from Piedmont, do you consider that an injury to Piedmont?—There is in Piedmont a disposition amongst the silk merchants, who are not silk throwsters, to obtain the means of exporting raw silk; and I should suppose there is a disadvantage to Piedmont in not having free exportation of silk as I see that they smuggle a portion of their raw with some difficulty and some expense, which of course they would export freely, more willingly, if allowed to do so; I suppose they smuggle about seven per cent. or less of their crop in raw white silk, which comes from Novi mostly, and is mostly exported to England.

5385. Does that smuggling take place chiefly on the Milan side?—I believe they smuggle it to Milan.

5386. Do you know the cost?—My recollection is, that it costs about two francs per pound; but it is difficult, as I have nothing to do with those transactions, to ascertain the cost; I suppose from ten to fifteen per cent. The increase in Lombardy, and principally in Tyrol, seems to have been about 30 per cent. on the former growth in the last nine years, and seems to be likely to increase as much, and probably more, in the next six years, judging from the quantity of mulberry trees planted; there has been probably some increase at Naples in silk generally, but particularly in good silk; they reel a better sort of silk, they used to reel a very coarse sort of silk, not adapted for this country; now they have improved the nature of their silk, and probably there will be a great increase of the quantity of good silk they produce, though perhaps there will not be a great increase of the total quantity of silk produced; for it requires a greater number of cocoons to produce a pound of fine silk than a pound of coarse one; I cannot give any answer as to Tuscany.

5387. In accounting for the want of increase in the Roman States, you have spoken of the want of capital, are you aware that the Jews of Pesaro are a very rich body of men?—Yes, they are; but circumstances have taken place in the Roman States, which have deprived the country of that very resource, which was a very great one; there were some very rich Jew houses in Pesaro, but there has been a sort of persecution by the Roman government against the Jews, and most of them have emigrated and gone to Tuscany, in consequence of that persecution.

5388. If they have gone to Tuscany, they have carried their resources to that country?—I suppose they have carried their money with them; I should think that industry has by that means been reduced, but that it might have been increased if the laws had been better; I know that the reeling of silk is not confined to the merchants there, but that the nobility take pride in the reeling good silk; some propositions have been made to me, which I was obliged to decline, for I knew a case in which the Pope had given an indemnity to a man not willing to pay his debts not to pay for five or six years, and no foreigner will run the risk of that.

5389. Where do you include the silk of Ancona?—In the Roman States.

5390. Have you been accustomed to purchase the cocoons in Italy?—Never.

5391. Nor been accustomed to the reeling of silk there?—Never; my business has been the receiving the silk consigned to my house in London.

5392. As a silk merchant, you are necessarily acquainted with the state of trade in Italy, and the operations going on there?—I must be aware of the abundance or scarcity of silk, and the state of the merchants generally there.

5393. Without having any of that particular knowledge which a person engaged

in

Mr.
*Andrew Martin.*

15 May,
1832.

in the purchase of cocoons would have, have you a better and much greater knowledge than such a person would have ?—I must have a general knowledge.

5394. You have stated that it is your opinion, that the Piedmontese are injured by the export of raw silk being prohibited ?—I should think the Piedmontese grower is injured by not being allowed to export his silk to the most advantageous market.

5395. You say that about seven per cent. of the growth of Piedmont is smuggled out of the country in a raw state ?—Yes, that I take to be the outside quantity.

5396. You conceive it is principally sent to England ?—Yes ; the best white silk is, I think, principally.

5397. Do you know for what purposes it is used here ?—I have no acquaintance with the manufacturing business.

5398. Do you not know that they use it for Persian warps, and that they cannot make Persian without it ?—I cannot give an opinion upon that subject ; we sell our silk at the market price, without knowing for what it is to be employed ; and the manufacturers, generally speaking, do not tell us for what they mean to employ it.

5399. Can you state how much organzine and tram is made in each country ?—In Piedmont, the whole of the produce, except what is smuggled, is made into organzine and tram, or consumed for their own manufactory ; in Lombardy, probably from five-eighths to two-thirds of the produce is converted into thrown ; at Naples I should say very little is thrown, only a very small quantity for their own manufactures ; they convert more silk into sewing silks for exportation. In Tuscany I suppose they throw part of what they produce, as they have themselves some silk manufactories ; in the Roman States, I do not think they throw anything considerable for exportation ; the great throwing is in Piedmont, and in Lombardy.

5400. To what countries do the Italians export silk, and in what proportions to France and England ?—I believe that Naples exports one-third of its fine silk to France, and two-thirds to England ; they export principally fine silk, the quantity probably is about 250,000 lbs. English ; Piedmont exports about 650,000 lbs. English to France, thrown of course ; 160,000 to Switzerland and Germany.

5401. Can you distinguish the quantities exported to Switzerland and to Germany ?—I cannot ; the account is taken at Milan, through which it passes to both countries, and there is no distinction made of the country to which it passes in my memoranda ; 50,000 to England, 300,000 are used for the Piedmontese manufactures, which are increasing. Lombardy and Tyrol export about 1,200,000 to England, that is about three-eighths of the total produce of Lombardy, of which one-third is thrown in those States of that export to England ; 750,000 to Switzerland and the Rhine, almost all thrown ; 270,000 to Vienna, all thrown ; 150,000 to Lyons, about half thrown and half raw ; 70,000 to Russia, perhaps more ; now this leaves about 600,000 lbs., which I suppose is consumed at home or sent elsewhere.

5402. To what period do those returns refer ?—I should say 1829 to 1830.

5403. From what sources do you obtain this information ?—We have documents sent by the principal carrier of Milan ; I cannot say that this is perfectly accurate, but I might get it perfectly accurate ; it is important for us to know what silk has gone in certain quarters, and we obtain the information as matter of business.

5404. What are the duties levied on the exportation of raw and thrown silks from France and Italy ?—From France, raw is not allowed to be exported, but thrown is exported without any difficulty ; to my knowledge I am not aware of any difficulty in exporting thrown, and I should say that I believe it is allowed to be exported.

5405. Of the best qualities, as well as the worst ?—Of any quality ; from Naples raw silk is exported free of duty, it was not five or six years ago ; from Piedmont, the exportation of raw is prohibited ; thrown is allowed to be exported at the duty of 50 centimes per lb., which I make equal to about five-pence and three quarters per lb. English ; the duty on the exportation of silk from Lombardy is Austrian livres 241 and a fraction per hundred kilogrammes, which is equal to $8\frac{3}{4}d.$ per lb. English ; Lombardy, on thrown, the duty is one half, or $120\frac{1}{2}$, equal to $4d. \frac{3}{8}$ths.

5406. You say that you know that thrown silk is exported from France ?—My impression is, that it can be exported without any difficulty.

5407. Is that silk grown in France, or Italian silk thrown there ?—I cannot ascertain whether the thrown silk is Italian or French ; I believe it is done without the least difficulty, I know that the exportation of raw silk is prohibited, but still

678.

Mr.
*Andrew Martin.*

15 May,
1832.

it comes to this country; there is of course a difficulty about that, but I am not aware of any difficulty about the thrown silk.

5408. In France they allow the transit of Italian silk?—Yes.

5409. Do you mean to state that there is no law prohibiting the export of French thrown silk?—I am not aware of any difficulty in exporting thrown silk, for I have received some without any difficulty; my impression is that that can be exported, I may be mistaken.

5410. Have you any doubt that the thrown silks, which you get, or which are exported to your knowledge, occasionally from France, are the produce of French raw silks?—I cannot say whether they are French raw silks thrown in France, or Italian raw silks thrown there.

5411. You are not aware of any law prohibiting French silk when it is thrown, being exported?—I am not; I believe there is no difficulty.

5412. You state that French raw silks come to this country sometimes as a matter of speculation?—Yes.

5413. They must necessarily be smuggled out of France?—They are, or exchanged for Italian raws.

5414. That must be attended with considerable expense, must it not?—I should think so.

5415. When it comes to this country with this expense added to it, how do you find the price as compared with that of Italian silk of the same quality?—It is difficult to judge; those silks imported into this country were not known, and were sold not nearly so high as I should have expected; I do not think that the purchaser did justice to the silk, that he paid so much for it as it was entitled to receive.

5416. Will you name the price of the Italian and the French?—The silk was not identically the same; my impression is, that they would have been worth more to manufacturers; it is not uncommon that the manufacturers do not appreciate silk fully at first.

5417. So that a manufacturer buying Italian silk, and buying also French silk, the price for that was not so high as you think it was entitled to?—Just so; I suppose that it was not smuggled, but that it was exchanged for Italian silk.

5418. You do not think there was more expense attending the import of that silk than Italian silk?—The act of exchanging those raws for Italian raws which were in bond, must have been attended with some expense. I suppose that a person must have fee'd some custom house officer for going out of the regular course.

5419. Do you know whether any difference exists at Lyons between the price of Italian throwns and French throwns?—I cannot answer that satisfactorily; but my impression is, that Piedmont thrown is worth more than French thrown; and in this country we have received some French thrown which were not so well liked as Piedmont thrown.

5420. Are French throwns well known as an article of trade in London?—Yes; the quantity coming is very small.

5421. When you say French thrown, you mean silk thrown in France?—Yes; and probably from French silk.

5422. Are you acquainted with the extent of manufacture of silk goods at Milan?—I am not.

5423. Are you acquainted with the extent of manufacture of silk goods at Como?—I am not.

5424. Can you state the extent of manufacture of silk goods at Turin and Genoa?—I think I stated it to be about 300,000 lbs. which they consumed.

5425. Are you informed that every State of Italy has a peculiar manufacture of silk goods of its own?—Not sufficiently to give any interesting information upon that subject.

5426. Have you reason to suppose that from any part of Italy manufactured silks are exported to England?—I should suppose, but really my answer is not worth taking down, that some velvets may have been imported into England from Genoa.

5427. You have stated the production of silk in Italy to be 4,000,000, how do you know that, if you do not know the extent of the manufacture in different places?—The silk is produced and employed afterwards to be manufactured into stuffs, or into goods; the production of silk goods from the cocoon, and afterwards its manufactory into stuffs, are two very distinct processes. Silk is first reeled from the cocoons, then that silk is thrown, and afterwards it is woven into stuffs; a man
may

may know the production of cotton in America without knowing the sort of goods that are made from it, and I cannot give any information whatever of the process of manufacture.

5428. Can you state what have been the variations of prices of raw and thrown silks in Italy and in England?—I have a few memoranda of the prices in different years from 1819 to 1832, those prices of course are approximated.

5429. From what source are those prices taken?—From the price currents of the respective countries; Lombardy organzine 24 to 28 deniers; in 1819 it appears that the price was here about 57 s., and the duty then was about 14 s. 8 d.; 1823, 42 s.; in January 1824, 36 s., that was the time when it was expected the alteration of the duty would take place, which took place in July; then the duty was reduced to 7 s. 6 d., and the price became, with the duty 30 s.; there was already an impression that some change would take place. In February 1825, 45 s.; the price then got up 15 s. after the reduction of duty. In November 1825, when the duty was reduced to 5 s. the price was 31 s.; that fall was probably owing to the crisis, to the reduction of duty and to the unsettled state of trade. In 1826, it was 28 s.; in 1827, 29 s. 6 d.; in 1828, 29 s.; in June 1829, when the duty was reduced to 3 s. 6 d. it was 26 s.; in November 1830, 24 s. 6 d.; in 1831, 21 s. 9 d. I will state the prices of Lombardy organzine at Bergamo, for the same size 24–28 deniers; in 1823 it was 23 livres; in 1824 it was 21½; in 1825, 29; in 1826, 25; in 1827, 26; in 1828, 26; in 1829, 22½; in 1830, 22, and in 1831, 20; I believe about the same periods I have referred to as to England. As to Milan raws, 4 to 5 cocoons, in 1819, 39 s.; in 1823, 28 s., the duty was then, I believe, 5 s. 6 d. per lb.; in January 1824, 24 s.; in July 1824, when it was reduced to 3 d., it was 18 s.; in February 1825, 26 s.; in November 1825 it was 22 s. 6 d.; in 1826, 21 s.; in 1827, 21 s. 6 d.; in 1828 the same, 21 s. 6 d.; in 1829, 17 s. 6 d.; in 1830, 17 s. 6 d.; in 1831, 16 s. 3 d.; in 1832, 17 s. In Lombardy the price of the same raws was in 1823, 18½ livres; in 1824, 17; in 1825, 23; in 1826, 20½; in 1827, 22¼; in 1828, 22¼; in 1829, 17½; in 1830, 19; in 1831, 16¼.

5430. What is the exchange of the Milan livre?—About 34 Milan livres are equal to 20 s., and 100 lbs. of Lombardy produce 70 lbs. English.

5431. The great decrease of price appears to have taken place in the last three years, is there any thing in the nature of the crops accounting for that?—The crops have not been very abundant, but the production has increased materially, and that of course has reduced the price; but prices had been nearly as low in Lombardy in 1823 and 1824.

5432. Can you inform the Committee what have been the prices at Lyons?—I understand that the Cevinnes silk, or I believe Alais silks, are worth three francs per kilogramme, or 12 per cent. more than the best Milan raws at Lyons; those silks are probably peculiar to France. It appears there is no such silk reeled in any other country; as to the prices at Lyons and London, my information is very imperfect. I have the prices of December 1831 in both places, which I will state; the Lombardy organzine in December 1831, of 24 to 28 deniers, was worth 28 ½ francs, with 12 ½ per cent. discount. In London, the same article was worth 22 s.; I have two prices current, one from Lyons, and another from Messrs. Durant of London, about the same date, which I will give in if it is wished; Italian trams of 24 to 28 deniers were at Lyons 28 ½ francs, with 12 ½ per cent. discount, and in London, 20 s.; the best Milan raw of three to four cocoons, 26 francs; in London 17 s.

5433. Are you speaking of silks of precisely the same quality?—I should suppose they are nearly of the same quality; in the silk trade they would be considered to be of the same quality, or nearly so.

5434. You spoke of Lombardy silks, of from 24 to 28 deniers, as being worth in Lyons 28 francs, was that the English pound?—The French pound; it seems from a very rapid calculation, that the prices, if they are correctly taken, would be dearer at Lyons than in London; I have had lately some French thrown silk sent to my house from Lyons to be sold in London; as I could not get a price which would have repaid the French silk merchant, he ordered me to send it back to him, and it has been reshipped to Calais.

5435. What are the duties paid on the import of Foreign raw and thrown silk into France?—The duty on silk derived from India, is 55 centimes per kilogramme, equal to about 2⅓ d. per lb. English; raws from other countries, 156 centimes, equal to about 7 d.; throwns 242 centimes per kilogramme, equal to about 10 ½ d.

678. English.

Mr.
*Andrew Martin.*

15 May,
1832.

English. In the last season they proposed to reduce it to 5 centimes on raw, and 10 centimes on throwns.

5436. Are the French, buyers of Bengal silk in this market?—I do not think they are to any extent, they have been; they have tried it, and two houses in London had a large order from several houses in Lyons, who united to make a large purchase of Indian silk in this market, I believe in 1826 or 1827; at that time India silk was extremely cheap in this country, the merchants in Lyons thought it would be a good time to make a trial of Indian silk; they bought about 300 bales of Bengal silk through two houses in London, and forwarded to Lyons; but I understood that that speculation did not answer, that they lost considerably by it, though Indian silk was that year almost as low as they had ever been in this country; the throwsters were not in the habit of using that silk, and refused to work it, it might have been prejudice or want of skill, but they made more waste than was expected; and upon the whole, I think it was a losing speculation.

5437. Did your mercantile transactions with respect to the exportation of raw and thrown silks from Italy necessarily include any knowledge of the reeling of silk in Italy?—I do not think it is necessary to have seen the operation of reeling silk to be a good judge of silk, of course every man who goes to Italy interested in the silk business, wishes to see the reeling of silk, and every one desirous to increase his own information; but there are gentlemen in London perfectly qualified to judge of the goodness of silk (silk brokers) who have very probably never seen it reeled in their life, the manufacturer finds it out also; he knows what are the defects of silk, without having seen it reeled, though the man who has sent it reeled may be better able to state from what the defects have arisen.

5438. You do not know what are the advantages the throwsters in Italy may derive from having the silk of their own reeling?—I should think there is always some advantage in winding silk which has been recently reeled; besides a man who has reeled his own silk, knows better what are the real qualities of the silk; even a good judge of silk may be mistaken in silk when he has not reeled it himself.

5439. Therefore it is a great advantage for a man to reel his own silk?—I should not say a great advantage, but it is an advantage undoubtedly.

5440. How are Switzerland and other places on the Continent supplied with silk, and of what kind?—Switzerland and Germany are mostly supplied from Piedmont and Lombardy, and nearly all the silk exported to those countries is in the thrown state; the quantity of raw is very small indeed; there is no duty in Switzerland on silk imported into Switzerland in the raw or the thrown state.

5441. Are there any duties on the importation of silk into Austria, Russia or Germany?—I am not able to answer that question; I should think if there is it is small; I have no doubt I should be able to get that information for the Committee in a short time.

5442. Has any improvement, in your opinion, taken place in the quality of raw silk in Italy since 1824?—I should think there has been improvement in Lombardy, and particularly at Verona and Tyrol, at Naples also there has been an improvement, that is they reel a much larger proportion of fine silks than they used to do; they originally used to reel very coarse silks in long skeins, which made them unfit for the consumption of this country; but within these few years they have begun to reel silks on the Piedmont system; silk worth probably 30 to 50 per cent. more than the coarse silk they reeled, and the quantity has been increasing gradually; they have reeled into fine silk the cocoons they used to reel into coarse silks.

5443. There has been no improvement in the finer silks of Italy?—I should think they have improved, generally speaking, in Lombardy; the quantity of good silk produced in Italy is much larger than it was in 1824.

5444. Do you suppose the quantities, which you say have been given by carriers from Italy, can be depended upon?—I believe the account is correct; it is the quantity, I apprehend, on which the duties have been paid, but my statement is only one approximating to the truth.

5445. Can you inform the Committee what is the price paid for throwing silk in Piedmont?—I find from my documents this statement, which I shall be able to correct if I get better and more recent information; the Piedmont price, including waste, which generally varies from three to six per cent., was for 22 to 24 deniers from 4s. 3d. to 4s. 6d. per lb. English; and from 26 to 30 deniers, 3s. 9d. to 4s. per lb. English. In France, including waste, the organzine of 20 to 22 deniers,

4s. 6d.

Mr.
*Andrew Martin.*

15 May,
1832.

4 s. 6 d. per lb. English; 24 to 26 deniers, 4 s. 4 d.; of 28 to 30 deniers, 3 s. 9 d., this, I understand, leaves to the throwster about 3 d. per lb. English profit; they throw the silk for the manufacturer, and I understand those prices leave about 3 d. per lb. profit.

5446. Can you state of what that consists, how much in wages, and how much in machinery, and other things?—No, my information is derived from Frenchmen who I believe are able judges; I did not ascertain the throwing myself, except having seen the mills.

5447. Can you state the prices in Lombardy and in France?—In Lombardy, at Milan, the prices were, not including the waste, which varies from three to six per cent., that is about eight to ninepence a pound on an average, for organzine 28 to 32 deniers, the price appears to be about 2 s. 3 d. per lb. English; for throwing 20 to 22 deniers, 2 s. 5 d. In abundant years, of course, there is more raw to be thrown, and the throwster tries to take advantage of it in those years of abundant crops; for the first eight months after the silk is reeled, prices are generally about 2 d. per lb. dearer; and I understand also, that from 2 d. to 4 d. per pound more is paid only for second rate silks, as they are more difficult to work, and then there is more waste.

5448. Is all the information you have given to the Committee respecting throwing, information you have received, and not practical information?—No, practical information; I have visited the mills, and obtained a good deal of my information from the throwsters on the spot.

5449. You have stated the price of raw silk in Italy averaged 18½ livres in 1823?—I stated, that that was the price at that particular time; I believe I have, since 1823, at least generally stated the prices in Lombardy in September, a time when there the silk is sold generally at the fairs; the price was about 17 livres in September 1824; I was myself in Italy at that time, and saw the fairs.

5450. In 1825, when the 5 s. 6 d. duty was taken off the import, it rose to 23 livres?—That might depend upon the crops and various causes, as England is only a part of its market. The abundance of the produce has a great effect upon the price, the crop in 1823, had been abundant, in 1824 very abundant; so that the price was of course lower, which is generally the case; in 1825 the crop probably was not so abundant, and prices had risen in England, and of course the prices partook of it in Italy.

5451. In 1823, before the reduction of duty from 5 s. 6 d. to 3 d. the price of raw was 18½ livres; when reduced to a penny, in 1827 and 1828, the price was 22¼ livres, and has been so lately; the difference has been a gratuity given by this country to the Italian grower, has it not?—I suppose that is the deduction of the Honourable Member; I cannot give an opinion upon that subject; it is evident that if the Italian received for one pound of silk 17 s. nett in 1823, and he received 23 s. nett in 1825, he received 6 s. more per pound for his silk.

5452. Have you reason to suppose, that the import of Italian thrown silks has been more profitable since the duty was reduced than before?—I conceive it has been more profitable to the Italian immediately after the reduction of duty in 1824, but for a short time.

5453. Might not that have taken place whether there was any alteration of duty on the thrown silk or not?—Certainly.

5454. Has the alteration of the law which took place in 1824 to 1826, and down to the present time, had the effect of increasing or decreasing the capital which is employed in the manufacture of silk?—I am utterly unable to answer that question.

5455. You sell silk to manufacturers?—I do.

5456. Do you consider them to be as prosperous and as worthy of credit now as they were five or six years ago?—I should think that the great manufacturers are rather better off; I am afraid the smaller ones are worse off, that is what guides me in giving credit.

5457. Do you think there has been an increase of capital among the large manufacturers?—I do not think I can give a more detailed answer than my last answer.

5458. To what charges is silk subject in the shape of commission to the manufacturer?—None; brokerage is paid by the merchant.

5459. Suppose you sell silk, what is the charge for commission?—Two per cent. and two per cent. *del credere* charged to the Italian merchant.

5460. Is there any charge beyond that?—No, I am not aware of any other,

678.

in

in the shape of commission and *del credere*; there are charges of course of land-ing the goods and putting them in the warehouse; there is the brokerage.

5461. What is that?—Five-eighths per cent. we sell to a broker and charge that to our correspondent in Italy.

5462. What is the credit on silk, or the discount?—Five months or $2\frac{1}{2}$ per cent. discount if paid in fourteen days.

5463. The credit was longer, was it not?—Yes, it was ten months formerly; it has been reduced gradually.

5464. There is very little credit given upon silk is there, now, is not cash gene-rally paid?—No, I should have expected that there would have been more cash paid than there is, owing to the great advantage of discounting at half per cent. per month, I am surprized at finding that so few pay cash.

5465. The temptation is not sufficient to produce the money?—So it appears. I should say when the discount takes place, the profits of the merchant in London are reduced necessarily.

5466. You say the extent of credit was gradually reduced, are you able to state the periods at which such reductions took place; for instance, you state that there was a period when the credit was at ten months, can you fix the date when it was reduced?—I cannot precisely; I believe it was reduced first to eight months, and then it was reduced from eight to five after the crisis of 1826, that may not be the last reduction, but I believe there was a reduction at that time on account of the failures which had taken place at that time among the purchasers of silk; the silk merchant, finding that the losses exceeded the *del credere*, did not choose to go on guaranteeing for so long a period at the *del credere* they received, they reduced it to five months, and my impression is, that it must be reduced still further, as it is at Lyons; at Lyons there is $12\frac{1}{2}$ per cent. discount; but if a man takes the credit of, I believe, three months generally, they do not sell to him again.

5467. The first considerable reduction took place in or about the year 1826?—That is my impression; I think there has been a reduction within the last ten years, from ten to five months, which has taken place gradually; I think it was re-duced from ten to eight and from eight to five.

5468. The year 1826, being the year in which the trade was thrown open to the foreigner?—The failures took place in the year 1825 and 1826, after the mad speculations entered into in England, and that accounts, I think, for the rise in price; after the reduction of the duty the prices rose.

5469. Do you consider that the foreign throwster has imported during the last four or five years at a gain or at a loss to himself?—It is almost impossible to give a positive answer, some men reel their silk and throw it, others purchase it, and generally speaking, we silk merchants do not know the price they have paid for their silk, they merely send the silk to London to be sold at a fixed limit, or at the best price we can get; if I judge from their complaints, they have been losing money for several years, for two or three years.

5470. Do you consider, that during that period it has been most to the advan-tage of the Italian to import raw or thrown?—I should say, to import raw de-cidedly; the quantity of raw imported is doubled, and of the quantity of thrown there has been a great change in the proportion, and there were much more throwns imported 20 years ago than raws; now it is reversed.

5471. Having stated that you conceive it has been more to the advantage of foreigners to import the silk in a raw than a thrown state for some years past, do you not consider that the duty upon the thrown has, in point of fact, been paid out of the pocket of the foreigner, and is at this time?—I should think in part; I believe it will be found generally, that duties fall in part on the consumers of the country, and in part on the importers; I do not suppose the whole of the duty is paid by the foreign throwster; I should think duties in general are divided and supported in part by the foreigner and in part by the consumer in this country.

5472. Did the merchants make a reduction of credit from the losses they sus-tained, or did they make it at the request of the trade?—I am not aware of any request of the trade having been made to the silk merchants to reduce the credit.

5473. Was it in consequence of the losses they sustained?—That is my im-pression.

5474. Were you residing in England at the time?—I should think I was; I have been residing in England since 1824, but I have been occasionally absent.

5475. If

Mr.
*Andrew Martin*.

15 May,
1832.

5475. If you were not absent for any length of time, of course you were here at the time spoken of?—I think I have been here at one or other of the two changes that have been made, one from ten to eight, and another from eight to five months; but I cannot say which.

5476. Were you engaged in the silk trade before 1824?—No.

5477. You say the great manufacturers are better off, and that the little ones are worse off; do you mean that the prosperity of the richer house has been purchased by the ruinous state of the little ones, or by increased profit?—I am utterly unable to answer this question; I answered as to my impression, that I should be inclined to trust the great manufacturers more than the smaller ones; I am afraid the smaller ones have been suffering of late years.

5478. The trade of Spitalfields has got into fewer hands, has it not?—That appears to me to be the probable effect of the alterations of the silk law.

5479. You mean that it is getting into the hands of large capitalists?—Yes.

5480. Did you reduce your credit at the end of last year?—I was not in England at the latter end of the last year, but I think my house did; there have been exceptions of course, there are certain houses we should be happy to trust still.

5481. Was that owing to the failures which had taken place?—To the apprehension of failures, not only on account of the state of the silk trade, but on account of the political appearance of things at that time, and also to the fear of the cholera.

5482. Are you aware that during the last two years, a larger proportion than usual of thrown silk has been imported into England; can you by any means account for that?—There may have been some increase of importation when the duty was reduced to 3*s*. 6*d*.; and since that, the expectation of a fresh reduction of duty might have produced some importation also; that was the hope of the Italian certainly, he hopes a reduction of duty may enable him to sell some thrown in this country at a profit.

5483. Had you any knowledge of the silk trade before 1826, and for how many years?—From 1824.

5484. Were there many failures before 1826?—I should say a great many at the end of 1825 or the beginning of 1826; it was in those years that the great failures took place at Macclesfield.

5485. Have there been many failures since?—There were a great many after the speculations of 1825; after the reduction of duty, men of small capital probably, set up mills in Macclesfield and bought our silks, but did not pay for them; they bought them at very high prices, and made I understand enormous losses; I understand some other men at Macclesfield bought those very silks extremely cheap and made large profits.

5486. Do you know that the manufacturers now give less credit than they did five or six years ago?—I am not aware of the manufacturers' business.

5487. Have you had an opportunity of looking into many bankrupts' estates?—Not myself; one of my partners has been more in the habit of attending to those things than myself.

5488. Since the manufacturers sell for cash, do not bankrupts' estates yield little or nothing for the creditors?—Fortunately as I did not trust much of late, I cannot say what is the case; fortunately I have had no losses lately.

5489. Is it a complaint of your house that the bankrupts' estates pay very little?—I am not aware of that, as I have had but little to do with those matters of late.

5490. Do not the larger brokers very often guarantee to the merchant payment for the silk they sell?—I should say very seldom, if ever, in my experience.

5491. The very dear silk you have spoken of as belonging to France is particularly adapted for marabout, is it not?—I am not aware positively of that; I understand it is, but I must say again that I am no judge of the manufacturing business.

5492. Supposing that to be the case, the Lombardy silk being adapted to marabout, should you not make your comparison with some kind of Italian silk adapted for marabout?—I must leave that question to the manufacturer, I do not understand the manufactory; I do not know whether silk is adapted for that particular kind of manufacture or not.

5493. The best fine white silks adapted for marabout, sell at how much more than Lombardy raw?—I really cannot answer that question, for I do not know positively what sort of silk is adapted for marabout.

5494. Do you know the difference between white Novi and Lombardy?—There

678.                                                                                          is

Mr.
*Andrew Martin.*

15 May,
1832.

is very little Lombardy white silk produced, Milan produces very little, if any, white silk, which is nearly equal to Novi; it is very seldom mentioned.

5495. How much more does the best white Novi silk adapted for marabout sell for than the Lombardy raw?—This will be answered by the price current, having no reference to the colour of the silk, which has some influence without doubt; in most times Novi silk, the best white, is quoted at eighteen and nineteen shillings, the best Bergamo sixteen and seventeen shillings, that is two shillings.

5496. To what countries are the best raw and thrown silks sent, and in what proportion?—I find that Piedmont sends to France about 650,000 pounds, which I have stated already; England receives a very small proportion of Piedmont thrown, which are considered to be very superior, whilst France imports very large quantities of Piedmont, about one-fifth of her presumed consumption, whilst England takes a very small proportion, not one-ninetieth part of its consumption, and Switzerland and Germany takes much more Piedmont silk thrown than England does (three times as much), and France eleven times as much Fossembrone; and Naples send their best raws mostly to England; Naples sends twice as much to England as to France; Milan sends about three-eighths of its produce to England, one-third in the thrown state, one third in the raw state, and sends very little to France, except in one particular year, when the crop was bad in France, and then they bought the very best Lombardy silks, and the value of those silks has been thought to be superior to what it was thought before; they have been obliged to use them when their crop was very short, and they have given higher prices than they used to give before.

5497. Speaking generally are the Piedmont organzines imported into France of a coarser kind than the French organzines?—I understand there is a great deal of thrown silk imported into France which runs from 30 to 34, and from 36 to 40 deniers, that is hardly saleable in England, while in France they obtain high prices for those numbers, those which are generally imported into France are of very superior quality.

5498. Is this the case generally with the Piedmontese organzines, are they generally of a coarser kind than the French organzines?—I cannot answer that question; there are a variety of sizes manufactured in Piedmont, and it depends upon the demand and the quantity manufactured, but it is a remarkable thing, that they import into France 30 to 40 deniers, and pay larger prices for them, while we import generally from 20 to 30 deniers only in England.

5499. What effect would be produced, in your opinion, on the price of thrown silk by a reduction of duty from 3 s. 6 d. to 1 s.?—I should suppose that the price of foreign thrown silk would be lowered, but not to the extent of the whole difference.

5500. Has France any silk superior to the silk of Italy?—I understand that they have a peculiar sort of silk called the Cevinnes or Alais silk, very superior in certain respects to any silk almost produced; it has more elasticity, and has peculiar qualities rendering it fit for certain articles; I understand the quantity produced there is from one-sixth to one-seventh of the total production of silk in France; there is another sort of silk for which I believe the French are superior, almost to any other country, the Provence silk from which they make their trams, which are considered to be the best in the world on account of their peculiar elasticity, but the remainder of the silk of French growth is probably equal to second rate Lombardy silk.

5501. What do you estimate to be the total production of France?—I conceive it to be 1,800,000 pounds English.

5502. Have you reason to suppose there will be any difficulty in obtaining those fine silks in the thrown state in England?—I cannot answer that question decidedly; I do not suppose there would be any difficulty; my impression is, that there is no difficulty in exporting throwns from France; I have not imported any into England myself, but it has been sent to me without any apparent difficulty, but I shall be happy to clear up that point.

5503. As a merchant, have you received any of those superior silks of France?—I have received some raw white silk, which I suppose came from that quarter.

5504. What is the quantity of raw and thrown silk imported into France?—I understand the quantity imported into France is about 1,200,000 pounds English, making the total consumption of France about 3,000,000; of those 1,200,000 pounds imported, about 700,000 may be in a thrown state.

5505. When you state the sizes of raw silk imported from Piedmont into France being

Mr.
*Andrew Martin.*

15 May,
1832.

being of 30 to 34 deniers, are you aware that also in this country raw silks of Italy of that size, such as the Turin and Vertua sell at very high prices?—I am aware of that, but they are raw and not thrown.

5506. You are understood to say, that you have no practical knowledge of what relates to the manufacturer or the throwster, either with reference to this country or to foreign parts?—Yes, just so.

5507. Consequently you are to be understood, that the statements you have made with reference to prices and to profits have been made upon hearsay only, and such information as you have been able to collect in a general manner, but you do not offer them to the Committee with any means of being able to vouch for their accuracy?—My impression is, that my information is generally accurate, that is the impression my mind has received, but I am very far from stating that it is perfectly accurate, the subject is so important, and the time given to answer those questions so short, that I should request to be permitted to get accurate information on which I can depend, at present I believe I can depend upon that which I gained at the time I was in those countries, as coming as near as possible to the truth.

5508. You have received this information as a merchant, and you believe it to be as correct as any information you have received?—Yes, I can only say, that as a merchant I should act upon that information as correct.

---

*Jovis, 17° die Maii, 1832.*

EDWARD AYSHFORD SANFORD, ESQUIRE, in the Chair.

Mr. *Andrew Martin*, called in; and further Examined.

Mr.
*Andrew Martin.*

17 May,
1832.

5509. THE Committee understand that you are desirous of adding to the Evidence you gave on a former day?—I have received some Evidence from Lyons, from a high authority as a merchant, stating the present prices of throwing there, which I believe may be depended upon. He states that the price for throwing there may be taken to be 6 francs per half kilogram of organzine, 20 to 22 deniers, (waste 10 per cent. included,) which I find to be equal to 4 s. 4 ½ d. per lb. English; this calculated at the exchange of 25 francs per pound sterling, and at 110 lbs. English for 50 kilogrammes. The throwing of organzine, 28–32 deniers, is 4 francs and 80 centimes, (waste 5 per cent. included,) equal to 3 s. 6 d.; tram, 22–24 deniers 5 francs, (waste 8 per cent. included,) equal to 3 s. 7 ¼ d. per lb. English; tram, 30 to 34 deniers 3 francs and 75 centimes, (waste 5 per cent. included,) equal to 2 s. 8 ¾ d. I got, by the same friend, a statement of what they considered to be the importation into France. I stated it already at 1,200,000 lbs. English, from a document which was laid before the French House of Deputies in March last, and which was, I believe, official. The statement of this Lyons merchant shows the great difference of the quantity of raw imported in 1829, when the crop was rather indifferent in France, and the price of cocoons very high. The French at that time imported a large quantity of Italian raws, and that quantity imported in a year of an indifferent crop in France may perhaps be useful to arrive at an approximate valuation of the French crop, which I believe cannot be ascertained officially. When I was in France I was led to believe that the quantity was about 1,800,000 lbs., but my correspondent does not state it in his letter; he only gives the quantity of foreign silk entered for home consumption in France. He states it to be, on an average per annum, from 1824 to 1831, of thrown silk, from 340,000 to 350,000 kilogrammes, equal to about 770,000 lbs. English; and the raw, in 1827 to 1828, was upon an average per annum 130,000 kilogrammes, equal to about 286,000 lbs. English. Now, in 1829, when the crop was deficient in quantity, and the price of cocoons very high, they imported 392,000 kilogrammes, equal to about 860,000 lbs. English.

5510. How many pounds English is the kilogramme?—Two pounds and two-tenths of a pound nearly.

5511. Are you able to inform the Committee what the crop has been in France in 1830 and 1831?—I stated, that my belief was, that the crop in France had been for the three last years past about 1,800,000 lbs. weight. With the permission of the Committee, I should like to correct my statement as to my impression that the

678.                                                                                    prices

Mr.
*Andrew Martin.*

17 May,
1832.

prices were higher in Lyons than in London in December last, which arose from an erroneous calculation. I stated, that, from a Price Current of Lyons, in December 1831, the price of Lombardy organzines, 24 to 28 deniers, was 28½ francs, which I take to be for the half kilogramme. Now, calculating the exchange at 25 francs, and the weight at 110 lbs. English for 50 kilogrammes, I find that this is equal to 20 *s.* 8 *d.* per lb. English. To compare it with the price in London, there is to be deducted from that the discount given at Lyons, which is 12½ per cent. ; but in this country the purchaser would have 2½ per cent. discount ; so that I deduct 10 per cent., and that 10 per cent. amounts upon 20 *s.* 8 *d.* to 2 *s.* 1 *d.* which leaves 18 *s.* 7 *d.*

5512. What was the price in England at that time ?—In London I find the Lombardy organzines quoted at 22 *s.* at that time, duty included.

5513. In what way do you make 28½ francs equal to 20 *s.* 8 *d.* ?—Calculating the exchange at 25 francs per pound sterling, and 110 lbs. English for 50 kilogrammes. Perhaps I had better state the date of the two Price Currents I have referred to. The quotation from Lyons was dated the 14th of December 1831, and the quotation from London of Messrs. Durant is dated the 8th of December 1831.

5514. Are you able to state to the Committee what the quotation of Piedmont organzine is ?—I cannot at present, but I hope I shall be able to ascertain it in a short time.

5515. Would it not be more correct to put the Piedmont organzine in comparison with the French organzine, than to put the Lombardy organzine in comparison with the French ?—I am not able to answer that question, not having sufficient knowledge of the qualities of French organzine.

5516. Upon the 18 *s.* 7 *d.*, which is the cost price at Lyons of the Lombardy organzine, what is the import duty from Lombardy into France?—I have stated the import duty into France to be 242 centimes per kilogramme, equal to about 10½ *d.* per pound English.

5517. Do you not conceive that the disturbances which were taking place at the time of your quotation at Lyons, might have produced an effect in lowering the price very considerably ?—I should think it must have affected business.

5518. And may not the disease which was running through the Continent have had the same effect?—It might.

5519. Do you mean to state that the price at Lyons was 18 *s.* 7 *d.*, minus the 10 *d.* of Italian duty, and therefore that 17 *s.* 8½ *d.* was the price at Lyons ; and in the same way in London, 2 *s.* was the price, which, taking off the duty, would leave 18 *s.* 6 *d.* as the price, exclusive of duty ; so that, in point of fact, the same silk was at Lyons 17 *s.* 8½ *d.*, and in London 18 *s.* 6 *d.* ?—That is the price which the Italian receives, without deducting charges for carriage and selling ; but I do not mean to say that it is what the manufacturer pays. It appears to me that it may be taken in two different ways ; one, the nett proceeds to the Italian ; and the other, the costs to the manufacturer, which I believe will be found to be different.

5520. Do you think that the Lyons manufacturer does not get his silk at 17 *s.* 8½ *d.* ?—No, he gets it at 20 *s.* 8 *d.*, less 12½ per cent. discount, viz. 18 *s.* 1 *d.* nett.

5521. In your opinion, can there be a different price for silks of the same quality in Lyons and in London, beyond the cost of the transport from one place to the other?—I should think not, except there was a greater consumption of one sort of silk at Lyons than in London ; for instance, I suppose that is the case from Piedmont. It appears to me that the Piedmontese must find a greater advantage in sending their silk to Lyons than to London, as they do not send it to London. I suppose it is that the price is higher ; at the same time there may be other causes ; for instance, the Piedmontese may be under advances to the Lyons merchant, who enables him, by those advances in money, to reel his silk. I should not think that can be the case to any great extent, because houses in London would be very happy to make advances to houses in Piedmont ; I have done it myself, but we do not find that there is that demand here for Piedmont which seems to exist at Lyons ; and therefore it seems likely that the Piedmontese get a better price for their silk at Lyons, or find a greater sale for it there, than they do in London ; but there may be other circumstances which have the effect of attracting more Piedmont silk to Lyons than to London.

5522. Is it not absolutely essential in some branches of manufacture, that they should have the Piedmontese silk?—I am not sufficiently informed to give any opinion of the manufacturing process.

5523. Can

Mr.
*Andrew Martin.*

17 May,
1832.

5523. Can you state to the Committee whether the French organzine, or the Piedmont organzine of the same size, sells at the highest price in the Lyons market? —I cannot.

5524. Can you state which is the best article?—My impression is, that the Piedmontese is superior to the French; but I am not sufficiently acquainted with French throwns and their prices to give a positive opinion.

5525. You stated that the Italian would have one price paid to him, and the manufacturer would pay another; who would receive the benefit of that difference? —I mean to say that, for instance, here, when we sell the organzine at 22 s., the manufacturer pays 22 s., less 2 ½ per cent. discount; that is the cost of the silk to him; he has nothing to do with the duty; but the Italian does not receive those 22 s., he receives those 22 s., less 3 s. 6 d. duty, and all the charges of bringing his silk to London, and the charges also of the merchant, and of the brokers who sell his silk in London; therefore whilst the manufacturer in London pays 22 s., less 2 ½ per cent., which leaves about 21 s. 5 d., the Italian receives only 22 s., less 3 s. 6 d. duty, and besides the charges for bringing his silk to market and selling it; therefore the Italian, after deducting charges paid in London, receives only about 17 s. for the thrown, with costs to the manufacturer here 22 s., with 2 ½ per cent. discount, or 21 s. 5 d. nett; the Italian bearing besides the charges from Italy to London, which are not included in this calculation.

5526. You have been asked about the distress at Lyons in December last; was not the silk trade in England greatly depressed in October, November and December last?—I should think it was.

5527. Have you any means of accounting for the Italian throwster sending his silk here under those disadvantages?—I should state, that I believe that the import of raw has been more profitable to the Italian than of the thrown, generally speaking; and the import of raw from Lombardy appears to me to have been of late years about twice the quantity of thrown.

5528. Are you aware that it appears by the official returns that the quantity of thrown silk introduced into this country from Italy, has very considerably increased within the last two years?—I should think it has not increased so much as that of raw since 1824. The proportion will, I believe, be found about two-thirds of raw and one-third of thrown; now if it was more advantageous to them to send thrown than raw, I suppose that they could send more thrown than they occasionally do. There may be mills in Italy which want a market for the surplus of their produce; they may make a profit on what they send to Vienna, and Elberfeldt, and the Continent at large; but if those countries cannot take the whole of the produce of the mills, they may perhaps at times want to realize it even at a loss, and for that purpose send it to England. There are, I believe, somewhat similar instances in this country of manufacturers who send to the Mediterranean markets their old or surplus stocks, in order to realize it.

5529. You are understood to say, that the Italian throwster throws silk chiefly for Vienna and other markets, not that of England; but that occasionally, when he has miscalculated the demands of those markets, and there is an over production, he sends that additional quantity to England, and sells it at a loss in this market, rather than keep it on his hands?—That is very nearly my impression; I suppose there are cases in which a throwster in Italy, to keep his mills in activity, may go on working, and he may perhaps find himself saddled with organzines, which he may wish to turn into money immediately; and if the market in Lombardy is slack, he may be more inclined to try the London market.

5530. Do you think that if it was more advantageous to the Italian to send thrown silk to this country, he would be able to throw a greater quantity than he does?—I should think he would, for the production of raw silk is greater than what he throws, as he exports in the raw state a large quantity.

5531. You have stated, that there are advances made by Lyonese manufacturers to the Piedmont throwsters; are you aware of any advances made by English merchants to throwsters in Italy?—I know instances; my house itself has made advances to the Piedmontese throwsters some years ago; and there may be other instances of advances being made, but I believe it is not very generally the case.

5532. Are those advances made by the manufacturers at Lyons, or by merchants?—I should think by the merchants; the merchants at Lyons are in the same case as the merchants in London; the silk merchants in London are ready to make advances of a portion of the value of silk on receiving it, or on having advice of its being sent to them. I suppose the question refers to advances for

678.                                                                         reeling

reeling before they have any pledge in their hand; that may be the case, and there are several houses at Milan to whom I should be happy to make advances, if they chose to avail themselves of that facility.

5533. Do you conceive that advances are made to a greater extent by the Lyonese merchants than by the English?—I think the Lyonese make advances to the Piedmontese, and I do not think they make any advances of any importance to the Milanese.

5534. Is it in anticipation of the manufacturer being able to dispose of the manufacture, that the merchants are induced to make those advances to the throwster at Piedmont?—It is in anticipation of being enabled to sell the silk at Lyons, and of course it supposes the manufacturers will be in want of silk. The silk merchants want to get that silk consigned to them, in order to gain a commission upon its sale to the manufacturer.

5535. Is it not for the purpose of securing the crop?—It is for the purpose of having the silk of that crop consigned to them.

5536. Is that owing to the rivalry of the merchants at Lyons?—Yes, I presume it is so in many cases, and also generally as an accommodation to the Piedmontese.

5537. Is not a large quantity of the silk produced in Italy sold at the fairs in Italy?—It is generally the case. In years, however, in which the crop is not abundant, or when the price of cocoons is considered to be high, of course the demand of the producers of the silk being often higher than what the purchaser is inclined to give, in such a case only a few contracts may be made at the fairs; but generally speaking the large sales are made at the fairs, where there is a general meeting of both sellers and purchasers; and this settles, in some measure, the price of silk.

5538. Can you state the date of those fairs?—At Brescia about the middle of August, and Bergam at the end of August. The cocoons are generally gathered in the north of Italy in the beginning of June, and a great proportion of the silk is reeled before the end of August.

5539. Is it not sent to those fairs after being reeled?—It is, and there it is purchased, either what is ready or what is to be delivered later.

5540. How is the price of cocoons regulated between buyers and sellers?—Cocoons are bought like other goods. I wish to add, if the question applies to the terms of the contract between buyer and seller, that I believe that the prices in Lombardy are not generally fixed immediately; but it is agreed, that the cocoons are bought at a price to be settled later, according to certain aggregates of prices, or to the price to be obtained by some particular person.

5541. At those fairs is the silk sold generally in a raw state?—There is generally more business done in raws than in throwns, as the new raws are then coming in.

5542. Have you been in the habit of purchasing cocoons yourself?—No.

5543. If individuals make their own bargains for cocoons, may not the prices vary very much?—They may vary.

5544. Do not the merchants, who attend at those fairs generally, purchase the silks, of which some are sent to England in a raw state, and some are thrown in the mills in Italy, and are they not both purchased upon the same terms?—I presume so; of late years, as the market of England is very important for Lombardy, some of the first sellers of silk in Lombardy have been in the habit of not selling their raw silk in Italy, but regularly sending them to London; their mark is known, their silk is liked, and in some instances they would rather refuse a high price at Milan, than not send it to England in order to keep up the reputation o₂ their mark.

5545. Can you state, whether a person purchasing silk to be thrown in Italy has any advantage over a person purchasing silk which is to be thrown in England?—I do not think he has any advantage in purchasing the raw silk, for there are a great many men in Lombardy that are silk merchants and throwsters at the same time, who have part of it thrown there, and send part of it to England to be sold here; it is generally consigned to England by the Italian merchants.

5546. Will not a man, who sends thrown silk and raw silk to London, naturally use the better sorts of silk for his own throwing rather than send them here?—I should think that a man who means to throw silk will naturally take the silk that will give the least waste; but at the same time, if I was a merchant in Milan, and

if

Mr.
*Andrew Martin.*

17 May,
1832.

if I thought that I could make more profit by sending my raw silk to England than by making it into thrown, I would do so.

5547. Is not that silk, which the throwster in Italy has an opportunity of selecting when it is made into organzine, the best?—I should say, that there is a probability that the silk which is of superior quality will make a better article; that silk which is reeled with care is not so liable to break, and is likely to produce a better article; but of course that raw silk of better quality must be paid dearer.

5548. Supposing that in the English market there is a demand for that superior kind of Italian silk, is there any difficulty in that silk being obtained in the English market by the English manufacturer upon the same terms upon which it is obtained by the Italian manufacturer?—I should think there is no difficulty except the possibility of the case, in which some men reel their own silk in order to use it themselves.

5549. If they reel for the purpose of throwing it themselves, and if they will not sell it to the English merchant because they want it themselves, does not that show that they see an advantage in keeping it?—It is very likely.

5550. Are the cocoons ever brought to this country?—There has been one instance, for a sort of experiment.

5551. Did you make that experiment?—I did not.

5552. Is not the silk that is thrown immediately after it is reeled, of a better appearance than that which is thrown after it has had the voyage from Italy to England?—I do not think I could distinguish it myself.

5553. Is there anything else you wish to explain to the Committee with reference to your former Evidence?—I have given the parity in English money and weight of organzine at Lyons, but I have not given the price of trams. I find the trams, 24–26 deniers, quoted at Lyons, the 14th December 1831, at 29 to 28¼ francs; 28¼ appears to be equal to 20s. 8d. per lb. English, subject to 12½ per cent. discount. I find the same article quoted in London from 19s. to 20s., subject to 2½ per cent. discount. I find the raw best, 9 to 10 deniers, was quoted at Lyons, the lowest price 26 francs, which upon the same basis, formerly stated, would be equal to 18s. 10d. English money, and from this deducting 12½ per cent. discount at Lyons, is reduced to 16s. 6d. On the 8th December 1831, the best Bergam was quoted in London from 16s. to 17s., reduced, by deducting 2½ per cent. discount, to 15s. 7d. and to 16s. 7d. I might add, that the comparison is not perhaps very well selected, and I think that the comparison of Piedmont organzine would be much better than Lombardy organzine, of which there is so little consumed at Lyons. I ought also to state, that the quotation at Lyons for best raw of Italy, probably applies to a superior quality to what is quoted in London as best Bergam raw. I was asked the other day what was the time at which the credit had been altered in England; I find that it was in March 1826, after numerous failures in the silk trade, that the present credit of five months, or 2½ per cent. discount for cash in fourteen days, was established. Before that time, eight months credit was granted, or 4 per cent. discount. The credit had been previously ten months, and was, I believe, reduced in 1821, to eight months, or 4 per cent. discount.

5554. What was the discount when the credit was ten months?—My impression is, that it was one half per cent. per month, and I understand it was 5 per cent. when the credit of ten months was not taken. In my last Evidence I stated, that I thought I was positive that raw silks could not be exported from France, but that I was not aware of any difficulty in the exportation of French thrown, as my house had received some sent from Lyons without any apparent difficulty, whilst I was aware that those who consigned raw silks from Lyons found difficulty in exporting them. I have not received an answer from Lyons yet, but upon inquiry in London, I have found that by the French tariff of 1822, both raw and thrown silks are prohibited, and it is now my impression, that that is the case at the present time.

5555. Is it your opinion, that the agitation of this question from time to time is injurious to the trade?—I think very injurious; our experience since 1824 has been, that every time there has been any agitation of an alteration of duty, it has unsettled business for several months; and even this Committee has unsettled business materially since the month of March. I speak here of my business as a silk merchant.

5556. Do you think that the business has been in a worse state since this

678. Committee

Mr.
*Andrew Martin.*

17 May,
1832.

Committee was formed than it was before the question was agitated ?—I am unable to answer, for I do not know what are the profits of the manufacturer.

5557. Do you not know, that in point of fact the people in Spitalfields are better employed now, and have been since this Committee was formed, than they were before ?—I am not aware. I mean to state, that since the Committee has been agitated, the silk merchants in London who had the prospect of an active sale in March, which seemed the general opinion after the India sale in February, have found their sales less active, and that it has been attributed to the agitation of the question ; and that is my opinion.

5558. Then your answer to the last question has merely a reference to the state in which the silk merchants and the silk brokers find themselves ?—Yes; and the whole of my Evidence has been intended to be confined, as much as possible, to my impression as a silk merchant.

5559. You know of course that the silk merchants were not the complaining parties, at whose instigation this Committee was formed ?—I am not aware of the merchants having made any complaint.

5560. Can you state what is the state of the trade now ?—I cannot state what is the situation of manufacturers, but I say that I found the demand for silk almost entirely suspended in March last.

5561. What has it been during the last four weeks ?—It revived a little, but I know that in March, since the Committee was instituted, we have found it more difficult to sell our silks.

5562. Were you compelled in March to take a lower price, in order to force a sale of your commodity ?—There was no demand at that time.

5563. Did you submit to a reduction in the price of silk in the month of March ?—I found sales more difficult.

5564. Did you sell any silk in the month of March ?—I think I did.

5565. Did you sell that at a lower price than you did in November ?—I cannot, and I do not like to state prices from memory ; but I shall be able to furnish the Committee with the price currents at that time. I must add, that in November I was in Italy, I was not in England. What I have stated is this, that I believe that at the end of February the merchants expected an active sale in March, and that at the beginning of March, after this Committee originated, the demand has slackened, and we have not had those active sales in March which we expected.

5566. Did you sell any silk in February ?—I think I did.

5567. From the time of your sales in the month of February down to the latest sale you made, has the price increased or diminished ?—I cannot, and I should not like to state prices from memory ; but I repeat that in the beginning of March, our prices became flatter ; we found it very difficult to effect sales ; in the month of April there was a tendency to improve, and we did more business ; and until of late, things were again paralysed by the agitation of political questions.

5568. Is not the month of March the month in which you generally make your largest sales ?—I should not say that ; January and February may be rather better months, when no unfavourable circumstances affect the demand for silk.

5569. But you anticipated an improvement in the month of March, which did not take place ?—Yes.

5570. Immediately after the appointment of this Committee, was it not generally apprehended that the duty would be taken off immediately ?—I should suppose that the expectation in general was, that the duty would be reduced.

5571. And that produced an immediate effect upon the sales ?—We experienced less demand, and I may conceive how a manufacturer would, if he could, postpone purchasing, on account of the possibility of a reduction of duty.

5572. Do you speak of price, or quantity, when you say that the sales decreased ?—When I speak of the sale decreasing, I speak of quantity.

5573. When this improvement took place in the month of April, had not that apprehension in some measure subsided ?—I understood, and it was the opinion of eminent silk brokers, who act as intermediaries between the silk merchants and the manufacturers, that the fresh demand in April arose from manufacturers having effected sales of their goods for the spring trade.

5574. Do you happen to know that this Committee was formed in consequence of complaints from the throwsters and the weavers, of the distress of the trade ?—I have heard so.

5575. Do you not know that one part of their complaint was, that the throwsters and

and the workmen are depressed, because they have not a sufficient protection against foreign thrown silk?—I understand that that was their motive.

5576. Then upon what ground could they form an opinion, when this Committee was formed, that there would be a reduction of this duty?—I think that in general, what we have seen in England since 1824, would lead to that conclusion, for we have had the duty reduced first from 14 *s.* 8 *d.* to 7 *s.* 6 *d.*, and then again reduced to 5 *s.*, and then again reduced to 3 *s.* 6 *d.*, and we have never seen it increased; and I should suppose therefore, from these precedents, that the expectation was, that (if the throwsters' interest might allow of its further reduction) it would be desirable to have it reduced; for if the manufacturer could get his silk cheaper, he would be able to produce his article cheaper.

5577. When the throwsters are complaining of the want of sufficient protection, upon what ground do you suppose that they expected they should have further cause of complaint given to them, by having the protection they have removed?— I believe the impression of the trade was, that the result of the inquiry would rather be a reduction of the duty than an increase.

5578. What do you mean by the trade?—A general impression is conveyed to us, through the brokers, and through what is transacted in the market. I find that after this Committee was appointed, our sales were more difficult, and attribute it to an anticipation of the reduction of the duty among our purchasers.

5579. Are you quite sure that the French raw silk has been as high as 26¾ francs the kilogramme?—In the Price Current of Messrs. Tournu, Bossan & Co. at Lyons, on the 14th December 1831, I find the best Italy raw silk, 9–10 deniers quoted from 26 to 27 francs, to be 26. I may add, that I find at the bottom of that Price Current, that the discount of Lyons on those prices is 12½ per cent., and the payment to be made in 30 to 40 days. If the Committee will allow, I will deliver in those two price currents.

[*The Witness delivered in the same.*]

5580. You have stated that the Italian throwster carries on a losing trade with this country, and that the Italian throwster sends some throwns to this market every year; does he then content himself with a certain loss upon those throwns every year?—I think it would be better to ascertain that from an Italian throwster himself; my impression is, that they have been often losing money upon their throwns of late years.

5581. You have stated, that the thrown silk trade is a less profitable one than the trade in raw; then how do you account for the smaller importation of raws the two last years in comparison with thrown?—I think I have not stated that the throwing trade is less profitable; I said that I believed the imports into this country of raw silk had been more profitable to the Italian than the import of thrown. It appears, errors excepted, in looking over an official Return of imports into this country, which has just been handed to me, that the importation of raw from Italy in 1830–31, was 3,000,000 lbs., and in 1828–29, 2,250,000 lbs.; and the import of throwns seems to have been in 1830–31 about 820,000 lbs.; in 1828–29, 675,000. I should think from this account there has been a reduction in the import of raw, and an increase of thrown. With respect to the latter part of the question, I confess I am unable to account for it; there are a variety of causes which may influence the import into the country in particular years. I wish to add, that the last reduction of duty here may, in a great degree, have acted as an encouragement to the import of thrown silk into England.

5582. Is it reasonable to suppose that a losing trade will increase?—No.

5583. Do not you think, that the events which happened in July 1830 had an effect upon the sales in the autumn of that year?—I should think it likely; England probably, at that time was considered the safest market, and I speak not only of Lyons, but the Continent generally; for I suppose, if the people of Lombardy gave up entirely sending their silk to Lyons, as it does not exceed 150,000 lbs. English, that would not have made any very material difference; but, I believe at that time, the state of France created an anxiety for the tranquillity of the Continent altogether, and that England was considered a country where property was safer than the Continent.

5584. Do not you suppose, that the apprehension of war, and of the cholera, in the North of Europe, may have diminished the demand for silk in Russia and Prussia, and upon the Rhine?—It may possibly at first. As to the cholera, I under-

stand

Mr.
*Andrew Martin.*

17 May,
1832.

stand that at Vienna, when it was daily expected, there was no disposition to buy, but when it made its appearance business resumed its activity.

5585. You account for the increase here in July 1830 by the French Revolution; how do you account for the increase in February, March and April?—It is very difficult to form any judgment from the imports of one month or two months.

5586. Do you consider that the Italian throwsters are increasing their trade?—I should think not; though I am not able to judge of the cost of throwing, nor to give an opinion upon the throwing trade, yet, from my intercourse with the Italian merchants or throwsters (for many of the Italian merchants are throwsters), my impression is, that I have heard them complain of prices of thrown in England more than of the raws; and I have heard them state that they considered the trade with England as not likely to increase for thrown, and that under the present duties they were under apprehensions of the superiority of machinery which they supposed to exist in England.

5587. Were the increased importations of raw silk into England last year of Piedmont organzines, or were they chiefly of Lombardy organzines or trams?—The quantities imported from Piedmont of thrown I take to be small; I think there is no great increase.

5588. Have you any interest whatever in this question other than as a merchant?—None whatever, to my knowledge; and I hope I have shown that my only object has been to get at the facts as much as I could.

5589. You have put in two Price Currents; are they to be considered as authentic documents?—As far as a Price Current can be. I give them merely as those which I found most readily, of not too distant a date, and without meaning to state that the proportion of price they establish between London and Lyons is constantly the same.

5590. You have stated, that in your opinion the increased importation of silk into England did not consist principally of Piedmont; must it not then have consisted of Lombardy?—There may have been a general increase altogether.

5591. Do you import thrown silks from any other country besides?—A trifle from Modena.

5592. Do you import any thrown from Constantinople?—Not to my knowledge.

### Mr. *William Stone*, called in; and Examined.

Mr.
*William Stone.*

5593. YOU are a partner in the house of E. Durant & Company?—Yes, I am.

5594. Your house are extensively engaged as silk brokers?—They are.

5595. How many years have you yourself been acquainted with the silk trade?—I have been acquainted with the trade for 17 years as a silkman, and partly as a manufacturer for seven years, and as a broker for ten years.

5596. In the course of that 17 years, have there not been great alterations in the silk trade in this country?—There have; there has been a considerable increase in the consumption of the article.

5597. And the trade has extended very much into the country?—It has.

5598. In what parts of the country has it extended?—In Lancashire, at Sudbury, and various places, but more particularly in Lancashire.

5599. In your character as a silk broker, have you not almost daily intercourse both with the merchant and manufacturer?—I have.

5600. Have there not during the 17 years that you have been acquainted with the trade, been very frequent alternations of good and bad trade?—There have.

5601. Do you recollect the periods of bad trade, and can you name them to the Committee?—It is rather a difficult question to answer, as to a particular period; but there have been considerable fluctuations in the trade.

5602. Have you known it at any time to have been as bad, or worse than it has been during the last few months?—I have known it quite as bad.

5603. Have you not reason to believe that it was worse at some former periods within your recollection, than it has been within the last few months?—I think it has been worse at other periods.

5604. Taking the period of nearly six years which has elapsed since the French manufactured goods were admitted, have you reason to believe that the trade has been during that time as good as it had been in the previous six years?—I have stated that for ten years I have known the trade as a broker, and previously to that I knew it as a silkman; and consequently my means of general information as

to

Mr.
*William Stone.*

17 May,
1832.

to former periods of the trade were not so good as they have been for the last ten years.

5605. Will you have the goodness to state, taking the period of ten years during which you have been acquainted with the trade as a broker, whether the first or the last five years was upon the whole the best trade ?—If the question refers to the point of consumption merely, it has been an increasing trade; but if it be considered, on the other hand, that the material has become amazingly depreciated in value, it is possible that the trade may not have been on the whole a profitable trade. When I state that I have known it as bad as of late, I particularly refer to my own experience while a silkman; I know that the trade was then getting exceedingly bad in that particular department.

5606. When do you speak of?—The seven years previous to the last ten.

5607. From your intercourse with the silk merchants, have you reason to believe, from what has been stated to you, that the Italian throwster has found this a profitable market?—I can only answer that question from hearsay and observation, but not from experience; but upon the broad scale, I think it has been a losing business.

5608. Have you reason to suppose that the Italian throwster has been receiving more or less since 1829?—Estimating it by the whole mass of thrown silks imported, and the prices at which they have been sold since 1829, I am of opinion that he has been a considerable loser,

5609. Do you believe that the Italian throwster has any advantage over the English throwster in the purchase of his material in Italy?—Of course a man who is upon the spot has certain advantages, but upon the whole, taking it upon the broad scale, I conceive that the English throwster has quite as good a market here for selecting his silks as the Italian throwster has.

5610. What are the local advantages to which you have just alluded?—A man being upon the spot, and well knowing the character of the silk, and judging pretty accurately of the result; those are advantages which I think are of some importance, but this selection of the silk is a matter of judgment, which is to be attained in the country by experience and attention.

5611. Would not an English merchant or an English throwster, having an agent there for the purchase of silk, have the same advantage?—If a man here were to employ an agent upon the spot to select a particular silk, undoubtedly he would have the same advantage, subject to a charge for that person.

5612. Can you estimate in money the advantage which you consider the Italian throwster has?—Independently of the duty, I should think it cannot amount to much, because we import silks here that upon the whole expense of waste do not exceed 3 or 4 per cent., and it might be a trifle less in Italy, but it could not be more than 1 or 2 per cent.

5613. At what period of the year do you generally receive the first silks in England?—In August.

5614. Have you ever been in Italy?—No.

5615. Do you think you can judge of the local advantages, never having been in Italy?—I think it may be estimated, that if the whole loss in waste, &c. does not exceed 3 or 4 per cent. here, that must be the utmost extent of the local advantages.

5616. Can you state at what period you generally receive the first parcels of Italian thrown silk?—The raws in August, and the thrown shortly afterwards; being the produce of the new crop, it must take time to work it; I should think the importation of the thrown might commence after one or two months, or three months; probably three months.

5617. The question refers to your experience as a broker, at what time you generally receive the first parcels of raw silk and the first parcels of thrown silk?—In the middle of autumn, or towards Christmas, we receive usually the first parcels of thrown silk; a good deal depending upon the state of this market, the usual course is to give a sufficient time for throwing.

5618. So that in fact you have Italian silks thrown in England, in the market as soon as you have Italian silk thrown in Italy?—Yes.

5619. You have been intimately acquainted with the throwing trade of this country, first as a silkman, and subsequently as a broker?—Yes, I have.

5620. During the last ten years, has there been a considerable increase in the number of mills and in the quantity of machinery; and where has that increase taken place?—I believe they have increased considerably in Lancashire particu-

678.                                                                                    cularly;

cularly; also at Derby and other places, I believe, speaking from the result of what I have seen, and the operations going on.

5621. Have there been any new mills erected since 1826, and where, if any?—I cannot state particularly whether new mills have been erected, but I should think there has been an increase since 1826 in Manchester.

5622. Do you know whether any have been built at Macclesfield since 1826?—I do not know it positively.

5623. Can you inform the Committee what has been the state of the throwing trade during the last five years, as compared with the previous five years?—I believe there has been an increase; whether profitable or not, I cannot possibly so enter into the balances of the parties as to state.

5624. Can you state what has been the price paid to the English throwster for throwing any particular kind of silk in each year?—I am not prepared with any information of that sort, but can probably get it. I can state what I used to pay formerly, also what are the prices now paid.

5625. Do you recollect what price was paid to the throwster during the seven years you were a silkman?—From 10 s. and upwards for fine organzines.

5626. Can you state what was the price paid in 1821?—I cannot recollect.

5627. Can you state the price paid in 1823 and 1824?—Not from memory.

5628. Do you recollect the state of the throwing trade in 1825?—In the year 1825 there was an immense demand both for the raw material and the thrown; there was an immense business going forward in 1824 and 1825.

5629. Do you recollect the state of the throwing trade in the spring of 1826?—That was the period of the result of the crisis; it was then in a bad state.

5630. Do you remember the price of throwing in the spring of 1826?—No, I do not.

5631. Have you any means of knowing the price paid for throwing in 1829?—No; I have not the means of knowing it, except by report, because it is not our business; it is the business of the dealers.

5632. Can you inform the Committee the state of the throwing trade in 1830?—At the beginning of 1830 it was exceedingly prosperous, I presume from the advances that took place in the thrown article.

5633. Have you reason to believe that the trade of the throwster was a good trade?—It can be only by comparison; I suppose it must be good on the whole, or else men would not persevere in it.

5634. Do you remember whether there was any difficulty upon the part of some manufacturers at Spitalfields to get their silk thrown?—There has been considerable difficulty.

5635. Is it within your knowledge, that with respect to certain silks of very fine quality, they could not get any person to throw them, and they were obliged to wait some months?—That was undoubtedly the case.

5636. Will you explain to the Committee how the present duties on thrown silk affect Spitalfields, and how they affect Manchester?—The effect must be a tax upon Spitalfields, inasmuch as they are the large consumers of the article.

5637. In your experience as a broker, what is the proportion of the foreign thrown silks which you have sold in Spitalfields, compared with what you have sold at Coventry, Manchester and elsewhere?—Taking the proportions in 1831, I find it to be in London 2-3ds, in Manchester 1-8th, in Coventry 1-12th, in Norwich 1-12th, in Macclesfield 1-17th.

5638. In the manufacture of what articles are the foreign thrown silks used?—In London for broad goods, and at Coventry for ribbons; at Manchester for broad goods, and at Norwich for mixed goods, such as bombazine goods; and that may also apply to Manchester.

5639. Are they not employed generally in the manufacture of a finer description of articles, such articles as are imported from France?—Certainly they are.

5640. In your opinion, is the price paid for thrown silks in England determined by the competition at home, or by the competition from abroad?—Both must have their influence; the thrown abroad, if it is brought into this country, must have a considerable influence upon English, and the English upon foreign.

5641. Which do you conceive is the chief cause?—The large proportion of English must be the basis, or at least the chief determining cause, whatever the proportions may be.

5642. Have you not seen that the price paid to the English throwster has been

falling

Mr.
*William Stone.*

17 May,
1832.

falling within the last two or three years, and at the same time the remuneration to the Italian throwster has been diminished ?—The difference of prices shows that.

5643. And therefore have you not reason to believe that it is a competition of that kind which has brought down the price to the Italian as well as the English throwster ?—There is no doubt that the two must operate together.

5644. What, in your opinion, would be the effect of lowering the duty upon foreign thrown silk to 1 s. per pound ?—The immediate effect to the English throwster must be detrimental, beyond doubt.

5645. Supposing 2 s. 6 d. taken off the duty, what effect do you think that would have upon the price ?—It would have a tendency to lower the price.

5646. To what extent, to the full extent or less than the full extent ?—I think it would be a mixed question, the result of which could not be shown immediately ; it must be the effect of time to prove what the ultimate result would be as to the price, but the immediate consequence must be a tendency to deprive the British throwster of the supply of raw silks ; if, as is the fact, silks in a thrown state are received under a duty of 3 s. 6 d., if you reduce the duty, the immediate tendency must be an increase of foreign thrown silk.

5647. Will the Italian continue to send thrown silk here unless he derives a profit from it ?—I should think certainly not.

5648. It has been stated to this Committee, that the price paid in Italy for throwing silks is 3 s., and by others it has been stated at 4 s. ; and they have been informed, that the price paid for throwing in England now is from 3 s. 6 d. to 4 s. ; do you concur in the latter statement ?—I think that is very fairly stated.

5649. Then the difference being 1 s. a pound, would not a duty of 1 s. leave the Italian throwster a bare remuneration ?—I think it must be a matter of figures. The question is, whether a shilling will give a sufficient protection to the British throwster at the different rates that have been stated. The price paid to the British throwster is said to be from 3 s. 6 d. to 4 s., and exclusive of waste, the medium will be 3 s. 9 d. The price paid to the Italian throwster is said to be 3 s. including waste ; then there is the waste to be deducted, which will reduce it to 2 s. 6 d. paid in Italy, and 3 s. 9 d. in England, not losing sight of the protection that the Italian throwster derives ; the figures will show the difference, and prove whether it is a protection or not. I think that taking those relative figures, the shilling is not a protection.

---

*Veneris, 18° die Maii,* 1832.

### EDWARD AYSHFORD SANFORD, ESQUIRE, in the Chair.

*John Benjamin Heath,* Esq., called in ; and further Examined.

*John B. Heath,*
Esq.

18 May,
1832.

5650. CAN you, in relation to the growth and produce of silk in France, give the Committee the grounds upon which you formed your opinion, stated in your former evidence ?—I can only, in confirmation of my former evidence upon that subject, state to the Committee the source from which I derived the information. I procured a return of the production at Lyons in July last, and I have since had it confirmed by correspondence ; I stated to the Committee, and here is the point upon which my evidence has been, I believe, misunderstood ; I stated to the Committee that the average import of France from 1825 to 1830, both inclusive, was 540,000 kilogrammes, which according to the usual mode of calculation, namely, 51 kilogrammes for 112 lbs. gave 1,186,719 lbs. ; and that, comparing notes with other gentlemen since I was before the Committee, I find confirmed within a fraction. Then with regard to the produce of France, from the same source, I got the particulars in France. The average in three years, 1829, 1830 and 1831, was 1,000 bales of 200 lbs. each, weighing 826,000 kilogrammes, which, by the same mode of calculation make 1,750,000 lbs. English.

5651. In your evidence you have stated the growth of silk in France to be 1,750,000 lbs. English weight ; and the document furnished by Mr. Doxat on his examination, showing the importation of silk into France to be upon an average 1,073,000 lbs., which, added together, would show the consumption of France at no more than 2,823,000 lbs., whereas an official statement published by the French Customs in 1830, of the exports in 1829 of silk goods of French manufacture,

678. (exclusive

John B. Heath,
Esq.

18 May,
1832.

(exclusive of goods made from waste silk) exhibits the weight of silk consumed in the manufactures of that kingdom exported to amount to 2,882,000 lbs.; now placing this 2,882,000 lbs. by the side of 2,823,000 lbs., it will appear that the whole of the silk, which you assign to the whole manufacture of France, is absorbed by that portion which is exported; and I presume as the consumption of silk goods is very considerable in France, and must form a large feature of the manufacture of that kingdom, does not it appear you have formed an erroneous estimate of the quantity of raw silk produced in France?—The estimate is none of mine; the particulars of the quantities I have stated to the Committee are such as I procured upon the spot, and I have every reason to believe they are correct, particularly as since I was here I have seen a printed document in the hands of Mr. Morrison, in which my statement is corroborated. With regard to Mr. Doxat's statement, how he can possibly say that the quantity of silk goods exported from France, weighs precisely so much, I am unable to state, because I do not know any thing of the details of the manufacture, or the quantity of silk it takes to make a piece of goods; but I should add further, that in the quantities I have given of the imports, I have taken the average of six years, and I have taken an average of three years for the production; now Mr. Doxat's document, of which I have an extract here, only goes to show what was done in 1829, and therefore, with all submission to Mr. Doxat's opinion, I do not see how my evidence is at all invalidated by it.

5652. Is that information obtained from private sources or public official documents?—I have already stated I obtained it at Lyons in the course of communication with some of my correspondents there. I was extremely anxious to ascertain, whether there was a probability or not of the French Government taking off the restriction that exists upon the exportation of French thrown silk. I took a great deal of information upon the subject, and I found that many of the data I received were collected for the purpose of being submitted to a Committee that was appointed by the Government of France to examine and investigate the question; therefore I have reason to believe that the information is correct.

5653. Is the whole of the silk which is grown in France sent to Lyons?—To the different places where the silk manufacture takes place, I know of no other than Lyons and St. Etienne.

5654. You know the manufacture of sarsenets at Avignon?—Yes, I have heard of it, as well as of others in different parts of France, I cannot tell the particular places. I should add further, that I have since understood, though I have no personal knowledge of the fact, that a great deal of manufactured silk has been imported into France from Germany and Switzerland. I repeat, I do not know the fact, but it may throw some light upon the subject.

5655. You have referred to the names of other merchants who have given you their estimates of silk produced in France, will you give the variations in their estimates, and their names?—I must decline to give their names; all that has passed has merely been to say, " from the documents you have, what is the estimate " you form of the import or the export of this or that." I took no notes, it was a matter of mere conversation.

5656. You have referred to a printed document you saw in the hands of Mr. Morrison, and stated, that the growth of silk in France was 1,600,000 lbs. in 1824; do you think that the growth of silk in France has only increased 150,000 lbs. since that time?—I have already stated, that the return I saw was founded upon the average of three years.

5657. How was it you obtained that information from which you derive a return of 1,750,000 lbs.?—I have already stated, that I obtained it at Lyons from notes, conversations and documents.

5658. It has been estimated that the looms of France are 60,000; now giving 70 lbs. to a loom for consumption, there would be 4,200,000 lbs. of silk?—I have already said that I do not know any thing of the details of the manufacture, and therefore any questions of that nature can only obtain for answer, that I know nothing about it; I never heard how many looms there are in France.

5659. Have you been accustomed to purchase the cocoons in Italy, and to concern yourself in the reeling of the raw silk?—I never purchased a cocoon in Italy.

5660. Have you been concerned in the reeling of the raw silk in Italy?—Never personally.

5661. Have

*John B. Heath,*
Esq.

———

18 May,
1832.

5661. Have you any knowledge of the different results of throwing one kind of raw silk from another?—Not from personal observation.

5662. Do you know any thing about the advantages resulting to the throwster in Italy, from throwing the raw silk of his own reeling, compared with the throwing of the raw silk purchased at the fairs of Bergamo, Brescia, and other places?—No, I do not; I know nothing about them.

5663. Are you acquainted with the extent of the manufacture of silk goods at Milan?—I am not aware there is any manufacture of silk goods there.

5664. Are you acquainted with the extent of the manufacture of silk goods at Como?—I never saw a manufacture at Como.

5665. You might know the fact notwithstanding?—I do not.

5666. Are you enabled to state to the Committee the extent of the manufacture of silk goods carried on at Turin and Genoa?—I know that silk goods are made at Turin, and velvets and other stuffs at Genoa; but I cannot state any thing as to the extent.

5667. Are you informed that every state of Italy has a peculiar manufacture of silk goods of its own, some to a greater extent than another?—I have no precise knowledge upon the subject, I know that silk stuffs are made at Turin, Genoa, in Tuscany, and some at Naples, particularly in the royal fabric at San Leucio; but I have no precise data.

5668. Have you obtained any information respecting the quantity of silk consumed by the several manufacturers of Italy, including those carried on in the kingdom of Naples?—No, I have not.

5669. You have been understood to state, the Italians are pursuing a losing trade in thrown silk sent to this country, can you state whether they are pursuing a profitable trade in raw silk consigned to this country?—What I stated with respect to thrown silk was this, that the persons who had sent thrown silk for sale to the London market, for the last four or five years, had lost money by it.

5670. Can you state whether the Italians are pursuing a profitable trade in raw silk consigned to this country?—More so in raw than in thrown.

5671. Have you any correspondents who send you raw silk as well as thrown silk for sale?—I have.

5672. What do you consider to be the reason that the Italian raw silk has paid the Italian better than thrown silk has?—Because the prices of raw silk in this market have been higher of late years than those of thrown, in proportion.

5673. Previous to 1830 and 1831, was the exportation of thrown silks to England profitable to Italians, or not?—It has occasionally been profitable; I am not an importer on my own account, I merely receive it to sell upon commission; I am not generally acquainted with the cost of it, further than examining from time to time the quotations sent to me.

5674. How do you account for the increase of thrown, and the decrease of the raw material, during the last two years?—I have already answered that on a previous day; I said then, I cannot account for it; but I can give an opinion upon the subject at least as far as regards the importation of thrown silk into this country, immediately after July 1830; I stated then, that a considerable quantity of silk which was lying in the warehouses at Milan and other places, not destined perhaps for this market, was, upon the alarm of the revolution, and the fear that property might not be safe, sent here more as a matter of security than speculation.

5675. The throwns were principally of Lombardy growth, which were not generally sent to France?—There were Lombardy thrown and Piedmont throwns also.

5676. Was there more Piedmont than Lombardy?—I had more Piedmont silk in my warehouse at that period than I had had for some time.

5677. How do you account for their not sending an increased quantity of raw?—This is a repetition of a question asked before; these occurrences took place at a time when the stock of raw silk was exhausted, it was the beginning of a new crop, and it was natural that the stock on hand should consist chiefly of thrown silks.

5678. Presuming the quality the same, that is, the thrown to have been made from a portion of the same filature, and that you have also received some in the raw state, what is the nett difference of price between the raw and the thrown which the Italian expects to realize from your sales?—It is impossible to answer that without reference to my books.

5679. When the thrown silk is from the parties own filature or reeling, does not the Italian expect, and do you not stand out for a higher price?—It depends upon the quality of the silk; if it is a filature that is well known in this market, of course

678.

I do,

*John B. Heath,*
Esq.

18 May,
1832.

I do, but then the person purchasing it has an additional advantage in the result; the silk makes less waste, and reels quicker and better.

5680. The Italian throwster therefore may be supposed to consider it an advantage to reel his own silk, because, year after year he continues to do so, and experience proves his own reeling to be the most valuable to him?—I have no doubt the Italian throwster finds an advantage in reeling his own silk, but in many cases the proprietors of filatures are not throwsters, and on the other hand many proprietors of mills do not reel silk.

5681. As your house are consignees, it is not supposed that you can know anything about the cost, and not having any reeling or throwing operations of your own, your opinions of profit and loss to the Italian can be but conjectural?—I do not see that at all, because I have stated whenever I have made a calculation I have taken the price current of the day, furnished to me from different places in Italy where the silk is sold, I have stated I know nothing of the details of the filature and the cost of reeling silk.

5682. To have an intimate knowledge of the properties of silk, does it not require great attention and long practical experience?—Yes, it does.

5683. If the knowledge of silk is not easily acquired, is it not difficult to distinguish the profits or losses of the Italians, skilled as they are in their own natural product of silk, and is it not likely when they, that is the Italians, repeat their consignments to this country, they find their account in so doing, while you may be fancying they are losing their money?—It is impossible to answer that series of questions in one breath, there are three or four questions in one.

5684. If the knowledge of silk is not easily acquired, is it not difficult to distinguish the profits or losses of the Italians, skilled as they are in their own natural product of silk?—I should say that a mere knowledge of the article of silk has nothing to do with the latter part of the question; I have stated it requires the experience of years to be a good judge of silk, which is one of the most difficult articles to understand thoroughly.

5685. And is it not likely that when they, that is the Italians, repeat their consignments to this country, they find their account in so doing, while you may be fancying they are losing their money?—If they did not find their advantage in it, they would not send them.

5686. In order to understand thoroughly the local advantages enjoyed by the Italian throwster over the throwster of Italian silk in this country, should not a skilful knowledge of silk be required as well as the experience of reeling, buying, selling and throwing the silk of Italy?—No doubt of it; and in answer to a question of the same nature, I stated that the observations I made were matters of opinion, and not founded upon practical knowledge of the filature or throwing mill.

5687. In answer to the question put the other day, How do you account for so many English throwsters failing? you answered, That it arose from their want of capital, did you not?—Not in that way, certainly; I was asked why I thought so many throwsters failed, and I stated I did not conceive there was any article so susceptible of variation in price from the caprices of fashion, and from the circumstances of the times, as silk; and many throwsters who have set up mills have done so without any capital whatever; as long as the throwing remunerated them they went on, but the moment any reverse came, they, having nothing to go back upon, and not being able to wait till a re-action took place, consequently failed.

5688. Do the commission throwsters fail also?—I do not know what is meant by commission throwsters.

5689. One who throws silk for hire?—If it does not remunerate him, and he has no money to draw upon, he naturally fails.

5690. Do you know whether persons employed in that way have failed?—Those of whom I have some knowledge, have been persons who have dealt with me, and it is upon the investigation of their affairs after failure, that I have formed that opinion.

5691. Have those persons been partly commission throwsters?—I dare say they have, but I have no knowledge of the fact myself.

5692. You stated in your last examination, that the production of silk in all Italy is from 5 to 6,000,000 of Italian pounds, will you state the quantity in English weight; and having understood from your evidence, the information you have given has been obtained from some Italian Custom-house returns, cannot you arrive nearer at the mark than within 20 per cent., or a fifth part?—I should state

that

*John B. Heath,*
Esq.

———

18 May,
1832.

that the details, as far as I can give them, are already in the evidence I have given; the only really official part was, that which concerns Lombardy; with regard to the Roman States, Naples, and Sicily, it was from information procured, but not from official documents.

5693. You have apportioned in your estimate 335,000 lbs. as the consumption of Berlin and Vienna, are you aware that that statement must refer only to the silk passing through the Milan Custom-house, destined for those places, and that you must have omitted the other silks sent direct from their places of growth to Berlin and Vienna, the latter place being understood to consume more than you have assigned to both those places?—I must have been misunderstood, because I stated distinctly as to the exports to Berlin and Vienna, that it was merely that from the Milan Custom-house in 1831.

5694. How have you been able to ascertain what other silks are the growth of parts of Italy, about which you can obtain no accurate returns, so as to arrive at a conclusion that the whole production has been from 5 to 6,000,000 of pounds?— With regard to the export from Piedmont, there is no difficulty in obtaining it; and I estimated that at 1,250,000 lbs.

5695. Upon being questioned by an Honourable Member on your last examination, respecting the quantity you place down as exported from Lombardy to the English market, namely, 2,250,000 Italian lbs., which is equal to 1,575,000 lbs. English weight, this statement appears correct, for by adding 175,000 for the export from Italy to England through the out-ports of Italy, we arrive at the fact, that about 1,750,000 lbs. English weight is imported annually upon an average into England. It is also pretty well known that France is accustomed to import from Italy about 1,000,000 of English lbs., which makes the quantity to France and England two millions and three quarters English lbs.; considering therefore the consumption of all Europe besides, and the quantity necessary for the manufactures carried on in Italy, about some of which you have spoken this morning, does not it appear you have underrated the production of silk in Italy?—I have no reason to alter my opinion, I am certain that the official part of this statement is correct; the computations have been made of the quantities exported at the different ports, and a calculation of the weight of each bale made.

5696. Is silk adapted to make organzine of the size of 18 to 22 deniers, imported in its raw state, in large quantities from Italy?—There is a large quantity.

5697. What proportion is brought of that fine quality, comparing it with the whole quantity of raw silk imported from Italy?—A great deal depends upon the season; sometimes it is reeled finer than at others; I cannot state any proportion; the greater proportion imported is in the middling and coarse sizes.

5698. Do not the best raw silks imported come from the throwing districts in Italy, when you have put aside some of the Fossembrones?—Undoubtedly they do; the throwing districts of Italy and Lombardy, I should say, produced the largest quantities.

5699. Does not your house receive some of the most accredited thrown silks of Italy?—I believe so.

5700. Do you receive much thrown silk of 18 to 22 deniers size?—I receive a certain proportion; of late years I have not received much.

5701. What proportion of that size do you receive, compared with the quantity of raw which would result to that size, when thrown into organzine?—It depends upon a variety of circumstances; there is no rule by which I can state what qualities my correspondents will consign to me.

5702. What do you conceive has caused a reduction of the importation of that fine description of silk?—I do not think it is quite so current of sale. One of the chief places of consumption is almost entirely stopped; I mean Norwich, where they used to consume a considerable quantity of the finest silk of 18 to 22 deniers. We sell very little at that place now.

5703. What has caused that decrease?—The article for which it was used is bombazine; it has gone very much out of fashion, and the manufacture has decreased very considerably at Norwich; I take it that must be the cause.

5704. You have given in evidence the prices of throwing silk in Italy, inclusive of the waste, can you state the price exclusive of the waste?—I could give the price in Italian money, I have not it here; the waste varies according to the goodness of the silk.

5705. You have spoken of the price in Italy of throwing organzine of the size of 18 and 22 deniers; is it not a fact, that very little of that size in organzine is

678. thrown

*John B. Heath,*
Esq.

18 May,
1832.

thrown in England?—I cannot state the precise quantity, but if the raw silk, calculated to make that size, comes to England, it must naturally be thrown.

5706. Do you know whether much of that size does come?—I conceive a considerable quantity.

5707. Is it fair to compare the price of throwing fine organzine in Italy, with that of throwing coarser organzine in England?—I do not know whether it is fair or not; I have given different prices for the different sizes.

5708. In the English market the marks upon the bales go a great way, and you gentlemen consignees are in the habit of estimating the value of the silk by the marks. That the Committee may understand what those marks are, will you inform them what they are supposed or intended to represent?—All I shall be able to answer is, that I scarcely ever recollect having sold silk without its being examined previously by the buyer, and in nine cases out of ten samples taken away and tried before it is purchased. Some brokers are so very particular as to require a sample from each bale in a parcel. I have silk, the marks of which is very well known to be that of the very best filature; my house has received the whole of that for years past, it was marked with the initials of my firm, three letters, when there were three partners, and now with two.

5709. Will you state the custom of your trade as respects credit and charges upon silk from the consignors' hands to your own, and the mode in which this trade is generally conducted, so that the Committee may form an idea of the consignee's or silk merchant's business?—Our business is to receive silk from Italy consigned here for the purpose of sale, and when we have sold it we render an account of the sales, deducting the charges, which include the commission, and the *del credere* for the buyer, whom we in most cases trust for five months.

5710. Then do the silk merchants sell the silk consigned to them, or is the business done by a broker?—The business takes place through a broker, we do not sell to the buyer directly.

5711. What is the brokerage?—Five-eighths per cent.

5712. Do the brokers ever guarantee their buyers, and receive an extra commission for so doing?—It used to be done more formerly than now; the remuneration was and is one per cent.

5713. Do brokers ever buy silks upon their own account?—They are better able to answer that than I am.

5714. You conceive they ought not?—Most assuredly they have sworn not to do it.

5715. Do they ever sell silk on their own account?—I give the same answer.

5716. Do you ever sell them silk in their own names?—Never, except for the principal, where the buyer does not wish to be known.

5717. Do they not often buy silk in the first instance from the merchant, and then seek buyers for it?—I am not able to inform you distinctly upon that subject.

5718. Is it not a notorious fact that they do so?—It does sometimes happen that a buyer for three or four bales will buy the whole parcel of six or eight to get them a trifle cheaper, taking upon himself the risk of placing them afterwards.

5719. Then he sells for principal?—No; suppose a broker could not find a buyer, after he has taken them upon himself, and return them in a reasonable time allowed for the delivery, the invoice would be made to principal, and he must take them.

5720. Do you not know that those transactions have gone to a great extent?—I do not know it; I have heard of it, and I can only say that I regret it.

5721. Have you any knowledge of the quantity of waste silk imported into this country?—No.

5722. You said the produce of Italy was 5 or 6,000,000 lbs. of raw?—Yes.

5723. And that they export of that silk about 1,500,000 lbs. of raw?—I have given the details already.

5724. Then if the waste imported into this country be from 6 to 700,000 lbs., the quantity of silk thrown in Italy is not much more than 4,000,000 of lbs.?—I do not know that fact; I have not stated any opinion as to the weight of thrown silk, except in Piedmont. Waste silk comes from other countries besides Italy; I have received some from Spain myself. It has occasionally come from India.

Mr. *Thomas*

Mr. *Thomas Stone*, called in ; and Examined.

5725. YOU are a manufacturer in Spitalfields?—I am.

5726. What is the name of your firm?—Stone & Brooks.

5727. How many years have you been engaged as a silk manufacturer?—More than six years; I ought to say that I am not immediately concerned in the department of the manufacture of silk, I manage more the cash department; I mention this, lest any question relating to the manufacture of the article should be asked me, and I should not be able to give any answer to it. I may also add, that being suddenly called to examination to day, I have not brought with me some documents which are necessary to give answers in detail.

5728. Are you engaged solely in the manufacture in London, or do you employ any persons in the country?—We employ throwsters; we have no weavers in the country, they are all in London.

5729. What are the articles you are in the habit of making?—Broad goods.

5730. Describe them?—Gros de Naples, some satins, and some broad figured goods, and likewise some velvets.

5731. Can you give the Committee any idea of the proportions of each?—The figured goods are small in comparison to the others; I may mention, that altogether, we have about 700 looms going.

5732. Do you use the Jacquard looms?—We do.

5733. What number of looms have you of the Jacquard description?—I should say between 40 and 50, but I cannot answer the question precisely, not being much in the manufactory.

5734. What wages do you pay for the manufacture of gros de Naples?—For what is called the three double, 6½ d.; and for the three single 5 d. a yard.

5735. What price do you pay for the manufacture of satins?—It depends very much upon the count; I do not know that I can give a full answer unless I had the document with me.

5736. The figured goods you are in the habit of making, are figured gros de Naples?—Yes.

5737. What price do you pay?—One shilling a yard is the price now, I believe.

5738. Is that a rich article?—No, we do not make very rich figures.

5739. Have you any means of knowing the price paid in Manchester for that article?—No.

5740. What do you pay for making velvets?—It depends upon the count, from 3 s. up to 4 s. per yard.

5741. What has been the state of the trade in Spitalfields since you have known it, generally?—I should say latterly it has become much worse than it was when I first knew it.

5742. You began at what time?—About six years ago.

5743. That was prior to the introduction of the French goods?—Yes, I began rather prior to the introduction of French goods.

5744. Was the trade good after the introduction of French goods?—For a time it was.

5745. Did it continue so during the years 1827 and 1828?—To the best of my recollection the trade became worse at the commencement of 1827.

5746. Do you recollect the state of the trade in 1827?—I think I may say it was not so good as in 1826, still I should not call it bad.

5747. What was the state of it in 1828?—In 1828 it was much as in the year 1827, to the best of my recollection.

5748. And in 1829?—1829 was with us a bad year; I speak as far as we are concerned.

5749. You make that an exception, was it generally so?—I did not know much about what other persons were doing, I confine myself very much to my own department of business; as regards ourselves it was a bad year.

5750. Are the wages you have now stated as being paid by your house, the same wages as have been paid since 1826?—No.

5751. State what alterations have taken place?—At the latter end of 1825, the house I belong to gave 11 d. for three doubles, for which we now pay 6½ d.

5752. Was the singles in about the same proportion?—The price was about 9 d.; in 1829 they were very likely 9 d.; in 1826 I have a memorandum that they were 8 d.; the double in 1826 was 9 d., and the single 8 d.; then in 1829 (1828 I have

678.                                                                              not

not got) the doubles 7 *d.*, and the singles 6 *d.* ; in 1830, 7 *d.* and 6 *d.* ; in 1831 6½ *d.* and 5 *d.*, which is the same now.

5753. Has the reduction been in the same proportion upon the other articles ?—I believe precisely in the same proportion, except velvets, they have not been so much reduced.

5754. What was the price of the manufacture of figured gros de Naples in 1826 ?—I think it was 1 *s.* 6 *d.* ; we did not make any figured goods in 1826.

5755. When did you begin to make them ?—I could not answer that correctly without I had some other papers. I believe about three years ago.

5756. During those six years has the manufacture of silk goods increased very considerably in the country ?—Very considerably, I think.

5757. In what place ?—Lancashire chiefly ; and there are other places where the manufacture of broad goods is carried on, for instance, at Sudbury in Suffolk.

5758. What effect has the increase of silk manufacture in Lancashire and other places had upon the wages of Spitalfields ?—I should say the effect has been injurious ; our operatives are working at prices that will scarcely allow of their subsisting, with the additional labour, probably of four hours in a day more than a man was accustomed to work some years ago.

5759. Do you know the price paid at Manchester for the making of these single and double gros de Naples ?—Not from any documents. I have heard it said as low as 3½ *d.* for singles.

5760. Are they of equal qualities with those made at Spitalfields ?—As far as I may judge, I have seen some patterns of singles from Manchester that were pretty much the same as our goods of that description.

5761. Is it within your knowledge that some Spitalfields manufacturers have removed and established themselves at Manchester ?—A gentleman who lived next door to us has gone down to Manchester and settled, but he was not the principal but his son : I do not know of any other persons out of the Fields, but it is very likely some have gone.

5762. And you attribute the fall in the rate of wages in Spitalfields to the competition at Manchester ?—I think it has greatly to do with it. I do not attribute it entirely to that, other circumstances have borne upon it, particularly the introduction of French goods, and the bringing French goods into this country illegally, all these have borne upon the reduction of wages.

5763. Is it your opinion there have been, during the last six years, as many weavers employed in Spitalfields, speaking of the average, as there were in the previous six years ?—Certainly not.

5764. Can you state the reduction in the number ?—I have information from persons who are in the habit of visiting the poor in the Fields, and it is supposed about one-third of the looms are now unemployed.

5765. Can you state what number of manufacturers there are now in Spitalfields ?—Not from any certain knowledge ; I have heard that out of about 147, or some such number, 47 have been obliged to quit business ; the fact is, they have been ruined ; that would leave about 100, but I merely give it as what I have heard, not from any positive information.

5766. Are not several of the manufacturers in Spitalfields now throwsters ?—Yes, some of them are.

5767. More than there were when you first went into business ?—That I do not know.

5768. Is it not the practice of manufacturers in Spitalfields to pay cash for their silks to a much greater extent than was the case formerly ?—I should think it was ; as regards our own house we always do it. I never allow a bill to be drawn upon us for silk.

5769. Have you reason to suppose that the manufacturers upon the whole have more capital in the business than formerly ?—That is a question I am unable to answer ; some of the manufacturers who have been established a long time have abundance of capital, many of the others I should think have very little, but it is mere matter of opinion.

5770. Has not the tendency of the business during the last six years been, to throw the business into the hands of a few manufacturers in Spitalfields ?—That would appear from what I have already said, as so many have gone out of the business.

5771. Did they go out of the business from having made their fortunes ?—No, they were ruined, as I have stated before.

5772. Do

Mr.
*Thomas Stone.*

18 May,
1832.

5772. Do they manufacture satins at Manchester?—I should think they did, but I am not sure.

5773. Have you ever been at Manchester?—No.

5774. Do they manufacture velvets?—I believe not; I think that manufacture is confined to the Fields; I know they make satins in other parts of the country.

5775. What was the state of trade at Christmas last year in Spitalfields?—There were very great complaints of trade then: as far as regards our own manufacture, I should say we were going on pretty much as usual.

5776. Was there any improvement in the month of January or February?—There were a good many sales made in January and February.

5777. Did you as a manufacturer anticipate an improved trade this spring?—Yes, we expected a good trade this spring.

5778. Did the establishment of this Committee affect the trade in Spitalfields?—Yes, it had its effect for a time; there was an opinion that the duty would probably be taken off silk, and there was a great talk among the buyers that such would be the case, and they were sparing in their purchases.

5779. How long did that effect continue?—I should say some few weeks, not long, for there soon became a demand for goods; and as far as we are concerned, we had a good sale for goods.

5780. Is it not the fact, that in the last month, the saleable goods in Spitalfields were generally sold?—As far as we are concerned, I should say our stock was very much diminished by that time; we did not retain more than 3-11ths of it.

5781. But for recent political circumstances, would you have had reason to expect a good trade during the summer?—We hoped for a good trade, and acted under that impression at the latter end of last year, and laid in a considerable stock of silk.

5782. Do you know the price of raw and thrown silks in February?—I do not recollect precisely; in February I know pretty nearly what they were.

5783. Had the establishment of this Committee any effect upon the price of raw and thrown silk?—I do not know that there was much effect produced; I am not able to answer that; we had not occasion to purchase in that month.

5784. Up to what period was it you had sold this large proportion of your stock?—I think about the end of March we had diminished our stock considerably.

5785. Have you reason to suppose that this is the case with the other manufacturers at Spitalfields?—Yes, we are pretty much affected in the same way.

5786. But trade was particularly brisk a fortnight ago?—Rather longer ago than that; about a month ago trade was very brisk.

5787. You have been a manufacturer for more than six years, but you had been acquainted with the trade prior to that?—No, I was not the least acquainted with the trade.

5788. Have you understood there have been other periods of distress in Spitalfields?—Yes.

5789. Will you have the goodness to state what, in your opinion, is the effect of the duty upon Italian thrown silks upon the manufacturers in Spitalfields?—I think it is injurious to them, inasmuch as it puts them in a worse situation than the foreign manufacturers.

5790. In what state does it place them in comparison with the manufacturers of Manchester?—The Spitalfields manufacturer has to throw his own silk by sending it to the throwster, while the manufacturer at Manchester, in many cases, has a throwing mill of his own.

5791. The question referred to the effect of the duty upon the two branches?—If we purchase foreign thrown silk, we pay duty upon it; and the manufacturer of Manchester, if he throws his own silk, gets it without.

5792. He does not get it thrown for nothing?—No, he must have an outlay for that.

5793. Is it your opinion that the duty falls upon Spitalfields chiefly?—It is.

5794. Can you recollect what may have been the average amount of claims you have had to make upon the Italian merchants, for damage done to thrown silk on the passage from Italy to England?—They are very trifling (the amount I cannot recollect, they are so trifling); we should think it hardly necessary to keep it in memory.

5795. What proportion of foreign thrown silk might you use in your manufactory?—I cannot state it precisely, but not a very great proportion; we have thrown most of our trams, having used very little foreign thrown trams; some foreign

678.                                                                  organzine,

organzine, generally Piedmont; but the article in most use with us is English thrown organzine.

5796. Have you had your silk thrown in the West of England, or the North of England?—In both places.

5797. Can you inform the Committee the prices you have paid in each of the six years for throwing?—I could by the books; but I can state that what we are paying now for trams, is 2 s. 3 d.; we have not thrown any organzine a considerable time past.

5798. You purchase Italian organzine?—Yes, some of it; but we purchase a good deal of English thrown organzine.

5799. Can you state the price you paid for trams in 1831 or 1830?—In 1830 and 1831 the price was about 3 s. 6 d.; but I cannot state the precise months, there have been several alterations.

5800. Is it within your knowledge that the throwsters were very well employed in the year 1830?—Yes, I think they were; there was a time that they were very well employed, and I think it was in 1830.

5801. Had you any difficulty in getting your silk thrown?—Yes, we had; we wanted to make arrangements with more than one, to get a certain quantity thrown per week; I am speaking of a particular time, I do not say it was the latter end of 1830 or the beginning of 1831; but there was a time when we wanted to make arrangements with the throwsters for a supply of so much per week, but we tried in vain.

5802. How long did this difficulty of getting your silks thrown last?—I should think, stating it from memory, about four months.

5803. Can you give any reason for it?—The reason I heard was they were all full of silk.

5804. Had they been before that time without silk?—I think that three months before that time they were very slack of business.

5805. There was a great depression in the previous year?—Yes.

5806. Therefore when the trade suddenly came upon them for a short time there was a difficulty in obtaining a supply?—Yes, there was.

5807. Was not there a very short quantity of foreign thrown imported in 1829? —There appears by a document I have seen to have been a small quantity.

5808. Would not those two reasons account for the briskness in the beginning of 1831, the shortness of the supply and the throwsters being out of employment previously?—No doubt they would have their effect.

5809. During that time, when the English throwsters were so well employed, was not the price of Italian thrown silk very high in this market?—Yes, I think it was.

5810. You have stated, that the mills have not been adequately employed previously to that period?—Yes.

5811. If the hands had been dispersed through the parishes, and been sent to their homes, would n t there be some difficulty in re-collecting them to commence work again?—Not any great difficulty.

5812. It might have occasioned delay?—Yes, it might, if they had done it; but I should say, that the information that I have received from time to time has been to the effect, that there has been no difficulty in getting hands.

5813. You have probably understood, there were periods of distress among the throwsters prior to 1826?—No, I cannot state it.

5814. Can you state to the Committee any information you possess as to the import of silks from France?—No; I really do not know any thing upon the subject as to quantities; I know that they are imported, and I believe they have a very injurious effect upon our trade.

5815. Of the two circumstances to which you attribute the reduction of wages in Spitalfields, namely, the imports from France, and competition from Manchester, which of those causes has been the most injurious?—I should say competition in our own country.

5816. Explain that?—Because when we are told by all the buyers and parties we have to do with, that they are making goods in the country at a 1 d. or 2 d. per yard lower than we are in the Fields, there is the greatest difficulty, or rather impossibility for the work people to get a better price for their labour than we are paying at the time, however low it may be, and there is an equal difficulty for their masters to get a better price for the works, however necessary that may be.

5817. Have you not understood, that the hands employed in the silk manufacture

at

at Manchester were previously employed in the manufacture of muslins?—I have heard that they had been employed in the cotton trade.

5818. You know nothing of this yourself?—No; I have stated that I have never been in Manchester, and I know nothing of it.

5819. Have you any reason to suppose there would be any difficulty in a man transferring his labonr from one employment to the other?—Very little, from what I have heard.

5820. That being the case, do you not conceive, that the wages paid for weaving gros de Naples in Manchester, must be governed by the price for weaving cotton goods?—I have always heard that it has its effect.

5821. Do you believe the manufacturers in Spitalfields can continue to pay higher wages than the manufacturer pays at Manchester?—Yes; he would be able to pay higher, but the low wages at Manchester makes it necessary that the wages at Spitalfields should be as low as possible.

5822. How much higher do you believe the Spitalfields manufacturer can afford to pay them than at Manchester?—It is generally considered there is at least a penny difference.

5823. And consequently, whenever the wages fall at Manchester, they must also fall at Spitalfields?—It has its effect beyond a doubt.

5824. Can you state that is positively the case; can you state that the wages are never high at Manchester when they are low at Spitalfields?—I never heard of it.

5825. If higher wages than those you have mentioned be paid in Spitalfields, they must be paid out of the profits of the manufacturer?—Yes, or out of his losses.

5826. Do you not know that they are a different description of goods manufactured at Manchester?—They are the goods we have spoken of, but I have seen patterns of goods to be compared to our singles.

5827. Do you not know that the great bulk of goods manufactured at Manchester are manufactured of a lower description of silk?—I believe the Manchester singles are made of Bengal silk, and ours are the same; we may use more China.

5828. Did you make, six years ago, what you call Manchester singles with Bengal silk in Spitalfields?—In 1826 we made many singles.

5829. From Bengal silk?—Yes.

5830. Such things as they make now at Manchester?—Yes; they may have been a little better.

5831. Have you any doubt that the manufacturers of Manchester can make goods as well as they are made at Spitalfields?—Judging from what I have heard, more than what I have seen myself, I should say they can make as good.

5832. You have been asked, if the hands at Manchester cannot readily change from the making of cotton goods to silk goods, and that if they could earn more at making silk goods, would they not therefore make silk goods in preference to the cotton goods, and you have stated they certainly would?—I have heard that they do change from one to the other.

5833. You were asked if the wages of the cotton trade must not govern the silk trade?—I do not recollect that that was put to me.

5834. Could the wages of the silk trade in Mancheste be higher than the wages of the cotton trade there?—They are a little higher; and that is an inducement for them to leave the cotton trade.

5835. They have left the cotton trade because it was depressed?—The reason they left the cotton trade was, because they got a little more wages in the silk trade.

5836. Do you know there are some branches of the cotton manufacture at Manchester in which a man will earn a guinea a week, and a man in the very next house will earn only 7s. a week?—No, I do not know it.

5837. Supposing the price of 22s. for foreign thrown Italian organzine to be the price of the day inclusive of the duty of 3s. 6d. and the duty to be reduced to 2s.; do you consider the price of the thrown silk would then be 20s. 6d. to the manufacturer in Spitalfields?—I think it probable it would be a little higher than 20s. 6d.

5838. How much higher?—It is a mere question of surmise on the part of any body, and my information is such, that it would not make my opinion worth having.

678.

5839. When

Mr.
Thomas Stone.

18 May,
1832.

5839. When the duty was reduced, would not the price of Italian raw and thrown be nearer to each other?—I should think they might for a time.

5840. Would not the Italian seller thus be enabled to maintain a higher price for the raw?—Certainly; if the price was better for the raw, he would maintain it for a time at a better price, that follows.

5841. You think only for a time?—It would find its level; there would be reason for its finding its level.

5842. What reasons?—Such as the price of throwing.

5843. Surely the Italian having 1 s. 6 d. less duty to work it at, he can give a better price for the raw, and thus a better price would be maintained for the thrown without the benefit to the manufacturer?—I should think the market price for the raw would be a fair one in Italy; and it would not be greatly affected by the alteration of the duty, it might a little, but not to any great extent.

5844. Were you at all acquainted with the silk trade before 1826?—I have said no; it was a very little while before 1826 that I became acquainted with the trade.

5845. You have no practical knowledge of the business of a silk manufacturer, except what you have obtained in the last six years?—No, none whatever.

5846. Nor of manufactured goods?—No.

5847. You know that the weavers of Spitalfields are much distressed?—Yes, very much.

5848. Have you had opportunities of seeing them at their own houses?—Occasionally.

5849. Can you devise any means by which this distress can be mitigated or relieved?—I should merely be inclined to suggest what appears to me very likely to mitigate the distress; the causes of it I have said to be the admission of French goods both legally and illegally, and likewise competition in our own country; if you were to remove part of the causes, if that could be done, we should have less distress.

5850. What part of those causes?—If the prohibition of French goods were again granted, no doubt there would be much more labour for our own weavers; again, if smuggling was prevented, there would be much more labour for our own weavers, and certainly if there was less competition in our own country, there would be more labour for the operatives in Spitalfields, but I would not recommend the relief of the latter to be obtained at the expense of the former.

5851. Do you suppose the larger quantity of French silks to be admitted legally or illegally?—From what I have heard I should think illegally.

5852. Do you think smuggling can be prevented without total prohibition?—I should think it probable that it might.

5853. Do you think with prohibition it could be?—I have my doubts of this. I know an instance where some silk goods were brought to a manufacturer, a native of France, that he might distinguish whether those goods were French or whether they were English, and he could not say that they were not French, and it would follow, that if they were French they must have been smuggled into this country.

5854. He did not know?—No, he did not know, though he was of French extraction, and had been concerned in manufacturing silk in this country many years.

5855. Can you distinguish the French silks?—No.

5856. Then you think total prohibition would be an advantage to the silk trade of Spitalfields?—It would lessen the distress, as there would be more labour for the hands.

5857. In the event of a prohibition, there would be smuggling?—There is great probability there would; there was smuggling before, and most likely it would continue.

5858. Do you believe from your experience of any absolute facts you are acquainted with, that a greater quantity of smuggling has taken place since the prohibition has been removed, than previously to the law being altered?—I could not say from any thing that has come directly under my knowledge that that is the case.

5859. Do you not believe that smuggling, like any other matter of trade, is determined by the profit; and that so long as smuggling is profitable, it will continue?—I am afraid it will.

5860. Under the state of the law, which compels any person in whose house goods might be found, to prove that they were of English manufacture, and in the event of his not being able to do so, that they should be condemned as French,

and

and he should suffer severe penalties; do you not think that would be sufficient to deter persons bringing in any quantity of goods illegally?—That would follow from the last question and answer; if he was detected, and he was to suffer large penalties, and forfeit the goods, it would not be profitable.

5861. Do you know the state of the law at present as regards smuggling?—It is generally considered a very illegal thing to smuggle, but it is done.

5862. In the event of a seizure of French goods, would not the person have to prove either that they were manufactured in England or that he had paid the duty upon them?—I suppose he would have to do that if the thing was fairly brought to the test; but there have been cases where that has not been the case, but the person has submitted to the fine.

5863. Suppose that you were to import legally 20,000 *l.* worth of French goods, and then sell 18,000 *l.* worth of those out of your warehouse, and the next day you import 18,000 *l.* worth illegally, if the officers were to come and take the whole, how would he be able to prove which goods had not paid the duty; the Custom House officer would be immediately nonsuited upon the mere showing of the Custom House receipt that you had paid the duty upon the 20,000 *l.* of goods; the possibility of ascertaining the identity of those goods would be lost; they had passed through the Custom House as gauzes, or any other articles, and you would only have to take care to import the same sort of goods; is not that so?—Yes, I dare say it is quite correct.

5864. If foreign manufactured silks were prohibited, would not the consequent increased demand of labour relieve the silk trade from the effects of the present injurious home competition to which you have referred?—It would have this effect; there would be more employment generally in the silk trade.

5865. Was there the same degree of distress existing when you entered into the business?—No, certainly not; the wages were different, and the distress less.

5866. Was it much less?—A good deal less.

5867. Did you, when you entered the silk trade, take a business that had been already established?—I did.

5868. Of whom did you take that business?—Of Mr. Levesque.

5869. Was not Mr. Levesque in the fancy and figured branch of the silk trade when he parted with his business?—No, he was making no fancy goods.

5870. Was not the description of commodity he made, superior to any thing you make now?—Perhaps generally his goods would be considered as superior, but we make some goods equally as good as he made.

5871. What is the reason you did not continue to make that superior commodity for which he was celebrated?—The trade that he carried on was amongst the retail customers at the West end of the Town, and it soon became unpleasant to me to carry it on; and therefore I took in a partner, and our trade was quite altered.

5872. Have you any reason to believe that the persons who used to purchase that description of goods from Mr. Levesque, are able now in any house in London to supply themselves with that description of commodity?—There is a change in the article; at that time the goods were mostly shot soft, and without they give an order to that effect, they would not obtain such goods.

5873. You mean that the shot soft commodity was superior to any thing you make now?—It was a dearer article, and cost us as manufacturers more, but it is a matter of taste, for many people say that the goods shot suple are preferable.

5874. Was not it a more sterling commodity, inasmuch as it really seems to be what it was?—Yes, so far as regards a sterling commodity, it was, no doubt.

5875. The commodity now made in Spitalfields is not actually so good as was then made, if you speak of sterling quality?—No.

5876. You have already said he had a connexion for the disposal of his goods you did not choose to follow up?—Yes.

5877. Do you think that those persons he used to supply, do sell the superior commodity in English manufacture that he then made?—I should think not; because there is no order given for that description of goods so far as I know; the taste is altered.

5878. Is it not because they supply themselves with a superior commodity from France?—I should think not altogether so; if any body would give us an order for such goods, we should be glad to make them.

5879. If they can get that commodity from France in a better and more saleable article than you can make here for the same price, is it not likely they will buy

678.                                                                    from

Mr.
*Thomas Stone.*

18 May,
1832.

from France?—If they can get the goods cheaper in a legal way, or if they choose to submit to the degradation of getting them in illegally, they certainly will prefer them from France.

5880. Do you not know that the parties your house used to supply, do purchase principally French silks?—I do not know it from personal knowledge; and I should say, I believe a good many of those silks which you are assuming to be shot soft because they are of a superior kind, perhaps are not shot soft but shot suple.

5881. The question refers to the superior commodity that used to be made in Spitalfields, that is not now made except in a more trifling degree?—As far as our own manufactory is concerned, we do not make that description of goods to the extent that Mr. Levesque did; we have altered our trade, and therefore we have been obliged to make a different description of goods.

5882. How long did you carry on a similar description of manufacture after you took the trade of Mr. Levesque?—About six months.

5883. Did you not in fact pay him a premium for his trade?—I did.

5884. What was the object of paying him that premium if you intended so soon to abandon it?—His business was considered valuable; then you are to take into account there was all the material for carrying it on, and those who were considered competent judges by myself, thought the sum he named was a fair one; the real object was to get into a business at the time that was ready made, and at a fair price, taking the materials all ready for one's hand.

5885. You wished to come into a trade where every thing was furnished to your hand, and where you had a certain connexion?—The connexion had its influence.

5886. Did you abandon the connexion or did the connexion abandon you?—I abandoned it completely.

5887. Was it because they declined to give you orders?—No; it was because I found the trade exceedingly troublesome, I had not been accustomed to trade, and it was particularly troublesome, especially as to the credit they took.

5888. What was the credit?—Generally what is called six and six months credit, which came to about 14 months.

5889. Was it houses of respectability at the West end of the Town, that Mr. Levesque formerly supplied?—Yes.

5890. Was Mr. Levesque remarkable for his attention to his business?—I believe he was very attentive to his business till he became ill; I have heard he has been in his manufactory many hours in a day, and constantly till he became very ill.

5891. What description of goods was it which Mr. Levesque made, of which you gave up the manufacture?—During the latter part of the time Mr. Levesque was in business he made what are called rich three-doubles, and that description of goods we still make, but they were then what is technically called shot soft, now that description of goods is shot suple.

5892. Why is it not now made?—The demand for it does not exist, they prefer suple.

5893. Is that description of goods not sold in the shops?—I think not; I am not very well acquainted with what is sold at the West end of the Town, but I think very few of that description.

5894. You do not think that the reason for those goods not being made in Spitalfields is in consequence of their being introduced from Manchester or France?—No; I think it is because there is an alteration in the taste; we made them for some time, till we found the demand ceased, and that if there were two or three sorts of goods on the counter, the shot suple would be selected if they were equally good.

5895. You have spoken of making single gros de Naples, did Mr. Levesque ever make single gros de Naples?—I think not.

5896. You used English thrown silks?—Yes.

5897. What quantity of velvet can a man make in a week?—A good workman would make about six yards of velvet.

5898. He would earn about 18 *s.* a week?—Yes.

5899. Have not the finer branches of silk goods been generally manufactured at Spitalfields?—Yes.

5900. And the finer fancy articles?—Yes, I believe what you call the rich fancy goods.

5901. Do

Mr.
*Thomas Stone.*

18 May,
1832.

5901. Do you not know that there is a prejudice in favour of French fashions, and that the introduction of fine fancy French goods had been the means of affecting the trade in Spitalfields?—I have heard there is a prejudice in favour of French goods, and that is supported by some other things I have heard.

5902. It has been stated to this Committee that that has been one means of driving the Spitalfields manufacturers to a lower article that brings them more into competition with Manchester?—It has reduced price which would have that effect.

5903. Do you not happen to know that the French people receive orders for the goods sent here?—Yes, I have heard so.

5904. Does not that give them an advantage over the manufacturer here, who makes them at his own risk?—It does.

5905. You have said that Manchester comes into competition with Spitalfields; do you not happen to know that the principal part of the China and Turkey silks are used at Manchester?—Yes.

5906. And that a quantity of waste is mixed with them?—Yes.

5907. If it should happen that the competition of Manchester or Sudbury should greatly interfere and press upon the profits and wages in Spitalfields, would not that be a reason why we should not increase that competition, by admitting the foreign article?—I have already said that I think the prohibition of French goods coming into this country, would be a benefit to the manufacture of Spitalfields, and to the country at large.

5908. Do you conceive that the introduction of foreign manufactured silk goods has a prejudicial effect upon the general labour in the silk trade in this country?—As far as it prevents our people being employed; every piece of French goods takes a certain time to make, and as there must be a certain time employed upon it, so far you injure the people here.

5909. Do you not know that the best profits, and the best wages, are upon fine articles?—Yes, I have reason to believe that the best profits are derived from the best articles.

5910. The 700 looms you employ are upon commoner goods, and therefore those finer articles do not interfere so much with you?—Not so much.

5911. But they do in some respects?—In some cases they do greatly.

5912. You stated before, that in the commencement of 1830 the thrown trade was brisker?—I said I believe that was the time.

5913. At that time was not the duty reduced; and do you think it was a remunerating price for the throwster?—The duty was reduced in 1829, when the throwing trade became brisker; there is no doubt that the throwster's trade was a good one at that time.

5914. Do you apprehend that the throwsters get a remunerating price at present?—All I have heard would tell me no; I am not a throwster myself, nor do I know any thing about the particulars of their business.

5915. Connected with the trade, it can hardly be otherwise than for you to know that there is a great deal of distress existing amongst them?—No doubt; and I should say the present price is not a remunerating price.

5916. If they only get half the money they used to get, and are doing a great deal more business, it may be attended with a loss instead of an advantage?—In some cases I have heard there is a loss.

5917. The more a man may do the worse it may be?—He has got his mill and machinery, and it is necessary for him to go on with business a little, that he may not make a very great loss by that machinery standing idle.

5918. It may be necessary for him to go on with machinery, though it is not a getting business?—Yes.

5919. But if it is a losing business, the more he does, the more he must lose?—Yes, unless a greater loss would arise from the machinery doing nothing.

5920. Is not there a great deal of capital embarked among the throwsters?—I believe there is.

5921. They employ a great many women and children?—No doubt of it.

5922. If the trade is not a remunerating trade at the present time, a reduction on foreign thrown silk must put them in a worse condition?—No doubt of it.

5923. Would not it have a tendency to destroy all the capital embarked in such mills?—It would destroy some of it.

5924. And have a tendency to throw them out of the trade?—Yes, and the hands must seek employment elsewhere.

678.

5925. Do

Mr.
*Thomas Stone.*

18 May,
1832.

5925. Do you happen to know, during the Milan Decrees, there was a great want of foreign thrown silk; that our manufacturers could not get it to manufacture?—I do not know much of it; I have never known a time since I have been in business, when we could not get foreign thrown silk.

5926. If our throwsters were destroyed and we had to depend upon the foreign throwster, would it not put us very much in his hands?—We should be in his hands if our own throwsters were destroyed, there can be no doubt about it.

5927. You said you gave up your connexion at the West end, from the necessity of giving six months' credit?—I said that it was a troublesome business.

5928. Has that been the case with other manufacturers besides yourself?—I do not know that it has.

5929. You do not know that other manufacturers have objected on that account? —No, I do not.

5930. Do you believe that the other manufacturers do give that credit?—I should think, if they have much to do with the West end of the Town dealers, they must give that credit.

5931. Therefore you think they do it?—Yes, I should think they must.

5932. You have given up the West end of the Town trade?—Yes.

5933. Your buyers were formerly from the West end of the Town?—Yes, chiefly so.

5934. To what buyers do you sell now?—Buyers from the city principally.

5935. Persons who pay you cash principally?—Yes, principally.

5936. You began business some time before the legal importation of French goods?—Yes.

5937. And previous to Mr. Levesque leaving business, he had discontinued the manufacture of fancy goods?—Yes.

5938. Do you happen to know why he discontinued the manufacture of fancy goods?—I should think the same reason that would induce any other manufacturer, because he had not the demand.

5939. Do you know whether he was influenced in doing it by the smuggling from France?—I do not know that he was.

5940. The articles he manufactured at that time are not now in demand?—No, not at our house, or else we should make them.

5941. Have you reason to believe that the same sort of goods are imported from France?—I do not know from any personal knowledge; I have heard that they are to a great extent.

5942. You have spoken of the discontinuance of the manufacture of an article here, shot soft; is not the introduction of suple in consequence of the French having used it?—I have said, that I conceive the goods shot suple are now preferred, and I believe this description of goods first came from France.

5943. You gave up a particular trade in which Mr. Levesque was employed, because you did not like his connexion, or the credit he gave?—I did not like the mode we were obliged to carry on the business altogether; it was very troublesome, and I should say did not pay quite so well as another kind of business.

5944. Was not the demand ceasing?—Yes, in part, certainly, but that was not the reason that influenced me.

5945. But that was one reason why Mr. Levesque gave it up?—No; that is, as to the fancy article; I believe there was a want of demand.

5946. You say, that as far as you are concerned, figured silks are not now made?—No, I do not say that, because I have already said we have some looms employed on those goods.

5947. Since 1826, have you not constantly seen figured silks in the shop windows of all the principal houses in the metropolis?—Whenever I have happened to pay attention to the subject, I have seen figured silks.

5948. Do you not know, from the common observation that every man makes, that the ladies do wear a great deal of figured silk?—No doubt they do.

5949. Have you a concern at Sudbury?—No, we have not.

5950. You have said, that Mr. Levesque was in the habit of giving credit for six and six months?—Yes.

5951. That system is almost discontinued?—With us it is discontinued altogether; we have not a single dealer with us that pays in that way.

5952. Is it discontinued generally?—I believe there are some manufacturers who have been established a long time, who make it answer to give the credit agreed upon, whether six and six I cannot tell.

5953. The

Mr.
*Thomas Stone.*

18 May,
1832.

5953. The practice, in general, in Spitalfields, is to sell the goods to be settled at the end of a month, with bills at two months?—It is what we call one and two months' account.

5954. How do you reconcile that with saying more capital is required?—I have said no such thing.

5955. The manufacturer, instead of having his capital in his book, as book debts, is now enabled to buy his material upon cash, and throw his own silk, or is enabled to have mills of his own?—He has his capital at command, and he does with it as seemeth good to him.

5956. The capital is differently disposed of to what it was formerly?—Yes.

5957. You stated, you preferred the system that has been recently introduced?—Very much.

5958. You prefer short credit to long credit?—Yes; and the mode of doing business is much less troublesome.

5959. Will you state what you mean by the mode of doing business?—Now we can sell, perhaps 50 or 100 pieces to one purchaser, while we have had to send up to the West end of the Town, it may be three or four times, about as many pieces, i. e. three or four.

5960. You mean to say, formerly you sold to a great number of houses to a small amount, and now the whole is absorbed in one house to a large amount?—No, I do not mean to say that, but that there are many people to whom we now sell many pieces to at one time.

5961. How many persons are there in the city of London who could come and buy 150 pieces of silk, and pay you ready money in one purchase?—A very great many in the city of London, but not a great many in the silk trade.

5962. Are there many purchasers in the city of London who can buy 150 pieces of silk in one purchase, and pay ready money?—When I said 150 pieces, I did not say we sold that number very frequently, but our mode of doing business, and that we like, is selling largely to a few houses.

5963. How many manufacturers in Spitalfields possess throwing mills?—I do not know.

5964. Can you not buy the throwns cheaper than you can buy the raws?—Certainly not, in a general way.

5965. Did Mr. Levesque assign any reason to you for giving up his business?—His health was very much injured; he had made a very good fortune, and thought fit to retire.

5966. Do you not think that one reason was an apprehension that the change in the laws would be injurious to the silk trade?—It might have influenced him, but the other reasons were the chief ones; his health had become very much injured.

5967. You state that at present, instead of selling to a variety of persons you sell very large quantities to one?—I did not exactly express myself so; I said we sold large quantities at a time, but not to one person in particular.

5968. Selling very large quantities to one person, do you find as many purchasers of small quantities as there were before this new system sprung up?—As far as the West end of the Town customers are concerned, to which I apprehend the question applies, we have nothing to do with them, they do not deal with us.

5969. You were understood to say there is an alteration of the system that has sprung up of late years?—I said that as applicable to our own house.

5970. And it was understood to consist in this, that you found now that the demand came upon you in a large quantity from one individual purchaser in a greater degree than it used to do formerly?—I did not confine myself to one, two, or three or four purchasers.

5971. But a small number?—Yes.

5972. Instead of a considerable number of small purchasers?—The connexions that Mr. Levesque had at the West end of the Town did not consist of many, but it was that kind of business that three or four journies might be made to the West end of the Town about three or four pieces; whereas now we can often sell 40 or 50 pieces in a few minutes.

5973. It is more convenient supposing you sell the same quantity of silk to one individual, rather than selling the same quantity to a number of different persons residing in different places?—Certainly.

5974. Is that what you mean by the advantage of this new system?—I have endeavoured to express myself as distinctly upon that subject as I can; I have

678.
stated

Mr.
*Thomas Stone.*

18 May,
1832.

stated that the former kind of business was very troublesome, and therefore we gave it up, and that the present business we do is a very different kind and far less troublesome.

5975. What has become of those more numerous purchasers of that class with whom you used to have dealings?—I have stated that the class was not very numerous, but they continue to deal with some of the persons in the Fields who choose to go on upon the same system.

5976. You do not know that they buy from those large houses, that you in the first instance supply with your goods?—I dare say that they do.

5977. Do you suppose that those persons find an advantage in the system, by means of which, instead of purchasing directly from one of the manufacturers, they are obliged to purchase through the medium of a warehouseman, who of course must have his profit upon the transaction?—If I understand the question right, it is this; do I understand it is preferable to these dealers at the West end of the Town to deal with the large warehouseman or with the manufacturers?

5978. Yes?—I should say that they have found it to their advantage, or they would not have done it.

5979. Do you consider that it has been completely a matter of option on their side?—As far as I know the business, I should say it is matter of option.

5980. Because, so far as respects yourself, it has not been completely matter of option, because you have declined that mode of dealing, and found it more preferable, and more for your own interest to carry the dealing on according to this new system, that is to say, by a channel that takes it through the hands of the warehouseman?—The answer I gave was, though not in these words, because I chose it, and that was an option.

5981. Do the warehousemen give six and six months credit?—I do not know.

5982. You said Mr. Levesque's business was in the West end houses?—Yes.

5983. And he made a large fortune?—Yes.

5984. What reason had you for giving it up?—I have given an answer to that as distinctly as I can.

5985. Do the West end houses buy French goods in small quantities?—They buy according to their demand.

5986. Can you recollect about the number of customers that Mr. Levesque had upon his books?—I should not think that Mr. Levesque had, among his principal customers in London, more than twenty.

5987. How many may you have about?—I should think we have, of our principal customers, from fifteen to twenty.

5988. When you spoke of houses buying occasionally 150 pieces of silk, you did not mean to confine that to two or three houses?—No, nor did I wish that number to be taken for what frequently occurs ; but it was the mode in which we do business, it being preferable to me.

5989. Whatever number of persons you choose to give credit to, they visit you in their rounds in Spitalfields almost every day?—Yes, whenever they think proper. Our door is open, and we are always glad to see them.

5990. When goods are taken, he that comes first gets the goods?—Yes, those that are out earliest in the morning.

5991. And, when trade is bad, and there are many goods. he who gives you the most money gets the goods?—Yes, we sell them as well as we can.

5992. If the system to which allusion has been made had not been more profitable upon the whole, you would not have adopted it?—It was much more pleasant to me. The trade we now do is much more pleasant than the trade we formerly did ; and that had great influence with me.

5993. If a stranger was to come to your house, and offer to purchase 50 *l.* worth of goods, and even to offer you a check for the amount, you would not sell them, would you?—Should not we? We should be very glad to sell them.

5994. Can you state whether the goods now manufactured in Spitalfields are of as good a quality as they were some time ago ; for instance, when you commenced business?—As far as our manufacture is concerned, we make more low goods than was generally made before the time alluded to ; certainly, as far as Mr. Levesque was concerned ; I never knew that he made that description of goods to any extent.

5995. What has made you increase your manufacture of low goods?—The demand for them.

5996. That

Mr.
*Thomas Stone.*

18 May,
1832.

5996. That is to say, if all your looms were employed in making rich goods you could not sell them?—No, certainly not to advantage.

5997. You have stated that the making rich goods is most profitable?—I should beg to state, that if we sell rich goods at a fair price, inasmuch as there is more capital employed, it would yield a larger profit; one piece of rich goods sold fairly, would yield a larger profit than a piece of low goods.

5998. If rich goods were much in demand, would not the competition of the manufacturers bring the rate of profit down to what generally exists now?—Yes.

5999. Do you mean the rich goods are not used now to so great an extent?—Yes.

6000. Who supplies the market?—We do in part: we do not discontinue making them by any means.

6001. In point of fact, are you not constantly interfered with by superior articles that come from France?—We have reason to believe that we are.

6002. Can you, by possibility, make these goods that come from France?—Yes, no doubt we can.

6003. Equally good?—Yes; except probably some few.

6004. Do you consider that the greatest number of looms are employed by the largest capitalists in Spitalfields?—I should think, perhaps not; but some of the large capitalists may not choose to do a large wholesale business; they may be content with a small business at the West end of the Town, and find it profitable to them; they have had the connexion a long time, and they have the means of giving that credit; in short, they may find it answer their purpose.

6005. Are there not as large or larger capitals in Spitalfields employed in a small number of looms?—That would follow as matter of course to those who, possessing large capitals, choose the business.

6006. If the trade is profitable, how do you reconcile that with the fact, that the largest capital is not employed in the largest number of looms?—They may prefer going on with their West end of the Town customers.

6007. Do they prefer going on with a trade less profitable?—It may be more profitable; I mean to say, that my objection is such as I have stated.

6008. The change was rather a matter of taste?—There was no absolute necessity, we did not like that kind of business.

6009. The class of persons at the West end of the Town, who used to take the long credit, have been considerably diminishing?—I do not know how they do their business now, whether they give that long credit or not.

6010. It appears by the official papers, that a considerable quantity of plain goods is imported from France; and in the last six months, upon plain goods it should seem that the duty paid was 21,000*l.*, whereas the duty paid upon the whole was not above 80,000*l.*, were you aware of that?—No; I was not aware of that.

6011. You have stated, you buy a portion of the Italian raw silks, and get them thrown, and you principally buy British thrown organzine; is it not important to you who buy the raws, that the throwster, who supplies you with British thrown organzine, should have a good supply of raws, from which you can both make your selection?—No doubt it is important that both should have a good supply of raws, otherwise the throwster could not send out good organzine, nor we procure good trams through him.

6012. Is the selection of Italian thrown organzine in this country great?—Yes; there is a great variety of organzine.

6013. Italian thrown?—Yes.

6014. Which do you prefer, the Italian thrown or the British thrown?—The British thrown for our own manufacture.

6015. Do you use much Piedmont organzine or Lombardy?—Not a great deal, very little Lombardy; and not a great deal of Piedmont.

6016. When you commenced business, had you any Jacquard looms?—We had none going at that time.

6017. Has the Jacquard engine much increased in Spitalfields?—I think not, but decreased; I speak from what I have heard of it in former times.

6018. Had you, at any period, more than 50 Jacquard looms at work?—Never, that I know of.

6019. Is there a greater degree of profit obtained by working a Jacquard loom than by working the common engine?—When you take into account the expenses of the Jacquard, it is pretty much the same profit.

6020. You say labourers used to earn 1*s.* 6*d.*?—Yes.

678.

6021. At

Mr.
*Thomas Stone.*

18 May,
1832.

6021. At the same period the price for working plain was 11 *d.* ?—Yes.

6022. In working the figures could a man obtain better wages ?—Yes, I think he could ; when using the Jacquard loom more skill is required, a man ought therefore to be better paid, and is generally paid more ; labour and skill find their value.

6023. What is the earning of a workman at this time, a fair average workmen, working plain at 6½ *d.* ?—Taking the necessary deductions into the account, I should think a good workman, upon the three doubles, would make 4½ yards at twelve hours a day.

6024. Four yards and a half a day ?—Yes.

6025. That is about 15 *s.* a week ?—You must take into the account the necessary deductions he has to pay for ; I should take the necessary deductions at about 3 *s.* or 3 *s.* 6 *d.* a week, from which I exclude rent and coals.

6026. You are speaking of the deductions from his labour ?—Yes, turning on the cane, twisting in, and quilling, &c.

6027. He must work pretty hard to do that ?—A good workman would make the quantity working at twelve clear hours a day.

---

*Lunæ, 21° die Maii, 1832.*

### EDWARD AYSHFORD SANFORD, ESQ. IN THE CHAIR.

Mr. *William Stone,* called in ; and further Examined.

Mr.
*William Stone.*

21 May,
1832.

6028. CAN you inform the Committee what have been the prices of Italian raw and thrown silk of the same quality in this market during the last 10 years ; stating the price of raw and the price of thrown, and the amount of duty in each year, and the nett proceeds to the Italian throwster.

[*The Witness delivered in the following Statement, which was read.*]

A TABLE

Mr.
*William Stone.*

21 May,
1832.

A TABLE showing the Comparative Nett Proceeds of One Pound English of ITALIAN RAW and ORGANZINE THROWN SILK (not dyed) Imported during the Years 1822 to 1831 (both inclusive), the Amount of Duty and Charges incidental to Import deducted.

QUANTITY BERGAM RAW, 4 to 5 Cocoons; ORGANZINE ranging between 22–28 Deniers.

### RAW.

| YEAR. | AVERAGE PRICE, including Duty per pound. (s. d.) | DUTY. (s. d.) | CHARGES, including Duty. (s. d.) | Nett Proceeds, with Duty and Charges off. (s. d.) | Proceeds to the Italian Throwster, for working the Raw into Organzine. (s. d.) |
|---|---|---|---|---|---|
| 1822 | 31 – | 5 6 | 8 7 | 22 5 | 7 2 |
| 1823 | 26 5 | 5 6 | 8 3 | 18 2 | 4 6 |
| 1824 to 25 March | 24 3 | 5 6 | 8 2 | 16 1 | 2 3 |
| 1824 after | 19 2 | – 3 | 2 7 | 16 7 | 5 8 |
| 1825 | 23 4 | – 3 | 2 10 | 20 6 | 8 4 |
| 1826 to 5 July | 19 8 | – 3 | 2 7 | 17 1 | 6 10 |
| 1826 after | 20 8 | – 1 | 2 6 | 18 2 | 2 7 |
| 1827 | 21 4 | – 1 | 2 7 | 18 9 | 2 4 |
| 1828 | 21 9 | – 1 | 2 7 | 19 2 | 2 5 |
| 1829 | 18 6 | – 1 | 2 5 | 16 1 | 5 1 |
| 1830 | 17 6 | – 1 | 2 4 | 15 2 | 3 4 |
| 1831 | 17 4 | – 1 | 2 4 | 15 1 | 3 1 |

### ORGANZINE.

| YEAR. | AVERAGE PRICE, including Duty per pound. (s. d.) | DUTY. (s. d.) | CHARGES, including Duty per lb. (s. d.) | Nett Proceeds, with Duty and Charges off. (s. d.) |
|---|---|---|---|---|
| 1822 | 48 2 | 14 8 | 18 7 | 29 7 |
| 1823 | 40 10 | 14 8 | 18 2 | 22 8 |
| 1824 to 25 March | 36 3 | 14 8 | 17 11 | 18 4 |
| 1824 after | 32 8 | 7 6 | 10 5 | 22 3 |
| 1825 to 18 Nov. | 39 7 | 7 6 | 10 9 | 28 10 |
| 1825 after | 31 9 | 5 1 | 7 10 | 23 11 |
| 1826 | 28 5 | 5 1 | 7 8 | 20 9 |
| 1827 | 28 9 | 5 1 | 7 8 | 21 1 |
| 1828 | 29 3 | 5 1 | 7 8 | 21 7 |
| 1829 to 5 July | 28 9 | 5 1 | 7 8 | 21 1 |
| 1829 after | 25 4 | 3 6 | 5 11 | 19 5 |
| 1830 | 24 1 | 3 6 | 5 11 | 18 2 |
| 1831 | 23 1 | 3 6 | 5 10 | 17 3 |

London, May 21st, 1832.    (Errors excepted.)

The average price of Bergam Raw, 3 to 4 Cocoons, between 1st August and the end of the year 1830, was 19 s.
The average price of Organzine, 18–22 Deniers, for the year 1831, estimated at 24 s. (result of the Crop of 1830.)

|  | s. | d. |
|---|---|---|
| Organzine | 24 | – |
| Charges | 6 | – |
|  | 18 | – |

|  | s. | d. |
|---|---|---|
| Raw | 19 | – |
| Charges | 2 | 6 |
|  | 16 | 6 |

1s. 6d. Net Profit to Italian Throwster.

6029. The whole of this Paper is drawn up on silk of the same quality in every year?—Precisely; taking the price currents at which they make up their accounts.

6030. By whom are these accounts or averages made?—By Messrs. Grandolfi & Co.

6031. You have stated the expenses on the raw silk to have been different in different years; what were the expenses in 1822?—The expenses were 8 s. 7 d.

6032. Of what does the 2 s. 7 d. in 1828 consist?—Of the charges made in coming from Italy here, including the Austrian duty, the charges and expenses of carriage, insurance and commission, and every expense attending the sale.

6033. Can you give us the items?—It would be rather difficult for me to give you the precise items; I will give you the principle on which it is done; it is done on a bale or certain quantity of foreign raw silk reduced to English pounds, that is 240 pounds, which is the usual size of a bale of raw; the price is taken at 26 s. 5 d., the duty at 5 s. 6 d. amounts to 66 l. 13 s. on the 240 lbs.; the small charges 2 l. 6 s., interest at six months at 4 per cent., taking it on the supposed and usual average of the sale, 1 l. 7 s. 7 d.; the sea insurance, fire insurance, brokerage, commission, *del credere*, makes up a charge of 16 l. 12 s. 10 d.; land carriage in Italy and export duty makes 13 l., making altogether 99 l. 19 s. 5 d., and that divided by 240 will give the net charges 8 s. 3 d.; that is the principle on which this is done.

6034. Are those of 1830 and 1831 calculated in the same way?—Precisely; if there is a variation of duty of course there would be a variation of so much, and the commission would be less according to the value, it must be varied because there is an *ad valorem* commission charged.

6035. Are we to understand that deducting the amount of duty and commission, that 2 s. 4 d. in 1831 will bear the same proportion as the 8 s. 7 d. did in 1822?—Exactly.

6036. On what denomination of raw and thrown are the averages made?—This is taken from a four to five cocoon, and the average of the thrown is 22 to 28 deniers.

6037. Is it Milan or Bergam?—It is not of the least consequence.

6038. Can you give us the particulars of the expenses on a bale at the present rates of duty?—On the present duty of 3 s. 6 d. per pound, the price 23 s. 1 d., it amounts to 43 l. 6 s. on a bale of thrown; the small charges on that are 2 l. 6 s. the interest at six months would be 18 s. 5 d.; sea insurance, fire insurance, brokerage, commission, *del credere*, would be 14 l. 10 s. 10 d.; land carriage in Italy and export duty 9 l., leaving the charges to be deducted 5 s. 10 d.

6039. How is the difference of the charge in the land carriage in Italy from 13 l. to 9 l. accounted for, have they made an alteration?—I cannot explain that; I think the name that I have given will satisfy every one that it is perfectly correct.

6040 Is the raw silk at Milan of a four to five cocoon, of no greater value than raw at Bergam of the same size?—I take the average of Bergam and Milan raw of a four or five cocoon; there may be various qualities of this description, but I do not think it affects the question; there was a question put to me bearing on this point, which was, whether the Italians had lost money in their throwing trade, and I stated, I believed they had, although I had not the means at hand of answerng the question.

6041. Do you conceive that 2 s. 3 d. is not a remuneration to the Italian throwster for throwing the silk?—According to the figures that have been given to this Committee.

6042. Does this 2 s. 3 d. include waste?—Yes, certainly, this includes every thing; in addition to that, I think I may fairly state to bear out my opinion, that the price of the raw taken from the 1st of August 1830 to the close of the year, of the finest class, say 3–4 cocoons, (it would not be until the following year that the result would be known; they cannot arrive in the market until towards Christmas); I find the averages of the raw 19 s. and the organzine 24 s., and deducting the charges on the same principle as we have done it before, it leaves to the Italian throwster 1 s. 6 d.

6043. Do you mean that on the whole sales in 1831?—Yes, only 1 s. 6 d.; I have made it out on the finer qualities in this instance, the result of which would be 18 to 22 deniers.

6044. Do you state that on the same authority, Messrs. Grandolfi?—I only
gave

Mr.
*William Stone.*

21 May,
1832.

gave the authority on the charges. I take the value of the article from my own knowledge as a broker.

6045. Is it your opinion that the Italian only receives 1 s. 6 d. for throwing silk in Italy, when he has to pay here a duty of 3 s. 6 d. ?—It is. The answer applies to the last two years. It must be borne in mind that 3-4 cocoon is the finer article.

6046. Is there any difference of charge in bringing raw and thrown silk from Italy?—There is a certain difference: as far as I can explain it, it will arise in the duty. The difference of the charges is, that on a bale of thrown silk it will be 13 *l.* ; and, on the bale of raw, it will be 9 *l.* These are the actual nett charges to the Italian from his own door. It is fair to suppose that any stock of thrown silk that would be on hand from the 1st of August to the 30th of December, would have the advantage of this market; the stock was exceedingly small; that bears on the question put to me, whether for the last two or three years it had been a favourable or unfavourable result to the Italian throwster.

6047. Do you conceive it is unfavourable to the Italian throwster because he is in closer competition with this country. So long as he pays 3 s. 6 d. duty, and the price of throwing is not more than 4 s., he receives only 1 s. 6 d?—I meant to explain. The price given for this class of throwing is said to be 4 s. by the Italian.

6048. Do you know what is given as the estimate for throwing silk of this quality in England at the present time?—I should think this quality, of the best class, might be done for 3 s. 9 d. or 4 s. a pound, exclusive of waste. The waste should be taken probably at four per cent. or five; that would make about 1 s.; and consequently it would be 4 s. 9 d. to 5 s.

6049. If then the Italian now only obtains 1 s. 6 d. per lb. when he is in close competition with England, supposing the whole duty of 3 s. 6 d. to be repealed, in what situation would the Italian be then?—It would put him in a better situation of course: 3 s. 6 d., added to 1 s. 6 d., would make it 5 s.

6050. His situation would be very much improved?—No doubt of it.

6051. The English throwster consequently would be fighting constantly against him, and ultimately be compelled to throw as cheaply as the Italian, to reduce the price of throwing to 1 s. 6 d. per lb. ?—Supposing that to be the case, of course he would.

6052. Can you state whether the imports for the present year, of Italian thrown silk, are considerable or otherwise?—They are not; they have fallen off considerably, it was put to me from August to August, which is the silk season, and I think the only fair principle upon which you can arrive at a conclusion; it applies to Italian silk, and is from August to August. If you do not follow this principle, you may, as I think has been the case in 1831, possibly misconceive the question. You may get two seasons of a crop of thrown silk into one current year ; therefore we always take it from August to August.

6053. That is the way on which you have formed these averages?—No, it does not apply in that case. From 1st of August 1829 to 1st of August 1830, I find the import of bales to be 3,376 of raw silk, and I find the import of organzine to be 568; that is 17 per cent., which is the lowest per centage we have had for a long time. From 1st August 1830 to 1st August 1831, we received 4,819 bales of raw, and of organzine 3,032, leaving a per centage of 63, which is a very great increase. Taking the import of raw up to the 1st of May 1832, it is 3,018 bales, the import of thrown is 594, reducing the per centage to about 19 per cent.

6054. Do you think that you have now in, all the silk of the season?—Nearly so. There may be some still to come, but nothing of any moment. There is evidence that the stocks are very low in Italy, and I believe they are.

6055. How do you account for the large difference in exportation?—By the very great advance which took place here in the thrown silk.

6056. About what time?—In August 1830.

6057. Did the prices of the thrown silk in the latter part of 1831 decrease?— In nearly the whole of 1831, the prices diminished considerably. I account for the importation by the circumstances that occurred in 1830; you will observe that we had the whole of the supply of the raw, and at the back of that a very large increase of thrown, which must have been brought here by the state of the market. A question was put to me, whether I did not know there was great distress at that time for the thrown article; and whether the manufacturers here were not obliged

678.

to

to wait for their supply of thrown silk; that was the fact, and that induced this large importation of thrown silk.

6058. That being followed by the lowering the price of thrown silks they have ceased to send?—Yes.

6059. Were the bales in 1830 and 1831 of the same weight as the bales of the present year?—As far as my remembrance goes, some of the bales in 1830 and 1831 were lighter, inasmuch as I think there was an increased supply of Piedmont silk, but not to any very great extent.

6060. You stated that in 1830 there was a great demand by the throwsters, do you not know that for many months before they had been in great distress for want of employment?—I have no doubt that was the fact, from looking at the import of the thrown from 1829 to 1830.

6061. You say that in 1830 there was a great demand for silk to be thrown?—Yes.

6062. And that induced an increased supply afterwards?—Yes.

6063. Previous to the commencement of the year 1830, do you not know that the throwsters were mostly unemployed, and in great distress for want of work?—I believe they were very much distressed.

6064. And many of them ruined?—Many of them failed, certainly.

6065. Were the throwsters doing well or ill in 1831, when there was this large importation?—In 1831 I think they were doing very badly.

6066. That would be a necessary consequence of the large importation from Italy?—Yes.

6067. Did the throwsters in 1830 get increased prices?—Yes.

6068. What did they get then?—In many cases in the latter part of the year they got an increase of nearly cent. per cent.

6069. You have stated, that at this particular time in the year 1830, the throwsters, including waste, got 3 s. 9 d. for throwing?—That was exclusive of waste; it is so stated for the throwing of tram.

6070. What did the English throwsters get in the year 1830, when you say they were distressed?—I should think their terms would be pretty much their own.

6071. I wish to know the exact price in 1830, that the English throwster got for throwing silk?—I think the price got up from 2 s. 6 d. to 3 s. 9 d. for the working of tram, and in the same proportion for the working of organzine; it is more particularly applicable to tram.

6072. We import a very small quantity of tram, do we not?—In 1829 to 1831 tram was a large feature.

6073. Are not our throwsters mostly employed in tram rather than organzine?—I think they are not.

6074. Do we not import more organzine than tram?—Yes, we do.

6075. I want to know what you paid in 1830 for throwing organzine and tram in this country?—For tram in the latter part of 1830, I conceive it to be about 3 s. 9 d. I am now giving the best evidence I can without any documents before me.

6076. What is it now?—Two shillings and three pence.

6077. What was it on organzine?—I cannot at this moment state; I think it would be increased though not so much.

6078. You must have some idea of what the prices were?—I have no doubt it increased considerably.

6079. You have given as a reason, that the very extraordinary price was the inducement for a large importation; you should tell us what the extraordinary price of the English throwster was?—At the close of 1831, the prices of the throwster, I apprehend, so far from being high, would be low.

6080. What were they?—I can only answer that question by analogy.

6081. State what you suppose to have been the price of organzine and tram in 1830?—I should think the price at the close of 1831 would be 2 s. 6 d. for tram, and for organzine 4 s.

6082. Very nearly what the prices are at this moment?—Exactly so.

6083. How could 4 s., which is the price paid now, be the great inducement for this importation?—It would be too late to operate.

6084. How early in 1830 was it that the very high prices were obtained here?—Taking the probable time it would opertae, in about July 1830; the price of the foreign thrown silk was very high.

6085. What

Mr.
*William Stone.*

21 May,
1832.

6085. What did they get for throwing here?—I can only do it by analogy; we approximate so near in price, it would be as 17 s. 6 d. to 26 s.

6086. State what you conceive at that time was the price for throwing organzine and tram in England?—I have no doubt it was very high, though I have not the exact figures before me; I have the figures of the foreign thrown silk before me.

6087. You have no power of answering the question?—Not authentically.

6088. I understood you to state generally, that the Italians got less in proportion for their organzine than the raw material?—I did.

6089. And then you say that at this particular period, foreign thrown was very high?—It was.

6090. Then they must have had a larger price for their thrown?—Yes; I said it was fair to suppose, that towards the close of 1830 the Italians would be reaping the advantage; it was on a very bare market that the prices got up to what I have stated, and induced this importation.

6091. And July 1830 was the time that you say the English throwing fetched the highest price?—I infer that to be so.

6092. As you have stated that about July 1830 the English throwsters got a good price, and as you have stated that the high price of English thrown has been the cause of the very large importation of foreign thrown, I should like to know about what time this rush of foreign thrown came into the market in consequence thereof?—It came into the market at the beginning of 1831.

6093. Nearly a year after?—Not a year after; about a fair time to allow it to come in.

6094. How many months in 1830 did the high prices of thrown silk continue?—The first alteration that took place was in October from a reduction by the price currents; there appears to have been a little reduction to the extent of 1 s. upon the price of thrown, from 26 s. 28 s., to 25 s. 27 s., that is in foreign thrown.

6095. As you cannot tell the price of English thrown in July 1830, I should like to know the exact price the foreign throwster got at that time; was it the extra-ordinary high price of foreign thrown that induced this large importation?—Yes, it was; if we make the calculation for three or four months, you will find the tempta-tion very strong for him to send to this market.

6096. You have stated in 1829, at one period of that year, that it was 5 s.; be good enough to state to the Committee in what months it was that the nett proceeds to the Italian throwster were 5 s.?—From the 1st of January to the 1st of July.

6097. Be good enough to tell us what were the variations in the price of thrown silk in 1830?—In the beginning of 1830 the prices were 23 s. 24 s., 22 s. 24 s., 22 s. 24 s., 23 s. 24 s.; in March 22 s. 24 s., 22 s. 23 s.; in April 23 s. 24 s., 23 s. 24 s., 22 s. 24 s.; in July 23 s. 25 s., 23 s. 24 s., 23 s. 24 s., 25 s. 26 s.; the variation was from 23 s. to 26 s. in July alone; in August it is 25 s. 26 s., 24 s. 26 s., 24 s. 25 s., 26 s. 27 s., 26 s. 27 s., 25 s. 26 s., as high as 27 s., and that for the coarser size; in September there was no variation; in October the prices were from 24 s. 26 s., 24 s. 25 s., or an average of 25 s. or 24 s. 6 d.

6098. You have stated that up to the 5th of July 1829, the foreign throwster got 5 s.; you have then stated, that from July 1829 he got 3 s. 4 d., and then you have stated that in 1830 he got about 3 s.?—That was a part of my reason for supposing that he lost money.

6099. And in 1831 he got 2 s. 3 d.; so far from the high price the foreign throw-ster got in 1830 being an inducement, it appears that he got less than he did in 1829?—The principle of 3 s. is taken for the whole of the year. If I give you the prices from February the lowest price is 22 s. 6 d., and the highest price on organ-zine is 26 s. 6 d.

6100. You have stated in what you have given in, that in six months from July 1829, the average was 3 s. 4 d. and in 1830 the average was only 3 s.; therefore there is a fall in the price instead of an increase?—That does not follow; if the price of the raw in 1829 should be 18 s. 6 d., and the price of the raw in 1830 should be 17 s. 6 d., that makes 1 s.; and if the price of the thrown should correspond with it, I think it would bear itself out.

6101. The fall is from 18 s. 6 d. to 17 s. 6 d. on the raw, and on the thrown from 25 s. to 24 s. 1 d.?—In 1829, the whole of that year, the raw is 18 s. 6 d.

6102. You have arrived in your estimate at the conclusion you have given in evidence that the high price of foreign thrown silk in 1830 induced the Italians to send in an increased importation in 1831; and you have also stated that in one year they got 3 s., and in another 3 s. 4 d.; now they must have got 4 d. less in 1830

678.                                                                                          than

Mr.
*William Stone.*

21 May,
1832.

than they did in 1829?—I did not exactly state that; I stated that we had received our supply of raw; and in addition to that, the high price of thrown in this market induced a further supply of thrown silk; I think that was my statement.

6103. The Italians are guided a great deal by the information they receive from the merchants; do you believe that the merchants would induce the Italians to make an enormous large importation, merely from a casual briskness arising from a want of trade in this market?—Yes, I think they would, and they would be very fairly borne out in doing it.

6104. How do you account for the great increase of thrown in the year 1830–31, the nett price of the thrown silk to the Italian having diminished?—The way in which I account for it is this; in the autumn we received our principal supply of raw, and advices would go out that this market was favourable to the introduction of foreign thrown silk, which foreign thrown silk we should not get without sufficient time; I believe it will be found that the bulk came at the commencement of 1831.

6105. Do you know that the price in August 1830 was 25*s*. to 27*s*.?—Yes.

6106. And at that time advices went out that increased the importation?—Yes.

6107. Do you not know that there was a great increase even in the year 1830?—I do not.

6108. It appears by official documents, that a great increase of the importation of Italian thrown silks took place in the year 1830, and a further increase in the year 1831. I want to know, as these foreign silks take some time in preparation for this market, and it also requires some time for them to receive information of the state of this market, how it does happen that any high price in July 1830 would have caused the increase of importation in the same year?—It appears by the principle upon which I take this data, that from August 1829 to August 1830, which is the season, the importation was only 568 bales of foreign thrown silk.

6109. When did that terminate?—It commenced the 1st of August 1829, and terminated 1st August 1830.

6110. Where did you take that account from?—From ships' reports, which we have access to, and which have been given in evidence before by one of the witnesses.

6111. You have stated, that this great importation took place from August 1829, when the fact is, that the great importation was from July to December in the year 1830?—I do not object to that.

6112. Have you, in your hand, a return of the number of bales imported from the ships in the year 1830?—I have got the gross number.

6113. But not in the different amounts?—No.

6114. If I understand you, you mean this, that the prices were remarkably high in the months of July and August 1830, and that that caused a great importation in the following six or seven months, which increase swelled the accounts to the amount you have mentioned?—Yes, that is my position.

6115. What was the price in August 1830 for thrown silk?—Twenty-four shillings and one penny the average.

6116. That is the average of the year, is it not?—I beg pardon, it is 25*s*. 7*d*.

6117. How long would goods, ordered in that month, be in coming to England?—They would be here towards and the beginning of next year.

6118. Suppose you ordered silk in August, how many days does the transit from Italy here take?—I am not acquainted with that, the mere transit would be 30 or 40 days; then they have got to work it.

6119. If I sent out an order on 1st August for thrown silk, supposing the silk to be ready, how long would it take to execute that order?—I imagine you would get it in October; but I am not sufficiently prepared to answer that question.

6120. In the month of August 1830 the price was 25*s*. 7*d*.?—Yes.

6121. The price in the preceding three months was 25*s*. 4*d*., which gives a nett profit to the Italian throwster of 3*s*. 4*d*., according to the same calculation, 25*s*. 7*d*. ought to give him a nett profit of what?—There is an alteration of the duty from 5*s*. to 3*s*. 6*d*.

6122. Are you correct in that?—I think so, with all due deference; in 1829 the duty was 5*s*. and it was reduced to 3*s*. 6*d*.

6123. Therefore the duty was the same at the period I am alluding to; you make your calculation from 1st January to 1st July?—Yes; then there was a duty of 5*s*.

6124. In

Mr.
*William Stone.*

21 May,
1832.

6124. In the same period in 1829, the duty was still 3 s. 6 d.?—In the latter part of 1829 the proceeds were 3 s. 4 d.

6125. The duty being 3 s. 6 d.?—Yes, exactly so.

6126. In August 1830 the duty was 3 s. 6 d., and the price of thrown silk 25 s. 7 d., therefore the proceeds ought to be about 3 s. 7 d.?—In the latter part of 1829 the average of the raw is 18 s. 6 d., the thrown 25 s. 4 d., leaving the proceeds 3 s. 4 d. In the next year we take the whole of the year, raw 17 s. 6 d., a shilling less; and thrown, 24 s. 1 d.

6127. What would the nett proceeds to the Italian manufacturer be in the month of August 1830, when the price of thrown silk here was 25 s. 7 d., the price of raw being 17 s. 6 d.?—It would leave the Italian 4 s. 6 d.

6128. And that you conceive would be a sufficient remuneration to induce the Italian to send here a great quantity of thrown silk?—According to the evidence we have it would.

6129. Can you state to the Committee what was the price the Italian obtained here in June and May, the two months preceding in the year 1830?—In April the price was from 22 s. to 24 s., that is the extreme; then 23 s. and 24 s., and 22 s. and 24 s., which makes an average of 23 s. 4 d.; the operation is this, it leaves only nett proceeds of 2 s. 4 d., consequently there was no temptation for the Italian to send his thrown silk here; in April and May you have the quantity of raw; in August the prices got up to 24 s. 7 d. The position which I put was this; you received the full complement of raws, and at the back of that the state of your market tempted them to send an additional quantity of thrown; that is the way I accounted for the additional quantity of thrown; and I wished to account for the answer I gave, that the Italians must have lost money.

6130. I ask you again, how could this high price in August, 1830, be an inducement for their sending an increased importation in 1830?—It came at the latter end of 1830, and the beginning of 1831. That is not the importation you have before you; that is what is entered for home consumption.

6131. Was not there an increased importation in the year 1830?—It must have been the latter part, after August.

6132. Were not the prices of British thrown silks high about December 1829, and January 1830?—If they were high, no doubt they fell immediately after.

6133. Why should not the high prices at the close of that year cause a similar effect, occasioning an increased importation as the high prices at a subsequent period?—The close of 1829 and the beginning of 1830 does not show it, it leaves 3 s. 4 d. It went down from 5 s. to 3 s. 4 d. For the whole of 1830, it went down to 3 s. Whatever English throwns might be, the average of foreign does not show that to be the case.

6134. When I asked you whether the prices of British throwns were not high, I understood you to say, yes?—The price of raw is considerably higher. I supposed it was the case as to thrown; but it does not appear to be the case on further examination.

6135. Have you any doubt that the English throwster has had more employment since 1826 than he had before?—I should have very little doubt that such was the case.

6136. Can you state what effect the transfer to the North has had on the throwing mills in the West of England?—That of depressing them, decidedly.

6137. Can you state how it has produced that effect?—It is exceedingly difficult to state how it has been produced, but I will give you a reason, from which you may infer that it must occur from the transplanting of the throwing mills to another part of the country; inasmuch as this was shown by one of the witnesses examined here the other day, a most respectable man, of the name of Wilmott. He had been in the trade for a number of years, is a most respectable man, and always did his work remarkably well. He had also been in the habit of throwing an article of Turkey silk, and was fully employed formerly. Our importations in former years we thought good at 400 bales: since that we have got up to 2,500 bales in the year; and yet this man has not been able to get work to employ him. It must have gone to some other parts. I can account for it in no other way.

6138. The silk you have mentioned is used frequently at Coventry, is it not?—Yes.

6139. How long have you known Mr. Wilmott?—Seventeen years, or thereabouts; and I believe, for the early part of that period, he was fairly and fully employed in Brussa silk.

678.

6140. Did

Mr.
*William Stone.*

21 May,
1832.

6140. Did you know his place or his mills?—I know that he lives in the West of England; and our house has received Brussa singles from him for some years past.

6141. Are the Brussa silks thrown into organzine?—No, into singles and trams.

6142. If competition has brought the price down to 3 s. 9 d., you think that is as low as they can come?—I fully concur with you in thinking that there is enough competition in this country.

6143. If deprived of all the Italian raw silks, would not that militate against the prosperity of this country?—The immediate effect would be injurious to the throwster of Italian silk.

6144. Did you not state that you believed they could throw in Italy for 2 s. 3 d.? —I said that the prices were fairly stated at 2 s. 6 d.; it being added that the Italian selected the very best silk for his object.

6145. You have never been in Italy?—Never.

6146. Do you believe there would be any difficulty in their throwing a much greater quantity of silk in Italy than they do at present?—I do not see any difficulty in their increasing their mills.

6147. Have you calculated how much the throwster has, clear of all expenses, for throwing Brussa?—I have not.

6148. Is there any analogy as to the uses in working between Brussa and Italian silk?—None whatever.

6149. The manufacturers of Coventry, who chiefly use this Brussa silk, now employ throwsters elsewhere?—I have no doubt they do.

6150. Do you know whether the cost of throwing is more or less at Mr. Wilmott's than elsewhere?—I do not know; but I believe Mr. Wilmott's prices are quite as low as those of any body else; that is my impression.

6151. Your reason for supposing the throwing trade is transferred to the North is, that the manufacture of silk has gone there?—Wherever it may be I do not pretend to say, whether in the North or not.

6152. Is what you have stated with respect to the West of England true also as regards the mills near London?—It would apply to them if they are unemployed, and to all other mills in the same situation. It must be the increased mills or the increased means of throwing.

6153. Can you state how many manufacturers in Spitalfields are throwsters?— I cannot; several.

6154. But more of them are throwsters than were throwsters formerly?—I should think the increase of the throwsters of late years in London is very moderate.

6155. Are not the large Macclesfield and Manchester manufacturers generally throwsters as well?—They are generally.

6156. Do you not know, that silk has been sent from Manchester to the West of England to be thrown?—Yes, for that very reason; the extraordinary difficulty of getting work done induced them to send from Manchester to the West of England.

6157. In what year was that?—In 1830.

6158. You do not mean to say that that was the only reason?—I think so; that was one of the rare cases.

6159. Have you any authority for saying that?—No authority beyond matter or opinion or belief.

6160. You have never known it done at any other time?—No.

6161. Has the price of English thrown silk been generally higher or lower than foreign thrown silk for the last three or four years, of the same quality?—Of the same quality latterly, I think it has been higher, the English higher; it must come under the term description; the quality must be matter of judgment or opinion.

6162. Is that owing to the English having improved in their mode of throwing silk or the Italians having deteriorated?—I think owing to the English having improved, and also very much improved in their selection of the material.

6163. Has the foreign thrown deteriorated, or is it nearly the same?—The quality of Italian thrown silk has I think of late years remained stationary, in former years I think it improved.

6164. Has the quality of Italian raw silk improved of late years?—I think it has.

6165. Do you speak generally of Italy?—Yes, I do.

6166. The

Mr.
*William Stone.*

21 May,
1832.

6166. The thrown silk of Piedmont is estimated the best, is it not?—Yes.

6167. Has that maintained its high character?—I think the higher class of it has maintained its high character the same as heretofore.

6168. Do the higher classes of Piedmont thrown silk come to this country?—I think the very fine classes do not; the higher classes that would be useful for the manufacturers of this country do not arrive in sufficient quantities.

6169. You have stated that Italian raw silk has improved, but that Italian thrown silk has remained stationary?—I have.

6170. Can you account for that?—It may be accounted for in this way, that their better classes of raw are making their way to this market.

6171. What is the state of the market here at this time, with respect to the supply of raw and thrown silk?—It is very moderate.

6172. Of what?—Of Italian; I supposed the question referred to Italian solely.

6173. Is it moderate in raw or both?—In both.

6174. Do you mean as compared with former years at this period, or only one or two years?—I think it is rather scarce at this time; I cannot fix my mind on a particular period; I was going to say more scarce this time two years; it is getting into the same position it then was in.

6175. Are prices looking up?—They are rather that way than otherwise.

6176. Do you consider at present that the supply is rather bare?—I do.

6177. More so than usually at this period of the year?—It is.

6178. Do you attribute that to increased consumption, or deficiency in the supply?—The supply up to this time has been small.

6179. Was the crop bad?—It is so reported, and it may have arisen from that cause; still we do not place reliance on the accounts given to us; the result has shown that the supply is small that we have received from last August, compared with previous years.

6180. Are there plenty of inferior raw silks in the market?—A fair supply; a better supply of inferior raws decidedly than otherwise.

6181. A greater proportion of inferior raws?—Certainly, at this moment.

6182. Can you state what proportion of Piedmontese and Lombardy thrown silk comes to this country?—I cannot do that; there are gentlemen here much more capable of doing that than myself.

6183. Can you inform the Committee to what uses the Bengal silks are applied generally?—Principally to the manufacturing of coarser goods; principally for bandannas, sewing silks and stockings, hosiery, and a variety of things of that sort.

6184. I believe some part of it is thrown into organzine?—Yes.

6185. Can you state what proportion of Bengal silk is usually thrown into organzine?—I cannot tell you exactly; there must be a good proportion of it thrown into organzine; for instance you cannot make the best bandannas without organzine.

6186. Is one-fourth of the whole of the Bengal silks applied, in your opinion, in that way?—I should think there can be no doubt of that; I mean into organzine.

6187. Do you not know that there are other organzines used with the Bengal?—I am not aware of that; they use Bengal organzines with other silks; that is the more usual course.

6188. Are not the superior Bengals, some of them, equal to the Italians, or the inferior Italians?—Some of them to the inferior, and much more suitable to some objects than the Italian.

6189. And to a considerable extent the Bengals and the Italians can be applied to the same purpose?—To a considerable extent they may; I conceive Bengal silk to be extremely beneficial to our manufactures in this country.

6190. Do you undertake positively to say, that the Bengals are applied to the same purposes as the Italian?—I never said so.

6191. However Bengals may be substituted for inferior Italians, do you imagine they can be to an extensive degree used as a substitute for Italians?—It would be a very inferior substitute if they were.

6192. Are you aware that they are used?—They are used as a substitute for Italian beyond a doubt to a great extent, and can be; but then it is mixed with Italian.

6193. What quality in deniers is the Bengal in organzine thrown into?—Into all sizes.

6194. What is the finest?—Some as fine as 28 deniers.

6195. What quantity do you suppose the Bengal of 28 deniers?—A very small quantity.

678.

6196. What

Mr.
*William Stone.*
———
21 May,
1832.

6196. What is the average quantity?—I should think 50 deniers.

6197. Is the price paid for the organzining of the fine Bengal silk as high as that paid for Italian?—There are some of the finer classes of Bengal silk, but to a very limited extent indeed, that would bear such a construction.

6198. Has the quality of the Bengal silk improved of late years?—I think not.

6199. It is not true, if it has been stated here, that they require but one-third of the labour that some of the finer Italian silks do?—I think the very finest quality of Bengal silk requires a good deal of labour; but taking the standard at 50 deniers, there is no comparison between that and the Italian.

6200. The labour of throwing and weaving is much less?—The labour I believe in the weaving must be the same, but that is a practical question applicable to a manufacturer, not to myself.

6201. It has been stated by some witness, that in the coarser Bengal silks to the throwster and the weaver, there is not a third of the labour required?—It depends on what it is applied to: it is self-evident that the working up of coarse Bengals must require less labour than the working up of fine Italian silks.

6202. The quantity of raw silk consumed is not an exact criterion of the quantity of labour employed?—Certainly not.

6203. What is the average in deniers of the Bengal silk imported into this country?—I can only speak from supposition; I should suppose between 60 and 70 deniers; probably near 70.

6204. To what of our fine manufactures is Bengal silk applied?—To the working of broad goods for instance.

6205. In any large proportion?—Not in any large proportion, nor so much as it was by any means since the introduction of China silk.

6206. Is China thrown into organzine?—Yes.

6207. Chiefly?—A very considerable portion of it.

6208. What is the quality in deniers of that?—I should think from 40 to 50 deniers; it is an exceedingly useful silk, and likely to be highly beneficial to this trade; for it is an increasing article, and will, I have no doubt, be extended very largely indeed.

6209. Where is the Bengal silk chiefly thrown?—Usually in Macclesfield and Manchester.

6210. Are you aware of any efforts made to improve its quality in Bengal?—I am not aware of any.

6211. Do they make any satins or velvets or silks of Bengal?—I believe not.

6212. Any of the richer articles of dress?—I think not; in waistcoating and such articles it is exceedingly useful; it makes exceedingly rich goods, and may be very beneficially employed.

6213. When you speak of the benefits to be derived by the silk trade from the use of Bengal or China silks, you speak of these coarse silks?—I do.

6214. It can but little interfere with the Italian silk, in the use of making superior articles of consumption?—I think it may materially interfere.

6215. Be good enough to tell the Committee what is the average of deniers used in the Italian organzine?—Probably 28 deniers.

6216. You spoke of the very finest Bengal of that size only in very small quantities?—Certainly; you coupled China with Bengal, and a quantity of China silk is thrown into organzine which is applicable to standard goods—to goods the consumption of which we have a considerable call for, mixed with Italian silk; it will very much affect the consumption of that article.

6217. They are used for the shutes while the Italian is used for the warps?—The reverse.

6218. In making the coarse gros de Naples, and those common things principally the production of Manchester and its neighbourhood?—Of Manchester, no doubt, and very largely used in Spitalfields too.

6219. You have been trying for some years to improve the quality of Bengal?—We have.

6220. You think you may improve it still more?—I hope so.

6221. At present the quantity you receive of a quality that interferes with the Italian is very small?—Certainly.

6222. You think the Chinese will more interfere?—It has, and does beyond a doubt.

6223. Has not the quality of Chinese silk improved since the free trade to
India?

Mr.
*William Stone.*

21 May,
1832.

India ?—The quantity o Chinese silk of the finest class has greatly increased of late years.

6224. Has the price decreased at the same time ?—Certainly.

6225. Can you give the general average of Chinese in deniers ?—I just now stated, from 40 to 50 deniers, taking, probably, four-fifths of it.

6226. So that, if you were to estimate the increase of the trade, as far as regarded employment, in pounds weight, it would be necessary to have nearly two pounds of Bengal or Chinese for one of Italian ?—That might apply to Bengal, but I do not think it does to China.

6227. If a bale of Chinese will average about 80,000 yards, and a bale of Bergam would be 160,000, it takes nearly double the quantity ?—To work it in labour; the labour part of it; it might abridge labour to a certain extent.

6228. Therefore you would not infer the prosperity of the silk trade from the amount of pounds weight of silk consumed in the trade, but from the fineness and nature of the works into which the silk was used ?—The relative bearings should be brought upon it certainly: all I meant to convey was, that the working of China silk is not so light as the working of Bengal; for instance, it occupies a great deal more machinery and time and expense to work Chinese than it does to work Bengal.

6229. So that those districts in England principally employed in making the coarse description of commodity we have been making for the last few years may be in a state of prosperity, while Spitalfields, where you are used to consume Italian silks in making velvets and figured articles, may not be in a state of prosperity ?—Certainly, it may be so.

6230. Is not that the fact ?—I should think it is the fact.

6231. Does not the same observation apply to Coventry ?—I can hardly venture to go so far as that, but I think it a very probable case that it may

6232. Bengals are said to be thrown for bandannas; are they, in point of fact, thrown for bandannas ?—I believe they are; I am in the habit of selling a great deal of Bengal organzine for bandannas.

6233. Are they not used unthrown for bandannas ?—They may, for aught I know to the contrary.

6234. To what use are the China silks applied ?—Principally to the weaving of plain gros de Naples.

6235. Is it not very important to the English manufacturer, that the supply from China should go on increasing ?—Most important, I think.

6236. Is it an article of more importance than Bengal silk, for the uses to which you have alluded ?—To the uses I have alluded I think it is; they are both useful in their respective operations.

6237. But for the fine manufacture the China is of more importance than the Bengal ?—For the working of plain gros de Naples, it is.

6238. Are fine raw Italian silks necessary to work up the Bengal organzine and China, at Manchester and other places ?—Certainly; it is absolutely necessary to have a supply of Italian silk.

6239. Are you acquainted with French thrown silk in this market ?—I have seen them; they are an article of rare occurrence.

6240. When you say French throwns, do you mean silks thrown in France or of the growth of France ?—I believe both, as far as my judgment will go.

6241. How are you able to determine on the one and the other ?—It is only on my own opinion, as matter of judgment.

6242. How do you arrive at a conclusion ?—By comparison, knowing the qualities of other silks.

6243. Do you perceive any superiority in the French silks ?—No, I do not; I think rather the other way.

6244. You have no doubt the silk you are alluding to was French silk?—No doubt of it.

6245. Were they silks approved of by our manufacturers ?—They were not.

6246. If French thrown silk, or raw silk, either of them, be prohibited in France, must not the export of it be attended with some additional expense more than that which would be necessary to convey Italian silk to this country ?—Certainly.

6247. If it comes at the same price as Italian silk, to what conclusion can you arrive, but that it must be cheaper at Lyons than Italian silk?—If it does come.

6248. Have the relative qualities of what you received been higher than Italian?—I think not.

678.                                                                 6249. How

Mr.
*William Stone.*

21 May,
1832.

6249. How are you aware that the silk you saw was of French growth? – Only from my own judgment.

6250. Have you ever been at Lyons?—Never.

6251. Why might it not have been Italian silk thrown in France?—It might have been; I do not say to the contrary.

6252. On what does your judgment proceed?—On general observation.

6253. Have you seen a great quantity of raw French silk?—Not a great quantity, a few bales; the import has been very small indeed.

6254. Are they smuggled?—If they are prohibited, they must come out in a contraband way some how or other, either by changing them for Italian silks in the depôt, or they must come out in some other way, as the Sardinian silk does.

6255. Is the quality of the French silk so different to the Piedmontese, so as to be able to discover it as a merchant?—I did those that were shown to me.

6256. Do you conceive this was of the finest description of French silk?—That I cannot tell.

6257. As you have never been in France and are not acquainted with the general quality of French silks, how can you feel competent to give an opinion on merely seeing a small quantity?—I do give that opinion.

6258. Was there any particular mark or sign about it?—I would remark, that it was done up as Piedmont, which of course drew my attention to it; it was shown to me as a Piedmont organzine, and I at once told the merchant that I believed it to be French, and he admitted it was.

6259. Are these likely to be of the best or worst quality?—I think of the best.

6260. To what uses were they calculated?—Calculated as a substitute for Italian organzine.

6261. To what extent was this?—To the extent of a very few bales.

6262. To the extent of how many?—Not many.

6263. The quantity of French organzine was quite trifling?—To the extent of about 20 bales; it was mere experiment.

6264. What silks are used here for the purpose of being thrown into marabout?—I believe white silk.

6265. What is the price of that now in the market?—I believe it is 19 s.

6266. And subject to what?—A discount of 2 ½ per cent.

6267. Have you ever seen any foreign marabout in this market?—Never.

6268. You know nothing of the silks used in France for the purpose of making gauze ribbons?—Nothing more than samples shown to me; we have had a very few white French raws.

6269. I think you stated that Italian thrown silks had been exported from this country lately?—They have.

6270. To what ports have they been exported?—I believe Russia, to a small extent, not exceeding 50 bales in the whole.

6271. Have they any throwing mills in Russia?—Not that I am aware of.

6272. Have you known instances of silk being sent from here to Lyons?—I have.

6273. Have you known instances of Italian silk being sent from Lyons to London?—That is the usual course.

6274. And the price cannot be different at London and Lyons for any length of time beyond the cost of conveying it from one place to another?—There is a question rests there; the home growth of France, which must materially assist them in their prices, not being allowed to be exported, that must of course have its effect, it is possible that the market may be under us from that cause; the importation of Piedmont silk in a measure counteracts that conclusion.

6275. The price of Piedmont silk cannot be different in the two countries?—Certainly not.

6276. Have you any doubt that the price of Piedmont silk determines the price of French of the same quality?—I should think so.

6277. Are you sure of that?—I understood the question was, whether the importation of Piedmont silk, of a similar quality, regulated the price of silk in France. I think it does.

6278. It has been stated here, that the Piedmont fetches a higher price than the French?—So it may, but it must be in relative proportion.

6279. It has been stated here, that the silk sold at Lyons to the French being wanted to mix with their own, frequently fetch higher prices than their own silks, though of inferior quality?—That is a very likely thing indeed.

6280. If

Mr.
*William Stone.*

21 May,
1832.

6280. If so the Italian silk cannot always regulate the price of the French?—It cannot always; the question is, whether it would regulate a similar quality.

6281. Having never been at Lyons you cannot know from practical experience?—I never wish to go to Lyons for such an object as that, or to Italy either. It must be a matter of opinion, acquired by experience, and general knowledge and information.

6282. If Piedmontese silks be used for the making of velvets, as you well know they principally are—Not principally.

6283. But for the making of satins?—And gros de Naples.

6284. If Piedmontese silks be used for any purpose for any article of fashion, and that article ceases to be used, Piedmont silk will not be required?—Not for that article.

6285. And they might not interfere with the French silks, if the supply of French silks of native growth was sufficient for the supply of the Lyons market?—Such a supposition is self-evident, but they do import and use it.

6286. How do you arrive at the fact, that the importation of Piedmont silk into Lyons regulates the price of the silk of the growth of France?—Because it is imported and used.

6287. Is it used in large quantities at Lyons?—The importation appears to me to be exceedingly large.

6288. What is the importation?—Six hundred thousand pounds.

6289. If the growth of France should be equal to 7–8ths of her consumption, and that it should serve for 7–8ths, and she have no necessity at all to use silk of a foreign growth, do you mean to say that the mere transit of silk through Lyons, at a different price would have any influence on the French market?—No, I do not; it would be very light indeed.

6290. Supposing the silk of France to supply 7–8ths of a year, and to be 2 s. a pound less, and the French grower having no opportunity to dispose of it to an Englishman, would that circumstance advance the price of the whole of the growth of France to the price of the silk passing in transit through Lyons?—It might not, taking it in the position in which you put it.

6291. Does the largest quantity regulate in general the price of the smaller quantity?—I think it does.

6292. It is more than probable, that the smaller quantity, passing through Lyons, if the Lyonese require it, must drop to the price of the French, rather than that the French be lifted up?—I think that a small quantity passing through France would be of little consequence one way or the other.

6293. The silk goes to Lyons, and might be there bought for any of the markets in Europe?—I believe it may.

6294. The French silk remains there without any such opportunity of so disposing of it?—Certainly.

6295. If the growth of France was equal to the consumption of the French manufacturer, he would not use the other material while he can obtain the cheaper?—Certainly not.

6296. Do you not think such a thing is quite possible?—I think it must turn on the relative qualities. If you were to take half of the French growth as an inferior quality, it would be a distinct question by itself. If you put it on equal qualities, I doubt the position extremely. I think the Piedmont silks form a large proportion of their best qualities.

6297. The French growth being more than the consumption, in such a case what would be the operation on the market in Lyons?—That they would not use Piedmont silk in that position.

6298. At the same time that the growth of Italy must be smaller than is required for the other markets of Europe, what would be the effect; would not the silk of Italy get higher in price, because the demand was greater than the supply?—Certainly.

6299. If the reverse of that position is applied to silk of French growth in Lyons, would not that have a tendency to reduce the price?—Certainly.

6300. In such a case how can prices be equal?—In such a case I do not see how they can.

6301. When you stated just now that the price of Italian silk regulated the price of French silk of the same quality, your answer supposed that the French did actually every year import the silk from Italy?—Yes, and consume it.

6302. The question put, supposes the French manufacture to give for the similar

678.                                                                      quantity

Mr.
*William Stone.*

21 May,
1832.

quantity of Piedmontese silk a less price, because of the large quantity produced in France; in that case, the silk would be sent to England, if the price here was higher than in Italy?—If I were a seller, and possessed of two articles, I would sell them alike, and endeavour to approximate the price to the qualities as much as I could.

6303. Then you mean that the prices of Piedmontese silk in Lyons would be the average price of the same silk in England, making allowance for the difference of carriage?—If Piedmont silk was cheaper than Italian, we should import Piedmont.

6304. The duty being in England 2 s. 6 d. more than it is in France on the import of Italian thrown silk, must not the price here be permanently to the manufacturer 2 s. 6 d. higher than to the French manufacturer?—Certainly.

6305. Would it not extend the consumption of goods manufactured in England, if the duty was lowered here to the price paid by the Frenchman?—Certainly it would.

6306. It would increase the demand for labour, and improve the condition of the weaver?—Certainly, in Spitalfields, I think so.

6307. In two ways; by lowering the price of the material to the manufacturer, and shutting out the goods now legally or illegally brought in from France?—I should think so.

6308. You stated the other day that you consider a duty on thrown silk a tax on Spitalfields. Will the Italian throwster, with reduced duty, supply Spitalfields with foreign thrown silk cheaper than the manufacturer can now buy Italian thrown silk, with the duty of 3 s. 6 d. per lb.?—In the present position, the Italians are supplying this market at a considerable loss; and I have no idea that will continue, it cannot possibly in the nature of things. If you take off a duty, your prices may still remain where they are. If you do not take off the duty, the prices of Italian thrown silk must advance, or else not come into the market at all. You must supersede the use of them; and that you must do by importing the raw and throwing it here.

6309. Will the Italian throwster, with reduced duty, supply Spitalfields with foreign thrown silk cheaper than the manufacturer can now buy Italian thrown silk?—The answer I have made was, I think, applicable to that. At present, the Italians must be losing, consequently you must improve the proceeds to them, either by taking off the duty or raising the price, or else they will not send it. The manufacturer, it is possible, may not get it one fraction cheaper than at present.

6310. Would the manufacturer receive a benefit, supposing the 3 s. 6 d. taken off?—He might not, in the present position of things; for the future, it is quite a distinct question. The Italian throwster is carrying on, if I am correct in my showing, a very considerable losing trade, which he must stop. If you take off the duty, the question is, how much of that must go to him to induce him to keep on sending, before you arrive at that conclusion.

6311. Supposing the price of 1822 for foreign thrown Italian silk to be the price of the day, inclusive of the duty, and the duty is reduced to 2 s. per pound, do you consider the price of thrown silk would then be 20 s. 6 d. to the manufacturer in Spitalfields?—The position must change: if the raw material goes down, I think they will have the benefit; at present, it is likely you will advance; but that you will not continue to receive throwns without some alteration, I am convinced.

6312. Do you think such a reduction would throw them out of employment?—I think the immediate effect of such a reduction would be that, except it is counteracted.

6313. If you thought it would throw them out of employ, you cannot calculate at what price the Italian thrown silk would arrive here?—There would be a competition with the Piedmont organzine; that is, a feature of a million pounds weight of organzine; and what we have received from Italy is, at the utmost, four cwt. per year. If the prices get up in Lombardy, of course you would apply to Piedmont.

6314. When the duty was reduced, would not the price of Italian thrown and raw be nearer to one another, and the Italian be thus able to maintain a higher price for the raw?—That must resolve itself into a question of price of throwing; if the Italian can throw cheaper than the Englishman, they will keep their price; if they cannot, they will send the raw in.

6315. You gave that answer, alluding to the prices of raw and thrown which they bear when sent here?—That was the question put to me.

6316. The Italian having 1 s. 6 d. per pound less duty to pay, surely he can give a better price for raw, and thus the same price will be maintained for the thrown,

without

Mr.
*William Stone.*

21 May,
1832.

without benefit to the manufacturer?—No doubt the reduction of duty of 1 *s.* 6 *d.* is an advantage to the Italian throwster.

6317. Would not a large importation of Italian raw silk be better for the manufacturer than a large importation of foreign thrown silk?—If you exclude foreign wrought silk, undoubtedly.

6318. Would it be cheaper?—It would.

6319. And would it not be better to produce that large importation of raw silk by an increased duty on thrown?—That would have the effect of doing it; but you will recollect, that is a protection to the throwster, not to the manufacturer; it is a protection to the throwster and the manufacturer combined. If you should grant our trade a very grand thing—prohibition, then it might be quite another question.

6320. A duty of 5 *s.* on thrown would enable England to give a better price for the raw in proportion to the thrown, and Italy would direct its attention to supply England with good raw silk?—Yes.

6321. And an increased duty on thrown would consequently work better for the manufacturer than a reduced duty on throwns, by the location of the market in England; and as the foreign thrown markets of Italy are already sufficiently acted upon by the various continental manufacturers, to the disadvantage of the English manufacturers, why advocate a reduction of the duty, which, in effect, seems to place the English manufacturer more in the power of the Italian?—There is a middle part of that question, that is not quite clear " it is quite acted on by the foreign demand," I presume, for the article; if it is, it must be to raise the price of it.

6322. If you shut out the Italian thrown silks from England, would not that lower the price of thrown silk in Italy, and give the foreign manufacturer a great advantage over the English manufacturer?—I think so.

6323. By a small additional duty, just sufficient to save the throwing trade of this country, the manufacturer may retain to himself the material, and regulate the price of it relatively, with the price of his goods?—That resolves itself into a question between the throwster and the manufacturer; between the country and the London and the Coventry manufacturer without mills; the latter are placed between the country manufacturer with mills on the one hand, and the Frenchman on the other; they have two competitors, but it is far better that they should have the internal than the external competition.

6324. Whatever protection is given to the home throwster will raise the price of silk to the home manufacturer, as compared with the foreign manufacturer?—That is the tendency beyond a doubt, by the same principle as lowering the duty has a tendency to increase the quantity of foreign thrown silk, and of course to injure the British throwster.

6325. In proportion as the duty in England has been lowered, have the Italians got more or not; have not the profits of the Italians decreased in proportion as our import duty increased?—It has so occurred, but it has not arisen from the reduction of duty.

6326. It therefore shows that the causes which operate to affect the price of Italian silk have been quite independent of any alteration of duty here?—It shows so far as this, that your British throwster has made immense strides, whether at the expense of his working people, is not the question.

6327. Has the actual reduction of the duty on thrown silk in England affected the price of the thrown here?—The result has shown that it has not.

6328. Do you mean to say, that the reduction of the duty on the foreign silk has not lowered the price of the thrown here?—I do not mean to say it has not; it would be extraordinary if it had the contrary effect; the effect of taking off the duty now would be to lower the prices. I think there are circumstances to prove that an alteration must take place, and consequently that you must reduce it; still the tendency of taking off the duty must be injurious to the British throwster.

6329. Then you have stated that the foreign throwster is not selling to an advantage?—That is my opinion.

6330. Do you conceive that is not the case with the British throwster?—To a great extent it may be.

6331. Do you not happen to know they are in great distress, and hands are out of employ?—Generally, (I know there are very great exceptions to that) I believe so.

6332. Within the last two years?—Within the last two years.

6333. Do

6333. Do you mean to say when the prices are reduced from 5 *s*. to 3 *s*. 6 *d*., and the proceeds on the labour reduced in the same proportion that the manufacturer can carry on a beneficial trade?—The throwster may, in the position you have put it, on your own showing; if you mean the operative, it is certainly otherwise.

6334. The broker gets a per centage for what he does?—Yes.

6335. You get a larger amount for the per centage for 200 *l*. than 100 *l*.?—Certainly.

6336. Do you not suppose that every man calculates his profits on the amount of his returns?—I do not, as a manufacturer; I think it is a very distinct thing. A broker might, or a commission man, or a warehouseman.

6337. Do you mean it is the general course for a man in trade, whether he be a broker, a merchant, or a salesman, not to calculate and aim at a certain per centage on his goods?—Yes, I do mean to say they aim at a per centage.

6338. Do you imagine that when a throwster, admitting he does the same quantity of business, is reduced from 5 *s*. to 3 *s*. 6 *d*., must not experience a loss to that extent, either to himself or the person he employs?—No doubt, and to those he employs, unless it is counteracted by the capability of his mill.

6339. I ask you now, whether you do not believe that a great deal of distress to the throwster and his workmen has arisen from the reduction of prices, independent of the falling off of business?—I think so, certainly.

6340. If the foreign throwster requires a remunerating price, the British throwster does also?—Certainly.

6341. Do you not know, that there has been a great deal of distress in the weaving districts also?—I have no doubt of it.

6342. And much distress in Spitalfields?—No doubt there has.

6343. Do you think there is a depreciation of profits?—In some cases I think so; but I think men are making money there.

6344. Do you not suppose, generally, that there is a great depreciation in the profits of the working classes, both here and at Coventry, and elsewhere?—I have no doubt there has been considerable difficulty in carrying on the trade.

6345. Do you not know that there has been great reduction in the profits, and consequent distress?—I understand so, and I believe it.

6346. You have stated, that you have known the trade as bad, or worse?—I did.

6347. Can you state any particular period when the weaving business was worse than it is now, taking it in all its branches, and can you assign any cause for it?—I do not go so far as to state any particular department, but we have constantly known distress in Spitalfields, and have contributed to its relief: we have had soup societies, and a variety of other things, and an equal extent of distress as we have now.

6348. But for so long a period?—I am not prepared to say for so long a period, by any means.

6349. Have you known any period of very great distress which has continued so long either in Coventry or elsewhere, among the weaving branches generally?—I think, generally speaking, the complaints are very considerable, and I think there are very considerable exceptions as to the profits of the master; I think the workmen work exceedingly low, and must be suffering considerably.

6350. Do you ever remember any period in which the distress was so severe, and for so long a continuance as the present?—I never knew the country in so bad a state, as far as opinion goes generally.

6351. Do you not happen to know, the distress in former periods has arisen from particular circumstances, such as in 1818, when almost every branch of trade suffered, for instance, the watch trade at Coventry, which arose from peculiar circumstances?—I cannot tell the circumstances; that there have been these things I know; I believe the distress is exceedingly great at this time, and I think it is very likely there are men more capable of answering this question than I am.

6352. You have stated before, that you had known the trade as bad, and as much distressed?—I meant in my own department.

6353. It has been stated by several witnesses, that the silk trade, with the exception of those fluctuations that must take place in all large manufacturing trades, was generally increasing and prosperous up to 1826; do you believe that to be a true statement?—I believe there were a very considerable number of failures,
                                                                                                but

Mr.
William Stone.

21 May,
1832.

but I think the trade was increasing up to 1826 ; the consumption of the article proves that.

6354. It is stated that though the trade did not decline to a great extent after 1826, it ceased to be so prosperous ?—A considerable degree of distress occurred in 1828, but we have since got over it.

6355. After 1829, did not the distress increase ?—I think the trade rather improved.

6356. What, since 1829! since the rednction of the duty ?—I think 1830 was a very good silk year for the masters employed in it, who understood their business ; 1831 I think a bad year.

6357. Then to what do you attribute all this distress, when the consumption of the article was increasing, and fashion extending ; how do you account for it ?— It is exceedingly difficult to account for it, as in the case of Mr. Wilmott, whom I mentioned ; that man has been greatly distressed, but then the work has been done in the country ; it may also apply to other parts ; the country is in a bad state ; labour is exceedingly low, 20 or 25 per cent. lower at Manchester than at Spitalfields at this moment, and consequently that most presses on Spitalfields.

6358. Do you not apprehend there are sufficient workmen to supply the whole demand ?—I do.

6359. And sufficient competition at home ?—Yes.

6360. Do not you think the introduction of a large quantity of foreign goods, put into competition with our own labour in our market, must have been one great cause of this distress ?—I do believe that to be so ; I believe if you could have shut out foreign goods effectually, trade would never have been in a more flourishing state than now, with the present rate of duties.

6361. You do not know of any practical advantages that the measure has produced ?—Except that the taking off the duty has lowered the price of the material exceedingly, and extended the consumption of it very largely.

6362. If the raw material is sold at one half, and wages and profits are also reduced, must not the returns of the manufacturer, unless he sell double the quantity, fall off one half ?—Certainly.

6363. Can any manufacturer get more than a fair and remunerating profit with this competition ?—Certainly not.

6364. If his returns be reduced to one half, unless he can double the quantity he sells, must it not reduce his profits ?—In the end, certainly it must.

6365. Do not you suppose that if the foreign silk was here, it must tend to distress, if not ruin a great many of the throwsters ?—I think it would have that tendency.

6366. If that be the case, and supposing they are so ruined, and we imported foreign thrown silk to a large extent, would not that in a great measure put us in the hands of the foreigner ?—I think that is a much more extended question ; we are, for instance, in the hands of the foreigner for the raw material altogether ; we do not grow it here, consequently we are in the hands of the foreigner ; in the nature or order of things it will come here if you buy it ; the Frenchman, your competitor, cannot get it unless he pays as much as you.

6367. It is said that our English throwsters have been the cause of the depression of the foreigner, must not that operate much worse ?—It must operate badly.

6368. If you had not the competition of the foreigner, all these people you employ would be more prosperous ?—Provided you worked the same quantity of goods.

6369. It has been stated by a gentleman who brought all the silk to our standard, the coarse and the fine, and who made out that it had declined three per cent., instead of having increased ; do you believe that to be the fact ?—That is a question beyond my understanding for the moment.

*Mercurii, 23° die Maii, 1832.*

EDWARD STRUTT, ESQUIRE, IN THE CHAIR.

Mr. *William Stone*, called in; and further Examined.

6370. IS the throwing of silk a component part of the manufactory?—The silk cannot be worked into goods without being thrown; that is the usual course.

6371. Is it an advantage to the manufacture; and is it of importance to keep the component parts together or to separate them?—That must depend upon circumstances.

6372. Do you consider that the throwing of Italian silk can be preserved in England with a lower rate of duties upon the importation of foreign thrown silk?—That must depend upon the price that the British throwster can work it for, if I am to give an opinion whether the British throwster can work under less protection or not (I am not a throwster.) I should think that could be proved, even according to the evidence we have heard in this room. It is possible, and I believe it to be the case that one throwster is able to work for less than another; but I think it is fair and proper to suppose the competition to be such that the British throwster throws at the lowest possible price it can now be done for.

6373. Were you alluding to some one individual?—No.

6374. Was it the certain rate you allude to?—The rate stated in this room, which I said was fairly stated; viz. 3 s. 9 d. per lb.

6375. Supposing that to be the rate, do you think the throwing Italian silk can be preserved in England with a lower rate of duties on the importation of foreign thrown silk?—I think it can. I think the figures would show that certainly.

6376. Would reduced or augmented duties on thrown, act the best towards producing a larger importation of Italian raw silk?—An increase of duty on thrown silk must have a tendency to increase the supply of the raw material.

6377. As a protection to the throwster?—Certainly.

6378. Do you know the parties in Italy who send silk to this country under the marks D. S. and the initials of D. S. with an S. through the D.?—I know them by name. The one with the D., with an S. separate, we believe to be a man of the name of Starango who is since dead; and I think what I have heard bears out the opinion I gave the other day that the Italian has been losing money. It has been stated that letters have been received from the executors of Starango last week, that within the last few years he has reduced his property from 45,000 l. to 30,000 l., which I believe to be the effect of his trade with this country.

6379. Do you believe the Italian merchant has been trading at a great loss the last few years?—Yes, in thrown and raw too.

6380. Do you state that those losses were on the thrown or the raw?—On his general trade, without any distinction.

6381. When did Mr. Starango die?—I cannot state the date; but the first letters were received, I believe, during the last week—within five or six weeks, or it may be less.

6382. The initial of D., with an S. through it, is whose?—Stainer.

6383. Is he dead?—No, I believe not.

6384. Are those parties silk merchants, residing in Italy?—Yes, they were.

6385. Do you happen to know whether they are considerable silk merchants, and many years accustomed to the silk trade in England?—I believe they were.

6386. Can you state the quantity each party is in the habit of sending annually to this market, from the 1st of January to 31st of December?—I cannot.

6387. Should you think 150 bales the annual average importation from each?—I think it is probable; but without returns I cannot state it; I never so particularly noticed the thing as to know what one man sends and what another.

6388. Do you think any parties might be selected, better able to demonstrate the working of the trade between Italy and England, than those men who have in their hands so considerable a part of the whole silk trade from Italy to England?—I think they are very excellent authorities.

6389. Can you state the quantity of thrown silk, compared with the quantity of raw, sent to England by those two Italian merchants during the last four or five years?—I cannot.

6390. Does

Mr.
*William Stone.*

23 May,
1832.

6390. Does your own house keep an account of the raws and throwns sent to this market from Italy, according to the marks on the bales representing the Italian proprietor ?—No, we do not.

6391. Do you know that those two Italian merchants have of late years increased their importations of thrown silk ?—I do not.

6392. You not having had any experience in Italy in the reeling and throwing and buying and selling silk, may not it be possible that those gentlemen, finding advantage in sending thrown silks to England, notwithstanding the competition, conceive they may not have been pursuing a losing trade ?—It is a possible case, but a very improbable one I think.

6393. You have stated that during the seventeen years you have known the silk trade, there have been periods of greater distress than the past wir ter; be pleased to state what period you refer to ?—I stated it in my own particular department. If I recollect right I qualified it with that; if I did not, I beg now to qualify it in reading over the evidence afterwards. I have it still in my recollection that it appeared so; my experience, as a silk man, for the first seven years, did not give me that general means of information which the last ten years have done.

9394. Have there been any periods of distress within the last ten years ?—There have been repeated fluctuations and distress, as far as my recollection and opinion go, without fixing on any particular period.

6395. Do you mean distress, or that fluctuation which exists in the silk trade from change of season ?—There have been a number of failures, and we have heard of great distress in Spitalfields; we have heard of soup societies, and things of that sort, which indicates distress.

6396. Do you mean that in the last ten years, there has been distress to compare with the distress of the last year among the operatives generally ?—I think it is probable, but will not undertake to say that has been the case.

6397. Do you think it ever continued half the time this has continued ?—I think it is possible that may not have been the case; I will not undertake to say it has been half or a quarter of the time.

6398. You mean to say you have known periods of as severe suffering within the last 10 years, as the last winter ?—I do not intend to convey anything so pointedly as that; my observations did not extend I think to the operatives; I think I was asked generally, and I remarked upon the state of the silk trade generally, as to the complaints we have heard; but not from my intimate knowledge.

6399. The question refers to the actual distress among the work-people in Spitalfields ?—I do not know the fact from my own knowledge; I believe it to be the fact.

6400. Have you any idea of the number of looms now not in work in Spitalfields ?—No, I have not.

6401. Did you ever know a month of May before, in which there were so many looms unemployed ?—I cannot say.

6402. Do you believe there have ever before been so many hands unemployed as now ?—I doubt whether there are now any good hands unemployed.

6403. Do you believe that there are any unemployed ?—I have no doubt of that fact.

6404. You state that the throwing mills of this country have increased very considerably within the last ten years, are there more spindles now in work than there were on the 1st of January 1826 ?—I cannot state that; I have stated that I think there is more silk consumed, the consumption will show the importations and the sales generally, I meant it to apply that way; as to my personal knowledge whether there are more mills or not, I do not pretend to say.

6405. Do you form your conclusions as to the state of the trade, from the sales of silk, and judging from the pounds weight ?—Certainly, from the consumption.

6406. Is it not the case, that one bale of Bergamo silk will find twice the quantity of work that one bale of Bengal will find, for the throwster ?—Taking them generally, which is the fair way, certainly the Italian silk takes a great deal more labour than the Bengal.

6407. You have stated that the throwing trade has gone from the West of England to the North, can you say to what towns in the North it has gone ?—I have said it was exceedingly difficult to answer that question; I instanced the case of Mr. Wilmott, as a circumstance, to show the difficulty of ascertaining it; that the silk is worked in the country there can be no doubt; that it has increased in quantity there can be no doubt; the official reports show that to be the case.

678.                                                                                    6408. Has

Mr.
*William Stone.*

23 May,
1832.

6408. Has any of it gone to Macclesfield or Congleton?—I should think it has gone of late years to Macclesfield and Congleton.

6409. Do you know the present state of those two towns, as compared with 1823?—No, I do not.

6410. Can you assign any reason for the throwing trade declining in Macclesfield and Congleton; are the wages high, or is throwing not well understood there, or what other reason can you assign?—I cannot assign either of those reasons; all I can say is, that the silk is increasing in consumption, therefore I take for granted, either the mills are capable of turning out a larger quantity of work, or it is done at Manchester or elsewhere; I can only do it from inference.

6411. Is the increase in the throwing mills at Manchester since 1826 equal to the decrease in Congleton and Macclesfield?—That I cannot tell.

6412. The Italian raw silk imported into this country is in great part thrown into tram, is it not?—A very large quantity must be thrown into tram.

6413. Until the last two or three years, were not the importations of tram very small?—Till the season of 1830 to 1831, decidedly so.

6414. Were not the importations of Italian tram very large during the year 1831?—During the season of 1830 and 1831, they were.

6415. You have stated that the account of the prices of raw thrown, &c. given in the list on your examination, was made up by Messrs. Gondolfin & Company; have not they since increased very much their importation of thrown, as compared with their importation of raw silk?—I am not aware of the fact, but from 1830 to 1831, I conceive, as merchants, their importations of thrown, it is fair to suppose, were equal to 63 per cent. on their raw; taking it as a general question, I can only answer it as a general question.

6416. Did not their importations of thrown silk in 1831, equal, or nearly so, their importations of raw?—I must answer that question in the same way as before, I have no other mode of doing it; during the season of 1830 to 1831, their importations of throwns, I conceive to have been 63 per cent.; I do not know whether it was more or less.

6417. Was this alteration in the trade brought about by the advice given to them by your house?—I do not know that it was; but it was evident that the market would produce that result.

6418. It is usual for men to consult their brokers?—They would ask their broker, and he would answer them, let him be who he might.

6419. Did not they import one-third of the foreign thrown tram imported last year?—I cannot say, they may have done it for aught I know.

6420. You have given in an account, showing the average prices of raw silks and thrown silks into this country, from 1822 to the present time, and have deduced from it an account of the price per pound the Italian throwster got in each year for throwing; to enable the Committee, however, to arrive distinctly at the price he obtained for throwing, should not you have given the price of raw silk in Italy?—I have nothing to do with that, I took it merely on the principle of this market, what a man would have got for the one or for the other if he sent to this market.

6421. You do not know at what he purchases the silk?—Certainly not.

6422. So that where he seemed to be losing 3 s. he might be losing only 1 s. 6 d.?—And on the other hand where he appeared to be getting 1 s. 6 d. he might be getting 3 s.

6423. Do you know what were the prices in Italy?—I do not.

6424. You have stated that the nett proceeds to the Italian throwster in 1831 were 2 s. 3 d. per lb., that of course includes waste?—That includes waste, all he gets is 2 s. 3 d. to cover every thing.

6425. You have stated the price of throwing organzine in England to be 3 s. 9 d. per lb,, do you include waste in that?—I do not include waste.

6426. Then whatever the loss by waste may be that must be added to the 3 s. 9 d.?—Yes.

6427. What do you allow for waste?—That depends upon the silk.

6428. It varies from 3 to 15 per cent., does it not?—It may, but I should doubt whether 15 per cent. is common now.

6429. Do you think 10 per cent. is common now?—No, I should take it upon the average of all the Italian silk put together, it would not exceed six to seven per cent.

6430. You have stated, that within your knowledge some English throwsters did well last year, was there not something peculiar in the circumstances of that
trade

Mr.
*William Stone.*

23 May,
1832.

trade so as to take them out of the general rule ?—I am not aware of that exception; their local advantages may have been such, but I am not aware of any peculiar advantages.

6431. Out of your extensive connexion how many throwsters, can you say, did well last year ?—In my extensive connexion I should hope most of them did well; but I should also have added, I believed 1831 to have been a bad silk year; and so I think still.

6432. What do you mean when you say a bad year ?—A bad year as to profits.

6433. Did any of them work organzine ?—No doubt of it.

6434. Did any advantage, supposing there to be an advantage, arise from the working of the lowest Italian silks ?—I think that is one cause of the ruin of the throwster, working bad Italian silk in this country.

6435. Bad Italian silk does come to this country?—Certainly it does.

6436. There is but a small proportion of the silk imported you would call good, is there?—There is a pretty fair proportion, and it has been increasing of late years.

6437. What proportion do you think ?—I should think, perhaps, two-fifths would be of the highest quality.

6438. Do not those silks waste very little ?—They do.

6439. Cannot a throwster turn off a large quantity of this silk from its working freely ?—Yes.

6440. And it is an excellent article when finished ?—Yes.

6441. Do you think the throwsters, who have worked upon the common run of Italian silks, have retained a remuneration ?—I doubt it very much.

6442. Have there not been a great many failures among them ?—There have.

6443. More than in any preceding year ?—Not more than in 1826, nor so many I think.

6444. Do not the districts, where the Italian plan of throwing is understood, generally speaking, produce better raw silks than those districts where they are ignorant of throwing ?—I think they do, as it applies to Lombardy.

6445. You have stated, that if the duty on thrown silk should be continued at their present rates, the quantity imported will decrease; how do you reconcile this opinion with the fact, that since the reduction of the duties in 1829, there has been an increased importation of organzine, and that trams have, for the first time, been imported to any extent ?—I explained that, or endeavoured to explain it, from the circumstances of this market; in 1830 the prices were very high, they afforded a considerable temptation to the Italian to send his thrown silks here, which applies equally to trams; since that period they have considerably decreased as it regards tram; as the question has been introduced, I believe 706 bales were imported, they have fallen to 62 bales during the present season.

6446. Do you think there would have been more if the duty were increased ?—Certainly not.

6447. Must not that depend upon whether it is profitable to him or otherwise ?—If I am asked whether the tendency of the reduction of duty has been a greater inducement to him to send silk, the thing is self evident.

6448. If in consequence of the duty the importation of foreign thrown silk should decrease, do you think the importation of raws would decrease also ?—No, I think they would not decrease.

6449. If there should be a diminished importation of thrown silk, and an increased importation of raw, would that not give additional employment to the English mills?—Certainly.

6450. Are the best filatures of foreign thrown silk better than the generality of English silk?—Yes; the best of the thrown silks of Italy as compared with the generality of thrown silks of England, certainly are better.

6451. Do you attribute this superiority chiefly to the silks which are used, or to the operation of throwing?—To the silk they are thrown from.

6452. Then at all events the Italian throwster has the advantage of having the best silk to throw?—He has an opportunity of buying the best silk, certainly.

6453. Will you explain the business of a silk broker, and the sources of his information?—As an agent between buyer and seller.

6454. Is it not necessary to be a sworn broker to practise in your trade?—According to the rules of the City of London it is.

6455. Are you a sworn broker?—That is one of the questions I decline to answer.

678.

6456. Is

6456. Is it any part of the broker's business to deal in silk for his own account?—Certainly not.

6457. Do you buy any silk from the Italian merchants for principals?—Yes.

6458. Do you arrange for the throwing of this raw silk for the principal with the throwster?—Yes, frequently.

### Mr. *John Hall*, called in; and Examined.

6459. IN what business are you engaged?—A silk throwster and silk manufacturer.

6460. How long have you been in the silk trade as a throwster?—About fourteen years.

6461. Were you engaged in the silk trade before that period?—I commenced business under the firm of Haycock, Sawer & Hall at Christmas 1806, as manufacturers of ribbons.

6462. As a throwster, what description of silk do you now throw, and where have you your mills?—My mills are situate at Coggeshall, in the county of Essex; the article I generally throw is Italian organzine.

6463. Do you throw any other silk but Italian organzine?—Occasionally; but I do not wish to enter into the explanation of other silks.

6464. Do you throw the Italian silk on your own account or for others?—I throw on my own account.

6465. In the purchases you make of raw, what advance do you consider necessary on the raw to remunerate you for the wages, waste, and other expenses attending the throwing?—That is a question which embraces so many sizes, that before I could give you an answer it will be necessary to fix upon a particular size, say a 30 denier silk, 5 s. upon cost.

6466. How much do you throw in a week?—Five cwt. is my usual average; 400 of organzine, and 100 of tram; that is what my machinery is calculated to do regularly.

6467. What is the total amount of wages for throwing that quantity?—Five shillings per lb. would cover all expenses attending it, and leave a profit to the throwster.

6468. Does that include waste?—It includes waste, wages, expenses, brokerage, exchange, interest of investment, and every thing from the first cost of the raw, say 17 s., and sold at 22 s.

6468. It includes profit also?—Yes.

6469. And tear and wear of machinery?—Yes, every thing, as I before stated.

6470. If 1 s. 6 d. were taken off the duty now payable of 3 s. 6 d., would that prevent your throwing?—I think not; for I commenced under the protection of 14 s., made a large investment with my late partner, Thomas Sawer, above 10,000 l.; afterwards we were reduced to 7 s., and we said we should be ruined, but we found ourselves exactly in the same situation. It was then reduced to 5 s., and from that to 3 s. 6 d.; and at 3 s. 6 d. duty I find myself in a better situation than I was before; therefore, if 1 s. 6 d. was taken off, my opinion is, the demand would be increased, and no injury arise to the throwster.

6471. Has the reduction of your expenses arisen from the reduction of wages paid, or from other economical arrangement in the manufactory?—A great and principal reduction in my annual expense arises in the first instance from a reduction of about twenty per cent. on wages; in the second, by making less waste; and lastly, by the reduction in the prices of coals and candles.

6472. What are the class of persons you employ in your mills; are they grown up persons or children?—I begin with girls about nine years of age; and many have continued with me ever since the mill was established.

6473. Are there any men?—Only one for each room, to overlook and keep them in order.

6474. What are the range of wages from the time they enter, until they are able to do full work?—I begin with children at 1 s. 6 d. to 2 s. a week; I bind them for three years, advancing them every year.

6475. That is 3 s at the end of three years?—Yes; then I go on with a second binding at 3 s. 6 d., 4 s. and 4 s. 6 d., that is taking the highest I give.

6476. Do you employ any boys?—Very few, only to clean the work.

6477. Are the overlookers paid by piece work, or by the week?—I pay by the week.

6478. Do

Mr.
*John Hall.*

23 May,
1832.

6478. Do you consider that you would actually require a protection of 2 s. per lb. on organzine silk ?—I think so; for in the first place there is a duty on the other side, which would require 1 s.; in the next place the silks in the raw state, after having been conveyed from Italy to this country, makes about 1 s. difference in point of waste and condition, which would give the Italian throwster an advantage over me. In every other respect I should say I want no duty, because my organzine, from the same filature, will sell for 1 s. per lb. more than that of any Italian throwster.

6479. Would it be worth more than that of other home throwsters ?—I do not say that.

6480. Are you speaking of 30 denier silk ?—Of any size.

6481. Have you frequent opportunities of comparing our silk with that of the foreign throwster; and do you consider your own better ?—Yes, better cleaned, and better worked generally, in consequence of better machinery; it makes less waste after it has been dyed.

6482. Do you consider that your capability of throwing at the rate you mention, is confined to your own mills; or do you consider that other mills in the county of Essex throw on the same terms ?—Certainly they could; I know one that does; I do not know any other.

6483. What one mill is that ?—The owner's name is Mr. S. Brown, in Colchester; his manager was many years with me.

6484. Do you work by water or steam ?—By both.

6485. That is included in your expense ?—Yes.

6486. Has Mr. Brown steam or water ?—Only steam.

6487. You say you should consider 5 s. as a remunerating price for organzine; what would you charge for tram ?—I should require 4 s.; but I would rather throw organzine at 5 s.

6488. Do you mean the 4 s. tram of 30 denier silk ?—Yes.

6489. What difference would 22 denier make in the charge ?—Twenty-two denier 7 s.; 26 denier 6 s.; 30 denier 5 s. It would require 2 s. a pound more to leave an equal remuneration to the throwster.

6490. Are you enabled to state what proportion of the silk is thrown in England at 22 to 26, and what proportion at 30 ?—No.

6491. Can you state what in your view are the component parts of the 5 s.; can you give the Committee any idea how much is for wages, how much for machinery, how much for capital, and how much for profit ?—I cannot dissect it correctly.

6492. Do you charge interest upon the whole outlay you have laid out ?—No, I have lately worked it down to what I consider a healthy price, so as to meet the present bad times.

6493. Do you consider it now worth 2,000 l. or what amount ?—I beg to decline answering that question.

6494. At what period did Mr. Brown erect his machinery at Colchester ?—In 1826 he commenced.

6495. Did he erect it himself or was it erected for him ?—He bought an acre of freehold ground and built the mill upon it.

6496. Does he throw at the same prices as you do ?—I know his wages are as low, and living in a more populous town, I should say lower than mine.

6497. Is he throwing silk at the present time in this mill, which he himself erected ?—He does, I have heard about 800 lbs. on the average per week, he works night and day, and so do I.

6498. With respect to that mill, you have charged yourself with what you consider a fair rent for the mill at the present time ?—Yes; I charge it according to what I think it would sell for.

6499. Do you think you could erect a mill now with all your experience, at the amount at which you value this mill, at the present moment, sufficient to throw the quantity you do at the same rate, and yet have a profit ?—If things are permitted to remain as they are, I would invest 10,000 l. in another mill, double the size of my present one.

6500. Would you erect another mill at Coggeshall ?—No, but I would erect one in a situation where I should have more hands.

6501. What do you charge for throwing 30 denier ?—I should be happy to do it at 5 s. a pound.

6502. Do you obtain that price now ?—I do.

678.

6503. Twenty-

Mr.
*John Hall.*

23 May,
1832.

6503. Twenty-two to twenty-four denier you should charge 2*s*. more for?—I should.

6504. What should you charge for 20 to 22?—I should expect 7*s*.; it would depend upon the quality of the silk.

6505. What is the size most used in the trade?—The size as much thrown as any is 26 to 28 deniers; I always find that very marketable.

6506. At what would you throw 26 to 28 denier?—At 5*s*. 6*d*. per lb. including waste, &c.

6507. Are you in the habit of seeing the best foreign thrown silk?—I am in the habit of seeing samples of foreign thrown silks of most descriptions by way of comparison only.

6508. You state that you would undertake to throw a silk which would be 1*s*. per pound better than any foreign silk?—Yes, from the same bale.

6509. Do you get that price for the silk you throw?—I believe I do, and more.

6510. What proportion of your silk is thrown on commission, and what proportion on your own account?—I have no commission work. I pay cash for all the silk I throw.

6511. What proportion of the silk you throw do you use in your own manufacture?—Last year I used only one third.

6512. Are the Committee to understand, that the 5*s*. you affix to the raw silk is partly a profit on the thrown silk, partly charges for throwing, and a profit for throwing, or is it simply confined to throwing?—For every expense and profit at the end of the year, to put me in a situation that I should be satisfied to go on.

6513. Having bought the raw silk, and sold the thrown at those prices, you have a remunerating profit?—Yes.

6514. Do you work night and day?—Yes, all the year.

6515. Have you a change of hands?—Yes.

6516. You state that you throw silk better than any Italian you see?—Any that comes under my notice.

6517. How do you account for the importation of Piedmont organzine?—Piedmont is a silk that we do not get the good raws; therefore I have no experience upon that; I am comparing 30 denier silk of good Bergamo Italian silk.

6518. You say that things remaining equally good as at present, you would expend 10,000*l*. in another mill?—I would.

6519. And yet you are compelled sometimes to take against your will silk of 22 to 26 deniers?—When I see the market runs upon those sizes, and I think I shall make a larger profit, I sometimes buy them, but they do not always answer my expectations.

6520. And yet you say you throw silk better than any person except Mr. Brown?—The proof is, that I can get a better price for the same filature than I see others are obtaining.

6521. Why should you who work so well, be obliged to take silk you do not want?—I am not obliged, but I do work it occasionally, expecting to make a profit.

6522. Why do you not always take that at 30 deniers; is not that always to be had?—Not always.

6523. Those silks of 22 deniers you cannot throw at less than 7*s*.?—Not to leave a satisfactory profit.

6524. You state that you would build another mill where hands are more plentiful, what is your object in that?—To make a living for my family.

6525. Do you expect to get wages at a lower rate?—No, I do not wish to have the wages lower, but to have a larger supply of hands.

6526. You could not get a change of hands at the same price?—Not in my present situation

6527. Silk at 22 to 24 deniers you would not like to throw at 5*s*.?—No, I would sooner shut up than do that.

6528. You speak of throwing the best silk at 5*s*. a pound, would you like to throw the ordinary quality at 5*s*. a pound?—I should not.

6529. Every body can obtain this superior quality of silk you throw?—Every one can if he pleases; the market is open to them as well as to me.

6530. You have the same opportunity as every other man?—Yes, and every man the same as me.

6531. Do you ever throw on commission for others?—No; if they will give me my price I should prefer that work.

6532. Do

Mr.
*John Hall.*

23 May,
1832.

6532. Do you mean to say you always buy the silk and sell it, and that it is not sent to you at a certain payment for throwing?—All the silks I purchase I buy *bonâ fide*; a broker may say at the time, I can obtain a customer at such a price for it in organzine; if it is satisfactory I agree to sell it.

6533. There are persons in the habit of purchasing silks, and sending to be thrown at a certain price; have any persons sent you silk to be thrown, and given you those prices?—I have not thrown for hire.

6534. Has any weaver sent silk to be thrown by you for which you have received that payment for the throwing?—I have no manufacturing customer that I recollect.

6535. Do you not take silk on commission, the terms being working, and the waste?—I agree to buy the raws, and take a price for the organzine; say the former 16s., the organzine 21s.

6536. Have you paid brokerage in that case?—Yes, of course; for I have bought the silk myself, and have to sell it again; and brokers will not sell without brokerage.

6537. That broker gets double brokerage?—Yes, but not from me.

6538. That is included in your 5s.?—Brokerage upon the thrown silk is.

6539. Is any of your own silk now in your agent's hands for which you cannot get customers?—I have not an ounce of silk which is not at my mills or at the dyers.

6540. You are a throwster, and depend upon your throwns?—Yes.

6541. Is it not important to have a good supply of Italian raw silk, from which you should make a selection for your throwing?—I think so; the better the market is supplied, the better chance of getting a good article.

6542. To secure this, is it not desirable to throw impediments in the way of those good raws being used by the throwsters in Italy?—It is.

6543. Do you consider the duty now levied on organzine one of the greatest impediments to a good market?—That is a question I am not capable of explaining what are the impediments; I am quite out of the way of importing throwns.

6544. You are desirous of having a good market, and plenty of choice, in order to have a good selection?—Yes.

6545. Do not you now get on an average about 3s. 9d. and 4s. for that you charge and get 5s. on?—Others may; I have no commission work.

6546. Can you state what is the nett amount per lb. remaining to you for throwing, whether 3s. 6d. or 4s., or what?—The nett amount for throwing must depend upon the waste, which varies from three to five per cent.

6547. At how much do you estimate the actual expense of throwing divesting it of brokering and profit, and so on?—I should say 1s. 6d. the pound for bare wages.

6548. Eighteen pence upon the nett wages?—As near as I can average it.

6549. Do you mean to say you get 1s. 6d. per lb. profit over the capital employed, and over wages and other expenses?—Certainly not; I should say 1s. 6d. more for waste and interest of investment, leaving 6d. per lb. for profit.

6550. Do you mean to say this 1s. 6d. is the whole of your expense?—For one portion of expense as near as I can recollect.

6551. You charge 5s.?—Yes, the whole may make 4s. 6d., and that will leave 6d. profit.

6552. What is the other 1s. 6d.?—Coals, candles, brokerage, rent, &c.

6553. In point of fact, without any of those contingencies or extras, you can throw your silk, as far as labour is concerned, at 1s. 6d.?—I can, merely wages to hands employed in that department.

6554. You say there are other expenses, bringing the expenses to 3s.?—Yes, carriage, overlookers and other charges.

6555. In this 3s. you do not include the interest of capital?—No, I have before stated that charge, with waste, investment, &c.

6556. Are there other mills in Essex?—Yes.

6557. Have you ever heard of any parish in Essex lending money to London manufacturers to assist them in building a mill in which their pauper poor might be employed?—No, not in Essex; I know of one in Suffolk, that of Mr. Duff's. I have heard they gave him the ground, and carted the material to build his mill, in order to find employment for the poor of the parish.

6558. Have the goodness to say whether any of your hands receive parochial relief?—I do not know that I have a hand that receives parochial relief.

678.

6559. Do

Mr.
*John Hall.*

23 May,
1832.

6559. Do the parents of the children you employ receive parochial relief?—I have no doubt they do in many instances.

6560. Is there any understanding between you and the parish officers of your own and any other parish ; and do you receive any thing from the parishes as a part remuneration for employing them?—Nothing from any parish.

6561. Do you never, in giving relief to the parent, take into consideration the wages received by the children ?—Invariably.

6562. Have you reduced the wages of your children ?—About twenty per cent. the last two years.

6563. You have stated that you give to the poor and to the sick parents of these children; do you ever give to a healthy parent ?—The four overseers, of whom I am one, give according to the scale fixed by the magistrates ; they have what they are entitled to, sick or not.

6564. So that in the end the earnings of the children are taken into consideration, and then you give what you consider a sufficient support for the family ?—Yes.

6565. Is that the general rule in your parish ?—It is ; and I should think in all parishes.

6566. When the parents are employed, and their children are employed, do they receive any parochial relief in addition ?—I do not employ the parents, I employ the children.

6567. Do you know of any instance where the parents are employed, and the children are employed, in which they receive additional relief from the parish ?—Yes.

6568. You have reduced your wages twenty per cent., and the parents, many of them receive parochial relief?—Yes.

6569. Do any of the parents of the children you employ receive parochial relief? —I have just stated they do.

6570. As you have stated that you live in a small parish, where you have only 4,000 inhabitants, and also you have stated that you have reduced the wages twenty per cent., and the parents of many of these children receive parochial relief, yet you have a difficulty in getting hands, and in getting them at so reasonable a rate as they do in other places ?—The supply is not sufficient for my demand.

6571. You state that the parents of the children you employ are principally agricultural labourers ; when they have full employment, are they in the habit of having parochial relief ?—No.

6572. It is only where they have not full employ that they receive parochial relief ?—Yes.

6573. Is there any means of employing the number of children but for your mill ?—No.

6574. But for your mill they would be all idle and on the parish?—Yes, I believe so.

6575. Do you employ all the members of any one family ?—I think not ; I do not know that I do.

6576. Do you employ one, two, or three orphans, of one family ?—I have only one instance where I have two orphans.

6577. Do these orphans receive any thing in addition to the pay you give them ?—They reside in the poor-house, and are sent to me by the overseers at fair wages.

6578. Do you pay the parish their wages ?—No, I pay the children.

6579. What are the average wages you pay ?—The average is 3 s. a week.

6580. You say if it was not for that mill a great many children would be out of employ and thrown upon the parish ?—I believe so ; so I found them when I first went to Coggeshall.

6581. You think it of importance that the throwing trade should be kept in this country ?—Yes, I think so.

6582. Suppose your mill was not there, you would have to increase the relief to the parents ?—Yes, very much.

6583. Would it be increased in nearly the proportion that you pay to the children ?—In many instances to the full ; others might leave the place.

6584. Are there any of those persons you employ in the country who can subsist upon the wages they receive from you ?—I believe the majority do subsist upon the wages they receive from me.

6585. Do

Mr.
*John Hall.*

23 May,
1832.

6585. Do you mean to say that any of them can live on 3*s.* a week?—Yes; 3*s.* a week, in our parish, will keep a child if lodged by its parents.

6586. How many hours a day do those children work?—Eleven.

6587. Different children come on at night?—We do not work children at night, but grown women.

6588. What wages do you give them?—Half as much more as by day.

6589. What is the average you give to the women?—The women average 5*s.* per week.

6590. Are the children bound to you by the assent of the parish officers?—No.

6591. Have the parish officers no knowledge of the fact of their being bound to you?—No, an Act of Parliament exists, called Mr. Hobhouse's Act, which requires that every person who enters a mill to work, shall have their names entered in a book, and that shall be signed by the contracting parties, and those contracting parties are compelled to fulfil the contract, which are, the parent, the child, and myself.

6592. Are the parish officers cognizant of the agreement which the children enter into?—They never wish to know any thing of the kind, and never ask it.

6593. Do the parish officers know you take them in that way?—They may have heard of it.

6594. You say that in the 3*s.* you have referred to, you do not include interest on your capital?—I divided the whole of my expense into three portions, making 4*s.* 6*d.*; it is in the 18*d.* after the wages.

6595. Are you a manufacturer of silk goods?—I am.

6596. Of what kind of silk goods?—I manufacture gros de Naples, velvets, and ribbons.

6597. Are you at all acquainted with the manner in which the same kind of work is got up at Coventry?—I am aware of the wages paid in Coventry, and the system by which business is conducted there, having been engaged in a concern in Coventry 20 years, and in the habit of going backwards and forwards to take stock, and give directions what to manufacture.

6598. Can you state what are the prices you pay now, and what are the prices paid at Coventry?—I pay two-thirds of the Coventry prices.

6599. What description of looms do you use?—I believe the most improved that are known of, they are called the rack and pinion system, a power-loom.

6600. Are the goods made in your looms as good as those at Coven ry?—Better, with the same material.

6601. And made at two-thirds of the wages?—Yes.

6602. Are any of the same kind of looms used at Coventry?—I believe an attempt was made to introduce them a little time ago; Mr. Merry sent down one, and the next day the place was burnt; I am not aware of any other, except one Mr. John Herbert has; whether it is at work or not I cannot tell, it is the same as Messrs. Ames & Atkinson's looms.

6603. Are the Committee to understand, that you can afford to sell the same kind of goods for one-third less than the people at Coventry can?—By no means; there is only the reduction of labour; the material costs me as much; it may make five per cent. difference upon the goods when manufactured.

6604. Are you acquainted with any Coventry manufacturers, and can you state why they do not introduce the same kind of looms there?—I know many, and there are parties in Coventry at the present moment writing in the Coventry Herald, and other papers, to excite the men against machinery of all kinds, which they call the poor man's enemy, although his best friend; it is the interest of some of the manufacturers in Coventry to bolster up the old system of manufacturing, called undertaking, whereby they keep totally clear of all machinery; if the improved looms are once fairly introduced, the trade will get into the hands of men of skill and capital, who will only supply the market according to the demand.

6605. When you were connected with Coventry, were you acquainted with those looms you now use?—Part of the time.

6606. Why did you not introduce those looms into Coventry?—Because we feared that they would have been destroyed, and our persons insulted; the times are now altered, and no doubt the competition with France will compel them to accept the best looms.

6607. How many years is it since you introduced those looms?—About five.

6608. Are they using them now in other parts of the country?—Only at Ames & Co.'s factory. A gentleman of large capital, in Manchester, has promised to see

mine

Mr.
*John Hall.*

23 May,
1832.

mine at work; if he approves of them, he has a large factory ready to place them to steam power; I could supply them to any extent.

6609. Perhaps you would like to sell the manufactory as well as the looms?— I am desirous of doing so at a fair price.

6610. Have you not advertised the factory?—I have, in order to attract observation to those looms.

6611. Is not this your advertisement " To broad silk and ribbon manufacturers; To be let on lease, 40 miles from London, rent 80*l.* per annum, and all taxes and repairs, except broken glass, paid by landlord, a factory, consisting of three floors, 130 feet by 24; warping room 30 feet by 30; good warehouse and lobby, 30 feet by 30; carpenters' shop and store room, containing 30 rack and bar looms in full work, at two-thirds the prices paid in Coventry; 70 broad looms, all complete with new reeds and harnesses; five warping mills, winding engines of 500 spindles; the whole of which may be rented, or bought at a low price; also 20 cottages at 2*s.* per week if required, for further particulars" and so on?—Yes, that is my advertisement; I have another factory, same size, adjoining my house.

6612. This is the way you took to give publicity to your bar looms?—Yes; I think that would give publicity to them.

6613. Is not this factory in the same place as the throwing mill?—The mill, unfortunately, is a mile distant from the factory, they are in different parishes.

6614. Notwithstanding you say the advantages you possess are five per cent. beyond those of Coventry, on the manufacture and the whole cost of the goods, yet you are disposed to get rid of that factory; are the Committee to understand that?—Yes, I am disposed to let it, if any person will agree to my terms. I have another very near of equal size.

6615. Then the Committee are to conclude that it is not a very profitable concern? —The manufactory is not very profitable to me, because I have to pay an agent five per cent. for disposing of my goods, besides the attention my mill requires will not allow me time to attend properly to the manufactory.

6616. As far as regards labour you have the advantage of Coventry, you have the advantage of using those looms without any danger of life or limb, and yet you are desirous of giving it up?—Yes, as I am so fully employed with another business which engrosses my whole attention.

6617. Did not you state a little while ago, that if things remained as they are you should like to expend 10,000*l.* in erecting another throwing mill in another place?—Yes.

6618. How many years were you engaged in travelling through the country for orders previous to your residence at Coggeshall?—Twenty years.

6619. Did you reside at Coventry?—Mr. Haycock, the senior partner, resided there till the day of his death in 1812, and was succeeded by Mr. Thomas May as manager.

6620. If you did not reside there, what was the fear you had of your life?— When there is great excitement in Coventry, I have known my late partner, within the last 12 months, go into Coventry at night and compelled to leave the town before daylight in the morning; when a reduced price for weaving is proposed, they insult all the masters who first sign it.

6621. Your partner, Mr. Haycock, resided there?—Yes.

6622. And he resided there during the whole of the time you were travelling about the country?—No, he died in 1812.

6623. In what way did you conduct the manufactory at Coventry after he died? —By a confidential servant, Mr. Thomas May, who was 40 years in the concern.

6624. And you were travelling about the North of England?—Previous to 1826, not since.

6625. Does it occur to you as possible that from your being travelling about the country your business did not succeed so well as that of others?—It did succeed equal to most others; I always had a first rate connexion, which is known to all the trade.

6626. Did not you abandon it?—I left it to take the management of the throwing mills, our manager having joined Mr. Brown of Colchester.

6627. Mr. Sawer was very glad to get rid of it, was not he?—No; for Mr. Sawer is as largely engaged in the country trade as ever.

6628. Was he concerned in the throwing mill?—Yes.

6629. Was not he very glad to get rid of that?—That is best known to himself, I proposed to separate, in consequence of the bad debts he made in selling silk; we

agreed

Mr.
*John Hall.*

23 May,
1832.

agreed to divide the concern; I took the mills and manufactory, and he the London warehouse and Coventry manufactory.

6630. But he wanted to relinquish that concern?—I have no reason to think so, as the proposition for a dissolution of partnership originated with me.

6631. Are the goods you now manufacture at Coggeshall the same kind of goods as are now manufactured at Derby and Congleton by power?—I have no acquaintance with any mills there, and cannot answer that question.

6632. If you can do it with two-thirds of the labour, you do it with less hands?—Those looms are calculated to make twice the quantity of goods that the old looms can.

6633. If your labour is reduced two-thirds, is it not by having fewer hands to do the same work?—Fewer hands can do as much work.

6634. That system would not require the whole of the hands of course?—Unless there was a greater demand.

6635. Would not a fall in price increase the demand?—That is my opinion.

6636. What description of ribbons do you make?—Only black ribbons.

6637. Do you use any of the thrown Italian silk?—I use all English thrown.

6638. What effect on the price of ribbons would the repeal of the duty paid on Italian organzine have upon 100*l.* worth of black ribbons, what per centage cheaper could you afford them?—If the whole 3*s.* 6*d.* could be saved to the manufacturer it would make full five per cent. reduction.

6639. Are not many of those ribbons used as shoe strings?—I believe not; they use doubles.

6640. Is any of your thrown used in black ribbon?—Yes, all the warp.

6641. You do not make coloured ribbons?—No.

6642. Why do you not make colours?—I cannot manufacture sufficient to keep a stock, I have only 30 looms, and situate as I have been sometimes with hands, it is impossible for me to carry the business to the extent I otherwise might if in Coventry.

6643. Is there not a great advantage you have by throwing your own silk, and selecting the silk most suitable for your purposes of manufacture?—I do not think it is, in the present state of the market.

6644. Have the goodness to describe your loom, the way in which it operates, and the advantage there is in using it, over the common loom?—The rack and bar loom will make double the quantity of goods in the same period that the original loom can.

6645. And produce it well?—I believe better, so the best judges have acknowledged, with less material.

6646. Have you ever applied the Jacquard machine to this loom?—I have; but I do not make fancy goods at present.

6647. Do you believe that steam power can be beneficially applied to the manufacture of fancy ribbons?—I do.

6648. Do you not employ horse power in your ribbon manufactory?—Only in the winding part.

6649. To what use are the sort of ribbons you make applied?—The narrow ones are used for bindings, strings to dresses, and the broad ones to trimming bonnets, &c.

6650. You think five per cent. would occasion an additional number of black strings for bonnets, and strings for dresses to be used?—Five per cent. would not; 10 to 15 per cent. may be saved, which will secure the American market.

6651. Did you ever express a desire to remove your throwing machinery to France or to Manchester?—I may in conversation have said, that if we are to be ruined here, we must have permission from Government to go somewhere else.

6652. What reason had you to think you should be ruined?—Because I hear the manufacturers say they shall all be ruined by the smugglers, and if they are ruined, I must cease to throw silk or remove to a better market.

6653. What effect do you think the taking off the duty of 3*s.* 6*d.* on foreign thrown organzine would have upon your mill property?—I think if the whole 3*s.* 6*d.* was taken off, the mills in this country would not be able to work at all, but that is only my opinion.

6654. Would not that be destructive to a great deal of property, and throw many hands out of employ?—I think so, but that is my own opinion.

6655. When you spoke of the apprehension of ruin, did you speak to the manufacture having been established at Manchester?—No, by the great distress created

678.

in the trade, owing to houses in the city of large capitals being so deeply engaged in the smuggled trade as they notoriously are.

6656. Do you mean to say that if the manufacturers of silk goods in this country were ruined, you would not have a demand for your goods?—The demand for thrown silks would cease.

6657. Do you know anything of the ribbon trade of Coventry?—I have been in the habit of having them manufactured under my direction.

6658. Do you think if there is a want of labour and fear of being ruined, it can very much benefit them to have an influx of foreign manufactured goods brought into the market?—Certainly not, if they can be kept out.

6659. Must it not tend to depress the prices?—I should think so; all we have to do is to meet the evil and beat them out of our market.

6660. Will not the English manufacturer stand a fair chance of being employed by having his material as cheap as that of the French?—I fear that he never can have, the French producing the silk in their own provinces, and in consequence of the very low wages that are paid in France in the mills, they possess great advantages over us.

6661. Do you know what wages they pay?—I hear by report that the wages are very low, not exceeding half of what we pay.

6662. What do you pay for a gros de Naples of three singles?—Four pence a yard.

6663. What do you pay for weaving three doubles?—Five pence a yard.

6664. Is that done in the best kind of work?—I could not boast; I think Spitalfields would make it much better; if I had to begin a broad silk manufactory I would begin in Spitalfields in preference to any other part of England.

6665. They pay a penny more in Spitalfields, and it is a penny better?—I may fairly say two pence.

6666. It is not always desirable to do things in the cheapest way?—If I had my looms in Coventry and the best hands working cordially with them, I would defy France, and supply all the world with ribbons.

6667. Can you state the prices you pay at Coggeshall for the two, four, six, eight, ten, and twelve ribbons?—In Coventry the goods are furnished by undertakers generally; the prices paid to the undertaker, who again employs the journeymen under him at very reduced prices, of which we know nothing; the price we pay the undertaker for the two-penny sarsenet is 2s. 4d., at Coggeshall we pay 1s. 8d.; four-pennies in Coventry 3s., in Coggeshall 2s.; six-pennies, 4s. at Coventry, in Coggeshall 2s. 6d.; eight-pennies in Coventry 5s., in Coggeshall 2s. 8d.; ten-pennies in Coventry 6s. 4d., in Coggeshall 3s. 6d.; twelve-pennies in Coventry 7s. 8d., in Coggeshall 3s. 6d.

6668. Are these articles as well manufactured by you as they are at Coventry? —They are and ought to be better. I observed when we first commenced, those employed by us were in correspondence with Coventry committees, they come with a determination to spoil their work, because they did not like a manufactory to be established out of Coventry.

6669. What reduction do you reckon on as between Coventry and you?— One and three pence, we take our scale as high as thirty-penny. I will state the whole scale if it is wished; fourteen-penny at Coventry 10s. 6d., at Coggeshall 5s. 2d.; sixteen-penny, 10s. 4d. at Coventry, at Coggleshall 7s. 4d.; twenty-penny at Coventry 13s. 4d., at Coggeshall 10s., there we come nearer, these require good hands; twenty-four-penny at Coventry 16s. 4d., at Coggeshall 12s.; thirty-penny at Coventry 20s., at Coggeshall 16s.; upon the whole round it comes to 98s. 8d. in Coventry, and at Coggeshall 66s. 4d.

6670. You admit that the quality is not so good at Coggeshall?—They are not all expert hands, the goods are not all so good as they would be if made by Coventry weavers in the same looms.

6671. Then you have no advantage over Coventry?—I should prefer working these looms in Coventry to any other place if they could be introduced with safety; but I have a letter from a friend there, stating that he dare not attach his name to that advertisement lest they should injure his person or destroy his property.

6672. Do you include in the prices you have stated at Coventry and Coggeshall, the expenses of winding, weaving, filling, and loom hire?—When I have stated that the business at Coventry is done by undertakers, the prices I have named include all the expenses. I get the profit upon the winding and warping here, and the manufacturer in Coventry gives that to the undertaker.

6673. Though

Mr.
*John Hall.*

23 May,
1832.

6673. Though you state in your advertisement that labour is one-third less, there is scarcely any difference?—There is a disadvantage, in the first place, for want of better hands, in the next by being out of the market.

6674. You actually get the work performed at a lower price, but in a much worse manner?—My own opinion is, that the manufacture of ribbons will not succeed out of Coventry, unless it gets into Manchester, and if it gets there, Coventry will be pauperized and ruined. The large capitals they have, added to their skill and industry, beat any thing, and whenever they begin with a new manufactory they will go on upon an extensive scale, so as to monopolize the whole market.

6675. Did you ever reside for any time in Manchester?—Three times a year for twenty years; I have spent a week or ten days each time, and am acquainted with some of the first manufacturers in the place; I have had an opportunity of observing their progress, and their ability to undertake the ribbon trade.

6676. Are the rack and bar looms the same as those called a-la-bar looms?—No, they are not.

6677. Will a rack and bar loom make a checked ribbon?—Every kind of ribbon, the most expensive that can be put to work, better than any others, they are steady and sure, the shuttles cannot fly back to injure the work as in the Coventry looms.

6678. You state, that you think that if those rack and bar looms were generally introduced you could defy France or any other country?—I think we should make ribbons for all the world.

6679. You are of opinion that if rack and bar looms were generally in use you could export ribbons to all parts of the world, and to France among the rest?—If they would take them, the prices would enable us to do so.

6680. When were the rack and bar looms introduced?—I think in 1825.

6681. Where were they invented?—By a person in St. Etienne; a late servant of mine saw them at work, and first gave the idea to Mr. Guilliotte, who could not get them to work; we bought one, and altered it until it was perfect, since which I have made several others that are preferred to Guilliotte's plan by experienced workmen, who have worked upon both.

6682. Why do we not now export to all parts of the world?—On account of the great difference between our labour and that of France and Switzerland. The rack loom will obviate this, better machinery will place us on a level, our capital will do the rest.

6683. On account of the dearness of labour you cannot export?—That is the greatest obstacle.

6684. If you procure the rack loom here, do not you think it probable that the foreigner will procure them?—Not to the same extent.

6685. Why not?—Because I do not believe they have got the same amount of capital to invest, they are expensive, and the first outlay alarms beginners.

6686. Do not you know that this is a French invention?—Yes.

6687. Do not you know that they have them in France?—In one manufactory.

6688. Do not you know that in all the silk manufactories in France they have abundance of machinery, that they possess large machines which they now have in the greatest abundance, and if so, what is your reason for thinking that any deficiency of capital would prevent their using that machinery which you have borrowed of them?—We have borrowed it of them, and have had it some years, but I never heard of its being in more than one factory, and I believe that is kept very secret; I do not know of any man in the trade, except a servant of mine, who has been over that factory.

6689. Are you not satisfied, from the ribbons that come here, that they are made by machinery?—With the Jacquard machine they are.

6690. Could you make them without machinery?—No ribbons can be made without machinery.

6691. Do not the ribbons which come in from France assure you they are made from machinery?—Yes, certainly, as I have before stated, with the Jacquard.

6692. Then what makes you think that the French should be deficient in respect of this machinery?—Because they have not used it to any extent, though it is answering the purpose of the person who possesses it extremely well.

6693. Have you ever been in France?—I have not, but I have had the best of information from those who have.

6694. What do you know of their capital?—Only from those who have been there.

678.

6695. Do

Mr.
*John Hall.*

23 May,
1832.

6695. Do not you know that they have large capital in Switzerland?—Yes, I have been informed they have.

6696. Have you ever heard of a person of very large capital at Basle?—I have not.

6697. Are you aware of looms similar to those you use at Basle?—I know they use the a-la-bar loom.

6698. Do they apply power to those rack and bar looms in France?—I believe not.

6699. Can it be applied in England?—Yes, they are better adapted for power than any loom yet invented.

6700. Do you think this country would have that advantage in the use of it?—I have stated it would, by getting a great export trade.

6701. You state that if the Manchester manufacturer took advantage of the ribbon trade, you think they would ruin Coventry?—I do, they possess so many advantages.

6702. What will be the effect of their taking up the plain goods upon the Spitalfields district, where they have been made?—As to plain gros de Naples, we all know the effect which has been produced by their supplying the market; that they have all felt the effect that it had; and I attribute a great deal of the distress in my own district and others, to the large supplies from Manchester, by men of large capital; I speak from my own knowledge of the immensity of goods which have been poured into the market, for a season; and I have seen perfect goods, cost above 2 s. 2 d., sold at 2 s.; I have seen them go down to 21 d. and then to 18 d., and down to 14½ d., entirely from an over supply.

6703. Have they not sold at a loss?—At a loss of 30 per cent.

6704. Then Coventry must be between two fires; the foreigner making the fine goods, and Manchester the worst, or plain?—That is the reason I think they will be ruined, unless they improve their means of production without delay.

6705. You have been asked if the duty of 3 s. 6 d. were taken off the importation of foreign thrown silk, whether the mills of this country would not be ruined?—I think they would; I have before stated they would cease to work; it would drive capital to France, Italy and Switzerland.

6706. You were asked whether, if the English manufacturer was destroyed, your mills would not stand still?—They would; no use to throw if the looms stand still.

6707. Would not taking off the protecting duty of 3 s. 6 d. per pound on Italian silk be destructive to the English throwster?—It would; I have before answered that.

6708. What effect will taking off the 3 s. 6 d. have upon the manufacturer?—About five per cent., provided the manufacturer gets the benefit of it; but I do not believe that he would; instead of having his organzine at a guinea a pound, he would have to pay 25 s.; it is the competition in England which keeps down the price.

6709. If you say the taking off the duty on the organzine would ruin the throwster, that is on the presumption that the foreign thrown silk will fall in proportion?—In case it falls 2 s. 6 d.; his having the first pick of the raws and cheap labour, we could not stand against him.

6710. If it did not fall, but maintained its price, are the consumers here benefited, or does the benefit go to the foreigner?—The profit would go to the foreigner, and the consumer no way benefited.

6711. You state that Manchester, you think, will take away the trade of Coventry; do you mean that they will apply power to the machinery at Manchester, and thus undersell them?—Yes, quickly; in the only profitable articles they at present make, plain ribbons.

6712. Why should they not apply power at Coventry?—If they would adopt the newest improvements cordially in Coventry, they are so excellently taught in the business, every hand would have regular employment, and no man in Manchester would dare oppose them.

6713. You think their real difficulty is, that they will not adapt the best machinery, whilst at Manchester they would be willing to do it?—If you can prove to a Manchester manufacturer the certainty of a fair return for his outlay, he goes to work directly.

6714. How many men do you employ in your manufactory?—I have about 70 men.

6715. Have

Mr.
*John Hall.*

23 May,
1832.

6715. Have most of those parochial settlements in the parish?—About half are parishioners. My good hands working on the rack looms, average 25 s. per week; in Coventry, at the high wages, about 12 s.; they have asked permission to work from 6 A. M. to 9 P. M., which would enable them to produce double the quantity.

6716. Do you mean to state that from six in the morning till nine in the evening they could make 50 s. a week?—I believe they can on a double rack loom.

6717. Do they make that on the gros de Naples?—They do not make 10 s. a week on them, when quill filler, &c. is paid.

6718. Have the goodness to state what is the article on which they can make the 50 s. a week?—Twenty-four and thirty lutestring.

6719. How many hours a day must they work to earn 25 s.?—They do not work above forty-eight hours during the week.

6720. Working four days per week they obtain 25 s.?—They do.

6721. Is not that an article of limited sale?—Provided I had more time to attend to it, and could make it in all colours, I should have unlimited orders for it.

6722. How do you account for so many men being out of work?—I have gone to Coventry and found a good many out of work; I give them two guineas to go to Coggeshall, they have gone and staid a week, and they would stay no longer; they had a combination among them, and would rather keep those men out of employ, to keep up their bad machinery, than suffer them to work for me. I have tried that within the last two years; during the worst time of distress, I had many men from Coventry come to me, and the moment they had got enough to travel back they have gone.

6723. What wages had been paid in Coventry when you were concerned in the trade?—I think eight years ago the men would some of them earn 3 l. a week, but 40 and 50 shillings, when working on gauzes or rich figures.

6724. Do you know the fact of those earnings?—We have paid those prices; and Messrs. Ames & Atkinson, and Mr. Cox, have paid the same, as I was told.

6725. What do the agricultural labourers earn in your neighbourhood?—About 9 s. a week in winter, 12 s. in summer.

6726. How is it you do not employ them, and give them 11 s. a week?—I have tried them, they cannot become good weavers.

6727. Do you mean to say that men who earn only 9 s. a week, come to you, and that when they can earn 11 s. or 12 s. a week, they will not earn the 11 s. or 12 s.?—They will spoil the work; we cannot take an agricultural workman into a ribbon manufactory to make saleable goods.

6728. You mean to state that you are compelled to give the Coventry men 25 s. a week for work, and that you cannot get it done for less?—I have never tried to get it done for less. I give two-thirds of Coventry price; if I was to offer less all my good hands would turn out immediately.

6729. Are not the hands you have had from Coventry bad hands?—When we first commenced at Coggeshall, we had some very bad hands come no doubt, for the purpose of spoiling our work, and to try to make us put down the looms; at present I have several very good hands.

6730. Have you offered your rack and bar looms to Manchester?—I have a person in negociation with me, who has promised to come and look at them next month; and if they answer the description I have given, I may agree with him for a lot.

6731. What is the difference of cost of the rack and bar looms?—The price of an a-la-bar loom is about 80 l.; a rack loom, 100 l. to 120 l. each.

6732. When you state that you give a certain price for labour, do you include the interest and wear and tear of the loom?—I do.

6733. You state that the rack and bar loom is in only one factory in France?—I believe so.

6734. Why have not they increased the number during the ten years they have had them?—My belief is that they are short of capital.

6735. France not using more of this machinery, may it not be presumed that the manufacturer there may not approve of it?—I know for a fact the person who uses them is always full of orders; the quality of Messrs. Ames & Co.'s figures proves nothing ever yet equalled them.

6736. You purchased those looms at 100 guineas a loom?—We paid Guilliotte about 1,200 l. for ten looms, stamping machine, and warping mills.

6737. You have more than those?—I have thirty, inferior to none.

678.                                                                         6738. They

6738. They cost you less probably ?—They cost less to make than buy.

6739. What do you ask now for your looms ?—For the whole concern together, 50 *l.* per loom.

6740. When you were at Coventry, what was the highest rate of wages you ever paid to any one man?—I stated that on fancy ribbons we have paid to one man as much as 60*s.,* per week; I have paid more for wages than goods are now worth in the market.

6741. Whilst men were earning such high wages, was there ever distress among the weavers ?—We employed a man at those prices only in February and ended in May, we had no machinery there, and sent them to what is called the right about, and there is considerable distress for a month or two, unless they can work at the harvest work; then they had the same wages again when the season returned ; there was more briskness in the trade formerly than there is now.

6742. Those high wages were earned only by very few on very good articles ?—Yes, on something superior, in fancy patterns.

6743. What was the average rate when you were paying thirty or forty or fifty shillings to particular men ?—The average rate of wages would be only 15*s.* on the common articles.

6744. Why did not the men who made 15*s.* come to you and obtain their share of employ, in the line in which they were making the higher wages ?—Because they had neither the skill nor the machinery; at times the briskness was such that manufacturers used to go down and send the bellman about to invite the weavers to dinner or supper at a public house at Nuneaton, for instance, to proclaim that a leg of mutton was provided and plenty of turnips, and when they got good hands there, used all the arguments they could to induce them to take their silk in preference to their old masters; we sometimes trusted them the value of a loom, 6 *l.* to 8 *l.,* so took it a little at a time.

6745. In what year was that?—In 1814 up to 1825.

6746. There were times in which you were slack also, what did you do then ?—Then we left them to sell their looms, &c., to get subsistence where they can; if the masters owned the machinery they would be more regularly employed.

6747. Times have been altered since that ?—I believe so; but having gone to Coggeshall for the last seven or eight years I have not known so much of this.

6748. During the prohibition they were better off?—During the prohibition there was no difficulty in making profits; money was in abundance; operatives scarce ; we are now placed in a different situation. A lady can go from London to France one day and return the next clothed in French silks ; once say they shall not have them at all, and every man will turn smuggler to please the ladies ; therefore let the operatives open their eyes to their own interest, invite men to furnish them with good machinery, and we will beat them out of the market.

6749. There was no war at the time you speak of ?—No, but there was prohibition.

6750. What do you think the ordinary workmen at Coventry now earn ?—I should think on the ordinary machinery they can earn 12*s.,* working six days a week.

6751. Have you paid more than 60*s.* a week ?—I dare say we have ; in 1825 we paid 80*s.* per gross for very common twenty-two-penny gauzes; in my looms a man would make a gross per week.

6752. That is more than the goods would now sell for you say ?—About the value of wages and silk altogether at present.

6753. Does not that prove a very great alteration in the state of the trade ?—Yes.

6754. Did you ever pay a second man as much ?—I could not enumerate the number without having our pay books here.

6755. Have you employed many at those wages at the same time ?—As many as we could procure ; good hands got all they asked.

6756. Do you make gauze ribbons at Coggeshall ?—No, I do not.

6757. Do you know how many pieces of the different widths a man can manufacture in a week in gauze ribbons, twelve-penny for example ?—So much depends upon the pattern ; about six pieces in a bar loom with 12 shuttles.

*Veneris*, 25° *die Maii*, 1832.

EDWARD AYSHFORD SANFORD, ESQUIRE, in the Chair.

Mr. *Robert Clay*, called in; and Examined.

Mr.
*Robert Clay.*

25 May,
1832.

6758. IN what branch of the silk trade are you engaged?—An importer of foreign manufactured goods.

6759. How long have you been in that line?—Since 1826, when the trade was opened.

6760. Before that period in what branch of the business were you employed?—Principally confined to French cambrics and kid skins.

6761. Since you were engaged in the French trade, have you visited Lyons, Saint Etienne and Chaumont, where the manufacture is carried on?—Yes.

6762. What kind of French goods have you principally dealt in?—In 1826 and 1827 in plain broad goods only; since then in ribbons; and in fact every description of manufactured goods.

6763. Are there many houses engaged in the import of French manufactured goods?—I should say very few direct importers from the manufacturers; there are numbers who buy goods in Paris, but very few engaged as direct importers from the manufacturers.

6764. How are the French goods purchased, are they purchased at Paris or from manufacturers?—It is very rarely that we purchase them, we principally order them from patterns, and samples produced by the manufacturers.

6765. In what manner are the patterns shown to you, are they shown in London, or do you go to Paris to see them?—We go to Paris or to the French manufactories; sometimes only to Paris, or at other times to Lyons, Saint Etienne and Chaumont.

6766. Are you yourself in the habit of going, or do you send an agent?—I usually go myself.

6767. When you go to Paris, do not the manufacturers from Lyons and Saint Etienne sometimes meet you there?—Frequently.

6768. Are there not many English purchasers of French goods that never purchase direct from the manufacturers at Saint Etienne?—Certainly, those that purchase of Paris houses; none of the Paris houses are manufacturers; I meant to say that there are very few, comparatively speaking, that are importers directly from the manufacturers.

6769. Will you state to the Committee what in 1826 and 1827 was the state of the trade in French goods imported by you, was it profitable, or in what state was it?—In 1826 there was a ready sale for every description of French goods; in 1827 the competition was greater, and of course the sale was not so ready.

6770. During those years were the profits good?—Exceedingly small at all times; I speak now of the articles of plain broad silks.

6771. In that year did you export to any considerable extent?—Yes.

6772. In 1828 what was the state of the trade as regards the imports?—In 1828 our trade became more general, instead of being merely importers of plain articles, it became more general; we imported ribbons and fancy silks.

6773. Did the prices received in 1826 and 1827 keep up till 1828?—Certainly not, they considerably declined.

6774. How was the demand for the various articles in that year?—Towards the latter end of 1828, the demand for plain silks considerably decreased.

6775. What has been the relative rate of prices between the English and French of goods of the same quality, as nearly as possible?—I am not able to answer that question; I am merely an importer, and I do not sell English goods.

6776. Then the reduction of price you mention was a reduction in the value of the same kind of French goods?—Certainly.

6777. What was the extent of reduction of price?—The same article that I first imported in 1826, which was the only article that I sold, plain gros de Naples, we then paid 5 francs and 25 centimes, and in 1827 they were reduced to 4 francs 75 centimes, nearly 10 per cent. reduction.

6778. What was the cause of that reduction?—I am not aware precisely; I imagine merely from the decline in the price of the raw material.

678.

6779. Of

Mr.
Robert Clay.

25 May,
1832.

6779. Of course not dealing in English goods you are not aware how far the competition of English goods had any effect?—No, I merely judge upon that subject from representations that have been made.

6780. Did you, in point of fact, find more difficulty in getting rid of your French goods in 1828 than you had done in 1826 and 1827?—Certainly in 1828 it was impossible to obtain a profit upon the plain silks.

6781. In 1828 what prices did you get for the same articles?—In 1828, in the early part of the year they were reduced about five per cent. more, to about 4 francs 50 centimes.

6782. Although you have not dealt in English goods have you had any opportunity of examining them to judge of the style and order in which they are got up? —We have certainly formed an opinion upon that subject, that the English are very slovenly in the finishing the goods, and in many instances we attribute the sale and the price of French goods more to the appearance, and the way in which it was got up, than to the intrinsic value; there is no question that the French are more particular in the way in which they turn out the goods from the manufactory.

6783. With respect to your customers that have purchased goods of you, what have been the qualities they have principally looked for in the French goods?—In the former years, 1826 and 1827, they were principally lower priced articles that we imported, and we gradually got to a richer article.

6784. In 1829 how were your purchases of silks?—Quite opposite to what they were in the preceding year; the article of gros de Naples, which was the principal part of our trade in 1826 and 1827, we did not import at all in 1829.

6785. Did you continue to buy any of that which had been reduced to 4 francs 50 centimes, in 1828 and in 1829?—To a very small extent indeed; not one hundredth part.

6786. What price did that which had been 5 francs 25 centimes in 1827, bear in 1829?—To the best of my recollection they were about 4 francs 25 centimes.

6787. Then in 1829, were your dealings more extended to the narrow fancy goods than they had been before?—Certainly.

6788. And a decrease in the plain?—Decidedly, or else I must have shut up my house.

6789. Then you began the fancy articles in 1828, did they keep up their price in 1829?—The price went on well established in 1829, they had been gradually decreasing from 1826 to 1829.

6790. In the narrows, what were the principal articles you imported?—Ribbons.

6791. What kind of ribbons have you principally been able to sell?—Principally gauze ribbons.

6792. Have you tried the sale of any other ribbons?—Of satin ribbons.

6793. How do they sell?—Like many other fancy articles, they sometimes bear a very large profit; and a month after they will be sold perhaps 40 or 50 per cent. loss.

6794. Can you state what quantity of each pattern, upon the average, you are able to sell?—My practice is to order the smallest quantity I can of each pattern.

6795. With respect to those fancy goods which you had began with in former years, had their price been kept up in 1830?—The prices were pretty well established in 1829, and I found very little difference between 1829 and 1830; in fancy articles they certainly decline, especially in gauze ribbons.

6796. Then are the Committee to understand that the trade in silk has been extremely various, subject to fluctuation?—Not much subject to fluctuations, but to a gradual decline ever since I have had any thing to do with it.

6797. Has it been a profitable trade generally, since you have had to do with it?—As far as I am able to judge, there is no business that returns the capital so seldom as that of the French trade, and few businesses that are so little productive.

6798. Can you state what is generally the quality of the goods you have bought; are they of a finer or of a coarser kind?—Decidedly of the best kind; all the low priced goods are prohibited in fact by the duty, and they are never imported.

6799. Are you aware of a practice existing of what is called jobbing; that is, sending a quantity of goods after they have passed the fashion for some time, to this country?—Jobs very frequently arise from our own orders; for instance, when I go over, I give orders to be delivered from three to six months, fixing the patterns, and fixing the quantities; for instance, at the present moment, I am going to-morrow, and I shall order goods as far as November; then many causes for jobbing arise from our rejecting those. After seeing 100 patterns of ribbons, it is very

likely

likely that out of those 100 patterns, I may refuse from 20 to 30 patterns, depending upon circumstances; I speak of patterns either taken entirely, or rejected; I do not receive part of a pattern.

6800. What are the grounds upon which you are allowed to reject, after you have ordered the goods?—In giving an order, the manufacturer is always expressly tied down to deliver his goods by such a day; if he is after his time, we of course have the privilege of rejecting them; if they are not manufactured equal in quality to the pattern, we have likewise the privilege of rejecting them; those goods once rejected by the house that orders them, must unquestionably become job goods.

6801. Do you keep a pattern of all that you order, in order to compare?—Certainly.

6802. In your own experience, has the proportion been so high as 25 or 30 per cent. of all the orders you have given?—I rejected in the goods that I ordered in the spring trade. more than 25 per cent. in the fancy goods; it is not so with the broad silks, we reject very few of them comparatively.

6803. Do you consider that most of the jobbed goods that come over, arise from that cause?—No, not most; because many of those goods may arise from a sudden stop in Paris, and from the goods ordered in foreign countries; for instance, goods ordered for Germany or America, must come into this market if they are rejected; for instance, a ribbon may be exceedingly well manufactured, and very saleable, and on the 10th of May, or the 20th perhaps, it is not worth so much by 25 per cent.

6804. Has any considerable change taken place in the kind of ribbons manufactured in France since you began, for instance, in the cut ribbons?—At first, when I had any thing to do with the trade, there was only one good manufacturer in France for the cut ribbons, that was at Chaumont; there was only one man that I could trust an order to for the first rate quality, what we call Coupé ribbons.

6805. Have the number of those manufacturers increased?—There are now 20, 30 or 50 perhaps, that I could give orders to with as much confidence in Saint Etienne and Chaumont; they are now almost all become manufacturers of Coupé ribbons.

6806. Can you state whence that demand has arisen?—There is a great demand no doubt in this country, and a very great demand for America, likewise for Germany, but the best of all the goods come to this country and to the Paris market.

6807. Do you continue the same extent of business now as you did in 1827, although in a different article?—I certainly do consider to the same extent, but I am a dealer now in perhaps ten articles, when I was a dealer only in one then.

6808. What is the state of the market now as regards the sale of plain French goods and plain English goods?—I consider that there is no sale for plain French goods, there is no such thing imported; I mean that it is on so small a scale that it is scarcely worthy of observation.

6809. Then you think the English manufacture is now competing with the French in plain goods?—There cannot be a doubt of it, the English manufacturers have beat the French entirely out of the plain, it is only by a continued succession of novelties that we can sell any thing in French goods.

6810. When you speak of plain French goods, do you mean gros de Naples without the figure?—Yes, not figured.

6811. Then are the Committee to understand that the plain French goods have been beat out of the English market?—Decidedly; the plain French goods have been beat out by the English.

6812. Do you consider the watered silk plain or figured?—That is certainly plain, but the watered silk must be of a richer quality; and in making use of the word plain, I was then alluding to low priced articles, namely, the article of gros de Naples. In speaking of watered silks, there is a different name used, they call them de soie, that is a rich quality, those are still imported, and they have been this season by myself.

6813. What is the proportion of the fine silks imported in this year and the last year, as compared with 1826-27?—That is very difficult to come to any conclusion upon; this year there has been more than the usual quantity of rich plain silks imported; when I say rich plain silks, I mean watered silks, but it is from the peculiar circumstance that watered silks have become the fashion of the season.

6814. In the patterns of narrow goods, is it the quality or is it the novelty only

678. that

that recommends them to this market?—The novelty, and having a great assortment; when we introduce a French pattern, the pattern is complete in all its colours.

6815. Have not you the same in England at Coventry?—I never heard of it.

6816. Do you mean to say that you as a merchant, going to buy French ribbons, have a better stock to look over than if you buy English ribbons?—As I do not order English goods, I am not capable of speaking upon that subject. With respect to the French goods I order them from a pattern, and I order them to be delivered at such a time.

6817. In 1831, what was the state of the trade in French goods imported?—I should say that in 1831 every man engaged in the trade to any extent must have lost money, especially upon broad silks.

6818. Did that arise from the high prices or from the large quantity imported?—From the great competition that exists with the English; the fact is, the moment we give the English manufacturer time to produce a pattern we can no longer sell ours, we merely sell ours from the novelty.

6819. You speak of fancy goods?—What we call armures.

6820. Are the Committee to understand, that if you give a pattern to an English manufacturer and ask for a supply, he will soon compete with the French article?—Since I have been in business there is no instance in which I could keep a single pattern at work at Lyons for three months, my only object is to bring in the quantity at once; I cannot bring in part the beginning of a month, and part at the end, if I do, it is copied here before the remainder arrives.

6821. Then are the Committee to understand that the English, by having the pattern, are soon able to copy and shut out the French goods?—No doubt of it.

6822. You do not order English goods yourself?—No; but I can only speak from experience, that in several articles which I have endeavoured to confine to myself, those articles have been invariably copied; till they were copied, I got a profit upon them, but the moment they were copied by the English, they have been sold for less than mine cost me.

6823. Was not that because they were more numerous in the market, and because the pattern was no longer a novelty?—I should say decidedly that it does not arise from that cause, but because the English produce them at a lower price, because the very article I am alluding to now, is manufactured by the English at the present moment.

6824. Do any of your customers deal in French as well as English goods; and are you able from them to learn what is the state of the market, although you do not yourself deal in English goods?—The very men that come into my house tell me that the English goods are decidedly lower than mine; that they will and can buy them so much under the prices; that they merely come to me for the assortment of such things as they cannot obtain. Those very men go to the English manufacturers, and say we cannot buy your goods; we can go to the French houses and buy them ten or fifteen per cent. under those prices. Now how can we come at the truth in such a case.

6825. Which statement do you think is nearest to the fact?—My decided opinion is, that there is a preference at all times given to English goods from their being cheaper.

6826. Is there ever an opportunity given to the manufacturers to make those goods at a cheaper rate by having sufficient time?—For the spring, but there is not for the autumn.

6827. In how short a time after the arrival of a French pattern have you known it copied by an English manufacturer?—I have frequently known a pattern copied before I have been able to deliver my own goods.

6828. What has been the effect upon your sale?—A competition instantly.

6829. Then are the Committee to understand that English goods have been made from the French pattern?—From the French pattern; any man here ordering a few pieces obtains a pattern of it.

6830. If you were aware of any English manufacturer preparing a pattern, would you order any of that pattern in France or not?—I should never order if I knew that it was in the course of manufacture here.

6831. In fact, your decided opinion is, that it is the novelty of the patterns that enables you to sell your goods; and that you cannot compete with the English manufacturer when he has no opportunity of competition?—In my opinion there

is

Mr.
*Robert Clay.*

25 May,
1832.

is not a doubt that it is novelty, and novelty alone, that sells the French goods; if that was not the case, why does an article decline 25 per cent. in a short time after it has been introduced, when it is of equal merit with one that has been selling five and twenty per cent. higher.

6832. Is not that the case also in articles not copied by the English manufacturers?—It is.

6833. You stated that those patterns can be copied by the English in a short time; why do not you then give them to be copied by the British manufacturers?—Because it would prevent the sale of my own goods.

6834. When you order a pattern from France, are you restricted from ordering that silk to be manufactured in England?—Certainly not.

6835. You give an order now for goods to be delivered in November, and you will have the patterns delivered to you by the French manufacturer; do you consider that you are at liberty to put that pattern into the hands of an English manufacturer to be made immediately?—Certainly, if I liked; but I never do it.

6836. Can you state what was the extent of consumption of French goods in the year 1830, in France?—In 1830, there is no doubt that the revolution in July stopped the home trade altogether in France; therefore the goods ordered by the French houses were compelled to be exported.

6837. Do you consider that that threw a great quantity of French goods into this market?—To a certain extent no doubt.

6838. What effect had that stoppage of the home trade upon the price of the French goods?—It has always this effect, that the manufacturer may be brought at a lower price than you can order them; for all fancy goods, generally speaking, become jobs.

6839. Then is it your opinion that a large proportion of the French goods so taken out of their original destination, and thrown upon England, were sold here at a loss to the manufacturer?—No doubt of it.

6840. What is the state of the silk trade now, in your opinion, with regard to French goods now in England?—In my opinion, at Lyons a very great decline has taken place; but from St. Etienne and Chaumont I think they have in all probability increased.

6841. At what relative price are the fancy goods imported this year, compared with the years 1827, 1828 and 1829?—There has been a gradual decline of price up to the year 1830; since 1830 the price has been very stationary; I speak of the price we ordinarily sell at.

6842. What are the kinds of goods coming in now; are they of the very best, or are they of all kinds?—So far as I am engaged in the business, the very best.

6843. Can you give the Committee an idea, since 1826–27 up to the present period, what is the decrease generally on plain goods, and what is the decrease of price on fancy goods, taking the same qualities in each year?—I partly answered the question before when I stated, that an article which in 1826 sold for 5 francs 25 centimes, had declined in 1829 to 4 francs 25 centimes, from 20 to 25 per cent. on plain goods; on ribbons from 25 to 30.

6844. Can you state, generally, what is the rate of duty which you consider you pay upon the imported value of French goods, stating the different descriptions of goods?—Upon plain goods I should say, the average rate of duty is 31 per cent.; on figured silks about 37½.

6845. Do you consider that that rate of duty can be collected at the Custom House, or does it lead to smuggling?—It certainly has led very considerably to smuggling; but there are other goods which pay a much higher rate of duty. The rate of duty upon what we call de coupé ribbon is also about 37½ per cent. I am speaking now of goods of the best quality; upon a striped gauze ribbon, the average duty is about 49 per cent.; upon velvets 45, upon crapes 47½, upon the article of tulle 100 per cent.

6846. What is the duty upon crape lisse?—That is no longer imported.

6847. What rate of duty would the de soie pay?—Thirty per cent.

6848. Are those rates of duty the rates now paid at the present prices, or are they the rates paid at the time the Act passed fixing those duties?—The present prices.

6849. Were they higher or lower at the time the Act passed?—Lower considerably.

6850. Then in proportion as the prime cost of every article imported is lowered, the duty consequently has become higher?—Certainly.

678.                                                                       6851. Has

Mr.
Robert Clay.

25 May,
1832.

6851. Has not the duty been once altered to meet that fall in the price of the goods?—It was altered, to the best of my recollection, in 1828 or 1829.

6852. To what extent did that meet the fall?—It placed them much upon the same footing that they were originally intended to be.

6853. Since 1828, in consequence of the reduction of the price of all the different articles, has the per centage again increased?—Certainly, especially on ribbons.

6854. What is the rate at which each of those different kinds of articles which you have mentioned can be smuggled into England?—The price of smuggling has generally been governed by the amount of duty paid upon each article; if the duty has been 40 per cent. the smuggler would perhaps demand 30; but if the duty is lowered to 20, the smuggler then is bound to lower his rate. I consider it possible, that plain silk goods might be smuggled over at from 20 to 22½ per cent., certainly not under 20 per cent.

6855. In what manner have you become acquainted with the rate at which different goods can be smuggled into England?—From offers that are continually made to me both in Paris and in Calais.

6856. Then you consider that there is a regular rate each year?—Certainly, and a regular insurance.

6857. What is the lowest rate at which you have known any of those goods smuggled?—I have never known of silk being smuggled at less than 20 per cent.

6858. What amount of duty do you consider could be collected fairly upon the importation of silk goods, so as to put an end to smuggling?—Twenty-five per cent. upon all broad silks; upon gauze ribbons I should say 30 per cent.

6859. Then if the duty on all broad silks was reduced to 25 per cent., and on all narrow goods to 30 per cent., is it your opinion that that duty could be collected, and that smuggling would be put an end to?—I have no doubt of it.

6860. Will you explain what tulle is?—It is a silk net, originally made in Nottingham, and it is now made in Lyons from a Nottingham frame; the only reason we can import it at all is, that it is a superior dress, the article itself is made better at Nottingham.

6861. Do not you import a great deal of it to sell to the people at Nottingham to work upon?—I formerly did, but not now, the consumption of tulle is very little now.

6862. Before you began the silk trade in 1826, you were extensively concerned in cambrics?—I was.

6863. What was the rate of duty you paid upon French cambrics per piece?—I merely speak from recollection, I think it was 11s. or 11s. 6d. for eight yards.

6864. At that time are you aware whether any smuggling existed of cambric?—To a very great extent indeed; I think the alteration took place before 1826.

6865. What was the reduction that took place in the duty upon that article?—From whatever the duty originally was upon plain articles, it is reduced now to 6s.

6866. Was not it a dozen years or more since it was reduced?—No, it is not a dozen years.

6867. Can you state what per centage the 11s. 6d. bore to the price of the article then, and what per centage the 6s. bears to the price of cambrics now?—It will be observed that at the time the high rate of duty existed upon cambrics they were only the low priced goods that were smuggled, the fine still paid duty; therefore it is a very difficult question to form an idea of the per centage that each paid at the time; there are so many different qualities of cambrics; you may have a cambric worth only 20 francs and one that is worth 100.

6868. Do you mean that the 11s. 6d. was paid as duty upon a piece of cambric of eight yards, whatever the value of it was?—Yes, and the same upon handkerchiefs.

6869. Would not the price of cambrics run from 3s. per yard here up to 20s.?—Yes, and the duty was the same upon each.

6870. Is the duty now the same upon cambrics of all qualities?—There is a distinction now made in handkerchiefs, but upon plain cambrics it is all the same.

6871. What is the range of price at the present moment of plain cambrics upon which the duty is paid?—I am not engaged in French cambrics now.

6872. Do you believe there is as great a variety now as there was then?—No doubt.

6873. Did

Mr.
*Robert Clay.*

25 May,
1832.

6873. Did the reducing the duty one half check or put an end to smuggling?—It put an end to it entirely.

6874. You believe that no cambric is smuggled now?—No question of it.

6875. Do you mean that when the duty was reduced to 6 s., there was no smuggling of cambrics?—Never, after they were reduced to 6 s. I consider it impossible.

6876. As far as you know, what was the state of smuggling in French goods in the year 1826, and what is the state of it now with respect to the same articles, first as to the kind of articles smuggled in 1826?—In 1826 I imagine that the principal articles smuggled were silk ribbons, gloves, lace and jewellery.

6877. Do not you apprehend, that the low French cambric has been almost entirely superseded by the manufacture of Irish?—There is no doubt of it at the present moment; but I am not conversant now with the cambric trade sufficiently to give an opinion upon it.

6878. Might not that be one cause why it would not answer the purpose to smuggle the low French cambrics?—I should conceive that it would never answer their purpose; formerly the Act ran, that you should pay such a duty upon a piece of cambric not exceeding eight yards in length or seven-eighths of a yard in width; the duty is now levied upon the square yard, which makes a very great difference indeed.

6879. Before 1826, in addition to cambrics smuggled, was there any smuggling in India handkerchiefs and bandannas?—To an extraordinary extent in bandannas.

6880. Can you state the amount of premium paid upon smuggling that?—It depended entirely on the facility of the smuggler; that is, the portable description of the article that he had to bring over; I should think upon bandannas, at that time, the premium would be 35 per cent.

6881. Since the importation of bandannas was permitted on a duty paid, have any been smuggled?—Certainly not.

6882. Are you satisfied that no smuggling exists?—So satisfied am I upon that, that there is no demand scarcely for the article; they are selling now at a lower price than what they used to sell for in India.

6883. Does that arise from the English competition?—It does.

6884. Were not the bandannas, at the time you speak of, when prohibited, commonly sold along the coast at from 50 s. to three guineas a-piece?—Yes.

6885. So that their sale at that price could not have a very prejudicial effect upon the English manufacture of bandannas?—I should say it could have no prejudicial effect at that price.

6886. Do you know the price of them at the present moment?—I do not at present.

6887. Are not a great number of bandannas imported in the white, and printed here?—No doubt.

6888. Has not the entire alteration in the fancy, and in the patterns, superseded the sale of the Indian printed bandannas in this market?—No doubt; there is a large importation of English bandannas to France.

6889. Previous to 1826 were you acquainted with any men that carried on smuggling to any great extent?—Yes.

6890. Can you state the amount?—It is difficult to do that, the smuggling was generally carried on through two or three houses at Calais, and there is no difficulty in ascertaining the amount of goods that have been smuggled from Calais in any year, because they must be entered at the Custom House, and those returns must be open for inspection; and if they are not entered in the books of the Custom House they must be smuggled out of France.

6891. Comparing the extent of smuggling in silk goods in 1826, and in each year up to the present, what do you consider to be the comparative amount?—I should think the quantity of silks smuggled now into England is not five per cent. of what it was in 1826. I mean to say, that before the alteration of the duty took place there were 100 pieces smuggled where there are only five now.

6892. Have you any knowledge of what was the state of the glove trade then and what it is now?—I am not a glover, but I believe there is no smuggling in gloves.

6893. Did you, before 1826, know any house that ever smuggled to the extent of 100,000 l. in one year?—I think I did.

6894. Have you any idea of any house smuggling to that extent now?—Certainly not.

678.

6895. In

Mr.
Robert Clay.

25 May,
1832.

6895. In speaking of silk goods, do you apply your observations to French silk goods?—Yes.

6896. Were there any China silks smuggled?—Not China, but Italian thrown silks were no doubt smuggled before the alteration.

6897. You mean that thrown silk, which paid 14s. duty, was smuggled into this country?—Yes.

6898. How was it smuggled?—It came on transit from Italy, and was lodged in a depôt in France, and then shipped and smuggled into England.

6899. You say that no smuggling exists now in cambrics, and none in gloves, does any exist in lace?—I should think there must be smuggling in lace.

6900. What is the duty now on lace?—Thirty per cent.

6901. Are you able to state what rate of duty could be collected on lace, so as to prevent smuggling?—The duty on lace must be reduced at least one-half.

6902. What is the state of smuggling with regard to jewellery?—I cannot state.

6903. Do you know whether any is smuggled?—I believe there is, because I have received accounts from Calais giving me different items that are smuggled, and amongst them there is jewellery.

6904. Then are the Committee to understand, that by the Custom House books at the port of Calais, and other ports along the coast, by a return of the export of French silk goods to England, the amount might be ascertained pretty correctly of the smuggling that has taken place in each year?—No doubt of it.

6905. Could any individual obtain it, or would it be necessary for Government to apply?—It might be obtained by an application through a correspondent at any of the sea ports.

6906. In what manner would you propose to put an end to smuggling in French silks?—There is only one mode of doing it, that is to reduce the duty; reduce the duty upon broad silks to 25 per cent., and the duties upon ribbons, and there will be little or no smuggling.

6907. Would you propose stamping the French goods?—The idea appears to me to be absurd, if a stamp were required you could import them already stamped; you could have them stamped upon the other side.

6908. How is the duty now collected, is it by value or by weight?—Principally by weight.

6909. Would you suggest any alteration in the present mode, in order to produce the utmost amount of duty?—I think I should not; at the same time it is to be observed, that if you reduce the present amount to an *ad valorem* duty it stops the smuggling altogether; but the *ad valorem* duty is always difficult to collect; experience has taught us, that one man may put the value of 30s. upon an article and another man may put 20s.

6910. Might not a person versed in silk goods be employed at the Custom House with good effect?—I think it is impossible, and in my opinion it ought to remain as it is, a rate of duty; if you intend to do all that you can for the collection of it, if you wish to protect the interest of the British manufacturer, decidedly have a rate a duty, because it prohibits the lower classes from coming in; if you have an *ad valorem* duty it may enable me to import an article that I cannot now obtain a profit upon, because instead of paying a duty of 30 per cent. I shall have it perhaps at 20 or 10.

6911. Upon what do you form the opinion that smuggling has decreased at the present time, as compared with 1826?—From the accounts I have received from Calais.

6912. When you visited Calais or Paris, had you an opportunity of ascertaining the rate at which smuggling would be carried on?—There are regular places at Calais known to every person that goes over.

6913. Are there respectable houses that will guarantee the goods?—Yes; the most respectable men in Calais, and in Boulogne, are smugglers.

6914. Is it not then considered any disgrace?—It is considered no disgrace there; it is no affair of theirs; they sell the goods and they get the money for the

6915. Are there any respectable houses in England that smuggle?—Speaking of respectability, it is no disgrace to a man in France to smuggle; but perhap an individual might not be considered respectable in England that did smuggle.

6916. You stated that there was one house which, previous to 1826, smuggled to the amount of 100,000l., do you think there were many houses that did it to that extent?—I think not another.

6917. Or

Mr.
*Robert Clay.*

25 May,
1832

6917. Or to half that extent?—Nor to half that extent.

6918. Do not you know of several considerable houses who smuggle to a great extent now?—I do not know, nor do I believe there is any such house in existence at the present moment.

6919. Was that your opinion before the seizure of Leaf's?—No, it was perfectly notorious; but they were the only extensive smugglers at the time.

6920. Do not you know there are persons in France who will deliver the goods to agents here, through whom some of the large houses in the silk trade get their goods?—No doubt about it; but speaking of smuggling we draw our conclusions by comparison.

6921. Do you believe that there is not a house now that gets smuggled articles to the extent of 100,000 *l.*?—I deny the possibility of such a house being in existence.

6922. Do you think it possible to put down smuggling by any means whatever, but that of reducing the duty to the expense of smuggling?—There is no other means of doing it.

6923. Do you think that any per centage beyond the rate of smuggling could be collected?—Certainly; five per cent. upon plain silks, and ten per cent. upon ribbons.

6924. Are the Committee to understand, that in order to put down smuggling, the expense of smuggling should be ascertained, and that that amount, with perhaps five per cent. more, might be fairly levied as a duty upon every one of those articles?—I have no doubt of it.

6925. Had not the house that you say smuggled to the extent of 100,000 *l.*, before 1826, several very large seizures?—No doubt about it.

6926. When French goods were prohibited, was not it necessary to keep them concealed, and to be very cautious in the disposal of them?—No doubt of it.

6927. If French goods should be smuggled now, is there the same danger of detection, and the same facility of detection as when such prohibition existed?—There is no danger at all now.

6928. Do you think that prohibition, or the present state of the law, is most favourable to smuggling?—The present state, certainly.

6929. If prohibition should take place again, would the smuggling be put an end to, or go on?—It would be increased.

6930. What is your reason for that opinion?—The reasons, according to my ideas, are exceedingly plain; if you cannot obtain an article legally, you do it illegally by smuggling.

6931. Do you mean, that under the present state of the law, there is less risk in smuggling, but at the same time there is less inducement?—Exactly.

6932. When did you first begin to import French goods?—In 1826.

6933. Have your dealings increased or diminished during the last six years?—They have fluctuated a good deal; in the year 1830 they decreased more than one-third; last year, in 1831, we partially recovered.

6934. You are speaking of the amount of your return?—Yes.

6935. If the goods are lower in price, must not you have sold a much greater quantity to keep up your return?—No doubt of it.

6936. What is the state in this year?—It is the same up to the present time; my opinion is, that the silk trade altogether is upon the decline, as far as regards imports.

6937. Do you import any plain French goods, or are they chiefly figured and fancy goods?—No, low priced French goods; but many that are plain are rich, I mean watered silks.

6938. Have there not been many rich watered silks worn in this country this year?—No doubt.

6939. If you take an English and a French watered silk of the same richness, which sells in preference?—I do not sell English; as a general principle, the preference is given to the English manufacture; but in that particular article, I think the preference would be given to the French.

6940. How do they make watered silks in England?—It is merely a plain silk, pressed with an iron going over it.

6041. Do you import any rich plain satin to any amount?—Yes.

6942. Were silk goods smuggled to any extent previous to 1826?—I should say they were to a very great extent.

678.

6943. Do

Mr.
*Robert Clay.*

25 May,
1832.

6943. Do you know any thing of the manner in which smuggling was then carried on?—Yes.

6944. Was it not then very dangerous to have foreign silk goods in your possession?—I should imagine it was.

6945. Before 1826, were there not frequent prosecutions and convictions for smuggling?—I have no doubt of it.

6946. Do you happen to know whether the principal smuggling transactions were generally prosecuted?—I do not know; it is impossible for me to answer that question.

6947. Did you ever hear of cases in which persons of an inferior description and grade of life got caught where the principals were let off?—You cannot of course prosecute a man that has any thing to lose; of course a man that has any thing to lose will not keep the things in his possession.

6948. Do not you remember a case happening in the City of London, in which a porter of the name of Wright was prosecuted for a considerable amount of goods found in his possession?—Certainly not.

6949. Do you remember one since 1826?—Yes.

6950. What situation of life was he in?—A ticket porter.

6951. Was he condemned in any penalties?—Yes.

6952. Did he pay those penalties?—Yes.

6953. You have stated the amount of duties now collected upon broad plain silks to be 31 per cent.; will you state the price of some plain broad article you have lately imported, and the duty you have paid upon it?—In the article of plain gros de Naples, I have imported a few pieces. Those goods cost me, in Lyons, three francs, 90 centimes; the duty upon those was 33 per cent.

6954. Are the calculations you have given of the per centage of the duty, *ad valorem*, or upon the weight?—They are all upon the weight; and therefore the higher the value of the goods, the lower the rate of duty.

6955. Where are the watered silks you have imported made?—At Lyons.

6956. But you say that the Lyons manufacture has decreased?—Yes.

6957. Has not this large increase of the watered silk re-animated the trade?—When you speak of animating a whole manufacturing town by the operation of three or four manufacturers, it is extraordinary. I mean to say that the manufacturers at Lyons have decreased very considerably; and because there has been one article in demand a few months that would never revive the manufacture of a town.

6958. Have you any idea of the number of looms in the town?—No, the manufacture is very extensive, but the whole of my business in plain articles is done with about four houses; and in articles of a more fancy description, with four more, so that I have not absolutely twelve accounts at Lyons. They are the best manufacturers that manufacture goods for this country.

6959. Are not the manufacturers at Chaumont and St. Etienne very extensive also?—I consider them, generally speaking, very numerous, but small manufacturers.

6960. Do you consider that the quantity of French goods sold now, whether smuggled or legally imported, is greater or less than it was before 1826?—There cannot be a doubt that it has increased to a very great extent.

6961. Do you think that it is four or five times as much?—I think it is.

6962. Has not the general use of silk goods since 1826, greatly increased?—I should think generally it has, but not to that extent.

6963. You have stated that the smuggler's price is regulated by the amount of duty; has the smuggler then lowered his charge as the duty has been reduced?—Certainly.

6964. To how great an extent do you think the smuggler will lower his charge?—As far as I can ascertain from information at Calais, the lowest rate of premium that there would be any chance of being taken would be 20 per cent.

6965. What does that 20 per cent. include?—I imagine it includes all charges, from the time of shipping to the delivery.

6966. Should the price of silk goods rise again, would it not bring the rate of duty down again to the rate intended in the year 1829?—It would.

6967. Do you consider the disturbed state of Paris in 1830, and the cholera on the Continent in 1831, and the reform in England in 1832, have all had an effect in reducing the price of French silk goods?—I would rather decline answering a question so general.

6968. To

Mr.
*Robert Clay,*

25 May,
1832.

6968. To what causes do you attribute the decline in the price of French silk goods?—To the decline in the raw material.

6969. To what do you attribute the decline in the price of raw silks?—The same cause that produces the decline of cotton.

6970. Did you not assign as a reason for the large importation of foreign silks into this country in the year 1830, the state of France in that year?—Not to the increased amount; but I alluded particularly to the quantity of goods that were bought at the low prices; there were a great many goods brought in from Paris in that year.

6971. You stated that when you first went to St. Etienne, there was only one house that made one description of goods; namely, the de coupé, fit for the English market, and that they have since improved their manufacture very much, what has induced them to improve their manufacture?—The article being in general demand.

6972. Do they find any competition in England?—I should suppose there is less competition of the English against that article than any other.

6973. But they were stimulated by the chance of sale in this country to improve their manufacture?—I conceive that every manufacturer is stimulated to improve his manufacture as far as he can, for his own advantage.

6974. Do you think that French goods have decidedly improved in value since 1826?—Decidedly.

6975. Have they not found it necessary to reduce their prices, and to improve their make, in order to keep a footing in the English market?—There is no question that they have been compelled both to reduce prices and to improve the manufacture.

6976. What is the description of French goods which, after being brought into this country, are beaten by English goods?—I should say all low priced goods up to the price of four francs, can be manufactured in this country decidedly cheaper than they can be imported from France.

6977. Do you mean to say, that the British public prefer new English fancy goods to new French fancy goods of the same kind?—Certainly not; I applied what I said to plain goods.

6978. In fancy goods do you not always import from France in the first instance, or would you take a pattern from England and get it made in France?—I have frequently done it, we frequently compose our own patterns and take them over with us.

6979. Why do you give them the patterns to make, in preference to the English manufacturers?—I have had nothing to do with the English trade.

6980. Have you ever taken a pattern from an English silk, and given it to a French manufacturer to make?—Never.

6981. You have stated, that the English can easily copy the French patterns; that they can make them cheaper than the French, and produce them very quickly; why then, as the English goods are the cheapest, do you not get the patterns, or at any rate only a small quantity of the goods from France, and have the bulk of the goods made in England?—The reason I do not do that is simply this, from France I have very little competition, we know very well that it can only come from a few houses, but if I give an English manufacturer an article it is dispensed throughout the trade at once; that circumstance causes a competition between those houses, and prevents you from obtaining a profit.

6982. Do you mean that if you give a pattern to an English manufacturer, it is shown about, and becomes quite common?—No doubt of it.

6983. Could you not enter into an agreement with the manufacturer to keep it to himself?—In all probability this might be done, but I do not deal in a single article that is not French; I have quite as much to attend to in my business, and it requires as much capital as I have to employ; I cannot engage in both; I do not interfere with the English trade, and I know nothing about it.

6984. If you thought it more to your advantage to deal in the English trade, probably you would deal in the English trade?—Probably I should, but I fancy I understand the French business tolerably well, and I know nothing about the English.

6985. How do you know the English goods to be cheaper?—Merely by competition, from my customers bringing the goods into my own house, the same patterns that I have imported two or three months before, they bring into my house at a much lower price than I can get them at.

678.

6986. What

Mr.
*Robert Clay.*

25 May,
1832.

6986. What description of articles do you refer to ?—I am now alluding to what we call armures.

6987. Are those that are made in England made in Manchester or in Spitalfields ?—I do not know ; I do not know any thing upon this subject from my own knowledge.

6988. When you state that after you have imported French goods you frequently see them in the market imitated by the British manufacturer cheaper ; does that arise from their being able to make them cheaper, or because the novelty was gone off ?—There is no doubt the English can manufacture them cheaper than the French, with the duty paid.

6989. Does that observation apply to the fine articles as well as to the coarse ?—In articles of fancy, I think the French most decidedly have a preference.

6990. Do you mean that they can manufacture them cheaper without the duty, or cheaper than they will come upon paying the duty?—I mean to say, that the French manufacture them decidedly cheaper than the English without the duty, but the duty being so heavy makes the French goods much higher.

6991. Do you think that there is a sufficient quantity of gauze ribbons introduced from France illicitly to lower the price of the French gauze ribbon to the fair dealers?—No, I do not; those are circumstances that are very prejudicial to every fair trader, and what you are always subject to ; but my opinion is, that an article that has paid the duty is so much more valuable than the one that is smuggled, that 19 times out of 20 that article will sell at a higher price on account of the condition.

6992. Then, independently of price, is there not such a preference given to French fashions, the French goods would sell before the English ?—I am decidedly of opinion that there is a preference given in point of fashion to the goods of France; there is one thing I wish to give an opinion upon, relative to the French ribbons ; when we bring a set of ribbons in, the ribbon is complete in all its colours; the consequence is, that if a retailer comes into my house, he can buy a regular assortment in that pattern of every colour he wants ; but if I understand rightly from the information I have received, he cannot do so in Coventry, they introduce only a few pieces at a time, and from week to week. Now if we introduce a pattern on the 1st of May, and again on the 24th, that pattern is not worth so much to us by 20 or 25 per cent. ; and why should not that be the case with the Coventry goods. If a man that goes into a Coventry house can only get a piece of black or a piece of white, he says no, I must go and buy them where I can get a regular assortment.

6993. You stated that you thought a duty of 25 per cent. would be sufficient to prevent smuggling, and you stated that you thought they might be brought in for 20; to a person who is in a large way of business, would it not be worth his while if he could have those goods delivered to him insured against all risk, to receive them by making an advance of five per cent. ?—Certainly not; it must be against his interest to do so.

6994. If he can get them five per cent. cheaper by having them introduced in that way, would it not be worth his while to save the five per cent. ?—No, and I will state the reason ; if a man smuggles his goods there is no certainty of the time when he is to receive them, for instance, if a smuggler ships 1,000*l.* worth of goods, and I send at the same time to an agent to ship me 1,000 *l.* regularly, I shall receive mine probably in seven days, and perhaps in six or seven weeks they will receive the smuggled goods ; and, independently of the time that has elapsed, there is a great difference in the condition of the goods, from the different mode of packing, and therefore my goods are worth nearly five per cent. more to me, exclusive of the time.

6995. Are they not worth more on account of the preference that is given to new articles ?—Decidedly, and therefore that is another reason why you cannot smuggle under those circumstances.

6996. Is it not the case that a manufacturer at St. Etienne may sell 120 garnitures of gauze ribbon to you, and he may also sell 120 garnitures to an Austrian buyer, to an American, to a Swiss, and also to the home market in Paris, and that he will thus make no less than 700 garnitures of one pattern, and the whole quantity shall be so placed as not to interfere with the interests of the various buyers ; is not that the case ?—I think not.

6997. Do you think that the French manufacturers confine themselves to making the quantity ordered for the English market?—Generally speaking they do ; but
you

you observe the lengths that we ordered our ribbons, are not calculated for any other market; I want my goods of a different length from what they want them for Germany; the German wants them of a different length from what they have wanted for America; and therefore the manufacturer very seldom makes more than the extent of the order; I have never understood that it has been the interest of the manufacturer to manufacture another set on his own account, after he has manufactured for the order. If I discover that an article has been made for any other house than myself, any loss I sustain upon that pattern, would be reimbursed by that house.

6998. Is it not the case, that a great quantity of French goods made for the American market, and rejected there, are sold as jobs in this country?—Certainly not.

6999. If orders were given to the Coventry ribbon makers in the same way as you give them to St. Etienne, would there not be a regular assortment made at both places?—No doubt of it.

7000. You stated that previous to the reduction of the duty upon the thrown silk, from 14s. 8d. to 7s. 6d., a considerable quantity was smuggled; did you state that of your own knowledge?—My knowledge upon that subject arises from the information I have received from respectable houses at Calais: I have written over for the amount of goods that have been exported, and I have received an answer, extracted from the Custom House books.

7001. Were they smuggled in large quantities?—I do not know.

7002. Do you know whether they were smuggled in bales?—I do not know; I should imagine they must have been in small packages.

7003. What period do you allude to when those transactions took place?—I cannot state.

7004. In what year was it?—I cannot say.

7005. When was the duty reduced upon thrown silk?—I do not know.

7006. Does the smuggler enter at the Custom House at Calais the goods he proposes to smuggle to England?—Not the smuggler himself, but the agent.

Mr.
*Robert Clay.*

25 May,
1832.

Mr. *William Stone*, called in; and further Examined.

7007. HAVE you prepared the Statement you were requested to prepare?—I have; the numbers I am about to state are from the best sources I have, there may be some variation, but it will be but trifling. In 1828 the number of raws received in this market, under the mark DS, was 170 bales, and the number of throwns under the same mark was 37; 96 bales of raw marked ℔, and 20 bales of thrown. For 1829 DS 165 bales of raw, thrown 3; ℔ 79 bales of raw, none of thrown. For 1830 DS 123 bales of raw, and 33 bales of thrown; ℔ 94 bales of raw, and 24 bales of thrown. 1831, DS 176 bales of raw, and 34 bales of thrown; ℔, 55 bales of raw, and 30 bales of thrown. 1832, DS, 20 bales of raw, and 14 bales of thrown; ℔ 5 bales of raw, and 3 bales of thrown.

Mr.
*William Stone.*

[*The Witness delivered in the following Paper, which was read.*]

A TABLE

A TABLE showing the MONTHLY IMPORTATIONS of ITALIAN RAW and THROWN SILK, during the Years 1830 and 1831 to the 1st May 1832.

| | Organzine. | Tram. | Raw. | Waste. |
|---|---|---|---|---|
| **1830 :** | | | | |
| January | 17 | - - | 174 | 31 |
| February | 18 | - - | 54 | 12 |
| March | 19 | - - | 91 | 32 |
| April | 35 | - - | 109 | 16 |
| May | 212 | 2 | 486 | 158 |
| June | 129 | 5 | 219 | 148 |
| July | 52 | 2 | 133 | 80 |
| August | 89 | 8 | 307 | 59 |
| September | 230 | 13 | 694 | 77 |
| October | 389 | 38 | 1,094 | 64 |
| November | 367 | 18 | 979 | 123 |
| December | 163 | 24 | 231 | 53 |
| | 1,720 | 110 | 4,571 | 853 |
| **1831:** | | | | |
| January | 241 | 29 | 262 | 93 |
| February | 511 | 115 | 394 | 164 |
| March | 395 | 177 | 348 | 222 |
| April | 420 | 181 | 287 | 218 |
| May | 141 | 64 | 74 | 90 |
| June | 61 | 20 | 36 | 110 |
| July | 25 | 18 | 111 | 48 |
| August | 52 | 4 | 462 | 36 |
| September | 59 | 12 | 471 | 65 |
| October | 94 | 9 | 622 | 33 |
| November | 66 | 10 | 567 | 86 |
| December | 38 | 5 | 194 | 62 |
| | 2,103 | 644 | 3,828 | 1,227 |
| **1832:** | | | | |
| January | 24 | 2 | 140 | 66 |
| February | 81 | - - | 196 | 81 |
| March | 87 | 2 | 196 | 82 |
| April | 40 | - - | 68 | 131 |
| | 232 | 4 | 600 | 360 |

7008. Do you include waste in the raws?—I do not.

7009. Do not those quantities show those parties to have increased their trade in organzine, since the 3 s. 6 d. duty upon organzine came into operation?—From the year 1828 up to the present time it would appear that they have increased it. In the season of 1830 to 1831 the importation of raws of DS was 168, of throwns 65; and the Ɖ 99 bales of raw, and 54 bales of thrown. From the 1st of August 1831, up to the beginning of May 1832, for DS the raws are 128, and the throwns 14 bales; for Ɖ the raws are 39 bales, and the throwns 3. I think this statement bears out the opinion I have already given, of the great falling off in foreign throwns this season.

7010. Have you got the account of trams?—No; but in my last examination I stated, that the importation of the season, from the 1st of August 1830 to the 1st of August 1831, for trams of all qualities, was 706; and from the 1st of August 1831 to the 1st of May 1832 it has fallen to 62 bales.

7011. Can you give the same account with regard to trams that you have given with regard to organzines?—For 1830 we received trams of DS 16 bales, none of Ɖ. For 1831 we received of DS 54 bales, and of Ɖ 2 bales; now the whole of this, except three bales, were received from August 1830 to August 1831.

7012. What do you consider to have occasioned that increase?—The price obtained for the article in the thrown state in this country during the summer of 1830.

7013. Does it not appear from this, that the parties are importing raws and throwns in more equal quantities?—No; it is as 128 bales of raw to 14 bales of thrown in the one case, and 39 bales of raw to 3 bales of thrown in the other.

7014. As both those parties in the year 1830–31, sent the raws and throwns in more equal quantities than they did in 1829, is it not a fair inference that the price

of

Mr.
*William Stone.*

25 May,
1832.

of the one may aid the price of the other, and that they find an advantage in sending thrown silk to England?—I do not think the facts bear out the question; I stated, in a former examination, that the markets in 1830 towards August onwards, induced a great importation of thrown, and it appears that these men commenced sending from that period to that time in 1831; to August 1830, DS only sent 2 bales, JÞ nothing; and I suppose the strong inducement arising from the state of this market at the commencement of August 1830, tempted them to embark in the thrown.

7015 Is it not sometimes the practice for the broker to take the raw silk when thrown from the throwster, and sell it for the principal?—That was one of the questions that was put to me before, and I beg leave to submit that it is one of the questions that should not remain on the Evidence, nor any thing relating to my own business as a broker; as to other men's business, as brokers, they must answer for themselves.

7016. You said that the broker's commission is five-eighths per cent.; if the merchant is not satisfied with the person to whom you sell, do not you guarantee one per cent.?—I beg leave to decline answering that question.

7017. Is the silk usually sold on a credit of five months?—It is.

7018. If paid for in cash does not the merchant allow 2½ per cent.?—He does.

7019. That is, if paid for within 14 days?—Yes.

7020. If the silk is then thrown, and returned from the throwster to the broker for sale to the consumer, is not a further guarantee for sale usual?—That I must decline answering.

7021. Is not the credit for thrown silk six months?—No, five months.

7022. What is the usual discount upon thrown silk?—Upon foreign thrown silk 2½ per cent., upon English thrown silk 3 per cent.

7023. Do not the manufacturers in Spitalfields generally pay cash for their silk?—Generally.

7024. Was that the case formerly?—Not so much as it is now.

7025. Have you reason to know, that the manufacturers generally sell their manufactured goods for cash?—I believe they do.

7026. You have stated, that you think the duty upon foreign thrown silk is a tax upon the manufacturer in Spitalfields; upon the supposition of the continuance of the present duties, what will be the effect upon the manufacturers of Spitalfields?—I think the tendency will be to cause the trade to go into the country, unless it is counteracted by preventing the importation of foreign goods, either by prohibition, or any other method that may be thought proper.

7027. What will be the effect upon the commission throwster?—It depends upon the place where the commission throwster may be situated; if he is in the North the more trade there is in that part the better he will be circumstanced; if in the West it must be certain destruction to him.

7028. Do any of the commission throwsters live in the North now?—I believe a great many.

7029. Do the Manchester manufacturers throw their silk themselves or by commission throwsters?—Both ways.

7030. Is it your opinion, that the Manchester manufacturers have already injured the trade in Spitalfields?—The trade having extended there, of course they have obtained a portion of it, and so far it must be to the prejudice of the London manufacturers; but this is fair competition.

---

*Lunæ, 28° die Maii, 1832.*

EDWARD AYSHFORD SANFORD, ESQUIRE, in the Chair.

Mr. *Francesco Caffi*, called in; and Examined.

7031. WHERE do you reside?—At Bergamo, near Milano, in Lombardy.

7032. How long have you been employed in the silk trade, and in what branch?—I have been from twelve to fifteen years in the silk trade, in reeling silk from the cocoons, in throwing, and as agent to a mercantile house in England.

7033. Did you in Italy raise any cocoons yourself, or buy them?—We raised some ourselves, but the most part we bought.

Mr.
*Francesco Caffi.*

28 May,
1832.

678.

7034. Will

7034. Will you state whether those merchants who throw and sell, are generally those who raise the cocoons, or whether they generally buy them?—The reeler buys the cocoons in the public market, at the price of the day, and by private contract, to pay three or four months after; but some give the money in advance, it depends upon the condition of the person, whether he is rich or poor.

7035. Is Bergamo, where you resided, one of the principal places for throwing silk?—Yes.

7036. What is the general manner of buying the cocoons?—In open market; and by private contract, three or four months before the crop is ready.

7037. Do the landlords there frequently make advances to those who raise the cocoons, and what are the general terms?—Some advance one-third, and then they send the cocoons to the reeler, and after the price is settled, they give the remainder of the money to some labourers; they give half the price of the cocoons.

7038. Do you mean for the supply of the mulberry trees?—The landlord is obliged to keep leaves and seed.

7039. It is a sort of partnership between the labourer and the landlord?—Yes.

7040. What portion does the landlord get, and what portion does the labourer get?—Half each.

7041. What does the landlord supply?—Mulberry leaves and eggs.

7042. Does he supply houses?—Sometimes he does, sometimes not; there are some of the tenants who are proprietors and labourers at the same time, and do the whole.

7043. In what months of the year is the reeling done?—In June, July, August, and September; the crop in cocoons is over in June, and the reeling goes on till September, and sometimes till October, if the crop is good.

7044. Does the crop vary much in different years?—Yes, by the season, which is sometimes later, sometimes earlier; if there is a hailstorm or frost, it effects the general produce.

7045. Will you state who are the parties that reel the cocoons off, and what are the expenses charged for reeling?—There are a great many persons who reel for others, some reel for themselves.

7046. What is the expense of reeling?—The expense for reeling silk from three to four cocoons are from six to seven Italian livres; and from four to five cocoons, six livres.

7047. How many deniers weight will the first be, and how many the last?—The three to four cocoons will be 20 to 24 deniers, the four to five will be 24 to 28, and the five to six 26 to 32, depending on the quality of the cocoons.

7048. What is the value in English money of the Italian livre?—Seven-pence halfpenny.

7049. In what manner is the reeling paid for, and what is the amount by the pound?—The woman employed at the boiler receives one livre and five sous per day, with bed and board; and the girl who turns the reel gets thirteen sous per day, and the same board and lodging; the quantity reeled differs according to the season, for in June and July they work both earlier and longer than at a later period of the year. In June and July, and till the middle of August, they work from four in the morning till eight at night, and they then do perhaps a rubo per day; but later in the year, not much more than half a rubo.

7050. What is a rubo?—It is ten pounds, and a rubo of cocoons gives about two pounds of raw silk.

7051. Of Italian weight?—Yes; an Italian pound is not quite three quarters of an English pound.

7052. You say that the people work a certain number of hours in June and July, and receive certain wages; are they paid the same wages in those months in which they cannot work so many hours in the day?—In August, September and October, they receive one-third less.

7053. Have you any statement of the expenses, in addition to the wages of the woman and girl which attend the operation?—The other expenses are for rent, taxes, repairs, &c.

7054. To what do they amount in addition?—With the 25 sous, and the 13 (calculating 20 sous, to the livre) it will make, with other expenses, six to seven livres in all per rubo, differing according to the quality.

7055. Can you state to what it will amount per pound weight of 16 ounces, in English?—Four livres and a half, about 2 s. 10 d. English.

7056. The

Mr.
*Francesco Caffi.*

28 May,
1832.

7056. The livre you speak of is always the Italian livre?—Yes; 7½ d. English, or 20 sous of Lombardy.

7057. Will you state the cost in English money for an English pound of sixteen ounces?—At six livres for the rubo, it is equal to 2 s. 6 d. per English pound of 16 ounces; and 2 s. 11 d. when the rate is seven livres.

7058. Will you state what are the charges for throwing tram, and what is paid for winding, doubling, twisting and waste, and what is the duty?—Forty Italian sous per Italian lb., that is one shilling and three-pence.

7059. How much of that do you pay for winding?—Fifteen sous per pound.

7060. What do you pay for doubling?—Ten sous; and for twisting fine, five sous; other expenses, rent, taxes, &c. computed at five sous, to which, add profit five sous, making together 40 sous, equal to 1 s. 3 d. English.

7061. How much is the waste?—Nearly three per cent. on tram, that will be about eight sous on an Italian pound, deducting the value of the waste.

7062. That is all that is paid, except the duty?—Yes; the duty is nine sous, about 3½ d. English; but the raw silk on export from Lombardy pays double.

7063. That will, together, be 1 s. 9½ d. in the money of this country?—Yes.

7064. How much would you add to make it up to the English pound?—Per English pound 2 s., exclusive of duty on export.

7065. Are the Committee to understand that those 40 sous are for an Italian pound of 12 ounces?—Yes.

7066. Are the Committee to understand that the whole expense in winding, doubling, twisting and waste for an English pound, is three livres and four sous, equal to 2 s.?—Yes, 48 sous to an Italian pound, or 64 for an English pound of 16 ounces, exclusive of export duty.

7067. What are the expenses of throwing organzine?—The winding is the same, 15 sous, or 5⅝ d.; doubling 10 sous, or 3¾ d.; twisting and throwing 13 sous, or 4¾ d.; rent, water power, taxes and repairs 12 sous, or 4½ d.; making 2 livres and 10 sous, or 1 s. 6¼ d. English; then there is profit of 10 sous, or 3¾ d.; making a total of 3 livres, or 1 s. 10½ d. English.

7068. How much do you add for waste?—The waste in throwing organzine is generally five per cent., that is 16 sous per lb. Then there is the duty of 9 sous on coming out of Lombardy.

7069. What do you allow for the difference of weight to make it English?—One livre and 5 sous; making, with duty, 5 livres and 10 sous.

7070. That is equal to 3 s. 2 d. English, for the English lb. of 16 ounces?—Yes; omitting the Austrian export duty, which is 9 sous the Italian lb., or 12 the English; adding the 12 sous, or 4½ d., the amount will be 3 s. 6½ d.

7071. At what number of deniers do you calculate this silk?—At an average throughout the year of from 24 to 28 deniers.

7072. Do the throwsters for this amount guarantee against all damage and loss, and engage to return weight for weight?—Yes, they do; including the waste.

7073. Is the amount you have stated the average charge to the person sending the raw silk to the throwster?—Yes.

7074. May that be taken to be the general price throughout Lombardy?—Yes; we throw from July to December at 3 livres and 5 sous per lb.; and then from January till June we throw at from 50 to 55 sous.

7075. Do the throwsters throw all the year, or for how many months?—For eight or nine months.

7076. Why do they not throw the remaining four months?—Because the greater part of the raw silk is sent to France and England; but Switzerland takes only about 50 bales of raw.

7077. Are you aware what the charges of throwing in Piedmont are?—I think 10 or 15 sous more than in Lombardy.

7078. Why are they more in Piedmont than in Lombardy?—Because there the exportation of raw silk is not allowed; and they are obliged to give it to the throwster, and he gets high prices; besides that, it is better thrown in Piedmont than in Lombardy. There is some in Lombardy well thrown, but it is better generally in Piedmont, as they have particular regulations respecting the reeling and throwing of silk there.

7079. What laws are there respecting the throwing silk in Piedmont?—There are laws that require the silk to be reeled of certain qualities, clean and good, and every thing necessary to be done must be done to get it up well.

678.

7080. Have

Mr.
*Francesco Caffi.*

28 May,
1832.

7080. Have they public examiners?—Yes, there are such persons; but in Lombardy there are no regulations, every body does as he pleases.

7081. You consider the Piedmont silk as better thrown than that of Lombardy? Yes.

7082. Can you account for its being better done; because there is a better demand?—Piedmont thrown has always had a high character.

7083. Has there been any law in Lombardy passed in your recollection to prevent the exportation of raw silk?—There was, in about 1816; my father was charged by the throwsters to present a petition to the Emperor of Austria, who is King of Lombardy.

7084. Was he in the same business with you?—Yes, he was; and he was charged to present a petition to the Emperor of Austria, praying that he would prohibit the exportation of raw silk. It was complied with, and exportation prohibited; but afterwards the landlords and tenants petitioned the Emperor to remove the prohibition, because it tended to lessen the growth of silk in the country. Lombardy produces three or four times more silk than they are able to throw.

7085. How long did that prohibition continue?—Only a few months.

7086. Has there been any prohibition since?—There has been a great many petitions, but prohibition has not since been granted.

7087. What is the lowest price at which you have known organzine to be thrown in Lombardy?—Fifty sous at the poor mills, they must pay rent and keep the persons employed; thus they are obliged sometimes to keep on at a low price.

7088. You have stated that the mills do not work the whole year in Lombardy? —No.

7089. What becomes of the work people in those mills during those months?— They do nothing at all; we are obliged to give them a certain sum, 100 livres the part of the year they are not employed, in advance.

7090. Is that deducted from their wages?—At the end of every week they leave 2 or 3 livres when they are at work.

7091. What is the regulation on that head?—There is a law that allows them to advance during the time they are not working, 100 livres to each labourer, and 50 to the women.

7092. That money is repaid during the season when they work?—Yes; and if they go to another mill, the master who takes up that person is obliged to pay the advance.

7093. What is the reason that the mills do not work all the year round?—Because the raw silk finds a better profit from selling in France or England.

7094. The land owners were incorrect in their petition, when they stated that the mills could not throw the whole?—In part they were correct, because the crops differ very much; one year is as much as three years at another time.

7095. On the average, could the mills in Italy, if worked the whole year, throw all the silk produced in Italy?—No, not half.

7096. Must not the quantity thrown in Lombardy depend upon the price which thrown and raw silk bear in England and other parts of the Continent?—Yes, if Germany and France give good profits for them, they will send them there.

7097. Have you any idea of the quantity of silk thrown in Lombardy?—No, there is no account.

7098. You have stated that the mills throw from eight to nine months, and that they do not throw after that time, because the raw silk finds a better market; why does the raw silk find a better market at the expiration of that eight months, and not before?—There are a great many reelers; they are obliged to give the raw silk to the throwsters because they advance money.

7099. They advance money to the reelers for certain quantities?—Yes, and this silk is always thrown.

7100. If the price of thrown silk in Germany or England or France afforded a profit better than the sale of raw silk, would they not continue working all the year?—Certainly.

7101. In point of fact do they usually work more than the eight or nine months? —About two-thirds of the year.

7102. They could not work the whole year round?—Yes, if the price of organzine was better.

7103. If

Mr
*Francesco Caffi.*

28 May,
1832.

7103. If they did so, do you think they would be able generally to throw all the crop?—No, only half.

7104. If they could get a better price for the organzine they would work more?—Yes.

7105. Has it always been the case that they worked only two-thirds of the year?—There are some years when organzine is in great demand in France and Germany, and then they have worked more.

7106. Have you a regular account of the sales of silk in the different parts of Europe at Bergamo?—Yes, every week.

7107. Is it your opinion that the quantity of thrown manufactured depends upon this price current?—Upon the orders we receive.

7108. Are you certain that the mills, if worked the whole year, could not throw the whole of the silk produced?—Quite clear they could not.

7109. Can you state the quantity of silk worked by the Italian mills?—No, we have no register.

7110. Can you state on an estimate or average, the quantity of pounds of silk produced in all Lombardy?—That will be about three millions of Italian pounds in all.

7111. Do you mean on an average of years?—Some years there are more, some years less.

7112. Of that quantity how much is thrown?—That depends upon the year, in some years more than half, in some years one-third; it depends upon the price and the demand.

7113. Does the quantity thrown depend on the crop in Italy, or does it depend also on the crop in France?—It depends partly on the crop in France.

7114. In what manner does the deficiency or excess of crop in France affect the exports from Italy?—Sometimes they get two-thirds of the crop of Italy when the crop in France is deficient, and when the trade is going on brisk; but when the crop is large in France, the demand is smaller, and we send more to England, or Switzerland, or Germany.

7115. Do you consider the prices you have named of 2 s. for the English pound of tram, and 3 s. 2 d. for organzine for the English pound, a remunerating price to the Italian throwster?—Yes, they would be glad to work all the year for that price.

7116. Do other branches of manufacture or agricultural labour receive the same profit as that which is gained by the labour in silk?—It is less than any other branch.

7117. Are the wages of labour in throwing silk larger than in any other business?—The earnings are nearly equal.

7118. Are the Committee to understand, that the quantity of silk thrown or raised will depend upon the relation it bears to other kinds of produce of the country, that if grain is dear there will be more grain raised; or if silk is dear there will be more silk raised?—Yes, but not in the same year, for it requires five or six years to raise the mulberry tree, they cannot gather leaves before three years ingrafted.

7119. Is there not some advantage to the throwster in working the silk fresh from the cocoons?—Yes, there is a little advantage, but it is not much.

7120. Does not the Italian throwster generally avail himself of that advantage in obtaining those sorts of silks?—That lasts only three or four months during the time of reeling; afterwards you must buy from the merchants.

7121. Do not they get them from the reelers?—The throwster is not the buyer, he receives the raw silk from the merchants, from private individuals for the most part.

7122. Do the mulberry leaves ever fail?—Yes, very often.

7123. On that depends the supply of the crop?—Yes.

7124. If the mulberry trees come out late in the season the crop is injured, is it not?—Yes, and if they come too early, the frost injures them, and if late, then they are injured by the heat.

7125. Of the three millions of pounds, can you state to what countries, and in what proportion the exports generally go?—It depends upon the crop in France, whether it is good or bad, how much is sent there, and the state of trade, whether it is going on briskly. If England calls for raw in preference to thrown, raw is sent; and as Germany, Russia and Switzerland order, so exports are made to those

678.                                                                                     countries.

Mr.
*Francesco Caffi.*

28 May,
1832.

countries.　Now we are sending organzine to Russia, there being a profit of 2 *s.* more on sending it to Russia than to England.

7126. Can you state, on the average, how many bales of each sort go to the countries you have mentioned ?—No, I cannot.

7127. Can you tell, on an average, how many pounds weight of raw are sent to England every year?—No, I cannot, because there are a great many smuggled.

7128. Can you tell the total quantity that goes to France and England together? —No, I cannot.

7129. Have you any means of giving that information to the Committee ?— From Italy.

7130. Do you know the amount of all the trade of Italy ?—That of Piedmont is 2,000,000 lbs. Italian, that we know, for it is registered.

7131. Do you know the amount of the produce of all the other states of Italy ? —No.

7132. Are you aware that in 1830 a very considerably increased quantity of organzine was sent to England, and if so, do you know the reason ?—Because the Revolution of France made such an impression in Italy, they were afraid of losing it by sending it there.　The Italians, generally, are sending in England, because they draw for three-fourths of the value, and they pay four per cent. interest, while the interest in Italy is six per cent.

7133. Could the same reason operate in 1831 ?—No.

7134. There was a larger increase then?—Then the manufacturing was not going on, and they were obliged to send here ; if any one will look at the prices at that time, it will be found, there was a loss of 1 *s.* and 1 *s.* 6 *d.* a pound sending here.

7135. If that was the reason for sending the thrown silk here on account of the revolution, and the state of France, would not the very same reason operate to induce them to send the raw also ?—No ; because the crop was in June, July, August or September ; we had it thrown at that time.

7136. Did you send any silk here in 1830 and 1831 ?—Yes.

7137. Is any silk smuggled out of Piedmont ?—Yes, a great deal of raw.

7138. Is any smuggled into Lombardy?—Yes.

7139. What is the premium for smuggling from Piedmont at which silks can be conveyed out of the country?—From 10 to 15 per cent.

7140. Does that per centage depend upon the number of military there ?—Yes ; the police officers or custom house officers now form a cordon sanitaire, in consequence of the fear of the cholera morbus.

7141. What is the inducement to smuggle the raw silk of Piedmont into Lombardy ?—Because they get a better price in Lombardy and England than they do in Piedmont.

7142. It is not for the purpose of throwing it there ?—No, but to send it to other countries in a raw state.

7143. Do you know for what particular kinds of manufacture the raw silk of Piedmont is essentially necessary ?—I am not acquainted with the manufacture of goods ; but I know that it is for ribbons and crapes.

7144. Is it white or yellow ?—White.

7145. Is the silk you speak of what is called Novi ?—Yes.

7146. With regard to the raw article, what are the largest mills for throwing silk in Italy ?—Mills to throw from 10,000 to 12,000 lbs. in the year.

7147. Do you mean mills that would throw that in the whole year ?—Yes.

7148. Can you state what will be the rent of such mills ?—From sixty to ninety pounds, depending on circumstances whether in a town or out of a town.

7149. Are they worked by water?—Yes.

7150. There is no steam power?—No.

7151. Have there been any improvements in the machinery of late ?—There has been a little improvement in doubling the thread, and in winding ; but the people are prejudiced against the introduction of machinery, but there are some now for doubling.

7152. Is the whole done by hand?—Yes, principally ; some improvements in doubling have been introduced lately.

7153. Has any improvement taken place in the quality of silk within the last ten years ?—Yes.

7154. To what is that owing?—It is owing to greater attention, and to taking
better

Mr.
*Francesco Caffi.*
—————
28 May,
1832.

better care in the working; they get up a better article, and a better price being obtained, every one is endeavouring to improve the quality.

7155. Is there any improvement in the throwing of organzine?—No, only in the tram.

7156. Are the persons who own the mills generally men of capital?—Middling. To carry on the throwing four or five thousand pounds is sufficient capital for a large mill to make advances to the reelers, who are generally needy.

7157. Are there many reelers who are spinners also?—A few.

7158. You say a mill throwing off 10,000 to 12,000 lbs. a year, would let for 60 l. to 90 l. a year, does that rent include all the taxes?—The taxes and repairs are all charged separately, that was in the 12 sous.

7159. What additional charges are there on a mill (taxes, repairs, water power, &c.) paying a rent of 75 l.?—Twelve sous a pound; the profit and water power, and tax, and every thing is included in the 12 sous; I have before stated, that includes superintendence also.

7160. Does France use large quantities of Lombardy organzine and tram, or does she chiefly import Piedmont organzine?—That depends upon the quality and fashion of the silk goods.

7161. She will take that which is most adapted for her trade?—Yes; but for ribbons it is all Piedmont.

7162. Are all sorts of thrown silk sent to Russia?—Generally the best qualities.

7163. Very fine, and very good?—Yes.

7164. Are they finer than those sent to England?—No.

7165. Are not the best raws required for those thrown silks?—To make good organzine good raws are required.

7166. You spoke of some alteration made in the manner of throwing trams lately, was not that alteration made to adapt the trams to the English market?—Yes; it was only in case England should want tram to be able to send it here, but there is no profit at all from the sending tram to this market.

7167. If you worked the mill the whole year round, you would not pay an additional rent for it?—No; the mills are always let for a lease of nine years.

7168. So that in point of fact you might throw one-third more silk without any increased cost in rent?—Yes; there is no alteration in rent, but some years some mills may have little or none to throw.

7169. Who are the parties; are they men, women or children, who are employed in winding?—Women.

7170. Who are the parties who reel the silk?—All women.

7171. Do they do it in their own houses or in factories?—In factories.

7172. How much can they earn a week?—In June and July they do eleven pounds Italian per week from the cocoons.

7173. Do they work six days in the week?—Yes.

7174. A woman will receive, exclusive of her board, seven livres and a half, or 4 s. 8 d.?—Yes.

7175. Will you state at what you estimate the weekly expense of board and lodging for a woman who receives 4 s. 8 d. in cash per week?—Seven-pence or eight-pence a day, a great number living together.

7176. What does she receive for her 7 d. or 8 d.?—Breakfast, consisting of a piece of white bread and cheese, and wine, that is at seven or eight o'clock in the morning; for dinner at twelve, two pieces of bread, soup, meat, and wine; and at three o'clock two pieces of bread, and some fruit and wine; in the evening sometimes they have Indian corn made into a kind of pudding.

7177. What meat do they receive, and how much?—Two or three ounces in the day.

7178. Of what meat?—Sometimes of mutton, sometimes of beef; they have not always the same kind of meat.

7179. Would this be the ordinary food of a peasant?—No; the silk workers must be kept well, because it is very tiresome to work from three or four in the morning till nine at night.

7180. This is better than the ordinary food of the labouring classes?—Yes.

7181. You know that this is the diet upon which they live for those three or four months?—Yes.

7182. Are the children who wind fed in the same manner?—Yes; all the persons employed in winding, reeling and turning the cocoons, are fed in the same manner.

7183. If the board of a grown up person cost 8 d. a day, what do you reckon

678.                                                                                          the

Mr.
*Francesco Caffi.*

28 May,
1832.

the board of the girls to cost?—There is not much difference, the children are from eleven to twelve years old, sometimes more; they go in the place of the boiler alternately.

7184. Are they fed on Sunday too?—Yes.

7185. They do not eat meat on the fast days, of course?—No.

7186. Those are pretty frequent, are they not?—Yes, twice a week, Friday, and Saturday.

7187. They eat dried fish then?—Some dried fish, and some sweet food, with vegetables.

7188. When you state 8*d.* per day as the expense of keeping those people, do you not think that is over-rated?—I think not.

7189. Do you consider that it will cost 8*d.* a day to keep persons of this description in Lombardy?—Yes, nearly; but it depends on the price of corn, meat, &c.

7190. How long does this harvest (silk) generally continue?—June, July, to the 17th of August; in August, September and October, a reduction takes place.

7191. As the autumn advances, they gradually diminish the time of work?—Yes.

7192. They receive the same food the whole of the time?—Yes.

7193. Is the reeling considered an unhealthy or hard labour?—It is a very hard labour; we are obliged to keep the persons in good health, and they must be in a good temperature.

7194. Are women principally employed in winding?—Yes, and all by hand.

7195. How many pounds in the week will they wind?—One pound and one-third, about 15 ounces and half per day.

7196. How much do they receive per pound?—Fifteen sous per pound, or 5⅝*d.* English.

7197. At that rate, how much will their wages be per week?—Six livres and 10 sous, or 3*s.* 9*d.*

7198. Do they board themselves?—Yes, they take the silk to their own houses.

7199. This is a nett money payment?—Yes.

7200. How do you manage as to the waste?—They bring the silk on the bobbins, and return the waste; each is separately weighed.

7201. What waste is there in the winding?—Generally half the waste on silk is in winding and half in throwing.

7202. On an hundred pounds, how much waste is there in winding and throwing?—There is on an average from four to five per cent.

7203. How many months in the year does the winding go on?—All the year.

7204. As long as the silk mills are employed, the winders are employed?—Yes; in the winter we have warm rooms and fires.

7205. The winding is done at their own houses?—Yes.

7206. The simple machinery they use is provided by themselves?—Yes.

7207. What have they of machinery beyond their swifts?—They have very little, the value of all is not above 30*s.*

7208. Is the operation performed by one woman only, or do their children assist?—Sometimes the girls assist, but they seldom require assistance; a girl of 15 years can do it herself.

7209. Who are employed in doubling?—They are generally girls.

7210. Where do they double, in the factories or at home?—In the factories.

7211. How many pounds per week will one girl do?—Twenty pounds.

7212. What is paid per week?—They are paid 10 sous per pound, making 10 livres or 6*s.* 3*d.*

7213. That is about 1*s.* a day?—Yes.

7214. Does one girl earn 6*s.* 3*d.* in a week?—Yes.

7215. Have you paid that yourself?—I have.

7216. What number of hours do they work for that?—As they do it by the pound, they come early in the morning and stay late; they make generally fourteen hours.

7217. Is there any expensive machinery furnished by the people themselves for doubling?—No, they only have to keep it clean and in order; if it is injured, they have to pay for that.

7218. Does it occupy any portion of their time to keep their machinery in order?—No, only two hours on the Saturday evening, the proprietor has it cleaned at the end of the season.

7219. Are

Mr.
*Francesco Caffi.*

28 May,
1832.

7219. Are the twisting and throwing done by men principally ?—Yes, there are some grown up lads, but no women.

7220. How many pounds per week will each man twist and throw?—Twenty pounds nearly.

7221. You speak of that on the average ?—The average may be a little less.

7222. Is that owing to their being inferior kinds of silk ?—It is owing principally to the season ; winter is not so favourable for this work as summer.

7223. How much is paid in winter ?—Thirteen sous per pound.

7224. That is 8 *s.* 1½ *d.* per week ?—Yes.

7225. What number of hours do they work ?—From six in the morning till 10 at night, 14 or 16 hours.

7226. What time do you allow for meals in that time ?—They take what they like, about two hours a day.

7227. So that they would actually be at work 14 hours a day ?—Yes.

7228. Do you consider that a fair average for wages, or a high average ?—A fair average.

7229. They work by the piece, and have no board ?—Yes, by the piece and no board.

7230. Exclusive of the three classes, you have a superintendent in each room, have you not ?—Yes, and a scaleman.

7231. Is your superintendent hired by the year ?—Yes.

7232. What wages does he get ?—Six hundred livres a year to 700.

7233. Does he board himself?—Sometimes he has his board, but not always.

7234. What wages does the foreman receive who takes in and sends out the goods received ?—Six hundred livres a year to 700.

7235. Do you include in the estimate you have given of 12 sous, you before referred to, the rent and water power, taxes, and every expense of that kind?—Yes.

7236. When you say that a man can perform this operation upon 20 lbs. in a week, do you mean that he can both twist it and throw it ?—Yes.

7237. Are not twisting and throwing distinct operations?—Yes.

7238. Supposing the silk to be intended to undergo both operations, do you mean that both operations can be performed on 20 lbs. in a week ?—Yes.

7239. Does the same man superintend the twisting and the throwing?—Yes.

7240. The doubling takes place after the twisting, and before the throwing?—Yes, there is six sous and a half for twisting.

7241. The twisting and throwing costing 8 *s.* 1½ *d.* for 20 lbs., how do you distinguish that from the doubling, inasmuch as that is an intermediate operation ; are the Committee to understand, that the silk is brought into the mill after being wound, that it is then twisted, that it is then doubled, that it is then thrown, but that it is twisted and thrown by the same person?—Yes, who receives the amount I have stated for doing it.

7242. How do you account for the paying a superintendent 600 livres to 700 a year, which amounts to little more than 1 *s.* a day, whilst a man throwing silk receives his 13 sous per lb. or 14 *d.* per day, will you explain how this is?—Because the superintendent has only light work, moving about, giving out and looking over the silk during a couple of hours in the day, and another couple of hours a day taking the work in.

7243. Is he in the factory all the day ?—No, only four or five hours.

7244. Is he answerable for the safety of the silk and every thing in the mill ?—No.

7245. Who is responsible for that ?—The men who throw.

7246. They are answerable for producing the quantity of silk ?—Yes.

7247. Are the superintendents engaged by the year ?—Yes.

7248. While the throwsters are only for the time they are employed?—Just so.

7249. Can you state in what manner the persons employed in the mills, while they are at work, are occupied when the mills are standing still?—They have a right to ask for the 100 livres in advance ; but if they find work in any place they do not call for it, but they generally ask for the money, and the shopkeepers let them have things for their subsistence during that time, and they run into debt, besides the 100 livres, trusting to repay when they get into work again ; the throwsters like to keep them a little in debt, as they are then sure of having them again when the season begins.

7250. Do

Mr.
*Francesco Caffi.*

28 May,
1832.

7250. Do the throwsters engage invariably to do the work by a certain day, when they receive silk to throw?—Yes; there is a stipulated time, one, two or three months, according to quantity.

7251. If they engage to deliver silk on the 1st of August, but should only deliver it on the 10th of August for instance, are they liable, in case of any change in the market, if the merchant loses by the market falling?—Yes, the throwster is liable; unless, as sometimes happens, the delay should arise from an accidental cause; such as a failure in the necessary supply of water.

7252. Would that be admitted?—Not by law, but a reasonable man would admit it.

7253. The law is imperative, if the party chooses to put it into execution?—Yes.

7254. Although the law is strict as to the penalty being paid in case of their being beyond the time, is it in point of practice often enforced?—Sometimes it is.

7255. Is it frequently called for?—It happens perhaps once or twice in a year.

7256. Who pays the carriage from the filatures to the mill and back again?—The proprietor of the silk, but that is trifling.

7257. You have been asked as to the respectability and wealth of the persons who throw silk; you state that some of them are persons worth 4,000 *l.* or 5,000 *l.* English, inasmuch as it is necessary that they should make advances to the reelers?—Yes, I said so.

7258. Are not some of them persons of very great wealth?—There are some of them that are.

7259. Are Bellarbio, Befani, Uboldi, and Brunati?—They are all persons of great wealth, and there are others also.

7260. Those persons, as well as many others, are persons of great wealth?—Yes.

7261. Do you think any of them are worth 100,000 *l.* English money?—Yes, and much more; but then the persons mentioned are merchants and bankers as well.

7262. Are there not some who are only throwsters, and are people of great wealth?—But few.

7263. The persons of great wealth are generally merchants and bankers, as well as throwsters?—Yes.

7264. Frizzoni, Carissime, Piazzoni, and Caroli?—They are all wealthy.

7265. Are there many of considerable wealth engaged in the throwing trade in Italy?—Some such are reelers and throwsters.

7266. The persons engaged in the trade may vary as to their wealth; but, generally speaking, they are thriving opulent persons?—Yes.

7267. The trade cannot be very well carried on without?—No.

7268. Is the information you have given respecting the throwing mills confined to the mills of Bergamo?—And of Milan.

7269. Do your observations extend to the whole of the mills of that district?—Yes, generally, Bergamo, Bressia, Milan, Como and Brianza.

7270. Is it white or yellow?—White.

7271. Will you state what expenses are charged to you as a shipper by the English merchant or agent in London, for a bale of organzine 240 lbs. English, taking the value at 25 *s.* (20 to 22 deniers)?—There is a printed statement I have with me, the duty is 42 *l.*, the carriage from Calais to London 12 *s.*, the London city duty of 1 *d.* per lb., 1 *l.* stamp, and other small expenses 2 *l.* 6 *s.*, assurance 1 *l.* 1 *s.*, insurance against fire 15 *s.*, making the expense in London altogether 47 *l.* 14 *s.*; the interest at 4 per cent. for four months, upon the expenses 12 *s.* 9 *d.*, brokerage 5-8ths per cent. 1 *l.* 17 *s.* 6 *d.* a commission and *del credere* 4 per cent. on 300 *l.* 12 *l.*, making 62 *l.* 4 *s.* 3 *d.*, that leaves 237 *l.* 15 *s.* 9 *d.*; two months interest, at 4 per cent. 1 *l.* 11 *s.* 9 *d.*, that leaves 236 *l.* 4 *s.* nett, to be received in London by a bill at three months. The expense from Italy down to Calais, including packing, carriage, &c., is 137 Austrian livres; duty out of Lombardy 135, making together 272 Austrian livres, or 9 *l.* 1 *s.* 4 *d.*, which, deducted from 236 *l.* 4 *s.* leaves 227 *l.* 2 *s.* 8 *d.* nett.

7272. What per centage is the whole amount of those charges, including the two months' interest upon the sale price in London?—Nearly 25 per cent.

7273. What is the difference in charge suppose you send raw silk here?—A bale

bale of raw silk of the same quality, consisting of 240 lbs., would be worth perhaps about 20 s. per lb., or 240 l.; the English duty is only 1 l. sterling, freight from Calais 12 s., London city dues 13 s. 6 d., agency and other expenses 2 l. 6 s., sea assurance 1 l., ditto against fire 12 s., making 6 l. 13 s. 6 d.; interest for four months about 4 s. 10 d., brokerage at 5-8ths per cent. 1 l. 10 s., commission and *del credere* 9 l. 12 s., making 17 l. 10 s. 4 d.; that being deducted from 240 l. leaves 222 l. 9 s. 8 d.; then there are the expenses from Lombardy to Calais, with duty out of Lombardy, 270 Austrian livres, or 9 l., packing, carriage, &c. 4 l. 13 s. 9 d., making 13 l. 13 s. 4 d., leaving 208 l. 16 s. 4 d. nett.

7274. Taking the expense from Milan to Calais, duty included, at 13 l. 13 s. 4 d., and the expenses to and in London at 17 l. 10 s. 4 d., together 31 l. 3 s. 8 d.. what per centage will that be on the 240 l.?—About 13 per cent.

7275. Is there any difference in the expenses on tram?—There is only 1 s. 6 d. difference in the English duty in Lombardy, the expenses are all the same.

7276. The expenses and charges on the thrown in London would be 63 l. 16 s., and on the raw 17 l. 10 s. 4 d.?—Yes, as the account shows.

7277. It appears that if the duty and expense, and the charges upon ir aw amount to 13 per cent., and upon the thrown to 25 per cent., the difference will be 12 per cent., as against the thrown?—Yes.

7278. Of that 13 per cent., how much is paid to the Italian government, and how much to the English government?—The duty on raw in coming from Lombardy is upon the bale 9 l.; and on the other to the English government 42 l.; the duty on organzine in Italy is 4 l. 10 s., on organzine in London it is 42 l.

7279. By the statement you have now made, it appears that the Italian throwster has been sending silk to this country, paying only about 1 s. 11 d. for throwing his silk, do you conceive that he has been sending it at a loss to this country when he has received only 1 s. 11 d. for throwing?—The difference is not in the throwing, but in the price of the market.

7280. At 25 s. as you have taken it, does he receive profit, or has he been selling at a loss?—He must calculate the price of the raw silk in Italy, and the price he gets here to ascertain that.

7281. Do you know the prices at which organzine and raw silk have been selling in this country, and whether those prices leave a profit to the Italian throwster?—The Italian throwster seldom sends.

7282. Has the Italian merchant been sending his silk here at a loss or at a profit?—At a loss for three or four years; it is not the throwster who sends it here, but the merchants generally.

7283. The Italian merchant, who has sent thrown silk here, has lost by it?—Yes.

7284. Does the merchant lose by the silks he sends in a thrown state to other countries as much as he loses by the silks he sends to this country?—Sometimes in Germany and Russia they get better prices; sometimes they have a great profit on the Continent, and sometimes not, it is now finding a better price in Russia; they have not sent here for the sake merely of sending, but hoping for a profit.

7285. Which is the best market to which you can send thrown silk at present?—Russia.

7286. What do you conceive to be the cause of this market being unprofitable to the importer of thrown silk?—Because the sale of raw silk is bad here.

7287. What is the cause of that?—They employ the raw silk here, and throw it themselves, probably cheaper than the throwster on the Continent.

7288. What would be the effect in the price of organzine and raw silk in this market, if the duty, which is now 3 s. 6 d., was reduced to 1 s.?—There would be more organzine sent here than raw; there would be a competition with the throwsters.

7289. Would that lead to a greater quantity of thrown being sent here than has hitherto been sent here?—Yes, till things come to a balance again; on the supposition that the prices of raw and thrown would form a relative value to each other, the price of organzine being now 23 s. 6 d., by the reduction they will reduce it to 21 s., which is all the same relatively to an Italian to receive 23 s. 6 d., if he has the duty of 3 s. 6 d. to pay, or 21 s. at 1 s. duty, he will save something certainly on the interest and commission paid in England.

7290. You are understood to say, that the duty of 3 s. 6 d. prevents thrown silk being imported into this country?—Yes; if the whole of the duty were taken off there would be a competition undoubtedly for a time.

678.

7291. If

Mr.
*Francesco Caffi.*

28 May,
1832.

Mr.
*Francesco Caffi.*

28 May,
1832.

7291. If the thrown silk be worth at Calais 21 *s.* 6 *d.* it ought to sell in London for 25 *s.*, because you pay 3 *s.* 6 *d.* duty; if the Italian could sell his silk at 21 *s.* 6 *d.*, what would he give for the raw in Italy, to throw it and sell it at 21 *s.* 6 *d.* ?—He must buy the raw at 18 *s.*, the raw silk in Italy is always higher in proportion than the thrown by at least 10 sous.

7292. How do you account for that ?—Because it is more in demand, the raw silk always bears a higher price in the Italian market; the reason is that raw is fit for any market, whereas, if once thrown it can be used only as thrown; for the same reason the raw is cheaper now in London than in Italy.

7293. Do you mean to say, that on the sale of raw silk in Italy there has been no profit ?—There has been a loss; there has been so great a competition in the purchase of cocoons.

7294. To what extent do you conceive the throwing in Lombardy can be increased? —It will not be increased because there is no profit attending it.

7295. Supposing that by removing the duty in this country a profit on a fair competition in this country could be created, to what extent do you conceive the throwing in Italy could be increased ?—They would not erect other mills till their own mills were employed all the year round.

7296. You conceive that one-fourth more might be thrown in those mills ?— Yes.

7297. In what state is the manufacture of silks in Lombardy at the present time? —There are some looms at Milan, and some at Como, I suppose not 2,000 looms altogether, employed chiefly in ribbons and gros de Naples, and Levantines; they do not work regularly, they are only as a cloak to introduce the French and English manufactures which are prohibited in Lombardy.

7298. Are manufactured goods sent from France, Switzerland and England allowed to be imported into Lombardy ?—No.

7299. How do they get manufactured goods into Lombardy ?—They are all smuggled in.

7300. Do any go through Vienna ?—They mostly go through Germany; they are smuggled in through Switzerland and Como.

7301. Do you get velvets from Genoa or Germany ?—We get them from Germany, and also from Genoa, on asking for a license, and paying a very high duty; the custom house officers in Lombardy have power to go and search for smuggled goods; the silk looms there are a sort of proof that they manufacture at home.

7302. Do you mean to say, that the principal part of the silk goods used in Lombardy are smuggled ?—Yes.

7303. They are not manufactured there ?—Only a small proportion.

7304. They are entirely prohibited by the Austrian government ?—They are.

7305. Will you state what agricultural labourers receive in Italy ?—In winter they receive 30 sous or 1 *s.*

7306. Is that without food ?—Yes.

7307. In summer what do they receive ?—In summer they get 2 *s.* during they harvest and the mulberry season.

7308. What is the average, not immediately during the corn crops ?—The harvest is three or four months, during the other months about 1 *s.* 6 *d.*; in most parts of the country there is a partnership between the landlords and the tenants.

7309. What do the workmen get in field labour ?—One shilling, about.

7310. What do the stone masons get per day ?—The best get nearly 3 *s.*, the ordinary ones 2 *s.* a day.

7311. They are not employed the whole year ?—No, only during half the year.

7312. What do the carpenters who work at common house work earn?—Common workmen earn 1 *s.* 6 *d.* a day, and the best 2 *s.* a day.

7313. Do those prices vary from year to year according to the price of corn ?— No, in proportion to the demand for labour.

7314. Do they drink tea and sugar ?—No, coffee.

7315. And wine ?—Yes, for common wine is very cheap.

7316. Is bread much cheaper than in this country ?—It is one-third cheaper.

7317. The climate is very superior to that of this country ?—Very superior indeed, and the prices of provisions are high, when we have a great many soldiers among us, as at present; they are about one-third less than the prices here.

7318. Have you any idea of what the rent of an agricultural labourer's cottage would be?—They pay 40 Milan livres or 1 *l.* 5 *s.* for a room in Milan, and out of the

the town half the price; they pay in some situations in the country more than in the town; for a common cottage they pay about 2 *l.* sterling per four chambers.

7319. Have they little gardens attached to their cottages?—Yes, plenty of garden.

7320. How many years is it before a mulberry tree is fit to supply the worms?—About five or six years from the seed.

7321. Are they raised from seed?—Yes.

7322. What value per annum do you reckon a mulberry tree of seven years of age?—At seven years the leaves may be worth 1 *s.*, at 30 years may be worth 30 *s.*, varying according to age and season.

7323. How much silk will an ordinary sized tree of that age produce?—The value varies according to the crop, sometimes we pay 2 *s.*, sometimes only 1 *d.* for a rubo weight of leaves, and to produce a rubo of cocoons (which rubo gives two Italian pounds of silk) we require 100 rubo of leaves. Sometimes we are obliged to strip the leaves to take the shade off the growing crops.

7324. Have there been any mulberry trees planted lately in Lombardy?—There have been a great many the last five or six years, and now they think to put a duty on each mulberry tree, and on that account the planting of them is stopped, the corn being a more profitable produce than mulberry trees.

7325. What will be the duty on mulberry trees?—The tax is proposed to be about 3 *d.* each tree.

---

*Mercurii, 30° die Maii,* 1832.

### THE RIGHT HON. THE EARL GROSVENOR, IN THE CHAIR.

Mr. *Richard Baggallay*, called in; and Examined.

7326. IN what branch of the silk trade have you been engaged?—As a dealer in ribbons and broad silks.

7327. How long have the house in which you are concerned been engaged in that trade?—I have been 28 years, the house much longer.

7328. Does your trade extend over England and Wales, or other parts of the United Kingdom?—Over England and Wales.

7329. Had you, before the year 1826, considerable dealings with Coventry, and were you also importers of goods?—We had considerable dealings with Coventry, but were not allowed to import at that time, and of course did not.

7330. Is it your department to attend to the purchases principally?—To overlooking the purchases.

7331. You judge as to the qualities and prices of the different articles you buy?—Yes.

7332. After the alteration of the laws in 1826, permitting the importation of foreign goods, did you become an importer of those articles, and to what extent?—We commenced partially in the year 1826; I went myself to Lyons and Switzerland.

7333. Are the Committee to understand that you have visited Lyons and Switzerland annually, in order to make purchases of the article you imported?—Yes, twice during the year.

7334. You have selected the articles yourself, such as you thought would suit the English market?—Yes.

7335. Can you give the Committee any statement of the proportionate quantities of goods purchased in each year of British manufacture, and the quantity purchased each year of Foreign manufacture?—I can give a statement in the year 1827, the first year we imported any of importance, and I can give the effect of it on our British purchases each following year; we are obliged to order there one season for the following; we cannot do as we do here, order at the moment, but must give the orders three or four months before we can obtain the goods; we order by pattern in the autumn of one year for the spring of the following year.

7336. In what manner does the delay of three or four months upon the purchases affect you as to expenses?—The effect is, that we are obliged to order one season for the following, which is to us often of great injury if fashion changes; or, as it

678. occasionally

Mr.
*Francesco Caffi.*

28 May,
1832.

Mr.
*Richard Baggallay.*

30 May,
1832.

Mr.
Richard Baggallay.

30 May,
1832.

occasionally happens, that if a death occurs in the Royal Family, there is a loss of 30 per cent. upon the goods in the fancy trade.

7337. You mean to say it is more convenient to you as a purchaser to buy at home?—It is more convenient in many respects; we can then see what we can buy; whereas by leaving orders we are obliged to take goods of inferior quality sometimes.

7338. Are you put to more expense in the ordering these goods?—Not to more expense, because a less expense than would take us over there to purchase would enable us to give the order.

7339. Do you incur an equal expense in purchasing English as French goods? —Certainly not; it would be impossible to go to Lyons in much less than six weeks to do any good there, while a week at home would answer the same purpose.

7340. That becomes an additional charge upon the price of French goods?— Yes, an additional charge, to the extent of five per cent., but the loss of time is of more importance than even the expense.

7341. The very ordering of the dealer at first is an inconvenience to the merchant dealing in French?—Yes, as compared with home.

7342. Will you state what effect the importation of French silks has had on British silks, as far as your own dealings have gone?—Our first dealings when we imported were in the year 1827, upon the article of plain sarsnet ribbons from Switzerland; our first year's importation, in 1827, reduced our Coventry purchases six per cent.; every 100 lbs. purchased in Coventry was brought to 94. In the year 1828 they were still further reduced 20 per cent. as compared with 1827, bringing them to 75.

7343. You purchased then less than you had done in the previous years?—Yes, in 1829 they were still further reduced by 30 per cent. on the 75, which I make 22 l. 10 s., bringing down the purchases of that year to 52 l. 10 s., as compared with the 100 l. originally; during the years 1829 and 1830, we found the Coventry were improving upon the Swiss. I confine myself entirely to Swiss ribbons; we improved in 1829 and 1830; the result was in 1830, that Coventry increased 30 per cent. upon 52 l. 10 s., bringing it back to 68 l. 5 s. In 1831, Coventry again increased upon the 68 l. 5 s. 12½ per cent., which I make 8 l. 10 s. 6 d., bringing it up 76 l. 15 s. 6 d. On Monday last I took out, up to that period in the month of May, our purchases as compared with the last year, and I find they are increasing this year 20 per cent. upon the 76 l. 15 s. 6 d., which I make 15 l. 7 s., bringing it up to 92 l. 2 s. 6 d.

7344. So that the result is that you now, in your dealings with Coventry, are within about eight per cent. of what you were in 1827?—Yes.

7345. Are the Committee to understand that in 1829, of every 100 l. of sarsnet ribbon which you sold, 52½ were English, and 47½ Swiss?—Yes.

7346. And now the proportion is 92 l. 2 s. 6 d. of English, and only 7 l. 17 s. 6 d. of Swiss?—Yes: and at this moment we order no plain Swiss at all, we think we can do better at home.

7347. Does that arise from the price of the Swiss ribbons having risen lately, or that of the Coventry falling?—The Coventry falling, not the rise of the Swiss.

7348. What has been the relative diminution of price, from the year 1827, of the sarsnet you imported, and also the Coventry?—I should say not above 10 to 12½ per cent. alteration on the Swiss, but the alteration in the British is considerable.

7349. Can you inform the Committee what was the price of a sarsnet of Swiss manufacture in 1827, and what the same ribbon would now cost?—I cannot speak positively, but probably there may be a difference of 10 to 12½ per cent. in the price of Swiss ribbons now, to what they were when first we imported them.

7350. What do you suppose to be the diminution in the English ribbon?—It is very considerable, perhaps 20 per cent.; but it is not only in the price, but in the manner in which they are made, and the material of which they are made; they are so much improved; when first we imported the Swiss, we imported them for their quality as well as their price; but we are now able to get at home what we conceive to be nearly or quite as good, and of less price than we then imported the foreign, paying the duty.

7351. Is the improvement in the manner of manufacture, or in the quantity of silk used in the ribbon?—Not being a manufacturer I cannot speak positively, but I think that it is probably from the more general use of the engine loom, and the improvement in the material.

7352. It appears that you imported the largest quantity of Swiss ribbons in the year 1829; was it not in that year that the duties were reduced to meet the fall
which

Mr.
*Richard Baggallay.*

30 May,
1832.

which had taken place in the price of the commodity, the duty being collected per pound weight?—I believe the alteration was in July; we are obliged to order them four or five months before we can get them, therefore my order would be given before my knowledge of that alteration.

7353. The duty being collected by the pound weight, if the prices fall, that duty will be relatively higher?—Yes.

7354. So that the duty at the present time may amount to a great deal more than 30 per cent.?—I can give the exact amount of duty; it will be 25 per cent., or rather more.

7355. Taking into consideration the bulk of the article, Swiss plain ribbons, compared with its value, the duty being only 25 per cent. when paid, it would be hardly worth while to smuggle them?—I never smuggled a piece myself, but I know they have been smuggled.

7356. Though the duty is so small, and the article so bulky?—They have been smuggled.

7537. Have you any idea what those ribbons could have been smuggled for?—I have an idea, I think they could be smuggled at 17½ per cent.

7358. Including insurance?—Yes.

7359. You judge from the price at which they have been sold in this country?—Yes, I have bought them here; when I see articles sold for less than we can import them for paying the duty, I fear that they have been smuggled.

7360. Do you purchase any plain sarsnet ribbons in France?—No, we do not.

7361. Why not?—The Swiss make them cheaper and better.

7362. Do you import any plain satin ribbons?—Yes, and I can state their relative price; we purchase them from Lyons.

7363. What has been the proportion of purchases of those since the year 1826?—I have not that statement of plain satin ribbons with me, but I can give their relative value with the English; I consider the English narrow ribbons to be about 12½ per cent. dearer than the French, I am speaking now without duty; then the wider widths are as cheap in Coventry as they are in France.

7364. Are they of the same quality?—As near as possible; we cannot make quite the quality; we cannot get the silk; they make it of their own silk.

7365. You attribute the inferiority of the English entirely to the difference in the quality of the silk?—Yes.

7366. Generally speaking, has the quantity of the plain satins increased or decreased?—Decreased latterly.

7367. Did they increase at the same time that the Swiss ribbon decreased?—They did increase, but not in the same proportion as the plain sarsnets; but they now decrease.

7368. Are your purchases of plain French now, more than they were in 1827?—Now our purchases of plain satin ribbons are very trifling; in the first instance, we purchased French satin ribbons; the increase was never so great as in plain sarsnets; they are now decreasing, and at this time we purchase very few plain.

7369. Will you state what changes have taken place in your purchases of foreign fancy ribbons?—In 1827, the Coventry were reduced from 100*l.*, 12½ per cent., bringing them to 87*l.* 10*s.*; in 1828 12½ more, for which I deduct 10*l.* 19*s.* 6*d.*, leaving it 76*l.* 10*s.* 6*d.*; in 1829, 7½ per cent., for which I deduct 5*l.* 14*s.* 6*d.*, leaving it 70*l.* 16*s.*; in 1830, we went rapidly on the increase in favour of Coventry, 37½ per cent., which I take at 26*l.* 11*s.*, bringing it up to 97*l.* 7*s.*; in 1831, a further increase of 15 per cent., 14*l.* 13*s.*, bringing it up to 112*l.*; we buy therefore 12*l.* more than before the introduction of French ribbons.

7370. Are the purchases going on?—Yes, increasing.

7371. You refer to fancy ribbons and gauzes?—Yes.

7372. You import, in fact, none now?—Scarcely any.

7373. Have you a French and English room for goods?—Yes.

7374. Do you ever mix the goods, and expose them together?—We have had instances in which we have mixed them together; what we could not sell as French we put into the English drawer, and sold for more than we could as French.

7375. Do you mean that the English public bought them as English?—When people go into a French warehouse, and see the patterns of this year, perhaps they will not buy those of last year; but in the English warehouse they sell.

7376. You sold it as a new English pattern, instead of an old French pattern?—I do not say that we sold it as a new English pattern, we put it there, and it was sold; they might take it for the one or the other; we have sent a French ribbon

678.

pattern

pattern to Coventry, and had it made, and sold it as well and at as good a price as we got for the French.

7377. Do not you think that shows a great preference in favour of French fashion, when you sent down patterns of that to the manufacturers of Coventry?— I should say it shows the power of the people of Coventry to make the goods equal; that they have more originality of taste in France is, I think, very possible; I have no doubt about it myself.

7378. Can you state what is the relative price of the goods made at Coventry from the pattern you imported from France and sent down to Coventry to be there copied, and what you are charged in France, excluding the duty?—My inquiry leads me to this conclusion, that the rich gauze ribbons require the amount of duty to bring them to the same price as the French.

7379. What is the amount of duty?—The present duty is about 33 per cent. on the most saleable widths, and it requires that duty to bring them to the foreign price.

7380. What proportion of the goods manufactured at Coventry do you consider to be under the denomination of rich gauze ribbon?—I have no means of answering that.

7381. What proportion of the whole do you buy?—I cannot tell that.

7382. Can you state the relative prices of the lutestrings and satins?—In the fancy lutestrings I make the duty 25 per cent.; that is, upon the average, some would be more and some would be less; but I believe there are very few at the present moment imported.

7383. What is the difference between the Coventry price and the French price? —I should say that the Coventry are cheaper; independently of duty, I believe that we can purchase cheaper in Coventry than in France; this year we have not one French.

7384. If neither paid the duty, the Coventry would be the cheapest?—If I had weight for weight there would be a style and fancy in the French, which would induce the customer perhaps to buy them, but I have not imported one piece this year.

7385. You do not mean to say, that if the two ribbons were bought, the one from France and the other made at Coventry, a person would buy the one as soon as the other for the same price?—So much would depend upon the expense and style in making them.

7386. You say that the fashion and the style would be in favour of the French ribbon?—I think it would, there is more invention.

7387. You were understood to state, that they were lower at Coventry?—I get the same weight of ribbon, but not the same style and fashion of finishing.

7388. Do you mean that in mechanical execution we equal them, but in the style of taste and finishing we do not?—Yes.

7389. Do you mean to say, that a piece of 36 yards of nearly the same quality could be bought at Coventry for less than in France?—Yes; but there would be a style of pattern, something in the execution of the pattern, which would give a preference to the French.

7390. Since the importation of the French ribbons, have not the Coventry manufacturers much improved?—Very much indeed with regard to colours; I would say I consider the English colours decidedly more permanent than the French.

7391. Will you state the proportion of fancy satins?—The duty is from 15 to 18 per cent.; but we have done nothing in foreign fancy satins the last year, we get them now from Coventry.

7392. You have ordered none for the spring fashion of this year?—No, we have imported none since last autumn.

7393. What were the relative prices when you last imported?—I should think that the French would be from 15 to 20 per cent. cheaper than the English without the duty, but of this I cannot speak confidently, and the duty is from 15 to 18 per cent.

7394. Have you found your customers, in the course of the last and the present year, less anxious to purchase French goods than formerly?—I should say decidedly so, that they are more disposed to purchase the English.

7395. Is that from the goods generally being heavier, or on what ground?— When the duty is paid upon the wide French gauze ribbons we cannot sell them so cheap as we can the English wide widths, and they prefer the English.

7396. The

7396. The difference of price, selling the one and the other?—Yes.

Mr.
*Richard Baggallay.*

30 May,
1832.

7397. Is not the duty on narrow gauze ribbons very high?—It depends upon whether they are striped or figured; in striped gauze we cannot do any thing in foreign, as the duty is from 40 to 50 per cent., the figured gauzes are sometimes from 30 to 40 per cent.

7398. It requires that amount of protection to enable the Coventry people to compete with the French?—Yes, in figured gauzes.

7399. You say that you have frequently known ribbons to be copied at Coventry?—We have.

7400. Do you not find that they are too late for the fashion when they return? —I think if we had the pattern we could have it copied in Coventry in three weeks, and it would be more than three weeks before we sold the French.

7401. With what class of persons does your trade chiefly lie, with persons at the West end of the Town or persons in the country?—Our trade is principally a country trade; it goes all over England and Wales; of course we have some customers at the West end of the Town, but we do not seek after that trade.

7402. Are the Committee to understand that the prejudice in favour of French ribbons no longer exists in the country among your customers?—I think there is a certain description of persons who, when they saw a thing decidedly superior in taste would buy it, but that is a very small proportion.

7403. Not because they are French?—No, but because they are better.

7404. You do not think that because you said one was French and the other was English, persons would prefer the French?—No, I think not.

7405. At what time have you gone to France to purchase for your summer trade?—The month of February or March, occasionally in June, August and September.

7406. If you could have a pattern copied in three weeks, why do you not have it copied earlier in the season?—If I had sent a pattern to Coventry to be copied, it would have been all over the town before I could have introduced my own from France.

7407. Can you state what is the amount of duty paid now on each kind of ribbons imported, by the existing law?—On plain sarsnets it is rather more than 25 per cent. at the present value of the goods, the last price at which we could buy; the next I have is plain satins from twopenny to sixpenny, 22 ½ per cent., on the wider widths 20 per cent.

7408. Can you state the relative price between the plain sarsnets manufactured in Switzerland of as near as possible the same quality as those manufactured in this country?—The Swiss are cheaper by 17 ½ per cent.

7409. Do you refer to the price in Switzerland, or the cost price in your warehouse here?—I speak of the cost price in my warehouse here independent of the duty.

7410. What proportion of the 17 ½ per cent. would you reckon for expenses?— On Swiss probably from two to three per cent.

7411. Do you mean covering the expenses of your journey?—Yes, I should not go for those alone, I conceive on the general average that would cover it.

7412. Will you state the relative cost of the plain striped ribbons?—Upon the striped gauze ribbons of a similar description to what are made at Foleshill, I make the present duty 50 per cent. on imported, and the value of those plain striped ribbons is about five per cent. dearer here than they are in France.

7413. Is there any reason then you can give for the distress at Foleshill?—The reason I would give is, that I believe at Foleshill they make by the single-hand loom, and there the distress is great; they are obliged to make it at Foleshill at the same price as they do at Coventry; unless they can produce them as cheap as they do at Coventry with the engines they use there, they cannot of course sell them; our first price in France would be only five per cent. cheaper than in Coventry.

7414. If the plain gauze ribbon is the same price at Coventry, or within five per cent., and at Saint Etienne, why does it require the 50 per cent. to protect it?—It does not require it, but when we import it we pay that.

7415. Are the gauze ribbons imported by the Custom House chargeable with the duty of 50 per cent.?—The duty we paid ourselves last autumn was 50 per cent.

7416. Is there any great quantity of that striped gauze brought into England?— Inasmuch as we lost 25 and 30 per cent. upon them we bring in no more, and I believe there are not many brought.

7417. Do

Mr.
Richard Baggallay.

30 May,
1832.

7417. Do you believe that any are smuggled?—I cannot conceive when there is only five per cent. difference why there should be smuggling.

7418. Do you know at all, from your knowledge of trade, what proportion of those ribbons is made at Foleshill, and what at Coventry?—I do not.

7419. Are the hands employed at Coventry in the manufacture of this particular description of ribbon said to be in distress?—My information, when at Coventry a short time since was, that they were not in distress, but that at Foleshill they are; the way in which they accounted for it was, that the one used the engine, and the other the single-hand loom.

7420. Will you proceed with your statement of the relative duties and prices?—On figured gauze ribbons the duty we pay is from 33 to 40 per cent.

7421. Do you believe that the duty is collected on the whole brought into this country?—I should say I am pretty sure not.

7422. Do you think the duty being so high encourages smuggling?—The duty so far encourages smuggling that we have had some repeatedly offered to us.

7423. What amount of duty would protect against the smuggling?—The figured gauze ribbons I have stated require almost the duty to protect them.

7424. What amount of duty could you collect, looking to their relative prices in England and abroad?—That depends upon the rate at which they are brought in by smugglers.

7425. At what price can they be smuggled?—I have no doubt they can be brought in for $17\frac{1}{2}$ per cent.

7426. All above $17\frac{1}{2}$ per cent. is an encouragement to smuggling in your opinion?—Decidedly so, in my opinion, not a week passes but patterns are laid before us, and we are asked to buy.

7427. Can you account for why this article should cost 30 to 40 per cent. more in Coventry than in France?—I should say, from information given me, by the higher price of labour paid for these figured gauze ribbons in Coventry.

7428. Is the rate of wages paid for this kind of goods, figured gauzes, more in proportion than the payment made for other goods?—Decidedly, in Coventry; this is from information I have obtained on the spot.

7429. Can you state what is the proportion more than is paid for any other kind of goods?—No, I cannot.

7430. You have stated, that you think if the Government is to collect a duty, that duty must be reduced?—Yes, upon some descriptions.

7431. You have also stated, that you conceive, to meet the present high rate of wages paid on the manufacture of those goods at Coventry, from 30 to 40 per cent. duty must be collected?—Forty is an extreme case; it is no uncommon thing on the spot abroad, to buy a lot of goods on better terms than the usual price, in which case the duty may be 40.

7432. Are the hands, in your judgment, employed in other branches of the manufacture of ribbons at Coventry, distressed or not?—When at Coventry the last month, that was one of the inquiries I made, and I was told there has been distress here, a reference to our poor rates would show it; but for our manufacture of fancy gauze ribbons of late the wages have been much higher than for any other branch.

7433. What will the men, working at plain striped gauze, the cost of which is only five per cent. more than the French, earn per week in Coventry; and what will they make working at figured gauze, the cost of which is about 33 per cent. more than that in France?—I can state it as I received it from two of the principal gauze manufacturers in Coventry; the quantity made in the Jacquard looms is ten pieces of sixteen-penny width, eight pieces of twenty-penny width, six and seven pieces of twenty-four-penny width, four, five and six upon the average; five of thirty-penny; if the weaver employs a picker up, to whom he pays 14s. a week, and also 4s. for filling, making 18s.; he can make 36 yards per week in one loom, in which there are ten of sixteen-penny, he can make ten times thirty-six yards, by that he will make 50s., from which he will have to deduct 18s.; the payment for the twenty-penny is 6s. 6d., and he can make eight, making 52s., leaving him 34s.; for the twenty-four-penny goods, six and sometimes seven, take it at six, at 8s. 6d., that is 51s., leaving 33s.; in thirty-penny, four, five and six, taking it at the average of five at 12s., that will be 60s., leaving 42s.; it must, however, be remembered, that during the time of putting in fresh warps he does not receive any wages.

7434. How

7434. How many hours must he work for that? ·They begin at six in the morning, and leave off at eight, taking their hours out for meals.

7435. Is it all done by piece-work, or by day-work?—By piece-work.

7436. There is none of that work done by the day?—No, except for the labour hired by the weaver.

7437. Can you tell how many looms the manufacturer who informed you of this employed?—The gauze manufacturer from whom I obtained this information, employed about 150 Jacquard looms, of which 80 were his own property; they cost from 25 *l.* to 27 *l.* each. The weavers in this employment are generally anxious to obtain a loom, and will in many instances pay off 10 *s.* a week from their earnings towards the payment for it, the 150 were originally the proprietors, but the 70 have been sold off to the work people for that payment, which is never refused when they desire it. In this manufactory 200 weavers are employed; and at the time I am referring to they were constantly at work.

7438. These 70 you understand to belong to the weavers?—Yes, having been purchased out of their earnings.

7439. Why should the weavers be anxious to obtain these looms when they can come upon their masters' premises and work there?—He said when the trade is not very good their master may not happen to have work for them, and when it is, they can work for whom they please; and they prefer being able to work for whom they please.

7440. No additional wages are paid to those who work their own looms?—Not while they work I presume for the same parties; but when the manufacturers have not looms of their own then they employ these persons.

7441. You say that at the time to which you are speaking, all these looms were employed?—So I understand.

7442. Were you there exactly at the time when business is most active?—I was there towards the end of April; I should conceive it is more active in February and March, in preparation for the spring, than later.

7443. Can you state what was generally the state of employment at Coventry when you were there?—Another manufacturer informed me that they were constantly employed.

7444. Did you understand that these gauze ribbon weavers had been employed generally during the year; or do you speak only of their employment during the last month?—One manufacturer informed me that he had employed them all the year round, and that he could have taken on more hands; and another, that if by chance one gave up a weaver, another was immediately ready to take him on. The 150 looms, and the 200, were all employed on this manufacture.

7445. Can you state whether these looms were employed on original patterns designed in Coventry, or on patterns supplied from France?—Those I saw were patterns designed in Coventry; it would be impossible for me to say there was nothing copied.

7446. Were any further statements made to you by any manufacturers when you were at Coventry; and if so, state what they were?—It was said by one gentleman, " In this manufactory there are 200 weavers employed at this time; they are constantly at work; in ordinary circumstances four pieces are warped at a time, and when these four are made, the weavers may be out of employ for two or three days, or at the utmost fourteen, to prepare the loom for fresh warps; the time will, in some measure, depend upon the pattern used in the looms; generally two or three patterns will serve for twelve months, but one pattern has been kept in the entire year."

7447. You have mentioned another manufacturer, did he confirm what you have now stated, or did he differ?—He confirmed it generally, but I have here a statement of the price paid for clipping, 2 *s.* 4 *d.* for twenty-four-penny width, and 3 *s.* 6 *d.* for thirty-penny width, a piece for 36 yards.

7448. Is that clipping to be deducted or added to the weaver's wages?—It is to be added to the weaver's wages; it is the cost of the manufacture.

7449. Does the price of that vary in different patterns?—I think he informed me it was the same all round.

7450. Have you any thing further to state respecting wages?—I heard also the wages of the winders and the warpers.

7451. Did you receive that from the same authentic source?—Yes, from the first manufacturer I found that the warpers earn from 12 *s.* to 14 *s.* a week, and this work is usually performed by girls and women: the last manufacturer employs his

678.                                                                              warpers

Mr.
*Richard Baggallay.*

30 May,
1832.

Mr.
Richard Baggallay.

30 May,
1832.

warpers by the year round, and pays them from 8 s. to 8 s. 6 d. per week ; when it is paid by the piece the hands earn from 20 s. to 25 s. per week.

7452. If employed by the year round, they earn from 8 s. to 8 s. 6 d. per week ; if employed when work is good they will be paid 12 s. to 13 s. ; and if by the piece they may earn from 20 s. to 25 s. ?—Yes, by the last manufacturer all the warpers are employed by the year.

7453. Have you the means of giving the particulars of the quantity of plain sarsnet ribbons made of different kinds ?—Of two-penny 24 pieces at one time, of four-penny 24, of six-penny 20, of eight-penny 16, of twelve-penny 14, of sixteen-penny 10, of twenty-penny 10, of twenty-four-penny 8, of thirty-penny 6 ; the smallest quantity ever made are 24 of two-penny, 20 of four-penny, 16 of six-penny, 14 of eight-penny, 10 of twelve-penny, 10 of sixteen-penny, 8 of twenty-penny, 6 of twenty-four-penny, and 5 of thirty-penny ; this I have in the manufacturer's own hand writing.   If the weaver makes a length, that is 36 yards, a week, which in the wide work is hard labour, he would receive from his master as follows, deducting for filling, loom-hire and loom-standing : for weaving two-pennies 10 s. a week, for four-pennies 16 s., for six-pennies 16 s., for eight-pennies 15 s., for twelve-pennies 21 s. 10 d., for sixteen-pennies 20 s. 10 d. for twenty-pennies 27 s. 4 d., for twenty-four-pennies 26 s. 8 d., and for thirty-pennies 24 s.   The manufacturer makes the remark, " In the single hand loom the prices are nearly the same, but the weaver can make but a piece and a half, while the engine-loom can make six."

7454. Are the Committee to understand, that the quantities you have stated can, with ordinary labour, be made in a week ?—Yes ; he says it is hard work for the wider widths.

7455. Were they performing that when you were at Coventry ?—Yes, they were.

7456. And receiving those wages from the gentlemen to whom you refer ?—Yes ; the manufacturer states ; " in consequence of the combination amongst the engine weavers, the prices are kept up in a bad trade, but the single-hand weavers do not so combine, and the prices are frequently in the winter reduced to a sum too small for the maintenance of life on the coarsest food ; 2 s. 6 d. a piece was paid last winter in the single loom, and 5 s. in engine looms where the hands had work."

7457. Has any improvement been made in the engine loom at Coventry of late ? —He states, " the construction of engine looms has been improving, as they make more pieces of a breadth at once than they used to do, this increase is in much greater proportion upon the wide ribbons ;" and ascribes to that cause the greater advantages which the Swiss have in the narrower breadths.

7458. Have you any means of knowing, from your communications with Coventry, that the machinery would be extended in Coventry, but for the combination which exists there ?—Only, as has been expressed, that there is an objection on the part of the weavers in Coventry to the use of new machinery.

7459. Can you state what have been the effects on the Coventry trade by the French competition, either in price or quality ?—No doubt there is a decided improvement in the manufacture of goods by our own sales being confined to Coventry instead of going to Switzerland.

7460. Have you visited Congleton, or any places where ribbons are manufactured by power ?—I have.

7461. Are you able to speak to the quality of ribbons manufactured by power-looms ?—No, I am not ; except the blacks the thing is not general.   I heard the other day in Manchester that they were about establishing a power-loom there, for the manufacture of plain sarsnet ribbon.

7462. Have you imported any broad silks from France ?—Yes.

7463. In what years ?—In the years 1827, 1828 and 1829.

7464. Do you purchase broad silks of English manufacture also ?—Yes.

7465. Are you enabled to state the proportions of broad silks of each manufacture ?—No I have not a statement of that kind made out, but for the last two years we have given up foreign broad silk entirely, doing better at home.

7466. In what year did you import most French silks ?—In the year 1828.

7467. Do Manchester and Spitalfields now compete so as to shut out the French ? —We can buy as cheap or cheaper the first price here than we can in France ; we can buy as good gros de Naples in Manchester as we can in Lyons at the same price.

7468. Of what class do you speak ?—I speak of the great bulk of the consumption from 2 s. to 3 s. a yard, and up to 3 s. 8 d. a yard.

7469. Do

Mr.
*Richard Baggallay.*

30 May,
1832.

7469. Do you mean that they are as cheap now here as they were at Lyons in 1829?—As cheap as they are now, I have had patterns very lately.

7470. What is the rate of duty now chargeable on the importation of French silks of that kind?—Thirty-three per cent.

7471. Is there much in your opinion imported through the Custom House?—I do not know, but I should think not many plain silks.

7472. Have you any opportunity of knowing whether any are smuggled?—I think some of the richer qualities are, but not of a price to 3 s.

7473. Can you speak of the richer figured silks?—I cannot speak to them, we do not deal in them now.

7474. Did you in 1829 import any figured goods?—Yes.

7475. Why did you not keep on importing?—Finding there was a loss upon them.

7476. Can you give an opinion as to the price of those richer goods made here, and those made in France?—No I cannot at a price higher than 3 s. 8 d., I consider that a very high price.

7467. Do you ever purchase any English plain goods above 3 s. 8 d. a yard?—Yes, we do occasionally.

7478. What is the highest price of plain goods?—We sometimes give as high as 5 s. 6 d. a yard, but that is very rare.

7479. What would be the price of that description of goods at Lyons?—I cannot say that; we should not sell one piece in a hundred, or one in two hundred; that is not a gros de Naples, it is a ducape; I should say 3 s. 8 d. is a high price.

7480. Have you lately purchased any of these plain goods made in Manchester and Macclesfield?—Last week.

7481. Do they interfere with the Spitalfields?—No doubt they do; the silk trade of Manchester is one that has sprung up within the last few years.

7482. Have they been engaged in Manchester in making any rich goods?—Yes.

7483. How long have they been so engaged?—It is gradually going on; they make every year more than the preceding year, they are gradually improving in that manufacture, and working better goods.

7484. Are any of the manufacturers in Spitalfields employed in making the gros de Naples and lower priced goods?—They are obliged to make lower priced goods than they did before, to meet the market.

7485. Have they been employed in making goods of an inferior fabric than they did formerly in Spitalfields?—No doubt they have, to enable them to sell them at a lower price.

7486. You say that the Manchester manufactory has sprung up within these few years?—Yes.

7487. What has been the progress of it?—Taking some of the cotton weavers to weave silk.

7488. What was the quantity of silk weaving in Manchester?—Twenty years back they scarcely knew it, alluding to the article of broad silks for dresses

7489. When were your first purchases of gros de Naples made at Manchester?—Perhaps a dozen or fifteen years ago, but I cannot speak particularly.

7490. The quantity of rich goods made at Manchester is very small, is it not, in comparison to the whole manufacture?—The demand for the inferior articles is of course greater in quantity, they make more of them.

7491. If the demand was for rich silks they could make them?—No doubt of it.

7492. May not the trade at Manchester be increasing without the trade in Spitalfields decreasing?—Yes, for the consumption is increasing greatly.

7493. Do you think that the trade in Spitalfields has much decreased?—I have no knowledge of that; I think that Spitalfields should have gone on increasing, but that they have given it away to Manchester.

7494. Is it not the fact, that the description of silk goods made at Manchester, generally speaking, is better calculated to interfere with cotton goods than with goods coming from France?—I do not see it so; I consider if I was to go to Lyons and buy the gros de Naples at three to four francs or four francs 25, I could go to Manchester and buy a better article at the same price.

7495. Is the gros de Naples made at 2 s. at Manchester, such as a fashionable lady would wear?—No.

678. 7496. Is

Mr.
*Richard Baggallay.*

30 May,
1832.

7496. Is not a greater proportion of the manufacture at Manchester of that description?—They make generally for the market.

7497. Do they make such goods in any quantity as fashionable women would wear?—They do not make a great quantity above 3 s.

7498. Do you think there are two houses employed who make any quantity above 3 s. a yard?—Yes.

7499. How many do you think?—I cannot fix the number.

7500. How many manufacturers are there who make silks altogether?—I cannot say.

7501. Do you think there are 120?—I really cannot give any idea of the number.

7502. What kind of silk is there made at Macclesfield?—Bandannas, black silk handkerchiefs, Persian sarsnets, gros de Naples; silk handkerchiefs used to be their trade.

7503. Do the French goods, so far as you have seen, come into competition with the Macclesfield?—Into no competition whatever.

7504. Have you been at Macclesfield lately?—I was through it lately.

7505. What is the state of trade there?—One branch of their trade, the bandanna trade, must be exceedingly good.

7506. Has the trade in fact increased?—I should think so, in the article of bandannas twenty to one; the Macclesfield manufacturers I am informed are constantly assisted by the bounty on exportation, they get a bounty on sending out bandannas, but the debentures are for different silk.

7507. They may purchase spun silk worth 3 s. a pound, weave it into bandanna and get a bounty of 3 s. 6 d.?—Yes, I think so.

7508. Can you give the Committee any information as to the foreign velvets, the quantity made, and the extent of labour on that article?—I can give that only by a letter from Germany as to the quantity made and the price paid for it.

7509. You were requested to apply for information upon that subject, were you not?—I was; I wrote to a house at Crefeld on the Rhine; I have received a letter from the house of Regal & Company.

7510. They are a respectable house?—Very much so.

*[The Letter was delivered in, and read, as follows:]*

Crefeld, April 9th, 1832.

Dear Sir,

I have just received your favour of the 2d instant, and shall reply to the different questions you ask. In the article of broad velvets, we only make one piece at the time in a loom.

The price we pay for weaving depends upon the quantity of threads which are both in web and pail.

| | s. | d. | |
|---|---|---|---|
| For 3,500 threads we pay | 1 | 9 | per yard. |
| 4,000 ,, | 1 | 10 $\frac{1}{4}$ | ,, |
| 4,200 ,, | 1 | 10 $\frac{1}{2}$ | ,, |
| 4,500 ,, | 1 | 11 $\frac{1}{4}$ | ,, |
| 4,800 ,, | 1 | 11 $\frac{3}{4}$ | ,, |
| 5,000 ,, | 2 | — $\frac{1}{2}$ | ,, |
| 5,400 ,, | 2 | 1 $\frac{1}{4}$ | ,, |
| 6,000 ,, | 2 | 2 $\frac{1}{2}$ | ,, |

Our weavers are about making 18 yards between three and four weeks, according to the man. In ribbons we make of

| No. 12 | Eight pieces in one loom and we pay at the time | 1 | 1 | for 36 yards. |
|---|---|---|---|---|
| 24. | Six ,, | 1 | 7 $\frac{1}{2}$ | ,, |
| 30. | Six ,, | 1 | 9 $\frac{1}{2}$ | ,, |
| 50. | Five ,, | 2 | 3 | ,, |
| 100. | Three ,, | 4 | 3 | ,, |
| 150. | Three ,, | 6 | 9 | ,, |

A man makes 36 yards in two weeks, taking the average. The ribbon weavers live in the country, and those who make the narrow numbers are miserably poor, though they make 288 yards in a fortnight. We only use Italian silk.

Mr. Baggallay.                          *J. F. Scheibler.*

7511. Do

Mr.
*Richard Buggallay.*

30 May,
1832.

7511. Do you know the quantity of velvets imported?—I do not; our importation of them is decreasing; the last year we bought considerably more in Spitalfields than previously.

7512. Is the quality here improving, or the price decreasing?—The quality is improving; we have many persons who will not buy the foreign velvets.

7513. How do the English velvets retain their colour, compared with the foreign? —Very much better.

7514. How is the comparative price at the present moment?—The German would be cheaper, but for the duty.

7515. What duty is paid?—From 45 to 47½ per cent.; and on ribbon velvets, 61; those we imported very lately.

7516. What duty did you pay on those?—I think 61½ or 62 per cent.

7517. What duty is paid on broad?—About 45 to 47½.

7518. Exclusive of the duty, what is the relative price of the velvets in England and Germany?—I cannot say precisely; but the objection is so great at the present time to German velvets, that I think those who have been over from Germany for orders, have got very few.

7519. Do you believe that there is any smuggling in velvets at that high duty?— I think it is very likely, I do not know it.

7520. Are you able to give any information on smuggling generally; what was the state of it before 1826, and now?—There must be much more than before 1826; before that time men would not smuggle the goods, because they might be followed; the foreign silks were prohibited, and no man would wish to have them in his possession.

7521. Were there not plenty of foreign silks sold before 1826?—No doubt they were sold, because we have constantly seen them.

7522. But not in such large quantities as now?—It is impossible to say; I cannot tell what is smuggled now; but those who smuggle can have it in their houses now; we cannot distinguish what have paid duty, and what have not.

7523. Can you state whether the manner in which the duty is now levied at the Custom House ought to be continued, or whether any other mode ought to be adopted to ensure the collection of the duty?—I think the best mode of duty is per pound weight, and not an *ad valorem* duty.

7524. What are the rates of duty which you think, as an importer, you could pay, and others would pay, to put an end to smuggling?—I cannot answer that question.

7525. Do you know the rate of insurance?—The last rate of insurance was, I believe, 17½ per cent.

7526. Are you aware what has been the rate of per centage since 1826?—No, but it has been since 1826 as high as 25 and 26 per cent.; I believe if they were brought in previous to 1826, they were brought in by private individuals, not for sale; individuals might bring them in in small quantities, but I should think not as matter of trade.

7527. Fifteen or twenty years ago the French goods were different altogether from the English, were they not?—Yes.

7528. The English have been gradually copying their colours and patterns, and style, until the articles manufactured in these two countries are very nearly assimilated?—Yes.

7529. They have been gradually assimilating since the trade was first opened with the Continent?—Decidedly.

7530. It will be now very difficult to distinguish a piece of goods made in England from one made in France, would it not?—I cannot give a better reply to that than by my former evidence, that we have bought foreign, and now buy English.

7531. Do you not say, that to a great extent the copying French patterns exists?—Not to a great extent; we have sent patterns to Coventry to be copied, but not to a great extent.

7532. Do you not believe that if the duty was reduced, the smugglers might yet be able, in a greater degree, to reduce the premium of insurance?—No, I think at 17½ per cent. the smuggler is reduced to the lowest amount at which he can do it, with a profit to himself.

7533. Does not competition in that, as in every other business, bring down the profit to the lowest amount?—Yes, I should think so.

7534. Can you imagine if French goods were again prohibited, notwithstanding their similarity, any respectable men would be so unwise as to deal in them?— I have seen lately so much what men will do for profit, that I cannot say.

678.                                                                     7535. You

Mr.
*Richard Baggallay.*

30 May,
1832.

7535. You are not inclined to think that persons in general would incur the risk, if the onus were thrown upon them, to show that they were English manufacture?—Yes, I think they would; we have had so much proof what persons will do, I do not think that it would be easy to distinguish the one from the other if the fag ends were cut off.

7536. You think that so long as there is a profit it will be done?—When we see what houses, called respectable, have done, I think they will do it again.

7537. You state, that the British manufactures are coming nearer to the foreign manufacture, would not therefore detection be more difficult?—Certainly.

7538. Are you aware of a large quantity of silk being seized in the year 1824, and a difficulty being felt in distinguishing them?—I am.

7539. Were they able to distinguish them?—De Ponilly, a Frenchman, who was over here was making goods in Manchester from the same pattern in every respect, so much like those he brought from Lyons, it was impossible to distinguish, there were French people over here making them.

7540. Did you see any part of those goods?—I saw De Ponilly's at Manchester, the whole was, I think, a cloak; a small parcel used to come up once or twice a week.

7541. Were not a large proportion smuggled?—No doubt of it.

7542. Since that period, have not the manufacturers of this country very considerably improved?—No doubt of it.

7543. If it was difficult to distinguish then, would not the difficulty be still greater now?—No doubt of it.

7544. You think that De Ponilly manufactured very few at Manchester, and smuggled the greatest part of those he sold?—That was my opinion; but that was only for a few months before the introduction of French goods.

7545. Do not you know, that he bought in warps and shute dyed in France?—I was not aware of that.

7546. Do you know Mr. Pellicar?—Yes.

7547. Did he ever inform you, when Mr. De Ponilly's goods were seized, that Government were completely imposed upon; that in point of fact the goods so seized were of French manufacture?—I have heard that Mr. Pellicar stated that.

7548. Are you aware, whether this particular silk, about which you have been asked, manufactured in Manchester by a French house, was a French silk dyed, wound and warped, and received into England by an Order in Council free of all duty?—No, I do not know that; I know he sold goods in London at the time. I once or twice called upon him in Manchester, there was apparently a warehouse for the selling goods, but I never saw any; I understood that he sent up a small parcel twice or three times a week.

7549. When you state the very great difficulty which existed in detecting the fact, as to the goods being French or English manufactured goods, you mean to state, that there was an exception to a general rule, and not a general rule to guide the Committee?—I think at that time the house of De Ponilly was an exception, not the rule; but I think now we should be troubled to know the difference.

7550. As a buyer in Spitalfields, have you had an opportunity of knowing the trade during the last few months?—I have.

7551. Has it, in your opinion, been very bad?—I should say not.

7552. Have there been large sacrifices made by manufacturers within your knowledge?—Not to my knowledge; if there had I think I must have known it.

7553. Have you known Spitalfields for as many years as you have been engaged in business?—I have.

7554. You have known distress formerly in Spitalfields?—Yes.

7555. Have you known it as great or greater?—I have known them in a state of greater distress than I believe they have been in the last year.

7556. Did you ever know the distress to be so severe, and for so protracted a period, as during the autumn and spring of this year?—Yes; I think I have known the distress in Spitalfields greater than during the last winter.

7557. Do you mean, in comparison to its duration, as well as its extent?—Yes.

7558. You have stated you do not know of any sacrifices being made by the manufacturers of Spitalfields?—No, I do not mean to say no sacrifices have been made; but I understood the question to be, whether the sacrifices have been as great in this year as in former; I meant that there have not been so large sacrifices made as in former years.

7559. Probably the goods did not accumulate late in the winter?—Probably not.

7560. If

Mr.
Richard Baggallay.

30 May,
1832.

7560. If the goods were not sacrificed they must have either been sold as they were made, or there must have been large stocks accumulated; in point of fact, was the trade of Spitalfields brisk through November, December and January?— My opinion is, that the manufacturers acted much more cautiously during the last autumn and this spring, than they have done in former years, the consequence of which was, that probably there was a less accumulation of stock.

7561. What do you mean by cautiously?—That they did not make beyond their consumption.

7562. Did not that occasion very great distress among the workmen?—I have not the means of knowing that, I think it is probable that a less quantity of goods was made.

7563. Did not the prudence which you take notice of on the part of the master manufacturers throw out of employment a great number of hands?—No doubt of it.

7564. What is the state of stocks in Spitalfields now?—I conceive they are not large.

7565. Do you believe there is a great quantity of silk goods now in the hands of the manufacturers?—I do not go into Spitalfields, but from my general knowledge of it I should say there are not large stocks.

7566. What has been the state of the persons to whom you sell goods during the last five years; has it been better or worse than formerly?—Since the year 1825 decidedly better; that is to say we have much less bad debts.

7567. You conceive the trade of the country, as connected with your trade, in a more healthy state?—Yes, than ever I knew it for the last twenty years; I do not mean to say there are such flashes and starts, but that the trade is more regular.

7568. You speak of the retailer?—Yes.

7569. Speaking with reference to the manufacturers, have you reason to suppose there is more or less capital among them than formerly?—There is a great accumulation of wealth in Manchester employed in the silk trade.

7570. Do you conceive the caution you just mentioned is evidence of a flourishing trade?—Trade is never so good as when conducted with caution.

7571. You referred to persons not giving such large orders as formerly; did you consider that a sign that trade was going on well?—The best proof in my opinion of trade going on well is, when there is never an excess of stock in the hands of the manufacturers or merchants.

7572. Have you reason to believe that the trade has been a beneficial one to the manufacturer of Manchester?—I presume so from the great increase; but the great competition necessarily destroys their profits.

7573. Have you known an instance of the failure of a broad silk manufacturer in Manchester?—I dare say I could find one, but not of any great importance; sometimes we hear of them privately; I heard of one last week, but in a very small way; I do not know of any one of any importance.

7574. What should you consider would be a proper rate of duty per lb. on importation to fix upon French goods?—That would require a long time to ascertain; it would require a different rate of duty, some would bear a higher and some a lower.

7575. What is your reason for preferring the duty per lb.?—If it is an *ad valorem* duty, it is more open to fraud.

7576. You contemplate a separation of the articles?—Yes.

7577. Do you consider that the wages in Spitalfields have been depressed by importations from France, or by competition from Manchester?—By competition from Manchester; I should think there have been very few importations of silk from France which have affected Spitalfields.

7578. Have not the hands in Spitalfields been principally employed in the manufacture of the superior branches of silks and velvets, and figured gros de Naples, and other articles of that kind; and have they made at Manchester many such goods in the years 1825, 1826, 1827, or even 1828, with very few exceptions? —Previous to the time spoken of, ten or twelve years back, the bulk of the silks were sold only to persons moving in the better spheres of life; now the lowest class of persons wear them, and the Manchester people are therefore increasing their manufacture, the great consumption being in articles of from 2s. to 3s. a yard.

7579. Do you not know, in point of fact, that the superior classes of society wear as much silk as they ever did?—I think, perhaps, there is as much silk

678.                                                                                   worn

worn by them, but they do not wear silk so much in proportion as the lower classes do.

7580. If they do not wear silks made in Spitalfields, what silks do they wear, Manchester and Macclesfield being now making silks which, in your opinion, the superior classes will not use?—I hardly know where to begin the superior class ; in former times gros de Naples at 3 *s.* 9 *d.* were considered tolerably cheap ; there are as good now bought at 2 *s.* 6 *d.* I believe that Manchester makes goods, used by the generality of persons, both low and respectable.

7581. Have you, on your recent visit at Manchester, seen any fancy silks in the course of being manufactured there ?—Yes, I saw some.

7582. Did you see any of a particularly good quality ?—I saw some very good ones certainly.

7583. The greater proportion of silks used in this country are of the lower prices ?—Yes, from 2 *s.* to 2 *s.* 6 *d.* a yard.

7584. Have not the rich silks been principally manufactured in Spitalfields till within the last three or four years ?—Yes, till the last few years.

7585. Have not the importations from France been of that description?—Decidedly, in broad silks which come in with the duty.

7586. These silks having been superseded in a great measure by silks brought in from France, how do you reconcile that with the statement that the competition in Manchester is that which has depressed Spitalfields ?—Because Manchester has sprung up ; they made only common goods ; but of late years they have made a great many fine goods.

7587. Are there many goods imported from France of the kind manufactured in Spitalfields ?—I do not think there are many.

7588. Are there many figured silks imported from France ?—I think very few.

7589. What are the articles principally imported ?—They have been principally crapes I believe.

7590. The Committee are to understand that the goods chiefly imported from France have been ribbons and goods not formerly made in England to any extent ? —Yes, they are.

## Mr. *John Dillon*, called in ; and Examined.

7591. TO what house of business in London do you belong ?—The house of James Morrison & Company.

7592. How long have you been engaged in trade in that house ?—Thirteen years.

7593. You are wholesale dealers ?—Yes.

7594. What articles in silks does your house embrace ?—Nearly every article.

7595. What part of the United Kingdom do you do business with ?—Every part of the United Kingdom. We have customers in, I believe I may say, every city or town in England and Scotland, and most of the towns in Ireland ; besides selling for export.

7596. As a wholesale dealer, will you state what is your general mode of doing business ?—Our general mode of business is, to buy of the manufacturers throughout the different districts in the country for cash, or at a very short credit, and to sell to the dealers throughout the country generally for cash also, or at a short credit.

7597. Do you do any thing in the export trade ?—We sell for export.

7598. Do you deal in French silks as well as in British manufactured silks ?—Yes, we have imported.

7599. Will you state the proportion of your purchases of English and French goods, making the distinction between broad silks and ribbons ?—I have made a calculation of our purchases of English broad silks and silk handkerchiefs for five years previous to the admission of French goods, in order to show the quantity that we bought in Spitalfields at that time, and the quantity that we bought elsewhere, that is, not in Spitalfields ; I have not stated the actual amounts, but taken the relative proportions, and I find, that from the 1st of August 1821 to the 1st of August 1826 we bought in Spitalfields 66 *l.* 10 *s.* 6 *d.* in every 100 *l.*, and at Macclesfield and elsewhere, 33 *l.* 9 *s.* 6 *d.*

[*The Witness delivered in the Statement as follows.*]

From

From 1st August 1821 to 1st August 1826.

| | | | | | | | | | |
|---|---|---|---|---|---|---|---|---|---|
| Bought in Spitalfields | - | - | - | - | £.66 | 10 | 6 | - - | in every £.100. |
| Ditto at Macclesfield, and elsewhere | - | | | | 33 | 9 | 6 | - - - | ditto. |
| | | | | | £.100 | - | - | | |

7600. You are speaking now solely of that portion of your business which is in silk?—I am speaking solely of that portion of our business which is in silks, and I am speaking of the five years previous to the admission of French goods.

7601. Your house does extensive business also in woollens and in other lines? —No doubt, but I am confining my attention not only to the silk branch but to the broad silk branch, as distinct from the ribbons. I have then taken a second series of five years, namely, from the 1st of August 1826 to the 1st of August 1831, being after the admission of French silks, and I find the proportion as follows: I may perhaps premise, that I here also take relative proportions instead of actual amounts, but that my calculations are founded upon very considerable amounts, several millions of pounds sterling. Our silk goods during this second term of five years, bought in Spitalfields, were in every 100*l.* as 53*l.* 6*s.*, those bought at Manchester, Macclesfield and other places in England, 44*l.* 2*s.* 8*d.*, those bought by ourselves in France 9*s.* 7*d.*; French goods bought by us in England 2*l.* 1*s.* 9*d.*; these will be found to make a total of 100*l.* It will be observed that the calculation just stated is of five years ending 31st July 1831. In all my calculations the year ends on the 31st July, because our books are made up annually to that day. A similar calculation has also been made for the nine months from the 31st of July 1831 to the 30th of April, the month which has just expired.

*[The Witness delivered in the Statement as follows.]*

| | Five Years ending 31 July 1831. | | | Nine Months ending 30 April 1832. | | |
|---|---|---|---|---|---|---|
| | £. | s. | d. | £. | s. | d. |
| Silk Goods bought in Spitalfields - in every 100*l.* | 53 | 6 | – | 54 | 17 | – |
| Ditto at Manchester, Macclesfield, and other places in England - ditto - | 44 | 2 | 8 | 44 | 16 | 10 |
| Ditto in France - - - - - - | – | 9 | 7 | — | | |
| Ditto French Goods bought in England - - | 2 | 1 | 9 | – | 6 | 2 |
| £. | 100 | – | – | 100 | – | – |

A similar calculation has been made as to ribbons. Previous to 1826 our purchases may be taken as all made at Coventry. I have therefore no Table similar to the first as to broad silks. Our purchases during the five years subsequent to the introduction of French goods from the 31st of July 1826 to the 31st of July 1831, are as follows:

| | Five Years ending 31 July 1831. | | | Nine Months ending 30 April 1832 | | |
|---|---|---|---|---|---|---|
| | £. | s. | d. | £. | s. | d. |
| Ribbons bought in Coventry, and elsewhere in England - in every 100*l.* | 88 | 8 | 6½ | 87 | 5 | 4 |
| Ditto bought in France - - ditto - | 9 | 1 | 8¾ | 10 | 19 | – |
| Ditto French Goods bought in England - - - ditto - | 2 | 9 | 8¾ | 1 | 15 | 8 |
| £. | 100 | – | – | 100 | – | – |

*Veneris, 1° die Junii, 1832.*

### EDWARD AYSHFORD SANFORD, ESQUIRE, in the Chair.

Mr. *John Dillon,* called in ; and further Examined.

Mr.
*John Dillon.*

1 June,
1832.

7602. HAVE you any thing to add to the answer to the last question that was put to you upon a former day?—In my last examination, I stated that the relative proportion of our purchases in French ribbons, to our purchases in English ribbons, for five years, had been 11 *l.* 11 *s.* per cent. and that our purchases during the last nine months have been 12 *l.* 14 *s.* 8 *d.* per cent.; as from that it might have been inferred that our purchases in French ribbons were increasing, I wish to explain that that is not the fact; our purchases in French ribbons for the nine months are, in fact, our purchases for the whole twelve months, as we shall not again visit France; whereas we shall continue to buy English ribbons for the remaining three months.

7603. Then are the Committee to understand that the per centage this year will be below 11 *l.* 11 *s.*, which you have stated to be the average of the preceding five years?—It will not be above it; as far as I can judge it will be below that per centage.

7604. You say that you shall not visit France again this year; shall you make any purchases in this country of French ribbons during the present year?—I cannot say that we shall not, most likely we shall not; but if we do, the purchases will be very small in proportion.

7605. Can you state the proportion of your whole French to your whole English trade in silks?—I find some difficulty in giving an answer to that question, without stating actual amounts; I have taken our last purchases in silk goods to the amount of 1,000,000 *l.*, and I find out of that million, we have bought of English goods 955,224 *l.*, and of French 44,776 *l.*; I make that four and a half per cent. upon our whole silk trade.

7606. Is that 1,000,000 *l.* within the last five years?—Within a very recent period; it is the last million of our purchases.

7607. Of every hundred pounds of French goods which you have purchased in the aggregate of the five years from July 1826 to July 1831, what was the proportion purchased in each year?—Taking 100 *l.* as representing our whole purchases of French broad goods during the five years from the 31st of July 1826 to the 31st of July 1831, we have bought in the following proportions:

|  | £. | s. | d. |
|---|---|---|---|
| In the Year ending 31 July 1827  -  -  -  - | 3 | 16 | 3¼ |
| ———  -  -  —  1828  -  -  -  - | 12 | 6 | 3¾ |
| ———  -  -  —  1829  -  -  -  - | 44 | 8 | 4¼ |
| ———  -  -  —  1830  -  -  -  - | 23 | 19 | 7 |
| ———  -  -  -  1831  -  -  -  - | 15 | 9 | 5½ |
|  | £. 100 | — | — |

The above refers to our broad silk purchases only; taking 100 *l.* as representing our whole purchases in French ribbons, we have bought as follows:

|  | £. | s. | d. |
|---|---|---|---|
| In the Year ending 1827  -  -  -  -  -  -  - | 8 | 12 | 10⅓ |
| ———  -  1828  -  -  -  -  -  -  - | 25 | 13 | 9¾ |
| ———  -  1829  -  -  -  -  -  -  - | 26 | 5 | 3½ |
| ———  -  1830  -  -  -  -  -  -  - | 21 | 15 | 11 |
| ———  -  1831  -  -  -  -  -  -  - | 17 | 12 | 1¼ |
|  | £. 100 | — | — |

It will be observed that our purchases increased up to 1829, and that from that period they have regularly decreased; I mean our purchases in French silks, broad and narrow.

7608. Can you state what were the proportions of every 100 *l.* of your purchases of English silks in the same years, taking broad silks and ribbons separately, in the same

same manner as you have stated the French separate?—Yes, the proportions have been as follows:

| | Broad Silks, &c. | | | Ribbons. | | |
|---|---|---|---|---|---|---|
| | £. | s. | d. | £. | s. | d. |
| Year ending 31 July 1827 - - - - - | 19 | 9 | 6¾ | 20 | 5 | 6 |
| ——— - - 1828 - - - - | 19 | 1 | 2¼ | 19 | 12 | 3 |
| ——— - - 1829 - - - - | 18 | 15 | 9½ | 18 | 19 | 11 |
| ——— - - 1830 - - - - | 22 | 14 | 10¾ | 21 | 18 | 7½ |
| ——— - - 1831 - - - - | 19 | 18 | 6¾ | 19 | 3 | 8½ |
| £. | 100 | — | — | 100 | — | — |

Our purchases of silk goods during the five years last past, as compared with our purchases of silk goods five years before the admission of French goods, have increased in actual amount by some hundred thousand pounds.

7609. What descriptions of broad silks have you recently purchased in France? —We have made no purchases of broad silks in France for a very considerable time past. We have not bought because we could not sell them.

7610. Has the sale of English broad silks increased in latter years?—Yes.

7611. Are the Committee to understand then that your sale is entirely now in British broad silks?—Yes; the paper I put in on the last examination, will show that our purchases in French broad silks were at the rate, during the last nine months, of 6 s. 2 d. per cent. upon our whole silk purchases.

7612. You say that your purchases of French silks have decreased since 1829. The Committee have had in evidence, that the West End large houses have been increasing their direct importations; does that account for your decreased trade in foreign goods?—I should say not; my belief, from all I hear in various quarters, being that the demand for French goods is altogether decreasing, and has very considerably diminished, in consequence chiefly of the very great improvement in the English manufactures.

7613. What kinds of ribbons have you bought from France, how much in gauzes, and how much in other kinds?—I have made a calculation as to the different proportions of the various kinds of ribbons we have imported from France, I have taken our purchases of last autumn and the present spring; the months most likely to give a fair average, and assuming our purchases in French ribbons during that period to be 100 l., the proportions will be as follows:

| | £. | s. | d. |
|---|---|---|---|
| Gauzes - - - - - - - - - | 56 | 1 | 6 |
| Satins - - - - - - - - - | 16 | 6 | 2 |
| Lutestrings - - - - - - - - | 1 | 8 | 6 |
| Petersham - - - - - - - - | 26 | 3 | 10 |
| £. | 100 | — | — |

It will be observed that that makes our purchases of gauze ribbons in France 56 per cent., on our whole purchases of ribbons in France. By a report, from what I consider a very good authority, which we received yesterday from France, I perceive that the calculated proportion of gauze ribbons to the whole production of ribbons in France, is 55 per cent.

7614. Where do you get that report from?—It is on the authority of an agent of ours; a party very competent to form an opinion.

7615. Can you now give a similar statement with reference to your purchases of English ribbons?—I have made a similar calculation of our purchases of English ribbons during the same period. Taking our purchases of English ribbons for the last autumn and the present spring trade at also 100 l. the proportion will be as follows:

| | £. | s. | d. |
|---|---|---|---|
| Gauzes - - - - - - - - | 12 | 11 | 8 |
| Satins - - - - - - - - | 31 | 13 | — |
| Sarsnets and Lutestrings - - - - - | 41 | 7 | — |
| Petershams, &c. - - - - - - | 4 | 8 | 1 |
| Galloons and Doubles - - - - - - | 9 | — | 4 |
| Velvets - - - - - - - - | — | 19 | 11 |
| £. | 100 | — | — |

7616. What

Mr.
*John Dillon.*

1 June,
1832.

7616. What were the actual months for which the calculations were taken?—The proportion of the French ribbons are taken from the months of August, September and October 1830, together with January, February and March 1832. The proportions of the English are taken from the months of September and November 1831, and February and March 1832.

7617. Do you import ribbons from any other part of the Continent besides France?—Not now.

7618. Do you import velvet ribbons from any other part of the Continent?—Not lately; we are not able to do it, we can buy English cheaper; we once bought plain ribbons from Switzerland, but they are now in a great measure, if not altogether, superseded by the English article.

7619. When you state your belief that the consumption of foreign goods is on the decline, do you form your opinion upon your own decreased trade, or upon reference to official documents?—I form it on the whole taken together, but chiefly upon the information of our customers from various parts of the country, of whom I have made inquiries; all unite in opinion that the preference given to the French goods is very materially on the decline. That is information which I have not collected merely with a view to this Committee, but because it is to our interest to know what goods will sell, and what goods will not sell. Having directed my attention very particularly for some time to that subject, I give it as my opinion, collected from various sources, that that is the case.

7620. Are you aware that by the official returns of ribbons imported, there appears to be an increase, as it appears that the amount imported in 1829 were 121,953 lbs. weight; in 1830, 126,370 lbs.; and in 1831, 148,729 lbs.?—I am not aware of that.

7621. Does it not appear from this that the direct imports have not decreased?—Yes, that the direct imports have not decreased; of course I can know of none but the direct imports.

7622. Have you any means of knowing whether any large quantity have been smuggled or not?—I have not; but I should think that the smuggling has decreased rather than increased.

7623. As far as complaints go, have you not heard that smuggling has been upon the increase?—My opinion is, that it is upon the decrease so far as I have heard.

7624. Is the decline in your demand for French silk goods occasioned by the improvement of the English manufacture, or by a very great reduction in price?—I should think both.

7625. Taking all the different kinds of ribbons separately purchased by your house, can you state how much of each kind has been English, and how much French?—I have formed an estimate: the former Tables I have put in show the proportion of each kind French, and the proportion of each kind English; but as our English purchases have been considerably more than our French, somewhere about nine times as great, the proportion of course is affected by that circumstance. Taking, therefore, as before, our purchases of French and English ribbons together as one mass, and as being represented by 100*l.*, the proportions of each country, and of each sort in each country, will stand thus:

|  | ENGLISH. | | | FRENCH. | | | TOTAL. | | |
|---|---|---|---|---|---|---|---|---|---|
|  | £. | *s.* | *d.* | £. | *s.* | *d.* | £. | *s.* | *d.* |
| Gauzes - - - - - - | 11 | 2 | 6 | 6 | 9 | 10 | 17 | 12 | 4 |
| Satins - - - - - - | 27 | 19 | 6 | 1 | 17 | 9 | 29 | 17 | 3 |
| Sarsnets and Lutestrings - - | 36 | 11 | 2 | – | 3 | 4 | 36 | 14 | 6 |
| Pads, Belts, Petershams, &c. - - | 3 | 17 | 10 | 3 | – | 7 | 6 | 18 | 5 |
| Galloons and Doubles - - - | 7 | 19 | 9 | - | - | - | 7 | 19 | 9 |
| Velvets - - - - - | – | 17 | 9 | - | - | - | – | 17 | 9 |
| £. | 88 | 8 | 6 | 11 | 11 | 6 | 100 | – | – |

7626. With regard to the prices of English and French gauze ribbons, do they bear any thing like a relative proportion?—I shall be prepared to show some samples of each, with a calculation of the prices.

7627. Are you able to state that this 11*l.* 2*s.* 6*d.* which you stated to be for English gauzes, and the 6*l.* 9*s.* 10*d.* for French gauzes, are relatively upon the

same

Mr.
*John Dillon.*

1 June,
1832.

same priced ribbon?— No, I am not prepared to state that the prices of the French and English gauze are the same.

7628. Can you give the Committee any estimate of the amount of the whole silk trade in England, and what the proportion of the whole French imported bears to it?—Any calculation I can make must be an approximation only. The whole silk trade of this country was estimated before the Committee of the House of Lords in 1821, at about ten millions. My own calculations, founded upon the extent of our returns in the several articles as compared with the whole business of the country in those articles (having some idea of the proportion of the one as compared with the other) would give the result of the silk manufacture of this country at six millions sterling. A party, better acquainted with the subject than I am, and who knows it in its mercantile relations as well as in connexion with our own business, I believe estimates it rather at seven than at six millions. With regard to the French goods imported into this country, if we had the returns of the duty paid in money at our Custom House, it might be assumed that the average duty paid was 37 per cent.; and thus, by means of the duty, you would arrive at the value of the import. The intention of the legislature I have understood was to make it 30 per cent. I have found that in practice (and that is confirmed by others with whom I have conversed) it has operated as a duty of 37 per cent. My own impression, or rather the result of my calculations, is, that the French annual import through the Custom House into this country, is from 450,000*l.* to 500,000*l.* sterling. As to the goods that come into this country, not through the Custom House, that is of course a still more difficult matter to estimate; but from what I have seen of the trade, it being impossible that any very large parcels of goods should be very frequently in this country without our knowing it, I can also of that form some estimate; and my impression is, that the quantity imported illicitly might increase the whole importation into this country to either 750,000*l.* or 800,000*l.*; that is including the importations through the Custom House.

7629. Are the Committee to understand, that you estimate the whole value of the silk trade in one year now, at between six and seven millions?—What I mean is this, that if the manufacturers' invoices throughout this country for one year were added together, their selling price to us, the warehousemen, would amount to six millions sterling.

7630. Can you abstract, in your comparison, the silk used in hosiery, sewing silk, trimmings and other weighty goods that have no reference to the ribbon and broad silk trade?—I could not do it on the spot; but I have the means of forming an approximation to that calculation, and I will endeavour to make it.

7631. Have you any means of knowing the proportion of ribbons made in France to the proportion of ribbons made in England?—I have understood that the ribbon manufacture of England is from 800,000 to 1,000,000 annually. In the report from France which I have previously quoted, I find it stated, that the ribbon manufacture of Saint Etienne and Saint Chaumont is from 30 to 32,000,000 of francs, and of Lyons from 1,000,000 to 1,200,000 francs, that is about 1,300,000*l.* sterling.

7632. From what data do you form that estimate in England?—From calculations made by manufacturers as to the quantity of raw silk consumed at Coventry, &c.

7633. Made at what period?—Within the last two months.

7634. From what you yourself judge good authority?—Yes, what I myself give credit to.

7635. And your authority for the amount of the French ribbon manufacture is a report of your agent received within a few days from the spot?—Received within a few hours.

7636. How did you obtain this information?—This is a report made by an agent of our's resident abroad, in consequence of certain questions sent to him, through me, by a member of this Committee.

7637. Since the year 1826, have your purchases of English silk goods increased or decreased?—They have very considerably increased.

7638. In what ratio?—Our purchases in Spitalfields in broad silk goods have remained nearly equal; they have rather diminished of the two, but inconsiderably; our purchases at Manchester and at Macclesfield have increased in the proportion of 11 to 8. I am now comparing the period subsequent to the admission of French goods, wit a similar length of time previous to the admission of

678.                                                                                 French

Mr.
*John Dillon.*

1 June,
1832.

French goods. Our purchases at Coventry in ribbons, in the last five years, as compared with the previous five years, have increased one-fourth.

7639. In what places in England are the goods manufactured, with which the French manufacturers come in competition?—Spitalfields, Manchester and Coventry, with the dependencies upon each; a considerable quantity of the goods sold in Spitalfields are manufactured at Sudbury and various other places, at factories belonging to manufacturers who reside in Spitalfields, and who sell the goods there.

7640. How many years is it since the Spitalfields manufacturers manufactured any portion of their goods at a distance from London?—I do not know.

7641. At what places are such goods made?—I believe that goods sold in Spitalfields are manufactured at Coggeshall, Sudbury, Andover, Taunton and Reading, and at some places in Derbyshire.

7642. Do you know whether, at the places where you have increased your purchases, the retail houses have diminished their's in proportion?—The retail houses do not visit the distant places of manufacture; the warehousemen are a sort of middlemen who buy the stocks and distribute them to the retail dealers; our increase cannot have affected the mode or extent of purchasing by retail houses.

7643. Was it not the case, that most of the manufacturers at Coventry had warehouses in Wood-street and other parts of London, prior to the year 1826?—Some of them have such warehouses now. I am not aware of any material decrease in that respect.

7644. Were there not a greater number prior to 1826 than there are now?—Probably there was.

7645. Was it not the practice for the retail houses of London to purchase more immediately from the manufacturers in Spitalfields, prior to the year 1826 than it is now?—I have understood that it was so, and that they have found it more economical not to do so now.

7646. Do you consider the public to be benefited by having an intermediate man between the shopkeeper and the silk manufacturer?—I do consider the public very considerably benefited, though I am certainly not prepared to say that that is the motive which induces such warehousemen to go into business, they have no doubt their own interest in view. A very short statement of the mode in which, for example, our business is conducted, will show, I apprehend, the extent and nature of the public advantage. We employ from 12 to 15 either principal or subordinate purchasers, who visit all the different markets in the kingdom, and as they purchase for ready money of the very largest manufacturers, the goods are brought in large quantities into our warehouse at the cheapest rates. If it were not for the existence of such houses as those in question, the retail dealers must, each of them, in his own person, visit all those different markets at a very great personal expense; he must buy small quantities at a much higher price than we buy them, and therefore the cost to the retailers, and through them the cost to the public must be very considerably increased. It is also of great advantage to the retailers, and they constantly express themselves as so feeling it, to find an assortment from all the markets of the kingdom under one roof. Such houses are, in fact, distributors only, and they distribute the goods of the manufacturers at a small rate of profit, which may be considered as a commission only. No doubt there is a great economy of time and of money in such a mode of distribution.

7647. Must not the sale price of the different articles be cheaper to the retail purchasers, and also the variety greater by that intermediate means?—Both results must happen in a very great degree.

7648. Would not a country draper, coming to London, find at your house all that he required, make his purchases in a few hours and go back again; so that a man might come from Bristol, for example, and make his purchases in one day, and go back again the following night?—He might.

7649. And seeing every article at the time he purchases?—Yes, we in fact hold the stocks of the manufacturers.

7650. When you talk of the public, do you consider the manufacturer and the artisan to form a part of the public?—Yes.

7651. Are they advantaged by your mode of business?—I apprehend that the manufacturers are; at least if I were a manufacturer, and had large quantities of goods to sell, I should feel benefited by large dealers, who bought those goods of me, and who paid me for them upon the spot.

7652. Is not the competition of the retail dealers in the market of the manufacturers

turers in a great measure shut out by this course, you being a middleman between the consumer and the manufacturer ?—Yes.

7653. How is the artisan benefited by this mode of doing business?—I do not know that the object of going into business is to advantage any body except the individual going into that business. I should be extremely happy to see all the artisans of this kingdom well paid, and well off; but I do not pretend to say that I go into business for the purpose of benefiting the artisan, or that a mode of business is adopted for their benefit; at the same time I would say, that any system of business which encourages both production and consumption must be beneficial to the artisan.

7654. Must not the circumstance of there being large capitalists ready at any time to purchase goods when brought to market, promote a regularity in the sale, and enable individuals to obtain cash for their goods, and thus continue the employment of the men who would not be able to do so if they had not the great houses to purchase the goods?—Certainly.

7655. You are of opinion that your mode of business lessens the expense of distributing the goods to the consumer, and therefore you consider that any means of diminishing that expense must be beneficial to the artisan who is the producer?—If indirectly it has the effect of extending the production and the consumption of the article, it must have that effect.

7656. During the period to which you have alluded since the year 1826, have the English silk goods in your opinion improved in quality or deteriorated?—My opinion is, that the English silk goods during that time have very considerably improved in quality. In evidence of that improvement there are many articles of English manufacture which now successfully compete with French goods which were excelled by the French at the time of their introduction in 1826; this is particularly the case in the ribbon trade, so much so, that French lutestrings and satins (in which the French at first excelled) are now almost superseded in this country by the English. In plain gros de Naples the English have now almost, if not altogether, superseded the French. Even in the richer and better kinds of broad silk goods there is, I believe, a decided improvement. Some watered gros de Naples are, I understand, still imported; I inquired of a person here employed in the watering of silk goods,—a person who says he has watered at the rate of 1,200 yards per diem for the last two months; he says that he watered last year, as he calculates, two yards French to one yard English, and that he has this year watered one yard French to two yards English. That must be taken with some allowance, because some French goods are imported ready watered, but still it should be taken for what it is worth, and it confirms my belief that the English silk trade, even in its better classes, is making rapid strides as compared with the French. We have scarcely this season been enabled to import figured lutestrings at all. I am now speaking again of ribbons. We have only imported two patterns, and of satins very few either plain or figured. Our sales in French goods are almost reduced to the single article of French gauzes and to a few peculiar articles. I have already alluded to the Swiss sarsnets which are now superseded by the English; this is, I admit, in some degree a question of price as well as of quality, but I have no doubt of the great improvement, on the whole, of our manufacture in point of taste as well as of skill. Some very superior patterns have certainly been produced from Coventry this season.

7657. When you speak of the improvement of the manufacture in England, do you not also know that the French have greatly improved in the manufacture of goods since the competition with England?—I believe they have.

7658. You spoke of the watering of gros de Naples; and you stated that last year a man watering two of French to one of English, might not that arise from that description of goods not being previously prepared in this country, as we are always obliged to follow the French; and consequently, not having the goods made, they could not be so watered, and that this year we were prepared by having that description of goods made, and therefore had an opportunity of watering them when required; might not that be the reason?—I admit that it might; I do not draw my conclusion from that fact alone; I form my opinion upon all the facts taken together, and chiefly upon the assurances of our customers from various parts of the country.

7659. In what estimation are French goods now held throughout the country as far as you are able to judge from the opinion of your customers who visit you?—As far as I am able to judge from those opinions, the preference for French silk

678.                                                                                    goods

goods has very considerably decreased, and is still diminishing.   I have asked several of those parties who used formerly to purchase largely in French goods, and they say that their purchases in French goods are very considerably diminishing, and others have ceased purchasing altogether.

7660. How long has that existed?—Those are answers chiefly given me within the last three months, that is, during the present spring trade.

7661. Do you think this diminution in the preference of the French silk goods has begun within a few months?—No; my opinion is, that it has been diminishing from the year 1829, or that at least it has been settling into a preference for certain particular articles, in which perhaps ultimately the French may continue to excel us, and thus to retain a trade here.

7662. What are those particular articles?—At present they are gauze ribbons; for example, crape and gauze handkerchiefs, and various articles in which taste is more particularly required.

7663. In the articles you have just enumerated, does not the labour form a great proportion of the value?— I apprehend it does.

7664. Is it not therefore a more valuable description of manufacture for a country to possess, where they want employment for their people?—It may be so, but that is a large question; and I am stating facts rather than giving opinions.

7665. Can you state what are the causes of the supposed prejudices in favour of French goods by your customers?—Some persons have stated that there is a prejudice in favour of French over English goods; my own opinion is, that there is no such prejudice at this time; there may have been a prejudice in favour of French goods whilst they were prohibited, and I think it probable that a prohibition would restore that prejudice.   There is a preference given to French goods in some articles, which appears to me to be well founded.   In the articles of gauze ribbons, and other things, they display more taste.   There seems to be more of taste, and more of the artist in their designs; but if English articles were made with as much taste, and as much skill as French ones, the English articles would stand on a par with the French, if not be preferred before them; I mean that there is generally no prejudice, at least I have found none in favour of French goods.

7666. And you think the preference is founded upon superiority of design in the French article?—Yes.

7667. Have the French articles any other superiority over ours?—I am aware of none.

7668. In colours, have the French any advantage over the English?—I believe they have not any advantage.   It has been supposed by some, but that is matter of opinion, that the French colours at first are superior to the English; but I understand from those very competent to judge (from our customers and others), that they do not wear so well, particularly in plain goods; so much so, that some persons will, for that reason, not buy French goods at all.

7669. By design, do you mean a great variety of colours in the patterns, or a more elegant finishing of the pattern?—The design I should call the drawing, the picture as it were, as distinct from the canvas.

7670. May not a picture be either a variety of colours, or plain and simple?— I apprehend that the French excel in taste in contrasting the colours, and also as draftsmen in making the design.

7671. What is the proportion of your sale as to country and town?—Our London sales have been, during the last five years, about one-sixth of our whole sales.

7672. What proportion of your sales do you export?—I am not prepared to answer that question, we never export ourselves; we sell for export, so that without some labour I could not tell.

7673. Do the goods sold for export come under the denomination of town sales? —They do not; they are not included in my calculation of the one-sixth.

7674. Is the proportion of French goods in the whole, greater in the country than in the town sales?—My opinion is, that the proportion, in our business, is about the same.

7675. What do you consider the town and country trade in the common acceptation to mean?—It is generally supposed that the trade of London is a rich trade, and that the trade of the country is a poor or coarse trade; I think that position to be a mistake in both its branches.   London is a very large place, containing upwards of a million of inhabitants, and the difference of proportion of rich goods sold in London, as compared with the rich goods sold in the country, is not so

great

great as is commonly supposed. Very rich goods, in very large quantities, are sold in country towns; those who have visited Dublin and Edinburgh, and the provincial towns of England during the race weeks, or the musical festivals, or the assizes, will have seen that very rich silks, and very expensive goods are there consumed. I do not believe that the highest classes in this country are those who wear the richest or most expensive goods; we sell very rich goods to the country towns. It is sometimes represented that one or two large houses, or one or two milliners at the West end of the Town, represent the whole silk trade of the country; I think they represent a very small part of it. Looking to the extent of our town trade, our business may be taken as a fair representation, I think, of both the country and the town trade.

7676. Is it not the custom for the higher classes in country towns to have their dresses from London milliners?—I dare say they often do, but I apprehend it can hardly be called the custom, from the numerous orders we have from the country towns to supply the materials, at the same time I have no doubt that they have to a considerable extent.

7677. Do not all the country milliners get all their goods from London?—No doubt they do their materials.

7678. Do not you supply many milliners with materials yourself?—We do, in some instances; but we rather supply the drapers who supply them; very few of the milliners come or send direct to London.

7679. Under the law at present, the duty is levied on goods by weight; are you prepared to state, what rate per cent. has been paid in the last year on each of the kinds of goods imported, according to the import value of the cost of the goods?—I am able to supply a calculation of the per centage of the various kinds of goods, according to the rates that they are charged by Act of Parliament. The duties we have paid during the last twelve months I estimate as follows: gauzes, striped and figured, at 27 s. 6 d. per lb., have come out from 32 to 50 per cent. on the cost.

7680. Do you mean on the cost, including all charges at the Custom House, or on the prime cost as invoiced at Saint Etienne?—I mean on the prime cost as invoiced to us, without the expenses. Figured silks or satins at 15 s. per lb., have come out from 20 to 37½ per cent. on the cost; plain ribbons at 11 s. per lb. have come out from 15 to 21¼ per cent.; crapes, plain and figured, at the rates of 16 s. and 18 s. per lb., from 25 to 50 per cent. on the cost.

7681. Are you aware at what rate any of those goods can be smuggled in?— No, I am not; I only know what may be considered as the gossip of the trade upon the subject; I have understood that they used to be smuggled at 15, with an insurance of 10 per cent., making 25 per cent. That has, I am told, been reduced to 20, perhaps to 15, but in so saying I am only repeating what I have heard at second or third hand, and I do not know that it is of any value as evidence.

7682. When you say, used to be smuggled, what period do you refer to?— When French goods were first admitted, that is, when the prohibition was removed.

7683. Are you prepared to state whether, in your opinion, any alteration ought to be made, and if so, what alteration in the duty in order to prevent smuggling in those articles?—It appears to me necessary that a reduction should take place, but I am hardly prepared to give an opinion as to the extent of that reduction. I have already stated, that in practice the duty comes out upon an average as high as 37 per cent., and that is much too high to protect the fair trader against the smuggler.

7684. In order to show the amount of protection necessary to put them on the same footing, can you state the cost price of ribbons in France, as compared with the cost price of nearly the same ribbons in England?—I will give the best information in my power upon that subject. I will first take gauzes. I have taken from our stock six patterns of gauzes French, and six patterns of gauzes English; these six patterns consist of the three numbers most in request in the two kinds of striped and figured gauzes. I have as nearly as possible taken similar articles in width and quality, and fair samples of price; I have prepared a statement exhibiting a comparison of the cost of each. I speak here of the cost at St. Etienne and the cost at Coventry, expenses being afterwards added to the French article.

678.

7685. Have

7685. Have the goodness to deliver in that statement.

[*The same was delivered in, and read as follows :*]

| French Number. | English Width. | STRIPED: | | FIGURED: | |
|---|---|---|---|---|---|
| | | Cost at St. Etienne, per 36 Yards. | Cost at Coventry, per 36 Yards. | Cost at St. Etienne, of 36 Yards. | Cost at Coventry, of 36 Yards. |
| 12 = 20 | | 10/ | 13/9 | 12/ | 18/ |
| 16 = 24 | | 13/9 | 17/ | 17/9 | 23/ |
| 22 = 30 | | 15/ | 21/ | 25/1 | 32/ |
| | | 38/9 | | 54/10 | |
| Add Expenses, 4 p' cent. | | 1/6 | | 2/2 | |
| | | 40/3 | 51/9 | 57/ | 73/ |

From the above it appears that a duty of 29 *l.* 13 *s.* 6 ½ *d.* per cent. on the striped, of 29 *l.* 3 *s.* 7 *d.* on the cut, and an average duty of 29 *l.* 7 *s.* 8 ½ *d.* per cent. on both, would raise the French to the English prices.

7686. Can you devise any means by which, if the smuggler is willing to bring such goods into this country at 20 per cent., the Government can collect 30 per cent. ?—Generally I should say that goods will not continue to pay a large duty while they can be smuggled for much less.

7687. The price you have given at Coventry is at the present time when the silks which they use for the raw material are subject to a duty of 3 *s.* 6 *d.* ?—Yes, these are purchases made in both cases for the present spring trade; and they are as fairly selected for the purpose of comparison as I could select them. I have brought with me patterns of the goods upon which the comparison was made (*producing the same*).

7688. Are you able to state the comparative weight of the two samples?—No, I have not weighed them.

7689. Have you made a similar comparison with respect to lutestrings?—Our purchases in lutestrings have been so few that I am not able to produce patterns. I have already said that we have bought but two patterns of French lutestrings for this season; and I have made this calculation which I will deliver in.

[*The same was delivered in, and read as follows :*]

COMPARISON of a Garniture of 36 Yards of French Figured Lutestring, with a similar Garniture of English.

| | French Numbers. | Cost at Lyons. | English Widths. | Cost at Coventry. |
|---|---|---|---|---|
| | | *s.* *d.* | | *s.* *d.* |
| A Garniture of 18 yards each | 16 & 30 | 46 2 | 24 & 30 | 48 – |
| Add Expenses, 4 p' cent. - | – – | 1 10 | | |
| | | 48 – | | 48 – |

By the above it appears that the French lutestring, when loaded with the expenses, but without any duty, costs the same as the English bought at Coventry; but I should in fairness add, that in taking the best comparison I could, the advantage of quality was certainly in favour of the French, but still the difference was hardly such as a customer would discover.

7690. Is there much difference in the style of finishing?—The superiority to which I have alluded was in that respect; so that of the two, I think the French would have been preferred, but not essentially to alter this calculation. With respect to satins, I have not the materials for making a calculation as in the other cases; but the result of a calculation, formerly made by our ribbon buyers, was to show

Mr.
*John Dillon.*

1 June,
1832.

show that 20 per cent. upon figured, and 10 per cent. upon plain, is necessary, to equalize the prices of French and English satins.

7691. Does that include all widths?—It is a general average of all widths.

7692. In making the selection of these striped and plain gauzes, did you consider that you have selected patterns from Coventry of the same quality as those from France; or if not, in what way did they differ?—I attempted to do that, and have done it as nearly as our stock would afford the means. I believe of the two, that the quality of the French, taking the whole six pieces, is finer than the quality of the English; and I am aware that that would disturb the calculation, but on various other occasions when we have made a calculation, and also when our French silk buyer has made the calculation, a similar result has been arrived at of about 30 per cent.

7693. Have you known a French pattern, copied at Coventry, destroy the sale of the French pattern imported?—No, I have not. I know we have very frequently supplied patterns to Coventry, and have afterwards sold the goods made from those patterns, but I do not remember any particular case.

7694. In what respect has the opening of the French trade been beneficial to the English manufacturer?—I cannot answer that question.

7695. In what way has the alteration of the law affected you as a warehouseman?—I should say that it has not operated beneficially to the warehouseman. We have no interest in the promotion of a silk trade with France; we prefer a near market to a distant one; it is every way more profitable to us; our buyers visit Spitalfields every day, Coventry every week, and Manchester nearly every fortnight in the year; whereas we can visit Lyons but three or four times in the year. As the principle of a large business must be quick returns and economy of time and expense, a near market must always be more advantageous than a distant one. For the same reason that we prefer a Spitalfields trade to a Manchester, we should also prefer an English to a Foreign trade, in buying. The Foreign trade has not been with us, nor I apprehend with the general warehousemen of this country, a matter of preference, but a matter of necessity. The dealers have come to town expecting an assortment of goods, and we were compelled to keep French goods because French goods were in demand, and because our opponents in trade kept them. If the demand should cease or lessen, it would be a very desirable thing for us; we are in no way interested in the increase of the French silk trade, but the contrary.

7696. Are you able to state whether the profits upon the sale of French goods are more than on the sale of English goods, taking the average of any given period?—The profits are not greater; but I believe some persons can tell, to their cost, that the losses are. I have understood from those who have dealt largely in French goods, that they have lately lost rather than gained by the trade.

7697. Since the opening of the trade, have you been exposed to gluts of goods from Paris?—There have been occasionally large imports of goods from France.

7698. Have there been more frequently jobs of French goods than of English goods?—As far as my own experience goes, certainly not. One of the inconveniences of our French trade is, that it is a trade of orders; as to gluts from Paris, they may occasionally happen from peculiar circumstances in France; but the kind of goods of which our manufacturers are afraid, I understand to be new goods, and excellent patterns; and I should think they have little to fear from other descriptions of goods.

7699. It has been represented to the Committee, that after goods have been in fashion perhaps in Paris for one or two months, it frequently happens that large quantities are sent over here called job goods, and sold at a very inferior price; what has been your experience in that respect?—I remember but one large parcel of goods that we bought from Paris; I have already stated that goods of a superior and beautiful kind are what generally come from France; I apprehend that our manufacturers would have little to fear from the refuse of the Paris market at the end of a Paris season.

7700. Then of your own experience that has not fequently happened?—Of my own experience in our business, that has not happened, although I have certainly heard of such goods being in the country.

7701. Can you state whether there have been more failures in dealers in silk since the change of the law in 1826, than there were in the preceding five or six years?—The question of failures is very much embarrassed by the circumstances of the times; failures generally since 1826, in all branches of trade, have been

678.                                                                                            **very**

Mr.
*John Dillon.*

1 June,
1832.

very numerous in this country, and have increased in their ratio. By a published return of the number of bankruptcies, I perceive that the annual number of commissions on an average of five years before 1826, was 1,129; and it has been estimated, that the annual number of commissions, on an average of five years since 1826, was 1,392; showing an increase of 11¼ to 14 nearly. I have in the above excluded the failures of 1826 from both these series; the commissions of that year alone were 2,583. Looking back to our transactions with the silk manufacturers for the last five years, I should say that there have been very few considerable failures amongst them; I only remember two or three failures of large manufacturers in Spitalfields within that period, and upon inquiring of one buyer who visits Manchester, he says that there has been only one large failure within the same period of a silk manufacturer with whom we have dealt; at the same time, I ought in fairness to state, that the silk manufacture appears to be concentrated into fewer hands. We now do the same business in Spitalfields with 60 manufacturers, which we formerly did with 100. As their number has decreased, it is fair to surmise that it has decreased by failures as well as of other causes; but I believe the failures have been amongst the smaller manufacturers, and not amongst the larger. Had the failures been caused by French competition, they would have been amongst the larger class of manufacturers, or those who make the richer descriptions of goods; but as the failures, or the persons who have gone out of business have been chiefly among the small makers, the change, I think, is owing to other circumstances; to a greater degree of competition for instance, particularly the competition with Manchester, and in a great degree to the fact that the large manufacturers of Spitalfields have themselves now embarked, as I have already said, at Coggeshall, Sudbury, and various other places; and also to the introduction of a system of cash payments. These things, and other causes that have been in operation, have, I dare say, very much concentrated the silk business; they have placed it in fewer hands, and caused the Spitalfields manufacture, and other manufactures (for it extends to the woollen and various other trades) to be carried on by a smaller number of persons, and by men of greater capital than formerly.

7702. Are not a great number of looms unemployed at Spitalfields at this moment?—I do not know; I know that we are buying largely at Spitalfields.

7703. Are you aware that there is any considerable stock of goods at Spitalfields?—I believe there are less stocks of goods at Spitalfields than usually at this time of the year.

7704. What you have said now relates to those of whom you buy; what is the state of the dealers in silk to whom you sell, have there been more failures among them of late?—Our own experience shows less failures. Taking the same periods of time that I have before given, from the year 1821 to 1825, and then the five years from 1827 to 1831, the number of persons in a connexion of several thousands who have stopped payment, in our debt, whether afterwards bankrupt or otherwise, have decreased, as from 23 to 21; and from various other circumstances, I am strongly of opinion that the drapers of this country to whom we sell are a more stable and solvent class of persons than they were at the previous period of five years before the introduction of French silk goods, that they are men of more capital than they formerly used to be.

7705. Do you mean to say, that your losses by the sales you have made have been less in the last five years than they were before?—I do.

7706. You have said that you pay cash in buying your goods, is that peculiar to your particular line, or has it become more general of late?—I believe that the payment of cash is not confined to our particular line, but even in our business I would remark, that the payment of cash, and the effects produced upon business by a cash system, have by no means been confined to the silk business, though it is of the silk I have chiefly spoken. We deal in articles of woollen, in lace, hose, gloves, and in many other articles, including the markets of Yorkshire and the West of England, Leicestershire, Nottinghamshire, Worcestershire and various other parts, and the same system of buying and selling for cash, or a short credit, instead of taking and giving a long credit, prevails in all those branches, and has produced the same effects upon them as in the silk trade.

7707. And therefore the answer you gave just now, as regarded the solvency of drapers generally throughout the country, relates also to those drapers being generally dealers in goods as well as dealers in silk?—Only that our staple article being silk,

Mr.
*John Dillon.*

1 June,
1832.

silk, our customers of whom I could more particularly speak, are that portion of the drapers that deal in silk goods, not for instance linen drapers.

7708. Do you attribute the more solvent and prosperous state of the drapers to the opening of the English ports to French silk goods?—No, that is too large an inference to draw. I state the fact, I believe that effect more to arise from the introduction of a cash system of carrying on business, so that the capital is more in the hands of the retailers than formerly.

7709. When you say you buy for cash, is it for bank notes at once, or payable by acceptances which have time to run?—Chiefly by money, in a very small degree in bills, but the answer is for cash as a system.

7710. Then you think that the opening of the ports has had nothing to do with producing this more solvent state of the dealers, but that it arises from the different systems of credit?—I do not see the connexion of the two things, or how the opening of the ports can have produced that effect; when I consider that the French silk business altogether is only 10 or 11 per cent. upon the whole silk business of England, I do not see how it can affect the solvency of the whole trade of this country, or its insolvency; it is the same thing to a dealer whether he retails French or English goods.

7711. Then this more prosperous state you consider to arise from a different system of credit?—I think it is chiefly to be attributed to that, at the same time I would say, I rather state the fact, and would leave it to the Committee to draw their own inferences.

7712. Is the present mode of carrying on business by cash favourable or not to speculation, or over-trading?—My opinion is, that a man will always be more prudent, and more careful with his own money, than with the money of other people; and that the healthiest mode of carrying on business is that of prompt payment through all its stages.

7713. Would not the effect of a transition from a system of credit to one of cash payment, be to prevent persons without capital continuing to carry on their trade?—The effect of any transition from one mode of conducting business to another mode, will be, whilst that transition is going on, to produce perhaps individual evil and suffering; for that reason I apprehend that the transition from a credit to a cash system, may have driven many persons out of business who had not capital to meet the new circumstances, this may account for many of the past failures; but when that transition has actually taken place it is a more healthy state of things, and is likely to produce great future benefit to individuals and to the community.

7714. It has been stated to the Committee, that there are certain great monopolists in London who buy large quantities of goods, and that although by buying those goods they may make the goods cheaper, yet they are injurious to the manufacturers; what is your opinion upon that subject?—I should find it extremely difficult to discover what injury large buyers can inflict upon manufacturers, unless the making large purchases and paying well for them be an injury.

7715. When great purchases are made, is not some inducement in reduced prices requisite?—I should not make a large purchase instead of a small one, unless some advantage were held out as an inducement; but whilst there is an open market, as there is in the silk trade, and competition amongst all the purchasers, who are very numerous, and many of them men of very considerable capital, the protection of the seller lies in the competition amongst the buyers.

7716. Can there be a combination among the buyers, those that are called the great houses in London?—Looking at the state of the silk trade for some years past, and as it now exists, I should say a combination is utterly impossible; the very fiercest competition has raged and is at this moment raging. I doubt whether in this country competition was ever carried to the height which it is at this time carried by the houses alluded to in the question; in the silk trade, as now conducted, combination has never taken place, and I think combination a moral impossibility; it is a contest of men of capital against men of capital.

7717. With so valuable a commodity as silk purchased at five months' credit, and sold so promptly for cash or bills with your indorsement, which the manufacturer gets discounted, may not a set of manufacturers go on for a long time supplying your establishment with cheap goods without doing any good to themselves?—It is quite evident that if a manufacturer buys his raw material at credit, and sells the manufactured article for cash, an effect like that referred to may take place.

　　　　　　　　　　　　　　　　　　　　7718. Do

7718. Do you think it does take place in many instances, or in any?—Whether manufacturers conduct their business with benefit to themselves or not, I cannot answer; I apprehend they would not continue manufacturers if they did not.

7719. When failures of silk manufacturers take place, have you ever heard that the low priced cash purchases for the warehousemen have consumed the merchants' property, and reduced the estate to a cypher?—I cannot state the causes of the failure of manufacturers, they are, I conclude, very various, and known to themselves and not to me; one of the causes of the failure of manufacturers probably has been, that they have sold their goods for less than they cost them; but I only know that from the probability of the thing.

7720. May not their so selling their goods for less than they cost them, arise from their having made those goods in a very slovenly manner?—Yes. It may arise from their having bought their materials at a bad market and at long credit; it may arise from their having made their goods in a slovenly manner, or of an unmarketable kind; it may arise from various causes; but if they sell those goods for the most they can obtain for them in open market, and where there is a fair competition, I apprehend that (although I speak as a buyer) no person can fairly attach blame to a purchaser, and that he can in no way be stated as being instrumental to the failure of the manufacturer, when he evidently gives more for the goods than any body else would give, or he would not become the purchaser.

7721. Is it usual in the silk trade to buy goods by the pound weight?—No.

7722. You buy them for their beauty, their quality and their colour?—From a combination of all these, and from their being a marketable commodity, and offered at a price at which they can be sold with a profit.

7723. And therefore a good manufacturer would take care to manufacture such goods as he was likely to sell, and make a profit upon?—Certainly.

7724. Might not a manufacturer make his goods injudiciously?—He might even make them good, and yet injudiciously; and of course he might make them neither good nor judiciously.

7725. Have not some of those who have failed in your trade, failed because they have sold goods cheaper than they bought them from you?—Very many, I have no doubt.

7726. Do not, in point of fact, very few large buyers take the greater part of the goods manufactured at Spitalfields?—I can hardly answer that question as to the proportion; I should think there are from twenty to thirty buyers who constantly visit Spitalfields, and each of them buys as largely as he can, or as largely as his trade demands.

7727. Are those all of them large buyers, or some large and some small?—There is a great variety in those twenty.

7728. Are you aware that any respectable manufacturers in Spitalfields have sold their goods at a loss, of late?—I am not aware of any such circumstance; the largest lot of goods we have bought in Spitalfields in the course of the present season, and which I believe was the cheapest because it was the largest, I have very good authority for saying, was not sold to us at a loss.

7729. Are the manufacturers in any case bound to the warehousemen as to the prices, and not to sell to other people?—In no way whatever, that I ever heard of.

---

*Lunæ, 4° die Junij,* 1832.

---

### EDWARD AYSHFORD SANFORD, ESQUIRE, in the Chair.

---

Mr. *John Dillon*, called in; and further Examined.

7730. THE Committee have understood that your house are buyers in many other branches in this country besides the silk, what has been the state of those branches during the last six months as compared with silk?—The state of business generally during the last six months has not been good; political circumstances, and the fear of disease, operated considerably upon all branches; but for those circumstances there would, I believe, have been an extremely good spring trade, as we call it. I am asked to compare the relative position of our silk business during the last six months with our other business during the same period; I may

observe

Mr.
*John Dillon.*

4 June,
1832.

observe that our silk business is little more than half of our whole transactions; our business is divided into eleven departments, of which the silk business, or that portion of the silk business which compares with the French trade, namely, broad silks in Spitalfields, broad silks, &c. at Manchester, and ribbons at Coventry, form three only; that is, three departments out of the eleven. Taking the six months just passed, and comparing them with the same six months of the last year, which is comparing an unfavourable with a highly prosperous year, I find that our purchases in the last six months have decreased about 9¼ per cent.; that decrease in the three departments of broad silks, &c. at Spitalfields and Manchester, and ribbons at Coventry, has amounted to 5$\frac{7}{10}$ per cent.; whilst in the other eight departments, which are in articles not comparing with French goods, the decrease has been 12¼ per cent. It is evident, therefore, that whatever circumstances may have caused a decrease in purchases this spring, as compared with last spring, the greater decrease, so far as our business is concerned, has been in those departments which have not been exposed to foreign competition.

7731. When you speak of the three departments of your business that constitute your silk trade, do you include the English and French trade?—I do not include the French; in the calculation from which I have given my last answer, the French articles are excluded altogether.

7732. You have given the Committee a comparative statement of your business for the last six months, could you give a similar statement with respect to the preceding six months?—Looking to the sales of the whole of our departments during the previous six months, and comparing the relative prosperity of the three silk departments with the other departments, I find that the silks were then below the others in point of prosperity, and not above them; as in the six months of which I have previously spoken, the depreciation of the one was to the depreciation of the other, as five to four.

7733. What have been the consequences of the removal of the prohibition of East India bandannas?—I understand that one of the consequences has been, a very considerable increase in the manufacture of English bandannas; the fact at least is, that the English manufacture has very considerably increased since the admission of India goods; I also understand from those quite competent to give an opinion, and who know the fact, that the importation of India bandannas has very considerably diminished; I can of course only speak of sales of India bandannas subsequent to their admission; on that subject, I speak chiefly on the authority of a broker who is well acquainted with the bandanna trade generally, who says that bandannas and corahs are almost exclusively the only silk manufactured goods that are cleared by duty for the home trade; about 50,000 pieces of the former, and probably 5 or 6,000 of the latter, are annually consumed. There is, he states, no chance of quantities, such as used to come previous to the opening of the ports, ever finding their way here, as British made handkerchiefs have largely now entered into consumption. From China, very few India silks can afford to pay duties, and even then only when they are at ruinous prices to the importers, &c. That India bandannas were used in this country very largely, I know from popular report and the notoriety of the fact. With regard to our own sales of bandannas, I should state, that on reference to our books, I find we bought in English bandannas, three years previously to the 1st July 1826, about 54,000 pieces, and that we bought in the three years subsequent to the 1st July 1826, in British and in India together, upwards of 160,000 pieces; coming down to the two years ending the 1st July 1831, we have bought of India 27,000 pieces, and of British, 117,000; but I ought to add, that in this last amount of British, is included corahs, which are India cloth printed in England. The relative proportion of these last I am not prepared to give, but it may be collected from the statement which I have already quoted.

7734. Are any bandannas manufactured of Italian silk?—I do not pretend to know any thing about the manufacture.

7735. Do you know at what price the corahs are commonly sold at the East India Company's sales?—I do not, at least sufficiently to state it in evidence.

7736. Are you aware that a piece of bandanna, weighing 14 ounces, can be imported from Bengal in the private trade, and that it can be sold here at 15*s.* and pay the importer a profit?—I am not aware of that.

7737. You have spoken of the Manchester silk manufacture having rapidly increased; what do you consider to have been the effect of that increase upon Spitalfields?—There is no doubt that the effect of that increase upon Spitalfields

678. has

Mr.
*John Dillon.*

4 June,
1832.

has been to reduce the price of the article; most likely also to reduce the profits of the manufacture in Spitalfields. Looking to the peculiar circumstances of Manchester, its large manufacturing population, and the fact, as I understand, that a very large number of the cotton weavers of Manchester who were working at low wages have turned their hands to silk; the operation of these circumstances must further be to lower the wages of Spitalfields, or rather to equalize the wages in all the places in which the silk manufacture is carried on. They are at this time making at Manchester a large proportion of the article most in consumption, the gros de Naples; they are not only making plain gros de Naples, but they are also making some progress in the figured gros de Naples. The competition between Manchester and Spitalfields may be illustrated by a fact which I will state to the Committee. Our Spitalfields buyer, in the course of last year, bought an article in small figures, for which he gave 3 s. 9 d. a yard; about the same time our buyer at Manchester bought an article sufficiently similar to interfere with the sale of the former at 3 s.; we then were of course compelled, in our future purchases of the Spitalfields article, to reduce our price. We made further purchases of that article at 3 s., but by that time the Manchester article was reduced to 2 s. 7 ½ d. These are patterns of Manchester figured goods. This one is an article we have received from Manchester since my last evidence. (*Producing five patterns.*)

7738. Was not one of the articles you have referred to called double and the other single?—No.

7739. Did you give 3 s. 9 d. in Spitalfields for a single?—I do not remember; it was in 1831; the one article was sufficiently near to interfere with the sale of the other.

7740. It has been stated that there have been disputes raised by the assignees of manufacturers, and that actions in two or three cases have been brought for the recovery of goods supposed improperly bought, and that compromises have been made, have such occurred to your knowledge?—I have heard that such have occurred.

7741. Do you know that they have occurred?—Only by hearing them talked of in the trade, no otherwise.

7742. Were the houses that bought the goods in question what you considered large, or the largest houses in your trade?—Whether such transactions have taken place with the largest houses is a comparative question; I do not wish to depreciate them; they may consider themselves as large, but the houses I have heard named I do not consider as in the first class, or as the largest houses in the trade. We, for example, may be considered in the class of the large or the largest houses, and no such transactions ever took place in connexion with our house.

7743. From your information, do you suppose that there are many foreign kid gloves imported into this country illicitly?—I believe not; judging from what passes in the trade, I should say that gloves are not smuggled; and that is the opinion of all the parties with whom I mix, who are most competent to judge.

7744. Are French gloves more profitable than English?—No; more frequently less so.

7745. Can you furnish the Committee with the prices of the five patterns you have exhibited to-day?—The prices are marked upon them. I should explain that they have not been selected with any view to cheapness or price, and that I do not put them in any way as samples of price, they are taken indiscriminately; one of them arrived only on Saturday last, and they are merely produced in illustration of the fact that figured goods are made at Manchester.

7746. Can you furnish the Committee with a copy of the Report with regard to the manufacture of ribbons in France, which you stated you obtained from your agent at Lyons?—I can; this is a Report which I have obtained in answer to questions forwarded through me by a member of this Committee to our agent at Lyons, who is a very competent and fit man to make such a report.

7747. Is he a general agent, or your own agent?—He is a general agent.

[*The Witness delivered in the same, which is as follows:*]

*Mai*

*Mai* 1832.

NOTICE sur la Fabrication des Rubans, à St. Etienne, à St. Chamond, et Lyon.

---

Question No. 1.—What number of looms is employed in the manufacture of ribbons?

Answer.—St. Etienne et St. Chamond - de 21,165 à 22,850.
Lyon - - - - - - 800 à - 900.

No. 2.—Are any of them *single* hand looms, or are all ENGINE looms?

St. Etienne et St. Chamond - 16,310 à 17,360, à *une seule* pièce.
- - - - - - 4,855 à 5,290, à plusieurs pièces, ou à LA BARRE.
A Lyon - - - - 800 à - 900 battans mécaniques à 4 pièces.

No. 3.—How many of the engine looms have the Jacquard apparatus attached?

St. Etienne et St. Chamond - 1,880 à 2,100; plus 80 à 100 à une seule pièce.
A Lyon - - - - 800 à - 900, la totalité des mécaniques des rubans dans cette ville.

No. 4.—What are the prices paid to the workmen for the manufacture of each number of each kind of goods?

St. Etienne et St. Chamond.—Satins et taffetas unis la pièce de 12 aunes:

| English No. - | – | – | 4 | 6 | – | 8 | – | 12 | 16 | 20 | 24 | 30 | 40 | – |
|---|---|---|---|---|---|---|---|---|---|---|---|---|---|---|
| French No. - | 1 | 1½ | 2 | 3 | 4 | 5 | 6 | 7 | 9 | 12 | 16 | 22 | 30 | 40 |
| Centimes | 19 | 20 | 25 | 30 | 35 | 40 | 65 | 95 | 105 | 130 | 150 | 180 | 205 | 230 |
| Gros grain et cordons, la pièce de 12 aunes - | | | | | | | 240 | 310 | 410 | 440 | 510 | 560 | 590 | 660 |
| Gazes rayées - - - ditto - - - | | | | | | | | 105 | 130 | 150 | 180 | 200 | 240 | 290 |
| Ditto, découpées - - ditto - - - | | | | | | | | 130 | 160 | 190 | 260 | 310 | 340 | 390 |

Les prix sont à-peu-près les mêmes dans tous les genres du même numéro, pour les métiers à une pièce comme pour les métiers à plusieurs pièces. (Voir la note, No. 9.)
La dévidage de la trame reste à la charge du maître ouvrier passementier.

Lyon: Rubans façonnées l'aune - - - - - No. 16 - - No. 30
Dessin en 900, 100 à 120 coups tramés, 2 tats l'aune - 45 cents. 60 cents.
D° - „ - 90 à 100 - ditto - 1 tat - - 30 - - 45
Cordons - - - - - - - - Nos. 10 et 12.
Dessin en 900, tramés 2 tats l'aune - - - - 60 cents.
D° - 600 „ 2 d° „ - - - - 50 „
D° 400 et 600 „ 1 d° „ - - - - 45 „
Le dévidage de la trame est au frais de l'ouvrier.

No. 5.—Are the prices stated in answer to question 4, for weaving only? If so, what is paid for warping and winding; what for cutting the gauzes; and what paid for any other kind of labour required in manufacturing?

It faut ajouter au prix de tissage plusieurs autres frais, dont le detail suit:
A St. Etienne et St. Chamond: *f.* *c.*
*Teinture,* 1 kilog. soye, couleur ordinaire, en commune - - - - - 3 -
*Dévidage,* 1 kilog. soye cuite - - - - - - - - - 3 -
„ 1 kilog. d° - écrue - - - - - - - - - 1 50
*Ourdissage,* 1 kilog. d° - cuite ou écrue - - - - - - - 1 -
*Nota.*—L'ourdissage se fait dans l'intérieur des fabriques par des femmes, qui sont payées de 1*f.* à 2*f.* par jour. Il n'y a point de dévidage à compter pour la trame; il est tout au compte de l'ouvrier.
*Découpage* se paie par pièce de 12 aunes, et varie selon que les dessins sont plus ou moins compliqués, et la largeur des rubans depuis 30 centimes jusqu'à 1*f.* 20*c.*, et quelquefois, mais rarement, 2*f.*
Quelque fabriquants ont des ateliers de découpage, et paient les ouvrières à tant par jour; cela revient plus cher que de les faire découper au-dehors. Le plus grand nombre envoie découper à Lyon, où il y a un grand nombre d'ouvrières habiles à ce genre d'ouvrage; elles gagnent de 90*c.* à 1*f.* 20*c.* par jour.

Les

Mr.
*John Dillon.*

4 June,
1832.

Les autres frais d'une fabrique des rubans sont ordinairement évalués de 5 à 6 %. Ils comprennent le loyer et les menus frais de magasin, patente, appointements de commis, tant ceux de magasin que de ceux qui vont visiter à cheval les metiers dans les montagnes, dessinateurs, cartons, &c. &c.

A Lyon :

|  |  |  |  |  |  |  |  |  | *f.* | *c.* | *f.* | *c.* |
|---|---|---|---|---|---|---|---|---|---|---|---|---|
| *Dévidage*, 1 kilog. soye cuite | - | - | - | - | - | - | - | - | 3 | 50 à | 4 | - |
| *Ourdissage*, 1 dº | - dº | - | - | - | - | - | - | - | 1 | 40 „ | 1 | 50 |

Frais divers d'une fabrique de rubans, de 8 à 10 %.
Les autre frais comme à St. Étienne et St. Chamond.

No. 6.—What number of pieces of ribbon is made at one time in each number respectively ?

A St. Etienne et St. Chamond :

| No. 1 et 1½ | - | - | - | - | - | de 28 | - - | à 30 pièces. |
|---|---|---|---|---|---|---|---|---|
| 2 – 3 | - | - | - | - | - | 24 | - - - | 26 ditto. |
| 4 – 5 | - | - | - | - | - | 20 | - - - | 22 ditto. |
| 6 – 7 | - | - | - | - | - | 16 | - - - | 18 ditto. |
| 9 | - | - | - | - | - | 14 | - - - | 16 ditto. |
| 12 | - | - | - | - | - | 12 | - - - | 14 ditto. |
| 16 | - | - | - | - | - | 10 | - - - | 12 ditto. |
| 22 | - | - | - | - | - | 8 | - - - | 10 ditto. |
| 30 | - | - | - | - | - | 6 | - - - | 8 ditto. |

Les métiers à une seule pièce font le plus ordinairement les Nos. larges, 16, 22 et 30. Il y a en outre quelques métiers dans le genre de Lyon qui font de 4 à 6 pièces.

A Lyon :
4 pièces dans tous les genres et tous les Nos.—(Voir la Note, No. 18.)
(Il y a 25 à 30 métiers à une pièce ceintures riches.)

No. 7.—What number of yards or ells does a man generally make in a week or month ?

St. Etienne et St. Chamond :

| Du No. 1 au No. 4 | - - | 8 aunes par jour | - - | 48 aunes par semaine. |
|---|---|---|---|---|
| Ditto 5 - - à 9 | - - | 6 aunes - ditto | - - - | 36 aunes - ditto. |
| Ditto 12 - - à 30 | - - | 4 aunes - ditto | - - - | 24 aunes - ditto. |

L'ouvrier à une seule pièce faite de } - 6 à 8 aunes - ditto - 40 à 45 aunes - ditto.

Lyon :
Tous les genres et numéros, de 1½ aunes à 2 aunes, 10 à 12 aunes, ditto.

No. 8.—How many hours do the weavers generally work ?

De 14 à 15 heures par jour.

No. 9.—What are the present usual earnings of workmen ?

A St. Etienne et St. Chamond :
Les ouvriers se divisent en deux classes :
    1º. Le maître ouvrier, chef d'atelier ou passementier.
    2º. L'ouvrier compagnon.

Le passementier possesseur de plusieurs métiers, se charge de la location, paye en outre le dévidage de la trame, le cannetage, la lumière, et tous les autres frais, entretien ou metier, &c. Les métiers, mecaniques, ustensiles, &c. lui appartiennent ; seul il est responsable envers le fabriquant, tant des matières qui lui sont confiées que de la bonne fabrication, quelques uns en outre (par une centaine environ) payent une patente d'environ 25 francs par an, ce qui leur donne le droit de roter pour la nomination des membres du conseil des prud'hommes. Il retient la moitié de la façon.

L'ouvrier compagnon est logé, mais il se nourrit et pourvoit à son entretien ; il n'a de rapports qu'avec le passementier.

Le gain d'un ouvrier compagnon varie selon le genre d'ouvrage et son habileté.

| Numéros - - | 1 | 1½ | 2 | 3 | 4 | 5 | 6 | 7 | 9 | 12 | 16 | 22 | 30 | 40 |
|---|---|---|---|---|---|---|---|---|---|---|---|---|---|---|
| Satins et Taffet. } unis - - } | 125 | 130 | 140 | 150 | 160 | 170 | 190 | 200 | 210 | 225 | 235 | 250 | 275 | 290 |
| Cordons et gr. grain, environ - - - |  |  |  |  |  |  | 210 | 225 | 240 | 260 | 275 | 300 | 320 | 340 |
| Gazes rayées - - ditto - - - - |  |  |  |  |  |  | 225 | 250 | 275 | 300 | 320 | 340 | 370 | 390 |
| Ditto découpées - ditto - - - - |  |  |  |  |  |  | 250 | 290 | 315 | 340 | 370 | 390 | 425 | 440 |

Le

Mr.
*John Dillon.*

4 June,
1832.

Le gain des ouvriers de la montagne est plus faible que celui des ouvriers à la barre ; il ne fait qu'une seule pièce à la fois tandis que les autres en font plusieurs ; ils ont quelques autres avantages, beaucoup moins de frais de metier et de tout genre, moins de dépense personnelle, moins de tems perdu ; il tisse le double de longueur, ainsi un ouvrier de barre faisant un No. 30. Gage rayée fait 3 aunes par jour à 6 pièces, 18 aunes ou 1½ pièce.

| | |
|---|---:|
| 1½ pièce gaze rayée, No. 30 - - à 2 *f.* 40 *c.* - - - - | 3 *f.* 60 *c.* |
| Moitié pour le passementier - - - - - - - | 1 80 |
| L'ouvrier de montagne fait 6 aunes ou ½ pièce à 2 *f.* 40 *c.* - - - | 1 20 |

Il ne partage pas avec un maître ouvrier, les métiers tiennent peu de place ; donnent peu d'embarras ; chaque ouvrier à la sienne ; les autres ouvriers employés à la fabrique de rubans, tels que les ouvriers teinturiers, apprêteurs, et gagnent de 1 *f.* 50 *c.* à 2 *f.* par jour ; les femmes la moitié environ.

Lyon :

Il y a comme à St. Etienne et St. Chamond le même maître ouvrier et le compagnon ; le compagnon gagne par jour de 2 *f.* 25 *c.* à 2 *f.* 50 *c.* (moitié de la façon.) Les autres ouvriers à-peu-près comme à St. Etienne.

No. 10.—What kinds or descriptions of ribbons are made ?

St. Etienne et St. Chamond :
Gazes rayées à bandes satin, et simatin ; ditto, façonnées et découpées.
Satins, taffetas, gr. grain, velours et unis ; ditto, façonnées.
Galons, lacets de tout genre, soye et calon, et enfin tous les genres, mais fort peu des articles riches, 2 tats qu' on fabrique à Lyon.

Lyon :
Rubans riches, grand façonné, 1 et 2 tats en satins gr. grain, &c. broches et chinés, &c.
Teintures riches 2 tats et façonné ordinaire, peu ou point de gazes.
Quelques qualités moindres dans les mêmes genres pour la consommation d'Amérique et d'Allemagne.

No. 11.—In what proportions are they made, satins, figured and plain, gauzes, &c. &c ?

St. Etienne et St. Chamond :

| | | |
|---|---:|---|
| Gazes rayés diverses - - - - - - | 30 | - ⎫ |
| Ditto - découpées - - - - - | 25 | - ⎪ |
| Taff. gr. grain satins façonnées - - - - | 15 | - ⎬ sur 100. |
| Cordons, divers - - - - - - | 10 | - ⎪ |
| Taff. et satins unis, &c. - - - - - | 20 | - ⎭ |

Proportion des divers genres de Métiers :

Métiers à la Barre.

| | | |
|---|---|---|
| 1500 à 1650 | Taffetas toutes largeurs et genres. |
| 750 à 850 | Satins unis forts et légers. |
| 175 à 200 | Velours, doubles pièces. |
| 450 à 500 | Façonnés anciens métiers à tambour (gazes rayées.) |
| 1900 à 2000 | ditto, à la jacquard - - - - - ⎫ Articles façonnés riches gazes |
| 80 à 90 | ditto, 4 à 6 pièces ditto genre de Lyon ⎬ ou autres. |

4855 à 5290

Métiers à haute lisse à une pièce.

80 à 100 à la Jacquard, ceintures et garnitures riches, satins et gr. grain.

230 à 260 ordinaire ceintures, gazes, brochées, &c. &c.

310 à 360

Métiers Casse lisse à une Pièce.

16000 à 17000 Ces métiers sont dans les montagnes autour de la ville ; ils fabriquent tous les genres de dispositions unis et raguses et petits desseins, &c.

Lyon :
Il y a trop de variété et de caprice dans les demandes pour pourvoir donner la proportion des divers genres de rubans à Lyon, articles pour la haute consommation ; ce seront des satins brochés, riches ou chinés, pour l'hiver, gr. grain ; idem pour le printems, ou les deux genres, en même tems, fort peu de gazes.

| | | Sur 100. |
|---|---|---|
| Satins brochés ou chinés grand façonné ⎫ | | |
| Gros grain - - do. - ⎱ditto - ⎭ - - - - | 75 *f.* à 78 *f.* |
| Teintures brochés ou - ditto - - - - | 20 à 25 |
| Gazes, &c. - - - - - ditto - - - - | 2 à 3 |

No. 12.

Mr.
*John Dillon.*

4 June,
1832.

No. 12.—Do the French continue to import plain sarsnet ribbons from Switzerland, and in what quantities?

La France importe de Suisse des rubans unis, taffetas et galons.

On suppose que la quantité est environ un tiers de sa consommation.

Il a été impossible d'obtenir des renseignemens satisfaisants.

No. 13.—What is the quantity of silk used in the whole ribbon manufacture?

St. Etienne et St. Chamond  -  de 325 à 340 mille kilog.
Lyon  - - - - - - - de 14 à 15 mille kilog.

No. 14.—What kinds of silk, and what proportions of each kind?

Il n'y a aucune règle fixe pour l'emploi des soyes dans la fabrique du rubans comme pour tous les tissus de soye en général; c'est indifféremment en soye de France ou soye etrangère, Piémont, Italie, ou toute autre, selon le genre d'articles ou les idées de chaque fabriquant. Il serait tout-à-fait impossible d'en donner les proportions.

No. 15.—What are the present prices of each?

Selon la Note ci jointe, cours du 20 Avril:

Organsin Piemont, jaune, 2<sup>me</sup> sorte, titre de 22–23 à 30–32 deniers, de 33*f*. à 28*f*. 50 *c*.
Organsin de Pays, jaune, 2<sup>me</sup> sorte, titre de 20–21 à 28–30 deniers, 34*f*. à 30*f*. 50 *c*.
Trame Piemont, jauue, 1<sup>re</sup> sorte, titre de 25–26 deniers, 29*f*. à 55*f*. 60 *c*. 24*f*. 50 *c*.
Grège Milan, titre de 9–10 à 18–20 deniers, à 27*f*. 50 *c*. à 23*f*.
Grège de France, 2<sup>me</sup> sorte, titre de 9–10 à 18–20 deniers, 28*f*. à 24*f*.

Prix pour la livre poids de marc, 492 grammes, avec escompte de 11 %, payable à 3 mois, ou 12½ %, payable comptant. (Il est rare que les fabriquants ne payent la soye comptant pour recevrir les 12½ %.) On appelle Don des soyes 1 %, qu'on donne sur les soyes grèges Françaises.

No. 16.—What is the present price of the silk used in manufacturing the gauze ribbons; is it more than 22 *s.* the English pound weight?

La livre poids de marc de soye montée en marabout, toute teinte et préparée pour la fabrication des gazes, vaut environ 35 à 39 francs escompte d'usage.

On nomme marabout la soye qu'on emploie à la fabrication des gazes. Ce sont deux organsins blancs du titre de 30–35 deniers, assez fortement tordus ensemble. On emploie indifféremment pour cet usage la soye de pays ou la soye étrangère; les organsins de Piemont sont estimés.

On fait d'abord teindre l'organsin; on le fait divider, et on l'envoie au moulin qui lui donne le tors voulu, et le rend sur des bobines (à-peu-près plié comme le fil de coton en peloton.)

La plûpart des moulins pour maraboutage est dans les environs de St. Chamond. Il y en a quelques uns à Lyon, qui consomme une grande quantité de soye montée en marabout, pour tous les genres d'articles dont la gaze est le fond.

Le maraboutage coute environ 5 à 6 francs le kilog: il y a en sus un faible déchet, ainsi:

| | | *f.* | *c.* |
|---|---|---|---|
| 1 Livre organsin, 30–32 deniers, blancs, vaut  -  -  - | | 31 | — |
| Teinture en cru - - - - - - - - - | | 1 | — |
| Dévidage - ditto - - - - - - | 125 | à 1 | — |
| Maraboutage - - - - - - - - | | 3 | — |
| 1 poids de marc, ou 492 gr. valent - - - - | | 36 | — |
| La livre Anglaise n'étant que de 454 gram. ne couterait que à déduise escompte d'usage, 11 %; plus 1½ % pour comptant, ci 12½ %  - - - - - - - - - | | 33 | 25 |
| | | 4 | 15 |
| Net  -  - | | 29 | 10 |
| Ajouter p<sup>r</sup> menus frais, &c.  - | | — | 25 |
| Francs  -  - | | 29 | 35 |

Or, the English pound weight, net, 23 *s.* 6 *d.*

No. 17.—What duties are paid in France on the silk used in the ribbon manufacture, or on the import of foreign manufactured ribbons?—

Les droits d'entrée sur les soyes pour rubans sont les mêmes que sur toutes les autres espèces de soye, parce qu'il n'y a point de genre de soye destiné particulièrement à la fabrication des rubans:

1*f*. 20 *c*. - - le kilog. soye grège.
2  40 - - - d° - d° moulinée.

Les rubans fabriqués à l'étranger payent à leur entrée en France 8*f*. 17 *c*. le kilog.; ce qui fait environ 15 à 17 %.

No. 18.

Mr.
*John Dillon.*

4 June,
1832.

No. 18.—Have any, and what improvements been recently made in the looms, or generally in the manufacture of ribbons?

Il y ad'as sez grands perfectionnemens apportés aux métiers de rubans, par l'effet de procédés qu'on a adaptés aux battans mécaniques, et qui rendent le passage de la navette beaucoup plus doux.

Le perfectionnement le plus remarquable est l'invention faite à Lyon il y a deux à trois ans, de battans mécaniques à quatre pièces et à plusieurs navettes. Ces articles riches, qui se fabriquaient à St. Etienne sur les anciens métiers à une seule pièce avec difficulté, et des moyens bornés, se font actuellement par 4 pièces, et la complication de broché ou lancé à plusieurs trames, jointe à toute la puissance de la mécanique à la jacquard, a créé un genre neuf qui est resté à Lyon, et que St. Etienne ne peut imiter :

1°.—Parce que les ouvriers de Lyon sont beaucoup plus habiles et plus intelligens pour les articles difficiles :

2°.—Parceque les dessinateurs de Lyon, accoutumés à vaincre toutes les difficultés par la complications des étaffes larges, gazes façonnés, &c. l'emportent de beaucoup sur ceux de St. Etienne pour le goût et la perfection des dessins :

3°.—Et enfin, par la faculté si précieuse d'adapter ces battans mécaniques à tous les métiers de façonné à Lyon, ce qui permet à l'ouvrier de faire des schalls ou tout autre espèce d'article, il lui suffit, aussi-tôt que la pièce est achevée, de changer le battans. Cet avantage est immense pour des articles de goût, qui perdent de leur valeur aussi-tôt qu'ils sont connus. St. Etienne, qui a essayé ces métiers, n'ayant que des rubans à fabriquer, ne pouvant les faire travailler toute l'année, ont été forcés d'y renoncer.

Par les raisons qui viennent d'être indiquées, Lyon peut avoir très facilement jusqu'à 15 ou 1800 métiers de rubans, et les réduire à volonté entre les saisons. C'est un article de plus en façonné, il peut s'arrêter, et se recommencer selon les caprices de la mode.

No. 19.—What is the supposed annual value of the ribbons made in France?

St. Etienne et St. Chamond, de 30 à 32 millions de francs.
Lyon, de 1 million à 1200 mille francs.

### Addition.

No. 20.—On a supposed value of 100 francs in ribbons, how much is the silk? how much the making and expenses, &c.?

#### St. Etienne et St. Chamond.

| | Soye. | Façons, &c. |
|---|---|---|
| | *f.* | *f.* |
| Gaze ord^re - - - - - | 50 à 55 - - - - | 45 à 50 |
| D° découpée - - - - | 40 à 45 - - - - | 55 à 60 |
| Articles pleins div^s - - - - | 60 à 65 - - - - | 35 à 40 |
| Lyon : | | |
| Façonnés ord^res - - - - | 65 à 68 - - - - | 32 à 35 |
| D° - - Riches melange de gaze et } grand chine - - -} | 45 à 50 - - - - | 50 à 55 |

---

### Mr. *Richard Bottrell*, called in; and Examined.

Mr.
*Richard Bottrell.*

7748. WHAT experience have you had in French and India manufactured silk goods?—An experience of upwards of 20 years.

7749. During that period you have resided both in London and on the Continent?—I have.

7750. Have you been in the habit of attending the Custom House sales of silks?—Constantly for the last 20 years.

7751. Have you ever been called in to examine goods which have been seized by the Custom House officers?—Yes, occasionally.

7752. Do you import?—No; we had a concern on the Continent, to which we sent the goods bought at the Custom House sales.

7753. Have you been acquainted with the extent and manner and cost of smuggling before 1826, and since 1826?—Yes, I know something of it.

7754. Do you imagine that smuggling is carried on to a greater extent now than formerly?—Certainly not; and in different kinds of goods altogether.

7755. What were the articles smuggled before 1826?—Gloves, cambrics and laces, vast quantities of plain and twilled silks, silk hose, India bandannas and taffaties and China crapes; these are the principal articles; but almost all kinds of French and India silk goods were smuggled largely previous to 1826.

7756. At what expense were they smuggled previous to 1826?—The expense varied according to circumstances. I have known Mechlin lace smuggled as low

as

Mr.
*Richard Bottrell.*

4 June,
1832.

as five to seven and a half per cent. Bandannas were generally passed over for 3 *s.* 6 *d.* a piece, and silks from half a franc to 75 centimes the ell, which was from 12½ to 18 or 20 per cent.

7757. Can you state the manner in which the business was conducted in India bandannas?—Bandannas were purchased at the India House, and some few at the Custom House sales, for exportation; shipped to Ostend, Calais, Dunkirk and Boulogne, and there opened and repacked in convenient packages, containing from 20 to 30 and 50 pieces each; each package having three envelopes, one of calico, another of oiled linen, and the outside of canvass, and slung like a knapsack that they might be rapidly removed the moment they were landed. These goods remained in the depôt at Calais, Boulogne, &c. and were taken out at a very small expense, as occasions offered, and sent over in lots of two, four or five hundred pieces at a time. India goods at one period left a much larger profit than French goods.

7758. What period are you speaking of?—I am speaking of the great smuggling period before 1826; after the battle of Waterloo principally. French silks are packed up in a similar manner as bandannas were, and in packages containing from six to twelve pieces each.

7759. If there had been a demand, could any quantity have been smuggled at the same price?—At that period there were large profits made; fifty to a hundred per cent. I believe as many were brought over as could be got over then.

7760. Supposing at that period there had been the power of introducing into this country ten times the quantity that were introduced, would there have been any difficulty in selling them?—Ten times is a large increase, but considerably larger quantities than were brought over could have been sold.

7761. If there was so large a profit as 50 per cent. how do you account for it, that there was not a greater quantity of smuggling carried on than what you represent?—I think they sent over nearly all the bandannas they could get; there were 50 or 60 houses along the coast that keep stocks of silk and other goods, and they were constantly occupied in sending to England.

7762. How did they dispose of those goods in England?—A great quantity no doubt was sold all round the English coast, and particularly at the watering places during the summer; London, Bath, Bristol and the other great towns took large quantities.

7763. Speaking of those that were disposed of at the watering places, was it not principally at the bathing rooms and the hair dressers' shops?—I should think not, compared with the whole quantity.

7764. Where were they disposed of in London?—At various shops and warehouses, and by various persons, almost all the servants of the nobility and gentry were dealers.

7765. Do you think the respectable shops and warehouses kept a stock by them?—Whether they always sold by pattern I cannot say, but many respectable concerns supplied their customers with prohibited goods.

7766. Have you any idea of the whole quantity sold in London in any one year?—The computation was, that in bandannas alone there was at least 50,000 pieces smuggled annually for some years.

7767. And what quantity of French silks?—I should suppose (at the least) to the extent of 400,000 *l.*; formerly there were very large sales, not only at the London Custom House but at various out ports, of French silks that had been seized, but now the sales are much smaller, and much less frequent.

7768. Were not the quantities seized generally in very small parcels?—We have purchased to the extent of 1,500 *l.* at one sale; and at the Custom House fire our loss exceeded 1,200 *l.* in gloves, silks and bandannas which had been purchased only a few days previous to the fire.

7769. Did you frequently buy whole pieces under such circumstances?—Frequently.

7770. What kind of silk do you speak of chiefly?—Florences, levantines, satins, &c.

7771. Do you think that the large houses at the West end of London sold considerable quantities of those silks?—No doubt of it; they were obliged to sell them.

7772. What is the largest seizure that you ever recollect?—I have known sales arising from seizures of from one to two and three hundred pieces of silk.

7773. What

Mr.
*Richard Bottrell.*

4 June,
1832.

7773. What is the highest amount of expense you have known, in any instance, of the smuggling of French goods prior to 1826?—About 25 per cent.

7774. Then the goods purchased at the Custom House sales did not form a very considerable part of the whole of the French silk goods imported?—But a small part.

7775. Did you ever know an instance in which it was necessary to sink silks?— Such a thing has occurred; spirits are now generally sunk, but they scarcely ever sink silks.

7776. Can you explain how French silks are brought over?—The general plan of getting them over is to ship them from the French port in a lugger, the lugger having a galley on board; they then proceed a certain distance, and according to the information they receive from other boats they are in correspondence with, either continue their voyage or return. It frequently happens once, and sometimes even twice, they come back without making a landing; at other times they proceed smoothly, and as they keep up good communications, they have at least two notices on their way home; the sea risk is not considered great.

7777. There is before the Committee a Parliamentary Return from the year 1816 to 1826, of a period of eleven years, in which the whole number of seizures is stated at 11,318, the total value of the whole so seized in all those years being no more than 107,000 *l.*, giving about 9 *l.*, as the value for each separate seizure; how do you reconcile that with your opinion, that frequently 300 pieces of goods were seized at a time?—I have known instances of from one to 300 pieces having been sold. I know an equally large quantity to have been shipped from Calais, and they were seized in three different places. There is no doubt that the goods for exportation were formerly sold very cheap, for I have bought French gloves as low as 3 *s.* a dozen; and then the Custom House sales were generally advantageous to the buyer. Within the last eighteen months I have purchased seized silk goods for less than one-third of their value. I did not sell them all in England, I shipped part to India, and part to Flanders, and the after sales was in accordance with my statement. The quantity of silk goods seized expressed in yards, or in lbs. weight, would enable the Committee to form a better opinion than the nett proceeds in money as sold at the Custom House sales.

7778. Were those goods sold for exportation?—They were.

7779. You have spoken of a purchase made when those goods were prohibited, at which you bought goods at one-third of their value, does not that prove that there was great difficulty and great danger in dealing in those goods, or you would have found persons to compete with you in the purchase of them?—I do not think that was the reason, because now when there is scarcely any profit to be made, we find a vast number of persons attending the Custom House sales. This may arise from there being a greater number of persons in business now than formerly; a greater competition, and a general diminution of profits in all branches of trade and industry.

7780. Is not it much easier to dispose of smuggled goods now than it was before 1826?—It is not so easy to dispose of them now, as during the period of prohibition.

7781. Was there not always a danger in having them in your possession?— There was.

7782. Does not the smuggler find it much easier to evade the laws now, in selling the goods than he did formerly?—A person that keeps a stock of silk goods does not run the same risk now that he did formerly.

7783. Prior to 1826 were not French goods, smuggled into this country, publicly sold in the shops in London?—They were sold by pattern to my knowledge; I do not recollect that I ever saw a piece exposed in a shop, but they were sold equally well by pattern.

7784. During the period from 1816 to 1826, did you ever see a piece of French ribbon exposed in a shop window?—I never saw any ribbons so exposed; nor had the French that variety of ribbons then that they produce now.

7785. What do you attribute that increased variety of ribbons to?—It must be owing to the changes in fashion, and the desire to have constant novelties.

7786. It has been stated to the Committee, that a great part of the import of ribbons are gauze ribbons, were gauzes manufactured in France to any extent before 1826?—I never saw any quantities of gauze ribbons before 1826, we have had craped gauzes, and plain gauzes in small quantities, and of very superior quality; plain and figured lutestring ribbons were followed and superseded by

678.                            the

Mr.
Richard Bottrell.

4 June,
1832.

the shaded ducapes and lutestrings; when they went out gauzes came in, and ever since (but particularly during 1830 and the early part of 1831), the country has been completely inundated with them.

7787. Are not a great proportion of the gauzes introduced into this country smuggled?—There are vast quantities smuggled, more perhaps in 1830 and 1831 than paid duty.

7788. You have stated that from 50 to 100 per cent. has been made upon French silk goods, how then do you account for the rate of smuggling being so low as 15 or 20 per cent.?—There were 50 persons to one engaged in smuggling formerly to what there are now.

7789. Do you not think the diminution is owing to the difficulty, hazard and disgrace of the thing?—There was no greater difficulty formerly, than now.

7790. How closely could a vessel approach the shore, without being liable to seizure, if she had French silks on board?—An English vessel, four leagues from the North Foreland, or Beachy Head; a foreigner, one league.

7791. At the present time may a vessel anchor off the Custom House?—She certainly may; but if you allude to the manifest of the goods, that makes an essential difference now and previous to 1826.

7792. If those persons could make 50 per cent. by smuggling, and yet the trade was not increased so as to diminish the profit, must there not have been something to prevent persons from entering that trade?—Business in general was more profitable formerly than it is now; so with the men who worked the goods, they soon became dealers, and purchased in small quantities for themselves, but they never sold at small profits.

7793. If the profit was so large, how was it that all the parties engaged did not participate more equally in the profit?—Some did; it often happened that the smugglers themselves subscribed as far as their means would allow, and thus in addition to freight, shared a part of the profit.

7794. If such a great profit was made, must not a proportionate risk have been incurred?—Certainly; you cannot at any time smuggle without some risk.

7795. When you say that you could bring over bandannas at 3s. 6d. a piece, do you mean that that was the cost of bringing them over, or that you could insure the bringing them over for that sum?—That was the freight for bringing them over when you employed a boat's crew yourself.

7796. What could you have insured their being brought over for?—From 5s. to 7s.

7797. Do you mean to say, that from the large profits you have mentioned, there is to be deducted the losses in consequence of seizures?—Certainly.

7798. Can you state the proportion of seizures at that time?—I cannot; but I know that many insurers made upwards of 15 per cent. profit per quarter.

7799. When you speak of silks being smuggled at from 15 to 20 per cent., do you mean to say that they were insured for that?—They were; but I have known an instance where a quantity of silk goods were sent over (without being insured,) and they were landed safe at less than five per cent.

7800. What period do you speak of?—Just after the battle of Waterloo.

7801. What is the present rate of smuggling on broad goods?—From 15 to 20 per cent.

7802. Do you think that our coast system was so well organized at the period of the battle of Waterloo as it has been since?—Certainly not; but I think the Custom House officers were more upon the alert then than they are now.

7803. What is the present rate paid for smuggling ribbons?—I think I could get ribbons at a rather less rate than broad silks; but they could be charged just as high as broad silks if you had them from any of the large houses in Calais.

7804. You have stated that the present rate is from 15 to 20 per cent., does that include every expense?—Twenty per cent. would include every thing delivered at any place in London.

7805. Before the year 1826, would it have been the same?—Just the same. But when profits were large, persons could afford to be liberal; and in cases of success, douceurs were given by way of encouragement to the men.

7806. Then in fact there is very little alteration?—Very little.

7807. Except that there is the advantage of being able to dispose of the goods more readily?—No, there is the great advantage of more safely keeping them, but not in selling more readily; there is not now the same demand or desire for them.

7808. You stated that there was an alteration in the description of goods that
are

Mr.
*Richard Bottrell.*

4 June,
1832.

are imported now from France, as compared with what were imported formerly?
—Formerly rich broad goods, and I think of a very superior quality to any that
come from France now; silk hose and kid gloves were then abundant, but now we
rarely see a pair of gloves, or a pair of stockings, and but few plain silks; gauze
ribbons and blond laces, are the principal articles now smuggled.

7809. You say that at that time it cost about 20 per cent. to smuggle, and that
now it costs about the same; if you smuggle gauze ribbons, are you not also to take
into consideration that gauze ribbons is an article much easier to smuggle than
broad silk would have been; and that therefore the price of smuggling broad silks
would be greater?—It would be rather more on broad silks, but a difference of a
few pounds weight on a large quantity would not be of much consequence.

7810. You stated that the rate of smuggling was from 18 to 20 per cent., and
that it is now from 15 to 20 per cent.; has it then decreased?—The rate varies
two and a half to five per cent., according to the circumstances of the case.

7811. Can silk goods be smuggled now at the same rate as when they were
prohibited?—It is about the same, but it will depend upon the quantity. If you
have a large quantity, you may make a bargain with the insurance company, and
two and a half per cent. may be reduced.

7812. Were the packages larger or smaller in 1826 than they are now?—
Sometimes in larger packages, but principally of about 30 or 40 lbs. weight, as
at present.

7813. Do you think that if the duties were reduced the price of smuggling
would be diminished?—I can hardly give an opinion; but it is certain the small
smugglers are nearly all annihilated in consequence of the diminution of profits.

7814. Do you think the amount of smuggling would be diminished?—I think
it would.

7815. Are not the goods which are entered at the Custom House for duty
examined at various places?—They are.

7816. Would it not be better, both for Government and the British manufacturer, that Foreign silks should be examined at one place and be subject to a
greater check and better examination than at present?—It would be decidedly
better than the present mode.

7817. What do you suppose to be the proportionate value of French manufactured silks smuggled into this country now, and before 1826?—The value was
generally estimated at 400,000*l.* a year; now but few plain broad silks are
smuggled.

7818. What do you suppose to be the quantity of ribbons now smuggled?—
I can hardly form an estimate.

7819. Do you suppose that it is above 400,000*l.*?—No, I should think not
above half that sum.

7820. Are any Indian bandannas smuggled at present?—None.

7821. What is the duty on Indian bandannas?—Twenty per cent.

7822. Taking the piece at the India House to be about 20*s.* per piece, the duty
then is 4*s.*?—It is.

7823. Did smuggling in Indian bandannas cease in 1826?—Immediately the
prohibitory laws were repealed.

7824. And you believe none have been smuggled since?—None from the
Continent; but a few pieces are brought occasionally by the East India ships.
We have India goods now in Flanders we cannot dispose of, that formerly com-
manded an immediate sale.

7825. Was the duty on bandannas always an *ad valorem* duty?—At the India
House the duty was first at the rate of 1*s.* the square yard, but it was soon altered
to the present duty.

7826. Do you think that upon the whole, at this moment, the price of smuggling
is dearer or cheaper than it was formerly?—I think the insurance companies would
charge rather more, because there is less to do, and fewer persons to do it. There
were formerly as many as 50 or 60 houses concerned in this business, and now
there are not one-tenth of that number.

7827. How do you mean concerned?—In keeping stocks to supply English
smugglers.

7828. Would not the business of that class of persons naturally expire with the
alteration of the law which allows every person to go to France and purchase his
goods?—Certainly; that and the consequent diminution of profits.

7829. Was not the value of the goods imported before 1826 greater than the value of the same quantity of goods now?—The value must have been greater previous to 1826.

7830. What reduction do you think there has been in the price of silk goods in France since 1826?—The reduction in price has not been so great I conceive as the reduction in the quality of the article; and this is partly occasioned by new systems of dyeing. I should think the reduction at least 25 per cent.

7831. Were not some of the silks formerly imported foreign thrown silk, and not manufactured silk?—Very little thrown; the greater part manufactured; the last lot of thrown silk smuggled was in 1823; and then only ten small ballots.

7832. Was foreign thrown silk smuggled to any extent formerly under the 14 s. 8 d. duty?—There was some, but no very great quantity.

7833. Do you recollect when the preventive service was first established?—I cannot now state the exact date.

7834. Do you remember whether at that time it increased the cost of smuggling?—It paralyzed it for a short time, but afterwards it seemed to re-assume its activity.

7835. Do you not consider the price of smuggling to be regulated by the duty? —I think the duty ought to have some effect upon it; but there are so many men round the coast out of employ, that if a profit could be made the goods would soon be got over.

7836. Can you inform the Committee whether smuggling is more advantageous to the smuggler now than formerly?—It is not at all advantageous now; they cannot sell the goods with any facility when they are got over; formerly they could always sell them and at a large profit; I think the insurers get their work done cheaper now than formerly.

7837. If the importers could not pay the present rate per cent., would the smuggler endeavour to do it for less?—On some goods he might; fancy goods and gauze ribbons still pay.

7838. Would they take 10 instead of 15 per cent.?—It would not answer the insurer's purpose; he could not make a profit by the business at such low rates.

7839. The parties directly engaged in the transaction, exposing themselves to great personal risk, and the parties insuring the goods to a pecuniary loss; must not the price paid for smuggling depend upon those two circumstances?—Certainly; and the reason it is increased now is, that the men are subject to so many risks, and to be sent on board a man-of-war.

7840. Will a man ever have occupation in smuggling unless he can smuggle at a less rate than the duty?—Certainly not.

7841. Are any cambrics smuggled now?—None.

7842. Can you state what the average duty upon cambrics is?—The duty is about 6 s. for six ells, from 8 to 15 per cent., varying according to quality; cambrics are very low in price, and not so much in fashion as formerly.

7843. Do you believe that any velvets or other manufactures of silks are smuggled from Germany?—None, the sea voyage is too long, and velvets too bulky to smuggle.

7844. Do you mean that they do not smuggle silks from Belgium or Holland, but only from the French ports?—To no extent, but from France; for unless you can keep up a telegraphic communication between the two shores, smuggling cannot be carried on to any advantage.

7845. Is that done between Calais and Dover?—It is.

7846. Will you state how?—The boat which leaves Calais with the goods communicates with other boats ostensibly engaged in fishing, and which do fish, and from them they receive intelligence as to the stations of the cutters, where cruizing, &c., and they have carried it to such perfection that they consider the sea risk to be scarcely anything; in fact, not one per cent. Besides, there is very little inducement for sailors of King's ships to look out for smugglers, for when the men of war make captures the men get scarcely any thing. I attended a sale at Deal some time ago, and was curious to know how the money would be divided; I found, on searching the London Gazette, (17th January 1831) that the captain in one case had 258 l. 3 s. 9 d., and the 8th class seamen 1 s. 5¼ d., 7th class 2 s. 11½ d., 6th class 4 s. 5 d. This was a seizure of silks, spirits and tea; and upon another occasion (the 10th January 1832) likewise silks, spirits and tea, the captain received 30 l. 6 s. 11 d., and the 8th class sailor had 7 d., 7th class, 1 s. 2 d., 6th class, 1 s. 9¼ d.; these facts speak for themselves.

7847. Is

Mr.
*Richard Bottrell.*

4 June,
1832.

7847. Is the difficulty greater in landing goods from France than formerly?—It ought to be greater than it was on account of the coast guard, but the difficulty in landing is much diminished in consequence of having such quick communication from coast to coast; the greater difficulty is in getting the goods up to London, and safely delivered.

7848. What kind of goods were formerly smuggled that are not smuggled at present?—Bandannas, and all descriptions of India goods, China crapes and taffetas, which formerly fetched from 7s. to 12s. a yard, and are now scarcely saleable at any price.

7849. What has been the effect of the repeal of our prohibitory laws at Ostend, Dunkirk and Calais, and other places along the opposite coast, as regards the sale of India and French silks?—There are no India goods sold, and but few French.

7850. What effect has smuggling generally upon the trade of this country?—It is my opinion that the quantity (except in fancy goods and gauze ribbons) has not been of so much consequence as the price at which they have been offered. Parties selling smuggled goods do great injury by jobbing the goods; thus reducing the standard of value, and depreciating similar articles in the public estimation.

7851. As you have resided in Belgium, are you aware whether any English goods are smuggled into France?—There are large quantities smuggled into France; it is estimated that Paris alone takes English goods through Belgium to the amount of ten millions of francs or 400,000 l. English; vast quantities of bobbin nets, muslins, printed cottons, fine shirtings, quiltings, hosiery, in fact almost all description of fine Manchester and Scotch goods, besides articles of Sheffield and Birmingham manufacture, and even some double milled kerseymeres and best English superfine blue cloths, are smuggled into France; the prohibited numbers of yarns are likewise passed in; last year when I was in the north of France a holder of yarns assured me, although cash had been paid for them in Manchester, the market was so well supplied they could not realize ten per cent. profit upon them.

7852. For what purpose are the fine muslins of twist used?—For weaving muslins in France.

7853. What is the expense of smuggling goods into France through Belgium?—The expense of smuggling must be greater in France than in England; I should think the expense exceeds 30 per cent. in getting English goods to Paris.

7854. Can you state what is the expense of getting them across the Belgian frontier?—It is impossible to state precisely; it differs according to the description of the goods, the quantity and the season of the year.

7855. You say that the price of smuggling is greater in France than in England; what is that owing to?—It is owing to their having so many Custom House officers, gens d'armes, and fortified towns.

7856. Does not the prohibition in France make it more difficult to smuggle into France than into England?—English goods have always been prohibited in France, yet they have been smuggled.

7857. Are all the articles you have mentioned prohibited in France?—All prohibited except some few numbers of yarns.

7858. You have stated, that there are so many people hanging about the English coast that have nothing to do, that they are glad to employ themselves in smuggling at a very low rate, what rate of duty could protect the English manufacturer against so much competition amongst the smugglers?—I am not prepared to answer the question relative to duty now, it will require much consideration. As regards the men who are hired to work the boats, they do not earn much; but the risk is so great on the part of the insurers that less than 15 to 20 per cent. would at no time pay them. In fact some silk goods are as cheap in England as in France, and whilst our manufacturers continue to sell at such small profits there is scarcely an inducement to smuggle plain silks.

7859. Do you consider that prohibition will better protect the trade than any rate of duty?—It evidently was the case, that during prohibition vast quantities of silk and other goods were smuggled from France, but then there was a profit to be made, the material being dearer here, and wages much higher than in France. Prices more generally approximating now, I do not think that smuggling would go on to the same extent as it did formerly.

7860. Is

Mr.
*Richard Bottrell.*

4 June,
1832.

7860. Is not the question of smuggling altogether a question of profit?—Certainly.

7861. At present, has not the competition existing among the insurance companies in France brought down the rate of smuggling to the lowest possible extent?—The diminution of profits has decreased the contraband trade, and consequently the number of the insurers, and not a competition amongst themselves.

7862. Do you not believe that a renewal of the prohibition would restore some of those companies that have now ceased to do business?—It would depend upon the relative price of silk goods in France and England.

7863. At the period when so much smuggling did go on under the prohibition, was it not under the circumstance that an immense profit was to be gained, which you have stated would not be so great now, even if the prohibition were renewed?—That is my opinion.

7864. Do you think that the competition among the British manufacturers would keep down smuggling, or at least keep it within moderate bounds?—It does so now in a variety of articles.

7865. Might not smuggling be prevented or rendered more difficult than it is at present?—I think it might by good regulations.

7866. Have you any suggestions to offer to the Committee upon that subject?—I have, in my hand, a copy of a paper which was forwarded to the Board of Trade, suggesting several regulations upon the subject, which I beg permission to deliver in.

[*The Witness delivered in the same, which is as follows:*]

MEMORANDUMS relative to a proposed Alteration and Amendment in the System of paying Duties on Foreign Silk Goods.

Two DUTIES to be levied:

1st, An *ad valorem* Duty of 10 per Cent.
2d, A Duty (additional) by Weight, according to the following Scale.

| | s. | d. | | | s. | d. |
|---|---|---|---|---|---|---|
| Silks - plain - - | 6 | – per lb. | RIBBONS: | | | |
| Do. - figured - - | 10 | – — | | | | |
| Satins - plain black - | 6 | – — | Gauze of all kinds - - | | 16 | – per lb. |
| Do. - white and coloured | 8 | – — | | | | |
| Do. - figured - - | 13 | 4 — | Figured, without Gauze - | | 13 | 4 — |
| Velvets, plain - - - | 13 | 4 — | All others, plain, without Gauze - - - | | 8 | – — |
| Do. - figured - - | 16 | – — | | | | |
| Crapes, Gauzes, Lisse, &c. of the Italian kind - | 16 | - -- | Velvet Ribbons, as Velvets. | | | |
| Crapes, Gauzes, Shawls, Handkerchiefs, Dresses, &c. of the China kind, plain - - - - | 16 | – — | Blonds, and all kinds of Lace, *ad valorem* of - - | | 15 per Cent. | |
| | | | Shawls, of Wool, of Wool and Silk, or Wool and Cotton - - - | | 25 per Cent. | |

Articles not decidedly plain to be considered figured.

When mixed with Thread, Cotton, or any inferior material, to pay the full Silk Duty.

All figured Ribbons exceeding 4 oz. to the piece of 18 yards, or 7 oz. to the garniture of 36 yards, to pay a further Duty of Two Shillings per oz. on the extra weight.

Gloves to remain at present Duties, but the Duty on Lamb and Kid Skins to be abolished.

All articles whatever worked with Silk, or printed, to pay an additional Duty of 50 per Cent. on the rate by weight; and all articles mixed with metal to pay the highest rate of Duty, *viz.* 16 *s.* and 50 per Cent.

## REGULATIONS.

1st.—An Annual License - - - - Importer - - - 10 guineas.
                                         Wholesale - - - 4 ditto.
                                         Retail - - - 2 ditto.
                                         Ship (quere) - -

All persons passing entries inwards for Foreign Silk goods above the value of 20 *l.* to be considered importers. Goods not to be delivered till license is produced.

2d.—All Silk goods to pay duty at one place or depôt to be entirely devoted to that purpose. The *ad valorem* duty (should the declared value be approved of) to be first levied, then the duty by weight; and every import to be fully and particularly
**entered**

entered in a journal and pasted into a properly ruled ledger. These, with the addition of a pattern book, would form a highly useful reference for the merchant and manufacturer.

3d.—Silks imported *via* " Dover," to be forwarded under seals of office to the *depôt in London*, where only silk goods should be examined for duty. British silk goods, entitled to " *bounty on exportation*," to be examined at same place.

4th.—All imports to be in cases ; and when a case shall not be fairly full, to be liable to seizure.

5th.—All silk goods to be accompanied with a " Consular Certificate," specifying "marks and numbers," measurement of each case, gross weight (case included), shipper and consignee. In default, goods to be forfeited.

6th.—The ship's manifest to be without erasure or interlineation ; and the particulars of all cases containing Silk goods to appear on the manifest in like manner, and to accord with the Consul's certificate. In default, forfeiture of goods and penalty. Consuls to forward to Custom House, London, duplicate certificates, and to sign their names to all manifests, in such a manner that *no* insertion can afterwards be made above their signature.

  *Note.*—The total number of packages, bales, cases, &c., written in words at length by the Consul when he signs, would render all manifests complete.

7th.—All Silk goods to be stamped.

———

7867. Are you not aware that under the present system goods are passed at a less rate per cent. at the Custom House, than was intended by law ?—I believe it to have been the case with some goods.

7868. Can you state how much below ?—The principal article is that of figured satin ribbons ; it was never intended by law that any figured goods should come in under 30 per cent., and figured satins have been passed at from 17 to 20 per cent. If two duties were levied, one an *ad valorem* duty of 10 per cent., and an additional duty by weight, such a thing could not have occurred ; but I beg to refer to the proposed regulations.

7869. Could the goods have been passed in the way stated at a less rate per cent. than 30, if the examiners had been more careful and attentive ?—They might not have been judges of the goods, or of the silk trade generally. If they had, however, made inquiries as to the value, they would have discovered that they were not getting the full duty.

7870. Do you think it possible in an article which must depend so much upon fancy and fashion, for the officers, merely looking at the article, to say what would be its value ?—The law allows a certain time to get information, and by communicating with the dealers in the articles they might obtain it. If the officer had sent to an English manufacturer, he would have cheerfully given his assistance, and the real value would have been discovered. It is important, as regards smuggling, to state, that no articles similar to those which have been passed at the Custom House at from 17 to 20 per cent. have been smuggled.

7871. Suppose those goods had been brought in at Dover, or any where else, would it be possible to call in the aid of a manufacturer ?—That is another difficulty for which the regulations provide. I have proposed that all silk goods should be forwarded to London under seals of office, in order that the manufacturers should have an opportunity of inspecting them when applied to. It frequently happens that goods pay duty at Dover, and that they are sent up to London with others that have been smuggled.

7872. Is there any check between the person that weighs the goods and the officer that takes the account ?—No check ; that is one of the faults of the system, the weigher might give a wrong weight, or the landing-waiter might enter a wrong quantity.

7873. Have you not had various communications with His Majesty's Government upon the subject ?—I have.

7874. In your communications with the Board of Trade, did you give them full information upon those points ?—I did.

7875. As it is important if our manufacturers cannot have foreign goods prohibited, that at least they should have the utmost extent of legal protection rigorously enforced, can you inform the Committee whether any alteration has taken place ?—I am frequently at the Custom House, and no alteration has yet taken place ; perhaps they are waiting the Report of this Committee.

678.                 7876. Would

Mr.
*Richard Bottrell.*

4 June,
1832.

7876. Would not a more detailed account, in fact an invoice of the goods, be advisable?—That is much wanted, and the *ad valorem* duty would insure a detailed account.

7877. Do you think if the trade generally had an opportunity of inspecting the entries at the Custom-House that it would be the best protection against the goods being undervalued?—Most certainly; a good understanding between the inspector and the manufacturers would be highly important.

7878. As it is at present, can the manufacturers refer, without trouble, to a detailed account of foreign silk goods imported?—They cannot.

7879. Do you think that the importation of French goods is owing to their being cheaper than the English, or to their being better in point of colour, manufacture and style?—Some are cheaper, others have certainly a better style.

7880. Can you state any reason why they should produce a superior style to the English?—Their pattern drawers are artists. The French have schools of design; we have not; until this deficiency is supplied, we must, in the generality of fancy articles, be their inferiors. In French figured gauzes, and gauze ribbons, there is generally a minute beauty, and general good effect, which the English have not yet attained.

7881. From what you know of the trade, legal and illegal, as well as the importation from England into France, as from France into England, do you believe that the balance is in favour or against this country?—The direct trade is greatly in favour of France; but we know by the exchanges, that the balance of industry is generally in favour of England; as a proof of it, the exchange is in favour of England, and one per cent. higher than gold.

7882. Have the Custom House officers ever stopped any of those goods, which instead of paying the minimum duty of 30 per cent., have really been passed at 15 or 20 per cent.?—Never.

7883. Mr. Dillon has stated to this Committee, that plain gros imported by his house, vary from 15 to 21¼ per cent. on the cost price; can you explain how this is, when the law has kept 25 per cent. in view as the minimum duty on plain gros?—I cannot account for it in any way; as the rate of duty is 11*s.* per lb., and calculated on a higher price than the present value of plain manufactured silks, the duty ought, as the value of goods diminished, to exceed 25 per cent. rather than fall below it.

7884. You saw the gauze ribbons exhibited on Friday last to the Committee, do you consider the twenty-penny English gauze to be of very good quality?—No, a very bad quality.

7885. The price was stated to be 13*s.* 9*d.* for 36 yards, and the approximating French ribbons, No. 12's, at 10*s.*, making a difference of 37½ per cent. in favour of the French; do you conceive the quality of the English ribbon to be a fair one for comparison?—Certainly not, the quality of the English gauze was very inferior; that of the French, one of the best I ever saw.

7886. Then an English ribbon of the value of even 10 per cent. more would make a considerable difference in the relative per centage of those two articles of French and English manufacture?—As the French is the lower priced and the best article, and the English the lower quality and the highest price, a better English ribbon brought against the French one would make the difference much greater than 37½ per cent. If you advance the English gauze 10 per cent., the difference would be 50 per cent. in favour of the French; but if you take 10 per cent. off the French price, and add 10 per cent. on the English, the difference would be above 66 per cent. in favour of the French gauze.

7887. Did you examine the qualities of all the English ribbons that were exhibited?—I did.

7888. Have you reason to think that the silk they were made from is of a different quality from that which the French use?—I should think the green gauze ribbon must have been made of a silk much inferior to any the French use.

7889. Did you examine and take an account at the King's warehouse of the goods seized from Messrs. Leaf & Co.?—I did.

7890. What description of goods were they?—They were principally gauze ribbons; there were some black satins and coloured gros de Naples, but principally gauze ribbons.

7891. Did the gauze ribbons in that seizure equal in quality the pattern of the French No. 12, exhibited by Mr. Dillon?—They were by no means equal in quality to that pattern.

7892. Did

Mr.
*Richard Bottrell.*

———

4 June,
1832.

7892. Did you inspect the other parcels of goods that have been seized within the last few months ?—Yes.

7893. Can you state what seizures have taken place, and of what description of goods they have been?—There have been no seizures of any consequence this year, except a few trifling things out of East Indiamen, and three cases of striped silks French manufacture.

7894. Have you the means of knowing whether the articles subjected to high duties have been more smuggled than others?—Such goods as offer the most advantage will be most smuggled; the higher the duty, the greater the chance of gain.

7895. One of the witnesses has stated to this Committee, that goods might be delivered in London by a dealer in Paris on his being paid at the rate of a shilling for each franc; what rate is this per cent., and what advantage would arise to a London buyer by his doing business in this way?—I see no advantage in making such a contract; at the present rate of exchange it would equal $27\frac{1}{2}$ to 30 per cent.; exchange 25 *f.* 50 *c.* would be $27\frac{1}{2}$ per cent.; exchange 26 *f.* would be 30 per cent.

7896. Can you give any information to the Committee upon the extent and present state of the silk manufacture in Russia?—I can; by inquiries that have been made, it is found that the quantity of silk manufactured at Moscow has more than doubled since 1820, the consumption of silk in 1820 was 10,000 poids, or 355,000 lbs. English; and in 1830, 25,000 poids, or 887,500 lbs. English; but manufactured silk goods in Russia have fallen in price 50 per cent. since 1820.

7897. Do you know what silk it consists of?—A great deal of China is used; but principally Italian thrown is imported into Russia.

7898. Is there not a large protecting duty imposed upon the entrance of manufactured silk goods in Russia?—There is.

7899. So that the Russian silk trade is thriving under a system of protection? —Increasing in quantity, and falling in price.

7900. Have they not increased the duties within the last 18 months?—The Russian tariff has been generally increased.

7901. Supposing the cost of smuggling 100 *l.* worth of goods to be 20 *l.*, how would you apportion that between the parties concerned, how much to the insurance, how much to the party undertaking to smuggle, and how much to the labourers actually engaged in it?—Above from one half to three-fourths goes to the insurers; there are many persons who employ boats without insuring, and it then costs them about 10 per cent.

7902. Do the insurers pay the penalty in case of a seizure?—In all cases.

7903. Do you know any thing of the wages paid in France in the silk manufacture?—I have made numerous inquiries, and have received very precise accounts from the manufacturing districts in France.

7904. Has the information you have received from different channels generally corresponded?—Generally; and they all agree on this point, that the cost for weaving plain silks in France is from one-sixth to one-fifth of the value of the article; or 16 to 20 per cent. My advices agree that at Lyons they are not at present making any quantity of low broad silk goods, and one great reason is, that the demand from America has almost entirely failed this year; that from the 1st of January to the 16th of April scarcely an order had been received.

7905. What is the rate of wages for figured goods?—It is impossible to draw a conclusion on figured goods, from 25 per cent. upwards; the difference is more in favour of France on figured goods than on plain. It appears that 100 cards ready cut for a Jacquard machine cost in Lyons only two francs and a half, or 2 *s.*; whereas the price in England is from 10 *s.* to 12 *s.*

7906. Are you acquainted with the comparative prices of weaving in France and in England?—I have examined the printed tariff which the prefect, M. Du Momart, agreed to, and although it does not exactly agree with the prices now paid, the difference is not very great on the articles sent to England. For making a gros de Naples at Lyons of the value of 4 francs 50 centimes, the wages are 90 centimes, which is just 20 per cent. On comparing this with the tariff, I find it to correspond. In light coloured satins of 11–24 width, they are paying 60 centimes, and the tariff quotes 70; for plain black cravats 31 inches square, they pay one franc the handkerchief; that is 31 inches French, and the English inch is less, being in the proportion of 8 to $8\frac{1}{2}$. For making 4-4 and 5-4 crape shawls, there is no difference between the tariff and the prices now paid. The

678. four

Mr.
*Richard Bottrell.*

4 June,
1832.

four quarter is one franc 40 centimes, and the five quarter 2 francs 25 centimes.

7907. Have the hands been tolerably well employed ?—In March they were better employed than in April. In March there were 1,324 ballots of silk sold at Lyons, but in April only 550.

7908. Do they make any remark as to the quantity of goods ordered for England this year?—They do not; in one of the letters it was mentioned that our English buyers had not found the market so favourable for purchasing as they had expected.

7909. And therefore it is supposed that the goods will come over into this country ?—Only in the event that other markets should prove bad, and the French manufacturer should make on speculation.

7910. What kind of goods are they now principally occupied on?—On heavy rich goods.

7911. For what market are those goods intended ?—For the principal cities of Europe; they had been likewise busy preparing for Leipsic fair.

7912. Do not you believe that they were principally intended for the London market ?—Not principally.

7913. Are not large quantities of crape imported into this country?—There are.

7914. Are similar articles made in Spitalfields ?—I never heard that they were.

7915. Then they are articles that do not come in competition with the manufacturers of those places?—They do not.

7916. Where are they made in this country?—They are principally made at Yarmouth and in Scotland.

7917. Do you believe that there is any considerable quantity of goods imported from France that come into competition with the manufactures of Spitalfields ?—All the broad goods that have been imported come into direct competition with Spitalfields. This season they have generally been rich goods, but the quantity has not been very great.

7918. Was it the case last year that they were rich goods?—I think they are more generally so this year.

7919. Are not the rich goods you speak of, the quality of goods that give most employment and require most labour ?—I do not know that they do require much more labour, but they of course consume a larger quantity of silk.

7920. Are they not now made in Spitalfields?—They are, and have long been; and in my opinion equal in every respect to the French, when the best silk is used.

7921. It has been supposed that France would send no other quality of goods into this country than the very rich goods, but if the French market should continue in the same stagnant state, is it not likely that the price will fall so considerably at Lyons, that considerable quantities of silk goods of other qualities will be brought here ?—No other than rich goods will be ordered for the English market. I have understood that Leipsic fair has turned out well; that stocks in France are not large; and that the French manufacturers are not inclined to make on speculation.

7922. What kind of goods do they send to Germany?—All kinds of plain and fancy goods; and generally articles superior to those made in Germany and Switzerland. I beg here to mention, from the information I have received from the South of France, that of the last year's crop of silk the stock on hand is very inconsiderable; and that notwithstanding the absence of orders from America organzine had risen from the 16th to the 27th May 50 centimes the half kilogramme

7923. Do they consider that a rise of some importance?—It appears so. It is likewise stated that the demand since March has not been great for manufactured goods; in raw silks there has been some speculation, owing to the small stock remaining of last year's crop.

7924. Can you tell the Committee the extent of the silk manufacture in France ?—I have discovered pretty nearly what the French have paid annually for raw and thrown silks imported into France; I have likewise collected from various sources the supposed quantity of silk grown in that country. The growth of 1831 exceeded 20,000 bales of 80 kilogrammes each; 1,600,000 kilogrammes give 3,527,675 lbs. English, as the quantity of silk grown last year in France.

7925. Do any of your French correspondents furnish you with the amount of the purchase of silk not of their own growth?—Yes; and it appears from their statements, and by the reports made to the Agricultural and other Societies of Arts and Industry in France during the last year, that the raw and thrown silk annually
imported

imported into France is of the value of from 36 to 40 millions of francs, which is about 1,500,000 *l.* English money.

Mr.
*Richard Bottrell.*

4 June,
1832.

7926. Can you state the number of looms at Lyons?—During the last few years they have spread very much into the country, but the number of looms is estimated in the city and neighbourhood at 30,000. St. Etienne is computed to possess 12,000 bar looms, besides single hand-looms, which are very numerous in the surrounding country. At Avignon the number of looms has much decreased; it is there where the Florences are made, of which the sale was so great formerly in England.

7927. Were the disturbances at Lyons owing to a dispute about the tariff?—Not as regards the tariffs signed by M. Du Momart, but it was in consequence of the previous low rate of wages.

7928. Did not the workmen wish to have a fixed, and on the whole an advanced price?—They did.

7929. Did that disturbance extend to St. Etienne?—No; there was some little agitation at St. Etienne, but nothing serious or similar to the affair at Lyons. The workmen at St. Etienne were in a different position; nearly all the bar looms at St. Etienne belong to undertakers.

7930. Do you know any public document relating to St. Etienne, which exhibits the state of prosperity or adversity in which they are?—No, I do not; but I have heard that they are alarmed at the great competition they experience, and that both wages and profits are exceedingly low.

7931. Have you not heard of their expressing their satisfaction?—I have not, although the quantity of silk consumed at St. Etienne has lately much increased.

7932. Did you ever see or hear any address from the mayor at St. Etienne to the French minister, stating that the people were at work for the British market?—No, I have seen no such address; but I have seen various publications from St. Etienne complaining of their prospects, and the low rate of wages.

7933. How do you reconcile the fact of their being in distress at St. Etienne with the increased consumption of silk?—That is a parallel case with our own; there is an increased consumption of silk in England, but no increase of wages.

7934. Do they manufacture a description of articles which consumes a great quantity of silk?—Their principal manufacture is gauze ribbons, but in large quantities.

7935. Besides what you have stated already upon the subject of smuggling, can you point out any other way in which the smuggling of silks may be prevented without any reduction of the duty. Would not stamping of the goods, and the personal punishment of smugglers, be effectual means?—Stamping has been recommended, but the Customs have reported against it, on the ground that it would be too tedious and consume too much time, besides being unnecessary. It is certain the quantity of goods seized formerly was very great, and there was not an article that was not stamped. If they stamped them then, I do not see why all imports should not be stamped now.

7936. Is there not a Board of Commissioners to superintend all the transactions at the Custom House?—There is.

7937. Do you know at what time in the morning those Commissioners come?—I believe their hours are from 10 till four.

7938. Is it your opinion that the officers whose duty it is to examine silk and other goods are adequately paid?—The landing waiters, and the surveyors particularly, are handsomely paid, but the weigher has a very small salary, and there is a sad disproportion in the pay of the superior and inferior officer; besides, as part is day-pay, the latter is subject to lose it in case of holiday, a fast-day, or any close day, whereas the annual and high salaries are not subject to such a deduction.

7939. So that the man whose duty it is to ascertain whether the account is correctly taken, may be tempted by a bribe which it would be well worth the while of some parties to pay?—I have understood cases to have occurred when offers have not been made to the officer, that the officer has made proposals to the parties attending. A circumstance occurred lately of this nature, but the transaction being exposed, the officer was discharged.

7940. Did you mention the occurrence of similar circumstances to the Board of Trade?—I did last year; and recommended that what are called " silk floors"

678. should

Mr.
Richard Bottrell.

4 June,
1832.

should be abolished, and that all silk goods should pay duty at one place, and be subject to a double check.

7941. Did they pay any attention to it?—All I know is, that the original system still continues of examining silks at various places. I understood the report from the Custom House was against the necessity of any change.

7942. Do not you think it would be a check against smuggling if all the silks, when embarked for import into this country, should have written upon them in large letters "silks"?—A certificate from the British consul would be better; this is provided in my proposed regulations.

7943. Will you state in what way the goods could be stamped without the liability of the stamp being imitated on the other side of the water?—By such a seal as was submitted to the Committee of silk manufacturers, and approved by them last January—a drawing of the impression was made by Mr. Ellis, of No. 15, Old Broad Street, and diagrams of the four sizes required, I beg to annex. The seal is a hand seal, and can be used with as much facility as a letter stamp. It contains five plugs, which are screwed in, or pinned, without trouble, and with little loss of time. The centre piece can, and is intended to be frequently changed, and may represent any number (at the option of the inspector), varying from 40 to 99; so that if 30 pieces of gros de Naples only were to be stamped, the centre plug might be changed, and the variable number altered three or four times, and in less than five minutes. Nothing can be more simple and effective, coupled with a pattern book as proposed in my regulation; and as to forgery, all chances thereof are removed, as no one could know what they would have to imitate. The other numbers represent the day, the month, and the year, the articles paid duty, and the right hand corner below, the importer's letter; viz. the 5th day, the 6th month, year 32.

DIAGRAMS of four Seals proposed by Mr. Bottrell for the purpose of Stamping foreign Silks, designed January 1832 by

Thomas Ellis, Engraver,
15, Old Broad Street, City.

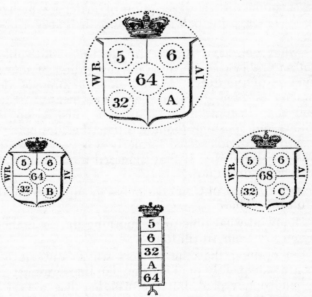

7944. If you could have all the duty that the goods now smuggled ought to pay, would you not be very happy to undertake all the trouble and expense of stamping them?—I should indeed; there are persons of the first respectability in London who would give security to any amount. The Government might require that the duty of examining Foreign silks should be well and faithfully performed, and the Government held harmless from any loss that might accrue by detaining silk goods, which competent judges and the trade might consider undervalued.

7945. Are you well acquainted with the kind of goods that were smuggled in the years 1826 and 1827?—Yes; I have attended nearly all the Custom House sales since 1810.

7946. Are they the same kind of goods that are now imported?—Not the same
kind

Mr.
Richard Bottrell.

4 June,
1832.

kind. The falling off from plain silk goods to gauzes was gradual; there are now large quantities of the latter, and but few of the former.

7947. What alterations have taken place in the goods imported from France?—The kinds of goods that used principally to be smuggled, and are not now, are the Florences.

7948. Can you state what articles were imported in 1827 and 1828, which it is no longer profitable to import?—It is no longer profitable to bring in any inferior kinds of broad silks.

7949. Is it your opinion that the duty ought to be levied *ad valorem*, or by the pound weight?—Both ways; there might be an *ad valorem* duty of 10 per cent., and an additional duty by weight; the first would insure a specific account or invoice of the goods, by which means the English manufacturer could refer to a detailed and correct account of all imports. The importations could certainly be put under much better regulations; indeed no other can be worse than the present system.

7950. Is it your opinion, that under all the circumstances a prohibition would be the best mode of protecting and extending the British silk manufacture?—I can scarce venture an opinion on a point of so much importance; there is no doubt, however, that every article of French manufacture brought in supplants a certain portion of British labour.

7951. Do you not believe that considerable improvements have taken place in the English manufactures in consequence of having the benefit of the French designs?—It appears to me that English silks are generally improved in style and colour.

7952. Do you know whether the Custom House officers have received any remuneration for the seizure of the goods belonging to Messrs. Leaf & Co., the prosecution of which was compromised?—They have not yet, I believe, received any compensation, and from not being paid I have understood that they have lost many opportunities of making seizures, not having the means of advancing money to informers.

7953. Is there not great dissatisfaction among the Custom House officers in consequence?—There certainly is; but it is not confined to that seizure, there is a general dissatisfaction throughout the House; the lower class of officers, who have often whole cargoes under their charge, not being (they consider) adequately paid, and I have heard it is in contemplation further to reduce the pay of the inferior officers; a measure which, in my opinion, would be highly injurious to the revenue.

7954. You have stated that there has been an improvement in the English manufacture in consequence of the removal of the prohibition?—I think so, as respects style and colour.

7955. Was there not an improvement before 1826?—Certainly there was, and very rich goods were made in Spitalfields long before 1826.

7956. Was it in as great a proportion as since?—Whenever good silk was used, good goods were produced, and this applies both to France and England. In dyeing of silk there is a greater deception now than formerly.

7957. Were crapes manufactured to any extent in England before 1826, of the kind now imported from France?—Of the Italian kind there were, but not of the China kind. The French have introduced the latter in a great variety, of a thinner and more elegant description than those imported from China, and the English have successfully imitated them.

7958. Have not the English manufacturers very much indeed lowered the price of crapes imported into this country from China?—Certainly; crapes from China are now at a mere nominal price.

7959. Have not the importers in consequence sustained very great losses?—They have.

7960. Are gloves, similar to those imported from France, manufactured now to any extent in England?—To a great extent.

7961. And that is a trade that has grown up entirely since 1826?—It has much increased; lamb and kid gloves having supplanted most other sorts of leather gloves.

7962. Do not various goods coming into general use, depend more upon fashion and demand than upon the ability of the manufacturer to produce them?—The English manfacturers can produce any article the public might fancy.

7963. Is it not the skill of the manufacturer that occasions what we call fashion?

—If

Mr.
*Richard Bottrell.*

_____

4 June,
1832.

—If the master has inventions, and the workmen skill, approved articles will doubtless be produced; the caprices of fashion cannot well be defined.

7964. Do you think that the goods that require the greatest skill will be always the goods most in fashion?—That depends whether the skill of the workman, and good taste in the pattern drawer, go hand in hand.

7965. Do you consider the artisan in a better condition now than formerly?—Decidedly not; he is obliged to work longer, and at less wages; but unfortunately it is the same in France and most other countries.

7966. Does not the condition of the manufacturer in Spitalfields depend rather upon the price of weaving at Manchester than at Lyons?—I should think in both he has rivals.

7967. Do you know of any mode or management by which goods can be got from the Custom House at less than the legal duty?—That is a question I cannot answer; all I can state is, as there is no check between the weigher and the landing waiter, a door is left open to possible fraud on the revenue. The best remedy is to be found in the regulation I have had the honour of proposing; the examination of all silk goods, to be superintended by competent persons, approved of by the government and the trade.

7968. Can you furnish the Committee with any information as to the manner in which individuals are occasionally employed, and how they are paid, and their duties at the Custom House?—I consider the employment of extra men at all to be very prejudicial to the revenue. The glut men are not employed at an average six days in a month, and when employed have only 3 s. a day; and it has happened that some of those men, with such a miserable and uncertain pay, have been in charge of the scale without any check; of course where there is such temptation, there is a possibility of fraud.

7969. Is not the amount of duties that is to be levied on the goods passing through the hands of the Custom House officers, sometimes very great?—Very considerable; for example, on merely 120 pounds of gauze ribbon the duty would be 165 l.

7970. Is it not the case that ships are often left in charge of a Custom House officer, who from their salaries being so small are under temptations to go home at night with small presents, leaving the vessel for an hour or more?—Such cases have occurred.

7971. You have stated that the protecting duties on silk goods in Russia have been increased; are you aware that the protecting duties in Prussia against foreign silks have been raised a crown a pound this year?—There has been an increase, but I do not know the extent of it.

_____

*Mercurii, 6° die Junii,* 1832.

_____

## EDWARD AYSHFORD SANFORD, ESQUIRE, in the Chair.

_____

Mr. *William Sedgwick,* called in; and Examined.

Mr.
*William Sedgwick.*

_____

6 June,
1832.

7972. YOU are a partner in the house of Howell & James?—I am.

7973. Are you large dealers in silk goods?—We are.

7974. Of what description?—Broad silks and ribbons.

7975. Do you deal in every description of silk, both Foreign and English?—Yes.

7976. How long have you been engaged in the business?—Myself ten years.

7977. Have you any calculations as to the quantities of silk, broad, figured, and ribbons, which you disposed of before 1826?—I have not.

7978. Have you of those you have disposed of since?—I have not.

7979. Before 1826 were you in the habit of selling French silks?—No, we were not; we sold English goods made from French patterns.

7980. Are you able to give the Committee any evidence with respect to smuggling before 1826?—I think it was carried on, but not to any very great extent.

7981. Were you aware of French silks being sold by other shops in the town, though not by yourselves?—Yes.

7982. What do you suppose was the quantity of French manufactured silks sold

at

Mr.
*William Sedgwick.*

6 June,
1832.

at that time?—I should think it was very small, but I cannot state the amount; perhaps fifty or sixty thousand pounds' worth in a year, perhaps not so much.

7983. What description of goods were they that were principally sold at that time?—Figured and fancy silks, and plain silks.

7984. Were they what are called the rich silks or the plainer?—The rich silks.

7985. What is the proportion of English and of French silks you now sell?—I should say two-thirds of our sales are English and one-third French; I speak of broad silks; of ribbons we sell scarcely any English.

7986. When you speak of ribbons, do you allude to one particular sort of ribbon or all sorts of ribbons?—All sorts of ribbons; the English-made lutestrings we do not sell at all, they are not an article in demand with our customers; gauze ribbons are more used.

7987. Is that description of goods of which you sell French manufacture of superior quality?—Yes, it is.

7988. Do you sell in broad goods much English figured silk?—Yes, we do, but the greater part of the broad goods are fancy goods.

7989. That which you sell of English manufacture is confined principally to plain goods?—Yes, formerly; though we are selling now English fancy goods, they are increasing in demand.

7990. Where are they manufactured?—They are manufactured in Spitalfields, and a portion manufactured in Manchester, but our principal consumption is from Spitalfields.

7991. Where are the best produced?—I think that the same goods may be produced in both places, but those in Manchester cheaper.

7992. For what reason?—From the difference in the price of labour.

7993. Do you purchase any gauze ribbons from Coventry?—No, we do not; we have no demand for them; the French are cheaper.

7994. That applies to all ribbons?—Generally speaking.

7995. Your sales consist chiefly of the newest goods?—Yes.

7996. As the inventions are in France, your trade is a good deal dependent upon the French?—Yes, it is.

7997. If a ribbon manufacturer from Coventry were to wait upon you with patterns, you would hardly venture to give him an order, though they might appear very beautiful, even more so than the French?—We could not.

7998. For what reason?—The English market is dependent upon the French taste.

7999. Independent of their cheapness, can they manufacture gauze ribbons equally well at Coventry as in France?—I do not think quite so well; I have seen some very nearly equal to French, but not quite.

8000. Do you include striped gauzes?—The striped gauzes may be made at Coventry equal to the French, but not the figured.

8001. Do you sell any of the English striped gauzes?—We have not for some time.

8002. Are the Manchester manufacturers gaining a profit upon their manufactures, or are they merely trying experiments?—That is a question I cannot answer, but I should think, in many cases, the profit must be very small.

8003. Do you sell any Manchester goods?—Very few indeed.

8004. When you say that the Coventry figured ribbons are inferior to the French, is that in taste or in quality?—In taste.

8005. Have the Coventry manufactures improved?—I think they have.

8006. Were you acquainted with the style of those manufactured in this country before 1826?—Not much.

8007. Do you think that great improvements have taken place in their manufactures since 1826?—I think there have.

8008. Do you not attribute that to the introduction of French patterns?—I think that has given a stimulus to the trade.

8009. Was it not your practice before that to introduce French patterns, and send them to Coventry to be made?—Yes.

8010. Have you ever seen any Manchester fancy goods equal to those you have lately seen made in Spitalfields?—I have.

8011. What prices have you given for articles of that description?—I could not state the prices from memory; 4s. a yard, perhaps, and as high as 4s. 9d.

8012. Did you buy them of the manufacturers, or a house in town?—Of a warehouseman in London; they were Manchester manufacturers.

678.

8013. You

Mr.
*William Sedgwick.*
———
6 June,
1832.

8013. You think them in general inferior in beauty of appearance to the goods made in Spitalfields?—Some of them are not so, but generally speaking they are.

8014. Their object there is to make cheaper for quantity, rather than to aim at excellence, is it not?—I think it is; I think they are more determined by the quantity they can sell; they depend upon that for their remuneration.

8015. You spoke of the description of goods you sell in your house; it is those generally sold by houses at the West end of the Town?—I should think it is; at least there are many houses at the West end of the Town sell the same goods.

8016. The consumption of the articles you speak of, such as French gauze ribbons, must be very large?—Yes.

8017. The English manufacturers used to make from their own designs, did they not?—They were generally copied from the French.

8018. Did they copy them quite to your satisfaction at the time?—Yes, they did copy exactly the pattern; they might have been better finished.

8019. You say that though the pattern might be even more beautiful than the French, if shown to you as an English design, you should not feel inclined to order it?—I should not, before we knew the state of the French market; this refers to ribbons.

8020. The extent of smuggling before 1826 you think was very small?—I think it was.

8021. The quantity sent was generally for patterns, was it not?—Yes.

8022. No respectable house sold French goods you think?—Not exposed on their counters.

8023. You think they were declined by houses called respectable?—Yes, in some instances.

8024. You have stated that the prices of Manchester articles you have bought, have been from 4 s. to 4 s. 9 d.; what description of articles were they?—Broad and figured silks.

8025. Did you purchase them from the manufacturer?—No, we did not.

8026. How do you know they were Manchester goods?—They were represented to be so, and I have every reason to suppose that they were so.

8027. Can you distinguish Manchester from other goods, by inspection?—I cannot.

8028. Have you any reason to suppose they were manufactured at Derby?—I have not the least.

8029. Have you ever seen any figured goods which were made at Derby?—No, I have not to my knowledge.

8030. Did you ever hear what was the cost of smuggling before 1826?—I suppose it might be about 25 per cent. at that time.

8031. Have you any idea what it is at this time?—Much about the same; but it is done at considerably less in some cases.

8032. Do you conceive that the quantity of goods smuggled into this country has increased since 1826?—It has increased considerably.

8033. To what do you attribute that increase?—That the goods thus obtained, can be sold much cheaper than those for which the regular duty has been paid.

8034. What rate of duty do you think would put an end to smuggling?—It would be difficult to say; the same competition may exist in smuggling that there is in dealing.

8035. Do you think there is sufficient competition among English manufacturers, to provide a supply at a moderate price?—I think there is.

8036. Do you consider that the competition is an impetus to improve the manufacture, as well as to render it cheap?—I think it tends more at present to render it cheap than to improve it, though it does a great deal towards improving it.

8037. Did you not see great improvement between 1821 and 1826?—I cannot state that I did.

8038. Do you not know that there was?—I do not of my own personal knowledge.

8039. Had you any means of observing?—Not much at that time.

8040. When you speak of figured silks made at Manchester, are there a large quantity made there?—I think there are a great quantity.

8041. Are they made in Jacquard looms?—I do not know.

8042. Are they large figures, or small?—Small figures generally.

8043. Do you think if French goods were excluded from our market, there would still continue sufficient competition among the manufacturers to produce
every

Mr.
*William Sedgwick.*

6 June,
1832.

every description of commodity, and with sufficient taste and excellence of design to satisfy the public?—I should hardly think there would.

8044. For what reason?—I think the English manufacturers require an impetus; I think when the competition ceased, there would not be altogether the same attention, and not the same variety of pattern produced.

8045. Did you see any patterns of French gauze ribbons before 1826?—No.

8046. Do you not understand it as a trade which has grown up principally in France since that time?—I cannot state that; I think the trade in ribbons in France was very considerable before that time.

8047. Were there many French ribbons smuggled before 1826?—I think not, not in proportion to the present quantity.

8048. Taking the proportions of broad goods and ribbons, what was the proportion you suppose smuggled before 1826; was it greater in broad than in narrow?—I do not suppose it was.

8049. Taking the total amount of goods smuggled, broad and narrow, was the greater proportion smuggled of broad, or of narrow goods?—I cannot state.

8050. Which do you suppose to be the greatest quantity smuggled at present?—Ribbons; I should think they are smuggled to a great extent.

8051. Supposing we were not to return to a system of prohibition, do you suppose that the kingdom would be continued to be supplied with English ribbons instead of French, as they were before 1826?—I think French ribbons would find their way into this country; before the year 1826, French goods were asked for, now they are not asked for.

8052. They were asked for as a rare commodity?—Yes.

8053. Now every body expects to find them?—Yes.

8054. Were they not more valued by the fashionable world, on account of their being a rare article?—I should think so.

8055. You do not mean to say they are not in the same esteem as they were?—No, but every body expects now to find them.

8056. You say there were goods smuggled previous to the year 1826; do not you think that as goods would be always smuggled, those which were, would be sufficient to give a kind of taste to our manufacture, supposing we were again to resort to prohibition?—The patterns might be obtained from the French if desired, and the English manufacturer might copy and improve upon them; the market is more open now, and there is scarcely a dealer in London who would not know where to go for French goods.

8057. Do you think there is a decided inferiority in the English ribbons now? Not in all the English ribbons; in some instances the English goods are equal to French; in fancy ribbons, the French are better.

8058. To any material degree?—The English might make their goods equal to the French.

8059. At the same price do you mean?—I cannot say that.

8060. Do you think there is much difference in the manufacture of the ribbons now shown to you and French ribbons of the same kind?—(*Some patterns being shown to the Witness*)—These, I should say, are as good as the French.

8061. What do you think would be the difference in price?—These belt ribbons are much cheaper made in England than in France; I do not know the price of the French.

8062. Has there been an increase since 1826, in the sale of French ribbons by your house, compared with the total amount of English ribbons sold by you?—Yes, there has been.

8063. Do you mean that that increase has gone on progressively from year to year?—Yes, it has.

8064. Are you selling a larger proportion or a less proportion now than last year?—The same proportion.

8065. Does not your answer apply chiefly to French gauze ribbons?—Yes, we sell very few others.

8066. When you speak of the consumption of English ribbons having decreased regularly from 1826, do you mean only the finer gauze ribbons or all ribbons generally?—I should say on all ribbons.

8067. What is the proportion between French and English ribbons which you sell?—I should say that the English is not an eighth part of the French.

8068. Has the sale by your house of English ribbons decreased, and of French ribbons increased?—It has.

678.                                                               8069. The

Mr.
*William Sedgwick.*

6 June,
1832.

8069. The Committee have heard a great deal about figured lutestring ribbons, will you inform the Committee whether the fashionable public use any figured lutestring ribbons?—I should say that they do not at present.

8070. If there are any made, they are sold in what you would call second rate trade?—Yes, in the common trade.

8071. The French having the superiority in the manufacture of gauze ribbons, take care to make that article richer, and the people of Coventry in vain attempt to cope with the French?—Yes, I think that is the case; the English market is so dependent upon the French taste, no English dealer will order goods until he knows what is the taste in France.

8072. Do not the importations of French goods at present very materially contribute to aggravate the pressure on the British artizan?—It depresses the English manufacturer certainly.

8073. Were there many broad goods smuggled before 1826, or only sufficient to stimulate British exertions and improve them?—I think only for that, the quantity was not large.

8074. And particularly for patterns to supply to the manufacturers?—Yes, to send to the manufacturers.

8075. Was it not very dangerous to deal in smuggled goods to any extent before 1826?—Yes, it was.

8076. You state that many respectable houses did deal in them however?—I cannot state that from my own knowledge; but it was generally supposed they did so, but not to any extent.

8077. When you say that fashionable houses chiefly deal in French ribbons, do you mean to say that only fashionable houses in London do so, or do you think fashionable houses in Edinburgh and different places in the United Kingdom, prefer French ribbons to English?—There are the same fashions prevailing in all parts of the kingdom, but more particularly in London.

8078. The fashionable houses, you think, in all parts of the kingdom, have that preference for French ribbons which the fashionable houses have in London?—Yes, undoubtedly.

8079. Suppose prohibition were again enacted, do you suppose it would be necessary for houses similar to yours to supply themselves with French silks to answer the demands of their customers?—I do not think it would, because they they might be made from French patterns.

8080. What are the articles now imported from France?—Principally fancy goods.

8081. What kind of ribbons?—The figured gauze ribbons and the striped gauze ribbons.

8082. Check and gauze ribbons?—Yes.

8083. What sort of broad silks are imported?—Figured silks.

8084. You mean figured gros de Naples?—Yes.

8085. Are there not great quantities of crapes imported?—I do not think there are; there is an article imported very much resembling the English crape, the Araphene.

8086. Of 100 l. worth of French goods which you might have imported, what proportion would be ribbons, and what proportion broad goods, in your opinion?—Our importations are principally ribbons and fancy silks and gauzes.

8087. Are more than one-half gauze ribbons?—Yes.

8088. Would you say 60 l. or 70 l. worth of the hundred?—Perhaps seventy.

8089. Of the remaining thirty, how much would be of the Araphene character?—A very small quantity.

8090. What would the remainder consist of?—Of figured silks and figured gauzes.

8091. Of that 30 l. how much do you imagine would interfere with the manufacture of Spitalfields?—I do not think the quantity of fancy broad silks imported from France does interfere materially with the English manufactures in broad silks.

8092. The gauzes are manufactured in Scotland, are they not?—We sell very few of English or Scotch.

8093. When you say that the ribbons you sell, and which the French are importing, are gauze ribbons, it is in that class of ribbons which are figured ribbons?—Yes.

8094. Do not you imagine that the French, having a superiority over us in

gauze

Mr.
*William Sedgwick.*

6 June,
1832.

gauze ribbons, will take care that ribbons, having more or less the character of gauze ribbons, shall be always made and introduced?—I do.

8095. Do you consider that the French manufacturer has got so considerable an influence in this market, that as things now stand the British manufacturer cannot successfully compete with him?—I think he can in broad silks, but not in ribbons.

8096. You say you have lately sold more English fancy goods than you did formerly?—Yes.

8097. For what reason have you turned your attention to the English in preference to the French?—From the feeling in favour of English manufacturers among our customers.

8098. Have the French fancy goods been made from French patterns, or from designs of the English manufacturers?—Some from French patterns.

8099. Have they been principally from French patterns?—I should think so; these (*producing some patterns*) are English manufactures made for us.

8100. Are those superior in quality to the French?—They are equal to the French.

8101. Were those made for you by a house in Spitalfields?—They were.

8102. It is a great object with you to have them well made?—It is.

8103. The customers who deal with you do not often care for 1 *d.* or 2 *d.* a yard provided they can have the article they desire?—Just so; provided it is of the best kind.

8104. Do you think that there are other houses that have customers who have the same desire to have that which others cannot procure?—Yes, there are other houses no doubt.

8105. It is not an object with some ladies whether they pay 3 *d.* more or less, so much as to have something produced which every body cannot possess?—Yes.

8106. When it comes to be an object with the Government to take care that the people shall have the greatest possible substance for money, that is not the greatest object with your customers?—It is not.

8107. You say that now the gauze ribbons are nearly the only ones demanded?—They are by our customers.

8108. You say in addition to that, that the reason is because gauze ribbons are the only ones now peculiarly fashionable?—Yes.

8109. Supposing that the fashion were to change in France, and that gauze ribbons were no longer to be fashionable there, and other ribbons were to become so, would their other ribbons have the same superiority in the English market now possessed by the gauze ribbons?—Not to the same degree.

8110. Have you generally, as a house of business, given the preference to the Spitalfields manufacturer that you have lately?—We are obliged to provide things according to the taste of the public; and the French goods generally having the first entrance into the market, we are obliged to supply ourselves with them. If there had been a feeling in favour of English goods we should have purchased the articles manufactured in this country, provided they were equal.

8111. Have you always given the preference to the English manufacturer which you have given in some instances lately?—We should if the English manufacturer had produced as good goods.

8112. Have you done so always?—I cannot answer that.

8113. You say you have lately sold more English fancy goods than you did some time ago; have you, since the opening of the ports, sold more English fancy goods than of French?—No; at the opening of the ports the balance turned in favour of the French.

8114. Were you with the same house before 1826?—Yes.

8115. You say you have lately sold more English fancy goods than of French; to what do you attribute this greater success of English trade?—These English goods are equal to the French; and there has been most demand for the English goods.

8116. Do you attribute that to the improvement in the English manufacture?—Yes.

8117. Do you think increased protection would best enable the British manufacturer to produce novelties that would please the public?—If they were sufficiently protected.

8118. Is there any particular species of protection you would recommend, provided we do not return to prohibition?—I should recommend that the goods should be stamped, it would be an inconvenience, but it would be a protection.

8119. Is

Mr.
*William Sedgwick.*

6 June,
1832.

8119. Is there any other protection you would recommend?—Perhaps they might be licensed as well—20*l.* license; this would in some measure prevent so many French agents from hawking goods from private house to house, which is now done.

8120. Can you state what house or houses make those English silks which you have sold lately?—Bridges & Campbell, and Ames & Atkinson are the principal.

8121. Were those patterns that you produced partly from one house and partly from another?—I think they were all from Bridges & Campbell's.

8122. How are those articles as compared in point of price, with the French?—I should say they are rather high in price.

8123. And yet the French goods have paid a duty of 30 per cent. probably?—Not so much as that I think.

8124. Were the English goods manufactured exclusively for your house, so as to enable you to keep particular patterns to yourselves?—They were.

8125. Can you always secure the patterns to yourself in French goods?—No, certainly not.

8126. Have your customers made any complaints since the introduction of French silks, that they do not wear so well as they did many years ago?—I never heard of it.

8127. Do you think it possible that the French, by introducing a new description of ribbons combined with gauze for the next season, might interfere with any arrangement you might make with Messrs. Bridges & Campbell, for a similar description of goods with those?—They might interfere with them.

8128. Would they not put those out of fashion then?—Yes, but as the patterns would not be obtained at another house, they would command a sale.

8129. To a certain extent you would be able to get through them without particular loss?—Yes, I should think so.

8130. But you would decline ordering such goods beyond a certain extent?—Yes.

8131. Was silk more precious before 1826 than now?—Yes.

8132. Then fifty or sixty thousand pounds worth of goods imported then would be a smaller quantity of goods than would be imported now for that sum?—Yes.

8133. Have you not many rich silks made entirely in Spitalfields?—We have purchased them.

8134. A large quantity?—Yes.

8135. Have not rich broad silks been used lately?—Very much indeed.

8136. Have not the larger part of those been French?—Certainly; but principally the fancy silks.

8137. Do you think as large a proportion of looms in Spitalfields is employed on silks fit for the consumption of the upper class of society as there used to be before French goods were introduced?—I cannot say; I should think not.

8138. Do you think that many other houses in the same line of business as your's have had their rich goods made in Spitalfields?—I have reason to think there are some.

8139. Many?—Not many; I do not think it is the custom in England now to give orders, especially for plain goods.

8140. Do you send any orders to St. Etienne or Chaumont?—Yes.

8141. Is not the bulk of the goods made in Spitalfields now of a low quality?—I do not think they are.

8142. You do now sell a great many French silks of the descriptions of which you formerly sold the English?—Yes.

8143. Therefore your sale in English articles of that description has been decreased?—Yes, but it is now again increasing.

8144. Do you think there are more or less than 100 looms making the finer descriptions of goods in Spitalfields?—I cannot say.

8145. Are there as many as 50?—I cannot say.

8146. Was it not the practice in your house previous to 1826, to give your orders in October, November and December for the articles for your spring trade?—Yes.

8147. Formerly houses in Coventry and Spitalfields were engaged during the winter in making the articles for your trade?—They were; now we give no orders to Coventry at all.

8148. Supposing prohibition were again resorted to, and French ribbons were still smuggled into this country, would they be ordered after the pattern of the English goods which were in the market?—I should think not.

8149. Would

Mr.
*William Sedgwick.*

6 June,
1832.

8149. Would not they be easily detected if they were not?—They would certainly be detected.

8150. These goods being imported would be either of a different pattern from the English, and thereby detected, or they would be the same pattern as the English; consequently, giving the advantage to the English manufacturer of the French manufacturer copying him, instead of allowing to the French manufacturer the advantage he now possesses of the English manufacturer copying him?—Yes.

8151. Do you conceive your house would sell less silk manufactures than they now do if prohibition were again enacted?—I do not think we should.

8152. Prohibition would then produce a benefit to the artizans and manufacturers of this country?—I think it would; but I do not think prohibition practicable unless by severe laws against smuggling.

8153. If the same laws were re-enacted as were in existence before 1826, would not there be the same security?—I think not, because the market is open and there is not an English dealer in London who does not know where to find the goods.

8154. Was there not, before 1826, a very great inducement to sell them, in the great difference of price between English and French manufactures?—Yes, there was.

8155. If the price more approximated, would there not be that inducement?—If the price of English and French were nearer together, I do not think there would.

8156. Under laws for prohibiting French goods, it was necessary they should have a large profit to remunerate them for the risk?—Yes.

8157. Do you give orders for the manufacture of fancy ribbons, for the coming season?—Yes; for French, not English.

8158. Do you give orders for French fancy broad silk goods?—Not to any great extent.

8159. Have you not generally given orders for English fancy ribbons to be made for you?—Yes, formerly.

8160. And also for English broad goods?—Yes.

8161. It is quite impossible for your house, or any other of a similar description, to sell any goods as fashionable, which are opposed to the style of those goods which are fashionable in France?—Yes, I should say so.

8162. In almost every principal town and city in England, are there not houses who find it absolutely essential to deal in the same description of goods which you deal in?—Certainly.

8163. And whose trade is very considerable?—Yes.

8164. Therefore it is not referrible only to your house, however large its dealings may be, taking into consideration that there are other houses similar to your own in London, and houses of a similar description throughout England, who feel it is necessary to deal in such goods; the aggregate amount of goods sold must be very large, must it not?—Yes.

8165. You have produced certain patterns of fancy goods from the house of Messrs. Bridges & Campbell; were orders given for those before March?—I believe in February.

8166: Why did you not give orders for those goods as formerly, in December and January?—By that time we know what the French will produce.

8167. Do you know what number of looms there are employed now in Spitalfields?—I do not.

8168. Were there any complaints in your business, on the part of your customers before 1826, of a want of articles of taste in the English manufactures?—I should say no very great complaints, because the articles were supplied; though we had not the French goods, we had the patterns, and had them copied in England.

8169. Can you recommend any measure to prevent smuggling?—I should recommend a stamp.

8170. There would be no great objection, if the goods were stamped in four or five different parts on the edge?—No. It would be a great deal of trouble to the Custom Hoose officers; but for myself, individually, I should not object.

8171. Do you think it would injure the fine goods?—I do not.

8172. What do you think it would increase the expense per yard?—A fractional part, a very trifling sum indeed.

8173. Supposing the consumer were compelled to bear the expense?—The consumer

sumer would not feel it if it was stamped at both ends, or it would be a very trifling expense if it was stamped in three places.

8174. Might not the stamp be imitated on the other side of the water?—At Goldsmith's Hall the stamp is varied frequently, to prevent imitation; no one knows the day beforehand what will be the stamp for the day.

8175. Do you not think that the lowering of the duty would be a much more effectual protection by putting an end to smuggling than stamping?—That would be met by competition from the smuggler; the smuggler would also lower his profits.

8176. Do you not know that the competition amongst the smugglers has brought down the profit to the lowest point?—I do not think it has.

8177. You think that smuggling is now carried on to a great extent?—I think it is.

8178. You have stated, that in your opinion 25 per cent. is the cost of smuggling, in some instances, now?—I should say it is.

8179. In some instances less?—Yes.

8180. What do you conceive to be the lowest?—I cannot say.

8181. Do you imagine it is done as low as 20 per cent.?—If smuggling silks, ribbons, &c. is done with the insurance, it cannot be at much less than twenty.

8182. Have you reason to think it is done, in any instances, as low as 20 per cent.?—I should think it may be.

8183. How much of that 20 per cent. do you imagine is paid for insurance?—I cannot say; I believe it to be about 25 per cent. upon the average; that includes the insurance.

8184. You do not know how much the insurance would be separately?—I do not.

8185. Do you think that the smuggler would continue his trade upon a very small profit?—I think he would, upon a very small profit.

8186. Has it been for many years 25 per cent.?—I should think it has.

8187. Has it not a tendency, when large profits are gained in trade, to induce persons to go into that trade?—It has a tendency, generally speaking.

8188. You have reason to believe that the smuggler would work for less, and that insurers, if compelled, would insure for less?—Yes.

8189. But as you state that smuggling was regularly transacted at 25 per cent. under the prohibitory law, do not you believe it might be done for half that amount, where there is no risk in bringing the goods into the Thames?—I think so.

8190. Do you think the skill of the manufacturer regulates the fashion, or the direction of the dealer or the milliner, governed by the taste of your customer?—I should say the dealer and miliner abroad, not in this country, and on that depends the English taste; and in all parts of Europe the fashion is regulated generally by the French.

8191. Do you consider that the communication of all classes of society with the Continent of late years, has tended greatly to increase and improve the English taste?—I think it has.

8192. Is there not more competition among English manufacturers than there used to be?—There is, as relates to prices.

8193. You have stated, that there is now, even in fancy goods, great competition between Spitalfields and Manchester?—Yes, there is.

8194. If French goods were prohibited, as they formerly were, do you not think there is sufficient competition amongst the English manufacturers to supply the public with goods of the best taste and quality, and at the lowest practicable price?—I should not say that there is as regards articles of taste, but quite sufficient as to price.

8195. Is not the trade of your house principally in articles made exclusively for your house, whether of French or of English?—It is to a great extent.

8196. Are you aware, that the importation of foreign silk goods has latterly become the more direct pursuit of the large retail houses, and less so of the large wholesale houses?—I should say that more of the large retail houses import than formerly; but I cannot answer as to the effect on the wholesale houses.

8197. Are not the importations by large retail houses in the West end of the Town, principally in job ribbons purchased in Paris after the season is over?—Certainly not.

8198. Does not your house, and do not other houses, either through an agent, or by visiting Paris, order from the French warehouseman goods in November and

December

Mr.
*William Sedgwick.*

6 June,
1832.

December to be delivered to you in March ?—We have an agent resident in Paris, orders are transmitted to this agent, and also to the manufacturer.

8199. Therefore you do not purchase job ribbons ?—We do not.

8200. Do you believe that the fashionable houses in the West end of London do purchase job ribbons ?—No.

8201. Is it understood among the trade, that smuggling exists to a considerable extent ?—Yes.

8202. Is it the fact, that foreign silk goods can frequently be bought cheaper in London than they can be imported ?—It is.

8203. Is it often considered necessary by the retail dealer in French goods to buy part in London, and to import the remainder, and thus make a cheaper average than if they imported the whole ?—I cannot say.

8204. How are the job goods left in Paris at the end of the season disposed of? —A great many of them find their way to the English market.

8205. At a ruinous rate to the English manufacturer ?—At prices at which the English manufacturer cannot compete with them.

Mr. *Emile Menetrier*, called in; and Examined.

Mr.
*Emile Menetrier.*

8206. YOU have been engaged for some years in the manufacture of silk ?— I have.

8207. In what branch ? —In all kinds of plain and fancy broad silks, but not in ribbons.

8208. In what place ?—In Lyons.

8209. When did you cease being engaged in the manufacture of silk at Lyons ? —In 1822 I quitted Lyons for Paris.

8210. Were you acquainted with the quantity of silk imported into this country before the prohibition was removed?—It is very difficult, I apprehend, to ascertain that.

8211. You know that silk was imported at that time into England ?—I know it well, because I was at a silk manufacturer's in Paris which received orders for England. Mr. De Ponilly, with whom I lived, had a manufactory at Lyons, as well as one in Paris; from Paris he sent me, in June 1825 to Manchester; there were orders given to us by English houses, and the goods were delivered to agents in Paris, who forwarded them to England.

8212. You had nothing to do with the importation of them into this country? —No.

8213. You know nothing of the expense and insurance for that importation, nor the nature of it as a smuggling transaction?—No.

8214. Are you aware of goods being imported into this country after 1826 in an illicit manner ?—Yes.

8215. Do you conceive that the opportunities of their illegal import into this country after 1826, increased or not?—I think so. Smuggling was active the first year or two, but I believe lately it has decreased very much.

8216. Before 1826, and since that period, were the goods smuggled into this country of the same description and quality?—I think plain goods decidedly better before 1826; there have been more plain goods of an inferior quality since the opening of the ports than before.

8217. You mean to say, there has been a great quantity since imported, but of an inferior quality to those imported prior ?—The qualities at first were much better than they have been since.

8218. Do you think that there has been an inferior quality of goods manufactured for the purpose of being smuggled in?—No, my opinion is, that it is to meet the English prices in the market. The French have been obliged to make articles to meet the market price.

8219. You think that has arisen from English competition?—No doubt of it.

8220. When such goods as you speak of first came into this country before 1826, there was a very great difference in the price, was there not ?—There have been variations in the prices of silks; silk varies according as the season is favourable or unfavourable.

8221. You mean in France?—Yes.

8222. You were in the house of De Ponilly & Company at the time they manufactured goods in England?—I was.

678.

8223. That

8223. That was since 1826, was it not?—Before and since; I arrived in Manchester 16th June 1825.

8224. Do you know any thing of a seizure made at that house?—No, I do not know the circumstances; I was at Manchester, and the seizure took place in London.

8225. Will you state what you know of the circumstances?—I cannot say any thing about it; I was quite ignorant of the transaction.

8226. Do you believe that those goods seized in London were made at Manchester?—All I know is, that a good many goods were sent up by us from Manchester to London; there were others made by our house in Spitalfields.

8227. Was it not the practice in De Ponilly's house to receive your silk dyed from France?—We received a certain quantity; but how much I do not know.

8228. So that if the warp came dyed, and the shute came dyed, there would be no difficulty in getting it wove in this country; and when it was, a person could not positively say whether the goods were of French or English manufacture?—It would be difficult; we had to contend with the prejudices of our weavers, and found it difficult to get them into our ways. Not finding the silk here good enough for some particular purposes, we were obliged to have the best Piedmont; but we likewise bought silk of houses in Manchester, in Macclesfield, and in London.

8229. Do you mean manufactured or unwrought silk?—Thrown silk for us to manufacture.

8230. Are you to be understood to say that a great part of that which De Ponilly & Company wove in this country was imported from France in the dyed state?—We had a great deal of silk dyed at Manchester, but I cannot say how much was dyed in London, nor what quantity the house had from France.

8231. Have you reason to believe that that you had was dyed in London?—The thrown we bought in this country was all dyed here; we received some dyed warps from France, and some white and ingrain, which were superior to the English.

8232. De Ponilly's house recovered those goods, did they not, and they were returned to them?—Yes, they were.

8233. Do you know any thing of the cost of smuggling goods into this country at the present time?—From what I know, I believe it to be about 20 to 25 per cent.; it is of course much lower when the goods are not insured, but then there is a great risk; on regular importation I believe many dealers have lost money.

8234. You have not much knowledge of it, but what people tell you?—It is from what I hear, and I see a good many people who are connected with smuggling, I do not believe there are any silk goods smuggled under 20 to 25 per cent., where the goods are insured.

8235. How long were Messrs. De Ponilly & Company manufacturers in this country?—Upwards of three years.

8236. Do you know why they gave up the manufacture?—Because they had manufactured a great many articles which were not in fashion here, although they were so in Paris; and they had imported goods in 1826, which likewise sold badly.

8237. Did they make the description of goods which were made in Paris?—Yes, they did.

8238. When they so made those goods, did they continue to make them for a longer period than the fashion continued in France for such goods?—Paris was always the standard as to fashion; but still there were some articles sometimes which did not take in England; and even when the article did not take in England, they often continued making it in Paris.

8239. Do you know whether the English Government gave to Messrs. De Ponilly & Company every facility for carrying on their operations successfully, by allowing them to import their silk free from duty, while organzine was subject to a duty of 14s. to the English manufacturer?—I cannot say.

8240. Were not they allowed a great many facilities?—I cannot say; I was residing at Manchester at the time.

8241. Did you hear that from your employer?—I did not.

8242. From whom did you hear any thing upon the subject?—I heard it spoken of, and I read of it in the newspapers.

8243. Do you know Monsieur Peleckat?—I knew him, but not intimately.

8244. Did

Mr.
*Emile Menetrier.*

6 June,
1832.

8244. Did he ever say any thing to you about that seizure made at Messrs. De Ponilly & Company's ?—Never.

8245. Do you know whether Messrs. De Ponilly & Company made some furniture for Windsor Palace ?—They did; or at least I have always understood it was for Windsor.

8246. Where was that made?—It was made in Spitalfields; I attended the weavers myself.

8247. Was any portion of that imported ?—I cannot say, having quitted the house before the order was completed; we had three looms in our own house in Church-street, Spitalfields, and some out of the house.

8248. How many looms had you in all ?—I cannot exactly say; we had, I think, about 300 looms at Middleton and other places in the neighbourhood of Manchester, of which about 60 were Jacquards; we had besides a manufactory in Spitalfields.

8249. How many looms had you in Spitalfields?—When I came to Spitalfields, they were winding up the concern; we had then 70 looms; there were many more looms previously.

8250. Have you ever imported thrown silk from France?—No; but some, I believe, direct from Italy.

8251. Was it not then that De Ponilly & Company were nearly ruined by the manufacture in this country ?—They lost money by having manufactured goods which went out of fashion.

8252. Can you state whether De Ponilly & Company gave up the manufacture, and the grounds of their desisting from manufacturing in this country ?—They commenced on too large a scale, and made a great many goods which did not answer, and when the panic came their losses were great.

8253. To what period do you refer ?—About six or seven years ago.

8254. Were they manufacturers in this country before the prohibition was removed?—Nearly two years before.

8255. At what time did Messrs. De Ponilly commence their manufacture in this country?—About two years before the importation was allowed.

8256. Did they bring any French workmen here ?—Very few; only four or five head men, to superintend the weavers and to put them in our way.

8257. Did they import any machinery from France ?—We had some Jacquards, but we had also some manufactured in Manchester, but not many.

8258. Were you a partner in the house ?—No, I was at the head of the manufactory at Manchester.

8259. Do you know what induced Mr. De Ponilly to establish himself in this country ?—He did not communicate to me what his intentions were.

8260. How many years did you carry on the manufacture in this country?—Altogether I should say from three to four years, but it was not carried to any extent after the first two years.

8261. It was an unsuccessful speculation?—It was.

8262. Did you find that they succeeded in their speculation in the two last years they were in this country?—The speculation at no time succeeded.

8263. Was not the general introduction of French goods allowed just after that panic?—I cannot say now whether it was a little before or after; we had a great many boxes of French goods imported and sold in this market after I came from Manchester.

8264. When did you come up from Manchester?—The 17th August 1826.

8265. They succeeded in their manufacture for about eighteen months ?—There was a great waste of money upon setting out on so large a scale; they expected it would answer, and it did in some few articles, but not on the major part; we had some weavers at Manchester that came from Paisley, who worked as well as any French weavers.

8266. In what articles ?—In gauzes particularly; we found them much more careful in weaving, and more attentive.

8267. You do not know whether the panic came before they allowed the importation of French goods generally, or afterwards ?—I cannot now say.

8268. You were allowed to manufacture goods in this country for two years before French goods were allowed to be sold ?—Yes; it was free to any one to manufacture.

8269. Did Messrs. De Ponilly & Company, or did they not, bring over any

678.

goods

Mr.
*Emile Menetrier.*

6 June,
1832.

goods in a manufactured state?—I cannot answer that, being at Manchester; if any goods came they must have come to London, and I was 180 miles from it.

8270. Did you not say there were several cases?—When the goods were allowed to be imported, I knew of several transactions of gros de Naples brought in legally.

8271. You do not know anything of goods brought in illegally at that time?—I was in Manchester previously, and afterwards; the goods were sold in the Poultry, and I was at the manufactory in Spitalfields; I was very little acquainted with the sales; I merely know some boxes of goods were legally imported.

8272. When did Mr. De Ponilly give up his establishment here?—In 1827, I believe.

8273. Both his establishments at Manchester and Spitalfields?—The Manchester one was given up first, and from Manchester Mr. De Ponilly sent me to Spitalfields, to wind up the manufactory there, which I did. I was there about eighteen months.

8274. Is Mr. De Ponilly carrying on the manufacture at present?—Yes; in Lyons.

8275. Is this the house the late Mr. Huskisson boasted of as coming from Lyons to establish itself in this country?—I do not know.

8276. Do not you know that an inquiry was set on foot into the silk you made for Windsor Palace, whether it had not been made in France, and in consequence of that inquiry was not some alteration made in the manufacture of it?—No alteration; we had five looms occupied in London on that order; but the extent of it I do not know.

8277. Do you know how much you made in Manchester?—None in Manchester; the order was given about the time we had given up at Manchester, and it was made in Spitalfields.

8278. Had you five looms occupied upon that work? —We had.

8279. Do you know how many yards were ordered?—I do not.

8280. How long were you allowed to make this work?—I do not know; there was plenty of time, I think, allowed.

8281. Did you have any silk dyed in Manchester?—Yes.

8282. Was there any thrown silk used by your house in Manchester which was bought at Manchester?—Yes.

8283. Can you tell of whom your thrown was bought?—Some was bought of Mr. Royle.

8284. To what extent?—I cannot say; I was not there at the beginning; there was a friend of mine there at the commencement whom I succeeded; I was in Manchester for about eighteen or twenty months; then I came to Spitalfields.

8285. When did you come to England?—In 1825; Mr. De Ponilly had begun manufacturing at Manchester about eight months before I arrived.

8286. You attribute the loss merely to the panic?—If there had been no panic there would still have been great loss, owing to the goods going out of fashion.

8287. What prevented the sale of the goods that Mr. De Ponilly had manufactured?—There were goods made of the Paris fashion, and Mr. De Ponilly thought the Paris fashion would be successful here, but it was not; and he had a great many materials dyed of that same article which we were employed on, and he was obliged to sell them at what he could get for them.

8288. In what way did the panic affect your house?—Because we sustained great loss, many bills becoming due which we were obliged to meet.

8289. Did you work the goods at Manchester from French patterns?—From our own patterns.

8290. Were they originally manufactured here?—Our drawers in Lyons and in Paris were making the same kind of figures; we made those we thought most likely to suit the English taste; there were some which suited only the consumption of France.

8291. Did you bring any of De Ponilly's designers to this country?—No, we never had any drawers from France in this country to my knowledge.

8292. You say that some of your throwns were bought of Mr. Royle; did you receive any bales of silk from London?—We bought silk at Macclesfield, but I do not recollect the name of the throwster.

8293. You do not know whether you received any from London?—We received the greatest part in the dyed state from London, and some clouded warps from Lyons.

8294. Did

8294. Did you not receive bales of silk in Manchester from London?—We did.

8295. Were those bought of the merchant through the broker?—I cannot say; we received a great many thrown Piedmont silks.

8296. They came from London?—Yes.

8297. What were the names of Mr. De Ponilly's partners?—Nourtier & Cohen.

8298. Was there not a Mr. Schirmer?—He was partner in the house in Paris; but not in the house in London.

8299. Was he not the designer of the patterns you made from?—He was at the head; but we had sometimes ten or twelve different designers.

8300. He met with some accident at Lyons, did he not?—He was killed at the late disturbance.

8301. Can you state the quantity of silk your looms consumed on an average in Manchester?—I cannot say.

8302. Were you here in London before the trade was opened for foreign goods?—I was in Manchester all the time of the prohibition.

8303. What goods were you selling before the sale opened for the French?—They were English; we sent our goods from Manchester to London; I do not know what the house in London made, but we sent up every week to London.

8304. What description of goods were they?—Every description, except ribbons; satins, gros de Naples, &c.

8305. Any levantines?—Yes.

8306. Can you give any information relative to the blond trade in France, and what they pay in coming into this country, through the Custom House?—They pay 30 per cent.

8307. Is much blond smuggled?—There is.

8308. At what rate?—Ten, twelve, and fifteen per cent.

8309. Does that include insurance?—Altogether it varies according to the demand, and the circumstances.

8310. What do you suppose to be the amount smuggled into this country altogether?—I should say full two-thirds of it.

8311. What is the gross amount, do you suppose, imported?—It is difficult to say.

8312. How do you know that two-thirds is smuggled?—Because so many houses in Paris sell their goods, to be delivered here.

8313. What is the relative price of English blond and French blond?—There is none made I believe in this country, or very little, according to what I have been told by lace manufacturers.

8314. Can you tell whether the quantity of plain silk goods smuggled, is large, as compared with gauzes?—I do not know, but there are hardly any plain broad silks smuggled; they have declined to a very great extent the last two years.

8315. Are there any other articles besides ribbons and blond, which you consider to be smuggled to any great extent?—No.

8316. Does smuggling employ a large number of people?—It is difficult to say; three or four years ago smuggling was carried to a great extent.

8317. Do not a great many people now live by smuggling?—No, I do not think many people do; but many have been ruined by it.

8318. What are they ruined by; is it from the competition?—They are ruined by the losses incurred in smuggling.

8319. In what way are those losses incurred?—Sometimes the goods have been forwarded without being positively insured; and the goods being seized, they have sustained heavy losses.

8320. They did not insure them?—No.

8321. Did the persons who smuggle, vary in their prices with one another, and so create competition?—I have heard it is nearly the same; there is no competition, as I believe; there are now but few insurers; insurance may be stated in general from 20 to 25 per cent.

8322. That covers the insurance, and the guarantee of delivery?—Yes; it is insured at from 20 to 25 per cent.

8323. Do you mean the article is to be delivered here?—Yes.

8324. You say two-thirds of the blond lace is smuggled?—Yes.

8325. Do you think two-thirds of the ribbons and silks are smuggled?—No; it was carried to a great extent about four years ago; but I think it has, since 1830, very much decreased.

8326. You think that the commodity has declined in quantity?—I believe the

678.                                                                  reason

Mr.
*Emile Menetrier.*

6 June,
1832.

Mr.
*Emile Menetrier.*

6 June,
1832.

reason of it is, the losses which have been sustained by the parties, has tended to prevent smuggling.

8327. You think that the smuggler does not get so much by smuggling silks at 25 per cent. as he does by smuggling lace at 10 per cent. ?—The profit is much lower on lace than on silk; but they carry what is most advantageous to them.

8328. You think that a great deal of the silk which does come, is smuggled? —Only in job goods; but as to fancy articles, I believe there are hardly any smuggled now; there are some houses, when they do not want the goods immediately, will buy job ribbons, to be delivered within a month or two; they want a cheap article, and they buy job ribbons on those terms.

8329. How many French houses are there now in London; warehousemen dealing in silks?—I do not know; I see very few of my countrymen here; there are some I believe at the West end, but I do not know them.

8330. Is it not the case that you will hear of a house this spring, but that you will not hear of that man next season; are there not several houses which were here two years ago, which are not to be found here now?—There are many people who come with small lots of silk and lace, but go away as soon as they have effected sales.

8331. Is not smuggling in blond done at eight per cent., because the dealers will not pay more?—Not to my knowledge.

8332. Is it at nine per cent.?—From what I know, it runs from ten to twelve, and fifteen.

8333. Is it not nearer ten than twelve?—It has been above ten for some time, I believe.

8334. You never knew it at seven and a half?—It might be, but in such a case as I mentioned before, goods that were not insured, then the whole might be lost.

8335. The 10 per cent. included the insurance?—Ten and a half altogether; that is the lowest I have heard of.

8336. The price of smuggling is regulated by the duties?—I suppose so; that must generally be the case.

8337. What duty would you recommend to prevent smuggling in blond?— From 12 to 15; if the duty was reduced to 15 per cent. I do not think there would be any smuggling in blond.

8338. What would you consider a fair protecting duty for French gauze ribbons, taking the price into consideration?—I believe few ribbons but job ribbons are smuggled; fashionable articles are wanted immediately, therefore they cannot resort to smuggling; I am told no smuggler will bind himself to deliver goods within a limited time.

8339. Are you in the silk trade now?—No, I very seldom do any thing in silks; some of my countrymen come with a lot sometimes and leave them for sale, and I sell them, but I am not regularly in the trade.

8340. How long have you left the silk trade?—About three years.

8341. What do you think would be the effect of inflicting a personal penalty on smugglers?—I think that when they are caught they are punished quite enough, by losing their property: the treadmill could not make the case much worse.

8342. Do you not think that the enactment of such a law would deter a person? —I think that those persons would not be much influenced by that; they would rather have six months at the treadmill, and not lose their money.

8343. The loss of the property is only the loss of the insurance?—The insurer has his claim upon the smuggler, and I have heard of instances of smugglers being obliged to deposit a certain sum of money for the security of the goods crossing; but the owner of the goods knows nothing of the smuggler.

8344. Whom do you mean by the smuggler; the man in France, or the person carrying on business here?—The parties who bring the goods over and land them here.

8345. The question referred to personal punishment on the person ordering the goods here; whether you do not think that the fear of personal punishment would deter such a person from ordering the goods?—Of course it would, if he is a respectable man.

8346. There would be no smuggling if there were not persons of that description who ordered the smuggled goods?—Certainly not.

8347. Those are the employers of the smugglers?—Exactly so.

8348. Therefore the way to prevent smuggling would be to discover some means
of

Mr.
*Emile Menetrier.*

6 June,
1832.

of deterring persons from ordering the smuggled goods?—Yes, that may be one way, or another would be to impose such duties as would remove the temptation of the smuggler to engage in the trade.

8349. Do you think that any regulation about stamping would be effectual in the prevention of smuggling?—I cannot say; a stamp might be imitated, and they could stamp them any where, if they knew what the stamp was.

8350. Have you ever heard of the plan of stamping by a letter to be changed every day, indeed two or three times during one entry?—No, I have not.

8351. If the smuggler was subject to such a punishment as has been alluded to, is it likely that English houses of large capital would continue to carry on the trade?—I must leave that to the feelings of others; I know I should not engage in it myself; it depends entirely on the feelings of parties, and their views of the matter.

8352. Do not you think it would tend much to prevent smuggling?—I think it might, in some instances.

---

*Veneris, 8° die Junii, 1832.*

---

THE RIGHT HON. THE EARL GROSVENOR, IN THE CHAIR.

---

Mr. *John Ballance*, called in; and Examined.

Mr.
*John Ballance.*

8 June,
1832.

8353. ARE you concerned in the silk trade?—I am a silk manufacturer; I wish in the evidence I am about to give, to confine myself as strictly as possible to show the operation upon the interests of the silk trade, of the change of the laws of 1824, agreeably to the Resolution of the House of Commons, appointing a Select Committee, &c. &c.

8354. Where do you carry on your manufacture?—In Spitalfields.

8355. How long have you been engaged in the trade?—Twenty-six years myself; my father, who is still with me, has been in it 60 years.

8356. Will you inform the Committee what was the condition of the silk manufacture in Spitalfields, before the year 1826?—It was a growing and a prosperous trade.

8357. How do you show this?—I show it in two ways, from the Custom House returns of raw silk, and from the rate of wages paid to the artisan for working up that silk; those returns trebled in 10 years previous to the opening of the ports, and the wages were such as enabled the artisan to live, without any dependence upon parish allowance. In the statement in my hand I have given averages of two years, for this reason, the importation of one year would hardly show the consumption of that year, and it often happens that the importation of one year forms part of the consumption of another.

" Custom House Returns of RAW SILK, between the years 1816 and 1825 inclusive, reckoning the average of two years, and exclusive of waste, knubs and husks, showing the increase per cent.

| | | |
|---|---|---|
| 1816 1817 | lbs. 1,108,247 | |
| 1818 1819 | 1,445,489 | 30 per cent. |
| 1820 1821 | 1,743,008 | 57 per cent. |
| 1822 1823 | 2,022,702 | 83 per cent. |
| 1824 1825 | 3,131,513 | 180 per cent." |

I select those 10 years because they were 10 years of peace on the Continent, when it is very evident our intercourse was much freer than during a season of warfare, and therefore, if smuggling were carried on to any extent it would have been likely to be carried on to a greater extent during the time of peace than that of warfare. Then as it regards the wages for working up this raw material the wages in Spitalfields, upon plain goods, averaged from 15s. to 16s. per week the year round from 1816 to 1826; I speak of nett wages to the workman. As it regards

678.

Mr.
*John Ballance.*

8 June,
1832.

regards fancy silks it is difficult to form an average; the average given to me, from a large fancy house, during that period, upon ordinary fancy goods, would be from 20*s.* to 25*s.*; I give this as the average of wages, not only for Spitalfields during that time. The accounts from Macclesfield, where silk goods were then manufactured, will exhibit a similar rate of wages; Manchester the same; of course I can speak to these only as the accounts were tendered to me.

8358. When you mention a similar rate of wages, do you mean a similar rate in proportion, or an exact similarity?—Varying perhaps from 1*s.* to 1*s.* 6*d.* a week; I suspect, as it regards fancy silks, the averages must be very general; but it is more strict with regard to plain goods, which vary less.

8359. The statement you have made as to wages applies to what you yourself gave, and what you believe to have been the wages given by others?—Just so, in fact we all paid the same price. I exhibit these Custom House returns in proof of the growing state of the trade during that period. I exhibit the wages given to the artisan in proof of its prosperity, and I take both in combination when I say that during those ten years it was a growing and prosperous trade.

8360. There were periods of distress in the silk manufactory prior to the year 1826, were there not?—Yes; but there are only two periods worthy of notice; the one in 1792 and the other in 1816, or running into part of 1817.

8361. Do you know the causes and the extent of distress at the periods referred to?—I well recollect the distress in 1792, that lasted for six months; from the autumn of 1792 to the spring of 1793, there were I believe about 4,000 looms out of work at that period, I say about, speaking in round numbers; the distress arose from a new article coming into general wear, that of printed cottons, which for a time displaced silk. The trade revived in the spring of that year; I am not aware of any distress, strictly speaking, of the silk trade, between that period and the latter period to which I have referred. Then in 1816 or the beginning of 1817, I beg to remark that was not a distress so much of the silk trade as a distress of the district in which the silk trade was carried on, that arose from a transition from war to peace; the disbanding of the army and navy threw a number of loose hands upon that district, which could not find immediate employment; the distress was equally felt in other branches of business, bricklayers, carpenters, and other descriptions of trades carried on there. There were very few weavers out of employment.

8362. Was smuggling carried on to any great extent under the prohibitory laws, as compared with what it has been since?—It was not. Smuggling was then confined to the coast; silks were brought in by stealth, in small quantities; there was great concealment practised; now since the ports have been opened, there has been what I call a regular wholesale trade in smuggling, and it is done openly and without disguise.

8363. What were the principal inducements to smuggling under the foreign system?—I consider that the chief inducement to smuggling, at that time, was the very high duties on the raw material, which gave a fictitious value to English manufactures, to which if you were to add wages paid, and, speaking in round numbers, I suspect there might be as much as from 70 per cent. difference between English and Foreign silks: the temptation, therefore, was great, on account of the relative difference in price; had the difference been less, I feel quite satisfied that under the law of prohibition there would have been scarcely any smuggling.

8364. What is the present condition of the silk manufacturer of Spitalfields?— I would, in speaking of the present, be understood to speak of the last nine or ten months; there has been great distress in this district; it is computed that there are about 16,000 looms in the district of Spitalfields; from five to 6,000 of those looms have been standing still for more than six months, taking the average from the latter end of September to the middle of April. I beg to add, that in the beginning of April there were three districts in the parish of Bethnal Green, visited house by house; the one known to be a very distressed district for want of work, another not so much distressed, and the other between both: in the distressed district, I think out of 500 looms visited, there were about 200 without work.

8365. What do you state to have been the duration of the distress?—This distress began in 1826, and lasted six months; it returned in 1828, and continued through the greater part of 1829; it has, however, been more severe this last winter than at the two former periods; I link these together, because the distress in each period was identically of the same character.

8366. What

Mr.
*John Ballance.*

8 June,
1832.

8366. What are the principal features of the distress?—A miserably reduced rate of wages, and great scarcity of employment.

8367. When was the price of labour reduced, and in what proportion?—From July 1826 to July 1829 it fell about 20 per cent.; from July 1829 to 1832 it has fallen about 20 per cent. more, making together 38 to 40 per cent. or thereabout, from 1826.

8368. How do you account for the price of labour falling in 1829, and continuing to fall to 1832?—The protecting duty of 15 s. upon foreign-wrought silks was reduced, in July 1829, to 11 s. and labour fell in consequence.

8369. What do you apprehend was the intention of Parliament in lowering the duties?—To prevent smuggling. That appears from a conversation I had with the then President of the Board of Trade, Mr. Vesey Fitzgerald; he told me—"We have received letters from Calais, stating that goods had been smuggled into this country at from 25 to about 28 per cent., if we reduce the duty to 25 per cent. we shall crush the smuggler;" and that was the reason the right honourable gentleman assigned for reducing the duty.

8370. Do you think the manufacturer has been benefited in any respect by the lowering of the duties?—No; the smuggler immediately lowered his price, and smuggling has been carried on to a greater extent than it was before; I need no further proof that the smuggler has lowered his price than the evidence before this Committee, which has stated it to be from 15 to 20 per cent.

8371. What are the present average weekly earnings of weavers?—The present average, if my weavers are to be taken as a sample, and I am inclined to think I pay rather more than others; in fact, I pay seven-pence a yard for making gros de Naples, and it has been given in here at six-pence halfpenny; I should think the average is from 9 s. to 10 s. per week for plain goods nett, taking it for the year round.

8372. Do you refer to the earnings of both sexes?—Yes, including men and women.

8373. This you state to be the average of the wages you yourself pay, notwithstanding you pay more than the general average?—Yes; when I say the year round, I mean that is what I pay the persons the year round, out of which they have got their own incidentals to pay; I am speaking of wages that go from our house to them, out of which they have to pay for twisting in, turning on, and incidentals; this 9 s. does not exclude, but includes those incidentals. I submit, in proof of the reduction of wages, a calculation of wages paid to my weavers on 5,000 lbs. weight of silk worked up in each year from 1816 to 1831 taken from our own books; these are wages paid to weavers only, not warpers and winders.

| | | | | | | | |
|---|---|---|---|---|---|---|---|
| " Lbs. 5,000 of Silk in 1816 cost weaving | - | - | - | £.3,362 |
| 5,000 - ditto 1817 - ditto | - | - | - | - | 3,273 |
| 5,000 - ditto 1818 - ditto | - | - | - | - | 3,356 |
| 5,000 - ditto 1819 - ditto | - | - | - | - | 3,357 |
| 5,000 - ditto 1820 - ditto | - | - | - | - | 3,390 |
| 5,000 - ditto 1821 - ditto | - | - | - | - | 3,256 |
| 5,000 - ditto 1822 - ditto | - | - | - | - | 3,253 |
| 5,000 - ditto 1823 - ditto | - | - | - | - | 3,304 |
| 5,000 - ditto 1824 - ditto | - | - | - | - | 3,290 |
| 5,000 - ditto 1825 - ditto | - | - | - | - | 3,170 |
| 5,000 - ditto 1826 - ditto | - | - | - | - | 3,146 |
| 5,000 - ditto 1827 - ditto | - | - | - | - | 2,842 |
| 5,000 - ditto 1828 - ditto | - | - | - | - | 2,480 |
| 5,000 - ditto 1829 - ditto | - | - | - | - | 2,267 |
| 5,000 - ditto 1830 - ditto | - | - | - | - | 2,214 |
| 5,000 - ditto 1831 - ditto | - | - | - | - | 1,944." |

8374. You have spoken of the reduction of wages consequent, in your opinion, on the state of the law, do you know the state of the parishes comprising the district commonly called Spitalfields?—I do; an account was taken in the beginning of March, of which the following are the particulars: in the district called Spitalfields there are included three parishes, St. Matthew Bethnal Green, Christchurch Spitalfields and Mile End New Town; previous to the appointment of this Select Committee we obtained from the parish officers the statement I will now read;

" STATE

Mr.
John Ballance.

8 June,
1832.

" STATE of the THREE PARISHES of Saint Matthew Bethnal Green, Christchurch Spitalfields and Mile End New Town, comprising the District called Spitalfields, taken from the Parish Acounts in February 1832 :

|  | Poor in the Workhouse. | Out-door Poor. |
|---|---|---|
| Bethnal Green | 1,100 | 6,142 |
| Christchurch | 460 | 418 |
| Mile End New Town | 161 | 552 |
| TOTAL | 1,721 | 7,112 |

Bethnal Green in 1825 had no debt.
    in 1832 is in debt £. 13,000.
    in 1825 Poor's Rate 2 s. in the Pound.
    in 1832 - ditto - 4 s.   ditto."

I beg to add the rate cannot be higher, if they increase the rate they bring the poor into the house.

| | | |
|---|---|---|
| Christchurch | in 1825 was in debt | £. 928. |
| — | in 1832 is in debt | 2,902. |
| Mile End New Town | in 1825 was in debt | 748. |
| — | in 1832 is in debt | 1,414. |
| — | in 1825, Poor's Rates 2 s. in the Pound. | |
| — | in 1832 - ditto - 6 s. - ditto." | |

8375. How did you become possessed of this document ?—About a week before the debate came on on the 1st of March, the committee sitting at Weavers' Hall sent circulars to the three parishes for information. This is an extract from the papers which they furnished to the committee.

8376. How were those papers furnished?—By the parish officers.

8377. Did you make that extract yourself?—I did.

8378. Were they signed by the parish officers?—Yes, that is an extract from papers signed by the parish officers; it must be very evident to the members of this Committee, that Bethnal Green exhibits a much larger account than Spitalfields and Mile End; if there be 16,000 looms in the district of Spitalfields, I apprehend it will be found that about 12,000 of those looms are located in the parish of Bethnal Green; the population of Bethnal Green is something about 60,000; giving three persons to a loom, we shall have very nearly 40,000 of that 60,000 directly engaged in the manufacture of silk, leaving the remaining 20,000 either for children or for persons that subsist by the earnings circulated among them. I therefore submit, that the Paper I am now about to produce, which is signed by the parish officers of Bethnal Green, will exhibit a sort of gauge, if I may so speak, of the condition of the silk trade in that parish; it is dated May 1832.

[*The same was delivered in and read, as follows:*]

### SAINT MATTHEW BETHNAL GREEN.

AN ACCOUNT of the Number of POOR in the WORKHOUSE of this PARISH, and likewise the Number of CASUAL POOR (or those receiving Out-door Relief,) from the Year 1821 to the present period, averaging the allowance per Head, One Shilling and Sixpence weekly.

| YEARS | Casual, or OUT-DOOR POOR. | NUMBER OF POOR in the House. |
|---|---|---|
| 1821 | 157 | 498 |
| 1822 | 196 | 526 |
| 1823 | 223 | 632 |
| 1824 | 289 | 721 |
| 1825 | 326 | 588 |
| 1826 | 984 | 842 |
| 1827 | 638 | 956 |
| 1828 | 1,319 | 796 |
| 1829 | 2,487 | 1,092 |
| 1830 | 4,693 | 1,380 |
| 1831 | 4,958 | 1,013 |
| 1832 | 6,218 | 1,160 |

May 1832.

R. Entwistle,
Master of Workhouse.

Mr.
*John Ballanee.*
___
8 June,
1832.

The increase will be perceived to be within the last four years; the casual poor are those who go twice a week, I should say Tuesdays and Fridays, to receive their pittance when they have no work to do.

8379. What is the population of that district?—I take the population of those three parishes at 100,000; I give about 60,000 to Bethnal Green, I give about 20,000 to Spitalfields, and I give about 20,000 to Mile End, I ought to give it at rather more. I have excluded the parish of Shoreditch, because though weaving is carried on there, it is carried on to a much smaller extent than in the other parishes.

8380. Is that population dependent on the silk manufacture for support?—About 50,000 of those are entirely dependent upon the silk manufacture for support; if there be 16,000 looms, it will be found that about three persons will subsist by each loom, that makes 48,000, and the remaining number, 50,000, are more or less interested, as they depend upon the wages that are circulated through this district.

8381. Have you made any comparison of the reduction in the amount of wages, circulated in that district, as compared with the period previous to 1826?—I am satisfied that I considerably understate what I am about to name, when I say that there is at the rate of 300,000*l.* per annum paid less in wages to the operatives of Spitalfields now than was paid to them before the opening of the ports in 1826.

8382. What has been the effect produced, so far as you have been able to observe, by the reduction of wages, on the character and habits of the population?—I should say, generally, very demoralizing effects, and I wish, if the Committee will allow me, to speak more particularly to this subject. The injury done to the labouring classes within the last six years, from the reduction of wages and the loss of work, has been very great. I have been well acquainted with the district of Spitalfields for forty years. I knew its former condition, and I know its present condition, and I have watched the change which has gradually been taking place since 1826, upon the general character and habits of its population. I could detail instances of suffering and wretchedness that would harrow up the feelings of this Committee; but I wish to confine myself rather to general effects, such as idleness, destitution, depraved habits, and I must add disaffection to the Government. In the winter of 1826, from the December of 1825 to the May of 1826, there were 7,721 looms thrown out of work to prepare for the introduction of foreign wrought silks in the month of July following; upon these looms there were 4,400 families dependent for support. I beg to add, this was taken by an actual survey from house to house, and the number put down in the whole district; then the distress began, some thousands parted with every thing they had to procure food for themselves and their children, and Spitalfields has never recovered from the blow which was then struck at it. The foreign manufacturer, from his ignorance of our markets could not immediately avail himself of all its advantages, and therefore trade revived a little in consequence of that, and the great scarcity of manufactured goods, from the abstraction of work; but by the end of the year 1827 and 1828, the knowledge, which the foreigner had obtained of our market, and his increased facilities for smuggling, began to give him a marked ascendancy; the consequence was, that the autumn of 1828, and the greater part of 1829, was a period of severe distress for the silk trade; wages were further reduced, and for nearly nine months there were about 5,000 looms unemployed. I say "about," for at that time we did not go from house to house, but took proportions; this long state of suffering produced a temporary re-action in 1830, but all the while manufactured silks, especially the richer fabrics, where labour is more largely expended, were being undermined by foreign manufacturers, and within the last nine months the distress of Spitalfields has been greater than at those periods to which I referred. I said that from five to 6,000 looms were standing the last winter, and that at once throws out of employment 18,000 persons; the point of difference between the distress of 1826 and now, is this, that those who had work were working at 10*d.* a yard, and those at work in 1832 have been working at 6*d.* and 7*d.* a yard. These repeated calamities have reduced the population to a very miserable and distressed condition; I allude now to many that have been kept at work during those periods. They are to be found in many instances without a bed, without furniture, with scarcely any clothes to cover them, a little straw heaped up in one corner of the room for the family to lie upon. I have known

678.                                                                                    instances

instances this last winter, I can give names, where a man has had to support himself, his wife, and three children, upon one loom's work, at 5 *d.* per yard, which yielded him about 7 *s.* per week, I have known his children crying for bread, and there has been none to give them, nor money to get it; yet those very persons could earn formerly, and did earn from 15 *s.* to 18 *s.* a week, they had the necessaries of life, and were contented and happy; and I must add further that this misery and wretchedness has produced an awful change in the public morals of the district. I speak from personal knowledge when I say, that the weavers of Spitalfields were formerly proverbial for good order and moral conduct, their children were decently clothed and educated; but their overwhelming distresses have produced a recklessness of character in which virtue and good principle are lost. The Sunday is not now as it used to be, a day of rest among them, it is a day of labour, and they say they must work seven days, or they cannot live. I must also observe upon their feelings towards the Government; they attribute to the measures of Government, I do not say whether they are right or wrong, but I speak to the fact, they do attribute to the measures of Government all their privations and miseries; and I do not in the least exaggerate when I say, there is a feeling of deadly hatred working in many thousands of them to the Government of their country, which presents a contrast as striking as it is painful to their former known loyalty and attachment.

8383. There has been during the years you have mentioned a large importation of raw silk, how do you reconcile the distress, you have been describing in Spitalfields to that circumstance?—Silk goods are made heavier now than they were formerly; if I work up a thousand weight of silk in goods, weighing one ounce to the yard, and I work up a thousand weight of silk in goods, weighing an ounce and a quarter to the yard, nothing can be clearer than that; I have one-fourth less in yards length, and paying the work people by the yard there is one-fourth less wages paid, but I do not wish to make this assertion without proof; and I hold in my hand an account of the produce of an hundred looms, from 1822 to 1831, showing the weight of silk worked up by them, with the wages paid in each year, including all charges. I am now exhibiting, not as formerly, the price for weaving only but that of winding and warping also. This is extracted from our accounts upon plain silks.

[*The said Account was delivered in, and read as follows:*]

| In 1822 | - - | 100 Looms worked up *lbs.* 5,964 | - | Total Wages paid £. 4,803 |
|---|---|---|---|---|
| 1823 | - - 100 | - - ditto - - 5,530 | - - - ditto - - | 4,294 |
| 1824 | - - 100 | - - ditto - - 5,516 | - - - ditto - - | 4,151 |
| 1825 | - - 100 | - - ditto - - 6,232 | - - - ditto - - | 4,690 |
| 1826 | - - 100 | - - ditto - - 5,543 | - - - ditto - - | 4,011 |
| 1827 | - - 100 | - - ditto - - 6,102 | - - - ditto - - | 4,010 |
| 1828 | - - 100 | - - ditto - - 7,210 | - - - ditto - - | 4,242 |
| 1829 | - - 100 | - - ditto - - 7,500 | - - - ditto - - | 4,150 |
| 1830 | - - 100 | - - ditto - - 7,730 | - - - ditto - - | 3,891 |
| 1831 | - - 100 | - - ditto - - 7,680 | - - - ditto - - | 3,490 |

This account shows nearly 2,000 lbs. weight of silk more worked up, and 1,600 *l.* less paid for it in 1822 than in 1831.

8384. Were the looms employed upon the same goods?—I have selected an hundred looms, that is a large number, in order to give a large surface; they consist of sarsnet, of gros de Naples, of ducapes and satins, an assortment of what I make. I make goods now selling from two shillings to seven shillings per yard.

8385. Have you taken the same proportions?—Precisely; I now beg to give the rate of wages per week that my weavers have earned from 1822 to 1831; from 1822 to 1826, their weekly earnings averaged 15 *s.* 6 *d.*; in 1826, 12 *s.* 10 *d.*; in 1827, 12 *s.* 6 *d.*; in 1828, 12 *s.* 10 *d.* in 1829, 12 *s.* 4 *d.*; in 1830, 11 *s.* 2 *d.*; in 1831, 9 *s.* 9 *d.*

8386. Is this the amount they earned when they were at work?—Yes, I am now giving averages; they may be fractionally a penny more or less.

8387. Can you give the highest and lowest earnings of any weaver?—The highest earnings of my weavers is 20 *s.* 8 *d.* per week, and the lowest is 6 *s.* 6 *d.* per week. The former is taken upon the richest black satins, which I make worth about 7 *s.* per yard. I had many of them going in 1826, but the subsequent importations from France, of rich satins, have compelled me almost to discontinue

making

Mr.
*John Ballance.*

8 June,
1832.

making the article. The same weavers are now upon works of a much lower description.

8388. Has there been any change in the description of silk goods manufactured in Spitalfields, at the present time, as compared with the time prior to 1826?—The staple manufacture of Spitalfields, before the opening of the ports, consisted of plain silks and fancy and figured silks, chiefly of fine and rich fabrics.

8389. Does that description apply to plain as well as the figured and fancy, were they generally rich fabrics?—Chiefly.

8390. Have any of those been discontinued?—Yes, especially the richer silks, and almost entirely the fancy and figured branch of the silk trade.

8391. Has the consumption of this description of silk fabrics been as considerable in Great Britain, within the last five years, as formerly?—The consumption of such silk in Great Britain has been much greater; no one will deny that who is at all acquainted with the trade.

8392. How then has this increasing demand been supplied?—From the Continent, especially from France.

8393. Has not Manchester supplied the demand as well as the Continent?—No; the staple silk trade of Manchester does not consist of the same sort of goods as were formerly made in Spitalfields, or are now imported from France.

8394. Are you able to inform the Committee what description of silk goods Manchester does manufacture?—Two sorts, silk goods mixed with cotton or worsted which certainly cannot be called a part of the silk trade; and the goods that she makes wholly of silk, are for the most part low priced, of coarser texture, and with reference to the plain articles more adapted for exportation.

8395. There are three terms used, plain, figured, and fancy, what do you mean them to designate?—Plain are those which have no pattern whatever; fancy is considered the higher class of figured goods, and figured is a technical term occupying a space between both.

8396. On what grounds are those fabrics you call fancy, do you refer to gauzes?—No.

8397. You speak in all cases of solid silk goods?—Yes, my observation is confined to the solid silk goods.

8398. Do you know an article called Gros de Tour?—Yes.

8399. Is that plain or figured?—I should call that plain; the sole difference between a gros de tour and ducape is, that one has about 70 or 80 shutes per inch, the other has between 50 and 60 per inch, the warp being proportionably richer.

8400. Is not the plain article an article that has an even surface?—Certainly; I do not know whether the question referred to the gros des Orleans, that is a figured article. I have said that silk goods, mixed with cotton and worsted, and silk goods chiefly of a low character and texture, whether they be figured or plain, constitute what may be called the staple silk trade of Manchester. I now exhibit two patterns, this is one I call silk mixed with cotton, which is not the silk trade. The Jacquard looms at Manchester are largely employed in making that article. As it regards goods, made wholly of silk, at Manchester, I exhibit this pattern of a figured [*showing a pattern.*] I apprehend the price to be from 3s. to 3s. 3d. per yard; the person who gave it me has had it in his warehouse since the 10th of March, he found it difficult to sell it, and in the interval has sold some hundreds of pieces of French silk, which had been preferred, though 2s. a yard dearer.

8401. Has Manchester carried on the silk trade for many years, or has it recently grown up there?—She has had this trade for a considerable number of years; a manufacturer told me the other day, that as far back as 1806, 1807 and 1808 he had 1,200 looms at work there, upon silk and silk mixed. I place this evidence against that of another witness, who said, that in the year 1819 there were not 50 looms at work at Manchester on silk; and I beg to add, the same manufacturer, who is now out of the trade, told me, and I give it on his authority, that he was not the only manufacturer that had looms at work on silk and silk mixed in 1806, 1807 and 1808; he gave me the names of six or seven other manufacturers at Manchester, who had likewise looms at work on silk and silk mixed, though not quite to the same extent.

8402. Is it not since the opening of the ports to foreign silk that the trade of Manchester has sprung up?—There was a steady increase of the manufacture of

678. silk

Mr.
*John Ballance.*

8 June,
1832.

silk goods and silk mixed, from 1806 to 1826, subject, of course, to occasional fluctuations.

8403. Was the trade of Spitalfields affected at that time by the increase of manufactures at Manchester?—I have said that the fabrics at Manchester and Spitalfields were essentially different, and they went to an entirely different class of consumers; in point of fact, throughout that period of 1806 to 1826 I have known seasons when the Manchester silk trade has been depressed and the Spitalfields trade has been active, but I recollect no instance of the reverse; generally speaking, the prosperity of the one indicated the prosperity of the other; I have it on the authority of Manchester manufacturers: one of them said to me—"We stood, before the opening of the ports, relatively with Spitalfields, as we now stand relatively with Lyons; formerly we watched the patterns that came out from the manufactures of Spitalfields for the spring sales in March and April, that we might instantly give them upon a lower coarse texture; we came in with those patterns about three months after, for a second class of consumers; thus Spitalfields was always ahead of us three or four months in respect of fashion, and took the lead of us in respect of quality: we now often do the same in relation to the patterns from Lyons."

8404. Is that description of silk goods you have mentioned as being made at Manchester confined to that place?—I have said that Spitalfields has lost its trade in rich silks, especially fancy and figured silks, and in some instances it has adopted the low Manchester trade, as a miserable substitute for what it has lost; if I may use the term, I will say Manchester has travelled to London, and hence a competition has arisen between those places, Manchester and Spitalfields, which was not felt before, or at least not to the extent, and which has injured both parties; I am speaking now of the staple trade of those places respectively; I do not mean to say that you will not find a single piece made in Manchester similar to Spitalfields, or in Spitalfields similar to Manchester, but I take the staple trade of the two places, as giving the character of the trade.

8405. You say the change has injured both parties?—I mean, that Spitalfields has taken up the Manchester trade more generally than it used to do; there is a competition existing between Manchester and Spitalfields on the low article, which did not before exist to the same extent.

8406. You state that you recollect no instance of depression in the trade of Spitalfields not felt at Manchester; has it been felt within the last nine months?—Manchester being a cotton manufacture principally, the population engaged in silk is comparatively small. I believe the population of Manchester is about 240,000; of that there are not, I am informed, one-tenth of them in silk, and of course the distress will not be so severely felt as that felt by the districts which are exclusively silk; but through the last winter Manchester itself was distressed; I will only advert to the town of Middleton, which is wholly a silk district, and it will appear in evidence that distress was very severely felt in that district.

8407. To what do you attribute the distress in the silk manufacture of Spitalfields?—I attribute it to the opening of the ports to foreign silk goods, in 1826.

8408. How do you prove that to be the cause of it?—I say, generally it greatly diminished the demand for labour; first, by the facilities which this measure has given to smuggling, which has ever since been carried on to a very great extent, and then, by the ruin, or nearly so, of the rich trade, especially the fancy and the figured branch of the silk trade, peculiar to Spitalfields. It must not be concealed, that the foreigner possesses strictly what may be called a monopoly of the English market, in respect to the fancy and figured branch of the silk trade, and we do ask the Legislature of our country to break down this monopoly, for we say it paralyzes industry in that district, and is producing misery and discontent.

8409. In your opinion the fancy silk goods have been supplied from France, and not from Spitalfields?—Yes.

8410. What advantages does France in particular possess over England?—The advantages of France and the Continent (I link them together, for I by no means restrict these advantages to France); France may have greater advantages than other parts of the Continent; but the other parts of the Continent have immense advantages over England, in relation to the silk manufacture; but to speak more particularly of France, I will mention four advantages, one is the raw material; another the low rate of wages for working up that raw material; another the large amount of her annual exports of manufactured silks; and the last is her possession

of

of foreign markets : before I enter upon these points, I wish to be distinctly understood that the stress I lay is upon the combination of all these ; that of the raw
material is only one element among several others ; and if that difficulty were removed, it would still leave us incumbered as much as ever with the three others ;
I do not mean to say that her possession of the raw material is not an advantage,
but it is only one element of her advantages, and if removed would still leave us
exposed to great difficulties.

The exclusive possession of the raw material secures to France two advantages ;
the one is in respect of quality ; there is a large proportion of that raw material,
which is the best in the world, and then it gives her an advantage in relation to
price, that superior silk is rendered to her manufacturers, in trams and organzines,
from $7\frac{1}{2}$ to 10 per cent. less than the best silks of Italy can be purchased in this
country by English manufacturers, independent of the import duties : in proof of
this I beg to produce this paper.

Mr.
*John Ballance.*

8 June,
1832.

[*The same was delivered in, and read, as follows* :]

COMPARATIVE VIEW of the Prices at Lyons of French Tram, the produce of French Raw, with the Prices
obtained in London at the same periods for Italian Tram, reckoning the size in both cases from 24–26 deniers;
the former taken from Quotations of Prices Current, and the latter from Sales effected, and given in Averages of
Three Months, from July 1827 to March 1832.

| Averages of Quotations of French Trams — 24–26 deniers. | Prices at LYONS, $12\frac{1}{2}$ p' % disct, and 1 Month. | | Computation into Sterlg p' lb. English Net, Cash 1 Month. | | Averages of Prices of Italian Trams in London — 24–26 deniers. | Sales effected in LONDON, including Duty and $2\frac{1}{2}$ p' % discount. | | Computation Less Duty Net, Cash 14 Days. | |
|---|---|---|---|---|---|---|---|---|---|
| 1827: | *f.* | *c.* | *s.* | *d.* | 1827: | *s.* | *d.* | *s.* | *d.* |
| *July, August, September - | 34 | 16 = | 21 | 8 | Three Months, p' Contra - | - 28 | – = | 24 | 5 |
| October, November, December | 24 | – = | 21 | 7 | Ditto - - ditto - | - 26 | – = | 22 | 7 |
| 1828: | | | | | 1828: | | | | |
| January, February, March - | 35 | 77 = | 22 | 8 | Three Months, p' Contra - | - 27 | – = | 23 | 5 |
| April, May, June - - - | 34 | 50 = | 21 | 11 | Ditto - - ditto - | - 27 | 6 = | 23 | 11 |
| July, August, September - | 35 | – = | 22 | 3 | Ditto - - ditto - | - 27 | – = | 23 | 5 |
| October, November, December | 35 | – = | 22 | 3 | Ditto - - ditto - | - 27 | 6 = | 23 | 11 |
| 1829: | | | | | 1829: | | | | |
| January, February, March - | 34 | 62 = | 22 | – | Three Months, p' Contra - | - 26 | 9 = | 23 | 2 |
| †April, May, June - - - | 34 | 40 = | 21 | 6 | Ditto - - ditto - | - 26 | – = | 22 | 5 |
| July, August, September - | 34 | – = | 21 | 4 | * Ditto - - ditto - | - 24 | – = | 21 | 5 |
| October, November, December | 33 | 75 = | 21 | 2 | Ditto - - ditto - | - 22 | 6 = | 20 | 6 |
| 1830: | | | | | 1830: | | | | |
| January, February, March - | 32 | 80 = | 20 | 7 | Three Months, p' Contra - | - 22 | – = | 19 | 6 |
| April, May, June - - - | 31 | 30 = | 19 | 7 | Ditto - - ditto - | - 22 | 6 = | 20 | – |
| July, August, September - | 31 | 30 = | 19 | 7 | Ditto - - ditto - | - 25 | – = | 22 | 5 |
| October, November, December | 29 | 90 = | 18 | 8 | Ditto - - ditto - | - 24 | – = | 21 | 5 |
| 1831: | | | | | 1831: | | | | |
| January, February, March - | 28 | – = | 17 | 6 | Three Months, p' Contra - | - 23 | 6 = | 21 | – |
| April, May, June - - - | 29 | 15 = | 18 | 3 | Ditto - - ditto - | - 21 | – = | 18 | 6 |
| July, August, September - | 29 | 25 = | 18 | 3 | Ditto - - ditto - | - 21 | – = | 18 | 6 |
| October, November, December | 28 | 75 = | 18 | – | Ditto - - ditto - | - 20 | 6 = | 18 | 1 |
| 1832: | | | | | 1832: | | | | |
| January, February, March - | 29 | 25 | 18 | 3 | Three Months, p' Contra - | - 20 | 6 = | 18 | 1 |

* Exche taken at 25. 25. to April 1829.
† Ditto - ditto 25. 60. from April 1829 to March 1832.

* The Duty was reduced from 3 s. to 2 s.

---

I have given to the Committee the relative prices for French tram, the produce
of French raw ; I will now give the relative prices of French organzine as compared with Piedmont organzine in this country during the same periods, reckoning
cash in both instances, for the manufacture of Lyons and the manufacture of
London.

[*The same was delivered in, and read.*]

COMPARATIVE

COMPARATIVE VIEW of the Prices at Lyons of French Organzine, the produce of French Raw, with the Prices obtained in London at the same periods for Piedmont Organzine, reckoning the size in both cases to be 22–24 deniers; the former taken from Quotations of Prices Current, and the latter from Sales effected, and given in Averages of Three Months, from July 1827 to March 1832.

| Averages of Quotations of French Organzine — of 22–24 deniers. | Prices at LYONS, 12½ p'°/₀ dis.ᵗ and 1 Month. | | Computation into Sterlᵍ p' lb. English Net, Cash 1 Month. | | Averages of Prices of Piedmont Organzine in London — 22–24 deniers. | Sales effected in LONDON, including Duty and 2½ p' °/₀ discount. | | Computation Less Duty Net, Cash 14 Days. | |
|---|---|---|---|---|---|---|---|---|---|
| | f. | c. | s. | d. | | s. | d. | s. | d. |
| 1827: | | | | | 1827: | | | | |
| *July, August, September - | 36 | 6 | = 22 | 11 | Three Months, p' Contra - | 32 | 6 | = 26 | 9 |
| October, November, December | 37 | 61 | = 23 | 11 | Ditto - - ditto - | 32 | — | = 26 | 3 |
| 1828: | | | | | 1828: | | | | |
| January, February, March - | 38 | 87 | = 24 | 8 | Three Months, p' Contra - | 33 | — | = 27 | 2 |
| April, May, June - - - | 36 | 88 | = 23 | 5 | Ditto - - ditto - | 33 | — | = 27 | 2 |
| July, August, September - | 37 | 34 | = 23 | 8 | Ditto - - ditto - | 31 | — | = 25 | 3 |
| October, November, December | 36 | 88 | = 23 | 5 | Ditto - - ditto - | 32 | — | = 26 | 3 |
| 1829: | | | | | 1829: | | | | |
| January, February, March - | 36 | 87 | = 23 | 5 | Three Months, p' Contra - | 32 | — | = 26 | 3 |
| †April, May, June - - - | 36 | 90 | = 23 | 2 | Ditto - - ditto - | 30 | — | = 24 | 3 |
| July, August, September - | 37 | 40 | = 23 | 6 | *Ditto - - ditto - | 29 | — | = 24 | 10 |
| October, November, December | 37 | — | = 23 | 2 | Ditto - - ditto - | 30 | 6 | = 26 | 2 |
| 1830: | | | | | 1830: | | | | |
| January, February, March - | 36 | 20 | = 22 | 8 | Three Months, p' Contra - | 28 | — | = 23 | 10 |
| April, May, June - - - | 33 | 85 | = 21 | 3 | Ditto - - ditto - | 28 | 6 | = 24 | 4 |
| July, August, September - | 32 | 75 | = 20 | 6 | Ditto - - ditto - | 28 | — | = 23 | 10 |
| October, November, December | 31 | 15 | = 19 | 6 | Ditto - - ditto - | 27 | 6 | = 23 | 4 |
| 1831: | | | | | 1831: | | | | |
| January, February, March - | 28 | 30 | = 17 | 9 | Three Months, p' Contra - | 25 | — | = 20 | 11 |
| April, May, June - - - | 31 | 30 | = 19 | 5 | Ditto - - ditto - | 25 | 6 | = 21 | 5 |
| July, August, September - | 31 | — | = 19 | 5 | Ditto - - ditto - | 25 | — | = 20 | 11 |
| October, November, December | 31 | 25 | = 19 | 7 | Ditto - - ditto - | 24 | — | = 19 | 11 |
| 1832: | | | | | 1832: | | | | |
| January, February, March - | 31 | 35 | = 19 | 8 | Three Months, p' Contra - | 25 | — | = 20 | 11 |

* Exchᵉ taken at 25. 25. to April 1829.
† Ditto - ditto 25. 60. from April 1829 to March 1832.

* The Duty was reduced from 5 s. to 3 s. 6 d.

Mr.
*John Ballance.*

8 June,
1832.

This exhibits sometimes 15 per cent. difference between French organzine purchased by manufacturers at Lyons, and Piedmont organzine purchased by manufacturers in London, exclusive of duty. I put this in verification of my declaration, that France, by her exclusive possession of the raw material, secures to herself an advantage of from 7½ per cent. to 10 per cent. I now advert to the second point, the low rate of wages paid for the working up of the raw material; these wages are now about 70 per cent. less than the wages paid in England.

8411. How do you acquire your information as to wages in France?—We sent over, in 1826, an agent to inquire into the state of the manufacture at Lyons previous to the opening of the ports. He brought back particulars of the prices of weaving, winding, &c.; the wages on ordinary works, say gros de Naples, were at 5¼ d. per yard, we were then paying 10 d. per yard; in 1829, there was an extensive correspondence conducted with different parts of France on the part of the Silk Committee; the wages then were reduced; the prices were from 3¼ d. to 4½ d. per yard; the same article in London was 8 d. per yard.

8412. Is the agent to whom you refer now in London, or is his attendance to be had?—I cannot say; I beg expressly to state that he went over in December 1825 or January 1826; he returned about February; it is from the accounts which he brought with him I give the statement as above for 1826 The wages for dyeing, winding, warping and weaving, at Lyons, in December and January last, were about 70 per cent. less than in Spitalfields; of course I do not bring into comparison the highest wages paid at Lyons with the lowest possible wages paid in Spitalfields;

Mr.
*John Ballance.*

8 June,
1832.

Spitalfields; I mean those wretched wages that compel the poor to subsist by the poor laws.

8413. You take the average rate of wages in Spitalfields and the tariff at Lyons? —They were working under the tariff; I come now to the third branch, and that is the exportation of French manufactured silks; I was requested by an honourable Member of this Committee to put in on my examination a paper as to what had been submitted in conversation by Mr. Doxat; I saw Mr. Doxat this morning, and requested him to come and put in this paper himself; he said he would come with pleasure if it was desired, but it would be extremely inconvenient; he therefore requested me to put in this paper for him; I beg to add that I have examined these items with the official printed Returns from the French Custom House for 1829, showing the weight and the value of their exports of manufactured silks, and the paper, so far as it is an extract from that official account, is correct; it exhibits this, that the exports of France for the year 1829 amounted in round numbers to 2,100,000 English pounds weight of French manufactured silks; manufacturers will bear me out in the declaration, that the original weight of raw silk producing these manufactured goods must have been very nearly three millions; at any rate I will take it according to the statement as under, 2,800,000 lbs.; then there is very nearly three millions pounds weight avoirdupoise raw silk manufactured in France for exportation, and I beg to add, that 1829 will, I apprehend, not appear a very large year for exportation; but that the other years will represent an amount nearly the same.

[*The same was delivered in, and read as follows* :]

The exports of manufactured silks from France alone, of their own manufacture, in the year 1829, appear to have been

Kilogrammes 958,000, amounting in value to - francs 111,156,000
Equal to lbs. 2,109,000 English, and to  - - - - £. 4,402,000 sterling.
*i. e.* The estimate of the prime cost in France.

But which would correspond to about £. 6,000,000 sterling, if we consider what would be the market value here of the high and very high classes of goods distinctly enumerated in the said mentioned official Returns of the Exports of French manufactured Silks.

It should be observed here, that according to every calculation that can be made of the correspondence that exists between lbs. 2,109,000 of manufactured silk goods of those high and very high descriptions, they would require even more than lbs. 2,800,000 of raw and thrown silks, at which Mr. Ballance has seen an estimate made by Mr. Doxat, of that corresponding quantity; and it should be further added, that considering the high and very high classes of the said goods, those lbs. 2,800,000 must be for the very major part composed of fine silks.

My argument is this; the export of France is nearly double the amount of Italian raw silk worked up in this country, for the manufacture of similar articles; the importation from Italy is about 1,500,000 pounds of silks of a high standard, calculated to make fine fabrics; France exports of manufactured silks, a quantity that would require very nearly 3,000,000 of raw silk of a similar standard to produce those goods; hence she exports very nearly double what we manufacture; I submit that this incontestibly proves the ability of France, in the event of any occasional obstructions of her commerce with other countries, to overwhelm this country at a given moment with silk goods. France it is well known sends this quantity to Greece, to the North of Europe, to America; and for the last six years, Great Britain has been her customer for those silks; and having this export trade, the possession of those markets, and the controlling influence of them by quantities, it is equally evident that there is a scope for the exercise of talent and skill, and industry, and a confidence in the application of it that must bear down the feeble opposition of the English manufacturer; I say feeble, not because the English manufacturer has not talent and skill, and industry, and capital equal to his rival, but solely that on account of his local disadvantages, he has no confidence in the application of his capital; he has tried it over and over again for the last five years, he has been beaten out of his own market with serious loss, not of profit only but of capital.

8414. With regard to the benefit which France has in the command of the markets, is there any peculiar advantage she has in the expense of the construction of patterns?—That grows out of her command of foreign markets, which is my fourth

Mr.
*John Bailance.*

8 June,
1832.

fourth point; her possession of all those markets gives that scope to her manufacture of any article, that necessarily reduces the price of the individual sales; if an article of fashion ceases to be fashionable here, she has instantly the markets of North America and Greece to which she can resort; the very reverse is the position of the English manufacturer, for he is compelled to sell an obsolete article to the very persons who have already been glutted, not only with this article, but with the foreign one likewise.

8415. Is there not also this advantage; supposing that you made a pattern, a fashionable article, if you made a great many of that same pattern of that fashionable article for one market, of course you will very much reduce the price, the price being very much in relation to the quantity of any fashionable article; has not the French manufacturer this advantage, that when he contracts for an English house to make a certain number of ribbons of a particular pattern, he can also contract with a German house, and an American house for instance, and consequently the expense of the pattern is spread over a much wider amount of ribbon than that of the English manufacturer, who having only the English market, must put all the expense of his pattern on a certain quantity of ribbon for the English market alone?—There can be no doubt of that, that the restricted supply of English silks, as compared wish the large consumption of French silks, must proportionably augment the price of the incidental charges.

8416. How do you propose to counteract those numerous advantages which you state the French to enjoy?—I say at once, and I say it boldly, because I know I am saying that which is strictly true; not by any lowering of duties. The only effectual relief is the exclusion of foreign manufactured silks; I lay great stress upon the word effectual, because I do not mean to say that there may not be partial relief; but I do say that there will be no effectual relief. This partial relief to the trade would be afforded in two ways, by extending the export trade, and by a better system of protection against smuggling.

8417. What description of silk goods are exported from this country?—Chiefly handkerchiefs, and low priced gros de Naples.

8418. How is the export of those articles beneficial to the trade generally?—By giving employment to the throwing mills, and relieving the market from the pressure of low priced goods. Since Spitalfields has been deprived of her rich trade, those coarser goods have been made more generally than formerly; and though the seat of this manufacture of low priced goods is in Manchester, if she could export them, she would not send them to London for sale.

8419. Having to contend with the great advantages you describe as peculiar to France, how can the export trade be extended?—We have been able to export by means of a debenture of 3 s. 6 d., which was granted in 1829; and if this debenture were 5 s. instead of 3 s. 6 d., the export of those articles, I apprehend, would be greatly extended.

8420. When you speak of a better system of protection against smuggling, would you propose to lower the present duties?—No; this measure would only aggravate the evil it is meant to cure; the smuggler would again lower his price, as he did in 1829, when the experiment was made.

8421. Have you made any calculation as to the amount of reduction that would take place in the cost of manufactured silks, by lowering the protecting duties upon foreign thrown silks?—Assuming that the English manufacturer received the full benefit of this reduction of duty, even in that case the cost upon heavy goods would be reduced not more than about five per cent., and upon rich and light fabrics, about three per cent.

8422. Would this reduction, in your opinion, meet the difficulties of the manufacturers, and enable them to come down to the smugglers' price?—By no means; it is evident in respect of fancy and figured silks, the question would not be in the least touched by it; and in respect of plain silks, there would still remain a difference between him and the smuggler of from 8 to 10 per cent.

8423. At what price per cent. do you consider broad silk goods can be smuggled into the country?—I am told at from 10 to 15 per cent., according to circumstances; but my calculation is upon the higher amount.

8424. When you say you are told, is that authority on which you can entirely depend?—I have no doubt of my authority, and this is further confirmed by my own inspection of the goods; I am satisfied at the price at which they are stated to me to be purchased, the per centage for smuggling cannot have been higher than 15.

8425. Do

8425. Do you advert to seizures?—No; I believe the system is of this kind, that they will offer to smuggle goods in at 20 per cent.; but the question is, on what value is the 20 per cent. taken? in most instances it is upon a reduced value, not the real value of the goods of course; by so much as the estimated value is reduced, by so much is the real price of the smuggler reduced in comparison with the duty that the importer would otherwise pay; therefore the rate per cent. may be 20, while the realization of that, in reference to the duty paid, may be 15 per cent.

Mr.
*John Ballance.*

8 June,
1832.

8426. You have stated that no benefit would accrue to the manufacturer from lowering the protecting duties; what do you suppose would be the effect, generally, on the trade, of such a measure?—I consider such a measure to be full of mischief; it would accomplish the ruin of the throwster as it regards Italian thrown silk; then a further reduction of the wages in the weaving branch, and a consequent accumulation of misery and wretchedness that one sickens to think of; I have said that the experiment was made in 1829, and the result has proved its mischievous tendency.

8427. Supposing the effect to be produced on the English throwsters which you apprehend, that they would be materially reduced in number and in power, what would be the effect on the manufacturers generally, of their being obliged to procure their supply of thrown silk from Italy?—I consider this to be most disadvantageous to them. The English manufacturer, it will be recollected, has now the choice of two markets, the English and Foreign; he then would be dependent on Italy; he can now select his raw silk and have it thrown just in the way that he requires it; he must then use what the Italians please to send him, and at their price too; this tells greatly against small manufacturers; and I do beg to draw the attention of the honourable Committee to this point. Bales of silk weigh about 240 lbs. whether they be raw or thrown. A manufacturer, as the case now stands, can purchase his bale of raw and have it thrown in two, three or four threads, as suits his purpose, having only fifty to sixty weight of each; but if he has no longer this advantage he must purchase 1,000 weight to get the same proportions. If it be answered he can get some merchant or middle man to divide those bales, my answer is, that he will have to pay for the accommodation; it tells greatly against small manufacturers, and throws every advantage into the hands of large ones.

8428. Do you consider it necessary for the manufacturer to have foreign thrown silk?—I say generally it is not necessary; I use but little myself, and not an ounce for rich goods.

8429. Would the English cost more or less than the foreign?—It costs me rather more than the foreign, as there is now only 3 s. 6 d. import duty.

8430. Are you a throwster?—I am not.

8431. The answers you give are as a manufacturer and not as a throwster?—Yes, speaking as a manufacturer only.

8432. As you consider that the lowering the duties on foreign thrown silk would be injurious, can you suggest any plan for the prevention of smuggling?—The only safe and effectual method to prevent smuggling under a system of protecting duties, is not to lower the duties, but to increase the risk of the smuggler.

8433. By what means would you propose to increase the risk of smugglers?—By good Custom House regulations properly enforced; and in that event I am satisfied that even more than the present amount of duty could be collected.

8434. What advantages would result to the silk trade by thus increasing the risk of the smuggler?—I submit, very great advantages; the throwing branch would be preserved, and that is no small advantage; wages protected; the poor better employed, and a measure of confidence restored to the manufacturer.

8435. Do you apply those advantages to the whole of the silk manufacture or to the plain branch principally?—I apply those advantages exclusively to plain silks.

8436. How are the figured and fancy branches to be preserved?—I believe, and I am bound to give an honest opinion, that this branch of the silk trade must be inevitably lost to this country unless foreign fancy and figured silks are prohibited.

8437. How do you come to that conclusion?—I come to it from the possession which the foreign manufacturer has of the English market in respect of fancy silks, and from the present consequent condition of this branch of the silk trade.

8438. What is the present condition of this branch of the silk trade?—From an

678.                                                                                          inquiry

Mr.
*John Ballance.*

8 June,
1832.

inquiry made in February last, it was found, that the number of fancy and figured looms was reduced to about 300.

8439. What was the condition of this branch of the trade prior to 1826?—The fancy and figured branch of the silk trade of course varies in extent according to the fashion; I therefore give only an average. If I take ten years prior to 1826, I apprehend the average will show at least one-fourth of the trade of Spitalfields to be upon the fancy and figured branch of it; therefore, upon 16,000 looms in Spitalfields, that will give an average of 4,000 looms: this is the estimate which manufacturers, exclusively in the fancy branch, have given to me; I am not a fancy weaver.

8440. Are the Committee to understand that, from the best information you have been able to acquire, there were 16,000 looms?—My opinion is, that there were about the same number of looms in 1826 as there are now.

8441. Do you believe that in any one year to which you have referred, in which it was probable there were 4,000 looms employed in fancy goods in Spitalfields, there were 400 employed in making poplins?—No, I think not.

8442. Do you consider Italian nets as fancy goods?—I do not.

8443. Will you state in what respect this branch of trade is of importance?— This branch of trade is important in respect of wages; if the proportion be one-fourth of the whole trade the wages would be as 40 to 100; then there is the talent and skill that would be called into exercise, which upon the present system will soon be lost to this country; and further, I think it will be found that the other branches of the silk trade will be active and prosperous, just in proportion as the fancy and figured branches of the trade are encouraged.

8444. Has the number of master manufacturers decreased since 1826?—Very considerably.

8445. Are you able to state particulars at the respective periods of 1826 and the present time?—In 1826 there were 167 manufacturers in Spitalfields, of these about 39 were in the fancy trade; there are now about 79 manufacturers, of these 66 are in the plain branch, and only 13 in the figured branch; those that are in the figured branch have not one-third of their former number of looms.

8446. There appears to be a reduction in the number of 88 manufacturers between the two periods?—Yes.

8447. Have they been obliged to discontinue business in consequence of failing in trade?—Sixty-seven of these have failed since 1826; 17 have retired from business; most of these 17 were men of capital. I mean to say that in the spring of 1826 there were 167 manufacturers in Spitalfields, and that in the spring of 1832 there are but 79 manufacturers, and that of the difference 67 have failed chiefly within the last three years; and that 17, who were men of capital, have retired.

8448. What is the condition of the people they then employed?—They are either reduced to a miserably low rate of wages or thrown upon the parish, and receive an allowance of 1 s. 6 d. a head.

8449. What do you conceive would be the condition of the other branches of the trade if the figured silk trade continued in the hands of foreigners?—I consider that the silk trade would not be worth following; its character and value would be lost; capitalists would withdraw from it, and the work people would become paupers.

8450. It is your opinion then that these branches of the silk trade have a common interest?—It is my firm conviction, grounded upon an observation of many years, that the supplanting of the one will issue in the ruin of the other. I call that trade ruined where profit and capital are sacrificed, and the labourer is reduced to a rate of wages which makes him dependent on parish allowances.

8451. Do you know any advantage derived by this country, generally, from the importation of foreign silk goods?—I do not.

8452. You stated that the number of casual poor in the parish of Bethnal Green, had increased from 157 in 1821 to 6,218 in 1832?—I believe that is the case.

8453. Are you aware of any increase of crime in consequence of this increase of pauperism in that district?—Yes, the increase of crime has been great.

8454. Are you prepared with any facts in corroboration of that statement?— I am not prepared with particular facts; but I have given in a statement, from which it appears that immorality has been increasing.

8455. Had

Mr.
*John Ballance.*

8 June,
1832.

8455. Had you any communication with Government in the year 1824, respecting the change of law relative to the silk trade?—Yes, I was one of a deputation that waited upon Lord Liverpool.

8456. What reasons were assigned at the time for the proposed change? They were principally two; the one to put a stop to smuggling, and the other was to give us the benefit of an export trade; it was said by the President of the Board of Trade that British silks, like British cottons, should find a market throughout the whole world.

8457. The benefits expected were, that smuggling would be diminished, and that you would obtain an export trade; did the trade concur in thinking that this advantage would be derived?—No; they could not understand how the taking off the mark of contraband, from foreign wrought silks, for a protecting duty, could possibly put a stop to smuggling; nor how the English manufacturer could have an export trade when he required 30 per cent. protection in his own market; nor how he could be benefited by having two markets open to the dealer, while there was only one to himself, his own, and that market glutted with foreign manufactures.

8458. Did you represent those objections to the system to the Government at that time?—Yes, strongly.

8459. Were there any conditions or propositions then made?—The throwster was promised 7 s. 6 d. protection; and it was afterwards reduced, I believe, at three days' notice, by a Treasury order, to 5 s.; the manufacturer was promised 30 per cent. upon foreign manufactured silks, and it was repeatedly said this duty can and shall be collected.

8460. The proposals made were, to the throwster 7 s. 6 d. protection, and to the manufacturer 30 per cent.?—Yes.

8461. Have you a protection of 30 per cent. as a manufacturer?—No; both those proposals were broken in 1829; the import duty on foreign thrown silks was again reduced from 5 s. to 3 s. 6 d. on organzine, and from 3 s. to 2 s. on trams, and the duty on foreign manufactured silks was lowered to 25 per cent.; it was found that smuggling, so far from being put a stop to, as was stated, had greatly increased. The distress of the silk trade at the time was attributed by Government to smuggling, which by letters from Calais, as I have said, was stated to be from 25 to 28 per cent. In order to remove the distress of the silk trade they reduced the duty to the smuggler's price.

8462. Did the silk trade make any remonstrance on those changes?—Yes, they remonstrated in 1824, and in 1826 and in 1829, but I am sorry to say without effect; they assured the Government at all those periods that no policy towards the silk trade could be permanent but that which would enable the throwster and the manufacturer respectively to give employment to their work-people; and that to attempt to settle this question upon any other basis is perpetually keeping it unsettled.

8463. Has it been kept unsettled?—Yes; the distress of the silk trade, it is very evident, has again opened the question; the appointment of this Committee is a proof of its having been forced upon the attention of the Legislature; but what has been the effect in the mean time? In the mean time the fancy branch is ruined, the plain branch is not worth following, and thousands of our poor have been starving.

8464. If you were to propose Custom House regulations which you thought would be effectual, what would be the kind of regulations you would suggest?—I should refer to two classes of regulation; I would say those that would affect the smuggler himself, and those which would apply to the receiver of smuggled goods; I submit criminal punishment for the former, and stamping of silk goods to throw difficulties in the way of the receiver.

8465. Do you think that those two regulations, a criminal punishment for the one, and stamping the goods as far as they could for the other, would be effectual?—I have no doubt that a duty of more than 30 per cent. could be collected upon their joint application; but I lay great stress on the stamping.

8466. Why so?—I believe this more than any other measure would close the market against the smuggler; and having to force his goods upon the buyer, who is weighing the increased risk against the advantage, he will not give the price for them he formerly did; I beg to deliver in to the Committee a paper containing my reasons for the stamping of foreign manufactured silks.

[*The same was delivered in, and read, as follows :*]

678.

REASONS

Mr.
*John Ballance.*

8 June,
1832.

REASONS submitted to the Select Committee on the SILK TRADE for the STAMPING of FOREIGN MANUFACTURED SILKS.

1.—UNDER a system of protecting duties, smuggling can be prevented only by regulations, which, while they increase the risk to the smuggler himself, shall enable the Custom House officers more easily to detect the *receiver* of smuggled goods.

2.—The fixing a stamp upon foreign manufactured silks, when they pass the customs, appears to be the only plan for securing the latter object.

3.—Whatever other provision may be made for the prevention of smuggling, without stamping the goods, the difficulty of distinguishing smuggled goods from others which have paid the duty will still remain, and present an insuperable obstacle to their being seized; and thus a safe and profitable market will be kept open to the smuggler, of which he will avail himself whenever he succeeds in safely landing his goods.

4.—While this market remains open for the purchase of smuggled goods, the effect of subjecting the smuggler to loss and punishment will not be to put down smuggling, but only to throw it into another channel. The principals will disappear, but the agency will remain.

5.—The acknowledged principle of equal justice requires, that if the *smuggler* be amenable to the law, effectual measures should also be adopted to detect, in order to punish, the *receiver* of smuggled goods.

6.—The inducement to purchase smuggled goods manifestly arises from the price at which they are obtained, relatively with those which have paid the duty; and as they are generally offered in large quantities, capitalists, who choose to avail themselves of this mode of purchase, do it to the serious injury of other dealers, whose means are not so abundant, or whose principles restrict them to the legal market.

7.—It may be expected that the advantages which have been derived by many persons from the wholesale trade which has been carried on in smuggling, will excite some opposition to the plan of stamping foreign silks.

8.—To an objection that the stamp will be counterfeited, and the measure thus rendered abortive, it is submitted, that whatever may be the case in a few instances, the general effect of such a regulation will be to deter both wholesale and retail dealers from holding smuggled goods, and thus to cut up the present *large* traffic in them. It is the general effect of a given measure that determines its utility. Besides,

9.—If the stamps be accompanied by a number, both fixed and moveable, and also a pattern book, it will be very difficult to succeed in counterfeiting the stamp, as so many other particulars must likewise correspond.

10.—The pressing solicitations of the silk trade for the stamping of foreign wrought silks, as a means of preventing smuggling, is most reasonable in itself; it interferes with no question of commercial policy; and any extra trouble that it may occasion to the customs, or to individuals, ought not for a moment to weigh against the miseries and wretchedness of a large suffering population in our silk manufacturing districts.

---

8467. Are those your reasons for that opinion?—Those are the reasons I submit.

8468. Supposing the system of stamping were allowed, do you not apprehend there would be considerable danger of the stamps being forged?—I think it is not likely; I should suggest collateral checks, which I will refer to presently; though those would not so effectually prevent smuggling as the law of prohibition, yet I feel satisfied that they would put a stop to the present wholesale trade in smuggling.

8469. Do you know what are the sentiments of the dealers in foreign silks upon this subject?—Yes, I do; and I beg leave to hand in a paper declaratory of their sentiments. A paper, of which this is a copy, was presented to the Board of Trade at the beginning of this year, at that time rather hastily got up, otherwise we could have obtained double the number of names.

*[The same was delivered in, and read, as follows:]*

THE undersigned dealers in silk goods of British and Foreign manufacture, understanding that a proposal has been made to Government to mark or stamp all Foreign silk goods upon the importation of them, and that some persons have objected to such a course as being inconvenient and vexatious, beg leave to state, that the contraband trade in Foreign silks is highly unjust and injurious to all those who deal fairly in them, and they are decidedly of opinion that the contraband dealing in Foreign silk goods will never be effectually stopped

unless

unless those regularly imported shall be stamped, and that the obligation to have them stamped will not be inconvenient or vexatious to those who deal in them.

Mr.
*John Ballance.*

8 June,
1832.

| | | |
|---|---|---|
| Moore, James, Tate & Co. | - - - | Cheapside. |
| Morrison & Co. | - - - - | Fore-street, Cripplegate. |
| Coster & Co. - | - - - - | Fountain-court, Milk-street. |
| Wynn Ellis | - - - - - | Ludgate-hill. |
| Leaf, Copling & Co. - | - - - | 8, Watling-street. |
| Bradbury & Greatorex | - - - | 6, Aldermanbury. |
| Mangham & Clark | - - - - | 37, Gutter-lane. |
| Lycett, Lawson & Davies | - - - | Gutter-lane, Cheapside. |
| Swan, Pearce & Co. - | - - - | 29, Saint Paul's Churchyard. |
| William Taylor | - - - - | Ludgate-street. |
| Edward Eyles & Co. | - - - | 5, Ludgate-street. |
| W. & D. Price | - - - - | 40, Margaret-street. |
| C. & G. Roberts | - - - - | 17, Saint Paul's Churchyard. |
| George & Bradley | - - - | 19, Holywell-street, Strand. |
| Griffiths & Crick | - - - - | Quadrant, Regent-street. |
| Howell, James & Co. | - - - | 9, Regent-street, Pall-mall. |
| Philip Cooper & Sons | - - - | 2, Waterloo-place. |
| Harding, Smith & Price | - - - | 82, Pall-mall. |
| Castle, Luck & Hyatt | - - - | 7, Love-lane, Wood-street. |
| Hitchcock & Rogers | - - - | 19, Ludgate-street. |
| Bailey, Milner & Co. | - - - | 77, Saint Paul's Churchyard. |
| George Hilditch | - - - - | 13, Ludgate-hill. |
| Welch, Gregory & Cubitt | - - - | 26, Skinner-street. |
| Townsend, Hardwick & Co. | - - - | 324, High Holborn. |
| John Stirling | - - - - | Conduit-street. |
| William Tinkler & Co. | - - - | 22, Old Bond-street. |
| Whitelock & Hickling | - - - | 166, Strand. |
| Nalders, Spall & Co. | - - - | 40, Cheapside. |
| Cooke, White & Bennett | - - - | Crown-court, Cheapside. |
| Bell, Bentley & Co. | - - - | 136, Cheapside. |

8470. As all parties and all opinions concur in the feeling that the stamping would be no vexation or inconvenience to them, what plan would you recommend?—The plans contained in the paper which I beg now to refer to the Committee.

[*The same was delivered in, and read.*]

### PLAN OF STAMPING.

THE stamps to be hand stamps, and the impression to be made by ink or paint on the fabric itself.

Each piece to be stamped with two separate stamps, one to denote the royal authority, and also to contain certain variable figures and letters, and the other to be simply a number.

The former of the two stamps to be thus:

The figures 21, signify the day of the month; the figure 1, the month itself; the figures 32, the year; the letter A the importer; and the figures 49, a variable arbitrary number, to be changed once a day, or oftener, as may be thought right. The stamp to be constructed as to allow of the change of letters and figures very easily.

The second stamp to impress a number, thus:

| 350 | 351 | 352 |
|---|---|---|

and so on up to 1,000, and then to begin again at 1; so that every piece imported shall have a separate number.

A pattern-book to be kept, into which a pattern cut from every piece imported shall be stuck, and in the margin of which book, opposite to each pattern, shall be impressed the two stamps, which have been impressed on the corresponding piece of goods.

No person to import foreign silk goods without a license, and every licensed importer to be known to the Customs by a certain letter, as A, B, &c., and that letter to be put in one of the quarters of the first stamp.

The stamps to be kept under proper locks, in the care of at least two superior officers, and the variable number in the centre to be changed at the pleasure of

8471. Those regulations would apply to plain goods?—They would.

8472. Would you confine them to plain goods?—Yes; there are contingencies affecting the fancy branch of the silk trade, which in my judgment cannot be met by an import duty; that branch cannot be preserved without a positive law of prohibition.

8473. If you recommend a positive prohibition of fancy and figured silks, do you not apprehend that the trade of the country would be great losers in point of style and fashion?—I apprehend not; the Parisian fashions could and would still be obtained as formerly; but they would be in silks of English manufactures; at the same time the encouragement thus given to British artists would in all probability soon enable them to rival French fabrics, and thus the British public would be gainers rather than losers; they would get French patterns, and at the same time give confidence to the British manufacturer to rival those patterns; at present he cannot do it; he goes to it with a halter round his neck.

8474. If they would not be injured in point of fashion, how would they be affected in point of price?—Doubtless wages would rise, as indeed they ought to rise, and must rise, or the misery must go on increasing; but I apprehend that the price to the consumer would not be much advanced, as the profits of the manufacturer and the dealer would then be more equalized.

8475. You have said that the amount of wages paid in the district of Spitalfields is 300,000 *l.* per annum less now than it was in the year 1826?—Yes, at least 300,000 *l.* a year less.

8476. If the poor workmen receive 300,000 *l.* less, do not the public derive the benefit of that 300,000 *l.*?—I should say that they get their silks somewhat cheaper in consequence, but not all the difference by any means.

8477. Can you give the Committee any notion of the proportion the public gets out of that 300,000 *l.*?—It is difficult to state the exact proportions.

8478. Who gets it; the manufacturer?—Not the manufacturer, for his profits are all gone, but the middle man between the manufacturer and the consumer, and if he be a man of large capital, he has profited abundantly by this change of system. I do not speak here of individuals, and I do beg to be distinctly understood, I am not alluding to individuals, but I do speak of the system, and of this system I say it has worked most oppressively towards the weaver, reducing him to want and wretchedness; it has worked very injuriously for the manufacturer, depriving him of profit and capital, but it has worked most profitably for the dealer, and the tendency of this system is to ruin the small capitalist, and to throw every advantage in the way of the large capitalist.

8479. You are understood to say, that if Custom House regulations were introduced, we might then collect a duty of 30 per cent. on plain goods?—I am satisfied of that.

8480. Taking that for granted, would you propose to return to the Schedule of Duties of 1826?—The reduction of duties which took place in 1829, I consider as unnecessary as it has been mischievous; and a duty of 5 *s.* on organzine and a duty of 3 *s.* on tram, with a corresponding increase of protecting duty on foreign manufactured silks, I conceive to be the only measure short of prohibition that would give confidence and health to the British manufacture.

8481. What do you mean by a corresponding increase?—My opinion is according to the different articles, from 2 *s.* to 3 *s.* for instance, the present duty on plain silk is 11 *s.*; I would say 13 *s.*

8482. Will you furnish a Table of the Duties which you consider would be sufficient as a protection to the trade?—I can furnish that for plain goods, but I do not consider that any thing less than prohibition would answer, as to figured and fancy goods; I think that by stamping foreign goods Government would be able to ensure the collection of the full amount of duty I have referred to, even 13 *s.* or 14 *s.* or 15 *s.* per pound. I have no doubt 40 per cent. might be collected were the goods stamped.

8483. Is it your opinion, that under such regulations it is still possible for the silk trade to prosper in this country, and that thus we should have a final adjustment of this question?—I have said that the most effectual remedy for the evils of the silk trade is to be found in the law of prohibition, and I am fully of opinion that had the consequences of the repeal of that law been foreseen by the Administration in 1824, that law would never have been touched; but looking at the silk trade as it now is, I am of opinion that if the fancy and figured branches of this

trade

Mr.
*John Ballance.*

8 June,
1832.

trade were protected by prohibition, as an exception to the general rule of commercial policy, and the other interests of the trade were protected by sufficient duties, it would instantly revive, and might become, to a certain extent, a flourishing manufacture. In a few months I apprehend the workpeople would get employment upon a rate of wages by which they could subsist, the manufacturer would have a portion of his profits restored to him, and gain confidence in what he does, and the throwster, who I beg to say has suffered most severely, would receive in the shape of increased employment, some little remuneration for the great loss of capital that he has been compelled to make ; but if these measures, or something like them, be not adopted, I feel satisfied that the silk trade will go floundering on till it shall exhibit a mere wreck of its former greatness and importance.

8484. You have stated a degree of distress that is quite astonishing ; the number of casual poor increased from 150 to upwards of 6,000 in the space of ten or eleven years ; you mean to say that the distress, which is likely to ensue if the present system be continued, is likely to aggravate the distress at present existing ?— My opinion is, that the late distress in the silk trade for the last nine months, producing as it must a scarcity of certain articles, will occasion a temporary activity. The looms may get employment for a time, but the consumption of this country cannot permanently take off both the importations from abroad and our own productions of silk goods ; and it is only for the silk trade to become a little active for four or five months, and the glut which will ensue will reduce it to its previous situation. Every excessive relapse aggravates the distress, because the poor become if possible poorer, have less furniture and less means of rallying ; the poor in Spitalfields, at this moment, are far more destitute than they were in 1826 ; then they had some little means to fall back upon, but now they have none.

8485. Do you apprehend, that if those regulations were adopted as to the plain silks, and prohibition as to figured silks, in that case Spitalfields and the silk district around would be restored to its former prosperity, and that quantity of wages which you say was once paid and which you state is now withdrawn, would be resumed ?—My opinion is, that such has been the shock and such the continuance of the distress, that it would take perhaps a year or two fully to restore Spitalfields to what it was : but I think eventually, at least two-thirds of that amount would be restored to Spitalfields.

8486. You do not consider Manchester as at all likely to come into competition with Spitalfields ?—Manchester now comes into competition with Spitalfields and Spitalfields with Manchester, because Spitalfields being deprived of her rich trade is thrown more upon the trade of Manchester than she was formerly, hence the collision.

8487. Supposing that the prohibition of the French figured and fancy goods should have taken place as you propose, do you not think that Manchester would have the same chance of coming into competition with Spitalfields in rich goods, it being open not only to Spitalfields but to the whole country to make them ?— It is very evident to me that Spitalfields, from its proximity to the West end of the Town, would always command, as it did before, the lead of the fashion, which would occasion a large quantity of the labour in Spitalfields to be taken up in the production of rich fabrics ; to make which, the operatives of Spitalfields are far better qualified than the cotton weavers of Manchester ; in proportion as labour is taken up in Spitalfields for the richer branches of the trade, would it diminish in the coarser branches, and therefore Manchester would then have restored to her a larger portion of that common trade in which she now comes into collision with Spitalfields ; thus three branches of trade would gradually revert to their former channels, Spitalfields would have the rich and fancy trade, and Manchester would have its own staple trade.

8488. You do not consider that the lowness of wages of the operatives, or the views of the manufacturers at Manchester, would bring them into competition with Spitalfields in rich goods ?—I think not ; because Spitalfields would have possession of the market.

8489. You mean to say, that the persons who may be said to regulate the fashion, would give their orders to the manufacturer in Spitalfields ?—Just so.

8490. That they would not send their orders and their designs to Manchester, their object being to keep the goods to Spitalfields, and not to send them to Manchester ?—My answer is, that there can be no doubt that they would send them to Spitalfields, from its proximity to the seat of fashion, and because the artisans of Spitalfields are accustomed to the manufacture of rich goods.

678.                                                                    8491. The

8491. The best weavers in figured goods are in Spitalfields?—The very best.

8492. Is the trade in Manchester in common goods advantageous to Manchester?—That I cannot answer.

8493. The rich fancy goods now making in England are now making in Spitalfields, are they not?—Yes; all the richest goods now made; the few which are made for West end houses are made in Spitalfields.

8494. The peculiar manufacture of Spitalfields has not been depressed by Manchester, but by France?—Certainly by France, not by Manchester.

8495. You say there has been a great decrease in the wages of the workmen; has there been a proportionate decrease in the price of goods to the public?—Not to the full amount, I apprehend.

8496. Has there been a proportionate diminution in the sale price of the manufacturer?—I should say a greater diminution; the profit of the manufacturer is nearly all gone.

---

## *Lunæ,* 11° *die Junii,* 1832.

### EDWARD AYSHFORD SANFORD, ESQUIRE, IN THE CHAIR.

### Mr. *John Ballance,* called in; and further Examined.

8497. YOU stated the other day that the exports of manufactured silk that came from France in one year amounted to 2,100,000 pounds weight, and you assumed that they must have consumed about 2,800,000 pounds weight of raw silk?—I said, that in order to export 2,100,000 pounds weight of manufactured silk, I considered it would require 2,800,000 pounds of raw silk to produce that quantity.

8498. You supposed the raw silk had been reduced in the hands of the dealer 25 per cent.?—My reason for that calculation came from my own experience of the process of manufacture in this country on silks of a high standard; we know that France works upon silk of a high standard; the silks made in Spitalfields were of a similar high standard; my own manufacture is in part of that standard; my calculation, therefore, is founded upon the process of throwing and manufacturing silks of that standard.

8499. In the manufacture of goods made from hard silk the reduction of weight in dyeing is inconsiderable, is it not?—In hard silk the reduction of weight is not an ounce.

8500. If the exports of France consist in great part of the articles made from hard silk, that will alter your calculation, will it not?—But I object to the assumption; it is very evident, that whatever manufactured silks are exported from France, from which the gum is not extracted, the reduction of waste will apply chiefly to the waste in the process of throwing, and to the waste in the subsequent process of manufacturing.

8501. Would the decrease be equal, supposing the exports were of hard silk?—There will be a reduction, but not to that extent.

8502. Does the book to which you referred the other day as containing an account of the weight of French manufactured silks exported, distinguish the different articles exported?—There are a variety of articles specified, but under a general character.

8503. Can you state what proportion of that was exported to England?—It is the total exports of France, without giving particulars to any country.

8504. That book does not contain an account of the quantity exported to England?—I did not observe that quantity particularly specified, it is included in the total amount.

8505. You stated that the agent who was sent to the Continent by the Trade Committee in 1825-6, had reported that wages in France were 70 per cent. lower than in England?—No, I stated what the agent said the rate of wages at Lyons actually was. We had two channels of communication at that time with Lyons, the one by the agent we sent over, and the other by means of correspondents altogether apart from the agent; when he arrived, we compared his report from Lyons with that correspondence, and the answer from the correspondents and his report agreed.

8506. Do

Mr.
*John Ballance.*

11 June,
1832.

8506. Do you mean that of 100 *l.* worth of goods manufactured, 70 *l.* consisted of labour?—No; the wages at that time for weaving gros de Naples three double at Lyons was 6¼ *d.* an ell, from which was to be deducted the expense arising to the weaver from winding his shute.

8507. Had you at the same time the prices paid at Zurich?—Yes, we had.

8508. Can you state the prices of weaving gros de Naples there?—I speak now from recollection, but I believe it was 4 *d.*

8509. Was that the three double?—I think it was; it was either 4 *d.* or 3½ *d.*; I could get the whole of these accounts, they were all minuted; I believe, taking the average of wages at Lyons, in the years 1826, 1829 and 1831, with the wages paid in England at those respective periods, the wages at Lyons appear from 70 to 80 per cent. less than in England.

8510. Can you furnish the Committee with a list of the English and Foreign prices at those periods?—I have them by me, but not here; I shall be happy to furnish them on another occasion.

8511. Does that include the broad and narrow goods, or only broad?—Only broad.

8512. Goods similar to those manufactured in Spitalfields?—Yes, from high standards of silk.

8513. Have the goodness to state when the book of prices was abolished in Spitalfields?—I think in 1824; there was an attempt made in 1823; I think it succeeded in 1824.

8514. Did wages fall immediately after that?—Wages rather rose than fell.

8515. How long did that advance in wages continue?—Upon the repeal of the Spitalfields Act, in June 1824, wages for a twelvemonth, I think, were rather higher than lower, and that arose from the demand for English manufactured silks, arising, unquestionably, from the remission of the duty, coupled with the continuance of the prohibition.

8516. Did wages fall considerably in 1825?—No.

8517. Did they fall in 1826?—Wages did not fall till, I think, the spring of 1826, and I will state the reason; we ascertained that upon the run of plain silks, one pound weight of manufactured silk would cost, in England, about 70 *s.*; the goods that we imported from Lyons in 1826, to ascertain the value of French silks, exhibited upon the average 50 *s.* per pound weight; that value, according to the proposal of 30 per cent. by the Government, would give us a protecting duty of 15 *s.*, raising the value of foreign manufactured silks in this market to 65 *s.* We placed before Mr. Huskisson those two facts, 65 *s.* on the one side, and 70 *s.* on the other, and we asked him how we were to get rid of the 5 *s.* still against us; his answer was, "The difference of 20 *s.* consists of many elements, and by abridging one and another you get rid of the 5 *s.*:" one of those elements was wages, and, in consequence, when French goods came into contact with English goods, we were compelled to get rid of the 5 *s.*, but it was done by reducing the wages.

8518. You stated on a former day that the trade was bad before French goods were admitted, from the apprehension of a large quantity coming in?—In 1826.

8519. Did that affect wages?—No; to the best of my recollection the looms that were employed received the same rate of wages as they had done two or three months previously. I wish to be understood, when I say that wages fell, that I cannot speak to the particular month.

8520. Can you state what the prices of weaving the gros de Naples were from 1824 to the opening of the ports?—The three double gros de Naples were from 10 *d* to 11 *d.* a yard.

8521. It fell in the spring of 1826 to how much?—I should think from 1 *d.* to 1½ *d.*; some would pay less, some more, according to circumstances.

8522. Did it rise at any time subsequent to that?—I think the price rallied a little in 1827, but not for any length of time.

8523. In 1828, which you have stated to be the period of better trade, wages again fell?—The silk trade began to languish in the spring of 1828, and it continued decreasing gradually in activity during the autumn of that year, and through the greater part of 1829. The wages during this time of gradual decay, settled down in the spring of 1829 to about 7½ *d.* and to 8 *d.* per yard; I mean that what was paid from 10 *d.* to 11 *d.* before, was paid about 8 *d.* per yard in 1829.

8524. Did it rise again during the period of good trade in 1829-30?—There was no good trade in 1829.

8525. Did it improve in 1830?—No, it did not; the duties were reduced the

678.                                                                5th July

5th July 1829, from 15 *s.* to 11 *s.*; this reduction was known to take place the April previous, and the manufacturers to prepare for this reduction in July, instantly reduced their labour from 8 *d.* to 6½ *d.*; the reduction was made to meet the importation in July.

8526. You mean that after the fall in 1828 wages never recovered?—After the fall in 1828, I am not aware that there was any re-action as to the average rate of wages upon the articles to which I have referred, plain silks.

8527. Were not gros de Naples manufactured after 1824, at Manchester, Sudbury, Coggeshall, Macclesfield, and some other places in the country?—They were manufactured in quantities before that time, not I believe more after than before.

8528. Do you know what prices were paid at each of those places for manufacturing the articles you have referred to?—To the best of my recollection the wages were higher at some periods in the North of England, Manchester and Macclesfield, for weaving plain silks, than they were in Spitalfields; I speak of periods from 1817 to 1825.

8529. Can you state what prices were paid at those places in the country subsequent to 1825?—I have no doubt I can obtain the information, but I am satisfied that on some occasions for some months they were actually higher.

8530. Did not the manufacture of plain goods extend very much in the country after the removal of the duties in 1824?—I am not aware that they extended greatly in the country; the duties were taken off the Bengal and China silk, and a species of what is called gros de Naples has since been generally made, in which there is a large proportion of India silks of a low standard, but that was not the trade of Spitalfields.

8531. Has a fall of wages in Spitalfields preceded or followed a fall of wages at Manchester?—That is a question I am not able to answer.

8532. Do the Spitalfields manufacturers regulate their wages by the reports they receive of the prices of wages in Manchester, Macclesfield, Coggeshall, and other places where the same description of goods are manufactured?—I apprehend that Spitalfields weavers regulate their wages essentially by the demand for their goods, combined with the prices which they get for them; and if that demand be not active, or if the price be ruinous, they try to get them made at as low a rate of wages as possible, irrespective of other places.

8533. How do you reconcile that answer with what you have already stated, that the activity which took place in 1830 had no influence in raising wages?—The activity of the trade was not to such an extent as to secure an advance of wages; it was active, as compared with 1829, but not active as compared with the years previous to the opening of the ports. I have said there was activity in the spring of 1830, but that was mainly with regard to black goods; there was an expectation of the death of his late Majesty, and it turned out upon inquiry that there were scarcely any black goods making in Spitalfields, because the sacrifices had been so tremendous on the sales which had taken place about three or four months before.

8534. Can you inform the Committee what prices are paid at Manchester, Sudbury, and other places in the country, for three double gros de Naples?—I do not know what prices are now paid. In London, the price given is 5 *d.* for three singles, 6½ *d.* for three doubles, and 8 *d.* for four doubles; I apprehend that there is very little variation; that there is not a variation of more than a halfpenny between that and the country.

8535. Do you mean of the same quality?—Of the same number of threads; but I apprehend that the quality turned out in the country is not of equal perfection.

8536. Can you state what is now paid for weaving the rich figured goods in Spitalfields?—I cannot state any thing as to figured goods.

8537. What is the state of the trade at this moment in Spitalfields?—I understand that the trade has improved as compared with its distressed situation last winter; this was to be expected from the extremity of the state of suffering, and the consequent scarcity of goods from the number of looms standing.

8538. You mean that this is another of those changes that occurred in 1827 and in 1830?—There have been two re-actions, the one after 1826, and the other after 1829, every re-action found the working classes still worse, and each relapse has been more severely felt than the former.

8539. There

Mr.
*John Ballance.*

11 June,
1832.

8539. There is a tolerable demand for goods in Spitalfields now, is there not?—I should say a fair demand for plain silks.

8540. Are wages higher now than they were in December 1831?—I made that inquiry last week, when I was told that the trade was improving; it has improved somewhat as to demand, but there is not a fractional improvement as regards wages.

8541. Has not the same alteration of good and bad trade, which you describe as having taken place in the silk trade, occurred in other branches of manufacture in this country?—I know nothing of other branches.

8542. Have you not understood, that in the cotton and woollen trades they have had those alternatives?—So far as report has come to my ears, I have heard of no instances of distress, at all equal to those which have afflicted the silk trade during the last five years.

8543. Do you know whether they are using the Jacquard loom in manufacturing silk goods in different places now?—I am told the Jacquard loom is used pretty generally at Manchester for the manufacture of palmarines, such as I exhibited here last Friday, a mixture of silk and cotton; the silk exhibits a figure which is made by the Jacquard loom.

8544. Are they in use at Derby as well as in Manchester?—I believe there have been two or three at Derby; but I cannot speak positively.

8545. Are there any at Sudbury?—I cannot say.

8546. Do you know that the weavers at Manchester, or in Lancashire, make two yards per day more than they do in Spitalfields?—I do not know that.

8547. What is the average number of yards made in Spitalfields of three double gros de Naples?—I apprehend, if the weaver make neat and good work, and work reasonable hours, he could not exceed three yards a day, unless he had assistance.

8548. Is depending entirely upon himself the most economical way of working? —I find it difficult to answer that question.

8549. Would it not be more advantageous to him to pay a person to assist him?—I think a very fractional difference; he might make, perhaps, an extra yard; but besides having to pay for such help, he would run the risk of having the work made worse.

8550. Do they use the fly shuttle in Spitalfields?—In some instances they do, I believe.

8551. Is it not generally used in the country?—I understand that they use it there.

8552. Is there any advantage in using the fly shuttle where the work is within the reach of a man's hand?—I should think not; they use the fly shuttle in the cotton looms in Lancashire, and perhaps they may in the silk looms; these are accidental circumstances in the manufacture of silk, to which I attach but very little importance.

8553. Do you not know that they are using Jacquards for making large damask table cloths?—No, I am not aware of that.

8554. Is the work produced by fly shuttle or hand loom the best?—That will depend a good deal, I should think, on what the work is.

8555. Can a weaver make rich goods with a fly shuttle?—I should not like to trust to him. I do not mean to say he could not do it, but there is a great deal in habit; what I mean to say is this, that I conceive there is no advantage either way, it is a point of trifling importance, and does not at all affect any general question of inquiry. Whether the Spitalfields weaver uses a fly shuttle or not he is equally at a distance from successful competition with France.

8556. Do you consider the competition with France a question of price, or a question of fashion and taste?—It is a question of price in relation to plain silks of middling qualities; it is a question both of price and taste in relation to the rich plain silks, and fancy and figured silks.

8557. How much cheaper do you think they can manufacture the plain silks in France than they can in England?—Before I can answer that question I must know the rate of wages I am to pay.

8558. At the present time three double gros de Naples will cost 3 s. in Spitalfields, what would it cost in Lyons?—I must know what I am to pay for the labour of those 3 s. gros de Naples.

8559. You have stated that at 7 d.?—If 7 d. be the price paid for the manufacture,

678.                                                                  I consider

Mr.
*John Ballance.*

11 June,
1832.

I consider it would require full 30 per cent. to protect the English manufacture against the manufacture of France.

8560. Does that arise from a difference in the rate of wages in Lyons and London, or the French obtaining their silks cheaper than they do in England?—It consists of two elements, one of which is the price of their raw material compared with that of England; the other resolves itself into a question of wages in relation to throwing, dyeing, warping, winding and weaving.

8561. Of 100 *l.* worth of three double gros de Naples manufactured in England how much per cent. is in wages?—I could not give the per centage at this moment; but I consider that it would cost from 20 *s.* to 22 *s.* including wages and waste, in the process to commute one pound of raw into a pound of manufactured silk in this country.

8562. Will you confine your answer to the prices in Spitalfields, excluding the throwing?—I cannot at this moment give any thing that would be correct.

8563. Is 3 *s.* a fair estimate of the price of a three double gros de Naples?—A three double gros de Naples will vary according to the quality, from 2 *s.* 9 *d.* to 3 *s.* 4 *d.* the cost price.

8564. Assuming the wages to be 7 *d.*, how much will that be per cent.?—About 20 per cent.

8565. Will the wages which enter into the manufacture of a piece of gros de Naples amount altogether to 25 per cent.?—I should say, speaking off hand, much more than 25 per cent.

8566. How much per cent. would you say would be a protection for the manufacturer in Spitalfields as against the French, independent of the throwster?—I have said that it requires full 30 per cent.; I lay stress upon the word full, because I believe it would require more in respect of plain goods to protect the English manufacturer against the foreigner. If he were to receive his silk free of import duty, he would require five-and-twenty per cent. to protect him against the difference of wages and waste in the process of manufacture.

8567. Will you state how much of that 25 per cent. you think the wages require?—It is impossible to give that fractionally, because different silks and different articles will waste more or less.

8568. Have you reason to think that the waste is less in France than in England, and if so, why?—I do not know any thing about the waste in the process of manufacturing in France.

8569. Have you any reason to believe that it is different?—The waste depends upon the character of the fabric, and as the character of the fabric in France is admitted to be superior to that of England, the waste will be less.

8570. What is the waste upon a yard of three double gros de Naples, will it be a penny?—I could not give it at the moment in money.

8571. Will it be a halfpenny?—I think it would be found, taking the average, that the waste is very nearly two ounces in the pound.

8572. Assuming the prices to be the same in the manufacture of a yard of three double gros de Naples in the two countries, the whole wages in Spitalfields being 20 per cent., how do you reconcile that with the supposition that 25 per cent. protection is necessary?—I have not said that the whole wages are 20 per cent.; I did not separate the waste from the wages; I have said that the cost of manufacturing, including these elements, would require a protection of at least 25 per cent. upon plain silks, middling quality.

8573. You have stated that three double gros de Naples is worth about 3 *s.* a yard, and that the wages upon that is 7 *d.*, is not that 20 per cent.?—That is the wages of weaving, but there is winding and warping and dyeing.

8574. How much per yard would the other expenses amount to, winding, warping and dyeing?—I could not give that fractionally without taking time; dyeing is 2 *s.* a lb.; it has been given here at 1 *s.* 3 *d.* to 1 *s.* 6 *d.* a lb.; I have tried dyeing at 1 *s.* 6 *d.* a lb., and have given it up, having had my silk spoiled; there is the winding the silk, 2 *s.* a lb.; the warping the silk, from 6 *d.* to 9 *d.* a lb. all to be added to the 7 *d.* and then there is waste to be added to the whole. I gave in to Mr. Vesey Fitzgerald, in 1829, the result of the items that the question put to me now calls for; and I have not the least objection to present it to this Committee.

8575. Have you any objection to state that the total wages of every description paid by the manufacturer in Spitalfields, independent of dyeing, amount to 25 per cent. on the article?—I mean to say this, that the cost of manufacturing that article,

including

Mr.
*John Ballance.*

11 June,
1832.

including all charges incidental to the manufacture, would make the price of that article when manufactured full 25 per cent. dearer than the French, independent of the import duty upon thrown silk.

8576. Do you believe that the wages, independent of throwing, altogether amount to 30 per cent. upon the article?—It requires full 30 per cent. protection to the English manufacturer against foreign competition. If he were relieved of the import duty on foreign thrown silk, that relief would be about five per cent., therefore he would require five-and-twenty.

8577. You have stated that he would require a protection of 25 per cent. on the score of wages and waste and incidental expenses, independently of dyeing?—No; I include every expense, from his purchase of the thrown silk, dyeing, winding, warping, weaving and waste, till it come out in manufactured silk for sale—the whole of these items, whatever price they may be.

8578. Will the charges on 100*l*. worth of manufactured silk, of three double gros de Naples, amount to 30*l*.?—Very considerably more; but I will make the calculation if desired. I cannot give it at this moment.

8579. Have you taken these points of comparison, when you state that 30 per cent. is required to protect the English manufacturer between England and France, both of them in an ordinarily good state of trade?—That is my point of comparison; I do not now include jobbed goods.

8580. You mean to say that under any circumstances we are not able to make those goods so as to compete with France, without a protection of 30 per cent.?—Unquestionably; I mean to state that this parallel is drawn under the ordinary state of trade, and the most favourable for France, when prices and profits are good there.

8581. Do you think there is any great difference, generally speaking, between the cost price and the selling price in this country?—If I were to answer that from what has taken place to my knowledge within these last nine months, I must say a large portion of the gros de Naples sold in Spitalfields has been sold at a loss; and if there was any doubt of that, I will add that I have sold gros de Naples at a great sacrifice, because I could not get a higher price for them.

8582. Therefore the cost price may be above the selling price?—Certainly.

8583. You would not continue making under those circumstances?—Certainly not; I have not continued to make for that reason; I had this time twelvemonth nearly double the number of looms I now have, because I do not choose to continue to sell at a loss.

8584. Is there a greater waste to the manufacturer in making rich, than in making poor goods?—Yes, according to the number of threads at work, and according to the high standard of the silk; if not of the very best description, there is more waste.

8585. Can you give the Committee an estimate of the probable total value of the whole manufacture in Spitalfields?—No, I cannot.

8586. Can you state what was the difference in price between the goods imported by the trade Committee, with the permission of Government, in the early part of 1826, and similar goods manufactured in Spitalfields?—It was as 50 to 70.

8587. Your manufacture consists principally of black goods?—Exclusively of blacks.

8588. Have there been any considerable quantity of black goods imported since 1826?—I am told that the importations from the Continent consist chiefly of coloured silks, fancy and figured silks, black satins and formerly velvets.

8589. Have you seen any French black gros de Naples?—Yes, I saw several in the seizure of Leaf & Company, at the Custom House.

8590. Did they differ from the English in colour; is the dye better or worse?—The goods which I saw at the Custom House appeared to be much of the same character.

8591. Is not the French black dye inferior to the English?—I am not able to speak to that of my own knowledge; I see them occasionally, but not sufficiently to speak to the comparison.

8592. Have you ever heard of any black goods being imported either from Florence or from Zurich?—I have not heard of the importation of black goods in respect of any places in particular.

8593. The quantity of black goods imported is understood to be inconsiderable, is it not?—I cannot answer that from my own knowledge.

8594. Is not black an article of very large consumption in this country?—

678.                                                          I believe

I believe that there are more black goods made than the country requires, large as the consumption may be.

8595. If there is a large consumption of black goods in this country, and if no considerable quantity are imported from abroad, is not that a proof that it is not a question of price and competition between Spitalfields and Lyons?—The greater bulk of consumption in this country of black silks, I apprehend to be of a low and coarse texture, and that is a description of goods with which the Continent, whether in black or coloured silks, does not interfere.

8596. Are there a large quantity of rich black satins imported?—I think there is, and I have felt its effects. At the opening of the ports, I had rather a large trade in black satins; perhaps I do not err when I say that one-third of my manufacture was in black satins; I found the competition with France in that article so serious, that I have now very few making.

8597. Do you happen to remember whether among the goods seized at Messrs. Leaf's, there were any considerable quantity of black satins?—I am not aware.

8598. Are the French black satins imported into this country of good colour?—What I have seen are of a very good colour, and I believe this to be their general character.

8599. If the price of making three double gros de Naples is lowered in colours, must it not be lowered also in black?—Yes, certainly.

8600. If the coloured goods come in competition with those made at home, and you are obliged to reduce the price of weaving coloured goods, the price of weaving black goods would fall as a necessary consequence, would it not?—It is unquestionable, that I can give no more for the manufacture of a piece of black gros de Naples than my neighbour gives for the manufacture of a similar piece of coloured goods.

8601. Did you ever see a pattern of Zurich levantine black?—I have seen foreign levantines, whether from Zurich I cannot say, and I have suffered from their introduction, for I should have sold some of my own instead.

8602. What you have stated on a former occasion respecting smuggling, you stated of course only as matter of gossip in the trade, not any thing from your own knowledge; you spoke it on the authority of other persons?—I spoke from my own inspection of the goods.

8603. Of the cost?—Yes.

8604. Have the goodness to state what you believe to be the actual cost of smuggling 100 l. worth of goods from France?—I speak of those goods that have been shown to me, coloured goods; in consequence of my being asked to manufacture in black a similar fabric at a certain price, I asked the price, and found it was within 15 per cent. of what I could produce it; and when I stated my difficulty, and my suspicion that those goods were smuggled, the answer was, "I did not smuggle them, but perhaps the person did of whom I bought them."

8605. Do you think that the competition which at present exists in this country in the black silk trade is at all owing to the success of the French manufacture in the coloured goods, which gives them a monopoly in that article?—I can point to several manufacturers who, before the opening of the ports, cared very little about the black trade; confining themselves to the rich trade, the coloured, figured and fancy trade, they have been beaten out of their own market, and rather than turn their weavers adrift, who had been working for them some 20 and 30 years, they have given them black to make; this has produced at times an unnatural competition in black goods, which has considerably injured the trade, reduced the profits, and reduced the wages of labour.

8606. Of an hundred looms employed in the manufacture of three double gross de Naples, how many do you believe are employed on black, and how many on colours?—I cannot tell; the proportion is not fixed, but will vary at particular seasons.

8607. If the cost of smuggling be 20 per cent., do you believe that a greater duty than 20 or 22 ¼ per cent. could be collected?—If His Majesty's Government are not more vigilant than they have been, not 20 nor 15 per cent. will be collected, but under good Custom House regulations there would be no difficulty in collecting a duty sufficient to protect the English manufacturer in plain goods.

8608. Supposing that by the precautions which you have alluded to, the cost of smuggling could be increased to 30 per cent., could a higher duty than 30 per cent. be collected?—Yes, there could be no doubt of that.

8609. How much higher duty than the cost of smuggling can, in your opinion, be

Mr.
*John Ballance.*

11 June,
1832.

be collected?—I should say generally, with good Custom House regulations, rigidly enforced, I think there would be no difficulty in collecting from 30 to 40 per cent.; I have very little doubt that the risk of the smuggler could be increased, so that the price of smuggling would come nearly up to the duty, though that duty were from 30 to 40 per cent.

8610. Do you believe that a higher rate of duty could be collected than the cost of smuggling?—I apprehend that the Custom House can command a higher duty, though perhaps but a fractional one, but the officers of the Customs can speak better than I can to that.

8611. What, in your opinion, is the reason why a higher duty than from 15 to 20 per cent. cannot be safely imposed by the Government, supposing, as the Committee are given to understand, that smuggling could be transacted for 20 per cent.?—In my opinion it arises from this circumstance, that no representation which we have made to His Majesty's Government for the last six years with relation to smuggling has been attended to; I do think it has been in the power of His Majesty's Government to prevent smuggling, had they but listened to our proposals.

8612. You stated on a former day, that in 1826 there were 167 manufacturers in Spitalfields, and that now there are only 79; did you speak of the manufacturers of broad silk goods only?—Yes, I spoke of the broad trade.

8613. You do not include narrow goods?—No; I have got the names of every manufacturer, and I will look over them to see whether there are any; I feel certain I have restricted myself to broad goods in both cases.

8614. You think that in 1826 there were 167 manufacturers of broad silk goods?—Yes, I believe I am quite correct.

8615. Can you state when that number was materially diminished, was it in 1826?—The far greater number, I believe, since 1828; there were several failures in 1829, but in the last three years a greater number than the former two.

8616. Can you state in what year any failed?—I can.

8617. Were they in general manufacturers of plain or of fancy goods?—That I cannot answer at this moment.

8618. Were not a great many of them small manufacturers, who had looms employed in making common gros de Naples?—Not altogether small manufacturers, there were some large ones; when I say large, I mean that they had a great number of looms.

8619. Can you inform the Committee whether the greater proportion of them were manufacturers of common gros de Naples or not?—Since the rich trade, peculiar to Spitalfields, has been surrendered by necessity into the hands of the foreigner, the great bulk of goods manufactured in Spitalfields have been of a low quality; the loss on those goods arising out of the competition in them, I think, has occasioned in great part the failure of those persons.

8620. Are there not a greater quantity of rich goods making in Spitalfields at this time than there were last year?—I do not know what others are doing; mine is considered a rich house; I am making less.

8621. What is the denomination of black satin mostly in use, is it called French black?—I should say, the best dye for black is almost exclusively what is called French black, the colour was introduced from France into this country, I think, about the year 1817.

8622. Is that the same which is used in France?—Yes, we had it from Lyons. There were two or three dyers who came over from Lyons and introduced the colour.

8623. Is it the same in appearance and durability?—I am not aware of any difference, the term French black, includes a variety of shades of black which obtain in this country as well as at Lyons.

8624. Can you inform the Committee what number constitute the committee at Weavers' Hall?—I do not recollect the exact number at this moment.

8625. What is the greatest number who have attended your meeting generally during the last six months?—Our committee has not met since this Select Committee have commenced their inquiry. It was formed in consequence of the distresses of the trade in October, and when, after successive interviews with Government, they obtained from the legislature this inquiry.

8626. Any meetings which have taken place have been meetings of private individuals?—There has been no business transacted; I believe the business was all arranged before hand.

8627. When

8627. When was that committee instituted?—In the latter end of October last or early in November.

8628. How were they appointed?—By a public meeting at Weavers' Hall.

8629. The members were proposed in the usual way?—They were.

8630. Can you state how many of that committee are interested in throwing?—I cannot.

8631. Are not the larger portion of them interested in throwing?—My impression is, a very small number are interested in throwing. I will not be certain, but I should think about three or four.

8632. When was the first committee appointed which met at Weavers' Hall? In 1815; a general association of the silk trade was formed in 1815.

8633. Have you a prospectus stating the objects for which that was formed?—I do not know whether there is a prospectus or not; that association was dissolved in 1824.

8634. Do the proceedings of that first committee or association exist?—It is only the master of the Court of Assistants of the Weavers' Company that can answer that question.

8635. Was not that committee formed chiefly for the purpose of preventing smuggling?—To look after smuggling was its main object, but it was formed, I should say, for the purpose of protecting the interests of the trade generally, of which that was a main part.

8636. And to get the duties on raw silk lowered?—I beg to say that was no part of the object of that association, it may have been the object of individuals being members of that association, but it was no part of the business of the association.

8637. If the minutes and documents of that committee were produced, would they not show that smuggling existed as far back as in 1815?—I believe if those documents were produced they would go to establish the statement I made last Friday, that smuggling at that time was confined to the coast, goods were brought in in small quantities by stealth. The minutes of that committee would fully establish this.

8638. What is your opinion of the present extent of smuggling?—I do not like to form an estimate, but if I were to judge from the number of smuggled goods that I continually meet with, my opinion would be that the amount smuggled exceeds the amount legally imported.

8639. What proportion do you consider the two combined quantities to bear to the general gross sales in this country?—I consider that this question is necessarily restricted to the sales of goods made from a high standard of silk, in other words, of fine fabrics manufactured from the silks of Italy, and not of coarse fabrics produced from the silks of India and China. The importation from Italy of raw and thrown silk for 1831, is about 1,600,000 lbs. A large portion of this silk is mixed with Bengal and China for the production of low priced gros de Naples of a worse texture, such as the Continent does not make. I consider that at least one-third of the Italian silk imported is thus appropriated, which for the purpose of the present calculation must be deducted from the total amount. Goods of a similar description to those imported from the Continent, if manufactured from the remaining quantity of raw and thrown silk, would cost in round numbers, at the present value of raw silk, about 2,200,000 *l.* Should it appear that manufactured silks, imported from the Continent and France, both legally and illegally, amount to 900,000 *l., the cost abroad,* (and I imagine it will appear that I understate this amount); when we add the duty and charges to represent the value of these goods in England as compared with those of British manufacture, we then have in answer to the question proposed, the proportions of these combined quantities to the gross sales in this country, stated in round numbers thus:—

| | |
|---|---|
| Goods manufactured in England of Italian silk value - - | £.2,200,000 |
| Manufactured goods imported from France and the Continent - - - - - -} | £. 900,000 |
| Average estimate of duty and charges, 34 per cent | 306,000 |
| | £.1,206,000 |

I submit that these proportions fully explain the cause of distress in the silk districts, more particularly of Coventry and Spitalfields, and show the pressure upon industry in those places as well as upon our throwing establishments throughout the country; and it is further evident, that by so much as I have understated the

amount

Mr.
John Ballance.

11 June,
1832.

amount of foreign silk goods imported, in that proportion will the pressure upon our silk districts be greater.

8640. Do you believe there is 100,000 *l.* worth imported from France which comes into direct competition with those manufactured in Spitalfields?—Yes, very far beyond that amount.

8641. Do you think that it is to the amount of 400,000 *l.* ?—I should think when one looks at the consumption of rich silks at the West end of the Town, and the similar consumption in all the principal towns of Great Britain, viz. Bristol, Edinburgh, Liverpool &c., there can be no question but that amount is under-rated.

8642. Are there any other articles in plain and figured gros de Naples in which they interfere?—These are the articles which constitute the principal manufacture of Spitalfields.

8643. Do you think that the quantity smuggled and that imported legally would throw about 100,000 persons out of employment, including throwsters, dyers, and so on?—Yes, I should think it would have the effect either of throwing fully that number out of employment, or of compelling them to make low priced goods, that do not come in competition with France, at a miserably reduced rate of wages, either they would be thrown out of employment or compelled to take work at a starving price.

8644. Are the Committee to understand that, in your opinion, there is imported from France legally and illegally, gros de Naples, plain and figured, to the amount of 400,000 *l.* ?—It is impossible that I can give a correct opinion without having data for it; from what I am continually seeing of foreign manufactured broad silks, plain and figured, there can be no question that the importation, legal and illegal, is to an amount that exceedingly interferes with the staple manufacture of Spitalfields. It is utterly impossible for me to speak to the precise quantity imported from loose calculations, but I gather it in a more certain way from the pauperizing effect of this importation upon the district itself.

8645. You see a great number of persons thrown out of employment in this particular branch in Spitalfields, and you see a large quantity of goods of this kind in the country?—Yes, I will give an instance; last December I was shown 30 pieces of figured gros de Naples, the purchaser told me that they were French, and the price which he had given for them; this price convinced me either that they were jobbed in France, or that they must have been smuggled at 15 per cent. Goods of a similar fabric and pattern, made in Spitalfields, had been offered to that dealer at a considerable sacrifice, within 2 *d.* per yard of what he had purchased these, and refused, in consequence of his being able to buy these French goods cheaper; thus the French were sold and the British not; had there been no such advantage obtained by the dealer, in respect of these goods, the English manufacturer would have disposed of his 30 pieces, though at a loss, and been induced to set his men to work; this is no solitary case. I could instance many others in proof that the foreign manufacturer essentially interferes with the British manufacturer, and especially with the artisans in Spitalfields.

8646. Can you state the number of looms that were employed in the manufacture of figured gros de Naples in 1825?—As far as my recollection goes, taking a series of years, 10 or 12 years, it will be found that the fancy and figured silk, of the higher branches of trade, formed about one-fourth of the whole.

8647. Do you throw your own silk?—No, I do not.

8648. Have you a mill of your own?—I had one.

8649. You do not possess it now?—I told Mr. Vesey Fitzgerald, in 1829, if he reduced the duty from 5 *s.* to 3 *s.* 6 *d.* I should give up that mill, I tried it for about nine months afterwards, and then I gave it up to the person who had superintended it for some years; I employ him as a throwster, but I have no interest in it.

8650. You consider the last reduction of duty as having had an injurious effect on the throwing trade?—I say a most injurious effect.

8651. You are interested in the throwing trade only as a mill owner?—My property lies there; I have given up the trade which I was very sorry to do.

8652. In regard to the committee at Weavers' Hall, was that appointed by a full meeting at Weavers' Hall?—Yes; a meeting was called by public advertisement the week before, and was fully attended.

8653. Have the English throwsters been worse off since the reduction of duty than they were before?—They have been far worse off.

8654. How has the bad condition of the English throwster shown itself?—In

the

the unexampled low price which he has been compelled to take for throwing, and in the consequent reduction of his wages to the work-people.

8655. Why does not he get a better price?—The manufacturer could not afford to give a higher price; it would not suit the manufacturer's purpose to have English thrown silk stand him in more than he could get Foreign thrown silk, for the difference between the price of raw and of thrown silk in this market must always constitute the protection of the throwster, that is what I call the common sense view of the question.

8656. Has there been a reduction in the wages of throwing?—The reduction of wages has varied in different places; I should say it has been from 25 to 40 per cent. since 1826. There are some instances in which it has been considerably more than that; in the North of England it has been considerably more.

8657. Do you conceive that this lowering the wages is to be attributed to the reduction of duty, or to competition between the throwsters themselves?—Certainly; from 1829 it has arisen not from the competition between the throwsters themselves, but from a reduction of the duty from 5s. to 3s. 6d., and from 3s. to 2s.; it works thus: As a manufacturer, I have the option of purchasing raw silk, or purchasing that silk in a thrown state from abroad. The price for the raw, say, is 18s. the price for thrown 23s. (I give the average difference since July 1829.) If I can get this bale of raw silk thrown, including waste, for about 5s., I buy it and send it to the throwster; if I cannot get it within that limit I purchase thrown silk; of course the price agreed between me and the throwster must have respect to the probable amount of waste in the process. It is well known that Italian raw silk will waste on an average from $7\frac{1}{2}$ to 10 per cent., which, deducted from 5s., will leave him scarcely 3s. 6d. per lb. for throwing fine organzine. This price is relatively much under the cost of throwing in Italy, notwithstanding all the advantages of the Italian throwster. In fact, under the present rate of duty the English throwster has no option but to refuse the offer altogether, or to take it at a price most ruinous to himself, and which compels him to give his work-people those miserable wages that drive them to have recourse for a part of their subsistence to the poor's rates; there is no alternative under the present state of things but this course for the throwster, or his machinery must stand idle. I press this upon the attention of the Committee, because I am quite satisfied that it is the difference of price in the market between raw and thrown silk that is substantially the protection of the throwster, and no other imaginary price founded upon any theoretical calculation whatever. I beg to refer here to a very valuable document submitted to this Committee by Mr. Doxat (No. 22), which shows the difference of price between raw and thrown silk from 1824; and I think establishes the fact, that this difference constitutes the throwster's protection, and which has been lessened as the duties have been lowered.

8658. Do you think it advantageous to the British manufacturer to have his silk thrown in this country rather than to be entirely dependent upon foreign thrown silk?—There exists no doubt of this among manufacturers of experience who understand their business.

8659. Do you think that goods, which are manufactured in this country of British thrown silk, are equally good with those which would be manufactured entirely of Italian thrown silk?—In some respects they are better; the satins are better.

8660. Why are they better?—They are made from the silk called Fossembrone, which we throw in this country in a peculiar way for satins.

8661. Do they throw it in that way in Piedmont also?—Piedmont silk does not give the lustre.

8662. You think that the silk thrown in this country is equal to silk thrown abroad?—Certainly, as regards the throwing.

8663. Supposing the throwing of silk had not hitherto been known in this country, do you think it would be desirable, in order to promote the general prosperity of the silk manufacture, that measures should be taken to introduce it?—It has always been my opinion, that so far from the weaving and throwing branches of the silk trade being at variance with each other, the prosperity of the British silk manufacturer is intimately connected with the prosperity of the throwing branch.

8664. The Committee have heard that it is cheaper to throw in Italy than in England, in consequence of the price of wages and other different circumstances; what do you conceive would be a protecting duty for the throwster on foreign thrown

Mr.
*John Bullance.*

11 June,
1832.

thrown silk?—I say at once to return to the schedule of 1826, 5 s. for organzine and 3 s. for tram.

8665. What, in your opinion, makes it necessary for the protection of the English throwster, that the duty on foreign organzine should not be less than 5 s. a pound, and on tram 3 s.?- The Italian throwster possesses many positive advantages, and those to a very great extent, and the English throwster has found, the last three years, by bitter experience, that a duty of less than 5 s. on organzine, and less than 3 s. on tram, is not sufficient to counteract those advantages.

8666. Are you aware of the difference of the cost of the plant and power between Italy and England?—It will be found generally as one to eight; a mill in Italy, the rental of which would be about 60 l. per annum, would turn off as much silk as a mill in this country which lets for 460 l. to 480 l. per annum.

8667. Are you aware of any difference in the price of wages?—I should say that the wages result in about one-third of what they are in England; they may not be actually one-third less, but the result to the throwster is one-third.

8668. Do you attach much importance to their being able to throw silks on the spot, and of their having a better selection of raws?—I consider it most important, and that in many respects it diminishes the quantity of labour, and it diminishes the quantity of waste. I cannot give a more striking proof of this than by a reference to the evidence of Mr. Caffi; I think it is in his evidence that a strong boy or man had received per week for nine months at the rate in English money of 7 s. 6 d., which amounts to 5 s. 6 d. per week per annum, could superintend spindles that turn off 20 lbs. weight of fine organzine per week; unless I am very much deceived, nothing of that kind can be done in this country; a proof that the material itself must be of excellent quality.

8669. What effect would a further reduction of duty have on the English throwster?—I am satisfied that Italian raw silk would not be thrown in this country, and the manufacturer would become dependent upon Italy.

8670. There would therefore be an increased importation of foreign thrown silk?—Undoubtedly; and that would reduce many respectable throwsters to great distress by destruction of the capital they have invested in mills and machinery, and what perhaps is still worse, it would fearfully augment the miseries of the labouring classes. A large portion of our female population are now employed in those mills.

8671. Do you not think the manufacturer would receive a corresponding benefit by this reduction?—I think not; because I think that the Italian would receive a portion of the benefit that would arise from the remission of the duty.

8672. Have you had the means of ascertaining the value of mill property employed in throwing silk in England at any given period?—There was a general inquiry instituted in the year 1826 as to the value of mill property by the committee sitting at that time at Weavers' Hall, it was instituted in consequence of the Treasury Order to which I have referred, the reduction from 7 s. 6 d. to 5 s.; and the expected opening the ports on the 5th of July; the inquiry extended over the whole kingdom; and the estimated value of mill property at that time was between 1,500,000 l. and 2,000,000 l. and nearer the latter amount; I do not mean what those mills did cost, but what they would have cost if they had been erected at that time.

8673. Have you any idea what the value of that property is at this time?—Not one-half certainly: this is one effect of the change of the laws of 1824.

8674. You stated, that if the protection be removed from the throwster, the manufacturer would be relieved to the extent of five per cent., do you apply this to English thrown Italian silks as well as Foreign thrown?—No; it appears on evidence that the English throwster already works at a loss, and if compelled to work at a greater loss, he would soon give up the throwing of Italian silks, and therefore I apply it only to foreign thrown silk.

8675. Under what circumstances would the reduction of five per cent. on the value of manufactured goods extend to the whole of the Italian silk imported, said to be about 1,500,000 lbs. weight?—The manufacturer would receive the full benefit of this five per cent. upon the whole quantity imported, only in the event of the English throwster being destroyed, and the Italian throwster taking no advantage of that circumstance.

8676. In the event of the importation of thrown silk continuing the same under the remission of the import duty, how would the manufacturer then be placed in respect of this five per cent.?—It is obvious, that in respect to the entire quantity

678. manufactured

Mr.
*John Ballance.*

11 June,
1832.

manufactured from Italian silks, his advantage would be reduced to 1¾ per cent. on heavy goods, and to one per cent on light goods.

8677. You have stated that you have been engaged in the silk trade for nearly 30 years, have you been in the habit of buying Italian raw silk all that time?—Yes; I may say almost every month throughout every year.

8678. What description of raw silk have you chiefly bought?—I buy Fossembrone raws and raws of Lombardy, commonly called Bergam raws, of the best quality.

8679. Of late have you found any difficulty in obtaining the best sorts of those raws?—I should say not so much in Fossembrone, but certainly in Bergam raws.

8680. Can you account for this difficulty?—I speak to the fact as what I have experienced, and this difficulty has been coincident with the late reduction of the import duty on foreign thrown silks.

8681. Are your purchases of Italian raw silk sufficient to give you a knowledge of the general state of the market in them?—We are, I may say, regular and rather considerable purchasers of raw silk, and I am in the habit of seeing samples of all the filatures that come into our market, of the best sorts of raw silk.

8682. Can you state why this difficulty has not applied to Fossembrone raws?—In Lombardy the Italians have throwing mills, and of course they have the option of sending either the raw or the thrown silk; that is not the case in the district of Fossembrone; I believe they have not yet any throwing mills.

8683. How would your manufacture in particular be affected, could you not obtain a good supply from Italy of the best sort of raw silk?—I should be inclined to give it up altogether; I mean to say my manufacture is of that description, if I were compelled to use the silks thrown in Italy, I think it would be of very little use my carrying it on.

8684. Do you think the lowering the import duty on foreign thrown silk would, by possibility, place you in those circumstances?—I have heard something of late that would make me fear it. Some London merchants, within the last two months, have written to their Italian correspondents upon this subject, and those Italians are now very much in doubt whether to send their best raws to this country, or to retain them to send them in a thrown state, as, in the event of a reduction of the import duty, they consider it would be more advantageous to them to send them thrown.

8685. In which case you would be of course entirely dependent upon them?—In which case we should have, to say the best, a very scanty supply of that description of raw silk, which I consider essential to the carrying on my manufacture; I may add, I have no recollection of the market ever being so bare as it is at this moment of the description of silk to which I have referred, the best raw silk.

8686. You have stated, that you give a preference to English thrown silk for the manufacture of the richest goods, do you prefer English thrown Italian organzine to Foreign thrown, independently of the prices of the two kinds?—Certainly; I have said that I use no Foreign thrown silk, except for some certain goods; all the richer goods are made exclusively from English throwns.

8687. The object being to supply the English manufacturer with thrown silk, cheap and good, which is the most likely method eventually to obtain that end, by keeping up a considerable duty upon foreign thrown silk, and encouraging the throwing trade in this country, or by lowering the protecting duties, and thus discouraging the throwing of Italian silk in England?—There can be no doubt that if we wish to have cheap and good throwing in this country, I mean cheap in proportion to foreign thrown silks, the only way to secure it is to give full protection to the throwsters. This will give them confidence in their business, which will secure to the manufacturer a regular supply in the market of good English thrown silk. I beg to add, this regular supply of English thrown silk can be obtained only by giving to the English throwster what I call a margin between the duty and his actual cost, to secure him against contingencies. This he had formerly; and the effect was, that in those years the price of English thrown silk was under that of Foreign thrown.

8688. It has been very often said, that Spitalfields suffers from the competition of Manchester, and not from that of France, what is your opinion upon that subject?—The most serious injury that Spitalfields receives is the competition with France and the Continent, that is the first and great injury. The competition with Manchester is incidental and grows out of it, but is altogether of a secondary nature.

8689. It has been stated to this Committee, that the distress of the silk trade has

not

Mr.
*John Ballance.*

11 June,
1832.

not been so great the last nine months as formerly; are you of that opinion?—I am entirely of a contrary opinion; and I apprehend that the persons who gave that opinion, being dealers only, are not qualified to give any opinion about it.

8690. It has been given in evidence, that there have been no sacrifices of profit this spring in the sales of silk goods, and that generally the manufacturers do not keep any stocks by them, is that the case?—I believe this evidence was given likewise by dealers who know very little of the sacrifices of manufacturers. I know there have been sacrifices, and I have myself made them, and have been compelled to do so; and as to keeping stocks, I may say generally, without offence, the manufacturers are too poor to keep them, they do not do it because they cannot do it.

8691. It appears in evidence, that the importation of plain silk goods from France was greater in 1827, 1828 and 1829, than it has been since, how do you account for that?—I answer this question by directing the attention of the Committee to the account I gave in last Friday from the parish of Bethnal Green; perhaps we have succeeded to some extent in stopping the legal importations of plain silks; but we have done it by reduced wages, that is pauperizing our workmen. As it respects the higher branches of plain goods, and the fancy and figured trade, even by that means we have not succeeded with them.

8692. It has been stated, that upon the work for which 6½d. was paid, a man can earn 13s. per week, how do you reconcile that with your statement of the average earnings of your weavers?—I can reconcile it only by saying, that no man could make the quantity that would realize 13s. per week. If he is paid only 6½d. per yard, he must either work 18 hours out of 24, or he must have assistance; his paying for which would of course reduce the 13s. I consider the calculation of the supposed quantity of work done altogether erroneous.

8693. Do you mean to say that the manufacturer's books are no criterion that the man who is paid 13s. a week has earned it all himself?—Certainly they are not.

8694. It appears in evidence, that in respect of the wages of silk manufactured goods, plain silks, manufactured in England are as cheap as those manufactured in France; is that your opinion?—In all silk goods quality as well as weight is to be considered; and I apprehend that the goods referred to were not made of the same materials; for example, if I make a piece containing 3,000 threads, each weighing 48 deniers, and I make another piece containing 6,000 threads, each weighing 24 deniers, I have the same weight per yard in both cases, but the one is of a low, and the other is of a high standard; and though those goods respectively weigh the same, they will not fetch within 9d. per yard in the market. If the one is worth 3s. the other will not be worth more than 2s. 3d. I therefore submit, that all calculations founded upon mere weight, are utterly fallacious.

8695. It appears that many large dealers in silk goods sell principally British silks, how do you account for this?—It is very obvious that every house has its particular connexion, and if that is mainly with the middling or lower classes, or what is called the country trade, the demand will be principally for low priced silks of English manufacture; but if the house supplies the upper classes of society, whether those classes of society are in London, or in the principal towns of England, there the demand will be principally for continental silks; therefore the comparative sales of any such houses are evidence only as it regards the sales of such houses, but not of the extent of trade as a whole.

8696. What description of silk goods does your house manufacture?—Plain black silks, and at a range of price from 2s. to 7s. per yard.

8697. You have said, that the remission of the import duty on foreign thrown silks, which would reduce the value of manufactured silks about five per cent., would not relieve the manufacturer in respect of smuggling; will you explain this?—I said that it requires a duty of full 30 per cent. to protect the English manufacturer in respect of plain silks, and I said this with reference to the ordinary state of trade at Lyons, excluding jobs. Goods are smuggled in considerable quantities at 15 per rent.; if the protection to the throwster were removed the manufacturer then would require 25 per cent., and it is obvious there would remain between him and the smuggler still the difference of ten per cent., which can be got rid of only by increasing the risk of smuggling. I am aware that it is very easy to get rid of smuggling by reducing the duty to the smuggler's price; but then we deprive the English manufacturer of the protection he requires, and thus get rid both of smuggler and manufacturer at once.

678.

8698. You

Mr.
*John Ballanse.*

11 June,
1822.

8698. You have alluded to certain checks in the plan of stamps, what are they?
—There are two; I alluded to the moveable number, and I alluded to a pattern-book; it is the pattern-book that secures those checks; if a pattern be cut off every piece as it passes the Custom House, and the pattern be entered in the book with a number attached, the piece suspected to be smuggled, which may have a forged stamp, must correspond in colour, in quality, in leizure, and likewise in the actual incision of the cut; these are coincidences that are scarcely ever possible to occur in reference to smuggled goods.

8699. How would this operate to prevent the forging of stamps?—I think in the way I have stated, that the difficulties thus thrown in the way would deter persons from forging those stamps.

8700. Have not watered silks been very fashionable this season?—Yes.

8701. Are they plain silks of very rich quality?—Yes.

8702. Have those silks been made in Spitalfields or imported from France?—They have been imported from France in very large quantities; one house at the West end of the Town told me the other day that very nearly one-fourth of their importations this year was in watered silks.

8703. What difference would it have made in Spitalfields had the demand been supplied from that district?—It would have kept in constant employ several hundreds of looms.

8704. And that upon the rich goods, where the earnings of the weaver would have been much greater?—Those workmen would have received from about 9 d. to 11 d. a yard making, and instead of which the poor fellows have been making works at 5 d. and 5½ d. per yard.

8705. In your evidence on Friday last, you exhibited some patterns of figured silks made at Manchester, should you state that the foreign silk manufacture interferes with the silk manufacture at Manchester?—The manufacturers of the Continent and of France work upon a high standard of silk, and such also is the staple manufacture of Spitalfields; but Manchester works uniformly on a coarser texture of silk, and a lower standard, and the manufactures of the Continent no more interfere with the staple manufacture of Manchester than did the manufacture of Spitalfields formerly interfere with that of Manchester; and I apply this even to furniture which is making at Manchester; it is well known that furniture is made of Bengal and China silks.

8706. Do you mean to say that Manchester has not suffered at all from the admission of foreign wrought silks?—She has undoubtedly suffered, but in an indirect way; the competition in low priced goods between Manchester and Spitalfields has been in consequence of the opening of the ports, which has deprived Spitalfields of her rich trade.

8707. Do not you think that Manchester would be benefited as well as Spitalfields by the prohibition of figured silks?—The legitimate trade once restored to Spitalfields, she would give up that competition with Manchester, and things would then revert to their former channels; Manchester would take her trade, and Spitalfields take her's.

8708. You have alluded to the raw silk of France as giving her manufacturers an advantage over us, how would that advantage stand could we obtain this raw material?—I have alluded to this raw material as only one element of advantage, if I may so speak, among many others; but could we obtain the raw material it is very evident there would still remain her low rate of wages; her very large export of manufactured silks, which is three-fourths of her whole production, and her control of fashion, and these conjoined would give that advantage to France as to render successful competition in the higher classes of the silk manufacture utterly impossible, even in the event of our having the raw material.

8709. Did not an Act exist formerly in Spitalfields which regulated the price of labour?—Yes.

8710. Were not the rates of wages higher then in consequence?—No, they were not higher on the plain branch; I conceive that the effect of the Act was to keep the price down in the plain branch; what it had to do with the figured branch I must leave to figured manufacturers to speak to.

8711. Has the price of labour increased since that Act was repealed?—The Act was repealed in 1824, and in 1825 there was an advance of 1 d. a yard; but I advert more particularly to that which took place in 1817, 1818 and 1819, when the Act was in force; I know instances in which a penny a yard more was paid in Manchester and Macclesfield for low goods than we paid in London, which is

decisive

decisive that the Act rather kept down the price of wages in plain goods than otherwise.

8712. When you stated that 300,300 *l.* are annually paid in wages less now among the poor in Spitalfields than formerly, do you make that calculation on the wages paid under the Act?—No; I take my calculation on the wages paid in 1826; and I beg to add that I made this calculation of 300,000*l.* paid less in Spitalfields now than in 1826 exclusively with reference to the reduction of wages in the plain branch, without including the figured trade; if I were to add the reduction in the figured branch, I should exhibit a much larger amount than 300,000*l.* per annum.

8713. When you speak of 30 per cent. upon foreign plain goods as the difference between the cost in England and France, is that founded on the regular cost of production of foreign goods, or taking into consideration the occasional glut of French goods and the consequent jobbing of those in the market?—My calculation is not made on job goods, but it is upon goods that may be ordered from Lyons in the regular way; and the calculation is made by working a certain quantity at their price, and the same quantity at our price, upon our present very low rate of wages.

8714. Do you not then require some greater protection than 30 per cent. against such goods which may be had in France occasionally at a less cost?— There can be no doubt that this is one very important element of the question. France, as I have said, exports in manufactured silks upwards of two millions of pounds weight. I have stated her markets to be in the North and South of Europe and America; should there be any obstruction to her sales in those places, the surplus must be poured into this country, consequently the English manufacturer becomes the victim of contingencies, which he neither can foresee nor control, and this destroys all his confidence. He may be preparing for his own market in the expectation of a good trade in the spring; there may arise contingencies from abroad, of which he knows nothing, and a glut of French silks may come in that will compel him to sell goods at a tremendous sacrifice.

8715. Are not the goods imported from France into this country chiefly of superior kinds?—My opinion is, that those imported of the superior kind, fancy and figured silks, more generally pay the duty, and that the smuggling is in plain goods of a more middling quality; I form this opinion from what I see around me.

8716. Is it not a great protection to our manufacturers that even the smuggling of those jobs must cost 20 per cent.?—No; and I do not think that it does cost 20 per cent., or any thing like it.

8717. State the grounds of that opinion?—From having seen the goods and the prices quoted.

8718. You do not know what the cost of the smuggler is, or the amount of insurance?—I am quite satisfied of one of two things, that either those goods were bought as jobs in the French market, or that if the regular price was paid for them there was not more than 15 per cent. paid to get them into this country. I do not care which it is, and I could not make them within 15 per cent.

8719. There is a difference between the article manufactured by you and the articles imported from France of 15 per cent.?—I mean to say that I have seen goods on which there has been a difference of 15 per cent.; and having stated this opinion to the purchaser, the answer was, though I did not smuggle them, I have very little doubt they were smuggled from the price at which I bought them.

8720. Does not that show that the 15 per cent. is sufficient to put the two manufacturers on a footing of equality?—I have said that it requires full 30 per cent. to protect the silk manufacturer in this country; the protection includes the price of labour to the artisan. If the manufacturer were to have but 15 per cent., the parishes in the silk districts would have to support all the work people.

8721. Are you not to be understood to say, that on comparing certain goods imported from France with goods manufactured in Spitalfields, you find a difference of 15 per cent.?—What I stated, or intended to state, was this, that the goods I saw I could not manufacture within 15 per cent.; the parties, when I objected to it, told me though they had not smuggled them, they suspected that they were smuggled, and at a charge of 15 per cent.

8722. Do you mean, when you state you could not make them within 15 per cent., to say the cost in Lyons or the cost in London?—I mean to say the cost in

678.

London,

*Mr.*
*John Ballance.*

11 June,
1832.

London, those goods having already paid the smuggler's charge to the amount of 15 per cent. and other expenses.

[*The Witness delivered in the following Comparative Statement, which was read:*]

COMPARATIVE STATEMENT of the Cost of manufacturing 500 Yards of Plain GROS DE NAPLES of Medium Quality in *London* and at *Lyons*; the former manufactured from English Thrown Italian Silk, and the latter from Thrown Silk of French growth. The Prices given as under for the Organzine and Tram at these Places respectively, are the Averages Prices of the last Three Months.

| LONDON: | | £. | s. | d. | LYONS: | | £. | s. | d. |
|---|---|---|---|---|---|---|---|---|---|
| *lb.* *oz.* | | | | | *lb.* *oz.* | | | | |
| 26  3 - - Warp, English Thrown Organzine - - } at 24/ | | 31 | 8 | 6 | 26  3 - - Warp, French Organzine - } - - at 19/8 | | 25 | -- | 7 |
| 19  2 - - Shute - ditto - Tram - at 21/ | | 20 | 1 | 7 | 19  2 - - Shute - ditto - Tram - at 18/3 | | 17 | 9 | - |
| 45  5      dyeing 45 *lb.* 5 *oz.* - at 2/ | | 4 | 10 | 6 | 45  5      dyeing 45 *lb.* 5 *oz.* - at 1/1 | | 2 | 9 | - |
| Winding 26 *lb.* 3 *oz.* Warp, reduced in dyeing to 19 *lb.* 8 *oz.* - - } at 2/ | | 1 | 19 | - | Winding 26 *lb.* 3 *oz.* Warp, reduced in dyeing to 19 *lb.* 8 *oz.* - - } at 1/3 | | 1 | 4 | 4 |
| Ditto - 19 *lb.* 2 *oz.* Shute - at 1/9 | | 1 | 13 | 5 | Weaver winds his own Shute. | | | | |
| Warping 500 yards - - - | | 1 | 5 | - | Warping 500 yards - - - | | - | 12 | 10 |
| Weaving 500 yards - at -/7 | | 14 | 11 | 8 | Weaving 500 yards - at -/4 | | 8 | 6 | 8 |
| | £. | 75 | 9 | 8 | | £. | 55 | 2 | 5 |

|  | £. | s. | d. |
|---|---|---|---|
| Cost of manufacturing 500 Yards of Gros de Naples in London - - - - } | 75 | 9 | 8 |
| Cost of - ditto - ditto - at Lyons - | 55 | 2 | 5 |
| £. | 20 | 7 | 3 |

500 Yards - - at £. 75  9  8 = per Yard to 3/-½ cost in England.

500 Yards - - at £. 55  2  5 = per Yard to 2/2½ cost in France.

£. 20  7  3 = 0 37 per cent. in favour of Lyons.

June 11.                    (Errors excepted.)                    *John Ballance.*

I have given above only the cost of production in both places without reference to profit in either case, and have calculated that in London upon English thrown silk, not Foreign thrown silk; the import duty upon which is 1 *d.* per lb. I speak with full confidence to the accuracy of this statement; and I submit that it more than supports the opinion which I have expressed. That in respect of plain silk goods of middling quality it requires a duty of full 30 per cent. to protect the English manufacturer. In respect of the higher description of plain silks, and of fancy and figured silks, the difference will be found to be from 40 to 50 per cent. against him.

---

*Jovis, 14° die Junii,* 1832.

JAMES A. STEWART MACKENZIE, ESQUIRE, IN THE CHAIR.

*John Bowring*, Esquire, LL.D. called in; and Examined.

*John Bowring,*
Esq. LL. D.

14 June,
1832.

8723. YOU have been for some time past in France, have you not?—Yes, I have been engaged for the last four or five months as a commercial commissioner at Paris, and it has been my business to examine, in all their bearings, the manufacturing and commercial relations of France, and I wish, with reference to this object, to make one preliminary observation to the Committee, which appears to me of great gravity and importance; it is this, that in investigating the state of exportations into France from England, and importations into England from France, we have discovered, that the amount of manufactured goods imported from France into England (upon the system which exists here), and imported from England into France (under the system which exists there), is about equal, but we have been very much struck by one remarkable fact, which is this; that in the goods

goods imported into France from England labour forms a great proportion of the cost of production, and in the goods introduced into England from France labour forms a small proportion of the cost of production; and hence one very obvious consequence will occur to the Committee, that in as far as any measure should prohibit the introduction of French goods into England, a much greater quantity of English labour must inevitably be displaced than the labour which is protected.

*John Bowring,*
Esq. LL. D.
___
14 June,
1832.

8724. Your attention, whilst you were a commercial commissioner in Paris was of course called, was it not, to the whole of the commercial relations between France and England?—Our business, in fact, was to examine the whole character of the commercial communications and relations between the two countries, and the task was of course a very laborious one, as it is well known that commercial intercourse had been minimized by the system which had been adopted by the two countries; but inasmuch as the French Government lent us the most cordial assistance for investigating every point, we were enabled, I think, to substantiate the facts of the case in a very satisfactory way.

8725. Your attention has been lately more immediately directed to the state of the silk trade in consequence of directions you received to inquire particularly into that branch, has it not?—Yes, specially so, inasmuch as, with reference to the relations between England and France, silk and silk goods have become very prominent topics; that is one of the points which necessarily required particular attention.

8726. In consequence of those directions you left Paris, did you not, and proceeded to Lyons and other places, in which the silk manufacture is carried on in France, and examined with the greatest care you could the state of the silk manufacture?—Yes, I left Paris in consequence of instructions received from home, and before I left Paris, having stated to the French Government the purpose of my mission, I received from them such introductions as were most likely to assist me in the object of my inquiries.

8727. Besides the means you received from the Government, did you possess any other means?—I had a large personal acquaintance in the district; I have been very familiar with France, and I will state to the Committee the character of the documents with which I was furnished, and the introductions I received. The President of the Council directed the Prefects to give me every assistance; the Minister of Finance instructed the Custom Houses to furnish me with any official returns I should desire; the Minister of Commerce introduced me to the Chambers of Commerce. I took with me, also, letters from the representatives of the different districts, and had myself a very considerable personal acquaintance among the most intelligent men in the Departments I visited.

8728. Had you sources of information amongst the operatives as well as amongst the other classes?—Very decidedly; my course all through was one of extreme frankness; I first visited the authorities, as I was bound to do, and stated that, as it was my intention to investigate this matter thoroughly, I hoped they would not take it amiss if I visited the workmen at their looms, and completely informed myself of the state of things; they not only approved of that conduct, but assisted me in every conceivable way. I was enabled to compare the official statements with the facts which I gathered from personal observation. I almost dwelt amongst the labourers for some time, and I think became perfectly familiar both with their habits of life and their social position. I am also desirous of putting into the hands of the Committee some evidence of the manner in which I was received in the silk manufacturing districts; some of the newspapers did all they could to frustrate my object; here is a newspaper containing an appeal to the manufacturers and to the workpeople, in order to prevent my obtaining information; the newspapers in general took a completely different course, stating that the period of secrecy had passed away, and that any individual who came to ascertain the facts of the case, and not to pillage their manufacturing secrets, was entitled to a cordial reception; and the workmen came in deputations, offering to communicate any information I might desire.

8729. Have you any reason to believe that this was a change from their former line of conduct, and that difficulties had been thrown in the way of obtaining information?—Undoubtedly the whole feeling in France, not only as connected with this particular topic, but connected with general commercial topics, has changed in a very extraordinary degree; the fact is, there is a strong English interest now spread over the country that is demanding a change, and that demand for the change in their commercial system is very greatly operating upon their

future

*John Bowring,*
Esq. LL. D.

14 June,
1832.

future plans of commerce, and more especially, as I am quite sure any examination of the subject will show, that the quantity of distress, the frightful crash and ruin which their prohibitory system has introduced into the whole of their manufacture will be such, that nobody can long resist the evidence of it.

8730. Will you state, in the first instance, what you consider to be the condition of the French silk trade generally?—The French silk trade is at this moment suffering under very considerable disadvantages: a portion of their general prohibitory system falls upon them; there is a tax upon raw silk in order to protect the French grower of silk; there is a heavy tax upon iron, an enormously heavy tax, in order to protect their iron masters; that tax upon iron has led to a great increase in the value of wood, so that as wood and iron enter into their machinery they suffer much from that circumstance, and as in the great towns the local taxation is also very heavy, the consequence has been, that except in cases in which taste and very long experience and aptitude enter largely into their manufacturing productions, their trade is passing away; that is very much the case with respect to plain goods at this moment, the trade is relieving itself a little by the migration of weavers from the towns into the country, that of Lyons has been more relieved by the violent expulsion of a great number of weavers.

8731. Have you any statement of the import of raw and thrown silk into France?—I have here an official statement which has been furnished me by the Minister of Finance from the Custom House of all the importations of raw and thrown silk from 1825 to 1831, a period of seven years, which I will deliver in; it will be seen that the great source of importations are the Milanese Provinces, standing under the head of Austria; the second in importance is Sardinia; the third in importance is Turkey; the fourth Naples and Sicily; in a former year there had been some importations from Egypt, the last two years there was none.

[*The same were delivered in, and read.*]

## FRENCH SILK TRADE.—IMPORTATIONS.

### Raw and Thrown Silk.

| COUNTRY WHENCE IMPORTED. | QUANTITIES IMPORTED (KILOGRAMMES). | | | | | | |
|---|---|---|---|---|---|---|---|
| | 1825. | 1826. | 1827. | 1828. | 1829. | 1830. | 1831. |
| England - - - - | 40,872 | 62,863 | 2,655 | 764 | 14,897 | 8,393 | 3,173 |
| Low Countries - - | 13 | 26,487 | 3,550 | 164,802 | 53,696 | 9,912 | 4,133 |
| Austria - - - - | 455,686 | 229,411 | 607,678 | 542,041 | 612,113 | 560,401 | 645,478 |
| Germany - - - | 666 | 2,129 | 86 | 313 | 464 | 82 | 986 |
| Switzerland - - | 15,488 | 10,207 | 16,182 | 17,566 | 15,273 | 18,671 | 25,379 |
| Sardinia - - - - | 277,316 | 411,546 | 368,127 | 276,264 | 335,556 | 344,683 | 296,652 |
| Tuscany - - - - | 5,911 | 1,259 | 4,882 | 5,038 | 8,141 | 4,863 | 1,854 |
| Naples and Sicily - | 45,126 | 48,575 | 49,200 | 39,735 | 57,250 | 40,398 | 30,439 |
| Spain - - - - | 42,673 | 10,480 | 25,024 | 18,547 | 9,227 | 10,325 | 23,104 |
| Turkey - - - - | 59,481 | 84,334 | 70,054 | 127,334 | 138,637 | 128,744 | 25,858 |
| Egypt - - - - | 764 | 308 | 673 | 12,286 | 551 | — | — |
| Barbary States - - | - - | 3,435 | 3,375 | 348 | 79 | 3,759 | 1,480 |
| United States - - | 123 | 4,153 | 1,262 | - - | - - | 2,113 | 244 |
| China and Cochin China - | - - | - - | 2,119 | 140 | 8,234 | - - | 6,146 |
| English India - - | - - | 1,227 | 23 | - - | 2,811 | - - | 435 |
| French India - - | - - | 139 | 436 | 1,054 | - - | 4 | 1,878 |
| TOTAL - - | 944,119 | 896,553 | 1,155,326 | 1,206,232 | 1,256,929 | 1,132,348 | 1,067,239 |

8732. The return refers to the gross import?— Yes.

8733. And includes the waste silk?—It does, I believe.

8734. Have you any statement of the exports of silk?—I have a similar statement, from the same source, of the exportation of raw and thrown silk, this is all foreign silk, the exportation of French silk being prohibited.

[*The same was delivered in, and read.*]

FRENCH SILK TRADE.—EXPORTATIONS.

*John Bowring,*
Esq. LL. D.

14 June,
1832.

RAW AND THROWN SILK.

| COUNTRIES TO WHICH EXPORTED. | QUANTITIES EXPORTED (KILOGRAMMES) | | | | | | |
|---|---|---|---|---|---|---|---|
| | 1825. | 1826. | 1827. | 1828. | 1829. | 1830. | 1831. |
| England | 466,814 | 216,687 | 701,490 | 773,340 | 396,260 | 609,497 | 669,605 |
| Low Countries | 6,711 | 4,517 | 5,585 | 6,097 | 4,660 | 4,065 | 3,094 |
| Prussia | 228 | - - | 20 | 147 | 13 | - - | 317 |
| Germany | 2,784 | 2,002 | 5,907 | 3,650 | 2,780 | 2,702 | 1,858 |
| Switzerland | 8,027 | 5,147 | 14,771 | 8,792 | 10,746 | 28,447 | 13,150 |
| Sardinia | 2,994 | 20,369 | 2,977 | 3,335 | 1,230 | 8,328 | 9,141 |
| Tuscany and Roman States | 416 | 379 | 1,974 | 3,358 | 668 | 2,527 | 745 |
| Spain | - - | 643 | 63 | 4 | 37 | 396 | 121 |
| Portugal | 31 | | — | — | | | |
| Turkey | - - | 380 | 137 | - - | 218 | 487 | 106 |
| Egypt | - - | - - | - - | - - | - - | 227 | 126 |
| Algiers | - - | | | | | - - | 3,724 |
| Barbary States | 570 | 1,806 | 1,534 | 7,120 | 4,558 | 1,368 | 598 |
| United States | 137 | - - | - - | - - | - - | 563 | 818 |
| Mexico | 654 | 579 | 1,941 | - - | 80 | 2,634 | 1,812 |
| Brazils | - - | 395 | 8 | - - | - - | 73 | — |
| TOTAL | 489,366 | 252,904 | 736,407 | 805,843 | 421,250 | 661,314 | 705,215 |

8735. Can you state the consumption of foreign silk in France?—That I have obtained from another source, by applying to the Minister of Commerce; the value of these documents consists in their coming from different and independent quarters; this is a document furnished me by the Minister of Commerce, as to the weight of silk imported for the consumption of the kingdom from the year 1820.

*[The same was delivered in, and read.]*

FRENCH SILK TRADE.

WEIGHT of SILK Imported for the Consumption of the Kingdom, from 1820 to 1831.

| YEARS. | AMOUNT IN KILOGRAMMES. | | | | | TOTALS. |
|---|---|---|---|---|---|---|
| | Cocoons. | Raw. | Thrown. | Dyed. | Bourre. | |
| | Kils. | Kils. | Kils. | Kils. | Kils. | Kils. |
| 1820 | 1,960 | 130,312 | 322,381 | 745 | 115,332 | 570,730 |
| 1821 | 2,914 | 77,314 | 251,406 | 668 | 85,299 | 417,601 |
| 1822 | 20,302 | 170,730 | 248,863 | 600 | 161,489 | 601,984 |
| 1823 | 4,062 | 118,439 | 234,474 | 333 | 168,323 | 525,631 |
| 1824 | 7,851 | 120,027 | 307,874 | 903 | 243,384 | 740,039 |
| 1825 | 22,496 | 145,407 | 337,770 | 740 | 182,102 | 688,515 |
| 1826 | 9,041 | 285,806 | 343,587 | 740 | 160,610 | 799,784 |
| 1827 | 14,031 | 130,430 | 338,948 | 873 | 186,309 | 670,591 |
| 1828 | 19,549 | 131,330 | 242,971 | 409 | 199,284 | 593,543 |
| 1829 | 14,177 | 396,520 | 371,416 | 380 | 239,374 | 1,021,867 |
| 1830 | 12,011 | 190,399 | 327,786 | 585 | 170,085 | 700,866 |
| 1831 | 14,428 | 111,968 | 292,232 | 1,170 | 104,982 | 524,780 |
| TOTAL | 142,822 | 2,008,682 | 3,679,708 | 8,146 | 2,016,573 | 7,855,931 |
| Average on 12 Years, per annum | 11,902 | 167,390 | 306,643 | 679 | 168,047 | 654,661 |

I have also an estimate of the Minister of Commerce of the value of the silks imported and employed for home consumption for the same years, by which it appears that from 1820 to 1830, the last period to which it is made up, the total weight in 1820 for foreign silk was 29 millions of francs and in 1830 it was 33 millions of francs.

*[The same was delivered in, and read.]*

FRENCH

*John Bowring,*
Esq. LL. D.

14 June,
1832.

FRENCH SILK TRADE.

ACCOUNT of the Importation of SILK for Home Consumption, from 1820 to 1830.

| YEARS | VALUE. | | | | | |
| --- | --- | --- | --- | --- | --- | --- |
| | Cocoons. | Raw. | Thrown. | Dyed. | Bourre. | TOTALS. |
| | f. | f. | f. | f. | f. | f. |
| 1820 - - | 5,880 | 5,510,858 | 21,963,890 | 70,779 | 2,039,608 | 29,591,015 |
| 1821 - - | 8,762 | 3,074,686 | 17,483,616 | 63,460 | 2,082,980 | 22,713,504 |
| 1822 - - | 60,906 | 6,805,334 | 17,362,198 | 97,000 | 2,724,196 | 27,049,634 |
| 1823 - - | 12,186 | 4,723,012 | 16,376,676 | 31,639 | 2,813,391 | 23,956,904 |
| 1824 - - | 23,553 | 4,774,680 | 29,703,988 | 89,789 | 4,042,109 | 38,634,119 |
| 1825 - - | 67,488 | 6,526,347 | 23,616,468 | 70,300 | 3,104,871 | 33,385,474 |
| 1826 - - | 27,123 | 12,854,340 | 24,020,310 | 70,300 | 2,770,437 | 39,742,510 |
| 1827 - - | 42,093 | 9,203,602 | 23,699,108 | 82,939 | 3,279,948 | 36,307,690 |
| 1828 - - | 58,647 | 9,247,756 | 16,943,998 | 38,899 | 3,370,921 | 29,660,221 |
| 1829 - - | 42,531 | 19,873,092 | 29,991,168 | 36,100 | 3,933,781 | 53,876,672 |
| 1830 - - | 36,033 | 7,611,394 | 22,900,992 | 99,979 | 2,983,441 | 33,631,839 |
| TOTAL - | 385,202 | 90,205,101 | 244,062,412 | 751,184 | 33,145,683 | 308,549,582 |
| AVERAGE - | 35,018 | 8,200,427 | 22,187,492 | 68,289 | 3,013,244 | 33.504,507 |

There is a document I also found possessed by the Minister of Commerce, of some value as connected with the earlier history of French trade, a Statement of the value of raw silks imported from 1800 to 1806, and of the quantities and value from 1815 to 1819. In the year 7, which was 1799, the estimated value was 1,789,500, and in 1819 it was 24 millions of francs; this document comes also from the Minister of Commerce, but from a source independent of the others; the value of this document arises out of the means of comparison which it gives.

[*The same was delivered in, and read.*]

ACCOUNT of the VALUE of RAW SILKS of all Sorts imported into France, from the Year 7 to the Year 1806, and of the QUANTITIES and VALUE from 1815 to 1819.

|  | *Francs.* |
| --- | --- |
| Year 7 - - - - - - - - - | 1,789,500 |
| — 8 - - - - - - - - - | 2,368,700 |
| — 9 - - - - - - - - - | 13,267,000 |
| — 10 - - - - - - - - - | 11,008,632 |
| — 11 - - - - - - - - - | 3,022.948 |
| — 12 - - - - - - - - - | 4,583,014 |
| — 13 - - - - - - - - - | 4,599,618 |
| — 14 - - - - - - - - - | 8,311,304 |

|  | QUANTITIES. | VALUE. |
| --- | --- | --- |
| | *Kilogrammes.* | *Francs.* |
| Year 1815 - - - | 289,432 | 14,793,690 |
| — 1816 - - - | 387,164 | 17,328,740 |
| — 1817 - - - | 492,614 | 26,376,180 |
| — 1818 - - - | 464,722 | 24,862,136 |
| — 1819 - - - | 464,198 | 24,301,399 |

8736. You stated that a considerable duty was charged upon the import of silk into France, have you any statement of the amount of duty levied in a series of years?—The Custom House have given me a Return from 1825 to 1830, which I have reduced to English lbs. and English money, for the convenience of the Committee.

[*The same was delivered in, and read.*]

FRENCH

*John Bowring,*
Esq. LL. D.

14 June,
1832.

### FRENCH SILK TRADE.

REPORT of the Importations of RAW and THROWN SILKS, and of the Duties levied during the following Years; reduced to English Weights and Measures.

| YEARS | QUANTITIES IMPORTED. | DUTIES LEVIED. |
|---|---|---|
|  | *Lbs.* | £.St$^s$. |
| 1825 - - | 1,065,439 | 39,202 |
| 1826 - - | 1,387,856 | 46,278 |
| 1827 - - | 1,035,012 | 38,595 |
| 1828 - - | 825,360 | 29,479 |
| 1829 - - | 1,693,353 | 54,286 |
| 1830 - - | 1,142,633 | 40,511 |
| TOTAL - - | *Lbs.* 7,149,652 | £. 248,351 St$^s$ |
| AVERAGE - | *Lbs.* 1,191,609 | £. 41,392 St$^g$ |

I have also a document showing the ports of exportation of raw silk to England for a certain number of years; Calais has become the principal port, and Marseilles secondary.

[*The same was delivered in, and read.*]

### FRENCH SILK TRADE.

| PORTS of EXPORTATION. | QUANTITIES OF RAW SILKS Exported from France for England, during the Years | | |
|---|---|---|---|
|  | 1828. | 1829. | 1830. |
|  | *Kil.* | *Kil.* | *Kil.* |
| Calais - - - | 751,947 | 375,772 | 570,171 |
| Havre - - - | 488 | — |  |
| Marseilles - - | 20,175 | 11,961 | 39,326 |
| TOTAL - - - | 772,610 | 387,733 | 609,497 |

All the above are Foreign Silks, and principally Italian, the export of French Silks being prohibited.

8737. You have stated what the import and consumption of foreign raw and thrown silk imported in France is, have you any means of ascertaining what the extent of consumption of French silk is?—As far as I could state from a good deal of correspondence and communication, the general estimate in the silk manufacturing district is, that the proportion is about three to one, which is the most current opinion of manufacturers; and I apprehend that that fact will be found very correct from two other data which I have; the report of the amount of the manufacture of France is, according to the best document, estimated at this moment about 140 millions of francs, of which 110 millions are exported, and 30 millions consumed in France, and the general calculation is, that 80 millions of that amount is in raw material; now if 20 francs per lb. be taken as the average of the value of that material, we shall find four millions of pounds as a result; and having ascertained that the importation is about one million, which all the documents prove, there remain three millions for the produce of France; as to that fact also, as it is a very interesting one, I have come to the same result from this estimate; there are in Lyons 30,000 looms, in the St. Etienne district 20,000, at Nismes 8,000, at Avignon 6,000, in other parts of France 6,000, making 70,000 looms in the country; the estimate of annual production is about 60 lbs. per loom, which also comes to the amount of 4,200,000 lbs.;

678.                                                                                  these

*John Bowring,*
Esq. LL. D.

14 June,
1832.

these facts go to show, that the amount consumed in France is about four millions of lbs., and the amount of French production three millions.

8738. Had you an opportunity of obtaining those communications from persons possessed of sufficient knowledge to be able to give full information upon the subject?—Yes; the almost universal impression at Lyons, and the neighbourhood, amongst intelligent persons is, that that is about the mark; they state that three parts of the silk they use is French, and one part foreign.

8739. Consequently the value of the 60,000,000 were the home produce?—Yes.

8740. What were the observations you were enabled to make on the quality of the French silk?—There can be no doubt there are certain districts which produce silk superior to any other silk produced in the known world; I have brought home for the Committee, some samples of that which may be considered the peculiar silk of France.

[*The Witness produced several samples of silk.*]

These are samples of the silk of the department of Cevennes, which are the most remarkable; there are three qualities there, they were bought in the open market; I will put in a document showing their cost.

### FRENCH SILK TRADE.

COST of Silk of which Samples accompany.

No. 1.

Ganges, 6/7 cocoons, white, being about 16 to 18 deniers:

| | | |
|---|---|---|
| 58 *f.* per kilog. say 100 kilog. - - 5,800 *f.* at 25 *f.* per £. sterling - | £.232 | - - |
| Deduct 12½ per cent. discount, at 3 months - - | 29 | - - |
| | £.203 | - - |

or 18/5 per lb. English avoirdupois.

No. 2.

S<sup>t</sup> Jean, 3/4 cocoons, yellow, say about 9 to 10 deniers:

| | | |
|---|---|---|
| 60 *f.* per kilog. say 100 kilog. - - 6,000 *f.* at 25 *f.* per £. sterling - | £.240 | - - |
| Deduct 12½ per cent. discount, at 3 months - - | 30 | - - |
| | £.210 | - - |

or 19/1 per English lb.

No. 3.

S<sup>t</sup> Jean, 5/6 cocoons, yellow = 14 to 15 deniers:

    at 58 *f.* per kilog. = as No. 1, gives 18/5 per lb. English.

These were the prices of 17th May 1832, at Lyons.

---

8741. You stated that 60 lbs. is the consumption in each loom, do you mean the consumption of silk, or do you mean the weight of the goods when manufactured?—The consumption of raw silk; the English estimate is considerably beyond that; but there are large districts in France, where the labour is not constant. Of this silk, which may be called the peculiar production of France, the quantity which the Cevennes give, is about 400,000 lbs. per annum; and those articles being purchased in the open market on the 17th of May, the price there came out at 18 *s.* 5 *d.*, 19 *s.* 1 *d.*, and 18 *s.* 5 *d.*; there is also an exceedingly small quantity of silk produced there, which sells as high as 100 francs per kilogram, or 2 *l.* sterling a pound. Some years ago, a peculiar worm was introduced into France, which they call the Sena worm; its produce is principally applied to the manufacture of blonde.

8742. Is the whole of the silk produced in Cevennes of fine quality?—The greater part of the Cevennes silk is of fine quality.

8743. What is the quantity of silk of this superior quality?—Four hundred thousand pounds is the present annual production of that which may be called the silk peculiarly French.

8744. Can you state the value of that silk, as compared with other silk imported?—It has universally the preference; the best way to show the superiority of this, will be to put in a price current, in which the particular qualities are quoted; this is the price current of the 26th of March last.

[*The same was delivered in, and read.*]

COURS

*John Bowring,*
Esq. LL. D.

14 June,
1832.

COURS des Soyes à Lyon, le 26 Mars 1832.

### Trames de France :

|        |   | f. | c. | f. | c. |
|--------|---|----|----|----|----|
| 24/26  | - - | 30 | - à | 30 | 50 |
| 26/28  | - - | 29 | -  | 29 | 50 |
| 28/32  | - - | 27 | 50 | 28 | 50 |
| 32/36  | - - | 26 | 50 | 27 | -  |
| 36/40  | - - | 26 | -  | 26 | 50 |
| 40/50  | - - | 25 | 50 | 26 | -  |
| 50/60  | - - | 25 | -  | 25 | 50 |
| 60/80  | - - | 24 | -  | 25 | -  |
| 80/100 | - - | 23 | -  | 24 | -  |

### Organsins de France :

|        |   | f. | c. | f. | c. |
|--------|---|----|----|----|----|
| 20/22  | - - | 33 | - à | 34 | -  |
| 22/24  | - - | 32 | -  | 33 | -  |
| 24/26  | -   | 31 | 50 | 32 | 50 |
| 26/28  | - - | 31 | -  | 32 | -  |
| 28/30 } 30/32 } | - - | 30 | -  | 31 | 50 |

### Grèges de France :

|              |   | f. | c. | f. | c. |
|--------------|---|----|----|----|----|
| Vivarais {3/4 cocons | | 26 | - à | 27 | - |
| ou {4/9 " | - | 25 | -  | 26 | - |
| Baguots. {5/6 " | - | 24 | -- | 25 | - |
| Provence ou {6/7 " | - | 24 | 50 | 25 | - |
| equivalente {7/8 " | - | 24 | -  | 24 | 50 |
| 8/10 " | - | 23 | 50 | 24 | - |
| 10/12 " | - | 22 | 50 | 23 | 50 |

### Organsins de Milan.

|        |   | f. | c. | f. | c. |
|--------|---|----|----|----|----|
| 18/22  | - - | 32 | 50 à | 33 | -  |
| 20/24  | - - | 32 | -  | 32 | 50 |
| 22/26  | - - | 31 | -  | 31 | 50 |
| 24/28  | - - | 30 | -  | 30 | 50 |
| 26/30  | - - | 29 | -  | 29 | 50 |
| 28/32  | - - | 28 | -  | 28 | 50 |
| 32/36  | - - | 27 | 50 | 28 | -  |
| 36/40  | - - | 26 | -  | 27 | -  |

### Trames de Milan et Lombardie :

|        |   | f. | c. | f. | c. |
|--------|---|----|----|----|----|
| 24/26  | - - | 29 | 50 |    |    |
| 26 28  | - - | 25 | -  |    |    |
| 28/32  | - - | 28 | - à | 28 | 50 |
| 32/36  | - - | 27 | -  | 27 | 50 |
| 36/40  | - - | 26 | -  | 26 | 50 |
| 40/50  | - - | 25 | -  | 25 | 50 |
| 40/60  | - - | 24 | -  | 24 | 50 |
| 60/80  | - - | 23 | -  | 23 | 50 |
| 80/100 | - - | 22 | 50 | 23 | -  |

### Grèges de France :

Soie des Cevennes, ou de quelques filatures d'ordres equivalentes.

|        |   | f. | c. | f. | c. |
|--------|---|----|----|----|----|
| 3/4    | - - - | 29 | - à | 30 | - |
| 4/5    | - - - | 28 | -  | 28 | 50 |
| 5/6    | - - - | 27 | -  | 27 | 50 |
| 6/7 } 7/8 } | - - - | 26 | -  | 26 | 50 |
| 8/10   | - - | point. | | | |
| 10/12  | - - | point. | | | |

### Organsins de Pièmont :

|        |   | f. | c. | f. | c. |
|--------|---|----|----|----|----|
| 21/22  | - - | point. | | | |
| 22/23  | - - | 32 | 50 à | 33 | -  |
| 23/24  | - - | 32 | -  | 32 | 50 |
| 24/25  | - - | 31 | 50 | 32 | -  |
| 25/26  | - - | 31 | -  | 31 | 50 |
| 26/27  | - - | 30 | 50 | 31 | -  |
| 27/28  | - - | 30 | -  | 30 | 50 |
| 28/30  | - - | 29 | -  | 29 | 50 |
| 30/32  | - - | 28 | 50 | 29 | -  |
| 32/36  | - - | 28 | -  | 28 | 50 |
| 36/40  | - - | 27 | 50 | 28 | -  |
| 40/49  | - - | 26 | 50 | 27 | -  |

### Grèges d'Italie.

|        |        |   | f. | c. | f. | c. |
|--------|--------|---|----|----|----|----|
| Milan  | { 3/4  | - - - | 26 | - à | 26 | 50 |
|        | { 4/5  | - - - | 25 | -  | 25 | 50 |
|        | { 5/6  | - - - | 24 | 50 | 25 | -  |
| Friout, Vicence, &c. | { 6/7 | - - - | 23 | 50 | 24 | - |
|        | { 7/8  | - - - | 23 | -  | 23 | 50 |
|        | { 8/10 | - - - | 22 | -  | 22 | 50 |
|        | { 10/12 | - - - | 21 | -  | 22 | -  |

### Grèges Royales de Naples :

|        |   | f. | c. | f. | c. |
|--------|---|----|----|----|----|
| 3/4    | - - - | point. | | | |
| 4/5    | - - - | 25 | -  | 26 | - |
| 5/7    | - - - | 24 | -  | 25 | - |

N. B.—Les prix de Lyon s'entendent ; la livre marc et conditionné à l'instar de Turin, sous escompte de 12½ % c'est-à-dire, de ⅛ du prix, terme 40 jours.

100 kilogrammes font lbs. 204¼ marc.

N. B.—La quantité de soies étrangères consommées dans nos fabriques varie considerablement d'année à année, puisqu'elle est subordonnée au prix plus ou moins élevé de ces soies comparativement aux nôtres ; c'est à Paris, et non ici, que l'on peut avoir le relevé exact d'entrée des soies en France ; l'administration générale des Douanes à Paris ne fait rien publier à cet égard, mais elle a necessairement le relevé des entrées des grèges et ouvrées, soit par mer, soit par terre. Le ministère a peut-être des données sur la quantité de production des soies en France, mais je ne vois personne ici qui puisse me la fournir.

---

8745. Had you any means of ascertaining whether the production of French silk is upon the increase or decrease?—It is very remarkably on the increase ; and I will say, that of all employments of capital at this moment in that country, no one is giving so great a return as the production of the mulberry tree. I have had occasion to examine many plantations, and also some books ; and I believe

678.

*John Bowring,*
Esc. LL. D.

14 June,
1832.

I believe the cultivation of silk is giving at this moment from 15 to 25 per cent. to the intelligent agriculturist. Perhaps the Committee will be interested in hearing a short statement I have made out, of the manner in which the silk reaches its reeled state. The price of eggs in France is, at this moment, two francs and a half per ounce ; one ounce of eggs will consume 1,500 weight of mulberry leaves, of which the general average cost is about three francs per hundred weight in a good year ; an ounce of the eggs will produce one hundred weight of cocoons, and the price of the cocoon is about one franc and a quarter per lb., that is, 125 francs for 100 lbs. ; the average I should judge is, that this 100 lbs. will give about 8 lbs. of silk, of which 18 francs may be considered the medium price. The average rate of winding by the women, employed in reeling off the cocoons, is about 25 lbs. of cocoons per day, or on the average two pounds of silk : the wages for winding is from 30 to 40 sous ; that is from 15 to 20 d. per day ; of the coarser silks, 100 lbs. will give a tenth, the general average, taking the whole of the silk district. I estimate that the mulberry tree will give one hundred weight of leaves, though there are trees which have been known to produce nearly 30 cwt. ; the cost of cultivation is estimated at a franc a hundred weight ; so that it is perfectly obvious they reap a very large profit ; the leaves are generally sold to the peasants, who " educate," as it is called, the worms. Some among them purchase the eggs, and cultivate themselves the mulberry tree for the food of the worm ; the cost of the mulberry tree is from 60 centimes to a franc, they are planted out at four years old : the peasantry will generally contract to plant them out at 80 centimes a tree ; at five years, they begin to produce for stripping ; they are cultivated now in ten or twelve departments of France ; they go on increasing in quantity for about 20 years. The increase of production of silk in France is extraordinary ; the mulberry tree interferes very little with other agricultural produce ; it is only of late years that the cultivation of the mulberry tree has been a subject of primary attention ; nobody had devoted himself to it as the principal means of profit, but solely as a secondary means ; but of late there has been a great change, and a great deal of capital is employed in the cultivation of the mulberry tree, with a view to the production of silk ; I have no doubt that the production of silk will become an object of constantly increasing attention ; the subject is becoming better and better understood.

8746. Do you speak of 18 francs as the average price of a pound of silk of native growth ?—Yes ; I make that statement on the authority of one of the principal growers ; I should scarcely consider myself justified in asserting, as my own opinion, that the estimate is precisely correct ; it is, however, that of a large proprietor in the neighbourhood of Nismes ; he may have referred to his own district ; the great difficulty is, to get at the correct statistical facts connected with production. In the Cevennes district, the cost would be very considerably higher.

8747. He gave you that as the net price, without discount, probably ?—Yes, most likely.

8748. Have you any objection to state the name of that person ?—M. Maigre.

8749. What do you consider as the tendency of the prices of raw silk in France ? —Most undoubtedly to decline ; the price of the silk which is obtained from the Cevennes, which is the most interesting district, and whose silks represent the most advanced state of cultivation, has been constantly tending downwards. I have here the price of cocoons and the price of raw silk from 1822 : I should remark, that the weights are very various in the silk districts by which silks are sold, and errors become inevitable, unless the local facts are known ; the pound by which this silk is sold, is a pound of which 242 make a hundred kilogrammes ; there is a difference of 21 per cent. in weight. In 1822, the price of cocoons, immediately after the harvest, was 1 $f$. 70 $c$. per Alais pound, and the raw silk, the Alais pound, was 31 $f$. In 1831, the price of cocoons was 1 $f$. 35 $c$., and the price of the Alais pound of silk, 21 $f$. 50 $c$. ; so that in 1822, the price of this silk was nearly 50 per cent. beyond the price in 1831. This document, which I have made official, by obtaining the sanction of the President of the Chamber of Commerce of Lyons to it, states, that in the Cevennes, 13 lbs. of cocoons will give 1 lb. of silk, wound at from four to five cocoons a thread, and the estimate of the expense of winding is about 3 $f$. 50 $c$. ; the silk is invariably sold by the Alais pound, which is the Languedocian, of former times.

[*The same was delivered in, and read.*]

FRENCH

*John Bowring*
Esq. LL. D.

14 June,
1832.

### FRENCH SILK TRADE.

PRICE of Cocoons and Raw Silk of Cevennes, at the period of the Harvest during the last Ten Years.

| YEARS | PRICE OF COCOONS, the Alais Pound. | | PRICE OF RAW SILK, the Alais Pound. | |
|---|---|---|---|---|
| | *f.* | *c.* | *f.* | *c.* |
| 1822 - - | 1 | 70 | 31 | — |
| 1823 - - | 1 | 50 | 22 | 25 |
| 1824 - - | 1 | 40 | 23 | — |
| 1825 - - | 1 | 70 | 28 | — |
| 1826 - - | 1 | 70 | 25 | — |
| 1827 - - | 1 | 50 | 23 | — |
| 1828 - - | 1 | 50 | 23 | 25 |
| 1829 - - | 1 | 45 | 23 | — |
| 1830 - - | 1 | 40 | 22 | 50 |
| 1831 - - | 1 | 35 | 21 | 50 |

The general estimate of the Cevennes silk is, that 13 lbs. of cocoons will give 1 lb. of silk, wound at from four to five cocoons a thread; and the estimate of the expense of winding is about 3 *f.* 50 *c.*

The Alais pound, universally employed in the Cevenne, is the old Languedocian weight, of which 242 lbs. make 100 kilogrammes.

8750. Are there any peculiar means for ascertaining the fineness of silk in France?—Yes; the means by which the fineness of silk is ascertained is by winding off the quantity of 400 ells, that is equal to 475 metres; they are wound off on a cylinder, which is an ell in circumference, the weight is expressed by grammes, 24 grammes are equal to one denier, 24 deniers an ounce, and 15 ounces make a pound, poids de marc, which is the Lyons mode of selling silk; the weight of which is somewhat less than the ordinary pound, or half kilogram; the weight of one thread of 400 ells is about two grammes and a quarter, at five threads, if reeled together, two of those so reeled be employed for the thread, it will give 21 grammes, which are called deniers, inasmuch as the operation takes place on only the twenty-fourth part; if 400 ells give 21 grammes, 9,600 will give 21 deniers; the calculation being made on 80 threads of 120 ells. I will state here, with reference to these weights, that the kilogram is 500 grammes; the pound weight used in the Lyons market is 492 grammes, and that the English avoirdupoise pound is 454 grammes.

8751. Are there any particular measures taken in France either by common consent or by the Government for the purpose of ascertaining the quality of silk previous to its being sold?—Yes; the Committee are perhaps aware that silk, when exposed to damp, imbibes a very considerable quantity of humidity, that its weight very much depends upon the atmosphere in which it is allowed to remain; the estimate in France is, that silk will imbibe in certain cases without any apparent change of quality, about 12 per cent. Before sales are effected in France, the silk is submitted to the temperature of from 18 to 22 degrees of Reamur. If during four-and-twenty-hours it lose two pounds and a half per cent. at Lyons and three pounds at Saint Etienne, it is again submitted to the temperature for another four-and-twenty hours, until its loss of weight is less than two pounds and a half per cent. per day; it is on the certificate of weight that this establishment (which is called, La Condition) gives, after exposure to this heated atmosphere, that the invoices are made out; I am not aware that any such experiments take place in this country; but in France they are the object of extreme attention; a committee is at present sitting and has been long sitting, to ascertain what measures can be taken to prevent frauds in the sale.

8752. Great importance is attached to that by way of giving security to the buyer?—Yes; except when the demand for raw silk is exceedingly active, all silk is bought with reference to the returns the Condition furnishes.

678.                                                                 8753. You

*John Bowring,*
Esq. LL. D.

14 June,
1832.

8753. You state to the Committee, that there is a prohibition of the export of raw silk in France?—Undoubtedly.

8754. Have you the means of ascertaining the state of public feeling with reference to that?—It is a question which has been agitated in most of their southern Chambers of Commerce, and certainly very violent opposition to the exportation of French silk has been elicited; and it has been very strongly represented to Government that their silk is of a peculiar quality, and that considerable injury might be done to the fabrics of France by consenting to its exportation; the growers of silk, however, have so decided an interest in its exportation, and generally speaking, the friendly feeling towards this country has so much increased, that I have reason to know it is the purpose of the French Government to consent to its exportation.

8755. What do you consider to be the state of the French silk manufacture?—I think the position that production has acquired, has grown mainly out of this circumstance, that it is of all the manufacturing interests of France, the least protected; that in consequence, by natural development, it has obtained for itself a very large foreign demand, it being an article in which that quality in which the French are so remarkably distinguished—taste, forms a very considerable portion in the cost of production; and that inasmuch as they have been constantly acted upon by foreign improvements, as foreign silks are admitted at a moderate duty, they have been enabled to maintain their position, and have undoubtedly a great superiority over their rivals in all matters where, as I said, taste is a considerable component part in the expense of production.

8756. Do you consider that the feeling in favour of French goods is on account of their superior quality, or that it is justified only by some prejudice?—I think the opinion of the superiority of French silk goods, where taste is a part, is no more a prejudice than a feeling in favour of the works of Raphael is a prejudice, and I can speak from the very large experience I have derived in almost every great market of Europe; it is in fact the common testimony to real superiority; as far as my experience goes, wherever a prejudice exists, it exists towards England, for the universal feeling is, that the manufacturing superiority of England is so great that the English manufacture has all the advantage of a strong prepossession in favour of its being much superior to and much cheaper than any other.

8757. You speak of these articles of manufacture of the finer descriptions, into which taste most enters?—Therein consists the great superiority of the French trade; as respects their means of manufacture, as respects the raw produce, as respects machinery, I believe they are in many particulars worse off than their competitors; but wherever taste is an element, there they have a decided advantage; I think no gentleman can have ever travelled in France without perceiving how much of taste is shown in the mere arrangement of a bed or the commonest clothing of the people; taste descends down to the lowest classes of the community, and there is a remarkable contrast between them and those of similar rank in this country in this particular; taste is in fact cheap in France, and is dear in England.

8758. By taste, you mean the taste in the selection of colours as well as in the designs?—Certainly; I take their taste to be that which produces beauty from both the arrangement of form and the disposition of colours. I conceive it to be that which the artist may be said to create, independent of the canvas on which he is working; the canvas will be equal in France and in England, but when wrought upon, it is the mind of the tasteful artist that produces the attractive result; so much of the question turns upon the creation of this taste, that I have made it a particular object of my inquiries to study its birth and follow its history.

8759. You state that the silk trade has less protection in France than almost any other trade; can you not state to what extent it is protected?—I have examined a great many invoices of foreign silks, in which the amount of protection was from 15 to 17 per cent. on the manufactured article; the amount of duty which the tariff gives is 17*f*. 60 *c*. per kilogram; it varies from 14 to 18 per cent. taking in all the silk articles which France imports.

8760. Have you any statement of the import of manufactured silks into France? —Yes, I have a statement which I will beg to give in upon that subject.

[*The same was delivered in, and read.*]

IMPORTATIONS

IMPORTATIONS into France of Manufactured Silks.

*John Bowring,*
*Esq.* LL. D.

14 June,
1832

| COUNTRIES Whence Imported. | QUANTITIES AND VALUE IMPORTED. | | | | | |
| --- | --- | --- | --- | --- | --- | --- |
| | 1828: | | 1829: | | 1830: | |
| | *Kil.* | *f.* | *Kil.* | *f.* | *Kil.* | |
| England - - - | 1,087 | 119,570 | 3,507 | 385,770 | 5,852 | 643,720 |
| Prussia - - - | 4,593 | 505,230 | 3,439 | 378,290 | 4,268 | 469,480 |
| Other Countries - | 596 | 65,560 | 329 | 36,190 | 234 | 25,740 |
| Totals - - | 6,276 | 690,360 | 7,275 | 800,250 | 10,354 | 1,138,940 |

From this it will appear that the importation of English silks into France has increased six fold; and I can state from an examination of different parties that that importation is going on increasing considerably.

8761. Do you know what is the description of silks imported into France?—The principal description from England is bandanna handkerchiefs.

8762. Is there any distinction between bandannas which may be the production of Asia, printed in this country, and imported, and British manufactures?—The importation of bandannas from Asia is prohibited in France from whatever country.

8763. Should you conceive that the importation of foreign silks, which according to your account goes on to a considerable extent in France, has been prejudicial to the French silk manufacturers, or the reverse?—On the contrary; there was very naturally a strong feeling in France against this measure; but I have obtained many facts which show that the importation of foreign silks is one of the primary sources of the prosperity of the French silk manufacture; one of the leading men of Lyons mentioned to me, that the result of the introduction of a number of foreign crapes into France, which were sold at a very low rate, was, that the low price carried them into very general consumption, in consequence of which the manufacture of crapes was taken up by the Lyonese manufacturers, and it has become now one of their most important productions.

8764. How did you obtain the amount of importations of British silk goods into France?—That is a Custom House document, and entitled to all respect as an official paper. We have had the best evidence of the authenticity of these statements, as on several occasions we have ourselves (the commissioners) examined the original books and found them always in accordance with the statements made. We did this sometimes for the purpose of avoiding the annoyance which the copying facts in detail would have caused, and we have had such evidence of their veracity as has been perfectly satisfactory to us; the readiness with which documents of so much importance have been given, documents which have been prepared solely at our request is in itself a great proof of the good faith shown by the French Government throughout in these matters.

8765. Is not the importation of British silks into France prohibited?—Certainly not; there is no prohibition in France of British silk manufacture; the silk manufacture is an exception to the general rule in France; it stands quite alone; and I will venture to state, in the broadest terms, that it is the only manufacture in France at this moment which is not in considerable distress, a distress whose hopelessness is far beyond anything we know of in this country. The silk is the only manufacture which has the benefit of competition with the foreigner.

8766. Have you any other facts to state, showing the advantage which has arisen in France, from the introduction of foreign silks?—A great portion of the silk trade in France is owing to foreigners; the great improvements which have been introduced have been almost all in consequence of discoveries which have been made in other countries; there has been the greatest conceivable opposition in France as elsewhere to all innovations; the bar loom, when it was introduced some years ago for the manufacture of ribbons, would have remained excluded but for the pressure of Swiss competition upon the French manufacturers.

8767. Do you know the history of the Jacquard loom?—The introduction and history of the Jacquard mechanism is certainly one of the most interesting and one of the most instructive facts connected with the silk manufacture. I was extremely desirous, having seen the beauty of the machine and the simplicity of its operation,

678.                                                                                     of

*John Bowring,*
Esq. LL. D.
——
14 June,
1832.

of some conversation with its inventor, and, accompanied by a number of gentle-men, I went to visit Jacquard, and was very much gratified on hearing from him a history of its invention, which is now generally recognized as one of extreme importance and value.    He told me he was originally a straw hat manufacturer; his attention had never been turned to mechanical topics till the Peace of Amiens opened the communication of France with England ; at that time an extract from an English newspaper fell into his hands, in which it was stated that a society here offered a premium to any man who should weave a net by machinery.    He told me that his thoughts were thus turned upon this subject, which, by the way, if there had been any interruption to intercourse would never have taken place : he did produce a net, which he threw aside for some time, and afterwards gave it to a friend as a thing of mere indifference.    The net by some means or other got into the hands of the authorities, and was sent to Paris.    When some time had passed. and Jacquard had completely forgotten his production, he was sent for by the Prefect, who said, " You have directed your attention to the making of nets by machinery,"    He did not immediately recollect it, but the net was produced to him, and that called it to his mind.    The Prefect said, " I require you to make the machine which led to this result:" he asked three weeks for its completion, and brought it to the Prefect, and desired him to strike with his foot, by which a knot was added to the net.    It was sent to Paris, and an order came for his arrest.    It was in Buonaparte's time, when things were done in a very rash and arbitrary way.    He found himself under the keeping of a gend'arme, and was not allowed even to go home to provide himself with the necessaries for his journey. He was required at Paris, in the Conservatory of Arts, to produce the machine in the presence of inspectors, which he did.    He was introduced to Buonaparte and to Carnot, who said to him, with a menace of incredulity, " Are you the man who pretend to do that which God Almighty cannot do, to tie a knot in a stretched string ?"    He produced the machine, and showed its operation.    This was Jacquard's first mechanical experiment.    He was afterwards called in to examine a loom on which 20 or 30 thousand francs had been expended, for the production of articles for the use of Buonaparte.    He offered to do that by a simple machine which they were attempting to do by a very complicated one, and, improving on a model of Vaucauson, he produced the mechanism which bears his name.    He returned to his native town, a pension of 1,000 crowns having been granted to him ; but so violent was the opposition made to the introduction of his machine, that he had three times the greatest difficulty in escaping with his life.    The Conseil des Prud-hommes, who are the conservators, ex officio, of the interests of the Lyonnese trade, broke up his machine in the public place; the iron (to use his own expression) was sold for iron, and the wood for wood, and he, its inventor, was delivered over to uni-versal ignominy.    It was only when the French were beginning to feel the effect of foreign competition that they were forced to employ this machine, which led to such great improvement in their manufacture, and, as every body knows, it is now extensively employed through the whole of the manufacturing districts of France.

8768. The bar loom, introduced subsequently to that, met with some difficulty also, did it not ?—Yes; that was a Swiss invention, and it was taken into the neighbourhood of St. Etienne by two brothers, who were themselves persecuted and abandoned to extreme misery ; the last of them died not long ago in a hos-pital, in consequence of the obloquy and neglect to which he was subjected. Since then the use of the bar loom has become nearly universal in the immediate neighbourhood of St. Etienne.

8769. You stated that the French manufacture of silk enjoys some peculiar advantages, does it also labour under any disadvantages ?—The disavantages under which it labours are very many ; I stated before, that there is a quantity of local taxation ; and I would also state, that at this very moment, some of the old regulations introduced by Colbert, are in operation, and I am quite sure must have a very considerable effect in increasing the price of production ; the general arrangement by which silk goods are manufactured is this ; the manufacturer who receives an order, sends to the man who is called a master, or a chef d'atelier ; he may be called a little loom proprietor ; he employs a man whom he calls a companion ; the wife of the chef d'atelier cooks the food of the companion ; and for the use of the loom, and for the services done in the house, takes half the wages, so that in fact it is said, and it is said with considerable truth, as compared with the state of things in Switzerland, that though the actual labouring weaver gets very small wages, in fact, he gets only half the price of the tarif, the manu-facturer

facturer pays a high rate, for he invariably pays double that which the weaver himself receives; that organization grew out of Colbert's regulations, which were very well intended in the infancy of the trade, but are now highly injurious; had the manufactures of Lyons not been encumbered by them, I have no doubt they would have been much more improved.

*John Bowring,*
Esq. LL. D.

14 June,
1832.

8770. Is not the silk manufacture under great disadvantage in the construction of the machinery in France?—Yes; there again the protective system interferes with the improvement of machinery; machinery pays a duty of from fifteen to thirty-three per cent. on its introduction into France, and the object of this is to protect the French machine maker, who has the same right to protection, inasmuch as he is obliged to pay 150 per cent. more for his iron, and much more for his wood, because the wood grower, and the iron master, are to be protected in their turn.

8771. You stated that trade is also under a disadvantage from local taxation, will you state the nature of that taxation?—Independently of the Government taxes, the towns of France are subject to taxes which are very oppressive, and fall very peculiarly on the labouring poor; taxes on food, and taxes on drink, and taxes on fuel, are imposed on their introduction into the towns, from which the inhabitants of villages, and the inhabitants of cottages on the mountains, are wholly exempt; one of the consequences is, that at this very moment, the trade both at St. Etienne and at Lyons is going into the mountains, for it cannot support the pressure of these local demands.

8772. Have you had any opportunity of ascertaining what is the opinion of well informed and sensible persons, in regard to the effect likely to be produced upon the future condition of the silk trade in France, by those changes of which you have spoken?—The feeling is so strong, that the Chambers of Commerce in the South have been making strong remonstrances to the Government as to the prejudice they are suffering from the present prohibitory system, and asking for relief from the prohibitory laws, which press upon their industry.

8773. Do they anticipate a competition from the manufacture of other countries, which will be fatal to them?—Yes; and many of the intelligent manufacturers at Lyons are under some alarm at the progress the silk manufacture in England is making; one of the highest authorities of the town told me, that if he had had to consult the interests of France, he would most rigidly prohibit the exportation of silk goods to England, such had been the progress made by the English manufacturer since 1825; I have heard that progress again and again the subject of discussion in Lyons; I have seen the articles exhibited by the manufacturers there, and have heard them express the greatest admiration at the advances made; I have had letters from numbers of them, some of them were in England not long ago, and they speak with astonishment of the great improvement they had witnessed here; I know from personal experience, that in old times, the contempt with which the silk manufactures of England were spoken of was boundless, and that the feeling towards it now is altogether changed, and that they are under great apprehension from English competition.

8774. Do you happen to know whether those apprehensions are well founded?—I believe they are.

8775. Do you mean to say that great improvements in the silk trade have taken place since 1825?—My opinion is, that since 1825 great improvements in the trade must have taken place.

8776. What means have you of stating that, not being a manufacturer?—I have said that the manufacturers of Lyons have stated that to be the effect upon their minds; and I have seen the articles produced then and now, and I apprehend and hope the fact cannot be denied.

8777. It has been stated generally by the manufacturers here, that no great improvements have taken place since 1825; do you happen to know that that is the fact, or not the fact?—I should say, if that be the fact I am very sorry for it; for in France very great improvements have taken place since 1825, and their belief is that very considerable improvements have taken place here. The best evidence of the true state of things is, that great quantities of manufactured silk have been lately exported from England, while formerly the export was trifling indeed.

8778. Does not it appear from our entries in the Custom House, that very few goods have been exported for France?—I have presented a document furnished to me by the Minister of Finance, which shows the amount of importation of silk manufacture into France. That document was obtained before this Committee was appointed, and obtained not with a view to be delivered here as evidence, but to

678. enable

*John Bowring,*
Esq. LL. D.

14 June,
1832.

enable us to ascertain the relative position of the English and French silk manufacture, when discussing our commercial relations generally.

8779. It has been stated to this Committee that very few exportations have taken place of silk goods from this country, and those of coarser goods, in consequence of the allowance of the debenture, and that there is no chance of our carrying on the trade but in the coarser articles and those mixed with cotton; do you know whether that is the fact?—I do not believe that it is the fact; for I find, that not only France, but other countries purchase largely of our silk goods. These purchases increase greatly, as the Custom House reports will show. I have put in a document, demonstrating that the exportation of English silk goods to France goes on at an accumulating rate.

8780. It has been stated by Mr. Hume, of the Custom House, that very few silks have been exported from this country, and those chiefly by reason of the allowance of the debenture and in the coarser silks; and that but for the debenture he apprehended there would be no exportation. In contradiction to that, how do you ascertain the facts you have referred to?—I have presented a document which has been furnished to me by the French Government; I am no further responsible for it than by stating that I have so received it. If they have furnished me with an erroneous statement the fault is with them not with myself; but I am bound to say I have had an opportunity of observing on many occasions the extreme sincerity of the French Government on this subject, and to that I must bear the most decided and undoubted testimony.

8781. You mean to say that your only knowledge is founded on the representation you had from the French Government?—I have made no such statement; I have made many inquiries of the manufacturers in the South, and they repeated again and again that the English manufacturer has made very great progress in the course of the last six years.

8782. You say that there has been a great export of English goods to France, and that they have expressed their astonishment at the improvement?—Yes.

8783. Do you mean to say that they are ribbons and fine fancy goods?—No, I do not believe that England can at all compete with France in ribbons and fine fancy goods. I stated, as a general principle, that where taste and beauty form a considerable part of the cost of production, there is no present and immediate chance of competition; and that it is precisely on account of their superiority that they are wanted here as a source of instruction and improvement.

8784. You say that the French people have found generally a great excellence in articles of our manufactories, and a great improvement in those articles in consequence of the introduction of their goods; are any ribbons and other fine fancy goods exported from this country to France?—A great many Frenchmen come here from the manufacturing districts; and it is not more easy to go from England to France, than to come from England to France.

8785. You are understood to have stated that it was the coarser and not the finer goods which were exported from England to France?—Undoubtedly.

8786. And the debenture operated most upon them?—I have not stated any thing as to the debenture; I have endeavoured to detail the facts which have come to my knowledge in France; I am responsible for my own opinions, but I cannot be answerable for the opinions of others.

8787. You have stated that one evidence of our improvement since the admission of French goods is, that a considerable quantity of our goods have been exported; do you know that otherwise than applying to goods of a low description?—I have again to state, that the export of English goods to France consists principally of low goods; I must repeat, in the strongest terms, my conviction that where competition is to be feared is precisely where taste forms a very considerable component part of the production; that the taste in France is by universal acknowledgement much more advanced than that of England.

8788. Do you mean to say that the preference which French goods would obtain over English depends upon their superiority and their excellence, and that prejudice is no part?—I have stated, that as far as prejudice goes, I think that prejudice through the world is in favour of England; and I may add that any one who denies to the French the superiority, is precisely like a man who says I am right, and all the world is wrong. If there is prejudice in England, no prejudice exists in Russia. I will put in a paper, showing the exports of France to all the countries in the world; it will be then seen whether the superiority of French goods,

such

such goods as have been spoken of, where taste forms a considerable portion, is a *John Bowring,* *Esq.* LL. D. mere foolish idle prejudice, or the concurring testimony of mankind.

8789. Have you any account that you can give in, of the exports of French manufactured silk to different countries?—I have here, in considerable detail, a Statement of the Exports of France, for the years 1828, 1829 and 1830; the Committee will be aware, that the quantities of matter which it has been necessary to examine, to get at these results, has been so great, that I could not easily get more than three years.

14 June, 1832.

8790. Will you state where you got this?—From the Custom House, under the direction of the Minister of Finance.

[*The same was delivered in, and read.*]

SILK MANUFACTURES Exported from FRANCE.

| DESTINATIONS. | AMOUNTS EXPORTED. | | | | |
|---|---|---|---|---|---|
| | 1828. | 1829. | 1830. | TOTAL. | AVERAGE. |
| United States - - - | 33,746,407 | 33,711,312 | 37,563,665 | 105,021,384 | 35,007,128 |
| Germany - - - | 18,285,633 | 19,374,808 | 18,309,636 | 55,970,077 | 18,656,692 |
| England - - - | 17,311,810 | 10,483,777 | 15,204,388 | 42,999,975 | 14,333,325 |
| Low Countries - - | 10,601,110 | 11,175,956 | 7,837,704 | 29,614,770 | 9,871,590 |
| Spain - - - | 6,184,268 | 7,253,207 | 4,673,174 | 18,110,649 | 6,036,883 |
| Sardinia - - - | 5,549,754 | 5,390,308 | 5,750,118 | 16,690,180 | 5,563,393 |
| Switzerland - - | 3,028,089 | 2,697,179 | 2,877,726 | 8,602,994 | 2,867,664 |
| Brazil - - - | 2,737,118 | 2,448,351 | 2,935,853 | 8,121,322 | 2,707,108 |
| Mexico - - - | 1,590,086 | 1,352,966 | 4,140,017 | 7,083,069 | 2,361,023 |
| Peru - - - | 2,967,410 | 2,524,882 | 824,350 | 6,316,642 | 2,105,547 |
| Other Countries - | 13,465,833 | 14,743,021 | 11,002,171 | 39,211,025 | 13,070,342 |
| TOTALS - - | 115,467,518 | 111,155,767 | 111,118,802 | 337,742,087 | 112,580,695 |

8791. What is the mode of valuation?—These are the official values; and I think they are not far remote from the real value; there may be a fluctuation of 10 per cent. above or 10 per cent. below, but they agree pretty well with the returns from the Chamber of Commerce; there is a classification of goods like that adopted here, for the classification of duty.

8792. Has that been established for some years, as ours has?—Yes; that is as it was modified a few years ago.

8793. Can you state the exports to England in 1826 and 1827?—In 1825, when the whole of the trade was a smuggling trade, it was six millions of francs; in 1826, it was seven millions and a half. I will call the attention of the Committee to a few facts connected with this Return, of the manufactured silks exported to England. In 1818, the manufactured silks exported to England, which were then wholly smuggled, amounted to 1,700,000 francs; it went on gradually increasing, till in 1825 it had reached 6,000,000 of francs. In 1826, the smuggling almost wholly ceased, the whole amount admitted was 7,500,000 francs. I estimate the amount for 1831 from 17 to 18 millions; this is also an official paper; it will be seen that the increase of smuggling up to 1826 was enormous; that it had advanced from a million and a half to six millions; that then, on the introduction of silk legally, it fell to almost nothing; that it again resumed its activity; and I think I shall be able to satisfy the Committee, that at this moment, the amount of smuggling is very nearly in amount what it was in 1825 before the prohibition.

[*The same was delivered in, and read:*]

**FRENCH SILK TRADE.**

**MANUFACTURED SILK exported to ENGLAND.**

| | Francs. | | | Francs. |
|---|---|---|---|---|
| 1818 - - - - - | 1,744,105 | 1825 - - - - | 6,104,103 |
| 1819 - - - - - | 2,713,583 | 1826 - - - - | 7,596,421 |
| 1820 - - - - - | 2,727,748 | 1827 - - - - | 11,460,119 |
| 1821 - - - - - | 2,815,178 | 1828 - - - - | 17,311,810 |
| 1822 - - - - - | 3,516,328 | 1829 - - - - | 10,483,777 |
| 1823 - - - - - | 2,901,670 | 1830 - - - - | 15,204,388 |
| 1824 - - - - - | 3,856,465 | | |

8794. Will

*John Bowring,*
Esq. LL. D.

14 June,
1832.

8794. Will you give the Committee information as to the state of trade in particular places, and the mode in which the trade has been carried on. The Committee understand that you have visited Lyons?—I have; I spent about five or six weeks in Lyons and the district.

8795. Do you know any thing of the early history of the Lyonese trade?—I looked a good deal into its early history; it owed, no doubt, a great deal to Colbert, whose regulations were perhaps beneficial in a moment of great ignorance; but they have been, in their consequences exceedingly fatal, having frequently subjected the silk trade at Lyons to great fluctuations and distress; there have been periods when that distress was almost unparalleled, flinging the whole labouring population into an abyss of suffering.

8796. There have been great fluctuations?—There have been; in the year 1700, there were a series of most oppressive regulations that drove the silk trade away from many of the towns in France, and acted most unfortunately on the foreign demand. In 1744 there were other regulations which prevented any persons, except Roman Catholics, engaging in it; and the extraordinary history of those fluctuations may be traced in the vicissitudes in the number of looms. In 1786, according to the best authenticated statement, there were 15,000 looms in Lyons. In 1789 they were reduced to half. In 1800 they were reduced to 3,500, the number of workmen was then only 5,800. In 1812 the number of looms was 10,720. In 1825 the number of looms was 20,101. I have had occasion also to consult a great number of curious documents connected with the town of Lyons, showing how the trade was struggling against the regulations under which it suffered.

8797. What is the number of looms now?—I do not wonder that the evidence given to this Committee should be very various; but the Prefect was so good as to direct a thorough examination upon the subject, and I am enabled to state precisely what it is from the account I will deliver in. I should observe this is the intra muros account, the account solely within the walls of the city; the surburban districts touch the town, the returns are as near as possible the same in number. The number of looms within the town is about 17,000, and the number of looms in the vicinity is also about 17,000, deducting the number which are out of employment; the number of looms that Lyons possesses at this moment is about 30,000. This is the document which was delivered to me by the Prefect.

*[The same was delivered in, and read:]*

### FRENCH SILK TRADE.

#### NUMBER of Looms in the Town of *Lyons.*

| | | | | | | | | | | | | |
|---|---|---|---|---|---|---|---|---|---|---|---|---|
| Plain | - | - | - | - | - | 10,855 | Ribbons | - | - | - | - | 473 |
| Jacquard | - | - | - | - | 2,911 | Not at work | - | - | - | - | 1,358 |
| Velvet | - | - | - | - | - | 711 | | TOTAL | - | - | - | 17,512 |
| Gauze and Crape | - | - | - | 359 | Deduct the looms not at work | - | - | 1,358 |
| Tulles | - | - | - | - | - | 614 | | Remains | - | - | - | 16,154 |

The looms are distributed among 7,000 workshops, in which the masters work 7,000, their children and apprentices 2,300, and the remaining 6,854 are worked by " compagnons."

The suburban Communes immediately adjacent to Lyons, which consist of La Guillotiere, Croix Rousse, Calaire and Vaize, are estimated to contain a number of looms about equal to those " intra muros."

---

8798. The Prefect, you state, had a survey made, and that that you give in is the result?—Yes, that is the case; this account was taken before the cholera had been ravaging Paris, and I have no doubt 3 or 4,000 more looms were thrown out of employ. I apprehend if 25,000 were taken now as the number of looms employed, that would be the full amount. Two circumstances have had a great effect on Lyons, the one the removal of the number of workmen in consequence of the disturbances in Lyons, and the stoppage of American demand has thrown out a great number, so that I should think that the quantity now employed is from 24 to 25,000.

8799. Have you any account of the imports and exports in the bonding warehouses in Lyons?—Yes; I have an account which contains a statement very much in detail of all the silk which is entered into bond there, all silk withdrawn from bond for home consumption, and the silk exported from the bonding warehouse at Lyons.

*[The same was delivered in, and read.]*

QUANTITIES

John Bowring,
Esq. LL. D.

14 June,
1832.

Custom House Account, Bonding Office.

QUANTITIES of SILKS imported from FOREIGN COUNTRIES, and which have entered the Bonding Warehouses of the Town of *Lyons*, up to 1st January 1832; showing also the Quantities entered for Home Consumption, and exported to other Countries.

| YEARS | ENTERED — SILK | | | | | FOR HOME CONSUMPTION — SILK | | | | | FOR EXPORTATION — SILK | | | | |
| | Silks. Raw. Douppions. | Others. | Thrown. Douppions. | Others. | Bourre, whether in mass or carded. | Silks. Raw. Douppions. | Others. | Thrown. Douppions. | Others. | Bourre, whether in mass or carded. | Silks. Raw. Douppions. | Others. | Thrown. Douppions. | Others. | Bourre, whether in mass or carded. |
|---|---|---|---|---|---|---|---|---|---|---|---|---|---|---|---|
| 1822 | 2,300 | 260,267 | 1,903 | 252,040 | 1,238 | 1,537 | 60,544 | 1,552 | 228,799 | - | 121 | 196,511 | - | 7,262 | 7,979 |
| 1823 | 2,084 | 272,144 | - | 241,251 | 4,793 | 665 | 47,157 | 419 | 215,244 | 1,988 | 482 | 223,930 | - | 10,169 | 2,332 |
| 1824 | 27,706 | 344,871 | 1,129 | 366,292 | 25,260 | 964 | 45,402 | 1,093 | 357,973 | 2,744 | 28,684 | 516,643 | - | 7,963 | 22,141 |
| 1825 | 15,489 | 403,493 | 1,014 | 430,911 | 42,676 | 236 | 41,743 | 814 | 329,951 | - | 15,581 | 352,998 | - | 97,555 | 42,577 |
| 1826 | 873 | 331,219 | 1,795 | 432,297 | 22,824 | 102 | 148,468 | 291 | 334,266 | 6,470 | 11 | 157,146 | - | 99,369 | 17,617 |
| 1827 | 1,142 | 531,596 | 577 | 548,689 | 48,415 | 1,326 | 37,119 | 687 | 334,965 | 1,593 | 796 | 525,165 | - | 219,713 | 46,813 |
| 1828 | 6,173 | 636,791 | 1,844 | 465,893 | 104,575 | 1,100 | 33,519 | 1,737 | 230,132 | 2,926 | 2,846 | 594,330 | - | 235,332 | 103,830 |
| 1829 | 3,293 | 575,224 | 988 | 469,273 | 51,360 | 3,262 | 212,176 | 988 | 367,831 | 341 | 165 | 322,688 | - | 89,209 | 50,160 |
| 1830 | 331 | 496,849 | 781 | 524,245 | 119,107 | 431 | 94,290 | 603 | 325,700 | 121 | - | 446,829 | - | 202,359 | 118,986 |
| 1831 | 811 | 444,556 | 211 | 598,583 | 133,468 | 208 | 39,836 | 315 | 292,686 | 181 | 603 | 396,424 | - | 293,326 | 133,287 |
| TOTAL | 60,202 | 4,297,010 | 10,242 | 4,329,474 | 553,716 | 9,832 | 760,254 | 8,499 | 3,017,527 | 16,364 | 49,289 | 3,732,664 | - | 1,262,257 | 545,722 |
| AVERAGE | 6,020 | 429,701 | 1,024 | 432,947 | 55,371 | 983 | 76,025 | 849 | 301,752 | 1,636 | 4,928 | 373,266 | - | 126,225 | 54,572 |

*John Bowring,*
Esq. LL. D.

14 June,
1832.

8800. Can this silk be resold for exportation?—Yes, it can be sold for exportation while in the bonding warehouse, but from the moment it is taken out of the bonding warehouse the hand of the buyer is tied, and he cannot export it, so that he suffers considerably from that restriction; and it is one of the causes of complaint, and a very natural one, if the silk is taken, as it is generally taken, and sent to the Condition in order to be examined, it must be used for the French manufacture; it becomes considered as French silk, and it is not allowed to be exported.

8801. Explain what La Condition is?—It is an establishment annexed to the Chamber of Commerce; it is intended to decide on the merchantable quality of silk, and to protect the buyer from the fraud of the seller, by ascertaining that no humidity or any thing extraneous to the quality of the silk is introduced; the silk is exposed in cases to the temperature of 18 to 22 degrees, which is a guarantee to the buyer; this Condition is also a source of a small revenue to the Chamber of Commerce; three francs per hundred kilogrammes are paid to the Chamber of Commerce; it is weighed on entering, it is weighed on exit, and the invoice is made out to the seller on the weight given by La Condition.

8802. Had you an opportunity of learning whether there have been great fluctuations in the Lyonese market for some years past?—I have obtained from authority the state of the Lyonese market since 1821, with reference to raw silks; and, in order that no difference of opinion might exist with respect to the quality, they have been so good as to furnish me with samples of French and Italian silks, arranged according to fineness by deniers, which, by comparison with the document, shows the comparative qualities of the organzines of Piedmont and Milan, and the trams both of France and Italy.

8803. Can you put in the present prices?—They are contained in this paper, and will show rather a curious fact, that though, upon the whole, the average price of French silk of the same quality is higher than Italian silk of the same quality, that is, with reference to its weight, there are cases in which the Italian is preferred; the general result, however, is a very considerable tendency downwards in price, and it is my opinion that the fall of silk is inevitable, in consequence of the great attention now paid in France to its cultivation.

[*The same was delivered in, and read.*]

#### FRENCH SILK TRADE.

STATEMENT of the Fluctuations in SILKS in the Market of *Lyons,*
from 1821 to the present time.

January 1821:

ORGANSINS.

| PIEDMONT. | | ITALY. | |
|---|---|---|---|
| | *f. c.* | | *f. c.* |
| 22/23 de<sup>rs</sup> - - 44 50 | | 22/23 - - - 39 50 | |
| 23/24 - - - 44 – | | 23/24 - - - 39 – | |
| 24/25 - - - 43 – | | 24/25 - - - 38 – | |
| 25/26 - - - 42 50 | | 25/26 - - - 37 50 | |
| 26/28 - - - 42 – | | 26/28 - - - 37 – | |
| 28/30 - - - 41 – | | 28/30 - - - 36 50 | |
| 30/32 - - - 40 50 | | 30/32 - - - 36 – | |
| 32/34 ⎫ | | 32/34 - - 35 – | |
| 34/36 ⎬ - 40 à 39 50 | | 34/36 - - 34 50 | |
| 36/40 ⎭ | | 36/40 - - 34 – | |

FRANCE.

| | |
|---|---|
| 22/24 | 30/32 |
| 24/25 | 32/34 |
| 25/26 | 34/36 |
| 26/28 | |
| 28/30 | |

January 1822:

TRAMS.

| FRANCE. | | ITALY. | |
|---|---|---|---|
| | *f. c.* | | *f. c.* |
| 26/28 - - - 34 – | | — - - - 33 75 | |
| 28/30 ⎫ | | — - - - 32 50 | |
| 30/32 ⎬ - - 33 – | | — - - - 32 25 | |
| 32/34 - - - 32 50 | | — - - - 31 50 | |
| 34/36 - - - 32 – | | — - - - 31 – | |
| 36/40 - - - 31 – | | — - - - 30 50 | |
| 40/50 - - - 30 50 | | — - - - 29 50 | |
| 50/60 - - - 29 50 | | — - - - 28 50 | |

*Note.*—THESE prices represent the lb. marc, and are reckoned subject to a discount of $12\frac{1}{2}$ per cent. The Italian Trams from 28/30 to 50/60 are less regular than those of France.

In 1821, there was a fluctuation of from 1 *f.* to 1 *f.* 50 *c.* per lb. At the close of the year they fell to the prices of the beginning, Italian organzines excepted, which remained from 75 *c.* to 1 *f.* above the January prices.

*John Bowring,*
Esq. LL. D.

14 June,
1832.

## January 1822:

### ORGANSINS.

| PIEDMONT. | f. c. | ITALY. | f. c. |
|---|---|---|---|
| 21/22 | - | | |
| 22/23 | - 42 50 | 22/23 | - - 40 50 |
| 23/24 | - 41 75 | 23/24 | - 40 - |
| 24/25 | - 41 - | 24/25 | - - 39 - |
| 25/26 | - 39 50 | 25/26 | - - 38 50 |
| 26/28 | - 38 50 | 26/28 | - 38 - |
| 28/30 | - 37 50 | 28/30 | - 37 - |
| 30/32 | - 36 50 | 30/32 | - 36 - |
| 32/34 } | | 32/34 | - 35 - |
| 34/36 } - 35 50 à 35 | | 34/36 | - - 34 - |
| 36/40 } | | 36/40 | - - 33 - |

#### FRANCE.

| | f. c. | | f. c. |
|---|---|---|---|
| 22/24 | - 40 - | 28/30 | - - 37 - |
| 24/25 | - 39 - | 30/32 | - - 36 - |
| 25/26 | - 38 - | 32/34 | - 35 à 34 50 |
| 26/28 | - 37 50 | 34/36 | - - 33 50 |

### TRAMS.

| FRANCE. | f. c. | ITALY. | f. c. |
|---|---|---|---|
| 26/28 | - - - 35 50 | — - - 36 - | |
| 28/30 | - - - 35 - | — - - 34 - | |
| 30/32 | - - - 34 50 | — - - 33 - | |
| 32/34 | - - - 33 50 | — - - 32 - | |
| 34/36 | - - 33 - | — - - 31 50 | |
| 36/40 | - - 32 50 | — - - 30 50 à 30 | |
| 40/50 | - - 31 50 | — - - 30 - à 29 | |
| 50/60 | - - 30 50 | — - - 28 50 | |

*Note.*—There was an increase in the value of organzines in the middle of the year of 6 to 8 f. per lb. and on trams of 6 to 9 f. At the end of the year there was a fall, leaving the advance one of 2 to 3 f. on organzines, and 4 to 5 f. on trams.

## January 1823:

### ORGANSINS.

| PIEDMONT. | f. c. | ITALY. | f. c. |
|---|---|---|---|
| 21/22 } | | | |
| 22/23 } | | 22/23 | - - 40 - |
| 23/24 | - - - 41 50 | 23/24 } | |
| 24/25 | - - - 40 50 | 24/25 } - - 39 - | |
| 25/26 | - - - 39 75 | 25/26 } | |
| 26/28 | - - - 38 50 | 26/28 | - - 38 - |
| 28/30 | - - - 37 50 | 28/30 | - - 37 - |
| 30/32 | - - - 36 50 | 30/32 | - - 36 - |
| 32/34 } | | 32/34 | - - 35 - |
| 34/36 } - 35 à 34 50 | | 34/36 | - - 34 50 |
| 36/40 } | | 36/40 | - - 34 - |

#### FRANCE.

| | f. c. | | f. c. |
|---|---|---|---|
| 22/24 | - - - 40 50 | 28/30 | - - 37 - |
| 24/25 | - - - 39 50 | 30/32 | - - 36 - |
| 25/26 | - - 39 - | 32/34 | - - 35 - |
| 26/28 | - - - 38 - | 34/36 | - - 34 - |

### TRAMS.

| FRANCE. | f. c. | ITALY. | f. c. |
|---|---|---|---|
| 26/28 | - - - 41 - | — - - - 39 50 | |
| 28/30 | - - - 40 - | — - - - 39 - | |
| 30/32 | - - - 39 - | — - - - 38 50 | |
| 32/34 | - - - 38 - | — - - - 37 50 | |
| 34/36 | - - - 37 - | — - - - 36 50 | |
| 36/40 | - - - 36 - | — - - - 35 - | |
| 40/50 | - 34 à 33 - | — - - 34 à 33 - | |
| 50/60 | - 32 à 31 - | — - - - 31 - | |

*Note.*—In May of this year prices rose, but fell again, so that at the end of the year there was a decline from 4 to 5 f. per lb. on organzines, and 6 to 7 f. on trams, Italian excepted, which not having advanced so much declined less.

## January 1824:

### ORGANSINS.

| PIEDMONT. | f. c. | ITALY. | f. c. |
|---|---|---|---|
| 21/22 | - - - 38 - | 22/23 | - - 33 50 |
| 22/23 | - - - 37 - | 23/24 | - - 33 - |
| 23/24 | - - - 36 - | 24/25 | - - 32 50 |
| 24/25 | - - - 35 - | 25/26 | - - 32 25 |
| 25/26 | - - - 34 50 | 26/28 | - - 32 - |
| 26/28 | - - - 33 50 | 28/30 | - - 31 - |
| 28/30 | - - - 33 - | 30/32 | - - 30 50 |
| 30/32 | - - - 32 50 | 32/34 | - - 30 - |
| 32/34 | - - - 32 - | 34/36 | - - 29 50 |
| 34/36 | - - - 31 50 | 36/40 | - - 29 - |
| 36/40 | - - - 31 - | | |

#### FRANCE.

| | f. c. | | f. c. |
|---|---|---|---|
| 22/23 | - - - 34 50 | 28/30 | - - 31 50 |
| 23/24 | - - - 34 - | 30/32 | - - 31 25 |
| 24/25 | - - - 33 50 | 32/34 | - - 30 50 |
| 25/26 | - - 33 - | 34/36 | - - 30 - |
| 26/28 | - - - 32 50 | | |

### TRAMS.

| FRANCE. | f. c. | ITALY. | f. c. |
|---|---|---|---|
| 26/28 | - - 32 - | 32 - - - 32 - | |
| 28/30 | - - - 31 50 | — - - - 31 - | |
| 30/32 | - - - 31 - | — - - - 30 50 | |
| 32/34 | - - - 30 75 | — - - - 29 50 | |
| 34/36 | - - 30 50 | — - - - 28 50 | |
| 36/40 | - - 30 - | — - - 28 - | |
| 40/50 | - - 29 50 | — - - - 27 50 | |
| 50/60 | - - 28 50 | — - - 27 à 26 - | |

*Note.*—In this year there was a gradual advance of 2 f. 50 c. to 3 f. per lb. on organzines. Trams remained all the year at about the same price, not fluctuating more than 50 c.

(*continued*)

*John Bowring,*
Esq. LL. D.

14 June,
1832.

## April 1825:

### ORGANSINS.

| PIEDMONT. | f. c. | | ITALY. | f. c. |
|---|---|---|---|---|
| 21/22 } | | | 22/23 | - - 41 |
| 22/23 } | | | 23/24 | - - 40 50 |
| 23/24 } | | | 24/25 } | - - 40 - |
| 24/25 - - - | 49 - | | 25/26 } | |
| 25/26 - - - | 47 50 | | 26/28 | - - 39 - |
| 26/28 - 45 à 44 | - | | 28/30 | - - 38 - |
| 28/30 - - - | 43 50 | | 30/32 | - - 37 - |
| 30/32 - - - | 41 50 | | 32/34 | - - 36 50 |
| 32/34 - - - | 40 50 | | 34/36 | - - 36 - |
| 34/36 - - - | 39 50 | | 36/40 | 35 à 34 50 |
| 36/40 - - - | 38 50 | | | |

### FRANCE.

| | f. c. | | | f. c. |
|---|---|---|---|---|
| 22/23 - - - | 44 - | | 26/28 | - - 41 - |
| 23/24 - - - | 43 50 | | 28/30 | - - 40 50 |
| 24/25 - - - | 43 - | | 30/32 | - - 40 - |
| 25/26 - - - | 42 50 | | 32/34 | - - 38 50 |

### TRAMS.

| FRANCE. | f. c. | | ITALY. | f. c. |
|---|---|---|---|---|
| 26/28 - - - | 37 - | | — - - | 37 à 36 - |
| 28/30 - - - | 36 50 | | — - - - | 35 50 |
| 30/32 - - - | 36 - | | — - - - | 35 - |
| 32/34 - - - | 35 50 | | — - - - | 34 50 |
| 34/36 - - - | 35 - | | — - - - | 34 - |
| 36/40 - - - | 34 - | | — - - - | 33 - |
| 40/50 - 33 à 32 | - | | — - - - | 32 - |
| 50/60 - - | 31 50 | | — - - - - | 31 |

*Note.*—DURING this year the fluctuations were not more than 1 *f.* per lb., except Italian organzines, which rose from 2 to 3 *f.* at the end of the year.

## January 1826:

### ORGANSINS.

| PIEDMONT. | f. c. | | ITALY. | f. c. |
|---|---|---|---|---|
| 21/22 - - - | 45 - | | 22/23 | - - 42 - |
| 22/23 - - - | 44 - | | 23/24 | - 41 - |
| 23/24 - - - | 43 50 | | 24/25 | - 40 - |
| 24/25 - - - | 43 - | | 25/26 | - - 38 50 |
| 25/26 - - - | 42 - | | 26/28 | - - 37 - |
| 26/28 - - - | 41 - | | 28/30 | - - 36 50 |
| 28/30 - - - | 39 50 | | 30/32 | - - 35 50 |
| 30/32 - - - | 39 - | | 32/34 | - 34 à 33 - |
| 32/34 - - - | 38 50 | | 34/36 | - - 32 50 |
| 34/36 - - - | 38 25 | | 36/40 | - 32 à 31 50 |
| 36/40 - - - | 38 - | | | |

### FRANCE.

| | f. c. | | | f. c. |
|---|---|---|---|---|
| 22/23 - - - | 43 - | | 28/30 | - - 39 - |
| 23/24 - - - | 42 50 | | 30/32 | - - 38 - |
| 24/25 - - - | 42 - | | 32/34 | - - 37 - |
| 25/26 - - - | 41 - | | 34/36 | - - 36 50 |
| 26/28 - - - | 40 - | | | |

### TRAMS.

| FRANCE. | f. c. | | ITALY. | f. c. |
|---|---|---|---|---|
| 26/28 - - - | 38 - | | — - - - | 35 - |
| 28/30 - - - | 37 - | | — - - - | 34 - |
| 30/32 - - - | 36 - | | — - - - | 33 - |
| 32/34 - - - | 35 - | | — - - - | 32 50 |
| 34/36 - - - | 34 - | | — - - - | 32 - |
| 36/40 - - - | 33 - | | — - - - | 31 50 |
| 40/45 - - - | 32 - | | — - - - | 31 - |
| 45/50 - - - | 31 50 | | — - - - | 30 - |
| 50/60 - - - | 30 - | | — - 29 à 28 | - |

*Note.*—PRICES in this year fell successively, so that at its close organzines were from 6 to 7 *f.* 50 *c.* lower than at the beginning. Trams fell, however, only 2 to 3 *f.* per lb.

## January 1827:

### ORGANSINS.

| PIEDMONT. | f. c. | | ITALY. | f. c. |
|---|---|---|---|---|
| 21/22 | | | 22/23 | - - 35 50 |
| 22/23 - - - | 38 50 | | 23/24 | - - 35 - |
| 23/24 - - - | 38 - | | 24/25 | - 34 - |
| 24/25 - - - | 37 - | | 25/26 | - 33 - |
| 25/26 - - - | 36 50 | | 26/28 | - 32 50 |
| 26/28 - - - | 36 - | | 28/30 | - 32 - |
| 28/30 - - - | 35 - | | 30/32 | - 31 50 |
| 30/32 - - - | 34 - | | 32/34 | - 31 25 |
| 32/34 - - - | 33 50 | | 34/36 } | |
| 34/36 - - - | 33 - | | 36/40 } | - - 30 50 |
| 36/40 - - - | 32 50 | | | |

### FRANCE.

| | f. c. | | | f. c. |
|---|---|---|---|---|
| 22/23 - - - | 35 50 | | 28/30 | - - 33 - |
| 23/24 - - - | 35 - | | 30/32 | - - 32 50 |
| 24/25 - - - | 34 50 | | 32/34 | - - 32 - |
| 25/26 - - - | 34 - | | 34/36 | - - 31 - |
| 26/28 - - - | 33 75 | | | |

### TRAMS.

| FRANCE. | f. c. | | ITALY. | f. c. |
|---|---|---|---|---|
| 26/28 - - - | 34 50 | | — - - - | 34 - |
| 28/30 - - - | 34 - | | — - - - | 33 50 |
| 30/32 - - - | 33 - | | — - 33 a' | 32 50 |
| 32/34 - - - | 32 50 | | — - - - | 32 - |
| 34/36 - - - | 32 - | | — - - - | 31 50 |
| 36/40 - - - | 31 50 | | — - - - | 31 - |
| 40/45 - - - | 31 - | | — - 30 a' | 29 50 |
| 45/50 - - - | 30 - | | — - - - | 29 50 |
| 50/60 - - - | 29 - | | — - - - | 28 50 |

*Note.*—IN this year there were many variations, principally in advance, so that at the close, organzines had risen from 2 to 3 *f.* per lb. and trams from 1 *f.* 50 *c.* to 2 *f.*

*John Bowring,* Esq. LL. D.

14 June, 1832.

### February 1828.

**ORGANSINS.**

| PIEDMONT. | | ITALY. | |
|---|---|---|---|
| | f. c. | | f. c. |
| 21/22 — — — 42 — | | 22/23 — — 38 — | |
| 22/23 — — — 41 50 | | 23/24 — — 37 — | |
| 23/24 — — — 40 50 | | 24/25 — — 36 — | |
| 24/25 — — — 39 50 | | 25/26 — — 35 50 | |
| 25/26 — 39 a' 38 — | | 26/28 — — 34 50 | |
| 26/28 — — — 37 75 | | 28/30 — — 34 — | |
| 28/30 — — — 35 50 | | 30/32 — — 33 75 | |
| 30/32 — — — 34 50 | | 32/34 — — 32 75 | |
| 32/34 — — — 33 50 | | 34/36 — — 32 50 | |
| 34/36 — — — 33 — | | 36/40 — — 32 — | |
| 36/40 — — — 32 75 | | | |

**FRANCE.**

| | | | |
|---|---|---|---|
| 21/22 — — — 41 — | | 26/28 — — 36 — | |
| 22/23 — — — 40 — | | 28/30 — — 35 — | |
| 23/24 — — — 39 — | | 30/32 — — 34 50 | |
| 24/25 — — — 38 — | | 32/34 — — 34 — | |
| 25/26 — — — 37 — | | | |

**TRAM.**

| FRANCE. | | ITALY. | |
|---|---|---|---|
| | f. c. | | f. c. |
| 26/28 — — — 35 50 | | — — — 35 — | |
| 28/30 — — — 34 50 | | — — — 34 — | |
| 30/32 — — — 33 50 | | — — — 33 — | |
| 32/34 — — — 33 — | | — — — 32 50 à 32 | |
| 34/36 — — — 32 50 | | — — — 31 — | |
| 36/40 — — — 32 — | | — — — 30 — | |
| 40/50 — — — 30 50 | | — — — 29 50 | |
| 50/60 — — — 29 — | | — — — 28 75 | |

*Note.*—A FALL took place in this year, of 2 to 3 f. on organzines, and 1 f. to 1 f. 50 c. on trams.

### February 1829.

**ORGANSINS.**

| PIEDMONT. | | ITALY. | |
|---|---|---|---|
| | f. c. | | f. c. |
| 21/22 — — — 38 50 | | 22/23 — — 37 — | |
| 22/23 — — — 38 — | | 23/24 } — — 36 50 | |
| 23/24 — — — 37 75 | | 24/25 } | |
| 24/25 — — — 37 — | | 25/26 — — 35 — | |
| 25/26 — — — 36 50 | | 26/28 — — 34 50 | |
| 26/28 — — — 36 — | | 28/30 — — 34 — | |
| 28/30 — — — 35 — | | 30/32 — — 33 75 | |
| 30/32 — — — 34 50 | | 32/34 — — 33 50 | |
| 32/34 } — — 34 — | | 34/36 — — 33 50 | |
| 34/36 } | | 36/40 — — 33 — | |
| 36/40 — — — 33 50 | | | |

**FRANCE.**

| | | | |
|---|---|---|---|
| 21/22 — — — 37 50 | | 26/28 — — 35 — | |
| 22/23 — — — 37 — | | 28/30 } — — 34 50 | |
| 23/24 — — — 36 50 | | 30/32 } | |
| 24/25 — — — 36 — | | 32/34 — — 34 — | |
| 25/26 — — — 35 50 | | 34/36 — — 33 50 | |

**TRAM.**

| FRANCE. | | ITALY. | |
|---|---|---|---|
| | f. c. | | f. c. f. |
| 26/28 } — — 34 — | | — } — 33 50 à 33 | |
| 28/30 } | | } | |
| 30/32 — — — 33 50 | | — — 33 à 32 50 | |
| 32/34 — — — 32 50 | | — — — 32 — | |
| 34/36 — — — 32 — | | — — — 31 50 | |
| 36/40 — — — 31 50 | | — — — 31 — | |
| 40/50 — 31 à 30 — | | — — — 30 — | |
| 50/60 — — — 29 50 | | — — — 28 50 | |

*Note.*—ORGANZINES and trams fluctuated this year about 1 f. 50 c. per lb. and at the end of the year they remained at about 1 f. higher than at the beginning.

### March 1830.

**ORGANSINS.**

| PIEDMONT. | | ITALY. | |
|---|---|---|---|
| | f. c. | | f. c. |
| 21/22 — — — 37 50 | | 22/23 — — 34 50 | |
| 22/23 — — — 36 50 | | 23/24 — — 33 — | |
| 23/24 — — — 35 50 | | 24/25 — — 32 50 | |
| 24/25 — — — 34 50 | | 25/26 — — 32 — | |
| 25/26 — — — 34 — | | 26/28 — — 31 50 | |
| 26/28 — — — 33 — | | 28/30 } | |
| 28/30 — — — 32 50 | | 30/32 } — — 30 50 | |
| 30/32 — — — 31 75 | | 32/34 } | |
| 32/34 — — — 31 — | | 34/36 — — 30 — | |
| 34/36 — — — 30 50 | | 36/40 — — 29 50 | |
| 36/40 — — — 30 — | | | |

**FRANCE.**

| | | | |
|---|---|---|---|
| 21/22 — — — 36 — | | 26/28 — — 32 — | |
| 22/23 — — — 35 — | | 28/30 — — 31 50 | |
| 23/24 — — — 34 — | | 30/32 } — — 31 — | |
| 24/25 — — — 33 50 | | 32/34 } | |
| 25/26 — — — 33 — | | | |

**TRAMS.**

| FRANCE. | | ITALY. | |
|---|---|---|---|
| | f. c. | | f. c. |
| 26/28 — — — 32 — | | — — — — 31 — | |
| 28/30 — — — 31 50 | | — — — — 30 50 | |
| 30/32 — — — 31 — | | — — — — 30 — | |
| 32/34 — — — 30 — | | — — — — 29 50 | |
| 34/36 — — — 29 — | | — — — — 29 — | |
| 36/40 — — — 28 50 | | — — — — 28 50 | |
| 40/45 — — — 28 — | | — — — — 27 50 | |
| 45/50 — — — 27 — | | — — — — 27 — | |
| 50/60 — — — 26 — | | — — — — 26 — | |

*Note.*—THERE were few variations in 1830, but a general tendency to a slight decline, so that at the end of the year, prices had fallen from 1 f. 50 c. to 2 f.

(*continued.*)

*John Bowring,*
Esq. LL. D.

———

14 June,
1832.

1831:—Observations:

In 1831, the demand for silk goods having slackened, there was a fall of from 4 to 6 *f.* on organzines, and 3 *f.* on trams; at the close of the year a slight advance of 1 *f.* to 1 *f.* 50 *c.* took place.

The lb. marc (which is the weight by which silk is sold at Lyons) is in the proportion of 102 lbs. 2 oz. to 50 kilogrammes.

The price of trams was long far beneath that of organzines, as inferior silks were mostly employed for them; but the demand for better and lighter stuffs has led to a demand for finer trams, and the rate of difference has become much less.

The Piedmontese had long a great advantage over other Italian silk; it was more regular, cleaner, and better prepared; of late however the general character of Italian silk has improved.

———

### May 1832.

| TRAMS OF FRANCE. | | *f.* | *c.* | ORGANZINES OF PIEDMONT. | | *f.* | *c.* | ORGANZINES OF FRANCE. | | *f.* | *c.* |
|---|---|---|---|---|---|---|---|---|---|---|---|
| 24 deniers - per lb. | | 29 | 50 | 20 deniers - per lb. | | 34 | — | 20 deniers - per lb. | | 33 | — |
| 26 — | | 29 | — | 22 — | | 33 | — | 22 — | | 32 | — |
| 28 — | | 28 | 50 | 24 — | | 32 | 50 | 24 — | | 31 | 50 |
| 30 — | | 28 | — | 26 — | | 31 | 50 | 26 — | | 31 | — |
| 32 — | | 27 | 50 | 28 — | | 30 | 50 | 28 — | | 30 | — |
| 34 — | | 27 | — | 30 — | | 29 | 50 | 30 — | | 29 | 50 |
| 36 — | | 26 | 50 | 35 — | | 27 | 50 | 35 — | | 28 | 50 |
| 38 — | | 26 | — | 40 — | | 27 | — | | | | |
| 40 — | | 25 | 75 | 45 — | | 26 | — | | | | |
| 45 — | | 25 | 50 | 50 — | | 25 | — | | | | |
| 50 — | | 25 | — | | | | | | | | |
| 55 — | | 24 | 75 | | | | | | | | |
| 60 — | | 24 | 50 | | | | | | | | |
| 65 — | | 24 | 25 | | | | | | | | |
| 70 — | | 24 | — | | | | | | | | |

8804. Are you able to account for the fall in the number of looms at Lyons, in the year 1789?—The cause of the rise after 1786 was probably the influence of the Commercial Treaty, which began then to be in operation; the decline after 1789 was the revolutionary movement, in which Lyons took a great part, and the siege of Lyons led to many of the manufacturers migrating: I beg to mention, that I have obtained from another source, independently of the Custom House, a statement of the quantity of foreign silk sold in the Lyonese market, and the average of that, for ten years, is 1,200,000. I state that as a commercial fact.

8805. You have stated that the principal export to France from England is bandanna handkerchiefs; are you able to inform the Committee whether they were British manufacture or Oriental manufactures printed in England?—I am not myself sufficiently cognizant of the case; but I have seen the quality of silk handkerchiefs used in France, and which are now extensively employed; they are precisely those I see in England; I am not aware of the fact as to those used in England, but I perceive no difference between the one and the other.

8806. You have stated the great superiority which, in your opinion, exists in the finer articles produced at Lyons over those produced in other places, will you state whether there are any circumstances to which you attribute, in particular, this superiority in taste and design?—I think that is the part of the question on which I may be enabled to throw most light; and I fear that it has not excited so much attention as it deserves. It is to the neglect of this, which may be called the germ of the French superiority, that I suspect the want of our superiority is principally to be traced. Up to the period in which the pattern is produced, I think the French have greatly the advantage over us; they have not a great superiority when the pattern is produced; when, in other words, the machine gets possession of the design; but the fact that struck me most in France was the way in which taste was formed, and I was exceedingly surprised at finding among the weavers themselves and among their children, and amongst every body connected with the production of patterns, an attention devoted to every thing which was in any way connected with beauty, either in arrangement or in colour. I have again and again seen the weavers walking about gathering flowers, arranging them in their most attractive shapes. I found them constantly suggesting to their masters improvements in their designs; and I learnt that in almost every case, where the manufacturer had great success, there was some individual in the fabric who was the creator of beautiful things;

*John Bowring,*
Esq. LL. D.

———

14 June,
1832.

things; there is at this moment scarcely any house of any considerable reputation in Lyons, which has not a partner who owes his position to his great success in the study of the arts; this has been treated as an object of so great importance, that they have, in the city of Lyons, a school of arts, to which the town itself gives 20,000 francs a year, and which takes possession of every lad who shows any great aptitude for drawing or for any other subject of study which is likely to be brought to bear on manufactures; all the painters and all the sculptors, and all the botanists at Lyons become manufacturers, and scarcely ever go out of the manufacturing circle. The town gives instruction in every thing which presents itself in the shape of art. I went to the school of St. Peter, which is one of the most remarkable schools of art, and I found there 180 students, and that to every one of those students the town was giving five years' gratuitous instruction in art; a great number of them were engaged in the study of anatomy; they had a surgical professor there, who was teaching them, not only the harmony of the human form, but all the wonderful organization of the human machine, as connected with the machinery of manufactures: I found a botanical professor, who had 30 or 40 boys under him studying flowers, and many flowers exceedingly beautiful: I found others attending to architecture; and, in fact, that all the departments of art, which could in any way be caught hold of for the production of tasteful things, had become objects of attention; and I found also a professor, the object of whose teaching was to show those young men how the machine could avail itself of their productions; that is to say, how by machinery they could produce, on a piece of silk cloth, that which they had drawn on a piece of paper. Those schools are not only the object of local attention, but they come immediately under the protection of Government; and I see by the general budget that the Government (that is the Minister of Commerce) allows 3,100 francs a year, independently of the endowment the town gives to this school. Although the Minister of Commerce makes a special grant for any purpose which is likely to advance those studies, the town is willing to consent to make supernumerary grants. The school supplies the student with every thing but the materials, and their works belong to the students themselves. Of late, which by the way is another evidence of the effect of competition, the school has become an object of very considerable attention, and the French, finding they are thrown more on their production of beautiful patterns, are giving to the schools of art a vast deal of their care and anxiety; the professor of painting of this school is a man of high distinction, very well known in the world of art. It is in this way that this taste, the testimony to which has been frequently called a prejudice, this admiration, this production of beautiful things, leads to the invention of works, which meet with the preferring acceptance of the consumer. I do not mean to say that there is not as much genius in England as in France, but there are not the same means of developing it. The French manufacturer considers that his pattern is the principal element on which he is to depend for his success: the mere art of manufacturing may be easily effected; but here is a taste-producing school which contains from 150 to 180 students; it has gone as high as 200. The manufacturer goes there, and he sees a boy who has passed through all the courses of study, who has in fact the appropriate knowledge, that boy's mind having been getting instruction in every shape, and applying it all to one particular end, namely, of manufacture, which he looks to as the means of future success. The manufacturers can pick out of these 200 boys the boy whose taste is most distinguished; that boy is admitted into his house, probably at a small salary. One manufacturer told me he had three such; to the lowest in rank he gave 1,000 francs, equal to 40*l.* The number of pieces produced, the object of a particular pattern, may be very small at first, but if his success is remarkable, in two years he may get 2,000 francs; after three or four years, if his success is great indeed, and the patterns he produces meet with great acceptance, he can obtain 3,000 francs: from the moment that his reputation is worth 3,000 francs his fame is established, and he has the offer of a partnership; and that is the history of a great many of the most prosperous manufacturers of Lyons.

8807. Is there more than one school?—There is but one principal school, which is the school of St. Peter. I have heard again and again, from manufacturers even of considerable reputation, that they are not in the habit of trusting wholly to themselves for the result of a pattern, it is to them a matter of great anxiety to hear the opinions of young men who are thus instructed; and as an evidence of the attention paid to the matter, I visited, not long ago, the house of a weaver, a man getting 30 or 40 sous a day; he turned over some hundreds of patterns, and

678.                                                                                          said,

*John Bowring,*
Esq. LL. D.

14 June,
1832.

said, I will give you my opinion of these; I was much struck with the correctness of his taste, and I found they were able to prophecy pretty correctly what the success of a pattern would be. In this way is the mind of the silk weavers of France devoted to that to which the mind of those of England is not devoted.

8808. Do you then mean to say, that the manufacturers here do not employ artists and give every attention they possibly can to the production of patterns?— I do not think they pay every attention to the production of patterns, because if they did we should see the same sort of schools established, and the same course pursued which has been so successful in France.

8809. Do not you know that there are a great number of individuals employed as pattern drawers, and paid liberally?—All I can say is, that there is a great superiority in France; the amount of payment to their artists is exceedingly various, the number of them is very great, the manufacturer does not depend on one or two or ten; the artist of genius will always find some manufacturer of sagacity who will buy his patterns of him.

8810. Is there a great competition to get into those schools?—No; the provisions are so large and liberal, that the school is constantly tolerably well filled, but the supply and demand regulate themselves there as elsewhere. The average of the school of Saint Peter is about 180 students, and the course of instruction lasts for five years. I do not mean to say there are not young men in this country who may not devote themselves to five years study, but that is the habit there.

8811. And the greatest possible attention is paid in Lyons to young men being educated for that purpose?—Yes; the greatest attention is paid to the production of a pattern, as the recompense of the successful manufacture of a new pattern or a new order of patterns, is full of encouragement. The subject of patterns is a frequent topic of conversation; for instance, the power of introducing patterns from a Kaleidescope, was, on one occasion, the object of my inquiry; I found that all the intelligent manufacturers agreed that the kaleidescope produces nothing but incongruities; there have been several attempts made to introduce oriental subjects, and some of the manufacturers endeavoured to blend those with Grecian designs, they failed altogether, the public taste being essentially pure and classical. I know a manufacturer who is at this moment occupied in adapting Persian patterns, and he is very much embarrassed by his attempts to blend the Persian taste with the European. So again, the study of what may be called the Grecian School, is essentially independent; in reference to the botanic part or the study of flowers as patterns, there will not be seen the inconsistencies in the French patterns which are so often found in the English patterns; they draw more correctly and observingly, and it were well if the same spirit existed here. I am satisfied that the instruction that comes from France is of the most valuable sort.

8812. The opinion then of the French manufacturers themselves is, that a great proportion of their superiority is owing to the attention they pay to the design?— Undoubtedly; the fact is, that is their primary feeling, and the true explanation of the whole question; it is the superiority in taste, which has grown out of their connection with all countries, and the study of many ages; no person can contend that the manufacturer here is in so advantageous a position as the Frenchman, who receives the taste of the whole world, since out of 140 millions which he manufactures, only 30 millions are for their own use, and the remaining 110 millions for exportation to other lands. There are collections of silk manufactures in France extending over the period of 4,000 years; I have seen in the Schools of Art in Lyons, the manufacture exhibited of every country, and have found men able to state how every particular pattern was produced from even the silks of the Egyptian mummies, to the most perfect productions of the last year; their history is known, they become the subject of instruction, and I should wish that our manufacturers should get into the same region of intellectual, artistical and historical study.

8813. Is not the manufacture of France essentially employed in the production of articles of taste?—Assuredly; therein consists their great success. I beg to state that the universal conviction in France is, that they are wholly dependent on the superior beauty of their productions for their foreign sale, and that is the great object of anxiety there, that every thing should be done to keep up that spirit; daily knowledge is gathered in from all quarters, and the universal desire among the manufacturers there is to do something which, in the regions of taste, shall be better than that which has been done by their neighbours, for they feel they are much behind hand in many other matters; that they do not possess the same

advantages

*John Bowring.*
Esq. LL. D.

14 June,
1832.

advantages for the production of their goods, after the taste is created; their looms for instance are frequently in a deteriorated and backward state, and nothing but the superiority they have on these matters of taste enables them to carry on a successful trade.

8814. Has the same spirit operated upon the operatives?—It has; the observations of the operatives are invaluable to the master; I have heard manufacturers again and again say that the masters who stood upon their own sagacity, and had not availed themselves of the hints of their dependants had failed.

8815. Are not very high sums paid to persons sometimes for the exercise of their ingenuity?—Yes.

8816. To what amount?—The highest sum I have ever heard of is 6,000 francs a year; but it is a better remuneration to give a talented young man a partnership than a salary of 4,000 a year, his assistance being so important for the production of a novel thing; in the same spirit is the manufacture carried on when the weaver gets hold of it; there are schools of weaving, as they are called, which are in many particulars the same in character as the schools of art. I have had conversations with the teachers of these schools, who are wholly devoted to the manufacturing branch; they have read its history, and are constantly executing difficult things. I have brought over from France some specimens of works of these teachers of weaving, which I am desirous should be seen as an evidence of the state of silk manufacturing art in that country.

8817. Will you describe the general establishment of these schools?—The schools of weaving are almost wholly individual schools, and consist sometimes of from sixty to eighty scholars; a pattern will be exhibited, and then their invention is put to the rack as to the best means of producing that pattern on a piece of silk goods; the master instructs them and removes the difficulties they find, and enables them to accomplish it. In the same way in which an artist obtains distinction and recompense for his success, a weaver will obtain it; he will of course easily get a little capital to enable him to become a chef d'atelier, and so obtain the benefit of any discovery he had made.

8818. Are the schools of weaving schools of design also?—No; there is a professor in the school of art whose object is the combination of mechanism with art, or the application of machinery to the transfer of a pattern.

8819. Are the schools of weaving under the same encouragement as the others? —No.

8820. Will you state how many professors, and what are the different branches taught in the school of art?—I think there are five or six professors; I will describe the course of things which is followed; there is the anatomical school which gets supplied with subjects with great facility, having the power of drawing on the hospitals as the other surgical schools have; then the school of the living human being; I found a very beautiful child, of three or four years old, with thirty or forty students sitting round it; they were employed in copying its locks, or engaged in the study of its features. I found in a third range the architectural students, they were copying different styles; and the great object of the master is to prevent confusion between different styles, and they find architecture of considerable importance for providing patterns of a stiff and formal character; thus their ornaments are correct and appropriate. Next comes the botanical school, in which the number of students is greater; they were engaged in copying the most beautiful flowers. A botanical garden is attached to the school; there were thirty or forty students, some of whom were engaged in arranging the flowers to show them in their most attractive shape. Then I think came what may be called a general professor, whose object was painting landscapes, and exhibiting art in its wider bearings; and last of all a professor whose object was the application of machinery to art, which takes possession of that which the boy has invented or produced, and teaches him how it is to be transferred to the silk manufacture. I found in that school a large collection of patterns, which had been deposited by the Prud'hommes after a certain number of years, those patterns come into the possession of that school, and are employed as helps for the production of new patterns.

8821. Do the parents pay any thing in this school?—Nothing at all; the instruction is purely gratuitous.

8822. Under what regulation are they admitted?—The Municipality have the power of putting them in, and the expense is defrayed by the Municipality, with the exception of the grant by the Minister of Commerce, which was only 3,000 francs the last year. There is also a department of natural history; I am

678.

desired

desired to obtain for them specimens of sculpture, for they thought they should probably find them of use; the Mayor requested I would send from hence, at the expense of the town, a copy of the Elgin marbles, for the service of the School of Art.

8823. Do you know what is the expense of the school?—In the year 1831 the city grant was 20,000 francs, the grant of the Minister of Commerce 3,100; the Mayor was so good as to give me the regulations of the school, which are contained in this paper.

*[The same was delivered in, and read.]*

### EXTRAIT du Réglement pour les Etablissemens Publics existant dans le Palais St.-Pierre.

Art. 1<sup>er</sup>.—En inscrivant les élèves qui demandent à entrer à l'Ecole, le secrétaire s'assure qu'ils réunissent les conditions prescrites.

Art. 2.—Les actes de naissance des élèves, ainsi que les certificats de vaccine, sont retenus et conservés au secrétariat.

Art. 3.—Les élèves qui, dans le courant de l'année, auraient le désir de passer dans une classe supérieure, devront en faire la demande à leur professeur. Cette demande sera soumise au Conseil, qui la rejetera, s'il ne reconnait pas l'élève capable de profiter des lecons dans la classe où il aspire à entrer; les mutations ont lieu à Pâques et à la rentrée.

Art. 4.—Les élèves des classes étrangères à l'Ecole, qui voudraient entrer dans une des classes, sans passer par celle des Principes, devront exécuter un ouvrage sous les yeux du professeur de la classe dans laquelle ils désirent être admis.

Si le professeur est satisfait de l'épreuve, il gardera l'élève dans une classe inférieure, le Conseil prononcerait, après avoir examiné l'ouvrage de l'élève.

Art. 5.—Tout élève admis contractera l'obligation de donner à l'étude tout le temps prescrit par l'article 11. Ceux qui s'y refuseraient seront rayés du rôle des titulaires, et leur place sera donnée à de nouveaux élèves.

Il est fait exception :

1°. En faveur des élèves externes du Collége Royal, lesquels pourront entrer à 10 heures et demie du matin, et sortiront à une heure, tant en hiver qu'en été. Ils devront être munis d'une carte du proviseur du Collége;

2°. En faveur des élèves de l'École de Sculpture, qui pourront entrer après neuf heures et jusqu' à midi; mais tous les élèves sortiront toujours à 2 heures.

Art. 6.—Si un élève était forcé de s'absenter de l'Ecole par maladie ou autre cause grave, les parens seront tenus d'en informer de suit le secrétaire, qui en donnera avis au Directeur et au professeur. A défaut par les parens de se conformer à cette disposition, l'élève perdra sa place après dix jours d'absence. Ils devront aussi, en cas de changement de domicile, donner leur nouvelle demeure au secrétariat.

Art. 7.—En cas d'insubordination ou autre faute d'un élève, le Directeur est autorisé à lui interdire l'entrée de l'Ecole; cette exclusion ne doit pas excéder quinze jours; une punition plus grave, et notamment le renvoi définitif, ne peut être ordonné que par le Maire.

Art. 8.—Les élèves doivent respect à leur professeur, être assidus aux leçons, et garder le silence pendant l'étude. Il leur est expressément défendu de salir les murs, et d'y tracer aucune espèce de figure.

Art. 9.—Personne ne peut communiquer, pendant les heures d'étude, avec les élèves.

Les élèves devront aussi être pourvus d'avance de tout ce qui leur est nécessaire, afin de ne pas sortir pendant la durée des classes.

Art. 10.—L'Ecole est ouverte tous les jours excepté les dimanches, les Jeudis et les jours de fêtes consacrées par le Gouvernement.

Art. 11.—Les classes sont ouvertes à 9 heures et finissent à deux, pendant toute la durée de l'année scolaire.

A neuf heures un quart, le portier refusera l'entrée du Palais aux élèves retardataires, le surveillant prendra note des absens, et en fera part au secrétaire avant midi, afin que les parens en soient instruits dans la journée.

Art. 12.—Dans chaque classe de l'Ecole des Beaux-Arts, et plusieurs fois dans l'année, s'il le juge à propos, le professeur fera un rapport au Conseil sur ceux de ses nouveaux élèves qu'il ne juge pas capables de suivre ses cours avec avantage. A l'appui de ce rapport, le dernier ouvrage de cet elève sera présenté au Conseil; et, s'il y avait lieu à un renvoi de l'Ecole, pour cause d'incapacité, la demande en sera faite au Directeur.

Art. 13.—Quand un élève quitte l'Ecole, il doit en faire sa déclaration au secrétariat, et en donner connaisance au Maître sous lequel il travaille. Il devra en même temps retirer tous les objets à lui appartenant; s'il avait négligé de les retirer un mois après sa sortie de l'Ecole, ils seront censés avoir été abandonnés au bénéfice du surveillant.

Art. 14.—Lorsqu'un ou plusieurs élèves auront perdu, dégradé ou détruit quelque objet appartenant au mobilier du Palais, l'auteur ou les auteurs seront renvoyés, et le dommage causé sera immédiatement mis à leur charge ou à celle de leurs parens.

Art. 15.—Le surveillant de l'Ecole est chargé de la police de la salle. Il rappelera au réglement les élèves qui s'en écarteront, et, en cas de récidive, il notera les indisciplinés.

Ces

*John Bowring*
Esq. LL. D.

14 June,
1832

Ces notes seront toutes les semaines déposées au secrétariat, où les parens des élèves pourront en prendre connaissance.

Art. 16.—Depuis le 1ᵉʳ Novembre jusqu'au 1ᵉʳ Mars, la classe du Modèle nu aura lieu de cinque à sept heures du soir; dans l'été, le Directeur déterminera l'heure des séances.

Art. 17.—Si des personnes étrangères à l'Ecole désirent étudier d'après le Modèle nu, elles peuvent y être admises, en présentant une permission signée du Directeur.
Les élèves titulaires sont seuls portés en tête sur la liste d'ordre d'entrée.

Art. 18.—Tous les élèves sont appelés à concourir: ceux qui ont remporté les premiers prix de la classe dont ils suivent les études, sont seuls exceptés de cette disposition.

Art. 19.—Tous les ans, au 1ᵉʳ Mars, les professeurs déterminent, pour chaque classe, les sujets qui devront être mis au concours; le choix de ces sujets est soumis à l'approbation du Maire.

Art. 20.—Immédiatement après l'approbation du Maire, les professeurs font connaître aux élèves de leur classe respective le programme qui a été arrêté, et ils signent les toiles ou les feuilles de papier sur lesquelles doivent être exécutés les ouvrages donnés au concours.

Art. 21.—Dans la classe des Principes, les élèves n'auront que quinze séances pour exécuter chaque dessin du concours.

Art. 22.—Les élèves ne peuvent travailler aux ouvrages du concours que dans l'intérieur de l'Ecole; il ne leur est permis, sous aucun prétexte, de passer de leur section dans celles où ils ne se sont point fait inscrire comme concurrens.

Art. 23.—Chaque concurrent écrit et scelle son nom derrière ses ouvrages, de manière qu'il soit impossible de lire ce même nom sans déchirer le papier qui couvre la signature: les élèves, dont les noms pourraient être reconnus, seront exclus du concours.

Art. 24.—Les ouvrages des concurrens sont remis, avant le 20 Août, au Directeur qui, en les recevant, s'assure que la formalité prescrite par l'article précédent a été remplie; ils seront fermés dans une salle disposée à cet effet.

Art. 25.—Pendant les trois jours qui suivent la distribution des prix, tous les ouvrages présentés au concours seront exposés publiquement dans la grand salle de l'Ecole.
Les élèves de la classe des Principes pourront ajouter à leur dessin du concours le meilleur de leur ouvrage fait dans le cours de l'année.

Art. 26.—Les ouvrages qui ont valu des médailles à leurs auteurs seront exposés toute l'année dans l'école, et lui demeureront acquis.
Ces ouvrages doivent être respectés par tous les élèves; et, s'il arrivait que quelques-uns d'entr'eux se permissent de les dégrader par quelques moyens que ce fût, ils seront renvoyés de l'Ecole, après avoir payé le dommage causé par eux.

Art. 27.—Les élèves titulaires de toutes les classes peuvent être admis à l'étude de la Perspective.

Art. 28.—Le cours de Perspective commence le 1ᵉʳ Avril, et a lieu de huit à neuf heures du matin.

Art. 29.—Les cours d'Anatomie sont obligatoires pour les élèves de l'école de Figure, et facultatif pour les autres élèves.

Art. 30.—Il y aura deux cours par année: le premier qui aura pour objet l'étude de l'Ostéologie et de la Myologie, sera ouvert pendant deux mois, du 1ᵉʳ Novembre au 1ᵉʳ Janvier; le second, qui traitera de la Physiologie comparée, sera de quatre mois, du 1ᵉʳ Mai au 30 Juillet.

Art. 31.—Les vacances commencent le 1ᵉʳ Septembre, et finissent le 30 Octobre.

---

This is a letter from the Mayor also, in which he tells me that they are intending to give this school much more developement, that they feel the pressure of necessity upon them, and that they have ordered a Report to be made of the Bresca school at Milan, to see whether any thing existing there can be advantageously introduced at Lyons; I mention that as an evidence of the anxiety and attention with which they look at these things. The manner in which the grant is made is precisely this; I hold in my hand the budget of the town of Lyons for 1831; in the year 1830 they granted 22,000 francs from the town, but this year only 20,000; the Mayor proposes the amount; it is then referred to the Municipal Council, to approve of it; it is then referred to the Prefect, and comes under the immediate cognizance of the King, so that the sanction of all the principal authorities is obtained, the town reserving to itself the right of making any supernumerary grant if it should be necessary; of late a very large legacy has been left by a French General of the name of Martin, who has directed that a considerable portion of it shall be applied to the establishment of an institution, whose objects are in many respects similar to those of the School of St. Peter; the amount altogether was not less, I believe, than two millions of francs, and the decision as to its application is as late as April 1831.

678.                                                                                      8824. The

8824. The operations of this school are intended with reference to the improvement of the silk manufactory?—Yes; but they do not exact that a boy there shall devote himself exclusively to the manufacture of Lyons; he gets gratuitous instruction as soon as he gives evidence of aptitude for those particular instructions; and it happens that in a town like Lyons, inasmuch as he gets an almost certain existence by applying his talents to the production of patterns, there are very few men who go into the higher walks of art, where there would be great uncertainty. Those men, devoting themselves to those studies for the purpose of improvement, calculate that when once they leave the school they can get a thousand francs, which is the first recompense of their labour. I was surprised to find that this school had not produced a greater number of artists and painters; but the simple fact is, the manufacture swallows them up, and it is on manufacture that their hopes are founded. I have said again and again, how is it you are not at Rome or at Paris, and applying your genius to something better; the answer was invariably, we have a certainty here; and thus it is that the manufacturer of Lyons avails himself of the talent which the neighbourhood produces.

8825. Are the Committee to understand that the students dissect the human body?—The instruction is precisely that given in any other anatomical school.

---

*Lunæ, 18° die Junii, 1832.*

---

### JAMES A. STEWART MACKENZIE, ESQUIRE, in the Chair.

---

*John Bowring,* Esq., LL. D. called in; and further Examined.

8826. DO you conceive that there is any thing in the national character of the French which renders them peculiarly apt in acquiring the superiority they testify in design?—It appears to me there is no national superiority, but their national education is undoubtedly much more friendly to the production of works of art than that of England; almost all the genius that exists among our labouring population is buried and barren, while in France it is productive.

8827. In those branches of the arts which we cultivate in this country we excel them, as, for instance, portrait and landscape?—Clearly; but in France there is a large proportion of the field of art dedicated to manufacturing industry.

8828. Did you ever see any thing produced in France equal to the shield of Achilles?—Certainly not in that department; I take it that one of the principal means of instruction which the French have is the accessibleness of all the works of art; there is scarcely any thing to be obtained in this country without paying a fee, more or less, and I am convinced the effect of that abuse on the mass of the population is fatal in the highest degree, and is a cause of indifference which operates very extensively and very banefully.

8829. Has not Lyons a gallery of pictures of very great merit?—There are many paintings there, but the subject does not require the study alone of paintings but of the works of art generally. Every traveller must have observed that the French people, as a people, treat art with great respect; they can be trusted every where, while the English people are mistrusted every where; art is out of their reach, and carelessness to its attractions is the consequence of their exclusion.

8830. Do you think that the superiority of which you have spoken extends to other branches besides silk goods?—Certainly; wherever art forms a part of the manufacture, it is turned to great account in France. I will mention an instance which struck me very much. I was accompanied to Paris by a Sheffield manufacturer of considerable eminence, who told me, that notwithstanding the double price of the raw material in France, if he could obtain the same workmen he had seen in France at any thing like the same wages, he should do wonders, and carry improvement much farther forward than it had been carried in England. He spoke of iron and steel works. The productions of the French in bronze have made their way in the same manner as their silk goods into all the markets of the world, and that is an article in which art forms a great part of the cost of the production.

8831. Is there any thing done by the Government to encourage the national taste?—What the Government has done is to make art universally accessible; all

collections

*John Bowring,*
Esq. LL. D.

14 June,
1832.

collections of art, whether in painting, statuary or engraving, in fact every thing which is likely to form the national taste, is opened to the people.

8832. All the establishments are open on a Sunday, are they not?—They are not only open on a Sunday, but they are crowded, and the labouring people go there; in France, I may say, there is an atmosphere of art, and into that atmosphere the nation is thrown.

8833. Have you any official returns from the " Condition " as to the silks used at Lyons?—I will put in a paper which has been furnished me, showing the quantities received into La Condition from the year 1806, and which exhibits the quantity of silk experimentalized on to ascertain its humidity.

[*The same was delivered in.*]

## FRENCH SILK TRADE.

### WEIGHT of Silk submitted to " The Condition."

Lyons.

| Year | kilog. | | Year | kilog. |
|---|---|---|---|---|
| 1806 | 348,448 | | 1821 | 527,645 |
| — 1807 | 362,557 | | — 1822 | 430,989 |
| — 1808 | 395,120 | | — 1823 | 467,385 |
| — 1809 | 401,652 | | — 1824 | 630,609 |
| — 1810 | 418,731 | | — 1825 | 564,542 |
| — 1811 | 352,085 | | — 1826 | 462,286 |
| — 1812 | 409,352 | | — 1827 | 634,988 |
| — 1813 | 433,460 | | — 1828 | 546,384 |
| — 1814 | 417,150 | | — 1829 | 587,137 |
| — 1815 | 386,202 | | — 1830 | 558,184 |
| — 1816 | 371,204 | | — 1831 | 586,268 |
| — 1817 | 367,479 | | | |
| — 1818 | 366,728 | | Total | 11,924,435 |
| — 1819 | 363,198 | | | |
| — 1820 | 534,652 | | Average on 26 Years, per annum | 458,624 |

8834. Can you state what the proportion of silk which is conditioned is to the whole quantity consumed?—Taking the whole period from that time, I find from three-fourths to four-fifths goes to the Condition; but, inasmuch as there is some delay when the demand for silk is very great, silk is sometimes sold without the necessity of being conditioned.

8835. There is no obligation on the vendor or the purchaser of sending it?—The purchaser has a great interest in sending it to the Condition, and it is generally done, except where it is of great consequence that the time should not be lost.

8836. Is it considered that the test applied by the Condition is a very accurate one?—I think it is not very accurate; and for some time a commission has been sitting nominated by the Chamber of Commerce, and a series of experiments made which will lead to some modifications. They propose hereafter to proceed in the same way in which gold is assayed, and have determined to come to what I may call the point of unity; they will extract from the silk every portion of humidity it contains, and allow a certain per centage for the average humidity, and then estimate the value of the silk by a calculation of the per centage above or below the marketable point of dampness: silk may then be said to be of as many carets fine as gold is. The difficulty now is, that when a great quantity of silk is exposed to the temperature of the Condition, the drier silks imbibe a certain portion of humidity from the silks which are less dry, so that the honest seller is under disadvantage in consequence of the knavery of the dishonest seller, the silk being put in cases that are adjacent. I think the test that they are about to apply is quite perfect. The proposal will minimize the humidity of silk as a standard, and then make a certain allowance for what may be considered the average merchantable humidity of the article.

8837. You stated on your last examination, that the Lyonese manufacturers assured you that they were greatly surprised at the improvement that had taken place in the English manufacture of silk since 1825; have you any facts which corroborate that assertion?—I have received many such assurances from the manufacturers, and from different members of the Chamber of Commerce, some of

678.

whom

*John Bowring,*
Esq. LL. D.

14 June,
1832.

whom had been in England; one, an eminently intelligent man, had been in England five times since 1825, and he stated that he had never seen, in the history of manufacturing improvement, any thing so rapid as the changes that had taken place in the English manufacture since 1826, and that he was struck with astonishment at the productions of some of our fabrics now, especially as contrasted with the productions of 1825; he thought the taste was improved, and the manufacture was improved. He is a very large manufacturer, and I have his statement in writing.

8838. Is this opinion formed on articles composed entirely of silk or on articles of a mixed quality?—Of silk entirely.

8839. As you are stating the opinion of this gentleman, perhaps you can state to what they attribute in France the increased demand for silks in England?—They attribute it principally to the introduction of their goods and the quantity of instruction thus communicated to the English manufacturer; secondly, to the extended demand which new articles have created in the English market; so that while their goods have been paid for at a high price by the rich, their adoption by the rich has led to a desire on the part of those less rich to wear silk articles: they think the introduction of their articles has mainly contributed to the increased production in England.

8840. Will you describe the operation of l'Ecole de Tissage?—The attendance of the scholars is wholly independent of the Government or the town; there are several instructors, whose business it is to take up students where the school of art has left them, and to show more practically the application of the loom to the designs which have been produced; they teach, in fact, not only the history but the practice of manufacture; they both give instruction, and themselves work at the loom for the instruction of those who desire information.

8841. Do they exercise any considerable influence over the state of the manufacture?—I find that the most intelligent, of whom I brought home some works, have from 60 to 80 students, but that is probably beyond the average number.

8842. Have you brought home any specimens of their work?—Yes, I have; that is a work [*handing it to the Committee*] produced by the Jacquard machine; I believe it is a master-piece in the art of weaving: it is that piece which obtained the weaving prize in France, and its beauty has been an object of great admiration; it is the production of one of the weaving masters, and is the will of Louis XVI. I believe it is one of the most extraordinary results of the loom; the other specimen is also considered a great triumph over complicated difficulties.

8843. Are these prizes annually offered at Lyons for the best work of art?—Yes; there is a yearly examination of students, and prizes are given by the town.

8844. Of what class of students?—The students of the school of which I have spoken, have from time to time prizes offered for their drawings.

8845. What is the nature of the prize?—It is generally a gold or silver medal.

8846. Is that found to excite much competition?—I think it acts principally on the students and the weaving masters as instructors; these works are produced rather as evidence of great aptitude than works likely to have a considerable sale in the market.

8847. The masters naturally feel very proud of their pupils carrying off prizes?—Undoubtedly. I hear some gentlemen, near me, deny that this is an extraordinary production: their opinion is not the opinion at Lyons; for the most intelligent manufacturers at Lyons quote these works as evidence of the very advanced state of manufacturing art. In the weaving of this work, there were 40,000 cartoons employed. I have here the report of the committee which examined the weaver and his works; and they state, that while under the old fabric there was difficulty in arranging 20 leishes, he had been able without any difficulty to arrange 400: he told me, that he did not believe that it was produceable by any other loom than the one which he had so improved.

8848. Do you consider that the emulation caused by giving prizes among the weaving masters, similar to what you have described, is very beneficial to the trade of Lyons?—All emulation is beneficial.

8849. Can you state what means exist in Lyons and in France for preserving to individuals the advantages of their ingenuity, in any discovery that they might make?—There is an establishment, which I will describe by and by, which has charge of the interests of the trade of Lyons: it is called the " Conseil des Prud' hommes." When a manufacturer has invented a pattern, he deposits it, sealed, in the

*John Bowring,*
Esq. LL. D.

18 June,
1832.

the archives of the Conseil des Prud'hommes; he pays a sum, varying from two francs to ten francs, which depends on the length of time he wishes to preserve the copyright; the Conseil des Prud'hommes exercises a direct jurisdiction, and has the power of inflicting fine, and even imprisonment for ten days; three invader of a right loses the illicit goods, and the Council has authority to amerce the offender according to the importance of the case.

8850. The process then of securing the copyright of a patent is exceedingly simple?—Exceedingly simple.

8851. The discoverer of a patent delivers a copy of it at the place appointed by the Conseil des Prud'hommes?—It is sealed, and the date of its deposition is recorded on the document; and priority of date decides priority of right.

8852. Is it found that practically there is very little difficulty for a man to assert his right to a patent?—I have been present at the discussion of a great many questions, and I have generally found them very equitably decided. I believe that the respectable manufacturers have strong and honourable feelings with regard to the impropriety of invading a copyright. Sometimes a weaver is employed by three or four houses for producing patterns long before the pieces are manufactured; and I have observed that the manufacturers who visit these looms cautiously avoid examining the patterns of their neighbours. There is a manufacture of patterns independently of the manufacture of goods; patterns are frequently offered to the buyer which do not represent goods actually manufactured; there is scarcely an instance of the invasion of a copyright among the better class of manufacturers, although there are a great many among the poor and surreptitious manufacturers.

8853. Generally speaking, there is no difficulty under this system, in any person who has invented a pattern, and registered it, preventing his right from being invaded?—Practically, I believe there is no difficulty.

8854. You have stated that this right is registered, and the proceedings carried on by what is called, "Conseil des Prud'hommes;" can you state the constitution of the Conseil des Prud'hommes?—The Conseil des Prud'hommes is one of the most popular and best organized institutions that exist in France. It is a tribunal charged with the discussion and settlement of all questions connected with the manufacturing interests of the country; and all the great manufacturing towns have their Conseil des Prud'hommes. They originated in a decree of Buonaparte's in 1806, which was the re-construction of the old manufacturing tribunal called the "Maître Garde." It is composed, as respects the silk trade of Lyons, of nine master manufacturers and eight weavers. The master manufacturers were chosen by the whole body of manufacturers, and the weavers were, till lately, chosen by the weavers who paid the patent duty. But the exclusion of the great body of weavers led to frequent misunderstanding, inasmuch as the number of weavers who paid the patent duty was comparatively small; and after the events at Lyons in November last, this being one of the great grievances of the weavers the institution was re-organized, and since January of the present year the weavers are represented by all the parties who have four looms of their own. The number of parties at Lyons who possess four looms at least, at this moment, is 778. The registration of their names has enabled me to obtain tolerably complete statistics as to the number of weaving operatives. There is only one weaver possessing thirteen looms. It has been supposed by some gentlemen who have given evidence here, that the quantity of capital possessed by the weavers must be very large, and that they hold a great number of looms, yet there is only one individual who has thirteen looms; there are four who have twelve, two who have ten, two who have nine, twelve who have eight, eight who have seven, fifty-three who have six, eighty-two who have five, six hundred and fourteen who have four, making in all 778 workmen possessing 3,000 looms; these are the weavers who are represented in the Conseil des Prud'hommes.

8855. Does the possessing of four looms give them the right of voting?—Yes.

8856. You have spoken of a change being made in the mode of election to the Conseil des Prud'hommes, by whom was that settled?—The points were submitted to the Government by the Prefect, and after an examination before the Minister of Commerce, the royal ordonnance was issued which I hold in my hand.

8857. So that in fact the Conseil des Prud'hommes is an establishment composed of the workmen and masters?—It is.

8858. Did you ever attend any of its sittings?—Yes; and I was much struck with the general good sense of their proceedings. The men who represent the

weavers,

*John Bowring,*
Esq. LL. D.

18 June,
1832.

weavers, appeared to me men of sound discretion and sober judgment. The tribunal sits in open court, and their discussions were an object of great interest, and their decisions gave general satisfaction; they act as a court of conciliation.

8859. Are all questions between masters and men settled by them?—All questions between masters and men, and masters and apprentices, and any questions that can in any way be brought to bear on the question of silk manufacture, are referred to the Conseil des Prud'hommes. Their business is to conciliate; they always examine the parties themselves; they have the power of summoning witnesses, and compelling their attendance.

8860. Is there any appeal from their decisions?—There is no appeal for any sum less than 100 francs; for any greater sum there is an appeal to the Tribunal of Commerce.

8861. Do they not take cognizance of matters between the manufacturer and the purchaser of goods?—No, their jurisdiction is wholly local; I should think they would take cognizance of questions with respect to quality between the inhabitants of a town, but not between the Lyonese seller and the foreign buyer.

8862. Generally speaking, the establishment gives satisfaction to both parties?—No doubt of it; I was a disinterested observer; I listened to the evidence given, watched the course of proceedings, and thought the Conseil exhibited appropriate knowledge, and applied it with a deal of sagacity.

8863. In questions between the masters and the purchasers of goods where the contract is not fulfilled, do not the Tribunal of Commerce refer to them for their opinion?—I have heard of frequent references to individual members of the Council.

8864. Do you mean that on the re-arrangement of this court, the number of master manufacturers remains the same as before?—Yes, before as now, all the manufacturers had the right of voting, but there were only 60 weavers who had that right; the relative number of manufacturers and weavers in the Council remains the same; the Ordonnance requires that the President should be chosen from among the manufacturers.

8865. Does the Conseil des Prud'hommes find difficulty, as we find in this country, owing to slight variations being made in the patterns?—No legislation would provide for that sort of neutral ground, where the questions of identity and similarity are slightly defined; I should say that, on the whole, it is one of the most popular institutions in France, and as far as I am able to judge of its operation, that few institutions in France have greater claims to regard.

8866. Are there frequent appeals from them?—I have a correspondence with the Mayor on the subject, and he states generally, that the number of appeals are very few indeed.

8867. Have they the power of inflicting fines in cases of violation of copyright?—Yes; and as I mentioned, they can inflict to the extent of three days imprisonment, which is frequently applied to refractory apprentices.

8868. Have they the power of settling disputes about wages?—Certainly, that comes immediately under their cognizance.

8869. With reference to what you state respecting the means of preserving the copyright and patterns, is a specification of the pattern given in, or is the pattern itself given in?—The identical pattern is delivered in; it is sealed; the date is written on the envelope, and it is deposited on the archives of the Conseil des Prud'hommes, where it may be referred to in case of dispute.

8870. Has it been found in practice whether there be any difficulty in discovering whether a pattern be original or not, with some slight variations?—The question would arise less frequently than the Committee would suppose; so rapid and unceasing is the production of novelties, and so slight the value of a pattern, where so many are daily in the course of birth. I am told on good authority that the average production in France of a particular pattern is not more than 25 pieces. There are many patterns which have never an existence in a piece, which in fact do not reach beyond the sample pattern.

8871. Of course, by the same pattern you mean the same colour?—The pattern may be the same with a variety of colours; the variety of colours is not supposed to change the character of a particular pattern. The number of pieces made of a particular pattern is naturally subject to great variations, but from the best information derived from a principal member of the Chamber of Commerce, I learn that there are a great number of patterns made by weavers which never appear in pieces, and a great number are manufactured in only one, two or three pieces, of

some

*John Bowring,*
Esq. LL. D.

18 June,
1832.

some the number produced is from 15 to 25; you will therefore have to take zero as the minimum, 25 as the medium, and 100 as the maximum of a particular pattern produced.

8872. You do not mean that the Conseil des Prud'hommes arrange the rate of wages?—Only in case of dispute, and this is done by fixing certain averages called Mercuriales.

8873. State to the Committee what are the arrangements under which silk is thrown at Lyons?—There are three modes of contracting for the throwing of silk in France; one where the waste is wholly for the account of the throwster, one where it is for the account of the owner, and third, one in which the owner and the throwster come to an understanding, as to what the probable waste will be. They agree on a value to be given to the silk, and if the throwster returns a greater quantity than agreed to between them, he is paid for it, whereas, if he return a less quantity, he is charged for it at the understood price. That is a plan now generally coming into use; the throwing establishments are generally small, and the quantity of capital employed in them is inconsiderable.

8874. Where are they situated?—Through the whole silk districts; it is not often that the grower of mulberries or the owner of silk worms is himself a throwster; there are a few of the manufacturers who have mills. From the report of the throwster themselves, they estimate the absolute cost of throwing to $3f.\ 50c.$ per pound, of which they calculate $1f.\ 50c.$ in the shape of labour, $1f.\ 50c.$ in the shape of waste, and 50 cents for wear, tear and profit; there are some throwsters who collect silk from the different agricultural producers of it. I could not find, in making inquiries over pretty large districts, that there are many throwing mills producing 1,000 pounds of organzine per annum, and there is perhaps not one throwing mill in which $5,000l.$ of capital is invested. The opinion in France is, that the throwing is in a retarded state and requires great improvements. Specimens of English thrown silk had been seen in France from England, and I was assured by manufacturers, that they were superior to their own thrown silk, of the same quality. It is a very prevalent opinion in France, that the time is not very far distant when thrown silk will be imported from England, inasmuch as our throwsters have very large capitals, and are able to improve their machinery, whereas machinery in France is very little advanced.

8875. Is the importation prohibited?—No; the importation in France is allowed at $2f.\ 40c.$ per kilogram.

8876. Is not the present state of French law as to the importation of iron, very unfavourable to the improvement of machinery?—Certainly.

8877. The expectation of importing thrown silk from England depends on the superiority of our machinery?—Yes; I have taken different statements of the prices paid for thrown silk; for organzines, $11f.$ is the general average; as to the throwing in general, they estimate the loss of from 4 to 6 per cent; but on the inferior silk of the country, and other silk, 6 to 10 per cent.; they have some silks of so exceedingly beautiful a quality, that I was informed by a large manufacturer at Nismes, he knew cases in which there was no loss at all in the shape of waste; this is the pure white silk which I before referred to. From another source I have this return; the average price of throwing organzine, where the throwster does not submit to loss, is $7f.$, that of tram, 4 to $5f.$ Where the throwster does submit, another account gives me from 10 to $11f.$ and for tram from 6 to $7f.$ There is a considerable difference in the price with respect to throwing, and it is difficult to get at it, inasmuch as the cost wholly depends on the waste and the quality.

8878. And the gain depends on the kind of silk?—Yes; the returns come to this, that generally speaking, the average cost of organzine is from 10 to 11 francs, and for tram from six to eight.

8879. Are you able to state, with regard to the silk which suffered no loss in throwing, at what period it was thrown after it was produced?—I believe very soon after the winding; it was mentioned to me as a most remarkable evidence of the great improvement in the cultivation of silks.

8880. Have you any reason to suppose, that the absence of waste depends on throwing it immediately after it is reeled?—None; I made the inquiry, and it loses nothing of its quality by ordinary delay.

8881. How is the reeling done?—The reeling is generally done by the peasantry, who probably are paid at about 25 sous per day. The cost per kilogram is estimated at four francs; the difference in cost is very considerable. I found from returns for a large period of time, that it has fluctuated from $3\frac{1}{2}$ francs to 5 francs.

678.                                                          8882. Is

*John Bowring,*
Esq. LL. D.

18 June,
1832.

8882. Is it reeled in skeins or in bobbins?—I believe principally in skeins.

8883. What is the price paid by the throwster to the persons employed in the mill?—I should think the estimate might be from 30 to 40 sous, or from 1 s. 3 d. to 1 s. 8 d. per day, that is for men, less for women certainly.

8884. Will you state any facts you are acquainted with relative to dyeing?—The average cost for dyeing is from three to four francs per kilogram; the price paid for white 6½ francs, for cherry 24 francs, for ponceau 42 francs, and for gall black four francs. The dyed silks are calculated to return 11–15ths of their weight for soft silk and light colours, and 14–15ths for supples—heavy colours; gall blacks give 16 to 18 or 25, and heavy blacks 18 to 22; labouring dyers are paid at 2 f. to 2 f. 50 c. per day, but are fed by their masters.

8885. Did you ever hear of any complaints being made as to the dishonesty practised by dyers?—Yes; I think that is one of the circumstances from which the manufacturers suffer very much; the quantity of silk robbed by the dyers is, according to the statements of the manufacturers, immensely great; and there is a contraband production going on of a very curious character. The weaver adds humidity to silk, and pillages a quantity equal to the weight of that humidity. The dyer adds weight by chemical applications, and robs the quantity whose weight he fraudulently introduces. The grievance is a subject of constant discussion, and several dyers at Lyons have made large fortunes by it. They say that the prices are so exceedingly low, that they cannot get themselves the means of subsistence; and the consequence is, they pay themselves by fraud. It is thus that there are always in the Lyons market a class of dishonest manufacturers who sell at prices under cost the goods woven out of the pillaged material.

8886. Did you ever hear their opinion respecting their superiority in dyeing to our's, or the reverse?—In some colours the belief is they are superior; I am informed, however, that some dyers at Lyons are settled in this country; I know that one or two individuals have asserted that there is very great improvement in dyeing in England.

8887. Do you conceive that they have any natural advantages for dyeing?—They have certainly a more beautiful climate and often clearer water.

8888. Is it true that they are at all particular in fixing the colour on a bright day only?—There is more thought of that than it deserves.

8889. Do you not in fact consider it to be a question of science altogether?—Clearly so; and that leads me to make an observation of some importance, that there is in France a class of men little known in England, whose trade it is to give manufacturers information. There are, for example, two or three principal chemists in Paris who receive their fees precisely as a physician does when he is called on to give his opinion as to a disease.

8890. Those are persons who make science a profession?—Yes, as applied to manufacturers; that is the case with a man very well known in the chemical world, Clement Desormes, a man whose business it is to be consulted in solving difficulties connected with his profession.

8891. Was the opinion of the Lyonese manufacturers that we had made great improvement in our colours within the last five or six years?—Yes, great improvement.

8892. Did you hear their opinion as to the comparative quality of their blacks?—I think there is a strong feeling that the English blacks are superior; the French blacks lost great reputation in foreign countries in consequence of fraud in dyeing black; some of them carried the trick so far, that I have understood the weight of silk was nearly doubled by drugs. The manufacture of Nismes was seriously injured by the loss of reputation which the overcharging their blacks brought with it. I know of a case where a quantity of silk caps was sent to Spain, and the dyers had so changed these silks, that when the black caps came to be worn, streams of ink ran over the forehead of the persons wearing them, and the manufacturers suffered serious damage in after life.

8893. The opinion generally is, that in blacks we are superior to them?—I think that opinion has gained ground very much.

8894. Is there any particular colour in which you consider them superior to us?—There is a general feeling that their colours are more varied and more tasteful than ours; they are more apt in seizing shades.

8895. But that depends on taste, not on chemical knowledge?—Certainly.

8896. Can you inform us what is usually paid to a professional chemist?—That wholly depends on the extent of the experiment; I believe the annual returns of

a man

*John Bowring,*
Esq. LL. D.

18 June,
1832.

a man of reputation would be as large as those of a professional man; an intelligent chemist would get as much as an intelligent physician.

8897. Do the French enjoy any superiority over us in their drugs?—On the whole the taxation on foreign drugs is higher than in England, and the French suffer more than we suffer from their absurd navigation laws, inasmuch as there are a great number of articles which they cannot import directly from England, but are obliged to do so from other countries; for instance, indigo. The consumption of indigo in France varies from 5,000 to 6,000 chests a year; the importation from the East is about 3,500, so that to the extent of 1,500 or 2,000 they have to supply their average wants; and they have a pernicious law which prevents their importing indigo from England, just as we also have a law preventing our importing indigo from France; but we are in a situation to import it direct, they get a large portion of their supply from England, and are obliged to pay two freights, sending it to Ostend instead of getting it direct; that is the fact with respect to every other drug not of European produce which they get from England, so that when they come into our market they are compelled to pay two freights.

8898. Do they mainly depend on this market for a supply of drugs?—They depend very much on this market.

8899. In fact they are decidedly under a disadvantage in procuring ingredients to work this?—Most assuredly; the only drug of considerable importance that they get from their own colonies is gum senegal, and more than three-fourths of that is made up for English account; France herself is, however, the producer of many dyeing drugs.

8900. Have you any facts to state as to the price of winding?—I have the return of the weavers, and they state it at 1 *d.* per ell.

8901. Will you state what is paid for the winding of the warp previous to its being put into the loom?—The winding the warp is charged 1 *f.* per kilogram, and 2 *f.* for fancy work.

8902. What are the prices of weaving?—I will put in the printed Tarif, and I consider it on the whole the very best evidence accessible; and I beg to state, that I have conversed with as many as 50 or 60 weavers, and not a less number of manufacturers, and I have in their hand-writing a statement that this Tarif may be considered as the average rates paid; there are a few cases in which the rates fluctuate from 10 per cent. above to 10 per cent below. The Conseil des Prud'hommes have made the Tarif the ground-work of many decisions; I have taken some trouble to look into it, and have found that the Tarif of 26th October 1831 may be considered to a great extent in actual operation.

[*The Witness delivered in the following Tarif.*]

### MAIRIE DE LA VILLE DE LYON.

TARIF au Minimum des Prix de la Façon des Etoffes de Soie, librement débattu et consenti entre les Délégués des Fabricans et des Ouvriers, dans la séance de la Chambre consultative des Arts et Manufactures de Lyon, du 25 Octobre 1831, à laquelle assistaient le Maire de Lyon et les Membres du Conseil des Prud'hommes, et qui était présidée par le Préfet du département du Rhône, pour recevoir son exécution à partir du 1er Novembre prochain.

*Draps de Soie.*

#### Doubles.

| | | | | | | | | f. | c. |
|---|---|---|---|---|---|---|---|---|---|
| Drap de Soie | - | - | - | 1/2 de 120 portées sur 8 lisses | - | - | - | 2 | 10 |
| Drap de Soie | - | - | - 11/24 de 110 | - | ,, | - | - | - | 1 | 80 |
| Drap de Soie | - | - | - 11/24 de 100 | - | ,, | - | - | .. | 1 | 70 |
| Drap de Soie | - | - | - 11/24 de 90 | - | ,, | - | - | - | 1 | 60 |
| Drap de Soie | - | - | - 11/24 de 80 sur 10 lisses | - | - | - | 1 | 50 |
| Drap de Soie | - | - | - 11/24 de 70 | ,, | - | - | - | - | 1 | 40 |
| Drap de Soie | - | - | - 11/24 de 60 | ,, | - | - | - | - | 1 | 25 |
| Drap de Soie | - | - | - 11/24 de 50 | ,, | - | - | - | - | 1 | 15 |
| Drap de Soie | - | - | - 7/16 de 45 à 40 | - | - | - | - | 1 | 5 |

#### Simples.

| | | | | | | | | f. | c. |
|---|---|---|---|---|---|---|---|---|---|
| Drap de Soie | - | - | - 11/24 de 80 portées sur 10 lisses | - | - | 1 | 40 |
| Drap de Soie | - | - | - 11/24 de 70 | ,, | sur 8 | - | - | - | 1 | 25 |
| Drap de Soie | - | - | - 11/24 de 60 | - | ,, | - | - | - | 1 | 15 |
| Drap de Soie | - | - | - 11/24 de 50 à 54 | ,, | - | - | - | 1 | 5 |
| Drap de Soie | - | - | - 7/16 de 40 à 45 | ,, | - | - | - | 1 | - |

*John Bowring,*
Esq. LL.D.

18 June,
1832.

*Draps de Soie, qualité d'Allemagne.*

### Doubles.

|  |  |  | f. | c. |
|---|---|---|---|---|
| Drap de Soie | - - - | 7/16 de 50 à 54 portées - - - - | 1 | 10 |
| Drap de Soie | - - - | 5/12 de 45 - - - - - - | 1 | 5 |
| Drap de Soie | - - - | 5/12 de 40 - - - - - - | — | 95 |
| Drap de Soie | - - - | 3/8 de 35 - - - - - - | — | 90 |

### Simples.

| Drap de Soie | - - - | 7/16 de 50 à 54 - - - - | 1f. à 1 | 5 |
|---|---|---|---|---|
| Drap de Soie | - - - | 5/12 de 45 - - - - - | — | 95 |
| Drap de Soie | - - - | 3/8 de 40 - - - - - | — | 85 |
| Drap de Soie | - - - | 3/8 de 35 - - - - - | — | 80 |

*Satins rayés.*

### Sur deux Rouleaux.

| Satin | - - | 11/24 de 110 à 120 portées de 3 bouts - - | 1 | 25 |
|---|---|---|---|---|

### Satin doubles pour la main.

| Satin | - - | 11/24 de 130 portées doubles sur 8 lisses - - | 2 | — |
|---|---|---|---|---|
| Satin | - - | 11/24 de 120 - „ - - - - | 1 | 90 |
| Satin | - - | 11/24 de 110 - „ - - - - | 1 | 70 |
| Satin | - - | 11/24 de 100 - „ - - - - | 1 | 50 |

### Satin simples pour la main.

| Satin | - - | 11/24 de 130 portées simples - - - | 1 | 80 |
|---|---|---|---|---|
| Satin | - - | 11/24 de 120 - „ - - - | 1 | 70 |
| Satin | - - | 11/24 de 110 - „ - - - | 1 | 55 |
| Satin | - - | 11/24 de 100 - „ - - - | 1 | 40 |

### Satins simples pour l'apprêt.

| Satin | - - | 11/24 de 130 - - - - - | 1 | 70 |
|---|---|---|---|---|
| Satin | - - | 11/24 de 120 - - - - - | 1 | 45 |
| Satin | - - | 11/24 de 110 - - - - - | 1 | 25 |
| Satin | - - | 11/24 de 100 - - - - - | — | 95 |
| Satin | - - | 11/24 de 90 - - - - - | — | 85 |
| Satin | - - | 11/24 de 80 - - - - - | — | 75 |
| Satin | - - | 7/16 de 70 à 75 - - - - - | — | 65 |
| Satin | - - | 7/16 de 60 à 66 - - - - - | — | 60 |
| Satin | - - | 7/16 de 50 à 54 - - - - - | — | 55 |
| Satin | - - | 7/16 de 40 à 45 - - - - - | — | 50 |

### Satins 4/4.

| Satin | - - | 4/4 de 160 portées de 2 à 3 bouts - - | 2 | 20 |
|---|---|---|---|---|
| Satin | - - | 15/16 de 155 à 180 - - - - | 1f. 90c. à 2 | — |
| Satin | - - | 4/4 de 150 - - - - - | 2 | — |
| Satin | - - | 15/16 de 145 - - - - - | 1 | 90 |
| Satin | - - | 7/8 de 135 à 140 - - - - | 1 | 80 |

*Serges.*

### Serge 4/4 double.

| Serge | - - | 4/4 de 80 portées de doubles 2 à 3 bouts - | 1 | 75 |
|---|---|---|---|---|
| Serge | - - | 15/16 de 75 - - - - - | 1 | 60 |
| Serge | - - | 7/8 de 60 à 70 - - - - - | 1 | 50 |

### Serge simple.

| Serge | - - | 4/4 de 80 portées de 2 à 3 bouts - - | 1 | 70 |
|---|---|---|---|---|
| Serge | - - | 15/16 de 75 - - - - - | 1 | 55 |
| Serge | - - | 7/8 de 60 à 70 - - - - - | 1 | 30 |

*Gros de Naples.*

### Triples.

| Gros de Naples | - | 11/24 de 60 portées triples de 4 à 5 bouts - | 1 | 40 |
|---|---|---|---|---|
| Gros de Naples | - | 11/24 de 50 - „ - 4 5 id. - | 1 | 30 |
| Gros de Naples | - | 7/16 de 40-45 „ - 5 6 id. - | 1 | 25 |
| Gros de Naples | - | 7/16 de 60 portées doubles de 4 5 id. - | 1 | 20 |
| Gros de Naples | - | 7/16 de 50 - „ - 3 4 id. - | 1 | — |
| Gros de Naples | - | 7/16 de 45 - „ - 3 4 id. - | — | 90 |
| Gros de Naples | - | 7/16 de 40 - „ - 2 3 id. - | — | 80 |
| Gros de Naples | - | 7/16 de 35 - „ - 2 3 id. - | — | 70 |

### Simples.

| Gros de Naples | - | 11/24 de 60 portées simples de 3 a 4 bouts - | 1 | — |
|---|---|---|---|---|
| Gros de Naples | - | 11/24 de 50 - „ - 4 5 id. - | — | 90 |
| Gros de Naples | - | 7/16 de 40 à 48 „ - 2 3 id. - | — | 75 |
| Gros de Naples | - | 7/16 de 30 à 45 „ - 2 3 id. - | — | 65 |

*Gros*

*John Bowring,*
Esq. LL. D.
————
18 June,
1832.

### Gros de Naples d'Allemagne.

| | | | | | |
|---|---|---|---|---|---|
| Gros de Naples | - | 7/16 de 40 à 45 portées doubles de 2 à 3 bouts | - | - 70 |
| Gros de Naples | - | 5/12 de 35 - - - - - 2 id. | - | - 65 |
| Gros de Naples | - | 3/8 de 30 à 32 - - - - 2 id. | - | - 60 |

### Simples, qualité d'Allemagne.

f.  c.

| | | | |
|---|---|---|---|
| Gros de Naples | - | 7/16 de 40 à 50 portées simples de 2 à 3 bouts - | - 70 |
| Gros de Naples | - | 5/12 de 35  40 - - - 1  2 id. - | - 65 |
| Gros de Naples | - | 3/8 de 30  35 - - - 1  2 id. - | - 55 |

### Lévantines.
#### Doubles en demi-aune.

| | | | |
|---|---|---|---|
| Levantine | - - | 1/2 de 45 portées doubles de 1 à 2 bouts - | - - 90 |
| Levantine | - - | 1/2 de 40 - - „ - - id. - - | - - 85 |

#### Simples en demi-aune.

| | | | |
|---|---|---|---|
| Levantine | - - | 1/2 de 45 portées simples de 1 à 2 bouts - | - - 80 |
| Levantine | - - | 1/2 de 40 - - „ - - id. - - | - - 70 |

### Serges.
#### Doubles en demi-aune.

| | | | |
|---|---|---|---|
| Serge | - - - | 1/2 de 45 portées doubles sur 8 lisses, 1 à 2 bouts - | - 95 |
| Serge | - - - | 1/2 de 40 - „ - sur 6 lisses - id. - | - 90 |
| Serge | - - - | 1/2 de 45 portées simples „ - - id. - | - 85 |
| Serge | - - - | 1/2 de 40 - „ - - „ - id. - | - 75 |

### Gros des Inde, Marcellines, et Gros de Naples divers.

f. c.   f. c.

| | |
|---|---|
| Gros des Indes doubles de 11/24 et 7/16 de 40 à 45 portées de 1 à 5 bouts | — 90 à 1 — |
| Gros des Indes triples 11/24 et 7/12, 45 à 50 portées de 1 à 8 et de 8 à 12 bouts | 1 —  1 35 |
| Marcelline double 11/24 à 1/2 aune de 24 à 35 portées - - - | - 90  1 — |
| Gros de Naples pour cravates, écossais riches, de 70 à 80 portées, la cravate | - 90  1 — |
| Gros de Naples doubles 7/8 de 90 à 100 portées de 2 et 3 bouts - | - 1 70  1 80 |
| Gros de Naples doubles 3/4 de 65 à 75 portées de 2 à 4 bouts - | - 1 20  1 30 |
| 15/16 meuble couleur de 110 à 120 portées simples de 3 à 4 bouts | - 1 90  2 — |
| 15/16 meuble couleur de 100 à 110 portées doubles de 3 à 4 bouts | - - — 2 25 |

### Cravates écossaises.

| | |
|---|---|
| Cravates écossaises à 1 fil en dent en 3/4 de 30 à 35 portées simples - la cravate | — 70 |
| Cravates écossaises à 1 fil en dent en 5/8 de 25 à 30 portées simples - „ | — 60 |

### Taffetas pour l'appret et pour la main.

| | POUR | | |
|---|---|---|---|
| | l'apprêt. | la main. | |
| | f.  c. | f.  c. | f.  c. |
| 4/4 de 110 à 120 portées simples de 1 à 2 bouts - - | 1 55 | — - à | 1 65 |
| 4/4 de 100 portées simples - de 1 à 2 id. | 1 40 | — - | 1 50 |
| 15/16 de 100 à 110 id. - - de 1 à — id. - | 1 70 | — - | 1 60 |
| 7/8 de 100 à 110 id. - - de 1 à 2 id | 1 25 | — - | - |
| 7/8 de 125 - - id. - - de 1 à 2 id. - | 1 40 | 1 40 | 1 60 |
| 3/4 de 100 à 110 id. - - de 1 à 2 id. - | 1 5 | 1 20 | 1 25 |
| 3/4 de 80 à 90 id. - - de 1 à 2 id. - | — 95 | 1 50 | 1 10 |
| 3/4 de 60 à 70 id. - - de 1 à 2 id. - | — 90 | 1 — | 1 5 |
| 5/8 de 70 à 80 id. - - de 1 à 2 id. - | — - | — 80 | — 90 |
| 5/8 de 50 à 60 id. - - de 1 à 2 id. - | — - | — 70 | — 75 |
| 7/12 de 70 id. - - de 1 à 2 id. - | — - | — - | — 80 |
| 7/12 de 50 à 60 id. - - de 1 à 2 id. - | — - | — 70 | — 75 |
| 1/2 de 70 id. - - de 1 à 2 id. - | — - | — - | — 80 |
| 1/2 de 50 à 60 id. - - de 1 à 2 id. - | — - | — 65 | — 70 |
| 1/2 de 40 à 45 id. - - de 1 bout - - | — - | — 55 | — 60 |
| 1/2 de 33 à 35 id. - - de 1 bout - - | — - | — 45 | — 50 |

### Gros Grains.

| | f.  c. | f.  c. |
|---|---|---|
| 7/8 de 100 à 110 portées de 4 à 6 bouts - | — - | — 1 80 |
| 3/4 de 90 à 100 id. de 3 à 5 id. - - | — - 1 40 à | 1 60 |
| 3/4 de 80 à 90 id. de 3 à 5 id. - - | — - | — 1 40 |
| 5/8 de 70 à 80 id. de 3 à 4 id. - | — - 1 20 à | 1 25 |
| 1/2 de 50 à 60 id. de 3 à 4 id. - | — - | — 1 10 |

678.

Parapluies.

*John Bowring,*
Esq. LL. D.

18 June,
1832.

Parapluies.

| | | | f. c. |
|---|---|---|---|
| 5/8 de 50 à 70 portées doubles et simples de 2 bouts | - | -   -   -   - | — 90 |
| 7/12 de 50 à 60    -   id.   -   de 2 id. | - | -   -   -   - | — 80 |
| 7/12 de 45 à 55   -   - id.   -   de 2 id. | - | -   -   -   - | — 75 |
| 3/24 de 40 à 45   -   - id.   -   de 2 id. | - | -   -   -   - | — 75 |
| 1/2 de 40 à 45    -   id.   -   de 2 id. | - | -   -   -   - | — 65 |
| 7/16 de 30 à 40   -   - id.   -   de 2 id. | - | -   —   55 à | — 60 |

*Velours façonnées, unis et Peluches.*     f. c.

1/2 aune. Velours plein façonné, fond Batavia, 55 fers au pouce { 1 lat } Un corps. { 8 25 / 8 75 / 9 25 } (2 lats; 3 lats)

1/2 aune { Velours ciselé, corps plein, fond taffetas { à mouches, de 38 à 40 fers au pouce - - - ; à bouquets - - id. - ; ciselé tout le long id. - } 1 lat } Un corps { 7 50 / 8 — / 8 50 }

Velours tout frisé, corps plein, fond taffetas - 1 lat } 6 —
Velours coupé, liseré, dit paysan, corps plein - 2 lats suivis } 6 —

Velours plein façonné, fond Batavia - } 
Velours ciselé, fond taffetas, à bouquets - - } 1 lat { Deux corps { 11 — / 9 50 / 10 50 }
Id. - - - id. - - - ciselé tout le long - }

Chaque lat en plus 50 cent. d'augmentation pour les articles désignés ci-dessus.

Velours façonné coupé, fond satin - }
Id. ciselé, fond satin, à mouches - }
Id. - - id. - - à bouquets } 40 fers au pouce - { Un corps { 7 — / 8 — / 8 — / 9 — }
Id. tout au long, fond satin - }

Velours ciselé, fond satin, à bouquets de 38 à 40 fers au pouce }
Id. - - - id. - ciselé tout le long, de 38 à 40 fers au pouce - - - - - - - } Deux corps { 9 — / 10 — / 9 — }
Id. fond satin, tout coupé, de 40 fers au pouce - }

*Articles Velours unis.*

1 1/24 Velours unis {
| | f. c. |
|---|---|
| 1 poil tramé cru, de 22 portées, de 60 à 65 fers au pouce - | 5 — |
| 1 poil 1/2 id. cru, de 22 - id. - de 60 à 65 - id. - - | 5 25 |
| 2 - id. - cru, de 22 - id. - de 60 à 65 - id. - - | 5 50 |
| 2 - id. cuit, de 22 - id. - de 60 à 65 - id. - - | 6 — |
| 2 - id. - cru, de 25 - id. - de 60 à 65 - id. - - | 6 50 |
| 2 - id. - cuit de 25 - id. - de 60 à 66 - id. - - | 7 — |
| 2 - id. - cru, de 28 à 30 id. - de 60 à 65 - id. - - | 7 50 |
| 2 - id. - cuit de 28 à 30 id. - de 60 à 65 - id. - - | 8 — |

Les couleurs à discuter entre Maître et Fabricans.

| | f. c. |
|---|---|
| 11/24 Velours ras frisé, de 24 à 26 fers au pouce - - - - - | 2 50 |
| 11/24 Velours ras frisé, à 2 coups, de 36 à 40 fers au pouce - - - | 3 50 |
| 1/2 aune Velours ras frisé, à 4 coups, de 24 à 26 fers au pouce - - - | 3 25 |

Velours armures et couleurs tendres à discuter entre les Maîtres et les Fabricans

| | f. c. |
|---|---|
| Peluches pour chapeau, de 18 à 20 fers au pouce - - - - | 3 — |
| Au-dessus de 20 fers, 25 cent. d'augmentation. | |
| Petites peluches, de 12 à 14 fers au pouce - - - - - | 1 75 |

*Popelines*

*Popelines façonnées, Courants pour Gilets et Courants divers.*

| GENRE D'ETOFFES. | LARGEUR. | CHEMINS. | LATS. | BOUTS. | COUPS au POUCE. | MILLES A L'AUNE. | PRIX au MILLE. f. c. | PRIX A L'AUNE. f. c. à f. c. |
|---|---|---|---|---|---|---|---|---|
| **POPELINES FAÇONNEES.** | | | | | | | | |
| Popelines tramées coton | 15 à 18 pouces | de 3 à 5 | 1 | 1 bout coton | de 60 à 70 | 2,640 à 3,080 | - 15 | - 40 à - 50 |
| Idem | 19 à 25 | 6 à 8 | 1 | Idem | 60 à 70 | 2,640 à 3,080 | - 20 | - 50 à - 60 |
| Popeline Muskovite pour gilets | 18 à 22 | 8 à 10 | 1 | Idem | 50 à 60 | 2,200 à 2,640 | - 30 | - 70 à - 80 |
| Popeline coton pour gilets | 15 à 18 | 6 à 8 | 1 | Idem | 50 à 60 | 2,200 à 2,640 | - 25 | - 60 à - 75 |
| **COURANTS POUR GILETS.** | | | | | | | | |
| Courants soie forts | 15 à 18 pouces | de 7 à 9 | 1 | 1 et 2 bouts | de 100 à 120 | 4,400 à 5,280 | - 20 | - 90 à 1 - 5 |
| Idem gilets soie | 19 à 22 | 10 à 12 | 1 | 2 et 3 id. | 100 à 120 | 4,400 à 5,280 | - 25 | 1 - à 1 - 25 |
| Idem - idem | 20 à 22 | 13 à 15 | 1 | 1 et 2 id. | 120 à 150 | 5,280 à 5,600 | - 30 | 1 - 40 à 1 - 75 |
| Idem - idem | 22 | 13 à 15 | 1 | 3 et 4 id. | 120 à 140 | 5,280 à 6,160 | - 35 | 1 - 75 à 2 - |
| Idem gilets simulés | 17 à 22 | 10 à 12 | 2 | 1 soie 1 coton | 70 à 80 | 3,080 à 3,520 | - 45 | 1 - 25 à 2 - 50 |
| Velouté pour gilets | 20 à 22 | 10 à 12 | 1 | 1 coton | 80 à 100 | 3,520 à 4,400 | - 30 | - 75 à 1 - |
| Velouté bosselé | 20 à 22 | 10 à 12 | 2 | coton gros fin | 100 - | 4,400 | - 35 | 1 - 50 à - |
| Idem bosselé lancé | 20 à 22 | 10 à 12 | 2 | 1 coton 1 soie | 90 - | 3,960 | - 40 | - 60 à - |
| Gilets lancé suivi | 20 à 22 | 10 à 12 | 2 | soie 2 et 3 | 100 à 120 | 4,400 à 5,280 | - 35 | 1 - 50 à 1 - 75 |
| Idem | 20 à 22 | 13 à 15 | 2 | idem 3 et 4 | 100 à 120 | 4,400 à 5,280 | - 40 | 1 - 75 à 2 - |
| Gilets gros de Tours lancé | 20 à 22 | 10 à 12 | 2 | soie 2 et 4 | 120 à 140 | 5,280 à 6,160 | - 40 | 2 - à 2 - 25 |
| Idem - idem | 20 à 22 | 13 à 15 | 2 | idem | 120 à 140 | 5,280 à 6,160 | - 45 | 2 - 25 à 2 - 75 |
| Velours simulé dit mosaïque | 20 à 22 | 9 à 12 | 3 | lancé soie et coton | 70 à 80 | 3,080 à 3,520 | - 50 | 1 - 50 à 2 - 75 |
| Gilets à corps et lisses | 20 à 22 | 10 à 12 | 1 | soie 2 et 3 | 100 à 120 | 4,400 à 5,280 | - 40 | 1 - 75 à 2 - |
| Idem | 20 à 22 | 13 à 15 | 2 | soie 3 et 4 | 100 à 120 | 4,400 à 5,280 | - 45 | 2 - à 2 - 25 |
| Idem | 20 à 22 | 12 à 15 | 2 | soie 2 et 3 | 120 à 140 | 5,280 à 6,160 | - 55 | 2 - 75 à 3 - 25 |
| Courants lamés à liage | 17 à 18 | 9 à 12 | 2 | lame et soie | 120 à 140 | 5,280 à 6,160 | - 60 | 2 - 60 à 3 - 25 |
| Courants lamés sans liage | 17 à 18 | 9 à 12 | 2 | idem | 120 à 140 | 5,280 à 6,160 | - 35 | 2 - 75 à 3 - 25 |
| Idem | 17 à 18 | 9 à 12 | 2 1/2 | idem | 100 à 120 | 4,400 à 5,280 | - 50 | 2 - 10 à 3 - |
| Idem | 17 à 18 | 8 à 10 | 2 | idem | 110 à 120 | 4,840 à 5,280 | - 50 | 2 - 30 à 2 - 40 |
| Idem | 17 à 18 | 8 à 10 | 1 1/2 | idem | 100 à 110 | 4,400 à 4,840 | - 45 | 1 - 75 à 2 - |
| **COURANTS DIVERS.** | | | | | | | | |
| Courants légers | 16 à 17 pouces | de 6 à 7 | 1 | 1 et 2 bouts | de 100 - | 4,400 | • | - 80 |
| Idem mandarine | 18 à 22 | 6 à 8 | 1 | soie | 90 à 100 | 4,000 à 4,400 | - 20 | - 80 à - 90 |
| Ombrelles corps plein | 17 à 20 | 7 à 10 | 1 | 1 et 2 bouts | 110 à 120 | - | - 20 | - 90 |
| Parapluies | 22 à 27 | Bordure - | 1 | 2 bouts | 90 à 100 | 4,000 à 4,400 | - 35 | 1 - 20 |

Augmentation de 5 centimes par mille dans le Courants et Gilets pour chaque Lat au-dessus de 2 lats, 5 centimes pour chaque Rouleau au-dessus d'un Rouleau, et de 5 centimes par mille pour les métiers montés en 600.

Réductions de 1 fr. pour les Lamés satin à deux coups de fond et un coup de lame, et de 50 centimes pour ceux à un coup de fond et un coup de lame.

678.

*Châles*

John Bowring,
Esq. LL. D.

18 June,
1832.

## Châles bourre de Soie.

|  |  |  |  | c. |
|---|---|---|---|---|
| Bordures | - - - | 5/4 en 400 ou 600, à fils | - - - le mille | 35 |
| Châles | - - - | 5/4 en 400 ou 600, à id. | - - - id. | 40 |
| Id. | - - - | 6/4 en 400 ou 600, à id. | - - - id. | 45 |
| Id. | - - - | 5/4 en 400 ou 600, à lisses | - - - id. | 50 |
| Id. | - - - | 6/4 en 400 ou 600, à id. | - - - id. | 55 |
| Id. | - - - | 5/4 ou quart simple | - - - id. | 55 |
| Id. | - - - | 6/4 ou quart en 1,200 ou 1,500 | - - id. | 62½ |
| Id. | - - - | 6/4 ou quart à rosace 1,500 | - - id. | 65 |
| Id. | - - - | 6/4 ou id. - id. 1,800 | - - id. | 67½ |

## Tissus dits Châly.

| Largeur. | Mécanique. | Pouces. | Coups. |  | Prix. |
|---|---|---|---|---|---|
|  |  |  |  | c. |  |
| 5/4, | 400, | 120, | 5,280, | à 37½ | le mille. |
| 5/4, | 600, | 120, | id. | à 40 | id. |
| 4/4, | 400, | 120, | id. | à 27½ | id. |
| 4/4, | 600, | 120, | id. | à 30 | id. |
| 3/4, | 400, | 120, | id. | à 22½ | id. |
| 3/4, | 600, | 120, | id. | à 25 | id. |
| 5/4 uni, |  | 120, | id. | à 35 | id. |
| 4/4 id., |  | 120, | id. | à 25 | id. |
| 3/4 id., |  | 120, | id. | à 20 | id. |
| 1/2 id., |  | 120, | id. | à 15 | id. |

## Tissus dits Thibet.

| Largeur. | Croisure. | Pouces. | Coups. |  |
|---|---|---|---|---|
|  |  |  |  | c. |
| 5/4, | 12  1/4, | 192, | 8,448, | à 35 le mille. |
| 4/4, | 12  1/4, | 192, | 8,448, | à 25 id. |
| 3/4, | 12  1/4, | 192, | 8,448, | à 15 id. |

## Châles brochéts et lancés laine.

|  |  |  |  | f. | c. |  |
|---|---|---|---|---|---|---|
| Large 6/4 ombré. | - | Mécanique 400 | à | — | 82½ | le mille. |
|  |  | Idem. 600 |  | — | 85 | id. |
|  |  | Id. 900 |  | — | 87½ | id. |
| Large 6/4. | - - | Id. 400 |  | — | 72½ | id. |
|  |  | Id. 600 |  | — | 75 | id. |
|  |  | Id. 900 |  | — | 77½ | id. |
| Large 5/4. ombré | - | Id. 400 |  | — | 67½ | id. |
|  |  | Id. 600 |  | — | 70 | id. |
|  |  | Id. 900 |  | — | 72½ | id. |
| Large 5/4. | - - | Id. 400 |  | — | 57½ | id. |
|  |  | Id. 600 |  | — | 60 | id. |
|  |  | Id. 900 |  | — | 62½ | id. |
| Large 4/4 ombré. | - | Id. 400 |  | — | 47½ | id. |
|  |  | Id. 600 |  | — | 50 | id. |
| Large 4/4. | - - | Id. 400 |  | — | 40 | id. |
|  |  | Id. 600 |  | — | 42½ | id. |
| Large 3/4. | - - | Id. 400 |  | — | 25 | id. |
|  |  | Id. 600 |  | — | 27½ | id. |

## Fichus Crépon.

|  |  |  |  | f. | c. |  |
|---|---|---|---|---|---|---|
| 26 à 28 Pouces | - | à chemin | - - à | — | 25 | le mille. |
|  |  | à tringles | - - à | — | 30 | id. |
|  |  | à lisses | - - à | — | 35 | id. |
| 34 à 38 Pouces | - | à chemin | - - à | — | 35 | le mille. |
|  |  | à tringles | - - à | — | 40 | id. |
|  |  | à lisses | - - à | — | 45 | id. |
| 45 à 49 Pouces | - | à chemin | - - à | — | 40 | le mille. |
|  |  | à tringles | - - à | — | 45 | id. |
|  |  | à lisses | - - à | — | 50 | id. |

Châles

*John Bowring,*
Esq. LL. D.

18 June,
1832.

### Châles 6/4.

#### Fond Satin, Indiens et Péruviens.

Larguer 57 pouces, liseré en 900, 1 lat, à 60 cent. le mille.
Idem,      id. en 1,200, 1 id., à 70   id.
Idem,      id. en 1,800, 1 id., à 75   id.
Idem,      lancé en 900, 2 id., à 75   id.
Idem,      id. en 1,200, 2 id., à 85   id.
Idem,      id. en 1,800, 2 id., à 95   id.
Idem,      id. en 900, 4 id., à 75   id.
Idem,      id. en 1,200, 4 id., à 85   id.
Idem,      id. en 1,800, 4 id., à 95   id.

### Fichus Mandarines.

| Larguer. | Portées. | | | | Prix. |
|---|---|---|---|---|---|
| 26 à 28 Pouces | 30 à 35, sans tringles | - | - | - | à 25 cent. le mille. |
| Idem | id. à tringles | - | - | - | à 30 id. |
| 34 à 38 pouces | 48 sans id. | - | - | - | à 33 ½ id. |
| Idem | id. à tringles | - | - | - | à 35 id. |
| 44 à 49 pouces | 70 sans id. | - | - | - | à 45 id. |
| Idem | id. à tringles | - | - | - | à 50 id. |

### Mouchoirs Brillantines 400 et 600.

#### 24 à 26 Pouces.

Mouchoirs brillantines fond et bordure liserés   -   -   - à 2 fils.   - 50 c. le mouch
Id.   id.   id.   id.   -   -   - à 4 id.   - 60
Id.   id. avec bordure poil traînant   -   -   - à 2 id.   - 60
Id.   id.   id.   id.   -   -   - à 4 id.   - 70

#### 28 à 29 Pouces.

Mouchoirs brillantines fond et bordure liserés   -   -   - à 2 fils.   - 70 c. le mouch.
Id.   id.   id.   id.   -   -   - à 4 id.   - 80
Id.   id. avec bordure poil traînant   -   -   - à 2 id.   - 85
Id.   id.   id.   id.   -   -   - à 4 id.   - 90

#### 30 à 33 Pouces.

Mouchoirs brillantines fond et bordure liserés   -   -   - à 2 fils.   - 85 c. le mouch.
Id.   id.   id.   id.   -   -   - à 4 id.   - 9
Id.   id. avec bordure poil traînant   -   -   - à 2 id.   - 01
Id.   id.   id.   id.   -   -   - à 4 id.   1 10

#### 36 à 39 Pouces.

Mouchoirs brillantines fond et bordure liserés   -   -   - à 2 fils. 1 20 c. le mouch.
Id.   id.   id.   id.   -   -   - à 4 id.   1 30
Id.   id. avec bordure poil traînant   -   -   - à 2 id.   1 30
Id.   id.   id.   id   -   -   - à 4 id.   1 40

#### 27 à 28 Pouces.

Cravates fond uni à bordure à poil   -   -   - ⎤
Bandes satin et filet cannelés   -   -   - ⎦ à 2 et 4 fils.   - 90 c. le mouch.

#### 31 à 33 Pouces.

Id.   id.   id.   -   -   -   -   -   - 1 20

### Crêpes de Chine et Zéphyrs.

| Larg. | Qualités. | Nombre de Coups au pouce. | Nombre de milles au mouchoir. | Prix du mille. | Prix du mouch. |
|---|---|---|---|---|---|
| | Unis. | 66 à 68 | 2,000 | - 30 c. | - 60 c. |
| 3/4 - | façonnes à tringles. | idem. | idem. | - 37 | - 75 |
| | id. à corps et à lissés | idem. | idem. | - 40 | - 80 |
| | Unis. | 68 à 70 | 2,870 | - 35 | 1 - |
| 4/4 - | façonnes à tringles. | idem. | idem. | - 45 | 1 25 |
| | id. à corps et à lisse | idem. | idem. | - 50 | 1 40 |
| | Unis. | idem. | 3,640 | - 57 | 1 90 |
| 5/4 - | façonnes à tringles. | idem. | idem. | - 65 | 2 25 |
| | id. à corps et à lisses | idem. | idem. | - 70 | 2 50 |
| | Unis. | idem. | 4,340 | - 65 | 2 75 |
| 6/4 - | façonnes à tringles. | idem. | idem. | - 75 | 3 - |
| | id. à corps et à lisses | idem. | idem. | - 80 | 3 25 |
| 3/4 - | - zephirs unis. | 86 à 90 | 2,490 | - 20 | - 50 |
| 3/4 | crêpes unis. ⎫ mouch. avec cadr. ⎭ | 80 à 84 | 2,600 | - 12 | - 30 |

*Echarpes*

*John Bowring,*
Esq. LL. D.

18 June,
1832.

*Echarpes Crêpe Zéphyr, façonnées.*

| | Le Mille pour le fond. | Le Mille pour le lancé. |
|---|---|---|
| | c. | c. |
| De 22 à 26 pouces à petites bordures poil lié, de 80 à 90 dents au pouce, sur 400 ou 600 cordes - - - - - - - - - | 25 | 40 |
| Id. id. à bordure, poil traînant sur 400 ou 600 cordes - - - - | 38 | 40 |

*Mouchoirs Crêpe Zéphyr façonnées.*

| | | |
|---|---|---|
| Petite bordure poil lié de 80 à 90 dents au pouce sur 400 à 600 cordes de 33 pouces - - - - - - - - - - - - - | 25 | 40 |
| De 33 pouces à petite bordure poil lié de 80 à 90 dents au pouce sur 750 à 900 cordes - - - - - - - - - - - - | 30 | 40 |
| De 33 pouces à bordure poil traînant, sur 400 à 600 id. - - - | 30 | 40 |
| Id.        id.        id.        sur 750 à 900 id. - - - | 35 | 40 |
| Id. à poil tout au travers,        sur 400 à 600 cordes - - | 60 | – |
| De 44 pouces à petites bordures poil lié, sur 400 à 600 id. - - - | 35 | 60 |
| Id.            id.        sur 750 à 900 id. - - - | 40 | 60 |
| Id.        à bordure poil traînant,    sur 400 à 600 id. - - - | 40 | 60 |
| Id.            id.        sur 750 à 900 id. - - - | 45 | 60 |
| Id. à poil tout au travers,        sur 600 - - - - - | 70 | – |
| De 55 pouces à petites bordures poil lié, de 400 à 600 id. - - - | 40 | 70 |
| Idem        id.        id.    de 750 à 900 id. - - - | 45 | 70 |
| Idem        à bordure poil traînant, de 400 à 600 id. - - - | 45 | 70 |
| Idem            id.    de 750 à 900 id. - - - | 50 | 70 |
| Idem        à poil tout au travers, - - - - - - - - | 90 | – |

Les colliers à dieux sur la largeur entreront dans la catégorie des Mouchoirs 3/4 zephyrs ci-dessus.

Les coups de broché sont assimilés aux coups de lancé.

*Etoffes pour Meubles.*

| | | | | f. | c. | |
|---|---|---|---|---|---|---|
| | ⎧ Satin liseré pour tenture de 80 à 100 portées - - | à | 2 | 25 | l'aune. |
| | ⎪ Id.  2 lats pour ornement.  id. - - - | à | 2 | – | id. |
| | ⎪ Damas sans envers, belle qualité - - - - | à | 3 | – | id. |
| | ⎪ Id.  id.  qualité ordinaire - - - - | à | 2 | – | id. |
| 11/24 - - ⎨ Damas trois couleurs - - - - - - | à | 4 | 50 | id. |
| | ⎪ Gallon broché - - - - - - - - | à | 4 | – | id. |
| | ⎪ Guirlande brochée et lancée - - - - - | à | 4 | – | id. |
| | ⎩ Gourgourand avec 12 lisses devant - - - - | à | 2 | – | id. |

*Marabous sur 400 ou 600.*

Les courants marabous à poil traînant - - - - - à 30 cent. le mille.
L'écharpe marabou - - - - - - - - - - à 25 id.
Id.     cru - - - - - - - - - - à 20 id.
Le tout sur un 35 à 45 portées de peigne en 11/24 le courant marabou
à poil de 90 dents à 100 au pouce - - - - - à 35 id.
L'écharpe marabou - - - - - - - - - - à 30 id.
Id.     cru - - - - - - - - - - à 25 id.

*Mouchoirs 26 à 28 pouces.*

D'un 50 à un 62 portées de peigne 3/4 le mouchoir avec bordure
ou petit poil - - - - - - - - - - - - à 32 cent. 1/2 le mille
Id. à poil traînant - - - - - - - - - à 35    id.
D'un 63 à 70 portées de peigne 3/4 le mouchoir avec bordure
ou petit poil - - - - - - - - - - - - à 37   1/2 id
Id. avec poil traînant - - - - - - - - à 40    id
D'un 71 à 80 portées toujours 3/4, l'augmentation est de 5 cent.
en plus au mille.
Les articles en cru - - - - - - - - - à 2   1/2 id.

*Mouchoirs 4/4, ou de 37 à 39 pouces.*

D'un 70 à 80 portées en 4/4 avec bordure ou petit poil - - à 55 cent. le mille.
A poil traînant - - - - - - - - - à 60 id.
Et progressivement de 5 cent. d'augmentation par 10 portées de peigne plus réduit.
Les lancés en 18 à 20 pouces - - - - - - 40 cent.
Id.  en 26 à 29 id. - - - - - - - 50
Id.  en 37 à 39 id. - - - - - - - 60
Lancé 2 lats 5 cent. de plus.
Le broché assimilé au lancé.
L'article damassé sera payé 10 cent. le mille en plus que les articles marabous en toute largeur.

*Rubans*

*Rubans façonnées.*

*John Bowring,*
Esq. LL. D.

18 June,
1832.

Satin de 110 à 120 Coups au Pouce    -    -    -    -    En Deux Navettes au brochés.

| | f. c. | | f. c. | |
|---|---|---|---|---|
| Nº 30, 2 lats en 900 - - - à - 70 l'aune. | - - 8 | 40 la 12 aunes. |
| Nº 16, 2 id. en 900 - - - à - 50 id. | - - 6 | - |

Satin de 100 à 120 Coups au Pouce    -    -    -    -    à 2 Navettes ou brochés.

Nº 30, 2 lats en 600    -    -    -    à  - 60 l'aune.   -    - 7  20 la 12 aunes.
Nº 16, 2 id. en 600    -    -    -    à  - 45 id.    -    - 5  40

Satin de 90 à 100 Coups au Pouce    -    -    -    à une Seule Navette.

Nº 30, 1 lat en 900    -    -    -    à  - 50 l'aune.   -    - 6  -
Nº 16, 1 id. en 900    -    -    -    à  - 35 id.    -    - 4  20

Satin de 90 à 100 Coups au Pouce    -    -    -    à une Seule Navette.

Nº 30, 1 lat  en 600    -    -    -    à  - 45 l'aune.   -    - 5  40
Nº 16, 1 lat  en 600    -    -    -    à  - 30 id.    -    - 3  60
Nº 16, 1 lat  en 400    -    -    -    à  - 30 id.    -    - 3  60

Taffetas de 100 à 120 Coups au Pouce  -    -    -    -    à 2 Navette, ou brochés.

Nº 30, 2 lat en 900 et 600    -    -    à     70 l'aune.   -    - 8  40
Nº 16, 2 id. en 900 et 600    -    -    à  - 50 id.    -    - 6  -

Taffetas de 70 à 80 Coups au Pouce  -    -    -    -    -    à une Navette.

Nº 30, 1 lat sur remisse, à poil    -    à  - 50 l'aune.   -    - 6  -
Nº 16, 1 id.     id.      id. -    -    à  - 35 id.    -    - 4  20

CORDONS DE 100 à 120 COUPS AU POUCE. -    -    -    à 2 Navettes ou brochés.

Nº 12 et 10, 2 lats en 900    -    -    à  - 60 l'aune.   -    - 7  20
Nº 12 et 10, 2 id.  en 600    -    -    à  - 60 id.    -    - 7  20

100 à 120 Coups au Pouce. -    -    -    -    -    à 1 Navette.

Nº 12 et 10, 1 lat en 900    -    -    à  - 45 l'aune.   -    - 5  40
Nº 12 et 10, 1 id. en 600    -    -    à  - 45 id.    -    - 5  40

Nᵒˢ 12 et 10, corps et remisse en 600 et 400 à  - 40 id.    -    - 4  80  { la piece de  12 aunes.

Certifié par le Conseiller d'Etat, Préfet du département du Rhône, et par le Maire de la ville de Lyon.

A Lyon, le 26 Octobre 1831.                    Le Préfet, *Du Molart.*
        Le Maire, *Boisset,* Adjoint.

---

8903. The paper you put in there describes what was the actual rate of wages when you were in Lyons?—It does.

8904. And the exact rate of the articles most commonly made?—Clearly so. My course was this: I sent for a number of weavers and conversed with them; I did the same with the masters, and ascertained that the prices which they paid and received were in nine cases out of ten the Tarif prices, and that where there was any distinction, it generally arose out of some peculiar circumstance: I came to this result, that on the whole the Tarif might be received as the most correct evidence of the present rate of wages: there are a few cases to which I have to refer, in respect to one or two other articles by-and-by, in which there is some slight difference.

8905. Is there any thing obligatory in the Tarif?—Not at all.

8906. It varies according to the supply and demand of labour?—Exactly so; the Tarif was the production of an active discussion, in which the masters and weavers took part; the discussion became very quarrelsome at last; the majority of the Conseil des Prud'hommes approved of the Tarif and recognized it; it was also recognized by the authorities as a Tarif, representing the average prices; and it is at this moment the representative (though not obligatory) of the wages paid in the town. After the troubles in November last, the whole of these acts were nullified.

8907. What was the origin of the November riots?—The origin of the November riots was an attempt to give to this Tarif the force of law. The authorities had compromised themselves, for the Tarif will be seen to have the signature of the authorities; there had been a great many discussions, and a number of masters and weavers met together: the Tarif had been the result of a very long deliberation, and the Prefect thought himself in a situation to give to the Tarif a legal character; but many masters refused to recognize his authority to settle the question of wages by any official mandate; the men insisted on what they called their recognized rights, and then the troubles broke out.

678.                                        8908. Although

*John Bowring,*
Esq. LL. D.

18 June,
1832.

8908. Although the authorities had been engaged in the discussions?—Not engaged in them; but they had given a certain sanction to their results. The Government, however, dismissed the Prefect, and reprehended the authorities for having gone much beyond their line of duty, and for becoming partisans of the Tarif.

8909. The whole of that arrangement was put an end to after the insurrection in November, and the Tarif now is a table of prices not recognized by the law, but by the common consent of the masters and the operatives, is it not?—It is so to a great extent; not that it could be enforced, but that it would be considered evidence of the average rate of wages. The Tarif having ceased to have the effect of law, it could not be referred to before the Conseil des Prud'hommes as a document to which every body is subjected; that to which the Conseil des Prud'hommes would subject disputants, is called "The Mercuriale."

8910. You have stated, that this Tarif is put in merely to express what is the state of prices in Lyons, and you have alluded also to what you call the Mercuriale; will you describe what the Mercuriale is?—The Mercuriale is the average rate of wages. In such a case as this, for instance; where a master shall have given to a weaver a certain quantity of silk to produce a certain article, and have agreed to pay him the market price, if there is any question or dispute between them, the matter is settled by the Conseil des Prud'hommes; the Conseil des Prud'hommes, for the settlement of such cases from time to time, make what they call a Mercuriale, or a record of the average prices, which, as I said before, do, in nine cases out of ten, represent the Tarif: they examine eight or ten masters and the same number of weavers, and having ascertained what was the price engaged to be paid by the master to the weaver, taking the average of these ten as representing the true state of things, they will, with respect to the particular article, regulate the dispute accordingly.

8911. Do they hold an examination on every occasion, where there is a dispute between the master and the men?—Not unless new facts are to be elicited.

8912. You stated, that the troubles in November last were caused by an endeavour, on the part of the Government, to make this Tarif a legal instrument?—No, the contrary; there was resistance offered on the part of certain manufacturers to the recognition of the Tarif: the weavers referred to the local authorities, who sanctioned the Tarif, and recognized the rights of the weavers to be paid the prices which the Tarif imposed: a great many manufacturers refused to pay these prices; the weavers assembled together in large bodies and applied to the authorities, who took their part, which strengthened their position; the quarrel became more and more violent between them, and the masters and their meetings increased in number and violence; they became an object of great anxiety, and troops were sent to disperse them; many of them said to me,—" We did not choose to be beaten, and we armed ourselves as well as we could." They armed themselves, beat the troops, and found themselves in possession of the place; not having any intention to rebel, but determined to resist any violence that was used towards them.

8913. That disturbance was quieted, and the Tarif was put an end to?—One of the first acts of the government of Paris, was to abrogate the Tarif, and annul all the proceedings of the Lyonese authorities.

8914. What effect was produced by these measures on the trade of Lyons?—The government were enabled to get rid of a considerable portion of the difficulty, by transporting a great number of workmen, so as to reduce the quantity of labour.

8915. You say they sent away large numbers of workmen?—Yes, both compagnons and chefs d'ateliers; the result was, that there was a rise in the price of labour. The government were easily able to effect that, inasmuch as Lyons being near the frontier, is always the abode of a number of strangers, whose removal the government had no difficulty in accomplishing.

8916. State what is the average production of the weavers in Lyons?—The average production of common satin, is from four to five ells a day; I have got here the estimate of 100 looms, and the average product of 100 looms is 357 ells, that is about three ells and a half a day per loom.

8917. Do you know what the hours of labour of the weavers generally are?—In Lyons from 16 to 18; and I have found many weavers who have laboured 20 hours a day.

8918. There must be some mistake; do you mean that a weaver labours sometimes as much as 20 hours a day?—I have known that, where there has been an

extreme

*John Bowring,*
Esq. LL. D.

18 June,
1832.

extreme demand for an article, and great pressure, in Lyons, almost the whole trade is a trade of order; the stocks are very small. It often happens that there is great precipitation in the demand, and great necessity for supplying that demand rapidly; the stock, except in plain goods, is always exceedingly small at Lyons.

8919. If persons are obliged to work 20 hours a day, there can be no want of labour?—In a late case, where some thousands of men were suddenly removed, when the demand came, the supply of labour was not equal to the demand; there are cases where men have been employed in particular manufactories, I allude to particular cases; I state this as an evidence of the extremely industrious disposition of the labourers.

8920. To what place did they transport these men?—A great number of them were Savoyards, and they returned to Savoy; a great many were inhabitants of the mountains, and they returned to their agricultural labour.

8921. How did they effect their removal?—They were turned out of the town, and they got home as they could.

8922. Do you happen to know how their removal was effected?—By an order of the magistrate; and if any resistance was offered, they would be marched off by the gend'armes.

8923. You stated that in consequence of the system of Lyons being a system of orders, the demand was extremely fluctuating; consequently, is not the demand for labour very fluctuating too?—Certainly.

8924. The operatives, then, are frequently without employment, or very little employment for some length of time, and then they again become employed to a great extent indeed, say 15, 16, or 20 hours during another short period of time?—Certainly; but for the removal of a great quantity of labour from the Lyonese market, the distress of late would have been perfectly frightful. When I was at Lyons, the presence of the cholera at Paris produced a cessation in the demand for articles of fashion; the American purchaser was almost wholly out of the market also, and unless there had been a great diminution in the supply of labour, the suffering would have been boundless.

8925. Have you had opportunities of observing the manner of life of the workmen?—I have seen a great deal of the workmen, and it occurred to me, that the most satisfactory way was, to allow them to speak for themselves. I think I explained before, that the general arrangement at Lyons is this; there is the chef d'atelier, who is a sort of superintending weaver, who has generally three looms; three looms are the average possession of a chef d'atelier through the whole of the district; the loom he does not himself employ, will be either used by an apprentice or by a companion; where it is used by an apprentice, the apprentice merely receives his food and clothing from the master weaver; where by the companion, the companion receives half the wages paid by the manufacturer, the consequence is, that the weavers are in a state of considerable isolation and independence; and at Lyons there is only one establishment where there are any large number of labourers under the same roof, belonging to the same establishment. The lien which the master weaver has over the companion, is only that which obliges the companion to complete any piece of work he has begun; and what the superintending weaver does for him, is to cook his food and provide soup. I find the average rental paid by the weavers, is from one hundred to two hundred francs a year; the houses are often vastly large at Lyons, and contain sometimes from 60 to 80, or 100 families; the town is much overbuilt, and rent has fallen considerably; the average wages is from 40 to 45 sous, which is from about 20*d.* to 22½*d.* In the establishment I spoke of, there are from 400 to 500 working people employed. The proprietors told me, that the average of weavers' wages was from 2*f.* 50*c.* to 4*f.* a day; it is principally a manufactory of shawls, and I have seen no labourers in Lyons whose appearance on the whole was so prosperous. They are fed at the establishment, and they pay six sous for a plate of meat, six sous for a bottle of wine, and one sou for a plate of soup.

8926. Does the average which you stated just now include women, or does the charge only apply to men?—That is the average for men.

8927. For how many hours of work?—I think they were working 14 or 16 hours, with two hours for meals.

8928. The average which you stated at 22½*d.*, was that for men only?—With reference to that particular estimate, I think the average was taken on the whole mass employed, including females.

8929. What are the taxes paid by the Lyonese weaver?—He is estimated to

consume

*John Bowring,*
Esq. LL. D.

18 June,
1832.

consume half a litre of wine per day, for which he pays a tax of 16 c.; then there is the direct personal tax, which, on a rental of 100 f., is 12 f. 50 c.; altogether, the Lyonese weaver pays 53 f. 95 c. in the shape of taxes.

8930. When you say that the wages were 2 f. 5 c. to 4 f., do you mean that only in regard to one establishment?—Yes; that was the only establishment where there was a large congregation of weavers, and the only opportunity I had of ascertaining what was the average rate paid in such circumstances. I am now going to read a statement from two very intelligent weavers; the Committee will understand that in all these matters men always make the worst of their own case. These are remarkably intelligent men, and give a very interesting account of the social condition of the workmen of Lyons. M. Falconnet, who was lately chosen by them as one of the Prud'hommes, is a very well-informed man: I gave him a series of questions, and desired his answer.

*[The Witness delivered in the following Document:]*

TRANSLATION of a LETTER from *Falconnet,* a Weaver, one of the Prud'hommes of Lyons to Dr. *Bowring*:

Sir,                                                                    Lyons, May 14, 1832.

I HASTEN to reply to the inquiries you did me the honour to address to me, and great is my satisfaction at being so requested to communicate; and I scarcely need begin by stating that from time immemorial Lyons has been the town where the workman has been most devoted to his labours, and where he leads the most sedentary of lives.

The workmen, who labour as companions, have their peculiar habits; their day's labour begins at five or six o'clock, and ends at eight in the evening, when they return to their abodes; they take one hour in the day for dinner; they gain from 2 f. to 3 f. 50 c. for their daily wages, and there are instances of the more able amongst them gaining four francs per day. Their average expenditure at their *auberge,* for breakfast, dinner, supper and a half litre of wine, is 30 sous, and the rest of their superfluous wages they spend in a few additional bottles of wine or beer, on the Sunday. The young men among them dress well, and visit the theatre. They are united in a general bond with the workmen of other towns of France, and when work is scarce they emigrate, and undertake what is called the tour of France. Their societies are organized under the title of the *Devoir*; they are all companions; they admit no masters, and they correspond with the principal towns of the country.

The organization of the weavers of silk goods differs essentially from that of other trades; as the business was imported into France by fugitive Italians, they had no rules of labour; it was their habit to give as much time as possible to their looms, so the weaver labours from 15, 16, 18 and even to 20 hours a day.

There are, it is supposed, 12,000 workshops in Lyons, containing 30,000 looms (this is the nearest estimate, for it is long since a census was taken.) The workshops have from two to six looms; there are few that have only one, and there are not fifty that have more than six. In many cases four looms are worked by the same family, father and children. In some workshops the looms are moved by apprentices; for some time there have been nearly as many apprentices as companions; but the apprentices decrease in number, as it is not worth the masters while to give them instruction. Formerly, when the conscription carried off our young men, we had few companions; their life was one of isolation; they eat, drank and dwelt with their masters, and seldom met in society. At that period the master weavers were forced to call in young women from the country, and the habit has continued; there are almost as many women as men employed; they weave the lighter stuffs, and the consequence has been a rapid decline in value; men have almost wholly abandoned this class of goods.

At the present moment the price of labour is the minimum fixed by the Tarif of October 1831. There are some exceptions, and the cholera has led to a reduction.

Formerly the gains of the masters and companions was more considerable on wrought than on plain silks; the prices are reduced 50 per cent. and the gains are about equal on the two.

When there are three looms the master generally works one of them, and the profits of the other two may give him about 900 f. per annum; he pays for rent an average of 150 f.; he lodges his workmen, which costs him yearly 80 f.; and there remains for himself and family, 670 f.; his children (especially the females) are called upon to work at a very early period, so that notwithstanding the efforts of philanthropy they are little instructed; if a father of a family have three looms, and two of his children can weave in them, he may gain from 1,500 to 1,600 francs per annum, and this is a period to him of great prosperity.

When the companion lodges with the master weaver his daily expenses are 1 ½ lb. bread, cost 30 c.; ¼ litre of wine, 12 ½ c.; a portion of meat or vegetables for dinner, 25 c.; 10 c. for cheese, 10 c. for supper; in all, from 80 to 90 c. Those who gain more than the average spend somewhat more.

The custom is to pay the companion one-half of the price of weaving. Of a stuff of which the rate is 1 f. the companion gets 50 c., but the master has the expense of putting up the loom, of winding, quills, &c. If the weaving price be 1 f. the master does not clear more than 20 c.; the average produce is 3 ells per day. The weaver would thus gain 1 f. 50 c., and if Sundays and other stoppages are deducted, it will amount from 350 f. to 400 f. per annum.

But

*John Bowring*
Esq. LL. D.
_____
18 June,
1832.

But there are many exceptions.   In new articles, such for instance as the ribbons and belts introduced three years ago, a weaver may gain from 2 *f*. 50 *c*. to 3 *f*. per day, and even now they gain from 2 *f*. to 2 *f*. 25 *c*.; and so they do on articles of difficult workmanship, on velvets (flowered), shawls, borderings, China crapes, &c.

The chef d'atelier may also gain more on these than on current articles, particularly if he need not alter his loom for six to eight months; but if the pattern is frequently changed, he does not get back his outlay, and this has been much the case of late, and concurring with falling prices, was one of the main causes of the riots of November.

Twelve months ago prices mounted, and 2,000 additional looms were put in motion; now those looms are for sale, and 100 workshops are to be disposed of.   Three-fourths of the masters and companions are in debt; in case of war, all our youth would be disposed to take up arms, and leave a trade which gives them no hopes for the future.

If you desire other information, it will be a gratification to me to communicate it to you.

I have the honour to be, your very humble servant,

(signed)     *Falconnet.*

---

There is a communication from another person, of whom I need only mention, that when the weavers met, after the events of November, to the number of 30,000, they chose two men to represent the state of things to Government, and this letter is from Charnier, one of the representatives, and of course must be taken as an authority.

[*It was delivered in, as follows :*]

EXTRACTS of a COMMUNICATION from *Charnier*, a Chef d'Atelier and Prud'homme of Lyons, dated 16th May 1832.

THE principal subject of unpleasant discussion with the manufacturer is the mounting new patterns.   The workman suffers from the mania of the manufacturer, who is constantly creating new designs.   It is a ruinous abuse, falling wholly on the chef d'atelier.

The chef d'atelier rents his own habitation; the furniture, the looms, the tools, are his; every thing in fact but the *remises* (gathering of the leishes,) and the *peignes* (reeds) which generally belong to the manufacturer.

Formerly, the chef d'atelier frequently undertook the patterns given him by the manufacturer; now the cartoons are delivered to him, he paying the expenses of stitching them together.

Apprentices generally mess in their masters' houses, who provide them with food, fire and light.

The companion is sometimes fed by the master, and pays from 45 to 55 *c*. per day for his meals; the general consumption is half a litre of wine, when his work is very laborious, or a quarter when the work is light.   The latter quantity is allowed to the apprentice by order of the Council of Prud'hommes.   The repasts last half an hour, and the hours of labour are from sixteen to eighteen hours.

An apprentice will be fed, lodged and washed for during three or four years; they are required to produce two-thirds of the worth of an ordinary weaver; for the excess they receive half the weaving price; they are compelled to fetch water, to sweep the apartment, &c.; they come into Lyons principally from the mountains of Savoy, Dauphinais and the High Alps.

In certain articles the companion receives two-thirds of the weaving of common goods, which is very low, so low that not more than 1 *f*. 50 *c*. per day is obtained for 6 ells produce.   One reason for this is, that the winding of the tram is on account of the manufacturer.   The consequence of the low wages is, that these goods are woven almost wholly by women and children.

In the thrown article (*lancé*) the weaver pays the wages of a boy of ten to fourteen years, who throws back the shuttle, and gets from 60 *c*. to 70 *c*.   The price paid to the weaver is 40 *c*. per 1,000 throws, and about 12,000 can be thrown per day, say 4 *f*. 80 *c*. of which 2 *f*. 40 *c*. is for the weaver.

In velvets, a weaver can get a higher price than in other articles.

The daily expenses of the weaver may be thus averaged :

| | |
|---|---|
| Bread, 2 lbs. at 4 *s*. - - - - - - - - | 40 *c*. |
| Meat - - - - - - - - - - | 50 |
| Wine, ¼ litre - - - - - - - - | 10 ½ |
| Oil, fire, light, &c. - - - - - - - | 7 ½ |
| Washing and other charges - - - - - | 10 |
| | *f*. 1  18 |

Of late many of our weavers have resumed the agricultural life they had abandoned.

*John Bowring,*
Esq. LL. D.

18 June,
1832.

8931. Are there any Saving Banks at Lyons?—There are, but they have very little influence there; I have no doubt that the confidence which existed has been much broken by the events which have taken place.

8932. Does any association exist among the labourers for the protection of labour?—These documents refer to a sort of association which exists among them, which is a trade union that has existed in France for many hundred years; the labourers in the different trades have communication with one another, and on the arrival of a stranger he immediately finds assistance from some men of the same trade settled in the town that he visits: that is the principal association existing among them; of late they have shown a very great desire to associate. The first association that adopted a better organization grew out of the expectation of the cholera.

8933. Is there any thing similar to our Trades' Union?—Nothing; if there were, I am convinced that the evils which are constantly occurring there for want of the means of expression of opinion would be got rid of.

8934. Has there been any great reduction of wages at Lyons of late years?— Yes, very considerable; there has been a considerable decline for the last 20 years; in 1810 the gros de Naples was from 90 c. to 1 f. 20 c. and 1 f. 22 c., while in 1832 it was paid from 50 c. to 70 c.; this is a weaver's statement, and I should say, no doubt the prices are represented at the minimum. I have here a memorandum from a weaver, in which, with reference to the trade, he says, that what is most complained of, is the price that is paid for the robe gros de Naples façonué, which is 20 c. for 1,000 shutes.

8935. What was the price paid in 1826?—I have not the return; there has been a constant tendency to depreciation from 1810 to 1832; the depreciation has been a gradual one.

8936. Is the market in Lyons for silks subject to very great fluctuation?—Not very great; the market for silk goods is less subject to it, in consequence of the fact that the stocks are very small.

8937. The fluctuation, of course, must be more in the wages than any thing else? —The fluctuation of wages does not operate so much upon the price of goods in stock as might be expected, in consequence of the stocks being so inconsiderable.

8938. Does not the fact of working to order arise from the working almost exclusively fancy goods and not plain goods?—To a great extent it does; but even to plain goods the question of colour is of considerable importance.

8939. Does not the application apply to new colours?—This is again the question of taste, which taste depends on such an immense number of contingencies, that the over production of goods of a particular colour might create as great an embarrassment as the production of a particular pattern.

8940. Have you any notion of what are the average profits of a manufacturer at Lyons?—My belief is, that the average rate of profit is about seven per cent.; where there is great success the profit is very considerable; where, for instance, a new pattern is introduced that captivates attention, the profit becomes very large; where it fails the loss is very large: it is precisely the region of production where the risks are greatest.

8941. Did the Lyonese manufacturers complain to you of their labouring under considerable disadvantages as regarded the Swiss and German manufacturers?— They consider themselves to be under a disadvantage of 11¼ per cent.; that is to say, on the importation of foreign raw silk three per cent.; they estimate a profit to the importer of three per cent., the fact being that the Swiss manufacturers are themselves importers of silk, while at Lyons a middle man almost always is employed; there is a brokerage on the purchase of three-fourths per cent. They estimate a difference on the loss in dyeing of three per cent., and a loss in weight of two per cent., making 11¼ in all: it is clear this is an exaggerated statement, though in some points it is true. It is true that they are under a disadvantage as regards the importation of foreign silk, and are under a disadvantage growing out of the want of capital; it is also true that they are subject to loss to a greater extent at Lyons than in Switzerland or Germany on dyeing, inasmuch as, from the extent of trade in Lyons, the quantity that can be gathered up from pillage is so large that a trade may be carried on with it: it would be very difficult in any of the Swiss towns to get so much pillaged silk as to set up business with it.

8942. Are they not subject to considerable heavy local taxation?—Very heavy: there is one other circumstance, the average interest on money in Switzerland and Germany, is nearly one per cent. lower than the average interest of money at

Lyons;

*John Bowring,*
Esq. LL. D.

18 June,
1832.

Lyons; that is also a disadvantage. With reference to a question I did not answer quite in detail before, I wish to state one fact of some importance. I asked a large manufacturer there, whether he would consent to open to me any one transaction, that I might trace it in the whole of its progress, and be able to report the precise circumstances; I have done that, and I will mention what I know to be the progress of the article. I took 500 ells of satin 7–16ths wide tram supple, at 6 *f.*, value 3,000 *f.*, weighing 60 grams per ell.

COST.

|  | *f.* | *c.* |
|---|---|---|
| 500 Ells; *i.e.* 12 grams of chain, or 12 kilo. organzine, soft and dyed; these 12 kilo. weighed, before dyeing, 17 kilo. 45 grams, at 50 *f.* | 872 | 50 |
| Throwing the organzine, at 11 *f.* | 191 | 95 |
| Dyeing the organzine (raw) at 3 *f.* | 51 | 35 |
| Winding the organzine, 12 kilo. at 4 *f.* | 48 | 00 |
| Warping, at 1 *f.* 50 *c.* | 18 | 00 |
| 500 Ells, at 36 grams of trams supple, 18 kilo. raw, at 47 *f.* | 846 | 00 |
| Throwing the tram, 7 *f.* | 126 | 00 |
| Dyeing - ditto, 3 *f.* | 54 | 00 |
| Weaving 500 ells, at 95 *c.* | 475 | 00 |
| Finishing 500 ells, at 10 *c.* | 50 | 00 |
|  | 2,732 | 80 |
| Proportion of expenses on 3,000 *f.* at 3 % | 90 | 00 |
|  | 2,822 | 80 |
| Profit | 177 | 20 |
|  | *f.* 3,000 | 00 |

In the weaving are included,

| Winding tram | 20 *c.* |
|---|---|
| Cannetage | 10 *c.* |
| Folding | 5 *c.* |

8943. Do you take into the calculation interest on the capital?—Yes; I should think that must be taken in.

8944. Then, practically, the Swiss and German manufacturers do undersell the Lyonese in many articles?—Certainly, in the plain articles.

8945. Have you any accounts of imports from Zurich?—I have some, but they are not official. The local taxation of Lyons in 1831 was 4,038,098 *f.* The last census at Lyons gave 145,675 individuals. The Octroi would produce 2,400,000 *f.*, so that there is a local taxation of 16½ *f.* or 13 *s.* 6 *d.* per head; that is a mere local tax, a municipal tax paid within the walls and not paid without.

8946. Do you mean each head of a family?—No; I take in the whole population.

8947. So that taking the average calculation of a family to be five persons, it applies to every one of the five?—Exactly so; here is a document of considerable interest, furnished me by the municipality, showing the bearing of the Octroi of the town of Lyons

[The Witness delivered in the following:]

OCTROI of the Town of Lyons (Intra Muros.)

YEAR 1830.

|  |  | QUANTITY. | TAX. | |
|---|---|---|---|---|
|  |  |  | *f.* | *c.* |
| Oxen | No. | 11,891 | 21 | 50 p' head. |
| Calves | ,, | 26,261 | 5 | 50 — |
| Sheep | ,, | 119,509 | 1 | 50 — |
| Lambs | ,, | 3,508 | — | 75 — |
| Pigs | ,, | 12,199 | 9 | — — |
| Butcher's Meat | Kilos | 166,281 | — | 20 p' kilo. |
| Fuel: |  |  |  |  |
| Hard Wood | Steres | 22,176 | 3 | — p' stere |
| White ditto | ditto | 2,658 | 2 | — — |
| Branches | per 100 | 4,591 | 4 | — p' 100. |
| Loads | ditto | 14,900 | 2 | — — |
| Faggots | ditto | 129,435 | — | 50 — |
| Turf | per 1000 | 4,201,200 | — | 25 p' 1000. |
| Charcoal | — | 176,286 | — | 40 — |

678.                                                              (*continued.*)

OCTROI of the Town of *Lyons* (Intra Muros), Year 1830—*continued.*

| | | QUANTITY. | TAX. | |
|---|---|---|---|---|
| | | | *f.* | *c.* |
| **Drink :** | | | | |
| Wine in wood - - - Hect. | | 190,262 | 5 | 50 p' hect. |
| Ditto in bottle - - - ditto | | 454 | 10 | — — |
| Vinegar - - - - ditto | | 4,421 | 5 | 50 — |
| Spirits - - - - ditto | | 780 | 14 | 70 — |
| Beer (Home) - - ditto | | 13,049 | 10 | — — |
| Ditto (Foreign) - - ditto | | 742 | 15 | — — |
| Light Wine - - - - ditto | | 792 | 5 | 40 — |
| | | | | |
| **Forage :** | | | | |
| Hay - - - - - Myr. | | 659,737 | — | 10 p' myr. |
| Straw - - - - - ditto | | 322,985 | — | 61 — |
| Oats - - - - - Hect. | | 43,339 | — | 50 p' hect. |
| | | | | |
| **Materials :** | | | | |
| Lime - - - - - Hect. | | 42,577 | — | 50 p' hect. |
| Mortar - - - - ditto | | 8,046 | — | 20 — |
| Plaster - - - C. Metr. | | 21,477 | — | 20 p' C. metr. |
| Cut Stone - - - Met. cub. | | 4,747 | 3 | — p' met. cub. |
| Blocks - - - - ditto | | 2,370 | 2 | — — |
| Rough Stones - - ditto | | 30,462 | — | 25 — |
| Paving Stones - - per 1000 | | 2,088,630 | 1 | 50 p' 1000. |
| Bricks - - - - ditto | | 1,811,740 | 2 | — — |
| Building Wood - - Met. cub. | | 11,395 | 2 | — p' met. cub. |
| Planks - - - - - per 100 | | 142,367 | 5 | — p' 100. |
| Oak Planks - - - ditto | | 6,358 | 8 | — — |
| Deal ditto - - - - ditto | | 406,280 | 1 | 50 — |

TOTAL PROCEEDS for the Year 1830.

| | | *f.* | *c.* |
|---|---|---|---|
| Gross Revenue - - - - - - - | | 2,307,330 | 32 |
| Expenses on collection, &c. - - - - | | 280,362 | 53 |
| Net Revenue - - - - | | 2,026,967 | 79 |

8948. State what is the average expense of changing each pattern in the loom ?— An individual who was very thoroughly informed on the subject, told me he was disposed to contract for the change at 25*f.*, it may happen that the modifications may be small in a pattern ; there are cases in which they are exceedingly expensive, the topic is constantly agitated, and it is the source of almost all the quarrels that exist at Lyons between the master and the labourer. The question of the mounting is one of a most embarrassing nature; the labourer is constantly stipulating, that before changing his loom he may be allowed to produce a certain quantity of pieces; the master is always interested in the production of novelty; of late they are beginning to understand the matter a little better. The complaint of the weaver is precisely this, he is made the victim of the ignorance of the master, who before he has thoroughly ascertained that what he gives to the weaver is likely to be acceptable to the public, engages the weaver to set up his machinery, if he is disappointed, the weaver is left without redress, not having been consulted as he formerly was (I mean many years ago), with respect to the pattern. The artist has become a much more important person of late years; the fact is, that in France every thing gives way to the creation of taste; the weaver has less to do with that than the inventor, and the consequence of the weaver having nothing to do with the invention of the pattern is, that he is the victim of its unpopularity.

8949. Did I not understand you to say, that the trade of Lyons was an order trade?—It is, to a very great extent.

8950. Then how can that apply; if it be an order trade of course the order must be given for a certain number of pieces?—It constantly happens, though the order is given, that the buyer refuses to take the goods, sometimes on account of delay in production, sometimes on account of change of fashion, sometimes for other causes which the dependence of the manufacturer on the buyer prevents his

appealing

*John Bowring,*
Esq. LL. D.

———

18 June,
1832.

appealing against; there is a vast quantity of uncertainty about the matter; the manufacturers are in fact much at the mercy of the buyer.

8951. The impression that we had here was, that an order trade was less speculative than one otherwise?—The quantity of speculation at Lyons is very small; the Lyonese manufacturers, even in this market, have almost always lost money when they sent goods on their own account; in two or three cases where experiments have been made on a large scale, the sum lost has been enormous; but the fancy trade is subject to many risks.

8952. You were stating what were the principal disputes between masters and men?—The great point of difficulty is this, that the weaver in Lyons is, to a great extent, at the mercy of the success of the master. Of ten quarrels which originate between the masters and the men, that is the primary cause of nine; the Conseil des Prud'hommes is at this moment endeavouring to legislate for such cases; that if the weaver be not guaranteed in the production of a given quantity of pieces, a certain consideration shall be allowed him, and the expense of mounting his loom be paid by the master who employs him.

8953. Does not the weaver sometimes pay the expense of the pattern, and sometimes the manufacturer?—Yes, but cases like this will arise; a manufacturer receives an order for a certain quantity of goods, and he may bargain with the weaver for mounting the loom for that particular pattern, by an understanding according to the circumstances of the case, that if the expense of mounting be inconsiderable the weaver shall undertake it on his own account, but if it be considerable he shall get something from the manufacturer. The master says, I have an order for 25 or a greater number of pieces; the weaver undertakes them; he delivers a part which are not found to answer, the foreign or Parisian buyer says to the manufacturer, I can take no more; the master is not in a situation to say to his correspondent, you shall take them; so he turns round on the weaver, who has incurred an expense, and says to him, I can take no more from you, I am already sacrificed.

8954. So that an order trade, although beneficial to the master, inasmuch as it does not involve him in so much risk as a speculative one, may be extremely injurious to the weaver?—Undoubtedly; I have put in a document from M. Charnier, and he told me that he would not, under any circumstances, take orders for any but plain goods, for any goods indeed which were liable to the modification of taste and the changes and caprices of the public.

8955. Do you conceive that the average of 25 f. for each mounting can be depended on?—The fact was given me by a member of the Chamber of Commerce; I do not consider my personal knowledge pledged to the amount; I have endeavoured, from the best sources, to collect facts, and I am merely putting those facts on record.

8956. Have you any account of the positive expense of changing the patterns, the highest and the lowest?—Yes, I have; I have known cases in which it has cost as much as 1,000 f. in regard to shawls of extreme beauty and costliness; it averages between almost nothing and the expense of 1,000 f. The case which led to the Jacquard invention was a case in which between twenty and thirty thousand francs had been expended in the mounting of a pattern.

8957. Do you know what the utmost expense is, that has been incurred in the changing a pattern which applies to the silk trade exclusively, independent of shawls?—I think I have heard of an expense of between 3 and 400 f. With reference to the stock of goods on hand at Lyons, I perceive before me a document from a member of the Chamber of Commerce, which states, that at no one period could he be able to collect 300 pieces of those classes of goods which may be considered as exposed to the fluctuations of fashion.

8958. What is the arrangement for the cost of mounting where the expense exceeds 100 f.?—When the expense exceeds 100 f. there is generally a special understanding between the master and the weaver, as to the way in which the expense shall be paid; wherever no specific understanding takes place, and there is a difference of opinion, the Conseil des Prud'hommes is appealed to.

8959. Is there any thing else you wish to state regarding the manufactory at Lyons before you proceed to St. Etienne?—I wish to state that I have only looked at the matter in its general bearings, and as a part and portion of the system of our commercial relations with France; but I am very desirous of putting the Committee in possession of one or two points connected with the change of opinion produced in France as respects their relations in general with England. I have some facts furnished me by the Chamber of Commerce, and I should not do justice to them, or to my own feelings, were I not to read them. I am stating the fact

generally,

*John Bowring,*
Esq. LL. D.

———

18 June,
1832.

generally, that the introduction of French goods into England has produced a most extraordinary change of opinion in France, and there is a disposition becoming stronger every day to enter into something like reciprocal legislation.

8960. Will you state from that document what your opinion is of the views of the Chamber of Commerce at Lyons upon this subject, as addressed by them to the Government ?—They represent to the Minister that " it is of the highest import- " ance that some forward steps should be taken, that the prohibitory regulations of " the Custom House system of France should be reconsidered, in order to show to " England that we are no longer indisposed to come to an understanding with her as " to the means of gradually removing the impediments that exist, and of extending the " amicable relations of the two countries." In another part they say, " the moment is " arrived in which opinion requires that our restrictive system should be revised, and " that which is hostilely prohibitory to the products of Great Britain should be " abandoned ; of these prohibitions, a great many have been shown us by long ex- " perience to have been unfortunate, and they are persisted in without any regard to " the changes which have taken place in the political situations of the two countries, " whom events daily bring more closely together. The whole system of prohibition " we consider as nothing more or less than a representation of the ancient theory " of national enmity, and look to a change in the system as the best ground of peace, " of union, and of sympathy, which could ally the two nations together."

8961. On leaving Lyons you proceeded to St. Etienne ?—I visited St. Etienne.

8962. You had an opportunity there of observing the state of trade ?—Yes.

8963. Did you enjoy the same facilities there which you met with at Lyons ?— I did. I had letters from the Government to the Authorities, and many individual letters to manufacturers.

8964. What is the principal silk manufacture of St. Etienne ?—The principal manufacture is ribbons.

8665. Has there been a great increase in the ribbon trade of St. Etienne ?— Very considerable ; in 1812 the number of looms was 9,000, in 1831 it was above 20,000.

8966. Has there been any migration of the trade of Lyons to St. Etienne ?— Some years ago there was a considerable migration of the trade from Lyons to St. Etienne, but there has been a migration of a portion of the trade back again to Lyons. One branch of the ribbon manufacture has been transferred there, in consequence of a new discovery, namely, the means of employing the broad loom in the production of ribbon. Taste is more developed at Lyons than at St. Etienne, and the manufacture of more costly ribbon has been removed to Lyons of late.

8967. Is there any establishment at St. Etienne similar to the Condition at Lyons? —It exists with a slight change as to the per centage allowed for humidity.

8968. Are there any schools of design ?—There is nothing that can be decidedly called a school of design. There is a great deal of attention paid to the subject of drawing ; there are many students not collected in the schools ; there are a considerable number of draftsmen at St. Etienne. At this moment there are 58 artists at St. Etienne, employed in the production of ribbon patterns.

8969. You have stated there has been a great increase in the ribbon trade, have you any documents exhibiting that ?—I have a document which shows a general result. I shall hereafter put in a return from the Government showing the fluctu- ations of the ribbon manufacture for some years. The number of looms have gone on increasing, but very irregularly, at the average rate of about 500 a year. Since I was last examined I have received from the French Government further returns of a detailed character as to the state of the silk trade ; and they have taken an immense deal of trouble to classify the facts under different heads.

8970. Can you state the number of looms in 1825 ?—I think generally the pro- gression has increased at about 500 a year. I shall endeavour to show the facts in accurate detail as to the progress of the ribbon manufacture ; the precise quan- tity of looms have, I believe, never been ascertained either at St. Etienne or Lyons until I produced the real statistics to this Committee. The information which has been previously given as to the quantity at Lyons or St. Etienne is not to be depended on. In fact there were till lately very imperfect means of knowledge, and the facts I put in of an official sort, of the number of looms in Lyons, is evidence of the inacuracy of all the previous statements. There are no positive facts to be gathered as to the quantity of looms in 1825, either in Lyons or St. Etienne. With respect to the statement of 1810, all I can answer for it is, that it is the best in- formation I could get from the most intelligent persons. The facts connected with 1831 are official.

*John Bowring,*
Esq. LL. D.

18 June,
1832.

8971. Have you a statement of the prices of silk at St. Etienne?—Yes; the price of yellow organzine, from 20 to 24 deniers, is 60*f.* per kilogram; white organzine, 62; the tram, generally employed for ribbons, 42; these three are French silk. The white Piedmont organzine, 61; the yellow Piedmont, 53; the Italian organzine at 20 deniers, 60*f.*; the foreign tram, 40; there is a difference of from one to two francs per kilogram in favour of the French silks of the same number of deniers.

8972. What proportion of foreign silk is used at St. Etienne?—About one-third.

8973. Is there any marabout silk used at St Etienne?—Yes; the silk twisted in the marabout manner, is used for gauze ribbons.

8974. What is the nature of the marabout silk?—It is twisted much more hardly than other silk, and employed principally for the making of the gauze ribbons; it is only a particular sort of throwing which gives it a greater hardness; the twist is tighter than in ordinary throwing; it is thrown twice.

8975. It has been stated here, that the price of marabout silk is 44 per cent. cheaper at St. Etienne than here; have you any means of verifying that fact?—I have a statement here of the facts given me, from which it appears that marabout silk, such as is used for the finest gauze ribbons, has been from 68 to 72*f.* per kilogram; the cost of the marabout silk of this quality, at this moment in the St. Etienne market, is about 27*s.* English; I take 70*f.* as the average. Throwing is 7*f.* 50*c.* to 9*f.*, take 8*f.* 25*c.* as the average loss on weight, 4°/₀ 2*f.* 75*c.* will give 81*f.*; deduct 12½°/₀ discount, leaves 71*f.*, to which add 4*f.* for dyeing, gives 75*f.* per kilogram, or 27*s.* per English pound; that is according to the statement of the President of the Chamber of Commerce of St. Chamond.

8976 Is it French or foreign silk that is thrown into marabout?—It is made indifferently of French and foreign. In consequence of a letter I received from a gentleman who attended this Committee, I wrote to inquire whether or not marabout was made wholly from French; great surprise was expressed at the question; Italian silk is used quite indifferently for it.

8977. Have the French any advantage whatever as to marabout, whether they obtain their own silk or not?—Only as respects that peculiar marabout which is used for gauzes; in other French silks the difference in prices at St. Etienne is from 1*f.* to 1½*f.* per kilogram above the Italian.

8978. When was the bar loom introduced at St. Etienne?—About 50 or 60 years ago; that is the period from which the prosperity of the town of St. Etienne may be traced.

8979. What sort of foreign silk is made into marabout?—My notes state only that it is Italian silk; I think it is Italian generally.

8980. You mean indiscriminately Italian and French?—Indiscriminately.

8981. Are we to understand that French silk is not better for marabout than Italian?—I stated that French silk of the same number of deniers, sells for 1*f.* to 1½*f.* higher than Italian; it is of course so much better.

8982. Has there been any great improvements since the bar loom at St. Etienne?—Some slight improvements; the circumstance of the bar loom fixing itself at St. Etienne, is similar to the introduction of the power loom at Ashton. At Lyons, where there is a great congregation of workmen, there has always been the strongest opposition to improvement; thus improvements have always sought some spot where the population was not dense; the population settled in the mountain district about St. Etienne was enough for the purposes of labour, and among them the bar loom was effectually introduced. The prosperity of the whole district may be said, to a great extent, to have grown out of its introduction; it was originally imported from Switzerland, and its importer, like Jacquard, was the subject of a great deal of persecution. Most of the improvements introduced in thinly peopled places have met with much less opposition than those in the more populous districts, or in larger towns.

8983. Will you explain to the Committee what you meant just now by the application of the broad loom to the manufacture of ribbons; this is a recent improvement?—Very recent; it is merely the power of introducing four small shuttles instead of one large one; in that way the broad loom of Lyons has been so applied, which it could not be before; I have a return from Lyons, stating what number of ribbon looms they have employed now; these have invariably four pieces woven from each, and there are now from 800 to 900 looms so employed.

8984. That can be applied to the manufacture of broad goods or ribbons?—Yes, the discovery gives every manufacturer two strings to his bow, and this is considered a matter of very considerable importance; in fact it has brought back a portion of the ribbon trade to Lyons, which had deserted it before this recent improvement.

678.                                                                                    8985. Are

*John Bowring*,
Esq. LL. D.

18 June,
1832.

8985. Are silks dyed at St. Etienne?—They are.

8986. What is the price of dyeing at St. Etienne?—The price of dyeing, for ordinary colours, is, at the rate of from three to four francs per kilogram.

8987. Is there any difference between the prices of Lyons and the prices of St. Etienne, as to warping and dyeing?—There is a slight advantage in favour of St. Etienne.

8988. On account of St. Etienne not being exposed to the same local taxes?—The local taxes at St. Etienne are less.

8989. You stated, just now, that the marabout silk was silk thrown in a particular way?—Yes; maraboutage only refers to a particular mode of twisting the silk; it is not necessary that the silk should be of a particular quality. The silk used in the finest gauze is the finest white organzine of the country.

8990. How many manufacturers of ribbons are there at St. Etienne?—There are 200 manufacturers of ribbons, who employ 500 clerks, independently of the weavers, and the daily produce is 350,000 ells of ribbon.

8991. Are the looms all of the same sort?—No, they are not; there are three sorts of looms used in the district; there is the low single-handed loom used only in the mountains, in the remoter districts, and limited to the manufacture of a single ribbon. I think I might state a very important fact, preliminary to this; that the weavers in almost the whole of the district are agricultural labourers, that they live for the most part on a small quantity of land, which is their own property; that they are not wholly dependent on their manufacturing labour for their subsistence, but they take to the loom or the mountain according to the demand for labour. So that in the whole district, taking in St. Etienne, St. Chamond, and St. Didier, there are generally a third of the whole quantity of looms not at work. When there are orders in the market the agricultural weavers (if I may call them so) apply to their looms, and when there are no orders they apply themselves to agriculture, constantly pursuing two occupations.

8992. Is that true of the people who reside in St. Etienne?—I speak of the mountainous district, where the inferior looms are. I am speaking of the single-handed looms, which cost only from 12 to 18 francs; in these districts there are 18,000 of these looms, and not more than two-thirds in action; they principally make the satin ribbons, and those called sarsnets.

8993. You spoke of 350,000 ells daily, did you include the whole of the district?—Yes; unless where I make a statement to the contrary, I speak of the whole district. As to the fact I am now stating relative to the ribbon manufactory concentrated in the St. Etienne district, the labourers seek orders from one place to another, as the demand changes. I have brought some samples of ribbons which come from the different machines that are now in work.

---

*Mercurii, 20° die Junii*, 1832.

### JAMES A. STEWART MACKENZIE, ESQUIRE, in the Chair.

*John Bowring*, Esq. LL. D. again called in; and Examined.

*John Bowring*,
Esq. LL. D.

20 June,
1832.

8994. HAVE you any further details to furnish to the Committee, respecting the looms at St. Etienne?—At the close of the last day of meeting, I stated that there were three classes of looms used in the ribbon manufacture of St. Etienne; the first was the old unimproved loom, called the basse lisse, which still continues to be much employed in the mountainous districts, of which looms there are about 18,000; they only produce one ribbon, and are principally used for satin and sarsnet plain ribbons. The class of workmen that generally employ these looms, are the class that I called agricultural weavers; they are occupied in the labours of the field when there is no demand for the sort of ribbon they produce, and they go into the towns of St. Etienne and St. Chamond in search of work when there are orders in those places. The second class of looms are also single handed looms, called haute lisse, they are generally applied to the production of large patterns; of these there are 500 at St. Etienne and St. Chamond, and to 100 out of these 500 the Jacquard machinery is applied; of this description there are 473 looms in Lyons, the greater part of which are employed in silk haberdashery (passementerie,) which I find by another return employs also 85 looms at St. Etienne. It was the improve-

nient

*John Bowring,*
Esq. LL. D.

20 June,
1832.

ment which I had occasion to speak of to the Committee, namely, the introduction of the bar loom, which has exercised so great an influence on the prosperity of St. Etienne; of these bar looms there are now about 5,000, 800 of which are employed in sarsnet ribbons, 200 in velvets, 700 for galoons of sarsnet, 800 for stout and light satin, and 2,000 Jacquard employed for any purpose for which that machinery may be required, and 500 for striped gauzes; of these 5,000, the estimate is, that there are habitually but two-thirds employed; that is the Return I obtained in May last. I have also a Return of 1828, if the Committee are interested in seeing the changes which have taken place within the last four years.

8995. Do you speak of St. Etienne only?—I am now speaking of the whole district, including St. Etienne, St. Chamond, St. Didier, and the neighbourhood.

8996. And these 5,000 are to be added to the 18,000 mountain looms?—Yes; the 18,000 are in the remoter parts of the district; the looms of the 2d and 3d classes are principally in the more immediate neighbourhood of the town, and in the town itself.

8997. Have the goodness to state what the ribbon looms employed at Lyons are?—There are from 800 to 900 ribbon looms at this time employed at Lyons, and they are, I believe, almost without exception, the Jacquard looms; and they have almost all grown out of the discovery to which I referred; namely, the application of the broad weaving looms to the production of ribbons. At Lyons, the number of ribbons made in a loom is four pieces, and they are the ribbons which generally lead the fashion, and are of a very superior quality and high price.

8998. Have you any particulars respecting the cause of the introduction of the ribbon trade at Lyons?—There was great difficulty in introducing improvements into Lyons, but at this particular moment, I believe there is more difficulty in introducing improvements into St. Etienne; for the Lyonese are the more intelligent people of the two; when this discovery was made, which enabled the Lyonese manufacturers to employ their broad looms in the production of ribbons, they, having superior draftsmen and superior patterns, were able to produce a ribbon so perfect and beautiful, that its reputation was very soon established, and there were considerable orders for it from Paris and elsewhere; the consequence is, that the trade which for some time before had wholly left Lyons, seems returning to it again. A few years ago, I understood that there was not a single ribbon loom remaining at Lyons; and when I was there in May, there were, as I said, more than 800. There are a very small number of looms, probably fluctuating from 20 to 40 at Lyons, which are single looms, employed only in the production of articles of very high character, and superior price and beauty.

8999. Can you state what are the present prices paid for manufacturing ribbons at St. Étienne?—I will put in a document which has been furnished to me by a man, of whom I may say without hesitation, that he is the best informed individual in the place as to local matters, and has been occupied for some years in statistical observations; he has written the only book of any merit which describes the silk trade of St. Étienne, its growth and progress; his name is Hedde, his writings may be consulted with great benefit by any gentleman interested in the history of that trade; for I beg to remark, it is extraordinary that there is a printed history of the ribbon trade of St. Etienne, though there is none of the greater silk trade of Lyons. In this document I have arranged the French numbers with the English, which will afford the means of comparison with considerable facility. I preferred the statement of Mr. Hedde, inasmuch as he is a witness perfectly disinterested, not being himself a manufacturer, but a man who has been consulted on many occasions, and who may be considered on the whole as the best authority in the neighbourhood; he is also in some respects an official organ, being one of those individuals who have given guarantees to Government for their conduct, and who have been appointed under ministerial auspices.

[*The Witness delivered in the following Return.*]

TABLE

*John Bowring,*
Esq. LL. D.

20 June,
1832.

St. Etienne, 22 April 1832.

TABLE of the WAGES paid to the WORKMEN per 12 Ells, for weaving.

| English numbers | 2 | 4 | 6 | 7 | 8 | 10 | 12 | 16 | 20 | 24 | 30 | 40 | 50 |
|---|---|---|---|---|---|---|---|---|---|---|---|---|---|
| French numbers | 1¼ | 2 | 3 | 4 | 5 | 6 | 7 | 9 | 12 | 16 | 22 | 30 | 40 |
| Satins and Tafetas | 20c | 30c | 40 | 50 | 60 | 75 | 90 | 1. | 1.25 | 1.50 | 1.75 | 2. | 2.25 |
| Cords (Cordons) | – | – | – | – | – | 2.50 | 3. | 4. | 4.50 | 5. | 5.50 | 6. | 6.50 |
| Striped Gauzes | – | – | – | – | – | – | 1. | 1.25 | 1.50 | 1.75 | 2. | 2.50 | 3. |
| Figured Gauzes | – | – | – | – | – | – | 1.25 | 1.50 | 2. | 2.50 | 3. | 3.50 | 4. |

The Rate paid for clipping, is as follows; 50, .50, .75, 1.0, 1.10, 1.25, 1.30, 1.40, per doz.

The finishing and watering of ribbon is performed in private workshops; the price for finishing is, 0.5, 0.5½, 0.6, 0.6½, 0.7, 0.7½, 0.8, 0.8¼, 0.9, 0.9½, 10, 11, 13, per doz. When the watering is done by the roller, it is paid at the same rate as the finishing (cilindrage), when by the press it is paid 1–3d more than the fixed rate.

---

I wish also to state, that I have from other sources, returns of the same sort. There is a fluctuation spread over the whole field, ranging from 7½ per cent. below to 7½ above, on these prices; but these may be fairly represented as the average prices of labour.

9000. Is not this gentleman connected with the silk trade?—By no means; he is wholly independant of that trade; he is not himself a manufacturer, but he is well acquainted with the manufacture, having been some years ago a professor, or lecturer on weaving in the schools of St. Etienne; as I showed to the Committee some specimens of the school of Lyons, I will beg to hand in a specimen of the ribbon produced by Mr. Hedde, of the school of St. Etienne.

[*The Witness handed it to the Committee.*]

9001. Is this remarkable for having gained a prize, or ever having been exhibited? —It was exhibited.

9002. Do the manufacturers at St. Etienne export for their own account?— I believe now in no instance; I heard of one or two cases, where in consequence of a great accumulation of stock, they sent ribbons to foreign lands; but they complained of serious losses wherever that had been the case; and I found they were more disposed to make sacrifices at home, than to run the risk of greater sacrifices in remoter countries.

9003. Can you form any estimate of the value of 1,000 kilogrammes of silk, when wrought into ribbon?—On that subject I have one or two returns. I have taken from two or three sources, estimates of the progress of the manufacture of 1,000 kilogrammes of silk. The manufacturer on a satin or sarsnet ribbon pays for dyeing 4,000 f.; for winding, 3,000; for warping, 1,500; for weaving, 52,000; for finishing, 1,500; in all, 62,000 francs; so that it is estimated that the ribbon, when manufactured, would cost 132,000 francs; that is to say, the value of the silk, when it had passed through the process of manufacturing, would be 132,000, taking 70,000 as the prime cost of the material. I have also some calculations in the case of gauzes; 1,000 kilogrammes of silk are estimated to cost 73,000 f.; the dyeing, 4,000; winding, 3,000; warping, 1,500; extra cost for maraboutage, 3,000; the finishing, 1,500; and weaving, 56,000, which makes together 69,000; so that the total cost of striped gauzes would be 142,000. I enquired at St. Etienne what was the case in which the greatest quantity of labour could be applied to a given quantity of silk, and on the richest figured gauze; they stated 1,000 kilogrammes of raw silk, thus manufactured, to be worth 162,000 f.; this is an additional value of labour, equal to 20,000 francs, given to the prime cost on the richest figured gauze; that is the manufacturer's statement of labour, added to a given quantity of raw material.

9004. Have you any further details respecting the portion of labour at St. Etienne, on a given amount of money?—I have endeavoured to trace the quantity of raw material, and the quantity of labour on a given value; taking 1,000 f. on an article of satin or taffetas, it is estimated that 469 francs would be paid in wages, and 531 for the raw material; in 1,000 f. value of striped gauze, 486 f. would be paid

for

*John Bowring,*
Esq. LL. D.

20 June,
1832.

for wages, and 514 for the material; in 1,000 f. value of rich figured gauze, 550 f. would be paid for wages, and 450 for the silk; in this very fine gauze one quarter of the silk is lost in clipping, which must be taken into calculation; in this case I speak merely of the richest gauze.

9005. What is the price paid for clipping ribbons?—No. 6 and 7, 50 c.; No. 9, 75 c.; No. 12, 1 f.; No. 16, 1 f. 10 c.; No. 22, 1 f. 25 c.; No. 30, 1 f. 30 c.; No. 40, 1 f. 40 c. per 12 elis. Cylindring and watering are paid at from 5 centimes to 13 per dozen; when the watering is done by the press, one-third more is paid. I have a return from St. Chamond, stating that in the very fine gauzes, as much as 5 f. per piece has been paid for clipping.

9006. As to the dyeing, there is also a loss in the weight of the silk; it will not come out of the loom 1,000 kilogrammes, it will come out only about 700?—That is a fact not peculiar to France, it exists equally in England; on my last examination I gave in a return of the loss on the different colours.

9007. Exclusive of the clipping, what loss would 1,000 kilogrammes suffer from any other cause?—The principal loss is in dyeing, and of that I made a return; it is as 4 to 15 in common colours; as far as respects cost, I have from another source, a statement in another shape; that in striped gauzes the silk may be estimated at from 50 to 55 f., the labour from 45 to 50; in other gauzes the silk from 40 to 45 f., and the labour, from 55 to 60; and in ordinary matters, the cost of the silk is about 65 per cent., and the labour 35; that comes from another and independant quarter.

9008. Will you state what are the prices paid at Lyons for weaving?—At Lyons the weaving is paid at the tarif price, except some richer articles which are paid from 5 to 10 centimes above; the only two numbers that were then being manufactured were Nos. 16 and 30; 45 c. was paid for 16, and for 30, 60 c.

9009. Will you state the quantity of pieces made in a bar loom at one time?—In Nos. 1 to 1½, there are from 28 to 30 pieces; in 2 to 3, from 24 to 26; in 4 to 5, from 20 to 22; in 6 to 7, from 16 to 18; in 9, from 14 to 16; in 12, from 12 to 14; and in 13, from 6 to 8.

9010. Is that an average number?—Yes, it is.

9011. What kind of goods are these?—This only has reference to width.

9012. Does it apply to a particular description of ribbons?—To all ribbons manufactured in the bar loom; the bar loom is used in France for the production of a great number of ribbons in the same looms.

9013. Are the gauze ribbons made in the bar looms?—Yes, I have myself seen them.

9014. And this applies generally?—Yes, generally.

9015. Can you state the quantity made per day?—From 1 to 4, the average is 8 ells per day; from 5 to 9, 6; and from 30, 3 to 4; that is the return of a weaver at St. Etienne's; at Lyons, where there are four ribbons only of a superior order, the quantity is from 1½ to 2 ells of that number.

9016. Can you state what are the daily earnings of a weaver at St. Etienne?—I stated, with reference to the manufactories at Lyons, that there are two classes of weavers, the superintendent weaver, the proprietor of the looms, who receives the whole pay, and who gives half of it to the dependent weaver. At Lyons, they are called the chefs d'atelier and compagnons; there is an organization very like it existing at St. Etienne's, where the proprietor of the looms calls himself the passementier, and the weaver is called the ouvrier. The question I take it refers to the gains of the labouring weaver. I have two documents on the subject; one states, that with respect to common ribbons, the daily gain of the working man will be about, 1, 125 c.; 1½, 130 c.; 2, 140 c.; 3, 150 c.; 4, 160 c.; 5, 170 c.; 6, 190 c.; 7, 200 c.; 9, 210 c.; 12, 225 c.; 16, 240 c.; 22, 250 c.; 30, 275 c.; 40, 290 c.; and that on the superior, which begins at 6, he will gain 220 c.; on 7, 230 c.; on 9, 240 c.; on 12, 260 c.; on 22, 320 c.; and on 40, 340: on striped gauzes, the gain of the labour will be, on No. 6, 225 c.; on 7, 250 c.; on 9, 275 c.; on 12, 3 f.; on 16, 320 c.; on 22, 340 c.; on 30, 370 c.; and on 40, 390 c.: on the richest gauzes, the gain will be, on 6, 250 c.; on 7, 290 c.; on 9, 320 c.; on 12, 340 c.; on 16, 370; on 22, 390; on 30, 425 c.; and on 40, 440 c.; by which it seems that the minimum daily earning of a ribbon weaver will be 1¼ f. which is just a shilling a day; and the maximum will be 4 f. 40 c. This is the return from the town of St. Etienne. It is stated that the gain of the mountain labourer is very much less from the circumstances I have described, of their not being constantly employed; it is a sort of auxiliary labour, the daily returns of which are

678.                                                                                       wholly

*John Bowring,*
Esq. LL. D.
_____

20 June,
1832.

wholly uncertain, and must be estimated considerably below the prices paid in the town for these superior articles; it is therefore impossible to state the daily gains of a mountain labourer, inasmuch as he has his farm to attend to, and the business of weaving is much dependant on his other engagements.

9017. Are these mountaineers paid a lower rate than the town people for the same article?—No; but their labour is less productive.

9018. In talking of the number of ells that were made per day, you said it was from one to four, do you mean eight ells from each piece?—The looms produce eight ells of every piece.

9019. Respecting the mountain district, have you any further information to give?—The passementier is in fact the individual who immediately comes in contact with the manufacturer; in many cases they employ dependents; there are a few cases in which the passementier has only his own loom; but in many he is the father of a family, and sometimes, especially in the town, he has five, six or eight looms under his roof; he then gets these looms employed as well as he can, giving to the weavers whom he engages half the weaving price; no man is called a passementier who is not the proprietor of a loom.

9020. Have you any thing further to state as to the companion?—The person who would be called a companion at Lyons is called an ouvrier at St. Etienne's.

9021. Can you state what is the proportion of the different class of ribbons manufactured at St. Etienne's?—It is estimated, taking 100 as the point of unity, that about 35 per cent. are striped gauzes; about 25 clipped gauzes; about 10 gros de Naples; about 4 grosgrains; I do not know the English name for that: it is a very thick pad; 12 per cent. for belts; and 14, including all other pieces of ribbon not in the particular estimate.

9022. Does this include those manufactured at Lyons?—No, at St. Etienne; at Lyons they are all of the higher quality.

9023. Can you state what duties are paid on the introduction of foreign ribbons in France?—The estimate of the duty on the introduction of foreign plain silk into France may be taken to be 15 per cent.

9024. Is there any introduced from any other place than Switzerland?—There is a small importation from Germany.

9025. Has there been any great hostility shown to the importation of it?—There is constantly a great show of hostility, but as far as I have been able to get at the sincere opinion of the ribbon manufacturers they own they are decidedly benefited by the influence of foreign competition; there are many men who do certainly, while among their neighbours, complain of the introduction of foreign goods, and speak of being tributary to strangers; but when you get at their honest conviction as to the general influence of foreign competition, they acknowledge it to have been exceedingly valuable; and though a different language may have been held openly, I believe the most intelligent would be sorry to hear of any legislative measure against foreign competition.

9026. Do you consider this introduction as being prejudicial to the French manufacture?—I think it has been beneficial in the highest degree; in whatever point of view I consider the question, it comes to this result, that the French manufacture owes its success very much to the influence of foreign competition; that it would never have introduced a single improvement but under the extreme pressure of some foreign rivalry.

9027. Do they import any figured goods at all?—Exceedingly few,

9028. Is the rivalry as regards plain or figured goods?—In both; the operation of the prohibitory system is precisely this: It is clear a nation never can go into a foreign market under a prohibitory system; because a prohibitory system, unless it elevates prices does nothing, the demand for prohibition being to elevate prices beyond the average cost of production in other countries. The silk manufacture, notwithstanding all the aptitude of the country for manufacture, notwithstanding the peculiar benefits of their soil and climate, and a very industrious and intelligent population, the silk manufacture, I say, is the only manufacture that has had the benefit of a foreign demand; the demand could never have been created under a prohibitory system. The manufacture, left thus to an unassisted natural developement, and having the constant impulse of foreign rivalry, has reached this extraordinary result, that of 140,000,000 *f.* of manufactured silk 110,000,000 *f.*, as I then believed, but as by document I have received since we last met, 120,000,000 *f.* goes into the foreign market, and it is impossible that one single franc's worth could ever go into the foreign market if there was an efficient prohibitory system, unless the public treasury were drawn on for the difference of price.

9029. Will

*John Bowring,*
Esq. LL. D.

20 June,
1832.

9029. Will you state what is the social condition of the St. Etienne weavers?
—Their situation, on the whole, is one of tolerable comfort, they are not so well
off as many portions of the French people; the climate is not a very agreeable
one, it is cold and mountainous; the wine is somewhat dearer and worse than in
other districts; and the population are not to be compared in intelligence with
those of Lyons; the quantity of instruction among them is decidedly less.

9030. You stated that the French consumed 30,000,000 *f.*, and you placed the
whole produce at 140,000,000 *f.*, and said that 110,000,000 *f.* were exported; are
the 10,000,000 *f.* to go to the increase of the manufacture in France, or to the
decrease of the consumption?—I think, in the last year, the demand in France may
possibly have diminished to the extent of 10,000,000 *f.*; the cholera, for many
months, stopped all purchases; the great demand in the Parisian market ceased,
which is for the grand display at Longchamps, which has not taken place this year;
for in consequence of the presence of the cholera there was a Royal Ordonnance
directing that the festival should not be held.

9031. You think that 10,000,000 *f.* less was consumed in France?—The mere
political agitation in France has certainly had much influence on the trade. I cannot be far off the truth in supposing, that the sale in France was at least 5,000,000
less in 1831 than in 1830.

9032. Has the export increased?—Slightly. I estimated the consumption of
France at 30,000,000 *f.*, if the consumption be considered at 25,000,000 *f.*, the increase of the manufacture would be about 5,000,000 *f.*, but the calculation cannot
be precise.

9033. You have occasionally mentioned St. Chamond, in what way is this connected with St. Etienne?—It is a small town near St. Etienne; there is a slight
difference in the price of labour there, the octroi is less, though the price of goods
is very near the same; the average profits at St. Chamond must be greater than
the average profits at St. Etienne, growing out of local advantages it possesses.
I do not know of any manufacturer of St. Etienne having amassed so large a fortune
as M. Dugas, of St. Chamond.

9034. Is there a Conseil des Prud'hommes at St. Etienne?—Yes; the Conseil des
Prud'hommes is less popularly constituted than that at Lyons, and less efficient in
its operation. At St. Etienne, the weavers stand in the old position, those only
being represented who pay the patent tax; at Lyons, every weaver possessed of
four looms has the right of voting.

The Conseil des Prudhommes at St. Etienne is composed of thirteen Members and two
Adjoints, viz.—

    5 Ribbon Manufacturers.
    2 Armourers.
    1 Hardware Manufacturer.
    1 Dyer.
    2 Mecaniciens (Machine makers.)
    3 Passementiers.
    1 Working Gunsmith.

9035. State the nature of this tax on patents?—The patent tax is a direct tax
paid to the Government; it is a source of considerable revenue, and comes under
the direct assessed taxes; it may be considered as a species of poll tax on those
who exercise certain professions; the towns are arranged according to their population, and there are also different orders of patents; patents by bankers, by merchants and by manufacturers claiming the right to exercise a profession.

9036. The passementier is not considered a profession?—He has the power of
rating himself; but it will be seen that at Lyons there were only sixty or eighty
weavers rated to the patent; they thought the honour cost them a deal too much.

9037. Have you any document showing the exact width of French ribbons, and
the number of reeds employed in the manufacture of each?—I put in a statement
which will give a great deal of information on this head.

*[The Witness handed in the following Statement:]*

DES PEIGNES employés a la Fabrication des RUBANS à ST. ETIENNE.

Pour établir la portée des peignes des rubans, on a pris la ligne pour mesure commune,
et le nombre des dents qu'elle renferme indique la portée du peigne.

La largeur du ruban, toujours prise d'une lisière à l'autre, est un peu diminuée, soit par
la tirée de la trame, soit par le rétrécissement du tissu dont la chaîne est plus ou moins
tendue. On y remédie en ajoutant à la largeur que l'on veut obtenir, un certain nombre de
lignes exigées par la nature du tissu.

Les

*John Bowring,* Esq. LL. D.

20 June, 1832.

Les peignes employés à la confection des rubans cordons sont ordinairement de quatre dents à la ligne, ceux de taffetas de quatre un quart à la ligne, ceux de satin de quatre et demi, ceux de gaze de six, six et demi à sept dents ; et enfin, ceux des velours, dont la foulée ou hauteur du peigne est proportionnée au travail des doubles pièces, sont de trois à trois dents et demie. Nous donnons ici un tableau destiné à faire connaître les diverses portées de peignes les plus usitées.

TABLEAU des diverses portées de Peignes employés à la Fabrication des RUBANS de tous genres.

| Numéros des Rubans. | Largeur du Ruban en lignes. | Largeur du Peigne. | Calculé à 4 dents à la ligne. | à 4 ¼ dents. | à 4 ½ dents. | à 5 dents. | à 6 dents. | à 6 ½ dents. | à 7 dents. |
|---|---|---|---|---|---|---|---|---|---|
| − ½ | 1 ½ | 2 | 7 | 8 | 9 | 10 | 11 | 12 | 14 |
| − ¾ | 2 ½ | 3 ¼ | 11 | 12 | 13 | 15 | 17 | 19 | 21 |
| 1 | 3 ½ | 4 ¾ | 16 | 17 | 18 | 20 | 24 | 26 | 28 |
| 1 ¼ | 5 | 5 ¾ | 22 | 23 | 25 | 28 | 32 | 36 | 40 |
| 1 ½ | 6 | 6 ¼ | 26 | 28 | 30 | 33 | 40 | 44 | 48 |
| 2 | 7 ½ | 8 ½ | 32 | 34 | 36 | 41 | 48 | 53 | 57 |
| 3 | 9 ½ | 10 ½ | 41 | 43 | 46 | 51 | 61 | 68 | 71 |
| 4 | 12 | 13 | 50 | 53 | 56 | 64 | 74 | 84 | 98 |
| 5 | 15 ½ | 16 | 63 | 66 | 70 | 80 | 96 | 106 | 124 |
| 6 | 17 ½ | 19 | 72 | 75 | 80 | 90 | 108 | 118 | 130 |
| 7 | 19 ½ | 21 | 80 | 85 | 90 | 100 | 120 | 130 | 140 |
| 8 | 22 | 24 | 92 | 97 | 102 | 113 | 132 | 148 | 154 |
| 9 | 24 | 26 | 99 | 104 | 110 | 125 | 150 | 160 | 172 |
| 10 | 26 | 28 | 108 | 114 | 121 | 134 | 162 | 176 | 188 |
| 12 | 29 | 31 | 120 | 127 | 134 | 150 | 180 | 200 | 212 |
| 14 | 32 | 34 ½ | 132 | 140 | 148 | 165 | 198 | 214 | 234 |
| 16 | 34 | 37 ½ | 144 | 153 | 162 | 176 | 216 | 234 | 254 |
| 18 | 38 | 40 ½ | 156 | 165 | 174 | 194 | 234 | 252 | 270 |
| 20 | 41 | 44 | 168 | 178 | 188 | 210 | 252 | 272 | 292 |
| 22 | 44 | 47 | 180 | 191 | 202 | 226 | 270 | 294 | 316 |
| 24 | 47 | 50 | 192 | 204 | 216 | 246 | 288 | 316 | 348 |
| 30 | 54 | 57 | 220 | 234 | 248 | 276 | 330 | 358 | 389 |
| 40 | 60 | 64 | 248 | 263 | 278 | 310 | 372 | 402 | 432 |
| 50 | 66 | 70 | 270 | 288 | 306 | 340 | 406 | 440 | 474 |
| 60 | 72 | 77 | 298 | 316 | 334 | 372 | 446 | 484 | 520 |

Portées des rubans-velours, fabriqués à la barre, à pièces doubles - - -

| | | | | | | | | | |
|---|---|---|---|---|---|---|---|---|---|
| Numéros - | 00 | 0 | 2 | 4 | 6 | 8 | 10 | 12 | 14 |
| Lignes - - | 1½ | 2 | 2½ | 3 | 3½ | 4½ | 5 | 5½ | 6 |
| Dents - - | 7 | 8 | 9 | 10 | 12 | 14 | 16 | 18 | 22 |
| Numéros - | 16 | 18 | 20 | 24 | 30 | 40 | 50 | 60 | 70 |
| Lignes - - | 6½ | 7 | 7½ | 8 | 9 | 10 | 11 | 12½ | 14 |
| Dents - - | 24 | 26 | 28 | 30 | 32 | 35 | 38 | 41 | 46 |
| Numéros - | 80 | 90 | 100 | 110 | 120 | 130 | 140 | 150 | 160 |
| Lignes - - | 15½ | 17 | 18½ | 20 | 21½ | 23 | 24½ | 26 | 27½ |
| Dents - - | 51 | 56 | 61 | 66 | 70 | 75 | 80 | 85 | 90 |
| Numéros - | 170 | 180 | 190 | 200 | 210 | 220 | 230 | 240 | 250 |
| Lignes - - | 29 | 30½ | 32 | 33½ | 35 | 37½ | 39 | 41½ | 43 |
| Dents - - | 95 | 100 | 106 | 112 | 120 | 130 | 140 | 150 | 160 |

9038. What is the population of St. Etienne?—Of St. Etienne, and the immediate district, 60,000.

9039. Of that number, how many are engaged in the ribbon trade?—I could not obtain any very correct estimate of that; there is so much of fluctuation in the immediate neighbouring district, that it is very difficult to come at an estimate other than by the quantity of looms forming some general average; I think that half the population in some way or other are connected with the silk manufacture.

9040. The weavers you stated are frequently proprietors of land?—Yes, the proprietorship of land is so common that in France, out of a population of thirty-four millions, more than six millions are rated to the land tax.

9041. Is the manufacturer obliged to take out the license in order to exercise the right of voting?—He is.

9042. What is the amount of octroi?—It varies according to the population in the different towns; the octroi always has reference to the population; that which is is a law at Lyons is not a law at St. Etienne. I was about to state to the Committee the different pressure of the octroi at St. Etienne from its pressure at Lyons.

9043. Is the amount of the patent tax the same on all parties?—No; there is a classification of different professions; the banker pays a higher patent than the merchant, and the merchant a higher patent than the manufacturer, who in turn pays a higher than the labourer; the great motive for the weaver to take out a license was the obtaining a right to vote in the Conseil des Prud'hommes, yet that motive operated so little that the number of weavers at Lyons who took it out did not exceed sixty or eighty; they asserted, and with reason, that the organization was a very bad one, and the prefect forwarded their complaints to the Government; on this representation a new ordonnance was issued by the Government and the King, and the Conseil des Prud'hommes at Lyons received a popular constitution, while at St. Etienne it remains in its former state, precisely as it was constituted during the imperial regime under Buonaparte.

9044. Are you aware that no merchant in London can exercise his trade without making himself free of the Weavers' Company?—I am.

9045. State the amount of octroi?—The population of St. Etienne being 60,000 the amount of octroi paid is 340,000 *f.* on food and drink for the municipal service, and 180,000 *f.* for state service, so that the octroi is 520,000 *f.* for the town, making about 9 *f.* a head, which is 40 per cent. less than the octroi at Lyons; at St. Etienne, the octroi is 3 *f.* 85 *c.* per hectolitre of wine, with an additional octroi of about 3 *f.* 50 *c.*, and there is an octroi of 15 *f.* per ox, which is a very heavy tax. It is a subject of great complaint that the octroi presses with peculiar severity on the labourer.

9046. Can you inform us whether other workmen in other parts are subjected to the same tax of octroi as you state the weavers in Lyons and St. Etienne are subject to?—No, there is no general tariff; and the complaint is that the burden of the octroi is always heavy in proportion to the population; the octroi of Paris is much more heavy than the octroi at Lyons, the octroi at Lyons is much more heavy than that at St. Etienne, and the octroi at St. Etienne is more heavy than that at St. Chamond; now as the octroi is always most costly in the large towns, there is throughout France a struggle on the part of the labourers to fix themselves in the country.

9047. My question is, whether in a town, with a population of 10,000, carrying on the cotton trade; 10,000 carrying on the iron trade, and 10,000 the silk trade, they would be all subjected to the same rate?—Certainly.

9048. Then is the conclusion from that, that all mountain labourers who work out of the town are not subject to this tax?—Certainly not, the octroi is a town-collected tax.

9049. In the 60,000 people of St. Etienne do you include the mountain population?—No, I include what is called the *banlieue*; a great many weavers live as much as 30 miles from the town; that class come down when their agricultural work is done, then they visit the town to ask for manufacturer's labour.

9050. They are not included in the 60,000?—Certainly not; some live at a remote distance.

9051. Of the 18,000 looms you spoke of, have you estimated the number included in this 60,000 population?—Of these 18,000 there is very small portion in the town.

9052. Can you estimate the comparative advantages the Swiss ribbon manufacturers possess over the French?—I put in the Lyonese statement of their disadvantages as contrasted with the French. The St. Etienne manufacturers consider the Swiss have an advantage of four to eight per cent. on the raw material; the loss on the silk, in passing through the different hands, the dyer, the spinner, the warper and weaver, is, they state, much less in Switzerland than in France, and they estimate the difference at five per cent.; thus they calculate that they are at an average disadvantage of 11 per cent. in competition with the Swiss, that is the St. Etienne statement; but were I asked my opinion on it, I should say the statement is exaggerated.

9053. On the subject of labour did you obtain any information, how does the 11 per cent. appear to consist?—I said that I believed the St. Etienne statement to be excessive; the real disadvantage they have is in the duty paid on foreign silk, and in the fact that in France the silk almost invariably passes into second hands for sale. The Swiss and German manufacturer is himself the importer of silk;

he

*John Bowring,*
Esq, LL. D.

20 June,
1832.

he is generally a man possessing greater capital than the French manufacturer, and in the same situation as every other manufacturer, who having a foreign connection may import his own silk, and save the profit of the importer. When they estimate six per cent. as an average difference I think that is an over estimate; perhaps on the whole the Swiss have a benefit of three or four per cent. on the raw material. The Swiss manufacturer has the silk without duty, and himself is the importer of it; the French manufacturer has to pay a duty on the silk, a profit to the importer, and a brokerage to the individual who buys the silk for him. But there are a great many of the operations which in France are carried on apart from the manufacturer, and which in Switzerland and Germany are done at home; the profit which the dyer, the throwster, the winder, or any other individual employed in the manufacture, would receive at St. Etienne, is a profit which goes into the pocket of the Swiss manufacturer who manages these details himself. Eleven, however, I think too high a rate of per centage; but I believe there is a difference of six or seven per cent. in favour of the Swiss manufacturer.

9054. Do you mean that the Swiss manufacturer pays no duty on thrown silk? —Neither on raw nor on thrown; and he has other circumstances in his favour of considerable importance in their bearings; he pays no duty on machinery, while the French pay a duty of from 15 to 33 per cent.; he pays no duty on iron, while the French duty is 150 per cent.; and the price of wood in Switzerland is on the whole not more than one-third of the price of wood in France; the increased cost of which has also grown out of the French prohibitory system; indeed the more the subject is traced the more advantages do you find possessed by the Swiss.

9055. In fact these disadvantages which the French manufacturer labours under, have almost all been created by the Government themselves?—They have almost all grown out of what is called the protecting system.

9056. Then the commercial prohibitory system in France operates generally as a bounty to the encouragement of silk manufacturers in Switzerland?—Certainly.

9057. Have you any estimate, derived from the lips of the weavers themselves, of their expenses?—I have here the result of many conversations I had with them, which will serve to corroborate or to compare with the facts I have mentioned; they estimate the average rate of wages at 40 sous per day, which is 1 s. 8 d. sterling. They state that none of them, even the most successful weavers, are at all as well off as the more successful men in other manufactures; there are instances of individuals employed in iron and coal works, who earn from 8 f. to 11 f. per day; the labouring people in the district eat three meals a day, of which soup forms the whole or a part; those who are employed in working richer ribbons eat animal food, and drink a bottle of wine of the average cost of 6 sous or 3 d. I have here, from a passementier, a statement of his monthly expenses: he says he pays for the preparation of the quills, 8 f. 67 c.; for rent, 5 f.; the cost of keeping the loom in repair, 5 f.; the tying together the cards, 2 f.; (that is one great ground of grievance; the cards are delivered to them separately, and the expense of fastening them together, both at Lyons and at St. Etienne, falls on the weaver); he estimates the interest, on the cost of his Jacquard loom, of 1,500 f. as 7 f. 50 c.; then there is soup twice a day, and lodging for the weaver, 6 f.; next there is 3 f. lodging for the quill-maker, and 33 c. for soap, which makes together an average of 37 f. 60 c.; then for the winter months, he adds, for 5 lb. of candles, 3 f. 75 c., and for fuel, 1 f. 50 c., that makes 42 f. 75 c. I find that the average number of looms possessed by the passementier are from two to five; the rooms which the weavers occupy are let at a rental of so much per croisée, which is the window space that allows the working of a loom, and that is paid from 60 f. to 80 f. per annum. This man himself had four looms, one was employed in making No. 30, which produced 6 pieces at 4 f. which would be 144 f.; 8 pieces, of No. 22, which would be 144 f.; 12 pieces, of No. 12, at 1 f. 75 c. would be 126 f.; 14 pieces, of No. 9, at 1 f. 25 c. would be 105 f. making 519 f.; he stated to me, that the profit of four looms, independent of his own, would be 103 f. 50 c.; of three looms, 99 f.; and of two, 90 f.; so that out of this he got, as he said, 292 f. and 50 c. I asked his return of daily earnings, and he said on the first and second loom he considered the average gain was 48 sous, which is 2 s.; on the third, 42 sous, which is 21 d.; and on the fourth, 35 sous, which is 17¼ d.; this is the return of the passementier as to the gain of the particular workmen employed by him on the above looms.

9058. Independent of his half?—Yes; and he gives the average production of the weaver at four ells a day; he says five and six have been produced by weavers, who were extraordinarily diligent and industrious. On a loom of No. 30,

making

*John Bowring,*
Esq. LL. D.

20 June,
1832.

making 2 doz. at 4 *f*. a doz. 8 *f*. have been gained of which he of course receives half, but this assumes uninterrupted labour. I find here a memorandum, which I made at the end of a days' visit to a district. I had returned from several devidages and questioned the labouring women ; a machine for winding costs from 20 to 40 francs, they can wind from half a pound to a pound of day, and they are paid from 20 to 30 sous ; the average is from 20 to 24 sous. I visited several ateliers and found that No. 12, the price paid was 30 sous for gauze, and the workmen could produce from four to five ells. If it were four-and-half, he would have to receive 6 *f*. 75 *c*. of which half went to the weaver and half to the owner of the loom. They say that a piece of ribbon, of 160 ells, No. 3, which is No. 6, English, requires 25 days labour at the rate of about six ells a day, with the common bar loom.

9059. In what part of France is the silk thrown that is used in the district of St. Etienne ?—It is thrown through the whole of the silk district on both sides of the Rhone.

9060. What distance is it conveyed after being thrown ?—The distance is frequently considerable, but on such an article as silk the cost of carriage cannot be much. The roads in the St. Etienne district are however most execrable ; there is nothing worse in Europe than the road from Lyons to St. Etienne.

9061. A rail road would be of use to them ?—They have got a rail road there which will soon be opened.

9062. Having stated that the passementier provides them with food, at the cost of 6 *f*. a month, do you consider that they are uniformly satisfied with that quantity of diet ?—He does not provide them with food, he only provides them with soup ; he is bound to furnish them with soup, and to dress their food.

9063. Is it not a very miserable sort of soup ?—Yes ; it is not such as an Alderman would enjoy.

9064. Is there any meat in the soup?—It is a mere lard soup ; boiled lard, in which there is a slight infusion of vegetables ; a bason of it is to be had for a penny. I have not represented the soup as the food on which the men live.

9065. In stating the disadvantages which the French manufacturer suffered, as compared with the Swiss manufacturer, you mentioned the charges on raw silk, that would be applicable of course only to a small proportion of the silk used ?—I think the price of silk in the French market depends on the importing price of Italian silk, the cost of foreign silk regulates the market price ; but the French will always pay so much more than the Swiss, in consequence of the duty which the French impose on foreign importation.

9066. This could only apply to a small portion of the silk purchased?—Yes ; inasmuch as the importation of Italian silk, with all its charges, regulates the value of French silk, the mercantile charges will fall on the French silk ; and as the Swiss manufacturer is himself the importer he saves the profit of the French importer. In France the manufacturer is not the importer of silk, but pays a profit to the importer.

9067. Do the Swiss throw their own silk or import it thrown ?—They import it thrown for the most part.

9068. If they import it thrown, what machinery is used ?—The heavy cost of machinery in France might give to the Swiss an advantage in throwing silk. There are also other machines beside throwing machines employed in the manufacture of silk, and it is a great question whether machinery might not be employed much more extensively in the silk manufacture. I have lately heard that while the French are placing difficulties in the way of the importation of machinery, the Swiss Government are giving encouragement to individuals for introducing machinery of different sorts.

9069. Have you visited any other towns in France where silk is manufactured ? —I visited Nismes and Avignon.

9070. State what are the number of looms at Nismes ?—The number is from 7,000 to 8,000.

9071. What is the principal manufacture there?—The principal manufactures are articles in which silk forms only a portion of the raw material ; there is also a manufacture of what may be called silk hosiery, such as caps and silk stockings are made of ; there is also a considerable manufacture of articles which are in imitation of the better sort of Lyonese goods.

9072. Can you state what is the rate of wages paid at Nismes ?—The rate of wages at Nismes is from 8 to 10 per cent. less than at Lyons.

9073. Does that arise from a decrease of the octroi ?—It arises from two causes ; the octroi is considerably lower at Nismes, and the neighbourhood of Nismes is

678.                                                                         more

*John Bowring,*
Esq. LL. D.

20 June,
1832.

more productive, and the general cost of existence is less. Rental is less expensive, so is food, and so is wine.

9074. Are there any other branches of labour to which the labourer can turn when the silk trade is slack?—None in the town.

9075. Is there any demand in England for that article?—Before 1825 there were a certain quantity of silk goods sent to England from Nismes. I visited the principal manufacturers there, and did not find one among them who now had any direct connection with England.

9076. Have you attended to the sarsnet trade of Avignon?—I visited Avignon, and inasmuch as I found there some interesting facts connected with the operation of our system on their productions, I took some pains to inform myself generally of the state of things.

9077. Have you any patterns that you wish to exhibit?—Those are the patterns (*handing them in*); this is the only produce of the Avignon trade, and its fluctuations may be easily traced.

9078. What is the article?—It is sarsnet.

9079. What is the quantity of raw silk produced in the Vaucluse Department? —The best estimate I could gain as to the present amount of production, is about 12,000,000 of francs. These patterns have been furnished me by a gentleman who has the largest manufactory in the whole of the district; he assured me, that in 1825 his sales were enormous for smuggling into England, both at Calais, Boulogne and Dunkirk; that of late years he had not sold a single piece, and that the trade with England in this article was now completely put an end to; that in 1825 the fraudulent trade had been very extensive, but that the improvements in England had been so great that they were now completely shut out of the English market. He put these specimens into my hand, as showing that notwithstanding the improvements they had introduced they had not been able to compete with England in this article; he attributed these improvements in England solely to the foreign competition, which had given such an energy to the exertions of our manufacturers.

9080. Did he state how many years previous to 1825 the trade had been carried on?—It had been carried on for several years; the trade had gone on increasing until 1825, when it reached its maximum; after 1826 he stated, that the demand considerably diminished, and at this moment it has wholly ceased.

9081. I wish to know the present prices of silk?—Of the twelve millions which the Vaucluse department produces, eight millions are consumed in the manufactures of Avignon, and the remainder goes to the Lyons market, with the exception of a small quantity that is sent to Nismes; for the last 15 years the manufacture of sarsnets has gone on progressively increasing; it received a momentary check by the Revolution of 1830, but it has already regained the vigour and taken up the position which it occupied before that period; a very intelligent friend of mine states, that he attributed the increased consumption of silk goods to the improved condition of society, and the increased appetite for luxuries which has grown out of accumulated wealth; that the desire for French fashions and productions has increased with the increase of connection with the different nations of Europe, and has been the consequence of the superiority of many of the French fabrics, which has created a demand for them, which removes them from the fear of foreign competition. The standard of silk in the Vaucluse department varies from 10 to 25 deniers; they may be reeled three, four and five to the thread, and are now selling in the Avignon market at from 17 to 17½ francs the local pound, which is equal to 41 and 42½ per kilogram. Silk from 18 to 20 deniers, obtains for the kilogram from 39 to 40; from 20 to 25 deniers, 14 to 15 francs, which makes the kilogram from 35 to 36.

9082. Is there any discount?—This statement I believe to be without discount.

9083. Can you supply the Committee with any details respecting the cultivation of silk?—The Vaucluse department is one in which considerable attention has been given to the cultivation of the mulberry tree; the larger proprietors have been making it an object of their peculiar care; some time back there was no individual in that department who looked at the production of silk as any other than accessary to the general rental of his estates; of late years a great change has taken place. In many departments of the district the cultivation of the mulberry tree is become the principal source of agricultural revenue. A few years ago, I learnt that there was no species of property, the return of which was so fluctuating and uncertain as that invested in the growth of the mulberry tree; of late no agricultural produce has given so regular and beneficial a return; they have done a great

deal

*John Bowring,*
Esq. ll. d.

20 June,
1832.

deal to improve the culture of the mulberry tree, to discover the mulberry tree most adapted to a particular soil; and they have done something to improve the caste of the silk worm, and the whole system of what is called the education of the silk worm has changed. It was in the hands of very ignorant peasants, but of late it has been taken up by more intelligent persons; a great number of works have been written on the subject, so that the business is now getting to be well understood, and the progress of improvement is very remarkable.

9084. Do you mean to say that science has been applied to the cultivation of the silk and the management of the worm?—I find, from an account given 20 years ago, so imperfect was the method then pursued for raising the silk worm, that that which was then considered a fair average, namely, six pounds for 80 or 100 pounds of cocoons, would now be considered a very bad return, for that double the quantity is ordinarily obtained at present.

9085. Has the quality improved also?—The quantity has increased and the quality has improved. The period of great improvement was the cessation of Buonaparte's reign. France then made a great start; much attention was devoted to the subject; Dandolo's book got translated, and there was much additional information circulated with reference to the particular aptitude of France for the production of silk. I may employ here an expression used by a local observer. He says, " the importance, certainty, and value of the results obained, are such as to excite the greatest astonishment in the minds of those who have traced them."

9086. You will now direct your attention to the subject of throwing?—It has not yet become a general custom in the southern departments of France for the growers to throw their silk; the habit of throwing their silk has been pretty generally introduced into the department of Ardeche, of which the present produce is twenty millions of francs; almost all the silk in the Vaucluse department is sold by the peasant or farmer to the throwster.

9087. By spinning is meant the winding from the cocoon?—Yes, it is.

9088. It is usually understood in this country as reeling?—Yes; the price for reeling is 2 *f.* per pound of the country, or 5 *f.* per kilogram. In the Vaucluse, they pay for throwing, from 3 *f.* to 4 *f.* for tram, and 7 *f.* to 9 *f.* for organzine; and they estimate the waste on silk, of their district, at from four to eight per cent.

9089. Can you state what is the labour?—The labourers in the Vaucluse district are engaged in a way rather different from the general usage of France; they are mostly yearly labourers, and receive from 250 *f.* to 350 *f.* a year, with food and lodging; from the best information I could get, the expense of food and lodging may be about the same amount, that is to say, the whole cost of a farming labourer there will be 8 *s.* or 9 *s.* a week.

9090. Is the farmer often, or generally, a reeler?—Very seldom in the Vaucluse, he is so in the Ardeche; the labourers, who are paid by the day, receive in money from 1 *f.* 25 *c.* to 1 *f.* 50 *c.* during six months of the year, and 1 *f.* 75 *c.* during the other six months; that is the price in fact of agricultural labour.

9091. You have no particular information regarding the wages paid for throwing silk?—No special information on that subject.

9092. What sized denier do you allude to?—This is the average of the district; the number of deniers is from 15 to 25.

9093. Can you inform the Committee whether women and children are chiefly employed in throwing silk, or men?—Men are, I believe, frequently employed in throwing; women and children are mostly employed in reeling. The habit of the labourers, in this district, is to work from sunrise to sunset; they are allowed two hours in winter for repose, and from three to four in summer; the heat being intense at mid-day.

9094. Are you quite sure that men are employed in throwing?—It was not an object of particular inquiry; I am not aware of the proportions.

9095. Is there anything unhealthy in the employment of the labourer engaged in raising the raw silk?—Not at all; one of the great improvements in what is called the education of the worm, is the discovery of the fact that it thrives best in the ordinary temperature; formerly the room was dark, and the temperature high, and the quantity of worms that perished was very considerable. Now the room in which the silk worms are kept is light and open to the ordinary currents of air, and an average temperature, and the disagreeable smell, which I remember in my boyhood, has very nearly passed away.

9096. Are the persons so employed ordinary peasants?—Ordinary peasants.

9097. Is the 15 to 25 denier the size of a single or double thread?—The single

678.                                                                               thread

*John Bowring,*
Esq. LL. D.

20 June,
1832.

thread I believe; I should take it the thread spun from three to five cocoons, but am not sure.

9098. Can you state how silk is sold in that country?—It is sold for ready money invariably, and sold by a local pound, the proportions of which I mentioned.

9099. Is it not also sold for local money?—No; francs are the universal money in France, no accounts are kept otherwise.

9100. In Ardeche and Vaucluse, are not the accounts kept in florins?—No.

9101. Can you state who pays the expense of the transport after the silk is thrown to the manufacturer?—That will always be the subject of specific bargain; the silk when it is thrown is generally taken to one of the great fairs, the fair of Beaucaire is the principal place of resort. I think it is held in the month of July; it is a great congregation of the silk growers, and the buyers receive it on the spot.

9102. After it is thrown?—Sometimes thrown, sometimes only reeled, and sometimes it is sold in cocoons; in all cases for ready money.

9103. The expense of transfer is generally one of specific agreement?—Yes.

9104. Is it purchased at these fairs by merchants or manfacturers?—Generally by manufacturers when thrown; some merchants lately thought of taking to themselves the business of throwing; one of the most distinguished merchants of Lyons, M. Dugas, has I know a project of establishing throwing mills on a larger scale than have yet existed in France.

9105. I thought you mentioned that it was calculated that shortly there would be an export trade from this country of thrown silk?—The opinion in France, certainly, is, that there is a superiority in the thrown silk of England; I have heard that opinion expressed very frequently; I am quite certain, that whatever the opinion be in France, their throwing machinery is in a rude state; I could not learn that there were any throwing mills in which a capital of 5,000 *l.* was vested.

9106. Have you any information to give on the subject of the expense of winding and warping in Vaucluse or Nismes?—At Avignon, the manufacturer is the winder and the warper; the price paid for winding depends on the quality of the organzine, and is from 275 cents to 375 cents per kilogram; the warping is paid at so much per piece of 100 to 110 ells, and the price is 1*f.* 50*c.* per piece.

9107. What is the food of the agricultural labourer?—The agricultural labourers in the Vaucluse department very seldom eat animal food; the bread is black bread, inferior to that usually eaten at Lyons and St. Etienne.

9108. Is not that partly owing to the fact that France is deficient in a supply of animal food?—Not deficient, but the quantity used is not considerable; it is a fruit country, which always interferes with the consumption of animal food. The labourers generally drink from half to a whole bottle of wine per day; the wine is excellent; a strong wine, and worth about 2*d.* a bottle. The rate paid for lodging is from 40 to 50 francs per annum. Their clothing has been a good deal improved of late years.

9109. What does the lodging consist of?—The lodging generally consists of a single room, in which a man dwells with his family; in France the number of families under the same roof is very considerable.

9110. Does the information about the sarsnets apply to Avignon?—That is the sole article made at Avignon; it is made in three qualities, and at this moment there are 5,000 looms employed in the manufacture of that article, of which 3,500 are within the walls, and 1,500 in the neighbouring district.

9111. Can you give us any information as to the number of hours the labourers work per day, their earnings, and general condition at Avignon?—The weaver receives from 45 to 60 cents per ell; the exact amount depends on the number of threads he has to throw into a given space: the Florentine of one thread is paid from 40 to 50 cents per ell; two threads, from 45 to 55; the Marsellinets, from 50 to 60; and the Marsellines, from 55 to 65. I have a return here of the number of pieces actually made; there are 60,000 per year, on an average of 55 ells each, which makes a produce of 3,300,000 ells. They take the average estimate of value to be about 2½ francs an ell. In reference to the English demand I mentioned, that one of the largest manufacturers there, stated that they formerly had a very large connection for the purpose of smuggling these goods into England, and that the sales for England had wholly ceased. This is corroborated by a manufacturer, who says, " Not only have we evidence of the cessation of the English demand by the cessation of all orders from the English smugglers, but in documents received from the depôts at Lyons and Paris, to the amount of many millions, we scarcely find the return of a sale to any English importer, either directly or indirectly; from

*John Bowring,*
Esq. LL. D.

20 June,
1832.

1810 to 1814 a fourth of the whole manufactory of Avignon was made for the English market; at that time the quantity of looms in existence at Avignon was not more than 2,500." The general demand for the article, therefore, has doubled since the number of looms has become 5,000, yet the English demand has been wholly put an end to.

9112. Do you understand that the manufacture of Avignon is now generally consumed in France?—Yes, very largely, and exported principally to America.

9113. Will you state what information you possess respecting the weavers at Avignon?—Of this manufacture a weaver can produce from four to six ells per day; the effect of the climate and other circumstances is such, and creates such an indisposition to labour, that I find by a return I have before me that one manufacturer, who has from 500 to 600 looms employed, states, that at the end of the year, he had not an average return of more than 1¼ ells per day, while the loom constantly employed would produce 6 ells. Inquiry was made as to the proportion of men and women employed in the Avignon manufactory: the quantity of men and women is about equal; the supply of weavers comes very much from the neighbouring districts, and of the whole persons engaged in the Avignon weaving business, there are not more than half who are hereditary weavers. They employ one child generally to three looms; the looms are, as at St. Etienne and Lyons, almost wholly in the houses of the weavers, and an industrious labourer is generally occupied from five in the morning until seven in the evening, and allows himself three hours for meals and rest. I had from the authorities a very honourable return as to the general good conduct of the workpeople there: it might be supposed, that where excellent wine is very cheap there would be a good deal of inebriety; perhaps there is no town in France in which inebriety is so unfrequent as Avignon. I beg to mention here, that the same thing which is occurring at Lyons and St. Etienne is operating at Avignon; there also is an octroi less heavy than that at Lyons, heavier than that at St. Etienne; and its operation on the labouring people is, that they are moving off in different directions from the town. I have a statement of their earnings in another shape; the best workmen earn from 2*f*. 50*c*. to 3*f*. a day; the next class, from 1*f*. 50*c*. to 1*f*. 75*c*.; the inferior, from 1*f*. to 1¼*f*.; so that you may suppose, from 800 to 900 francs is the maximum, and from 300 to 400 the minimum of their average yearly earnings. They state, that they suffer more than any others from the competition with Zurich in other countries, but they think they are sufficiently protected at home by the difference of the 15 per cent. duty, with which the foreign goods are visited.

9114. What do they state as to the competition with foreign markets?—They say, " It appears to us that foreign competition will force improvement upon us; it will lead to some reduction in the price of labour; and if that were accompanied with relief from our local taxes, we should have nothing to fear, and we are strongly impressed with this, inasmuch as we have an opportunity of comparing our relative position in the Dutch market with the position of the Swiss."

9115. Are the people in France desirous that the raw material should be exported?—Not desirous, but not unwilling in their present friendly disposition towards England to consent; the intelligent French manufacturers feel that if encouragement was given to the production of the raw material, they also would be benefited with the rest of the world. I called to their recollection the experiment made in England with respect to the export of long wool; that was looked on with great apprehension in this country, and it was supposed that much immediate calamity and inevitable ultimate destruction of the woollen trade would follow; the export of long wool has now become a very important trade, and with no injury to the woollen manufacturer; no doubt in the result both France and England would be greatly benefited by the export of raw silk from France.

9116. Does there exist a prejudice in France against exportation?—There has been a very strong prejudice.

9117. Do they use any foreign silk at Avignon?—A small quantity; they have made several experiments on foreign silk, and have imported some small quantity from India, some from Italy, and some from the Levant; they are in the habit of importing when there is a deficiency of supply.

9118. It has been stated here that a very great increase in the import of China silk from Sincapore has taken place into this country during the last few years; have the Avignon merchants turned their attention to the use of China silk?— I do not think they have; at Lyons, almost all the experiments made with China silks have failed; there have been three or four cases of large importations

from

from this market, and they have been unsuccessful ; and their opinion is, that inasmuch as our throwsters are much more accustomed to throwing that particular quality of silk than theirs, they the French had better not meddle with it ; to them it is as a new article, and they hardly know how to employ it, they have therefore abandoned its importation; one house told me they had imported 300 bales into Lyons, which were bought on peculiarly advantageous terms, yet they left a great loss to the Lyonese importer ; it was a sort of silk to which they were unaccustomed, and they had great difficulty in disposing of it ; the bales were imported raw, and imported for the purpose of making an experiment on a large scale.

*Veneris, 22° die Junii,* 1832.

### JAMES A. STEWART MACKENZIE, ESQUIRE, in the Chair.

*John Bowring,* Esq. LL. D. again called in ; and Examined.

9119. HAVE you any information you can give to the Committee relative to the ribbon trade in Switzerland?—I have obtained from authentic sources the following facts, as to the state of the ribbon trade at Basle : the number of looms is from 3,100 to 3,200; of which from 120 to 130 have the Jacquard machine; the number of persons employed is about 12,000 ; they are all agriculturists, and only seek manufacturing labour when the cultivation of the land leaves them free. It is estimated in that district they are employed in manufacturing from two-thirds to three-fourths of the year,    The ribbons they make are principally plain, and of the numbers from one to thirty,  the looms producing from 16 to 28 pieces, according to the breadth.   A good weaver will be occupied from four to five weeks in the completion of a chain of 10 pieces, which consists of 120 ells.   There is no standard as to price of labour,  every house making its separate bargain with every separate weaver; and from No. 1 to 8, at a chain of 120 ells, 21 sous are paid ; of No. 30, of the first quality, from 19 to 21 *f.* for the taffeta ; of No. 10, the fine cordons, from 32 to 34 *f.*   The return states, that the principal markets are the United States, Germany, England, Russia, the Havannah, Mexico, Belgium and France ; in 1831, the quantity of ribbons exported to the United States and to England was 454,000 kilogrammes; to France, Switzerland exported 8,709 kilogrammes; and they imported, in 1830, 11,480 kilogrammes : the fact is, that while Swizerland exports to France the ribbons of an inferior order, she pays herself in ribbons of a superior order, which she imports from France : of the quantity of silk consumed I have no means of making a correct estimate ; its price is as low as from 16 to 17 *f.* which I suppose must be for tram, and is from 30 to 35 *f.* for organzine, per pound.

9120. What effect has the introduction of French silk goods into England had on the French manufactures?—It has created considerable improvement, by introducing additional activity, and has operated on that part of their manufactures where their superiority is undoubted ; that is, on the production of the greater portion of fashionable articles ; and I draw from this the conclusion, that its improving effect is precisely on those qualities of silk whose introduction would be most beneficial to England ; that is, on the silks which represent the greatest quantity of taste knowledge and the greatest advance in the manufacturing article ; it seems to me, that at this moment the instruction that England is deriving from France is more and more useful and important.

9121. Were there any kinds of goods largely smuggled into England before 1826, which have ceased to be exported now ?—I mentioned that up to 1825 of the Avignon manufactures, consisting of sarsnets and Marseillines, the smuggled importation was very great : there was also a considerable exportation of black goods and many sorts of plain goods, the illicit introduction of which has, at this moment, nearly ceased.

9122. Have you any information respecting exports to England from Lyons and St. Etienne, before 1826?—The general fact that I could deduce from all the inquiries I have made is, that the English demand has been more and more thrown on the articles of which taste and fashion form the important feature, and more and more abstracted from the grosser and less difficult articles of fabric.

9123. Can

*John Bowring,*
Esq. LL. D.

22 June,
1832.

9123. Can you give the scale by which the official values of silk goods are calculated in France?—I have obtained from the Custom House their rates of calculation, which are averages by which silks are valued in the official estimates of the French Government: of raw silks, 40 $f$. per kilogram; thrown silks, 70 $f$. per kilogram; and the waste silk, 20 $f$. per kilogram. These are the returns on which the Custom House estimates the official value: the estimates of plain silks are 120 $f$. per kilogram; wrought silks, 130 $f$.; crapes, 88 $f$.; and plain, 120 $f$.

9124. What constitutes the plain, and what the wrought?—I shall have an opportunity of explaining that by-and-bye, and putting in a document which will show the whole bearing.

9125. Are these all the heads under which the exports are estimated?—These are the general heads: the French Government has taken the trouble, in consequence of a communication I made to them, to send me a number of documents, analyzing to a great extent their exportation in silk manufactures, which I will put in. I should state, that I applied to the Custom House, not with reference to the proceedings of this Committee, but generally to be able as a commercial commissioner to form a correct value of the trade of France; and to this end it was necessary to ascertain from the French Government the rate of official value they give to their imports and exports.

9126. Have you any official statement, showing the different species of silk goods exported from France?—I am now going to put in a document I have received within these few days, in answer to a communication, desiring the French Government to send me an analysis of their exportations. The analysis does not go into so many ramifications as might possibly be provided for the purpose; it is, however, an eminently valuable document, as it contains the whole history of the silk exportations of France since 1825, and it is brought down to 1831; the subdivisions are under the heads of plain, wrought and embroidered; then the embroidered with silk, or gold and silver, and with tinsel; then comes stuffs, in which there is a mixture of thread, cotton and wool; another head is counterpanes, an article which goes principally to South America and Spain; gauzes, crapes, net laces, hosiery and all the various classes which are known by the name, in France, of Passementerie, which are threads, cords, laces and so on. The whole exportation of manufactured silks from France are ranged under these heads; and thus they form curious points of comparison with the statements I put in before, where the arrangements were under the head of Countries, and not under that of Articles. It appears that in 1825, the exportation from France was 92,000,000 of francs; in 1826 90,000,000 $f$.; in 1827, 115,000,000 $f$.; in 1828, 115,000,000 $f$.; in 1829, 111,000,000 $f$.; in 1830, 111,000,000 $f$.; and in 1831, 120,000,000 $f$.: so it seems, therefore, that the trade has been nearly stationary for the last five years, with the exception of an increase of about 10,000,000 $f$. in 1831: it appears also, that the manufacture was not immediately increased, on the contrary, it was rather diminished, by the English demand on the opening of the English markets in 1826. There is this curious fact deducible thus, that notwithstanding the presence of the English as buyers in the French market, the official value of French exported silks had not much increased; the fact being, that the importation of French silk goods into England has been accompanied by the exportation of English silk goods to other countries, to an amount not much inferior to the amount which England takes from France; this will be found to be a fact, and a very instructive one it is.

*[The Witness delivered in the following Statement:]*

FRENCH

### FRENCH SILK TRADE.

#### MANUFACTURED SILKS Exported from *France.*

| DESCRIPTION of the GOODS. | VALUES EXPORTED: | | | | | | |
|---|---|---|---|---|---|---|---|
| | 1825. | 1826. | 1827. | 1828. | 1829. | 1830. | 1831. |
| Stuffs — Pure — Plain | 25,867,800 | 40,708,080 | 51,839,400 | 51,038,040 | 46,121,400 | 51,335,040 | 59,576,640 |
| Pure — Wrought | 22,668,620 | 13,957,710 | 19,675,370 | 18,312,710 | 17,395,300 | 19,021,600 | 17,825,860 |
| Embroidered — Silk | 710,970 | 3,266,510 | 906,620 | 330,330 | 564,330 | 275,210 | 189,540 |
| Embroidered — Gold and Silver — fine | - | - | 102,799 | 397,368 | 463,788 | 414,972 | 350,892 |
| Embroidered — Gold and Silver — tinsel | - | - | 182,700 | 229,860 | 290,160 | 219,960 | 117,900 |
| Mixed with thread, cotton & wool | - | - | 4,472,123 | 4,961,470 | 6,849,840 | 5,954,080 | 4,736,480 |
| Counterpanes | 2,600 | 45,840 | 11,960 | 20,920 | 23,160 | 11,040 | 320 |
| Gauze | 1,076,432 | 1,123,584 | 1,300,682 | 926,352 | 1,067,808 | 1,250,816 | 1,016,960 |
| Crape | 2,643,432 | 3,139,224 | 3,703,392 | 3,743,296 | 4,122,360 | 3,205,048 | 3,885,200 |
| Net | 1,111,360 | 1,228,080 | 981,600 | 819,040 | 767,600 | 610,400 | 398,400 |
| Lace | 740,744 | 657,095 | 941,441 | 792,100 | 758,879 | 749,480 | 606,522 |
| Bonnetry | 3,286,500 | 2,082,200 | 2,629,300 | 2,341,300 | 2,076,000 | 1,617,300 | 1,983,700 |
| Threads, Cords, &c. — Gold and Silver — fine | - | - | 279,099 | 986,616 | 833,505 | 544,824 | 582,930 |
| Gold and Silver — tinsel | - | - | 38,274 | 122,730 | 114,570 | 98,700 | 56,100 |
| Silk — Pure | 3,564,700 | 1,933,200 | 2,767,000 | 2,572,000 | 2,791,100 | 2,681,100 | 3,414,400 |
| Silk — Gold and Silver — fine | - | - | 342,382 | 77,046 | 57,037 | 48,342 | 74,503 |
| Silk — Gold and Silver — tinsel | - | - | 629,744 | 263,280 | 209,640 | 165,360 | 204,720 |
| Silk with other matters | - | - | 61,530 | 65,940 | 147,770 | 44,730 | 49,070 |
| Ribbons | 30,687,960 | 22,074,600 | 24,382,200 | 27,467,160 | 26,501,520 | 22,870,800 | 24,309,840 |
| TOTALS | 92,361,118 | 90,216,123 | 115,247,016 | 115,467,518 | 111,155,767 | 111,118,802 | 119,379,977 |

*John Bowring,*
Esq. LL. D.

———

22 June,
1832.

9127. Can you give the Committee any analysis of the manner in which the different quantities of French silk goods are distributed in different foreign countries?—This is the Return of the whole exportation from France in plain goods, in the same number of years; I should state, that not finding any better word for the word *uni* than plain, I have used the word plain in a very comprehensive manner; the best way would be to subtract the other articles from it which are particularly classified, and whatever does not come under these heads will be referred to this class of plain goods. By this statement of the exportation of plain goods, it will be seen that there is a considerable increase of demand from the richer countries for the better and more fashionable articles; in 1825, the United States and England took two-fifths of the whole produce of France in these articles; in 1826, they took three-fourths, and in 1831, four-fifths.

[*The Witness delivered in the following Statement :*]

FRENCH

FRENCH SILK TRADE.

MANUFACTURED SILKS Exported from *France*.

PLAIN GOODS:

| COUNTRIES To which Exported. | VALUES EXPORTED: | | | | | | |
|---|---|---|---|---|---|---|---|
| | 1825. | 1826. | 1827. | 1828. | 1829. | 1830. | 1831. |
| | *f.* | *f.* | *f.* | *f.* | *f.* | *f.* | *f.* |
| England - - - - | 4,884,000 | 4,901,760 | 7,536,720 | 13,336,680 | 7,532,040 | 11,637,720 | 12,992,280 |
| Netherlands - - - - | 7,060,800 | 5,408,280 | 5,563,920 | 4,890,120 | 6,284,040 | 3,791,280 | 2,326,680 |
| Russia - - - - - | 32,280 | 119,880 | 1,738,560 | 1,243,320 | 1,115,280 | 1,011,000 | 643,320 |
| Prussia - - - - - | 88,800 | 53,280 | 337,920 | 156,600 | 166,680 | 144,600 | 163,440 |
| Germany - - - - | 5,169,360 | 5,050,920 | 6,178,080 | 4,793,760 | 4,199,160 | 4,357,680 | 3,558,960 |
| Switzerland - - - - | 1,254,360 | 1,389,000 | 1,763,520 | 1,191,480 | 1,057,080 | 1,316,640 | 911,640 |
| Sardinia - - - - | 3,886,560 | 2,905,920 | 1,570,200 | 1,835,760 | 2,135,760 | 2,483,280 | 1,635,720 |
| Tuscany and Roman States - | 205,080 | 136,320 | 578,760 | 465,480 | 440,520 | 251,640 | 898,080 |
| Naples and Sicily - - | 874,080 | 829,320 | 788,680 | 800,400 | 851,640 | 943,080 | 681,120 |
| Spain - - - - - | 3,572,400 | 2,165,520 | 2,830,200 | 2,753,400 | 3,504,240 | 2,373,960 | 2,750,160 |
| Portugal - - - - | 332,280 | 477,120 | 375,720 | 379,800 | 456,480 | 254,280 | 228,120 |
| Turkey - - - - - | 411,960 | 291,360 | 235,080 | 105,840 | 299,040 | 616,560 | 547,920 |
| Barbary Powers - - | 252,720 | 215,880 | 256,680 | 193,080 | 230,760 | 96,840 | 405,240 |
| Danish Islands - - - | 460,440 | 344,400 | 127,560 | 201,240 | 351,000 | 147,000 | 130,320 |
| Spanish Islands - - - | 464,880 | 563,640 | 649,080 | 517,440 | 486,000 | 255,240 | 183,120 |
| United States - - - - | 16,496,280 | 8,536,080 | 15,330,960 | 12,095,400 | 11,009,880 | 15,659,760 | 28,114,560 |
| Mexico - - - - - | 1,323,840 | 1,460,640 | 1,071,480 | 601,080 | 685,200 | 2,187,240 | 1,608,960 |
| Brazil - - - - - | 979,080 | 909,600 | 1,123,800 | 1,293,480 | 828,960 | 1,208,640 | 355,560 |
| Chili - - - - - | 247,800 | 79,680 | 291,480 | 256,560 | 364,800 | 163,560 | 272,400 |
| Peru - - - - - | 585,840 | 1,356,000 | 504,720 | 1,575,120 | 1,043,040 | 436,920 | 68,160 |
| Buenos Ayres - - - | 1,860,840 | 1,113,240 | 135,720 | 165,720 | 262,200 | 79,800 | 235,800 |
| British India - - - | 442,200 | 512,280 | 655,920 | 727,320 | 1,035,120 | 615,360 | 192,840 |
| Spanish Islands - - - | - | - | - | - | - | 16,440 | 83,040 |
| French Colonies - - | 586,920 | 772,920 | 622,800 | 708,480 | 844,920 | 602,040 | 218,520 |
| Other Countries - - | 1,395,000 | 1,195,040 | 1,571,840 | 750,480 | 937,560 | 690,480 | 370,680 |
| Total - - *f.* | 52,867,800 | 40,708,080 | 51,839,400 | 51,038,040 | 46,121,400 | 51,335,040 | 59,576,640 |

The next document I have to deliver in comprises the classes which the French call *façonnées*, or figured, in which, of course, there is greater vicissitude, being more subject to the fluctuation of fashion ; I observe that in the year 1826, England imported ten times the amount of figured silks which she imported in 1825 ; while of plain goods she imported nearly the same amount ; in the two years, the changes in the United States' demand are also very striking ; in 1825, she imported 14,000,000 *f.*, the English being then in the market to a small amount ; in 1826, she imported only 4,000,000 *f.*, while England imported ten times the amount she had taken in the previous year ; in 1827, America took 8,000,000 *f.* ; in 1828 and 1829, 5,000,000 *f.* ; in 1830, she took 7,000,000 *f.* and a half ; and in 1831, nearly 9,000,000 *f.* ; in the year 1825, England began by taking 71,000 *f.* ; in 1826, she took 740,000 *f.* ; in 1827, 1,200,000 *f.* ; in 1828, 860,000 *f.* ; in 1829, 560,000 *f.* ; in 1830, 768,000 *f.* ; and in 1831, 511,000 *f.* The most extraordinary fluctuations are in the Mexican demand ; in 1825, Mexico took less than 30,000 *f.* ; in 1826, she took 131,000 *f.* ; in 1827, 184,000 *f.* ; in 1828, 214,000 *f.* ; in 1829, 250,000 *f.* ; in 1830, 720,000, *f.* ; and in 1831, 1,300,000 *f.* while in plain goods there has been much less fluctuation in the Mexican demand ; last year the United States took one-half the amount of all the exports of France in figured silks ; Germany, one-fourth ; Mexico, one fourth ; and Spain took 1-27th.

*John Bowring,* Esq. LL. D.

22 June, 1832.

[*The Witness handed in the following document :*]

FRENCH

FRENCH SILK TRADE.

MANUFACTURED SILKS Exported from *France*.

FIGURED OR WROUGHT SILKS (Façonnées.)

| COUNTRIES To which Exported. | VALUES EXPORTED: | | | | | | |
|---|---|---|---|---|---|---|---|
| | 1825. | 1826. | 1827. | 1828. | 1829. | 1830. | 1831. |
| | ƒ. | ƒ. | ƒ. | ƒ. | ƒ. | ƒ. | ƒ. |
| ENGLAND - - - - | 71,500 | 741,260 | 1,124,500 | 860,730 | 560,300 | 768,690 | 511,940 |
| Netherlands - - - - | 62,920 | 1,565,980 | 1,282,840 | 1,606,020 | 961,480 | 747,760 | 267,540 |
| Russia - - - - | 11,960 | - | 527,800 | 400,790 | 379,730 | 353,860 | 199,030 |
| Hanse Towns - - - | - | - | - | 45,630 | 54,730 | 38,480 | 76,960 |
| Austria - - - - | 13,390 | - | 70,200 | 94,250 | 75,530 | 121,810 | 57,070 |
| Prussia - - - - | 2,600 | 390 | 4,810 | 2,730 | 7,150 | 11,700 | 26,520 |
| Germany - - - - | 5,195,200 | 3,728,140 | 4,638,400 | 4,753,450 | 5,529,550 | 5,586,360 | 3,955,120 |
| Switzerland - - - | 7,280 | 329,000 | 419,900 | 804,310 | 671,970 | 708,110 | 662,740 |
| Sardinia - - - - | 235,820 | 1,255,800 | 1,102,140 | 1,225,510 | 661,180 | 869,830 | 544,440 |
| Tuscany and Roman States - | 7,280 | - | 28,080 | 102,570 | 55,120 | 51,480 | 118,040 |
| Naples and Sicily - - | 90,350 | 95,940 | 171,730 | 369,330 | 370,370 | 288,340 | 191,100 |
| Spain - - - - | 2,015,130 | 942,890 | 1,293,240 | 1,140,880 | 962,650 | 237,510 | 327,860 |
| Portugal - - - | 39,910 | 142,480 | 46,670 | 134,680 | 51,480 | 25,350 | 53,430 |
| Turkey - - - - | 10,400 | 10,010 | 3,120 | 6,500 | 5,460 | 10,920 | 31,070 |
| United States - - - | 13,993,850 | 4,160,130 | 8,035,820 | 5,059,210 | 5,430,100 | 7,460,570 | 8,824,270 |
| Mexico - - - - | 29,640 | 131,170 | 184,860 | 214,500 | 250,900 | 720,650 | 1,334,060 |
| Brazil - - - - | 196,300 | 249,730 | 398,710 | 516,100 | 449,410 | 518,830 | 276,250 |
| Chili - - - - | 13,390 | 56,550 | 41,210 | 312,650 | 240,760 | 86,450 | 129,740 |
| Buenos Ayres - - - | 103,480 | 196,690 | 48,100 | 26,000 | 2,470 | 21,840 | 111,280 |
| Peru - - - - | 59,280 | 137,150 | 57,330 | 326,430 | 239,980 | 123,630 | 40,950 |
| British India - - - | - | 6,500 | 17,550 | 112,320 | 113,880 | 115,050 | 38,220 |
| French Colonies - - | 30,030 | 40,560 | 16,380 | 13,650 | 187,330 | - | 17,550 |
| Other Countries - - | 78,910 | 171,340 | 161,980 | 184,470 | 133,770 | 154,080 | 30,680 |
| TOTAL - - ƒ. | 22,668,620 | 13,957,710 | 19,675,370 | 18,312,710 | 17,395,300 | 19,021,600 | 17,825,860 |

*John Bowring,*
Esq. LL. D.

————

22 June,
1832.

9128. Have you any particulars respecting crape?—Yes; here is a document which shows that of the crapes the United States took last year two-thirds of the whole exports, and the article has increased in exports nearly 50 per cent. since 1825; last year, Turkey was the second buyer in importance; England, third; Germany, fourth, and Egypt fifth.

[*The Witness handed in the following Statement :*]

FRENCH

## FRENCH SILK TRADE.

### MANUFACTURED SILKS Exported from *France*.

#### CRAPES.

| COUNTRIES To which Exported. | VALUES EXPORTED. | | | | | | |
|---|---|---|---|---|---|---|---|
| | 1825. | 1826. | 1827. | 1828. | 1829. | 1830. | 1831. |
| | *f.* | *f.* | *f.* | *f.* | *f.* | *f.* | *f.* |
| ENGLAND - - - - | 43,560 | 194,304 | 304,832 | 349,184 | 497,112 | 425,480 | 227,656 |
| Netherlands - - - | 89,232 | 103,048 | 149,600 | 127,248 | 93,104 | 61,776 | 80,168 |
| Russia - - - - | - - | - - | 24,112 | 11,880 | 26,928 | 19,888 | 13,288 |
| Hanseatic Towns - - | - - | - - | 176 | 3,960 | - - | 440 | — |
| Austria - - - - | - - | - - | 33,528 | 23,056 | 14,696 | 5,720 | 5,984 |
| Prussia - - - - | 968 | 12,672 | 528 | 440 | 6,688 | 4,136 | 9,944 |
| Germany - - - | 162,624 | 534,512 | 165,792 | 233,640 | 309,584 | 317,680 | 211,552 |
| Switzerland - - - | 19,272 | 19,448 | 27,896 | 50,248 | 19,448 | 20,592 | 1,936 |
| Sardinia - - - | 97,856 | 132,264 | 102,520 | 127,160 | 98,736 | 54,384 | 89,760 |
| Tuscany and Roman States - | 3,520 | 1,408 | 17,952 | 11,616 | 16,368 | 16,896 | 15,224 |
| Naples and Sicily - - | 52,712 | 7,656 | 11,968 | 32,120 | 15,400 | 41,008 | 4,928 |
| Spain - - - - | 21,736 | 115,808 | 72,336 | 30,888 | 64,680 | 74,096 | 63,360 |
| Portugal - - - | 4,752 | 20,768 | - - | 1,848 | | 176 | — |
| Turkey - - - - | 190,696 | 93,104 | 70,136 | 59,488 | 134,288 | 148,808 | 295,416 |
| Egypt - - - - | 52,888 | 30,624 | 1,584 | 3,960 | 20,768 | 40,568 | 127,512 |
| Barbary States - - | 5,368 | 20,944 | 46,728 | 28,600 | 21,472 | 9,856 | 56,496 |
| Danish Isles - - - | 5,280 | - - | 4,400 | 2,112 | 5,544 | 3,344 | 2,640 |
| Spanish Isles - - - | 6,600 | 1,496 | 8,008 | 11,528 | 13,464 | 44,352 | 1,760 |
| United States - - | 1,807,168 | 1,741,960 | 2,621,080 | 2,545,840 | 2,670,800 | 1,873,784 | 2,659,360 |
| Mexico - - - - | 3,520 | 17,072 | - - | 7,656 | 4,752 | 1,232 | 7,744 |
| Brazil - - - - | 16,192 | 17,776 | 3,432 | 23,672 | 28,072 | 10,648 | 1,232 |
| | - - | 13,640 | - - | 11,792 | - - | 2,904 | 1,056 |
| French Colonies - - | 36,784 | 19,888 | 13,288 | 42,592 | 29,128 | 27,280 | 264 |
| Other Countries - - | 22,704 | 40,832 | 23,496 | 2,728 | 31,328 | - - | 7,920 |
| TOTAL - - *f.* | 2,643,432 | 3,139,224 | 3,703,392 | 3,743,256 | 4,122,360 | 3,205,048 | 3,885,200 |

9129. Have you any returns as to ribbons?—I have a return as to ribbons; France produced of ribbons, in 1825, 30,600,000 *f.*; in 1826, it was 22,000,000 *f.*; in 1827, 24,000,000 *f.*; in 1828, 27,500,000 *f.*; in 1829, 26,500,000 *f.*; in 1830, nearly, 23,000,000 *f.*; and in 1831, 24,000,000 *f.*; the great increase in 1825 is solely attributable to the American demand of that year, in which America alone took 18,000,000 *f.* of ribbons, while in the following year she took less than 4,000,000 *f.* It will be seen from this Table that the increased demand exists only in the richer and more prosperous countries, such as England and the United States, and that is growing out of the fact, that the fashion of the French ribbons has been the principal cause of their sale; it is a curious circumstance, that the South American trade, which in 1826 was 3,280,000 *f.* was in 1831 only 1,100,000 *f.* being a gradual diminution to the extent of 2,000,000 *f.*; the Americans took, in 1831, half the exports, or more than 12,000,000 *f.*; the Germans took one-fifth, or nearly 5,000,000 *f.*; the English took one-twelfth, or nearly, 2,000,000 *f.*; the Spanish, took one-twentieth, or 1,200,000 *f.*; the Mexicans took one-fortieth, or 578,000 *f.*; the Sardinians, one-fiftieth, or 465,000 *f.*; and the Swiss, one-sixty-fifth, or 374,000 *f.*; in 1825 and in 1827, there was an exportation of ribbons to China, but since 1827 there has been no exportation to China from France; to British India, in 1829 and 1830, nearly 300,000 *f.* of ribbons were exported from France; but the export almost ceased in 1831.

*John Bowring,* Esq. LL. D.

22 June, 1832.

[*The Witness delivered in the following Statement:*]

MANUFACTURED

## FRENCH SILK TRADE.

**MANUFACTURED** Silks Exported from *France.*

RIBBONS.

| COUNTRIES To which Exported. | VALUES EXPORTED: | | | | | | |
|---|---|---|---|---|---|---|---|
| | 1825. | 1826. | 1827. | 1828. | 1829. | 1830. | 1831. |
| | f. | f. | f. | f. | f. | f. | f. |
| England - - - - | 437,400 | 952,560 | 1,395,360 | 1,798,320 | 1,210,440 | 1,658,640 | 1,949,760 |
| Netherlands - - - - | 1,084,800 | 2,997,960 | 2,219,400 | 2,225,640 | 1,805,160 | 1,560,000 | 1,076,400 |
| Russia - - - - | 92,640 | 1,560 | 124,320 | 138,240 | 119,400 | 74,040 | 76,800 |
| Germany - - - - | 3,995,400 | 5,545,680 | 5,588,400 | 7,064,760 | 7,458,600 | 6,693,600 | 4,781,760 |
| Switzerland - - - | 369,840 | 663,360 | 631,440 | 556,560 | 484,080 | 459,720 | 374,280 |
| Sardinia - - - - | 447,960 | 840,480 | 643,080 | 646,560 | 562,200 | 687,600 | 465,600 |
| Tuscany and Roman States - | 9,720 | 4,080 | 29,640 | 202,920 | 192,600 | 102,720 | 146,520 |
| Naples and Sicily - - | 193,680 | 159,360 | 77,040 | 156,360 | 154,920 | 166,440 | 123,960 |
| Spain - - - - | 1,219,320 | 1,813,200 | 1,389,120 | 1,323,120 | 1,358,880 | 1,062,720 | 1,220,760 |
| Portugal - - - - | 148,200 | 114,600 | 69,120 | 10,320 | 48,360 | 67,920 | 39,480 |
| Turkey - - - - | 17,520 | 20,880 | 45,600 | 6,600 | 32,760 | 51,480 | 29,400 |
| Haiti - - - - | 91,920 | 16,920 | 112,080 | 60,120 | 71,640 | 56,040 | 65,640 |
| Danish Isles - - - | 442,080 | 477,120 | 128,760 | 137,400 | 247,920 | 96,000 | 174,960 |
| Spanish Isles - - - | 144,000 | 294,600 | 159,480 | 323,640 | 117,360 | 91,200 | 31,080 |
| United States - - - | 18,142,080 | 3,918,720 | 9,302,160 | 10,058,040 | 9,726,000 | 7,560,360 | 12,269,280 |
| Mexico - - - - | 1,048,320 | 938,520 | 426,600 | 422,640 | 223,080 | 789,360 | 578,640 |
| Brazil - - - - | 525,120 | 285,240 | 379,440 | 569,400 | 692,760 | 809,160 | 339,960 |
| Columbia - - - | 858,600 | 724,920 | 134,280 | 97,920 | 155,040 | 117,840 | 37,800 |
| Chili - - - - | 100,440 | 79,080 | 151,080 | 202,920 | 115,440 | 65,280 | 189,720 |
| Peru - - - - | 260,880 | 1,248,720 | 288,120 | 619,200 | 791,040 | 154,800 | 4,800 |
| China and Cochin-China - | 24,840 | - | 63,960 | — | — | — | |
| British India - - - | 81,600 | 101,520 | 251,280 | 317,280 | 300,480 | 115,440 | 45,720 |
| French Colonies - - | 159,840 | 389,760 | 603,840 | 144,960 | 245,280 | 201,360 | 126,480 |
| Other countries - - | 991,760 | 485,760 | 168,600 | 384,240 | 388,080 | 220,080 | 161,040 |
| TOTAL - - f. | 30,687,960 | 22,074,600 | 24,382,200 | 27,467,160 | 26,501,520 | 22,870,800 | 24,309,840 |

*John Bowring,* Esq. LL. D.

22 June, 1832.

9130. **Do** you wish to submit to the Committee any facts growing out of those documents which you have handed in?—I have drawn out the more prominent facts which bear on the other branches of the silk trade, and those facts seem to me to be important as evidence of the great fluctuation of the trade. In the article of silk brocade, of which France exported, in 1826, 3,000,000 f. and in 1831, less than 200,000 f.; the United States, in 1825, took more than 1,000,000 f. and in 1831, less than 5,000 f.; in 1826, England took more than 140,000 f.; in 1827, more than 1,300,000 f., and in 1831 not a single piece. Of silk gauzes, the English demand has fluctuated as follows: in 1825, England took 230,092; in 1826, 110,544 f.; in 1827, 229,916 f.; in 1828, 148,960; in 1829, 918,040 f.; in 1830, 150,192 f., and last year only 9,296 f.; while, in America, the fluctuation has been in another direction; they took, in 1825, 426,700 f.; in 1826, 277,200 f.; in 1827, 385,100 f.; in 1828, 267,400 f.; in 1829, 423,600 f.; in 1830, 638,100 f., and in 1831, 761,000 f.; the whole quantity exported from France scarcely having fluctuated at all, there being almost a cessation of the English demand and a doubling of the American. In tulles there is also a striking falling off in the exports; in 1826, it was 1,200,000 f.; in 1831, it was less than one-third of that amount. England took, in 1825, 94,000 f.; in 1826, 279,800 f.; in 1827, 308,400 f.; in 1828, 260,800 f.; in 1829, 177,120 f.; in 1830, 82,700 f.; and in 1831, 24,800 f.; that is about one-third of the exportation to England in 1825. In the United States, the importation last year was less than one-third of what it was in 1825, it was then 342,800 f; in 1826, it fell to 88,800 f.; in 1827, to 99,600 f.; in 1828, 40,400 f.; in 1829, 99,100 f.; in 1830, 90,100 f., and in 1831, 10,190 f. In South America, it was, in 1825, 177,600 f.; in 1826, 168,300 f.; in 1827, 70,960 f.; in 1828, 116,700 f.; in 1829, 914,000 f.; in 1830, 67,200 f. and in 1831, only 37,000 f. In silk lace, the export, in 1831, was less by half than in 1825; in 1825, the amount was 322,850 f., and in 1831 it was only 160,690 f.; the exportation to England of French haberdashery was as follows; in 1825, 13,900 f.; in 1826, 104,300 f.; in 1827, 108,400 f.; in 1828, 107,500 f.; in 1829, 84,300 f.; in 1830, 147,300 f.; and in 1831, 140,000 f.

9131. This of course is all legal exportation?—I should state, that in France it is all legal exportation.

9132. It

*John Bowring,*
Esq. LL. D.

22 June,
1832.

9132. It includes that which is smuggled into this country?—Yes; these are the whole returns.

9133. The Committee are to understand, that the tulle which you have mentioned here is altogether made of silk?—Certainly, except when the return mentions any other mixture.

9134. Have you been able to analyze the different qualities of goods taken by England at different periods before and since the change of system?—I have taken the three years of 1825, 1828 and 1831, and these are the results which I have obtained. I will put in the document.

[*The Witness delivered in the following Statement :*]

### FRENCH SILK TRADE.

MANUFACTURED Silks exported from *France* to *England*, as far as can be collected under different Heads from Official Reports.

| 1825. | 1828. | 1831. | |
|---|---|---|---|
| *f.* | *f.* | *f.* | |
| 4,884,000 | 13,336,680 | 12,992,280 | - - - Plain Silks. |
| 71,500 | 860,730 | 511,940 | - - - Wrought Silks (*i. e.* Figured ) |
| 10,640 | 8,580 | - - - | - - - Stuffs brocaded with Silk. |
| — | 27,240 | 17,640 | - - - - Ditto with Gold and Silver. |
| — | 8,100 | 10,260 | - - - - Ditto with Tinsel. |
| — | 98,080 | 37,600 | - - - - Ditto with Thread, Cotton, &c. |
| 23,072 | 148,960 | 9,296 | - - - Silk Gauze. |
| 43,560 | 349,184 | 227,656 | - - - Silk Crape. |
| 194,080 | 266,880 | 24,800 | - - - Silk Net. |
| 332,351 | 192,526 | 160,692 | - - - Silk Lace. |
| 54,800 | 51,100 | 14,200 | - - - Hosiery (Bonneterie.) |
| — | 23,000 | 18,090 | - - - Silver and Gold Galoons. |
| — | 5,310 | 270 | - - - Tinsel Galoons. |
| 13,900 | 107,500 | 49,300 | - - - Silk Cords, Tapes, &c. |
| — | — | 900 | - - - - Ditto with Gold and Silver. |
| — | 7,920 | 23,400 | - - - - Ditto with Tinsel. |
| 437,400 | 1,798,320 | 1,949,760 | - - - Ribbons. |
| 6,071,303 | 16,990,010 | 16,048,084 | - - - Totals. |

The result is, that it confirms a fact which I have stated before, that the exportation to England in 1825, before the legal introduction, was 6,000,000*f.*, and that fact corresponds very much with the state of things I have gathered from other sources. In this return the articles are classified, in 1828 the amount was nearly 17,000,000*f.*, and in 1831, 16,000,000*f.*

9135. Have you any information as to the relative position of the English and French manufactures in the market of the United States?—I have some curious information derived from the United States. The English and French merchants are there on an equal footing; and it is certainly, of all countries, the country that affords the best ground for comparison, from the largeness of its imports. The operation of the different systems of legislation may be traced there with considerable accuracy; while French silks were prohibited in England, those of England were in so backward a state that she exported scarcely any manufactured silks to America. I have obtained, from official sources, the American returns of 1830, and I find that the United States imported from England of piece goods 249,860 dollars, of other silk manufactures 119,701 dollars, this is the legitimate importation without any reference to smuggling; in all 369,561 dollars of English silk goods were entered at the Custom House. The United States imported from France 2,256,529 dollars of piece goods, and 1,291,849 dollars of other silk goods, making 3,548,378 dollars. Now this is the state of export of a manufacture which has most of what is called protection in England; (assuming 30 per cent. for that protection, as it is the highest duty paid in England on any sort of stuff,) the same article is that which has the least of that which is called protection, in France, inasmuch as the duties on foreign silk goods in France, are less than half the duties paid in England on foreign silk goods; the protection of silk manufactures in England is thus double that which the silk manufactures have in France, while the exports of the article which has only half the protection are, it will be seen, nearly ten-fold greater than from England,

678. where

*John Bowring,*
Esq. LL. D.

———

22 June,
1832.

where the protection is double.   I wish that the Committee should have an opportunity of contrasting this with the American imports of those manufactures which in
France have most of the so-called " protection," namely, the absolute prohibition of
competing foreign goods, which, as I have repeatedly said, is only the protection which
enables an inferior article to obtain a superior price ; it is the encouragement given
to imperfection.   Now I would, in the markets of the United States, contrast the state
of that French article so protected, with the English article which has only a 10 per
cent. protection in England, I mean cotton goods.   By the same official document it
will be seen, that in 1830 the amount of cotton manufactures imported from England
was 5,295,294 dollars, and from France only 619,987 dollars, yet to support this
trade the French people are taxed with a premium or bounty to the exporter of cotton
goods equal to 40 s. English per cwt. though the duty  paid on the raw material in
France is only 8 s. 11 d., so that they receive from the Government on the exportation
of cotton manufactures nearly five times the amount the Government have received on
the raw material ; notwithstanding this, the French manufacturers declare they shall
be ruined unless they can obtain an additional bounty of 20 sous for plain, and
30 sous for printed cotton, and they demand that it shall be secured to them until
every difficulty is removed ;  they ask, too, a boon of 3,000,000 f. in the shape of an
additional bounty to enable them to export 5,000,000 kilogrammes.   Yet in spite of
this protection or encouragement given to the French manufacturer, the exportation
of cotton goods from France was in 1830 three-fourths of a million pounds less than in
1827.   Thus the Committee will see the influence of " protection," as it is called, on
foreign commerce ; and I will now state one or two of its effects on production.   While
according to the best calculation 7,000,000 of spindles are employed in England
to manufacture more than 240,000,000 lbs. of cotton ; in France, according to the
return of the Commission which reported on the cotton trade, 3,200,000 spindles are
employed to manufacture 66,000,000 lbs.   So that where the protected French
manufacturer produces only 66,000,000, the unprotected English manufacturer
would, with the same number of spindles, produce nearly 110,000,000 ; or if the
English manufacturer produced at the same rate as the French, instead of 240,000,000
he would only produce 144,000,000.   In England it is estimated, according to the
Parliamentary Returns, that 700,000 persons are engaged in different branches
of the cotton manufacture, and they produce nearly four times the quantity which is
rendered in France by 550,000 persons, according to the returns of the French Commission.   That protection has thus led to the waste of more than two-thirds of the
whole amount of labour employed on the protected articles.  The French cotton manufacturers have had the benefit of this prohibitory system ever since the peace, and according to the statement made by their Commission it costs the country 47,000,000 f.
per annum beyond the sum at which the same articles might be imported from
England ; this is the result of 18 years experience of protection, yet the testimony
of the French manufacturers is, that the very existence of their business is rendered doubtful from year to year.

9136. You have given the statement of the amount of importation to America in
1830 ; have you the import of the corresponding year in 1825 ?—I have not.

9137. Can you state to the Committee what was the state of the export of
of manufactured silk goods to England before 1826 ?—I have returns from the
year 1818.

| England took in | | | *f.* | England took in | | | *f.* |
|---|---|---|---|---|---|---|---|
| 1818 from France | - | | 1,744,105 | 1825 from France | - | | 6,104,103 |
| 1819 - | - | - | 2,713,583 | 1826 - | - | - | 7,596,421 |
| 1820 | - | - | 2,727,748 | 1827 - | - | - | 11,460,119 |
| 1821 - | - | - | 2,815,178 | 1828 - | - | - | 17,311,810 |
| 1822 - | - | - | 3,516,828 | 1829 - | - | - | 10,483,777 |
| 1823 | - | - | 2,901,670 | 1830 - | - | - | 15,204,388 |
| 1824 - | - | - | 3,856,465 | | | | |

and by another return it appears between 16,000,000 and 18,000,000 francs in
1831.

9138. That exclusively relates to the export of silk goods ?—Yes ; and the returns
show that there was a gradual yearly increase of exports from France under the old
prohibitory system of from 1,750,000 francs, which it was in 1818 up to 1825 when
it was 6,000,000 of francs ; that is, the smuggling then was at the rate of 240,000 l.
a year ; in 1826 the amount being 7,600,000 francs (equal to 300,000 l.) the duty
received was only 60,000 l.  If the whole had paid duty, supposing 25 per cent.,
the average would have been 75,000 l., so that smuggling in 1826 was only
60,000 l.

John Bowring,
Esq. LL. D.

22 June,
1832.

60,000 l. or one-fourth of what it had been in the previous year. The immediate effect of the legitimate admission of French goods was, that three-fourths of smuggling immediately stopped ; as the price of goods has declined, so has the duty increased, and smuggling has increased in the same proportion ; in 1830, 5,000,000 of francs more of goods were exported from France than in 1829, yet the duty paid in England was 8,530 l. less ; in 1831, 7,000,000 of francs more of goods were exported than in 1829, and the duty paid was 3,500 l. less ; in 1831, the amount exported from France was greater than in 1828, and the duty received in England was 57,670 l. less ; these are facts showing the stupendous increase of smuggling ; what I wish to submit is this, that from the earliest period of which we have returns, the smuggling became more and more active up to 1826 ; it then received a sudden check from the change of legislation. The annual returns may be a little more or less, but on the whole the important fact is, that up to that period smuggling went on increasing from year to year ; in 1826 it was much diminished, inasmuch as the importation into England was scarcely greater than the year before, previous to the legitimate introduction, and a large amount of duty was received ; from that period smuggling continued increasing ; and I shall show the Committee that at this moment the amount of smuggled goods introduced into the country is greater (that is the position I mean to take) than the amount of smuggling in 1826, from which I shall draw an inevitable deduction, inasmuch as it was then changed by a particular legislation, that it will be necessary now to check it by a similar interference. The same state of things which occurred before 1826 has occurred since that period ; and we are now very much in the same category, with a nominal duty of 30 per cent., in which we stood in 1825, under the system of prohibitory laws.

9139. Will you state what is the state of the smuggling trade in silks at present? —From the best information we have been able to gather, and which has been derived from a variety of sources, some of them confidential, from inquiries of smugglers, from the Custom House returns, and in fact, from information sought in all directions, I should estimate that at this moment the smuggling into England fluctuates from 250,000 l. to 350,000 l. a year ; the Committee will see that this result is altogether borne out by the French official statements ; they give at this moment an export of about 800,000 l. a year. It appears that from 450,000 l. to 500,000 l. of goods paid duty, which leaves 300,000 l. of goods for the clandestine trade. Now that result agrees with returns which the French Minister was so good as to communicate confidentially ; returns which I beg to say were made not with reference to the inquiries of this Committee, but previously when my colleague and I, as commercial commissioners, were engaged in investigating the general character of the relations between France and England. It was a matter of moment to ascertain in what manner England paid France for the goods which she took from her, and as it is notorious that immense quantities of English prohibited goods are introduced into France, we felt it necessary that the veil should be lifted up, and that we should be initiated into the secrets ; this enabled us to see, to a very great extent, the bearing of the whole contraband system ; and from a comparison of all the facts, I am convinced that the amount of smuggling is, as I said before, about 300,000 l. a year.

9140. Do you mean sterling pounds?—Yes.

9141. When you use the term pound, we wish you to state what pound you mean ?—It may be desirable to mention to the Committee, that some months ago, when it was found that the French Government was willing to reconsider their commercial system, and to extend their friendly relations with England, a commission was instituted, consisting of two French Councillors of State, both of them men distinguished in France, and of two English Commissioners, of whom I had the honour to be one. The meetings took place at the house of the Minister of Finance, and instructions were given to all the departments, that no facts connected with the commercial relations between the two countries should be concealed. The majority of documents which I have presented to this Committee, are documents not prepared with any reference to this inquiry, but documents we obtained in order to enable us to state what would be the natural course of the commercial relations between these countries, if we could eventually succeed in removing the restrictions upon them.

9142. Were these inquiries made previous to the existence of this Committee ?— Undoubtedly, and without any reference to it ; when this inquiry was suggested, I had a very strong feeling that the commercial interests of the country were bound together by what I may call a silk thread, inasmuch as of the imports into England

678. from

*John Bowring,*
Esq. LL. D.

22 June,
1832.

from France, the most important import is that of silk goods; and the question becomes one of very prominent importance with reference to the consideration of the whole field of commercial interchange.

9143. Will you state what in your opinion would be the consequence of a prohibition at present?—If a prohibition could be made efficient, which I consider quite a chimera, its temporary effect would be this: it would increase price in England by the increase of demand, and it would reduce price in France by the decrease of demand. Now the immediate consequence of that would be to give fresh motives in the shape of an additional premium to the smuggler; if there be a difference of 30 per cent. now under what is called the protecting system, it is probable that England being no longer a purchaser of the produce of France, the difference would soon become a difference of 60 per cent. thus the recompense to the smuggler would be doubled, and doubled would be his activity; my opinion is, that the progress of manufacturing industry, and manufacturing improvement, is precisely like the progress of any thing else. An inferior sculptor for instance, who had got possession of the English market, would be very sorry to see the works of Canova come into competition with his own; but any body who desired that the art of sculpture should be advanced, would be glad to encourage the introduction of the works of the master. I see no distinction whatever between the measures to be taken for the improvement of sculpture, and the measures to be taken for the improvement of manufacturing industry. What prohibition does is this, it alters the character of the smuggling transaction; under the state of things that exists in England the number of smugglers is small, and in order that it should be a beneficial trade the operation must be carried on on a vast scale. It is very well known that the number of directing individuals, engaged in the smuggling trade, is inconsiderable, and that the demoralization is proportionably small. In France you have no opportunity of seeing what the effect of prohibition is on smuggling in masses; you have not there smugglers by hundreds, but by thousands and tens of thousands; the whole frontier is in a state of frightful demoralization, and as I stated, so remarkable has been the effect of the prohibitory system, in maximizing the motives of smuggling, that the smuggling in France has taken quite another character, and has got a word which perfectly represents that character, for smuggling is now called filtration; the smugglers are engaged along the whole of the frontier in the introduction of illicit commodities of all kinds, and that would be the inevitable effect of prohibition here. The system of lowering duties has diminished the demoralization of smuggling, though it has no doubt improved the art; increasing duties, and prohibition above all will infallibly create a class of people similar to those in France and Spain, who are looked on as public benefactors, inasmuch as they procure for the public a class of enjoyments otherwise absolutely denied to them; you may thus excite the sympathies and friendly feelings of a whole nation towards a class of men whose existence depends on the violation of the laws. If any gentleman had the opportunity of seeing the frightfully contaminating effect that this system of prohibition produces on the national character, I cannot help thinking that the question would be decided with reference to its moral consequences alone.

9144. You say, that you consider the number of persons engaged in smuggling in this country is very small, do you consider it smaller than it was during the existence of the prohibitory system?—Undoubtedly; the effect of the alteration of the duties was, that smuggling became much more a trade than it was before; it is now in the hands of a few houses, whose operations are carried on on a large scale, and who find it their interest to be insurers on a calculation of many chances. In elucidation of that fact I would beg to mention, that in France, where the goods are charged with a high duty, the smuggler carries on his business on account of another, as is the case here; that he is a man who has a certain portion of respectability and capital, who himself deposits the money, and delivers the goods to the importer with whom he makes the contract for delivery. But wherever there are absolutely prohibited articles to be smuggled, or where the duties are inordinately high, as in the case of cotton twist or tobacco, the smugglers are men smuggling on their own account; men who introduce comparatively a small amount of the article, and who carry on the trade for themselves, being recompensed by the large profits. It is worth their while to run the risk of introducing 30 *l.* 40 *l.* or 50 *l.* worth of goods, where the premium on smuggling is maximized, as it is worth the while of the superior smuggler to contend against the duty on a large scale. This wholesale smuggler is only successful where he can carry on his business to a considerable

extent

*John Bowring*
*Esq.* LL. D.

22 June,
1832.

extent, and run the risk of introducing a large quantity of goods, with the chance of now and then a caption or a forfeiture.

9145. Do you consider that the number of persons engaged in smuggling is smaller than it was during the existence of the prohibition in England, but that they are better combined and organized; so that though a small number of persons be engaged in smuggling, they are enabled to introduce, as in fact they do, a much larger quantity of foreign goods?—Yes, that is my impression.

9146. You consider, therefore, that there is an advantage in this respect, that a smaller number of persons are engaged in an illegal manner?—Yes.

9147. But do you consider that there is any benefit to the manufacturer by this alteration, since, although fewer persons are engaged in the illicit trade by means of the better combination and organization you spoke of, they, in point of fact, introduce a larger quantity of goods which come in competition with the home manufacture?—Certainly, the sinister interest of the manufacturer is, that the least quantity of goods should be introduced; it is indifferent to him how they are smuggled if they come into the market.

9148. As far as regards the interest of the manufacturer he is in a worse condition from the present state of smuggling than he was during the time of the prohibition?—Undoubtedly, but prohibition now would not restore the state of things before 1826.

9149. Now, as comparing the smuggler in England with the smuggler in France, do you not consider that that which in reality occasions the great difference in the number of persons engaged in illicit trade in these countries, is regulated generally by the necessity which exists in this country, of the smuggler being provided with a mode of water-carriage for his goods?—The difficulties in France to the revenue officer are greater than in England, owing to the extensive land frontier; the Custom House regulations in France are much more severe. France has the advantage of a land and water frontier, and all the advantages we have as to water France has; the smuggler has the additional power of introducing goods along the land frontier of France to a great extent.

9150. Not only more easily but more cheaply?—The cost of smuggling into France is greater than the cost of smuggling into England. We have returns from every Custom House along the line, and along the coast; and the average cost of smuggling into France is undoubtedly from seven to ten per cent. greater than the cost in England. I will explain what the character of the French protection is. The French have three lines of Custom Houses, while in England we have only one; each of these lines of course exercises a certain control; when the goods have passed these three lines of Custom Houses they are still subjected to municipal examination; the goods cannot get into any town without being subject to the visits of the officers of octroi, so that in addition to the average cost of smuggling, there is an additional charge of five per cent. beyond the cost of introduction over the frontier, through the three lines into the towns, which is estimated as the value of the fraudulent introduction through the octroi; even though the cost of introducing the article into the country be the same in France as in England there is this additional charge to introduce them to the consumption of the greater towns. It is also known that the despotic power exercised by the French Government on these occasions is such as could never be employed here. In Bonaparte's time people were even visited by death; while it is perfectly notorious that with the heavy visitations of the law, under the most cruel persecution and violent acts of injustice, English goods were to be seen every where constantly introduced, and the prohibition, with all the terrors of legislation, and all the cruelties of despotism, was inefficient.

9151. You have said you consider in France the smuggler is regarded rather as a patriotic character, as one who furnishes to the population articles which otherwise they would not procure?—To a great extent, but I spoke of Spain more particularly.

9152. Do you not consider that the observation applies rather to the smuggling of what may be considered necessaries of life, than to smuggling of those articles which will come in competition with the national manufacture of the country?—There is no smuggling except where the article comes some way in competition with the manufacture of the country; the necessaries of life may be as much the production of the country into which they are smuggled, as the luxuries of life.

9153. Do you not consider that this feeling is confined to articles which are in fact necessary to the bodily sustenance of the inhabitants, rather than to articles of

678.                                                                                                    mere

*John Bowring,*
Esq. LL. D.

22 June
1832.

mere ornament or fancy?—To some extent; I have no doubt that the man who smuggled cattle into France would be looked on with greater interest and affection than the man who smuggled cotton twist, yet the man who smuggles cotton twist is considered a benefactor.

9154. Are you aware that during the period of the prohibition, and when the project was advanced for making the alteration made in our laws, it was advanced as one of the main arguments for that alteration, that if a duty was fixed, in lieu of prohibition, the smuggler would then become an odious character; and that the feeling previously existed rather favourable to persons following that illicit trade, would wholly cease, and that they would be considered a sort of enemy to their country?—I think it very likely that extravagant opinions have been expressed on the subject; I am convinced of this, that it will be in proportion to the efficiency of a protecting system, that the smuggler will be regarded as a public benefactor. If I understand a protecting system, it is a system which shuts out some object of desire; it diminishes human happiness in some shape or other.

9155. Do you consider that in point of fact any alteration has taken place in regard to the feelings entertained towards those who are engaged in this illicit trade by the removal of the prohibition, and the substitution of the duties?—My evidence has wholly gone to the state of things in France and Spain.

9156. But as a person of very general information, I put a question to you, whether you do consider that in point of fact that part of the expectation to which I have alluded, and which many persons certainly looked at with a great degree of hope has been realized in this country, namely, that it was thought a degree of odium would attach to the smuggler which would tend very much to the discouragement of his illicit trade after the removal of prohibition?—I think that expectation must have been an exaggerated one.

9157. Is it not a direct contradiction to any opinion that was so entertained, that in point of fact it is now stated, that a higher class of persons are engaged in smuggling, as I understand you to say, that smuggling is confined to fewer persons, but a higher and better organized class, with greater capital, who, by means of their greater capital and higher situation, are enabled to prevent the small smuggler from trading with advantage, which is the reason you give why fewer persons are, in point of fact, at this moment engaged in such illicit trade?—My opinion distinctly is this; that the completer organization of the smuggling system, which system has been growing better from day to day, gaining more activity and more knowledge, must undoubtedly bring with it one of two things; either a reduction of duties so as to diminish the profit of the smuggler, or unless that be remedied, and speedily by the Government, the legitimate trade between the two countries will be destroyed; I will state by-and-bye the effect of the prohibitory system in France on the public revenues; the absorption of capital, and the extremely small produce of the French Custom House; the French being an importing nation of thirty-four millions, it will strike honourable Members with astonishment when they hear from me to what an enormous extent smuggling has interfered with the Custom House revenues.

9158. Am I to infer that you consider the removal of the prohibitory system has not in point of fact thrown that degree of odium on the smuggler which some persons anticipated it would?—I have seen no increased odium falling on the smuggler; formerly the buyer of the article came more in contact with the smuggling adventurer, so that he might have a stronger feeling towards him than he has now, when the smuggling adventurer is a hired servant who is paid at a certain rate for carrying on a trading operation; the smuggler is, at the present moment, rather farther removed from the buyer of the smuggled commodity, inasmuch as the operation is carried on in gross, and in that respect, perhaps, some change of feeling has been created; that may be easily estimated by the change of position of the smuggler in gross and the smuggler in detail; the smuggler in detail in France and yet more so in Spain, I have seen the object of universal welcome; I have seen the peasantry rising to protect him; and have known them murder the Custom House officers who have gone in pursuit of him. Honourable Members can draw a deduction from such a state of things which is produced where the prohibitory system is in full vigour.

9159. Is not the profit of the smuggler greater now than in 1826?—I think it may be in the cases where the organization of the system is most complete; in the returns from the Custom House there are some curious facts; there are certain towns in France which the smuggler uses for the introduction of goods into

England,

*John Bowring,*
Esq. LL. D.

——

22 June,
1832.

England, where smugglers operating on the old system have completely failed, where for instance they had not capital sufficient to carry on smuggling on a great scale; I remember one town where there were three smuggling companies which have been extirpated, they having been in fact swallowed up by companies having greater capital, more business and knowledge of the way in which illicit goods could be introduced.

9160. Then I understand from you that smuggling is in fact more profitable at this time than during the prohibitory system?—More profitable to the more intelligent smugglers, but less so to the clandestine smugglers; if there are two grades, those who have the perfect machinery and those who have not, of course he who has the monopoly of a better machinery than his neighbour gets a greater profit out of it; the small smuggler is carrying on a bad trade, and the larger smuggler is carrying on a good one.

9161. You consider that smuggling is more profitable to the higher class of smugglers, and that in point of fact a higher class of persons are engaged in smuggling than were engaged during the existence of a prohibition?—Yes, I believe from facts that have come to my knowledge, that if it was desired by any individual to smuggle 50,000 *l.* of goods into England, there would be no difficulty in obtaining the deposit in gold before the goods were delivered into the hands of the smugglers, so efficient are their arrangements, and so much capital is employed in the introduction of the goods.

9162. Then I learn from you that persons of very large capital indeed are engaged in smuggling?—Yes, a very large capital in reference to such a profession; I believe that at this moment there would be no difficulty in obtaining a deposit of 50,000 *l.* for the introduction of silk goods into England, supposing there was a demand for that quantity of goods; and there can be no doubt the facilities of introduction would be increased, and the motives for introduction be maximized by prohibition; I have a distinct belief, from facts that have come to my knowledge, that if a prohibition at this moment was obtained for silk goods in this country, that smuggling in five years would be doubled or trebled.

9163. I understand, at the present day, that persons of very large capital and high credit are engaged in these transanctions?—Yes.

9164. Do you consider then that I am wrong in drawing an inference from the facts you have stated, that no additional degree of odium has attached to this illicit trade in consequence of the removal of the prohibition?—I really feel difficulty in expressing an opinion of that sort as to English minds; one must have had great intercourse with that class of people, and I have not come in contact with them in this though I have in other countries; I have observed that in proportion to the efficiency of the prohibitory system in other countries, the feelings of kindness and affection for the smuggler increase; the smuggler who smuggles against a duty of 30 per cent. has, it may be said, 30 per cent. value in the love and affection of the inhabitants; if against 60, he has so much more; and if against prohibition, he has the greatest portion of friendly regard that can be shown to him. In the course of my life I have more than once, in Spain particularly, travelled hundreds, I may say thousands of miles, in company with large bodies of smugglers, men who had introduced from 1,200 to 1,500 mule loads of English goods. I have gone with them over very large districts from Portugal to Spain, and across the country from Gibraltar. I have seen how they have been received with cordial welcome as the instruments of procuring for a whole people enjoyments, which but for them they would not have possessed. I conceive that human desires and human motives are pretty much the same all over the world; and that if you force the people of England to pay 50 per cent. more for silk goods than they can buy them elsewhere, he who sells them 50 per cent. less will infallibly be looked on with a friendly eye.

9165. Do you think, that when the public can have silk for 30 per cent. duty, the smuggler is considered a public benefactor?—I think he will be so considered. I should be sorry to seem to approve of the conduct of the smuggler, but if I was asked at this moment, if the smuggler be in reality a public benefactor, and whether he leads to the employment of a greater quantity of labour in England than would be employed if the smuggler did not exist, I think I could demonstrate that he does, and that I could put that part of my evidence in a way to bear conviction with it.

9166. You are aware that during the existence of a prohibitory system there was the power of seizure and of search, which in point of fact constituted the main protection, so that when the goods were landed and placed in the warehouse of the importer it was then that the danger in reality began. Now do you consider that

678.                                                                    persons

*John Bowring,*
Esq. LL. D.

22 June,
1832.

persons of large capital and credit, such as you have alluded to, would continue this illicit trade when exposed to the risk of information by some one of the many numerous persons they must employ, and when the risk of their credit would be the consequence of their detection?—Perhaps not; the only consequence would be, you would have 100 small importers instead of one large one.

9167. When the importers are numerous and small a smaller quantity is brought in?—Not necessarily so. In France the power of seizure exists as it existed in England, and may be exercised by domiciliary visits in a harsh manner, so much so that it would not be tolerated here; yet even then it is just as vain to attempt to stop the smuggling into France of English goods, as it would be to stop the smuggling into England of French goods. With respect to spirits, the enormous extent to which French spirits are smuggled into England, in consequence of a duty, which is almost a prohibition, is a remarkable evidence that there is no protection that can guard against it.

9168. You are aware that the seizure of spirits is very frequent?—It forms a small proportion to the quantity introduced.

9169. I presume you will admit, that the circumstance of having to cross the channel, does offer a difficulty to smuggling into England which does not occur to smuggling into Spain or France, from other parts of the Continent?—The smuggling into Spain is very much a coast smuggling. I should say *à priori* that the difficulty of smuggling into England ought to be greater; but you cannot resist the fact that the premium of smuggling into England is less than the premium of smuggling into France, which is evidence that though the natural difficulties are greater in England, yet that the real difficulties are greater in France. The only way one can estimate difficulties is by the cost of vanquishing those difficulties, and the cost of vanquishing them is in France greater than the cost of vanquishing them here; the premium of smuggling goods into France is greater than into England, and I take that as irresistible evidence that the difficulties are greater in France than in England, inasmuch as the same class of smugglers are employed for the same purposes; a great number of men are employed in the trade. If a man asks six or eight per cent. more for introducing goods into France than into England, I take it there must be more of difficulty to surmount; the only test in these cases is of course the cost.

9170. Do you consider that in France there is the class of persons of high credit and capital engaged in smuggling, which you have described?—No doubt; in Paris there are two or three houses at least; the extent of illicit introduction into France is extraordinary; we had an opportunity of seeing precisely on what articles it bears. Honourable Members will feel that, from the very moment you create an import of French goods into England, you create an export of English goods into France; these are events of twin birth, they grow up at the same time; it is impossible you can admit French manufacture without exporting English. I state these facts, with this observation, that the quantity of labour which enters into the production of English goods, is double the quantity of labour which enters into the goods we take from the French; that the raw material of the article of English export forms a small portion of the cost of production, and that the raw material in France forms a great portion of the cost of production, so that the result is (and I speak from examination on a very large scale,) the result is, that in our exports to France nearly double the amount of labour exists which exists in our imports from France; that even the protection of 30 per cent. which is given to the silk manufacturer is the sacrifice of 60 of English labour; and this must not be lost sight of, looking at the question not as a silk question only, but looking at its operation as bearing on the whole country.

9171. I ask not what quantity of labour is engaged, but what quantity of labour is engaged in the articles on which the silk imports are paid?—I may, as a looker on, venture to suggest that the legislature is bound to look very much into the situation of those whose labour may be affected by changes in themselves beneficial to the community. This object appears to me worthy of very serious attention. I omitted to state that among other important facts elicited, we have been able to trace the progress of payment by this country to France for the goods which England takes from France, and that there is an article prohibited in France, the exportation of which from England, and the clandestine introduction of which into France has gone on, I should say, *pari passu,* with the importation into England of silk goods; that article is cotton twist. According to all the returns from the Custom House large quantities are introduced into the countries adjacent to France, where it is left for clandestine introduction into France. In the year 1831
the

*John Bowring,*
Esq. LL. D.

22 June
1832.

the illicit importation of cotton twist into France was, I have little doubt, from 15 to 20,000,000 ƒ., and as a curious fact illustrative of the inefficiency of a prohibitory system, though the quantity of cotton twist introduced into France is probably now four or five times the amount which it was ten years ago, because it is the demand which has been produced in France for payment which has created the export from England; though the quantity of cotton twist is four or five times as much as it was ten years ago, the seizures are at this moment not half what they were at that period. Thus smuggling has organized itself, made itself more complete and more compact, and has arrested all the powers of legislation.

9172. Do I understand you to say, that the replies you have given as to smuggling have not been with reference to this as a mere subject of silk inquiry, but with reference generally to the trade and manufacture of the country?—Yes.

9173. And you consider that the question of the labour, which you admit has been displaced, is one that ought to call for attention?—Certainly.

9174. Am I right in understanding you to admit that a quantity of British labour, of a particular class, has been in fact displaced by the alteration of the law?—No doubt of it; every alteration must necessarily displace labour of a particular character, although you may have a great result of good on the whole; if your prohibitory system could have been efficient, and under that system the same desire for wearing silk could have existed, (which I do not believe possible) you might have had the manufacture of the article, which the French article has now supplanted; you might have had a greater quantity of silk weavers, but you would have less hands employed in the whole. My statement is, that you would have perhaps protected 2,000 silk weavers, but you would have sacrificed 4,000 cotton weavers infallibly; so that the loss to the labouring weaver would be, in fact, 50 per cent.

9175. Do I understand you to say, that you consider the smuggler a benefactor to his country, because, for every article of foreign manufacture introduced here, some article of home manufacture must be exported to replace it?—Not necessarily of home manufacture; though in regard to France it does happen that the payment is made in home manufacture. In the particular case of countries situated like France and England, where there is a particular manufacture and an aptitude for the production of certain articles, the probability is, the direct exchange will take place in the manufactured article, but that is not inevitable; it might take place in tobacco: if the markets of England were as advantageous as those of Holland, the probability is, that large quantities of tobacco would be introduced from England into France, though the tobacco must itself have been bought by English labour. In two countries, each having particular manufacturing fitness, where in England long attention has led to great improvement in particular departments, and in France, where a long series of experiments has led to the great developement of manufacturing aptitude of another class, the probability is, that the exchange would take place between those articles: for instance, I think that in almost all the articles of taste and fashion the French possess a superiority of between 30 and 40 per cent.: I think the English have a greater superiority than this in those manufactures, such as cotton, where mechanical aptitude is brought to bear. Now as such articles are susceptible of a greater variety of price than colonial produce, which both countries have the power of importing direct from the colony, it is clear the exchange would not take place in colonial produce, not in an article from the third country, but rather in articles the peculiar produce of each country.

9176. Supposing the exchange to take place in articles of manufacture imported into this country, and articles, the production of manual labour, exchanged by the exportation from this country of articles worked by machinery, do you still consider the importer of the foreign article a benefactor to the country?—Clearly. think machinery represents labour as much as any other manufacture of the country.

9177. Have you any thing more to state as to cotton twist?—I am in a position of some difficulty, as far as respects a good deal of information, which I have as a commissioner. The French Government have certainly opened to our view a great deal of the feebleness and inefficiency of their system; they have shown us the correspondence from the Custom Houses, and enabled us to know what the state of things is: I can therefore only add, that I have had evidence enough to satisfy me, in the peculiar position in which I was placed, that at the present moment the importation of cotton twist is from 15 to 20,000,000 ƒ. Honourable Members may

678. satisfy

*John Bowring,*
Esq. LL. D.

22 June,
1832.

satisfy themselves to a great extent, by looking at Parliamentary Returns of the export of cotton twist to the countries adjacent to France; the export to Italy, to Spain, and particularly the immense export of cotton twist to the Netherlands, and to the countries along the Rhine, a great portion of that is for ilicit introduction into France. I can also speak from my own personal knowledge of the large clandestine exportation of cotton twist from Switzerland into France. I have facts of another character; and although I feel great difficulty in giving publicity to many papers that I have before me, yet I will, to satisfy any honourable Member, show the documents connected with the French Custom House: these I hold confidentially; and I do not think myself justified, as a commissioner still engaged in an important inquiry, in detailing more than I have done, or putting those documents publicly forward.

9178. What do you conceive, from the inquiries you have made, would be a proper and sufficient protecting duty for the silk trade in this country?—I think 20 per cent. would destroy a very great portion of the smuggling trade; any thing beyond 20 is perfectly illusory; an increase of smuggling would infallibly go on.

9179. What would be necessary to protect the silk manufacturer from foreign competition?—I have only given evidence with respect to France; I think protection wholly illusory.

9180. What would be the effect on the silk manufacturer in this country of removing every sort of protection?—I think the silk manufacture in this country would ultimately increase to an enormous degree. I apply to the manufacture of silk that which applies to every other; as far as my experience goes, wherever ignorance and inferiority have remained unprotected, intelligence and superiority have taken their place.

9181. What would be the effect of entirely removing the protecting duty on cotton twist in France?—Bad; which is already the infallible consequence of prohibition. At this moment, of the capital invested in the production of cotton twist, I think I may state the great proportion is absolutely lost, and the loss of the rest is inevitable; I have had occasion to examine the operation of the system on a very wide scale, and I state as a general result on the details of which I should be able to give evidence to satisfy honourable Members, that their protective experiment has cost the French nation since the peace, 200,000,000 pounds sterling; and their prohibitory experiment has wholly failed in accomplishing any one object for which it was introduced. Wherever there are unfavourable circumstances, such as are now connected with the cotton twist trade in France, they can be no more subdued by protection than a geranium can be made to flourish in Iceland. I am satisfied that no industry can or will succeed that is not of natural growth; that all attempts to force industry have been ruinous and fatal to the nations that have made the attempt; I say thus much from observations growing out of an experience of a great many years, in almost all countries where manufactures are established.

9182. Do you not think there are natural difficulties opposed to the flourishing of the silk trade in this country in almost an equal degree as compared with France?—I think not; I think that France has exceedingly few advantages which England might not possess, and the English have a great many advantages France does not possess; and I believe if, by a gradual diminution of duty, the French goods had admission into this market, that in the course of 20 years, though the quantity of French goods imported might be increased, yet the quantity of English goods produced would be increased three or fourfold. The French would be for a very long time our instructors, and would bring more beautiful goods than we should be able to produce; they would only continue in this market by their superiority, and it is my most decided opinion that their being in this market, so far from being injurious to the English manufacture, would be beneficial in the highest degree; beneficial as a source of instruction—beneficial as introducing a constant variety of new patterns; for, as I mentioned before, the rapidity with which invention is at work in their manufacture is perhaps its great characteristic, and that the consequence of having these beautiful goods produced in France would be an extension of the desire on the part of the people to clothe themselves in silk goods, the demand for which would be greatly increased on the whole.

9183. Do you give that opinion, even supposing there should not be a reciprocal feeling on the part of the French with regard to permitting us to have the raw materials?—I repeat, that I think the English manufacturer has a great grievance in not being able to purchase the raw material in France; it is an evil to be remedied,

and

John Bowring,
Esq. LL. D.

22 June,
1832.

and it has been represented so strongly that I believe it will be removed; in that respect the Frenchman has now the advantage which monopoly gives him. I stated before, however, that the quantity of the superior raw material is very small, with reference to the whole production; the quantity of silk consumed in French manufacture is four millions of pounds; the quantity of superior silk produced in France is about 400,000, of which 400,000 I do not estimate that more than one-half is of that beautiful quality to which reference has been made: this is only one-twentieth of the whole of the silk consumed in France. To the extent in which it operates, it is clearly prejudicial to the English manufacturer.

9184. I put it to you in the higher branches of the silk trade, not as to the general consumption?—No doubt that is a very considerable disadvantage to the English manufacturer.

9185. Am I also to understand, that you conceive that cotton twist in France would be entirely destroyed, supposing it not to be protected?—No, I think what protection has done there for cotton twist is what protection would do here as to any other article; it destroys all motive to improvement. The manufacturer of cotton twist, if he can obtain the security of a certain price, does not improve his machinery; foreign competition might force him to do so.

9186. I want to know what, in your opinion, the effect would be?—It is certain if you did not take from France her silks, she would not take your cotton twist.

9187. Do I understand you to state it as your opinion that the price of French silk is generally governed by the price paid for Italian silk?—Yes, I think it is established by the document I presented, that, taking an average of the year, the French silk, of the same number of deniers as Italian, has an average superiority of from 20 to 30 sous per kilogram; but there are particular circumstances, where there is a demand for particular goods, in which Italian silk of the same number of deniers has sold for higher prices than French.

9188. If our manufacturer was enabled, by a reduction of duty on Italian thrown silks, to import the article at the same price as the manufacturer at Lyons, he would be on a footing of equality with the French manufacturer?—That is quite clear as respects that material.

9189. You were asked as to the displacement of labour by the introduction of French goods; if it should appear that the silk manufacture has increased since 1826, instead of diminished, there can be no displacement?—There may have been of labour employed in the production of a particular class of silk goods.

9190. If manufacture has increased, there can be no actual displacement of labour in that particular trade?—Not in that, certainly.

9191. As to the manner in which the balance of trade is adjusted between the two countries, have you any further information to give?—The trade at this moment fluctuates from three to four millions; I think the manufactures of the two countries very nearly adjust themselves. It would appear from official returns, that England takes a very large quantity of goods from France, and France a very small quantity of goods from England; that is not the fact; the amount of manufactured exports from France for England is about the amount of the imports of goods from England into France; but there is another indirect source of payment growing out of the French navigation laws: they cannot import colonial produce from England; the consequence of which is, that a considerable quantity of the colonial produce imported for French account goes to Antwerp, Ostend and the Italian Ports, inasmuch as they may import it from the Ports of the Netherlands or Italy, but cannot import it directly from England. Through that indirect means is the balance of trade principally adjusted; on the whole the result is, that a balance remains due to England; the proof of that will be found in the constantly rising state of the exchange, which is evidence of the increased demand for paper on England. For a considerable time, the rate of exchange has been from three to four per cent. above par.

9192. Have you any further information to give respecting smuggling into France?—I believe I have stated generally the facts of the case, that the principal article of illicit introduction at this moment is cotton twist; of finer cotton goods there is also a considerable fraudulent importation. There is a large importation of fine cutlery, of worsted goods, and of that waistcoating which is called quilting.

9193. Can you state what is the amount of protection afforded by the present system of French Custom House law?—I stated before what the organization of

678. the

*John Bowring,*
Esq. LL. D.

22 June,
1832.

the French Custom House is; they have three lines of Custom Houses, they employ 25,000 men in their preventive service, and according to the testimony of the Director in Chief of the Custom House, their power of protection does not go beyond 30 per cent. Against the difference of the price of 30 per cent. on manufactured goods, they have no means whatever of legislation; beyond that the smuggler comes into the field and they are helpless.

9194. Can you supply the Committee with any information respecting the Custom House revenues of France?—The operation of the restrictive system on revenues has been very remarkable. I stated, that wherever a protective system is entered into, the demand for protection always goes on increasing, when it gets to prohibition of course protection can go no further. It was found that high duties were not sufficient, and a prohibition was looked to and that failed; a few years ago the manufacturers came to the plan of exacting bounties. In the first year the sum granted was 80,000 *f.*; last year, in consequence of the constantly increasing distress, and the exactions of the manufacturers, no less than 14,000,000 *f.* were granted in bounties on the French manufactures. According to the last census France has 34,000,000 of inhabitants; the whole of the Custom House revenues in consequence of the diminution of trade, and the demand for bounties, was 70,000,000 *f.* or less than 3,000,000 *l.* sterling, produced by the Custom House returns.

9195. Can you state what are the modes adopted by the smuggler to get goods into France, is his collusion with the officer, one of them, or to any extent?—No doubt; when you increase the number of revenue officers you only increase the number of chances which the smuggler has; it is much more easy to find among 1,000 men some man to be corrupted, than among 500; the evil increases with the means you provide for its remedy.

9196. Have not the French Government lately had under consideration the increasing the bounty on silk exported?—It was suggested to them, but it has been rejected by the Council of Commerce.

9197. Was it not proposed to give it them in the shape of a drawback?—They made an attempt to get a bounty but they failed; they have lately seen the bearing of the system on a great number of circumstances, and they are not at all disposed to continue it. The Council of Commerce consists of Peers and Deputies nominated by the Government, to whom questions of commerce and legislation are referred previous to their introduction. Many members may be known to honourable gentlemen present, the Duke de Broglie is one, and Count Mollien is another.

9198. What has been the operation of the protective system in France?—My opinion may be very decidedly gathered from the different answers I have given to the Committee. The manufacturers are in a state of embarrassment and arrear, in proportion as the prohibitory system is brought to bear on them; generally their state is one of great distress; their machinery is more imperfect than ours, and the sufferings of the people are very great. A monopoly is created by the prohibition of a foreign article, the effect of it increases the prices, and they rise to an enormous height; enormous prices give enormous profits, and to that every body rushes; the effect of home competition is the bringing down the prices, and the capital invested at the time of the high prices is in consequence lost; there is no outlet, inasmuch as the element of a prohibitory system is, that it shall make the produce of a particular locality higher priced than the general produce of the world, or else it does nothing; the consequence is there can be no relief. If you manufacture an article above the average price you cannot get rid of it, there is no disposing of an article produced at 60 or 70 per cent. above the average value; it is soon found that more capital is employed in the production of a particular article than will supply the very narrow sphere to which the prohibition has limited the seller; then there is no resource in the general market; sufferings increase among the manufacturers and labourers, till the Government, in order to preserve the labouring classes from starvation, are forced to come forward and pay the extra cost in the shape of a bounty; this has been the course of things in France, and thus improvement is checked; the capital already invested is lost, and wherever the unnatural experiment has been made, it has brought ultimate ruin on the adventurers.

9199. Do these observations of your's apply particularly to the silk trade in France?—The silk trade has been suffering to a certain extent from the protective system; from the cost of iron and wood, from the duty on the import of the raw material, and from the local taxation; all these are disadvantages pressing on the French manufacturer; he is much injured by competition with Switzerland, and
with

*John Bowring,*
Esq. LL. D.

22 June,
1832.

with Southern Germany, and he has been saved simply by the possession of that quality which has enabled him to produce a fashionable and tasteful article.

9200. Do you consider the state of the silk manufacturer in France, as compared with the silk manufacturer in this country, to be better or worse?—I should think, on the whole, better; where the silk manufacturer has not misunderstood his position; I think the French silk manufacturer who is producing works of taste, and employing himself principally with a view to turn to account the advantages of his position, will be labouring successfully; not so in the coarser manufactures. In England, too, the silk manufacturer will be successful in the proportion in which he keeps to the article in which he has a superiority; it is a question of judgment. I conceive a deal of the prosperity in all countries to be owing to the manufacturer getting into a region where he has evident advantage; while on the other hand some men mistake their localities, and set about planting vine trees in temperatures too low to produce grapes.

9201. Is not the higher branch of the silk trade the most profitable?—No doubt of it; if there be any part of the field where the French have a monopoly, it is there; but that is growing out of superior knowledge, out of the habits of ages and circumstances, the ramifications of which I have endeavoured to explain.

9202. Will not your observations as to the vine, apply to the mulberry tree?— I think France will produce silk so much cheaper than England that it would be idle to cultivate the mulberry tree here.

9203. It forms no part of your contemplation that it would be practicable to raise the silk worm profitably in this country?—I think not; I think silk could be imported more cheaply from France than grown in this country; in France if I were asked my opinion with respect to many of their silk manufactures, I would say, you are on a false ground, abandon your looms, cultivate the mulberry tree, and you will get a much better return. Free trade opens to all countries their natural resources, and puts every body in his true position.

9204. Has the protective interest been injurious to the shipping trade of France? —I will mention a fact, showing what the operation of the protective system has been on the shipping trade of France. I have got a return here showing what the state of the shipping was in 1820; I have taken the country which on all occasions I find it convenient to use as a means of comparison, inasmuch as it is the country in which France and England meet on equal terms. In 1820 there were 137 French ships arrived from the United States, and there were 132 American ships. It is known that since 1820 France has increased the duties on iron; and this has doubled the value of wood; the first for the protection of masters of forges, and the other for the proprietors of forests. These two classes have had the benefit of the prohibitory system to its full extent. In 1820 these two nations started with an average number of shipping; in 1830 the last return, the number of French vessels that arrived from France was only 21; while of American vessels there were 325 engaged. Such is the operation of the system of protection on the shipping trade of France.

9205. Can you state what changes have taken place with regard to the importation of iron?—That has almost ceased; formerly there was a very large trade between Bordeaux and Sweden. The French said, we will not have your iron, because we can get iron of our own, though it costs us four times as much as your's. The Swedes say, if you do not take our iron we cannot take your wine; and the consequence is, that the trade, which was a very considerable one, has become comparatively null. The same circumstances have occurred in other countries; it is quite impossible to have an export without an import; and as it is equally impossible to have an import without an export, they are co-adjacent circumstances, born and bred together, and you do as efficiently provide for your exports to other countries, by allowing their importations, as you do by any treaty of commerce.

9206. Can a system of prohibition applied to the silk trade be made efficient against a considerable difference of price?—It is impossible; against a great difference in price and quality there can be no efficient protection.

9207. You have already stated in your evidence that under a system of prohibition, in the year 1818, we imported from France 1,744,000 value in francs, and that under a system allowing importation we have imported in the last year the extent of 17,000,000*f*, more than half of which you say is smuggled?—No; only 300,000*l.* worth.

9208. But we do smuggle more goods under a system allowing importation than under a system of prohibition?—No doubt; your trade with France has been constantly increasing.

9209. From

*John Bowring,*
Esq. LL. D.

22 June,
1832.

9209. From what you know of the state of manufacture in France and England, do you not believe that, in case we resorted to a prohibition again, the smuggling of silk goods from France would greatly increase?—It would to an incalculable degree; the organization of the smuggling system is every day more and more perfect.

9210. What is the state of the illicit trade in gloves?—I visited Grenoble, where I staid some days, and obtained returns; I found that the whole produce of glove at Grenoble fluctuates from about 250,000 to 300,000 dozen; about one-third of that number is taken by this country. In looking to an official return, I have formed a most distinct opinion, that the smuggling of gloves is not more than 5,000 dozen per annum, if it be so much; I have not made an accurate estimate of the duty levied on gloves; it seems to me that such a duty can be levied and is levied.

9211. What duty do you consider should be collected on gloves?—I imagine 20 per cent. might be collected.

9212. Can you suggest any means for ascertaining the invoice value of goods?— It seems to me that after all the only means of entering on a wise and judicious legislation would be to establish on the real value an ad valorem duty; I have no doubt that a vast deal of fraud is practised on the respectable trader; I think the levying of a regular importation duty, though lower than the present, would put the manufacturer in a better situation than he is in now.

9213. Have you any information as to the mode in which the Americans act?— The Americans have in Lyons accredited agents; they order attested certificates of the value to be brought with the invoices; these certificates are received at the Custom House as evidence of the value; they have also the power of taking the goods at the invoice price; they have a consul at Lyons, we have none; when goods are bought in Lyons for the United States, to the invoice a certificate of value from the consul is attached, that is admitted by the American Custom House; the power of taking the goods at the invoice price has been found a sufficient security against fraud.

9214. Have you reason to think that the duty actually paid is considerably above 30 per cent.?—Yes, that is a great ground of complaint; the duties require a new adjustment; and the feeling of discontent on this ground is certainly increasing at Lyons and elsewhere; I have not heard any accusation of want of good faith on the part of the English Government, but I have seen evidence perfectly satisfactory which shows the duties in many cases to be from 50 to 60 per cent.; I have had opportunities of comparing some invoices with the duties levied, and in some the duties levied have been much beyond 30.

9215. Have you made any estimate of the loss to England which the prohibition of French silk would bring with it?—I have been making a calculation with respect to the character of the trade between England and France; I estimate the importation from France at this moment of silk goods, at 800,000 *l.* of which I should take 500,000 *l.* to be material, 250,000 *l.* to be labour, and 50,000 *l.* profit; if 25 per cent. was taken, the revenue would receive of course, from 800,000 *l.*, 200,000 *l.* revenue; if 20 per cent., 160,000 *l.* I estimate a profit to the importer of 6 per cent. on the million, inasmuch as you add the 200,000 *l.* duty to the 800,000 *f.* the capital invested would be a million; this importation from France is paid for in cotton twist; the average numbers are above No. 180, the value, as before, 800,000 *l.*, into which the labour enters for at least 550,000 *l.*, so that if prohibition were to be successful it would destroy 300,000 *l.* value in labour; 200,000 *l.* in revenue, and 60,000 *l.* in profit.

9216. The object of reducing the duty is to lessen the profit of the smuggler, is it not?—The object of diminution of duty is to destroy the smuggling.

9217. Do you think the smuggler will not continue his trade if the duties are low?—I think his trade will be destroyed to a very great extent; smuggling, like every thing else, of course runs a risk; and, like other trades, it is at this moment, not giving more than something beyond the average return for the capital. It is clear that if you diminish the return the smuggler receives, you will be destroying a great deal of his trade; no duties can be long collected which are far beyond the average rates of smuggling; 20 per cent. is collected on the article of gloves, of which there is a importation of nearly 100,000 dozen per annum.

9218. Is smuggling carried on chiefly by the inclination of smugglers, or owing to the encouragement of the receiver of the goods in this country?—They are contemporaneous; the smuggler is willing to carry on a contraband trade, for he finds somebody willing to buy the goods; it is a question of demand and supply.

9219. The

John Bowring, Esq. LL. D.

22 June, 1832.

9219. The cost of silk being supposed to be 20 or 30 per cent., are there not articles better worth the attention of the smuggler than silks, such as brandy, that pays 700 or 800?—I mentioned that that was an article smuggled by petty smugglers; manufactured articles are articles which are wholly in the hands of the smugglers in gross; the whole of whose arrangements are left to those who run very little personal risk. The smugglers of such articles as brandy are individual smugglers for their own account, in consequence of the great profit they receive.

9220. If the receiver of the smuggler was checked, would the smuggler carry on his trade on his own account?—How can you change the desire to have a better thing for a lower price? If you destroy all human motives you may interfere with the buyer of the smuggled article; you cannot persuade a man that three is less than two, or that a good article is not preferable to a bad one, or that a cheap article is not preferable to a dear one.

9221. May you not so increase the risk as that no person of character will engage in it?—You may destroy the great smuggler by creating 100 little smugglers, the demoralization will go on in proportion to the risk. The great objection to the prohibitory system is this, that you cannot legislate against universal interests. Universal interests always take care of themselves as far as they can. It is very well known to what an enormous extent bandanna handkerchiefs were smuggled some years ago; it was hardly thought genteel to be without a bandanna.

9222. Are not English goods when within the boundary of the city of Paris protected from seizure?—No; they are obliged to protect cotton twist when it gets to the factory, otherwise the works would be stopped; and that is an exceedingly absurd position; they seize in the barriers, they seize beyond the barriers, they seize in the town, and they do not seize the cotton twist when it gets into the hands of the manufacturer, lest the weavers should turn out.

9223. Then how can you account for their exhibiting with impunity goods of English manufacture in the shop windows in Paris?—That is the greatest evidence that you cannot stop a trade for which there is such a demand.

9224. Is it within your opinion that in this country during the time of the prohibition silk goods were exhibited for sale in many of the shop windows in London; is that fact within your knowledge?—That is a fact of which I am not cognizant.

---

*Lunæ, 25° die Junii,* 1832.

JAMES A. STEWART MACKENZIE, ESQUIRE, IN THE CHAIR.

Mr. *William Harter,* called in; and Examined.

Mr. *William Harter.*

25 June, 1832.

9225. YOU are a silk manufacturer in Manchester, are you not?—I am.

9226. You are a mill owner also, are you not?—I have recently built a mill.

9227. You have signed a petition to Parliament, in which you express an opinion that it is " inexpedient to alter the present laws in regard to the silk trade," and desire " that they may continue as they are "?—That is the fact.

9228. Will you state to the Committee why you think it inexpedient to alter the law?—I think frequent changes in the regulations in any trade, are very injurious, and I cannot conceive any alteration in the present silk laws which would be likely to benefit the trade; all interests are as nearly balanced as they can be by any plan which has occurred to my mind.

9229. The present laws have for their object the protection of the English manufacturer; do you think he needs that protection?—Yes, protection in the shape of a moderate duty against the too free admission of foreign silks, but not prohibition.

9230. Will you state to the Committee why you think protection necessary?—Because in many respects the French and English manufacturers do not work on equal terms.

9231. State what you conceive to be the disadvantages of the English manufacturers, as compared with the French?—The disadvantages are many; in the first place, we have not so good a supply of the raw material, and that supply is heavily taxed before it reaches our shores.

678. 9232. Whence

Mr.
*William Harter.*

25 June,
1832.

9232. Whence do we derive our supply of raw silk?—From India, and China, and Italy, we have our chief supply; and we have also some from Turkey.

9233. With respect to the supply from India and China, how is that taxed?—By reason of the monopoly of the East India Company, it is taxed to a considerable extent.

9234. Do you conceive their monopoly to affect it?—I conceive it to be the effect of all monopolies to keep up the prices, limit the quantity, and prevent improvement in the quality.

9235. There is no China monopoly?—We cannot import it direct from China.

9236. Are you not aware that a large proportion comes from Sincapore direct?—If I leave out the word China, perhaps it may be more strictly correct.

9237. Our ships cannot go direct to Canton?—No; and I consider every impediment as operating as a tax, and that impediment is a consequence of the East India Company's monopoly.

9238. How is the Italian raw silk taxed?—By the Italians themselves; the Lombardy raw is subject to an export duty of about 9 d. a pound; Piedmont raw is prohibited from export, but is sometimes obtained through Lombardy, being first smuggled into that country at an expense of about 8 d. per pound, to which expense of smuggling must be added the Lombardy export duty of 9 d., making together 1 s. 5 d.

9239. Do you mean that the Piedmont raw silk is taxed about 1 s. 5 d. a pound, and the other 9 d. before leaving Italy?—Yes; besides which, there is an import duty of one penny a pound on coming into this country, making 1 s. 6 d. per pound in the one case, and 10 d. per pound in the other.

9240. Do you conceive that the average duty on Italian raw silk, before it reaches our shores, amounts to 1 s. 2 d. a pound to the English manufacturer?—Precisely so.

9241. Are there any other circumstances which you think operate to increase the price to the English manufacturer?—Yes, there are the charges of the consignee in London, amounting I believe to about six per cent., which, added to the duty of 1 s. 2 d. a pound, will raise the price from 12½ to 15 per cent. above the price in Italy.

9242. That is on the presumption that as much raw comes from Piedmont as from other parts of Italy, if less came from that part it would not be so high?—True, but as the Italian has so much better choice of market, it may be said still, that there is as much as from 12½ to 15 per cent. in his favour.

9243. At what do you estimate what you call the choice of market?—I think no manufacturer would reckon it less than 5 per cent.

9244. You have stated the disadvantage of the English manufacturer in respect of the supply of the raw material, does not the French manufacturer suffer in the same way?—By no means; the French themselves produce a very considerable quantity of raw silk, equal by some, it is said, to four-fifths of their consumption (I apprehend it is equal to that, though some state it to be only three-fourths) and the export is rigidly prohibited; they cannot therefore be taxed on more than one-fifth of their consumption, while we are taxed on all ours.

9245. What effect has this prohibition of export, in your opinion?—It must have the effect of frequently depressing, or at least preventing advance in the price of the raw material to the French manufacturer; and it also prevents the prices of silk being equalized between the French and the English manufacturer, to the manifest disadvantage of the latter.

9246. Are you aware whether the silk produced in France is of as good a quality as that which comes to England?—It is said to be, and I believe it is, superior to any which the English manufacturer can procure.

9247. Are there any other reasons than those you have already stated, for supposing that the French have a better market for their raw material than the English?—Yes, there is another reason, which to my mind is a very convincing one; the East India Company's sales of Bengal and China raw silk, are not frequented by the French or other continental manufacturers: the indigo sales are attended by the continental manufacturers, with the exception of the French, who themselves import largely of that article (indigo) direct from the place of growth; this is a proof, I think, that they have at least as good a market, if not a better than we, for their raw material.

9248. You wish the Committee to understand that it is your opinion, that the English manufacturer has not only a comparatively limited market for his raw silk,

but

but that it is heavily taxed, and that the quality is inferior to that possessed by the French manufacturer?—Yes, just so.

9249. Have you any other reason for thinking that the English manufacturer requires protection?—Yes; there is a deeply rooted prejudice in favour of foreign silk manufactures; in many fancy articles, the French have had much more experience than we, and their labour and food I believe is generally lower; Paris too, notoriously sets the fashion of female attire, and not in this country only, but in the United States, which is a great market, and elsewhere.

9250. Perhaps you think that on equal terms the Americans would be disposed to take our manufactures, that is, provided the prices were as low as the French?—It would be some time, I think, before they would do so. In this market I think the circumstance of fashion alone would give to the French a very great advantage; if their goods were admissible at a low duty, they would have what is called the cream of every season, that is the early part of it.

9251-1. Is it your opinion that the present duties on silk goods, are such as the manufacturer requires for his fair protection?—It is at all times difficult to fix the exact point of protection, properly so called, that is, to exact such a duty on foreign goods as will not act as a prohibition, and yet be a fair protection to the home manufacturer; I do not think prohibition at all desirable, but the contrary.

9251-2. Why do you not think protection desirable?—My reason is, that it would at once take away that stimulus to exertion which is necessary to success in all undertakings, and thereby prevent ours so soon being able to compete with the continental manufacturers in the Transatlantic markets.

9252. Would you have any objection to a reduction of the duty on foreign manufactured silks?—I do not ask for any additional duty, nor do I think a reduction necessary; it is abundantly proved, that the present laws are not prohibitory with respect to foreign silks, for sufficient find their way, not only to keep alive our energies, but in the opinion of many, to depress them, and furnish grounds for great complaints.

9253. Is it your opinion that if the duties were taken off foreign thrown silk the import would materially increase?—I understand that the Custom House returns, on the average of three years, do not warrant that inference; but I think nevertheless such would inevitably be the case. That it has not yet been so I think may be attributed to the trade having been so long unsettled, (I may say, indeed, ever since the year 1824, since when there have been many fluctuations,) but the certain ultimate consequence of a reduction of the duty must be to induce larger importations.

9254. What, in your opinion, would be the effect on the price of foreign thrown silk if the duty were repealed?—I do not think the price would immediately fall in this market, or at least very little; therefore the repeal of the duty would for some time operate merely as a bounty to the foreign throwster, and of course stimulate him to greater exertions to supply us.

9255. Supposing on the other hand, as appears to have been the case before from the Custom House Returns on an average of three years, no increase of importation were to follow a diminution or total repeal of duty, what effect would that diminution or repeal have on the price?—It appears to me that it would have no effect at all, unless there were a change either in the amount of consumption, or the amount of production of thrown silk in England; prices are always regulated by supply and demand.

9256. What is the import duty on foreign thrown organzine at present?—The duty is nominally 3 s. 6 d. per lb.; but virtually, with reference to the English throwster, only 2 s. 9 d. or thereabouts.

9257. How is that?—Both raw and thrown silks pay an export duty from Lombardy, but the raw pays double that which is levied on the thrown; the difference, therefore, between the export duties being so much upon the raw, and of course against the English throwster, must be deducted from the organzine import duty.

9258. Will you explain this more fully?—I have shown before that the average duty on raws may be considered 1 s. 2 d. per lb.; if from this we deduct 5 d. for the export duty on organzine, it leaves a difference of 9 d., which, deducted from 3 s. 6 d., leaves the duty 2 s. 9 d., which is consequently the duty on foreign thrown organzine.

9259. If the import duty were removed from thrown silk, the drawback on the export of manufactured silk would of course cease; what effect would that have

678.    on

Mr.
*William Harter.*
———
25 June,
1832.

on our export trade?—It would instantly give a serious check to our export trade; the drawback has put the export trade in motion, but it has not yet acquired sufficient strength to continue its career without the assistance of that force; the best proof of our not being able to export without the drawback is, that before it was allowed our export was very trifling, but it has since materially increased; there is yet abroad, as well as at home, a great difficulty to combat in the long-existing prejudice in favour of French goods.

9260. Would it not benefit the manufacturer to take the duty off foreign thrown silk?—It does upon a first view of the question, seem that the manufacturer would be benefited by the repeal of the duty on foreign thrown silk; but as I have before said, the repeal would for some time, if not permanently, operate merely as a bounty to the foreign throwster; for he would still be able to get the same price, or nearly so, for his organzine; but supposing for a moment that the price is reduced to the manufacturer by the amount of the duty repealed, what then becomes of the English throwster? To sell his organzine at the same price as the Italian would leave him nothing for throwing, or very little; the consequences are obvious; the English throwster must give up, the Italian would thus get possession of the market, and of course a better price, and then how would the manufacturer be benefited? I would add, that upon the present system, the English and Foreign throwsters keep each other in check, and by their competition keep down the price of organzine to the weaver.

9261. Have you any other reason for desiring to retain the duty on foreign thrown silk?—Yes, there is another very important reason to which I particularly wish to draw the attention of the Committee; it is the fact that organzine is not a raw material, but a partly manufactured article. This fact seems altogether to have been lost sight of, and it is a very important one to keep in view, when considering the principle on which it ought to be admitted into this country. I repeat that organzine is not a raw material, but to a certain, indeed to a considerable extent, a manufactured article. The French term ouvrée, designates the thing correctly.

9262. On that account you think it ought to pay a duty?—Exactly so; if one process be protected, the weaving for instance, I do not see why all should not; throwing is as much a process of manufacture as weaving; and if the Italians or French be permitted to throw for us without duty or restriction, I cannot see why they should not also be allowed to dye, to wind, to warp, and even to weave; the only difference between throwing and weaving is, that one is the first process of manufacture and the other the last.

9263. You mean that all labour is entitled to a certain degree of protection?—My main position is, that in every country there is more or less dormant labour, and that the grand desideratum of all commercial enactments is, or should be, to call that labour into action by every means in our power; and to this end all raw materials of manufacture should be not only admitted without duty, but their importation should be studiously encouraged from every possible source; manufactures at the same time should not be too rigidly excluded; a duty should be imposed on them to prevent their importation in sufficient quantities to depress our own; but that duty should not be so high as to render us indifferent to foreign competition.

9264. Do you not think that a duty on thrown silk is a tax on Spitalfields and Coventry for the benefit of Manchester?—I do not so consider it by any means; because in the first place it is not clear that the price of organzine is raised to the consumer by the amount of the duty, and therefore it is not clear that he is taxed to that amount. It is quite certain that in Spitalfields and Coventry they are not the only consumers of foreign thrown silk; a good deal is used in Manchester occasionally, and elsewhere. It is equally certain that in the two former places they use a large proportion of English thrown from Bengal, China, Italian and Turkey silk.

9265. Suppose in Spitalfields and Coventry their consumption is exclusively in foreign thrown silk, and that the price is raised by the amount of duty, is not the duty in that case a tax upon them for the benefit of others?—That is supposing what is not the fact; but admitting for a moment the two first assumptions to be well founded, it does not follow that the third is so, because if their consumption be limited to organzine thrown in Italy, and they do not choose to export their goods, having a better market at home, I do not see how they can be injured, but the contrary, by the goods of other manufacturers being exported. I conceive that if myself and my neighbour are manufacturers of gros de Naples for instance, and I

export

Mr.
*William Harter.*

25 June,
1832.

export my goods, my neighbour is equally profited with myself by having the home market thus cleared of so much ; this must be the case so long as prices are regulated by supply and demand.

9266. Is not the duty paid only on the silk used in this country ?—The duty is not paid on silks used exclusively in this country; a good deal is now exported in the shape of goods; more will be exported if the trade be not interfered with. Government have said they do not wish to derive a revenue from the silk trade; and I do not see how a duty, which has been previously paid by the trade, can be more profitably employed than in giving encouragement in the way of drawback to the export of every branch of that trade ; a trade too, which, on so many accounts, it is extremely desirable to maintain and promote.

9267. If goods manufactured exclusively from silk thrown in this country be exported, would not what is called a drawback in that case be really a bounty ?— I do not think it can justly be called a bounty, because the trade has previously paid the same amount in duty. I should rather say it is a drawback of that duty allowed on any portion of the trade for the benefit of the whole.

9268. Of course you think the export branch of the trade a very material portion of it ?—It is certainly an important feature in the silk trade, and especially if we regard it as an increasing one.

9269. Do you know what was the value of the silk manufactures exported last year ?—The value is computed at about 500,000 *l.*

9270. Can you state what number of persons this export trade would afford employment to if the goods were made from silk thrown in this country ?—I think I do not overstate the amount at 10,000 individuals for 12 months.

9271. How do you arrive at that conclusion ?—Of the total value exported, I reckon that 4-5ths, or 400,000, consisted of manufactures of silk only; the labour on the raw material of which I calculate at 80 per cent., which would produce 180,000 *l.* ; the remaining fifth, or 100,000 *l.*, I call mixed goods, on which I reckon the labour at 150 per cent.; this will produce 60,000 *l.* ; so that the total labour on the exports of the last year will amount to 240,000 *l.* This sum, at 8 *s.* per week, will afford employment to 11,537 individuals for 12 months; or, at 9 *s.* per week, to 10,255.

9272. If it found employment for so many, of course it would maintain a considerably greater number ?—Certainly ; inasmuch as this number comprises the heads of many families as well as children.

9273. Do you know the amount of drawback on the exports of silk manufactures in 1831 ?—Forty-six thousand six hundred and fifty-eight pounds.

9274. The manufacturing of the goods on which the drawback was allowed, would cause an expenditure in labour of 240,000 *l.* ?—That is my calculation.

9275. This drawback had been previously paid by the silk trade itself, in the form of duty ?—Yes.

9276. You say that the sum of 240,000 *l.* at the average rate of wages of 9 *s.* per week, would furnish employment to 10,255 individuals for 12 months, or at 8 *s.* per week, will afford employment to 11,537 individuals, and you think if the drawback were withheld, that employment would be withdrawn from the larger portion of the individuals you have named ?—I think there cannot be a doubt of that.

9277. Why do you think that ?—Because before the drawback was allowed our goods were considered dear by the shippers, and in consequence, during the five years that the drawback was withheld, our exports were very trifling, but increased on the drawback being allowed.

9278. Do you know what was the amount of export of British manufactured silk from 1821 to 1831 ?—Yes ; the official value shows a considerable increase in the amount of silk goods exported immediately on the drawback being allowed.

9279. What was the increase ?—It appears that in 1828, the export of manufactures of silk only, amounted to 81,636 *l.* ; in 1829, to 141,686 *l.* ; (1829 is the year that the drawback was allowed, it was allowed first in July 1829); in 1830, the amount exported was 348,761 *l.*, and in 1831 about 400,000 *l.*

9280. So that in the space of only two years and a half after the drawback was allowed, the export of silk goods increased from 81,636 *l.* to about 400,000 *l.* ?— Exactly so ; that is an increase of very nearly 400 per cent. in that time.

9281. You have stated that as the amount of exports of the manufacture of silk only in 1828 and 1831, what was the total amount of the exports including goods made of silk mixed with other materials ?—The total amount of exports of silk only

and

Mr.
*William Harter.*

25 June,
1832.

and silk mixed with other materials, was, in 1828, 179,053 *l.*, and in 1831, about 500,000 *l.*, being an increase of about 175 per cent.

9282. Is the silk manufacture a healthy employment?—It is particularly so; I cannot conceive any manufacturing employment more healthful, nor do I know any so much so.

9283. What temperature is necessary, does it require great heat?—A moderate heat is best, such as we like in our own houses.

9284. Is that the case in the mills?—It is so.

9285. Is there any article of silk manufacture we are not now able to export?—There is one which is an article of great consumption both here and abroad, namely, the article of sewing silk, but it is exported in very small quantities indeed.

9286. Whence are the American markets supplied?—The American markets are supplied from India and China, and very largely from Italy.

9287. Is the English sewing silk as good as that made elsewhere?—The best English sewing silk is the best in the world, so far as I have seen.

9288. Why then is it not exported?—Because it cannot be sold at near the same prices as that imported from other countries, nor can English sewing silk of the same quality as the foreign, be sold at the same prices.

9289. Is the drawback allowed on the export of sewing silk?—No.

9290. If it were, perhaps sewing silk could be exported?—It certainly could.

9291. Have you any expectation of being able to export sewing silk without the aid of drawback?—I know not what time may produce, but my only present hope is in the expected extinguishment of the East India Company's monopoly.

9292. You say it is exported very largely from Italy, cannot you get the thrown silk from Italy, and manufacture it as cheaply as the Italians?—I am not prepared to say whether we can manufacture it as cheaply or not, but by the time the silk could arrive in England it would stand in to our manufacturer much more than it does to the Italian manufacturer.

9293. How much more?—As I have stated before, from 12 to 15 per cent.

9294. You stated in the early part of your evidence that the effect of the East India Company's monopoly was to tax the price, limit the quantity, and prevent the improvement of the quality of raw silk; is that opinion formed from what you suppose to be the effect of monopolies in general?—That would be quite sufficient, I think, to justify the opinion I have given; but I have facts which I think will satisfy the Committee of the correctness of at least some of my conclusions; it appears that in 1823, the quantity of raw silk imported into England for home consumption from the East Indies, China, St. Helena, and the Cape of Good Hope, was 1,210,252 pounds, the four subsequent years averaged only 1,430,663 pounds, the next and last four years, namely, 1828 to 1831, averaged 1,637,486 pounds, showing an increase very small, in comparison with the increase from other quarters, whereof the trade is not monopolized by a company. The import from Turkey in 1823, was 195,855 pounds, in the four following years it averaged 319,528 pounds, in the four next and last years, 441,319 pounds. The import from other parts in 1823, was only 645,788 pounds, in 1824 to 1827, a space of four years, it averaged no less than 1,158,896 pounds, the four last years, 1,206,272 pounds, thus the average of the last eight years, shows an increase upon 1823, as follows; from the East Indies, China, &c., about 26 per cent. only; from Turkey, 94 per cent., and from other parts 83 per cent., the gross increase from all parts being in eight years, about 51 per cent.

9295. The East India Company do not now import China raw silk?—No; it is now left entirely to the private trade, and has been so ever since about the year 1824.

9296. Has there been any increase in the import since the relinquishment of the import by the Company?—There has been a considerable increase.

9297. Can you state the amount of that increase?—I am not aware of any official Returns, distinguishing the import of China silk from other silk from the East, but I think I have a document which will be quite satisfactory to the Committee; looking at the account of what has been sold at the East India Company's sales, it appears that on an average of five years, say 1821 to 1825, 2,465 bales have been sold; from that period to 1831, a period of six years, the average sales have been 3,413 bales. I will explain to the Committee the documents from which I have made this calculation. After each sale a price current is published by the brokers, in which is shown, not only the quantity of silk put up for sale, but the quantity

refused

Mr.
*William Harter.*

25 June,
1832.

refused and withdrawn, and the quantity actually sold; from these documents, which I conceive are pretty good authority, it appears that there has been the increase which I have named in the quantity of China silk sold at the East India Company's sales since the Company gave up the silk trade to China.

9298. Since the trade has been carried on by private traders, the import of China silk has increased nearly 50 per cent. ?—I think fully 50 per cent. or more, for large parcels of China silk are frequently sold without passing through the Company's sales at all.

9299. It would appear that the increase of 26 per cent. which you say has taken place from the East Indies, China, &c. since 1823, is chiefly the effect of the Company discontinuing to import China raw silk?—It certainly would appear so.

9300. Have you attended the sales this year?—I have.

9301. What is the relative price of the last sale as compared with the preceding? —The prices at this sale are in some cases rather higher, but in some less, there is not five per cent. difference I should conceive.

9302. How much per pound?—Speaking of Bengal silk, as the selling price varies from 10s. to 17s., the variations in the price per pound are not uniform, though the per centage may be so.

9303. Why do you select the year 1823 as the period of comparison?—Because it was the year before the duty was repealed.

9304. Can you give the Committee an account of the quantites sold at the East India sale this year, and the amount of the quantity sold at the East India sale last year?—I have no documents at hand to enable me to do so. I beg to add with respect to China silk imported, I have not had recourse to any Government official document to ascertain the quantity as distinguished from Bengal; I do not know that such a return exists, but I understand from a gentleman now in this room, who is likely to be well informed on the subject, that the increased import of China silk since the Company discontinued that branch of their trade, is not less than 200 to 300 per cent.

9305. Have you made any calculation of the increase of the last eight years since the duty on raw was repealed, compared with the previous eight years before the duty was repealed?—I have made that calculation, and the result is, that the imports from the East Indies, China, &c. have increased only 50 per cent., whilst during the same period, the imports from Turkey have increased 210 per cent.; and from other parts, meaning chiefly Italy, 172 per cent.

9306. Do you consider the comparatively small increase of raw silk, imported from the East, as the effect of the East India Company's monopoly?—I cannot assign any other reason.

9307. Can you state the gross increase of the last eight years, as compared with the previous eight years?—I make it about 95 per cent.

9308. In those calculations, have you taken into account thrown silk and waste? —Neither the one or the other.

9309. Is the quality of East India silk as good as the raw silk we procure from Italy?—No, certainly not.

9310. Do you think there has been any improvement in the quality of East India silk of late years?—If there has been a change in the quality, it certainly has not been for the better; I think I may say that it has deteriorated.

9311. Can you assign any reason for that deterioration, except that you have given, namely, the monopoly of the East India Company?—None whatever.

9312. You stated that the importation of raw silk from all parts, since 1823, has increased about 51 per cent. on the average of the last eight years; have you made an estimate of the increase of the year 1831, as compared with the year 1823, the year before the duty on raw silk was reduced?—I have made that calculation, and the result is, that the increase of the year 1831, as compared with 1823, is something less than 50 per cent.

9313. Does it appear that the consumption of silk on the Continent has increased in the same ratio as that in England, during the same period?—As far as I am informed, the consumption of silk on the Continent has increased in a much greater ratio than that of England; for instance, in Lyons, as has been lately given in evidence before the Committee, the number of looms in 1825 was about 20,000, now they are 35,000, being an increase in only six years of about 75 per cent., whereas our consumption has increased only 50 per cent. in eight years, I understand that at Elberfeld, the silk manufactures have increased fully one-third

since

Mr.
*William Harter.*
_____

25 June,
1832.

since the beginning of 1830. At Zurich I have no actual account; but it is stated that the increase has been most extraordinary.

9314. Are there any duties attaching to the silk trade, which you think ought to be removed?—Yes; there are some to which probably the Committee may not attach much importance, but they make a part of the whole; I should say the penny per lb. import duty upon the raw material, though it is a small duty, yet with a house of only moderate extent, would amount to from 150*l.* to 200*l.* a year; there is also a duty of half per cent. levied on the export of silk manufactures; I think both those duties should be taken off.

9315. Is the silk trade carried on to a considerable extent in Manchester?—It is, to a very considerable extent.

9316. Have you any idea of the quantity of silk consumed there annually?—It is very difficult to ascertain the exact amount; but I have taken some pains, and come to the conclusion, that it is between seven and eight hundred thousand pounds weight per annum.

9317. What proportion is that to the gross annual importation?—It is about one-fifth.

9318. Will you state the proportion of Bengal, China, and Italian silk, composing that fifth?—I could not state that, without applying to the manufacturers for an account of the quantity of each which they use; I have been told of one house consuming not less than 250 lbs. per week of Italian thrown organzine, that is about 50 bales per annum.

9319. How many silk mills are there in Manchester?—There are twelve in Manchester and the immediate neighbourhood; besides which there are three belonging to Manchester houses elsewhere; namely, one at Tring in Hertfordshire, one at Blackburn in Lancashire, and one at Macclesfield, belonging to a Manchester house, making 15 belonging to Manchester houses.

9320. Is not the mill at Tring shut up?—I have been told since I came to town, that it has been shut up till very lately; but is now opened again.

9321. Can you give any reason why a Manchester house should build a mill elsewhere than in the neighbourhood?—I cannot.

9322. Do you know how many mills have been erected since 1823?—I believe there have been erected and converted, seven or eight.

9323. When you speak of mills, do you mean that they are employed entirely in throwing, or are employed in the manufacture of silk?—I do not know any employed exclusively in throwing; they are chiefly employed in throwing and manufacturing; the manufactories are generally partly carried on in the buildings, or attached to them.

9324. State the number of those exclusively employed in throwing?—I cannot at this moment recollect one.

9325. Are not those mills at Manchester more matter of convenience than of profit?—The profits I cannot judge of, for I am not yet a throwster; I have built a mill, and am putting machinery into it; I do not expect to derive much benefit from throwing; I have never known a throwster get rich; I have built my mill more as a convenience for my manufactory, because in brisk times we often sustain great inconvenience from the want of thrown silk; we cannot always obtain the particular description which may be suited to our trade; different manufacturers have different modes of applying the material.

9326. Have you felt a difficulty in the getting silk thrown?—Frequently.

9327. Was that the case in 1830?—Yes, it was.

9328. Did you pay a much higher price at that time for thrown silk?—I paid a much higher price than I do now.

9329. How much more?—I think in some cases there might have been a difference of 50 per cent. more than now.

9330. In some instances, were not the manufacturers obliged to purchase silk from the throwsters not being able to get their own silk thrown?—That must have been the case.

9331. Therefore the throwing trade in 1830 was particularly good?—I conceive it was a good trade in 1830, so far as I can judge, not being a throwster.

9332. Can you distinguish those who have built for profit, and those who have built for convenience?—I cannot say any thing about the profit or loss, not being a throwster; but I judge from the result. I have known the trade ever since I was a boy, but never knew a mere throwster become rich; if a manufacturer has to wait for his organzines or trams, he will sustain material inconvenience; though the

Mr.
*William Harter.*

25 June,
1832.

the throwing mills may not be worked at a profit, a manufacturer may have orders or goods which may yield a profit, and he had better throw the silk without profit, than be prevented from making his goods.

9333. If he were to wait, he might sustain a loss ?—Certainly.

9334. If it is an inconvenience to have to go to places in England to get silk, that inconvenience would be still greater if you had to go to Italy ?—Certainly.

9335. How long did the difficulty of obtaining thrown silk last, in 1830 ?—I cannot state at this moment from memory.

9336. What had the state of things been for two years prior to 1830 ?—It had been very variable, but not good.

9337. There was a sudden glut of work following temporary pressure, and silk was not to be obtained ?—There was a sudden demand for work, which the throwster was unable to supply.

9338. Not having been previously at work ?—It might have been the case in some instances, that he was not previously at work; I believe there were several mills set to work, which had been previously closed.

9339. Is it the case now that you cannot get silk thrown ?—No, we can get it thrown now.

9340. Does that arise from there having been new mills erected since 1830 ?—There have been some built.

9341. Several mills have been shut up in consequence of the badness of the trade, previous to 1830 ?—Yes.

9342. It was at that critical time, 1830, you felt a pressure; that is, a difficulty in getting your silk thrown ?—I have at various times had difficulty in getting my silk thrown.

9343. You, as a manufacturer, wanted a particular sort of thrown silk ?—Yes.

9344. Therefore it may have reference to a particular kind of silk more than to thrown silk generally ?—Certainly, to both occasionally.

9345. Did not other manufacturers feel the same inconvenience you did ?—That is a question I cannot answer; I suppose they may have done so.

9346. Has there not been a great deal of new machinery set at work in throwing, since that time ?—I am not aware of any very great increase; my own mill is one; there is another building, I believe, to supply the place of an old one.

9347. Has not Mr. Royle increased his machinery since 1830 ?—I do not know; I do not think there has been any enlargement of the building since that period.

9348. At former periods you state you have experienced the same difficulty in obtaining thrown silk ?—I have.

9349. Has not the trade been subject to these periods of excitement and depression, every three years, during your experience ?—They have occurred frequently; I cannot state at what precise periods.

9350. Since 1829, it has been the principal trade at Manchester, has it not, and has prospered more there ?—No, not the principal trade, but it may have prospered more at Manchester than elsewhere.

9351. Have there been many failures of manufacturers engaged in the silk trade at Manchester ?—I think not many.

9352. Has there not been a greatly increased amount of capital employed in the trade since 1830 ?—There may be some, but I am not prepared to answer that question fully.

9353. Has not the trade generally increased ?—I am not prepared to say whether it has or not since 1830.

9354. It has since 1824 ?—Yes.

9355. You buy your silk for cash or short credit, and sell entirely for cash or short credit, do you not ?—That is my system.

9356. Must not a great additional amount of capital have been employed in the trade since 1824 ?—Certainly.

9357. You mentioned Mr. Royle's mill, do you know whether it is at full work ?—I do not.

9358. Do you know Mr. Benjamin Williams's mill at Broughton ?—Yes.

9359. Do you know that that has lately begun to work at short hours ?—That may be the case, but I am not acquainted with it.

9360. Do you not think that the most effectual way of getting good thrown silk, is to secure a good and cheap raw silk ?—I think the way to get a permanent supply of good thrown silk, is to secure a good supply of good raw silk.

9361. You have stated that you think the penny per lb. import duty on raw silk

ought

Mr.
*William Harter.*

25 June,
1832.

ought to be taken off; are the Committee to understand that you do not think it will be an advantage to have the duty taken off thrown silk?—Yes, because if the duty were repealed, we might become more dependent on the foreign throwster for a supply of organzine, inasmuch as we cannot throw, from the best information I can obtain, on any thing like the same terms as the Italian.

9362. Your opinion is founded on the idea that you pay more for throwing silk in England than they do in Italy?—We cannot throw silk in England so cheaply as they do in Italy, so far as I am informed.

9363. Have you been in the habit of having silk thrown for your manufacture?—Yes.

9364. Have you been in the habit of buying it raw to have it thrown?—Yes.

9365. What have you paid at different periods since 1823?—I am not prepared to answer that question.

9366. You state that in 1830 and 1831 you paid 50 per cent. more than you paid formerly; what did you pay in that year per lb.?—The prices of throwing vary of course according to the size and description of the silk; the price of throwing now may be said to vary from 1 s. 6 d. a lb. to 4 s., but 1 s. 6 d. is not the price for organzine; it is what is commonly called coarse tram or threads, not Italian tram. I think I paid for the same (I am speaking from memory now) in 1830, 2 s. 3 d.

9367. Was that Bengal and China?—Bengal alone.

9368. What did you pay for Italian?—I can scarcely charge my memory. L should think, for Italian organzine, the price in 1830 was from 5 s. to 6 s.; I cannot speak more closely to the price.

9369. You were understood to say that 1 s. 6 d. to 4 s. 6 d. were the extremes?—That was previous to 1830.

9370. What kind of silk did you pay 4 s. for?—That would be Italian, certainly; it might be a little more or a little less; I cannot speak precisely to the prices.

9371. You think in 1830 there was 50 per cent. difference?—Yes, I believe 50 per cent. in Bengals; that I perfectly recollect.

9372. Have you been in the habit of employing one mill or several?—I have employed several.

9373. Are you not able to state what were the prices at which you gave a preference of one over others?—I cannot go back so far, and state the prices more nearly.

9374. What have you been paying since January?—About the same prices. I paid before 1830, 1 s. 6 d. where I paid 1 s. 6 d. before, and 4 s. where I paid 4 s. before.

9375. You have been a manufacturer for some years; what kind of goods have you turned out?—I have manufactured chiefly what are called narrow goods, a species of ribbons, not technically called ribbons, but galloons and doubles.

9376. Have you manufactured no other goods than galloons and doubles?—Yes, I have made silk handkerchiefs and sewing silk.

9377. In what goods have you used Italian thrown?—I have used Italian thrown only in the finest narrow goods and handkerchiefs.

9378. What are your finest goods?—They are known under the same denomination as those I have already mentioned, but are of a finer texture, made of a finer material.

9379. Do they make any of those goods in Spitalfields?—They do.

9380. Do they make any of them in Coventry?—None that I have heard of; I do not know of any.

9381. You come principally in competition with Spitalfields?—Yes.

9382. Have you increased in the amount of your manufacture each year?—It has increased; I cannot state the exact ratio of increase.

9383. Have you attended to the machinery you employ, as compared with the machinery in Spitalfields; is it nearly the same?—I believe there is little or no difference; in Spitalfields they are almost entirely discontinuing the manufacture of narrow goods, and are employing looms in the country, some in Devonshire, some in Reading and other parts.

9384. Are you able to state the wages you pay as compared with Spitalfields?—I do not know what they pay in Spitalfields; I can state generally what the earnings of my weavers are.

9385. Can.

Mr.
*William Harter.*

———

25 June,
1832.

9385 Can you state per piece or per yard?—There is a great variety of classes; there is one class for which we pay 11 *d.* per gross.

9386. What is that?—Narrow galloons; I have not the list of the prices, I must do it from memory.

9387. Have you any rate or table of wages fixed at Manchester?—There is a rate fixed among ourselves, but not by an association of masters; if one master lowers the price, others are inclined to follow him of course.

9388. Is there any price fixed by the workmen; do they agree and print any table?—They do, but it is not always submitted to; there have been several contests with the description of weavers who work for me. I had a contest with my weavers some time ago.

9389. What was the result of that contest?—The result was, that after being out for between three and four mouths they came to terms; it was in the spring of the year, the looms were full of goods, the weavers thought they could do as they pleased under such circumstances, and they turned out for considerably higher prices.

9390. Are you aware what at that time were the prices for the same kind of goods in London?—No, I am not.

9391. There were none of the same kind of goods made in Coventry?—I believe not.

9392. Since that dispute, have the workmen worked at such prices as you fixed?—They have.

9393. Will you state the price of wages of some other description of goods?—I cannot go through the whole not having documents with me; and these are matters not always retained in the memory. There are others for which we pay 2*s.* 1 *d.*, those are a kind of broad galloons.

9394. Do you pay the same prices as are paid in other towns?—So far as I believe our prices are very similar to those paid for the same kind of goods elsewhere; and we come as nearly as we can to the prices paid by other towns if they be not higher than our own.

9395. Are those goods made in Spitalfields?—I believe so, but not to a great extent, and also at Derby.

9396. Do you employ men, women, or children?—Both men and women.

9397. What earnings do they make at those wages?—It depends of course upon the ability and industry of the operative. I may say, speaking of men and women, from 12*s.* to 23*s.* per week.

9398. How many hours do you reckon?—Twelve hours a day, except Saturday, when they do not work so long.

9399. Do you deduct any thing for the use of the loom, or are those the prices net to the weaver?—They are the prices paid to the weaver, we supplying the machinery.

9400. Are those looms power looms?—Yes, they are.

9401. Have you none but power looms?—I have a few, but not many.

9402. How long is it since you established power looms?--The first about two years and a half ago.

9403. Are you adding to them?—Yes.

9404. For what description of goods?—The same description of goods.

9405. You do not mean to make fancy gauze ribbons?—I have no present intention.

9406. What is the difference of the earnings of the weavers in winter?—Not much; of course the weaver has better light in summer, and will in consequence make more work.

9407. Are the weavers constantly employed?—I think in our trade they are.

9408. Do you find that when your trade has increased that you get any hands from the cotton trade?—I did when my hands turned out.

9409. Do you find that when your trade is slack they return to the cotton trade?—I endeavour to keep them on all the year round rather than lose good hands.

9410. How many hands do you employ, men and women?—Am I obliged to answer that question?

9411. How many 'mills have you got out of the twelve which have been stated to exist?—I have one.

9412. Can you tell how many spindles there are in the mills?--Mine has not at present any machinery; I cannot state the gross number of spindles in Manchester.

678.                                                    9413. Do

Mr.
*William Harter.*

25 June,
1832.

9413. Do you suppose the wages of the weavers in Manchester generally are of the average of yours?—In my trade they are; but I believe in the broad trade they must be much less.

9414. Why are they less in the broad trade?—It is more easy to state a fact than to give a reason for it.

9415. Do not the same persons work in broad and narrow?—Very rarely.

9416. You have done nothing in the broad way?—I do something in it now, but very little.

9417. Do you find that the earnings are less than those you employ in the narrow trade?—They certainly are.

9418. Is there more art required in the narrow than the broad?—I cannot say that there is.

9419. Is there more competition?—There cannot be more competition than there is in my own trade, except amongst the weavers themselves, because the broad are so much larger a body than the narrow weavers. The narrow weavers combine, and will often remain out a considerable time rather than submit to any infraction of their regulations.

9420. You conceive that may have an influence in keeping up the wages?—No, I am not prepared to say that; I mentioned the thing incidentally; on the contrary I beg to make one remark on the subject of turns out. I have seen a great many, and have invariably found that the result has been the lowering of the wages of the operative; that was the result in my own case.

9421. Have there been any great improvements of late years in the machinery?—We fancy that our machinery is as good or better than that elsewhere. The throwsters of other places deny it; whether they are right or we are right I cannot say, not being yet a throwster.

9422. Has there been any improvement in the weaving?—I am not aware of any peculiar machinery except in the narrow trade.

9423. You stated that a very considerable proportion of the silk worked up in Manchester is Italian; is the Italian thrown employed to make similar goods to those made up in Spitalfields?—Yes, they make similar goods; they make gros de Naples and handkerchiefs; I cannot say much about the qualities, not being a broad manufacturer.

9424. When you speak of the handkerchiefs, do you mean bandanna handkerchiefs?—And black handkerchiefs.

9425. There is no other house using a considerable quantity of foreign thrown silk but one, is there?—I cannot say.

9426. Do you export any of the goods you make?—I do.

9427. Do you obtain the bounty on them?—I do.

9428. You do not use any of the silk that pays the duty?—I do, a small proportion.

9429. Did not the export of goods begin after the duty was taken off; was there any before?—Speaking of my own trade, there was none before.

9430. At what time did you begin to export goods?—I began to export immediately on the drawback being allowed and not before, of particular goods of my manufactory.

9431. In what year did you begin to export?—In the year 1829; in the interval between the present drawback being allowed, and the large drawback which has been referred to, there was no export at all in certain goods of my manufacture, but under the old system there was.

9432. What do you mean by the old system?—By the old system, I mean when the duty of 4s. a lb. was paid on the Bengal silk, and 5s. 6d. on Italian, and 5s. 6d. on Turkey; at that time there was a considerable drawback allowed, I think about 12s. a lb.

9433. What is the drawback now?—Three shillings and sixpence.

9434. If you deduct from the 12s., being the amount of the drawback, the 5s. 6d. a pound, the amount of the import duty, that leaves 6s. 6d., whereas there is now only 3s. 6d., how is it you did not export goods, when the advantages were greater in exporting than they are now?—I have said that I did export under the old system; as to the exact rate of drawback, I beg to correct my answer, so far as to say I was speaking from memory in saying that it was 12s. per pound; I believe that would refer to broad silks alone, but at that time the duty on thrown silks was higher than now.

9435. Are not the principal goods exported now, by you and others, made from
the

the coarser silks, on which there is no duty paid at all?—I cannot say what others may do, mine makes but a very small proportion of the trade; I do not use as much foreign thrown as I do of English thrown, that I admit.

9436. Do you use one-tenth of Italian thrown, as compared with English thrown?—I should think not.

9437. Then you take a bounty on the Bengal silk which pays no duty; you receive the bounty on that kind of silk?—It may be put in that way.

9438. Do you still retain the opinion you have given, that 3*s.* 6*d.* a pound duty on organzine silk is no impediment to the manufacturer of fine goods, who works up that silk?—Yes, I am still of that opinion.

9439. Do you mean to say, that if the manufacturer gets his silk for 20*s.* instead of 23*s.* 6*d.*, he cannot make his goods cheaper?—No, I say he can make them cheaper.

9440. You think, that taking off the duty, would not lower the price?—Yes, or very little.

9441. Is it your opinion that the price of Italian thrown silk regulates the price of the English thrown here?—I think they regulate each other.

9442. If one was lower, you think the other would be lower too?—There is a point beyond which we cannot go; I have stated that if the price of organzine thrown silk was reduced to the manufacturer by the amount of duty repealed, the English throwster would of course be obliged to sell at the same price, or not to sell at all; and I say he cannot sell at the same price.

9443. To what countries do you export your goods?—They go to different markets.

9444. Do they go to the Continent or to America?—I export them wherever I can; across the Atlantic, or elsewhere.

9445. Do they come in competition with any French goods, or do the French make no goods similar to ours?—They come into competition with French and German goods.

9446. Made from the same silk?—I cannot say what they make their goods from.

9447. Do you export to a country where there is no competition?—I export to a country where there is great competition, but to which I could not export till the drawback was allowed.

9448. Do you not think that our manufacturers of broad goods, if they could manufacture 3*s.* cheaper, could export as well as you?—Yes, if they could manufacture 3*s.* cheaper. I have the drawback, or I could not export.

9449. You do not mean to say that the manufacturer of broad goods making at 3*s.* a pound less, would be able to export against France and Germany?—I had rather not give an opinion more decidedly upon broad goods, not calling myself a manufacturer of such goods.

9450. Do you know by experience, whether you should be able to do so yourself?—We do know that broad goods are exported, and that the export is increasing.

9451. What description of broad goods are exported?—I can speak from what I hear, of our gros de Naples.

9452. Of the best sorts, or otherwise?—I cannot say.

9453. Are they not of inferior kinds?—I conceive that generally for the foreign markets they will be the lower priced goods.

9454. Are they not made from Bengal silk, both warp and shute?—No, I think not; I think they are made of Italian silk, China silk and Bengal.

9455. Have you ever exported any of those you have manufactured?—Yes.

9456. Of what silk were they made?—Both of Italian and Bengal silk.

9457. Did they go to those markets to which you sent those narrow goods?—Yes.

9458. Is it not the case, that those broad goods which are exported, are sent frequently when there is a great depression, and at a sacrifice?—A good deal will depend upon the state of the American markets; if they are very bare of goods, they will of course give a better price for them than when their market is in a different state.

9459. Are the broad goods you manufacture all plain?—Yes, they are.

9460. You are understood to have stated, that a reduction of duty would not lower the price, has that been the case since the duty was lowered from 5*s.* to its present state; if 3*s.* 6*d.* was taken off what would keep it up?—If it were reduced

by

Mr.
*William Harter.*

25 June,
1832.

by the amount of the duty, the English throwster could not sell to a profit, and therefore he must give up the trade.

9461. The question relates to the manufacturer who works up the Italian silk; are you deliberately of opinion, that if this 3 *s*. 6 *d*. was taken off Italian thrown silk, the price would not be reduced?—I am deliberately of opinion, that if 3 *s*. 6 *d*. was taken off Italian thrown silk, the price would be very little reduced.

9462. What would keep it up?—It would be kept up, I think, in this way; the English throwster could not sell his silk at the same price as the Italian, and he must give up throwing.

9463. Are the Committee to understand that the price of thrown silk is regulated by what the English throwster can sell it for?—It is regulated by the supply and the demand; I mean to say, that if he does not sell to a profit, he must give up the trade; but he would not for some time come down in his price so low as not to leave him a profit; I shall be shortly both a throwster and a manufacturer, if I thought we should have foreign throwns considerably lower by the effect of the reduction of duty, I should not think of throwing my own silk, because I believe I could not throw at the same price as the foreign throwster.

9464. You were understood to say, that if the duty was taken off Italian thrown, the price of thrown would not fall, but the English throwster would keep it up; if so, does not the English throwster regulate the price?—I say that the English and Foreign throwster, by their competition, keep down the price of organzine to the weaver.

9465. You were understood to say, that if the duty was taken off, the price of Italian thrown would not decrease?—I say it would not fall immediately.

9466. What then is that which keeps it up?—The present duty may keep it up.

9467. Supposing the present duty of 3 *s*. 6 *d*. taken off, are you still of the opinion you gave, that the price of thrown silk would not come down, or would come down very little?—I think it would not come down much, and I explain it in this way; if that measure were put in force, the English throwster would see that he had a very poor chance in this market, and he would restrict his operations; I conceive we should have a very great additional supply of foreign thrown organzine, and the English throwster would see it come in at a price at which he could not afford to sell.

9468. You say that the English manufacturer has a disadvantage in paying 1 *s*. 2 *d*. in the pound more than the French, how do you make that out?—I think the answer was, that Italian raw silk costs so much more in this country than in Italy.

9469. The question referred to the advantage of the French manufacturer over the English; how is it that we in London pay more for silk than the French do at Lyons?—I admit that the French pay a duty on a small portion of their silk, say one-fourth or one-fifth, but we are taxed upon all ours.

9470. Are you able to say whether the duty paid on the importation of silk into France does not raise the price of all the silk consumed in France?—I am not able to answer that question.

9471. Are you aware of the quality of the bulk of silk used in France, as compared with the Italian imported?—It is said that they have a quality very superior to any produced in Italy or elsewhere.

9472. That is understood to be very small in quantity?—Yes; but taking into account its extreme fineness, the quantity cannot be called small.

9473. The question refers to the bulk of that used?—I am led to believe it is better generally, but I have no knowledge of the fact.

9474. You cannot state how the price of silk should be lower in France than in England, except that you believe that the small quantity imported from Italy pays a duty, you do not think that affects the rest?—I think the French have a better market at home, or why do not they go to the East Indies for their silk, or to China, or come to England for it, to our East India sales.

9475. You state, that we in England receive our Italian silk, paying 1 *s*. 2 *d*. more than the French manufacturers do, will you explain that?—I believe that we pay 1 *s*. 2 *d*. here more than the price in Italy.

9476. The importation of Italian silk into France is subject, as far as Italy is concerned, to the same duty as it is coming into this country, the only increase we have here is from the increase of charge?—I spoke generally, when I said that they had their silk cheaper than we had.

9477. You

Mr.
*William Harter.*

25 June,
1832.

9477. You have been asked why you thought that a reduction of duty on the thrown silk would not be followed by a diminution in the price of raw silk, will not every 6 *d.* per pound reduction of duty on thrown, add to the price of raw, and thus keep up the price of raw ?— It is difficult to say what may be the precise effect of a larger importation of thrown upon the import of raws, possibly it may have the effect the question supposes; I can answer the question only in this general way, if the Italians found a better market here for their thrown silk, of course they would throw more and send us less raw.

9478. What is your opinion with regard to the price of thrown, will not the price they can get for thrown depend upon the price they can get for their silk in other parts of the world ?—Certainly, in some measure.

9479. Then must not the London market be on a par with the other markets ?— Notwithstanding the organzine is subject to a duty of 3 *s.* 6 *d.* a pound, it comes in in considerable quantities, and I believe it does not pay that duty in other countries, therefore it comes here in spite of the duty.

9480. If it does not pay duty in other countries, why does not it go to those other countries ?—That is a difficulty I cannot solve.

9481. Every diminution of duty will raise the price of the raw in Italy, will it not?—That appears not unlikely to be the effect.

9482. If you did not export your goods, would they not add to the glut at home, and so far does not the drawback relieve the manufacturer for home market?— Undoubtedly.

9483. Did not your predecessors largely export goods before 1824, when there was a drawback or bounty on the export?—I exported myself previous to 1824.

9484. Your predecessors did before you?—I believe they did.

9485. In 1824, when this was discontinued, did not that export trade cease, or nearly so ?—It did, certainly.

9486. A great deal has been said about the a-la-bar loom; is that modern, or did you see it at work 20 years ago?—It has been at work 20 years to my knowledge.

9487. Do you not think if the a-la-bar loom was used at Coventry, they would be able to compete with France ?—I cannot say.

9488. Have you applied the a-la-bar looms to the fancy ribbons?—I do not make them.

9489. Were not the weavers of broad goods earning very low wages, and were they not in great distress during last winter ?—The wages of broad goods weavers are certainly not high, so far as I am acquainted with them, and they have a tendency to sink lower and lower; I believe they were very much distressed last winter.

9490. Do you think forty looms is the extent there has ever been in Spitalfields in galloons?—I think there were many more 10 years ago, but I cannot answer that question with certainty, for I am not informed.

9491. You are quite certain that the manufacture of galloons is carried on in Spitalfields?—It is carried on by Spitalfields' houses; I believe the manufacture is carried on by them now principally in other places, Reading, Devonshire, and so on; there are still some looms in Spitalfields, but I do not know how many.

9492. Do you know when the manufacture was carried on in Spitalfields to any extent?—No, I do not.

9493. You stated 4 *s.* as the price for the throwing Italian silk, you probably spoke of 26 to 30 deniers; do you think that 4 *s.* would be sufficient for throwing 18 to 22 deniers fine organzine?—I have stated before, that I am not a throwster, and therefore cannot answer those questions so accurately, but I should think 4 *s.* would be an exceedingly low price for that size of organzine.

9494. Have you had any from 18 to 22 thrown?—I do not know that I have, but I know pretty well what the thing is.

9495. Are there any 18 to 22 used at Manchester?—Eighteen is a very fine size; I should almost doubt it.

9496. You do not use any yourself?—No.

9497. What is the size you use?—All sizes, from 22 to upwards of 100.

9498. What is the price of throwing your ordinary size?—The trade has been so depressed among the throwsters latterly, that I could have it thrown almost at my own price.

9499. You say that your goods are chiefly manufactured by power-looms, and that you have introduced them about two years and a half, what proportion of

678.

Mr.
*William Harter.*

25 June,
1832.

persons are thrown out of work in your manufactory by working power-looms instead of hand-looms?—I do not think one; I employ as many hands, but they produce more goods.

9500. What increase of goods are you enabled to make by power-looms with the same number of hands?—It will not make a very great difference if a weaver is determined to work, though as it is much easier to weave by power, much less laborious than by hand, generally they will do more work by power than by hand; a man cannot have his mind and body always on the stretch.

9501. Do you pay the same wages to the man who superintends a power-loom as the man who superintends a hand-loom?—No, not so high wages.

9502. Does it require as good a workman?—Yes, very nearly.

9503. As experienced a man?—Yes, or very nearly.

9504. Do you employ the power-loom for your broad goods?—I do not.

9505. Have you heard of any case?—I have heard of one or two cases.

9506. Have you known it applied to the Jacquard loom?—No, I have not, nor do I think it is.

9507. What is the increase of throwing in Manchester and its neighbourhood? —Of the 12 I have named, one mill is not in work as far as relates to throwing; I cannot state the precise increase, I can state when the mills were erected, or pretty nearly so.

9508. What quantity of silk do you suppose the Manchester mills to turn off?— It has been stated to me that they may turn off about 350,000 lbs. per annum, that I think is pretty near the mark.

9509. How many horses' power is employed in all the silk mills at Manchester? —At almost all those mills they have more power than they use, what they call spare power; I suppose they could apply 300 horse power, but I should doubt whether more than half that is actually employed.

9510. Suppose the situation of 100 of your weavers making galloons and doubles under the old system, and making them in your mill, what would be the increase of quantity of work made in a week?—They would produce, I dare say, about one-fourth more.

9511. Not more than that?—Not more than that on the average, I should think.

9512. What proportion of the 350,000 turned out by mills at Manchester, is Italian?—I am not able to answer that.

9513. Do you think the proportion is large or small?—I think a large proportion.

9514. Have they not turned out a much larger quantity of silk when there was an increased demand?—I think that very likely, by working longer hours; I believe what I have stated is about the quantity they have thrown latterly. I do not know whether they have been in full work or not.

9515. You spoke of 350,000 lbs. thrown at Manchester, that is only one-tenth of the whole 3,500,000 lbs. consumed in this country. Manchester therefore has not absorbed the throwing trade of England?—It does appear to be about one-tenth of the whole quantity, but in the 3,500,000 the throwns are included.

### Mr. *Henry Tootal*, called in; and Examined.

Mr.
*Henry Tootal.*

9516. YOU are a silk manufacturer and throwster at Manchester, are you not?— I am; but I beg to observe that, not expecting to be called upon to-day, I have not brought with me some memorandums which I am anxious to have; however, if the Committee wish it I will go on.

9517. How long have you been engaged in those trades?—I commenced manufacturing in 1816.

9518. Have you a recollection of the general state of the trade in Manchester at that time?—The trade at that time was very limited, both in point of variety and extent.

9519. Do you recollect what description of goods were made at that time?— Silk handkerchiefs principally, as well as goods mixed with other materials.

9520. Were there any gros de Naples manufactured at that time?—None that I ever heard of.

9521. Were there any sarsnets?—Not that I am aware of.

9522. When were the first gros de Naples made at Manchester?—To the best of my recollection it might be in 1822; but it was not until 1824 that any quantity was produced.

9523. Do

Mr.
*Henry Tootal.*

25 June,
1832.

9523. Do you know what number of silk, and silk and cotton looms, were at work in Manchester in 1823?—On referring to a memorandum made some years ago, I find the looms employed in 1823 in weaving entire silk goods were about 2,500; and in making silk, mixed with other materials, about 3,000.

9524. What description of goods were made at this time?—Principally silk handkerchiefs and figured sarsnets; some gros de Naples were also made.

9525. Those were articles composed of silk only?—Yes; and in mixed goods, poplins, an article composed of silk and worsted, as well as silk and cotton goods, both for shawls and garments, &c.

9526. What do you mean by poplins?—An article made of silk and worsted, the manufacture of which had previously been principally confined to Dublin.

9527. Can you state the number of looms in 1824?—I cannot state the precise number, but it was very much increased over 1823.

9528. To what do you attribute this great increase?—To the reduction of duty on the raw material.

9529. Can you state the number of looms employed in 1828?—I estimate the number of looms in 1828 at about 8,000 for weaving goods composed entirely of silk, and of mixed goods about 4,000.

9530. Do you recollect the description of goods principally made at that time? —The principal article manufactured in the trade at that time was plain gros de Naples and a few figured ones also.

9531. Were not there many plain sarsnets making in Manchester from 1816 to 1823?—None that I am aware of; but for many previous years silk handkerchiefs had been made there.

9532. Was the Jacquard machine in use in 1828?—Partially, a few were in use; I should think the number did not exceed thirty, or thereabout.

9533. Can you state the number of looms in work at the present time?—I believe the number of looms now employed to be about 14,000; that includes mixed as well as entire silk goods.

9534. Can you state the proportions?—From eight to nine thousand entirely silk, and from five to six of mixed goods.

9535. What is the description of goods principally made now?—Principally plain gros de Naples, some figured also.

9536. Is the Jacquard machine much used now in Manchester?—The Jacquard is now getting into pretty general use.

9537. For the manufacture of silk goods or mixed?—Both.

9538. How many do you suppose are used in the manufacture of silk?—I should think not many; probably not more than sixty.

9539. The Jacquard loom is almost entirely used for figured goods, is it not?— Entirely so.

9540. What is the total number of Jacquard looms now employed?—I should say from 6 to 700 employed in Manchester and the neighbourhood.

9541. In what period has that increase taken place?—Since September last year two-thirds of them at least, or probably more than that.

9542. Are you of opinion that sixty are employed on goods all silk?—In giving that number, I must state that it is wholly from memory; I have no memorandum, that is the impression on my mind.

9543. Are the remaining number of 550, or whatever it may be, employed in the manufacture of goods, of which silk is a component part?—Certainly, entirely so.

9544. You say that increase has taken place chiefly since September 1831? —Yes.

9545. That goes to show a great increase of a particular description of articles in the trade?—Yes; the figured silks, and silk and cotton goods; a pattern of the latter I beg leave to show to the Committee.

9546. Taking a piece of that article, what drawback on export would it be entitled to; and supposing it to be made from foreign thrown silk, what duty on import would the silk in that piece pay?—The piece, of 42 yards, would weigh from three to three and a half lbs.; the drawback at 1 s. 2 d. per lb. would be from 3 s. 6 d. to 4 s., and the duty levied on the silk imported (being one lb. eight ounces, at 3 s. 6 d. duty) would be 5 s. 3 d.

9547. Are not those goods an invention of your own house?—I believe they are.

678.

9548. You

Mr.
*Henry Tootal.*
___

25 June,
1832.

9548. You do not expect them to interfere with the rich manufactured silks coming from France, do you?—They are calculated for the higher classes.

9549. What is the price per yard?—The lowest price we have ever sold at is 2 s.

9550. What is the price of the richest silk of France three double?—I can only say what I suppose it to be, probably 4 s. 6 d. per yard.

9551. Do you mean the selling or cost price?—I mean the selling price.

9552. What do you suppose to be the cost of the Jacquard machines when ready for work?—The cost will vary considerably, according to the extent of the pattern, from 15 l. to 30 l. each.

9553. Are there any very rich figured silk manufacturers at Manchester?—There are.

9554. What number of looms do you suppose are employed in that manufacture?—I do not know.

9555. Is there any considerable number employed?—I should think not, though we employ some ourselves; and here, with permission of the Committee, I would beg leave to present for their inspection a pattern of rich figured gros de Naples made by the Jacquard machine, and woven at Manchester, a dress of which the Queen has condescended to accept and wear; and I would also take this opportunity of stating, that though a good deal has been said about Manchester making nothing but inferior goods, yet if rich goods were wanted, her capability of making them is undoubted, as this pattern will prove.

9556. Will you state the rate of wages paid for weaving plain gros de Naples in 1823, 1828, and at the present time?—In the year 1823, for a twenty hundred three single gros de Naples, the price was 9 d.; in 1828, 6 d.; and now it is 4½ d. the same article.

9557. Equally well manufactured in each case?—Certainly.

9558. By the same machinery?—Simply the loom.

9559. No application of power?—None.

9560. How many yards do you conceive a fair workman would weave in a day?—An active workman will weave something more than six yards per day, between six and seven yards per day, which at 4½ d. will be from 13 s. to 14 s, a week.

9561. Do you supply the loom?—No; the weaver finds his own loom, we supply him with the harness and reed; out of that he will have to pay 1 s. 6 d. a week for winding, and it will occupy him, I calculate, half a day in the week to go to and from the warehouse for his work and to twist in his warp; that will require to deduct 1 s. 6 d. a week and the loss of half a day's labour, bringing down his weekly earning so much; a child of twelve years of age will wind for three looms.

9562. What number of hours would he work for that?—I consider that he would have to work from twelve to fourteen hours.

9563. Exclusive of stoppages for meals, or inclusive?—Inclusive.

9564. Is there any deduction for hire of the loom?—I am supposing the loom as belonging to the weaver, so that he has that outlay himself.

9565. Do you know at what the hire of a loom is reckoned?—I do not.

9566. What do you consider the loom standing to be worth; do you think he pays 5 l. a year more than he would merely for his own accommodation?—I cannot say; I think not so much.

9567. Do you make a deduction for candles?—I do not.

9568. Do the weavers earn as much less now as the fall in the price a yard would indicate?—I think not.

9569. Why not?—Because the weaver works a longer time now than formerly; he is compelled to do so.

9570. Is it not necessary that he should rent a room for his loom, and that he should be cleanly and use soap, and that he should have fuel, candles or oil; and will not all those form a considerable amount in the shape of deduction?—All those things enumerated will be necessary for him in order to do his work; as to room rent I do not know what that will be. In my former answer I supposed it to be the individual's own loom; a room for his loom must of course add to his expenses.

9571. Would there not be an increased consumption of those articles, oil, fire and so on, if he were required to work a greater number of hours per day?—Certainly, in the winter season.

9572. Has there been any diminution in the price of these at all corresponding
with

Mr.
*Henry Tootal.*

25 June,
1832.

with the reduction of his wages?—If I answer at all, I must answer on general principles; my impression is that most of those articles are lower than they were some years ago.

9573. Have they fallen 5c per cent. as his wages have?—I cannot answer that question.

9574. Can you inform the Committee what quantity of silk is annually consumed in Manchester?—That is a point which it is very difficult to ascertain; I have given myself some trouble to endeavour to do so, and my impression is, that it is between seven and eight hundred thousand lbs. per annum.

9575. What proportion does the quantity thrown in Manchester bear to the quantity of foreign thrown silk imported?—The quantity thrown in Manchester has been stated to be 350,000 lbs., I make it a little more; and the average of the last three years import is, by official documents, stated to be 374,000 lbs.

9576. Is any foreign thrown silk used in Manchester; and can you tell about what proportion, as compared with British?—Foreign thrown silk is frequently used in Manchester, but I cannot state the proportion. I know about the end of 1830, and the beginning of 1831, the quantity used was about 3,000 lbs. per week.

9577. Since that time it must have increased?—During some periods of 1831 the quantity would be larger than that.

9578. Are any goods exported which are made from foreign thrown silk?—Yes, certainly; gros de Naples are made from foreign thrown silk, and a good many of these goods are exported.

9579. Have you any means of stating what proportion of the value of manufactured silk goods you consider to be labour?—I believe that the amount of labour expended will be about 80 per cent. on goods made of silk entirely.

9580. Do you speak with reference to the present low rate of wages?—Yes; I also take the silk as raw, not as organzine.

9581-1. Then in the 80 per cent. is included the throwing?—Yes; in taking that 80 per cent. there must be a good deal of English thrown silk.

9581-2. British?—It must be all British thrown silk.

9582. What do you consider to be the proportion on mixed?—About 150 per cent.

9583. There is some difference when you say in the mixed, between that which is mixed with cotton and that which is mixed with woollen?—Yes, there is now very little mixture of silk with woollen in Manchester.

9584. The manufacture of poplin is given up?—Yes, it is worn out.

9585. Is there not an article called waste silk, worth from 3 s. to 3 s. 6 d. a lb., and which, on exportation, receives a drawback of 3 s. 6 d. a lb.?—Goods made from waste silk are frequently exported, and do receive a drawback as described, but this requires explanation. Waste, as its name implies, is waste caused partly in the process of throwing, after which it is spun over again, and in which process it loses one half its weight; so that two lbs. of waste will produce only one lb. of silk in the state in which it is applied to the manufacture before being exported; that calculation will show that, exclusive of labour, it is raised to double its original value; and before the goods are exported the labour expended upon them will be about 250 per cent., thereby raising the goods in value to the amount required by Act of Parliament to enable them to claim drawback. I thought it important to mention this point, as the article had been adverted to in former evidence, and not put in its true light.

9586. What description of manufacture does it employ?—Silk handkerchiefs mostly.

9587. Is it not employed in hosiery also?—I believe it is, as well as gloves.

9588. Do you know what number of throwing mills there were in Manchester, and the neighbourhood, in 1823?—The number of silk mills in 1823 was, I believe, only two.

9589. Do you know how many there are now in Manchester, and the neighbourhood?—I believe there are now ten mills at work, and two not yet completed.

9590. Can you state the number of spindles at work in those mills, and the number of hands employed?—I believe the number of spindles to be about 7,000 dozen, and the number of hands employed upon them from 3,500 to 3,700.

9591. Can you state what are the weekly earnings of persons employed in those mills?—The earnings vary materially, according to age and ability. I hold in my

hand

hand the particulars of a mill, containing about 700 dozen ; the number of persons, employed, and the rate of wages given in Manchester :

|  |  |  | s. | d. |  | s. | d. |  |
|---|---|---|---|---|---|---|---|---|
| No. 1.—Under 9 years of age - - - | 14 persons from | 1 | 6 | to | 2 | 6 | per week. |
| No. 2.—Above 9 and under 16 years - | 148 - „ - | - 2 | - | to | 5 | - | „ |
| No. 3.— - - - - - - - - - | 50 - „ - | - 2 | - | to | 8 | 6 | „ |
| No. 4.— - - - - - - - - - | 59 - „ - | - 2 | - | to | 9 | - | „ |
| No. 5.—Above 16 years old - - - - | 6 - „ - | - 8 | - | to 10 | - | „ |
| No. 6.— - - - - - - - - - | 57 - „ - | - 6 | - | to 10 | - | „ |
| No. 7.— - - - - - - - - - | 6 - „ - | - 12 | - | to 16 | - | „ |
| No. 8.— - - - - - - - - - | 8 - „ - | - 18 | - | to 27 | - | „ |

348

Commence working at six in the morning, and leave off at seven in the evening : allow for meals one hour and forty minutes.

No. 1.—Engine Piecers.
2.—          „
3.—Cleaners and Doublers.
4.—Throwing Lads (as well as spinning.)
5.—          „
6.—Doublers, Danters, &c.
7.—Sundry Men⎱Overlookers, &c. average under
8.—     „    ⎰  4s. 9d. each.

9592. Are not those earnings considerably less than in a cotton mill?—The average is lower than in a cotton mill, decidedly.

9593. Are you not of opinion the wages at Manchester, in the silk branch of the trade, are as low as they possibly can be reduced to allow of a man's living at all?—I should say that the wages are exceedingly low; I should be very glad to see them higher.

9594. When the people work short time, are their wages reduced?—I conceive so.

9595. What is the present condition of the silk trade in Manchester; is it very much depressed, or is it improving?—There is considerable activity in it just now, particularly in the plain trade; wages are low; but those in the trade are anxious to keep their workmen at work if possible; I should not say that it was otherwise than active.

9596. What are the wages this year, compared with what they were two or three years ago?—In 1828 and 1829, the prices paid would be pretty much alike; 1829 was a year of not so great activity, and workmen might have more waiting for work in consequence.

9597. Were the receipts of the principal workmen more than in the present year, do you think?—I should fancy not.

9598. What were they in 1830; were they more than they are this year — It is purely matter of memory, but I think they would be something more than now; the trade was in a state of great activity.

9599. Was it in 1831 in a state of greater activity than now?—Beginning about March 1831, the silk trade was in a very dull state, and continued so during all that year.

9600. Is it again more active this year?—It is.

9601. When you say they are in a state of great activity, do you allude to the present moment?—Yes.

9602. Were they not in a state of great depression from November up to March?—Probably not so long as that, but there was more activity after the February sale.

9603. Do you expect it to continue in its present state of activity?—I have no reason to think otherwise.

9604. What is the present state of the stocks of manufactured goods at Manchester?—I believe small.

9605. You have spoke of the earnings of these people per week; they were most of them out of work a considerable number of weeks during the last year, were they not?—A great many were out of work during the winter.

9606. Their

Mr.
Henry Tootal.

25 June.
1832.

9606. Their earnings being so small, they are in a state of great destitution when they are out of work?—Certainly.

9607. Do you export any of the plain goods you make yourself?—I cannot say we have not exported. In 1829, in consequence of the drawback system coming into operation, our house thought it very likely that we might be enabled to compete with the French manufactures; and, in consequence, we made several small adventures to various parts of the world, but more particularly to the Americas. Our object in doing so was, if the result were favourable, to exhibit those accounts to our friends, in order to induce them to ship (that being a business we do not wish to follow.) In some cases the results were favourable; in others not so.

9608. Were you able, as regards the price, to judge from those exports, how near you came to your competitors?—We got orders in consequence of those accounts; and those orders in many instances have been repeated.

9609. Do you mean orders for plain gros de Naples, or richer goods?—In plain gros de Naples, and in other goods also.

9610. Do not the Americans come to you who went formerly to France?—That is the case in a great many instances.

9611. Are those demands from America increasing?—The trade with America is understood not to have been good during the spring of this year; the export last year was very considerable, but in this not so much so.

9612. Have you had any quotation of the prices in America, of the articles sent from France and from this country?—It is very difficult to form an estimate of the two, without patterns; I can only say that the Americans are now taking gros de Naples and other articles, and the orders are repeated.

9613. If the duty was taken off on organzine, what effect do you think that would have upon your trade as a manufacturer?—If I could be quite certain that the taking off the duty would lower the article to the extent of 3 s. 6 d. a pound, it would be my interest to have it so, and I should wish it.

9614. You doubt whether there would be so much benefit by the taking off the duty, as you derive from the drawback?—I very much doubt whether the price would be lowered to that extent, by taking off the duty.

9615. Do you think the bounty has an effect in increasing the exportation of gros de Naples?—I think it has; I have no doubt of it.

---

## Mercurii, 27° die Junii, 1832.

### JAMES A. STEWART MACKENZIE, ESQUIRE, in the Chair.

*John Bowring,* Esquire, LL.D. again called in; and Examined.

John Bowring,
Esq. LL. D.

27 June,
1832.

9616. ARE not the silk goods imported into this country from France chiefly of the finer descriptions?—I should judge they are; but as I have put in Official Tables, I desire to refer, in all matters of fact, to those Tables, which will show the particular qualities as far as they can be ascertained.

9617. Are not the silk goods exported from England to France of a coarse and heavy description, particularly bandannas?—I believe so; but I should state, with reference to the importation of bandannas, that I understand from a French importer the improvements which have been made in England are so striking, that the demand had been continually increasing, and is at this moment greater than ever.

9618. Are you aware that the improvement is principally in the designs, and consequently in the printing?—All my evidence goes to establish the fact, that there has been a great improvement in this very particular since the introduction of French goods; and I stated, in illustration, that there was no importation of English bandannas into France before the period of the legal introduction of French goods into England.

9619. At all events, as far as the inquiry of this Committee is concerned, the proportion of labour in the goods exchanged between the two countries is the reverse of the statement you have made, is it not?—That may be as to one article, but the quantity of silk goods that France takes is, up to this moment, not large; my observation with respect to the importation by France of silk goods from England is, that that importation is going on rapidly increasing. I have not stated that in those particular silk goods there is a greater quantity of labour than in the silk goods England takes from France; my statement is a general statement, and it shows

that

*John Bowring,*
Esq. LL. D.
———
27 June,
1832.

that, taking in the whole amount of exports and the whole amount of imports, the proportion of manufacturing labour sent from England is double the proportion of manufacturing labour received from France.

9620. Are you aware that in the value of the bandannas labour forms a very small proportion of the value of the article exported?—I am not capable of giving an estimate with respect to an article into the manufacture of which I have not inquired.

9621. Are you aware that the value of a piece of bandanna when printed and completed is about 25 *s.*?—I should suppose so.

9622. Are you aware that a piece of bandanna will weigh about eight ounces?—I am not.

9623. Are you aware that the price of making that eight ounces of silk into a piece of bandanna is only 2 *s.*?—I am not cognizant of such facts as imply a knowledge of the details of English silk manufacture; I desire my evidence should be considered as having no other reference to England than as furnishing means of comparison between France and England; I have not at all examined the English silk manufacture, information respecting which can be better gathered from other sources. I give the opinions which I have formed from the investigation of the French silk manufacture. The whole amount of silks exported from England to France is indeed small, but it is an export that is considerably increasing. What I intended to show the Committee was this fact, that in consequence of improvement, demand had grown up in France for a particular English article; and as respects the general subject, I stated that the demand for English products in France was the consequence of a similar demand growing up in England for French articles; that in the English articles labour formed a very large proportion of its value, and that the raw material formed a very small proportion, while, as respected the imports into England from France, the raw material formed a very large proportion of the value, larger than in any other manufactured stuff with which I am acquainted, cashmire only excepted, and that the quantity of labour was relatively small.

9624. You do not mean to adhere to your last answer, with respect to our silk trade?—I have never said that the quantity of labour in English silk goods exported is equal to that in French silk goods imported; my representation as respects the imports into France of English silk goods is just this, that whereas a few years ago the demand was exceedingly small, it is now constantly increasing.

9625. You stated that the value of French silk goods exported to England last year was about 18 millions of francs, that the English silk goods exported to France was about 640,000, so that it appears, as far as respects the silk trade, the quantity exported from each country is 28 to 1 in favour of France, besides the disproportion of labour referred to in the last question?—Certainly; but there is one circumstance which bears upon that question, namely, that while the exportation from England to France is an increasing exportation, that is, compared with 1828, the importation into England was not larger in 1831 than in 1828; there has been a progressive increase of exports of silk goods into France from England, and not a progressive increase of exports into England from France. In 1828 the quantity of goods imported into England from France was about the quantity imported in 1831; whereas during the same period, if the French returns be compared, it will be found there has been a progressive augmentation in the importation of English silk goods into France. The fact is rather to be taken as evidence of the improvement, and an irresistible fact it is, than as proving any thing else; it shows that there has been some improvement introduced in the last five or six years in England, whether it refers to the loom or to the figure, which did not exist before, and which has led to an increased reputation of the English manufacture. I can speak from observation, that the English bandannas are altogether of a different character from the character they had before the importation of foreign silk goods was allowed: no gentleman did then wear an English bandanna; they were so worthless, that to carry them was almost disgraceful, and every body was supplied with a smuggled article. Now this is no longer the case; we buy the English bandannas, believing them to be better than the Oriental. Six or eight years ago we did not think so.

9626. Is it not the case, that in many instances those sold as English bandannas are imported plain, and printed here?—Perhaps that may be, but that very printing is the introduction of a portion of that skill which was wanting to our manufacture, and whose absence is felt in so many other departments; a great many impediments and restrictions have been removed, and a great impulse given to improvement; this

has

has operated beneficially every where, first upon the raw material, and afterwards on the whole course of production from beginning to end.

*John Bowring,* Esq. LL. D.

27 June, 1832.

9627. Are you aware that the increase in the quantity of silk used in the years immediately prior to the prohibition being removed was considerably larger than it has been since?—I should be very much surprised if the official returns show that.

9628. It appears in Mr. Hume's evidence, that in the years 1815, 1816 and 1817, the amount of raw silk imported was 1,095,000 lbs.; in the years 1821, 1822 and 1823, the quantity was 1,970,000 lbs.; in the last three years, 1829, 1830 and 1831, the quantity is 3,075,000 lbs.?—It appears to me, that the way to come to a correct estimate is to take the same number of years preceding and subsequent to the introduction of French goods; to form two averages from them, and then compare the results. It will then be seen whether the average amount was greater or not before the period of 1826 than it has been since, and I should anticipate that the facts will show a great increase since that period; the safest way to judge is to take as an average the same number of years before the legal entry which have passed since the removal of the prohibition; the number in each case being seven years, I find that the average before the removal of the prohibition will give somewhat less than two millions of lbs.; that the average importation since the introduction of French manufactured silk is about three millions of lbs.

9629. Are you aware that the previous seven years was burthened with a duty of 5s. 6d. on the raw silk and 14s. 10d. on the thrown?—Certainly; that is a circumstance to be taken into the account, and I do not think the old legislation is to be justified, since to oppress the raw material with a fiscal burden is exceedingly injurious to the developement of industry; but after all the great result is, that since the admission of French goods, there has been an average increase of importation of more than a million of lbs. of silk per annum.

9630. Is not the waste a much greater quantity in the latter period than the former?—Yes, it was inconsiderable in the first part of the period, and taking in the increased quantity of waste, the argument will be much stronger; for as I had not estimated the waste, if that be added to the calculation, the increased importation will be a million and a half instead of a million.

9631. You have stated that the French silk manufacture has obtained a foreign trade, because it has had less protection than other French manufactures have; do you really think that the acquisition of a foreign trade is to be attributed to this cause rather than to the great advantages you have already described as being possessed by the French manufacturer?—My statement is, that the existence of a foreign trade is impossible, or rather is wholly incompatible with the existence of a protecting system; this argument may be put in a shape that is absolute demonstration; protection implies the necessity of a price beyond the average price; if the price be not beyond the average price, protection is mere waste of words; now I stated with regard to France, that 11-14ths of her silk trade is foreign trade; that the whole consumption of silk manufacture in France being only 3-14ths, the great advantage they have is the demand of the whole world; now a home and protected trade is limited to the home demand; and if any gentleman is able to show, that to sell to 24 million of buyers in Great Britain is better than to be able to sell to all the buyers in the world at large, I shall agree that a limited protected home trade is a better one to the manufacturer than an unbounded but unprotected foreign trade; my opinion, grounded on the facts we possess, is far different.

9632. You stated that France has, owing to the want of protection, been obliged to adopt every foreign improvement, what foreign improvements or inventions do you refer to?—I stated not that she had been obliged to adopt every foreign improvement, but that every foreign improvement that had been adopted had been forced upon her by the unprotected position of her silk trade; the bar loom, which was a most remarkable improvement, was a foreign improvement; I mentioned that even the Jacquard machine was in reality the result of an English suggestion; and I also stated with reference to her schools of art, that most of the professors are travelled professors, who have visited foreign countries to gather information, which they turn to account at home.

9633. When you speak of the French silk trade as having so little protection, do you not think the following are great advantages, and operate to great protection: the possession of the best raw material in the world; the exclusive use of it; the public establishment of schools of design, painting, botany, &c. and the prohibition of the silk manufactures of China and Bengal, and of the mixed silk and cotton,

678. and

*John Bowring,*
Esq. LL. D.

27 June.
1832.

and silk and worsted goods of this country, and a duty upon the silk manufactures of all other countries sufficient to protect her from all injurious competition?—I must answer that seriatim; I should say generally that honourable Members will be aware there can be no trade at all, but a trade which represents some superiority; that unless a nation had an advantage over another nation it would never have any intercourse with another nation; that the result of equality would be the destruction of all barter, so that we should be compelled to do every thing ourselves and reduced to something lower than the primitive state. Unless we could find individuals possessing greater advantages than ourselves, there would be an end to every species of intercourse, whether trading or social; as to these particular points, I have stated that the French have a considerable advantage in the possession of the superior qualities of silk, and the exclusive use of it, and to that extent the privilege of a monopoly; but even this monopoly I conceive to be a benefit of a very temporary and doubtful character, for it is my belief that if restrictions were removed (and I have used that argument with some effect I believe to those who are concerned,) that if the impediments to the exportation of French silk were removed, it would be a boon to the silk growers, and ultimately a boon to the silk manufacturers themselves. The cultivation of their silk, which is even at this moment exceedingly valuable and productive to France, does not receive the developement of which it is capable in consequence of the impossibility of exporting the silk produced; there is thus a check on the growth of that article for whose production France is so singularly apt. With respect to the prohibition of China and Bengal manufactures, I hold it to be an unquestionable principle that any prohibition of a foreign article is in the long run baneful to the manufacture, for in truth that which is called protection is nothing more nor less than the shutting out the means of knowledge, and the throwing a protecting circle round ignorance and retardation; the same argument applies to the prohibition of cotton and worsted manufactures in France; the cotton and worsted manufacture in France is in great distress, a distress which arises mainly from the false direction given to labour by the interference of the Government.

9634. The silk trade of France is also protected by a duty, as against Germany and Switzerland?—Yes, but the duty is small.

9635. And it flourishes in a degree superior to any other country with the advantage of that protection, does it not?—It owes nothing to protection—nothing,—but as to duties, there is another matter involved in the consideration, which is the question of revenue, and it is a question which ought not to be lost sight of; I do not believe that so small a duty would have satisfied manufacturers who demanded protection; it may have been looked to as a source of revenue, and I think foreign manufactures might be reasonably made to pay a duty as an excellent means of providing revenue supplies; but I cannot admit the title of a manufacturer to put that duty into his pocket under the name of a protection, which might have been levied on the imported articles for the public benefit. It is in fact an absorption of the national resources by a private and sinister interest.

9636. You have stated that the number of looms in Lyons, in 1825, was 20,000, can you state what was the number at St. Etienne at that period?—I have no other facts on this subject than those I have given in.

9637. It appears that since the opening of the English ports to French silk, the number of looms at Lyons has increased from 20 to 35,000?—I have stated with respect to the returns previous to 1831, that great uncertainty prevails; I believe the first regular and official statistics were those made lately by the prefect, and which I have presented; previously to that period I am not sure that any official statement exists, and I think any conclusions founded on the former state of things would be liable to many errors.

9638. You conceive that the French manufacture has greatly increased?—I have no doubt it is increased in certain articles.

9639. Have you any doubt of its great increase at St. Etienne?—None at all.

9640. In what has it decreased?—It has decreased in the manufacture of low inferior articles, and even now a great many French manufacturers are making precisely the mistake which is made here, that is, they are endeavouring to retain possession of a species of manufacture where they labour against great disadvantages.

9641. You have given in evidence a return of the looms existing at Lyons, at particular periods, and at St. Etienne?—Always with the reservation that there are no accurate official returns of former periods; and I mention a curious circumstance connected with the silk trade of Lyons, that there is no authentic history of the town, nor any history of its silk trade.

9642. Have

*John Bowring,*
Esq. LL. D.

27 June,
1832.

9642. Have you at all calculated the quantity of thrown silk it takes, or the number of persons it employs to manufacture the eighteen millions of francs of French silks imported into this country?—I have not.

9643. Which do you think most beneficial to English artisans, the importation of raw silk, to be worked up in England, or the import of eighteen millions of francs of French manufactured goods?—I must first see how the eighteen millions are to be paid for; without all the facts, a question of that sort can lead to no useful result.

9644. With reference to the silk trade alone, would you say it was as beneficial to the operative to have the manufactured commodity brought into this country as to have the silk in the raw state, that he might manufacture it?—I state generally that the present state of things is in every respect better for the English operative; a much greater quantity of labour is employed in the present state of things than would be under a prohibitory state.

9645. You do not mean that with reference only to the silk trade?—No; I have not so examined the bearings of the silk question apart as to be able to give a decided opinion whether silk labour has been superseded, and to what extent; but I do know the exportation of French silks from France, and their importation into England have created a demand for English labour in another direction. If indeed it could be made out, that people would be as well pleased with inferior English silks as with superior French silks, and if a nation could be made to do that which no individual ever did in his own personal case, namely, to prefer an inferior garment to a superior one, it is possible that the protective system might be made operative, and a greater quantity of silk labour be demanded; but inasmuch as every body, in his particular case, prefers that which is good and cheap to that which is bad and dear, sound legislation would be grounded on the common sense and reasonable preference of the public. It is clear with reference to the silk manufacturer, that if there be an increased importation to the extent of a million and a half of raw silk, and that raw silk be employed in manufacture, there must be an increase of demand for labour sufficient to manufacture the million and a half so consumed.

9646. You would not consider that, by an increased import of French manufactured goods, there has been any extent of displacing the English operative labour, while facts prove that there is an increased extent of import of the raw material?—The result proves the contrary.

9647. Does not the finer description of silk require a vast deal more labour than the coarser?—Exactly.

9648. Has not the increase in the importation of silk been greatly in the coarser descriptions?—I suppose there may have been a greater increase in the coarser descriptions.

9649. Do you suppose that the quantity of the finer description of French manufacture, which has been introduced into this country, has not displaced that consumption of fine manufacture in this country?—No, I doubt that very much; I think the introduction of a superior article has increased general demand; it is my belief that if a taste had not been created in this country for silk apparel among the rich, which the beauty of the French manufacture has excited, there would have been a considerably less demand for English among the more numerous consumers.

9650. Are you not aware that the mode in which a certain quantity of silk is worked up, will make a very considerable difference in the quantity of employment to be afforded to the operatives?—Certainly.

9651. You are understood to have stated that the silk imported now is of a much coarser description than before the prohibition?—I think I made no such statement; I have stated, on the contrary, that the natural tendency of competition will always be towards improvement, and that this in fact has been the constant tendency of things; and that as a result the whole of the French manufacture is naturally and necessarily getting into the higher regions.

9652. You are not aware that the great proportion of silk imported now is much coarser than before the removal of the prohibition?—That is against all the facts I have gathered.

9653. The question refers to raw silk?—I beg pardon, I believed you referred to manufactures. In France the quality of raw silk is much improved rather than deteriorated; all the evidence shows the quality of the article has been mended by attention to it, and the same is the case in Italy; so in manufacture, the great

678. **struggle**

*John Bowring,*
Esq. LL. D.

27 June,
1832.

struggle is to produce a better article on cheaper terms, that is the manufacturer's triumph.

9654. Do you know what proportion of the six millions of francs of French silk manufactured goods which you state were exported to this country in 1825, were for the purpose of being warehoused in England previous to the opening of the ports in 1826?—The official returns will show.

9655. Are you aware what proportion of those goods were brought in under the privilege possessed by the house of Depoully & Company?—I should think a very small quantity; the means they possessed were not such as to enable them to command a large capital.

9656. You have stated some disadvantages which you conceive the French manufacture labours under, one of which is local taxation (octroi), have you ever compared that taxation with the English poors rate, watch rate, lighting rate, church rate, county rate, and other local charges?—The reason of my referring to the octroi was, that it was a burthen pressing peculiarly on the labourer; the octroi is a special tax on food and drink, and therefore specially a tax on labour; many of those taxes exist in France of which the question speaks, and I did not refer to them because they do not act immediately on the artisan.

9657. You have not thought any thing of the taxation of the food of Englishmen?—Yes; and if I were to be asked my opinion of the corn laws, I should say, the necessity for getting rid of them is most imperative.

9658. Have you ever compared the difference between the English and French labour, as it respects national taxation?—That resolves itself very much into a question of opinion as to the operation of legislation, by indirect taxation, on the price of food; I think there is no part of our legislation so vicious and so oppressive as that which increases the price of bread; but that same vicious legislation exists also, unfortunately, in France, for they have a system of corn laws built on ours, and I think that they cruelly suffer from them.

9659. Therefore you would do away with the corn laws, on the same principle of giving employment to the poor?—Truly.

9660. Suppose an English weaver to earn 25*l.* per annum, how much of that sum goes in direct and indirect taxation?—Those are calculations on which I should hesitate to give a hasty opinion; I have desired, throughout this examination, not to be considered as bearing testimony to the state of things here. On any question relating to English labour, except of a general character, I venture to suggest, that the Committee would be more safely guided by others.

9661. You have given an opinion and statement of facts as to the bearing of these things on the operatives of France, therefore you are asked, have you considered the bearing of those circumstances on the operatives of England?—I am sure the Committee will have the means of getting the information on matters connected with England from so much better sources, that it would be desirable they should look elsewhere. I have been asked my opinion with respect to local and national taxation; I stated why I brought in the local taxation of France, because it was a duty bearing so peculiarly on labour. It is a misfortune that so much indirect taxation should bear on labour as results from the operation of the English corn laws. The corn laws in France are also a great burthen, as the average price of corn there is much greater than the average European price.

9662. You have stated, that a French weaver is also under great disadvantage as to the construction of his machinery on account of the taxes on iron, &c.; are you not aware that in this country, every article of which the building and machinery of a manufactory is composed is much more heavily taxed?—Not more heavily taxed, certainly the duty on the import of foreign iron is small in England, in France it is 150 per cent. on the value.

9663. Iron enters in a very trifling degree into the expense of building in England?—Of course it must stand at its quantum valeat, whatever that may be.

9664. Mr. Royle stated, that he paid nearly 4,000*l.* in taxes on the articles used in the building of his mill?—He would have paid three times as much in France.

9665. You have stated, that Switzerland has greatly the advantage of France, because of the duty of 33 per cent. on machinery, and of 150 per cent. on iron in France; what machinery does Switzerland use in her silk manufacture?—Wherever those grievances pressing on France do not press on Switzerland, Switzerland has a great advantage, and machinery is used at every step of manufacture.

9666. Do the Swiss throw their own silk, or do they import it thrown?—I have
delivered

*John Bowring,*
Esq. LL. D.

27 June,
1832.

delivered in all the information respecting Switzerland which I possess, in a document. I have never visited that country with a view to this inquiry.

9667. Can you state from what you gathered that document?—It was a document gathered from various sources, the most intelligent sources in the country.

9668. Do they work many Jacquard machines in that country?—I should doubt that; they are applied more particularly to the production of the more complex patterns, and Switzerland is very little advanced in that branch of manufacture.

9669. Is there any thing in the silk manufacture that can fairly be called machinery, if you except the Jacquard, and what is used in the operation of throwing?—If a loom is not a machine I do not know what is.

9670. You have spoken of the cost of iron, are you aware that the cost of the iron in a loom is about 1 s. 6 d.?—If it be only 1 s. 6 d., the average cost of the common loom used in France I gave in evidence was less than 1 l., that which cost 1 s. 6 d. here, would be 4 s. 6 d. there, that on 20 s. would be between 20 and 30 per cent., a very serious consideration.

9671. Do you know how long a period a loom will last?—I should think a very considerable period.

9672. Half a century?—Very likely; but with respect to iron it enters so much into the daily uses of life, even for nailing up a door or a window, that it becomes in France an article of importance. I can safely say, that the iron monopoly occasioned a yearly loss to France of three or four millions sterling.

9673. You stated that France is under a disadvantage in the manufacture of her silk goods as compared with Germany and Switzerland, to the extent of 11¾ per cent., and that three per cent. profit to the importer of Italian silk into France is a part of this 11¼ per cent., what facilities have the manufacturers of Switzerland for importing silk from Italy which the French do not also enjoy?—My statement was, that the French represented the difference to be 11 per cent., but that I considered that exaggerated, and as far as I could form an estimate it went to the extent of seven or eight per cent., I then gave in particulars of the different sums of which I conceived the seven or eight to be composed. I stated that which is a fact of some importance, that the Swiss manufacturer will, for the most part, import the silk; there are but few instances of the French manufacturers being importers; the profit of importation would therefore be so much benefit to the Swiss manufacturer, independent of the circumstance of his paying no duty.

9674. If the Swiss manufacturer finds an advantage in importing his own silk from Italy, why does not the French manufacturer do the same?—It must be perfectly obvious, that the organization and habits of society are very different in different countries. I presume the Manchester manufacturer does not import his own silk; the importation of silk implies the possession of capital, foreign correspondence, and perhaps even the knowledge of certain languages not possessed by every body. The question is one which bears upon a peculiar division of labour; it may be desirable there should be that division under some circumstances and not in others.

9675. You state that brokerage is part of the cost, is not brokerage a customary charge in all countries?—There is no broker where a merchant or manufacturer receives his silk direct from the Italian or foreign producer, the brokerage is the cost of a transfer from the seller to the buyer in a particular market; it is the charge of agency, and clearly an additional cost.

9676. Are not brokers' and merchants' commissions paid in England?—Certainly.

9677. You have also spoken of the pillage of silk at Lyons as constituting a material disadvantage to the French, what reason have you to suppose that there is a less pillage in Zurich, with its 12,000 looms, or in Spitalfields with its 16,000 looms, than there is in Lyons?—I put that as the statement of the French manufacturers, of course all those statements must be taken for the value which honourable Members may attach to them. One reason for supposing that the pillage is more extensive in Lyons is, that there is a great deal of illicit manufacturing trade, it is a very large market, and there are a number of individuals who do gain their livelihood by the manufacture of that fraudulently obtained silk; now that trade could not exist in a very small market; there would not be enough of irregularity to enable a man to be fed from those irregular sources.

9678. You know nothing personally of Zurich?—I do not; the document I have put in is from Basle.

9679. You have already stated that the rate of interest is one per cent. higher at

678.                                                           Lyons

*John Bowring,*
Esq. LL. D.

27 June,
1832.

Lyons than at Switzerland, what is the present rate of interest at Lyons?—From five to six per cent.

9680. There are no usury laws in France?—No, six per cent. is the interest which in a court of justice would be given, provided there had been no special agreement.

9681. You have stated, that a member of the Chamber of Commerce at Lyons, who is himself a manufacturer, told you that he saw many articles in England in which the French suffered from competition, please to state what those articles were?—I have put in his evidence in the shape in which it was given; he stated certain facts in corroboration of it, that they had formerly a demand for America at Lyons, which he now found supplied from England.

9682. You speak with regard to the silk trade?—Yes; that certain articles which had been bought at Lyons were now bought in England, and that they have been accustomed to receive certain orders for America which were now supplied from England.

9683. Did he specify the particulars?—He did not.

9684. You have also stated, that he told you that the competition between France and England has produced in England various new articles; what are those articles?—I have not the means of judging precisely what the articles were; it would be very difficult, on a subject of that sort, for an individual not a manufacturer to give evidence in its minute details: I have no doubt at all, from the veracity of the individual, of the fact; but the way in which the evidence could be best substantiated would be to produce patterns of the article, which is not a practicable thing while Lyons is so far away.

9685. You have also stated, that he told you that the introduction of French silk goods into this country has improved the English manufacture, by the instruction which they have given to the English manufacturer; do you speak of fancy silk goods?—Certainly.

9686. You have said that the English manufacture has improved since the opening of the ports; that the improvement is astonishing, equal to 50 years?—Such was the language of that gentleman, who is undoubtedly one of the most intelligent men of the country. It is with unbounded surprise and regret I have heard it stated here, that there has been no improvement in the last seven years in England; sure I am that there has been great improvement in France.

9687. You saw many designs in France, have the goodness to look over that (*a pattern book*), and state whether there is not a great degree of fancy and beauty?—My opinion is of little value in such a matter; I rather prefer to cite the opinions of others, and the grounds of those opinions. In a question of superiority or inferiority reference must be made to universal opinion. If the English silk goods are equal to the French, I cannot account for the infatuation which prefers the French to the English, not only here but in every market of the world; and whence comes the demand for protection, if the French are not superior?

9688. Can you point out any pattern which you would say is French, or which is English?—No, I cannot.

9689. You state that the fact of the English silk trade asking for a protection of 30 per cent. is a proof that our manufactures are inferior to French manufactures; do not the English ask protection against the local advantages of the French?—That does not alter the matter: the evidence of our inferiority is, that the French come into the market and offer their goods 30 per cent. cheaper than the English; hence it is perfectly clear that the goods are to be had at 30 per cent. less.

9690. The cost may be less?—Yes, surely; it is obvious the French have, from some cause or other, something which enters into the production of goods at a cheaper cost than the English; if, for example, taste in France be cheaper than in England, that has its effect.

9691. May we not be able to produce quite as good an article in this country, but not quite so cheap?—Yes; but however the question may be shifted, still there is 30 per cent. less taken from the English public, if you give 30 per cent. less to the French than to the English, and, as a necessary consequence, 30 per cent. more will remain in their pocket; the 30 per cent. duty is at all events so much taxation on the public.

9692. If you increased the poor's rates in consequence 40 per cent. there would be no advantage?—I have demonstrated, I think, that as far as our relations with France are concerned, if you mean infallibly to render the poor's rates double, you should prohibit French silk.

9693. How

*John Bowring,*
Esq. LL. D.

27 June,
1832.

9693. How do you account for our requiring 30 per cent. which, you say, the public pay if they purchase English silks, with the fact you have stated that the French manufacturers of silk at Lyons complain that we are beating them out of the American markets?—In certain articles it appears that we have made that progress; one branch may be prosperous, and another declining.

9694. Do you not think, after all, you have been greatly misled at Lyons by the French manufacturer, as to the pretended superiority they have, and that the great improvement we have made in this country has resulted from our intercourse with them?—How can I be misled as to their great superiority, when I have the testimony of all mankind that in the foreign markets of all nations the French enter and we do not. That, to my mind, is incontestible evidence of superiority.

9695. Is it not evident that we are labouring under some disadvantage?—Yes; but to remove it, let the manufacturers of England consent to receive instruction from every source; to insist on its exclusion is to demand ruin. The protection they ask may serve a particular manufacturer, but will be most pernicious to the manufacture itself; it will be a barrier to all improvement, and certainly shut the door against all future success.

9696. Are you aware that from 1815 to 1825 the silk manufacture of this country had increased in consumption more than a million of pounds weight of silk, though burthened with 5 s. 6 d. on the raw silk and 14 s. 10 d. on the thrown, that in spite of all those difficulties and disadvantages it was flourishing, and that there were no complaints made in Spitalfields till after the introduction of French goods?—I must state the matter in the way in which it presents itself to my mind : the demand for prohibition of French silk goods is, after all, only a demand that England should not export cotton goods to France. If the two facts of export and import were represented contiguously, as they ought honestly to be, the question would be disposed of in the judgment of the least enlightened, who have not a sinister interest. I do not mean to say, if the silk manufacturer has a monopoly that he may not personally turn it to some account, but the true question is the question of loss and profit on the whole.

9697. Supposing your position, or the information you gained in France with regard to the improvement in the silk manufacture in this country is incorrect, the argument you have raised upon it falls to the ground?—No, the argument cannot fall to the ground, while there is evidence that England produces an inferior and France a superior article.

9698. Explain what you mean by inferior and superior; do you mean in quality or in price?—They will come to the same result. If English sellers exact a hundred for that which can be imported from another country for seventy, English buyers will suffer at the rate of 30 per cent. in all such transactions : now, no individual ever became rich by paying 30 per cent. more than he needed, nor did any nation ever so become rich. A judicious system of legislation would be one in which each nation should be thrown upon its natural aptitude for obtaining every thing at the least cost.

9699. You say that in this country, in consequence of the competition, the manufacture has wonderfully improved, from the information you received in France; supposing the manufacture has not improved in that degree, your argument with regard to the effect of competition upon our manufactures falls to the ground?—If the result is that the English manufacture has not improved, undoubtedly the argument founded on the supposition that it has improved has no basis.

9700. If there has been only that naturally progressive advantage which, from the state of the goods previously to that period manufactured in this country, of course the argument which has been raised upon that falls to the ground?—I should have thought that natural progression and non-improvement are not very compatible still less convertible terms.

9701. It has been given in evidence, that there were formerly about 4,000 looms in the district of Spitalfields alone, which were employed in the manufacture of figured silks, and that now there are not 300 ; do you call this an improvement?—I have no doubt that the silk manufacture, or any manufacture, must be very disadvantageously placed in such a situation as Spitalfields ; even in France, the manufacturer, to relieve himself, is getting out even of those towns where the cost of subsistence is much less than in the capital; when such a manufacture establishes itself in a very large city, it establishes itself in a situation from which it will infallibly be driven by the home competition of cheaper places.

9702. It is also in evidence, that in one of the parishes of that district the average number

*John Bowring,*
Esq. LL. D.

27 June,
1832.

number of weavers receiving parochial relief for five years previously to 1826 was 300, while the average number since have been upwards of 3,000 ?—I have no doubt a great deal of distress exists, and it demands all sympathy, but a great deal of distress does exist from the very fact that two and two make four; but it is not the less true that two and two make four because it causes distress

9703. You state that the export of silk goods from France to England has improved the French silk manufacture; is not the fair meaning of this alleged mutual improvement this, that the contest between the two manufacturing countries is reducing the operatives in both countries to the lowest point of subsistence ?—That is a question which, to answer properly, would require a vast number of details; it is, in fact, the great question of the quantity of labour in the market, which, like every other commodity, must be sold according to its value, that is according to the relative amount of supply and demand.    The cheapest labour will always be bought; and the best security against distress is, that the labour of a nation should be applied to natural and most improved production.    The relative situations and aptitudes of nations can be best judged of by the emulation which exists between the labourers in the fair unprotected field of competition.    But the general and complicated question of wages cannot be settled by reference to a single article; there may be on a single article a particular pressure, reducing wages below the average standard, but, taken upon the whole, there is always in the market a quantity of labour whose excess or deficiency regulates its price.    In manufacturing goods for a foreign market, the price of goods, and with it the price of labour must go down, if you remove the foreign demand, which you would do by prohibition of the foreign articles which pay for the goods you export: close any channel to the export of English labour by the prohibition of a foreign article, and a smaller quantity of English labour would be demanded.    Thus any new restrictions would increase the evil and increase the distress; that is the result to which you would inevitably come by prohibition.    You have a great deal of misdirected labour, and in some departments a great excess of labourers.    It appears to me, that nothing can give you relief on a great scale but the removal of the prohibitory system altogether; my confirmed belief is, that the suffering which exists even in this country is the natural consequence of attempts to force labour and capital into a false position, and that every effort to proceed in that direction must aggravate the evil.

9704. Are you aware that there was no distress in Spitalfields, and generally in England, till 1825 ?—Were it so, can any man say that the labour of Spitalfields, which is dear, can long compete with another labour which is cheap ? does not the cheap labour at Glasgow at 5 s. as much supplant the labour of Spitalfields at 10 s. as the labour of any other place, whether at home or abroad ?

9705. They say that the commodity which they made is now supplied from France, and that they desire to be enabled to supply the public with this; would it not be therefore to the advantage of Spitalfields that the French manufactured silks of the description which Spitalfields formerly made should be excluded from our market ?—It is possible that a particular place possessing a monopoly might gain by the prohibitory system, but the inevitable result would be, that upon the whole there would be a loss.

9706. The question before this Committee is upon the silk trade ?—But the consequences cannot be narrowed or confined to the silk trade.

9707. You state that the introduction of French novelties has increased the consumption of silk goods in England ; are you aware of the cause of the increased consumption of silk goods from 1821 to 1825, before those novelties were admitted? —That, again, is a question referring to the state of things in England, and connected with a branch of the subject on which I do feel myself much less competent to give opinions than other gentlemen who may be examined before this Committee.

9708. In 1821, according to Mr. Hume's evidence, the quantity of raw and thrown silk consumed in England was 2,460,898 lbs.; in 1825 it was 3,633,321 lbs. being an increase of above 50 per cent. in five years; or if you take 1824, it was 3,393,984 lbs. which is an increase of 40 per cent. in four years, though the trade was burthened with enormous duties ?—It appears to me, that the only way to make a correct estimate is to do that which the honourable Member did some time ago, take a certain number of years, average those years, and when those years are averaged take the result from that: as far as the question of importation is concerned, there has been an increase to the extent of more than a million and half of pounds since the admission of French goods.  These returns do, in truth, show

from

*John Bowring,*
*Esq.* LL. D.

———

27 June,
1832.

from 1814 to 1819 a considerable diminution; there were a million and a half of raw silk imported in 1814; in the following year there was only a million; in the following year only 870,000; in 1818 there was a less importation than in 1814; so that the increase was, at all events, most uncertain, irregular and capricious.

9709. What was the importation in 1815?—One million; that was 500,000 less than in the previous year

9710. The years 1814 and 1815 were years both of war and peace; will you refer to 1817?—In that year the importation for home consumption was 200,000 lbs. less than it was in 1814, and in 1819 it was not so much as it was in 1814; in 1820 and 1821 it was a little more than in 1819, so that for eight years it had made no progress at all, the quantity of raw and thrown silk being less in 1821 than in 1814; then there was only three years between that and the period of non-prohibition; in 1822 there was 400,000 more than in 1814; but if the whole of these eight years be compared with the great increase since 1825, the addition to the amount of imports will be very striking.

9711. Is it not the case, taking the Government returns of raw and thrown silk from 1814 to 1824, there has been a great increase in the manufacture of silk?—In 1824 there was an increase, but in the year previous to 1824 that increase was trifling, and there are many years in which the decrease was very remarkable.

9712. You have stated that there have been at Lyons some great improvements, by changing the broad silk loom into a loom weaving several breadths of ribbons; are those looms, when so altered, superior to any other ribbon looms to be met with at St. Etienne, or elsewhere in France, and if so, please to describe in what the difference in them consists?—Those looms which are the latest improvements are principally used for the production of ribbons of the highest price and most beautiful quality.

9713. Are they like the engine loom or the a-la-bar loom?—They are not, I think; the shuttle is thrown in the ordinary way.

9714. Can they produce more work than any other description of ribbon loom? —No, they produce, I believe, less.

9715. How many breadths of this sort of work does an engine loom make?— I have given in a statement of the particular number.

9716. Do you still adhere to the declaration that the price of marabout silk at St. Etienne is 27s. a lb.?—I delivered in the price given to me by the President of the Chamber of Commerce at St. Chamond; the evidence I then gave referred to the most beautiful description of silks used for the production of the most beautiful species of ribbons.

9717. Are the Committee to understand you to say that France uses indifferently raw silk of her own growth or Italian raw, for marabout?—Yes.

9718. Please to inform the Committee what kind of Italian raw she appropriates for this purpose?—I believe the Milanese silk, but I am not perfectly sure; I asked information in France, in consequence of an impression that Italian silk could not be used for making marabout; I was told that *maraboutage* represented a particular twist, and that the name was applied to it without any reference to the country where the silk was produced. I got a little laughed at for supposing that maraboutage was any thing but a peculiar way of preparing the silk.

9719. You have given in two calculations of the cost of ribbons in France, one of satins and taffetas and another of gauzes; in the former you state the price of the silk to be 70 francs per kilogram, and in the latter, being part of it, marabout, at 76 francs per kilogram; how do you reconcile those prices with the prices that you have before stated as those of silk in France?—Silk is of many qualities; but it is not my business here to reconcile incongruities; I have presented the facts I have received from different sources, and upon comparing the whole some deductions will be drawn; it was not for me to alter or to reconcile them. On the whole, when differences of quality and circumstances are taken into account, the differences will, I believe, be found not very great.

9720. You have stated that Avignon had formerly sent one-fourth of the goods made there to England, and that now she sends none, and you stated that that town is engaged in the manufacture of sarsnets; are you aware that sarsnet is an article which, at the time you speak of, was used very extensively for ladies' dresses, and that gros de Naples is substituted for it?—That is a question which, perhaps, might be more satisfactorily answered by others. I have a document here, which I obtained, after long discussions at Avignon, on the subject of their manufactures, from

678. the

*John Bowring,*
Esq. LL. D.

27 June,
1832.

the leading manufacturer there; he states the fact, and of his veracity I have not the slightest doubt.

9721. Are you aware that when these goods came to this country sarsnet was the prevailing wear, and that it is not worn now?—I am not.

9722. Is the trade at Nismes in a flourishing condition?—I should think not in a flourishing condition; they are tolerably well off.

9723. Are there not many goods made in Nismes of silk mixed with cotton and other materials?—Yes.

9724. Is not the importation of those articles prohibited from foreign countries? —Yes.

9725. Then the trade of Nismes is an exception to that general principle of not prospering under a system of protection?—The trade of Nismes·is little; there may be seven or eight thousand looms. Nismes is hardly in the export trade; I do not call it a very prosperous trade, for it cannot go beyond the barriers of the country where it is held, and that would lead me to observe this important circumstance, that Nismes does not export any of her produce, and why? because Nismes comes within the circle of protection; the articles that Nismes produces are articles which have not the benefit of this foreign competition, and one of the results is, that Nismes is without a foreign trade.

9726. Have the goodness to state where a full competition exists in the fine goods?—It exists in every place where the French goods find a market.

9727. Are they ever importing any fine goods from England?—No, clearly not, because they produce them cheaper at home.

9728. Then where is the competition?—It is to be seen in its effects on the production of these articles, which are very decidedly superior to their rivals. Competition must put some individual in a situation better than that of his fellow competitors; the next beneath him is his check against deterioration. All that competition does, when a production is raised to the highest state of perfection, is to keep it there; if there were any deterioration in the quality of French goods, that competition which hitherto has kept the French goods in the elevation they occupy, would begin to act and supplant them.

9729. What has been the effect of competition on coarse goods in France?— To assist them to struggle against the peculiar disadvantage under which France labours in producing them.

9730. Does not France labour under the same disadvantages with regard to fine goods?—No, for in respect of fine goods France has such a superiority, from her more exquisite taste and devotion to all those studies which invigorate and improve it as to neutralize the disadvantages she labours under from such parts of her prohibitory system as bear upon the finer articles.

9731. You think it is wholly in design she has the advantage?—No, I think she has an advantage in the raw silk; but her range of success will be found to be the widest wherever there is a demand for a supply of taste, fashion and novelty.

9732. Why do not the advantages which you say she derives from nature produce an effect upon her plain goods as well?—Because her advantages are counteracted by other disadvantageous circumstances; in the first place she pays a duty on the raw material which enters into a larger proportion of the value on the coarser goods; in the second place I have noted there are many circumstances connected with the social condition of her labouring population which are unfriendly to improvement. In finer goods her peculiar aptitude is greater, her peculiar difficulties less.

9733. Has not France obtained her present superiority in commodities from the advantages she has had in the competition with foreign countries, and has she not done so under a system of protection against the manufacture of other countries, and in the advantages of her own silks and of her designs?—On the contrary the result of my testimony will be to show, that it is not to that protection that France owes any thing but loss; of all the manufacturers of France the silk manufacture is the least protected, and that is the only one which has a tolerable chance for futurity, unless her system is changed.

9734. With what country has she been in competition in the superior manufactures?—The competition nearly acts as efficiently by its influence on the inferior branches, by compelling them to struggle for superiority; if France produces an article of greater beauty than England, the effect of English competition upon her is quite as active; if England comes into the market with an article the next in quality, it is quite as useful as if she came in with an article of the same quality.

9735. Did

*John Bowring,*
Esq. LL. D.

27 June,
1832.

9735. Did England come into France with any manufactures at all; did she compel her forward by any description of manufacture?—Certainly she did, and there is a remote and indirect, as well as a close and direct operation of competition; every country that produces silk goods is in a state of competition with France and every other country that makes them; competition may act through the coarse article upon the fine as decidedly, though more distantly, than through the fine upon the fine.

9736. Is there any other market into which France enters into competition with England for her finer description of goods besides the English market?—I should think, at this moment, England is not in a state to rival France in the more fashionable articles of French production, and the best evidence of that is, that she is an importer from France.

9737. Will you look at that extract from the Journal de Commerce, and translate it?—" Our manufactures, and those of Torquain are in a satisfactory state, because the manufacturers of Roubaix, who employ them, sell their woven goods easily; combed wools and woollen yarn are rather sought for, and their price is augmented 20 per cent.; within the last eight months the manufacturers of woollen yarn cannot supply the demands which are addressed to them; their profits are enormous, also the number of looms has been trebled in two months; woollen goods are in the same favourable state, and some have mounted from 375 cents to 5 francs, since the month of November; all labourers who wish to labour can find labour at 125 to 150 cents per day."

9738. Will you refer to an extract containing information from Nismes?—" Our manufacture continues to work with the activity of which it is susceptible; our silks are asked for, with a tendency to an advance in price; foreign silks are bought, and if demand continues, the old silks will be already exhausted before the new harvest." Is it the pleasure of the Committee to receive from me some information as to the state of manufactures in this Roubaix district?

9739. Is not the Journal de Commerce of some authority in France?—No doubt; if I had expected that the general state of manufactures in France would have been gone into, I would have brought some information which would show that the situation of the cotton manufacture is discouraging in the extreme; the expressions of distress which have emanated thence are stronger than have been ever heard even in this country. I have now found among my papers an address to the King, presented in the present year, from Mulhausen, the seat of one of the largest manufacturers in France, the first sentence of which is, " Our looms are wholly abandoned, and our labourers without food." Roubaix is a comparatively inconsiderable place.

9740. Did you, among the papers that had their origin in France, see any returns relating to Roubaix?—In the department of the North, I see Roubaix is the sixth town in manufacturing importance.

9741. When small places are in prosperity does it not follow that large ones, which usually employ those small ones, cannot but be well off?—The whole number of looms in the district du Nord was stated by Chaptal at 10,000; now, as evidence of the prosperity of that district, I will mention that in March last the cotton manufactory of Rouval-les-Doullens, established only four years ago by a well known individual (who came to England and visited our most improved establishments), at a cost of 1,400,000 francs, was sold for 308,000; there was a sacrifice therefore of between 70 and 80 per cent. of the whole invested capital.

9742. Can you state in what town of the northern districts the principal mart for cotton twist is?—The principal mart for English cotton twist is in the south, namely, the town of Tarare, in the department of the Rhone.

9743. Roubaix is not the place where the sale takes place?—No; Rouen is the great market for French cotton twist.

9744. If this trade was so distressed in March last, how do you account for this article in the Journal de Commerce so late as the 28th of March last?—It is impossible for me to account for the introduction of a particular article into a foreign newspaper.

9745. Do you think that, a mill having been built upon the most improved principles, and under the best circumstances, within the last five years, and which cost 10,000 *l.*, the silk trade can be considered as in a state of prosperity if that mill will not at the present moment sell for 500 *l.*?—If it is the fact that a mill which cost 10,000 *l.* will not sell for 500 *l.*, it is evidence of a great depreciation; it

678.                                                                                was

*John Bowring,*
Esq. LL. D.

27 June,
1832.

was an ill considered investment, and if there had not been protection that mill never would have been built.

9746. Did the manufacturer you alluded to just now visit our country to examine and carry home our last improvements?—He did, and he is a man of superior capacity.

9747. How do you reconcile this inquiry with your opinion that protection to the French cotton trade paralyzes its efforts towards improvement?—There is a frequent miscalculation of the value and extent of the power of protection. If he had not been protected he would not have vested his capital in this cotton mill; he ought to have seen that all manufactures are likely to fail which do not grow out of natural circumstances, but require for their support the interference of Government and the prop of monopoly: those alone have fair prospects before them which rise from the ordinary flow of capital; those who build factories under the auspices of a protective law are doomed to discover too late the insufficiency of that protection, and must prepare for the consequences. I am intimately acquainted at this moment with the proprietor of one of the largest factories in France for the production of cotton twist, and he has assured me that he considers seven-eighths of capital invested as irretrievably lost.

9748. Is there any duty on the importation of the raw cotton into France?—Yes; the duty is, I think, about seven-eighths of a penny per lb. English; it is a considerable duty, somewhat above the duty paid in England.

9749. Did not the cotton manufacture of this country rise to its eminence under a system of prohibition?—I believe the system of prohibition was never of any use to it at all, for of all the manufactures of England the cotton manufacture was the least protected. In our early legislation there was a penalty imposed on any one who should wear a cotton garment; and it is within the recollection of honourable Members, that it is only within the last few years the duty of 3 ½ d. per yard on printed cottons has been removed. So far from being considered worthy of protection, it is the manufacture against which our old protectionists made a dead set, and every attempt was encouraged to sacrifice it to the woollen and the linen trades: its great success is owing to its having surmounted those disadvantages in spite of every discouragement, and it is at this moment the least protected of any.

9750. Competition has not been the cause of that?—There has been always competition, even foreign competition, in the trade.

9751. With what countries were we in competition when it was rising?—We were in competition with France.

9752. Do you mean during the war?—Yes, there was great production of cottons there.

9753. Do they find their way into this country now?—Yes, wherever there is peculiar beauty; and notwithstanding the disadvantages under which the French labour, they bring some printed cotton articles of fashion into this market; Koechlin, of Mulhausen, a large manufacturer of cottons, has, I know, been a considerable exporter for this market.

9754. What is the duty on cottons?—Ten per cent.

9755. Is it not the fact, that as soon as any inventions took place in the cotton manufactory in this country they were carried to France, and manufactories established upon the same principle?—Yes, but not immediately.

9756. We did not borrow from them, but they were in a state of borrowing from us?—That is too general an expression; improvements emanate from various sources; we are greatly in advance on the cotton manufacture; but there are many disputes afloat as to priority of invention, and unsettled claims to discovery between Frenchmen and Englishmen.

9757. You have stated that the export of silk goods from France to England has been attended by an export of silk goods from England to other countries of a similar amount, do you mean to say that this export from England has been caused by the export from France to England?—Yes, to a great extent; the introduction of French goods is throwing our silk manufacturers into a more natural and safe position; and wherever they turn their attention to the manufacture of such articles as they can produce on better terms than the French, they have very little to fear from French rivalry; and the proof of this is, there is a considerably increasing export of manufactured goods; in the last year the amount was, I think, according to Mr. Hume's estimate, half a million of English silk manufactures exported.

9758. That

*John Bowring,*
Esq. LL. D.

———

27 June,
1832.

9758. That was to their prejudice of course?—Yes; but they have been bene-fited in other directions.

9759. You have stated that the manufactured goods exported from France to England balance the manufactured goods exported from England to France; but does not France export very largely of wines, brandies and other produce to Eng-land?—Certainly.

9760. Can you enumerate the principal sorts of manufactured goods made in England which France prohibited?—France prohibits the greater quantity of our manufactures.

9761. Then France does not at present act liberally towards England, but con-fines herself to entertaining liberal sentiments?—France acts very absurdly, both to England and to herself; but the important fact is, that England by consenting to the introduction of French produce, does as effectually force the French to receive English as if the French spontaneously opened their doors; but even in France a great change has taken place in opinion; this prohibitory system has been tried in all its bearings; its consequences are beginning to be felt; the people are gradually setting right their miscalculations, and the Government is beginning to feel its way. Among the circumstances which have created this change of opinion, that sort of English interest which has grown up in France in consequence of her Eng-lish relations ought not to be forgotten.

9762. Are any silk goods smuggled out of France, either with a view to escape the export duty, or to avoid information being given of the smuggling operations into England?—I should doubt that; the export duty is a mere registration duty; there is no motive for the risk.

9763. Has the general export trade of this country to France increased or fallen off since 1816?—Decidedly increased.

9764. You have stated that the importations of this country to France, and the exportations from thence are about equal; upon what authority do you make this statement?—First, from general knowledge; secondly, from the certainty that no person gives his goods for nothing: can any body be found who transfers his article without receiving its value, and nobody can deny that the whole trade between England and France is but the representation of all those articles together so bar-tered or exchanged.

9765. It appears by the Parliamentary Return of the 22d of August 1831, that the annual importation from France upon an average of four years, from 1826 to 1831, exceeded two millions and a half, whilst the exports of British and Irish manufactures for the same period amounted to less than half a million per annum; are you prepared to impugn this statement, or how can you reconcile it with your own?—I should think the French are not such wiseacres as to give us two millions and a half for our half a million; if France really consented to transfer to us two millions and a half of her produce for only half a million of ours, it is clear we are carrying on the most beneficial trade that ever existed since the world began; but independent of clandestine importation into France, France cannot receive colonial produce direct from England; the consequence is, that colonial produce, indigo for instance, of which she buys 1,500 chests a year, is returned in the Netherlands' account; thus of the balance, a portion is paid clandestinely, and a portion by a circuitous route.

9766. If the exportation were as large, British goods would be seen at Paris as the French goods are very well displayed here; it has been stated by a witness, a large buyer of English goods, who was in Paris two months for the purpose of settling there, if he could have introduced English goods, that he found it imprac-ticable, and that he saw scarcely any English goods in the shops there; are you prepared to invalidate this statement?--I am not called upon to prove or to repro-bate the statement of others, I mention a substantial fact, that the introduction of English goods into France is very great, and that their money value is very great; if a stranger go to Paris, he will be just as much lost as a stranger that comes to London; the sale of goods depends on connection; a man flinging himself into a new world may perhaps not be able in two months to follow all the windings of commercial intercourse.

9767. Did you yourself see many English goods exhibited in the shops in Paris? —Constantly.

9768. It has been stated by witnesses connected with some of the most fashion-able houses here, that such is the prejudice in favour of French goods, that if English articles were offered superior, and at a much less price, they would be rejected in

　　　　　　　　　　　　　　　　　　　　　　　favour

favour of French, are you prepared to deny this statement?—I have already stated my conviction that the preference is not matter of prejudice; that the universal testimony of universal opinion must be accepted as evidence of undoubted superiority.

9769. Is the value of English silk goods exported within the last six years, greater or less than of those exported within the six previous years?—I have no other information upon that subject than the official returns. The increase appears to have gone on very rapidly; for the last six years there has been a constant tendency to increase. I will take it from three years to three years. In 1821, 136,000 pounds; in 1824, 159,000 pounds; in 1827, 173,000 pounds; in 1830, 427,000 pounds; and in 1831, 500,000 pounds.

9770. Some questions have been put to you, of which the object was to show that the demand for labour in the silk trade in this country had declined; because, though the coarser manufacture might have increased, the finer had decreased; that is to say, that although there had been an increase in the importation of Bengal silk, there had been a falling off in the importation of French and Italian raw silk. The Committee have before them Returns of the Importations from France and Italy of Raw Silk, from the year 1820 to the year 1831, from which it appears, that previous to the year 1824, in no year did the importation amount to 600,000 pounds, while in no year since that year was it so little as 900,000 pounds; it thus appearing, that there has been an increase not only in the importation of the Bengal silk, but also in that of the French and Italian silk; are you of opinion that there can have been any decline in the demand for labour in the silk manufactures in this country?—Certainly not; those facts afford a decided answer to that question. The same tests must be applied to the two periods.

9771. Have not, in your opinion, the united effects of the increased importation of the finer and richer French manufactured silks, and the increased importation of all raw silks into England, been to add greatly to the employment of the operatives in this country, with other operatives not employed in the cotton or silk manufactures?—That is the deduction I should draw; my opinion upon that subject is so strong, that I believe a protection of 30 per cent. given to the silk manufacture has been the destruction of 60 per cent. of labour elsewhere, so that to the silk manufacturer at this moment a considerable sacrifice of British labour is made, and the sacrifice must be estimated by the amount of duty laid on; not that I am advocating an immediate admission of French silks without a duty; but if they were admitted without a duty, the effect on labour would be to increase the demand for British labour, and that to a very considerable extent.

9772. If the course of manufacture in this country is so changed that the operative is now employed only three days in weaving silk, when he used to be employed six days in a week, can there be any increase of employment when the quantity has increased only 25 per cent.?—The employment may have increased, but the labourers to be employed may have increased more rapidly. My position is, that prohibition would not ultimately benefit them in the smallest degree.

9773. You stated, in answer to a question, that the quantity of raw silk imported here before prohibition had not increased, but had diminished?—No; I stated, that taking the average of years, there was an increase from a million to a million and a half of pounds since the introduction of French goods.

9774. Have you not overlooked the Table of Averages of three years before and after?—I have taken the period of seven years, considering that as the safest data.

9775. The price of silk in France, and the price of silk in Piedmont, is not exactly the same?—The difference will be the profit to the importer.

9776. The price in France is generally less than the price in Piedmont, is it not?—No, or the French would not import a million of pounds in the year, and pay the duty on it. There must be an average profit upon it, or it would not come to be sold in the French market. I have, however, put in the prices for ten years.

9777. Have you compared them with the prices for the Avignon silk?—Yes; the result is, that there is upon the whole a difference of twenty to thirty sous in favour of the French silk per kilogram, except where, for particular purposes, the Italian silk sells for a higher price.

9778. The Italian silk brings down the price of the French?—Yes, or the French growers might create a monopoly.

9779. Are you aware of any monopoly that the French importers possess in Piedmont?—I cannot conceive there can be a monopoly in the Piedmontese market; the general usage is to send the silk to the Lyonese depôt; if it can be disposed of there at an average rate of profit, the Italian grower will sell rather in a nearer than

in

*John Bowring,*
Esq. LL. D.

27 June,
1832.

in a remoter market; but if the buyer releases it from bond, he may sustain a loss, inasmuch as the exportation of silk not in bond for the purpose of exportation is prohibited. The silk merchant at Lyons is thus under a certain disadvantage; because if he take the silk out of the depôt, and it does not suit the French market, he has no means of getting rid of it, not being able to export it.

9780. It is in evidence before the Committee that the French merchants are in the habit of advancing money to the Piedmont growers, would not that have the effect of giving them a species of monopoly in the Piedmont market?—I should think not; the Lyonese price and British price will be the same, adding to the latter the cost of transport; the importations into England prove there is no such monopoly.

9781. Are the English merchants in the habit of doing the same?—No, I believe not before the silk is produced; the merchants are in the habit of making advances as soon as the silk is sent forward in transit; I suppose they would make advances on silk in bond at Lyons; the advances of the English merchants are decidedly more extensive than the French.

9782. Do you think that the English enter into competition with the French, barring the question of the distance of the two?—Yes; and I should think upon the whole the facilities of disposing of large quantities of silk in London are greater than at Lyons.

9783. You have stated that all trades in France are suffering considerable distress?—I stated that the protected trades are in a state of great suffering.

9784. The silk manufacture you say is suffering distress, but in a less degree, how do you reconcile this distress in the silk trade with the fact, that the growth of raw silk of France now is so remunerative as to pay a profit of 20 or 25 per cent.?—I do not immediately see the bearing of the question; I do not perceive how the latter part of the question is associated with the former.

9785. How does it happen, while the trade is in this distress, that the manufacturer should be disposed to give so high a profit upon the silk to the grower?—I do not state that the silk trade is in a state of great distress; of all raw materials, silk finds the readiest sale, its price being fixed by foreign silk imported; I have stated, too, that there is much less comparative distress in the silk trade; besides the production of France is only three-fourths of her manufacture, so that there will invariably be a sale for her silk as long as France does not produce enough to supply her own demand.

9786. In the Northern Department of France, has not the cotton and woollen manufacture been exceedingly well occupied this year, particularly the woollen manufacture?—I believe there has been a little variation, but upon the whole the situation of French manufactures has been a very distressing one.

9787. The workmen in those trades have not been earning good wages?—I have not returns of their wages at so late a period in the Northern district.

9788. You have stated that within the last three years there has been an export of English silk goods to France, and that the exports consist chiefly of goods of a coarse description; are you aware that for precisely the same period a drawback has been allowed upon the exportation of such goods?—I believe that is the case; the amount has not been a very large one; but the drawback, I take it, has tended to remunerate the exporter for the duty on thrown silk; the less amount of duty paid by the French on thrown silk is a disadvantage under which the English manufacturer labours.

9789. Are the Jacquards in France the property of the master or the workmen?—Of the working weaver generally.

9790. Can you state the cost of Jacquard machines of different sizes?—They are very various; there have been some that have cost from three to four thousand francs; and I believe there are some as low as five or six hundred.

9791. Do you speak of the present value?—Yes.

9792. What is the lowest price of the Jacquard loom you are aware of?—I should think five or six hundred francs, but I speak with hesitation about it.

9793. What is the price in England?—That I cannot say, but the mechanism is very different for different objects; it may be applied to a very simple process or a very complex one, it is like determining the value of a watch, without specifying particulars.

9794. What would be the cost of a Jacquard of 400 cords?—That is a question which must be referred to a manufacturer.

678.

9795. Do

*John Bowring,*
Esq. LL. D.

——————

27 June,
1832.

9795. Do you know whether that would cost five or six hundred francs?—I do not know.

9796. What is the general practice, whether the master or the workmen is at the expense of preparing the patterns?—The pattern is always prepared by the manufacturer.

9797. Is not the pattern produced in the silk by the mere application of the prepared cards to the cylinder of the Jacquard?—Those are details which I am not competent to go into; those are minute particulars of manufacture upon which it is unlikely I should be informed, and I should much mislead the Committee if I did not state that I am unprepared to answer them.

9798. You have stated that the weavers at Lyons suffer great loss from the frequent changes of patterns, and that it is an object of great complaint amongst them; are you aware that one set of cards may be changed for another, so as to change the figure, and the loom is weaving in a few minutes, as the time on a hand organ may be changed at pleasure, by the substitution of one barrel for another?—I have understood both from masters and weavers, that whenever a change of pattern takes place at Lyons, it is a costly affair to both, or either, wherever it may fall; and if there be a discovery in England, so that the change can be made without cost, that is an advantage the English manufacturer has over the French.

9799. Can you state the cost per hundred of the cards used for figured weaving at Lyons?—I cannot.

9800. Are you not aware there is a heavy tax in England on the pasteboard on which the pattern is made?—And a heavy tax in France too.

9801. What is the tax in France?—I think, but am not sure, 50 or 60 per cent. on importation.

9802. Are you aware that the French silk manufacturers, before 1824, paid as much as 1,000 *l.* a year for cards?—They must have had a very large trade, then.

9803. You stated that the French Government lately sent away from Lyons a considerable number of weavers into the mountains?—No, I stated that the weavers who were sent away were foreigners, and that they were conveyed to the frontier; those who retired to the mountains were the native inhabitants, whom the Government had no power to send away.

9804. Can you suggest any way in which our Government can reduce the number of weavers in Spitalfields, Coventry and Macclesfield, until they shall not exceed the demand for their labour?—I stated, in reference to those fluctuations which have grown out of our restrictive and prohibitory system, that a great deal of distress must be the infallible consequence; the removal of that distress is an urgent case for the consideration of the legislature, but its discussion is, I fear, a question which would occupy too much time here.

9805. In England, when the weaver is out of work, or his wages are unduly depressed, are you aware of any resource he has except the poors' rates?—He has the poors' rates, and the unfortunate French weaver has no poor rate; in that particular the Englishman has, in all events, a resource denied to his French competitor.

9806. You stated that there is an expectation in France that they shall be able to import thrown silks from England; if that expectation be a well founded one, why, in your opinion, do they not now import them, seeing that throwing has been latterly done in England at so ruinous a rate?—I have only given the testimony of certain individuals, who stated there had been such an improvement in the art of throwing silks in this country, that they thought it very likely they should be in the English market for the purchase of thrown silks; the opinion was founded on what is asserted to be the superiority of the thrown silk of England.

9807. It is a mere opinion, not founded on any transactions?—It is an opinion founded on an examination of the samples of English thrown silk.

9808. Did you visit any of the throwing establishments in France?—The throwing mills are so inconsiderable in extent as to be scarcely entitled to the name of establishment; silk is thrown, in a great majority of instances, by small throwsters.

9809. Did you take opportunities of inspecting their throwing?—I saw their throwing, such as it existed: it appeared to me in a very little advanced state.

9810. Do you believe that a single bale of English thrown silk has found its way into France?—I have no knowledge of any thrown silk imported in quantities, but individuals who have seen specimens of English thrown silk state, that from the

superiority

John Bowring,
Esq. LL. D.

27 June,
1832.

superiority which machinery had obtained in England, they thought it exceedingly likely there would be an importation into France of silk thrown in England.

9811. Do not the French throw three millions of pounds of silk?—They throw the silk they produce. There are some individuals who are producing silk on a large scale; but through the whole of the silk district, almost every peasant cultivates a certain number of mulberry trees, or buys a certain quantity of leaves; but the cultivation is so diffused, that there is great difficulty in collecting all the minute facts.

9812. You are aware that this country does not throw three millions of pounds, or how then can France be an inconsiderable throwing country?—I have not said that they are an inconsiderable throwing country, but that her throwing mills are on a smaller scale than ours. The question of throwing is not a question that occupied my mind, except for the purpose of comparing prices, and those I have handed in.

9813. Have you visited throwing mills in England?—I have, but not with reference to this question. Manufacturing details must be referred to manufacturers. My opinion would be valueless. The point for me to ascertain was the point of price.

9814. You stated that there was no mill which would throw so many as 10,000 pounds?—Yes; it was stated to me that there was no one in which there was 5,000 l. invested.

9815. Did you see any one in which so small a quantity as 300 pounds was thrown?—That question is again of detail, and one which I cannot estimate. I have mentioned the price from several sources.

9816. You have stated the burthens of local taxation in France; after all this taxation, are not the prices of provisions there much lower than in England?—That is a question of locality. I have put in the local taxation, because it presses on provisions. If I were asked whether the price of provisions in Lyons were higher or lower than in Devonshire, I should say that the prices of provisions in Devonshire are as low as at Lyons. I cannot compare Lyons with Coventry, and places in a similar situation, as I am not acquainted with the state of their markets.

9817. In London?—The price of provisions in London is considerably higher.

9818. You stated that the number of looms at St. Etienne, in 1810, was 9,000, and in 1831 was 20,000; inform the Committee, as nearly as you can, what increase of the trade of St. Etienne, and of the size of the town, has taken place since 1825?—Those are facts on which I can give no more information than I have already given.

9819. You have stated that the great cause of the prosperity of St. Etienne was the introduction of the bar loom; has not that loom been known in St. Etienne for above 20 years?—Yes, and this is my authority; this is a statement in the handwriting of the individual who is the historian of St. Etienne. He says, " We owe our great superiority to the introduction of the bar loom." The bar loom, which is, as I described before, employed for the superior qualities of ribbons, while those woven in the mountains are made by the common looms.

9820. Have they not been used in St. Etienne for 20 years?—They were introduced from Switzerland as early as 1750. My informant says that there had been successive improvements, and to the introduction of those improvements the town owes its prosperity. That is the statement of a man who knows more about its prosperity than any other man.

9821. Is not the principal cause of the great prosperity and increase of the town of St. Etienne, the great extent of English orders for ribbons since the opening of the Ports?—All the documents showing the proportion of ribbons taken by England I have had the honour of presenting to the Committee, and the Committee is thus in the possession of the means of estimating the extent and importance of the English demand.

9822. Does not the price at which smuggling is performed bear some relation to the legal rate of duties at which goods may be imported?—None at all, at least only temporarily. The price of smuggling is that which gives the smuggler a profit.

9823. Then it will be no encouragement to the smuggler to increase the rate of duty?—If the rate of duty were increased, it would be an additional profit to the smuggler if he succeed in his enterprise; that is to say, his first operation would give the additional profit. The second operation would give less profit; and competition in this, as in every thing else, would bring down the charge for insurance to its average minimum value.

9824. You have stated, that the best way of protecting British manufactures

678.                                                                                  would

*John Bowring*,
Esq. LL. D.

27 June,
1832.

would be to reduce the protecting duties to 20 per cent. *ad valorem* ; how do you think that that rate of duty which would not realize above 18 per cent., can protect them better than the present law, under which, according to your own statement, 5-8ths of the goods imported pay a legal duty of from 25 to 50 per cent. and the other 3-8ths are subject to the smuggler's charges, which, according to your statement, averages 20 per cent. ?—I think the English manufacturer would always be much better off when he has to contend with a legitimate than an illegitimate trade ; that is the first reason. The second is, that the lowering of the duty would inevitably give a great impulse to improvement ; that if the quantity of goods now smuggled came legitimately into the market, that legitimate importation could be estimated and calculated upon, so that the fluctuations of the market would be less.

9825. The evidence you have given has resulted from your having been employed by the Board of Trade to make inquiries on the subject, with a view to your examination before this Committee ?—I have stated precisely the character of the evidence I have given ; a great part of it was collected without any reference whatever to this Committee ; but inasmuch as the proceedings of this Committee might possibly have had a bearing upon the general commercial relations of this country with France, and as any step unfriendly to France was likely to have a fatal influence on the discussions of our commission, I did, instructed by the Board of Trade, visit the silk district, to collect on the spot information of a more detailed character than I had before obtained as a commercial commissioner.

9826. Did you not from time to time receive information as to the evidence given before this Committee, and were you not instructed to collect facts to contradict that evidence ?—Certainly not ; I was instructed to collect the facts of the case, whatever their result might be, and I must for my own justification state that I am not here in any respect as a representative of the Board of Trade to advocate any particular system ; my own opinions I have stated openly ; they have grown out of my inquiries in France, and not out of instructions from England, and I cannot consent that my evidence shall be considered as the evidence of a partisan ; I came here with official documents which I leave to produce the impression which their importance and veracity demand.

9827. You were understood on a former day to state, that besides the official documents you have put in, you cannot yourself vouch for the truth of your information that the facts are only those which you have been told by others ?—I do not understand the question so presented ; in some cases my evidence is the result of personal observation, in others it is the result of facts collected from the best sources ; in others it consists of official documents furnished by the Government; in every case I have endeavoured to collect the best evidence which circumstances allowed, and I must leave the whole in the judgment of the Committee to estimate its value ; on several occasions there has been an anxiety to make me personally responsible for differing statements, but that responsibility I must respectfully disclaim ; the documents and statements which I have presented I believe to be the best procurable by me, since I applied to those who were in my judgment the most able to give me information of a decisive and trust-worthy character ; in fine, it is my desire only to say, that I have endeavoured to get the facts from the best sources, whether official, semi-official or extra-official.

---

*Veneris, 29° die Junii,* 1832.

---

EDWARD AYSHFORD SANFORD, ESQUIRE, IN THE CHAIR.

---

Mr. *Louis Schwabe*, called in ; and Examined.

Mr.
*Louis Schwabe*.

29 June,
1832.

9828. YOU are a silk manufacturer at Manchester, are you not ?—I am.

9829. What description of goods do you manufacture ?—Various descriptions of goods, as well low priced as costly.

9830. Do you manufacture furniture silks ?—I manufacture furniture silks, figured damask, tabbaretts, waistcoatings, and other fancy goods.

9831. Can you produce any patterns of furniture silks ?—Yes, I produce patterns of my manufacture. [*Producing several patterns, and at the same time producing a written*

Mr.
Louis Schwabe.

29 June,
1832.

*a written Statement, which was handed in to the Committee, a copy of which is as follows :*]—

" I BEG to produce, for the inspection of the honourable Members of the Silk Committee, patterns as specimens of the various fabrics manufactured by me in Manchester; but I beg it may be understood, they are not specimens of artificial weaving prepared for this occasion, but merely samples by which I solicit orders from the general trade; *viz.*

No. 1, 2, 3, 4, 5, 6, 7 - - - are entirely silk.

No. 8. - - - - - - is silk and worsted.

No. 9. - - - - - - is silk and cotton.

No. 1.—" Is gold-coloured figured silk Damask, manufactured entirely of British, *i.e.* Calcutta silk. The design is composed by myself, in imitation of Gessner's designs of his Idyls. The human figures are my composition, after the designs of Raphael's decoration of the Vatican. These figures are afterwards re-drawn by an artist, at the enormous expense of 1 *l.* 11 *s.* 6 *d.* per day. I allude to this, to show the considerable expense we are at for want of a School of Arts, which would enable us to obtain skilful labour of that description at a material reduction of price.

" The beauty of this pattern, as regards its manufacture, consists in its great variety, with only 600 cords employed; and I do assert, that no piece of workmanship, of the same fabric of cloth, can be exhibited to surpass it, in point of management, as regards the finish and saving of expense.

No. 2.—" Crimson and gold tissue Damask :—This is the same in design as No. 1. The warp is Italian silk, British thrown; the weft Bengal tram. I have, myself, adopted certain improvements to my Jacquard machines, by which I am enabled to complete this description of fabric at a considerable less expense and greater speed than to my belief can be produced, either in France or Spitalfields.

No. 3.—" Pattern of green silk Damask :—This is the copy from an East India design, which I submit to the inspection of the Committee, and beg to draw their attention to the fact, that East India manufactured goods, of the same quality, are of no more cost to the merchant at the East India House than the price which the warp and weft would stand the manufacturer of this country in; say 3½ ounces per yard, averaging 1 *s.* 6 *d.* per oz. would be equal to 95 *s.* per piece of 18 yards. This is a convincing proof that the East India Company must get an enormous profit upon the raw material imported into this country; and at all events adduces a reasonable conclusion, that Manchester suffers equally with Spitalfields by the present system of admitting foreign manufactured goods; so that we are not enabled to sell in competition with that Company, and until their monopoly is restricted, that branch of profitable labour will be lost to the operative of this country.

No. 4.—" Pattern of Tissue Satin, border crimson and gold, and amber :—The design is of an eminent English artist, an ornamental decorator. The warp is foreign thrown, organzine; the weft East India tram. In claiming the attention of the Committee to this specimen of workmanship, I beg to suggest the imperative necessity which exists, of giving protection to the British silk throwster, inasmuch as it often happens that the same implicit dependence cannot be placed in obtaining this article in so perfect a state as from the English throwster, owing to the variety of agents through whose hands it passes.

No. 5.—" Royal purple and gold Tissue Damask :—It has been manufactured to order for a nobleman, and is the copy of foreign manufacture of its best kind; the warp is foreign thrown silk, and is admitted to be as beautiful a specimen of tissue damask as can be produced in France; in short, this pattern has often been doubted whether it was the production of the English or French loom; it combines the firmness of plain weaving with the face of a rich satin, and exemplifies the ability of the English artizan in producing a perfect shade or wood-work, which gives additional effect to the figures.

No. 6.—" Green and white satin Damask :—This is an original design, in imitation of French fabrics; the drawing of the pattern is retained without injuring the surface of the ground-work. This is a specimen of British thrown Italian warp in its natural state, as it leaves the loom without the aid of the fiery process of the Spitalfields silk finisher, the advantage of which is, that it retains its beauty after being a long time in use, and not merely shows to advantage when new.

No. 7.—" Chinese corded Tissue Damask (pale green and cream colour :)—This fabric being exceedingly complex can only be produced by using the very best of silk, and employing the most skilful artizan. The warps of this specimen contain both English and Foreign thrown Italian organzine. The boldness of its execution adapts this work to rooms of great height, without losing any of the effect of the design, and is peculiarly suitable, both for day-light and candle-light. This pattern is my own drawing, and the texture is exclusively my own, to the best of my knowledge.

No. 8.

No. 8.—" Berlin Gros (plain dark green :)—I am the only manufacturer of this article; the beauty of this fabric is, that it emulates with velvet in its richness of appearance, and will fall in broader and more graceful folds than any other plain cloth. The warp of the best quality will contain about 9 lbs. of British thrown Italian organzine to 100 yards of cloth, and the worsted is of a description peculiar alone to this country.

No. 9.—" Silk Gobelin (crimson ground, imperial wreath :)—This is my own drawing, and is original. Though I do not pretend to exhibit specimens of artificial silk-weaving, it is my firm belief, that this species of workmanship exhibits the excellence of every process connected with the art of weaving, in as great a degree of perfection as any thing which can be produced by British artizans, where the silk weft solely is employed to produce the figure. The peculiar object of this workmanship is to imitate mosaic work; and where expense is of no object, any device which can be produced in mosaic work, can equally be effected by this description of weaving. This specimen is wrought with a draw-boy machine, but the narrower widths are made by the Jacquard loom; the peculiar mode of working the Jacquard loom is an invention of my own, and enables me to sell this fabric at a very moderate charge. I need only add, that the excellence of this article has procured me the distinguished patronage of Their Majesties, and what I have already delivered of it, along with other silk furnitures, has met with Their Majesties' entire approbation."

9832. Is the Bengal silk peculiarly adapted to fabric No. 1?—I believe it is well adapted.

9833. Does not the use of Bengal silk produce that roughness on the face which you, of course, as a manufacturer, would like very much to get rid of?—I should certainly prefer the Italian silk, if it was not much more expensive.

9834. Do you happen to know whether an article of that kind is now making in Spitalfields by any manufacturer?—[*Pointing to one of the patterns.* No. 3.]—I do not doubt but that they may manufacture a similar article in Spitalfields.

9835. Do not you, in point of fact, know of your own knowledge whether there are any manufactured there of that kind?—There are.

9836. Have you any objection to state to the Committee what you pay for weaving this per yard?—Yes; I have instructed some cotton weavers to weave this article, and having done so, I believe I can deliver the article somewhat cheaper than Spitalfields manufacturers can.

9837. The power loom is not applied to that in any degree?—I believe not.

9838. What prevents you from applying the power loom?—Speed would, in my judgment, interfere with the natural elasticity of the silk, therefore I conceive, by the application of the power loom, what would be gained by speed would be more than counterpoised by the injury done to the article manufactured and to the warp.

9839. Have you been at Lyons?—No, I never was in any manufacturing town abroad; I came to England very young, and what I know I learnt at Manchester.

9840. Are you acquainted with the sort of silk which they use in the manufacture of a similar article at Lyons?—I do not pretend to be in anywise acquainted with foreign manufacture.

9841. Do you not know that the English manufacturer has an advantage over the French, in having possession of the Bengal silk for the manufacture of such things?—No, because Bengal silk may, as I believe, be got as cheaply by the French manufacturer as it can be got by the English manufacturer; but when Bengal silk can be got by the English manufacturer at the rate it will cost when the injury to trade, resulting from the East India monopoly, ceases, my belief is, that the English manufacturer will have a decided advantage over the French.

9842. But when you speak of Bengal, these are China manufacture and not Bengal manufacture?—I believe silks are manufactured in the East Indies as well as in China.

9843. Did you ever see a China silk manufacture of these articles?—Yes, I have seen articles of the sort, said to have been made in China.

9844. Does it answer well for the purpose?—China silk answers exceedingly well.

9845. Do you consider that some of their superior kinds of silk are, for that purpose, equal to the Italian?—Decidedly so; some of them are.

9846. You stated that the persons who had been employed in manufacturing these articles you had taken from the cotton weaving; how long is it since they were weaving cotton?—Some about four years, some three years, and some two years;

Mr.
*Louis Schwabe.*

29 June,
1832.

years; but I may say very little instruction is necessary to make a clever cotton weaver a silk weaver.

9847. What branch of the cotton trade have you taken them from?—From weaving good cotton warps.

9848. Were they from figured or plain?—Both plain and figured.

9849. Is there any difficulty in a cotton weaver turning his hand to the manufacture of silks?—No, otherwise I believe many weavers now employed would be starving for want of employ.

9850. So that you mean to say the silk trade is absorbing hands heretofore employed in manufacturing single-hand weaving in the cotton trade, that were thrown out of employment by the power-looms?—Yes, I think so.

9851. And in that way the introduction of the silk trade has been a very great benefit?—Yes, at Manchester.

9852. And the persons are content to weave for very low wages?—I believe they are very well satisfied with what we have been giving them; of late there has been no complaint.

9853. How long have you been resident as a manufacturer at Manchester?—I have been residing at Manchester, as a merchant and exporter of manufactured goods, for the last 16 years, but I have not been a manufacturer all that time.

9854. How long have you been a manufacturer there?—About five or six years.

9855. What country are you a native of?—Of Dessau, in the neighbourhood of Leipsic.

9856. How many looms producing this kind of work which you exhibit, do you employ at Manchester?—As many looms as my orders and trade require.

9857. Have you any objection to state how many they are?—I think I am not called upon to do so, but I may state I can execute any order with as much dispatch as any manufacturer in Spitalfields.

9858. Have you more than 100 looms?—It does not depend on the number of looms.

9859. How many looms are there in Manchester, do you suppose, employed in that description of weaving, not of your own alone, but of other persons?—The Committee will please to observe it is not by the number of looms, or rather machines, but it is the quantity of gatings by which it can be judged what a manufacturer can do.

9860. What is the meaning of gatings?—The arrangement of the machinery.

9861. Do you mean the size and capability of the loom, its power to execute a pattern?—I mean the shafts, the comber boards, and the general arrangements of the machinery, to produce a pattern and peculiar fabric of cloth.

9862. The Committee wish to know what is the number of looms that you suppose is employed in manufacturing that description of silk goods at Manchester?—I really cannot say; I have very little personal acquaintance with other Manchester manufacturers, and I know nothing of their business; I find it quite sufficient to attend to my own concerns.

9863. Then you do not know the number of looms at Manchester, you only know your own number, which you decline to tell the Committee?—All that I wish to say is, that I can execute any order in my way of business as quickly and as well as any manufacturer in Spitalfields can.

9864. You state that you furnish employment for the operatives of Manchester; now will you tell the Committee whether you furnish employment for more than 200?—I decline to answer any question relating to my own private affairs; I may say, however, that I have two looms and upwards; that I have employed more than a hundred hands at one time; that I am not as rich as some of the Spitalfields manufacturers may be; but if I were, I may add, I think I could produce better things than what they have hitherto produced.

9865. You have been asked as to the advantages you have in the use of Bengal silk; are there any advantages you possess in the purchase of Bengal silk that the Frenchmen do not possess; cannot the French manufacturer come to the market and buy Bengal silk as well as you can, if it so answers his purpose?—Yes.

9866. Is not the market open to the French manufacturer as well as the English?—Yes.

9867. You stated you have used Bengal silk in this work because it is cheaper?—In this particular specimen (No. 1,) I used it; it was exhibited to the Board of Trade; afterwards it was shown to Mr. Huskisson, to convince him of the capability

678.                                                                                        of

Mr.
Louis Schwabe.

———————

29 June,
1832.

of the British manufacture of silk damask, entirely British, wove by British artisans, and of East India silk.

9868. The Committee understood you to say, that you used Bengal silk because it is cheaper than other silk; did you not say so?—It is cheaper than Italian silk.

9869. Can you state what is the price in France or on the Continent of the silk used in similar works there?—I only speak of my own works; I cannot speak positively as to what is paid abroad.

9870. Are you paying at Manchester for the weaving of this work, a lower or a higher price than is paid for the same work on the Continent?—I do not pretend to be acquainted with foreign prices, nor any thing of the kind.

9871. Are not some of the patterns you have shown to the Committee a mixture of silk or some other material?—It is so stated in the statement I have handed in.

9872. Then the patterns you have produced are specimens of a manufacture which is not a mannfacture actually carried on at Manchester to any extent?—I only know my own business; I know nothing of the business of my neighbours.

9873. How long is it since those patterns were made?—Some of them have been laid before the Board of Trade three or four years ago; some have been made for a particular order within the last six months, but none of them have been made to be exhibited on this occasion.

9874. Did you not say that some of them were made to show Mr. Huskisson what could be done by British manufactures?—I did.

9875. How many of those patterns have you had orders for?— Almost all.

9876. How many?—There is only one amongst them that I have not had an order for.

9877. Have you any objection to state how many yards you have sold from first to last of that description of article?—[*Pointing to one of the patterns*]—A great deal.

9878. That is not an answer to the question?—I have an objection to the question.

9879. Have you sold any lately?—Yes; there are some amongst the specimens which actually are sold.

9880. Have you sold them as specimens or as articles for use?—As articles for use, and also as articles to be exported; some of my fabrics have been exported by some of the trade in London.

9881. To what country have they been exported?—I have been informed that they have been exported to America.

9882. Is pattern No. 3, Foreign or English manufacture?—It is my own.

9883. That is your own manufacture at Manchester?—Yes.

9884. Do you know what an article similar to that may be purchased for at the East India Company's sales?—I have been informed at times for about 85 *s.* and at other times, 95 *s.*

9885. For a piece of what length?—Of eighteen yards.

9886. That is about 5 *s.* a yard; at what price can you make that to afford to sell it with a profit?—I have mentioned in my statement that the warp and weft cost me as much as about what it costs the merchant when he buys it at the East India House.

9887. Do you supply the London upholsterers with any of these articles of furniture?—Yes, many of them.

9888. Is there any reason why you do not supply them to a greater extent that you can name to the Committee?—Yes, there is.

9889. Will you state that reason?—Because the principle of business, in the trade carried on at Manchester, is totally different from the principle of the business as generally carried on in London. We at Manchester are all as much as possible for cash payments, and do not like to give long and indefinite credit. My terms are frequently objected to by London upholsterers, who require very long and indefinite credit. I have, however, among my customers, some most respectable London upholders, who buy for cash or short credit, and are satisfied with a moderate but reasonable profit.

9890. Do you know what the credit is which the London upholsterers require on the purchase from the Spitalfields manufacturer?—No; I only speak of some who require from six to twelve months; and twelve months credit has been required of me. I think three or four months credit reasonable.

9891. Then you conceive that the long credit required by many of the London
upholsterers

Mr.
*Louis Schwabe.*

———

29 June,
1832.

upholsterers is the reason why they would not deal with you?—It is so with some of them.

9892. And is a reason also why the consumer here has to pay a very high price for his articles?—Decidedly so; the longer the credit the higher the price.

9893. Do not you consider that these long credits are very injurious to any branch of manufactures?—Decidedly so.

9894. And that the nearer to a cash payment the better for every thing?—Decidedly, I am of that opinion.

9895. Now, do you mean to say that there are not houses in London in the furniture trade (in these articles) that would buy them at a short credit?—I have stated that some of the most respectable dealers and upholders in London pay cash, or are satisfied with my terms.

9896. Are there not a great number of houses in London who deal in articles of this kind, and who even supply the upholsterers in London?—Yes.

9897. Have you applied to those individuals, and have you sold any goods to them?—Yes; and I have sold goods to them.

9898. Can you mention any house in the furniture trade that you have sold these things to?—Yes, if it were necessary.

9899. There is a house of Waithman & Co. in Regent-street, that sells a good many of these things; did you apply to them?—I wish it to be perfectly understood I did not say or mean that the whole of the trade require credit. I only said and meant, that part of the trade require long credit; that is what I said, and one of the reasons I assigned for not doing more business.

9900. Do not you know that there are in London several houses of that description, who deal largely in these articles, and sell them to upholsterers, when buying them at a short credit is no object to them?—Decidedly, I said so.

9901. Have you applied to those individuals, and have you sold them any quantity?—I have applied to individuals for orders, and I have received orders.

9902. Can you mention any particular house that you have received orders from?—I do not wish to name my connexions; but if necessary I could.

9903. Do not you know that East India goods of this description are sold in the sales at cash, and that they must be paid for before they are cleared?—I am perfectly aware of that.

9904. Do you happen to know that there is not a house, even in Bond-street or the West end of the Town, and other places, that has not bought largely of these goods at the India House, and paid cash?—I do not doubt it; I know many of them are very wealthy.

9905. Well, then, can that be a reason; how do you account for your not selling these goods, because you say the length of credit has been the means of preventing you from selling these goods?—Many upholders will not buy without long credit; but that is not the only reason; one other reason is, that Spitalfields manufacturers, and upholders dependent on them, choose to decry Manchester goods.

9906. You stated just now that the reason why you did not sell these things in large quantities was, because the houses in London required a long credit?—I did not apply my observations to these particular patterns, and I only meant that that was one of the reasons.

9907. Without speaking of patterns at all, you were asked upon that whether these long credits were not a great disadvantage, and an extra charge to the consumer?—I did say so.

9908. Well, now you have been asked whether there are not houses that deal largely in these goods at the West end of the Town, the principal houses, that buy them and pay cash in the India House, as well as buying them at short credit in town?—I have not denied that such is the fact.

9909. Then the statement that you cannot sell these goods [*pointing to pattern No. 3.*] to individuals, because they give long credit, cannot be true?—I beg pardon; I did not state it with regard to this pattern; in fact, I stated distinctly that the warp and weft cost me as much money as what the piece would sell for at the East India House: that is what I say.

9910. All the evidence before the Committee goes to show, that the principle of credit in Spitalfields is very short; now how do you know that it is long, because you have stated it is long?—I am informed so by persons who are employed to sell for me.

678.                                                              9911. Then

Mr.
*Louis Schwabe.*

29 June,
1832.

9911. Then you know nothing of the fact, but as you are told?—I know that such has been the reason assigned to me by my agents.

9912. Then you do not know but as you are told?—I know that some persons have required very long credit of me.

9913. You know nothing of the fact yourself?—Yes, I have offered these very patterns, some of them at least, to certain parties, and it is to such that I allude, who say, " Pray, sir, what are your terms?" I tell them my terms, and then they turn round, and say, " We cannot do business on such terms."

9914. Might not that be a mere excuse, rather than telling you your goods are dearer or worse than other people's?—No, I know otherwise; my goods are neither dearer nor worse than other people's, and if required I can bring evidence of London dealers and upholders who will testify to the contrary.

9915. Now, have you ever offered these goods to large warehousemen in London that are capitalists, and that can afford to pay shortly?—I have.

9916. And have they sold them in considerable qualities?—These goods are not goods that any persons keep a large stock of.

9917. Did you not offer them to an upholsterer who did not like to buy them on your terms?—Yes.

9918. You do not know that the upholsterers hardly ever buy those goods at all, but they are supplied by the warehousemen in London, do you?—I do know respectable upholders who buy their goods from the manufacturer; I will not deny that there are tradespeople in London who know the London business better than myself.

9919. Are not the foreign goods which pass through the upholsterer's hands subject to the same difficulties of credit that your goods would be?—Decidedly so.

9920. In point of fact, the upholsterer does not recommend to his customers to purchase things of this kind, unless he can get a long credit on the article himself?— I believe that a prejudice, inimical to Manchester silk goods, has been industriously circulated in London by Spitalfields manufacturers, and tradespeople dependent on them, which is one reason why I do not sell my goods so easily as the Spitalfields manufacturers can.

9921. You do not happen to know that the Spitalfields people manufacture those particular articles infinitely better than down at Manchester, and infinitely better than those from the East Indies?—I am certainly not aware of that, and would willingly compete with any Spitalfields manufacturer.

9922. Have you any doubt that the people at Manchester can make them quite as well as the people at Spitalfields?—I think they make them better at Manchester.

9923. Do you mean to say that any man at Manchester can manufacture this sort of article equal to the house of Stephens Wilson?—I venture to say Stephens Wilson cannot produce a piece of cloth like this (No. 9.)

9924. Does it advance the respectability of the silk trade by introducing such a pattern as that?—[*Pointing to one of the patterns*]—That it is a very old pattern, and it is a good deal soiled.

9925. They are held probably by your agent, and shown to his customers?—Yes.

9926. And therefore have been in constant use?—Yes.

9927. How old is that pattern?—Let me see, the upholsterers for whom it was made failed in business; I think it is about two years and a half since that pattern was made.

9928. Do you know what credit the house of Stephens Wilson gives?—I have quite enough to do to manage my own business, and know nothing of theirs.

9929. But when you say long credit, you ought to know?—I have stated I only know what other people ask of me.

9930. Do you think they give any body more than six months?—I tell the Committee candidly I only mind my own business, and let other people mind theirs.

9931. When you say the London upholsterers have prejudices against the manufacturers at Manchester, do they refer to the goods or the sellers?—I must leave them to ~ide that.

9932. Supposing the gentlemen in Spitalfields wished a comparison should take place, and they have no objection to bringing goods here to be placed by the side of yours, should you have any objection?—Why, I am leaving London to-night.

9933. But

Mr.
*Louis Schwabe.*

29 June,
1832.

9933. But would you have any objection to leaving the goods?—I should not like to explain my particular mode of manufacturing in presence of my opponents.

9934. But what the Committee meant was this; that supposing any of the gentlemen of Spitalfields wished to place Spitalfields goods at one part of the room, and your goods were placed at the other, that the Committee would have an opportunity of comparing the two together at the same moment?—I really do not think that would be quite justice to myself, because I should have nobody to protect my interest as a manufacturer; I would, however, gladly compete with any Spitalfields manufacturer in producing any particular pattern of the articles manufactured by me.

9935. Then you refuse to have it done?—Unless I could be here to protect my own interest.

### *John Bowring*, Esq. LL. D. again called in; and Examined.

*John Bowring,*
Esq. LL. D.

9936. HAVE you any additional evidence to give of distinctions conferred by the French government on account of superior skill in the silk manufacture?—These patterns have called to my recollection a fact of some interest connected with that particular fabric. The man who has most advanced the production of furniture of that sort was made a member of the Legion of Honour by Buonaparte. An inquiry was instituted as to the individual who was considered to represent the Lyons manufacture in its state of greatest advancement; that individual's name is Grand, and he, in consequence, had that distinction conferred upon him.

9937. Are you aware in what light the French manufacturers view the present inquiry before this Committee?—With very considerable anxiety.

9938. Have not the French manufacturers at Lyons expressed their fear lest the Committee should recommend the prohibition of their manufactures, from the knowledge that that prohibition would produce great consequences to the commerce at Lyons. Just read that extract?

[*Dr. Bowring read the extract, which was as follows:*]

" We received from London a letter, dated the 11th of April, stating that, on the pressing solicitation, repeated a thousand times by English manufacturers, Ministers granted to them the formation of a Committee, composed of members of the House of Commons, whose object is to ameliorate the situation of the manufacturer. It is proposed to do nothing less than to prohibit French silks: Mr. Ellis is for prohibition, Mr. Morrison is against it, and they are both Members of Parliament. The Members of the Committee who are of Mr. Ellis's opinion, are for entire prohibition; those of Morrison's part of the Committee, of which Mr. Joseph Hume is at the head, desire, instead of a prohibition, to diminish duties, in order to counterbalance the benefit which the smugglers obtain, and to put an end, if it is possible, to their illicit traffic." The Editor says, " An absolute prohibition of French silks would be injurious to our manufacturers; but every thing induces us to believe, that the English Government will not lightly take so serious a determination."

---

9939. What is that from?—This is an extract, dated the 17th of April, from a Lyonnese paper.

9940. In fact, they are evidently persuaded that they have received a great benefit?—Clearly so.

9941. You have stated, that the total value of the produce of the silk manufactures of France is about five millions and a half sterling, and you have stated that the total amount of silks consumed in France, in the manufacture by looms, is 4,200,000 pounds weight, and you gather that from the various statements of the number of looms; now it has been stated by other individuals who have been examined before this Committee, that the quantity consumed is very much larger than that; and probably, if you make an allowance for the quantity used in manufacturing sewing silk and stockings...?—I returned the sewing silk and stockings.

9942. Not in your estimate of quantities?—Yes.

9943. You gave 70,000 looms, and you stated, when employed, that each loom consumed annually 60 pounds of silk, which gives 4,200,000 pounds; that excludes the quantity of sewing silk and stockings?—No, I beg to state it does not; a deduction must be made for looms not employed, and for other articles besides silk, which will, I suppose, be sufficient to cover the quantity of silk worked up without the intervention of looms. In the calculations of the whole silk manufactures of France, I mentioned before that all these calculations must be decidedly of an approximative character. The common estimate of the quantity of silk con-

*John Bowring,*
Esq. LL. D.

29 June,
1832.

sumed in France was four millions; then I corroborated that estimate from various different sources, and it appeared to me, from all these sources of evidence, that estimate could not but be a nearly accurate one.

9944. You stated that it was estimated from the best information you could obtain that each loom consumed sixty pounds weight of silk; then you stated there was 30,000 looms at Lyons; at St. Étienne, 20,000; 8,000 in different parts of France, and 2,000 at some other place, making 60,000; but in going more particularly into the inquiry, you have stated that Lyons and its neighbourhood has 35,000, and in the district round there are from 18,000 to 20,000 more?—My evidence stated, that though the number of looms at Lyons was about 33,000, that it was estimated the number of looms at this moment employed was from 24,000 to 25,000.

9945. You stated the probable quantity at work was 30,000, on account of the declining state, from the existence of the cholera at the present moment?— I stated that there had been 30,000 at work, but from the existence of the cholera that number was reduced 4,000 or 5,000, so that I estimate the number of looms at present in work at Lyons and its neighbourhood may be about 24,000 to 25,000.

9946. But if you mean to diminish the number of looms, and take an estimate of the quantity of pounds of silk consumed by each loom in the course of a year, and then say they shall be employed the whole of that time, that gives you a much larger average than sixty pounds; you state an ordinary weaver makes four ells per day; that in no ell is there less than five ounces, which, multiplied by six, gives thirty ounces per week, which is nearly 100 lbs. weight of silk for every loom?— I mentioned, among other facts, that in the Vaucluse District, the average return on a very large manufacture was only one ell and a half per day, and the Committee will also take into consideration that at Avignon as well as at Lyons, a quantity of other materials enter into the manufacture which I should think would very nearly counterbalance the quantity of silk not manufactured by the loom, but employed for other objects; at Nismes, for instance, there is a very considerable shawl manufacture, where cotton and wool enter into the article.

9947. Well, but take your own statement of 70,000 looms, and each loom consumes 60 pounds weight of silk, that gives 4,200,000 pounds; now, as matter of calculation, you can either reduce the value of these pounds into kilogrammes or take it pounds, just as you like, for the purpose of showing that there is a very great mistake in the estimated value of the manufactures of France; if you take, as you have stated you ascertained it from the manufacturer, that the kilogram of raw silk was at 70 *f.*?—Seventy francs!

9948. Yes?—I do not remember to have made any such estimate of general value; with respect to these details, I was not at all aware I should be again called upon to refer to documents, the whole of which I have delivered in, and feel great inconvenience in being thrown on my memory to justify calculations which I have presented in writing; in all these cases I have delivered in statements given me by others, always with a declaration, that I am not in any respect responsible for any incongruity, if incongruity there be. I have been asked for the French returns of the value of silk manufactures, and have delivered them in; if they are not correct, no responsibility falls upon me, nor can I be called to explain any results or any contradictions that may grow out of them; but I feel myself bound to say, and that after long experience, that the veracity and good faith of the French Government have been most exemplary, and I am compelled to bear earnest testimony to their disposition to give the most correct information; I was asked why I believed that four millions of silk were employed in France; I have obtained from numerous manufacturers their estimate, and in that they were nearly all concordant; I endeavoured to test it by other means, and it still appeared to me that the results I drew were correct; but if any individual should show that a Custom House return in this country is an incorrect return, the responsibility would fall on the individual who prepared that return, and not on the individual who presents it, or draws deductions from it.

9949. If you will reduce 4,200,000 pounds of silk into kilogrammes, and if you will then take the official value of the manufactures of France by the value fixed upon them by the Government, you will ascertain that it is nearly double the amount you have given of the value of the manufactures of France; the Committee are only desirous, as you have put this evidence before them, that you yourself should be convinced, that in stating the manufactures of France at five millions and a half, there is a great inaccuracy?—If the Committee will do me the

honour

*John Bowring,*
Esq. LL. D.

29 June,
1832.

honour of putting into my hand their estimates on paper, and showing that those estimates are irreconcileable with my evidence, I will very cautiously examine them, and explain as far as I am able the incongruity, or at once admit it; but I feel very great difficulty, without any previous notice of the nature and character of this cross-examination, in answering, off hand, objections which are really a complicated subject of figures and arithmetic; of course, if the Committee can impugn the official statement of the French Government, I am not responsible for that in any shape; I have myself no doubt at all, from the way in which on every occasion the French Government have communicated information to us, that they have given documents which they believe to represent the facts; if their veracity is disputed, I shall not object to communicate to the French Government a desire that they may be elucidated.

9950. You have stated that the official value of plain silks in France is 120*f.* per kilogram?—I have given the Custom House return.

9951. You have also stated that they give 130*f.* for wrought?—I believe so; but cannot immediately say from memory; the quantity of facts I have had to give in evidence is so numerous, that though I have no doubt my evidence may be correctly quoted by the honourable Member, I really must be allowed to refer to it before I can be expected to answer such questions as are grounded on quotations of figures, when I have not those figures before me.

9952. You have spoken of the number of looms, as particularly alluded to by Chaptal in his book; when was that published?—I cannot speak positively from recollection, but Chaptal's account does not come down to the present period.

9953. What does he estimate it at?—I am not quite sure, but I recollect I was struck with the smallness of his estimate when I read his book.

9954. The book was printed, when?—I think the first edition of his book was printed in 1819.

9955. And the last?—I am not sure whether there is another edition. I stated, with respect to all previous calculations of the looms of Lyons, that great uncertainty exists as to the numbers before 1831. I do not myself put any considerable confidence in previous statements. The census of the population, and an official estimate of the quantity of looms, were made when I was at Lyons; till then, I believe no official statements had been published.

9956. Do not you believe the looms have increased very much within the last few years?—I should think there has been, most decidedly, an increase of looms.

9957. Therefore what Mr. Chaptal has said cannot apply to the present state of things?—Clearly not.

9958. But it might have been corrected by the present time?—I have given the best information obtainable at the present time. When Chaptal was Minister of the Interior, he instituted certain inquiries as to the cultivation of silk. The increased cultivation is a matter to be estimated, inasmuch as it may be calculated in how many years a mulberry tree will be made productive, and I should think, that out of a reference to all the sources, probably a correct estimate might be formed of the present extent of the French production of raw silk.

9959. Do you consider the French authorities give you your information concerning the silk trade from a desire to serve England, and would therefore be cautious not to mislead the English silk manufacturer?—I do not believe the French Government had any other desire than to state the truth. When they gave me the information, they gave it solely with reference to the commercial commission that was then sitting; it was given as much to the French commissioners as to the English.

9960. Did you receive no information from the French authorities since it was known that you were inquiring into the silk trade?—A great deal. Many of the details that I put in, I stated grew out of the inquiry I had lately made, but the most important facts had all before come under the cognizance of the commission that was sitting at Paris.

[*Dr. Bowring was requested to come prepared, on a future day, to give the Committee an answer to the following :*]

9961. What is your reason for thinking that the value of the silk manufactures of France is only 5,500,000 *l.* when you state that the consumption of silk made into goods is 4,200,000 pounds, and when you show from information derived from manufacturers, that the expense of working up these goods is in no case less than 80 per cent. of the cost of the material, and in some instances reaching so high as 120, the great majority of goods being of that description on which the cost of labour is 90 per cent.

*Barrett Wadden,* Esq. called in; and Examined.

9962. ARE you a silk manufacturer?—I am.

9963. In Spitalfields?—In Spitalfields.

9964. How long have you been a manufacturer in Spitalfields?—Nearly ten years.

9965. Where did you reside before the time you came to settle in Spitalfields?—In Dublin.

9966. What was the cause, and what were the circumstances under which you removed to London?—I fear I shall be under the necessity of trespassing on the Committee, by giving a long answer to that question. At the time of the Union between Great Britain and Ireland, in the year 1800, there were fixed at that period what are called the Union Duties; which duties amounted to 10 per cent. on the importation of British manufactured silks into Ireland. About the year 1819, the Government of this country, desirous to amalgamate the two kingdoms into one and to unite and identify their respective interests, came to a determination to repeal the Union Duty, so called; and as long as I was a silk manufacturer in Dublin (which I believe I was for 14 years, and I have been 10 years here) the payment of 10 per cent. on British manufactured silks was, what in Dublin we silk manufacturers then considered a protection. I found by experience, that our warehousemen, our mercers, and our fashionable milliners in Dublin were constantly in the habit of visiting this Metropolis, three, four and in some instances, I believe, six times a year, in search of British goods and London fashions; and according as those things found their way into Dublin, brought in by the parties that I have already alluded to, we immediately set to work to bring out our imitations; for it was of very little importance how beautiful an article it might be that we could produce; it had no sale in our market unless it was stamped with British origin; unless it came amongst us as sanctioned by London fashion and taste. The result was, that when I was a silk manufacturer in Dublin, in common with all the other manufacturers there, we were constantly a season behind-hand, London taking the lead; and I was obliged to follow the imitations of those beautiful fabrics manufactured by Ames & Atkinson's house in London, and Campbell & Bridges, (they were the manufacturers that used to interfere with me then,) Bell & Winkworth, and another very eminent house that was in Broad-street, Adamson & Bell. We found that all our buyers came to London to those houses, and brought over some splendid specimens of British industry, and thus we required the protection of 10 per cent. to preserve us from the competition we were exposed to in this way. As soon as I discovered that the British Government had determined to repeal the Union Duties, I was appointed to be one of a deputation to wait upon the then Chancellor of the Irish Exchequer, and in company with some very influential persons, men of high character and great experience, we waited upon the Chancellor of the Exchequer, and at that interview he was assisted by Sir Henry Parnell, and by, I think, the late Lord De Vesci. We explained, on that occasion, that in our opinion, as soon as the Union Duties would be repealed, that the silk manufactures in Dublin would be destroyed; and as long as I have the use of reason, and the power of memory, I do not think I shall ever forget the answer that the Chancellor of the Exchequer then made to me: it was in these words, " You are wrong; the repeal of those duties will be to you a source of very considerable employment; for while there is a duty of 10 per cent. on British manufactures coming to Ireland, and a duty of 10 per cent. on your Irish poplins or tabinets going to England, so long you will be shut out from that market; but take away those duties, and for every ten weavers that you now employ in the production of Irish poplins or tabinets, you will in my judgment," says the Chancellor of the Exchequer, " be enabled to give employment a hundred fold." We begged leave to differ from him; however it was no great importance; they had it all their own way; the duties were repealed; and I have lived to see some of my best, my oldest and my most valued friends sent to prison, their families scattered East, West, North and South; the manufacture, as it relates to silk in the city of Dublin, almost annihilated, and the prophecy of the then Chancellor of the Exchequer exhibited, at least in my judgment, I think I am justified in saying, he was a very false prophet. Under these circumstances I came to London, determined that I would not remain there to be destroyed, and I find I was right; for I left men behind me, ten years ago, in the city of Dublin, engaged in manufacture of silk, that, on the day I left it, were worth their 14,000*l.*, their 20,000*l.*; and these men, I am sorry it grieves me to

the

*Barrett Wadden,*
Esq.

29 June,
1832.

the very heart to be compelled to speak it, they are gone; they are destroyed as manufacturers; they have lost their property, and I believe are not worth so many pence. Under these circumstances I came to Spitalfields; and now that I am here, I find a system by the same power is put in operation, that is placing me in a situation now, as it relates to France, somewhat similar to the situation that I was originally in as a Dublin manufacturer in relation to the fashions of London; that brings me till I came to Spitalfields.

9967. What was the condition of the silk manufacture at the time of your removal, the circumstances of which you have just stated, and what was the condition in which that manufacture remained up to the time of the opening of the Ports to foreign silk goods?—When I came to London, I knew, indeed common experience, common sense, pointed it out, that my first object should be to try and get a knowledge of the manners and the customs of the people, and having got that knowledge, to apply it to my own advantage. I was a good deal struck with the marked difference that I observed between the condition of the wretched silk weavers that I left behind me in Dublin, and a corresponding class of persons that I came amongst in Spitalfields. I found the weavers in Spitalfields in the possession of much more comfort than I was led to think I would find them possessed of. I observed that when Sunday came, their families made a respectable appearance, and went into the parish church, and that the men, at least as far as my knowledge went of them, presented a most respectable and orderly appearance; and here I will state a singular fact, that the first weaver I employed in London, when I came here, was a man whose appearance was so far above that class of persons that I was in the habit of seeing in Dublin. I was so much delighted with the appearance of the man, that I said to him, " I am extremely glad to see you so respectable; is it possible that you are enabled to maintain this appearance by your labour?" The answer he gave me was, " I have been for 24 years a hard-working man; I have gathered together 300*l.*, which I have in the funds, and that, with the continued renewal of my labour, enables me to preserve my family, and to appear respectable before you." I consider the weavers of Spitalfields, as a body, decidedly a very superior class of men to those that I left behind me; and I consider them as enjoying those necessaries and those comforts that are the best and perhaps the only guarantee for peaceable and good conduct that a parental Government ever need expect to have from the working part of the community.

9968. Did the alteration of the law, that is to say the opening of the Ports, produce any immediate bad consequences on the silk trade?—I found that it did; goods got amongst us at prices that I have no doubt on my mind left the first importers a very considerable profit, but at prices so far below those which we were in the habit of receiving in this market, that we really looked at each other as if we had got out of our graves. I, for instance (my eyes are never very good), but on that occasion I did open them, and looked at my brother manufacturers with the same amazement as I observed they were looking at me; we were all astonished at the state that the importation of goods was likely to bring us to, the price was so low; we almost immediately (I can speak for myself) turned round to see was there any thing left within my reach that would enable me by grasping it to come on a par with foreign production, and the first class of persons I found it necessary to grapple with were the working people. I proposed a reduction of wages, which they most reluctantly yielded to; but they were obliged, under the circumstances, to yield to a reduction of wages, and the manufacturers were obliged to yield to an alteration of their profits; and this state I believe has altogether grown out of opening the Ports to foreign manufactured goods.

9969. What has been the general condition of the silk manufacturers since the first opening of the Ports up to the present time?—It has been extremely unsettled; there do not appear to me to be any regular balance of preserving us; one time we have the appearance of briskness, another time we have all the horrors of want of employment staring our people in the face, and this producing such distress amongst our people, and such uneasiness among the manufacturers, that it is almost impossible for any man, I assert it as a fact, as it relates to myself, that I find the experience that I have gathered as a manufacturer for twenty-four years is an experience that fails me in the present condition in which I am placed; that I find my former experience no longer available to the pursuits of my business; that I am tossed into a new order of things, and that this new order of things places me in a situation as if I had almost only come into the world yesterday.

9970. You have spoken of a great reduction of wages which you were obliged to

678. resort

*Barrett Wadden,*
Esq.

——

29 June,
1832.

resort to, was it immediately after the admission of foreign silk goods that you found it necessary to begin to make that reduction?—I would say not immediately; as well as my memory serves me, the reduction was not an immediate one, for the Government, seeing that there were some difficulties in the way, they, I believe, altered their original design, and rendered it imperative upon the importer of foreign manufactured silks to bring them in at certain lengths. The French manufacturers at that time were not prepared for such an alteration, and consequently many of the productions which they had got ready for this market remained with them in their own; they were not admissible; they were not answering or corresponding to the lengths which the act of permission gave them; therefore, on the other hand, there was an enormous anxiety among the people of this country to get hold of foreign productions. Those foreign productions having been shut out for a great number of years, increased the anxiety of every lady in the land, and I would almost say of our servant maids, to get hold of something foreign. As soon as the Ports were open for the admission of those foreign goods, the public were in a great measure disappointed, for they did not come in in those quantities to satisfy the demand that was remaining for them, and the demand would not give way; it must be satisfied; and it required the continued import of the French goods from France, added to whatever stock we had in Spitalfields, and a continuation of employment, to satisfy the enormous demand that was then standing in expectation of being satisfied with foreign productions.

9971. Has the deterioration in the trade of which you have spoken, both as to wages and as to profits, been progressive up to the present time?—There was, I would say, a progressive decline of wages and of profits from the year 1825 to the latter part of 1826, and a further decline took place in both wages and profits from that period down to 1829, and it has been one series of drooping from 1829 down to the present time; therefore I am safe in saying, that the deterioration as to wages and profits has been progressive up to the present time.

9972. Do you consider that the English manufacturer made every practicable exertion to meet the foreign competition?—I think the English manufacturer has made every exertion which very considerable capital, great experience, and a determined industry on his part would enable him, that he would not be put down by foreign competition; but this capital, this industry, and this experience, so exerted by him, has failed.

9973. Are you in the plain or the fancy department of the trade?—Altogether in the manufacture of plain goods.

9974. Are you at all interested in the throwing of silk?—Directly, I am not; indirectly, I say, that I am; that is, I have an interest in common with every manufacturer of silk goods in this country, to uphold the British throwster; I myself am not connected with a mill, but common foresight points out this to my mind, that if the British throwster ceases to be protected by a fair preference given to him by the British silk manufacturer, that the British silk manufacturer must necessarily arrive at a period of time when he will cease to have the benefit that arises out of the competition carried on between the foreign throwster and the British throwster, and therefore I am most anxious to preserve the British silk throwster, knowing that as long as I do that I render a benefit to myself, and that is the explanation that I give to the term when I say that I am indirectly interested in the throwing mills of this country.

9975. You have spoken of the condition of the working class in Spitalfields at the time when you first came to reside among them; are the Committee to infer from what you say, you consider that they were at that time a highly respectable body of persons?—I considered them so respectable that it made a very strong impression upon my mind, and I put up my two hands and returned thanks to God for the change I saw; I came from a place where I saw a great deal of misery and wretchedness to a place where I found more respectable men, amenable both to the laws of their country and respectful to their masters.

9976. They were, then, at that time both an orderly and respectable body of persons?—I considered very much so.

9977. What has been their general condition since 1826, and what is their condition now?—Their condition is, I regret to say it, altered much for the worse; I consider their condition to be wretched in the extreme, and that wretchedness will appear more apparent when I present to this honourable Committee the papers that I have here. The first paper that I have the honour of submitting to this Committee is, " A Comparative View of the various Expenses of manufacturing

turing 232 lbs. of Italian organzine silk and 168 lbs. of Italian tram silk, British thrown, into 5,183 yards of plain gros de Naples, in the years 1824, 1826 and 1831 respectively, in Spitalfields." I must preface this document by this simple remark, that this is an account taken from my own books. In the year 1824 I paid the throwster, for throwing these 400 lbs. weight of silk, 134 *l.* 16 *s.*, dyeing it 64 *l.* 16 *s.*, winding 50 *l.*, warping 13 *l.* 1 *s.*, weaving 226 *l.* 15 *s.* 1½ *d.*; total, 489 *l.* 8 *s.* 1½ *d.*, making an expense per pound of 24 *s.* 5½ *d.* for converting it from the raw state into plain gros de Naples. In the year 1826 the Ports were opened for the admission of foreign manufactured silks, and the throwster fell to 97 *l.* 8 *s.*, the dyer to 49 *l.* 4 *s.*, the winder to 38 *s.* 11 *d.*, the warper to 10 *l.* 3 *s.*, the weaver to 172 *l.* 15 *s.* 4 *d.*; making a total, in the year 1826, of 368 *l.* 1 *s.* 4 *d.*, or 18 *s.* 4¾ *d.* per pound weight.

9978. That applies to the last half o the year 1826?—Yes. In the year 1831 the throwing further descended to 73 *l.* 4 *s.*, the dyeing to 40 *l.*, winding 32 *l.* 2 *s.*, warping 7 *l.* 19 *s.* 6 *d.*; weaving 151 *l.* 3 *s.* 5 *d.*; total, 304 *l.* 8 *s.* 11 *d.*, or 15 *s.* 2¾ *d.* on the pound weight of manufactured silk; so that the reduction in throwing since 1824 is 46 per cent., the reduction in dyeing 38½ per cent., winding 36 per cent., warping 38½ per cent., weaving 33½ per cent.; an average reduction presenting itself of 38½ per cent. Need the Committee be surprised, is it necessary that I should point out the state of degradation and the horrible misery that is inflicted on the working community, when I see the wages reduced 38½ per cent. since the year 1824, and when I accompany that document with one that I shall now read. As soon as I went in pursuit of those documents drawn from my own books, to ascertain what the reduction has been since the year 1824 in every department of our manufacture, my mind immediately went in search to see was there a corresponding reduction in the necessaries of life, and I here have an average price of the underwritten articles during the years 1824, 1826 and 1831; the years correspond to the years in my own accounts, and I find that the four pound loaf, in the year 1824, was 9¼ *d.*; in the year 1826, 8¾ *d.*; and in the year 1831, 9 *d.*; bread has fallen in that period 2¾ per cent. Meat has not varied; it was 6 *d.* and an eighth in the year 1824, and was 6 *d.* and an eighth last year. Coals, per chaldron, in the year 1824, were 52 *s.* 9 *d.*; in the year 1826 they were 50 *s.* 6 *d.*; and last year they were 43 *s.*, presenting a decrease of 17 per cent. Soap and candles remained, from the year 1824 to the 31st of December last, the same price, namely 7 *d.*; a reduction has since taken place, by the repeal of duty on candles. Potatoes, per hundred, have fallen from 3 *s.* per cwt. to 2 *s.* 6 *d.*, or 16¾ per cent. Bacon has not varied. Butter has advanced 9 per cent. Tea has fallen from 5 *s.* 4 *d.* to 4 *s.* 8 *d.* or 12½ reduction. Sugar has fallen from 6½ *d.* to 6 *d.* or 7¾ reduction; and porter has fallen 20 per cent.; so that the average reduction of bread, meat, coals, soap, potatoes, bacon, butter, tea, sugar, porter, such articles as our poor must have, let them get them what way they will, the average reduction since 1824 is 7½ per cent., while the reduction of their wages is 38½ per cent. If I am asked, is the state of the people in Spitalfields worse now than it was before the opening of the Ports, and is their condition wretched, my answer is, take 7½ per cent. from 38½ per cent., and they are 31 per cent. poorer now than they were then.

*Barrett Wadden, Esq.*

29 June, 1832.

COMPARATIVE VIEW of the various EXPENSES of Manufacturing 232 *lbs.* of ITALIAN ORGANZINE, and 168 *lbs.* ITALIAN TRAM SILK, British Thrown, into 5,183 Yards plain Gros de Naples, in the Years 1824, 1826, 1831, respectively, in *Spitalfields*.

| YEARS | Throwing. | Dyeing. | Winding. | Warping. | Weaving. | TOTAL. | Expense per lb. |
|---|---|---|---|---|---|---|---|
|  | £.   *s.*   *d.* | £.   *s.*   *d.* | £.   *s.*   *d.* | £.   *s.*   *d.* | £.   *s.*   *d.* | £.   *s.*   *d.* | *s.*   *d.* |
| 1824   -   -   - | 134  16  – | 64  16  – | 50  –  – | 13  1  – | 226  15  1½ | 489  8  1½ | 24  5½ |
| 1826   -   -   -  (This Year Foreign made Silks admitted.) | 97  8  – | 49  4  – | 38  11  – | 10  3  – | 172  15  4 | 368  1  4 | 18  4¾ |
| 1831   -   -   - | 73  4  – | 40  –  – | 32  2  – | 7  19  6 | 151  3  5 | 304  8  11 | 15  2¾ |
| Reduction since 1824 | 46 per cent. | 38½ p' cent. | 36 p' cent. | 38½ p' cent. | 33½ p' cent. | 38½ p' cent. | { Average Reduction. |

AVERAGE PRICE of the Underwritten ARTICLES during the Years 1824, 1826, 1831, in *Spitalfields*.

| YEARS | Bread 4 lb. Loaf. | Meat per lb. | Coals per Chaldron. | Soap and Candles per lb. | Potatoes per Cwt. | Bacon per lb. | Butter per lb. | Tea per lb. | Sugar per lb. | Porter per Quart. | |
|---|---|---|---|---|---|---|---|---|---|---|---|
| | d. | d. | s. d. | d. | s. d. | d. | d. | s. d. | d. | d. | |
| 1824 - - | 9¼ | 6⅛ | 52  9 | 7 | 3  - | 6½ | 11 | 5  4 | 6½ | 5 | |
| 1826 - - | 8¾ | 6¼ | 50  6 | 7 | 3  - | 6½ | 11 | 5  - | 6½ | 5 | |
| 1831 - - | 9 | 6⅛ | 43  - | 7 | 2  6 | 6½ | 12 | 4  8 | 6 | 4 | |
| Reduction since 1824 } | 2¾ p'cent. | - - | 17 p'cent | - - | 17 p'cent. | - - | - - | 12½ p' ct. | 7¾ p'cent. | 20 p'cent. | Average Reduction since 1824 is 7½ per cent. |
| Advance since 1824 - } | - - | - - | - - | - - | - - | 9 p' ct. | — | — | — | | |

*Barrett Wadden.*

*Barrett Wadden,*
Esq.

——

29 June,
1832.

9979. You have stated, that the weavers of Spitalfields are 31 per cent. worse now than they were in the year 1824; do you mean to say that they are not even worse than that sometimes, for want of employment?—The Tables which I have had the honour of handing in, are Tables extracted from my own books. What I am about to state is this; that I believe I may fairly say of myself, that there is not a silk manufacturer, either in Spitalfields or out of Spitalfields, that gives more permanent employment to the people that he employs than I do; that from Christmas to Christmas if they are a day idle, it is their own fault; and then when I say their condition is 31 per cent. worse now than it was then, I mean to say that that is the condition of a man working six days in a week, and every working day in the year.

9980. About what number do you employ?—I think when the Ports were open I had about 300, and now I have only between 60 and 70; I find it a very unprofitable trade.

9981. You employ about a fifth?—Yes.

9982. Are these calculations taken in any particular months of the year?—No; the average of the entire year: I had a good deal of difficulty in obtaining those; and I can assure the Committee, they are framed with a conscientious regard to truth.

9983. Have you had any opportunity of seeing the persons who work for you at their own houses, so as to judge more particularly of their condition?—I have had some opportunities of seeing the weavers at their own houses; and I regret to say, that I have oftentimes considered it almost unsafe to go into their dwellings, their condition was so truly wretched, many of them have their bed gone to the pawnbroker or taken away for the nonpayment of rent, and that their condition is one so truly altered, that it must present itself to the mind of every person in the habit of coming into Spitalfields; the first alteration that takes place in a weaver's family, that has enjoyed comfort, is, that the little article of superfluous dress that his wife may possess or himself, is the first article to find its way to the pawnbroker's shop; the next article that follows is something that the family actually want, but the time is arrived when they must part with it, and thus they go on parting with one article after another till, in very many instances, the midnight lamp has no longer oil in it; not that the wisdom of the weaver has vanished, but he is obliged to take it to the pawn-shop to borrow a few pence on it: the shuttles are gone to pawn; their whole condition is so altered that, absolutely, when persons have come strongly recommended to me for employment, and I now state a case, that occurred no later than last week; some persons came to me strongly recommended as to integrity, and as to ability to weave; I sent my clerk to examine what condition those weavers were in before I would entrust my work into their hands; and he reported to me, that their condition was so forlorn; nothing in their room but a loom and a pallet on the floor; no table, no chair; that as soon as the report was made to me, I said, " I cannot employ them; I run a risk in placing valuable work in the hands of men who have not the means to execute it in that

manner

manner that they would execute it had they those means, and were they in the situation of life that they were formerly in."

*Barrett Wadden,*
Esq.

29 June,
1832.

9984. Was there much smuggling going forward in respect of foreign silk goods, during the existence of the prohibitory laws?—I can only here state an opinion, my opinion is, that there was just that quantity of smuggling carried forward that gave a stimulus to manufacturers and to improvements, that the articles smuggled, I firmly believe, were more generally brought in by persons visiting the Continent than they were by persons in trade, for there were so many difficulties placed in the way of selling contraband goods, that I doubt very much that a man would expect to make it a profitable transaction to pursue it as a trade. But the persons visiting the Continent found means of bringing in occasionally certain fabrics, which, finding their way into the hands of milliners and of friends, we, in many instances, obtained our patterns from those productions so brought in, and received a stimulus that I am almost inclined to think was then of benefit to us; and here I will record a singular fact in Ireland; I was indebted to a most respectable house in Belfast that furnished me with the first piece of French dyed black gros de Naples that was brought into Ireland, and it was brought by a smuggler into Belfast; so that for the fourteen years that I was a manufacturer of silks in Dublin, I never knew of any smuggling taking place among traders, but that one instance; and it is a curious fact, that as soon as my customer in Belfast bought these half dozen pieces of silk upon that occasion brought in, they cut off a pattern, sent it to me, and abused me for the horrible colour which I had been selling to them as a good black. I sent for my silk-dyer; we pulled the pattern asunder, analyzed the colour, and discovered the ingredient used in the dyeing of it; and I am proud to say, I was manufacturing French black silks for about a year and a half before that colour appeared in London.

9985. Has smuggling increased in your opinion since the legal admission of foreign silk goods?—I believe that smuggling has increased, and I hope I am not out of order, to use a phrase made use of some time last January or February by the present Chancellor of the Exchequer, his words were, " smuggling has increased to such an enormous extent, that we can have no conception of it." I beg leave to say, that I believe the noble Lord the Chancellor of the Exchequer on that occasion spoke the truth.

9986. Is it your opinion that smuggling has been progressively increasing, and that it is now more extensive than it was after the time of the opening of the Ports?—I have no doubt but it is more extensive.

9987. To what do you attribute the reason that the fewer goods should be smuggled when there was no other way of obtaining them than now when they can be legally imported?—When the article was prohibited it was accompanied by the right of search, which rendered it extremely difficult and dangerous to sell, even in a clandestine manner, foreign manufactured silks; but now when the Ports are open (and I doubt whether I ought to use the word smuggler, the last Witness that has been before the Committee has given him the name of public benefactor); now that the Ports are open to the public benefactor in the character of smuggler, every man lays claim to that high character; and if business should continue much longer in the same state as it is, I am very much inclined to think I shall become a smuggler or a public benefactor.

9988. Was there not a general reduction of duties in the year 1829?—There was.

9989. What was the object proposed by that reduction?—The then Government assured the Silk Manufacturers' Committee, of which I had the honour of being a member, that they had but one object in view, and that object was to put an end to smuggling.

9990. Was it at that period stated what the smugglers' charge was considered to be?—It was stated by the then President of the Board of Trade that the smugglers' charge was from 25 to 28 per cent.

9991. Do you know in what manner the smugglers' price was at that period supposed to be ascertained?—I understood, and I believe it to be the fact, the price was ascertained by the then President of the Board of Trade corresponding with the public benefactor at Calais, and finding out what he would charge an occasional customer for smuggling goods.

9992. Were not the duties reduced at that period to the level of the smugglers' charge, in the belief, on the part of the Government, that by that means smuggling would be prevented?—It was; and I shall, with the permission of the Committee,

678.                                                                state

*Barrett Wadden*,
Esq.

29 June,
1832.

state now what I stated then ; I was one of a few gentlemen that had the honour of waiting upon the Duke of Wellington ; he was then Premier; and the Duke listened most attentively and most kindly to all the tale of distress that we had to unfold, and every thing that we said, the burthen of the song on the part of the Duke was, " Aye, but the smuggler, what are we to do with him ; we must lower the duties to get rid of him ;" and upon that occasion I took the liberty of taking from the ink-stand that was then on the noble Duke's table two pens, and, holding them as I do now, I said, " My Lord Duke, let those two pens represent two roads, and let my finger and thumb represent Lyons ; here are two roads from Lyons to England or Spitalfields, that on one road there is a toll-bar, which is kept by the smuggler ; and he has got up a board, and he says all goods coming this way shall be charged 25 per cent. ; the Government has got up a toll-bar on the other road, and on their board it is announced that all goods coming this way shall be charged 35 per cent., consequently we were injured by the smuggler bringing his goods into the market;" and the noble Duke at the head of His Majesty's Government found that he had very little to do at his toll-bar, for the smuggler was getting all the business. We went up and stated the amount of our wretchedness ; the Duke says, " Aye, the smuggler is the cause of it, and to relieve you from all this wretchedness, we will reduce our price to that identical price which the smuggler is charging you." " I beg leave most humbly but most respectfully to state, upon that occasion then we shall have injury inflicted upon us by two persons instead of one ;" that is absolutely the fact : the object which the Government had very properly in view, to put an end to illicit trade, has not done it, while it has brought us into a situation much worse than we were in prior to that change.

9993. Do you mean to say, that instead of the alteration having had the effect proposed, smuggling has not lessened, but on the contrary has increased, since the year 1829 ?—The conviction on my mind is, that the alteration has not produced the effect which the Government had contemplated, and that smuggling has very considerably increased since 1829.

9994. If a further reduction of duties should take place, do you think that the smuggler will still be able to carry on his trade, that is to say, do you consider that the smuggler can still afford to lower his charge ?—Should a further reduction of duty take place, I am quite satisfied that means will be devised for the smuggler to lower his charge, viewing, as I do, the character of that personage, altered from a smuggler into a public benefactor ; he will necessarily look around for some means of conferring the greatest benefit on the public ; and if he finds the public force his 25 per cent. charge down to 20, the probability is, that he will find out or discover means whereby he can descend to 15 per cent. I have heard much of the charge of smuggling ; it is far from me to say how far these accounts are right or wrong ; but I am rather inclined to think that smuggling can be carried on, and profitably conducted for a charge considerably less than 25 per cent. ; and I have only to add this, that the smuggler can afford to lower his price; that the smuggler in all human probability will not lower his price till he is compelled to do so ; need this honourable Committee consider me wrong in coming to this opinion, when I find that a box two feet long, twenty inches wide, and twenty inches deep, will contain plain gros de Naples to the value of 414*l.*, so that here is a quantity of property compressed into a compass so small that it can easily be got on shore.

9995. Have you had any opportunity of seeing goods which have been smuggled ?—I have seen a great deal.

9996. Of what sorts were those goods ?—They were plain, figured and fancy goods.

9997. Do you consider that the reduction of duties in 1829 was beneficial or injurious in its effect, on the whole, on the silk trade ?—I consider that the reduction of duties in the year 1829 was both beneficial and injurious in its effects, that is, the amount of benefit which it conferred was but a small per centage on the aggregate of injury it produced.

9998. Do you consider that a further reduction of duties will at all tend to relieve the trade from any of the disadvantages under which it now labours ?—Perhaps before I answer that question I may be permitted to explain to the Committee what I mean by the words beneficial and injurious.

9999. Yes, explain to the Committee in what respects you consider the alteration of the law in 1829 to have conferred a benefit, and in what respects it has been injurious ?—The injury that that change of law inflicted was this ; it reduced the duty from 5*s.* a pound down to 3*s.* 6*d.*, and compelled the silk throwster of

this

*Barrett Wadden,*
Esq.

29 June,
1832.

this country to turn round on the people in his employ and reduce their wages in a proportionate degree, so that I believe there are silk mills at work in this country where the wages of the people do not go beyond 2 *s.* 11 *d.* per week, and that 2 *s.* 11 *d.* per week was a state of wages forced upon the people by reducing the duties upon foreign thrown silks from 5 *s.* to 3 *s.* 6 *d.*; that reducing the duty from 15 *s.* to 11 *s.* on the pound weight of manufactured silk compelled the manufacturers in Spitalfields, of whom I am one, to turn round on our throwster, our dyer, winder, warper and weaver, and extract a reduction out of their united earnings to enable us to stand this competition; so far for what I mean by the term injury. Now as to what I mean by beneficial; the alteration which was then made was accompanied with an arrangement that I think I am justified in calling beneficial; that is, the law that changed or lowered the duties from 5 *s.* to 3 *s.* a pound conferred a benefit upon the persons exporting manufactured goods, by giving the original importer of foreign thrown silks a certificate or a debenture, which was a transferrable article representing 3 *s.* 6 *d.*, the amount of duty paid, and the man that could export a quantity of goods found those debentures in the market, which entitled him to receive a corresponding drawback; so that while the measure was a measure of injury to every man in the trade, that injury, I must admit, was lessened to what I will call a per centage on the aggregate of injury; it was lessened by encouraging an export trade, which export trade we could not have only for the formation of that thing which we call a certificate or debenture.

10000. Did those debentures give any advantage to the importers of Italian silks beyond the price for which the debentures were sold?—I should think not.

10001. Then that advantage accrued to the manufacturers who manufactured a different description of silk?—I shall come to that.

10002. Do you consider that a further reduction of duties will at all tend to relieve the trade from any of the disadvantages under which it at present labours? —I am satisfied that so far from relieving the trade by a further reduction of duties, I hope I am not wrong in giving an honest expression to my own feelings, but I must in justice to myself say, that I absolutely consider it a symptom of insanity for any man to recommend it.

10003. Are the goods which you manufacture of a low or of a rich quality?— All the goods I manufacture are of the best description, a rich quality.

10004. When you speak of the depreciation and difficulties of the silk trade of Spitalfields, do you mean to say that you find it difficult to sell those goods which you manufacture?—I am in the habit, and ever have been, of manufacturing the very best description of goods, and I find it very difficult indeed to sell my goods at a profit; I can sell any quantity of them, if I will sell them at a loss.

10005. Whence do you consider that difficulty to arise; is it from the Manchester goods that are in the market?—As far as it relates to my business, the difficulty does not arise to me from Manchester, it arises from the import of the better description of gros de Naples, which are the only description of goods I make.

10006. Of the description of goods you make, namely, rich plain goods, has there been a larger quantity made in Spitalfields of late than formerly?—I should say not, decidedly not.

10007. Has the use, on the part of the public, of such goods fallen off?—My opinion is, that the use on the part of the public of those goods has not fallen off.

10008. Then how do you consider that the consumption has been supplied?— A very considerable part of the consumption, I believe, has been supplied by the import of goods from France, through the legal imports and the occasional operation of the public benefactor supplying the public.

10009. Upon what description of goods are the looms of Spitalfields chiefly employed?—Principally upon plain low priced goods made from inferior silks, and those inferior silks rendered cheap by every species of craft and cunning in the introduction of heavy dyes.

10010. Has the trade of Spitalfields removed to Manchester?—I should say not, and I think that that will appear manifest, when a most respectable gentleman has appeared before this honourable Committee, the representative of I believe the first, decidedly the first house in London, if not in Europe; that witness has put it upon record that the sales of their great house have not diminished in Spitalfields, that they remain about the same; that circumstance—(I did not require to be assured of a fact that I know)—but that circumstance led me to believe that I was

678. perfectly

*Barrett Wadhen,*
Esq.

—————

29 June,
1832.

perfectly correct in believing the trade of Spitalfields has not gone to Manchester; I think we remain stationary in Spitalfields.

10011. Do you consider that the English manufacture has improved since the year 1826?—Here I am compelled to say that in my judgment, and that judgment scattered over 24 years experience, we have not improved in Spitalfields since the year 1826.

10012. You have before stated that every exertion has been resorted to by the manufacturer to compete successfully with foreign goods; how do you reconcile that answer with there being no improvement in the workmanship?—I have stated that every exertion which capital and unwearied diligence on the part of the manufacturers, and labour on the part of the working people have been made, but wages have fallen so low as to render it utterly impossible to preserve the condition of the working people; the consequence is, that our working people yield to the low wages, they become careless in the performance of their works, and justify that carelessness by the miserable wages they receive; and I am satisfied that, if reference be made to the magistrates, it will turn out that in some instances, when weavers have been brought before them charged with negligence, the magistrates, from motives of humanity, have refused to inflict punishment, on the ground that the wages of the people were so low that the working man had but his choice of evils, either to get through his work with all possible dispatch, and save his family from starvation, or to use that diligence that he was bound to use in the performance of his duty towards his employer, and become so exhausted as to be unfit to finish that work that he had commenced.

10013. Have you paid any attention to the quantities of the different sorts of silk goods imported?—I have paid some attention to try and find out what was the cause of our distress, and how far that cause could be relieved, and in examining the official imports I found that one article, namely, plain velvet and figured velvet imported into this country from the 5th of January 1830 to the 5th of January 1831 was what in my judgment was considerable; and my attention was called to the import of velvet on this ground, that the importation of velvet into this country from abroad only interferes with Spitalfields, for that velvets are not yet made in Manchester, notwithstanding the enormous improvements that have taken place there in other departments of weaving; those velvets are only made in Spitalfields, and my attention was turned to the official accounts, to ascertain what quantity of labour was supplanted in Spitalfields by the import of 13,475 lbs. weight of plain silk velvet, containing 3,369 pieces, each piece 32 yards long; also 1,372 lbs. weight of figured velvet, containing 240 pieces, each piece 30 yards long, being the quantity imported into this country from the 5th of January 1830 to the 5th of January 1831. I now solicit the attention of this honourable Committee to this important fact, that the plain velvets imported that year, the silk contained in them would cost me 15,662 *l.* 2*s.* 6*d.* and the wages would cost me 26,901 *l.* 1*s.* 6*d.*, which is 171¾ per cent. on the cost of the raw silk, or 63¼ per cent. on the cost of the goods: so far for the plain velvets. The figured velvets—(the injury that is inflicted on the weavers here is enormous)—the figured velvets contained silk that would cost me 1,600 *l.* 1*s.* 6*d.*, and the wages on this 1,600 *l.* 1*s.* 6*d.* would be 4,683 *l.* 8*s.* 6*d.*, so that the wages on those figured velvets imported, if they had been made in Spitalfields, would have amounted to 292⅔ per cent. on the cost of the raw silk, or 74½ per cent. on the price of the goods. Curiosity led me to inquire somewhat further, to ascertain what number of persons I should employ, if I were the fortunate manufacturer to receive an order to that extent from any of the highly respectable warehousemen of London, I would require a silk mill employing 600 persons, 22 dyers, 132 winders, 53 warpers, 922 weavers, 150 quillers, or a total of 1,882 people, whose labour during this period of importation has been supplanted, not by their labour going to Manchester, for Manchester has not even made velvets, but by a demand for their labour being transferred to the manufacturer abroad.

AN ACCOUNT

AN ACCOUNT showing the Cost of Raw Silk, Wages, and other Charges of Manufacturing 13,475 *lbs.* of Plain Silk Velvet, containing 3,369 Pieces, each Piece 32 yards long. Also, 1,372 *lbs.* of Figured Velvet, containing 240 Pieces, each Piece 30 yards, being the Quantity Imported into this Country from 5th January 1830 to the 5th January 1831.

*Barrett Wadden,*
Esq.

29 June,
1832.

| | £. | s. | d. | £. | s. | d. |
|---|---|---|---|---|---|---|
| 17,011 *lbs.* of Fossombrone Raw Silk, at 19 *s.* - - - | 16,160 | 9 | – | | | |
| 2½ per cent. for Cash 14 days - - - - | 404 | – | – | | | |
| | 15,756 | 9 | – | | | |
| Deduct, for Waste sold, 539 *lbs.* at 3 *s.* 6 *d.* | 94 | 6 | 6 | | | |
| | | | | 15,662 | 2 | 6 |
| Cash paid, throwing 16,337 *lbs.* Organzine, 5 *s.* per lb. - | 4,084 | 5 | – | | | |
| Ditto - dyeing - - - „ - - - „ - - | 1,505 | 4 | – | | | |
| Ditto - winding - - - - - - - | 1,350 | 6 | – | | | |
| Ditto - warping - - - - - - - | 673 | 16 | – | | | |
| Ditto - weaving - - - - - - - | 18,866 | 8 | – | | | |
| Ditto - wires - - - - - - - | 84 | 4 | 6 | | | |
| Ditto - Pasteboard Cases - - - - - | 336 | 18 | – | | | |
| | | | | 26,901 | 1 | 6 |
| The Wages is 171 ¼ per cent. on the cost of the Raw Silk, or 63¼ per cent. on the cost of the Goods. | | | | | | |

| | £. | s. | d. | £. | s. | d. |
|---|---|---|---|---|---|---|
| 1,739 *lbs.* of Fossombrone Raw Silk, 19 *s.* per lb. - - | 1,652 | 1 | – | | | |
| 2½ per cent. discount, Cash 14 days - - - | 41 | 6 | – | | | |
| | 1,610 | 15 | – | | | |
| Deduct for Waste sold, 61 *lbs.* 3 *s.* 6 *d.* - | 10 | 13 | 6 | | | |
| | | | | 1,600 | 1 | 6 |
| Cash paid, throwing 1,663 *lbs.* Organzine, 5 *s.* - - | 415 | 15 | – | | | |
| Ditto - dyeing - - - - - - - | 207 | 17 | 6 | | | |
| Ditto - winding - - - - - - - | 138 | 16 | – | | | |
| Ditto - warping - - - - - - - | 225 | – | – | | | |
| Ditto - weaving - - - - - - - | 3,660 | – | – | | | |
| Ditto - wire drawer - - - - - - | 12 | – | – | | | |
| Ditto - Pasteboard Cases - - - - - | 24 | – | – | | | |
| | | | | 4,683 | 8 | 6 |
| The Wages is 292 ⅔ per cent. on the cost of the Raw Silk, or 74 ½ per cent. on the Goods. | | | | | | |
| Total Cost of Plain and Figured Velvets - - - £. | | | | 48,846 | 14 | – |

*(left margin: 13,475 lbs. Plain Velvets. / 1,372 lbs. Figured Velvets.)*

| Sent to the Throwster, 18,750 *lbs.* Raw Silk. | | Sent to the Dyer, 18,000 *lbs.* Organzine Silk. | |
|---|---|---|---|
| | *lbs.* | | *lbs.* |
| Received back, thrown into Organzine | 18,000 | Received back, Dyed hard - - | 5,440 |
| Waste - - - | 600 | Dyed soft - - | 9,420 |
| Waste invisible - - | 150 | Weight lost in Dyeing | 3,140 |
| | 18,750 | | 18,000 |

These Velvets, if made in Spitalfields, would give active employment for Seven Months,—

| To Silk Mill, employing Persons - - - | 600 |
|---|---|
| Dyers - - - - - - - - | 22 |
| Winders - - - - - - - | 132 |
| Warpers - - - - - - - | 53 |
| Weavers - - - - - - - | 922 |
| Quillers - - - - - - - | 153 |
| Total - - - | 1,882 |

Besides Reed-makers, Thread-makers, Harness-makers, Wire-Drawers, Turners, &c. &c.

*Barrett Wadden.*

10014. Are you enabled to give the Committee any further calculations which you may have formed, as to the employment which some of the articles introduced from abroad would give to the British artisan?—If that question would be adjourned to a future period of my examination, the documents that I have are arranged so that they will come in order.

10015. Have you any knowledge of the rate of wages at Lyons, and of the cost of the various processes of manufacture at that place?—I have some knowledge of the rate of wages payable at Lyons, and that knowledge led me to draw out comparative accounts of the manufacture of plain goods and figured goods in Lyons,

678. and

*Barrett Wadden,*
·Esq.

———

29 June,
1832.

and in Spitalfields respectively, which accounts I shall now have the honour of submitting to this Committee. The account now before the Committee is a comparative view of the cost and expenses of manufacturing 100 kilogrammes of organzine, and 75 kilogrammes of tram silk into 5,296 yards of plain gros de Naples at Lyons and Spitalfields respectively. I thought it much better to present to this honourable Committee a quantity of silk manufactured, than to fix their attention on either a yard or on a pound weight, for that if we descend to the particulars attendant on either the yard or the pound weight, there are so many fractional parts, either to be laid aside or improperly used, as to prevent this honourable Committee from coming to a fair conclusion of the comparative cost that actually does exist between Lyons and Spitalfields. I will further, before I read this document, observe, that these accounts, or comparative views were framed by me last March, from information which I had from Lyons, on the 13th of the previous October and on the 11th day of the following December, and which accounts I find to stand a comparison with every channel of information that at least I am capable of getting at. I find that last December, for 100 kilogrammes of organzine silk at Lyons the price was 58 francs; that 75 kilogrammes of tram at Lyons could be had for 54$f.$; that these sums, when reduced by a discount of 12$\frac{1}{2}$ per cent., subject to one month's credit, is represented by 8,618$f.$ 75$c.$; that the dyeing of this silk at Lyons is 72 sous per kilogram: Dr. Bowring, the other day, gave in an account of the manufacture of 500 ells of satin, which I shall come to directly, and he represented the dyeing at 12 sous less than I do. The winding 75 kilogrammes organzine, at 60 sous; the warping is paid by the day, 30 sous; the weaving 4,236$\frac{4}{5}$ ells, at 55$c.$ per ell, gives an aggregate of 11,862$f.$ 99$c.$, which, taking the exchange at 25$f.$, is 474$l.$ 10$s.$ 5$d.$: a similar weight of Piedmont organzine silk manufactured at Spitalfields being equivalent to 220 lbs. 12 oz., and a similar weight of Italian tram, being equivalent to 165 lbs. 9 oz. of our weights: this silk was manufactured by me, and the prices I have here set down, and the prices that I am paying at this moment, the article, when produced by me, would cost me 662$l.$ 11$s.$ 7$\frac{1}{2}d.$, or 39$\frac{2}{3}$ per cent. on the cost price at Lyons. I believe the last Witness was not wrong when he stated the difference between the production of France and England took a range of between 30 and 40 per cent.

10016. The silks used here [*pointing to the Account*] are of the same fineness in both cases?—The same precisely.

December 1831.

**COMPARATIVE VIEW** of the Cost and Expenses of Manufacturing 100 Kilogrammes of Organzine, and 75 Kilogrammes of Tram Silk, into 5,296 Yards plain Gros de Naples, at *Lyons* and *Spitalfields* respectively.

### LYONS.

| | | *f.* | *c.* | *f.* | *c.* |
|---|---|---|---|---|---|
| 100 Kilogrammes Organzine Silk, at 58$f.$ - - | is - | 5,800 | – | | |
| 75 Ditto Tram Silk, at 54$f.$ | is - | 4,050 | – | | |
| 175 | | 9,850 | – | | |
| 12$\frac{1}{2}$ per cent. Discount, one month's credit - | | 1,231 | 25 | | |
| | | | | 8,618 | 75 |
| Dyeing Organzine and Tram - - - | 72 sous p' kilo. | | | 630 | – |
| Winding 75 kilo. Organzine - - | 60 | | | 225 | – |
| Warping paid - - | 30 – p' day | | | 59 | – |
| Weaving 4,236$\frac{4}{5}$ Ells. | 55 cents. p' ell | | | 2,330 | 24 |
| | *f.* | | | 11,862 | 99 |

Exchange, at 25$f.$ - - - £. 474. 10. 5.

### SPITALFIELDS.

| *lbs.* *oz.* | | £. | *s.* | *d.* | £. | *s.* | *d.* |
|---|---|---|---|---|---|---|---|
| 220 12 | Piedmont Organzine Silk, at 24/ p' lb. - | 264 | 18 | – | | | |
| 165 9 | Italian Tram Silk, at 21/6 p' lb. - | 177 | 19 | 7 | | | |
| 386 5 | | 442 | 17 | 7 | | | |
| | 2$\frac{1}{2}$ per cent. Discount, 14 days credit - | 11 | 1 | 5 | | | |
| | | | | | 431 | 16 | 2 |
| | Dyeing Organzine & Tram, at 2/ p' lb. | | | | 38 | 12 | 6 |
| | Winding 165$\frac{1}{2}$ lb. Organzine, – 2/ – | | | | 16 | 11 | 1$\frac{1}{2}$ |
| | Winding 165$\frac{1}{2}$ lb. Tram - - 1/9 – | | | | 14 | 9 | 9 |
| | Warping 59 pieces - - - 2/3 – | | | | 6 | 12 | 9 |
| | Weaving 5,296 yards - - /7 – | | | | 154 | 9 | 4 |
| | £. | | | | 662 | 11 | 7$\frac{1}{2}$ |

Or 39$\frac{2}{3}$ p' cent. on the cost price at Lyons.

*Bar^t Wadden.*

10017. And

*Barrett Wadden,*
Esq.

29 June,
1832.

10017. And the wages given in France are the wages paid in October?—The wages stated, are the wages paid on the 11th day of December, and the information which I previously had made the 13th day of October, fixes the price about three per cent. less than the price stated there.

10018. That was, the prices given here as the prices paid by you in Spitalfields, are the net prices?—The prices which I state in this account, I took Piedmont organzine at 24 s. and the best description of the Italian tram at 21 s. 6 d.; and reducing that by a payment of cash in 14 days, and taking off 2½ per cent. discount, reduces it to 431 l. 16 s. 2 d.; and as far as relates to all the other charges they are cash payments, not subject to any deduction whatever.

10019. And the prices which you have placed here as the wages for the different operations in England, are at the prices that you have described as a loss to the operative of 31 per cent., as compared with his former situation?—The prices contained in those comparative views are a loss to the people in my employment of 38½ per cent.; their condition relieved by a fall in provisions to the extent of 7½ per cent.

10020. Has any instance of comparison of silk goods come lately under your observation which confirms the statement you have just given in to the Committee?—The Committee will permit me to follow the papers that I have presented with others, for the papers I have now presented are plain gros de Naples; finding the difference to be so considerable in the manufacture of plain goods, in which there is no fancy, in which there is no skill or science required, in which there is no expensive establishment of designers to be employed, finding the difference so great in the production of plain goods, my mind went in pursuit of what difference may exist in the production of figured goods; and finding the difference to be something more in figured goods than in plain, I was most anxious to do what some of the celebrated painters of antiquity, I believe, have done, when they wanted to draw a monster, they drew him of large dimensions, and I therefore took the liberty of drawing out an estimate of the production of fancy goods on a quantity of silk double the weight of that in plain goods; as it relates to silk dyeing, winding and warping, the price in the figured department is the same, and the difference is to be found in the weaving. " Comparative Estimate of the cost and various expenses of manufacturing 200 kilogrammes of organzine and 150 kilogrammes of tram silk into 9,620 yards of figured gros de Naples, at Lyons and Spitalfields respectively, December 1831;" 7,696 ells of figured silk at Lyons answers to our 9,620 yards in Spitalfields. The silk at Lyons would cost me 17,237 f. 50 c.; the dyeing, 1,260 f.; the winding, 450 f.; the warping, 166 f. 50 c.; weaving at 85 c. per ell, 6,541 f. 60 c., presenting an aggregate of 25,655 f. 60 c., when reduced to English money at an exchange much lower than it has been for months back; I have taken the exchange all on that cost at 25 f., and I would be justified in taking it at 25 f. 60 c.; but taking the exchange at 25 f. it would be 1,026 l. 4 s. 6 d. and it would cost me to produce goods of the same quality and quantity, 1,506 l. 2 s. 7 d. making a difference between the cost of production at Lyons and Spitalfields, of 479 l. 18 s. 1 d., or 46½ per cent. on the cost price at Lyons.

COMPARATIVE

December 1831.

COMPARATIVE ESTIMATE of the Cost and various Expenses of Manufacturing 200 Kilogrammes of Organzine, and 150 Kilogrammes of Tram Silk, into 9,620 Yards Figured Gros de Naples, at *Lyons* and *Spitalfields* respectively.

## LYONS.

| | f. | c. | f. | c. |
|---|---|---|---|---|
| 200 Kilogrammes Organzine Silk, at 58 f. p' kilo. | 11,600 | – | | |
| 150 Ditto Tram Silk, at 54 f. p' kilo. | 8,100 | – | | |
| 350 | 19,700 | – | | |
| 12½ per cent. Discount, one month's credit | 2,462 | 50 | | |
| | | | 17,237 | 50 |
| Dyeing 350 kilogrammes at 72 sous p' kilo. | | | 1,260 | – |
| Winding 150 ditto Organzine – 60 – – | | | 450 | – |
| Warping ditto – – 30 – p' day | | | 166 | 50 |
| Weaving 7,696 ells – 85 cents. p' ell | | | 6,541 | 60 |
| | | | f. 25,655 | 60 |

Exchange at 25 f. - - - £.1,026. 4. 6.

## SPITALFIELDS.

| lbs. oz. | | £. | s. | d. | £. | s. | d |
|---|---|---|---|---|---|---|---|
| 441 8 | Piedmont Organzine Silk, at 24/ p' lb. | 529 | 16 | – | | | |
| 331 2 | Best Italian Tram Silk, at 21/6 p' lb. | 355 | 19 | 2 | | | |
| 772 10 | | 885 | 15 | 2 | | | |
| | 2½ p' cent. Discount, 14 days credit | 22 | 2 | 10 | | | |
| | | | | | 863 | 12 | 4 |
| | Dyeing 772 lbs. 10 oz. Organzine and Tram at 2/ p' lb. - | | | | 77 | 5 | – |
| | Winding 331 lbs. of Organzine - 2/ - - | | | | 33 | 2 | – |
| | Winding 331 lbs. of Tram - 1/9 - - | | | | 28 | 19 | 3 |
| | Warping 74 pieces, each 130 yards - 6/ p' piece | | | | 22 | 4 | – |
| | Weaving 9,620 yards - - 1/ p' yard | | | | 481 | – | – |
| | | | | £. | 1,506 | 2 | 7 |

Difference between Lyons and Spitalfields, £.479. 18. 1.; or 46½ p' cent. on the cost price at Lyons.

*Bar* Wadden.*

*Barrett Wadden, Esq.*

*29 June, 1832.*

10021. You have put down weaving at one shilling a yard for figured silk; what was the price paid at Spitalfields seven years ago?—The article that is there represented at one shilling a yard, seven years ago was paid 2 s. 3 d. for; I have paid 2 s. 4 d. myself for weaving hundreds of thousands of yards of them.

10022. Can you inform the Committee what is paid for weaving that article at Sudbury?—The article that these accounts refer to is not wove at Sudbury, and I doubt very much whether it is woven in any other part of the kingdom but Spitalfields; perhaps, for the satisfaction of the honourable Member that puts the question, I ought to state, that those goods are goods of the nicest fabric; they are not such goods as are generally made either at Sudbury or Manchester.

10023. You mean they are peculiar to Spitalfields?—Yes.

10024. That they are those goods that enter more peculiarly into competition with Spitalfields, being imported from abroad?—They are.

10025. Have you stated the whole of the advantages of which you are aware the French manufacturer has over the English?—I beg to remark, that I have not yet answered the last question that was asked me, which I understood to be, has any instance of importation of silk goods come lately under my observation that would confirm these statements.

10026. Is the Jacquard loom used in making of figured gros de Naples?—Yes; it would be an increased expense of labour to make it without the Jacquard; I am asked, has any instance of importation of silk goods come under my knowledge that would confirm this statement; a house that I believe does not stand second in point of respectability to any house in the empire, last March did import a case of plain goods precisely the quality that this comparative view is made upon; and the importer of this box of plain goods in last March had the candour to let me examine the contents of that box; to put into my hands the weight of silk contained in the goods in that box, and to show me the amount of money that he paid to the manufacturer at Lyons for those goods; and he had also the kindness to tell me a fact which is of very considerable importance, that the goods were made for him by an order that he had transmitted to Lyons in the previous December, and were not bought under any peculiar circumstances, such as very frequently occurs, and might lessen the real value of the goods, but that they were goods made by order. The case contained 3,302 ells, and their weight was 253 lbs. 2 oz., and the money the importer paid to the manufacturer at Lyons, was 423 l. 10 s. British; I was anxious

to

*Barrett Wadden,*
Esq.

29 June,
1832.

to ascertain how far my comparative accounts would stand the test of a comparison with this importation, and bringing with me the documents which were placed in my hands by a gentleman who, I am proud to say, I feel the kindness he has done me, and shall feel grateful to him for it; I drew out an estimate what those goods answering in quality and quantity would cost me in Spitalfields, and they would cost me 531 *l.* 8 *s.* 6 *d.* the particulars of which I suppose it is not necessary to read; my next object was, to try if I could discover by any process what profit the manufacturer of those goods had at Lyons, and I had only one way, a school-boy method of doing it; supposing my own calculations to be correct, I asked myself this question, if goods worth 662 *l.* in Spitalfields can be produced for 474 *l.* at Lyons, what would be the cost at Lyons to the manufacturer there of a parcel of goods that could be made in Spitalfields for 531 *l.* I find 380 *l.* 4 *s.* would be the cost; and if I subtract this cost from the 423 *l.* 10 *s.* which he received for the case of goods imported last March, I find the Lyons manufacturer had a profit of 43 *l.* 6 *s.* or ten per cent. on his sales.

---

### *Lunæ, 2° die Julii,* 1832.

### JAMES A. STEWART MACKENZIE, ESQUIRE, IN THE CHAIR.

*John Bowring,* Esquire, LL. D. called in; and further Examined.

*John Bowring,*
Esq. LL. D.

2 July,
1832.

10027. ARE you prepared to give an answer to the question which the Committee put to you on Friday last?—The question which the honourable Committee put to me was this: " What is your reason for thinking that the value of the silk manufactures of France is only 5,500,000 *l.*, when you state that the consumption of silk made into goods is 4,200,000 pounds, and when you show from information derived from manufacturers that the expense of working up these goods is in no case less than 80 per cent. of the cost of the material, and in some instances reaching so high as 120, the great majority of goods being of that description on which the cost of labour is 90 per cent.?" Now this question involves two very important results; one, the amount of silk consumed in the French manufacture; and the other, the value of the manufactured article. I have gone into considerable details, which I shall have the honour of submitting to the Committee, and which I think will show that my evidence is substantially correct. I must recall to the attention of the Committee, that no question put to me referred to the value added to the raw material with reference to the whole produce of the French manufacture, and I have made no observation hitherto which referred to the labour employed in the silk manufacture as a whole, but merely to the value of labour and other added values, as bearing on particular articles. In looking over my evidence, I find that there were only two articles respecting which any inquiries were put to me as to the added value of labour; the first respecting ribbons, and they were ribbons of a particular quality, the whole of the ribbon trade forming only one-sixth part of the French production; and it is true, as the honourable Member has stated, that I mentioned the additional value added to the raw material on those particular articles of ribbons, to which the question referred, was from 80 to 120 per cent., but in the statement I made as to satin from Lyons, the cost of the material will be found to amount to 2,036 francs 42 centimes out of 2,732 francs 80 centimes, so that less than 35 per cent. has been there added by labour; and it will also be seen by the result of the evidence I have given, that there are a great number of articles in which labour does not add 25 per cent. to the value of the material, such for instance, as the coarser and heavier articles; I stated the average value of common sarsnets, for example, from two francs and a half to three and a half per ell, to which not more than 60 centimes was added by labour, which will be about 20 per cent. Now from the facts given in my evidence, the additional value to the raw material—(I speak only of the facts to which my evidence refers)—the additional value to the raw material ought, on those facts, to be taken at 70 per cent. and not at 90, as the question proposes; but if all the silk manufactures are placed in view, the additional value will be very far less than that. In a calculation I have in my possession, made lately at Lyons, as to the value of 22 millions of francs, the proportions are regulated as follows; and I should state, that this is in answer to a question I proposed to a Member of the Chamber of Commerce, estimating particularly

*John Bowring,*
Esq. LL. D.

2 July,
1832.

particularly that species of articles which come into the English market, and taking any sum you please for a given amount. He has taken 22 millions. What will be the quantity of material, what of labour, and what of profit?—The return is this: material, 16 millions of francs; labour, five millions; profit to the manufacturer, one million; result, 22 millions, which, in fact, brings down the added value by labour to about 30 pent.

10028. Is this a calculation of goods made at Lyons?—Yes.

10029. And therefore includes none made at St. Etienne?—No; from another Lyons document I learn that in the average of ribbons manufactured there, the proportion of raw material on 100 $f$. is from 65 $f$. to 68 $f$., labour, profit and added value being 32 $f$. to 35 $f$. or an average of 50 per cent. on the whole; that in the richer articles of ribbons at Lyons, the proportions are 45 $f$. to 50 $f$ for silk, and 50 $f$. to 55 $f$. labour, &c. or 100 per cent. for added value; I think, therefore, taking into account the articles where 20 to 35 per cent. is added by labour and other cir-. cumstances, the average cannot be fairly estimated at more than 60 to 70 per cent. for added value; but if the calculation of waste is made, it will not be forgotten that in the process of dyeing, silk loses from 30 to 35 per cent., which of course must be deducted from the quantity of pounds of silk remaining to be manufactured, if any reference be made to the weight of silk; now taking the estimate of added value at 70 per cent. and supposing the amount of thrown silk to be four millions of pounds, and that 18 $s$. be taken as its average value, the amount will be 3,600,000 $l$., to which add 70 per cent. which I think may be thus divided: 30 per cent. for dyeing, interest, profit and expenses of all sorts, and there will remain 40 per cent. for labour specially; this is the whole cost: add to 3,600,000 $l$. 2,520,000 $l$., the 70 per cent. making 6,120,000 $l$., the value of the whole silk manufacture of France; I supposed about 18 $s$. was a fair average for the value of silk; but on looking into the matter more closely, I find it is too high; I had taken as an average, on the gross silks at Lyons, 35 deniers as the average for trams, and the lowest price at Lyons for those trams was about 26 $f$. 50 $c$.; I have taken 26 deniers as the average for organzine, and I find the value of that organzine 31 $f$., that makes 57 $f$. 50 $c$. of which the average will be 28 $f$. 75 $c$. per pound marc.; I have deducted from that amount 12½ per cent. for discount, and 9½ for the difference between French and English weight, between the pound marc. and the English pound, which makes 6 $f$. 32 $c$. leaving the average value 22 $f$. 43 $c$. the English pound, which at the exchange of to-day, or 25 $f$. 60 $c$. gives 17 $s$. 6¼ $d$. per pound at a close calculation. Now four millions of pounds of silk at 17 $s$. 6¼ $d$. will give about 3,500,000 $l$. sterling; add 70 per cent. for profit, expenses, labour, &c., that makes 2,450,000 $l$. sterling, and you come again at the result, being 5,950,000 $l$. sterling, the whole value of the silk manufactures of France. The last official return of exports is about 120 millions of francs; I estimated the home consumption at about 30 millions of francs, which is 150 millions of francs altogether, and that amount comes up to the same result of six millions sterling; I would state as my own conviction, that that is rather an over estimate of the value of the silk manufactures of France; that I have consulted every author to whom I have had access since I had the honour of meeting the Committee, and there is not one authority that averages it so high; I have collected, bearing on this question, such official facts as I have been able at different periods; in the most brilliant period before the Revolution, when Lyons was supposed to have from 15,000 to 20,000 looms, M. Verninac made a return to the Government of the value of the silk manufactures; he estimated the raw material at 70 millions of francs, 2,800,000 $l$. sterling; and he says at that period labour added for the additional value of a third, making 933,000 $l$.; the then value, according to his estimate of the silk manufacture of France was 3,733,000 $l$. Since that period, the price of silk has fallen, and the quantity of labour applied, as well as the value of labour, has somewhat increased; there have been a great number of fashionable goods produced, and there has been a slight increase in the value of labour, as comparing the present time with the period preceding the Revolution; but I do not imagine that the increase and manufactured value can in any case be taken at more than 60 per cent. on the whole; and if it be taken at 60 per cent. that again will bring us to the same result of six millions at present. I find, too, that in 1805, when Fourcroy was Minister of the Interior, the calculation of the amount of the whole of the French manufacture of silk goods, in a return made to him, was this: Silk stuffs, 35 millions; ribbons, gauzes, blonds, &c. 20 millions; and all that class of hosiery, &c. which the French call bonnetry, 20 millions;

making

*John Bowring*
Esq. LL. D.

2 July,
1832.

making 75 millions in the whole, which is three millions sterling: and I find this is a calculation adopted by Peuchet in his book on French Statistics; the population of Lyons, since 1805, has increased 50 per cent. and I do not think the productions can, under any reasonable calculation, have more than doubled in France since 1805. In 1819, there is another return, made under Chaptal's auspices; it is a return of French grown silk, and the grown silk in France, according to this, at this period, was less than a million of pounds; it was, in fact, 908,026 pounds. Now I cannot conceive it possible that the production in France of raw silks can have more than trebled itself in fifteen years, considering that four or five years are required to bring a mulberry tree into bearing. The general opinion in France is, as I stated, that the annual amount produced by the silk manufacture does not exceed 140 millions. Of this amount, eighty millions represents the silk, and sixty millions the added value, by labour, profit, &c. which also corroborates my estimate.

In 1788, the whole number of looms in France was estimated at about 50,000, the consumption of silk being two and a half millions of pounds; one author, Peuchet, estimates it at three millions: the number of looms employed and not employed at the present moment, may be fairly taken at from 70 to 80,000, somewhat above a third more, which again will bring the annual consumption to be about four millions of pounds. Calculate the export then as I have stated, and divide that by four millions of pounds, you have then 37 $f$. 50 $c$. as the average value of the manufactured article: now the average cost of silk appears to be 22 $f$. 43 $c$. per lb.; this result again gives 70 per cent. for added value, in labour, profit, &c.

I have submitted that calculation to another process, and I get at the same result; estimating the consumption of raw silk in France at four millions of pounds, and considering the various deductions to be made in the process of manufacture, I would take six per cent. for loss in throwing, 20 per cent. for loss on dyeing, nine per cent for loss by weaving, clipping, (which is a large loss in some articles), and other waste, which leaves 35 per cent. in all to be deducted from the weight of raw silk; 35 per cent. on four millions of pounds gives 1,400,000; so that there will be 2,600,000 lbs. of silk to be represented in the manufactured state. Now, since I had the honour of seeing the Committee, I have examined the weight of silk manufacture exported from France, according to the Custom House Returns, and they were in 1829, 998,885 kilogrammes; in 1830, 1,025,385 kilogrammes, making together 2,024,270 kilogrammes, which give an annual average export in weight of 1,012,135 kilogrammes, which, reduced to English pounds, make 2,226,697 lbs.: Now if, according to my data, one-fifth be added for home consumption of silk goods, that will be 445,340; the result will be 2,672,037 lbs., which almost exactly coincides with the previous estimate, and the result is got at by a process altogether distinct.

On another question, as to the proportion of labour which enters into the official calculations of France, (and I may here be allowed to say, that these inquiries have led me to a conclusion that these official values are more correct than I had before believed,) the French Custom House has taken as its standard, as I mentioned, 130, 120 and 88 $f$. per kilogram, the average being 113 $f$. per kilogram to the manufactured article. Now estimating the nett value of silk at 50 $f$. per kilogram, and adding 17 $f$. 50 $c$. for the loss of 35 per cent. in dyeing, weaving, clipping and other waste, you get 67 $f$. 50 $c$.; if you add four francs per kilogram for dyeing, three for interest, seven francs for profit, on 113 $f$., (which is about six per cent.) the expenses of establishment five per cent., those 19 $f$. more will give 86 $f$. 50 $c$. per kilogram, and there will be left for labour 26 $f$. 50 $c$., which is somewhat above 30 per cent. on the whole: that I would submit is another test by which the same result is got at.

From these calculations, derived from different independent sources and presented in different forms, it would appear that the estimate of four millions of pounds of silk employed to produce an average of from five and a half to six millions pounds sterling in manufactured value, is not far from the truth. Two other documents I desire to put in, as additional evidence of the veracity of the official returns. I should not have done so, but for an observation that the probability was, that those returns had been prepared for the occasion: I therefore will deliver to the Committee, taken from the receipts of the Minister of Finance, the account given, and for which he has reckoned to the nation for duties paid on imported manufactured silk: that will be considered quite independent evidence. In 1828, there were duties paid on piece goods, perhaps I had better put in the documents, merely stating, that in 1828

226,727 $f$.

*John Bowring,*
*Esq.* LL. D.

*2 July,*
*1832.*

226,727 *f.* were paid in France, and accounted for in the Budget of receipts for foreign manufactured silks. In 1829, 259,409 *f.*, and in 1830, 324,373 *f.* As an evidence too, that the exports of French silk manufactures are controlled, and appear in the Custom House books, I have copied from the same financial accounts, the receipts of the French Government on the export of French manufactured goods, merely to show that they have a motive in accurately estimating the exports of manufactured goods from France. In 1828, the Government received 26,339 *f.*; in 1829, 24,802 *f.*, and in 1830, 24,444 *f.* These documents I had better submit to the Committee, because they are of an official character.

[*The same were handed in.*]

DUTIES paid in *France* on FOREIGN MANUFACTURED SILKS
entered for Home Consumption.

|  |  | *f.* | *f.* |
|---|---|---:|---:|
| 1828 : Piece Goods | - - - - - - | 125,935 | |
| Ribbons | - - - - - - | 100,792 | |
|  |  |  | 226,727 |
| 1829 : Piece Goods | - - - - - - | 149,658 | |
| Ribbons | - - - - - - | 109,751 | |
|  |  |  | 259,409 |
| 1830 : Piece Goods | - - - - - - | 205,144 | |
| Ribbons | - - - - - - | 119,229 | |
|  |  |  | 224,373 |

For this sum as received under the above heads, the Minister of Finance is debited in the accounts of the foregoing years.

DUTIES received in *France*, on the Export of FRENCH SILK MANUFACTURES
to Foreign Countries.

| 1828 | - - - - - - - | *f.* 26,339 |
|---|---|---:|
| 1829 | - - - - - - - | 24,802 |
| 1830 | - - - - - - - | 24,444 |

There is one thing, which probably as it bears on some questions put to me, as to the state of reeling and throwing in France, I may be allowed to mention; I have found, with reference to that matter, a representation made by the town of Lyons, of which I have here a copy, which describes the extreme backwardness of that portion of the silk manufacture. They state in general result, that so much in arrear are the reeling and throwing establishments, and so very imperfect is the management of both reeling and throwing, that it is necessary the Government should interfere, in order to force improvement by penal legislature; and they give, at the same time the facts of the situation of things in Italy, as evidence that that species of penal legislation has been beneficial. Perhaps the Committee will not consider it as matter of intrusion, as several questions were asked me, as to the opinion respecting the prohibitory system in Lyons, if I state, that in going into this examination, I have found this sentence in the report made by Monsieur Dugas, who is the delegate of the town of Lyons, as to the operation of the system under which their manufactures have grown up. He says, " Upon premiums and prohibitions industry slumbers, superiority is lost, and protection, instead of a source of security, becomes the primary cause of ruin."

*Barrett Wadden,* Esq. called in; and further Examined.

*Barrett Wadden,*
Esq.

10030. YOU are perhaps aware that the first witness who was examined before this Committee on the part of the Coventry trade, gave it in evidence, that in 100 *l.* worth of gros de Naples, the amount of wages was 30 *l.*, are you able to state to the Committee the proportion of labour in plain gros de Naples and in figured gros de Naples?—I am; I shall present to this Committee an account, showing the cost of silk and wages paid for manufacturing the same into 5,296 yards of plain gros de Naples in Spitalfields; the cost of the silk in the first instance (silk of this quality), this is silk in the raw state, the value of the silk was 361 *l.* 10 *s.* 3 *d.*, about 18 *s.* a pound weight; when I speak of raw silk, I mean silk that has undergone no process of manufacture, that I call raw silk; I do not call thrown silk raw silk, for it has undergone a very material process of manufacture.

The

Barrett Wadden, Esq.

2 July, 1832.

The silk cost me 361 *l.* 10 *s.* 3 *d.*; I paid for throwing the warp for organzine, 49 *l.* 13 *s.* 4½ *d.*, for throwing 220¾ lbs. of organzine silk; cash paid for throwing 165½ lbs. of tram, 20 *l.* 12 *s.* 6 *d.*; for dyeing the silk, 38 *l.* 12 *s.* 6 *d.*; winding it, 31 *l.* 0 *s.* 10½ *d.*; warping it, 6 *l.* 12 *s.* 9 *d.*, and weaving it at 7 *d.* a yard, 154 *l.* 9 *s.* 4½ *d.*; so that the whole of amount of money expended in converting the silk from its raw condition into manufactured goods, is 301 *l.* 1 *s.* 4½ *d.* which is 45½ per cent. on the first cost of the goods, or 83⅜ per cent. on the value of the raw silk. In that calculation no incidental charge is made whatever, such as those charges arising out of the expenses of the necessary establishment. I find that the value of silk contained in the yard of goods so made, is 1 *s.* 4¼ *d.* and the fraction of a farthing, and that the value of wages of each yard is 1 *s.* 1½ *d.* I called the attention of the Committee to an account somewhat similar, but applicable to figured gros de Naples; the cost of the raw silk in this figured gros de Naples, I find to be 723 *l.* 0 *s.* 4 *d.*; and putting that silk through the various processes of throwing, dyeing, winding, warping and weaving, I find the net amount of wages upon 723 *l.* worth of raw silk, is 783 *l.* 2 *s.* 3 *d.*; so that the wages on that figured gros de Naples, is 52 per cent. on the first cost of the goods, or 108¼ per cent. on the value of the raw silk; so that in each yard of those goods, when made, the silk is worth 1 *s.* 6 *d.* 1,456 out of 9,620 parts of a farthing, the value of the wages per yard, is 1 *s.* 7½ *d.* 1,428 out of 9,620, the first cost 3 *s.* 1½ *d.* with some fraction.

[*The same was handed in.*]

AN ACCOUNT showing the Cost of Silk and Wages paid for Manufacturing the same into 5,296 yards plain Gros de Naples, in *Spitalfields*.

| | £. | s. | d. | £ | s. | d. |
|---|---|---|---|---|---|---|
| Cash paid for Raw Silk - - - | | | | 361 | 10 | 3 |
| Ditto, throwing 220¾ *lbs.* Organzine, 4 *s.* 6 *d.* - | 49 | 13 | 4½ | | | |
| Ditto, 165½ Tram, 2 *s.* 6 *d.* | 20 | 12 | 6 | | | |
| Ditto, dyeing - - - | 38 | 12 | 6 | | | |
| Ditto, winding - - - | 31 | - | 10½ | | | |
| Ditto, warping - - | 6 | 12 | 9 | | | |
| Ditto, weaving - - | 154 | 9 | 4½ | | | |
| Net amount of Wages - - - | | | | 301 | 1 | 4½ |
| | | | £. | 662 | 11 | 7½ |

The Wages is 45½ per cent. on the first cost of the goods, or 83⅜ per cent. on the value of the Raw Silk.

| | s. | d. |
|---|---|---|
| Value of Silk contained in each yard - - | 1 | 4¼ $\frac{2812}{5296}$ |
| Value of Wages in each yard - - - - - | 1 | 1½ $\frac{3042}{5296}$ |
| First cost per yard - - - | 2 | 6 $\frac{558}{5296}$ |

AN ACCOUNT showing the Cost of Silk and Wages paid for Manufacturing the same into 9,620 yards figured Gros de Naples, in *Spitalfields*.

| | £. | s. | d. | £. | s. | d. |
|---|---|---|---|---|---|---|
| Cash paid for Silk - - - - - | | | | 723 | - | 4 |
| Ditto, throwing 441½ *lbs.* Organzine, at 4 *s.* 6 *d.* - | 99 | 4 | 6 | | | |
| Ditto, 331 Tram, 2 *s.* 6 *d.* | 41 | 7 | 6 | | | |
| Ditto, dyeing - - - | 77 | 5 | - | | | |
| Ditto, winding - - | 62 | 1 | 3 | | | |
| Ditto, warping - - | 22 | 4 | - | | | |
| Ditto, weaving - - | 481 | - | - | | | |
| Net amount of Wages - - - | | | | 783 | 2 | 3 |
| | | | £. | 1,506 | 2 | 7 |

The Wages is 52 per cent on the first cost of the goods or 108¼ per cent. on the value of the Raw Silk.

| | s. | d. |
|---|---|---|
| Value of Silk contained in each yard - - | 1 | 6 $\frac{1456}{9620}$ |
| Value of Wages in each yard - - - - | 1 | 7½ $\frac{1428}{9620}$ |
| First cost per yard - - | 3 | 1½ $\frac{2884}{9620}$ |

*Barrett Wadden.*

Perhaps I may be permitted to accompany the document which I have now presented, with another, to which I attach considerable importance, and I think the importance of my next document will appear visible when I state that it is one founded upon a calculation put in by Dr. Bowring, and those calculations, as put in by him, were furnished to him by a silk manufacturer at Lyons, who, with great candour, and I have no doubt great simplicity, opened his books and let the learned Doctor take from those books, an extract of the various costs and prices of manufacture, through which a certain quantity of silk was put before it arrived in the shape of 500 ells of satin. I hope I am not out of order in soliciting the attention of the Committee to the document that I am now about placing on record; it is a document arranged by me on the same plan of those comparative accounts, showing the cost of production at Lyons and in Spitalfields respectively, and which I have had already the honour of presenting to the Committee. Dr. Bowring has also, if his evidence be examined, put upon record the cost of certain raw silks purchased by this manufacturer for the purpose of being worked by him into

*Barrett Wadden,*
Esq.

————

2 July,
1832.

into 500 ells of satin, he has given in the various costs of the raw silk, and all the processes of throwing, dyeing, winding, warping and weaving, and the only alteration that I have undertaken to make in the account as tendered by the learned Doctor, is to correct some of his figures, where I have found them to be arithmetically wrong. I hope in doing that, I have done justice to his account, which if not corrected by me, would stand a record, that even the learned Doctor himself had put upon the Minutes of your Evidence some most erroneous calculations. He states that the manufacturer gives 50 *f*. per kilogram, for 17½ kilogrammes of silk, and the item set down as amounting to 872 *f*.; I find that according to school boy arithmetic it is 875 *f*.; he goes on to put it through the process of throwing, which he states cost the manufacturer 11 *f*., I do not dispute it, for throwing the tram 7 *f*., for dyeing, 3 *f*. per kilogram; for winding, 4 *f*. per kilogram; for warping the whole 500 ells of satin, 18 *f*., and for weaving the 500 ells of satin, 475 *f*., altogether amounting to 2,471 *f*. 88 *c*., which taken at the exchange of 25 *f*. turns out to be worth 98 *l*. 17 *s*. 6 *d*. I find that in Spitalfields, goods manufactured of equal weight and of equal length and similar in quality, would cost me 139 *l*. 9 *s*. 3 *d*., or the cost of working the silk through its various processes, agreeable to those calculations which I made last March, and which I have already had the honour of submitting to this Committee; so that the cost of production between Lyons and Spitalfields in the manufacture of those 500 ells of satin, as given in evidence by the learned Doctor, the difference between Lyons and Spitalfields is 40 *l*. 11 *s*. 9 *d*. or 41 per cent. above the cost price at Lyons; and I now am about placing before the mind of this honourable Committee a point that its attention has not yet I believe been called to. I am anxious to ascertain if the whole of the duty at present payable upon thrown silks coming into this country were abolished; if the authorities that be, have made up their minds to render the silk mills of this country of no value, by letting into this country foreign thrown silk free of duty, how much then would this 40 *l*. 11 *s*. 9 *d*. which is now the difference between Lyons and Spitalfields on the production of 500 ells of satin, how much less would that difference be. I find that I have paid duty upon 38 lbs. 9 oz. of organzine silk, and duty on 39 lbs. 11 oz. of tram, the united amount of these duties is 10 *l*. 14 *s*. 3 *d*., so that if I had my material without the payment of one farthing duty, the balance between Lyons and Spitalfields in the manufacture of these 500 ells of satin, would be 29 *l*. 17 *s*. 6 *d*. or 30⅛ per cent. above the cost price at Lyons, and yet with this fact, half of this fact, I may say, as relates to Lyons, put on record by the learned Doctor; and another important fact put on record also by him, namely, that he found that there was a difference between the cost of production in France and in Spitalfields, amounting to between 30 and 40 per cent., I say in the midst of these glaring facts, he has informed your honourable Committee that 20 per cent. would be a protection against foreign manufacturers; when I have thus shown from his own figures on one side, and my own on the other, that if I could be relieved altogether from the entire payment of duty on the article I consume, the difference then will be between Lyons and Spitalfields, 30⅛ per cent. I have now to make one other observation upon this document, and upon the half of this evidence, as furnished me by the learned Doctor, that this satin so manufactured at Lyons, is made by a party who acknowledged to the learned Doctor, that he had his 10 per cent. profit; for his evidence is, that the satins would sell for 3,000 *f*., that is, yielding the French manufacturer 10 per cent. profit, and the material was furnished to that manufacturer by a grower getting from 15 to 25 per cent. profit on the production of the raw material; is it necessary for me to add another word to what I have stated, to show that there is a power between the grower and the producer of silk in France, where the manufacturer has on the manufactured goods 10 per cent. and the grower 20 per cent., here then is 30 per cent. possessed between the grower and the manufacturer out of profits so large, they may well afford to lower their price whenever pressed upon by any further reduction of the protection, such as it is, which we now have, or further lowering the wages of our working people, and if our people are to be forced down to a state of existence more degrading than their present position, and if our property is to be annihilated, upon the Government then be the responsibility; I am told I am to stand a competition against two parties, whose united profits are 30 per cent.; I admit the price of their labour is not very high, but it is sufficiently high and large to keep them in the production of their raw material, and in the perfection of their works. I beg pardon of the Committee for not accompanying the Statement with the counter parts.

[*The Witness then handed in the Account.*]

COMPARATIVE

COMPARATIVE VIEW of the Cost and Wages paid for Manufacturing 17½ Killogrammes of Organzine, and 18 Kilogrammes of Tram Silk, into 500 Ells of Satin at *Lyons* and *Spitalfields* respectively.—As given in Evidence by Dr. Bowring.

| LYONS. | | | | | SPITALFIELDS. | | | | |
|---|---|---|---|---|---|---|---|---|---|
| | *f.* | *c.* | *f.* | *c.* | *lbs. oz.* | | £. | *s.* | *d.* |
| 17½ Kilogrammes Raw Silk, at 50 *f.* per kilo. } - is | 875 | – | | | 17½ Kilo. equal to 38 9 Organzine, at 25*f.* p'lb. | | 48 | 4 | – |
| 18 Ditto · ditto at 47*f.* · - · is | 846 | – | | | 18 - - - 39 11 Tram, at 21 *s.* 6 *d.* p' lb. | | 42 | 13 | 4 |
| 35½ | 1,721 | – | | | 35½ 78 4 | | 90 | 17 | 4 |
| 12½ per cent. Discount one month's credit } - | 215 | 12 | | | 2½ per cent. discount - - | | 2 | 5 | 4 |
| | | | 1,505 | 88 | | | 88 | 12 | – |
| Throwing Organzine, 17½ Kil. at 11*f.* } - | 192 | 50 | | | Dyeing 78 lbs. 4 oz. Silk at 2 *s.* per lb. - - - } 7 16 6 | | | | |
| Throwing Tram, 18 Kil. at 7*f.* - - - } - | 126 | – | | | Winding Organzine, 29 lbs. at 2 *s.* - - - - } 2 18 – | | | | |
| Dyeing Organzine, at 3*f.* - | 52 | 50 | | | Winding Tram, 39½ lbs. at 1 *s.* 9 *d.* - - - } 3 9 7½ | | | | |
| Dyeing Tram, at 3*f.* - - - | 54 | – | | | Warping 5 pieces, each 125 yards, at 6 *s.* - - } 1 10 – | | | | |
| Winding Organzine, 12 Kil. at 4*f.* - - - - } | 48 | – | | | Weaving 625 yards, at 1 *s.* - 31 5 – | | | | |
| Warping - - - | 18 | – | | | Dressing ditto, at 1½ *d.* - 3 18 1½ | | | | |
| Weaving 500 ells - - | 475 | – | | | | | 50 | 17 | 3 |
| | | | 966 | – | | | | | |
| | *f.* | | 2,471 | 88 | | £. | 139 | 9 | 3 |

Exchange at 25*f.* is £. 98. 17. 6.

Cost of Production in *Spitalfields* over *Lyons* - 40 11 9
Suppose the whole of the Duty on the above Silk were taken away, what would the difference then be?
38½ lbs. Organzine, at 3 *s.* 6 *d.*, and 39¼ lbs, Tram, at 2 *s.* - - - - } 10 14 3

The difference would be - - - 29 17 6

*Barrett Wadden.*

10031. At the close of your last examination you were engaged in stating those advantages which you considered the French manufacturer to possess over the English; have you any thing to add to that statement?—I have only to add that I consider the French manufacturer has a most important advantage over me; and that is, that in the first place he is furnished with a raw material that is acknowledged to be the best silk in the world, that the possession of that material is preserved to him by the Government under which he lives, not permitting a pound weight of that material to leave the country; and consequently, the grower of French silk not having any other market for the sale of his commodity, he must take whatever price that market yields. And here is an extraordinary fact, that at the time we are told that the silk manufacture of France is depressed, the grower that furnishes that depressed market with the material, is pocketing a profit on an average of 20 per cent. That is one important advantage. The other is, that the Frenchmen work with positive orders, we do not. It is one continued series of speculation with us from one end of the year to the other. The Frenchmen also has got an ability to export, which I should be extremely glad to see that we possessed; and I have little doubt upon my mind, before I shall take my leave o this honourable Committee, that I will be able to put some mode before the honourable Committee, by which an export trade of this country may be increased to a very considerable extent.

10032. Do you consider that these advantages on the part of the French manufacturer, are in any degree counteracted by the protection which the English manufacturer at present possesses?—They are counteracted as far as the duties collected go. I consider that they are counteracted to that extent; but that even with the collection of duties he has the advantages which I have already alluded to, and which we do not and cannot possess.

10033. What, in your opinion, would counteract those advantages which the French manufacturer possesses?—Having the evidence and the experience of fourteen years residence in the city of Dublin as a manufacturer, working against the influx of British manufactured fabrics coming in there, I come to this opinion,

*Barrett Wadden,*
Esq.

2 July,
1832.

and

*Barrett Wadden,*
Esq.

———

2 July,
1832.

and I can come to none other, that as far as the fancy or figured trade of France is concerned, nothing short of positive prohibition will save us from the effects of the competition to which we are now exposed.   It is unnecessary for me to go into the particulars of what I am inclined to think I could produce to show the truth of my position, but it is quite enough for me to say, that the ability on the part of the people of France to weave and to produce fabrics, seems to partake of a kind of playfulness, that they actually as it were play with the threads over which they operate, and form it into those beautiful designs which in a great measure the national character of France partakes of: and that taste, aided and assisted by science, and that science lending itself to the silk weaver to imitate even the operations of nature.   I need scarcely say that it is impossible for any gentleman to have visited the tapestry manufactory in the suburbs of Paris, without seeing the enormous benefit that is conferred on the manufacturers of the country, by the Government of that country upholding an art that would be destructive to an individual, but which, when supported by a Government, opens a school of knowledge to every silk weaver in the country, that either he may get the means of hearing it, or seeing it, or of reading it.   When I see the persons in that manufactory at work upon productions that were lent them for the occasion; the most splendid pictures taken from the Louvre, and brought down to be imitated in tapestry; when I see the Government protecting a trade, I say this trade so protected must decidedly be a prosperous trade, and be urged on to a state of perfection that it is almost needless to suppose that persons can expect to arrive at; for when I was in France every thing was open to me without my hand in any one instance going into my pocket; whereas here I live in such a state of things that I can see nothing without paying for it; no, I cannot even see the royal lions in the Tower without giving my 5*s.* or 6*s.*; nothing is to be seen in this country without payment; whereas in Paris every school of knowledge that Paris possesses, is thrown open to every man that is in pursuit of that knowledge.   I have only to add, that as far as the prohibition of fancy goods goes, I am quite satisfied that nothing else will protect us.   It is a question of fashion united to a question of price.   As far as the introduction of plain goods goes I am not prepared to say so; because in plain goods there is no skill of design wanted, there is no taste required, it is the production of the plain article.   And then I should say that I think we could be fairly protected if means were devised of putting an end to smuggling; for I am quite satisfied that if the duties were properly levied, and those duties added to the various other expenses of transit, that it would amount to something in the shape of protection to us from the being inundated by foreign productions.   But the question then solves itself into this difficulty; can any means be devised of securing a revenue to the country, and at the same time procuring protection to me as a manufacturer?   I would say, yes.   If the Government be anxious to secure employment to our people, I then say to the Government, punish the smuggler beyond any thing that the law now imposes, but make a law that would punish the smuggler when detected in importing foreign goods.   I have always considered, and perhaps the honourable Committee will bear with me when I say it, that I do consider that the law of man ought to approach as near as man can approach to the law of God; and when I know this fact, that the law of God is no respecter of persons, neither ought the law of man; but as the law now stands, the urchin that filches from my pocket a handkerchief worth 2*s.* 6*d.* is transported, while the man dealing in thousands may filch from the public pocket and he escapes now, by putting his hand into a pocket already too heavy to carry the quantity of property it possesses, and dealing out some few paltry thousand pounds, which does not diminish his comfort or his luxury to the value of a hair of his head.   I would then say to this honourable Committee, and I entreat this honourable Committee to solve this matter seriously, and see, could not something in the shape of imprisonment; could not something in the shape of the tread mill be applied to the great smuggler; for here I would not call him the public benefactor;  I will say he is a man doing so much mischief, that the law ought to take hold of him, be he who he may, and punish him, as a man that is scattering ruin on the community, while he is pocketing his thousands.

10034.  Are you aware that the several points relative to the advantages enjoyed by the foreign manufacturer, and the possibility of protecting the English manufacturer, were the subjects of negociation by the Board of Trade during the past winter?—They were.

10035.  How long did that negociation last?—Full three months; the negociation lasted, I think, something better than three months; and at all the interviews
that

that we had with the President, assisted by the Vice-President of the Board of
Trade, we urged upon that honourable Board the positive necessity of giving us
a protection such as would arise out of the stamping of goods; we urged upon that
honourable Board to provide for us a protection such as would arise by making
smuggling a penal offence, and after a lapse of three months we were decidedly
led to believe that we would be successful in both those points, for the first point,
that of stamping goods, came urged on the mind of that honourable Board with
as strong a recommendation as respectability, great experience, and enormous
wealth could give.    There was a memorial presented to that honourable Board
which has been already alluded to by a former witness, and the first signature to
that memorial was the house of James Morrison & Company, followed by the
most influential houses in this metropolis; and what did that memorial pray for,
or what did it recommend? The stamping of goods.    We were therefore led to
believe, that a recommendation coming from such a quarter would be attended to,
and that if attended to would be decidedly most efficient as far as it went in protecting us.    We were also led to believe that His Majesty's Government would turn
its attention to see how the smuggling transactions could be put an end to, and
we asserted then, what to-day's experience proves to be a fact, that unless you
visit the smuggler with some penal punishment, if he is to be only punished by the
payment of fines, you will let a system be pursued that will not be checked, and
that until it is checked the evils that press upon us must continue.    The honourable
Board of Trade at length gave us to understand that they could do nothing for us
(a very polite way of getting rid of us), for that, upon consulting the Customs they
found—that is the Board of Trade found, that if our recommendation was urged
into practice it would be troublesome to the officers, and it would be inconvenient
to the importers.    We stated that, as far as the trouble that it gave to the officers
went, that it was absurd to talk of it; if there was not a sufficient number of officers
to discharge an increased duty, it would be very easy to add some few to their
number, whereas it must be recollected that, according to the Government itself,
admitting that there were smuggling transactions carried on to the extent of about
300,000*l.* a year, if, by the exercise of a judicious arrangement in the Customs,
200,000*l.* a year of these smuggling transactions could be secured through a legal
channel, about 70,000*l.* a year would be then received in the shape of duties added
to the revenue of the country, and 100,000*l.* a year would then be the whole
amount of the smuggling transactions.    But, no! no! such was the spirit of our
Government, they were so disposed to economy, that they would not employ a few
additional officers, even at the chance of receiving an increased annual revenue of
70,000*l.*    As to the inconvenience it would be to the importers, the Committee
will be surprised when I tell them, that the whole importers of French goods into
this country does not exceed 60 persons, and these persons only importing at the
distance perhaps of once a fortnight; so that, for the convenience of 60 individuals
importing goods once a fortnight, sooner than give trouble to some half dozen
officers very well paid in the Customs, the whole trade is to be left exposed to this
injurious system of contraband dealing; hence, we were told by the Committee
they could not do any thing for us; we were told we should have a decided answer
on the following Monday, nay, some of our Members were requested by the
President of the Board of Trade to receive their answer at two o'clock on the
following Monday, and after a lapse of ten weeks we were told, that the thing was
surrounded with such difficulty, that it imposed too much trouble on the officers and
too great an inconvenience on the importers, and we were left to have no other
alternative than to go in the attitude of petitioners to your honourable House, and
request your interference in our behalf.    Thus I have stated the transactions, as far
as I know of them, with the Board of Trade, and in so doing I believe I have
strictly regarded truth.    I will state to the Committee as to the statement that was
then made by the Board of Trade, that I have written down on a slip of paper
before me, the exact words as uttered by my Lord Auckland, the President of that
honourable Board, in answer to a question that was put to him by one of our
members that had the honour of forming a deputation to wait upon him; the
question was put, " My Lord, we hope that His Majesty's Government have not
any intention of reducing the duties now payable upon foreign manufactured silks,
or upon the materials that we work;" and my Lord Auckland's words were these:
" It is not the intention of Government to proceed upon the principle of the reduction of duties."    I hold myself personally responsible for those words, for I had
them

them written before me, and an assurance to that effect was given to us by the Board of Trade.

10036. Do you conceive that an increase of the amount of duty would be the means of preventing smuggling or decreasing it, in your opinion?—I have this fact staring me in the face, that the amount of smuggling since 1829 is greater than it was before 1829; and then with that fact before me, I ask myself this question, What was the amount of duty payable upon the material we work and the goods that we have to compete with prior to the year 1829? and I find that thrown silks, which we have to work, were then subject to a duty of 5s. per pound weight, tram subject to a duty of 3s. per pound weight, and the pound weight of plain manufactured foreign silks subject to a duty of 15s. per pound weight, and the pound weight of figured manufactured foreign silks subject to a duty of 20s. per pound weight; and therefore I am of opinion, that if we could regain the position as to the amount of duties we have lost, there would be less smuggling; if we could regain that position, that in all human probability would find smuggling decrease, provided strict regulations were enforced, to whatever extent it was in prior to the year 1829; and I am quite satisfied that every calm and reflecting mind will, indeed the Government have acknowledged that smuggling since that period has gone on to an extent that could not have been anticipated.

10037. Then you would consider smuggling as likely to be in proportion to an increased amount of duties, would not you?—I consider that if the duty on the pound weight of manufactured silk was raised from 11s. to 15s. that we would be then placed in the situation that we occupied between the years 1826 and 1829; and that there was less smuggling between the years 1826 and 1829, than there has been between the years 1829 and 1832.

10038. Do you know the rate of smuggling now?—No, personally I do not; I am informed by a house whose confidence I am in, and they in mine, that the ribbons which they import are brought through the Customs of London at ten per cent.; and the article of tulle, which they import through the Customs of London, is smuggled at eight per cent.

10039. Is there more than one partner in that house that you just alluded to?—There are several partners.

10040. Do you consider that the quantity of smuggling depends upon the competition of the London houses, which are endeavouring to undersell each other in French goods, more than it does on the higher or lower rate of duties?—The house that has already given me the information which I have now alluded to has assured me, that on their arrival at Lyons or in Paris they are surrounded by a class of persons, all smugglers, competing with each other for the custom of the persons that have just arrived in their market; and there is such competition among these persons as reduces the charge of smuggling to the London houses; but that there is a very considerable competition, and I would say an enormous competition, amongst the great London houses; as relates to our manufacture, the competition is prodigious, and I have no doubt whatever, as relates to foreign manufacture, there is a similar competition; they have discovered a mode by which they screen themselves, and that is, by not smuggling the things themselves directly, but buying it upon condition that it is to be delivered to them at a certain place, or at a certain time, in London, the smuggler no doubt undertaking the risk, and thus conscience becomes reconciled.

10041. You have spoken of the great distress that is existing in that particular branch of the trade in which you are concerned, do you consider that that distress is confined to that branch of the trade as to Spitalfields?—When we were petitioners to your honourable House, I believe that distress then existed in the silk trade, such as the silk trade never before experienced, and I am satisfied that Coventry partook more of the extreme wretchedness of the silk trade than any other part of the country where the silk trade is carried on; that the great bulk of the distress, I would say the overwhelming distress of the silk trade chiefly was exhibited in Spitalfields and in Coventry; there was distress in Macclesfield, in Manchester, in Middleton, and in Sudbury; and the reason that I state so is, that I am almost in weekly communication with those places, and I think I have in my possession a letter which to my mind is conclusive of the state of distress in the neighbourhood of Manchester.

10042. What is the nature of the information which the letter you have referred to contains?—The letter which I now hold, and which I shall have the honour of handing in, is a letter from the Overseer of the Poor of Middleton; Middleton,
I believe,

I believe, is within two or three miles of Manchester, and is that immediate suburb of Manchester that is employed in weaving the better description of gros de Naples, or the description of work that stands between the general manufacture of Manchester and the general manufacture of Spitalfields; so that if a traveller wants to get an article between those two extremes, he is likely to find it at the town of Middleton; the letter which I hold in my hand is a letter from the Overseer of the Poor of Middleton, dated Middleton, 17th March 1832; this letter was written in reply to a letter sent down by our Committee to the town of Middleton, to ascertain in what condition their silk trade was; were they as bad as we were, and if they were, to let us know the amount of their distress.

*Barrett Wadden,*
Esq.

2 July,
1832.

*[The same was delivered in and read, as follows :]*

Sir,                                                        Middleton, 17 March 1832.

In answer to your inquiries, I must say it is true that distress for want of employment among the silk weavers of this town has been such, during six months up to February, as was never before experienced; the extreme privations, and I may add the unexampled patience of the poor sufferers, excited the compassion of the more wealthier portion of the inhabitants of this town and neighbourhood, and a most munificent subscription was raised for the relief of those, who, notwithstanding their sufferings, would not apply for parochial relief; and here I may observe by the way, that the increase of poors' rates or the number of applicants for relief, will not go far to prove the extent of the distresses of the labouring class in a parish or the kingdom, for these very obvious reasons; in the first place, nearly one-half of the rates collected, go for other purposes than the relief of the poor, (our church expenses included;) I suppose it is nearly the same throughout the kingdom; again, let the trade be ever so good, there are many poor who cannot, and others who will not help themselves: on the other hand, when distress prevails, there are very many who would almost perish with hunger before they would ask for parochial relief; during the late distress I have witnessed numerous instances of this, in cases where I have been informed of families who were suffering in silence extreme distress; when I have asked them why they did not apply for relief, I have been answered with a magnanimity that deserves to be recorded, ' No, I would sooner die for want;' others more mildly, but more forcibly, would reply, ' We will try to do without a little longer.' From the above named subscription we were enabled to relieve 600 families per week, for five weeks successively, with from 6 lbs. to 18 lbs. of meal, and from 15 lbs. to 30 lbs. of potatoes, each. It appears by the different statements brought in by the parties who then inspected the township, that out of 1,454 silk weavers, 929 were out of employ. I have had some difficulty in obtaining the necessary information, otherwise I should have answered your letter sooner.

I am, Sir, your's obediently,

To Mr. Phipps.                                          *Sam.* Pilkington,
Overseer of the Poor, Middleton.

---

10043. Did you ever hear of rich silk goods of any sort, such as are used by the wealthier classes, being made at Manchester?—I believe that they are not made; when I say not made, I have no doubt there are some few exceptions; I have seen an odd piece of silk now and then that I have been told was bought at Manchester, and that I would say was as well made as we could attempt to make it in Spitalfields.

10044. Has it been the habit of Manchester silk manufacturers to imitate any sort of fancy silk goods that may have been made in Spitalfields?—I believe it has been their habit.

10045. You have said that you confine yourself to the plain branch of trade?—I do.

10046. Do you know what state the rich figured and fancy trade of Spitalfields is now in?—As to the rich figured and fancy trade of Spitalfields, I consider it is almost extinct; there are some rich figured silks making in Spitalfields, but the amount of labour employed in those productions is not as one loom to every thousand. If I say that there are 15,000 looms employed in Spitalfields, I am about exhibiting productions upon which there are not 15 employed. [*The Witness produced three or four splendid specimens of the production of Spitalfields.*] These are works wove in Spitalfields, by our oldest manufacturer, Mr. Harn; I am just told his house is about 150 years established; and so high is the character of the man, that if he were here, and the question was asked him, " How many looms have you at work on those goods?" he would immediately answer it.

10047. Do you say not more than 15 looms are at work upon this particular work?—I should think not; and I doubt very much if there is half that number at work at Manchester in those particular goods.

678.                                                      10048. What

*Barrett Wadden,*
Esq.

———

2 July,
1832.

10048. What do you call this?—[*Pointing to one of the specimens.*]—I call that a satin damask with velvet flowers.

10049. Is it a recent production?—It is a recent production, weaving at present in Spitalfields.

10050. For any particular order?—For a particular order.

10051. What order is it for?—It is weaving for His Majesty's use at Windsor Palace.

10052. In what colour?—In a full rose colour.

10053. Were there many figured and fancy silks made in Spitalfields before the opening of the Ports?—I have every reason to believe that there were, for I am personally acquainted with three houses that, prior to the opening of the Ports, had between them 900 looms at work on figured goods, and those three houses now have not between them 80 looms. The falling off in our fancy and figure trade in Spitalfields is prodigious; and while it is so, I deeply regret to find that the foreign manufacturer has taken it from us.

10054. Is that description of commodity still in use to as large an extent as it was formerly?—By commodity I am to understand figured silks?

10055. Yes?—I think there is no diminution on the part of the public consumption in figured silks, and that there is as great a demand for it now as there has been within my memory.

10056. Then what, in your opinion, is the reason that those articles, of which you say there is as great a consumption, are not now made in Spitalfields?—The Ports of this country being open to foreign productions, and those foreign productions having arrived to a state of excellency that I must, as a manufacturer, say they are very superior to ours, they have got hold of this market, and indeed they must get hold of every market into which those productions go, for if science is regarded, and perfection admired, French productions are sure to find a sale go where they will; they are so perfect in their designs, and so beautiful in their execution, and therefore they have got hold of this market; the fashions are introduced; we are obliged to follow those fashions, and some of us, I fear, somewhat like Saint Peter, we follow afar off, at least it is my opinion, and we are likely to continue in that fallen attitude, at a loss to every man that pursues it; however, I am determined I shall not be one of those, and therefore I shall keep to the plain branch of weaving.

10057. Do you think sufficient efforts are made by the British manufacturer to provide fancy goods for the higher ranks of the community of London?—I believe sufficient effort has been made, at least an effort sufficient to prove the ruin that must follow it if it be continued. As I before stated, the fact is, France leads the fashion; our milliners, our first-rate dress makers, our warehousemen, import it, and we follow it; as long as this is the case, I regard it as hopeless to enter into a successful competition against foreign productions in the fancy trade.

10058. Do you, in the generality of your manufactures, use English or foreign thrown organzine?—I use both; but the great bulk of the goods which I manufacture are made from British thrown silks.

10059. Do you find the English answer your purpose as well as the foreign?—I find it does in a great range of works. If I am asked in what cases I prefer it, or why I prefer it, I say, that in the article of satin, for instance; I consider our British thrown silks, generally speaking, are superior to foreign thrown silks, and I am now about stating a fact that perhaps will be valuable to the gentlemen by whom I am surrounded: It is in evidence by Dr. Bowring, and a most valuable piece of information it is, that the manufacturer of France, amongst the difficulties that he describes himself as having to contend with, classes a difficulty which he says arises from the stealth that takes place in the article that he introduces to the dyer's care. The honourable Committee, no doubt, will immediately recollect to what part of Dr. Bowring's evidence I refer. I am now about stating a fact, which I think will be beneficial, not only to the gentlemen manufacturers in whose presence I speak, but beneficial to every manufacturer in the kingdom; that will have the means of getting at a knowledge of the fact that I am now going to put on record. Amongst the advantages which I find to arise to me as a manufacturer from using British thrown silk is this very important one; I beg leave most distinctly to state, that what I am now about uttering is not to be considered or regarded as a charge made by me against that class of persons called dyers, than whom I am not acquainted with a more upright or a honourable class of men; but from the nature of the employment they give, and the number of persons in their respective dye-houses, the

article

*Barrett Wadden,*
Esq.

2 July,
1832.

article passing through their hands is very subject to be either wasted by negligence, design or by fraud; and I think that the man that points out a method to put an effectual lock upon his property while in the hands of the dyer, confers upon society a lasting benefit: that lock I am this day going to describe. I will point out a method to my brother manufacturers, whether they live in Spitalfields, in Coventry or in Manchester, that if they follow it, all the property that they send to their dyer they are sure to receive back; for out of the thousands of pounds weight of silk that I have dyed since I came into this country, I am safe in saying I have not lost a single ounce; and that declaration I would not be able to make, if, through the vigilance of my mind, looking round to see how I could be secured against any species of low cunning, or fraud or trick, that I had not discovered an effectual mode of preserving my property. Amongst the reasons why I give a decided preference to British thrown silk is this one: I have stated that the skein of raw silk is silk that has gone through no process of manufacture; this skein of silk that I am now exhibiting is produced from that raw, and I have that silk (I had a good deal of difficulty in getting the check brought to perfection when I came into this country,) but I have that silk thrown for me by one of the first throwsters in the country, and the plan that I strike out, to put an effectual security or bond upon my property, while out of my hands and in the possession of the dyer, is simply this: to have all the slips that each knot (I call this a knot or hank); to have the respective skeins that are contained in each hank about the same length or size, and to have then a certain number of those skeins put into each hank, I find that I am enabled to send, for instance, I sent the other day 186lbs. weight of silk in this state to my dyer, containing 1,807 knots or hanks, each knot containing four skeins; the skein as here exhibited is as it comes off the throwster's mill, and round this original skein is a strong thread of silk tied, and round every four there is a coarse cotton band tied; so that all I have to do is to reckon how many of those knots or hanks I give to my dyer, and when I get them back, ascertain, does every knot, (for he has my positive instructions never to break or violate one of those knots)—and therefore all I have to do, is to take a skein of dyed silk and ascertain, are there in that skein the same number of original skeins or slips that he received when they were given by me to dye: so that if manufacturers were to adopt this system, I go so far as to say, they need scarcely use a scale or weights; that it would be a better system, and a more complete one, to give to the original skein of silk taken off the throwster's mill, have a given quantity of those original skeins put into a knot, and to reckon those to the dyer. I have done it for years, and to that extent, which is perhaps a very considerable one, I have been successful in, and that is one great reason that I give a preference to British thrown silks, for I cannot get foreign thrown silks banded in a similar manner. Whenever I buy a bale of foreign Piedmont for instance, I am under the necessity of going back to the original slips, bind them all, and get them up into the state which I have represented.

10060. Do you think the English throwster capable of producing as good an organzine as the throwster of Piedmont?—I think he is, when receiving a price that will compensate him for his care and trouble, and the outlay of capital.

10061. Do you consider that he has as good raw silk as is to be found in Italy? —Indeed I think, generally speaking, he has not; there is one class of silk which I believe the throwster of this country has the whole throwing of; that class of silk is called Fossembrone; but the reason why I think that in the other description of silks he is not in the habit of getting the better description of them is, that it must appear self-evident to any reflecting mind, that the foreign throwster having the pick and cull of his own market before the English throwster can get to those silks, that he has a decided preference in making that selection out of a very large stock, and thus the English throwster or manufacturer is obliged to take into his work the refuse of a stock, or the remainder of a stock that has been already picked and culled by the foreign throwster. That is my opinion, as far as it relates to the general run of Italian silk, making two distinctions; one distinction is the Fossembrone, which comes to this country, and the other distinction is, that the article of Piedmont raw does not come here at all; that it is a prohibited article.

10062. Does the Fossembrone silk come to England in a thrown state?—I believe it comes to England in a raw state; unthrown, I believe, the whole of it.

10063. You have said, that you believe nearly the whole of the Fossembrone silk comes to this country?—I believe it does.

10064. Is Fossembrone chiefly thrown into organzine in this country?—I should say that the great bulk of it is thrown into organzine, such as the skein that I

678. have

*Barrett Wadden,*
Esq.

———

2 July,
1832.

have exhibited ; this is the organzine silk ; and the honourable Members will bear with me, if I just request their attention, if they will take that skein of silk, and hold it between them and the light, they will see what constitutes organzine ; it is the thread ; here is the thread of raw silk ; this thread of raw silk is first twisted, this thread also is twisted, and those two threads when twisted receive another twist together, which is organzine. Now this skein of silk is what we call tram, and the process of making tram is simply this : that the original single thread is not twisted at all ; but that the two threads are simply and softly twisted together, so that in organzine there is a double twist, that silk being used in warp ; it receives a strength that fits it to undergo the process of working, whereas it is only necessary to twist this thread in a sufficient manner to bear the process of throwing it across the work, which work is performed by the weaver's shuttle ; there are then sixteen twists on the single thread, and from twelve to fourteen on the double thread ; I am not a throwster, but as far as I am capable of examining those things with the assistance of a magnifying glass, I believe that to be the truth ; this is tram, and if the Committee will just hold this between them and the light, they will see it does not contain the same labour in it that the other does.

10065. Is that the same species of silk ?—Yes ; that not twisted is the best description of Italian raw silk ; the article I am now showing is the Fossembrone ; they are both British thrown. While I am in possession of the attention of the Committee, perhaps this is a proper time to give some information relative to the silk called Marabout, to which the attention of the Committee has been called to ; the skein of silk which I now hold is a skein of white Novi raw, from which marabout is made ; it is a silk coming from the worm in the colour that it now exhibits, whereas this is also the natural colour of the silk coming from the worm, and the value that this silk bears in the market is a value put upon it because it is suited for receiving the dye without discharging the gum, and receiving a colour more clear and pure, which this silk can never attain ; for here is a silk originally yellow, here is a silk originally white, and to put a pure and delicate shade of colour upon this yellow gum silk, it is unfitted for the purpose ; whereas this silk is peculiarly fitted for that purpose, that is Novi raw : now for the purpose of describing the process of marabout, which I shall do in a few words ; I should state to the Committee that article is first thrown into tram, and when thrown into tram it goes to the dyer, and here is some of it in a dyed state [*handing it to the Committee.*] After it is dyed, the throwster gets its back, and has to re-wind it, and to re-throw it, into the process that I now exhibit here, it is marabout ; and if the honourable Committee will examine that, and hold it between them and the light, they will see it is like the hardest twist of whipcord. I shall now beg leave to add, that that article of white Novi is this day worth 19 *s.* 6 *d.* cash ; that the price for throwing it into tram is 2 *s.* 6 *d.* ; the price for dyeing it is 2 *s.* ; and the price for re-winding and re-marabouting it after it is dyed is 5 *s.* ; to that add 10 per cent. waste, or 2 *s.* and you have the present value of a pound weight of silk marabouted, 31 *s* per lb.

10066. The 19 *s.* 6 *d.* then is exclusive of all these operations ?—Yes, that is the cost of the raw silk ; and 31 *s.* the value of that silk marabouted.

10067. You say that the Fossembrones make a very excellent organzine ?—A very excellent one.

10068. And for many purposes will stand in the place of Piedmont organzine ? —For a great many purposes I think it superior, and for other purposes I think it inferior ; here is an article which I beg leave to exhibit ; it is one of my own manufacture, and this is altogether made of Fossembrone silk ; every bit of that is Fossembrone [*handing it up to the Committee.*] I was determined to try an experiment ; I heard some of my friends say they were beaten to pieces in this market by French productions, and I determined to try ; the Jacquard that wove that cost me 21 *l.* ; I made about a thousand yards of it, and I sold it at a loss, after offering it to some houses with which I was in the habits of the most intimate friendship ; men that would give me a decided preference ; and they said, " Wadden, we are extremely sorry to see you wasting your property in this manner, but the French are beating you hollow, taking price into consideration."

10069. What price can you produce that at ?—I can produce the thing, if I can get a sale for it ; allow me to say, I think the general run of French manufactured silks coming into this country are, I must acknowledge, superior to ours ; but that if I am encouraged, and that a profit is insured to me that will enable me to buy the best description of materials, and to pay fairly every man that I employ to manufacture that material into goods, I will let my head be severed from my body

if

if I will not undertake to manufacture goods as perfect in Spitalfields as they can be produced elsewhere.

10070. Was this beautiful fabric which you have produced an experiment on your part?—It was a mere experiment on my part, for the avowed purpose of ascertaining was the fact correct as stated to me by some of my brother manufacturers, that they were cut out in this market by the introduction of foreign productions; I determined to try the experiment; I paid 21 *l.* for the Jacquard, and when I produced the work, I have actually sold it at a loss, and I was the entire of the 21 *l.* out of pocket besides.

10071. You did not throw the cost of the Jacquard on the commodity?—Not one farthing.

10072. Was there any other difficulty in selling it beyond the price of it?—None whatever; it was an imitation of one of those silks that we had the honour of manufacturing and presenting as a present to the Queen of Great Britain from Spitalfields.

10073. Were similar articles selling at the time?—Yes, in large quantities.

10074. When was it that you made this?—I had a man employed weaving that work, I think, from July last up to the month of April.

10075. Do you consider the style of this equal to any thing you have seen from France?—The pattern, as there exhibited, is altogether of Spitalfields production; the design is Spitalfields, the execution is Spitalfields, and the materials of which it is made is of British thrown silk.

10076. Have you seen any thing of this description in French superior in appearance to this?—I think that I have seen some French silks that I would consider as more beautiful than that; I am here covered with a modest feeling; I do not like to extol my own productions, which I would if I were to say they were superior to others.

10077. What is the difficulty that you complain of in this instance, as that which prevented you obtaining a profit when you sold this commodity?—The French maker is able to give an ell, or 1¼ yard, for the same price that I should get for one yard, and that yard leaving a loss to me.

10078. Is not a great quantity of French silk of that description, but of an inferior quality, sold in this country?—I believe a great deal of silk, inferior in quality to this, and a great deal very superior to it in quality, is imported into this country and sold.

10079. If the duty should be taken off foreign thrown silk, do you think that Fossembrone silk in the raw state will be continued to be imported into this country? —My opinion is, the British silk mills would have no other employment but that arising from the throwing of such silks as the East India Company import, and that they would not have any supply of the finer silks of Italy. In other words, the finer silks would be retained in Italy to be thrown by the silk mills of Italy, and be sent into this country in a thrown condition.

10080. You consider that the manufacturer, as well as the throwster, would sustain injury by such a change?—I cannot for a moment separate the interest that binds the manufacturer to the throwster, and the throwster to the manufacturer; in fact they are dependent upon each other, and therefore, as I cannot separate them, I am inclined to think that should the duty be taken off, or even reduced, that the throwster will be sacrificed, and that if sacrificed, the manufacturer in course of time will fall in for a portion of that sacrifice.

10081. Do you think that throwing has improved in England of late?—I think it has not. I think that neither throwing nor weaving has improved in England of late.

10082. In what respect do you consider the throwing has rather deteriorated as you intimate?—I attribute the deterioration to the low price that is paid to the throwster; the same cause (low wages) which converts a good weaver into a careless one, the same cause is at work with the silk throwster; and hence the silk throwster, undertaking to work the silk at a certain price, sooner than see his mill and machinery all idle, which price, in most instances, includes the waste, he is compelled to leave in the original skein of silk what we call nibs or gouts; that to prevent an increased loss to him, such as would arise from a deficiency of weight occasioned by waste, he is obliged to leave the nibs or gouts in the silk to return as much weight to his employer as the silk is capable of producing; and thus, whenever that is the case, the grossest act of injustice is then done to the weaver, for the article cannot be wove by the weaver till all those original nibs or

678.                                                                                            gouts

*Barrett Wadden,*
Esq.

————

2 July,
1832.

gouts are taken out of it; and therefore we apply the term cleaning (not that the silk ever was dirty), but the term cleaning applies to the removing of those things which we call nibs or gouts, which if not removed by the throwster must be by the weaver. If it is removed by the throwster it makes the price of weaving to the weaver more easy; if it is not removed by the throwster it increases the already difficult situation in which the weavers are placed; and owing to the low wages that the throwster receives, I think that the silks generally thrown now are not as well cleaned nor as well thrown as they were when the throwster had a much better price for his operation.

10083. How do you account for the low wages and consequent distress in the trade of the throwster, at a time when there is so large an importation of raw silks, and so general a consumption of silk goods in this country?—I think the distress arises out of what I would denominate an unnatural competition, according as we force down wages, as it relates to forcing down the price of labour on those persons under us, and according as our profits are forced down by the buyers who are above us. This forcing down of wages and profit has a natural tendency to increase our productions; for if a man finds that his wages and his profits are reduced, he immediately tries to increase his business by an increase, just in about the same proportion as that property that he finds himself losing; and hence, in a great number of instances, we are compelled to go on with our productions till those productions absolutely outrun the demand, and produce such a stagnation in trade, such distress amongst ourselves and amongst our people, that we are all unfortunate monuments of the condition that we are placed in.

10084. You have stated in an early part of your evidence, that the condition of the silk weavers of Spitalfields is at this time very wretched; can you give any statement as to the number of them who may be at this time out of employment?—When this honourable Committee was appointed, I have reason to believe that there were about 5,000 looms in Spitalfields out of employment, and I should think that owing to the time of year, which always brings round employment to a certain extent, that of the 5,000 weavers that were out of employment when this honourable Committee was appointed, in all probability from 1,000 to 1,500 of them have fallen in to employment; and I should in round numbers suppose that there are 3,000 or thereabouts still out of employment; and while I am on this part of my evidence I would say, and I say it with feelings of extreme sorrow, that since the opening of the Ports to foreign productions, a new species of crime has sprung up in Spitalfields. I would wish here to be considered as bearing my testimony to the character of the weavers of Spitalfields, taken as a body, that, taking into consideration the enormous quantity of property which is continually in their hands, (I estimate the property at all times in the hands of the weavers of Spitalfields at about 160,000 *l.*) and considering that this property is placed in the hands of some 12 or 15,000 people, there is not on the habitable earth, and it must be a proud consolation to the Government of this country to know, that the weavers of Spitalfields have ever been remarkable for their honesty; that if I look, as I sometimes do, at the violation of trust that takes place, it is a violation of trust only to the extent of some isolated cases; and I am now about stating an important fact, that will show that the alteration of the law has given birth to a species of crime in Spitalfields unknown in Spitalfields prior to the alteration of the law. Those documents which I have now to show, will show the crime to which I already allude; here are published documents, offering various rewards for the apprehension of weavers who have violated their trust, that have run away with their master's property. I am sorry to find, that among the sufferers are some gentlemen present; and no later than within the two last months here are two weavers who have absconded with property to the extent of between, I believe, eight and nine hundred yards of manufactured goods. Why have they absconded? I find there is a prevailing opinion amongst the people of Spitalfields, and that opinion is, that the Government of this country has abandoned the silk trade, and given it up to destruction; that if the weavers can only get out of this country, and plant their feet upon American ground, they are sure to find valuable employment; and hence it comes, that some of those persons who have absconded with their employer's property have, on their arrival in the United States of America, written home letters requesting their families to follow them out, for that they were at length on a soil in which labour and industry had its reward. I exhibit those as proofs that a species of crime has sprung up that is in operation upon some few unfortunate men,

and

*Barrett Wadden,*
Esq.

———

2 July,
1832.

and among the few I find my own countrymen, (for the seven or eight hundred yards of property that was made away with within the two last months is by two Irishmen, one in my own employment;) that therefore this arises out of a state of distress, the working people imagining there is no spot for them to anchor their hopes upon, they look round, and while in possession of their employer's property, they finish it, sell it, and with the produce they get themselves transported to foreign land, there to live superior to any thing they can enjoy through the medium of their own labour at home.

10085. In what manner are those weavers who are out of employment in Spitalfields supported?—The great bulk of them, I believe, are thrown on their respective parishes; others of them, in my rambles through Spitalfields, I have seen, several of them standing at the corners of streets selling matches; some sell fruit when in season, others hawk fish, and more of them are attended by their wretched families, with their hearts almost ready to break within them, trying to catch a penny from the passenger by imitating the song of joy. I have seen such a state of suffering, that I am afraid to trust my feelings to describe it; they are at all times alive to the distresses of the people, and when I see those distresses produced, not by the people themselves, but produced by circumstances over which they have no control, that is the only excuse that I can offer to the Committee if I exhibit any degree of warmth of mind or feeling.

10086. You stated a new species of crime had sprung up since the prohibition, which was the weavers making goods and then selling them, and running away; do you mean that that never happened before the prohibition was taken off?—I have made it my particular business to inquire most anxiously into their condition, and I cannot find a single record in which a violation of faith took place when the people's labour was protected.

10087. Have you any knowledge of the goods which were some time since seized belonging to Messrs. Leaf & Company?—I have some knowledge of them.

10088. Can you state what proportion of those goods was broad silks and what ribbons?—I think I can; I received a letter from the Commissioners of Customs some time last November, requesting my attendance down at the Custom House, to examine some goods which were then under seizure, and which were reported to be the property of Messrs. Leaf & Company. In examining those goods, I found that they contained 7,919 pieces of ribbon, measuring 218,869 yards, and that there were amongst those goods 369 pieces of broad silks, measuring 25,541 yards.

10089. You are aware that those goods have been restored, in pursuance of some arrangement between Messrs. Leaf & Company and the Government?—I am.

10090. Now do you know whether those goods have been since sold for home consumption?—I have reason to believe that all the goods that were so restored have been since sold for home consumption, in common with the goods which that house is in the habit of selling.

10091. Is that in accordance with the law?—I am placed in such a situation now as I never was placed in before in all my life. I am asked a question of law; however I shall give my opinion. I believe that the goods ought not to have found their way into our home market; for I find by a reference to the Act of George the Fourth, c. 23, there is this Clause:—" And whereas it is expedient that greater re-
" wards than heretofore should be granted to officers upon the seizure of foreign
" silk goods; Be it Enacted, That upon the seizure and condemnation of any such
" goods, for the breach of any law now made or hereafter to be made, relating to
" the revenue of Customs, or for the prevention of smuggling, there shall be paid
" to the officer seizing the same, in lieu of the rewards granted by any former Act,
" the whole value of such goods, exclusive of the duty thereon: Provided always,
" That such goods shall be sold for exportation only."

10092. Do you know that they have been sold?—I have no doubt whatever, the goods were returned to Messrs. Leaf, and they got them into their stock and sold them.

10093. Do you know whether, in the compromise that took place, they saved the duty or paid the duty; were the goods restored to them on their paying the duty, or without paying the duty?—The goods, I understood, were restored to them, on their paying 20,000*l.*; and that compromise, I must add, took place at about ten o clock on the night previous to the question being brought into His Majesty's Court of Exchequer: that that compromise took place although a pledge, as solemn as a pledge could be made, was given by the Vice President of the Board of Trade to the country, that justice should not be compromised with the parties.

678.

10094. Do

10094. Do you know when these goods were returned whether they entered into any bond, and whether the Government entered into any arrangement with them, by which they, on their own parts, made a compromise that they would not prosecute for any previous offence committed before that?—I am not able to give any information whatever on that subject; I know nothing of it.

10095. Did you hear this pledge that you speak of, made by the Vice President of the Board of Trade?—The pledge, as made by the Vice President of the Board of Trade, and to which I have now referred, is a pledge that I have read in the various publications of the day, as uttered by the Vice President in a certain place, that it would be a violation of my duty to be more explicit upon; I read it as matter of history.

10096. Did the trade generally understand it as a pledge?—The trade, I believe, to a man, understood it as a pledge.

10097. Did the trade, from the publicity that was given to the statement, consider themselves able to reckon upon it with certainty?—They considered the declaration that was reported to have been made by the Vice President of the Board of Trade, as a certain guarantee that ample justice should be done to the trade by punishing the parties, as far as the law would permit.

10098. Did the trade consider that the very large sum of money exacted from Messrs. Leaf in this compromise, was in any way adequate to the benefit which the trade imagined they would have derived by the pursuance of the prosecution?—The trade, generally speaking, considered that the payment of money, no matter how large, ought not to have been accepted; but that a more ample scope of justice would have been afforded to the general manufactures of the country and the trading interests of the country by punishing to the utmost extent of the law, and getting recorded, on the roll of the court, the fact that the parties had been convicted; for I believe the result would be, that if detected in any circumstance somewhat similar, that the second offence would place them in a situation, subject to such an infliction of penalty, as would leave them beggars, be their property to what extent it might; and that by avoiding the conviction which might have taken place, they have avoided that situation which they would have been placed in if a conviction had been recorded; and that they, the second time, had the misfortune to commit the same offence.

10099. Do you not consider that a public conviction would have been a very great and a very beneficial circumstance to the manufacturers generally?—Most assuredly.

10100. Do you not believe, that if it had not been for that pledge to which you allude, the trade would have taken some steps to obtain a distinct pledge to that effect?—I think they would.

10101. You do not happen to know yourself, do you, the circumstances of the compromise?—No; but I have good authority for saying, the sum paid was 20,000 *l.*

10102. You have stated, that you have reason to know that these goods, so returned to Messrs. Leaf, did, in point of fact, come into the English market?—They did.

10103. Are you aware whether the Government, in the arrangement which they made with Messrs. Leaf, have made it a part of the stipulation that those goods should not be sold in this market?—That I know nothing whatever about; I am not able to answer the question.

10104. Do you not consider that the circumstance of those goods being sold in the home market, independently of the quantity of British manufacture which may have been displaced by their being so sold, has also had the ill effect of operating very much to the discouragement of the manufacturer, by depriving him of that protection which he thinks he has a right to rely upon?—That is my opinion.

10105. Do you know whether the exportation of silk goods from this country has of late increased?—I believe the export of silk goods from this country has very considerably increased.

10106. To what do you consider that this circumstance is to be attributed?—The increase of our export trade can be traced to a drawback or bounty that is now given to the men that can find out an export market for our goods; that is, here is a sample of one of the most beautiful foreign thrown silks of Piedmont that I ever saw in my life; that article coming into this market pays 3*s.* 6*d.* duty; the Government, or an Act of Parliament rather, gives to the exporter of a pound weight of manufactured goods, a drawback equivalent to the import duty which the

Government

*Barrett Wadden,*
Esq.

2 July,
1832.

Government has received on the pound weight of thrown silk, and that consequently we are indebted to that debenture or drawback for our export trade; take away that debenture, your export trade ceases; increase it if you can devise a means for increasing it, and you stand the best possible chance of increasing the employment of the people, by giving them an increased export trade.

10107. You have stated that the present drawback on the exportation of silk goods has been the principal cause of increase in the export of such goods within the last two or three years, how then do you account for their not having a large export formerly, when the drawback was a much larger one than at present?—When the drawback was much larger than it now is; I suppose that the honourable Member refers to that period of time when thrown silk paid a duty of 14 s. 8 d.; if that be the case, when foreign thrown silk paid a duty of 14 s. 8 d. per lb. the silks of Bengal paid a duty of 4 s. per pound, and every other description of raw silk paid a duty of 5 s. 6 d. per pound; so that if I wanted to manufacture this article or that article, I could manufacture no article, no not even the bit of silk that lines this hat, but from silk that had paid a duty, and that silk worked up subject to the payment of wages which were then high, prevented us from having an export trade at all like that which we now have, for we are now manufacturing goods out of silks that have only paid a penny a pound duty. Our principal exports arise from the manufacture of the silks of Bengal and China, with a mixture of Italian raw silk; so that our export trade altogether is carried on from the manufacture of silks that have only paid one penny a pound duty, and getting a drawback or bounty derivable from a fund created by an impost on foreign thrown silks coming into this country that have paid 3 s. 6 d. a pound duty; here perhaps I may be permitted to state, that in a conversation which I had with the late President of the Board of Trade, who assured me that the duty payable upon foreign thrown silks was not a question of revenue at all; that the arrangement was to protect the silk mills of this country, and to give back to the silk trade whatever amount of duty they received on thrown silks; we will give it back to you if you find out a foreign market for your productions, caring not one straw whether the goods you manufacture are made of silks that have paid a duty, or made of silks of your own production from raw, that we give you subject to a penny a pound duty.

10108. Are you of opinion, that without the debenture the export of silk goods would continue?—I have already stated, and I state again, that take away the debenture and your export trade will immediately cease; that it is a trade that cannot exist otherwise.

10109. Does the export tend to the relief of the trade in general?—I should think very much; for if through the medium of low wages and wretched profits, profits that are sometimes called shades, and as long as I have lived in the world I never could ascertain how many shadows make a substance, or profits that are called shades, have a natural tendency to increase production; this production when increased outruns demand, and therefore it is of the utmost importance that we should have an export trade to take away the overplus whenever we can find a vent for it, and that vent I do fearlessly assert never can be obtained if you take away the drawback which the exporter of silk goods now has, and which constitutes his profits; for I do not hesitate to say, that English manufactured silks are to be found in the shops of New York at as low a price as they are to be found in any draper's window in the city of London; that the cost of transit and the charges, and the profit, is one arising out of the drawback.

10110. Assuming that the duty on the foreign thrown silk was taken off, and no debenture allowed, do you think it would be practicable to export silk goods from this country?—I think it would not be practicable.

10111. Are you able to state the amount of duty received in any one year on the import of thrown silk in this country, and the amount of drawback in the same year returned on the exportation of silk manufactured goods?—I hold in my hand an account published by order of the House of Commons of the 21st of September 1831, and it is headed " Raw, waste, thrown and manufactured Silk for Home Consumption in the United Kingdom, from the 5th of January 1830 to the 5th of January 1831." The duty received upon thrown silks for that year amounted to 73,551 l. 0 s. 8 d.; and upon a reference to the same document, exhibiting an amount of drawback paid in the United Kingdom on British silk manufactured goods exported in the year ending the 5th January 1831, I find the total amount of drawback on stuffs or silks, or ribbons of silk, is 24,973 l. 4 s., and the drawback paid on stuffs, or ribbons of silk and cotton mixed, 9,296 l. 10 s. 11 ¼ d.; stuff, or

ribbons

*Barrett Wadden,*
Esq.

———

2 July,
1832.

ribbons of silk and worsted mixed, 2,420 *l.* 13 *s.* 6½ *d.*; so that the total of the drawback paid that year was 36,690 *l.* 8 *s.* 7 *d.* The honourable Committee will pardon me if I call their attention to a circumstance which I am not capable or able to satisfy my own mind upon, but I think it is worth the attention of some more acute mind than I possess; we are set down here as receiving a drawback amounting to 24,973 *l.* 4 *s.*, which, at 3 *s.* 6 *d.* a pound, would represent exports to the amount of 142,704 lbs. weight of manufactured silk, and upon a reference to the quantity of silks that we are in another part of the account exhibited as exporting, the weight is 182,994 lbs. I state this extraordinary circumstance, hoping that the gentleman whose signature is to this, namely, William Irving, Inspector General of Imports and Exports, will be able to account for this extraordinary circumstance, namely, that if you try to ascertain the quantity of goods that you have exported by the amount of drawback you have received, you can scarcely imagine a case where a man would be idiot enough to export goods and not ask for the drawback, and therefore if the amount of goods exported be measured by the amount of drawback received, it is actually 142,704, and we are represented by another part of this document as exporting 182,994, a difference of upwards of 40,000 lbs. weight of silk.

10112. You would not get the drawback on the unmanufactured silk, would you?—Decidedly not; every 3 *s.* 6 *d.* which is received on a pound weight of foreign thrown silk is put by to form a fund for the encouragement of an export trade, and thus we are here represented as having exported manufactures of silk only to the extent of 182,994 lbs., and when I come to ascertain the quantity we exported by the amount of drawback received, I find a difference of above 40,000 lbs. in weight. But again, when I come to examine the drawback received on the export of silk mixed with cotton, and the drawback received upon the export of silk mixed with worsted, I find that here the difference is monstrous; the whole of the amount of drawback, amounting to 36,690 *l.* 8 *s.* 7 *d.*, represents goods exported to the extent of 377,925 the weight; whereas, in the official document, we are held up to the public as exporting goods to the amount of 472,340 lbs. weight, or nearly 100,000 lbs. weight of goods exported beyond what is represented by the drawback paid.

10113. Are you able to suggest to this Committee any means by which the export trade in silk goods might probably be extended?—This is a question which I consider of extreme difficulty and of extreme importance. After giving the subject as much attention as I had either time or wish to do, I came to two conclusions, that there are two ways by which the export trade may be increased to a very great extent. The first of those ways would be to increase the drawback; and I think there are two ways by which that might be done: the first might be to raise the duty from 3 *s.* 6 *d.* to 5 *s.*, giving an increased protection to the silk mills of this country; but that protection referred back again to the silk trade of the country, encouraging them to export their manufactures. For if I find, according to this document, that there is 89,544 *l.* in money received as duty on the import of silks, every guinea of which it is the wish of the Government we should draw out of their hands. They have told us so over and over again, that they do not regard it as a question of revenue, but as a question of protection; and that they, in other words, open a kind of account for the silk trade. They say, we will give you credit for all the money we receive for the payment of duties on foreign thrown silk, and we will debit you with all the money that you call upon us to pay for the export trade until, or at least to the extent, so as to balance the accounts; and I find that the amount of money paid in this year on the import of silk was 89,544 *l.* 0 *s.* 5 *d.*; and the whole amount of drawback they were called upon to pay only reaches, as I before stated, 36,690 *l.* Now I come to this conclusion, and I defy the mind of any rational man to come to any other, that 3 *s.* 6 *d.* is not a drawback sufficient to take away out of this market goods equal to the weight of foreign organzine silk imported. For the duty on the foreign organzine silk is only 3 *s.* 6 *d.*, the drawback is only 3 *s.* 6 *d.*; and while the Government receive, as I before stated, 89,544 *l.* they are only paying out of that 36,690 *l.* It is self-evident that the drawback, as it now stands, is not sufficiently large to give us an export trade equivalent to the import duty we pay, which is decidedly the object of the Government. And then if I am asked how is that to be done, I would say at once, if by any process that you can raise the amount of drawback to a price above 3 *s.* 6 *d.*, in whatever proportion you ascend with that price in an equal ratio you send our manufactured silks abroad, and you get a beneficial export trade. Now

there

*Barrett Wadden,*
Esq.

2 July,
1832.

there is another way of doing that, which I would suggest to the Committee. I admit that it is a question of great difficulty; for if I am to be left exposed to stand a competition with foreign productions, the cheaper I can get my material the better for me; but, as I now stand, I am in an attitude to get my material as cheap as I can ever expect to get it; for the only duty that it pays is 1 *d.* per lb., that is upon all raw silks; but when I come to work up foreign thrown silks they are burthened with 3 *s.* 6 *d.* I do not believe that they are burthened sufficiently to protect the mill property of this country; and I am satisfied that if that duty was raised to what it was prior to the alteration of 1829, namely, 5 *s.*, and that 5 *s.* given back to us upon the export of our manufactured goods, that we would have a larger export trade, and a much greater one than we have now. If I am asked to what extent, I would say decidedly treble, or fourfold the extent; because if we are enabled to export a given quantity of goods with a 3 *s.* 6 *d.* debenture, we would be enabled decidedly to export a much greater quantity of goods with a 5 *s.* debenture; but the question in my judgment is this, how is the 5 *s.* debenture to be obtained. Is it to be obtained by raising the present rate of duty on foreign silk up to 5 *s.*, or can any other means be devised? I think that I could furnish some other means, that I could devise a method. According as the matter now stands, the debenture or certificate continues in existence but for two years from its date; that is, that if I import a bale of silk, pay the duty, get an acknowledgment in the shape of a certificate from the Government that I have paid the duty, I can transfer that, I can sell it for any period within two years; but if I do not sell it within two years it becomes of no value to me. I would suggest that a great benefit could be conferred on the export trade of the country if the debentures were to continue in existence, and to have no limitation as to time; I may then be told that if that plan were adopted it would place the Government in a difficulty of keeping open the accounts, and they tell me over and over that the money received is not a question of revenue. I would suggest in a few words, let the money which the Government receives in payment of duties on foreign thrown silks be paid into the Bank of England to the credit of an account to be opened, to be called the British Silk Export Trade of the country, and let the person presenting a certificate or debenture then receive a drawback to be monthly declared by any competent board that might examine into the state of our imports and exports for the debenture, to be raised from 3 *s.* 6 *d.* up to 5 *s.*, and to stop whenever the amount of drawback would come up to the amount of duty received. In my humble judgment the export trade of the country could be greatly enlarged in this kind of manner; and by how much it is enlarged will give valuable employment to that portion of the community that are so anxious to have it.

10114. Then you think that the duties of 1829 on thrown silk, given in the form of debentures, tended to increase the export trade of the country, and that if the duties on thrown silk were raised and the debenture raised also, that would give an additional impulse to the export trade?—It is my opinion that it would; it is my opinion, after many many hours very serious consideration and close examination.

10115. Do not you consider that the reduction of duty on thrown silk would augment the price of raw silk in Italy, or that it would keep up the price of thrown silk to the English manufacturer?—I should think that it would: if you increase employment for the throwing mills of Italy, you increase competition among the throwsters of Italy for the raw material.

10116. Whereas if you augment the duty on thrown silk you would diminish the price in Italy, and keep up the price of thrown silk to the English manufacturer?— My sincere and candid opinion is this; that it would be a preservation to the silk mills of this country, and that it would afford increased employment to the people; and that if the system be managed so as to give us back, in the shape of drawback, all the money we pay in the shape of import duties, that while we are benefiting by it the revenue will remain as the Government wish it to remain, not deriving any benefit from our trade.

10117. The Committee understand you to say, that, according to your belief, there is one branch of the smuggling which is carried on from the Customs at a very low rate, so low as eight and ten per cent.; are you enabled to give any explanation to the Committee upon that subject?—When goods are brought through the Custom House, paying only 10 per cent. that should have paid 30, it is as I under-stand, and I am told so by the parties that are engaged in the transaction, that it is done by using I cannot say false weights, but announcing that certain packages of

*Barrett Wadden,*
Esq.

2 July,
1832.

goods weigh much less than they do actually weigh ; as for instance, if a package of goods that weighs three hundred weight be represented as a package only weighing one hundred weight, although that one hundred weight is charged with 30 per cent. according to the law, yet the three hundred weight find their way into the warehouse at 10 per cent. ; that is the way.

10118. It ought to be charged 90 per eent.?—Yes.

10119. Do you consider then, that the existing regulations of the Custom House are not adequate to the prevention of frauds of the nature to which you allude?—Sometime last September, an officer in the Custom House in London, a gentleman I believe holding a very important situation, assured me, that the arrangements of that establishment were so conducted that it would be possible for a vessel to arrive in the Thames in mid-day laden with silks, and to begin unloading them without the payment of the duty ; I asked him to describe it to me, for I could not understand the thing ; and he said, " My dear friend, I am in a hurry ; but if I had time, I could put you in possession of the way of doing the thing."

10120. The answer that you have given refers to a different species of smuggling ; the question related more particularly to that which is carried on by means of the false weights?—My opinion is, that such a system is in operation in the Custom House.

10121. Do you think that the arrangements in the Custom House are such as cannot prevent what you consider a use of false weights?—I think it is the negligence of arrangement.

10122. The Committee understand it then to be the impression of your mind, that according to the present system, it is practicable for a person both to defraud the revenue in the way of weight, and also by landing goods without the payment of any duty at all at the present time?—My decided opinion is, that it has been practised, but how far it is practised now I am not prepared to say.

10123. Have you any reason to suppose that the large smuggling transaction, in which Leaf & Company were engaged, was carried on with any connivance on the part of persons employed in the Customs?—Indeed I should think not.

10124. Is it your opinion that the smuggling transaction, in which Leaf & Company were engaged, is to be considered as a mere isolated case?—I should think it is not an isolated case ; but that they found it necessary to embark largely in those kind of transactions, and no doubt reconciled the matter to their own mind, on the ground that they were entering into competition with houses that were similarly circumstanced.

10125. You said that 20,000*l.* was paid to compromise the matter ; do you know at all what was done with the 20,000*l.*, or if the officers received any part of it, which they ought to have received?—I can only state what I have heard, and what I believe to be the fact, that the 20,000*l.* so paid has never been divided amongst the officers ; that they have got, in some few instances, 50*l.* 40*l.* 30*l.* and 100*l.* ; but that the great bulk of the money is in the hands of the parties who received it: however, I am bound to state this fact, that the house that owns the goods, namely, Leaf & Company, did memorial the Lords of the Treasury to refund them back their 20,000*l.*, on the ground that the goods so seized were not smuggled at all, and that consequently the Lords of the Treasury or His Majesty's Commissioners of Customs may hold back this 20,000*l.* until the subject-matter of that memorial is ultimately settled. Therefore when I understand that the officers have not got the reward to which the law entitles them, the reason may arise out of the circumstance I have stated, that the parties are claiming back the 20,000*l.* ; not that I believe they will ever get a penny of it.

10126. You have stated, that the smuggling transaction in which Leaf is said to have been engaged and others, have arisen from neglect or from bad arrangements at the Custom House, do those bad arrangements still continue, or have they been altered or improved in any respect?—The arrangements are so shockingly loose there, that I know one gentleman, and he has told me, that by giving the man at the scales a sack of flour and a flitch of bacon, he will let him go through.

10127. Then you think the arrangements are still very loose?—I should think so.

10128. Would you not consider the mode of taking the goods altogether very defective, if such a system is allowed ; would not you think some other mode of arranging the duties would be better?—I am not prepared to submit to the honourable Committee a mode of arranging duties, but when I know this important fact, that persons in high authority will not make most valuable changes for the

benefit

benefit of the community, on the ground that those changes if made would be troublesome to the officers, I can find an excuse for the officers being negligent; my opinion is, that the officer or the man who receives the public money ought to work with a degree of fidelity and integrity suitable to the rank of life that he holds.

*Barrett Wadden,*
Esq.

2 July,
1832.

10129. You would not palliate his dishonesty by any opinions of a Government? —Most assuredly not.

10130. Then this system of passing a large package of goods through the Customs rated at only a small quantity, may account for the immense quantity of foreign goods which inundates this market?- -I think there is no other way of accounting for it.

10131. Then taking the annual official or declared value of the goods passing into this country through the Custom House at 600,000*l.*, adding to this the indirect smuggling through the Customs, as well as direct smuggling, the import would be treble the sum, or about two millions?—I am extremely fearful to hazard any opinion that my mind has not been dwelling upon, and through the medium of calculations I may get myself involved upon; but it is quite enough for me to say, and to quote the words of my Lord Althorp, he stated in my presence, that we had not a remote idea to what extent the smuggling of foreign manufactured silk goods was carried on; and if the noble Lord, the Chancellor of the Exchequer, has not a remote idea of the quantity of smuggling that is done, it follows as a matter of course, that I cannot possess that knowledge of it.

10132. It has been stated by Dr. Bowring, that the average value of raw silk of France, of the finest growth, is about eighteen francs per pound, which at the present rate of exchange is equal to about 14*s.* a pound English; do you know the price of good Italian raw silk in this country?—The present price, I take it, ranges from 17*s.* 6*d.* to 18*s.*

10133. There appears then to be full 3*s.* a pound difference in favour of French manufacture, notwithstanding the grower of the silk himself gets a profit of 25 per cent.?—Above 3*s.* a pound difference on the price that Dr. Bowring has been referring to.

10134. It has been stated by Dr. Bowring, that the number of looms at Lyons has increased 10,000 since 1825, and that at St. Etienne and St. Chamond there are now 23,000, do you know the number of looms at these places in 1825?—I have seen a letter written in the year 1825, and bearing that date, in which the number of looms at St. Etienne the writer puts down as 12,000 in the year 1825.

10135. Was that letter from a competent authority, do you think?—An authority that I place an unlimited reliance upon, in the hands of a man of as honourable a mind and as upright heart as any human being I believe can possess.

10136. Then it appears that since opening the Ports to the French silks in 1826, there has been an increase at Lyons of 10,000 looms, and in the district of St. Etienne 11,000 looms, with what district in England does their manufacture most interfere?—The looms at Lyons interfere with Spitalfields; the looms at St. Etienne interfere with Coventry, and I believe those are the two districts that the foreign manufactories interfere with.

10137. It has appeared in evidence, that both in Spitalfields and Coventry, there has been distress to an extent utterly unknown in former years, do you think that the prodigious increase of the looms at St. Etienne, St. Chamond and at Lyons, has had any thing to do with that distress?—I should think that as the British public have not fallen off in the demand and consumption of articles of silk dress, and that as employment has awfully diminished in Spitalfields, and more awfully again diminished in Coventry, that by how much the people of those two places have lost employment, the people at Lyons and St. Etienne have increased employment, and that the British public are thus supplied while our own artisans are wandering about like mendicants.

10138. Do not the Swiss and German manufacturers also send goods to this country, and thereby increase the distress?—They send goods; but not to any considerable extent; the official return of goods imported from those towns do not exceed 15,000 or 18,000 pounds weight.

10139. If, with all the advantages possessed by France in respect of her raw material and low rate of wages, she considers it necessary for the due protection of her manufacture, to levy a duty of 15 per cent. on silk goods of Switzerland and Germany, do you think that the English manufacturer has great cause to complain at being forced into competition with the Continent as well as with France at a duty

of

*Barrett Wadden,*
Esq.

———

2 July,
1832.

of 30 per cent. ?—I think it is self evident that if France finds it necessary to protect her manufacture by imposing a duty of 15 per cent. on Swiss and German silks, and that England finds it necessary to levy a duty of 30 per cent. on French manufacture to preserve the English weaver, it must appear evident to any reflecting mind that the duty on Swiss and German goods in this market ought to be 45 per cent.

10140. You have directed your attention to the loss of labour occasioned by the introduction of certain silk goods of foreign manufacture ; it has been stated by Dr. Bowring that the proportion of French silks for three years was about 18 millions of francs, which he has estimated at 800,000 *l.* ; can you inform the Committee the amount of labour which has been displaced in our silk districts by this importation ?—I really cannot ; I am at present engaged in wading through a mass of calculations which I have no doubt will enable me before long to arrive with some degree of certainty, so as to answer the question that is asked me, and I should not like to hazard an opinion at a time that I am getting through those calculations that will give value to that opinion, if expressed by me founded on those calculations.

10141. We have been told by Dr. Bowring that a fourth of the produce of the looms of Avignon used to be sent to England, and now none of these goods are sent here ; the article made at this place were sarsnets ; is that article called sarsnets still fashionable here, or is some other article substituted for it ?—The article called sarsnets is gone out of use among us, and those that are now manufactured are principally used as the linings for muffs and cloaks, and therefore sarsnet has, in fact, gone out, and the article called gros de Naples has come in.   Formerly we manufactured our sarsnets with silk of a much lighter fabric ; the fashion is now, that a lady's sleeve is not fashionable unless it forms a ponderous balloon about her shoulder, and that cannot be produced without using a stronger fabric — a thing that when it gets the puff will retain it, whereas sarsnets, if they get the puff, would exhibit, I will not say the shape of a lady's arm, but would exhibit her, perhaps under a very ponderous dress, as having a very slight arm.

10142. It has been stated to the Committee, that the silk trade is suffering under competition between Spitalfields and Manchester ; do you think that the introduction of foreign silk goods, by rendering labour abundant, has produced this unnatural competition ?—It must be evident, that if there is a great competition carried on amongst ourselves, and that a foreigner gets in amongst us, that he must add to that competition ; if two coaches are running between the Bank and Paddington, and they are carrying on a competition, and then a third and a fourth coach comes in, it necessarily increases their embarrassment.

10143. Does it not, then, appear to you as a proof of great inconsistency, not to say of cruelty, to attribute the distress of the throwster and of the manufacturer to home competition, rather than to the lowering of import duties, whereby a larger quantity of thrown and manufactured silks may be brought into the English market to increase the home competition ?—I really think that the public are best served when a successful and an honourable competition is encouraged amongst ourselves ; by the word honourable, as applied here, I would mean a competition with my Manchester neighbour, determined to outrival him if I can, expecting that he is making a corresponding exertion to outrival me, and the public standing by ready to receive the benefit ; by the term successful competition I mean that operation that will afford a fair profit to the manufacturer for his works when produced, and that I would designate as a competition fully efficient for all the public service ; and to add to that competition, or to throw us into a situation whereby we have more difficulties to struggle and encounter, is, in my opinion, neither very fair nor just.

10144. It appears by the evidence of Dr. Bowring, that he admitted that there was a difference in the cost of French and English silk goods of from 30 to 40 per cent., and yet he recommended an *ad valorem* duty of 20 per cent. on the admission of silk goods of foreign manufacture ; what is your opinion of this recommendation, coupled with this admission ?—I fear that the Doctor's recommendation there is something like the recommendation which a great many quacks occasionally give, that if followed produce not only disease, but in very many instances death ; and I am quite satisfied, that if the fact be as recorded by Dr. Bowring, that there is a difference between the productions of the two countries, and that difference amounting to from 30 to 40 per cent., and that the duties by any stratagem or device be reduced to 20 per cent., I then turn to those men, poor and miserable

as

as they are, I say they are rich, when compared to the situation which they will be compelled to descend to.

*Barrett Wadden,*
Esq.

2 July,
1832.

10145. You have alluded to a promise given to the deputation of the silk trade respecting the import duty, and that you told the President of the Board of Trade you would then consider any proposal to lower the import duties not only as increasing the miseries of the silk trade, but as in violation of an express promise?—Having written down the words of that promise, any lowering of duties, or any deviation below the present amount of duty, I would regard, most assuredly, as a violation of the promise that has been made to us.

10146. Can you afford the Committee any evidence why an increased quantity of silk, speaking of its weight, is not always an increased quantity of employment afforded to the operative?—I exhibit two canes, as our weavers call them; I call them warps; each warp is the same length, 100 yards. This warp contains 6,600 threads of silk, and it weighs 3 lbs. 2 oz. 8 drs.; the price for weaving it is seven-pence. This warp is 100 yards long; it contains 4,400 threads; it weighs 4 lbs. 8 oz. 8 drs.; the price for weaving it is seven-pence; so that while the man is weaving this, his employment is not increased, nor the value of his labour increased one farthing, although he is working up nearly as much more silk.

10147. Has his employment within the last three or four years been universally of the heavier silks?—The great bulk of the employment of the people in Spitalfields and at Manchester is on those coarse silks which are no index of increased employment, but are an index of increased work to the labourer, giving him a material that is very inferior to this.

10148. Is the proportion of those heavy warps on the whole much greater than heretofore?—Decidedly much greater.

10149. Is it the finer or the coarser that is manufactured at Lyons?—The finer.

10150. What is the general term of credit in Spitalfields?—It can scarcely be said there is credit in Spitalfields; we are in the habit of selling our goods at one month's running account and two month's credit, but I would say that 7–8ths of the goods manufactured in Spitalfields are sold for money payable in the following month. I will state a fact, that when I sell goods, and I would most anxiously give credit to the parties buying them, that in very many instances the parties send requesting me to call on them to receive the money, allowing them simple interest at the rate of five per cent. per annum for the number of days my account has to run: there is abundant capital in the trade among our warehousemen.

10151. What is the credit that you understand is taken by the large warehousemen?—They have the name of taking two months' credit; but I believe that in most cases they pay their accounts the following month, deducting two months' interest.

---

*Mercurii, 4° die Julii,* 1832.

### LORD DUDLEY COUTTS STUART, IN THE CHAIR.

Mr. *Francois Felix Bouillon,* called in; and Examined.

10152. OF what country are you a native?—France.

Mr.
F. F. Bouillon.

4 July,
1832.

10153. In what house of business are you engaged at present in London?—No. 12, Princes-street, Hanover-square; the firm of the house is Maradan, Carson & Company, in which I am a partner.

10154. Does that house deal largely in silk goods of foreign manufacture?—Not very largely; the amount of our sales is generally between forty and fifty thousand pounds a year.

10155. Does your house deal both in fancy silk goods and also in plain silk goods of foreign manufacture?—At present, during the last two or three years, we deal more in the fancy goods than in the plain.

10156. Do you not also sell a large quantity of foreign ribbons?—Yes.

10157. In point of fact, is not the whole or a very large proportion of the silk sold by your house, foreign silk?—It is.

10158. Can you inform the Committee about what proportion the fancy goods you have sold this year bear to the plain goods sold by you within the same period?—We have sold very little plain goods this year; we have sold far more of fancy goods, and of plain goods a very small quantity indeed this year.

678.

10159. Fancy

Mr.
F. F. Bouillon.

4 July,
1832.

10159. Fancy goods are very much the fashion now?—Yes.

10160. Fashionable ladies will wear fancy goods?—Yes; those generally used are the plain goods, but not those sold by our house; we have sold a great many more fancy goods than of plain.

10161. You sell many more of fancy goods than of plain, because the genteel and opulent females who come to your house generally use them?—Yes.

10162. You sell no British fancy goods?—No, our house does not sell any.

10163. If you saw any British fancy goods you would feel no inclination to deal in them?—Yes I would, with pleasure; but as a house, for several years, we have been obliged to come into competition with the English manufacturer; we import a great many French goods; we were obliged to have our own patterns made, paying very dear, to have less competition; for that cause we are trying to do every thing we can to push the sale of our own goods, or those fancy goods, which are very high in price.

10164. Could you sell British goods if they were equally good, in your house, as well as French?—Certainly.

10165. Is not the fashion uniformly set by the designs that come from France? —Yes; but a good many designs have been copied in England; they come out almost as soon as the French.

10166. Would not your customers prefer the French goods to the British?—For several years the ladies have not thought so much of asking me whether the goods are Foreign or English, they choose the goods, and do not ask whether they are French or English.

10167. They come to your house as a house of fashion, and expect to find goods of French fashion and French fancy; they take that as a matter of course? —Certainly.

10168. If you import fancy silks to the amount of 100 l., how much plain silk do you import in those?—Not an eighth part; we cannot sell foreign plain goods in this country in competition with the English; some English goods come a good deal cheaper than the French plain goods; it is only the design and the beautiful quality of these which enables us to make a profit.

10169. Do not you import a good many watered silks?—Yes.

10170. Do you consider them as plain goods?—Yes; it is done in this country as well as in France, now.

10171. The ribbons sold by you are French?—Yes; the gauze ribbons I am bound to say are a great deal superior to the English.

10172. Would you have any objection to state about what is the annual value of foreign silk goods which you sell; you state the whole to be about 40,000 l. or 50,000 l., a part of those goods are English?—Yes, and there is the profit included; we have about eighty people at work at our house, and the labour is to be paid for.

10173. Out of that sum how much is expended on French goods?—Fourteen or fifteen thousand pounds a year; we are obliged always to have a large stock; our goods from France, silks and ribbons, amount to about fourteen or fifteen thousand pounds a year.

10174. Do your house import the goods you sell, or do you purchase them in this market after they have been imported by others?—We import almost every thing ourselves.

10175. Are there not other houses having a similar business to yours in London? —Yes, English houses.

10176. Do you believe that they have been lately carrying on their business very much in the same classes of goods?—Yes; but every year for the last two or three years, most houses have reduced their purchases in France a great deal.

10177. How do you know that?—I hear that in the market.

10178. It is a matter of opinion?—I speak from what I hear from others in the French market.

10179. Do you speak of the decline in purchases of plain goods?—Yes.

10180. You find when you purchase plain goods from France the cost of duty is 35 per cent. do you not?—Yes; from 25 to 30 per cent. expenses included.

10181. If you could get them in at 15 per cent. you would find it worth your while?—Yes, that is the thing to be prevented.

10182. Is the stock you have on hand consigned to you for sale, or do you import it on your own account?—On our own account.

10183. Should you find any great inconvenience in having your goods stamped
by

Mr.
F. F. Bouillon.

4 July,
1832.

by the Customs in London when they were imported?—I think that will perhaps prevent some part of the smuggling, but I think it will be very difficult for the officer who comes to visit the goods to ascertain whether the stamps have been put on after the pieces are cut; if I have cut up the half of my piece, he could not ascertain whether what remained came from such a piece; and I think it would give trouble to the officers and fail in accomplishing the object.

10184. Do you think it would be a material injury to the goods if they were stamped or printed in about four or five or six places in the side?—It will certainly alter the width of the piece, and occasion a certain loss on the piece.

10185. Supposing it to be about every twelve yards, do you think that would be a serious injury?—I think it would.

10186. Do you think the amount of duty now imposed on foreign silk is sufficient to protect the English manufacture?—On some it is sufficient, on some other it is not, in my opinion.

10187. Have the goodness to mention those articles in which you think it is not sufficient?—I think the duty on gauze ribbons and on gauzes in general is not high enough; the reason is, that I think the Coventry manufacturers are very far behind our own, as the gauze ribbons cannot be conveniently pressed; it would be difficult to smuggle them; if they are pressed, they are entirely spoiled; and I think if the duty were raised upon the gauze ribbons, that would protect the manufacturer here; it would perhaps prevent the job goods coming over, which I will explain; the ribbons of France are made in very great quantity; each manufacturer brings out his patterns, and executes a large quantity of ribbons, but in a month after those goods have been brought into the market in Paris, they do not sell; then the rest must be sold, for when they become stale things, they are of no use in France; they renew so often the pattern of their things, that when the things have been seen they must be sold; the consequence is, that they are sent into this country, and sold at a very low rate indeed.

10188. Do you speak of fancy silks and gauze ribbons, when you speak of things that must be sold?—Yes; in ribbons particularly.

10189. Do you think they call a pattern old, after it has been seen in Paris six weeks?—Yes, six weeks or two months certainly.

10190. What do you think of the duty on figured satin ribbons?—It is very heavy; it is heavy enough for the satin ribbons and the sarsnet ribbons; they make them in this country a good deal better than the gauze ribbons.

10191. You speak of the extent of manufacture of ribbons in France, have you any idea what the value of manufactured ribbons in France is?—No, I cannot say; but I know one house, Dugas, frères, before the competition came against them; that house took stock five years back, and they made 26,000l. profit in that year. Warehousemen were obliged almost to beg goods from them, and they were obliged to give orders six or seven months before-hand.

10192. There are a good many large houses in St. Etienne and St. Chamond, manufacturers, are there not?—Yes; that is the reason the quantity of looms is larger in those places.

10193. Have you an idea what was the value of the business transacted by Messrs. Dugas, frères, in the course of any one year?—I am told that Messrs. Dugas, frères, had at least 20 per cent. profit altogether, but now it is quite different. Warehousemen are no longer compelled to entreat them to supply them; but, on the contrary, they must be very careful themselves to execute the orders, for now there is a great deal of competition against them.

10194. You were asked what you thought of the duty on satin ribbons; you say it is very heavy; what is your opinion on the duty of figured satin ribbons?—The plain satin ribbons are not much used in England; the quantity is very small; but it must be the brocade ribbon; that is the only one you have from France in a large way; they charge very high in France for it.

10195. Is the duty heavy upon it?—It is 30 per cent. on the cheap ones.

10196. Have you any idea of the extent of smuggling?—No but I am sorry to say I believe it is very largely carried on.

10197. Do you believe that there are as many goods smuggled as are entered in the regular way?—I cannot say; but it is a thing that spoils the market, certainly.

10198. Do you find your goods, when you have imported them, occasionally interfered with by others who have been smuggling them?—Yes.

10199. You think it is carried on to a great extent?—I think so.

10200. Do

10200. Do you know a house at the West end of the Town who smuggle a hundred and fifty or two hundred thousand pounds worth a year?—I cannot say, indeed.

10201. Have you an opinion upon that fact?—I cannot say; I think that certainly the smuggling is going on very largely; but when once the smugglers get the goods over, in the present state of the law, the affair is quite settled; I mean the goods cannot be detected.

10202. Suppose that French goods were prohibited again, do not you think there would be very great danger of not keeping them out?—There would be great danger for some time to come, having had great quantities of goods over for several years, and having paid the duty on them, every house would have accommodation for receiving others.

10203. The novelties would be detected at once, would they not?—If there was a difficulty in getting French goods over, the wish to purchase would become dilatory, I am afraid.

10204. In what year did you come over?—In 1821.

10205. Were you acquainted with Mr. Pelican?—Merely to meet him in company.

10206. Did you never sell goods through his agency?—No.

10207. Do you think that if total prohibition was enacted, that would not go a great way to prevent smuggling?—I think it would be a long while before they could be prepared to prevent smuggling; if there was a fine for it, and that fine only money, I do not think that it would prevent smuggling.

10208. You would recommend, perhaps, that a man should be sent to the tread mill for it?—Something of that kind might prevent it; but the loss of 200 l., or any sum of that kind, would never do.

10209. Smuggling is now carried on by some very large houses, is it not?—I think so.

10210. Formerly, before the prohibition, was not the smuggling principally carried on in small quantities, and by private individuals?—No; I think it was in a great quantity and not a small one; there were a great many goods in London, but the people were so afraid to have them in their possession, that the ladies paid a good deal more for them.

10211. No person would dare to keep a large stock of goods at that time, would he?—Yes; they would keep them concealed.

10212. They were not offered to the public in all the shops as they are now?—No; but the ladies were not so difficult as they are now; if a pattern-book was taken to them, that would be sufficient.

10213. You do not think there was any thing like the quantity of French goods sold then which there is now, do you?—I think there was.

10214. Do you mean to say, that looking at the ladies in the Metropolis, you saw as many French goods in wear as there are now?—I am certain that every where less French goods come from France now. The house of Carez Vacossin & Company, who used to come twice a year, do not feel it worth their while to come over any more.

10215. Do you not know that they are connected with the house of Robert & Thomas Clay, and therefore having an agency house in London, there is no necessity for their coming to sell their goods in London now?—I do not think the arrangement with Mr. Robert Clay is what is supposed; they are not prevented selling goods for their own account.

10216. Do you not know that Carez Vacossin & Company have lately visited Paris to meet Mr. Clay there?—Yes; that is on other business; the Merino business.

10217. Do you not think a prohibition, if enforced, would be beneficial to the silk trade?—If it could be; but to enforce the prohibition, you must find a way to prevent smuggling, and I do not think that could be done.

10218. You say your house deals largely in French fancy silks; if they could be prohibited, there would be an end of the trade of your establishment?—I would not say so; for if there was no way to get French goods by any means, I would certainly try and go to Lyons, have the patterns very early, and give them to English manufacturers, and beg them to make such a thing and such a thing for me under my direction, and I am certain they could do it.

10219. That would be very beneficial to the English manufacturer, would it not?—Certainly.

10220. You

Mr.
F. F. Bouillon.
————
4 July,
1832.

10220. You have said that plain broad goods were made in this country better and cheaper than in France ?—I did not say better, but cheaper; this [*producing a sample*] came to me at 3 s. a yard, duty paid; in Manchester, they make it at 2 s. 5 d. and 2 s. 6 d. a yard, the same quality as I am told; I am told I could not get (now that the pattern is known) from any body more than 2 s. 2 d. a yard, if I go offer it to the English merchant.

10221. The price you speak of, 3 s. 5 d. is the price of the new fashioned article ? —Yes.

10222. It is copied in Manchester in a cheaper article ?—Yes.

10223. The article is therefore decidedly interfered with by the copy made here ?—Yes.

10224. That produced in this country cheaper, is inferior to that article, is it not? —Yes.

10225. Have you seen as good as this made for 2 s. 6 d. a yard ?—I have not; but I have been told that it is done.

10226. If you take it at 3 s. 1½ d. per yard, you take off 11 per cent. which is 4 d., reducing it to 2 s. 9½ d. the ell, reducing that ell into yards, by taking off one-fifth, that reduces it to 2 s. 3 d.; then there is the rate of exchange, 6¼ in favour of this country, so that it could be bought in Lyons at 2 s. 1 d. per yard ?—Then there are the expenses and the duty; but I call these fancy goods; I speak upon the plain goods, which never give any loss; these goods will always give a loss, for they are fancy goods.

10227. You have stated the price of that article as at the beginning of the season, can you state the price of such articles at the close of the season ?—That is what I call fancy goods; they may be got as a job 25 per cent. cheaper after the first month is over. The price I have stated is the price I have paid to have it early in the season before any body else.

10228. Have you not reason to think, that while it is fashion the manufacturer who sent it to you would of course insist upon having a good profit ?—Certainly.

10229. Are any broad silk goods imported from this country into France ?— No; I think they are prohibited there; but at all events the duty is such as to prevent the importation.

10230. Are any smuggled into France?—The smuggling into France is very difficult; our coast is so well guarded.

10231. No smuggling of these articles takes place in consequence of the excellent regulations of the Custom House which exist in your country ?—I will not say none, but very few.

10232. It follows that it would be possible to establish in this country such efficient Custom House regulations as would prevent any smuggling from France? —I think a great many alterations may be made in this country.

10233. What is accomplished in one country may be also in another ? —Yes, I suppose so.

10234. You have stated the amount of annual sales in your house to be forty or fifty thousand pounds, have the goodness to state the proportion of English?—As a French house, we sell very few English goods; we sell only sarsnets and plain gros de Naples, and several things which we can procure in this country cheaper than we can in France.

10235. Do your sales of English goods amount to 2,000 l. a year ?—Yes, thereabouts, perhaps.

### Mr. *John Dubois*, called in; and Examined.

Mr.
John Dubois.
————

10236. ARE you a broad silk manufacturer ?—I am.

10237. Are your goods made in Spitalfields?—They are.

10238. How many years have you been in the trade ?—About thirty.

10239. Has not your family been many years engaged in the silk manufacture of Spitalfields ?—Above a century.

10240. What description of goods have you been accustomed to make, fancy or plain ?—Both fancy and plain.

10241. Have you made chiefly the rich or the lower description of goods ?—Of middling and rich quality.

10242. How many looms did you formerly employ?—From 120 to 150.

10243. To what class of persons were your goods chiefly sold ?—The higher classes.

10244. Have

10244. Have you supplied the mercers at the West end of the Town?—Principally the mercers.

10245. What proportion of your trade was fancy and what plain?—About one-fourth fancy and three-fourths plain,

10246. Were your fancy goods generally made to order?—They were.

10247. Were you able then to employ your hands better through dull seasons of the year, and with greater regularity, than it is possible for the manufacturer to do who does not work to order?—Yes; we generally received our orders in the month of January for the spring trade, and in the month of July for the winter trade.

10248. Was the branch of trade in which you were employed, that of rich fancy goods, in a state of prosperity up to the time of the opening of the Ports for French goods in the year 1826?—It was.

10249. Had the opening of the Ports to foreign silk goods in 1826 any effect upon your trade?—It prevented my getting my orders in the usual way.

10250. Was the effect immediate or has it been gradual?—It has been gradual.

10251. You have stated that formerly you were enabled to employ your hands with great regularity from the orders you received to prepare goods for the seasons, are you still in the habit of receiving such orders, or have they been discontinued?—They have been discontinued.

10252. Why do they not now give you orders as formerly?—Because they get the goods from the foreign market; some of the most fashionable houses go over to Paris regularly every two months; others buy their goods of the travellers that come over here, and others buy them again of houses that are established here; and I have been informed by some of them that are very respectable men, that they can buy them at least 10 per cent. cheaper than they can import them.

10253. You have, in fact, ceased to supply those parties with goods?—I have.

10254. Speaking still of rich plain and fancy goods, you consider that it is from that market your former customers supply themselves?—They get supplied from the foreign markets.

10255. Do they supply themselves from Manchester with any of those English goods?—I believe not.

10256. What effect have all those circumstances had upon your trade?—To do it away entirely.

10257. What is at present the general condition of the fancy trade at Spitalfields?—It is very flat, I believe, except in the waistcoat line.

10258. Can you give the Committee an idea of the proportion of looms which Spitalfields formerly employed in the fancy branch?—I believe from one-fourth to one-fifth, 40 or 50 years ago.

10259. Were there many fancy silks made in Spitalfields of a very splendid description and requiring immense skill both in design and execution?—There were; here are some patterns of silk which were made 60 or 70 years ago [*producing some patterns*]; these are Spitalfields manufacture.

10260. Dr. Bowring has stated in his evidence, that there is an opinion in France that the improvement in English figured silks since the opening of the Ports is prodigious, equal to fifty years, as you have shown the Committee specimens of English manufacture, and such as were made for many years prior to the opening of the Ports, and you had been engaged in the rich fancy trade; will you say whether the opinion of Dr. Bowring is correct or not?—I think it is not correct.

10261. You have stated that you have formerly been a fancy manufacturer as well as a manufacturer of plain goods, do you mean to say you have entirely given up the fancy trade?—Entirely.

10262. And that from want of orders from those customers who used formerly to give you those orders?—Yes.

10263. Do you think Spitalfields was formerly equal to France in the fancy branches of the silk manufacture?—I do.

10264. Do you know whether the productions of Spitalfields in those days were imitations of foreign patterns or from original designs?—They were, I believe, from original designs.

10265. Were there then regular designers in Spitalfields?—There were; each house kept a pattern drawer, and they paid him from 300 *l.* to 500 *l.* a year for the patterns that were drawn.

10266. Are designers employed now in a similar manner?—They are not.

10267. To what do you attribute that change?—There is not sufficient employment for them; I do not think that any manufacturers in London could afford to

pay

Mr.
John Dubois.

4 July,
1832.

pay the expense of 500 l. a year for a pattern drawer or designer, now several houses pay according to the figure which they have done, and according to the work it is for.

10268. Have you any thing to add?—I consider that as the manufacturers of this country can afford an abundant supply, every importation we have from the foreigner is throwing so much British capital and British labour out of employment, and will in the end, I have very little doubt, tend to ruin our manufactures altogether.

10269. Are you of opinion that if we were to return to a prohibitory system there would be any difficulty in detecting French goods?—I think not.

10270. Though there might be some inconsiderable quantity of smuggling before the opening of the Ports to the admission of French silks, was it not so inconsiderable as to be altogether unworthy of notice?—Yes; and I think the stamping of them would be of service, because, though a piece might be cut at both ends, I think it might be identified, though the stamp at the end might be cut off.

10271. You refer to their continuing to pay the duty on admission, as now?—Yes, just so.

10272. You have shown some very splendid patterns; do you think it is possible for the fancy silk trade to continue in this country without a prohibition of importation from France?—I do not think it is; as Mr. Wadden said the other day with respect to Ireland, so we are with respect to France; it is impossible for an English manufacturer to know what is going on in France, or what will come over; there are some houses here who have some rich silks going, and Mr. Cooper told me they were obliged to stop their figures, because the French watered silks were introduced by the French milliners and French dress makers; and Madame Carson and Madame d'Arvie are doing nearly all the trade in millinery and dress making at the West end of the Town, while our own people are walking about unemployed.

10273. You spoke of Mr. Cooper; he is a highly respectable mercer, living in Waterloo-place?—Yes, he is.

10274. He is engaged in the trade which supplies the higher classes with goods?—Yes.

10275. He was obliged to stop his orders for figured silks because watered silks were introduced from France?—Yes.

10276. Must it not also effectually prevent persons from giving orders, under the expectation of the foreign fashions interfering?—Yes.

10277. It has the effect of preventing the sale, and depreciating the price of the goods?—It has.

### Mr. *Joseph Grout*, called in; and Examined.

Mr.
Joseph Grout.

10278. WHERE do you reside?—At Stamford Hill, in the county of Middlesex.

10279. Are you engaged in the manufacture of silk goods?—I am.

10280. How long have you been engaged in this manufacture?—Twenty-six years.

10281. What articles do you make?—Every sort of crape, namely, China, Italian and French.

10282. What description of silk do you use in your manufacture?—We purchase three kinds of raw silk in about equal proportions, one-third Bengal, one-third China, and one-third Italian.

10283. Do you use either foreign or English thrown tram or organzine in your manufacture?—We never use either foreign or English thrown tram or organzine.

10284. In what places have you carried on your manufacture within the last 10 or 12 years?—We have had establishments in the following places within that period, viz. one at Norwich, one at North Walsham, one at Great Yarmouth in Norfolk, one at Bungay, one at Mildenhall in Suffolk, one at Saffron Walden, one at Bocking and Braintree, one at Sible Hedingham in Essex, one at Glasgow and Paisley in Scotland, and one at Ponder's End in Middlesex; also a selling warehouse in London. We also had, within this period, a filature or reeling establishment in Bengal.

10285. What number of persons do you usually employ in your various establishments, and what rate of wages do you pay them?—We have made out an average statement for the last ten years, commencing with the year 1822 and closing with the year 1831, to the last day of December in each year. I wish it to be understood decidedly by the Committee, that in this statement of the number of persons, they are all directly employed by us; the name of every person appears upon our books,

678.    except

Mr.
*Joseph Grout.*

4 July,
1832.

except carpenters, bricklayers, millwrights, stone masons, and those we employed in Bengal, who are not included; this is the average number of persons employed, and the average rate of wages paid for each person.

*[The Witness delivered in the same, which was read as follows :]*

| YEARS | Average Number of Persons employed. | Average Rate of Wages paid each Person per Week. | |
|-------|-------|:---:|:---:|
| | | *s.* | *d.* |
| 1822 | 2,747 | 7 | 6 |
| 1823 | 2,974 | 8 | – |
| 1824 | 3,594 | 8 | 1 ½ |
| 1825 | 3,908 | 8 | 8 ½ |
| 1826 | 3,516 | 6 | – |
| 1827 | 3,164 | 5 | 7 |
| 1828 | 2,818 | 4 | – |
| 1829 | 1,540 | 3 | 11 ½ |
| 1830 | 1,624 | 4 | – |
| 1831 | 1,871 | 3 | 8 ½ |

Persons employed in the above establishments are from ten to sixty years of age, and their weekly average rate of wages is from 1 *s.* 6 *d.* to 20 *s.*

10286. You state that the persons you employ are of the ages of from 10 to 60 years; do you not employ, in some of your factories, a considerable number of young women of from 16 to 24 years of age?—Yes.

10287. What was their general character and conduct before the change in the law, and before the great reduction in wages which has taken place?—Very different from what they are; they were very respectable in their apparel: observations have been made in the public papers on the people we employed, when at church, that they were dressed very respectably; since that, I am sorry to say, that many of them have sunk into a degraded and dissipated state.

10288. The question refers to the morals and conduct of those young people; was not it a matter of observation that their conduct was consistent with their appearance?—Most certainly.

10289. That it was quite respectable, and such as you would desire to see in young people?—Yes.

10290. Has there been any change in regard to their morals and character since this great reduction of wages?—Very great; it is not only the reduction of wages, but we have discharged a great number; some of the men have emigrated, others have gone to the poor house, and many of the females have gone, I fear, to a state of prostitution; and every time I go into my manufacturing districts, it is attended with a considerable expense, from my meeting those people whom I have been in the habit of employing, and their asking some little relief.

10291. Their condition is most abject, and much to be pitied?—It is.

10292. You probably are of opinion, that though some part of the community may purchase commodities to deck themselves somewhat cheaper, when you take into consideration the demoralizing effects and consequences to the poorer classes of the community, that is a matter not altogether to be lost sight of in a question of this kind?—Certainly not.

10293. Is the proportion of persons you now employ, as to men, women, and children, similar to what it was formerly?—Yes, they bear the same proportions.

10294. Where are your mills situate for winding and throwing your silk?—We have mills at Norwich, Great Yarmouth, Bungay and Mildenhall.

10295. Do you work your mills by steam or water power?—We work them by both; we have 15 horses power by water, and 116 horses power by steam, making a total of 131 horses power.

10296. What number of spindles have you at work in your establishments, and have you any objection to state the speed at which you drive them?—Not the least; we had four distinct throwing mills in 1822, and since; I will give in an account of the number of spindles, and the hours they worked.

*[The Account was delivered in, and read :]*

NUMBER

NUMBER of Spindles going in all our Mills at *Norwich* and *Yarmouth*, in the following Years.

| YEARS | Number of Spindles. | |
|---|---|---|
| 1822 - - | 59,754 | Working 22½ hours per diem. |
| 1823 - - | 59,754 | Working 22½ hours per diem. |
| 1824 - - | 63,756 | Working 22½ hours per diem. |
| 1825 - - | 86,664 | Working 22½ hours per diem. |
| *Mem.*—Night Work discontinued from this time. | | |
| 1826 - - | 77,384 | Working 12½ hours per diem. |
| 1827 - - | 78,522 | Working 12½ hours per diem. |
| 1828 - - | 83,352 | Working 12½ hours per diem. |
| 1829 - | 60,024 | Working 12½ hours per diem. |
| 1830 - - | 59,616 | Working 12½ hours per diem. |
| 1831 - - | 59,616 | Working 12½ hours per diem. |

*Mem.*— 31,326 - - Spindles going at fast speed of 2,476 revolutions per minute ;

and 28,290 - - Spindles going at slow speed of 1,584 revolutions per minute.

TOTAL - 59,616 - - Going.

27,048 - - Standing.

GROSS NUMBER - 86,664 or 7,222 Dozens.

### DETAILED STATEMENT.

Norwich Water Mill contains - - 15,456 Spindles.
Norwich Steam Mill contains - - 20,976 ditto.
Yarmouth South Steam Mill contains - 28,704 ditto.
Yarmouth North Steam Mill contains - 21,528 ditto.

86,664 or 7,222 Dozens.

10297. Have you had any spindles standing still within the last few years?—Yes, we had in the year 1826, none previous, 9,280; in 1827, we had 8,142; in 1828, 3,312; in 1829, 26,640; in 1830, 27,048; and in 1831, 27,048.

10298. Previously to the year 1826 all your spindles were at work?—Every one, and every one working night and day with a double set of hands.

10299. Has not your machinery been erected within the last few years, and is it not upon the most improved principles?—We think it is.

10300. Have you any objection to state the amount of the capital your concern has invested for ground to build upon, buildings, steam engines, and machinery, in your various establishments?—No, not the least: before I proceed with this, I ought to explain, we keep our cash perhaps rather differently from most persons; in our concern, in our cash ledger, we have only two accounts, one of our permanent expenses, such as wages, for silk purchased, for repairs; even if we replace old machinery with new, now that goes into what we call the permanent expense account. We have another account, we call the non-permanent expense account; whenever we purchase ground and build a mill, and fill it with machinery, we ascertain the cost price of that, and carry it to that account, therefore that shows exactly what is the amount of our non-permanent account. The total outlay of capital invested in ground for building on, buildings, steam engines, and machinery, in the various establishments in our concern, and charged to non-permanent account, is 143,546 *l.*; we also had an establishment in Bengal (since given up), where the outlay for a silk filature was 3,300 *l.*; we also rent a mill at Norwich, and the late barracks at Yarmouth, for which we pay between 600 *l.* and 700 *l.* a year.

10301. Does your concern employ any power looms?—Yes, we have put up at various times 462.

10302. Have you any objection to state the cost of those power looms?—No, the cost of the power looms, with reeds, harness, and driving gear prepared fit for

678. working,

Mr.
*Joseph Grout.*

4 July,
1832.

working, with room to contain it, exclusive of the steam engines to drive it, is 34 *l.* 10 *s.*; I multiply 462 by 34 *l.* 10 *s.* and that brings the amount to 15,939 *l.*

10303. Have you any hand looms at work?—Yes, we have 420.

10304. Have you any hand looms standing still?—Yes; I have a letter here from one of my partners, stating the number; I wrote him a few weeks ago, requesting he would send me the particulars of all that were standing still. This letter is signed William Martin, and dated Norwich, 27th June 1832: " Dear Sir, Agreeably with your wishes, I have looked over our books, and think the following statement is as nearly correct as possible: hand looms out of use in the years 1829 1830 and 1831; 243 formerly used at North Walsham, 140 ditto at Sible Hedingham, 700 at Saffron Walden, 402 at Bocking and Braintree; making 1,485; and 102 power looms standing still at Yarmouth; making the total number of 1,587 looms unemployed."

10305. You state that there are 1,587 out of employ; does not this arise from other crape looms having been put up in other parts of the kingdom, which have had the effect of displacing some of yours?—No, I have taken some pains (with the assistance of several gentlemen in the crape trade) to make myself acquainted with this fact; and I find, that so far from any increase in the number of crape looms at work in this country, that there is a decrease of 265, exclusive of our own, since the year 1825; for in that year there were 1,450 looms at work, exclusive of ours, and in 1831 only 1,185, working in the following places; *viz.* Taunton, Shepton Mallet and Dassell, Devises, Reading, Haslemere and Hammerpond, Macclesfield, Kettering, Bullock Smithy and Leigh; by which the Committee will see at once that our unemployed looms have not been displaced by any others having been put up in this country; and I beg to state, most distinctly and decidedly, that the lessened demand for our manufactures is occasioned solely by the introduction of the product of foreign looms.

10306. Do you get your weaving done at lower prices by power than by hand looms?—We do not pay quite so much for the piece woven by power as by hand.

10307. Then you appear to have an advantage by employing power looms?—I do not think there is any advantage, at the present price of hand weaving, in using the power loom, for inasmuch as we save in the price of weaving done by power, we lose by interest of capital on the first cost of the power looms, the additional waste of silk, and heavy expense of wear and tear, and wages of mechanics employed to keep them in order.

10308. Suppose you were about to increase your number of looms, would you put up power in preference to hand looms?—Certainly not, at the present price of hand weaving.

10309. Do you know whether there are any power looms used on the Continent for weaving the article you manufacture?—Yes; I received a letter in April 1829 from a gentleman, a silk throwster in the neighbourhood of Lyons, upon that subject; some extracts from which I will read by permission of the Committee:—" For nearly twelve months we have supplied an establishment with crape silk (four leagues from us) provided with power looms, which are worked by means of a waterfall; it is the only one of the kind in France; there are an hundred looms in activity which perform perfectly well, and they are about to increase the number to 300." " If you are inclined to entertain my proposals, and your occupations will allow you to visit the establishment I have completed, and which I now superintend and direct, I dare to hope you will discover some new ideas; the neighbouring establishment by water power may likewise be interesting to you."

10310. How does it happen that your trade has so fallen off, that in the year 1831 you did not employ half so many persons as in the year 1825?—I have shown, that in 1826 we began to feel the depression, as in July in that year, our ports were opened for the reception of foreign manufactures, and we, at once, lost a great part of our white and coloured trade. Every succeeding year it became worse, and last year we had not a single loom going, with either white or coloured crape; whereas previous to the year 1826, we had in the spring as many looms employed on whites and colours as on blacks; so that full one half of our trade is lost.

10311. How has your trade in black goods been effected by the admission of foreign manufactures?—I do not think there is any great quantity of black crapes brought into this country, in consequence of the ruinous prices at which English crapes are selling.

10312. Is it your opinion, that you can compete with the foreigner, as far as regards your black trade?—I think as long as we can purchase Bengal raw silk a

little

Mr.
Joseph Grout.

4 July,
1832.

little below the cost price of raising it, and our operatives are willing to work at starvation prices, and we, the manufacturers (when the goods are finished) sell them at a loss, we shall be able to compete with the foreigner, but no longer, even in black crapes.

10313. Will any manufacturer continue to carry on a losing trade?—Not generally, I should think; but as we have above 100,000*l.* invested in buildings and machinery, which capital will be lost, unless we continue to work, the Committee will see that we have no alternative, we must go on.

10314. How do you account for the silk manufactures of this country being in so depressed a state, while there continues to be an increased importation of raw silk?—I think I can explain to the Committee, that in the weaving of our article of crape the weaver works up a greater number of ounces of silk for but little more than half the wages he earned for a lesser number of ounces previous to the admission of foreign manufactured goods; for instance, in the year 1822, we paid 12*s.* for weaving a piece weighing 20 oz.; whereas we now pay but 7*s.* for a piece of the same length and breadth, weighing 24 oz.

10315. How would it affect your trade if the duty were to be taken off from foreign thrown silks imported into this country?—It would not affect us directly, as we never, by any chance, use foreign thrown silks; although such a measure would be indirectly very prejudicial in this way: I have stated to the Committee, that we use in the proportion of one-third Italian silk in our manufacture, and we purchase the best quality we can get. Supposing the duty to be taken off the thrown, it would most likely induce the Italians to select their best silks to throw for this country, and we must content ourselves with paying a high price for the inferior raw silk, even supposing we obtain it, which would be very injurious to our trade.

10316. Is it your opinion, that if this country were to return to the prohibitory system, smuggling would be encouraged by such a measure?—I wish to call the attention of this honourable Committee most distinctly to that point; I think I may positively assert that for the last ten years, during the prohibitory laws, there was not in amount 20*l.* worth of crape smuggled into this country.

10317. And your crape trade was not injured at that time by the importation of smuggled goods?—We did not suffer from the smugglers certainly.

10318. Have you reason to think that the facilities for getting in goods were not so great as have been represented?—Certainly not.

10319. Do you speak of the Chinese crape?—No; the Italian and French.

10320. What has been the effect, since the admission of foreign-wrought silks, with respect to smuggling; is it your opinion that there is a less or greater quantity run in?—I think there has been an immense quantity run in during the last five or six years.

10321. What measures would you recommend, with a view to restore the silk trade of this country to its former state of activity?—I am of a decided opinion that nothing short of entire prohibition would have that desirable effect, and I think it is putting the industry of the operatives of this country to a severely cruel test, to oblige them to compete, not only with the foreign nations of Europe but with China also, where all the necessaries of life may be purchased at one-twelfth the price paid in England, besides the local advantages they possess in raising the silk on their own soil.

10322. You have stated, that you had a silk filature, or reeling establishment in Bengal; will you inform the Committee the cost price of raising raw silk in India, of the best quality?—That to which I am about to refer is the only document I saved from my fire, of all my Bengal papers. In the year 1818, we had it in contemplation to establish a silk filature or reeling establishment in India, with a view to the raising of raw silk of the best quality, to supply our home manufactures; and in 1819, one of my partners went to France, to make himself perfectly acquainted with the best mode of reeling in that country; he stopped a considerable time at Avignon and Vaucluse, and had access to all the reeling establishments in the neighbourhood; in the same year he left England for India, taking with him drawings and plans of the French reeling-houses, and also black and white mulberry trees, which he intended to plant in Bengal; also about 80 tons of machinery, such as boilers, steam apparatus, and pans for the purpose of reeling. As soon as he arrived in Bengal he had an interview with our agents, Messrs. Alexander & Company, who recommended him premises suitable for our purpose, situate at Bhartiparra, on the banks of the Ganges, between Nattore and Moorshedabad,

678.                                                                                    about

about 140 miles up the country, from Calcutta, very near the Company's filatures at Santipore, Bauleah, Cossimbuzar and Jungypore, which are the principal silk districts of Bengal, where he commenced building a filature or reeling establishment, with cocoonery, on the French principle, and made the first shipment of thirty-nine bales of raw silk of the best quality, per Mellish and Susan, some on the French, and some on the Bengal principle of reeling, on 2d April 1822; and he afterwards made ten other shipments of raw silk of the best quality, the cost of raising which is shown by the following Statements; which calculations are made by taking the sicca rupee at the exchange of 2 s. 6 d.; although the Company, I believe, took it at 2 s. 2 d. or 2 s. 3 d. at that time. I will give statements of eleven shipments; *viz.*

No. 1.—Shipment of 39 bales of Raw Silk, part reeled on the French and part on the Bengal principle, per *Mellish* and *Susan*.

|  | s. | d. |  |
|---|---|---|---|
| Cost at Bhartiparra | 16 | ⚊ | per lb. |
| Government Duty and Commission on the River Hooghley to Calcutta, Charges, Commission, Freight, and Insurance to London, say 15 per Cent. | 2 | 5 | ⚊ |
| Total Cost | 18 | 5 | ⚊ |

No. 2.—Ten bales of Raw Silk, as before, per *Susan*.

|  | s. | d. |  |
|---|---|---|---|
| Cost at Bhartiparra | 14 | 2 | ⚊ |
| Charges, as before | 2 | 1½ | |
| Total Cost | 16 | 3½ | ⚊ |

No. 3.—Eight bales of Raw Silk, as before, per *Kent*.

|  | s. | d. |  |
|---|---|---|---|
| Cost at Bhartiparra | 14 | 6 | ⚊ |
| Charges, as before | 2 | 2 | ⚊ |
| Total Cost | 16 | 8 | ⚊ |

No. 4.—Four bales Raw Silk, as before, per *Lord Hungerford*.

|  | s. | d. |  |
|---|---|---|---|
| Cost at Bhartiparra | 14 | 10 | ⚊ |
| Charges, as before | 2 | 1 | ⚊ |
| Total Cost | 16 | 11 | ⚊ |

No. 5.—One bale Raw Silk, as before, per *Lord Hungerford*.

|  | s. | d. |  |
|---|---|---|---|
| Cost at Bhartiparra | 14 | ⚊ | ⚊ |
| Charges, as before | 2 | 1 | ⚊ |
| Total Cost | 16 | 1 | ⚊ |

No. 6.—Sixteen bales Raw Silk, as before, per *Prince of Orange*.

|  | s. | d. |  |
|---|---|---|---|
| Cost at Bhartiparra | 18 | 7 | ⚊ |
| Charges, as before | 2 | 8 | |
| Total Cost | 21 | 3 | |

No. 7.—Sixteen bales Raw Silk, as before, per *Resource*.

|  | s. | d. |  |
|---|---|---|---|
| Cost at Bhartiparra | 14 | 9 | ⚊ |
| Charges, as before | 2 | 2 | ⚊ |
| Total Cost | 16 | 11 | ⚊ |

No. 8.—Twenty-two bales Raw Silk, as before, per *Exmouth*.

|  | s. | d. |  |
|---|---|---|---|
| Cost at Bhartiparra | 15 | 2 | ⚊ |
| Charges, as before | 2 | 3 | ⚊ |
| Total Cost | 17 | 5 | ⚊ |

No. 9.—Seventeen bales Raw Silk, as before, per *Mellish*.

|  | s. | d. |  |
|---|---|---|---|
| Cost at Bhartiparra | 17 | ⚊ | ⚊ |
| Charges, as before | 2 | 6 | ⚊ |
| Total Cost | 19 | 6 | ⚊ |

No. 10.

Mr.
*Joseph Grout.*

4 July,
1832.

No. 10.—Nine bales Raw Silk, as before, per *Asia*.

|                           |     | s. | d. |         |
|---------------------------|-----|----|----|---------|
| Cost at Bhartiparra       | - - - - - - - - - | 15 | 5 | per lb. |
| Charges, as before        | - - - - - - - - - | 2 | 4 | — |
| Total Cost                | - - - - - - | 17 | 9 | — |

No. 11.—Thirty-four bales Raw Silk, as before, per *Victory*.

|                           |     | s. | d. |   |
|---------------------------|-----|----|----|---|
| Cost at Bhartiparra       | - - - - - - - - - | 16 | 6 | — |
| Charges, as before        | - - - - - - - - - | 2 | 6 | — |
| Total Cost                | - - - - - - | 19 | — | — |

These eleven shipments average 18 s. 4 d. per pound. In this calculation of the cost, as we intended these silks for our own consumption, we made no charge for interest from the time of their leaving Calcutta, nor on their arrival in London any allowance for the East India Company's charges of one per cent., rent, fees, &c.; nor broker's charges, or loss in the weight of silk, all of which may be reckoned at rather more than 6 per cent. on the cost price; nor are the expenses of the resident partner at Bhartiparra included in this calculation of cost.

10323. Is it your opinion, that if great care and attention were bestowed on the raising of raw silk in India, it could be produced of equal quality and as cheap as the French or Italian?—No, certainly not; I do not think it possible for all the skill, experience, ingenuity and industry that human agency could bestow, to raise silk on the soil and with the climate of Bengal to within from 18 to 23 per cent. in quality as silk produced in France and Italy, owing to the great advantages which the latter countries possess in their beautiful climate, and fitness of the soil for the production of the cocoon; our object in the establishment of a filature in India was not only with a view to improve the quality of raw silk raised in that country, but had also reference to cheapness, and I am sorry to say that, with all the practical knowledge my partner possessed of Bengal saw silk, which he had been working in our own concern for nine years previous to his going to India, and the further advantage of his having made himself acquainted with the French mode of reeling, added to his indefatigable exertions in India, with a view to forward these two objects, we failed entirely in both of them.

10324. You have said that you formerly had an establishment in India for the purpose of raising raw silk, did the East India Company throw any difficulties or obstructions in your way?—Not the least; so far from it, we had the benefit of the professional services of one of the Company's architects without any charge being made to us.

10325. Is it your opinion that the monopoly enjoyed by the East India Company is injurious to the silk trade, and that it would be benefited if the India trade were entirely thrown open?—I do not know that it is a monopoly; but if so, it must be a losing one to the Company; and I should be exceedingly sorry, as a large consumer of Bengal silk, to see the Company decline the raising of it, for I am sure that if it gets into the hands of individuals, we shall have very little raw silk imported into this country from India in future; human life is so uncertain in that climate, that out of three persons sent out by our establishment two died in less than three years, and in all probability my partner would have died also had he staid but a few weeks longer in India.

10326. In point of fact, you are able to purchase Bengal silk at the Company's sales for less than you can raise it for yourself in India?—Certainly.

10327. Therefore you conclude, that not being successful in your own speculations, having all the advantages of capital and experience, others would be as unsuccessful as yourself in raising it at a price which would answer your purpose?—I do not think it would answer the purpose of any person, whatever might be his capital, however talented and however plodding, for without the latter and a great deal of attention it would be impossible to carry on a silk filature in India, for human life is so uncertain, that if you send out an establishment of eight or ten individuals they may probably be all dead in a few years.

10328. Did your partner attempt to introduce the silk worm from Europe?—He had both mulberry trees and eggs; the origin of the worm came from the Eastern part of the globe; the worm improves in Italy and France; but take it back again into the Eastern part of this globe, such as Persia and India, and it degenerates; in Europe, the cocoon is globular, and the thread runs about 630 yards, tapered

678. from

from one end to the other; whereas the Bengalee cocoon is oblong, and the thread runs only 580 yards, of a very much finer and more delicate and less valuable texture.

10329. It is weak and wants fibre?—Yes.

10330. You are understood to state that you have obtained your silks more advantageously through the Company's sales than you could otherwise have done?—Most certainly; I have the average of what I have paid for the last five years, 17 s. 6 d., and my own cost me, exclusive of six per cent., 18 s. 4 d., and I have the pick of the Company's sales.

10331. You spoke of the knowledge of your parner, have the goodness to state how he obtained this knowledge of the proper mode of raising and reeling silk?—He served seven years apprenticeship to it in working at our mills and arranging the silk for the mills at Norwich; then he stopped two years longer, taking the management of the concern at Norwich, and from thence he went to France to make himself acquainted with the French mode of reeling.

10332. To what part of France?—Avignon and Vaucluse.

10333. Did he become well acquainted with the silk of the district of Vaucluse?—Perfectly.

10334. What is the character of that silk?—Excellent.

10335. Did he at any time inform you the price for which that silk was selling?—Yes; he wrote me from Avignon, stating the price that silk was worth at Avignon in July 1819; the price of the very best silks at that time was 13 s. per pound English.

10336. What difference is there, in your opinion, between that silk and that you have spoken of as purchased from the East India Company's sales at 16 s. 6 d.?—I take the highest quality of French silk, to make the comparison, and the highest quality of Bengal, and there is a difference in favour of France of from 18 to 23 per cent. in quality.

10337. The silk similar to that selling in Vaucluse at 13 s. per pound could be purchased, at what price here?—I do not know that there is a price for it; the exportation from France of that silk is prohibited; but silk of that size and quality would sell for 20 s. here in the raw state.

10338. It has appeared in evidence that there are 7,000 dozen of spindles at Manchester, do you mean to say that you have 222 dozen of spindles more than there are in all the town of Manchester?—The statement I have given shows that fact.

10339. Then Manchester has not drawn to itself your branch of the silk trade?—Most certainly not; I do not think there is a single crape loom going at Manchester.

10340. Is there as large a consumption of white and coloured crapes in this country as at the time you are speaking of?—The official returns state, crape white and coloured, in 1826, 5,496 lbs. 13 oz.; in the year 1827, 16,381 lbs.; in the year 1828, 24,951 lbs. 13 oz.; in the year 1829, 22,786 lbs. 11½ oz.; in the year 1830, 28,880 lbs. 4 oz.; in the year 1831, 19,669 lbs. 5 oz.: therefore it appears there was a very considerable consumption of crape, and unfortunately it fell on the French and other foreign productions.

10341. Do you know whether there has been a great reduction in the price at which the Frenchman offers his crape, as compared with three or four years ago?—I cannot say.

10342. Had the silk trade any interviews with Government previous to the appointment of this Committee, and were you present at such interviews?—The silk trade had several interviews with Lord Auckland, and I attended as one of the deputation.

10343. Were any promises made to the silk trade at any of these interviews respecting the import duties?—Yes; Lord Auckland distinctly told us that it was not the intention of His Majesty's Government to proceed upon the principle of reduction of the import duties, and we immediately communicated this to the silk trade on our return.

10344. Have there not been a large number of crape looms at Manchester abandoned within the last two or three years, the manufacturers finding it impossible to continue the manufacture to a profit?—I believe there have.

10345. Do you not consider that the Company's periodical sales of silk are a great object to the British manufacturer in giving him due notice of what he shall offer for sale?—Certainly; I consider them very beneficial to the silk trade of this country.

10346. Do

Mr.
*Joseph Grout.*

4 July,
1832.

10346. Do not they generally put up their silk at a low taxed price, leaving it to fair competition to give the market value for their silk?—I think the Company put up their silk below the cost price, in some instances considerably so.

10347. They put it up at a taxed price?—Yes, which is a very fair price.

10348. They do not use any reserve upon it, but if it goes at one penny per pound more than the taxed price it is sold?—Yes, nothing can be more fair than the Company's sales.

10349. You have been asked some questions as to the form in which the East India Company put up their silk, is there not a distinction in respect to that put up on account of private dealers; that they can withdraw, and do withdraw, their silk, whenever it does not reach such a price as meets their views, is not that the case? —I think the East India Company are nothing more than servants of the public; suppose I have a shipment of silk comes into the St. Katharine's Docks, I try to make a sale, and if I cannot effect a sale a few days before the Company's sale comes on, I desire this silk to be removed from St. Katharine's Dock to the Company's warehouses; they are bound to take it in and to print it in the catalogue with that of the Company; then the day before the declared sale comes on, they may say to the Company, I withdraw that, though it is printed in your catalogue, and send it back from the Company's warehouses to St. Katherine's Dock; when the Company put up the sale it is put up at a certain price, and it is sold if it sells for a penny above that price.

10350. When the laws affecting the silk trade, in 1826, passed, you were led by representations made by Government to expect considerable advantages, were you not?—We were led to expect that, but unfortunately we have never seen it.

10351. If you could have foreseen all the changes you have described which have affected the trade, would you have laid out the property you have in the erection of mills and machinery?—I do not think we have made any outlay since that time, except building some large sheds to stow away our unemployed looms; we stopped then; I saw the necessity of stopping; I was certain the silk trade could never be carried on otherwise than at a loss in this country under those laws.

10352. If you could have seen, before the passing of those laws, the changes which have been made, would you have laid out this money in machinery?—Certainly not.

10353. If you could have foreseen the consequences which have occurred, would that have deterred you from embarking so large a capital in the erection of machinery?—Most certainly it would.

10354. Would not the consequences have been, that that would have thrown a great many of your hands out of employ, and caused great distress?—Yes; and that I have been obliged to do since from necessity.

10355. It appears by calculation, from the statements you have put in, that you employed in the year 1823 not by any means of the largest number of persons in every year; but 3,000 persons, at the average of 8*s.* per week each, which will give a total of 60,000*l.* earned in the year by those persons; it appears in the year 1830, you employed somewhere about 1,600, the average earnings 4*s.* giving as a total of earnings 16,000*l.* for those persons; is that correct?—It is.

10356. Can you inform the Committee in what way the deficiency of earnings has been made up to those people, or whether those who have been wholly unemployed since, have been seeking in vain for other employment?—Those people who continued the employment at a reduced rate of wages are of course suffering great privations; a great number of them have got more employment; some have obtained it, others could not do it; a great number of them were females; and, as I said before, some of them, perhaps, have gone to the workhouse, and others have gone into prostitution from necessity, and some were formerly as worthy people as ever lived.

10357. They did not find any employment in making any goods which France has received in exchange for commodities we have taken from her?—Certainly not.

10358. So far as your experience goes, it has been decidedly injurious to all the towns where your manufactories were erected?—Most decidedly.

10359. Did you build your mills on the faith of protecting duties?—Most decidedly we did.

10360. Have you ever applied to Government for compensation, for the losses you

Mr.
*Joseph Grout.*
———
4 July,
1832.

you have sustained?—I have had it in contemplation very frequently, but never yet have made a direct application; I think the justice of our case demands it.

10361. Have you an idea of the value of the mill property of yourself and other persons, and what sort of claim you should make on the Government for compensation, if the present system be continued?—I could not state the amount exactly; it has been variously stated.

10362. Do you think it is less than two millions?—Certainly not; I think it is very much more.

10363. If the duties were further reduced, and the free importation of foreign manufactured silks be allowed, are you of opinion that property will be entirely destroyed and valueless?—There can be no doubt of it.

10364. Have you ever been disappointed at the East India sales, at seeing a quantity of private trade silk suddenly withdrawn, because the price offered has not been sufficient to remunerate the importers?—Very frequently.

10365. Have you ever found the Company withdraw their silk from sale, though they might sell for low prices?—Certainly not for the last 20 years; I can speak to that positively.

10366. You spoke of your partner taking over mulberry trees to India; had he an opportunity of making the experiment whether they would flourish?—He took them first to the Botanical Gardens of Calcutta; they were taken care of there, and taken up the country; he planted them there; and I think I have heard him say, that in a very few weeks they were seven feet high; the mulberry plant in Bengal is very different from that of France and Italy; in France and Italy it is a mulberry-tree, but in Bengal it is brushwood; it is let out to the ryots (the little farmers) five or six acres each; they sell this brushwood to the peasantry, for the purpose of feeding their worms from the leaves: there is no such thing as a mulberry-tree in Bengal; the climate will not admit of it; a ryot may go to-day and mow down his brush-wood and sell it to worm-feeders, and the day after to-morrow he will go and mow it again; so that a very small space of mulberry ground is sufficient in Bengal, as compared with other countries; but the leaf from the brush wood is very inferior to that from the tree in Europe.

10367. Do you think that arises from the nature of the soil or the climate?—The soil and climate both.

10368. It has been stated, that the value of silk mills and machinery in Manchester is about 200,000*l.*; does not the capital you have invested in mills and machinery amount to three quarters of that sum?—It would appear so. I will beg to state one fact, with the permission of the Committee, to show, that in our concern we have not lost sight of the improvement of silk in our own colonies. Here are nine bales of silk raised in Bengal: six bales reared on the French principle by way of experiment, and three reared on the Bengal principle; when they came to London, I took my broker and one or two other persons to examine them, and report on the quality; I also examined them and reported upon them, and these are my private marks upon those nine bales; and I made the Bengal reeled silk precisely the same quality as the French reeled silk; a great deal of pains was taken with this experiment, with a view to satisfy ourselves.

10369. You are understood to say, that the thread from the Bengal cocoon is very considerably smaller in substance than the thread of the Italian cocoon; can you state the number of threads of the Bengal silk which you consider would be equal to another given number of threads of the Italian silk, so as to form the same substance?—Yes; I would say four cocoons of French and Italian silk would make a thread quite as round as six and a half or nearly seven threads of Bengal cocoons.

---

*Veneris, 6° die Julii*, 1832.

---

JAMES A. STEWART MACKENZIE, ESQUIRE, in the Chair.

---

Mr. *William Bridges*, called in; and Examined.

Mr.
*William Bridges.*
———
6 July,
1832.

10370. HOW long have you been engaged in the silk trade?—Twenty-five years.
10371. What is the name of your house?—Bridges, Campbell & Co.
10372. Have you been manufacturers principally of plain or fancy goods?—The greater part fancy goods.

10373. Where

10373. Where is your manufacture?—In Spitalfields.

Mr.
William Bridges.

6 July,
1832.

10374. Are you well acquainted with the silk trade?—I am, having been engaged in it from my youth up to the present time.

10375. Was the trade in a flourishing state up to the time of the opening of the Ports to foreign silk in 1826?—In a very flourishing state.

10376. Were the silk goods which you made of the best quality?—Of the best quality.

10377. You furnished silk goods to the principal retail houses at the West end of the Town?—I did so.

10378. Did you make at that time many rich plain goods for the same class of customers?—All the plain goods that we made were of a rich quality; some seasons we made more plain than others; but most of our goods were figured.

10379. About what number of looms were you in the habit at that time of employing?—Three hundred or three hundred and fifty.

10380. What proportion of those were employed on figured and what on plain?—There were two-thirds figured, and the remainder plain.

10381. What periods are you speaking of?—Prior to 1826.

10382. Have you any personal knowledge whether goods the produce of your manufacture, were worn by ladies of high rank in this country?—Most certainly; they were worn by the Royal Family, and by the nobility in general.

10383. Were the silks made from designs by English artists, or did you copy French patterns?—By English artists, drawn expressly to our instructions.

10384. Do you think there was any want of taste and skill on the part of the English manufacturer at that time, as compared with the French?—Certainly not; and I beg leave to show a few patterns of what we made in 1822 and 1823 [delivering them in]; the two first in the corner are the first production of the Jacquard in this country.

10385. How many Jacquard looms did you at any one time employ; what was the greatest number?—About 140.

10386. At what period was that?—That was in 1824 and 1825.

10387. Immediately on the introduction of the Jacquard into this country, you availed yourself of it?—Yes, and made large purchases.

10388. If you had been encouraged to continue a manufacture of figured silks, would you have used your Jacquard looms most extensively?—Most certainly.

10389. Did it make any alteration in the wages, the introduction of the Jacquard looms?—I paid for the work 3s. previous to the introduction of the Jacquard, and after that 2s. 4d.

10390. What do you pay now?—Thirteen pence, that is 1d. more than is generally paid; the prices have been coming down since 1822.

10391. Have you a specimen of the article you are now making at 1s. 1d.?—Yes; I beg to exhibit this shawl, which is very costly; the getting of it up cost me 80l., that is the machinery, before I could get any thing made from it; the person was three months in getting it ready, and the labour on this cost three-fourths of the value.

10392. When did you make this shawl?—In 1822 and 1823.

10393. Have you made any of these lately?—No.

10394. Nothing so costly as to the labour?—Nothing; the whole of the gauze trade has left this country; I had fifty looms, and now I have not one.

10395. Do you happen to know the number at Paisley?—I have no knowledge of Paisley whatever.

10396. Is not the fabric made at Paisley of a different nature and character?—Yes.

10397. Are you acquainted with Mr. Fulton's goods?—Yes.

10398. Does he not make many beautiful goods?—Yes.

10399. Are they of a description similar to this?—I believe not.

10400. Have you any doubt of their capacity to make them?—I question if they would go to the expense.

10401. You feel reluctant to say, that they would not be able to do what you yourself have done?—I should not wish to say so; but I mean to say there was no want of taste at that time.

10402. But the nature and character of his manufacture is totally different from that which you now exhibit?—Certainly.

10403. What you are now making is different to what you made in 1823?—Yes.

678.

10404. Do

Mr.
*William Bridges.*

6 July,
1832.

10404. Do you know whether there has been any rich gauze goods introduced from France?—I have never seen any thing so costly as far as that goes; the outlay was 80 *l.* and I think very few would have gone to that expense.

10405. Is that article now imported from France?—I believe it is.

10406. Are not the articles imported from France, crapes rather than gauzes?—I believe there are some of each; I have seen some of each.

10407. Recently?—Yes.

10408. Are the figured goods made in Scotland of a character different to some which you have probably seen introduced from France?—Yes.

10409. Then rich gauze goods do still come from France? —I believe they do.

10410. Do you find that they have such an advantage and superiority over you in the manufacture and the price at which they render this commodity, as to exclude you from all chance of success in any attempt to compete with them?—I do find it so; and I for one shall never try to make such a costly thing again till I have the command of my own market.

10411. Is it then the French or the Scottish manufacturer which has interfered with your trade, in the article now before us?—The French.

10412. What quantity might have been imported of that during the last year, in value?—I do not know.

10413. I now show you four patterns of gauzes which you made in 1823 and 1824?—Those patterns were manufactured by me in the two years you named.

10414. Do you now make such articles?—No.

10415. Is it because they are made in Scotland, or that you found your trade interfered with by the goods that come from France?—By the goods that come from France.

10416. Do such goods come into the market from France?—They do.

10417. Are such goods as these made in Scotland?—Certainly not.

10418. The patterns exhibited here are of figured gauzes suited for dresses; was there any considerable quantity of these articles imported in the last year?—I should think there was; no doubt about it; I have seen some; I have some in that I made last year, and I shall be glad to sell them at two-thirds of the price.

10419. Do you mean to say that they are still fashionable?—I believe they are, for evening dresses.

10420. But not greatly in demand?—There is no great consumption.

10421. When you speak of them as an article of manufacture, you mean an article made quite for the superior classes?—Yes; for evening parties.

10422. Have you referred to the French tariff of prices now paid for work at Lyons?—I have not.

10423. You are not able to state what is paid at Lyons, for the article which you now state you are paying 13 *d.* for in Spitalfields?—Not exactly; I believe it has been given in.

10424. Did you, at the time that you made the patterns that you have exhibited, make your goods chiefly from private orders, or for general sale?—Chiefly from orders; I used to exhibit patterns from which orders were given, that employed my looms for the ensuing season.

10425. At what time of the year were these orders given?—About November, for the following spring, and about the present time for the autumn.

10426. Had you large accounts with the first houses at the West end of the Town?—Yes; I think three of the principal houses together used to order of me to the amount of 20,000 *l.* a-year in fancy silk, and a large City house at that time used to take generally 10,000*l.*

10427. In the manufacture of these silk goods what description of silk did you use?—Silk thrown at the mill of Mr. John Ward, of Bruton.

10428. Is that a silk of a superior quality?—Very superior.

10429. Did it answer your purpose as well as Piedmontese organzine?—Decidedly better.

10430. You purchased raw silk and had it thrown for your own use?—I did.

10431. Was it thrown as well as the Piedmontese silk?—I consider Mr. Ward's throwing quite equal to the Piedmontese.

10432. Do you generally buy your silk in the raw, and employ a throwster to throw it for you?—Always.

10433. Can you state the extent of employment that you give to the throwing mills?—Not exactly; but I can state that I have paid Mr. Ward as much as 3,000*l.* in a year for throwing.

10434. Is

Mr.
*William Bridges.*

6 July,
1832.

10434. Is not the English thrown silk better than the Italian thrown silk?—It is used by many; some gentlemen think the Piedmontese organzine to be far superior; I do not use it; I consider English thrown silk to be quite equal to it; and I can make all my works of it.

10435. It has been stated here by a witness, that English thrown silk is worth 1 *s.* more than Italian thrown silk; do you agree in that opinion?—Whichever was cheapest I should avail myself of, as a manufacturer, the quality being taken into consideration; in rich satins, I should not use Piedmontese organzine.

10436. Do you apprehend that two bales of equal quality, purchased in Lombardy and thrown, the one there and the other in England, that the English would be worth more than the Italian?—I should prefer it; there is more confidence to be placed in the English throwster.

10437. Is it not essential that the raw silk should be of a very good quality?—Most assuredly; we generally select those silks of the best quality.

10438. In your judgment, is it not essential that you should do every thing in your power to encourage the importation of good raw silk?—Certainly.

10439. Did you at that time make velvets?—Yes.

10440. Did you generally use Piedmontese?—No; I generally used organzine, made of Fossembrone raw silk.

10441. You stated, that up to the time of the opening of the Ports, in 1826, your trade was in a flourishing state, be pleased to inform the Committee what is the state of your manufacture at the present moment?—It is greatly altered; the fancy part of the trade is nearly destroyed.

10442. What quantity of fancy looms do you employ?—Only from sixty to seventy.

10443. Has this decrease in your fancy trade been gradually coming on ever since the opening of the Ports?—It has.

10444. Besides the experience of your own house, do you know what is the state of the fancy trade generally in Spitalfields?—There is scarcely any of it left.

10445. To what do you attribute this gradual decline in the fancy branch of British silk manufacture?—From the great quantity of French goods that are brought into the market.

10446. In what way does the foreign fancy silk interfere with you?—Instead of my receiving orders as I used to do, I find that the principal buyers of fancy goods are in the habit of going to Lyons for French fashions, so that notwithstanding the excellency of the goods which we make here there is no chance of my selling them against the French.

10447. You think it a matter of fashion, not of price?—French will sell while English goods will lay by; if the market is thin, then mine will come in.

10448. Do you mean that if yours were introduced and offered as French, they would sell though they do not sell as English?—That may be done in some houses, but respectable houses will not do that.

10449. You think that might be done if they were so introduced, but you do not think the French cheaper than yours?—Yes, I do; they come into the market and displace ours.

10450. Do they sell these in preference to yours because they are cheaper?—They are cheaper, and that will be the cause in some instances.

10451. To what do you attribute their being cheaper?—They have advantages that we have not.

10452. Will you state what these advantages are, in your opinion?—I am not aware of them; but I am convinced they must have them.

10453. Is it not a great advantage that they should obtain silk at a less duty?—I do not consider that is much advantage.

10454. Do you think it an advantage to the manufacturer to obtain silks 2 *s.* 6 *d.* cheaper?—Certainly, I should like to get my silks cheaper.

10455. Would it not be a great advantage to you as a manufacturer, and your labourers as journeymen, if you could obtain your Foreign thrown silk 2 *s.* 6 *d.* cheaper than you now do?—I would like it; but it is a question if you remove the duty whether we should have it.

10456. Supposing the duty removed, would not the price paid by the French manufacturer and the price paid by you be the same?—I question if the duty was taken off whether it would not go into the Italian's pocket.

10457. He would not charge the French less than you?—I am not anxious to try that.

10458. You

Mr.
*William Bridges.*
———
6 July,
1832.

10458. You do not want the advantage of obtaining silks on the same terms as the French do?—I will not say that.

10459. Perhaps you will like to pay for your raw silks at the same price as the French do?—I have heard some say so.

10460. Have you not heard it stated by a gentleman sent out by Government to obtain information, did he not afford you that sort of information that leads you to suppose that their silk is from 2 *s.* to 3 *s.* a pound cheaper than your raw?—I understood so.

10461. The Italian having the markets of Lyons and London both open to him, might he not obtain the same price for his articles in both?—I question it; it has been given in by some gentleman more conversant with that part of it than I am.

10462. Do you believe, if the Italian could get a higher price in London for his silk, that he would sell it at Lyons for a less price?—Perhaps by coming to this market he would avail himself of a higher price if he could; but our throwster will keep him from getting too high a price.

10463. You have spoken of some large buyers who formerly gave you orders, are they the same description of persons that formerly gave you large orders who have now ceased to give you these orders?—Yes; the French fashion is in the way of their giving me any orders.

10464. You spoke of one house in the city with whom you transacted business to the extent of 10,000 *l.* a year in fancy silks, do you in point of fact take an order for any goods from that house at present?—I have not a single order from that house.

10465. Are your accounts closed, or nearly so, with that house?—Nearly so; there is one house that I formerly, in fancy silks, had an account of 12,000 *l.* a year with, and last year I had an account of only 153 *l.*; and I beg further to state, that this house, up to 1825, averaged at 12,000 *l.* a year.

10466. Are there a large quantity of fancy goods still used?—Yes; greater than ever.

10467. How do you know that?—From my own observations, and from what has been told me by large buyers.

10468. How do you account for the French manufacturers having got such entire possession of the market for fancy goods?—The feeling here for French fashions is so strong, that notwithstanding the excellence of British goods the French will sell in preference to them.

10469. Is that not through want of taste or exertion on the part of the English manufacturer?—There has been every exertion made without avail. Last year in consequence of the announcement that the Queen would hold eight drawing rooms I made a considerable proportion of fancy silk goods for the purpose, but the French silks were almost entirely used, some of our goods we got off at a loss and others remain on our hands unsaleable; I beg to produce some of these silks which I made for the drawing-rooms, one of them was made for the Queen's coronation dress.

[*The Witness exhibited them to the Committee.*]

10470. What was the price of this coronation dress?—Twenty-three shillings per yard.

10471. What proportion of that was labour?—About 4 *s.*

10472. What difference in cost would it have made to you if the duty was repealed on foreign thrown silk?—Not 2 *d.* a yard.

10473. How did this speculation answer your purpose?—I have the greater part of them left on my hands; the first drawing-room I was rather successful, and sold thirty dresses; on the second, not five, and afterwards not any; as soon as the French found it out they came into the market, and we had no chance with them.

10474. At what price do the French import articles of a similar pattern and quality?—After the drawing-rooms continued, they supplied them at a much lower rate than I could.

10475. Is the price at which they now supply them equal to one-third of the price at which you can supply them at?—Nearly so.

10476. You say that you made a considerable quantity of these; are they all silk?—Not one half; these are what we are now making. [*Exhibiting some others.*]

10477. The rich figured silks which I now hold in my hand are some which you have made within the last two or three years?—Yes.

10478. Do

10478. Do you find a ready sale for them?—No.

10479. Do you, as a manufacturer and as a judge of these articles, consider them quite equal to the French in style, in taste and in manufacture?—I do in every point.

10480. These large patterns are some which you do now make?—Yes.

10481. And a few of them perhaps to order?—Some few to order; I sold three lots of goods last year, on which I lost 20 per cent.

10482. If a manufacturer, on speculation, was to employ 100 looms in the making of plain silk goods, and there was not a very good sale, could he at a trifling loss, at 1 *d.* or 2 *d.* per yard, dispose of them at once?—That is the case.

10483. If he was to manufacture fancy goods to a smaller extent, and did not find a ready sale, would not his loss be more considerable?—Yes, from 20 to 30 per cent. on many articles of fancy goods.

10484. When there is a scarcity of rich French silks, is there ever a momentary demand?—Yes; a friend of mine who went over to France could not see any thing to his mind. I received a large order from him in consequence; that was late in the spring; my looms had been standing from November till the end of February before they were employed; had I had my orders in the usual time, there would have been no complaint in Spitalfields.

10485. Under the circumstances, your labourers had some trifling employment?—Yes; living near the seat of fashion.

10486. You being near the seat of fashion had some orders, while other houses in Spitalfields had nothing to do?—I believe I have the greater part of the trade now, bad as it is.

10487. Are you of opinion, that any thing short of exclusion would restore the silk trade to its former state?—I am decidedly of opinion, that nothing short of total exclusion will ever restore the trade to its former state.

10488. At such a state as would employ your people?—At such a state as would employ my working people, that I might lay my goods by, knowing that the approaching spring would clear me out.

10489. You think there is no desire, on the part of the operatives, to go back to the 2 *s.* 4 *d.* a yard?—I think they would be satisfied with considerably less than that.

10490. Do you consider the present wages at Spitalfields not sufficient to remunerate the operative?—I think they are below the starving point.

10491. Do you think such an advance in wages as I have spoken of, would interfere at all with the consumption of goods in this country?—It would, no doubt, interfere in some measure; a less advance would satisfy the operatives.

10492. You do not think that 2 *d.* or 3 *d.* per yard is any bar to the sale of rich figured goods to persons, in a price of something like 4 *s.* 5 *s.* or 6 *s.*?—It cannot be.

10493. Do you think it would be a material relief if the duty was taken off foreign thrown silk?—No; I do not use foreign thrown silk; and besides, I believe if the duty was taken off, it would go into the pocket of the Italian.

10494. Are the Committee to understand, that the improvements that have taken place in the manufacture of foreign silk is chiefly to be attributed to the introduction of the Jacquard looms, some years before the opening of the Ports for foreign silks?—Most certainly.

10495. In the patterns which you have exhibited, some of which were made before 1826, and others about that time, you show us evidence that the improvement in the figured branches of the silk trade were much greater before the opening of the Ports than they have been since?—That is my decided opinion.

10496. This being your experience as a manufacturer, extensively engaged for a series of years in the rich figured trade, what do you think of an opinion stated by Dr. Bowring to exist in France, that the improvements in English figured silks since 1825, has been equal to 50 years?—I consider this opinion to be entirely fallacious.

10497. You have stated, that your house has scarcely one-third of its former number of figured and fancy works going; and it has been given in evidence, that in all Manchester there are not more than 60 Jacquard looms, and that these are chiefly making low-priced silks; therefore your house alone, although reduced to its present number, has as many rich figured silks still going, as are making in all Manchester, of every description?—Certainly.

10498. Then Manchester has not taken away the figured silk trade which Spitalfields has lost?—Undoubtedly not.

678.                                                                           10499. Do

Mr.
*William Bridges.*

6 July,
1832.

10499. Do you conceive that England is on a fair ground with France, while the latter country produces three millions of her raw silk, grown at from 15 to 25 per cent. cheaper than the Italian, if the information, which has been received, has been correct on that point?—Certainly she is not on a fair footing with France; but with that I am not acquainted.

10500. You stated, that you had only 60 or 70 looms employed in fancy goods?—Yes.

10501. Are they employed to order?—Part of them; the greater part.

10502. Are these on the table specimens of the goods you have now in your looms?—They are.

10503. Although the French has interfered with you, they have not actually annihilated your trade?—They have interfered as much as this, that instead of paying 16,000 *l.* a year for labour, it is now something like 6 or 7,000 *l.*

10504. Did you, in executing the order received in February of which you have spoken, sustain a loss, or did you make a profit?—The profit was very small, but the order has been doubled since; I thought it would have been a loss, but these 30 pieces have been made something like 90.

10505. You made them so well, and so much to the satisfaction of the person who ordered them, that he repeated his order?—Yes.

10506. The first cost of the outlay of the money was reimbursed by being thrown over the greater number of yards?—That is the case.

10507. Do you also manufacture plain goods?—I do.

10508. Do you find that the French interfere in the plain gros de Naples?—In making plain goods; I do it chiefly to keep my hands employed that I am desirous of retaining, and I believe that in so doing I interfere with a good many gentlemen.

10509. You have not found the same difficulty in competing with the French in plain as you do in figured?—If any gentleman will give me the cost price for the plain, I take it.

10510. Are you a member of the Trade Committee?—I am.

10511. How many gentlemen compose that committee?—I think it does not exceed 15.

10512. What number have generally attended their meetings?—About 10.

10513. Of these how many of them are unconnected with throwing or throwing mills?—I should think from 10 to 12 or 15 are unconnected with throwing.

10514. Do you know when the committee last assembled?—I do not think it has met since the end of January or February.

10515. You have not assembled since this Committee was appointed by the House?—Certainly not.

10516. Do you believe that the committee of manufacturers, as such, have had any thing to do with the evidence brought before this Committee? —Not the least, in any shape or way whatever.

10517. The committee has not met as a committee at their usual place of meeting, Weavers' Hall?—They have not.

10518. Have not certain members of the committee been the persons chiefly engaged in getting up evidence before this Committee?—No, but inquiries have been constantly made as to the proceedings of this Committee.

10519. Is not Mr. Brocklehurst a member of the committee?—He is.

10520. And Mr. Moore?—Yes.

10521. And Mr. Grout?—Yes.

10522. Have you been in the habit of meeting these gentlemen, since the Committee met, on the subject of the proceedings that have taken place here?—I have met Mr. Grout, but not in an official manner; I have inquired of him to know what would be the result of this Committee, but we have never had a meeting.

10523. You have inquired of him, knowing that he generally attended the meetings of this Committee?—Yes.

10524. Have you ever met Mr. Brocklehurst more than once since January?—I have never met Mr. Brocklehurst in a single instance.

10525. Nobody has attempted to influence you as to any opinion you may give?—Not the least.

10526. Do you believe they have influenced other persons?—No.

10527. You are not a throwster yourself?—No.

10528. Would you undertake to say that a majority of the committee are not interested in throwing?—I think that a majority are not interested in throwing in any shape or way.

10529. Do

Mr.
*William Bridges.*

6 July,
1832.

10529. Do you think that nine-tenths of the silk manufacturers in London agree with you in your opinion, whether they are throwsters or not, as to the operation of the introduction of French silk goods on your manufactures in Spitalfields ?—No doubt full nine-tenths are of the same way of thinking as myself.

10530. Out of the 60 manufacturers in Spitalfields, perhaps five or six take a different view ?—That may be so.

10531. You think that there are certain manufacturers in Spitalfields who are anxious that the duty should be taken off thrown silks ?—I believe there are five or six, perhaps 10, but not more.

10532. Are they not the largest manufacturers ?—I think not.

10533. Are not the large manufacturers in Spitalfields engaged in throwing, or interested in the throwing mills ?—I am not aware of that.

10534. You have exhibited some patterns, did you yourself make any of these goods on speculation ?—A few of them.

10535. What is your reason for not making many of them on speculation ?—Because I have not the command of my own market; if I had, I should have no opposition at all in preparing them for the spring trade.

10536. Do you apprehend that if you made goods on speculation, you would be interfered with by any other market, and sustain a loss rather than get a profit ?—If I had the command of my own market, I should have no fear of any one infringing on me, so as to injure my own sale.

10537. Do you mean by that, to say that you want the exclusive control of the fancy silk trade in Spitalfields ?—I have no objection to fancy silks being made in Manchester, or any where else, only keep the foreigner out of the market.

10538. Do you know whether any persons now in Spitalfields makes that description of commodity which you have exhibited to the Committee, on speculation ?—I do not think there are six looms of the sort going in Spitalfields.

10539. Will you tell the Committee why you do not set such looms to work ?—Unless I do it on a broad scale, it is of no use at all; what is left of the better trade, I believe I have; and at present it is not worth the while of any house to take it up.

10540. Is there hardly any other house than yours which is now making rich silk figured goods in Spitalfields, or in fact in England ?—I really do not think there is.

Mr. *George Stephens*, called in; and further Examined.

10541. HAVE you been examined on a former day ?—Yes.

10542. Can you give some additional information to the Committee ?—Yes; on a previous examination I alluded to ribbons; I will now speak of broad silks.

10543. Do you live with Halling, Pearce & Stone ?—Yes.

10544. Are you a buyer of Spitalfields and Manchester silks ?—Yes.

10545. And were you before the admission of French silks ?—I was.

10546. What kind of goods did you buy of Spitalfields manufacture before French silk goods were admitted ?—A variety of kinds of goods; I have a list, if I may be permitted to read it.

10547. Those you now speak of were manufactured in Spitalfields ?—Yes, they were in 1825; there were gros de Naples, twill sarsnets, satins, figured satins, velvets, figured velvets, cut figured gauzes, gold and silver tissues, figured gauze handkerchiefs, scarfs, plushes, Italian nets, figured plushes, poplins, figured poplins, and lustres.

10548. What kind of goods do you now buy of Spitalfields manufacture ?—We buy at present very few, not half the number we used to buy; they are gros de Naples, low satins, and low black velvets.

10549. You have named ten or twelve articles which you were in the habit of receiving from Spitalfields before the admission of foreign goods, and you now receive only three or four; do you receive most of the others from other parts of England ?—No, we receive nearly the whole of them from France.

10550. What silks do you buy of Manchester manufacture ?—Low gros de Naples and sarsnets; of mixed goods we buy palmyrines, shawls, crape handkerchiefs, &c.

10551. The latter articles are a mixture of cotton and silk, or silk and worsted ?—They are.

10552. Are many of these goods made in Jacquard looms ?—I believe some of them are; the mixed goods are.

Mr.
*George Stephens.*

10553. Are

Mr.
George Stephens.

6 July,
1832.

10553. Are there not some kinds of goods made at Manchester, that were made in Spitalfields, previous to the admission of foreign goods?—No.

10554. Does not Manchester produce very beautiful articles for ladies dresses? —Not any very beautiful, many very cheap. I have before me two or three patterns of the best things ever had from Manchester.

10555. Has not Manchester produced many kinds of goods since the opening of the Ports which have prevented the sale of French fancy silk goods?—No, it has not; Manchester has produced different sorts of goods, but none good enough in any case to prevent the sale of rich French goods.

10556. Do you come into immediate contact with Manchester manufacturers? —Yes, they frequent our house for French patterns almost every month in the year.

10557. Do they not often copy French articles and sell the articles made in imitation as French goods?—They sell them as fancy goods; they copy from them sometimes at a very great loss; there was an instance this spring in which a considerable sum of money was lost; it was in the article of shawls, which we imported about the end of February, and the Manchester manufacturers took them down to copy; they cost us 28 f. in Paris, and we thought they might be produced in England for 10 s. 6 d., and in three weeks from that time we had them from Manchester at 12 s. 6 d.; immediately after that there was a large lot sent over from Paris, which we bought at 10 s.

10558. So after the French had supplied you with a considerable quantity at 28 f. you found there was a large influx suddenly at 10 s.?—Yes, they send them all over Europe at the first price, and then send the jobs to London.

10559. Does not the convenience of sending goods from Paris to London induce them generally to send their jobs to this market?—I think most of the Parisian jobs come to this country.

10560. Is it not a great interference with the general manufacture of London? —It is impossible to guard against so great an evil as that; at the present time I can buy in London 2,000 garnitures of a particluar kind of ribbon (decoupé gauze) at about 30 s. for which we paid from 50 f. to 60 f. in Paris, in April last.

10561. And equally good?—Equally good.

10562. Do you consider these goods to be smuggled?—I think some are smuggled; some are sold at a sacrifice.

10563. Can you name the fancy goods that have been made in Manchester since 1826?—There are a variety of kinds; those I have handed in are some of them; there are very few rich goods; they are almost all different kinds of mixed goods.

10564. In nearly all descriptions of mixed goods which come from Manchester there is a consumption more or less of silk?—Yes; but within these last four months a figured silk has been sent up which had a very limited sale indeed.

10565. In all these goods where there is a considerable quantity of silk mixed with cotton or worsted, are they called silk goods generally?—They are.

10566. Are they made by houses principally in the silk trade?—Yes; they are called silk manufacturers.

10567. Do you believe that any of the goods that are made at Manchester interfere with the superior French goods which are introduced into this country?—Not in silk goods, or what are called the superior articles of silk goods; this is an article [*exhibiting it*] for which we pay a large sum every year to France; it has never been produced in Manchester; it is cut figured gauze.

10568. What is this selling at now?—From 4 s. to 6 s. a yard, eighteen inches wide.

10569. Do you call this a fashionable thing now?—Yes, some of the patterns are not a month from Paris.

10570. In what respect do they differ from the goods made by Messrs. Fulton? —They are very different; Messrs. Fulton's sell from 4 s. to 6 s. a yard, thirty-six inches wide; these are from 4 s. to 6 s. a yard, eighteen inches wide; and we sell these to our first-rate customers; Messrs. Fulton's we do not.

10571. Messrs. Fulton's goods are wider?—Yes, they are; but not so costly; they have not the rich appearance these have.

10572. Do you import these goods at the present moment?—Yes.

10573. You have seen a rich gauze shawl exhibited this morning to the Committee?—I have.

10574. Are gauzes of that sort made in Scotland?—Not such gauze as that.

10575. Are

Mr.
*George Stephens.*

6 July,
1832.

10575. Are gauzes of that sort made in France?—Yes.

10576. Are any gauzes now worn in England of that fabric, not confining the enquiry to shawls?—Yes, for dresses, handkerchiefs and shawls; but not so large as that.

10577. Are the rich gauzes imported from France?—Yes; they come from Lyons.

10578. Has it been the French or the Scottish gauzes that have interfered with the gauze trade of Spitalfields?—The French decidedly; ladies who will buy these things will not buy the Scottish because they are too cheap.

10579. Are not a considerable quantity of Scottish gauzes sold?—A considerable quantity.

10580. Are they made any where else but at Paisley?—Not any where else to my knowledge.

10581. Do you sell any of the English crape handkerchiefs?—Yes, we do.

10582. In what respect do they differ from the French?—They are softer.

10583. Are they better or inferior?—By some people their softness is thought a quality in their favour.

10584. How long have they been made to any extent in England?—I think about three years.

10585. In 1825, there were very few or none made in this country?—I think none exactly like them.

10586. It is now a branch of trade, in imitation of the French?—Yes.

10587. Are they cheaper or dearer than the French?—There are different qualities of each kind; the lower priced English ones are not so high as the high priced French, and we have some English that are higher than the French.

10588. Do they sell in your warehouse and shop along with the French?—Yes.

10589. What proportion do you sell of each; as many English as French?—I cannot say in the particular article of the zephyr handkerchief what the proportion is.

10590. Do you not know that this handkerchief is a new article as regards France?—I do not.

10591. Did you ever see an article of this kind worn in this country before 1826?—I have no recollection of it.

10592. Is it not a recent invention, copied here as soon as it was procured?—It is possible it might be.

10593. Do you think the manufacturers would have made as many fancy goods if no French silk had come into the market?—Yes; from our coming into immediate contact with them, I have observed that they would have embarked more money in fancy goods if it had not been for the French goods coming here.

10594. Do you not think it likely, that a deal of the speculation at Manchester was owing to the reduced price of silk as compared with the years 1822 and 1823?—I believe that at Manchester they made silk goods in consequence of silk being lowered, with a view of selling goods that had displaced certain mixed articles that were once sold; for seven years, before 1826, poplins, figured and plain, were sold greatly; then the manufacturers made a low priced gros de Naples, from 1 s. 6 d. to 2 s. 6 d., which caused this article to go out.

10595. That was the substitution of plain silk instead of silk and worsted?—Yes, it is an inferior class of the community that consumes the Manchester silks.

10596. Have the manufacturers now a chance of getting a good price for a novelty?—No; we do not think of giving the Manchester manufacturers a good price for a novelty; we know pretty nearly what it will cost them, and we never think of giving a great price.

10597. You have little confidence in giving an order to a Manchester manufacturer, for a considerable quantity of an article when he has first produced it?—We do not do so.

10598. Do you act in the same manner with regard to French goods?—No; we are obliged to give for new French goods any price that the person who offers them asks; we give in many instances three times the cost of the material and labour; we pay for fashion besides the cost of the labour on the raw material. I have some patterns of Manchester manufactures and French mixed, the Manchester we are buying under 2 s. a yard; for this French article, I hold in my hand, we paid 5 f., and I do not think it worth 2 s. 6 d.

10599. I put into your hand a pattern of an article (figured palmyrine) made at Manchester, and another made in France, will you inform the Committee the price

678.

at

Mr.
*George Stephens.*

6 July,
1832.

at which the two articles sell in this country, whether you believe the cost of one is greater than the other, or why one sells for more than another?—This article from Manchester I know may be bought under 2 *s.* a yard; and when I look on the other, and see that there is not any greater labour, I do not think it would cost more; but it is a French article, and we know that French fashion will sell at any price; that therefore is the reason we give a great price for it.

10600. What is the cost of that French article?—Five francs. We are not able to sell it under 5 *s.*; I believe that is the exact retail price.

10601. Do you believe that if a lady were to purchase a dress of either sort, that one would last any longer in wear than the other?—Not at all longer.

10602. Do you find that there is a wish to purchase French commodities?—Yes.

10603. Is not the French article, which you now hold in your hand, in better taste than the English?—It is in better taste.

10604. What you mean is, that the French manufacturer has a much better taste than the Manchester manufacturer?—I have seen more tasty goods from France than I have from Manchester.

10605. An article which costs the same money would, if it be made in France, for that reason, sell at a higher price in your shop?—Yes.

10606. Have you seen French goods and Manchester goods more tasty than Spitalfields?—Of late years I have seen more tasty articles from France; but I have seen some very good from Spitalfields.

10607. Why do you not give your orders to Spitalfields?—We are obliged to have French fashions; we are governed by the fashions there, and we are obliged to have new patterns.

10608. You have spoken of your giving orders for French silk goods, and of your not giving orders for goods from Manchester, what is the reason you do not act with Manchester as you do with France?—Because we can always sell those we order from France; we are not so certain that we shall sell those we order from Manchester.

10609. Do you think that would have been the case if the Manchester manufacturer had made better goods?—The Manchester manufacturers have always been afraid to embark their capital, conceiving they would do it at a loss.

10610. Has not the admission of French silk goods caused a great deal of improvement in English silk goods?—No; I think they improved as much from 1821 to 1825, as from 1826 to 1831.

10611. Can you name any articles of the kind?—I would mention an article which we used to call ducape; the ducape of 1825 was better than the Spitalfields gros de Naples of 1831; the Spitalfields manufacturers have followed the French in the make, and their silk has lost the richness which it once had; the majority of the Spitalfields silks now have a harsh feel about them.

10612. Have any of the Spitalfields manufacturers made such gauzes, since 1826, as you spoke of?—We have known several in Spitalfields, who have tried since 1826 to make fancy goods, such as cut gauzes, scarfs and shawls, but they have never sold at a profit.

10613. Do you now buy any figured silk goods from Spitalfields?—We now only buy black and white, no coloured figured silk except they be a job.

10614. Is there a peculiarity about the colour of both black and white, in the English manufacture and the French manufacture, which prevents your purchasing the French?—Yes, it is a peculiar shade of black and of white which we buy.

10615. Do you not buy any rich plain silks from Spitalfields?—No; all from France.

10616. Why do you buy them in France in preference to England?—We are led by the colours; we can get them in France immediately the fashion is adopted.

10617. Whereas if you ordered them in England, you would have to wait for them?—Yes.

10618. Do you think there is an extensive sale of such goods?—I do.

10619. Can you inform the Committee what proportion your French stock bears to your English?—Dividing it into 100 parts, it is about 40 to 60.

10620. Do you mean silk goods and ribbons?—Ribbons are excluded.

10621. The English are 60, and the French 40?—Yes.

10622. Does the French part consist of more expensive goods than the English?—Much more expensive.

10623. Does the sale of French fancy goods increase?—It does.

10624. What

Mr.
*George Stephens.*

6 July,
1832.

10624. What proportion do the French sales bear to the English in silk goods?—I think it is nearly half.

10625. Does that include ribbons?—It does.

10626. Did not your house furnish the Board of Trade with a paper, showing the proportion of French and English goods sold by your house?—Yes, it did.

10627. What period did this Return refer to?—To the year 1830.

10628. What were the proportions stated in that Return?—They vary a little; generally about 16 and four, divided into 20 parts.

10629. For what period?—The six months ending the 30th June 1830.

10630. How do you reconcile this Return with the proportion of half and half which you have just now stated?—The Return to the Board of Trade was made up from the invoices; we purchased low gros de Naples for country concerns, and they are not sold to first class customers in London.

10631. Your town trade is about half and half of French and English silk goods?—It is.

10632. And that in the country is principally Manchester silks?—In the country there are more Manchester silks sold.

10633. And Spitalfields also?—Yes.

10634. Do you not sell some French goods in the country?—Yes.

10635. Will you name the kind of French silk goods you now buy?—Plain gros de Naples, watered ditto, figured ditto, clouded ditto, gros des Indies, plain satins, figured ditto, rich velvets, figured ditto, plushes, cut gauzes, plain ditto, tissue on crape dresses, tissue on gros de Naples, ditto ditto on satins, ditto cut gauze handkerchiefs and scarfs, zephyr shawls, handkerchiefs and scarfs, crape shawls, handkerchiefs and scarfs, embroidered silk dresses, ditto handkerchiefs, shawls and scarfs, ditto crape shawls, scarfs and handkerchiefs, tissue handkerchiefs, scarfs, grenadine scarfs, shawls and handkerchiefs, mousline de Soie, shawls, scarfs and handkerchiefs, ditto for dresses, Aerophane crêpe crepè, silk shawls.

10636. These you now buy?—Yes.

10637. Do you know the duty that these things pay?—They should pay 30 per cent. and upwards.

10638. Do they pay such duty?—They do not always.

10639. Do you mean, that such goods go through the Custom House, paying less than the legal rate of duty?—Since I was last examined here, I have seen goods which it is plain must have come through the Custom House at less than the legal rate; one article in particular, which must have come through the Custom House at a less rate than ours did, I will name, it is called Petersham. I bought the same sort of article in the city one morning, at 54s., and on the same day I received some which came from Paris direct to us, and they cost us 63s., they are got generally in Paris; the very article which I bought in the city from the importer the same day that ours came, was 15 per cent. lower.

10640. Do you know whether the manufacturer sold them at the same price to the buyer?—I know he sold them at the same price, we have ascertained that since; we know the channel they came through, they left the manufactory the same day, and arrived in London the same morning; we bought ours in Paris, the city buyer bought his at Lyons.

10641. Might not the London house have bought cheaper than the Paris house?—Not at all; he is not a large buyer; he has given us the information, that he bought at the same price.

10642. You have ascertained that fact?—Yes, we have gone through every part of it; it cannot be otherwise.

10643. You are perfectly satisfied that the French manufacturer who purchased these goods did pay the same price for them?—I believe it as firmly as I believe that I exist.

10644. Do you know if these goods had been rendered into this country without an intermediate profit at Paris, if he could not have sold them to you within 15 per cent. of what you did purchase them at the London market?—He could not.

10645. Do you believe that the person you bought them of in London, is a responsible man?—I know he is a responsible man.

10646. You know that he did not sell them at a loss?—I know that he did not; I have his word for it.

10647. Can you account for the difference arising in these two purchases, both having passed through the Custom House?—I have the word of the importer for

678. it,

it, that the goods left the manufactory on the same morning, and arrived in London on the same morning, and came direct through the Custom House.

10648. Did the English importer say to you that they came through the Custom House?—Yes, he did.

10649. Did he lead you to suppose that he passed them at a less duty than he ought?—Yes, he does not mind admitting that he did pass them at less; I believe he gave a nominal value for the goods he was passing, and they passed at a less rate.

10650. Is the Table of Duties upon weight or value?—It can be taken by weight or value.

10651. You have no doubt these goods were not smuggled, but that, in point of fact, they passed through the Custom House?—I have no doubt of it.

10652. The article which you allude to was a Petersham, which is very heavy?—It is very heavy.

10653. Do you know that goods are ever passed through the Custom House *ad valorem*?—They pass *ad valorem* often.

10654. At whose discretion is it?—I believe the officer who stands at the desk.

10655. Is it within your knowledge that the same kind of silk goods that are passed one time by weight, are passed another time *ad valorem*?—I believe such to be the case.

10656. You were told by the importer that he passed his goods at a less rate of duty than he ought to have paid?—Yes, he admitted that to me.

10657. How long since is this transaction?—It was about the beginning of May.

10658. Was it by weight or value?—I do not know.

10659. Do you mean that the party from whom you purchased those goods, admitted that a fraud had been committed on the Custom House?—Yes, he admitted that to me.

10660. Can you state on what day the transaction took place?—I cannot state the day.

10661. Could you not, by reference to your books, give the date?—It would be possible to confirm the fact, that goods do pass through the Custom House on one day at one rate and another day at another; I could give another instance.

10662. In addition to this instance, have you any confirmed opinion as to the practice of goods passing through the Custom House without paying the legal rate of duty; do you believe that it is a common occurrence?—I believe it is a common occurrence.

10663. To what particular description of goods do you refer in the opinion you give, that they do not always pay the legal rate of duty?—I have instanced the plain Petersham, and I know others; plain silk goods come in without paying any duty whatever; I have the best possible proof that plain silk goods are smuggled.

10664. You do not mean smuggled through the Custom House?—No.

10665. What proof have you of goods being smuggled, not through the Custom House?—I have a general opportunity of knowing that goods are smuggled.

10666. Have you reason to suppose it is profitable to smuggle gloves at present?—I do not think it is profitable.

10667. Then the rate of duty paid on gloves is a rate that is actually collected?—I think even a greater could be collected; I think 1 s. a dozen more could be easily collected on gloves without creating smuggling.

10668. Do you know what the rate is upon the value?—Habits, 4 s.; men's, 5 s.; long, 7 s.

10669. Do you happen to know what it would average per cent. on the value?—In one instance it is 20 per cent.

10670. Would it not be more than 20 on the cost?—It would; the average cost of habits is 20 f.

10671. Can you explain why it is that silks can be smuggled at a less expense than gloves?—I think gloves are liable to injury from damp.

10672. Are there not many colours in silks that are equally liable to injury from damp?—Yes, there are.

10673. If it appears that 22½ can be collected on gloves, why should not 22½ be collected on silk also?—I cannot say why; I think that gloves could be smuggled if persons were disposed to smuggle them, but where they can get things more profitable they will not smuggle them.

10674. If a case of gloves of a given size should be worth 100 *l.* and a case of silks of the same size be worth 200 *l.* does it not follow that one might be smuggled

for

for half the cost of the other?—Yes, I think the bulk of the article regulates the price of smuggling.

10675. Do you think that the house you alluded to smuggles other kinds of goods besides silk goods?—I think a great many of other descriptions.

10676. What description of goods besides silk?—I know that they smuggle some gloves, and I have the best possible information that they smuggled tea, spirits and tobacco.

10677. In fact, they are regular smugglers?—Regular smugglers.

10678. Do you know of other houses who carry on that system?—I know that others do.

10679. Do you believe it is carried on to any extent?—I believe to a great extent.

10680. Is it not possible for the Custom House officers to prevent it?—Not to prevent the smuggling in silks; they have not the means of knowing the state of the stocks of silk goods in London.

10681. Could not regulations be adopted, or laws enacted, which would very much check smuggling?—I think it might be entirely stopped.

10682. Do you think that giving larger rewards to informers would enable the Government to collect larger duties than are now collected?—Yes; on gloves and other articles.

10683. Are you in the habit of going to Spitalfields several times in the course of the week?—Yes.

10684. Therefore you are pretty well acquainted with the state of things in Spitalfields?—Yes.

10685. Do you happen to know the general condition of the stocks in Spitalfields; are they heavy or light?—We do not buy of many houses in Spitalfields; I cannot speak as to the general stocks.

10686. You do not know the state of employment, or of the stocks either?—I do not.

10687. Have you been in the habit of going to Manchester often?—We do not go to Manchester; Manchester manufacturers come to our house.

10688. Do you know whether, in Spitalfields, there are more or less of rich plain gros de Naples made now than was made a year or two ago?—I do not think there is more made than there was three years since.

10689. Do you think that 1 s. more per dozen might be collected on French gloves, and would that be a great advantage to the workmen, or would it not?—I think it would gradually diminish the quantity of French gloves sold; it would have a great effect on the quantity sold.

10690. Would it induce the retail dealer to introduce English manufactured goods rather than French, with a view to his own profit?—It would.

10691. If the smuggler was required to smuggle on his own account, would it be in gloves and silk, or spirits, tobacco and tea?—I believe it would all continue.

10692. Are not some houses driven into the system of smuggling in self defence, because other persons do it?—Entirely so. I knew a lace importer about two years since; he came to a gentleman who was speaking to me, and said he was going to the Board of Trade, to ask for some alteration in the duty on blond; the gentleman laughed at him, and said, he might just as well stay at home; he did not go; and he has been as great a smuggler as others since.

10693. He overcame his scruples from necessity?—Yes.

10694. Do you think it would give some check to smuggling if it were made penal against the receivers and encouragers?—If 1,000 l. was offered to persons who could inform the Government where smuggled goods were to be found, (and a great many could give such information now,) it would have a great effect in checking smuggling.

10695. You mean, not confining it to the Custom House officer?—Yes.

10696. If the goods found were given to the informer, do you not think it would be very unsafe for any shopkeeper to deal in smuggled goods, when the young men in his employment might give information?—The value of the goods would not be enough; it would not be sufficient to pay for the loss of the situation, which would be the consequence; the value of the goods would not be enough.

10697. Would not the objection raised by the honourable Member, as to the liability of the master of the establishment, be got rid of by having the goods stamped?—Yes; that would prevent such importations; we once kept printed cotton stamped.

Mr.
*George Stephens.*

6 July,
1832.

10698. In point of fact, if prints were found on you unstamped, you were subject to a penalty?—Yes.

10699. You always dealt in those goods?—Yes.

10700. And yet never had an instance of that kind?—No.

10701. In your house you have not less than 70 or 80 young persons?—We have as many as that.

10702. Would not the temptation be greater in silk than in cotton?—I think it would.

10703. Do you not think that the most effectual way of putting down smuggling is to lower the duties to the cost of smuggling?—That would be the most preventive means to stop smuggling.

10704. Would not the English manufacturer be better able to compete with the French, if the duties upon thrown silk were reduced?—It would be about 2 d. a yard in his favour; it would not touch fancy goods.

10705. On plain gros de Naples?—It would reduce the price 2 d. a yard on that article; a great many French goods are governed by colour; we sell the French gros de Naples at 5 s., the Spitalfields, at not more than 3 s. 6 d.; 2 d. or 3 d. would not be felt on the sale of French goods.

10706. Is not 2 d. or 3 d. a yard a pretty good profit?—It is on a silk of 3 s.

10707. You do not believe that 2 d. reduction on the price of English goods would induce a sale of them against French?—Reducing the price of English from 3 s. to 2 s. 9 d. would not prevent the sale of the French goods at 4 s. or 5 s.

10708. Is it only the difference of the colour, or are not the French, after paying the duty, much dearer than the English?—If they pay the duty they are.

10709. Independent of the duty, taking the articles made at Spitalfields and at Lyons, how do they stand?—We do not pay Spitalfields more than 3 s., except for blacks; I therefore cannot speak of the rich coloured silks of Spitalfields.

10710. In the present state of trade, when profits are reduced to the lowest amount, is not 2 d. an important consideration?—To the buyer and seller it is.

10711. Or to the manufacturer, is it not?—I cannot answer that question.

10712. Would it not make a little difference in the sale to the consumer?—If we reduced our silks at 3 s. to 2 s. 9 d. it would not affect the sale at all.

### Mr. *Richard Bennett*, called in; and Examined.

Mr.
*Richard Bennett.*

10713. ARE you a silk manufacturer?—I am.

10714. Where do you carry on your manufacture?—The goods are manufactured at Spitalfields; the silk is thrown at Macclesfield.

10715. How long have you been engaged in the silk manufacture?—Twenty-one years.

10716. Is yours the plain or the fancy branch of the trade?—The plain branch exclusively.

10717. What was the condition of the manufacture previous to the opening of the Ports in 1826?—Previous to that time we were generally in an improving condition; we could give fair wages to the weavers, and the manufacturers also had a remunerating profit; the returns of the imports of silk up to 1826 would prove its progressive increase.

10718. What has been the state of the trade since that time?—It has been very unstable, attended with frequent fluctuations, and a gradual change for the worse.

10719. Did the admission of foreign silk produce any immediate bad consequence to the silk trade?—It caused an almost immediate reduction of wages and profits in every department of the trade; this reduction commenced in the following autumn.

10720. Has the reduction of wages and profit been gradual since 1826 up to the present period?—It has.

10721. What was the condition of the operatives previous to 1826?—Quite the reverse to what it is now as regards their comfort; for so numerous a class, they were considered the most respectable body of artizans.

10722. What has been their condition since that period?—Miserably altered for the worse; their low wages, combined with their more frequent want of employment, has subjected them to great privations and distress.

10723. Has this change produced ill effects on their morals and general demeanour?—Decidedly; their morals are much altered for the worse, and our own men are often obliged to work on a Sunday, which was not formerly the case.

Pilfering

Mr.
*Richard Bennett.*

6. July,
1832.

Pilfering is going on to a great extent. Formerly there used to be but little pilfering; now there are many instances where persons embezzle a whole piece, or two or three pieces, to the value of 40 *l.* or 50 *l.*

10724. Are they driven to that?—Yes; from their low wages and general distress.

10725. Do you attribute that distress to foreign competition?—I am decidedly of opinion that that is the chief cause.

10726. From the circumstance of trade being so unsteady, you are not able to give that constant employment you formerly did?—Most undoubtedly not; in former times we were in the habit of employing hands, for many years, on the same description of goods; trade was more steady, and the hands then produced their work in a better style than they do now.

10727. What description of goods are chiefly made in Spitalfields?—Principally the rich plain and fancy figured silks.

10728. Are there as many goods now made in Spitalfields as there were formerly?—Most certainly not.

10729. Has this decline in the manufacture arisen from a decline in the consumption?—Quite the reverse; of late years the consumption of silk goods has materially increased.

10730. Are you acquainted with the description of goods made in Manchester?—Yes; from every opportunity I have had of seeing the Manchester goods, they consist chiefly of a low class of goods, and also of mixed goods of silk and worsted, and silk and cotton.

10731. Does not Manchester supply goods suitable for the wear of the higher ranks of society?—I think not; there are few goods sold above 2 *s.* 6 *d.*; the greater portion are from 1 *s.* 9 *d.* to 2 *s.* 3 *d.*

10732. How do you account for the distress in Spitalfields at a time when the consumption of silk goods has greatly increased, and the public are not supplied with silk goods from Manchester?—The dealers in the higher classes of goods get supplied chiefly from abroad.

10733. Is there no competition between Spitalfields and Manchester?—There is a competition; for since the manufacturers of Spitalfields have been deprived of the manufacturing the better class of goods, they have turned their attention to the manufacturing of the lower description of goods, similar to those which are made in Manchester.

10734. Are you of opinion that the competition with Lyons, and not with Manchester, has caused the distress in Spitalfields?—Most decidedly.

10735. Do you think that every exertion has been made on the part of the trade to meet that foreign competition?—I think that every exertion has been made; from a calculation I made, it appears that silk goods are reduced in value full 25 per cent. by the reduction in wages, profits, dyeing, throwing, and in every other department of the trade, in order to meet the foreign competitor.

10736. This is without reference to the fall in the price of raw silk?—Yes.

10737. Is it possible to make any further reduction?—I think not.

10738. Are you of opinion that goods are as well woven now as formerly?—I should say there is no want of capability on the part of the weavers; but I think, from the low rate of wages which they receive, they do not do their work so well as they did formerly; their low rate of wages compels them to work so many hours, that in weaving a great length of work it is rarely made so perfect.

10739. At what do you estimate the average weekly earnings of a weaver?—I think their nett earnings do not exceed 8 *s.* or 9 *s.* a week; it used to be on plain goods, from 14 *s.* to 17 *s.*

10740. What effect did the alteration of the duties, in 1829, produce on the silk trade?—It caused a still further reduction to take place in the price of labour and profits, and also reductions in every other department of the trade.

10741. What was the object proposed?—The prevention of smuggling.

10742. Has that object been realized?—It has not.

10743. What ground have you for thinking that smuggling has increased in the country?—The fact of the large seizure that took place some time back is a convincing proof that smuggling is going on to a great extent. There are several parties in London who are avowed importers of foreign goods, whose names are never seen in the entries at the Custom House.

10744. What would be the effect of a further reduction on foreign thrown silk?

678.							—It

—It would produce very little benefit to the manufacturer, and almost a total ruin to the throwster.

10745. Do you think that smuggling was carried on to an extent during prohibition, so as to be injurious to trade?—I never heard of smuggling being carried on to an extent that was injurious to trade.

10746. Yet at that time there was a very great difference in the price between the French and English manufactured goods?—Much greater than now.

10747. Has the increase of smuggling been progressive?—I think it has.

10748. Do you think there are houses in the habit of smuggling now, who, during the existence of the prohibitory laws, would not have incurred the risk or the disgrace of smuggling?—I decidedly think so.

10749. Would you deem it prudent to embark any capital in the manufacture of figured silks in the present state of the trade?—I should deem it very imprudent in the present state of the law.

10750. In what manner does the importation of fancy and figured silks interfere with your branch of the trade, so as to induce you to come to that conclusion? —In the first place the taste of the public is entirely regulated by foreign fashion; it is impossible for the manufacturer here to have his new goods in the market at the same time that the French have theirs, so that the French take the lead.

10751. In the event of a reduction of duty, you cannot be protected from the market being visited with those goods technically called jobs?—Decidedly not.

10752. Has the manufacture of figured silks much declined since 1826 in Spitalfields?—I think there is not a tenth of the number of looms on figured silks there were a few years back; there used to be about 3,000 or 4,000 looms in figured and fancy goods; I think the utmost number now is from 300 to 500.

10753. From your knowledge of Spitalfields for 21 years, do you think that your statement of from 3,000 to 4,000 looms before the admission of foreign goods, is correct or not?—I think it is; that opinion is founded on a census taken of the number of looms employed at former periods.

10754. Would you think it prudent in a manufacturer to provide a stock of fancy silks for the spring or autumn trade?—Decidedly not; he would have to incur the same expense to produce a pattern as a whole piece; if he did not get any orders he would be all the expense out of pocket.

10755. Do you think the fancy branch is likely to become extinct by the continuance of the present system?—I think it would in time; if the manufacture dwindles away to the extent of the last six or seven years, people possessing knowledge and talent will back out of the trade, and turn their attention to something else; in a few years the fancy trade will be extinguished.

10756. Are you of opinion that in the event of prohibition there would be a sufficient home consumption to protect the public against extravagant prices for their silks?—I am of that opinion; there was sufficient competition before the introduction of foreign goods to answer that purpose.

10757. Is the home competition less now than it was then?—I think it has rather increased, and in addition to that we have also the competition with the foreigner; when the profits were reduced the trade endeavoured to make it up a little by increasing the quantity.

10758. You have no objection to any competition with English manufacture?— Decidedly not; that is all fair; we are all on the same footing.

10759. If your trade had the protection of the exclusion of foreign silks, do you think it would stimulate the manufacturer to make any exertion to produce goods possessing taste and skilful design, and be the means of extending the trade?—I am quite satisfied it would tend to improve the manufacture of fancy and figured silks, because the manufacturers would then possess greater encouragement; as it is now, he has no security for the capital he may expend in new and skilful designs, as he cannot obtain orders from the buyers.

10760. If the fancy branch could be extended, would that produce any beneficial effect on the plain branch of the trade?—Undoubtedly; it would relieve the plain branch by a number of persons who were formerly in the fancy trade, turning their attention to their legitimate trade of figured silks, and there would be less pressure on the plain branch than there is now.

10761. Would it not also relieve the operatives in Spitalfields, by taking the excessive supply of labour, which is now wholly confined, to the plain trade?— Decidedly.

10762. What

Mr.
*Richard Bennett.*

6 July,
1832.

10762. What advantage do the French possess over the English?—The advantage of growing about 3,000,000 lbs. of silk.

10763. Is the French manufacturer supplied with the silk so grown, at a lower price than you can purchase the raw material?—I am not in possession of any evidence as to price, but we infer so from the fact, that when our goods come into competition with theirs, they undersell us even with paying the duty.

10764. Might not that depend on less wages for labour?—France being a cheaper country, that has its influence on every department of trade.

10765. What in your opinion would be the best means of extending the Spitalfields manufacture?—The best plan would be an entire exclusion of foreign goods; a duty of 5 s. on foreign organzine, and 3 s. on tram, and some further protection against smuggling. Why should not the person who employs the smuggler, be subject to the same law himself?

10766. Would it not be a good penalty, that the person who wore smuggled goods should be placed in the pillory?—That depends on whether he has a knowledge of their being smuggled or not.

10767. Do you think it possible for a person to buy goods, without knowing whether they are smuggled?—The public know nothing of the matter.

10768. Yet you say they prefer French silks?—Decidedly, because they are cheaper.

10769. And how do they prefer French silks if they do not know them?—They are sent to them as French silks; there is a difference in the mode of getting them up; all French goods are folded in flat pieces like linen, while ours are generally on blocks.

10770. If a lady was sold a particular commodity, being French, selling at a less price, would she not be wholly blameless?—Yes.

10771. Is it the practice to tell the public that goods are smuggled, or to say nothing about it?—To say nothing about it.

10772. When you speak of prohibition, do you mean entire prohibition, or only a fancy and figured article?—Entire prohibition would be most beneficial, but if there were proper Custom House regulations entered into, with an anxious desire on the part of the Government to protect the trade against smuggling, the exclusion of figured goods, and the admission of plain goods, at a rate of duty, might serve us materially.

10773. Do you know the rate at which smuggling is now conducted?—I do not.

10774. Do you consider that it depends on the scale of duties paid for imported articles?—No doubt that has some influence.

10775. Short of a prohibition, you do not conceive the trade would be protected?—That is my firm opinion.

10776. What will improve the trade of this country, would you increase the price of the article, or in what way would improvement take place?—We should have the manufacture of those goods which are imported.

10777. In what way would prohibition operate?—It would be beneficial in one respect, by acting as a stimulus to trade, which would afford a little advance to the operative and a little profit to the manufacturer.

10778. Would it also increase the price to the consumer?—Undoubtedly it would tend to increase the price of the article; it would be at the expense of the rich instead of the poor.

10779. Would not that lessen the quantity to be used?—It would have little or no effect on the consumption.

10780. Lowering ribbons from 10 d. to 8 d., or from 1 s. to 10 d., would have no effect on the consumption?—Very trifling.

10781. Would it have an effect if it was 20 per cent.?—Decidedly.

10782. It is a matter of degree with you?—Where a person goes to a shop to buy three or four yards of ribbon, whether it comes to 3 s. 4 d. or 4 s. is of little importance.

10783. Do not the public indulge themselves in silk articles of greater cost than are made in England?—Decidedly.

10784. Whether they pay five per cent. more or less is no consideration with them, and would not deter them from the purchase of it?—Certainly not.

10785. Do not persons indulge themselves in this way without reference to the absolute value of the thing they purchase?—No doubt of it.

10786. Is it not the case sometimes, that an article which will afford little practical advantage is sold at a higher price than a commodity which, if the wear

678. and

and durability was looked at, would afford twice the quantity ?—There is no question of it.

10787. People coming to buy a fancy article look to fancy more than quality ?—Most undoubtedly.

10788. Are you concerned in a throwing mill ?—I am.

10789. What circumstance induced you to become a throwster ?—Formerly our trade was to that extent that we sent to our throwsters 5 or 6,000 *l.* worth of raw silk, in order to secure a sufficient supply when thrown; but finding that our profits were gradually diminishing, we were induced to combine the profits of a throwster by investing that capital in a silk mill, which would require a much less stock of raw silk than by employing several throwsters.

10790. Is it your opinion that English thrown organzine is equal to foreign ?—I think it is better.

10791. Is the consumption of Piedmontese organzine very great ?—No, I think the consumption is somewhere from 60,000 to 80,000 lbs. per annum.

10792. What description of Italian raw silk do you consider the best ?—The Fossembrone.

10793. Is that applicable to every description of figured silk ?—There is hardly an article of the rich plain or figured silks in which it may not be used to advantage, equally as well as Piedmontese silk.

10794. If the duties of foreign thrown silk were further reduced, would they send a greater quantity of raw here ?—If you give further encouragement to the Italian throwster, it will be an inducement to him to establish mills and export the Fossembrone in a thrown state, some portion of which would go to other markets.

10795. Do you think the Italian would continue to send as large a quantity of good raw as he now does, if the duties were further reduced ?—Decidedly not; it would be an inducement to him to throw more silk; there are many throwsters in Italy who are also growers of silk.

10796. Would not the Italian send his silk to the place where he could get the highest price ?—If he had a mill he would keep his own mill employed and take the chance of the market.

10797. Have the Italians mills, who grow the silks ?—Most of them have. I am in the habit of buying thrown and raw, and I know that both thrown and raw come from the same party.

10798. Does the party throw it himself or buy it thrown ?—There are very few exceptions, where the exporter of thrown silk is not a throwster.

10799. Do you mean that the persons who send the silk here are throwsters ?—Decidedly so.

10800. To what part of Italy do you allude ?—Bergamo. I wish to correct what I said before in reference to the growing of silk; the cocoons are taken to the markets there, the persons who purchase the cocoons are reelers and throwsters and they export it here in a thrown state.

10801. Is silk thrown in Italy at a less price than in England ?—Considerably less, from the difference of the rate of wages between the two countries, and also from the circumstance that Italian thrown silk is imported here at a much less price than I can work for.

10802. Can you state what the wages are there ?—From the best information, I believe it can be thrown at Bergamo for from 2*s.* 6*d.* to 3*s.* per pound, while I cannot do it for 5*s.* to afford me any profit as a throwster.

10803. If the Italian can send the silk to this country at 16*s.* in the raw state, and at 18*s.* 6*d.* thrown, if the duty is repealed, will you be able to get the raw at 16*s.* when he can introduce his thrown at 18*s.* 6*d.*?—Decidedly not.

10804. What did you pay per pound before you built your own mill ?—It varied from 7*s.* to 8*s.* 6*d.*

10805. Cannot you have it thrown now for 4*s.*?—I could not do it for 4*s.*; I know that Italian organzine is thrown for 4*s.* and even under that, but when a man is ground down in his price he attempts to do it without performing the whole of the process; some is done that is not even cleaned.

10806. Is it not also the case that you are obliged to depress the wages of the people you employ ?—Of course.

10807. Are those who throw organzine at 4*s.* getting a profit, or is it only to keep their machinery going ?—I believe to keep their machinery going.

10808. Do you think the silk is thrown so well now as it used to be ?—I think
the

Mr.
*Richard Bennett.*

6 July,
1832.

the bulk of the silk is not thrown so well as it used to be; when men are ill paid they cannot afford to do it so well as when they were better paid.

10809. If the throwster had a large protecting duty would he make it better than he does now?—Certainly.

10810. Is the throwing of silk materially altered since the duty was lowered?—It has had the effect of compelling the throwster to do his work at that price which will not allow him to do it so well as he would were he better paid.

10811. Was it better under a protecting duty?—I think it was.

10812. In point of fact, do you think that the throwing in this country has gone back?—I think generally it has, from a want of a remunerating price.

---

*Lunæ, 9° die Julii*, 1832.

EDWARD AYSHFORD SANFORD, ESQUIRE, IN THE CHAIR.

Mr. *William Wallis*, called in; and Examined.

Mr.
*William Wallis*

9 July,
1832.

10813. ARE you a silk weaver?—I am; I have been in the trade about 28 years.

10814. In what branch of the silk trade?—I was some years ago in the fancy branch; but of later years I have been more engaged in the plain branch; since 1824, particularly so.

10815. Where do you reside?—In the parish of St. Matthew Bethnal Green. I have lived in my present abode more than 21 years.

10816. Are you acquainted with the situation of the working classes in Spitalfields?—With the working classes of Bethnal Green more particularly; living more immediately among them. The situation of the silk weavers of the district called Spitalfields, is pretty much the same with those of Bethnal Green. The parish of Spitalfields itself contains a very small number of weavers comparatively.

10817. Do you live in Bethnal Green or Spitalfields?—In Bethnal Green.

10818. What is the condition of the Spitalfields population at present, taking in all the district?—Distressed in the extreme. The condition of the weavers, generally speaking, at the present moment, is below any thing I ever saw. I have seen distress in those districts certainly, many years ago; but never any thing like what it is at present. I have had, from time to time, the honour of having interviews with the Board of Trade; and I confess here, as I have done there, that the distress has progressively increased since the introduction of the new laws, to a greater extent than it has ever done before. The people, from the time of the alteration of the system of importation, have been continually reduced; from a reduction in wages, and a consequent reduction in their situation to meet that reduction in wages, they are wretched in the extreme. The last winter was such a one as I have never yet seen, and if the trade has to undergo such another winter, in point of employment, as the last, hundreds of thousands will feel the effect of it, and thousands will die of want. The parish is in that state of distress that they can no longer support the people. Within the last six years the parish have incurred a debt of 13,000l.; previous to 1824 they had no debt. Now, as I have stated, they have one of 13,000l., with no means of discharging any of it. I beg leave to put in a Statement of the Number of Out-door and In-door Poor receiving relief.

10819. From whence did you obtain this document?—It is obtained from the Vestry Clerk of St. Matthew Bethnal Green. An Account of the number of Poor in the Workhouse of this parish, and likewise the number of Casual Poor, or those receiving out door relief, from the year 1821 to the present period, averaging the allowance per head 1 s. 6 d. weekly. In 1821, the casual out door poor were 157; in the house, 498: 1822, out door, 196; in the house, 498; 1823, out-door, 223; in the house, 526: 1824, out-door, 289; in the house, 633: 1825, out-door, 326; in the house, 721: 1826, out-door, 984; in the house, 588: 1827, out-door, 638; in the house, 842: 1828, out-door, 1,319; in the house, 956: 1829, out-door, 2,487; in the house 796: 1830, out-door, 4,693; in the house, 1,092: 1831, out-door, 4,958; in the house, 1,380: 1832, out-door, 6,218; in the house, 1,160. The next paper I beg to put in is from the same authority; namely, the Vestry Clerk, and the

678.				reference

reference to 1822 from a document in my possession obtained at the time in 1822. It is an Account of the Number of Pensioners on the four divisional books; I mean those who receive regular weekly pay, independent of the casual out-door poor. In 1822, the number in the division called the Green Division was 61; the Church Division, 107; the Town Division, 103; the Hackney Road Division, 99: total, 371. In 1832, up to the present time, the Green Division was 274; the Church Division, 125; the Town Division, 147; the Hackney Road Division, 125: making a total of 621. They average each family as consisting of four persons; some have families of six or seven children; some of two or three, and some are single persons; but they average each family at four, making the total number of persons who receive this relief, 2,684.

10820. To what date is this paper made up?—It is made up to last January. I have a paper here, differing a little from the last; I obtained it from the master of the workhouse, stating the number of persons in the poor-house on the 26th March 1822, which was 469; on the 21st of May, 463: on the 25th of March 1823, 548; 20th May, 517: on the 23d of March 1824, 639; on the 18th of May 593: in 1825, March 22d, 521; 17th May, 465: in 1826, March 21st, 745; 16th May, 699: in 1827, March 20th, 687; 15th May, 644: in 1828, March 18th, 659; 13th May 637: in 1824, March 24th, 1,015; 19th May, 1,014: in 1830, March 23d, 1,215; 18th May, 912: in 1831, March 22d, 906; 17th May, 908: in 1832, January 3d, 940; 28th February, 843; 27th March, 725; on the 24th of April, 650; May 29th, 625; June 24th, 620; July 4th, 675. There is an explanation required here; in the early part of the year, owing to the sickness breaking out in the Metropolis, which showed its appearance in the workhouse of St. Matthew Bethnal Green, there was a direct order from the Secretary of State to clear the house; at that time there were from 12 to 1,300 people in the house; and it is not calculated, with comfort, to hold more than 600 or 700. A large room in the house, that had been a workshop, was fitted up and applied to the purpose of a sort of infirmary; and in addition to which, they were compelled to turn out all the able-bodied young men, with a sort of pension, to keep them out of the house, and prevent an extension of the disorder; that accounts for the difference in the paper in the present year, as compared with former years.

10821. The first paper you put in contains a period of 12 years; taking the first six, am I correct in finding that the number of in-door poor was 3,807, and for the last six years 6,397?—I have no hesitation in saying that it is correct, from my own opinion as to the appearance of the district; but I take it for granted that the vestry clerk has made the return from the official books.

10822. It also appears by this paper, that the out-door or casual poor were, on an average for the first six years, 2,175, and for the last six years 20,313?—That I am sorry to say, I can very fairly corroborate from appearances which came under my own observations; the Board day is twice a week; and I am sure I often go out of my way to avoid passing the house and witnessing the scenes of misery which are to be seen on that spot of ground, of persons trying to get this relief; they are relieved on Tuesdays and Thursdays, and there is a double Board sitting for eight or nine or ten hours, with scarcely time to take any refreshment. I have no hesitation in saying, that this return is quite correct.

10823. To what cause do you ascribe the increased distress?—I attribute it to no other cause than the introduction of foreign wrought silk; because the distress has been progressive from that time up to the present period; I have no hesitation in saying, that from 1826 up to the present period, however persons may appear out of doors, if you saw them in their own dwellings they are not the same people compared with those of 1824, 1825 and 1826; their furniture, in hundreds of instances is entirely gone, and their homes made desolate, and without the common necessaries for use.

10824. Was the distress in Spitalfields, at any former period within your recollection, so great as it was last winter?—I have known distress in Spitalfields at very distant periods; there was distress 22 years ago, but it arose from a different cause and was transient; the people had the means within themselves to fall back upon resources that they had been able to obtain during their employment at reasonable wages.

10825. State the periods at which you have known distress?—About 1812 I thing there was a period of very great distress; about 1816 there was a great deal of distress, but that distress was not felt by the silk trade generally; wherever it fell among the silk weavers it arose from the circumstances of there being a number

of

Mr.
*William Wallis.*

9 July,
1832.

of persons discharged from the army and navy, but the trade generally was pretty good, as I see by looking back to returns and accounts which I have in my possession; the persons in employment were in good circumstances, and the parish of Bethnal Green was not in the state that it is now; in fact they were not more than ordinarily distressed at that time. There has been considerable distress from time to time in consequence of the change of fashion, but nothing to equal the present in its intensity.

10826. Was the other period subsequent to 1816?—I do not recollect any other period in particular; I know we have had slight distress for a few months, but I cannot recollect the exact period.

10827. From 1812 to 1816 are the subsequent periods, which was the greatest distressed?—The subsequent period is not to be compared to either of the others. At the former periods people recovered from their distress when they got into full employment, since the repeal of the prohibitory laws that has not been the case; in proportion as employment has fell off they have not been able to recover their lost circumstances, and if they got into arrears of rent and lost their goods they had no opportunity when they got into work to purchase fresh ones, and they remained in the same state of destitution; for the last six years the state of distress has been progressive and alarming, and if we are to undergo a similar winter to that which we endured last, the scenes in Bethnal Green and Spitalfields will be truly horrible.

10828. In point of fact you never knew any period in which the distress was so great as it was last year?—Never.

10829. When was the book abolished?—In 1824.

10830. In the previous periods of distress wages could not have been lowered before the book rates?—In the previous periods of distress, although wages never were high, most people had the means to recover themselves, and had not this been followed by a repeal of the prohibitory laws, and trade remained under that fostering protection which it had before received, the people would have recovered their lost ground; as a proof of that, in consequence of the arrangement of Government in 1824 to meet the difficulties in 1826 by allowing the trade two years to prepare for the introduction of foreign goods, the consequence was, that the trade revived from the transient distress occasioned by the discussion of the question in 1824; that was accompanied by a slight advance in the wages then paid, but as soon as the introduction of foreign goods began, then the reduction of wages commenced, and from that period they have never been able to recover from the distressed state of things which they were thrown into, and which has progressively increased from time to time up to the present. I do not attribute that distress to the book of prices, which I think was always misunderstood, but to the repeal of the prohibitory laws. Whatever necessity there was for an alteration in the rate of wages between master and man, on any given kind of work, the regulations were always made by a mutual agreement, and, under the influence of the Act of Parliament, made binding on all persons in the district by an order of Sessions, and the Act had no influence on raising or lowering the rate of wages, it had only the influence of protecting the trade, both masters and men, from that cutting competition that exists by one man receiving $4\frac{1}{2}d$. while another man was receiving $6d$. or $7d$. for the same description of work, and thus destroying one another.

10831. From 1824 to 1826 the prices given to the weavers were the book prices?—They were.

10832. Was that the case during a considerable part of 1826?—I think not; they began to reduce either early in 1826 or at the latter end of 1825.

10833. The effect of the book was only to ratify and legalize an agreement between the master and the workmen?—Unless there was a dispute between the parties as to the settlement, and then the question was decided at quarter sessions after an inquiry, in the usual way.

10834. Were not all the weavers employed at one time in 1830?—It is possible they might be; I believe there was rather a brisk trade.

10835. Has the trade for the last six years increased in Spitalfields?—I think it has not much altered; the number of looms, from the best means I have of ascertaining them, is rather more; I think the number was greater in 1824 and 1825, in consequence of the stimulus given by the Government delaying the importation from 1824 to 1826, and allowing the drawback on goods on hand; it has been nearly stationary since; my own opinion is, there is nearly 17,000 in the district.

10836. Were there as many as that six years ago?—No doubt, full as many as that.

678.                                                                                    10837. You

Mr.
*William Wallis.*

9 July,
1832.

10837. You speak of the whole district ?—Yes.

10838. How many are there in the parish of Bethnal Green ?—From the best evidence I can obtain, about 12,000.

10839. What was the number six years ago?—Not quite as many ; Bethnal Green has been progressively increasing in buildings, owing to its being a more airy situation than the parish of Spitalfields.

10840. Do you apprehend that the quantity of looms has not increased for the last six years in the whole district?—I think there is not likely to be the means within the district of Spitalfields of enlarging the number of looms, for the trade is so ill protected; Spitalfields always had an ambition to make the first class of work.

10841. What are the rate of wages now paid?—I hold in my hand a statement of the rates of wages paid at different periods; it is for one given quality of work all through, not taking the lowest or the highest, but steering a middle course. In 1769, for a 1,000 single sarsnet, 20 inches, it was $5\frac{1}{2}d.$; in 1795, $6d.$; in 1806, $6d.$; in 1825, $6\frac{1}{2}d.$; and in 1832, $4d.$ I have ascertained the rate of prices of the present year from the best of all possible authorities, from the actual existence of wages we are now paying.

10842. Do you mean to say, that in 1769, it was $5\frac{1}{2}d.$, and that in 1832, it is reduced to $4d.$?—That is the fact.

10843. What would be the average earnings of a fair workman?—For a double sarsnet, of the same description two double threads, in 1769, it was $6\frac{1}{2}d.$; in 1795, $7\frac{1}{2}d.$; in 1806, $8d.$; in 1825, $8d.$; and in 1832, $4\frac{1}{2}d.$: 1100 three threads, in 1769, $7d.$; in 1795, $8d.$; in 1806, $9d.$; in 1825, $10d.$; and in 1832, $5d.$: for a three double the gros de Naples,* in 1825, $12d.$; and in 1832, $6\frac{1}{2}d.$: the 1000 four thread mantua, in 1769, $7d.$; in 1795, $8d.$; in 1806, $9d.$; in 1825, $10d.$; and in 1832, $6d.$: the four double ducape, in 1769, $9d.$; in 1795, $10d.$; in 1806, $12d.$; in 1825, $12d.$; and in 1832, $9d.$: the 1500 four thread mantua, for umbrellas, 24 inches in width, in 1769, $10d.$; in 1795, $12d.$; in 1806, $13d.$; in 1825, $14d.$; and in 1832, $8d.$: satins, the 1000, five thread, in 1769, $8d.$; in 1795, $9d.$; in 1806, $10\frac{1}{2}d.$; in 1825, $10\frac{1}{2}d.$; and in 1832, $6d.$: the 1000 six thread, in 1769, $8d.$; in 1795, $9d.$; in 1806, $10\frac{1}{2}d.$; in 1825, $10\frac{1}{2}d.$; and in 1832, $6d.$: 1000 eight thread, in 1769, $10d.$; in 1795, $12d.$; in 1806, $14\frac{1}{2}d.$; in 1825, $14\frac{1}{2}d.$; and in 1832, $10d.$: 1000 ten thread, in 1769, $14d.$; in 1795, $15d.$; in 1806, $17d.$; in 1825, $17d.$; and in 1832, $12d.$: the 1000 twelve thread, in 1769, $16d.$; in 1795, $18d.$; in 1806, $21d.$; in 1825, $21d.$; and in 1832, $16d.$: velvets, that is in 1825, $4s.$; and in 1832, $2s.$ $6d.$; 1200 velvets, two threads, in 1825, $4s.$ $6d.$; and in 1832, $3s.$ $3d.$; that requires a great deal of skill and ingenuity, as will be seen by the pattern which I exhibit, it was made by one of the best workmen in the trade, and after working 16 hours, he could not make more than three quarters of a yard, and he had to employ a person to attend him at the rate of $18d.$ a week to keep him on.

> \* This work was not known in 1769 or 1795, or in 1806, to any extent.

10844. Are the prices paid for weaving velvets now the same as you have now given ?—Yes.

10845. Are the velvet weavers, at this moment, all employed or not?—There is rather an early trade in velvet weaving; they are beginning to put them up.

10846. Has there been any advance in the wages of weaving velvets ?—I have not heard of greater prices than were given last year. I believe the last year may be a criterion for the prices of this year; the statement which I hold in my hand, shows a progressive decline in the price of weaving since 1825; that takes in figured goods, 1100 three single, in 1827, $8d.$; in 1828, $7d.$; in 1829, $6d.$ and $5d.$; in 1830, $6d.$ and $6\frac{1}{2}d.$; in 1831, $5d.$; and in 1832, $5d.$: 1100 three double, in 1827, $9d.$; in 1828, $8d.$; in 1829, $6d.$ and $7d.$; in 1830, $7d.$; in 1831, $6d.$; and in 1832, $6\frac{1}{2}d.$; 1000 four single, in 1827, $9d.$; in 1828, $8d.$; in 1829, $7d.$ and $8d.$; in 1830, $7d.$; in 1831, $6d.$; and in 1832, $6d.$; 1200 velvets, in 1827, $4s.$ $6d.$; in 1828, $4s.$ $3d.$; in 1829, $3s.$ $9d$; in 1830, $3s.$ $6d.$; in 1831, $3s.$ and $3s.$ $3d.$; and in 1832, $3s.$ $3d.$: 400 cords Jacquard, in 1824, was paid $2s.$ $2d.$; in 1825, $2s.$; in 1826, $1s.$ $10d.$; in 1827, $1s.$ $10d.$; in 1828, $1s.$ $8d.$; in 1829, $1s.$ $6d.$; in 1830, $1s.$ $4d.$ in 1831, $1s.$ $3d.$; and in 1832, $1s.$ $1d.$ and $1s.$

10847. Generally speaking, has there been an advance on wages ?—No advance; rather a depression than an advance, to my knowledge, at the present time.

10848. But the weavers are employed ?—They are getting into work in the velvet branches; this is rather an early date for velvets, they are worked up for winter consumption.

10849. Are

Mr.
William Wallis.

9 July,
1832.

10849. Are the weavers, generally, at Spitalfields, pretty well employed?—I am afraid not as well as a month ago; I have heard a great many accounts lately of persons going out of work, and several houses will not take in more hands. I was told on Saturday, of one house in Spital-square, turning out all their hands.

10850. Is it not the part of the year at which there is generally the greatest demand for labour?—The period just passed, including the last two months, is certainly so; but just at present there is generally a change of fashion.

10851. In the paper which you have put in, giving the statement of prices, I suppose it is the three doubles which are the articles of the greatest consumption?—No, the three singles; the three singles and the three doubles are the same article, but one is of a richer texture than the other.

10852. These are the greater articles of manufacture in that district?—They comprise three-fourths of the looms of Spitalfields at the present time.

10853. Am I correct in understanding from this paper that the price of the three singles was, in 1825, 1826 and 1832, 5 d., and that the price of the double was, in 1825, 12 d. and in 1832, 6 ½ d.?—These are prices taken from books in my own possession.

10854. Am I to understand that in the great articles of manufacture in Spitalfields, the prices have fallen since 1825?—They have.

10855. When was the Jacquard loom introduced into Spitalfields?—In 1822; the prices paid under the Jacquard, show the progressive decline better. In 1824, the four-double made under a Jacquard was 2 s. 2 d.; in 1825 it fell to 2 s.; in 1826, to 1 s. 9 d.

10856. That is what would be called a richer article?—Yes, it is; this is the article I allude to [exhibiting it.] Here are the prices paid to one man for one kind of velvet, in 1827, 1828 and 1829, he was paid the same all through; 1830 and 1831, the velvet was a richer one. He was a very excellent workman; in 1827 he received for the work 4 s. 6 d., and so in 1828; in 1829, 3 s. 9 d.; in 1830, 3 s. 6 d.; in 1831, 3 s. 3 d. and 3 s., and he does the same work now at 3 s.

10857. There were several articles made in Spitalfields prior to 1824, the whole of which has been transferred to the country?—The article of Italian nets has been entirely taken away; I had a deal to do in that some years ago, and earned a good livelihood by it. I worked 13 years for one house, that was famous for that and lustres.

10858. Was not that transferred to the country?—Not till it went out of fashion in London.

10859. Has not the article of figured lustres been transferred to the country?—Not till it was out of fashion; perhaps the Committee will allow me to show a progressive rate of patterns from the earliest period up to the present time, to show that there was always a progressive inclination to improvement throughout the silk trade, before the opening of the Ports; since the opening of the Ports, we have not gone on faster in improvement than we did before. We made as good works previous to the commencement of 1821, 1822 and 1823, without the Jacquard as were imported from France through illicit trading, with the Jacquard.

10860. Has not the article of figured handkerchiefs been lost to Spitalfields since 1824?—It was never made to any extent in Spitalfields in my remembrance, it was made a great many years ago, but it has gone to Macclesfield, and made way for the more substantial article of gros de Naples.

10861. Do you remember bombazines being made in Spitalfields?—Yes, I do.

10862. That article has left Spitalfields a great many years?—Yes; not from want of being able to accomplish the work, but owing to the change of colour; I do not think the difference between the prices in Spitalfields and in Norwich was the cause, but a change of fashion to French instead of the original English black. A dyer in London, knowing the particular means of dyeing in a peculiar manner, the colour desired, but the alteration in fashion gave the Norwich manufacturer the means of dyeing them at home instead of sending them to London, and thereby save the expense; this with other facilities in the manufacture of bombazines peculiar to Norwich, finally drew the trade from London.

10863. Do you remember gauzes and crapes being manufactured in Spitalfields?—Yes.

10864. Have not they left Spitalfields for a great many years?—Yes; for the same reason that the other articles have.

10865. It was prior to 1824 that there was any change?—Whenever change of fashion took place in any particular article, and when the first sale of it was over,

a larger

a larger quantity at a cheaper price was manufactured, generally by Macclesfield, Manchester or other places.

10866. You would not call Italian crapes or bombazines fashionable articles?—Not now; they were at one time much in demand, as fashionable articles for mourning; there was a peculiar feature in the bombazines. It was quite common at that time that the goods made at Norwich should be carried up to London to be dyed and dressed, and that was in a great measure the cause of the trade being carried on to a certain extent, for they saved the expense of a great portion of the work; when a change of colour took place, then the bombazines went to Norwich, the silk weaver never thought fit to look after it, for it was an article very little manufactured among us.

10867. Gros de Naples are not subject to such fluctuations of prices in Spitalfields?—I believe not.

10868. Has not that rendered it more easy to transfer the trade to the country?—It might have been in some respects, but I do not see the effect of that; the rich gros de Naples would not answer the Manchester manufacturers; the three-single they manufacture in the greatest abundance, the articles of a richer description are those in which we are interfered with by France.

10869. Do they not manufacture goods equal to those manufactured at Spitalfields?—I have seen goods equal in quality, but no manufactures are equal to this; I have never seen any thing so rich as this [*exhibiting it*] from Manchester.

10870. Are not some of the weavers removing from Spitalfields to Manchester?—I am not aware of any to any extent.

10871. Are you aware that some masters have removed?—I know of no one, and one only; and the last time I heard of him in 1828, was, that he was doing scarcely any thing.

10872. Do you know that satins are now making at Manchester?—I wrote to Manchester to ascertain that fact, and I could not get any one to say they were.

10873. Have you heard that velvets are now making there?—I have been told that they are not making there; it is the Manchester plain goods that come in competition with us.

10874. In the alteration in the trade in Spitalfields, have the lower classes of goods increased in quantity, as the superior classes diminished?—The lower classes have increased, and the high or richer fabrics diminished in consequence of the importation of foreign goods.

10875. Have the quantity of goods which formerly were manufactured, of a superior description in Spitalfields, given place to the manufacture of an inferior description of goods in Spitalfields?—It certainly has; more inferior goods are made in Spitalfields now than were formerly.

10876. Does a weaver earn more in manufacturing superior goods, than he does in manufacturing the inferior class?—Considerably so; but the wages for weaving figured goods have been reduced in a larger proportion that the wages for weaving plain.

10877. In the instances in which there has been a change, in which an article formerly made in Spitalfields has been removed to the country, has it ever occurred that the cause of that was, that it had gone entirely out of fashion, and ceased to be an article of consumption, and that it was revived in distant country places?—It might have been so; I am inclined to think, from all the observations I can make on that subject, that no articles have left Spitalfields while in full protection and demand. The Manchester manufacturers have taken up an article in gros de Naples, and are now commencing a manufacture, some samples of which I have from a house in the city; they do not interfere with the gros de Naples made in Spitalfields; the quality of them would not sell to a great extent in London; these are the best goods which I could get at Manchester, and it will be easily seen that they do not interfere with us at all.

10878. Will the best goods that are obtained at Manchester, compete with the French goods?—No, for the same reason that they will not compete with Spitalfields; the class of persons that purchase French goods, purchase them for the excellence of their fabric and texture.

10879. What is the proportion of three doubles in Spitalfields, to three singles?—Somewhere about one-third.

10880. Has the trade been more liable to fluctuation since the alteration than it was before?—Very considerably so; the fluctuation was nothing, compared to the present moment; there is scarcely a question about the excellence of the workmanship

manship as there used to be; I mean he who was a good workman, was sure to be retained in his employment; that is not the case now, if there is any slack, every one is turned out of employment indiscriminately, without reference to length of service, or good workmanship.

Mr.
*William Wallis.*

9 July,
1832.

10881. What was the character of the silk weaver before the alteration?—Generally his character was industrious and sober; the best way I can describe, is by appealing to their conduct on former questions, when the repeal of the prohibitory laws was agitated; when they made their appearance in this neighbourhood in such large numbers, their conduct was such as became them as a large body of men to a great extent.

10882. Does it appear that any material alteration has taken place since 1824 and 1825?—I see no resemblance in hundreds, to what there was at that time.

10883. Do you think the reduction of wages and distress has had an evil effect on their morals and habits?—No doubt of it; a discontented mind, arising from want of means to keep up their appearance, and the constant weight of petty demands on them without the means of discharging them; that very circumstance and not being able to send their children to a place of worship or a Sunday school, are all of them circumstances that have not only affected their morals, but their particular character; they begin to lend an ear to any thing that may be said against the Government, and are subject to make use of disrespectful expressions, when I am sure that a few years ago nothing of the kind would have occurred; distress makes a man say what he would never think of under easier circumstances; from the want of means to put themselves in possession of the right cause, they ascribe the whole cause of the distress to the Government, as well as the taxes, and a repeal of the prohibitory laws, and feel an enmity where they ought to feel a confidence.

10884. You have stated that there are about 12,000 looms in the parish of Bethnal Green, how many of these were out of employ at the commencement of this year?—Unfortunately we have no regular statement, not having the means to obtain it without considerable expense and trouble; from the best information I can gain, there were from 5,000 to 6,000 in Bethnal Green alone; in 1826, there were 7,721 looms out of employ; in 1832, from the best estimate I could form, and from a comparative calculation made from 1,500 looms taken in three separate districts, one a good one, one an inferior one, and one rather a bad one, there were about 7,000 in the whole out of work; that is rather over than under the mark.

10885. Has the competition with Manchester, or the competition with France been most detrimental to the trade of Spitalfields?—Competition with France, for the reasons before stated, I do not consider Manchester in competition with us; I consider we are in competition with Manchester, being obliged to take up those articles which we ought to be able to lay down.

10886. What proportion of looms do you consider are engaged in the fancy trade in Spitalfields, at the present time, and what in the plain?—I take it, throughout the whole of the trade, not more than 250 are engaged in the figured and fancy branches; another portion are engaged in the rich kind of plain works, that is an article which would come under the class of superior articles; there is a branch of the trade which for some time has been very prosperous, that is the figured waistcoat branch; that has maintained its station better than most branches in the trade, owing to the little interference with foreign competition; the average earnings on that kind of work during the last twelve months have been from 16 *s.* to 18 *s.* or 20 *s.*, working from sixteen to eighteen hours, and sometimes on a Sunday, at a price of 2 *s.* 4 *d.* which they are now reducing to 2 *s.*; that is a branch of trade which requires a great deal of strength as well as skilful workmanship to accomplish.

10887. Are there only 150 looms employed on figured silks?—Not more than from 150 to 200.

10888. What was the proportion formerly?—Full a third; and I have known, when the fancy branch of the trade was in full demand, nearly half the looms to be employed on figured silks.

10889. What is the proportion now?—I think about one-eighth; there has been an impression made on this Committee that we owed our excellence to the circumstance of the importation of French goods; I am desirous to show that we made figured silks for many years before French goods were thought of.

10890. Is it true that you have derived considerable advantage in the trade from the patterns you received from France?—I think not; we were progressively improving quite as fast or faster before French goods were introduced, and it is true

678.                                                                                        that

Mr.
*William Wallis.*

9 July,
1832.

that we have under very depressed circumstances followed them and kept pace with them.

10891. Do you think that you were progressively increasing as much before the alteration as you have in the subsequent period?—I think more so; I beg to exhibit a pattern of brocade made about the year 1750; these patterns that I exhibit have the date written on them when they were made and by whom, and they show a change of pattern and improvement of figure; here are others of the same man's production, which are marked on the edge; these were made for ladies' scarfs, and were very fashionable at that time.

10892. Is this not composed of Bengal silk?—Yes it is; and it is more applicable to that work than a better kind of silk; I have a pattern here of a silk which was made sixteen years ago for a house in Bow-lane, Cheapside, for oriental turbans, and I beg to hand in some velvet patterns from sixty to seventy years old; I have also some patterns of gauze made from twenty-five to forty years ago; that is a branch of trade which is entirely lost to Spitalfields.

10893. Are you aware that a large quantity is made at Paisley?—I am.

10894. Do you think that a higher rate of wages can be continued to be paid to the weavers in Spitalfields than is paid at Manchester?—I have no doubt of it at all, if we were protected against French goods; I think we pay a higher rate of wages now than Manchester.

10895. Do you think that in the event of a prohibition there would be a greater difference than there is now between the wages at Spitalfields and Manchester? —About the same difference as there always has been.

10896. Do you not conceive, that if the same sort of work was made in Spitalfields as at Manchester, the same price would be paid for it?—I think not.

10897. Suppose you removed your loom to Manchester, and that you were working with superior kinds of goods, would you not pay the same wages which you now pay in Spitalfields?—I think not, there might be a shade difference.

10898. Where do you receive the most?—In Spitalfields.

10899. Why do you conceive that will be the case?—An article in full demand as a fashionable article would be started at Spitalfields, and Manchester would be placed in the exact relative condition that we are placed as regards France; the first introduction of a fancy article always commands a higher price.

10900. If it was merely a plain article, in which fancy had nothing to do, then of course it would be just the same in Spitalfields as at Manchester?—The colour would make a slight difference; this which I now hold in my hand has been made in Spitalfields, and succeeds there; if Manchester interferes with Spitalfields at all, it is for the country trade, and not in rich goods.

10901. Is it not true, that in every branch of manufacture a town-made article fetches a higher price than a country-made article?—I do not know that, that applies to Spitalfields in particular.

10902. Do you think there is any difficulty in a man's turning from weaving a piece of fine muslin to the manufacture of gros de Naples?—Not a great deal of difficulty.

10903. Do you think that the rate of wages paid in Manchester would be the same as those obtained by a person employed on a muslin?—Very like it might, that would depend entirely on circumstances; if there was a demand for silk, the muslin weaver would get better wages for silk, and he would go to it. In Spitalfields there are two or three who were originally muslin weavers, that are now in the silk trade: unless a man can earn more by silk than muslin, he will not go to it.

10904. You think that a man might earn a trifle more in weaving silk than cotton?—I should think so.

10905. If the wages for cotton were to fall, would not the wages for weaving silk also fall?—That is possible.

10906. Do you imagine that the number employed in the silk trade in Lancashire is one-tenth of what is employed in the cotton trade?—I have no idea of that.

10907. Do you not believe that it is a very inconsiderable number compared with those employed in the cotton trade?—I should think so.

10908. Do you not therefore think, that the wages for weaving silk depends on the state of the labouring classes employed in the manufacture of cotton goods?— It depends on the same circumstances as it does in Spitalfields; if there is a great depression in trade, people are glad to take what work they can get; the Manchester people themselves are best able to answer that question.

10909. Can a cotton weaver manufacture fancy goods?—I should think not.

10910. Will

Mr.
*William Wallis.*

9 July,
1832.

10910. Will your observation apply to the plain trade?—It goes to that description.

10911. Are you acquainted with the article called the Cambra?—Yes, there are figured and plain.

10912. Have there not always been a quantity of mixed figured goods made at Manchester?—Yes, it is the link between the two trees; the cambra forms a portion of the cotton trade, being part cotton and part silk.

10913. Could not a person accustomed to weave silk and cotton, easily make an article of pure silk?—Very likely.

10914. That being the case, do you think that in the event of a prohibition, the wages at Spitalfields for working the common article would advance?—I think they would a little; they are lower now than ever they were.

10915. Do you not think that Spitalfields, being connected with, as it is at Manchester, the condition of the weavers, must improve or deteriorate, according as the condition of the weavers in the country improves or otherwise?—I think if that had been the case, they would have been better off than now, for I have known the cotton trade to be in worse circumstances than it is now.

10916. Did not the book prevent that on former occasions?—I do not think the book ever interfered with it; the book kept the prices in Spitalfields at a regulated rate, but never had that effect in Manchester; if it had been a barometer of price paid for weaving silk, that would have driven the silk trade in Manchester much below what it was; that is one proof Spitalfields and Manchester will never rival one another to their ruin in this particular branch of trade. Ten years ago there were facilities to the cotton weavers at Manchester to encourage the silk trade to the ruin of Spitalfields.

10917. Did they not in fact, make large quantities of figured lustres at Manchester?—They did, after they were done with in London, but of a very inferior quality.

10918. Was not the effect of their being made largely in Manchester the reason of their being given up in Spitalfields?—No, it was from their ceasing to be an article of fashion.

10919. Was not this article made at Sudbury?—There was a house or two in Spitalfields that had houses at Sudbury.

10920. What was the price paid?—The price for the blue article was 1 *s.* 3 *d.*

10921. You do not remember what was paid at Sudbury?—From 1 *s.* to 1 *s.* 3 *d.*

10922. Do you remember the year?—In 1816.

10923. Were they made in 1821?—I think there were none made in 1821 at Sudbury.

10924. Were not immense quantities used about 1821 and 1822?—Of the lower class there might be.

10925. Do you believe that a considerable quantity of plain goods are now imported from France?—I think there are of the finer quality.

10926. The price for weaving gros de Naples is 6½ *d.*?—Yes.

10927. Do you know what is the cost per yard of smuggling French goods?—I never made any calculation of that.

10928. What is the value of a gros de Naples per yard?—I am not conversant with the selling price of goods, but they are very low.

10929. If it costs 6 *d.* to smuggle the article, how would that interfere with the wages of that of Spitalfields?—It would only interfere by its being so much below Spitalfields, in some way or other as to the material.

10930. Is there a prejudice in favour of plain or figured silk?—If it is French, people will give so much the more for it.

10931. Do you not think the prejudice would be stronger if there was a prohibition?—I think not.

10932. Do you think there is less feeling of that kind than there was formerly?—I think not, even if the same prejudice existed, we should meet the prejudice as before; I know that in 1821, 1822 and 1823, the man who made these patterns had worked for four or five years on goods that were sold in all the houses in London for French made goods, they were made on French patterns and on French principles, and sold to the public at a high rate of price, in many under the rose, as foreign goods actually smuggled.

10933. Were not smuggled goods hawked along the coast, and sold as French goods?—We reaped the benefit of it; the great mass of goods thrown on us now by

the

Mr.
*William Wallis.*

9 July,
1832.

the fair and the foul trader prevents us from getting our goods off, and causes that distress we complain of.

10934. Do you not think that many goods manufactured in Spitalfields were offered at the West end of the Town as French?—I rather doubt that; a house might not have sufficient integrity to avoid it; when a lady fancied a pattern, and they believed because it was English she would not have it, where had it been French she would have taken it, they might probably pass it off that way as French.

10935. Are there many rich velvets imported from the Continent?—I do not think there are; at one period there were.

10936. Are not the velvets imported, chiefly the low German velvets?—They interfere more than the higher ones.

10937. Do you think this is owing to competition with France?—Yes; for this reason, that persons employed in these works, while there was no competition in the richer articles of plain works, are compelled of necessity to get the best wages they can; perhaps there are three times the number of weavers that never find employment in velvet; there was a period, within my remembrance, when it was divided into distinct branches; when some made lustres, plain and figured; some made fine silks, and some made velvets. A man is compelled to take any thing, and he must be master of every branch to enable him to obtain any work.

10938. Do you believe that the fall in the price of figured gros de Naples, has a tendency to lower the price of velvets?—I believe it has.

10939. If the competition with the cotton weavers at Lancashire has the effect of lowering the price of low gros de Naples, must it not lower the price of all weaving in Spitalfields?—I think they never would interfere with us to any great extent.

10940. You fear the competition with France more than with Manchester?— Decidedly so. If I was convinced with the fact, that the manufacturers of Manchester or any other part of England were making these kind of goods, to the full extent they are made in Spitalfields, I should never have stood forward to trouble the Government or the Parliament with this question. My countrymen being better in that quarter, I should have the liberty to go there, and having the experience both of a figured and plain weaver in Spitalfields, I should command that respect from a master that would obtain me employment, and I could live there cheaper than in Spitalfields.

10941. Do you not think that of late years, in consequence of the increase of the manufacture in a particular sort of goods, Spitalfields is more interfering with Manchester than Manchester is interfering with Spitalfields?—I think that is so.

10942. Do you think that the goods manufactured in Spitalfields now, are inferior in quality to what were made some years ago?—I think they are very much so; not in point of workmanship but in the article made use of, for the sake of obtaining them cheaper.

10943. Are there not, at this moment, a larger quantity of rich gros de Naples making than were made two years ago?—There has been a demand for richer goods, and we have endeavoured to meet that.

10944. Has not the quantity of rich goods increased?—It has in quantity a little, but not in price, for weaving.

10945. Are you acquainted with the sort of goods imported from France?—To a certain extent.

10946. Are you acquainted with the article called French Crapes?—I am; it is a small handkerchief.

10947. Have they been made in Spitalfields?—Not in any quantity.

10948. The importation of that does not affect Spitalfields?—I do not think it does; if the article had been in demand and been a profitable one, we should have had our share in it.

10949. You do not think the people of Paisley, Norwich, Yarmouth or Braintree have underworked you in that article?—I do not.

10950. What is the article imported from France, that you think injurious to the weaver of Spitalfields?—The rich figured gros de Naples and other fancy silk goods.

10951. It has been stated, that few plain goods are imported?—I believe there are a great many rich plain goods, and from inquiry on Saturday last, I am confirmed in that opinion.

10952. If it should appear there are few plain gros de Naples imported from France, the evil would be confined to the figured goods?—Yes, it would.

10953. Do

Mr.
*William Wallis.*

9 July,
1832.

10953. Do you not think that the duty on thrown silk is injurious to the weaver of silk?—I think not.

10954. Will you explain why?—Having been 28 years in the trade, I remember a period when foreign thrown silk was almost the only kind made use of in fine goods, and I worked for a house in Cheapside, not now in the trade, where they used scarce any thing else than Piedmont silk for the finer kinds of gauzes and figured fancy goods; the effect of the Milan Decree of Buonaparte on that house was dreadful; they reduced their hands from 250 or 300 down to about 15; and I was one of the 15 who had the honour of being allowed to remain; they were compelled to give up the whole of their manufacture for several months, in every branch of trade except velvet.

10955. Was that occasioned by the impossibility of getting a supply from Italy?—It was occasioned by the Milan Decrees; after some time, an improvement took place in the Bengal silk, and there came up a species of goods of the description I hold in my hand, that allowed the Bengal silk to be used with greater effect; Bengal silk was then in demand, and there has been a progressive improvement in the throwing of Bengal silk from that time; within a few years there was a considerable improvement in throwing of that silk; I do not believe, that since the reduction of duty, there has been any thing like such good English thrown silk as there was eight or nine years ago.

10956. The Milan Decrees rendered it as difficult to get raw as thrown silk?—Of course; I was going to observe, that since the alteration of the duties, and the distress among the people engaged in throwing, I have noticed a very great alteration in the quality of the silks I have had to work up; there has been a great deal more pickings or roughness, which is obliged to be cleared away, and this arises from the circumstance, in my opinion, that under the excessive low rate of pay, they are not able to pay sufficient attention to the work.

10957. What was the nature of the difficulty the manufacturers experienced after the Milan Decrees, was it as to the quality of the silk?—The difficulties were two-fold; first, in the want of material to a very great extent, and next in the quality of that which they did obtain.

10958. There was no difficulty in getting the silks thrown that we could obtain here?—I think not, there was so few, that of course the throwsters were very slack of work.

10959. Can you state how much the duty on thrown adds to the cost of a yard of gros de Naples?—I am not conversant with that question; I always consider, that when any thing is well paid for, it is more likely to be well done than when it is badly paid for.

10960. If it should amount to 2 d. a yard, would not the manufacturer be in the same situation as he now is with regard to the competition with France?—No, I think not.

10961. Will you state how?—I should think that the manufacturers calculate their business by the cost of the material they have to work up; I do not think the present duty on thrown, amounts to 2 d.; but whatever the amount may be, he could not, I think, raise his wages to that amount; it is possible he might.

10962. Is the same sort of loom used in Manchester as is used in Spitalfields?—I think so, certainly.

10963. Do you use the fly shuttle there?—Yes.

10964. Can you make the same description of silk with the fly shuttle as you do with the hand?—I do not think the work would be so good; from the appearance that I have observed in the Manchester and country goods generally, there seems to me to be something of a dress on their goods that is not applied to the goods in Spitalfields.

10965. Does it require more experience to use a hand loom than a fly shuttle?—Not at all; the fly is used for the sake of facility; it is applicable to all wide works, to which it is of great advantage; when a man gets used a little to the fly, he can make as good work as any other man in that way; the hand loom throws the shute more correctly, and makes the work more true, giving it a better face than the fly shuttle.

10966. To what do you attribute the increase of trade in 1824 and 1826?—To the stimulus given to the trade by reduction of duty, and the drawback allowed, and to the knowledge, that in 1826, there would be an importation of French goods.

10967. Has there been any great increase of the number of looms in Spitalfields since 1826?—I do not think there has.

678.

10968. You

Mr.
*William Wallis.*

9 July,
1832.

10968. You say there are about 17,000, are they all employed?—Certainly not.

10969. How many are out of employ?—From 2,000 to 4,000.

10970. Do you know how many were out of employ in 1825?—There were more generally employed then, than there are now.

10971. What is the average rate of wages now earned per week by a weaver?— About 7 s., not more, rather less than more; but that is the general average of single and double.

10972. How many hours must he work a day for that?—The average hours in Spitalfields are about 16.

10973. Are there any deductions to be made from that 7 s.?—The common deductions for attendance, which it is very difficult now to get at; people are obliged to employ their own families, because they cannot afford to pay for assistance; a man who has two looms takes a third person to keep them going; these two looms on a three single, earn about 13 s. per week; with the three single and double together, it would amount throughout the year to perhaps 14 s. or 15 s. per week.

10974. What was the average rate of wages in 1825 for the same description of work?—The average earnings in 1825, upon the same kind of work, amounted to from 16 s. to 17 s., subject to the same deductions.


Mr. *John Poyton*, called in; and Examined.

Mr.
*John Poyton.*

10975. ARE you engaged in the silk trade?—Yes.

10976. In what particular department?—I am at present in the plain line; I was formerly in the figured.

10977. How long have you been in the silk trade?—Upwards of forty years.

10978. Have you known the trade for forty years in Spitalfields?—Yes, I have been in Spitalfields the whole of that time.

10979. Did you ever know a period in those forty years in which the distress was so great as during the last winter?—I have known distress at different times in the course of that period, but none like the distress that has existed since 1826; the trade prior to that time was always more steady; the figured and fancy branches, which were the most profitable part of the trade, are now of little value, and the plain branch is subject to many more fluctuations than formerly; there are frequently thousands of weavers out of employ, and at all times their wages are so low that while in employ they cannot obtain the common necessaries of life; formerly it there was distress it arose from want of work, not price; but since 1826 there has been much more distress for want of work than prior to that time, and a perpetual distress for want of price.

10980. Has there been a deduction in the price of labour since 1826?—The reduction in the price of labour since 1826 has been upon the average nearly one-half in the plain branches, and considerably more than one-half in the figured branch, on some articles as much as two-thirds; for instance, what we term hat shags, that used to be a very profitable part of the trade, and employed a good many hands; it would take two feet to make a hat, for which 4 s. 10 d. used to be paid per yard; 1 s. 6 d. is now paid for it; and there are many other works in proportion.

10981. Was the trade in Spitalfields on the decline prior to 1826?—A statement of a few facts I should consider quite sufficient to prove that it was very rapidly on the increase prior to 1826; in the early part of my connexion with the trade the men and their sons were generally engaged in weaving, and their wives and daughters used to employ their time principally in the winding of silk, and there never was any complaint of there not being sufficient to supply the demand; but in process of time, at the early period of the present century, there was a very great complaint, because the trade had so increased that the supply was completely insufficient for the demand; the manufacturers to remedy that evil introduced the present winding machines, and being of a very expensive description, the journeymen had not sufficient capital to purchase them; the manufacturers then generally purchased them, and factories were established for the winding of silk; there was a prejudice in the minds of the winders against working in factories, and the consequence was that the trade of silk winding has gone into a new channel, or a new set of hands; these winders being thrown out of work, they transferred their labour from the winding to the weaving of silk; notwithstanding this great influx of hands,

there

there never was any complaint of a superabundance. About the years 1817 and 1818, and from that to 1823, there was a continual and perpetual influx of people from Ireland, who had been engaged in silk weaving and other branches, and notwithstanding that increase there was no complaint of a superabundance of hands; again, there was a great increase of hands through the regular increase in the general way of population; it was the custom up to that time for a man who had a family to have the whole of them employed in weaving; I know two instances of men who were married about sixty years ago, who have now upwards of fifty of their offspring in the trade; and notwithstanding the influx from these circumstances, there was never any complaint from the superabundance of hands prior to 1826.

10982. To what cause do you ascribe the present distress?—I ascribe the present distress to the repeal of those protecting laws that existed prior to 1824; I know that up to that time it was on the increase, and in a flourishing and profitable state; and when a proposition was made to repeal those laws, the journeymen generally felt alarmed, and anticipated the evils which would be the natural result, and all the evils that we did anticipate have come to pass; it is a very natural conclusion for us to ascribe the evil to the cause from which we anticipated such result.

10983. Was there any hope of benefit to the working classes held out at the time of the alteration?—At the time the alteration was made, feeling alarmed at the evils likely to come upon us, we applied to the Board of Trade, and had several interviews with Mr. Huskisson and several Members of Parliament, who told us that our fears were ill grounded; that when the new laws were brought into operation, we should feel the reverse effects result from the measure from what we anticipated; the principal design they said was to extend our export trade, by extending our export trade we should not be the slave of fashion, as we were up to that time; and it was being so completely the slave of fashion that produced the fluctuations in our trade prior to that time, which we should not be exposed to after the new law came into operation; there might be some little alteration, they said, in the rate of wages, but still it would produce that constancy of employment that would secure us a better return for our labour at the year's end than what we experienced before; so far from any of these benefits being realized, we find the measure has operated quite the reverse; I had an interview with Mr. Ricardo on the subject, when the measure was first introduced; he said your fears are altogether groundless; so far from it producing the evil you expect, universal prosperity will be its natural result, and I shall be happy to see you in a twelvemonth after it has been in operation, and so far from your thinking me an enemy, you will consider me one of your best friends, and thank me for the part I have taken.

10984. His Majesty's Ministers told you, that prosperity and constant employment, and benefits of all sorts would be the result, you told His Majesty's Ministers that ruin and diminution of labour and wages would be the result, is that the fact?—We had several interviews with the Board of Trade on the subject; distress was our constant theme, and prosperity they ever predicted.

10985. Which, as it turns out, by experience, knew your business best, you or His Majesty's Ministers?—If we judge from the result we must be considered to be the truest prophets.

10986. What were your reasons, as a body, for opposing the repeal of the laws?—First, because we knew we could make enough silk to supply the utmost demand without recourse to the foreigner for a supply; secondly, because we knew that an over supply would necessarily be destructive to the value of our labour, which over supply we naturally expected would be the result; thirdly, we knew the contest would be unfair, the foreigner having advantages over us, both natural and political, which we never expected to possess; fourthly, we knew that foreign competition would be much more destructive to our interests than home competition; fifthly, we knew that every time when the system had been tried, even when the country was in a much better condition to compete with a foreigner than at present, yet notwithstanding the same destructive effects were its results; sixthly, the conviction on our mind was, that under any rate of duty, when the sale of foreign manufactured silks were legalized, smuggling would greatly increase, by which means our difficulty to compete would become greater; seventhly, we did expect, when the value of labour was reduced in this country, that would produce a reduction in the price of weaving on the Continent; yet we had no idea the reduction would have been carried to the extent it has been carried on the Continent, a proof this that our fears have been more than realized.

678.                                                                                    10987. Has

10987. Has there not been an increased exportation of silk goods of late?—There has been an increase in the export in quantity, but there has been no increase in value; in fact there has been less exported in value, under the present sytem, than there was in the same given time under the former system. The value of goods exported in the five years previous to the repeal of the laws, was 1,919,964*l.*; in the last five years, since 1826, the total export was only 1,448,536*l.* being a decline in the value exported of nearly 500,000*l.* The quantity of goods have been nearly doubled; the benefits to be derived from an export trade regards the value not the quantity; 100*l.* on the official value, under the former system,. was worth 273*l.*; but under the new system, for the last five years, it only amounts to 128*l.*, so that there has actually been a decline of 150*l.* on every 100*l.* of official value exported.

10988. Has not the country derived some benefit from the exportation in point of revenue?—If you look at the thing as it is presented by the official documents, you will find it quite the reverse; for in the seven years prior to the alteration of the law, the amount of duty that was received by this country, upon raw and thrown silk, amounted to 4,516,000*l.* Since the alteration of the law, the whole duty that has been collected, on the raw and thrown silk, amounts to 931,000*l.*; the duty collected on manufactured silks, to 865,000*l.*; making a total of 1,796,000*l.* that the Government has received in the shape of duty; whereas, in the former period, before the alteration of the law, it was 4,516,000*l.* so that there has actually been a decline in the amount of revenue, received by Government, of 2,720,000*l.*

10989. Supposing the present system to continue, do you think the silk trade can continue to live in this country?—If it lives in the country it cannot live profitably; it must continue its existence by starvation prices for the operative, and ruinous profits to the masters. I consider the prices which the operatives are now receiving, are in thousands of instances altogether inadequate to support them; thousands are compelled to apply to the parochial authorities for support, and numbers have received it even when in full employ; some of the best of our artisans have emigrated to foreign nations. I know several that have gone to America with the determination to establish the silk trade there; I know one family, that lived close by me, who were so reduced by poverty and disease, brought on them by incessant labour, that they threw themselves on the parish for support; they belonged to one of the city parishes, and the parish finding they were likely to be saddled with a very heavy burthen, for there was a man and his wife and seven children, agreed to advance the money to send them to America, and they went about three weeks ago. That is a system not likely to be beneficial to the silk trade when you drive away its artisans, for it amounts to nothing short of commercial persecution. When a man cannot live by his labour, it is productive of precisely the same effects as religious persecution; the only difference between the one and the other is, that the one leaves his country because he cannot bear the grumbling of his belly, the other because it cannot bear the grumbling of his conscience; the effect is the same in both cases.

10990. Has there not been an increase of consumption of raw and thrown silk?—There has been increased consumption since 1824, but no increased consumption if you take the average of 25 and 26; it is admitted that there must have been an increase in the importation of raw and thrown silks, but it is consumed in articles that require little labour; formerly all the silk we used to work up, even in plain work, was worked in this way, say a plain common sarsnet, that has given way to what we call a three-single, and in a three-single a man can work up nearly double the weight to what he could in the sarsnet. There are other works in which we used to consume a small quantity of silk, that have gone entirely out of use, such as the gauzes; they were made on a principle that consumed so little, that one pound of silk would make about 70 yards, which would give a man employment for at least 16 or 17 days; it would take him that time to work up one pound of silk, whereas in the works that are generally now made, a man can work up very near four ounces a day, in some cases more. I am convinced, when you take into account the transfer of labour from the light and fancy branches to the plain and heavy, so far from there being an increase of labour in the silk consumed in this country, there has been an actual decrease of labour.

10991. You do not think that the consumption of the weight of silk is a fair criterion of the prosperity of the trade?—By no means; a pound of silk that was worked up in the way I have just alluded to, the value of the labour when it was made in the district of Spitalfields was upwards of 3*l.*, whereas the working up a pound

pound of silk at present would be only about 6 *s.* 8 *d.*; the two articles I have just alluded to, were extreme cases; if you look at the difference between a figured gros de Naples and the plain one, there is double the labour consumed in the one to what there is in the other, and yet there is the same quantity of yards to a pound weight.

10992. Has not the repeal of the duties benefited Lyons as much as it has injured Spitalfields?—I should consider if I took a review of the history of Lyons, and I can only get information historically on the subject, that so far from Lyons being benefited by the alteration in our laws, it has been actually injured, and that for the following reason; when this measure was introduced, the French manufacturer expected, I believe, to have realized a very considerable benefit by being allowed to come into our market, and they prepared accordingly for that measure, and the reason why they prized our market so much was, that England, it is well known, is a country that consumes a great deal of silk of all manufacturers; the French manufacture a great deal and consume very little; they depend principally on the export trade for the existence of the trade of France; and when they found there was a duty of 30 per cent. laid on silk imported into this country, they considered it necessary to turn their attention towards the meeting of the difficulties they had to encounter, and the first expedient they had recourse to was the reduction of the value of labour; the French artisans not being very much pleased with the idea of having the value of their labour reduced, they protested against it, and the consequence was, that the manufacturers established the trade in districts where it had never existed before; and according to Doctor Lardner's statement in 1829, there were two-thirds of the looms then in Lyons out of employ, in consequence of the trade emigrating to adjacent places for the sake of getting their labour done cheaper than in Lyons; the reduction was kept on up till 1831, and it was under the control of these circumstances; as the value of labour decreased in this country, they were under the necessity of depressing the value of labour in France. It appears that in 1831, the cry of the French people was, give us a tariff to secure a reward for our labour, or give us a bayonet in our vitals, for our lives are now become a burden to us. I do not think the system has been more beneficial to the artisans of Lyons than to those of Spitalfields.

10993. Do you think it possible, by any contrivance, to prevent smuggling?—I know of no plan that is likely to succeed; when we waited on the Board of Trade, Mr. Huskisson avowed it was his intention to press this law, for the purpose of doing away with smuggling; he said, smuggling had increased to a very great extent; that it was not only a growing evil but a grievous burthen on the silk trade, and some steps ought to be taken to put an end to it. The Chancellor of the Exchequer and Mr. Charles Grant were present; and he stated, that if such rules and regulations were introduced, he would pledge his existence that it would prevent smuggling altogether: we told him, we much doubted it; and a regulation introduced was for the avowed purpose of remedying the evil altogether. In 1829 it was admitted, that the same evil existed, and an alteration in the rates of duty was proposed and carried, and that was said by the then President of the Board of Trade to be quite sufficient to cover the evil; but we see, notwithstanding all the remedy that has been applied to the disease, that the evil still exists; and so far from it being diminished, we have every reason in the world to believe that it increases, to a most enormous extent: I ground that opinion upon the returns that have been made to Parliament, and from the Custom House of France; one statement was published by the House of Commons, the other was brought before the Committee by Doctor Bowring. Doctor Bowring's statement is, that the Custom House returns show, that in 1828 the French exported from France to this country, silks to the amount of nine million francs in value. In 1830, there was an increase of six millions of francs; by comparing this statement with the returns laid before Parliament, in the first year referred to, there was imported from France into this country, through the Custom House, 150,000 lbs. weight of silk, and an equal proportion in value; but in 1830 the quantity of silk diminished, and there was only imported, through the Custom House, from France, 115,000 lbs; whereas, according to Doctor Bowring's statement, the importation had increased six millions of francs; so that if both statements are correct, it is quite clear one half of the silk imported is brought here by the smuggler.

10994. Can you state the number of persons who are receiving relief in the Spitalfields districts, who are in full work?—No, the information I can collect on

that

that subject is only from individuals; all the parochial authorities in those districts set their faces against it.

10995. Have you reason to suppose that there are a great number of persons who receive relief, being in full work?—I have no reason to suppose the number is very great, because I know that there is a dislike on the part of most people to receive parochial relief; that was a general principle at one time; but I am sorry to say that the morals of the people are very materially degenerated, under the influence of the present laws.

10996. You heard the questions that were put to the other witness as to the rate of wages; does your opinion coincide with the one which he gave on that subject? —Yes; I am perfectly satisfied with his statements on the subject, and I believe they are perfectly correct.

## Mr. *Robert Bolter*, called in; and Examined.

10997. WITH what part of the silk trade are you connected?—Chiefly with the plain branch.

10998. Did you serve your apprenticeship in Spitalfields?—I did.

10999. How many years is it since it concluded?—Twelve years.

11000. Having served an apprenticeship of seven years, and been in the trade twelve, can you now earn a fair subsistence by your trade?—I cannot; it is impossible under the present rate of wages for any man in Spitalfields to earn any thing like a livelihood, and we only drag on a very miserable existence indeed.

11001. What do you take to be the average rate of wages?—From the best information I can collect, it is from 6 *s.* 8 *d.* to 7 *s.* a week, not more.

11002. I suppose you were apprenticed to the trade at a time when the rate of wages was not so low as it is now?—When I was bound apprentice, the rate of wages was higher, and the work more constant than it is at present; it was considered at that time that a man might be able to earn a comfortable livelihood when he had the work to do; far different is it at the present time; when I was bound apprentice, the Government of the country had protected the trade, and I considered were bound to protect it; I thought I had done the same as purchased an annuity for life, as something by which I should be enabled to get a living for a family; I consider that the Government ought to have protected the same, as every other species of property; but I am sorry to my cost, and the cost of those in Spitalfields, that they have not kept good faith.

11003. Have the workmen in Spitalfields derived any benefit at all from the alteration of the law?—No, quite the reverse; the district of Spitalfields has been very much injured by a repeal of the prohibitory laws; it is an injury to the whole district, for there are a great number of shop-keepers who now cannot do any thing; instead of its being a benefit, it has been a very serious injury.

11004. What do you consider would be the best mode of relief?—The best mode of relief would be to prohibit the importation of foreign silk goods into this country, and to punish the smuggler most severely. When I went to the Board of Trade, before Mr. Poulett Thomson and Lord Auckland, a question was asked, how we would prevent smuggling; I stated, by fine and imprisonment; and if they continued the duties, putting it under the Excise; let the excisemen take the stock now and then, the same as at a tobacconist or tea warehouse; but they considered that to be too much trouble.

11005. Are the wages in Spitalfields lower now than they were seventy years ago?—They are lower, generally, from 1½ *d.* to 2 *d.*

11006. Do you know the price paid in 1769 for plain goods?—I do.

11007. What is the difference between the price paid at that time and the price now paid?—For a four thread mantua, 1769, was 7 *d.* per yard; 1832, 6 *d.* ditto: ducape, 1769, 9 *d.* per yard; 1832, 8 *d.* ditto: gros de Naples, 9 *d.* and 10 *d.* in 1823, and 5 *d.* and 6 *d.* in 1832. This is the general average rate of wages that are paid in Spitalfields; some manufacturers pay more than others.

11008. If the silk trade is so extremely depressed as you and the other witnesses describe it, why do you not remove from that into some other branch of trade?— That is a question that has been often asked by honourable Members, why you cannot find employment in some other branch of industry; it may be very well with men of capital to remove their capital and enter into some other branch of manufacture; but it is not so easy for a workman after he has learned his trade to

remove

Mr.
*Robert Bolter.*

9 July,
1832.

remove and find other means of employ; other trades must be learned, and it is very hard for a man after he has served seven years that he should not be able to get a living, but be thrown on the wide world to seek that employment he can hardly find.   I consider that a working man cannot find employment after he has once served his time to a particular trade in any other; if we went to labouring work, we should never be able to return to weaving, for our hands would be in that state that we should not be able to handle the silk.

*Mercurii, 11° die Julii*, 1832.

## GEORGE BANKES, ESQUIRE, in the Chair.

*John Ballance*, Esquire, called in; and further Examined.

*John Ballance,*
Esq.

11 July,
1832.

11009. YOU wish to make some addition to the evidence you gave on a former occasion; you gave it as your opinion on a former occasion, that smuggling, under the prohibitory laws, was very trifling as compared with what it had been since those laws were repealed; are you still of the same opinion?—The opinion which I then gave was founded upon the information which from time to time was furnished to the Committee of the Silk Trade, of which I was a member; I have since seen Dr. Bowring's statement of the exports of silk goods from France from 1818 to 1825, and so far as any dependence is to be placed upon those accounts, I find that they confirm the opinion which I then gave.   From these accounts it appears that smuggling remained almost stationary till 1824, and that the apparent great increase in smuggling took place in 1824, and chiefly in 1825; it was in March 1824 that the laws relative to the silk trade were repealed, and the Committee will observe the coincidence between the change of the laws and the increase of smuggling; for besides the facilities for smuggling referrible to the Warehousing Act, by which foreign silks were allowed to come into this country under bond for exportation, it is well known that the immediate effect of the alteration of the law in 1824 was to give encouragement to smuggling.   In expectation of the Ports being shortly opened to foreign silk goods, there was a relaxation of the laws; little or no vigilance was exercised on the part of the officers of the Crown, and smuggling went on without control, as the transactions of Depouilly's house fully prove.   I submit, therefore, to this honourable Committee, that to form a correct estimate of the extent of smuggling under the prohibitory laws, 1824 and 1825 must either be left out of the calculation, or be taken at the average of the six years preceding, for it is most unjust to adopt measures of which smugglers may instantly take the advantage, and then use the rapid increase of smuggling in those years as an argument for the continuance of the present system; and I will just add, that if the six preceding years be taken, that is from 1818 to 1824, according to this statement the average rate of smuggling for those six years is about 106,000*l.*, that is before the change in the law took place.

11010. Does that include the year 1824?—It excludes 1824; it is from 1818 to 1824; the change of the law took place in March 1824.

11011. Have you made a calculation of what would be the average, taking the six years preceding, and taking the years 1824 and 1825 both inclusive?—I have not made that average, but I can very easily make it.

| | £. |
|---|---|
| Average Value, per annum, of the Exports of Silk goods from France to England, from 1818 to 1823 inclusive, according to Dr. Bowring's statement, 16,300,000 francs, for six years, equal per annum - - | 106,000 |
| Ditto - - - ditto - - - ditto, from 1818 to 1825 inclusive, 26,100,000 francs, for eight years, equal per annum - - - - | 128,000 |

11012. You say also, that the admission of French silk for the purpose of warehousing afforded great facilities to the smuggler; perhaps you can tell the Committee why it afforded great facilities?—This measure was introduced by Mr. Huskisson; the committee of the silk trade very strongly opposed it, upon the opinion that, under the cloak of bringing in foreign silks under bond for exportation, the

smugglers

John Ballance,
Esq.

11 July,
1832.

smugglers would avail themselves of the opportunity to carry on with greater facility the contraband trade.

11013. They might either warehouse them or land them, as best suited their purpose?—Just so; that was the ground of an opposition to it, and we resisted it very strongly, but without effect; and it is to be observed that immediately after that, according to Dr. Bowring's statement, smuggling increased considerably.

11014. Have you any information to make with reference to the extent of smuggling since 1826?—If I were to gather the extent of smuggling from the Statement which has been given to this Committee, of exports from France since 1825, I must conclude that it has been carried on to a very limited extent, indeed that it scarcely exists. This appears by comparing these Accounts with our own Custom House Returns of duty paid on silks imported from Europe; the comparative view which I have drawn out is as follows [*handing in an Account.*]

| DR. BOWRING's Statement of Exports from *France* to *England*, of SILK GOODS, in Francs. | | | | | Valued in sterling. |
|---|---|---|---|---|---|
| 1826 | - - | *francs* 7,596,000 | - | Answer, | £. 301,000 |
| 1827 | - - - | 11,460,000 | - - - | - | 453,000 |
| 1828 | - - - | 17,311,000 | - - - | - | 685,000 |
| 1829 | - - - | 10,483,000 | - - - | - | 414,000 |
| 1830 | - - - | 15,204,000 | - - - | - | 602,000 |
| 1831 | - - - | 18,000,000 | - - - | - | 712,000 |

DUTY paid upon IMPORTS of SILKS, from *Europe*, for the Years as under:

| | Duty paid. | Computation of cost Abroad. | Difference supposed smuggled. |
|---|---|---|---|
| 1826 - | £. 55,259, at 30 p' ct. - | £. 184,197 | 116,813 |
| * 1827 - | 138,125 - - - - | 460,417 | — |
| 1828 - | 198,404 - - - - | 661,347 | 23,653 |
| † 1829 - | 144,144, at 30 & 25 p' c. | 524,160 | — |
| 1830 - | 135,988, at 25 p' ct. - | 543,952 | 58,148 |
| 1831 - | 140,414 - - - - | 561,656 | 150,344 |

* This year no smuggling!

† This year about £. 100,000 more paid Duty than Dr. Bowring states was exported from France.

The Committee will observe, that according to this Account, there had been smuggled in 1826, 1827 and 1828, only about 140,000 pounds; that in 1827 there was no smuggling; in 1829 there was not only no smuggling, but an excess of imports beyond the amount of exports from France, stated by Dr. Bowring, of about 100,000*l.*; and the two last years, 1830 and 1831, according to the same Accounts, show an average amount of smuggling of only 104,000*l.* I am aware that these Custom House Returns include the duty on all silks coming from the Continent, but as the duty paid upon those which pass the Customs from other parts of Europe besides France, is of trifling amount, the principle of this calculation is not disturbed by it. I believe, however, that Switzerland and Germany do send considerable quantities of silk goods to this country; what I mean is, that the proportion of those which pay duty is too inconsiderable to affect the Statement which I have delivered in. The Custom House Returns have generally given the duty paid upon silks from Europe, so that we have not been able in every instance to separate those which come from France only; but as a guide to ascertain what the proportions may be, I have before me two years, that of 1828 and that of 1830, where the Accounts are kept separate, and I find that the value of goods that passed through the Customs from other parts of Europe in 1828, besides France, was about 30,000*l.*, and in 1830, about 13,000*l.* It is evident, therefore, that the question under consideration cannot be affected by these fractional entries. I therefore submit that these Accounts of Exports, when stated to exhibit the total exports of silk goods from France to England, carry with them their own refutation, for all this is directly contrary to the fact. It is notorious that smuggling did increase in 1827 and 1828, that it was made the subject of complaint to Government, and that they reduced the duties in 1829 in consequence; and it is equally well known that since that reduction, smuggling has been carried on to a greater extent than ever; the conclusion therefore is irresistible, that either there is an error in these Accounts, or what I imagine will prove to be the case, that large quantities of silk goods now find their way into this country without being cleared out at the French Customs, and therefore these Returns of Exports neither do nor can show the extent of smuggling.

11015. You mean in fact, that they are smuggled out of France?—Yes, smuggled out of France. I consider that is shown by these Accounts.

11016. Then you would think it not an impossible thing that they might be sent out of France as a case of eggs, in order to prevent the possibility of its being known

whether

whether it was a case of eggs or really was silk?—Certainly; I have heard of such instances.

11017. There might be an understanding, might there not, between the officers of the Customs at Calais and London, to inform them of any cases of silks exported from Calais, and if there was an object to conceal on the part of the smuggler on this side of the water, that this case should not be known really to contain silks, it would be desirable to keep it equally secret at Calais, and therefore he would have a motive besides for inducing the officer of the Custom House here also to pass those commodities as if they really were eggs?—I think that certain letters that have passed from Calais, will quite establish the view the honourable Member has taken of it.

11018. It has been given in evidence that the total value of the silk trade of France is about six millions sterling, is this your opinion?—Am I to understand this question as referring to a calculation which has been given in evidence before this Committee? the witness to which I refer stated as follows: " Now taking the estimate of added value for labour at 70 per cent., and supposing the amount of thrown silk to be 4,000,000 of pounds, and that 18 s. be taken as its average value, the amount will be 3,600,000 l., to which add the 70 per cent. as above, which I think may be divided thus, 30 per cent. for dyeing, interest, profit and expenses of all sorts, and there will remain 40 per cent. for labour specially; this is the whole cost; add to 3,600,000 l. 2,520,000 l. the 70 per cent. making 6,120,000 l. the value of the whole silk manufactory of France." The same witness has made it even less than this, by giving 17 s. 6 d. as the average price of thrown silks; that is, 16 s. for tram and 19 s. for organzine.

I differ essentially from this calculation, in respect both of the quantity and price of the thrown silk and the amount of labour, stated to be 40 per cent. for manufacturing it; the Committee will allow me to advert to those items; it is in evidence by the same witness that there are 70,000 looms in France, which consume on an average 60 pounds of silk per annum; and from the same evidence we have been told the number of ells per diem made in these looms when at work. Now speaking as a manufacturer, and making every allowance for the occasional stoppage of these looms, I am satisfied that they will consume more than 60 pounds of undyed silk; and I apprehend the error lies in substituting the weight of undyed silk consumed by these looms for the weight of the goods produced by them; this would give 4,200,000 pounds in manufactured goods, and will correspond with 4,800,000 pounds of thrown undyed silk; and I am the more confirmed in this opinion as it harmonizes with the declaration of the same witness in another part of his evidence, where he states it to be a prevailing opinion in France that three-fourths of her silk manufacture is of silk of native growth, and one-fourth of silk imported; this importation is said to average about 1,200,000 pounds, which makes the total quantity consumed in the manufacture to be as before stated, 4,800,000 pounds. It will also appear that 18 s. a pound for organzine and tram, which the witness assigns to the four million pounds of thrown silk, as the average value, is not the average value, but approaches nearer to the minimum value; in proof of this I adduce the evidence of the same witness, who stated that a manufacturer at St. Etienne gave 70,000 f. for 1,000 kilogrammes of thrown silk, which is equal to 25 s. per pound, and this for the manufacture not of gauze but of satin ribbons, an ordinary article. Again, the value of 18 s. is assigned to the whole quantity of four millions of pounds weight, whereas one-fourth of this quantity is silk imported, of which about 700,000 pounds weight is Piedmont organzine, the nett cash price of which at this moment at Lyons is 20 s. 5 d.; and it is here worthy of remark, that 18 s. for thrown silk at Lyons is less than the price of Italian raw silk of good quality in London. I apprehend the witness was not aware of this circumstance, as it places in a striking view one of the advantages of France, and shows up the folly of the expectation of our sending thrown silks to that country; with respect to the 40 per cent. on the 18 s. which is assigned in the above statement as the cost of labour specially, I have the same remark to make upon it, that it is not the average cost; this 40 per cent. upon 18 s. represents 7 s., which is about the cost upon plain gros de Naples of from 2 s. 3 d. to 2 s. 5 d. a yard; the cost on figured silks is nearer 9 s., and upon gauze ribbons considerably more; and as the fancy and figured trade form a large proportion of the French manufacture, the average per centage of the whole labour and cost in this department cannot, I apprehend, be reckoned safely at less than 50 per cent.; putting then these quantities together and their values together, it must be evident that the silk manufacture of France is very considerably above 6,120,000 l. But there is another

678.                                                                                         test

*John Ballance,*
Esq.

11 July,
1832.

test to which I submit this inquiry, and it is as easy and simple as it is conclusive : if 18 *s.* be really the average price of thrown silk, and 70 per cent. be really the average cost, including profit and interest, and expenses of all sorts, 30 *s.* will be the total value of the pound ; from which deduct about three ounces for loss of weight in dyeing and waste, this will give 33 *s.* 6 *d.* or thereabouts, as the average value of manufactured silks exported from France. Now I ask, is this the fact ? is this the average value per pound weight of silk goods imported from France ? or do they gain as they cross the channel ? The following statement which I have received from an importer, and which he is ready at any time to confirm, will answer this question :—

| | |
|---|---|
| Plain silks, purchased at Lyons, free of duty - - | 35 *s.* to 37 *s.* per lb. |
| Figured silks - - ditto - - ditto - - - | 45 *s.* to 47 *s.* per lb. |
| Gauze ribbons, purchased at St. Etienne - ditto - | 52 *s.* to 54 *s.* per lb. |
| Cut gauzes - - ditto - - ditto - - - - | 65 *s.* per lb. |

So that even plain silks are from 2 *s.* to 3 *s.* above the average assigned by this witness to the whole manufacture of France.

Now if we divide the silk manufacture of France into ten parts, and give only one-tenth to gauzes, which is a small proportion, and take the plain goods as five-tenths, and the figured as four-tenths, this will give an average not of 33 *s.* 6 *d.* but of 42 *s.* 6 *d.* ; and this average, spread over the French manufacture, will give a very different result from 6,120,000 *l.* I must also observe, that the witness is mistaken in stating, that from 30 to 35 per cent. is the loss in dyeing. The average loss (excepting in the article of sarsnets) is about 14 per cent., and he himself has shown this from the instance he has given of the manufacture of 500 ells of satin at Lyons.

Bearing also upon the question of the value of the French silk trade, is the evidence given by this witness of the number of ells produced by the looms when at work. At Lyons it is said they make from four to five ells per day, and a similar length I believe is assigned to the engine looms at St. Etienne ; now, I apprehend, that if this calculation is pursued, it will appear either that this quantity is not made, or that the looms of France consume much more than 60 pounds of thrown silk per annum. The ell of silk will average, and I am giving a low average, about an ounce and a quarter ; take it at four ells per day, that will give one pound 14 ounces per week, or 97 pounds per annum of manufactured silk, so that without assigning any silk at all to the gauze ribbon looms, and taking the sarsnet looms at Avignon, at the quantity specified, the other silk looms of France to consume only of thrown silk, 60 pounds per annum, must not work more than eight months in the year. I here offer one general remark, upon the evidence to which I have alluded, that where particular instances of the French silk manufacture are given, the value is taken at a high rate ; but when the question refers to the entire manufacture of France, the value is reckoned in the reverse proportion ; and to this I attribute many of the discrepancies which appear in the evidence of this witness.

---

11019. Do you consider this inquiry into the value of the silk trade of France, of any importance?—Yes ; I consider it intimately connected with the great interests of the silk trade of this country. It has been stated, that France exports four-fifths of her silk manufacture : it follows then, that in proportion to the extent and value of that manufacture, will be its pressure on the silk trade of Great Britain. On a former occasion, I considered there might be imported, legally and illegally, silk goods from the Continent to the amount of 900,000 *l.* sterling. The witness to whom I have referred, admits that 800,000 *l.* comes from France alone. Taking, therefore, into account his low estimate of the value of the French manufacture, the Committee, I apprehend, will fully concur with me, that the 900,000 *l.* attributed as exports from the Continent, must now be considered as much underrated ; indeed as the very minimum amount of silk goods exported from the Continent to England, and that the maximum amount of importation extends far beyond this, and is not capable of being reduced to accurate calculation ; but here I submit to the consideration of this honourable Committee a very important question. What is the amount of labour displaced in our silk districts, even by this minimum importation? It is in evidence, that the Continent manufactures 40 per cent. cheaper than England ; this, of course, must be added to the 900,000 *l.* to give the value of these goods if manufactured in England ; 40 per cent. on
900,000 *l.*

*John Ballance,*
Esq.

11 July,
1832.

900,000 *l.* will give a total value of 1,260,000 *l.*,\* and the labour required for the production of this amount of silk goods will be from 800,000 *l.* to 850,000 *l.* : this sum, I observe, is directly displaced ; but the honourable Committee will observe, that the effect of this displacing of labour will be to render it very abundant. The indirect effect, therefore, will be, to reduce the price of labour in the manufacture of all other silk goods ; and this, in the district of Spitalfields alone, has withdrawn from the work-people at least 300,000 *l.* per annum. If then I add a similar effect upon Coventry and Macclesfield, and upon the throwing of Italian silk in different parts of the kingdom, the total loss in wages will much exceed 1,500,000 *l.* Indeed I am satisfied that I do not over-state this total loss to all our silk districts in wages, especially from these destructive measures, in assigning two millions annual loss sustained by them ; and may I ask, what compensation has there been for this frightful loss of wages to our artisans ? the witness to whom I have referred has said, that cotton twist is smuggled into France, and that upon examining smugglers he conjectures, that the quantity thus introduced amounts to 800,000 *l.*, and considers that 550,000 *l.* of this is labour ; in which, in another part of his evidence, he reckons machinery ; and this he traces to the importation of French silks. The argument, then, of such a theory is this ; that it is wise and just for a paternal government to suffer the continuance of a positive and extensive injury, inflicted upon one class of persons, that a mere contingent benefit might accrue to another class ; even though the positive injury should be threefold that of the conjectured good. I speak not thus strongly on my own account ; I plead not for myself, for I am beyond the reach of these destructive measures ; but I do plead for many a distressed throwster and manufacturer, and especially for their more distressed work-people ; and I ask permission to quote the opinion of one of the highest authorities of our country ; it is an opinion which I have always held, which every year's experience strengthens, and which I imagine I shall never abandon. It is found in the Report of the Lords Committee on Foreign Trade, in 1821, and is as follows : Their Lordships observe, "It appears certain, that without some artificial support, this (silk) manufacture could not, in former times, have been introduced or maintained with any success in this country ; and as long as our principal supply was derived from a part of Europe, so much nearer to France as Italy, all competition in its own favourite branch of manufacture with the former country, (which produces at the same time so large a portion of the raw silk which it consumes,) must have appeared entirely hopeless." The evidence before this Committee has shown, that the silks of Bengal and China cannot be applied to the manufacture of fine silk goods ; that the British manufacture is as dependent as ever on the silks of Italy ; and therefore, that the conclusion which their Lordships drew in 1821, remains as strong as ever.

11020. Are the Committee to understand that you dispute the statement given in by Dr. Bowring, which shows that the labouring class of England gained by the importation of French silks, and by the exportation of a greater quantity in labour in cotton goods ; do you dispute that statement ?—I have said that the importations of silk from the Continent, take them at the lowest calculation, have displaced directly and indirectly in the silk districts of this kingdom, a far larger proportion of labour than has been assigned by the Doctor to that amount of cotton twist, which upon the examination of smugglers, he suspects has been imported into France ; but I may go farther than this, and return a direct affirmative to the question of the honourable Member. Dr. Bowring, in the answer to which I referred, has given 800,000 *l.* as the value of the exports of silk goods from France to England ; 500,000 *l.* he calls material, and 300,000 *l.* he considers labour and profit ; that is 60 per cent. upon the material ; and his hypothesis with respect to the export of cotton twist, is built upon this proportion ; but 60 per cent., which is here assigned as the cost of production, is at variance with the former evidence of this witness. Ribbons, it is well known, form a considerable part of this importation ; and his statement of the sort of manufacturing ribbons at St. Etienne, exhibits 90 and 100 per cent. upon the value of thrown silk ; besides, his estimate of the average cost in the respect of the whole silk trade of France, is 70 per cent. upon thrown silk, to which must be added from his own evidence, about 20 per cent. more, as the expense of throwing. There is therefore a discrepancy at the least of
30 per

---

\* In my former statement of 900,000 *l.* I added 34 per cent., but then I was speaking of duty and charges ; now I am referring to cost, and the duty does not cover the cost.

30 per cent. between those statements, which to my mind throws a doubt over the whole calculation about cotton twist; and it will also strike this honourable Committee, that the comparison of imports and exports, to have been a fair one, should have been drawn not between cotton twist, but manufactured cotton goods and French silks; cotton twist corresponding with thrown, and not with manufactured silks.

11021. Have you examined his statements and calculations?—The Doctor assigns 550,000*l.* to have been expended in labour upon the cotton twist; I take it merely as his declaration, and then show that the silk districts have been injured to three times the extent, even upon the lowest estimate of importation.

11022. Five hundred and fifty thousand pounds upon what; the silk goods imported, or the cotton exported?—The cotton exported.

11023. Is not silk of all materials the most valuable used in manufacture?—As compared with cotton.

11024. Or linen?—Yes.

11025. Or woollen?—It is considered so.

11026. Does it not therefore follow that 100*l.* worth of silk goods will contain 100*l.* worth less of labour, than 100*l.* worth of either of the other articles?—In the production of cotton twist, there is a very large portion of machinery, which I do not call labour; besides, I am speaking of labour displaced in England, not labour expended in France.

11027. What will the amount of labour be in 100*l.* worth of gros de Naples?—I have answered that question before; it depends on the weight.

11028. What do you consider the usual exports of this country in manufactured goods?—I offer no opinion upon the general exports of the country.

11029. Do they not consist largely of earthenware and iron, and hardware?—I wished my evidence to be restricted to the question of the labour displaced in our silk districts, by the importation of foreign manufactured silks; and I never should have alluded to cotton, had the subject not been introduced by the Doctor himself; but as he has thought proper to make the comparison, I think it is of immense importance to the silk trade to show, which is very easily done, that far more labour has been destroyed in our silk districts, than even according to the Doctor's statement, which is after all conjectural, has been taken up in cotton.

11030. Supposing that in return for 100*l.* worth of manufactured goods we export earthenware, should we not in that case export a much larger quantity of labour?—I do not touch the subject of political economy; it is quite enough for my argument, that I see misery and wretchedness around me in all the silk districts, and that that misery did not exist six years ago.

11031. But you consider it the fairest method, to take into account the labourers who may be thrown out of employment in one part of the country, and not to take into account the labourers that may not be brought into employment in another?—I have taken both into account in the comparison which I have exhibited; but further, I am quite satisfied that the thousands of persons who have been thrown out of employ in Coventry and in Spitalfields, could not become cotton spinners; and I am equally certain that there would be no room for them there if they could.

11032. Then are the Committee to understand that you consider there are fewer labourers employed now in the silk trade, than there were before 1826?—Taking the average of the last six years, not only fewer labourers, but at a less rate of wages.

11033. Did not Mr. Wallis, at the last meeting of the Committee, state that there were a greater number of looms in Spitalfields now than formerly?—No, I think his evidence was about the same.

11034. Do you doubt the fact, that there are a greater number employed out of London than there were before 1826?—I have reason to know that the difference, which ever way it is, is very trifling.

11035. You believe that there are no more employed at Manchester than were employed before 1826?—I think the Committee will have evidence to prove that in a day or two.

11036. You are not aware that weavers, who were formerly employed in weaving calicoes, are now employed in weaving silks?—That was the case in 1806, 1807, 1808, and up to 1824; it is no new feature of the silk trade of Manchester.

11037. Are you aware when the great body of cotton weavers went from that trade into the silk trade?—They did not go in a body, they went gradually; and I believe a more considerable number before 1826 than since.

11038. Do you believe that before 1826 there were many looms employed in
the

*John Ballance,*
Esq.

11 July,
1832.

the manufacture of gros de Naples at Manchester?—Many looms, yes! if they were not employed in gros de Naples, they were employed in silks of other descriptions.

11039. Will you state what description?—It is well known, that from the time the silk trade began in Manchester, which I think was about 1803 or 1804, that Manchester manufactured those articles that were then in demand. Sarsnets had a very considerable run from that time until about 1818 or 1819, and then gros de Naples gradually took their place.

11040. Do you believe there were a great number of looms employed in manufacturing sarsnets at Manchester formerly?—Whatever was in demand in low priced silks, Manchester had a portion of that then, as well as now.

11041. The articles of manufacture in Spitalfields are now nearly all of pure silk, are they not?—Yes, they are.

11042. Do you mean that there were many looms manufacturing pure silk before 1824?—Yes.

11043. It has been stated by Mr. Tootal, that there are now 9,000 looms employed on gros de Naples at Manchester, do you believe there were 1,000 before 1824?—I believe it will be found that there are now not 9,000, and that before 1824, there were many more than a thousand.

11044. Do you believe there were 2,000?—Yes; it is not difficult, I apprehend, to know the number pretty nearly. I think the Committee will soon be in possession of it.

11045. What number would you state, as your opinion, were engaged before 1824?—I decline answering the question as to the exact number; I never wish to answer questions of opinion only, except generally.

11046. You have no opinion whether one half or one quarter of the quantity were employed before 1824?—The silk trade of Manchester increased up to 1826, but it has made, I believe, little or no progress since in quantity, and it has greatly declined in wages.

11047. Are you of opinion that the Manchester looms are now making low gros de Naples, as a substitute for the silk and cotton chambras, that were in fashion before 1823, the period when gros de Naples came out?—Yes, it accords with the declaration I have just made that they change with the fashions.

11048. You think that the altered value of silks has placed the commodity of gros de Naples within the range of a lower class of the community than before could enjoy that commodity?—Yes.

11049. Do you think Manchester might safely be employed in manufacturing that commodity for that particular class of the community, without any injury to Spitalfields, provided that Spitalfields had not been interfered with by France?—The whole nature of my former evidence supports that view; the trade of Manchester, take it as a whole, is a low trade with which the silks of France do not directly interfere; they interfere with it indirectly, inasmuch as they increase the competition between Spitalfields and Manchester in that article.

11050. So that there would have been all that consumption of silk by the particular class of the community alluded to, and which silk might have been so manufactured at Manchester without any injury to Spitalfields, which would not have been desirous of having to receive any of that particular description of commodity, provided she had not had that superior commodity which she formerly manufactured interfered with by the manufacturers of France?—As the low silks of Manchester find a ready sale throughout the country, notwithstanding the large importation of French silks, I think it is conclusive that if Spitalfields had supplied these silks instead of France, they would have found as ready a sale notwithstanding the Manchester low goods.

11051. Are you aware that there is a considerable quantity of crapes imported from France?—Yes.

11052. Are those articles manufactured in Spitalfields?—There has been a crape manufacturer here who has stated that his trade is essentially injured, and his people reduced to a state of pauperism and wretchedness by that importation, and therefore all that it proves is this, that other silk districts besides Spitalfields have been greatly injured by the importations of the Continent, and of course that distress is in proportion to the pressure of those fabrics upon the places in England, where similar fabrics are manufactured.

11053. Did not that same witness state, that so far from his manufacture having been interfered with by Manchester, that there were at the present time 243 looms

678.                                                                                              less

less employed in the manufacture of crapes than there were before the year 1826?
—Yes.

11054. Are you acquainted with the article that is imported from France under the name of crape?—I have never seen it.

11055. Do you know whether the article imported from France is an article that was imported into this country before 1820, or an article made altogether since?—I beg to say, I can give no evidence on the subject of crape.

11056. But whatever quantity of crape is imported from the Continent does in fact interfere with Spitalfields?—I am not aware that crape is manufactured at Spitalfields any more than ribbons are.

11057. Was there a manufacture of crape in Spitalfields in the year 1824?—I am not aware that crape has formed part of the silk manufacture of Spitalfields for this 20 years.

11058. Then the articles that interfere with Spitalfields are gros de Naples, plain and figured, imported from France?--What interferes with Spitalfields of imported silk goods, are those silk goods which used to be made in Spitalfields, and always have been considered the staple article of Spitalfields whatever they are.

11059. Do you believe there is any other article now imported from France, the importation of which has annihilated any branch of the trade of Spitalfields?—It has been given in evidence, that before the opening of the Ports, taking a series of years, there were 4,000 looms on figured silks in Spitalfields; another witness has stated, that in some parts of that period half the trade was in fancy silks, according as fashion led to fancy or plain. It is now in evidence, that of the 300 looms the greatest number that can be found in Spitalfields on such silks, not 120 of that 300 are upon rich figured silks, and that the remaining number are making singles in imitation of Manchester.

11060. Then the Committee are to understand, that formerly one-half of the looms manufacturing in this country of pure silk were employed on fancy goods?—I have not said so; I have said it has been given in evidence (I did not give that evidence,) that at certain periods, according as the fashion led to fancy or plain silks, there was one-half of the manufacture of Spitalfields employed in those silks.

11061. Of the whole consumption of silk goods in this country, what proportion do you think are figured gros de Naples; the consumption of foreign and English?—It is not possible for me to answer this question. With respect to foreign silks, I suspect it will be found that the great bulk of silk goods imported from the Continent are of a rich description, and that a larger proportion of fancy silks than of plain came in.

11062. How many looms do you think the figured silks imported from France would employ in Spitalfields?—I must first of all know the quantity imported.

11063. Is it your opinion that about one-fourth of the looms formerly at work in Spitalfields were employed in making figured silks?—Yes, taking the average of years.

11064. Is that your opinion?—That is my opinion.

11065. Do you believe that there are less fancy silks consumed in this country than there were at the period alluded to?—I am quite satisfied that the consumption is much greater.

11066. Can you then inform the Committee where they were made in England if they were not made in Spitalfields?—They were made no where in England; there is not a place to which I can assign the manufacture of those silk goods, nor do I believe any place can be found; I speak of rich silks.

11067. Then it is understood that it is your opinion that there are now consumed in this country as many figured gros de Naples as would employ more than 4,000 looms?—I think so; I beg to observe that the trade in those rich goods was steadily advancing from 1822 to 1825, and in all probability, taking the experience of past years, would as steadily have increased had not foreign silk goods been admitted. This trade receded in 1826, and has been drooping ever since.

11068. Do you think there are as many figured gros de Naples consumed in this country as would employ 5,000 looms in Spitalfields?—I think it highly probable.

11069. Do you think there are as many silks consumed in this country as would employ the same number of looms that before were employed in that particular manufacture, looking at the quantity which is now consumed by the public?—I am quite satisfied, that taking the calculation upon the minimum amount of importation which I have stated, were it stopped, instant and active employment would be given to all the looms that were before employed on a similar fabric.

11070. But

*John Ballance,*
Esq.

11 July,
1832.

11070. But do you believe as many are now used in this country as would employ 5,000 looms in Spitalfields?—I should think there were; it is impossible to speak except to round numbers.

11071. How many yards of rich figured gros de Naples would a loom produce per week?—That varies altogether according to the figure and description of work.

11072. What would be the average of the Jacquard loom?—I cannot give the average, for I am not a fancy weaver.

11073. A witness having stated that each loom would produce eighteen yards per week, will you have the goodness to say what you think those eighteen yards would be worth?—No, I cannot speak to the value of figured silks, for I am not a figured weaver.

11074. Do you think that 650,000*l.* was the value of figured silks formerly consumed in this country, or that at the present moment are consumed in this country; do you think that that is an excessive quantity, and a quantity not likely to be consumed in this country?—I have no doubt that there is a much larger quantity consumed in this country.

11075. When you spoke of 4,000 looms having been engaged on figured and fancy silks, you did not mean to say that these were all engaged in figured gros de Naples, but on all sorts of figured and fancy goods?—I spoke of the fancy trade, whatever be the specific article manufactured.

11076. You mean to include figured gros de Naples, satins, gauzes, velvets, sarsnets, furnitures, crapes and brocades?—Certainly, the entire fancy trade.

11077. There were 4,000 looms employed formerly?—That supposes the manufacture took a series of years.

11078. And you think at the present time there is more consumed in that article than formerly?—Yes, but not produced in Spitalfields.

11079. Therefore it follows, does it not, that if there was no importation from foreign parts there would be a larger number of looms employed than formerly?—Yes; if there was no importation of these fancy and figured silks from France, a greater number of the looms in Spitalfields than formerly would very shortly be employed in the production of them, and, as I before said in respect of style and fashion, would produce them equally well.

11080. You are of opinion that there is now a larger quantity of figured and fancy goods consumed in the United Kingdom than there was at the time when 4,000 looms were employed in the production of Spitalfields, is that so?—My impression is, that the quantity has rather increased than diminished.

11081. What proportion has it increased, do you apprehend?—It is very difficult for me to determine the proportion.

11082. What is your impression that it has increased?—As these goods are imported from the Continent, together with plain silks, &c. both legally and illegally, to an extent which, as I have before said, cannot be reduced to accurate calculation, I should only mislead in the attempt to give exact proportions.

11083. Do you think that five pounds for the production of each loom per week would be a high estimate of the value of goods manufactured in fancy goods?—That would depend upon the value of the article, which varies very much.

11084. If each loom produces 18 yards a week, have you any doubt each yard would be worth 5*s.*?—I believe the average worth of fancy silks is now from 4*s.* 6*d.* to 4*s.* 9*d.*; but I speak under correction, for I am no fancy weaver.

11085. Do not you know that at the present moment the description of goods which we are now talking of, (rich figured silks,) are to be bought at Lyons at rather less than 3*s.* a yard?—Yes, I have seen the patterns and prices annexed; they are four doubles, and manufacturers will know what I mean by four doubles. They can be bought at this time in Lyons (figured silks) from 3*s.* to 3*s.* 1*d.* a yard.

11086. Taking the weeks at fifty in the year, and taking twenty yards as the production of each loom, that will give you one thousand yards for the production, as the quantity produced by each loom in a year; multiply that by four thousand, and you will find it will produce four millions of yards, which at 3*s.* a yard will give 600,000*l.* as the value in France?—Yes.

11087. Now from your knowledge of the silk trade, the quantity of this description of commodity produced, and from the opinion that you have given this day before the Committee, as to the total value of the silk manufacture of France, do you think that 600,000*l.* is at all too much to place as the value of figured silks imported from France, on the principle upon which you have just made this calculation?—I consider it much under the amount imported.

11088. Then do you believe that more than 600,000*l.* worth of figured silks are annually imported from Lyons?—I have very little doubt of it; I have very little doubt that more is imported now than was manufactured in Spitalfields before the opening of the Ports, and my reason is this; the increase of population must occasion an increase of consumption, and the looms would have increased in Spitalfields as the demand increased, had we not been supplied from a foreign market.

11089. Do you think there are 800,000 *l.* worth of goods imported?—I have said that I cannot give any thing like an accurate calculation.

11090. You have no doubt that it is more than 600,000 *l.*?—I have very little doubt that that is the minimum amount.

11091. Can you give any opinion as to the probable value of gros de Naples, imported from Lyons?—I have stated that the value is from 36 *s.* to 38 *s.* per pound manufactured, and the richer ones will run from 40 *s.* to 42 *s.*

11092. Do you think of all sorts of broad silk goods imported from France, the value will equal the value of the figured articles?—No; I apprehend the value of the figured is greater than the value of the plain silks imported.

11093. Perhaps you do not think any plain goods come from France worth the notice of the trade at the present moment?—So far from this being the case, a considerable number of plain silks do come from France, and this spring especially, there has been a very large proportion of plain watered silks.

11094. If more than 600,000 *l.* worth of figured silks be imported from Lyons, must not the total import of broad silk approach nearer a million in value; a million sterling, that is?—I have said that the total amount of the importation of foreign silk goods cannot be accurately calculated. It is quite sufficient if we can ascertain the minimum value of this importation, and prove that even this importation is displacing labour directly and indirectly to the amount of 1,500,000 *l.*; and if this be the effect of the lowest calculation of our importations, I leave any honourable Member of the Committee to make his own calculation of the effect produced in our silk districts by the maximum importation.

11095. But must it not, in your opinion, exceed a million sterling, if the quantity of figured is 600,000 *l.*? My opinion is, that the importations from the Continent do exceed a million sterling, reckoning the cost abroad.

11096. Have you any doubt, from the evidence you have heard in this room, of the total imports, one half at least must be in ribbons?—I have not attended to the evidence sufficiently to form an opinion. The ribbon question did not attract my attention; I was not then so frequently in attendance, as during the broad silk question; and I wish to restrict myself more particularly to my own department, of which I can speak with more certainty.

*Ambrose Moore,* Esquire, called in; and Examined.

11097. YOU are a silk manufacturer, I believe, in the firm of Wilson, Moore & Company?—I am.

11098. How long have you been in the trade?—I have been in business on my own account above 20 years; I have known the trade above 30 years.

11099. Has there not latterly been great distress in the silk trade?—There has; I should state that the principal part of our business is carried on at Spitalfields, but we have a mill at Derby, and we also employ some looms in that town.

11100. Has there not been formerly also great distress in the silk trade?—There has occasionally been great distress for short periods.

11101. Has there been more distress in the silk trade, and has it been of a more permanent nature since 1826 than before that period?—Yes, that is the character of the distress that has existed in the silk trade since 1826, and the distress that has existed since that period may, by its permanency and continuance, be contrasted with that of former times.

11102. It is now of greater extent, and more permanent in its character?—It is so; it formerly generally continued only for a few months, and was occasioned by some changes of fashion or scarcity of silk that affected the trade.

11103. Can you show that there is any connexion between the existing distress and the change of system which took place at the period adverted to, 1826?—Yes, I apprehend that it is solely to be traced to the change of system; the great quantity of foreign manufactured silk goods which now come into this country causes a great want of employment amongst all classes of people in the silk trade, and the effect of that change of system has been to turn the manufacture of England more upon the coarser and lower description of goods, which afford less employment, and to take them from the finer, more difficult and more complicated works; and to these

must

*Ambrose Moore,*
Esq.

11 July,
1832.

must be added, the enormous increase in the smuggling of foreign silks, which, whatever may be said to the contrary, is an undoubted fact.

11104. Is there any thing in the present condition of the trade which has not occurred over and over again at different periods, and which is not perhaps inherent in the nature of the trade?—I apprehend that distress is not at all inherent in the nature of the silk trade; I think the consumption of silk in this country has become now so regular, and is so much worn by all classes, that it is almost an article of necessity as much as cotton is, and that therefore there is nothing in the nature of the trade that should cause distress to arise. Formerly the trade was much more confined to the supply of the upper classes, and was consequently subject to interruptions from changes of fashion, which caused great distress possibly for a few months, but the character of the trade I think now is changed, and silk is an article of such regular consumption that constant employment might be expected in the silk trade, if our Government would give it proper protection against foreign goods; indeed, I do not know any trade more likely to afford regular and steady employment to the work-people engaged in it, nor one more likely to increase, than the silk manufacture of England would do under those circumstances.

11105. Silk has now become a permanent and steady consumption?—Yes, it has; it is worn by all classes.

11106. Has the distress in the silk trade latterly been confined to Spitalfields or Coventry, or has it extended to other places where the silk trade is carried on?—It has been co-extensive with the trade itself; some towns have felt it more than others; Spitalfields and Coventry, I believe, have not been more distressed than Macclesfield and Manchester; the persons engaged in the trade at Manchester have felt great distress. The manufacturers of Manchester will be best able to tell their own story, but if they would tell of their losses during the last year, the Committee would see that they have felt distress, whatever may have been asserted to the contrary; and if the Committee will inquire of the Manchester operatives, which they probably will do, they will find that they also have been in great distress.

11107. You have gone into the subject generally and accurately, no doubt; are you quite convinced the distress has extended to Manchester as well as other places?—I have not the shadow of a doubt of it; I happen to have a copy of a memorial which was presented to the Lords of Trade; it has been mentioned to the Committee before, but I will quote a part of it, that the Committee may perceive I speak correctly. The memorial stated—" It having been represented at your Board, that the throwing trade of Macclesfield and elsewhere has come from those places to Manchester, we the undersigned principal mill-owners of Manchester, beg to remove this erroneous impression; our throwing mills have been unprofitable, and we have, ever since the reduction of duty in 1829, considered their cost as a total loss of the capital used in their erection; and beg to add, that the silk trade at Manchester and its vicinity is in a very depressed and ruinous state."

11108. Is that document signed by the manufacturers of Manchester generally or individually?—It is signed by eight or ten of the principal ones.

11109. Has the distress been in the manufacturing department only, or in other branches of the silk trade also?—It has been in the throwing department quite as much as the manufacturing; there is not a department of the trade that has escaped.

11110. Can you see, as respects the throwing trade, any connexion between the existing distress and the change of system?—I apprehend the mere circumstance of lowering the duties on foreign thrown silk, with such rapidity, is sufficient to connect the distress with the alteration of system; that the Government should expect that no ill effects upon the throwing trade should follow from so rapidly reducing the protection of 9 s. 2 d. per lb. down to 3 s. 6 d. on one sort of silk, and 2 s. on another, seems to me quite unreasonable, and this cause alone is sufficient to connect the distress with the change of system. The throwing trade has also, as I have already stated with respect to the manufacturing branches of the trade, been in some measure diverted by the treatment of this trade by Government, from the working of the finer sorts of silk, to the coarser and inferior sorts which afford much less employment.

11111. Was there not a great extension of the throwing trade in 1824, and subsequently?—I know it is alleged against the throwing trade, that they very imprudently increased their throwing operations in the face of the law, for admitting foreign silk goods; but if they did do so, the Government of that day, and other

678.

public

*Ambrose Moore,*
Esq.

———

11 July,
1832.

public men who now censure the trade for so doing, by their speeches, urged on the very steps they now condemn. They told the trade that " the cords were now cut which had kept it bound to the earth," and that there was nothing to prevent the silk trade being extended in a manner similar to that of cotton. It can be no matter of wonder that some effects should have been produced by such exhortations. There was not, however, subsequently to the alteration of the law in 1824, any thing like such an extension of the trade as the Government represent, and such extension as did take place has long since been contracted again, so that for a long time past there has been less machinery at work upon silk; and if the fineness of the silk then used is taken into consideration, there is now less throwing done, by a considerable quantity, than was done before the Ports were opened to foreign silks, or even than was done in 1824. The Committee will allow me to instance the town of Macclesfield. There are in that town fewer factories, fewer spindles, and fewer people employed in throwing than there were in 1824; and the machinery at work in that year, it should be borne in mind, could not have been erected after the alteration of system as is often pretended. Factories and machinery are not built and put to work in a short time, but require a long time to prepare, and therefore those at work in 1824 must have been built in 1823, or before. I believe that the same will be found to be the case in other districts, in the West of England, and at Congleton. At Macclesfield it is very striking.

11112. But did not the Macclesfield throwsters, in 1824, or some subsequent year, advertise for 5,000 hands; at least it was so stated in Parliament by Mr. Huskisson?—It was so stated in Parliament certainly, and one house did advertise; their hands were rather unruly at the time, and it was with a view to keep them in order, but it produced no effect in bringing hands into the town, for not a single hand came in consequence of it, nor was it in fact ever intended to produce such effect. All these circumstances, relative to that advertisement, were stated before Mr. Huskisson even mentioned it in Parliament, and it has been more than once mentioned against the whole throwing trade of England as a specimen of their folly, when in point of fact it was the act of an individual house, and merely to accomplish the purpose I have stated of frightening their hands on the moment, because they were acting unreasonably.

11113. You mean it was a local transient act, and not at all characteristic of the state of the trade generally?—Certainly, it was not the act of Macclesfield, but only of an individual.

11114. There has been, however, since 1823, a great increase in the quantity of raw silk imported into this country?—Yes, undoubtedly there has, since 1823, been an increase in the import of raw silk. The silk trade had been regularly increasing, and was in a very prosperous state before 1824, although it was then burthened with duties, which yielded I believe about three quarters of a million to Government. It is worthy of remark, that that increase was always in the raw and not in the thrown silk; and that circumstance shows, that the effect of the duty on the thrown was to produce an importation of raw silk; and it also accounts for the regular and gradual increase of throwing mills in England previous to that time. This tendency to increase had been for years checked by the very high prices of silk, as well as the heavy duty on the raw silk; but as soon as the circumstances of the times had brought silk down to a moderate price, an increased consumption of it began to be apparent. This was the state of the case in 1824 when the Government first announced its intention to reduce the duties on raw silk, and that reduction undoubtedly assisted in the extension of the trade. The excitement which the Government itself created in the trade had some effect, but it is not in my opinion consistent with the fact to attribute in any but the slightest degree, the increased consumption of silk in 1824 and 1825 to any thing else than that increasing desire for silk goods which had long manifested itself, and which had then become much stronger than at any former period. It should also be remarked, that before foreign goods were admitted, the increase in the importations of silk was chiefly in Italian, a proof that the trade was extending principally in the manufacture of the better sorts of goods; but that since that period the use of Italian silks has very much fallen off, and there has been an increase in the use of those of the East Indies and Turkey. The total average quantity, however, of all sorts imported since 1825, falls short of the average of 1824 and 1825, and so large a proportion of it being coarse, it does not afford near so much employment for the mills, as the finer sort imported from Italy, besides that a considerable quantity is used for

purposes

*Ambrose Moore,*
Esq.

————

11 July,
1832.

purposes with which neither weavers nor throwsters have any thing to do, such as sewings, trimmings, fringes, &c. &c. The hosiery trade has also increased, and uses a larger proportion of the silk imported than it used to do.

11115. Was not there a larger proportion of knubs and waste than formerly?— I have not taken that into account.

11116. Do you believe that the quantity of sewing silk manufactured in this country has increased?—I apprehend it has.

11117. Are you aware that Mr. Harter, who is a manufacturer, stated that there were considerable exports before 1824, and that there had been none since?—I was not aware of that; I have not looked at it with reference to exports, but as to the quantity made now. I have understood, and I believe it, that more sewing silk is made in this country than used to be.

11118. Do you mean that the home consumption is increased to an extent greater than the previous export?—I know nothing of the export, and therefore I do not wish to give an opinion about it; but I believe the manufacture of throwing silk has increased, from what inquiries I have made. I understand sewing silk very much more used in this country than it used to be, the low price causes it to be applied to a vast many purposes which it was not used to be applied to.

11119. You have stated, that there has been a great increase of the importation of coarser kinds of silk which you have accounted for, has there not also been a great increase in the importation of Italian silk since the year 1824?—I am talking of the importation of Italian silk since then.

11120. Of raw silk?—Taking raw and thrown together.

11121. What has been the importation of Italian raw silk since the year 1824; as compared with the time previous to that year?—It is larger, undoubtedly.

11122. And putting the years 1824 and 1825 entirely out of the question, has not the importation subsequent to the year 1825, been very much larger than the year previous to 1824?—Of course it is my duty to answer the question; but I do not think in an examination of this question, the Committee ought to leave the years 1824 and 1825 out of the calculation. I always must protest against that view of it, because it is unjust and injurious to the silk trade. The general importation of raw silk since 1826, is greater than it was previous to 1824, but there is one year, 1826, in which the importation is less than it was before 1824. The silk trade unquestionably, speaking generally, has been on the increase for many years, but that increase has not continued since the opening of the Ports to foreign goods, on the contrary, since then it has gone back both in quantity and also in the quality of its productions. The importation of Italian raw silk had been gradually increasing for many years previous to 1823, and in that year the quantity of raw imported from Italy, was nearly double what it had been ten years previously, indeed if you take the average of 1814, 1815 and 1816, the importation of raw silk in 1823 had trebled, and this increase was before there was any idea of taking off the duties, or of making any alteration of the system; I think that all this shows there was a great tendency to increase, quite independent of the plans of Government.

11123. The raw silk had been previously burthened with a considerable duty, and it was expected on the removal of that duty, the trade would increase?—I perfectly recollect the period, and I am satisfied from all the appearances at that time, that if the duty had not been taken off the silk trade would still have very much increased; but I consider that taking off the duty on raw silk of 5 s. 6 d. a pound, very much assisted in the extension of the manufacture, as the prohibition continued for two years longer. I think the fairest way of looking at the effect that foreign competition has on our manufacture, is to compare the present condition of the trade with what it was in 1824 and 1825, after the burthen of duty was removed, and before foreign goods were let in, for I cannot consider it at all fair to compare its present state, that is, as to its extent, with the period when it was burthened with enormous duties and when the price of the material was from other causes so high. The comparison I propose, will show distinctly and separately the effect of taking off the duty on the raw material, and also the taking off the prohibition against foreign goods, which I think ought not to be mixed up together.

11124. But if on the other hand you take the prohibition united with the reduction of the duty on raw silk, it appears that the effect of the two united, has been rather to increase the consumption of Italian silk than diminish it?—I think not; but that the circumstance of taking off the duty, or the burthen under which the silk trade lay, showed what the silk manufacture of this country was capable of.

11125. Are

*Ambrose Moore,*
Esq.

11 July,
1832.

11125. Are the Committee to understand this as your opinion, that the silk trade has been a progressively increasing manufacture in this country, that you felt yourself entitled to infer it would continue to increase, and that when the duty was removed on the raw material, that it would increase with a still greater rapidity than it had done before; and that in fact it has not increased in proportion, so rapidly since as it had done before the duty was removed?—Certainly the taking off the duty, and letting the prohibition remain, gave the silk trade of this country an opportunity of showing that it was capable of expanding in a great degree; and this is to be seen by the importation and consumption of silk in 1824 and 1825.

11126. If the price of silk had been the same that it has been since 1824, and there had been no importation of manufactured goods from France, do you think that the consumption of silk would have been greater than it is now, by all that difference which the weight of manufactured goods imported from France would give?—I am quite satisfied it would.

11127. Did the increase from 1821 to 1826 depend on the material, or a growing taste on the part of the public?—I believe there was a growing inclination to wear silk, and it arose partly from the reduction in the price of silk, which had been at a very high price during the war, and particularly while the intercourse with the Continent was very much interrupted. It was, at one time, as high as 120 s. a pound; it had been more valuable than silver; and it was not likely, whatever might be the taste of the public for silks, they could be very extensively worn while that was the price of the material: but as soon as the interruption, occasioned by the war, had ceased, and the price became low, there was then a tendency to increase, quite independent of the French manufacture, and of all the goods she was making or could send here. I should be glad to put before the Committee what was the consumption of the years 1824 and 1825, and to compare those two years with the six years that have elapsed since then; I know it is always contended by the Government, that we should leave out of view 1824 and 1825; but it is my duty to contend, that 1824 and 1825 ought to be taken into the account; and I wish respectfully to call the attention of the Committee to this point.

11128. Do not you think that the great increase of manufacture that took place in the years 1824 and 1825, after the reduction of the price of silk, is an evidence of the great increase of consumption and the great prosperity that would have taken place had it not been for the interruption, and the admission of French silk goods?—Certainly all the goods were sold as fast as they could be made.

11129. Are you aware that the years 1824 and 1825 were years of great speculation and excitement?—They were in mining companies, foreign loans, and many most absurd schemes; there was no silk company; no speculation in silk; silk was bought and wove, and sold and worn; there was no speculation in silk.

11130. Then you do not believe there was an increased manufacture of silk goods at that time, in consequence of the great excitement that prevailed among the trading and commercial world generally?—I believe not. The great increase had commenced before the Government plan was known, and was in full operation before any of the speculations and excitement in the commercial world took place.

11131. I think you stated the goods were sold as fast as they were made; and therefore it was not a speculative manufacture?—They were sold as fast as they could be made; and those who bought them of the manufacturer sold them as fast to the public. I myself very well recollect that that was the case.

11132. In point of fact there was no speculation, and in consequence there was no loss?—Certainly.

11133. Was that the time that the Hibernian Silk Colonial Company took place?—There was a company of that sort; but it had no immediate effect on the silk trade, nor had the silk trade any thing to do with it. I believe Mr. Huskisson was one of the promoters of it; what his ideas were of conferring advantages upon the silk trade by it I do not know.

11134. Did not the price of the material advance very much in 1825?—Yes; because there was an increased demand for it.

11135. And was not the spring of 1826 a time of extraordinary bad trade at Macclesfield?—I do not know whether it was at Macclesfield particularly, I believe it was; it was in London.

11136. Did not that arise from the anticipated admission of French goods, which were to be allowed to come in in July?—Entirely, in my judgment; there was no buyer of goods that I ever addressed myself to in that half year, wanting him to

buy

buy goods, who did not give this answer "the French goods will be in in July, and we will not buy till we see the effect their coming in will produce;" that was the invariable answer.

*Ambrose Moore,*
Esq.

11 July,
1832.

11137. At what period was that?—The latter end of 1825, and the first half of 1826.

11138. Did not the distress prevail at Macclesfield at the end of 1825, and at the early part of 1826?—I do not know, I think it is probable; but it was the latter end of 1825, and the early part of 1826, that distress existed in London.

11139. Was not the cotton trade bad at that time in your recollection?—No, I do not know that it was.

11140. Do you remember a discussion in the House of Commons, in 1826, on the state of Macclesfield?—On the state of the silk trade, there was a discussion.

11141. Then it is your opinion, that the general excitement that preceded the panic, had no influence on the silk trade?—I believe none; I believe every body was rather in better spirits that year in all their transactions, certainly in much better spirits than they are now; but that it had any material effect on the silk trade, I entirely deny; and the best proof I can give is, that the goods were regularly disposed of to the public as they were made.

11142. From the circumstance of the manufacture having been worked up for consumption and not for speculation, you think the manufacture could not be embarrassed?—Certainly.

11143. Do not you think the small importations of silks in 1826, was occasioned by the state of things which then existed in England?—I think it was occasioned by the state the silk trade was in at that time.

11144. Do you remember the state of the silk trade immediately after the French goods were admitted?—Yes, I remember the whole of that year was a very bad one.

11145. Was not the trade very brisk after those goods were admitted?—Not in 1826.

11146. Not in the winter of 1826?—Taking 1826 generally, it was what I call a bad year; it was found by experience, a bad year by the silk manufacturers.

11147. Was not the fact, that so large an importation of French goods as had been anticipated, did not take place, because the description of commodity prepared by the French manufacturers was not precisely that which the English had been accustomed to?—The anticipated evil was mitigated partly from the circumstance the honourable Member has referred to in his question, and partly by an arrangement made by the Board of Trade, to admit goods only of certain lengths; which arrangement was intended expressly to prevent the coming in of any large quantity of goods which the French might have ready to pour into this market upon the opening of the Ports, and which by coming in suddenly might very greatly aggravate the distress then existing in the silk trade.

11148. The Government by that Act, seemed to be afraid of their own measure, did they not?—I apprehend they were.

11149. At any rate they did not wish to bring it into operation with too great rapidity?—No, it was a good scheme to prevent too great a quantity of French goods coming in at first.

11150. Do not you think that the French manufacturer was sufficiently acquainted through the smuggler, with the demand in England for proper articles suited to the English market?—No, I do not think he had any thing like the knowledge of the English market that he now has; I think from the underhand way in which the silk trade between England and France was carried on at that time, by means of smuggling, it was not at all likely that the French manufacturer should acquire the same knowledge of the demand by the English public, as he has now the opportunity of doing.

11151. Were persons of as large capital at that time concerned in smuggling as it is stated are now?—I believe not, I should say certainly not.

11152. Do you not consider it to be the business of this Committee to inquire into the joint effects of the two changes that have taken place in the silk laws; namely, the removal of prohibition and the reduction of duty on raw silks?—I consider the Committee should inquire into both, but I do not think they should join them together; they are not necessarily connected, and to understand the subject perfectly, they should inquire into the effect of each separately.

11153. Then do you consider it a fair mode of inquiring into the joint effect of the two, to take the two years, when one of these changes had been effected, and

678.                                                                          the

*Ambrose Moore,*
Esq.

———

11 July,
1832.

the other had not, rather than take a series of years previous to the two, and a series of years subsequent to the two?—I think they ought to be separated, and for this reason, unless you do so you will not see which of the two measures has had a good and which a bad effect upon the English silk manufacture. I have already shown that the goods made in 1824 and 1825 were made for actual consumption, and were sold and used as fast as they were made, and this proves what was the demand of the English public for silk goods; a very greatly increased demand as soon as the duty was taken off raw silk; which demand would have been continued to be supplied by the English silk manufacturer had not French goods been allowed to be imported; as I have shown that there was no speculation as to the silk used in 1824 and 1825, I think I am entitled to 'ask the Committee to look at the two questions separately.

11154. How does the average of the years 1824 and 1825 compare with the last six years?—The total average consumption of the years 1824 and 1825, of thrown and raw silk, was 3,642,969 lbs. and the total average consumption of the six following years was 3,612,522 lbs., showing a falling off of 30,000 lbs. per annum, instead of there having been any increase.

11155. And comparing Italian with the other sorts of silk?—Comparing Italian with the other, the coarser sorts of silk, it will be found that the consumption of Italian silk has been decreasing, and the consumption of the coarse description of silk, that is the East India and Turkey silks, has been increasing; the average of the consumption of Italian silk for the years 1824 and 1825, is 1,937,094 lbs., and the average consumption of the six subsequent years in Italian silk is 1,626,816 lbs., showing a falling off in the use of Italian silks, which are applied to the making of the finer description of works, of above 300,000 lbs. per annum. Then the average consumption of 1824 and 1825, in coarse silks, is 1,705,875 lbs., and of the six subsequent years 1,985,706 lbs.; so that the effect of the alteration in the laws has been to deteriorate the silk manufacture of Great Britain in this respect that it has turned it from the manufacture of the richer sort of goods, such as are calculated to uphold a manufacture in the estimation of the public, to the manufacture of coarse and inferior goods; besides the consideration of the smaller quantity of employment which these coarse silks give to all persons engaged in the trade.

11156. You have stated that there are several branches of manufacture in which silk is used to a greater extent now than heretofore, and which has nothing to do with throwing or weaving?—Yes.

11157. Then it follows that, if the finer kinds of silk manufacture had continued as prosperous as heretofore, taking into account the increase of the population, the cheapness of the article and the taste of the public for silk goods, there ought in your opinion to have been a greater increase than now appears?—If after the duties had been taken off raw silk, the prohibition had been continued for some years longer against foreign goods, I do not doubt that the manufacture of Great Britain would have very much increased, and particularly in that class of goods which would have been made from the finer and better sorts of silks, and that the importation of Italian raw silk would have very much increased instead of falling off as it has done; the falling off in the importation of Italian raw silk is as much as the whole of the silk mills of Manchester can throw; I may here be allowed to remark that these Manchester mills, which it is said have ruined all the rest of the throwing trade in England, cannot throw more than 300,000 or 350,000 lbs. per annum, and that partly of coarse and partly of fine silk.

11158. Did the throwsters generally extend their operations in the face of the new system adopted in 1824, which they said they were so alarmed at?—No; I believe that there has been no great increase in the throwing establishments of England since, but that the great increase took place before 1824, and was occasioned by the gradual increase of the trade. The Committee can have better evidence from Macclesfield upon that subject than I can give them; but I will just advert for a moment to what is the state of that town: in 1824, there were fifty-eight mills at work, and there are now forty-one at work, that is the state of the town of Macclesfield; therefore no mills that have been erected there since, nor any thing they can have done there since, can possibly account for their having fewer mills at work than they had in 1824.

11159. Has there been such an importation of raw silk into England, as would satisfy the mills of England which were in existence before the change of system in 1824?—I believe not; I believe if every mill was destroyed that has been erected since, or if the mills in England were put into the condition they were at that

moment,

*Ambrose Moore,*
Esq.

11 July,
1832.

moment, that they would not have now full employment, the kind of silk that we have chiefly to throw being so much coarser, and some of it not being thrown at all.

11160. Still you must admit that the quantity of raw silk now imported is much larger than it was before the alteration of the system in 1824; how then is it that the mills are not so well employed as they were at that period?—I think the answer to the last sufficiently answers this question; but if, instead of looking at the weight of silk imported, the Committee would for a moment consider it as a matter of length, if we look at it as a thread, to be measured by yards, instead of looking at it as so many pounds weight, it will be quite clear that from the coarseness of the great part of the raw silk now imported, there is very diminished employment for the silk mills of England. Those who wish to make out that it is not foreign competition, and not the change of system in the silk trade, that has destroyed the English throwster, are constantly referring to the weight of silk imported; but it is not fair to look at the question in that way, and it is still more unfair to do so after this explanation of the apparent inconsistency between the weight of silk and the quantity of employment it gives, has again and again been made.

11161. You have stated there is a great quantity of silk now imported not thrown at all, or only partially thrown, and that there is a larger quantity of it thrown coarse than before?—Yes; the thread of silk is much coarser than it was, and a considerable quantity is used for purposes that require little or no throwing.

11162. It has been said that the real mistake was the levying any duty at all on the thrown silk; that the whole of it should have been taken off, and that if it had the importation would have been just the same as now, neither more nor less; is that your opinion?—No; I have no doubt at all that the importation of thrown silk depends on the duty on thrown silk. It has been repeatedly and confidently stated that we are never to expect more than about the same quantity; it is said to be " a curious fact," that we have always had the same quantity of foreign thrown silk in under all circumstances; but it will be found that the quantity of foreign thrown silk that comes into this country will depend on the degree of duty that there is on it; and that as you lower the duty on thrown and encourage its importation, you will discourage and will lessen the importation of raw; and if it were not so, there would be no way of accounting for our having been standing still for sixty or seventy years in the import of thrown silk, while the silk manufacture of Great Britain has so extended itself, and the imports of raw have kept pace with that extension. It was the duty on thrown silk that encouraged the original building and the gradual increase of silk mills in England, and made it the interest of the Italians to raise silk to send to this market in a raw state; but as the duty has been gradually lowered, the Committee will perceive that the importation of Italian thrown silk has been increasing, and that of raw has been diminishing; and if the present system should be followed up, we shall in the end have all our silk from Italy in a thrown, and none of it in a raw state.

11163. From the amount of the average quantity of silk consumed in the last six years, does it not appear that while France has been increasing in her silk manufacture during the same period 50 per cent. this country has not increased?—Certainly that is the case.

11164. It has also been said, that the introduction of thrown silk into this country arises not from its superior cheapness, but from the necessity of having a certain quality of that silk from Italy which cannot be thrown in this country; are you of that opinion?—No, I am not at all of that opinion; the assertion has often been made at the Board of Trade and other places, that it is necessary to have a given quantity of foreign thrown silk, and that that quantity and no other quantity will come, but there is not the slightest foundation in fact for the assertion.

11165. Has it been explained why it was necessary to have a certain quantity of that silk, by those who held that opinion?—No, I have never heard it explained. It is stated sometimes that foreign thrown silk is necessary to make velvets, at another time that it is necessary to make satins; but the fact is not so. It is a matter of price; if at any time foreign thrown silk can be had in the market cheaper than English thrown silk, it will be bought, but not from any preference because it is foreign; that is the general course; a few persons may be prejudiced in favour of one or the other; but that is the general feeling. As to foreign thrown silks being necessary for any branches of the English silk manufacture, it is entirely a mistake; the richest and best works are made with English thrown.

11166. Is the distress in the throwing trade local or general, arising from the transfer from one town to another; for instance, from Macclesfield to Manchester?
—I believe

*Ambrose Moore,*
Esq.

11 July,
1832.

—I believe it is general; it certainly does not arise from the transfer of it from one place to another. It has been attempted to account for the distress of Macclesfield by saying the trade has gone to Manchester; when during the last winter, we complained of distress in the throwing trade, the Government replied to us, that the distress of Macclesfield was easily to be accounted for from its transfer to Manchester, and that Manchester had upwards of 300 horse-power applied to silk throwing; while the fact is, that there are not above 150 horse-power applied to it in that town, and that the falling off, in the throwing trade of Macclesfield alone, is greater than the whole throwing trade of Manchester. I do not know any part of England where the throwing trade is carried on, to which the depression in that trade has not extended.

11167. At this moment can you buy the foreign thrown silk cheaper than you can buy the raw of an equal quality, and throw it yourself?—At this moment I can buy the foreign thrown silk cheaper than I can buy the raw, and throw it.

11168. Are you aware that any improvement has taken place in silk machinery, either in throwing or weaving, since 1826?—I believe there were quite as good throwing machinery put up before 1826 as has been put up since; and as to weaving machinery, there is only the Jacquard worth speaking of; and that was introduced and was at work in England before 1824, and there has been no improvement in it since.

11169. Has the skill of our artisans improved since?—No; I think their workmanship has fallen off; such, at least, is the case in Spitalfields.

11170. What do you attribute that to?—I attribute it the low prices that are paid in Spitalfields, which have induced great slovenliness of workmanship. The Committee need not, I think, travel further than their own minds to know that that must inevitably be the case; whenever you pay a low price, you generally get an inferior article; and it will be the case with workmanship as with every thing else; in short, my experience is that workmanship is worse than it was.

11171. In both departments do you mean, or only in the weaving?—I was then referring to the weaving; but I think that silk, generally speaking, is not thrown so well in England as it was when the prices were higher.

11172. As to capital; is the capital of manufacturers and throwsters greater or less now than it was?—There is decidedly less capital employed in both branches of the silk trade than there used to be before the alteration of the system; very far less. Most of the throwsters are ruined, and a great many manufacturers also, and some of them are men of capital; but a great many of them are men of no capital.

11173. Then it follows that the three points, on which Mr. Huskisson is supposed mainly to have relied, namely, the superiority of our machinery, the skill of our artisans, and the extent of our capital, have entirely failed?—I consider it an entire failure, as far as those three principles are concerned.

11174. Had not you in 1824, when the alteration of the law was under consideration, some intercourse, personally, with some of the members of Government, on the subject of that alteration?—Yes; I had several interviews with some of the members of Government.

11175. What, in your opinion, led the Government of that day to a change of system in the silk trade?—I believe they were led to the consideration of the question of the silk trade chiefly from the Committee appointed by the House of Lords in 1821, on the Foreign Trade of the Country. They wished to extend the silk manufacture of this country, and there was some expectation on their part, that they could give us an export trade. They also wished to prevent smuggling, though I believe that was not by any means their principal motive.

11176. Were the operations of Government founded, do you apprehend, on the abstract principle of free trade, or on the less sound though more practical principle of putting an end to the contraband trade?—I have already stated what I believe were the views of Government, the advocates of the present system now always pretend, that there was such a dreadful degree of smuggling that the object of Government was to put a stop to it, and that that was the sole object; but I apprehend their views were of a more general nature, and that putting a stop to smuggling was not their principal motive.

11177. Did the proposal for altering the system excite much alarm at that time in the trade?—Yes; there was generally, with the exception of a very few individuals, great alarm in the silk trade at the proposed alterations.

11178. What was the ground of alarm?—There was in the trade, an opinion that the French silk manufacture was a very powerful and extensive one, and in that respect their alarm was a well grounded one, they seemed to have a correct notion

of

of the extent and importance of the French manufacture; another ground was, that our trade had, up to that period, been burthened with heavy duties which had kept silk dear in this market, and our labour in the principle weaving districts of Spitalfields had been regulated and restricted by the magistrates of the districts, so as to keep down improvements in the richer branches of the trade. They considered the advantages which the French were in possession of from the growth of their own raw material, their low wages, the perfection they had attained to, while we had been kept under burthens and restrictions, and from their already enjoying the markets of all the civilized world, and that consequently there was a probability that this market would be overwhelmed with French goods; these were the general impressions of the trade, and their grounds of alarm.

11179. But was not time asked for persons engaged in the trade to withdraw their capital and to save themselves from the extraordinary and unequal competition that was expected?—It was certainly asked that time should be given; the object of some individuals was undoubtedly to retire from the trade, but the general motive in asking for time, was the better to enable the trade to meet the competition that was coming on.

11180. What time did the trade require from Government to get out of that sort of artificial burthensome state which the trade appeared up to that time to have been kept in?—The trade was very much pressed for a period of seven years between the time of being disburthened from the duties, and having to enter into competition with a trade which had never been burthened at all.

11181. What time was granted?—Two years and a quarter; viz. from March 1824 to July 1826.

11182. From your subsequent experience, do you think that time was sufficient for the purpose?—No; I am of opinion that it was by no means sufficient, it was quite impossible for the trade to get out of such a state as the silk trade then was in, into that state which should make it safe and reasonable for them to compete with the French. I know there are persons who do not enter into the subject considerately and who do not understand the subject, but pursue a theory regardless whom it may injure, who say that no time ought to have been granted; these persons have no mercy on those who have property embarked in the trade, who have capital invested which cannot be turned to any other purpose, they have no consideration for such things at all, but contend that a Government may tax and burthen, and restrict a manufacture as long as they please, and encourage persons under such a system to invest large sums in manufactories, protected to a given extent by law, and that as soon as ever it is the pleasure of Government to remove these burthens and restrictions, they may also at the same moment remove all protections, and require you to jump out of this artificial into a natural state all at once, and be prepared to compete with all the world. The proposal must strike every person as unreasonable and unjust, to say nothing of its being unwise. To extricate the silk manufacture of England from the effects of the high duties, the restrictions on its labour and all its old habits, and to prepare it safely for competition with such a manufacture as that of France, a long period should have been given, and if it had, I do not doubt that a very much more successful result would have been attained; as it was, the two years' interval I have mentioned was absorbed almost entirely by the efforts of excitement made by the Government of the day, and afterwards, as the time approached for the letting in of French goods, by the greatest alarm and panic. If I might venture to say what I think has been the great mistake of Government in this question, I would say, that it has been the great impatience always shown to hurry the silk trade on to a state of freedom from protection faster than the matter was capable of, and this only ultimately retards the very object aimed at.

11183. The Government, of course, at that period removed all the existing restrictions on the labour and the mode of working?—Not at all, it was no part of their plan; the Spitalfields Act was left in force, and the Government proposed we should actually go into this contest with our hands tied up as to labour, and without the possibility of making any improvements in our manufacture. It has been stated before the Committee, that a "higher order of intellect is applied to the silk trade in France than is so applied in England." I do not think the remark a very civil or a very judicious one towards a large manufacture in which there are a number of most intelligent persons, and mechanics of great talent, but I think it is rather applicable to the respective Governments than to the persons engaged in the manufacture. There was, in my opinion, very little intellect displayed by our

*Ambrose Moore,*
Esq.

11 July,
1822.

678. Government

*Ambrose Moore,*
Esq.

———

11 July,
1832.

Government in the way in which they should set up and have carried on this competition. That the Government should first begrudge us any time to prepare, then give us two years for the purpose, and then, by continuing in force a law such as the Spitalfields Act, attempt to prevent our improvement, would seem almost impossible; but such was the fact. The regulations under the Spitalfields Act, among other things ordained, that if any thing was woven by machinery, it should be paid as if done by manual labour, restricted the number of threads to the inch, said that if an article were made partly with cotton it should be paid as if made wholly with silk, forbid you to ornament any but certain sorts of velvet with a bias edge, and directed that works should be made this way or that, according to the judgment of the magistrates at quarter sessions; and these regulations were all enforced under a penalty of 50 *l.* for every violation. The forcing of us into competition with France with these restrictions upon us, might justify the remark I have alluded to as applied, not to the trade, but the Government; I think it presents, at all events, a contrast very strikingly in favour of the Government of France, which always seems to take pleasure in listening to the wants and wishes of the silk trade of that country, and in promoting every improvement in it, while in England the silk trade is on all occasions treated with the greatest distrust and suspicion, and every preference shown to the French.

11184. Was not the Spitalfields Act repealed soon after?—Yes, it was repealed, but it was by the exertions of about half a dozen persons in the trade, and it was at an expense to these persons, of about 1,500 *l.* Is not that a proof of what I stated, that the trade owes no gratitude to the Government? This 1,500 *l.* was expended in obtaining the repeal of a law, which if left in force, would have prevented the least chance of successful competition with France, and it was paid out of our pockets, and part of it given in fees to the Lord Chancellor and other officers of the two Houses of Parliament. This surely was not the way to treat the silk trade of this country, and at the same time lay claim to credit for enlarged and enlightened views respecting it; and as we are now petitioners before Parliament, and have an opportunity of stating our grievances, I hope it will not be taken amiss if I state that the silk trade is never looked upon or treated with that consideration and favour which I think we are entitled to from our own Government.

11185. Your statement is, that the repeal of the Spitalfields Act formed no part of the plan of Government in the alteration of the law?—The complaint I mean to lay before the Committee on the part of the silk trade is, that we are charged with having had time to prepare for entering into this competition, and that we made none but a bad use of the time, whereas in point of fact, the Government proposed we should go into it with our hands tied up as to labour, from which restriction they refused to release us, that we effected our release ourselves at a great expense, and we did it not only with Government not assisting us, but actually with the Cabinet Ministers opposing us and canvassing against us.

11186. In the various statutes that passed connected with the alteration of the law, the repeal of the Spitalfields Act was not one of them?—Certainly.

11187. But it was an Act that passed in consequence of the private solicitation of the manufacturers of Spitalfields and London, who thought themselves interested in the repeal of the Spitalfields Act?—Yes.

11188. And in its repeal, you were not assisted but opposed by the Cabinet Ministers?—I know that three Cabinet Ministers canvassed against us to get votes against us in the House of Lords.

11189. Did that Act pass as a private Act?—It did.

11190. With all the expense incident to a private Act?—Yes, with the usual fees paid on private Bills to the officers of the two Houses, and great expense in hiring counsel.

11191. It had been attempted before had it not?—Yes.

11192. And was thrown out after a Committee had sat on the silk trade in the House of Lords, and approved of the repeal?—Yes; it was introduced at first, with the assistance of Mr. Huskisson, who was then President of the Board of Trade, into the House of Commons, and it passed the House of Commons, and it went up to the Lords; and in consequence of the opposition of the Cabinet Ministers, it was referred in the House of Lords to a Select Committee, that Select Committee heard counsel and witnesses, and reported in favour of the Bill; but notwithstanding that report in favour of the Bill, the parties to whom I have referred, opposed it in the House; and it was altered on the third reading in such a way as to render it perfectly nugatory, and therefore it dropped that session. The next

session

*Ambrose Moore,*
Esq.

———

11 July,
1832.

session it was introduced, and carried in opposition to the canvass of three Cabinet Ministers, who got all the peers they could to vote against the Bill.

11193. There is no doubt of the propriety of the repeal of that Act?—None at all.

11194. And you complain that there was not that paternal solicitude on the part of the promoters of the great change, as there ought to have been, or they would have proposed to repeal the Spitalfields Act as part of the measure?—I complain of it in two respects; I say it shows our Government neither took a kind nor an enlightened view of this question as respects the trade, and it shows that they are not entitled to complain that we have not done all we could to meet the competition with France, since they not only not put us in the way, but they actually opposed our getting freed from this restriction; that although the weavers of Spitalfields were much prejudiced in favour of the Act, I do not think they had generally taken any unreasonable advantages of it in respect of the wages they obtained. If the Act had not been in existence, I think the greater part of the time they would have obtained higher wages. The greatest objections to it were, its interference with the manner in which the works were to be made; and the prices also that were fixed by it were much higher than could possibly be given now.

11195. It was injurious to you, as fettering your arrangements with regard to particular articles?—It was incompatible with the state of the trade, as it was in future to be carried on. A competition with a foreign manufacture, while that law existed, was out of the question.

11196. Did not the Government express to the trade their intention and confident expectation that the regulations should be such, that no greater quantity of French goods should come in after the removal of the prohibition than had previously been smuggled into this country?—They did; Lord Liverpool stated that it was not the wish or intention of Government, that the quantity of French silk goods coming into this country should be increased, but only that they should come in in a legal instead of an illegal manner.

11197. And in point of fact it has resulted, has it not, that the quantity introduced, by illicit means alone, now greatly exceeds what was introduced by illicit means prior to the prohibition?—Yes, undoubtedly the quantity smuggled has greatly increased; and as to the whole importation, those who state it at the lowest, and who think the alteration of the system a favourable one, admit that four times the amount is sent from France to England than was sent before the alteration of the system; and I have no doubt that it is double that, that is, that eight or ten times as many French goods now come as were smuggled in before the alteration.

11198. In your negociation with Government, was that a matter of most anxious solicitude on your part, and that of the other persons engaged in the silk trade?—It was.

11199. And did the Government at that time express themselves most confident and decidedly on that point, that there would not be any greater quantity imported than was then smuggled?—Certainly, it was stated over and over again.

11200. Were you convinced that such would be the case at the time?—My own impression was different from that of others in the trade; I was rather sanguine in my expectation of benefit from the change.

11201. You supposed Government had means of information not possessed by the trade in general, and therefore you were disposed to place confidence in their repeated assertions?—I placed confidence in this, that they could and would collect 30 per cent.; an engagement which they have never fulfilled.

11202. But you believed they had the power?—I believe then and still believe that they have the power; I do not mean to say, that the Government at that day had any idea of encouraging a smuggling trade; but I do say this, that it is the duty of the Government to prevent it, that they have the power of doing so in great measure if they please, and that they have never tried in good earnest to do it.

11203. When you say they have not carried into effect their intention of collecting 30 per cent., what do you mean?—I mean that there are so many goods coming into this country, smuggled in at a much lower rate, perhaps 15 per cent.

11204. But does not the rate in some cases much exceed that?—I am not speaking of the legal rate. What I complain of is, that they do not collect the duties, that there is no sufficient endeavour used to prevent smuggling.

11205. So that in point of fact so much as 30 per cent. is not collected?—Certainly not, on an average. The goods that pay the duty may average that, but a

**very**

very large proportion of the silk goods imported are smuggled, so that the law is in great measure a dead letter.

11206. Do you consider that when the Government undertook to reduce the duties, they had taken means to provide against smuggling?—Smuggling has increased ever since the alteration of the system, and therefore I am inclined to think Government never did take any means to stop it.

11207. That is what you mean when you state Government have not fulfilled their engagement?—Yes, as far as protecting the silk trade goes, by collecting a duty of 30 per cent. I remember Mr. Huskisson's words were, that Government " both could and would collect 30 per cent." That was a distinct pledge to the silk trade, and it was also a part of the plan of Government; and I think I may fairly say that it was part of the engagement which they entered into with the trade, that the throwsters should be adequately protected; they started with a duty of 7 s. 6 d. a pound on thrown silk, and they kept to that engagement but a very short time; and I consider that a distinct breach, I will not say of a written treaty, because I cannot put my finger on an actual written engagement, and say here is a breach of it; but the fair understanding was, that they would make such regulations that there should be no greater importation of goods into this country than there had been already smuggled in, and that they would protect the English throwster, in short that they would protect both classes of the trade.

11208. You believed that some extraordinary regulation would be adopted in order to ensure the collection of 30 per cent.?—Certainly that was what Government undertook to do.

11209. You knew you had the good faith of Government pledged, and you thought they would have the power, if they chose to exercise it, of carrying it into effect?—Certainly, it was the expectation of the trade, and I consider the Government fairly bound to do that which they undertook, and which they at the time declared their ability to perform.

11210. You have stated you were concerned in the alteration of the law in 1824, did you concur in the reduction to 5 s. in the pound in 1825?—No, it came by surprise on the trade; it was done by a Treasury Order, sent to the Customs, to reduce the duty from 7 s. 6 d. to 5 s. It was, I believe, a great injury to some individuals, as it affected their stocks on hand, and I consider it a departure from the engagement that Government had entered into to protect the throwster; at all events I considered it was the very lowest point the Government could reduce the duty to, if they meant to have any regard to their engagement.

11211. Then did you, in 1829, concur in the reduction of that duty from 5 s. to 3 s. 6 d. a pound in organzine, and from 3 s. to 2 s. on foreign tram?—Certainly not; I had nothing to do with it either on one side or the other; but I certainly disapproved of it, and thought it would be, as it has proved, most ruinous to the trade.

11212. Was the trade, to your knowledge, consulted on the reduction of the duty in 1829?—There was a great many representations made to the trade and to Government against the reduction of the duties; I believe a few individuals, not interested in throwing mills, and who thought they should individually benefit by getting thrown silk cheaper, represented to Government that it would be a desirable thing to take off the duty.

11213. When you say representations were made, do you mean they were made before the reduction or afterwards?—Before it had taken place.

11214. Were you consulted at all at that time, having been consulted before, and what is your opinion of the effect of the change in the duties which took place in 1829?—I was not at all consulted.

11215. But you were consulted in 1824?—In 1824 I was, by Mr. Huskisson; but in 1829 I was not consulted at all.

11216. What is your opinion of the effect of the change which took place in the duties in 1829?—The whole alteration that took place in 1829, both the lowering the duties on foreign goods and lowering the duties on foreign thrown silk, has been most injurious to the silk trade, and accounts, in a great measure, for the distress that has existed in the trade the greater part of the period that has since elapsed.

11217. Can you explain to the Committee the nature of the understanding that was ultimately had between Government and the trade in 1824, as to terms upon which the Ports should be open to foreign silk goods?—The terms settled eventually by the Government, and which the Government are in fairness bound to keep were, that there should be a duty of 7 s. 6 d. a pound on foreign thrown silks, and that foreign goods should pay a duty of at least 30 per cent. with an assurance

from

*Ambrose Moore,*
Esq.

11 July,
1832.

from Government that they both could and would collect that duty of 30 per cent., and would secure the trade against smuggling.

11218. That you speak of as the understanding that was actually come to between Government and the trade at that time?—Yes, that was the ultimate understanding.

11219. How long was this engagement kept on the part of Government?—I consider it was quite an infringement of that engagement that the duty on thrown silk should be reduced to 5s. in the very next year, without any consultation with the trade, and without any circumstances to justify the alteration; this was a violation of it as far as the stipulated protection for the throwster is concerned. As to the quantity of foreign goods brought in, I will, with the permission of the Committee, state what appears from the official accounts from France (which I have reason to believe the Committee have seen), to have been the quantities of French silk goods sent into this country from France before and since the opening of the Ports, so that the Committee may see how far the understanding we had with Government, that no more goods should come in under the new system than came in under the old, has been kept. It appears by the French official accounts of the exports of silk goods from France to England, from the year 1821 to 1825, both inclusive, that the average annual amount was 3,838,749.f. in value, and that the average of the next five years, that is the five years after the Ports were open, was 12,411,303f. in value, showing that the quantity had been more than trebled. And in the former average, that is I have included that year (1825) in which there was a great increase in the importation from France, arising, as I believe, entirely from the laxity that had arisen in the execution of the laws for the prevention of smuggling, occasioned by the near approach of the period when the goods would be legally admitted; and but for the admission of this year into the calculation, the quantity of silk goods smuggled in from France before the opening of the Ports would appear considerably less. The exportation from France to England in the last year (1831) which is not included in that statement, is very much larger still, amounting to, I believe, 20,000,000 of francs, so that it has increased six or seven fold.

11220. What was your individual opinion at the time of the arrangement respecting the prospects of the silk trade of this country under the alteration?—I was anxious individually to see the silk trade relieved from the duties with which it had been burthened, and which I had always thought were a great impediment to its increase.

11221. You speak of duty on the raw material?—Yes; on raw silk. I thought that taking off that duty was calculated to extend the trade very much; and the Government would not take off the duty, without coupling with it a measure for admitting foreign silk goods. I was therefore willing to take the two together as better than continuing the duties upon raw silk; I was certainly at that time very ignorant of the advantages which the French possess in the silk manufacture. The growth of her own raw silk is an immense advantage, and that circumstance I neither fully considered, nor if I had, should I then have been aware of the great advantage it is of to France; and further, which is the most striking feature of the inquiry before the Committee, I had no idea of the effect that mere fashion produces on this trade; the rage for French fashion is quite independent of all price, and all perfection.

11222. What is your opinion now of the further reduction which took place in 1829?—I have already stated it generally. It has been very injurious to every branch of the silk trade; and I consider it was a very unnecessary measure; it has been quite ruinous to the throwster, and I think it has retarded the general prosperity of the trade; I consider it has thrown back the trade at least twenty years, or more, in the course of improvement. It has increased the importation of thrown silks, and has diminished the importation of Italian raw silks. It was always likely that the reduction of duty from 5s. to 3s. 6d. should produce that effect, and if the duty were reduced still lower, that effect would be still more apparent; so that we should import all thrown silk and no raw silk from Italy: and as to its effects on the manufacturing department of the trade, it has discouraged the making of the better class of goods, and obliged the manufacturer to turn his attention to the lower and coarser description of goods; and as to producing the effect proposed from it, that of checking smuggling, smuggling has been carried on more extensively since than ever.

11223. Do you suppose that the duties of 5s. on organzine and 3s. on tram, as they existed in 1829, would have kept up the supplies of Italian raw silk?—Yes;

I do

*Ambrose Moore,*
Esq.

———

11 July,
1832.

I do not doubt that the importation of Italian raw silks would have been greater than they have been since, had that duty continued, provided also that Government had not reduced the duties on goods, and that they had taken some better means to prevent smuggling, for if they reduced the duty on foreign goods, as they did in 1829, and allowed so many foreign goods to be smuggled, I do not mean to say raw silk to a larger extent would have come in, for the more foreign goods we have the less silk we want.

11224. Do you find as good Italian raw silk now as formerly, when the duties on thrown silk were higher than they are now?—I think the quality of Italian raw silk has not been so good the last year or two; I find more difficulty in getting good raw silk; no doubt there is good Italian raw silk imported, but not so much good in proportion as there used to be.

11225. Do you believe Italy produces less good raw silk now than she did formerly?—The view I take of it is, that she has been inclined to send more thrown silk; I think the circumstance of the duties being lowered in this country has led her to send rather more of thrown silk and rather less of raw silk.

11226. Do you consider the Italian has any local advantages as a throwster which you have not in England?—Yes, I do; I think that the being on the spot where the raw silk is to be had, where it is first reeled, gives him some great advantages; many of the Italian throwsters also reel their own silk.

---

*Veneris,* 13° *die Julii,* 1832.

### EDWARD AYSHFORD SANFORD, ESQUIRE, IN THE CHAIR.

---

*Ambrose Moore,* Esq. called in; and further Examined.

*Ambrose Moore,*
Esq.

———

13 July,
1832.

11227. WHAT has been the state of the trade during the last two or three years, that is to say, since the alteration in 1829?—As far as the effect of the alteration in 1829 on the throwster is concerned, I may say, that it has been most mischievous, and consequently has been very injurious to the trade at large; it obliged the throwster immediately to reduce the wages of his hands as one of the elements of the economy which he was obliged to observe, and this produced great distress among the working hands in that department of trade, and in those parts of the country where throwing is carried on, it has had the effect of driving the poor who work in the mills, upon the poor's rate. In 1830 (the following year), there was what may be called a re-action in the throwing trade, arising in my opinion, altogether out of the previous depression, brought about by the reduction of duties, the effect of the reduction of those duties had been so to discourage throwing, and to ruin so many persons engaged in it, and so to contract the operations of others, that in the course of the year 1830, it was found that the supply of thrown silk was not adequate to the consumption of it by the looms, and the consequence was, that for a few months in 1830, there was a great demand for thrown silk, particularly tram, and the price of throwing rose, and was for a few months in a pretty good state, and if it had but continued, it would have been all that the throwsters could have wished; but as this temporary scarcity was undoubtedly occasioned merely by the injudicious manner in which the Government reduced the duties, so it was rectified in a few months by the great influx of foreign thrown silks, occasioned by the advance of price and the low duties, and these two concurrent operations very speedily again reduced the throwster to the same distress as he had been in before the advance of price took place. In the weaving department also the same distressing reduction of wages was the consequence.

11228. The wages are now miserably low in most of the throwing establishments, are they not?—Yes.

11229. Has it become the practice to make up the wages of the hands employed in mills from the poor's rates?—In many parts of the kingdom that is the case, when the price at which throwing can be done in England is stated, and a comparison is instituted with the price of throwing in Italy, with a view to show that we approach the Italians in price very nearly, and want but little protection, two circumstances are left out of sight, one is, that at the prices that have been quoted before this Committee as the market prices of throwing in England, the English throwster

*Ambrose Moore,*
Esq.

13 July,
1832.

throwster looses, although the parish assists him to pay the wages of his hands; and the other is, that the prices quoted as those of Italy, afford a profit to the throwster of that country. When the question is, what is sufficient protection, it appears to me important to consider these circumstances; one thing is quite clear, that when the parish pays half the wages, the cost of throwing is not to be taken at what it may appear to cost the throwster. Then as to the effect of this alteration of duties in 1829, on the manufacturing branch of the trade, it has let in foreign goods at lower rates than before; I speak of those which have come through the Custom House, and so far from effecting the object which it was stated the Government had of preventing smuggling, I believe the fact to be, that there has been more smuggling since then than there was before.

11230. What was the state of trade, particularly during the year 1831?—It was in a declining state the whole year, and towards the close of it there were thousands of persons thrown out of employment, from the inability of the manufacturers to dispose of their goods; great sacrifices on manufactured goods were made, and more distress existed in Spitalfields at the close of that year, than I ever recollect to have heard of there before; and although there was less public display made about the distress of Spitalfields, upon this occasion, (no public subscription was entered into for its relief, and it was not brought before the public in that form which upon some former occasions it had been,) yet it must not be inferred that it was not equal to the distress on former occasions; it was in fact much greater, but it seemed to be of that permanent nature, arising out of a system deliberately adopted by the Government, that it was treated as a hopeless case, for which there was no cure, unless Government would alter the system applicable to the silk trade.

11231. Was this state of the trade occasioned by any change of fashion or decline in the consumption of silk goods?—Not at all; the distinction between the distress I am now speaking of, and that of all former periods is, that it used formerly to arise from some falling off in the consumption of silk goods; but in this case I believe the consumption was as large as ever, and the supply of all the better sort of goods came from France. According to the French official accounts, the exports of silk goods from France to England last year, was greater than in any former year; I am not at all disposed to believe those accounts are correct, and have not a doubt that a much larger quantity of silk goods than they exhibit, find their way to England; but taking those accounts as they are, you will see that there was last year sent to England a much larger quantity than had ever been sent before, and at least seven times the amount that was sent on an average of five years previous to the opening the Ports.

11232. From the observation you have now made, you are supposing that there was a great quantity of goods imported into this country which were smuggled out of France?—I believe so; I do not doubt it.

11233. Have you any means of being able to prove that?—I have nothing that could be called positive proof of it, but I am quite satisfied that it is so; in the first place, the accounts of the French Government of the export of silk goods from that country to this, do not account for the obvious quantity of French goods that are constantly in this market, and secondly, I think it is so unlikely to be the course of business for a smuggler, whose transactions require concealment, and whose operations might often be detected if they were known, to pass all his goods regularly through the Custom House of France, when they are intended to be smuggled into this country, in the middle of boxes of eggs, and large packages of Dutch baskets, and all kinds of ways; and therefore whatever may be said by Calais houses, and parties having an interest in concealing the real state of this branch of the inquiry, I do not believe that the French official accounts of exports of silk goods to this country give us the true amount, nor any thing near it.

11234. Is the nonpayment of the export duty a sufficient temptation to them to smuggle their goods out of France?—I am not aware what is the exact amount of that export duty, I should think it is but small, and perhaps it might not be worth their while, for the mere object of avoiding that payment; but at the same time, if it be so small, it will make it in another point of view more likely that they would pass their goods otherwise than through the Custom House, because it is not worth the vigilance of the French Government to prevent them.

11235. Do you believe that in any year since 1826, any thing like so small a quantity in value as 400,000*l.* worth of French manufactured silks have been imported into this country, do not you believe the quantity must have been very much

678.                                                                                 larger

*Ambrose Moore,*
Esq.

———

13 July,
1832.

larger than that?—I have no doubt it has been very much larger in every year since then; in several of the last years, I am quite sure that such a quantity of goods as I have seen about, could not be comprised within such a sum as 400,000*l.*

11236. In point of fact, do you believe it is perfectly notorious, that there are some two or three houses in London, whose transactions in French silks would alone make more than that?—I have no doubt of that at all; if you look to the number of French houses that there are, and look to the very large quantities of business they are doing, it is quite clear they could make no returns at all if it were to be comprised within such an amount.

11237. Did you in consequence of the state of trade, which you have spoken of as occurring in 1831, make any representations to the Government about it?—Yes; the trade became so much distressed towards the latter part of last year, that about October a committee was formed, which had various communications with Government until the month of February.

11238. What was the nature of the representations made to Government?—The general nature of the representations was, that the trade was in great distress, and that it was attributed to the very inadequate protection that it received against foreign competition; and that without better protection it was quite in vain to expect that the employment of persons engaged in the manufacture could continue. We also represented particularly the difficulties that existed in the fancy department of the silk trade. We represented as one of the modes of mitigating the evil, that foreign silk goods, upon their importation into this country, should be stamped, and that some more efficient means should be taken to put a stop to smuggling; that it had been quite clear, that pecuniary penalties were not sufficient to prevent smuggling, for that men of large capital had engaged in it as a regular trade, and who were of a class that would not engage in it if the offence itself was made a disgraceful one; and I think we were justified in taking that view of the necessity of fixing some stigma upon the offence of smuggling, from what I have heard has been given in evidence before this Committee, viz. that in France, and it is not quite clear whether it was not meant also in England, that a smuggler is looked upon as a public benefactor, and if so it is quite time that that character of the smuggler should be changed, and that he should be held up by the law as a criminal. We represented particularly, as the opinion of the committee of the silk trade, that in dealing with the question, on this occasion, that they would not attempt a cure which would be worse than the disease, by pursuing a similar course to that adopted in 1829, when the protecting duties were reduced; that on the contrary, both as it respects thrown silks and manufactured goods, we would not consent to proceed on any such principle. We did not mean to dispute that some goods might not be in the Schedule too high and others too low, but the principle should not be of curing smuggling by a reduction of duties. We recommended, in order the more effectually to prevent smuggling, that the importation of foreign goods should be limited to one Port, and that there should be one warehouse, or one department of the Customs at that Port, for the housing and examination of those goods, and that with a view still further to prevent frauds and secure the collection of the duties, some person should be appointed as an inspector by the Government, who should either be recommended by the trade, or be a person in whom the trade had confidence. On one of these occasions we quite understood the President of the Board of Trade to state that they were prepared to go with us on the principle of not reducing the duties.

11239. Why do you think it is important that criminal punishment should be inflicted on persons engaged in smuggling transactions?—Because it will prevent men of capital and character from engaging in the smuggling trade. The necessity for such a law is apparent from a transaction which came to light in the course of last autumn, from which it appeared that a house of large capital had been engaged in that trade. When men of large capital engage in this trade it tends to reduce the rate of smuggling. When men with 200,000*l.* or 300,000*l.* capital engage in any trade they can afford to carry it on, and always do carry it on, at a small per centage profit; and therefore it is of the greatest possible importance, in my opinion, to make it a trade which it is disgraceful to be concerned in, that it may fall into the hands of small dealers, and so the rate of smuggling may be raised. The payment of such a sum as 20,000*l.* as a compromise by that house, may seem a large sum and a sufficient punishment, but they had probably made a profit of 40,000*l.* by their smuggling transactions; and therefore looking at the matter as

one

*Ambrose Moore,*
Esq.

13 July,
1832.

one of mere profit and loss, there is no security whatever from pecuniary penalties that they will not go on with it.

11240. Would not the only effect of inflicting criminal punishment be, that men of capital would nominally withdraw from the silk trade, at the same time as they employed others to conduct it for them?—I think it would, unless the plan of stamping was also a part of the regulation; but if a man of capital should set up another establishment, nominally distinct from his own, but in reality to carry on his smuggling operations for him; if the goods were stamped at the Custom House, you would be able to trace those goods, and detect them if they had not paid the duty; and I apprehend that the two measures are necessary; the one for the other. I do not think stamping altogether effectual although useful, without criminal punishment, and criminal punishment would not be effectual without stamping, because a man of straw, who would run the risk of imprisonment and hard labour, might be the nominal smuggler; but if the goods, by means of stamping, could be traced to the real smuggler, I think the remedy would be complete.

11241. Do you think a system of stamping might be adopted, to effect the purpose you propose?—I have no doubt at all of that. I believe you have had in evidence, the particulars of stamping, which were recommended by the trade to Government; but I have no doubt, from having considered that plan, that it would be perfectly efficient. You will recollect it does not proceed on any notion that a stamp may be made so perfect that it cannot be forged; that idea is quite abandoned; and it proceeds on a perfectly different principle; which is, that a fresh stamp shall be adopted every day; that it shall have certain changeable letters and figures in it, which shall make it quite unknown to all the world what stamp is going to be put on the goods: the stamp shall have on it the date of the day on which it was put on the goods, and it shall be accompanied (and this is quite a necessary part of the plan) by a pattern-book, to be kept at the Custom House, and that a pattern shall be cut from each piece of goods imported and stuck into that book: and there shall be a progressive number separate from the stamp, on each piece; for instance, one shall be 300, another 301, another 302, another 303, and so on; and those numbers shall be placed against the pattern in the pattern-book; so that if a person should have imported ten pieces of a particular pattern on a particular day, and then having ascertained the stamp put on them, should go over to Calais, and should smuggle in 100 more of the same description exactly, and should copy the stamp, it would then be seen there would have been 110 pieces marked, and the Custom House pattern-book would show only ten pieces had passed; and that I apprehend would be a means of detection, and the very fear of it would deter persons from attempting to copy the stamp.

11242. It would throw great difficulties in the way?—Yes, it would throw great difficulties in the way, and would very much check smuggling, if it did not entirely stop it.

11243. Why do you think stamping of so much importance?—Without goods are stamped it is impossible, in 99 cases in 100, to prove they have not paid the duty. Nothing is more common than for an importer to pass one case of goods through the Custom House, and smuggle in twenty others; and to make the one which has paid duty father all those which have not. If goods were stamped, and patterns kept at the Custom House, this could not be done.

11244. Is it your opinion, that foreign goods may be stamped without much trouble or difficulty? —There is no doubt that they may; if the duty was 30 per cent. on goods, it is quite clear, as a matter merely of profit, it must be very well worth the while of the Government to have them stamped, in order to secure the collection of the revenue. We submitted some plan of stamping to the Custom House, which was a very difficult and tedious one; and although it was so, yet the inventor of it said he would contract for the stamping of each piece with this stamp at a farthing a piece; I mention this, to show that the expense of so difficult a stamp as we never should have thought of recommending, was so small a per centage on the goods; then it is said it causes great delay and inconvenience; I believe there is no pretence for such an allegation: it would be necessary to employ a few more persons, but if the Government were to have an apartment in the Custom House, a large room, such as the King's Warehouse, for the purpose of examining and passing and stamping silk goods, there would be no reason at all why they should not employ a sufficient number of persons to stamp all the goods that came, without putting the importer to any delay or inconvenience at all; and the duty they

678.                                                                                          would

*Ambrose Moore,*
Esq.

———

13 July,
1832.

would get on the goods would much more than cover any expense occasioned by employing extra hands.

11245. But whatever delay there would be, the whole trade would feel it alike, one man would not have an advantage or preference over another, and therefore you think it is not a thing which importers ought to complain of?—Certainly; if there were some inconvenience to importers, when it is considered how many thousands of men are thrown out of work in consequence of smuggling, I think that inconvenience should be borne for the sake of the greater good accomplished by the plan; but I submit there will be no inconvenience in it but what is capable of being avoided by good arrangement.

11246. Do you think the main objection against stamping goods, because stamps are easily forged, does not apply to the plan you recommend?—I am satisfied that the plan is a perfectly secure one, admitting that it is most easily forged; indeed, the stamp submitted to Government was of a very simple nature in its form, and it would appear, when stamped on paper, that it could be easily forged, but the forgery would not, I apprehend, facilitate smuggling at all.

11247. How were these representations received by the Board of Trade?—We had a great many interviews, and there was every appearance of giving consideration to our representations. I have already stated, that the President of the Board of Trade was understood by every one of us on one occasion to say, that Government did not intend to proceed on any principle of reducing the duties either on thrown silk or on goods; this I wish distinctly to state to the Committee, because the trade generally do deprecate extremely any reduction of duties, as it would be inflicting a most unnecessary and grievous evil. We understood Lord Auckland also to assent to the necessity of inflicting some punishment on smugglers that should withdraw men of capital from the trade.

11248. Do you remember the period at which that interview took place?—I do not recollect exactly, but I believe it to have been the latter end of December last. With respect to our representation as to stamping, there was in our opinion an evident objection to its adoption; the objection stated was chiefly that the best experience had always proved that stamps could be forged; we again and again stated that we proceeded on a different principle, but still we were met with the objection that stamps could be forged; I believe that was, as far as principle was concerned, all the objection that was made. The question of stamping was so far under consideration, that a communication was addressed to me from the Custom House by the Surveyors General, to desire a few of the trade to attend there to discuss with the officers the plan of stamping, and which we submitted to them. What report they made to the Board of Trade upon it we do not know, but the result was, that the plan of stamping, criminal punishments, and all the other suggestions made on the part of the trade were rejected, without any reasons whatever being assigned.

11249. Do you conceive that there is that difference between French manufactured silk and English manufactured silk that would enable you to discover the difference between them?—If a quantity of French goods are looked at together, and a quantity of English, there would be no difficulty whatever in saying which are French and which are English. If you look at a dress or a small piece of silk, I do not think in many cases you would be able to tell, but certainly taking the French goods in the bulk, the texture, appearance and style of the work, and there is no difficulty whatever in distinguishing them from English. I went to the Custom House to see those goods which were seized from Leaf & Company: no man in the trade could have any hesitation in saying those were a lot of French goods. In like manner Manchester goods may be known from Spitalfields goods, and yet I should not like to say I could always tell whether the dress a lady has got on is of Manchester or Spitalfields manufacture; but if I saw goods in a quantity, or done up in pieces, I should have no difficulty in distinguishing them.

11250. You do not think that there would be any difficulty in making the discovery, supposing there was an understanding between the manufacturer in this country and the smuggler?—No, I think there would not be any difficulty at all.

11251. You understand the drift of the question?—Yes.

11252. If a smuggler in France or a manufacturer in this country chose to connect himself with a smuggler in France, and worked the same pattern in England as he knew was working in France, then the person who would have to sell it would say, " This was manufactured in Spitalfields or Manchester," or wherever it might be, be, " and I can bring you the man who worked it to prove that he had work in his loom of this pattern;" you think that the manufacture would be so different as to enable you to judge of the two?—If evidence was brought in a court of justice of the sort alluded to, and if a man was produced to swear he made those goods in Manchester or Spitalfields, the decision would be probably, that they were made at Manchester or Spitalfields, however persons in the trade might differ in opinion from that evidence. I believe an instance of that sort has already occurred in the case of Depouilly & Company; I do not doubt in the least that the goods seized were smuggled goods, and yet evidence of the sort now referred to was obtained, and a charge was made against the silk trade that they had acted with jealousy and illiberality towards that house.

11253. In point of fact it would turn out, in a state of prohibition, the French manufacturer might copy a pattern for its novelty, when it came into the market, then you might immediately detect it; the novelty would detect the manufacture, would it not?—Certainly; I addressed my remarks to the present state of the intercourse; a state of prohibition would have the effect of producing dissimilarity between the two manufactures, in many of those particulars that would enable us to know French goods from English.

11254. What settlement of the question between the Government and the trade were you led to expect would take place?—I have already stated that the trade objected to any arrangement founded upon the principle of a reduction of duties. This we understood was conceded to us. We wanted more protection than we had, and not that the existing protection should be reduced. We particularly urged the necessity of taking better measures than had ever up to that been adopted to put a stop to smuggling, and the stamping of goods, and the punishment by imprisonment and hard labour of all persons engaged in smuggling transactions, were the suggestions we made to effect the object; and we had considerable hope, from the urgency with which we pressed these points, as well as from what fell from the President of the Board, that they would have been adopted.

11255. At what time did this negociation finally terminate?—It was in the month of February that one of our committee was sent for, and was told that nothing could be done; that a Committee of the House of Commons would probably be appointed to consider the question of smuggling, and that nothing further could be said to us.

11256. Were there no reasons against stamping founded on the objection to the retail trade?—A deputation of the retail dealers waited on the Board of Trade, and made some objections to stamping; the committee of the silk trade took pains to ascertain, both from the Board of Trade and also from the gentlemen who were deputed by the retail trade, what the nature of those objections were, and they never could learn more than these two; supposing a piece of silk to have the stamp at one end, a lady would sometimes have a fancy to have a dress cut from that end, which would cut off the stamp, and so leave the rest of the piece liable to seizure; and this fancy must be complied with, or the lady would leave the shop without purchasing what she intended. The other objection was, that it would be in the power of any shopman who wished to do an injury to his master, to cut off the stamps from foreign goods, and so render them liable to seizure; the objections amounted to no more than these. To set off against these objections, we had a declaration in favour of the plan, presented to the Board of Trade, signed by the largest dealers in foreign silks, both wholesale and retail, and which we could have got much more numerously signed if we had thought it necessary; but we thought it quite sufficient proof of the plan being unobjectionable if it was signed by a few of the most eminent houses. I am therefore led to conclude that the objections stated by the retail dealers were not the objections which operated on the minds of those who have the direction of these matters, they never could have come to the conclusion, that for the sake of such trifling objections as these thousands of the English weavers were to be kept in a state of starvation; and therefore I again am obliged to come to the conclusion, that there were other more powerful reasons operating in the minds of those who have the direction of these affairs.

11257. Do you think the removal or the lowering of the duties on foreign thrown silks would relieve the manufacturer from his present difficulties, and enable him the better to compete with the manufacturer on the Continent?—If all the duty were to come off, and then if the silk were to sell just so much lower than it did before the duty was taken off, I submit that even then there would be no cure at all for

the

*Ambrose Moore,*
Esq.

———

13 July,
1832.

the evil that is felt in the silk trade. I think you may take the case of Coventry, and apply this reduction to the silk consumed there, and you will find it will not make a difference of two per cent. on all the ribbons there produced; and if you look at its application to that branch of the Coventry trade which suffers most from competition with France, that is the gauze and fancy branches, it would be quite a drop in the bucket as to any kind of relief, and perfectly inadequate to the end proposed; and if our Government would condescend to look at it really with a view to ascertain whether it would be a remedy or not, it would be seen to be no remedy at all; that it may answer the purpose of making manufacturers who are not throwsters believe, that they might, at the expense of the throwsters, get some personal advantages to themselves, and so divide the trade into parties, and set one party against another party, I do not doubt; and it has on former occasions produced that effect, but the expected advantage has by experience been found no advantage at all; as duties have been lowered, the manufacturers have been further from successful competition than ever. I have been speaking upon the supposition, that if the duty were to come off, it would make all the difference in the price; but in point of fact, it would make a very little difference in the price of the thrown silk; I believe the greater part of the duty that would be taken off, would be just so much in the pocket of the Italian. I do not deny that foreign thrown silk would for a time sell for something less in this market, just so much less as would serve to destroy the English throwster; and when the English throwsters were a sufficient number of them destroyed, the price would then rise again, and the Italian would take so much more of the throwing trade to himself. It would also prevent Italian raw silk from coming to the English market; that silk would come in a thrown state. The effect of a reduction of duty would be very trifling upon rich goods. I would take this silver tissue as an instance of what I mean; the reduction of a shilling or two in the pound on the price of silk, makes so trifling an affair in the whole cost of this article when finished, that it would produce no effect in relieving the English manufacturer from the disadvantages under which he is, as compared with France.

11258. But would not the lowering of the duties on foreign thrown silk be a benefit to the silk manufacturer in this country, by placing more within his reach the excellent thrown silks of Piedmont and Lombardy?—No, I do not think it would; I do not consider that Piedmont organzine, as is so often represented, or that any foreign thrown organzine, is at all essential to any branch of silk manufacture in this country; I believe you could find no branch of the silk manufacture, whether velvet or satin, or any other, but that in the manufacture of it some persons would prefer foreign thrown silk and some English thrown silk; it is an entire mistake, not to call it a misrepresentation, to say that a certain quantity of foreign thrown silk is essential to the English manufacture, and that the English manufacturer will take no more than that quantity. The fact is, that foreign thrown silk is not at all essential; that if you can get good raw silk in this country, you can get as good or better organzine thrown from it in this country than the majority of the thrown silk of Italy; and that the true policy of the country is to take that course that should bring good raw silk here; it is equally a mistake to say that there is something curious that nobody can describe in the fact that a certain uniform quantity of foreign thrown silk always comes into this country let the duty be what it may. This curious thing, which has been so often referred to, and which seems to me to be no subject of wonder whatever, is, that for the last 60 or 70 years there has annually been from about 350,000 to about 500,000 pounds weight of foreign thrown silk imported, and that the quantity should not have varied more, considering that the silk manufacture of this country has so much increased during that period. The fact is that the duty on foreign thrown silk encouraged the building of throwing mills in England, and made it the interest of the Italians to send their silk in a raw state, because they could get more by sending it raw than by sending it thrown; and although that duty was reduced, first to 7 s. 6 d. and then to 5 s., the quantity of thrown silk imported was not increased; because the English throwster strove to keep it out by working for a price which was a great loss to himself, and by inflicting great misery and wretchedness upon those persons who worked for him, but still he did it; the English throwster succeeded in keeping down the importation of foreign thrown silk as long as there was a duty of 5 s. remaining; but the Committee will perceive, the moment the duty was reduced from 5 s. to 3 s. 6 d. the fact, which is better than a thousand theories, is seen, that foreign thrown silk came in in

great

*Ambrose Moore,*
Esq.

13 July,
1832.

great quantities.    Foreign tram came in for the first time when the duty was made 2 *s.* ; as long as the duty on foreign tram was kept the same as on foreign organzine we did entirely without foreign tram.    A bale of foreign tram, I dare say, did not come into this country once in twenty years; but now foreign tram comes in, and I appeal to that fact to prove that the importation of thrown silk is a question of duty; it is a question whether so much labour shall be performed in this country, or whether it shall be performed in foreign countries.

11259.  Then you infer that by a total repeal, if such a thing could be enacted, of the duty on foreign thrown silk, the Italians would cease to send their raw, and would supply you with thrown silk?—My belief is, that by degrees they would send it thrown, instead of sending it raw.

11260.  And there would be that consequent want of employment for the people, and that destruction of property that is vested in the mills of this country?—It appears to me, without any benefit to the manufacturer arising from it, that it would be the transfer of so much employment from the labour of this country to the north of Italy.

11261.  You were speaking of the encouragement of throwing in England, do you consider the present duty sufficient for the encouragement of throwing of Italian silk?—No, I have just this moment stated that ever since the reduction of the duties from 5 *s.* to 3 *s.* 6 *d.*, the throwing trade of this country has been discouraged, and that more Italian thrown silk has been sent in than was before; and I believe if the duty continues at 3 *s.* 6 *d.* that this effect will be progressively increased ; that more thrown silk will come in and less raw ; it will be seen that while Italian thrown silk has been increasing, Italian raw has been diminishing.    And the official accounts show, taking raw and thrown together, that the whole quantity of Italian silk annually consumed has been on the decline since foreign goods were admitted.

11262.  Do you think that the reduction of the import duties on foreign thrown silk, would, on the whole, be prejudicial or injurious to the silk manufacture of Great Britain?—I think it would be decidedly injurious to the silk manufacture of Great Britain, taken as a whole; not separating one branch from the other, but taking this country as a silk manufacturing country, I apprehend it would be a fatal blow to it to discourage the throwing of silk in this country.    There was a time, a century ago, when the silk manufacture was not a very important one, but still the Government of that day thought it would be advantageous if they could introduce throwing into this country, and throwing was protected and encouraged for a series of years until it has become a very large trade ; I am not an advocate for the continuance to that amount of duty that was once upon it; I do not want 7 *s.* 6 *d.* or 9 *s.* but I am satisfied it is the true policy of this country to protect throwing, so as to encourage the extension and protection of it, for I am satisfied without it, the silk manufacture of this country, as a whole, will decline in its extent, its perfection, and in the character of the goods ; and in fact I do not believe, on the whole, it will be near so extensive, it will be a dwindling one.   I look upon the large supply of good raw silk as being at the very foundation of the prosperity of the silk trade of this country ; I do not think that any country will successfully carry on a silk trade unless that country throws her own silk ;  look at the large silk manufacturing countries in the world, and you will perceive they all throw the greatest part of their own silk.    Take France, which is at the head of the silk manufactures of the world, it has been stated by those who do not wish to magnify the advantages of France, that that country raises, in her own territory, at least three-fourths of the silks she uses, she of course herself throws that which she raises.    The next silk manufacture in extent is that of England, at present we throw seven-eighths of the silk we use.    Then if we take Vienna and Italy together, because they are under the same Government, the thrown silk used in the silk trade of that country is derived from the Austrain States of Italy ; if you take away those three instances there will remain no extensive silk manufacturing country in Europe.

11263.  You spoke of the dwindling state of the silk trade of this country, do you consider a well adjusted scale of duties would be the most effectual means of increasing the silk manufacture?—Yes, I do.    Deprive England of her throwing trade, and of a good supply of Italian raw silk, and instead of enabling us the better to compete with France, you send us to a much greater distance from her, we shall then be less on an equality with France than we are now ; we shall then be hardly able to say that we have a great silk manufacture, in the proper sense of the word, in this country ; we shall not have the whole operation in our hands, we shall be

678.                                                                                                      merely

*Ambrose Moore,*
Esq.

13 July,
1832.

merely weavers.   In order to exemplify more fully what I mean, I will take the liberty of exhibiting the different stages of the silk manufacture to the Committee; I will first show a skein of raw Fossembrone silk as imported from Italy; that is the state in which it is imported (*exhibiting it.*)   Secondly, a skein of Fossembrone organzine, which has been thrown in this country; that is the next stage of the manufacture (*exhibiting it.*)   The third is a skein of Fossembrone organzine, in a dyed state (*exhibiting it.*)   Then the fourth stage is this, having the silk wound on a bobbin (*exhibiting it.*)   And the fifth stage (*exhibiting it,*) is what is called a cane, or in other words a warp.   This has been prepared to make satin.   Those are the several processes of the manufacture previous to the work going into the loom, and there remains only the last process, which is the weaving.   Now what I contend for is, that there is no more reason why our Government should draw a line here, having on the one hand the skein of raw and the skein of organzine, and on the other hand the skein of dyed, the silk on the bobbin, and the silk in a cane or warp prepared for the loom, and say that all on the one hand shall be done out of the kingdom, and all on the other hand done in the kingdom, than that they should draw the line between any other two of the processes.   If the Government insist that for the benefit of the weaver all silk shall be thrown out of the kingdom, the next stage will be that all shall be dyed out of the kingdom, and then wound and warped out of the kingdom; and I should like then to know what reason there can be why silk should not be wove out of the kingdom any more than that it should not be warped, wound, dyed and thrown there.   I cannot see why the weaving more than the other processes should be protected.   There are some great advantages in the detail of the manufacture from throwing silk in this country.   The wants of a manufacturer as to the kind of thrown silk are constantly varying, and if we have the silk in a raw state we can throw it in this country to supply those varying demands; we can throw it into organzine or into tram; we can throw it into two threads or three threads; we can give it a slack or a hard throw; and then as to one of the grand advantages also of throwing in this country, it makes us so much more independent of a foreign country.   If we drew the whole of our supply of thrown silk from abroad, we might in case of a war have our manufacture almost totally and quite suddenly suspended, and this is not a mere case of supposition, but it is that which has already happened.   I remember very well the Berlin and Milan decrees, at which time it was exceedingly difficult to get thrown silk, or silk in short at all.

11264.   It was equally difficult at that time to get raw, was it not?—Undoubtedly it was; but if it is wished to secure the trade of this country against contingencies of that sort, it will be found that there will be practically less difficulty in getting raw than thrown silk.   On the occasion to which I have referred, there was really great difficulty indeed in supplying the English looms with silk; it was smuggled in very small and irregular packages through Holland, when any silk arrived it was a subject of rejoicing, and I remember on one occasion some talk of an illumination in Spitalfields; whether that was really in contemplation or not, it will show the Committee there was great difficulty in getting silk for the supply of the manufacture.   I think it is clearly our interest to encourage the importation of Italian silk in a raw state rather than a thrown, as it would be less probable that there would be an interruption in case of war, to our obtaining raw silk.   It is very likely the cultivation of silk both in France and in Italy will increase; now if we go on encouraging the Italians to send us their silk in a raw state, it is probable the cultivation of raw silk in Italy will outstrip their capability of throwing; I know at present they can throw more silk than they do, but if at a future time the cultivation of raw silk should have very much increased, they probably would not be able to throw it, if we had been in the habit of taking it from them in a raw state; but if we take the opposite course and discourage the import of Italian raw silk into this country, and encourage the Italians to throw it in Italy, if war should arise and interrupt the intercourse, it will find us dependent upon them; and as the markets of France, Russia and Vienna will be all open to them, their Governments will be less unwilling to close the English market to them, but if they had been in the habit of sending only raw silk to England, they would not have mills enough in Italy to throw it, and their Governments would be the more likely to afford facilities for sending it to this country, as there would be no other market to which it could be sent, and therefore I infer it is very much the interest of the silk manufacture of this country, that we should be constantly in the habit of throwing as much as possible of our own silk.

11265.   Do

*Ambrose Moore,*
Esq.

13 July,
1832.

11265. Do you think that the present low prices paid for throwing in England are favourable or unfavourable to the protection of silk?—My opinion is, that throwing generally is not so perfectly done as when the price was higher. There are some persons throw it now very well, probably as well as ever, but speaking generally, I believe silk is thrown in a more negligent manner than when the price paid for it was such as would enable them to bestow more care upon it. The object now is to get it done at as little cost as possible.

11266. Are you aware that a notion prevails that the speed may be increased without injury; do you think the speed of throwing silk may be increased without the probability of injury to the material?—I think silk is thrown better as the speed is slower, but I do not believe that speed can be usefully applied to silk so as to cheapen the throwing of it materially; speed is only applicable to two of the processes of throwing, it is applicable only to what is called the spinning or twisting part, and what is called the throwing part, and the wages in those two departments do not (I am speaking now merely from recollection,) amount to above one-third or one-fourth of the whole cost of throwing, so that if you quicken the speed you only quicken one-fourth of the actual cost of it.

11267. Do you think the present duties sufficient to give due encouragement to the British throwster?—I think there has been quite a retrograde movement in the throwing trade in this country; I believe it is not in the efficient state it was before those duties were reduced.

11268. Have the low duties on foreign thrown silks depressed the wages of our people in silk mills or caused them to work an additional number of hours?—It has depressed the wages very much. The regulations that are introduced into the Cotton Factories Bill are quite needless at present for silk mills, but I cannot conceive anything more likely than the forcing down the rate of throwing, to induce people to resort to the employment of children who are too young, that they may work at less wages than the older ones can, and to make them work an additional number of hours, and thus to make it necessary for the legislature to interpose for the protection of these children, though at present there is no necessity whatever for applying such regulation to the silk mills, yet nothing is more likely to bring us into that state to want it than the course our Government has pursued respecting the throwing trade.

11269. When was your throwing mill at Derby built?—It was completed and began to work in July 1823.

11270. What was the duty on thrown silk at the time your mill was built?—The duty on raw silk was 5 s. 6 d. and on thrown silk, 14 s. 8 d., leaving a difference in favour of the English throwster of 9 s. 2 d.

11271. What was your inducement for embarking in the throwing trade?—It appeared to me, that at that period there was a great tendency to increase in the silk trade of this country; I had no knowledge of the means that Government were going to resort to then, to alter the system, for that was not announced until the following year; but the silk trade showed indications of increase. After the termination of the war silk had fallen in price, and silk goods had been getting more and more into consumption, and I thought that there was a fair prospect of the silk trade of this country extending. Our house had also been one of those, having no mill, that had suffered great inconvenience from the irregular supply of thrown silk during the war. Sometimes it was at an enormous price, and those who had mills of their own could throw it with great advantage: I was also desirous of making our manufacture as perfect as I could by throwing silk to my own mind, and adapting it to the various purposes I wanted to apply it to in goods; these were my principal reasons; but if I could have thought it possible, when I was investing that property under the then protection of 9 s. 2 d. in the pound, that the Government, in a way that I think is really unjust to those persons who acted on the faith of the existing law, could possibly have so very hastily and greatly, and with so little regard for the interest of those whose capital was invested in silk mills, have reduced that protection, I am quite sure I never should have embarked in it.

11272. Then you mean to claim protection for the throwster, on the ground that he has large capital invested in buildings and machinery, which you say would be useless for any purpose than for throwing mills?—I feel very strongly that the English throwster has a great claim on the Government to a reasonable degree of protection; and as a throwster, I do wish that the case of the throwster should be considered by Parliament in that light.    I think it is but a matter of common jus-tice that property invested in a manner that cannot be available to any other pur-pose, should not be sacrificed by an alteration in the law in a way that nobody, when they invested their capital in that way, could have foreseen.    I hold it would be quite unjust for the Government to hold out a temptation to people to build mills, and then turn round and say, " Now we think it for the good of the weaver that your mills should be destroyed :"  I confess I do not think that is just; and I have endeavoured to show, by exhibiting the different processes of manufacture, that there is no correctness in that view of it.  I feel that the throwster and the capitalist, who have employed money in the throwing trade, are as much entitled to protection as the weaver.    A great many have been ruined undoubtedly, and their invested capital very much deteriorated or destroyed from this change in the law, and that it should be carried further merely to benefit, as they say, the weaver, whom I believe it would not benefit, is I think most unjust.

11273.  Can you inform the Committee what would be the effect upon the price of the manufactured article in this country, were so much of the duty on thrown silk removed as would make the export duty of the thrown silk from Italy equiva-lent to the export duty of the raw silk from Italy ?—Upon the supposition that it should make the whole difference in the price of the silk when the duty was taken off, which I do not believe would be the effect of taking off the duty, it would make a difference of from five to six per cent. in the cost of some goods, but considerably less upon others ;  I believe upon none more than from five to six per cent., I speak on the supposition that they are made of foreign thrown silk.    It would make the greatest difference on the lower description of those goods ;  the lowest description of goods made in this country are composed, the greater part of East India silk with a mixture of Italian ;  but the lowest sort of goods made of foreign thrown silk is what I speak of as that class of goods in which it would make the greatest difference.    Upon the higher description of goods, velvets for instance, nearly one half of the cost is the price of weaving ;  it would make a very small reduction indeed on those goods, not above three per cent. ;  in the gauze fabrics, it would not make a difference of more than one per cent.

11274.  Do you think every exertion has been made on the part of the manufac-turer of this country, in the first instance, to prepare for, and afterwards to meet the competition with France ?—It has been very difficult for the silk trade to know what course it ought to pursue, so as to escape from the reproach of having done wrong.    There was time given it to prepare, and there were great inducements held out to the trade, to believe that the measures of Government were calculated to promote its extension and prosperity, and that it would do very wisely if it availed itself of the new state of things, to increase the trade ;  and captivated by such enticing recommendations, a great number of persons did rather extend their opera-tions ;  they were justified certainly by the public inclination for silk, in so doing, and went on prosperously enough in that course, and amidst the commendations of, I believe, all the influential men in Government and in Parliament, until the French goods came in ;  then the interference of the French with our trade caused great distress, and ungenerously enough I must say, we were reproached with having made those exertions to which we had been before urged on, and were told " time was given you to withdraw your capital, and yet has any body ever heard that you availed yourselves of the opportunity, on the contrary you have extended your operations, and have only yourselves to blame ;" and therefore as a very sensible operative observed to me one day, it is not possible to pursue a blameless course, whether the manufacturers make exertions to increase the quantity of goods they produce, or whether they lie on their oars and let the French have the possession of the market, they never can satisfy the Government.  In the first case the Govern-ment say " you have overdone it," and in the other case " you let the French occupy the ground."  I speak with all seriousness of the difficulty the trade has been in, to know exactly what course to take.    However, they have made, I think, every exertion that could be made ;  they have exerted themselves with quite activity enough in one direction ;  they have reduced the wages of the people that worked for them as much as any body could desire ;  I do not think they will be charged with having been at all negligent in that particular.  You have had it proved, that the rate of wages has been reduced by 40 per cent. ;  I am not sure whether that evidence given before you, applied to the country as well as to London ;  but I know that that reduction has taken place all over the kingdom in the silk trade, and in

every

*Ambrose Moore,*
Esq.

13 July,
1832.

every branch of the silk trade.   The manufacturers of silk have not been inattentive to every improvement that they could make; I think dyeing has improved considerably, but I will state that that has been no consequence of the introduction of French goods, for the dyeing was in a course of improvement, and had very much improved before the French goods did come in ; and I believe that every thing in the way of economy, of which the silk trade was susceptible, I believe by all their arrangements of all sorts, the manufacturers generally, and the throwsters, have endeavoured to improve their manufacture ; I do not wish it to be inferred from that that there has been any greater skill in the manufacture now than formerly ; I do not think there is so much skill, if you except the intelligent manufacturer, Mr. Bridges, who has exhibited some patterns, and one or two others, you will find that there is hardly any person who knows how to make the higher description of articles now.   I beg to show a specimen of Spitalfields manufacture, which fell within my reach a few days since (*exhibiting it*;) it shows that a good many years ago, they were able to make what was difficult to execute ; it was made in Spitalfield 70 years ago ; it was intended as the hangings for a room that the then Prince of Wales was fitting up, though the intention of fitting it up with that description of silk was afterwards given up ; it is every bit of it wove, not embroidered at all.   The " School for Design" happens to have been in China, and had not the benefit of the taste of Lyons ; but I exhibit it to you for its execution ; it was the fancy, in short, of the Prince of Wales at the time ; he chose the style.

11275. This of course was manufactured by a simple hand loom ?—Yes, it was before the Jacquard loom was invented ; in fact, in those days the Spitalfields manufacturer quite outran the Lyons manufacturers in the employment of artists ; it was not at all an unusual thing for an artist to be retained for a particular house, at a salary of 200*l.* or 300*l.* a year ; I have heard, I think, of instances in which pattern drawers lived quite like gentlemen ; it was a flourishing trade, and they were well paid, because they were good designers.

11276. In point of fact, was not the silk trade induced, from the representations which had been made in certain speeches delivered in Parliament, to enter into speculations, erect mills and machinery for the purpose of improving and extending their manufacture, and for which they were afterwards reproached by the very same parties in Parliament ?—Undoubtedly, that has been the case ; some persons of better judgment than others, or at least who fancied they had better judgment than others, availed themselves of the interval to withdraw ; and others led on by the public speeches referred to, built mills, and extended their operations in silk manufacturing ; and it is certainly true that they were then reproached for so doing ; but it should be borne in mind, that the machinery of all sorts, whether looms or any thing else in operation now, is not so great as it was before the admission of foreign silks ; therefore it is not true that we are depressed from having such a great power of machinery at present brought to bear on the silk trade, for the production of the English looms is not so great, nor do the silk mills of this country perform so much work as they did before the admission of foreign silks ; and what we are now suffering, does not arise from the continued operation of those new mills and new factories, because there are fewer mills at work than there were in 1824 ; I believe there is not above one half the number of spindles at work in Macclesfield that there were in 1824.   And here is another point whereon we are unfairly dealt by, that is as to what machinery was at work in 1824 ; when we speak of what was at work in 1824, we are told, oh ! it was the excitement and the speculative feeling that were abroad generally, and the excitement in the silk trade particularly, forgetting that a mill cannot be built and brought into operation without a considerable length of time being allowed ; and therefore the machinery actually in operation in 1824, I think it fair to conclude, must have been erected previously to 1824.

11277. You have spoken of the reduction of wages being 40 per cent. ; that calculation was made on plain goods, was it not ?—Yes.

11278. And had no reference to figured ; therefore, if you take into consideration a general average reduction of wages, the reduction of wages would be much greater than 40 per cent., would it not ?—Yes, certainly, if you take the amount paid for wages, the amount is much greater than 40 per cent.

11279. How has the reduction in wages been effected ?—It has been effected to the extent I have already stated, and the effect on the operatives has been that of

678.                                                                                   reducing

*Ambrose Moore,*
Esq.

———

13 July,
1832.

reducing them to the greatest state of destitution; they, in fact, possess nothing, if I may so speak, really beyond the extent of their own skins; they do not seem to possess a shadow of property in the world; I believe many of the operatives in Spitalfields are without any thing approaching to the character of furniture—without a bed: nothing is more common than to hear that such a man cannot leave his home and come to the warehouse of his employer, because he has nothing to come out in; he sends his child or his wife. I met with an instance during the last winter, in the case of one man whom I had been obliged to turn off, but whom I was afterwards induced to give some work to again. I asked him how he had been living?—Why, he had 2 *s.* or half-a-crown a week, and some friend or other had occasionally given him a shilling—some friend in his own trade—a poor man like himself, and he had several children; he got from the workhouse 1 *s.* on a Tuesday, and 1 *s.* 6 *d.* on a Friday or Saturday, and that was the way he had been carrying on his existence for several months, and this was at the time when we were making these representations to the Board of Trade, urging on them to do something that should relieve the silk trade from the great pressure that was then on the working part of the people, to say nothing of the ruin that was among the manufacturers themselves.

11280. Has not the general effect been to produce great demoralization, and a total recklessness as to the consequences, among the operatives in Spitalfields?—Yes, there is a great alteration in that respect; they are not the respectable body, in any sense, that they once were. As far as I can learn, they take very little interest in any thing that goes on between the trade and the Government; they say they see no chance of obtaining any relief, and they feel no interest in supporting their committee, or in doing any thing that shall be calculated to bring redress. They are not the people in appearance that they once were; looking at a number of them together, as I sometimes do on my own hands, and recollecting what kind of appearance they presented 25 years ago, I am struck with the contrast. They appeared then no better than poor working men, but they were decently clad, and had an appearance about them of living as working men should do, but not better than they should do; but now, if you look at them, at the first glance you will see a most wretched squalid race of people, badly clad and fed, and almost, I might say, diminished in size. Allow me to state, with respect to this effect upon them, that there is a degree of dishonesty that there did not used to be. It is a matter of frequent occurrence now, that a man decamps with the work he has got to do; several instances have occurred lately, in which men have got work in the loom from one or two different masters, and when they have finished their piece they run away. There are several instances of people having gone to America; that seems to be the place they like to go to. I am told, and I believe it to be the fact, that in America there is rather a different view of the silk trade to what there is in England; that they are encouraging people to come to America. I met with a publication a short time back, in which there was a recommendation to different classes of artisans as to what point they should make for in America, and there was a direction to silk weavers where they should go; and so a little manufactory is there nursed, and they intend to form a silk manufactory, which the policy of our Government is assisting all they can, by driving our weavers away from England. Two or three of my hands have gone, and taken property I had entrusted to them with them.

11281. Did they take their looms with them?—I do not know that; I should think not; the loom was not worth taking, excepting they had a Jacquard machine, and that would be too heavy to take; but the loom itself is as simple as can be.

11282. Do the weavers make their own looms in any case?—They provide the looms; in most cases they hire them of what are called loom brokers.

11283. Is this a new species of dishonesty, or have you not experienced the same thing occurring before, before the reduction of the duty?—No; 20 or 25 years ago such a thing was never heard of; there was a little pilfering in small quantities, but weavers absconding with their work was scarcely ever heard of.

11284. When was the first instance of it that came to your knowledge?—I cannot recollect exactly, but the crime has very much increased within the last 12 months.

11285. Did it not occur before the duties were reduced, before the change in the duties?—I do not recollect any instance; I should not be very willing to say no such case occurred; it was a very rare occurrence before, and there have been a great many cases since: it is quite a frequent occurrence now. Some manufacturers

*Ambrose Moore,*
Esq.

1ß July,
1832.

turers are obliged to resort to the plan of having general contributions of their hands, to pay for the defalcations of others; we take them on that condition, so that they guarantee each other's honesty.

11286. It has been stated to the Committee by former witnesses that the fancy branch of the trade had suffered most, and in Spitalfields that there are but few looms of that description remaining, to what do you attribute the loss of the figure trade?—I consider the supply of fancy goods from abroad to be the cause; there is a consumption of fancy goods, but they are not made in Spitalfields; they come in almost universally from France.

11287. Do you know from your own observation that fancy silks are very extensively worn?—Very extensively, from my own observation of the shops and warehouses where I happen to go on business; I see such large quantities that I am assured both that there is a large quantity smuggled and a large quantity worn in this country.

11288. Do you know of any fancy silk goods being made to any extent in any place in England not in Spitalfields?—None, except quite a low description; there are a few Jacquards at work in different parts of the kingdom; a few at Manchester and Sudbury, and one or two other places, but they are not making rich goods, such as you had shown you by Mr. Bridges; such as used to be made in Spitalfields, and such as are now made at Lyons, and imported into this country.

11289. With very few exceptions they are what you call four singles, rather than three or four doubles?—The great bulk are three singles, made of coarse East India warps, so that the silk may be heavy; but the most inexperienced persons in such matters would at once discover the great difference between the rich goods of Spitalfields and Lyons and these goods that are made in Jacquards at Manchester and Sudbury, and one or two other places.

11290. Do you think that there is a prospect of reviving the fancy branch of the silk trade under the present system?—It certainly is a point of difficulty; I feel it so, and I dare say it is generally so considered; but I confess I see very little chance for this branch of the trade while the present system is continued. I confess also, that I once thought differently; in the year 1824, when the alteration was first proposed, I was a very great advocate for that alteration, because I thought that taking off the duties on raw silk would assist in extending the trade very much; but I had no idea, I confess, at that time, that the fancy trade of this country would have been so cut up by the change. I could not have believed that there would be so little ground for the English fancy silk manufacturer to stand upon, and that the whole ground would be so occupied by the French; that the whole current of fancy and of caprice, if I may say so, for French goods would have been carried to the extent that it is. I wish to state distinctly to the Committee, I do not at all agree that there is this high order of intellect in the French manufacturer, and none of it in the English manufacturer; but if the present system be continued, I do not doubt but that there will very soon be very little skill left in the English silk trade, that is, in the higher departments of it; that there is at present no want of skill I am sure; but that there is a determination on the part of those who set the fashions, to have French goods; ladies of rank have French milliners, they recommend French fashions, and they will not have to do with any goods but such as are French, either figured or plain. Then the large dealers who supply them would tell you if they were asked, that it is no use their giving orders for English goods, and they would not in my judgment, be men of business if they did; they would say I am quite sure " we can sell French goods; there is a taste for them, and therefore as a matter of safe speculation, we go to France and order our goods; we have no motive for ordering Spitalfields, and therefore we must take that course, as tradesmen, which is most likely to be successful." Now that is the state of the fancy trade; and without some better protection than we now have, I do not see how the ground we have lost can be recovered in that branch of the trade; I am quite satisfied, if a committee of taste were appointed, and they were without any knowledge as to which were French and which English, upon the respective productions of Lyons and Spitalfields, and were to decide in favour of the English, that still the English would not sell, and the French would.

11291. You give the latter part of that answer without reference to price?—Quite so; I put it entirely as matter of fashion and as matter of colour; I wish I had brought a pattern of the colour that prevailed last winter; it is the most in-

678.                                                                                  consistent

*Ambrose Moore,*
Esq.

13 July,
1832.

consistent with good taste that it is possible to be; if it had been produced in Spitalfields, I am quite sure we should have been told greater stupidity was never discovered by any manufacturer than to suppose that ladies could wear such a colour, and yet it was quite the fashion, because it came from France.

11292. Have you considered the subject of the very unequal competition between France and England, with reference to the raw silks of France, independent of the price of labour between the two countries?—I do not profess to have very correct information on that subject; I know generally, that France possesses a great advantage in having her own raw silk, and that the exportation of it being prohibited, produces this effect, that silk is lower in France than in England; I do not speak of thrown silks, nor of any thing at all connected with the duty on thrown silk in this country. Quite independent of that, France has always her raw silk at an average very considerably lower than we have, the greater part of it being of her own growth; added to which she has the monopoly of it, and although it is told to you that that is impossible to be the case, while she draws part of her supply from Italy, I believe if you look into the fact as it exists, you will find that the statement I make, is true. The price of French and Italian silk is the same sometimes, no doubt. Silk will at times get up in France to the price of Italian silk. The Italian silk France uses is not precisely of the same kind as her own silk. At the time when a fresh, and perhaps a very abundant crop of silk comes into the market in France, the French manufacturers will not resort to Italian silk, the monopoly they have of French silk enabling them to get that silk lower than they can get silk in the Italian market. That fact is not at all irreconcileable even with theory; and that in the greater number of instances, the French manufacturers get French raw silk cheaper than we can get Italian raw silk, is a fact that is undeniable.

11293. How many years, to your knowledge, has the assaying machine for the trial of silk been known in this country?—I have known it for thirty years; we have one of Swiss make, with the date of 1759 upon it, which was in my uncle's possession before my own, at least forty years ago.

11294. Then a witness was in error, when he supposed it was an advantage that the French possessed that we did not possess?—Every person in the trade, except the witness, knew that such things were quite ancient.

11295. Are there any other local advantages besides those you mentioned, supposed to be enjoyed by France, which England has not?—The most striking advantages are the growth of her own silk, cheapness of labour, and the possession of the markets of all the civilized world.

11296. With reference to France producing so large a quantity of raw silk, do you not consider that, preceding any rates of duty, a law should go forth to the effect, that silk manufactured goods should not be imported into England from any country or countries producing and not exporting raw silk?—I think it but equal justice to the English manufacture, that such should be the arrangement, and that we should not be called upon to take her silk goods unless she will let us have her raw silk; I should have thought Government would, as a matter of national fairness, independent of all regard to the interest of the silk manufacture, have long since taken the same view of it; but besides that, it places the silk manufacture under a positive disadvantage, as compared with the price of silk goods manufactured in the two countries, because giving France the monopoly of her own silk, it enables her manufacturers to get it at a cheaper rate; and it should be a subject for the consideration of this Committee, whether French silks ought to continue to be imported into England, unless France allow us her raw silk, and that free of all charge upon it; if she should refuse to accede to this proposal, then she would in fact prohibit the exportation of her own goods in this country.

11297. And in the other view of the question, if she admitted it?—Then that argument against the competition would be taken away from us, but it would leave in full force all the other disadvantages under which we labour, and for which we should still require very high protection; but I hold it to be unanswerable, that while she will not let us have her raw silk, and that free of duty, we ought to take none of her goods.

11298. But supposing her to allow the exportation of raw material, what rate of duties would you recommend on the manufactured article?—I do not see any reason, even in that case, that we should take less than the Government promised us when the Ports were first opened ; nor do I, considering all the other advantages which France would still possess, think that we could do with less.

11299. That was *bonâ fide* 30 per cent. ?—Yes ; independent of the question of fashion, which is so powerful, that unless the Government of this country should feel itself at liberty to deal with it by way of prohibition, I can suggest no other than that it must be dealt with in the way of still higher duties ; so that if people will have French fashions they must be made to pay something higher for them, and as to the Government being unable to collect higher duties, I am perfectly incredulous about that.

11300. When you say 30 per cent. you mean 30 per cent. on plain goods ?—Yes.

11301. And what would you recommend on figured goods, or would you recommend a higher duty?—Without pledging myself to any duty I think a higher duty might be collected ; and that either a higher duty or prohibition must be resorted to.

11302. By placing a higher duty, how would you propose to counteract the advantages, which to a certain degree that would give the smuggler ?—By stamping ; by punishing people in their persons who are engaged in smuggling; and by some other regulations which cannot well be gone into before the Committee. That smuggling, even at a duty of 40 per cent., might be kept within such a small compass as to be a matter of no importance I have no doubt.

11303. And if France should impose a duty on the export of her raw silk, would you add that to the amount of duty on the manufactured article ?—I should say that while she will not allow her raw silk to come quite free I would not have any of her goods, such would be no violation of the public policy of this country. It has been felt as a great injustice by all classes, from the operative to the most intelligent person in the silk trade, for several years past, that instead of France and England being placed on a fair footing of dealing equally with each other, the silk trade of this country should be kept in a starving state for the benefit of the silk trade of France, while no trade of an advantageous nature to England is allowed by France between England and that country.

11304. Perhaps you could hardly expect France to allow the exportation of her raw material without duty when other countries impose a trifling duty, and if she were to impose a small duty, would you not recommend that that should be imposed on the manufacture too ?—I know no reason why she should not do it without any duty at all. If perhaps it were a very small duty it would be a matter of very little importance.

11305. Then you would add that to the goods ?—If it were a very small one, it might be comprized within any duty that you put upon it, or you might put a higher duty on French goods than you do on goods coming from any other part of the world.

11306. Might not the additional tax on the raw material, supposing the French Government were to allow its export to this country, might not the additional tax be more in amount than any duty which the Government could collect on the manufactured goods of France when entering this country?—When I speak of its being admissible that there should be any duty, I am supposing some small duty that would be very trifling in its effects, but if it were a large one it would probably be as bad as the prohibition of the exportation of the silk.

11307. Can China and Bengal silk be substituted for the raws of Italy, or do they best work up together ?—To work them up together advantageously, you must have a portion of Italian silk which is imported raw and thrown in this country.

11308. But can China and Bengal silks be substituted for the raws of Italy ?—Very few goods can be made wholly of either China or Bengal, all goods almost require that part of the silk used in them should be Italian.

11309. You have then found from considerable experience as a silk manufacturer, that there is no substitute for Italian silk, and having given your opinion, the present duties on thrown silks are placed too low to draw from Italy a large and regular supply of their best silk ; do you recommend a return to the duty of 5 *s.* a pound on organzine and 3 *s.* on tram, as the best means of making England a more important market for the raw material ?—Yes, that is distinctly my opinion; it was very bad policy to lower the duties on organzine below 5 *s.* and 3 *s.* on tram, and the true policy would be, to return to that amount of duty; I believe that is the most likely way to bring a large supply of raw silk, and eventually, if people are not in too great a hurry for the accomplishment of a good object, eventually to produce cheap thrown silks for the use of the English looms.

11310. Are

*Ambrose Moore,*
Esq.

———

13 July,
1832.

11310. Are you of opinion that the Italian having sent a less quantity of raw during the present low duties on thrown silk, and a larger quantity of thrown to this country, is a proof that he has gained more by the raws than by the throwns?—No, I cannot take it as a proof of any such thing; I take it he has considered it most for his interest to send it in a thrown state.

11311. Can such a conclusion be drawn?—There are persons in the world that seek to convince people that such is to be the inference; I think that the lower you make the duties on thrown silk, the probable effect on the Italian's mind would be, that he should say " now is the time to send my silks thrown," and if you raise the duty to 5 s. I think he will find it his interest to send it in a raw state.

11312. With respect to gauzes, do you consider any duty sufficient to protect the manufacture of Coventry, or that the manufacture of gauzes can go on in this country without prohibition?—I am not personally much acquainted with the Coventry trade, but I have a general knowledge of it, and that leads me to the conclusion that they cannot go on with their manufacture of fancy gauze ribbons in the present state of the law.

11313. Do you think they can go on without prohibition?—I have an impression that prohibition is essential to the fancy gauze ribbon trade.

11314. Do you think that the additional amount placed upon the thrown silk when imported, would be injurious to the home manufacture?—I think it would not be injurious; if I were a manufacturer and had no throwing mill, I feel convinced I should be of that opinion; I feel confident that the silk manufacture of this country would be benefited by it. It is the best way to provide cheap thrown silk if we could get the Italians in the constant habit of sending plenty of good raw silk, and by keeping the duty not less than 5 s., they would be induced to send us large supplies of good raw silk; this would be the way really to benefit the English silk manufacture, and I cannot think that that is an enlightened view of the question that would destroy the throwster under a pretence of making thrown silk cheap.

11315. On a trade affecting the employment of people in this country, whether would you consider the throwing branch or the manufacturing branch as of the greater importance?—In respect of their extent?

11316. In respect of their existence as employment for people in this country; whether, if it were a question of the annihilation of one of the two, or not even to that extent, if it were a question of benefiting one at the expense of the other, which should you consider most important to preserve?—It is quite clear that if one only is to be preserved it must be the weaver, because a throwster is of no use without he has somebody afterwards to weave up the silk he throws; but this is no necessary view of the question, as the interests of the two are quite consistent with each other. If the numbers engaged in each branch were the only consideration, the balance would preponderate in favour of the weavers; but then, if you take into account the amount of invested capital of the throwster, he has by far the stronger claim. The Government has no moral right to destroy the capital which they encouraged us to invest in throwing mills; it would be an act of cruelty, without a very much stronger case than our Government can make out, to sacrifice that property. The great distinction between the throwster and the weaving manufacturer is this, that a weaving manufacturer has no capital at all invested in his business, at least I reckon that for every thousand pounds a throwster has invested a manufacturer would not have fifty, so that although even if it were injurious to the manufacturer's trade it would not involve any sacrifice of his property, as his capital is invested merely in goods and debts, and therefore if, from the trade being an unprofitable one, he was induced or indeed obliged to give it up, he would have nothing to do but to collect his debts and sell his stock of goods, and he would be safely landed; but how would the throwster be off, with many, perhaps 20, 30 or 40,000 l. invested in buildings and machinery? his trade would not only be destroyed, but himself entirely ruined.

11317. They would both be in the same situation, with the addition of the throwster having lost the whole of his capital?—Yes; and supposing his capital to have been partly borrowed, which would be the case in many instances, he would not only be ruined, but would be under the disgraceful necessity of compounding with his creditors.

11318. Is the Committee to understand it as your opinion, that the prosperity of the silk trade of England depends on the rate of duties fixed on the importation of

foreign

foreign thrown silk?—I think it does, in a very much greater degree than credit is generally given for.

*Ambrose Moore,*
*Esq.*

13 July,
1832.

11319. And that the silk trade never can be prosperous with the present low duties on silks imported into England?—Never so prosperous as it might have been and would have been if the duties had not been lowered from what they stood at previously to the reduction of them in 1829.

---

## *Lunæ, 16° die Julii,* 1832.

### LORD DUDLEY COUTTS STUART, in the Chair.

*John Brocklehurst,* jun. Esquire, called in ; and Examined.

11320. YOU are a partner of the firm of John & Thomas Brocklehurst, of Macclesfield?—I am.

*J.Brocklehurst,*jun.
Esq.

16 July,
1832.

11321. What is your line of business?—We are general silk manufacturers, that is, manufacturing the raw silk through all its processes of throwing, dyeing and weaving into goods.

11322. Are you acquainted with these respective branches in your own neighbourhood?—So far as I have had an opportunity of acquiring the experience of 24 years as a manufacturer, and 15 of them as a banker.

11323. What may have been the state of the throwing interest before November 1826?—The throwsters were carrying on a very moderately remunerative, but steadily increasing, branch of manufacture.

11324. What was the condition of the population employed in the throwing mills up to that period?—They were employed at reasonable wages; they were diligent, sober, well conducted, and they were then very contented.

11325. What may have been the state of the throwing interests since 1826?—Involved in ruin ; the value of their property (invested on the faith of protecting duties) totally annihilated ; and many families once in a very respectable condition of life reduced to poverty, and dependent on that rate to which they were once cheerful contributors.

11326. Can you state what might be the number of persons employed in the throwing mills of Macclesfield in 1824?—Ten thousand two hundred and twenty-nine.

11327. In 1828?—Five thousand two hundred and fifty-four.

11328. In 1831?—Three thousand seven hundred and sixty-two ; and the commencement of this year only 3,622.

11329. In 1824 how many spindles might there be at work at Macclesfield?—Two hundred and seventy-six thousand.

11330. In 1828?—One hundred and fifty-nine thousand seven hundred and sixty-two.

11331. In 1831?—One hundred and twenty-two thousand one hundred and ninety-six.

11332. In January 1832?—Only 117,192. I must here remark, the remaining spindles are standing still, and the people are unemployed.

11333. What may be the usual hours of work in the silk mills?—They commence at six and work till twelve, taking twenty minutes at eight for breakfast ; the mill closes at twelve for dinner, it resumes at one ; the people have a quarter of an hour or twenty minutes for tea at five, and work till six ; then they are allowed to work two hours extra if they wish it, and this is done every day in the week but Saturday ; then they work only ten hours and forty minutes.

11334. What were the average earnings of the mill people in 1824?—Eleven shillings per week for the full hours of work, or 1¼d. an hour.

11335. In 1828?—Five shillings and five-pence per week for sixty hours, or 1d. an hour.

11336. In 1831?—Two shillings and ten-pence halfpenny for forty-four hours, or three farthings an hour ; thus showing that the wages of the mill people were 75 per cent. higher in 1824 than in 1828, and 125 per cent. higher than at present, and that their actual earnings (the true index of their condition) are now 75 per cent. lower than in 1824, or only one-fourth part of what they earned at that period,

678.                                                                                              the

J. Brocklehurst, jun.
Esq.

———

16 July,
1832.

the protecting duty on foreign thrown organzine in 1824 being 9 s. 2 d. now 3 s. 6 d. ; on tram, 9 s. 2 d., now 2 s. I have a table in which those things are comprised in a small compass, which I will beg to deliver in.

[*The same was delivered in, and read, as follows :*]

### STATEMENT of Number of SPINDLES and MILL PEOPLE, WAGES and EARNINGS at these Periods.

| In 1824 | - - - | Spindles - | - | - | - | - | 276,000 |
| | | Mill People | - | - | - | - | 10,229 |
| 1828–9 | - - | Spindles - | - | - | - | - | 159,792 |
| | | Mill People | - | - | - | - | 5,254 |
| Dec. 1831 | - - - | Spindles - | - | - | - | - | 122,196 |
| | | Mill People | - | - | - | - | 3,762 |
| Jan. 1832 | - - - | Spindles - | - | - | - | - | 117,192 |
| | | Mill People | - | - | - | - | 3,622 |

WAGES for 76 Hours, (in fact actual Earnings,) in 1824.

| | MEN. | | Young Men, of 15 to 20 Years. | | Young Women, of 15 to 20 Years. | | Children, 10 to 15 Years. | | Children, 7 to 10 Years. | |
|---|---|---|---|---|---|---|---|---|---|---|
| | s. | d. | s. | d. | s. | d. | s. | d. | s. | d. |
| 1824 - - - | 18 | – | 14 | – | 12 | – | 7 | 6 | 3 | 6 |
| 1828 - - - <br> Average employment only 66 hours, or 11 hours a day. | 8 | 6 | 7 | 3 | 6 | – | 3 | 6 | 1 | 9 |
| 1831 - - - <br> Employed only 44 hours per week. | 4 | 7 | 4 | – | 3 | 1 | 2 | – | 1 | – |

As regards the Spindles, as well as the people, they are here ready to be employed if work could be had, and have fluctuated in the amount employed in the intervals.

11337. How do the hands out of employment subsist?—Chiefly on the poor-rates of the town and adjacent townships; some receive their pittance from a distance; and I am sorry to observe the general tendency towards cheapening our goods to be by a levy on the land.

11338. What improvements have been made in throwing machinery since 1824? —I know of no improvements since 1824; increased speed and the great improvements in and extension of machinery took place from 1819 to 1823, for it appears that the progress in these respects was such, that in the year 1824 the mills and machinery worked up 6,263,026 lbs. of raw silk, showing that at that period the silk trade had reached its highest point of perfection; for by a Table I will put in, I find that before the change took place in 1826, the annual average of the two preceding years appears to be 3,131,613 lbs. of raw silk worked up by the mills, made into goods, and consumed; and I find that after the change, during the last six years, we have annually consumed only 3,235,606 lbs. of raw silk; but there has been a great decline, both in the style of goods and the quality of the work, which may be seen by the great diminution in the quantities of fine silks worked up subsequently to that period; for, in 1824 and 1825, we worked up, of fine, raw and thrown Italian silk, 3,874,188 lbs. the annual average of those two years being 1,937,094 lbs. taken into home consumption; and for the last six years, that is, since the change of system, the raw and thrown Italian silk altogether taken into consumption amounts to 9,760,896 lbs., the annual average consumption being 1,626,816 lbs.; showing a decreased consumption of fine silk, on the average for the last six years, of 310,278 lbs. a year. By this it is evident that the silk trade are justified in the complaints they have made, and it is equally evident that the whole character of the silk trade of this country is changed, from fine goods giving great employment to the mills, and to the weavers, to a coarse description of goods giving

less

less employment to the mills and to the weavers, and withal the consumption of *J. Brocklehurst,* jun.
material only equalled the consumption of preceding years, when we were working    Esq.
on fine goods and with fine silk.

16 July,
1832.

*[The Witness delivered in the Table referred to by him.]*

TOTAL SILK imported and taken into Home Consumption.

|  | Lbs. |
|---|---|
| In the Year 1824 - - - - - - - - - | 3,414,520 |
| — - 1825 - - - - - - - - - | 2,848,506 |
|  | 6,263,026 |

|  | Lbs. |
|---|---|
| *Before the change, the annual average of Silk consumed* - - - | 3,131,613 |
| Total taken into Home Consumption during the last six years, under the new system - - - - - | 19,413,639 |
| *Since the change, the annual average of Silk consumed* - - - | 3,235,606 |

But the following Table will show the change that has taken place in the Silk Manufacture having gone from the finer branches to a coarser trade.

|  | Lbs. |
|---|---|
| Italian Raw and Thrown Silk taken into consumption in 1824 and 1825 | 3,874,188 |
| *Or before the change the annual average of Italian Raw and Thrown Silk consumed* - - - - - - - - - - - | 1,937,094 |
| Total Italian Raw and Thrown, taken into consumption, during the last six years - - - - - - | 9,760,896 |
| *Or since the change, the annual average consumption of Raw and Thrown Italian Silk* - - - - - - - - - - - | 1,626,816 |
| *Or a total annual decrease since the change* - - - - - | 310,278 |

11339. You have given the average consumption of silk for two years, 1824 and 1825; is it your opinion that the silk trade of this country would have consumed that quantity of silk or a greater quantity, had it not been interfered with by the manufactures of France?—I am of opinion that the consumption of silk goods in this country has increased at least 30 or 40 per cent. since that period, and if we had had the making of those goods, our trade would have been 30 or 40 per cent. more.

11340. Do you think the sudden increase previous to the year 1824, and subsequent to that period, arises from the alteration in the duty, and the consequent lowering of the price of the commodity?—There was no actual lowering in the price of silk goods after the repeal of the duties; for I find immediately after the duties were repealed, that raw silk advanced the amount of the duty repealed; so that the argument, which was advanced, that the consequent prosperity of the silk trade was occasioned by the repeal of the duties, was totally fallacious. I have here a price current of the Bengal silk, sold at the East India Company's October sale in 1824; the repeal of the duties took place in March, but the measure was not completed till about midsummer; at the midsummer sale, Bengal silks were selling at 17 s. a pound, taking for instance the first silk on the list; and at the October sale it sold for 21 s. 2 d. the duty repealed, being 4 s. a pound, which is just the difference of the duty.

11341. Though there was a great increased consumption of silk in 1824 and 1825, the price of that silk had not fallen?—It had not.

11342. Was the consequence of that, large stocks of manufactured goods remained on hand, or were they taken up by consumption?—There was no speculation at all in silk, the goods came into the market and were consumed as fast as they were made; they were taken into consumption, which was the case up to 1826, when the shopkeepers diminished their stocks, and prepared for the reception of foreign goods.

678.                                                                                          11343. So

J. Brocklehurst, jun.
Esq.

16 July,
1832.

11343. So that in anticipation of the introduction of manufactured goods from France, in the spring of 1826, the shopkeepers became cautious in their purchases, and there was a flatness experienced for the first time in the silk trade?—The flatness generally commenced about October or November in 1825, and more remarkably so in Bengal silk, in consequence of a large accumulation of Indian bandannas and other oriental silk goods, in the India warehouses, waiting the period when they would be admitted to home consumption.

11344. You believe, up to the period of which you speak, all the goods manufactured from that increased quantity of silk, had been taken up by shopkeepers, and disposed of to the consumers?—I am fully convinced there were no stocks of English silks in the market when the French were admitted; there is another fact shows that circumstance perhaps in a clearer light, for at the latter end of 1825 we took less silk into consumption, which makes the quantity taken into consumption that year, less than in the year 1824.

11345. You did not take silk into a course of manufacture, because you apprehended injury from the goods to be received from France, and also from the large quantity which you knew to be in the India warehouses?—We had notice in 1824, our customers were buying India goods, and storing them in the India warehouses; but the demand for British goods was such in England that we went on without fear, and consumption took off the goods as fast as we made them; but in the latter end of 1825, knowing that the time was approaching, our customers said we will sell off to the last yard, to be prepared for the foreign goods which are in bond.

11346. Then from that period your trade received a great check, wages began to decline, and they have continued in a declining state since that period?—The silk trade has been in a drooping state from that period; there has been several reactions, but the tendency of the whole has been to decline year by year.

11347. Have you known the silk trade, for a great many years, from the earliest period you have known it till 1824, to have been a gradually progressive trade?—I have known it to be a progressive trade from 1808, when I first became acquainted with it; we have had occasional changes in consequence of the scarcity of silk and advances in prices, but the general tendency was, upon the whole, an improvement on the preceding year.

11348. Has it been a progressively increasing trade, from the first period of your knowing it till 1824?—Yes, it has.

11349. From 1824 to 1826, in consequence of the favourable state of the silk trade, from the remission of duty, and the taste for silk gradually increasing, did it make a still more rapid advance?—On the one hand there was a taste for silk in the country progressively increasing, and on the other hand there was a great improvement in the manufacture of silk; the taste on the one hand had encouraged the manufacturer, and the manufacturer on the other hand encouraged the taste.

11350. You were led to expect there would be a very large increase by the alteration of the law?—The Minister told us we should go on and make the silk equal to the cotton trade; he only considered the silk trade to be the younger sister, and that he should soon place the silk trade on a par with her sister; that was one expression of Mr. Huskisson's.

11351. In the year 1826 the new measure came into operation?—Yes.

11352. Has the silk trade continued progressively to increase in the same proportion from 1826 to the present time, that it had done in the eight or nine years preceding?—The consumption of raw silk has continued only the same in quantity as it was previously, but certainly attended by a great deterioration in the species of manufacture and the quality of goods made since that period; and though I have seen some very good things made since, still they are merely exceptions.

11353. The quality of the goods, generally speaking, which have been manufactured since, have been rather of an inferior character than otherwise, as compared with what they were before; there has been a larger proportion of coarser and heavier articles, and of course they consume more silk?—They do, and the goods have been of a lower and inferior character.

11354. Even making allowance for this, has there been a proportionate increase even in the quantity of silk used, as compared with what it was the eight or nine years before?—The annual average for the last six years does not surpass the average of the two years preceding the change.

11355. So that there has not been a progressive increase?—The silk trade of
England

England has stood still, while the silk trade of the Continent has made an advance in some instances of 60 and 70 per cent.

11356. If the consumption of silk has been in coarser and heavier silks, must not the quantity of employment for the operatives have been diminished since 1825?—The increase has taken place in the strength of the goods, and not in the length or breadth, it has been more silk and less wages; I can show to the Committee the difference when we make it heavier and lighter. When silk is low, we put in double the quantity; one piece of these goods [*producing a piece of silk goods*] is made of the same length and breadth, and has only consumed eight ounces of silk; the other piece I present to the Committee takes 24 ounces to make the same length and breadth, and as silk becomes cheaper we put more of the material into the goods, which explains to the Committee the increased consumption of Bengal silk while our general manufacture has been sinking in regard to Italian silk.

11357. Does it not resolve itself into this, that, if over a certain space you consume a greater quantity of silk, and that the total quantity of silk so consumed is not more than it was in the year 1824 or 1825, the quantity of employment to the operative must be diminished?—The quantity of employment of the operative is, to a very great extent, diminished. I will, on my next examination, produce a Table which will show the increased quantity of silk worked up for a diminished amount of wages; but before I leave this question entirely I wish to call the attention of the Committee to this; the fine raw Italian silk used in the years 1824 and 1825, amounted to 2,851,275 lbs., and for the last two years, 1830 and 1831, the quantity of fine Italian raw silk amounted to only 2,255,018 lbs., showing a decrease in the finer branch of Italian consumed in this country of 25 per cent.; and I may here add, at the same period, that whilst a decrease has been taking place in England, France has increased her looms at Lyons from 25,000 in 1825 or 1826 to 35,000 in 1832, and the rest of the silk trade of France has increased in the same proportion.

11358. That increase is in the finer fabrics, which afford most labour?—Certainly; that increase in France has been entirely in the fine silks.

11359. What number of throwing mills may there be at Macclesfield?—Seventy-one.

11360. When were they erected?—Up to 1814 there had been erected 32; from 1814 to 1823, 26 were erected; from 1824 to 1826, the alleged period of our great increase, 12 mills were erected, but only four of those were filled with machinery; and since 1826, only one solitary mill, in the year 1829.

11361. How many mills were at work in 1824?—I have a statement to hand in, showing, in the first nine years, from 1814 to 1823, the annual average increase amounted to three mills, and in the three following years the increase, that is, from 1824 to 1826, was little more than one mill and a quarter a year.

11362. Were those mills built since the year 1824 larger than they had been accustomed to build previously to that period?—No, the parties built mills to suit their own convenience; men with a larger capital build a proportionate mill, and men of less means build a smaller mill; but this statement shows, that notwithstanding all the assertions of Mr. Huskisson, that the over-trading, over-building and wild speculations of these years were the causes of the distress that overtook the trade in 1826, this Right honourable Gentleman never admitted the true cause, namely, the precipitate competition into which his measures had forced the silk trade; he was impatient, and unwilling to wait till the trade should evince some symptom of its capability to compete with a rival of whose powers it knew no more than he did. However, the Government having confidence in its own arrangements, and contemning the ignorance of the manufacturer and the representations of practical men, they rejected the petitions of the trade in 1826 for inquiry, taunting the trade with its superfluous fears, predicting in glowing colours the unbounded progress this emancipated silk trade would make, and what has it all ended in, but the sacrifice of a valuable source of revenue derived from a luxury, the ruin of many hundred manufacturers, dyers and throwsters, and other contingent trades, overwhelming with distress and misery many thousands of work people, and, in fact, disorganizing the whole trade, and suspending all progress during the last six years.

11363. How many mills were at work in 1824?—Fifty-eight.

11364. How many now?—Forty-one mills; I beg to deliver in a Statement showing the proportionate increase each year of factory building in Macclesfield, from 1814 to 1824, from 1824 to 1826, and also during the last six years; there are now

*J. Brocklehurst,*jun. Esq.

16 July, 1832.

*J.Brocklehurst,*jun. Esq.

16 July, 1832.

now only 41 at work, the remaining 30 standing still, or 17 less at work than in 1823, and only nine more than in 1814.

[*The same was delivered in, and read.*]

| | | |
|---|---|---|
| Number of Factories built in Macclesfield and the neighbourhood up to 1814, and occupied as Silk Factories - - - - - - - - | 32 | *Average annual increase, from 1814 to 1823.* 3 *mills.* |
| Ditto - - up to the year 1823 - - | 58 | *From 1823 to 1826,* 1¼ *mills.* |
| Ditto - - up to the year 1826 - - | 70 | *From 1826 to 1832,* 1 *mill in six years.* |
| (Only four of these increased twelve have been filled with machinery.) | | |
| Ditto - - up to the year 1832 - - | 71 | *Decrease of mills at work, since 1823, of* 17 *mills.* |
| Number of Silk Factories occupied in Macclesfield and the neighbourhood, in 1832 - - - | 41 | |
| Ditto - - unoccupied - - - - | 30 | *Decrease, since 1826, of* 29 *mills.* |

11365. What may be the horse power of the mills at Macclesfield?—About 550; several of the mills being partly turned by water, it is difficult to be precise.

11366. Do you know the probable cost of those mills?—About 400,000 *l.* or 500,000 *l.*, computing the mills now standing, and those not put to work.

11367. Are those mills and machinery convertible to any other kind of manufacturing?—They are not. Silk machinery being adapted to its peculiar purpose; the buildings also are not of proportions suited for cottons; the engines are too small, and the gearing of too slight a construction.

11368. Do you consider the throwing of silk to be confined to Manchester, Macclesfield, Congleton, and the West of England?—Far from it, it is spread over the whole kingdom; silk mills are established in twenty counties, and about fifty towns; and to remove any doubts of this, I have taken the pains to obtain the names of mill proprietors in all the number of towns I have mentioned. It has been so much the practice lately to treat this important and useful property as of no consequence; but when one of the most severe afflictions of the country, is its present mass of unemployed people, I would ask, is this interest to be further trifled with by political economists,whose extent of knowledge has been obtained in a class of M'Culloch's, unconfirmed by practical knowledge of the state and condition of a body of work people, whose bread would be swept away by a stroke of their pen.

11369. How many horse power do you understand to be employed in the throwing of silk now, at Manchester?—I have heard from various sources; one of the principal mill owners at Manchester (Mr. Williams) informed me, that he computed the horse power of Manchester to be 138.

11370. Have you reason to believe, from other inquiries that you made, that that is correct?—I believe that is quite the extent of it, and I believe 138 horse power at Manchester does not throw more silk than 138 horse power would do at Macclesfield.

11371. Macclesfield alone, according to your statement, has about four times as much power applied to silk as Manchester?—Yes, the Manchester mills have been estimated at from 10 to 12, and the mills at Macclesfield are from 60 and 70.

11372. Do you know of any advantage there is possessed by the silk throwsters at Manchester, above those of Macclesfield and Congleton, and the neighbourhood?—The reverse, I believe; that silk is not thrown so cheap at Manchester as in other towns, but that it is a convenience to have a mill attached to their manufactory; in proof of this, they have stated in their memorial to the Board of Trade, that they consider their mill property a total sacrifice to the change which took place in 1829, when the duties were reduced from 5 *s.* to 3 *s.* 6 *d.* on thrown silk.

11373. From the reduction of the protecting duty, and the severe competition in the trade, have those mills that were placed in inferior situations, where they could not procure water power or coals cheap, been generally thrown out of use?—I think that the mills alluded to have not been thrown out of work in consequence of the dearness of coals or scarcity of water, but because Italy has taken away their employment.

11374. If

J. Brocklehurst, jun.
Esq.

16 July,
1832.

11374. If Italy sending her thrown silk here, induces a competition that lowers the price of silk throwing, will it not necessarily fall more severely on those mills where the labour or moving power is the dearest?—I think they have been thrown out of employ in consequence of their being less to be thrown, and that we have lost the throwing of that silk.

11375. If in consequence of the increased importation of thrown silk from Italy, there be less work for our own silk mills, must not those that throw that silk at a dearer rate, be of course the first of those thrown out of employ?—It probably may have that effect to a limited extent.

11376. All other things being the same, is not that the effect?—An increased quantity of thrown silk from Italy must have a general tendency to injure all the mills in England.

11377. Supposing a mill, in which the expense of working be 5,000 *l.* a year, and another in which the expense of working was 4,000 *l.* a year, doing the same quantity of work; and supposing the profit of one expending 5,000 *l.* a year to be 1,000 *l.*, and the profit of the other would be 2,000 *l.* would it not?—Precisely.

11378. If the profit of throwing silk was increased to give to that mill which expended 4,000 *l.* a profit of only 1,000 *l.* that would leave the other without any profit?—Yes.

11379. Would not the necessary consequence be, that that would discontinue working?—Yes; but that is not the cause of their being thrown out of employment; whatever rate the work may be proposed to be done at, the throwster would do it, it being in fact paid out of the poor rate; whenever wages will not do it, it is taken from the poor rate.

11380. You think there are some mills kept at work by the deficiency being paid out of the poor rate?—I consider that the present basis of our throwing to be the poor rate; I do not consider that any mills are in a bad situation where they have labour free, as the water and the coals form a very small proportion of the expense; it depends upon the quantity of work to be done, and that, having diminished since 1824, peculiarly in the fine silks, we can trace at once the cause of their not being in work. There is not the work to be done, and even those which are at work are in such a desperate state of competition, that whichever gets most from the poor rate is best off.

11381. It is not the quantity of silk which is to be taken into consideration only, but the fineness of the silk?—Yes, up to 1824, the throwsters had generally fine silk in hand, which they worked according to their convenience; but there is now a scarcity of that kind of fine silk for throwing.

11382. What has been the annual amount of poor rates expended at Macclesfield from the 25th of March 1821 to the latest period you know of?—In the year commencing March 25th, 1821 and ending March 25th, 1822, the expenditure was 4,208 *l.* and it was about the same up to 1826. In 1827, it was 7,810 *l.* and in 1832, 8,467 *l.* 10 *s.* 5 *d.*, and if the allowance to the poor were now what it was in 1821, the expenditure on the poor's rate would amount to nearly 12,000 *l.*

11383. Is the practice of giving a smaller pecuniary amount to the poor almost universal now?—No; it is not the case in an adjoining township, in which there is a large extent of land, and whilst the land can bear to pay any thing, there is not that disposition to grind down the poor to the smallest mite on which they can subsist.

11384. Can you state the number of families in Macclesfield receiving relief for the last ten years?—From about 1821 up to 1826, the average number of families was 56. In 1826, soon after the change took place, the families receiving relief amounted to 332, and in 1829, 320; but another change occurred in 1829; and in 1831, I find the families receiving relief amounted to 511; now the great increase of 56 families to 511 shows the diminution of allowance; for the year preceding 1826, the whole amount of poor's rate was but 4,200 *l.*, and in 1832, 8,000 *l.*, the amount is not doubled though the families increased to about nine times the number.

11385. So that the relief given to each family has been greatly reduced?—Yes; I find before 1826, the allowance to the poor was calculated at 2 *s.* per head per week, but that they have latterly reduced them to 10 *d.*, and in general they require the able part of the family to break stones, sweep the streets, draw coals, and any almost superfluous work they can contrive for them. In the adjoining township of Hurdsfield containing about 3,500 inhabitants, the money expended upon the poor for the five years preceding the 25th of March 1826, amounted to 1,190 *l.* 15 *s.* 11 *d.*, and for the last five years, the expenditure has been 3,300 *l.*; this Table will contain the

678.

*J. Brocklehurst*, jun. the whole of the information upon the subject, the number of poor receiving relief
    Esq.    and the proportionate amount of poor's rates collected.

16 July,
1832.

[*The same was delivered in, and read.*]

### GROSS EXPENDITURE of the POOR RATES.

|  | £. | s. | d. |
|---|---|---|---|
| From the 25th March 1821 to 25th March 1822 - - - - - | 4,208 | 3 | - ½ |
| That is to say, for the year 1822–1823 - - - - - | 4,165 | 16 | 5 |
| Ditto - - - 1823–1824 - - - - - | 3,827 | 10 | 6 |
| Ditto - - - 1824–1825 - - - - - | 4,201 | 18 | – |
| Ditto - - - 1825–1826 - - - - - | 4,478 | 19 | – |
| Ditto - - - 1826–1827 - - - - - | 7,810 | 11 | 4 |
| Ditto - - - 1827–1828 - - - - - | 6,067 | 18 | 8 |
| Ditto - - - 1828–1829 - - - - - | 6,458 | 16 | 6 |
| Ditto - - - 1829–1830 - - - - - | 8,670 | 17 | 5 ½ |
| Ditto - - - 1830–1831 - - - - - | 6,673 | 8 | 2 |
| Ditto - - - 1831–1832 - - - - - | 8,467 | 10 | 5 ½ |

THE allowance is now reduced from 1 s. 6 d. to about 1 s., and some instances only
10 d.; and the able part of the family required to sweep the streets, to break stones
and wheel coals; otherwise the last year would have been about 12,000 l. or three times
the amount before the absurd change took place.

---

### NUMBER of FAMILIES receiving RELIEF.

| At Christmas - - | 1821 | - - - - - - | 73 families. |
|---|---|---|---|
| | 1822 | - - - - - - | 47  – |
| *The reduced Allowance per head* | 1823 | - - - - - - | 51  – |
| *will account for the fact of the number* | 1824 | - - - - - - | 50  – |
| *relieved and the amount expended, not* | 1825 | - - - - - - | 56  – |
| *preserving the former proportions.* | 1826 | - - - - - - | 332  – |
| | 1827 | - - - - - - | 174  – |
| | 1828 | - - - - - - | 199  – |
| | 1829 | - - - - - - | 320  – |
| | 1830 | - - - - - - | 216  – |
| | 1831 | - - - - - - | 511  – |

THE Township of Macclesfield only is comprised in these statements, exclusive of
Sutton and Hurdsfield, containing about 10,000 inhabitants, and which separately support their own poor.

The Overseers of Hurdsfield (containing about 3,500 inhabitants) state the money
expended on the Poor, for the five years ending the 25th March }
1826 - - - - - - - - - - as }   £. 1,190 15 11

And for the Five years ending the 25th March 1831, as -   **£. 3,303 10 9 ½**

---

11386. Have you any Comparative Table of the Weekly Expenditure before and
since the alterations of the laws respecting the silk trade?—During the beginning
of 1823, the weekly expenditure for the casual poor amounted to 7 l. 1 s. 8 ½ d.
In 1832, it amounts to 88 l. 15 s. 9 d., showing an increase in nine years of 1,150 l.
per cent., producing a state of distress to which I know no parallel. I have here
an authentic document signed by the Chief Magistrate of Macclesfield and by
the Overseers, showing a progressive increase of the amount paid to those poor.

[*The same was delivered in, and read.*]

THE

Macclesfield, 9th May 1832.  *J. Brocklehurst*, jun. Esq.

THE WEEKLY PAYMENTS to the CASUAL and regular OUT-POOR of the Township of *Macclesfield*, in the year 1832, have been as follow:

16 July, 1832.

| CASUAL POOR: | £. | s. | d. | THE WEEKLY OUT-POOR: | £. | s. | d. |
|---|---|---|---|---|---|---|---|
| Week ending | | | | | | | |
| January 28, 1832 - | 94 | 4 | 5 | Same week - - - | 18 | 5 | 6 |
| February 4 - - - | 93 | 18 | 9 | Ditto - - - - | 12 | 7 | 6 |
| — 11 - - - | 94 | 6 | 5 | Ditto - - - - | 11 | 11 | 11 |
| — 18 - - - | 97 | — | 3 | Ditto - - - - | 10 | 13 | 6 |
| — 25 - - - | 94 | 17 | 11 | Ditto - - - - | 10 | 14 | 6 |
| March - 3 - - - | 84 | 8 | 9 | Ditto - - - - | 10 | 14 | 6 |
| — 10 - - - | 89 | 19 | 4 | Ditto - - - - | 11 | 1 | — |
| — 17 - - - | 89 | 13 | 7 | Ditto - - - - | 10 | 18 | 6 |
| — 24 - - - | 86 | 10 | 8 | Ditto - - - - | 10 | 17 | 6 |
| — 31 - - - | 84 | 8 | 7 | Ditto - - - - | 10 | 12 | 6 |
| April - 7 - - - | 88 | 11 | 8 | Ditto - - - - | 10 | 9 | 6 |
| — 14 - - - | 82 | 16 | 2 | Ditto - - - - | 11 | — | 6 |
| — 21 - - - | 83 | 10 | 4 | Ditto - - - - | 11 | 17 | — |
| — 28 - - - | 78 | 3 | 11 | Ditto - - - - | 10 | 11 | 6 |
| (14 | 1,242 | 10 | 9 | (14 | 161 | 15 | 5 |
| Weekly Average in 1832 | 88 | 15 | 9 | Average in 1832 - | 11 | 11 | 1 |

| CASUAL POOR: | £. | s. | d. | OUT-POOR: | £. | s. | d. |
|---|---|---|---|---|---|---|---|
| Similar Payments in 1823. | | | | | | | |
| Week ending | | | | | | | |
| January 25, 1823 - | 7 | 13 | — | Same week - - - | 17 | 10 | 6 |
| February 1 - - - | 6 | 12 | 2 | Ditto - - - - | 15 | — | 6 |
| — 8 - - - | 7 | 4 | — | Ditto - - - - | 15 | 5 | — |
| — 15 - - - | 6 | 12 | — | Ditto - - - - | 13 | 16 | — |
| — 22 - - - | 7 | 9 | — | Ditto - - - - | 14 | 1 | 5 |
| — 29 - - - | 7 | 10 | 8 | Ditto - - - - | 18 | 2 | 10 |
| March - 8 - - - | 8 | 1 | 5 | Ditto - - - - | 16 | 16 | 5½ |
| — 15 - - - | 10 | 9 | 8 | Ditto - - - - | 16 | 11 | 6 |
| — 22 - - - | 7 | 16 | 10 | Ditto - - - - | 23 | — | 6 |
| — 29 - - - | 5 | 18 | — | Ditto - - - - | 15 | 5 | 6 |
| April - 5 - - - | 5 | 17 | 6 | Ditto - - - - | 14 | 17 | 6 |
| — 12 - - - | 5 | 17 | 8 | Ditto - - - - | 16 | 9 | 6 |
| — 19 - - - | 6 | 2 | — | Ditto - - - - | 15 | 14 | — |
| 26 - - - | 6 | 2 | — | Ditto - - - - | 14 | 19 | 6 |
| (14 | 99 | 5 | 11 | (14 | 227 | 10 | 8½ |
| Weekly Average in 1823 | 7 | 1 | 8½ | Average in 1823 - | 16 | 5 | —½ |

THE Population of the Township of Macclesfield, between 1823 and 1832, has increased one-fourth, as near as can be ascertained: then since 1823, the Population has increased about 25 per cent., whilst the payments to Casual Poor have increased about 1,150 per cent.; or, *including the Out-Poor, about* 335 *per cent.* The payments to the Casual Poor in 1823 were at the average of 2 s. per head per week: those in 1832 do not exceed 1 s. 3 d. per head per week. These payments are independent of payments to Out-Poor residing in other Townships, of coal, clothing, bedding, and the expense of the House.

The Out-Poor consist principally of the aged, infirm, cripples, and those unable to work.

The Casual Poor consist of those unable to procure work, but who, for the most part, are not considered permanently on the books.

Since 1823 the Overseers have, as far as possible, transferred cases from the Out to the Casual Poor Statement. This will account for the payments to the regular Out-Poor being less in 1832 than 1823.

The number of persons in the workhouse, in the year 1821 and 1822 was 69; in 1824 and 1825 was 59. The number in the House in 1832 is about 135 or 140.

The account of Poor in the House, for 1822, 1823 and 1824 have been mislaid, and cannot at present be found.

I have examined the books, and believe this statement to be as correct as it well can be.

*George Ainsworth.*     *Jos^b Fawkner,*
*Lazarus Hardom.*     Assistant Overseer.
Signed in the presence of *W^m Hopes,* Mayor.

J. Brocklehurst, jun.
Esq.

———

16 July,
1832.

11387. Can you state the weekly relief afforded to the casual poor paid the first week in each year during the last ten years?—In 1821, 7 *l*. 5 *s*. 6 *d*. a week was expended; in 1827, the year after the change, 45 *l*. 17 *s*., and at the commencement of this year 85 *l*. and increased by the 1st of February this year to 96 *l*.

11388. In these statements do you comprehend the adjoining townships?—No; Hurdsfield and Sutton contain about 10,000 inhabitants, and maintain their own poor. I have however reason to know that the poor in those townships press heavily upon the people.

11389. Are there many empty houses in Macclesfield?—The last return by the collectors of poor rates state them to be 484.

11390. Are there many houses, the occupiers of which do not contribute to the poor's rate?—For the year 1831, the occupiers of 1,646 houses paid no poor's rates.

11391. You have been charged at Macclesfield with over trading previous to 1826, was it the fact?—I should say not; as a proof of it, our house as bankers, lost nothing up to the period of foreign goods being admitted to home consumption. In 1826, the panic produced no inconvenience to the banks at Macclesfield, they were both run upon like the rest of the bankers, they took up their notes and one of them burned the whole of his issue, indignant at the charge of overtrading; I should think 100 *l*. covered our loss in obtaining gold and conveying it to the country, also the whole of our losses in 1826; if there had been so much over-trading at Macclesfield, the bankers would have lost by it. Government wishing to rid themselves of the odium of their currency follies, very unjustly charged them to the account of the bankers over issues.

11392. Did not the manufacturers and throwsters at Macclesfield advertise for 5,000 hands?—It was so stated by the late Mr. Huskisson, he had procured a printed copy of the advertisement, and being delighted with such an opportunity of defending his own views by charging them on the silk trade, he could not forbear telling his secret before hand, and though I along with others undeceived him as to the object of the advertisement being to induce an individual manufacturer's hands to return to work, still to our surprise the subject was alluded to in a way, and in an assembly where we had no opportunity of explaining the circumstance.

11393. That was a matter of a local and temporary nature, and not at all indicative of the state of the trade?—The advertisement came from an individual who employed only 100 hands, he would not give them the terms they asked, and he put forth that advertisement.

11394. Did not the manufacturers build a great many houses at that time?—No, certainly not; in 1822 several building societies among the work people were formed, and during that and the two following years, an increase of houses, keeping pace with the increase of the trade, took place, all that was done was warranted by the circumstances of the trade, and had nothing to do with speculation.

11395. Were the empty houses you have mentioned ever occupied?—Yes, before 1826, by people engaged in the silk trade; and Macclesfield being particularly a silk district, the desertion of these houses has the same cause as the closing of the factories; besides, the 1,646 houses paying no poor's rates, but too faithfully exhibit the state of the silk trade.

11396. You have mentioned a very great reduction in the wages which has taken place at Macclesfield; bread, and the general necessaries of life remain pretty stationary, do they not?—The average price of corn at that time was from 60 *s*. to 65 *s*., and it is the same now.

11397. What has been the condition since 1826 of the people employed in the mills?—In 1826, when they were overtaken by the change, they were living in comfortably furnished houses, and they were amply provided with clothing, and when distress first assailed them, their only want was food, they fell back upon their little properties around them, which have since been gradually disposed of. They are now reduced to a state of destitution, hundreds of them without a change of clothes, and in many instances without any thing like a bed left in their cottage, sleeping on straw, covered with the clothes worn during the day, huddled together for the sake of warmth this was the case last winter, when I left Macclesfield). Demoralization of every kind has been the result, and the once respectable and well-conducted artisan is now broken-hearted and reduced to pauperism; two-thirds of the people were found to be in want of the common conveniences and necessaries of life.

11398. Have you observed whether that has had an injurious effect upon their morals?—To the greatest extent; I know one individual instance where a mother
and

J. Brocklehurst, jun.
Esq.

16 July,
1832.

and two daughters of 18 or 20, have 3 s. a week for the three to subsist on; they paid 1 s. for rent, 6 d. for coals, and had 6 d. per head to subsist on.

11399. Is that case within your own personal knowledge?—Yes, it is; it was found out by the committee inquiring into the state of the town.

11400. Were the people employed in the silk trade orderly and decent people?—I do not know any class of working people in the country so orderly as the people in the silk mills generally; it is a neat trade; it is what I should call the drawing-room trade of the country.

11401. They have undergone a remarkably injurious change?—Yes, they are a poor ragged and miserable people.

11402. Were the mother and two daughters you speak of well-conducted previously?—They were very respectable, well-conducted people, in their rank of life, indeed; it was one of the teachers of the Sunday school described to me this scene of distress, among many others he had witnessed on the day appointed to visit the houses of the poor; he said he should not recover the shock it had given to his feelings for a long time; the girls had for some years attended the school, and he had known their conduct up to the time he discovered their situation.

11403. In what state have these circumstances placed the town of Macclesfield?—In 1826, in addition to various acts of Royal munificence and liberal subscriptions raised throughout the kingdom, the shopkeepers and innkeepers came forward and contributed very cheerfully towards the relief of the distressed portion of the town, not only of those belonging to the town, but of those who had settlements elsewhere; since that time great numbers of these contributors have also fallen into ruin, and the remainder find themselves so overwhelmed with poor rates, that they feel it difficult to raise the means of going on. Money has been borrowed on the poor rates, and the overseers, both in Macclesfield and the adjoining townships, have lately been obliged to borrow money on their own personal security. A memorial from the overseers, describing these circumstances, has been presented at the Board of Trade, and a petition for relief, from the shopkeepers, was presented to the House of Commons by my Lord Grosvenor, I believe, in the month of March last.

11404. Can you state how many failures occurred between 1814 and 1826, of silk throwsters and manufacturers?—They were of so rare occurrence, I can only recollect one or two; and though a banker the last nine years of the time, I should think 9 l. would cover our losses.

11405. Since 1826, how many have failed?—Somewhere about 40, as nearly as my recollection serves me, besides a great many in minor trades.

11406. How large a proportion is that of the whole?—Two-thirds at that time.

11407. How many establishments may there be at the present time?—There are now about as many left as have failed; I have a list of the parties who failed, but I think it is not desirable to go into those particulars.

11408. To what do you attribute so many failures?—Some few might probably have been from unsuccessful competition, but I am confident the bulk of these have been ruined by the reduction of duties on foreign thrown silks, and the general bad effects of the measures that came into operation in the year 1826.

11409. They were in it, and could not get out of it?—Men cannot get out of a trade they are embarked in so rapidly as some political economists imagine.

11410. If you had 20,000 l. invested in a silk mill, do you know any mode of realizing your property when the throwing of silk is unprofitable?—At the time when individuals wish to get out of a trade, they find that the moment, of all others, no one wishes to get into it.

11411. Does not that observation peculiarly apply to manufacturing establishments, where there are large buildings, a plant and machinery, peculiarly adapted to that trade?—Yes, but political economists conceive that we can turn from the manufacture of cotton or silk, or any thing else, with the rapidity they proceed to conclusions.

11412. Can the machinery be applied to any purpose?—To no purpose but fire wood; I have seen property sold (if in fact it may be so called) that cost 60 s. for 3 s.

11413. Do you know any instance of mill property being offered for sale?—I know an instance of a mill originally costing 6,000 l. or 7,000 l. that was purchased in 1827 for 1,700 l., and I stated the fact to the Board of Trade in 1828 or 1829; a few weeks ago I met the late proprietor in London, and asked him what that mill actually cost him; he said 7,000 l. independently of machinery, and that

678.                                                                              the

J. *Brocklehurst*, jun.
Esq.

16 July,
1832.

the machinery cost him above 4,000*l.* more; altogether that property, which cost 11,500*l.* was knocked down for 1,700*l.* and about 200*l.* for the machinery.

11414. When was that mill erected?—In 1822, I believe.

11415. It was not old or worn out?—No, it was and is still as good and as perfect a mill as any in the kingdom.

11416. Was that man ruined?—He was, and has since been reduced to the necessity of trying to maintain himself and his family by keeping a petty shop in London.

11417. Supposing that mill to be erected in 1827, as it was in 1822, what would it have cost to have built that mill and stored it with machinery?—Perhaps 10 per cent. less.

11418. It would have cost about 10,000*l.* in the year 1827?—Yes, and it would now.

11419. What may be the prices of throwing silk at Macclesfield?—There are no fixed prices; throwsters who engage work are too often obliged to take the prices offered without reference in any way to cost, and then find themselves compelled to turn round on their wages and expenses, to see whether they can make their contract pay.

11420. Can wages be reduced any lower?—Most assuredly not; for at this time they do not afford subsistence or common household necessaries, much less clothing, putting aside rent.

11421. Can you state the cost of throwing a pound of Italian organzine?—There are two modes in England of estimating the cost of throwing: the one, if part of the wages be paid by the poor rate, making no allowance for wear and tear; but if a man must pay his way, and give fair wages to the work people, the cost would be about 5*s.* exclusive of waste; this does not include the finer sorts, some of which would cost 7*s.*

11422. Is it not thrown at a less price?—I believe it is; and for some time past I have observed a number of throwsters who have attempted these low prices either timely finding out their error and suspending their throwing, or falling into ruin. Various opinions have prevailed with regard to the prices of throwing silks in this country and in Italy, and various rates of protection have been proposed; but I am convinced of this, that the protection to the throwster should be 5*s.* and upwards on organzine, for although it may be supposed from some statements that have been made of the price of throwing silk in Italy, a less degree of protection would be sufficient, from what I know of the silk market and the prices at present, I am convinced a less price than that would not protect the English throwster. It is evident the Italian has gained such a footing in this market now that it will require the degree of protection I have named to reinstate the British throwster in his own market, for the Italian in his process has these peculiar advantages, he sends raw and thrown in the first instance with the prices attached to them, say 17*s.* for the raw, and 1*l.* 3*s.* for the thrown; upon arrival, the market prices are 18*s.* for the raw, and only 1*l.* 2*s.* for the thrown, in consequence of the larger supply of thrown and the smaller supply of raw; the supplies of thrown increasing, and raws still diminishing, the raws rise to 18*s.* 6*d.* and the throwns fall to 1*l.* 1*s.* 6*d.*; the merchant determines to sell for account of the Italian at these prices, which results the same thing to the Italian as 17*s.* for the raw, and 1*l.* 3*s.* for the thrown; whereas the English throwster, buying the raw at 18*s.* 6*d.* and expending the work upon it of 5*s.* 6*d.* for throwing and waste, makes his organzine cost him 24*s.* which is 2*s.* 6*d.* above the price the Italian is selling at in this market; so that in effect, at this time, 21*s.* 6*d.* having paid the duty of 3*s.* 6*d.* in order to protect the English throwster, the duty at this moment should be 6*s.* per pound.

11423. What is the cost of throwing Italian tram?—A throwster, to keep his factory and machinery in repair, and pay his way, should have 4*s.* and upwards, exclusive of waste.

11424. Do your house throw silk by commission?—We do not; up to the beginning of 1831 we sold Italian tram and organzine of our own throwing.

11425. Why did you abandon this branch?—The Italian throwster began to undersell us in 1830, and we deemed it prudent to give up a losing competition; circumstances soon justified the step, as we witnessed the ruin of several throwsters, and much sacrifice on throwsters' stocks.

11426. Is the throwing of Italian silk of importance to England?—Of the first consequence, as it affords so much employment on account of its being of a fine size, and consequently considerable wages. Independent of this, Italian raw silk

is

J. *Brocklehurst*, jun.
Esq.

16 July,
1832.

is absolutely requisite to ensure the consumption of the raw silk imported from China and Bengal; and I may here state with regard to a trade I know something of, where 100,000 lbs. of Bengal and China silk is consumed, 50,000 lbs. of Italian silk is requisite to work it up into manufactured goods.

11427. Do you consider the throwing in this country advantageous to the silk manufacture generally?—I am satisfied the silk trade of the country depends upon the extent of our thowing operations, for where the throwing shall be conducted, the natural tendency is a concentration of the stock of raw material.

11428. Would it not be equally advantageous to the manufacturer to be supplied with foreign throwns?—Judging merely as a manufacturer, I should say decidedly not, for we find it of the first importance that we should be enabled to regulate the throw of our material according to its purpose; not only the perfection but the very power of our making any peculiar article, depends upon our having the raw material at hand for selection; throwing being in effect the first stage of manufacturing.

11429. In what other view do you consider it important to retain the throwing of Italian silk in England?—It would tend to insure a larger stock of material at steady prices, the manufacturer would have as it were three stocks of Italian silk to trust to; stock of raw in the merchants' hands, stock in the mills, and the customary stock of foreign throwns as heretofore.

11430. Would not the stock of foreign throwns be increased?—At times it might; but the Italian throwster having other customers for his throwns would merely feed this market, and should any sudden demands arise abroad we should be deprived of a supply until we had outbid them, thus losing a season, and suspending our consumption of Bengal and China silk. It is of peculiar advantage that the British manufacturer should have two markets at home for raw and thrown Italian silk, having only one market consisting of throwns, his own purchases would raise the market against himself, besides being more subject to the interference of speculation when the supply should be temptingly small.

11431. Have not the throwsters of Italy the control of your supply of raws already?—Since 1829, it appears to me, that their influence has, in this respect been extended; but there are districts in Italy which produce raw silk, and have no throwing mills. Now as the rest of the Continent are not buyers of Italian raws, these districts are very beneficial to this country; though during the last two years, I have an impression that part of their supplies have fallen off, and may be going into the Italian throwsters' hands; but I must add these districts furnish a very small supply towards the quantity required in this country to work up other silks.

11432. Do you attribute this to the reduction of duties on throwns in 1829?—I do; and there is a very important and in my mind an alarming diminution taking place in the supplies of raws from the direct throwing districts of Italy. To place this point more clearly before the Committee, I have made an extract from an intelligent Broker's Books of Account, (Messrs. Brockwell & De Lannoy,) showing the amounts of raws and throwns annually sent by every merchant reeler and throwster in Italy, each of these parties send their bales of silk under peculiar marks. The selection I have made consists of between 20 and 30 of the general senders of raws and throwns from the throwing districts, which will show the change which has taken place in their operations since the alteration of duties in 1829. I put in the Table, which shows the three last annual imports of raws and throwns, of these respective marks, demonstrating that when the duties on throwns were reduced in 1829, the raws have progressively decreased, and the throwns have increased in the importation from Italy. The total number of raws, arising from 26 Italians, who trade regularly with England in raws and throwns, are, in 1829, 691 bales of raws, 127 bales of throwns; in 1830, 660 bales of raws, 336 bales of throwns; in 1831, 558 bales of raws, 589 bales of throwns; and to the 25th May, this year, 45 bales of raws, 46 bales of throwns; showing, that in 1829, there were 444 per cent. more raws than throwns; in 1830, 96 per cent. more raws than throwns; in 1831, five per cent. more throwns than raws.

*[The Witness delivered in the same:]*

| Mark | 1828 Raw | 1828 Thrown | 1829 Raw | 1829 Thrown | 1830 Raw | 1830 Thrown | 1831 Raw | 1831 Thrown | 1832 (to May 25.) Raw | 1832 Thrown |
|---|---|---|---|---|---|---|---|---|---|---|
| E.B. C.&C. | 32 | 13 | 30 | 13 | 3 | 7 | 15 | 25 | - | - |
| P.B. | 18 | 5 | 8 | 5 | 6 | 12 | 1 | 10 | - | - |
| W.C. | 6 | - | 16 | 1 | 7 | 16 | 2 | 21 | - | - |
| L.F.B. | 2 | 1 | 5 | - | 8 | 16 | 14 | 53 | 3 | 5 |
| ℐℰ | 8 | - | 8 | 1 | 7 | 19 | 2 | 20 | - | 4 |
| (G.B.C.) | 13 | 5 | 16 | 2 | 11 | 10 | 6 | 13 | - | 1 |
| B.G. | 32 | 6 | 30 | 3 | 28 | 4 | 5 | 24 | 1 | - |
| C. di B.G. | 64 | 1 | 42 | 3 | 17 | 1 | 15 | 19 | 1 | 2 |
| G.T. | 35 | 1 | 26 | - | 40 | 10 | 44 | 20 | 5 | - |
| (P) | 48 | 6 | 61 | 6 | 37 | 15 | 28 | 15 | 5 | - |
| L.C. | 103 | 50 | 22 | 43 | 33 | 31 | 19 | 51 | - | 5 |
| ℌ | 74 | - | 101 | - | 88 | 40 | 74 | 29 | 6 | 3 |
| D.S. | 101 | 1 | 152 | 3 | 118 | 42 | 140 | 99 | 14 | 14 |
| G.V. | 29 | - | 12 | - | 28 | 1 | 10 | 9 | - | - |
| C.D. | 6 | - | 13 | - | 17 | 5 | 3 | 5 | - | - |
| G.B.P. | 33 | 1 | 33 | 4 | 45 | 7 | 23 | 16 | 5 | - |
| A.P. | 6 | - | 9 | - | 3 | 6 | 5 | 3 | - | - |
| F.G.M. | 5 | - | - | 3 | 5 | 6 | 4 | 14 | - | - |
| P.N.G. | 4 | - | 8 | - | 10 | - | 6 | 9 | - | - |
| A.F. | 14 | - | 3 | 2 | 29 | 14 | 13 | 9 | - | 6 |
| G.M. | 11 | 9 | 21 | 21 | 36 | 16 | 23 | 29 | 5 | 1 |
| F.M.C. | 2 | - | - | - | 14 | 3 | 7 | 12 | - | 1 |
| G.B.C. | 28 | 4 | 35 | 5 | 26 | 16 | 45 | 14 | - | 4 |
| F.B. | 13 | - | 19 | - | 21 | 8 | 52 | 51 | 2 | - |
| D.B. | 14 | 6 | 19 | 10 | 18 | 18 | - | 9 | - | - |
| Pq.L. | 4 | 3 | 2 | 2 | 5 | 13 | 2 | 10 | - | - |

| Importation of 26 Marks | RAW. (Bales.) | THROWN. (Bales.) | PER CENT. More Raw than Thrown. | Less Raw than Thrown. |
|---|---|---|---|---|
| in 1829 | 691 | 127 | 444 | - |
| 1830 | 660 | 336 | 96¼ | - |
| 1831 | 558 | 589 | - | 5½ |
| 1832 (to 25 May) | 45 | 46 | - | 2 |

J. *Brocklehurst*, jun.
Esq.

16 July,
1832.

11433. Do most of the Italians, who consign silk to this market, consign both thrown and raws?—No; there are several who send only raws, but the largest number send both.

11434. Are the trade accustomed to reason upon such facts as these?—I fear not, for if they were the throwing question would be better understood; it would then be guided by solid reasoning instead of vague and inconsistent opinions.

11435. Have these facts been useful to you so as to enable you to regulate your own transactions?—I have found them eminently useful, inasmuch as they early indicated what were the effects of the change of duty in 1829. The broker who usually selects for me the samples of raw and Italian silk, and proposes them for purchase, up to that period was in the habit of supporting his proposals, by saying he could sell such and such proportions when manufactured into organzine and tram; but in 1830 he ceased to suggest his prospects of sale, his advice changed; these tables and his experience showed him the coming collision of Italian and British throwsters; his observations now were, if you can use up so and so in your manufacture all very well, but do not buy with a view to sell this silk in a thrown state; the Italian throwster, with his peculiar advantages, can undersell you. We followed his advice, and contracted our throwing; it saved us from a severe loss by the competition that came on in 1831, though we would have followed up the operation of throwing for sale for the sake of our work people, giving them the use of the steam-engines, mills and machinery, if the returns would have paid their wages. To this day we are ready to resume the trade when bare cost can be obtained.

11436. Have you any information as to the capability of throwing silk in this country?—This country is already prepared to throw, I believe, to a very great extent, with its present mills and machinery, and a large unemployed population, well acquainted with the throwing of silk.

11437. Do you consider the present low duties, on thrown silks, a disadvantage to the silk manufacturer generally of this country?—Certainly they are, because they are placed too low, as I have previously shown, to draw a large and regular supply of the best raw silks from the throwing districts of Italy, and which are evidently every day becoming more essential to the silk manufacture of this country.

11438. Do you consider the silk manufacture of this country capable of great increase, provided the duty on thrown silks were well adjusted?—I consider the silk trade of this country to be comparatively in its infancy; if well managed by our Government, every thing depending upon its obtaining increased protection, to enable the throwster and manufacturer to regain the ground they have lost since 1826; the first point requiring protection is the securing the throwing mills of England ample supplies of raws, and trusting to competition, among themselves, to supply the manufacturer with a large and excellent choice of throwns at moderate prices; the next important point is to secure to the manufacturer a profitable and secure market at home, and the certain consequence will be an increasing export of the surplus, if without profit, or at a loss for a time it would be of little consequence, so long as he has profits at home to counterpoise the losses on his export.

11439. Are not the present duties upon thrown silks adjusted in a manner to enlarge the silk trade in England?—No, they are not; for most assuredly they check instead of promote an ample supply of the raw silks of Italy.

11440. By what mode would you obtain an increased supply of the better kinds of raw silk from Italy?—By restoring the duties on thrown silks to what they were in 1829, coupled with the principle that thrown silk should only be admissible from those countries exporting their raw silk.

11441. To what do you attribute the diminished supply of the better raw silks of Italy?—To the Italians retaining more for the purposes of throwing at home, confirmed by the Table I have just referred to, and to the increased trade of the various continental manufactures.

11442. Do you consider there are sufficient mills and machinery in England to carry on a more extensive trade in the throwing of Italian silk, than at present?—In 1824 the mills of England threw 50 per cent. more Italian raw silk than in 1831; in addition to this, it is well known that there are thousands of people who understand the throwing of silk, who are in a state of starvation for want of employment.

11443. What was the proportion of raw and thrown imported from Italy during the years 1827 and 1828, while the 5s. duty prevailed?—The average proportions were 180 per cent. more raws than throwns.

11444. If the duty on throwns had not been reduced, would these proportions

of

of raws and throwns been continued to be imported?—I can see no reason to the contrary.

11445. What was the proportion of raws and throwns imported from Italy during the years 1830 and 1831?—The average for those two years ending December 1831, was 84 per cent. more raws than throwns.

11446. It having been stated in evidence, that other causes were given for the large importation of thrown silk during the years 1830 and 1831, than the reduction of duty to 3 s. 6 d. per lb., can you state the proportions of imports of raws and throwns for the first six months of the present year?—For the six months just terminated, that is from 1st January to the 30th June, the proportions are only 68 per cent. more raws than throwns; thus showing the conspicuous diminution from 180 per cent. since the last reduction of duties.

11447. Is there, in your opinion, any other cause than the low rates of duty, to have induced the Italian to be still sending these increased proportions of throwns to England?—I attribute it entirely to the present inadequate duty.

11448. If the duties on throwns were restored to 5 s., do you calculate on excluding the foreign throwns?—Certainly not, it would not be requisite to do so; past experience proves that we had a certain convenient supply when the duty was 14 s. 6 d., or in reality 9 s. 2 d.; and when it was 5 s. there was a supply; and I have no doubt there would, with that duty, still be the usual supply; my object would be to keep that supply in reasonable check, the great and good effects of which would be the maintaining, and eventually increasing a supply of good Italian raws to this market; our silk trade would then rest on a secure foundation, it would be an entire manufacture in all its processes; for to me it is very evident, that to where the throwing can be successfully carried on, all subsequent processes have a natural tendency.

11449. Do you consider the present low prices for throwing as tending to improve or deteriorate the manufacture of silk in this country?—The present low price compels the throwster to do his work in the cheapest readiest way, without paying due attention to the clearing of the silk of its imperfect places; this is a great injury to the weaver, enhancing the cost of weaving, by impeding his progress, and increasing the faults and imperfections on the surface of the silk when woven; I consider the silk manufacture generally of the country to be degenerating.

11450. What might be the condition of the weavers before 1826?—From 1808, when I first became acquainted with the trade, it was steadily increasing to 1816, from which time it made rapid progress up to 1826, and gave occupation to a large influx of cotton weavers. It is a singular fact, that from about 1817 to 1824, there were few, and no material fluctuations of prices of weaving or quantity of employment, and by this time the greater part of the cotton weavers had been absorbed by the silk trade, and I should say it was a steady progressive trade both in figured and plain silk weaving through the whole period up to 1826.

11451. What has been the condition of the weavers since 1826?—Since 1826 their condition has undergone such a transition from comfort and regular employment to so great a degree of distress as hardly to be known to be the same trade as it was before interfered with.

11452. Have you any statement of wages that will show the alteration you describe?—I have a Table of some of the principal articles made at Macclesfield, and the prices from 1821 to 1831, which I will deliver in; the average earnings of the weavers in 1821 to 1826 amounted to 16 s. 6 d., but as soon as the change took place, their earnings decreased to 7 s. 9 d., and they are now reduced to 6 s. per week. These statements of wages of weavers include the weaving of the richer kinds of handkerchiefs not made by all manufacturers, and therefore rather exceed the actual average of earnings of the weavers.

[*The same was delivered in, and read.*]

STATEMENT

STATEMENT of leading ARTICLES made at *Macclesfield*.

*J. Brocklehurst*, jun.
Esq.

16 July,
1832.

| — | Mounture Handkerchiefs. | Figured Stage Harness of 100 Shafts. | Black Figured Handkerchiefs. | Grey Bandanna Handkerchiefs. | Single Sarsnets. | Gros de Naples. | Average Earnings, clear of all Deductions. |
|---|---|---|---|---|---|---|---|
| | Per Doz. s. d. | Per Doz. s. d. | Per Doz. s. d. | Per Piece. s. d. | Per Yard. d. | Per Yard. s. d. | s. d. |
| 1821 | 30 – | 14 – | 10 – | 3  6 | 9 | 1  1 | 16  6 |
| 1822 | 30 – | 13 – | 10 – | 3  6 | 9 | 1  1 | 16  – |
| 1823 | 24 – | 14 – | 10 – | 3  6 | 9 | 1  1 | 16  – |
| 1824 | 22 – | 12  6 | 9  – | 3  6 | 9 | 1  – | 15  6 |
| 1825 | 24 – | 13  6 | 9  6 | 3  6 | 9 | 1  – | 16  7 |
| 1826 | 16 – | 12  – | 8  – | 2  6 | 8 | –  10 | 7  9 * |
| 1827 | 14 – | 12  – | 7  6 | 2  6 | 6 | –  8 | 7  4 |
| 1828 | 14 – | 12  – | 7  – | 2  6 | 6 | –  8 | 7  4 |
| 1829 | 12 – | 10  – | 6  6 | 2  6 | 5 | –  6 | 7  – |
| 1830 | 11 – | 9  – | 6  6 | 2  3 | 5 | –  7 | 6  6 |
| 1831 | 9 – | 7  6 | 6  3 | 2  3 | 4 | –  6 | 6  – |

* The falling off in earnings in 1826, and subsequently, is accounted for by the scarcity of work, and the frequent changes of it the weaver has been subjected to, as well as by the reduced *rate* of wages.

For several months past, both here and at Manchester, &c. the weavers have not been allowed to bring in more than a given quantity of work, besides being kept waiting for warps and shute.

The 7th column condenses the weekly earnings on the average of *all the* different descriptions of work in the other columns.

---

11453. Does the Table you have handed in contain a list of all the articles made at Macclesfield?—In addition to the handkerchiefs, sarsnets, gros and Persians already enumerated, crapes are made, also figured gros, velvets and satins have been at different times and subsequently relinquished.

11454. Do the manufacturers of the Continent interfere with you?—It is to this interference I attribute the abandonment of these articles, checking the progress of this most valuable part of the silk manufacture, placing the whole trade of Macclesfield and the country around in competition, as it were, on only a few articles of a lower grade.

11455. Do you think that if your trade had been better protected it would have been more extensive and in a more advanced state?—Seeing around me a great increase of consumption of foreign manufactured silk goods, it is evident that if these goods had been manufactured in England, the silk trade would have been so much the larger; but our Government have never seemed to understand the interests of the silk trade, and I may observe the importation of the silk manufacturers from France last year, was to an extent that the fine raw material would have distributed an enormous amount of wages among the English artisans.

11456. What description of goods did you make before 1826?—Before 1826, besides handkerchiefs, we made rich gros de Naples for the West end retail houses; the goods were of net bright silk, both warp and shute, these houses merely buy linings of us latterly, but unwilling to be driven out, we are making low goods, substituting in competition with others dye stuff for silk, and the dyer who can load the silk most is in the highest repute.

11457. Do these houses buy goods from you now?—Since 1826, our trade with these houses has gradually declined; we have often had the mortification to see them use our capital in payment for foreign silk goods, knowing the validity of the parties, it was the preferable evil to locking up our capital without interest, to give them the use of it at a certain rate, but I must do the parties the justice to say, that they have stated (and I believe it), that it is with regret that they are obliged in self defence to encourage foreign manufactures, that to this day they wish the admission of them was under more restrictions, these are the wishes of some of the most respectable houses in the trade at the West end of the Town.

11458. Do weavers lose more time than formerly?—Much more, I am sorry to say; I know but too many instances where weavers with families wait several weeks at a time for work, they are nominally employed by being allowed to retain their reeds and harnesses in the hope of something arising in their favour, hence manufacturers often find themselves with 1,200 weavers on their list of workmen, and in reality only a portion (700 or 800) at work.

11459. When weavers and artisans are thrown out of work do they take to other

employment?

*J. Brocklehurst*, jun.
Esq.

———

16 July,
1832.

employment ?—No, there seems no opening ; a weaver or millman in general knows nothing of agriculture; in and round Manchester and Macclesfield the land being chiefly grass land, but little labour is required to keep it in order. From 1816 to 1826, the cotton weavers whom the power loom had displaced, found employment in silk, and on that account I think it most important to retain the silk manufacture to this country as affording an asylum for people thrown out of other employments. On reading the evidence of a gentleman on the 17th February 1831, before the Select Committee of the House of Commons, on the affairs of the East India Company, as to the extent of interference of the great export of cotton fabrics to India from Great Britain with the native manufacturers, he there stated that the interference had been very considerable, and that it had destroyed the cotton manufacture in many places in India. The next question he was asked was, " Has the export produced distress among the weavers and artisans of India ?" his reply is a remarkable one, " Not to the extent that might have been supposed, for the weavers in that country are also cultivators of land, and turn their labour from one employment to another without that shock which might be felt in other countries." But in regard to Macclesfield and that neighbourhood, I have known instances where the people thrown out of employment have been unable to obtain any thing to do for 18 months or two years at a time.

11460. Do you employ many Irish ?—We do, indiscriminately with other weavers ; steady characters and having skill in their avocations, are a sufficient recommendation.

11461. Are the Irish weavers subject to more distress than other weavers ?— Most unfortunately they are ; not having even the wretched resource of a parish.

11462. Do you know what may be the state of silk weaving in Dublin ?—I am led to believe it is very bad, for I saw the poor Irish in Macclesfield pass the last winter in great distress, but I never heard of any of them attempting to return to their own country ; and I am confirmed in this belief by a letter I received a month ago from a gentleman, a member of a relief committee in Dublin, which with the permission of the Committee I will refer to : his letter is dated Dublin, the 8th of June 1832. " Sir,—As a member of a committee sitting now in Dublin, of which the " Lord Mayor is chairman, for the assistance of the poor, and as I find several silk " weavers are now out of employment here, I take the liberty of requesting to know " from you whether there be an opening for such persons to get work in Maccles- " field ; if so, endeavours would be made to assist in providing the means for such " persons to get over. In the year 1830, I was a member of a committee then in " existence, and we sent several silk people to Macclesfield and other manufac- " turing towns in England, where employment offered itself, and who were generally " successful ; there are persons here who are in want of employment in both broad " and narrow branches. It is to be hoped that a reformed Parliament will see into " the necessity of altering a system which is giving employment to France while " Great Britain and Ireland are the sufferers, France being a country which will " give no reciprocity in return. I have to apologize for this trouble, and shall at " all times be happy to render your firm any service in Dublin." I wrote him a reply in these words,—" London, June 16th, 1832. Sir,—Your favour has been " forwarded to me, and in reply I regret my inability to hold out any prospect of " Dublin weavers obtaining employment in Macclesfield for the present; certainly, " in 1830, owing to a miserable state of the silk trade in 1829 and previously, a " momentary re-action on the demand for labour occurred, yet I well remember " a portion of the weavers who came over at the time (bringing with them their " scanty all, consisting of an old loom) who never succeeded in obtaining any direct " employment; but they raised a few shillings on this moveable, perhaps the value " of it as old timber, and since that time they have occasionally obtained a short " job as journeymen ; in too many sad instances living huddled six or eight together " in a small room or cellar, without furniture or a bed, their wives and children " obliged to subsist on charity."

11463. What would be the effects of opening the trade to India, as to increasing or improving your supply of Bengal raw silk ?—I believe it is already open for all the purposes of individual enterprize as to growing, buying and exporting raw silk to England.

11464. What would be the effect of the East India Company's relinquishing their trade to private individuals ?—The silk trade derive incalculable advantages from the large and steady supply periodically put up for sale (thrice a year) by the Company at low tax prices ; their long previous notice of sale, quantity, quality, &c.

checks

J. *Brocklehurst*, jun.
Esq.

16 July,
1832.

checks speculation, and should they abandon their trade, for years to come, in my opinion, the culture of silk in India would decline both as to quantity and quality.

11465. Do you consider it desirable that the East India Company should continue their growth of silk?—If, as it is understood, that the revenue of the Company must come here in some medium, there cannot be a better than in raw material, the growth of India.

11466. Are the importations of silk goods from India injurious to any party?—Up to 1829, the duties on India goods were rated per yard, per piece or per pound, and under those rated duties the British trade was protected, and public wishes for India bandannas fully satisfied; all the evidence the Committee have received, and my own experience confirms the fact, that there had been no smuggling under the previous regulations of 1826; I have here the official returns of seizures of smuggled goods, and there are scarcely fifty pieces of bandannas enumerated from the year 1826 to the year 1829; but the change to an *ad valorem* duty in 1829 has already had the effect of increasing the sale of Indian bandannas for home consumption, which is attributable to the encouragement the present *ad valorem* duty affords to the importer; for when the British manufacturer requires most protection, he obtains the least; the present price the piece of India bandanna sells for at the East India Company's sale being 20 s., the *ad valorem* duty of 20 per cent., would be 4 s.; but when the price falls, and the piece sells but for 15 s., the protecting duty falls to 3 s.

11467. Under what further disadvantage does this system place the trade?—At Liverpool, these bandannas are cleared by valuation; and last February when the prices at the East India Company's sale was 19 s. to 20 s. a piece, the Custom-house at Liverpool allowed this description of goods to pass at the valuation of 15 s.; thus the duty in Liverpool was but 3 s. at the time it was near 4 s. in London.

11468. Do you know whether the *ad valorem* duties are inconvenient to the importers of goods from India?—A bill to regulate the collection of duties is about to pass into a law, and a memorial has, I believe, been presented by some London merchants to the Board of Trade, desiring to be put on the footing of Liverpool, that is, to have the power to clear by valuation, as they feel an inconvenience in the delay of their goods being obliged to pass the East India Company's sales, to ascertain their value.

11469. Do you see any objection to this being granted?—None, provided all these goods were placed under a rated duty sufficient to protect the British manufacturer against India and China.

11470. Are they not protected by the present regulations?—Up to 1829 they were, but by the official returns of India bandannas taken into home consumption, there appears a progressive increase, showing that the protection is not sufficient. In 1829, Indian bandannas taken into home consumption were 67,465 pieces; in 1830, 77,953 pieces; in 1831, 101,023 pieces, being an increase of 47 per cent. in two years; and I must here remark, these India goods are brought home as a return and sold without any reference to cost, and when they come into the market British goods are always laid aside, Indian goods having the preference, and the lower they fall the worse the situation of the British manufacturer. I have seen a time when a piece sold for 13 s., and the *ad valorem* duty upon that would be very small indeed.

11471. What remedy would you recommend?—A rated duty of 8 d. per yard; until 1829 the duty on bandanna handkerchiefs was 1 s. per yard, but to favour India it was reduced from 30 to 20 per cent., the exact proportion 8 d. bears to 1 s. Under a rated duty, the importers might be allowed to clear their goods at their own convenience.

11472. Are the India Company's imports of silk goods materially injurious?—Certainly both to the manufacturer and to themselves; the manufacturer is obliged to watch the amount of imports, consequently dares not make and hold any stock; he continually hears that the Company and private traders are enlarging their orders for goods in India; and as regards the India Company's profit and loss by their double proceeding of importing both goods and the raw material to make a similar article, sooner or later they will discover that their goods and raw material are in competition in this market to their mutual disadvantage. I have here a statement of the Company's profit and loss upon their silk transactions from the year 1816 to the year 1830; it is a certain fact, that up to 1825, with the exception of one year, the Company were making a liberal profit upon their silk transactions, and since

678.                                                                    that

J. *Brocklehurst*, jun.
Esq.

16 July,
1832.

that time they have had a loss every year but one year; except the last year, they gained 3,000*l.* out of all their silk from India.

11473. How do you arrive at the facts?—This is from a copy of the Papers (Appendix, fol. 656.) laid before Parliament, and ordered to be printed, on the 11th October 1831; it is headed, "Account of Profit and Loss upon the Sales of Bengal Raw Silk sold by the East India Company in the following Years."

[*The same was delivered in.*]

[*See* No. 22 of the Papers, (Appendix, folio 656) laid before Parliament, (Commons,) and ordered to be Printed, 11th October 1831.

(Extract.)

ACCOUNT of Profit and Loss upon the Sales of *Bengal* Raw Silk, sold by the *East India* Company, in the following Years:

|  | PROFIT. | LOSS. |
|---|---|---|
|  | £. | £. |
| 1816–17 - - | 255,755 | — |
| 1817–18 - - | 244,547 | — |
| 1818–19 - - | 80,431 | — |
| 1819–20 - - - | — | 53,967 |
| 1820–21 - - | 43,223 | — |
| 1821–22 - - | 63,861 | — |
| 1822–23 - - | 73,830 | — |
| 1823–24 - - | 101,138 | — |
| 1824–25 - - - | — | 75,109 |
| 1825–26 - - - | — | 32,105 |
| 1826–27 - - | 45,123 | — |
| 1827–28 - - - | — | 40,634 |
| 1828–29 - - - | — | 22,165 |
| 1829–30 - - | 3,152 | — |

Account for 1831 not made up.

India Bandannas taken into Home Consumption, from an Official Statement, &c. &c.

In 1829 - - - 67,465 pieces.
1830 - - - 77,953 —
1831 - - - 101,023 – being an increase of about 47 per cent. in two years.

11474. Do you believe that their manufactured goods, coming into this country, come in competition with the raw silk they import?—Yes, certainly.

11475. What may be the accumulation of Bengal raw silk in the Company's warehouses?—There has latterly been a great accumulation.

STOCK of Raw Silk in the East India Company's Warehouses:

1829: January 1st,  7,043 bales, about 150 lbs. per bale  - lbs. 1,056,450
1830: January 1st,  8,541 - - - — - - - - - 1,281,150
1831: January 1st,  9,795 - - - — - - - - - 1,469,250
1832: January 1st, 10,233 - - - — - - - - - 1,534,950

This account shows an accumulation of 50 per cent. in the East India Company's warehouses since 1829.

11476. Was any of their silk refused at the sales in 1831?—In 1831 the Company offered for sale 8,000 bales, of which 2,726 were refused by the trade.

11477. Was any refused at their sale in February last?—Owing to the large quantity refused at previous sales, the Company diminished the usual quantity offered for sale by 200; still 472 were refused, making in reality 672 as not being taken by the trade.

11478. To what do you attribute this decreasing consumption of Bengals?—Partly to the Company importing manufactured goods, tending to displace so much material which otherwise would be manufactured into the same description of goods in England.

11479. If

J. *Brocklehurst*, jun.
Esq.

———

16 July,
1832.

11479. If the object in view were the benefit of India, are you of opinion that that object would be best promoted by increasing the importation of raw silk or of manufactured silk goods?—That is a question to be decided by political economists, who advocate cheap buying and selling, though our artisans accustomed to make these goods be starving; but as labour is so superabundant in this country, I think there can be no doubt the duty of our Government would be to promote the importation of raw material and not manufactured goods, even from our own colonies.

11480. Have not the imports of manufactured goods of that sort had the effect, greater or less, to depress the price of their raw silk?—It has had that effect; they (the East India Company) are sustaining a loss upon their imports of raw silk.

11481. Then would it not be more for the advantage of the East India Company, not to import manufactured goods?—I had a conversation a short time ago with a gentleman, high in the management of the India Company's trade; I observed to him, " so I understand you have ordered 20,000 pieces of India goods to be sent home, where you ordered 5,000 before; why do you do this, you will only reduce the price of your silk, and it is only displacing a certain quantity of manufacture in this country;" his answer was, " if we do not import them, the private trader will;" I replied in anwer, " is there any difficulty in there being a duty to regulate that?" he said he thought that it would be very desirable, that is, to have a rated duty, not an *ad valorem* duty; now we do not wish to displace the goods from India entirely, but to keep them at their present quantity; it being rather alarming to have an increase of imported bandannas, of nearly 50 per cent. within two years.

11482. At the time that bandannas and other manufactured silks of India were not admitted to home consumption in this country, they were not sold at a much higher price than they are now, were they?—They were sold at about a guinea a piece, as at present.

11483. At the time that they were sold for exportation, and not allowed to be consumed in this country, the raw silk of India did fetch a much higher price per pound than it does at present?—Frequently double the present price.

11484. Does it not appear, that since the manufactured silk goods of India have been admitted into this market for general consumption, the raw silk sent from India to this market has been sold at a loss by the Company?—Ever since 1824, as will be seen by the Return of the Company's profit and loss on silk, already before the Committee, it is shown they have been losers in every year but one.

11485. Are you aware what the exports to France may consist of?—It has been stated by various parties, and I believe correctly so, that the export in value consists of 26,000*l*. a year to France; and I know one house who have made and sold 15,000*l*. of the 26,000*l*.; it has been stated by a gentleman, sent by the Board of Trade to make inquiry into the silk trade of France, that he scarcely saw a shop in that country, wherein he did not see English manufactured silks exhibited, but he never stated what kind of silks; now it is well known, that it is customary for all shops to exhibit handerchiefs in their windows, and I dare say he would, from want of minuter scrutiny, come away with the conclusion, that we had a large trade to France; but we have no silk trade to France, except in a few bandanna handkerchiefs, amounting to 26,000*l*. a year; and it is equally certain that this gentleman may be mistaken in saying that only 800,000*l*. worth of silks come from France; it is not to be supposed that he has a clearer account of the extent of imported French silk goods; my belief is, that double the quantity comes from France; it has also been stated, that the trade of this country requires foreign goods to stimulate it to improvements; now I have here some patterns of bandannas which have never had any well printed foreign goods to compete with; I can exhibit a pattern of these goods of one house in this city, which I believe to be unequalled by any manufacturer in the world [*producing some patterns of bandannas*]; this house has no foreign competitor to propel it forward in improvements; on the same ground, it may be justly observed, that England only wants protection to improve her silk manufactures generally, and obtain a large silk trade.

11486. When were these printed?—Some of these designs were made in 1823, 1824, and from that time up to the present period; I have one piece of handkerchiefs here, the designing of the patterns upon this piece cost 800*l*.

11487. If you had an importation of that commodity from France, do you believe that any person would have undertaken to incur an expense of 800*l*. to perfect these patterns?—Certainly not; improvement and extension of any branch of trade must grow out of profits. There exists too great a desire in this country to advance; we do not require the aid of foreign competition in our own market,

it

*J. Brocklehurst,* jun.
Esq.

16 July,
1832.

it is too evident that this competition has only paralyzed British exertion during the last six years. Every country abroad seem disposed to protect and promote the interests of their manufacturers. I know in Belgium, there has been a proposition under the consideration of their Government, to give their printers the entire monopoly of their own market against England. [*The Witness exhibited another piece of handerchiefs,*] I do not wonder, if a gentleman going to France, should frequently see this Paul Pry figure in all the shops, and thus be led to suppose that we have a large export to France. I exhibit this piece to show the perfection to which printing has arrived; this is acknowledged, by competent judges, to be the best work ever produced by block printing.

11488. Do you believe, that if the other fancy branches of the silk trade were protected, a similar outlay of capital would take place for the purpose of producing whatever can be required as matter of taste, and with as great skill in the execution of that taste?—It being done in this instance, there can be no doubt, that with our immense capital and population, means would be found to produce articles of taste equal to those of other countries, if we had but adequate protection.

11489. Do you believe that the reason these things are not undertaken in the other branches of the trade, is, that they have not this protection?—Yes, it is simply for want of protection that the trade languishes at present; I am satisfied, if it possessed the home market, we might soon have an extended export trade.

11490. That would then permit an improvement in the superior branches of your manufacture, and the inferior might be sold, either with a profit on the goods or at a trifling loss, which the profit on the better branches of that trade would enable you to sustain?—Yes, I am decidedly of that opinion; for if we were making the better articles I have no doubt we should occasionally export a portion of these better articles, and having made a profit in the beginning of the season, the surplus stock we should export, and thus eventually we should cultivate the taste for our articles in other countries.

11491. You do not think it is from that want of taste we do not succeed in foreign countries?—I think if our trade were protected our taste would soon be found equal to that of other countries. I have heard a great deal of Schools of Art in France, and I must own, with some regret, that the want of protection disables us from forming similar establishments, particularly as regards the silk trade.

11492. How is the trade now carried on by France with this country?—I believe that she monopolizes all the valuable branches, and that without a general return to a better system we shall lose the silk trade.

11493. Have you considered the applicability of the power loom to the weaving of broad silk?—I have for several years past attentively watched the various efforts to apply the power loom to the weaving of broad silk made by enterprizing individuals, and I may add, that I have seen the attempts in more instances than one accelerate the ruin of the parties, this was a favourite crotchet of the late Mr. Huskisson. I remember in 1824 he was present at one of our interviews with the Board of Trade, and predicted the successful application of power looms, and that we should beat all the world; he knew nothing about the matter, and in fact he and his successors have, as regards the silk trade, gone on from mistake to mistake, till they have at last dragged it down to its present ruined condition.

11494. Is the power loom applicable to silk weaving at all?—It has been successfully applied to weaving common narrow ribbons down to a shoe-string, for several years; in the a-la-bar, of which we have heard such absurd tales of its utility as an invention, I saw weaving tapes and ferrets 20 years ago, we had them at work ourselves. It is useful in weaving these narrow things, 24 pieces in a row, because one or two shuttles being suspended, the moving power is still beneficially going on, but in weaving broader goods so much depends upon the handling and trimming of the silk, a great waste of power must necessarily occur.

11495. Is not the power loom applied to the weaving of crape gauze?—In this article also it is valuable; the crape thread being hard twisted and capable of bearing the friction of this mode of weaving.

11496. Why is it not equally applicable to broad goods?—It is not applicable to broad goods, the thrown silk goes through the process of dyeing preparatory to weaving, and according to colour is subject to more or less injury; for instance, in all grain and fast colour stronger acids or alkalies are applied, these less or more deeply penetrate the fibre of the silk and render it tender or brittle, and sometimes the process chafes or ruffles the surface of the thread, so that the next process of winding it from the skein and in warping it, that is preparing it for the weavers's use,

are

J. Brocklehurst, jun.
Esq.

16 July,
1832.

are very tedious, the silk having many broken places repaired by knots, this renders the weaving proportionally more difficult; hitherto no certain process has been discovered to ensure silk from injury in the course of dyeing; this silk consequently requires great care and attention on the part of the weaver to produce a faceable article when woven; now in weaving cotton the yarn of the warp is dressed with a preparation of paste, to make the thread firm, and able to resist the friction of the reed and harness through which it passes, and the calico or cloth is afterwards cleansed by boiling, washing and bleaching, or in dyeing or printing; but broad silk goods are required to come from the loom perfect in colour, texture, brilliancy and fit for use, and any defect in these respects is destructive of its value, dressing the silk in any way totally spoils it.

11497. What other obstacles are there to the introduction of the power loom?— Power loom weaving does not admit of the introduction of a variety of colours or stripes in the shute requisite to make a piece either of fancy ribbon or broad silks, what is usually described as plaided or checked; and in weaving figured goods, should any imperfection in the pattern arise by threads out of their place, the power loom still proceeds, and would often waste a far greater proportion of valuable material than the power is worth.

11498. Are there any more obstacles?—The economy of power loom weaving is, one person to attend to two or more looms, and in cotton weaving, he can do so as his warp undergoes a preparation not applicable to silk, and which obviates all tediousness of working; his principle employment is to feed the looms with shute or weft, and of course the looms are constantly in action, but in silk weaving, the chief process is, in neatly trimming the warp, and were tedious trimming occupies a much greater portion of time than is taken up by merely the weaving or making of the piece, and here the saving of the moving power is lost.

11499. Are there any other difficulties?—The quantity of threads contained in the warp require the greatest nicety on the part of the weaver to produce a faceable surface, these threads are so crowded, that the weaver makes but two or three to four yards a day, but the advantage derived in weaving cotton by power is, that each loom turns out 60 yards a day, and a person attends two looms. Calico weaving may be pursued through the year, calico being always a convertible article, but in silk goods, the frequent changes of fabric silk, &c., would often throw the looms totally out of use, thus incurring a great loss on capital expended. I mention these facts with a view to remove some of the notions entertained at the Board of Trade in 1824, and subsequently, that we must apply power looms, and then we should be on right principles. I despair of ever applying power looms. This spring one of the most intelligent and most ingenious mechanics in Lancashire, set up a power loom and commenced weaving silk with it, about a month ago he removed the loom and gave out the silk to be woven by a hand loom weaver, saying it could not be accomplished; if a man in Europe could have accomplished it, that gentleman would have succeeded.

11500. You have shown some very beautiful specimens of printing in the silk handkerchief trade, and have mentioned that as much as 800 l. was expended in the preparation of the patterns, have the goodness to state whether in your opinion, the same taste of skill and exertion would be applied to other fancy branches of the silk trade, provided the protection given to those branches were adequate to secure a suitable remuneration?—I have no doubt as high a degree of perfection in the manufacture of the finest and most tasty silk goods would be attained in this country as could be produced in any part of the world, provided we were protected, and some security afforded by the Government as to a fair remunerative return on the application of skill and capital requisite to the production of figured and fancy silks. I feel fully confirmed in this opinion, by reference to the beautiful styles the English, and silk and cotton printers have attained, both in designs and engraving, we are not behind the rest of the world in many other articles of taste I could enumerate. I am satisfied, therefore, that Spitalfields and Coventry would, under wise protective laws, very soon show their ability to rival foreign productions.

11501. You mean that they would rival them in taste as well as in execution?— Yes; if our Government, like their neighbours, would but display the same disposition to encourage rather than disparage her own manufacturers.

11502. Do you consider smuggling to be injurious to you?—Smuggling is injurious to the manufacturer, by displacing his productions at a lower price than what the law may recognize as the necessary protection in the shape of duty; it

678.                                                                    enables

*J. Brocklehurst*, jun.
Esq.

———

16 July,
1832.

enables the dealer in smuggled goods to undersell the fair trader, and smuggled goods come into competition with our own goods at ruinously low prices.

11503. Who are the promoters of smuggling of silk goods?—I do not think the regular smugglers, for the risk of getting 30 or 40 per cent., would enter into the traffic in silk goods on their own account, whilst spirits and tobacco offer profits of six to 1,200 per cent. The channels for the disposal of silk are inconvenient, and the article not understood by the smuggler, he must have a receiver to take the goods in proper season; the delay as to delivery of spirits is no injury to the quality, rather the reverse; the promoters are to be found among the dealers, who are in reality the smugglers, through mere servants, and when one house smuggles it compels many others to do so in self defence.

11504. What would be the remedy, in your opinion?—Imprisonment and hard labour. All respectable houses wish for such a law for their mutual protection; it would be effectual if merely suspended over the parties, and I believe would seldom, if ever, require to be put in force.

11505. Would stamping foreign goods be beneficial?—Highly so, first in aid of detection of fraud, and it would enable the public, when disposed to encourage their own manufacturers, to discriminate the goods of other countries.

11506. Are you aware of the advantage that would result to this country by transferring the silk trade to France, in exchange for their taking cotton yarn from us?—I see no advantage, for they take the yarn as absolutely necessary to their manufacture of lace, not out of any reciprocal feelings, for I understand that they cannot spin these fine sizes for want of the peculiar damp climate of Manchester; now I do not see any such necessity existing for our taking silk goods from France, surrounded as we are by a great body of unemployed artisans who are able to make these silk goods if adequately protected.

11507. Have you ever been invited to establish a silk manufacture on any part of the Continent where a silk manufacture had formerly flourished, and been destroyed?—Many inducements were held out to me in 1829, after the harsh treatment we had experienced at the hands of our own Government.

11508. By what country where you invited?—In that year I visited Bruges, Ghent, Brussels, Mecklin, Antwerp, and the cities and towns on the Rhine, &c. I had an introduction to a gentleman at Brussels, at that time connected with the Government; he informed me of the anxiety of the Netherlands Government to see the silk trade re-established in the country, from whence it had gone to England.

11509. Had you an opportunity of judging of what progress they had made towards its re-establishment?—At Antwerp I saw a manufacture of silk carried on, but the proprietors could not extend or vary their productions, owing to their want of choice of material, and the want of the means of adapting their silk to the varying purposes, by throwing it accordingly. The manufactured silk I saw was denominated Antwerp black silk; it was a fabric they had made for several years; they made the same quantity, I believe, ten years ago as they are making now.

11510. Did you hear of the cost of the manufacture?—I saw a weaver, who told me he earned what I estimated to be 7 d. a day, weaving this heavy stout black silk, and I should say a man in England would be very ill paid at half-a-crown a day for the same work, and would not be able to support his strength and pay his way with less wages.

11511. All the necessaries of life in that country are unprotected; there is a free export and import of them?—In Belgium I believe that to be the case.

11512. Are there any corn laws?—Not to my knowledge; they may have some trivial duty.

11513. As the Government of the Netherlands were desirous to recover this trade, had you any proposal made you?—The gentleman I allude to offered to introduce me without delay to Prince William, and promised to ensure me his personal patronage; that the Prince would take a direct interest in the establishment; that his proportion of advance should be 2,000*l.* to my 1,000*l.*, to any extent I pleased to lay out money, but if I was inclined to embark capital sufficient for the undertaking, he would insure to me, for a long period of years, the exclusive right of the population capable of working silk at Ghent or Bruges, but particularly Bruges, the population being between 30 and 40,000, and any legislative enactments that I might require, to give me protection against foreign competition.

11514. Is the establishment of silk throwing and manufacturing very practicable at these places?—During my stay at Bruges I had the means of ascertaining the condition and temper of the population; I had also pointed out to me the very

great

J. Brocklehurst, jun. Esq.

16 July, 1832.

great advantages that could be derived from a stream of water that was evidently capable of turning a throwing mill to any reasonable extent; I perceived also that the population in general were very short of employment, and were very scantily paid; I have therefore no doubt that it would be very beneficial to any party competent to undertake it.

11515. Do you know any thing of the disposition of the present Government?—I believe they are as much disposed to encourage an extension of trade as the former one; they have lately had under consideration certain regulations in favour of their own silk printers, with a view to enable them to buy on favourable terms the silk handkerchiefs in a grey or unfinished state, and to print them in the vicinity of Brussels.

11516. Then we should have the making and selling the grey silk cloth to them in an unprinted state?—It is usual for a trade, to use a common expression, " to creep, and then go ;" and so soon as they have secured a printing trade, they can more safely proceed to make the cloth for themselves.

11517. What progress have they made?—Hitherto they have copied the English patterns, and succeeded, for we find their orders for unprinted silk cloth on the increase.

11518. Is it not possible that some of those goods which were seen in the shops in France were printed in the Netherlands?—It is possible, certainly, that a few may have been sent from the Netherlands, being printed there.

11519. Do you know what may be the extent of the British export trade in silk goods?—I understand it amounted to about 500,000 *l.* in value last year.

11520. Do you consider the export trade to be of advantage to the silk trade?—I think the export trade very beneficial, inasmuch as it carries off the surplus productions; it is always understood to be serviceable to any branch of trade, as it relieves the home market of what would otherwise embarrass the manufacturer and depress the prices at times below their proper level; for though the surplus goods be exported at an apparent loss, yet this may in reality be counterbalanced by a profit on that portion of the goods that may have been sold at home; thus, to a manufacturer possessing the home market, an export trade would be of considerable advantage; it is the remedy for gluts, and the French have found the utility of this market to clear off their job goods, in addition to their large regular trade to this country.

11521. To extend the export trade, you are of opinion the manufacturer should possess the home market?—When the duties were taken off the raw material in 1824, we were expressly told it was with a view to enable us to extend the export trade, and if the repeal of duties had not been followed by the fatal measure of letting in foreign goods, I have no doubt we should have had by this period a prosperous trade at home, and a growing demand from abroad; instead of this being the case, when foreign goods were admitted in 1826, though the effect was to diminish the value of material and to force down wages 50 per cent., yet our export trade diminished; for, in 1825, the export of silk goods, according to the official value, was 150,886 *l.* and in 1826 only 106,931 *l.*, showing a falling off of about 30 per cent. : so much for Mr. Huskisson's plan of forcing the export trade by foreign competition in the home market; and though half the trade had been ruined by 1828, the export had increased the difference only betwixt 159,670 *l.* in 1824, and 179,053 *l.* in 1828, an increase not worth consideration in comparison with the immense sacrifices the Government and the trade had been called to make, and which I calculate to be four millions of revenue, and as much of private property or more.

11522. When did the export trade begin to increase?—In July 1829 the debenture was first granted; it had not time to effect a material change in the export during that year; but in the year 1830 it increased beyond 1829 about cent. per cent., and in the year 1830 another 50 per cent.

11523. What per centage on the exports do you consider the debenture?—The debenture is nominally 3 *s.* 6 *d.* per pound on exported silk goods; but deducting what may be paid for the debenture, loss of debentures running out of date, and so on, it is reduced to about 3 *s.* a pound, or 5 to 7 ½ per cent. on the value of goods.

11524. If 5 to 7 ½ per cent. can have had the effect of increasing the exports to such an extent, do you see any means of still further increasing the export?—From what I know of the export trade, a very little addition to the drawback would ere long be found to have a beneficial effect.

11525. Would a debenture of 5 *s.* per pound increase the trade?—It is the opinion of others besides myself, that if the drawback were 5 *s.* the exports would

678.                                                                                 rapidly

*J. Brocklehurst,* jun.
Esq.

———

16 July,
1832.

rapidly increase, and thus act in favour of the home trade, which would then in turn extensively participate in the advantages of export.

11526. Do you not believe the export of goods has been profitable to manufacturers when you put out of view bandannas?—I am inclined to think not.

11527. But it has been a relief to the manufacturer, from the superabundance of stock he finds it desirable to get rid of?—I am afraid that the export hitherto, instead of being a proper and natural export, has been an export of those goods which were sold at half price. Eventually we may have an export at times with a profit; the course most likely to be successful is, to send out small adventures to all promising markets, instead of large masses of goods at very low prices, and to support these adventures the manufacturers should have profits in the home market. By this time the country must be convinced of the folly of attempting to force a bankrupt trade to extend its exports.

11528. You are of opinion probably, that the export trade in England might be similar to that now exercised by France with regard to her goods, that when she has supplied the home market with a superior commodity, the refuse, which she could not get rid of without injuring the home market, would be exported?—That is precisely my view, and I think that the export trade would extend, and that it might eventually become a profitable trade; for I well recollect that the export trade in these goods, bandanna handkerchiefs, commenced at a loss on almost every thing we sent out; it was preferable to export all goods we sold at a loss, especially all goods that were imperfect; for if we had sold them in the home market at a loss, the buyers would afterwards turn round upon us, and expect to have all other goods at the same price. The French invariably stipulate that the goods they sell at a loss shall be exported, so as not to come into subsequent injurious competition with their newer productions.

11529. Where do you export them to?—One house made 15,000*l.* worth of the 26,000*l.* exported to France; two other houses, who export perhaps 10,000*l.* worth more of the same article, making 25,000*l.* out of the 26,000*l.* that are stated to have gone to France; the remaining portion of the 500,000*l.* go to all parts of the world; and all the reciprocity we obtain from France is as 26 is to 500.

11530. Would not the throwster be exposed to greater competition by the Italian throwster when the debentures should be at a higher price?—It appears to me that the high price of the debenture obtained by the consumer of foreign thrown would not be of any advantage to the Italian throwster; my opinion is, that the high price of the debenture would only benefit the first party; for the high price of the debenture would imply a brisk export, of course a demand for goods, and this must naturally be accompanied by a brisk demand for throwing, and thus benefit the throwster.

11531. Did you ever know the debenture to sell at a price to be of service to the consumer of foreign throwns?—In 1830, before the Italians deluged this market under the 3*s.* 6*d* duty, debentures sold for 6*d.* to 9*d.* a pound, and if the 5*s.* duty had not been disturbed in 1829, so as to encourage the Italian throwster to send such a glut in 1830, my belief is, that debentures would now be selling at a price worth the consideration of the consumer of foreign throwns, and our export trade would have been advanced most conspicuously; and if once this debenture could acquire a buoyancy of value, they would be found to help all parties in turn; viz. the consumer of foreign thrown, the exporter and the British throwster.

11532. Do you not consider the debenture a tax on Spitalfields?—I do not; it belongs first of all to the Government of our country, to protect the throwster by a duty, and that duty goes to the Revenue; but if the Government see fit to return it to the exporter, they do a service to Spitalfields and Coventry, by enabling him to carry out of the country a certain portion of goods which would otherwise only add to an overloaded market; any imperfectly made goods would be the first to be exported, being the cheapest; there is no manufacturer gives out the same class of silk to the weavers, but he will have different qualities of goods brought in, and it is the inferior qualities that would be first exported. On referring to the official returns as to the channels through which the drawback flows, it will be seen that the last year, 23,360*l.* was paid on goods quitting the Port of London, and 23,292*l.* paid on goods passing the Out-ports, such as Liverpool, &c. whence a good portion of the Manchester and country goods are shipped, by which it appears that the benefits are pretty equally divided.

11533. So that in effect many of the goods manufactured for the home trade, are shipped for the export trade?—Undoubtedly.

11534. What

11534. What goods do you understand to be generally exported?—Bandannas and other handkerchiefs, the low gros de Naples of Spitalfields, and Manchester job goods, and mixed goods; and an eminent manufacturer at Coventry informs me, that the debenture last winter had carried off a great many of the jobbed ribbons of Coventry; I am sure that if the Government really wish to do all they can for the silk trade, they have it in their power, by advancing the duties, so as to benefit all parties; and by increasing the debenture, increase the export trade.

11535. Do you suppose the British silk trade have obtained any established markets abroad?—I believe not, but a great many assay parcels are sent out to every market where we think there exists a chance of success; and by means of the debenture, if increased, I entertain hopes of obtaining a footing for English silks abroad; though at present we have very strong prejudices in favour of France and India to contend against. There is a circumstance to which I will call the attention of the Committee, that is the comparison of the India bandannas and the British bandannas; there has been an increased export of the India goods, and British goods at the same period have remained at the amount; of 1829, I see 13,979 pieces of India goods were sold, and 10,828 British; in 1830, 17,922 of India goods and 21,000 British; in 1831, 40,000 of India goods and 20,000 of British sale; these are the exports of one house, showing that we are not making that progress in export of our own goods which we might do, while others are increasing.

11536. Do these appear in the official returns of goods exported from this country?—No; these were the private transactions of one house as exporters.

11357. How do those goods, which are only printed in this market, and which are of foreign manufacture, appear in the returns of exports?—They are printed in bond; they are not entered as articles of export; they are exported from a bonding warehouse.

11538. Would there be any considerable export of bandannas, without the drawback of 3 s. 6 d. now allowed?—I think that the export of all silk goods would again dwindle to what it was before 1829; Mr. Hume, in his evidence, has given a very decided opinion on this point, that without debenture there would be no export.

11539. In the weaving of bandannas and other silk goods, you say that a part of the wages is paid by the poor's rate?—It is becoming too much the case for wages of silk manufacturing to be made out by the poor's rate.

11540. Then a bounty is given by the parish?—I think the parish is now paying one-third of the wages of labour.

11541. So that in fact what may appear as profitable export trade, may be made up of wages and the revenues of the parish?—That is my decided opinion.

11542. Should you see any difference between a bounty given by the parish, and a bounty paid by the Treasury, except that the one is local and the other national?—I see no difference at all.

J. Brocklehurst,jun.<br>Esq.<br><br>16 July,<br>1832.

---

Mercurii, 18° die Julii, 1832.

<h2 style="text-align:center">LORD DUDLEY COUTTS STUART, IN THE CHAIR.</h2>

---

John Brocklehurst, Jun. Esq., called in; and further Examined.

11543. HAVE you any further information to give to the Committee, or any Table that you wish to put in?—I have a Table here of the earnings of weavers in our employ, their comparative earnings in 1824 and 1831, showing also the quantities of silk consumed at each period. In 1824, I find from our books, that 500 weavers, in one week, worked 620 lbs. of silk, and their wages amounted to 370 l.; the average earnings being 15 s. a week, from which have to be deducted the usual expenses for a quill winder, loom standing, and other incidental expenses of 2 s. 6 d., their earnings would then be 12 s. 6 d.; the quantity of silk used in each loom averaged 1 lb. 4 ozs.; the cost of weaving that silk would be 9 d. per ounce. In 1831, taking the average work of that year, I find that 500 weavers worked up 875 lbs. of silk per week, and that their wages was 171 l.; the average earnings of these weavers would be 7 s. a week, from which are to be deducted the same expenses of quill winding, loom standing, and other incidental expenses, leaving the net earnings of 500 weavers to be 4 s. 6 d. per head; at this period they worked up

J. Brocklehurst,jun.<br>Esq.<br><br>18 July,<br>1832.

*J. Brocklehurst,* jun.
Esq.

———

18 July,
1832.

1 lb. 12 ozs. each loom; the cost of weaving would be 3 *d.* per ounce; in 1824 it was 9 *d.* per ounce. By this, it appears, that they now consume 40 per cent. more silk than in 1824, and that their present wages are about one-third of what they then were. As to the other manufacturers, who have lately turned their attention to the making of plain goods, I am satisfied their books would, in such instances, show the weavers to be working up an immense proportion of material, at a very low rate of wages, to what they did before the change of system, in some instances eight times the quantity for the same money.

11544. Having spoken of the beneficial effects of the East India Company's periodical sales, I would ask whether the Company can render their silk more serviceable to the general purposes of the silk manufacture?—During the last 24 years, I have observed all the various kinds of silk that have been imported from India, and though some of it often appears superior in quality, in the raw state, yet in no instance have I ever seen a skein of India silk, when worked and dyed, fit to compare with the staple and quality of French or Italian silk, or similarly applicable to the finer branches of manufacture. But there might be an important improvement in arranging and describing the sizes of reeling and assorting India silk, which would be of great convenience to the buyers, and the consequent difference of price would remunerate the Company for the application of the requisite skill and trouble. For several years the India Company described the various sizes of their raw silk by three letters, A., B. and C., A. being intended to describe the finest; but latterly they have extended their description to A. 1, 2 & 3, B. 1, 2 & 3, and C. 1, 2 & 3, A. 1, being the finest. Now the system in this country, in the various branches of spinning wool, cotton or linen, is to describe the size of the yarn by a number, say No. 30, which indicates that a certain number of yards weighs a pound. But as regards India silk, it is well known, that the raw silks coming from the different filatures, vary so much altogether, that one district may send A. 1 silk as coarse in size as the silk of the C. size of another part of India; and as seasons and methods of reeling vary in India, the A. size one year is often as coarse as the B. of the preceding year; this is a great disadvantage to the purchasers, who from the way the samples are exposed for sale, have no means of judging of the actual size but by the eye. To remedy this the Company have merely to follow the Italian and French method, which describes 400 ells of silk thread to weigh so many deniers, this would be preferable to adopting the practice of a descriptive number used in the other articles referred to, particularly as France and Italy have already a similar system, and it would be preferable therefore for the East India Company to adopt the same instead of attempting to convert those countries to any new one of their own projecting.

11545. What is your opinion of the change of measures in 1824 and 1826?— I consider it a most ill-judged change, grounded on the Report of the Committee of the House of Lords, made in 1821, which sat with the view to extend the foreign trade of the country; they made some inquiries into the silk trade, and unfortunately the Committee of that day made a Report on very imperfect information.

11546. In what way do you so consider it?—The Report was unfortunately acted upon, and the result has proved a total failure, and the subsequent change in 1829 has only aggravated the evil. The trade regret to find that the Board of Trade are still too much inclined to be influenced by the advice of persons not well acquainted with manufacturing and its details, and with all its difficulties, theoretic and speculative persons who have not displayed skill in the management of their own affairs, persons who have no stake in the trade or in the country, but are very ready to offer bold suggestions to the Government, and who to this day receive more attention than the representations of manufacturers who have still property to protect, and a mass of people around them whom they wish to see rescued from distress.

11547. What do you consider to be the worst features of the several alterations? —No equivalent hitherto for the sacrifice of a large revenue readily collected upon an article of luxury; in 1824, a remission of the duties on raw and thrown silk, annually amounting to upwards of 700,000 *l.*, a return of duty to the trade on stock amounting to 470,000 *l.*; in 1826, a remission of annual duty on printed silk handkerchiefs of from 50 *l.* to 100,000 *l.*, also the duties on soap, dye, stuffs, &c.; and last not least, the galling fact, that the silk trade, if left untouched, would now in all probability be producing 1,000,000 *l.* to 1,500,000 *l.* of revenue a year, instead of which, the change has merely been productive of the ruin of hundreds of respectable men engaged in this trade, involving thousands of honest industrious artisans in the same wreck.

11548. Has

J. Brocklehurst, jun.
Esq.

18 July,
1832.

11548. Has the depression complained of in the silk trade been more severely felt in the other branches of manufacturing industry?—Though the return to cash payments may have had an effect in throwing out of employ a great mass of the labouring and manufacturing classes of the country, yet during the same period, there have evidently been a growing taste for, and greatly increased consumption of silk goods here and throughout the civilized world. I am therefore confident that there would have been no permanent depression in the silk trade during the last six years, and I have every reason to believe, that if the silk trade had been properly protected, ere now we should have had a large export trade out of profits from our home trade, (as I have already explained in a former part of my evidence,) instead of which, the present position of the silk trade is reduced to a pitiful contest between the starving artisan and the wealthy nefarious trader, that is, the people with large capital who encourage smuggling, a state of things bitterly aggravated by the doubt as to which party the Government look most favourably.

11549. Do the evils complained of extend to every branch of the silk trade?—They do.

11550. Explain how every branch of the silk trade is affected by the evils complained of?—The distress I complain of, as felt by the silk trade, extends to every branch of it. The merchants have lost hundreds of thousands since the experiment was tried, the manufacturers are more than one-half of them swept away, the throwing mills of the country are more than half closed, half the artisans are out of employ, and no person connected with the silk trade has benefited by this change except some of the wholesale dealers, who contrive to keep down the few manufacturers left in the trade, by applying the great lever of foreign competition to overturn one after another, as they attempt to obtain remunerative prices.

11551. Do you see any remedy for the evils complained of by the silk trade?—I know of no remedy so effectual as extended protection, but certainly I have heard a sweeping remedy suggested from rather high authority; the same remedy was promised in 1826, as forming a part of the new system, and in my judgment it ought to have preceded the change, for if the means of subsistence had been first reduced to the work people, they would have been placed in a position to enter into competition on more equal ground with their foreign rivals, who it is acknowledged live at half the expense this country will admit of, and they would have been without the great cause of complaining, the injustice of their being called upon to contend on disadvantageous and cruel terms as to the first necessaries of life.

11552. Would the reduction of the prices of subsistence have benefited the silk trade?—I fear that ere long these favourite low prices we have been descending to for the last few years, will be found to be a cause of much of the general prevailing distress. We have certain engagements which we are bound to fulfil at a fixed price, and to enable us to do so without pressure on any interest, all other prices should be maintained in a relative degree; and with respect to the fallacy of cheap bread being a remedy, I have observed every reduction hitherto has tended only to place the loaf and the artisan at a greater distance from each other; so long ago as in 1826, the land-owners were warned of their danger, but from some cause they could not see any analogy between corn and the silk manufacture, but I feel convinced that in 1826, if the trade had had a committee of inquiry granted, much of the distress, ruin and discontent that at present exists, might have been obviated.

11553. Do you then consider the land-owners to be interested in the result of the inquiry?—I am of opinion that the silk trade forms one of the great outworks of defence to the property of the land-owner; he cannot long expect to have cheap manufactured goods, and a high price for corn; indeed, in 1826 we were often assured by the Government that ere long the system of free trade would be extended to corn, and I should say the land-owners must begin to feel they are drawing near such a reduction of their protection as will ultimately sweep away all rent, in the same corresponding ratio that the reduction of the protection once possessed by the silk trade has destroyed all its profits and wages.

11554. Then you do not advocate low priced provisions, as the remedy for the distress of the silk trade?—If the landed interests take no direct steps towards protecting the industry of the country against unjust foreign competition (for I cannot lose sight of the protection corn growers enjoy of from 50 to 60 per cent., whilst industry has but from 20 to 30 per cent.), I see no choice left but to join the desperate, and it will ere long be found irresistible, cry of "No Corn Laws;" but I would much rather see the land-owners come forward promptly and unanimously, to crush the

further

*J. Brocklehurst*, jun.
Esq.

———

18 July,
1832.

further ruinous schemes of political economists, and to raise up industry to their own necessary level of protection.

11555. Do you consider the dealers in silk goods capable of giving the best advice to the Government for the general welfare of the silk trade?—Some of them, who for some years have had the ear of Government, seem unable to understand how a trade can be ruinous to the manufacturer and the workpeople so long as they (the dealers) are buying and selling; but it would appear to any one accustomed to live among the work people, that the best criterion of the welfare of a trade is the condition of the people employed, whether they are paying their way, or whether parishes and capitals are not furnishing the means of this cheap buying and selling. From this general censure, I am happy to say, there are some honourable exceptions, who, setting aside their own immediate interests, evince great candour in the investigation of a question involving the future condition and prosperity of a large branch of manufacture.

11556. How do you justify the opinion you have given, that the silk trade in this country is in its comparative infancy?—I am of opinion that the silk trade of England, under judicious and better protection than it has obtained for the last six years, may yet become a most valuable and extensive source of profitable employment; but it is to be regretted, that the silk manufacture of England has been stationary in quantity, and has retrograded 50 per cent. in the finer branches during the last six years, whilst the silk manufacture on the Continent has in the same period been shown to have advanced 50 per cent. in quantity and proportionately in excellence. From all the information I have collected, there seems to exist no limit to the extent of the growth of the raw material; and as it declines in price, I cannot but imagine that the general consumption of silk will continue to increase. It is well known, that but a few years ago the cotton trade was looked down upon by the more staple linen and woollen trades, but to what an important state has the cotton trade arrived since the Arkwrights and the Peels applied their great mechanical powers of mind towards its improvement and promotion, under ample protection? I know it has been said, that it were well this country had never possessed a silk trade; but I would ask, should the prediction I have ventured as to its future extensive progress be verified, and should other countries only, who may have wisely cherished this trade in its infancy, be at this future period enjoying the benefits resulting from such a prosperous manufacture, what would be the bitter regrets of a narrow-minded policy that would either drive or have excluded entirely from our shores this now so persecuted silk trade. Now, with respect to the present production of the raw material in Europe, there is Italy producing seven and France three to four millions of pounds. I cannot but regret to find so insignificant a portion as one-sixth part fall to the share of England, possessing, as I have shown she does, mills, machinery, and an immense unoccupied population skilled in the throwing and weaving of silk, and a consumption of silk goods greater in this than in any other country; and I may once more be allowed to repeat, that the most likely way to obtain our proportionate share of this rising manufacture will be to give the trade such a degree of protection as shall enable it to feel confidence in its own market: grant it but this, and it will soon be seen that as its means increase, so will its enterprise. But this line of reasoning might extend too far, and occupy too much of the time, for the Committee to complete the evidence before them; and seeing the necessity that the labours of this Committee should be brought to a close, I am unwilling to prolong my examination, and in preference I beg to recommend, that the artisans from the country may be allowed to detail their own circumstances; and I have now only, with all respect, to state, that there is a growing anxiety on the part of the trade to have an early Report made by this Committee; it will allay much alarm, and tend to inspire considerable confidence.

### Mr. *Thomas Johnson*, called in; and Examined.

Mr.
*Thomas Johnson*.

———

11557. WHAT part of the trade are you engaged in?—The silk throwing trade.

11558. What number of mills are in your neighbourhood?—Forty-five mills; 58 concerns; the same establishment sometimes are occupied by two persons.

11559. What is the horse power?—About 316.

11560. Do you know generally the value of the mills?—I believe the value is about 140,000 *l.*

11561. How many has been erected since 1824?—Fourteen; six of them have
been

Mr.
*Thomas Johnson.*

18 July,
1832.

been converted to other purposes; the greater part of them were erected soon after that year.

11562. How many are now employed?—Twenty-one.

11563. What number of spindles were at work in 1823, and what number are now at work?—In 1823 there were 146,352 spindles at work; in 1832, 97,860 spindles.

11564. What wages did you pay in 1823, and what in 1832?—The wages for a man in 1823 was 15 s.; for a young man from 15 to 20, about 8 s.; for a young woman from 15 to 20, 7 s.; children from 10 to 15, about 5 s.; and children from 7 to 10, about 2 s. 9 d.. In 1832 the wages of men were about 10 s., young men 5 s. 6 d.; a young woman from 15 to 20, 5 s.; children about 3 s., and the younger children 1 s. 6 d.; that is for six days per week; but as they have been at a reduced time, the wages have been reduced in proportion.

11565. What was the number of hands employed in 1823, and what is the present number?—In 1823 there were 3,961, and in 1832 2,219.

11566. How many hands are out of employment?—From the best information I can obtain, about 1,700; probably not quite that number; they have been getting a little more into work since the East India Company's sale.

11567. How do these hands subsist?—Some on the poor's rate, others by begging, others by thieving, and many of the females by prostitution.

11568. What is the state of your town with respect to the poor rates?—I have an authenticated statement from the assistant overseer, it comprises the 10 years from 1821 to 1832. In 1828 there was 678 *l*. 2 *s*. 5 *d*. paid to the regular poor, and 70 *l*. 10 *s*. paid to the casual poor, making 748 *l*. 12 *s*. 5 *d*.; there are different sums paid every year, up to 1832; the amount paid to the regular poor and casual poor in 1831–1832, is 1,520 *l*. I beg to deliver this Table in.

[*The same was delivered in, and read.*]

STATE of the Poor in the Town of *Congleton*, from the Year 1821 to Lady-day 1832.

Population, according to the Census in 1821 - - - - 6,405
Population, according to the Census in 1831 - - - - 9,352

| YEARS | Average Number of Casual Poor receiving Relief Weekly. | Average Allowance per Head per Week. | Number of Poor in the Workhouse. | Annual Rate per Pound. | Annual Amount paid to the Regular Poor. | | | Annual Amount paid to the Casual Poor. | | | TOTAL. | | |
|---|---|---|---|---|---|---|---|---|---|---|---|---|---|
| | | d. | | s. d. | £. | s | d. | £. | s. | d. | £. | s. | d. |
| 1821 | 37 | 7 | 32 | 2 11 | 678 | 2 | 5 | 70 | 10 | – | 748 | 12 | 5 |
| 1822 | 26 | 9 | 35 | 2 4 | 591 | 1 | 2 | 49 | 8 | 1 | 640 | 9 | 3 |
| 1823 | 54 | 8¼ | 38 | 3 2½ | 492 | 2 | 8 | 100 | 3 | 4 | 592 | 6 | – |
| 1824 | 35 | 8½ | 35 | 2 4 | 499 | 4 | – | 64 | 7 | – | 563 | 11 | – |
| 1825 | 88 | 8¼ | 52 | 2 4 | 506 | 9 | 3 | 161 | 18 | 6 | 668 | 7 | 9 |
| 1826 | 420 | 8¼ | 56 | 5 11½ | 558 | 8 | 3 | 765 | 8 | 2 | 1,323 | 16 | 5 |
| 1827 | 165 | 8¾ | 40 | 3 - | 573 | 5 | 9 | 364 | 2 | 3 | 937 | 8 | – |
| 1828 | 253 | 6¼ | 49 | 3 3½ | 533 | – | 6 | 336 | 1 | 3 | 869 | 1 | 9 |
| 1829 | 540 | 7¼ | 50 | 5 10 | 719 | – | 4 | 834 | 2 | 8 | 1,553 | 3 | – |
| 1830 | 292 | 7¼ | 60 | 5 10 | 734 | 19 | 8 | 458 | 7 | 3 | 1,193 | 6 | 11 |
| 1831 to 1832 | 561 | 6 | 52 | { 5 10 / 5 10 } | 699 | 9 | 6 | 521 | 6 | 8 | 1,520 | 16 | 2 |

I hereby certify, That the Statement, as above, showing the condition of our working people since 1821, is a true and accurate account.

*Oliver Buckley,*
Ass^t Overseer.

14 July 1832.

11569. Are any of the hands employed in the mills supported by the parish?—This statement will show that they are.

11570. How long has this been the case?—Since 1826, with few exceptions.

11571. What do you consider the reason of it?—A reduction of wages and scarcity of employment, forced upon the masters by a reduction of the duty on foreign silks.

11572. Have you made any improvement in machinery since 1824?—Yes; a gradual improvement has extended through the machinery; we are continually

678. endeavouring

Mr.
*Thomas Johnson.*

18 July,
1832.

endeavouring to make our machinery better, and the old machinery is being replaced with new.

11573. To what part of the machinery does the increase of speed apply?—To all, more or less.

11574. What benefit is derived from the increase of speed?—Very little; a little factory room may be all the benefit which we have derived from the increase of speed.

11575. Is there an increase in the application of machinery now used, for the labour of persons that were formerly employed in the mills?—Wherever we increase the speed, we require a greater number of hands.

11576. What has been the effect of the reduction of the import duty on foreign thrown silks in 1829, from 5s. to 3s. 6d.?—An increase of the importation of Italian thrown silk; secondly, a less quantity of Italian raws; thirdly, they will take care, in my opinion, indeed the fact proves it, to keep the best silks for their own mills, and send us the worst; fourthly, Italy is able to supply the whole of this market with thrown silk; fifthly, many more of the throwing mills in this country will be out of work, and their operations transferred to Italy, and by degrees the whole trade of throwing in Italian silks will be lost to this country.

11577. What would be the effect of a still further reduction of the import duty?—Destruction of the British throwster; we are all but annihilated as it is; our property is made useless. I have a capital of 15,000*l*. sunk in a silk mill and machinery; the mill is of no more value to me than this piece of paper; it gives me no return; I have not only sacrificed my own labour, but I have sacrificed funds, and property which I derive and draw from other sources; it all seems to sink, and I am keeping this mill in action in hopes of better and improved times.

11578. When did you erect this mill?—In 1810.

11579. Is your mill as favourably situated as any other?—It is beautifully situated as a mill, and has water power; nothing can excel the situation.

11580. Is the labour as cheap with you as in other parts of the kingdom?—Most decidedly.

11581. Is it as cheap as it is at Manchester?—Cheaper, I should think.

11582. Have the Italian States now the power of supplying this market more abundantly with thrown silk?—I believe they have.

11583. When did you feel the effect of lowering the duties of foreign thrown silk?—In 1826, the first effects were that we fell back in wages and profits.

11584. By 1829, had you by reduced wages, &c. in some degree accommodated yourselves to the then times?—Yes; for in 1830 we were getting round, if I may use the term; the last reduction to 3s. 6d. had not had time to fetch the thrown silk from Italy; at the end of the year it arrived, and ever since that we have been in a state of ruin.

11585. Out of the fourteen mills which have been built since 1826, how many have been built since 1829?—Not any.

11586. Were they all built between 1826 and 1829?—They were all built from 1824 to 1826.

11587. Were the whole of the fourteen which you have stated to have been built subsequent to 1824, built prior to the year 1829?—I think they were all built previous to 1826.

11588. Out of these fourteen, six are converted to other purposes?—Yes.

11589. Do you throw so much Italian silk in Congleton as formerly?—No; good Italian silks are not in the abundance they were formerly, nor does it pay us to work them.

11590. Are the mills and machinery at Congleton principally employed in the coarser silks?—Yes, they are.

11591. Can you state what may be the condition of the throwster relative to his affairs, or in what way have the alterations affected you personally?—The condition of the throwster, as far as I am able to see by looking around me, is one of great privation and distress; the little he had seems to have been lost; instead of being a respectable individual, he is sinking fast into a state of degradation, and a very little longer will annihilate him as a practical man; as far as regards myself, I am losing my capital daily.

11592. Does this state of things affect the land in the neighbourhood?—Yes; for if we have not wages to pay the poor, the poor must fall on the parish rates.

11593. Having stated that your own mills return you no profit, do you consider the other mills are in a better condition than your own?—Certainly not; for I have

an

Mr.
*Thomas Johnson.*

18 July,
1832.

an antimate and friendly acquaintance with my neighbours, and they would one and all be glad to relinquish them at a most terrible sacrifice; as I am deputed by them, I have their permissson to make this general statement relative to that fact.

11594. I think it is quite plain from your evidence, that you view an increase of duty on the importation of foreign thrown silk as an object of the throwster of this country, is it not so?—Yes, a great objeet.

11595. State to the Committee what you would consider the amount of duty that would be, in your estimation, a protection to the throwster of England?—I should like to return to the old duty.

11596. Which was?—Fourteen shillings, and 9s. on the raws.

11597. Would nothing less satisfy you?—Yes, most decidedly.

11598. State what you consider, in your opinion and that of others, would satisfy the throwsters in and around Congleton?—I believe they would be satisfied with the duties previous to the last alteration.

11599. Will you name them?—Five shillings on organzine and 3s. on tram.

11600. You consider that 3s. 6d. does not protect the throwster?—We have been sinking fast into ruin since the alteration was made.

11601. Do you look much to the advantage derived from the export trade?—I confine myself to my own situation; I know what I was doing previous to the alteration, and I know where I have been going fast since; I do not wish to enter into the other part of the question; I know how the alteration has affected me, and I speak to that only.

11602. You stated that out of the fourteen mills built since 1824, that six had been converted to other purposes; have any of the mills built prior to 1824 been converted to other purposes, or are any of them now standing still?—My answer is more applicable to the fourteen particular mills which have been built since 1824; but in answer to your question, I should say there are some standing still.

11603. So that though there may be an increase in the number of mills, some of them are quite out of work?—Quite out of work.

11604. Has the quantity of employment much increased in Congleton since 1824?—Quite the reverse.

11605. How many mills are there now at work?—Only twenty-one.

11606. All at work?—Twenty-one all at work.

11607. Forty-five is the gross number?—Forty-five is the gross number, but there are fifty-eight concerns; some establishments have two proprietors in one mill.

11608. Sometimes two establishments belong to the same mill with a separate name?—Yes.

11609. Out of forty-five, fourteen of which have been built since 1824, and twenty-one are now at work, so that there are ten less at work now than there were prior to the year 1824?—Exactly so; but even the twenty-one that are at work till within these few weeks, have been working short time only partially; although my own mill may be considered a mill at work, it is half standing; the hands were only working three or four days a week until lately.

11610. The quantity of employment to the operatives has very greatly decreased?—Decidedly.

11611. The operatives are in a very distressed and demoralized condition?—They are sinking fast in a state of degradation; their wants press on them in various ways, their bellies go half full, their backs half clothed, and the people feel no inclination to send their children to school; and a state of degradation and immorality is fast overtaking them.

11612. There is nothing like comfort about their dwellings?—If they have comfort about their dwellings, pride naturally causes them to seek other comforts; if they have food, they seek for clothing; when they can get clothing, and can appear decently among their neighbours, they seek for education. There are many instances around me, when I have corrected the parents for not sending their children to school, their answer has been that they were ashamed to send them, for they had not decent clothing to send them in.

11613. When you built your mill in 1810, what description of silk did you usually employ?—We had a great variety of silk at that time; we threw a good deal of Italian silk, we seldom touch it now.

11614. Was the large proportion of silk that you threw Italian?—At that period it was.

11615. What is the description of silk that you now throw?—Coarser silks; Bengal silks or coarse Chinas.

11616. For

Mr.
*Thomas Johnson,*

18 July,
1832.

11616. For what market did you usually throw silk when you commenced?—For the London market.

11617. For what market do you now throw?—Chiefly for Manchester.

11618. Which is the most preferable to the throwster, the throwing fine or coarser silks?—It is all a matter of chance; if we get a fair price for round silks, we probably prefer them; but if we get fine silks, and get fairly paid, it does not much matter.

11619. In which is the greater waste?—The finer silks make the largest quantity of waste, and give a larger quantity of work; I could as soon work three pounds of coarse silk as I would one pound of fine.

11620. Is there more work required in throwing the coarser silks or the finer silks?—The coarser silks do not require the same work as the finer.

11621. The finer silks require more work than the coarser?—Decidedly.

11622. You say there are only 45 mills, and that 14 have been erected since 1824?—Yes; they were erected from 1824 to 1826.

11623. And also say that there are now 21 at work?—Yes.

11624. If the 14 were deducted from the 21, it leaves only 7?—If the 14 are deducted from the 45, it leaves 31.

11625. There are 10 less at work now than there were in 1821?—No; we have 21 now at work.

11626. Do you mean to say, that the new mills that have been built since 1824, are employed, and that all those that have gone out of employ are the old mills?—No; I say that we have only 21 mills at work.

11627. How many mills are not employed at this moment?—I cannot say.

11628. There are 18 standing still, and six converted to other purposes, making 24, and there are 21 at present at work?—That is my opinion.

11629. Of those 18, are they or are they not the old established mills that existed between 1810 and 1824?—There are some of both.

11630. You said that six of these mills had been converted to other purposes, have they been so converted at great loss to the proprietors?—Two-thirds of their value I should think.

11631. Is not one great difference between the Italian silks and the coarser silks from China and Bengal, that the finer silks affords much more employment to the throwster?—Most decidedly.

11632. Is it not therefore very decidedly, in order to promote the employment for the throwing mills of this country, desirous that the importation of Italian thrown silks should be discontinued?—Decidedly; one pound of Italian raw silk will give as much employment as three pounds of another sort.

11633. Do you consider it of importance to get raw silk from France imported here?—Yes.

11634. At the present rate of duty that it is imported into Italy?—Certainly.

---

*Jovis, 19° die Julii,* 1832.

## THE RIGHT HON. THE EARL GROSVENOR, IN THE CHAIR.

### Mr. *John Prout*, called in; and Examined.

Mr.
*John Prout.*

19 July,
1832.

11635. ARE you a silk weaver?—Yes.

11636. Where do you reside?—At Macclesfield.

11637. How long have you been employed in the silk trade?—Including the period of my apprenticeship, 34 years.

11638. Are you prepared to give evidence before this Committee as to the state of your trade before the alterations in the law, and since the introduction of foreign raw silk?—I am prepared with facts connected with our case, and proved by my own experimental knowledge, to show the injury our trade has sustained, and I trace it to that part of the laws which introduced foreign wrought silks at reduced duties.

11639. What was the staple trade of Macclesfield when you first began to work?—The manufactures consisted of bandannas and black figured handkerchiefs till about the year 1809, when the figured and fancy trade was introduced.

11640. Can you state to the Committee a brief view of the improvement in the silk

Mr.
*John Prout.*

19 July,
1832.

silk manufactures of Macclesfield?—From the year 1809, till the years 1824 and 1825, there was a great deal of improvement in the beauty and texture of the silk manufactures took place, during that period industry was rewarded and ingenuity encouraged. The fancy trade made very great improvements, a great number of looms were employed in weaving the light and valuable part of the trade and by the introduction of a process peculiar to the manufactures of Macclesfield; our light fabrics obtained a superiority by the operation of steam, chiefly confined to our manufactures, it enabled us to finish goods in a superior way, and we had great advantages in our department from it; they endeavoured to make the fabrics manufactured in Macclesfield rival any part of the world, although it was stated that competition would improve our genius, brighten our faculties, make us better workmen, and contradict the degrading refutation of slothfulness attached to the character of a silk weaver of Britain, nothing will more refute the imputation than the character given of our manufactures in the opinion expressed by certain American gentlemen, as detailed in the Report of Evidence delivered in 1821, in the House of Lords Committee; namely, that with respect to the quality of the silk manufacture, stated not only by persons interested in the trade, but by American gentlemen, that setting the question of price aside, it is in many respects fully equal to the French, equal in the article of piece goods, superior in gloves and hosiery, as well as poplin and other mixed manufactures.

11641. What improvement has taken place in the trade since 1824 and 1825?—I am not aware of any; the object has been to produce a cheap article for the reason that the maximum price of English silk goods must be the price which enabled them to sell in the market in competition with the French manufacturer, and any attempt to raise the price above that, would injure the workmen and manufacturers.

11642. In what part of the trade were you chiefly employed?—In the figured and fancy trade which since suffered so severely; before the alterations of the laws came into operation, I was employed in weaving a description of fancy goods, for which I received for every 16 ounces of silk, 1 *l.* 16 *s.* 3 *d.*; at the present period I am employed in weaving another description of silk goods; for every 20 ounces of silk I consume, I receive only 6 *s.*; thus in the former case, for every 100 lbs. of silk I consumed in weaving, I received 176 *l.* 10 *s.*, and in the latter instance, only 20 *l.*, or in other words, the price of weaving in the former case was 2 *s.* 3 *d.* per ounce, and in the latter instance only 3 *d.* I have to make an observation; I wish to state that although this may be considered an extreme case, it must be considered generally applicable to the whole number of looms I then had under my employ, having no such a thing as a plain article in my possession for a great number of years previous to the alteration.

11643. Is your case a particular instance, or does it apply to any extent as far as regards the situation of the Macclesfield weavers?—It is not a particular instance; although it has been urged that competition excites to improvement, it has been demonstrated, that such a competition as we have been subject to is destructive of it. As a proof of that, a great number of looms were employed in weaving a light and valuable article, which consumed from 16 to 20 ounces weekly, for which the workmen received from 20 *s.* to 30 *s.* per week; that branch of our trade is nearly annihilated, and instead of this description of goods, we are now employed in weaving bandannas and other petty articles, which consume from 40 to 50 ounces weekly, for which workmen receive as wages, from 7 *s.* to 9 *s.* weekly, subject to incidental expenses connected with their employment. I will, with permission, make an observation here that I think bears strongly to elucidate our distress, without taking the extreme case of the raw material, that the present amount is upwards of three millions. I believe that in the year 1832, the amount was not much greater than in 1824–5, and take that for granted, and then consider that although our articles have been of that description as not only to reduce the value of manufactured articles, but lower the value of wages of labour in a proportion of six to one, you see that the raw material has not corresponded in importation in proportion to the decay of that valuable part of our trade, it accounts for the existing privation among us; only consider with reference to this particular case, a case founded on truth; a case that bears the strongest scrutiny, that I have most lamentably to complain of, if I weave that quantity of silk with as much labour for 3 *d.* as formerly I did for 2 *s.* 3 *d.*

11644. What country has taken from you your figured and fancy trade?—The decline of our fancy trade is coincident with the introduction of fancy articles from

France, and as there never was any exportation of fancy articles to any great extent, the just inference to be deduced is, that our fancy articles have been superseded by the French, and I conceive it will appear clear when it is considered there is a decay of our native manufactures, and at the same time a consumption of fancy articles.

11645. Can you produce any proof that a change of fashion had not caused a decay of the light fabrics of your trade?—The plain facts of the case are these, that although there must, from any change in the demand, be a variation in the article manufactured, yet the most valuable part of our trade declining with the introduction of foreign manufactured articles, it at one view I think shows, that it was not a change of fashion but foreign competition which caused that decay, when it is proved that there is equally a demand, and that these fancy articles are greatly worn when not made by us.

11646. Was there not a great excitement and rise of wages in the years 1824 and 1825?—There was not a great excitement, considering the circumstances of the case: the trade was relieved of a very heavy duty upon the raw material; that, as a natural result, produced a cheaper article, while at the same time a prohibitory enactment continued, and we enjoyed the home market; yet it cannot be denied there might have been some excitement in the minds of some manufacturers, though, from the repeated declarations made by the Chancellor of the Exchequer, they had their expectations raised that nothing could shake until the evil came upon them, and although the manufacturers have been repeatedly blamed for not withdrawing their capital and preparing themselves for the altered circumstances into which the trade was to be plunged, yet the injustice of such an imputation will be found, when the declaration then made by Mr. Robinson is considered, who expresses the firmest confidence in the prosperity and stability of the trade. The substance of the speech was, that we had fertilized the world with our commerce; that we should henceforth enjoy a period of uninterrupted prosperity. I should have been happy if such had been the case. There was no great rise of wages at that period, though it has been often stated there was a rise of wages: it was stated that a great influx of hands took place into the town; that was not the fact. I shall prove, in its proper place, that during a period of 25 years the staple article of the trade was at a lower price in 1825 than it was in 1810.

11647. Can you state to the Committee an account of the price of labour in the silk weaving trade?—I have prepared a Table, exhibiting a comparative view of the prices of labour in the years 1810, 1819, 1825 and 1832. I have selected, not the whole of the works, but that part of the trade that was the staple industry of the town; and I have chosen those periods when the most excitement was stated to prevail, as well as those periods when the greatest depression prevailed. In the bandannas there was comparatively a stationary amount of wages; that was the staple trade of the town, and all others must be derived from it; that was, in 1810, 4*s.*, and in 1825, 3*s.* 6*d.*; while, in the short space of seven years, from 1825 to 1832, it decreased to 2*s.* 3*d.* for seven yards. The plain sarsnet articles remained at a comparatively stationary price from 1810 to 1825, and from 1825 to 1832 they reduced from 9*d.* to 4*d.* The gros de Naples were reduced, in the same period, from 13*d.* to 6*d.*; the small figured handkerchiefs were reduced from 8*d.* to 4*d.*; and the rich mountures from 24*s.* to 9*s.* during the same period.

[*The Witness delivered in the following Statement:*]

|  | 1810: | 1819: | 1825: | 1832: |
|---|---|---|---|---|
| Bandannas   -   - | 4*s.* 1*d* per cut. | 3*s.* 6*d.* & 4*s.* per cut. | 3*s.* 6*d.* per cut. | 2*s.* 3*d.* per cut. |
| Plain Sarsnets -  - | 10*d.* per yard. | 9*d.* per yard. | 9*d.* per yard. | 4*d.* per yard. |
| Gros de Naples -  - | -   -   - | -   -   - | 1*s.* 1*d.* per yd. | 6*d.* per yard. |
| Black Bars   -   - | 11*s.* 6*d.* per doz. | 10*s.* 6*d.* per doz. | 9*s.* per doz. | 6*s.* 3*d.* per doz. |
| 8 Shaft Figures -  - | -   -   - | 8*s.* per doz. | 8*s.* per doz. | 4*s.* per doz. |
| 100 ditto -   -   - | -   -   - | 14*s.* per doz. | 13*s.* 6*d.* per doz. | 7*s.* per doz. |
| Mountures, &c. -  - | -   -   - | 30*s.* per doz. | 24*s.* per doz. | 9*s.* per doz. |

You

Mr.
*John Prout.*

———

19 July,
1832.

You will perceive that during a period of 25 years the wages of labour in the silk trade remain comparatively stationary: taking the years when excitement was stated to prevail, and taking the highest price at the last named period, it will show that the price, when contrasted with the year 1810, is rather lower in some instances; yet, during a short period since, our labour has fallen in some instances from 50 to 60 per cent. According to the most correct statement that could be made in the year 1824, our average wages were near 19*s.* per week; in 1825 they were much about the same; but from that are to be deducted the incidental expenses. It appears that in 1825 the number of looms, from the most correct statement that could be made, was 5,325, and that the weekly amount paid in wages was 5,214*l.* From the last estimate we made, in endeavouring to ascertain the correct amount of the looms now employed, there appeared to be about 3,500, and the average wages appeared to be about 6*s.* a week, it might amount to 6*s.* 6*d.*; that is the extreme highest rate that we could fix on. I estimate the loss of labour of the trade of Macclesfield, contrasting it with the number of looms, to be about 189,000*l.* annually.

11648. How many persons are there employed in each loom?—A loom is estimated to give employment to four persons, but it does not do that accurately.

11649. Is the 6*s.* 6*d.* per week the nett wages of the weaver?—I consider it to be the nett wages of the workman deducting the incidental expenses; at the same time, I wish to state, it is the highest rate that could possibly be fixed on, not only that, but I have further to state that these are the wages when fully employed, not taking into account the casualties that take place.

11650. What do you call the incidental expenses?—Every weaver must have a quill winder; that is an expense.

11651. How much does he receive a week?—I cannot get a good winder under 1*s.* per week.

11652. Is the 6*s.* 6*d.* the nett wages of the weaver?—I consider it as such.

11653. Without any deduction?—Yes, without any deduction.

11654. In the 5,214*l.*, do you include the wages of the throwster?—No.

11655. Nothing but that which is paid to the weaver, and the persons attendant on the weaver and his loom?—Yes.

11656. Is it your opinion, that the silk weavers of Macclesfield have suffered through the alteration in the laws, and can you show any reasons to prove the same? —It is my opinion they have suffered extremely through the alteration in the laws; and I have only to state their past and present situation to show the truth of that remark. Previous to the alteration in the laws, there was a degree of comfort attached to the situation of a weaver of Macclesfield; their wages were never to any great amount, but yet it appeared to afford them the competency that might be considered sufficient to produce the comforts of life. Since the alteration in the laws their situation has gradually and progressively deteriorated, their condition is such that I should be inadequate to describe; their clothing, a great part of it is deposited in the pawn shops; their children are, in numberless instances, obliged to go barefoot, and they present a spectacle of misery in their countenances. If one sees a weaver that one has not seen before for some time, when you see him again his appearance indicates the extreme of human misery. A great number of them that formerly attended places of divine worship on a Sunday, are now prevented from doing so from the want of decent apparel to appear in, and a great number have applied to the parish for relief, and break stones on the highway, and are even loth to leave such a degrading occupation to return to the looms, although their allowance from the parish is only 1*s.* per day; this has been aggravated by other circumstances. Their employment has been continually so irregular, and although wages appear exceedingly low, yet the diminished employment has aggravated their situation; every succeeding year has produced a fresh convulsion in the trade, and each succeeding season has produced a great depression, and the means of charity are now decaying that formerly relieved their wants; for my own part I feel a difficulty in introducing any particular situation of my own before this honourable Committee, but I have suffered in common with my fellow workmen; I feel at the same time that poverty does not necessarily infer degradation, because we may be poor from causes over which we have no control. I can say that previous to the alteration in the laws, I was enabled to contribute to the parochial rates and assessments; I could support my family with the decency that becomes an honest and industrious man, but since that period my own condition has been considerably deteriorated. I have been exempted from the payment of poor rates and parochial assessments on

Mr.
*John Prout.*

19 July,
1832.

account of the poverty of my situation; and without entering at length into such a painful subject, I beg to assure this honourable Committee, that when I have seen my children surrounding the table, and heard their cries for food, embittered with the reflection that I had none to give them, I have frequently wished that a protracted life of misery might be closed by premature disease. I appeal to this honourable Committee, as guardians of our rights and liberties, whether industry does not deserve a better fate; having thus very inadequately stated the situation of my fellow workmen, in connexion with my own, I feel at the same time a duty incumbent on me, to show to the Committee the reasons of this distress emanating from the alteration in the laws. I hope and trust, as I speak the voice of my fellow labourers, and as my interest is identified with theirs, that this Committee, which has been appointed to inquire into the state of their distress, will allow me to go through my reasons: I know it has been stated, that the silk question is a particular question as regards this branch of manufacture; but I conceive it, as a general question, received in connexion with the commercial policy of the country, and having stated these premises, with the permission of the Committee, I will show the reasons why the alteration of the laws must have had that effect; there is the disadvantage we labour under with reference to the competition with France, there is the cheapness of the article; the comparative price of provisions; all these are subjects which have been disposed of; but I would submit to this honourable Committee, that all laws which are made on a partial principle must be unjust. One reason why the alteration in the laws has most severely caused us to suffer is this, that it is a perversion of principle that should identify justice as the basis of legislative enactment, for under the policy of free principles, we have imported wrought silks at nominal duties, of from 25 to 30 per cent., articles which we do not want from the foreigner and can produce ourselves, while articles which we do in reality want, and which could not be brought into competition with British labour, and which would constitute proper equivalents for our exports, are subject to duties ranging from 60 to 200 per cent. I will give another reason why the alteration in the laws has caused this distress, the alteration in the laws, by importing foreign wrought silk at the before mentioned duties, have not only diminished our employ, but it aggravates the situation of the labouring population by reducing the value of labour, without any equivalent in the reduction of the price of provisions, thus doubling the pressure of taxation; and the inevitable result is, entailing want and misery on the labouring population, of whom I form a part.

11657. Do you not imagine that the competition of the Lancashire cotton weavers has greatly caused a reduction in your wages?—The competition of the Lancashire cotton weavers existed before the alterations in the laws, and no such effect was produced; the weaving of seven yards of bandannas in the year 1792, was 3 s. 9½ d.; in 1825, from 3 s. 6 d. to 4 s. 1 d.; thus during a period of near 30 years, in the article which the cotton weavers might most easily weave, our wages remained comparatively stationary; while in another description of goods, the black fringe article, it increased from 7 s. to 10 s. 6 d.; and yet during a period of seven years since the alteration of the laws, bandannas have been reduced to 2 s. 3 d., and the black fringe to 6 s. 3 d.; thus clearly proving that our distress has arisen from other causes than the competition of the cotton weavers.

11658. Are you informed of the various depressions that have taken place in your trade?—In the year 1826, there was a general depression of the silk trade; not only did the measures then coming into operation appear most materially to affect the capitalist in the diminished employment of his labourers, but to meet the competition in the market, wages were seriously reduced. In the latter part of 1829, the trade was again fluctuated; wages then, as compared with 1824 and 1825, had fallen four per cent.; diminished employment followed; and notwithstanding the general misery of the labouring population, representations as fallacious as unjust were set forth, that as the raw material had increased in the importation, our misery would be only temporary; the fabrics manufactured had been changed from light to heavy goods; from 1829 to the present time, every succeeding season has produced a further reduction in labour, and diminished employment.

11659. What do you propose as a remedy for the evils that afflict the silk trade?—We claim the protection due in reference to our circumstances, and those of our foreign rivals; we claim an effective protection to that extent, and I believe that could not be obtained without returning to prohibitory enactments; and while the principle of the corn law recognizes the justice of protection to the corn grower, we require an application of that principle to the silk trade. It does appear that

the

Mr.
*John Prout.*

19 July,
1832.

the silk trade will always suffer in every general case which affects the commercial industry of the country; it appears equally clear that there is a specific evil to contend with, a competition in our own market, with a foreign rival possessing the greatest advantages over us. In order to place the silk trade on the same basis as the other branches of industry, we should enjoy the home market, and this can only be accomplished by the protection before named.

11660. Have you no other remedy to propose, short of prohibition?—I certainly should prefer an increase of the duties on plain goods to 30 per cent. and a seclusion of the figured branch of trade from the market; at the same time I am bound to state, that we have a right to that protection that will secure us.

11661. You stated the amount of wages at 6 s. or 6 s. 6 d.; has not the weaver to pay sundry expenses necessarily incident to his employment, such as keeping the loom in repair, purchasing tackle, procuring quill winders, &c. out of the amount which you have stated as his nett earnings?—No, I should conceive I had deducted the whole expenditure connected with that department; they took a census which ranged from 5 s. to 6 s. 6 d.; I do not wish to make an overstrained case of distress, so I name the highest sum.

11662. So that in point of fact the weaver does not receive so much as 6 s.?—In many cases.

11663. When he receives 6 s. 6 d. he has not that to spend, but he must deduct some of it for necessary expenses; is that so?—In some cases, I cannot apply it generally.

11664. Can you put in a Table showing the number of looms, and the earnings of the weavers, and the amount of the wages of these weavers by the week in 1824 and 1825; at Macclesfield also, the same account and number of looms and earnings to the present, concluding with the calculation of how much is the falling off from the value of weavers' wages?—

[*The Witness delivered in the same.*]

TABULAR VIEW, exhibiting the Amount paid for LABOUR in the WEAVING DEPARTMENT of the SILK TRADE of *Macclesfield,* in 1825 and 1832; likewise showing the Average Wages of the Weavers, Weekly Amount, and Annual Loss in the before named periods.

PER WEEK:

|  | Number of LOOMS. | Average Wages per Week. | Weekly Amount paid in Labour. |
|---|---|---|---|
|  |  | s.    d. | £.      s.    d. |
| In 1825 - - - - | 5,214 | 19    7 | 5,214    1    3 |
| In 1832 - - - - | 3,500 | 9    - | 1,575    -    - |

THE loss on the Amount paid for Labour in 1832, as compared with 1825, is upon the most moderate calculation, upwards of 189,000 *l.* annually; and as it may in all probability appear to this honourable Committee, that there is some discrepancy in the Statement of 9 s. per week, it must be observed, that this applies to the weaver when fully employed, and includes the incidental expenses connected with his employment, and which, when deducted from the before-named sum, will reduce his wages in both periods near 3 s. per week, and in the latter instance to about 6 s.; and as the whole amount of wages paid to the weaver is distributed in the Town, every abstraction from the same is an evil, and the foregoing Statement will at one view show and account for the general decaying state of the retail traders and shopkeepers, who have every year increased burdens with diminished means, until the fearful prospect of utter ruin presents itself to their view.

---

11665. Before the period of which you now complain, have you known any other periods of distress in your branch of the trade?—I never knew any period of distress which might be considered of any permanency; any previous depression that arose in the trade, was only of temporary duration; further, it appears obvious from the Table I put in, that prior to 1825, wages had remained 50 or 60 per cent. higher than they are at present.

11666. You are aware there is a duty on thrown silk?—I am.

11667. Supposing the duty was removed, have you ever turned it in your own

mind

mind what benefit is likely to be derived to the weaver?—I have considered the subject, but I have never considered that it would permanently benefit the weaver; the duty on thrown silk, I believe, amounts to about five per cent. on manufactured goods, admitting that the fabrics are composed two-thirds of tram, and one-third of organzine. In Macclesfield, where my children are dependent on the throwing establishments, and the population are dependent on it for their support, the diminished deduction in the throwster's wages must materially aggravate our situation.

11668. Do you think that 3 s. 6 d. amounts to as much as five per cent. on manufactured articles?—In some cases; I take the heavy fabric, not the light valuable articles, for on them it would be about 2 ½ per cent.

11669. Has there been any new trade introduced into Macclesfield since the alteration of the system and the reduction in the price of wages?—There has been a few more Jacquard machines introduced, but they were introduced previous to the alteration; they commenced in 1824; there has been no new trade since.

11670. I mean unconnected with the silk trade?—None at all; the trade has gradually declined, and the wealthy and prosperous appearance of the inhabitants has changed. There is one circumstance I wish to mention, it has had a great effect on the peaceable and loyal disposition of the people; at the last public meeting that was called to memorialize His Majesty's Ministers and the Board of Trade, the people would not have the word " praying " inserted in the petition; but I took care to have it inserted; when I sum it up in a few words it has produced poverty; poverty has produced demoralization, and demoralization disaffection to His Majesty's person and government; in short, we are obliged now to have soldiers to keep the peace, whereas the constables formerly did it.

11671. You alluded to a particular method of manufacture at Macclesfield?—This is a simple process called steaming, which is similar to calendering, which is only applicable to handkerchiefs; this did not come in competition with the manufactures of Spitalfields. It was a peculiar process in the first instance of our own, and I was employed wholly in that department of the trade.

11672. Has it not been adopted in other parts?—Yes, latterly; but some of these fabrics have been abolished by the introduction of foreign articles.

11673. Is the manufacture at Macclesfield of a finer or coarser description than it used to be in the years 1824 and 1825?—It is greatly changed to a coarser description; I can instance it in reference to my own employment; formerly I was employed in the light and valuable fabrics of the trade; I have nothing now in my possession but plain goods, and these of a heavy description. The work I formerly made at from 1 s. 6 d. to 2 s. 3 d. per ounce, I now make at about 3 d. per ounce.

## Mr. *Joseph Smith*, called in; and Examined.

11674. WHAT is your profession?—A silk weaver.

11675. Residing where?—At Macclesfield.

11676. Are you acquainted with the present state of the artisans employed in the silk trade?—I am; I have been a silk weaver for twelve or thirteen years, and have had some experience among them, and I believe I can speak pretty correctly as to the general circumstances of the persons employed in the trade.

11677. Is there a great amount of distress among the operatives unemployed in that branch of the manufacture?—There is a very great amount of distress among the operatives, and I believe that those who are in constant employment participate in the distress as well as those who are not at work; I know instances of persons who have two or three small children that cannot work, and of course are dependent on them for subsistence out of their small earnings; although they are in constant employment, they cannot procure comforts for even themselves, much more their family, and I know that great privations are endured by these persons; I suppose the average earnings of the weaver to be between 6 s. and 7 s. per week, and frequently the man has a wife and two or three children to support out of that.

11678. Do you consider the depression experienced in the silk manufacture to be of a temporary or permanent character?—According to the facts I have witnessed of late years, I consider it to be of a permanent character, for the depression has been greatly increasing; I have not witnessed any periods at which we could say we have been returning backwards to prosperity; every thing appears to me to be getting worse and worse; every struggle the men make to better their condition proves fruitless, and from these circumstances I am led to conclude that it is of a permanent character.

11679. Do

Mr.
*Joseph Smith.*

19 July,
1832.

11679. Do you recollect the condition of the persons employed in the manufacture of silk prior to the admission of foreign wrought silk into the market?—I do; and, generally speaking, I believe that persons employed in the silk manufacture were as well and as comfortably situated as persons in any other branch of manufacture whatever. A year or two prior to the introduction of foreign silk the people were remarkably well off; they had got clothes and furniture, and comforts of almost every description that appertains to the condition of workmen; but now their furniture has disappeared from their houses, the bulk of them have no clothes to go out in on a Sunday, and they cannot even procure a little recreation of any kind, but are compelled to sit at home and witness their own poverty and destitution.

11680. Has the situation of the operative greatly deteriorated since the measure first came into operation?—As I observed before, I have witnessed a gradual deterioration in the condition of the operative generally, and I believe that deterioration will increase unless some measures are adopted to arrest its progress.

11681. To what cause do you ascribe the deterioration in the circumstances of the persons employed in the silk manufacture?—I ascribe it to the introduction of foreign wrought silks, which come into competition with the home manufacture; the English artisan is compelled to manufacture at the same price as the foreigner, otherwise he would find his employment taken from him; this would entirely deprive him of the means of subsistence, therefore he is compelled to submit to work at the same price as the foreigner, although his wages will not yield him comfort, or even a mere subsistence.

11682. Are you acquainted with the opinion of the operatives, generally, as to the causes which have produced this lamentable change in their condition?—I am; I believe that the general opinion among the operatives is, that it arises from the circumstances I have mentioned; I believe that, owing to the repeated applications they have made for redress of grievances having proved fruitless, an opinion is generally prevailing among them that the Government of the country is totally indifferent to their situation, and I know that representations would be more frequently made were not this the case, but many of them appear to have totally given up all hope, and do not care what comes next.

11683. Do you believe that the privations endured by the artisans employed in the silk manufacture has a tendency to deteriorate their moral character?—Yes, I have known many instances of persons who, while they could get a comfortable living, were considered respectable characters, but now, owing to all attempts to procure a comfortable living having proved fruitless, they have sunk into a state of despair, and do not seem to care what becomes of them.

11684. From your intimate and extensive knowledge of the character and condition of persons engaged in the silk manufacture, perhaps you can inform the Committee if there are any means of arresting the progress of this moral degradation to which you have alluded?—If I am confined to any specific remedy, I should say, prevent the introduction of foreign wrought silks, which compete with our goods; that would be the most effectual, as respects the silk trade.

11685. Do you believe there is a strong inclination to acquire knowledge among the working classes, which is nullified by the state of destitution to which they are now reduced?—Yes, I know a number of persons most anxious to obtain information, but who are totally precluded from obtaining it by the circumstances in which they are placed; I know many persons who formerly had small libraries by them, and while their circumstances would admit were continually increasing them, but owing to the pressure of the time they have been compelled, however reluctantly, to part with the works they then possessed, and now they have given up all hope of being able to purchase any works at all; their thoughts are solely engrossed by the more necessary demands of nature.

11686. Do you think that if they had the means of procuring these comforts which they formerly possessed, a great improvement in their moral character would be the consequence?—Certainly.

11687. Are the artisans of Macclesfield able to produce as good an article as the artisans of any other town?—I should think that in the branch of manufacture in which they have been more particularly employed they would exceed the artisans of any other town.

11688. You do not consider their distress arises from want of knowledge or ability, but from other causes over which they have no control?—Certainly; I conceive if there was a probability of their being placed on an equal footing with the artisans of any other town or any other country, I believe the artisans of Macclesfield would rival those of any other place whatever.

11689. Can

Mr.
*Joseph Smith.*

19 July,
1832.

11689. Can a workman earn more money when employed in some particular branches of silk manufacture, than when employed in other branches?—There are particular branches, such as the fancy branches, in which a workman can earn more money than he can when employed in the manufacture of coarser articles; but there is a gradual deterioration in the condition of even this class of workmen, and I believe they are fast approaching to the situation of their fellow workmen; those who are the most skilled feel a kind of indifference as to whether they continue in such kind of employ or not; it requires a little more care and attention, and perhaps a little more skill, but finding they are not rewarded in proportion to their skill and attention, they feel rather inclined to accept of the lower kinds of work, and I believe that the finer kinds of work, unless encouraged, will gradually grow into disuse.

11690. Do you consider that the tendency of the circumstances in which the workmen are at present placed, is to deteriorate the quality of the silk manufactured?—I certainly do, for the reasons before assigned.

11691. Do you not think if the artisans were properly encouraged, great improvements may be made in the silk manufacture?—I certainly do; for I know that while the artisans were encouraged, improvements were continually taking place, their reward was a stimulus to improvement, but now the most valuable kind of labour is continually falling in value; they plainly see that in a while they will be reduced to a level with their brethren who have not so much skill as themselves, consequently they feel a kind of apathy to continue these kind of works in existence, and I believe that unless some means are taken to reward skill where it is found, that it will totally disappear from among the workmen.

11692. Can you state whether the weavers wait for work, and how long, and if out of place, how long they are before they can obtain fresh employment?—I believe that a weaver on an average waits about one-sixth or one-seventh of his time, I mean those who are in work, but there are a considerable number, I suppose one-third, constantly out of work.

11693. When you state 7*s.*, you mean that as the wages of those who are in work?—Yes; not including the time they wait for work. With the permission of the Committee, I will state a circumstance that has come under my own observation, to show the demoralization that prevails among the workmen, and the impositions practised on the parish in consequence of the workmen being reduced to such a state of destitution. I happened to be in a room where there were five or six looms, and there were two persons present whose gains were so small that they were obliged to receive relief from the parish, in a smuggled way of course; I observed these persons going from their work at the time when they were required to be in attendance by the parish to receive their pay, and they afterwards returned to their work to make up sufficient to obtain a subsistence. This practice has been very prevalent in Macclesfield, of late years, the men feel they are all circumstanced alike, they are compelled to adopt this stratagem in order to obtain a subsistence, and I believe they would not divulge the secret for any consideration whatever.

Mr. *Thomas Cope*, called in; and Examined.

Mr.
*Thomas Cope.*

11694. WHAT is your profession?—A silk weaver.

11695. Where do you live?—At Macclesfield.

11696. How long have you been employed in the silk trade?—Since 1817, to the present time.

11697. Have you been employed by the same master since 1817?—Yes.

11698. Is the employment under that master as regular as that of others?—My employment under him has been more regular than most others in the town.

11699. How were you employed, and what were your earnings from 1817 to 1823 inclusive?—During that time my employment was steady and regular, with the exception of a few weeks in the summer of 1818, at which time the weaving department of the silk trade was rather slack, but not to any serious amount; my earnings from 1817 to the beginning of 1819, were rather less than afterwards, because during that time I was employed in making plain goods or chiefly so, but taking into my account the time which is unavoidably lost in this department of our trade, I would earn 15*s.* or 16*s.* per week. In the commencement of 1819, I began weaving fancy work and continued to do so for several years, so that my earnings from that time to 1823, were upwards of 20*s.* per week.

11700. What do you mean by time being unavoidably lost in the weaving department of your trade?—I mean that time which a weaver loses in waiting for warps
and

and shute. It is commonly the case that when a weaver has finished his warp he waits a week, sometimes a fortnight, and seldom less than two or three days even in good trade, and besides which it often happens that a weaver has to wait for shute, and I think it may fairly be said, that weavers, taking them as a whole, lose one-fifth part of their time unavoidably; I intend this to apply to the weaving department of our trade; since 1826 to the present time, trade has been so precarious from the introduction of the free trade measures, that weavers lose one-fifth part of their time unavoidably.

11701. What causes them to wait for the shute?—The unsteadiness of the trade and not knowing what to prepare.

11702. You could do more work if you had it?—Of course we could.

11703. How were you employed in 1824 and 1825, and what were your earnings?—In those years my employment was regular, and my earnings much the same as in the preceding period, with a small advance in 1825, but which lasted but a very short time.

11704. How have you been employed since 1825 to the present time?—My employ since 1825 has been very unsteady and irregular, and has met with several interruptions and long depressions, which have caused me and my family to suffer very severe privations.

11705. What have been your earnings during this latter period?—During this latter period my earnings have rapidly decreased, so much so, that if I were fully employed I cannot live as a working man ought to do, and pay my way honestly. If I take into my account the difference of the work at which I am now employed as compared with that at which I was formerly employed, my earnings are reduced considerably more than one half.

11706. How much can you earn a week?—It is a very difficult thing to ascertain the precise average earnings of weavers, so many variations take place in their employment, and the description of work they make, that it is a very difficult point to come at; it may be estimated at somewhere about 6 *s.*

11707. What was the condition of the silk weavers at Macclesfield generally, from 1817 to 1825?—Comparatively easy and prosperous; they were then not only enabled by their industry to feed and clothe themselves and families respectably, but they were enabled to lay something by for a rainy day; in proof of which I beg leave to say, that between 1820 and 1826. several building societies were formed; the principal part of the members of these building societies were men employed in the silk trade, by which societies there have been built I suppose not less than three or four hundred houses; but unfortunately for the members of these societies, the principal part of the houses so built have fallen into other hands, in consequence of the depressions in our trade, which have taken place since 1825.

11708. What has been the condition of the silk weavers at Macclesfield from 1825 to 1832?—The condition of the silk weavers of Macclesfield has been gradually declining; their wages have been reduced from 30 to 50 per cent. upon plain works; their employment has been very irregular and deficient; their fancy trade since 1825, has been, as they suppose, superseded by the foreigner, and they are now compelled to labour upon the poorest and worst paid works: their clothing, bedding and furniture, are nearly exhausted, so that now, every period of distress that overtakes them, finds them in a worse condition than before to endure its hardships; our workhouse is filled with paupers, and our streets with beggars; the stimulus to industry is now destroyed, and it is become a matter of indifference with some men whether they have employment or not, because they find by experience that they can live as well upon parish allowance as they can by their own labour; I remember a circumstance which occurred in Macclesfield last winter, which will illustrate their condition; a weaver employed by a respectable house, when he had finished his piece, instead of taking it home to his employer, he took it off and sold it, and when he was brought before the Court, and asked why he had committed the crime, he said, " I have worked hard, I have been careful in expending my money, and still I find that I cannot pay my way and live; in fact, I find my affairs going worse and worse every week, and therefore I have committed the crime in order that I may be transported beyond the sea."

11709. To what do you ascribe the want of regular employ, and the reduction of your wages?—To the introduction of foreign wrought goods into our market.

11710. Does not the distress of the weavers in other manufactures equal yours? I am not acquainted with other manufactures, and therefore I cannot speak to them.

11711. Does

11711. Does not the increase of silk weaving in Lanchashire account for your distress, and is not the manufacture prosperous, both as regards master and men?—I will not say there has been no increase in Lancashire, but I will venture to say that the increase has been very small, as compared with what it has been stated to be ; and likewise, that the increase which has taken place in Lancashire (admitting that there is an increase) does not account for the depression of the trade in Macclesfield and Spitalfields ; whether the trade is prosperous or not as it regards the masters, I do not know, but according to my notion of prosperity, I am sure it is not so with the workmen, nor can they ever be in a prosperous state, supposing them to be fully employed, unless they have more wages for their work, or otherwise their provisions, rents and clothing, cheaper. It is the opinion of some men, that if the people have plenty of work, they must be well off ; but this is far from being the truth, for it is quite possible for the people to be fully employed, and still to be in a very poor condition, in consequence of the price of their labour not being proportioned to the price of provisions, rent, clothing and taxes ; the people do not merely want employment, but they want to be paid for that employment in such a manner as will enable them to live as Englishmen have been accustomed to do, by the fruits of their industry ; before I proceed to lay before this Committee the state of the Lancashire silk trade, I think it will be proper to state the reason why any inquiry was instituted respecting that trade.

11712. Are you acquainted with the trade?—I think I am. In March last, when the motion was made for this Committee of Inquiry, we were informed by the public newspapers that the Right honourable Mr. Poulett Thomson had said, that the silk trade in Lancashire was prosperous ; that in 1824 there were 6,000 looms in Manchester, and that the number had increased from that time to the present to 15,000. In consequence of having read this statement, the Weavers' Committee determined to ascertain if possible whether it was correct or not ; accordingly they sent myself and another man down into that country ; our business was to inquire what number of looms there were going in Lancashire, in the neat silk and mixed trades ; what description of goods they were making ; what reductions had taken place in their wages since the free trade measures were introduced ; what number of Jacquards there were employed ; whether in the silk or mixed trade ; how they had been employed during the last winter, and what was the general condition of the Lancashire silk weavers. With these instructions we set off to Manchester, and from there to all the principal places in Lancashire where the silk trade is carried on. At Manchester, including Salford and Harfieldsay, we found 950 looms ; in the Middleton district, including Broadman-lane, Jumbo-Tongue, Chadderton, Whitgate, Moston and the town of Middleton, we found 2,121. In the Failsworth district, including Failsworth, Hollinwood, Taunton, Droilsden, Woodhouses, Newton, Garton, Swinton and Eccles, 2,623. In the district of West Leigh, including Leigh, Pennington, Beaford, Atherton, Tilsey and Astley, 3,000. At Stockport and the Moor, 270, making a total of 8,964 ; about 3,000 of these looms are employed in the mixed trade ; so that it appears by this statement that there are not quite 6,000 looms employed in the neat silk trade in Lancashire. The description of goods made in Lancashire is as follows : grey bandannas, principally made of spun silk, and of an inferior quality ; single sarsnets, three and four singles (these latter are called the lowest or poorest description of gros de Naples); I believe these descriptions of work are from the principal part of the manufacture of Lancashire ; in the neat silk trade, there may be some few gros de Naples of a finer texture, and besides these I believe there are a very few florets in factories. In Manchester, there is some little of the handkerchief trade carried on, but not to any extent ; those looms employed in the mixed trade I leave out of the question, because I do not consider them as belonging to the silk trade at all ; their wages have been reduced 50 to 60 per cent. since the free trade measures have been introduced ; the number of Jacquards employed in the neat silk trade, in March last, was about fifty, and about 300 in the mixed trade ; during the last winter distress prevailed to a very great degree in Manchester ; we were informed that there had not been more than one-third of the looms employed, and those employed had not had more than half work. In Middleton, out of about 1,400 looms, there had been 900 of them unemployed for more than three months of the winter. In the Failsworth district, their sufferings had not been quite so great, in consequence of being employed in the mixed trade. In the Leigh district, the people had had very little to do during the winter ; and if we must judge of their condition by their appearance, their clothing and household furniture, they are wretched beyond any thing

ever

*Thomas Cope.*

19 July,
1832.

ever experienced by them at any former period. When we asked them how it was that they had not made their case known to the Government, they said they did not believe that Government cared any thing about them; that it was of no use to petition them; that the only aim of Government was to aggrandize themselves, no matter what became of the working classes: this opinion generally prevails among the working people of the North.

11713. Has not the amount of hand labour thrown out of employ by the cotton power loom, occasioned the depression in your wages, and your want of employment?—I do not think so; I am aware that the great majority of the weavers now weaving silk in Lancashire were formerly employed in the cotton; but I am likewise aware that the greater part of these had fled to the silk trade before the introduction of the measures which opened our market to the foreigner, but without having occasioned any perceptible inconvenience to us, either as to wages or our employment.

11714. How do you prove that your want of employment and the reduction in your wages arise from foreign competition, when the consumption of the raw material is so much increased since the introduction of the measures in 1824?—I do not know that any thing which I have to offer will amount to a complete proof of my opinion; but there are several circumstances connected with the silk trade, which if they do not amount to a complete proof, will appear to be very strong presumptive evidence of the fact. The first is the fact, that before the introduction of the measures in 1824, the silk trade steadily, but progressively advanced in its magnitude, notwithstanding the partial and temporary embarrassments with which it met, and which for the moment impeded but did not arrest its progress, which will be seen by referring to the Custom House Returns. In the second place, it appears that the trade, notwithstanding the improvements in our machinery, our increased speed, the reductions in our wages, and the efforts of both masters and men to compete with their foreign rival, has decreased, as will be seen by the Return, alluded to above. Thirdly, from 1817 to 1825, our wages were little reduced, but since 1825 they have been reduced 30 to 50 per cent. Again, during the former period, up to 1825, the trade suffered very little distress, but since then the silk trade has undergone three very serious depressions, all in the compass of five or six years.

11715. Have not workmen generally better means of informing themselves as to the number of the looms than their masters?—I believe they have; there is one circumstance I might mention: in 1829 there was a very formidable union of the silk weavers in Lancashire; they had books, and sent men round to all the different places, villages and hamlets, to ascertain the number of looms there were in Lancashire, and they put the names of the places and the number of looms down in the book wherever any weaving was going on: from these books we have obtained the number of looms. Our next inquiry was, as to whether any increase had taken place since the year 1829, and whether any new houses had been built; we found there had been a very inconsiderable increase since that time, therefore I think the result justified us in relying on the number of looms we obtained from that source.

11716. Why is it that the workmen can give better information on this point than their masters?—In Lancashire it is the prevailing practice to have more harnesses (the apparatus by which the work is performed) in their workshops than they have actually at work; that I believe to be pretty generally the case as far as that county is concerned. Supposing this to be so, and one person has eight harnesses and only five looms, the manufacturer makes a return of eight looms, while in reality he has only five employed.

11717. How long were you in Lancashire?—Five days.

11718. Although you were there only five days, were you acquainted with the county previously?—Yes.

11719. Was your companion a native of Lancaster?—Either a native, or bordering on it.

### Mr. *David Rowbotham*, called in; and Examined.

Mr.
*David Rowbotham.*

11720. WHAT is you trade?—A silk weaver, residing in Macclesfield. I was the person who accompanied the last Witness through Lancashire, and can bear testimony to the truth of what he has stated.

11721. How long have you been a silk weaver?—Seventeen or eighteen years.

11722. How were you employed before?—I have been employed in nearly all

678. the

Mr.
David Rowbotham.

19 July,
1832.

the various sorts of fancy goods made of cotton and spun silk, and in the common fabrics of cotton as well.

11723. What induced you to leave the cotton and go to the silk?—I was one of many thousands at that time whose employment was superseded by the operation of the power loom, many of whom found an asylum in the silk trade, which at that time afforded a very fair remuneration for labour.

11724. Was there a great increase of silk weavers at that period?—I believe there was as great an increase from the year 1816 to 1820 as there has been in the same number of years at any subsequent period; this increase came from the cotton trade.

11725. Was that attended by a great reduction of wages?—I am not aware there was any reduction of wages during the years I speak of; the supply of work remained very steady, therefore no material injury was done to those who had been before employed.

11726. Was there not a great depression in the years 1818 and 1819?—I believe there was a slight depression about that time, but it was so trifling, as compared with what we have experienced since, that it is scarcely remembered by the workmen, while those of 1826, 1829, and last winter made an impression never to be erased; the depressions in 1818 and 1819 were temporary, and soon passed away.

11727. What was the state of the silk trade, as far as your experience went, during the period you allude to, and up to 1823, as it regards the silk weavers generally, and particularly as to yourself?—From the time I commenced the trade, in 1815, up to 1823, the trade seemed to be steadily advancing, particularly the fancy trade; we experienced very little inconvenience from want of employ. A silk weaver might in those days maintain his proper rank in society, as an honest industrious man and a good member of the community; as to myself, my condition was such as to enable me to gain a comfortable living, and make some provision for the decline of life.

11728. How were you situated in 1824 and 1825?—About the same; in 1825 I considered myself to be worth 150*l.*; now, I do not know that I am worth 10*l.* My money is all gone; my property is rendered of very little value.

11729. How has the trade been since 1825?—As far as my experience goes, it has been very unsettled, and rapidly sinking; the condition of the workmen has generally been wretched in the extreme.

11730. Can you state what the reduction in price has been in the five years prior to 1826 and the five years subsequent to that period?—I believe it is impossible to know precisely what the reduction has been on all the various descriptions of work made in the trade, but I think I have a statement here which will place the matter in as clear a light as it can be placed; whether this statement is exactly similar to that which has been given before I do not know, but it is a statement I have been at considerable pains to collect and ascertain the correctness of.

[*It was delivered in.*]

THE following Scale of Reductions will best serve to show when the heaviest pressure fell upon the Trade.

| YEARS. | Mountures, per Dozen. | | Figured Stage Harness of 100 Shafts, per Dozen. | | Black Handkerchiefs, per Dozen. | | Bandannas, per Cut. | | Single Sarsnets, per Yard. | | Gros de Naples, per Yard. | |
|---|---|---|---|---|---|---|---|---|---|---|---|---|
| | s. | d. | s. | d. | s. | d. | s. | d. | s. | d. | s. | d. |
| 1821 | 30 | – | 14 | – | 10 | – | 3 | 6 | – | 9 | 1 | 1 |
| 1822 | 30 | – | 13 | – | 10 | – | 3 | 6 | – | 9 | 1 | 1 |
| 1823 | 24 | – | 14 | – | 10 | – | 3 | 6 | – | 9 | 1 | 1 |
| 1824 | 22 | – | 12 | 6 | 9 | – | 3 | 6 | – | 9 | 1 | – |
| 1825 | 24 | – | 13 | 6 | 9 | – | 3 | 6 | – | 9 | 1 | 1 |
| 1826 | 16 | – | 12 | – | 8 | – | 2 | 6 | – | 7 | – | 7 |
| 1827 | 14 | – | 12 | – | 7 | 6 | 2 | 6 | – | 7 | – | 7 |
| 1828 | 14 | – | 12 | – | 7 | – | 2 | 6 | – | 5½ | – | 8 |
| 1829 | 12 | – | 10 | – | 6 | 6 | 2 | 6 | – | 5 | – | 7 |
| 1830 | 11 | – | 9 | – | 6 | 9 | 2 | 3 | – | 4½ | – | 6 |
| 1831 | 9 | – | 7 | 6 | 6 | 3 | 2 | 3 | – | 4 | – | 6 |

I only

I only wish to make one observation: yet with all these reductions our supply of work has greatly fallen off, and numbers have been wholly thrown out of employ, and those that are in work cannot, by their utmost exertions, shield themselves from poverty and want; in fact, there is no stimulus to industry, for he that lives upon the parish is as well off as he that works for his living. In proof of that, I have been acquainted for many years with a man with whom I served in the army, and whom I always considered a very respectable man; I have noticed him sweeping the streets, and I have asked him how it was that he continued to sweep the streets; he said, " I cannot do any better." I said, " Cannot you get any more by your trade than by sweeping the streets?" " No," says he, " I cannot get so much; if I go to the loom, that may not be so regular; I may have many a blank week, and there are many operatives who cannot obtain work; I do not wish the overseers to come at a knowledge of this, for if they do they will force me to work."

11731. How do you reconcile the fact, of an increased importation of silk since 1823, with the falling off of the trade?—That question has been so often asked, and answered in general terms, that I think I cannot do better than to put in the comparative view of my workshop, taken last March, compared with what it was in March 1823, which statement will show, that in March 1823, I received for work, made in my garret, 1 s. 10½ d. per ounce; at the present period I receive 5½ d.

*Mr.*
*David Rowbotham.*

19 July,
1832.

[*It was delivered in.*]

A COMPARATIVE VIEW of my WORKSHOP, in the Years 1823 and 1832.

### MARCH 1823.

| Nº of Looms. | Wages. | Weight. | Description of Workmen. | Age. | |
|---|---|---|---|---|---|
| | | Oz. | | | |
| 1 | 28/ | 18 | Myself - - | 40 | |
| 2 | 24/6 | 16 | Apprentice | 19 | |
| 3 | 27/ | 12 | Journeymen | 40 | For weaving Silk, 1 s. 10½ d. per oz. |
| 4 | 26/ | 12 | ditto - - | unknown. | |
| 5 | 26/ | 12 | ditto - - | ditto | |
| 6 | 23/ | 12 | Wife - - | 30 | |
| | 154/6 | 82 | | | |
| | 12 | | | | |

82) 1854 (22
164
—————
214
164
—————
50
4
—————
82) 200 (2
164
—————
36

s. d.
154 6 Gross Wages.

s.
Deduct for Journeymen's
Wages, and Quill Winder } 74
Rent, Taxes, Coals and Candles, 11
————— 85 -
————
69 6

Here I have £. 3. 9. 6. to maintain a Family of eight persons with, or about 8 s. 8 d. per head.

### MARCH 1832.

| Nº of Looms. | Wages. | Weight. | Description of Workmen. | Age. | |
|---|---|---|---|---|---|
| | | Oz. | | | |
| 1 | 8/3 | 20 | Myself - - | 49 | |
| 2 | 12/4½ | 30 | Daughter - | 20 | |
| 3 | 10/ | 18 | Son - - | 18 | For weaving Silk, 5½ d. per oz. |
| 4 | 9/9 | 12 | Journeyman | 21 | |
| 5 | 11/3 | 25 | ditto - - | 18 | |
| 6 | 10/ | 28 | Wife - - | 39 | |
| | 61/7½ | 133 | | | |
| | 12 | | | | |

133) 739 (5
665
—————
74
4
—————
133) 296 (2
266
—————
30

s. d.
61 7½ Gross Wages.
Deduct ⅓ for waiting for Canes - 8 9½
————
52 10

Paid to Journeymen and } s.
Quill Winder - - } 18
To Rent, Taxes, Coals and } 10
Candles - - - }
————— 28 -
————
24 10

Here I have £. 1. 4. 10. per week to maintain a family of seven persons with, or about 3 s. 6 d. per head; and we are one of the best situated families that I know of: there are hundreds that have not a third part of the income that we have; we are all workers but one. I do not know only one other in Town as well off as I am.

*D. Rowbotham.*

11732. Do

Mr.
*David Rowbotham.*

19 July,
1832.

11732. Do you consider this a fair criterion whereby to judge of the general state of the trade?—Perhaps not exactly so; it is not an exaggerated statement. If I was asked to give an opinion of the fact, generally, I should say that it required twice the quantity of silk to employ the same number of looms, and four times the quantity to afford the same amount of wages.

11733. Having been a Lancashire weaver, you are probably acquainted with the silk trade of that county?—I have always kept up a correspondence with my friends, and I have recently been through all the manufacturing districts, and made inquiry into the state of the trade and the condition of the workmen.

11734. What is the result of that inquiry?—The information that we obtained was that the trade had suffered a greater degree of depression during the last two years, and last winter in particular, than it had ever experienced before; the people had suffered more than they had ever done previously, and had it not been for the extraordinary crop of potatoes, they had last summer, they must have literally starved. They complained grievously of oppression from all quarters, and heaped the bitterest imprecations on those who had brought about the changes which had reduced them to their present condition.

11735. Did you find much of the higher branches of the trade in Lancashire?—Very little; we heard of some few looms of florets and figured handkerchiefs, but nothing of any importance.

11736. What did their trade principally consist of?—There is a considerable diversity of goods; but from the observations I made, as well as my former knowledge, I conclude that the better half of the trade is an inferior description of gros de Naples, the remainder consists chiefly of a light texture of mixed goods, in my opinion not calculated to interfere with the manufactures of Spitalfields or of Macclesfield. I admit that a few substantial goods are made in the mixed trade, but they are two-thirds cotton, and cannot be considered as part of the silk trade; I know that their fancy trade has gradually declined under the present system; I know, from my own personal experience, that the fancy trade has declined in Manchester.

11737. Do you know whether the rich figured trade of Spitalfields, the ribbon trade of Coventry, or the handkerchief trade at Macclesfield, are carried on at Manchester?—It is impossible these branches of trade could have been carried on there without its coming to my knowledge; and I have no hesitation in saying, they are not carried on there to an extent to be sensibly felt in other places; if they deal in these goods, they must be made elsewhere, probably at Lyons.

11738. Has the manufacture of silk goods, or goods made from silk and cotton, been recently introduced into Lancashire?—No, it is of very long standing; my mother-in-law was bound apprentice to a silk weaver, in Lancashire, more than 70 years ago. I have some printed lists of prices, which were her's, and which in some degree show the progress of the trade at remote periods; here is a list, that bears date 1786, of the prices of the Manchester trade at that period; I compare that with one of 1796, which displays a gradual increase of the trade; there are a greater number of works, of different sorts, principally of silk mixed goods, it bears the signatures of 15 manufacturers in the silk trade, at Manchester, in 1796. If you compare that with 1810, you will see that there is a very great increase of the different descriptions of goods that are made, so that it appears the trade of Manchester has been progressively increasing.

11739. Did you meet with any ribbon weavers in Lancashire when you were making this inquiry?—We did not find a single ribbon loom or ribbon weaver in Lancashire, nor had they ever heard of any; I made particular inquiry into that branch of trade.

11740. Has not the cotton weaver derived an advantage, equal to your loss, under the present regulation?—Certainly not; they derived considerable advantage before these regulations came into operation, but none since; in my opinion, in our fall, we dragged them along with us. I conceive that no portion of the community has been benefited by the new system except the wealthy, and particularly those who have fixed money incomes. These measures appeared to me to be based on that passage in holy writ, which says, " He that hath nothing even that which he hath shall be taken away, and he that hath much, more shall be added unto him."

11741. Are there many cotton weavers in Lancashire and Cheshire, that can easily turn their hand to silk if it was advantageous to them?—The number susceptible of the change is now very limited; cotton weaving is a branch of industry that is fast falling into decay, and silk weaving seems to be on the same road.

11742. To what cause do you ascribe the difficulty which you complain of?—In
my

Mr.
*David Rowbotham.*

19 July,
1832.

my opinion there are various causes to which they may be ascribed; all of them, I am sorry to say, appear to me to have originated in the building in which I now stand; the most prominent is, that our home market is supplied by other countries; the flower is given to the Frenchman, and nothing but the dry stem which it grows on is left for us.

11743. Has not the introduction of the Jacquard machine been of great service to you?—The Jacquard machine was a benefit in 1824 and 1825; but I have never been able to use mine to any advantage since that time. If I attempted to do any thing in the fancy trade, I was invariably a loser by it; if I got a cane, and put it into the loom, it almost invariably stopped at the end of it; that has been a great inconvenience to me, for I was trained to the fancy trade from my infancy, and never worked a piece of plain goods from the time I was fourteen years of age up to 1826, and I am now near fifty years old.

11744. You have not experienced any distress hitherto in your own family?—I have only been sheltered from the distress by what I saved in better times; other branches of my family have suffered in common with my fellow workmen. I would beg to introduce one instance; I have a relative residing in Macclesfield, who, if the Lancaster trade had been so very beneficial, would have remained there; so far from its being prosperous, it was such as to induce him to believe he would do better at Macclesfield; he came to Macclesfield about twelve months ago, and got into employment; he very soon felt that his condition was not bettered; he is a timid shy man, and one of those not willing to make a display of their poverty; I was unacquainted with his situation until his family, by actual starvation, had been reduced to that state of health that three of his children were ill of a fever; he was obliged then to make application to me, and I found them in the most wretched condition that the imagination of man can conceive; they had nothing in the house; I had to strip my own beds to shelter them in their sickness; and I discovered that at that period they had not had more than 4 s. to subsist on for a fortnight.

11745. Has not home competition been the cause of all this?—I cannot possibly conceive that home competition can be charged as the cause of it; if that be an evil that is calculated to lower our wages and do us injury, I should conceive the evil must be greatly aggravated when it extends to country against country; if the competition of one manufacture against another, and one town against another, be calculated to reduce our wages, it must be a great aggravation of the evil to extend the competition to country against country.

11746. Do you consider that a repeal of the duty on foreign thrown silk would have the effect of benefiting the trade?—I think very far from it; I have found by experience that lowering the duties on foreign thrown silk subjects us to considerable inconvenience; the silks that we have had to work since the duties have been lowered have not been so well thrown as before; we have had more trouble with them. The circumstance of taking away the duties would be a matter that could not be kept a secret; the buyers would take advantage of it, and I believe we should be materially injured by the measure.

*John Wright*, called in; and Examined.

*John Wright.*

11747. ARE you an operative silk throwster at Macclesfield?—I am.

11748. Do you consider distress inherent in the silk trade prior to the alteration in the duties?—I know of no distress from 1801 up to the year 1826, save and except between the year 1815 and 1816, which arose from the sudden transition from war to peace.

11749. What was the condition of the hands employed in the throwing mills at Macclesfield up to 1825?—The condition of the labouring classes was remarkably fair; the price of labour was good; the work people were contented and happy; we had bread enough and to spare, and there was no complaining in our streets.

11750. What alteration has taken place since, both as respects regularity of employment and amount of wages?—The trade is so subject to fluctuation that we are in jeopardy almost every season; we sometimes thought we were going to drive all before us, when the operation of the free trade system, like a mighty tornado, had almost swept all before it, and left us, the operatives, in a most destitute and forlorn condition; indeed I cannot fully describe the amount of the misfortunes that have befallen us, although I was appointed in the year 1826 to distribute the charity; and I think the state and condition of the working classes was at that time
withou

without a parallel; it seem to rain from one end of Macclesfield to the other, and as far as my researches went, I have often seen men eating their food with their tears, and while they have been eating their scanty morsel, tear after tear, like a plentiful shower, have dropped from their eyes; as regards wages, our earnings are from 50 to 60 per cent. less than they were in 1824; and I am sorry to say we look forward to a further reduction.

11751. How do you attribute your distress to the alteration of the law?—In the year prior to the alteration we had only one enemy to contend with, which was the Italian throwster; but observe we have now three, namely, the regular trader from France, bringing his wrought silks; the regular trader from Italy, bringing his thrown silks, and the smuggler.

11752. Had you not the smuggler before the prohibition?—Allow me to say that smuggling was carried on upon a very small scale till after the alteration of the duties, nothing of any consequence.

11753. What improvements have been made in silk machinery, about what time and where?—It is my opinion that the country is indebted to Macclesfield and Congleton for the many improvements that have been made in silk machinery. The Doublin frame was invented upwards of 25 years ago; this machine was incomplete until a person in Macclesfield invented the cleaner, also the roller in the room of a star in the winding process was the improvement of Macclesfield and Congleton conjointly. Speed is sometimes called an improvement, this we had as early as 1818.

11754. What difference is there betwixt what is termed Macclesfield and Manchester machinery?—Macclesfield is on a par with Manchester as respects machinery, we have all sorts and all speeds, so has Manchester; that which is termed in particular Manchester machinery, is made of metal enjoying no advantage over that made of wood, having a cylinder and cords instead of a drum and straps; this we had in Macclesfield 15 years ago.

11755. Do you consider that silk can be thrown better and cheaper on the new machinery, with extra speed, than on good machinery of the old construction, and at a slower speed?—I am fully persuaded that silk is thrown worse with a cylinder and cords than with a drum and straps, for this very reason, cords naturally either give or take according to the weather, and being frail and tender, compared with the straps, are subject to break, and the silk is invariably more irregular in its spin and throw by cords and cylinder than by drum and straps, cheaper it cannot be thrown on what is stated to be Manchester machinery, all things considered; in the first place, there is double the cost on the Manchester machinery compared with that which is termed the Macclesfield; in the second place, more waste is made with extra speed; in the third place, there is extra expense in turning; in the fourth, more hands are necessarily required, and there is more expense in the wear and tear; in the last place, there must be a more costly silk, and great speed is only applicable to the best qualities.

11756. What is the amount of horse power employed in the throwing of silk in Manchester, and what is the horse power idle in Manchester and Congleton alone? —Here I appear to tread on very delicate ground; it seems according to the statement that lies before me, that I am about to make a sweeping remark on a very marvellous statement that caught my eye sometime ago in Macclesfield; a friend called on me and put into my hand the Mirror of Parliament, wherein I found it stated that the horse power of Manchester was 342; it struck my mind very forcibly that nine or ten mills never could hold machinery employing that number of horse power. I was deputed by the operatives committee to go to Manchester to ascertain the fact, I and my colleague took nothing on second hand, we went direct to the mill, and all the information I am about to lay before the Committee on this subject, I received from every manager or every master; the horse power of Manchester employed in the throwing of silk is 138, it having been stated to be 342.

11757. You mean mills actually at work?—Actually at work. I will now mention what is idle at Macclesfield and Congleton alone, to say nothing of the many mills all round the country; the idle horse power at Macclesfield is 331; at Congleton, 157; total, 488.

11758. As you reside in the neighbourhood of Manchester, what do you know of the condition of the throwing trade of that place?—In January last, the operatives of Manchester sent a Memorial to the Board of Trade, stating the reduction in their earnings to be 40 per cent. less than in 1826; when I and another went

to

*John Wright.*

19 July,
1832.

to Manchester, and inquired of the operatives what was their then condition, they stated that it was considerably worse, with the expectation of a further reduction; the first gentleman throwster that we waited on, was Mr. Longworth; we asked him if the silk trade was in a healthful condition, and whether it had been so since the alteration in 1826; his reply was, we went on fair and prosperously till 1826, but since then, there has been nothing but distress; the second gentleman we saw, was Mr. Taylor, of the firm of Harrop, Taylor & Pearson; he informed us, that their mills in the last year, worked for about four or five months four days per week, and a short time some part of this; he said he was half inclined to stop his mill altogether; the next gentleman we were honoured with speaking to, was Mr. Smith, we asked him if the throwsters' protection were removed, could he compete with the foreigner; he was quite sure he could not; we asked, would there be an export trade if the duty on Italian thrown silk was removed, and of course the drawback; in reply, he stated that the exportation of silk would come to an end entirely; we also desired the two last gentlemen to say whether they could throw silk cheaper than Macclesfield and Congleton; we made the same inquiry at Broughton mill; they all with one consent declared, they could not; at the last mentioned place we learned that distress had thrown its gloomy mantle over every mill in Manchester, not excepting Mr. V. Royles. At Messrs. Occleston's we met with the same information precisely, we inquired of Messrs. Taylor, Smith, Occlestone & Williams how it was, since they could not throw cheaper than the above mentioned places, they ventured such amazing capital in building and machinery; they candidly owned that the erection of their mills was under the fostering care of Government at a time when the silk trade was making rapid advances, and it was difficult to get silk thrown; therefore the erection of our silk mills was mere convenience, as being attached to our looms. I was much struck with what fell from the lips of the Right honourable Gentleman, that Manchester was sucking up the trade of Macclesfield and Congleton; I think we discovered that the thing lay very easy on their stomachs, and that they would, if they could obtain back again their outlay, throw it upon the shores of the Bollin.

11759. Cannot the throwster exist if his protection be removed, and how would it affect the manufacturer?—First, the fact of the trade having suffered so much already by a reduction of duties from 7 s. 6 d. to 3 s. 6 d., our earnings having sunk from 50 to 60 per cent., and the profits of our employers gone, which has been clearly shown; without multiplying words, I think it is evident to the Committee from what has been stated, that if the duty was lowered or taken away, the throwster would be annihilated at once; I beg further to state, that owing to circumstances over which we have no control, we are not prepared successfully to compete with the Italian throwster; namely, the great and pressing national burthens, we are in patience and in common honesty bound to sustain, until some equitable means be devised to emancipate us from them; till then, protection is absolutely necessary; again, the difference of the price of labour in the two countries is decidedly in favour of the Italian; the wages of a man in Italy being 8 d. per day, in England 2 s., making a difference of nearly 70 per cent., to which add poor rates and taxes on the materials used in building and machinery. The second part of the question is, how would it affect the manufacturers; I think it appears to be the intention of Government to take care of the manufacturer; it shall be mine, as far as my slender ability goes; the repeal of the duties would be directly opposed to political economy; the English throwster being destroyed, the manufacturer must look to a foreigner for the supply of his looms; a monopoly would of course be created, and that entirely in the hands of strangers; and when the English throwster was gone to ruin and decay the Italian would ask what he thought proper for his thrown silk. I do not know how it could be otherwise, seeing that there would be no check upon him, he having the command of the throwing trade of Europe. If Government intends to ensure a cheap pound of thrown silk for the British weaver, allow the existence of the English throwster to be a check upon the Italian.

11760. How is it that you complain of want of employment, when it is stated that a large quantity of raw silk has been imported latterly?—Since the alteration in the silk duties, a complete revolution has taken place in the silk trade; a change from light to heavy goods, and of course from fine to round silk.

*Veneris,* 20° *die Julii,* 1832.

EDWARD AYSHFORD SANFORD, ESQUIRE, in the Chair.

*John Wright,* called in; and further Examined.

11761. HOW is it you complain of want of employment, when it is stated that a larger quantity of raw silk has been imported latterly?—I stated yesterday that a complete revolution had taken place in the silk trade, a change from light to heavy, from fine to round silks. From my own observation I find, that although there may be an increase of raw material to this country since the alteration to some small amount, yet the labour on that is considerably less than we derived from the fine silks; I observe, that according to the present circumstances we are pursuing in the silk trade, one machine will do as much as two formerly did, which were employed in the throwing of fine silks. We have been told frequently that we lose nothing, because we have the export trade; but as the present system only gives about half employ to the hands employed in throwing silk, I think it is quite clear there is no room for boasting concerning the large quantity of raw silk imported into this country since the alteration; the change of system has been to us like changing a hen for an owl; there is a great deal of boasting that the export trade has been a beneficial thing to us; that is my simple idea of it.

11762. Has the throwster any right to protection?—Yes, for various reasons: first, the silk throwster erected his mills on the faith of Government, the protection afforded to the silk throwing trade of the country in its infancy and afterwards; secondly, the amazing outlay of capital entitles him to protection, there being, according to the estimate taken in 1826, no less a sum than two millions of outlay in building and machinery.

11763. Where is that estimate taken from?—It was made by the London Committee in 1826. The reason that the throwster has a right to protection is, that the land-owner is protected; fourthly, and if I am rightly informed, the cotton spinner has a protecting duty of 10 per cent.; and in the fifth and last place, I believe that the importance of the great staple commodity of the country is in a great measure owing to the existence of the English throwster. It has been stated by a great but now lamented statesman, that the cotton and silk trades were sisters; I beg to say, that the silk trade is the eldest sister, and that Sir Robert Arkwright might have had on his escutcheon to this day, if he chose, what were the implements of his father's employment, if the principle of the cotton system had not been taken from the throwing machines. We had then our dames spinning cotton and flax by wheel and distaff, and the throwing machine, all ranged, spinning like they are now employed in the spinning of cotton, now employed by drum and strap and cylinder and cord, I remember seeing when I was a little boy, I think, which is one grand reason why the silk throwing of this country ought to be preserved, if it were only a relic of the importance it has given in the suggestion of the principle of spinning cotton, of such consequence and importance to this country.

11764. Can other trades give employ for the silk hands if their trade be destroyed by the removal of their protection?—No, they cannot, for turn which way you may you will see no prospect of admittance into other trades; and on the supposition that we could learn another business as speedily as we could say, as some time is said in the art of legerdemain, " Fly, Jack," there is no room for us; to make this appear, I direct your attention to the present state of circumstances; firstly, I look in the face the overwhelming surplus of the people, and ask them whether these are times to turn a whole trade upon them; secondly, turn your thoughts to the alarming increase of pauperism and of poor rates, and ask the overseers and rate-payers whether it is good policy to turn a whole trade on them at once. I think I can further show that other trades cannot find employ for us, from the labouring and bending of great minds in the Upper House, in order to find employment for the overplus labourers in the corn-growing districts; also the Emigration Committee arrayed before the Board of Trade, &c. Again, the silk throwing and weaving has been an asylum to hundreds, if not thousands of persons once engaged in the cotton trade, but, owing to the invention and improvement of machinery have been thrown out of employment, and turned to the silk trade for a morsel of bread.

11765. What do you know of smuggling, and what is your opinion concerning the smuggler?—I know nothing of it practically.

11766. Are

John Wright.

20 July,
1832.

11766. Are you particularly acquainted with the qualities and kinds of silk thrown in this country as compared with those imported from foreign parts as thrown silk, and what is your opinion of the mode of throwing in this country, is it inferior to the works on the Continent?—It is rather superior.

11767. In case the finest silks from France and other parts of the Continent could be brought into England in a raw state at as low a duty as the Italian raw silks are now brought, do you believe that your mills and the mills of the country could throw their raw silks into as good thrown silk as is now imported from Italy? —I believe we could, rather better.

11768. Has there been any change in the sort of silk and the mode of throwing within the last few years?—Yes, a very great change.

11769. Before the alteration of duty, what was the mill you were acquainted with, and what was it in the habit of throwing?—One mill I have the oversight of was, prior to the alteration, employed principally, if not altogether, with the very best Bergam silks.

11770. For what market were those silks thrown?—For the London market; for a gentleman of the name of Christie.

11771. Since that period has there been any change?—There has been a very great change; we have been obliged to throw all sorts of inferior silks, coarse round silks of Bengal and China and Persia, giving less employ, less wages, and less profits.

11772. For what market are they thrown?—Some for London, some for Manchester; the inferior goods are a sort of gros de Naples.

11773. Are you aware whether your master threw on the account of manufacturers before 1824, or on his own account?—It was principally by commission for manufacturers at a distance.

11774. Does he throw on his own account now or by commission?—Both.

11775. Has he very much ceased to throw the Italian raw silks?—Scarcely a bale comes; the little fellows dance for joy when they see an Italian bale come in; the employer seems to be overjoyed when he sees Italian silks come into his warehouse.

11776. How many hands are there employed in the mills you superintend?— Ninety-five.

11777. What is the average rate of wages paid to them?—The average rate of wages are about 4 s. 6 d.

11778. What are the ages?—They are from seven years old to 40.

11779. What is the lowest rate of wages, and what is the highest?—The lowest rate of wages is 1 s. per week, and the highest is 10 s.; in 1824, the highest rate of wages was 20 s. and the lowest was about 2 s. or 2 s. 6 d.

11780. Was the rate of wages the same for some years previous?—I remember wages remarkably steady; in 1810, I had 10 s. for piecing, at what is called spinning mills; in 1824, there was paid about the same price for the same work.

11781. Then there had been little alteration from 1810 to 1824?—No great deal.

### John Middlehurst, called in; and Examined.

John Middlehurst.

11782. ARE you employed as an operative throwster at Macclesfield?—I have been employed in that business about 24 years.

11783. Can you state to the Committee whether the throwing trade has been steady or otherwise during the time you have been so employed?—It was a steady and remunerative employment prior to the legislative interference of 1826.

11784. Do you consider the distress of the silk trade to have been occasioned by the operation of these laws?—I do; for in the first place it has destroyed the finer fabric of manufacture, and thereby diminished the demand for the finer qualities of thrown silk; in the second place, the rate of duty on foreign thrown silk is so low that it gives the Italian throwster, coupled with the advantage of a first pick of silk, the exclusive command of the British market.

11785. Do you think if there was a higher duty imposed on foreign thrown silk so as to prevent the importation of it, the manufacturer would get as good silk in point of quality and workmanship, as he now gets from Italy?—I am of opinion the manufacturer would get a better article, for this reason, the English throwster would then get good raw silk from Italy, and from my own knowledge of the two, there is no comparison in point of workmanship, between the Italian and English thrown silk, and I have past a great quantity through my hands lately, and remarked

678.                                                                                                  to

*John Middlehurst.*

20 July,
1832.

to the person who owned it, it would be exceedingly lessy in consequence of its being so badly got up; the party said he was aware of it, but the price and quality was a sufficient inducement. My opinion is, if the Government goes on to encourage the Italian throwster, he will get the better of this imperfection, and then I do not know what we shall do.

11786. To what extent have the wages of people employed in the silk trade of Macclesfield been reduced?—The workmen have been reduced from 50 to 70 per cent since the legislative interference of which I before spoke, thousands are thrown out of employ and have nothing to subsist on but what they get from the parish, and the applicants for relief have been so numerous that the overseers have been obliged to refuse relief to those applicants who could earn 2 s. 6 d. per week.

11787. Do you not think that the reduction in wages has been greater than the state of the trade required?—I believe it has not; in my opinion the master throwsters have been the greatest sufferers.

11788. What means have you of knowing that such a necessity does exist on the part of the master throwsters?—The situation I hold is such that my employers necessarily put confidence in me; I can state from my own knowledge that the price paid for throwing Italian silk has been reduced from 60 to 70 per cent., in addition to this, the poor rates have been trebled, and they frequently have to stand still for three or four months for want of silk. I know many throwsters who came into the trade with a capital of some hundreds who are now dependent on the parish for support, and others are obliged to work at any thing they can get however humble, to prevent further degradation; I may just mention one throwster who had several hundred pounds embarked in the throwing trade, was sweeping the streets as a common scavenger, on the day that I left Macclesfield to give evidence before this Committee, he came to me and desired I would impress on the Committee the necessity of extending relief to the trade, by which alone he could ever expect to be relieved from his present degradation and misery which had been his lot for three years. I know one spirited proprietor who, in 1829, actually gave the throwsters who occupied his mills the use of the mill and engine to work for themselves, they accepted the offer, and worked it as long as they could, at last they were under the necessity of asking the proprietor to put the engine in repair, being themselves unable to do so.

11789. What mill was that?—The Soho mill at Macclesfield, which is a very large mill, and is capable of doing a great deal of work, the machine there is uncommonly good, and is able to throw silk as cheap as any other throwing mill provided it was protected.

11790. What was the horse power employed in the throwing trade of Macclesfield in 1824, and up to the present period?—In 1824, it was 575; in 1828, 333; in 1831, 255; and in 1832, 244, being a diminution of the horse power from 1824 to 1832, of 331.

11791. What were the number of hands employed in 1824, and what at the present period?—In 1824, it was 10,229, whose actual earnings were 11 s. per week; in 1828 and 1829, 5,254, whose net earnings were 5 s. 5 d.: I must remark here, that the time was reduced from 76 to 66 hours per week; in 1831, 3,762; the earnings at the usual time of working 76 hours might have been 5 s., but their being reduced to 44 hours, the average earnings were two-elevenths in 1832 of what they were in 1831, only the number of hands had decreased to 3,610.

11792. Is not the throwing trade of Macclesfield distressed in consequence of its being transferred to some other place?—I do not believe the trade has been transferred to any other place but Italy; I know there has been a great deal said about Manchester's absorbing and sucking in the trade of the country; I know that the throwing trade of Macclesfield has not been distressed by Manchester; there has been no material increase there since 1824. I am aware there are two new mills built very lately, but one of them is to supplant an old one, and the other for the purpose of manufacturing ferrets, galloons, and doubles by steam, and only a small portion to throw such a silk as will enable them, the proprietors, to complete small orders; such orders as it is not worth while to give out small quantity of silk to throw to enable them to complete.

11793. When you say galloons, do you mean shoe-strings?—I think ferrets are more usually used for shoe-strings; galloons are what they bind shoes with.

11794. Do you know what has been the horse power at work in the silk mills at Manchester?—The horse power at Manchester was 138 in May last.

11795. How

*John Middlehurst.*

20 July,
1832.

11795. How did you ascertain that?—By going to the several proprietors of the mills, who gave me their horse power, where I could see the proprietors; in many instances, where I did not see the proprietors, I took it from the managers.

11796. How many horse power is there out of work at Macclesfield?—Three hundred and thirty-one.

11797. Do you think that the trade has been very little carried from Macclesfield to Manchester?—I do, and I have the best authority for thinking so; when I heard it stated that there was a superiority in the Manchester manufacture, which gave them a decided advantage, I went there to ascertain how such an assertion was borne out by facts; I had access to several mills, and I found the principle exactly the same at Macclesfield, being merely a transfer from wood to iron, and from leathern straps to cotton bands.

11798. There is no improvement of any importance?—Of no actual importance; I also went to several proprietors, and they all told me they could not throw silk as cheap as they could get it thrown at Macclesfield.

11799. What is the difference of speed at Macclesfield and Manchester?—The difference is nothing; we have machinery at Macclesfield going as rapid as any at Manchester

11800. Did you see all the mills at Manchester?—I saw several.

11801. Did you see Mr. Royle's?—I was in it but I did not see the machinery; other mills boasted of having as good machinery as Mr. Royle's, and told me their speed was exactly the same as his.

11802. Were you ever in treaty with any of the Manchester throwsters for the superintendance of their mills?—I was, but I did not engage, the wages offered not being sufficient; the party told me he should be glad to give me what I wanted, but the trade was in such a state, owing to the unjust interference of Government, that he should be glad to dispose of his machinery at a very great sacrifice.

11803. In what year was that?—In 1827; I wish to observe, I got a friend of mine to see how cheap he would throw a pound of silk of 30 deniers, he put the persons he worked to throw it at the lowest wages, and when the people know it is piece work that is a necessary stimulus to exertion, it cost him 2s. 9d. labour, besides rent and turning, and incidental expenses.

11804. What is the difference between the price of wages at Macclesfield and Manchester?—There is not any material difference.

11805. In what way can you throw silk cheaper at Macclesfield than at Manchester?—I do not know whether it is in consequence of the better judgment of the Macclesfield people. In proof of the distress of themselves, at various times, I took a statement from a Macclesfield throwster, he allowed me to examine his books from 1818 to the present period.

*[The Witness delivered in the following Table:]*

### SILK into ORGANZINE.

| Year | s. | d. | Year | s. | d. |
|---|---|---|---|---|---|
| 1818 | 8 | 6 | 1826 | 5 | – |
| 1819 | 8 | – | 1827 | 4 | 6 |
| 1820 | 8 | – | 1828 | 4 | – |
| 1821 | 8 | – | 1829 | 4 | – |
| 1822 | 8 | – | 1830 | 5 | – |
| 1823 | 8 | – | 1831 | 3 | 6 |
| 1824 | 7 | 6 | 1832 | 3 | 6 |
| 1825 | 10 | 6 | | | |

11806. You are at present engaged in a mill?—I am.

11807. What number of hands are employed in it?—I do not know the precise number of hands.

11808. But about what?—I am what is termed a maker up, and I make up for more persons than one; I have access to two or three mills, and I enjoy the confidence of the whole, therefore I can speak more generally.

11809. Did not the silk people at Manchester go to cotton, when their wages were too low?—I believe they did, they originally came from the cotton; when they are not sufficiently remunerated in silk, they return to cotton again.

11810. And the silk people at Macclesfield do the same?—No; they have no other means of living but by silk weaving.

11811. Are

*John Middlehurst.*

20 July,
1832.

11811. Are the wages liable to be lower at Macclesfield than at Manchester?—I think they are, owing to that circumstance.

11812. Did you hear last year of a very large house at Manchester stopping when the mill was turning off hands, and buying foreign thrown at a cheaper price than they were throwing?—I did.

11813. Did you know that was the case?—I knew that was the case.

### *John Kelly,* called in ; and Examined.

*John Kelly.*

11814. WHERE do you live?—At Manchester.

11815. Did you sign the petition presented to the House of Commons, from the silk weavers of Manchester?—I did.

11816. You are a silk weaver?—Yes.

11817. How long have you been a silk weaver?—Twenty-seven years.

11818. What length of time have you been in Manchester?—Since 1819.

11819. Can you inform the Committee what has been the state of the silk weavers in Manchester, from that period to the commencement of the free trade system?—In 1819, the state of the broad silk weavers gradually increased until 1825; in those years the weavers were generally employed, and the prices for weaving afforded themselves and their families a comfortable subsistence to live upon.

11820. What was your average earnings per week from 1819 to 1825?—I was for three or four years employed in the figured branch of neat silk weaving, it simply means this, it is not spun silk. My earnings for these years were upwards of 1 *l.* per week, clear of all deductions for winding, candle-light, and so forth. When I was employed in the plain work, my average earnings were from 16 *s.* to 17 *s.* per week, clear of all deductions.

11821. What are your average earnings per week at this time?—For the last two years my average earnings have been 6 *s.* 9 *d.* not deducting candle light, &c.

11822. Is that in plain or figured goods?—The plain branches.

11823. What was the average earnings of silk weavers generally, before the free trading system commenced?—They have been nearly the same as my earnings, when both in the figured and plain branches.

11824. What are the average earnings of silk weavers generally at this time?—From 6 *s.* to 7 *s.*, varying only as they are more or less employed, not deducting for winding, candle light and so forth.

11825. To what cause do you attribute your present distress, and the low prices paid for weaving?—Principally to the introduction of foreign wrought silks, which have had a tendency to reduce the price of weaving above one-half since 1825, a list of which I hold in my hand, and will give in; I beg leave to make one or two observations on this list. When the introduction of foreign wrought silks came in, in 1826, then our prices fell, and the weavers feeling they had so much taken from their wages, in 1827 they formed a union, and in consequence of the union we advanced our prices, and maintained that until the duty came off again in 1829, and then we were reduced to the prices here stated in 1831 and 1832.

[*The Witness delivered in the following Lists.*]

| | Inches. | Reed. | Price for Weaving, per Shawl. | | | | | | | | |
|---|---|---|---|---|---|---|---|---|---|---|---|
| | | | 1822. | 1827. | 1832. | 1825. | 1827. | 1832. | 1824. | 1826. | 1832. |
| | | | *s. d.* | *s. d.* | *s. d.* | *s. d.* | *s. d.* | *s. d.* | *s. d.* | *s. d.* | *s. d.* |
| Damask shawls - | 56 | 1,800 | 4  6 | 2  10 | 1  9 | — | — | — | — | — | — |
| Canton Crape Shawls, Centre pattern - - | 71 | 1,800 | - - | - - | - - | 12 - | 5 - | 3 - | — | — | — |
| Genappe Shawls 4 pattern - - | 56 | | - - | - - | - - | - - | - - | - - | 6 - | 4 - | 1  9 |
| Cord Shawls - - | 60 | 1,800 | - - | - - | - - | - - | - - | - - | 6 - | 3  3 | 1  4 |

*John Kelly.*

20 July, 1832.

| NAMES OF WORKS. | Inches. | 1822-3-4. | 1826. | 1827. | 1829. | 1831. | 1832. |
|---|---|---|---|---|---|---|---|
| | | s. d. | s. d. | s. d. | s. d. | s. d. | |
| 4 Doubles Gros de Naples | - - | - 11 | - 6 | — | | | — |
| 3 Ditto - - ditto - - | - - | - 11 | - 5½ | - 7 | - 5½ | - 5 | — |
| 3 Singles - ditto - - | - - | - 10 | - 5 | - 6½ | - 5 | - 4½ | — |
| 2 Ditto - - ditto - - | - - | - 7 | - 4 | - 5 | - 4 | 3½d. to 3d. | — |
| White and Coloured Persians - - - | 18 | - 4½ | - 2½ | - 3½ | 3d. to 2½d. | 2½d. to 2d. | — |
| Black ditto - - - | - - | - 5 | - 3½ | - 4 | - 3 | - 2½ | — |
| Black fringed Handkerchiefs, per doz. - - | 29 | 6 6 | 5 - | 5 9 | 4 - | 3 - | — |
| Ditto - - - | 31 | 7 6 | 6 - | 6 3 | 4 6 | 4 - | — |
| Ditto - - - | 33 | 8 6 | 6 6 | 6 9 | 4 9 | 4 6 | — |
| Ditto - - - | 35 | 9 6 | 7 - | 7 6 | 5 6 | 5 3 | — |

Three Threads, paid and reduced in the same proportion.

| NAMES OF WORKS. | Inches. | 1822-3-4. | 1826. | 1827. | 1829. | 1831. | 1832. |
|---|---|---|---|---|---|---|---|
| Turbans, Handkerchiefs - | 29 | 8 - | 5 9 | 6 - | 5 - | 4 6 | — |
| Ditto - - - | 30 | 8 6 | 6 - | 6 6 | 5 3 | 4 9 | |
| | 34 | 10 - | 7 6 | 8 - | 6 - | 5 6 | |

Breadth under and over, paid and reduced in same proportion.

| NAMES OF WORKS. | Inches. | 1822-3-4. | 1826. | 1827. | 1829. | 1831. | 1832. |
|---|---|---|---|---|---|---|---|
| Romal Handkerchiefs - | 27 | 6 6 | - - | 4 9 | - - | 3 - | — |
| Ditto - - - | 29 | 7 3 | - - | 5 3 | - - | 3 3 | — |
| Ditto - - - | 31 | 8 3 | - - | 5 10 | - - | 4 - | — |
| Ditto - - - | 34 | 10 - | - - | 7 6 | - - | 4 6 | — |

Nothing for Shuttles now, let there be ever so many.

| NAMES OF WORKS. | Inches. | 1822-3-4. | 1826. | 1827. | 1829. | 1831. | 1832. |
|---|---|---|---|---|---|---|---|
| Stitch Romals - - - | - - | - - | - - | - - | - - | 8 - | 6s. to 5s. |

| NAMES OF WORKS. | Inches. | 1822-3-4. | 1826. | 1827. | 1829. | 1831. | 1832. |
|---|---|---|---|---|---|---|---|
| Welsh Shawls - - - | 31 | - - | - - | 6 9 | - - | 4 9 | — |
| Ditto - - - | 33 | - - | - - | 7 3 | - - | 5 3 | — |
| Ditto - - - | 35 | - - | - - | 7 10 | - - | 5 9 | — |

Three Threads, paid and reduced in the same proportion.

| NAMES OF WORKS. | Inches. | 1822-3-4. | 1826. | 1827. | 1829. | 1831. | 1832. |
|---|---|---|---|---|---|---|---|
| Barcelonas, figured - - | 24 | - - | - - | 4 6 | 2 9 | 2 6 | — |
| 8 Shafts - ditto - - | 26 | - - | - - | 5 - | 3 - | 2 9 | — |
| Coloured, twilled - - | 26 | 6 - | - - | 4 9 | 4 - | 2 6 | — |
| Culgees, per cut - - | 36 | 3 - | - - | 2 6 | - - | 2s. to 1s. 9d. | — |
| Ditto - - - | 40½ | 4 1 | - - | 2 9 | - - | 2s. 3d. to 2s. | — |
| Cop Culgees - - - | - - | 2 6 | - - | 2 - | - - | 1s. 2d. to 1s. | — |

In the second place, we have not been as well employed since these measures came into operation. I have taken a calculation for two years since they came into operation; I find I have waited for work nearly six months in two years, and the weaver generally has been in the same situation.

11826. When you speak of a second reduction of duties, you allude to 1829?—Yes.

11827. If the silk weaving in Manchester and its neighbourhood be so unprofitable why do you not leave it?—There are some to whom an opportunity has presented itself, and they have availed themselves of it; others, I am sorry to say, have taken their employers' work, and have sold it to support themselves and families until they could obtain a better employment; but generally speaking, a poor weaver, with his family, cannot shift, particularly when he is in debt with his neighbours and friends, taking into account that he has no cash to shift with, therefore he is compelled to bear the burthen that others have placed on him; and his case is still aggravated to believe the cotton weaver better off than himself.

11828. If the silk trade of this country has a greater protection given to it by law, in your opinion, would that have a tendency to increase employment?—I should think so; and as a proof of this, I have only to refer to the prosperity and comfort the trade yielded to the masters and workmen in those years when we had a protection by law; the workmen could then obtain a fair remuneration for their labour on all goods made, whether they were of the same description of goods made in London or not; from these circumstances, coupled with the facts of the case which have been laid before this honourable Committee, I am therefore of the same

678.                                                                 opinion

opinion with those on whose behalf I now appear before you, that if we have not a greater protection given to us as a trade generally, our case is hopeless, and we shall be doomed to misery and starvation all the days of our life. Permit me here to make a remark, at the present time a silk weaver is a person looked on with contempt; if I am asked the reason why, it is not because they are dishonest generally, but because he has no money, and the means of obtaining so small a pittance weekly; this was not the case before the measures of 1826 came into operation; then they could pay their way and appeared respectable, and formed a part of civil society which did credit to themselves. Since the introduction of the free trade measures, he has been obliged to go to the parish to receive a small pittance to maintain himself and his family. I may say scores have been placed in that situation.

11829. You mean to say that he is obliged to make up out of the poor rates for the deficiency of what he receives for his labour?—Yes.

11830. Are you aware that in former times the silk weavers in Manchester and Macclesfield, and Spitalfields, used to have premiums given to them by respectable tradesmen to teach their sons the art of weaving?—Yes, I have known instances of that; I myself served my time to a silk weaver, and I have known cases where money has been given by way of premium to teach persons.

11831. Is that the case now?—No; on the contrary, as many as could find any sort of employment endeavour to leave it.

11832. You say, if you had more protection, it would tend to increase your wages, in what way?—If fewer foreign goods were to come in, and the foreigner was compelled to pay a higher duty than at present, there would be more for us to make; and the foreign goods, being dearer, would as a matter of course tend to so increase our wages.

11833. Can you remember when the silk weaving was at the greatest extent in Manchester?—I should think in 1823, 1824 and 1825; and had it not been for the introduction of foreign wrought silks, I am of opinion its prosperity would have continued.

11834. Do you consider that in the last year as many goods have been made at Manchester as in the years 1823, 1824 and 1825?—No, if that had been so, there would not have been so many hundreds of persons walking about the streets, both in town and country. I beg leave here to make an observation: previous to the introduction of foreign wrought silks, when we took our work home weekly, we had to wait three, four, five or six hours before our work was taken in to the warehouse and we received our wages; at the present time a weaver may get fitted in an hour or an hour and a half, which proves there are not so many workmen employed as formerly.

11835. Were the silk goods in 1823, 1824 and 1825 for garments, or of what description mostly?—For garments chiefly, also figured and plain gros de Naples, also handkerchiefs and figured shawls.

11836. Is the figured branches at Manchester on the increase or decrease?—On the decrease; at the latter end of 1823 I worked for Messrs. Wilson & Williams; they at that time lent me 10*l.*, to put a figured scarf to work; I did so, and paid for the machinery, and obtained a good living: for these last eight years it has been laying useless.

11837. Were the goods made in 1823, 1824 and 1825 of as good a quality as those made at present?—No.

11838. Do you see handsome rich silks in the shop windows at St. Ann's-square at Manchester?—Yes, of various descriptions, plain and figured, with labels on them; rich French silks.

11839. Did you ever see any of this description making by the weavers in your neighbourhood?—No.

11840. Are there not many manufacturers employing looms that were not known in 1825?—Yes, but that does not prove that the trade has increased, for this reason: the same manufacturers have left the weaving department, either in the whole or part, also many old establishments do not employ half as many weavers as they did before our trade was thrown open to foreign competition, so that the new manufacturers employ only a part of the looms thrown out of work, and the rest remain idle.

11841. What description of broad silks were you employed in before 1826?—Previous to 1826 I was employed in making figured scarfs half a yard wide, and figured garments a yard wide, and figured handkerchiefs.

11842. Were

11842. Were these of the highest description of figured silks?—Yes, especially the handkerchiefs and the garments.

11843. What description of silk was used in the manufacture?—Those I made into handkerchiefs and garments was Piedmont, especially by the master, to accomplish his own orders.

11844. Do you consider that the quality of plain goods manufactured now in Manchester is superior or inferior to the quality of plain goods manufactured before 1826?—Inferior.

11845. Is the silk employed in this manufacture Piedmont or Bengal?—I am not able to speak to that at the present moment; in 1823 and 1824 we had neat silk dyed; we have now supples, that is to say, the silk has not the whole of the gum boiled out of it.

11846. Are the figured goods now made in Manchester of neat silk, or a mixture?—I am not aware that there are any making of neat silk; there may be some few, but they are very few in comparison with what were made previously.

*John Kelly,*

20 July, 1832.

## *John Scott*, called in; and Examined.

11847. ARE you a silk weaver residing at Manchester?—Yes.

11848. How long have you been a silk weaver?—Better than 15 years.

11849. When did you come to Manchester?—In the beginning of 1821.

11850. Did you sign a petition presented to the House of Commons?—I did.

11851. Where did you live before you came to Manchester?—In Dublin.

11852. Were you engaged in the silk trade there?—Yes, about three years.

11853. What was the state of the silk trade of Dublin before you came to Manchester?—In a most depressed condition; indeed it was almost annihilated.

11854. And to what cause do you ascribe that great depression?—To the repeal of the protection duties, for while they existed the manufacturer could make goods at some profit, but no sooner were they repealed than all the mercers' shops were crowded with English silks; nearly all the manufacturers became insolvent; the weavers were thrown destitute of employment, and compelled to seek work in Manchester and elsewhere; but for that reason I would not have been here: my father was in business at that time; he fell a victim to the free-trade system which was brought about between England and Dublin.

11855. When you came to Manchester, did you find the silk trade in a prosperous state?—Yes, so much so that I found not the least difficulty in obtaining employment; I had work that I could earn 18 s. a week at, and if I had the same work now I could not earn half that sum; it was the best silk that could be got, whereas what we have now is of the coarsest sort.

11856. What length of time did that state of things continue?—It continued with growing prosperity until near 1826.

11857. What was the general condition of the Manchester weavers prior to 1826?—Their condition was vastly better than what it is now; they had constant employment and a reasonable price for doing it.

11858. Have not the weavers been as well employed since the free trade measures, as they were before?—No, quite the reverse; for before that time as the weavers increased in number employment kept pace with the increase, and we seldom waited for warps; and as a proof that our employment was more permanent, and not subject to these great fluctuations which we have since experienced, I will relate an incident that will substantiate what I say; it was customary to stile the weavers by the particular branch to which they had been confined, such as those who wove black handkerchiefs, were called black handkerchief weavers, and those who wove sarsnet or gros de Naples, were called sarsnet or gros de Naples weavers, from the length of time that they were known to weave that work without changing to other descriptions, and it was the same with the other branches of weaving; but it is far different now, for the weavers generally, and particularly in the handkerchief branch, not only have to wait a considerable time for work, but are kept in suspense as to what kind they must start next; so that when a weaver gets a different sort, which is almost invariably the case, he undergoes an additional loss of time and expense before he can earn a penny for himself.

11859. What is the present condition of the weavers at Lancashire?—Their condition is most distressing, though many of them may have work now, their wages are so trifling, that they are not able to procure a sufficiency of the coarsest necessaries of life, much less repair the evils they have rendered while out of employment.

*John Scott.*

ployment.

*John Scott:*

20 July,
1832.

ployment. I perhaps have a better opportunity of knowing their condition than many; a few weeks since I visited nearly all the weavers' places in Manchester and Salford, and I cannot describe the misery I witnessed; their garrets were without furniture, in many instances there was no bed, and nothing but their looms; previous to 1826, I very well recollect, that the weavers generally used to provide themselves with a week's provision at once, now that is not the case; they have to make a meal after meal just as they can.

11860. How do you know the condition of so large a population, spread over the weaving districts of Lancashire?—I very well know their condition; I am acquainted with numbers from all parts, their appearance, together with their complaints, and the many times I have been in their districts, afford me a better opportunity than most men of knowing their situation, and I must say that it is hard for such a number of honest, peaceable and industrious artisans to be plunged into such a depth of misery and want which they have been ever since the admission of foreign wrought silks. I know there are some, who endeavour to prove, that the evils we complain of arise from different causes to what we ascribe them, and that others go so far as to say that the silk trade is not at all in such a distressed condition as is represented; but it is impossible to make a reflecting mind believe, that the great reduction, which has been made in his wages, proceeded from any other cause than that which we assign, namely, the introduction of foreign wrought silks; knowing as we do that cheap labour was the primary object of those who brought about the system.

11861. You have alluded to having gone through the country on business relative to the union, what did you mean by that?—Relative to the union of the silk weavers, formed to protect their wages.

11862. Do you consider the master manufacturer as good a judge of the condition of his work people as a workman is?—I do not; for a weaver will never disclose the particulars of his situation to his employers, which he will freely do to a fellow sufferer, and even if he would, experience makes a deeper impression than a mere knowledge of the case can.

11863. Is there any difference of opinion among the weavers, as to the cause of their present distress?—I do not know that there is; I am inclined to believe there is not among the thinking part of the weavers of Manchester.

11864. How do you know there is no difference of opinion in Manchester as to the cause of your present condition?—From frequent intercourse among them, and from petitions that have been sent to Parliament.

11865. Can you inform the Committee how many looms there were weaving for Manchester, previous to 1826?—From the best of my knowledge there were about 9,000 in 1824 and 1825.

11866. How many looms do you suppose there are now?—Not more than 9,000 or 10,000 when they are all at work.

11867. Do you mean silk looms, or silk and mixed?—The 9,000 in 1824 and 1825 were mixed, and neat silk looms, and the same now.

11868. Can you state the number of silk looms, at both periods, as distinguished from silk and cotton?—There were about 5,000 or 6,000 in 1824 and 1825.

11869. Can you state how many there are now of that description?—About the same.

11870. Do you mean to say there are 5,000 or 6,000 employed in silk only, and the remainder in silk and mixed?—Yes.

11871. How can you prove there are no more looms at work in Manchester now than there were in 1824 and 1825?—I do not consider that the introduction of French silk had at all a tendency to increase the number of looms, but rather the contrary effect: and as a proof that they have not increased in Lancashire, I will relate a circumstance that took place there. In 1826 we commenced our union, in which we inrolled about 6,000 looms, and it was computed, that with the bandannas, the shawl, and a few others that were never in the union, there could not be less than 3,000, making in all 9,000.

11872. How was that computed?—It was calculated that the bandannas and shawl looms, and some few others, that were unwilling to join the union, were about 3,000.

11873. Did you take the numbers, or how was it managed?—We had meetings, at stated times, composed of delegates from every district; I have been there some scores of times, and the delegates gave in the numbers of those in their districts who were in, and those who were out of the union.

11874. It

John Scott.

20 July,
1832.

11874. It has been stated that Manchester employs 15,000, is it not possible for them to have increased to that number since 1826?—It was also stated then that there were but 6,000 weaving for Manchester in 1824, and as I have endeavoured to show that in 1826 there were 9,000, it is very difficult to account for the great reduction that took place in the price of weaving, seeing that labour must have increased one-half in the demand, and consequently should have prevented the reduction; and it is yet more difficult to account for the still greater reduction in wages when we find that from 9,000 they have increased to 15,000; but the truth is, there can be no such number, for when I come to calculate the weight of silk that 15,000 looms would work up in a year, I find that it would take nearly double the quantity of silk to what I apprehend is worked up by Manchester. Suppose there to be 9,000 gros de Naples looms, each weaving twenty-four yards a week, at 1 oz. to a yard; 2,500 bandanna looms at four cuts each, or 32 oz. per week; 3,500 mixed and other neat silk goods, such as black handkerchiefs, Welsh shawls, romals and some few other looms of neat silk goods, 3,500 at an average of 12 oz. of each per week, the weight of silk for fifty weeks will be 1,056,250, allowing the weaver to earn from 6s. to 8s. including expenses of every kind. I have stated the number to be 9,000 or 10,000, and supposing 10,000 to be regularly employed, making the same length and weight of work, for instance, gros de Naples looms, 4,500; bandannas, 2,500; mixed and other goods, 3,000; the weight these looms would work up in fifty weeks is 700,000 lbs. The mills of Manchester are reckoned to throw 350,000 lbs. per annum, and reckoning them to purchase 200,000 lbs. which is as much as they do, 10,000 looms must play more than one-fourth of their time; and the honourable Committee must recollect I have not taken into account the small ware trade, the fringe trade, and the sewing trade, which would take perhaps 60,000 or 70,000 lbs. more; neither have I taken the silk wholly in the raw, so that according to this calculation there cannot be the number of looms that have been stated.

11875. Are not all the looms fully at work?—No, they are not, particularly in the handkerchief branch; and I would here inform the honourable Committee that that part of the trade has become nearly extinct when compared with what it was.

11876. You do not mean bandannas?—No, silk handkerchiefs that are not made for printing; they come out of the loom ready to wear; they are made from dyed silk.

11877. But does not the increase in the gros de Naples stand as a substitute for the handkerchief branch?—I do not believe there are a greater number of gros making now than there were of other descriptions making then for the same purpose, the greater part of which are not making now, and consequently the gros cannot be a substitute for the handkerchief trade.

11878. What were the descriptions of goods making then which you say the gros have substituted?—There were vast quantities of figured sarsnet, yard wide, plain and figured sarsnet dresses, which have all gone down; three and four doubles, very few of which are making at present, and a great many three singles, called gros now.

11879. Did you make rich gros, or three and four doubles, so far back as 1822?—I made three and four doubles, in 1822, for Messrs. Benjamin & Thomas Williams, and I know they had a great many making at that time.

11880. Were they of a better quality in 1822 as compared with what are making now?—I think there is but little comparison, they were made of a far superior silk, and I know the weavers liked them better.

11881. Do you consider that a weaver has a better knowledge of the quality generally making, than a master can have individually?—He must necessarily have a better knowledge generally of what is making, and also of the quality, for while a master sees only his own work, a weaver has an opportunity of seeing the work of all the masters, by going into the weavers' workshops, as they frequently do.

11882. What are the description of goods making at present at Manchester?—Gros de Naples, two thread sarsnets, black handkerchiefs, romals, turbans or negligees, bandannas, Welsh shawls and some few looms of other kinds, besides the mixed looms of various sorts.

11883. What do you mean by romals?—The striped silk handkerchiefs that gentlemen wear round their necks.

11884. Are there not some rich figured gros making at Manchester?—I cannot state the exact number; I should think there are not many; the weavers told me

678.                                                                    that

*John Scott.*

20 July,
1832.

that the masters were stopping some, and the men were giving up others on their own account, for the prices were reduced.

11885. Are there any steam looms working silk in Manchester?—There was an attempt made by a very eminent person in Manchester, Mr. Royle, a man well respected by his work people and a very ingenious man; he made an attempt to start a steam loom; I know the person who worked on it while it was in operation; that loom has stopped, and the weaver is now weaving the warp in his own place; he lives in the same street that I do.

11886. How long is it since that loom stopped?—About six or seven weeks ago, as near as I can recollect.

11887. Have you ever seen any produce of that loom?—I have not.

11888. Has the weaver that worked at it told you what it made?—I do not know what was the cause of the loom being stopped; he told me it would not do; it was for weaving bandanna handkerchiefs.

11889. It was not in the higher branches of the trade?—No, the silk is of a superior quality, and it is picked and dressed ready for the steam loom; I do think, if there is a man in Lancashire capable of weaving silk by steam it is Mr. Royle; he is a very ingenious man.

11890. How many out of the 9,000 employed in weaving silk are employed on neat silk?—I believe between 5,000 and 6,000.

11891. In the figured branches of trade at Manchester are they chiefly employed in mixed or in neat silks?—Nearly all in mixed goods.

11892. Of a light description?—Yes.

11893. In which a very small quantity of silk was used?—Very small; they are two-thirds cotton; in some cases more.

11894. What is the quality of the figured manufactured silk now made at Manchester?—China and Bengal alone.

11895. What may be the selling price of it?—I cannot say.


*Jonathan Sisson*, Esq. called in; and Examined.

*Jonathan Sisson,*
Esq.

11896. WHERE do you reside?—In Dublin.

11897. Are you engaged in the silk trade?—In the early part of my life I was engaged in the silk trade, and at subsequent periods I was for several years an importer of raw and organzine silks.

11898. Were you ever in the throwing line?—Never.

11899. How long were you engaged in the silk trade?—For several years in the importation of raw and thrown silk to Dublin, which I sold to the silk manufacturers; I am not at present connected in trade.

11900. Did you continue to be a manufacturer at the time you were a merchant?—Certainly not.

11901. When you commenced business as a silk merchant, how long did you continue in it?—I commenced about 1816 or 17, and continued in it about nine or ten years.

11902. When did you give up the business?—I continued importing till the year 1826.

11903. What induced you to give up your connexion with the trade?—I found the silk trade rapidly declining in Dublin and persons preparing to quit the business, besides which there was little or no profit to be realized; on the last silk I imported there was a considerable loss.

11904. What reason do you assign for your importations of raw and thrown silk being less profitable than formerly so as to induce you to abandon it?—The operation of two measures; the first was the sudden and unexpected repeal of the union protecting duties and the admission of foreign silk into Great Britain and Ireland; the effect of the former was to inundate Ireland with the British fabric, and the effect of the latter with French fabrics; there was consequently little room left for the existence of either the importer or the manufacturer in Dublin, besides which, the British manufactures about this time were sent to Dublin in large quantities and sold by auction at destructive prices.

11905. To what do you attribute the latter circumstance?—To the distress among the silk trade of England, who improved the opportunity then opened of getting rid of their heavy stocks.

11906. What was the cause of the loss on the importation of silks to which you allude?—Some of my former answers have in a great degree replied to that question,

but

but there is another which goes to what has mainly contributed to this loss; namely, the sudden reduction of duties on thrown silk by Treasury order in November 1825, from 7 s. 6 d. to 5 s. per pound; the effect of such an additional shock as this being 50 per cent. on the duty, almost paralyzed the exertions of persons in the silk trade in holding on against such continued injurious legislative enactments; there was a want of confidence naturally created when such important changes were made without previous notice or Acts of Parliament being passed for their adoption.

*Jonathan Sisson,*
Esq.

———

20 July,
1832.

11907. Was the last importation of your's thrown or raw?—It was thrown; there were different bales, and of different descriptions.

11908. Have you since the period you allude to continued to inform yourself of the state of the silk trade in Dublin?—I am one of the representatives of the Corporation of Weavers in the Common Council of the city of Dublin, and it is my duty to attend to the trading interests of my constituents, besides which, permit me to say, though not personally interested, I could not but deeply deplore the calamitous appearances which presented themselves among the manufacturers of Dublin generally, particularly the silk ones. I therefore have devoted as much of my time as possible to ascertain the causes and extent of that distress, and if possible provide some remedy for the suffering state of a once prosperous and healthy trade.

11909. Having continued to inform yourself of the state of the trade in Dublin, what is it?—It continues still in a very depressed state; I believe I can best answer that question by giving in a statement I brought over here in the year 1824, of the number of looms then employed in Dublin; there was at that time in Dublin from the best computation I could make 1,200 broad silk looms of different kinds, and there were 996 ribbon machines; I took an account prior to leaving Dublin of the present number, and of broad, narrow and every description of loom, and there were only 150.

11910. Are you able to distinguish those that are used entirely for silk and those used for mixed goods?—The broad silk loom was principally engaged in the making sarsnets, velvets and Irish tabinets, and which we call part of our silk trade.

11911. Could you say out of the 1,200 what was used for silk goods, such as velvets and sarsnets, and what for tabinets and poplins?—I think if I was to say 400 it would be about the number; there was a good deal of throwing going on in Dublin in 1824, and there were about 10 silk mills then engaged, at the present time I think there is two.

11912. Was any computation ever made of the value of property invested in thrown silk in Ireland?—I do not think there was any particular computation, but generally speaking there was a very large proportion in the silk throwing; we had some very extensive factories; the trade was rapidly increasing in 1824, and exclusive of the mills which were in operation, a great number of silk mills were erected that have never come into use, but have gone to perfect destruction; I know one silk mill that cost something like 2,000 l. and the factory was sold in the year 1829 for under 50 l.; there was another factory, as extensive, and arriving to very great perfection; it was making Italian organzine silks very well indeed; the person became bankrupt, and the whole of that machinery, which cost about 4,000 l. was sold for 62 l.; when we look at the effects, we must charge them to the causes which we consider to have produced them, happening as they did so short a time before; the extent of distress in 1826 it is almost impossible for me to enumerate; in that year it was indeed an awful thing to go through the Liberties of Dublin. A meeting was called by a requisition to the Lord Mayor, and a large subscription made for these persons; the effect of the distress was tremendous; the number of beings huddled together as they were, without any thing to support them, created a famine; the dreadful fever of 1826, then called the famine fever, was the consequence, and Government was obliged at the end of that year to erect hospitals even in the fields to receive these people. What became of them it is difficult to say; great numbers fell a sacrifice to a premature death, others have amalgamated themselves into the common distress that Ireland abounds with, and have endeavoured to obtain some other kind of employment, I have seen them as news vendors and sweeping the streets; the Mendicity Institution in Dublin contains several of them. I was speaking to a throwster some time ago, and asking him how his business was going on, and whether he was doing any thing; he said he had some ten hands employed. I asked him where he got these persons when he wanted them; why, said he, whenever any stir of business comes, I send to the Mendicity, where I find these

678. people,

people, and instead of being engaged in an elegant nice trade like the silk trade, pulverizing oyster shells to manure the land.

11913. Can you state what has been the effects on the moral habits of females and others who formerly were employed at mills and other branches of the silk trade?—The effects on the moral feelings of the country are very awful; numbers of young females who were turned out of bread, and had no possible means of getting any support, were obliged to turn to prostitution; several have left the land of their nativity to seek employment in different parts of England, where I believe they have always been received with very great kindness, but still encountered great difficulties, as they had no claim on the poor laws of England, and were often disappointed in obtaining work. Some of them, who were obliged to come back from want of employment, are amalgamated, I may say, in one common mass of ruin and desolation.

11914. Were you ever engaged in any committees in Dublin to raise subscriptions to enable distressed weavers to find refuge in England?—Yes; in the year 1826, I was one of a committee under the Lord Mayor; in 1829, there was another scene of distress and another meeting called, and a committee was formed, who devoted part of the subscriptions received to that purpose, at the request of the operatives. In 1832, a meeting was also called, of which committee I am also a member, who allocated some of the funds for a similar purpose, but to a very trifling extent, as the accounts received from England did not hold out encouragement, from the low state of the silk trade there; the persons principally sent over were those who had friends or relations in England that could be of some assistance to them.

11915. Did these meetings more particularly relate to general distress, or the distress of the silk trade?—They related to general distress among the trades; but when we came to ascertain who were the principal persons seeking relief, we found the majority were persons who were or had been earning a support from the silk trade. It may not be amiss to mention that the last committee was for the purpose of providing against this lamentable evil the cholera morbus; as a member of that committee, I have not the least doubt that the disease was increased in the Liberty of Dublin by the distress to which I have already referred; I found the disease at the worst also in Ringsend, another part of Dublin, which had suffered in the same way from loss of employment, and trades that formerly existed there, which confirms my former opinion. In Ireland, the business is not so much carried on by factories as it is in England; each person is in the habit of having his loom at his own residence. As all the silk manufacture was carried on in that part of Dublin called the Liberty, something like Spitalfields, the house property which a great many of the silk weavers were possessed of has become almost valueless; there are whole streets nearly desolated; when the houses have fallen down they have not been considered worth rebuilding or preserving.

11916. Were these houses occupied by persons connected with the silk trade?— They were inhabited by persons of different trades, perhaps mostly by the silk branches; there are particular places, called Fordham's Alley and Skinner's Alley, which I walked through the other day, and most of the houses are down or falling; these places were formerly occupied principally by persons in the silk trade, and an extensive throwing factory of long standing had been established there; the occupier, a most respectable man, died lately, having lost his property, consisting chiefly in his factory and expensive machinery, which became nearly valueless since the changes in the duties on Italian thrown silks. Some gentleman in this country, who owned property in the Liberty, walked up lately to see where his property stood, but he could find no vestige of houses whatever. I possess some property there, and I begin to tremble even for the ground rents; I believe it would be as valuable to the Earl of Meath, who is the owner of it, if it were growing grass.

11917. Was not there distress, in former times, in the Liberty of Dublin?— Certainly.

11918. What was the cause of the former distress among the silk weavers of Dublin?—There were different causes; famine sometimes made its appearance in Ireland, and then of course distress was felt for a time; or the change of fashion, muslins for instance being worn instead of silks, was sometimes a cause. but when the causes ceased the effects ceased also, and trade returned to its natural prosperity; one of our late Secretaries, Lord Levison Gower, while in office, during this distress, said that there was no particular distress in Dublin but what had existed for 100 years, since the days of Bishop Pulter; that having been stated to the people of England, from whom I have always perceived the best feeling towards

Ireland,

*Jonathan Sisson,*
Esq.

20 July,
1832.

Ireland, when made truly acquainted with her real state and interests, I think it right to say that such was not the fact, the noble Lord was misinformed. There never was a period of any distress in the Liberty of Dublin, that lasted as it has now done since 1826 for six years, to the almost total extinction of its manufactures, the ruin of that part of the city where such manufactures exist, and the pauperism of so many thousands of its once prosperous inhabitants. I beg further to say, that some of the evidence taken by the late Committee on the state of the Irish poor, went nearly to the same effect, and also charges the decline of the silk trade of Dublin to the arrangement of wages under an Act analogous to the Spitalfields Act. This I beg to say is also incorrect, for the silk weavers of Dublin, in the year 1826, fearful of the importation of French silks, broke through all these former arrangements, and at a public meeting, where the Lord Mayor presided, of their own accord, agreed to reduce 15 per cent. on the prices then existing; and since that time the prices of weaving silk goods have been reduced still further, 30 to 40 per cent. The prices of weaving in Dublin, at present, are about the same as Macclesfield and Manchester. While on this subject, I beg to state, that there is a circumstance which the people of Ireland feel deeply as an additional cause of the present existing distress in the silk trade. A committee of manufacturers sat at my house, the day before I came here, under orders from this honourable Committee, and they said do state this fact: we feel it very severe that France should inundate us with her fabrics. I assure you there was no unkindly or jealous feeling among them, although they believe that the superior advantages and capital of England is more than Ireland can compete with. They referred particularly to French manufacture, and said, is it not a severe circumstance that we are inundated with the produce of the Lyonese loom, that we see our former customers clad in that fabric, and yet France will not take our commodity in return. I particularly allude to the Irish tabinet, which was actually prohibited. Since I came to town I have heard of some amelioration, but which if it be fact, still amounts to almost prohibition, as being, I am informed, between 50 and 60 per cent. duty on the value. In the year 1829, when I found the distress continuing, I came over at the suggestion of the silk manufacturers and operatives of Dublin, with a petition to Parliament, for an increase of duty on French silks, and remonstrating on the want of reciprocity in France; I waited on the then Prime Minister, the Duke of Wellington, and also on the then President of the Board of Trade, Mr. Vesey Fitzgerald, I particularly stated how Dublin would be benefited if an opening could be made for our manufacture into France. Since then I have been endeavouring to show the necessity of something of the kind being done, or that fabric which Ireland still excels in, will be altogether extinct in a little time. The silk trade of Great Britain petitioned, and remonstrated at the same period against a decrease of duty, and in favour of an increase on French silks, but I regret to say without effect.

11919. Do you think it would be a great advantage to the manufacturer of Ireland, if there was a reciprocal feeling on the part of France to receive the tabinets of Ireland?—May I be permitted to state a fact, which occurred just before I left Ireland. A lady of very great patriotism, who had been in France a short time before, waited on one of the manufacturers, to inform him, that if an opening could be made for Irish manufacture, she would herself find persons who would take 300 dresses which would be about 700 *l.*

11920. Do you think it would be a great advantage to the manufacture of Ireland?—So convinced were the Parliamentary Commissioners, appointed in 1821, and who sat in Dublin, on the necessity of upholding the tabinet manufacture, that in their Report it was recommended, that some change should be made for the encouragement of the export of that fabric; and I beg to submit, that in this view of the case, the subject is particularly connected with the present almost prohibitory regulations of France; permit me to say that no nation is justified in expecting commercial advantages to the detriment of that country whose liberality she does not think proper to imitate. For while Great Britain and Ireland are inundated with French manufactures, to the consequent loss of employment of the home operative weaver, the manufactures of Great Britain and Ireland (unless in some partial instances) are strictly prohibited from French Ports. Such an arrangement, may I be allowed to say, does not merit the appellation of free trade; it is free alone to the foreigner. A nation that principally involved the British Empire in the present enormous debt, is permitted commercial advantages which she denies to the British Empire, though that very debt is one cause of her inability to cope

678.                                                                                                   with

with other nations less incumbered and taxed than Great Britain, unless where in some cases British skill, perhaps aided by machinery, but with a sacrifice on profits, endeavours to support the unequal conflict.

11921. How long has the silk trade been established in Dublin?—It commenced in Dublin about the same time that it did in Spitalfields, and from the same causes. It was under the reign of Louis the Fourteenth, at the time the Protestants came over here.

11922. To what extent have you known the silk trade to flourish in Dublin?— I take the period of 1783, and in the average three years, 1781, 1782 and 1783, there were 114,525 lbs. of raw and thrown silk imported, which shows it to have been a trade of some moment; the imports of three years, was but 86,443 lbs.; from the year 1801 to 1821, the average amount of raw and thrown silk imported into Dublin annually, was 70,654 lbs., so that it appears to have been an increasing trade; from the number of looms at present employed partially, the amount of silk imported annually cannot exceed 7,000 to 8,000 lbs.

11923. From what countries did you import?—I believe from the same countries as London; from Italy, Turkey, and from the East Indies, &c.; but all payments came through London, and the silks are generally forwarded by the same channel, as few ships came direct, this raises the price on the Dublin manufacturer by commissions, transit of goods, &c.

### Mr. *William Beckwith*, called in; and Examined.

11924. IN what profession are you?—A silk manufacturer.

11925. Where do you carry on your business?—In Spital-square and Coggeshall in Essex.

11926. How long have you been engaged in the silk trade?—About 23 years, with the exception of four years, when I was engaged as a silk warehouseman.

11927. What has been the greatest number of looms you have employed?— About 250.

11928. In what branch of business have you employed your looms?—In nearly all the branches of the broad silk trade, but principally in the article of serge for coat linings, and in fancy waistcoatings and velvets.

11929. Have you ever been an importer of silks and fancy velvets?— I have, from Germany and France.

11930. Do you continue to import?—No, I left it off because I found that other importers could supply me at from 15 to 20 per cent. less than I could import for myself.

11931. Were they smugglers from whom you bought these cheap goods?—I have no direct knowledge of that; but I must presume that such was the case as I purchased for ready money.

11932. What description of goods were they?—Figured velvets for waistcoats, and figured silks.

11933. Are these the same description of goods you say you can purchase at a cheaper rate?—I did purchase the identical patterns from 15 to 20 per cent. cheaper; so much so, that I took the advantage of a contract being ten days behind time, to decline having the parcel.

11934. Were these cheap goods bought from large warehouses in London?— The largest, the very largest establishments.

11935. Do you mean that they were houses on a large scale, and of great business in this town?—Decidedly, the largest houses in the trade.

11936. Have you any objection to give their names?—Messrs. Morrison & Company, Leaf & Company, and the agents of foreign houses, Spencely & Lynch and others. I beg most distinctly to state, that I do not charge these houses with being smugglers.

11937. Has your practice of buying of these houses been so frequent as to satisfy you that they do not sell their goods at a loss?—About two years ago a Frenchman came to me, and asked me if I would give him a large order for the autumn; 30 or 40 yards is considered a large quantity, but in this instance he tied me down to give him an order for 90 or 100 yards of each pattern, to be delivered the first week in October. I gave him an order for a few hundred pounds' worth. In September the identical patterns were offered to me 15 or 20 per cent. below my contract. In order to protect those I had coming, I thought I could not do better than purchase of these large houses; I did so, and made a second purchase.

At

Mr.
*William Beckwith.*

20 July,
1832.

At last my own came, 20 per cent. dearer than the job houses were enabled to supply me: I was then protected, by buying up all that I could, as well as importing my own.

11938. What do you mean by job houses?—Houses that have very extensive dealings, and only purchase at a great sacrifice, excepting in the brisk time of the year, at spring or autumn. At the present time the jobbers are in the market; I might this morning have sold a parcel at 30 per cent. cheaper than I could manufacture them, for the custom was, 15 years ago, to write up, "Job warehouses," but the parties having become rich they discontinued this operation; they now all call themselves respectable honest dealers, and feel offended with the word "jobber," which used to be a premium for them to do their business.

11939. They are persons who profess to purchase goods from the manufacturer, the manufacturer making a sacrifice?—Yes; I remember an instance of a large dealer stating that he would not keep his warehouses open without he could supply his customers 10 or 15 per cent. below the manufacturing prices; I believe it is a fact that he continues to do so at the present time. What I referred to applies more particularly to a French importer. I have another instance of goods imported from Germany, where the agent who sold me the goods, when they arrived at the Custom House, offered to take my money, and save me 15 or 20 per cent. in the duties, the duties being 47 on figured velvets. I was very much annoyed at this, for my opponents went round to my customers and stated, that whatever my price was, they could supply them at 15 per cent. less. To prove the fact, I advanced the money, and sent my warehouseman down with the German agent: my young man told me, that he managed it with the lighterman or some other parties, and he got them through the Custom House; it was an understood thing; he passed goods for several houses to a large extent, and offered to contract with me at 15 per cent.; I told him I had understood it was done at 10 or 12; he said his price was 15. I paid the regular duty, and gave up the trade of importer, and got out of it as soon as I could. It had the effect of stopping all my looms, and I was ruined as an importer.

11940. How recently was your last transaction with such an agent as the German agent?—Two years.

11941. Has the rate of smuggling decreased since?—I asked him a few days ago, when I met him, and I think he said it was 15 or 20 per cent. on velvets at the present time.

11942. There has been no change?—No, I think not.

11943. What, in your opinion, would be the effect of lowering the duty to 15 per cent. on manufactured goods?—He said, if the duty was lowered on velvets this autumn, he thought that at 20 or 25 per cent. they would be able to inundate the market, with low goods in particular.

11944. Have you been in the habit of making large stocks for the spring and autumn trade?—I have; I held a large stock of fancy waistcoating last August, and should have continued a great many looms upon that article but for a large importation of Messrs. Leaf & Company, which caused such a sudden glut in the market as to affect my stock full 15 per cent. in less than 10 days, as nearly all my best customers became acquainted with the circumstance, and would only purchase mine as a job lot, which I partly submitted to in this market, and risked the others on consignments to several foreign markets.

11945. You do not continue to manufacture fancy velvets?—I have given that trade up altogether.

11946. On what are your looms employed now?—They are principally employed on the lowest description of works, the three singles, serges, and other works by which the weavers can earn 7 s., 8 s., or 10 s. a week, with so many reductions, they grumble dreadfully. I used to give them 2 l. a week; then they were well clothed, comfortable and happy.

11947. In what branch was that?—In weaving rich fancy silks and velvets. I was driven, by the high rate of labour, from Spitalfields, and I established a factory in Essex. I used to pay 2 s. 6 d. for an article in Spitalfields, which I now make and sell at 2 s. 4 d. per yard; I give 7 d. or 8 d. for weaving it now. I stopped all my looms about a month or two ago, and offered a reduction of wages of 25 to 30 per cent., which necessity has compelled them to accede to, but I have only been able to supply a small portion of my looms at that price. About two years ago I made a similar reduction of wages, and I received a letter signed "Swing," stating, that if I did not advance my labour in two days, my factory

678. should

Mr.
*William Beckwith.*
———
20 July,
1832.

should be burnt down. As I was not then insured, I paid men to watch, and as a proof the threat was not sham, two houses were destroyed at that time. I was refused by two offices an insurance; I now have got my factory insured, with some difficulty, at 11 s. per cent., and the weavers could not do me a greater favour than to burn it down. I put it up to auction on one occasion, and would have sold it at 65 or 70 per cent. loss, but rather than submit to that I was disposed to work it a little longer, to wait for better times.

11948. Have you been an exporter of silks?—Yes, to 20 different markets.

11949. Did any of these markets answer your purpose?—Only some two or three, but the drawback is too small to continue the trade.

11950. What did you export?—All description of goods, from the lowest to the richest; from some markets my returns were of a ruinous description.

11951. Were those velvets that you purchased here for exportation or home manufacture?—All home manufacture; I am sending off some old foreign velvets this week at 50 per cent. loss; I have exported some thousands of pounds, and my answers have invariably been that although your goods are stouter and heavier than the French we can only sell them at a great sacrifice, as the French novelties, although thin and flimsy invariably have the preference; I have a letter from Philadelphia to that effect, another from Rio, and another from Valparaiso, as to the Cape, there are only some few particular description of goods that the French have not interfered with me, so that I have been fortunate enough to realize a profit, but as regards the competition with French goods in other markets it is quite out of the question.

11952. Can you suggest what would create a better export trade?—I take the liberty of suggesting that you should increase the debenture to 7 s. on goods made only of silk, leaving the silk and cotton and the silk and worsted mixed as they now are; *viz.* silk and worsted, 7 d. per pound; silk and cotton, 14 d. per pound; silk only, 3 s. 6 d.; that would have the effect of exporting all the old fancy stocks at the end of each season. I think I could now make light flimsy articles all silk, both waistcoatings and garments that would beat the French, and by sending them fresh out of the loom of the same quality as theirs, with a drawback of 7 s., I see no difficulty to contend with them in the American and other markets; at present our patterns are exposed two or three months, and foreigners look upon them as old goods and beat us with French novelties.

11953. You mean that should take place for one year?—I should like it to be permanent, at all events for two or three years, so that we might obtain a footing in the different markets, which would afterwards be difficult to drive us out again.

11954. Is your markets principally American?—No; I send to the Colonies, North and South America, New York, Malta, Rio, Cape of Good Hope, Lisbon, Valparaiso, Cadiz, Demerara, Palermo, Vera Cruz; I have tried them from 50 l. or 60 l. up to 500 l. worth.

11955. Would your proposal affect any fancy silk goods now mixed with cotton?—It would have the effect of stopping my looms on three singles and serges, and I would venture to make figured goods all of silk, thus retaining the double chance of the home trade or the export trade; the present drawback on silk and cotton is so trifling that it is not worth while to look after the debenture.

11956. Are umbrellas and parasols now allowed any drawback?—No, they are not, but they ought to be in my humble opinion, as they are about the only article exported made from thrown silk, and they are mounted so superior in this country that no doubt the trade would increase to a considerable extent if that was allowed; I believe this is the only article made from thrown silk with a prospect of profit on exportation.

11957. What is the present price of silk debentures?—They are almost value- less, I sold them as low as a farthing per pound last week; it was my misfortune to loose by the dates expiring, something like 2,000 or 3,000 pounds; last week I sold 1,500 pounds weight at a farthing per pound; parties are always looking after them when they are going to export, and they want one of my unfortunate dates, one that is just expiring.

11958. Do you know whether the Custom House officers have been remunerated for the late seizure of smuggled silks?—The officers lately informed me they had not yet got a shilling; it became a matter of secondary consideration whether they should not look to other parties for remuneration, if silk goods were presented at the Custom House, in fact, one man came to me who is a poor miserable fellow, that was once a captain of a ship, but who is now reduced to be one of the hangers

on

Mr
*William Beckwith.*

20 July,
1832.

on about the Custom House, he considers himself fortunate to get employed four or five half days at 3 *s.* 6 *d.* a day, he was placed in the situation to weigh three or 400 pounds of silk ; a certain importer made him a liberal offer, being in a half starved state, I told him I thought he had better make sure of something for himself, and let me know who was the party ; I went with his name to the Board of Trade, but they declined seeing him ; I was very persevering with his case, for he is really an intelligent man, and though others do it, he would not hurt his conscience by touching any bribery money ; his name is Allan Fraser, a man well known, and I think who deserves to be better taken care of.

11959. Do you believe that smuggling continues ?—I believe that man could prove the fact, that 300 lbs. or 400 lbs. of silk are passed in the scales, and 100 lbs. or 150 lbs. is called out, and then the 500 *l.* a year clerks reckon up the correct duties ; he could throw immense light on smuggling.

11960. Is there any body else connected with smuggling, whom you yourself know, that could give us any information on that subject ?—I think I could find some ; the thing is notorious.

11961. I think your opinion of free trade was once different ?—It was.

11962. Be good enough to tell me the reasons you have for changing it ?— Practical experience, great losses ; nothing goes on at a profit ; I contended with my men for a reduction of wages ; I thought the price of labour in Spitalfields was exceedingly high ; I could not sell my goods at a profit, and I thought the duties on thrown silk might be reduced.

11963. Before the alteration, were you not in the habit of giving advice and suggesting to the Board of Trade the advantages likely to be derived from an open trade ?—Yes ; I got up two petitions to both Houses of Parliament on that occasion.

11964. Have you, since your change of mind, memorialized them in any way, stating that your opinion was altered, and that the results had not been exactly what you expected ?—Yes ; I waited on all the parties who had been the means of leading me into this serious error ; I stated that I had been seriously deceived ; Lord Goderich and Mr. Huskisson I saw half a score times ; they promised, if it was only persevered in, to reduce the duty ; they would take care that I should have cheap corn by and by, and a repeal of this, that and the other ; that it would be all honey and God-sends. I since took the liberty of calling on his Lordship, and stating that it had answered my purpose miserably bad ; and I went to the Board of Trade, and tried to make a better bargain with them, but they still kept to the reduction of duties on foreign thrown silk ; I said further reduction might benefit the manufacturer but it would ruin the throwster. I might reduce my labourer further till I was ashamed to go amongst my weavers.

11965. As far as your experience goes, the alteration which you desired has been productive of very great disadvantage to the silk trade of this country ?—Very great indeed ; scarcely a manufacturer is so well off as he was a few years ago ; there are one or two large houses loth to acknowledge the fact. I should be glad to get out of my trade if I could get the cost price for my machinery ; but not at 60 per cent. loss. I must still live in hopes of getting this cheap corn, and some other such God-sends by and by.

11966. Do you consider it a free trade when there is 30 per cent. duty levied on it ?—I never thought it was a free trade.

11967. You do not consider the 30 per cent. is collected ?—Certainly not ; I should say not in two-thirds of the trade.

11968. Do you know this of your own knowledge ?—I believe it is so.

11969. In what way would you suggest such an alteration should be made as would place the law on that footing which it was intended to be, viz. that the 30 per cent. should be collected, I mean what changes or alterations would you make as to the Custom House ?—I am in hopes of total exclusion of the fancy or figured branch, or it will soon be lost here ; I would say to collect the 30 per cent. there might be stamping, a pattern book and a few other strict regulations ; and one port, the port of London only, one warehouse, and some persons who know what silk goods really are. If you go down there, you see a man who perhaps never saw a piece of silk in his life before he had the luck to get such an appointment there ; he is taking the duty on all sorts of fancy toys, clocks and other things. The German agent told me that goods worth 12 *s.* a yard could be passed at 4 *s.* There are some men there who pass goods without knowing the value, &c. &c.

11970. Would it satisfy your view if the 30 per cent. was *bonâ fide* collected, or would you consider a more extended protection or prohibition on foreign goods requisite ?—

678.

Mr.
*William Beckwith.*

20 July,
1832.

requisite?—If the 30 per cent. was collected, that might do upon plain silks, with a stamp; I think 40 per cent. ought to be put on the figured; I am now making a few.

11971. Then with import duties to the extent of 30 or 40 per cent. and strict regulations at the Custom House so as to prevent the dishonest importation by smuggling, you would be satisfied without having recourse to prohibition?—Yes; I put it at 40 per cent. on figured goods, with a certificate from the Consul abroad, and the importer's name to be entered. When I say 40 per cent. on fancy goods, I mean with reference exclusively to my own particular branch, but not to apply to ribbons, gauzes or the fancy and figured trade generally.

11972. You restrict this to fancy waistcoatings?—Yes; figured silks and velvets for waistcoats.

---

*Sabbati, 21° die Julii, 1832.*

---

### EDWARD AYSHFORD SANFORD, ESQUIRE, in the Chair.

---

Mr. *William Beckwith*, called in; and further Examined.

Mr.
*William Beckwith.*

21 July,
1832.

11973. WHAT do you think would be a check to smuggling?—My answer to that question would be, immediate exposure before a magistrate; at present it is a long process of 12 or 18 months in the Exchequer before an exposure takes place. I once detected the largest smuggler that ever was in the trade.

11974. Do you mean the exposure of the goods, or the exposure of the man?—An exposure of the man; immediate exposure, or immediate judgment. If he was examined before the Lord Mayor of the city of London, the name of the parties and the house would be published, and the firm would be held in disgrace by the trade; then the whole trade might be aware of the circumstance. Fine and imprisonment for the first offence, and I think it would not be too hard if we ask for transportation for the second, or for the treadmill, and all partners to be liable who belonged to the firm; it might be very hard for partners living at a distance with property (they might live at Brighton or other places), but we say that the profits would reach him, and therefore we would say that the losses ought to reach all partners.

11975. In the same way as with a banker?—Yes. About nine or ten years ago I purchased some smuggled thrown silk on the part of the trade, and we made a seizure of one bale. I think it was full 18 months before the case came on in the Court of Exchequer; we convicted the smuggler; his name was Little. He had been a smuggler for many years, in cambrics and thrown silks more particularly. At that time thrown silk paid 14s. 7d. per lb. duty, and I think the value of the silk at that time was worth 35s. or 36s. per lb. The market price was 50s., duty paid, I believe, and I purchased it at 42s. He stated, at that time, that he had got 40 or 50 bales coming, and I believe he stated he sold 140,000l. per annum to his customers. Some of the aldermen were impeached, and some of the first houses in the trade, and they were very much annoyed by the exposure; but it was nearly 18 months afterwards that we got into the Exchequer for final conviction, and a more complete case, the Judge said, was never made out. It ruined the man in his smuggling transactions, and we heard no more of him. The duty was afterwards reduced to 7s. 6d. I ought, however, to state, that in the mean time the man took the opportunity of traducing my character, stating that he would not have cared but I was a private friend, and that I boarded with him for three days a week, and so forth, whereas I had never seen the man in my life before this transaction, and knew nothing of him.

11976. How are your weavers now employed at Coggeshall?—Very badly indeed, many of them upon low works, such as three singles, serges, and a few upon figures; the remainder, I believe, are out of work, and have been for the last three or four weeks. I am fearful to speculate upon fancy silks in the autumn, lest I may be served the same trick as I was last year, when I did so; Messrs. Leaf & Company imported a great quantity from France for this market, and caused mine to be sold at 15 per cent. loss.

11977. How do these men live when they are out of work?—By parish rates, begging, thieving, poaching, &c.; it is no uncommon thing for me to have two or

three

Mr.
*William Beckwith.*

21 July,
1832.

three hares offered me at a time; they would steal any thing at an hour's notice when they are out of work: as to the poor girls, they are prostitutes by dozens. There is only one more factory there, belonging to Mr. Hall, and he gets the people to work night and day for him; he has one set of hands for the night and the other for the day, and that is the way he makes up better wages for some of his hands than I can afford to give. Some of the girls, of 16 or 18 years of age, only earn as low as 3 s. 6 d. or 4 s. per week.

11978. How can he, by employing them night and day, give them more wages? —He does not give them more; he gets more labour out of them; his business is of a throwing description, he does not weave at nights.

11979. Is there any other information which you would wish to give to the Committee?—I wish to produce a few patterns, in illustration of my evidence of yesterday. [*The Witness produced the same, some handsome figured and fancy waistcoat silks and velvets.*] I was speaking, in my last day's evidence, about the drawback, that if the drawback was increased to 7 s. per lb. on all silk goods, which would about draw back the surplus Government hold on thrown silks imported, I should be able to make new and light flimsy figured goods, and export them to the foreign markets; at present I make them heavy, for the home trade only, and in consequence of the old patterns going in competition with the light flimsy novelty of the French, they beat me; I have no inducement now to send the light flimsy goods there: letters from all my correspondents state that that is the fact; my old goods, though stouter and better, do not sell against the light French goods. I have also a sample of Manchester goods, which is said to be better than ours; I leave the Committee to decide whether it is or not. [*The Witness produced the same, a thin shabby silk and cotton waistcoat silk.*]

11980. Is that a silk for waistcoats?—Yes, we make it of silk and cotton. The Manchester manufacturer is allowed to obtain a drawback of 14 d. a lb. upon that thin article, which is equal to my getting about 7 s. per lb. upon all silk; I ought to have at least 7 s. upon my silk, to enable me to export against the French.

11981. What is the duty paid upon this?—[*Witness produces a pattern of French silk.*]—It ought to be 30 per cent., but from the price at which it is sold in the London market at this time, I should think they do not pay above 15 per cent. I have another sample, I beg to show to the Committee, of Manchester goods, which claims the drawback of 14 d. a pound; I should imagine it has half an ounce of silk in half a dozen yards. [*The Witness produced the same.*] I have a sample made in Spitalfields about 50 or 60 years ago; if I had encouragement of a good drawback of 7 s. per lb., I think I should revive that trade. [*The Witness produced the same, a beautiful rich figured silk.*]

11982. What was this made for?—I should imagine for Court dresses; they are attempted to be brought in by houses at this time, and I dare say we shall succeed if we have encouragement in making them. I was yesterday asked, whether I was once a free trader, which I acknowledge; but I have been deceived by not having the Corn Bill repealed and smuggling checked, &c. &c. An article I have with me, I once paid for weaving it 2 s. 6 d. per yard; I was under the necessity of reducing it in Essex to about 6 d. or 7 d.; I can now only obtain 2 s. 6 d. per yard in the market for it on this day. [*Producing the same, a black figured silk and cotton.*] It is of that description that I cannot afford to export it with a 14 d. drawback; if I had a larger drawback I would make it all silk, or make a flimsy novelty which I should find a good encouragement for.

11983. The drawback of 3 s. 6 d. upon that would not be sufficient if it were made all of silk, would it?—No, it would not; 7 s. would about do it. Here is an article of figured velvet, [*producing the same.*] That is a trade that I once employed 50 or 60 men upon; the French have now all that trade.

11984. What is this a yard?—If they paid proper duty it would have stood me in 24 s. per yard.

11985. You state that, to your knowledge, while the duty was 14 s. 7 d. upon thrown silks, there was a considerable quantity smuggled, and you stated further, that you did not think there was that smuggling in thrown silks now?—No, I think not in thrown silk.

11986. That being your opinion, as to the facts in both cases, would you not think that any considerable increase in the present rate of duties upon thrown silks, would rather tend to encourage smuggling again?—I do not know how far that might go; I think with proper regulations, with regard to Custom Houses, and so forth, it would be prevented; but I have always considered it as wilful negligence.

678.                                                              There

There is one part of my evidence of yesterday, I beg to make an observation upon, having stated that 30 per cent. upon plain goods, and 40 upon figured, would be a protection. I have a calculation with me this morning, made by one of the most intelligent manufacturers, and I think a good calculator too, who states that he thinks the difference in plain goods is 39 per cent., and on figured 46 per cent., and I have gone into the calculation myself, and concur in his opinion.

11987. You have been asked whether raising the duty on foreign thrown silk would not encourage smuggling, do you think 5 s. a pound on thrown silk is as likely to encourage smuggling as the duty of 14 s. 7 d. did ?—No, certainly not; I said that if it was raised to 14 s. 7 d. it might have that effect.

11988. Not at 5 s. ?—Not at 5 s.; I have no objection to go back to the old times and take our chances; I presume if there was no smuggling at 3 s. 6 d. there would be none at 5 s.; but if you go back to the old system I have no doubt that the trade would revive again.

### Mr. *Thomas Pittifor*, called in; and Examined,

11989. HAVE you had opportunities of learning the usual amount of the earnings of weavers in the Jacquard loom ?—Yes, I have had frequent opportunities of learning it.

11990. In what situations have you been placed ?—I have been employed for the last two or three years as designer and draftsman in Jacquard looms, and as the general manager of the fancy business of Morris & Oswin; I have been employed for a much longer period than that in the same way in other situations.

11991. What do you conceive the amount of the earnings of weavers to be ?—About 14 s. a week upon the average; I think that is the highest average we could possibly take.

11992. Do you mean by that to include the time at which they are out of employment throughout the year, or do you mean to say that that is the amount when employed ?—I mean that that is the amount when employed; I do not take into account the time when they have no employment at all.

11993. Have you found in your inquiries upon this subject, any exception to this general rule, which you lay down in regard to the average of wages ?—I have found a great many below it, but I have found very few over; but if the Committee will allow me, I will read a paper, which I obtained from Mrs. Dresser, who employs a great number of hands in the Jacquard looms.

11994. Those are the cases of persons that receive more than 14 s. a week, are they not ?—Yes; I have obtained a list from Mrs. Dresser, of eight persons, and they include all those of her hands, (and she employs more than 200) who have obtained more than that sum. I had a great deal of conversation with Mrs. Dresser upon the subject, and she was of opinion that a higher sum than 14 s. could not be taken as the average, and she had never given any information to any person which could lead to a supposition that it was higher.

11995. And those are the cases that she mentioned to you of persons receiving more than 14 s. ?—She gave me a list, five of them received more than 14 s. a week, and the rest received about that average.

11996. Will you state the circumstances under which they receive more than 14 s. ?—Yes, I have it written down here, the way in which they obtained it, and it is from their own personal communication. Samuel Franklin has earned in twelve months 71 l. 10 s., from which 5 l. 10 s. must be deducted for quill winding or filling, which would leave 65 l. or 25 s. a week; during the whole time he has constantly employed an assistant or picker up, and he has made the utmost exertions. But the only circumstance which enabled him to earn the money was this, that as he became indebted to Mrs. Dresser, at the time his loom was put to work, a sum amounting to nearly 20 l., a written agreement was entered into, binding him to repay the money within a certain time, and binding Mrs. Dresser to find him constant employment for that period without alteration of pattern. Joseph Francis's earnings, are stated in Mrs. Dresser's account at 63 l.; but there appears to be some error in this, he himself believes his earnings to have been, as nearly as possible, an average of four lengths in six weeks, or 276 pieces of 20 d. clipped gauze, at 6 s. 6 d. per piece, amounting to 89 l. 14 s., from which, deducting filling, 6 l. 18 s., there is left 82 l. 16 s. To produce this, two persons have been constantly employed 13 hours every day, and if one is called away for any purpose, such as going to the warehouse to fetch out warps, or to take in the work, or in picking or making it up a third

person

Mr,
*Thomas Pittifor.*

21 July,
1832.

person supplies his place. In this way two persons are constantly and another occasionally employed, and the earnings of the whole amount to 31 *s.* 10 *d.* per week; the loom has been exceedingly well employed, and there has been no alteration of pattern in the whole time. C. Benn has made 102 pieces of 30 *d.* clipped gauze, at 12 *s.* per piece, amounting to 61 *l.* 4 *s.*, from which, deducting filling, 4 *l.* 5 *s.* leaves 56 *l.* 19 *s.*, or 21 *s.* 11 *d.* per week; he has several times employed a picker-up, and has had no alteration of pattern; he is a tenant of Mrs. Dresser, and at the beginning of this time was indebted to her 7 *l.* or 8 *l.*, and has been favoured for employment to enable him to pay it; he assured me that for a long time previous to the last twelve months, he did not earn more than 7 *s.* or 8 *s.* per week. Thomas Hulm has made 126 pieces of 24 *d.* clipped gauze, in 53 weeks, at 8 *s.* 6 *d.* per piece, deducting filling, 4 *l.* 10 *s.*, leaves 49 *l.* 1 *s.*; he paid for assistance, 1 *l.* 16 *s.*, and for the use of his loom, 5 *l.* 6 *s.*, which leaves 41 *l.* 19 *s.* or 15 *s.* 10 *d.* per week. William Payne has made 72 pieces of 20 *d.* gauze, at 6 *s.* 6 *d.*, and 72 pieces 24 *d.* at 8 *s.* 6 *d.*, amounting to 54 *l.*, from which, deducting filling, 4 *l.* 4 *s.*, leaves 49 *l.* 16 *s.* or 19 *s.* 2 *d.* per week, from which should be deducted the payment of an assistant for eleven weeks. These are the only hands of Mrs. Dresser which will show a higher rate of wages than I have named.

11997. From those cases which you have given in it appears, that in the first place, owing to a debt which they had contracted with their employer, it was the interest of the employer to give them constant employ, and from the list it appears also that very often where it is stated that a person is gaining so much, he is not in fact gaining that, because he has to pay out of what he is getting so much to the persons he is employing?—Yes, that is the case in all those cases, and very frequently in others.

11998. For instance, in one case where you state a person is getting 31 *s.* 6 *d.* a week, from that you must deduct the sum which he of course is obliged to give to the other two persons, and the one person occasionally that he employs?—Yes.

11999. Which would make it about what?—I should think it would make about 16 *s.* or 18 *s.* a week remaining.

12000. And the reason of his obtaining 16 *s.* or 18 *s.* a week upon the whole, which would be without any deduction of time when he was at work, that it had become the peculiar interest of his employer to give him peculiar employment?—In the case of Franklin it was, but not in this case; but I have no doubt that this pattern sold well, and therefore it was the interest of the employer to get as much of it done as possible; under ordinary circumstances it could not have been the case.

12001. It is a rare thing that a pattern continues for any length of time without change, is it not?—Yes.

12002. Therefore it was under very rare circumstances that he got this sum?—Yes.

12003. Have you obtained a list of the sums earned by the weavers from any other manufacturers?—Yes, I have obtained a list from Mr. Hands.

12004. Are these cases of exception also?—Yes; the list is as follows:—John Brown made, from March 26th, 1831, to March 23d, 1832, twenty pieces of 30 *d.* damask, at 13 *s.* and 115 pieces of 30 *d.* gauze at 12 *s.* amounting to 82 *l.*, from which deducting filling, 6 *l.* 19 *s.* leaves 75 *l.* 1 *s.* or an average of 1 *l.* 8 *s.* 10 *d.* per week. Brown informed me that during the greater part of the time mentioned he had no employment for any other loom, and as he had permission from Mr. Hands to make as much as he pleased in this, the exertions of three or four persons, including himself, and his son, twenty-four years of age, were used to get as much out of it as possible; and he assured me that for a long period as much was produced in it as is usually produced from two; John Cole, made from March 11, 1831, to March 17, 1832, 20 pieces of 30 *d.* damask at 13 *s.* and 62 ½ pieces 30 *d.* gauze at 12 *s.* making 50 *l.* 10 *s.*, from which deducting filling, 4 *l.* 4 *s.* 6 *d.* leaves 46 *l.* 5 *s.* 6 *d.* or 17 *s.* 5 ½ *d.* per week. John Cox has made from March 6, 1831, to March 10, 1832, 64 pieces of 20 *d.* striped gauze at 4 *s.* 4 *d.* and 110 pieces 30 *d.* at 12 *s.*, making 87 *l.* 17 *s.* 4 *d.*, 7 *l.* 10 *s.* deducted for filling, leaves 80 *l.* 7 *s.* or 1 *l.* 10 *s.* 4 *d.* per week. The work was hurried forward by order of Mr. Hands, and for a part of the time the loom was kept going nearly day and night; two persons were constantly employed upon it and sometimes three. This person I had not an opportunity of seeing personally, but I had this information from a person who did see him, and on whose accuracy I can rely. Henry Hulm made from February 12, 1831, to February 18, 1832, 152 pieces of 24 *d.* gauze at 8 *s.* 6 *d.*

678. per

Mr.
*Thomas Pittifor.*
———
21 July,
1832.

per piece, amounting to 64 *l.* 12 *s.*, filling, 6 *l.* 7 *s.* 6 *d.*, would leave 58 *l.* 4 *s.* 6 *d.*, or 1 *l.* 1 *s.* 11 ½ *d.* per week; he has constantly employed an assistant or picker-up the whole time. Benjamin Kimberley, made from March 15, 1831, to March 20, 1832, 164 ½ pieces of gauze at 8 *s.* 6 *d.* per piece, amounting to 69 *l.* 18 *s.* 3 *d.*, filling, 6 *l.* 17 *s.* would leave 63 *l.* 1 *s.* 3 *d.*, or 1 *l.* 3 *s.* 9 ½ *d.* per week; this person assured me that there were always two or three persons employed on this loom. Dusson and Pickard made from February 15, 1831, to February 14, 1832, 164 pieces of 20 *d.* gauze at 6 *s.* 6 *d.* per piece, making 51 *l.* 6 *s.*, filling, 3 *l.* 1 *s.* 6 *d.*, leaves 48 *l.* 4 *s.* or 18 *s.* 6 *d.* per week; Dusson worked in the loom one part of the year and Pickard another. Samuel Shilton has made from March 4, 1831, to March 3, 1832, 160 pieces of 20 *d.* gauze, at 6 *s.* 6 *d.* per piece, making 52 *l.*; deduct filling, 4 *l.*, leaves 48 *l.*, or 18 *s.* 6 *d.* per week; he has always employed a picker-up. The earnings of the eighth, William Walsh, amounts exactly to the sum I have named, 14 *s.* per week.

12005. Did you not state at the commencement that that was a statement which you had received from Mr. Hands?—Yes; Mr. Hands has also appended to it a statement of what he conceives to be the average quantities of gauze made by gauze weavers that were regularly employed; he thinks, in a ten shuttle loom, of 16 *d.* gauze, five pieces per week at 5 *s.*, 1 *l.* 5 *s.*, deduct for filling, 2 *s.*, 1 *l.* 3 *s.*; in an eight of 20 *d.* ditto, four pieces at 6 *s.* 6 *d.*, 1 *l.* 6 *s.*, deduct for filling, 2 *s.*, 1 *l.* 4 *s.*; in a six of 24 *d.* ditto, three pieces at 8 *s.* 6 *d.*, 1 *l.* 5 *s.* 6 *d.*, deduct for filling, 2 *s.*, 1 *l.* 3 *s.* 6 *d.*; in a five of 30 *d.* ditto, two and a half pieces at 12 *s.*, 1 *l.* 10 *s.*, deduct for filling, 2 *s.* 6 *d.*, 1 *l.* 7 *s.* 6 *d.*; and from this Mr. Hands would deduct one-fourth for time lost in alteration of pattern and putting in fresh warps, which would leave to the weaver of 10 *d.*, 17 *s.* 3 *d.* per week; of 20 *d.*, 18 *s.*; of 24 *d.*, 17 *s.* 7 ½ *d.*, and of 30 *d.*, 20 *s.* 7 ½ *d.* This statement Mr. Hands assured me was the one he made to Mr. Baggallay; he told me that was what he conceived would be about their earnings.

12006. Under the most favourable circumstances?—Yes, with complete work all the year through.

12007. He did not state that those were the earnings now, but what they might be under favourable circumstances?—Yes, with a good hand well employed.

12008. Do they receive that at this moment?—I do not know; I do not think that they do.

12009. Does Mr. Hands say they do?—No, he does not.

12010. Has Mr. Hands taken into that calculation the time that is lost in putting in the warps?—Not in the quantity first taken.

12011. You are not laying this down then as the profits of the weavers under all circumstances in those looms, but as the profit which would occur in the most favourable circumstances to a weaver who was only out of employment in the times when it was necessary to change the warps?—Yes; I think that the hands could not earn more than that under the most favourable circumstances; but I do not think the circumstances are so favourable as this statement supposes; Mr. Hands, I think, does not deduct sufficient for the time lost.

12012. What difference is there between your calculation and that contained in the paper?—I should think the average was nearer five months than three.

12013. Do you apply that to the present period?—I mean within the period of the last two or three years, if trade was good it would be the interest of the manufacturer to get things ready, and there would then not be so much time lost.

12014. There would be only three months under such circumstances lost?—I think three months would still be lost even under the most favourable circumstances.

12015. You have given in exceptional cases of the highest amount of wages which any weavers receive?—Yes, the very highest.

12016. And you have been taking the high cases without taking all the cases, and merely stating the particular circumstances under which those persons who receive more than 14 *s.* receive those wages?—Yes.

12017. In the statement which you have given in, it is understood that those are not ordinary cases, but cases of exception which you have collected together and which are examples of the highest rate of wages which any persons receive?—Yes, precisely so.

12018. And which you account for in most cases by being under very particular circumstances?—Yes; I wish to show by this the way in which a great deal of delusion takes place with regard to the earnings even in Coventry itself, for these circumstances are things sometimes unknown to the manufacturer himself, he only knows the sum paid to the person who takes out the work.

12019. In

Mr.
*Thomas Pittifor.*

21 July,
1832.

12019. In most of those cases you have given in, you have not only received the statement from the persons to whom you allude, but you also have been to the individuals themselves to whom those particulars refer, and you have got a corroboration of the statement from them, which you are now giving in to the Committee?—In all, except the one that I referred to.

12020. When you speak of 14 s. as the average, you take that from your information also?—Yes, certainly.

12021. You have given the average of 14 s. according to your own information and your own observation?—Yes.

12022. For what time do you take this average?—I should take it for the last two or three years. In May last I had occasion to make out a statement of the earnings of four of our best hands in order to send them up to Mr. Morris, who was then in London, there was a dispute between him and the hands, and I wished to let him know what their real earnings were, two of them have been taken at 12 months, and the other two for the whole time they had worked for us; had I taken our other looms, I am sure they must have shown considerably less, but circumstances had prevented them from being so regularly worked as to draw any fair inference from them; the earnings of one hand averaged 10 s. 9 d. a week, of another, 14 s., of another, 15 s. and another, 18 s. 6 d.; they had then just finished their spring patterns, and they have since lost more than a month in alteration.

12023. Those were the four persons who had the best employment?—Yes, under the most favourable circumstances I could find.

12024. Did they receive that throughout the year or only in the time during which they were employed?—Throughout the year; but I made no deduction for the assistance which they received, they received assistance, but I could not tell for what period, but if I were to deduct the time which they have since lost it would be considerably lower; if I were to take it for the last 12 months from the present date it would make it considerably less.

12025. You have neither deducted the time which they have since lost in consequence of the want of their former employment, nor the loss which they received by the assistance which they received?—No.

12026. You know that they received assistance?—I know that they received assistance frequently.

12027. But you do not know the amount paid for that assistance?—No; neither do I suppose they could themselves tell.

12028. The whole of your evidence on this branch would go to prove that when the manufacturer states what he has given to his weaver he does not know what is the amount of the wages that weaver receives and puts into his pocket?—No. This statement surprised Mr. Morris very much, he had no idea their earnings were so low.

12029. But the weaver getting employment, and he finding a number of other persons out of employment, gets others to assist him whom he has to pay?—Yes.

12030. You say that a great deal of time is necessarily lost, how is it that so much time is necessarily lost?—Owing to the continual alterations of pattern; we are continually obliged to change our pattern, and especially where we find so much competition and so little demand.

12031. It is the want of demand in a great measure?—It is that in a great measure which causes it, but there must be always a great change of pattern under the most favourable circumstances, and wherever the demand is bad the changes will be greater.

12032. Therefore, taking into account the various changes of the patterns, during which the weavers must be necessarily out of employment, they must receive higher wages when they are employed?—Yes, certainly.

12033. Would it not be possible while one pattern is making to make such arrangements for the next pattern as to prevent a great deal of the loss of time now incurred?—Undoubtedly there might, and would be, if the demand were more certain; but the state of trade has usually been such for some years past as rather to make the manufacturers afraid than anxious to commence for a new season; and to enable them to arrange their next patterns while the present ones are making, they must be designed a considerable time before hand; but this they are often afraid of, as they naturally apprehend that when they are finished the French may introduce some new style which will cast theirs into the shade; or at least a different style, if not a new one, which may lead the fashion into a direction contrary to

678.                                                                                    what

Mr.
*Thomas Pittifor.*

21 July,
1832.

what they had expected.    They therefore find it safer to follow in the path of the French than to strike out into any new one of their own; and a great deal of time is lost in endeavouring to find what direction the French are taking.    In this way the hands not only lose the time required in the alteration of a pattern, but also that which is lost in determining upon it.

12034. They cannot make arrangements previous to the time at which they ascertain what the French patterns are likely to be?—No; our season begins much later than it would but for those circumstances.

12035. Do you work to order or not?—It is not at all common in the English market; I believe it is customary with the French, but not with us.

12036. They cannot receive orders if they have to wait for the patterns?—No; before orders would be given by warehousemen in London, he would be of course himself anxious to know what the French were doing.

12037. How often do those alterations occur of which you have been speaking?—Under the most favourable circumstances, they would occur twice in the year, for the spring and winter seasons; but I have known them to occur as often as four or five times in the year.

12038. What time does it at present take to make an alteration of pattern?—If the loom, for instance, were making figured gauze, and the alteration was to another pattern of figured gauze, and the arrangement of the silk in the harness was such as to suit both patterns, if the cards were got ready while the other pattern was making, the change might be effected in a few minutes; but if the arrangement of the threads were different, and which is usually the case, the time would be prolonged according to the difference there was in that arrangement; but if the change were from figured gauze to satin figure, or to lutestring, or double figure, or from satin figure or lutestring figure to gauze, or any alteration of that kind, the time lost would be from one to two or three months.

12039. Are those alterations requiring one or two or three months which most frequently occur?—I cannot say that those requiring two or three months most frequently occur; but those that require less time than a month are not very frequent; I should think the average of the time lost in alteration would be a month at least.    In fact, the time lost in the alteration of some patterns is very great indeed, exceeding even three months; I have known a longer time than three months employed in getting out a single pattern.

12040. But taking the average of patterns you would say about a month is required for an alteration?—Yes.

12041. If a French pattern comes over here it requires a month before we can have manufactured goods to the same pattern?—Yes, to get the pattern ready, not to manufacture the goods.

12042. How long would it take to manufacture the goods?—That would depend upon the quantity wanted; a loom can only produce two or three or four pieces in a week.

12043. If there were a foreign demand, how long would it require to supply that demand by the English manufacturer?—It would depend upon the facility of the patterns, and the number of looms that the manufacturer could put upon them; if he could put a quantity of looms upon them, he would finish them of course more quickly.

12044. Are grosses or half grosses usually warped for figures by you?—Half grosses in most cases.

12045. Would it not save time if you were to warp whole grosses?—Many persons imagine that it would, but they are not so well acquainted with the trade as we are; the hand would no doubt have to wait less frequently for his warps; but the advantages would not be so great to him as it appears to be, for if the silk is at all of inferior quality or badly warped, the warps become so much crossed and entangled towards the latter end, that more time is lost in clearing and disengaging them than would have been incurred in twisting in fresh warps for the latter half; at the same time it is often very inconvenient to the manufacturer, for often when he has occasion to stop the pattern he may find a great quantity of work in the looms, and it does not enable him to make that variety of colours which is desirable; if he puts in grosses he must have four pieces of every mixture of colours, which is very inconvenient where only a small quantity is made.

12046. Therefore you do not think upon the whole that much time would be gained by employing whole grosses instead of half?—I do not think there would be much advantage; but the disadvantages would be very great.

12047. Is

Mr.
*Thomas Pittifor.*

21 July,
1832.

12047. Is the loss of time much greater in the preparation of fancy ribbons than of plain ones?—Yes, very much greater; a plain ribbon consists of only a single warp, or at most of two, which are of one colour, while a fancy ribbon sometimes consists of many warps, perhaps five or six, and it is possible that they may be each of a different colour, and therefore if one of those is wanting, the whole loom may be standing for want of it; and as fancy colours are dyed in small quantities, as they remain in fashion for only a short time, therefore those colours are sooner exhausted and are oftener wanted than the colours used in the plain trade, which are in regular demand, and dyed in large quantities; casualties and hindrances arise from this source much more frequently than in the plain trade.

12048. Upon the average it takes more time to get a pattern of fancy goods than it would plain goods?—Yes, a pattern of plain goods may be got in a very short time.

12049. You have stated that in most of those cases where the persons received more than 14s. a week they have been employing a picker-up?—Yes.

12050. What would a person give a picker-up?—I should think it would generally amount to about a third part of the earnings; it would depend entirely upon agreement.

12051. Therefore, if the person was nominally receiving 24s. a week, and employing a picker-up, he would only be getting 16s.?—Yes.

12052. And if he were employing two, he would only receive 8s.?—That is a case which could hardly be expected to occur; but it is a very inconvenient and unpleasant method, and cannot be carried on to any extent when trade is good. No person will be employed as a picker-up who can get employment of his own.

12053. Do not the hands often purchase the looms of their masters?—Yes, they do sometimes, but it is not so much that they wish to have the looms as that they imagine that while they are paying for them they may be so much favoured for employment as would make nearly a remuneration to them for all they pay their master for the loom.

12054. Then it is in fact inducing the master to employ them?—Yes, the master employs those that buy the looms of him, because he is more sure of having his money.

12055. Do you consider there is any undue proportion between the earnings of plain weavers and figured weavers?—No, I do not; I do not think there is that proportion that there ought to be; the weaving of figures requires a great deal more skill than the weaving of plain goods, and I certainly think there is not that paid to them which is sufficient to pay for that additional skill, and the plain weavers have this additional advantage, that their earnings are more regular; all the earnings of the fancy weavers are so irregular, that at times he is sinking to the brink of starvation, though at other times he is getting more than the plain weavers; I think nothing can be more disadvantageous to him; if he received his earnings more regularly, he could more easily regulate his expenses.

12056. The plain weavers are divided into two classes, those that are old and those that are young—apprentices, boys?—The making of narrow sarsnets is principally confined to women and apprentices, men are not able to earn a living upon them; but in the better articles in the plain trade I think there is very little difference between the weaver and the fancy weavers, certainly not so much as there ought to be. The fancy weavers ought to get more, and not the plain weavers get less.

12057. The same proportion exists between the better class of plain weavers and the worst class of plain weavers as there does between the better class of plain weavers and the weavers of fancy goods?—I think the difference between the earnings of the lower and the better class of plain weavers is greater than between the better class of plain weavers and the figured weavers.

12058. Do you think that the present prices of the figured weavers would be sufficient, if part of the delay they are now subject to could be removed?—If the demand were made more certain, and there were a fairer profit, I should have no doubt that the manufacturers themselves would take such measures as to prevent that delay, but it would be an expensive method, and such as I believe the manufacturers now cannot afford; but if such regulations could be made as would increase the demand—(I do not attempt to point out what is the best mode of doing so)—I am quite sure that this very great evil would be avoided, and the present prices would enable a workman to live in comfort.

12059. Are not the delays of two descriptions, one necessary from the necessary

work

Mr. *Thomas Pittifor.*

21 July, 1832.

work in which the weavers of fancy goods are employed, and the other consequent on the want of demand, which operates so as to make those causes act more strongly?—Yes.

12060. Have you yourself made any calculations at all as to what would be the difference between the cost, calculating according to the wages of a French article and the cost of an English article of about a similar description?—Yes.

12061. What are the data on which you found the cost of the French article?—The Tables were furnished to me by the manufacturers of Coventry, and given to me in French prices; I was requested to turn them into English money, and to contrast them with the prices paid in England, and to take a per centage upon them.

12062. How do you know that those French prices are correct?—I cannot say that they are; they were furnished to me; I cannot prove their authenticity.

12063. Have you reason to know that they are authentic in any way?—Yes, I understand that some evidence which was laid before this Committee in the French language was sent down by a member of the Committee, with a view that it might be translated; it was put into my hand to translate, and I was requested at the same time to make this statement to the Committee.

12064. You do not know those prices to be originally correct?—I cannot answer for their original correctness; they might have been incorrect when they were laid before the Committee; I cannot say that those prices are paid in France.

12065. You can answer for the paper which you have translated being the paper that was laid before the Committee?—Yes.

[*The Witness delivered in the same, which was read.*]

| | French Numbers. | English Widths. | French Prices, from Dr. Bowring's Tables. | | | French Prices, from Mr. Dillon's Tables. | | | English Price. | | | English Prices per cent. more than Dr. Bowring's. | English Prices per cent. more than Mr. Dillon's. |
|---|---|---|---|---|---|---|---|---|---|---|---|---|---|
| | | | £. | s. | d. | £. | s. | d. | £. | s. | d. | | |
| Plain Satins, the English piece of 36 yards. | 1½ | 2 d. | – | – | 4¾ | – | – | 4¾ | – | 1 | 6 | | |
| | 2 | 4 d. | – | – | 7¼ | – | – | 6 | – | 1 | 10½ | | |
| | 3 | 6 d. | – | – | 9½ | – | – | 7¼ | – | 2 | 3 | | |
| | 5 | 8 d. | – | 1 | 2½ | – | – | 9½ | – | 2 | 10½ | | |
| | 6 | 10 d. | – | 1 | 6 | – | 1 | 3½ | – | 3 | 6 | | |
| | 7 | 12 d. | – | 1 | 9½ | – | 1 | 10¾ | – | 4 | 1½ | | |
| | 9 | 16 d. | – | 2 | – | – | 2 | 1¼ | – | 5 | – | | |
| | 12 | 20 d. | – | 2 | 6 | – | 2 | 7¼ | – | 6 | – | | |
| | 16 | 24 d. | – | 3 | – | – | 3 | – | – | 7 | – | | |
| | 22 | 30 d. | – | 3 | 6 | – | 3 | 7¼ | – | 8 | 6 | | |
| | 30 | 40 d. | – | 4 | – | – | 4 | 1¼ | – | 11 | – | | |
| Not made in England. | 40 | 6 inch | | — | | | — | | | — | | | |
| AGGREGATE AMOUNT - £. | | | 1 | 1 | 3½ | 1 | – | 10¾ | 2 | 13 | 7½ | 151¾ | 156¾ |
| Striped Gauzes | 7 | 12 d. | – | 2 | – | – | 2 | 1¼ | – | 4 | 1½ | | |
| | 9 | 16 d. | – | 2 | 6 | – | 2 | 7¼ | – | 4 | 6 | | |
| | 12 | 20 d. | – | 3 | – | – | 3 | – | – | 5 | 6 | | |
| | 16 | 24 d. | – | 3 | 6 | – | 3 | 7¼ | – | 6 | 6 | | |
| | 22 | 30 d. | – | 4 | – | – | 4 | – | – | 8 | – | | |
| | 30 | 40 d. | – | 5 | – | – | 4 | 9½ | – | 9 | 6 | | |
| AGGREGATE AMOUNT - £. | | | 1 | – | – | 1 | – | 1¼ | 1 | 18 | 1½ | 90½ | 90 |
| Clipped Gauzes | 9 | 16 d. | – | 3 | – | – | 3 | 2½ | – | 7 | 6 | | |
| | 12 | 20 d. | – | 4 | – | – | 3 | 9½ | – | 9 | 9 | | |
| | 16 | 24 d. | – | 5 | – | – | 5 | 2½ | – | 12 | 9 | | |
| | 22 | 30 d. | – | 6 | – | – | 6 | 2½ | – | 18 | – | | |
| | 30 | 40 d. | – | 7 | – | – | 6 | 9½ | 1 | 2 | 6 | | |
| AGGREGATE AMOUNT - £. | | | 1 | 5 | – | 1 | 5 | 2½ | 3 | 10 | 6 | 182 | 180¼ |

OF these prices, the English Weaver receives two-thirds, and pays for his Quill-winding; the Undertaker retains one-third for the winding and warping of the Warp, the winding of the Shute, and the use of the Looms.

The French Weaver receives half; the other half is retained by the Undertaker, for the winding of the Shute, the use of the Looms, and some small accommodations to the Workman.

Mr. *Thomas Pittifor.*

21 July, 1832.

| | Mr. Dillon's Evidence. s. | d. | | s. | d. | Per Cent. more than French. |
|---|---|---|---|---|---|---|
| French Native Organzine, per lb. of 16 oz. 28 to 30 deniers net | 20 | 6 | English Fossembrone and Organzine, net. | 24 | – | 17 |
| French Tram - - - - | 16 | 2 | Italian Tram in England, net. | 21 | 10 | 35 |
| French Marabout - - - There appears to be an error in Dr. Bowring's calculation. | 23 | 6 | English Marabout - | 36 | – | $53\frac{1}{4}$ |
| French Soft Warp, winding, per lb. of 16 oz. Dr. Bowring's price is not taken, as he appears to confound Winding and Warping. | 1 | 2 | English Soft Warp, winding. | 2 *s.* to 2 *s.* 4 *d.* average 2 *s.* 2 *d.* | | $86\frac{1}{4}$ |
| French Marabout, winding, per lb. | – | 7 | English Marabout, winding, per lb. | 1 | 6 | 157 |
| French Warping, per lb. - - | – | $4\frac{1}{2}$ | English Warping, per lb. | 1 | 4 | 255 |
| French Gauze, clipping, per piece of 36 yards, average. | – | 10 | English Gauze, clipping, per piece, average. | 2 | – | 140 |
| French Dyeing - - - | 1 | 2 | English Dyeing, average | 1 | 8 | $43\frac{1}{2}$ |

ENGLISH SATINS:

| To make | | oz. | dr. | | £. | s. | d. |
|---|---|---|---|---|---|---|---|
| 1 piece, 2 *d.* | Would require | 45 | 12 | of undyed Warp, at 24/ per lb. of 16 oz. net - | 3 | 8 | $7\frac{1}{2}$ |
| 1 – 4 *d.* | | 29 | 10 | Italian Tram, 21/10 per lb. net | 2 | – | $8\frac{3}{4}$ |
| 1 – 6 *d.* | Dyeing, | 75 | 6 | at 1/8 per lb. - | – | 7 | $10\frac{1}{4}$ |
| 1 – 8 *d.* | | | | Making - - | 2 | 10 | $1\frac{1}{2}$ |
| 1 – 12 *d.* | | | | $41\frac{3}{4}$ per cent. higher than the French. £. | 8 | 7 | 4 |
| 1 – 16 *d.* | | | | | | | |
| 1 – 20 *d.* | | | | | | | |
| 1 – 24 *d.* | | | | | | | |
| 1 – 30 *d.* | | | | | | | |
| 1 – 40 *d.* | | | | | | | |

FRENCH SATINS, Mr. *Dillon's* Prices:

| | | oz. | dr. | | £. | s. | d. |
|---|---|---|---|---|---|---|---|
| 1 piece, N° $1\frac{1}{2}$ | Would require | 45 | 12 | undyed Warp, at 20/6 per lb. of 16 oz. net - | 2 | 18 | $7\frac{1}{2}$ |
| 1 – 2 | | 29 | 10 | Tram, at 16/2 per lb. - - - | 1 | 9 | 11 |
| 1 – 3 | Dyeing, | 75 | 6 | at 1/2 per lb. - | – | 5 | $5\frac{3}{4}$ |
| 1 – 5 | Winding, | 45 | 12 | at 1/2 per lb. - | – | 3 | $4\frac{1}{4}$ |
| 1 – 7 | Warping, | 45 | 12 | at $4\frac{1}{2}$ *d.* per lb. - | – | 1 | $-\frac{3}{4}$ |
| 1 – 9 | | | | Making - - | – | 19 | $7\frac{1}{4}$ |
| 1 – 12 | | | | £. | 5 | 18 | $-\frac{1}{2}$ |
| 1 – 16 | | | | | | | |
| 1 – 22 | | | | | | | |
| 1 – 30 | | | | | | | |

ENGLISH STRIPED GAUZES:

| | | oz. | dr. | | £. | s. | d. |
|---|---|---|---|---|---|---|---|
| 1 piece, 16 *d.* | Would require | 17 | 13 | undyed Warp, at 24/ per lb. net | 1 | 6 | $8\frac{1}{2}$ |
| 1 – 20 *d.* | | 13 | 6 | dyed Marabout, at 36/ per lb. - | 1 | 10 | 1 |
| 1 – 24 *d.* | Dyeing, | 17 | 13 | Warp, 1/8 per lb. | – | 1 | $10\frac{1}{4}$ |
| 1 – 30 *d.* | | | | Making - - | 1 | 14 | – |
| 1 – 40 *d.* | | | | 46 per cent. higher than French. £. | 4 | 12 | $7\frac{3}{4}$ |
| The only Widths made in England, | | | | | | | |

FRENCH STRIPED GAUZES:

| | | oz. | dr. | | £. | s. | d. |
|---|---|---|---|---|---|---|---|
| 1 piece, N° 9 | Would require | 17 | 13 | undyed Warp, at 20/6 per lb. 16 oz. net | 1 | 2 | $9\frac{3}{4}$ |
| 1 – 12 | | 13 | 6 | dyed Marabout, 23/6 per lb. net | – | 19 | $7\frac{1}{4}$ |
| 1 – 16 | Dyeing, | 17 | 13 | Warp, 1/2 per lb. | – | 1 | 4 |
| 1 – 22 | Winding, | 17 | 13 | ditto, 1/2 per lb. | – | 1 | 4 |
| 1 – 30 | Warping, | 17 3 | 13 – | Soft Warp, Marabout used in the Warp, $4\frac{1}{2}$ *d.* per lb. | – | – | $5\frac{3}{4}$ |
| Corresponding Widths. | | | | Making - - | – | 18 | – |
| | | | | £. | 3 | 3 | $6\frac{3}{4}$ |

ENGLISH CLIPPED GAUZES:

| | | oz. | dr. | | £. | s. | d. |
|---|---|---|---|---|---|---|---|
| 1 piece, 20 *d.* | Would require | 17 | 11 | undyed Warp, at 24/ per lb. net | 1 | 6 | $6\frac{1}{4}$ |
| 1 – 24 *d.* | | 13 | 4 | dyed Marabout, at 36/ per lb. - | 1 | 9 | $9\frac{3}{4}$ |
| 1 – 30 *d.* | Dyeing, | 17 | 11 | Warp, at 1/8 per lb. - - - | – | 1 | $10\frac{1}{4}$ |
| 1 – 40 *d.* | | | | Making - - | 3 | 3 | – |
| The Widths usually made. | | | | Clipping, at 2/ per piece - | – | 8 | – |
| | | | | 83 per cent. more than the French. £. | 6 | 9 | $2\frac{1}{4}$ |

FRENCH CLIPPED GAUZES:

| | | oz. | dr. | | £. | s. | d. |
|---|---|---|---|---|---|---|---|
| 1 piece, N° 12 | Would require | 17 | 11 | undyed Warp, 20/6 per lb net | 1 | 2 | 8 |
| 1 – 16 | | 13 | 4 | dyed Marabout, 23/6 per lb. - | – | 19 | 5 |
| 1 – 22 | Dyeing, | 17 | 11 | Warp, at 1/2 p' lb. | – | 1 | 4 |
| 1 – 30. | Winding, | 17 | 11 | Warp, 1/2 per lb. | – | 1 | 4 |
| | Warping, | 17 3 | 11 – | Soft Warp, Marabout used in the Warp, $4\frac{1}{2}$ *d.* p' lb. | – | – | $5\frac{3}{4}$ |
| | | | | Making - - - | 1 | 2 | – |
| | | | | Clipping, 10 *d.* p' piece | – | 3 | 4 |
| | | | | £. | 3 | 10 | $6\frac{3}{4}$ |

Dr. Bowring's prices have not been taken in these calculations, as some particulars are not mentioned by Dr. Bowring at all, and some others he seems to confound together.

The calculation is made on the supposition that the French and English weights would be equal, though from the superiority of the French silk, there is no doubt that a better quality than the English might bemade from a smaller weight.

*Ambrose Moore*, Esq. called in ; and further Examined.

12066. IN what respect do you consider the alteration of system in the silk trade has miscarried?—I think the reason why the alteration of system has in a great measure miscarried, is to be found in the over great haste with which it has been sought to bring this trade from its former artificial state, occasioned by taxation and restrictions into a state to compete with foreign manufactures ; by not at first giving a longer time after the duty was taken off raw silk, before foreign manufactured goods were admitted into this country, so that we should have had a better opportunity of preparing for that competition, by not at the time of the opening of the Ports to French goods when the system was first changed, insisting upon having the export of French raw silk allowed from that country to this, and by the rapid succession of reductions in the duties on thrown silk by which the throwing trade of this country has been so much injured and retarded.

12067. Do you think that that protection has been given to the trade since 1824, which it was led to expect it would receive?—I apprehend that it has not.

12068. In what respect?—The compact has been broken which was entered into with the trade when the Ports were opened ; and that protection has been withheld which was stipulated for by both branches of the trade ; a duty of at least 30 per cent. was to be collected, smuggling was to be put down, and the throwsters protected. Instead of protection being given to the united interests of the silk trade, endeavours are made to divide it by its being represented to manufacturers that their interests are opposed to those of the throwsters, and by sacrificing the latter to the former, instead of protecting the trade as a whole.

12069. Will you state to the Committee what amount of duty upon foreign thrown silks you would consider a reasonable protection for encouraging throwing silk in this kingdom?—With a due consideration to the interests of the whole silk manufacture of Great Britain, and with a view to promote the best interests and the extent of that manufacture, I should say that 5 s. on foreign thrown organzine and 3 s. on foreign thrown tram, are the lowest duties that are consistent with those interests, and I think that they are sufficient. I think it was an error to reduce the duties in 1829, below the rates I have just mentioned.

12070. In the opinion of the trade have the most effectual measures been taken to repress smuggling?—The opinion of the trade generally is, that little or no endeavours have been made to suppress smuggling.

12071. What reason is there for that opinion?—The belief is, that the wish of Government is, that French silk goods should come in considerable quantities to this country, and that they had rather have them come smuggled than not at all. If high duties were enforced the quantity of goods imported would be less, which might, it is supposed, prevent so much cotton twist or other English goods being smuggled into France in return ; and that the object of Government in not preventing smuggling while the duties remain as high as they are at present, is to get the duties on French silk goods reduced to a point which shall let in still larger quantities than at present ; whether this impression is right or wrong I know not, but it exists in the trade to a great extent, and is supported by the refusal to recommend to Parliament the stamping of foreign silk goods, and to attach some sort of criminal punishment to the offence of smuggling, in addition to the pecuniary penalties to which the smuggler is now liable ; on this last mentioned point it is supposed a difficulty is felt, lest there should be retaliation on the part of foreign Governments, and by that means smuggling of English goods into other countries should be checked ; notwithstanding that smuggling is notoriously carried on in silk goods to an enormous extent, and they are to be met with in almost every direction, yet scarcely any instances of detection occur ; and when a very flagrant case of this kind came to light a few months ago, the prosecution of it was compromised ; no matter what high fine was paid as the condition, a compromise of any kind gives colour to the belief that no great anxiety was felt to put down smuggling in silks. I do not mean to impute any unworthy motives, I dare say the public good is the object in view, but still I believe ever since 1824, there has been no intention to take any energetic measures to prevent smuggling ; in short my opinion upon this subject and that of the trade is founded upon this, that the Government do not wish to check the smuggling of English goods into France, and that for that reason they are backward in putting down the smuggling of French goods into England.

12072. The Committee have been informed that there is a considerable local taxation in France which is a burthen upon manufacturers there, do you think that

the

*Ambrose Moore,*
Esq.

21 July,
1832.

the local taxation of France is greater than that of England?—I think that the local burthens of all classes in England are much greater than the local taxation in France, and that the real question for the consideration of the Committee upon this point is, the relative cost of living of the English and French artisans, and not the mere point of what tax a French artisan may happen to pay upon a bottle of wine or a loaf of bread.

12073. There is a heavy duty, the Committee are told, upon iron in France, which operates to enhance the price of wood, and thus to injure the silk trade, by making the machinery expensive; do you think that the French manufactures suffer very much from that circumstance?—With all those points of the French manufacture which at all enter into competition with the silk manufacture of this country those duties have nothing to do, and can have no effect whatever upon them; they can apply only to the throwing branch of the trade, and not in the least to the weaving; and as far as throwing establishments are concerned, all the necessary buildings and plant in a throwing establishment in England are infinitely more costly than similar establishments in France.

12074. There is a tax upon raw silk imported into France; is this, do you think, a great disadvantage to the French manufacture?—The duty is but small, and the Committee will recollect that it can apply only to a small part of the silk the French use, three-fourths of it, and upwards, being the growth of their own country; and it is a fact proved beyond contradiction, that they get their own raw silk very much cheaper than we get Italian raw silk in England.

12075. Do you then, or do you not think that, taking altogether the disadvantages mentioned in the three foregoing questions, they are such that, excepting the cases in which taste and long experience and aptitude enter largely into their productions, their merit either is passing away or is likely to pass away?—My opinion is, that the circumstances referred to in the three preceding questions are not producing that effect, and cannot produce any such effect.

12076. The Committee understand that the French manufacturers are under considerable disadvantages as compared with those of Switzerland, as it respects the commissions upon the import of silk from Italy, brokerage, the pillage of silk at Lyons, &c.; do you think this is a correct opinion?—So far from the French being under any such disadvantage as it respects the cost of their silk, the fact is, that they get their raw silk very much cheaper than the Swiss manufacturers get theirs; the Swiss manufacturer derives his silk from Italy, and the French manufacturer gets the larger part of his from the growers of silk in his own country, and it is a well-known fact that the French silk, on an average, is considerably cheaper than Italian can be obtained, for as to the commission paid in Switzerland upon the importation of Italian silk, I believe the Swiss manufacturers have no means of getting their Italian silk that are not equally open to the French manufacturers; I do not believe that they have any advantage, even in respect to the obtaining Italian silk, over the French. As far as brokerage is concerned, it is always worth the while of a manufacturer to pay a brokerage; it is no loss to me if I employ a broker to buy silk for me; it is better worth my while, as a matter of profit, to pay his commission, than to have the trouble and loss of time in purchasing it myself; and therefore, if the Swiss do not pay a brokerage, and the French do, the former are no gainers by that circumstance; and as to pillage, I confess I can see no possible advantage that a large town in Switzerland, such as Zurich, with its 12,000 looms, can have over a large town in France: I have no doubt that there is pretty much the same degree of honesty and dishonesty in all manufacturing places.

12077. Do you think there is a strong English feeling in France with respect to trade with England?—I believe there is a strong disposition in France to sell goods to the English, but I believe there is no English feeling beyond that. I had occasion to hear a person who went to France to buy silk goods speak of this strong English feeling; it was soon after the dethronement of Charles the Tenth, and when the French trade was in consequence in a state of great embarrassment: he told me how very happy the French were to see him, saying, that England was their best customer, and that she was looked upon by the French silk trade in a very much more favourable light than any of the French people used to look upon her, because she took so many of their French goods; but there is no feeling in favour of any fair and honourable reciprocal trade with England.

12078. Do you think that such an institution as the Conseil des Prud' hommes can be of any advantage to the silk manufacture of England, as it regards the com-

678.                                                                      petition

*Ambrose Moore,*
*Esq.*
_____

21 July,
1832.

petition with other countries?—None whatever, as it regards the competition between England and other countries; it may be a useful institution, but it can have nothing to do with the course of inquiry before this Committee; there is nothing in it which enables the French, or if we had a similar institution in England there could be nothing in it which would enable the English to enter better into foreign competition.

12079. Do you attach any importance to the plan the French have of ascertaining the condition of silk at Lyons?—As I said, in reply to the last question, this institution also may be useful; whether it is more useful than the plan we have I am not quite sure; the plan in England is, that if silk is out of condition, a broker, who is supposed to be a person understanding silk well, and the condition that it ought to be in, is employed between the parties, to determine the state and condition of the silk, and if it be not in good condition, to award such an allowance to the buyer as he thinks right. I never found any disadvantage in that plan, but it has nothing to do with the main question of inquiry before this Committee.

12080. Is it not surely an improvement upon the ascertainment of the quality and condition of the silk?—It has nothing to do with ascertaining the quality of the silk, it only determines the condition, and even in that respect I do not consider it of any importance.

12081. In point of fact, has this plan any thing whatever to do with the quality of the silk?—I believe not with the quality, only with the condition; the condition is perfectly distinct from the quality.

12082. Do not the manufacturers here adopt the same system of ascertaining the condition as is pursued at Lyons?—In some cases I believe they do; different people have different ways; there is no public institution of the kind.

12083. Is there not the same system in the trade of examining the condition when the silk is received from the throwster?—Yes, its result is the same; if I buy a bale of silk, and I ascertain that it is damp, or not in a right condition in any respect, I send for the broker. who examines it, and he adjusts the matter between the seller and the buyer.

12084. Is it your opinion that the success of the French in their competition depends at all upon such regulations as have been mentioned in the preceding questions?—Not at all; I consider them quite beside the question; and if the Committee should allow their attention to be drawn to them as to matters of importance, it would lead them away from the principal features of the case.

12085. To what do you consider their success is owing?—To the exclusive possession of their own raw silk; the low rate at which they can afford in France to perform all the operations of manufacture; their having, as it respects taste and excellence, the prejudice of all the world in their favour; their being in actual possession of all the markets of Europe and America, and the consequent certainty and confidence with which they carry on all their operations. This certainty and confidence encourage and enables them to employ the best artists and to incur expense in the preparation of works of skill and fancy, in a way the English never can venture upon while they have no better protection than at present.

12086. What is your opinion as to the total quantity of foreign silk goods that find their way to this country?—From my own observation and all the inquiry I could make, I am of opinion that the amount of French goods which some how or other find their way into this country is at least double that which the French official accounts of exports would show.

12087. Has the use of silk goods in this country increased 50 per cent. and has the importation of the raw material increased in the same proportion?—I have no doubt that the use and the wear of silk goods in this country has increased at least 50 per cent. since the year 1826, while the average imports of raw and thrown silk for the last six years have actually fallen off as compared with those of 1824 and 1825.

12088. Would you consider it an important benefit to the silk manufacture of this country if the prohibition to export raw silks into France was done away with, and if a nominal rate of duty was levied upon their import into England, similar to that levied on imported Italian raw silks?—I consider that it would be a great advantage in point of price to obtain the French raw silk, as it would tend to equalize the prize of silk in France and in England, but still it would not give to England all the advantage which the manufacturers of France would still have from being on the spot where the silk is raised, in like manner that the Italian throwsters have an advantage over the throwsters of this country, from the power they have of getting the choicest of the raw silk; it would moreover leave the French in

possession

possession of all their other advantages, such as have been enumerated in the answer I gave to a former question.

### Alexis James Doxat, Esq., called in ; and further Examined.

*Alexis Doxat,*
*Esq.*

21 July,
1832.

12089. IT has been mentioned, on your part, by Mr. Ballance, in the course of the first day of his examination, June the 8th, that you communicated confidentially to two Members of this Committee, on the 9th of May last, a detailed Statement of the exports of French manufactured silks, drawn from official Returns of their Customs, with computations into English weight and money, and circumstancial notes thereon, of which Mr. Ballance gave an abstract only to the Committee, because it was judged more in order that you should yourself, on some other occasion, deliver in that document which had been adverted to already in Mr. Heath's evidence on the 11th May. You, being present on the second day of Mr. Ballance's examination, when reference was again made by him to that document, expressed to the Committee that you were ready to deliver in that statement, but that you had received other documents on which you were then occupied, and which you were desirous to deliver in conjointly, as also some other papers referrible, (and as an appendix) to your examination, on the 11th, 13th, 17th, 18th and 19th of April last; will you now deliver in those papers, and accompany them with such observations as may appear to you necessary in connexion with their subjects ? —I will, and in so doing I shall endeavour to be as brief and concise as the importance of the subject will allow me. I have the honour to deliver in the paper in question, No. 26, extracted from the Returns of French Customs, of their exports of French manufactured silks for 1829, it presents a distinct statement of every description of those goods, their weights in kilogrammes, and their total value in francs, as also the official value assigned to each denomination of goods per kilogram ; and then my computations into English weights and money, not only as regards the totals, but the prime cost in France per pound weight and per ounce English. In that statement will be found also an approximative estimate of the quantity of pounds weight of raw silk, the very major part fine raw silk, (much finer than the standard on which our silk manufacturers have worked for some years past,) that may have been required to produce the quantity of kilogrammes, 958,000 equal to 2,108,000 pounds English of manufactured silks of high and very high descriptions, namely, about 2,882,000 pounds English of fine raw silks. It is right to observe here, that those 958,000 kilogrammes, comprise 85,000 kilogrammes of silks, mixed with cotton, &c. of high descriptions however ; but those 958,000 kilogrammes are exclusive of various items of export, such as silk umbrellas, modes, and woollens mixed with silk, of which I have specified the quantities, &c. at the foot of the said statement of exports for 1829, having collected them from various parts of the said official Customs Returns for that year, and they more than compensate for the portion of cotton contained in the said 85,000 kilogrammes. There are besides some quantities of goods manufactured with waste, which I have also indicated, and which likewise are not comprised in the general statement of 958,000 kilogrammes above mentioned. I will now beg leave to read some brief notes which I have made on that statement, explanatory of its principles and bearings. (*See* notes at the bottom of the statement, for 1829, down to " above mentioned, 9th May.") I should observe here, that I received those official returns for 1829, about a year ago or more, and that they appeared to me to present so interesting an arrangement and classification, that I sent them not long after I had received them, to one of the principal officers of His Majesty's Customs, for his inspection. I have the honour to put in three papers, No. 27, 28 and 29, which present similar returns of exports of French manufactured silk goods, for the years

*See* p. 862.

*See* p. 862.

*See* pp. 863, 864,
865.

> (No. 27.) - - - - - 1827 ⎫
> (No. 28.) - - - - 1828 ⎬ with similar computations ;
> (No. 29.) - - - - - 1830 ⎭

and to which the notes and observations attached to the Returns for 1829, I have just read, are equally applicable. I further have the honour to put in a Paper No. 30, which presents an abstract recapitulation of those Returns, for 1827, 1828, 1829 and 1830, in order to bring them under one distinct view. At the foot of this paper will be found an abstract, which I have made of the exports of manufactured silks from waste, of silk umbrellas, modes, and woollens mixed with silk, to which I have just alluded. Further, a Paper, No. 31, containing a detailed statement of the imports of foreign manufactured silks into France, for home consumption, for the years 1827, 1828, 1829 and 1830. And a Paper, No. 32, which is an estimate

*See* p. 866.

*See* p. 867.

*See* p. 868.

of

*Alexis Doxat,*
*Esq.*

———

21 July,
1832.

*See* p. 869.

*See* p. 870.

of the total amounts of the silk manufactures of the United Kingdom, for the periods 1815–17, 1818–20, 1821–23, and 1824–25, distinguishing the amounts of duties, of wages, profits, &c. of the cost of raw and thrown silk, waste, &c., and the rates per pound on an average, of the various descriptions of silks consumed, inclusive of waste, &c. Also, Paper, No. 33, which is a similar estimate for 1826 to 1831, distinguishing the averages for the last three years, 1829 to 1831, Also, a Paper, No. 35, which is an abstract statement of the exports of French silk manufactures, for the years 1827 to 1830, conjointly with an abstract view of the total amounts of the silk manufacture of the United Kingdom, for the years 1826–31, 1829–31, and 1815–17 to 1824–25. It will be observed, that the average amounts of the market values here of the silk goods, declared out, exported from France in the years 1827 to 1830, is 6,280,000 *l.* on an average, per annum, independently of the considerable quantities exported from the other Continental silk manufactures, constituting in the aggregate an enormous amount of silk manufactures of various descriptions, disposable for export (independently of the quantities retained for home consumption, which latter quantities are but limited in regard to Switzerland, the Rhenish provinces, &c.)—disposable for export, I say ; no inconsiderable portions of which continually press upon us, but with increased intensity under contingent circumstances, frequently adverted to in the course of my examination in April last. The magnitude of the amounts of foreign silk manufactures will be more evident when compared with the total amounts to which the British silk manufactures have been reduced during the last three years, an amount, the average of which I have overstated at 5,244,000 *l.* ; an amount contrasted with the rapid increase of the years

| | | | | |
|---|---|---|---|---|
| 1815–17 | - | - | - | at £.4,000,000, |
| 1818–20 | - | - | - | at   5,290,000, |
| 1821–23 | - | - | - | at   6,085,000, |
| 1824–25 | - | - | - | at   7,811,000 ; |

*See* p. 939.

all which amounts, for the years 1815–17 to 1824–25, are considerably understated, for the reasons particularized in my printed paper, No. 4, delivered in to this honourable Committee on the 11th of April last. And here I may be allowed to repeat, that there is no saying to what extent this branch of our national industry would have attained, had we remained protected by the laws of 1766, jointly with the benefit of reduced duties to 5 *s.* on thrown silks, and 1 *d.* per pound on raw silks, with wages in the ratio of 8½ *d.* per yard for weaving well neat gros de Naples, of the description frequently alluded to in the course of my evidence. According to every comparative point of view, whether it be on that basis, or on the former gradations relative to the periods of high duties and wages, at the moderate rate of 10½ *d.* for weaving the same description of goods, we ought to have been at the amount of more than 10,000,000 *l.*, of which 6,000,000 *l.* and more of wages, &c., and duties, for the years 1829 to 1831, contrasted with about 5,250,000 *l.*, their actual amount, 2,500,000 *l.* of which is the amount of wages, &c., and duties, at which I have over estimated the result of those three years. Had we manufactured at those low duties, with that rate of wages, and the benefit of a continuance of our protective laws, I am convinced that the comparatively little smuggling that took place previously to 1826, would have been almost entirely done away with.

12090. Under what point of view do you consider those amounts raised by the silk trade ?—As taxes on luxury, and as a transfer from the superfluities of the rich and easy to industrious employment, and that by most equable gradation, according to the respective means ; whilst it is well known that in regard to the cotton and most other articles of manufacture, the lower classes of society consume of them in far greater relative quantities than of silks ; but on these subjects, a letter received from Calais, dated 4th of June last, furnishes some curious data : the quantities exported from that port to England are stated thus in that letter.

| | Kilogrammes of Plain Silks. | Kilogrammes of Figured Silks. | Kilogrammes of Ribbons. | Value of Blondes. |
|---|---|---|---|---|
| | | | | *f.* |
| For 1831 - - - - | 95,971 | 208 | 10,984 | 96,517 |
| For 1832 to 29th May - - | 44,216 | 120 | 5,623 | 71,496 |

Now the quantity alone of plain silks, 95,971 kilogrammes, is equal to 211,000 pounds English ; and by reference to our Custom House Returns for 1831, No. 205, House
of

*Alexis Doxat,*
Esq.

21 July,
1832.

of Commons, 27th February 1832, and Customs same date, it will be seen that the whole quantity of silk goods from all parts of Europe, plain, figured, gauze, crape, ribbons, fancy goods, &c., was only 148,729 pounds in weight; this of course, exclusive of certain quantities of net, tulle, millinery, and unenumerated goods, entered by square yards, by the numbers and by valuation, the whole of which would appear to constitute a small aggregate only in weight : and here there opens to us another field for most important observation in the value, abstractedly, in the value alone, of those 95,971 kilogrammes of plain goods declared out at Calais for England, which at the official rate of the French Customs of 120 francs per kilogram for plain goods is 11,516,520 francs, constituting alone about two-thirds of the amount of 18,000,000 of francs, stated by the official returns of the French Customs as the whole of the exports of French silk manufactures to this country for that year : now there is reason to believe that a large proportion, that is about two-thirds of the silk goods which we receive from France, is composed of various descriptions which do not come under the denomination of plain silks " Etoffes unies," which would constitute the remaining one-third. We see by the official returns of exports from the port of Calais, that the goods declared out of other descriptions than plain, amount to only 1,440,637 francs, compared with the amount of 11,516,520 francs, referrible to plain goods alone. What does this show ? That not only considerable quantities, even of those goods which are declared out from France for England, do not pass through our Custom Houses, but beyond this, that immense amounts of goods sent to this country are never declared out. If the returns from Calais present us with such a case, and *nota bene,* the quantities of plain silks alone declared out from that port, show an amount at once of two-thirds of the 18,000,000 francs, stated as the whole amount of French silk goods exported to this country. If the returns from Calais present us with such a case for the year 1831, fully corroborated by the subsequent returns from that port up to the 29th May 1832, as before enumerated, what must we judge of the collective amounts of the actual exports from the whole line of the French coast, so many parts of which offer, for obvious reasons, much greater facilities still than the port of Calais, for the purposes of illicit trade with this country, although we have seen by the premises what considerable portions even of the quantities declared out from Calais have been introduced here clandestinely. On this particular point I must notice here, that whilst the declared exports of plain silk goods from Calais for 1831, the declared alone, show 95,971 kilogrammes equal to 211,000 pounds English; the whole quantity of plain goods from all parts of Europe which appear in our Custom House Returns for that year, is only from 50 to 60,000 pounds weight, that is only about one-fourth part even of the declared exports, the declared exports alone, of plain silk goods at Calais for this country. But speaking again abstractedly on the subject of quantities of raw and thrown silks, waste, knubs and husks consumed in our manufactures, I beg leave to deliver in a Paper (No. 37), which I have arranged since I had the honour to be before this Committee in April last, which brings this subject in all its bearings into one condensed point of view.

See p. 873.

12091. You state at the head of the first column of your Paper (No. 37), that the quantities indicated therein of raw and thrown silks, waste, and knubs and husks, duty paid, are taken from Parliamentary Returns only, and I observe that that column presents a progress of 36 per cent. from 1815–17 to 1818–20, whilst in the adjoining column of quantities which you have estimated as actually brought into consumption, and which you have computed into one standard, that of Italian silks, you show a less progress during the same period, that is of 31 ¼ per cent. compared with the 36 per cent. you draw from Parliamentary Returns; how do you account for that difference which you show against your view of the question ?—On this particular, I beg to refer to the note adjoined to my Paper (No. 1), relative to the mode in which I have established my estimates of consumption, all of which it will be seen by the said Paper, are brought to one ultimate amount, which is balanced for the whole series of years by Parliamentary Returns, a mode of analysis which I have adopted in order to bring into one form the whole subject in the most correct point of view, and by which means every quantity of the various descriptions of silks, duty paid, that is entered for home consumption, and actually brought into consumption at the various periods, can be traced step by step.

See p. 873.

See p. 932.

12092. In your former examination you have stated that on an average the manufacturers in France are provided with fine raw and thrown silks, at lower rates than we import them from Italy, and than they can be imported into France from Italy, owing to the manufacturers in France being so greatly provided with silk of their own growth, and consequently that there was for the major part no analogy

678.                                                                                                                between

*Alexis Doxat*, Esq.

21 July 1832.

between the prices of silks at Lyons and those of Italy, and in this country; can you furnish the Committee with any statement corroborative of your view of this subject?—I have the honour to put in a paper (No. 36) relative to this point; and in order to detain the Committee as little as possible on this subject, which has already taken up so much time, I will confine myself in explanation of the principles on which this paper is grounded, to the reading of two notes joined to it. The title of the paper is "Statement intended to show the Differences which range between the prices of silks at London and at Lyons," with an Appendix, to show the range of differences in the prices between Milan and Bergam and Lyons. I shall only further observe here, in abstract, that the differences in the first part of this comparative statement, that is, between London and Lyons, are,

*See* pp. 871, 872.

| *s.* | *d.* | | *s.* | *d.* | |
|---|---|---|---|---|---|
| 4 | 1 | - - - in 1826 | 2 | 2 | - - - in 1830 |
| 1 | 8 ¾ | - - - in 1827 | 1 | 5 | - - - in 1831, and |
| – | 8 | - - - in 1828 | 1 | 8 | - - - in 1832. |
| 3 | 6 ½ | - - - in 1829 | | | |

I shall only add with respect to the Appendix, that the differences it shows between Milan, &c. and Lyons, are,

| *s.* | *d.* | | *s.* | *d.* | |
|---|---|---|---|---|---|
| 2 | 10 | - - - in 1826 | 1 | 9 ¾ | - - - in 1830 |
| 1 | 5 | - - - in 1827 | 1 | 7 ¼ | - - - in 1831, and |
| 1 | – ½ | - - - in 1828 | 1 | 3 ¾ | - - - in 1832. |
| 4 | 4 ¼ | - - - in 1829 | | | |

12093. You stated in evidence before this Committee, in April last, that you assigned about 5,500,000 lbs. weight. of raw and thrown silks to the manufacture in France, are you still of the same opinion?—I am.

12094–5. It has been mentioned in evidence that that consumption consists of only 4,000,000 lbs. weight of raw and thrown silks, and that the quantity of manufactured silks of all descriptions, including sewings, trimmings, &c. does not exceed in weight 2,600,000 lbs. to 2,671,000 lbs., of which about 2,226,000 lbs. weight exported, and 445,000 lbs. weight for home consumption. How do you reconcile those estimates with that you have just now again mentioned?—I will endeavour to answer that question as briefly as possible; and in the first place I shall observe, that by reference to my Table, No. 30, it will be seen that it nearly coincides with the quantity of 2,226,000 lbs. weight stated as the official returns of exports of French manufactured silks, which official returns however I should repeat here (conformably with the notes to my Paper, No. 26) do not comprise the whole of the quantities exported. Now I would recal to the recollection of this honourable Committee, that which has been frequently stated, that there is no duty whatever collected in France, directly or indirectly, on silk of their own produce; and that on every inquiry which for some years I have sedulously made through various channels from which I conceived the best information on these subjects could be derived, I have been informed that no exact estimate of the quantities of raw silks produced in France could be formed, as there were no adequate means whatever to that effect; consequently the various accounts which I have received at different periods and from various quarters on this subject present some differences and discrepancies in the several modes in which those estimates have been established, it is on this account that (as I had the honour to state before to this honourable Committee) I have not thought myself justified in giving in those statements as part of my evidence; I shall only state here that the average of the various statements embracing the years 1820 to 1828 presented an amount of 5,342,214 lbs. English weight as the consumption of silks in France per annum, and of 5,710,000 lbs. per annum for the years 1824 to 1828. It is from the aggregate result of those inquiries that I thought myself justified in my communications with the Board of Trade, in 1829 and 1830, in stating that I understood the consumption of silks by the French manufacturers to be about 5,500,000 lbs. weight per annum. On this subject I have not made any further particular researches of late, convinced from all the results of my previous inquiries, that they could not have been productive of any data more valid, and that it would have been causing needless trouble to our correspondents. I should add on this subject, that I fully coincide with the opinion given in evidence before this Committee, that the cultivation of silk in France has been for some years past in a course of rapid increase, that cultivation being very beneficial, as I understand, in those extensive parts of France which are so peculiarly favourable to it. Having stated those particulars, I now return to the quantity of

*See* p. 866.

*Alexis Doxat,*
Esq.

21 July,
1832.

of 445,320 lbs. weight of manufactured silks to which this question refers, as having been given in evidence as the total of French manufactured silks retained for home consumption, to which I beg to observe it will, in fairness, be necessary to add 45,000 lbs. import of foreign manufactured silks in France for home consumption to which I have before adverted; and this would give a total of 490,320 lbs. English of French and foreign manufactured silks (inclusive of every description of silks, sewings, trimmings, furniture, &c.) for the consumption of a population of 34 millions, that is from one-fourth to one-fifth part of an ounce per head; and in money, 77 c. per head in France, equal to 7 ¼ d. sterling per head; computed (speaking in round numbers):

upon - - 490,000 lbs. English,
equal to - 223,000 kilogrammes,
valued at - - 118 francs per kilogram.
equal to 26,314,000 francs.
equal to £.1,028,000 sterling;
say 7 ¼ d. per head in France,

contrasted with 6 s. 2 d. per head in the United Kingdom;

that is, 10 to 1: and this ratio, computed only upon the amount which we had attained in our own manufactures in 1824–5, (considerably under-stated by me; *vide* my Papers, No. 4, delivered in by me on the 11th April, and No. 33, delivered in to-day,) at 7,811,000 l. from which I have deducted 456,000 l. for silk and even mixed goods, exported per annum during the last three years, over-stated in value, leaving the amount of 7,355,000 l. spread over 24,000,000, inclusive of the population of 8,000,000 in Ireland, of which only a very small fraction can touch that article of luxury; in other words, an amount of 1,028,000 l., distributed over 34,000,000 in France, and an amount (under-stated) of 7,355,000 l. distributed over 24,000,000 in this country   Having exhibited these results, I think all comment upon them superfluous; there are many other points of importance towards which I would feel anxious to solicit the attention of this honourable Committee, but I will not further trespass on their indulgence.   Before I withdraw from their presence, however, I would beg leave earnestly to draw once more their most deliberate attention to the analysis which I have had the honour to place before them, of the researches which it has been in my power to make into this important branch of our national industry, in my various Tables, but more particularly in that (No. 2,) which I have delivered in on the 11th of April; and I beg leave to recal here, abstractedly, in the most brief way, some numbers contained in that Paper: they relate to a comparative view of the respective progresses of THE SILK and THE COTTON TRADES in this country, in regard to *quantities alone,* from 1815–17 to 1824–25, that is previously to the removal of our protective laws to the silk trade of 1766; which progresses were as follow;

*See* pp. 939 & 869.

*See* p. 934.

Three years, from 1815–17 to 1818–20, 31½ per cent. the Silk, against 22 per cent. the Cotton;
Six years - from 1815–17 to 1821–23, 70 per cent. the Silk, against 48 per cent. the Cotton;
Eight years, from 1815–17 to 1824–25, 156 per cent. the Silk, against 83 per cent. the Cotton;

whilst those progresses have been INVERTED thus:

In the last six years, 1826 to 1831, compared with the medium of 1821–23, 1824,–25,
19½ per cent. the Silk, against 41½ per cent. the Cotton;

although the progress of the cotton trade itself during the last six years has been a little less than during the former periods.   Then in regard to the average amount of wages, duties, profits, &c., the silk trade presents, abstractedly, the following results;

In those two periods, 1815–17 to 1824–25, and 1826 to 1831, say,
For 1815 to 1817, three years, at the average of £ 2,073,000 per annum,
1818–20 - - three years - - - 2,719,000 —
1821–23 - - three years - - - 3,514,000 —
1824–25 - - two years with low duties and⎱4,263,000 —
the same rate of wages, at the average of -⎰

(The Amounts for these eleven years under-stated, respecting which, *see* my Table, No. 4.)
Whilst the average per annum of the last six years
1826–31, has been about - - - - £.2,685,000; and that
of the last three years 1829–31, has been about - 2,534,000;

*See* p. 939.

(The Amounts for these last six years over-stated, as noticed in the course of my evidence;)

instead of the rate of about 6,000,000 l. at which we ought to have been for the last three years, according to several comparative Estimates, made in various ways and grounded on various antecedents; and this is the trade that has been pointed out as exhibiting a triumphant proof of the successful application of the principles of Free Trade.

[*The Witness delivered in several Accounts, &c., which were read,
and are as follow:*]

678.

*1,932,450 ⎫ Grammes,
2,778,350 ⎬ reduced into
316,870 ⎭ kilogrammes.

1829.　(Fo. 48.)

(Mr. *Alexis Doxat*'s Paper, No. 26.
Delivered in 21st July 1832, to the Select Committee on the Silk Trade.)

## ADMINISTRATION DES DOUANES.

### EXPORTATIONS des TISSUS de SOIE de FABRIQUES FRANÇAISES.

| TISSUS DE SOIE. | Quantités. | Kilos. | Valeurs. | Frs.p' Kilo. | Computation into English Weight & Value | | | |
|---|---|---|---|---|---|---|---|---|
| | | | | | Lbs. English. | £. Sterling Value. | Per lb. 16 oz. Engh. | Per oz. English |
| | Kils. | | Frs. | | | | s. d. | s. d. |
| Etoffes — Pures — Unies | 384,345 | – | 46,121,400 | 120 | 845,559 | 1,826,590 | 43 2½ | 2 8 |
| Façonnées | 133,810 | – | 17,595,300 | 130 | 294,382 | 688,923 | 46 9¾ | 2 11 |
| Brochées — de Soie | 4,341 | – | 564,330 | 130 | 9,550 | 22,350 | 46 9¼ | 2 11 |
| d'or ou d'argent — fin | *1,932 | – | 463,778 | 240 | 4,250 | 18,368 | 86 5¼ | 5 4 |
| faux | 1,612 | – | 290,160 | 180 | 3,546 | 11,491 | 64 9¾ | 4 - |
| Mêlées de fil, coton ou d'autres matières | †85,623 | – | 6,849,840 | 80 | 188,370 | 271,281 | 28 9¾ | 1 9 |
| Couvertures | 579 | – | 23,160 | 40 | 1,273 | 917 | 14 5 | - 10 |
| Gaze de Soie pure | 9,534 | – | 1,067,808 | 112 | 20,974 | 42,289 | 40 4 | 2 6 |
| Crêpe | 46,845 | – | 4,122,360 | 88 | 103,059 | 163,261 | 31 8 | 1 11 |
| Tulle | 9,595 | – | 767,600 | 80 | 21,109 | 30,400 | 28 9¾ | 1 9 |
| Dentelle de Soie, dite blonde | (Francs.) | Valeur Kilos. | 758,879 | – | - | 30,055 | — | — |
| Bonneterie | 20,760 | | 2,076,000 | 100 | 45,672 | 82,218 | 36 - | 2 3 |
| Passementerie — d'or ou d'argent — fin | *2,778 | – | 833,505 | 300 | 6,111 | 33,010 | 108 - | 6 9 |
| faux | 3,819 | – | 114,570 | 30 | 8,401 | 4,537 | 10 9½ | - 8 |
| de Soie — Pure | 27,911 | – | 2,791,100 | 100 | 61,404 | 110,539 | 36 - | 2 3 |
| mêlée d'or ou d'argent — fin | *316 | – | 57,037 | 180 | 695 | 2,259 | 65 - | 4 - |
| faux | 1,747 | – | 209,640 | 120 | 3,843 | 8,303 | 43 2½ | 2 8 |
| mêlée d'autres couleurs | 2,111 | – | 147,770 | 70 | 4,644 | 5,852 | 25 2½ | 1 6 |
| Rubans, même | 220,846 | – | 26,501,520 | 120 | 485,861 | 1,049,565 | 43 2½ | 2 8 |
| | 958,504 | | 111,155,767 | | 2,108,703 | 4,402,208 | | |
| | (Kilogrammes) | | (Francs.) | | (English lb. of manufactured silks.) | (Sterling) Prime cost in France. | | |

equal to 2,882,000 lbs. of Raw Silk, the very majoi
part fine Raw Silk, at the rate of 12¼ ounces o;
Manufactured Goods, on the average of those high
descriptions of goods, per lb. 1s. 0¾d., of Raw Silk.

Note.— † Some Silk goods mixed with Cotton, &c., but of high descriptions, as may be seen by the Official
Value of 80 francs per kilogram, compared with those of 120 francs for Plain Silks ⎫
130　　–　　– Figured – ⎬　and I have not added
120　　–　　– Ribbons ⎭
any Weight for the Silk blonde - - - - - - - value £.30,055 sterling above-mentioned,
nor for 18,382 kils. = 40,439 lbs. of Manufactured Waste - - — 42,677 — at p. 47,
nor for 93,473 - = 205,638 - of Manufactured Wool and Silk (no Value assigned) at p. 52.

£.

Besides £.34,272 Sterling Value of Silk Umbrellas, at p. 51 ⎫ Douanes.
and - 101,735 — Modes - - ibid. ⎭
(Minute made 9th June.)

Note.—It would appear by the Preamble ("Avertissement"), p. 2. of the "Administration des Douanes, 1829," that the French Official Values were fixed in 1825, and definitively confirmed on the 29th May 1826, at which period the prices of Raw and Thrown Silks were on an average much higher than of late years, and the rates of weaving were somewhat higher on an average; but those Official Values were, as it would appear, fixed low at the time, considering those circumstances, and the classes of Silk goods exported from France, many of the Plain being in delicate costly colours, some of light textures, many more yards of which to the lb. than the thicker descriptions. The Figured seem to have been valued at low relative rates, and the Ribbons at very low rates, that is at 120 francs per kilogram, which is the same as Plain goods, whereas the Ribbons are on an average higher, and considerably higher, when we take into account the class of light or highly finished Gauze Ribbons, of which France exports large proportions.

Query.—Are all the Silk goods exported from France included in these Returns? The Export Duty being at a small fraction only, it is possible that the French Customs are not very particular in regard to declarations of them; and under these circumstances, are all the goods exported for the purpose of being smuggled into this country included in those Returns? if not, then those quantities short declared would have to come in addition to the considerable quantities and amounts of Exports enumerated in these Returns.

If we consider the high classes of goods of which the Exports from France are composed, we shall find that an amount of 4,400,000 l. sterling would represent a market value here of more than 6,000,000 l. sterling, independently of the very large amounts of goods which the Swiss and the Rhenish manufacturers export.

Finsbury Square, ⎫
9th May 1832. ⎭
(signed)　　*Alexis James Doxat.*

[This Paper was communicated confidentially to two Members of the
Honourable Committee on the day above-mentioned, 9th May.]

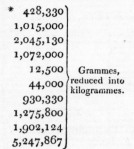

* 428,330
1,015,000
2,045,130
1,072,000
12,500
44,000
930,330
1,275,800
1,902,124
5,247,867
} Grammes, reduced into kilogrammes.

(Mr. *Alexis Doxat*'s Paper, No. 27, Delivered in to the Select Committee on the Silk Trade, 21st July 1832.)

1827. (Fo. 40.)

## ADMINISTRATION DES DOUANES.

### EXPORTATIONS des TISSUS de SOIE de FABRIQUES FRANÇAISES.

| Marchandises Exportées de l'Intérieur Seulement. | | | | | Computation into English Weight & Value. | | | | | |
|---|---|---|---|---|---|---|---|---|---|---|
| TISSUS DE SOIE. | Quantités. | Kils. | Valeurs. | Per Kilo. | Lbs. English. | £. Sterling English. | Per lb. 16oz. Engh. | | Per oz. English. | |
| | Kils. | | Frs. | Frs. | | | s. | d. | s. | d. |
| Etoffes – Pures – Unies | 431,995 | – | 51,839,400 | 120 | 950,389 | 2,053,041 | 43 | 2 ½ | 2 | 8 ⅜ |
| Etoffes – Pures – Façonnées | 151,349 | – | 19,675,370 | 130 | 332,968 | 779,223 | 46 | 9 ¾ | 2 | 11 ⅛ |
| Etoffes – Pures – Brochées – de Soie | 6,974 | – | 906,620 | 130 | 15,343 | 35,906 | 46 | 9 ¾ | 2 | 11 ⅛ |
| Etoffes – Pures – Brochées – d'or ou d'argent – fin | * 428 | – | 102,799 | 240 | 942 | 4,071 | 86 | 5 ¼ | 5 | 4 ⅞ |
| Etoffes – Pures – Brochées – d'or ou d'argent – faux | * 1,015 | – | 182,700 | 180 | 2,233 | 7,236 | 64 | 9 ¾ | 4 | – ⅝ |
| Etoffes – Mêlées – de fil, de coton ou d'autres matières | † 49,692 | – | 3,975,360 | 80 | 109,322 | 157,440 | 28 | 9 ¾ | 1 | 9 ⅝ |
| Etoffes – Mêlées – de fil, et d'or ou d'argent – fin | * 2,045 | – | 368,123 | 180 | 4,499 | 14,579 | 64 | 9 ¾ | 4 | – ⅝ |
| Etoffes – Mêlées – de fil, et d'or ou d'argent – faux | * 1,072 | – | 128,640 | 120 | 2,358 | 5,095 | 43 | 2 ½ | 2 | 8 ⅜ |
| Couvertures | 299 | – | 11,960 | 40 | 658 | 474 | 14 | 5 | – | 10 ⅞ |
| Gaze – de Soie pure | 11,546 | – | 1,293,152 | 112 | 25,401 | 51,214 | 40 | 4 | 2 | 6 ¼ |
| Gaze – mêlée d'or ou d'argent – fin | * 13 | – | 2,250 | 180 | 29 | 89 | 64 | 9 ¾ | 4 | – ⅝ |
| Gaze – mêlée d'or ou d'argent – faux | * 44 | – | 5,280 | 120 | 97 | 209 | 43 | 2 ½ | 2 | 8 ⅜ |
| Crêpe | 42,084 | – | 3,703,392 | 88 | 92,585 | 146,669 | 31 | 8 | 1 | 11 ¾ |
| Tulle | 12,270 | – | 981,600 | 80 | 26,994 | 38,875 | 28 | 9 ¾ | 1 | 9 ⅝ |
| Dentelle de Soie dite blonde | — | Frs. | 941,141 | – | - - | 37,273 | — | | — | |
| Bonneterie | 26,290 | Kils. | 2,629,000 | 100 | 57,838 | 104,119 | 36 | – | 2 | 3 |
| Passementerie – d'or ou d'argent – fin | * 930 | – | 279,099 | 300 | 2,046 | 11,053 | 108 | – | 6 | 9 |
| Passementerie – d'or ou d'argent – faux | * 1,276 | – | 38,274 | 30 | 2,807 | 1,515 | 10 | 9 ½ | – | 8 ⅛ |
| Passementerie – de Soie – pure | 27,670 | – | 2,767,000 | 100 | 60,874 | 109,584 | 36 | – | 2 | 3 |
| Passementerie – de Soie – mêlée d'or ou d'argent – fin | * 1,902 | – | 342,382 | 180 | 4,184 | 13,560 | 64 | 9 ¾ | 4 | – ⅝ |
| Passementerie – de Soie – mêlée d'or ou d'argent – faux | * 5,248 | – | 629,744 | 120 | 11,546 | 24,940 | 43 | 2 ½ | 2 | 8 ⅜ |
| Passementerie – de Soie – mêlée d'autres matières | 879 | – | 61,530 | 70 | 1,934 | 2,437 | 25 | 2 ½ | 1 | 6 ⅞ |
| Rubans, même de velours | 203,185 | – | 24,382,200 | 120 | 447,007 | 965,632 | 43 | 2 ½ | 2 | 8 ⅛ |
| | 978,206 | | 115,247,016 | | 2,152,054 | 4,564,234 | | | | |
| | (Kilogrammes) | | (Francs.) | | (Lbs. English of manufactured Silks.) | (£. Sterling, Prime cost in France.) | | | | |

equal to 2,942,604 lbs. of fine Raw and Thrown Silk.

(*See* Statement for 1829.)

† Some Silk goods mixed with Cotton, &c. but of high descriptions, as may be seen by the Official Value of 80 francs per kilogram, and those Weights and Amounts are exclusive of

| | | | | | | |
|---|---|---|---|---|---|---|
| Fo. 40.—Tissus de Bourre & Fleurets, 16,259 kils., | 887,000 frs. | = | 35,770 lbs. Engh | = | £.35,130 | sterling. |
| – 34.—Silk Umbrellas, No 49,901 - - - | 749,000 – | = | — | = | 29,644 | — |
| – 34.—Modes - - - - - - | 2,299,000 – | = | — | = | 91,061 | — |
| Woollens mixed with Silk not specified in 1827 - - - - | — | = | — | = | — | — |
| | | | | | £. | |

(*See* Minutes at the bottom of Statement for 1829.)

| | | |
|---|---|---|
| *1,655,700<br>1,277,000<br>661,500<br>3,288,720<br>4,091,000<br>428,030<br>2,194,000 | Grammes reduced into Kilogrammes. | |

(Mr. *Alexis Doxat's* Paper, No. 28. Delivered in to the Select Committee on the Silk Trade, 21st July 1832.)

1828.

(Fo. 48.)

## ADMINISTRATION DES DOUANES.

### Exportations des Tissus de Soie de Fabriques Françaises.

| MARCHANDIZES Exportées de l'Intérieur du Royaume, en payant des Droits, en Franchise ou avec prime. | | | | | Computation into English Weight and Value. | | | | | |
|---|---|---|---|---|---|---|---|---|---|---|
| TISSUS DE SOIE. | Quantités. | Kilos | Valeurs. | Fr. p' Kilo. | Lbs. English. | £. sterling value. | Per lb. 16 oz. Engh. | | Per Ounce English. | |
| | *Kilos.* | | *Francs.* | | *Lbs.* | *£.* | *s.* | *d.* | *s.* | *d.* |
| Etoffes — Pures — Unies - - - - | 425,317 | – | 51,038,040 | 120 | 935,697 | 2,021,309 | 43 | 2½ | 2 | 8⅜ |
| Etoffes — Pures — Façonnées - - - - | 140,867 | – | 18,312,710 | 130 | 309,907 | 725,256 | 46 | 9¾ | 2 | 11⅛ |
| Etoffes — Pures — Brochées — de Soie - - | 2,541 | – | 330,330 | 130 | 5,590 | 13,082 | 46 | 9¾ | 2 | 11⅛ |
| Etoffes — Pures — Brochées — d'or ou d'argent — fin | * 1,656 | – | 397,368 | 240 | 3,643 | 15,737 | 86 | 5¼ | 5 | 4⅞ |
| Etoffes — Pures — Brochées — d'or ou d'argent — faux | * 1,277 | – | 229,860 | 180 | 2,809 | 9,103 | 64 | 9¾ | 4 | –⅝ |
| Etoffes — de Fil, de Coton ou d'autres matières - - - - | † 60,530 | – | 4,842,400 | 80 | 133,166 | 191,778 | 28 | 9¾ | 1 | 9⅝ |
| Etoffes — de fil, et d'or ou d'argent fin - | * 662 | – | 119,070 | 180 | 1,456 | 4,716 | 64 | 9¾ | 4 | –⅝ |
| Couvertures - - - - - - | 523 | – | 20,920 | 40 | 1,151 | 829 | 14 | 5 | – | 10⅞ |
| Gaze de Soie pure - - - - - | 8,271 | – | 926,352 | 112 | 18,196 | 36,687 | 40 | 4 | 2 | 6¼ |
| Crêpe - - - - - - - | 42,537 | – | 3,743,256 | 88 | 93,581 | 148,248 | 31 | 8 | 1 | 11¾ |
| Tulle - - - - - - - | 10,238 | – | 819,040 | 80 | 22,524 | 32,437 | 28 | 9¾ | 1 | 9⅝ |
| Dentelle de Soie dite Blonde - - | blank. | francs. | 792,100 | – | - - | 31,370 | — | | — | |
| Bonneterie - - - - - - | 23,413 | kilos | 2,341,300 | 100 | 51,509 | 92,725 | 36 | – | 2 | 3 |
| Passementerie — d'or ou d'argent — fin | * 3,289 | – | 986,616 | 300 | 7,236 | 39,074 | 108 | – | 6 | 9 |
| Passementerie — d'or ou d'argent — faux | * 4,091 | – | 122,730 | 30 | 9,000 | 4,861 | 10 | 9½ | – | 8⅛ |
| Passementerie — de Soie — Pure - - | 25,720 | – | 2,572,000 | 100 | 56,584 | 101,861 | 36 | – | 2 | 3 |
| Passementerie — de Soie — Mêlée d'or ou d'argent — fin | * 428 | – | 77,046 | 180 | 942 | 3,051 | 64 | 9¾ | 4 | –⅝ |
| Passementerie — de Soie — Mêlée d'or ou d'argent — faux | * 2,194 | – | 263,280 | 120 | 4,827 | 10,427 | 43 | 2½ | 2 | 8⅜ |
| Passementerie — de Soie — Mêlées d' autres matières - | 942 | – | 65,940 | 70 | 2,072 | 2,611 | 25 | 2½ | 1 | 6⅞ |
| Rubans, même de Velours - - - | 228,893 | – | 27,467,160 | 120 | 503,565 | 1,087,808 | 43 | 2½ | 2 | 8⅜ |
| | 983,389 | | 115,467,518 | | 2,163,455 | 4,572,970 | | | | |
| | Kilogrammes. | | (Francs.) | | lbs. English of manufactured Silks. | £. sterling prime Cost in France. | | | | |

Equal to 2,958,193 lbs. of fine Raw and Thrown Silks.
(*See* Statement for 1829.)

† Some Silk Goods mixed with Cotton, &c. but of high descriptions, as may be seen by the Official Value of 80 *f.* per kilogram, and those Weights and Amounts are exclusive of

| Fol. | | | | | | |
|---|---|---|---|---|---|---|
| 40 | Tissus de Bourre de Soie et Fleurets, kilo. 28,288, | *f.* 1,045,816 | lbs. 62,234 | Engh = | £. 41,417 | sterling. |
| 34 | Silk Umbrellas - - No. 41,705 - | — 625,575 | — | = | 24,755 | – |
| 34 | Modes - - - - - - - | — 2,465,979 = | — | = | 97,663 | – |
| 43 | Woollens mixed with Silk - - - - 82,122 | — | 180,668 | | Blank. | |
| | | | | | £. | |

(*See* Minutes at the bottom of Statement for 1829.)

(Mr. *Alexis Doxat's* Paper, No. 29.
Delivered in to the Select Committee on the Silk Trade, 21st July 1832.)

1830. (Fo. 48.)

* 1,729,050 } Grammes
1,816,080 } reduced into
268,565 } Kilogrammes.

## ADMINISTRATION DES DOUANES.

### Exportations des Tissus de Soie de Fabriques Françaises.

| FABRICATIONS Marchandizes Françaises. | | | | | Computation into English Weight and Value. | | | | | |
|---|---|---|---|---|---|---|---|---|---|---|
| TISSUS DE SOIE. | Quantités. | Kilos. | Valeur. | Fr. p' Kilo. | Lbs. English. | £. sterling value. | Per lb. 16 oz. Engh | | Per Ounce English. | |
| | *Kilos.* | | *f.* | | *Lbs.* | £. | *s.* | *d.* | *s.* | *d.* |
| Etoffes — Pures — Unies - - - - - | 427,792 | – | 51,335,040 | 120 | 941,142 | 2,033,071 | 43 | 2½ | 2 | 8⅜ |
| Etoffes — Pures — Façonnées - - - - | 146,320 | – | 19,021,600 | 130 | 321,904 | 753,331 | 46 | 9¾ | 2 | 11⅛ |
| Etoffes — Pures — Brochées — de Soie - - | 2,117 | – | 275,210 | 130 | 4,657 | 10,899 | 46 | 9¾ | 2 | 11⅛ |
| Etoffes — Pures — Brochées — d'or ou d'argent — fin | * 1,729 | – | 414,972 | 240 | 3,804 | 16,435 | 86 | 5¼ | 5 | 4⅞ |
| Etoffes — Pures — Brochées — d'or ou d'argent — faux | 1,222 | – | 219,960 | 180 | 2,688 | 8,711 | 64 | 9¾ | 4 | –⅝ |
| Etoffes — Mêlées de fil, coton ou d'autres matières | † 74,426 | – | 5,954,080 | 80 | 163,737 | 235,805 | 28 | 9¾ | 1 | 9⅝ |
| Couvertures - - - - - - | 276 | – | 11,040 | 40 | 607 | 437 | 14 | 5 | – | 10⅞ |
| Gaze de Soie pure - - - - - | 11,168 | – | 1,250,816 | 112 | 24,570 | 49,537 | 40 | 4 | 2 | 6¼ |
| Crêpe - - - - - - - | 36,421 | – | 3,205,048 | 88 | 80,126 | 126,933 | 31 | 8 | 1 | 11¾ |
| Tulle - - - - - - | 7,630 | – | 610,400 | 80 | 16,786 | 24,174 | 28 | 9¾ | 1 | 9⅝ |
| Dentelle de Soie dite Blonde - - | blank. | francs. | 749,480 | – | - - | 29,682 | — | | — | |
| Bonneterie - - - - - - | 16,173 | kilo. | 1,617,300 | 100 | 35,581 | 64,051 | 36 | – | 2 | 3 |
| Passementerie — d'or ou d'argent — fin | * 1,816 | – | 544,824 | 300 | 3,995 | 21,577 | 108 | – | 6 | 9 |
| Passementerie — d'or ou d'argent — faux | 3,290 | – | 98,700 | 30 | 7,238 | 3,909 | 10 | 9½ | – | 8⅛ |
| Passementerie — de Soie — Pure - - | 26,811 | – | 2,681,100 | 100 | 58,984 | 106,182 | 36 | – | 2 | 3 |
| Passementerie — de Soie — Mêlée d'or ou d'argent — fin | * 269 | – | 48,342 | 180 | 592 | 1,915 | 64 | 9¾ | 4 | –⅝ |
| Passementerie — de Soie — Mêlée d'or ou d'argent — faux | 1,378 | – | 165,360 | 120 | 3,031 | 6,549 | 43 | 2½ | 2 | 8⅜ |
| Passementerie — de Soie — Mêlées d' autres Couleurs - | 639 | – | 44,730 | 70 | 1,406 | 1,771 | 25 | 2½ | 1 | 6⅞ |
| Rubans, même de Velours - - - - | 190,590 | | 22,870,800 | 120 | 419,298 | 905,774 | 43 | 2½ | 2 | 8⅜ |
| | 950,067 | | 111,118,802 | | 2,090,146 | 4,400,743 | | | | |
| | (Kilogrammes) | | (Francs.) | | (lbs. English of manufactured Silks.) | £. sterling prime Cost in France. | | | | |

Equal to lbs. 2,857,955 of fine Raw and Thrown Silks.

(*See* Statement for 1829.)

† Some Silk Goods mixed with Cotton, &c.; but of high descriptions as may be seen by the official Value of 80*f.* per Kilogram, and those Weights and Amounts are exclusive of

| Fol. | | | | | | |
|---|---|---|---|---|---|---|
| 51 | Tissus de Bourre et Fleurets, | kilo. 16,270, | *f.* 828,336 = | lbs. 35,794 | Engh = | £. 32,805 sterling. |
| 51 | Silk Umbrellas - | No. 46,186 | — 692,790 = | — | = | 27,437 |
| 51 | Modes - - - - - - | | — 2,152,813 = | — | = | 85,260 |
| 52 | Woollens mixed with Silks - | 108,849 | — = | 239,468 | | Blank. |
| | | | | | | £. |

(*See* Minutes at the bottom of Statement for 1829.)

(Mr. *Alexis Doxat's* Paper, No. 30.
Delivered in to the Select Committee on the Silk Trade,
18 July 1832.)

RECAPITULATION of the ANNUAL EXPORTS from *France*, in the Years 1827, 1828, 1829 and 1830, of FRENCH MANUFACTURED SILKS, of every description; showing their Quantity in FRENCH WEIGHT and VALUE in FRANCS, computed into English Weight and Value.

| | | | Kilogrammes. | Valeurs, Francs. | Computations into | | |
|---|---|---|---|---|---|---|---|
| | | | | | Lbs. English of Manufactured Silks, | and £. Sterling, Prime cost in France. | |
| Folios. | | | | *Frs.* | *Lbs.* | *£.* | |
| 1827. 40 | Tissus de Soie - | * | Kilo. 978,206 | 115,247,016 | 2,152,054 | 4,564,234 | |
| 1828. 40 | Ditto - - | * | – 983,389 | 115,467,518 | 2,163,455 | 4,527,970 | |
| 1829. 48 | Ditto - - | * | – 958,505 | 111,155,767 | 2,108,703 | 4,402,208 | |
| 1830. 48 | Ditto - - | * | – 950,067 | 111,118,802 | 2,090,146 | 4,400,703 | |
| 1827. 40 | Tissus de Bourre et Fleuret - - | | kilo. 16,259 | 887,024 | 35,770 | 35,130 | Exclusive of Woollens mixed with Silk. |
| 34 | Silk Umbrellas - | | No. 49,901 | 748,515 | - - - | 29,644 | |
| 34 | Modes - - - | | - - - | 2,299,307 | - - - | 91,062 | £. 155,836 - - Exclusive of quantities and value of Woollens mixed with Silk. |
| – | Woollens mixed with Silk - - - | | - - - | - - - | - - - | - - - | (Woollens mixed with Silk not distinguished before 1828.) |
| 1828. 40 | Tissus de Bourre et Fleuret - - | | kilo. 28,288 | 1,045,816 | 62,234 | 41,417 | |
| 34 | Silk Umbrellas - | | No. 41,705 | 625,575 | - - - | 24,755 | |
| 34 | Modes - - - | | - - - | 2,465,979 | - - - | 97,663 | £. 163,835 - - Exclusive of value of Woollens mixed with Silk. |
| 43 | Woollens mixed with Silk - - - | | kilo. 82,122 | - - - | - - - | - - - | |
| 1829. 47 | Tissus de Bourre et Fleuret - - | | – 18,382 | 1,077,584 | 40,440 | 42,667 | |
| 51 | Silk Umbrellas - | | No. 57,692 | 865,380 | - - - | 34,272 | |
| 51 | Modes - - - | | - - - | 2,568,821 | - - - | 101,735 | £. 178,684 ditto. ditto. |
| 52 | Woollens mixed with Silk - - - | | kilo. 93,472 | - - - | - - - | - - - | |
| 1830. 47 | Tissus de Bourre et Fleuret - - | | – 16,270 | 828,336 | 35,794 | 32,805 | |
| 51 | Silk Umbrellas - | | No. 46,186 | 592,790 | - - - | 27,437 | |
| 51 | Modes - - - | | - - - | 2,152,813 | - - - | 85,260 | £. 145,502 ditto. ditto. |
| 52 | Woollens mixed with Silk - - - | | kilo. 108,849 | - - - | - - - | - - - | |

\* *Note.* In the above quantities of

Kilo. 978,206 ⎫
983,389 ⎬ are comprised
958,505 ⎪
950,067 ⎭
of some Waste, &c.,) which more than make up for the difference that would arise from a portion of Cotton, &c.

⎧ Kil. 49,692 ⎫ of Silks mixed with Cotton, &c. (of high value, see Notes, &c.
⎨ 60,530 ⎬ 1829;) but on the other hand, I have not taken into account, in
⎪ 85,623 ⎪ the said quantities and values, the quantities and values of Silk
⎩ 74,426 ⎭ Umbrellas, Modes, and Woollens mixed with Silk (independently

(N.B.—*See* Notes at the bottom of the Returns for 1829.)

1827 to 1830 : (Mr. *Alexis Doxat's* Paper, No. 31.
Delivered in to the Select Committee on the Silk
Trade, 21 July 1832.)

## DOUANES ROYALES DE FRANCE.
IMPORTS of FOREIGN MANUFACTURED SILKS into *France* for Home Consumption.

| IMPORTATIONS définitivement pour la Consommations intérieure du Royaume. | Fol. | Kilogrammes. | Valeurs, Francs. | Taux d'Evaluations. |
|---|---|---|---|---|
| **1827.**     TISSUS DE SOIE : | | | | |
| Etoffes, Schalls et Mouchoirs   { unis - - | 18 | kil   5,281 | fr.   640,310 | fr. 110 |
| { façonnées - | – | –   188 | –   22,560 | – 120 |
| Gaze de Soie pure - - - - - | – | –   33 | –   3,696 | – 112 |
| Crêpe - - - - - - - - | – | –   - | – | – 64 |
| Dentelles - - - - - - - | – | –   - | –   2,904 | valeur |
| Bonneterie - - - - - - | – | –   3 | –   300 | fr. 100 |
| Rubans de toutes sortes - - - - | – | –   9,008 | – 1,080,360 | – 120 |
|     TISSUS DE FLEURET : | | | | |
| Bonneterie - - - - - - | – | 1,286 | –   51,440 | – 40 |
| | | kil.   16,339 | fr. 1,801,570 | |
| Computed into English weight and value - - | – | lbs.   35,946* | £. 71,349† | |
| **MARCHANDISES** admises pour la Consommation avec Paiement des droits. | | | | |
| **1828.**     TISSUS DE SOIE : | | | | |
| Etoffes, Schalls et Mouchoirs   { unis - - | 18 | kil.   6,276 | fr.   690,360 | fr. 110 |
| { façonnées - | – | –   122 | –   14,640 | – 120 |
| Gaze de Soie pure - - - - - | – | –   50 | –   5,600 | – 112 |
| Crêpe - - - - - - - - | – | –   4 | –   256 | – 64 |
| Dentelles - - - - - - - | – | –   - | –   3,835 | valeur |
| Rubans de toutes sortes - - - - | – | –   11,205 | 1,344,600 | fr. 120 |
|     TISSUS DE FLEURET : | | | | |
| Bonneterie - - - - - - | – | –   683 | –   27,320 | – 40 |
| | | kil.   18,340 | fr. 2,086,611 | |
| Computed into English weight and value - - | – | lbs.   40,348* | £. 82,638† | |
| **MARCHANDISES** mises en Consommation. | | | | |
| **1829.**     TISSUS DE SOIE : | | | | |
| Etoffes, Schalls et Mouchoirs   { unis - - | 26 | kil.   7,275 | fr.   800,250 | fr. 110 |
| { façonnées - | – | –   251 | –   30,120 | – 120 |
| Gaze de Soie pure - - - - - | – | –   91 | –   10,192 | – 112 |
| Crêpe - - - - - - - | – | –   2 | –   128 | – 64 |
| Dentelles - - - - - - - | – | –   - | –   31,100 | valeur |
| Rubans de toutes sortes - - - - | – | –   12,202 | – 1,464,240 | fr. 120 |
|     TISSUS DE FLEURET : | | | | |
| Bonneterie - - - - - - | – | –   1,300 | –   52,000 | – 40 |
| Passementerie et Rubannerie - - - | – | –   71 | –   2,982 | – 42 |
| | | kil.   21,192 | fr. 2,391,012 | |
| Computed into English weight and value - - | – | lbs.   46,622* | £. 94,694† | |
| **MARCHANDISES** mises en Consommation. | | | | |
| **1830.**     TISSUS DE SOIE : | | | | |
| Etoffes, Schalls et Mouchoirs   { unis - - | 26 | kil.   10,354 | fr. 1,138,940 | fr. 110 |
| { façonnées - | – | –   312 | –   37,440 | – 120 |
| Gaze de Soie pure - - - - - | – | –   83 | –   9,296 | – 112 |
| Crêpe - - - - - - - | – | –   1 | –   64 | – 64 |
| Dentelle de Soie dite Blonde - - - | – | –   - | –   29,339 | valeur |
| Rubans, même de Velours - - - - | – | –   13,259 | – 1,591,080 | fr. 120 |
|     TISSUS DE FLEURET : | | | | |
| Bonneterie - - - - - - | – | –   1,572 | –   62,880 | – 40 |
| Passementerie et Rubannerie - - - | – | –   11 | –   462 | – 42 |
| | | kil.   25,592 | fr. 2,869,501 | |
| Computed into English weight and value - - | – | lbs.   56,303* | £. 113,643† | |

    * Lbs. English of Manufactured Silks.      † £. Sterling prime Cost in France.

(Mr. *Alexis Doxat*'s Paper, No. 32.
Delivered in to the Select Committee on the Silk Trade, 21st July 1832.)

AN ESTIMATE of the TOTAL AMOUNTS of the SILK MANUFACTURE of the United Kingdom, during the Periods 1815-17, 1818-20, 1821-23, and 1824-25, (understated in regard to Wages, in these Periods; respecting which, *see* my Paper, No. 4, delivered in to this Honourable Committee, on the 11th April.)

N. B. Papers, Nos. 2 & 3, were delivered in on the same day.

## AVERAGES PER ANNUM.

| | Amounts of Duties. | Amounts of Wages, &c. (understated.) | Consumption of all descriptions of Raw, Thrown, and Waste, &c. | Rates of Wages per lb. of all descriptions. | Amount of Duties, Wages, &c. Collectively. (Wages understated.) | | Cost of Silk of all Descriptions, exclusive of Duties. (a) | | Total Amounts of Duties, Wages, &c. and of Silk. |
|---|---|---|---|---|---|---|---|---|---|
| | | | | | Of the various descriptions imported. | See Paper, No. 3 | Aggregate Amounts. | Averages. | Amount of Manufacture. (Understated in regard to Wages.) |
| | *See* Paper, No. 3. $\frac{3}{B}$ £. | *See* Paper, No. 3. $\frac{3}{B}$ £. | *See* Paper, No. 2. on lbs. | *See* Paper, No. 3. $\frac{3}{B}$ per lb. s. d. | *See* Paper, No. 3 $\frac{3}{A}$ per lb. s. d. | $\frac{3}{A}$ £. | £. | per lb. s. d. | £. per lb. s. d. |
| 1815-17 | 465,000 | 1,608,000 | 1,484,000 | at 21 8 | at 27 11 much understated. | 2,073,000 | 1,927,000 at 25 11 | | 4,000,000 at 53 10 |
| 1818-20 | 599,000 | 2,120,000 | 1,931,000 | „ 22 - | 28 2 | 2,719,000 | 2,571,000 „ 26 7 | | 5,290,000 „ 54 9 |
| 1821-23 | 729,000 | 2,785,000 | 2,463,000 | „ 22 7 | 28 6 | 3,514,000 | 2,544,000 „ 20 8 | | 6,058,000 „ 49 2 |
| 1824-25 | 272,000 | 3,991,000 | 3,611,000* | „ 22 1 | 23 7 | 4,263,000 | 3,548,000 „ 19 8 | | 7,811,000 „ 43 3 |
| Averages of 1821-23 1824-25 | 500,000 | 3,388,000 | 3,037,000 | „ 22 4 | at 26 2 | 3,888,000 | 3,046,000 „ 20 2 | | 6,935,000 „ 46 4 |

* By reference to my Paper, No. 2, it will be seen that the Quantities, Duty paid, as per Parliamentary Returns, of all descriptions of Raw and Thrown Silks, Waste, &c. in 1824-25, were equal to those in 1826-31, on an Average; and by the same Paper, that the same is the case in regard to the quantities brought into consumption, computed into Italian Standard, in those two periods:

| | Quantities, Duty paid, as per Parliamentary Returns, (of all descriptions of Waste, Knubs, and Husks.) | | Quantities consumed, brought into one Standard, that of fine Italian Silks. | Computed Differences between the Quantities of all descriptions brought into consumption, and those Quantities, computed into fine Italian Standard. |
|---|---|---|---|---|
| | *lbs.* | *lbs.* | *lbs.* | |
| Averages per Annum, *viz.* 1824-25 - | 3,807,000 | 3,611,000 | 2,783,000 - - being 23 per cent. less. | |
| Ditto - - - 1826-31 - | 3,819,000 | 3,813,000 † | 2,765,000 - - „ 27½ „ less. | |

Quantities of all descriptions, brought into consumption according to Mr. Doxat's Tables, Nos. 1 & 2, delivered in on the 11th April.

† N. B. Large Quantities of Waste, &c. in the last six years, and also large proportions of coarse Silks.

(a) Taken from a Statement which I have made from period to period, of "Approximate Prices and Amounts of Raw and Thrown Silks, Waste, &c. consumed in Great Britain, from 1815-17 to 1831."

(Mr. *Alexis Doxat's* Paper, No. 33.
Delivered in to the Select Committee on the Silk Trade,
21st July 1832.)

AN ESTIMATE of the TOTAL AMOUNTS of the SILK MANUFACTURE of the United Kingdom, during the Years 1826, 1827, 1828, 1829, 1830 and 1831. (Overstated in regard to Wages in these Years; respecting which *see* the course of my Evidence and my Paper, No. 4, delivered in to the Committee on the 11th of April.)

N.B. Papers Nos. 2 & 3 were delivered in on the same day.

| | Amounts of Duties. | Amounts of Wages, &c. (Overstated.) | Consumption of all Descriptions of Raw, Thrown, and Waste, &c. | Rates of Wages per lb. of all descriptions | Amounts of Duties, Wages, &c. Collectively, (Wages overstated.) | | Cost of Silk of all Descriptions exclusive of Duties. (b) | | Total Amounts of Duties, Wages, &c. and of Silk. |
| | | | | | Of the various Descriptions imported. | | Aggregate Amounts. | Averages. | Amount of Manufacture. (Overstated in regard to Wages.) |
| | See Paper, No. 3. $\frac{3}{B}$ £. | See Paper, No. 3. $\frac{3}{B}$. £. | See Paper, No. 2. on lbs. | See Paper, No 3. $\frac{3}{B}$ per lb. s   d | See Paper, No. 3. $\frac{3}{A}$ per lb. s. d. | See Paper, No. 3. $\frac{3}{A}$ £. | £ | per lb. s. d. | per lb. £.   s. d. |
|---|---|---|---|---|---|---|---|---|---|
| 1826 - | 82,000 | 1,859,000 | 2,493,000 at 14  11 | at 15  7 | 1,941,000 | 2,060,000 | at 16  6 | 4,001,000 at 32  1 |
| 1827 | 128,000 | 3,519,000 | 4,392,000 ,, 16  - | 16  7 | 3,647,000 | 3,940,000 (c) | 17  11 | 7,587,000 ,, 34  6 |
| 1828 | 111,000 | 2,811,000 | (a)4,028,000 ,, 13  11 | 14  6 | 2,922,000 | 3,612,000 (c) | 17  11 | 6,534,000 ,, 32  5 |
| 1829 | 45,000 | 1,787,000 | 3,038,000 ,, 11  9 | 12  1 | 1,832,000 | 2,150,000 | 14  2 | 3,982,000 ,, 26  3 |
| 1830 | 90,000 | 3,092,000 | (a)4,654,000 ,, 13  3 | 13  9 | 3,182,000 | 3,196,000 | 13  9 | 6,378,000 ,, 27  6 |
| 1831 | 95,000 | 2,493,000 | (a)4,272,000 ,, 11  8 | 12  1 | 2,588,000 | 2,785,000 (d) | 13  -½ | 5,373,000 ,, 25  1¼ |
| Averages of 1826-31, 6 years | 92,000 | 2,594,000 | 3,813,000 * | | | 2,685,000 | 2,957,000 | | 5,642,000 |
| Averages of 1829-31, 3 years | 77,000 | 2,457,000 | 3,988,000 | | | 2,534,000 | 2,710,000 | | 5,244,000 |

* By reference to my Paper, No. 2, it will be seen that the Quantities, duty paid, as per Parliamentary Returns, of all descriptions of Raw and Thrown Silks, Waste, &c. in 1824-25, were equal to those of 1826-31, on an average; and by the same Paper, that the same is the case in regard to the Quantities brought into consumption, computed into Italian Standards in those two periods.

678.

**Computed Differences between the Quantities of all Descriptions brought into Consumption, and those Quantities computed into fine Italian Standard.**

Quantities consumed brought into One Standard, that of fine Italian Silks.

| lbs. | |
|---|---|
| 2,783,000 -- being 23 per cent. less. | |
| 2,765,000 -- being 27½ per cent. less. | |

Quantities, Duty Paid, as per Parliamentary Returns, (of all Descriptions.)

| lbs. | lbs. |
|---|---|
| 3,611,000 | 3,807,000 † |
| 3,813,000 | 3,819,000 ‡ |

Averages per annum, viz. 1824-25 †
Ditto - 1826-31
† Inclusive of waste, knubs and husks.

‡ Large Quantities of Waste Silk, &c. in the last six years, and also large proportions of coarse Silks.

(a) Very large quantities of Waste in those years.

(b) Taken from a statement which I have made from period to period of "Approximative Prices and Amounts of Raw and Thrown Silks, Waste, &c. consumed in Great Britain, from 1815-17 to 1831."

(c) The prices of Raw and Thrown Silks were higher in 1828 than in 1827, but the much larger quantity of Waste, &c. in 1828 brought down the average to the same rate of 17 s. 11 d. per lb. of all descriptions.

(d) The low rate of 13 s. 0½ d. per lb. for the average of Silks of all descriptions, in 1831, arises not only from some fall in the prices since 1824-25, but from the larger proportions in late years of coarse descriptions, and particularly of Waste Silks and Knubs and Husks, the value of which being comparatively very little, has the effect of lowering the average price of Silks collectively of all descriptions.

The Scale of per Centages joined to this Table of Prices, indicates in a great measure the degrees of fineness of the Standard on which we have worked at various periods; it will be seen that up to 1824-25 inclusive, we gradually worked on a finer standard, whilst the inverse, on an average, has taken place since that period; and beyond this I should observe here again, that of late years we have applied Silks of the same Standard to lower descriptions of Goods on an average; for example, large quantities to the Manufacture of plain Goods, which used to be worked into figured and fancy Goods.

| | Prices of 3-4 to 4-5 Cocoons, Milan and Bergam Raw Silks, exclusive of Duties. s. d. | Total Average of Raw, Thrown, Waste, &c. (i.e.) of Silks of all Descriptions, exclusive of Duties. s. d. | Differences per Cent. between those relative Prices. s. d. |
|---|---|---|---|
| 1815-17 - | 32  - | 25  11 | 6  1=to 19 p'ct. |
| 1818-20 - | 31  4 | 26  7 | 4  9= 15 |
| 1821-23 - | 24  4 | 28  8 | 3  8= 15 |
| 1824-25 - | 21  9 | 19  8 | 2  1= 10 |
| The protective Laws of 1766 removed. | | | |
| 1826 - | 20  9 | 16  6 | 4  3=to 20 p'ct. |
| 1827 - | 21  8 | 17  11 | 3  9= 17 |
| 1828 - | 22  9 | 17  11 | 4  10= 21 |
| 1829 - | 18  5 | 14  2 | 4  3= 23 |
| 1830 - | 17  6 | 13  9 | 3  9= 21 |
| 1831 - | 17  3 | 13  0½ | 4  2½= 25 |

(Mr. *Alexis Doxat*'s Paper, No. 35,
Delivered in to Select Committee on the Silk Trade,
21st July 1832.)

AN ABSTRACT STATEMENT of the EXPORTS of FRENCH SILK MANUFACTURES, for the Years 1827 to 1830 ; conjointly with an ABSTRACT VIEW of the TOTAL AMOUNTS of the SILK MANUFACTURES of the United Kingdom, for the Years 1826–31, 1829–31, and 1815–17 to 1824–25.

| Folios of Printed Returns. | Quantities of Manufactured Goods, mostly of high and very high descriptions. | Valued in Francs at | Computations into English | | Approximate Estimates of what would be the Value of those high descriptions of Goods in our Markets, taken at 40 per Cent. above Prime Cost in France. |
|---|---|---|---|---|---|
| | | | WEIGHTS and | VALUE. | |
| | *Kilogrammes.* * | *Francs.* | *Lbs. English.* † | *£. Sterling.* | *£. Sterling.* |
| 40 - - 1827 | 978,000 | 115,247,000 | 2,152,000 | 4,564,000 | 6,390,000 |
| 40 - - 1828 | 983,000 | 115,468,000 | 2,163,000 | 4,573,000 | 6,402,000 |
| 48 - - 1829 | 959,000 | 111,156,000 | 2,109,000 | 4,402,000 | 6,163,000 |
| 48 - - 1830 | 950,000 | 111,119,000 | 2,090,000 | 4,401,000 | 6,161,000 |

*N. B.* These Exports are independent of the considerable Quantities exported from the other Continental Silk Manufactures.

---

The Total Amounts of our Silk Manufactures have been

In 1826–31 - - 6 years, per Annum £. 5,642,000 ⎫ Taken at Estimates *Overstated*
   1829–31 - - 3 ditto - - ditto - 5,244,000 ⎭      in regard to Wages.

Previously to the removal of our Protective Laws of 1766, they were

In 1815–17 - - 3 years, per Annum £. 4,000,000 ⎫
   1818–20 - - 3 ditto - - ditto - 5,290,000 ⎪ Taken at Estimates very much *Understated*
   1821–23 - - 3 ditto - - ditto - 6,058,000 ⎬ in regard to Wages, respecting which,
   1824–25 - - 2 ditto - - ditto - 7,811,000 ⎪ see my Paper No. 4, delivered in to
                            ⎪ the Committee on the 11th of April,
Medium ⎰ 1821–23 - - ⎱ 5 years, per Annum £. 6,935,000 ⎭ relative to the mode in which I have
       ⎱ 1824–25 - - ⎰                              made my Estimates.

---

* Those Quantities of French Manufactured Silks Exported, comprised some Silk mixed with Cotton ; viz.

                                   ⎧ But of high descriptions ; and those portions of Cotton which they may contain, are more than compensated by various Items of Exports, such as Silk Umbrellas, Modes, and Woollens mixed with Silk ; besides Goods made with Waste, &c. none of which are comprised in these Statements, as they are introduced under various distinct heads, in the Returns of the French Customs ; all of which I have also made Abstracts for each Year, from the said Returns ; respecting which I beg leave to refer, in order to avoid superfluous repetitions, to the circumstantial notes joined to the detailed Returns for the Year 1829.

*Kilo.* 50,000 in 1827
      61,000 - 1828
      86,000 - 1829
      74,000 - 1830

† It is estimated that those Quantities of Manufactured Silks of high classes, would require about

    *lbs.* 2,943,000 English ⎫
        2,958,000 ditto   ⎪ Of Raw and Thrown Silks, mostly
        2,882,000 ditto   ⎬      of fine Standard.
        2,858,000 ditto   ⎭

(Mr. *Alexis Doxat's* Paper, No. 36,
Delivered in to the Select Committee on the Silk Trade,
21st July 1832.)

STATEMENT intended to show the DIFFERENCES which range between the PRICES of SILKS at *London* and at *Lyons*.

| | Prices Current of Milan and Bergam Raw Silk, of 3-4 to 4-5 Cocoons, at London. | | PRICES CURRENT of French Organzine of 24-25 Deniers at Lyons. | | PRICES CURRENT of French Trams, of 24-26 Deniers at Lyons. | | AGGREGATE of French Organzine, 24-25 Deniers, and Trams of 24-26 Deniers. | | DIFFERENCES between the Prices Current of Milan and Bergam Raw Silk of 3-4 to 4-5 Cocoons in London, and the Aggregate of French Organzine of 24-25 Deniers, and Trams of 24-26 Deniers, at Lyons. | |
|---|---|---|---|---|---|---|---|---|---|---|
| | | Cash, 14 Days. | Discount 12½ per Cent. and 1 Month. | Computation into Sterling Cash, 1 Month. | Discount, 12½ per Cent. and 1 Month. | Computation into Sterling Cash, 1 Month. | | Cash, 1 Month. | | |
| | | *s. d.* | *f. c.* | *s. d.* | *f. c.* | *s. d.* | | *s. d.* | * * *s. d.* | |
| 1826. | * | 20/3¼ | 40 – | 25/2 | 38 75 | 24/4½ | * | 24/9¼ | 4/6 | |
| | | 18/1 | 36 75 | 23/1¼ | 37 – | 23/3¼ | | 23/2¼ | 5/1¼ | |
| | | 20/0½ | 38 25 | 24/0½ | 37 50 | 23/7 | | 23/9¾ | 3/9¼ | |
| | | 20/2¼ | 36 90 | 23/2¼ | 36 85 | 23/2 | | 23/2 | 2/11¾ | |
| | *s. d.* 19/7¾ | | *f. c.* 37 95 | 23/10½ | *f. c.* 37 50 | 23/7¼ | 23/8¾ | | | 4/1 |
| 1827. | | 21/5¾ | 37 15 | 23/4 | 38 – | 23/11 | | 23/7½ | 2/1¾ | |
| | | 20/7 | 37 20 | 23/4¼ | 36 35 | 22/10¼ | | 23/1¼ | 2/6¼ | |
| | | 20/9¼ | 35 70 | 22/5 | 33 90 | 21/4 | | 21/10½ | 1/1¼ | |
| | | 21/ | 36 60 | 22/10 | 34 15 | 21/6¼ | | 22/2 | 1/2 | |
| | 20/11½ | | 36 65 | 22/11¼ | 35 60 | 22/5 | 22/8¼ | | | 1/8¾ |
| 1828. | | 21/9¾ | 38 10 | 24/0 | 35 80 | 22/6¼ | | 23/3 | 1/5¼ | |
| | | 22/0½ | 36 75 | 23/1¼ | 34 35 | 21/7¼ | | 22/4¼ | 0/3¾ | |
| | | 22/1¼ | 36 60 | 23/0½ | 34 95 | 21/11½ | | 22/6 | 0/4¾ | |
| | | 21/11½ | 36 50 | 22/11¼ | 35 – | 22/0 | | 22/5¾ | 0/6¼ | |
| | 21/11¾ | | 37 – | 23/3 | 35 – | 22/0¼ | 22/7¾ | | | 0/8 |
| 1829. | | 21/ | 36 75 | 23/1¼ | 34 60 | 21/9¼ | | 22/5¼ | 1/5¼ | |
| | | 18/5½ | 35 70 | 22/4 | 34 40 | 21/6¾ | | 21/11¼ | 3/5¾ | |
| | | 17/6 | 36 60 | 23/0 | 34 – | 21/4 | | 22/2 | 4/8 | |
| | | 17/3¼ | 36 – | 22/7½ | 33 75 | 21/2¼ | | 21/10¾ | 4/7½ | |
| | 18/6½ | | 36 25 | 22/9¼ | 34 20 | 21/5½ | 22/1¼ | | | 3/6½ |
| 1830. | | 17/4½ | 34 90 | 21/11¼ | 32 80 | 20/7 | | 21/3 | 3/10½ | |
| | | 17/5 | 32 95 | 20/8¾ | 31 30 | 19/7¾ | | 20/2¼ | 2/9¼ | |
| | | 18/10 | 32 10 | 20/2 | 30 80 | 19/3¼ | | 19/8½ | 0/10½ | |
| | | 17/8¾ | 30 50 | 19/1½ | 29 20 | 18/8¾ | | 18/11 | 1/2¼ | |
| | 17/10 | | 32 60 | 20/5¾ | 31 5 | 19/6¾ | 20/0¼ | | | 2/2 |
| 1831. | | 17/7¼ | 28 – | 17/6¼ | 28 – | 17/6¼ | | 17/6¼ | Raw at London higher than Organzine & Trams at Lyons 0/1 | |
| | | 16/11¼ | 30 40 | 19/0¾ | 29 15 | 18/3¼ | | 18/8 | 1/8¾ lower. | |
| | | 16/10½ | 30 40 | 19/0½ | 29 25 | 18/3¾ | | 18/8 | 1/9½ do. | |
| | | 16/5¼ | 31 – | 19/5 | 28 75 | 18/0 | | 18/8½ | 2/3¼ do. | |
| | 16/11½ | | 29 95 | 18/9 | 28 80 | 18/0¼ | 18/4¾ | | 5/9½ | |
| | | | | | | | | | 1 higher as above. | |
| 1832. | | 16/11½ | 30 25 | 18/11½ | 29 25 | 18/3¾ | | 18/7½ | 5/8½ (¼=1/5 | |
| 4 Months. | 16/11½ | | 30 25 | 18/11½ | 29 25 | 18/3¾ | 18/7½ | | | 1/8 |

*Notes.*—The point of comparison has been taken between the prices of Milan and Bergam Raw Silks of 3-4 to 4-5 Cocoons at London; and of French Organzines of 24-25 deniers } collectively, at Lyons.
Ditto, Tram - - 24-26 ditto }
because quotations of French Raw Silks are but seldom received in London, besides our being but imperfectly acquainted with their denominations. I should observe, that I have reason to believe that French Organzine and Tram are made with Raw Silks of qualities superior on an average to the range of the qualities of Milan and Bergam Raw Silks of 3-4 to 4-5 Cocoons comprised in our Prices Current.

This Scale being made for the whole series of years on the same descriptions of Raw Silks at London, and of Thrown Silks at Lyons, it answers all the ends required as an index of the relative variations in prices that have taken place in those two markets, from quarter to quarter and year to year, for the reasons which I have stated in various instances during the course of my Examinations before this Honourable Committee, on the 11th, 13th, 17th, 18th and 19th of April last.

## APPENDIX TO PAPER (No. 36.)

| | Prices Current of Milan and Bergam Raw Silk, of 3-4 to 4-5 Cocoons. Cash, 14 Days. | | Corresponding to, at Lyons, With Discount 12½ per Cent. and 1 Month. | | Computation into Sterling Cash, 1 Month. | | Aggregate of French Organzine, of 24-25 deniers, and Trams of 24-26 deniers. | DIFFERENCES between the Prices at which Milan and Bergam Raw Silk, of 3-4 to 4-5 Cocoons, stand in at Lyons, and the Aggregate of French Organzine, of 24-25 deniers, and Trams of 24-26 deniers, at Lyons. |
|---|---|---|---|---|---|---|---|---|
| | *l. c.* | | *f. c.* | | *s. d.* | | | |
| 1826 - - | 22 2 | = | 34 25 | = | 21/8 | | | |
| | 19 10 | = | 30 55 | = | 19/2½ | | | |
| | 21 14 | = | 33 70 | = | 21/3½ | | *s. d.* | *s. d.* |
| | 21 17 | = | 33 85 | = | 21/4½ | | | |
| | | | | | | 20/10¾ | 23/8¾ | 2/10 |
| 1827 - - | 22 16 | = | 34 55 | = | 21/9¼ | | | |
| | — | = | — | = | — | | | |
| | 21 10 | = | 32 25 | = | 20/4 | | | |
| | 22 19 | = | 34 50 | = | 21/7¾ | | | |
| | | | | | | 21/3¼ | 22/8¼ | 1/5 |
| 1828 - - | 23 2 | = | 34 50 | = | 21/9¼ | | | |
| | — | = | — | = | — | | | |
| | 22 16 | = | 34 5 | = | 21/6 | | | |
| | 22 16 | = | 34 5 | = | 21/6¼ | | | |
| | | | | | | 21/7¼ | 22/7¾ | 1/0½ |
| 1829 - - | — | = | — | = | — | | | |
| | 18 17 | = | 28 60 | = | 18/0 | | | |
| | 18 6 | = | 27 75 | = | 17/5 | | | |
| | 18 14 | = | 28 40 | = | 17/10 | | | |
| | | | | | | 17/9 | 22/1¼ | 4/4¼ |
| 1830 - - | 18 8 | = | 27 95 | = | 17/6¾ | | | |
| | 18 14 | = | 28 35 | = | 17/10 | | | |
| | 20 4 | = | 30 40 | = | 19/1½ | | | |
| | 19 5 | = | 29 15 | = | 18/4 | | | |
| | | | | | | 18/2½ | 20/0¼ | 1/9¾ |
| 1831 - - | 17 17 | = | 27 20 | = | 17/1¼ | | | |
| | 18 - | = | 27 45 | = | 17/3 | | | |
| | 17 2 | = | 26 10 | = | 16/5¼ | | | |
| | 17 - | = | 26 - | = | 16/4¼ | | | |
| | | | | | | 16/9½ | 18/4¾ | 1/7¼ |
| 1832 - - 4 Months. | 18 2 | = | 27 55 | = | 17/3¼ | 17/3¼ | 18/7 | 1/3¾ |

*Notes.*—In order to extend this point of view, and to render it more comprehensive, I present herewith the Prices Current at Milan and Bergam of Raw Silk of 3-4 to 4-5 Cocoons, with the computation of the prices at which those Silks would have stood imported at Lyons; and the differences which they present in the various periods, with the collective prices at Lyons of French Organzine of 24–25 deniers, and Trams of 24-26 deniers, will show again how erroneous must be the idea expressed of an analogy, in general, between the prices of Silks in Italy and in France, and that the prices in Italy govern those of France; while I contend that the partial Imports of Italian Silks operate only as moderators in favour of the French manufacturers, who can always have recourse to them when the prices of their own Silks ascend to the points at which Italian Silks can be imported, and that in general they obtain the Silks of their own produce, both Raw and Thrown, at lower prices (speaking of relative qualities) than they can import the produce of Italy.

| | | *s. d.* | | *s. d.* |
|---|---|---|---|---|
| We see by the Comparative Table between London and Lyons, differences ranging at various periods of - - | | 4 1 | to | - 8 |
| And from Milan and Bergam } and Lyons - - ditto - - ditto - - | | 4 4¼ | to | 1 0½ |

So that it is not, in respect to our market alone, that those differences fluctuate so considerably; but with respect to Italy itself, notwithstanding its great proximity to the Lyons market, than which nothing more can show how essentially the French manufacturer rests on the produce of its own soil, and what vast advantage accrues to that manufacture, from its having reserved for it the exclusive consumption of that produce, both in respect of prices and qualities.

(Mr. *Alexis Doxat*'s Paper, No. 37.
Delivered in to the Select Committee on the Silk Trade, 21st July 1832.)

AN ABSTRACT VIEW of the Progress of the Silk Trade of *Great Britain* and *Ireland*, from 1815–17 to 1821–23, 1824–25, and to 1826–31, (in regard to Quantities.)

AN ABSTRACT VIEW of the Progress of the Cotton Trade, in *Great Britain* and *Ireland*, during the same periods.

(In regard to Quantities.)

Raw and Thrown Silks, Waste, and Knubs and Husks.

| Conformably with Parliamentary Returns only. (*Vide* my Paper, No. 1, delivered in on the 11th of April.) | | Conformably with Computations made by Mr. Alexis Doxat. *Vide* my said Paper, No. 1. | | | |
|---|---|---|---|---|---|
| QUANTITIES on which Duties have been Paid. (Large Quantities of Coarse Silks, and considerable Quantities of Waste in the last six years.) | PROGRESS in Quantities, in the respective Periods. | QUANTITIES brought into Consumption, computed into Italian Standard. | PROGRESS in Quantities of Italian Standard, in the respective Periods. | | |
| | *Lbs.* | | *Lbs.* | | *Lbs.* | |
| 1815–17 | 1,417,000 | - - - - | 1,085,000 | - - - - | 94,000,000 | — |
| 1818–20 | 1,932,000 | 36 p' c$^t$ over 1815–17, or 12 p' c$^t$ p' ann. over 1815–17. | 1,426,000 | 31½ p' c$^t$ over 1815–17, or 10½ p' c$^t$ p' ann. over 1815–17. | 115,000,000 | 22 p' c$^t$ over 1815–17, or 7⅓ p' c$^t$ per ann. over 1815–17. |
| 1821–23 | 2,413,000 | 70 p' c$^t$ over 1815–17, or 8⅓ p' c$^t$ p' ann. over 1818–20. | 1,848,000 | 70 p' c$^t$ over 1815–17, or 10 p' c$^t$ per ann. over 1818–20. | 137,000,000 | 48 p' c$^t$ over 1815–17, or 6⅓ p' c$^t$ p' ann. over 1818–20. |

Duties Lowered on Raw and Thrown Silks, and Waste, and Knubs and Husks.

| | | | | | | |
|---|---|---|---|---|---|---|
| 1824–25 | 3,807,000 | 169 p' c$^t$ over 1815–17, or 29 p' c$^t$ p' ann. over 1821–23. | 2,783,000 | 156 p' c$^t$ over 1815–17, or 25 p' c$^t$ p' ann. over 1821–23. | 172,000,000 | 83 p' c$^t$ over 1815–17, or 12¾ p' c$^t$ p' ann. over 1821–23. |
| 1821–23 } 1824–25 } | 3,110,000 | 119 p' c$^t$ over 1815–17, or 16 p' c$^t$ p' ann. over 1816–20. | 2,315,000 | 113 p' c$^t$ over 1815–17, or 16 p' c$^t$ p' ann. over 1816–20. | 155,000,000 | 65 p' c$^t$ over 1815–17, or 9 p' c$^t$ p' ann. over 1816–20. |

PROGRESSES INVERTED.

Duties further Lowered, and our Protective Laws of 1766 removed.

| | | | | | | |
|---|---|---|---|---|---|---|
| 1826–31 | 3,819,000 | 22¾ p' c$^t$ over { 1821–23, 1824–25 } or 3¾ p' c$^t$ p' ann. over { 1821–23, 1124–25 } | 2,765,000 | 19½ p' c$^t$ over { 1821–23, 1824–25 } or 3¾ p' c$^t$ p' ann. over { 1824–25 } | 219,000,000 | 41 p' c$^t$ over { 1821–23, 1824–25 } or 6⅞ p' c$^t$ p' ann. |

During 1815–17 to 1821–23, we worked at moderate Wages, and very high Duties.

1824–25 - - - - same Wages, and much lower Duties.

1826–31 - - - - low and wretched Wages, and lower Duties, with large proportions of low Works.

(*Vide* my Paper, No. 4, delivered in to the Committee 11th April, qu. 4047. of my Evidence.)

ABSTRACT of my Paper, No. 2, delivered in to the Committee on the 11th of April.

| | Quantities, Duty paid, as per Parliamentary Returns, (of all Descriptions, inclusive of Waste, Knubs and Husks.) | Quantities of all Descriptions, brought into Consumption, as per Mr. Doxat's Tables, Nos. 1 & 2, delivered in on 11th April. | Quantities consumed, brought into one Standard, that of fine Italian Standard. | Computed Differences between the Quantities of all Descriptions, brought into Consumption, and those Quantities computed into fine Italian Standard. |
|---|---|---|---|---|
| | *Lbs.* | *Lbs.* | *Lbs.* | |
| Averages per Annum, viz. 1824–25 - | 3,807,000 | 3,611,000 | 2,783,000 | being 23 p' c$^t$ less. |
| Ditto - - - - - 1826–31 - | 3,819,000 | 3,813,000 * | 2,765,000 | „ 27½ „ ditto. |

\* N.B. Large quantities of Waste, &c. in the last Six years, and also large proportions of coarse Silks.

*Lunæ, 23° die Julii,* 1832.

### EDWARD AYSHFORD SANFORD, ESQ. in the Chair.

*Allan Fraser,* called in; and Examined.

12096. HAVE you been employed at the Custom House?—Yes.

12097. In what capacity?—As an extra weigher occasionally.

12098. Are you now so employed?—When there is plenty of business, not being a class weigher, I am obliged to wait for my turn.

12099. What is the rank or class of officer you have served under?—Landing waiter.

12100. What is the duty of a landing waiter?—To see all the goods duly weighed and tallied as they are landed from the ship or in warehouses.

12101. What is the rank and class of officer next above a landing waiter?—Surveyors.

12102. What is the duty of a surveyor?—To check the landing waiter occasionally in the course of the day, and to sign his book as a proof that he has been there.

12103. You have been engaged at a wharf weighing and examining cargoes occasionally, have you not?—Yes.

12104. Was more than one vessel discharging at the same time?—Sometimes two, sometimes three, I have known.

12105. How many scales are there generally at the wharf?—Frequently two.

12106. How many men to each scale?—There ought to be two, but very often there is but one; I have to attend to two scales myself.

12107. Has there been any alteration lately made in that respect, are there fewer men to the scales now than there used to be sometime before?—Yes.

12108. When was that alteration made?—I believe within the last two or three years.

12109. How long have you been employed?—Two years.

12110. Was it before you began?—I understood from other officers who had been longer in the service than myself, that there used to be frequently three at the scale, and when there ought to have been two in my own time there has frequently been only one.

12111. How are those men paid?—Three shillings a day, when they are called upon by turn.

12112. Their employment is not constant?—No, I had but 87 days from the 14th of June 1831, to the 31st of December.

12113. Do you receive any pay exclusive of that?—No, I have been obliged to wait six weeks after that before I got my money.

12114. Whose duty is it to superintend the weighing?—It is the landing waiter's duty to superintend.

12115. Whose duty is it to inspect their conduct?—The landing waiter's.

12116. How frequently does he do that?—He is supposed to do it all the day from eight or nine o'clock in the morning.

12117. Is he always there?—Sometimes he is away; perhaps he has got duties to attend to in the warehouse when we are alongside the ship.

12118. Are you ever left so long as half an hour?—Yes, and sometimes an hour.

12119. May you, during that time, pass many parcels of goods?—Yes; but they must not go away till he has given his judgment and signed the warrant for their removal.

12120. Does he ever insist on his return on those things being re-weighed?—Sometimes I have seen them re-opened after they were examined and packed, but not in all cases.

12121. During the hours of business particularly whilst ships are open or goods lying about unexamined in the quay, does the landing waiter ever quit his post?—Sometimes.

12122. Can he evade the surveyor?—Yes, he can.

12123. How many scales does a landing waiter superintend?—Sometimes he superintends two, and one pair of scales has been totally out of his sight by being

placed

placed in a different position when there were other goods weighing, the weigher likewise himself has been obliged to come and report to him the weight or the tale.

12124. Could you, if you had been so minded, have sent away those cases without his knowing it?—No, that would have been prevented at the dock gates.

12125. Would he have known whether the weight you returned was correct or not?—Not unless he saw it weighed over again.

12126. Was there any check upon you?—Only the landing waiter.

12127. Were you serving as a landing waiter?—No, as a weigher.

12128. In order that there might be fraud, there must be collusion between the weigher and landing waiter?—Yes, certainly in some cases.

12129. Is there any case in which you are left quite alone or not?—Yes; it has devolved upon me to be sent into a warehouse, perhaps at the London docks, to examine cases of toys and music, the landing waiter whom I have been under, and who has signed my certificate when the duty has expired, I have known come only occasionally, he has stepped up and taken the tale and has entered the number of articles those cases contained.

12130. Those were toys, not silk?—Yes, generally speaking cases of toys and cases of glass.

12131. Has that ever occurred with regard to silk?—No, I cannot take upon myself to say that it has.

12132. In order that there should be fraud in the weighing of silk goods, it is necessary there should be collusion between the weigher and the landing waiter?—Yes; there is a check clerk belonging to the Dock Company, who is also a check on the landing waiter.

12133. Do you believe that there are frauds committed on the Customs in the entry of silk goods?—I have no hesitation in saying that I am positive there have been.

12134. State the grounds on which you entertain that belief?—In my experience not being a very great judge of silk, I know disputes have arisen upon the value of it between the merchant that it belonged to, the Dock Company's clerk and the landing waiter, the surveyor, they have all disputed, and not been able to come to an opinion whether the value put upon it was right in regard to the revenue and the justice of the merchant.

12135. What reason have you to suppose there was any fraud committed, you not being conversant with the value of silk?—I know that it is probable that it would take place, I have had to weigh that silk.

12136. All you can speak to is, that you have heard there have been disputes regarding the value of silk?—Yes, after the entry made of the value.

12137. Have you any reason to believe that silks are passed at a less weight than they actually weigh?—I cannot take upon myself to say that they are from my own experience of weighing, though I have weighed a great many bales.

12138. You have no reason to believe there is a fraud in that respect?—I know there is a possibility of it; in some cases the judgment of the revenue officer has been given up to the judgment of the merchant, who was obliged to be satisfied with the entry as made.

12139. Have you reason to believe that the entry of the merchant was not correct?—Certainly I cannot take upon myself to say that.

12140. Then how can you be sure that fraud was committed in consequence of that difference?—I am perfectly certain there has been.

12141. Has any proof of that come within your knowledge?—No; but I am certain it has been often so on account of what the merchant contended at the time.

12142. Will you state any case of that nature you have seen?—I cannot state any one in particular; I should not wish to state any other but what has come home to my own knowledge.

12143. Has any case come under your own immediate notice?—Not as to the actual fraud that I cannot take upon myself to say; but I am positive that it took place from that difference of opinion between the merchants and the revenue officers.

12144. What reason have you to believe there was fraud on account of that difference of opinion?—Because it is very probable there was more value than it was entered at.

12145. Have you any reason to believe that it was so?—No, not particularly.

12146. Do you speak of bales of thrown and raw silk, or silk goods?—Of both.

12147. Do you speak of manufactured goods?—Not manufactured goods; I mean bales of raw and thrown silk.

12148. Do

*Allan Fraser.*

23 July,
1832.

12148. Do you know anything respecting silk manufactured goods?—I have seen a great many passed.

12149. Have you had any thing to do with the weighing of them?—Yes, but not very frequently.

12150. In what manner are they weighed, is it in any particular place?—In what is generally considered the silk warehouse on the quays.

12151. Are they all weighed in the same place?—No, not all.

12152. Are there scales for the weighing these situated in different places?—Yes.

12153. Does it ever happen that the same landing waiter is employed to look at more than one of these scales at the same period?—Yes.

12154. Do you mean to say that the same landing waiter may be employed to superintend two sets of scales, that are so situated that he cannot see them both at the same time?—I do mean to say so.

12155. You mean to say so with respect to silk manufactured goods?—In some cases; sometimes the silk is not landed till the surveyor comes.

12156. He comes, of course, for further security?—Yes, that is his duty every day to go round to the landing waiters.

12157. Then the security is increased by his attendance?—Yes; the landing waiter submits to him what he is about, and takes his judgment upon it.

12158. Does the surveyor keep a book?—No.

12159. In what way is the entry made?—By reporting it to the landing waiter.

12160. Is that merely a verbal report?—Yes, except tallying the scales, then of course I bring the report how many the bale contains.

12161. Do you bring the report in writing?—Yes; but I have no book because I have no commission.

12162. You bring it on a sheet of paper?—Yes.

12163. When you put down the weight on paper, you do not consider the setting it down as part of your regular duty, but set it down because the landing waiter is not present at the moment you weigh it?—Yes, he asks of course whether my account is correct.

12164. Whom does he ask?—The weigher who keeps a memorandum.

12165. In that case he has nothing to depend upon but the word of that person who has weighed it, unless he chooses himself to see it weighed over again?—Just so.

12166. Does he often see it weighed over again?—No.

12167. Do you mean to say that the landing waiter does not see the goods weighed?—Not always.

12168. The goods are passed without the landing waiter actually checking the weighed goods?—Unless he chooses to have them weighed over again, when there are two scales going at once.

12169. How can it be ascertained, that the landing waiter takes down weight except by the weigher?—By reference to the books in the office, which they receive in the morning, and return at night.

12170. The landing waiter keeps a book in which he takes down the weights given him by the weigher?—Yes.

12171. How can it be ascertained that the weights he puts down are the real weights given him by the weigher; what check have you?—None whatever, except that when the surveyor comes round he supposes that that is correct; he is supposed to have seen what the landing waiter has done all day.

12172. Do you know any case in which the surveyor has weighed goods again after the weight has been taken down by the landing waiter?—Yes; in some cases perhaps he will weigh one cask or two casks under his own eye.

12173. Is that common?—Not every day.

12174. Supposing a person weighs 300 lbs. what should prevent the landing waiter putting down 200?—Nothing whatever.

12175. Did you ever see goods which the surveyor weighed after the landing waiter?—Yes, the surveyor has made me do it frequently; but it has been merely where there was a number of casks or cases, he has said bring one back which he selected, and weighed it over again.

12176. Has any error been discovered in such case?—Sometimes.

12177. Do you know of any errors in silk manufactured goods having been discovered in that way?—Not particularly in silk goods.

12178. Do you know Mr. Beckwith?—Yes, that was the gentleman that introduced my name.

12179. Have

*Allan Fraser.*

23 July,
1832.

12179. Have you ever been offered money by a merchant, to whom silk has belonged when weighing it?—Yes.

12180. On what occasions?—To falsify the weight, and I have refused it with indignation.

12181. Did you not report what had happened to the surveyor when that offer was made to you?—No.

12182. Why did you not?—Because I did not know the person; he was off, and sent another person to superintend.

12183. Who went away?—The person that offered the bribe.

12184. Was it not the merchant who came to clear the goods?—The merchant's clerk I suppose.

12185. Should you not think it your duty at once to report that circumstance to the surveyor?—I should have considered it my duty, and I endeavoured to ascertain the man's name, but could not.

12186. Has that happened to you more than once?—Yes, I may say frequently.

12187. You did think it your duty to convey it to the surveyor?—I should have represented it to the landing waiter, but I could not find him, he went away.

12188. Was not it in your power to have mentioned, that the merchant or his clerk had offered you without giving his name?—I believe they pretty well understand one another upon that.

12189. Why did not you report it?—Because I had not an opportunity; I was employed in keeping 42 men at their work.

12190. Why did you not do it after the day was over?—I considered that I had no inducement.

12191. Have you, then, no duty to perform?—I have performed my duty in strict justice, and have refused bribes, considering that my duty as superior.

12192. What instructions had you when placed on duty?—None whatever; we are told where to go when we are appointed in the morning; one or two landing waiters send for us. If I am taken as an extra man, I am informed where to go to, either on the quays or in the docks; I have my particular duty, and the landing waiter says, you may take this or the other duty; I know nothing of any instructions.

12193. What is your duty?—To weigh them, or take the number.

12194. That is all you do?—Yes, and the landing waiter signs the warrant form as to those of us who have been employed, as he is supposed to be responsible for the duty performed by the weighers that day, and by means of that certificate we get the money six weeks afterwards.

12195. Have you any other income but the 3s. per day for the days you are employed?—No.

12196. If a bribe is offered, you do not consider it your duty to report that matter to your superior officer?—I have no inducement to do so: I would if the man had stopped there, but he went away, and I could not go away to look after him.

12197. The fact was you did not report it?—No.

12198. Do you consider it your duty to report such things?—I do.

12199. And you did not perform your duty?—In that case I could not, while I had to attend to so many men employed belonging to the quays.

12200. Could you not have reported this after the hours of labour were over?—Yes.

12201. But you did not?—No.

12202. Do you recollect such a circumstance as between three and four hundred being passed in the scales, and only 150 called out?—No.

12203. It has been given in evidence, that you are able to prove the fact that three or four hundred pounds are passed, and only 150 entered?—No, I rather think there is an error in that.

12204. If that has been given in evidence before this Committee, you do not consider it correct?—No, I do not.

12205. You cannot prove that fact?—I cannot; I will not take upon me to do it.

12206. Is your name Allan Fraser?—It is.

12207. Is there any instance in which you have ever known the quantity of silk reported less than the actual amount weighed?—I am not aware of it.

12208. Have any bribes ever been received within your knowledge?—I have not seen it, but I know that the parties have met for that very express purpose after the day's labour was closed.

12209. What

*Allan Fraser.*

————————

23 July,
1832.

12209. What parties?—The Custom House officer who had consented to accept the bribe.

12210. How do you know that the Custom House officer has consented to accept the bribe?—Because I have seen them drinking together frequently.

12211. Is that the only evidence you have of it?—Yes, because I have not wished to intermix with them, to know the full particulars.

12212. Then it is only suspicion, you have no direct proof?—I have never seen the money pass.

12213. Has any body ever told you they have received money?—Yes.

12214. Who has told you that they have received money?—Several officers, whose names I choose to withhold, and I have said to them that they have incurred a great responsibility.

12215. If you charge this against officers, you must state their names, as an act of justice to those who are not guilty?—I will not involve the responsibility of any one, nor will I charge any man wrongfully, but I know it has been done at the wharf repeatedly; but I am disposed to withhold any thing else but that I know that they met for eating and drinking.

12216. The question put to you is this, whether any public officer has told you he has received money as a bribe to alter the amount?—Yes, one in particular, but unfortunately he was one, I was going to say, of the same class I was; but he was an extra officer for twelve years, and he died about a month ago through starvation, or something very much like it.

12217. At what period was the transaction with that person who is now dead?—Previous to the month of March 1831.

12218. Do you mean to say he is now dead?—Yes.

12219. What was his name?—Hine.

12220. You stated before that there were several?—He expressly told me, and I believe, that it was from real necessity he did it.

12221. State any other?—I will not mention any others by name, if you please.

12222. You stated to the Committee, that several persons have actually told you that they had received money; one, you say, is now dead: in justice to the department you belong to, you must state the names of the others?

[*The Witness was directed to withdraw.*]

[*Strangers were directed to withdraw.*]

[*The Witness was again called in.*]

12223. The Committee consider, that after the charge you have made on several parties, it is their duty to ascertain who those parties were that told you they had received money as bribes?—I must beg the same liberty to be allowed to me which has been to some others, of not giving names, but perhaps it has come within the knowledge of the Committee that one party has been discharged within the last 12 months who was in the silk floor, but that is not within my knowledge.

12224. What is his name?—His name is Bodman, who was employed in what is called the silk floor.

12225. Was he one of the parties who told you he had taken money?—No, he did not tell me that.

12226. Are any of those parties who told you they had received money now in the Custom House?—Occasionally, as I am myself employed, as landing officers; no otherwise.

12227. Is there any one who is a regular officer who has told you so?—No.

12228. The parties who told you they had received bribes were not regular Custom House officers?—Not by salary; such as weighers are considered to have a salary, the first class 45 *l.*, then the next 35 *l.*

12229. They were persons like yourself, casually employed?—Yes.

12230. Have you any objection to state their names?—Yes, I should be held up to disrespect by them for charging them with this.

12231. Does not it appear to you to be much more unjust to the whole class to which you belong to have cast a stigma upon them, by stating that individuals among them had told you they had received bribes, than to state the names of the individuals who told you so?—No, I do not conceive so.

12232. Do you mean to say, you would not think it unjust for a person to accuse the whole of your class when only one was the guilty man?—It may appear to the minds of the Committee singular, but I mean no personal injury to any one, and I beg not to give their names because it has been dire necessity that has induced

them

*Allan Fraser.*

23 July,
1832.

them to accept of it, to make up the dreadful deficiency when they had but 15 or 20 pounds a year.

12233. How many parties have told you they have received money?—I can say as many as three.

12234. Are they still living?—Two of them, and one of them is dead.

12235. Is that one who is dead the one you mentioned before as being dead?—Yes.

12236. You were understood to say, that he had not told you he had received money?—Yes, he told me so expressly.

12237. What was the sum they told you they had received?—I had not the sum mentioned.

12238. What did they state to you?—That they had been offered money, and had taken it; that is all.

12239. For doing what?—For foregoing their duty, I suppose.

12240. They did not state to you for what particular purpose this money had been given?—No.

12241. Did they state by whom it had been given?—No; there are a number of persons employed on the wharfs, such as merchants' clerks, agents and others, to do business for them.

12242. What did they state to you?—That they had been offered money, and had taken it.

12243. For what purpose?—I suppose to make short weight; that is what I understood by them.

12244. When did this happen?—Months ago.

12245. How long ago?—Last year, not this year; for I have had but seven days employment in the Custom House this year.

12246. What time of the year?—That I cannot say; it might be somewhere about this time last year.

12247. About July?—Yes.

12248. Was it a matter of conversation between these two persons and yourself?—No, not particularly, it only came out in casual conversation, as it might arise where officers are sometimes an hour or two together.

12249. Casually in conversation, they stated that they had made a good job?—No, I do not say that; but that they had been offered money, and in some instances had taken it.

12250. Did they tell you in what way they managed to get the goods free?—No; but in the one instance I mentioned just now it was done; the goods were sent home, and the house thought it was a snare laid for them, and they returned the goods; and in consequence of that it came out, and he was discharged.

12251. Those parties did not state to you the manner in which they had done the business?—No.

12252. What reason had you to suppose it was for the passing short weights?—Because they had no other means of doing it; we are never two days in one place at the Custom House, or very rarely; nor yet with the same landing waiters two days, and particularly the extra weighers; we are with a different landing waiter every day. I believe one month last year I had twenty-three days, when they were very busy at the London Docks.

12253. You know no particulars regarding those transactions?—No.

12254. You only know generally, that those people told you they had taken a bribe?—That is all I know about it.

12255. You do not know the amount?—No, I do not.

12256. You do not know the particular branch of duty required?—No, conscientiously I do not.

12257. You state that the persons who told you they had been offered money did not tell you for what purpose it had been offered?—Not expressly.

12258. Then why do you think it was a bribe?—Because I am certain of it, they being on duty at those places; had they not been on duty they would not have had it.

12259. All those persons told you they had been offered money without stating for what purpose?—Yes.

12260. You conclude it was for some improper purpose?—They told me that; but not the particular business they had been on.

12261. Did they tell you it was for the purpose of making short weight?—Yes, and I have had bribes offered to myself for the express thing.

678.                                                                   12262. You

12262. You positively refuse to state the names of the parties who communicated this to you?—Yes, I do, on the very grounds I have claimed the indulgence on, because I shall be held up to disgrace from every officer if I do it.

12263. Do not you think you will be held up to much more disgrace for having passed a general stigma upon those people?—I do not think it is a general stigma; it is merely those three instances which have come within my knowledge; they took it, and my case was the exception, it having been offered to myself; those men perhaps were no more in distress than I was, but still I myself had a different feeling.

12264. Do not you think, that if the Custom House is satisfied of the truth of that you have stated with regard to conversations between yourself and two extra officers, they will feel it their duty to discharge every extra officer, in order to get rid of the men who had been guilty of this act?—I think it might be more just on one ground; but I am satisfied from the responsibility which has fallen upon those extra officers, equal sometimes to that of the class officers, if there is a sound classification of officers that evil will be removed.

12265. If you consider that as part of the duty of the Custom House, do you not think you are inflicting a great hardship on all the innocent officers by refusing to give up the names of the men who are alone guilty out of the whole number?—That is not my intention.

12266. Do not you see that you cast suspicion upon the whole number of 100, as no one can know who are the three who have been guilty of this?—They never will know it from me; I am not aware that it was ever offered or ever taken by any of the others; I have never extorted a confession from any of them; when that was the case it was voluntarily said to me by those to whom I refer when we were waiting for duty.

12267. Have you any value for your own employment or not; you cannot possibly suppose that the Government can continue you in employment if you, being a servant of theirs, shall conceal from them the knowledge of those persons who have defrauded the revenue?—I would say, as a matter of right and of conviction, I feel the importance of that duty I have had to perform and should have to perform again; if I were continued, I should feel it my duty on all occasions to report to my superior officers in a case of that description, though I have not done it, though I hold no commission; but it is very little consideration whether I am continued or not, nor do I come here to say what I do from any motive of interest.

12268. Why did you not do it on the surveyor coming to you, referring to the goods which were probably then there?—The surveyor was gone; he is not there above five minutes, then he is off to the next landing waiter's box.

12269. Did not he come again the next day?—Next day I was in another part, and there might be another surveyor.

12270. Did you set aside the goods and report them to the landing waiter?—I did not do that.

12271. Do you know what particular goods the offer was made to you respecting?—No; for there were three or four different kinds of goods landed at the same time; it is impossible for the weigher to know about it.

12272. You have referred to other persons having been excused giving names, other persons who may have requested not to give up names are not placed in the same situation you are; they were asked as to the names of private individuals, you are asked in consequence of a charge being made against a public servant?—That may be true, but still I wish not to answer to the names.

12273. It comes to your knowledge that frauds have been committed against the Crown; you being a paid servant of the Crown, during the time of your employment, do you not feel yourself called upon, in the performance of your duty, to give the names, otherwise the House of Commons may feel themselves bound to enforce the giving the names?—Very good.

12274. Do you remember any case in which a liberal proposal was made to you to pass goods by an importer of silk goods, which you communicated to Mr. Beckwith?—Not particularly silk; I wish it to be understood, that I never wished Mr. Beckwith to say that respecting silk, I said with different goods where I have been engaged.

12275. You never stated to Mr. Beckwith that a liberal offer had been made to you to pass silk goods?—No, not silk goods, certainly.

12276. Did you state to him that a liberal offer had been made to you to pass other goods?—Yes, I did.

12277. What goods were those?—Different goods.

12278. What

*Allan Fraser.*

—— ——

23 July,
1832.

12278. What goods ?—Toys, and different descriptions of fruit.

12279. What have you stated to Mr. Beckwith?—I told him that bribes had been offered to me frequently, but that I had rejected tnem.

12280. Did you state that they had been offered to you to pass a smaller quantity of goods ?—I have frequently.

12281. Did you say that a bribe had been offered to you to pass a certain quantity of goods ?—That I might call less weight ; I have no power to pass the goods, that is done by warrant, but to call less weight.

12282. State how that applies to toys; toys are not weighed?—They are numbered.

12283. Would it then be for altering the tally?—Yes, certainly ; we very often have the power to do that, giving a less number.

12284. What was Mr. Beckwith's answer to you?—I do not know what his answer was, it was sometime before that conversation took place ; he asked me what had come out during the time I had been employed, not that I thought I should have come here.

12285. Did Mr. Beckwith **apply to** you to give evidence before the Board of Trade?—No, not that I am aware of; I do not recollect it ; I believe I recollect he said something to me, in case he should wish it, whether I should have any objection, and I said no.

12286. Would you have any objection to give the names of those parties to the Board of Trade?—Certainly, I should have equally as here, from the very motive I have mentioned.

12287. Coming up before the Board of Trade, you would not have thought it right to give them all the information in your power?—Yes, I should, with the exception of withholding the names, which I do from a personal feeling.

12288. Of what use would that information be if it fell short of affording them the means of discovering the fraud?—It would only tend to prove that such things do exist, and have existed.

12289. What is the use of the proof, if means are not afforded of doing away with the evil ?—The Committee can draw their own conclusions from that, from the thing having existed.

12290. You mean to say that different merchants, or their agents, have offered you bribes to pass goods, calling the weight less than it was, or calling a tally less number ?—Yes.

12291. Do you believe that to be frequently done ?—Not very generally, but there are opportunities where a weigher has, on his own responsibility, to attend a case ; he comes up into the warehouse, and goes on taking the weights till the whole is weighed.

12292. How many days in a year do you say you are employed ?—I think 87 I calculated last year.

12293. How much a day did you get?—Three shillings.

12294. In the course of your employment, when you had to see the goods weighed, have there not opportunities occurred when you could commit frauds in the weights you have had to specify?—There have.

12295. You believe there are those temptations in the way of those individuals, who have only that small remuneration for performing their duty ?—I do.

12296. Have you reason to believe, that from the poverty of those individuals, the opportunities which are afforded to them are numerous ?—Yes.

12297. And also from the knowledge that money has been offered by those individuals to yourself?—Yes, that is true.

12298. After the Government business has been over for the day, have you ever been sent on errands by your superior officer ?—Very generally.

12299. What had you generally to do on such occasions ?—Sometimes to carry parcels of goods to some acquaintance, with different things, which had been drawn as samples, presents made by merchants.

12300. Are you to be understood to say, you had to carry for your superior officer, different things made presents of by the merchants?—Yes, trifles, not to any extent of value, certainly ; but those are things which we could not in prudence refuse.

12301. What reason had you to know those things were presents that you carried ?—Because I have known them from this reason, that where the merchants have been in the same warehouse, or their agents, they have drawn so many small

678.                                                                                          articles

*Allan Fraser.*

23 July,
1832.

articles out of the box; instead of their being put in again, they have been out of compliment given to the landing waiter.

12302. Have you seen that done?—Yes, but not to any great value.

12303. Of what did they consist?—I cannot tell, there have been different things in bags and paper parcels.

12304. State any one thing?—I cannot undertake to state any one thing.

12305. You have carried the parcels, you have seen the things given, and you must be able to state what they were?—Sometimes some little mock cut glass, an article not larger than this inkstand, or an article to put soap in, or one which was a little cracked, which no duty was paid on.

12306. Where were they brought to?—On the quays from London Bridge to the Tower.

12307. What landing waiter have you ever given such a thing to?—I have been employed under every one.

12308. How often have you seen such things?—Not above two or three times.

12309. What was the value of the article?—Not five shillings perhaps; perhaps the article was cracked.

12310. Did you say by whose desire you took it?—No, when those things were left out, if there is more than could be put in, or one is a little broken, it is not considered of any value, nor any fraud upon the revenue; they are generally things which have got a little injured by packing or unpacking.

### Mr. *George Stephens*, called in; and further Examined.

Mr.
*George Stephens.*

12311. HAVE you any information to give to the Committee as to the mode in which silks are passed at the Custom House?—No, I have not any information to give upon that point.

12312. You mentioned to a Member of this Committee a letter you had seen?—I made some communication to some silk manufacturers to-day, respecting a letter I saw on Saturday last in the hands of a person accustomed to attend the Custom House.

12313. Have you that letter?—I have not that letter, it was a private communication which I have reason to believe was sent from a Custom House officer to a person used to attending the Custom House for the passing of silk.

12314. What was that letter?—It was an invitation to attend a breakfast given yesterday morning by a Custom House officer when private matters it was said were to be arranged.

12315. A private breakfast?—I apprehend so.

12316. Did you see the letter?—I did.

12317. Did you read its contents?—I did; I am not sure as to the exact words of it, but it was requesting his attendance at a breakfast to-morrow morning, when matters should be arranged.

12318. Did any conversation pass between you and him before the letter was shown to you?—Yes, the conversation led to his producing the letter.

12319. Have the goodness to state the conversation that you had upon the subject?—It was with a person with whom I am in the habit of doing business, he is serving in a large silk house.

12320. Can you mention his name?—I cannot; in the conversation I said to him, your business will be shortly put an end to; I trust we shall see Orders in Council that will take your business out of your hands; he said, we are prepared for it, it will make no difference to us; I said, whatever your expedients may be I am convinced that this will quite overthrow you; he said, I do not care, we know what will be done, we are quite prepared, we have something beyond that (referring to his system of business); he then showed me the letter, and said, do you see how we manage things here; he told me it was from a Custom House officer, but he held his hand over the name.

12321. You pronounce his words as if he was a foreigner?—Yes, he is a foreigner.

12322. What do you mean by their system of business?—That which I meant was this; he does not hesitate to inform me he can pass silks lower than we can, and I know that he can pass silks lower than we can.

12323. How do you know that?—We have made repeated observations, we have had silks of the same kind which have come from the same place, and within a week of the same time, and they have been always lower than ours.

12324. Do

Mr.
*George Stephens.*

23 July,
1832.

12324. Do you know how they came in?—We know in some cases they came through the Custom House.

12325. Have you ever ascertained whether they paid the same duty for those articles that you have done?—I have not.

12326. It is not within your knowledge that they come through the Custom House paying a smaller duty than your's?—No, but he has not hesitated to acknowledge that they can get them through the Custom House lower.

12327. You have not ascertained whether that is the fact?—No.

12328. Do you know the mode in which he gets them through lower?—No.

12329. Did he ever say to you that he paid smaller weight than the goods really weighed?—No, he has not said in what way he does it.

12330. Do you believe it has been the practice with that house to do so?—Yes, I believe it has.

12331. To a great extent?—Yes.

12332. Why do you believe that?—From the quantity of goods they import, from their always selling them lower than we can import them, and from the regularity with which they have their goods to the time they name; the regularity of their arrival.

12333. That is not the case with smuggled goods in general?—No.

12334. Is this a house at the West end of the Town or in the City?—I hope I shall not be compelled to answer that.

12335. You have made a charge against a public department, you must either state the name of the officer if you know it, or of the individual?—I did not see the name of the officer.

12336. Unless you come to individuals there is no opportunity in the Committee of tracing the transaction to the foundation?—That is very just; I should be very glad to give this Committee or the Government any information, but I do not know the name of the officer.

12337. But you know the name of the party who spoke of this as a system carried on, and that though Government might change the persons, they were prepared to evade any new system, or any alterations, that is very important information?—Yes, it is; but I hope I shall not be compelled to give the name; I was assured, before my last examination, I should not be compelled to give the name, if I gave information on this subject.

12338. You stated that you could buy goods in this market considerably lower than you could import them?—I did.

12339. You stated that in some instances those goods were smuggled?—Yes.

12340. You stated, in other instances your belief that they must have been passed through the Custom House under the regular duties, by reason of your buying them of those individuals who import them at a much less price than you could pass them through the Custom House?—Yes, I stated that I believed certain goods had come through the Custom House.

12341. But you gave as your reasons for your belief, that you were in the habit of buying them at a much less price than you could import them?—Yes, and some other circumstances which I have stated as to the times of the arrivals.

12342. There is no certainty as to the time of arrival of smuggled goods?—There is not.

12343. That is a disadvantage?—Yes.

12344. With respect to those other goods from the time of their arrival you were convinced they had passed through the Custom House?—Yes, and from other circumstances.

12345. State what those other circumstances were?—Those I stated on the last examination; in one case I went into the particulars; I was resolved if possible to ascertain whether any goods came through the Custom House lower, and I satisfied my mind, as far as those circumstances could satisfy me, that that was the case, a lot of goods were bought by an English importer, and another lot by a French buyer of Paris at the same time in Lyons; they left Lyons, for each party on the same day, arrived in London on the same day, we having bought some of them in Paris of the French buyer; they arrived on the same morning, they came by the same vessel, and we could buy them in London at 15 per cent. lower than we could import them, and I had the person's word that they came through the Custom House.

12346. Have you any other reason than this for supposing the goods came in at shortweights?—No, but I have that they came in at lower duty.

678.                                                    12347. You

12347. You mean that they came in at short weights?—No; that they came in for less duty than ours did.

12348. By what means do you believe that those goods passed through the Custom House for less than the legal duty?—I apprehend from their being taken *ad valorem* and less amount given.

12349. Do you mean by the goods being entered at less than the actual weight?—At less than their value.

12350. How did you enter your goods?—They came by weight.

12351. Do you know how their goods were entered?—I am not sure how the others came, whether *ad valorem*, or by weight.

12352. Is it optional as to the same goods?—I believe it is optional with the officers.

12353. The only reason you have for supposing those goods came in fraudulently, or paid less duty than they ought to have done was, that they were sold at a cheaper rate than you could afford to sell yours?—That is the fact; and that they left at the same price, and arrived on the same day ours did.

12354. You did not ascertain that they left at the same rate, did you?—Yes; we ascertained that.

12355. Do you not believe that the house in London might be induced to sell them to you at a sacrifice?—No; they were quite new; I saw them opened, and made a purchase immediately.

12356. Persons may sacrifice, you know, for particular reasons sometimes; had you reason to suppose that that house is ever placed in such a situation as to require money immediately, and that they did in that case?—No, I think not; it is a respectable house.

12357. Were they fresh fashioned goods, such as a person would be able to find a market for immediately?—Yes.

12358. They were not job goods?—No, they were not job goods.

12359. What was the difference of price, considerable?—It was 15 per cent.

12360. Have you any reason to believe, that those goods coming in in that way, came in by fraud or connivance with the officer?—I do not know by what means it is done; they came through the Custom House, I believe.

12361. Have you any other instances where you suspect goods have been run through the Custom House at a lower duty?—I have not.

### Mr. *William Beckwith*, called in; and further Examined.

12362. YOU were asked about imported goods, " Were they smugglers from whom you bought those cheap goods;" the answer was, " I have no direct knowledge of that, but I must presume such was the case:" you then mentioned Messrs. Morrison & Company, Spencely & Company, and others, (foreign houses) as the houses from which you bought those goods referred to in the answer you have given; then you answered to a second question, " I do not charge those houses with being smugglers." How do you reconcile those two answers; first, that you bought cheap goods from houses that you presume must have been smuggled, and you afterwards say, that you do not accuse those houses of being smugglers?—There must be some mistake in the report; as I distinctly stated at the same time, that I ceased being an importer of foreign silk goods, because I could purchase from some of the largest houses in the city of London for 15 or 20 per cent. lower than I could import myself, though I paid ready money, and that on large parcels of some hundreds of pounds.

12363. You stated that you left off because you found other importers could supply you at 15 per cent. less than you could import for yourself; you were then asked, were they smugglers from whom you purchased, and you said you must presume they were, because you purchased for ready money; you were asked to name the persons, and you named those whose names have been read, and you add, that you do not charge those houses with being smugglers, though you had previously said, that they were smugglers?—No. I stated, that I left to the Committee to judge how those houses could supply me at 15 or 20 per cent. less; I have since called upon one of those who supplied me last year, to know whether they could repeat that sort of business; he said he had a large quantity coming in about ten days, and for that reason I am now not making a single loom of figured velvet, because I anticipate that that house alone will be able to supply me, I will venture

to

Mr.
*William Beckwith.*

23 July,
1832.

to say, at full 20 per cent. less than any honest houses can import, and pay the proper duty.

12364. Do you mean that those houses from whom you bought those goods did smuggle those goods?—I believe I distinctly stated, that I could not prove the houses to be smugglers, but I leave it to the Committee to judge how they could supply me at 15 to 20 per cent. less.

12365. In one part of your evidence you stated, you could not conceive those could have been so sold except by a smuggling transaction, but in another part you state, you do not wish to have it understood that the persons from whom you bought were smugglers?—I distinctly stated, that I did not wish to charge the parties with smuggling; I stated the fact of my own transaction, that I did once give an order about midsummer to a certain French house, to supply me with figured velvets, and deliver them in October.

12366. Have you any other grounds for believing those goods were smuggled than that you could purchase them cheaper from those houses than you could import them?—I have, from a very respectable source at the Custom House, ascertained that certain large houses were in the habit of passing figured silks for the duty on plain; I do not attend to that sort of business myself.

12367. Do you mean to say that the information you obtained from the Custom House led you to believe those houses had passed figured goods for the duty on plain goods?—There is a strong impression upon my mind, which leads me to believe that is the case. I handed a letter to Mr. Ballance, as a member of the Silk Committee, which states that many houses had repeatedly passed figured silks for plain. I have known the individual for nearly twenty years who signs the letter, and believe him to be respectable.

12368. Are the Committee to understand that you distinctly state as your opinion that the houses of Messrs. Morrison & Co., and Leaf & Co., and others named by you, do defraud the revenue?—No; I have distinctly stated that I do not charge any house with smuggling, but that there are ways and means of employing agents, that do such things. What am I to understand when I am obliged to leave off my business as an importer, and purchase from these houses? I beg to leave the matter to the Committee to form their own conclusions as well as I do.

12369. Will you be able to produce the parties from the Custom House who have given you the information?—I believe I can do so.

12370. Is it your wish to bring the subject before the Committee?—I have no objection. The letter to which I refer was addressed to the Silk Committee.

12371. You have stated that you had bought goods from large houses at 15 and 20 per cent. lower than you could import them; is that the reason you believe that they must have been smuggled?—I can only make my own conjectures; I would wish to leave that to the honourable Committee to judge for themselves.

12372. Have you any other reason for believing it?—Yes; a certain agent in the Custom House told me that I should not stand on the same footing as other persons, unless I allowed him to bring in some goods in the regular way, which I understood him to say was at low duties. I declined doing so; and the agent who sold me the goods on the part of his master, afterwards called upon me and said, that he was agent for passing silks upon the best terms; and if I did not have my goods so introduced, other houses would have an advantage over me.

---

*Mercurii, 25° die Julii,* 1832.

### THE RIGHT HON. THE EARL GROSVENOR, IN THE CHAIR.

Mr. *William Fairclough*, called in; and Examined.

Mr.
*W. Fairclough.*

25 July,
1832.

12373. YOU are a landing waiter in the Customs?—I am.

12374. You have been for some time accustomed to be on the silk floor, have you not?—I have.

12375. Can you, from experience yourself, describe the process of weighing and examining silk goods on their landing, by the officers of the Customs?—I can; when the packages are brought to the silk floor for examination, on being opened, it is customary to count the number of inner packages, so as to be enabled, when the different articles are selected, to see that we have the whole; they are then opened,

Mr.
W. Fairclough.

5 July,
1832.

opened, and the different descriptions of silk are selected, so as to have each description put into the scale at once; the weight is then taken by the landing waiter, and entered into a blue book similar to that I hold in my hand; the operation is then finished as far as the landing waiter is concerned, until he is superintended by the landing surveyor, whose business it is to re-weigh after the landing waiter, and to make a calculation of the weight of the boxes, for the allowance of the tare called tareing, which is always done by the landing surveyor; the operation is carried on in the mode of selecting certain paper parcels, according to the number there are, so as to get as accurately as we can at the allowances of tare; when that is done, the landing waiter, in connexion with the agent of the merchant, or the merchant himself, casts out the allowances which are made, deducting them on each description of silk from the weight in gross, and after that deduction, the nett quantity is ascertained on which the duties are charged.

12376. Is it the practice on the silk floor that one landing waiter should have to attend to more than one pair of scales?—It is not.

12377. You are not aware that any instance has occurred, in which that has been the case?—I am not aware that it has ever occurred, at two of the floors it would be impossible, for there is not convenience enough to put up two pair of scales.

12378. It has been stated to this Committee, that a landing waiter has frequently to attend to two pair of scales at once, can that possibly be the case?—It cannot.

12379. That has never come within your knowledge?—No, nor do I think it has ever been the practice; it is on only one of the floors out of three that there is an opportunity of putting up two pair of scales.

12380. Do you conceive that if the landing waiter attends to his duty, it is possible for the weigher to commit a fraud?—I think it is impossible for the weigher to commit a fraud.

12381. It is only therefore by connivance with the landing waiter, that a fraud could be committed by the weigher?—I should think so.

12382. Do you know any way in which such negligence could occur on the part of the landing waiter, as to permit a fraud by the weigher?—I know no instance, except by concealment of a package or a fraud of some kind on the part of the weigher, and it is scarcely possible, because the landing waiter is generally in attendance on the package as the different articles are taken out of it.

12383. In fact, the weigher by himself cannot defraud the revenue, supposing the landing waiter to do his duty?—He cannot.

12384. Is it the practice to allow the same landing waiter constantly to remain on the silk floor, or are they changed?—They are changed monthly.

12385. Are they changed irregularly?—They are from station to station.

12386. It has been stated to this Committee, that instances have occurred of the weighers receiving bribes to defraud the revenue, do you conceive that it would be of any advantage to bribe the weigher, unless arrangements could also be made for the landing waiter being bribed?—I think it would be impossible almost, that he could carry on the trade under such circumstances if the landing waiter did his duty, because, as I have before stated, he is in attendance on the whole of the operation, and it is not his duty and his practice generally to take the weight as called out, but to see the weight, for in silk we weigh to an ounce.

12387. Is the landing waiter always present?—Yes.

12388. You have never known him absent?—No.

12389. Have you ever known any instance in which the scales have been left to the weigher, without the attendance of the landing waiter?—No, and I doubt its being possible.

12390. Do you think it possible that the weigher could call out 150 pounds when there were 200 in the scale, without the landing waiter being aware of it?—It is impossible.

12391. Does the landing waiter always go and weigh the package?—Always; he sees it weighed; he does not put the weights into the scale, but he calculates the weights which are put in, himself.

12392. He never trusts to the calling out of the weigher?—Never.

12393. If it was reported that he had so trusted, would that lead to his reprimand or removal?—Certainly, and very deservedly in my opinion.

12394. You cannot undertake to say such a thing never happened?—No, I cannot, I can speak for myself, and I believe I can for my brother officers.

12395. Frauds might be committed by collusion?—Certainly that is possible.

12396. Is there not also a check over the landing waiters by the surveyor?—
Constantly,

Mr.
*W. Fairclough.*

25 July,
1832.

Constantly, and at uncertain times; in fact the landing waiter never knows when the supervision is taking place; the surveyor, according to the state of business, is at his back at any moment of the day, and re-weighs and examines after the officer, so that that sort of operation would be a very doubtful one for a man to lend himself to.

12397. The surveyor makes it a practice, does he not, to attend, and frequently when parcels of silk are being weighed, to have a particular parcel that has passed the scale, but an uncertain parcel, re-weighed?—Frequently.

12398. Supposing there were collusions between the weigher and the landing waiter, it would be very difficult indeed, or at all events a great risk for them to run, to attempt to pass a parcel at short weight, as it might be at once discovered by the surveyor on ordering that particular parcel to be re-weighed?—Certainly he would run that risk and be certain of detection, unless there was a means of conveying a parcel of goods out of the warehouse, which we do not conceive there is.

12399. Do you conceive, in case of collusion between the landing waiter and the weigher, it would be next to impossible for a man to pass goods at short weights?—I do not say it would be impossible, but it would be next to impossible; the probability is, that the surveyor would detect a thing of that description.

12400. What is the salary of a landing waiter?—They are various; there are three or four classes, the first is 400*l.* a year.

12401. So that a man inclined to assist in a fraud of that kind, would be risking so good a place as that, with a tolerable certainty of being discovered?—I think almost with a certainty of that.

12402. If therefore such a statement as this has been made to the Committee, that the same landing waiter is employed to superintend two sets of scales that are so situated that he cannot see them both at the same time, you would say that statement is positively false?—I should consider that it is positively false; I know in one room only they can put up two scales, and when there have been those two put up, there has been an officer in attendance on each.

12403. It is only on one floor out of three that that can be done?—Yes, there is not convenience for putting up two; two have been worked on some occasions but very seldom.

12404. Have there ever been attempts to pass figured goods for plain?—I cannot say there has not been an attempt, the selection is generally made by the officer previous to the goods going to the scale.

12405. Such a thing might be done?—Then I should say, that the officer must be very unenergetic in his examination, they are very easily known.

12406. If an attempt of that kind were made, to pass figured goods for plain, would the parties passing them not be subject to some control as in the case of the weights?—Decidedly.

12407. They would be subject to the supervision in the first instance of the landing waiter, and secondly of the surveyor?—Yes.

12408. Do you open every package?—Yes, sometimes there are as many as 50 or 60 in a large case.

12409. Do you find more goods passed through the Custom House since the large seizure which took place a few months ago?—No, the business is complained of as being slack.

12410. In what manner are toys and other goods that pay duty by tale, counted or examined?—In the same manner that silks are, the whole goods are taken out of the package, and when they pay an *ad valorem* duty, a calculation is made of the value of the article.

12411. Do they ever count the articles or examine them without a landing waiter being present in any process?—Frequently, some of those cases.

12412. In that case may not the persons so employed report a short number?—No, I think not.

12413. If he is left alone to do that?—They are tied up in parcels and we make the weigher take out the number of parcels, the whole of them, so that the officer can count them as well as the weigher, so that if the weigher under such circumstances was inclined to commit a fraud and cheat the officer, we have the means of checking him, it is only by a selection of the numbers we know what they are, and see the number contained in them.

12414. Does not that person frequently count over the packages when the landing waiter is not present?—No.

12415. Are you sure that he never can in one floor count over and report to you

when

Mr.
W. Fairclough.

25 July,
1832.

when you are in another?—There are some descriptions of things which he does, kid skins and those sort of things, which are taleable.

12416. And toys?—Toys are taken by the count in the paper.

12417. That cannot be the case as regards silk?—No, certainly not; the operation is quite different as to silk.

12418. You think the officer so employed may report short those articles taken by tale?—He may partly, but he would be checked by the officer, each parcel of goods are selected and put by the weigher, so that the officer can see the number of the articles if he supposes the weigher has told him wrong and endeavoured to impose upon him, he can check him himself.

12419. Could he do so without examining the contents of the case?—Yes.

12420. Do you mean to say no case undergoes examination without the landing waiter seeing the case?—Not without his seeing the package; skins are articles rather excepted, because they are tied in bundles, we have a number of bundles and we make the weighers go on counting the number of skins in a bundle; with regard to silk it is quite different.

12421. Generally speaking, are the Committee to understand that the landing waiter has a check even on articles, the duty on which sums is paid by the tale?—We do not trust wholly to the weighers, but even in taleable articles like skins we tell some bundles over again.

12422. Is it possible that any person could make a present of any portion of those toys to any trifling amount?—He might a dog and butcher, or a dog, or something of that kind, there may be 300 little dogs and toys and so on, and put it into his pocket, being so small.

12423. You could not miss hundreds or miscount hundreds?—No, certainly not.


Mr. *Joseph Beals*, called in; and Examined.

Mr.
Joseph Beals.

12424. YOU are a landing surveyor in the Customs?—I am.

12425. Will you state to the Committee the nature of the checks which the landing surveyors have upon the landing waiters in the examination of silk goods?—We make uncertain visits upon the landing waiters on duty, and when we go on we re-weigh what has been done and re-examine, and examine the landing waiters' books to see that the correct denomination has been made to the goods which had been examined and weighed.

12426. Is it the constant practice with yourself and other surveyors, to attend during the time the silk goods are weighed occasionally and at uncertain intervals, and to have parcels re-weighed in order to compare with the weights delivered to you?—Yes, it is our duty to do so.

12427. You would consider that you would be neglecting your duty if you did not do that?—Yes, certainly.

12428. You believe that to be the constant practice enforced in the Custom House?—I do.

12429. Have you ever known an instance upon re-weighing goods after the landing waiter of finding that a wrong weight had been put down, so as to lead you to suspect connivance or fraud had been attempted?—No, I do not remember an instance of it.

12430. How long have you held your present situation?—Eight years; I have been 27 years in the service.

12431. You do not mean to say a mistake may not happen by accident?—It has never come to my notice that there has been a misweight called.

12432. It might be done by accident?—No case either by accident or fraud has come under my notice.

12433. You never in your experience have had occasion to believe that erroneous weights have been delivered to you by the landing waiters for a fraudulent purpose?—No, I never had reason to suspect such a thing.

12434. Is it the practice to change the landing waiters frequently in the silk warehouse?—Yes, it is, they are changed monthly, there are two stations, and the landing surveyors change stations monthly, one takes the upper station one month and then he goes to the other the next month; one landing surveyor is not constantly in the same situation

12435. Do you equally think it your duty to turn your attention to the qualities of the goods, whether goods are plain or figured?—Certainly; we always examine

to

Mr.
*Joseph Beals.*

25 July,
1832.

to see whether they are correctly returned in the book, we look at them ourselves to see that they are so, and make a selection when we visit the officers.

12436. Do you examine all the parcels, or at uncertain periods?—We make our visits at uncertain times, and after they are taken out the quantity is put by itself, different descriptions; and we examine them, and select them out for weight or for tale.

12437. It is your duty officially to weigh for the tare?—Yes.

12438. That is a duty never left to the landing waiter?—Never.

12439. You tare down to half an ounce do not you?—We tare down to a quarter of an ounce, we bring it to as great a nicety as possible, even standing weight we take it; there are a great many internal packages, which require a great deal of nicety, they are selected out, and we make one or two trials, just as we think sufficient, according to the number, and the weight is put down and cast out by us.

12440. Though you attend very frequently, and at uncertain times, may it not be possible that frauds may be committed sometimes in your absence?—Certainly, it is possible if there is the connivance of the officers; I superintend other officers, not only one department; one cannot be constantly in one place.

12441. They might avail themselves of particular occasions if they were inclined to commit fraud?—Yes; but they are liable to my coming, and re-weighing, it would be at a great risk; I do not say that it is not possible.

12442. You have said, that you never knew erroneous weights delivered to you by the landing waiter?—They do not deliver them to us, but they are entered regularly in their book.

12443. You mean to say, in the course of the number of years you have been in the service, you never heard of such a thing as erroneous weights being given in by the landing waiter?—No, I never did in silk goods.

12444. Would you not consider that a landing waiter was running a very dangerous risk, if he were, by collusion with the weigher, to attempt to pass goods at an under weight?—Certainly.

12445. Would he not be risking the very good place which he has but for a moderate consideration?—No doubt he would, if he were detected he would be dismissed.

12446. Do you think there is any pecuniary consideration which it would be worth while for parties desirous of passing goods at short weights to offer to the landing waiter, which would be sufficient to remunerate him for the risk of the loss of his place in case of discovery?—I think not.

12447. You think if he had a good place of from 200*l.* which is the lowest, to 400*l.* a year, the chance he has of passing the goods unknown to you fraudulently, would be so little, as not to make it worth while for him to risk the loss of that place?—Certainly; I should think not.

12448. You would consider, that although he might perhaps succeed with one, or half a dozen parcels, on the second or seventh he might be discovered, and that there would be every probability of his being discovered?—Certainly; if he made it a common practice, I have no doubt he would be discovered.

12449. Are not goods frequently entered below their value?—Yes, and I frequently make detections.

12450. Are you not liable, in fine fancy goods, to be deceived?—We take the best care we can of that; if we have any doubt about it we apply to the trade.

12451. If you suspect it you take to the goods, allowing the parties a certain per centage, do not you?—We do not do that unless we get information from the trade that they are undervalued.

12452. Have you reason to believe that those goods have been frequently entered considerably under value; and yet when you have so detained them, and allowed the parties a per centage of 10 per cent. you have lost by them?—If they are brought to sale they have brought the 10 per cent. sometimes.

12453. Have you, in all cases been able to make the amount?—If they are detained as undervalued the merchant gets his return of the duty, and 10 per cent., when they are put up to sale; there have been instances where the goods have been sold for the amount; circumstances may arise that may prevent that.

12454. Do you think, if a man entered his goods at 20 per cent. less than the value, the great chance would be, that on sale you would not obtain the money?—Goods are not often detained and sold for 20 per cent. under value, they are frequently made 50 per cent. and even more than that.

12455. When

12455. When they are seized and sold, having been entered at 50 per cent. under value, it is very seldom you can realize the value, is it?—Yes, repeatedly more, I detained some silk goods some time ago, which were sold at more than the price entered, and the duty and the 10 per cent. paid to the merchant.

12456. Was that the case with any considerable quantity?—About 150*l.* or 160*l.* worth.

12457. Do you recollect whether they were purchased by any persons in the trade?—I do not know, they were sold at the public sale.

12458. Does it not more frequently happen that the goods do not fetch their value?—Sometimes it has happened from a change of market, or combinations in the trade, or circumstances of that kind.

12459. Do not the people in the trade often set their face against the seizure, and form a sort of combination?—Sometimes I believe there is a combination of the trade, and they will not buy the goods at the sale, and they frequently do not fetch their value at those sales; sometimes they fetch more than the value, sometimes not the value.

12460. When you have reason to suspect that a quantity of silk goods are entered below their value, you in the first instance stop those goods, and take the opinion of persons in the trade as to their value?—Yes.

12461. So that you have, in the first place, the security of the opinion of persons in the trade regarding the goods before you finally determine on seizing them?—Yes; we do not seize them in the first instance until we have satisfied ourselves by inquiring of the trade of their value.

12462. Is not that a great security to you against loss, inasmuch as you have, before you undertake the responsibility of the goods, the advice of the trade as to their value?—Yes.

12463. When you call on persons in trade as to the value of those goods, when they are not common articles, do not you find often a difficulty or variance in the valuation?—We have certainly great difficulty in ascertaining the true value of goods frequently.

12464. Persons in the trade have a difficulty in agreeing as to the value within 10 or 15 per cent. have they not?—We frequently have differences of opinion as to their value.

12465. You say they are sometimes entered 40 or 50 per cent. under value?—Yes, there have been such cases.

12466. Supposing they are entered at 20 per cent. under value, do you not think you should have considerable difficulty in some cases in proving that fact?—It is a very unpleasant thing for the officers, we get such various opinions that sometimes we do not know how to act.

12467. Upon the whole are you of opinion that you are enabled, with the assistance and the advice of the trade, which you have in the first instance prior to the seizure of the goods, to force the importer of the goods to value them at about the just price?—I think generally; the undervaluings are very few comparatively with the number of goods we pass.

12468. You are anxious to detain them, if you have reason to believe the goods are undervalued, inasmuch as a profit arises from doing so?—We participate in the profit; the Crown takes half, and the officers take the other moiety.

12469. Does that difference amount to much?—That depends upon the amount on the sale of the goods.

12470. Generally speaking, do you get much by it?—No; we do occasionally in some instances.

12471. Do you not get quite enough to induce you to be anxious to make the seizure if possible?—Certainly.

12472. With all the difficulties you have described in ascertaining the real value yourself, and a difficulty of the persons in the trade in ascertaining the value when they are called on, if a man is inclined to enter his goods only 10 or 15 per cent. under value, do not you think his goods would be passed without detection?—No doubt, 10 or 15 per cent.; we could not be justified in seizing them for that difference.

12473. When the goods are stopped, and the parties have 10 per cent. allowed upon them, the parties can run no great risk?—No; we should not stop them for 10 or 15 per cent.

12474. Then the probability is, that in all cases they may enter those goods 10 or 15 per cent. under value?—That may be done.

12475. Does

12475. Does your experience lead you to believe that the goods are considerably under valued, they being allowed to be entered 10 per cent. under value, inasmuch as 10 per cent. is allowed by the Crown in case of seizure; do you conceive they are entered much below that 10 per cent?—Not generally; some merchants will risk; but I do not think that is often done.

Mr.
*Joseph Beals.*

25 July,
1832.

*Lunæ, 27° die Julii,* 1832.

EDWARD AYSHFORD SANFORD, ESQUIRE, IN THE CHAIR.

Mr. *John Manning*, called in; and Examined.

12476. YOU are Surveyor General of the Customs?—Yes; one of them.

Mr.
*John Manning.*

27 July,
1832.

12477. Can you state to the Committee whether there were not some misrepresentations made at the latter end of last year by anonymous letters sent to the Chairman of the Customs stating the writer could prove that frauds to the extent of 50,000 *l.* per annum were practised upon the Customs by passing silks at wrong weights; letters signed under the name of Veritas?—Yes, there were; they were private and confidential; all those papers, all the communications, and all the correspondence, was private and confidential, to the Chairman of the Board of Customs; they were addressed in the first instance to Lord Auckland.

12478. They were addressed in the first instance to Lord Auckland, and by him forwarded to the Chairman of the Board of Customs?—Yes.

12479. Are you aware that any investigation took place in consequence of these representations?—There was an inquiry; perhaps I may be permitted to read from memorandums the particulars that I ascertained, and which I know of my own knowledge during the time that that correspondence between Veritas and the Chairman was in progress. The writer was called upon to substantiate the facts, and transmitted to the Chairman an account of 24 packages of silk goods, imported at sixteen different periods in the last year.

12480. Those 24 packages were not of the value of the 50,000 *l.* which was stated, were they?—No. He did not appear personally at all in the correspondence.

12481. So that the writer of that letter, in the first instance having stated that he could prove frauds to have been committed to the extent of 50,000 *l.* annually, came down to this accusation of twenty-four cases?—Of twenty-four cases containing the marks and numbers of each importation, and requested that it might be returned to him filled up with the weights in each package of each description of silks, and the quantity of duty paid; these particulars were prepared from the landing waiters' books, in which the original examination of the goods were entered by him, and a copy of the account sent by the writer was filled up, and returned to him by the Chairman as requested. In a few days (three or four days) after this, an account was received from the writer of the particulars of eight of the packages.

12482. Eight out of the twenty-four?—Yes, No. 22, and upwards of three of those importations, from which it would seem that the goods in those eight packages were passed at a considerable less weight than the writer's account specified. This not being considered satisfactory proof of the alleged fraud, the writer was then called upon, and subsequently produced invoices of the goods, but I am not prepared to say whether those invoices contained the weights of the silks; and another specification of the weights of the goods in each of the eight cases before mentioned as weighed by the importers when they received them into their warehouses, between which and their former account there was a trifling difference, as they stated, a mere clerical error; those are the particulars so far on that point.

12483. They were compared with the weights which were charged from the landing waiter's book?—They were.

12484. And they were manufactured silks?—Yes, they were.

12485. Not organzine?—No; manufactured silk goods of two or three descriptions, I believe gauzes and those subject to the higher rate of duty and to the lower rate of duty.

12486. Is it usual for the invoices of silk goods to contain the weights of the different descriptions in each package?—They are not usually produced to the

678.                                                                                        landing

landing officers, but I understand from inquiry of the importers that mode is general since this transaction, that the weights of the goods are not inserted in the invoices.

12487. Did the invoices sent to the Custom House of these eight packages contain the weights?—The invoices were forwarded to the Custom House by the party.

12488. Could not these invoices have been made out subsequently to the account being furnished?—They might, I think; there was time after the particulars were given from the landing waiters' books to have obtained invoices from Paris; I do not however mean to say that such was the fact; but an affidavit was sent from Paris dated the 14th of February, that is nearly two months after they were produced.

12489. Can you state to the Committee what the amount of the difference of the duty was between that taken on the landing account on these parcels, and what should have been taken, according to the statement of the weights received by the importers, provided those weights had been correct?—Between 280*l.* and 290*l.*; about 285 or 286 lb.

12490. On those eight cases?—Yes; the difference of duty admitting the proofs produced by the writer to be correct, the difference of duty to the prejudice of the Crown was between 280*l.* and 290*l.*

12491. Have you reason to believe at the Customs, that these weights given in in the invoices were correct?—There was an affidavit of the importers who received them at their warehouses; there was also an affidavit produced at the latter end of February from the manufacturer or the party at Paris, from the house at Paris from whom they were received. An affidavit was sent from Paris, dated the 14th of February, and produced by the writer Veritas, in proof of the correctness of a statement thereon of the particulars of the goods in the eight cases (No. 22 and upwards) which exactly corresponded with the writer's specification of them. There is a circumstance I discovered in looking over the papers yesterday, which I think important to state if I may be allowed : it is singular that this affidavit in French hand writing, with the particulars of the goods in English hand on the other side, that they are written on a sheet of foolscap paper with the maker's name, " J. Coles, 1830," precisely similar paper to that on which Veritas's long correspondence is written. In comparing the paper of this French affidavit, it was written on precisely the same paper indeed as the specification ; it may be therefore inferred that a copy of Veritas' specification was sent to Paris for the purpose of obtaining the affidavit thereto.

12492. You would infer from that, that the weights stated in that by Veritas were most likely the weights which were filled up after he had received the real landing weights from the Customs?—Certainly; the weights in his two specifications which I have been speaking of before those weights were transmitted to the Chairman subsequent to the information given him from the landing officer's books; and this affidavit was dated the 14th of February, and transmitted to the Chairman about the 20th or 21st of February; and on comparing that paper, it was exactly as the copy of the specification was written by the English dealer in the same handwriting (the English hand-writing) on precisely similar paper to all the different letters of Veritas, which amounted to about twenty.

12943. Then the only proof that you have of the weights being really correct weights, was this affidavit taken in France, which appears to have been made out in England?—There was an affidavit, also, accompanying the letter of Veritas. When he transmitted the affidavit there was also an affidavit of the importers of these eight cases to the same effect, stating that these specifications were correct, and those were the weights received in their warehouses.

12494. But did not you state that you had received from the importers, through Veritas, an account of weights as the goods were delivered into their warehouses, which tallied within a very trifling difference with the weights of the Custom House?—No, I beg pardon; the first account received from Veritas, and a subsequent specification as he called it, but made out in a very different form, more minutely, those two documents correspond with a trifling variation, mere clerical errors as I stated.

12495. But the result of this investigation, and of the charge brought by Veritas, beginning with an assertion that he could prove that 50,000 *l.* annually was fraudulently introduced into this country, ended at last in proof being adduced, adduced only of eight cases, and upon those, from the facts submitted to you, very great doubt was entertained?—Certainly I should not receive that as proof, even if any mistake arises and the goods are delivered out of the custody of the officer of the Crown; merchants of the highest respectability in London would get no redress from any subsequent examination or affidavit on their part of the correctness; even if it is admitted there is an error, it is never acknowledged, consequently it is not deemed satisfactory proof of fraud, because the importers of these goods, who were parties connected with Veritas all through the transaction it seems, their account would not be taken certainly, without it was confirmed by some other proof.

12496. Are you aware from your communication, and from the manner in which the Chairman employed you in part of this business, that the greatest pains were taken at the Custom House to investigate the whole of the transaction alluded to by Veritas?—Veritas's remarks were general; therefore there was no point on which we could trace, except these eight cases, and then the landing books were produced, and the accounts appeared to be regularly taken; and on one or two occasions subsequently to that transaction, the Chairman directed me to visit the silk floors, which I did, and in several instances I saw what were the proceedings of the landing officers, and I re-examined several packages which I found to be correct after they had gone through this examination, but it happened at a time when there was a slackness of business, and it was confined to these particular marks that he gave, and there were very few impositions subsequent to that period.

12497. From your investigation of this matter, are you of opinion that with regard to those eight cases even fraud was committed?—It is a difficult thing for me to say, I can only say, from the general character of the officers who examined these goods, that I should think it could not be correct, but certainly it is possible. From the general respectability of the officers who are employed in the examination of those goods, I should almost think it impossible that an officer will so commit himself, holding a respectable situation, for any paltry consideration made to him, even if it were 100 *l.* or 200 *l.* or 300 *l.*, that would not be a compensation for the chance of the loss of his situation, which it is most likely would be the consequence, because a thing of that sort could not long escape detection.

12498. But the result of this investigation was not produced by Veritas, was it? —Certainly not; the whole extent of the alleged frauds, at least according to his own statement, was upon these eight packages, and the difference was about 280 *l.*; the amount of duty paid was between 700 *l.* and 800 *l.*, and Veritas's statement was about 1,000 *l.* or 1,100 *l.*

12499. What was the difference of the duty that ought to have been paid?— Between 280 *l.* and 290 *l.*; but as regards the officers, in perusing Veritas's statement, I think it important, if I may be allowed to state, " That on a remark in one of the Chairman's letters to the writer, namely, that if there are any officers in the establishment who have betrayed their trust, they should at least be known." The writer replied, in a subsequent letter, it would be treachery to make known the individual or individuals who were parties to the frauds practised in the eight cases, No. 22 and upwards, set forth by him, particularly as they are not your officers, though all his correspondence in which he presumes those extensive frauds have been practised, the officers of the Customs are accused of being in connivance with the parties, and instrumental in effecting them, but yet in these eight he says, as I said before, they are not your officers.

12500. So that after having stated that great frauds were committed by the connivance of the Custom House officers, when brought to the proof he is only able to adduce one single instance, and that fraud he states was not committed by the connivance of the Custom House officers?—That is his own statement, though his grounds of assertion are, that the officers of the Customs are in connivance with the parties, and instrumental in effecting them; that was the result of all this inquiry.

12501. The Committee understand you to say, that the amount of duty received by the Customs on these eight cases was about 800 *l.* when they ought to have received 1,040 *l.*; now does not that amount to nearly 30 per cent. on the duty alone? —I should think it does.

12502. So that it is a very serious saving, though it will not appear a very considerable thing; but if the amount of the duty be something less than 100 *l.* received by the Custom House on each case, and it should be 135 *l.* that is clearly a saving of 35 per cent. on the amount of duty?—Admitting the fraud to have taken place, certainly.

12503. Which you do not admit?—It cannot be admitted, because there is no proof other than the affidavit of the parties; and that is a bare statement of the precise net weight. Now there is a great process in the examination of these goods by taking the rollers and weighing them, and allowing a tare; now all this did not appear; it was not a detailed statement but merely a general statement.

12504. With

Mr.
*John Manning.*

27 July,
1832.

12504. With regard to the class of men employed by you as occasional officers for weighing, you are aware many are employed from day to day as they are required; what are the wages allowed to them?—There are several classes, I think 35; perhaps 25; I cannot exactly say; there are three classes.

12505. But speaking of the wages of the lowest class?—They have a fixed salary and a rate of payment per day when employed.

12506. You mean to say that there are no persons occasionally employed who have not a fixed salary?—In the importation of the goods generally there are a considerable number above the established officers, but in the examination of silks I do not know that an instance has ever occurred of a man that is not an established officer being employed on that duty; indeed they are selected as the most worthy and best men.

12507. Do you know a man of the name of Allen Fraser?—No, I do not.

12508. Have you had occasion to make inquiry respecting him?—I suggested, when the man was named, that I would inquire as to the character of this man, and what he was; the result of that inquiry is, that he was appointed as what was termed a glut weigher; that is, when all the established men are employed, men by the Commissioners on recommendation are approved of and paid when employed at the rate of, I believe, 3 s. a day; this man was first appointed in June last.

12509. Have you brought with you a statement from the Custom House books of the number of days, and of the dates of the employ of that man?—I have; not at the docks but the quay station, where these goods are usually, and indeed always examined.

12510. Where alone silk goods are examined?—Yes.

12511. Does it appear from that statement that Allen Fraser could ever have been employed in weighing silk manufactured goods?—It has been ascertained on examination of the books, there is always an account kept of the duty that each man is employed on, and I have procured an account of that for the information of the Committee; and it appears, that the man has been employed about 12 or 14 days since August last on the quay station. At the docks no account was taken, and if I may be permitted, I can state on what duty he was employed on each of those occasions. It does not appear that he has ever been employed in the examination or weighing of silk. A man of that description would not be employed in that.

12512. That is a statement of the wages, and of the dates, as well as of the places at which that man was employed?—*(Producing a paper)*—It is.

[*The same was handed in, and read.*]

The following is a STATEMENT of the DAYS upon which *Fraser* has been employed on the Quays where Silk Goods are examined only, and it does not appear that he has ever been employed in the examination or weighing of Silk Goods.

| DAYS. | STATION. | DUTY. | Under whose SUPERVISION. |
|---|---|---|---|
| 9 August - 1831 | Coxe's Quay - - | Weighing Flax - - | Mr. Green. |
| 10 - - - | Globe Yard - - | Tallying Skins - - | Mr. Diggs. |
| 1 Sept. - - | Fresh Wharf - - | Shipping sundry Goods | Mr. Arnaman. |
| 2 - - - - | Ditto - - | Ditto - - - | Mr. Coxe. |
| 1 Oct. - - | Brewer's Quay - - | Ditto - - - | Mr. Kennedy. |
| 4 - - - - | Custom House Quay, (Ground Floor) | Opening Cases * - | Mr. Hammond. |
| 5 - - - - | Ditto - - - | Ditto - - - | Ditto. |
| 3 Nov. - - | Brewer's Quay - - | Tallying Apples - - | Mr. Rowen. |
| 5 - - - - | Fresh Wharf - - | Ditto Skins - - | Mr. Arnaman. |
| 9 - - - - | Coxe's Quay - - | Ship of Fruit - - | Mr. Poer. |
| 14 Dec. - - | Custom House Quay (Ground Floor) | Opening Cases - - | Mr. Johnson. |
| 16 - - - - | Botolph Wharf - - | Tallying Skins - - | Mr. Blake. |
| 19 - - - - | Custom House Quay (Ground Floor) | Opening Cases - - | Mr. Pocock. |
| 20 - - - - | Brewer's Quay - - | Tallying Apples - - | Mr. Hervey. |
| 27 April - 1832 | Custom House Quay (Ground Floor) | Tallying Skins - | Mr. Field. |
| 28 - - - - | Galley Quay - - | Opening Cases (Clocks) | Mr. Green. |
| 10 May - - | Custom House Quay - | Ditto - - (Eggs) | Mr. Ferguson |

* *N.B.* It has never been the practice to examine Silks on the Ground Floor at Custom House Quay.

*The Witness.*]—It appears he was only employed three days at the quays.

12513. And those three days on which he was employed at the quays he was employed on the ground floor where no silk goods are ever opened ?—It is only on the several occasions that I mention in this Account (about four days) that he was employed in opening cases on the ground floor of the warehouse under the silk floor, where no silk goods are ever opened, if they are it must be a casual thing; it probably may happen, in a case where the contents are unknown, they may commence opening, but from the situation of the place it is not a suitable place for it.

12514. Has Allan Fraser any fixed salary ?—He has not.

12515. And what allowance did he receive for each of the days' work, and how many hours was he employed ?—The hours of attendance are according to the season; in the winter from nine to four, and in the summer eight to four ; and I think he received 3 *s.* a day.

12516. Do you consider 3 *s.* a day, under such circumstances, sufficient wages for a man on whom you are to place confidence in taring weights ?— He is immediately under the eye of the landing waiter, the officer does not trust him ; he merely puts in the weights and balances the scale, the landing waiter sees to a pound what the goods weigh.

12517. Are we to understand, in all such cases, the landing waiter is the person who takes the tare or keeps the weight, and the other party merely his labourer ?— In such goods as skins, a merchant will enter 20 bales of skins with an endorsement of the contents of each bale ; in that case the landing waiter knows that the bale is endorsed as 100 ; he will trust that man ; he is present and sees it ; but he does not perform the operation himself of turning over the skins, but this man tallies them and announces there are 100 in that bale, then the landing waiter selects another bale, and if he is satisfied he will discharge the 20 bales on the examination of one, two, three, four or five, as the case may be.

12518. What is your duty at the Custom House ?—Surveyor general for investigation of cases generally, and occasionally to go on to the quays.

12519. Your duty is that of a surveyor general, to see generally that the surveyors, as you call them, do their duty ; is it not ?—Not particularly ; we are employed in matters generally, all cases ; it does not often occur that we have an opportunity of going out, but occasionally to see that no more officers are employed than are necessary, and that the officers are on duty ; and if we visit the docks we see that the landing waiters and surveyors are acting in the due performance of their duty.

12520. The landing surveyors are the parties charged with the immediate superintendence of the landing waiters ?—They are; they are instructed to re-weigh, re-examine and to settle all tares on goods of every description, and no case of silk goods is ever discharged without the immediate examination and supervision of the landing surveyor as well as landing waiter.

12521. Do you mean to say that every package of silk goods is re-weighed and re-examined by the landing surveyor ?—No, it is not delivered without the supervision of the officer ; there is no case of silk goods scarcely, but what requires a tare, and they are all laid out on a table similar to this ; the whole contents of the case ; the landing surveyor goes and takes the landing waiter's book, in which there is a specification of each description ; he sees those, and he selects from the blocks and the different figured silks, a certain number, for the purpose of ascertaining the tare, and then he sees the contents ; indeed they are frequently weighed in his presence.

12522. Has it come to your knowledge that there had been any defect in ascertaining the particular kinds of manufactured goods, to charge them agreeably to the Schedule in the Act ?—In fancy articles of silk goods there have been sometimes doubts on the part of the officers, but whenever they entertain a doubt, they always consult the trade ; there is a diversity of opinion even among the trade, and then of course a representation is made to the Board, and it is decided by the prevailing opinion.

12523. Have you formed any opinion whether the appointing of a person bred to the trade, and a weaver, as a judge of manufactured silk goods, would facilitate the entries and proceedings of the Customs ?—I think it would not ; I think the practical officers of the Customs, from day to day, in the course of their examination, know every article of importation, perhaps from experience and practice, as well as an individual bred up in the trade ; in short, I think with submission, that that would not be a good arrangement, for that individual, particularly in regard to the goods to be valued, might be interested ; if that individual is consulted, that individual would be liable to be biassed more than an officer who had no interest

either

either in the trade, or any other person, but whose interest it is to protect the revenue.

12524. But the Committee are supposing a person to be appointed to protect the revenue as much as any other Custom House officer, without any connexion in trade, or with any manufacturer?—I do not think that that individual could know, or give such good information as the officers attain from the merchants in the trade generally. I remember there was once a skin inspector; there were skins of different descriptions; there were great varieties of them; that skin inspector did not know so well, although he was appointed on purpose, as many of the officers; we did not send to him, because he did not know from time to time, and we always referred it to the trade. If a new case occurs in the importation of silk goods, where there is a doubt, the officers apply to the trade, and they are not satisfied with applying to one, two or three.

12525. Are the Committee to understand you to say, that no advantage would be derived by appointing a person who is qualified?—I think it would be an injury to the revenue. That individual's opinion would be taken perhaps, and it would be an erroneous one, and the officers would be relieved from their responsibility.

12526. But do not you find the opinions of persons called in very often erroneous?—They differ, and it is impossible to say which is right, until it is ultimately decided one way or the other; therefore that party that it is decided against, it is presumed, gives an erroneous opinion.

12527. But do they not differ, to a very great degree very often, as to the value of goods; have you known the difference of opinion?—It is not in my practice, but the landing surveyors; but there are cases frequently in our department for further inquiry.

12528. In making the inquiry, with regard to the cases alluded by Veritas, would not the investigation have been much more easy, supposing the goods had been stamped?—That would have led to nothing; it was a transaction that had gone by.

12529. You examined it by the invoices of the importer?—No, the goods were not examined by any document produced by the merchants.

12530. The investigation took place by your having the invoices of the importer handed to you?—There was no investigation of the transaction, other than an inquiry to lead to whether his allegation was correct; whether his statement of frauds was correct, and we could not trace that during the whole of the inquiry, and during the correspondence and his repeated allegations of those frauds, he could not substantiate, or at least did not attempt to establish that any fraud had been committed but this one.

12531. Had not you the invoices of the goods handed to you by Veritas?—They were handed in, but not to me.

12532. Were they not handed to the Customs by Veritas?—They were; this was after the transaction.

12533. Were not those invoices handed in subsequently, when they might have been made up for the purpose?—They might have made invoices.

12534. It should seem, from the nature and tenor of your evidence, that you had a suspicion on your mind, that the invoices were made up for the occasion?—I am not prepared to insinuate as much as that.

12535. If there had been an opportunity of comparing those invoices with the goods in the possession of the importer, and the goods had been stopped, would not the investigation have been much more easy?—The merchant might have had an importation of a similar description of goods the week before, you could not identify them after they were once out of the custody of the Crown; but if goods were required to be stamped generally, any goods found in a merchant's possession not stamped, would of course be liable to seizure.

12536. But supposing the goods were corresponding in the stamps, that the stamps were made of such a description as to be able to identify the goods according to the invoices, in that case would not the investigation have been more easy?—The mere fact of discovering the goods to have been stamped, would have been satisfactory proof that the duty was paid.

12537. But supposing the stamps did not correspond with the invoice?—The stamps contain nothing, that I am aware of, to lead to any comparison of the invoice; the invoice is merely a statement of the particulars of the goods, the number of pieces and lengths, or whatever they may be, and the price of the article; but as to the stamp, it has no reference to any thing of the sort.

12538. Does

Mr.
*John Manning.*

27 July,
1832.

12538. Does the landing waiter ever superintend more than one scale?—Not that I am aware of. Of silk goods, certainly not; there are no means in the silk floors; there is only one scale fixed in the silk floors.

12539. And a landing surveyor only superintends one floor?—During the whole of the legal hours he is moving from one floor to another at the different stations: the landing surveyor.

12540. But a landing waiter?—The landing waiter remains, and never leaves a case when the lid is taken off; he never leaves that case till he has ascertained the whole contents of it.

12541. And at that period he is never supposed to be superintending another scale?—Never.

12542. You stated that the letter of Veritas was in some degree confirmed by an affidavit made by the importers?—Yes, there was an affidavit.

12543. And also by an affidavit made by a Frenchman?—Yes.

12544. So that if he were inaccurate those affidavits must both of them have been false?—Certainly, if he were incorrect.

12545. Then either there must be some mismanagement, some error or connivance in the Custom House, or those two affidavits must have been sworn falsely?—Yes. It does not prove that there was fraud on the part of the officers, but there must have been some error on the part of the officers; it would not prove the fact of fraud. It is quite possible, during the examination of goods, for a person to put a small parcel under the table or under the counter; such a thing is possible, but I should hardly think that such a thing is done.

12546. You know nothing of the examination of goods yourself?—I have known it forty years.

12547. Because you mention there is a difficulty in ascertaining the tare; do you know that French ribbons are not imported on wooden blocks, as you stated?—They are imported on rollers, or something of that sort.

### Mr. *William Beckwith*, called in; and further Examined.

Mr.
*William Beckwith.*
—————

12548. IN your evidence before this Committee, you have stated that you purchased velvets of Morrison & Co.?—Yes.

12549. And you have stated that you purchased them for fifteen per cent. cheaper than you could import them, although you imported them for ready money?—Yes; and upon that part I beg to correct a little error I have fallen into in stating it without my documents at the time. I am now ready to correct it by the documents themselves; it appears the velvets were 25 or 30 per cent. cheaper instead of 10 or 15 per cent., as appears by my invoice, from Lyons, and Messrs. Morrison & Co.'s invoice in one instance—[*producing the invoices, marked B. C. D.*].

(B.)

LONDON, Oct. 15, 1828.

Mr. W. Beckwith,
    Spital Square,

*Bought of JAMES MORRISON & Co.*

Z Day Book, fol. 185.                Conveyance_____

| 30 ⅛ | 30 | | | | £. s. d. |
|---|---|---|---|---|---|
| 30 ¼ | 29 ¾ | } 178 ⅞ Yards French Figured Silk Velvet - | 15/6 | | 138 12 6¾ |
| 30 ½ | 28 ¼ | | | | *W. W. P.* |

3 Months from date.
Allowed for damage, 2 s. .      *W. C.*

N. B.—The above were equal in pattern and quality of a parcel I imported, which cost me 19 s. 8 d. per yard.      *W. B.*

LYONS,

(*C.*)

Lyon, 24 Sept^bre 1828.

Monsieur W. Beckwith de Londres,

*Bois à FELIX VERNER de Lyon.*

Les Marchandises ci-après payables à Lyon expediées par l'entremise de
Messieurs Ch^es Devaux C^ie.

Velours ½ au Liserè.

2621      3,192 au. 24
2620      3,193  „  24 ⅛

$\qquad$ 48 ⅛ au à 19 *s.*  -  -  -  -  £.45. 14. 4.

C. B.

Oct. 18th. Paid by Cheque  -  -  -  £.61. 3. 0.

Duty included,
To Devaux & Co.

---

(*D.*)

London, 17 Oct. 1828.

Mr. Beckwith,

*To C. DEVAUX & Co.*

Charges on Two Pieces of Velvet ex Superb, at Calais.

|  | £. | s. | d. |
|---|---|---|---|
| Duty 10 lbs. 1 oz. Figured Velvet  -  -  -  27 s. 6 d.  -  -  - | 13 | 17 | — |
| Custom House Entry and Warrant  -  -  -  -  -  -  - | — | 5 | — |
| Freight from Calais, and Charges there, including Carriage from Lyons, Shipping, &c.; Wharfage, Landing, &c.  -  -  - | 1 | 8 | 7 |
| Cartage  -  -  -  -  -  -  -  -  -  -  -  -  - | — | 2 | — |
| Postages  -  -  -  -  -  -  -  -  -  -  -  - | — | 3 | 6 |
| Agency  -  -  -  -  -  -  -  -  -  -  -  -  - | — | 7 | 6 |
| £. | 16 | 3 | 7 |

Omitted in the Account of the Four Pieces:

| Carriage from Lyons to Calais, Shipping there, Commission, &c. - | 1 | 6 | — |
|---|---|---|---|
| £. | 17 | 9 | 7 |

Amount of Bill, Two Pieces  -  £.45  14  4
Three Month's Interest  -  -  11  4

$\qquad$ £.45  3  —

13  17  —
2  3  —          Rec^d by Cheque, £.61. 3. 0.

16  —  —          For C. Devaux & Co.

Oct. 18, 1828.                              *E. Hutton.*

I have made a double mistake, Morrison & Co. supplied me at three month's credit,
while I paid ready money at Lyons, which makes another difference which ought
to be taken into consideration; instead of 15 it should be nearly 30 per cent.

12550. Have you made any other purchases of foreign goods at Morrison & Co.'s?
—Yes, several.

12551. What was the date of that purchase by the invoice?—Fifteenth October
1828.

12552. Did the evidence which you gave first here allude to that transaction, or
to any other transaction?—To this transaction, and others as well, but this is one
case I thought sufficient to illustrate, without bringing all.

12553. What were the others?—Some other velvets.

12554. And at what period?—About the same period.

12555. Where these other velvets part of the same parcel, or were they different?
—Different, and of course they were a different date and a different invoice.

12556. Now what is the date of the second?—I have not brought the second;
I believe it was previous to this; I think so.

12557. Now

Mr.
*William Beckwith.*

27 July,
1832.

12557. Now what was the transaction of velvets, stated in your first evidence to have been purchased by you at 15 per cent.; was that the identical transaction you allude to, or any other?—I should say, there is a doubt on my mind that it is not; that the other will be about 15 per cent., and this proves to be about 30. I think if I had brought the other document probably it would not have been so strong a case as this one.

12558. Did you not afterwards state, that from their cheapness you inferred that they could not have paid the regular duty?—I think I did.

12559. Now in consequence of having said so, had you ever any communication with any of the partners of Morrison & Co.'s house?—I had. I had a long letter or two from Mr. Dillon.

12560. Did you see the invoice of those goods that you considered to have bought so very cheap; at the time that you had an interview with Mr. Dillon, were you shown the invoice of the goods and the accounts at the Custom House?—I did not look at them and examine them minutely, I did look at a great book that was produced, and I said that I would not go into the question as to how fair and honest Morrison & Co. had come by them; I could not doubt but what they had got them in a proper manner.

12561. But do you recollect whether Mr. Bridges or any gentleman accompanied you to that house?—Yes; but not for that purpose; I remember the case, that I received a letter from Mr. Dillon one morning as I went from the Silk Committee; on my return home, I called on him to know what his letter referred to.

12562. Is Mr. Bridges a partner in the house of Bridges & Campbell?—Yes.

12563. Have you no recollection of his being present at the time when this conversation passed between you and Mr. Dillon, with respect to those invoices and charges?—Yes. Mr. Crow was also present.

12564. Did you not at that time declare yourself perfectly satisfied?—Yes, as much as I am now, that they had got them cheaper than I could.

12565. Now did you not at that time express your regret at having expressed a doubt of these goods having been smuggled, and not regularly entered?—No; I never expressed any regret about the matter, nor do I now regret it; it is a matter of profit, and I saved a great deal of trouble by going to Fore-street instead of sending to Germany, or anywhere else.

12566. Did you not, having charged the house with having got those goods in a smuggled way——?—I stated, in my former evidence, I never charged the house with smuggling; I never did, and do not mean it now.

12567. But did you not express a doubt, of those goods, which were bought so cheap, having paid the regular duties?—Yes, I doubt it now; if mine had paid that duty they would have been seized, I have no doubt.

12568. Did you not at that interview, when Mr. Bridges was present, expressly declare having seen the invoices, you were perfectly satisfied you were in error?—No; had I paid the duty, and entered mine at 10 s. per yard, they would have been seized. How am I to reconcile the point of goods that are entered at a difference of 50 per cent.? I entered mine at 15 s. per yard, and theirs must have been entered at 10 s. per yard, to allow them to supply me at 15 s. 6 d. per yard.

12569. The question is this, did you or did you not, having once charged the house with an illegal transaction, did you not express yourself satisfied you had been wrong?—No, I did not; I never charged the house with smuggling.

12570. The Committee is alluding to the conversation which took place with a partner of that house, as regards that transaction, and not at all to what passed in evidence, this is a prior period?—I deny having charged the house with any illegal proceeding.

12571. Did you declare that you thought your suspicions were incorrect?—My suspicions then and now are, that they must have been entered at an inferior value, or they could not possibly have come in at the proper duty.

12572. Did you not express your regret at that time at having stated to any body that you suspected that house of an illegal transaction?—I never regretted it either then or now.

12573. You never expressed it?—I do not know that I did.

12574. Not in conversation?—If I did, I said I was sorry Mr. Dillon felt himself charged with smuggling; I should be sorry if he felt that imputation of being a smuggler; I do not charge him with it, I state the fact, and leave the honourable Committee to draw their own conclusions from the invoices now produced.

678.                                          12575. Did

12575. Did you, in that conversation, express any regret at having stated suspicions against the house?—I have not stated them that I am aware of. Will Mr. Dillon state that I did to any other party or to any person.

12576. The question is simply this : if you will attend to it, you can answer it aye or no. Did you, in the conversation with Mr. Dillon, express a regret that you should have, to any other parties, stated a suspicion that the transaction of the entry of the velvets by that house had not been regular?—I will acknowledge that I have indirectly made such an observation; I think I wrote him a letter to that effect, that if I had, I would go with him to any person that considered it an imputation of smuggling against the firm, and set the matter right. The fact is, I wrote that letter with the advice of some persons in Mr. Dillon's establishment, on purpose that I might continue to deal with Morrison & Co. and save a law suit. I distinctly say now, I do not charge Morrison & Co. with being smugglers, but leave the honourable Committee to form their own opinions.

12577. Will you answer the Committee this question; will you state to the Committee whether you did or did not at that time express your suspicions of these goods having been illegally introduced?—Who did I express that to?

12578. Did you or not express that opinion?—Who was it to? There was only Mr. Dillon that I had any conversation with, he made a charge upon me, he said, " You have circulated a report that we are smugglers," and that is an unpleasant thing. I said, " No, I have not. Perhaps I may have stated this transaction of velvets to one or two in the trade, but I will make a point of seeing those individuals and explain the matter," and I did so ; Mr. Dillon did not ask me for the names of any party he charged me with having circulated the report to.

12579. Are the Committee to understand that you had expressed your suspicions to others of those goods being illegally introduced?—No, I do not wish the Committee to infer any thing of the sort; I had my suspicions then, and I have now, and as such I kept purchasing instead of importing.

12580. The question is, whether you expressed those suspicions to others?—I am not aware that I did, except in my own establishment perhaps.

12581. Did you not, at the interview which the Committee have alluded to, state your regret that you should have mentioned any such suspicions, and offered to write a letter to the house expressly stating that regret?—I do now charge my memory, and I regret very much that I destroyed Mr. Dillon's correspondence ; it is only a fortnight ago that I destroyed it. Since my examination, I thought it was done with ; and in those letters I recollect there was this observation. " I would not have cared," says Mr. Dillon, " for any observation upon such an occasion as this, had not the allusion come from a respectable manufacturer like yourself; if it had come from a discarded servant I should not have cared."

12582. Read that letter, and say whether you have any recollection of such a letter.—(Handing a letter to the witness.)—In the first place, what is the date of that letter?—The 2d of December 1831.

12583. Now just run over it, and say whether you recollect any such letter?—I remember a letter something to this effect.

12584. Well, that is a letter from Mr. Dillon to you?—It is a letter asking me whether I had been up to Lord Auckland, or any of the members of the Board of Trade, stating they were smugglers, to which I said I had not.

12585. Is that a copy of the letter which you say you destroyed lately?—Before I give a direct answer to that question, I had better read it all through. There was also another long letter from Mr. Dillon.

[The Letter was handed in, and read, as follows:]

Dear Sir,                                                    " Fore-street, December 2d, 1831.

" Since I saw you here, I have more fully investigated the matter as to the velvets. As I understand it, you expressed an opinion to our Mr. Kirsop, that the silk velvet you bought of us in September and October 1828, could not have been duty paid on account of the low prices at which we invoiced them to you, you having ordered similar goods from France about the same time at much higher prices. Under ordinary circumstances this is a matter which I should not have felt any disposition to explain or enter upon. That we should astonish our customers by the cheapness of our goods is no new matter ; but I think there are at present reasons why I should more fully explain to you the matter, and call upon you for an explicit declaration respecting it. The facts are these ;—we sold you as follows: September 10th, 1828, 268 yards figured silk velvet 18s. 241 l. 4s. October 15th, 1828, 178 ⅞ of ditto, 15s. 6d. 138l. 12s. 6d. These velvets formed the greater portion of two lots, the bought invoices of which now lie before me ; viz. August 13th, 1828. Bought by us, of
C. V. Turbe,

C. V. Turbé, Lyons, in English money, 171 *l*. 6 *s*. 9 *d*. September 10th, 1828, Bought *of* the same, 86 *l*. 7 *s*. 10 *d*. We paid duty on these, September 5th, 1828, 49 lbs. figured silk velvet 27 *s*. 6 *d*. 67 *l*. 7 *s*. 6 *d*. October 13, 1828, 28 lbs. 15 oz. ditto ditto, 27 *s*. 6 *d*. 39 *l*. 16 *s*. The first lot came in three cases ex Belfast; the last in a case ex Heros, Calais to London; the duty in both cases being paid by our agent, Mr. J. W. Wilkinson. The original document you and Mr. Bridges saw when last here, and may again see if you please; as at that time you expressed yourself satisfied of your mistake, the matter might have dropped here, but as you so fully believed it that you could name it to one of our buyers, it is highly improbable but that you should also, during the course of three years, have named it in some other quarter. I must call on you, therefore, to state in the same quarter, that you are now fully satisfied that your impression was a mistaken one. This is a matter which I may, perhaps, feel more personally than as affecting the house, which may well disregard such reports, though even as affecting the house, whilst there are parties who either from interest or bad feeling have a disposition to misrepresent us, it is desirable that in all respectable quarters such misrepresentations should be done away. You know that a French trade forms a very small part indeed of our business; that in French broad silks we do next to nothing, and that it is quite as much our interest as it is that of the English manufacturers that smuggling should be put down. The best trade for us is a home trade; and that is the business which we have always cultivated. A statement similar to the one you made, had it come from a discarded servant, or from any party who sought to injure others, in order to cover his own misconduct, I should not have stooped to have noticed; but coming from a respectable manufacturer like yourself, I have thought it right, in the first place, to undeceive you, and, in the second place, to call upon you as a matter of justice, to explain the matter correctly in every quarter where, whilst labouring under a mistake yourself, you may have misrepresented it to others.

" I remain, dear Sir, awaiting your reply,

" Your's, very truly,

" *John Dillon*,"

Mr.
*William Beckwith*.

———

27 July,
1832.

---

12586. Have you any recollection of receiving a letter nearly to the same purport as that?—I have; but before I give the answer to that letter, you had better have the other letter read, because that letter of mine, I believe, was in answer to both.

*[The Letter of the Witness, in answer to Mr. Dillon's letter, was handed in, and read, as follows:]*

" Dear Sir, Spital Square, Dec. 5th, 1831.

" My absence from town till a late hour on Saturday night, prevented me the pleasure of acknowledging the receipt of your letter of the 2d instant. I am very sorry for your uneasiness respecting the figured velvets, which I am now satisfied came regularly through the Custom House; and I shall therefore make a point of informing the few friends I had mentioned the matter to, and this I trust will fully satisfy you. But should you know of any person to whom I have named it, and you think yourself or your Firm injured by it, I shall have great pleasure in accompanying you to correct any mis-statement I have erroneously made. Having been always on friendly terms with your Partners, I trust you will not attribute any such unworthy motives to me, as to think me capable of misrepresenting your House in any quarter, to cover my own misconduct.

" I remain, dear Sir, your's truly,

" *W. Beckwith*."

" To John Dillon, Esq. Fore-street."

---

12587. That letter is dated three years subsequently, is it not, to the purchase you made?—Yes.

12588. Having heard that letter and answer, how do you reconcile the statement in that letter with the evidence you gave before this Committee, that you still suspected these goods were smuggled, and that you left the Committee to draw what conclusion they thought proper?—I stated that I did not charge the house with smuggling, either then or now; and with regard to that letter, I beg to state, that before I wrote that letter I had written a very long one, with the intention of answering Mr. Dillon's, defending my suspicions as far as I could. I am perfectly aware Mr. Dillon states in his letter that the French trade forms a very small proportion of their business; I remember perfectly well writing the letter, and stating, instead of that, my suspicion was a little confirmed by one of their firm, Mr. Crow, being in France the major part of the year, purchasing goods; and I then stated, that another part of my suspicions was that their house, like many others, had greatly increased since Leaf's affair, and I destroyed that letter. I was defending my suspicions, and, by the advice of some friends, they thought, as the business was dying away, it would be more to my interest and advantage to let the matter drop; and then it was that I wrote that letter.

12589. Do

Mr.
William Beckwith.

12589. Do you mean to say, when you wrote that letter, you wrote that which you did not believe at the time you wrote it?—Yes; leaving Mr. Dillon to draw

Mr.
William Beckwith.

27 July,
1832.

12625. Were you not shown that?—I dare say I was, but I was fatigued, and paid but little attention to it.

12626. Did he or not offer to show you that?—I dare say he did, a large quantity of documents were brought forward.

12627. Mr. Dillon having stated the duty was paid by weight, and he having offered to show you the document in which it was shown it was paid by weight, and the duty on your goods having also been paid by weight, how do you now reconcile this with your former statement, respecting the circumstance of the goods having been entered at a different value?—My suspicions are founded on the difference of price.

12628. Then although Mr. Dillon stated they were entered by weight, and offered to show you the document; and although you knew yours were entered by weight also, you thought you were justified in calling on the Committee to presume their's must have been entered at a different valuation?—It does not even alter my opinion now, any figured velvet manufacturer would express the same doubts which I have.

12629. Did you not see the invoice of the goods you bought from Messrs Morrison & Co. the invoice of those goods bought at Lyons?—No, I am not sure that I did; Mr. Crow acknowledged afterwards, that he got six or eight per cent. profit by the transaction, when I was since talking to him about it, and then I stated to him, I remember, that the Frenchman must have been a great rogue to serve me in the way he did.

22630. Have you any recollection of having seen the invoice?—I do not recollect it.

12631. But it was offered to you?—I do not recollect that, they offered books and papers, which I did not choose to look at, because they could not convince me further than I was convinced.

### *John Dillon*, Esquire, called in; and Examined.

John Dillon,
Esq.

12632. YOU are a partner in the house of Morrison & Co.?—I am.

12633. There is a letter there dated the 2d December 1831, purporting to be signed by you, is that your hand writing?—This is a copy of a letter I wrote to Mr. Beckwith, after the interview I had with him.

12634. Well now what passed at that interview which led to the witing of that letter?—Perhaps I may be allowed to state what led to the interview; one of our buyers told me that Mr. Beckwith, in the course of conversation with him, had said, that from the cheap price at which he had bought the velvets of us two or three years before, he believed that they were not duty paid; I was a little startled by the information : and I deliberated and I believe consulted with my partner, Mr. Crow, as to whether it was or was not worth while taking notice of such an imputation; we determined however to take notice of it, and to convince Mr. Beckwith of the falsehood of his suspicions. It happened that Mr. Beckwith, accompanied by Mr. Bridges, called upon us, and in the presence of my partner, Mr. Crow, I repeated to him what he had stated, and I said, Now, Mr. Beckwith, we are desirous of putting you in possession of the facts, and you are quite at liberty to see them; I will show you, with regard to those velvets, the original purchase, and all the documents connected with them.

12635. Do you allude to the velvets which you sold to Mr. Beckwith in 1828? —I do; the only velvets that we ever sold him.

12636. And it is respecting those velvets that Mr. Beckwith had entertained suspicions with regard to the regular entry of the goods?—Yes; I began by asking Mr. Beckwith the ground of his suspicions; he stated that he had ordered velvets which were so much dearer than those he bought of us; that he inferred from that circumstance that we could not have paid the duty; and upon comparing notes, and my mentioning the name and producing the invoice, he said he had bought them of the very same man. I then said, I will now convince you that the duty was paid on those goods, and we searched and found the two original invoices, for there were two transactions occuring within a month of each other; I produced to him then what I produce now (*producing two invoices.*)

12637. These are the original invoices?—These are the original French invoices, by which we discovered, as he said, that we had bought them of the same man as he had bought them. We bought ours of Charles V. Turbé, of Lyons.

12638. Now

*John Dillon,*
Esq.

———

27 July,
1832.

12638. Now where is Mr. Beckwith's invoice?—I never saw Mr. Beckwith's invoice; he informed me it was the same man, and he abused the man for selling to us at a rate so much lower than he had sold to him.

12639. Then, if these invoices are from different houses, of course Mr. Beckwith must have been in error, in supposing they were supplied from the same house?—He must have been so; he certainly did so state to me, and was very indignant with the Frenchman for having charged him 30 or 40 per cent. more than he charged us.

12640. However, you produce now the original invoices to you of those velvets purchased by you at Lyons, part of which you sold to Mr. Beckwith?—Yes, the greater part of which we sold to Mr. Beckwith.

12641. Your letter is dated the 2d of December 1831, on what day did Mr. Bridges and Mr. Beckwith call on you?—It was some three or four days before; I expected to hear again from Mr. Beckwith, and after an interval of three or four days not hearing from him, I addressed that letter to him.

12642. Now did you show to Mr. Beckwith and Mr. Bridges these original invoices which you now produce?—I showed them to Mr. Beckwith, Mr. Bridges was standing by.

12643. Did you show the value or the weight; did you show the entry or any document to satisfy him of their having gone through the Custom House?—I showed him the only document which we possessed, the account of our agent, in which the duty was paid.

12644. Who is your agent?—Our agent's name is Wilkinson; and I stated to Mr. Beckwith that if he wanted to see the original entries, they were made by Mr. Wilkinson on such a day, mentioning the date and giving the marks of the package, and every clue by which he might make the necessary inquiry, producing the vouchers for our payment of the duty.

12645. Then did Mr. Beckwith at that conversation express to you any alteration of his opinion, or that his suspicions were removed, if suspicions he had entertained of this being an irregular transaction?—He did most unreservedly.

12646. Well now, in that letter you state your readiness, if he is not satisfied, again to show him all the documents?—I do.

12647. Will you look at that letter of Mr. Beckwith's; is that the answer which you received from Mr. Beckwith to your letter of the 2d?—It is.

12648. Does that letter contain any expressions of regret different from those which, in conversation, Mr. Beckwith expressed?—Certainly not at all different in their purport; he owned himself, in the conversation with me, perfectly satisfied with the documents I showed him; he expressed regret for having entertained such suspicions, and was willing to explain it in any quarter in which he had made those mis-statements; and it was in consequence of that declaration of his that he would make the explanation in other quarters, and three or four days having elapsed, and he having made no such explanation, that I wrote him this letter.

12649. Now subsequent to that letter did you ever understand that Mr. Beckwith had again stated his suspicions or charged your house with irregular proceedings?—I never did.

12650. You are aware that doubt has been expressed in his evidence given before this Committee?—I am.

12651. Now did you write any other letter, and did you receive from Mr. Beckwith any other letter respecting that transaction than those two that are now produced?—I wrote Mr. Beckwith two other letters subsequent to the receipt of this; I see my first letter was dated on the second, and his reply on the fifth; on the sixth therefore (the next day) I wrote, " Dear Sir,—In reply to yours of yesterday, I beg most unequivocally to assure you, that when speaking of parties who misrepresented others in order to cover their own misconduct, I in no way whatever referred to you, as you may be assured by a reference to my former letter. The very fair and friendly tone of your letter is gratifying to me, and what I should have expected from you ; as you state that whilst labouring under a misapprehension you mentioned the matter to a few friends, and now express a willingness to explain the truth to them; I beg to know the names of the individuals in question, as I can then form a better judgment of the steps which ought to be taken. When the matter first arose Lord Auckland's name was mentioned; I shall be obliged by your saying whether the fact in question, or the opinion which it appears you entertained, was mentioned by you to that nobleman, or in any way conveyed to him, or to any party connected with the Board of Trade. After the candid declaration in

678.                                                                                    your

your letter I cannot doubt your readiness to give every information, and to do any thing in your power to remedy any mischief which may have arisen. Fully sensible of the fairness and propriety of which, I remain, dear Sir, yours truly, John Dillon."

12652. Did you receive any answer to that letter?—To that I received no answer; I waited for some days and consulted with my partner (Mr. Morrison I believe was out of town at the time)—with my partner Mr. Crow, as to whether we should or not take any steps to compel an answer, and after the interval of some days (that is from December the 6th to the 17th) I addressed this letter to Mr. Beckwith. " Dear Sir,—I beg to remind you of my letter of the 6th, to which you have not yet favoured me with an answer. Your's truly, John Dillon." To that also I got no answer, and there the matter dropped.

12653. Then you have never received any other letter from Mr. Beckwith respecting his suspicions on that transaction, except the one which has been shown you dated the 5th?—I have not. In every thing Mr. Beckwith wrote and said to me, up to this moment, he always conveyed to my mind that he was perfectly satisfied with the matter; and if I did not know from undoubted information that he had given such evidence, I could not have believed it, it is so inconsistent with all that he has ever said or written on the subject. I have two remarks to add; one is, that I at that time showed Mr. Beckwith by calculations, or offered to enter into calculations to show him, that after we had bought those goods at the invoice prices, and paid the duty and expenses, that we still got a profit on them, and I wish also to explain, on the subject of weight, that there is no option on the part of the purchasers as to entering by weight or by value; the option is on the part of the Government, and not on that of the importers, and the Government at that time always collected the duty by weight.

12654. You paid duty on that parcel of goods by weight, did you not?—We did, by weight, and we had no power or option to do it otherwise, we always do it by weight, and so does every body else.

12655. Now will you examine Mr. Beckwith's invoices of the 24th, and your's of the 23d of September, as it is understood the velvets were of the same pattern and the same quality, and state what is the difference per cent. between the price charged to Mr. Beckwith, and the invoice price charged to you?—Our invoice prices of September the 23d, are at the two prices of 15 francs and 18 francs, and Mr. Beckwith's invoice of the succeeding day (the 24th) is at 19 francs.

12656. Now what proportion of your's was at the 15 francs?—I really cannot say, for I perceive that in other invoices some of our's were 21 francs; the price depends on the width, quality, &c.

12657. Does it not depend also on the person who they are bought of?—Certainly.

12658. Your's may have been bought from the manufacturer and the others from an agent?—Yes.

12659. With the profit of the intermediate dealers is not that so?—Yes; besides that one manufacturer may sell much dearer than another, and the same manufacturer may sell much dearer to one person than he does to another.

12660. Will not those two invoices explain a difference of 20 or 30 per cent. in prime cost, and account for the difference of price at which Mr. Beckwith seems surprised?—On the face of the thing I should say that does appear so.

12661. Look at that invoice of Mr. Beckwith's, were those goods, according to that invoice, bought from the manufacturer at Lyons or from an agent in London?—From the fact of its being written in the French language, and with a French pen, I should say that the goods were bought in France.

12662. Who were they bought of?—Mr. Beckwith's?

12663. Yes?—The invoice says, Felix Vernet of Lyons.

12664. Is not there another importer below?—No, that is the charge of Devaux.

12665. Look at the heading of the invoice?—The heading of the next invoice is, " Mr. Beckwith to C. Devaux" it is for charges on two pieces of velvet by the Superb from Calais.

12666. Do those appear by the invoice to have been bought through an agent, or of the original manufacturer?—They were shipped only by Devaux; I should infer from this invoice, that the goods were bought from the manufacturer at Lyons.

12667. Is Mr. Crow a partner of your's?—He is.

12668. Is the person who acts as your agent in France, and who is stated to have been resident there nine months, a partner of your's?—He is not a partner,

he

he is the brother of our partner, and certainly never was resident there nine months in any one year, or any thing like it.

### *William Banbury*, Esq., called in; and further Examined.

*William Banbury,*
Esq.

27 July,
1832.

12669. IN your former evidence you alluded to some compromises said to have been made by several large houses whom you did not particularize, are you prepared to point out the houses that you then alluded to, or do you wish to withdraw the evidence, or what do you wish to be done about it?—I would rather withdraw the evidence than mention names. When I was examined before, I said, I hoped I should not be called upon to name any house, because it would be extremely unpleasant to me, and I did not wish to do it, and then I was not pressed any further on the subject; I do not know that that evidence at all relates to this inquiry, and it was the only part of my examination that I found myself unpleasant in, and extremely sorry I am that I was led into it, and made any observation of the sort, and if it can be withdrawn I shall be very happy.

12670. Well, do you in that evidence refer to a particular transaction, namely, that of Marshall of Watling-street, or do you refer to other matters of the same sort that came under your notice?—Several things of this kind have come under my notice, but I did not mention any names; and I do not wish to mention any names I am sure. I have been told it was supposed I alluded to the honourable Member there (*pointing to Mr. Morrison*) but I certainly can say I did not allude to him nor to his house. I did not allude to the honourable Member for Leicester. I have two that I could allude to; I should be very sorry to mention their names, because I had not it from authority, mine is only hear say; I have not been an assignee, or heard the trials or any thing.

12671. The Committee understand you to say that you do not allude to the two honourable Members who are Members of this Committee, and engaged in that trade?—No, I say it does not apply to them.

12672. But that you feel a difficulty in pointing out the houses to which you do allude?—There is a man, I suppose he would not mind if I mentioned his name; but I would rather not, because he tells me when he meets me, " Well Banbury when do you get out of business, because I have had a good deal of your money, and if you do not get out I will have more yet." Somebody has had it for I have lost 25,000 *l.* in business.

12673. Then there are two or three houses to which you do allude, but you do not allude to the respectable manufacturers of London generally?—Certainly not.

12674. But who the houses are, are pretty notorious in the trade?—I was very glad I was not before compelled to mention the names; I said it would be extremely hurtful to my feelings to do it, and I was not pressed any further.

12675. How many houses were there in that case of Marshall & Company in Watling-street?—Upon my word I do not know really.

12676. In the case of Marshall & Company, were there not four houses against whom actions were brought?—Upon my word I forget; I am sure there was one I know in Cheapside, or in that neighbourhood, and one or two in the country.

12677. Do you know of any other instances in which actions have been ever threatened or brought against individuals, or where actions have been compromised? —I think I have heard of such things, but they do not come within my own knowledge.

12678. You were asked " Do you mean to apply that charge of making those compromises, to all the great dealers in the city?" and your answer is, " I believe it is pretty general."—There have been a great many I know nothing about; there have been actions I have seen in the newspapers. Sometimes people that have had actions brought against them have had verdicts in their favour, and sometimes they have been convicted, but I do not recollect, I am sure, all these transactions.

### Mr. *Thomas Stone*, called in; and further Examined.

Mr.
*Thomas Stone.*

12679. It is understood you wish to make some further addition to your evidence in explanation of that which you have already stated, have you any papers to produce, or any statement to make in explanation or confirmation of your former evidence, and to what part of your evidence does that allude?—It alludes to the duties on foreign thrown silk. I consider that at present this Committee have not a fair statement of the Spitalfields case before it; I consider that the operatives in Spitalfields would be injured if the Committee were now to decide on

678.	the

the evidence, as far as I understand it, (and I have been here regularly attending upon it) unless they had the case more fully stated on the part of the Spitalfields weavers. I have taken pains to take the opinions of some of the most respectable, and the most extensive manufactures in the Fields, and I have got a paper with their signatures attached to it, and they, together with Mr. Gibson and myself, employ at least 3,500 looms. Now I believe that the Trades' Committee have not, altogether, so many as 500 looms in Spitalfields, independent of those who are throwsters. My reason for mentioning this is, that 500 looms is nothing in comparison with 3,500 or 3,700.

12680. But have you any thing to state in explanation or in confirmation of the opinions which you gave respecting the importation of thrown silk?—I consider this Paper highly confirmatory of it.

12681. What part of your evidence does that allude to?—To that part in which I have stated my opinion, that if French wrought goods were still to come into this country, the duties on Foreign thrown silk should be removed to enable the master weavers in Spitalfields to compete with the French manufacturers.

12682. In what part of your evidence have you so stated?—I have stated in my evidence, it was decidedly my opinion that that should be the case.

12683. Now the 3,700 looms that you speak of as employed by yourself and other manufacturers in Spitalfields, how many of them are Spitalfields looms?—More than 3,000.

12684. And you have also stated, that what you call the Trades' Committee (you perhaps know best what you mean by the expression) employ only 500 looms, is that statement correct?—I believe, as respects Spitalfields, it is correct in respect to the manufacturers who are for an increase of duties, except that they are throwsters; but I believe, even if I were to include them, that it would amount to but a few more.

12685. Have you not stated in your evidence, that you believe the throwsters are now working for a loss, and if the duty were further reduced they must be destroyed, and a great part of their property destroyed?—I have stated, in my evidence, that I consider the throwsters are now in a very depressed situation, and I do not wish to lessen the force of that admission. My only desire is to have a fair statement of the case before the Committee, and then I shall be satisfied with the decision the Committee may come to; at present I think they have not a fair statement.

12686. What is the paper which you were about reading?—" We, the under-" signed silk manufacturers, are of opinion that the removal of the duties on foreign " thrown silk would be a great benefit to us. Signed, Peter Bedford & nephews. " As a manufacturer I fully agree to the above, but as a throwster should prefer " the duties remaining as they now are. Signed, J. J. Buttress," (a man that employs 520 looms. " Charles Rugg, Fore-street."—" We think nothing will sub-" stantially benefit the silk trade but prohibition; if that is not granted we think " it would be most desirable to remove the duty entirely from Piedmont organzine. " Duff, Brooks, Emerson & Co."—" We think the same. J. & W. Robinson " and Co.; Robert Graham & Sons, W. Brandon, Spital-square; W. Wilson & Co., " 11, Fort-street; W. Soker, 16, Fort-street, Spital-square." I am certainly within the mark when I say, that these gentlemen employ 3,700 looms, our own and Mr. Gibson's included.

12687. Are any of those gentlemen members of the Trades' Committee?—I believe that Mr. Emerson was one of the Members of the Trades' Committee.

12688. None of the others?—Really I am not sure.

12689. How many of the 3,700 looms are employed in Spitalfields?—I have answered that question, I said 3,000.

12690. How many looms are there altogether in Spitalfields, Bethnal Green, and the neighbourhood?—Something like 16,000 looms altogether, and about one-third of those are out of employ.

12691. Do you mean to state, that the gentlemen composing the Trades' Committee, and holding opinions in unison with theirs, do not employ more than 10,000 looms?—I mean to say, that they do not employ 1,000; that is to say in Spitalfields.

*Lunæ, 30° die Julii, 1832.*

**EDWARD AYSHFORD SANFORD, ESQ. IN THE CHAIR.**

Mr. *Thomas Stone*, called in; and further Examined.

12692. HAVE you any thing further to say in confirmation or explanation of your former evidence?—Having been favoured with the permission of seeing my former evidence, the part that I should refer to is No. 5789; what I said the other day is in confirmation of that. There were some more questions put to me on that subject, I had no copy of the evidence, therefore I could not exactly say that that was the case; I should have said more if more questions had been asked me on the subject at the time; but I believe that this is quite sufficient to show that I hold the opinion which I have now endeavoured to confirm. I do not wish to say any thing more unless there was some further question put to me.

12693. Have you any explanation to give on the subject of the average earnings of your weavers in Spitalfields?—I believe the weavers on three singles, after necessary deductions are made, are earning something like 7 s. a week, not more.

Mr. *Robert Graham*, called in; and Examined.

12694. WHERE do you live?—Spital Square.

12695. What are you?—A manufacturer, of Spitalfields only.

12696. What number of looms do you employ?—About 400.

12697. How many years have you been a manufacturer, and how many years have you been acquainted with Spitalfields?—I have been 25 years a manufacturer, and have been acquainted with it all my life.

12698. Have you been in the habit of employing throwsters during the whole of the period since you have been a manufacturer?—A very great portion of the time within the last 20 years, and perhaps a little longer, I am not quite sure.

12699. Have the prices which you have paid for throwing silk varied very much during that time?—Yes, very much.

12700. What was the price that you were paying for throwing silks the last year?—I have taken the statement from 1826 to the present time, from my own silk book; the prices which I paid for fine Italian silks from 1826 to March 1828 was 3 s. 6 d. per tram.

12701. Is that taken on an average?—It is taken from my own silk book; during the whole of that time I paid 3 s. 6 d.

12702. Without variation?—Yes; and then from March 1828 to May 1829, I paid 3 s., and from May 1829 to May 1830, I paid 2 s. 9 d., and from May 1830 to January 1831, I paid 3 s. 6 d., and from January 1831 to the present time, 3 s.; this is for the best and finest silks deniers 24-26. In January 1826 I paid 6 s. 6 d. for organzine, which continued till February 1827.

12703. Do those prices per tram include the waste?—No; from February 1827 to January 1828, I paid 6 s.; and from that time to January 1829, it was 5 s., and from January 1829 to February 1830, 4 s. 6 d.; from February 1831 to January 1831, 5 s. 6 d., and from January 1831 to April 1831, 5 s., and from April 1831 to March 1832, 4 s. which is the present price.

12704. That is also exclusive of waste?—Yes; I do believe that many have worked at lower prices.

12705. You have no account of the prices paid before 1826?—I have not them with me; but I can remember 10 years ago we paid 8 s., or about 8 s. was the price.

12706. Do you recollect it being lower than the price you have given in before?—I think it very probable it ranged from 8 s. down to 6 s. 6 d.

12707. Has any alteration taken place in the price recently?—Not with me.

12708. What is your opinion of the effect of the duty on thrown silk in the trade of Spitalfields?—I believe, under the present regulations, that we ought to be placed on similar terms with all other competitors, if we are to have this powerful competitor, the French, it appears to me we ought to be enabled to go into the market on similar terms.

12709. Do you not consider that the lowering or the total removal of the duty on thrown silk would be very satisfactory both to the manufacturer and the operative

678.                                                                                          in

Mr.
*Thomas Stone.*

30 July,
1832.

Mr.
*Robert Graham.*

portion to other goods, the price was 4 s. 6 d.; in July 1826, in the same year, they were reduced to 4 s., and they continued till September 1828, and of course through the season, at 4 s.; in 1829, we paid 3 s. 9 d.; then in July 1829 they were advanced to 4 s.; in June 1830, 3 s. 6 d.; and they remain at the same price now.

12794. Have not velvets been made as low as 2 s. 3 d.?—Not by me; I have stated the lowest price I have paid.

678.                                                                              12795. Do

1829, it was 6 *d.*; in November 1829, it was 5 *d.*; in March 1830, it was 5 ½ *d.* and from August 1831 to the present period 5 *d.*; this is the lower kind of goods.

12752. But do you apprehend that the throwing has been latterly a very profitable thing to the throwster or otherwise?—I know nothing of throwing except the price that I paid.

12753. You do not know whether the profits and wages are reduced?—Yes, I have stated that.

12754. Do you happen to know in consequence of that there has been a good deal of distress?—I think it very probable.

12755. Have any of the throwsters that you have been in the habit of employing discontinued their business and allowed their mills to stand still?—None of the

Appendix (C.)

## Appendix (D.)

### RETURNS OF THE AMOUNT OF POOR RATES AND RATE OF ASSESSMENT.

### Appendix (D.)—No. 1.

AMOUNT of Poor Rates collected in the United Parishes in the City of *Coventry*, by Twelve Rates in each Year, and the Amount in the Pound.

| YEAR | No. of Rates. | St. Michael's Parish. | | | In the £. | | Trinity Parish. | | | In the £. | | TOTAL. | | |
|---|---|---|---|---|---|---|---|---|---|---|---|---|---|---|
| | | £. | s. | d. | s. | d. | £. | s. | d. | s. | d. | £. | s. | d. |
| 1815 | 12 | 6,113 | 5 | 9 | 9 | – | 3,040 | 10 | – | 6 | – | 9,153 | 15 | 9 |
| 1816 | – | 10,667 | 8 | 9 | 15 | 6 | 5,028 | 8 | 3 | 10 | – | 15,695 | 17 | – |
| 1817 | – | 12,415 | 7 | 3 | 19 | – | 6,417 | 1 | 9 | 13 | 9 | 18,832 | 9 | – |
| 1818 | – | 10,096 | 17 | – | 16 | – | 5,489 | 2 | 7 | 11 | 6 | 15,585 | 19 | 7 |
| 1819 | – | 9,589 | 19 | – | 15 | – | 4,729 | 5 | 1 | 9 | – | 14,319 | 4 | 1 |
| 1820 | – | 9,258 | 6 | – | 13 | 3 | 4,188 | 17 | 6 | 7 | 6 | 13,447 | 3 | 6 |
| 1821 | – | 9,053 | 16 | 3 | 12 | – | 4,929 | 15 | 6 | 8 | 9 | 13,983 | 11 | 9 |
| 1822 | – | 7,567 | 9 | 9 | 9 | 6 | 3,639 | 15 | 3 | 6 | – | 11,207 | 5 | – |
| 1823 | – | 7,321 | 1 | 9 | 9 | 3 | 3,422 | 9 | – | 6 | – | 10,743 | 10 | 9 |
| 1824 | – | 6,494 | 15 | 6½ | 8 | 1 | 3,525 | 19 | 7 | 5 | 9 | 10,020 | 15 | 1½ |
| 1825 | – | 6,016 | – | 8 | 7 | 8 | 2,908 | 15 | 10 | 5 | – | 8,924 | 16 | 6 |
| 1826 | – | 9,432 | 11 | 1 | 12 | 8 | 4,213 | 15 | 8 | 7 | 9 | 13,646 | 6 | 9 |
| 1827 | – | 7,847 | 1 | 11 | 9 | 2 | 3,693 | 1 | 11 | 5 | 8 | 11,540 | 3 | 10 |
| 1828 | – | 5,425 | 11 | 4 | 6 | 6 | 3,463 | 8 | 11 | 5 | 4 | 8,889 | – | 3 |
| 1829 | – | 10,369 | 7 | 8 | 15 | 2 | 5,720 | 5 | 9 | 10 | 7 | 16,089 | 13 | 5 |
| 1830 | – | 13,170 | 6 | 9 | 15 | 6 | 7,009 | 10 | – | 11 | 3 | 20,179 | 16 | 9 |
| 1831 | – | 10,265 | 5 | 7 | 13 | – | 5,644 | 13 | 1 | 9 | 9 | 15,909 | 18 | 8 |

## Appendix (D.)—No. 2.

AMOUNT of Poor Rates collected in the Parish of *Bedworth*; with the Number of Rates, the Rate of Assessment, and Gross Amount of Property Assessed.

| Ending at LADY DAY | Number of RATES. | Rate of ASSESSMENT. | | AMOUNT COLLECTED. | | | Gross Amount of Property Assessed. | | |
|---|---|---|---|---|---|---|---|---|---|
| | | *s.* | *d.* | £. | *s.* | *d.* | £. | *s.* | *d.* |
| 1815 - - | 6 | 5 | 9 | 1,133 | 4 | 2 | 4,982 | — | — |
| 1816 - - | 6 | 5 | 6 | 1,102 | 10 | 5 | 4,982 | — | — |
| 1817 - - | 11 | 13 | — | 2,448 | 10 | 4 | 5,018 | — | — |
| 1818 - - | 10 | 12 | 6 | 2,383 | 16 | — | 5,048 | — | — |
| 1819 - - | 12 | 12 | 6 | 2,384 | 16 | — | 5,048 | — | — |
| 1820 - - | 11 | 10 | 3 | 1,961 | 1 | 10 | 5,045 | — | — |
| 1821 - - | 11 | 10 | 6 | 2,000 | 2 | 3 | 5,045 | — | — |
| 1822 - - | 8 | 7 | 6 | 1,450 | 12 | 3 | 5,048 | — | — |
| 1823 - - | 6 | 5 | 6 | 1,066 | — | 10 | 5,048 | — | — |
| 1824 - - | 6 | 6 | — | 1,214 | 6 | 6 | 4,940 | — | — |
| 1825 - - | 5 | 5 | — | 1,123 | 11 | 1 | 4,940 | — | — |
| 1826 - - | 6 | 6 | — | 1,300 | — | 5 | 4,940 | — | — |
| 1827 - - | 7 | 7 | — | 1,431 | 18 | 6 | 5,220 | — | — |
| 1828 - - | 5 | 5 | — | 1,156 | 18 | 4 | 5,874 | — | — |
| 1829 - - | 5 | 5 | — | 1,182 | 1 | 6 | 5,940 | — | — |
| 1830 - - | 8 | 8 | — | 1,882 | 1 | 1 | 5,940 | — | — |
| 1831 - - | 6 | 6 | — | 1,434 | 18 | 6 | 5,942 | — | — |
| 1832 - - | 10 | 10 | — | 2,355 | — | 4 | 5,942 | — | — |

The Increase in 1827 was in consequence of the Canal which runs through the Parish being charged. The decrease in 1824 through the stoppage of some Coal Mines.

*John Neale*, Churchwarden.

*John Paxford Shaw*,⎫
*John Siddown*, ⎬ Overseers.

## Appendix (D.)—No. 3.

RETURN of the Property Assessed in the Parish of *Stoke*, in the County of *Warwick*, with the Number of Rates, Rate of Assessment, and Gross Amount on all Property Assessed in the said Parish of *Stoke*, from the Year 1815 to the Year 1832 inclusive.

| YEAR. | Number of RATES. | Rate of ASSESSMENT. | | | | AMOUNT OF LEVY. | | | TOTAL. | | |
|---|---|---|---|---|---|---|---|---|---|---|---|
| | | | | *s.* | *d.* | £. | *s.* | *d.* | £. | *s.* | *d.* |
| 1815 - - | 5 | 4 | at | 1 | — | 348 | 6 | 3 | 391 | 19 | — |
| | | 1 | at | — | 6 | 43 | 12 | 9 | | | |
| 1816 - - | 4 | 3 | at | 1 | — | 265 | 16 | — | 396 | 14 | 7½ |
| | | 1 | at | 1 | 6 | 130 | 18 | 7½ | | | |
| 1817 - - | 5 | 4 | at | 1 | — | 354 | 10 | — | 398 | 19 | 6 |
| | | 1 | at | — | 6 | 44 | 9 | 6 | | | |
| 1818 - - | 5 | 4 | at | 1 | — | 364 | — | — | 494 | 17 | 3½ |
| | | 1 | at | 1 | 6 | 130 | 17 | 3½ | | | |
| 1819 - - | 5 | 5 | at | 1 | — | 454 | 7 | 6 | 454 | 7 | 6 |
| 1820 - - | 4 | 4 | at | 1 | — | 369 | 10 | — | 369 | 10 | — |
| 1821 - - | 4 | 4 | at | 1 | — | 376 | 8 | — | 376 | 8 | — |
| 1822 - - | 3 | 3 | at | 1 | — | 289 | 2 | 6 | 289 | 2 | 6 |
| 1823 - - | 3 | 3 | at | 1 | — | 289 | 3 | 6 | 289 | 3 | 6 |
| 1824 - - | 2 | 2 | at | 1 | — | 203 | 2 | — | 203 | 2 | — |
| 1825 - - | 3 | 2 | at | 1 | — | 209 | — | 6 | 282 | 5 | 6 |
| | | 1 | at | — | 9 | 73 | 5 | — | | | |
| 1826 - - | 3 | 3 | at | 1 | — | 302 | 9 | — | 302 | 9 | — |
| 1827 - - | 3 | 2 | at | 1 | — | 204 | 4 | — | 285 | 11 | 6 |
| | | 1 | at | — | 9 | 81 | 7 | 6 | | | |
| 1828 - - | 3 | 3 | at | 1 | — | 335 | 13 | — | 335 | 13 | — |
| 1829 - - | 3 | 3 | at | 1 | — | 330 | 2 | — | 330 | 2 | — |
| 1830 - - | 3 | 3 | at | 1 | — | 328 | 11 | — | 328 | 11 | — |
| 1831 - - | 3 | 3 | at | 1 | — | 328 | 14 | — | 328 | 14 | — |
| 1832 - - | 2 | 2 | at | 1 | — | 216 | 19 | — | 216 | 19 | — |
| | | | | | | | | | 6,074 | 8 | 11 |

*John Bray*, Overseer of Stoke.

## Appendix (D.)—No. 4.

AMOUNT of POOR RATES collected in the Parish of *Shilton*, in the County of *Warwick*; with the Number of LEVIES, and AMOUNT collected in each Year from 1815 to 1832; and the GROSS AMOUNT of all PROPERTY ASSESSED.

|  |  | £. | s. | d. |
|---|---|---|---|---|
|  | 5 - - - in 1815 - - - - - - | 220 | 1 | 3 |
|  | 9 - - - in 1816 - - - - - - | 376 | 15 | 3 |
|  | 8 - - - in 1817 - - - - - - | 352 | 4 | – |
|  | 7 - - - in 1818 - - - - - - | 330 | 3 | 9 |
|  | 7 - - - in 1819 - - - - - - | 328 | 17 | 6 |
|  | 7 - - - in 1820 - - - - - - | 307 | – | 9 |
| Number of | 3 - - - in 1821 - - - - - - | 164 | 9 | 8 ½ |
|  | 4 - - - in 1822 - - - - - - | 175 | 9 | – |
| LEVIES | 4 - - - in 1823 - - - - - - | 175 | – | – |
|  | 4½ - - - in 1824 - - - - - - | 197 | 16 | 1 ½ |
| in each Year. | 4 - - - in 1825 - - - - - - | 175 | 11 | – |
|  | 6 - - - in 1826 - - - - - - | 263 | 18 | 6 |
|  | 6 - - - in 1827 - - - - - - | 312 | 12 | 6 |
|  | 7 - - - in 1828 - - - - - - | 349 | 10 | 9 |
|  | 7 - - - in 1829 - - - - - - | 350 | 17 | 3 |
|  | 7½ - - - in 1830 - - - - - - | 314 | – | – |
|  | 6½ - - - in 1831 - - - - - - | 221 | 16 | 4 |

1832 - - - RETURN of the Gross Amount of all Property Assessed - £. 915 15 –

*John Johnson.*

## Appendix (D.)—No. 5.

AMOUNT of POOR RATES collected in the Parish of *Nuneaton*; with the Amount of ASSESSMENT, RATE in the POUND, and NUMBER of LEVIES, from the Year 1821 to the Year 1832.

| PERIODS. | ASSESSMENT. | | | RATE, at 1 s. in the Pound. | | | Number of LEVIES. | TOTAL AMOUNT. | | |
|---|---|---|---|---|---|---|---|---|---|---|
|  | £. | s. | d. | £. | s. | d. |  | £. | s. | d. |
| From Lady-day 1821 to 1822 | 7,816 | – | – | 390 | 16 | – | 7 | 2,735 | 12 | – |
| 1823 | 7,816 | – | – | 390 | 16 | – | 5 | 1,954 | 12 | – |
| 1824 | 7,816 | – | – | 390 | 16 | – | 6½ | 2,540 | 4 | – |
| 1825 | 7,816 | – | – | 390 | 16 | – | 6 | 2,344 | 16 | – |
| 1826 | 8,182 | – | – | 409 | 2 | 4 | 5 | 2,045 | 11 | 8 |
| 1827 | 8,257 | – | · | 412 | 17 | – | 6½ | 2,683 | 11 | 3 |
| 1828 | 8,853 | – | – | 442 | 13 | 8 | 6 | 2,656 | 2 | – |
| 1829 | 8,890 | – | – | 444 | 10 | 11 | 5½ | 2,445 | – | – ½ |
| 1830 | 8,984 | – | – | 448 | 14 | – | 11⅓ | 5,160 | 1 | – |
| 1831 | 9,034 | – | – | 451 | 14 | 4 | 7½ | 3,387 | 15 | 9 |
| 1832 | 9,034 | – | – | 451 | 14 | 4 | 12 | 5,420 | 12 | – |

Sir,                                                                 Nuneaton, June 4th, 1832.

IN obedience to your command, I have transmitted to you our Assessment and Rate from 1822 to 1832, the period which I have been assistant overseer; I have applied to the person whom I succeeded in office, who served under various overseers, some of whom are dead, and some have left the town, so that we cannot come clearly to the Assessment beyond the above dates.

I am, Sir, &c. &c.

*Thomas Ralphs,*
To E. A. Sanford, Esq. M. P.                    Assistant overseer of Nuneaton.

## Appendix (D.)—No. 6.

AN ACCOUNT of the DISBURSEMENTS of the Parish of *Bedworth*, in the County of *Warwick*, for Ten Years, to the COUNTY RATES and the POOR.

| | COUNTY RATE. | | | CASUAL POOR. | | | In the House of Industry. | | | TOTAL. | | |
|---|---|---|---|---|---|---|---|---|---|---|---|---|
| | £. | s. | d. | £. | s. | d. | £. | s. | d. | £. | s. | d. |
| From 25th March 1822 to the 25th March 1823 | — | | | — | | | — | | | — | | |
| From 25th March 1823 to the 25th March 1824 | — | | | — | | | — | | | — | | |
| From 25th March 1824 to the 25th March 1825 | 92 | 8 | – | 772 | 3 | – | 302 | 19 | – | 1,167 | 10 | – |
| From 25th March 1825 to the 25th March 1826 | 93 | 7 | 3 | 789 | 9 | 11½ | 285 | 6 | 4½ | 1,168 | 3 | 7 |
| From 25th March 1826 to the 25th March 1827 | 103 | 8 | – | 982 | 16 | 7¾ | 334 | 13 | –¾ | 1,420 | 17 | 8½ |
| From 25th March 1827 to the 25th March 1828 | 85 | 4 | 6 | 793 | 2 | 4 | 282 | 3 | 8 | 1,160 | 10 | 6 |
| From 25th March 1828 to the 25th March 1829 | 91 | 12 | 3 | 762 | 13 | 9 | 278 | 13 | 5 | 1,132 | 19 | 5 |
| From 25th March 1829 to the 25th March 1830 | 97 | 8 | – | 1,393 | 17 | 11 | 403 | 2 | 5 | 1,894 | 8 | 4 |
| From 25th March 1830 to the 25th March 1831 | 103 | 9 | 9 | 1,094 | 5 | 5 | 332 | 11 | 6 | 1,530 | 6 | 8 |
| From 25th March 1831 to the 25th March 1832 | 133 | 18 | 6 | 1,764 | 18 | 2½ | 339 | 7 | 5½ | 2,238 | 4 | 2 |

BESIDES the great increase of the Poor's Rates, the Poor have been supplied gratis with fuel by some of the more respectable inhabitants and proprietors of land, &c. of the parish. The Poor were supplied with soup and bread at very near half the cost price, both in 1829 and 1831. Both the poor and middling classes are at this time decidedly in a much worse state than they ever were for the last twenty years: there are numbers of the poor without bed or bedding for themselves and their families to lie upon; and the Poor Rates press so heavily upon the rate-payers, (who are so much reduced in numbers from the depressed state of the trade,) that it is impossible for them to afford that relief which the necessities of the poor absolutely require; and it is my firm belief, that another year like the past will reduce most of the middling class of the parishioners to a state of pauperism. The number of summonses that have been issued this year against the payers to the Poor Rates for non-payment thereof, has been unprecedented in my recollection. The Poor's Levy collected on each rate up to 1829, amounted to from 230 *l.* to 240 *l.*; at the present time it does not amount to more than 190 *l.* or 200 *l.* The Magistrates having taken into consideration the distressed state of the rate-payers, have considerably reduced the allowance formerly granted to the poor; at the present time, each pauper has only 1 *s.* 6 *d.* per week, formerly they had 2 *s.* 6 *d.* per week allowed them; but the effect has been severely felt by many of the farmers, not less than 50 sheep having been stolen in the parish within the last twelve months, besides numbers that have been stolen from the parishes adjoining, which amount to a considerably greater number than those stolen in this parish during the same period. There are now numbers of families who are obliged to receive relief from the parish, although the man and woman are both in full employment, their earnings being so very small, that it is impossible for them to get as much as the Magistrates allow for their earnings to be made up to.

*John Yates.*
Acting Overseer.

678.

Appendix (E.)

STATE of the SILK TRADE of *Dublin*, 1824.

NUMBER of Broad Looms employed, including Tabinets     -     -     -   1,200
Broad and narrow Ribbon Engines     -     -     -     -     -     -     -     996
                                                                      ⎯⎯⎯⎯
                                                                      2,196

Ten silk mills at work in 1824.

If I take into account the other trades depending on the silk manufacture, such as the winder, warper, throwster, dyer, &c. I think the number of persons employed, and who were receiving subsistence dependent thereon, to be about 6,000; and this statement agrees with a return made at that period, which gave the number 6,280.

I beg further to state, that the number of looms which I have said are now employed in Dublin, are but partially so, from six to nine months in the year. In the throwing branch, I have ascertained that but 50 to 60 persons are employed, and that but occasionally. The prices of weaving, throwing, &c. are about 50 per cent. lower than 1824.

I have not said any thing about the ribbon-engine branch; it appears so almost annihilated, that, scattered as the few engines are through the liberties of Dublin, it was difficult to ascertain the number in the short time I had to prepare, but I am quite sure that the number cannot exceed 30 to 40. I think I over-rate, and would prefer doing so.

I find, by a return received from the Room-Keepers' Charitable Society, that the number of families receiving assistance in 1824 was     -   4,765
                                            1826   -   -   -   6,497
                                            1831   -   -   -  13,149.

This statement corroborates the former evidence I have given, for it was to such institutions that the destitute silk weaver was led first to look for assistance, the families being regularly visited, and, of course, the weaver had not the same feelings applying there as to the Mendicity Institution, where the mode of relief was different, but to which asylum refuge was at last taken by many; and I find that in 1824, the numbers were, in that Institution, but 1,448, while in the year 1831, the numbers increased to 3,004; proving increasing manufacturing as well as other distress.

I now beg leave to mention a further fact; that so prosperous was the silk-throwing trade of Dublin in 1824, prior to the reduction of duty on Italian thrown silks, and the opening of our ports to French manufactures, that raw silks were sent from England to be thrown, not only in Dublin, but the mills being full there, large quantities were sent to a place called Tullymore, 40 miles from Dublin, where a factory had been erected for many years, for both throwing and manufacturing of silk. This factory, with another about 7 miles from Dublin, have been since given up, proving unsuccessful. One proprietor, I am informed, is gone to America, and the other, a very old and respectable silk manufacturer, has embarked into another way of life, having lost the whole of his capital in the silk trade.

I know of no regular importer of silks into Dublin; at present there is no opening for the trade. Our principal importers have embarked into other pursuits, or retired altogether. Some silk manufacturers have become principally importers of British and French silks, and others, who had realized property, have quitted a pursuit which they could not carry on successfully, while the operative has been mainly thrown on the public for support, or become an alien from his country, to seek for employment elsewhere.

A very few manufacturers still continue to labour against the current, but to a small extent. I have known some to continue their weavers merely to give them bread, while little or no demand existed for the goods thus made.

I beg further to state, that notwithstanding the injury inflicted on the silk trade of Dublin by the loss of the Union protecting duties, yet it appeared to have been the determination of some of the trade (however hopeless) to have grappled, if possible, in a competition with the English silks; and the trade was, in point of fact, however unprofitable, carried on in a degree after such protecting duties had ceased. But whatever feeling of that description had existed to make the trial, it appeared to have been almost wholly given up, when the effect began to be felt of the importation of French silks, which followed shortly after, but
                                                                      particularly

particularly in 1829, when, against the continued remonstrances and petitions of Great Britain and Ireland, the *reduction* of duty took place on French silks. The Irish manufacturer had then a *twofold* difficulty to contend with, in both English and French manufacture, which they were wholly unable to contend against; and the result has been the almost total extinction of the silk manufacturers in Dublin, save a *remnant* of the tabinet fabric. To such a state are the manufacturers of Dublin reduced, that societies are forming to promote the wear of native manufacture. I had a letter from a respectable and extensive manufacturer in Dublin last week, which stated that he had laid by almost all his looms, and would never be able to manufacture in Ireland with success under the present existing state of things.

It is a remarkable fact, that the same remonstrances that are now made by the silk manufacturers of *England* against the want of sufficient protection for their trade with *France,* were made use of by the *Irish* silk manufacturers against the withdrawing of the protecting duties which their trade then possessed with *Great Britain*; and the consequences were then predicted which have since happened. There appears a strong analogy between the two cases.

May I be permitted to state another fact, which appears to me to bear strongly on the present inquiry; it is part of an examination which took place before a Committee of The Lords, in 1785, on the Silk Trade, as printed.

" Q. I understand the witness to say, that while French silks were permitted to be imported here under a very high duty, the importation was to such an amount as to be almost ruinous to the English manufacturer; the question I will now ask is, whether that importation has or has not diminished since the *prohibitory* duties were changed into *absolute* prohibition; that is, is the importation less *now* than it was *before*?—*A.* I believe a great deal less."

I shall not trouble this Honourable Committee by making any comment; the circumstance speaks for itself.

May I be allowed further to submit, that if France relaxed her almost prohibitory system against British and Irish commerce, then there could be no objection to open a fair treaty of commerce, and admit her silks, but so as to *protect* SUFFICIENTLY the British and Irish manufacture, particularly against the *smuggling* system of France; and I have no doubt that some of the manufacturing distress in Dublin would be relieved in part by an export of her staple article, (assisted by bounty, as silks are now from Great Britain) as well as many parts of England and Ireland, whose different manufactures are now prohibited. But permit me to say, that the present system of free trade (so called), undefined as it is in its objects, appears an absurdity in practice, and most injurious to the nation that adopts it.

I beg most respectfully to refer to the Parliamentary Committee that sat in Dublin in 1821, which has been before adverted to; and would submit, that had a Committee, formed on such principles, but more extended, been appointed to act permanently in Dublin (for temporary Committees can have little time or opportunity to receive information), and to extend its inquiries, not to the silk trade only, but the general interests of Ireland, of which England at present can know but little, and reported from time to time, much labour would be saved now and at all times to Parliament, and to the Government of Ireland. Enactments which have passed, so injurious not only to the silk trade, but the general interest of Ireland, would not have been proposed; while the valuable information therein afforded would probably have led to measures that would have alleviated the distresses under which Dublin and Ireland generally labour, affording means of employment in the development of her great internal resources, have promoted consequent peace and happiness; for it is evident that want, if suffered to exist, will create discontent, and discontent produces greater evils.

On this subject, if I am not incorrect in referring to it, permit me to say, I have already communicated my opinions to the Noble Lord at the head of His Majesty's Government.

*Jonathan Sisson.*

Appendix (F.)—No. 1. -  -  -  -  -  -

*Statement made in March and April* 1830, *for* 1814 *to*
1829 ; *and continued to* 1831, *in March* 1832.

*N. B.*—The small quantities of Manufactured
Goods exported, are comprised in these
Amounts of Consumption.

COMPENDIUM OF  -  -  -

### ESTIMATES OF CONSUMPTION OF RAW AND THROWN SILKS, AND WASTE AND KNUBS AND HUSKS, from 1814 to 1831.

PER ANNUM.
DIVISION OF THE VARIOUS DESCRIPTIONS.

| | Bengal and China. | Italian, &c. | Turkey. | Waste, &c. Rates of Computation. | Thrown. | Totals, Per Annum. | Grand Totals, Raw, Thrown, and Waste, &c. |
|---|---|---|---|---|---|---|---|
| | *lbs.* | *lbs.* | *lbs.* | *lbs.* | *lbs.* | *lbs.* | *lbs.* |
| 1814 - - - | 971,000 | 277,000 | 57,000 | 28,000 | 587,000 | 1,920,000 | 1,920,000 |
| Averages : | | | | | | | |
| 1815–17 - - | 856,000 | 236,000 | 73,000 | at $\frac{1}{2}$ 24,000 | 295,000 | 1,484,000 | 4,450,000 |
| 1818–20 - - | 1,011,000 | 400,000 | 120,000 | ,, 57,000 | 343,000 | 1,931,000 | 5,796,000 |
| 1821–23 - - | 1,137,000 | 632,000 | 243,000 | ,, 62,000 | 389,000 | 2,463,000 | 7,390,000 |

DUTIES LOWERED on RAW and THROWN  -  -  -  -  -

| | | | | | | | |
|---|---|---|---|---|---|---|---|
| 1824–25 - - | 1,349,000 | 1,269,000 | 334,000 | ,, 178,000 | 481,000 | 3,611,000 | 7,225,000 |

DUTIES FURTHER LOWERED, AND OUR  -  -  -  -  -

| | | | | | | | |
|---|---|---|---|---|---|---|---|
| 1826 - - - | 1,173,000 | 718,000 | 221,000 | ,, 92,000 | 289,000 | 2,493,000 | 2,493,000 |
| 1827 - - - | 1,862,000 | 1,463,000 | 405,000 | $\frac{5}{12}$ 209,000 | 453,000 | 4,392,000 | 4,392,000 |
| 1828 - - - | 1,456,000 | 1,340,000 | 429,000 | $\frac{1}{3}$ 418,000 | 385,000 | 4,028,000 | 4,028,000 |
| 1829 - - - | 1,471,000 | 825,000 | 338,000 | $\frac{5}{12}$ 235,000 | 169,000 | 3,038,000 | 3,038,000 |

DUTIES on THROWN SILKS  -  -  -  -  -  -

| | | | | | | | |
|---|---|---|---|---|---|---|---|
| 1830 - - - | 2,070,000 | 1,202,000 | 460,000 | $\frac{1}{2}$ 485,000 | 437,000 | 4,654,000 | 4,654,000 |
| 1831 - - - | 1,632,000 | 1,026,000 | 338,000 | $\frac{5}{12}$ 762,000 | 514,000 | 4,272,000 | 4,272,000 |

CONSUMPTION  -  -  - lbs. 49,659,000

lbs. 49,659,000

March 1832.                    (Errors excepted.)

- - - - - Appendix (F.)—No. 1.

* Computation with Reference to the Rates of Wages, &c. which various Descriptions of Silks, Waste and Knubs and Husks, afford respectively,—

| | ESTIMATED AT | | |
|---|---|---|---|
| Bengal & China's and - | $3/5$ of fine Italians | | 1814 to 1829 |
| | $16/25$ ditto | | for 1830 |
| Turkey - - | $2/5$ ditto | | 1814 to 1831 |
| Waste - - - | $1/2$ ditto | | 1814 – 1830 |
| Waste with Knubs & Husks | $5/12$ to $1/3$ ditto | | 1814 – 1830 |

- TABLES, (A.) (B.) and (C.)

PARLIAMENTARY RETURNS.
Dated 30th April, } 1829.
— 5th May, }
From 1814 to 1828, & subsequently.

### ESTIMATES OF CONSUMPTION.

Computation of various Descriptions, to the Standard of Italian, Raw and Thrown.

Amounts of Duties.

| Grand Totals, Raw, Thrown, and Waste, &c. | Raw and Waste Totals. | Thrown Totals. | DUTY PAID. Totals. | Averages per Annum. | Averages per Annum. |
|---|---|---|---|---|---|
| lbs. | lbs. | lbs. | lbs. | lbs. | £. |
| 2,120,000 | 1,533,000 | 587,000 | 1,484,000 | 1,484,000 | 780,000 - 1814 |
| ,250,000 | 3,366,000 | 884,000 | 3,256,000 | 1,085,000 | 465,000 - 1815-17 |
| ,796,000 | 4,767,000 | 1,029,000 | 4,279,000 | 1,426,000 | 599,000 - 1818-20 |
| ,240,000 | 6,133,000 | 1,107,000 | 5,535,000 | 1,848,000 | 729,000 - 1821-23 |

- - - AND WASTE AND KNUBS AND HUSKS.

| | | | | | |
|---|---|---|---|---|---|
| ,615,000 | 6,592,000 | 1,023,000 | 5,566,000 | 2,783,000 | 272,000-1824-25 |

- - - PROTECTIVE LAWS OF 1766 REMOVED

| | | | | | |
|---|---|---|---|---|---|
| ,253,000 | 1,964,000 | 289,000 | 1,845,000 | 1,845,000 | 82,000 - 1826 |
| ,213,000 | 3,759,000 | 454,000 | 3,317,000 | 3,317,000 | 128,000 - 1827 |
| ,548,000 | 4,163,000 | 385,000 | 2,909,000 | 2,909,000 | 112,000 - 1828 |
| 892,000 | 2,720,000 | 172,000 | 2,090,000 | 2,090,000 | 45,000 - 1829 |

- - FURTHER LOWERED IN JUNE 1829.

| | | | | | |
|---|---|---|---|---|---|
| 694,000 | 4,257,000 | 437,000 | 3,391,000 | 3,391,000 | 90,000 - 1830 |
| 312,000 | 3,798,000 | 514,000 | 3,037,000 | 3,037,000 | 95,000 - 1831 |

933,000 IMPORTS, DUTY PAID, as per Parliamentary Returns.
    40,000 lbs. (about) re-exported in 1827 and 1828, after having paid Duties.
    217,000 - ditto - ditto - in 1829-30-31 - - - ditto.
257,000 Deduct quantities exported as above.*—( See Note to the right.)
676,000

(signed)      *Alexis James Doxat.*

678.

---

*Minutes made in March and April* 1831.

The quantities consumed, as set forth in this Table, in the respective periods and years, are taken from the Compendious Parliamentary Table, dated *Customs,* 28th April,—*Parliamentary,* 5th May, 1829,—

" An Account of Total Quan-
" tities of Raw and Waste and
" Thrown Silks, entered for
" Home Consumption in Great
" Britain and Ireland, in each
" year, from 1814 to 1828,
" both years inclusive, and
" Rates of Duty thereon:"

and subsequent Return. Whilst former Statements were unconnected,—published under heads varying from each other, without sequel as to their application,—and showing a greater increase than the above, from 1815-17 to 1821-23;—that published on the 5th and 8th May, 1829, of " Imports and Exports of Thrown and Raw Silks, and Waste Silks, from 1814 to 1828," shows an increase of 102 per cent. in the years 1815-17 to 1821-3.

The above-mentioned Parliamentary Returns of Quantities, *duty paid,* from 1814 to 1828 and to 1831, presenting under *one* column, all the various descriptions of Raw Silks, with the addition of Waste Silk, and Knubs and Husks, which descriptions are so greatly differing from each other, with regard to the amounts of Wages of Labour, &c. accruing from them respectively,—I have *investigated,* and *separated them* into their several Classes ; —*viz.* Bengal and China Raw Silks,—Italian, &c. Turkey,—Waste and Knubs and Husks,—and Thrown Silks; and computed them into one Standard,—that of fine Italian Raw Silks.

I have also taken into consideration, in the amounts consumed in the respective periods, the state of Stocks (Duty paid) greater or less, which remained on hand, as nearly as it has been in my power to ascertain them from various sources.

I have brought all those Estimates of Quantities to an ultimate Balance with the said Parliamentary Returns (Duty paid), as may be seen by this Table ;—which is a Compendium of all the Documents from which I have established those dissected Returns.

---

* Besides those quantities which have been exported after having paid Duties, (*i. e.* entered for Home Consumption,) I believe that about
    50,000 lbs. were exported, Duty paid also, in 1825 ; and about
    60,000 - ditto - ditto, in 1826 ; but I have not any exact Returns of those Exports; and I have not noticed them, in deductions, on either side, as those two quantities,—referrible to two different periods—1821-25, and 1826-31,—nearly balance themselves.

| Of which the<br>lowing are the<br>AMOUNTS<br>of<br>DUTIES<br>comprised in<br>he preceding<br>Column. | PROGRESS<br>in regard to<br>DUTIES, WAGES, PROFITS,<br>&c. |
|---|---|
| £.<br>465,000 | |
| 599,000 | 1818–20 - 31 p' ct. over 1815–17 |
| 729,000 | 1821–23 - 69½ - - 1815–17 |
| 272,000 | 1824–25 - 105 - - 1815–17 |
| 500,000 ) | 1821–23<br>1824–25 } (87) - - 1815–17 |
| 82,000 | |
| 128,000 | |
| 111,000 | |
| 45,000 | |
| 90,000 | |
| - - | 1826–30 - 30 p' ct. *under* { 1821–2<br>1824–2 |
| 95,000 | 1831 - 33½ p' ct. *under* ditto |
| - - | 1826–31 - 31 p' ct. *under* ditto |

s of 1766 not been altered.—*See* on this
Progression, made in May 1831.

R K S :

on, that the PROGRESS of the SILK TRAD
821–23 } previously to the removal of our Pr
824–25 }

d to DUTIES, WAGES, &c. in the ratio of

Cent. per Annum, IN FAVOUR OF SILK,

per cent. in 8 Years, 1815–17 to 1821–23, 1824–25.)

821–23 } the situations of those Trades have
824–25 }
TED thus :

per Cent. per Annum AGAINST SILK.

34¾ per cent. in 5 Years, { 1821–23<br>1824–25 } to 1826–30.

Besid

| BRIEF MINUTES RELATIVE TO THESE COMPARATIVE STATEMENTS OF THE SILK AND THE COTTON TRADES, FROM 1815 TO 1831. | QUANTITIES CONSUMED. |
|---|---|
| | Total Deliveries of Cotton Wool for the Consumption of our Manufacturers,—of which large Quantities exported in Goods, and from ⅕ 1815–17,—to ¼ 1826–30,—progressively in a Spun State only. |
| | AVERAGES PER ANNUM. |

The COTTON TRADE *has often been adverted to of late years, as without parallel in its progress; and the* SILK TRADE *has as often been mentioned in contradistinction, as " Dwindling, Sickly, &c." previously to the alterations in our Laws relative to this Branch of our National Industry.—Observations so contrary to the real state of the case, would not have occurred, had a nearer comparative view of the respective Progresses of the Silk and of the Cotton Trades been taken, as will appear by these Statements and Recapitulations.*

|  | lbs. |  | Approximative Rates of Duties, Wages, &c. p' lb. s.  d. |  |
|---|---|---|---|---|
| 1815–17 - | 94,000,000 | - | 5   — | |
| 1818–20 - | 115,000,000 | - | 4   5 | 181 |
| 1821–23 - | 137,000,000 | - | 3   10¾ | 182 |
| 1824–25 - | 172,000,000 | - | 3   6¼ | 182 |
| Average of 1821–23 1824–25 | (155,000,000 | - | 3   8½) | |
| 1826 - | 165,000,000 | - | 3   2¾ | |
| 1827 - | 211,000,000 | - | 3   —¼ | |
| 1828 | 218,000,000 | - | 2   10 | |
| 1829 - | 222,000,000 | - | 2   8 | |
| 1830 - | 242,000,000 | - | 2   6 | |
| Average of 1826–30 | 212,000,000 | - | 2   10 | 182 |
| 1831 - | 259,000,000 | - | 2   4¼ | 18 |
| Average of 1826–31 | 219,000,000 | - | 2   7⅝ | 18 |

\* *N. B.*—In the above Estimates
more r

Besides which, according to various comparative Estimates, gr
the average Amount of Wages, &c. in { 1821–23  1824–25 } which was

Per Annum.
of about - - - £. 3,900,000,\* would have been
more than - - 6,000,000, in 1829–31 ;—
instead of - - - 2,530,000, which is the actual

A decrease this, the more lamentable in its consequences on
it has been attended with frequent and extraordinary variations
our Manufacturers having no control whatever on the various
changing abroad, which occasion a variety of degrees of intensi
they experience from the produce of Foreign Manufactures (b
Quantities) in this important branch of our NATIONAL INDUSTR

Not only have the greatly reduced Returns of 1826–30, averag
and 1829–31 - -
greatly fluctuated from year to year during that period of six ye
opened to Foreign Competition, but the variations in the course
extreme.

\* £. 3,900,000 for { 1821–23  1824–25 } I have taken at very r

(Errors excepted.)

## Appendix (F.)—No. 3. - - - - - -

(A.)

### A COMPENDIOUS COMPARATIVE VIEW of the respective PROGRESSIONS at the various Periods of 1815–17 to {1821–23 / 1824–25} - - -

(*a*) Rates of Wages of Silk, computed per lb. of Italian standard.
(*b*) Ditto - - - - - - - - - per lb. of all descriptions.
(*c*) Ditto on Cotton - - - - - per lb.
(*d*) The rates and amounts of Wages in the Silk Trade, are under-rated for the first eleven years.

### IN REGARD TO QUANTITIES.

| SILK, OF ITALIAN STANDARD. | | | | | | | | | | COTTON. |
|---|---|---|---|---|---|---|---|---|---|---|
| | Averages per Annum. *lbs.* | (*a*) *s.* | *d.* | (*b*) *s.* | *d.* | | | (*c*) *s.* | *d.* | *lbs.* |
| 1815, 1816, 1817 - - - - | 1,084,000 | 38 | 2 | 27 | 11 | | | 5 | – | 94,000,000 - - - |
| | | | | | | Per cents over 1815–17. | | | | |
| 1818, 1819, 1820 - - - - | 1,426,000 (*i. e.* $10\frac{1}{2}$ p' ct. p' ann. over 1815–17.) | 38 | 1 | 28 | 2 | $31\frac{1}{2}$ | 22 | 4 | 5 | 115,000,000 - - - (*i. e.* $7\frac{1}{3}$ per cent per annum over 1815–17.) |
| | | | | | | SILK. | COTTON. | | | |
| 1821, 1822, 1823 - - - - | 1,848,000 (*i. e.* 10 p' ct. p' ann. over 1818–20.) | 38 | – | 28 | 6 | 70 | 48 | 3 | $10\frac{3}{4}$ | 137,000,000 - - - (*i. e.* $6\frac{1}{3}$ per cent per annum over 1818-20.) |
| 1821–23, 1824–25 Medium - - | 2,315,000 (*i. e.* 16 p' ct. p' ann. over 1816–20.) | (33 | 3) | (26 | 2) | (113) | (65) | (3 | $8\frac{1}{2}$) | (155,000,000) - - - (*i. e.* 9 per cent per annum over 1816–20.) |
| 1824, 1825 - - - - | 2,783,000 (*i. e.* 25 p' ct. p' ann. over 1821–23.) | 30 | 7 | 23 | 11 | 156 | 83 | 3 | $6\frac{1}{4}$ | 172,000,000 - - - (*i. e.* $12\frac{3}{4}$ per cent per annum over 1821–23.) |
| | | | | | | Per ct. | Per ct. | | | |
| | | | | | | Per Cents over {1821–23 / 1824–25} - - | | | | *lbs.* |
| 1826 - - | lbs. 1,845,000 | 21 | – | 15 | 7 | | | 3 | $2\frac{3}{4}$ | 165,000,000 |
| 1827 - - | – 3,317,000 | 22 | – | 16 | 7 | | | 3 | $-\frac{1}{4}$ | 211,000,000 |
| 1828 - - | – 2,909,000 | 20 | 1 | 14 | 6 | Progressions INVERTED: | | 2 | 10 | 218,000,000 |
| 1829 - - | – 2,090,000 | 17 | 6 | 12 | 1 | SILK | | 2 | 8 | 222,000,000 |
| 1830 - - | – 3,394,000 | 18 | 9 | 13 | 9 | *under* COTTON. | | 2 | 6 | 242,000,000 |
| 1826–30 - - - - - | lbs. 2,710,000 | 19 | 11 | 14 | 5 | 17 | $36\frac{3}{4}$ | 2 | 10 | *lbs.* 212,000,000 |
| (5 Years.) | (*i. e.* $3\frac{2}{3}$ p' ct. p' ann. over {1821–23 / 1824–25) | | | | | Per ct. | Per ct. | | | (5 Years.) (*i. e.* $7\frac{1}{3}$ per cent per annum over {1821–23.) / 1824–25.) |
| 1831 - - - | lbs. 3,037,000 | 17 | $-\frac{1}{2}$ | 12 | $1\frac{1}{3}$ | 31 | 67 | 2 | $4\frac{1}{4}$ | *lbs.* 259,000,000 |
| 1826–31 - - | lbs. 2,765,000 | 19 | 5 | 14 | – | $19\frac{1}{2}$ | $41\frac{1}{3}$ | 2 | $7\frac{5}{8}$ | *lbs.* 219,000,000 |
| | | | | | | SILK. | COTTON. | | | |
| (6 Years.) | (*i. e.* $3\frac{1}{2}$ p' ct. p' ann. over {1821–23) / 1824–25) | | | | | | | | | (6 Years.) (*i. e.* $6\frac{1}{3}$ per cent per annum over {1821–23.) / 1824–25.) |

## - - - - - - - Appendix (F.)—No. 3.

(A.)

of the SILK and the COTTON TRADES in *Great Britain*,

- - - to 1826–30, and 1826–31.

N. B.—*See the Heading to my General Statement, respecting Amounts of Wages in the Cotton Manufacture; their Decrease occasioned by a concurrence of causes.*

### IN REGARD TO AMOUNTS OF DUTIES, WAGES, &c.

| SILK. | | | | | | COTTON. | |
|---|---|---|---|---|---|---|---|
| | (*d*) £. | | Per cents over 1815–17. | | | £. | |
| 1815–17 | 2,073,000 | | | | | 23,500,000 | 1815–17 |
| 1818–20 | 2,719,000 ($10\frac{1}{3}$ p' ct. p' ann. over 1815–17.) | 31 | Increase | Increase | 8 | 25,396,000 ($2\frac{2}{3}$ p' ct. p' ann. over 1815–17.) | 1818–20 |
| 1821–23 | 3,514,000 ($9\frac{3}{4}$ p' ct. p' ann. over 1818–20.) | $69\frac{1}{2}$ | ditto | ditto | $13\frac{1}{2}$ | 26,686,000 ($1\frac{2}{3}$ p' ct. p' ann. over 1818–20.) | 1821–23 |
| Medium. {1821–23 / 1824–25} | (3,888,000) ($11\frac{2}{5}$ p' ct. p' ann. over 1816–20.) | (87) | ditto | ditto | $21\frac{1}{8}$ | 28,483,000 ($3\frac{1}{10}$ p' ct. p' ann. over 1816–20.) | Medium. {1821–23 / 1824–25 |
| 1824–25 | 4,263,000 ($10\frac{5}{8}$ p' ct. p' ann. over 1821–23.) | 105 | *ditto | ditto | $28\frac{3}{4}$ | 30,279,000 ($6\frac{1}{2}$ p' ct. p' ann. over 1821–23.) | 1824–25 |
| | | Per ct. | (*Duties on Raw and Thrown Silk, &c. lowered.) | | per ct. | | |
| £. | | | | | | | £. |
| 1,941,000 | | | Progressions INVERTED: | | | | 26,640,000 |
| 3,647,000 | | | | | | | 31,870,000 |
| 2,922,000 | | | SILK. | COTTON. | | | 30,883,000 |
| 1,832,000 | | | Decrease. | Increase. | | | 29,600,000 |
| 3,182,000 | | | | | | | 30,250,000 |
| 1826–30 | 2,705,000 (5 Years.) (6 p' ct. p' ann. under {1821–23.) / 1824–25.) | 30 | MINUS - -{1821–23 / 1824–25} | - PLUS | $4\frac{3}{4}$ | 29,849,000 (5 Years.) (1 p' ct. p' ann. over {1821–23.) / 1824–25.) | 1826–30 |
| 1831 | 2,588,000 | $33\frac{1}{2}$ | MINUS - - ditto | - - PLUS | 7 | 30,486,000 | 1831 |
| 1826–31 | 2,685,000 (6 Years.) ($5\frac{1}{8}$ p' ct. p' ann. under {1821–23.) / 1824–25.) | 31 | MINUS - - ditto | - - PLUS | 5 | 29,955,000 (6 Years.) ($0\frac{5}{8}$ p' ct. p' ann. over {1821–23.) / 1824–25.) | 1826–31 |
| | | Silk. | | | Cotton. | | |



(*continued*)

Appendix (F.)—No. 3.—*continued.*

## (B.)

APPENDIX to the annexed COMPARATIVE STATEMENT of Amounts of DUTIES, WAGES, &c. accrued from the SILK TRADE at various Periods.

HAVING been requested by a Member of the Honourable Committee to show, in a distinct Statement, the Rates and Amounts of DUTIES, and of WAGES, &c., I have drawn out the following TABLE.

| AMOUNTS of DUTIES. | | AMOUNT of Wages, &c. | RATES of Wages, &c. per lb. of Italian Standard. | | Per lb. of all Descriptions. | | Per Centages in respect to Amount of Wages. |
|---|---|---|---|---|---|---|---|
| | £. | £. | s. | d. | s. | d. | |
| 1815⎫ 1816⎬ 1817⎭ | - - 465,000 | 1,608,000 | 29 | 8 | 21 | 8 | |
| 1818⎫ 1819⎬ 1820⎭ | - - 599,000 | 2,120,000 | 29 | 9 | 22 | – | = 32 per cent *over* 1815-17. |
| 1821⎫ 1822⎬ 1823⎭ | - - 729,000 | 2,785,000 | 30 | 2 | 22 | 7 | = 74 per cent *over* 1815-17. |
| Medium. 1821-23⎫ 1824-25⎭ | (500,000) | (3,388,000) | (29 | 5) | 22 | 4 | = (108) *over* 1815-17. |
| 1824⎫ 1825⎭ | - - 272,000 | 3,991,000 | 28 | 8 | 22 | 1 | = 142 per cent *over* 1815-17. |
| 1826 | - - 82,000 | 1,859,000 | 20 | 2 | 14 | 11 | = 53 per cent *under* 1824-25. |
| 1827 | - - 128,000 | 3,519,000 | 21 | 3 | 16 | – | = 12 per cent *under* ditto. |
| 1828 | - - 111,000 | 2,811,000 | 19 | 4 | 13 | 11 | = 30 per cent *under* ditto. |
| 1829 | - - 45,000 | 1,787,000 | 17 | 1 | 11 | 9 | = 55 per cent *under* ditto. |
| 1830 | - - 90,000 | 3,092,000 | 18 | 3 | 13 | 3 | = 23 per cent *under* ditto. |
| 1826-30 | - 91,000 | 2,614,000 | 19 | 2 | 13 | 6 | 34 per cent *under* 1824-25. |
| | (5 Years.) | * | | | | | * (5 Years.) |
| 1831 | - - 95,000 | 2,493,000 | 16 | 3 | 11 | 8 | = 40 per cent *under* ditto. |
| 1826-31 | - 92,000 | 2,593,000 | 18 | 8 | 13 | 2 | = 35 per cent *under* 1824-25. |
| | (6 Years.) | ** | | | | | ** (6 Years.) |

## (C.)

AN ABSTRACT COMPARATIVE VIEW of the respective PROGRESSES of the SILK and COTTON TRADES, During 15 Years,—1816-20, 1821-23, 1824-25, and 1826-30.

### SILK.

**QUANTITIES (of Italian Standard.)**
Averages per Annum.
lbs.

1816-20 - 1,289,000

Medium of
1821-23 ⎰ 2,315,000 = 79½ p' ct. increase.
1824-25 ⎱

1826-30    2,710,000 = 17 p' ct. increase.

Decrease in progress⎰ 62½ p' ct. decrease
of Quantities - -⎱ Silk in quantities. *

**AMOUNT OF DUTIES, WAGES, &c.**
Averages per Annum.
£.

2,461,000

3,888,000 = 58 p' ct. increase (inversion.)

2,705,000 = 30 p' ct. decrease.

Decrease Silk in Duties,⎰ 88 p' ct. decrease
Wages, &c. - -⎱ †

### COTTON.

**QUANTITIES.**
Averages per Annum.
lbs.

1816-20 107,000,000

Medium of
1821-23 ⎰ 155,000,000 = 45 p' ct. increase.
1824-25 ⎱

1826-30 212,000,000 = 36¾ p' ct. increase.

Decrease in progress⎰ 8¼ p' ct. decrease
of Quantities - -⎱ Cotton in quantities. *

**AMOUNT OF DUTIES, WAGES, &c.**
Averages per Annum.
£.

24,637,000

28,483,000 = 15½ p' ct. increase.

29,849,000 = 5 p' ct. increase.

Decrease Cotton, in Progress⎰ 10½ p' ct.
of Duties, Wages, &c. - -⎱ †

March 1832.          (Errors excepted.)          (signed)   *Alexis James Doxat.*

*Minute made in April* 1831.

## Appendix (F.)—No. 4.

(*\* This Heading has reference to the General Statement of June* 1830.)

(*The Estimate of* 1830 *was made in March* 1831.)

AN ABSTRACT OF ESTIMATES contained in the foregoing Columns* (No. 1 to 13) of the Consumption of Raw and Thrown Silks, and Waste, and Knubs, and Husks, during a period of 15 Years, *viz.*

From 1815 to 1823, with very high Duties, and moderate Rates of Wages, *i.e.* 10½ *d.* for weaving Plain Gros de Naples " 10 to 1100, 3 double," neat London make, and other Wages in proportion; (good proportions of Figured and Fancy Goods in those years):

and from 1824 to 1825, with reduced Duties, same Wages, with the continuance of exclusion of Foreign Manufactured Silks; (good proportions of Figured and Fancy Goods in those years):

and from 1826 to 1829, when the Duties were further reduced, and the Rates of Wages reduced to 7½ *d.,* 8 *d.,* 7 *d.,* and 6 *d.* (1830, 6¼ *d.*; 1831, 6 *d.*); but our Ports were opened to Foreign Manufactured Silks. (Reduced and greatly reduced proportions of Figured and Fancy Goods in these last Four years).

In these Estimates the same Rate of Profits has been calculated during the whole Series of Years, from 1815 to 1829—

that is - - 5 per Cent. on Plain Goods, and 10 per Cent. on Figured ;
Incidentals 3    ditto    on    ditto    and 6    ditto    on    ditto.

Waste at the Mills - - - - - - - - ¼ of an Ounce on lb. 1. 0¾ ;

Ditto in the ulterior processes of manufacture ½    ditto    on 12 Ounces of Silk dyed all bright, or on 13½ Ounces of half bright Dye, and half Souple.

The Castings of the amount of Wages, &c. during the whole period of 1815 to 1829, have been made on the supposed same price of fine Raw Silk, that is 20 *s.,* although the prices were much higher in the former years, which would also have contributed to add to the amount of the Estimate of Wages, and other Charges of Manufacture and Profit. The amounts of Cost of the Raw, and Thrown and Waste Silk, &c. have been cast at the real approximate prices of those respective articles.

Various deductions have been made in those Castings from the rates in former years, paid for throwing, winding, as also in the weaving of Figured Silks, referrible to improvements made in subsequent years in our Machinery, and with regard to more economical Processes and Management.

No account has been taken in these Estimates of considerable additions that accrued to the amount of Wages of Labour, &c., from our Silk Manufacturers making, in former years, great quantities of Goods mixed with Cotton and Wool, such as Chambrays (figured and plain), Poplins, Bombazeens, &c. &c., which branches of manufacture have been reduced to comparatively very small quantities of late years.

Under all these circumstances, it is obvious that the present Estimates are considerably under-rated for the years 1815–17 to 1824–25.

March 1832.                         (signed)    *Alexis James Doxat.*

*Minutes made on the 1st and 2d Weeks in April 1831.*

## Appendix (F.)—No. 5.

### PLAIN SILK GOODS.

COMPARATIVE VIEW of various respective Costs of Manufacture, at LONDON and at LYONS, of Accounts to be manufactured,

lb. 1 $-\frac{3}{4}$ of Raw Silk, worked into $\frac{1}{2}$ lb. of Organzine and $\frac{1}{2}$ lb. of Tram } into

N. B. Of late years a very large proportion of Goods is manufactured

The Silk Manufacture in France being, for the major part, employed for the Export Trade, is liable to great and sudden her Consumption, on an average, are supplied with Silks of her own Growth, of which the Exportation is strictly prohibited. avoirdupoise p' annum. With regard to these contingent variations, against which we have to contend, in addition to the ordinary

#### AT LONDON:

| | Estimate (1) LONDON. | (2) | (3) | (4) |
|---|---|---|---|---|
| | s. d. s. d. | s. d. s. d. | s. d. s. d. | s. d. s. d. |
| Raw Silk, lb. 1 $-\frac{3}{4}$ | at 17 6 - 18 4 | at 17 6 - - - 18 4 | at 17 6 - - - 18 4 | at 17 6 - - - 18 4 |
| Throwing Organzine / Ditto Tram | at 6 − / 3 6 } 4 9 | at 5 6 / 3 6 } - - 4 6 | at 5 − / 3 − } - - - 4 − | at 4 6 / 2 10 } - - - 3 8 |
| | 23 1 | 22 10 | 22 4 | 22 − |
| Dyeing 1 lb. | at 1 8 | at - - 1 7 | at - - 1 6 | at - - 1 5 |
| Winding 6 oz. Warp | at 2 6 - - 11$\frac{1}{4}$ | 2 3 − 10 | 1 9 − 7$\frac{3}{4}$ | 1 6 − 6$\frac{3}{4}$ |
| Ditto 7$\frac{1}{2}$ Shute Souple | 2 3 - 1 −$\frac{1}{2}$ | 2 − − 11$\frac{1}{4}$ | 1 6 − 8$\frac{1}{4}$ | 1 4 − 7$\frac{1}{2}$ |
| Warping 6 oz. | - 1 - - - 4$\frac{1}{2}$ | 1 − − 4$\frac{1}{2}$ | − 10 − 3$\frac{3}{4}$ | − 9 − 3$\frac{1}{4}$ |
| Weaving 13 yards | - - 8$\frac{1}{2}$ 9 2$\frac{1}{2}$ 13 3 | − 7$\frac{1}{2}$ 8 1$\frac{1}{2}$ 11 10 | − 7 7 7 10 9 | − 6 6 6 9 4 |
| | 36 4 | 34 8 | 33 1 | 31 4 |
| | s. d. s. d. | s. d. s. d. | s. d. s. d. | s. d. s. d. |
| Incidentals, at 3 p'Ct. | on 36 4 - 1 1 | on 34 8 1 −$\frac{1}{2}$ | on 33 1 1 − | on 31 4 − 11$\frac{1}{4}$ |
| Interest on, at 2 p'Ct. | - 37 5 - − 9 | 35 8$\frac{1}{2}$ − 8$\frac{1}{2}$ | 34 − − 8$\frac{1}{4}$ | 32 3 − 7$\frac{3}{4}$ |
| Profit, at 5 per Cent. | - 38 2 - 1 10$\frac{1}{2}$ - 3 8 | 36 5 1 9$\frac{3}{4}$ 3 7 | 34 9 1 8$\frac{3}{4}$ 3 5 | 32 11 1 7$\frac{3}{4}$ 3 3 |
| Cost of 13 oz. manufactured into 13 yds. | 40 − | - - 13 oz. - - 38 3 | - - 13 oz. - - 36 6 | - - 13 oz. - - 34 7 |
| | s. d. | s. d. | s. d. | s. d. |
| Of which { Silk | - 18 4 - - - | - - 18 4 - - | - - 18 4 - - | - - 18 4 - - |
| Of which { Wages, &c. | 21 8 - - - | - - 19 11 - - | - - 18 2 - - | - - 16 3 - - |
| Cost of 16 oz. manufactured into 16 yds. | 49 3 | - - 16 oz. - - 47 1 | - - 16 oz. - - 44 11 | - - 16 oz. - - 42 7 |
| Of which { Silk | - 22 7 - - - | - - 22 7 - - | 22 7 - - | - - 22 7 |
| Of which { Wages, &c. | 26 8 - - - | - - 24 6 - - | - - 22 4 - - | - - 20 − |
| Cost of plain manufactured Silks in common Colours - - } per Yd. | s. d. 3 1 | - - - 1 Yard s. d. 2 11$\frac{3}{8}$ | - - - 1 Yard s. d. 2 9$\frac{5}{8}$ | - - - 1 Yard s. d. 2 8 |

RECAPITULATION of Total Differences of Costs of a good PLAIN *Gros de Naples*, 10 to 1100 threads, 3 double;

| At LONDON and at LYONS. Rates of Weaving, &c. and Cost of fine Raw Silk. | | | | | Differences. Per Yard. | Per lb. | Per Cent. |
|---|---|---|---|---|---|---|---|
| | s. d. | s. d. | s. d. | s. d. s. d. | s. d. | s. d. | |
| Cost per Yard, 3 1 | (at − 8$\frac{1}{2}$ per yard, | − 5$\frac{1}{2}$) | 2 4$\frac{3}{8}$ | | - - − 8$\frac{5}{8}$ | - 11 5 | - 30 |
| | (at 17 6 per lb. | - 17 − ) | | 2 2$\frac{3}{8}$ | - - − 10$\frac{5}{8}$ | - 14 − | - 40 |
| 2 11$\frac{3}{8}$ | (at − 7$\frac{1}{2}$ | − 5$\frac{1}{4}$) | 2 2$\frac{7}{8}$ | | - - − 8$\frac{1}{2}$ | - 11 3 | - 31 |
| | (at 17 6 | 16 − ) | | 2 1 | - - − 10$\frac{3}{8}$ | - 13 9 | - 41 |
| 2 9$\frac{5}{8}$ | (at − 7 | − 4$\frac{3}{4}$) | 2 1$\frac{3}{8}$ | | - - − 8$\frac{1}{4}$ | - 11 1 | - 33 |
| | (at 17 6 | 15 6 ) | | 1 11$\frac{5}{8}$ | - - − 10 | - 13 5 | - 43 |
| 2 8 | (at − 6 | − 4 ) | 1 11$\frac{3}{8}$ | | - - − 8$\frac{5}{8}$ | - 11 6 | - 37 |
| | (at 17 6 | 14 6 ) | | 1 9$\frac{5}{8}$ | - - − 10$\frac{3}{8}$ | - 13 8 | - 47 |

Charges at Lyons, and of transmission to London, at 6 per cent. - 1 *s.* 9 *d.* to 2 *s.* 3 *d.*

Import Duty - - - 11 *s.*

When for Illicit Imports, the Charges to Lyons and to Paris are - 1 *s.* 2 *d.* to 1 *s.* 6 *d.* *i. e.* 4 p'cent.

March 1832.

## Appendix (F.)—No. 5.

### PLAIN SILK GOODS.

*ood Gros de Naples, of common Colours,* " 10 *to* 1100—3 *double,*" neat Make; estimated in these
t either Place, from

3 Yards { weighing 13 Ounces, if Shot Souple, = 1 Ounce per Yard.—
11½ - if all Bright Dye = 14⅙ Drams - ditto.

" *Shot Souple,*" *i. e.* with a portion of the Gum left in the Silk.

luctuations, both in regard to the Charges in the various processes of Manufacture, and to the Prices of Silks; about 4-5ths of
t is estimated that, on an average, the Consumption of Silks in France for some years past has been about lbs. 5,500,000
nd considerable pressure of that Competition, I refer to my Letter of 28th April 1829, to the Right Hon. Vesey Fitzgerald.

### AT LYONS:

| | s. d. | s. d. | s. d. | s. d. | s. d. | s. d. | s. d. | s. d. |
|---|---|---|---|---|---|---|---|---|
| Raw Silk, lb. 1 – ¾ | - at 17 - - | 17 9 | at 16 – | 16 9 | at 15 6 - - - | 16 2 | at 14 6 - - - | 15 2 |
| Throwing Organzine | - at 3 9 | 3 – | at 3 8 | - - - 2 11 | at 3 4 | - - - 2 8 | at 3 – | - - - 2 5 |
| Ditto Tram | - - 2 3 | | 2 2 | | 2 – | | 1 10 | |
| | | 20 9 | | 19 8 | | 18 10 | | 17 7 |
| Dyeing 1 lb. | - - - at 1 1 | | at - - 1 – | | at - - - 11 | | at - - - 11 | |
| Winding 6 oz. Warp at 1 7 | - - 7 | | 1 6 – 6¾ | | 1 4 – 6 | | 1 3 – 5½ | |
| Ditto 7½ Shute | - - – - - - – | | – – – – | | – – – – | | – – – – | |
| Warping 6 | - - - 7 - - 2½ | | – 6½ – 2¼ | | – 6 – 2¼ | | – 6 – 2¼ | |
| Weaving 13 yards | - - 5½ 5 11½ | 7 10 | – 5¼ 5 8¼ | 7 5 | – 4¼ 5 1¼ | 6 9 | – 4 4 4 | 5 11 |
| | (1 lb. = 35 3) 1 yard 2 2⅜ * | 28 7 | (1 lb. = 33 4) 1 yard 2 1 * | 27 1 | (1 lb. = 31 6) 1 yard 1 11⅝ * | 25 7 | (1 lb. = 28 11) 1 Yard 1 9⅝ * | 23 6 |
| See at Foot * | | | | | | | | |
| ncidentals at 1¾ p'Ct. on 28 7 | – 6 | | on 27 1 – 5½ | | on 25 7 – 5¼ | | on 23 6 – 5 | |
| nterest on, at 2 p' Ct. 29 1 | – 7¼ | | 27 7 – 6½ | | 26 – – 6¼ | | 23 11 – 5¾ | |
| rofit, at 3½ per Cent. 29 8 | 1 – ½ | 2 2 | 28 1 – 11¾ | 2 – | 26 6 – 11¼ | 1 11 | 24 5 – 10¾ | 1 9 |
| Cost of 13 oz. manufactured into 13 yds. | | 30 9 | - - 13 oz. - - | 29 1 | - - 13 oz. - - | 27 6 | - - 13 oz. - - | 25 3 |
| Of which { Silk - | - 17 9 | | - - 16 9 | | - - 16 2 | | - - 15 2 | |
| Wages, &c. | 13 – | | - - 12 4 | | - - 11 4 | | - - 10 1 | |
| Cost of 16 oz. manufactured into 16 yds. | | 37 10 | - - 16 oz. - - | 35 10 | - - 16 oz. - - | 33 10 | - - 16 oz. - - | 31 1 |
| Of which { Silk - | - 21 10 | | - - 20 7 | | - - 19 10 | | - - 18 7 | |
| Wages, &c. | 16 – | | - - 15 3 | | - - 14 – | | - - 12 6 | |
| Cost of Plain manufactured Silks in common Colours - - } p' Yd. | | 2 4⅜ | - - - 1 Yard | 2 2⅞ | - - - 1 Yard | 2 1⅜ | - - - 1 Yard | 1 11⅜ |
| And without the Charges of Incidentals, Interest, and Profit, as above * } | * 16 oz. 35 3 | 2 2⅜ | * 16 oz. 33 4 | 2 1 | * 16 oz. 31 6 | 1 11⅝ | * 16 oz. 28 11 | 1 9⅝ |
| | Estimate (1 . 1) Lyons. | | | (2 . 2) | | (3 . 3) | | (4 . 4) |

Range of differences presented in an INVERTED order.

| Cost at LONDON: | Rates of Weaving, &c. and Cost of fine Raw Silk. | at LYONS. | | | Differences. Per Yard. | Per lb. | Per Cent. |
|---|---|---|---|---|---|---|---|
| s. d. | s. d. | s. d. | s. d. | s. d. | s. d. | s. d. | |
| Cost per Yard, 3 1 | (at – 6 per Yard, | – 5½) | 1 11⅜ | | - - 1 1⅝ - | 18 | 2 - 58 |
| | (at 17 6 per lb. | - 17 – ) | | 1 9⅝ | - - 1 3⅜ - | 20 | 4 - 70 |
| 2 11⅜ | (at – 7 | – 5¼) | 2 1⅜ | | - - - 10 - | 13 | 3 - 39 |
| | (at 17 6 | 16 – ) | | 1 11⅝ | - - - 11¼ - | 15 | 7 - 49 |
| 2 9⅝ | (at – 7½ | – 4¾) | 2 2⅞ | | - - - 6¾ - | 9 | 1 - 25 |
| | (at 17 6 | 15 6 ) | | 2 1 | - - - 8⅝ - | 11 | 7 - 35 |
| 2 8 | (at – 8½ | – 4 ) | 2 4⅜ | | - - - 3⅝ - | 4 | 9 - 13 |
| | (at 17 6 | 14 6 ) | | 2 2⅜ | - - - 5⅝ - | 7 | 4 - 21 |

Charges at Lyons, and of transmission to London, at 6 per Cent. - 1 *s.* 9*d.* to 2 *s.* 3*d.*
Import Duty - - - 11 *s.*

When for Illicit Imports, the Charges at Lyons and to Paris are - 1 *s.* 2*d.* to 1 *s.* 6*d.* *i.e.* 4 p' Ct.

(Errors excepted.) (signed) *Alexis James Doxat.*

(D.)

STATEMENT, by which may be seen at one View the Proportions in which the
Wages of Manufacture,

Supposing 11 ounces 8 drams of Gros de Naples, all Bright Die (16 oz. for 12, and ½ oz. Waste)
Or    12  -  11  -  -  ditto  -  Shot Souple  (Warp 16 oz. for 12 Bright)  -  -
Souple Shute 16 oz. for 14½  -  -

## COST OF ORGANZINE.

| Average of Charges for Throwing Organzine in Piedmont and various parts of Italy. | | | | | s. | d. |
|---|---|---|---|---|---|---|
| | | Cost of 1 lb. good Italian Raw Silk of 22/24 drs.——Average of 17 months, from October 1827 to February 1829, as per my Statement A. - - - - - - - - - | | | 22 | – ½ |
| | | Add Waste at 6¼ per Cent. = 1 ounce - - - - - | | | 1 | 4½ |
| | | Depressed Charge for *good* Work of 1 lb. Organzine of 22/24 drs. suitable for making a neat Gros de Naples - - - - - | | | 6 | – |
| s. | d. | | s. | d. | | |
| 1 | 9½ | Thus | 3 | 5 | Wages of Labour thereon. | |
| – | 3½ | | – | 7 | Part of the Rent, of Taxes, of Rates, and general Expenses of Establishment. | |
| – | 5 | | – | 10 | Charges referrible to Machinery and Incidentals, inclusive of Part of the Rent and Taxes, &c. | |
| – | 1 | | – | 5 | Charges referrible to Power. | |
| – | 6 | | – | 9 | Throwster's Profit. | |
| 3 | 1 | | 6 | – | Total Charge at depressed rates for working well 1 lb. Organzine 22/24 drs. | |
| | | Cost of 1 lb. English Organzine of 22/24 drs. worked from superior Italian Raw Silk - - - - - - - - - | | | 29 | 5 |

(Errors excepted.)

(D.)

[p]rime Cost of the Silk, the Wages of [T]ganzine and Tram, and on usual moderate  
[fr]om 1815–17 to 1824–25.

[and] some Waste } to be made entirely [c]harges be, constituting the Total Cost of those 13 Yards?  
and of good Engli[sh]

COST OF TH[ROWING]

| | [SI]LK. | WASTE. | Wages of Labour. | Part of Rent, Taxes, and Expenses of Establishment. | Machinery, Incidentals, and Part of Rent and Taxes and Power. | IN-TEREST. | PROFIT. |
|---|---|---|---|---|---|---|---|
| | d. | s.  d. | s.  d. | s.  d. | s.  d. | s.  d. | s.  d. |
| Cost of 1 lb. good Italian R[aw] ——as per Statement A. | –¼ | –  8¼ | 1  8½ | –  3½ | –  7½ | –  – | –  4½ |
| Add Waste at 5½ per Cent. | 9¾ | –  7¼ | 1  1¼ | –  1½ | –  3¾ | –  – | –  3 |
| | 10 | 1  3½ | 2  9¾ | –  5 | –  10¾ | –  – | –  7½ |
| Depressed Charge for good V[...] 24/26 drs. suitable for m[...] Naples | –  – | –  – | –  11 | 1 including Ingredients and Profit. | –  – | | |
| Thus 2  2½ Wages of Lab[our] | –  – | –  – | 1  7 | –  – | –  2¼ | | |
| –  3 Part of the Ren[t] and general [Establish]ment. | –  – | –  – | –  4½ | | | | |
| –  4 Charges referri[ng] Incidentals, [and] Rent and Ta[xes] | –  – | –  – | 10  10 | | | | |
| –  2½ Charges referri[ng] | –  – | –  – | | 1  3½ | | | |
| –  6 Throwster's Pr[ofit] | –  – | –  – | –  – | –  – | –  10¾ | | |
| 3  6 Total Charge [for] working well | –  – | –  – | –  – | –  – | –  – | –  10¾ | 2  3 |
| | | 1  3½ | 16  6¼ | 2  8½ | 1  1 | –  10¾ | 2  10½ |

21  10  Prime Cost of the Raw Silk.

1  3½  Charge for Waste.

23  1½

– 16  6¼  Wages of Labour on the various Processes, i. e. depressed Wages on the Throwing operations, and moderate usual Wages of Manufacture, from 1815-17 to 1824-25.

– 2  8½  Part of Rent, of Taxes, and Expenses of Establishment and Dyeing Ingredients, &c. and Incidentals.

– 1  1  Machinery and Power, and part of Rent and Taxes, &c. relative thereto, and Incidentals.

– – 10¾  Interest on Manufacture.

– 2  10½  Profits on Throwing and Manufacturing, except Dyeing.

47  2½  Cost of 13 yards, weighing 11 oz. 8 drs. if all Bright Dye,  
or, 12  11  if Shot Souple.

Cost of 1 lb. English Tram [...] from good Italian Raw Si[lk]

[Organ]zine or Tram, do not constitute any part, as the

[...] Tram, worked in France from French Raw.

(E.)

ENGLAND.

and our Charges for Throwing Organzine and Tram, at depressed Rates against usual Rates of Throwing in France.

| ON. | SILK. | | WASTE. | | WAGES of LABOUR. | | Part of Rent, Taxes, and Expenses of Establishment. | | Machinery, Incidentals, and part of Rent and Taxes and Power. | | INTEREST. | | PROFIT. | |
|---|---|---|---|---|---|---|---|---|---|---|---|---|---|---|
| s. d. | s. | d. | s. | d. | s. | d. | s. | d. | s. | d. | s. | d. | s. | d. |
| - 14 8 - of which | 11 | -¼ | - | 8¼ | 1 | 8½ | - | 3½ | - | 7½ | - | - | - | 4½ |
| - 13 2 - - | 10 | 9¾ | - | 7¼ | 1 | 1¼ | - | 1½ | - | 3¼ | - | - | - | 3 |
| 27 10½ | 21 | 10 | 1 | 3½ | 2 | 9¾ | - | 5 | - | 10¾ | - | - | - | 7½ |
| 11 | | | | | | | - | 11 | 1 including Ingredients and Profit. | | | | | |
| 6 | | | | | | | 1 | 3¾ | - | 2¼ | | | | |
| 4½ | | | | | | | - | 4½ | | | | | | |
| 7 | | | | | 7 | 7 | | | | | | | | |
| 2 | | | | | | | | | 1 | 2 | | | | |
| 9¾ | | | | | | | | | | | - | 9¾ | | |
| -¾ - 15 5 | | | | | | | | | | | | | 2 | -¾ |
| - 43 3½ | | | 1 | 3½ | 13 | - | 2 | 7 | 1 | 1 | - | 9¾ | 2 | 8¼ |

|  | s. d. | per Ct. | s. d. | |
|---|---|---|---|---|
| of 43 3½ | 50 4/10 | | 21 10 | Prime Cost of the Raw Silk. |
| | 3 | | 1 3½ | Charge for Waste. |
| | | | 23 1½ | |
| | 30 | | 13 - | Wages of Labour on the various Processes,—*i. e.* depressed Wages on the Throwing operations, and very low Wages of Manufacture. |
| | 6 | | 2 7 | Part of Rent, of Taxes, and Expenses of Establishment, and Dyeing Ingredients, &c. including Incidentals. |
| | 2 5/10 | | 1 1 | Machinery and Power, and part of Rent and Taxes, &c. relative thereto, and Incidentals. |
| | 1 9/10 | | - 9¾ | Interest on Manufacture. |
| | 6 2/10 | | 2 8¼ | Profits on Throwing and Manufacturing, except Dyeing. |
| | | | 43 3½ | Cost of 13 yards, weighing 11 oz. 8 drs., if all Bright Dye, or 12 oz. 11 drs., if Shot Souple. |

e difference of 37¾ per cent. is increased to 48 per Cent., as under, when owing to some great falling-off of the demand port, the Lyons Manufacturer (who depends greatly on the Export Trade) is obliged to make a sacrifice, in the sale of ods, of the charges of Incidentals, Interest and Profit.

s. d.
31 4½ Cost at Lyons, as on the other side, of 13 yards, weighing 12 oz. 11 drs. Shot Souple, from which deducting
- 6¼ Amount of Incidentals on Manufacture.
- 7¼ Ditto Interest on ditto.
1 -¾ Ditto Profit on ditto.
2 2¼ together.

29 2¼ Cost at Lyons, at usual Rates of Throwing, and low Wages of Manufacture, less the three above items.

s. d.
36 10 per lb. against 54 7¼ London Cost, at depressed rates of Throwing, and very low Wages of Manufacture.

2 3 per yard 3 3 9/10 per yard.

Difference of Costs 17 9¼ per lb. = 48 per Cent. on Prime Cost at Lyons, 29 s. 2¼ d.

(signed) ALEXIS JAMES DOXAT.

## OMMON COLOURS.

de Naples, 10 to 11 hundred, 3 Doub

bout 4/5ths of her Consumption, on an a
e ordinary and considerable pressure of

e Charges, both at LONDON and LYON

| Weaving, per Yard. | Incidentals - 3 p |
|---|---|
| | Interest - - 2 |
| | Profit - - 5 |

| | Lyons. | | London. | Lyo |
|---|---|---|---|---|
| Lo | d. d. | | s. d. | s. |
| | ,, 5½=5=70 per Ct. | | 3 8 ,, 2 | |
| | | | 9½ per Ct. on the cost of 40s. | |
| | ,, 5¼=4¾=58 | – | 3 7 ,, 2 | |
| | ,, 4¾=4¼=64 | – | 3 5 ,, 1 | |
| | ,, 4 =3½=71 | – | on 13 yards 3 3 ,, 1 | |
| | ,, – 1½ | | | |
| Ct. = 30 per Ct. | | | | |

In 1821–23
1824–25

| | d. d. | | d. |
|---|---|---|---|
| | ,, 6¼=5¾=83 per Ct. | | 3/3=3 per Yd. |
| zin | ,, – 4=0 3½ | | = 9⅜ per Ct. |
| th | | | on the |
| N | In 1831. | | LONDON |
| ch | | | Cost of |
| sa | Ct. = 39 per Ct. | | s. d. |
| 4 | | | 34 7 |
| 2 | | | |
| 2 | er Yd.=72*Cts. p' Aune. | | |
| | itto =69 ditto. | | |
| | itto =63 ditto. | | |
| | itto =53 ditto. | | |
| | times per French Ell. | | |

Manufactured Silks, with
low and wretched Wages,
h competition, as may be
Paper, as also of Papers
der the graduated Scale),

of 8½ d. for Weaving, well
emuneration for work well
the Weaver, upon whose
—The Rate of Wages for
7 to 1824–25, with very
our national industry, so
1815–17.

d.)

# I N D E X.

[In the following Index, the Figures following the Names, refer to the Number of the
Question in the Evidence; and *App.* to the Page of the Appendix.]

## A.

## B.

*Baggallay, Richard* (Analysis of his Evidence)—*continued.*

than the French, 7390——Duty on fancy satins, which are now got from Coventry, 7391–7393——Preference of consumers latterly in favour of English goods, 7394–7396, 7401–7404——Amount of duty necessary to enable Coventry to compete with the French, 7397, 7398——French pattern could be copied at Coventry in sufficient time for the fashion, 7399, 7400——If pattern sent to Coventry to be copied, it would be public before the French goods come over, 7406——Duty on each kind of ribbon imported, 7407——Comparative prices between Switzerland and England, and proportion for expenses on plain sarsnets, and plain striped ribbons, 7408–7412——Reason of distress at Foleshill, 7413, and not at Coventry, 7419——Duty on plain gauze ribbons imported, 7414, 7415——Striped gauze ribbons not imported from loss thereby, 7416, 7417——Duty on figured gauzes, 7420, 7421——Duty necessary thereon to prevent smuggling, 7422–7426——Wages higher for the manufacture of that article than others, 7427–7429——Duty necessary to meet high rate of wages thereon, 7430, 7431 ——Comparison as to earnings of weavers at Coventry upon plain and figured gauzes, and quantity of work, and hours of labour, 7432–7437.

Preference of weavers for their own looms, and methods of purchasing them, 7437–7440 ——Weavers fully employed at Coventry, 7441–7446——Amount paid for clipping, 7447–7449——Wages of winders and warpers, 7450–7452——Quantity of plain sarsnets made at Coventry of different kinds at one time, with rate of wages, 7453–7456—— Improvements in the engine loom, 7457——Machinery would be extended in Coventry, but for the objection by the weavers to the use of new machinery, 7458——How far improvement in Coventry manufacture from foreign competition, 7459——Intention to establish power looms at Manchester, for the manufacture of plain sarsnet ribbons, 7461 ——Manchester and Spitalfields shut out the French at present in the manufacture of broad silks, 7462–7469——Duty on French broad silks, 7470——How far they are smuggled, 7471, 7472——Importation of rich figured goods given up from loss thereon, 7473–7475——Price thereof, 7476——Price of English plain goods, 7477–7479—— Manner in which the silk trade at Manchester interferes with Spitalfields, description of goods made at Manchester, 7480–7501——Description of trade at Macclesfield, 7502–7507——Letter from Germany upon the manufacture of velvets, 7508–7511—— English velvets improving, 7512, 7513——Comparison of prices and duty upon German and English velvets, 7514–7518——Greater facilities for smuggling now than before 1826, 7519–7522——Duty would be better collected by weight than *ad valorem*, 7523, 7575, 7576——Rate of insurance upon smuggling, 7525, 7526——Assimilation of style between France and England, since opening the trade, 7527–7531——Rate of insurance could not be lowered if duty reduced, 7532, 7533——Smuggling would be attempted even under prohibition, 7534–7537——Difficulty in distinguishing between certain French and English goods in 1824, and greater difficulty now, 7538–7549——Distress in Spitalfields not so great lately as formerly, 7550–7565——State of trade among retailers more regular and better at present than for some years, 7566–7568——State of trade among manufacturers better, few large failures at Manchester, 7569–7573——Difficulty of ascertaining a proper rate of duty upon importation of French goods, 7574——How far Manchester trade, and not importations from France, have affected the Spitalfields trade, 7577–7590.

*Ballance, John* (Analysis of his Evidence.) Silk manufacturer in Spitalfields, 8353–8355 ——Spitalfields trade growing and prosperous, previous to 1826, 8356——Custom House returns of raw silk and wages, 1816–1826, 8357–8359——Causes of distress in the silk trade, 1792 and 1816, 8360, 8361——Increase of smuggling since removal of prohibition, 8362, 8363——Distress of Spitalfields weavers, and periods thereof, 8364–8366—— Periods of reduction in wages, and proportion thereof, 8367, 8368——Reduction of duty upon foreign wrought silks did not prevent smuggling, from the smuggler reducing his profits, 8368–8370——Present rate of wages of weavers, 8371–8373——Amount of wages paid on 5,000 lbs. of wrought silk, 1816–1831, 8373 ——State of the poor in three parishes of St. Matthew Bethnal Green, Christchurch Spitalfields, and Mile End Old Town, comprising the district called Spitalfields, taken from parish accounts in February 1832, 8374–8378——Poor in the workhouse and casual poor of the parish of St. Matthew Bethnal Green, 1821–1832, 8378——Population of the Spitalfields district, 8379—— Number dependent on silk manufacture, 8380——Estimate of how much less wages paid in Spitalfields now and before 1826, 8381——Effect of reduction of wages on the character and habits of the Spitalfields population, and in causing them to be disaffected to Government, 8382——Account, showing manner in which less wages are paid for working up a larger quantity of silk, 1822–1831, 8383, 8384——Rate of wages per week, 1822–1831, 8385–8387——Manufacture of richer silks abandoned since 1826, 8388–8390 ——Consumption thereof in England has increased, but is supplied from France and not from Manchester, 8391–8393, 8409——Description of goods made at Manchester, 8394, 8400——Description of the term plain, figured and fancy goods, 8395–8400—— Silk trade at Manchester has been in existence since 1806, 8401, 8402——Before the opening the ports, prosperity of either Manchester or Spitalfields, showed prosperity of the other, 8403——Spitalfields has since been obliged to adopt the Manchester trade to the injury of both, 8404, 8405.

Distress at Manchester not so great as in Spitalfields, from its being partly cotton manufacture, 8406——How distress in Spitalfields attributed to opening the Ports, 8407,

*Ballance, John* (Analysis of his Evidence)—*continued.*

8407, 8408——Detail of advantages possessed by France and the Continent over England, 8410——Comparative view of the prices at Lyons of French tram, the produce of French raw, with price in London at the same periods for Italian tram, in averages of three months, from July 1827, to March 1832, 8410——Comparative view of the prices at Lyons of French organzine, the produce of French raw, with prices obtained in London at same periods for Piedmont organzine, in averages of three months, from July 1827 to March 1832, 8410——Advantages in favour of France from rate of wages being lower, difference in 1826 and 1829, 8410-8412——Advantages to France from its exports of manufactured silks, with particulars thereof in 1829, 8413——Advantage to France, from expense in construction of patterns, grows out of her command of foreign markets, manner thereof, 8414, 8415——Exclusion of foreign manufactured silks, the only effectual counteraction for those advantages, 8416——Benefits of export trade, and how it might be extended by increasing the price of debentures, 8417–8419——If duties lowered, smuggler would again lower his profits, 8420——Lowering duty on foreign thrown would not enable the manufacturer to come down to the smuggler's price, 8421, 8422——Present rate of smuggling, 8423–8425——Lowering duties on foreign thrown would ruin throwsters, and cause great mischief, 8426——Disadvantages of being dependent upon Italy for thrown silk, 8427——Not necessary for a manufacturer to use foreign thrown, 8428—— English costs rather more than foreign, 8429——Under good Custom House regulations, properly enforced, smugglers' risk would be increased, and more duty than the present amount collected, 8432, 8433——Advantages to the plain silk trade, by increasing the risk of the smuggler, 8434, 8435.

Fancy branch can only be preserved by prohibition, 8436, 8437——State of the fancy trade prior to and since 1826, 8438–8442——Importance of the fancy branch to the silk trade, 8443——Reduction in the number of manufacturers since 1826, 8444–8447—— Consequent distress of the weavers employed by them, 8448——Supplanting one branch will be the ruin of the others, 8449, 8450——No advantage to this country from the importation of foreign silk goods, 8451——How far increase of crime from the distress of the weavers in Bethnal Green, 8452–8454——Distress of the silk trade from reductions of duty and increase of smuggling, remonstrances to Government thereon, 8455–8463 ——Proposed regulations against smuggling, that of criminal punishment for the smuggler and stamping goods to detect the receiver, 8464, 8465——Necessity for stamping, 8466 ——Reasons submitted to the Committee for stamping silks, 8466, 8467——Certain checks should be used to prevent stamps being forged, 8468——Paper with signatures declaratory of the sentiments of the silk trade in favour of stamping, 8469, 8470——Plan for stamping in order to prevent forgery, 8470——Regulations applicable to plain goods, 8471——Prohibition the only preservation for the fancy branch, 8472——Why in that event the English would not lose in point of taste and fashion or pay higher price, 8473, 8474——Manner in which the middle man between the manufacturer and consumer has benefited by the decrease of wages and the present system, 8475–8478—— Duties that might be collected on plain goods under proposed regulations, 8479–8482 ——Manner in which the silk trade would revive thereunder, 8483——Manner in which it would remove the existing distress in Spitalfields, 8484, 8485——Spitalfields competes with Manchester from being deprived of her rich trade, 8486——How both would be restored to their former trade under proposed regulations, 8487–8490——The best English fancy goods are made in Spitalfields, 8491, 8493——The peculiar manufacture of Spitalfields has not been depressed by Manchester, but by France, 8494——Decrease of wages has not reduced price to the fullest extent to the consumer or manufacturer, 8495, 8496.

(Second Examination.)   Reduction in the weight of silk in the process of manufacture in France, 8497–8504——Comparison of wages in France and Switzerland, 8505–8512 ——Rate of wages in Spitalfields, 1824–1831, 8513, 8526——Rate of wages in other manufacturing districts, 1817–1825, 8527–8530, 8534, 8535——By what Spitalfields wages regulated, 8531–8533——Present state of Spitalfields rather better, 8537–8540—— Cotton and woollen trades have not been subject to similar distress as the silk trade, 8542——Places where the Jacquard at present in use, 8543–8545——Number of yards per day weavers can make, 8546–8549——Examination as to the use of the fly-shuttle, 8550–8555——Examination upon the competition with France, and protecting duty necessary for the English manufacturer, 8556–8583——More waste in the manufacture of poor than rich goods, 8584——Difference in price of goods imported by the trade committee and similar goods made at Spitalfields, 8586——Importation of black goods 8587–8593——Consumption thereof, 8594, 8595——Competition with France in black satins, their colours, 8596–8598——Price of black goods, 8599–8601——Cost of smuggling, 8602–8604——Manufacturers who have been beaten out of the market in the fancy trade employ their weavers on black goods, 8605, 8606——Duty that might be collected and smuggling prevented by proper Custom-house regulations, 8607–8611—— Failures of manufacturers of broad goods, 8612–8619——Less rich goods making than last year, 8620——Description of French black satin mostly in use, 8621–8623——Appointment of the Committee at Weavers'-hall, its object and number of members interested in throwing, 8624–8635, 8652——Not part of the business of the Association to get the duties on raw silk lowered, 8636——Their minutes will show that smuggling in 1815 was limited and confined to the coast, 8637——Smuggling at present exceeds the amount

legally

*Ballance, John* (Analysis of his Evidence)—*continued.*

legally imported, 8638——Proportion of legal and illegal imports to the gross sales of the country, 8639——Amount imported from France that interferes with Spitalfields, 8640-8642——Hands thrown out of employment by foreign importations, legal and illegal, 8643-8645.

Proportion of fancy trade to the whole previous to 1825, 8646 ——Injury to throwsters from reduction of duty in 1829, 8647-8651, 8653-8655——Reduction of wages for throwing from reduction of duty, 8656, 8657——How throwsters' price regulated, 8657 ——Advantage of silk being thrown in this country, 8658-8663——Duty necessary to protect throwster, 8664, 8665——Advantages in favour of Italy of less expense in throwing and in the selection of raw silk, 8666-8668 ——Reduction of duty would cause dependence upon Italy, 8669——Ruin throwsters and augment misery of labouring classes, 8670——Italian would be benefited thereby, 8671——Value of mill property in 1826 and at present, 8672, 8673——Amount per cent. the manufacturer would be relieved by lessening the protection of the throwster, 8674-8676——Cause of the difficulty in getting the best description of Italian raw silk, 8677-8682——Witness must give up manufacture if he could not get English thrown silk, 8683-8685——Advantages of English thrown silk and of encouraging throwster, 8686, 8687——Greatest injury to Spitalfields is from the Continent, competition with Manchester is of a secondary nature, 8688——Distress of the silk trade greater than formerly, 8689——Sacrifices made by manufacturers, 8690——Reduced wages has partly stopped legal importation of plain goods, 8691——Calculation as to earnings of weavers, 8692, 8693——Calculations founded upon weight are fallacious from difference in value, 8694——Description of goods whether of British or foreign manufacture depend upon the class of customers to be supplied, 8695——Reducing duty to the smugglers' price gets rid of both smuggler and manufacturer, 8697——Operation of stamping and manner of preventing forgery, 8698, 8699——Importations of watered silks from France and labour displaced thereby, 8700-8704——Manchester has not suffered so much from foreign importations as Spitalfields, 8705, 8706——Manchester and Spitalfields would both be benefited by prohibition, 8707——Other advantages of France would counterbalance ours had we her raw material, 8708——Wages in Spitalfields and effect thereon by repeal of Act regulating labour, 8709-8712——Contingencies the English manufacturer liable to and protection necessary, 8713-8715——Amount per cent. more cost to English manufacturer of goods manufactured, than smuggled or jobbed in from France, 8716-8722——Comparative statement of the cost of manufacturing 500 yards of plain gros de Naples in London and at Lyons, 8722.

(Third Examination.)  Increase of smuggling in 1824, 11825—— From French goods being warehoused previous to the opening the Ports in 1826, 11009-11013——Comparison of Dr. Bowring's statement of exports from France with duty on imports into this country, showing limited smuggling, 1826-1831, and how far contrary to the fact, 11014——Silk goods smuggled out of France, and method thereof, 11016, 11017—— Examination in answer to Dr. Bowring's evidence upon the value of the silk trade, and labour consumed therein in France, 11018-11020——Injury to the silk trade from exports of cotton, 11021-11026——Labour displaced in the silk trade not taken up by the cotton trade, 11027-11031——Examination upon the employment of weavers in the silk and cotton trade at Spitalfields and Manchester previous to and since 1826, 11032-11045—— Manchester would have kept its low trade if Spitalfields had not been interfered with by France, 11046-11050——Importations of crapes from France interfere with those places where they are manufactured in England, 11051-11057——Number of looms that would have employment in the event of their manufacturing the goods imported from France, 11058-11072, 11075-11079——Quantity of figured silks consumed in this country, 11073, 11074——Increase in the consumption of fancy goods, 11080-11082——Value of foreign importation, 11083-11096.

*Banbury, William* (Analysis of his Evidence.)  Partner in the house of James Vere & Co., 4403-4408——Period of Acts passing prohibiting the importation of foreign wrought silks and velvets and manufactured ribbons, 4409, 4410——Bad effects of their repeal, 4411——Beneficial effects of their operation, 4412, 4413——Increase of manufactures and employment of operatives under them, 4414-4416——Account of the progressive increase of duty on foreign thrown silk, 1660-1768, 4417-4420——Account of the progressive variation of duty on raw silk, 1660-1786, and from 1784-1825, 4420——Injury to capital invested in mills and machinery in consequence of the repeal of the prohibitory laws, 4421-4423, 4425——Up to period of the repeal, silk trade progressively improving, 4424——Reason for submission to high duties on thrown silk, 4426, 4427——Trade still increased, notwithstanding heavy duties on thrown silk, 4428-4432——Present bad state of the throwing trade, 4433-4440——To what attributed, 4441-4446——Bad effect of the reduction of duty on organzine, 4447——Bad effect of further reducing duty on foreign thrown silk, 4448——Bad effects of reducing duty thereon by a Treasury order in 1825, 4449-4455——Necessity for encouraging the throwing Italian silk in this country, 4456——Difference of credit on sales before reduction of duty, and at present, 4457-4461——Duty that would protect throwsters, 4462-4465, 4481-4483——Effect of the duty remaining as it is, 4466-4470——Rise in the price of foreign silk, if throwing trade here destroyed, 4471——Expense of importing silk from Milan, 4472-4474——Remuneration

*Banbury, William*—continued.

neration to the throwster, and difference in price between raw and thrown silk, 4475–4480 ——Reason for importation of thrown silk at present, 4484–4488——Reasons for low rate of wages, 4489–4491——Expense of throwing latterly paid out of capital, 4492—— Importation of thrown silk decreasing at present, 4493–4501.

Trade at present improving, but will not continue, 4502——How the importation of manufactured goods affects the throwster, 4503, 4504——Bad state of silk manufacturers at present, and how affected by large houses purchasing under prime cost, 4505–4515 ——How far short credit and bad profits beneficial to the consumer, 4516–4525—— Trade has not flourished since fair profits ceased to be obtained, 4526——How far a few large buyers depress the market, 4527——In the event of failures, actions are brought against those houses purchasing under prime cost, 4528–4534——Injury done to manufacturers by those houses, 4535——How far those houses operate to continue a man in insolvency, 4536–4542——Compromises between creditors and those houses, 4543–4545 ——How far trade in a better state at present, 4546–4551——Credit and discount at present allowed, 4552–4565——Plan of guarantee pursued by brokers and per centage thereon, 4566–4580——Effect of the Berlin and Milan decrees upon the silk trade, 4581–4588——Inconvenience of being dependent upon Italy for silk, 4589——Necessity for protecting the throwing trade, 4590, 4591——Prohibition the only remedy for the present distress, 4592, 4601——Reason why raw silk from Piedmont prohibited, 4593– 4596——France prohibits the export of all silk except manufactured, 4597——Importance to obtain French raw silk, 4598–4600——Good effect of prohibition, 4602–4605 ——Benefits of high duties, 4606–4610——How far prohibition would stop smuggling, 4611–4622——Italian silk for manufacture equally good as the French raw, if that cannot be obtained, 4623–4634, 4639——Advantage to the French manufacturer from the cheapness of the article he uses, 4629, 4635–4637, 4655–4658——At what period thrown silk sold at a less price than raw, 4640, 4641——Italian silk can be as well thrown in England as in Italy, 4642, 4643, 4645——Approximation of prices, 4644——Improvements in silk throwing, 4646–4650——No improvement in quality of Bengal silk, 4651 ——Some good China silk, 4652——Importation of waste, and in what state exported, 4653, 4654.

(Second Examination.)  Examination upon job houses who have had actions brought against them, and compromises made between them and creditors, with witness declining to mention their names, 12669–12678.

*Bandannas.*  No smuggling bandannas at present, premium thereon formerly paid, *Clay* 6879–6888; *Bottrell* 7820–7825——Effect of removal of prohibition upon East India bandannas upon increasing the manufacture of English, *Dillon* 7733–7736——Duty thereon, *Bottrell* 7820–7825——Examination upon importation of India bandannas, duties thereon, and alterations necessary therein, *Brocklehurst* 11466–11471——Exportation of British and India bandannas, 1829–1832, *Brocklehurst* 11535–11538.

*Bank of England.*  Unsteadiness of trade at Manchester caused by Bank circulation, *Royle* 3233–3238——Account of promissory notes and post bills of the Bank in circulation every week, from 10th April 1830 to 7th January 1832, *Royle* 3235.
  See also *Currency.*

*Basle.*  State of the ribbon trade at Basle, and method of conducting it, to what countries exported, and proportions, *Bowring* 9119.

*Beals, Joseph* (Analysis of his Evidence). Landing surveyor in the Customs, 12424—— Their duty, and manner in which they check the landing waiters, 12425–12428——No recollection of finding a wrong weight put on goods, through fraud, on weighing, 12429– 12433——Landing waiters' stations changed periodically, 12434——Examination as to the quality of the goods, 12435, 12436——Method of weighing for the tare, 12437–12439 ——Possibility of fraud from connivance of officers, but great improbability thereof, 12440–12443——Improbability of collusion on the part of the landing waiter from the value of his situation, 12444–12448——Goods sometimes entered under the value, detained and sold, and fetch more than the value, 12449–12458——Sometimes they do not fetch their value, 12459——Reference to persons in the trade to ascertain value of articles out of the common course, 12460–12464——Goods generally valued very near the value, 12465–12467——Division of profit on goods seized, and consequent inducement for seizing, 12468–12471——Amount per cent. goods allowed to be entered under value, 12472–12475.

*Beck,* Mr.  See *Looms.*

*Beckwith, William* (Analysis of his Evidence). Silk manufacturer at Spital-square and Coggeshall, 11924–11926——Greatest number of looms employed, and on what description of goods, 11927, 11928——Importation of certain goods discontinued, from being able to purchase them cheaper in London, 11929–11933——Description and names of job-houses, and their method of transacting business, 11934 11939——Rate of smuggling, 11939–11942——Effect of lowering duties on manufactured goods on smuggling, 11943 ——Bad effects of importation by Leaf & Co. on certain goods manufacturing by witness, 11944, 11945——Description of goods on which looms at present employed upon, and
678.                                                 reduction

*Beckwith, William* (Analysis of his Evidence)—*continued.*

reduction in wages, 11946, 11947——Manner in which the French interfere with the export trade, 11948–11951——Manner of increasing the export trade by increasing the price of debentures, 11952–11957——Custom House officers have not been remunerated for the late seizure, and are imperfectly paid, 11958——Manner in which smuggling is carried on at the Custom House, 11959, 11960——Witness's opinion formerly in favour of free trade, and reasons for changing it; great disadvantage to the silk trade from last alterations, 11961–11965——Amount of duties that ought to be collected on plain and figured goods, 11966–11972.

(Second Examination.) Method to be adopted for preventing smuggling, 11973–11975——Witness's weavers at Coggeshall employed upon low works, their dishonesty and immorality from distress, 11976–11978——Alteration that should be made in the amount of drawback, 11979–11983——Amount of duty necessary for protection, and its effect upon increasing smuggling, 11984–11988.

(Third Examination.) Supposition of smuggling transactions by certain houses, from their selling goods in London lower than they could be imported for, 12362–12365, 12369–12372——Supposition that certain houses in the habit of passing figured goods for duty on plain, 12366, 12368.

(Fourth Examination.) Production of invoices of certain goods bought of Morrison & Co. showing how much per cent. goods bought cheaper than imported for, 12548–12551——Other transactions with Morrison & Co. of a similar nature, 12552–12557——Examination as to witness's having expressed regret for previously inferring that Morrison & Co. had not come properly by those goods, 12558–12580——Examination upon the correspondence that took place between witness and Morrison & Co.'s house relative to that transaction, 12581–12587——How far the goods would have been regularly passed though the Custom House although entered lower than their regular duty, 12588–12599—— Difference in the duty on goods imported by witness and sold to him by Morrison & Co., 12600, 12601——Supposition that one of Messrs. Morrison & Co.'s partners being at Paris, induced the manufacturer to supply their house instead of witness with goods he had ordered, 12602.——Witness did not charge Messrs. Morrison & Co.'s house with smuggling, 12603, 12604——Purchase of goods 30 per cent. lower than import price, proof of the manufacturer cheating witness, or that Morrison & Co. must have passed their goods lower than witness, 12605–12613——How much per pound weight witness's goods entered at; how far both parcels of goods being entered by weight would affect their value. 12614–12631.

*Bedworth Parish* :

Amount of the Poor Rates collected in the parish of Bedworth, with the number of rates, the rate of assessment and gross amount of property assessed, *App.* p. 927.

An Account of the disbursements of the parish of Bedworth, in the county of Warwick, for ten years, to the County Rates and the Poor, *App.* p. 929.

*Belgium.* See *Smuggling.*

*Bengal,* establishment of a filature, and reeling establishment there; cost price of silk raised thereat, and reason of the establishment not answering, *Grout* 10322–10324, 10331–10334——Comparison of quality of the Bengal silk reeled upon the Bengal and the Italian principle, *Grout* 10368.

*Bengal and China Silk,* consumption thereof, *Royle* 3204——Drawback acts as a bonus on the use of, *Royle* 3357, 3358——Increase in the importation of China silk, *Brockwell* 3567——Importation of China, Turkey and Bengal silk, *Brockwell* 3690–3693——For what Bengal silks are used in France, *Doxat* 4113, 4114——Importation of Bengal and China silk, *Doxat* 4278——China silks have improved, but not Bengal, *Doxat* 4302; *Banbury,* 4951, 4652——Purposes to which Bengal and China silk applied, and its comparative quality, *Stone* 6183–6198, 6203–6213, 6217, 6218, 6232–6234——How far Bengal silk affects the consumption of Italian, *Stone,* 6214–6217, 6221——Chinese silk interferes more with the Italian, *Stone* 6222——How far cheaper than the Italian, *Schwabe* 9867–9870——Difference as to substance between Bengal and Italian silk, *Grout* 10369——Improvement in the quality of Bengal silk, *Stone* 6219, 6220——Quality of East India silk has deteriorated, *Harter* 9309–9311——Increase in quantity and decrease in price of Chinese silk, *Stone* 6223, 6224——Importance of increasing the supply of China silk, *Stone* 6235——Its comparison with Bengal silk, *Stone* 6236, 6237——Loss to the French from importation of China silk, *Bowring* 9118——Imports of China silk and increase therein since the Company discontinued its importation, *Harter* 9295–9299, 9304——Price and quality of Bengal and China silk for making certain articles, *Schwabe* 9841–9845——Market for Bengal silk open to the French as well as the English, *Schwabe* 9865, 9866.

See also *East India Company. Importation,* 2.

*Bennett, Richard* (Analysis of his Evidence.) Silk manufacturer at Spitalfields, 10713–10715——Progressive increase of the plain branch previous to 1826, 10716, 10717——Bad consequences to trade from the admission of foreign goods, 10718–10720——Distress of weavers since, and bad moral consequences therefrom, 10721–10726——Rich plain and

*Bennett, Richard* (Analysis of his Evidence)—*continued.*

and fancy silks formerly made in Spitalfields, 10727——Not as many goods now made there as formerly, 10728——Increase of consumption of silk goods, 10729——Description of Manchester goods, and their prices, 10730, 10731——Competition with France, and not with Manchester, the cause of the distress in Spitalfields, 10732–10734——Every exertion made to meet foreign competition ; reduction of prices of goods, 10735–10737——Weavers do not work so well from working more hours, 10738——Weekly earnings of weavers formerly and at present, 10739——Reduction of wages and profits by alteration of duties in 1829, 10740——Smuggling not prevented thereby, 10741, 10742——Increase thereof, 10743——Further reduction would little benefit the manufacturer, and to ally ruin the throwster, 10744——Smuggling during prohibition was not injurious to trade, 10745, 10746—— Houses in the habit of smuggling now who would not have incurred risk under prohibition, 10747, 10748——Manner in which the French regulate the fashion and lead the market, 10749, 10750——Reduction of duty will not protect the market against jobs, 10751——Decline in the fancy trade ; number of looms formerly and at present, 10752–10755——Under prohibition, home competition would be a sufficient protection as to price and quality, 10756–10759.

Benefit to the plain branch and operatives by extending the fancy trade, 10760, 10761——Advantage of France from growth of silk and cheapness of labour, 10762–10764——Spitalfields manufacture might be extended by prohibition, certain duties on organzine and tram, and further protection against smuggling, 10765–10771, 10775——Entire prohibition most beneficial, but plain goods might be admitted under proper Custom House regulations, 10772——Influence of duties upon rate of smuggling, 10773, 10774——How prohibition would benefit trade, 10776, 10777——Small increase of price would not lessen consumption, 10778–10787——Necessity of commencing throwing, from diminished profits of manufacture, 10788, 10789——English thrown organzine better than foreign, 10790——Consumption of Piedmont organzine, 10791——Fossembrone the best Italian raw, 10792, 10793——Reduction of duty on thrown would be a greater inducement to Italians to send more thrown and less raw, 10794–10796—— Parties who grow and throw silk in Italy, 10797–10800——Silk thrown in Italy at a less price than in England, 10801–10805——Reducing price of throwing in England prevents its being properly done, and causes reduction of wages, 10805, 10806, 10808——No profit upon the throwing organzine at the present rate, 10807——Under a larger protecting duty silk would be better thrown than at present, 10809——Throwing has gone back for want of a remunerating price, 10810–10812.

*Berlin,* consumption of Silk therein, *Heath* 5693.
　　See also *Milan.*

*Bethnal Green.* See *Spitalfields District.*

*Black Goods.* Importation of black goods, *Ballance* 8587–8593——Consumption thereof, *Ballance* 8594, 8595—— Competition with France in black satins, their colours, *Ballance* 8596–8598——Price thereof, *Ballance* 8599–8601——Manufacturers who have been beaten out of the market in the fancy trade employ their weavers on black goods, *Ballance* 8605, 8606——Description of French black satins mostly in use, *Ballance* 8621–8623.
　　See also *Crape.*

*Black Ribbons.* See *Ribbons,* 2.

*Blonde.* Duty on blonde lace from France, *Menetrier* 8306——Amount smuggled, and rate of smuggling, *Menetrier* 8307–8313, 8331–8335——Duty that would prevent smuggling in blonde, *Menetrier* 8336, 8337.

*Board of Trade,* witness's letter to, *Royle* 3123——Cause of it, *Royle* 3263, 3438——Examination upon memorial to the Board of Trade, and petition to the House of Commons, as to the state of the Silk Trade at Manchester, *Royle* 3254–3262——Copy, memorial, *Royle* 3262——Same names signed to both memorial and petition, *Royle* 3426, 3427——Negociations with the Board of Trade, with regard to stamping goods and making smuggling a penal offence, and answer by the Board in the negative, *Wadden* 10034, 10035——Witness's application to the Board of Trade in 1829 for reduction of duty on foreign thrown silk, *Graham* 12769–12772, 12776–12778, 12780.
　　See also *Duty on Importation. Smuggling.*

*Bolter, Robert* (Analysis of his Evidence.) Impossibility of earning a livelihood in Spitalfields at present, 11000——Average wages, 11001——Government have not protected the trade as they were bound to do, 11002——Injury to workmen and shopkeepers in Spitalfields from repeal of prohibitory laws, 11003——Relief would be given by prohibition, punishing the smuggler severely, or by putting duties under Excise, 11004——Difference in wages in 1769 and at present, 11005–11007——Difficulty of weavers obtaining work in other branches after serving an apprenticeship, 11008.

*Bombazines,* decrease in the importation of certain silk used in the manufacture thereof, *Heath* 5696–5703.
　　See also *Norwich.*

*Bottrell,*

*Bottrell, Richard* (Analysis of his Evidence.)   Smuggling not carried on to a greater extent now than formerly, and in different goods, 7753-7755, 7945-7948——Expense of smuggling previous to 1826, 7756, 7773——Method of conducting smuggling prior to 1826, great profit thereon, and who were purchasers, 7757-7765——Quantities of smuggled goods, by whom bought, and amount of seizures, 7766-7772, 7774——Present method of smuggling from France, 7775, 7776——Seizures, 1816-1826, 7777——Not so easy to dispose of smuggled goods now as during the prohibition, but less risk in keeping them, 7778-7783, 7807——Greater variety of French goods now than during prohibition, 7784-7786, 7808——More gauze ribbons smuggled in 1830 and 1831 than paid duty, 7787——Reason of diminution in the rate of smuggling, 7788, 7789——How close a vessel could approach the shore formerly and at present with smuggled goods, without seizure, 7790, 7791——Further examination upon the profits and risk of smuggling formerly, 7792-7800——Comparison of present and former rate of smuggling, 7801-7811—— How far reduction of duty would decrease smuggling, 7813, 7814——Necessity for foreign goods being examined at one place and subject to a greater check, 7815, 7816 ——Proportionate value of French broad silks smuggled now and before 1826, 7817—— Of ribbons now smuggled, 7818, 7819——No smuggling in bandannas at present, duty on them, 7820-7825——Fewer persons concerned in smuggling now from diminution of profits, 7826-7828——Reduction in price and quality of French goods since 1826, 7829, 7830——Very little thrown silk smuggled prior to 1826, 7831, 7832——Preventive service only stopped smuggling for a time, 7833, 7834——How far smuggling would be carried on if duty reduced, 7835-7840——No smuggling in cambrics; duty thereon, 7841, 7842——Sea voyage too long to smuggle velvets from Germany, 7843——Silks are not smuggled from Belgium or Holland, 7844——Manner in which communication for smuggling is carried on between Dover and Calais, 7844-7846——Small encouragement to King's sailors to effect seizures; small amounts received by them, 7846—— Greater risk in inland carriage than sea voyage, 7847——Goods that were formerly, but are not now smuggled, 7848——Effect of repeal of prohibitory laws upon the French coast, 7849——Quantity of smuggled goods of not so much consequence as the low price at which they are jobbed, 7850.

Large quantities of English goods smuggled into France through Belgium; description of them, and expense attending it, 7851-7857——Low rate of profit upon smuggling has diminished it; how far it would be renewed if prohibition revived, 7858-7864—— Suggestions of regulations and duties for the prevention of smuggling, 7865, 7866, 7967 ——Manner in which goods have been passed at the Custom House lower than at their proper rate of duty, 7867-7869, 7882——Necessity for inspector at the Custom House being in communication with manufacturers to ascertain the value of goods, 7870-7878 ——Reason of taste and design being in favour of France, 7879, 7880——Comparison of advantages between France and England, both in legal and illegal trade, 7881—— Variation in duty on plain silks, 7883——Examination upon the qualities of certain gauze ribbons exhibited to the Committee, to show amount of duty between French and English, 7884-7888——Description of goods seized from Messrs. Leaf's, 7889-7892—— Small amount of seizures this year, 7893——Greater encouragement to smuggle under high duties, 7894——No advantage in smuggling paying shillings for francs, rate of exchange thereby, 7895——Increase of silk manufacture in Russia since 1820, 7896, 7897——Increase of duties upon importation into Russia, 7898-7900——How profits upon smuggling divided, 7901, 7902——Comparison of wages between France and England, 7903-7907——Articles the French at present employed upon, and for what market intended, 7908-7912——French crapes do not come into competition with Spitalfields manufacture, 7913-7916——Broad goods of France come into competition with Spitalfields, 7917-7920——Only rich French goods ordered for the English market, 7921——Description of goods sent by France into Germany, 7922——Rise in the price of French organzine from small stocks on hand, 7922, 7923.

Extent of silk manufacture of France; importation, growth and number of looms, 7924-7926——Origin of the disturbances at Lyons about wages, 7927, 7928——Did not extend to St. Etienne, 7927——Bad state of the weavers at St. Etienne, and from what causes, 7930-7934——Advantages of stamping goods to prevent smuggling, 7935—— Hours of attendance of the Commissioners of Customs, 7936, 7937——How far certain Custom House officers are open to bribery from the amount and manner of paying their salaries, 7938, 7939——Necessity for silks paying duty at one place, 7940, 7941—— Certificate of British Consul should be sent with silks imported into England, 7942—— Method by which silks might be stamped without risk of forgery; diagrams of four seals for that purpose, 7943-7944——Duty should be levied both by *ad valorem* and by weight, 7949——How far prohibition would protect British manufacture, 7950——How far English manufactures improved since French goods imported, 7951, 7954-7956—— Dissatisfaction among the Custom House officers from not being remunerated properly, 7952, 7953——Losses upon importation of China crapes from their being superseded by the French, and successfully imitated by the English, 7957-7959——Increase in the glove trade since 1826, 7960, 7961——Upon what fashion depends, 7962-7964——Artisans in most countries in a worse situation than formerly, 7965——Spitalfields manufacturer has rivals both at Manchester and Lyons, 7966——Temptations to Custom House officers from badness of pay and only occasional employment, 7968-7970——Increase of import duties into Prussia, 7971.

*Bouillon,*

*Bouillon, Francis Felix* (Analysis of his Evidence). Dealer in foreign silk goods, 10152–10157——More fancy than plain goods sold this year, 10158–10161——Reason for not dealing in British goods, 10162–10167——English plain goods come into the market as cheap as the French, 10168–10170——Gauze ribbons a great deal superior to the English, 10171——Amount of French goods sold per annum, 10172–10175——Purchases in France in plain goods have been latterly reduced, 10176–10179——Duty on importation, 10180, 10181——Difficulties in the way of stamping, 10182–10185——Increasing the duty on gauzes would prevent jobbing, 10186–10189——Duty sufficient on satin and sarsnet ribbons, 10190–10194, 10195——Extent of the manufacture of ribbons by certain houses in France, 10191–10193——Extent of smuggling, 10196–10201——Facilities less for receiving smuggled goods under a prohibition than at present, 10202, 10203——Punishment instead of fine must be used to prevent smuggling, 10207–10209——Whether smuggling not carried on to a greater extent under prohibition than at present, difficulties in the way of it, 10210–10217——Under prohibition, French patterns would be obtained and manufactured by English manufacturers, 10218, 10219——Certain plain goods made in this country from French patterns cheaper than in France, 10220–10226——Goods are jobbed cheaper after the fashion is over, 10227——English broad silks are prohibited in France, 10229——French Custom House regulations prevent smuggling, 10230, 10231——Alterations might be made in English Customs regulations, 10232, 10233——Proportion of English sales by witness's house annually, 10234, 10235.

*Bounties.* Additional bounties on exportation by Act 59 Geo. 3, c. 112, *Hume* 60——Amount of bounty and drawback paid in the United Kingdom on British manufactured silk goods exported, *Hume* 64——Manner in which drawback and duties affect different branches of the silk trade, *Hume* 92–99——How far drawback acts as a bounty on exportation, *Hume* 103–112——How far duty and drawback is a tax upon one manufacturing district for the benefit of another, *Hume* 113-119.
See also *Drawback.*

*Bowring, John,* LL. D. (Analysis of his Evidence). Proportion of labour to the cost of production between goods imported into France and England from each other, 8723——Means by which witness obtained information as to the state and condition of the silk trade in France, 8724–8729——Disadvantages under which the French silk trade is suffering at present, 8730, 8769–8771——Importations into and exportations from France of raw and thrown silk, 1825–1831, 8731——Account of the weight of silk imported for the consumption of France, 1820–1831, 8735——Account of the value of silk imported for consumption of France, 1820–1831, 8735——Account of the value of raw silks, all sorts, imported into France from the year 7 to the year 1806, and of the quantities and value, 1815-1819, 8735——Report of the importations of raw and thrown silks, and of the duties levied 1825–1830, reduced to English weights and measures, 8736——Ports of exportation from France and quantities of foreign silks exported, 1828–1830, 8736——Extent of consumption of French silk, 8737–8739——Superiority of French silk at Cevennes, and cost thereof, 8740, 8741——Annual production thereof, 8742, 8743——Value of silks in France, shown by price current, 8744——Production of French silk increasing, 8745——Method of the silk production and manufacture, from its earliest stage, 8745——Price of silk of native manufacture, and how far on the decline, 8746–8749——Price of cocoons and raw silk of Cevennes, 1822–1831, 8749.

Method taken in France to ascertain the quality and weight of silk, 8750–8752 —— French Government intend to allow the exportation of raw silk, 8753, 8754——Advantage to France from their superior taste, 8755–8758——Extent of protection to the French silk trade, 8759——Importation of foreign manufactured silks into France, and how far beneficial to it, 8760–8766——History of the invention of the Jacquard machine, 8767——Also, of the introduction of the bar loom, 8768——Improvements that have taken place in English silk manufacture since 1825, and fear of the French from English competition, 8772–8777——Importation of English manufactured silks into France, 8778–8787—— Superiority assigned to French goods is not through prejudice, 8788——Account of silk manufactures exported from France, 1828–1830, 8789, 8790——Mode of valuation, 8791, 8792——Increase of smuggling from France, 8793——Imports of manufactured silk to England, 1818–1824, 8793——Fluctuations in the silk trade at Lyons, 8794–8796——Number of looms employed therein at different periods, 8796–8798——Quantities of silk imported from foreign countries which have entered the bonding warehouses of Lyons, 1822–1832, showing quantities entered for home consumption, and exported, 8799——Establishment of La Condition, for ascertaining the weight and quality of silk, 8800, 8801—— Statement of the fluctuations in the price of silks in the market of Lyons, 1822–1832, 8802, 8803——Cause of the fall in the number of looms at Lyons in 1789, 8804——Quantity of foreign silk sold in the Lyonese market for 10 years, 8804——Description of handkerchiefs exported from France to England, 8805—— Reasons for superiority of French taste, particularly from the establishment of schools of art and weaving schools, and encouragement given to talent, 8806–8825.

(Second Examination.) National taste in France for works of art encouraged by all public works of art being open to public inspection; other branches of art in which France excels England, 8826–8832——Weight of silk submitted to La Condition, 1806–1820, 8833——Proportion of silk sent to La Condition and sold without, 8834, 8835——

Modifications

*Bowring, John,* LL. D. (Analysis of his Evidence)—*continued.*

Modifications about to be made in the tests applied by La Condition, 8836——To what improvement in English silk manufacture attributed by the French, 8837–8839—— Operation of l'Ecole de Tissage, specimens of their work and prizes given therefor, 8840– 8848——Means of preserving the rights of patents through the establishment of the Conseil des Prud'hommes, 8849–8853, 8869–8871——Constitution of the Conseil des Prud'hommes, their sittings and duties, 8854–8868, 8872——Price of throwing silk in France, 8873–8878——Absence of waste does not depend on its being thrown directly after being reeled, 8879, 8880——Wages to reelers and persons in throwing, 8881–8883 ——Prices paid for dyeing, 8884——Frauds by French dyers and weavers, 8885—— Comparison of superiority between English and French as to dyeing, 8886–8895—— Professional chemists in France, 8889, 8890, 8896——Disadvantage from the French being prevented getting their drugs from England, 8897–8899——Wages paid for wind- ing, 8900, 8901——Tariff of weavers' wages at Lyons, 8902–8904——Tariff not obli- gatory, riots in November 1831, from endeavouring to make it so, 8905–8908—— Manner in which the Conseil des Prud'hommes settle disputes as to wages, 8909–8911 ——Means by which riots put an end to, by removal of weavers, 8912–8915——Manner of their removal, 8920–8922——Average production of weavers per day at Lyons, 8916 ——Hours of labour of weavers in Lyons, 8917–8919——Fluctuation in the demand for labour at Lyons, 8923, 8924——System of work pursued by the weavers, their wages and cost of living, 8925–8928——Amount paid by the Lyonese weaver for taxes, 8929—— Communications from two weavers relative to the method of living; hours of labour, wages, &c. of weavers at Lyons, 8930 ——Saving banks have little influence, 8931.

New poor association among labourers, for their protection, 8932, 8933——Rate of wages, and their operation upon the price of goods at Lyons, 8934–8938——Profit and loss to a Lyonese manufacturer, their disadvantages from foreign competition, 8940–8944 ——Local taxation of Lyons, 8945–8947——Expense of changing patterns, and disputes between masters and weavers thereupon, and how affected by order trade, 8948–8958—— Change of opinion in France with regard to its commercial relations with England, 8959, 8260——Facilities for ascertaining the state of the trade of St. Etienne, 8961–8963—— Increase of the ribbon trade there, 8964, 8965, 8969, 8970——Migration of trade between Lyons and St. Etienne, 8966——How far establishment of la Condition exists at St. Etienne, 8967——Artists employed there, 8968——Prices of silk there, 8971——Pro- portion of foreign silk used there, 8972——Nature and price of marabout silk, and advan- tages of the French thereby, 8973–8977, 8979–8981, 8989——Introduction of the bar loom into St. Etienne, 8978——How far improvements therein, 8982–8984——Compari- son of prices of warping and dyeing between Lyons and St. Etienne, 8985–8988—— Number of ribbon manufacturers at St. Etienne, 8990——Daily produce of ribbons, 8990, 8993——Looms are not all of the same sort, 8991——Ribbon weavers at St. Etienne district are also agricultural labourers, 8991, 8992.

(Third Examination.)   Description of looms employed at St. Etienne, 8994–8996—— Number and description of ribbon looms employed at Lyons, 8997——Cause of the intro- duction of the ribbon trade at Lyons, 8998——Wages of weavers at St. Etienne, 8999– 9001——St. Etienne manufacturers do not export on their own account, 9002—— Examination upon the proportions of labour, raw material and cost of manufacture at St. Etienne, 9003–9007——Prices of ribbon weaving per piece at Lyons, and number of pieces manufactured, 9008–9015——The like at St. Etienne, 9016–9020——Proportion of different classes of ribbons manufactured at St. Etienne, 9021, 9022——Duties on importation of foreign ribbons into France, 9023——Benefits to France of foreign com- petition, 9024–9028——Social condition of the St. Etienne weavers, 9029——Decreased consumption in France, and increased export, 9030–9032——How St. Chamond is con- nected with St. Etienne, 9033——Conseil des Prud'hommes at St. Etienne less popularly constituted than at Lyons; of what it consists, 9034——Nature of the tax on patents, 9035, 9036, 9043——Table of the width of French ribbons, 9037——Population of St. Etienne, and number connected with the silk trade, 9038, 9039.

Population of France rated to the land tax, 9040——Manufacturer must take out a licence to vote, 9041——Amount of octroi, and manner in which it depends upon the population, 9042, 9045–9051——Advantages of the Swiss over the French in ribbon manufacture, 9052–9056, 9065–9068——Calculation of expenses and earnings of French weavers, 9057, 9058——Where silk thrown, and its conveyance to St. Etienne, 9059– 9061——Description of diet of weavers, 9062–9064——Population, and state of trade at Nismes, 9069–9075——Patterns handed in of sarsnets from Avignon, 9076–9078—— Production of raw silk in the Vaucluse department, 9079——Improvements in English manufacture shut out the smuggling trade from Avignon, 9079, 9080, 9111, 9112—— Consumption of silk, and prices in the Vaucluse department, 9081——Increase in the cultivation of silk in the Vaucluse department, 9083–9085——How far French growers throw their own silk, 9086——Price of reeling and labour, 9087–9090——Men employed in throwing, women and children in reeling, hours of labour, 9093, 9094——Improved manner of rearing the worm makes the employment more healthy, 9095——Size of deniers, 9092–9097——Manner in which the silk is sold, 9098, 9104——Superiority of English thrown silk over French, 9105——Price paid for winding and warping at Avig- non, 9106——Food, clothing and lodging of labourers, 9107–9109——Number of looms at Avignon, 9110——Hours of labour, earnings and general condition of weavers at
Avignon,

*Bowring, John,* LL. D. (Analysis of his Evidence)—*continued.*

Avignon, 9111–9113——Their opinion as to competition with foreign markets, 9114——
Both France and England would be benefited by the export of French raw silk, 9115, 9116
——How far foreign silk used at Avignon, 9117——Loss to the French upon importa-
tion of China silk, 9118.

(Fourth Examination.)  State of the ribbon trade at Basle, and mode of conducting it;
to what countries exported, and proportions, 9119——Effect of the introduction of French
silk goods into England upon French manufactures, 9120——Goods that were smuggled
into England previous to 1826 that have ceased since, 9121——English demand is for
articles of taste, 9122——Official value of silks exported from France, 9123–9126 ——
Analysis of the manner in which the different quantities of French silks, plain and figured,
are distributed in foreign countries, 9127——The like of crapes, 9128——The like of
ribbons, 9129——Examination upon the foregoing statements, 9130–9133——Qualities
of the different French goods taken by England, 1825, 1828 and 1831, 9134——Relative
position of the English and French manufactures in the United States, 9135——Export
of manufactured silks from France to England, 1818–1830, 9137, 9138——Increase of
smuggling, 9138, 9139——Institution of a commission in France for considering its relations with this country, 9141, 9142——Disadvantages of prohibition by increasing
smuggling, 9143——Smuggling in fewer hands than under prohibition, and how it places
the manufacturer in a worse situation, 9144–9148 ——Greater difficulty in smuggling into
France, and greater severity of the Custom House and municipal regulations, 9149, 9150
——Manner in which the smuggler in France is considered a public benefactor, 9151–
9153——How far expectation realized, that upon changing prohibition for duties, odium
would attach to the smuggler, 9154–9158——Profits of the higher class of smugglers,
great extent of smuggling, and large capital employed therein, 9159–9163, 9170——
Better feelings of the people towards smugglers according to the greater risk they run,
9164–9165——How far prohibition would change the smugglers from a few large to a
great many small ones, 9166–9168.

Premium of smuggling higher into France than England, 9169——Difference in the
proportion of labour between English and French goods, 9170——Smuggling cotton twist
into France in the same manner as silk into England, 9174——Question of displacing
labour should be looked at with a view to the manufacture of the country, and not the silk
manufacture only, 9172–9174——Further examination as to the smuggler being a public
benefactor, and as to the exchange of exports between France and England of silk and
cotton, 9175, 9176——Amount of importation of cotton twist into France, 9177——
Amount of duty that would decrease smuggling, 9178——Protection to the silk manufacturer illusory, 9179——Silk manufacture would increase by removing all protection,
9180——Great expense to France of its protection of its cotton twist trade, without any
effect, 9181, 9185, 9186——Advantages of France and England from admitting French
goods at a low duty and obtaining the raw material, 9182–9184——How far price of
French silk regulated by the price paid for Italian silk, 9187——Reduction of duty on
thrown would place English manufacturer on equal footing with the French, 9188——
If silk trade has increased there is no displacement of labour, 9189, 9190.

Balance of trade between England and France against England, 9191——Articles
smuggled into France, 9192——Their Custom House regulations, 9193——French
Custom revenues, 9194——Increasing number of revenue officers gives a greater
chance for smuggling, 9195——Bounty and drawback on exportation of silk from France
rejected by the Council of Commerce, 9196, 9197——Disadvantages of the protective
system to France, 9198, 9199——Natural advantages of France for producing fine goods
and of England for coarser, 9200, 9201 ——Not profitable to cultivate the mulberry tree
in this country, 9202, 9203——Disadvantages of protective interest to shipping trade of
France by increasing the duties on iron, 9204, 9205——How smuggling would be increased under prohibition, 9206–9209——Small amount of smuggling in gloves, 9210——
Duty that might be collected therein, 9211——Advantages of an *ad valorem* duty on
importation, 9212——Plan of the Americans with regard to invoices sent with their goods
from France, 9213——How much above their proper rate duties are levied in England,
9214——Calculation of loss to England by prohibition of French silks, 9215——Reducing duty on importation will destroy smuggling, 9216, 9217——Encouragement
given by receiver of goods cannot be checked, 9218–9221——Seizure and protection
therefrom of English goods in France, 9222, 9223.

(Fifth Examination.)  Importations between France and England, and proportion of
labour in the manufactures of each, 9616–9626 ——Importations of silk previous to and
since removal of prohibition, 9627–9630——How far France has obtained a foreign
trade in silks from its home trade being unprotected, 9631, 9632——How far the advantages of France act as a protection, 9633–9635——Increase and decrease of Lyons and
St. Etienne silk trades, 9636–9642——How far the importation of silk manufactured
goods from France tends to displace English labour, 9643–9650——Improvement in
quality of French and Italian raw and French manufactured silks imported since removal
of prohibition, 9651–9653——Proportion of silk manufactured goods imported in 1825
that were warehoused against the opening the ports in 1826, 9654, 9655——Comparison
of French and English labour as regards local taxation, 9656, 9657——As regards national
taxation, 9658–9661——Taxes on iron and machinery for building mills dearer in France
than England, 9662–9664, 9670–9672——Advantage of Switzerland over France as to

*Bowring, John,* LL. D. (Analysis of his Evidence)—*continued.*

taxation of machinery, 9665–9669——Reasons for the French not importing silk from Italy as well as the Swiss, 9673, 9674——No brokerage upon receiving silk direct from the foreign producer, 9675, 9676——How far pillage of silk greater at Lyons than in other countries, 9677, 9678——Rate of interest in France, 9679, 9680——Complaint in Lyons of England supplying the American market, 9681–9683——How far English manufactures have improved from competition with France, 9684–9688——Superiority of the French and inferiority of English silk manufactures, and disadvantages of prohibiting importation of French manufactures, 9689–9706——Increase of consumption of silk in England, 1821–1825, 9707, 9708.

Comparison of importations, 1814–1825, 9708–9711——Improvement in ribbon looms in Lyons, 9712–9715——Price of marabout in France and how manufactured, 9716–9718——Difference in prices of certain silks and ribbons, 9719——Whether sarsnets manufactured at Avignon are worn now, 9720, 9721——State of trade at Nismes, without export trade from being protected, 9722–9725——Competition between France and England, and advantages and disadvantages with respect to fine and coarse goods, 9726–9736——State of trade in certain districts in France, 9737–9744——Loss of capital in mills from insufficient protection, 9745–9747——State of the cotton trade in England, and how far it has prospered from being the least protected, 9748–9756——Further examination as to importation between France and England, 9757–9765——How far English goods exposed in the shop windows in France, 9766, 9767——Preference in favour of French goods is from their superiority, and not prejudice, 9768——Increase in exportation of English silk goods in certain years from 1821, 9769——Further examination as to the decline or increase of English labour from importations from France, 9770–9774——Relative prices of French and Italian silk in France, 9775–9778——Advances by the French and English merchants to the Piedmont growers, 9780–9782——Comparison of distress in the silk and other trades in France, 9783–9787——How far export of coarse silks to France in consequence of the drawback, 9788——Value of Jacquards in England and France, 9789–9795——Expense of changing patterns in France and England, 9797–9802——Destination of weavers sent away from Lyons, 9803——Advantage of the English weaver over the French from poors-rates, 9804, 9805——Comparison of throwing between France and England, with improvement of the latter from improved machinery, 9806–9815——Prices of provisions in France and England, 9816, 9817——State of trade at St. Etienne, and how far its superiority to be attributed to the bar loom, 9818–9821——Price of smuggling and its connection with duties, 9822–9824——Character of witness's evidence, and from what sources obtained, 9825–9827.

(Sixth Examination.)  Distinction conferred by the French Government for superior skill in silk manufacture, 9936——Extract from a letter showing the fear of the French manufacturers that the Committee will recommend the prohibition of their manufactures, 9937–9940——Further examination upon the produce of silk manufactures and consumption and number of looms in France, 9941–9960.

(Seventh Examination.)  Further examination upon the value of silk manufactures and consumption in France, and of cost for labour, materials, &c., 10027–10029——Duties paid in France on foreign manufactured silks entered for home consumption, 1828–1830; Duties received in France on the export of French silk manufactures to foreign countries, 1828–1830, 10029——Backwardness of the throwing and reeling establishments in France. 10029.

*Bribery.*  See *Custom House.*

*Bridges, William* (Analysis of his Evidence.)  Silk manufacturer at Spitalfields in the fancy trade, 10370–10374——Flourishing state of the silk trade, and description of goods made before opening the Ports in 1826, 10375–10378, 10426, 10439, 10440——Number of looms employed, with proportion on figured and proportion on plain goods, 10379–10381——Goods manufactured by witness worn by the Royal Family, 10382——Patterns drawn by English artists, 10383——No want of taste and skill on the part of the English manufacturer, 10384——Number of Jacquard looms employed upon their introduction, 10384–10388——How far reduction of wages thereby, 10389, 10390——Description of goods made under present wages, 10391–10393——Reduction of looms from the gauze trade having left the country, 10394——Comparison of witness's and Mr. Fulton's goods, 10395–10403——Import of gauzes from France, and manner in which they interfere with the English trade, 10404–10421——Goods made from orders formerly, 10424, 10425——Preference by witness in favour of English thrown silk, and value thereof, 10427–10436——Necessity for encouraging the importation of good raw silk, 10437, 10438——Decrease of the fancy trade from the importation of foreign goods, 10441–10449, 10463–10468, 10500–10509——Advantages to the French that make their goods cheaper, 10450–10452——Disadvantages of removing duty on importation of thrown, and as to the French obtaining their raws cheaper than the English, 10453–10462, 10493.

Pattern of the Queen's coronation dress, and dresses for drawing-rooms, manufactured by witness, and loss thereby, through the importation of foreign goods, 10469–10475——Facility for disposing of plain and fancy goods at a loss, 10476–10483——Sometimes temporary employment for looms when French goods scarce, 10484–10486——Prohibition the

*Bridges, William* (Analysis of his Evidence)—*continued.*

tion the only means of restoring the trade, 10487, 10488——Advance of wages that would satisfy the operatives, 10489–10491——Pence not an object in price to the consumer of figured goods, 10492——Improvements in manufacture attributed to the Jacquard looms, previous to and not since the opening the Ports, 10494–10496——Manchester has not taken fancy trade from Spitalfields, 10497, 10498——England not on a fair footing with France, 10499——Composition of the Trade Committee ; how far they are interested in throwing, 10510–10515——They have not interfered with the evidence to be given before this Committee, 10516–10528——Different views of silk manufacturers as to importation of French goods, 10529, 10530——Not large manufacturers, who are anxious for removing duty on thrown silks, 10531–10533——No fear of home competition, if foreigner kept out, 10534–10540.

*Broad Silk.* See *Silk,* IV. *Spitalfields Trade.*

*Brocklehurst, John,* jun. (Analysis of his Evidence.) Silk manufacturer at Macclesfield, 11320–11322——Throwsters' trade increasing before 1826, 11323——Good condition of the operatives at that period, 11324——Ruin of throwing interests since 1826, 11325 ——Number of persons employed in the throwing mills at Macclesfield, 1824–1832, 11326–11328——Number of spindles at work 1824–1832, 11329–11332——Hours of work in silk mills, 11333——Their wages 1824–1832, 11334–11336——Statement of the number of spindles, and mill people and wages, at Macclesfield, 1824, 1828, 1831, 11336 ——Subsistence of hands out of employment, 11337——Annual consumption of silk prior to and since 1826, showing decreased consumption in the latter period, 11338—— Increase of consumption of silk goods but for interference of the French, 11339——Price of silk not lower after repeal of duties in 1824, 11340, 11341——No stocks of English silks on hand when the French were admitted, 11342–11345——Yearly decline of trade since 1826, 11346——Progressive increase from 1808–1826, 11347–11349——Ministers expected the alteration would place the silk trade on a level with the cotton trade, 11350 ——If consumption of silk has increased since 1826, the goods manufactured have been of an inferior quality, 11352–11354——Advance in the silk trade of the continent over that of England, 11355——Decreased amount of wages upon manufacture of a larger quantity of silk, 11356, 11357——Decrease in consumption of Italian raw, 1824–1831, 11357——Increase of looms at Lyons over England, 11357, 11358——Number of throwing mills in Macclesfield, and number erected, 1814–1824, and 1824–1832, 11359–11364—— Power thereof, 11365——Cost thereof, 11366——Mills and Machinery not convertible to other manufacture, 11367——Number of counties in England in which silk mills are established, 11368——Power of mills at Manchester, 11369, 11370.

Comparison of power and advantages of silk mills at Macclesfield and Manchester, 11371, 11372——Mills that are out of employment are, from throwing trade being transferred to Italy, and not from disadvantageous situations of mills, 11373–11380—— Scarcity of fine silk for throwing at present, 11381——Annual amount of poor rates at Macclesfield, 1821–1832, 11382, 11385——Number of families receiving relief, 1821– 1832, and reduction in the amount of allowance, 11383–11385——Average increase in weekly expenditure to the poor, 1832 over 1823, 11386——Statement of weekly payments to the casual and regular out poor of Macclesfield, 1832 and 1823, 11386——Weekly relief to casual poor, 1821–1831, 11387, 11388——Empty houses and houses not contributing to the poors' rate, 11389, 11390——Charge of overtrading against Macclesfield prior to 1826, unjust, 11391——Advertisement for increased hands at Macclesfield was only of a local and temporary nature, 11392, 11393——How increase of houses built in 1822 warranted, 11394——Desertion of houses show the state of the silk trade, 11395 ——Price of corn nearly the same, 11396——Distress of operatives, and bad moral effect therefrom, 11397–11402——Distressed state of the town of Macclesfield in consequence, 11403——Number of failures, 1814–1826, and since, and causes thereof, 11404–11408—— Difficulty of removing capital invested in machinery, or converting machinery to other purposes, 11409–11412——Deterioration in mill property, 11413–11418——Wages for throwing cannot be reduced lower, 11419, 11420——Cost of throwing, and amount of protection necessary for the British throwster, 11421–11423——Throwing trade given up from loss from foreign competition, 11424, 11425——Importance of the throwing trade, 11426–11430——Statement of decreased importation of Italian raw, and increased thrown, from reduction of duties, in 1829, 11431, 11432——Examination thereupon, 11433–11435——How the silk manufacture might be increased under proper duties, 11436–11442——Importation of foreign raw and thrown silk, 1827–1832, and effect of present duty thereon, 11443–11448—Tendency of low prices to degenerate the silk manufacture, 11449.

Statement of the leading articles made at Macclesfield, with rates of wages, 1821–1831, showing reduction therein, and consequent distress of weavers, 11450–11453——Progress of manufacture checked by interference from the Continent, 11454——How the silk trade would have improved under better protection, 11455——Description of goods made before and since 1826, and loss of trade since, 11456, 11457——Loss of time by weavers more now than formerly, 11458——They have no other employment when out of work, 11459——Distressed state of the Irish weavers, and the silk trade in Dublin, 11460–11462——Advantages from the East India Company's sales of silk, 11463–11465 ——Examination

678.

*Brocklehurst, John,* jun. (Analysis of his Evidence)—*continued.*

——Examination upon importation of India bandannas, duties thereon, and alterations necessary therein, 11466–11471——Manner in which the Company's imports of silk goods acts injuriously to the manufacturer and to themselves, 11472——Account of the profit and loss upon the sales of Bengal raw silk sold by the East India Company, 1816–1830, 11473——Their manufactured goods come into contact with their raws imported, 11474——State of raw silk in the East India Company's warehouses, 1829–1832, 11475——Quantity of silk refused at the Company's sales, 1831 and 1832, and causes thereof, 11476–11478——Duty that would effect, and advantages that would result from the Company importing raw material instead of manufactured goods, 11479–11484——Importation of English silks into France, 11485——No necessity for foreign competition as a stimulus to improvement of manufacture in England, shown by the production of certain patterns, 11485–11487——No want of taste, if trade properly protected, 11488–11491, 11500, 11501——Monopoly by France of the valuable branches which will eventually cause the loss of the silk trade, 11492——Obstacles in the way of the employment of power looms to broad silks, 11493–11499——Injury to trade by smuggling, and who are the promoters of it, 11502, 11503——Remedy therefor by imprisonment and hard labour, and stamping goods, 11504, 11505——No advantage in transferring silk trade to France in exchange for its taking our cotton yarn, 11506——Offers to witness to establish himself in the silk trade in the Netherlands, and state of the silk trade there, 11507–11518——Value of the British export trade, 1831, 11519——Advantage thereof, and state thereof, from alteration of the law, 11520, 11521——Effect of debentures thereon, 11522–11525——Manner in which the export trade might be made more profitable, 11526–11528——Proportion of exports between France and other parts of the world, 11529——Effect of debentures on throwsters and consumers, 11530, 11531——Why debenture not a tax on Spitalfields, 11532——Goods that are generally exported, 11534——British silk trade has no established markets abroad, 11535——Exportation of British and India bandannas, 1829–1832, 11535–11538——How far wages upon goods exported, paid by the parish, 11539–11542.

(Second Examination.) Wages of weavers, 1824–1831, showing greater quantity of silk worked up at reduced wages, 11543——Benefits that would be derived by the East India Company altering the description of the arrangement of their silks, 11544——Evils arising out of the alterations in the laws in 1824, 1826 and 1829, 11545–11550——Effect of the price of provisions, and corn laws upon the silk trade, 11551–11554——How far dealers capable of advising Government upon the state of the silk trade, 11555——Necessity for protection to obtain increase in the silk trade; tendency of low priced raws to increase it; increase in the cotton trade, and manner the silk trade might equally increase, 11556.

*Brockwell, Thomas* (Analysis of his Evidence.) Silk broker in London and Manchester, 3439–3447——No difference in the price per pound of throwing silk in Italy during the high duties, and at present, 3448–3453——Price in England does not regulate the price in Italy, 3454——Germany and her own people, the largest customers of Italy, 3456——France a large customer to the King of Sardinia, 3457——Quantity of silk produced in Italy, 3458, 3459——Proportion grown in Italy, 3460——England hitherto the largest customer for raw silk, 3462——Importation of Italian raw silk diminishing, 3463–3468——Increase of thrown silk imported, 3469, 3470——Reducing duty would cause Italy to throw more, 3471, 3472——Ruin of English throwsters will throw the trade more into the hands of Italy, 3472, 3473——Quantities of Italian raw and thrown silk imported into different countries, 3474–3476——Consumption of foreign thrown silk, 1828–1831, 3477–3482——Reduced duty on foreign trams, not a sufficient protection to the English throwster, 3483, 3484——Ruin to throwsters from the low prices of throwing Italian silk in England, 3485–3489——Failures of manufacturers and throwsters last year, 3490–3493——Interest of the manufacturer, that the throwster should gain instead of loose, 3494——Those manufacturers who want foreign silk without duty, have small vested interest in the silk trade, and would be ruined, 3495–3497——Who have the vested interests, 3498——Silk trade will flourish as the throwster is protected, 3499, 3500——Regulations that should be adopted to prohibit the importation of French and Swiss manufactured goods, or compel the French and Swiss to export their raw silk, 3501–3515.

Necessity for encouraging export trade, 3516, 3517——If French raws exported, and manufactured goods admitted, differences in the prices of labour might be afterwards regulated, 3518, 3519, 3525——Method of trade adopted by the French manufacturer, 3520–3524——Piedmont silk, the best thrown exported from Italy, 3526–3528——Greater proportion of the best quality of Piedmont silk exported to France than England, 3529–3532——Prices of Milan raw and thrown silk 1819–1831, 3533–3539——Difference in price to the Italian grower, between raw and thrown since 1819, 3540, 3541——Price of Italian thrown silk acts on that of English, 3542, 3543——Prices of throwing, 3544–3548——Difference of price that remunerates the Italian and that which will not remunerate the English throwster, 3549–3553——Italian would not send raw silk to England if he could not obtain a remunerating price for throwing it, 3554, 3555——Trade of Italy with England, France and Germany, 3556–3559——How far the price of raw silk can be maintained in England, 3560–3562——Capability of Italy to increase the

*Brockwell, Thomas* (Analysis of his Evidence)—*continued.*

the raw material is limited, and that of increasing thrown greater, 3563–3566——Increase in the importation of China silk, 3567.

(Second Examination.) How price of Italian thrown silk in the British market affected by that of British Italian thrown, 3568, 3569——Advantages possessed by the Italian throwster over the English, 3570–3572, 3681——Why the English have not similar advantages, 3573–7577——How the purchase of silk between Italy and England is carried on, 3578–3581, 3592–3594——How far price obtained regulates the sales, 3582–3584——Different qualities of Italian silk in the same bale, 3585, 3586——Advantage to the Italian therefrom, and from selecting silks not liable to waste, 3587–3591, 3683 ——Italians retain their best quality of silk themselves, 3595, 3596, 3682——Effect of reducing the duty on thrown silk on price and quantity of Italian raw silk, 3597–3600—— Average difference of price between Italian raw and thrown silk, 3601–3608——How far a remuneration to the Italian throwster, 3609–3614—— Different style of thrown silk in each country, 3616—— Importations of raw and thrown silks, 1824–1831, 3619——Average weight of a bale of silk, 3620–3626—— Importation and consumption of foreign thrown silk and duty, 1819–1831, 3627–3636——English mills can produce as good thrown silk as any other country, 3637–3642——Ruin of throwsters by reducing duty on foreign thrown, 3643——Prices of throwing in England, 3646–3650——Reasons why British throwster cannot compete with Italian, 3644, 3645, 3651–3654——Protection that should be given to English throwsters, 3655–3657——Expenses of throwing mills, 3658, 3669——Quality of Fossembrone silk, and its importation into this country, 3661–3667——How the importation of thrown silk has been checked, 3668–3675.

How far improvement has taken place in the quality of Italian raw silk imported, 3675–3679——Difference in the expense of throwing according to the quality of the silk, 3680——Difference in the price of raw and thrown silk if duty repealed, 3684–3686—— Greater distress to the operatives if duty taken off, 3687, 3688——Increasing duty would cause a greater supply of Italian raw silk, 3689——Importation of China, Turkey and Bengal silks, 3690–3693——Increase of waste silk, 3694, 3695——Necessity in the Manchester trade for the best Italian silks to mix with China, 3696–3698——Necessity of debentures for the export trade, 3699–3703——Process of exportation by debentures, 3704, 3705——Quantity of waste silk imported, and from whence, 1828–1831, 3706–3710——Inducement of debentures to increase certain branches of trade, 3711——Effect of duty upon the importation of foreign thrown silk, 3712–3716——Stock of silk in Italy low at present, 3717–3722.

*Brokers.* Plan of guarantee pursued by brokers, and per centage thereon, *Banbury* 4566–4580——Commission and brokerage, *Martin* 5458–5461 ; *Heath* 5711; *Hall* 6536–6538——They seldom guarantee, *Martin* 5490——Business of a silk broker, and sources of their information, *Stone* 6453–6458 ; and how far they purchase on their own account, *Heath* 5713–5720——Examination upon broker's commission ; sale, credit and discount upon silk sales, *Stone* 7015–7025——Extra commission for guaranteeing, *Heath* 5712 ——No brokerage upon receiving silk direct from the foreign producer, *Bowring* 9675, 9676.

See also *Discount.*

*Bronze.* Productions of the French in bronze have made their way in the same manner as their silk goods into all the markets of the world, *Bowring* 8830.

*Brunskill, William* (Analysis of his Evidence.) Distress of the ribbon trade caused by foreign competition, 121——Beneficial effects of prohibiting foreign ribbons, 122—— Difference in the causes of the distress in 1817 and at present, 123——Prohibition the only remedy for the distress, 124——French ribbons would be imported at 20 per cent. higher duty, 125–128——Same description are made at Coventry, 129——Rate of duty upon different description of ribbons, and upon what it depends, 130–133——Reason why an *ad valorem* duty would not answer, 134–136——Great increase of smuggling since the repeal of the prohibition, and reasons for it, 137–144——Methods of checking smuggling, 145, 146——Price of debentures, 147–149——Effect of lowering the present rate of duty to an amount that would prevent inducement to smuggle, 150——Present rate at which goods can be smuggled for, 151——Rate at which smuggled by Messrs. Leafs, 152–154——Method adopted by them, and amount paid those employed, 155–163——Not the same extent of stock prepared as formerly, the consumption at Coventry is much the same, but a commoner article, taking less labour, 164–170, 444–446—— Extent to which English manufacture has improved by the admission of French goods, 171–173——Comparison of skill in different branches with France, 174–178——Period of introduction of machinery, and where used, 179–188——Who would be benefited by increased price in the event of a return to the prohibitory system, 189–194, 486——Morals of the work people worse, from the poverty to which they are reduced, 195—— Distress of the Spitalfields' trade through foreign competition, 196–200——Extent to which the Spitalfields' trade is affected by the Manchester trade, 201–205——Demand for foreign plain goods so great, that they sell in preference to English goods of the same quality, and much cheaper, 206–224——Quantity of velvets imported from Germany, 225–229——Rate of duty thereon, 230–233——*Ad valorem* duty can be collected on heavy articles, but not on fancy articles, 234——Duties not sufficiently high for protection, 235——Spitalfields' trade would revive if prohibition granted, 236——Advantage

678.　　　　　　　　　　　　　　　　　　　　　　　　　　　　　to

*Brunskill, William* (Analysis of his Evidence)—*continued.*

to France by the use of machinery, 237, 238——In the event of prohibition there would be an increase of machinery in Coventry, 122, 289-241——Objection to power looms there, one destroyed, 242, 243, 245-247——Wages in France cheaper for fancy articles, 244——Particulars of the forming the list of prices for wages, and how they affect engine work and hand work, 248-268——In what the French manufacture excels the English, 269-272.

Ineffectual attempt to get the article at Coventry equal to that of the French, through the refusal of the work-people from the lowness of the wages, 273-316——English goods are cheaper than French goods can be imported for, 317-321——Cost of machinery a bar to its general introduction, 323 ——The similarity of wages for plain and fancy work at St. Etienne approach nearer than at Coventry, 324, 325——Effect of machinery in equalizing wages for different descriptions of work, 326-328——How much per cent. English goods are worse than French, and manner of making them equal, 329-331—— Different rates of wages, 332-338——Distress of the weavers, particularly the single-hand looms, number of looms unemployed, 339-342, 455, 456——Difference in quantity of work and wages of the engine loom and single hand, 343-348——Employment in the black ribbon trade, 349-353—— Raw article in France costs less than here, 354—— How far obtaining material cheaper would enable the giving better wages, and producing the article cheaper, 355-363——Prohibition more necessary than reducing the duty on foreign thrown silk, 364-366——Quantity of British and foreign thrown silk consumed at Coventry and Spitalfields, 367-370——For some purposes English thrown silk answers better than foreign, 371-373——No duty could protect the fancy branch, it being entirely governed by the French fashions, 374-377——Increase in the silk manufacture at Coventry has not been in proportion to the population, 378-382——Possibility of distinguishing between French and English manufactured goods, although difficult in some cases, 383-400 ——English dye their goods equally well with the French, 401-405 ——How far the distress of the Spitalfields' trade is to be attributed to competition with Manchester, 406-426——Difficulties the fancy trade have to deal with from the prevailing fashion in favour of foreign goods and a glutted market, 427-443——The smuggling which took place formerly on a small scale was beneficial, 447-450——How far reducing the duty on certain manufactured goods would relieve one party at the expense of another, 451-454.

Bad effects upon trade from the opening the Ports in 1824, 457-463——How far debentures assist in exportation, 464-468——How far the general use of cottons has interfered with the silk trade, 469, 470, 475-479——Small remuneration upon the exportation of silk, 471-474——Suspicion of smuggling for some time, but none found out till the case of Leaf's, 480-485——Rate of wages at Coventry, 487-492——English wages double those of foreign, 493, 494——Employment of the weavers till the foreigners found out the channels of trade, 495, 496——Effect of removing the protecting duty upon the price of thrown silk, 497-501——Effect of the duty on foreign silk in the price of ribbons, 502, 503 ——Preference given to foreign thrown silks over English, 504-511 —— Beneficial effect of taking off the duty on foreign thrown silk, and lowering that of manufactured silks, 512-514——Usual method of smuggling, 515-520——Gauzes formerly manufactured, and at present, 521——Rate of insurance in cases of smuggling, 523-530——Increase of smuggling since 1826, 531——Manufacturers who thought well of the alteration in 1826 that have changed their opinion since, and left the trade, 532-536——Proposition of a fine was the main cause of not being able to get the work-people to do the quantity of work required, 537-545——Description of foreign silk used at Spitalfields and Coventry in the manufacture, 546-551——Amount of duty that would be sufficient protection against smuggling plain goods, 552-556——Nothing but prohibition will answer for fancy articles, 557.

(Second Examination.) Amount of extra expenses in importing goods from France beyond what they would cost in England, 558-562——That amount is so much additional, but not a sufficient protection to the English manufacturer, 563-565——Amount per cent. the value of labour in England exceeds that of France, 566-575, 593-610—— Amount that per centage on labour bears to the value of the article, 576-578——Proportion of wages to the cost of the article at Coventry, 579-582——Amount per cent. the duty causes the English manufacturer to pay over the French manufacturer upon importation of Italian thrown silk, 583-592——Causes that have reduced the wages in Spitalfields, 611-622——Reasons for Spitalfields struggling against Manchester, 623-625—— Articles that are manufactured at Manchester, and their quality, 626-631, 637-639—— Importation of velvets from France, 632——And from Germany, 633——Importation of satins from France, 634, 635——Importation of velvets has increased, 640-642—— Method of manufacture of velvets at Elverfeldt and Crefeldt, 643-646——Certain ribbons made in England cannot be made equal to the French from their not allowing the material of which they are made to be exported, 647-654——In what cases French patterns are copied, 655-660——Reasons for Swiss ribbons not being imported to the same extent af formerly, 661-663——Duty thereon, and how collected, 664-668—— Causes of English fancy goods being worse than the French, 669——French raw silk superior to any other, 670-672——English manufacture of fancy articles will not equal the French from the cost of machinery preventing its use, 673-679——Reason for goods now manufacturing at Coventry being better than they usually are, 680-683.

Amount

*Brunskill, William* (Analysis of his Evidence)—*continued.*

　　Amount per cent. at which Leafs' smuggled their goods is only conjecture, 684, 685
——Prices obtained for French goods, 686-688——Time taken for preparing loom, and
expense of setting the pattern and manufacturing goods in imitation of French goods,
689, 690, 727-733——Quantity and description of foreign silk annually consumed in
Coventry, 691-702——Amount per cent. the protecting duty causes the Coventry manufacturer to pay more for his silk, 704-707——No increase or improvement in machinery from its cost, 708-712——Best method of preventing smuggling, 713-715——
Quality of different machinery, 716-719——Method of making purchases in France, 722-
726——Reason why prohibition the only protection for the fancy trade, 734-736——
Smuggling can never be entirely stopped but can be reduced to a sufficient extent to prevent injury, 737, 738——Patterns here are cheaper and as good as the French, but the
taste is in favour of the French, 739-746——Disadvantage to the English manufacturer
from keeping a stock on hand, 747-749——There were more orders for ribbons formerly
than at present, 750-753——Competition is that of fashion, 754——Large imports of
plain goods now, 755.

*Bruton*, increase of poor's rate at, *Ward* 3983.

# C.

*Caffi, Francesco,* (Analysis of his Evidence.)　Manner of buying coccons in Italy for
reeling, 7031-7036——Method of advances between the landlord and labourer, 7037-
7042——Period of reeling, and by whom done, 7043-7045——Expense of reeling and
weight of the silk, 7046-7057——Value in English money of the Italian livre, 7048-7056
——Expenses of throwing tram, with weight per lb. English, 7058-7066——The like for
throwing organzine, 7067-7071, 7087——Prices of throwing, and during what periods,
7072-7076——Charges for throwing more in Piedmont than Lombardy from its being
better done, caused by the raws not being allowed to be exported, 7077-7082——Attempts
to get exportation of raws prohibited from Lombardy, 7083-7086——Method of paying
operatives when throwing mills not at work, 7088-7092——Mills if worked all the year
could not throw all the silk produced in Italy, 7093-7095, 7108——Advances by throwsters to reelers, 7096-7099——Mills would work all the year if they could get a better
price for throwing, 7100-7105——Quantity of silk produced in Lombardy, and quantity
thrown, 7106 7112——Manner in which the crop of France affects the exports from Italy,
7113-7114——How far price of throwing remunerates the throwsters, 7115——Comparison of wages and profits in silk and other businesses, 7116, 7117——Manner in which
quantity of silk thrown or raised bears to other kinds of produce, 7118——Advantage to
the throwster in working the silk fresh from the cocoons, 7119-7121——Care required in
the cultivation of mulberry leaves, 7122-7124——Exports from Italy to different countries,
7125-7136——Premium for smuggling raw silk from Piedmont, 7137-7141—— Description of the silk, and for what purposes used, 7142-7145——Size of mills, their rents and
power, 7146-7150——Improvements in machinery, 7151, 7152——Improvement in the
quality of silk, 7153-7155.

　　Capital of mill-owners ; taxes and out-goings of mills, 7156-7159——Descriptions
of silk sent to different countries, 7160-7165——No profit in sending trams to England,
7166——Rent would not increase if mills worked all the year, 7167, 7168——Wages,
diet and cost thereof of women and children employed in reeling, 7169-7192——Necessity for keeping them in good health, 7193——Wages of women employed in winding, and where done, and amount of work per week, 7194-7208——Operation of doubling,
and wages, 7209-7218——Operation of twisting and throwing, hours of labour, wages
and amount of work, 7219-7229, 7236-7241——Wages of superintendents, 7230-7234,
7242-7248——Manner of subsistence of operatives when mills not at work, 7249——
Liability of throwsters if work not delivered at the day named, 7250-7256——Great
wealth of persons engaged as throwsters, 7257-7268——Calculation of charges upon a
bale of thrown and raw silk from Italy to London, 7271-7278——Losses latterly to
Italian merchants sending thrown silk here, 7279-7283——How far other countries pay
better, 7284, 7285——Italian raw being thrown here the cause of sending Italian thrown
being unprofitable, 7286, 7287——If duty reduced, a greater quantity of thrown would be
sent here, 7288 7290——Raw silk in Italy higher than thrown, 7291-7293——Quantity
of thrown that would be increased if duty reduced, 7294-7296——French and English
manufactures are smuggled into Lombardy, 7297-7304——Wages of agriculturist and
other labourers in Italy, 7305-7313——Prices of provisions, 7314-7317——Rents of
cottages, 7318, 7319——Period at which mulberry tree fit to supply the worms, 7320
——Value of leaves, 7322, 7323——Planting mulberry trees stopped from an intention to
impose a duty, 7324, 7325.

*Cambrics.*　Duty in 1826 on French cambrics, *Clay* 6862-6872——How far reducing duty
prevented smuggling in cambrics, *Clay* 6873-6878——No smuggling in cambrics ; duty
thereon, *Bottrell* 7841, 7842.

*Cape of Good Hope.*　See *Importation,* 2.

*Capital,* sufficiency thereof for the purpose of importation, *Cheeper* 902, 903——Difficult to transfer capital invested in machinery, *Jacombs* 1767, 1768; *Brocklehurst* 11409–11412 ——There are not more men of capital employed in the business now than formerly, *Cox* 2212——Injury to capital invested in mills and machinery, in consequence of the repeal of the prohibitory laws, *Banbury* 4421–4423, 4425——Expense of throwing latterly paid out of capital, *Banbury* 4492——Comparison of capital, 1824–1826 and to 1831, in the silk trade, *Royle* 3102; *Martin* 5454–5457; *Stone* 5769——How far additional capital in trade since 1824, *Harter* 9352–9356——Loss of capital in mills from insufficient protection, *Bowring* 9745–9747——Amount of capital invested in buildings and machinery, *Grout* 10300——Capital invested causes the necessity of continuing manufacture, though at a loss, *Grout* 10313——Less capital since alteration of system, *Moore* 11172.
　　See also *Roman States.*

*Carriage.* Rate of carriage of goods, *Swift* 3765–3770——Manchester has no advantage from rate of carriage, *Swift* 3774.

*Cash Payments.* More cash payments than formerly, *Stone* 5768, 5959–5962——Manner in which cash payments and short credit act favourably to trade with regard to solvency, *Dillon* 7706–7713.
　　See also *Bank of England. Credit.*

*Cevennes.* See *France.*

*Chamond, Saint,* manner in which it is connected with St. Etienne, *Bowring* 9033.

*Cheeper, Anthony.* (Analysis of his Evidence.) Calculations of the proportion of the value of labour in the manufacture of ribbons, and upon what founded, 758–770—— Quantity of ribbons imported in the quarter ended 10th October 1831, and amount of duty paid, 771–777——Per centage paid according to the present duty, 778–780——Articles that are smuggled, 781——Amount of duty that might be collected, 782–784——Smuggling would take place but to small extent under prohibition, and who would be likely to carry it on, 785–807——Difficulty of disposing of smuggled goods, 808–812, 847–851 ——Possibility of an English manufacturer making a small quantity of goods here and smuggling a larger quantity from France, 813–815——Smuggler or disposer of smuggled articles is at the mercy of his customers and servants, 816–819——Trade depressed at Coventry, 820–822——Not half employment for the operatives, 823–825——Injury to the trade from glut in the market, and means of preventing it, 826, 827——Disadvantages of contending with the French fashions, 828–832——Trade was increasing up to the admission of foreign goods, 833–835——But for foreign competition, English goods would equal the French, 836——Losses to English manufacturer from change in the fashion, 837–846——Increase of smuggling since 1826, and amount of loss of English labour thereby and by foreign importation, 852–857——Description of benefit that would be derived from the small amount of smuggling under prohibition, 858–861——In the event of prohibition, the standard of taste would cease to be regulated by France, 862–865—— Improvement in taste not to be attributed solely to France, 866–868——Benefit to English manufacturers from a variety of patterns, 869, 870.
　　Foreign colours have not superseded the English, 871–873——Quantity of goods smuggled, and from what source information obtained, 874–876——Internal competition necessary to protect the public, but not foreign competition, 877–887——Beneficial effects of prohibition over duty, and amount that would be smuggled under it, 888–896 ——Bad effects of jobbing, from the large stocks on hand, 897–901——Number of large importers, and sufficiency of capital for that purpose, 902, 903——Period the Coventry weavers have been in their present distress, 904–907——Difference in the amount of insurance upon smuggling under prohibition and protecting duty, 908–912——Possibility of distinguishing between French and English manufacture, and persons who would be likely to do so, 913–929——Amount of duty upon foreign importation compared with labour, 930–932——Description of English goods that were made superior than at present before foreign goods allowed to be imported, 933–935——Increase and improvement in machinery, 936–939.

*Children.* See *Operatives.*

*China.* See *Bengal and China. East India Company. Importation,* 2.

*Clay, Robert* (Analysis of his Evidence.) Importer of foreign manufactured goods; number engaged in the trade, 6758–6763——Method of purchasing goods in Paris, 6764–6768 ——State of import trade from 1826, 6769–6774——Reduction in the price of French plain goods between 1826 and 1828, 6775–6781——Comparison between French and English in the manner of finishing their goods, in favour of the French, 6782——Change in the import trade from plain to fancy goods, and prices thereof since 1829, 6783–6795, 6841–6843——Unprofitableness of the French import trade, 6796, 6797——Goods are all of the best kind, 6798, 6842——Manner in which jobbing arises, from goods being rejected after orders given, 6799–6803——Increase in manufacture of cut ribbons, 6804– 6807——English plain goods have beat the French out of the market, 6808–6811—— Watered silks are imported, 6812, 6813——Necessity for selling French goods immediately they come over, from their being immediately copied by the English and sold much cheaper, 6814–6835——Revolution in France stopped the home trade, and caused the exportation of goods at a loss to the manufacturer, 6836–6839——State of trade with
　　　　　　　　　　　　　　　　　　　　　　　　　　　　　　　　　　　regard

*Clay, Robert* (Analysis of his Evidence)—*continued.*

regard to French goods in England, 6840——Rate of duty upon French goods, and manner it operates upon smuggling, 6844–6853——Rate of insurance upon smuggling, 6854–6857——Duty that might be collected that would prevent smuggling, 6858, 6859, 6922–6924——Description of tulle, and where made, 6860, 6861——Duty in 1826 upon French cambrics, 6862–6872——How far reducing duty prevented smuggling in cambrics, 6873–6878——No smuggling bandannas at present; premium thereon formerly paid, 6879–6888——Smuggling greater before alteration of duty than at present, 6889–6891, 6893, 6894——No smuggling in gloves, 6892——Articles that were smuggled formerly and at present, and duties on them, 6895–6903, 7000–7006——How return might be obtained from the French Custom House books, which would show the extent of smuggling into England, 6904, 6905——Reducing duty the only mode of preventing smuggling, 6906——Stamping goods would not answer, 6907.

Why rated duty more advantageous than *ad valorem*, 6908–6910——Number of houses in France who guarantee the goods, and number in England who smuggle them, 6911, 6912——Danger in smuggling under a prohibition, but not at present, 6925–6927——Smuggling would be increased if prohibition revived, 6928–6931——Silk trade on the decline as regards imports, 6932–6936——Preference to French watered silks over English, 6937–6941——Prosecution of parties for smuggling who have not the chief interest in the goods, 6942–6952——Price of certain plain goods, and duty thereon, 6953, 6954——Number of manufacturers at Lyons of whom bought, 6955–6959——Quantity of French silks sold now greater than in 1826, 6960, 6961——Use of silk goods increased since 1826, 6962——Smugglers' price regulated by the amount of duty, 6963–6965——Causes of the decrease in the price of silks, 6966–6970——Reason for the French improving their manufacture in cut ribbons, 6971–6973——French have been compelled to reduce their prices and improve their manufacture, 6974, 6975——English beat the French in low priced plain goods, 6976——Competition in England causes the French manufacturer to be employed instead of the English, though upon English patterns, 6977–6987——Duty on the French causes the English manufacture to be cheaper, 6988–6990——Goods that have paid the duty are more valuable than those smuggled, 6991, 6993–6995——Reason of preference given to French goods, 6992——French merely manufacture to the extent of their order from England, and not for other countries from the same pattern, 6996–6999.

*Clipping,* Amount paid for, *Baggallay* 7447–7449.

*Coarse Goods.* See *Labour.*

*Cocoons.* See *Italy. Reeling.*

*Coggeshall.* See *Wages,* 2.

*Collusion.* See *Custom House.*

*Colonies.* Manufacture to which silk grown in English possessions is applied, *Doxat* 4296, 4297.

*Colours.* Foreign colours have not superseded the English, *Cheeper* 871–873—— English goods have been varied as much in colour as the French, *Jacombs* 1699, 1700——Colours the French are in the habit of producing, *Stephens* 2975——Would not be bought if made in England, *Stephens* 2982, 2983——English colours more permanent than French, *Baggallay* 7390.

*Commission.* See *Brokers.*

*Competition.* Is both home and foreign, *Jacombs* 1694–1696——Home competition would be met on equal terms, *Jacombs* 1749–1752; *Cox* 2215–2217; *Swift* 3908; *Doxat* 4063; *Bridges* 10534–10540— –Foreign competition causes home competition, *Jacombs* 1721–1723; *Ratliff* 1956——In the event of prohibition, competition in England would increase the use of machinery and amount of wages, *Cox* 2218–2229——There was always competition; the greatest competitor is the foreigner, *Sawer* 2395, 2396——Home competition gives a fair security to the public, and will allow a fair profit, *Sawer* 2415–2418——Home competition more important than French, *Gibson* 4832, 4833——Profits of manufacture and wages determined by competition, *Gibson* 5049——Too many mills and competition too great here, *Heath* 5301——Whether Foreign or English competition regulates the market here, *Heath* 5304——Competition in this country sufficient, *Stone* 6142——Tendency of English competition more to render goods cheap than to improve them, *Sedgwick* 8034–8039——Under prohibition, home competition would be a sufficient protection as to price and quality, *Bennett* 10756–10759.
See also *Fashion. Foreign Competition. France. Manufacturers. Spitalfields. Throwsters.*

*Condition La.* Establishment of La Condition for ascertaining the weight and quality of silk, *Bowring* 8800, 8801——Weight of silk submitted to La Condition, 1806–1820, *Bowring* 8833——Proportion of silk sent to La Condition and sold without, *Bowring* 8834, 8835——Modifications about to be made in the tests applied by La Condition, *Bowring* 8836——How far establishment of La Condition exists at St. Etienne, *Bowring* 8967——Such an establishment would be no benefit to England, and is not of importance to this inquiry, *Moore* 12078–12084

678.                                                        *Congleton,*

*Congleton,* Amount of Population, 1821 and 1831, *Johnson* 11568 ——State of the poor's rate, and allowances therefrom, 1821 and 1831, *Johnson* 11568——How far hands employed paid by the parish, *Johnson* 11569–11571.
 See also *Wages* 3.

*Conseil des Prud'hommes.* Means of preserving the rights of patents through the Establishment of the Conseil des Prud'hommes, *Bowring* 8849–8853, 8869–8871——Constitution thereof at Lyons, their sittings and duties, *Bowring* 8854–8868, 8872——Manner in which they settle disputes as to wages, *Bowring* 8909–8911 —— It is less popularly constituted at St. Etienne than at Lyons; of what it consists, *Bowring* 9034——Nature of the tax on patents, *Bowring* 9035, 9036, 9043——Manufacturer must take out a license to vote, *Bowring* 9041——Institution of the Conseil des Prud'hommes, and that for ascertaining the condition of silk in France would be no benefit to England, and is not of importance to this inquiry, *Moore* 12078–12084.

*Consuls.* Certificate of British Consul should be sent with silks imported into England, *Bottrell* 7942.

*Consumers.* How the higher classes of consumers benefit by reduction of wages and profits, *Stephens* 2825–2831——Public prefer a large house to deal at from the great variety, *Stephens* 2843, 2844——How far short credit and bad profits beneficial to the consumer, *Banbury* 4516–4525——Description of goods, whether of British or Foreign manufacture, depend upon the class of customers to be supplied, *Ballance* 8695.
 See also *Higher Classes.  Lower Classes.*

*Consumption of Silk.*  See *France* IV.  *Silk* I.

*Cope, Thomas* (Analysis of his Evidence.)  Silk weaver at Macclesfield, 11694–11698—— Earnings, 1817–1823, 11699; and in 1824 and 1825, 11703——Manner in which weavers unavoidably lose time in their work, 11700–11702——Irregularity of work and rate of wages since 1825, 11704–11706——Prosperous state of weavers, 1817–1825, 11707—— Distressed condition and dishonesty of them, 1825–1832, 11708——From introduction of foreign goods, 11709, 11714——Increase of silk trade in Lancashire does not account for distress at Macclesfield, 11711——Number of looms and description of trade in the silk districts in Lancashire, 11712——Cotton trade has not depressed silk weavers wages, 11713——Why workmen have better means of informing themselves of the number of looms than their masters, 11715–11719.

*Corn.* Price of corn nearly the same as in 1822, *Brocklehurst* 11396——Effect of the price of provisions and corn laws upon the silk trade, *Brocklehurst*, 11551–11554.

*Corn Laws.* Necessity for getting rid of them, imperative, *Bowring* 9657.

*Cost Price* of manufacture.  See *Etienne, St.,* France III. 2.

*Cottages,* rent thereof in Italy, *Caffi* 7318, 7319.

*Cottons and Cotton Trade.* How far the general use of cottons has interfered with the silk trade, *Brunskill* 469, 470, 475–479——Effect of taking off the duty on printed cottons on the silk trade, *Royle* 3059, 3060——Comparison of protection between the silk throwster and cotton spinner, *Royle* 3112——How cotton trade affects wages in Manchester, *Royle* 3239–3243, 3247-3249——Comparison of the silk and cotton trade, *Doxat* 4036, 4037 ——Calculations as to duties, wages, profits, &c. upon silk and cotton, 1814–1831, *Doxat* 4038——Comparison of the consumption of silk in periods of five years, 1816–1830, as compared with cotton, *Doxat* 4046, 4047——Progress of the silk trade over the cotton to 1826, and contrary effect since, *Doxat* 4140——Cotton and woollen trades have not been subject to similar distress as the silk trade, *Ballance* 8542——Importation of cotton twist into France, *Bowring* 9175–9177——State of the cotton trade in England, and how far it has prospered from being least protected, *Bowring* 9748–9756——Injury to the silk trade from exports of cotton, *Ballance* 11021 11026——Cotton trade has suffered with the silk from the present regulations, *Rowbotham* 11740——Observations upon the progresses of the silk and cotton trade, 1815–1832, *Doxat* 12094.
 See also *Duty on Importation. France. Labour. Manchester. Silk trade,* 2. *Smuggling. Wages. Weavers.*

*Country trade.* Prevalence of taste for French goods in the country towns, *Sawer* 2356—— Ready sale of goods formerly in the country trade, *Sawer* 2412–2414——Manufacturers formerly frequented country towns with patterns of ribbons, *Stephens* 2702.

*Coventry,* the consumption of silk at, is much the same, but a commoner article, taking less labour, *Brunskill* 164–170, 444–446——In the event of prohibition there would be an increase of machinery at, *Brunskill* 122, 239–241—— Ineffectual attempt to get English manufacture equal to the French caused by refusal of weavers from the lowness of wages, *Brunskill* 273–316, 537–545——The similarity of wages for plain and fancy work at St. Etienne, approach nearer than at Coventry, *Brunskill* 324, 325——Increase of the silk manufacture has not been in proportion to the population, *Brunskill* 378–382 ——Trade depressed at, *Cheeper* 820–825——Ribbon trade and watch trade the principal manufactures at, *Poole* 945—— Greatest number of persons employed in the ribbon trade, *Poole* 946—— Articles made at Coventry are finer than those made at other
places,

*Coventry*—continued.

places, *Poole* 1124——Increase and decrease of population, 1821–1831, *Poole* 1165–1173——Principally consumes foreign organzine, *Dorat* 4219–4224——Disdadvantages to Coventry ribbon trade by introduction of foreign manufactured goods, *Hall* 6657–6659——With witness's looms at Coventry, and hands working cordially, France might be defied, *Hall* 6666——Ruin to Coventry if ribbon trade gets to Manchester, *Hall* 6674, 6675, 6701.

Disadvantages to Coventry from having to compete with Manchester and the foreigner, *Hall* 6704——If Coventry would adopt improvements it would prevent Manchester hurting it, *Hall* 6711–6713——Combinations prevent Coventry men working for witness, *Hall* 6722——Reduction of purchases of ribbons from Coventry, 1827–1829, from importations from Switzerland and recovery by Coventry from 1829–1831, *Baggallay* 7342–7346, 7369–7372 ——Diminution in price and improvement in quality of Coventry over Switzerland, *Baggallay* 7347–7351——Coventry can manufacture equal to France, though France has more original taste, *Baggallay* 7377——Improvement in Coventry manufacture, *Baggallay* 7390; *Sedgwick* 8005——Amount of duty necessary to enable Coventry to compete with the French, *Baggallay* 7397, 7398——Examination as to copying French patterns, *Baggallay* 7399, 7400, 7406; *Dillon* 7693; *Sedgwick* 8009, 8017, 8018 ——How far improvement in Coventry manufacture from foreign competition, *Baggallay* 7459——Increase in the purchase of ribbons at Coventry, *Dillon* 7638——Inferiority of Coventry ribbons is in taste, *Sedgwick* 8004——No orders given to Coventry at present, *Sedgwick* 8147——Account of the sums expended in the united parishes of the city of Coventry, by weekly payments, to the permanent and casual poor in each year, 1815–1831, with gross amount of parish expenditure for each year, also average price of wheat, *Poole* 965.

> *Papers laid before the Committee :*

Amount of the Poor Rates collected in the united Parishes in the City of Coventry, by twelve rates in each year, and Amount in the pound, *App.* p. 926.

See also *Fancy trade. Foleshill. Jacquard Machine. Looms. Manufacturing Districts. Sarsnets. Silk trade. Wages,* 4. *Weavers,* 3.

*Cox, Richard Saurey.* (Analysis of his Evidence.) Loss of witness's business in the gauze and finer branches of the trade since the introduction of foreign goods, 2051, 2052——Number of gauze looms in 1826 and 1831, 2053, 2054——Number of looms generally, and persons employed therein, 2055–2057——Comparison of prices of certain articles in 1824 and at present, 2058——Wages of plain, engine and Jacquard weavers, 2059, 2060——Number of Jacquard looms in 1824, 1826 and at present, 2061, 2062——Quantity of time lost by the men in fixing their work, and what assistance they have, 2064–2071——Looms sometimes quite out of employment, 2072——Advantage in the manufacture in the application of engine over single hand looms, 2073—— Masters supply the looms, and are subject to their wear and tear, 2074–2076——Expense of Jacquard looms for changes of pattern, and yearly average per loom, 2077, 2078——How far the style and quality of goods has improved since the admission of French goods, 2079–2082——Distress at Coventry attributable to the introduction of French goods, 2083——Duty on foreign fancy goods is no protection, 2084——Advantage of prohibition, 2085——Loss of trade with a particular house since the admission of French goods, that being entirely supplied with them, 2086–2094——Cause of the disadvantage of competition with the French, 2095, 2096——French ribbons find their way every where, 2098——Quantity of foreign silk used in English manufacture, 2099, 2100——No difficulty in discovering between home and foreign manufacture, 2101, 2102——Proportion of the value of labour to the value of material in different articles, 2103.

(Second Examination.) Average wages of single-hand weavers, 2104——Increased consumption of silk does not benefit the labourer, 2105, 2106——Calculation of the cost of labour upon one pound of silk, 1824–1831, 2107–2111——Difference in the price of labour between France and England is very considerable, 2112——How far single-hand weavers employed, and amount of wages, 2113, 2114——Description of goods for which witness's house pays a higher price than others, and reasons, 2115–2119——Advantage to the master by employment of engine-looms, 2119, 2120——In what the advantage of employing an undertaker consists, 2121–2123——In the event of a prohibition there would be no difficulty in ascertaining between Foreign and English goods, 2124–2131——There would be great risk in distributing a large quantity of French goods over the country, 2132–2136——Difficulty of smuggling under it, 2137–2144——There could be a sufficient quantity and variety of goods manufactured at home for supply of the home market, 2145——Manner in which the introduction of foreign goods causes a glut in the market, and compels the manufacturers to job their goods, 2146–2149——Loss by manufacturing goods upon a guess of the French patterns in the event of any variation, 2150–2152——Those who now order their goods in France used formerly to order them in England, 2153, 2154——Extent of goods made to order at present in Coventry, 2155–2157—— From what patterns ordered goods used formerly to be made, 2158–2160——Some goods at present are sold to the large houses, 2161, 2162——Conversation with Lord Auckland, showing how the French set the fashions here, 2162–2164——Fancy trade requires a prohibition, 2165——Extent of duty that would protect the plain trade, 2165–2168——Quantity of silk manufactured, 1824 and 1831, 2169—— Manufacture of gauzes predominated, 1824–1827, and were then partly discontinued from the French

*Cox, Richard Saurey* (Analysis of his Evidence)—*continued.*

importing them, 2170–2176——How far the Coventry trade affected by change of fashion before opening the trade, 2177–2185——Ribbons are more universally worn now than formerly, 2186——How far changes in the market, according to the fashion, affect speculations, 2187–2190——Proportion the higher branches bear to the whole trade in ribbons, 2191, 2192——Prohibition should extend to all French fancy ribbons, 2193–2195——In calculating profits allowance is made for any sacrifice that may take place, 2196–2198——Lower classes are supplied by persons in that particular branch ; fancy goods are not made with any view to show, 2199——No good answered by the introduction of foreign goods while weavers are out of employment, and wages inadequate, 2200.

More failures in Coventry since the introduction of foreign goods, 2201, 2202——Quantity of French goods imported, and number of hands they would have employed if made in England, 2203, 2204——Preference for French goods is owing to the taste, not the price, 2205——Superior articles made, 1822–1825, than since, 2206, 2207, 2211——Dependence on the French fashions for the quantity of ribbons used, 2208, 2209——There are not more men of capital employed in the business now than formerly, 2212——Present duty not a protection for plain goods, 2213, 2214——Competition in England would not be more injurious than competition with France, 2215–2217——In the event of prohibition, competition in England would increase the use of machinery, and amount of wages, 2218–2229——How far French goods are paid for by British labour, 2230–2234——If many inferior gauzes are made, the French will soon supply the whole country, as no one will buy the English, 2235–2243——How far they may suit exportation, 2244–2247——Proportion of foreign silk used in manufacture, and how affected by duty, 2248–2257——Comparative quality of different foreign thrown silks, and English thrown, 2258–2260——Best thrown silk is used for the finer purposes, 2261——British thrown Italian silk is better than Italian thrown, 2262–2266——In what the superiority in throwing consists, 2267——Not much improvement in the quality of British thrown silk since 1823, 2268, 2269——No silk thrown out of England is superior to British thrown silk; Piedmont silk is used for particular purposes, 2271——Disadvantages of being dependent upon the Italian throwster, 2270–2274——There is now a fair competition in price for marabout silk, 2275–2279——Its quality has retrograded, 2280——Where it comes from, 2281.

Drawback allowed upon exportation of ribbons, 2282——Comparison of English and French designers, and reason for the French being able to employ a superior class, 2283–2292——Average value per pound of silk used at Coventry, 2293——During 1813 and 1814 there were as many pieces of ribbon used, but not of the same description, 2294——Introduction of the Jacquard loom into England, 2295——Description of goods it can make, 2296——French did not use it in 1813, 2297——Engine looms are not much increased with the exception of the Jacquard, 2298——Breadths were not required formerly, or they could have been made; same quantity could have been made formerly as are at present made with the Jacquard, 2299–2304——Jacquard is only for peculiar patterns, 2305——Effect of reducing the duty upon foreign thrown silk, 2306–2310——On what the prices of English and Italian thrown silk depends, 2311–2319——Number of looms employed and wages paid in Spitalfields, 1814–1827, in the manufacture of broad silks, 2320–2327——Discontinued in 1827, from being superseded by the French fancy goods, 2328——Manufacture at Manchester or in any other part of England did not interfere with that branch, 2329–2331——Description of goods made, 2332, 2333——French goods of that description are not intrinsically so good as those made here formerly, 2334–2337——French import something new in large quantities every season, 2338–2341——How far goods would be made at Manchester in the event of prohibition, 2342–2345——To what extent supleing is carried by the French, 2346–2348——Importation of French silks has increased lately, 2249——Generally takes place to a large extent at the present time of the year, 2351——Anxiety of the silk trade to prevent smuggling, 2352.

*Crape.* Not so easily smuggled as plain silk, *Hume* 13——French crapes do not come into competition with Spitalfields, *Bottrell* 7913–7916——Losses upon importation of China crapes from their being superseded by the French, and successfully imitated by the English, *Bottrell* 7957–7959——Description of raw silk used in the manufacture of different crapes, *Grout* 10278–10283——English black crapes selling at ruinous prices ; present foreign competition therein, *Grout* 10311, 10312——Consumption of white and coloured crapes, 1826–1831, from French and other foreign productions, *Grout* 10340——Comparison of quality and price of English and French crape handkerchiefs, *Stephens* 10581–10592——Importation of French crapes, or manufacture thereof, in certain parts of England does not interfere with Spitalfields, *Wallis* 10945–10949——Importation of crapes from France interfere with those places where they are manufactured in England, *Ballance* 11051–11057.

*Credit.* Difference of credit on sales before reduction of duty and at present, *Banbury* 4457–4461; *Gibson* 5095–5100; *Stone* 5950–5958——How far short credit beneficial to consumer, *Banbury* 4516–4525——Credit at present allowed, *Banbury* 4552–4565 ; *Martin* 5462, 5463; *Wadden* 10150, 10151——Reasons for reducing credit, *Martin* 5466, 5467, 5472–5475, 5480, 5481——When period of credit altered in England, *Martin* 5533——Present method of transacting business arising from difference of credit, and benefit thereof, *Stone* 5967–5993.

See also *Brokers. Cash Payments. Consumers.*

*Creditors.*

*Creditors.* In the event of failures, actions are brought by creditors against houses purchasing goods under prime cost, *Banbury* 4528–4534——How far those houses operate to continue a man in insolvency, *Banbury* 4536–4542——Compromise between creditors and those houses, *Banbury* 4543–4545.

*Crifeldt.* See *Velvets.*

*Currency,* how silk trade affected by change in, *Royle* 3055–3058.
See also *Bank of England.*

*Custom House.* Manner in which goods are sometimes imported through the Custom House at less than their proper duty, and how to be prevented, *Stephens* 2779–2787, 2973, 2974, 2976–2981, 2984–2996, 10639–10649; *Bottrell* 7867–7869, 7882; *Wadden* 10117–10122, 10126–10129; *Beckwith* 11959, 11960; *Beals* 12472–12475——Articles purchased at the Custom House for exportation, and smuggled in for home consumption, prior to 1826, *Stephens* 2854–2861——Necessity for foreign goods being examined at one place, and subject to a greater check, *Bottrell* 7815, 7816, 7940, 7941——Suggestions of regulations and duties for the prevention of smuggling, *Bottrell* 7865, 7866, 7967——Necessity for inspector at the Custom House being in communication with manufacturers, to ascertain the value of goods, *Bottrell* 7870–7878 —— Hours of attendance of the Commissioners of Customs, *Bottrell* 7936, 7937——How far certain Custom House officers are open to bribery, from the amount and manner of paying their salaries, *Bottrell* 7938, 7939, 7968–7970——Dissatisfaction among Custom House officers from not being properly remunerated, *Bottrell* 7952, 7953; *Beckwith* 11958——Under good Custom House regulations, properly enforced, smugglers' risk would be increased, and more duty than the present amount collected, *Ballance* 8432, 8433, 8607–8611——French Custom House regulations, *Bowring* 9193, and revenues, *Bowring* 9194——Increasing number of revenue officers gives a greater chance for smuggling, *Bowring* 9195——How much above their proper rate duties are levied in England, *Bowring* 9214.

Leaf's transaction was not done with the connivance of the Custom House officers, *Wadden* 10123——It is not an isolated case, *Wadden* 10124——Officers have not received the compromise money, and reasons, *Wadden* 10125; *Beckwith* 11958——Extent of smuggling to be partly accounted for by the looseness of the Customs regulations, *Wadden* 10130, 10131 ——Alterations might be made in English Customs regulations, *Bouillon* 10232, 10233——Manner of levying duties at the Custom House; fraud a common occurrence, *Stephens* 10650–10662 ——Duty of landing waiters, *Fraser* 12099, 12100—— Duty of surveyor, *Fraser* 12101, 12102——Number of ships discharging at one time, *Fraser* 12103, 12104——Number of men at the scales and reduction in the amount thereof, *Fraser* 12105–12110——Pay of extra weighers; not constant employment, *Fraser* 12111–12113, 12195——Examination as to opportunities of removing goods during absence of landing waiter, *Fraser* 12114–12124.

Fraud must be caused by collusion between the weigher and landing waiter, *Fraser* 12125–12128, 12132——Instance of weighers being left alone, *Fraser* 12129–12131—— Disputes between Custom House officers and merchants as to the value of silk, *Fraser* 12133–12136——No knowledge of silk being passed at less than the actual weight, *Fraser* 12137——Possibility of fraud from value being left to the judgment of the merchant, *Fraser* 12138–12147——Method of weighing silk manufactured goods, and difficulty from landing waiter attending two sets of scales, *Fraser* 12148–12154——Examination, showing the responsibility of the weigher, and want of check upon the landing waiter, *Fraser* 12155–12171——Instances of goods being re-weighed by the surveyors, *Fraser* 12172–12177——Refusal of bribes by witness, and reasons for not reporting their offer to the landing waiter, *Fraser* 12179–12191, 12196–12201, 12268–12271, 12274–12289——No instructions given to extra weighers when going on duty, *Fraser* 12192 ——Duty of extra weighers, *Fraser* 12193, 12194——No recollection of a smaller number being entered than that actually passed, *Fraser* 12202–12207——Examination upon the fact of the commission of bribery among the Custom House officers, *Fraser* 12208–12212 ——Examination as to the names of officers who have told witness of their receiving bribes for not doing their duty, with witness declining to mention them, *Fraser* 12213–12249, 12262–12267, 12272, 12273——Supposition that the bribe was for passing short weights, *Fraser* 12250–12261——Opportunities of committing fraud from the poverty of extra weighers, *Fraser* 12290–12297——Presents of small value to landing waiters from merchants, *Fraser* 12298–12310——How far a trifling present might be made of toys, *Fairclough* 12422——Examination as to a letter from a Custom House officer, with inference of bribery therefrom, *Stephens* 12311–12320——Silk passed through the Custom House lower than if done by a fair trader, *Stephens* 12321–12333, 12338–12345——Witness declines giving the name of his informant, or the Custom House officer, *Stephens* 12334–12337——Knowledge of goods coming in under *ad valorem* duty at less than their proper value, *Stephens* 12346–12361——Supposition that certain houses in the habit of passing figured goods for the duty on plain, *Stephens* 12366–12368——Difficulty of such an attempt, *Fairclough* 12404–12408.

Process of weighing and examining silk goods on their landing, *Fairclough* 12375—— Landing waiters do not attend to more than one pair of scales, *Fairclough* 12376–12379 ——Difficulty of the weigher committing a fraud without connivance with the landing waiter, *Fairclough* 12380–12383——Landing waiters changed periodically, *Fairclough* 678.                                                                                                12384,

*Custom House—*continued.

12384, 12385; *Beals* 12434——No advantage to bribe the weigher without the landing waiter, *Fairclough* 12386——Landing waiter always present, *Fairclough* 12387, 12388 ——Not possible for the scales to be left to the weigher without the attendance of the landing waiter, *Fairclough* 12389——Landing waiter never trusts to the weigher, but always calculates the weight himself, *Fairclough* 12390–12392——He would be removed if he did, *Fairclough* 12393, 12394——Frauds might be committed by collusion, *Fairclough* 12395——Operation of the check of the surveyor upon the landing waiter, *Fairclough* 12396, 12397——Which would prevent collusion between the landing waiter and weigher, *Fairclough* 12398, 12399——Salary of landing waiters, *Fairclough* 12400—— Consequent improbability of their being open to fraud, *Fairclough* 12401——Not often two scales in use at one time, but when so there is an officer to each, *Fairclough* 12402, 12403——Not more goods passed through the Custom House since the last seizure, *Fairclough* 12409——Manner of examining and counting other goods not silk, showing difficulty of improperly counting, *Fairclough* 12410–12421, 12423.

Duty of landing surveyors, and manner in which they check landing waiters, *Beals* 12425–12428——No recollection of finding a wrong weight put on goods through fraud on re-weighing, *Beals* 12429–12433——Examination as to the quality of the goods, *Beals* 12435, 12436——Method of weighing for the tare, *Beals* 12437–12439——Possibility of fraud from connivance of officers, but great improbability thereof, *Beals* 12440–12443 ——Improbability of collusion on the part of the landing waiter from the value of his situation, *Beals* 12444 12448——Goods sometimes entered under the value, detained and sold, and fetch more than the value, *Beals* 12449–12458——Sometimes they do not fetch their value, *Beals* 12459 ——Reference to persons in the trade to ascertain the value of articles out of the common course, *Beals* 12460–12464——Goods generally valued very near the value, *Beals* 12465–12467——Division of profit on goods seized, and consequent inducement for seizing, *Beals* 12468–12471——Amount per cent. goods allowed to be entered under value, *Beals* 12472–12475.

Examination upon an investigation in consequence of a letter signed "Veritas" and addressed to Lord Auckland, alleging a fraud upon the Customs, and difference in the proper amount of duty, and that paid, *Manning* 12477–12500——Amount per cent. of saving upon the amount of duty, admitting a fraud to have taken place, and reasons for not admitting that as a fact, *Manning* 12501–12503——Employment of extra men, and how paid, *Manning* 12504–12506——Only established officers employed in the examination of silks, *Manning* 12506——Allan Fraser never employed in examining silks, *Manning* 12507–12511——Statement of the dates, station, duty, and under whom Fraser employed on the quays where silk goods are usually examined, *Manning* 12512——Silk goods not usually opened on the ground floor where Fraser employed, *Manning* 12513 ——Wages received by Fraser, and number of hours labour, *Manning* 12515——How far his situation a place of trust, when he is immediately under the superintendence of the landing waiter, *Manning* 12516, 12517——Duties of surveyors general, *Manning* 12518, 12519——Duties of landing surveyors, particularly with regard to silk goods, *Manning* 12520, 12521——Manner in which doubts entertained by the Custom House officers are cleared up by reference to the trade, *Manning* 12522, 12526, 12527—— Why appointing a person on purpose to judge goods, and charge them according to their value, would not be beneficial, *Manning* 12523–12525——Examinations of the allegations of Veritas, by the invoices which might have been made up for the occasion, *Manning* 12528–12534——Landing waiters only attend one scale, and never leave a case after the lid is off till they know its contents, *Manning* 12538–12541——Statement by Veritas confirmed by affidavits, which would be false if fraud not proved against officers; manner in which officers may be liable to error, *Manning* 12542–12547.

*Cut Ribbons.* See *Ribbons,* 3.

# D.

*Damages.* See *Italy.*

*Debentures,* sales thereof, *Hume* 97–99——Price thereof, *Brunskill* 147–149; *Doxat* 4307; *Gibson* 5079——Value of debentures would depend on the proportion of thrown silk imported, as compared with the quantity of British goods exported, *Hume* 100—— Advantages of debentures to the export trade, *Hume* 101, 102; *Brunskill* 464–468; *Brockwell* 3699–3703; *Wadden* 9997–9999; *Brocklehurst* 11530, 11531 ——Process of exportation by debentures, *Brockwell* 3704, 3705——Inducement of debentures to increase certain branches of trade, *Brockwell* 3711—— Raising the price of debentures by diminishing imports or increasing exports, will benefit the manufacturer at the expense of the throwster, *Gibson* 5084–5094——Benefits of export trade, and how it might be extended by increasing the price of debentures, *Ballance* 8417–8419; *Beckwith* 11952– 11957——Debentures no advantage to the importers of Italian silk, beyond the price of the debentures, *Wadden* 10000——Effect of debentures on export trade, *Brocklehurst* 11522——Why debenture not a tax on Spitalfields, *Brocklehurst* 11532.

See also *Exportation. Manchester.*

*De Ponilly* & Co. Witness ignorant of the circumstances attending a seizure at Messrs. De Ponilly's, *Menetrier* 8222–8226, 8243, 8244——Whether silks used by De Ponilly's houses were

*De Ponilly* & *Co.—continued.*
were dyed in France or in England, *Menetrier* 8227-8231——Articles manufactured by De Ponilly & Co., that were fashionable in France but not in England, caused them to give up their manufacture here, *Menetrier* 8235-8238, 8250-8253, 8285-8288——Whether the English government allowed De Ponilly & Co. to import organzine free of duty, *Menetrier* 8239-8242——Furniture made by De Ponilly & Co., at Spitalfields, for Windsor Castle, *Menetrier* 8243-8247——Number of looms employed by De Ponilly & Co., *Menetrier* 8248, 8249——A few of the head weavers brought from France, *Menetrier* 8256——Their Jacquards partly brought from France and partly manufactured at Manchester, *Menetrier* 8257——How far their speculation succeeded, *Menetrier* 8261-8265——Some weavers employed from Paisley as good as the French weavers for gauzes, *Menetrier* 8265, 8266——Importations by De Ponilly & Co. legally, *Menetrier* 8269-8271——Number of looms employed on the order for Windsor Castle, *Menetrier* 8276-8280——Where thrown silk obtained, *Menetrier* 8282-8284, 8292-8296——Goods manufactured at Manchester from French patterns, *Menetrier* 8289-8291——Names of De Ponilly's partners and designer, *Menetrier* 8297-8300.

*Designs.*   Fashion set by the designs that come from France, but many copied in England, and come out as soon as the French, *Bouillon* 10165.

*Designers,* nature and employment of them, *Perkins* 1559, 1560——Comparison between French and English, *Jacombs* 1674-1677 ; *Cox* 2283-2292——How far fluctuation in trade affects designers, *Jacombs* 1688-1691——Reason for the French being able to employ a superior class, *Cox* 2283-2292——Designers used to be employed in the Spitalfields trade formerly at high salaries, *Dubois* 10263-10267——Patterns drawn by English artists, *Bridges* 10383.
     See *France.*

*Dillon, John,* (Analysis of his Evidence.)   Description of the mode of transacting business by the house of James Morrison & Co. 7591-7597——Statement of purchases of broad silks and silk handkerchiefs at Spitalfields and other English manufactories, for five years previous to 1826, 7598-7600——Similar statement for five years and nine months since 1826, 7601——The like as to ribbons, 7601.

(Second Examination.) Proportion of purchases of French and English ribbons, 7602-7604—— Statement of proportion, per 100*l.* of whole French trade in silk, 1827-1831, 7605-7607——The like in ribbons, 7607——The like of English silks and ribbons, 7608——French trade decreasing from the great improvement in English manufactures, and reduction in price, 7609-7612, 7624——Statement of proportion, per 100*l.* of different descriptions of French ribbons bought, 7613——Per centage gauze ribbons bear to the whole production of French ribbons, 7613, 7614——Statement of proportion, per 100*l.* of different descriptions of English ribbons, 7615——Month which calculation taken, 7616——Velvets and Swiss ribbons superseded by English articles, 7618——How far consumption of foreign goods on decline when official documents show an increase, 7619-7621——Smuggling has decreased, 7622, 7623——Proportion of each kind of ribbon purchased in France and England per 100*l.*, 7625-7627——Estimate of the amount of the silk trade of England, and proportion the French imports bear to it, 7628-7639——Proportion of ribbons made in France and in England, 7631-7636——Increase in the purchase of English broad silks, and from what parts since the admission of the French, 7637, 7638——Increase in the purchase of ribbons at Coventry, 7638——Places where goods sold at Spitalfields are manufactured, 7639-7641——Manner in which the warehouseman's business is conducted, and how far a benefit to the public, 7642-7655.

Improvement in English over French manufacture, demand for French goods diminishing, and in what goods French likely to retain a superiority over the English, 7656-7662——Manner in which the French excel the English in superiority of taste and design, 7663-7670——Opinion as to town and country trade as to the sales of rich or coarse goods, 7671-7678——Amount of present rate of duty collected by weight, 7679, 7680——Rate of premium, for smuggling, 7681, 7682——Reduction of duty necessary as a protection against smuggling, 7683, 7686——Comparison of cost price of striped and figured gauzes in France and England, 7684, 7685, 7687, 7688——Similar comparison of French and English lutestrings, 7689——Superiority thereof rather in favour of the French, 7690——Duty necessary to equalize the prices of French and English satins, 7690——How far striped and plain gauzes of the same quality, 7691, 7692——French patterns copied at Coventry do not destroy the sale of the French pattern imported, 7693——French trade has not been beneficial to trade from the distance of the market, 7694, 7695——Profits not greater upon the sale of French than English goods, but losses are, 7696——Why gluts in the market from French job goods do not hurt the English manufacturer, 7697-7700——Reason for failures being reduced in the silk manufacture, 7701——Less goods at Spitalfields now than usually at this time, 7702, 7703——Fewer failures among the retailers latterly, 7704, 7705——Manner in which cash payments and short credit act favourably to trade with regard to solvency, 7706-7713——Examination upon the purchases by large warehousemen, and how they act upon profit or loss to the manufacturer, 7714-7729.
     678.                                                                    (Third

*Dillon, John,* (Analysis of his Evidence)—*continued.*

(Third Examination.) Comparison of silk trade with that of other departments for certain periods, 7730–7732——Effect of the removal of prohibition upon East India bandannas, upon increasing the manufacture of English, 7733–7736——Interference of Manchester with the Spitalfields trade, 7737–7739, 7745——How far actions have been brought, and compromises made with assignees of manufacturers and warehousemen respecting goods supposed to be improperly bought, 7740–7742——Gloves are not smuggled, 7743——French gloves less profitable than English, 7744——Report from France with regard to the manufacture of French ribbons there, 7746, 7747.

(Fourth Examination.) Witness's account of interview with Mr. Beckwith, in which witness produced proof of certain velvets sold him having paid duty, 12632–12637——Examination as to the production of invoices to Mr. Beckwith, and his expressing his alteration of his previous opinion, 12638–12646——Correspondence between Morrison & Co.'s house and Mr. Beckwith as to the latters charge against the former of irregular proceedings, 12648–12653——Duty on witness's parcel paid by weight, 12654——Difference in price between the two parcels, and how far from being bought of different persons 12655–12666——Witness's agent in Paris is not a partner; period of his residence in Paris, 12668.

*Discount,* rate of, at present allowed, *Banbury* 4552–4565; *Martin* 5464, 5554——Not sufficient to produce cash payment, *Martin* 5464, 5465.
　　See also *Brokers.*

*Distress.* See *Coventry. Fancy Trade. Manchester. Operatives. Ribbons,* 7. *Silk Trade. Spitalfields District. Spitalfields Trade. Throwsters. Weavers.*

*Doubling.* Operation of doubling, and wages, *Caffi* 7209–7218.

*Doxat, Alexis James,* (Analysis of his Evidence.) Silk merchant in London, importing from Italy, 4031–4034——Imports and consumption, 1814–1831; situation of the trade before and since the importation of foreign manufactured silks; comparison of the silk and cotton trade; duties on silk and cotton; rate of wages per yard, 4036, 4037——Silk duties easily collected, 4037——Calculation as to duties, wages, profits, &c. upon silk and cotton, 1814–1831, 4038——Degree of distress in the silk manufacturing districts, 4039——Advantage of low duties on the importation of raw, and high duties upon thrown, 4040——How price of the raw material would have been affected thereby, 4041–4043——Increase of wages, 1815–1825, and decrease to 1831, 4045——Comparison of consumption in periods of five years, 1816–1830, 4046——Compared with cotton, 4047——Comparison of wages and duties, 4047——Decrease of manufacture of fancy goods, 4049–4051——Comparative cost of manufacture at London and Lyons, 4051–4052.

(Second Examination.) Comparison of quantity of labour and rate of wages at London and Lyons, 4053–4055, 4073–4079——Rate of wages per yard, 1815–1825, 4056–4061——Deductions in wages since 1826, and variation in the quantity of employment, 4062——State of trade at home regulates itself, 4063——Description of low and mixed trade carried on at Manchester to take advantage of debentures for exportation, 4064——How fluctuations in the silk trade in France act detrimentally to English industry, 4066–4068, 4073——Quantities of silk consumed at France and Switzerland, and proportion therein, 4074–4078——Statement of import of raw, thrown and waste silk into France, 4078——Quality of French silks, and improvement in reeling, 4079, 4080——Looms employed in Switzerland and Spitalfields, 4081——Importations into France from Switzerland of velvets and plain goods, 4082——Method of levying duty on importations into France, 4083, 4085——Difficulty of getting at the total quantity of exports from Italy, 4086, 4087——Importations into Switzerland, 4088, 4089——Quality of silks imported into England, France and Switzerland, 4090–4092.

Importation of Swiss ribbons into France, 4093–4096——Cheapness of manufacture in Switzerland, 4094——Duties on Importation into Switzerland and Germany, 4097, 4098——Imports and exports to and from Vienna, 4099–4101——Articles worked at Vienna for the Levant, 4103——Comparative quality of silk imported into England and other countries, 4104–4110——Comparative statement of the quality of silk used in England and France, 4111, 4112——For what Bengal silks are used in France, 4113, 4114——Coarse goods require a mixture of fine with them, 4115——Description of raw silk that fetches the highest price in London at present, 4116–4118——Superiority of French silk, 4119–4121——Attributed to superior reeling, 4119–4121——For what Piedmont silk required, 4123——Why the English do not reel as well as the French, 4124——Estimate of quantities of raw silks consumed in England, 1824–5, and in 1826–31, 4125——Increased importation of raw silk does not show prosperity of the throwster, from the labour being less on coarser descriptions, 4126–4130——Comparative view of the quantities of Italian thrown and raw silks consumed, 1815–31, 4131——Taking off the duty on organzine has increased importation of thrown silk, 4132——But not after every deduction, 4133——Variation in the importation of thrown silk at different periods since 1763 and causes, 4134–4140.

(Third

*Doxat, Alexis James,* (Analysis of his Evidence)—*continued.*

(Third Examination.) Reasons for prosperity at Manchester, and distress at Spitalfields, 4140——Progress of silk trade over cotton to 1826, and contrary effect since, 4140—— Reduction in wages of the Spitalfields trade owing to foreign imports since 1826, 4141, 4143——Extent of smuggling, 4144-4147——Bills drawn from France for payment thereof, 4148-4155——How far Manchester trade interferes with Spitalfields, 4156-4160 ——Effect of foreign competition thereon, 4161, 4162——Improvement of the Spital-fields trade, 1815-1825, 4163——Great distress since, and causes, 4164-4168——On what the competition between France and Spitalfields depends, 4169, 4170——Difference in price of materials and wages between Lyons and Spitalfields and Manchester, 4171– 4183——Variations in the price of silk between Lyons and London, and causes thereof, 4184-4193——Price of Italian organzine in Lyons and London, 4194-4202——Disad-vantages of the English manufacturer competing with the French, 4203-4207——Impor-duties and charges upon raw silk into Lyons and London, 4208-4213——The like upon thrown, 4214, 4215, 4217, 4218——Method of assaying a bale of silk in France, 4216—— Spitalfields consumes principally English organzine; Coventry foreign, 4219-4224—— Higher price paid by the English than the French weaver, 4225——Proportion of import duty to the price of Italian thrown, 4226-4229——Advantages of the French weaver in manufacture, 4229——Protection required by English throwsters, 4229-4234——Ruin to the throwster by removing the duty on foreign thrown silk, 4235-4237——Disadvantages of being dependent upon foreign throwsters, 4237, 4238——Why the Swiss do not suffer disadvantage therefrom, 4239, 4240——Greater importation of Italian thrown, if duty reduced, 4241-4244.

Advantages of the Italian throwster over the English, 4245-4247——Increased im-portation of thrown from reduction of duty in 1829, 4248——Variation in importation of Piedmont organzine, 4249——Further disadvantages of reducing duty, 4250, 4251—— Prices of silk in France are lower than in England, independent of duty, 4252, 4253—— Silk thrown equally well in England as in Italy, 4254, 4255——Italian silk comes over on consignment, 4256——Export of Piedmont raws prohibited, 4257——Price of Italian silk thrown in Italy and England, 4258——Increase in the produce of French silks, and less necessity for importing Italian, 4259-4263——Difference in price of silk in Lyons and Italy, 4264-4269——Difference of price at which the manufacturers at London and Lyons is supplied with material for manufacture, 4270——How duty on importation of Italian thrown silk affects price in England and France, 4271-4275——How English manufacture relatively cheaper than Italian, 4276——Advantage from water in Italy, 4277——Importations of Bengal and China silks, 4278——Abridged recapitulation of comparative cost of manufacture at London and Lyons, 4279——On legal and illegal imports, 4279.

(Fourth Examination.) Price of Italian raw silk imported into Lyons, 4280-4286—— Marabout not thrown in Italy, 4287——Advantages of the French over the English throwster, 4288-4290——How far the importation of French raw silks would be bene-ficial, 4291-4295——Manufactures to which silk grown in English possessions is applied, 4296, 4297——Proportion of wages on silk grown in the Colonies and in Italy, 4298—— Relative increase since alteration of duty in the importation of Italian with other silks, 4299-4301——China silks have improved, but not Bengal, 4302——Relative increase in manufacture of coarse goods since 1825, and consequent diminution of labour, 4303– 4305 ——Diminution in the price of silk in the home market corresponding with the reduction of duty on imported thrown silk, 4306, 4307——Price of debentures, 4307—— Comparison of the reduction of wages between cotton and silk, 4308-4311.

(Fifth Examination.) Further examination as to the price of silk at Lyons and in London, 4312-4315; and importation of foreign silk into France, 4316-4318——How far the silk trade of France improving, 4319-4322——How far certain natural and political causes have affected import of thrown silk into England, 4323-4325—— How far prices of French manufactured goods imported last year sufficient to remunerate manufacturer, 4326-4329——Quantity of manufactured goods exported from France and consumed therein, 4330——Advantage to the French in the price of Italian raw silk, 4331——In what instances the French use Italian raw, and prices, 4332-4344, 4357-4374——Effect of import of Italian silk into France on prices and consumption of French silk, 4341-4352 ——Raw and thrown silk dearer in England than in France, 4533-4356——Price of Pied-mont organzine in London and quantity imported, 4375-4378——Price of coarse silks in France, 4379, 4380——Depression of throwing trade from the importation of foreign thrown, 4381—— How sale price of Italian silk regulated on commission, 4382-4389, 4393——Exportation to other countries if the market depressed, 4390, 4391——Approxi-mation in price of Italian and French silk at Lyons, 4392——With the exception of dif-ference of duties and charges, French pay the same for foreign silk as other parts of the world, 4394—— Statement respecting the great reduction of wages, and table, showing rates at London and Lyons, 4395——Difference in 1825 and 1831 in the price of throwing between Lyons and England, 4396——Comparative view of the market price at London of certain raw silks, 1824-1832, 4397——Remuneration to the throwster, 1824-1831, 4398-4402——Statement of cost of manufacture of plain goods at London and Lyons, 4402.

(Sixth Examination.) Documentary evidence put in by witness as to French and English imports and exports, and silk manufactures generally, and examination thereon, 678.                                                                                          12089-

*Doxat, Alexis James,* (Analysis of his Evidence)—*continued.*

12089-12092——Exports of silks from Calais to England, 1831, 1832, 12090; and examination showing inference of smuggling from official exports, 12090——Examination as to difference of price of raw and thrown silk at London and Lyons, 12092—— Examination as to consumption of silk in France as shown by certain documentary evidence, 10293-10295 —— Observations upon the progresses of the silk and cotton trade, 1815-1832, 12094.

Administration des Douanes ; Exportation des Tissus de soie de fabriques Françaises, with computation into English weight and value, *Doxat* 12094 —— Marchandises Exportées de l'Intérieur Seulement, *Doxat* 12094 —— Marchandises Exportées de l'Intérieur du Royaume en payant des Droits, en Franchise ou avec prime, *Doxat* 12094.

Recapitulation of the Annual Exports from France, 1827-1830, of French manufactured Silks of every description ; showing their quantity in French weight and value in francs, computed into English weight and value, *Doxat* 12094.

Douanes Royales de France; Imports of foreign manufactured Silks into France for home consumption, *Doxat* 12094.

Estimate of the total Amounts of Silk Manufacture of the United Kingdom, during periods 1815-1817, 1818-1820, 1821-1823, and 1824-1825 (understated in regard to wages in these periods), *Doxat* 12094.

Estimate of the total Amounts of Silk Manufacture of the United Kingdom, 1826-1831 (overstated in regard to wages in these years), *Doxat* 12094.

Abstract statement of French Silk Manufactures for the years 1827-1830, conjointly with an abstract view of the total Amounts of the Silk Manufactures of the United Kingdom at different periods during 1815-1831, *Doxat* 12094.

Statement intended to show the differences which range between the Prices of Silks at London and at Lyons, *Doxat* 12094.

Abstract view of the progress of the Silk Trade of Great Britain and Ireland at different periods between 1815 and 1831 (in regard to quantities,) *Doxat* 12094——Similar abstract view of the Cotton Trade, *Doxat* 12094.

Papers delivered in by Mr. Alexis Doxat, at his examination before the Committee, on the 11th, 13th, 17th, 18th, and 19th of April 1832, *App.* pp. 932-945.

*DRAWBACK :*

　　　1. *Generally.*
　　　2. *Papers laid before the Committee.*

1. *Generally.*

Evils thereof, *Royle* 3205-3207, 3211-3214 —— Amount of drawback, by whom received, and for what goods, *Royle* 3314-3323 ; *Gibson* 5074-5078 ; *Harter* 9273-9275 ——Effect of withdrawing the drawback, *Royle* 3324-3327——Is a bonus on the use of Bengal and China silk, *Royle* 3357, 3358——Necessity for the drawback for the export trade, *Harter* 9266-9268——Manner in which drawback, causing export, relieves the manufacturer for the home market, *Harter* 9482-9485——Drawback on exportation of a certain article produced, *Tootal* 9545-9549——Drawback on waste silk, and manner the silk is worked up to claim it, *Tootal* 9585-9587——Bounty increases exportation of gros de Naples, *Tootal* 9615——How far export of coarse silks to France, in consequence of the drawback, *Bowring* 9788——Increase in exportation from the drawback, *Wadden* 10105, 10106, 10108——Amount of duty and drawback, 1830, *Wadden* 10111 —— Inaccuracy of the return to Parliament showing the above, *Wadden* 10111, 10112—— Alteration that should be made in the amount of drawback, *Beckwith* 11979-11983—— Reason why drawback does not counteract the effect of the duties, *Graham* 12738, 12739. See also *Bengal and China silk. Bounties. Exportation.*

2. *Papers laid before the Committee.*

Account of the Drawback paid each quarter, from 5th January 1830 to 5th January 1832, upon the exportation of British manufactured Silk Goods ; distinguishing the amount paid upon Stuffs or Ribbons of Silk only, upon Stuffs or Ribbons of Silk and Cotton, and upon Stuffs or Ribbons of Silk and Worsted mixed ; and distinguishing London from the other Ports, *App.* p. 920.

*Dublin.* Distressed state of the Dublin silk trade, *Brocklehurst* 11460-11462——Witness's connection with the silk trade in Dublin, *Sisson* 11896-11902——Decline of the silk trade in Dublin, from reduction of duties on British goods, and afterwards from reduction of duties on foreign goods imported into Ireland, *Sisson* 11903-11907—— Number of looms and description of goods made therein, in Dublin, in 1824 and at present, *Sisson* 11908-11911——Great destruction of property in 1826, and distress in that year, *Sisson* 11912——Demoralized state of the lower classes in consequence, *Sisson* 11913——Examination upon the formation of committees in Dublin for subscriptions to transplant weavers out of work to England ; deterioration in value of houses formerly occupied by persons in the silk trade, *Sisson* 11914-11916——Distress in Dublin of longer duration

*Dublin*—continued.

duration now than at any former period, *Sisson* 11917, 11918——Silk trade established in Dublin at the same time as in Spitalfields, *Sisson* 11921——Years in which Dublin silk trade most flourished, and imports thereinto, 1781–1821, *Sisson* 11922–11923.

> *Paper laid before the Committee.*

State of the Silk Trade in Dublin 1824, *App.* p. 930.
  See also *Union Duties.*

*Dubois, John,* (Analysis of his Evidence.) Broad silk manufacturer in Spitalfields, 10236–10239——Quality of goods manufactured, 10240, 10241——Number of looms employed formerly, 10242——Description of trade formerly, 10243–10247——Bad effect of opening the ports on Spitalfields fancy trade, 10248–10256, 10261, 10262——Proportion of looms formerly employed, and description of work, 10258, 10259——Not an improvement in English figured silks since the opening the Ports, 10260——Designers used to be employed in the Spitalfields trade formerly at high salaries, 10263–10267——Foreign competition will tend to ruin our manufactures altogether, 10268——There would be no difficulty in detecting French goods under a prohibition, 10269——Smuggling inconsiderable before opening the Ports; stamping would be of service, 10270, 10271——Impossible to continue the fancy trade without prohibition from France, 10272–10277.

*Duties.*  See *Silk Trade, 2.*

*Duty on Importation.*  Principles of Acts of 1824 and 1826, and Tables of 1826, that of substituting a protecting duty of 30 per cent. in lieu of prohibition, *Hume* 3–8——Incorrectness of the Table, from the alteration of value in goods, *Hume* 9——Attempted to be remedied in 1829, *Hume* 10, 11——Witness's instructions in drawing up the Tables, *Hume* 32–34——Causes of alteration from the value of 30 per cent., *Hume* 13–30, 69, 70——In 1829 officers were allowed to take an *ad valorem* duty, or a duty per pound at their pleasure, *Hume* 27——Division of silk goods into three different principles of per centage, *Hume* 31——Table of 1829 increased the protection as compared with 1826, *Hume* 35, 36——Negociations of the silk trade with Government for a protecting duty in 1829, *Hume* 37–41——Table of the duties on the importation of manufactured silk, showing the rates of the duties, and the amount of the same upon the value of the articles, *Hume* 42——Duty on the importation of waste silk, 1815–1831, *Hume* 50——Duties payable on the importation of raw, waste and thrown silk, showing the changes which have been made therein since 1824, *Hume* 52.

Traders would rather pay Government than smugglers, duties regulated to meet the alternative, *Hume* 80–83——Manner in which duties and drawback affect different branches of the silk trade, *Hume* 92–99——How far duty and drawback is a tax upon one manufacturing district for the benefit of another, *Hume* 113–119——Duty not sufficiently high for protection, *Brunskill* 235——How far reducing the duty on certain manufactured articles would relieve one party at the expense of another, *Brunskill* 451–454——Reducing duties has not expanded commerce, *Merry* 2542——Evils of further reducing duty, *Wadden* 10144——It would be in violation of the promise of the Board of Trade, *Wadden* 10145; *Grout* 10342, 10343——Amount of duty compared with labour, *Cheeper* 930–932——Duties on silk and cotton, *Doxat* 4036, 4037——Small duty on importation into Austria, Russia and Germany, *Martin* 5441——*Ad valorem* duty can be collected on heavy articles but not on fancy goods, *Brunskill* 234——Why rated duty on manufactured goods more advantageous than *ad valorem*, *Clay* 6908–6910——Duty would be better collected by weight than *ad valorem*, *Baggallay* 7523, 7525, 7576.

Difficulty of ascertaining a proper rate of duty upon importation of French goods, *Baggallay* 7574——Amount of present rate if duty collected by weight, *Dillon* 7679, 7680——Duty should be collected both by *ad valorem* and by weight, *Bottrell* 7949——Advantages of an *ad valorem* duty on importation, *Bowring* 9212——How far present duties necessary on foreign manufactured goods, *Harter* 9252——Certain duties attaching to the silk trade which should be removed, *Harter* 9314——Further reduction of duty will be an entire destruction of property, *Grout* 10363——Duty paid at the commencement of the season on all goods that come in the regular way, *Stephens* 2752——Decrease in revenue from amount of duties collected since repeal, *Poyton* 10988——Necessity for a well adjusted scale of duties, *Royle* 3178; *Moore* 11263——How far silk manufacture might be increased under proper duties, *Brocklehurst* 11436–11442——Amount of duties that ought to be collected on plain and figured goods, *Cheeper* 782–784; *Beckwith* 11966–11972——Amount of duty on plain goods, and generally, *Stone* 6010; *Bouillon* 10180, 10181——Amount of duty necessary for protection, and its effect on increasing smuggling, *Beckwith* 11984–11988——Examination upon duties on foreign thrown and manufactured silks, and protection necessary for manufacturers and throwsters, *Graham* 12781–12783.

> *Papers laid before the Committee.*

Amount of Duty paid on all Raw and Waste Silk imported and entered for home consumption, 1814–1832; distinguishing from whence, *App.* p. 918, 932.
  See also *Coventry. Ribbons,* 6. *Silk,* VII. 2. *Smuggling,* V. 2. *Spitalfields.*

678.                                                                                          *Dyeing*

*Dyeing.* English dye their goods equally with the French, *Brunskill* 401–405——Quantity of silk dyed at Coventry, 1824–5 and 1830–1, *Ratliff* 1833——Comparative price of dyeing at London and Lyons, *Gibson* 5158——Comparison of advantages of dyeing between the French and English, *Gibson* 5160–5166——Prices paid for dyeing in France, *Bowring* 8884——Frauds by French dyers and weavers, *Bowring* 8885—Comparison of superiority between English and French as to dyeing, *Bowring* 8886–8895——Professional chemists in France, *Bowring* 8889, 8890, 8896——Disadvantage from the French being prevented getting their drugs from England, *Bowring* 8897–8899.

# E.

*East India Company.* How importation of China silk taxed through the monopoly of the East India Company, *Harter* 9233–9237——Effect of East India Company's monopoly in checking the import of raw silk shown by amount of imports from different parts, 1823–1827, *Harter* 9994, 9305–9308——Imports of China silk and increase therein since the Company discontinued its importation, *Harter* 9295–9299, 9304——Variation in price at the Company's sales, *Harter* 9300–9302——Examination upon certain patterns produced, their sale or export, and prices of similar articles at East India Company's sales, *Schwabe* 9871–9886——Benefits of silk raised by the East India Company, and difficulty of other persons attempting it, *Grout* 10325–10327, 10330——Advantages to the manufacturer from the Company's sales, *Grout* 10345; *Brocklehurst* 11463–11465——Price at which they put up their silks, *Grout* 10346–10348——Method adopted with regard to goods of individuals advertized at the Company's sales, *Grout* 10349.

Company do not withdraw their silk, even though sold at low prices; individuals do, *Grout* 10364, 10365——Manner in which the Company's imports of silk goods acts injuriously to the manufactures and to themselves, *Brocklehurst* 11472——Account of profit and loss upon the sales of Bengal raw silk sold by the East India Company, 1816–1830, *Brocklehurst* 11473——Their manufactured goods come into contact with their raws imported, *Brocklehurst* 11474——State of raw silk in the East India Company's warehouses, 1829–1832, *Brocklehurst* 11475——Quantity of silk refused at the Company's sales, 1831 and 1832, and causes thereof, *Brocklehurst* 11476–11478——Duty that would effect, and advantages that would result from the Company's importing raw material instead of manufactured goods, *Brocklehurst* 11479–11484——Benefits that would be derived by the East India Company altering the description of the arrangement of their silks, *Brocklehurst* 11544.

See also *Bengal and China Silk.*

*East Indies.* Unhealthiness of the climate renders human life uncertain, *Grout* 10325–10327.

See also *Importation,* 2.

*Elverfeldt.* See *Velvets.*

*Eggs.* Silk sometimes smuggled over from France as a case of eggs, *Ballance* 11016, 11017.

*Engine Looms.* See *Looms. Wages.*

*English Goods.* Statement of the purchases of broad silks and silk handkerchiefs at Spitalfields and other English manufactories, for five years previous to 1826, *Dillon* 7598–7600——Similar statement for five years and nine months since 1826, *Dillon* 7601——Statement of proportion, per 100 *l.* of purchases of English silks and ribbons, 1827–1831, *Dillon* 7608——Velvets and Swiss ribbons superseded by English articles, *Dillon* 7618——Feeling in favour of English manufactures at present, *Sedgwick* 8096, 8097——Some English fancy goods equal to the French, *Sedgwick* 8098–8102——Preference in favour of English manufacture, from improvement therein, *Sedgwick* 8110–8116——Improvements that have taken place in English manufacture since 1825, and fear of the French from English competition, *Bowring* 8772–8777——To what improvement in English manufacture attributed by the French, *Bowring* 8837–8839.

How far English manufactures have improved from competition with France, *Bowring* 9684–9688——Reason for not dealing in British goods, *Bouillon* 10162–10167——Proportion of English sales by witness's house annually, *Bouillon* 10234, 10235——English silks have not improved since admission of the French, *Stephens* 10610–10612——Preference in favour of English black and white silk goods over French, *Stephens* 10613, 10614——Improvement in manufacture not to be ascribed to the importation of French goods, *Wallis* 10889–10893——No stocks of English silks on hand when the French were admitted, *Brocklehurst* 11342–11345——No necessity for foreign competition as a stimulus to improvement of manufacture in England, shown by the production of certain patterns, *Brocklehurst* 11485–11487——Improvements would be made in silk manufacture if artisans properly encouraged, *Smith* 11690, 11691.

See also *Avignon. Colours. Coventry. France,* III. *Retailers. Ribbons,* 4.

*Etienne,*

*Etienne, St.* State of the silk and ribbon manufacture, and situation of weavers at, *Bowring* 8961–9821.

See also *Wages. Weavers,* 8. III.

*Exportation.* Official value of British manufactured silk exported each year, 1821–1830 *Hume* 64——Export of British silk has increased since 1826, *Hume* 85——Quantity exported 1826, 1830, 1831, *Hume* 86, 87——Effect in the change of the law in 1829, on the export of silk, *Hume* 88–91——Manner in which drawbacks and duties affect different branches of the silk trade, *Hume* 92–99——Value of debentures would depend on the proportion of thrown silk imported as compared with the quantity of British goods exported, *Hume* 100——How far drawback acts as a bounty on exportation, *Hume* 103–112 ——How far duty and drawback is a tax upon one manufacturing district for the benefit of another, *Hume* 113–119——Small remuneration upon the exportation of silk, *Brunskill* 471–474——Drawback allowed on the exportation of ribbons, *Cox* 2282——How far the French have possession of the foreign markets over the English, *Merry* 2498–2502 ——Advantages of the French with regard to exportation, *Merry* 2533–2536——Extent of the export trade of France, *Stephens* 2680, 2681——Necessity for encouraging export trade, *Brockwell* 3516, 3517——Value of silk manufactures exported last year, *Harter* 9269——Number of persons export trade would employ if goods made from silk thrown in this country, *Harter* 9270–9272——Exports 1821–1831, and increase therein upon allowance of drawback, *Harter* 9276–9281——Description of goods exported when export commenced, and drawback allowed, *Harter* 9426–9437——Countries to which narrow goods exported, *Harter* 9444–9447——How far broad goods could be exported if manufactured for less, *Harter* 9448–9459.

Increase in exportation of English silk goods in certain years from 1821, *Bowring* 9769 ——Exports are of goods manufactured from Bengal and China silk, *Wadden* 10107—— How exportation relieves trade, *Wadden* 10109——Not practicable to export if duty on thrown silk taken off, and no debenture allowed, *Wadden* 10110——Manner of increasing the export trade by raising duty on importation and drawback on exportation, and taking off limitation of time upon debentures, *Wadden* 10113–10116——Increase in the quantity of goods exported since repeal of prohibitory laws, but decline in value, *Poyton* 10987——Value of British export trade in 1831, *Brocklehurst* 11519——Advantage thereof, and state thereof from alteration of the law, *Brocklehurst* 11520, 11521—— Manner in which export trade might be made more profitable, *Brocklehurst* 11526–11528 ——Proportion of exports between France and other parts of the world, *Brocklehurst* 11529——Goods that are generally exported, *Brocklehurst* 11534——British silk trade has no established markets abroad, *Brocklehurst* 11535——Less labour in working cost goods, and showing the export trade not so valuable as supposed, *Wright* 11761—— Manner in which French interfere with export trade, *Beckwith* 11948–11951.

See also *America. Debentures. France,* VI. *Lombardy.*

*Extra Weighers.* See *Custom House.*

# F.

*Factories Regulation.* Injurious tendency of Factories Regulation Bills, *Royle* 3145–3149, 3175–3177.

*Failures.* More in Coventry since the introduction of foreign goods, *Cox* 2201, 2202—— Failures and compositions attributable to a glutted market, and the introduction of foreign goods, *Stephens* 2739–2745——Failures of throwsters and manufacturers last year, *Brockwell* 3490–3493——Cause of failures 1825 and 1826, *Martin* 5484, 5485——Reasons for failures being reduced, *Dillon* 7701——Number of failures in Macclesfield 1814–1826 and since, and causes thereof, *Brocklehurst* 11404–11408.

See also *Creditors. Manchester. Manufacturers. Throwsters.*

*Fairclough, William,* (Analysis of his Evidence.) Landing waiter in the Customs, 12373 ——Process of weighing and examining silk goods on their landing, 12375——Landing waiters do not attend to more than one pair of scales, 12376–12379——Difficulty of the weigher committing a fraud without connivance with the landing waiter, 12380–12383—— Landing waiters changed periodically, 12384, 12385——No advantage to bribe the weigher without the landing waiter, 12386——Landing waiter always present, 12387, 12388——Not possible for the scales to be left to the weigher without the attendance of the landing waiter, 12389——Landing waiter never trusts to the weigher, but always calculates the weight himself, 12390–12392——He would be removed if he did, 12393, 12394——Frauds might be committed by collusion, 12395——Operation of the check of the surveyor upon the landing waiter, 12396, 12397, which would prevent collusion between the landing waiter and weigher, 12398, 12399——Salary of landing waiters, 12400—— Consequent improbability of their being open to fraud, 12401——Not often two scales in use at one time, but when so there is an officer to each, 12402, 12403——Difficulty of any attempt to pass figured goods for plain, 12404–12408——Not more goods passed through the Custom House since the last seizure, 12409——Manner of examining and counting other goods not silk, showing difficulty of improperly counting, 12410–12421, 12423——How far a trifling present might be made of toys, 12422.

*Fancy Trade.* *Ad valorem* duty can be collected on heavy articles, but not on fancy articles, *Brunskill* 234——Wages on fancy articles are cheaper in France, *Brunskill* 244——No duty could protect the fancy branch, it being entirely governed by the French fashions, *Brunskill* 374-377, 557; *Cox* 2165——Difficulties the fancy trade have to encounter from the prevailing fashion in favour of foreign goods and a glutted market, *Brunskill* 427-443——Causes of English fancy goods being worse than the French, *Brunskill* 669——They will not equal the French, from the cost of machinery preventing its use, *Brunskill* 673-679——How far importation of the fancy trade affects the plain trade, *Goode* 1228-1232, 1238-1245——Fancy branch in Coventry has increased, and would increase further but for foreign competition, *Goode* 1233, 1237, 1248-1250——Figure branch worse last year than the year before, *Smith* 1262——More skill required in making figured than plain ribbons, on account of extra machinery, *Smith* 1263.

Distress of the fancy trade from foreign competition, *Brunskill* 437-443; *Goode* 1233-1237, 1248-1250; *Marston* 1418-1424; *Jacombs* 1598; *Merry* 2473-2486; *Doxat* 4049, 4051; *Dubois* 10248-10256, 10261, 10262; *Bridges* 10441-10449, 10463-10468, 10500-10509; *Moore* 11286-11289; *Prout* 11644, 11645——Fluctuation in the value of fancy articles according to the time they are brought out, *Jacombs* 1678-1685 ——Proportion the higher branches bear to the whole trade in ribbons, *Cox* 2191, 2192——Fancy goods are not made with a view to the lower classes, *Cox* 2199——Successful sale of spring goods, but loss at the end of the year from introduction of French goods in the autumn, *Merry* 2473-2486——Comparison of quantity and value of fancy goods made at Coventry five years previously and subsequent to 1826, *Merry* 2605-2609——Few English fancy ribbons sold, *Stephens* 2642——Little improvement in English fancy goods since 1826, *Stephens* 2669-2671——Before removal of prohibition sacrifices could be made after sale of spring stock without ruin, *Stephens* 2731, 2732—— Decrease of fancy trade attributed to the public using more plain articles than formerly, *Gibson* 5133-5141.

Fancy articles made in England cheaper than in France, *Gibson* 5142-5147 ——Figured silks much worn at present, *Stone* 5946-5948——Importation of rich figured goods given up from loss thereon, *Baggallay* 7473-7475——Price thereof, *Baggallay* 7476—— Description of the term plain, figured and fancy goods, *Ballance* 8395-8400——Fancy branch can only be preserved by prohibition, *Ballance* 8436, 8437, 8472——State of the fancy trade prior to and since 1826, *Ballance* 8438-8442——Importance of fancy branch to the silk trade, *Ballance* 8443——Proportion of fancy trade to the whole previous to 1825, *Ballance* 8646——Prohibition the only protection for the fancy trade, *Wadden* 10033; *Dubois* 10272-10277——More fancy than plain goods sold this year, *Bouillon* 10158-10161——Effects of opening the Ports on the Spitalfields fancy trade, *Dubois* 10,248-10256, 10261, 10262——Not an improvement in English figured silks since the opening the Ports, *Dubois* 10260——Difference in the quality of certain fancy goods made in France and by Messrs. Fulton, *Stephens* 10570-10572——More money would have been embarked by manufacturers in the fancy trade but for French goods, *Stephens* 10593——Decline in the fancy trade, number of looms formerly and at present, *Bennett* 10752-10755——Benefit to the plain branch and operatives by extending the fancy trade, *Bennett* 10760, 10761——Quantity of figured silks consumed in this country, *Ballance* 11073, 11074——Increase in the consumption of fancy goods, *Ballance* 11080-11082—— Few fancy goods made in England that are not made at Spitalfields, *Moore* 11286-11289 ——Difficulty of reviving the fancy trade while fashion in favour of France, *Moore* 11290, 11291.

See also *Black Goods. Fine Goods. Gauzes. Ribbons. Silk Trade. Steam.*

*Fashion.* Competition is that of fashion, *Brunskill* 754——Loss to the English manufacturer from change in the fashion, *Cheeper* 837-846——How far Coventry trade affected by a change of fashion before opening the trade, *Cox* 2177-2185——How far change of fashion affects speculations, *Cox* 2187-2190——Silks are more fashionable, and are used in a greater variety of articles than formerly, *Merry* 2537-2538——Quick succession of, in Paris, obliged, and early sale of goods, *Stephens* 2697, 2698 ——Under prohibition, English fashions did not follow the French so rapidly, *Stephens* 2699——Upon what fashion depends, *Bottrell* 7962-7964.

See also *France. Taste.*

*Fine Goods.* Increase in the manufacture of fine silks up to 1826, and decrease since, *Willmott* 4731-4736——Parts of England in which the finer description of plain goods are made, *Gibson* 4810-4813——Mills at present at work turn off more fine silks than those formerly in existence, *Gibson* 5119, 5120——Manufacture of rich goods more profitable than low, but less demand for them, *Stone* 5994-6000——From competition with France, *Stone* 6001——Less rich goods making than last year, *Ballance* 8620.

See also *Fancy Trade.*

*Fly Shuttle.* See *Weavers.*

*Foleshill Parish.* Evidence concerning the poors' rate of the parish, *Marston* 1349-1413, 1502-1505——Reason for distress at Foleshill, *Baggallay* 7413, and not at Coventry, *Baggallay* 7417.

See also *Wages, 4.*

*Foreign*

*Foreign Competition*, distress of the ribbon trade, caused by, *Brunskill* 121; *Smith* 1308, 309; *Marston* 1370, 1371; *Merry* 2552, 2554–2557——Distress of the Spitalfields' trade through, *Brunskill* 196–200——Foreign plain goods sell in preference to English goods of the same quality, and much cheaper, *Brunskill* 206–224——Foreign goods cannot be imported so cheap as English goods can be made, *Brunskill* 317–321——Difficulties the fancy trade have to deal with from the prevailing fashion in favour of foreign goods and a glutted market, *Brunskill* 427–443——But for foreign competition, English goods would equal the French, *Cheeper* 836——Internal competition necessary to protect the public, but not foreign competition, *Cheeper* 877–887——It supplies the demand for manufactured goods, and drives the manufacturer and workman to a lower description of goods, *Poole* 1132–1134——New patterns could be obtained, and variations could be made, but the fashions would not lead, from the anxiety to know what patterns will come from abroad, *Smith* 1310——No good answered by the introduction of foreign goods while weavers are out of employment and wages inadequate, *Cox* 2200.

Manner in which foreign competition obstructs business, *Sawer* 2419——Diasdvantage from the introduction of foreign goods when the market could be supplied at home, *Sawer* 2420–2426——Admission of foreign silks has rather done good than harm, *Royle* 3273——Advantage to operatives if foreign competition removed, *Stone* 6368——How far consumption of foreign goods on the decline when official documents show an increase, *Dillon* 7619–7621——No advantage to this country from the importation of foreign silk goods, *Stephens* 2746, 2747; *Ballance* 8451——Examination upon competition with France, and protecting duty necessary for English manufacturer, *Ballance* 8556–8583 ——Foreign competition will tend to ruin our manufactures altogether, *Dubois* 10268 ——Loss of half trade from introduction of foreign coloured goods, *Grout* 10310—— Value of foreign importation, *Ballance* 11083–11096——Importation of certain goods discontinued, from being able to purchase them cheaper in London, *Beckwith* 11929–11933——Manner in which foreign competition operates against labour, *Graham* 12747–12750.

See also *Competition. France. Prohibition. Ribbon Trade. Silk Trade.*

*Foreign Countries.* See *Wages*, 8. *Weavers*, 8.

*Fossembrone Silk.* Quality thereof, and its importation into this country, *Brockwell* 3661–3667——It is generally thrown in this country, *Wadden* 10061–10064——How far it is superior to Piedmont in making organzine, *Wadden* 10067, 10068——It is the best Italian raw, *Bennett* 10792, 10793.

*FRANCE:*

    I. *Generally.*
    II. *Silk Trade therein.*
    III. *Intercourse with England.*

      1. Generally.
      2. Advantages of France.
      3. Disadvantages of France.

    IV. *Consumption of Silk therein.*
    V. *Imports of Silk into, quality and value.*
    VI. *Exports of silk from.*
    VII. *Production of Silk therein, quality and value thereof.*
    VIII. *Raw silk.*
    IX. *Thrown Silk.*
    X. *Imports of manufactured goods into.*

I. *Generally.*

Benefits to France from foreign competition, *Bowring* 9024–9028——Population of France rated to the land tax, *Bowring* 9040——Great expense to France of its protection of its cotton twist trade without any effect, *Bowring* 9181, 9185, 9186——Disadvantages of the protective system to France, *Bowring* 9198, 9199; and to the shipping trade of France by increasing the duties on iron, *Bowring* 9204, 9205——Rate of interest in France, *Bowring* 9679, 9680.

II. *Silk trade therein.*

Method of trade adopted by French manufacturers, *Brockwell* 3520–3524——Method of assaying a bale of silk in France, *Doxat* 4216——How far silk trade of France improving, *Doxat* 4319–4322; *Moore* 11163——Extent of silk manufacture of France; importation, growth and number of looms, *Bottrell*, 7924–7926; *Bowring* 9941–9960 ——Means of obtaining information as to silk trade in France, *Bowring* 8724–8729—— Disadvantages under which the French silk trade is suffering at present, *Bowring* 8730, 8769–8771——Extent of protection of the French silk trade, *Bowring* 8759——How far France has obtained a foreign trade in silks from its home trade being unprotected, *Bowring* 678.

*FRANCE*—continued.

### II. *Silk Trade therein*—continued.

*Bowring* 9631, 9632——How far advantages of France act as a protection, *Bowring* 9633–9635——State of trade in certain districts in France, *Bowring* 9737, 9744——Comparison of distress in silk and other trades in France, *Bowring* 9783–9787——To what the success of the French silk trade is owing, *Moore* 12085——Abstract Statement of French silk manufactures for the years 1827–1830 conjointly, with an abstract view of the total amounts of the silk manufactures of the United Kingdom at different periods during 1815–1831, *Doxat* 12094.

### III. *Intercourse with England.*

#### 1. Generally.

Description of English goods sold in France, *Stephens* 2914–2930——Change of opinion in France with regard to its commercial relations with England, *Bowring* 8959, 8960——Institution of a commission in France for considering its relations with this country, *Bowring* 9141, 9142—— Examination as to exchange of exports between France and England of silk and cotton, *Bowring* 9175, 9176, 9757–9765——Advantages to France and England from admitting French goods at a low duty, and obtaining the raw material, *Bowring* 9182–9184——Comparative statement of the quality of silk used in England and France, *Doxat* 4111, 4112——For what Bengal silks are used in France, *Doxat* 4113, 4114——Reason why French do not buy Bengal silk in the English market, *Martin* 5436——Instance of French thrown silk being obtained here, *Heath* 5332–5339——Quantity coming to London is very small, *Martin* 5420, 5421——No feeling in France in favour of any fair and reciprocal trade with England, *Moore* 12077——Documentary evidence put in by witness as to French and English imports and exports and silk manufactures generally, and examination thereon, *Doxat* 12089–12092——Exports of silks from Calais to England, 1831–32, and examination, showing inference of smuggling from official reports, *Doxat* 12090——No advantage in transferring silk trade to France in exchange for its taking our cotton yarn, *Brocklehurst* 11506.

#### 2. Advantages of France.

Comparison of advantages between France and England, *Brunskill* 237, 238, 244, 354, 566–575, 593–610; *Ratliff* 1855–1858, 1869–1872, 1893–1898; *Doxat* 4331; *Bottrell* 7881; *Ballance* 8410–8415; *Harter* 9231–9250; *Wadden* 10031; *Bennett* 10762–10764; *Moore* 11291–11295——Other advantages of France would counterbalance ours, had we the raw material, *Ballance* 8708——Disadvantages of England over France from taxation of the raw material, *Harter* 9231, 9247, 9248——Advantage to the French from use of machinery, *Brunskill* 237, 238——From price of Italian raw, *Doxat* 4331——From exportation of raw being prohibited, *Royle* 3399–3407; *Harter* 9244, 9245——From setting the fashions, *Cox* 2162–2164; *Harter* 9249, 9250; *Bennett* 10749, 10750; *Moore* 11291, 11292——Working for orders, *Wadden* 10031——From cheap labour, *Brunskill* 244; *Bennett* 10762–10764——From the growth of raw, *Brunskill* 354; *Ratliff* 1855–1858, 1889–1892; *Harter* 9244, 9245; *Wadden* 10031; *Bridges* 10453–10462, 10493; *Bennett* 10762–10764; *Moore* 11291, 11292——How far advantages of France counteracted by the amount of duty collected in England, *Wadden* 10032——England not on a fair footing with France, *Bridges* 10049—— French sell only one pattern to one house in different countries, and thereby lessen the cost of manufacture, *Ratliff* 1872——French merely manufacture to the extent of their order from England, and not for other countries from the same pattern, *Clay* 6996–6999——Comparative cost of manufacture at London and Lyons, *Ratliff* 1965–1969; *Doxat* 4051, 4052; *Hall* 6660, 6661——Abridged recapitulation thereof, *Doxat* 4279——Statement of cost of manufacture of plain goods at London and Lyons, *Doxat* 4402——Comparison of quantity of labour, cost of material, and rate of wages at London and Lyons, *Brunskill* 566–575, 593–610; *Doxat* 4053–4055, 4073–4079, 4171–4183; *Bowring* 8723, 9170, 9616–9626, 10027–10029——Examination in answer to Dr. Bowring's evidence thereupon, *Ballance* 10018–10020——Table showing the comparative cost of manufacture between French and English goods, *Pittifor* 12060–12065.

How fluctuations in the silk trade in France act detrimentally to English industry, *Doxat* 4066–4068, 4073——On what the competition between France and Spitalfields depends, *Doxat* 4169, 4170——Variation in the price of silk between Lyons and London, and causes thereof, *Ratliff* 1961; *Doxat* 4184–4193——Import duties and charges upon raw and thrown silk into Lyons and London, *Doxat* 4208–4218——Prices of silk in France are lower than in England, independent of duty, *Doxat* 4252, 4253, 4353–4356——Further examination on price of silk at Lyons and in London, *Doxat* 4312–4315; *Martin* 5511, 5521; *Harter* 9468–9470, 9474–9476——Difference in weaving and dyeing in favour of France, *Gibson* 4842–4847——Charges of transport of raw silk from Lyons, *Heath* 5342——Preference of the French for their own silk, *Ratliff* 1889–1892; *Heath* 5342, 5350——Advantages of France from its exports of manufactured silks, with, particulars thereof in 1829, *Ballance* 8413——Balance of trade between England and France against England, *Bowring* 9191——Natural advantages of France for producing fine goods, and of England for coarser, *Bowring* 9200, 9201——Competition between France and England, and advantages and disadvantages with respect to fine and coarse goods,

*FRANCE*—continued.
  III. *Intercourse with England*—continued.
    2. Advantages of France—*continued.*
goods, *Bowring* 9726–9736——Obtaining French raw silk would not counterbalance all
the disadvantages of France over England, *Moore* 12088——Advantages to the French
by the duty on foreign thrown silk here, *Graham* 12719——Statement intended to
show the differences which range between the prices of silks at London and at Lyons,
*Doxat* 12094.
  See also *Orders.*

  *Papers laid before the Committee* :
Detailed Costs of the manufacture of good plain Silk Goods in common colours at
London and at Lyons; also a recapitulation of the differences of those Costs per lb. and
per cent., and estimates of the Charges of import through the Custom House and by
smuggling, *App.* p. 940.

Abridged comparative view of Costs at London and at Lyons of good plain Silk Goods
in common colours, and statements relative to their legal imports and to their illicit
imports, *Evidence* p. 243.

Costs and Statements presented in an inverted view, *Evidence* p. 263.

Statement (made in 1829), showing every charge of the Silk Manufacture dissected, and
the relative proportions in regard to wages of labour, to machinery, &c.; also the
relative charges abroad for throwing dissected, *App.* p. 942.

Statement, (made in April 1829,) Idem, grounded on a lower rate of Charges for
weaving, &c.; Charges for throwing the same, *App.* p. 944.

A nearer view of the respective Charges of every item of the manufacture of good plain
gros de Naples, in common colours, at London and at Lyons, with remarks as to their
effect or rates of labour, &c., and on quantities of work, *App.* p. 945—— Statement in
which Charges relative to every process of the manufacture of good plain goods at London
and at Lyons in 1821–1825, and in 1826–1831, are placed next to each other, with their
respective differences set forth in per centages, *Evidence* p. 258.

    3. Disadvantages of France.
Taxes on iron and machinery for building mills dearer in France than in England,
*Bowring* 9662–9664, 9670–9672——Advantage of Switzerland over France as to taxation
of machinery, *Bowring* 9665–9669——Backwardness of throwing and reeling establish-
ments in France, *Bowring* 10029——France not under disadvantages compared with
Switzerland, *Moore* 12076.
  See also *French goods.*

  IV. *Consumption of Silk therein.*
Extent of consumption of French silk, *Bowring* 8737–8739——Decreased consumption
and increased export, *Bowring* 9030–9032——Total consumption of raw and thrown in
France, *Martin* 5504——Examination as to consumption of silk in France as shown by
certain documentary evidence, *Doxat* 12093–12095.

  V. *Imports of silk into, quality and value thereof.*
Quantities of silk consumed in France and Switzerland, and importation therein, *Doxat*
4074–4078——Statement of imports of raw, thrown, and waste silk into France, *Doxat*
4078——Quality of silk imported into, *Doxat* 4090–4092——Price of Italian raw imported into Lyons, *Doxat* 4280–4286, 4331, 4332, 4344, 4357–4374——How far regulated by the quantity introduced, *Heath* 5364——Importation of foreign silk into France,
*Doxat* 4316–4318; *Heath* 5255, 5263–5267, 5371; *Martin* 5504, 5509, 5510; *Heath*
5650–5658—— Importations into, and exportations from France of raw and thrown silk,
1825–1831, *Bowring* 8731——Weight thereof, 1820–1831, *Bowring* 8735——Value
thereof, 1820–1831, *Bowring* 8735——Account of the value of raw silks of all sorts
imported into France from the year 7 or 1800 to 1806, and the quantities and value, 1815–
1819, *Bowring* 8735.

Report of the importations of raw and thrown silks, and of the duties levied, 1825–
1830, reduced to English weights and measures, *Bowring* 8736——Quantities of silk
imported from foreign countries which have entered the bonding warehouses of Lyons,
1822–1832, showing quantities entered for home consumption and exported, *Bowring*
8799——Quantity of foreign silk sold in the Lyonese market for 10 years, *Bowring*
8804—— Effect of import of Italian silk into France on prices and consumption
of French silk, *Doxat* 4341–4352; *Heath* 5663——Approximation in price of Italian
and French silks at Lyons, *Doxat* 4392——With exception of difference of duties
and charges, French pay the same for foreign silk as other parts of the world, *Doxat*
4394——Quantity of Italian imported, *Heath* 5256, 5257——From whence information
of French imports obtained, *Heath* 5260, 5261——Sales of Italian silk registered in
France, *Heath* 5270, 5271——Reasons for the French importing fine Italian raw silks,
*Heath* 5273–5275——Consumption of foreign organzine at Lyons is principally Piedmont, *Heath* 5351——Quality thereof, *Martin* 5497, 5498——Reasons for the French
not importing silk from Italy as well as the Swiss, *Bowring* 9673, 9674.
                                    *Papers*

*FRANCE*—continued.

V. *Imports of Silk into, quality and value thereof*—continued.

*Papers laid before the Committee.*

Statement of the Quantities of Raw and Thrown Silks imported into France from Italy and other parts, during the years 1825, 1826, 1827 and 1828, also Imports of Waste Silks, *Evidence* p. 218.

VI. *Exports of Silk from.*

It prohibits the export of all silk except manufactured, *Ratliff* 1882, 1883; *Banbury* 4597; *Martin* 5404, 5554——Thrown silk allowed to be exported from France, *Martin* 5404, 5406–5411——Ports of exportation from France, and quantities of foreign silks exported, 1828–1830, *Bowring* 8736——Bounty and drawback on exportation of silk from France rejected by the Council of Commerce, *Bowring* 9196, 9197——Administration des Douanes: Exportation des Tissus de soie de Fabriques Françaises, with computation into English weight and value, *Doxat* 12094——Marchandises exportées de l'intérieur seulement, *Doxat* 12094——Marchandises exportées de l'intérieur du royaume en payant des Droits, en Franchise ou avec prime, *Doxat* 12094——Recapitulation of the annual exports from France, 1827–1830, of French manufactured silks of every description, showing their quantity in French weight, and value in francs, computed into English weight and value, *Doxat* 12094.

VII. *Production of Silk therein, quality and value thereof.*

Proportion superior silk bears to the whole produce of France, *Heath* 5368——Annual production, *Heath* 5365; *Martin* 5501, 5511; *Bowring* 8742, 8743——Value of silks in France shown by price current, *Bowring* 8744——Production of French silk increasing, *Doxat* 4259–4263; *Bowring* 8745——Method of production and manufacture of silk, from its earliest stage, *Bowring* 8745——Price of silk of native manufacture, and how far on the decline, *Bowring* 8746–8749——Price of cocoons and raw silks of Cevennes, 1822–1831, *Bowring* 8749——Method taken in France of ascertaining the quality and weight of silk, *Bowring* 8750–8752——Statement of the fluctuations in the prices of silk in the market at Lyons, 1822–1832, *Bowring* 8802, 8803——How far French growers of their own silk, *Bowring* 9086——Improved manner of rearing the worm makes the employment more healthy, *Bowring* 9095——Size of deniers, *Bowring* 9092–9097—— Manner in which silk is sold, *Bowring* 9098–9104——Price of coarse silk in France, *Doxat* 4379, 4380——Price and quality of certain French silks, *Heath* 5339–5341, 5343.

VIII. *Raw Silk.*

Regulations that should be adopted to prohibit the importation of French and Swiss manufactured goods, or to compel the French and Swiss to export their raw silk, *Brockwell* 3501–3515——If French raws allowed to be exported, and manufactured goods admitted, differences in the price of labour might be afterwards regulated, *Brockwell* 3518, 3519, 3525——Necessity of prohibiting importation of manufactured goods from France unless she allows the importation of raw silk; amount of duty on manufactured goods in that event, *Moore* 11296–11301——In the event of France putting a duty on the importation of raw, whether that amount should be added to the manufactured goods, *Moore* 11303–11306——Quality of French silks, and improvement in reeling, *Doxat* 4079, 4080——Superiority of French silk attributed to superior reeling, *Doxat* 4119–4121.

Why English do not reel silk as well as the French, *Doxat* 4124——Importance to obtain French raws, *Banbury* 4598–4600——Description of French silks that are superior to the Italian, *Martin* 5500——Higher price of French raw than Italian, *Heath* 5348; *Martin* 5579——In what superiority in French silk consists, *Heath* 5367–5372—— Manner in which raw silks are smuggled out of France, *Martin* 5412, 5413——Expense attending it, *Martin* 5414, 5418——Superiority of French silk at Cevennes, and cost thereof, *Bowring* 8740, 8741——French silk superior to any English manufacturer can procure, *Brunskill* 670–672; *Ratliff* 1854, 1878; *Harter* 9246, 9471–9473——French government intend to allow the exportation thereof, *Bowring* 8753, 8754——Both France and England would be benefited by the export of French raw, *Bowring* 9115, 9116—— Duty on raw silk imported into France is small, and the French use principally silk of their own growth, *Moore* 12074——Advantage of being enabled to get French raw silks, *Moore* 12088.

IX. *Thrown Silk.*

Comparison as to quality of French thrown silk, *Stone* 6239–6245, 6248——Expense of conveying them to this country, *Stone* 6246, 6247——Means of ascertaining French silk, *Stone* 6249–6253, 6255–6258——How obtained, *Stone* 6254—— For what purposes calculated, *Stone* 6259–6263——Rise in the price of French organzine from small stocks on hand, *Bottrell* 7922, 7923.

X. *Imports of manufactured goods into.*

Importations into France from Switzerland of velvets and plain goods, *Doxat* 4082 ——Importations of Swiss ribbons into France, *Doxat* 4093–4096——Importation of foreign manufactured silks into France, and how far beneficial to it, *Bowring* 8760–8766 ——Importation of English manufactured silks into France, *Bowring* 8678–8787; *Brocklehurst* 11485——How far English goods exposed in shop windows in France, *Bowring* 9766, 9767——Necessity for getting an opening in France for reception of

Irish

*FRANCE*—continued.

X. *Imports of manufactured goods into*——continued.

Irish tabinets, *Sisson*, 11918–11920——Duty on importations into France, *Doxat* 4083–4085; *Heath* 5255, 5263–5267; *Martin* 5435; *Bowring* 9023, 10029——Douanes Royales de France; Imports of foreign manufactured silks into France for home consumption, *Doxat.* 12094.

See also *America. Avignon. Bengal and China Silk. Chamond, St. Condition, La. Conseil des Prud'hommes. Cottons. Country Trade. Coventry. Crape. Dyeing. Etienne St. Exportation. Fancy Trade. Gauzes. Germany. Italy. Jobbing. Labour. Lyons. Manchester. Orders. Piedmont Silk. Prices. Sardinia. Smuggling*, VI. *Throwsters. Watered Silks.*

*Fraser, Allan*, (Analysis of his Evidence.) Extra weigher at the Custom House, 12096–12098——Duty of landing waiters, 12099, 12100——Duty of surveyor, 12101, 12102 ——Number of ships discharging at one time, 12103, 12104——Number of men at the scales, and reduction in the amount thereof, 12105–12110——Pay of extra weighers, not constant employment, 12111–12113, 12195——Examination as to opportunities of removing goods during absence of landing waiter, 12114–12124——Fraud must be caused by collusion between the weigher and landing waiter, 12125–12128, 12132—— Instances of weighers being left alone, 12129–12131——Disputes between Custom House officers and merchants, as to value of silk, 12133–12136——No knowledge of silks being passed at less than their actual weight, 12137——Possibility of fraud from value being left to the judgment of the merchant, 12138–12147——Method of weighing silk manufactured goods, and difficulties from landing waiter attending two sets of scales, 12148–2154,

Examination, showing the responsibility of the weigher and want of check upon the landing waiter, 12155–12171——Instances of goods being reweighed by the surveyors, 12172–12177——Refusal of bribes by witness, and reasons for not reporting their offer to the landing waiter, 12179–12191, 12196–12201, 12268–12271, 12274–12289——No instructions given to extra weighers when going on duty, 12192——Duty of extra weighers, 12193, 12194——No recollection of a smaller number being entered than that actually passed, 12202–12207——Examination upon the fact of the commission of bribery among the Custom House officers, 12208–12212——Examination as to names of officers who have told witness of their receiving bribes for not doing their duty, with witness's declining to mention them, 12213–12249, 12262–12267, 12272, 12273—— Supposition that the bribe was for passing short weights, 12250–12261——Opportunities for committing fraud, from poverty of extra weighers, 12290–12297——Presents of small value to landing waiters from merchants, 12298–12310.

*Fraud.* See *Custom House.*

*FRENCH GOODS:*

1. *Generally.*
2. *Importation thereof.*
3. *Advantages of their Importation.*
4. *Disadvantages of their Importation.*
5. *Comparison of manufacture between France and England.*
6. *Preference in favour of.*
7. *Prices*
8. *Prohibition thereof.*

1. *Generally.*

Quantity of manufactured goods exported from France and consumed therein, *Doxat* 4330——Increase in the manufacture of cut ribbons, *Clay* 6804–6807——Articles the French at present employed upon, and for what markets intended, *Bottrell* 7908–7912 ——Account of silk manufactures exported from France, 1828–1830, *Bowring* 8789, 8790——Mode of valuation, *Bowring* 8791, 8792——Imports of manufactured silk to England, 1818–1824, *Bowring* 8793——To 1830, *Bowring* 9137, 9138——Effect of the introduction of French silk goods into England, upon French manufactures, *Bowring* 9120——English demand is for articles of taste, *Bowring* 9122——Official value of silks exported from France, *Bowring* 9123–9126——Analysis of the manner in which the different quantities of French silks, plain and figured, are distributed in foreign countries, *Bowring* 9127. The like of crapes, *Bowring* 9128. The like of ribbons, *Bowring* 9129 ——Examination upon the foregoing statements, *Bowring* 9130–9133——Qualities of different French goods taken by England in 1825, 1828 and 1831, *Bowring* 9134.

2. *Importation thereof:*

Method of purchasing French goods, *Brunskill* 722–726; *Jacombs* 1601–1609; *Clay* 6767–6768——Quantity of French goods imported, *Cox* 2203–2204——French import something new in large quantities every season, *Cox* 2338–2341——Greater variety of French goods now than during prohibition, *Bottrell* 7829, 7830——Importation of French silks has increased lately, *Cox* 2349——Generally takes place to a large extent at the present time of the year, *Cox* 2351——Few goods in France at present, *Stephens* 2685, 2686——Increase of French stocks by wholesale dealers since 1828, *Stephens* 2950–678.                                                                                     2955,

*FRENCH GOODS—* continued.

### 2. *Importation thereof—* continued.

2955, 2969, 2970——Revolution in France a cause of greater importation into England since July 1830, *Heath* 5305–5314——Tendency of any convulsion in France to cause importation into England, *Heath* 5308–5312 — Number of persons engaged in importation of foreign manufactured goods, *Clay* 6758–6763——State of import trade from 1826, *Clay* 6769–6774——State of trade with regard to French goods in England, *Clay* 6840——Silk trade on the decline as regards imports, *Clay* 6932–6936——Quantity of French silks sold now greater than in 1826, *Clay* 6960, 6961——Goods that have paid duty are more valuable than those smuggled, *Clay* 6991, 6993-6995——Only rich French goods ordered for the English market, *Bottrell* 7921——Proportion of silk manufactured goods imported in 1825 that were warehoused against opening the Ports in 1826, *Bowring* 9654, 9655-——Different views of silk manufacturers as to importation of French goods, *Bridges* 10529, 10530——French goods coming to this country double the amount shown by French account of official exports, *Moore* 12086.

### 3. *Advantages of their Importation.*

Extent to which English manufacture has improved by their admission, *Brunskill* 171–173; *Cox* 2079, 2082; *Bottrell* 7951, 7954-7956; *Sedgwick* 8006-8008——Who are benefited by their introduction, *Gibson* 5037-5040——How far importation of silk manufactured goods from France tends to displace English labour, *Bowring* 9643-9650 ——Improvement in the quality of French manufactured silks imported since the removal of prohibition, *Bowring* 9651-9653.

### 4. *Disadvantages of their Importation.*

Disadvantages of contending with French fashions, *Cheeper* 828-832; *Jacombs* 1743 ——Introduction of French ribbons has shut out the English manufacturer from both town and country trade, *Jacombs* 1613–1615, 1697, 1698——Contract for a particular pattern not fulfilled from French goods coming over previous to its execution, *Jacombs* 1618–1628——Loss from the imitation of French patterns, *Jacombs* 1635–1639—— Loss by the manufacture of certain ribbons by their being superseded by the French, *Jacombs* 1656, 1657; *Cox* 2051, 2052, 2086-2094——Superiority of silk, and nature of the principle of business in France checks home trade, *Ratliff* 1873, 1874——Dependence on French fashions for the quantity of ribbons used, *Cox* 2208, 2209; *Sedgwick* 7995-7998, 8071, 8072——How far French goods are paid for by British labour, *Cox* 2230-2234.

Destruction of trade from their introduction, *Sawer* 2397-2399——Account showing loss of retail trade since 1826, through admission of French goods, *Merry* 2450-2456, 2545-2547——Interference of the French in other branches of the trade, *Merry* 2466-2468——French goods supersede English of a superior quality, *Merry* 2528—— Expense and loss of time in purchasing French over English goods, *Baggallay* 7333-7341; *Dillon* 7694, 7695——Fashion commands a higher price to be given for French than Manchester goods of the same quality, *Stephens* 10598-10606——Orders given to France instead of Spitalfields and Manchester in consequence thereof, *Stephens* 10607-10609—-Description of French goods at present bought, *Stephens* 10635——Duty that should be paid thereon, *Stephens* 10637——Expectation by Government that a larger amount of French goods would not come in after the alteration, than were smuggled in previously, with contrary result, *Moore* 11196-11200, 11219——Rich goods in the shop windows in Manchester marked French, *Kelly* 11838, 11839.

### 5. *Comparison of Manufacture between France and England.*

French manufactured goods not so distinguishable from English as formerly, *Hume* 68; *Brunskill* 383–400; *Cheeper* 913–929; *Ratliff* 1849–1853; *Cox* 2101, 2102, 2124–2131; *Stephens* 2667, 2668, 2901–2907; *Stone* 5853-5855; *Baggallay* 7538-7549; *Moore* 11249–11253——Comparison of skill in different branches with France, *Brunskill* 174–178——There would be no difficulty in detecting French goods under a prohibition, *Dubois* 10269——In what French manufacture excels the English, *Brunskill* 269-272, 329-331; *Ratliff* 1860——How much per cent. English goods are worse than French, and manner of making them equal, *Brunskill* 329-331——English dye their goods equally with the French, *Brunskill* 401-405; *Stone* 6002, 6003——British goods equally cheap and durable, *Jacombs* 1716-1719.

Difference in quantity and quality of silk used in manufacturing the same article in France and England, *Ratliff* 1847, 1848——Difference in the number of pieces of a pattern made in France and England, *Ratliff* 1870, 1871——Reasons for French fancy goods being superior to the English, *Sawer* 2427, 2428——Rivalry dare not be attempted, *Sawer* 2429-2431——Comparison between French and English in the manner of finishing their goods in favour of the French, *Clay* 6782——Assimilation of style between France and England since opening the trade, *Baggallay* 7527-7531——French trade declining from the great improvement in English manufactures and reduction in price, *Dillon* 7609-7612, 7624——Improvement in English over French manufacture, demand for French goods diminishing, and in what goods French likely to retain a superiority over the English, *Dillon* 7656-7662——Superiority of the French and inferiority of the English manufacture, and disadvantages of prohibiting importation of French manufactures, *Bowring* 9689-9706.

6. *Preference*

*FRENCH GOODS*—continued.

### 6. *Preference in favour of.*

French goods would be imported at 20 per cent. higher duty, *Brunskill* 125–128——French plain goods will sell in preference to English of the same quality, and much cheaper, *Brunskill* 206–224——Taste in favour of French ribbons, and its effect upon our manufacture, *Jacombs* 1601–1609, 1698, 1716–1719——No reduction in the price of English goods could drive the French out of the market, *Ratliff* 1875——French ribbons find their way every where, *Cox* 2098——Preference for French goods is owing to taste, not price, *Cox* 2205——Proportion French and English ribbons bear to each other in purchases from manufacturers, *Stephens* 2639–2641——Proportion during prohibition, *Stephens* 2654–2666——Preference for French goods, and reasons for it, *Cox* 2205; *Stephens* 2648–2653, 2956–2961; *Clay* 6992; *Bowring* 8788, 9768——In the event of a change of pattern in French goods they can still be sold as such, and accepted as new goods, *Stephens* 2696.

Goods obliged to be disposed of quickly in consequence of the quick succession of fashions in Paris, *Stephens* 2697, 2698; *Clay* 6814–6835——French goods sometimes sold for English, *Stephens* 2708; *Baggallay* 7373–7376——French would have preference, even if English of equal perfection, *Stephens* 2709——Goods are all of the best kind, *Clay* 6798–6842——Statement of proportion per 100*l.* of whole French trade, 1827–1831, *Dillon* 7605–7607——Amount of French goods sold per annum, *Bouillon* 10172–10175 ——Proportion of different description of goods imported from France, *Sedgwick* 8080–8090——Impossible for fashionable houses to sell goods opposed to the style fashionable in France, *Sedgwick* 8161–8164——French regulate the fashion in all parts of Europe, *Sedgwick* 8190——Superiority assigned to French goods is not through prejudice, *Bowring* 8788 ——Monopoly by France of the valuable branches will eventually cause the loss of the silk trade, *Brocklehurst* 11492——Merit of the French silk manufactures not likely to pass away from the disadvantages they labour under, *Moore* 12075.

### 7. *Prices.*

Amount of extra expenses in importing goods from France beyond what they would cost in England, *Brunskill* 558–562——That amount so much additional, but not a sufficient protection to the English manufacturer, *Brunskill* 563–565——Prices obtained for French goods, *Brunskill* 686–688——How French prices ascertained, *Ratliff* 1859, 1962–1964——Question between French and English is one of price as well as fashion, *Ratliff* 1948——French goods can be bought much cheaper in London than imported, *Stephens* 2757, 2758; *Sedgwick* 8202, 8203——Offers by French warehousemen to deliver to English purchaser free of expense, *Stephens* 2908–2913——How far prices of French manufactured goods imported last year sufficient to remunerate manufacturer, *Doxat* 4326–4329——Reduction in the price of French plain goods between 1826 and 1828, *Clay* 6775–6781——Changes in the import trade from plain to fancy goods, and prices thereof since 1829, *Clay* 6783–6795, 6841–6843——Unprofitableness of the French import trade, *Clay* 6796, 6797——Revolution in France stopped the home trade, and caused the exportation of goods at a loss to the manufacturer, *Clay* 6836–6839—— French have been compelled to reduce their prices and improve their manufacture, *Clay* 6974, 6975——Reduction in price and quality of French goods since 1826, *Bottrell* 7829, 7830——Sale price of the richest French silks, *Tootal* 9550, 9551——Advantages to the French that make their goods cheaper, *Bridges* 10450–10452.

### 8. *Prohibition thereof.*

They should be prohibited, or French raws allowed, *Brockwell* 3501–3525——Benefits to be derived by the prohibition, *Stone* 5905–5909——Calculation of loss to England by prohibition of French goods, *Bowring* 9215——Extract from a letter, showing the fear of the French manufacturers that the Committee will recommend the prohibition of their manufactures, *Bowring* 9937–9940.

See also *Fancy Trade. Gauzes. Handkerchiefs. Jobbing. License. Manchester. Orders. Prices. Prohibition. Smuggling. Throwsters. Watered Silks.*

*French-houses.* Number thereof in London, *Menetrier* 8329, 8330.

# G.

*Gauzes.* Gauzes that were formerly manufactured, and at present, *Brunskill* 521——French gauzes now sold in this country for less than operatives paid for making similar in 1824–1826, *Marston* 1371, 1372——How foreign brocade gauzes can be distinguished from English, *Marston* 1458–1460——When fine gauzes first manufactured, *Marston* 1510—— Quantity of silk used and cost of manufacture of gauze fancy ribbons in 1823 and at present, *Jacombs* 1629–1634——Cost of manufacture of gauze ribbons in 1823, from their being a new article, *Jacombs* 1668–1673——Advantage of the French in the manufacture of gauze silk, from the cost of the material, *Ratliff* 1855–1858——Gauze trade nearly abandoned at Coventry, *Ratliff* 1863——Manufacture of gauzes predominated 1824–1827, and were then partly discontinued from the French importing them, *Cox* 2170–2176 ——If many inferior gauzes are made, the French will supply the whole country, *Cox* 2235–2243——How far they may suit exportation, *Cox* 2244–2247——Taste in favour

*Gauzes*—continued.

of French gauzes; comparative price thereof, *Sawyer* 2373–2378——Rich cut gauzes were made in 1825 and 1826, *Merry* 2459, 2460——Were discontinued from interference of the French, and not being able to get material for making them so good as the French, *Merry* 2461–2463——Fewer houses make gauzes now than in 1824–1826, *Merry* 2600, 2601——Principal part of ribbons imported from France are gauze, *Merry* 2612, 2613 ——Proportion English gauze ribbons bear to the French, *Stephens* 2642——Proportion of the trade that consists of gauzes, *Stephens* 2819

Number of pieces of gauze ribbons of a certain width a man can manufacture a week, *Hall* 6757——Duty on plain gauze ribbons imported, *Baggallay* 7414, 7415——Striped gauze ribbons not imported from loss thereby, *Baggallay* 7416, 7417——Duty on figured gauzes, *Baggallay* 7420, 7421——Duty necessary thereon, *Baggallay* 7422–7426, 7430, 7431——Per centage gauze ribbons bear to the whole production of French ribbons, *Dillon* 7613, 7614——Comparison of cost price of striped and figured gauzes in France and England, *Dillon* 7684–7688, 7690–7692——More gauze ribbons smuggled in 1830 and 1831 than paid duty, *Bottrell* 7787——Examination upon the quantities of certain gauze ribbons exhibited to the Committee to show amount of duty between French and English, *Bottrell* 7884–7888——Striped gauzes at Coventry equal to the French, but not figured, *Sedgwick* 8000——If fashion in France changed against gauze ribbons, the prevailing fashion would not have the same superiority in the English market the gauze now have, *Sedgwick* 8017–8019——French gauze ribbons a great deal superior to the English, *Bouillon* 10171——Increasing the duty on gauzes would prevent jobbing, *Bouillon* 10186–10189——Import of gauzes from France, and manner in which they interfere with the English trade, *Bridges* 10406–10421——French gauzes, and not the Scotch, that interfere with Spitalfields, *Stephens* 10573–10580——Whether the fancy gauze trade can go on without prohibition, *Moore* 11312, 11313.

See also *Scotch gauzes*.

*Germany*, duties on importation into, *Doxat* 4097, 4098——Description of French goods imported into, *Bottrell* 7922.

See also *Duty on Importation. Italy. Switzerland.*

*Gibson, Thomas Field*, (Analysis of his Evidence.)  Broad silk manufacturer at Spitalfields, 4805–4807——Benefits to the Spitalfields trade by reduction of duties on raw and thrown silks, 4808, 4809, 4814, 4815——Other parts of England in which the finer description of plain goods are made, 4810–4813——Increase of competition between Lancashire and Spitalfields, 4816——Its effect on masters and workmen, 4817——No fixed rule of wages in Spitalfields, 4818–4822——Manufacture of velvets entirely, and satins principally confined to Spitalfields, 4823, 4824——Variation of the book price of weaving velvets, 4825, 4826——Proportion of the different kinds of silk manufactured at Spitalfields, 4827——All reductions of duty beneficial to the Spitalfields manufacturer, looking to competition with France, 4828–4830——Home competition more important than the French, 4832, 4833——Increased value per cent. the present duty adds to the goods, 4834–4836——If duty taken off it would equalize the prices in this and the foreign market, 4837, 4838——Advantages possessed by the French manufacturer over the English, 4839–4841.

Difference in weaving and dyeing in favour of France, 4842–4847——Silk thrown as well in England as imported from Italy, 4848——Italian thrown silk not improved, 4849——Operation of throwing in England improved of late years, 4850–4852—— Quality of silks imported from Italy, 4853, 4854——Cost of throwing organzine in Lombardy, 4858, 4859——Cost in England, and which does not remunerate the throwster, 4860–4877——Taking off the present duty would not ruin throwsters, 4878– 4882——They would get a better price, 4883——Price of Italian silk regulates that of the English, 4884, 4885——Reasons why reducing the duty would not increase the importation of foreign thrown, 4886–4889——Italians could not rapidly, or to any extent, increase the import, 4890–4892——Difference in the price between raw and thrown in this country does not remunerate the throwster, 4893–4895——Quantity or quality of Italian silk will diminish unless the throwster obtains a fair return for labour, 4896–4898——Cost of reeling silk in Italy, 4899–4905——Advantage of throwing immediately after reeling, 4907, 4908——Price at which Italian throwster would throw to order, 4909–4912——More profitable to the Italian to import raw, 4913——Total abolition of duty would place more advantages in the hands of the Italians, 4914–4919 —— English cannot produce thrown at the same price as the Italian, 4920——Duty that would protect, 4921–4924, 4927.

Decreasing scale of duty will increase amount of importation, 4925, 4926—— Machinery better in England than in Italy, 4928——Wages higher in England, 4929—— Rate of wages in Italy, 4930–4933——When silk is reeled in Italy, 4934——Increase in the importation of thrown silk did not increase after reduction of duty till last year, 4935 ——Decreasing duty would not decrease price of Italian thrown, 4936–4941——Reason of Italian throwster losing in the English market, 4942——If duty reduced he could introduce it at a profit, 4943——Duty that might be collected to protect Spitalfields manufacturer of plain goods against the French manufacturer, 4944–4947——Not much smuggling plain goods, 4948——Amount to which duty might be decreased to prevent smuggling, 4949–4951——Reasons for the Italian increasing his importation at a loss, 4952–4954, 4960

*Gibson, Thomas Field,* (Analysis of his Evidence)—*continued.*

4960——Increase of throwing mills in what years, 4955, 4956——Distress of the throwster attributed to home competition, 4957–4959——Produce of silk in Italy, and to what countries exported, 4961–4973——How far reducing duty would act as a bounty on the importation of Italian thrown silk, 4974–4981——Why causes which induce the importation of thrown silk would not act upon the raw, 4982, 4983——Whether reduction of duty would benefit the foreigner at the expense of the English throwster, 4984–4999—— Parties who have been benefited by changes in the law since 1829, 5000–5005——On what returns profits calculated, 5006–5011——Whether greater amount of goods selling now than in 1826, 5012–5017——Why goods are manufactured cheaper at Lyons than in England, 5018——Advantages to the French from their orders for fancy goods, 5019– 5027——Effect of the introduction of French goods on English prices, 5028–5036—— Who are benefited by their introduction, 5037–5040——Why reduction of duties would not prejudice the operative, 5041, 5042——Always a sufficient supply in the English market to answer the demand without foreign importation, 5043–5048—— Profits of manufacture and wages determined by competition, 5049——Proportion of labour to the value of plain goods, 5050, 5051——Smuggling would not be put down by prohibition, 5052–5055——Advantages of the Italian over the English throwster, 5056–5060.

(Second Examination.) Descriptions of thrown silk imported from Italy, and to what uses applied, 5061–5066——Broad goods imported from France, 5067, 5068——How taking off the duty would benefit the Spitalfields manufacturer, 5069, 5070 ——How far it would increase consumption and the demand for labour, 5071–5073——Duty paid on the fine goods of Spitalfields, and the drawback allowed on the common goods of Manchester, 5074–5078——Low value of debentures, 5079——Difference in the price between Italian thrown and raw silk, 5080——Small profit to the Italian to import at present price, 5081, 5082——Imports will be diminished if present price continues, 5083—— Raising the price of debentures by diminishing imports or increasing exports will benefit the manufacturer at the ruin of the throwster, 5084–5094——Difference in credit in Spitalfields formerly and at present, 5095–5100——Destruction of the trade of silk men, 5095–5108——Reasons why duties remaining as they are there will be less foreign thrown silk imported, 5109–5112——Comparison of importation of Italian thrown and raw silk during the last three or four years in favour of raw, 5113, 5114 ——Reason for a larger importation of thrown during last year, 51 5, 5116——Proportion of home thrown silk to meet it, 5117.

Causes that operated to reduce the price of trams, 5118——Mills at present at work turn off more fine silk than those formerly in existence, 5119, 5120——Any reduction of duty would be an advantage to the Italian throwster, 5121——Serious evil taking off the whole duty, 5122–5124——Alteration that might be made in the duty, 5125—— British thrown silk in the market to meet foreign, 5126–5128——Loss of fancy trade attributed to the public using more plain articles than formerly, 5133–5141——Fancy articles made in England cheaper than in France, 5142–5147——Articles to order are manufactured according to the pattern of each house, 5148–5151——Rates of weavers wages at London and Lyons, 5152–5157——Comparative price of dyeing at London and Lyons, 5158, 5159——Comparison of advantages of dyeing between the French and English, 5160–5166——In what articles smuggling at present carried on, 5167–5172——Advantages the Italian throwster possesses over the English, 5176–5180——Why the English has a better market for his silk than the Italian, 5181, 5182——Silk of the same quality is thrown as well in England as Italy, 5183, 5184——Increased speed in throwing mills is not an injury to the silk, 5185, 5186——Duty that might be collected as a protection to both manufacturer and throwster, 5187–5192——Not a common practice in Italy for those who reel to be also throwsters, 5198——Present rate of wages to witness's hands, 5199, 5200, 5202–5207——Wages higher during prohibition, 5201.

*Gloves.* They are not smuggled, *Stephens* 2797–2803; *Dillon* 7743——State of operatives in the glove trade, *Willmott* 4801–4803——French gloves less profitable than English, *Dillon* 7744——Increase of the glove trade since 1826, *Bottrell* 7960, 7961——Small amount of smuggling gloves, *Bowring* 9210——Duty that might be collected therein, *Bowring* 9211; *Stephens* 10666–10674——Advantage of an extra duty on gloves, *Stephens* 10689–10691.

*Glutted Market.* See *Stock.*

*Gondolphin,* Messrs. See *Importation.*

*Goode, Edward,* (Analysis of his Evidence.) Two branches in the ribbon trade, 1200 ——Number of persons employed in the plain branch, and present distress, 1201– 1208——Average wages, and reduction therein since 1804, 1209–1213——How far fixed rate of wages departed from according to circumstances, 1214–1216——How far reduction attributed to the importation of foreign manufactured ribbons, 1217–1228 ——How far importation in the fancy trade affects the plain trade, 1228–1232, 1238– 1245——Decline of the plain branch, and in the value of its machinery, 1246, 1247—— Fancy trade has increased in Coventry, and would increase further but for foreign competition, 1233–1237, 1248–1250——Ribbons can be made as good in Coventry as in France, 1251——Workmen wish to keep to the tables of wages as closely as possible, though they do not afford a living, 1253.

*Good Hope, Cape of.* See *Importation,* 2.

*Government.* Views of Government in altering the system, *Moore* 11174–11176——Time granted by Government to prepare for change not sufficient, *Moore* 11179–11182—— Restrictions on labour, and mode of working not removed by Government, *Moore* 11183——Promise by Government that they would collect a 30 per cent. duty, which they have not done, *Moore* 11201–11209, 11217–11219——Representations made to Government by the silk trade on the distress therein, and on the necessity for inflicting criminal punishment on smugglers, and stamping goods, and means of preventing forgery in stamping, and rejection by Government of plans offered, *Moore* 11238–11248—— Final answer of Government, *Moore* 11254, 11255.

*Graham, Robert,* (Analysis of his Evidence.) Manufacturer in Spitalfields, number of looms employed by witness, 12694–12697——Prices paid for throwing silk at different periods, 12698–12707——Effect of removing the duty on thrown silk to the manufacturer and operatives, 12708, 12709——Competition for labour in Manchester, and its effect on lowering the wages in Spitalfields, 12710–12712——How far prohibition of French goods would raise wages in Spitalfields, 12713, 12714——Competition with Spitalfields weavers not only in London districts but with cotton weavers, 12715——Fear that material improvement cannot take place in the rate of wages in Spitalfields, 12716 ——Advantage given to the French by the duty on foreign thrown silk here, 12719 —— Per centage duty on foreign thrown silks increases the cost of manufacture, 12720– 12728——For what foreign thrown silks employed, and proportion used in Spitalfields, 12729–12737——Reason why the drawback does not counteract the effect of the duty, 12738, 12739——Improvements that have taken place in silk weaving and throwing, 12740——Period of introduction of the Jacquard loom, and whether more or less used than formerly, 12741–12746——Manner in which foreign competition operates against labour, 12747–12750——Falling off in wages within the last few years, 12751——Distress of the throwing trade, and from what causes, 12753–12755.

Opinion that prohibition is the most substantial means of benefiting the silk trade, 12756– 12762——State of the silk trade, 1827–1831, 12763–12768——Witness's application to the Board of Trade in 1829, for reduction of duty on foreign thrown silk, 12769–12772, 12776–12778, 12780——And for a rated instead of an *ad valorem* duty on velvets, 12773– 12775, 12779—— Examination upon duties on foreign thrown and manufactured silks, and protection necessary for manufacturers and throwsters, 12781–12783——Looms employed in the manufacture of fancy silks in Spitalfields, 12784–12787——If duties reduced throwing would not be discontinued in this country, 12788–12791——Manner in which Manchester is the primary cause of low wages in Spitalfields, 12792–12795—— Valuation of velvets at the Custom House by witness, and his causing them to be detained, and afterwards sold by public auction, 12796–12800——Throwster as much right to protection as the weaver, 12801, 12802——Throwster the greater amount of fixed capital, 12803——Proportion of foreign and English thrown silk used by witness, 18804, 12805.

*Grout, Joseph,* (Analysis of his Evidence.) Description of raw silk used in the manufacture of different crapes, 10278–10283——Number of places in which manufacture carried on, 10284——Average number of persons employed, and average rate of wages per week, 1822–1831, 10285——Respectable condition of young people formerly employed, and change in their morals and character since the reduction of wages, 10286–10292—— Proportion of persons now employed as to men, women and children, similar to what it was formerly, 10293——Situation of mills for winding and throwing silk, and what power worked by, 10294, 10295——Number of spindles at work in 1822–1831, and their speed, 10296–10298——Machinery on improved principles, 10299——Amount of capital invested in buildings and machinery, 10300——Number of power looms, and cost thereof, 10301, 10302——Hand looms out of employ, and how far displaced by foreign labour, 10304, 10305——Comparison of advantages of power and hand looms in favour of the latter at present, 10306–10308——Power looms in use at Lyons, 10309——Loss of half trade from the introduction of foreign coloured goods, 10310——English black crape selling at ruinous prices; present foreign competition therein, 10311, 10312——Capital invested causes the necessity of continuing manufacture, though at a loss, 10313——Less wages paid for more work since the admission of foreign goods, 10314——Injurious effect of taking off duty on foreign thrown silk, 10315——Great increase of smuggling since removal of prohibition, 10316–10320——Entire prohibition the only means of reviving trade, 10321——Establishment of a filature and reeling establishment at Bengal, and cost price of silk raised there, and reason of the establishment not answering, 10322– 10324, 10331–10334.

Benefits of silk raised by the East India Company, and difficulty of other persons attempting it, 10325–10327, 10330——Silk worm improves in Italy and France, but degenerates if taken back to its native place, India or Persia, 10328——Comparison of price of French and Bengal silk, 10335–10337——Manchester has no crape trade, shown by number of looms employed by witness more than in the whole town of Manchester, 10338, 10339——Consumption of white and coloured crapes, 1826–1831, from French and other foreign productions, 10340——Promise by the President of the Board of Trade, that there should be no reduction of import duties, 10342, 10343——Abandonment of crape looms at Manchester, 10344——Advantages to the manufacturer from the

*Grout, Joseph,* (Analysis of his Evidence)—*continued.*

the Company's sales, 10345——Price at which they put up their silks, 10346–10348——
Method adopted with regard to goods of individuals advertized at the Company's sales,
10349——Advantages promised from change of law in 1826, and disadvantages resulting therefrom, 10350–10354, 10358, 10359——Comparison of earnings in 1823 and
1830, and distress of the work people from reduction, 10355–10357——Amount of loss
from the present law, and as to claim upon government, 10360–10362——Further reduction of duties will be an entire destruction of property, 10363——Company do not withdraw their silk even though sold at low prices; individuals do, 10364, 10365——Difference in the mulberry plant between Bengal, and France and Italy, 10366, 10367——
Comparison of quality of the Bengal silk reeled upon the Bengal and the Italian principle, 10368——Difference as to substance between Bengal and Italian silk, 10369.

*Guarantee System.* See *Brokers.*

# H.

*Haberdashers.* Interest of the large haberdashers to continue the present system, and how
far it causes a monopoly, *Stephens* 2804–2817——Small dealers have not increased so
much as large houses have increased the amount of their returns, *Stephens* 2821–2823
——Reasons why the agents in London selling for the manufacturers will not serve a
small house under 5 per cent. higher than a large house, *Stephens* 2832–2842——Public
prefer a large house to deal with from the great variety, *Stephens* 2843, 2844——Proportion French and English ribbons bear to each other in purchases from manufacturers,
*Stephens* 2639–2641——Before removal of prohibition sacrifices could be made after sale
of spring stock without ruin, *Stephens* 2731, 2732.

See also *Howell* & *James.　Morrison* & *Co.　Retailers.*

*Hall, John,* (Analysis of his Evidence.) Silk throwster and manufacturer at Coggeshall,
6459–6461——Description of silk thrown, and situation of mills, 6462–6464—— Amount
necessary to cover expenses, and give a profit to the throwster, 6465–6469, 6487–6493,
6501–6506, 6512–6515, 6527, 6528, 6594, 6732——Why reduction of duty would not
injure throwsters, 6470——Of what reduction of expenses consist, 6471——Description
of persons employed, method of hiring and rate of wages, 6472–6477——Duty necessary
to protect throwster, 6478——English organzine better than Italian, 6478–6480, 6507–
6509, 6516, 6517——Examination as to other mills in Essex, 6482–6486, 6494–6497
——Value of mills at present, 6498–6500——Proportion of silk thrown by witness used
in manufacture, 6511——Reasons for taking certain sized silks without always obtaining
a profit, 6518–6523——Larger supply of hands could not be obtained in witness's present
situation, 6525, 6526——Market for good silk open to every person, 6529, 6530——
Method of transacting throwing business, 6531–6535——Amount of brokerage, 6536–
6538——Necessity of having a good supply of raw silk for throwing, 6539–6544——
——Rate of throwing, 6545–6555——Mill in Suffolk assisted to be built by the parish,
for the purpose of employing the poor, 6557.

Parochial relief to some parents of children employed by witness, 6558–6580——Rate of
wages, 6579, 6584, 6585——Importance to keep up the throwing trade of this country,
6581–6583——Number of hours children work, 6586——Children not worked at night,
6587——Women's wages, 6588, 6589——How far parish officers cognizant of the manner
in which children are hired, 6590–6593——Superiority of witness's machinery over that
used at Coventry, and reasons for similar not being introduced at Coventry, 6597–6620——
Reason of witness giving up his Coventry manufactory, and keeping his throwing mill in
Essex, 6621–6630——Fewer hands employed by witness's machinery, 6631–6635——Only
English thrown silk used for making black ribbons, 6636, 6637, 6640——Effect of repeal
of import duty on value of black ribbons, 6638——Reason for not manufacturing coloured
ribbons, 6642——Not an advantage to throw silk for manufacture in the present state of
the market, 6643 ——Advantage of the rack and bar loom over the original looms, 6644–
6646——Steam power can be beneficially applied to the manufacture of fancy ribbons,
6647——Uses to which ribbons made by witness applied, 6649——Duty that would
secure the American market, 6650——Necessity for removing machinery, if manufacturers ruined, 6651, 6652——Bad effect of repealing duty on mill property, 6653, 6654.

Distress to trade by large capitalists being engaged in smuggling, 6655——Demand
for thrown silks would cease, if manufacturers ruined, 6656——Disadvantages to Coventry
ribbon trade by introduction of foreign manufactured goods, 6657–6659——Advantages
of the French from cheapness of cost of manufacture, 6660, 6661——Rate of wages for
plain goods, 6662, 6663——Preference to Spitalfields for broad silk manufacture, 6664,
6665——With witness's looms at Coventry, and hands working cordially, France might
be defied, 6666——Difference in wages at Coggeshall and Coventry, 6667, and comparison of goods, 6673——Ruin to Coventry if ribbon trade gets to Manchester, 6674,
6675, 6701——Rack and bar looms not the same as a-la-bar looms, 6676——Advantage
of the rack and bar looms, and by whom invented, 6677–6681——Dearness of labour
prevents export trade, 6682, 6683——Causes that would prevent the French using
the rack and bar looms, 6684–6697——They are better adapted for power than any loom
invented, 6699——Export trade would be gained by their use in this country, 6700——
Distress caused by glut in the market from Manchester, 6702, 6703——Disadvantage to
Coventry from having to compete with Manchester and foreigner, 6704——Ruin to the
678.　　　　　　　　　　　　　　　　　　　　　　　　　　　　throwster

*Hall, John,* (Analysis of his Evidence)—*continued.*

throwster by repealing import duty, 6705-6707——How far it would benefit the manufacturer, 6708——Profit by reduced price of thrown silk would go to the foreigner, 6709, 6710.

If Coventry would adopt improvements, it would prevent Manchester hurting it, 6711-6713——High rates of wages to those employed on rack and bar looms, 6714-6721——Combinations prevent Coventry men from working for witness, 6722——Wages formerly paid at Coventry, 6723, 6724——Wages of agricultural labourers, 6725——Reasons they cannot be employed as weavers, 6726, 6727——Rate of wages given to Coventry men working for witness, 6728, 6729——Negociation with a person at Manchester for witnesses' rack and bar looms, 6730——Difference in cost of rack and bar loom and a-la-bar loom, 6731——Reasons for the French not using the rack looms, 6733-6735——Cost of looms, and present worth, 6736-6739——High rate of wages at Coventry formerly, and difficulty of procuring hands, 6740-6747, 6751-6755——Advantages of former prohibition, 6748, 6749——Wages ordinary workmen can earn at present at Coventry, 6750——Number of pieces of gauze ribbons of a certain width a man can manufacture per week, 6757.

*Handkerchiefs.* Description of handkerchiefs exported from France to England, *Bowring* 8805.

*Harter, William,* (Analysis of his Evidence.)  Silk manufacturer and mill owner at Manchester, 9225, 9226——Witness's signature to a Petition to Parliament against altering the present silk laws, 9227——Too frequent changes in any trade injurious; interests in the silk trade at present well balanced, 9228——Moderate protection, not prohibition, necessary to the English manufacturer, 9229, 9230——Disadvantage of England over France, from taxation of the raw material, 9231, 9247, 9248——From whence the supply of raw derived, 9232——How importation of China silk taxed through the monopoly of the East India Company, 9233-9237——Duties on Piedmont and Lombardy silks, 9238-9240——Other charges increasing the price to the English manufacturer, 9241-9243——Advantage to the French from their growth of raw silk, and exportation being prohibited, 9244, 9245.

French silk superior to any the English manufacturer can procure, 9246——Advantage to the French from setting the fashions, 9249, 9250——Prohibition not desirable, 9251——How far present duties necessary on foreign manufactured goods, 9252——Effect of reducing duty on foreign thrown silk, on import and price, 9253-9255——Amount of duty thereon at present, 9256-9258——Removal of duty on foreign thrown, and of drawback on export, would reduce export trade, 9259——Reduction of duty would not eventually benefit the manufacturer from ruin of English throwster, 9260——Necessity for retaining the present duty on foreign thrown, 9261-9263——Why duty on thrown silk is not a tax on Spitalfields and Coventry, for the benefit of Manchester, 9264, 9265——Necessity for the drawback for the export trade, 9266-9268——Value of silk manufactures exported last year, 9269——Number of persons export trade would employ if goods made from silk thrown in this country, 9270-9272——Amount of drawback on exports in 1831, 9273-9275——Exports 1821-1831, and increase therein, upon allowance of drawback, 9276-9281——Silk a healthy employment, and carried on in a moderate temperature, 9282-9284.

Reason why English sewing silk not exported, 9285-9288——It could be exported if drawback allowed upon it, 9289-9291——Why it cannot be manufactured so cheap in England as in Italy, 9292, 9293——Effect of the East India Company's monopoly, in checking the import of raw silk, shown by amount of imports from different parts, 1823-1827, 9294, 9305-9308——Imports of China silk, and increase therein, since the Company discontinued its importation, 9295-9299, 9304——Variation in price at Company's sales, 9300-9302——Quality of East India silk has deteriorated, 9309-9311——Increase in the importation of raw silk from all parts, 1831 over 1823, 9312——Increase of consumption on the Continent in a greater ratio than in England, 9313——Certain duties attaching to the silk trade which should be removed, 9314.

Annual consumption of silk at Manchester, and of what description, 9315-9318——Number of mills at Manchester and belonging to it, and number exclusively employed in throwing, 9319-9324——How far profitable, 9325, 9332——Inconvenience sometimes felt from the want of thrown silk, and higher price paid for it, 9325-9330, 9333-9338, 9342-9345, 9348, 9349——How far increase of mills and machinery, 9340, 9346, 9347——How far throwing trade has prospered at Manchester since 1829, 9350, 9351——How far additional capital in trade since 1824, 9352-9356——Permanent supply of thrown best obtained by a good supply of good raw, 9360——Removing duty on foreign thrown would cause dependence on foreign throwster, 9361——Silk cannot be thrown so cheaply in England as in Italy, 9362——Prices of throwing, 1830 and 1831, 9363-9374——Manufacture of narrow goods, Italian thrown used therein, and competition therein with Spitalfields, 9375-7383——Wages at Manchester; contests with weavers; hours of labour; description of looms, 9384-9407, 9413-9420——Employment of weavers between silk and cotton trade, 9408, 9409.

How far improvements in machinery, 9421, 9422——Italian thrown used at Manchester is for similar goods to those made at Spitalfields, 9423-9425——Description of goods exported, when export commenced and drawback allowed, 9426-9437——Taking off duty on thrown would not lower its price, and the throwster must give up, 9439-9442, 9460-9467——Countries to which narrow goods exported, 9444-9447——How far broad goods

*Harter, William,* (Analysis of his Evidence)—*continued.*
goods could be exported if manufactured for less, 9448-9459——How far the English
pay more for their silk than the French, 9468-9470, 9474-9476——Quality of silk used in
France better than any other, 9471-9473——How far reducing duty on thrown, will add
to the price of raw, 9477, 9481——How far price of Italian thrown depends upon price
obtained for silk in other parts of the world, 9478-9480—Manner in which drawback
causing export, relieves the manufacturer for the home market, 9482-9485——A-la-bar-
loom at work 20 years ago, 9486-9488——Distress of weavers of broad goods last winter,
9489——How far manufacture of galloons carried on in Spitalfields, 9490-9492——Prices
of throwing at present, 9493-9498——Manufacture by power looms has not thrown
workmen out of employ, 9499-9505——Power not applied to the Jacquard loom, 9506
——Quantity of silk thrown by the Manchester mills, proportion thereof Italian, 9507-
9515.

*Hawking.* See *Licence.*

*Health.* Improved manner of rearing the worm, makes the employment more healthy,
*Bowring* 9095——Silk a healthy employment, and carried on in a moderate temperature,
*Harter,* 9282-9284.

*Heath, John Benjamin,* (Analysis of his Evidence). Produce of silk of different states
in Italy during 1829-1831, 5211-5213——Most of them capable of increase, 5214——
Proportion of increase during the last eight or ten years, 5215, 5216——On what the
price of silk depends, 5217, 5218——Proportion made into organzine and tram, 5219-
5221-——Exports from Lombardy States to different countries, 1831, 5222——Description of manufactured silks exported, and from what parts of Italy, 5223, 5224——Different sizes of silk, but of the same description, 5225——Expense of throwing organzine
and tram in Italy, 5226-5235——Export duty paid in different parts of Italy, 5239, 5240
——From whence sewing silk exported, 5241-5243——From whence largest import of
thrown silk, 5245, 5246——How far imports come through France, 5247-5249——Quality
of silks imported vary, 5250-5254——Imports of silks into France and duty paid, 5255
——Quantity of Italian, 5256, 5257——Quantity that comes to England, 5258.

From whence information of French imports obtained, 5260, 5261——Proportion of
raw and thrown, 5262——Duties paid on import into France, 5263-5267——Sales
of Italian silk registered in France, 5270, 5271——Reasons for the French importing
fine Italian raw silks, 5273-5275——Imports of silk into Switzerland free of duty,
5276——Getting silk duty free in Switzerland gives small inducement to throw, 5278-
5280, 5357-5361——Description of goods manufactured at Zurich, 5281——How
far Italian throwster has been a loser by imports to England, 5285-5289, 5302——
English throwster has more advantages in the selection of silk than the Italian, 5290-
5293——Reasons for failure of English throwsters, 5294, 5306——Period occupied in
throwing in Italy, 5295, 5296——Piedmont silk the best of Italy, 5297——Lombardy
silk sometimes imported into Piedmont to be thrown, 5298——From what the superiority
of Piedmont silk arises, 5299——How far an advantage to the Italian throwster, 5300
——Too many mills and competition too great here, 5301——Whether foreign or
English competition regulates the market here, 5304.

Revolution in France a cause of greater importation since July 1830, 5305, 5314——
Increase of English throwing mills, 5307——Tendency of any convulsion in France to
cause importation of silk to England, 5308-5312——England the principal mart for
importation of raw silk of Italy, 5313——Method of smuggling a certain description of
Piedmontese silk, 5316-5324——Degree of improvement in Italian silk, and from what
parts, 5325-5327——Best silks of France bear an increased price over the best silks of
Italy, 5328-5331——Specimens of French silk produced, 5330——Instance of French
thrown silk being obtained here, 5332-5339——Price and quality of certain French
silks, 5339-5341, 5343——Charges of transport of raw silk from Lyons, 5342——Description of silk for making marabout, 5346, 5347.

Higher price of French raw silks than of Italian, 5348——Preference of the French for
their own silks, 5349, 5350——Consumption of foreign organzine at Lyons is principally
Piedmont, 5351——From whence silk imported into Switzerland, 5355, 5356——Imports into Switzerland from England of China and Bengal silk, 5362——How far the
price of Italian silk affects the price of French silk at Lyons, 5363——How far price of
Italian is regulated by the quantity introduced, 5364——Average production of silk in
France for the last three years, 5365——In what superiority of French silk consists, 5367,
5372-——Proportion the superior silk bears to the whole produce of France, 5368——
Imports of foreign silk into France, 1825-1830, 5371——Increased production of silk in
Italy since the peace, 5373, 5374.

(Second Examination.) Further examination as to imports into and produce of silk
in France, 5650-5658——Examination upon the manufacture in different parts of Italy,
5659-5668——Reason of imports in raw silk being more profitable than thrown to the
Italians, 5669-5673——Reason for a greater importation of thrown than raw in 1830,
5674-5677——Advantage to the Italian from reeling his own silk, 5678-5680——How
profit and loss to the Italian calculated, 5681——Knowledge of silk difficult to be acquired, 5682, 5684——But it has nothing to do with calculating profits of Italians,
5684——Italians find advantage from sending consignments to this country, 5685——
678.                                                                          Knowledge

*Heath, John Benjamin,* (Analysis of his Evidence)—*continued.*

Knowledge of silk and experience in reeling, &c., necessary to determine local advantages of Italian throwster, 5686——Reasons of failures among throwsters, 5687–5691——Production of Italy, 5692, 5694——Consumption of Berlin and Vienna, 5693——Exports from Lombardy to France and England, 5695——Decrease in the importation of certain silk used in the manufacture of bombazines, 5696–5703——Prices of throwing in Italy exclusive of waste, 5704——Comparison with England, 5705–5707——Value of silk ascertained from examination, and not from marks on the bales, 5708——Method of conducting business of a silk merchant, 5709, 5710——Amount of brokerage, 5711——Extra commission for guaranteeing, 5712——Business of brokers, and how far they purchase on their own account, 5713–5720——Importation of waste silk, 5721–5724.

*Helena, St.* See *Importation,* 2.

*Higher Classes.* Manner in which they benefit by reduction of wages and profits, *Stephens* 2825–2831.
See also *Consumers.*

*Holland.* See *Smuggling.*

*Home Consumption.* See *Importation* 2.

*House of Commons.* Effect of the appointment of the present Committee on the silk trade, *Royle* 3061, 3062——Examination upon petition thereto as to the state of the silk trade at Manchester, *Royle* 3254–3262——Copy petition, *Royle* 3262——Names signed thereto, *Royle* 3426, 3427.

*Howell & James.* Witness a partner in their house, *Sedgwick* 7972–7976——Description of goods sold prior to 1826, *Sedgwick* 7979——Articles made exclusively for the house, *Sedgwick* 8195.

*Hume, James Deacon.* First changes which took place in the laws relating to silk was in 1824, 2——Principles of Acts of 1824 and 1826, and tables of 1826, that of substituting a protecting duty of 30 per cent. in lieu of prohibition, 3–8——Incorrectness of table from the alteration of value in goods, 9——Attempted to be remedied 1829, 10, 11——Causes of alterations from the value of 30 per cent, 13–30, 69, 70——In 1829 officers were allowed to take an *ad valorem* or a duty per pound, at their pleasure, 27——Divisions of silk goods into three different principles of per centage, 31——Witness's instruction in drawing up the tables, 32–34——Table of 1829 increased the protection, as compared with 1826, 35, 36——Negotiations of the silk trade with the Government for a protecting duty, 1829, 37–41.

Tables of duties on the importation of manufactured silk, showing the rates of the duties, and the amount of the same upon the value of the articles, 42——Period at which prohibition took place, 43–45——Average importation of raw and thrown silk, 1765–1767, 46, 47——From 1785–1831, 48——Of waste silk, 49——Duty on waste silk, 1815–1831, 50——Quantities of raw silk, waste silk and thrown silk imported at certain periods, 1765–1831, 50——Quantities of raw, waste and thrown silk imported into the United Kingdom from 1814, with the quantities entered for home consumption, and quantities exported during the same period, 51——Duties payable on the importation of raw and waste silk and of thrown silk, showing the changes which have been made therein since 1824, 52——Importation of thrown silk did not increase in proportion to the increase of raw silk, 53——Views taken by the silk trade, and applications to the Board of Trade from different places at different periods as to the cause of their distresses, 55–60——Additional bounties on exportation by Act 59 Geo. III. c. 112, 60——Complaints against smuggling, 62, 63——Account of all silks, separately, imported from July 1826, 64.

Official value of manufactured silk imported each year since the repeal of the prohibition, 1826, distinguishing European and East Indian, 64——Amount of bounty and drawback paid in the United Kingdom on British manufactured silk goods exported, 64——Official value of British manufactured silk exported each year from 1821–1830, both inclusive, 64——Prohibition more effectual against smuggling than protecting duty, 66, 68——French and English manufactured goods not so distinguishable as formerly, 68——Reduction of duty on plain goods would have prevented smuggling, but the high rate on gauzes, &c. enables assorted cargoes still to pay for smuggling; plain silks are not smuggled alone to any extent, 71–76.

Smuggling has lately increased, owing to the distress in France, which has thrown large quantities of goods on the market at prices under the market value, 77–79——Traders would rather pay to Government than smugglers, duties regulated to meet the alternative, 80–83——Export of British silk has increased since 1826, 85——Quantity exported, 1826, 1830, 1831, 86, 87——Effect of the change of law in 1829 on the export of silk, 88–91——Manner in which drawback and duties affect different branches of the silk trade, 92–99——Value of debentures would depend on the proportion of thrown silk imported, as compared with the quantity of British goods exported, 100——Advantages of debentures to the export trade, 101, 102——How far the drawback acts as a bounty on exportation, 103–112——How far duty and drawback is a tax upon one manufacturing district for the benefit of another, 113–119.

*Husks.* See *Importation,* 2.

                                                                        IMPORTATION

*IMPORTATION:*          **I.**

> 1. *Generally.*
> 2. *Papers laid before the Committee.*

**1. *Generally.***

Period at which the prohibition took place, *Hume* 43–45——Average importation of raw and thrown silk, 1765–1767, *Hume* 46, 47——From 1785–1831, *Hume* 48—— Of waste silk, *Hume* 49——Quantity of raw silk, waste silk and thrown silk imported at certain periods, 1765–1831, *Hume* 50——Quantity imported, 1814–1831, with quantities entered for home consumption, and re-exported during the same period, *Hume* 51——Importation of thrown silk did not increase in proportion to the increase of raw silk, *Hume* 53——Account of all silks, separately, imported from July 1826, *Hume* 64——Official value of manufactured silk imported each year since the repeal of the prohibition, 1826, distinguishing European and East Indian, *Hume* 64——Quantity of ribbons imported in the quarter ended 10th October 1831, and amount of duty paid, *Cheeper* 771–777——Number of large importers, and sufficiency of capital for that purpose, *Cheeper* 902, 903——Quantity of ribbons imported 1831, *Ratliff* 1836.

Manner in which imports and exports of this country should be regulated, *Ratliff* 1958– 1960——Comparison of importation of raw and thrown silk, *Royle* 3118, 3119——Imports and consumption, 1814–1831, *Doxat* 4036, 4037——Qualities of silk imported into England, France and Switzerland, *Doxat* 4090–4092——How far imports of silk from Italy to England come through France, *Heath* 5247–5249——Quantity of Italian silk that comes to England, *Heath* 5258——Proportion of raw and thrown silk coming to England, *Heath* 5262——Reason for large imports into England during 1830–31, *Martin* 5580–5585, 5587, 5590——Importations by Messrs. Gondolphin, *Stone* 6415–6419—— Inferior quality of goods imported into England since removal of prohibition to meet prices in English market, *Menetrier* 8216–8221——Proportion of legal and illegal imports to the gross sales of the country, *Ballance* 8639——Importations of silk previous to and since removal of prohibition, *Bowring* 9627–9630——Comparison of importations, 1814– 1825, *Bowring* 9708–9711——Quality of silk, and not weight, should be looked to as to importations, the coarse diminishing employment of mills, *Moore* 11159–11161.

**2. *Papers laid before the Committee.***

Return of all Raw and Waste Silk imported and entered for home consumption in each year, from 1814 to 5th January 1832; distinguishing the importations from the East Indies, China, St. Helena, the Cape of Good Hope, and Turkey, from other parts; and stating separately in each year the quantity of Raw, Thrown and Waste, including Knubs and Husks, and the amount of duty separately, *App.* p. 918.

An Account of the several kinds of Silk imported; distinguishing the quantity of Raw from Italy, the Levant, Bengal and China; also of Thrown, distinguishing Organzine from Trams and Singles, from the same places, in each of the years from 1830–1831, *App.* p. 922.

The various descriptions of Raw and Thrown Silks, and Waste and Knubs and Husks, imported 1814–1831, separated and computed into one standard; all balanced by the Parliamentary Return of quantities, duty paid, *App.* p. 932.

See also *Bengal and China Silk.     Duty on Importation.     France,* v.    *French Goods. Italy.     Silk.     Silk Trade.*

*India.*    See *East Indies.*

*Insolvency.*    Manner in which houses purchasing goods under prime cost continue a man in insolvency, *Banbury* 4536–4542.

*Insurance.*    See *Smuggling.*

*Intercourse* between France and England.    See *France,* III.

*Italy.*    No difference in the price per lb. of throwing silk in Italy during the high duties, and at present, *Brockwell* 3448–3453——Price in England does not regulate the price in Italy, *Brockwell* 3454——Germany and her own people the largest consumers of Italy, *Brockwell* 3456——Quantity of silk produced in Italy, *Brockwell* 3458, 3459——Proportion grown in Italy, *Brockwell* 3460——England hitherto the largest customer for raw silk, *Brockwell* 3462——Ruin of English throwsters will throw the trade more into the hands of Italy, *Brockwell* 3472, 3473——Quantities of Italian raw and thrown silk imported into different countries, *Brockwell*, 3474–3476——Difference in price to the Italian grower between raw and thrown since 1819, *Brockwell* 3540, 3541——Price of Italian thrown acts on that of English, *Brockwell* 3542, 3543——Difference in price that remunerates the Italian, and that which will not remunerate the English throwster, *Brockwell* 3549–3553 ——Italian would not send raw silk to England if he could not obtain a remunerating price for throwing it, *Brockwell* 3554, 3555——Trade of Italy with England, France and Germany, *Brockwell* 3556–3559——Capability of Italy to increase the raw material is limited, and that of increasing thrown greater, *Brockwell* 3563–3566——Advantages possessed by the Italian throwster over the English, *Brockwell* 3570–3572, 3681 ; *Swift* 3912–3921 ; *Ward* 3963–3971 —— Why the English have not similar advantages, *Brockwell* 3573–3577.

678.                                                                                              **How**

*Italy*—continued.

How the purchase of silk between Italy and England is carried on, *Brockwell* 3578–3581, 3592–3594——How far the price obtained regulates the sales, *Brockwell* 3582–3584 ——Different qualities of Italian silk in the same bale, *Brockwell* 3585, 3586——Advantage to the Italian therefrom, and from selecting silks not liable to waste, *Brockwell* 3587–3591, 3683——Italians retain their best quality of silks themselves, *Brockwell* 3595, 3596, 3682 ; *Swift* 3799 ; *Ward* 3985–3987——Effect of reducing duty on thrown silk on price and quality of Italian raw silk, *Brockwell* 3597–3600——Average difference of price between Italian raw and thrown silk, *Brockwell* 3601–3608——How far a remuneration to the Italian throwster, *Brockwell* 3609–3614——Stock of silk in Italy low at present, *Brockwell* 3717–3722——Quality of Italian silk not improved, *Swift* 3758–3762——Advantage to the Italians by their silks not being injured by carriage, *Swift* 3798——Difficulty of getting at the total quantity of exports from Italy, *Doxat* 4086, 4087——Italian silk comes over on consignment, *Doxat* 4256——Advantage of water in Italy, *Doxat* 4277——How sale price of Italian silk regulated on commission, *Doxat* 4382–4389, 4393——Exportation to other countries if the market depressed, *Doxat* 4390, 4391——Produce of silk in Italy, and to what countries exported, *Gibson* 4961–4973——Not a common practice in Italy for those who reel to be also throwsters, *Gibson* 5198.

Produce of silk of different States in Italy during 1829–1831, *Heath* 5211–5213—— Most of them capable of increase, *Heath* 5214——Proportion of increase during the last eight or ten years, *Heath* 5215, 5216——Proportion thereof made into organzine and tram, *Heath* 5219–5221——Description of manufactured silks exported, and from what parts of Italy, *Heath* 5223, 5224——Export duty paid in different parts of Italy, *Heath* 5239, 5240——Period occupied in throwing in Italy, *Heath* 5295, 5296——Increased production of silk in Italy since the peace, *Heath* 5373, 5374——Gross produce of silk in Italy, and detail of countries from which produced, *Martin* 5376–5383——How far produce of Italy likely to increase, and what countries particularly, *Martin* 5381, 5383, 5386, 5387——Different descriptions of silk manufactured in each country in Italy, *Martin* 5399——To what countries Italians export, with proportions to each, *Martin* 5400–5403——Reasons for knowing the production of Italy without knowing the manufacture of different places, *Martin* 5422–5427——In what parts of Italy improvement has taken place in raw silk, *Martin* 5442, 5443——How far importation of thrown profitable to the Italian since the reduction of duty, *Martin* 5452, 5453——Import of raw most advantageous to the Italian, *Martin* 5470——Whether difficulty in obtaining superior quality of French thrown silks in Italy, *Martin* 5502, 5503——Possible for the Italians to throw a larger quantity, *Martin* 5530 ; *Stone* 6146.

Sales of silk at fairs in Italy, and how far prices regulated thereby, *Martin* 5537–5543 ——Advantage of the English market to the Italians, *Martin* 5544——How far best Italian silk retained by Italian manufacturer for his own use, *Martin* 5547–5549—— Cocoons have been brought to England by way of experiment, *Martin* 5550, 5551—— Present state of the market with regard to the supply of Italian raw and thrown silk, *Stone* 6171–6181——Loss by the Italian merchants from trade with this country, *Stone* 6378–6380——Imports of silk by certain Italian throwsters, *Stone* 6381–6392, 7007–7014——Reason why apparent loss to the Italian throwster may not be actual loss, *Stone* 6420–6423——Examination upon the manufacture in different parts of Italy, *Heath* 5659–5668——Reason of imports in raw silk being more profitable to the Italians than thrown, *Heath* 5669–5673——Reason for a greater importation of thrown than raw in 1830, *Heath* 5674–5677——Advantage to the Italian from reeling his own silk, *Heath* 5678–5680——How profit and loss to the Italian calculated, *Heath* 5681——Knowledge of silk has nothing to do with calculating profits of the Italians, *Heath* 5684——Italians find advantage from sending consignments to this country, *Heath* 5685.

Knowledge of silk, and experience in reeling, &c., necessary to determine local advantages of Italian throwster, *Heath* 5686——Production of Italy, *Heath* 5692, 5694—— Claims against Italian merchants for damage on transit from Italy are trifling, *Stone* 5794 ——Manner in which crop of France affects exports from Italy, *Caffi* 7113, 7114—— Manner in which quantity of silk thrown or raised bears to other kinds of produce, *Caffi* 7118——Exports from Italy to different countries, *Caffi* 7125–7136——Improvement in the quality of the silk, *Caffi* 7153–7155——Description of the silk sent to the different countries, *Caffi* 7160–7165——Calculation of charges upon a bale of thrown and raw silk from Italy to London, *Caffi* 7271–7278——Losses latterly to Italian merchants sending thrown silk here, *Caffi* 7279–7283——How far other countries pay better, *Caffi* 7284, 7285——Italian raw being thrown in England the cause of sending Italian thrown being unprofitable, *Caffi* 7286, 7287——Advantages in favour of Italy of less expense in throwing and in the selection of raw silk, *Ballance,* 8666–8668——Italian would be benefited by reduction of duty on thrown, *Ballance* 8671——Parties who grow and throw silk in Italy, *Bennett* 10797–10800——Silk thrown in Italy at a less price than in England, *Bennett* 10801–10805——Italians have the power of supplying the market abundantly with thrown silk, *Johnson* 11582.

See also *Bengal and China Silk. Importation,* 2. *Lombardy. Operatives,* 2. *Provisions. Reeling. Rent. Throwing mills,* 2. *Throwsters ,*2.

*Jacombs,*

# J.

*Jacombs, William,* (Analysis of his Evidence.)  Account of the general expenses of the parish of Nuneaton, 1581——Number of persons depending upon the ribbon trade, and number of looms, principally single hand, 1582–1587——Reduction of wages since 1826, 1588, 1589——Depreciation in the value of Jacquard looms, from the low profits upon the fancy trade, 1590–1597, 1660–1665——Attributed to the introduction of French ribbons, 1598——Which has checked improvement in the manufacture, 1599, 1600, 1666, 1667, 1686, 1687——Taste in favour of French ribbons, and practice with regard to purchasing them, and its effect upon manufactures here, 1601–1609, 1698——Expense of putting a French pattern to work, 1610——Ribbons are more worn now than formerly, 1611, 1612——Introduction of French ribbons has shut the English manufacturer out from both town and country trade, 1613–1615, 1697, 1698——Reason why steam would not do for the manufacture of fancy ribbons, 1616, 1617.

Contract for a particular pattern not fulfilled, from French goods coming over previously to its execution, 1618–1628——Quantity of silk used, and cost of manufacture of gauze fancy ribbons in 1823 and at present, 1629–1633——Which manufacture abandoned since 1828, 1634——Loss by the imitation of French patterns, 1635–1639——Number of looms fully employed up to 1828, 1640–1648——State of trade in different years since 1820, 1650–1656——Loss by the manufacture of certain ribbons, from their being superseded by the French, 1656, 1657——Cost of manufacture of gauze ribbons in 1823, in consequence of their being a new article, 1668–1673——Comparison between the French and English designers, 1674–1677——Fluctuation in the value of fancy articles, according to the time they are brought out, 1678–1685——How far fluctuation in trade affects the designers, 1688–1691——Depression in the trade generally, 1692, 1693——Competition is both home and foreign, 1694–1696——English goods have been varied as much in colour as the French, 1699, 1700.

Examination upon the cost of labour and material in manufacture, 1701–1715——British goods equally cheap and beautiful, but the fashion is in favour of French goods, 1716–1719——Manufacturers' profits decreased, 1720——Foreign competition causes home competition, 1721–1723——Relief to trade by prohibition of French goods, 1724–1737——Proportion of foreign silk consumed in English manufacture, 1738, 1747——Impossible to compete with the French, from the prejudice in their favour, 1743——No duty would protect, 1748——Home competition would be met on equal terms, 1749–1752——Improvement in the silk trade in 1823 was not owing to French patterns, 1753–1757——To what improvement attributed, 1758–1761——Few houses willing to engage for English goods, 1762——Profits in any trade affected by the competition in it, 1763–1766——Difficult to transfer capital invested in machinery, 1767, 1768——Increase of Jacquard looms at Coventry since 1826, and depreciation in their value, 1769–1774.

Similar description of loom used now as in 1823, as regards the Jacquard, 1775——Quantity of work performed per week, and price paid in a single hand and engine Jacquard loom, showing the rate of wages, 1776–1784——Object of the Tables of Wages in 1829 and 1831, and how far conformed to, 1785–1793——None work at a lower rate than that fixed by the Table, 1794–1800——Parochial relief more in some instances than wages, 1801–1804——Wages are inadequate, from weaver's necessary expenses, 1805–1813——Wages that would be adequate, 1814——At which the French could not be competed with, 1815——Prohibition would cause a higher rate of wages; increased price would not be felt by the consumer, 1816–1820——How far protecting duty not sufficient for competition with the French; seldom English articles made cheaper, from the cheapness of French living, 1821——In what years profits were better than at present, 1822——Better to work at a lower rate than the Table than receive parochial relief, 1824, 1825——Effect of the Table has not been felt by the parish yet, 1826–1828——Increasing the price of ribbons by the reduction of wages would not afford more employment, 1829.

*Jacquard machine.*  Number of Jacquard looms, 1823 and 1826, *Smith* 1264——In 1832, *Perkins* 1537; *Cox* 2061, 2062——Introduction of the Jacquard loom, and alteration of plain looms to enable its use, *Smith* 1281–1292, 1312–1315; *Perkins* 1532; *Cox* 2295; *Graham* 12741–12746——Its introduction has changed the mode of figure weaving, *Smith* 1293, 1294, 1316——No improvement in the Jacquard loom since its introduction, *Smith* 1295, 1296——Number of Jacquard and engine looms in use, 1826 and 1831, *Smith* 1297, 1298——Increase of the Jacquard looms decreased the use of other looms, *Smith* 1299; *Perkins* 1533–1536——Increase of Jacquard looms at Coventry since 1826, *Jacombs* 1769–1774——Necessity for using the Jacquard loom to imitate the French patterns, *Smith* 1321, 1322——Whether more or less used than formerly, *Graham* 12741–12746——Distress not attributed to the Jacquard engine, *Marston* 1378——Jacquard apparatus can be applied to the engine loom, *Perkins* 1540——Number of looms in 1818, and number that have the Jacquard apparatus, *Perkins* 1541–1545.

Depreciation in the value of Jacquard looms, from the low profits upon the fancy trade, *Jacombs* 1590–1597, 1660–1665, 1769–1774——Similar description of loom used now as in 1823, as regards the Jacquard, *Jacombs* 1775——Jacquard looms have been put up in large quantities in this country, but not lately, *Ratliff* 1880, 1881——Sometimes quite out of employment, *Cox* 2072——Description of goods made by it, *Cox* 2296, 2305——French did not use it in 1813, *Cox* 2297——Advantages thereof, *Merry* 2469–2471

678.                                                                                  ——Handsome

*Jacquard machine*—continued.

——Handsome goods made previously to its introduction, *Merry* 2472——Comparison as to quality of work made in a single hand and an engine loom, each with Jacquard machinery, *Merry* 2587, 2589——Use of the Jacquard decreased in Spitalfields, *Stone* 6016-6019——Places where the Jacquard at present in use, *Ballance* 8543-8545—— History of the invention of the Jacquard machine, *Bowring* 8767——Power not applied to the Jacquard machine, *Harter* 9506——Cost of Jacquard looms, *Cox* 2077, 2078; *Tootal* 9552——Value of Jacquards in England and France, *Bowring* 9789-9795—— Number of Jacquard looms employed upon their introduction, *Bridges* 10384-10388—— Of little use since 1825, *Rowbotham* 11743.

See also *De Ponilly & Co. Looms.*

*Jobbing.* Bad effects thereof, from the large stocks on hand, *Cheeper* 897-901——Caused by glut in the markets through foreign goods, *Cox* 2146-2149——Injury to the trade by jobbing French goods, *Stephens* 2672-2674——Great quantity of job goods sent over just after the French revolution, *Stephens* 2675-2679, 2683——Manner in which jobbing French goods prevent sale of the English, *Stephens* 2733-2736——The French will not job their own goods in their own markets, *Stephens* 2737, 2738——Goods are jobbed in during the season at half the price paid for them at the commencement of the season, *Stephens* 2753-2756——Not as many English goods jobbed as French in proportion to the capital employed, *Stephens* 2818——How silk manufacturers affected by large houses purchasing under prime cost, *Banbury* 4505-4515, 4535——How far a few large buyers depress the market, *Banbury* 4527——In the event of failures, actions are brought against those houses purchasing under prime cost, *Banbury* 4528-4534, 12669-12678——How far those houses operate to continue a man in insolvency, *Banbury* 4536-4542——Com- promises between creditors and those houses, *Banbury* 4543-4545.

Manner in which jobbing arises from goods being rejected after orders given, *Clay* 6799-6803——Why gluts in the market from French job goods do not hurt English manufacturer, *Dillon* 7697-7700——How far actions have been brought and com- promises made with assignees of manufacturers and warehousemen respecting goods supposed to be improperly bought, *Dillon* 7740-7742——Quantity of smuggled goods of not so much consequence as the low price at which they are jobbed, *Bottrell* 7850—— West end large houses do not deal in job ribbons, *Sedgwick* 8197, 8199, 8200——French job goods find their way into the English market at prices at which the English manufac- turer cannot compete with them, *Sedgwick* 8204, 8205——Goods are jobbed cheaper after the fashion is over, *Bouillon* 10227——Facility for disposing of plain and fancy goods at a loss, *Bridges* 10476-10483——Inconvenience of French job goods of the same quality and lower price, *Stephens* 10559-10562——Reduction of duty would not protect the market against jobs, *Bennett*, 10751——Description and names of job houses, and their method of doing business, *Beckwith* 11934-11939.

See also *Creditors.*

*Johnson, Thomas,* (Analysis of his Evidence.) Number of mills; their power; value; number erected since 1824, and spindles at work at Congleton, 1823-1832, 11557-11563—— Wages paid in 1823 and 1832, 11564——Number of hands employed, 1823 and 1832, 11565——Number unemployed and method of subsistence, 11566, 11567——Amount of population of Congleton, 1821 and 1831, 11568——State of the poors' rate and allow- ances therefrom, 1821-1831, 11568—— How far hands employed paid by the parish, 11569-11571——Improvements in machinery, and increase of speed therein since 1824, 11572-11575——Disadvantages from reduction of duty on foreign thrown in 1829, 11576——Destruction of throwster by farther reduction, 11577——Sacrifice of captial and labour in the erection of a silk mill, 11577-11579.

Labour cheaper at Congleton than Manchester, 11580, 11581——Italians have the power of supplying this market abundantly with thrown silk, 11582——Bad effect of reducing duty on thrown silk, 11583, 11584——Mills principally built between 1824 and 1826, 11585-11588——Not much Italian now thrown; mills principally employed in the coarser silks, 11589, 11590, 11613-11617——Ruinous state of the throwsters at present, 11591-11593, 11601——Duty necessary to protect the throwster, 11594-11600 ——Less number of mills at work now than prior to 1824, 11602-11609, 11621-11630——Distressed and demoralized condition of the operatives, 11610-11612——Finer silks require more work than the coarser, 11618-11621——Necessity for discontinuing the importation of thrown silk, the fine silk giving more valuable employment to the operatives, 11631, 11632 ——Necessity of getting raw silk from France at same duty as upon Italian importation, 11633, 11634.

## K.

*Kelly, John,* (Analysis of his Evidence.) Silk weaver at Manchester, and signed petition to the House of Commons, 11814-11818——Increase in the broad silk trade, and prosperity of the weavers, 1819-1825, 11819-11825——Their wages at that time and since, 11820- 11824——Distress attributed to the introduction of foreign goods, 11825——Prices of weaving 1822-1832, 11825, 11826——Reason silk weavers cannot shift their trade, 11827——Necessity for protection to the silk trade, and distress of weavers from its
repeal,

*Kelly, John,* (Analysis of his Evidence)—*continued.*

repeal, 11828, 11829——Premiums formerly given to weavers to learn the art, 11830, 11831——Why protection would tend to increase wages, 11832——State of the silk trade at Manchester, and description of goods made, 1823–1825, and at present, 11833–11837, 11841–11843, 11846——Rich goods in the shop windows at Manchester marked French, 11838, 11839——How certain looms employed now that were not employed in 1825, 11840——Quality of plain goods manufactured at Manchester inferior to that made before 1826, 11844——Description of silk used in the manufacture now and formerly, 11845.

*Knubs.* See *Importation,* 2.

# L.

*Labour.* Comparative prices of labour in England and France, *Brunskill* 566–575, 593–610; *Ratliff* 1864, 1865; *Cox* 2112——Means of ascertaining the relative prices of labour between Switzerland and England, *Ratliff* 1903, 1904——Amount per centage on labour bears to the value of the article, *Brunskill* 576–578; *Merry* 2569, 2570; *Gibson* 5050, 5051——Calculations of the proportion of the value of labour, and upon what founded, *Cheeper* 758–770——Loss of English labour by smuggling and foreign importation, *Cheeper* 852–857——Amount of Duty upon foreign importation, compared with labour, *Cheeper* 930–932——Number of hours labour per day, *Poole* 981; *Merry* 2625–2629; *Swift* 3743-3757——Additional labour required in consequence of the Jacquard looms in getting in the warps, *Smith* 1336——Examination upon the cost of labour and material in the manufacture, *Jacombs* 1701–1715; *Cox* 2103——Calculation of the cost of labour upon one pound of silk, 1824–1831, *Cox* 2107-2111——Labour much dearer in England than France, though now reduced to its lowest ebb, *Merry* 2525.

Tendency of the cotton and silk trades to equalize labour, *Royle* 3330–3336——If French and Swiss raws exported and manufactured goods admitted, difference in the prices of labour could be afterwards regulated, *Brockwell* 3518, 3519, 3525——Advantage to the foreigner from the cheapness of labour, *Swift* 3903–3905, 3909–3911——Consequent necessity for low wages, *Swift* 3906, 3907——Diminution of labour from increased manufacture of coarse goods since 1825, *Doxat* 4303–4305; *Willmott* 4727–4730——How far removing duty on thrown silk would increase the demand for labour, *Gibson* 5071–5073——Less labour required in working Bengal silk, *Stone* 6199–6201——Consumption of raw silk no criterion of the amount of labour employed, *Stone* 6202——Examination as to the quantity of labour employed in manufacturing different descriptions of silk, *Stone* 6225–6231——Labour lower at Manchester than Spitalfields, *Stone* 6357——Italian silks takes more labour than Bengal, *Stone* 6406——Prohibition of manufactured goods would cause more employment here, *Stone* 5864——Dearness of labour prevents export trade, *Hall* 6682, 6683.

Hands thrown out of employment by foreign importations, legal and illegal, *Ballance* 8643–8645——Fluctuation in the demand for labour at Lyons, *Bowring* 8923, 8924——Question of displacing labour should be looked at with a view to the manufacture of the country, and not the silk manufacture only, *Bowring* 9172–9174——If silk trade has increased, there is no displacement of labour, *Bowring* 9189, 9190——Proportion of labour to the value of the goods, *Tootal* 9579–9584——How far importation of silk manufactured goods from France tends to displace English labour, *Bowring* 9643–9650, 9770–9774——Comparison of French and English labour as regards local taxation, *Bowring* 9656, 9657——As regards national taxation, *Bowring* 9658–9661——Expense of labour on figured gros de Naples would be increased without the Jacquard, *Wadden* 10020–10024——Increased quantity of silk does not always show increased profit to the labourer from there being more labour in coarser silk, *Wadden* 10146–10149——Labour displaced in the silk trade not taken up by the cotton trade, *Ballance* 11027–11031——Labour cheaper at Congleton than Manchester, *Johnson* 11580, 11581——Finer silks require more work than the coarser, *Johnson* 11618–11621——Statement of the price of labour in Macclesfield 1810, 1819, 1825 and 1832, and examination thereupon, *Prout* 11647–11655, 11661–11663.

See also *Etienne, St.   France.*

*Labouring Classes.* See *Agricultural Labourers.   Silk,* VII. 2.

*Lace.* See *Blonde.*

*Lancashire.* Number of looms and description of trade in the silk districts in Lancashire, *Cope* 11712——Depression of the Lancashire trade, and decline of the fancy trade therein, *Rowbotham,* 11733–11736——Silk trade of Lancashire if long standing, comparison of prices, 1786, 1796 and 1810, *Rowbotham* 11738.

See also *Spitalfields.*

*Landing Waiters.* See *Custom House.*

*Land Tax.* Population of France rated thereto, *Bowring* 9040.

*Large Houses.* See *Haberdashers.   Jobbing.*

678.

*Laws*

*Laws relating to the Silk Trade.*   First change therein in 1824, *Hume* 2——Present regulations do not require alteration, *Royle* 3067, 3073-3075, 3199, 3200——Parties who have been benefited by the changes in the law since 1829, *Gibson* 5000-5005——Witness's signature to a Petition to Parliament against altering the present silk laws, *Harter* 9227——Too frequent changes in any trade injurious; interests in the silk trade at present well balanced, *Harter* 9228——Advantages promised from change of law in 1826, and disadvantages resulting therefrom, *Grout* 10350-10354, 10358, 10359——Amount of loss from the present law, and as to claim upon Government, *Grout* 10360-10362——Failure of the three principles of the alteration, superiority of machinery, skill of artisans, and extent of capital, *Moore* 11173——Evils arising out of the alteration in the laws in 1824, 1826 and 1829, *Brocklehurst* 11545-11550——Only the wealthy have been benefited by the present regulations, *Rowbotham* 11740.

> *Papers laid before the Committee.*
> Various remarks as to the calamitous results which have attended the changes in our protective laws of 1765, effected in 1826, and opinion expressed as to the ultimate view which the Right honourable William Huskisson would have taken of those results, *Evinence*, p. 258.

See also *Duty on Importation.*

*Leaf & Co.*   See *Custom House.   Smuggling.*

*L'Ecole de Tissage.*   See *Taste.*

*Levant, The.*   See *Importation,* 2.

*Licence.*   British manufactures should be protected by a £.20 licence to prevent French agents hawking goods, *Sedgwick* 8117-8119.

*Livre.*   Value in English money of the Italian livre, *Caffi* 7048-7056.

*Local Taxation.*   Amount of octroi and manner in which it depends upon the population, *Bowring* 9042, 9045-9051——Local burthens of all classes in England are greater than the local taxation of France, *Moore* 12072.

> See also *Labour.   Lyons.*

*Lombardy.*   Exports from Lombardy States to different countries, 1831, *Heath* 5222, 5695 ——Duties thereon, *Martin* 5405; *Harter* 9238-9240——Attempts to get exportation of raws prohibited from Lombardy, *Caffi* 7083-7086——Quantity of silk produced in Lombardy and quantity thrown, *Caffi* 7106-7112——French and English manufactures are smuggled into Lombardy, *Caffi* 7297-7304.

> See also *Silk,* VII. 3.

*Looms.*   Dutch looms used in the plain branches of the engine trade, *Poole* 1004——Number of widths an engine loom can make, *Poole* 1005, 1006——Nature of the a-la-bar loom, *Poole* 1007——Examination upon destruction of steam looms at Coventry last November, *Poole* 1012-1046——Manufacture by engine looms, and how long they have been in use, *Poole* 1047-1050——There are articles made in the hand loom that cannot be made in the engine loom, but not the contrary, *Poole* 1080; *Marston* 1381, 1382——Comparison of quantity made between an engine and a hand loom, *Poole* 1085-1089; *Perkins* 1552, 1553——Extent to which there is more employment for the engine weavers than the hand loom weavers since the list of prices, *Poole* 1106-1114——Quality of the hand loom articles preferable, *Poole* 1120, 1121, 1135-1137——How far single hand feels depression in the trade first, *Poole* 1122, 1123——How far the engine loom tends to throw workmen out of employment, *Poole* 1129, 1130; *Marston* 1492, 1493.

The two principal machines for weaving at Coventry are the engine loom and the Jacquard machine, *Poole* 1140-1144——Same description used in France as used at Coventry, *Poole* 1145, 1146——Proportion that Mr. Beck's steam machine would have made to other machines, *Poole* 1148-1152——Mr. Woodhouse's loom was for plain goods, *Perkins* 1547——Number of looms in Coventry, *Poole* 1174-1177——Number of engine looms employed in 1826 cannot be ascertained, *Poole* 1192——Number at present unemployed, *Poole* 1193-1196——But little increase lately from foreign competition, *Smith* 1265, 1266——Improvements in single hand engine would increase if foreign ribbons were excluded, *Marston* 1379, 1380——Depression of trade since the introduction of the engine machine has prevented its being much used, *Marston* 1425——Extent to which the cheapness in the manufacture in the engine loom has acted upon the employment of the single hand looms, *Marston* 1437-1447——Number of fancy looms employed before 1823, *Perkins* 1539.

Number fully employed up to 1828, *Jacombs* 1640-1648——Number of gauze looms in 1826 and 1831, *Cox* 2053, 2054——Number of looms generally, and persons employed therein, *Cox* 2055-2057——Advantage of the engine over the single hand looms, *Cox* 2073, 2119, 2120——Masters supply the looms and are subject to their wear and tear, *Cox* 2074-2076——Engine looms are not much increased with the exception of the Jacquard, *Cox* 2298——Breadths not required formerly, or they could have been made, *Cox* 2299-2304——Same quantity could have been made formerly as at present made with the Jacquard, *Cox* 2299-2304——A-la-bar loom at Coggeshall erected by a French

artist;

*Looms*—continued.

artist; unsuccessful attempt to make satins therein, *Sawer* 2379–2387, 2400–2409——
Great deal of excellent work done by hand looms, *Sawer* 2410, 2411——Power loom
does not answer, *Sawer* 2434——Improved looms began to be made about the year
1820, *Merry* 2457, 2458——Looms employed in weaving silk and silk mixed with other
articles, 1819 and 1831, *Royle* 3038–3045, 3264–3267.

Advantage of the rack and bar looms over the original looms, *Hall* 6644–6646——
Rack and bar looms not the same as a-la-bar looms, *Hall* 6676—— Advantage of the rack
and bar loom, and by whom invented, *Hall* 6677–6681—— Causes that would prevent
the French using the rack and bar looms, *Hall* 6684–6697, 6733–6735——They are
better adapted for power than any loom invented, *Hall* 6699——Export trade would be
gained by their use in this country, *Hall* 6700——Negociation with a person at Manchester for witness's rack and bar looms, *Hall* 6730——Difference in the cost of the rack
and bar loom, and a-la-bar loom, *Hall* 6371——Cost of looms and present work, *Hall*
6736–6739——Preference of weavers for their own looms, and methods of purchasing
them, *Baggallay* 7437–7440——Improvements in the engine loom, *Baggallay* 7457
——History of the introduction of the bar loom into France, *Bowring* 8768——A-la-bar
loom at work 20 years ago, *Harter* 9486–9488.

Manufacture by power looms has not thrown workmen out of employ, *Harter* 9499–
9505——Speed by power looms would be injurious to the silk, *Schwabe* 9838——Number
of power looms and cost thereof, *Grout* 10301, 10302——Hand looms out of employ,
and how far displaced by foreign labour, *Grout* 10304, 10305——Comparison of advantages of power and hand looms in favour of the latter at present, *Grout* 10306–10308——
Sometimes temporary employment for looms when French goods scarce, *Bridges* 10484–
10485——Comparison of the number of looms in and since 1824, in the whole Spitalfields
district, *Wallis* 10835–10837, 10840——Comparison of number in the parish of Bethnal
Green, *Wallis* 10838, 10839——Looms out of work at the beginning of this year, *Wallis*
10884——Proportion of looms at present and formerly employed in the figured and plain
branches, *Wallis* 10886–10889——Looms in Spitalfields not increased since 1826, *Wallis*
10967——Number unemployed, *Wallis* 10968–10970.

Number of looms that would have employment in the event of their manufacturing the
goods imported from France, *Ballance* 11058–11072, 11075–11079——Obstacles in the
way of the employment of power looms to broad silks, *Brocklehurst* 11493–11499——
Why workmen have better means of informing themselves of the number of looms than
than their masters, *Cope* 11715–11719——How certain looms at Manchester employed
now that were not employed in 1825, *Kelly* 11840——Number of looms at Manchester,
1824–1826, and at present, *Scott* 11865–11871——Examination against the increase of
looms in Manchester since 1826, shown by the quantity of silk worked up, *Scott* 11874,
11875——Greatest number of looms employed by witness at Spitalfields, and on what
description of goods, *Beckwith* 11927, 11928, 11946, 11947——Weavers purchase looms
of their masters as a means of keeping in employment, *Pittifor* 12053, 12054——Number
of looms in Spitalfields, number out of employ, and number employed by the trades committee, *Stone* 12690, 12691——Number of looms employed by witness in Spitalfields,
*Graham* 12694–12697——Looms employed in the manufacture of fancy silks in Spitalfields, *Graham* 12784–12787.

See also *Avignon.   De Ponilly & Co.   Etienne, St.   Jacquard Loom.   Machinery.
Steam.   Switzerland.*

*Lost Time.*  See *Weavers*, 2.

*Lower Classes.*  They are supplied by persons in that particular branch, fancy goods are not
made with any view to them, *Cox* 2199.

See also *Consumers.*

*Lustres.*  Manufacture of figured lustres at Sudbury and prices paid, *Wallis* 10919–10924.

*Lutestrings.*  Comparison of cost price of French and English, *Dillon* 7689, 7690——
Figured lutestrings only used in the common trade, *Sedgwick* 8069, 8070.

*Lyons.*  Origin of disturbances at Lyons about wages, *Bottrell* 7927, 7928——Fluctuations
in the silk trade at Lyons, *Bowring* 8794–8796——Number of looms therein at different
periods, *Bowring* 8796–8798——Cause of the fall in the number of looms at Lyons in 1789,
*Bowring* 8804——Riots in November 1831 from endeavouring to make the tariff for wages
obligatory, *Bowring* 8905–8908——Means by which riots put an end to by removal of
weavers, *Bowring* 8912–8915——Manner of their removal, *Bowring* 8920–8922——
Their destination, *Bowring* 9803——Profit and loss to a Lyonese manufacturer, their disadvantages from foreign competition, *Bowring* 8940–8944——Local taxation of Lyons,
*Bowring* 8945–8947——Number and description of ribbon looms employed at Lyons,
*Bowring* 8997——Cause of the introduction of the ribbon trade at Lyons, *Bowring* 8998.

Prices of ribbon weaving per piece at Lyons, and number of pieces manufactured,
*Bowring* 9008–9015——Increase and decrease of Lyons silk trade, *Bowring* 9636–9642
——How far pillage of silk greater at Lyons than in other countries, *Bowring* 9677,
9678——Improvement in ribbon looms at Lyons, *Bowring* 9712–9715——Comparative
view of the cost and expenses of manufacturing certain organzine and tram in plain gros
de Naples at Lyons and Spitalfields, *Wadden* 10015–10019——Confirmation thereof,
678.                                                                    *Wadden*

Lyons—continued.

*Wadden* 10026——The like comparative view on figured gros de Naples, *Wadden* 10020–10024——Number of looms at Lyons and St. Etienne show they interfere with Spitalfields and Coventry, *Wadden* 10134–10138——Power looms in use there, *Grout* 10309—— Lyons has been as much injured as Spitalfields, *Poyton* 10992——Increase of looms at Lyons over England, *Brocklehurst*, 11357, 11358.

See also *America. Dyeing. Etienne, St. France*, III. 2. *Weavers*. 8. IV.

# M.

*Macclesfield.* Description of trade there, *Baggallay* 7502–7507——Annual amount of poor's rates at Macclesfield, 1821–1832, *Brocklehurst* 11382, 11385——Number of families receiving relief, 1821–1832, and reduction in the amount of allowance, *Brocklehurst* 11383–11385——Average increase in weekly expenditure to the poor 1832 over 1823, *Brocklehurst* 11386——Statement of weekly payments to the casual and regular poor, 1832 and 1823, *Brocklehurst* 11386——Weekly relief to casual poor, 1821–1831, *Brocklehurst* 11387, 11388——Empty houses, and houses not contributing to the poor's rate, *Brocklehurst* 11389, 11390 —— Charge of over trading against Macclesfield prior to 1826, unjust, *Brocklehurst* 11391——Advertisement for increased hands at Macclesfield was only for a local and temporary nature, *Brocklehurst* 11392, 11393——How increase of houses built in 1822, warranted, *Brocklehurst* 11394——Desertion of houses show the state of the silk trade, *Brocklehurst* 11395——Distressed state of the town from distress of operatives, *Brocklehurst* 11403.

Statement of leading articles made at Macclesfield, with rates of wages, 1821–1831, showing reduction therein, and consequent distress of weavers, *Brocklehurst* 11450 11453 ——Description of goods made before and since 1826, and loss of trade since, *Brocklehurst* 11456, 11457——Improvement in the silk trade at Macclesfield, 1809–1824, but not since 1825, *Prout* 11639–11641——No new trade has been introduced at Macclesfield since alteration of the system, and the trade has gradually declined, *Prout* 11670—— Method of manufacture called steaming, peculiar to Macclesfield, *Prout* 11671, 11672 ——Coarser description of goods at Macclesfield than formerly, *Prout* 11673——Artisans of Macclesfield will exceed those of any other town in their own manufacture, *Smith* 11687, 11688——Increase of silk trade in Lancashire does not account for distress at Macclesfield, *Cope* 11711.

See also *Manufacturing Districts. Silk Trade. Wages*, 5. *Weavers*, 5.

*Machinery.* Period of introduction of machinery, and when used, *Brunskill* 179–188—— Advantage to France by the use of machinery, *Brunskill* 237, 238——In the event of prohibition there would be an increase of machinery, *Brunskill* 122, 239–241 ; *Ratliff* 1879 ; *Merry* 2527——Objection to power looms at Coventry, one destroyed, *Brunskill* 242, 243, 245, 247——Cost of machinery a bar to its general introduction, *Brunskill* 323, 673–679——Effect of machinery in equalizing wages for different descriptions of work, *Brunskill* 326–328——Difference in the quantity of work and wages of the engine loom, and single hand, *Brunskill* 343–348——No increase or improvement in machinery from its cost, *Brunskill* 708–712——Quality of different machinery, *Brunskill* 716–719 ——Increase and improvement in machinery, *Cheeper* 936–939——Machinery used in the fancy branch has not increased, *Poole* 948, 949——Improvements in machinery were received by the working classes with alacrity, *Poole* 950, 1009, 1015–1018——Reasons why machinery not more generally used, *Poole* 951 —— Foreign competition has latterly prevented improvements in machinery, *Poole* 953, 954——The same description of machinery that is used in France is used at Coventry, *Poole* 1145, 1146——Decline in the value of machinery, *Goode* 1246, 1247——Newly introduced expensive machinery not used from the superior advantages of the French, *Ratliff* 1876—— In the event of prohibition competition in England would increase the use of machinery, *Cox* 2218–2229.

Sale of certain machinery by witness at a sacrifice, *Sawer* 2358–2366——Offer of sale of certain machinery at Stratford-le-Bow, but no purchaser ; cost price thereof, *Sawer* 2367–2372——Witness's machinery at Coventry superintended by a servant, which plan formerly succeeded, *Sawer* 2392–2394—— Expense of machinery, and value of goods turned out, *Merry* 2566–2568——No improvement in machinery since 1825, *Merry* 2852 ——Exportation of English machinery into Lombardy, *Royle* 3132, 3133——Applications for leave to export machinery, *Royle* 3136–3142——Comparison of English and French and Italian machinery, *Royle* 3151–3159——Necessity of exporting machinery and labour if duty on foreign silk removed, *Royle* 3306–3313——Certain machinery not perfected from supposed alterations in the silk trade, *Swift* 3728——Machinery better in England than in Italy, *Gibson* 4928——Superiority of witness's machinery over that used at Coventry, and reasons for similar not being used at Coventry, *Hall* 6597–6620 ——Necessity for removing machinery if manufacturers ruined, *Hall* 6651, 6652—— Improvement of machinery in Italy, *Caffi* 7151, 7152——Machinery would be extended in Coventry but for the objection by the weavers to new machinery, *Baggallay* 7458—— How far improvements in machinery, *Harter* 9421, 9422——Machinery on improved principles, *Grout* 10299——Difficulty of converting machinery to other purposes, *Brocklehurst* 11409–11412——Improvements in machinery, and increase of speed therein since 1824 at Congleton, *Johnson* 11572–11575——Improvements in machinery due to

Macclesfield

*Machinery*—continued.

Macclesfield and Coventry, *Wright* 11753——Comparison between Manchester and Macclesfield machinery, *Wright* 11754——Duties on implements of machinery in France have no effect as compared with England, *Moore* 12073.

See also *Capital. Coventry. France*, III. *Looms*, 2. *Switzerland. Throwing Mills.*

*Manchester.* Articles that are manufactured at, and their quality, *Brunskill* 626–631, 637–639——How far goods would be made there in the event of prohibition, *Cox* 2342–2345 ——Number of throwing mills erected there since 1819, *Royle* 3025–3029, 3046–3050 ——Quantity of mills employed in throwing, and quantity in weaving, *Royle* 3034–3036 ——Peculiarities of the Manchester trade, *Royle* 3201, 3202——Comparison of quality of Manchester and Spitalfields goods, *Royle* 3208–3210——Difference in the manufacture between Manchester and Spitalfields, *Royle* 3408–3418——Increased demand for goods could be met at Manchester, *Royle* 3215——Effect of alterations in the law upon the silk trade at Manchester, *Royle* 3222, 3223——Few failures therein, *Royle* 3224, 3225; *Baggallay*, 7569–7573——Complaints from Manchester have been instigated from other quarters, *Royle* 3226–3228——No distress at Manchester, *Royle* 3230–3232—— Unsteadiness of trade since July 1830; how caused by the Bank circulation, *Royle* 3233–3238——Rate of wages, and how affected by the cotton trade, *Royle* 3239–3243, 3247–3249——Account of poors' rates in Manchester, 1826–1832, *Royle* 3244——French goods have not interfered with the Manchester trade, *Royle* 3245, 3246——Examination upon memorial to the Board of Trade, and petition to the House of Commons as to the state of the silk trade at Manchester, *Royle* 3254–3262——Copy, memorial, *Royle* 3261 ——Copy, petition, *Royle* 3262——Same names signed to both memorial and petition, *Royle* 3426, 3427.

Silk thrown at Manchester is worked up at Coventry and Spitalfields, *Royle* 3293—— Necessity in the Manchester trade for the best raw Italian silk to mix with the China, *Brockwell* 3696–3698——Manchester not superior to the West of England for throwing, *Brockwell* 3731–3734; *Ward* 3997–4001——Silk sent from Manchester to the West of England for throwing, *Swift* 3731–3734——It is not sent, *Ward* 4004——Manchester has no advantage in rate of carriage, *Swift* 3774——Description of the low and mixed trade carried on at Manchester, to take advantage of debentures for exportation, *Doxat* 4064——Reason for prosperity at Manchester and distress at Spitalfields, *Doxat* 4140 ——Duty paid on the fine goods of Spitalfields, and the drawback allowed on the coarse goods of Manchester, *Gibson* 5074–5078——Distress caused by glut in the market from Manchester, *Hall* 6702, 6703——Intention to establish power looms at Manchester for the manufacture of plain sarsnet ribbons, *Baggallay* 7461——Manner in which silk trade at Manchester interferes with Spitalfields; description of goods made at Manchester, *Baggallay* 7480–7501——Profit of Manchester manufacturers very small, *Sedgwick* 8002——Manchester manufacturers generally inferior in beauty to Spitalfields, but some of them equal ; their prices, *Sedgwick* 8010–8014, 8024–8029——Quantity and description of goods manufactured at Manchester *Sedgwick* 8040–8042; *Menetrier* 8303–8305; *Ballance* 8394, 8400.

Silk trade at Manchester has been in existence since 1806, *Ballance* 8401, 8402—— Before opening the ports, prosperity of either Manchester or Spitalfields showed prosperity of the other, *Ballance* 8403——Distress at Manchester not so great as in Spitalfields, from its being partly cotton manufacture, *Ballance* 8406——Manchester and Spitalfields would be both benefited by prohibition, *Ballance* 8707——Annual consumption of silk at Manchester, and of what description, *Harter* 9315–9318——Number of mills at Manchester and belonging to it, and number exclusively employed in throwing, *Harter* 9319–9324——How far profitable, *Harter* 9325, 9332——How far throwing trade has prospered at Manchester since 1829, *Harter* 9350, 9351——Manufacture of narrow goods, Italian thrown used therein, and competition therein with Spitalfields, *Harter* 9375–9383 ——Italian thrown used at Manchester is for similar goods to those made at Spitalfields, *Harter* 9423–9425——Quantity of silk thrown by the Manchester mills; proportion thereof Italian, *Harter* 9507–9515——State of trade at Manchester, description of goods manufactured, and number of looms employed from 1816, *Tootal* 9517–9535——Number of Jacquard looms employed at Manchester, and on what goods, *Tootal* 9536–9544—— Capability of Manchester for the production of rich goods; pattern of a dress made for the Queen produced, *Tootal* 9553–9555.

Consumption of silk in Manchester, *Tootal* 9574——Quantity of silk thrown in Manchester, and quantity of foreign thrown imported, *Tootal* 9575——Quantity of foreign thrown silk used in Manchester, *Tootal* 9576–9578——Throwing mills at Manchester in 1823 and at present; number of spindles and weekly earnings of operatives, *Tootal* 9588–9591——Activity in the silk trade at Manchester at present, *Tootal* 9595, 9602, 9603—— Patterns produced of witness's manufacture at Manchester, and statement in explanation thereof, *Schwabe* 9829–9836——Examination as to the number of looms in Manchester, and in witness's employ, with witness's declining to answer as to his own, *Schwabe* 9853–9864——Examination upon certain patterns produced, their sale or export, and prices of similar articles at East India Company's sales, *Schwabe* 9871–9886——Reasons for not doing a larger business with the London upholsterers from long credit taken by them, and prejudice raised by Spitalfields manufacturers against Manchester goods, *Schwabe* 9887–9920——Articles not manufactured better at Spitalfields than Manchester, *Schwabe* 678.

*Manchester*—continued.

9921–9923——Further examination as to credit, the production of similar goods by Spitalfields weavers, and refusal by witness to have his goods examined by Spitalfields manufacturers, *Schwabe* 9924–9935——Rich silk goods are not made at Manchester, with some exceptions, *Wadden* 10043, 10045——Manchester has no crape trade, shown by the number of looms employed by witness more than the whole town of Manchester, *Grout* 10338, 10339——Abandonment of crape looms at Manchester, *Grout* 10344——Articles of Manchester manufacture now bought, *Stephens* 10550–10554, 10563–10566.

Quality of Manchester goods not sufficient to interfere with the sale of rich French goods, *Stephens* 10555, 10567–10569——Loss to Manchester from copying French goods, and being met in the market by French job goods, *Stephens* 10556–10558—— Inferior class consume the Manchester silks, *Stephens* 10594–10595——High prices not given to Manchester manufacturers, *Stephens* 10596, 10597——Description of Manchester goods and their prices, *Bennett* 10730, 10731——Satins and velvets not making at Manchester, *Wallis* 10872, 10873——Manchester would have kept its low trade if Spitalfields had not been interfered with by France, *Ballance* 11046–11050——Particular description of goods made at Spitalfields, Coventry and Macclesfield, not carried on at Manchester, *Rowbotham* 11737——Prosperous state of Manchester throwing trade to 1826, and depression therein since, *Wright* 11758——State of the silk trade at Manchester, and description of goods made, 1823–1825, and at present, *Kelly* 11833–11837, 11841–11843, 11846——Quality of plain goods manufactured at Manchester inferior to that made before 1826, *Kelly* 11844——Reason for the handkerchief branch becoming nearly extinct, *Scott* 11875–11877——Description of goods formerly made in Manchester for which gros de Naples have been substituted, *Scott* 11878–11880——Description of goods now making in Manchester, *Scott* 11882–11884, 11890–11895.

See also *Carriage. Manufacturing Districts. Silk Trade. Spitalfields. Wages,* 6. *Weavers,* 6.

*Manning, John,* (Analysis of his Evidence.) Surveyor General of Customs, 12476——Examination upon an investigation in consequence of a letter signed " Veritas," and addressed to Lord Auckland, alleging a fraud upon the Customs, and difference in the proper amount of duty, and that paid, 12477–12500——Amount per cent. of saving upon the amount of duty, admitting a fraud to have taken place, and reasons for not admitting that as a fact, 12501–12503——Employment of extra men, how paid, 12504–12506—— Only established officers employed in the examination of silks, 12506——Allan Fraser never employed in examining silks, 12507–12511——Statement of the dates, station, duty, and under whom Fraser employed on the quays where silk goods are usually examined, 12512——Silk goods not usually opened on the ground-floor where Fraser employed, 12513——Wages received by Fraser, and number of hours of labour 12515—— How far his situation a place of trust when he is immediately under the superintendence of the landing-waiter, 12516, 12517.

Duties of Surveyors General, 12518, 12519——Duties of landing surveyors, particularly with regard to silk goods, 12520, 12521——Manner in which doubts entertained by Custom House officers are cleared up by reference to the trade, 12522, 12526, 12527 ——Why appointing a person on purpose to judge goods and charge them according to their value would not be beneficial, 12523–12525——Examination of the allegations of Veritas by the invoices, which might have been made up for the occasion, 12528–12534 ——How far stamping goods would be beneficial, 12535, 12536——Stamping would have no reference to invoices, 12537——Landing-waiters only attend one scale, and never leave a case after the lid is off till they know its contents, 12538–12541——Statement by Veritas confirmed by affidavits which would be false if fraud not proved against officers; manner in which officers may be liable to error, 12542–12547.

*Manufactured Goods.* See *France,* X.

*Manufacturers.* Manufacturers of spring goods with good machinery do not generally stop in May, but single-hand looms do, *Merry* 2487——They do not prepare for the autumn as early as May, *Merry* 2488——Number of failures and withdrawals from business of manufacturers since the introduction of foreign goods, *Stephens* 2751——Reasons why their agents in London will not serve a small house under five per cent. higher than a large house, *Stephens* 2832–2842——Power of the Italians with regard to manufacture over the English, *Royle* 3100, 3101——Difference in the value of fixed property between a throwster and manufacturer, *Royle* 3106–3108——Protecting duty to manufacturers if trade of throwster destroyed, *Royle* 3116, 3117——How far other countries protect their manufacturers more than the English, *Royle* 3144——Failures of manufacturers last year, *Brockwell* 3490–3493——Interest of the manufacturer that the throwster should gain, *Brockwell* 3494——Those manufacturers who want foreign silk without duty have small vested interests in the silk trade, and would be ruined, *Brockwell* 3495–3497.

Disadvantages of the English manufacturer competing with the French, *Doxat* 4203–4207——How far prices of French manufactured goods imported last year sufficient to remunerate manufacturer, *Doxat* 4326–4329——Bad state of silk manufacturers at present, and how affected by large houses purchasing under prime cost, *Banbury* 4505–4515, 4535——Advantage to the French manufacturer from the cheapness of the article he uses, *Banbury* 3629, 4635–4637, 4655–4658——Advantages possessed by the French manufacturer

*Manufactures*--continued.

manufacturer over the English, *Gibson* 4839-4841——Number at present in Spitalfields, and number who have been ruined, *Stone* 5765, 5771——Some have turned throwsters, *Stone* 5766, 5767——How far reducing duty would benefit the manufacturer, *Hall* 6708.

Number of manufacturers at Lyons of whom plain goods bought, *Clay* 6955-6959 ——Competition in England causes the French manufacturer to be employed instead of the English, though upon English patterns, *Clay* 6977-6987——State of trade among manufacturers better, *Baggallay* 7569-7573——Reduction in the number of manufacturers since 1826, *Ballance* 8444-8447——Failures among manufacturers of broad goods, *Ballance* 8612-8619——Amount per cent. the manufacturer would be relieved by lessening the protection of the throwster, *Ballance* 8674-8676——Sacrifices made by manufacturers, *Ballance* 8690——Contingencies English manufacturer liable to, and protection necessary, *Ballance* 8713-8715——Amount per cent. more cost to English manufacturers of goods manufactured than smuggled or jobbed in from France, *Ballance* 8716-8722 ——Comparative statement of the cost of manufacturing 500 yards of plain gros de Naples in London and Lyons, *Ballance* 8722——Moderate protection, not prohibition, necessary to the English manufacturer, *Harter* 9229, 9230——Exertion of the English manufacturer to meet foreign competition has failed, *Wadden* 9972-10057——Possibility, if protected by price, of English manufacture equalling the French, shown by witness's experiments, *Wadden* 10068-10078——Different stages of manufacture, *Moore* 11263 ——Difficulties the manufacturers have had to contend with to meet competition with France, *Moore* 11274.

See also *America. Debentures.*

*Manufacturing Districts.* Applications from different, to the Board of Trade relative to the causes of their distress, *Hume* 57——How far duty and drawback is a tax upon one manufacturing district for the benefit of another, *Hume* 94, 113-119; *Brunskill* 451-454——Degree of distress in the silk manufacturing districts, *Doxat* 4039; *Wadden* 10041——Distress has been felt at other manufacturing districts as well as Spitalfields, particularly Manchester, *Moore* 11106-11108.

*Marabout.* French will not allow it to be exported, *Brunskill* 647-654——There is now a fair competition in price for it, *Cox* 2275-2279——Its quality has retrograded, *Cox* 2280——Where it comes from, *Cox* 2281——Its price much reduced, *Merry* 2602, 2603 ——Process of manufacture thereof, and prices, *Swift* 3811-3837——Advantage of France over England in the manufacture of, *Swift* 3838-3846——Quantity annually thrown, *Swift* 3847-3851, 3868-3870——Reason throwing marabout does not give a larger profit than other silk, *Swift* 3852-3854——Increased employment to operatives in throwing marabout, *Swift* 3875, 3876——It is not thrown in Italy, *Doxat* 4287—— Description of silk for making, *Heath* 5346, 5347——Comparison of prices of silk adapted for the manufacture of marabout, *Martin* 5491-5495; *Stone* 6264-6267—— Nature and price of marabout silk, and advantages to the French thereby, *Bowring* 8973-8977, 8979-8981, 8989——Price of marabout in France, and how manufactured, *Bowring* 9716-9718——Description thereof, and process of throwing it, *Wadden* 10065 ——Price thereof, raw and thrown, *Wadden* 10065, 10066.

See also *Organzine.*

*Market.* See *Stock.*

*Marston, Joseph,* (Analysis of his Evidence.) Operative in the single hand in the ribbon business, 1348——Guardian of the poor of Foleshill, 1349——Meaning of an undertaker, 1352——Number of operatives in Foleshill employed and unemployed, and how the account obtained, 1353-1357, 1361, 1362——Distress of that branch, it has been declining for the last four years, 1358-1360——Average earnings, when in full employment, previous to and since making lists in November last, 1363-1369——Distress attributable to foreign competition, 1370, 1371——French gauzes now sold in Coventry for less than operatives paid for making them in 1824-1826, 1371, 1372——Increase of the poors' rates in Foleshill, 1373——Account of monies actually paid to the permanent and casual poor in the parish of Foleshill, 1819-1831, 1374——Reasons for the establishment of the list of prices in November last, 1375——Not a fair remuneration, 1376—— Reasons for the manufacturers not giving better, 1377——Distress not attributed to the Jacquard engine, 1378——Improvements in the single hand engine would increase if foreign ribbons were excluded, 1379, 1380.

Articles that are made in the single hand loom which cannot be made in the engine loom, 1381, 1382——Increase in the population since 1821, within what years the increase took place, and how far employed, 1383-1392, 1501——Cause of the distress in 1818, and proportion it bore to the present, 1393-1396——State of trade in 1827 and 1828, 1397, 1398——How the difference in the amount of poors rates in certain years accounted for, 1399-1402——Benefits obtained by the local Act rating proprietors of houses to the poor rates instead of the occupiers, 1403, 1404——Number of houses built and uninhabited since 1825, 1405-1407, 1501——Allowances to persons not in the workhouse, 1408-1413——Increase or depression of the weaving trade, 1814-1818, 1414-1417—— Distress in the fancy branch of the trade from foreign competition, 1418-1424—— Depression of trade since the introduction of the engine machine has prevented its being much 678.

*Marston, Joseph,* (Analysis of his Evidence)—*continued.*

much used, 1425——Full employment in 1826 in the manufacture of brocade gauzes which have since been made abroad, 1426–1436.

Extent to which the cheapness in the manufacture in the engine loom has acted upon the employment of the single hand looms, 1437–1447——Rise in the wages upon certain articles since the table of prices was fixed, 1448–1450——Trade has partially improved since November 1831, but the distress is so great, improvement is not perceived, 1451–1457——How foreign brocade gauzes and figured satins can be distinguished from English, 1458–1460——Object of the list of November to equalize the wages of the hand loom and engine loom weaver, 1461, 1467–1469——Reasons for the manufacturer being better able to pay the increased wages upon that list, 1462, 1463——More uniformity in the present list than in any former one, 1464–1466——Number of people employed by the undertakers, and amount of the undertakers' profits, 1470–1475——Amount of work apprentices formerly taxed to perform, and amount at present, 1476–1486——Want of work and low wages always accompany each other, 1487——Present rate of wages, although a rise, are quite inadequate, 1488——Greater employment of engine looms would throw more people out of employment, 1492, 1493——Comparison of the state of weavers formerly and at present from the rate of wages, 1494–1500——Number of men employed upon the roads, 1502——Who are paid by a composition rate, which will be spent, in addition to the poors' rate, 1502–1505——Comparison of wages 1818 and at present, 1506–1508——Silk used by the undertakers is always in a dyed state, 1509——When the fine gauzes first manufactured, 1510——Specimens of silks produced by the witness, with examinations upon the manufacture, cost and weight of each description, 1511–1528.

*Martin, Andrew,* (Analysis of his Evidence.)   Gross produce of silk in Italy, and detail of countries from which produced, 5376–5380——How returns obtained, 5382, 5383——How far produce of Italy likely to increase, and what countries particularly, 5381, 5383, 5386, 5387——Injury to Piedmont, from the export of silk not being allowed therefrom, 5384, 5394——Manner in which silk is smuggled thereout, and amount and cost thereof, 5384–5386, 5395, 5396——Reason for want of capital in the Roman States, 5387, 5388——Information upon which witness's evidence furnished, 5389–5393, 5506–5508——Different descriptions of silk manufactured in each country in Italy, 5399——To what countries Italians export, with proportions to each, 5400–5403——Export of raw silk not allowed from France, 5404——Or from Piedmont, 5405——Duties on exportation of thrown from Piedmont and Lombardy, 5405.

Thrown silk allowed to be exported from France, 5404, 5406–5411——Manner in which raw silks are smuggled out of France, 5412, 5413—Expense attending that course, 5414, 5418——Comparison of price thereof with Italian silk, 5415–5417——Piedmont thrown worth more than French thrown, 5419——Quantity of French thrown silk coming to London is very small, 5420, 5421——Reasons for knowing the production of Italy without knowing the manufacture of different places, 5422–5427——Prices of raw and thrown silks in Italy, England and France, (1819–1831), 5428–5434, 5449–5451——Duties on importation of foreign raw and thrown silk into France, 5435——Reasons why the French do not buy Bengal silk in the English market, 5436——Not necessary to have been acquainted with the reeling of silk, to judge of its qualities, 5437——Advantage to Italian throwsters from reeling their own silk, 5438, 5439.

Description of silk supplied to Switzerland and Germany, and from whence, 5440——No duty on importation into Switzerland, 5440——Small duty on importation into Austria, Russia and Germany, 5441——In what parts of Italy improvement has taken place in raw silk, 5442, 5443——Price of throwing in Piedmont, France and Lombardy, 5445–5447——How far importation of thrown profitable to the Italian since reduction of duty, 5452, 5453——Comparison of capital, 1824–1826 and to 1831, in the silk trade, 5954–5457——Commission and brokerage, 5458–5461——Credit at present given, 5462, 5463——Amount of discount allowed, but not sufficient to produce cash payments, 5464, 5465——Reasons for reducing credit, 5466, 5467, 5472–5475, 5480, 5481——Rise in price after reduction of duties in 1826, 5468.

Loss to Italian throwster from imports for several years, 5469——Import of raw most advantageous, 5470——Proportion of import duty paid by foreign throwster, 5471——Spitalfields trade getting into the hands of a few large capitalists, 5478, 5479——Tendency of reduction of duty to increase importation of thrown, 5482——Cause of failures in 1825 and 1826, 5484, 5485——Brokers seldom guarantee, 5490——Comparison of prices of silks adapted for manufacture of marabout, 5491–5495——Countries to which the best raw and thrown silks are sent, and in what proportions, 5496——Quality of Piedmont organzines imported into France, 5497, 5498——Effect of reduction of duty on price of foreign thrown, 5499——Description of French silks that are superior to the Italian, 5500——Estimated production of France, 5501——Whether difficulty in obtaining superior quality of French thrown silks in Italy, 5502, 5503——Imports of thrown and raw into France, and total consumption, 5504——Particular sized raw silks of Italy that sell high in England, 5505.

(Second Examination.)   Correct information as to price of throwing in France, 5509——And of importations of Italian silk into France, 5509, 5510——Amount of French crop for last three years, 5511——Comparison of prices in London and Lyons 1831, 5511–5521——How far Piedmont thrown superior to the French, 5524——Difference in
price

*Martin, Andrew,* (Analysis of his Evidence)—*continued.*

price paid by the manufacturer and that received by the Italian, 5525——Distress of the silk trade in England during the latter end of 1831, 5526——Comparison of importations of raw and thrown, and reasons for Italian throwster importing thrown, 5527-5529—— Possible for Italians to throw a larger quantity, 5530——Advances made by merchants at London and Lyons to foreign throwsters, 5531-5536——Sales of silks at fairs in Italy, and how far prices regulated thereby, 5537-5543——Advantages of the English market to the Italians, 5544 ——Comparison of advantage in purchasing silk to be thrown in England and Italy, 5545, 5546——How far best Italian silk retained by Italian manufacturer for his own use, 5547-5549——Cocoons have been brought to England by way of experiment, 5550, 5551——Silk cannot be distinguished that has been reeled immediately, and that which has had a voyage to England, 5552——Price of trams at Lyons and London 1831, 5553——When period of credit altered in England, 5553——Discount on long credit, 5554——French tariff of 1822 prohibits exportation of both raw and thrown silks, 5554——Bad effect upon trade from agitation of the silk question, and appointment of the present Committee from fear of further reduction of duty, 5555-5578 ——Price of raw silk in France 1831, 5579——Price currents given in, 5579——How far authentic, 5589——Reason for large imports into England during 1830 and 1831, 5580-5585, 5587, 5590——Why trade of Italian throwster not likely to increase, 5586.

*Menetrier, Emilie,* (Analysis of his Evidence.)    Manner of smuggling goods into this country prior to 1826, 8210-8213——Opportunities for smuggling increased after 1826, but smuggling has decreased latterly, 8214, 8215——Inferior quality of goods imported into England since removal of prohibition, to meet prices in English market, 8216-8221 ——Witness ignorant of circumstances attending a seizure at Messrs. De Ponilly & Co.'s, 8222-8226, 8243, 8244——Whether silks used by De Ponilly & Co.'s house were dyed in France or in England, 8227-8231——Rate of smuggling at present, 8233, 8234—— Articles manufactured by De Ponilly & Co. that were fashionable in France but not in England caused them to give up their manufacture here, 8235-8238, 8250-8253, 8285-8288——Whether English government allowed De Ponilly & Co. to import organzine free of duty, 8239-8242——Furniture made by De Ponilly & Co. for Windsor Castle, at Spitalfields, 8245-8247——Number of looms employed by De Ponilly & Co., 8248, 8249——A few of their head weavers brought from France, 8256——Jacquards partly brought from France and partly manufactured at Manchester, 8257—— How far speculation succeeded, 8261-8265.

Some weavers employed from Paisley as good as the French weavers for gauzes, 8265, 8266——Importations by De Ponilly legally, 8269-8271——Number of looms employed on the order for Windsor Castle, 8276-8280——Where thrown silk obtained, 8282-8284, 8292-8296——Goods were manufactured at Manchester from French patterns, 8289-8291 ——Names of Mr. De Ponilly's partners and designer, 8297-8300——Description of goods manufactured at Manchester, 8303-8305——Duty on blonde lace from France, 8306——Amount smuggled, and rate of smuggling, 8307-8313——Smuggling plain broad goods has declined latterly, 8314, 8315——Ruin of smuggling from losses, 8316-8320—— Rate of insurance upon smuggling, 8321-8323——On what articles smuggling continues, 8324-8328——French houses in London, 8329, 8330—— Rate of smuggling in blonde, 8331-8335——Duty that would prevent smuggling in blonde, 8336, 8337——Fashionable articles are not smuggled, 8338—— Loss of property a sufficient punishment without personal punishment of the smuggler, 8339-8343——Who the smuggler is, 8344—— Punishing persons ordering the goods or lowering duties would prevent smuggling, 8345-8348, 8351, 8352——Stamp might be imitated if known, 8349, 8350.

*Merchants.*    Merchants in London cannot exercise their trade without being free of the Weavers' Company, *Bowring* 9044.

*Merry, William,* (Analysis of his Evidence.)

Account, showing loss of retail trade since 1826, through admission of French goods, 2450-2456, 2545-2547 ——Improved looms began to be made about the year 1820, 2457, 2458——Rich cut gauzes were made in 1825 and 1826, 2459, 2460——Were discontinued from the interference from the French, and not being able to get material for making them so good as the French, 2461-2463——They produce their goods at a lower price, 2464, 2465——Interference by the French in another branch of the trade, 2466-2468——Advantages of the Jacquard machine, 2469-2471——Handsome goods were made previously, 2472——Successful sale of spring goods, but loss at the end of the year from introduction of French goods in the autumn, 2473-2486——Manufacturers of spring goods, with good machinery, do not generally stop in May, but those with single hand looms do, 2487——They do not prepare for the autumn so early as May, 2488—— Expense of getting up patterns; how far the French are at the same expense, 2488-2491 ——English cannot get orders from the prejudice in favour of the French, 2492-2496 ——Under a prohibition the English would go to every expense to produce goods equal to the French, 2496, 2497.

How far the French have possession of the foreign markets over the English, 2498-2502 ——Comparison of the price of French and English goods after payment of duty on the French, 2503-2524——Labour much dearer in England than France, though now reduced to the lowest ebb, 2525——In the event of prohibition more machinery would be used, 2527

*Merry, William,* (Analysis of his Evidence)—*continued.*

——French goods supersede English of a better quality, 2528——Advantages of the French from previous orders, 2491, 2529–2532, 2537–2539——Advantages of the French with regard to exportation, 2533–2536——Smuggling has increased since lowering the duties, 2540, 2541——It has not expanded commerce, 2542——Depression of wages since 1826; Comparison of 1823–1825, with 1829–1831, 2543, 2544——Under prohibition as many novelties could be produced, and as many designers employed as in France, 2548 ——Business was increasing, and could have been carried on profitably under a prohibition, 2549–2551.

Sufficient capacity in this country to supply any quantity that might be required, 2553——Present distress entirely caused by foreign competition, 2552, 2554–2557—— Silks are more fashionable and are used in a greater variety of articles than formerly, 2557, 2558——Reasons for supposing smuggling is carried on to a great extent, 2560, 2561——Reasons why the present list of wages should be abided by, 2562–2565—— Expense of machinery, and value of goods turned out, 2566–2568——Proportion of labour to the value, 2569, 2570——Quantity of certain goods turned out in a given time, showing the average rate of wages, 2572–2586——Comparison as to the quality of the work made in a single hand and an engine loom each with Jacquard machinery, 2587– 2589——Making plain satins given up from its being a bad trade, 2590——English manufacturers do not now receive orders for their goods, 2591–2595.

Description of goods that are made at Reading, 2599——Fewer houses making gauzes now than in 1824–1826, 2600, 2601——Price of marabout much reduced, 2602, 2603—— Heavy goods are cheaper than the French, and but for prejudice in their favour, would be sold, 2604——Comparison of quantity and value of fancy goods made at Coventry five years previously and subsequent to 1826, 2605–2609——More men have been employed since 1826, but at lower wages, 2610, 2611——Principal part of the ribbons imported from France are gauze, 2612, 2613——Comparison of the prices of silk of the same quality in France and in England, 2614–2617——Improvement in manufacture previous to introduction of French goods, and cause of improvement since, 2618–2624——Average wages, and number of hours of labour, 2625–2629——Means of improving manufacture through the French patterns, during prohibition, 2630–2636.

(Second Examination.) Cost price of French goods less than the English, and profits much larger, 2846–2852——Wages lower than in 1825, 2852——No improvement in machinery since 1825, 2852.

*Middlehurst, John,* (Analysis of his Evidence.) Throwing a remunerative employment prior to 1826, 11783——Distress occasioned by the alteration of the laws in that year, 11784——Higher duty on foreign thrown silk would cause a better description of silk to be thrown in England, 11785——Reduction of wages, 11786, 11787——Necessity for reduction and distress of throwsters, 11788, 11789——Reduction in horse power at Macclesfield, 1824–1832, 11790——Number of hands employed, and rate of wages, 1824–1832, 11791——Throwing has been transferred to Italy and not to Manchester, 11792, 11793, 11797——Horse power at work at Manchester, 11794, 11795——Horse power out of work at Macclesfield, 11796——Comparison as to superiority between Manchester and Macclesfield, 11797–11801——Wages for throwing at Macclesfield 1818–1832, 11802–11805——Manchester people alternately work between silk and cotton, according to the wages in either trade, 11809——Macclesfield people have no other means of living but by silk weaving, 11810——Wages liable to be lower at Macclesfield than Manchester, 11811——Instance of a mill at Manchester stopping and buying foreign thrown silk cheaper than they could throw it, 11812, 11813.

*Middleton.* Letter from the Overseer thereof, showing the state of distress there, *Wadden* 10042.
   See *Silk Trade.*

*Milan.* Expense of importing silk from, *Banbury* 4472–4474——Effect of Berlin and Milan Decrees upon the silk trade, *Banbury* 4581–4588——Injurious effect of the Milan Decrees upon importation of Italian silk, and subsequent improvement of Bengal silk therefrom, *Wallis* 10954–10958——Effect of the Milan Decrees in causing difficulty of obtaining silk, *Moore* 11263, 11264.
   See also *Prices.*

*Mile End Old Town.*  See *Spitalfields District.*

*Mills.*  See *Capital.  Competition.  Throwing Mills.*

*Moore, Ambrose,* (Analysis of his Evidence.) Distress of the silk trade greater, and of more permanent character since 1826, than previously, attributed to opening the Ports, 11099–11105——Distress has been felt at other manufacturing places as well as Spitalfields, particularly Manchester, 11106–11108——Manner in which distress of the throwing trade has been caused by the reduction of duty on foreign thrown silk, 11109–11113—— Increase in the importation of raw silk since 1823, caused by high duty on thrown, 11114, 11115——Manufacture of sewing silk has increased, 11116–11118——Importation of Italian raw previous to and since 1824, 11119–11122——Increase in the silk trade for several years up to the opening the Ports, and decrease since, 11122–11134——State of the silk trade immediately previous to the admission of French goods, and means adopted

*Moore, Ambrose,* (Analysis of his Evidence)—*continued.*

adopted to prevent too large a quantity coming in at first, 11135–11151——Effects of removal of prohibition and reduction of duty on raw silk should be inquired into separately, 11152, 11153——Consumption of silk, 1824 and 1825, and since, 11153–11156 ——Prohibition should have been continued some years after duty taken off raw silk, 11157——No increase in throwing establishments since 1824, decrease in number thereof at Macclesfield, 11158——Quality of the silk, and not the weight should be looked at as to importations, the coarse diminishing employment of mills, 11159–11161—— Encouraging importation of thrown by lowering duties, diminishes the importation of raw, 11162——Increase of silk manufacture in France during the last six years over England, 11163——No necessity for foreign thrown ; richest and best works made from English thrown, 11164, 11165——Distress in the throwing trade is general, and not arising from the transfer from one town to another, 11166.

Foreign thrown silk cheaper than the raw can be bought and thrown for, 11167——No improvement in throwing or weaving since 1826, 11168——Workmanship has fallen off both in throwing and weaving, from low prices, 11169–11171——Less capital since alteration of system, 11172——Failure of the three principles of the alteration, superiority of machinery, skill of artisans and extent of capital, 11173——Views of the Government in altering the system, 11174–11176——Alarm in the trade before the alteration, and on what grounded, 11177, 11178——Time granted by Government to prepare for the change not sufficient, 11179–11182——Restrictions on labour and mode of working not removed by Government ; evils of the Spitalfields' Act, 11183, 11194, 11195—— Spitalfields' Act repealed at the expense of private parties in the trade, 11184——Repealed as a private Act, with all the expenses attendant thereon, and although opposition by certain Cabinet Ministers, 11185–11193——Expectation by Government that a great amount of French goods would not come in after alteration than were smuggled in previously, with contrary result, 11196–11200, 11219——Promise by Government that they would collect a 30 per cent. duty, which they have not done, 11201–11209, 11217–11219—— Evils of reduction of duty in 1829, 11210–11216, 11222——Advantages of reducing the duty on the raw material, 11220, 11221——Advantages to France from the growth of her silk, and leading the fashion, 11221——Less supply of good Italian raw silk now than previous to reduction of duties, from inducement to the Italian throwster to send more thrown, 11223–11225——Local advantages of Italian throwsters over the English, 11226.

(Second Examination.) Distress of throwing trade since alteration in 1829, by reducing profits and wages, and reducing the operatives to assistance of the poors' rate, 11227– 11230——Distress of trade occasioned by French importations, 11231——Examination upon smuggling goods out of France, 11232–11236——Representations made to Government by the silk trade on the distress therein, and on necessity for inflicting criminal punishment on smugglers; and stamping goods, and means of preventing forgery in stamping; and rejection by Government of plans offered, 11238–11248——Means of discovering French goods from English, and difficulties in the way of it, 11249–11253 ——Final answer of Government, 11254, 11255——Statement by the retail trade of difficulties in the way of stamping, 11256——Evils of reducing or removing duties on foreign thrown silk, from being an advantage to the manufacturer over the throwster, and causing the Italians to send all thrown silk, and no raw, 11257–11262——Necessity of a well adjusted scale of duties, 11263——Different stages of manufacture, 11263—— Effect of the Milan Decrees in causing difficulty of obtaining silk, 11263, 11264——Necessity for encouraging the importation of raw over thrown silk, 11264——Low prices cause imperfection in the throwing, 11265——Speed in throwing cannot be increased without injury, 11266——Throwing trade retrograded since reduction of duties, 11267—— Low duties on foreign thrown have reduced wages in throwing, 11268——Commencement of throwing by witness, duty on thrown at the time, and reasons for embarking in throwing trade, 11269–11271——Throwster should be protected on account of the capital vested in machinery, which machinery can be applied to no other purpose, 11272——Effect upon the price of the manufactured article of reducing so much duty on thrown as would make export duty on thrown from Italy equal to export duty on raw, 11273.

Difficulties the manufacturers have had to contend with to meet competition with France, 11274——Not so much skill in manufacture now as formerly, from not being able to employ so high a class of designers as formerly, shown by a pattern exhibited made 70 years ago, 11274, 11275——Inducements for building mills and increasing machinery; not so many in work now as before 1824, 11276——Reduction in wages, and consequent destitution of weavers therefrom, 11277–11279——Instances of dishonesty in consequence, by absconding of weavers to America with their employers' manufactured property, 11280–11285——Loss of the fancy trade from importations from France ; few fancy goods made in England that are not made in Spitalfields, 11286–11289——Difficulty af reviving the fancy trade while fashion in favour of France, 11290, 11291—— Advantage to France from her raw silk, 11292——How long the assaying machine for the trial of silk has been known in this country, 11293, 11294——Other advantages of France, 11295——Necessity for prohibiting importation of manufactured goods from France, unless she allows the importation of her raw silk, and amount of duty on manufactured goods in that event, 11296–11301——Means of preventing smuggling in that case, 11302——In the event of France putting a duty on the importation of her raw, whether that amount should be added to the manufactured goods, 11303–11306——

678.　　　　　　　　　　　　　　　　　　　　　　　　　　　　　　　　　　Necessity

*Moore, Ambrose,* (Analysis of his Evidence)—*continued.*

Necessity for Italian silk in working up Bengal and China silk, 11307, 11308——Duty on thrown that is necessary to ensure a good supply of Italian raw, 11309–11311—— Whether the fancy gauze trade can go on without prohibition, 11312, 11313——Additional duty on thrown silk would be beneficial to the home manufacture, 11314—— Greater degree of distress by ruining the throwster than the manufacturer, from his having a larger vested capital, 11315–11317——Prosperity of the silk trade depends upon the duties on the importation of thrown silk, 11318, 11319.

(Third Examination.) Reason why the alteration of system in the silk trade has miscarried, 12066——Protection not given to the silk trade which it was held out it would receive in 1824, 12067, 12068——Protecting duty necessary for throwsters, 12069—— Reasons why effectual measures have not been taken to repress smuggling, 12070, 12071 ——Local burthens of all classes in England are greater than the local taxation of France, 12072——Duties upon implements of machinery in France have no effect as compared with England, 12073——Duty on raw silk imported into France is small, and French use principally silk of their own growth, 12074——Merit of the French silk manufactures not likely to pass away from the disadvantages they labour under, 12075——France not under disadvantage as compared with Switzerland, 12076——No feeling in France in favour of any fair and reciprocal trade with England, 12077——Institution of the Conseil des Prud'hommes, and that for ascertaining the condition of silk in France, would be no benefit to England, and is not of importance to this inquiry, 12078–12084——To what the success of the French silk trade is owing, 12085——French goods coming to this country double the amount shown by French accounts of official exports, 12086——Increase in the use of silk goods in this country, and falling off in importation of raw and thrown, 12087——Advantage of being enabled to get French raw silks, 12088——But it would not counterbalance all the advantages of France over England, 12088.

*Morrison, James* & *Co.* Description of the mode of transacting business by their house, *Dillon* 7591–7597——Introduction of invoices of certain goods bought of Morrison & Co. showing how much per cent. goods bought cheaper than imported for, *Beckwith* 12548–12551——Other transactions with Morrison & Co. of a similar nature, *Beckwith* 12552–12557——Examination as to witness's having expressed regret for previously inferring that Morrison & Co. had not come properly by those goods, *Beckwith* 12558– 12580——Examination upon the correspondence that took place between witness and Morrison & Co.'s house relative to that transaction, *Beckwith* 12581–12587——How far goods would have been regularly passed through the Custom House, although entered lower than their regular duty, *Beckwith* 12588, 12589——Difference in the duty on goods imported by witness and sold to him by Morrison & Co. *Beckwith* 12600, 12601—— Supposition that one of Messrs. Morrison & Co.'s partners being at Paris induced the manufacturer to supply their house instead of witness with the goods he had ordered, *Beckwith* 12602——Witness's agent in Paris not a partner; period of his residence in Paris, *Dillon* 12668——Witness did not charge Messrs. Morrison & Co.'s house with smuggling, *Beckwith* 12603, 12604——Purchase of goods 30 per cent. lower than import price proof of the manufacturer cheating witness, or that Morrion & Co. must have passed their goods lower than witness, *Beckwith* 12605–12613——How much per pound weight witness's goods entered at; how far both parcels of goods being entered by weight would effect their value, *Beckwith* 12614–12631.

Witness's account of interview with Mr. Beckwith, in which witness produced proof of certain velvets sold him having paid duty, *Dillon* 12632–12637——Examination as to the production of invoices to Mr. Beckwith, and his expressing his alteration of his previous opinion, *Dillon* 14638–12646——Correspondence between Morrison & Co.'s house and Mr. Beckwith as to the latter's charge against the former of irregular proceedings, *Dillon* 12648–12653——Duty on witness's parcel paid by weight, *Dillon* 12654—— Difference in price between the two parcels, and how far from being bought of different persons, *Dillon* 12655–12666.

*Mortality.* Unhealthiness of the climate in India renders human life uncertain, *Grout* 10325–10327.

*Mulberry Leaves.* Care required in the cultivation of mulberry leaves, *Caffi* 7122–7124 ——Period at which the mulberry tree fit to supply the worms, *Caffi* 7320——Value of the leaves, *Caffi* 7322, 7323——Planting of mulberry trees stopped from an intention to impose a duty, *Caffi* 7324, 7325——Not profitable to cultivate the mulberry tree in this country, *Bowring* 9202, 9203——Difference in the mulberry plant between Bengal and France and Italy, *Grout* 10366, 10367.

## N.

*Narrow Goods.* See *Ribbons.*

*Necessaries of life* are higher at Coventry than in France, *Ratliff* 1974.

*Netherlands.* Offers to witness to establish himself in the silk trade in the Netherlands, and state of the silk trade there, *Brocklehurst* 11507–11518.

*Nismes.* Population and state of trade thereat, *Bowring* 9069–9075——Without export trade from being protected, *Bowring* 9722–9725.

*North*

*North of England.*   See *Throwing Mills.*

*Norwich.*   Reason for Norwich taking the bombazine trade, *Wallis* 10861, 10862.

*Nottingham.*   See *Manufacturing Districts.*

*Nuneaton Parish.*   Account of the general expenses of the parish, *Jacombs* 1581——
Number of persons depending upon the ribbon trade principally single hand, *Jacombs*
1582–1587——Effect of the table has not been felt in the parish yet, *Jacombs* 1826–
1828.

> *Papers laid before the Committee.*

Amount of Poor Rates collected in the Parish of Nuneaton ; with the Amount of Assessment, Rate in the pound, and number of levies, 1821–1832, *App.* p. 928.

# O.

*Octroi.*   See *Local Taxation*

**OPERATIVES.**
 In throwing mills.
>  1. Generally.
>  2. In Italy.

 1. *Generally.*

Number employed, *Ward* 2936–2938——Hands partly dependent on the poor's rate,
*Ward* 3981——Number out of employ, *Ward* 3979, 3980, 4009——Principally females
employed, *Ward* 4005——Throwing a healthy and domestic employment, *Ward* 4006,
4007——No means of subsistence if dismissed, *Ward* 4008——Employment of hands
before 1826, *Willmott* 4665–4669——Decrease in the employment of hands since
1829, and causes, *Willmott* 4670, 4671——Mill people more important than winders,
*Willmott* 4712, 4713——What other employment for the people besides silk winding,
*Willmott* 4714–4718——Description of persons employed, method of hiring, and rate of
wages, *Hall* 6472–6477——Larger supply of hands could not be obtained in witness's
present situation, *Hall* 6525, 6526——Number of hours children work, *Hall* 6586——
They are not worked at night, *Hall* 6587—— How far parish officers cognizant of the
manner in which children are hired, *Hall* 6590–6593——Fewer hands employed by
witness's machinery, *Hall* 6631–6635——Average number of persons employed, and
average rate of wages per week, 1822–1831, *Grout* 10285——Respectable condition of
young people formerly employed, and change in their morals and character since reduction of wages, *Grout* 10286–10292——Proportion of persons now employed as to men,
women and children, similar to what it was formerly, *Grout* 10293—— Comparison of
earnings in 1823 and 1830, and distress of the work people from reduction, *Grout* 10355–
10357——Good condition of operatives prior to 1826, *Brocklehurst* 11324——Number
of persons employed in throwing mills at Macclesfield, 1824–1332, *Brocklehurst* 11326–
11328——Subsistence of hands when out of employment, *Brocklehurst* 11337——Distress of operatives and bad moral effect therefrom, *Brocklehurst* 11397–11402——Number
of hands employed at Congleton, 1823 and 1832, *Johnson* 11565——Number unemployed, and method of subsistence, *Johnson* 11566, 11567——Distressed and demoralized
condition of the operatives, *Johnson* 11610–11612.

 2. *In Italy.*

Method of paying operatives when throwing mills not at work, *Caffi* 7088–7902——
Operation of twisting and throwing, hours of labour, wages and amount of work,
*Caffi* 7219–7229, 7236–7241——Wages of superintendents, *Caffi* 7230–7234, 7242–7248
——Manner of subsistence of operatives when mills not at work, *Caffi* 7249.

See also *Doubling.   Reeling.   Throwing Mills.   Winding.*

*Orders.*   Advantage to the French by previous orders, *Merry* 2491, 2529–2532, 2537–2539;
*Gibson* 5019–5027 ; *Stone* 5903, 5904 ——English cannot get orders from prejudice in
favour of the French, *Merry* 2492–2496——English manufacturers do not now receive
orders for their goods, *Merry* 2591–2595 ; *Stephens* 2690, 2695——When orders for
French goods usually given, *Stephens* 2688, 2689——Articles to order are manufactured
according to the pattern of each house, *Gibson* 5148–5151——Orders for fancy articles
being given to particular English houses will prevent French goods entirely superseding
the sale of those orders, *Sedgwick* 8120–8130——When orders formerly given for the
spring trade, *Sedgwick* 8146——Orders now given for French fancy ribbons, *Sedgwick*
8157—Orders formerly given for English fancy ribbons and broad goods, *Sedgwick* 8159,
8160——Orders for English goods given later now than formerly to ascertain what the
French are likely to produce, *Sedgwick* 8165, 8166——Method of ordering goods in
France, *Sedwick* 8198——Goods made from orders formerly, *Bridges* 10424, 10425.

See also *America.   Coventry.   France*, III.

*Organzine.*   By whom first mill for throwing organzine introduced into England, *Swift*
3726——Process of manufacture of marabout organzine and tram, and prices thereof,
*Swift* 3811–3837——Distinction between organzine and tram, *Wadden* 10064, 10065.

See also *Importation*, 2.   *Italy.   Silk*, VII. 3

# P.

*Patents.* See *Conseil des Prud'hommes.*

*Patterns.* Benefit to English manufacturers from a variety of patterns, *Cheeper* 869, 870 ——Manufacturers provide patterns, *Perkins* 1557, 1558——Improvement in the silk trade in 1823, was not owing to French patterns, *Jacombs* 1753–1757——From what patterns ordered goods used formerly to be made, *Cox* 2158–2160——Expense of getting up patterns ; how far the French are at the same expense, *Merry* 2488–2491——Means of improving manufacture through French patterns during prohibition, *Merry* 2630–2636—— In the event of a change of pattern in French goods they can still be sold as such, and accepted as new goods, *Stephens* 2696——No encouragement now to lay out money in producing novelties, *Stephens* 2730——How far French patterns could be obtained to give taste to English manufacture in the event of prohibition, *Sedgwick* 8056 ; *Bouillon* 10218, 10219——Advantage to French from expense in construction of patterns grows out of her command of foreign market ; manner thereof, *Ballance* 8414, 8415.

See also *Coventry. Manufacturers. Orders. Weavers.*

*Perkins, James,* (Analysis of his Evidence.) Introduction of the Jacquard machine merely a change in the fancy looms, 1532——Number of fancy looms superseded by the use of the Jacquard machine, 1533–1536——Number of Jacquard machines now at Coventry, 1537——Number of fancy looms employed before 1823, 1539—— Jacquard apparatus can be applied to the engine loom, 1540——Number of looms in Coventry in 1818, and at present, and number that have the Jacquard apparatus, 1541– 1545——Mr. Woodhouse's loom was for plain goods, 1547——Proportion of extra work of an engine loom over a single hand loom, 1552, 1553——Average wages, 1554–1556 ——Manufacturers provide the patterns, 1557, 1558——Nature of the employment of designers, 1559, 1560——Time taken in getting the work into the loom, 1563——Number of weeks unemployed in the last year, 1565, 1566——Amount per week witness formerly taxed to earn as an apprentice, 1569——There are satin figures now making, but of a different style and quality, 1570——Description of goods witness at present employed upon, 1571–1573——Quantity made in a certain time, and price thereof, showing the average rate of wages when in full work, 1574–1579.

*Peter, St.* Examination upon the method of conducting the school of St. Peter in France for the encouragement of Arts, *Bowring* 8806–8825——Extrait du Réglement pour les Etablissemens Publics existant dans le Palais St.-Pierre, *Bowring* 8823.

*Piedmont Silk.* Extent of importation thereof into France, *Ratliff* 1908, 1909——Is used for particular purposes, *Cox* 2271——Is the best thrown exported from Italy, *Brockwell* 3526–3528——Greater proportion of the best quality of Piedmont silk exported to France than England, *Brockwell* 3529–3532——For what Piedmont silk required, *Doxat* 4123——Variation in importation of Piedmont organzine, *Doxat* 4249——Export of Piedmont raws prohibited, *Doxat* 4257——Reasons why, *Banbury* 4593–4596 ; *Martin* 5405——Price of Piedmont organzine in London, and quantity imported, *Doxat* 4375– 4378——Piedmont silk the best of Italy, *Heath* 5297——Lombardy silk sometimes imported into Piedmont to be thrown, *Heath* 5298——From what the superiority of Piedmont silk arises, *Heath* 5299——Injury to Piedmont from the export of silk not being allowed therefrom, *Heath* 5384–5394——Manner in which it is smuggled thereout, and amount and cost thereof, *Heath* 5384–5386, 5395, 5396——Duties on exportation from Piedmont, *Martin* 5405——How far Piedmont thrown superior to the French, *Martin* 5524——Premium for smuggling raw silk from Piedmont, *Caffi* 7137–7141——Description of the silk, and for what purposes used, *Caffi* 7142–7145——Duties thereon, *Harter* 9238–9240 ——Advances by the French and English merchants to the Piedmont growers, *Bowring* 9780–9782——Consumption of Piedmont organzine, *Bennett* 10791.

See also *Silk,* VII. 3. *Smuggling.*

*Pillage.* See *Lyons.*

*Pittifor, Thomas,* (Analysis of his Evidence.) Examination upon the earnings of weavers, 11989–12028——Examination upon the time taken in making alterations in a pattern, and loss to the weaver thereby, and whether less time would be occupied therein, 12029– 12043——There would not be much more time or advantage gained by warping whole grosses than half grosses, 12044–12046——Loss of time greater in the manufacture of fancy than plain ribbons, 12047, 12048——Expense of assistance required by weavers, reducing the amount of their earnings, 12049 12052——Weavers purchase the looms of their masters as a means of keeping in employment, 12053, 12054——Not an undue proportion between the earnings of plain and figured weavers, 12055–12057——Delay in weavers' work how far necessary, and method of prevention, 12058, 12059——Tables showing the comparative cost of manufacture between French and English goods, 12060–12065.

*Plain Silks* were more frequently smuggled than fancy silks, *Hume* 11—— Are not smuggled alone to any extent, *Hume* 71–76 ; *Gibson* 4948——Demand for foreign plain goods so great that they sell in preference to English goods of the same quality and much cheaper, *Brunskill* 206–224——Large imports of plain goods now, *Brunskill* 755——No importation of plain ribbons from France, *Poole* 1125–1128——How far importation in the
fancy

*Plain Silks—continued.*

fancy trade affects the plain trade, *Goode* 1228–1232, 1238–1245——Decline in the plain branch, *Goode* 1246, 1247——Plain goods the best branch for throwsters, *Royle* 3095—— Statement of cost of manufacture of plain goods at London and Lyons, *Doxat* 4402——— Proportion of labour to the value thereon, *Gibson* 5050, 5051——More plain articles used now than formerly, *Gibson* 5133–5141——English plain goods have beat the French out of the market, *Clay* 6808–6811, 6976——Price of certain plain goods and duty thereon, *Clay* 6953, 6954 ; *Baggallay* 7477–7479——Variation in duty on plain silks, *Bottrell* 7883 ——Description of the term plain, figured and fancy goods, *Ballance* 8395–8400—— Advantage to the plain trade by increasing the risk of the smuggler, *Ballance* 8434, 8435.

Regulations against smuggling applicable to the plain branch, *Ballance* 8471—— Duties that might be collected on plain goods under proposed regulations, *Ballance* 8479, 8482——Reduced wages has partly stopped legal importation of plain goods, *Ballance* 8691 ——Plain trade may be protected if the smuggler detected and punished, *Wadden* 10033 ——English plain goods come into the market as cheap as the French, *Bouillon* 10168– 10170——Purchases in France in plain goods have been latterly reduced, *Bouillon* 10176–10179 —— Certain plain goods made in this country from French patterns cheaper than in France, *Bouillon* 10220–10226——Reasons for buying plain silks from France, *Stephens* 10615–10618——Plain goods are smuggled, *Stephens* 10663–10665 ——Progressive increase of the plain branch previous to 1826, *Bennett* 10716, 10717.
See *Duty on Importation.*

*Poole, Benjamin,* (Analysis of his Evidence.)  Ribbon weaver at Coventry, 940–942 ——Distress of the working classes, 943, 944——Ribbon trade and watch trade the principal manufactures at Coventry, 945——Greatest number employed in the ribbon trade, 946——No improvement in the manufactures since the introduction of foreign manufactured ribbons, 947, 948, 1002, 1003——Machinery used in the fancy branch has not increased, 948, 949——Improvements in machinery were received by the working classes with alacrity, 950, 1009, 1015–1018——Reasons why machinery not more gene-rally used, 951——Want of employment attributed to foreign competition in certain branches, 952——Which has latterly prevented improvements in Machinery, 953, 954 ——General rate of wages and reductions latterly, 955–960——Causes of the distress at Coventry, 1815–1817, 961–963——Amount of poor rates at Coventry, 1831, 964, 965 ——Account of the sums expended in the united parishes of the city of Coventry by weekly payments to the permanent and casual out poor in each of the years ending April 1815–1831, with the gross amount of parish expenditure for each year; also the average price of wheat, 965——Account of the average weekly earnings of weavers having full employment in the plain ribbon trade, including satins and sarsnets, 1815– 1830, 965——Working classes do not contribute to the poors' rates, 966——Reasons for difference in the amount of poors' rates between 1830 and at present, 967——Distress greater now than in 1818, 968–979——Average wages for the whole year, 980——Num-ber of hours labour per day, 981——Difference in the rate of wages in 1818 and at present, 982–990——More out of employment now than in 1818, 991, 992——Wages received by journeymen from the undertakers the same as from the manufacturers, 993, 994——Nature of the undertaker, 995——Undertakers superseded by the engine looms, 996–1001——Dutch loom used in the plain branches of the engine trade, 1004—— Number of widths an engine loom can make, 1005, 1006——Nature of the a-la-bar loom, 1007——Engine looms have been worked by steam, 1008, 1011.

Destruction of steam looms last November, 1012, 1019, 1022——Meeting of the workmen in November, 1013——Particulars of the meeting, its objects being equal rate of wages, 1019–1024, 1051, 1052——No knowledge by whom the factory was burnt, 1024, 1025——Probable reasons for its destruction, that it would have produced a greater quantity of goods in a given time, and at greater cost than by hand labour, and kept the workmen out of employment, 1026–1042——No expression of dissatisfaction at its ex-istence at the meeting, 1043——Promise of the proprietor not again to apply steam to the manufacture of ribbons in Coventry, 1045——No attempt at its introduction since, 1046——Manufacture by engine looms, and how long they have been in use, 1047–1050—— List of prices between 1816 and 1831, and in what instances departed from, 1053–1061—— Reduction in the wages of single hand loom weavers between 1829 and 1831, 1062–1064 ——List of prices of engine loom work agreed to at a meeting of manufacturers held at the Castle Inn, in the City of Coventry, on Thursday, November 10th, 1831, and to com-mence the following day, 1064——Resolutions of a meeting of the Committee of Ten appointed at the general meeting to make a new standard, held at the Castle Inn, on the 9th November 1831, for deviating from the standard 1822, and regulating the width of sars-nets, 1064——List of prices of single hand work agreed to at a meeting of manufacturers held at the Castle Inn, in the City of Coventry, on Thursday, November 10th, 1831, and to commence the following day, 1064——Meetings at which the above prices were settled, 1065–1067——Comparison of wages earned by the engine and single hand loom weaver, 1068–1070, 1075–1079, 1084, 1117–1119——Discontent among the weavers from some of the masters wanting a further reduction of wages between 1829 and 1831, 1071–1074 678.                                                                  ——There

*Poole, Benjamin,* (Analysis of his Evidence)—*continued.*

————There are articles made in the hand loom that cannot be made in the engine loom, but not the contrary, 1080————Many hands out of employment at that time, 1081———— Single hand list includes winding and warping but not the engine list, 1082, 1083———— Comparison of quantity made between an engine and a hand loom, 1085–1089———— Engine loom weaver receives less per piece than the single hand, 1090, 1091————How far the lists were for the purpose of equalizing the wages between an engine loom and single hand loom weaver, 1092–1105.

Extent to which there is more employment for the engine loom weavers than the hand loom since the list of prices, 1106–1114————Wages should continue to be paid according to the prices in the lists, 1115, 1116————Quality of the hand loom articles preferable, 1120, 1121, 1135–1137————How far the single hand feels any depression in the trade first, 1122, 1123————Articles made at Coventry are finer than those made at other places, 1124————No importation of plain ribbons from France, 1125–1128————How far the use of the engine loom tends to throw workmen out of employment, 1129, 1130————Greater consumption of silk at present than ever known, 1131————Foreign competition supplies the demand for manufactured goods, and drives the manufacturer and workmen to a lower description of goods, 1132–1134————Articles made at Reading are not made at Coventry, 1139————The two principal machines for weaving in Coventry are the engine loom and the Jacquard machine, 1140–1144————The same description of machinery that is used in France is used in Coventry, 1145, 1146————Proportion that Mr. Beck's steam machine would have made to other machines, 1148–1152————Examination upon the poor rates and distress from 1815, 1153–1164————Increase or decrease in the number of weavers and population, 1821–1831, 1165–1173————Number of looms in Coventry, 1174–1177———— How many months full employment for the weavers last year, 1178–1182————How far a weaver's family assist him, 1183, 1184————Extent to which the consumption of silk will tend to show the beneficial employment of the operative, 1186–1191————Number of engine looms employed in 1826 cannot be ascertained, 1192————Number at present unemployed, 1193–1196.

*Poor's Rates.* Amount of poor's rate at Coventry, 1831, *Poole* 964, 965————Account of the sums expended in the united parishes of the city of Coventry, by weekly payments, to the permanent and casual poor, in each of the years ending April 1815–1831, with gross amount of parish expenditure for each year; also, average price of wheat, *Poole* 965———— Working classes do not contribute to the poor's rate, *Poole* 966————Reasons for difference in the amount of poor's rate between 1830 and at present, *Poole* 967———— Examination upon poor's rates and distress from 1815, *Poole* 1153–1164————Increase of the poor's rates in Foleshill, *Marston* 1373————In Bruton, *Ward* 3983————Account of monies actually paid to the permanent and casual poor in the parish of Foleshill, 1819– 1831, *Marston* 1374————How the difference in the amount of poor's rates in certain years accounted for, *Marston* 1399–1402————Account of poor's rates in Manchester, 1826– 1832, *Royle* 3244 ————Increase of poor's rates in Sherborne, *Willmott* 4672–4679, 4724, 4800————Amount of assessments for poor's rate, 1816–1832, *Willmott* 4679————Parochial relief to some parents of children employed by witness, *Hall* 6558–6580————Examination as to the poor's rate in Macclesfield, *Brocklehurst* 11382–11390————At Congleton, *Johnson* 11568–11571.

### Papers laid before the Committee.

Amount of Poor Rates collected in the United Parishes in the City of Coventry, by Twelve Rates in each year, and the Amount in the Pound, *App.* p. 926.

Amount of Poor Rates collected in the Parish of Bedworth;' with the Number of Rates, the Rate of Assessment, and Gross Amount of Property assessed, *App.* p. 927.

Return of the Property assessed in the Parish of Stoke, in the County of Warwick; with the Number of Rates, Rate of Assessment, and Gross Amount on all Property assessed in the said Parish of Stoke, from the year 1815 to the year 1832 inclusive, *App.* p. 927.

Amount of Poor Rates collected in the Parish of Shilton, in the County of Warwick; with the Number of Levies, and Amount collected in each year from 1815 to 1832, and the Gross Amount of all Property assessed, *App.* p. 928.

Amount of Poor Rates collected in the Parish of Nuneaton; with the Amount of Assessment, Rate in the Pound, and Number of Levies from the year 1821 to the year 1832, *App.* p. 928.

Account of the Disbursements of the Parish of Bedworth, in the County of Warwick for Ten Years, to the County Rates and to the Poor, *App.* p. 929.

See also *Weavers.*

*Population,* increase therein since 1821 : within what years the increase took place, and how employed, *Marston* 1383–1394, 1501.

*Post Bills.* See *Bank of England.*

*Power looms.* See *Machinery.*

Poyton

*Prices*—continued.

reduced price to the fullest extent to the consumer or manufacturer, *Ballance* 8495, 8496 ——Difference in the price of goods imported by the Trade Committee and similar goods made at Spitalfields, *Ballance* 8586 —- Operation of wages upon the price of goods at Lyons, *Bowring* 8934-8938——How far price of French silk regulated by the price paid for Italian silk, *Bowring* 9187—— Other charges increasing price to the English manufacturer, *Harter* 9241-9243——Difference in prices of certain silks and ribbons, *Bowring* 9719——Relative prices of French and Italian silk in France, *Bowring* 9775-9778- — Comparative price of French and Bengal silk, *Grout* 10335-10337——Small increase of price would not lessen consumption, *Bennett* 10778-10787——Price of silk not lower after repeal of duties in 1824, *Brocklehurst* 11340, 11341——Examination as to difference of price of raw and thrown silk at London and Lyons, *Doxat* 12092.

*Papers laid before the Committee.*

Comparative View of the London Market Prices of Milan and Bergam Raw Silks of four to five cocoons, and of Milan and Bergam Organzines of 26 to 28 deniers at various periods, from June 1824 to February and April 1832, with Notes thereon as regards the British Throwster, *Evidence*, p. 261.

See also *French Goods*, VII. *Italy. Silk*, VII. 3.

*Prime Cost.* See *France*, III. *Jobbing.*

*Production of Silk.* See *France*, VII.

*Profits.* Profits in any trade affected by the competition in it, *Jacombs* 1763-1766 ——Manufacturers' profits decreased, *Jacombs* 1720——In what year profits better than at present, *Jacombs* 1822——Great profits of the French manufacturer over the English, *Ratliff* 1866-1868——Greater profit to the dealer on French than English goods, *Ratliff* 1945-1947——Decrease of profit since 1826, and how affected by giving higher wages, *Ratliff* 2027-2030 ——In calculating profits, allowance is made for any sacrifice that may take place, *Cox* 2196-2198——Profits upon French goods much larger than on English, *Merry* 2846-2851——Profits of French dealers and manufacturers, *Stephens* 2936-2947 ——Effect of competition on profits, *Royle* 3219-3221——How far the throwster and manufacturers consider each other's profits, *Royle* 3389-3391——How far bad profits beneficial to the consumer, *Banbury* 4516-4525 — ·Trade has not flourished since fair profits ceased to be obtained, *Banbury* 4526——Reduction of profits and labour by previous reduction of duties, *Willmott* 4740-4744——On what returns profits are calculated, *Gibson* 5006-5011 ; *Stone* 6334-6338——Profits of manufacturer and wages determined by competition, *Gibson* 5049——Comparison of profits in silk and other businesses, *Caffi* 7116, 7117——Profits are not greater upon the sale of French than English goods, but losses are, *Dillon* 7696.

See also *Competition. Consumers. France. Silk Trade*, 2.

*Prohibition.* Period at which prohibition took place. *Hume* 43-45 ; *Banbury* 4409, 4410 ——Prohibition more effectual against smuggling than a protecting duty, *Hume* 66, 68 ; *Cheeper* 888-896——Beneficial effects of prohibition, *Brunskill* 122 ; *Jacombs* 1724-1737 ; *Cox* 2085 ; *Banbury* 4412-4414, 4602-4605——Prohibition the only remedy for the distress, *Brunskill* 124 ; *Ratliff* 1844-1846 ; *Banbury* 4592-4601—— Who would be benefited by increased price in the event of a return to the prohibitory system, *Brunskill* 189-194, 486——Prohibition more necessary than reducing the duty on foreign thrown silk, *Brunskill* 364-366——Spitalfields' trade would revive if prohibition granted, *Brunskill* 236——In the event of prohibition there would be an increase of machinery, *Brunskill* 122, 239-241 ; *Ratliff* 1879 ; *Merry* 2527——Bad effects upon trade from opening the ports in 1824, *Brunskill* 457-463——Manufacturers who thought well of the alteration in 1826 that have changed their opinion since, and left the trade, *Brunskill* 532-536 — -Prohibition the only remedy against smuggling fancy articles, *Brunskill* 557, 734-736 ; *Ratliff* 1910-1916, 1930, 1931, 1934-1940——In the event of prohibition, the standard of taste would cease to be regulated by France, *Cheeper* 862-865——Every description of ribbon should be prohibited, *Ratliff* 1917——Prohibition would place France in the same situation England now is with regard to the ribbon trade, *Ratliff* 1918-1925——Prohibition should extend to all fancy French ribbons, *Cox* 2199-2195 ——Under a prohibition the English would go to every expense to produce goods equal to the French, *Merry* 2496, 2497——As many novelties could be produced and as many designers employed as in France, *Merry* 2548——Business was increasing and could have been carried on profitably under a prohibition, *Merry* 2549.

Sufficient capacity in this country to supply any quantity that might be required, *Merry* 2533——Proportion French goods bore to English during prohibition, how obtained, and difficulty and risk in selling, *Stephens* 2654-2666——It might benefit, *Royle* 3068-3071——Bad effects of repealing Prohibitory Acts, *Banbury* 4411——Increase of manufactures and employment of operatives under prohibitory laws, *Banbury* 4414——Injury to capital invested in mills and machinery in consequence of the repeal of the prohibitory laws, *Banbury* 4421-4423, 4425——Up to the period of the repeal the

*Prohibition*—continued.

the silk trade progressively improving, *Banbury* 4424——Benefits derived from former prohibition, *Hall* 6748, 6749——How far prohibition would protect British manufacture *Bottrell* 7950——Prohibiting French goods would weaken the stimulus for improvement in English manufacture, *Sedgwick* 8043, 8044——Under prohibition English goods might be made from French patterns, *Sedgwick* 8079——Prohibition would be a benefit under severe laws against smuggling and approximation of price between French and English goods, *Sedgwick* 8148–8156——In the event of prohibition there is sufficient competition in England for supply of goods as to price, but not taste, *Sedgwick* 8192–8194.

Exclusion of foreign manufactured silks the only effectual counteraction for the advantages possessed by France, *Ballance* 8416; *Grout* 10321; *Bridges* 10487, 10488; *Bennett* 10722, 10776, 10777; *Graham* 12756–12762——Why, in the event of prohibition, the English would not lose in point of taste and fashion, or pay higher price, *Ballance* 8473, 8474——Moderate protection, not prohibition, necessary to the English manufacturer, *Harter* 9229, 9230——Prohibition not desirable, *Harter* 9231——Entire prohibition most beneficial, but plain goods might be admitted under proper Custom House regulations, *Bennett* 10772——Distress attributed to the repeal of the protecting laws which existed prior to 1824, *Poyton* 10982——Contrary result of the repeal of those laws from that held out by Government, *Poyton* 10983–10985——Statement of reasons for opposing repeal of those laws, *Poyton* 10986—— Prohibition should have continued some years after duty taken off raw silk, *Moore* 11157——State of the silk trade, 1827–1831, *Graham* 12763–12768.

See also *Bandannas. Fancy Trade. French Goods,* 8. *Importation. Smuggling,* V. 3.

*Promissory Notes.* See *Bank of England.*

*Protections.* See *Cotton. Silk Trade.*

*Protecting Duty.* See *Duty on Importation. Smuggling.*

*Prout, John,* (Analysis of his Evidence.) Silk weaver at Macclesfield, 11635, 11636—— Injury to weavers from introduction of foreign wrought silk, 11638——Improvement in the silk trade at Macclesfield, 1809–1824, but not since 1825, 11639–11641——Decrease in the amount of wages paid upon the manufacture of coarse goods over the fine goods, 11642, 11643——Fancy trade has declined not from the change of fashion, but the introduction of foreign goods, 11644, 11645——State of trade in 1824 and 1825, 11646 ——Statement of the price of labour in Macclesfield 1810, 1819, 1825 and 1832, and examination thereupon, 11647–11655, 11661–11663——Distress and demoralization of the weavers through the alteration in the laws, 11656, 11669, 11670.

Competition with cotton manufacturers did not reduce wages of weavers, 11657—— Depression of trade in 1826 and 1829, 11658——Protecting duty necessary for the silk trade, 11659, 11660——Tabular view exhibiting the amount paid for labour in the weaving department of the silk trade of Macclesfield in 1825 and 1832, with average wages, weekly amount and annual loss, 11664——Distress previous to 1825 not permanent, 11665——Disadvantages of removing the duty on foreign thrown silk, 11667, 11668——No new trade has been made at Macclesfield since alteration of the system, and the trade has gradually declined, 11670——Method of manufacture called steaming peculiar to Macclesfield, 11671, 11672——Coarser description of goods made at Macclesfield than formerly, 11673.

*Provisions.* Price thereof in Italy, *Caffi* 7314–7317——Comparison of price between France and England, *Bowring* 9816, 9817.

*Prussia.* Increase of import duties into, *Bottrell* 7971.

## Q.

*Quality of Silk.* See *France,* VII. *Silk,* II.

*Queen.* See *Manchester.*

## R.

*Ratliff, Cleophas,* (Analysis of his Evidence.) Ribbon manufacturer at Coventry, 1830–1832——Quantity of silk dyed in Coventry, 1824, 1825, 1830 and 1831, 1833—— Different leading ribbons manufactured at Coventry in 1824–25 and 1830–31, 1834—— Distress of the ribbon trade attributed to the great importation of French ribbons, 1835 ——Quantity of ribbons imported 1831, and calculation of the employment the making them would have given the British manufacturer, 1836——More plain satins at present introduced into England than formerly, 1837, 1838——English manufacturer can produce as good an article as the French, 1839–1843——Prohibition the only means of enabling the English manufacturer to make goods; the abolition of the import duty on foreign silk would not affect him, 1844–1846——Difference in the quantity and quality of silk used in manufacturing the same article in France and England, 1847, 1848—— Whether difficulty in distinguishing between French and English goods, 1849–1853——

678.  Difficult

*Retail Trade.* Account showing loss thereof by admission of French goods, *Merry* 2450–2456, 2545–2547——State of trade among retailers more regular and better at present than for some years, *Baggallay* 7566–7568——Fewer failures among retailers latterly, *Dillon* 7704, 7705——Description of goods sold prior to 1826, *Sedgwick* 7979——Proportion of French and English goods at present sold, *Sedgwick* 7985–7987, 8015; *Stephens* 10619–10034——Retail houses import more than formerly, *Sedgwick* 8196.

See also *Haberdashers.*

*Returns.* Increase by large houses of the amount of their returns, *Stephens* 2821–2823, 2950–2955, 2969, 2970.

*RIBBONS :*

      1. *Generally.*
      2. *Black.*
      3. *Cut.*
      4. *English.*
      5. *Foreign.*
      6. *Duty on Importation.*
      7. *Distress of the Ribbon Trade.*

### 1. *Generally.*

Are more worn than formerly, *Jacombs* 1611, 1612; *Cox* 2186——During 1813 and 1814 there were as many pieces of ribbon used, bu7 not of the same description, *Cox* 2294——Uses to which ribbons made by witness applied, *Hall* 6649——Manufacture of narrow goods Italian thrown used therein, and competition therein with Spitalfields, *Harter* 9375–9383——Countries to which narrow goods exported, *Harter* 9444–9447.

### 2. *Black.*

Only English thrown silk used for making black ribbons, *Hall* 6636, 6637, 6640——Effect of repeal of import duty on value of black ribbons, *Hall* 6638.

### 3 *Cut.*

Increase in the manufacture of cut ribbons, *Clay* 6804–6807——Reasons for the French improving their manufacture thereof, *Clay* 6971–6973.

### 4. *English.*

Similar description to the foreign are manufactured at Coventry, *Brunskill* 129——Certain ribbons made in England cannot be made equal to the French from their not allowing the material of which they are made to be exported, *Brunskill* 647–654——In what cases French patterns are copied, *Brunskill* 655–660——Reason for goods now manufacturing at Coventry being better than they usually are, *Brunskill* 680–683——Time that would be taken for preparing loom, and expense of setting pattern, and manufacturing goods in imitation of the French goods, *Brunskill* 689, 690, 727–733; *Smith* 1323–1335; *Jacombs* 1610——Patterns here are cheaper and as good as the French, but the taste is in favour of the French, *Brunskill* 739–746——There were more orders for ribbons formerly than at present, *Brunskill* 750–753——Description of English goods that were made superior than at present before foreign goods allowed to be imported, *Cheeper* 933–935——No improvement in the manufacture since the introduction of foreign manufactured ribbons, *Poole* 947, 948, 1002, 1003——It has been checked thereby, *Jacombs* 1599, 1600——Ribbons can be made as good in Coventry as in France, *Goode* 1251——Jacquard looms make the article better in point of taste but not quality, *Smith* 1317–1320——Necessity for using Jacquard looms to imitate French patterns, *Smith* 1321, 1322——State of trade in different years since 1820, *Jacombs* 1650–1656 ——Depression in the trade generally, *Jacombs* 1692, 1693——Examination upon the cost of labour and material in the manufacture, *Jacombs* 1701–1715.

Few houses willing to engage for English goods, *Jacombs* 1762——Seldom English articles made cheaper from the cheapness of French living, *Jacombs* 1821——Different leading ribbons manufactured at Coventry, 1824–5 and 1830–31, *Ratliff* 1834——With same advantages, the English manufacturer can produce as good an article as the French, *Ratliff* 1839–1843——Production of some patterns equal to the French made in the looms of Mr. Henry Atkins, of Coventry, *Ratliff* 1841–1843——Difficult to distinguish between different English manufacturers' goods, *Ratliff* 1852——There could be sufficient quantity and variety of goods manufactured at home for supply or the home market, *Cox* 2145——Loss by manufacturing goods upon a guess of the French patterns, in the event of any variation, *Cox* 2150–2152——Orders are now given in France that used to be given in England, *Cox* 2153, 2154——Extent of goods at present made to order in Coventry, *Cox* 2155–2157——Superior articles made, 1822–1825, than since, *Cox* 2206, 2207, 2211——English goods are not sold as French, they are not so good or so cheap, *Stephens* 2703–2707——French goods sometimes sold as English when English are asked for, *Stephens* 2708——If there were equal perfection in English goods, French would have preference, *Stephens* 2709——Reason for not manufacturing coloured ribbons, *Hall* 6642——English narrow ribbons dearer than the French, *Baggallay* 7362, 7363 678.                                    ——Inferiority

*RIBBONS*—continued.

   **4.** *English*—continued.

——Inferiority of English from not being able to get French silk, *Baggallay* 7364, 7365.

Decrease in the quantity of plain satin ribbons purchased, *Baggallay* 7366–7368—— Effect of duty upon the price of French and English ribbons; English cheaper without duty, *Baggallay* 7378–7389——Preference of consumers latterly in favour of English goods, *Baggallay* 7394–7396, 7401–7404——Statement of purchases of English ribbons for five years and nine months, since 1826, *Dillon* 7601——Proportion of purchases of French and English ribbons, *Dillon* 7602–7604——Statement of proportion per 100 *l.* of different description of English ribbons, *Dillon* 7615——Proportion of each kind of ribbon purchased in France and England, per 100 *l. Dillon* 7625–7627——Proportion of ribbons made in France and in England, *Dillon* 7631–7636——Beauty in English ribbons would not carry weight as to their purchase, without knowing the French market, *Sedgwick* 8019——Influence of the French in ribbons over the English market prevents competition by the English manufacturer, *Sedgwick* 8092–8095.

   **5.**—*Foreign.*

Beneficial effects of prohibiting them, *Brunskill* 122, 125–128——Reason for Swiss ribbons not being imported to the same extent as formerly, *Brunskill* 661–663——Statement of the proportion per 100 *l.* of whole French trade in ribbons, 1827–1831, *Dillon* 7607——Statement of the proportion per 100 *l.* of different descriptions of French ribbons bought, *Dillon* 7613——Report from France with regard to the manufacture of French ribbons, *Dillon* 7746, 7747——Proportion of ribbons now smuggled, *Bottrell* 7818, 7819 ——French ribbons cheaper than English, *Sedgwick* 7993, 7994——Ribbon trade in France considerable before 1826, *Sedgwick* 8046——Whether proportion of ribbons smuggled greater in broad or narrow, *Sedgwick* 8047–8050——Greater demand for French ribbons during prohibition, from their being a rare article, *Sedgwick* 8051–8055——Comparison of quality between French and English ribbons, and as to price, *Sedgwick* 8057– 8061——Increase in the sale of French, and decrease of English ribbons since 1826, *Sedgwick* 8062–8068——Fashionable houses in all parts of the kingdom have the same preference for French ribbons, *Sedgwick* 8077, 8078——Table of the width of French ribbons, *Bowring* 9037——Extent of the manufacture of ribbons by certain houses in France, *Bouillon*, 10191–10193.

   **6.**—*Duty on Importation.*

French ribbons would be imported at 20 per cent. higher duty, *Brunskill* 125–128—— Rate of duty upon different descriptions of ribbon, and upon what it depends, *Brunskill* 130–133——Reason why an *ad valorem* duty would not answer, *Brunskill* 134–136—— Effect of lowering the present rate of duty to an amount that would prevent inducement to smuggle, *Brunskill* 150——No duty could protect the fancy branch, it being entirely governed by the French fashions, *Brunskill* 374–377; *Jacombs* 1748; *Cox* 2165——Duty on Swiss ribbons, and how collected, *Brunskill* 664–668——Amount per cent. the protecting duty causes the Coventry manufacturer to pay more for his silk, *Brunskill* 704– 707; *Cheeper* 778–780.

Amount of duty paid on ribbons imported, in the quarter ended 10th October 1831, *Cheeper* 771–777——How far protecting duty not sufficient for competition with the French, *Jacombs* 1821; *Cox* 2084——Extent of duty that would protect the plain trade, *Cox* 2165–2168——Present duty not a protection for plain goods, *Cox* 2213, 2214—— Amount of duty that would prevent smuggling in ribbons, *Stephens* 2759–2762—— Manner in which goods are sometimes imported through the Custom House at less than their proper duty, and how to be prevented, *Stephens* 2779–2787, 2973, 2974, 2976, 2981, 2984–2996——Reasons why duty would not prevent smuggling, *Stephens* 2893–2896—— Duty on each kind of ribbon imported, *Baggallay* 7407——Duty sufficient on satin and sarsnet ribbons, *Bouillon* 10190, 10194, 10195.

   **7.**—*Distress of the Ribbon Trade.*

Is caused by foreign competition, *Brunskill* 121; *Ratliff* 1835, 1955; *Cox* 2083; *Merry* 2552, 2554–2557——Difference in the causes of the distress in 1817, and at present, *Brunskill* 123——Prohibition the only remedy for it, *Brunskill* 124——Cause of distress at Coventry, 1815–1817, *Poole* 961–963; *Marston* 1393–1396——It is greater now than in 1818, *Poole* 968–979; *Marston* 1393–1396——It is greater since 1826 than five years previously, *Ratliff* 1950–1955——Examination relative to distress from 1815, *Poole* 1153– 1164.

See also *Black Goods. Duty on Importation. Drawback,* 2. *Etienne, St. Smuggling.*

*Riots.* See *Lyons. Wages.*

*Roads.* Number of weavers now employed upon the roads, and how paid, *Marston* 1502– 1505.

*Roman States.* Reason for want of capital therein, 5387–5393, 5506–5508.

*Rowbotham, David,* (Analysis of his Evidence.) Silk weaver at Macclesfield, 11720—— Previous employment in the cotton trade, and reasons for leaving it for the silk trade, 11722, 11723——Increase of weavers from the cotton trade, 1816–1820, did not hurt the
                                silk

*Rowbotham, David,* (Analysis of his Evidence)—*continued.*

silk trade or much reduce wages, 11724–11726——Severe distress from reduction of wages, 1829–1831, 11726–11744——Prosperous state of weavers up to 1825, and distressed state since, 11727–11729——Scale of reductions of wages, 1821–1831, 11730 ——Weavers can obtain more by sweeping the streets than at their work, 11730—— Comparative view of prices per ounce obtained by witness for his work, 1823 and 1832, 11731, 11732——Depression of the Lancashire trade, and decline in the fancy trade therein, 11733–11736.

Particular descriptions of goods made at Spitalfields, Coventry and Macclesfield, not carried on at Manchester, 11737——Silk trade in Lancashire of long standing, comparison of prices, 1786, 1796 and 1810, 11738——No ribbon weavers in Lancashire, 11739——Cotton trade have suffered with the silk from the present regulations; only the wealthy have been benefited by the present regulations, 11740——Few cotton weavers can now turn their hand to silk weaving, 11741——Distress attributed to introduction of foreign goods, 11742——Jacquard machine of little use since 1825, 11743——Home competition not the cause of the distress, 11745——Injury by further reducing duty on foreign thrown silk, 11746.

*Royle, Vernon,* (Analysis of his Evidence.) Silk throwster and manufacturer at Manchester, 3022–3024——Number of throwing mills erected at Manchester since 1819, 3025–3029, 3046–3050——Steam power at present employed in the mills, 3030–3032 ——Probable quantity of thrown silk that could be produced by them, 3033—— Quantity of mills employed in throwing, and quantity in weaving, 3034–3036——Value of the mills, 3037——Looms employed in weaving silk, and silk mixed with other articles, 1819 and 1831, 3038–3045—— State of the silk trade, 1819–1830, 3051–3054—— Depression in 1831, and how affected by change in the currency, 3055–3058——Effect of taking off the duty on printed cottons on the silk trade, 3059, 3060.

Effect of the appointment of the present Committee on the silk trade, 3061, 3062—— Silk trade chiefly home trade, 3063——Proportion of foreign silks thrown, 3064–3066—— Present regulations do not require alteration, 3067, 3073–3075, 3199, 3200——Prohibition might benefit, 3068–3071—— Duty on foreign thrown silk, 3076——Ruin to the throwsters by taking off the duty, 3077–3088, 3104, 3105——Increased importation thereby, 3077, 3106, 3196——Reason for foreign thrown silk being cheaper than the English, 3084–3087——Throwsters might survive taking off the duty by becoming manufacturers, 3088–3091——Italian throwster would be a greater gainer than the English by taking off the duty, 3092–3094——Plain goods the best branch for throwsters, 3095——How price of foreign silk regulated in England, 3097–3099, 3103——Power of the Italians with regard to manufacture over the English, 3100, 3101——Capital in the silk trade, similar at present to 1826, 3102——Difference in the value of fixed property between a throwster and a manufacturer, 3106–3108——Number of operatives employed by the Manchester mills, 3109——Amount of taxes on materials of throwsters, 3110.

Compensation to throwsters if their trade destroyed, 3111—— Comparison of protection between silk throwster and cotton spinner, 3112——Protection by the French to their throwsters, 3113–3115——Protecting duty to the British manufacturer if the trade of throwster destroyed, 3116, 3117——Comparison of the importation of raw and thrown silk, 3118, 3119——Alleged distress of the throwsters, 3120—— Reduction of men and wages in cases of pressure, 3121, 3122——Letter by witness to the Board of Trade, 3123——Effect of lists for wages, there are none at Manchester, 3124–3126——Regulation of wages in Italy, 3127–3131——Exportation of English machinery into Lombardy, 3132, 3133——Italians do not keep their best raw silks at home, 3134, 3135——Applications for leave to export machinery, 3136–3142——How far other countries protect their manufacturers more than the English 3144——Injurious tendency of factories regulation Bills, 3145–3149, 3175–3177——Importation of thrown silk does not show prosperity of the silk trade, 3150.

Comparison of English with French and Italian machinery, 3151–3159——Advantages of Italian and French in throwing and wages, 3160, 3161, 3251–3253——Wages in Italy, 3164–3170, 3250——Charge per pound for throwing, 3162, 3163, 3171–3174——Rate of duty should be settled, 3178——Importation of Italian thrown silk, and duty thereon, 3179–3187——Price of Italian thrown silk, 3188–3195——English thrown silk equal to the Italian, 3197, 3198—— Peculiarities of the Manchester trade, 3201, 3202—— Cause of increase in the silk trade, 3203——Consumption of Bengal and China silk, 3204——Evils of the drawback, 3205–3207, 3211–3214——Comparison of quality of Manchester and Spitalfields goods, 3208–3210——Increased demand for goods could be met at Manchester, 3215——Degree of distress at present, 3216–3218.

Effect of competition on profits, 3219–3221——Effects of alterations in the law upon the silk trade in Manchester, 3222, 3223——Few failures therein, 3224, 3225——Complaints from Manchester have been instigated from other quarters, 3226–3229——No distress at Manchester, 3230–3232——Unsteadiness of trade since July 1830, how caused by the bank circulation, 3233–3238——Account of promissory notes and post bills of the Bank, in circulation, every week from 10 April 1830 to 7 January 1832, 3235——Rate of wages, and how affected by the cotton trade, 3239–3243, 3247–3249——Account of poor's rates in Manchester, 1826–1832, 3244——French goods have not interfered with the Manchester trade, 3245, 3246——Examination upon memorial to the Board of Trade, and petition

678.

*Royle, Vernon,* (Analysis of his Evidence)—*continued.*

petition to the House of Commons, as to the state of the silk trade at Manchester, 3254–3262——Copy Memorial, 3261——Copy Petition, 3262——Cause of witness's letter to the Board of Trade, 3263.

(Second Examination.) Number of looms at Manchester, and on what employed, 3264–3267——Increase of the silk trade, and how affected by change in the law, 3269–3272——Admission of foreign silks has rather done good than harm, 3273——Medical certificate of the cleanliness and healthiness of witness's mills, 3274, 3275——Disadvantage to the English throwster by taking off the duty on Italian thrown silk, 3276–3279——Evils of further reduction, 3280——Possible to manufacture fancy goods by power, 3281–3283——Power of the mills at present at work in Manchester, 3284–3289——Certain mills at Manchester will be worked when finished, 3291, 3292——Silk thrown at Manchester is worked up at Coventry and Spitalfields, 3293.

Number of persons dependent upon witness's mills for employment, 3294–3305——Necessity for exporting machinery and labour if duty on foreign silk removed, 3306–3313——Amount of drawback, by whom received, and for what goods, 3314–3323——Effect of withdrawing the drawback, 3324–3327——Weavers would be benefited by taking off the import duty, 3328, 3329——Tendency of the cotton and silk trade to equalize labour, 3330–3336——Effect of reducing duty on foreign thrown silk on weavers and throwsters, 3337–3356——Drawback, a bonus on the use of Bengal and China silk, 3357, 3358——Necessity for a higher protecting duty for the English weaver and throwster than the French, 3359–3388——How far the throwster and manufacturer consider each others profits, 3389–3391.

Whether English or Italian thrown silk regulate the price of each other, 3392–3398——Advantage to the French manufacturer from French silk, not being allowed to be exported, 3399–3407—— Difference in the manufacture between Manchester and Spitalfields, 3408–3418——British weaver should not be dependent upon the Italian throwster, 3420——Reasons for extending mills and increasing machinery, 3421–3425——Same names signed to both Memorial and Petition, 3426, 3427——Depressed state of trade in January last, 3428–3432——Witness has commenced weaving, 3433——Reduction of wages if duty on foreign thrown silk taken off, 3435, 3436——Knowledge of intention of removing duty would have prevented increase of machinery, 3437——Reasons for witness's letter to the Board of Trade, 3438.

*Russia.* Increase of silk manufacture in Russia since 1820, *Bottrell* 7896, 7897——Increase of duties upon importation into Russia, *Bottrell* 7898–7000.

See also *Duty on Importation.*

# S.

*Sardinia.* France a large customer to the King of Sardinia, *Brockwell* 3457.

*Sarsnets.* Quantity of plain sarsnets made at Coventry of different kinds at one time, with rate of wages, *Baggallay* 7453–7456.

See also *Avignon.*

*Satins.* Importation of satins from France, *Brunskill* 634, 635——How foreign figured satins can be distinguished from English, *Marston* 1458–1460—— There are satin figures now making, but of a different style and quality, *Perkins* 1570——More plain satins at present introduced into England than formerly, *Ratliff* 1837, 1838——No difficulty in distinguishing between French and English plain satins, *Ratliff* 1849–1853——Making plain satins given up from its being a bad trade, *Merry* 2590——Manufacture of satins principally confined to Spitalfields, *Gibson* 4823, 4824——Where manufactured, *Stone* 5772–5774——Duty on fancy satins which are now got from Coventry, *Baggallay* 7391–7393—— Duty necessary to equalize the prices of French and English satins, *Dillon* 7690——Use of satins supplanted by the use of gros de Naples, *Wadden* 10141.

*Savings Banks* have little interest in France, *Bowring* 8931.

*Sawer, Thomas,* (Analysis of his Evidence.) Prevalence of the taste for French goods in the country towns, 2356——Sale of certain machinery by witness at a sacrifice, 2358–2366——Offer of sale of certain machinery at Stratford-le-Bow, but no purchaser; cost price thereof, 2367–2372——Taste in favour of French gauzes; comparative price thereof, 2373–2378——A-la-bar loom at Coggeshall erected by a French artist; unsuccessful attempt to make satins therein, 2379–2387——Witness's machinery at Coventry superintended by a servant, 2388, 2389——Which plan formerly succeeded, 2392–2394——There was always competition; the greatest competitor is the foreigner, 2395, 2396——Destruction of trade from the introduction of French goods, 2397–2399.

Expected advantages by the introduction of the a-la-bar loom, but which were not realized, 2400–2409——A great deal of excellent work done by the hand looms, 2410, 2411——Ready sale for goods formerly in the country trade, 2412–2414——Home competition gives a fair security to the public, and will allow a fair profit, 2415–2418——Manner in which foreign competition obstructs business, 2419——Disadvantages of the introduction of foreign goods when the market could be supplied at home, 2420–2426——Reason for the French fancy goods being superior to the English, 2427, 2428——Rivalry dare not be attempted, 2429–2431——How far reduction of duties has had the effect of putting down smuggling, 2432, 2433——Power loom does not answer, 2434——Description of silk used in manufacture, 2435–2440——Duty on foreign thrown silk has

*Sawer, Thomas,* (Analysis of his Evidence)—*continued.*

has no effect upon the greater proportion used at Coventry, 2441——Necessity for encouraging the throwing Italian silk here, 2442, 2445.

*Schools.* Establishment thereof in France for the encouragement of the arts, *Bowring* 8806.

*Schwabe, Louis,* (Analysis of his Evidence.) Silk manufacturer at Manchester, 9828—— ——Patterns produced of witness's manufacture, and statement in explanation thereof, 9829–9836——Speed by power looms would be injurious to the silk, 9838——Price and quality of Bengal and China silk for making certain articles, 9841–9845——Little diffi-culty in cotton weavers being employed in silk weaving, 9846–9852——Examination as to the number of looms in Manchester, and in witness's employ, with witness's declining to answer as to his own, 9853–9864——Market for Bengal silk open to the French as well as the English, 9865, 9866——How far it is cheaper than Italian, 9867–9870—— Examination upon certain patterns produced, their sale or export, and prices of similar articles at East India Company's sales, 9871–9886——Reasons for not doing a larger business with the London upholsterers from long credit taken by them, and prejudice raised by Spitalfields manufacturers against Manchester goods, 9887–9920——Articles not manufactured better at Spitalfields than Manchester, 9921–9923——Further exa-mination as to credit, the production of similar goods by Spitalfields weavers, and refusal of witness to have his goods examined by Spitalfields manufacturers, 9924–9935.

*Scotch Gauzes.* They have not interfered with the trade of Spitalfields, though a considera-ble quantity are sold, *Stephens* 10578–10580

*Scott, John,* (Analysis of his Evidence.) Silk weaver at Manchester, and signed Petition to the House of Commons, 11847–11850——Distressed state of the Dublin silk trade from removing duties on importation of English goods into Ireland, 11851–11854——Pros-perous state of weavers at Manchester to 1826, and distress since, 11855–11861—— Weavers know each other's distress better than master manufacturers can, 11862——No difference of opinion among the weavers as to the cause of their distress, 11863, 11864—— Number of looms at Manchester, 1824–1826, and at present, 11865–11871——Com-mencement of union among Manchester weavers in 1826, and manner of conducting it, 11871–11873——Examination against the increase of looms in Manchester since 1826 shown by the quantity of silk worked up, 11874, 11875——Reasons for the handker-chief branch becoming nearly extinct, 11875–11877——Description of goods formerly made in Manchester for which gros de Naples have been substituted, 11878–11880—— Why weavers have a better knowledge of the quality of silk working up than masters, 11881——Description of goods now making at Manchester, 11882–11884, 11890–11895 ——Ineffectual attempt by Mr. Royle to weave by steam, 11885–11889.

*Sedgwick, William,* (Analysis of his Evidence.) Partner in the house of Howell & James, 7972–7976——Description of goods sold prior to 1826, 7979——Extent of smuggling prior to 1826 in rich goods, 7980–7984, 8020–8023——Proportion of French and English goods at present sold, 7985–7987, 8015——Increase of sale in English broad fancy goods, 7988, 7989——Principally manufactured at Spitalfields, 7990——But can be manufac-tured at Manchester cheaper, 7991——From difference in price of labour, 7992—— French ribbons cheaper than English, 7993, 7994——Dependence of the English market upon the French fashion, 7995–7998, 8071, 8072——Striped gauzes at Coventry equal to the French, but not figured, 8000——Profit of Manchester manufacturers very small, 8002——Inferiority of Coventry ribbons is in taste, 8004——Improvement in Coventry manufactures, 8005——Improvement in English manufactures, from introduction of French goods, 8006–8008.

French patterns sent to Coventry to be manufactured prior to 1826, 8009, 8017, 8018 ——Manchester manufactures generally inferior in beauty to Spitalfields, but some of them equal their prices, 8010–8014, 8024–8029——Beauty in English ribbons would not carry weight as to their purchase, without knowing the French market, 8019——How far cost of smuggling less now than prior to 1826, 8030, 8031——Increase of smuggling, from goods being cheaper than those paying duty, 8032, 8033——Difficulty to say rate of duty that would put an end to smuggling, 8034——Tendency of English competition more to render goods cheap than to improve them, 8034–8039——Quantity and descrip-tion of goods manufactured at Manchester, 8040–8042——Prohibiting French goods would weaken the stimulus for improvement in English manufacturers, 8043, 8044—— Ribbon trade in France was considerable before 1826, 8046——Whether proportion of ribbons smuggled greater in broad or narrow, 8047–8050——Greater demand for French ribbons during prohibition, from their being a rare article, 8051–8055——How far French patterns could be obtained, to give taste to English manufacture, in the event of pro-hibition, 8056.

Comparison of quality between French and English ribbons, and as to price, 8057– 8061——Increase in the sale of French and decrease of English ribbons since 1826, 8062– 8068——Figured lutestrings only used in the common trade, 8069, 8070——Smuggling previous to 1826 only sufficient to stimulate and improve British exertion, 8073, 8074—— Danger of dealing in smuggled goods under prohibition, and how far resorted to by respectable houses, 8075, 8076——Fashionable houses in all parts of the kingdom have the same preference for French ribbons, 8077, 8078——Under prohibition, English goods might be made from French patterns, 8079——Proportion of different description of goods imported from France, 8080–8090——Importation of fancy broad silks from 678.          France

*SILK*—continued.

   I. *Consumption of*—continued.
*Stone* 6404, 6405; *Clay* 6962; *Bennett* 10729——Consumption of richer silks in England has increased, but is supplied from France and not from Manchester, *Ballance* 8391–8393, 8409——Increase of consumption on the Continent in a greater ratio than in England, *Harter* 9313——Increase of consumption in England, 1821–1825, *Bowring* 9707, 9708 ——Consumption of silk 1824 and 1825, and since, *Moore* 11153–11156——Annual consumption of silk prior to and since 1826, showing decreased consumption in the latter period, *Brocklehurst* 11338——Increased consumption of silk goods, but for the interference of the French, *Brocklehurst* 11339——If consumption of silk has increased since 1826, the goods manufactured have been of an inferior quality, *Brunskill* 164–170, 444–446; *Poole* 1131–1134; *Ratliff* 1949; *Brocklehurst* 11352–11354——Increase in the use of silk goods in this country, and falling off in importation of raw and thrown, *Moore* 12087.
   *Papers laid before the Committee.*

Comparative View of the Quantities of Italian Thrown Silks, and of Italian Raw Silks consumed in this Country 1815–17 to 1829–31, *Evidence*, p. 227.

Minute relative to throwster's work, showing the consumption of raw silks of all descriptions in the years 1824–25, and in the years 1826–31, dissected and computed into one standard, and compared with regard to the rates of labour and profit they have afforded to the throwster; also remarks thereon, *Evidence*, p. 224.
   See also *Bengal and China Silk. Coventry. France*, IV. *Manchester. Spitalfields.*

   II. *Quality of.*
Qualities of silks imported into England, France and Switzerland, *Doxat* 4090–4092 ——Comparative quality of silk imported into England and other countries, *Doxat* 4104–4110——Comparative statement of the quality of silk used in England and France, *Doxat* 4111, 4112——Coarse goods require a mixture of fine with them, *Doxat* 4115—— Quality of silk imported from Italy, *Gibson* 4853, 4854; *Heath* 5250–5254——Different sizes of silk, but of the same description, *Heath* 5225——Degree of improvement in Italian silk, and from what parts, *Heath* 5325–5327——Not necessary to be acquainted with the reeling silk to judge of its qualities, *Martin* 5437——Countries to which the best raw and thrown silks are sent, and in what proportions, *Martin* 5496——Proportion of good silk imported, *Stone* 6436–6440——Districts where Italian plan of throwing is understood produce better raw than those where they are ignorant of it, *Stone* 6444—— Best thrown silks of Italy are better than the generality of English thrown, *Stone* 6450–6452——Opinion as to town and country trade as to sales of rich or coarse goods, *Dillon* 7671–7678——Manufacture of richer silks abandoned since 1826, *Ballance* 8388–8390 ——Scarcity of fine silk for throwing at present, *Brocklehurst* 11381——Description of silk used in manufacture now and formerly, *Kelly* 11845.
   See also *France*, VII.

   *Papers laid before the Committee.*
Minute relative to the degrees of fineness or the various descriptions of silks on which our manufacturers have worked during the last six years, 1826–1831, *Evidence*, p. 221.

   III. *Value.*
Average value per lb. of silk used at Coventry, *Cox* 2293——Knowledge of silk difficult to be acquired, *Heath* 5682–5684——Value of silk ascertained from examination, and not from marks on bales, *Heath* 5708——Silk more valuable before 1826 than at present, *Sedgwick* 8131, 8132——How long assaying machine for the trial of silk has been known in this country, *Moore* 11293, 11294.
   See also *France*, VII.

   IV. *Broad.*
Number of looms employed and wages paid in Spitalfields 1814–1827, in the manufacture of broad silks, *Cox* 2320–2327——Discontinued in 1827 from being superseded by the French fancy goods, *Cox* 2328——Manufacture of Manchester, or in any other part of England did not interfere with that branch, *Cox* 2329–2331——Description of goods made, *Cox* 2332, 2333——French goods of that description are not intrinsically so good as those made here formerly, *Cox* 2334–2337——Broad goods imported from France, *Gibson* 5067, 5068——Manchester and Spitalfields shut out the French at present in the manufacture of broad silks, *Baggallay* 7462–7469——Duty on French broad silks, *Baggallay* 7470——How far they are smuggled, *Baggallay* 7471, 7472——Increase in the purchase of English broad silks, and from what parts since the admission of the French, *Dillon* 7637, 7638——Proportionate value of French broad silks smuggled now and before 1826, *Bottrell* 7817——Broad goods of France come into competition with Spitalfields, *Bottrell* 7917–7920——Increase of sale in English broad fancy goods, *Sedgwick* 7988, 7989——Principally manufactured at Spitalfields, *Sedgwick* 7990——But can be manufactured at Manchester cheaper, *Sedgwick* 7991——From difference in the price of labour, *Sedgwick* 7992——Importation of fancy broad silks from France do not much interfere with English broad silk manufacture, *Sedgwick* 8091——Smuggling plain broad goods has declined latterly, *Menetrier* 8314, 8315——English broad silks are prohibited into France, *Bouillon* 10229.
   See also *Exportation. Spitalfields.*

*SILK*—continued.

### V. *Foreign.*

Description of foreign silk used at Spitalfields and Coventry in the manufacture, *Brunskill* 546–551, 691–702——French raw silk superior to any other, *Brunskill*, 670–672——Proportion of foreign silk consumed in English manufacture, *Jacombs* 1738–1741 ; *Cox* 2099, 2100, 2248–2257; *Stone* 5637——Description of foreign silk manu factured, and how obtained, *Ratliff* 1884, 1885; *Sawer* 2435–2440——Proportion o foreign silk thrown, *Royle* 3064–3066——How price of foreign silk regulated in En gland *Royle* 3097–3099, 3103——For what articles foreign silks used, *Stone* 5638, 5639.

### VI. *Raw.*

Comparative importation of raw and thrown silk, *Royle* 3118, 3119——Italians do not keep their best raw silks at home, *Royle* 3134, 3135——England hitherto the largest customer to Italy for raw silk, *Brockwell* 3462——Importation of Italian raw silk diminishing, *Brockwell* 3463–3468——How far the price of raw silk can be maintained in England, *Brockwell* 3560–3562——How far improvement has taken place in the quality of Italian raw silk imported, *Brockwell* 3675–3679——Cost thereof, *Swift* 3855——Injury to Italian raw silks in their transit from Italy, *Swift* 3914–3922; *Ward* 3988–3989——Inducement of profit to the Italian to send his raw silk here, *Ward* 4028——Advantage of low duties on importation of raw, and high duties on importation of thrown, *Doxat* 4040——How price of raw material would be affected thereby, *Doxat* 4041–4043——Description of raw silk that fetches the highest price in London at present, *Doxat* 4116–4118—— Estimate of the quantity of raw silk consumed in England, 1824–5 and 1826–1831, *Doxat* 4125——Import duties and charges upon raw silk into Lyons and London, *Doxat* 4208–4213——How far the importation of French raw silk would be beneficial, *Doxat* 4291–4295; *Banbury* 4598–4600——Italian raw as good as French, if that cannot be obtained, *Banbury* 4623-4634, 4639——Comparative view of the market price at London of certain raw silks, 1824–1832, *Doxatt* 4397——Account of the progressive variation of duty on raw silk, 1660–1786, and from 1784–1825, *Banbury* 4420.

More profitable to the Italian to import raw, *Gibson* 4913——Why causes which in duce the importation of thrown will not act upon raw, *Gibson* 4982, 4983——More raw than thrown silk imported from Italy during the last two years, *Gibson* 5113, 5114—— England the principal mart for the importation of raw silk of Italy, *Heath* 5313——Particular sized raw silks of Italy that sell high in England, *Martin* 5505——Improvement in Italian raw silk, and to what attributed, *Stone* 6164–6170——Necessity for a supply of Italian raw silk, *Stone* 6238——Necessity for having a good supply of raw silk for throwing, *Hall* 6539–6544——Raw silk in Italy higher than thrown, *Caffi* 7291–7293—— Custom House returns of raw silk, 1816-1826, *Ballance* 8357–8359——Not part of the business of the Trade Association to get the duties on raw silk lowered, *Ballance* 8636 ——Cause of the difficulty in getting the best description of Italian raw silk, *Ballance* 8677–8682——Whence the supply of raw silk derived, *Harter* 9232——Increase in the importation of raw silk from all parts, 1831 over 1823, *Harter* 9312——Improvement in the quality of French and Italian raw imported since removal of prohibition, *Bowring* 9651–9653——Price of French and Italian raws, *Wadden* 10132, 10133.

Necessity for encouraging the importation of good raw silk, *Bridges,* 10437, 10438—— Increase in the importation of raw silk since 1823 caused by the high duty on thrown, *Moore* 11114, 11115——Importation of Italian raw previous to and since 1824, *Moore* 11119–11122——Advantages of reducing duty on the raw material, *Moore* 11220, 11221 ——Less supply of good Italian raw silk now than previous to reduction of duties, from inducement to the Italian throwster to send more thrown, *Moore* 11223–11225—— Necessity for encouraging importation of raw over thrown silk, *Moore* 11264——Necessity for Italian silk in working upon Bengal and China silk, *Moore* 11307, 11308—— Decrease in consumption of Italian raw, 1824–1831, *Brocklehurst* 11357——Necessity for getting raw silk from France at the same duty as upon Italian importation, *Johnson* 11633, 11634.

*Papers laid before the Committee.*

Return of all Raw and Waste Silk imported and entered for home consumption in each year, 1814–1832; distinguishing from whence, and Amount of Duty, *App.* p. 918.

An Account of the several kinds of Silk imported; distinguishing the Quantity of Raw from Italy, the Levant, Bengal and China; also of Thrown, distinguishing Organzine from Trams and Singles, from the same places, in each of the years 1830–1831, *App.* p. 922.

Various descriptions of Raw and Thrown Silks, and Waste Knubs and Husks, imported 1814–1831, separated and computed into one standard; all balanced by the Parliamentary Return of Quantities, Duty paid, *App.* p. 932.

Comparative view of the Quantities of Italian Thrown Silks, and of Italian Raw Silks, consumed in this country, 1815–1831, *Evidence,* p 227.

Minute relative to Throwsters' work; showing the consumption of Raw Silks of all descriptions in the years 1824–25, and in the years 1826–31, dissected and computed into one standard, and compared with regard to the rates of labour and profit they have afforded the Throwster; also remarks thereon, *Evidence,* p. 224.

Comparative

*SILK*—continued.

> VI. *Raw*—continued.
>
> *Papers laid before the Committee*—continued.

Comparative view of the London market prices of Milan and Bergam Raw Silks of 4 to 5 cocoons, and of Milan and Bergam Organzines of 26 to 28 deniers at various periods from June 1824 to February and April 1832 ; with notes thereon, as regards the British Throwster, *Evidence*, p. 261.

See also *Crapes. Fossembrone. France*, VIII. *Importation. Italy. Labour. Manchester. Throwsters.*

> VII. *Thrown.*
>
>> 1. *Generally.*
>> 2. *Duty on Importation.*
>>
>>> i. Generally.
>>> ii. Disadvantage of reducing.
>>> iii. Necessity for increasing.
>>
>> 3. *Prices of throwing and Thrown Silk.*

### 1. *Generally.*

Quantity of British and foreign thrown silk consumed at Coventry and Spitalfields, *Brunskill* 367–370 ; *Doxat* 4219–4224 ; *Graham* 12729–12737——Comparative quality of different foreign thrown silks and English thrown, *Brunskill* 371–373, 504–511 ; *Ratliff* 1886–1888 ; *Cox* 2258–2266, 2271 ; *Royle* 3197, 3198 ; *Gibson* 4848 ; *Swift* 8928 ; *Hall* 6478–6480, 6507–6509, 6516, 6517 ; *Bowring* 9105 ; *Wadden* 10058 ; *Bridges* 10427–10436 ; *Bennett* 10790 ; *Moore* 11164, 11165 ; *Wright* 11766, 11767——Best thrown silk is used for finer purposes, *Cox* 2261 ; *Swift* 3867——In what the superiority in throwing consists, *Cox* 2267——Not much improvement in the quality of British thrown silk since 1823, *Cox* 2268, 2269——Improvements in English thrown, and to what attributed, *Stone* 6161–6163——Duty on foreign thrown silk has no effect upon the greater proportion used at Coventry, *Sawer* 2441——Necessity for encouraging the throwing Italian silk here, *Sawer* 2442, 2445 ; *Banbury* 4456 ; *Ballance* 8658–8663, 8686, 8687——Proportion of foreign silk thrown, *Royle* 3064–3066.

Different style of thrown silk in each country, *Brockwell* 3616——Importation and consumption of foreign thrown silk and duty, 1819–1831, *Brockwell* 3469, 3470, 3477–3482, 3627–3636——How the importation of thrown silk has been checked, *Brockwell*, 3668–3675——Reason for small increase in the importation, *Ward* 4025——Variation in the importation of thrown silk at different periods since 1765, and causes, *Doxat* 4134–4140 ——How far certain natural and political causes have affected import of thrown silk into England, *Doxat* 4323–4325——Expense of importing silk from Milan, *Banbury* 4472–4474——Reason for importation of thrown silk at present, *Banbury* 4484–4488——Importation decreasing at present, *Banbury* 4493–4501——Italian thrown silk not improved, *Gibson* 4849——Reasons for Italian increasing his importation at a loss, *Gibson* 4952–4954, 4960——Descriptions of thrown silk imported from Italy, and to what uses applied, *Gibson* 5061–5066——Comparison of importation of Italian thrown and raw silk, *Gibson* 5113–5116 ; *Martin* 5527–5529—— Proportion of home thrown silk to meet it, *Gibson* 5117, 5126–5128——From whence the largest import of thrown silk, *Heath* 5245, 5246 ——Period of the year at which Italian raw and thrown silk received in England, *Stone* 5616, 5617——English thrown is in the market as soon as Italian, *Stone* 5618——Imports of Italian thrown silk, and at what period the year should be calculated from, *Stone* 6052–6058.

To what place Italian thrown silk exported from this country, *Stone* 6268–6271——. Proportion of foreign thrown used in manufacture, *Stone* 5795——Market for good silk open to every person, *Hall* 6529, 6530——Demand for thrown silks would cease if manufacturers ruined, *Hall* 6656——Very little thrown silk smuggled prior to 1826, *Bottrell* 7831, 7832——No necessity for a manufacturer to use foreign thrown, *Ballance* 8428 ——Witness must give up manufacture if he could not get English thrown, *Ballance* 8683–8685——Inconvenience sometimes felt from the want of thrown silk, and higher price paid for it, *Harter* 9325–9330, 9333–9338, 9342–9345, 9348, 9349——Permanent supply of thrown best attained by a good supply of good raw, *Harter* 9360——Means taken by witness to prevent pillage in dyeing, *Wadden* 10058, 10059——Necessity for discontinuing the importation of thrown silk, the fine silk giving more valuable employment to the operatives, *Johnson* 11631, 11632——Italian silk formerly thrown, but now changed for Bengal, very little Italian silk now thrown, *Wright* 11768, 11775——Proportion of foreign and English thrown silk used by witness, *Graham* 12804, 12805.

### 2. *Duty on Importation.*

> i. Generally.

Amount thereof at present, *Royle* 3076, 3179–3187 : *Harter* 9256–9258——Effect of duty remaining as it is, *Brockwell* 3712–3716 ; *Banbury* 4466–4470 ; *Gibson* 5109–5112 ; *Stone* 5636, 7026–7028 ; *Harter* 9261–9263 —— Alteration that might be made therein,

678.

*SILK*—continued.

    VII. *Thrown*—continued.

        2. *Duty on Importation*—continued.

            i. Generally—*continued.*

therein, *Gibson* 5125——Why not a tax on Spitalfields and Coventry for benefit of Manchester, *Harter* 9264, 9265——Not injurious to the weaver, *Wallis* 10953——Import duties and charges into Lyons and London, *Doxat* 4214, 4215——Per centage duty on foreign thrown silk increases the cost of manufacture, *Brunskill* 583–592; *Graham* 12720–12728.

            ii. Disadvantages of reducing.

It will ruin English throwsters, *Royle* 3077–3083, 3104, 3105, 3276–3279; *Brockwell* 3643; *Swift* 3764, 3877–3880; *Ward* 3972–3975; *Doxat* 4235–4237; *Willmott* 4739; *Hall* 6705, 6707; *Ballance* 8426, 8670; *Harter* 9260; *Wadden* 10079–10080; *Bennett* 10744; *Johnson* 11577; *Wright* 11759——And cause Italy to throw more, *Brockwell* 3471, 3472, 3689; *Swift* 3902; *Caffi* 7288–7290, 7294–7296; *Bennett* 10794, 10796; *Moore* 11257, 11262——And cause dependence upon Italy, *Brockwell* 3472, 3473; *Gibson* 4914–4919, 5121; *Stone* 5925, 5926, 6365, 6366; *Ballance* 8669; *Harter* 9361; *Wright* 11759——And cause distress of operatives, *Royle* 3337–3356; *Brockwell* 3687, 3688; *Ballance* 8670——Disadvantages of being dependent on Italian throwster; *Cox* 2270–2274; *Royle* 3420; *Doxat* 4237, 4238; *Banbury* 4589; *Ballance* 8427——Disadvantages generally of removing or reducing duty, *Cox* 2306-2310; *Royle* 3280; *Doxat* 4250, 4251; *Banbury* 4447–4449; *Gibson* 5122–5124; *Stone* 5644–5649; *Wadden* 10002; *Grout* 10315; *Bridges* 10453–10462, 10493; *Johnson* 11583, 11584; *Prout* 11667, 11668; *Rowbotham* 11746——Effect of removing duty on price, *Brunskill* 497–501; *Brockwell* 3684–3686; *Stone* 5837–5843; *Harter* 9253–9255, 9439–9442, 9460–9467, 9477–9481; *Tootal* 9613, 9614; *Wallis* 10959–10961; *Moore* 11273; *Graham* 12720–12728.

How duty affects price in England and France, *Doxat* 4271–4275—— Reduced duty on foreign trams not a sufficient protection to the English throwster, *Brockwell* 3483, 3484 ——Duty that would protect throwsters, *Swift* 3874; *Banbury* 4462–4465, 4481–4483; *Gibson* 5187–5192——Whether the throwing Italian silk can be continued in this country with a lower rate of duty, *Stone* 6370, 6375——If duties reduced, throwing would not be discontinued, *Graham* 12788–12791——Removing duty has increased importation, *Doxat* 4132——But not after every reduction, *Doxat* 4133; *Gibson* 4935——Effect of reduction in 1826 on price of throwing and wages, *Willmott* 4747–4750——Evils of reduction of duty in 1829, *Doxat* 4248, 4299–4301; *Gibson* 4925, 4926; *Ballance* 8647–8651, 8653–8655; *Wadden* 9997–9999; *Moore* 11210–11216, 11222; *Johnson* 11576——How far taking off duty would increase consumption and demand for labour, *Gibson* 5071–5073 ——Advantages, or otherwise, of reducing duty on importation, *Brunskill* 512–514; *Stone* 6305–6312, 6445–6448——How it would affect importation of Italian raw and thrown, *Royle* 3077, 3104, 3196; *Doxat* 4241–4244; *Gibson* 4886–4892, 4974–4981; *Martin* 5482; *Stone* 6313–6318.

Reduction of duty would place English manufacturer on equal footing with the French, *Bowring* 9188——Removal of duty on foreign thrown and of drawback on exportation will reduce export trade, *Harter* 9259——Not large manufacturers who are anxious for the removal of duty on thrown, *Bridges* 10531–10533——Reduction of duty thereon would not prevent the sale of French goods, *Stephens* 10704–10712——Encouraging importation of thrown by lowering duties diminishes the importation of raw, *Moore* 11162 ——Duty on thrown that is necessary to ensure a good supply of Italian raw, *Moore* 11309–11311——Statement of decreased importation of Italian raw and thrown from reduction of duties in 1829, *Brocklehurst* 11431, 11432——Examination thereupon, *Brocklehurst* 11433–11435——Importation of foreign raw and thrown, 1827–1832, and effect of present duty thereon, *Royle* 3179–3187; *Brocklehurst* 11443–11448——Statement of the opinions of different manufacturers as to the removal of duties on foreign thrown silk and on prohibition, *Stone* 12686–12689——Effect of removing duty on thrown silk to the manufacturers and operatives, *Graham* 12708, 12709.

            iii. Necessity for increasing.

Necessity for a higher protecting duty for the English weaver and throwster than the French, *Royle* 3359–3388——Advantage of high duties, *Doxat* 4040; *Banbury* 4426, 4427, 4606–4610——Account of progressive increase of duty 1660–1786, *Banbury* 4417–4420——Effect of increasing duty on manufacturer and throwster, *Stone* 6319–6323——Tendency of increased duty on thrown to increase supply of raw, *Stone* 6376, 6377——Additional duty on thrown would be beneficial to home manufacture, *Ward* 3990, 3991; *Moore* 11314——Higher duty would cause a better description of silk to be thrown in England, *Wright* 11785.

    See also *Duty on Importation. Exportation. Importation. Spitalfields*

    3. *Prices of throwing and of Thrown Silk.*

On what prices of English and Italian thrown silk depend, *Cox* 2311——Reason for foreign thrown silk being cheaper than English, *Royle* 3084–3087——Price of Italian thrown, *Royle* 3188, 3195—— Whether English or Italian thrown silk regulate the price of each other, *Royle* 3392–3398——No difference in the price per pound of throwing silk in Italy during the high duties and at present, *Brockwell* 3448-3453——Ruin to throwsters from the low price of throwing Italian silk in this country, *Brockwell* 3485–3489 ——Prices

*SILK*—continued.

VII. *Thrown*—continued.

3. *Prices of throwing and of Thrown Silk*—continued.

——Prices of throwing, *Brockwell* 3544-3548, 3646-3650; *Swift* 3856-3860; *Ward* 3947-3949; *Graham* 12698-12707——Difference in the price that remunerates the Italian throwster, and will not remunerate the English, *Brockwell* 3549-3553——How price of Italian thrown silk in the British market affected by that of British Italian thrown, *Brockwell* 3568, 3569——Difference in the price of raw and thrown silk if duty repealed, *Brockwell* 3684-3686——Reduction in the prices of throwing, *Swift* 3741, 3742; *Ward* 3950——Impossible for throwster to reduce the prices of throwing, *Swift* 3763——Charges that would remunerate the throwster, *Swift* 3796——Difference in the price of throwing certain silks, *Swift* 3923-3926; *Willmott* 4788, 4789.

Price of Italian organzine in Lyons and London, *Doxat* 4194-4202——Proportion of import duty to the price of Italian thrown, *Doxat* 4226-4229——How duty on importation of Italian thrown affects price in England and France, *Doxat* 4271-4275——Difference in 1825 and 1831 in the price of throwing between Lyons and England, *Doxat* 4396——Rise in the price of foreign silk if throwing trade here destroyed, *Banbury* 4471——Approximation of prices between Italian silk thrown in Italy and England, *Banbury* 4614——Cost of throwing organzine in Lombardy, *Gibson* 4858, 4859—— Cost in England, and which does not remunerate the throwster, *Gibson* 4860-4877.

Price at which Italian throwster could throw to order, *Gibson* 4909-4912——English cannot produce thrown at the same price as the Italian, *Gibson* 4920——Decreasing duty would not decrease price, *Gibson* 4936-4941——Small profit to the Italian to import at the present price, *Gibson* 5081-5083——Imports will be diminished if the present price continues, *Gibson* 5083——Why the English has a better market for his silk than the Italian, *Gibson* 5181, 5182——Expense of throwing organzine and tram in Italy, *Heath* 5226-5235——Piedmont thrown worth more than French thrown, *Martin* 5419—— Price of throwing in Piedmont, France and Lombardy, *Martin* 5445-5447.

Effect of reduction of duty on the price of foreign thrown, *Martin* 5499——Correct information as to the prices of throwing in France, *Martin* 5509——Manner in which the price of thrown silk in England determined, *Stone* 5640-5643——Decrease in the price of thrown, 1831, *Stone* 6057——Prices obtained by the throwster in 1830, *Stone* 6067, 6068—— Price of thrown silk and duty in 1830, and manner they increased importation, *Stone* 6079-6134——Effect of duties on the price of foreign and English thrown silk, *Stone* 6324-6328——Prices of throwing in Italy, exclusive of waste, *Heath* 5704 ——Comparison with England, *Heath* 5705-5707.

Prices of throwing during the last six years, *Stone* 5797-5799——Amount necessary to cover expenses and give a profit to the throwster, *Hall* 6465-6469, 6487-6493, 6501-6506, 6512-6515, 6527-6528, 6594, 6732——Rate of throwing, *Hall* 6545-6555—— Profit by reduced price of thrown silk from reduction of duty would go to the foreigner, *Hall* 6709, 6710——Expenses of throwing tram in Italy, and weight per pound English, *Caffi* 7058-7066——The like for throwing organzine, *Caffi* 7067-7071, 7087——Prices of throwing, and during what periods, *Caffi* 7072-7076——Charges of throwing more in Piedmont than Lombardy, and causes thereof, *Caffi* 7077-7082——How far price of throwing remunerates throwsters, *Caffi* 7115.

Comparative view of the prices at Lyons of French tram, the produce of French raw, with price in London at the same periods for Italian tram, in averages of three months, from July 1827 to March 1832, *Ballance* 8410——Comparative view of the prices at Lyons of French organzine, the produce of French raw, with prices obtained in London at same periods for Piedmont organzine in averages of three months, from 1827 to March 1832, *Ballance* 8410——English costs rather more than foreign, *Ballance* 8429——How throwster's price regulated, *Ballance* 8657——Prices of throwing silk in France, *Bowring* 8873-8878——Silk cannot be thrown so cheaply in England as in Italy, *Harter* 9362 ——Prices of throwing, 1830 and 1831, *Harter* 9363-9374, 9493-9498.

How far price of Italian thrown depends upon price obtained for silk in other parts of the world, *Harter* 9478-9480——Reducing prices of throwing in England prevents its being properly done, and causes reduction of wages, *Bennett* 10805, 10806, 10809—— No profit upon throwing organzine at the present rate, *Bennett* 10807——Foreign thrown silk cheaper than the raw can be bought and thrown for, *Moore* 11167——Instance of a mill at Manchester stopping, and buying foreign thrown silk cheaper than they could throw it, *Middlehurst* 11812, 11813——Comparative view of the London market prices of Milan and Bergam organzines of 26 to 28 deniers at various periods, 1824-1832, *Evidence*, p. 261.

See also *France*, III. 2.

*Papers laid before the Committee.*

Comparative View of the Quantities of Italian Thrown Silks consumed in his Country, 1815-17 to 1829-31, *Evidence*, p. 227.

See also *France*, IX. *Importation. Italy.*

VIII. *Waste.*

Increase of waste silk, *Brockwell* 3694, 3695——Quantity imported, and from whence, 1828-1831, *Brockwell* 3706-3710——Importation of waste, and in what state exported, *Banbury* 4653, 4654; *Heath* 5721-5724.

*SILK*—continued.

VIII. *Waste*—continued.

*Papers laid before the Committee.*

Return of all Raw and Waste Silk imported and entered for Home Consumption in each year, 1814–1832; distinguishing from whence, and Amount of Duty, *App.* p. 918.

The various descriptions of Raw and Thrown Silks, and Waste, and Knubs and Husks imported 1814–1831, separated, and computed into one standard; all balanced by the Parliamentary Returns of Quantities, Duty paid, *App.* p. 932.

See also *Fossembrone. Importation. Labour. Prices. Sewing Silk.*

**Silk Men.** Destruction of the trade of silk men, *Gibson* 5095–5108.

**Silk Merchants.** Method of conducting the business of silk merchants, *Heath* 5709, 5710.

*SILK TRADE.*

  1. *Generally.*

  2. *Papers laid before the Committee.*

  1. *Generally.*

Views taken by the silk trade, and applications to the Board of Trade from different places at different periods as to the cause of their distress, *Hume* 55–60——Trade was increasing up to the admission of foreign goods, *Cheeper*, 833–835; *Banbury* 4424; *Willmott* 4775, 4787; *Wallis* 10860; *Bridges* 10375–10378, 10426, 10439, 10440; *Moore* 11122–11151; *Brocklehurst* 11347–11349 —— State of trade, 1627 and 1828, *Marston* 1397, 1398——1819–1830, *Royle* 3051–3054——1826–1831, *Stone* 5600–5606, 6357——1824 and 1825, *Prout* 11646——Depreciation of trade since 1826, *Royle* 3055–3058, 3428-3432; *Brockwell* 3738,3739; *Swift* 3881–3883; *Willmott* 4724, 4767; *Doxat* 4039, 4140; *Martin* 5526; *Wadden* 9969, 10041; *Wallis* 10880; *Brocklehurst* 11346; *Prout* 11658; *Wright* 11748–11750——To what attributed, *Brockwell* 3740; *Stone* 6357–6364; *Hall* 6702, 6703; *Ballance* 8455-8463; *Wadden* 10142, 10143; *Moore* 11231; *Rowbotham* 11742, 11745; *Wright* 11751——Cause of distress. 1792 and 1816; *Ballance* 8360, 8361.

Trade has partially improved since November 1831, but the distress is so great the improvement is not perceived, *Marston* 1451–1457——Specimens of silks produced by the witness, with examination upon the manufacture, cost and weight of each description, *Marston* 1511–1528——Description of goods witness at present employed upon, *Perkins* 1571–1573——To what improvement in trade in 1823 attributed, *Jacombs* 1758–1761—— Quantity of silk manufactured, 1824 and 1831, *Cox* 2169——Sufficient capacity in this country to supply any quantity that might be required, *Merry* 2553; *Stephens* 2729; *Gibson* 5043–5048——Improvement in manufacture previous to the introduction of French goods, and cause of improvement since, *Merry* 2618-2624——Effect of taking off the duty on printed cottons on the silk trade, *Royle* 3059, 3060——Effect of the appointment of the present Committee on the silk trade, *Royle* 3061, 3062; *Martin* 5555–5578.

Silk trade chiefly home trade, *Royle* 3063——Importation of thrown silk does not show prosperity of the silk trade, *Royle* 3150——Cause of increase in the silk trade, *Royle* 3203——How affected by change of the law, *Royle* 3269–3272——Parties that have vested interests in the silk trade, *Brockwell* 3498——Silk trade will flourish as the throwster is protected, *Brockwell* 3499, 3500——Situation of the trade before and since the importation of foreign manufactured silks, *Doxat* 4036, 4037——Comparison of the silk and cotton trade, *Doxat* 4036, 4037——Calculation as to duties, wages, profits, &c. upon silk and cotton, 1814–1831, *Doxat* 4038 – –Progress of the silk trade over the cotton to 1826, and contrary effect since, *Doxat* 4140.

Trade increased notwithstanding high duties, *Banbury* 4428–4432; *Willmott* 4790–4795 ——Trade at present improving, *Banbury* 4502, 4546–4551——Trade has not flourished since fair profits ceased to be obtained, *Banbury* 4526——Effect of Berlin and Milan Decrees thereon, *Banbury* 4581–4588—— Whether greater amount of goods selling now than in 1826, *Gibson* 5012–5017——Extension of the silk trade, and in what countries, *Stone* 5596-5598——Comparison of distress formerly and at present, *Stone* 6393-6403; *Ballance* 8689; *Moore* 11099–11105——How far a certain description of goods that were made formerly, and not at present, is from taste being altered, or from foreign or English competition, *Stone* 5867–5895, 5936–5945——Estimate of the amount of the silk trade in England, and proportion the French imports bear to it, *Dillon* 7628–7630 ——Comparison of silk trade with that of other departments for certain periods, *Dillon* 7730-7732——Supplanting one branch will be the ruin of the others, *Ballance* 8449, 8450.

Remonstrances to Government thereon, reduction of duty and increase of smuggling, *Ballance* 8455–8463——Manner in which the silk trade would revive under certain duties and regulations, *Ballance* 8483——Protection to the silk manufacturer illusory, *Bowring* 9179——Silk manufacture would increase by removing all protection, *Bowring* 9180 ——Interests in the silk trade at present well balanced, *Harter* 9228——Certain duties attaching to the silk trade which should be removed, *Harter* 9314——Overwhelming distress in Spitalfields and Coventry, and distress in Macclesfield, Manchester, Middleton

and

*SILK TRADE*—continued.

**1.** *Generally*—continued.

and Sudbury, *Wadden* 1041——Improvements in manufacture attributed to the Jacquard looms previous to and not since the opening the ports, *Bridges* 10494–10496 ——Bad consequences to trade from the admission of foreign goods, *Bennett* 10718– 10720——To what increase of trade in 1824 and 1826 attributed, *Wallis* 10966——Bad state of the silk trade if the present system continues, *Poyton* 10989.

Government have not protected the trade as they were bound to do, *Bolter* 11002—— Relief would be given by prohibition, punishing the smuggler severely, or putting duties under excise, *Bolter* 11004——State of the silk trade immediately previous to the admission of French goods, and means adopted to prevent a large quantity coming in at first, *Moore* 11135–11151——Effects of removal of prohibition and reduction of duty on raw silk should be inquired into separately, *Moore* 11152–11156——Alarm of the silk trade before the alteration of the law, and on what grounded, *Moore* 11177, 11178—— Ministers expected the alteration would place the silk trade on a level with the cotton trade, *Brocklehurst* 11350——Advance in the silk trade of the Continent over that of England, *Brocklehurst* 11355——Tendency of low prices to degenerate silk manufacture, *Brocklehurst* 11449——Progress of silk manufacture checked by interference from the Continent, *Brocklehurst* 11454.

How silk trade would have improved under better protection, *Brocklehurst* 11455—— How far dealers capable of advising Government upon the state of the silk trade, *Brocklehurst* 11555——Necessity for protection to obtain increase in the silk trade; tendency of low priced raws to increase it; increase in the cotton trade, and manner the silk trade might equally increase, *Brocklehurst* 11556—— Protecting duty necessary for the silk trade, *Prout* 11659, 11660; *Kelly* 11128, 11129——Distress previous to 1825 not permanent, *Prout* 11665——Prohibition the most effectual remedy, *Smith* 11684—— Since reduction of duties silk trade has changed from light to heavy goods, and from fine to round silk, *Wright* 11760——Witness's opinion formerly in favour of free trade, and reasons for changing it; great disadvantage to the silk trade from last alterations, *Beckwith*, 11961–11965——Reason why alteration of system in the silk trade has miscarried, *Moore* 12066——Protection not given to the silk trade which it was held out it would receive in 1824, *Moore* 12067, 12068——Examination upon the progress of the silk and cotton trade, 1815–1832, *Doxat* 12094—— Abstract view of the progress of the silk trade of Great Britain and Ireland at different periods between 1815–31, in regard to quantities; similar abstract view of the cotton trade, *Doxat* 12094.

Estimate of the total Amounts of Silk Manufacture of the United Kingdom during periods, 1815–17, 1818–20, 1821–23 and 1824–25, understated in regard to wages in these periods, *Doxat* 12094.

Estimate of the total Amount of Silk Manufacture of the United Kingdom, 1826–1831, overstated in regard to wages in these years, *Doxat* 12094.

Abstract Statement of French Silk Manufactures for the years 1827–1830, conjointly with an Abstract view of the total Amounts of the Silk Manufactures of the United Kingdom at different periods during 1815–1831, *Doxat* 12094.

**2.** *Papers laid before the Committee.*

Large comparative view of the Silk and Cotton Trades in regard to their respective and relative progress, both in quantities and in Duties, Wages, Profits, &c. from 1815–17 to 1821–23, 1824–25 and 1826 to 1831, and various remarks thereon, *App.* p. 934.

Compendious comparative view of the Silk and the Cotton Trades in regard to quantities, and to duties, wages, &c. during the same periods, *App.* p. 936.

Distinct Statement of the Amounts of Duties, and of the Amounts and Rate of Wages, &c., accruing from the Silk Trade during those periods, *App.* p. 938.

Comparative view of the progress of the Silk and Cotton Trades during 5—5, and 5 years:

1816 to 1820; 1821 to 1825, *i. e.* Medium of $\left\{\begin{array}{l}1821-23,\\1824-25,\end{array}\right\}$ and 1826 to 1830.

*App.* p. 938.

Explanation of the principle upon which Estimates of the Silk Trade grounded, from 1815–17 to 1821–23, 1824–25, and from 1826 to 1831, *App.* p. 939.

See also *Cotton. Dublin. Duty on Importation. Fancy Trade. France*, II. III. 2. *Importation*, 2. *Laws. Manchester. Spitalfields Trade* .

*Silk Worm.* It improves in Italy and France, but degenerates if taken back to its native place, India or Persia, *Grout* 10328.

*Singles.* See *Importation*, 2.

*Single hand Looms.* See *Looms. Wages.*

*Sisson, Jonathan,* (Analysis of his Evidence.) Witness's connection with the silk trade in Dublin, 11896–11902—— Decline of silk trade in Dublin from reduction of duties on importation of British goods, and afterwards from reduction of duties on foreign goods imported into Ireland, 11903–11907——Examination generally upon the former prosperity and present distress of the silk trade in Dublin, 11908–11923.

*Smith, Joseph,* (Analysis of his Evidence.)   Silk weaver at Macclesfield, 11674–11676——Average wages of weavers, their present distressed state, and former comfortable situation attributed to introduction of foreign manufactured goods, 11677–11681——Examination generally as to the condition of the silk weavers at Macclesfield, 11682–11693.

*Smith, David,* (Analysis of his Evidence.)   Number of Jacquard weavers at Coventy, 1257——Distress in that department caused by the irregularity of employment, 1258——Average earnings per week if in full employ, 1259——Number of weeks unemployed last year. 1260——Figure branch worse last year than the year before, 1262——More skill required in making figured than plain ribbons on account of extra machinery, 1263——Number of Jacquard looms 1823 and 1826, 1264——But little increase latterly in consequence of foreign competition, 1265, 1266——Highest rate of wages earned by figured loom weaver, and at what period, 1267–1270——Jacquard trade as good in 1826 as at any other time, 1271——Employment of the Jacquard weavers, 1826–1831, 1272–1280——Introduction of the Jacquard loom and alteration of plain looms to enable its use, 1281–1292, 1312–1315——Its introduction has changed the mode of figure weaving, 1293, 1294, 1316——No improvement in the Jacquard loom since its introduction, 1295, 1296——Number of Jacquard and engine looms in use, 1826 and 1831, 1297, 1298.

Increase of the Jacquard looms decreased the use of other looms, 1299——Principal employment for the weavers now is in altering patterns, for which there is no wages, 1300–1307——Distress in Coventry at present owing to foreign competition, 1308, 1309——New patterns could be obtained, and variations could be made, but the fashions could not lead from the anxiety to know what patterns will come from abroad, 1310——Which decreases the amount of wages, 1311——Jacquard looms make the article better in point of taste but not quality, 1317–1320——Necessity for using the Jacquard loom to imitate the French pattern, 1321, 1322 ——Time occupied in setting and changing patterns, and how that work affects the rate of wages, 1323–1335——Additional labour required in consequence of the Jacquard looms in getting in the warps, 1336——Amount of wages earned when the loom is fully prepared for work, 1337——Time taken in preparing the work is a loss to the workmen, besides in some instances the want of work altogether, 1338–1340——Proportion time lost in changing patterns, bears to the time taken in making the article, 1341–1346.

SMUGGLING:

    I.   *Generally.*
    II.  *Extent thereof before opening the Ports.*
    III. *Increase thereof since opening the Ports.*
    IV. *Present method thereof and rate of smuggling and Insurance.*
    V.  *Means of prevention.*

       1. *Generally.*
       2. *By increasing or reducing Duties.*
       3. *By Prohibition.*

          i.  Advantages thereof.
          ii. Disadvantages thereof.

       4. *By stamping Goods.*
       5. *By punishment of parties.*

    VI. *Smuggling into France.*

    I.  *Generally.*

Not much smuggling in plain goods, *Hume* 71–76; *Gibson* 4948——Suspicion of smuggling for some time but none found out till the case of Messrs. Leaf's, *Brunskill* 480–485——Articles that are smuggled, *Cheeper* 781; *Stephens* 2880–2892; *Gibson* 5167–5172; *Clay* 6895–6903, 7000–7006; *Menetrier* 8324–8328; *Stephens* 10675–10679——Goods that were formerly but are not now smuggled, *Bottrell* 7848; *Bowring* 9121——Anxiety of the silk trade to prevent, *Cox* 2352—— Bills drawn from France for payment thereof, *Doxat* 4148–4155 —— Larger quantity of French silks admitted illegally, *Stone* 5851——Distress to trade by large capitalists being engaged in smuggling, *Hall* 6655——How return might be obtained from the French Custom House books, which would show the extent of smuggling into England, *Clay* 6904, 6905——Silks are not smuggled from Belgium or Holland, *Bottrell* 7844.

Fashionable articles are not smuggled, *Menetrier* 8338——How far competition of the London houses in underselling each other in French goods induces smuggling, *Wadden* 10040——Supposition of smuggling transactions by certain houses from their selling goods in London lower than they could be imported for, *Beckwith* 12362–12365, 12369–12372——Quantity of ribbons and broad silks seized belonging to Messrs. Leaf's, *Wadden* 10087, 10088——Their subsequent restoration, and being brought into home consumption, *Wadden* 10089, 10090, 10102——How far contrary to law, *Wadden* 10091——Amount of compromise, although in defiance of a pledge by the Vice President of the Board of Trade that justice should be done *Wadden* 10092–10097, 10101——Why a conviction would have been more beneficial to the trade, and which they would have

tried

*SMUGGLING*—continued.

IV.—*Present method and rate of Smuggling and Insurance*—continued.

——No advantage therefrom; rate of exchange thereby, *Bottrell* 7895——Method of smuggling a certain description of Piedmont silk, *Heath* 5316-5324——Number of houses in France who guarantee the goods, and number in England who smuggle them, *Clay* 6911, 6912——Rate at which Swiss ribbons have been smuggled, *Baggallay* 7355-7359——Rate of insurance could not be lowered if duty reduced, *Baggallay* 7532, 7533——Reasons for diminution in the rate of smuggling, *Bottrell* 7788, 7789.

Comparison of present and former rate of smuggling, *Bottrell* 7801-7812——Fewer persons concerned in smuggling now from diminution of profits, *Bottrell* 7826-7828——Manner in which communication for smuggling is carried on between Dover and Calais, *Bottrell* 7844-7846——Greater risk in inland carriage than sea voyage, *Bottrell* 7847——How profits upon smuggling divided, *Bottrell* 7901, 7902——Ruin of smuggling, from losses, *Menetrier* 8316-8320——Profits of the higher class of smugglers; great extent of smuggling, and large capital employed therein, *Bowring* 9159-9163, 9170——Better feelings of the people towards smugglers, according to the greater risk they run, *Bowring* 9164, 9165——Influence of duties upon the rate of smuggling, *Bennett* 10773, 10774——Silk goods smuggled out of France, and method thereof, *Ballance* 11016, 11017; *Moore* 11232-11236.

V. *Means of Prevention.*

1. *Generally.*

Methods of checking smuggling, *Brunskill* 145, 146, 713-715——Smuggling can never be entirely stopped, but can be reduced to a sufficient extent to prevent injury, *Brunskill* 737, 738——Premium should be offered for the discovery of smuggled goods, *Stephens* 2897-2900——Preventive service only stopped smuggling for a time, *Bottrell* 7833, 7834——Small encouragement to King's sailors to effect seizures; small amounts received by them, *Bottrell* 7846——Description of goods seized at Messrs. Leaf's, *Bottrell*, 7889-7892——Small amount of seizures this year, *Bottrell* 7893——Encouragement given by receiver of goods cannot be checked, *Bowring* 9218-9221——Method to be adopted for preventing smuggling, *Beckwith* 11973-11975——Reasons why effectual measures have not been taken to repress smuggling, *Moore* 12070, 12071——Smuggling might be stopped, and rewards to informers would enable higher duties to be collected, *Stephens* 10680-10682——Rewards that would check smuggling, *Stephens* 10694-10696.

2. *By increasing or reducing Duties.*

Amount of duty considered necessary by the silk trade for protecting them against smuggling, *Hume* 37-41; *Brunskill* 552-556; *Clay* 6858, 6859, 6922-6924——Reduction of duty on plain goods would have prevented smuggling, but the high rate of duty on gauzes, &c. enables assorted cargoes still to pay for smuggling, *Hume* 71-76——Traders would rather pay Government than smugglers, duties regulated to meet the alternative, *Hume* 80-83——Effect of lowering the present duty to an amount that would prevent inducement to smuggle, *Brunskill*, 150——Reduction of duty would not prevent smuggling, as smuggler would lower his profit, *Sedgwick* 8175-8189; *Ballance* 8368-8370, 8420——Amount of duty might be decreased to prevent smuggling, *Brunskill* 150; *Gibson* 4949-4951; *Clay* 6906; *Dillon* 7683, 7686; *Bottrell* 7813, 7814, 7835-7840; *Menetrier* 8345-8348; *Bowring* 9178, 9216, 9217.

Manner in which rate of duty on French goods operates upon smuggling, *Clay* 6844-6853——Smuggler's price regulated by the amount of duty, *Clay* 6963-6965——Greater encouragement to smuggle under high duties, *Bottrell* 7894——Difficulty to say rate of duty that would put an end to smuggling, *Sedgwick* 8034——Reduction of duty on foreign thrown would not enable manufacturer to come down to smuggler's price, *Ballance* 8421, 8422——Reducing duty to the smuggler's price gets rid of both smuggler and manufacturer, *Ballance* 8697——How far expectation realized, that upon changing prohibition for duties odium would attach to the smuggler, *Bowring* 9154-9158——Reduction of duties in 1829 increased smuggling instead of reducing it, as was intended, *Wadden* 9988-9993; *Bennett* 10741, 10742——Effect of increasing duties on smuggling, *Wadden* 10036, 10037——Duties should be reduced to the cost of smuggling, *Stephens* 10703——Effect of lowering duties on manufactured goods on smuggling, *Beckwith* 11943.

3. *By Prohibition:*

    i. Advantages thereof.
    ii. Disadvantages thereof.

  i. Advantages thereof.

Prohibition more effectual against smuggling than protecting duty, *Hume* 66, 68.——Nothing but prohibition will prevent smuggling fancy articles, *Brunskill* 557, 734-736——Smuggling would take place but to small extent under prohibition, and who would be likely to carry it on, *Cheeper* 785-807——Difficulty of disposing of smuggled goods, *Cheeper* 808-812, 816-819, 847-851——Possibility of an English manufacturer making a small quantity of goods here, and smuggling a larger quantity from France, *Cheeper* 813 815——Smuggler, or disposer of smuggled articles, is at the mercy of his customers
and

*SMUGGLING*—continued.

    V. *Means of Prevention*—continued.

      3. *By Prohibition*—continued.

        i. Advantages thereof—*continued.*

and servants, *Cheeper* 816–819——Description of benefit that would be derived from the small amount of smuggling under prohibition, *Cheeper* 858–861——Amount that would be smuggled under prohibition, *Cheeper* 888–896; *Cox* 2137–2144——There would be great risk in distributing a large quantity of French goods over the country under a prohibition, *Cox* 2132–2136——Great risk of smuggling during prohibition, *Stephens* 2724, 2725; *Clay* 6925–6927——Proper prohibition would prevent smuggling, *Stephens* 2760; *Banbury* 4611–4622; *Wilmott* 4796–4799——Means of preventing smuggling under a prohibition, *Stephens* 2962–2968, 3008–3014——State of the law as to smuggling with regard to the proof of French goods, *Stone* 5860–5863——Danger of dealing in smuggled goods under prohibition, and how far resorted to by respectable houses, *Sedgwick* 8075, 8076.

        ii. Disadvantages thereof.

Prohibition would not put down smuggling, *Gibson* 5052–5055; *Stone* 5852–5859; *Baggallay* 7534–7537——Smuggling would be increased if prohibition revived, *Clay* 6928–6931; *Bowring* 9143, 9206–9209——Low rate of profit upon smuggling has diminished it; how far it would be renewed if prohibition revived, *Bottrell* 7858–7864——Smuggling in fewer hands than under prohibition, and how it places the manufacturer in a worse situation, *Bowring* 9144–9148——How far prohibition would change smugglers from a few large to a great many small ones, *Bowring* 9166–9168.

      4. *By stamping Goods.*

Why stamping would not answer as a preventive against smuggling, *Clay* 6907——Advantages of stamping goods to prevent smuggling, *Bottrell* 7935; *Ballance* 8466——Method by which silks might be stamped without risk of forgery; diagrams of four seals for that purpose, *Bottrell* 7943, 7944——British manufactures should be protected by the goods being stamped, *Sedgwick* 8117–8119——Means of preventing smuggling by stamping the goods; expense would not be felt by the consumer; stamp must be varied to prevent imitation, *Sedgwick* 8169–8174——Stamp might be imitated if known, *Menetrier* 8349, 8350——Proposed regulations against smuggling; that of criminal punishment for the smuggler, and stamping goods to detect the receiver, *Ballance* 8464, 8465.

Reasons submitted to the Committee for stamping silks, *Ballance* 8466, 8467——Certain checks should be used to prevent stamps being forged, *Ballance* 8468——Paper with signatures declaratory of the sentiments of the silk trade in favour of stamping, *Ballance* 8469, 8470——Plan for stamping in order to prevent forgery, *Ballance* 8470, 8698, 8699——Negociations with the Board of Trade with regard to stamping goods, and answer by the Board in the negative, *Wadden* 10034, 10035——Difficulties in the way of stamping, *Bouillon* 10182–10185——Stamping would be of service, *Dubois* 10270, 10271; *Stephens* 10697–10702——Statement by the retail trade of difficulties in the way of stamping, *Moore* 11256——How far stamping goods would be beneficial, *Manning* 12535, 12536——Stamping would have no reference to invoices, *Manning* 12537.

      5. *By punishment of Parties.*

Prosecution of parties for smuggling who have not the chief interest in the goods, *Clay* 6942–6952——Loss of property sufficient punishment without personal punishment of the smuggler, *Menetrier* 8339, 8343——Punishing persons ordering goods would prevent smuggling, *Menetrier* 8345–8348——Plain trade may be protected if the smuggler detected and punished, *Wadden* 10033——Negociation with the Board of Trade as to making smuggling a penal offence, *Wadden* 10034, 10035——Punishment instead of fine must be used to prevent smuggling, *Bouillon* 10207–10209——Remedy therefor by imprisonment and hard labour, and stamping goods, *Brocklehurst* 11504, 11505.

    VI. *Into France.*

Effect of repeal of prohibitory laws upon the French coast, *Bottrell* 7849——Large quantities of English goods smuggled into France through Belgium; description of them, and expense attending it, *Bottrell* 7851–7857——Greater difficulty of smuggling into France, and greater severity of the Custom House and municipal regulations, *Bowring* 9149, 9150; *Bouillon* 10230, 10231——Manner in which the smuggler in France is considered a public benefactor, *Bowring* 9151–9153, 9175, 9176——Premium for smuggling higher into France than into England, *Bowring* 9169——Smuggling cotton twist into France in the same manner as silk into England, *Bowring* 9171——Articles smuggled into France, *Bowring* 9192——Their Custom House regulations, *Bowring* 9193——Seizure and protection therefrom of English goods in France, *Bowring* 9222, 9223.

    See also *Avignon. Bandannas. Cambrics. Consuls. Crape. Custom House. De Ponilly* & Co. *France,* III. 2. *Gloves. Jobbing. Piedmont. Silk.*

*Spindles.* See *Throwing Mills.*

*Spitalfields Act.* Evils thereof, *Moore* 11183, 11194, 11195——It was repealed at the expense of private parties in the trade, *Moore* 11184——It was repealed as a private Act with all the expenses attendant thereon, and although opposed by certain Cabinet Ministers, *Moore* 11185–11193.

*Spitalfields District.*   State of the poor in three parishes of St. Matthew Bethnal Green Christchurch Spitalfields and Mile End Old Town, comprising the district called Spitalfields, taken from parish accounts in February 1832, *Ballance* 8374-8378 ——Examination upon the population and state of the poor generally in that district, *Ballance* 8379-8454 ; *Wallis* 10818-10822.
    See also *Weavers,* 7.

*Spitalfields Trade.*
    State thereof and causes of distress therein, and whether greater formerly or at preser.., *Brunskill* 196-200 ; *Doxat* 4163-4168 ; *Stone* 5741-5749, 5775-5777, 5780-5786, 5865, 5866 ; *Baggallay* 7550-7565 ; *Ballance* 8356, 8537-8540 ; *Wadden* 10011, 10012 ; *Poyton* 10981.
    It is getting into the hands of a few large capitalists, *Martin* 5478, 5479 ; *Stone* 5770, 6004-6009——How long affected by the appointment of the present Committee, *Stone* 5778, 5779.
    Methods of improving, *Brunskill* 236 ; *Gibson* 4808, 4809, 4814, 4815, 5069, 5070 ; *Ballance* 8484, 8485, 8707 ; *Bennett* 10765-10771, 10775.
    How affected by competition with France and foreign competition generally, *Brunskill* 196-200 ; *Doxat* 4141-4143, 4161, 4162, 4169, 4170 ; *Gibson* 4828, 4830, 4944-4947 ; *Stone* 5787-5793, 5899-5902, 12692 ; *Bottrell* 7966 ; *Ballance* 8407, 8408, 8640-8642, 8705, 8706 ; *Wadden* 10003-10008, 10015-10026, 10053, 10056, 10394, 10469-10475 ; *Stephens* 10549 ; *Bennett* 10735-10737 ; *Wallis* 10885, 10950-10952.
    How affected by competition with Manchester and home competition generally, and comparison of goods, *Brunskill* 201-205, 406-426, 623-625 ; *Royle* 3208-3210, 3408-3418, 4140 ; *Doxat* 4156-4160 ; *Gibson* 4186, 4187, 5074, 5078 ; *Stone* 5826-5831, 7030 ; *Baggallay* 7577-7590 ; *Dillon* 7737-7739, 7745 ; *Bottrell* 7966 ; *Ballance* 8403-8406, 8486-8490, 8494, 8688, 8707 ; *Wadden* 10010 ; *Bennett* 10732-10734 ; *Wallis* 10857-10859, 10863-10871, 10877-10879, 10917, 10918, 10939-10941.
    Description of manufacture and of silk consumed therein ; manufacture of velvets entirely and of satins principally confined to Spitalfields, *Gibson* 4823, 4824——Proportion of the different kinds of silk manufactured at Spitalfields, *Gibson* 4827 ; *Stone* 6011-6015——Description of goods manufactured and number of looms employed, *Stone* 5728-5733——Reference to Spitalfields for broad silk manufacture, *Hall* 6664, 6665——Places where goods sold at Spitalfields are manufactured, *Dillon* 7639-7641——Fewer goods at Spitalfields now than usually at this time, *Dillon* 7702, 7703—-How far rich goods manufactured at Spitalfields now ; not much by orders, *Sedgwick* 8133-8145 ; *Wadden* 10046-10052——The best English fancy goods made at Spitalfields, *Ballance* 8491-8493——How far manufacture of galloons carried on in Spitalfields, *Harter* 9490-9492——Spitalfields chiefly employed upon plain low priced goods made from inferior silks, *Wadden* 10009.
    Proportion of looms formerly employed and description of work, *Dubois* 10240-10247, 10258, 10259 ; *Bridges* 10379-10381——Goods manufactured by witness worn by the Royal Family, *Bridges* 10382——Description of goods made under present wages, *Bridges* 10391-10393——Comparison of witness's and Mr. Fulton's goods, *Bridges* 10395-10403——Pattern of the Queen's coronation dress and dresses for drawing rooms manufactured by witness, and loss thereby through the importation of French goods, *Bridges* 10469-10475 ——Goods bought at Spitalfields formerly and at present, *Stephens* 10545-10548——Not more rich plain goods made in Spitalfields than three years ago, *Stephens* 10688——Rich plain and fancy silk formerly made in Spitalfields, *Bennett* 10727——Not so many goods now made there as formerly, *Bennett* 10728——Figured handkerchiefs never made to any extent in Spitalfields, *Wallis* 10860——More inferior goods now manufactured in Spitalfields and reduced wages therefor, *Wallis* 10874-10876——Inferiority of article manufactured in Spitalfields, but not in workmanship, *Wallis* 10942——Increase of rich goods now making but not in price for weaving, *Wallis* 10943, 10944.
    Account showing the cost of silk and wages paid for manufacturing the same into plain gros-de-Naples, *Wadden* 10030.
    See also *Crape Fancy Trade.   Manchester.   Manufacturers.   Manufacturing District. Silk,* IV. *Silk Trade.   Switzerland.   Wages,* 7.   *Weavers,* 7

*Spring Goods.*   See *Fancy Trade.*

*Stamping Goods.*   See *Smuggling,* V. 4.

*Steam.*   Engine looms have been worked by steam, *Poole* 1008, 1011——Reason why it would not do for the manufacture of fancy ribbons, *Jacombs,* 1616, 1617——It can be beneficially applied in their manufacture, *Hall* 6647——Power might be applied to the coarser but not the finer fabrics of silk, *Ratliff* 2045-2047——Steam power employed in throwing mills at Manchester, *Royle* 3030-3032——Possible to manufacture fancy goods by power, *Royle* 3281-3283——Ineffectual attempt by Mr. Royle to weave by steam, *Scott* 11885-11889.
    See also *Looms.*

*Stephens, George.* (Analysis of his Evidence.)   Witness with Halling & Co. of Cockspur-street, 2637, 2638——Proportion French and English ribbons bear to each other in purchases from manufacturers, 2639-2641——Few English fancy ribbons sold ; proportion English

*Stephens, George*, (Analysis of his Evidence)—*continued*.

English gauze ribbons bear to the French, 2642——Price of the article not an object, 2643–2646——Preference for French goods, and reasons for it, 2648–2653——Proportion French goods bore to English during the prohibition, how obtained, difficulty and risk in selling, 2654–2666——Witness can distinguish between French and English from a lot of goods, but not from a pattern, 2667, 2668——Little improvement in English fancy goods since 1826, 2669–2671——Injury to the trade by jobbing French goods, 2672–2674——Great quantity of job goods sent over just after the French Revolution, 2675–2679, 2683——Extent of the export trade of France, 2680, 2681——Few goods in France at present, 2685, 2686——When orders for French goods usually given, 2688, 2689——Orders were given to English manufacturers during the prohibition, but would not be now, 2690–3695——In the event of change of pattern in French goods they can still be sold as such, and accepted as new goods, 2696——Goods obliged to be disposed of quickly in consequence of the quick succession of fashions in Paris, 2697, 2698—— Under prohibition the English fashions did not follow the French so rapidly, 2699.

Manufacturers formerly frequented country towns with patterns of ribbons, 2702—— English goods are not sold as French, they are not so good or so cheap, 2703–2707—— French goods are sometimes sold as English when English are asked for, 2708——If there were equal perfection in English goods the French would have preference, 2709—— Increase of smuggling; method of doing it; rate per cent. of insurance ; how far done openly, 2710–2723——Great risk of smuggling during prohibition, 2724, 2725——It is generally now considered that goods are safe when once deposited, 2728——Home manufacture could supply the market without the introduction of foreign goods, 2729—— No encouragement now to lay out money in producing novelties, 2730——Before removal of the prohibition sacrifices could be made after sale of spring stock without ruin, 2731, 2732——Manner in which the market is constantly glutted, and the jobbing French goods prevent the sale of English, 2733–2736——The French will not job their own goods in their own market, 2737, 2738——Failures and compositions attributable to a glutted market, and introduction of foreign goods, 2739–2745——No new channel of trade or of employment for weavers, caused by the introduction of French goods, 2746, 2747——Difference in the price of ribbons smuggled and that pay duty, 2748–2750—— Number of failures and withdrawals from business of manufacturers since the introduction of foreign goods, 2751——Duty paid at the commencement of the season of all goods that come in the regular way, 2752——Goods are jobbed in during the season at half the price paid for them at the commencement of the season, 2753–2756.

French goods can be bought much cheaper in London than imported, 2757, 2758—— Amount of duty that would prevent smuggling in ribbons, 2759–2762——Proper prohibition would prevent smuggling, 2760——Recent case of smuggling and per centage of insurance, 2763–2771——Offer by a French house to smuggle in some goods to be purchased for francs and delivered in London for shillings, including insurance, 2772–2778 ——Manner in which goods are sometimes imported through the Custom House at less than their proper duty, and how to be prevented, 2779–2787——General rates of insurance upon smuggling, and what it includes, 2788–2796——Gloves are not smuggled, 2797– 2803——Interest of the large haberdashers to continue the present system, and how far it causes a monopoly, 2804–2817——Not as many English goods jobbed as French in proportion to the capital employed, 2818——Proportion of the trade that consists of gauzes, 2819——Small dealers have not increased so much as large houses have increased the amount of their returns, 2821–2823——How the higher classes of consumers benefit by reduction of wages and profits, 2825–2831——Reasons why manufacturers' agents in London will not serve a small house under five per cent. higher than a large house, 2832– 2842——Public prefer a large house to deal at from the great variety, 2843, 2844.

(Second Examination.)   Articles purchased at the Custom House for exportation and smuggled in for home consumption prior to 1826, 2854–2861——Reasons why new goods not passed through the Custom House could not be smuggled, 2862–2868—— Rates of premium for smuggling, 2869–2879, 2971, 2972——Description of goods usually smuggled, 2880-2892——Reasons why duty would not prevent smuggling, 2893–2896 ——Premium should be offered for discovery of smuggled goods, 2897–2900——Possibility of discovering French from English goods, 2901–2907——Offers by French warehousemen to deliver to English purchaser without expense, 2908–2913——Description of English goods sold in France, 2914–2930——The French would reduce the price of their goods if the English did, 2932–2935——Profits of the French manufacturers and dealers, 2936–2947——Ribbons worn by ladies are not supplied cheaper than if made in England, 2949— —Increase of French stocks, and returns by wholesale dealers since 1828, 2950–2955, 2969, 2970——Reasons for the preference given to French goods, 2956–2961 ——Means of preventing smuggling under a prohibition, 2962–2968, 3008–3014——Less than the proper duty sometimes paid at the Custom House, 2973, 2974, 2976–2981, 2984–2996——Colours the French are at present producing, 2975——Would not be bought if made in England, 2982, 2983——Accounts opened with a greater number of wholesale dealers formerly than at present, 2997–3007, 3016–3050.

(Third Examination.)  Goods bought at Spitalfields formerly and at present, 10545– 10548——Those not now bought there come from France, 10549——Articles of Manchester manufacture now bought, 10550-10554, 10563-10566——Quality of Manchester,

678.

*Stephens, George,* (Analysis of his Evidence)—*continued.*

chester goods not sufficient to interfere with the sale of rich French goods, 10555, 10567–10569——Loss to Manchester from copying French goods, and being met in the market by French job goods, 10556–10558——Inconvenience from job goods of the same quality and lower price, 10559–10562——Difference in quality of certain fancy goods made in France and by Messrs. Fulton, 10570–10572——French gauzes and not the Scotch that interfere with Spitalfields, 10573–10580——Comparison of quality and prices of English and French crape handkerchiefs, 10581–10592——More money would have been embarked by manufacturers in the fancy trade but for French goods, 10593 ——Inferior class consume the Manchester silks, 10594, 10595——High prices not given to Manchester manufacturers, 10596, 10597——Fashion commands a higher price to be given for French than Manchester goods of the same quality, 10598–10606——Orders given to France instead of Spitalfields and Manchester in consequence thereof, 10607–10609——English silks have not improved since admission of French, 10610–10612.

Preference in favour of English black and white silk goods over French, 10613, 10614 ——Reason for buying plain silks from France, 10615–10618——Proportions of buyings and stock, French and English, 10619–10634——Description of French goods at present bought, 10635——Duty that should be paid thereon, 10637——Instance of goods coming in through the Custom House lower than their proper rate of duty, 10639–10649—— Manner of levying duties at the Custom House, fraud a common occurrence, 10650–10662——Plain goods are smuggled, 10663–10665——Extra duty might be collected on gloves without creating smuggling, 10666–10674——Extent of smuggling and of general description of goods, 10675–10679——Smuggling might be stopped, and rewards to informers would enable higher duties to be collected, 10680–10682——Not more rich plain goods made in Spitalfields than three years ago, 10688——Advantage of an extra duty on gloves, 10689–10691——Persons driven to smuggling in self-defence, 10692, 10693——Rewards that would check smuggling, 10694–10696——Benefits of stamping goods, 10697–10702——Duties should be reduced to the cost of smuggling, 10703—— Reduction of duty on foreign thrown silk would not prevent sale of French goods, 10704–10712.

(Fourth Examination.) Examination as to a letter from a Custom House officer, with inference of bribery therefrom, 12311–12320——Silk passed through the Custom House lower than if done by a fair trader, 12321–12333, 12338–12345——Witness declines giving the name of his informant or the Custom House officer, 12334–12337——Knowledge of goods coming in under *ad valorem* duty at less than their proper value, 12346–12361.

*Stock.* Disadvantage to the English manufacturer from keeping a stock on hand, *Brunskill* 747–749——Injury to trade from glut in the market, and means of preventing it, *Cheeper* 826, 827——Bad effects of jobbing from the large stocks on hand, *Cheeper* 897–901——Manner in which the market is constantly glutted, and the jobbing French goods prevent the sale of English, *Stephens* 2733–2736.

*Stoke Parish.* Return of the Property assessed in the Parish of Stoke, in the County of Warwick, with the number of Rates, Rate of Assessment, and gross Amount on all Property assessed in the said Parish of Stoke, 1815–1832, *App.* p. 927.

*Stone, Thomas,* (Analysis of his Evidence.) Spitalfields manufacturer, 5725–5727——Description of goods manufactured, and number of looms employed, 5728–5733——Rate of wages, 5734–5740——State of the Spitalfields' trade, 1826–1829, 5741–5749——In 1831 and 1832, 5775–5777, 5780–5786——Reduction in wages since 1826, 5750–5755 ——Increase of the silk manufacture in other parts of England, and injury thereby to wages in Spitalfields, 5756–5758, 5761, 5762——Wages at Manchester, 5759, 5760—— Reduction in the employment of weavers during the last six years, 5763, 5764——Manufacturers at present in Spitalfields, and number who have been ruined, 5765, 5771—— Some have turned throwsters, 5766, 5767——More cash payments than formerly, 5768, 5959–5962——How far capital in the silk trade equal to formerly, 5769——Spitalfields trade thrown into the hands of a few manufacturers, 5770——Where satins manufactured, 5772–5774——How long the Spitalfields' trade affected by the appointment of the present Committee, 5778, 5779——Injurious effect of the duty upon Italian thrown silks upon the manufacturers of Spitalfields, 5787–5793——Claims against Italian merchants for damage on transit from Italy are trifling, 5794.

Proposition of foreign thrown silk used in manufacture, 5795——Price of throwing during the last six years, 5797–5799——Period of briskness in the throwing trade, and difficulty in getting silk thrown, 5800–5813——Manner in which competition with Manchester and the wages given there acts injuriously upon the wages in Spitalfields, 5814–5825——Comparison of articles manufactured at Manchester and Spitalfields, 5826–5831 ——Comparison of wages between the silk and cotton trade at Manchester, and transfer of hands from one to the other, 5831–5836——Effect of reducing duty on Italian thrown to the Italian seller and Spitalfields' manufacturer with regard to price, 5837–5843—— How distress of Spitalfields' weavers to be alleviated, 5847–5850——Larger quantity of French silks admitted illegally, 5851——Difficulty of ascertaining between French and English silks, 5853–5855——Prohibition would not effectually prevent smuggling, 5852–5859——State of the law as to smuggling with regard to the proof of French goods, 5860–

*Stone, Thomas,* (Analysis of his Evidence)—*continued.*

5860–5863——Prohibition of manufactured goods would cause more employment here, 5864——Distress in Spitalfields less formerly than at present, 5865, 5866——How far a certain description of goods that were made formerly and not at present, is from the taste being altered, or from foreign or English competition, 5867–5895, 5936–5945.

Quantity of velvet one man can manufacture in a week and wages earned thereby, 5897, 5898——How far the fancy trade of Spitalfields affected by the introduction of French goods, 5899–5902——Advantage of the French over the English manufacturer from previous orders, 5903, 5904——Benefits to be derived from the prohibition of French goods, 5905–5909——Throwsters do not get a remunerating price at present, 5910–5919—— Reduction of duty would destroy throwsters' capital, and throw their hands out of employment, 5920–5924——Ruin of English would cause dependence upon foreign throwsters, 5925, 5926——Figured silks much worn at present, 5946–5948——Difference of credit, 5950–5958——Present method of transacting business arising therefrom, and benefits thereof, 5967–5993——Manufacture of rich goods more profitable than low, but less demand for them, 5994–6000——From competition with France, 6001——Goods can be made here equal to those coming from France, 6002, 6003——Manner in which capital in Spitalfields employed, 6004–6009——Amount of duty on importation of plain goods, and generally from France, during the last six months, 6010——Description of silk used in Spitalfields' manufacture, 6011–6015——Use of the Jacquard loom decreased in Spitalfields, 6016–6019——Earnings of weavers at present, 6020–6027.

(Second Examination.) Examination upon the case of the Spitalfields' weavers not being properly before the Committee, and upon the number of looms employed by manufacturers and by the Trades' Committee, 12679–12685——Statement of the opinions of different manufacturers as to the removal of duties on foreign thrown silk and on prohibition, 12686–12689——Number of looms in Spitalfields, number out of employ, and number employed by the Trades' Committee, 12690, 12691.

(Third Examination.) Confirmation of witness's opinion, Question 5789, 12692—— Average weekly earnings of weavers in Spitalfields, 12693.

*Stone, William,* (Analysis of his Evidence.) Partner in the house of Durant & Co., 5593– 5595——Extension of the silk trade, and in what counties, 5596–5598——Fluctuations therein in different years, 5600–5606——Italian throwster a loser since 1829, 5607–5608 ——Small advantages of the Italian over the English throwster, 5609–5612, 5615—— Period of the year at which Italian raw and thrown silks received in England, 5616, 5617 ——English thrown is in the market as soon as Italian, 5618——Period of increase of mills and machinery in England, and where, 5619–5622——How far throwing trade increased, 5623——State of the throwing trade, and prices of throwing 1821–1830, 5624– 5635——Effect of duties on thrown silk on Spitalfields and Manchester, 5636——Proportions of foreign silks used in different manufacturing districts, 5637——For what articles foreign silks used, 5638, 5639——Manner in which price of thrown silks in England determined, 5640–5643——Effect of lowering duty on foreign thrown silk, 5644–5649.

(Second Examination.) Table showing the nett proceeds of one pound of Italian raw and thrown silk, deducting duty and charges (1822–1831), 6028–6030——Principle upon which calculations made, 6031–6039——Italian throwster not sufficiently remunerated, 6040–6047——Advantage of Italian over English throwster, if duty repealed, 6048–6051 ——Imports of Italian thrown silk, and at what period the year should be calculated, 6052-6058——Decrease in the price of thrown 1831, 6057——Weight of bales of 1830 and 1831 lighter, 6059——Bad state of the throwsters in certain years, 6060–6066—— Prices obtained by the throwster in 1830, 6067–6078——Prices of thrown silk, and duty in 1830, and manner they increased importation, 6079–6134——Depression of mills in the West, from transfer thereof to the North of England, 6139–6141, 6147–6160——Competition in this country sufficient, 6142——Italians might throw more silk, 6146—— Improvement in English thrown silk, and to what attributed, 6161–6163——Improvement of Italian raw silk, and to what attributed, 6164–6170——Present state of the market with regard to the supply of Italian raw and thrown silk, 6171–6181——Purposes for which Bengal silk applied, and its comparative quality, 6183–6198, 6203, 6204, 6209– 6213, 6217, 6218, 6232, 6233——Less labour required in working it, 6199–6201—— Consumption of raw silk no criterion of amount of labour employed, 6202——Use to which China silks applied, and their quality, 6205–6208——How Bengal silks affects the consumption of Italian, 6214–6217, 6221——Improvement in the quality of Bengal silk, 6219, 6220——Chinese silk interferes more with Italian, 6222.

Increase in quality and decrease in price of Chinese silk, 6223, 6224——Examination as to quantity of labour employed in manufacturing different descriptions of silk, 6225– 6231——Application of China silk, 6234——Importance of increasing the supply, 6235 ——Its comparison with Bengal, 6236, 6237——Necessity for a supply of Italian silk, 6238——Comparison as to quality of French thrown silks, 6239–6245, 6248——Expense of conveying them to this country, 6246, 6247——Means of ascertaining French silk, 6249–6253, 6255–6258——How obtained, 6254——For what uses calculated, 6259–6263 ——Price of silk used for making into marabout, 6264–6267——To what place Italian thrown silk exported from this country, 6268–6271——Prices of Italian silk in London and Lyons, and how regulated and affected by the home growth of France, 6272–6304 ——Advantages or otherwise of reducing duty on importation, 6305–6312——How it

678.                                                                                        would

*Stone, William*, (Analysis of his Evidence)—*continued.*

would affect the importation of Italian raw and thrown, 6313–6318——Effect upon the manufacturer and throwster of increasing duty on thrown, 6319–6323——Effect of duties on the price of foreign and English thrown silk, 6324–6328——How far distress of throwster in consequence of reduction of prices, 6329, 6333, 6339, 6340——How profits calculated, 6334–6338——Distress of weavers, in consequence of reduction of profits, 6341–6345——Whether it has been greater, and of longer duration formerly than at present, 6346–6352——State of trade, 1826–1831; Difficult to account for distress, 6357——Labour lower at Manchester than Spitalfields, 6357——How far distress attributed to admission of foreign manufactured goods, 6358–6364——How far ruin of throwsters would cause dependence upon foreigner for thrown silk, 6365, 6366——Advantage to operatives if foreign competition removed, 6368.

(Third Examination.) Whether the throwing Italian silk can be continued in this country with a lower rate of duty, 6370–6375——Tendency of increased duty on thrown to increase supply of raw, 6376, 6377——Loss by Italian silk merchants from trade with this country, 6378–6380——Imports of silk by certain Italian throwsters, 6381–6392——Comparison of distress formerly and at present, 6393–6403——Greater consumption of silk now than formerly, 6404, 6405——Italian silk takes more labour than Bengal, 6406——Towns in the North to which the silk trade has been transferred from the West, 6407–6411——Importations of tram 1830 and 1831, 6412–6414——Importations, 1830 and 1831, by Messrs. Gondolphin, 6415–6419.

Reason why apparent loss to the Italian throwster may not be actual loss, 6420–6423——Allowance for waste, in calculating nett proceeds of throwsters, 6424–6429——How far throwster did well 1831, 6430, 6431——The year 1831 a bad year for profits, 6431, 6432——Disadvantage to throwsters of working bad Italian silk, 6433–6435——Proportion of good silk imported, 6436–6440——Doubt as to English throwsters, of common run of Italian silk having obtained a remuneration, 6441——Failures among them, 6442, 6443——Districts where Italian plan of throwing is understood produce better raw than those where they are ignorant of it, 6444——Effect of increasing or decreasing duties upon importation of thrown and raw silk, 6445–6448——Smaller importation of thrown and greater importation of raw would give additional employment to English mills, 6449——Best thrown silks of Italy are better than the generality of English thrown, 6450–6452——Business of a silk broker, and sources of his information, 6453–6458.

(Fourth Examination.) Importation, 1828–1832, by certain Italian merchants, 7007——Monthly importations of Italian raw and thrown, 1830 and 1832; examination upon the increased or decreased importation of those parties, 7008–7014——Examination upon broker's commission, sale, credit and discount upon silk sales, 7015–7025——Effect of continuance of present duties upon manufacturers and throwsters, 7026–7028——Extent to which Manchester has interfered with Spitalfields is but fair competition, 7030.

*Stuffs.* See *Drawback*, 2.

*Sudbury.* See *Silk Trade.*

*Supleing,* extent to which it is carried by the French, *Cox* 2346–2348.

*Surveyors.* See *Custom House.*

*Swift, Lamech,* (Analysis of his Evidence.) Silk throwster in Somerset and Devon, 3723–3725——By whom first mill for throwing organzine introduced into England, 3726——Machinery not perfected, from supposed alterations in the silk trade, 3728——Manchester not superior in throwing to the West of England, 3730——Silk sent from Manchester to the West of England for throwing, 3731–3734——Description of silk thrown, and for whom, 3735–3737——Depreciation of trade since 1826, 3738, 3739——To what attributed, 3740——Reduction in the prices of throwing, 3741, 3742——Rate of wages, and hours of labour, 3743–3757——Quality of Italian silk not improved, 3758–3762——Impossible for throwster to reduce the prices of throwing, 3763——Ruin to throwsters, by taking off the duty on foreign thrown silk, 3764——Rate of carriage of goods, 3765–3770——Other charges, 3771, 3772——Reason for distance from London, the obtaining water power and cheap labour, 3773——Manchester has no advantage in rate of carriage, 3774.

Wages not sufficient without parish assistance, 3775–3781, 3786–3790——Hands have no other means of employment but silk mills, 3782–3785——Only females employed; their ages, 3791–3795——Charge that would remunerate throwster, 3796——Waste of silk, 3797——Advantage to the Italians by their silks not being injured by carriage, 3798——Italians reserve the best silks for themselves, 3799——Greater wages could be given if throwster paid a remunerating price, 3800–3802——Silk mills near London have been worse off than those in the West of England, 3803, 3804——Average wages of artisans and agricultural labourers, 3805–3810——Process of manufacture of marabout, organzine and tram, and prices thereof, 3811–3837——Advantage of France over England in the manufacture of marabout, 3838–3846——Quantity of marabout annually thrown, 3847–3851, 3868–3870——Reason throwing marabout does not give a larger profit than other silk, 3852–3854——Cost of raw silk, 3855——Cost of throwing, 3856–3860.

Difference in the expense of throwing finer and coarser articles, 3861–3866——Finer description that are imported, 3867——To what distress of throwsters attributed, 3871——Time occupied in throwing a quantity of Bengal or Turkey silk would not be more than

*Swift, Lamech,* (Analysis of his Evidence)—*continued.*

than consumed in throwing half the quantity of Italian, 3872, 3873——Duty that would be a sufficient protection to the throwster, 3874——Increased employment to operatives in throwing marabout, 3875, 3876——Bad effects to throwster of reduction of duty, 3877–3880——Distressed state of trade since the introduction of French goods, 3881–3883 ——How far country throwsters affected by the establishment of mills near town, 3884–3889——How affected by the importation of foreign silk, 3890–3901——If duty removed more Italian thrown will be imported, 3902——Advantage to the foreigner from the cheapness of labour, 3903–3905, 3909–3911——Consequent necessity for low wages, 3906, 3907——,Home competition rights itself, 3908——Advantages of the Italian throwster over the English, 3912–3921——Injury to raw silks in transit from Italy, 3914–3922——Difference in the price of throwing certain silks, 3923–3926——Water power used by the Italians for throwing, 3927——Distinction with regard to the quality of silks thrown, 3928——Increase of mills and machinery, in consequence of promises of prosperity held out to the silk trade, but which were not realized, 3929–3933.

*Switzerland,* supersedes France in the manufacture of sarsnet ribbons, *Ratliff* 1899–1902; *Baggallay* 7360, 7361——The Swiss manufacture from Italian grown silk, *Ratliff* 1903—— Swiss goods are imported into England, *Ratliff* 1905——Regulations that should be adopted to prohibit the importation of Swiss manufactured goods, or to compel Swiss to export their raw silk, *Brockwell* 3501–3515——In that case difference in the prices of labour could be afterwards regulated, *Brockwell* 3518, 3519, 3525——Quantities of silk consumed, and importation therein, *Doxat* 4074–4078——Looms employed in Switzerland and Spitalfields, *Doxat* 4081——Importations into Swirzerland, *Doxat* 4088, 4089 ——Quality of silks imported into England, France and Switzerland, *Doxat* 4090–4092 ——Importation of Swiss ribbons into France, *Doxat* 4093–4096——Cheapness of manufacture in Switzerland, *Doxat* 4094——Duties on importation into Switzerland and Germany, *Doxat* 4097, 4098——Why the Swiss do not suffer inconvenience from being lependent upon foreign throwsters, *Doxat* 4239–4240.

Imports of silk duty free into Switzerland, *Heath* 5276; *Martin* 5440——Causing small inducement to Swiss to throw, *Heath* 5278–5280, 5357–5361——Description of goods manufactured at Zurich, *Heath* 5281——From whence silk imported into Switzerland, *Heath* 5355, 5356——Imports into Switzerland, from England, of China and Bengal silk, *Heath* 5362——Description of silk supplied to Switzerland and Germany, and from whence, *Martin* 5440—— Comparative prices between Switzerland and England, and proportion for expenses on plain sarsnets and plain striped ribbons, *Baggallay* 7408–7412 ——Advantages of Swiss over French in ribbon manufacturer, *Bowring* 9052–9056, 9065–9068——Advantage of Switzerland over France as to taxation of machinery, *Bowring* 9665–9669——Duty that should be levied on Swiss and German goods, according to the duty levied thereon by France, *Wadden* 10139.

See also *Coventry. English Goods. Smuggling.*

*Sudbury.* See *Lustres.*

# T.

*Tables of Duties.* See *Duty on Importation.*

*Taste.* In the event of prohibition, the standard of taste would cease to be regulated by France, *Cheeper* 862–865——Improvement in taste not to be attributed solely to France, *Cheeper* 866–868——Taste in favour of French ribbons, *Jacombs* 1601–1609, 1698; *Ratliff* 1893–1898; *Baggallay* 7377–7389——Manner in which French excel the English in superiority of taste and design, *Dillon* 7663–7670; *Bottrell* 7879, 7880——Why no complaint of want of taste in English manufacture previous to 1826, *Sedgwick* 8168; *Bridges* 10384 ——Improvement of English taste latterly from communication with the Continent, *Sedgwick* 8191——Advantages to France from superior taste, *Bowring* 8755–8758.

Reasons for superiority of French taste, particularly from the establishments of schools of art and weaving schools, and encouragement given to talent, *Bowring* 8806–8825—— National taste in France for works of art encouraged by all public works of art being open to public inspection; other branches of art in which France excels England, *Bowring* 8826–8832——Operation of L'Ecole de Tissage; specimens of their work and prizes given therefor, *Bowring* 8840–8848——Distinction conferred by the French Government for superior skill in silk manufacture, *Bowring* 9936——Not so much skill in manufacture now as formerly from not being able to employ so high a class of designers as formerly, shown by a pattern exhibited, made 70 years ago, *Moore* 11274, 11275——No want of taste if trade properly protected, *Brocklehurst* 11488–11491, 11500, 11501.

*Taxation.* See *Labour.*

*THROWING MILLS.*

      1. *Generally.*

      2. *Italy.*

   1. *Generally.*

Erection thereof, at what periods, and whether increase therein, *Royle* 3025–3029, 3034–3036, 3046–3050, 3291, 3292, 3421–3425, 3437; *Swift* 3929–3933; *Ward* 3942–3946, 3977–3978, 3984; *Willmott* 4663, 4763–4766; *Gibson* 4955, 4956; *Heath* 5307; 678.                                                                                          *Stone*

*THROWING MILSS*—continued.

### 1. *Generally*—continued.

*Stone* 5619-3622 ; *Harter* 9340, 9346, 9347 ; *Grout* 10296-10298; *Moore* 11158, 11276; *Brocklehurst* 11329-11332, 11336, 11359-11364 ; *Johnson* 11557-11563, 11585-11588, 11602-11609, 11621-11623.

Situation of mills, number out of employment, and whether caused by disadvantages of situation, *Swift* 3773, 3803, 3804 ; *Ward* 4002, 4003, 4021-4023 ; *Willmott* 4754, 4755 ; *Stone* 6139-6141, 6147-6160, 6407-6411 ; *Hall* 6462-6464, 6482-6486, 6494-6497, 6621-6631 ; *Grout* 10294, 10295 ; *Brocklehurst* 11373 11380——Comparison of mills in different parts of England, *Willmott* 4768-4774 ; *Brocklehurst* 11368, 11371, 11372 ——Mill in Suffolk assisted to be built by the parish for the purpose of employing the poor, *Hall* 6557——Sacrifice of labour and capital in the erection of a silk mill, *Johnson* 11577-11579.

Power thereof, *Royle* 3030-3032, 3284-3289 ; *Willmott* 4663 ; *Grout* 10294, 10295 ; *Brocklehurst* 11365, 11369, 11370 ; *Johnson* 11557-11563 ; *Wright* 11756, 11757 ; *Middlehurst* 11790-11796——Probable quantity of thrown silk that could be produced by them, *Royle* 3033.

Speed thereof and increase therein, *Ward* 3952-3962 ; *Willmott* 4758-4761 ; *Moore* 11266——Increased speed not an injury to the silk, *Gibson* 5185, 5186.

Extent of improvement therein, *Ward* 3951, 4019, 4020 ; *Banbury* 4646-4650 ; *Gibson* 4850-4852 ; *Willmott* 4757 ; *Stone* 5623 ; *Bowring* 9806-9815 ; *Wadden* 10081, 10082 ; *Bennett* 10809-10812 ; *Moore* 11168-11171, 11265, 11267 ; *Graham* 12740——English mills can produce as good thrown silk as any other country, *Brockwell* 3637-3642 *Doxat* 4254, 4255 ; *Banbury* 4642, 4643, 4645 ; *Gibson* 5183.

Value thereof, and depreciation therein, *Royle* 3037 ; *Ward* 4011, 4012 ; *Hall* 6498-6500, 6653, 6654 ; *Ballance* 8672, 8673 ; *Brocklehurst* 11366, 11413-11418 ; *Johnson* 11557-11563——Mills and machinery not convertible to other manufacture, *Brocklehurst* 11367.

Expenses thereof, *Royle* 3162, 3163, 3171-3174 ; *Brockwell* 3658, 3669, 3680 ; *Swift* 3765-3772, 3861-3866 ; *Stone* 5624-5635——Advantages of the Italian and French in throwing and wages, *Royle* 3160, 3161, 3251-3253 ; *Gibson* 4907, 4908 ; *Martin* 5545, 5546.

Description of silk thrown, and loss by coarse silks, *Swift* 3735, 3737, 3872, 3873 ; *Ward* 4013-4017, 4024 ; *Willmott* 4751-4753 ; *Stone* 6449 ; *Johnson* 11589, 11590, 11613-11617——Waste of silk in throwing, *Swift* 3797.

Number and description of operatives employed therein, *Royle* 3109, 3294, 3305 : *Swift* 3791-3795 ; *Brocklehurst* 11336——Medical certificate of cleanliness and healthiness of witness's mills, *Royle* 3274, 3275——Hands have no other means of employment but silk mills, *Swift* 3782, 3785——Hours of labour, *Brocklehurst* 11333.

### 2. *In Italy.*

Water power used by the Italians in throwing, *Swift* 3927——If mills worked all the year they could not throw all the silk produced in Italy, *Caffi* 7093-7095, 7108——Mills would work all the year if they could get a better price for throwing, *Caffi* 7100-7105 ——Size of mills, their rents and power, *Caffi* 7146-7150——Capital of mill-owners, taxes and outgoings of mills, *Caffi* 7156-7159.

See also *Operatives.*

*Thrown Silk.* See *France*, IX. *Importation. Silk*, VII.

*THROWSTERS :*

### 1. *Generally.*
### 2. *In Italy.*
### 3. *Papers laid before the Committee.*

### 1. *Generally.*

Their distress, and to what attributed, *Royle* 3120-3123 ; *Brockwell* 3481-3489 ; *Swift* 3871, 3884-3901 ; *Ward* 4029, 4030 ; *Doxat* 4381 ; *Banbury* 4433-4441, 4503, 4504 ; *Willmott* 4762 ; *Gibson* 4957-4959 ; *Stone* 6060-6066, 6329, 6333, 6339, 6340, 6430-6435 ; *Wadden* 10083 ; *Moore* 11109-11113, 11106, 11227-11230 ; *Brocklehurst* 11424, 11425 ; *Johnson* 11591-11593, 11601 ; *Middlehurst* 11784, 11788, 11789, 11792, 11793, 11797 ; *Graham* 12753-12755——Failures of throwsters, *Brockwell* 3490-3493 ; *Heath* 5294, 5306, 5687-5691 : *Stone* 6442, 6443.

Necessity for protecting the British throwster, *Brockwell* 3494, 3499, 3500 ; *Banbury* 4590, 4591 ; *Hall* 6581-6583 ; *Wadden* 9977 ; *Brocklehurst* 11421-11423, 11426-11430 ——Protection that should be given to the British throwster, *Brockwell* 3483, 3484, 3655-3657 ; *Swift* 3874 ; *Ward* 4010 ; *Doxat* 4229-4234 ; *Banbury* 4462-4465, 4481-4483 ; *Willmott* 4737, 4738 ; *Gibson* 4921-4924, 4927 ; *Hall* 6478 ; *Ballance* 8664, 8665 ; *Johnson* 11594-11600 ; *Moore* 12069——Protection more necessary to throwster than manufacturer from fixed capital being greater; *Royle* 3106-3108, 3110 ; *Moore* 11315-11317, 12272 ; *Wright* 11762, 11763 ; *Graham* 12801-12803——Comparison of protection between English throwster and cotton spinner, *Royle* 3112——Protection by the French

to

*THROWSTERS*—continued.

### 1. *Generally*—continued.

to their throwsters, *Royle* 3113–3115; *Doxat* 4288–4290——Reason why British throwster cannot compete with the Italian, *Brockwell* 3644, 3651–3654.

State of trade and remuneration to throwsters, formerly and at present, *Ward* 3992–3995; *Doxat* 4126–4130, 4398–4402; *Banbury* 4475–4480, 4492; *Willmott* 4665–4669; *Gibson* 4893–4898; *Stone* 6424–6428, 6441, 5800–5813, 5910–5919; *Hall* 6518–6523, 6643; *Wadden* 10060, 10061; *Bennett* 10788, 10789; *Moore* 11269–11271, 11318, 11319; *Brocklehurst* 11323; *Middlehurst* 11783——Effect of removing duty on foreign thrown silk on trade of throwsters, *Gibson* 4879–4883, 4984–4999; *Stone* 5920–5924, 6048–6051; *Hall* 6470, 6471; *Moore* 11318, 11319——Compensation to throwsters if their trade destroyed, *Royle* 3111——Protecting duty to British manufacturer if trade of throwster destroyed, *Royle* 3116, 3117——Ruin of English throwsters will throw the trade more into the hands of Italy, *Brockwell* 3472, 3473——Inducement to the throwster to continue, *Royle* 3088–3091, 3976.

### 2. *In Italy*.

Italian throwster would be a greater gainer than the English, by removing duty on thrown silk, *Royle* 3092–3094; *Gibson* 4984–4999; *Stone* 6048–6051——Advantages of the Italian throwster over the English, *Brockwell* 3644, 3651–3654; *Doxat* 4245–4247; *Gibson* 5056–5060, 5176–5180; *Heath* 5290–5293, 5300; *Martin* 5438, 5439; *Stone* 5609–5612, 5615; *Caffi* 7119–7121; *Moore* 11226——Reason for Italian throwster losing in the English market; *Gibson* 4942; *Heath* 5285–5289, 5302; *Martin* 5469; *Stone* 5607, 5608, 6040–6047——If duty reduced he could introduce it at a profit, *Gibson* 4943——Proportion of import duty paid by foreign throwster, *Martin* 5471——Advances made by merchants in London and Lyons to foreign throwsters, *Martin* 5531–5536——Why trade of Italian throwster not likely to increase, *Martin* 5586——Liability of throwster if work not delivered at the day named, *Caffi*, 7250–7256——Great wealth of persons engaged as throwsters, *Caffi*, 7257–7268.

### 3. *Papers laid before the Committee*.

Minute relative to Throwsters' Work; showing the consumption of Raw Silks of all descriptions in the years 1824–25, and in the years 1826–31, dissected and computed into one standard, and compared with regard to the rates of labour and profit they have afforded to the Throwster; also remarks thereon, *Evidence*, p. 224.

Comparative view of the London market prices of Milan and Bergam Raw Silks, and Organzines at various periods, from June 1824 to February and April 1832, with notes thereon as regards the British Throwster, *Evidence*, p. 261.

See also *Debentures*. *Silk*, VII. 2.

*Tootal, Henry*, (Analysis of his Evidence.)　Silk manufacturer and throwster at Manchester, 9516——State of trade at Manchester and description of goods manufactured, and number of looms employed from 1816 to the present time, 9517–9535——Number of Jacquard looms employed at Manchester, and on what goods, 9536–9544——Drawback on exportation and price of a certain article produced, 9545–9549——Sale price of richest French silks, 9550, 9551——Cost of Jacquard looms, 9552——Capability of Manchester for the production of rich goods; pattern of dress made for the Queen produced, 9553–9555——Wages of weavers, their hours of labour, quantity produced per day, and deduction for necessary expenses, 1823, 1828 and 1832, 9556–9573——Consumption of silk in Manchester, 9574——Quantity of silk thrown in Manchester, and quantity of foreign thrown imported, 9575.

Quantity of foreign thrown silk used in Manchester, 9576–9578——Proportion of labour to the value of the goods, 9579–9584——Duty on waste silk, drawback on exportation, and manner in which it is worked up to claim the drawback, 9585–9587——Throwing mills at Manchester in 1823, and at present; number of spindles, and weekly earnings of operatives, 9588–9591——Average wages lower than in a cotton mill, 9592——Rate of wages, 9593, 9594——Activity in the silk trade at Manchester at present, 9595, 9602, 9603——Comparison of wages, 1828–1831, 9596–9606——Exportation to America, increase therein, instances of orders to England formerly given to France, 9607–9612——Doubt whether taking off duty on organzine would lower manufactured article to that amount, 9613, 9614——Bounty increases exportation of gros de Naples, 9615.

*Trade Committee*.　Difference in the price of goods imported by the trade committee, and similar goods made at Spitalfields, *Ballance* 8586——Appointment of the Committee at Weavers Hall, its object, and number of members interested in throwing, *Ballance* 8624–8635, 8652; *Bridges*, 10510–10515——They have not interfered with the evidence to be given before this Committee, *Bridges*, 10516–10528——Not part of the business of the association to get duties on raw silk lowered, *Ballance* 8636.

*Trams*.　Causes that operated to reduce the price of trams, *Gibson* 5118——Price of trams at Lyons and London, 1831, *Martin* 5553——Importations of tram 1830–31, *Stone* 6412–6414——No profit in sending trams to England from Italy, *Caffi* 7166——Distinction between organzine and tram, *Wadden* 10064, 10065.

See also *Importation*, 2. *Italy*. *Organzine*. *Prices*. *Silk*, VII. 2.

*Tulle.*  Description of tulle, and where made, *Clay* 6860, 6861.

*Turkey Silk.*  See *Bengal and China Silk.  Importation*, 2.

*Twisting.*  See *Throwing.*

## U.

*Undertakers.*  Nature of the undertaker, *Poole* 995; *Marston* 1352——They are superseded by the engine looms, *Poole* 996-1001——Amount of the undertakers' profits, *Marston* 1470-1475—— Silk used by the undertakers is always in a dyed state, *Marston* 1509——In what the advantage of employing an undertaker consists, 2121-2123.

*Union Duties.*  Ruin of Dublin silk manufacturers by the repeal of the Union duties, or 10 per cent. on introduction of English silk manufactures into Ireland, *Wadden*, 9966; *Scott* 11851-11854; *Sisson* 11903-11907.
      See also *Dublin.*

## V.

*Value of Silk.*  See *Custom House.  France*, VII.  *Silk*, III.

*Vaucluse Department.*  See *Avignon.*

*Velvets.*  Quantity of velvets imported from Germany, *Brunskill* 225-229, 633——Rate of duty thereon, *Brunskill* 230-233——Importation of velvets from France, *Brunskill* 632——Importation of velvets has increased, *Brunskill* 640-642——Method of manufacturing velvets at Elverfeldt and Crifeldt, *Brunskill* 643-646—— Manufacture of velvets entirely confined to Spitalfields, *Gibson* 4823, 4824——Variation in the book price for weaving velvets, *Gibson* 4825, 4826——Quantity of velvet one man can manufacture in a week, and wages earned thereby, *Stone* 5897, 5898——Letter from Germany upon the manufacture of velvets, *Baggallay* 7508-7511——English velvets improving, *Baggallay* 7512, 7513.
      Comparison of prices and duty upon German and English velvets, *Baggallay* 7514-7518——Sea voyage too long to smuggle velvets from Germany, *Bottrell* 7843——Importation of foreign silk velvets, 1830-1831, and British labour displaced thereby, *Wadden* 10013——Account showing the cost of raw silk, wages and other charges of manufacturing certain plain and figured velvets imported, 1830-1831, *Wadden* 10013——Importation of velvets, and of what description and prices, *Wallis* 10935-10938——Witness's application to the Board of Trade for a rated instead of *ad valorem* duty on velvets, *Graham* 12773-12775, 12779——Valuation of velvets at the Custom House by witness, and his causing them to be detained and afterwards sold by public auction, *Graham* 12796-12800.
      See also *English goods.*

*Veritas.*  See *Custom House.*

*Vienna.*  Imports and exports to and from, *Doxat* 4099-4101——Articles worked at Vienna for the Levant, *Doxat* 4103——Consumption of silk therein, *Heath* 5693.

## W.

*Wadden, Barrett,* (Analysis of his Evidence.)  Silk manufacturer in Spitalfields, 9962-9964 ——Ruin of Dublin silk manufacturers by the repeal of the Union duties, or 10 per cent. on introduction of English silk manufactures into Ireland, 9966——Good condition of the Spitalfields' weavers ten years ago, 9967, 9975, 9976——Reduction of wages upon the opening of the Ports, 9968——Unsettled state of trade since, 9969——Why reduction of wages not immediate upon opening the Ports, 9970——Deterioration of wages and profits progressive to the present time, 9971——Exertion of the English manufacturer to meet foreign competition has failed, 9972——Necessity for supporting the British throwster, 9974——Alteration for the worse of the condition of the Spitalfields weavers, 9977——Examination with statements showing distress of weavers, 9977-9983 ——Smuggling before repeal of the prohibition a benefit to the manufacturer, 9984 ——Great increase of smuggling since, 9985, 9986-9994——Disadvantage to the trade by reducing duty in 1829 from lowering wages and profits, and advantage to the export trade thereby from debentures, 9997-9999.
      Debentures of no advantage to the importers of Italian silk beyond the price of the debentures, 10000——Disadvantage to trade from a further reduction of duty, 10002 ——Difficulty in disposing of the rich quality of plain goods manufactured in Spitalfields from the demand for them being supplied legally and illegally from France, 10003-10008——Spitalfields chiefly employed upon plain low-priced goods made from inferior silks, 10009——Spitalfields trade has not removed to Manchester, 10010——Improvement has not taken place in Spitalfields manufacture from the low wages since 1826, 10011, 10012——Importation of foreign silk velvets, 1830-1831, and British labour displaced thereby, 10013——Account showing the cost of raw silk, wages and other charges of manufacturing certain plain and figured velvets imported, 1830-1831, 10013——Comparative view of the cost and expenses of manufacturing certain organzine and tram in plain gros de Naples at Lyons and Spitalfields respectively, 10015-10019——The like
comparative

*Wadden, Barrett,* (Analysis of his Evidence)—*continued.*

comparative view on figured gros de Naples, 10020–10024——Expense of labour on figured gros de Naples would be increased without the Jacquard, 10026——Confirmation of the comparative view of cost of manufacture on plain gros de Naples, by calculations on a subsequent importation, 10026.

(Second Examination.) Account showing the cost of silk and wages paid for manufacturing the same into plain and figured gros de Naples in Spitalfields, 10030——Advantages of the French manufacturer over the English, 10031, 10032——Prohibition the only protection for the fancy trade; plain trade may be protected if the smuggler detected and punished, 10033——Further examination as to smuggling, and means of prevention, 10034–10040——Overwhelming distress in Spitalfields and Coventry; and distress in Macclesfield, Manchester, Middleton and Sudbury, 10041, 10042 ——Rich silk goods are not made at Manchester, with some exceptions, 10043–10045——Small number of looms employed in rich figured and fancy goods in Spitalfields, specimens produced, 10046–10052——Fancy trade in Spitalfields diminished from the introduction of French goods; their superiority, 10053–10056——Efforts of British manufacturer unavailing while France leads the fashion, 10057——Preference in favour of British thrown silk, and means taken by witness to prevent pillage in dyeing, 10058, 10059.

English throwster can produce as good an organzine as the Piedmont throwster if properly compensated, 10060——He has not generally as good raw as the Italian, from the latter having the choice of the market, 10061——Fossembrone silk generally thrown in this country, 10061–10064——Manner of throwing and distinction between organzine and tram, 10064, 10065——Description of marabout and process of throwing it, 10065 ——Price thereof, raw and thrown, 10065, 10066——How far Fossembrone superior to Piedmont in making organzine, 10067, 10068——Possibility, if protected by price, of English manufacturer equalling the French, shown by witness's experiments, 10068–10078——How throwster and manufacturer would be sacrificed if duty on thrown silk removed or reduced, 10079, 10080——Neither throwing or weaving has improved in England of late, 10081——Manner in which low wages causes deterioration in throwing, 10082——Reason for low wages and distress of throwsters while large importation of raw silks and greater consumption of silk goods, 10083——Number of Spitalfields weavers out of employment, and instances of their absconding to America with their employers' manufactured property, 10084–10086.

Quantity of ribbons and broad silks seized belonging to Messrs. Leaf & Co., 10087, 10088——Their subsequent restoration, and being brought into home consumption, and evils thereof, 10089–10104 ——Examination upon, exportation and drawback thereon, 10105–10116——Negligence of arrangement at the Custom House by which goods get in at less than their proper duty, 10117–10122, 10126–10129——Leaf's transaction not done with connivance of Custom House officers, 10123——It is not an isolated case, 10124——Officers have not received the compromise money, how far in consequence of a memorial from Leaf's to get the money back, on the ground of the goods not being smuggled, 10125——Extent of smuggling to be partly accounted for by the looseness of the Customs regulations, 10130, 10131——Price of French and Italian raws, 10132, 10133——Number of looms at Lyons and St. Etienne, and how they interfere with Spitalfields and Coventry, 10134–10138——Duty that should be levied on Swiss and German goods, 10139——Use of satins supplanted by gros de Naples, 10141——Distress attributed to the introduction of foreign goods, 10142, 10143——Evils of further reducing the duty on importation, 10144——Lowering duties would be in violation of the promise of the Board of Trade, 10145——Increased quantity of silk does not always show increased profit to the labourer from there being more labour in coarser silk, 10146–10149——Rate of credit of Spitalfields trade, 10150, 10151.

*WAGES.*

      1. *Generally.*
      2. *At Coggeshall.*
      3. *At Congleton.*
      4. *At Coventry.*
      5. *At Macclesfield.*
      6. *At Manchester.*
      7. *At Spitalfields.*
      8. *In Foreign Countries.*

  1. *Generally.*

Rate of wages; reductions therein, and causes thereof, *Doxat* 4045, 4047, 4062, 4395; *Banbury* 4489–4491; *Willmott* 4698–4711, 4720; *Gibson* 4929, 5152–5157, 5201; *Hull* 6579, 6584, 6585, 6588, 6589, 6662, 6663, 6714–6721, 6740–6747, 6751–6755; *Baggallay* 7427–7429, 7450–7452; *Ballance* 8367–8373, 8385, 8387, 8527–8530, 8534, 8535, 8656, 8657, 8692, 8693; *Bridges* 10389, 10390; *Bennett* 10739, 10740; *Wallis* 10841–10856, 10971–10974; *Poyton* 10980; *Bolter* 11001–11007 *Brocklehurst* 11334–11336, 11543; *Rowbotham* 11730–11732; *Wright* 11776–11781; *Middlehurst* 11786–11791; *Kelly* 11820–11826; *Pittifor* 11989–12028——Effect of 678.

lists

*WAGES*—continued.

### 1. *Generally*—continued.

lists for wages, *Royle* 3124, 3126——Reduction of wages if duty on thrown silk taken off, *Royle* 3435, 3436——Wages not sufficient without parish assistance, *Swift* 3775–3781, 3786–3790; *Ward* 3981; *Brocklehurst* 11539–11542——Greater wages would be given if throwster had a remunerating price, *Swift* 3800–3802——Average wages of artisans and agricultural labourers, *Swift* 3805–3810; *Willmott* 4745, 4746; *Hall* 6725 ——Work cannot be continued at present wages, *Ward* 4026, 4027; *Brocklehurst* 11419, 11420——Proportion of wages on silk grown in the Colonies, and in Italy, *Doxat* 4298 ——Comparison of reduction of wages between cotton and silk, *Doxat* 4308–4311.

Statement respecting the reduction of wages and tables showing rates at London and Lyons, *Doxat* 4375; *Gibson* 5152–5157——Women's wages, *Hall* 6588, 6589—— Wages of winders and warpers, *Willmott* 4698–4711; *Baggallay* 7450–7452——Account showing manner in which less wages are paid for working up a larger quantity of silk, *Ballance* 8383, 8384; *Grout* 10314; *Brocklehurst* 11356, 11357, 11543——Number of yards per day weavers can make, *Ballance* 8546–8549——Advance of wages that would satisfy operatives, *Bridges* 10489–10491——Decrease in the amount of wages paid upon the manufacture of coarse goods over fine goods, *Prout* 11642, 11643; *Smith* 11689—— Average wages do not include the time they wait for work, *Smith* 11693——Cotton trade has not depressed silk weavers' wages, *Cope* 11713; *Rowbotham* 11724–11726 ——Why protection would tend to increase wages, *Kelly* 11832——Expense of assistance required by weavers reducing the amount of their earnings, *Pittifor* 12049–12052—— Not an undue proportion between the earnings of plain and figured weavers, *Pittifor* 12055–12057.

### 2. *At Coggeshall.*

Difference in wages at Coggeshall and Coventry, and comparison of goods, *Hall* 6667–6673——Rate of wages to Coventry men working for witness at Coggeshall, *Hall* 6728, 6729.

### 3. *At Congleton.*

Wages paid to throwsters in Congleton, 1823–1832, *Johnson* 11564.

### 4. *At Coventry.*

Particulars of forming a list of prices for wages, and how they affect engine work and hand work, *Brunskill* 248–268——Effect of machinery in equalizing wages for different descriptions of work, *Brunskill* 326–328——Difference of wages for engine loom and single-hand work, *Brunskill* 343–348; *Poole* 1068–1070, 1075–1079, 1084, 1090, 1091, 1117–1119——How far obtaining material cheaper would enable the giving better wages, *Brunskill* 355–363——Rate of wages, *Brunskill* 332–338, 487–492; *Poole* 955–960, 965, 980–990, 1062–1064; *Goode* 1209–1213; *Smith* 1259, 1337; *Marston* 1363–1369, 1495, 1500, 1506–1508; *Perkins* 1554–1556, 1574–1579; *Jacombs* 1588, 1589, 1776–1784; *Cox* 2059, 2060, 2104, 2113, 2114; *Merry* 2543, 2544, 2572–2586, 2625–2629, 2852; *Swift* 3743; *Doxat* 4036, 4037, 4056–4061; *Willmott* 4685–4697, 4721–4723; *Gibson* 5199, 5200, 5202–5207; *Hall* 6723, 6724, 6750; *Baggallay* 7432–7437——Proportion of wages to the cost of the article, *Brunskill* 572–582——Account of the average weekly earnings of weavers having full employment in the plain ribbon trade, including satins and sarsnets, 1815–1830, *Poole* 965——Wages received by journeymen from undertakers the same as from manufacturers, *Poole* 993, 994.

Meeting of the weavers in November for the purpose of equalizing the rate of wages, *Poole* 1019–1024, 1051, 1052, 1065–1067——List of prices between 1816 and 1831, and in what instances departed from, *Poole* 1053–1061; *Goode* 1214–1216; *Ratliff* 2040, 2041——List of prices of engine loom work agreed to at a meeting of the manufacturers, held at the Castle Inn, in the city of Coventry, on Thursday, Nov 10th, 1831, and to commence the following day, *Poole* 1064——Resolutions of a meeting of the Committee of Ten, appointed at a general meeting to make a new standard, held at the Castle Inn, on the 9th Nov. 1831, for deviating from the standard of 1822, and regulating the width of sarsnets, *Poole* 1064——List of prices of single hand work agreed to at a meeting of manufacturers, held at the Castle Inn, in the city of Coventry, on Thursday, Nov. 10th, 1831, and to commence the following day, *Poole* 1064——Discontent among the weavers from some of the masters wanting a further reduction of wages between 1829 and 1831, *Poole* 1071–1074——Single hand list includes winding and warping, but not the engine list, *Poole* 1082, 1083——How far the lists were for the purpose of equalizing the wages between an engine loom and single hand loom weaver, *Poole* 1092–1105; *Marston* 1375, 1461, 1467–1469; *Jacombs* 1785–1793; *Ratliff* 1975–1979——Wages should continue to be paid according to the prices in the lists, *Poole* 1115, 1116; *Merry* 2562–2565.

How far reduction attributed to the importation of foreign manufactured ribbons, *Goode* 1217–1228; *Smith* 1311——Workmen wish to keep to the tables as closely as possible, though they do not afford a living, *Goode* 1253; *Marston* 1376, 1488——How time occupied in setting and changing patterns affects the rate of wages, *Smith* 1323–1335, 1338–1340——Reasons for the manufacturers not giving better wages, *Marston* 1377 ——Rise in the wages upon certain articles since the table of prices was fixed, *Marston*

*WAGES*—continued.

### 4. *At Coventry*—continued.

1448–1450, 1462, 1463——More uniformity in the present list than in any former one, *Marston* 1464–1466——Want of work and low wages always accompany each other, *Marston* 1487——None work at a lower rate than fixed by the table, *Jacombs* 1794–1800——Parochial relief more in some instances than wages, *Jacombs* 1801–1804, 1824, 1825——Wages inadequate from weavers' necessary expenses, *Jacombs* 1805–1813; *Ratliff* 1970–1973, 1980–2015——Wages that would be adequate, *Jacombs* 1814, 1815.

Prohibition would cause a higher rate of wages, and increased price would not be felt by the consumer, *Jacombs* 1816–1820; *Cox* 2218–2229——The list does not prevent the man of capital exercising his own judgment with regard to wages, *Ratliff* 2016–2018 ——It secures against bad work, *Ratliff* 2019——Neither the public nor the weaver would benefit by lower wages, *Ratliff* 2020, 2026——Comparison between allowing the price of raw silk to find its level, and that of wages, *Ratliff* 2031–2039——Manufacturer departing from agreement would have his goods made worse, *Ratliff* 2042——Description of goods for which witness's house pays a higher price than others, and reasons, *Cox* 2115–2119.

### 5. *At Macclesfield.*

Statement of the price of labour in Macclesfield, 1810, 1819, 1825 and 1832, and examination thereupon, *Prout* 11647–11655, 11661–11663——In 1817–1823, *Cope* 11699 ——In 1824 and 1825, *Cope* 11703——Competition with cotton manufacturers did not reduce wages of weavers, *Prout* 11657——Tabular view, exhibiting the amount paid for labour in the weaving department of the silk trade of Macclesfield in 1825 and 1832, with average wages, weekly amount, and annual loss, *Prout* 11664——Wages for throwing at Macclesfield, 1818–1832, *Middlehurst* 11802–11805——Wages more liable to lower at Macclesfield than Manchester, *Middlehurst* 11811.

### 6. *At Manchester.*

There are no lists there, *Royle* 3124–3126——How wages in Manchester affected by the cotton trade, *Royle* 3239–3243, 3247–3249——Rate of, *Stone* 5759, 5760; *Harter* 9384–9407, 9413–9420——Comparison of wages between silk and cotton trade at Manchester, and transfer of hands from one to the other, *Stone* 5831–5836——Wages of weavers at Manchester, their hours of labour, quantity produced per day, and deduction for necessary expenses, 1823, 1828 and 1832, *Tootal* 9556–9573, 9588–9594——Average wages lower than in a cotton mill, *Tootal* 9592——Comparison of wages, 1828–1831, *Tootal* 9596–9606——How wages in the silk trade at Manchester affected by those in the cotton trade, *Wallis* 10904–10916.

### 7. *At Spitalfields.*

No fixed rule of wages in Spitalfields, *Gibson* 4818–4822——How regulated, *Ballance* 8531–8533——Rate of, *Stone* 5734–5740, 6020–6027——In 1816–1826, *Ballance* 8357–8359——1824–1831, *Ballance* 8513–8526; *Stone* 12693——Reduction therein since 1826, *Stone* 5750–5755——Injury of the increasing silk manufacture in other parts of England, to wages in Spitalfields, *Stone* 5756–5758, 5761, 5762——Manner in which competition with Manchester, and the wages given there, acts injuriously upon wages in Spitalfields, *Stone* 5814–5825; *Wallis* 10894–10916; *Graham* 12710–12712, 12792–12795——Estimate of how much less wages paid in Spitalfields now and before 1826, *Ballance* 8381 ——Effect on wages in Spitalfields by repeal of Act regulating labour, *Ballance* 8709–8712——Reduction of wages in Spitalfields, and causes thereof, *Brunskill* 611–622; *Doxat* 4141–4143; *Wadden* 9968–9971; *Moore* 11277–11279; *Beckwith* 11946, 11947; *Graham* 12751——Operation of book prices, and when abolished, *Wallis* 10829–10833 ——Manner in which smuggling gros de Naples would interfere with wages in Spitalfields, *Wallis* 10925–10129——How far prohibition of French goods would raise wages in Spitalfields, *Graham* 12713, 12714——Fear that material improvement cannot take place in the rate of wages in Spitalfields, *Graham* 12716.

### 8. *In Foreign Countries.*

They are cheaper in France, on fancy articles, than in England, *Brunskill* 244——The similarity of wages for plain and fancy work at St. Etienne, approach nearer than at Coventry, *Brunskill* 324, 325——English wages double those of Foreign, *Brunskill* 493, 494; *Gibson* 4927; *Bottrell* 7903–7907——Regulation of wages in Italy, *Royle* 3127–3131——Wages in Italy, *Royle* 3164–3170; *Gibson* 4930–4933——Advantages of Italian and French in wages, *Royle* 3160, 3161, 3251–3253; *Ballance* 8410–8412——Comparison of wages and profits between silk and other businesses in Italy, *Caffi* 7116 ——Wages of agricultural labourers in Italy, *Caffi* 7305–7313——Origin of disturbances at Lyons about wages, *Bottrell* 7927, 7928——Did not extend to St. Etienne, *Bottrell* 7929——Comparison of wages in France and Switzerland, *Ballance* 8505–8512—— Wages to reelers, winders and persons in throwing in France, *Bowring* 8881–8883, 8900, 8901——Tariff of weavers' wages at Lyons, *Bowring* 8902–8908——Rate of wages at Lyons, *Bowring* 8934–8938——Of ribbon weavers, *Bowring* 9008–9015——At Saint Etienne, *Bowring* 8999——Of ribbon weavers, *Bowring* 9016–9020.

See also *Clipping. Competition. Conseil des Prud'hommes. Coventry. Doubling. Fancy Trade. France. Labour. Operatives*, 2. *Profits. Reeling. Sarsnets. Silk Trade*, 2. *Winding.*

678.　　　　　　　　　　　　　　　　　　　　　　　　　　　　　　*Wallis,*

*Wallis, William,* (Analysis of his Evidence.) Silk weaver formerly in the fancy branch, but latterly in the plain, residing in Bethnal-green, 10813–10815——Distressed state of the Spitalfields weavers since importation of foreign goods, 10816–10818——State of the poor in the parish of Bethnal-green, 10818–10822——Distress attributed to the introduction of foreign wrought silk, 10823——Periods of distress formerly, but none so great as at present, 10824–10828——Operation of the book prices, and when abolished, 10829–10833——How far all the weavers employed in 1830, 10834——Comparison of number of looms in and since 1824, in the whole district, 10835–10837, 10840——Comparison of number in the parish of Bethnal-green, 10838, 10839——Statements of rates of wages, 1769–1825, 10841–10847, 10851–10856——Extent of employment of weavers at present, 10848–10850.

When articles formerly made in Spitalfields transferred to the country, 10857–10859, 10863–10868——Progressive inclination to improvement in the silk trade up to opening the Ports, 10859——Figured handkerchiefs never made to any extent in Spitalfields, 10860——Reason for Norwich taking the bombazin trade, 10861, 10862——Richer goods manufactured at Spitalfields than Manchester, 10869——Few removals of masters or weavers from Spitalfields to Manchester, 10870, 10871——Satins and velvets not making at Manchester, 10872, 10873——More inferior goods now manufactured in Spitalfields, and reduced wages therefor, 10874–10876——Gros de Naples made at Manchester do not interfere with those made in Spitalfields or France, 10877–10879.

More fluctuation in trade since alteration than previously, 10880——Alteration for the worse in the habits and moral character of the Spitalfields weaver since alteration, 10881–10883——Looms out of work at the beginning of this year, 10884——Competition with France most detrimental to the trade of Spitalfields, 10885——Proportion of looms at present and formerly employed in the figured and plain branches, 10886–10889——Improvement in manufacture not to be ascribed to the importation of French goods, 10889–10893——How wages in the silk trade at Manchester affected by those in the cotton trade, and how it acts upon the wages in Spitalfields, 10894–10916——Manufacture of figured lustres at Spitalfields not given up from their being made at Manchester, 10917, 10918——Manufacture thereof at Sudbury and prices paid, 10919–10924——Manner in which smuggling gros de Naples would interfere with wages in Spitalfields, 10925–10929——Smuggling a benefit under prohibition, 10930–10934.

Importation of velvets, and of what description and prices, 10935–10938——Spitalfields more interfering with Manchester than Manchester with it, 10939–10941——Inferiority of the article manufactured in Spitalfields but not in workmanship, 10942——Increase in quantity of rich goods now making, but not in price for weaving, 10943, 10944——Importation of French crapes, or manufacture thereof, in certain parts of England, does not interfere with Spitalfields, 10945–10949——French fancy goods injurious to Spitalfields, 10950–10952——Duty on thrown silk not injurious to the weaver, 10953——Injurious effect of the Milan Decrees, upon importation of Italian silk, and subsequent improvement of Bengal silk therefrom, 10954–10958——How much duty on thrown adds to the cost of manufacture, 10959–10961——Examination upon the use of the fly shuttle, 10962–10965——To what increase of trade in 1824 and 1826 attributed, 10966——Looms in Spitalfields not increased since 1826, 10967——Number unemployed, 10968–10970——Average rate of wages, 1825 and at present, deductions therefrom, and hours of labour, 10971–10974.

*Ward, John Sharrer,* (Analysis of his Evidence.) Throwster at Bruton in Somersetshire, 3934——Number of hands employed 3936–3938——Average wages, 3939–3941——Number of spindles at work in 1823–1829, 3942–3945——Price of throwing, 3947–3949——Means by which price reduced, 3950——Improvement in machinery trifling since 1823, 3951——Increased rapidity in machinery and extra employment therefrom, 3952–3962——Advantages possessed by the Italian throwster, 3963–3971——Ruin to throwsters by removing import duty, 3972–3975——Inducement to the throwster to continue, 3976——Number of mills formerly and at present, 3977, 3978——Loss to proprietors, the mills being out of employ, 3979, 3980——Hands partly dependent on the poor rate, 3981——Number out of employ, 3982——Increase of poor's rate at Bruton, 3983——Number of spindles at work, 3984——Italians keep their best silk themselves, 3985–3987——Injury to raw silk in the transit, 3988, 3989.

Necessity for increasing the duty on foreign thrown silk, 3990, 3991——More advantageous to work on commission than for private use, 3992–3995——Silk not thrown better at Manchester than in the West of England, 3997–4001——Manufacture could not be carried on so cheap near London as in the West, 4002, 4003——Silk not sent from Manchester to the West lately for throwing, 4004——Principally females employed, 4005——Healthy and domestic employment, 4006, 4007——No means of subsistence if dismissed, 4008——Number who have been dismissed, 4009——Protection that should be granted to the throwster, 4010——Depreciation in the value of machinery, 4011, 4012——Bengal and Turkey silks do not afford employment for mills in the West of England, 4013–4017——Improvement in throwing in the last sixty years, 4019——Means of competing with disadvantages thereby, 4020——Mills disadvantageously situate are thrown out of employ, 4021–4023——Bengal silk would not employ so many as half the quantity of Italian, 4024——Reason for small increase in the importation of thrown silk, 4025——Work cannot be continued at the present wages, 4026, 4027——Inducement of profit to the Italian to send his raw silk here, 4028——How importation of foreign manufactured goods affects the throwster, 4029, 4030.

*Warehousemen.*

*Warehousemen.* Manner in which warehousemen's business is conducted, and how far a benefit to the public, *Dillon* 7642–7655——Examination upon the purchases by large warehousemen, and how they act upon profit or loss to the manufacturer, *Dillon* 7714–7729——Manner in which the middle man between the manufacturer and consumer has benefited by the decrease of wages and the present system, *Ballance* 8475, 8478.
　　See also *Jobbing.*

*Waste.* More waste in manufacture of poor than rich goods, *Ballance* 8584——Absence of waste does not depend on its being thrown directly after being reeled, *Bowring* 8879, 8880——Duty on waste silk and drawback on exportation, *Tootal* 9585–9587.
　　See also *Importation. Silk,* VIII.

*Watered Silks.* Are imported from France, *Clay* 6812, 6813 ——Preference of French watered silks over English, *Clay* 6937–6941——Importation of watered silks from France, and labour displaced thereby, *Ballance* 8700–8704.

*WEAVERS.*

　　　1. *Generally.*
　　　2. *Time lost by them.*
　　　3. *At Coventry.*
　　　4. *At Foleshill.*
　　　5. *At Macclesfield.*
　　　6. *At Manchester.*
　　　7. *At Spitalfields.*
　　　8. *In Foreign Countries.*

　　　　　i. Generally.
　　　　　ii. At Avignon.
　　　　　iii. At St. Etienne.
　　　　　iv. At Lyons.

　　1. *Generally.*

They would be benfited by taking off the import duty on foreign thrown silk, *Royle* 3328, 3329——Why reduction of duty would not prejudice the operative, *Gibson* 5041, 5042——Reduction in the employment of weavers during the last six years, *Stone* 5763, 5764; *Wadden* 9980, 9981——Consequent distress of weavers from reduction of manufacturers, *Ballance* 8448——Examination as to the use of the fly shuttle, *Ballance* 8550–8555; *Wallis* 10962–10965——Advantage to the English weaver over the French from poor's rates, *Bowring* 9804, 9805——Little difficulty in cotton weavers being employed in silk weaving, *Schwabe* 9846–9852——Calculation as to wages and to price of food, 1824, 1826 and 1831, showing how much per cent. the weaver is worse off than before opening the Ports, *Wadden* 9977–9979, 9982.

How weavers out of employment are supported, *Wadden* 10085——Distress of weavers since the admission of foreign goods, and bad moral consequences therefrom, *Stone* 6341–6345; *Wadden* 9983; *Bennett* 10721–10726; *Wallis* 10816–10818, 10823, 10881–10883; *Prout* 11638, 11656, 11669, 11676; *Smith* 11683; *Cope* 11708; *Kelly* 11825–11829; *Beckwith* 11976–11978——Whether distress greater or of longer duration formerly than at present, *Stone* 6346–6352; *Wallis* 10824–10828——They do not work so well working more hours, *Bennett* 10738——How far all the weavers employed in 1830, *Wallis* 10834——Extent of employment of weavers at present, *Wallis* 10848–10850.

Feeling among them that Government is indifferent to their situation, *Smith* 11682——The acquiring information by them superseded by the demands of nature, *Smith* 11685, 11686——Proportion of time they have to wait for work, and number constantly out of employment, *Smith* 11692——Instance of receiving parish relief when in work, *Smith* 11693——Irregularity of work and rate of wages since 1825, *Cope* 11704–11706——Previous employment in the cotton trade, and reasons for leaving it for the silk trade, *Rowbotham* 11722, 11723——Increase of weavers from the cotton trade, 1816–1820, did not hurt the silk trade, or much reduce wages, *Rowbotham* 11724–11726——They can obtain more by sweeping the streets than at their work, *Rowbotham* 11730——No ribbon weavers in Lancashire, *Rowbotham* 11739.

Few cotton weavers can now turn their hand to silk weaving, *Rowbotham* 11741——Increase of the broad silk trade, and prosperity of the weavers, 1819–1825, *Kelly* 11819–11825——Reasons silk weavers cannot shift their trade, *Kelly* 11827——Premium formerly given weavers to learn the art, *Kelly* 11830, 11831——Weavers know each others distress better than master manufacturers can, *Scott* 11862——No difference of opinion among weavers as to the cause of their distress, *Scott* 11863, 11864——Why weavers have better knowledge of the quality of silk working up than masters, *Scott* 11881——Witness's weavers at Coggeshall employed upon low works, *Beckwith* 11976–11978.

　　2. *Time lost by them.*

Time occupied in preparing work is a loss to the workman, besides in some instances the want of work altogether, *Smith* 1338–1340——Proportion time lost in changing pattern bears to the time taken in making the article, *Smith* 1341–1346; *Perkins* 1563; 678.　　　　　　　　　　　　　　　　　　　　　　　　　　　*Cox*

*WEAVERS*—continued.

### 2. *Time lost by them*—continued.

*Cox* 2064–2071——Loss of time by weavers more now than formerly, *Brocklehurst* 11458
——Manner in which they unavoidably lose time in their work, *Cope* 11700–11702——
Examination upon the time taken in making alterations in a pattern and loss to the
weaver thereby, and whether less time could be occupied therein, *Pittifor* 12029–12043,
12058, 12059——There would not be much more time or advantage gained by warping
whole grosses than half grosses, *Pittifor* 12044–12046——Loss of time greater in the
m anufacture of fancy than plain ribbons, *Pittifor* 12047, 12048.

### 3. *At Coventry.*

Morals of the work people are worse from the poverty to which they are reduced,
*Brunskill* 195——Their distress and causes thereof, *Brunskill* 339–342, 455, 456;
*Cheeper* 823–825, 904–907; *Poole* 943, 944, 952; *Goode* 1201–1208; *Smith* 1258;
*Marston* 1358–1360——Their employment in the black ribbon trade, *Brunskill* 349–353
——Difference in the quantity of work of the engine loom and single hand, *Brunskill*
343–348——Employment for them till the foreigners found out the channels of trade,
*Brunskill* 495, 496——More out of employment now than 1818, *Poole* 991, 992, 1081
——Meeting of them in November, *Poole* 1013——How far the use of the engine loom
tends to throw workmen out of employment, *Poole* 1129, 1130; *Marston* 1492, 1493——
Increase or decrease in the number of weavers and population, 1821–1831, *Poole*
1165–1173——How many months full employment for them last year, *Poole* 1178–
1182——How far a weaver's family assist him, *Poole* 1183, 1184——Extent to which
the consumption of silk will tend to show the beneficial employment of the operative,
*Poole* 1186–1191——Number of persons employed in the plain branch, and present
distress, *Goode* 1201–1208——Number of Jacquard weavers at Coventry, *Smith* 1257
——How long unemployed last year, *Smith* 1260, 1272–1278; *Perkins* 1565, 1566——
Jacquard trade as good in 1826 as at any other time *Smith* 1271.

Principal employment of the weavers now is in altering patterns for which there is
no wages, *Smith* 1300–1307, 1323–1335——How far increase of population employed,
*Marston* 1383–1392, 1501——Increase or depression of the weaving trade, 1814–1818,
*Marston* 1414–1417——Full employment in 1826 in the manufacture of brocade gauzes
which have since been made abroad, *Marston* 1426–1436——Number of people employed by the undertakers, *Marston* 1470–1475——Comparison of the state of weavers
formerly and at present from the rate of wages, *Marston* 1494–1500——Increasing the
price of ribbons by reduction of wages would not afford more employment, *Jacombs* 1829
——Calculation of employment to the British manufacturer that has been lost by importation of French ribbons in 1831, *Ratliff* 1836; *Cox* 2203——Increased consumption
of silk does not benefit the labourer, *Cox* 2105, 2106——How far single hand weavers
employed, and amount of wages, *Cox* 2113, 2114——More men have been employed
since 1826, but at lower wages, *Merry* 2610, 2611——Weavers fully employed at Coventry, *Baggalluy* 7441–7446.

### 4. *At Foleshill.*

Number of operatives at Foleshill employed and unemployed, and how the account
obtained, *Marston* 1353–1357, 1361, 1362.

### 5. *At Macclesfield.*

They have no other employment when out of work at Macclesfield, *Brocklehurst* 11459;
*Middlehurst* 11810——Distressed state of Irish weavers at Macclesfield, *Brocklehurst*
11460–11462——Average wages of weavers at Macclesfield, their present distressed state
and former comfortable situation attributed to the introduction of foreign manufactured
goods, *Smith* 11677–11681; *Cope* 11707–11709, 11714; *Rowbotham* 11726–11729,
11744.

### 6. *At Manchester.*

Contests with weavers at Manchester, hours of labour, and description of looms, *Harter*
9384–9407, 9413–9420——Employment of weavers at Manchester between silk and
cotton trade, *Harter* 9408, 9409——Distress of weavers of broad goods last winter,
*Harter* 9489——Manchester people alternately work between silk and cotton according
to the wages in either trade, *Middehurst* 11809——Prosperous state of weavers at Manchester to 1826, and distress since, *Scott* 11855 11861——Commencement of the union
among the Manchester weavers in 1826, and manner of conducting it, *Scott* 11871–
11873.

### 7. *At Spitalfields.*

How distress of Spitalfields' weavers to be alleviated, *Stone* 5847–5850——Distress of
Spitalfields' weavers, and periods thereof, *Ballance* 8364–8366——Good condition of
Spitalfields' weavers ten years ago, and alteration for the worse since, *Wadden* 9967,
9975–9977——Number of Spitalfields' weavers out of employment, and instances of their
absconding to America with their employers' manufactured property, *Wadden* 10084–
10086; *Moore* 11280–11285——Distress of Spitalfields' weavers greater since 1826 than
formerly, from their being more want of work and want of price, *Poyton* 10979——
Extent of parish relief to weavers, *Poyton* 10994, 10995——Impossibility of earning a
livelihood